D0776832

COMPACT AMERICAN

SPANISH DICTIONARY

Spanish-English

English-Spanish

HOUGHTON MIFFLIN COMPANY
BOSTON • NEW YORK

Library of Congress Cataloging-in-Publication Data

Compact American Spanish dictionary : Spanish–English, English–Spanish.
        p.   cm.
        Updated ed. of: The concise American heritage Spanish dictionary. 1992.
        ISBN 0-395-96215-3 : $14.00
        1. Spanish language—Dictionaries—English. 2. English language—Dictionaries—Spanish. I. Concise American heritage Larousse Spanish dictionary. II. Houghton Mifflin Company.
PC4640.C56 1999
463'.21—dc21

        99-11861
        CIP

Manufactured in the United States of America

STAFF

David R. Pritchard • *Senior Project Editor*
Jacquelyn Pope • *Associate Editor*
NSI Media, Inc. • *Computer Terminology*
Javier Mateu • *Consultant*

Managing Editor
Christopher Leonesio

Production Supervisor
Elizabeth Rubè

Senior Manufacturing Assistant
James Mitchell

EDITORIAL DEVELOPMENT STAFF

Editors
Diane Traynor Senerth   J. Mauricio Sola

Contributing Editors
Lois Grossman   David Weeks

Ida Calero Fernández
Hélène Houssemaine-Florent
David A. Jost

Craig A. Lapine
Grisel Lozano-Garcini
Fernando A. Pfannl

CONTENTS / ÍNDICE

PREFACE

The *Compact American Spanish Dictionary* is an authoritative, easy-to-use bilingual dictionary from the editors of the American Heritage® Dictionaries. The vocabulary has been selected for practicality and up-to-dateness, with special attention to the evolving language of computers and high technology. The English usage and spelling is that of the United States, with British variants clearly marked, while the Spanish represents both "pan-Hispanic" usage and the diverse special forms and senses found throughout Latin America. The various meanings of a word are identified by synonyms and labels, with clear typographic distinctions observed throughout the entry, enabling the user to quickly locate a precise equivalent for the particular sense that is wanted. Idioms, phrases, and example sentences have been kept in generous numbers, offering invaluable help in the idiomatic use of both languages.

GUIDE TO THE DICTIONARY

Entry words All entry words are divided into syllables. Words that are identical in spelling but that constitute separate entries are entered with superscript numbers (**haber¹, haber²**).

Inflected entry words Nouns and adjectives that inflect for gender are entered under the masculine form. The feminine ending is separated from the masculine form by a comma (**ca·í·do, a**). When the feminine form contains a syllable break that is different from the masculine, the break is indicated (**cal·cu·la·dor, ·ra**), as is any change in the written accent (**ca·be·zón, o·na**).

Variants Variant spellings of an entry word are indicated with parentheses or with a bold slash (**fe·mi·n(e)i·dad; gla·dia·dor/tor**). Syllable breaks and gender differences are fully shown (**gla·dí·o·lo/dio·lo; ba·rran·co** m./**ca** f.; **gen·ti·li·dad** f./**lis·mo** m.). The form to the left of the slash always represents a complete word, though an inflected feminine ending after the slash applies to both the entry word and its variant (**gaz·mo·ñe·ro/ño, a**). When the inflected ending applies only to the main entry and not to the variant, it is placed before the slash (**gor·je·a·dor, ·ra/je·an·te**).

Cross-references When a variant form of an entry word does not occur close enough to the main entry to be combined in a single entry, a cross-reference is given (**sicología** f. var. of **psicología**). Feminine nouns that are semantically related to a masculine form are treated under the masculine entry. When a feminine noun falls more than five lines away from its masculine entry in alphabetical order, a cross-reference is given (**justa** f. see **justo, a**).

Irregular verbs All irregular verbs are referenced to the Spanish Verb Table with a boldface section number (**dar §20**). The number corresponds to the appropriate model verb in the Table. Common irregular verb forms are entered in the Dictionary along with cross-references to their infinitives (**estuviera, vo** see **estar**).

Organization of entries Equivalents of the entry word are given in roman type. Synonymous equivalents are separated by commas. Different senses are separated by semicolons. The various senses of an entry word are distinguished by either of two features: (i) a synonym or phrase in the language of the entry word, given in italic type within parentheses, or (ii) a field label printed in small capital letters (CHEM., ECON.). When the first equivalent of an entry word is the most frequent translation or an obvious cognate, no discrimination is given for that sense.

Labels are also used to indicate levels of appropriate usage (COLL., SL.) or restriction to a geographic region (AMER., MEX.). Regional meanings are placed after all other senses for a particular part of speech and are grouped by general region first, then specific countries. Example phrases are enclosed within angle brackets following the sense to which they apply. Note that when the entry word is used within the entry with no change in spelling, it is abbreviated to its initial letter.

Idioms, phrases, and plurals Common idioms and phrases are listed as run-on entries at the appropriate part of speech. The first run-on is introduced by a bold diamond (♦). Additional items follow in alphabetical order and are separated by bold bullets (•). Equivalents or idioms involving the plural usage of the entry word are grouped after a bold diamond followed by the plural label (♦ pl.) Plurals that follow the diamond are abbreviated to their initial letter.

PREFACIO

Este diccionario bilingüe de alta calidad y de uso fácil está presentado por la editorial de los diccionarios *American Heritage*®. El vocabulario ha sido seleccionado teniendo en cuenta las necesidades prácticas del usuario y refleja la lengua actual. Se ha dado atención especial al lenguaje de computadoras y de tecnología avanzada. El uso del inglés y su ortografía son los correspondientes al inglés de los Estados Unidos, mientras que las variaciones británicas aparecen claramente identificadas. El castellano representado en este diccionario incluye las diversas formas y acepciones que pueden encontrarse en el habla de Latinoamérica. Los artículos han sido organizados con el fin de ofrecer al lector el equivalente preciso de la palabra o frase que necesita encontrar. Los modismos, frases y ejemplos abundan en esta obra, ofreciendo al lector una ayuda invaluable en el uso idiomático de ambas lenguas.

GUÍA PARA EL USO DE ESTE DICCIONARIO

Vocablos Todos los vocablos han sido silabeados. Las palabras cuya ortografía es idéntica pero cuyos significados son diferentes se incluyen en forma separada, acompañadas de un índice sobrescrito (**like¹, like²**).

Fonética La guía para la pronunciación de los vocablos ha sido basada en el sistema usado por *The American Heritage Dictionary*. (Véase la Guía para la Pronunciación Inglesa.) En este sistema los acentos tónicos primarios (′), secundarios (′) y la indicación de una sílaba no acentuada (-) aparecen a continuación de la sílaba que modifican: **generosity** (jĕn′ə-rŏs′ĭ-tē). En esta obra hemos utilizado estos símbolos no sólo para indicar la acentuación sino también para reemplazar las sílabas que se repiten en las palabras derivadas. Por ejemplo, dada la pronunciación del vocablo **humid** (hyōō′mĭd), hemos abreviado la pronunciación de **humidifier** de esta forma: (-′ə-fī′ər), en donde (-) reemplaza a la sílaba no acentuada (hyōō-) y (′) reemplaza a la sílaba acentuada (mĭd). De haberse escrito en su totalidad, **humidifier** se transcribiría (hyōō-mĭd′ə-fī′ər). La sílaba o la combinación de sílabas que se pronuncia igual que el vocablo que las precede han sido abreviadas con el símbolo (:). En el caso del vocablo **humidify** (:ə-fī), el símbolo (:) reemplaza a (-′) de la palabra que antecede. De haberse escrito en su totalidad, **humidify** se transcribiría (hyōō-mĭd′ə-fī).

Variantes Las variaciones ortográficas de un vocablo aparecen entre paréntesis o separadas por una vírgula en negrilla (**adz(e)**; **con·vey·er/or**). Los cambios en el silabeo se indican con claridad (**con·vert·er/·tor**), así como el cambio en la pronunciación de una variante (véase **coupe/·pé**). No ofrecemos, en cambio, la pronunciación de las variaciones en los casos de adjetivos con terminación **-ic/i·cal** (-ĭk/ĭ-kəl) o sustantivos con terminación **-ence/en·cy** o **-ance/an·cy** (-əns/ən-sē) ya que se consideran variaciones regulares.

Formas irregulares Cuando el vocablo inglés tiene una irregularidad, ésta se indica en letra negrilla. Las formas comparativas y superlativas de los adjetivos se muestran de la siguiente manera: 1) **big** adj. **-gg-**, para indicar **bigger, biggest**; 2) **happy** adj. **-i-**, para indicar **happier, happiest**; 3) **ample** adj. **-er, -est**, para indicar **ampler, amplest**. No hemos indicado la irregularidad de los adjetivos de una sola sílaba que terminan en consonante (como **hard, low**) ya que usualmente forman su comparativo y superlativo agregándosele **-er** y **-est**. La información referente a la formación de plurales irregulares aparece en corchetes (**knife** [pl. **-ves**]).

En cuanto a los verbos, las formas irregulares del pretérito y del participio pasado se indican en la siguiente forma: **sing** intr. **sang, sung** (el gerundio se incluye solamente en los casos en que se repite la última consonante). Nótese que cuando el pretérito y el participio pasado coinciden en forma, la forma irregular aparece solamente una vez (**make** tr. **made**). En otros casos indicamos solamente la irregularidad ortográfica, evitando así la repetición: 1) **step** intr. **-pp-**, para indicar **stepped, stepped, stepping**; 2) **hew** tr. **-ed, -ed** o **-n**, para indicar **hewed, hewed** o **hewn**; 3) **mimic** tr. **-ck-**, para indicar **mimicked, mimicked, mimicking**. Los verbos cuya terminación **y** cambia por **i** se consideran regulares y no aparecen en el artículo (**try**, tried, tried, trying).

Organización de los artículos Los equivalentes del vocablo a definirse y sus sinónimos aparecen en letra redonda y están separados por una coma. Las diferentes acepciones del vocablo aparecen separadas por un punto y coma. Las distintas acepciones de cada palabra se han diferenciado por medio de (i) un sinónimo o frase escrita en el idioma del vocablo, en cursiva y entre paréntesis, o, (ii) un rótulo impreso en letras mayúsculas pequeñas (ECON., QUÍM.). Estas convenciones no han sido utilizadas cuando el primer equivalente del vocablo es de uso muy frecuente o cuando su traducción es un cognado directo.

Los rótulos se usan frecuentemente para indicar el uso apropiado del vocablo (FAM., JER.) o para circunscribir su uso a un país determinado (E.U., G.B.). Los ejemplos aparecen entre corchetes angulares, inmediatamente después de la acepción que ilustran. Nótese que el vocablo inglés se abrevia cuando aparece en el ejemplo exactamente como cuando encabeza el artículo.

Modismos, locuciones y formas plurales Los modismos de interés general y las locuciones aparecen en la parte de la oración a la que corresponden, precedidos por un rombo en negrilla (♦), y separados en forma alfabética por el símbolo (•). Ciertos equivalentes y locuciones que demandan el uso del vocablo en su forma plural han sido agrupados en forma similar (♦ pl.). Las formas plurales que se ofrecen en esta sección se abrevian con la inicial del vocablo que encabeza el artículo.

ABBREVIATIONS / ABREVIATURAS

abbr.	abbreviation	CUEBC. FIC.	ciencia ficción
abr.	abreviatura	CIENT.	científico
ACC.	accounting	CINEM.	cinema/cinematografía
ACOUS.	acoustics	CIR.	cirugía
ACÚS.	acústica	COLL.	colloquial
adj.	adjective/adjetivo	COM.	commerce/comercio
adv.	adverb/adverbio	comp.	comparative/comparativo
AER.	aeronautics/aeronáutica	COMPUT.	computers/computadoras
AGR.	agriculture/agricultura	conj.	conjunction/conjunción
AMER.	America	CONSTR.	construction/construcción
ANAT.	anatomy/anatomía	contr.	contraction/contracción
ANT.	antiguo	COST.	costura
ANTHR.	anthropology	CRIMIN.	criminology/criminología
ANTROP.	antropología	CUL.	culinary/culinario
ARCH.	archaic	def.	definite/definido
ARCHEOL.	archeology	dem.	demonstrative/demostrativo
ARCHIT.	architecture	DENT.	dentistry
ARM.	arms/armas	DEP.	deportes
ARQ.	arquitectura	DER.	derecho
ARQUEOL.	arqueología	DEROG.	derogatory
art.	article/artículo	DESPEC.	despectivo
ARTE.	bellas artes	DIAL.	dialect/dialecto
ARTS	fine arts	DIB.	dibujo
ASTROL.	astrology/astrología	DIPL.	diplomacy/diplomacia
ASTRON.	astronomy/astronomía	ECOL.	ecology/ecología
ASTRONAUT.	astronautical	ECON.	economics/economía
ASTRONAUT.	astronáutica	EDUC.	education/educación
AUTO.	automobile/automovilismo	ELEC.	electricity/electricidad
aux.	auxiliary/auxiliar	ELECTRON.	electronics
AVIA.	aviation/aviación	ELECTRÓN.	electrónica
BIBL.	Bible	ENGIN.	engineering
BÍBL.	bíblico	ENTOM.	entomology/entomología
BIOCHEM.	biochemistry	EQUIT.	equitation/equitación
BIOL.	biology/biología	esp.	especially/especialmente
BIOQUÍM.	bioquímica	E.U.	Estados Unidos
BKB.	bookbinding	EUFEM.	eufemismo
BOT.	botany/botánica	EUPH.	euphemism
CARP.	carpentry/carpintería	f.	feminine/femenino
CERAM.	ceramics	FAM.	familiar
CERÁM.	cerámica	FARM.	farmacia
cf.	consulte	F.C.	ferrocarril
CHEM.	chemistry	FIG.	figurative/figurado

FILOS.	filosía
FIN.	finance/finanzas
FÍS.	física
FISIOL.	fisiología
FONÉT.	fonética
FORT.	fortificación
FOTOG.	fotografía
G.B.	Great Britain/Gran Bretaña
GEOF.	geofísica
GEOG.	geography/geografía
GEOL.	geology/geología
GEOM.	geometry/geometría
GEOPH.	geophysics
GRAM.	grammar/gramática
HER.	heraldry/heráldica
HIST.	history/historia
HORT.	horticulture/horticultura
HUM.	humorous/humorístico
ICHTH.	ichthyology
ICT.	ictiología
IMPR.	imprenta
indef.	indefinite/indefinido
INDUS.	industry/industria
ING.	ingeniería
interj.	interjection/interjección
interrog.	interrogative/interrogativo
intr.	intransitive/intransitivo
inv.	invariable/invariable
IRÓN.	irónico
JER.	jerga
JEWEL.	jewelry
JOURN.	journalism
JOY.	joyería
LAW	law
LIT.	literature/literatura
LOG.	logic
LÓG.	lógica
m.	masculine/masculino
MACH.	machinery
MAQ.	maquinaria
MARIT.	MARITIME
MARÍT.	marítimo
MAS.	masonry
MAT.	matemáticas
MATH.	mathematics
MEC.	mecánica
MECH.	mechanics
MED.	medicine/medicina
METAL.	metallurgy/metalurgia
METEOROL.	meteorology/meteorología
MIL.	military/militar
MIN.	mineralogy/mineralogía
MITOL.	mitología
MUS.	music
MÚS.	música
MYTH.	mythology
NUMIS.	numismatics/numismática
ODONT.	odontología
OFTAL.	oftalmología
OPHTHAL.	ophthalmology
OPT.	optics
ÓPT.	óptica
ORNIT.	ornitología
ORNITH.	ornithology
p.	past/pasado
PAINT.	painting
PALEON.	paleontology/paleontología
part.	participle/participio
PERIOD.	periodismo
pers.	person, personal/personal
PHARM.	pharmaceutics
PHILOS.	philosophy
PHONET.	phonetics
PHOTO.	photography
PHYS.	physics
PHYSIOL.	physiology
PINT.	pintura
pl.	plural/plural
POET.	poetry, poetic
POÉT.	poética
POL.	politics/política
pos.	posesivo
poss.	possessive
prep.	preposition/preposición
pres.	present/presente
pret.	preterite/pretérito
PRINT.	printing
pron.	pronoun/pronombre
PSIC.	psicología
PSYCH.	psychology
QUÍM.	química
RAD.	radio/radio
RAIL.	railway
reflex.	reflexive/reflexivo
REG.	regional/regional
rel.	relative/relativo
RELIG.	religion/religión
RET.	retórica
RHET.	rhetoric
R.P.	Río de la Plata
S.	sustantivo
SCI.	science
SEW.	sewing
sing., sg.	singular/singular
SL.	slang
SOCIOL.	sociology/sociología
SPORT.	sports
subj.	subjunctive/subjuntivo
superl.	superlative/superlativo
SURG.	surgery
TAUR.	bullfighting/tauromaquia
TEAT.	teatro
TEC.	tecnología
TECH.	technical
TEJ.	tejeduría
TEL.	telecomunicaciones
TELEC.	telecommunications
TELEV.	television/televisión
TEN.	teneduría de libros
TEO.	teología
TEX.	textiles
THEAT.	theater
THEOL.	theology
TIP.	tipografía
TOP.	topography/topografía
tr.	transitive/transitivo
U.S.	United States
v.	verbo
var.	variant/variante
VET.	veterinary/veterinaria
ZOOL.	zoology/zoología

SPANISH PRONUNCIATION GUIDE

Let-ter	Spanish Example	English Example	Description
a	pata	father	
b	boca	bib	At the beginning of a word
	cabo		Between vowels, closer to *v*
c	calco	cat	Before *a, o, u,* like *k*
	cedro	cedar	Before *e, i* like *s*; in much of Spain pronounced like *th* of *thick*
ch*	chiste	church	
d	dar	die	At the beginning of a word
	cada		Between vowels, like *th* of *rather*
e	leche	café	
f	fácil	fat	
g	gente		Before *e, i,* like *h* of *ha!*
	guerra	guide	With *u* before *e, i,* a hard *g*
	gato	got	Before *a, o, u,* a hard *g*
h	honor		Always silent
i	silla	machine	
j	jugo		Like *h* in *ha!*
k	kilo	kite	
l	listo	list	
ll*	llama		In Spain, like *lli* of *million;* elsewhere like Spanish consonant *y* (see below)
m	mamá	mum	
n	nona	none	
ñ	año		Like *ny* of *canyon*
o	solo	so	
p	papa	pipe	
q	quita	raquet	
r	caro		Like *dd* of *ladder*
rr	carro		Strongly trilled
s	soso	sass	
t	tonto	tight	
u	luto	lute	
	agüero	anguish	
v	vino		Identical to initial Spanish *b*
	lava		Identical to intervocalic Spanish *b*
w	wat		Pronounced either like English *v* or *w*
x	éxito	exit	Exception: in "México" *x* is like Spanish *j*
	mixto		Before a consonant, may be pronounced *s*
y	y		Like *i* of *machine*
	yeso	yes	In River Plate, like *s* of *vision*
z	zona		Like *s* in *sass;* in much of Spain, like *th* of *thick*

*In 1994 the Spanish language academies eliminated *ch* and *ll* as separate letters of the alphabet. The alphabetic listings in this Dictionary reflect this change, so that words containing these letter combinations are ordered as they would be in English. For phonological purposes, however, it is convenient to continue to think of *ch* and *ll* as individual letters with unique pronunciations.

GUÍA PARA LA PRONUNCIACIÓN INGLESA

Símbolo	Ejemplo inglés	Ejemplo español	Sonido aproximado
ă	pat	—	entre la *a* y la *e*
ā	pay, mate	rey	
âr	care, hair	—	parecido a *ea* en *brea* (con la *r*)
ä	father	año	
b	bib	boca	
ch	church	chico	
d	deed, milled	dar	
ě	pet, feather	el	
ē	bee, me, piece	mil	
f	fife, phase, rough	fama	
g	gag	gato	
h	hat	joya	
hw	which	juez	
ĭ	pit	—	entre la *i* y la *e*
ī	pie, by	aire	
îr	pier, dear, mere	—	entre *ía* en *día* e *íe* en *fíe* (con la *r*)
j	judge	—	entre la *y* inicial y la *ch*
k	kick, cat, pique	casa	
kw	quick	cuan	
l	lid, needle	luz	
m	mum	muy	
n	no, sudden	no	
ng	thing	inglés	
ŏ	pot, swat	la	
ō	toe, go, boat	solo	
ô	caught, paw, for	corre	
oi	noise, boy	oigo	
o͝o	took	—	parecido a la *u* en *yogur*, más breve
o͞o	boot, suit	uno	
ou	out, cow	auto	
p	pop	pan	
r	roar	—	una *ere* con la lengua curvada hacia atrás
s	sauce	sapo	
sh	ship, dish	—	una *che* suavizada, más como la *ese*
t	tight, stopped	tu	
th	thin, path	—	parecido a la *ce* de Castilla
th	this, bathe	cada	
ŭ	cut, rough	—	parecido a una *o* que tira a la *a*
yo͞o	use, few	ciudad	
ûr	urge, term, firm	—	parecido a una *e* que tira a la *o* (con la *r*)
v	valve	—	una *efe* sonora
w	with	cual	
y	yes	yo	
z	zebra, xylem	mismo	
zh	vision, pleasure	—	parecido a la *ll* de Argentina
ə	about, item, edible, gallop, circus	—	parecido a una *e* muy breve que tira a la *i*

SPANISH VERB TABLE

The following Table presents model conjugations for all regular and irregular Spanish verbs. These models include only those tenses in which an irregular conjugation occurs. All irregular forms are printed in bold type.

§01 REGULAR VERB CONJUGATIONS:

-AR Verbs: AMAR	-ER Verbs: VENDER	-IR Verbs: PARTIR

Present

AM-o	VEND-o	PART-o
-as	-es	-es
-a	-e	-e
-amos	-emos	-imos
-áis	-éis	-ís
-an	-en	-en

Imperfect

AM-aba	VEND-ía	PART-ía
-abas	-ías	-ías
-aba	-ía	-ía
-ábamos	-íamos	-íamos
-abais	-íais	-íais
-aban	-ían	-ían

Preterit

AM-é	VEND-í	PART-í
-aste	-iste	-iste
-ó	-ió	-ió
-amos	-imos	-imos
-asteis	-isteis	-isteis
-aron	-ieron	-ieron

Present Subjunctive

AM-e	VEND-a	PART-a
-es	-as	-as
-e	-a	-a
-emos	-amos	-amos
-éis	-áis	-áis
-en	-an	-an

Imperfect Subjunctive

AM-ara/ase	VEND-iera/iese	PART-iera/iese
-aras/ases	-ieras/ieses	-ieras/ieses
-ara/ase	-iera/iese	-iera/iese
-áramos/ásemos	-iéramos/iésemos	-iéramos/iésemos
-arais/aseis	-ierais/ieseis	-ierais/ieseis
-aran/asen	-ieran/iesen	-ieran/iesen

Future/Conditional

AMAR-é/ía	VENDER-é/ía	PARTIR-é/ía
-ás/ías	-ás/ías	-ás/ías
-á/ía	-á/ía	-á/ía
-emos/íamos	-emos/íamos	-emos/íamos
-éis/íais	-éis/íais	-éis/íais
-án/ían	-án/ían	-án/ían

Imperative

ama/amad	vende/vended	parte/partid

Present Participle

amando	vendiendo	partiendo

Past Participle

amado	vendido	partido

§02 ADQUIRIR

Pres.	adquiero	adquirimos
	adquieres	adquirís
	adquiere	adquieren

Pres.	adquiera	adquiramos
Subj.	adquieras	adquiráis
	adquiera	adquieran

§03 AGORAR

Pres.	agüero	agoramos
	agüeras	agoráis
	agüera	agüeran

Pres.	agüere	agoremos
Subj.	agüeres	agoréis
	agüere	agüeren

§04 ALZAR

Pret. **alcé**, alzaste, etc.
Pres. Subj. **alce**, etc.

§05 ANDAR

Pret.	anduve	anduvimos
	aduviste	aduvisteis
	anduvo	anduvieron

Imp. Subj. **anduviera/iese**, etc.

§06 ARCAIZAR

Pres.	arcaízo	arcaizamos
	arcaízas	arcaizáis
	arcaíza	arcaízan

Pret. **arcaicé**, arcaizaste, etc.

Pres.	arcaíce	arcaicemos
Subj.	arcaíces	arcaicéis
	arcaíce	arcaícen

§07 ARGÜIR

Pres.	arguyo	argüimos
	arguyes	argüís
	arguye	arguyen

Pret.	argüí	argüimos
	argüiste	argüisteis
	arguyó	arguyeron

Pres. Subj. **arguya**, etc.
Imp. Subj. **arguyera/iese**, etc.
Pres. Part. **arguyendo**

§08 ASIR

Pres. **asgo**, ases, etc.
Pres. Subj. **asga**, etc.

§09 AVERGONZAR

Pres.	avergüenzo	avergonzamos
	avergüenzas	avergonzáis
	avergüenza	avergüenzan

Pret. **avergoncé**, avergonzaste, etc.

Pres.	avergüence	avergoncemos
Subj.	avergüences	avergoncéis
	avergüence	avergüencen

§10 AVERIGUAR

Pret. **averigüé**, averiguaste, etc.
Pres. Subj. **averigüe**, etc.

§11 BENDECIR like DECIR in all
forms *except* Fut./Cond.:
bendeciré/bendeciría, etc.

§12 BRUÑIR

Pret.	bruñí	bruñimos
	bruñiste	bruñisteis
	bruñó	bruñeron

Imp. Subj. **bruñera/ese**, etc.
Pres. Part. **bruñendo**

§13 BULLIR

Pret.	bullí	bullimos
	bulliste	bullisteis
	bulló	bulleron

Imp. Subj. **bullera/ese**, etc.
Pres. Part. **bullendo**

§14 CABER

Pres. **quepo**, cabes, etc.

Pret.	cupe	cupimos
	cupiste	cupisteis
	cupo	cupieron

Pres. Subj. **quepa**, etc.
Imp. Subj. **cupiera/iese**, etc.
Fut./Cond. **cabré/cabría**, etc.

§15 CAER

Pres. **caigo**, caes etc.

Pret.	caí	caímos
	caíste	caísteis
	cayó	cayeron

Pres. Subj. **caiga**, etc.
Imp. Subj. **cayera/ese**, etc.
Pres. Part. **cayendo**
Past Part. **caído**

§16 COLGAR

Pres.	cuelgo	colgamos
	cuelgas	colgáis
	cuelga	cuelgan

Pret. **colgué**, colgaste, etc.

Pres.	cuelgue	colguemos
Subj.	cuelgues	colguéis
	cuelgue	cuelguen

§17 CONOCER

Pres. **conozco**, conoces, etc.
Pres. Subj. **conozca**, etc.

§18 CONSTRUIR

Pres.	construyo	construimos
	construyes	construís
	construye	construyen

Pret.	construí	contruimos
	construiste	construisteis
	construyó	construyeron

Pres. Subj. **construya**, etc.
Imp. Subj. **construyera/ese**, etc.
Pres. Part. **construyendo**

§19 CONTAR

Pres.	cuento	contamos
	cuentas	contáis
	cuenta	cuentan

Pres.	cuente	contemos
Subj.	cuentes	contéis
	cuente	cuenten

§20 DAR

Pres. **doy**, das, etc.

Pret.	**di**	**dimos**
	diste	**disteis**
	dio	**dieron**

Pres.	**dé**	demos
Subj.	des	deis
	dé	den

Imp. Subj. **diera/iese**, etc.

§21 DECIR

Pres.	**digo**	decimos
	dices	decís
	dice	**dicen**

Pres. Subj. **diga**, etc.
Imp. Subj. **dijera/ese**, etc.
Fut./Cond. **diré/diría**, etc.
Imperative **di**, decid
Pres. Part. **diciendo**
Past Part. **dicho**

§22 DEDUCIR

Pres. **deduzco**, deduces, etc.

Pret.	**deduje**	**dedujimos**
	dedujiste	**dedujisteis**
	dedujo	**dedujeron**

Pres. Subj. **deduzca**, etc.
Imp. Subj. **dedujera/ese**, etc.

§23 DELINQUIR

Pres. **delinco**, delinques, etc.
Pres. Subj. **delinca**, etc.

§24 DESOSAR

Pres.	**deshueso**	desosamos
	deshuesas	desosáis
	deshuesa	**deshuesan**

Pres.	**deshuese**	desosemos
Subj.	**deshueses**	desoséis
	deshuese	**deshuesen**

§25 DISCERNIR

Pres.	**discierno**	discernimos
	disciernes	discernís
	discierne	**disciernen**

Pres.	**discierna**	discernamos
Subj.	**disciernas**	discernáis
	discierna	**disciernan**

§26 DISTINGUIR

Pres. **distingo**, distingues, etc.
Pres. Subj. **distinga**, etc.

§27 DORMIR

Pres.	**duermo**	dormimos
	duermes	dormís
	duerme	**duermen**

Pret.	**dormí**	dormimos
	dormiste	dormisteis
	durmió	**durmieron**

Pres.	**duerma**	**durmamos**
Subj.	**duermas**	**durmáis**
	duerma	**duerman**

Imp. Subj. **durmiera/iese**, etc.
Pres. Part. **durmiendo**

§28 EMPELLER

Pret.	**empellí**	empellimos
	empelliste	empellisteis
	empelló	**empelleron**

Imp. Subj. **empellera/ese**, etc.
Pres. Part. **empellendo**

§29 EMPEZAR

Pres.	**empiezo**	empezamos
	empiezas	empazáis
	empieza	**empiezan**

Pret. **empecé**, empezaste, etc.

Pres.	**empiece**	**empecemos**
Subj.	**empieces**	**empecéis**
	empiece	**empiecen**

§30 ENVIAR

Pres.	**envío**	enviamos
	envías	enviáis
	envía	**envían**

Pres.	**envíe**	enviemos
Subj.	**envíes**	enviéis
	envíe	**envíen**

§31 ERGUIR

Pres.	**irgo***	erguimos
	irgues*	erguís
	irgue*	**irguen***

*[alternate forms: **yergo**, etc.]

Pret.	**erguí**	erguimos
	erguiste	erguisteis
	irguió	**irguieron**

Pres. Subj. **irga/yerga**, etc.
Imp. Subj. **irguiera/iese**, etc.
Pres. Part. **irguiendo**

§32 ERIGIR

Pres. **erijo**, eriges, etc.
Pres. Subj. **erija**, etc.

§33 ERRAR

Pres.	**yerro**	erramos
	yerras	erráis
	yerra	**yerran**

Pres.	**yerre**	erremos
Subj.	**yerres**	erréis
	yerre	**yerren**

§34 ESCOGER

Pres. **escojo**, escoges, etc.
Pres. Subj. **escoja**, etc.

§35 ESPARCIR

Pres. **esparzo**, esparces, etc.
Pres. Subj. **esparza**, etc.

§36 ESTAR

Pres.	**estoy**	estamos
	estás	estáis
	está	**están**

Pret.	**estuve**	**estuvimos**
	estuviste	**estuvisteis**
	estuvo	**estuvieron**

Pres.	**esté**	estemos
Subj.	**estés**	estéis
	esté	**estén**

§37 FORZAR

Pres. **fuerzo**	forzamos
fuerzas	forzáis
fuerza	**fuerzan**

Pret. **forcé**, forzaste, etc.

Pres. **fuerce**	**forcemos**
Subj. **fuerces**	**forcéis**
fuerce	**fuercen**

§38 GARANTIR [defective]

Pres. ---	garantimos
	garantís
---	---

Pres. Subj. ---
Imperative ---, garantid

§39 HABER

Pres. **he**	**hemos**
has	habéis
ha	**han**
Pret. **hube**	**hubimos**
hubiste	**hubisteis**
hubo	**hubieron**

Pres. Subj. **haya**, etc.
Imp. Subj. **hubiera/iese**, etc.
Fut./Cond. **habré/habría**, etc.
Imperative **hé**, habed

§40 HACER

Pres. **hago**, haces, etc.

Pret. **hice**	**hicimos**
hiciste	**hicisteis**
hizo	**hicieron**

Pres. Subj. **haga**, etc.
Imp. Subj. **hiciera/iese**, etc.
Fut./Cond. **haré/haría**, etc.
Imperative **haz**, haced
Past Part. **hecho**

§41 IR

Pres. **voy**	**vamos**
vas	**vais**
va	**van**

Imperfect **iba**, etc.

Pret. **fui**	**fuimos**
fuiste	**fuisteis**
fue	**fueron**

Imp. Subj. **fuera/ese**, etc.
Imperative **ve**, id
Pres. Part. **yendo**

§42 JUGAR

Pres. **juego**	jugamos
juegas	jugáis
juega	**juegan**

Pret. **jugué**, jugaste, etc.

Pres. **juegue**	**juguemos**
Subj. **juegues**	**juguéis**
juegue	**jueguen**

§43 LEER

Pret. leí	**leímos**
leíste	**leísteis**
leyó	**leyeron**

Imp. Subj. **leyera/ese**, etc.
Pres. Part. **leyendo**

§44 LUCIR

Pres. **luzco**, luces, etc.
Pres. Subj. **luzca**, etc.

§45 OÍR

Pres. **oigo**	**oímos**
oyes	oís
oye	**oyen**
Pret. oí	**oímos**
oíste	**oísteis**
oyó	**oyeron**

Pres. Subj. **oiga**, etc.
Imp. Subj. **oyera/ese**, etc.
Pres. Part. **oyendo**
Past Part. **oído**

§46 OLER

Pres. **huelo**	olemos
hueles	oléis
huele	**huelen**
Pres. **huela**	olamos
Subj. **huelas**	oláis
huela	**huelan**

§47 PAGAR

Pret. **pagué**, pagaste, etc.
Pres. Subj. **pague**, etc.

§48 PEDIR

Pres. **pido**	pedimos
pides	pedís
pide	**piden**
Pret. pedí	pedimos
pediste	pedisteis
pidió	**pidieron**

Pres. Subj. **pida**, etc.
Imp. Subj. **pidiera/iese**, etc.
Pres. Part. **pidiendo**

§49 PENSAR

Pres. **pienso**	pensamos
piensas	pensáis
piensa	**piensan**
Pres. **piense**	pensemos
Subj. **pienses**	penséis
piense	**piensen**

§50 PERDER

Pres. **pierdo**	perdemos
pierdes	perdéis
pierde	**pierden**
Pres. **pierda**	perdamos
Subj. **pierdas**	perdáis
pierda	**pierdan**

§51 PLACER

Pres. **plazco**, places, etc.

Pret. plací	placimos
placiste	placisteis
plació*	placieron*

*[alternate forms: **plugo**, **plugieron**]
Pres. Subj. **plazca**, etc.
Imp. Subj. **placiera/iese***, etc.
*[alternate form: **plugiera/iese**]

§52 PLEGAR

Pres. **pliego** plegamos
pliegas plegáis
pliega **pliegan**
Pret. **plegué**, plegaste, etc.

Pres. **pliegue** **pleguemos**
Subj. **pliegues** **pleguéis**
pliegue **plieguen**

§53 PODER

Pres. **puedo** podemos
puedes podéis
puede **pueden**
Pret. **pude** **pudimos**
pudiste **pudisteis**
pudo **pudieron**
Pres. **pueda** podamos
Subj. **puedas** podáis
pueda **puedan**
Imp. Subj. **pudiera/iese**, etc.
Fut./Cond. **podré/podría**, etc.
Pres. Part. **pudiendo**

§54 PONER

Pres. **pongo**, pones, etc.

Pret. **puse** **pusimos**
pusiste **pusisteis**
puso **pusieron**
Pres. Subj. **ponga**, etc.
Imp. Subj. **pusiera/iese**, etc.
Fut./Cond. **pondré/pondría**, etc.
Imperative **pon**, poned
Past Part. **puesto**

§55 QUERER

Pres. **quiero** queremos
quieres queréis
quiere **quieren**
Pret. **quise** **quisimos**
quisiste **quisisteis**
quiso **quisieron**
Pres. **quiera** queramos
Subj. **quieras** queráis
quiera **quieran**
Imp. Subj. **quisiera/iese**, etc.
Fut./Cond. **querré/querría**, etc.

§56 RAER

Pres. **raigo*** raemos
raes raéis
rae raen
*[alternate form: **rayo**]
Pret. raí **raímos**
raíste **raísteis**
rayó **rayeron**
Pres. Subj. **raiga***, etc.
*[alternate form: **raya**]
Imp. Subj. **rayera/ese**, etc.
Pres. Part. **rayendo**
Past Part. **raído**

§57 REGIR

Pres. **rijo** regimos
riges regís
rige **rigen**

Pret. regí regimos
registe registeis
rigió **rigieron**
Pres. Subj. **rija**, etc.
Imp. Subj. **rigiera/iese**, etc.
Pres. Part. **rigiendo**

§58 REÍR

Pres. **río** **reímos**
ríes reís
ríe **ríen**
Pret. reí **reímos**
reíste **reísteis**
rió **rieron**
Pres. Subj. **ría**, etc.
Imp. Subj. **riera/iese**, etc.
Pres. Part. **riendo**
Past Part. **reído**

§59 REÑIR

Pres. **riño** reñimos
riñes reñís
riñe **riñen**
Pret. reñí reñimos
reñiste reñisteis
riñó **riñeron**
Pres. Subj. **riña**, etc.
Imp. Subj. **riñera/ese**, etc.
Pres. Part. **riñendo**

§60 REUNIR

Pres. **reúno** reunimos
reúnes reunís
reúne **reúnen**
Pres. **reúna** reunamos
Subj. **reúnas** reunáis
reúna **reúnan**

§61 ROER

Pres. roo* roemos
roes roéis
roe roen
*[alternate forms: **roigo** or **royo**]
Pret. roí **roímos**
roíste **roísteis**
royó **royeron**
Pres. Subj. **roa***, etc.
*[alternate forms: **roiga** or **roya**]
Imp. Subj. **royera/ese**, etc.
Pres. Part. **royendo**
Past Part. **roído**

§62 SABER

Pres. **sé**, sabes, etc.

Pret. **supe** **supimos**
supiste **supisteis**
supo **supieron**
Pres. Subj. **sepa**, etc.
Imp. Subj. **supiera/iese**, etc.
Fut./Cond. **sabré/sabría**, etc.

§63 SALIR

Pres. **salgo**, sales, etc.
Pres. Subj. **salga**, etc.
Fut./Cond. **saldré/saldría**, etc.
Imperative **sal**, salid

§64 SEGUIR

Pres.	**sigo**	**seguimos**
	sigues	seguís
	sigue	**siguen**

Pret.	seguí	seguimos
	seguiste	seguisteis
	siguió	**siguieron**

Pres. Subj. **siga**, etc.
Imp. Subj. **siguiera/iese**, etc.
Pres. Part. **siguiendo**

§65 SENTIR

Pres.	**siento**	sentimos
	sientes	sentís
	siente	**sienten**

Pret.	sentí	sentimos
	sentiste	sentisteis
	sintió	**sintieron**

Pres.	**sienta**	**sintamos**
Subj.	**sientas**	**sintáis**
	sienta	**sientan**

Imp. Subj. **sintiera/iese**, etc.
Pres. Part. **sintiendo**

§66 SER

Pres.	**soy**	**somos**
	eres	**sois**
	es	**son**

Imperfect **era**, etc.

Pret.	**fui**	**fuimos**
	fuiste	**fuisteis**
	fue	**fueron**

Pres. Subj. **sea**, etc.
Imp. Subj. **fuera/ese**, etc.
Imperative **sé**, sed

§67 SITUAR

Pres.	**sitúo**	situamos
	sitúas	situáis
	sitúa	**sitúan**

Pres.	**sitúe**	situemos
Subj.	**sitúes**	situéis
	sitúe	**sitúen**

§68 TAÑER

Pret.	tañí	tañimos
	tañiste	tañisteis
	tañó	**tañeron**

Imp. Subj. **tañera/ese**, etc.
Pres. Part. **tañendo**

§69 TENER

Pres.	**tengo**	tenemos
	tienes	tenéis
	tiene	**tienen**

Pret.	**tuve**	**tuvimos**
	tuviste	**tuvisteis**
	tuvo	**tuvieron**

Pres. Subj. **tenga**, etc.
Imp. Subj. **tuviera/iese**, etc.
Fut./Cond. **tendré/tendría**, etc.
Imperative **ten**, tened

§70 TOCAR

Pret. **toqué**, tocaste, etc.
Pres. Subj. **toque**, etc.

§71 TORCER

Pres.	**tuerzo**	torcemos
	tuerces	torcéis
	tuerce	**tuercen**

Pres.	**tuerza**	**torzamos**
Subj.	**tuerzas**	**torzáis**
	tuerza	**tuerzan**

§72 TRAER

Pres. **traigo**, traes, etc.

Pret.	**traje**	**trajimos**
	trajiste	**trajisteis**
	trajo	**trajeron**

Pres. Subj. **traiga**, etc.
Imp. Subj. **trajera/ese**, etc.
Pres. Part. **trayendo**
Past Part. **traído**

§73 TROCAR

Pres.	**trueco**	trocamos
	truecas	trocáis
	trueca	**truecan**

Pret. **troqué**, trocaste, etc.

Pres.	**trueque**	**troquemos**
Subj.	**trueques**	**troquéis**
	trueque	**truequen**

§74 VALER

Pres. **valgo**, vales, etc.
Pres. Subj. **valga**, etc.
Fut./Cond. **valdrá/valdría**, etc.

§75 VENCER

Pres. **venzo**, vences, etc.
Pres. Subj. **venza**, etc.

§76 VENIR

Pres.	**vengo**	venimos
	vienes	venís
	viene	**vienen**

Pret.	**vine**	**vinimos**
	viniste	**vinisteis**
	vino	**vinieron**

Pres. Subj. **venga**, etc.
Imp. Subj. **viniera/iese**, etc.
Fut./Cond. **vendrá/vendría**, etc.
Imperative **ven**, venid
Pres. Part. **viniendo**

§77 VER

Pres. **veo**, ves, etc.
Imperfect **veía**, etc.

Pret.	**vi**	vimos
	viste	visteis
	vio	vieron

Pres. Subj. **vea**, etc.
Past Part. **visto**

§78 VOLVER

Pres.	**vuelvo**	volvemos
	vuelves	volvéis
	vuelve	**vuelven**

Pres.	**vuelva**	volvamos
Subj.	**vuelvas**	volváis
	vuelva	**vuelvan**

Pres. **yazco***, yaces, etc.
*[alternate forms: **yazgo** or **yago**]
Pres. Subj. **yazca***, etc.
*[alternate forms: **yazga** or **yaga**]
Imperative **yaz** or yace, yaced

§80 IRREGULAR PAST
PARTICIPLES
In addition to verbs already mentioned
in this section, the following verbs and
their compounds have irregular past
participles.

abrir	**abierto**
cubrir	**cubierto**
escribir	**escrito**
freír	**frito**
imprimir	**impreso**
romper	**roto**

VERBOS IRREGULARES DEL INGLÉS

La siguiente lista de verbos da el infinitivo, el pretérito y el participio pasivo de los verbos irregulares del inglés. No se incluyen las formas compuestas con los prefijos be-, for-, mis-, over-, out-, re-, with-, un-, under-, que tienen la misma conjugación.

abide abided *o* abode, abided *o* abode
arise arose, arisen
awake awoke, awaked
be was, been
bear bore, born *o* borne
beat beat, beaten *o* beat
begin began, begun
bend bent, bent
beseech besought *o* beseeched, besought *o* beseeched
bet bet *o* betted, bet *o* betted
bid bade *o* bid, bidden *o* bid
bide bided *o* bode, bided
bind bound, bound
bite bit, bitten
bleed bled, bled
blend blended *o* blent, blended *o* blent
bless blessed *o* blest, blessed *o* blest
blow blew, blown
break broke, broken
breed bred, bred
bring brought, brought
build built, built
burn burned *o* burnt, burned *o* burnt
buy bought, bought
cast cast, cast
catch caught, caught
chide chided *o* chid, chided *o* chid
choose chose, chosen
cleave cleft *o* cleaved, cleft *o* cleaved
cling clung, clung
clothe clothed *o* clad, clothed *o* clad
come came, come
cost cost, cost
creep crept, crept
crow crowed *o* crew, crowed
curse cursed *o* curst, cursed *o* curst
cut cut, cut
deal dealt, dealt
dig dug, dug
dive dived *o* dove, dived

do did, done
draw drew, drawn
dream dreamed *o* dreamt, dreamed *o* dreamt
drink drank, drunk
drive drove, driven
dwell dwelled *o* dwelt, dwelled *o* dwelt
eat ate, eaten
fall fell, fallen
feed fed, fed
feel felt, felt
fight fought, fought
find found, found
flee fled, fled
fling flung, flung
fly flew, flown
forsake forsook, forsaken
freeze froze, frozen
get got, got *o* gotten
gild gilded *o* gilt, gilded *o* gilt
gird girded *o* girt, girded *o* girt
give gave, given
go went, gone
grind ground, ground
grow grew, grown
hang hung, hung
have had, had
hear heard, heard
hew hewed, hewed *o* hewn
hide hid, hidden *o* hid
hit hit, hit
hold held, held
hurt hurt, hurt
keep kept, kept
kneel knelt *o* kneeled, knelt *o* kneeled
knit knit *o* knitted, knit *o* knitted
know knew, known
lade laded, laded *o* laden
lay laid, laid
lead led, led
lean leaned *o* leant, leaned *o* leant
leap leaped *o* leapt, leaped *o* leapt
learn learned *o* learnt, learned *o* learnt
leave left, left
lend lent, lent
let let, let
lie lay, lain
light lighted *o* lit, lighted *o* lit

lose   lost, lost
make   made, made
mean   meant, meant
meet   met, met
mow   mowed, mowed *o* mown
pay   paid, paid
prove   proved, proved *o* proven
put   put, put
quit   quit *o* quitted, quit *o* quitted
read   read, read
rend   rended *o* rent, rended *o* rent
rid   rid *o* ridded, rid *o* ridded
ride   rode, ridden
ring   rang, rung
rise   rose, risen
run   ran, run
saw   sawed, sawed *o* sawn
say   said, said
see   saw, seen
seek   sought, sought
sell   sold, sold
send   sent, sent
set   set, set
sew   sewed, sewn *o* sewed
shake   shook, shaken
shave   shaved, shaved *o* shaven
shear   sheared, sheared *o* shorn
shed   shed, shed
shine   shone *o* shined, shone *o* shined
shoe   shod, shod *o* shodden
shoot   shot, shot
show   showed, shown *o* showed
shrink   shrank *o* shrunk, shrunk *o* shrunken
shut   shut, shut
sing   sang, sung
sink   sank *o* sunk, sunk
sit   sat, sat
slay   slew, slain
sleep   slept, slept
slide   slid, slid
sling   slung, slung
slink   slunk, slunk
slit   slit, slit
smell   smelled *o* smelt, smelled *o* smelt
smite   smote, smitten *o* smote
sow   sowed, sown *o* sowed
speak   spoke, spoken
speed   sped *o* speeded, sped *o* speeded

spend   spent, spent
spill   spilled *o* spilt, spilled *o* spilt
spit   spat *o* spit, spat *o* spit
spin   spun, spun
split   split, split
spoil   spoiled *o* spoilt, spoiled *o* spoilt
spread   spread, spread
spring   sprang *o* sprung, sprung
stand   stood, stood
stave   staved *o* stove, staved *o* stove
steal   stole, stolen
stick   stuck, stuck
sting   stung, stung
stink   stank *o* stunk, stunk
strew   strewed, strewed *o* strewn
stride   strode, stridden
strike   struck, struck *o* stricken
string   strung, strung
strive   strove *o* strived, striven *o* strived
swear   swore, sworn
sweat   sweat *o* sweated, sweat *o* sweated
sweep   swept, swept
swell   swelled, swelled *o* swollen
swim   swam, swum
swing   swung, swung
take   took, taken
teach   taught, taught
tear   tore, torn
tell   told, told
think   thought, thought
thrive   throve *o* thrived, thrived *o* thriven
throw   threw, thrown
thrust   thrust, thrust
tread   trod, trodden *o* trod
wake   woke *o* waked, waked *o* woken
wear   wore, worn
weave   wove *o* weaved, woven *o* weaved
wed   wedded, wed *o* wedded
weep   wept, wept
wet   wet *o* wetted, wet *o* wetted
win   won, won
wind   wound, wound
wrap   wrapt *o* wrapped, wrapt *o* wrapped
wring   wrung, wrung
write   wrote, written

PLACES, PEOPLES, AND LANGUAGES

♦ (of) place, people, nationality   ◊ language

A·dri·at·ic Sea   Mar Adriático
Ae·ge·an Sea   Mar Egeo
Af·ghan·i·stan   Afganistán
   ♦ Af·ghan   afgano
Af·ri·ca   África
   ♦ Af·ri·can   africano
African American   afroamericano
Al·ba·ni·a   Albania
   ♦◊ Al·ba·ni·an   albanés

Al·ge·ri·a   Argelia
   ♦ Al·ge·ri·an   argelino
Al·giers   Argel
Alps   Alpes
Am·a·zon   Amazonas
A·mer·i·ca   América; *(U.S.A.)* Estados Unidos
   ♦ A·mer·i·can   americano; *(of U.S.A.)* estadounidense, norteamericano

American Indian   indio americano
Am·er·ind/in·di·an   amerindio
An·da·lu·sia   Andalucía
♦ An·da·lu·sian   andaluz
An·des   Andes
♦ An·de·an   andino
An·glo   angloamericano
An·glo-A·mer·i·can   angloamericano
Ant·arc·ti·ca   Antártida
♦ Ant·arc·tic   antártico
Ar·ab   árabe
A·ra·bia   Arabia
♦ A·ra·bi·an   árabe
Ar·a·bic   arábigo, árabe
Arc·tic Ocean   océano Ártico
Ar·gen·ti·na   Argentina
♦ Ar·gen·tine, Ar·gen·tin·i·an   argentino
A·sia   Asia
♦ A·sian   asiático
At·lan·tic Ocean   océano Atlántico
Aus·tral·a·sia   Australasia
Aus·tra·lia   Australia
♦ Aus·tra·lian   australiano
Aus·tri·a   Austria
♦ Aus·tri·an   austríaco
A·zores   Azores
Az·tec   azteca
Bal·e·ar·ic Islands   Islas Baleares
Bal·kans   Balcanes
♦ Bal·kan   balcánico
Bal·tic Sea   Mar Báltico
♦ Baltic   báltico
Ban·gla·desh   Bangladesh
Basque   vasco
Bed·ou·in   beduino
Bel·gium   Bélgica
♦ Bel·gian   belga
Be·lize   Belice
Beth·le·hem   Belén
Bo·he·mi·an   bohemio
Bo·liv·i·a   Bolivia
♦ Bo·liv·i·an   boliviano
Bos·ni·a-Her·ze·go·vi·na   Bosnia Herzegovina
Bra·zil   Brasil
♦ Bra·zil·ian   brasileño
Brit·ain   Gran Bretaña
♦ Brit·ish   británico
♦ Brit·on   británico
British Isles   Islas Británicas
Brit·ta·ny   Bretaña
♦ ◊ Bret·on   bretón
Bul·gar·i·a   Bulgaria
♦ ◊ Bul·gar·i·an   búlgaro
Cam·bo·di·a   Camboya
♦ Cam·bo·di·an   camboyano
Ca·na·da   Canadá
♦ Ca·na·di·an   canadiense
Ca·nar·y Islands   Islas Canarias
Car·ib   caribe
Car·ib·be·an Sea   Mar Caribe
♦ Caribbean   caribe
Cas·tile   Castilla
♦ Cas·til·ian   castellano
Cat·a·lo·nia   Cataluña
♦ Cat·a·lo·nian ♦ ◊ Cat·a·lan   catalán
Celt   celta
♦ ◊ Celt·ic ♦ céltico ◊ celta

Central America   América Central
♦ Central American   centroamericano
Chi·ca·no   chicano
Chil·e   Chile
♦ Chil·e·an   chileno
Chi·na   China
♦ ◊ Chi·nese   chino
China, People's Republic of   República Popular de China
China, Republic of   República de China (Taiwán)
Co·lom·bi·a   Colombia
♦ Co·lom·bi·an   colombiano
Con·go, Democratic Republic of   República Democrática del Congo (Zaire)
♦ Con·go·lese   congoleño, congolés
Cos·ta Ri·ca   Costa Rica
♦ Cos·ta Ri·can   costarriqueño, costarricense
Cro·a·tia   Croacia
♦ ◊ Cro·a·tian   croata
Cu·ba   Cuba
♦ Cu·ban   cubano
Cy·prus   Chipre
♦ Cyp·ri·an   chipriota
Czech Republic   República Checa
♦ ◊ Czech   checo
Dan·ube   Danubio
Den·mark   Dinamarca
♦ Dane ♦ ◊ Dan·ish   dinamarqués, danés
Do·min·i·can Republic   República Dominicana
♦ Dominican   dominicano
Dutch   holandés
East Indies   Indias Orientales
Ec·ua·dor   Ecuador
♦ Ec·ua·dor·ian   ecuatoriano
E·gypt   Egipto
♦ E·gyp·tian   egipcio
El Sal·va·dor   El Salvador
♦ Sal·va·do·ran/ri·an   salvadoreño
Eng·land   Inglaterra
♦ ◊ Eng·lish   inglés
English Channel   Canal de la Mancha
Eur·a·sian   eurasiático
Eu·rope   Europa
♦ Eu·ro·pe·an   europeo
Fi·li·pi·no   filipino
Fin·land   Finlandia
♦ Finn   finlandés
♦ ◊ Finn·ish   finlandés
France   Francia
♦ ◊ French   francés
Gael·ic   gaélico
Ga·li·cia   Galicia
♦ Ga·li·cian   gallego
Ger·ma·ny   Alemania
♦ ◊ Ger·man   alemán
Goth·ic   gótico
Great Britain   Gran Bretaña
Greece   Grecia
♦ ◊ Greek   griego
Gua·te·ma·la   Guatemala
♦ Gua·te·ma·lan   guatemalteco
Gui·a·na   Guayana
Guy·a·na   Guyana
♦ Guy·a·nese   guyanés
Gyp·sy   gitano

Hague, The La Haya
Hai·ti Haití
 ♦ Hai·tian haitiano
Ha·van·a La Habana
 ♦ Ha·van·an habanero
He·brew hebreo
Hel·len·ic helénico
Hin·di hindi
Hol·land Holanda
 ♦◊ Dutch holandés
Hon·du·ras Honduras
 ♦ Hon·du·ran hondureño
Hun·ga·ry Hungría
 ♦◊ Hun·gar·i·an húngaro
I·be·ri·a Iberia
 ♦ I·be·ri·an ibérico
Ice·land Islandia
 ♦ Ice·land·er ♦◊ Ice·land·ic islandés
In·ca inca
 ♦ In·can incaico
In·di·a India
 ♦ In·di·an indio, hindú
Indian Ocean océano Índico
In·dies Indias
In·do·chi·na Indochina
In·do·ne·sia Indonesia
 ♦◊ In·do·ne·sian indonesio
I·ran Irán
 ♦ I·ran·i·an iraní
I·raq Iraq
 ♦ I·raq·i iraquí
Ire·land Irlanda
 ♦◊ I·rish irlandés
Is·ra·el Israel
 ♦ Is·rae·li israelí, israelita
It·a·ly Italia
 ♦◊ I·tal·ian italiano
Ja·mai·ca Jamaica
 ♦ Ja·mai·can jamaiquino, jamaicano
Ja·pan Japón
 ♦◊ Jap·a·nese japonés
Je·ru·sa·lem Jerusalén
Jor·dan Jordania
 ♦ Jor·da·ni·an jordano
Ken·ya Kenya
 ♦ Ken·yan keniano
Ko·re·a Corea
 ♦◊ Ko·re·an coreano
Korea, Democratic People's Republic
 of República Popular Democrática de
 Corea (Corea del Norte)
Korea, Republic of República de Corea
 (Corea del Sur)
La·os Laos
 ♦◊ La·o·tian laosiano
Lat·in ♦ latino ◊ latín
Latin America América Latina,
 Latinoamérica
 ♦ Latin American latinoamericano
Leb·a·non Líbano
 ♦ Leb·a·nese libanés
Lib·y·a Libia
 ♦ Lib·y·an libio
Lon·don Londres
 ♦ Lon·don·er Londinense
Lux·em·bourg Luxemburgo
 ♦ Lux·em·bourg·i·an luxemburgués
Ma·drid Madrid
Ma·gel·lan, Strait of Estrecho de

Magallanes
Ma·jor·ca Mallorca
Ma·lay·sia Malasia
 ♦ Ma·lay·sian malasio
Ma·ya, Ma·yan maya
Med·i·ter·ra·ne·an Sea Mar
 Mediterráneo
 ♦ Mediterranean mediterráneo
Mex·i·co México
 ♦ Mex·i·can mexicano
Mi·nor·ca Menorca
Mon·go·li·a Mongolia
 ♦◊ Mon·gol, Mon·go·li·an mongol
Mo·roc·co Marruecos
 ♦ Mo·roc·can marroquí
Neth·er·lands Países Bajos
New World Nuevo Mundo, América
New York Nueva York
 ♦ New York·er neoyorquino
New Zea·land Nueva Zelandia
 ♦ New Zea·land·er neozelandés
Nic·a·ra·gua Nicaragua
 ♦ Nic·a·ra·guan nicaragüense
Ni·ge·ri·a Nigeria
 ♦ Ni·ge·ri·an nigeriano
Nile Nilo
North America América del Norte,
 Norteamérica
 ♦ North American norteamericano
North Pole Polo Norte
Nor·way Noruega
 ♦◊ Nor·we·gian noruego
Oc·ci·dent Occidente
Old World Viejo Mundo
O·ri·ent Oriente
Pa·cif·ic Ocean océano Pacífico
Pak·i·stan Pakistán
 ♦ Pak·i·stan·i pakistaní
Pal·es·tine Palestina
 ♦ Pal·es·tin·i·an palestino
Pan·a·ma Panamá
 ♦ Pan·a·ma·ni·an panameño
Par·a·guay Paraguay
 ♦ Par·a·guay·an paraguayo
Par·is París
 ♦ Pa·ri·sian parisiense
Per·sian ♦ pérsico ◊ persa
Persian Gulf Golfo Pérsico
Pe·ru Perú
 ♦ Pe·ru·vi·an peruano
Phil·ip·pines Filipinas
 ♦ Phil·ip·pine filipino
 ♦◊ Fil·i·pi·no filipino
Po·land Polonia
 ♦ Pole ♦◊ Po·lish polaco
Pol·y·ne·sia Polinesia
 ♦ Pol·y·ne·sian polinesio
Por·tu·gal Portugal
 ♦◊ Por·tu·guese portugués
Puer·to Ri·co Puerto Rico
 ♦ Puer·to Ri·can puertorriqueño
Pyr·e·nees Pirineos
Quech·ua quechua
Rocky Mountains Montañas Rocosas
Rome Roma
 ♦ Ro·man romano
Ru·ma·ni·a o Ro·ma·ni·a Rumania
 ♦◊ Ru·ma·ni·an o Ro·ma·nian rumano
Rus·sia Rusia

◆◇ Rus·sian ruso
Sal·va·do·ran, Sal·va·do·ri·an
  salvadoreño
Sau·di Arabia Arabia Saudita
  ◆ Saudi, Saudi Arabian árabe saudita
Scan·di·na·vi·a Escandinavia
  ◆ Scan·di·na·vi·an escandinavo
Scot·land Escocia
  ◆ Scot, Scotch, Scot·tish escocés
Sem·ite semita
  ◆ Se·mit·ic semítico, semita
Ser·bo-Cro·a·tian serbocroata
Slav·ic eslavo
Slo·va·ki·a Eslovaquia
  ◆◇ Slo·vak eslovaco
Slo·ve·ni·a Eslovenia
  ◆◇ Slo·vene esloveno
South Africa África del Sur
  ◆ South African sudafricano
South America América del Sur,
  Sudamérica
  ◆ South American sudamericano
South Pole Polo Sur
So·vi·et Socialist Republics, Union of
  Unión de Repúblicas Socialistas
  Soviéticas (antes de 1990)
Soviet Union Unión Soviética (antes de
  1990)
  ◆ Soviet soviético
Spain España
  ◆ Span·iard español
  ◆◇ Span·ish español
Spanish America Hispanoamérica
  ◆ Span·ish-A·mer·i·can
  hispanoamericano
Su·ri·nam Suriname
  ◆ Su·ri·na·mese surinamés
Swe·den Suecia
  ◆ Swede sueco
  ◆◇ Swed·ish sueco
Swit·zer·land Suiza

◆ Swiss suizo
Syr·i·a Siria
  ◆ Syr·i·an sirio
Tai·wan Taiwán
  ◆ Tai·wan·ese taiwanés
Thai·land Tailandia
  ◆◇ Thai tailandés
To·ky·o Tokio
Tol·tec tolteca
tropic of Can·cer trópico de Cáncer
tropic of Cap·ri·corn trópico de
  Capricornio
Troy Troya
  ◆ Tro·jan troyano
Tur·key Turquía
  ◆ Turk turco
  ◆◇ Turk·ish turco
U·ru·guay Uruguay
  ◆ U·ru·guay·an uruguayo
U.S.A. EE. UU., E.U.
U.S.S.R U.R.S.S
United Arab E·mir·ates Emiratos
  Árabes Unidos
United Kingdom Reino Unido
United States of America Estados
  Unidos de América
Vat·i·can Vaticano
Ven·e·zue·la Venezuela
  ◆ Ven·e·zue·lan venezolano
Viet·nam Viet Nam
  ◆◇ Viet·nam·ese vietnamita
Wales Gales
  ◆◇ Welsh galés
West Indies Indias Occidentales,
  Antillas
  ◆ West Indian antillano
Yid·dish yiddish
Yu·go·sla·vi·a Yugoslavia
  ◆ Yu·go·sla·vi·an, Yu·go·slav
  yugoslavo

LUGARES, PUEBLOS E IDIOMAS

◆ (de) lugar, pueblo, nacionalidad   ◇ idioma

A·dri·á·ti·co, Mar Adriatic Sea
Af·ga·nis·tán Afghanistan
  ◆ af·ga·no Afghan
Á·fri·ca Africa
  ◆ a·fri·ca·no African
África del Sur South Africa
  ◆ su·da·fri·ca·no South African
a·fro·a·me·ri·ca·no African American
Al·ba·nia Albania
  ◆◇ al·ba·nés Albanian
A·le·ma·nia Germany
  ◆◇ a·le·mán German
Al·pes Alps
A·ma·zo·nas Amazon
A·mé·ri·ca America
  ◆ a·me·ri·ca·no American
América Central Central America
América del Norte North America;
  (E.U.) United States
América del Sur South America
América Latina Latin America
a·me·rin·dio Amerind, Amerindian
An·da·lu·cí·a Andalusia
  ◆ an·da·luz Andalusian

An·des Andes
  ◆ an·di·no Andean
an·glo·a·me·ri·ca·no Anglo-American
An·tár·ti·da Antarctica
  ◆ an·tár·ti·co Antarctic
An·ti·llas West Indies
  ◆ an·ti·lla·no West Indian
A·ra·bia Arabia
  ◆◇ á·ra·be ◆ Arab, Arabian
  ◆◇ Arabic
A·ra·bia Sau·di·ta Saudi Arabia
  ◆ á·ra·be sau·di·ta Saudi Arabian,
  Saudi
a·rá·bi·co/go ◆ Arabian ◇ Arabic
Ar·gel Algiers
Ar·ge·lia Algeria
  ◆ ar·ge·li·no Algerian
Ar·gen·ti·na Argentina
  ◆ ar·gen·ti·no Argentine, Argentinian
Ár·ti·co, océano Arctic Ocean
A·sia Asia
  ◆ a·siá·ti·co Asian
At·lán·ti·co, océano Atlantic Ocean
Aus·tra·la·sia Australasia

Aus·tra·lia   Australia
♦ aus·tra·lia·no   Australian
Aus·tria   Austria
♦ aus·trí·a·co   Austrian
A·zo·res   Azores
az·te·ca   Aztec
Bal·ca·nes   Balkans
♦ bal·cá·ni·co   Balkan
Ba·le·a·res, Islas   Balearic Islands
Bál·ti·co, Mar   Baltic Sea
♦ báltico   Baltic
Ban·gla·desh   Bangladesh
be·dui·no   Bedouin
Be·lén   Bethlehem
Bél·gi·ca   Belgium
♦ bel·ga   Belgian
Be·li·ce   Belize
bo·he·mio   Bohemian
Bo·li·via   Bolivia
♦ bo·li·via·no   Bolivian
Bos·nia Her·ze·go·vi·na   Bosnia-Herzegovina
Bra·sil   Brazil
♦ bra·si·le·ño   Brazilian
Bre·ta·ña   Brittany
♦◊ bre·tón   Breton
Bri·tá·ni·cas, Islas   British Isles
♦ bri·tá·ni·co   British, Briton
Bul·ga·ria   Bulgaria
♦◊ búl·ga·ro   Bulgarian
Cam·bo·ya   Cambodia
♦ cam·bo·ya·no   Cambodian
Ca·na·dá   Canada
♦ ca·na·dien·se   Canadian
Ca·nal de la Man·cha   English Channel
Ca·na·rias   Canary Islands
Ca·ri·be, Mar   Caribbean Sea
♦ caribe   Carib, Caribbean
Cas·ti·lla   Castile
♦ cas·te·lla·no   Castilian
Ca·ta·lu·ña   Catalonia
♦◊ ca·ta·lán   ♦ Catalonian   ♦◊ Catalan
cel·ta   ♦ Celt   ◊ Celtic
cen·tro·a·me·ri·ca·no   Central American
chi·ca·no   Chicano
Chi·le   Chile
♦ chi·le·no   Chilean
Chi·na   China
♦◊ chi·no   Chinese
China, República de   Republic of China
(Taiwan)
China, República Popular de   People's
Republic of China
Chi·pre   Cyprus
♦ chi·prio·ta   Cypriot
Co·lom·bia   Colombia
♦ co·lom·bia·no   Colombian
Con·go, República Democrática del
Democratic Republic of Congo (Zaire)
♦ con·go·le·ño/lés   Congolese
Co·re·a   Korea
♦◊ co·re·a·no   Korean
Corea, República de   Republic of
Korea (South Korea)
Corea, República Popular Democrática
de   Democratic People's Republic of
Korea (North Korea)
Cos·ta Ri·ca   Costa Rica
♦ cos·ta·rri·cen·se/que·ño   Costa
Rican

Cro·a·cia   Croatia
♦◊ cro·a·ta   Croatian
Cu·ba   Cuba
♦ cu·ba·no   Cuban
Da·nu·bio   Danube
Di·na·mar·ca   Denmark
♦◊ da·nés, di·na·mar·qués   ♦ Dane
♦◊ Danish
do·mi·ni·ca·no   Dominican
E·cua·dor   Ecuador
♦ e·cua·to·ria·no   Ecuadorian
EE. UU., E.U.   U.S.A.
E·ge·o, Mar   Aegean Sea
E·gip·to   Egypt
♦ e·gip·cio   Egyptian
El Sal·va·dor   El Salvador
♦ sal·va·do·re·ño   Salvadoran,
Salvadorian
E·mi·ra·tos Á·ra·bes U·ni·dos   United
Arab Emirates
Es·can·di·na·via   Scandinavia
♦ es·can·di·na·vo   Scandinavian
Es·co·cia   Scotland
♦ es·co·cés   Scot, Scotch, Scottish
es·la·vo   Slavic
E·slo·va·quia   Slovakia
♦◊ slo·va·co   Slovak
E·slo·ve·nia   Slovenia
♦◊ esloveno   Slovene
Es·pa·ña   Spain
♦◊ es·pa·ñol   ♦ Spaniard   ♦◊ Spanish
Es·ta·dos U·ni·dos   United States
Estados Unidos de América   United
States of America
♦ es·ta·dou·ni·den·se   American, of
the United States of America
eu·ra·siá·ti·co   Eurasian
Eu·ro·pa   Europe
♦ eu·ro·pe·o   European
Fi·li·pi·nas   Philippines
♦◊ fi·li·pi·no   ♦ Philippine   ♦◊ Filipino
Fin·lan·dia   Finland
♦◊ fin·lan·dés   ♦ Finn   ♦◊ Finnish
Fran·cia   France
♦◊ fran·cés   French
ga·é·li·co   Gaelic
Ga·les   Wales
♦◊ ga·lés   Welsh
Ga·li·cia   Galicia
♦ ga·lle·go   Galician
gi·ta·no   Gypsy
gó·ti·co   Gothic
Gran Bre·ta·ña   Great Britain, Britain
Gre·cia   Greece
♦◊ grie·go   Greek
Gua·te·ma·la   Guatemala
♦ gua·te·mal·te·co   Guatemalan
Gua·ya·na   Guiana
Gu·ya·na   Guyana
♦ guyanés   Guyanese
Ha·ba·na, La   Havana
♦ ha·ba·ne·ro   Havanan
Hai·tí   Haiti
♦ hai·tia·no   Haitian
Ha·ya, La   The Hague
he·bre·o   Hebrew
he·lé·ni·co   Hellenic
hin·di   Hindi
His·pa·no·a·mé·ri·ca   Spanish America

♦ his·pa·no·a·me·ri·ca·no   Spanish-American
Ho·lan·da   Holland
♦◊ ho·lan·dés   Dutch
Hon·du·ras   Honduras
♦ hon·du·re·ño   Honduran
Hun·ga·ria   Hungary
♦◊ hún·ga·ro   Hungarian
I·be·ria   Iberia
♦ i·bé·ri·co   Iberian
in·ca   Inca, Incan
In·dia   India
♦ in·dio   Indian
In·dias   Indies
Indias Occidentales   West Indies
Indias Orientales   East Indies
Ín·di·co, océano   Indian Ocean
in·dio   Indian
indio americano   American Indian
In·do·chi·na   Indochina
In·do·ne·sia   Indonesia
♦ in·do·ne·sio   Indonesian
In·gla·te·rra   England
♦◊ in·glés   English
I·rán   Iran
♦ i·ra·ní   Iranian
I·raq   Iraq
♦ i·ra·qí   Iraqi
Ir·lan·da   Ireland
♦◊ ir·lan·dés   Irish
Is·lan·dia   Iceland
♦◊ is·lan·dés   ♦ Icelander ♦◊ Icelandic
Is·ra·el   Israel
♦ is·ra·e·lí/li·ta   Israeli
I·ta·lia   Italy
♦◊ i·ta·lia·no   Italian
Ja·mai·ca   Jamaica
♦ ja·mai·qui·no/ca·no   Jamaican
Ja·pón   Japan
♦◊ ja·po·nés   Japanese
Je·ru·sa·lén   Jerusalem
Jor·da·nia   Jordan
♦ jor·da·no   Jordanian
Ken·ya   Kenya
♦ ke·nia·no   Kenyan
La·os   Laos
♦◊ la·o·sia·no   Laotian, Lao
la·tín   Latin
la·ti·no   Latin
La·ti·no·a·mé·ri·ca   Latin America
♦ la·ti·no·a·me·ri·ca·no   Latin-American, Latin American
Lí·ba·no   Lebanon
♦ li·ba·nés   Lebanese
Li·bia   Libya
♦ li·bio   Libyan
Lon·dres   London
Lu·xem·bur·go   Luxembourg
♦ lu·xem·bur·gués   Luxembourgian
Ma·drid   Madrid
♦ ma·dri·le·ño   of Madrid
Ma·ga·lla·nes, Estrecho de   Strait of Magellan
Ma·la·sia   Malasia
♦ ma·la·sio   Malaysian
Ma·llor·ca   Majorca
Ma·rrue·cos   Morocco
♦ ma·rro·quí   Moroccan

ma·ya   Mayan, Maya
Me·di·te·rrá·ne·o, Mar   Mediterranean Sea
♦ mediterráneo   Mediterranean
Me·nor·ca   Minorca
Mé·xi·co   Mexico
♦ me·xi·ca·no   Mexican
Mon·go·lia   Mongolia
♦◊ mon·gol   Mongol, Mongolian
Ni·ca·ra·gua   Nicaragua
♦ ni·ca·ra·güen·se   Nicaraguan
Ni·ge·ria   Nigeria
♦ ni·ge·ria·no   Nigerian
Ni·lo   Nile
Nor·te·a·mé·ri·ca   North America
♦ nor·te·a·me·ri·ca·no   American, North American
No·rue·ga   Norway
♦◊ no·rue·go   Norwegian
Nueva York   New York
♦ ne·o·yor·qui·no   New Yorker
Nueva Ze·lan·dia   New Zealand
♦ ne·o·ze·lan·dés   New Zealander
Nuevo Mundo   New World, America
Oc·ci·den·te   Occident, West
O·rien·te   Orient, East
Pa·cí·fi·co, océano   Pacific Ocean
Pa·í·ses Ba·jos   Netherlands
Pa·kis·tán   Pakistan
♦ pa·kis·ta·ní   Pakistani
Pa·les·ti·na   Palestine
♦ pa·les·ti·no   Palestinian
Pa·na·má   Panama
♦ pa·na·me·ño   Panamanian
Pa·ra·guay   Paraguay
♦ pa·ra·gua·yo   Paraguayan
Pa·rís   Paris
♦ pa·ri·sien·se   Parisian
per·sa   Persian
Pér·si·co, Gol·fo   Persian Gulf
Pe·rú   Peru
♦ pe·rua·no   Peruvian
Pi·ri·ne·os   Pyrenees
Po·li·ne·sia   Polynesia
♦ po·li·ne·sio   Polynesian
Po·lo·nia   Poland
♦◊ po·la·co   ♦ Pole ♦◊ Polish
Po·lo Norte   North Pole
Polo Sur   South Pole
Por·tu·gal   Portugal
♦◊ por·tu·gués   Portuguese
Puer·to Ri·co   Puerto Rico
♦ puer·to·rri·que·ño   Puerto Rican
que·chua   Quechua
Rei·no U·ni·do   United Kingdom
Re·pú·bli·ca Che·ca   Czech Republic
♦◊ che·co   Czech
Re·pú·bli·ca Do·mi·ni·ca·na   Dominican Republic
♦ do·mi·ni·ca·no   Dominican
Ro·co·sas, Mon·ta·ñas   Rocky Mountains
Ro·ma   Rome
♦ ro·ma·no   Roman
Ru·ma·nia   Rumania or Romania
♦◊ ru·ma·no   Rumanian or Romanian
Ru·sia   Russia
♦◊ ru·so   Russian
sal·va·do·re·ño   Salvadoran

se·mi·ta Semite
 ♦ se·mí·ti·co/mi·ta Semitic
ser·bo·cro·a·ta Serbo-Croatian
Si·ria Syria
 ♦ si·rio Syrian
so·vié·ti·co Soviet
Su·da·mé·ri·ca South America
 ♦ su·da·me·ri·ca·no South American
Sue·cia Sweden
 ♦◊ sue·co ♦◊ Swede ♦◊ Swedish
Sui·za Switzerland
 ♦ sui·zo Swiss
Su·ri·na·me Surinam
 ♦ su·ri·na·més Surinamese
Tai·lan·dia Thailand
 ♦◊ tai·lan·dés Thai
Tai·wán Taiwan
 ♦ tai·wa·nés Taiwanese
To·kio Tokyo
tol·te·ca Toltec
trópico de Cán·cer Tropic of Cancer
trópico de Cap·ri·cor·nio Tropic of
 Capricorn

Tro·ya Troy
 ♦ tro·ya·no Trojan
Tur·quí·a Turkey
 ♦◊ tur·co ♦ Turk ♦◊ Turkish
U.R.S.S. U.S.S.R.
U·nión de Re·pú·bli·cas So·cia·lis·tas
 So·vié·ti·cas Union of Soviet Socialist
 Republics (before 1990)
Unión So·vié·ti·ca Soviet Union (before
 1990)
 ♦ so·vié·ti·co Soviet
U·ru·guay Uruguay
 ♦ u·ru·gua·yo Uruguayan
vas·co Basque
Va·ti·ca·no Vatican
Ve·ne·zue·la Venezuela
 ♦ ve·ne·zo·la·no Venezuelan
Viejo Mundo Old World
Viet Nam Vietnam
 ♦◊ viet·na·mi·ta Vietnamese
yid·dish Yiddish
Yu·gos·la·via Yugoslavia
 ♦ yu·gos·la·vo Yugoslavian, Yugoslav

Geographic Labels / Rótulos Geográficos

AMER.	America/América
ARG.	Argentina
BOL.	Bolivia
C. AMER.	Central America/América Central
CARIB.	Caribbean/Caribe
CHILE	Chile
COL.	Colombia
C. RICA	Costa Rica
CUBA	Cuba
DOM. REP.	Dominican Republic/ República Dominicana
ECUAD.	Ecuador
E.U.	Estados Unidos
G.B.	Great Britain/Gran Bretaña
GUAT.	Guatemala
MEX.	Mexico/México
NIC.	Nicaragua
PAN.	Panama/Panamá
PAR.	Paraguay
PERU	Peru/Perú
P. RICO	Puerto Rico
R.P.	River Plate/Río de la Plata
SALV.	El Salvador
S. AMER.	South America/Sudamérica
SP.	Spain/España
URUG.	Uruguay
U.S.	United States
VEN.	Venezuela

COMPUTER TERMINOLOGY

The basic vocabulary of computers, such as *hardware, processor,* and *diskette,* is included in the main body of the Dictionary. The following list contains newer or less familiar terms, especially the vocabulary of home computers and the Internet. In some cases, such as *mouse* and *screen,* a ready equivalent exists in Spanish, but for many other terms there is no single translation that has yet gained universal acceptance. The translations given here are the most common ones in actual use today, including many anglicisms and neologisms.

backup I. n. copia de reserva *o* respaldo *o* seguridad, backup *m* **II.** tr. **♦ back up** hacer una copia de reserva (de) <back up a file to diskette *hacer una copia de reserva de un archivo en un diskette*>.
bandwidth n. ancho de banda.
boot I. tr. butear, iniciar, arrancar <boot a computer from a systems disk *butear una computadora con un disco del sistema*> **II.** n. autoarranque *m.*
browse tr. *(the Internet)* navegar (por); *(a list)* hojear.
browser n. navegador *m,* explorador *m.*
bulletin board n. pizarra (electrónica), tablero.
chat I. intr. charlar, chatear **II.** n. charla, chat *m* **♦ chat room** sala *o* canal *m* de charla.
circuit board n. placa *o* tarjeta de circuitos.
click I. n. click *m,* clica, pinche *m* **II.** intr. pulsar, pinchar, clickear <click on File to get the menu *pulsar sobre File para ver el menú*> **♦ double-click** pulsar doblemente, hacer un double-click.
cookie n. galleta.
crash I. intr. colgar, caer, chocar <we lost all our data when the disk drive crashed *perdimos toda nuestra información cuando la unidad de disco se colgó*> —tr. tumbar <a series of commands that crashed the computer *una secuencia de comandos que tumbó la computadora*> **II.** n. fallo (de sistema).
cut and paste tr. cortar y pegar.
cyberspace n. ciberespacio.
default I. n. (por) defecto <the default was set to on *estaba prendido por defecto*> **II.** intr. ser por defecto <the setting will default to zero *la propiedad será cero por defecto*>.
desktop publishing n. autoedición *f.*
directory n. directorio (de archivos).
disk drive n. unidad *f* de disco.
dot matrix n. matriz *f* de puntos.
download tr. bajar, descargar.
drag tr. arrastrar <drag the selected text into the next column *arrastrar el texto seleccionado hasta la próxima columna*>.
drive n. unidad *f* de disco.
driver n. controlador *m,* manejador *m.*
e-mail I. n. correo electrónico, email *m* <a whole screen of unread e-mail *una pantalla llena de correo electrónico sin leer*> **II.** tr. enviar *o* mandar por correo electrónico <please e-mail me with your answer *por favor envíame un correo electrónico con tu respuesta*>.
file n. archivo, fichero **♦ filename** n. nombre *m* de archivo *o* fichero.
file server n. servidor *m* de archivos.
firewall n. cortafuegos *m.*
format tr. formatear.
freeware n. programas *m* gratuitos.
graphics n. gráficos *m.*

hack intr. hackear, jaquear **♦ hack into** sabotear <hack into a computer system *sabotear un sistema de computación*>.
hit n. hit *m,* golpe *m.*
home page n. página principal, página inicial.
hyperlink n. enlace *m,* hiperenlace *m.*
hypertext n. hipertexto.
interface n. conectador *m* entre unidades (sistema).
Internet n. Internet *m,* Red *f.*
joystick n. palanca (de juego).
laptop n. portátil *m,* computadora portátil.
log intr. **♦ log in** or **on** conectarse *o* entrar (al sistema) **• log out** or **off** desconectarse *o* salir (del sistema).
motherboard n. placa madre.
mouse n. ratón *m* **♦ mousepad** n. alfombrilla de ratón.
newsgroup n. grupo de noticias, grupo de discusión.
overwrite tr. sobre-escribir.
password n. clave *f* (de acceso), contraseña, pasapalabra.
post I. tr. enviar, poner <post a message to a newsgroup *enviar una nota a un grupo de noticias*> **II.** n. mensaje *m,* nota.
reboot tr. apagar y prender, reiniciar.
record n. registro.
run tr. ejecutar, correr <the computer is running three applications simultaneously *la computadora está ejecutando tres aplicaciones simultáneamente*>.
save tr. grabar, salvar, guardar <save a file to disk *grabar un archivo a un disco*>.
scan tr. escudriñar <scan the hard disk for possible errors *escudriñar el disco duro buscando errores*>; *(a photograph)* escanear.
screen saver n. salvapantallas *m.*
scroll intr. enrollar **♦ scroll bar** barra de enrollar.
search engine n. buscador *m.*
spam I. n. correo basura, espam *m* **II.** tr. enviar correo basura a, espamear.
spreadsheet n. hoja de cálculo.
taskbar n. barra de tareas.
toolbar n. barra de herramientas.
trackball n. seguibola.
unformatted adj. sin formatear.
upgrade I. n. actualización *f,* upgrade *m* **II.** tr. actualizar —intr. hacer una actualización.
upload tr. subir <upload a file to the main server *subir un grupo de archivos al servidor principal*>.
username n. nombre *m* de usuario.
virtual reality n. realidad *f* virtual.
World Wide Web n. Red *f,* Telaraña mundial **♦ Web page** página web **• Website** sitio web, website *m.*
workstation n. consola, estación *f* de trabajo.

Spanish/English

A

a, A f. first letter of the Spanish alphabet.
a prep. *(dirección)* to, into, forward; *(destino)* in, at; *(lugar)* at, on, to; *(distancia)* to, up to; *(hora)* at, in; *(método)* on, in, by, with, according to; *(tasa)* at, per, a, by.
á·ba·co m. abacus.
a·bad m. abbot.
a·ba·de·sa f. abbess.
a·ba·dí·a f. abbey.
a·ba·jo I. adv. down; *(en una casa)* downstairs; *(posición)* below, underneath ♦ **echar a.** to demolish; POL. to overthrow • **hacia a.** downward(s) II. interj. down with <*¡a. el rey!* down with the king!>.
a·ba·lan·zar §04 tr. & reflex. to fling, hurl (oneself).
a·ba·li·zar §04 tr. to mark with buoys.
a·ba·lo·rio m. glass bead(s).
a·ban·de·ra·do m. standard-bearer.
a·ban·de·ra·mien·to m. registration (of a ship); POL. joining a cause.
a·ban·de·rar tr. to register (a ship); POL. to join (a cause).
a·ban·de·ri·zar §04 tr. to divide into factions —reflex. AMER. to join (a cause).
a·ban·do·na·do, a adj. abandoned; *(descuidado)* careless; *(desaliñado)* slovenly.
a·ban·do·nar tr. to abandon, desert; *(desertar)* to leave; *(renunciar)* to give up; *(descuidar)* to neglect —reflex. *(entregarse a)* to abandon oneself to; *(descuidarse)* to become slovenly.
a·ban·do·no m. abandonment; *(descuido)* neglect; *(desenfrenamiento)* abandon.
a·ba·ni·car §70 tr. & reflex. to fan (oneself).
a·ba·ni·co m. fan; MARIT. winch.
a·ba·ra·jar tr. R.P. *(parar)* to block, parry (a blow); *(agarrar)* to catch (in flight).
a·ba·ra·tar tr. to reduce (prices) —reflex. to become cheaper.
a·bar·car §70 tr. *(contener)* to embrace, cover; *(abrazar)* to embrace; *(divisar)* to take in; AMER. to stockpile.
a·ba·rra·mien·to m. *(lanzamiento)* hurling, hurtling; *(sacudimiento)* shaking.
a·ba·rran·car §70 tr. to form ditches in —intr. to run aground —reflex. *(caerse)* to fall into a ditch; *(atascarse)* to get into a fix.
a·ba·rro·ta·do, a adj. full, crowded.
a·ba·rro·tar tr. *(fortalecer)* to bar up; *(llenar)* to fill up; *(exceso)* to overstock; AMER. *(acaparar)* to stockpile.
a·ba·rro·te m. bundle ♦ pl. AMER. *(comestibles)* groceries; *(tienda)* grocery store.
a·ba·rro·te·rí·a f. C. AMER. hardware store.
a·ba·rro·te·ro, a m.f. AMER. hardware storekeeper.
a·bas·tar·dar tr. to bastardize —intr. to degenerate.

a·bas·te·ce·dor, ·ra m.f. supplier.
a·bas·te·cer §17 tr. to supply, provide *(de* with).
a·bas·te·ci·mien·to m. *(provisión)* supply; *(aprovisionamiento)* supplying.
a·bas·to m. supplying ♦ **dar a.** to produce to capacity • **no dar a. (a)** not to be able to keep up (with) ♦ pl. supplies, provisions.
a·ba·ta·tar·se reflex. AMER. to become embarrassed.
a·ba·ti·ble adj. collapsible, folding.
a·ba·ti·da·men·te adv. despondently.
a·ba·ti·do, a adj. despondent.
a·ba·ti·mien·to m. low spirits.
a·ba·tir tr. *(derribar)* to knock down, demolish; *(desanimar)* to depress, discourage —reflex. *(desanimarse)* to become discouraged; *(aves)* to swoop.
ab·di·ca·ción f. abdication.
ab·di·car §70 tr. & intr. *(resignar)* to abdicate.
ab·do·men m. abdomen.
ab·do·mi·nal adj. abdominal.
ab·duc·ción f. abduction.
ab·duc·tor I. adj. abducent II. m. abductor.
a·be·cé m. alphabet; *(rudimentos)* rudiments.
a·be·ce·da·rio m. alphabet.
a·be·dul m. birch.
a·be·ja f. bee.
a·be·jar m. apiary, beehive.
a·be·jo·rro m. bumblebee; *(pesado)* pest.
a·be·rra·ción f. aberration.
a·ber·tu·ra f. opening; *(hendidura)* crack, fissure; *(franqueza)* frankness; PHOTOG. aperture.
a·be·to m. fir.
a·be·tu·nar tr. *(embrear)* to tar; *(los zapatos)* to polish.
a·bier·to, a I. see abrir II. adj. open; *(raso)* open, clear; *(franco)* candid; *(sincero)* sincere; S. AMER. generous.
a·bi·ga·rra·do, a adj. variegated, multicolored.
a·bi·ga·rrar tr. to mottle, variegate.
a·bi·sa·grar tr. to hinge.
a·bi·se·lar tr. to bevel.
a·bis·mal adj. abysmal.
a·bis·mar tr. to overwhelm, depress —reflex. to yield, give oneself up *(en* to).
a·bis·mo m. abyss ♦ **estar al borde del a.** to be on the brink of disaster.
ab·ju·ra·ción f. abjuration, renunciation.
ab·ju·rar tr. to abjure, renounce.
a·blan·da·bre·vas m.f.inv. COLL. good-for-nothing.
a·blan·da·mien·to m. softening.
a·blan·dar tr. to soften; *(suavizar)* to mollify; *(mitigar)* to mitigate —intr. *(el viento)* to calm down; *(la nieve)* to thaw —reflex. to soften; *(calmarse)* to calm down.
a·blan·de m. AMER., AUTO. break-in (period).
a·blan·de·cer §17 tr. to soften.
a·bla·ti·vo m. ablative.
a·blu·ción f. ablution, washing.

ab·ne·ga·ción f. abnegation.

ab·ne·ga·do, a adj. unselfish.

ab·ne·gar §52 tr. to abnegate, renounce —reflex. to deny oneself.

a·bo·ca·do, a adj. involved, engaged (*a* in); (*vino*) mild, smooth.

a·bo·ca·mien·to m. (*acción*) biting; (*acercamiento*) approaching; (*reunión*) meeting.

a·bo·car §70 tr. (*asir*) to bite; (*escanciar*) to decant; (*acercar*) to bring near —intr. MARIT. to enter a channel —reflex. (*aproximarse*) to approach; ARG. to engage (*a* in).

a·bo·car·dar tr. to widen, ream.

a·bo·chor·na·do, a adj. suffocating; (*avergonzado*) ashamed.

a·bo·chor·nar tr. to suffocate; (*avergonzar*) to embarrass; (*hacer sonrojar*) to make blush —reflex. (*avergonzarse*) to become embarrassed; (*sonrojarse*) to blush; AGR. to parch.

a·bo·fe·te·ar tr. to slap.

a·bo·ga·cí·a f. law (profession).

a·bo·ga·do, a m.f. lawyer, attorney ♦ **a. del diablo** devil's advocate.

a·bo·gar §47 intr. (*defender*) to advocate, plead; (*interceder*) to intercede.

a·bo·len·go m. ancestry, lineage; (*patrimonio*) patrimony.

a·bo·li·ción f. abolition, repeal.

a·bo·li·cio·nis·ta m.f. abolitionist.

a·bo·lir §38 tr. to abolish, repeal.

a·bo·lla·do, a adj. dented; AMER., COLL. (*sin dinero*) penniless, broke.

a·bo·lla·du·ra f. dent.

a·bo·llar tr. to dent —reflex. to become dented.

a·bol·sar·se reflex. (*la ropa*) to become baggy; (*la piel*) to sag.

a·bom·ba·do, a adj. convex; AMER. (*aturdido*) stupefied; (*comida*) bad, spoiled.

a·bom·bar tr. to make convex; AMER. (*aturdir*) to stupefy —reflex. AMER. to go bad.

a·bo·mi·na·ble adj. abominable, detestable; (*desagradable*) abominable, disagreeable.

a·bo·mi·na·ción f. abomination.

a·bo·mi·nar tr. to abominate, detest.

a·bo·na·ble adj. payable, due.

a·bo·na·do, a m.f. subscriber, season ticket holder; (*viajero*) commuter.

a·bo·nar tr. (*acreditar*) to vouch for, guarantee; AGR. to fertilize; (*subscribir*) to subscribe to; (*pagar*) to pay ♦ **a. cuenta** to pay in installments —reflex. to subscribe.

a·bo·no m. (*estiércol*) fertilizer; (*billete*) subscription; AMER. payment, installment.

a·bor·dar tr. MARIT. to board; (*acercar*) to approach; (*emprender*) to tackle (a problem) —intr. MARIT. to dock.

a·bo·ri·gen adj. & m.f. aboriginal.

a·bo·rre·cer §17 tr. to hate, abhor.

a·bo·rre·ci·ble adj. hateful, abhorrent, loathsome.

a·bo·rre·ci·mien·to m. hatred, loathing.

a·bor·tar tr. & intr. to abort.

a·bor·to m. abortion; FIG. failure; COLL. (*feo*) ugly person.

a·bo·to·nar tr. & reflex. to button (up) —intr. to bud.

a·bo·ve·da·do m. ARCHIT. vaulting.

a·bo·ve·dar tr. to arch, vault.

a·bo·za·lar tr. to muzzle, put a muzzle on.

a·bra·ca·da·bra m. abracadabra.

a·bra·sa·dor, ·ra/san·te adj. burning, scorching.

a·bra·sar tr. (*quemar*) to burn; (*calentar*) to overheat. —intr. & reflex. to burn up.

a·bra·za·de·ra f. (*zuncho*) clamp, bracket; PRINT. bracket.

a·bra·zar §04 tr. to embrace, hug; (*ceñir*) to clasp; (*adoptar*) to adopt, embrace —reflex. to embrace (each other).

a·bra·zo m. embrace, hug.

a·bre·bo·ca m.f. ARG. absent-minded person, featherbrain.

a·bre·car·tas m.inv. letter opener.

a·bre·la·tas m.inv. can opener.

a·bre·va·de·ro m. watering hole *or* trough.

a·bre·var tr. to water (livestock); (*mojar*) to wet, soak.

a·bre·via·ción f. abbreviation, shortening; (*libros*) abridgement.

a·bre·via·do, a adj. (*breve*) brief, short; (*libros*) abridged, shortened.

a·bre·viar tr. (*reducir*) to abbreviate; (*libros*) to abridge; (*acelerar*) to shorten, hasten.

a·bre·via·tu·ra f. abbreviation; (*compendio*) compendium, résumé.

a·bri·dor, ·ra I. adj. opening II. m. (*abrelatas*) can opener; AGR. grafting knife.

a·bri·gar §47 tr. (*proteger*) to shelter; (*cubrir*) to keep warm; (*sospechas*) to harbor —reflex. to wrap oneself up.

a·bri·go m. (*protección*) shelter, cover; (*sobretodo*) overcoat; MARIT. harbor ♦ **al a. de** protected by.

a·bril m. April.

a·bri·llan·tar tr. AMER. to glaze (fruit).

a·brir §80 tr. to open; (*desplegar*) to spread out; (*empezar*) to open, begin; (*encabezar*) to lead, head; (*horadar*) to dig ♦ **a. el apetito** to whet the appetite • **a. la mano** to extend one's hand • **a. paso** to make way • **en un a. y cerrar de ojos** in the twinkling of an eye —reflex. to open; (*aclarar*) to clear up (weather); (*florecer*) to blossom; (*hender*) to split, crack; (*desviarse*) to swerve ♦ **a. con** to confide in, open up to.

a·bro·cha·dor m. (*abotonador*) buttonhook; S. AMER. stapler.

a·bro·char tr. (*con botones*) to button (up); (*con broches*) to fasten; (*zapatos*) to lace, tie; S. AMER. to staple.

a·bro·gar §47 tr. to abrogate, repeal.

a·bro·jo m. thistle, caltrop.

a·bro·que·lar tr. & reflex. to protect (oneself).

a·bru·ma·do, a adj. overwhelmed.

a·bru·ma·dor, ·ra I. adj. overwhelming, oppressive II. m.f. oppressor.

a·bru·mar tr. to overwhelm, oppress —reflex. to become foggy.

a·brup·to, a adj. abrupt; (*escarpado*) craggy, rugged.

abs·ce·so m. abscess.

ab·sen·tis·mo m. absenteeism.

ab·so·lu·ción f. absolution.

ab·so·lu·to, a I. adj. absolute; (*sin mezcla*) pure (alcohol) ♦ **en absoluto** absolutely not, not at all • **lo a. de** absolute II. f. (*proposición*) dogmatic assertion; MIL. discharge.

ab·sol·ver §78 tr. to absolve; LAW to acquit.

ab·sor·ben·te adj. absorbent; (*cautivante*) absorbing.

ab·sor·ber tr. to absorb —reflex. to become absorbed *or* engrossed.

ab·sor·ción f. absorption.

ab·sor·to, a I. see **absorber** II. adj. engrossed, entranced.

abs·te·mio, a I. adj. abstemious, teetotaling II. m.f. teetotaler, non-drinker.

abs·ten·ción f. abstention.

abs·te·ner·se §69 reflex. to abstain, refrain.

abs·ti·nen·cia f. abstinence.

abs·trac·ción f. abstraction; *(preocupación)* preoccupation.

abs·trac·to, a adj. & m. abstract ♦ **en a.** in the abstract.

abs·tra·er §72 tr. to abstract —reflex. to become withdrawn *or* lost in thought.

abs·tra·í·do, a I. see **abstraer** II. adj. *(distraído)* absorbed; *(retirado)* withdrawn.

abs·tu·vie·ra, vo see **abstenerse.**

ab·suel·to, va, ve see **absolver.**

ab·sur·di·dad f. absurdity.

ab·sur·do, a I. adj. absurd, ridiculous II. m. absurdity.

a·bu·che·ar tr. to boo, hiss.

a·bue·la f. grandmother.

a·bue·lo m. grandfather; *(viejo)* old man ♦ pl. grandparents.

a·bu·lia f. abulia, lack of will power.

a·bul·ta·do, a adj. large, bulky.

a·bul·ta·mien·to m. *(aumento)* increase; *(hinchazón)* swelling.

a·bul·tar tr. *(engrosar)* to enlarge; *(hinchar)* to swell —intr. to be bulky.

a·bun·dan·cia f. abundance.

a·bun·dan·te adj. abundant, plentiful.

a·bun·dar intr. to abound.

a·bur·gue·sar·se reflex. to become bourgeois.

a·bu·rri·do, a adj. *(cansado)* bored; *(tedioso)* boring, tiresome.

a·bu·rri·dor, ·ra adj. boring, tedious.

a·bu·rri·mien·to m. boredom, tedium.

a·bu·rrir tr. to bore —reflex. to become bored.

a·bu·sa·dor, ·ra adj. AMER. abusive.

a·bu·sar intr. to go too far, exceed ♦ **a. de** to abuse, misuse.

a·bu·so m. excess; *(injusticia)* injustice.

ab·yec·to, a adj. abject, low.

a·cá adv. here, over here ♦ **a. y allá** here and there, everywhere • **más a.** closer.

a·ca·ba·do, a I. adj. finished; *(perfecto)* complete, consummate; *(arruinado)* ruined II. m. finish.

a·ca·bar tr. to finish, complete; *(perfeccionar)* to put the finishing touches on; *(pulir)* to give a finish to; *(consumir)* to use up —intr. to end, stop; *(morir)* to die ♦ **¡acabáramos!** finally!, at last! • **a. con** to put an end to, destroy • **a. de** to have just • **a. por** to end up —reflex. to end, terminate; to run out of <*se me acabó el tiempo* I ran out of time> ♦ **¡se acabó!** that's the end of that!

a·ca·che·te·ar tr. to slap, hit.

a·ca·cia f. acacia.

a·ca·de·mia f. academy.

a·ca·dé·mi·co, a I. adj. academic II. m.f. academician.

a·ca·de·mis·ta m.f. academician.

a·ca·e·cer §17 intr. to happen, occur.

a·ca·e·ci·mien·to m. happening, occurrence.

a·ca·lam·brar·se reflex. to get cramps.

a·ca·llar tr. to hush, quiet; FIG. to placate.

a·ca·lo·ra·do, a adj. heated, warm; *(enardecido)* heated, animated.

a·ca·lo·ra·mien·to m. *(ardor)* ardor, heat; *(entusiasmo)* vehemence, passion.

a·ca·lo·rar tr. to warm up; *(alentar)* to encourage —reflex. to heat up; *(hacerse vivo)* to get heated; *(irritarse)* to get excited.

a·ca·lo·ro m. var. of acaloramiento.

a·cam·pa·mien·to m. *(acción)* camping; *(lugar)* camp, encampment.

a·cam·pa·na·do, a adj. bell-shaped.

a·cam·pa·nar tr. to shape like a bell.

a·cam·par tr., intr., & reflex. to camp.

a·ca·na·la·do, a adj. fluted, striated.

a·ca·na·lar tr. to striate, flute.

a·can·ti·la·do, a I. adj. *(abrupto)* steep; *(escalonado)* shelved (coastline) II. m. cliff.

a·ca·pa·ra·dor, ·ra I. adj. hoarding II. m.f. *(acumulador)* stockpiler, hoarder; *(monopolizador)* monopolizer.

a·ca·pa·ra·mien·to m. *(acumulación)* hoarding; *(monopolio)* monopoly.

a·ca·pa·rar tr. *(acumular)* to stockpile, hoard; *(monopolizar)* to monopolize.

a·cá·pi·te m. S. AMER. *(párrafo)* paragraph; *(subtítulo)* subheading.

a·ca·ra·me·la·do, a adj. *(bañado)* caramelized; *(color)* caramel-colored; *(melifluo)* sweet.

a·ca·ra·me·lar tr. to caramelize —reflex. to be *or* become extremely sweet.

a·ca·ri·ciar tr. to caress; *(abrigar)* to cherish, hold dear.

a·ca·rre·ar tr. *(transportar)* to cart, transport; *(ocasionar)* to occasion, cause.

a·ca·rre·o m. cartage, transportation.

a·ca·so I. m. chance, accident II. adv. perhaps, maybe ♦ **por si a.** just in case.

a·ca·ta·mien·to m. respect, reverence.

a·ca·tar tr. *(respetar)* to respect; *(obedecer)* to observe, comply with.

a·ca·ta·rrar·se reflex. to catch a cold.

a·cau·da·la·do, a adj. wealthy, rich.

a·cau·da·lar tr. to accumulate, amass.

ac·ce·der intr. *(consentir)* to agree, consent; *(al trono)* to accede.

ac·ce·si·ble adj. accessible.

ac·ce·so m. *(entrada)* access, entry; *(accesibilidad)* accessibility; *(arrebato)* outburst, fit; MED. attack, fit.

ac·ce·so·rio, a adj. & m. accessory.

ac·ci·den·ta·do, a I. adj. rough, uneven II. m.f. accident victim.

ac·ci·den·tal adj. accidental.

ac·ci·den·tar·se reflex. to have an accident.

ac·ci·den·te m. accident; *(del terreno)* roughness, unevenness; MED. fit, spell ♦ **por a.** by chance.

ac·ción f. action; *(hecho)* act, deed; *(efecto)* effect; *(judicial)* legal action, lawsuit; MIL. battle; COM. share (of stock); LIT., THEAT. action, plot; THEAT. gesture ♦ **a. de gracias** thanksgiving • **a. ordinaria** COM. common stock.

ac·cio·nar tr. to work, operate —intr. to gesticulate.

ac·cio·nis·ta m.f. shareholder, stockholder.

a·ce·char tr. to watch, spy on.

a·ce·cho m. watching, spying.

a·ce·ci·nar tr. to cure (meat).

a·ce·dar tr. to make sour.

a·cé·fa·lo, a adj. acephalous; FIG. leaderless.

a·cei·tar tr. to oil, lubricate.

a·cei·te m. oil ♦ **a. combustible** *or* **de quemar** fuel oil • **a. de hígado de bacalao** cod-liver oil • **a. de ricino** castor oil • **a. de linaza** linseed oil.

a·cei·te·ro, a I. f. AMER. oil cruet II. adj. oil III. m.f. oil vendor.

a·cei·to·so, a adj. oily.

a·cei·tu·na f. olive.

a·cei·tu·na·do, a adj. olive-green.

a·cei·tu·no, a I. m. olive tree II. adj. olive.

a·ce·le·ra·ción f. acceleration.

a·ce·le·ra·da f. acceleration.

a·ce·le·ra·dor m. accelerator.

a·ce·le·rar tr. to speed up; *(facilitar)* to expedite —intr. to hurry; *(motores)* to race.

a·cel·ga f. chard, beet.

a·cen·to m. accent; *(signo)* accent mark; *(tono)* tone ♦ **a. ortográfico** written accent.

a·cen·tua·ción f. accentuation.

a·cen·tua·do, a adj. accented.

a·cen·tuar §67 tr. to accent; *(hacer resaltar)* to accentuate —reflex. to stand out.

a·cep·ción f. meaning.

a·cep·ta·ción f. acceptance; *(aprobación)* approval.

a·cep·tar tr. to accept; *(admitir)* to believe in; *(aprobar)* to approve of.

a·ce·quia f. irrigation ditch.

a·ce·quiar intr. to dig irrigation ditches.

a·ce·ra f. sidewalk.

a·ce·ra·do, a adj. steel, steely.

a·ce·rar tr. *(cubrir)* to cover with steel; *(aceras)* to pave; *(fortalecer)* to strengthen.

a·cer·bi·dad f. *(sabor)* sourness; *(severidad)* harshness.

a·cer·bo, a adj. *(agrio)* sour; *(severo)* harsh.

a·cer·ca de prep. about, concerning.

a·cer·ca·mien·to m. approach.

a·cer·car §70 tr. to bring near —reflex. to approach, draw near.

a·ce·rí·a f. steel mill.

a·ce·ri·co m. *(almohada)* small pillow, cushion; *(alfiletero)* pincushion.

a·ce·ro m. steel; *(arma)* blade, sword ♦ **a. fundido** cast steel.

a·ce·ro·la f. BOT. haw (fruit).

a·cé·rri·mo, a adj. staunch, stalwart.

a·ce·rro·jar tr. to bolt, lock.

a·cer·ta·do, a adj. correct, accurate.

a·cer·tar §49 tr. *(adivinar)* to guess correctly; *(encontrar)* to find, hit upon —intr. *(tener razón)* to hit the mark, be correct; *(lograr)* to succeed ♦ **a. a** to happen to • **a. con** to come upon or across.

a·cer·ti·jo m. riddle.

a·cer·vo m. *(montón)* pile, heap; *(patrimonio)* common property.

a·ce·ta·to m. acetate.

a·ce·ti·le·no m. acetylene.

a·ce·to·na f. acetone.

a·ce·tre m. *(caldero)* water bucket; RELIG. font.

a·cha·car §70 tr. to attribute, to impute.

a·cha·co·so, a adj. sickly, frail.

a·cha·pa·rra·do, a adj. stocky, stubby.

a·cha·que m. ailment, illness ♦ pl. C. AMER. morning sickness • **a. de la edad** ailments of old age.

a·cha·ro·la·do, a adj. resembling patent leather.

a·cha·ro·lar tr. to varnish, enamel.

a·cha·ta·do, a adj. flat, flattened.

a·cha·tar tr. to flatten, squash —reflex. to become flat.

a·chi·ca·du·ra f./**mien·to** m. *(disminución)* reduction; MARIT. bailing.

a·chi·car §70 tr. *(disminuir)* to reduce; *(humi-*

llar) to humiliate; *(ropa)* to take in; MARIT. to bail out —reflex. *(disminuirse)* to get smaller, shrink; *(acobardarse)* to shrink back.

a·chi·cha·rran·te adj. *(quemante)* scorching; *(bochornoso)* sweltering.

a·chi·cha·rrar tr. to scorch —reflex. *(quemarse)* to burn; *(calentarse demasiado)* to get overheated.

a·chi·co·ria f. chicory.

a·chis·pa·do, a adj. tipsy, slightly drunk.

a·chis·par tr. COLL. to make tipsy —reflex. to get tipsy.

a·cho·char·se reflex. to become senile.

a·cho·la·do, a adj. AMER. *(mestizo)* half-Indian; *(avergonzado)* red in the face.

a·cho·lar AMER. tr. to embarrass —reflex. *(acriollarse)* to adopt mestizo ways; *(avergonzarse)* to be ashamed.

a·chu·bas·car·se §70 reflex. to become threatening or overcast (the sky).

a·chu·ra f. AMER. offal.

a·chu·rar/re·ar tr. AMER. to gut, disembowel; COLL. *(matar)* to stab to death.

a·cia·go, a adj. fateful, unlucky.

a·ci·ca·la·do, a adj. spruced up.

a·ci·ca·lar tr. & reflex. to dress or spruce up.

a·ci·ca·te m. *(espuela)* spur; *(incentivo)* spur, incentive.

a·ci·ca·te·ar tr. to spur, incite.

a·ci·dez f. acidity.

á·ci·do, a I. adj. acid; *(agrio)* sour, tart II. m. acid; COLL. L.S.D.

a·cí·du·lo, a adj. acidulous, sour.

a·cier·te, to see acertar.

a·cier·to m. *(logro)* good shot, hit; *(éxito)* success; *(cordura)* good sense; *(habilidad)* skill, dexterity, knack ♦ **con a.** *(con éxito)* successfully; *(con destreza)* skillfully.

a·cla·ma·ción f. acclamation, acclaim.

a·cla·mar tr. to acclaim, hail.

a·cla·ra·ción f. clarification, explanation.

a·cla·ra·do m. rinse, rinsing.

a·cla·rar tr. to clarify; *(explicar)* to explain; *(aguar)* to thin; *(enjuagar)* to rinse —intr. *(clarear)* to clear up; *(amanecer)* to dawn —reflex. *(hacerse inteligible)* to become clear; *(clarear)* to clear up ♦ **a. la voz** to clear one's throat.

a·cla·ra·to·rio, a adj. clarifying, explanatory.

a·cla·re·cer §17 var. of aclarar.

a·cli·ma·tar tr. to acclimatize, acclimate —reflex. to become acclimatized or acclimated.

ac·né f. acne.

a·co·bar·da·mien·to m. cowardliness.

a·co·bar·dar tr. to intimidate —reflex. to become intimidated.

a·co·ce·ar tr. to kick.

a·co·dar tr. *(apoyar)* to rest; CARP. to square —reflex. to lean or rest one's elbows on.

a·co·ge·di·zo, a adj. easily adaptable.

a·co·ge·dor, ·ra adj. *(cordial)* welcoming; *(cómodo)* inviting, cozy.

a·co·ger §34 tr. *(dar bienvenida)* to welcome; *(amparar)* to shelter; *(aceptar)* to accept —reflex. *(refugiarse)* to take refuge ♦ **a. a** to have recourse in, resort to.

a·co·gi·da f. *(recibimiento)* reception, welcome; *(amparo)* shelter, refuge ♦ **tener buena a.** to be well received.

a·co·go·tar tr. COLL. to knock down (with a blow to the back of the head).

a·col·cha·do, a I. adj. padded, quilted II. m. *(relleno)* padding; ARG. bedspread.

a·col·char tr. *(rellenar)* to quilt; *(muebles)* to upholster.

a·có·li·to m. RELIG. acolyte; *(monaguillo)* altar boy; *(discípulo)* disciple, follower.

a·co·me·ter tr. to attack; *(intentar)* to undertake; *(dominar)* to overcome.

a·co·me·ti·da f. attack, assault.

a·co·mo·da·do, a adj. *(rico)* well-off; *(moderado)* reasonable.

a·co·mo·da·dor, ·ra m.f. usher.

a·co·mo·dar tr. *(arreglar)* to arrange, put in order; *(adaptar)* to adapt; *(colocar)* to accommodate —intr. to suit, be suitable —reflex. AMER. to set oneself up.

a·co·mo·da·ti·cio, a adj. *(acomodadizo)* accommodating, obliging; *(conveniente)* suitable.

a·co·mo·do m. *(empleo)* job; *(alojamiento)* lodgings; AMER. connections.

a·com·pa·ña·mien·to m. accompaniment; *(comitiva)* retinue.

a·com·pa·ñan·te, e I. adj. accompanying II. m.f. companion; MUS. accompanist —m. escort —f. chaperon.

a·com·pa·ñar tr. to accompany; *(escoltar)* to escort; *(agregar)* to enclose ♦ **a. en el sentimiento** to express one's condolences • **a. con** or **en** MUS. to accompany oneself on.

a·com·pa·sa·do, a adj. *(rítmico)* rhythmic; *(pausado)* slow-paced.

a·com·pa·sar tr. to give rhythm to.

a·com·ple·ja·do, a I. adj. suffering from a complex II. m.f. person who suffers from a complex.

a·com·ple·jar tr. to give a complex to —reflex. to get a complex.

a·co·mu·nar·se reflex. to unite, join forces.

a·con·di·cio·na·do, a adj. conditioned ♦ **aire a.** air-conditioning • **bien, mal a.** in good, bad condition.

a·con·di·cio·na·dor m. conditioner ♦ **a. de aire** air conditioner.

a·con·di·cio·na·mien·to m. conditioning.

a·con·di·cio·nar tr. *(disponer)* to prepare; *(reparar)* to repair; *(el aire)* to air-condition.

a·con·go·jar tr. to distress —reflex. to be distressed.

a·con·se·ja·do, a adj. sensible, prudent.

a·con·se·jar tr. to advise, counsel —reflex. ♦ **a. con** or **de** to consult with, get advice from.

a·con·te·cer §17 intr. to happen, occur.

a·con·te·ci·mien·to m. event, occurrence.

a·co·pia·dor, ·ra I. adj. gathering, collecting II. m.f. gatherer, collector.

a·co·piar tr. to gather, collect.

a·co·pio m. gathering; *(provisiones)* stock; AMER. *(abundancia)* abundance.

a·co·pla·do m. AMER. trailer.

a·co·pla·mien·to m. coupling, joint.

a·co·plar tr. *(unir)* to couple, join; *(aparear)* to mate; *(conciliar)* to reconcile —reflex. to mate.

a·co·ra·za·do, a I. adj. *(blindado)* armored, armor-plated; *(endurecido)* hardened, inured II. m. battleship.

a·co·ra·zar §04 tr. & reflex. to armor (oneself).

a·cor·da·do, a adj. agreed (upon).

a·cor·dar §19 tr. *(concordar)* to agree; *(decidir)* to decide; *(conciliar)* to reconcile; *(recordar)* to remind; AMER. to grant, accord —intr. to harmonize, go together —reflex. *(recordar)* to re-

member; *(convenir)* to agree, come to an agreement ♦ **si mal no me acuerdo** if my memory serves me right.

a·cor·de I. adj. *(conforme)* in agreement; *(con armonía)* harmonious II. m. chord.

a·cor·de·ón m. accordion.

a·cor·do·nar tr. *(rodear)* to cordon off, surround; *(atar)* to tie or lace (up).

a·co·rra·lar tr. *(encerrar)* to pen; *(atrapar)* to corner; *(intimidar)* to scare.

a·cor·tar tr. to shorten, reduce —reflex. to become shorter.

a·co·sa·mien·to m. harassment.

a·co·sar tr. *(perseguir)* to harass; *(un caballo)* to spur.

a·cos·ta·do, a adj. in bed, lying down.

a·cos·tar §19 tr. to put to bed; MARIT. to bring alongside —intr. to reach shore —reflex. to go to bed; *(inclinarse)* to list; MARIT. to go alongside ♦ **a. con** COLL. to sleep with • **a. con las gallinas** COLL. to go to bed early.

a·cos·tum·bra·do, a adj. *(habituado)* accustomed or used to; *(habitual)* customary.

a·cos·tum·brar tr. & reflex. to accustom (oneself) —intr. to be accustomed to.

a·co·ta·ción f. *(comentario)* remark; THEAT. stage direction; TOP. elevation mark ♦ **a. al margen** marginal note.

a·co·tar tr. *(amojonar)* to stake out; *(fijar)* to set limits on; *(anotar)* to annotate; *(notar)* to remark; *(admitir)* to admit; TOP. to indicate elevations on.

a·cre[1] m. acre.

a·cre[2] adj. acrid.

a·cre·cen·ta·mien·to m. increase, growth.

a·cre·cen·tar §49 tr. *(aumentar)* to increase; *(avanzar)* to promote —reflex. to increase, grow.

a·cre·di·ta·ción f. accreditation.

a·cre·di·ta·do, a adj. accredited; *(ilustre)* reputable.

a·cre·di·tar tr. *(embajador)* to accredit; *(afamar)* to make famous; *(asegurar)* guarantee, vouch for; COM. to credit —reflex. **a. de** to develop a reputation as.

a·cre·e·dor, ·ra I. adj. worthy, deserving II. m.f. creditor.

a·cri·bi·llar tr. *(agujerear)* to riddle (a with); *(molestar)* to hound.

a·crí·li·co, a adj. & m.f. acrylic.

a·cri·so·lar tr. *(aclarar)* to clarify; METAL. to refine, purify.

a·cro·ba·cia f. acrobatics.

a·cró·ba·ta m.f. acrobat.

a·crós·ti·co, a adj. & m. acrostic.

ac·ta f. *(informe)* record; *(minutas)* minutes; *(certificado)* certificate ♦ **a. notarial** affidavit • **levantar un a.** to draw up a certificate.

ac·ti·nio m. actinium.

ac·ti·tud f. attitude.

ac·ti·va·ción f. activation.

ac·ti·va·dor m. activator.

ac·ti·var tr. to activate; *(acelerar)* to expedite —reflex. to become activated.

ac·ti·vi·dad f. activity ♦ **en (plena) a.** in (full) operation.

ac·ti·vis·ta adj. & m.f. activist.

ac·ti·vo, a I. adj. active II. m. COM. assets.

ac·to m. act ♦ **a. seguido** immediately after • **a. de presencia** token appearance • **a. reflejo** reflex action • **en el a.** at once.

ac·tor, ·ra I. m. actor —m.f. LAW plaintiff
II. adj. acting.

ac·triz f. actress.

ac·tua·ción f. performance; *(acción)* action ♦
pl. LAW proceedings.

ac·tual adj. present-day, current.

ac·tua·li·dad f. *(ahora)* present (time); *(estado)*
current situation ♦ **en la a.** nowadays ♦ pl.
news, current events.

ac·tua·li·zar §04 tr. to modernize.

ac·tual·men·te adv. at present, nowadays.

ac·tuar §67 tr. to actuate —intr. *(obrar)* to
act; THEAT. to to perform ♦ **a. de** to act as.

a·cua·re·la f. water color.

a·cua·re·lis·ta m.f. water colorist.

a·cua·rio m. aquarium.

a·cuar·te·lar tr. MIL. to quarter, billet.

a·cuá·ti·co, a/til adj. aquatic.

a·cua·ti·za·je m. AMER. landing on water.

a·cua·ti·zar §04 intr. AMER. to land on water.

a·cu·chi·lla·mien·to m. *(apuñalamiento)* stabbing, slashing; CARP. surfacing (of wood).

a·cu·chi·llar tr. *(apuñalar)* to slash, cut; *(herir)*
to knife, stab; CARP. to plane, scrape.

a·cu·ciar tr. to hasten, goad.

a·cu·cli·llar·se reflex. to squat, crouch down.

a·cu·dir intr. *(presentarse)* to go, come; *(valerse)* to appeal, to have recourse; *(asistir)* to
attend, show up ♦ **a.** to turn to • **a. en ayuda
de** to go to the aid of.

a·cue·duc·to m. aqueduct.

a·cuer·de, do see acordar.

a·cuer·do m. *(convenio)* agreement, accord;
(dictamen) opinion, ruling ♦ **de a. con** in
agreement or accordance with • **de** or **por común a.** of common accord • **vivir en perfecto
a.** to live in absolute harmony.

a·cues·te, to see acostar.

a·cui·dad f. acuity, sharpness.

a·cu·llá adv. (over) there, yonder.

a·cu·mu·la·ción f./**mien·to** m. accumulation,
gathering.

a·cu·mu·la·dor, ·ra I. adj. accumulative **II.** m.
storage battery.

a·cu·mu·lar tr. to accumulate, gather.

a·cu·mu·la·ti·vo, a adj. accumulative.

a·cu·nar tr. to rock, cradle.

a·cu·ñar tr. *(monedas)* to coin, mint; *(meter cuñas)* to wedge, key.

a·cuo·so, a adj. watery, aqueous.

a·cu·pun·tu·ra f. acupuncture.

a·cu·rru·car·se §70 reflex. to curl up; FIG. to
crouch.

a·cu·sa·ción f. accusation, charge.

a·cu·sa·do, a adj. & m.f. accused.

a·cu·sa·dor, ·ra I. adj. accusing **II.** m.f. ac-
cuser.

a·cu·sar tr. to accuse; *(denunciar)* to give
away; *(indicar)* to acknowledge —reflex. to
confess.

a·cu·sa·ti·vo m. accusative.

a·cu·sa·to·rio, a adj. accusatory, accusing.

a·cu·se m. acknowledgment ♦ **a. de recibo** acknowledgment of receipt.

a·cús·ti·co, a I. adj. acoustic, acoustical **II.** f.
acoustics.

a·da·gio m. *(refrán)* adage; MUS. adagio.

a·da·lid m. MIL. military leader, commander;
FIG. *(jefe)* leader, head (of a party).

a·dán m. FIG., COLL. ragamuffin, scruffy fellow
♦ **A.** Adam • **ir en traje de A.** to be naked.

a·dap·ta·bi·li·dad f. adaptability.

a·dap·ta·ción f. adaptation, adjustment.

a·dap·ta·dor m. MECH. adapter.

a·dap·tar tr. & reflex. to adapt, adjust (oneself).

a·de·ce·nar tr. to divide into groups of ten.

a·de·cua·ción f. fitting, adjustment.

a·de·cua·do, a adj. *(apropiado)* appropriate,
suitable; *(suficiente)* adequate, sufficient.

a·de·cuar tr. to make suitable, adapt.

a·de·fe·sio m. COLL. *(persona)* mess; *(traje)*
ridiculous or gaudy outfit.

a·de·lan·ta·do, a adj. *(precoz)* precocious, advanced; *(reloj)* fast ♦ **por a.** in advance.

a·de·lan·tar tr. *(avanzar)* to move forward;
(acelerar) to speed up; *(anticipar)* to advance;
(aventajar) to surpass; AUTO. to overtake, pass;
(relojes) to set ahead or forward —intr. *(avanzar)* to advance, go forward; *(relojes)* to be
fast; FIG. *(progresar)* to make progress —reflex. to get ahead ♦ **a. a** to get ahead of.

a·de·lan·te adv. forward, ahead ♦ **¡a.!** come in!
• **de aquí en a.** from now on • **más a.** farther
on.

a·de·lan·to m. *(de paga)* advance; *(progreso)*
progress.

a·del·ga·zar §04 tr. to make slim or thin
—intr. to lose weight, become slim.

a·de·mán m. gesture ♦ **en a. de** as if about to
• **hacer a. de** to make a move to ♦ pl. manners.

a·de·más adv. besides, in addition.

a·den·tro I. adv. within, inside ♦ **ser de tierra
a.** AMER. to be from the interior **II.** m.pl. the
innermost self.

a·dep·to, a I. adj. supportive **II.** m.f. follower.

a·de·re·zar §04 tr. *(condimentar)* to season;
(adornar) to adorn; *(arreglar)* to prepare, get
ready; TEX. to treat.

a·de·re·zo m. *(condimento)* seasoning; *(adorno)*
adornment; *(arreglo)* preparation; TEX. starch,
gum.

a·deu·dar tr. *(deber)* to owe; ACC., COM. to
debit —reflex. to get into debt.

ad·he·ren·cia f. adherence, adhesion.

ad·he·ren·te adj. & m.f. adherent.

ad·he·rir §65 tr. to affix, stick on —intr. &
reflex. *(pegarse)* to stick, adhere; *(consentir)* to
support, adhere.

ad·he·sión f. adhesion, adherence.

ad·he·si·vo, a adj. & m. adhesive.

a·di·ción f. addition; AMER. bill, check.

a·di·cio·nal adj. additional, added.

a·di·cio·nar tr. to add (to).

a·dic·to, a I. adj. addicted; *(dedicado)* fond,
attached **II.** m.f. addict; *(partidario)* follower.

a·dies·tra·do, a adj. trained.

a·dies·tra·dor, ·ra m.f. trainer, coach.

a·dies·tra·mien·to m. training.

a·dies·trar tr. *(instruir)* to train, coach; *(guiar)*
to guide, lead —reflex. to teach or coach oneself.

a·di·ne·ra·do, a adj. wealthy, affluent.

a·diós interj. & m. good-by.

a·di·po·so, a adj. adipose, fatty.

a·di·ta·men·to m. *(añadidura)* addition; *(accesorio)* attachment ♦ **por a.** in addition.

a·di·ti·vo, a adj. & m. additive.

a·di·vi·na·ción f. prediction; *(conjetura)*
guessing ♦ **a. del pensamiento** mind reading.

a·di·vi·na·dor, ·ra adj. & m.f. diviner.

a·di·vi·nan·za f. riddle, puzzle.

a·di·vi·nar tr. *(predecir)* to predict; *(conjeturar)* to guess; *(el pensamiento)* to read; *(resolver)* to solve ♦ **dejar a. algo** to hint at something.

a·di·vi·no, a m.f. fortuneteller.

ad·je·ti·var tr. *(poner adjetivos)* to qualify; *(usar como adjetivo)* to use as an adjective —reflex. to be used as an adjective.

ad·je·ti·vo, a I. adj. adjectival II. m. adjective.

ad·ju·di·ca·ción f. adjudication, awarding.

ad·ju·di·ca·dor, ·ra m.f. awarder.

ad·ju·di·car §70 tr. to award —reflex. to appropriate (for oneself).

ad·ju·di·ca·ta·rio, a m.f. awardee.

ad·jun·tar tr. to attach, enclose.

ad·jun·to, a I. adj. attached, enclosed; *(persona)* assistant, adjunct II. m.f. associate.

ad·mi·ní·cu·lo m. instrument, gadget ♦ pl. emergency equipment.

ad·mi·nis·tra·ción f. *(dirección)* administration, management; *(oficina)* headquarters.

ad·mi·nis·tra·dor, ·ra I. adj. administrative II. m.f. administrator, manager.

ad·mi·nis·trar tr. *(dirigir)* to manage; *(conferir)* to administer, give.

ad·mi·nis·tra·ti·vo, a adj. administrative.

ad·mi·ra·ción f. admiration; *(sorpresa)* surprise, wonder; GRAM. exclamation point.

ad·mi·ra·dor, ·ra m.f. admirer.

ad·mi·rar tr. to admire; *(sorprender)* to surprise, amaze —reflex. to marvel at.

ad·mi·si·ble adj. admissible.

ad·mi·sión f. *(acción)* admission; *(aceptación)* acceptance; ENGIN. intake.

ad·mi·tir tr. *(entrada)* to admit; *(aceptar)* to accept; *(reconocer)* to acknowledge; *(tener cabida)* to hold ♦ **admitamos que** supposing.

ad·mo·ni·ción f. admonition, warning.

ad·mo·ni·to·rio, a adj. warning.

a·do·ba·do m. marinated meat.

a·do·bar tr. *(aderezar)* to marinate; *(preservar)* to pickle; *(pieles)* to tan.

a·do·be m. *(ladrillo)* adobe.

a·do·bo m. *(salsa)* marinade; *(de pieles)* tanning.

a·doc·tri·na·mien·to m. indoctrination.

a·doc·tri·nar tr. to indoctrinate, instruct.

a·do·le·cer §17 intr. to fall ill ♦ **a. de** to suffer from, have.

a·do·les·cen·cia f. adolescence, youth.

a·do·les·cen·te adj. & m.f. adolescent, youth.

a·don·de conj. where.

a·dón·de adv. & conj. where.

a·don·de·quie·ra adv. wherever, anywhere.

a·dop·ción f. adoption.

a·dop·tar tr. to adopt.

a·dop·ti·vo, a adj. adoptive, adopted.

a·do·quín m. paving stone; FIG., COLL. dunce, idiot.

a·do·qui·na·do m. *(pavimento)* pavement; *(acción)* paving.

a·do·qui·nar tr. to pave.

a·do·ra·ción f. adoration, worship.

a·do·rar tr. & intr. to adore, worship.

a·dor·me·cer §17 tr. to put to sleep —reflex. to doze off, get sleepy.

a·dor·me·ci·do, a adj. *(soñoliento)* sleepy, drowsy; *(un miembro)* numb, asleep.

a·dor·me·ci·mien·to m. *(acción)* dozing off; *(sueño)* sleepiness; *(modorra)* drowsiness.

a·dor·mi·lar·se/tar·se reflex. to doze, drowse.

a·dor·nar tr. to adorn; SEW. to trim; CUL. to garnish; FIG. to embellish.

a·dor·no m. adornment; SEW. trimming; CUL. garnish ♦ **de a.** decorative.

a·do·sar tr. to place *or* lean against; *(unir)* to join; AMER. *(agregar)* to attach.

ad·qui·ri·do, a adj. acquired ♦ **mal a.** ill-gotten.

ad·qui·ri·dor, ·ra m.f. acquirer, buyer.

ad·qui·rir §02 tr. to acquire, buy.

ad·qui·si·ción f. acquisition, purchase.

ad·qui·si·ti·vo, a adj. acquisitive, purchasing.

a·dre·de adv. on purpose, deliberately.

a·dre·na·li·na f. adrenaline.

ads·cri·bir §80 tr. *(atribuir)* to attribute, ascribe; *(designar)* to assign.

ads·cri(p)·to, a I. see **adscribir** II. adj. *(atribuido)* ascribed; *(designado)* assigned.

a·dua·na f. customs.

a·dua·ne·ro, a I. adj. customs II. m. customs officer.

a·du·cir §22 tr. to adduce, cite.

a·due·ñar·se reflex. to take over *or* possession.

a·du·la·ción f. adulation, flattery.

a·du·la·dor, ·ra I. adj. adulating, flattering II. m.f. adulator, flatterer.

a·du·lar tr. to adulate, flatter.

a·du·lón, o·na COLL. I. adj. fawning, flattering II. m.f. flatterer, fawner.

a·dul·te·ra·ción f. adulteration.

a·dul·te·ra·dor, ·ra I. adj. adulterating II. m.f. adulterator.

a·dul·te·rar tr. to adulterate —intr. to commit adultery.

a·dul·te·rio m. adultery.

a·dúl·te·ro, a I. adj. *(infiel)* adulterous; *(corrompido)* corrupt II. m. adulterer —f. adulteress.

a·dul·to, a adj. & m.f. adult.

a·dul·zar §04 tr. to sweeten; METAL. to soften.

a·dus·tez f. austerity, harshness.

a·dus·to, a adj. *(austero)* austere, severe; *(quemado)* scorching, burning hot.

ad·ve·ne·di·zo, a I. adj. foreign, alien II. m.f. *(extranjero)* immigrant, foreigner; *(nuevo rico)* parvenu.

ad·ve·ni·mien·to m. *(llegada)* advent, arrival; *(accesión)* accession.

ad·ve·nir §76 intr. to come, arrive.

ad·ven·ti·cio, a adj. adventitious.

ad·ven·tis·ta adj. & m.f. Adventist.

ad·ver·bio m. adverb.

ad·ver·sa·rio, a m.f. adversary, opponent.

ad·ver·si·dad f. adversity, misfortune.

ad·ver·so, a adj. *(desfavorable)* adverse, unfavorable; *(opuesto)* opposite.

ad·ver·ten·cia f. *(admonición)* warning; *(consejo)* advice; *(noticia)* notice; *(prefacio)* preface, foreword.

ad·ver·ti·do, a adj. *(avisado)* informed, warned; *(capaz)* capable, skillful.

ad·ver·tir §65 tr. *(fijar)* to notice; *(avisar)* to warn; *(aconsejar)* to advise —intr. to notice.

ad·vi·nie·ra, no see advenir.

ad·ya·cen·cia f. adjacency, contiguity.

ad·ya·cen·te adj. adjacent.

a·é·re·o, a adj. air, aerial; *(leve)* light.

a·e·ro·bús m. airbus.

a·e·ro·di·ná·mi·co, a I. adj. aerodynamic, aerodynamical II. f. aerodynamics.

a·e·ro·di·na·mis·mo m. aerodynamism.

a·e·ró·dro·mo m. airdrome, aerodrome (G.B.).

a·e·ro·fo·to·gra·fí·a f. *(técnica)* aerial photography; *(foto)* aerial photograph.

a·e·ro·gra·ma f. aerogram, air letter.

a·e·ro·lí·ne·a f. airline.

a·e·ro·li·to m. aerolite, meteorite.

a·e·ro·mo·de·lis·mo m. airplane modeling.

a·e·ro·mo·zo, a m.f. flight attendant —m. steward —f. stewardess.

a·e·ro·nau·ta m.f. aeronaut.

a·e·ro·náu·ti·co, a I. adj. aeronautic, aeronautical II. f. aeronautics.

a·e·ro·na·ve f. airship.

a·e·ro·pla·no m. airplane.

a·e·ro·pos·tal adj. airmail.

a·e·ro·puer·to m. airport.

a·e·ro·sol m. aerosol.

a·e·ros·pa·cial adj. aerospace.

a·e·ros·tá·ti·co, a I. adj. aerostatic, aerostatical II. f. aerostatics.

a·e·ro·te·rres·tre adj. air-land, air-to-ground.

a·fa·bi·li·dad f. affability, geniality.

a·fa·ble adj. affable, genial.

a·fa·ma·do, a adj. famous, renowned.

a·fán m. *(fervor)* eagerness, zeal; *(anhelo)* urge, desire.

a·fa·nar·se reflex. strive, toil.

a·fa·no·so, a adj. *(fervoroso)* eager, zealous; *(trabajador)* hard-working, diligent; *(agitado)* hectic, feverish.

a·fe·ar tr. to make ugly, deform.

a·fec·ción f. affection.

a·fec·ta·ción f. affectation.

a·fec·ta·do, a adj. affected; *(fingido)* feigned.

a·fec·tar tr. to affect; *(impresionar)* to move; *(influir)* to influence; *(dañar)* to afflict —reflex. *(impresionarse)* to be moved or affected.

a·fec·to, a I. adj. *(cariñoso)* affectionate; *(que gusta)* fond *(a* of) II. m. affection, fondness.

a·fec·tuo·si·dad f. affection.

a·fec·tuo·so, a adj. affectionate, loving.

a·fei·ta·da f. shave, shaving.

a·fei·ta·do·ra f. electric razor or shaver.

a·fei·tar tr. & reflex. to shave (oneself).

a·fei·te m. make-up, cosmetics.

a·fel·pa·do, a I. adj. plush II. m. doormat.

a·fe·mi·na·do, a adj. effeminate.

a·fe·mi·nar tr. to make effeminate —reflex. to become effeminate.

a·fe·rra·mien·to m. *(asimiento)* grasping; *(insistencia)* insistence.

a·fe·rrar §49 tr. *(asir)* to grasp; *(agarrar)* to hook; *(amarrar)* to moor —reflex. to cling *(a* to); *(insistir)* to persist *(a* in).

a·fian·za·mien·to m. securing, strengthening.

a·fian·zar §04 tr. *(garantizar)* to guarantee; *(asegurar)* to secure —reflex. *(asegurarse)* to steady oneself; *(establecerse)* to establish oneself.

a·fi·ción f. *(inclinación)* inclination, liking *(a* for); *(aficionados)* fans, enthusiasts.

a·fi·cio·na·do, a I. adj. fond *(a* of); *(novicio)* amateur II. m.f. *(diletante)* fan, enthusiast; *(novicio)* amateur.

a·fi·cio·nar tr. to inspire a fondness *(a* for); —reflex. to become fond *(a* of).

a·fie·bra·do, a adj. feverish.

a·fie·brar·se reflex. AMER. to become feverish.

a·fie·rra, rro see aferrar.

a·fi·la·do, a adj. sharp.

a·fi·la·dor, ·ra I. adj. sharpening II. m. *(persona)* sharpener; *(máquina)* sharpening machine.

a·fi·la·lá·pi·ces m.inv. pencil sharpener.

a·fi·lar tr. to sharpen; AMER., COLL. to woo —reflex. to grow or become thin.

a·fi·lia·ción f. affiliation.

a·fi·lia·do, a m.f. affiliate, member.

a·fi·liar tr. to affiliate —reflex. to become affiliated, join *(a* with).

a·fín adj. *(próximo)* adjacent; *(parecido)* similar.

a·fi·na·dor, ·ra m.f. tuner —m. tuning key.

a·fi·nar tr. *(perfeccionar)* to refine; *(purificar)* to refine; MUS. to tune —intr. *(cantar)* to sing in tune; *(tocar)* to play in tune.

a·fin·car §70 intr. to acquire real estate —reflex. to establish oneself.

a·fi·ni·dad f. affinity.

a·fir·ma·ción f. affirmation.

a·fir·ma·do m. roadbed.

a·fir·mar tr. *(declarar)* to affirm; *(afianzar)* to secure —reflex. to steady oneself.

a·fir·ma·ti·vo, a I. adj. affirmative II. f. affirmative answer or statement.

a·flau·ta·do, a adj. high-pitched.

a·flic·ción f. affliction.

a·fli·gi·do, a adj. distressed; *(por muerte)* bereaved.

a·fli·gir §32 tr. *(apenar)* to cause pain; *(pesar)* to trouble, distress —reflex. to be troubled or distressed *(con, de, por* by).

a·flo·jar tr. to loosen, slacken; *(entregar)* to give up —intr. *(disminuir)* to diminish; *(decaer)* to grow lax, slack —reflex. to become loose or slack.

a·flo·ra·mien·to m. emergence.

a·flo·rar intr. *(aparecer)* to emerge; GEOL. to outcrop.

a·fluen·cia f. *(de gente)* crowding; *(abundancia)* affluence; *(facundia)* fluency; *(de sangre)* flow.

a·fluir §18 intr. *(manar)* to flow; *(acudir)* to flock.

a·fo·far·se reflex. to become soft or fluffy.

a·fo·ní·a f. aphonia (loss of voice).

a·fó·ni·co, a or **á·fo·no, a** adj. aphonic, hoarse; PHONET. voiceless, silent.

a·fo·rar §19 tr. to measure, gauge; COM. to appraise, assess.

a·fo·ris·mo m. aphorism.

a·fo·ro m. measurement; COM. appraisal.

a·for·tu·na·do, a adj. fortunate, lucky; *(feliz)* happy.

a·fre·cho m. bran.

a·fren·ta f. affront.

a·fren·tar tr. to affront.

a·fren·to·so, a adj. insolent, offensive.

a·fro·di·sia·co, a adj. & m. aphrodisiac.

a·fron·ta·mien·to m. confrontation.

a·fron·tar tr. to face (up to), confront.

a·fue·ra I. adv. out, outside; *(en público)* in public II. interj. scram!, get out of here! III. f.pl. outskirts.

a·fue·re, ro see aforar.

a·ga·cha·da f. stooping, crouching.

a·ga·char tr. to bow, bend ♦ **a. las orejas** to hang one's head, be crestfallen —reflex. to crouch, squat.

a·ga·lla f. ICHTH. gill; BOT. nutgall ♦ pl. FIG., COLL. guts, courage.

á·ga·pe m. banquet.

a·ga·rra·de·ra f. AMER. handle, holder.

a·ga·rra·do, a I. adj. COLL. *(mezquino)* stingy; *(en los bailes)* cheek-to-cheek II. m.f. COLL. cheapskate —f. COLL. quarrel.

a·ga·rrar tr. *(asir)* to grab, grasp; COLL. *(enfermedad)* to get, catch; *(conseguir)* to get, wangle; AMER. *(vehículo)* take —intr. *(pegarse)* to take hold, stick; *(arraigar)* to take root ♦ **a. para** S. AMER. to head for —reflex. *(asirse)* to cling, hold on; *(pelearse)* to grapple, come to blows.

a·ga·rre m. grabbing; FIG. *(valor)* guts; AMER., COLL. influence.

a·ga·rro·ta·do, a adj. stiff, tense.

a·ga·rro·tar tr. *(estrangular)* to garrote; *(atar)* to bind tightly —reflex. to become stiff.

a·ga·sa·ja·dor, ·ra adj. *(acogedor)* welcoming; *(obsequiante)* attentive.

a·ga·sa·jar tr. *(festejar)* to entertain; *(regalar)* to lavish gifts on.

a·ga·sa·jo m. entertainment; *(regalo)* present.

a·ga·za·par·se reflex. *(agacharse)* to squat; *(esconderse)* to hide out.

a·gen·cia f. agency; *(oficina)* bureau.

a·gen·ciar tr. & intr. to manage, obtain.

a·gen·cio·so, a adj. diligent, industrious.

a·gen·da f. notebook.

a·gen·te m. agent ♦ **a. de bolsa** stockbroker, broker • **a. de policía** policeman.

á·gil adj. agile, nimble.

a·gi·li·dad f. agility, nimbleness.

a·gi·li·tar tr. *(hacer ágil)* to render agile *or* nimble; AMER. to activate, hasten.

a·gi·li·zar §04 tr. to make agile *or* nimble.

a·gio m. speculation.

a·gi·ta·ción f. agitation; *(alboroto)* excitement.

a·gi·ta·dor, ·ra I. adj. agitating **II.** m.f. *(provocador)* agitator —m. stirring rod.

a·gi·tar tr. to shake; *(alborotar)* to excite —reflex. to wave, flutter; *(perturbarse)* to be agitated; MARIT. to get rough *or* choppy.

a·glo·me·ra·ción f. agglomeration; *(gentío)* crowd.

a·glo·me·ra·do m. agglomerate; *(combustible)* coal briquette.

a·glo·me·rar tr. to agglomerate —reflex. to be amassed *or* heaped together; *(apiñarse)* to crowd.

a·glu·ti·na·ción f. agglutination.

a·glu·ti·nan·te adj. & m. agglutinant.

a·glu·ti·nar tr. to agglutinate, bind.

ag·nós·ti·co, a adj. & m.f. agnostic.

a·go·bia·do, a adj. *(cargado de espaldas)* bent over, stooped; *(fatigado)* exhausted, weary.

a·go·bia·dor, ·ra adj. *(sofocante)* stifling; *(agotador)* backbreaking; *(abrumador)* overwhelming.

a·go·bian·te adj. *(sofocante)* stifling *(agotador)* backbreaking.

a·go·biar tr. *(cargar)* to weigh down; *(cansar)* to weary; *(deprimir)* to depress —reflex. to bend, stoop.

a·go·bio m. *(carga)* burden; *(fatiga)* fatigue.

a·gol·pa·mien·to m. *(cúmulo)* pile; *(gentío)* crowd, crowding.

a·gol·par·se reflex. *(apiñarse)* to flock; *(venirse encima)* to come all at once.

a·go·ní·a f. agony, anguish.

a·gó·ni·co, a adj. dying; *(angustiado)* in agony.

a·go·ni·zan·te adj. dying.

a·go·ni·zar §04 intr. to be at death's door; *(sufrir)* to be in agony; *(extinguirse)* to fade.

a·go·rar §03 tr. to augur, foretell.

a·go·re·ro, a I. m.f. *(adivino)* soothsayer; *(profeta)* prophet of doom **II.** adj. ominous, foreboding.

a·gor·go·jar·se reflex. to become infested with weevils.

a·gos·tar tr. to parch; *(arar)* to plow in the summer —intr. to graze in the summer.

a·gos·to m. August; *(cosecha)* harvest ♦ **hacer su a.** FIG., COLL. to feather one's nest.

a·go·ta·do, a adj. exhausted; *(libros)* out-of-print; COM. sold-out; AMER. dead (battery).

a·go·ta·dor, ·ra adj. exhausting, tiring.

a·go·ta·mien·to m. *(abatimiento)* exhaustion; *(disminución)* depletion.

a·go·tar tr. to exhaust —reflex. to be used up *or* depleted; *(cansarse)* to be exhausted; *(libros)* to be out of print.

a·gra·cia·do, a adj. good-looking, attractive.

a·gra·ciar tr. *(embellecer)* to embellish; *(favorecer)* to grace; *(premiar)* to award.

a·gra·da·ble adj. agreeable, pleasant.

a·gra·dar tr. & intr. to please —reflex. to like one another.

a·gra·de·cer §17 tr. to thank; *(sentir gratitud)* to be grateful for.

a·gra·de·ci·do, a adj. & m.f. grateful, thankful (person) ♦ **muy a.** much obliged.

a·gra·de·ci·mien·to m. gratitude, thanks.

a·gra·do m. *(placer)* pleasure; *(gusto)* taste, liking.

a·gran·dar tr. to enlarge; *(exagerar)* to exaggerate —reflex. to grow larger.

a·gra·rio, a adj. agrarian, agricultural.

a·gra·va·ción f./**mien·to** m. aggravation, worsening.

a·gra·van·te I. adj. aggravating **II.** m. aggravating circumstance.

a·gra·var tr. & reflex. to worsen.

a·gra·via·dor, ·ra/vian·te I. adj. insulting, offensive **II.** m.f. offender.

a·gra·viar tr. to offend; *(perjudicar)* to harm —reflex. to take offense.

a·gra·vio m. offense; *(perjuicio)* injury.

a·gra·vio·so, a adj. insulting, offensive.

a·gre·di·do, a adj. assaulted, attacked.

a·gre·dir §38 tr. to attack, assault.

a·gre·ga·do, a I. adj. aggregate **II.** m. aggregate; *(añadidura)* addition; P. RICO day laborer ♦ **a. militar** military attaché.

a·gre·gar §47 tr. *(añadir)* to add, attach; *(unir)* to gather, collect —reflex. to join.

a·gre·miar intr. to form a union, unionize.

a·gre·sión f. aggression.

a·gre·si·vi·dad f. aggressiveness.

a·gre·si·vo, a adj. aggressive.

a·gre·sor, ·ra I. m.f. aggressor **II.** adj. aggressive.

a·gres·te adj. rustic; FIG. uncouth.

a·griar tr. to (make) sour; *(amargar)* to embitter; *(irritar)* to annoy —reflex. to become sour.

a·grí·co·la *or* **a·gri·cul·tor, ·ra I.** adj. agricultural, farming **II.** m.f. agriculturist, farmer.

a·gri·cul·tu·ra f. agriculture, farming.

a·gri·dul·ce adj. bittersweet.

a·grie·ta·mien·to m. cracking; GEOL. crack.

a·grie·tar tr. & reflex. to crack, split.

a·gri·men·sor, ·ra m.f. surveyor.

a·gri·men·su·ra f. surveying.

a·grio, a I. adj. sour; *(áspero)* rude, disagreeable **II.** m. sourness, acidity.

a·gro m. agriculture, farming.

a·gro·no·mí·a f. agronomy, agronomics.

a·gro·nó·mi·co, a adj. agronomical.

a·gró·no·mo, a I. adj. agronomical **II.** m. agronomist.

a·gro·pe·cua·rio, a adj. ♦ **la industria a.** agriculture and livestock industry.

a·gru·mar tr. & reflex. to curdle, clot.

a·gru·pa·ción f./**mien·to** m. *(grupo)* group; *(asociación)* association, union.

a·gru·par tr. & reflex. to group, cluster (together).

a·gua f. water; *(lluvia)* rain; ARCHIT. slope ♦ **a. corriente** running water • **a. de borrajas** trifle, nothing • **a. de colonia** toilet water • **a. nieve** sleet • **a. oxigenada** CHEM. hydrogen peroxide • **a. salobre** *or* **salada** salt water • **claro como a.** crystal-clear • **con el a. al cuello** in trouble • **hacer a.** to leak • **hacerse a. en la boca** to melt in one's mouth • **hacérsele a. la boca** to make one's mouth water • **sin decir a. va ni a. viene** suddenly, unexpectedly ♦ pl. *(reflejos)* wavy pattern; *(destellos)* sparkle; *(orina)* urine • **a. abajo, arriba** downstream, upstream • **entre dos a.** undecided.

a·gua·cal m. whitewash.

a·gua·ca·te m. avocado.

a·gua·ce·ro m. downpour.

a·gua·chen·to, a adj. AMER. thin.

a·gua·cil m. var. of **alguacil.**

a·gua·de·ro, a I. adj. waterproof **II.** m. watering trough *or* hole.

a·gua·do, a adj. diluted, watered-down; *(abstemio)* abstemious.

a·gua·fies·tas m.f.inv. killjoy.

a·gua·fuer·te m.f. etching (print or plate).

a·gua·ma·ri·na f. aquamarine.

a·gua·nie·ve f. sleet ♦ pl. wagtail.

a·guan·ta·dor, ·ra adj. AMER., COLL. patient.

a·guan·tar tr. to endure, tolerate; *(sostener)* to hold up; *(contener)* to hold, retain —reflex. to control *or* contain oneself.

a·guan·te m. *(paciencia)* tolerance; *(fuerza)* endurance.

a·guar §10 tr. to water down; *(malograr)* to spoil, mar —reflex. to become watery; *(arruinarse)* to be spoiled.

a·guar·dar tr. to wait for, await —intr. to wait.

a·gua·rrás m. turpentine oil.

a·gua·te·ro m. AMER. water carrier.

a·gu·de·za f. sharpness; *(ingenio)* wit.

a·gu·di·za·ción f. *(agravación)* worsening; *(aumento)* intensification.

a·gu·di·zar §04 tr. to sharpen; *(empeorar)* to worsen —reflex. to become serious.

a·gu·do, a adj. sharp, pointed; *(chillón)* shrill; *(perspicaz)* keen; MUS. high-pitched; GEOM., GRAM. acute.

a·güe·ro m. prediction; *(señal)* omen.

a·gue·rri·do, a adj. experienced, seasoned.

a·gue·rrir §38 tr. to accustom to war.

a·gui·jar tr. to goad.

a·gui·jón m. ENTOM. sting; BOT. thorn; *(punta)* goad; *(estímulo)* spur.

a·gui·jo·na·zo m. sting, prick.

a·gui·jo·ne·ar tr. to sting; *(estimular)* to goad.

á·gui·la f. eagle; *(condecoración)* emblem; *(persona)* wizard, whiz.

a·gui·le·ño, a adj. aquiline, hook-nosed.

a·gui·lón m. MECH. jib; ARCHIT. gable; *(caño)* clay drainpipe; *(teja)* beveled tile.

a·gui·nal·do m. Christmas bonus.

a·gu·ja f. needle; *(de sombreros)* hatpin; *(del*

reloj) hand; ARCHIT. steeple ♦ **a. de gancho** crochet hook • **a. magnética** compass.

a·gu·je·rar/re·ar tr. to pierce, perforate —reflex. to be pierced *or* perforated.

a·gu·je·ro m. hole.

a·gu·je·ta f. *(cinta)* lace ♦ pl. MED. soreness.

a·guo·so, a adj. watery, aqueous.

a·gu·sa·nar·se reflex. to get wormy.

a·gu·za·do, a adj. sharpened.

a·gu·zar §04 tr. to sharpen ♦ **a. los dientes** *or* **el apetito** to whet one's appetite • **a. el ingenio** to sharpen one's wit • **a. las orejas** *or* **los oídos** to prick up one's ears.

¡ah! interj. ah!, ha!

a·he·cha·du·ras f.pl. chaff, siftings.

a·he·char tr. to sift, winnow.

a·he·cho m. sifting, winnowing.

a·he·rrum·brar tr. & reflex. to rust.

a·hí adv. there ♦ **a. no más** right over there • **de a. que** hence • **por a.** thereabouts.

a·hi·ja·do, a m.f. godchild —m. godson —f. goddaughter.

a·hi·jar tr. to adopt; *(imputar)* to attribute to.

a·hi·la·do, a adj. *(suave)* gentle, soft; *(tenue)* faint.

a·hi·lar tr. to line up —intr. to go in single file —reflex. *(desmayarse)* to faint; *(adelgazar)* to become thin; BOT. to grow tall and slender.

a·hin·ca·do, a adj. earnest, zealous.

a·hin·car §70 intr. to urge, press —reflex. to hurry, rush.

a·hín·co m. eagerness, zeal.

a·hí·to, a adj. stuffed.

a·ho·ga·do, a I. adj. stifling **II.** m.f. drowned person.

a·ho·gan·te adj. stifling.

a·ho·gar §47 tr. to drown; *(sofocar)* to choke; *(oprimir)* to oppress; AGR. to drown, soak (plants) —reflex. to drown; *(sentir sofocación)* to choke ♦ **a. en un vaso de agua** to make a mountain out of a molehill.

a·ho·go m. *(en el pecho)* shortness of breath; *(angustia)* anguish.

a·hon·dar tr. to go deeper into —intr. to go deep.

a·ho·ra I. adv. now; *(pronto)* soon; *(hace poco)* just now, a few moments ago • **a. bien** *or* **pues** well, now then • **a. mismo** right now • **hasta a.** until now • **por a.** for the time being **II.** conj. now then, well then.

a·hor·ca·do, a m.f. hanged person.

a·hor·ca·jar·se reflex. to sit astride, straddle.

a·hor·car §70 tr. & reflex. to hang (oneself).

a·ho·ri·ta adv. COLL. right now, this minute.

a·hor·mar tr. to mold, fit.

a·hor·nar tr. to put in the oven —reflex. to bake *or* burn on the outside only.

a·hor·qui·llar tr. to shape like a fork; AGR. to prop up.

a·ho·rra·dor, ·ra m.f. economizer, saver.

a·ho·rrar tr. to save; *(evitar)* to spare —reflex. to save *or* spare oneself.

a·ho·rra·ti·vo, a adj. thrifty.

a·ho·rro m. saving ♦ pl. savings.

a·hu·cha·dor, ·ra m.f. hoarder.

a·hue·ca·do, a adj. hollow.

a·hue·ca·mien·to m. hollowing-out.

a·hue·car §70 tr. to hollow out; *(mullir)* to fluff up; *(la voz)* to make deep —intr. ♦ **a. el ala** COLL. to beat it, split.

a·hue·va·do, a adj. egg-shaped.

a·hu·ma·do, a I. adj. CUL. smoked, cured; *(con humo)* smoky; *(color)* smoke-colored **II.** m. CUL. smoking, curing.

a·hu·mar tr. CUL. to smoke, cure; *(con humo)* to fill with smoke —intr. to be smoky —reflex. *(ennegrecerse)* to be blackened by smoke.

a·hu·yen·tar tr. to drive *or* scare away; *(desechar)* to dismiss —reflex. to flee, run away.

ain·dia·do, a adj. Indian-like.

ai·ra·do, a adj. angry, irate; *(licencioso)* licentious.

ai·rar tr. to anger, annoy.

ai·re m. air; *(viento)* wind; *(apariencia)* air, appearance; *(gracia)* grace; MUS. air, tune; MED., COLL. crick, stiff neck ♦ **a. acondicionado** air conditioning • **al a. libre** in the open air • **darse aires** to put on airs • **estar en el a.** RAD., TELEV. to be on the air; FIG. to be up in the air • **tener un a. con** to resemble.

ai·re·a·ción f. ventilation, air circulation.

ai·re·a·do, a adj. ventilated, aired out.

ai·re·ar tr. to ventilate, aerate; *(discutir)* to discuss, air out —reflex. to take in the air.

ai·re·o m. airing, ventilation.

ai·ro·si·dad f. grace, elegance.

ai·ro·so, a adj. gallant.

ais·la·cio·nis·ta adj. & m.f. isolationist.

ais·la·do, a adj. isolated; *(solo)* alone; *(apartado)* remote; ELEC. insulated.

ais·la·dor, ·ra m. ELEC. insulator.

ais·la·mien·to m. isolation; *(retiro)* seclusion; ELEC. insulation.

ais·lan·te adj. insulating.

ais·lar tr. to isolate; *(retirar)* to seclude; ELEC. to insulate —reflex. to withdraw.

¡a·já! interj. *(aprobación)* sure!; *(sorpresa)* aha!

a·jar tr. to crumple, wrinkle —reflex. to get crumpled *or* wrinkled; BOT. to wither.

a·je·dre·cis·ta m.f. chess player.

a·je·drez m. chess; *(piezas)* chess set.

a·jen·jo m. absinthe.

a·je·no, a adj. another's, someone else's; *(libre)* free, devoid; *(impropio)* inappropriate ♦ **a. de sí** detached, aloof.

a·je·tre·ar tr. & reflex. *(apresurar)* to rush, hurry; *(fatigar)* to tire.

a·je·tre·o m. bustle, rush.

a·jí m. [pl. **-íes**] red *or* green pepper.

a·jo m. garlic; *(diente)* garlic clove.

a·jon·jo·lí m. [pl. **-íes**] sesame.

a·juar m. trousseau.

a·jui·ciar tr. *(hacer juicioso)* to bring to one's senses; *(enjuiciar)* to judge.

a·jus·ta·do, a adj. tight.

a·jus·tar tr. to adjust, adapt; *(modificar)* to alter, fit; *(reconciliar)* to reconcile; *(apretar)* to tighten; *(precios)* to fix; *(contratar)* to hire; COM. to settle; MECH. to fit —intr. to fit —reflex. *(acomodarse)* to adjust, conform; *(acordarse)* to come to an agreement.

a·jus·te m. adjustment; *(modificación)* alteration, fitting; *(arreglo)* arrangement; COM. settlement; MECH. fitting.

a·jus·ti·cia·do, a m.f. executed criminal.

a·jus·ti·cia·mien·to m. execution.

a·jus·ti·ciar tr. to execute.

al contr. of **a** and **el**.

a·la f. wing; *(del sombrero)* brim; *(de la hélice)* blade; ARCHIT. eave; MARIT. sail ♦ **cortarle las alas** to clip someone's wings • **dar alas a** to encourage.

a·la·ba·dor, ·ra adj. praising, laudatory.

a·la·ban·za f. praise.

a·la·bar tr. to praise, laud —reflex. to boast, brag.

a·la·bas·tro m. alabaster.

a·la·ce·na f. cupboard, closet.

a·la·crán m. scorpion.

a·la·cri·dad f. alacrity, eagerness.

a·la·do, a adj. winged.

a·lam·bi·que m. still, alembic.

a·lam·bra·da f. wire netting.

a·lam·bra·do m. chicken wire fence.

a·lam·brar tr. to fence in with wire.

a·lam·bre m. wire ♦ **a. de púas** barbed wire.

a·lam·bris·ta m.f. tightrope walker.

a·la·me·da f. poplar grove; *(paseo)* boulevard.

á·la·mo m. poplar.

a·lar·de m. show, display.

a·lar·de·ar intr. to boast, brag.

a·lar·de·o m. boasting, bragging.

a·lar·gar §47 tr. to lengthen; *(extender)* to extend, prolong; *(estirar)* to stretch (out); *(cuerda)* to play out —reflex. to get longer; DEROG. to drag out.

a·la·ri·do m. yell, howl.

a·lar·ma f. alarm; *(inquietud)* anxiety ♦ **a. aérea** air-raid warning • **dar la a.** to sound the alarm.

a·lar·ma·dor, ·ra/man·te adj. alarming.

a·lar·mar tr. to alarm; *(asustar)* to scare —reflex. to become alarmed.

a·lar·mis·ta adj. & m.f. alarmist.

a·la·zán, a·na adj. & m.f. sorrel, chestnut.

al·ba f. dawn, daybreak; RELIG. alb ♦ **al a.** at dawn • **al romper el a.** at dawn.

al·ba·ce·a m. executor —f. executrix.

al·ba·ñal m. sewer, drain.

al·ba·ñil m. bricklayer, mason.

al·ba·ñi·le·rí·a f. masonry.

al·ba·ri·co·que m. apricot.

al·ba·yal·de m. white lead.

al·be·drí·o m. free will; *(capricho)* whim, fancy.

al·ber·ca f. *(tanque)* reservoir, tank; MEX. swimming pool.

al·ber·gar §47 tr. to lodge, house; *(una esperanza)* to cherish; *(una duda)* to harbor —intr. & reflex. to stay, take lodgings; *(refugiarse)* to take shelter.

al·ber·gue m. *(alojamiento)* lodging; *(refugio)* shelter, refuge; *(cubil)* den, lair.

al·bi·no, a adj. & m.f. albino.

al·bo, a adj. POET. white.

al·bón·di·ga f. meatball.

al·bor m. whiteness; *(alba)* dawn.

al·bo·ra·da f. dawn; *(toque)* reveille.

al·bo·re·ar intr. to dawn.

al·bor·noz m. *(capa)* burnoose; *(bata)* bathrobe.

al·bo·ro·ta·do, a adj. *(agitado)* excited; *(ruidoso)* rowdy; *(atolondrado)* rash; *(el mar)* rough.

al·bo·ro·ta·dor, ·ra m.f. troublemaker; *(niño)* unruly child.

al·bo·ro·tar tr. *(agitar)* to agitate; *(incitar)* to incite; *(excitar)* to excite —intr. to make a racket —reflex. to get excited *or* agitated; *(el mar)* to become rough.

al·bo·ro·to m. *(jaleo)* uproar; *(ruido)* racket; *(motín)* riot; MEX. *(alegría)* joy.

al·bo·ro·za·do, a adj. jubilant, overjoyed.

al·bo·ro·zar §04 tr. to delight —reflex. to be elated, rejoice.

al·bo·ro·zo m. joy, jubilation.
al·bri·cias interj. great!, congratulations!
al·bur m. risk, hazard ♦ **jugar** or **correr un a.** to take a risk.
al·ca·cho·fa f. artichoke.
al·ca·hue·te, a m.f. COLL. gossip; AMER. squealer —m. pimp —f. madam.
al·ca·hue·te·ar tr. to procure —intr. (ser alcahuete) to pimp; COLL. (chismear) to gossip; (soplar) to squeal.
al·ca·hue·te·rí·a f. pimping ♦ pl. **andar con a.** COLL. to squeal on people.
al·cal·de m. mayor.
al·cal·dí·a f. (cargo) mayoralty; (oficina) mayor's office.
al·ca·li·no, a adj. alkaline.
al·ca·loi·de m. alkaloid.
al·can·ce m. (distancia) reach; (extensión) range, scope; (talento) talent ♦ **al a.** accessible, within reach (de to, of) • **al a. del oído** within earshot • **dar a. a** to catch up with • **de gran a.** FIG. far-reaching.
al·can·cí·a f. piggy bank.
al·can·for m. camphor.
al·can·fo·rar tr. to camphorate.
al·can·ta·ri·lla f. (cloaca) sewer, drain; (en un camino) culvert.
al·can·ta·ri·lla·do m. sewers, drains.
al·can·ta·ri·llar tr. to lay sewers in.
al·can·zar §04 tr. to reach (up to); (tomar) to catch; (conseguir) to attain; (comprender) to grasp; (igualar) to catch up with; AMER. to pass, hand over —intr. to reach; (durar) to be sufficient or enough ♦ **a. a** to manage to, be able to.
al·ca·pa·rra f. caper.
al·cau·cil m. artichoke.
al·cá·zar m. castle, fortress.
al·ce m. elk, moose.
al·cis·ta FIN. **I.** m.f. bull **II.** adj. bullish ♦ **mercado a.** bull market.
al·co·ba f. bedroom.
al·co·hol m. alcohol.
al·co·hó·li·co, a adj. & m.f. alcoholic.
al·co·ho·lí·me·tro m. alcoholometer.
al·co·ho·lis·mo m. alcoholism.
al·co·ho·li·zar §04 tr. to alcoholize.
al·cor·no·que m. cork oak; FIG. blockhead.
al·cor·zar §04 tr. to frost, ice (a cake).
al·cur·nia f. ancestry, lineage ♦ **de noble a.** of noble birth.
al·cu·za f. cruet.
al·da·ba f. (picaporte) (door) knocker; (barra) crossbar, bolt; (de caballería) hitching ring.
al·da·ba·da f. knock.
al·da·be·ar intr. to knock at or on the door.
al·da·be·o m. knocking, rapping.
al·da·bo·na·zo m. loud knock (on a door).
al·de·a f. village, hamlet.
al·de·a·no, a **I.** adj. village; (campesino) rustic **II.** m.f. peasant.
¡a·le! interj. come on!, let's go!
a·le·a·ción f. alloy.
a·le·ar[1] intr. to flap, flutter; FIG. to get better.
a·le·ar[2] tr. to alloy.
a·le·a·to·rio, a adj. aleatory, uncertain.
a·lec·cio·nar tr. (enseñar) to instruct, teach; (amaestrar) to train.
a·le·da·ño, a **I.** adj. bordering, adjoining **II.** m. boundary, border ♦ pl. outskirts.
a·le·ga·ción f. allegation; AMER. argument.

a·le·gar §47 tr. to allege; (aseverar) to claim —intr. to argue.
a·le·ga·to m. allegation; AMER. argument.
a·le·go·rí·a f. allegory.
a·le·gó·ri·co, a adj. allegorical, allegoric.
a·le·grar tr. to cheer; (avivar) to enliven —reflex. to rejoice, be happy; (achisparse) to get tipsy.
a·le·gre adj. happy, glad; (jovial) cheerful, sunny; (brillante) lively, bright; (achispado) tipsy.
a·le·grí·a f. happiness, joy.
a·le·grón m. COLL. joy.
a·le·ja·do, a adj. distant, remote.
a·le·ja·mien·to m. removal, withdrawal; (enajenación) estrangement; (distancia) distance.
a·le·jan·dri·no adj. & m. POET. alexandrine.
a·le·jar tr. to put farther away; (enajenar) to estrange —reflex. to move away, withdraw.
a·le·la·do, a adj. stupefied, bewildered.
a·le·lar tr. to stupefy, bewilder —reflex. to be stupefied or bewildered.
¡a·le·lu·ya! interj. alleluia!, hallelujah!
a·len·ta·dor, ·ra adj. encouraging.
a·len·tar §49 intr. to breathe —tr. to encourage, inspire —reflex. to cheer up.
a·ler·gia f. allergy.
a·lér·gi·co, a I. adj. allergic ♦ **ser a.** to be allergic to **II.** m.f. allergy sufferer.
a·le·ro m. eaves.
a·le·rón m. aileron.
a·ler·ta I. adv. on the alert ♦ **¡a.!** watch out! **II.** m. alert, warning.
a·ler·tar tr. to alert, warn.
a·ler·to, a adj. watchful, vigilant.
a·le·ta f. ICHTH. fin; (hélice) blade; MECH. leaf; ANAT., ARCHIT. wing.
a·le·tar·ga·mien·to m. lethargy.
a·le·tar·gar §47 tr. to make drowsy.
a·le·te·ar intr. to flutter, flap.
a·le·te·o m. fluttering, flapping.
a·le·vo·sí·a f. treachery, perfidy.
al·fa·bé·ti·co, a adj. alphabetical.
al·fa·be·ti·za·ción f. alphabetization; EDUC. literacy instruction.
al·fa·be·ti·zar §04 tr. to alphabetize; EDUC. to make literate, teach literacy skills to.
al·fa·be·to m. alphabet ♦ **a. Morse** Morse code.
al·fa·nu·mé·ri·co, a adj. alphanumeric.
al·fa·re·rí·a f. pottery.
al·fa·re·ro m.f. potter, ceramist.
al·féi·zar m. window sill.
al·fe·ñi·que m. sweetened almond paste; (persona) weakling.
al·fé·rez m. second lieutenant.
al·fil m. bishop (in chess).
al·fi·ler m. pin ♦ **a. de gancho** AMER. safety pin • **no caber un a.** COLL. to be filled to the brim • **pegado** or **prendido con alfileres** COLL. shaky.
al·fi·le·rar tr. to pin.
al·fi·le·ra·zo m. pinprick; FIG. dig, gibe.
al·fi·le·te·ro m. pincushion.
al·fom·bra f. carpet; (tapete) rug, mat.
al·fom·bra·do m. carpets, carpeting.
al·fom·brar tr. to carpet.
al·for·ja f. knapsack; (provisión) supplies.
al·for·za f. pleat, tuck.
al·for·zar §04 tr. to pleat, tuck.
al·ga f. alga, seaweed.
al·ga·ra·bí·a f. uproar, din.

al·ga·rro·ba f. BOT. *(planta)* vetch; *(fruto)* carob bean.

ál·ge·bra f. algebra.

al·ge·brai·co, a adj. algebraic.

ál·gi·do, a adj. icy, cold.

al·go I. indef. pron. something; *(en negaciones e interrogaciones)* anything; *(cantidad)* some ♦ **a. es a.** something is better than nothing • **por a.** for some reason II. adv. somewhat, a little.

al·go·dón m. cotton ♦ **a. de azúcar** cotton candy • **a. en rama** raw cotton • **a. hidrófilo** absorbent cotton.

al·go·do·nal m. cotton plantation *or* field.

al·go·do·ne·ro, a I. adj. cotton II. m. cotton plant.

al·go·rít·mi·co adj. ♦ **lenguaje a.** ALGOL.

al·go·rit·mo m. algorithm.

al·gua·cil m. sheriff; R.P. dragonfly.

al·guien indef. pron. someone, somebody; *(en negaciones e interrogaciones)* anyone, anybody.

al·gún adj. some —see **alguno.**

al·gu·no, a I. adj. some; *(en negaciones e interrogaciones)* any ♦ **a. vez** sometime II. indef. pron. someone ♦ **a. que otro** a few, one or two ♦ pl. some.

al·ha·ja f. jewel, gem.

al·ha·jar tr. to bedeck with jewels; *(amueblar)* to furnish.

al·ha·je·ra f./o m. AMER. jewelry box.

al·ha·ra·ca f. fuss, ado.

al·he·lí m. [pl. **-íes**] BOT. wallflower, stock.

al·he·ña f. henna.

al·hu·ce·ma f. lavender.

a·lia·do, a I. m.f. ally ♦ **los Aliados** the Allies II. adj. allied, confederate.

a·lian·za f. *(unión)* alliance; *(anillo)* wedding ring; BIBL. covenant.

a·liar §30 tr. to ally, join —reflex. to become allies.

a·lias adv. & m. alias.

a·li·bí m. alibi.

a·li·ca·í·do, a adj. *(débil)* haggard; *(deprimido)* depressed.

a·li·ca·tes m.pl. pliers, pincers ♦ **a. de uñas** nail clippers.

a·li·cien·te m. incentive.

a·lie·na·ble adj. alienable.

a·lie·na·ción f. alienation.

a·lie·na·do, a adj. & m.f. insane, mentally deranged (person).

a·lie·nar tr. to alienate.

a·lien·te, to see **alentar.**

a·lien·to m. breath; *(valor)* courage ♦ **dar a.** to encourage • **cobrar a.** to take heart • **sin a.** breathless.

a·li·ge·rar tr. to lighten; *(acelerar)* to quicken.

a·li·ma·ña f. pest, vermin.

a·li·men·ta·ción f. *(acción)* feeding; *(comida)* food; *(manutención)* support ♦ **a. deficiente** malnutrition.

a·li·men·tar tr. to feed, nourish; *(mantener)* to support; *(fomentar)* to nurture —reflex. to take nourishment ♦ **a. con** to feed on.

a·li·men·ta·rio, a adj. alimentary, nutritional.

a·li·men·ti·cio, a adj. nourishing, nutritious.

a·li·men·to m. food, nourishment ♦ pl. alimony, support.

a·lin·dar tr. to set boundaries to —intr. to be contiguous *or* adjacent.

a·li·ne·a·ción f. *(línea)* alignment; *(colocación)* aligning; SPORT. line-up.

a·li·ne·a·do, a adj. aligned ♦ **no a.** POL. non-aligned.

a·li·ne·ar tr. & reflex. to align, line up.

a·li·ñar tr. to straighten, tidy; CUL. to season.

a·li·ño m. tidiness; CUL. seasoning.

a·li·sar tr. to smooth; *(el pelo)* to slick.

a·li·sios adj. trade <*vientos a.* trade winds>.

a·lis·ta·mien·to m. listing; MIL. recruitment.

a·lis·tar tr. to list; MIL. to recruit —reflex. to enlist; AMER. to get ready.

a·li·te·ra·ción f. alliteration.

a·li·viar tr. to alleviate, ease; *(aligerar)* to lighten; *(acelerar)* to quicken —reflex. to get better.

a·li·vio m. alleviation, easing; *(aligeramiento)* lightening; *(cese)* relief.

al·ji·be m. cistern.

a·llá adv. there, over there; *(en tiempo remoto)* way back ♦ **a. tú** that's your business, it's up to you • **más a.** farther • **más a. de** beyond • **por a.** over there.

a·lla·na·mien·to m. raid ♦ **a. de morada** search of premises.

a·lla·nar tr. *(nivelar)* to flatten; *(invadir)* to raid; *(superar)* to overcome.

a·lle·ga·do, a I. adj. *(cercano)* near, close; *(emparentado)* related II. m.f. *(pariente)* relative, relation; *(partidario)* supporter, adherent.

a·lle·gar §47 tr. to place near, gather —reflex. to approach.

a·llen·de POET. I. adv. beyond II. prep. on the other side of.

a·llí adv. there ♦ **por a.** *(sitio)* over there; *(camino)* that way.

al·ma f. soul; *(individuo)* human being, soul; *(centro)* crux; TECH. core; CONSTR. web; ARTIL. bore ♦ **a. de Dios** COLL. good soul • **a. mía** dearest, darling • **caérsele el a. a los pies** to be disheartened • **con toda el a.** with all one's heart • **no tener a.** to be heartless • **partir el a.** to break someone's heart • **tener el a. en un hilo** to have one's heart in one's mouth.

al·ma·cén m. store; *(depósito)* warehouse; ARTIL. magazine; S. AMER. grocery store.

al·ma·ce·na·je m. *(costo)* storage charge; *(almacenamiento)* storage ♦ **a. frigorífico** cold storage.

al·ma·ce·na·mien·to m. storage.

al·ma·ce·nar tr. to store, warehouse; FIG. to stock up (with).

al·ma·ce·ne·ro m. warehouseman; S. AMER. grocer.

al·má·ci·ga f. *(resina)* mastic; *(semillero)* nursery, seedbed.

al·má·ci·go m. mastic tree; *(semilla)* nursery seed; *(semillero)* nursery, seedbed.

al·ma·na·que m. calendar.

al·ma·za·ra f. oil mill.

al·me·ja f. clam.

al·men·dra f. almond ♦ **a. garrapiñada** praline.

al·men·dra·do, a I. adj. almond-shaped II. m. *(pasta)* almond paste; *(macarrón)* macaroon —f. almond milk.

al·men·dro m. almond tree.

al·mí·bar m. syrup.

al·mi·ba·ra·do, a adj. syrupy.

al·mi·ba·rar tr. to candy; FIG. to sweet-talk.

al·mi·dón m. starch ♦ **dar a.** to starch.

al·mi·do·na·do, a I. adj. starched; FIG. smart, dapper II. m. starching.

al·mi·do·nar tr. to starch.
al·mi·ran·te m. admiral.
al·miz·cle m. musk.
al·mo·ha·da f. pillow ♦ **consultar con la a.** to sleep on it.
al·mo·ha·di·lla f. (cojincillo) small cushion; (para sellos) inkpad; AMER. pincushion.
al·mo·ha·di·llar tr. to pad, stuff.
al·mo·ha·dón m. cushion.
al·mo·rra·nas f.pl. hemorrhoids, piles.
al·mor·zar §37 intr. to eat lunch, lunch —tr. to eat for lunch, lunch on.
al·muer·zo m. lunch.
a·lo·ca·do, a adj. thoughtless, crazy.
a·lo·car §70 tr. to drive crazy or insane.
a·lo·cu·ción f. allocution, address.
a·ló·ge·no, a adj. of a different race.
a·lo·ja·mien·to m. lodging(s); (vivienda) housing.
a·lo·jar tr. to lodge; (albergar) to house —reflex. to lodge, stay.
a·lo·jo m. AMER. var. of **alojamiento.**
a·lon·dra f. lark.
a·lon·gar §16 tr. to lengthen, stretch.
a·lo·pa·tí·a f. allopathy.
al·pa·ca f. alpaca.
al·par·ga·ta f. rope-soled sandal.
al·pi·nis·ta m.f. mountain climber.
al·pi·no, a adj. alpine.
al·pis·te m. birdseed; FIG., COLL. alcohol.
al·qui·lar tr. to rent, lease; (personas) to hire —reflex. to be for hire ♦ **se alquila** to let, for hire.
al·qui·ler m. (acción) renting, hiring; (renta) rent ♦ **a. de coches** car-rental service • **de a.** for rent.
al·qui·mia f. alchemy.
al·qui·mis·ta m. alchemist.
al·qui·trán m. tar, pitch.
al·qui·tra·na·do, a I. adj. tarred II. m. MARIT. tarpaulin.
al·qui·tra·nar tr. to tar, cover with tar.
al·re·de·dor I. adv. (en torno) around; (cerca de) about, approximately II. m.pl. (cercanías) surroundings; (afueras) outskirts.
al·ta f. see **alto, a.**
al·ta·men·te adv. highly, extremely.
al·ta·ne·rí·a f. arrogance, haughtiness.
al·ta·ne·ro, a adj. high-flying; FIG. arrogant, haughty.
al·tar m. altar.
al·ta·voz m. loudspeaker.
al·te·ra·ción f. alteration; (alboroto) disturbance; (disputa) altercation; (del pulso) irregularity.
al·te·ra·do, a adj. altered; (perturbado) upset; (enfadado) angry.
al·te·rar tr. to alter; (perturbar) to upset; (enfadar) to annoy —reflex. to change; (perturbarse) to get upset.
al·ter·ca·ción f./do m. altercation, argument.
al·ter·ca·dor, ·ra adj. & m.f. argumentative.
al·ter·car §70 intr. to argue, quarrel.
al·ter·na·do, a adj. alternate.
al·ter·nan·te adj. alternating.
al·ter·nar tr. & intr. to alternate ♦ **a. con** to mix.
al·ter·na·ti·va f. alternative, choice ♦ **tomar una a.** to make a decision.
al·ter·na·ti·vo, a adj. alternating, alternate.
al·ter·no, a adj. alternating; BOT., GEOM. alternate.

al·te·za f. Highness; (altura) height.
al·ti·ba·jos m.pl. ups and downs.
al·ti·llo m. (colina) hillock; S. AMER. (desván) attic.
al·ti·me·trí·a f. altimetry.
al·tí·me·tro m. altimeter.
al·ti·pla·ni·cie f. high plateau, altiplano.
al·tí·si·mo, a adj. very high, most high ♦ **El A.** God, the Almighty.
al·ti·tud f. altitude, height.
al·ti·vez/ve·za f. haughtiness, pride.
al·ti·vo, a adj. haughty, proud.
al·to, a I. adj. high; (estatura) tall; (piso) upper; (voz) loud; (crecido) swollen; (ideales) lofty; (traición) high, serious; (precio) high ♦ **a. costura** haute couture • **a. fidelidad, frecuencia** high fidelity, frequency • **a. horno** blast furnace • **altas horas** late hours • **en a.** on high II. m. height, elevation; MUS. alto; MIL. halt, stop; AMER. pile, heap ♦ **de a.** high • **de lo a.** from on high, from above • **hacer a.** to stop, come to a stop ♦ pl. AMER. upper floors —f. MED. discharge; (ingreso) entry ♦ **dar de a.** MIL. to admit; MED. to discharge III. adv. (arriba) up high, above; (en voz fuerte) aloud, loudly ♦ **pasar por a.** to overlook, omit IV. interj. halt!, stop! ♦ **¡a. al fuego!** cease fire!
al·to·cú·mu·lo m. altocumulus.
al·to·par·lan·te m. loudspeaker.
al·truis·ta I. adj. altruistic II. m.f. altruist.
al·tu·ra f. height; (altitud) altitude; (nivel) level; FIG. loftiness ♦ **estar a la a. de las circunstancias** to be worthy of the occasion ♦ pl. the heavens • **a estas a.** at this point or stage.
a·lu·bia f. French or kidney bean.
a·lu·ci·na·ción f. hallucination.
a·lu·ci·na·dor, ·ra I. adj. hallucinatory II. m. hallucinogen.
a·lu·ci·na·mien·to m. hallucination.
a·lu·ci·nan·te adj. hallucinating; (extraordinario) extraordinary.
a·lu·ci·nar tr. & intr. to hallucinate.
a·lu·ci·na·to·rio, a adj. hallucinatory.
a·lu·ci·no·gé·ni·co, a adj. hallucinogenic.
a·lud m. avalanche.
a·lu·di·do, a adj. abovementioned, referred to.
a·lu·dir intr. to allude, refer (a to).
a·lum·bra·do, a I. adj. lighted, lit II. m. lighting.
a·lum·bra·mien·to m. lighting; (parto) childbirth.
a·lum·brar tr. to light (up), illuminate; FIG. to enlighten, illuminate —intr. to give light; (dar a luz) to give birth.
a·lum·bre m. alum.
a·lu·mi·nio m. aluminum, aluminium (G.B.).
a·lum·na·do m. student body.
a·lum·no, a m.f. pupil, student.
a·lu·na·do, a adj. R.P., COLL. grouchy.
a·lu·na·ra·do, a adj. spotted, dotted.
a·lu·nar·se reflex. AMER. (herida) to fester; R.P., COLL. to get grouchy.
a·lu·ni·za·je m. lunar landing.
a·lu·ni·zar §04 intr. to land on the moon.
a·lu·sión f. allusion.
a·lu·vión m. flood; (sedimento) sediment; FIG. flood.
al·ver·ja f. vetch; AMER. pea.
al·ver·ji·lla f. sweet pea.
al·za f. rise, increase; ARTIL. backsight ♦ **en a.** on the rise.

al·za·do, a I. adj. raised, elevated; *(en celo)* in heat; *(rebelde)* mutinous **II.** f. height.

al·za·mien·to m. POL. uprising.

al·zar §04 tr. to raise, lift (up); *(recoger)* to gather; MARIT. to hoist ♦ **a. cabeza** COLL. to get back on one's feet • **a. el codo** COLL. to have a lot to drink —reflex. to rise, get up; POL. to rebel, rise ♦ **a. con** COLL. to make off with, steal.

a·ma f. *(señora)* lady of the house, mistress; *(dueña)* proprietress ♦ **a. de case** housewife • **a. de cría** or **de leche** wet nurse • **a. de llaves** housekeeper.

a·ma·bi·li·dad f. kindness.

a·ma·ble adj. kind.

a·ma·do, a adj. & m.f. beloved, dear (one).

a·ma·dri·nar tr. *(uncir)* to couple; AMER. to train (horses) to follow the lead.

a·ma·es·tra·dor, ·ra m.f. trainer.

a·ma·es·tra·mien·to m. training.

a·ma·es·trar tr. to train.

a·ma·gar §47 tr. *(amenazar)* to threaten *(a, con* to); *(fingir)* to feign.

a·ma·go m. *(amenaza)* threat; *(señal)* sign; MIL. mock attack.

a·mai·nar tr. MARIT. to lower —intr. to die down, let up.

a·mal·ga·mar tr. & reflex. to amalgamate, mix.

a·ma·man·ta·mien·to m. suckling, nursing.

a·ma·man·tar tr. to suckle, nurse.

a·ma·ne·cer §17 **I.** intr. to dawn; *(despertar)* to wake up, to start the day **II.** m. dawn, daybreak ♦ **al a.** at dawn or daybreak.

a·ma·ne·ci·da f. dawn, daybreak.

a·ma·ne·ra·do, a adj. mannered, affected.

a·ma·ne·ra·mien·to m. affectation.

a·ma·ne·rar·se reflex. to become affected.

a·man·sa·dor, ·ra m.f. AMER. horsebreaker —f. R.P. a long wait.

a·man·sa·mien·to m. breaking, taming.

a·man·sar tr. *(un animal)* to tame; *(un caballo)* to break; FIG. to soothe —reflex. to calm down.

a·man·te I. adj. fond, loving **II.** m.f. lover.

a·ma·nuen·se m.f. amanuensis.

a·ma·ña·do, a adj. *(falsificado)* fixed, falsified; *(diestro)* clever, skillful.

a·ma·ñar tr. DEROG. to fix, falsify —reflex. to manage.

a·ma·ño m. *(maña)* skill; *(arreglo)* scheme.

a·ma·po·la f. poppy.

a·mar tr. to love.

a·mar·fi·la·do, a adj. ivory-like.

a·mar·ga·do, a adj. bitter, embittered.

a·mar·ga·men·te adv. bitterly.

a·mar·gar §47 tr. FIG. to make bitter —intr. & reflex. to become bitter or embittered.

a·mar·go, a I. adj. bitter; FIG. painful **II.** m. bitterness; AMER. sugarless maté.

a·mar·gor m. bitterness; FIG. pain.

a·mar·gu·ra f. bitterness; FIG. sorrow ♦ **¡qué a.!** what a pity!

a·ma·ri·lle·ar intr. to yellow, turn yellow.

a·ma·ri·llen·to, a adj. yellowish; *(de tez)* sallow.

a·ma·ri·llo, a adj. & m. yellow.

a·ma·rra·de·ro m. *(poste)* hitching post; MARIT. *(poste)* bollard; *(sitio)* mooring.

a·ma·rrar tr. to tie (up), fasten; MARIT. to moor.

a·ma·rre m. tying; MARIT. mooring.

a·ma·rre·te adj. ARG., PERU stingy.

a·mar·ti·llar tr. to hammer; *(un arma)* to cock.

a·ma·sar tr. to knead; FIG. to amass.

a·ma·si·jo m. CUL. dough; *(tarea)* task; ARG., COLL. thrashing, beating.

a·ma·teur adj. & m.f. amateur.

a·ma·tis·ta f. MIN. amethyst.

a·ma·to·rio, a adj. amatory, love.

a·ma·zo·na f. MYTH. Amazon; FIG. *(mujer varonil)* amazon; *(caballista)* horsewoman.

a·ma·zó·ni·co, a adj. Amazonian.

am·ba·ges m.pl. circumlocution ♦ **hablar sin a.** not to beat around the bush.

ám·bar m. amber ♦ **a. gris** ambergris.

am·ba·ri·no, a adj. amber.

am·bi·ción f. ambition.

am·bi·cio·nar tr. to aspire to, strive for.

am·bi·cio·so, a adj. & m.f. ambitious.

am·bi·dex·tro/dies·tro, a adj. ambidextrous.

am·bien·ta·ción f. atmosphere; LIT. setting.

am·bien·tar tr. to give atmosphere to; LIT. to set —reflex. to adjust oneself.

am·bien·te I. adj. surrounding, ambient ♦ **el medio a.** the environment **II.** m. atmosphere; FIG. ambiance; R.P. room.

am·bi·güe·dad f. ambiguity.

am·bi·guo, a adj. ambiguous.

ám·bi·to m. *(perímetro)* boundary, limit; *(campo)* field.

am·bi·va·len·cia f. ambivalence.

am·bos, as adj. & indef. pron. both.

am·bu·lan·cia f. ambulance.

am·bu·lan·te I. adj. traveling, itinerant **II.** m. AMER. peddler; MEX. ambulance driver.

am·bu·lar intr. to ambulate, amble.

am·bu·la·to·rio, a adj. ambulatory.

a·me·ba f. amoeba.

a·me·dren·tar tr. to scare, frighten —reflex. to become scared or frightened.

a·mén I. m. amen ♦ **en un decir a.** FIG. in an instant **II.** adv. ♦ **a. de** besides, in addition to.

a·me·na·za f. threat, menace.

a·me·na·za·dor, ·ra/zan·te adj. threatening.

a·me·na·zar §04 tr. to threaten, menace —intr. to threaten, be imminent.

a·men·guar §10 tr. to diminish.

a·me·ni·dad f. amenity, pleasantness.

a·me·ni·zar §04 tr. to make pleasant; FIG. to enliven.

a·me·no, a adj. pleasant, agreeable.

a·me·ri·ca·nis·mo m. Spanish-American word, custom or trait.

a·me·ri·ca·ni·zar §04 tr. to Americanize —reflex. to become Americanized.

a·me·ri·ca·no, a adj. & m.f. American —f. jacket.

a·me·tra·lla·do·ra f. machine gun.

a·me·tra·llar tr. to machine-gun.

a·mian·to m. amianthus, asbestos.

a·mi·ga·ble adj. amicable; FIG. harmonious.

a·mi·gar §47 tr. *(amistar)* to bring together; *(reconciliar)* to reconcile —reflex. *(amistarse)* to become friendly; *(reconciliarse)* to make up.

a·mi·ga·zo, a COLL. **I.** adj. close (friend) **II.** m.f. buddy, pal.

a·míg·da·la f. tonsil, amygdala.

a·mig·da·li·tis f.inv. tonsilitis.

a·mi·go, a I. m.f. friend ♦ **a. íntimo** or **del alma** close friend, bosom buddy • **a. de lo ajeno** COLL. thief • **hacerse a. de** to make friends with • **hacerse amigos** to become friends **II.** adj. friendly; FIG. fond of.

a·mi·go·te m.f. COLL. great friend, pal.
a·mi·gui·sí·mo, a adj. very friendly.
a·mi·la·na·do, a adj. intimidated.
a·mi·la·nar tr. to frighten, intimidate; FIG. to dishearten, discourage —reflex. to become frightened *or* intimidated; FIG. to become disheartened *or* discouraged.
a·mi·no·á·ci·do m. amino acid.
a·mi·no·rar tr. to reduce, diminish ♦ **a. el paso** to walk more slowly.
a·mis·tad f. friendship ♦ **trabar** *or* **estrechar a.** to make friends ♦ pl. friends, acquaintances • **hacer las a.** to reconcile, make up • **romper las a.** to quarrel.
a·mis·tar tr. to make friends with; *(reconciliar)* to reconcile —reflex. to become friends; *(reconciliarse)* to make up.
a·mis·to·so, a adj. amicable, friendly.
am·né·si·co, a adj. & m.f. MED. amnesiac, amnesic.
am·nis·tí·a f. amnesty.
am·nis·tiar §19 tr. to grant amnesty to.
a·mo m. master; *(dueño)* owner, proprietor.
a·mo·blar §19 tr. var. of **amueblar.**
a·mo·do·rra·mien·to m. sleepiness.
a·mo·la·dor m. AMER. grinder, sharpener.
a·mo·lar §19 tr. to grind, sharpen; FIG. to irritate, annoy.
a·mol·da·mien·to m. fitting; FIG. adaptation.
a·mol·dar tr. to mold, model; FIG. to adapt, adjust —reflex. to adapt oneself.
a·mo·nes·ta·ción f. *(represión)* reprimand; *(advertencia)* warning.
a·mo·nes·tar tr. *(reprender)* to reprimand; *(advertir)* to warn.
a·mo·nia·co/ní·a·co m. *(gas)* ammonia; *(goma)* gum resin.
a·mon·to·na·mien·to m. *(acción)* heaping, piling up; *(montón)* accumulation; *(de gente)* crowding.
a·mon·to·nar tr. *(apilar)* to heap *or* pile (up); *(acumular)* to accumulate, gather; *(riquezas)* to hoard —reflex. *(apilarse)* to pile up; *(acumularse)* to crowd (together).
a·mor m. love; *(afecto)* affection; *(querido)* darling, beloved ♦ **a. propio** pride • **hacer el a.** to make love • **¡por a. a Dios!** for goodness sake! • **sin a.** loveless ♦ pl. *(amoríos)* love affairs, romances; *(requiebros)* endearments • **de mil a.** COLL. gladly, with pleasure.
a·mo·ra·li·dad f. amorality.
a·mo·ra·ta·do, a adj. purplish; AMER. black-and-blue, bruised ♦ **a. de frío** blue with cold.
a·mo·ra·tar tr. to make blue *or* purple; AMER. to bruise —reflex. to turn blue *or* purple; *(magullarse)* to bruise, turn black-and-blue.
a·mor·da·zar §04 tr. *(una persona)* to gag; *(un perro)* to muzzle; FIG. to silence, gag.
a·mor·fo, a adj. amorphous, shapeless.
a·mo·rí·o m. fling, love affair.
a·mo·ro·so, a adj. loving, affectionate; *(enamoradizo)* amorous; AMER. charming.
a·mor·ta·jar tr. to shroud; TECH. to mortise.
a·mor·te·cer §17 tr. *(golpes)* to cushion; *(ruidos)* to muffle; *(luces)* to dim; *(colores, música)* to soften.
a·mor·ti·gua·ción f. var. of **amortiguamiento.**
a·mor·ti·gua·dor, ·ra I. adj. *(de golpes)* cushioning; *(de ruidos)* muffling; *(de luces)* dimming; *(de colores, música)* softening **II.** m. AUTO. *(dispositivo)* shock absorber; *(paracho-*

ques) bumper ♦ **a. de luz** dimmer • **a. de ruido** muffler.
a·mor·ti·gua·mien·to m. *(de golpes)* cushioning; *(de ruidos)* muffling; *(de luces)* dimming; *(de colores, música)* toning down.
a·mor·ti·guar §10 tr. *(golpes)* to absorb; *(ruidos)* to muffle; *(luces)* to dim; *(colores, música)* to tone down; FIG. to alleviate.
a·mor·ti·za·ción f. LAW amortization; *(de un bono)* redemption; *(de una deuda)* repayment.
a·mor·ti·zar §04 tr. LAW to amortize; *(un bono)* to redeem; *(una deuda)* to repay, pay off.
a·mos·car·se §70 reflex. COLL. to get angry.
a·mo·ti·na·do, a I. adj. rebellious; MIL. mutinous **II.** m.f. rebel; MIL. mutineer.
a·mo·ti·na·mien·to m. uprising; MIL. mutiny.
a·mo·ti·nar tr. to incite to riot —reflex. to rebel; MIL. to mutiny.
am·pa·rar tr. to protect; *(defender)* to defend —reflex. to protect oneself; *(acogerse)* to seek protection.
am·pa·ro m. protection; *(defensa)* aid.
am·pe·ra·je m. amperage.
am·pe·rí·me·tro m. ammeter, amperemeter.
am·pe·rio m. ampere ♦ **a. hora** ampere-hour.
am·plia·ción f. *(extensión)* extension, expansion; PHOTOG. enlargement.
am·pliar §30 tr. to expand; *(desarrollar)* to elaborate on; *(aumentar)* to increase; *(ensanchar)* to widen; PHOTOG. to enlarge.
am·pli·fi·ca·ción f. *(aumento)* amplification, magnification; PHOTOG. enlargement.
am·pli·fi·ca·dor, ·ra I. adj. amplifying **II.** m. ELEC., RAD. amplifier; *(altavoz)* loudspeaker.
am·pli·fi·car §70 tr. *(aumentar)* to amplify; *(con microscopio)* to magnify; PHOTOG. to enlarge.
am·plio, a adj. *(espacioso)* spacious, roomy; *(extenso)* ample, broad; *(ancho)* full, wide.
am·pli·tud f. *(anchura)* fullness; *(extensión)* extent ♦ **a. de miras** broad-mindedness • **de gran a.** far-reaching, of large scope.
am·po·lla f. blister; MED. ampoule.
am·po·llar tr. & reflex. to blister.
am·po·lle·ta f. hourglass.
am·pu·lo·si·dad f. pomposity.
am·pu·lo·so, a adj. pompous, bombastic.
am·pu·ta·ción f. amputation.
am·pu·ta·do, a m.f. amputee.
am·pu·tar tr. to amputate, cut off.
a·mue·blar tr. to furnish.
a·mue·ble, blo see **amoblar.**
a·mu·je·ra·do, a adj. effeminate, womanish.
a·mu·le·to m. amulet, charm.
a·mu·ra·lla·do, a adj. walled.
a·mu·ra·llar tr. to wall, fortify with walls.
a·mus·tiar tr. & reflex. to wither.
a·na·bap·tis·ta adj. & m.f. Anabaptist.
a·na·ca·ra·do, a adj. pearly, mother-of-pearl.
a·na·car·do m. cashew.
a·na·cro·nis·mo m. anachronism.
á·na·de m.f. duck.
a·na·de·ar intr. to waddle.
a·ná·fo·ra f. anaphora, repetition.
a·na·gra·ma m. anagram.
a·na·les m.pl. annals.
a·nal·fa·be·to, a adj. & m.f. illiterate.
a·nal·gé·si·co, a adj. & m. analgesic.
a·ná·li·sis m.inv. analysis ♦ **a. de orina** urinalysis • **a. de sangre** blood test.
a·na·lis·ta m.f. analyst; *(historiador)* annalist.

a·na·lí·ti·co, a I. adj. analytical II. f. analytics.

a·na·li·zar §04 tr. to analyze, examine.

a·na·lo·gí·a f. analogy ♦ **por a.** by analogy.

a·ná·lo·go, a adj. analogous, similar.

a·na·ná(s) m. [pl. **-na(s)es**] pineapple.

a·na·quel m. shelf.

a·na·ran·ja·do, a adj. & m. orange.

a·nar·quí·a f. anarchy.

a·nár·qui·co, a adj. anarchic, anarchical.

a·nar·quis·ta I. m.f. anarchist II. adj. anarchistic.

a·nar·qui·zar §04 tr. to make anarchic —intr. to propagate anarchism.

a·na·te·ma m. anathema.

a·na·te·ma·ti·zar §04 tr. to anathematize, excommunicate; (maldecir) to curse, condemn.

a·na·to·mí·a f. anatomy.

a·na·tó·mi·co, a adj. anatomic, anatomical.

a·na·to·mi·zar §04 tr. ARTS. to delineate.

an·ca f. (grupa) croup, rump; (nalga) rump, buttock.

an·char tr. & intr. to widen, broaden.

an·cho, a I. adj. wide, broad; (holgado) loose, full ♦ **de a.** wide • **estar** or **ponerse muy a.** COLL. to boast • **quedarse tan a.** to remain unworried II. m. width, breadth ♦ **a sus anchas** as one pleases.

an·cho·a f. anchovy.

an·chu·ra f. width, breadth; (amplitud) fullness.

an·cia·ni·dad f. old age.

an·cia·no, a I. adj. old, elderly II. m. old or elderly man; RELIG. elder —f. old or elderly woman.

an·cla f. anchor.

an·clar/co·rrar intr. to anchor, drop or cast anchor.

an·da·da f. (pan) thin, crisp bread; (caminata) long walk ♦ **volver a las andadas** FIG., COLL. to be up to one's old tricks.

an·da·dor, ·ra I. adj. (veloz) fast-walking; (andariego) wandering II. m.f. (caminante) walker (person); (andariego) wanderer ♦ pl. straps (to support an infant learning to walk).

an·da·du·ra f. (acción) walking; (manera) gait.

an·da·mio m. scaffold; (tablado) platform.

an·da·na·da f. MARIT. broadside; (gradería) covered grandstand ♦ **soltar una a.** FIG., COLL. to scold, reprimand.

an·dan·te I. adj. walking, traveling ♦ **caballero a.** knight errant II. m. & adv. MUS. andante.

an·dan·za f. (suceso) occurrence, event; (aventura) adventure ♦ **volver a las andanzas** to be up to one's old tricks.

an·dar¹ §05 intr. to walk; (marchar) to go, move; (funcionar) to work, function; (transcurrir) to go by, elapse; (estar) to be; (sentirse) to be, feel ♦ **¡anda!** (como exhortación) get going!, move along!; (expresando admiración) no kidding! • **¡ándale!** COLL. hurry up! • **a. con cuidado** or **con pies de plomo** to be careful, tread cautiously • **a. de broma** to be joking • **a. en** (envolverse) to be mixed up or engaged in; (escudriñar) rummage through, search; (en edad) to be going on, be about • **a. por las nubes** to be absent-minded • **a. tras** to go after, pursue • **¿cómo andas de salud?** how is your health? —tr. to travel, go —reflex. to leave, go away ♦ **a. en** to be mixed up in • **a. por las ramas** to beat around the bush.

an·dar² m. pace, gait ♦ **a todo a.** at full speed.

an·da·rie·go, a I. adj. wandering, roving II. m.f. wanderer, rover.

an·da·ri·vel m. (balsa) cable ferry; (maroma) ferry cable; MARIT. lifeline, safety ropes.

an·dén m. station or railway platform; (parapeto) parapet, railing.

an·di·nis·ta m.f. mountain climber.

an·dra·jo m. tatter, rag; DEROG. wretch.

an·dra·jo·so, a adj. tattered, ragged.

an·dro·ce·o m. androecium.

an·dró·gi·no, a I. adj. androgynous, hermaphroditic II. m.f. androgyne, hermaphrodite.

an·droi·de m. android.

an·du·vie·ra, vo see **andar¹**.

a·néc·do·ta f. anecdote.

a·nec·dó·ti·co, a adj. anecdotal.

a·nec·do·tis·ta m.f. anecdotist.

a·ne·ga·ble adj. floodable, subject to flooding.

a·ne·ga·ción f. flooding.

a·ne·ga·di·zo, a adj. subject to flooding.

a·ne·ga·mien·to m. flooding.

a·ne·gar §47 tr. to flood, inundate —reflex. be inundated; MARIT. to sink ♦ **a. en llanto** to dissolve into tears.

a·ne·jar tr. to join, attach.

a·ne·jo, a I. adj. attached, annexed II. m. annex; LIT. appendix.

a·né·mi·co, a adj. & m.f. anemic.

a·nes·te·sia f. anesthesia.

a·nes·te·siar tr. to anesthetize.

a·nes·té·si·co, a adj. & m. anesthetic.

a·nes·te·sió·lo·go, a m.f. anesthesiologist.

a·nes·te·sis·ta m.f. anesthetist.

a·ne·xar tr. to join; (documentos) to enclose.

a·ne·xo, a I. adj. joined; (documento) enclosed II. m. (suplemento) annex; (apéndice) enclosure.

an·fe·ta·mi·na f. amphetamine.

an·fi·bio, a I. adj. amphibious, amphibian II. m. ZOOL. amphibian.

an·fi·bo·lo·gí·a f. amphibology, amphiboly.

an·fi·tea·tro m. amphitheater.

an·fi·trión, o·na m. host —f. hostess.

án·fo·ra f. amphora.

an·ga·ri·llas f.pl. (andas) stretcher; (camilla) packsaddle with panniers.

án·gel m. angel ♦ **a. custodio** or **de la guardia** guardian angel • **tener a.** to have grace or charm.

an·gé·li·co, a/cal adj. angelic, angelical.

an·ge·li·to m. (ángel) little angel, cherub; (niño) cherub, small child.

an·ge·lo·te m. (niño) chubby child; ICHTH. angelfish.

an·gli·ca·no, a adj. & m.f. Anglican.

an·gli·cis·ta m.f. Anglicist.

an·glo·fo·bia f. Anglophobia.

an·glo·par·lan·te adj. English-speaking.

an·glo·sa·jón, o·na adj. & m.f. Anglo-Saxon —m. (idioma) Anglo-Saxon.

an·go·ra adj. & m. Angora, angora.

an·gos·tar tr., intr., & reflex. to narrow.

an·gos·to, a adj. narrow, tight.

an·gos·tu·ra f. narrowness; (paso estrecho) narrow passage or place; MARIT. narrows, strait; BOT., CUL. angostura.

án·gu·lo m. angle; (esquina) corner, angle ♦ **de á. ancho** PHOTOG. wide-angle • **en á.** at an angle.

an·gu·lo·si·dad f. angularity.

an·gu·lo·so, a adj. angular, sharp.

an·gu·rria f. AMER. (hambre) hunger; (avaricia) greed.

an·gu·rrien·to, a AMER. adj. (avaro) greedy; (hambriento) starved.

an·gus·tia f. anguish.

an·gus·tia·do, a adj. anguished.

an·gus·tiar tr. to anguish, cause anguish —reflex. to become anguished or distressed.

an·gus·tio·so, a adj. anguished; (penoso) distressing.

an·he·lan·te adj. (ansioso) yearning; (jadeante) gasping, panting.

an·he·lar intr. to yearn or long to; (jadear) to gasp, pant —tr. to yearn or long for.

an·he·lo m. yearning, longing.

an·he·lo·so, a adj. longing.

an·hí·dri·do m. anhydride ♦ **a. carbónico** carbon dioxide • **a. nítrico** nitric oxide • **a. sulfúrico** sulfur dioxide.

a·ni·dar intr. to nest; (habitar) to live —tr. to shelter —reflex. to nest.

a·ni·llar tr. (dar forma) to shape into a ring; (sujetar) to fasten with rings.

a·ni·llo m. ring; ZOOL., ANAT. annulus, ring ♦ **a. pastoral** bishop's ring • **caer** or **venir como a. al dedo** COLL. to be just right.

á·ni·ma f. soul, spirit; (de las armas) bore.

a·ni·ma·ción f. (viveza) liveliness; (movimiento) animation.

a·ni·ma·do, a adj. (vivo) lively; (activo) bustling; (movido) motivated; ZOOL. animate; AMER. better of health).

a·ni·ma·dor, ·ra I. adj. (excitador) enlivening; (alentador) inspiring **II.** m.f. (de ceremonias) master of ceremonies; (artista) entertainer.

a·ni·mad·ver·sión f. animadversion.

a·ni·mal I. adj. animal **II.** m. animal; FIG. beast.

a·ni·ma·la·da f. COLL. foolish or silly thing.

a·ni·ma·lu·cho m. ugly beast.

a·ni·mar tr. (dar vida) to give life to; (avivar) to enliven; (estimular) to stimulate; (alentar) to encourage —reflex. (avivarse) to become animated or lively; (atreverse) to feel encouraged ♦ **a. a** to decide to, get in the mood to.

á·ni·mo m. spirit; (energía) energy, vitality ♦ **¡a.!** courage! • **caerse los ánimos** to lose heart • **dar á. a** to encourage • **estar** or **tener ánimos para** to be in the mood to.

a·ni·mo·si·dad f. animosity, enmity.

a·ni·mo·so, a adj. spirited, courageous.

a·ni·ña·do, a adj. (pueril) childlike; (infantil) childish.

a·ni·ñar·se reflex. to be childish.

a·ni·qui·la·ción f. annihilation, destruction.

a·ni·qui·la·mien·to m. var. of **aniquilación**.

a·ni·qui·lar tr. to annihilate, destroy —reflex. to be annihilated or destroyed.

a·nís m. anise; (grano) aniseed; (licor) anisette.

a·ni·sa·do m. anisette.

a·ni·ver·sa·rio, a adj. & m. anniversary.

a·no m. anus.

a·no·che adv. last night, yesterday evening.

a·no·che·cer §17 I. intr. to get dark, fall (night); (llegar) to arrive at nightfall **II.** m. nightfall, dusk.

a·no·che·ci·da f. nightfall, dusk.

a·no·ma·lí·a f. anomaly.

a·nó·ma·lo, a adj. anomalous.

a·no·na·da·ción f. depression, dejection.

a·no·na·dar tr. to overwhelm, dishearten —reflex. to be overwhelmed or disheartened.

a·no·ni·ma·to m. anonymity.

a·nó·ni·mo, a I. adj. anonymous **II.** m. (anonimato) anonymity; (carta) anonymous letter.

a·nor·mal adj. abnormal.

a·nor·ma·li·dad f. abnormality.

a·no·ta·ción f. (acción) noting; (nota) note.

a·no·ta·dor, ·ra I. adj. annotating, noting **II.** m.f. annotator.

a·no·tar tr. (poner notas) to annotate; (apuntar) to make note of.

an·qui·lo·sa·mien·to m. MED. stiffening; FIG. paralysis.

an·qui·lo·sar tr. MED. to stiffen —reflex. to become stiff; FIG. (paralizarse) to be paralyzed.

án·sar m. goose.

an·sia f. (inquietud) anxiety; (angustia) anguish; (anhelo) yearning.

an·siar §30 tr. to yearn or long for.

an·sie·dad f. anxiety.

an·sio·so, a adj. (preocupado) anxious; (deseoso) eager.

an·ta·gó·ni·co, a adj. antagonistic.

an·ta·go·nis·ta I. adj. antagonist, antagonistic **II.** m.f. antagonist, rival.

an·ta·ño adv. in days gone by.

an·te¹ m. ZOOL. elk.

an·te² prep. (delante de) before, in front of; (considerando) in view of, regarding.

an·te·a·no·che adv. the night before last.

an·te·a·yer adv. the day before yesterday.

an·te·bra·zo m. forearm.

an·te·cá·ma·ra f. antechamber, anteroom.

an·te·ce·den·te I. adj. preceding **II.** m. antecedent ♦ pl. background.

an·te·ce·der tr. & intr. to precede, antecede.

an·te·ce·sor, ·ra I. adj. former **II.** m.f. (predecesor) predecessor; (antepasado) ancestor.

an·te·da·tar tr. to antedate, backdate.

an·te·de·cir §11 tr. to foretell, predict.

an·te·di·cho, a adj. aforesaid, aforementioned.

an·te·di·lu·via·no, a adj. antediluvian.

an·te·la·ción f. ♦ **con a.** in advance • **con a. a** prior to.

an·te·ma·no adv. ♦ **de a.** in advance.

an·te·na f. ZOOL. antenna; RAD., TELEV. antenna, aerial; MARIT. lateen yard.

an·te·no·che adv. var. of **anteanoche**.

an·te·o·je·ra f. ♦ pl. blinders.

an·te·o·jo m. telescope ♦ **a. de larga vista** binoculars ♦ pl. (gafas) eyeglasses; (anteojeras) blinders; INDUS., SPORT. goggles.

an·te·pa·sa·do, a I. adj. before last **II.** m.f. ancestor.

an·te·pe·cho m. (baranda) rail, railing; (alféizar) window sill.

an·te·pe·núl·ti·mo, a adj. antepenultimate.

an·te·po·ner §54 tr. (poner delante) to place in front; FIG. to put before.

an·te·pro·yec·to m. draft, blueprint ♦ **a. de ley** draft bill.

an·te·pues·to, ta, pusiera, puso see **anteponer**.

an·te·rior adj. previous, before (a to); ANAT., ZOOL. front, fore.

an·te·rio·ri·dad f. ♦ **con a.** beforehand, in advance • **con a. a** prior to.

an·te·rior·men·te adv. previously, before; (con antelación) beforehand, in advance.

an·tes I. adj. & adv. before; (antiguamente) previously, formerly; (más bien) sooner ♦ **a. de** before, prior to • **a. de ayer** the day before yesterday • **a. que** before; (en vez de) rather than **II.** conj. rather, on the contrary.

an·te·sa·la f. anteroom ♦ **hacer a.** to cool one's heels.
an·te·úl·ti·mo, a adj. penultimate.
an·te·vís·pe·ra f. the day before yesterday.
an·ti·á·ci·do, a adj. & m. antacid.
an·ti·a·é·re·o, a adj. antiaircraft.
an·tia·me·ri·ca·no, a adj. & m.f. anti-American.
an·tia·tó·mi·co, a adj. antinuclear.
an·ti·bi·ó·ti·co, a adj. & m. antibiotic.
an·ti·can·ce·ro·so, a adj. anticarcinogenic.
an·ti·ci·pa·ción f. anticipation ♦ **con a.** in advance.
an·ti·ci·pa·da·men·te adv. in advance.
an·ti·ci·pa·do, a adj. advance, advanced ♦ **por a.** in advance.
an·ti·ci·pa·dor, ·ra adj. anticipatory.
an·ti·ci·par tr. to advance, move forward; (prestar) to advance; S. AMER. to foresee, anticipate —reflex. to be or arrive early ♦ **a. a** to get ahead of.
an·ti·ci·po m. anticipation; (dinero) advance (payment).
an·ti·cle·ri·cal adj. & m.f. anticlerical.
an·ti·co·a·gu·lan·te adj. & m. anticoagulant.
an·ti·com·bus·ti·ble adj. & m. noncombustible.
an·ti·co·mu·nis·ta adj. & m.f. anticommunist.
an·ti·con·cep·ti·vo, a adj. & m. contraceptive.
an·ti·con·ge·lan·te I. adj antifreezing II. m. antifreeze.
an·ti·cua·do, a adj. (en desuso) antiquated; (pasado de moda) old-fashioned.
an·ti·cua·rio, a I. adj. antiquarian II. m. antique dealer.
an·ti·cuer·po m. antibody.
an·ti·de·mo·crá·ti·co, a adj. undemocratic.
an·ti·de·pre·si·vo, a adj. & m. antidepressant.
an·ti·di·lu·via·no, a adj. var. of antediluviano.
an·tí·do·to m. antidote.
an·tie·co·nó·mi·co, a adj. uneconomical.
an·ties·té·ti·co, a adj. unaesthetic, unsightly.
an·ti·faz m. mask.
an·ti·gás adj. (against) gas.
an·ti·gua·lla f. COLL. relic, old-fashioned item.
an·ti·gua·men·te adv. (antes) formerly, once; (en tiempos remotos) in ancient times.
an·ti·guar §10 intr. to acquire seniority —reflex. to become old-fashioned.
an·ti·güe·dad f. (vejez) old age; (época) ancient times; (en el empleo) seniority ♦ pl. antiques.
an·ti·guo, a I. adj. (viejo) ancient, old; (anterior) former ♦ **a la a.** in the old-fashioned way II. m. old-timer ♦ **los antiguos** the ancients.
an·ti·hi·gié·ni·co, a adj. unsanitary.
an·ti·in·fla·cio·nis·ta adj. anti-inflationary.
an·tí·lo·pe m. antelope.
an·ti·ma·te·ria f. antimatter.
an·ti·mo·nár·qui·co, a adj. antimonarchist.
an·ti·na·tu·ral adj. unnatural.
an·ti·nu·cle·ar adj. antinuclear.
an·ti·pa·tí·a f. antipathy, dislike.
an·ti·pá·ti·co, a adj. disagreeable, unpleasant.
an·ti·pa·ti·zar §04 intr. AMER. to dislike.
an·ti·pa·trió·ti·co, a adj. unpatriotic.
an·ti·po·li·lla m. moth killer.
an·ti·rrá·bi·co, a adj. antirabies, antirabic.
an·ti·rra·cis·ta adj. & m.f. antiracist.
an·ti·se·mi·ta I. adj. anti-Semitic II. m.f. anti-Semite.

an·ti·se·mí·ti·co, a adj. anti-Semitic.
an·ti·sép·ti·co, a adj. & m. antiseptic.
an·ti·so·cia·ble adj. antisocial, unsociable.
an·ti·so·cial adj. antisocial.
an·ti·sub·ma·ri·no, a adj. antisubmarine.
an·ti·su·do·ral adj. & m. deodorant, antiperspirant.
an·ti·te·rro·ris·mo m. antiterrorism.
an·tí·te·sis f.inv. antithesis.
an·ti·té·ti·co, a adj. antithetical, antithetic.
an·ti·tó·xi·co, a adj. antitoxic.
an·ti·to·xi·na f. antitoxin, antibody.
an·to·ja·di·zo, a adj. capricious.
an·to·jar·se reflex. (gustar) to fancy, feel like; (parecer) to seem.
an·to·jo m. (capricho) whim; (de comida) craving; (lunar) birthmark ♦ **a su a.** as one pleases.
an·to·lo·gí·a f. anthology ♦ **de a.** COLL. great.
an·to·ló·gi·co, a adj. anthological.
an·to·ni·mia f. antonymy.
an·tó·ni·mo, a I. m. antonym II. adj. antonymous.
an·to·no·ma·sia f. antonomasia.
an·tor·cha f. torch; FIG. guide ♦ **a. a soplete** blowtorch.
an·tra·ci·ta f. anthracite, hard coal.
an·tro m. grotto; FIG. den, lair ♦ **a. de corrupción** den of iniquity.
an·tro·pó·fa·go, a I. adj. anthropophagous II. m.f. cannibal.
an·tro·po·gra·fí·a f. anthropography.
an·tro·poi·de adj. & m. anthropoid.
an·tro·po·lo·gí·a f. anthropology.
an·tro·po·ló·gi·co, a adj. anthropological.
an·tro·pó·lo·go, a m.f. anthropologist.
an·tro·po·me·trí·a f. anthropometry.
an·tro·po·mór·fi·co, a adj. anthropomorphic.
an·tro·po·mor·fo, a adj. anthropomorphous.
a·nual adj. annual, yearly.
a·nua·li·dad f. annual payment.
a·nua·rio m. yearbook, annual.
a·nu·ba·rra·do, a adj. cloudy, overcast.
a·nu·blar tr. to cloud; FIG. to darken, tarnish —reflex. to become cloudy or overcast; FIG. to be tarnished.
a·nu·dar tr. (hacer nudos) to tie in knots; (atar) to tie together —reflex. to become stunted ♦ **a. la lengua** FIG. to become tongue-tied.
a·nu·la·ción f. annulment, nullification ♦ **a. del juicio** LAW mistrial.
a·nu·lar[1] I. adj. annular, ring-shaped II. m. ring finger.
a·nu·lar[2] tr. to annul; (desautorizar) to remove from power.
a·nun·cia·ción f. announcement.
a·nun·cia·dor, ·ra I. adj. (declarativo) announcing; (publicitario) advertising II. m.f. (persona) announcer; (empresa) advertiser.
a·nun·cian·te I. adj. advertising II. m.f. advertiser.
a·nun·ciar tr. to announce; (publicar) to advertise; (presagiar) to foreshadow.
a·nun·cio m. announcement; (cartel) poster; (señal) sign; COM. advertisement ♦ **anuncios clasificados** classified advertisements.
an·ver·so m. obverse.
an·zue·lo m. fishhook; FIG. lure ♦ **tragarse el a.** COLL. to swallow the bait.
a·ña·di·do m. addition.
a·ña·di·du·ra f. addition ♦ **de a.** for good measure • **por a.** besides.

a·ña·dir tr. to add; *(aumentar)* to increase; *(conferir)* to lend.

a·ñe·ja·mien·to m. aging, maturing.

a·ñe·jar tr. & reflex. to age, mature.

a·ñe·jo, a adj. aged, mature.

a·ñi·cos m.pl. bits, pieces ♦ **hacerse a.** to break into pieces.

a·ñil I. m. BOT. indigo; *(para lavado)* bluing **II.** adj. indigo, blue.

a·ñi·lar tr. to dye indigo *or* blue.

a·ñi·nos m.pl. *(piel)* lambskins; *(lana)* lambswool.

a·ño m. year ♦ **a. bisiesto** leap year • **a. económico** fiscal year • **a. lectivo** school year • **a. en curso** current year • **a. luz** light-year • **el a. verde** COLL. never • **en el a. de la nana** COLL. way back • **entrado en años** advanced in years • **tener ... años** to be ... years old.

a·ño·ran·za f. nostalgia.

a·ño·rar tr. & intr. to long, yearn (for).

a·o·jar tr. to give the evil eye to, jinx.

a·o·jo m. evil eye, jinx.

a·o·va·do, a adj. oval; BOT. ovate.

a·o·var intr. to lay eggs.

a·o·vi·llar·se reflex. to roll up into a ball.

a·pa·bu·lla·mien·to m. var. of **apabullo**.

a·pa·bu·llar tr. to crush, squash.

a·pa·bu·llo m. COLL. crushing.

a·pa·cen·ta·de·ro m. pasture.

a·pa·cen·ta·dor, ·ra I. adj. grazing **II.** m. shepherd —f. shepherdess.

a·pa·cen·ta·mien·to m. *(acción)* grazing, pasturing; *(pasto)* pasture, grass.

a·pa·cen·tar §49 tr. & reflex. to graze, pasture.

a·pa·che m.f. Apache; FIG. *(malhechor)* thug, bandit —m. MEX. raincoat.

a·pa·ci·bi·li·dad f. calmness, gentleness.

a·pa·ci·ble adj. calm, gentle.

a·pa·ci·gua·dor, ·ra I. adj. appeasing, pacifying **II.** m.f. appeaser, pacifier.

a·pa·ci·gua·mien·to m. appeasement, pacifying.

a·pa·ci·guar §10 tr. *(sosegar)* to appease; *(un dolor)* to relieve —reflex. to calm down.

a·pa·dri·nar tr. *(patrocinar)* to sponsor; *(apoyar)* to support; *(a un niño)* to be godfather to; *(en una boda)* to be best man for; *(en un desafío)* to act as second for.

a·pa·ga·do, a adj. *(extinguido)* extinguished; *(apocado)* shy; FIG. dull, subdued.

a·pa·gar §47 tr. *(el fuego)* to put out; *(la luz)* to turn out; *(la cal)* to slake; *(el ruido)* to silence; *(el color)* to tone down —reflex. to fade.

a·pa·ga·ve·las m.inv. candle snuffer.

a·pa·gón m. blackout, power failure.

a·pa·la·brar tr. to agree to.

a·pa·le·ar tr. to thrash; AGR. to winnow.

a·pa·le·o m. thrashing; AGR. winnowing.

a·pan·di·llar tr. to form into a gang —reflex. to band together.

a·pa·ñar tr. *(asir)* to grasp; *(apoderarse)* to seize; COLL. *(abrigar)* to wrap up; *(reparar)* to repair, mend; ARG., PERU to cover up for, protect; MEX. to excuse, forgive —reflex. *(darse maña)* to manage.

a·pa·ño m. *(acción)* grasping; COLL. *(remiendo)* patch; *(habilidad)* knack; *(lío)* mess, trouble; *(amante)* lover.

a·pa·ra·dor m. *(armario)* sideboard, cupboard; *(taller)* studio; *(escaparate)* window.

a·pa·ra·to m. apparatus, device; FIG. pomp, show; ANAT., ZOOL. system; MED. bandage ♦ **a. de televisión, de radio** television, radio set • **aparatos de mando** controls.

a·pa·ra·to·si·dad f. showiness, ostentation.

a·pa·ra·to·so, a adj. pompous, ostentatious.

a·par·ca·mien·to m. *(acción)* parking; *(garaje)* parking lot, garage.

a·par·car §70 tr. *(estacionar)* to park; MIL. to deposit (arms).

a·par·ce·rí·a f. sharecropping.

a·par·ce·ro, a m.f. sharecropper; AMER. comrade.

a·pa·re·ar tr. to match up, pair off; ZOOL. to mate, breed.

a·pa·re·cer §17 intr. & reflex. to appear; *(mostrarse)* to show up, turn up.

a·pa·re·ci·do m. ghost, phantom.

a·pa·re·ci·mien·to m. appearance.

a·pa·re·ja·do, a adj. apt, fit ♦ **ir a. con** to go hand in hand with • **traer a.** to mean, involve.

a·pa·re·jar tr. to prepare, make ready; *(los caballos)* to harness; MARIT. to rig —reflex. to get ready.

a·pa·re·jo m. preparation; *(arreo)* harness; *(poleas)* derrick; MARIT. rigging; PAINT. priming; CONST. bonding; AMER. saddle.

a·pa·ren·tar tr. *(fingir)* to pretend, feign; *(parecer)* to seem, look.

a·pa·ren·te adj. *(presumible)* apparent, seeming; *(visible)* apparent, visible.

a·pa·ri·ción f. *(acción)* appearance; *(fantasma)* apparition, specter.

a·pa·rien·cia f. appearance ♦ **en a.** apparently • **salvar las apariencias** to keep up appearances, save face.

a·par·ta·de·ro m. sidetrack, siding.

a·par·ta·do, a I. adj. remote, isolated **II.** m. *(casilla postal)* post office box; *(párrafo)* paragraph, section.

a·par·ta·men·to m. apartment, flat (G.B.)

a·par·ta·mien·to m. *(separación)* separation; *(aislamiento)* isolation.

a·par·tar tr. *(separar)* to separate; *(llevar aparte)* to take aside; *(alejar)* to put aside —reflex. to withdraw, move away.

a·par·te I. adv. *(por separado)* apart, separate; *(a un lado)* aside, to one side ♦ **a. de** besides, apart from **II.** m. paragraph; THEAT. aside.

a·par·theid m. apartheid.

a·pa·sio·na·do, a adj. enthusiastic, intense.

a·pa·sio·nan·te adj. exciting, thrilling.

a·pa·sio·nar tr. to enthuse, excite —reflex. to become enthused *or* excited.

a·pa·tí·a f. apathy, indifference.

a·pá·ti·co, a adj. apathetic, indifferent.

a·pá·tri·da I. adj. stateless, without a country **II.** m.f. stateless person, one without a country.

a·pe·a·de·ro m. *(poyo)* mounting block; *(fonda)* inn; RAIL. way station.

a·pe·a·mien·to m. *(de un caballo)* dismounting; *(de un vehículo)* getting out; ARCHIT. bracing; SURV. surveying.

a·pe·ar tr. *(bajar)* to lower; *(árbol)* to fell; *(caballo)* to fetter; *(rueda)* to chock; *(tierras)* to survey; ARCHIT. to prop up —reflex. *(de un caballo)* to dismount; *(de un vehículo)* to get out of; AMER. to stay, lodge.

a·pe·chu·gar §47 intr. ♦ **a. con** COLL. to put up with, face.

a·pe·dre·ar tr. *(lanzar)* to hurl stones at; *(matar)* to stone to death —intr. to hail —reflex. to suffer damage from hail.

a·pe·gar·se §47 reflex. to become attached *or* fond (*a* to, of).

a·pe·go m. FIG. attachment, fondness ♦ **cobrar a. a** to become attached to *or* fond of.

a·pe·la·ble adj. appealable.

a·pe·la·ción f. LAW appeal; (*recurso*) recourse ♦ **interponer a.** to (file an) appeal.

a·pe·lar intr. to appeal ♦ **a. a** *or* **ante** to appeal to.

a·pe·la·ti·vo, a I. adj. appellative II. m. AMER., COLL. last name, surname.

a·pe·lli·dar tr. to call, name —reflex. to be called *or* named.

a·pe·lli·do m. last name, surname; (*apodo*) nickname ♦ **a. de soltera** maiden name.

a·pel·ma·za·do, a adj. compact, compressed; FIG. dull, stodgy.

a·pel·ma·zar §04 tr. to compress, compact.

a·pe·lo·to·nar tr. to form into balls *or* tufts —reflex. (*hacerse bolitas*) to form balls *or* tufts; FIG. (*apiñarse*) to cluster, throng.

a·pe·nar tr. to grieve, pain —reflex. to be grieved *or* pained.

a·pe·nas adv. (*casi no*) scarcely, hardly; (*con dificultad*) hardly, with difficulty; (*enseguida que*) as soon as.

a·pen·dec·to·mí·a f. appendectomy.

a·pén·di·ce m. appendage; ANAT. appendix.

a·pen·di·ci·tis f.inv. appendicitis.

a·per·ci·bir tr. (*disponer*) to make ready; (*advertir*) to warn —reflex. to prepare oneself.

a·per·ga·mi·na·do, a adj. parchment-like; FIG. dried-up.

a·per·ga·mi·nar·se reflex. COLL. to become wizened, dry up.

a·pe·ri·ti·vo, a I. adj. CUL. appetizing; MED. aperitive II. m. CUL. apéritif, appetizer; MED. aperitive.

a·pe·ro m. (*utensilios*) equipment, gear; AGR. draft animals; AMER. riding gear.

a·per·so·nar·se reflex. to present oneself.

a·per·tu·ra f. (*principio*) opening, commencement; (*de un testamento*) reading; (*ajedrez*) opening move; POL. opening.

a·pe·sa·dum·brar tr. to grieve, distress —reflex. to be grieved *or* distressed (*de, por* by).

a·pes·tar tr. (*contaminar*) to infect (with the plague); COLL. (*fastidiar*) to annoy —intr. to stink —reflex. (*ser contaminado*) to be infected with the plague.

a·pes·to·so, a adj. (*fétido*) stinking; COLL. (*fastidioso*) annoying.

a·pe·te·ce·dor, ·ra adj. appetizing, tempting.

a·pe·te·cer §17 tr. (*ansiar*) to long for, crave; FIG. to desire —intr. to be appealing *or* attractive.

a·pe·te·ci·ble adj. appealing, appetizing.

a·pe·ten·cia f. (*hambre*) appetite; (*deseo*) desire.

a·pe·ti·to m. appetite ♦ **abrir, dar** *or* **despertar el a.** to whet one's appetite.

a·pe·ti·to·so, a adj. appetizing, delicious.

a·pia·dar tr. to move to pity —reflex. to (have) pity ♦ **a. de** to take pity on.

á·pi·ce m. (*cima*) apex, top, pinnacle; FIG. (*nonada*) iota, whit ♦ **no ceder un a.** not to give an inch.

a·pi·cul·tor, ·ra m.f. beekeeper, apiculturist.

a·pi·cul·tu·ra f. beekeeping, apiculture.

a·pi·lar tr. to pile *or* heap.

a·pim·po·llar·se reflex. to bud, sprout.

a·pi·ña·do, a adj. (*cónico*) conical; (*apretado*) crammed *or* packed together.

a·pi·ña·mien·to m. (*acción*) crowding; (*aprieto*) crush.

a·pi·ñar tr. & reflex. to cram, jam.

a·pio m. celery.

a·pi·so·na·do·ra f. (*aplastadora*) flattener; (*de carretera*) steamroller.

a·pi·so·na·mien·to m. (*acción*) flattening; (*de carretera*) steamrolling.

a·pi·so·nar tr. (*tierra*) to pack down; (*carretera*) to steamroller.

a·pla·ca·mien·to m. appeasement, placation.

a·pla·car §70 tr. to appease, placate.

a·pla·na·dor, ·ra I. adj. flattening II. f. steamroller.

a·pla·na·mien·to m. leveling, flattening.

a·pla·nar tr. (*allanar*) to level, flatten; COLL. (*pasmar*) to stun —reflex. (*venirse abajo*) to collapse; FIG. to lose heart.

a·plas·tan·te adj. (*agobiador*) overwhelming; (*cansador*) exhausting.

a·plas·tar tr. (*estrujar*) to crush; (*vencer*) to overwhelm; COLL. (*apabullar*) to stun —reflex. AMER. (*desanimarse*) to become discouraged; (*cansarse*) to get tired.

a·plau·dir tr. to applaud; FIG. to applaud, commend.

a·plau·so m. (*palmas*) applause, clapping; FIG. applause, praise.

a·pla·za·mien·to m. postponement.

a·pla·zar §04 tr. (*diferir*) to postpone, put off; AMER. to fail, flunk.

a·pli·ca·ble adj. applicable.

a·pli·ca·ción f. application; (*adorno*) appliqué; (*esmero*) diligence.

a·pli·ca·do, a adj. diligent.

a·pli·car §70 tr. (*poner*) to apply, put on; (*designar*) to assign; (*usar*) to use, employ —reflex. to apply oneself.

a·pli·que m. light fixture.

a·plo·ma·do, a adj. poised.

a·plo·mo m. aplomb; (*verticalidad*) vertical alignment.

a·po·ca·do, a adj. diffident, timid.

a·po·ca·líp·ti·co, a adj. apocalyptic.

a·po·co·par tr. to apocopate, elide.

a·pó·co·pe f. apocope, elision.

a·pó·cri·fo, a adj. apocryphal.

a·po·dar tr. to nickname.

a·po·de·ra·do, a I. adj. empowered, authorized II. m.f. (*poderhabiente*) attorney, proxy; (*empresario*) manager, agent.

a·po·de·ra·mien·to m. (*autorización*) authorization; (*apropiación*) seizure.

a·po·de·rar tr. to grant power of attorney to —reflex. ♦ **a. de** (*apropiar*) to take possession of; (*dominar*) to overwhelm.

a·po·do m. nickname.

a·po·ge·o m. ASTRON. apogee; FIG. height.

a·po·li·llar·se reflex. to be moth-eaten; AMER., COLL. to snooze, doze.

a·po·lí·ti·co, a adj. & m.f. apolitical (person).

a·po·lo·gis·ta m.f. apologist, defender.

a·pol·tro·nar·se reflex. to get lazy.

a·por·car §73 tr. to hill, earth up (plants).

a·po·rrar intr. COLL. to be left speechless.

a·po·rre·a·do m. CUBA beef stew.

a·po·rre·ar tr. (*golpear*) to beat; (*instrumento*) to bang on; (*insistir*) to harp on —reflex. FIG. to break one's back.

a·por·tar intr. MARIT. to arrive; (*llegar por ca-*

sualidad) to arrive *or* end up by chance —tr. *(traer)* to bring; *(contribuir)* to contribute.

a·por·te m. AMER. contribution, donation.

a·po·sen·tar tr. & reflex. to lodge.

a·po·sen·to m. *(habitación)* room; *(hospedaje)* lodging.

a·po·si·ción f. apposition.

a·pos·tar §19 tr. *(jugar)* to wager; *(colocar)* to post —reflex. to position oneself.

a·pos·ta·tar intr. to apostatize.

a·pos·ti·lla f. marginal note, annotation.

a·pós·tol m. apostle.

a·pos·to·la·do m. apostolate.

a·pos·tó·li·co, a adj. *(de los apóstoles)* apostolic; *(del papa)* papal, pontific.

a·pós·tro·fe m. *or* f. RHET. apostrophe.

a·pós·tro·fo m. GRAM. apostrophe.

a·po·te·ca·rio m. apothecary.

a·po·teg·ma m. apothegm, maxim.

a·po·te·ó·si·co, a adj. *(glorificador)* deifying; *(glorioso)* magnificent.

a·po·te·o·sis f.inv. apotheosis, FIG. glorification.

a·po·te·ó·ti·co, a adj. magnificent.

a·po·yar tr. *(estribar)* to lean, rest; *(ayudar)* to aid, support; *(confirmar)* to uphold; MIL. to reinforce —intr. to lean, rest —reflex. to lean, rest; FIG. to rely on.

a·po·yo m. *(soporte)* support; *(fundamento)* basis; *(protección)* aid.

a·pre·cia·ción f. *(valorización)* appraisal; *(aprecio)* appreciation.

a·pre·ciar tr. to appraise; *(estimar)* to appreciate; *(considerar)* to consider.

a·pre·cia·ti·vo, a adj. appraising.

a·pre·cio m. COM. appraisal; *(estima)* esteem; MEX. attention ♦ **no hacer a. a** MEX. not to pay attention to.

a·pre·hen·der tr. *(apresar)* to apprehend; *(confiscar)* to seize; *(concebir)* to apprehend.

a·pre·hen·sión f. *(apresamiento)* apprehension; *(embargo)* seizure; *(comprensión)* comprehension.

a·pre·hen·si·vo, a adj. apprehensive.

a·pre·mian·te adj. pressing, urgent.

a·pre·miar tr. *(acelerar)* to press; *(oprimir)* to oppress; LAW to compel.

a·pre·mio m. *(urgencia)* urgency; LAW judicial order.

a·pren·der tr. to learn *(a* to).

a·pren·diz, ·za m.f. apprentice.

a·pren·di·za·je m. apprenticeship.

a·pren·sión f. *(miedo)* apprehension; *(sospecha)* suspicion.

a·pren·si·vo, a adj. apprehensive.

a·pre·sar tr. *(aprisionar)* to capture; ZOOL. to grasp; MARIT. to capture.

a·pres·tar tr. *(preparar)* to make ready; TEX. to size —reflex. to prepare oneself.

a·pres·to m. *(preparación)* making ready; TEX. sizing.

a·pre·su·ra·mien·to m. hurry, haste.

a·pre·su·rar tr. to hurry, hasten —reflex. to hurry, make haste *(a, por* to).

a·pre·ta·do, a adj. *(comprimido)* cramped, tight; COLL. *(arduo)* difficult; *(mezquino)* stingy ♦ **estar muy a.** COLL. *(problemas)* to be in a jam; *(dinero)* to be short of money • **estar a. de trabajo** to be up to one's neck in work.

a·pre·ta·mien·to m. var. of **aprieto.**

a·pre·tar §49 tr. *(nudo)* to tighten; *(estrujar)* to squeeze; *(comprimir)* to compress; *(abrazar)* to hug; *(apremiar)* to urge ♦ **a. la mano** to shake

hands • **a. los dientes** to grit *or* clench one's teeth —intr. *(los zapatos)* to pinch; *(la ropa)* to be too tight; *(empeorar)* to worsen, get worse.

a·pre·tón m. grip, squeeze ♦ **a. de manos** handshake.

a·pre·tu·jar tr. *(apretar)* to squeeze; *(apiñar)* to cram.

a·prie·te, to see **apretar.**

a·prie·to m. jam, fix ♦ **poner a alguien en un a.** to put someone on the spot.

a·pri·sa adv. quickly, swiftly.

a·pri·sio·nar tr. to bind.

a·pro·ba·ción f. approval; LAW ratification.

a·pro·ba·do, a I. adj. approved **II.** m. passing grade.

a·pro·bar §19 tr. *(consentir)* to approve of; *(examen)* to pass; LAW to ratify —intr. to pass an examination.

a·pro·ba·to·rio, a adj. approving.

a·pron·tar tr. *(disponer)* to have ready; *(entregar)* to deliver at once.

a·pron·te m. R.P. *(de caballos)* trial (race); FIG. dry run.

a·pro·pia·ción f. appropriation.

a·pro·pia·do, a adj. appropriate, suitable.

a·pro·piar tr. AMER., FIN. to earmark —reflex. to take possession *(de* of).

a·pro·pin·cuar·se reflex. to draw near.

a·pro·ve·cha·dor, ·ra I. adj. opportunistic **II.** m.f. opportunist.

a·pro·ve·cha·mien·to m. use, utilization.

a·pro·ve·char intr. to be useful —tr. to make good use of —reflex. ♦ **a. de** to take advantage of.

a·pro·vi·sio·na·mien·to m. *(acción)* supplying; *(provisiones)* supplies.

a·pro·vi·sio·nar tr. to supply, provision.

a·pro·xi·ma·ción f. *(proximidad)* nearness; *(estimación)* approximation.

a·pro·xi·ma·da·men·te adv. approximately, about.

a·pro·xi·mar tr. to bring near —reflex. to draw near.

a·prue·be, bo see **aprobar.**

ap·ti·tud f. aptitude ♦ pl. gift, talent.

ap·to, a adj. *(hábil)* competent; *(conveniente)* fit.

a·pues·te, to see **apostar.**

a·pues·to, a I. adj. elegant **II.** f. bet, wager.

a·pu·nar·se reflex. AMER. to be overcome by altitude sickness.

a·pun·ta·dor, ·ra I. adj. observing, noting **II.** m.f. THEAT. prompter; MIL. pointer, gunner.

a·pun·ta·la·mien·to m. propping, shoring.

a·pun·ta·lar tr. to prop up, shore up.

a·pun·tar tr. *(arma)* to aim, point; *(señalar)* to point to *or* at, indicate; *(tomar nota)* to make a note of; *(sugerir)* to cue, clue; *(insinuar)* to hint at, suggest; THEAT. to prompt —intr. to begin to show —reflex. to begin to turn sour.

a·pun·te m. *(nota)* note, notation; THEAT. prompter ♦ **llevar el a.** R.P., COLL. *(escuchar)* to pay attention; *(en el galanteo)* to accept someone's attentions.

a·pu·ña·lar tr. to stab, knife ♦ **a. a alguien con la mirada** to look daggers at someone.

apu·ñar tr. to seize in one's fist.

a·pu·ñe·(te·)ar tr. COLL. to punch.

a·pu·ra·do, a adj. AMER. in a hurry.

a·pu·rar tr. AMER. to hurry, press; *(purificar)* to refine; *(agotar)* to use *or* finish up; *(enfadar)* to annoy —reflex. AMER. to hurry.

a·pu·ro m. hurry ♦ **estar en apuros** *(dificulta-des)* to be in a jam; *(dinero)* to be hard up (for money).

a·que·jar tr. to afflict, distress.

a·quel, ·lla dem. adj. [pl. **-llos, -llas**] that (. . . over there) ♦ pl. those.

a·quél, ·lla dem. pron. [pl. **-llos, -llas**] that one (over there); *(el primero)* the former ♦ pl. those.

a·que·llo neut. dem. pron. that, that matter ♦ **a. de** that business about.

a·que·ren·cia·do, a adj. MEX. in love, fond.

a·que·ren·ciar·se reflex. ♦ **a. a** to become fond of *or* attached to.

a·quí adv. *(en este lugar)* here; *(ahora)* now; *(entonces)* then, at that point ♦ **de a. en ade-lante** from now on, from here on in • **por a.** *(alrededor)* around here; *(por este lado)* this way.

a·quie·tar tr. to calm, soothe —reflex. to calm down, become calm.

a·qui·la·tar tr. JEWEL. to appraise; FIG. to ap-preciate.

a·ra f. *(altar)* (sacrificial) altar; *(piedra)* altar stone —m. macaw ♦ **en aras de** for the sake of.

a·rá·bi·co/go, a adj. ♦ **número a.** Arabic nu-meral.

a·rác·ni·dos m.pl. arachnids.

a·ra·da f. *(acción)* plowing; *(tierra)* plowed land; *(labranza)* farming.

a·ra·do m. *(máquina)* plow; *(acción)* plowing.

a·ran·cel m. tariff, duty.

a·ran·de·la f. MECH. washer; AMER. frills, flounce.

a·ra·ña f. spider; *(candelabro)* chandelier ♦ **a. de mar** spider crab.

a·ra·ñar tr. *(rasgar)* to scratch, scrape; COLL. *(recoger)* to scrape together.

a·ra·ña·zo m. scratch.

a·rar tr. to plow.

a·rau·ca·no, a adj. & m.f. Araucanian.

ar·bi·tra·je m. arbitration; COM. arbitrage.

ar·bi·trar tr. to arbitrate; SPORT. to referee, um-pire; *(proceder libremente)* to act freely —intr. to arbitrate.

ar·bi·tra·rie·dad f. arbitrariness.

ar·bi·tra·rio, a adj. arbitrary.

ar·bi·trio m. *(voluntad)* will; *(recurso)* means; *(juicio)* judgment.

ár·bi·tro m. arbiter, arbitrator; SPORT. referee.

ár·bol m. tree; MECH. axle; MARIT. mast; ARCHIT. crown drive shaft ♦ **á. de levas** camshaft • **á. motor** drive shaft.

ar·bo·la·do, a I. adj. wooded **II.** m. grove.

ar·bo·lar tr. MARIT. to rig; *(poner derecho)* to set upright —reflex. to rear (a horse).

ar·bo·le·da f. grove, wood.

ar·bo·re·to m. arboretum.

ar·bo·ri·cul·tu·ra f. arboriculture.

ar·bo·ri·zar §04 tr. to forest, plant with trees.

ar·bus·to m. bush, shrub.

ar·ca f. *(cofre)* chest ♦ **a. de agua** reservoir • **a. de la Alianza** BIBL. Ark of the Covenant • **a. de Noé** BIBL. Noah's Ark ♦ pl. coffers.

ar·ca·buz m. *(arma)* harquebus; *(arcabucero)* harquebusier.

ar·ca·da f. ARCHIT. arcade; *(de un puente)* span; *(basca)* retch.

ar·cai·co, a adj. archaic, old-fashioned.

ar·ca·ís·ta m.f. archaist.

ar·cai·zar §06 tr. to make archaic.

ar·cán·gel m. archangel.

ar·ca·no, a I. adj. arcane **II.** m. mystery.

ar·ce m. maple (tree).

ar·chi·du·que m. archduke.

ar·chi·du·que·sa f. archduchess.

ar·chi·mi·llo·na·rio, a m.f. multimillionaire.

ar·chi·pié·la·go m. archipelago.

ar·chi·va·dor, ·ra m.f. filing clerk —m. filing cabinet.

ar·chi·var tr. *(clasificar)* to file, put into a file; FIG. to shelve.

ar·chi·ve·ro, a/vis·ta m.f. archivist.

ar·chi·vo m. archives; *(de oficina)* files; COMPUT. file.

ar·ci·lla f. clay ♦ **a. figulina** potter's clay.

ar·ci·llo·so, a adj. clay-like, clayey.

ar·co m. GEOM. arc; ARCHIT., ANAT. arch; ARM., MUS. bow; SPORT. goal ♦ **a. iris** rainbow • **a. voltaico** ELEC. arc lamp.

ar·der intr. to burn; FIG. to glow, blaze ♦ **a. de** *or* **en** FIG. to rage *or* be ablaze with.

ar·did m. ruse, scheme.

ar·dien·te adj. *(quemante)* burning; *(al rojo)* glowing; FIG. ardent.

ar·di·lla f. squirrel ♦ **a. listada** chipmunk.

ar·di·te m. old Spanish coin of little value ♦ **no valer un a.** COLL. not to be worth a cent.

ar·dor m. heat; FIG. zeal.

ar·do·ro·so, a adj. hot; FIG. ardent.

ar·duo, a adj. arduous, difficult.

á·re·a f. area.

a·re·na f. sand; *(redondel)* ring; *(campo de ba-talla)* battlefield ♦ **arenas movedizas** quicksand.

a·re·nal m. *(terreno arenoso)* sandy ground; *(arena movediza)* quicksand.

a·re·nar tr. *(enarenar)* to cover with sand; *(fro-tar)* to sand.

a·re·ne·ro, a m.f. *(vendedor)* sand merchant —m. RAIL. sandbox.

a·ren·ga f. harangue; FIG. sermon.

a·ren·gar §47 tr. & intr. to harangue.

a·re·ni·lla f. calculus; *(polvo)* blotting powder.

a·re·nis·co, a I. adj. sandy **II.** f. sandstone.

a·re·no·so, a adj. sandy.

a·ren·que m. herring.

a·re·te m. *(aro)* hoop, ring; *(pendiente)* earring.

ar·ga·ma·sa f. mortar, plaster.

ar·ga·ma·sar intr. to mix mortar —tr. to mortar, plaster.

ar·gen·ta·do, a adj. *(bañado)* silvered, silver-plated; *(color)* silver, silvery.

ar·gen·tar tr. to silver, silver-plate.

ar·gen·ta·rio m. silversmith.

ar·gén·te·o, a adj. *(de plata)* silver; FIG. silvery.

ar·gen·te·rí·a f. gold *or* silver embroidery.

ar·gen·ti·nis·mo m. Argentine word *or* expres-sion.

ar·gen·to m. POET. silver ♦ **a. vivo** quicksilver.

ar·go·lla f. ring; S. AMER. *(anillo)* wedding *or* engagement ring; MEX., COLL. luck.

ar·go·nau·ta m. MYTH. Argonaut; ICHTH. argo-naut, paper nautilus.

ar·got m. slang, jargon.

ar·gu·cia f. subtlety.

ar·güir §07 intr. to argue —tr. *(deducir)* to deduce; *(probar)* to prove.

ar·gu·men·ta·ción f. *(acción)* arguing; *(argu-mento)* argument.

ar·gu·men·ta·ti·vo, a adj. argumentative.

ar·gu·men·tar intr. to argue.

ar·gu·men·tis·ta m.f. CINEM. script writer.

ar·gu·men·to m. *(razonamiento)* line of reason-ing; *(trama)* plot; *(sumario)* summary.

ar·gu·ya, yo, yera, yó see **argüir.**
a·ria f. aria.
a·ri·dez f. aridity, aridness.
á·ri·do, a I. adj. arid, dry; FIG. dry, dull
II. m.pl. dry goods.
a·rie·te m. MIL., HIST. battering ram.
a·rio, a adj. & m.f. Aryan.
a·ris·co, a adj. *(desabrido)* unfriendly; *(salvaje)* wild.
a·ris·ta f. GEOM. edge; BOT. beard, awn; ARCHIT. arris.
a·ris·ta·do, a adj. BOT. bearded; *(con borde)* with edges.
a·ris·to·cra·cia f. aristocracy.
a·ris·tó·cra·ta m.f. aristocrat.
a·ris·to·crá·ti·co, a adj. *(noble)* aristocratic; *(distinguido)* distinguished.
a·ris·to·té·li·co, a adj. & m.f. Aristotelian.
a·rit·mé·ti·co, a I. adj. arithmetical, arithmetic II. m.f. arithmetician —f. arithmetic; *(libro)* arithmetic book.
ar·le·quín m. harlequin, clown.
ar·ma f. weapon, arm ♦ **a. blanca** bladed weapon ♦ **a. de fuego** firearm ♦ pl. *(instrumentos)* arms, weapons; *(ejército)* troops, army; FIG. *(medios)* means ♦ **¡a las a.!** to arms! ♦ **alzarse en a.** to rise up in arms ♦ **parar por las a.** to shoot ♦ **presentar a.** to present arms.
ar·ma·do, a I. adj. armed; CONSTR. reinforced II. f. armada, (naval) fleet.
ar·ma·du·ra f. MIL. armor; *(armazón)* frame, framework; ELEC. armature; MUS. key signature.
ar·ma·men·tis·ta adj. arms, armaments.
ar·ma·men·to m. *(acción)* armament; *(armas)* weapons.
ar·mar tr. *(dar armas)* to arm; *(aprestar)* to prime; *(montar)* to assemble; *(dar fuerza)* to reinforce; MARIT. to equip; FIG. to create ♦ **armarla** to cause a scandal —reflex. to arm oneself; S. AMER. to strike it rich, get lucky.
ar·ma·rio m. closet, wardrobe.
ar·ma·tos·te m. *(algo tosco)* monstrosity; *(palurdo)* hulk.
ar·ma·zón m. or f. framework, frame.
ar·me·lla f. eyebolt.
ar·me·rí·a f. *(museo)* military museum; *(tienda)* gunsmith's shop; *(fabricación)* gunsmithing.
ar·mi·ño m. ermine.
ar·mis·ti·cio m. armistice.
ar·mo·ní·a f. harmony.
ar·mó·ni·ca·men·te adv. harmonically, harmoniously.
ar·mó·ni·co, a I. adj. harmonic, harmonious II. m. harmonic —f. harmonica.
ar·mo·nio m. harmonium.
ar·mo·nio·so, a adj. harmonious.
ar·mo·ni·za·ción f. MUS. harmonizing; *(reconciliación)* reconciliation; *(de colores)* coordinating.
ar·mo·ni·zar §04 tr. & intr. to harmonize.
ar·nés m. armor ♦ pl. harness.
a·ro m. *(círculo)* hoop, ring; R.P. earring; BOT. arum ♦ **entra por el a.** COLL. to yield unwillingly.
a·ro·ma m. aroma, scent; *(del vino)* bouquet.
a·ro·mar tr. to perfume, scent.
a·ro·má·ti·co, a adj. aromatic.
a·ro·ma·ti·za·ción f. perfuming, scenting.
a·ro·ma·ti·za·dor m. AMER. atomizer.
a·ro·ma·ti·zan·te adj. perfuming.
a·ro·ma·ti·zar §04 tr. to perfume; CUL. to flavor.

a·ro·mo·so, a adj. aromatic, fragrant.
ar·pa f. harp ♦ **a. eolia** Aeolian harp.
ar·pí·a f. harpy; COLL. shrew, hag.
ar·pi·lle·ra f. burlap, sackcloth.
ar·pis·ta m.f. harpist.
ar·pón m. harpoon; ARCHIT. clamp.
ar·po·nar/ne·ar tr. to harpoon.
ar·que·a·da f. MUS. bowing.
ar·que·ar tr. *(curvar)* to curve; MARIT. to gauge —intr. AMER. to audit —reflex. to curve.
ar·que·o m. *(acción)* curve; MARIT. gauging; COM. audit.
ar·que·o·lo·gí·a f. archaeology.
ar·que·o·ló·gi·co, a adj. archaeological.
ar·que·ó·lo·go, a m.f. archaeologist.
ar·que·ro m. *(soldado)* archer; *(tonelero)* cooper; SPORT. goalie.
ar·que·ti·po m. archetype.
ar·qui·dió·ce·sis f.inv. archdiocese.
ar·qui·tec·to, a m.f. architect.
ar·qui·tec·tó·ni·co, a adj. architectural.
ar·qui·tec·tu·ra f. architecture.
ar·qui·tec·tu·ral adj. architectural.
a·rra·bal m. slum ♦ pl. outskirts.
a·rra·ba·le·ro, a I. m.f. COLL. common, coarse person II. adj. COLL. coarse, common.
a·rra·ci·ma·do, a adj. clustered, bunched.
a·rra·ci·mar·se reflex. to form a bunch.
a·rrai·gar §47 intr. BOT. to take root —tr. AMER., LAW to limit or restrict movement —reflex. BOT. to take root; *(establecerse)* to establish oneself; *(vicio, virtud)* to become deeply rooted.
a·rrai·go m. BOT. rooting ♦ **tener a.** to have a sense of belonging.
a·rram·blar tr. *(cubrir de arena)* to cover with sand (receding waters); *(arrastrar)* to sweep away; COLL. *(arrebatar)* to make off with.
a·rran·ca·cla·vos m.inv. claw (of a hammer).
a·rran·ca·da f. sudden start.
a·rran·ca·dor, ·ra I. adj. starting II. m. AUTO. starter —f. AGR. lifter, picker.
a·rran·ca·du·ra f. *(desarraigo)* uprooting; *(extracción)* extraction.
a·rran·car §70 tr. *(de raíz)* to pull up; *(con violencia)* to pull out; *(conseguir)* to obtain, seize —intr. *(salir)* to get started; *(provenir)* to stem *(de* from); AUTO. to start (up); RAIL. to pull out.
a·rran·que m. *(acción)* uprooting; *(toma)* seizure; *(principio)* outset; *(arrebato)* outburst; *(ocurrencia)* witty remark; AUTO. starter.
a·rra·sa·do, a adj. satiny, satin-like.
a·rra·sa·du·ra f. leveling, smoothing.
a·rra·sar tr. *(allanar)* to level; *(arruinar)* to destroy —intr. & reflex. to clear (the sky) ♦ **a. en** or **de lágrimas** to fill with tears.
a·rras·tra·di·zo, a adj. *(a rastras)* trailing; *(trillado)* frequented.
a·rras·tra·do, a I. adj. wretched II. m.f. rogue.
a·rras·trar tr. to pull, drag; *(los pies)* to drag, shuffle; *(atraer)* to attract —intr. to crawl; *(colgar)* to hang down —reflex. to crawl, grovel.
a·rras·tre m. dragging; FIG. influence, pull.
a·rra·yán m. myrtle.
a·rre·ar tr. *(ganado)* to herd; *(estimular)* to urge on; *(poner arreos)* to harness; AMER. to steal —intr. to move along.
a·rre·ba·ta·di·zo, a adj. excitable, impetuous.
a·rre·ba·ta·do, a adj. *(impetuoso)* impetuous; *(sonrojado)* flushed.

a·rre·ba·ta·dor, ·ra adj. *(cautivante)* charming; *(excitante)* exciting.

a·rre·ba·tar tr. *(arrancar)* to snatch; FIG. *(conmover)* to move, stir; AGR. to parch, dry up —reflex. FIG. *(enfurecerse)* to get carried away; AGR. to become parched *or* dry; CUL. to burn.

a·rre·ba·to m. *(arranque)* fit; *(furor)* rage; *(éxtasis)* ecstasy.

a·rre·bol m. *(color)* red glow; *(afeite)* rouge.

a·rre·bo·lar tr. to make red —reflex. to turn red.

a·rre·ciar intr. *(empeorarse)* to worsen; *(el tiempo)* to blow *or* rain harder.

a·rre·ci·fe m. reef.

a·rre·drar tr. to scare *or* frighten away —reflex. to be scared *or* frightened.

a·rre·gla·do, a adj. orderly, neat.

a·rre·glar tr. *(ordenar)* to put in order; *(acomodar)* to tidy up; *(ajustar)* to fix up; *(reparar)* to repair; *(solucionar)* to resolve; MUS. to arrange; ARG., MEX. to settle (a debt) ♦ **¡ya te arreglaré yo!** I'll fix you! —reflex. *(conformarse)* to adjust; *(ataviarse)* to get dressed (up) ♦ **arreglárselas** COLL. to manage.

a·rre·glo m. *(acción)* arrangement; *(orden)* order; *(convenio)* understanding; *(compostura)* repair; MUS. arrangement ♦ **con a. a** in accordance with.

a·rre·lla·nar·se reflex. to lounge.

a·rre·man·ga·do, a adj. turned-up.

a·rre·man·gar §47 tr. *(levantar)* to lift or tuck up; *(las mangas)* to roll up —reflex. COLL. to become determined.

a·rre·me·dar tr. to imitate, copy.

a·rre·me·te·dor, ·ra adj. & m.f. COLL. determined, resolute (person).

a·rre·me·ter tr. *(atacar)* to attack; COLL. *(emprender)* to go at.

a·rre·me·ti·da f. *(ataque)* assault; *(empujón)* shove.

a·rre·mo·li·nar·se reflex. *(apiñarse)* to crowd about; *(el agua)* to swirl.

a·rren·da·dor, ·ra m.f. *(propietario)* landlord; *(inquilino)* tenant.

a·rren·da·mien·to m. *(acción)* rental; *(alquiler)* rent.

a·rren·dar §49 tr. *(alquilar)* to rent; *(atar)* to tie up, hitch (horses).

a·rren·da·ta·rio, a I. adj. renting II. m.f. tenant.

a·rre·o m. AMER. herd, drove ♦ pl. harness.

a·rre·pen·ti·mien·to m. repentance.

a·rre·pen·tir·se §65 reflex. to repent; FIG. to regret.

a·rres·ta·do, a adj. arrested.

a·rres·tar tr. to arrest, place under arrest.

a·rres·to m. *(detención)* arrest; *(reclusión)* imprisonment; *(audacia)* boldness.

a·rriar §30 tr. MARIT. to lower; *(aflojar)* to slacken.

a·rri·ba adv. above; *(en una casa)* upstairs; *(en lo alto)* overhead ♦ **¡a.!** *(para animar)* get up!, come on!; *(para victorear)* hurrah for ...! ♦ **a. citado** abovementioned ♦ **de a.** from above; AMER., COLL. free, gratis ♦ **de a. abajo** COLL. *(de cabo a rabo)* from top to bottom; *(desde el principio al fin)* from beginning to end; *(completamente)* from head to foot ♦ **más a.** higher *or* farther up ♦ **para a.** upwards, up.

a·rri·bar intr. to arrive ♦ **a. a** to manage to.

a·rri·be·ño, a AMER. I. adj. highland II. m.f. highlander.

a·rri·bis·ta I. adj. social-climbing II. m.f. social climber.

a·rri·bo m. arrival.

a·rrien·de, do see **arrendar**.

a·rrien·do m. *(acción)* renting; *(precio)* rent; *(contrato)* lease.

a·rrie·ro m. muleteer.

a·rries·ga·do, a adj. *(peligroso)* risky; *(audaz)* daring.

a·rries·gar §47 tr. to risk, venture ♦ **a. el pellejo** to risk one's neck —reflex. to risk.

a·rri·mar tr. to bring *or* draw near; *(arrinconar)* to ignore ♦ **a. el hombro** to lend a hand —reflex. to lean; *(juntarse)* to join together; COLL. *(vivir juntos)* to shack up ♦ **a. al sol que más calienta** COLL. to know which side one's bread is buttered on.

a·rri·mo m. *(sostén)* support; *(pared)* partition.

a·rrin·co·na·do, a adj. *(apartado)* distant; *(desatendido)* neglected.

a·rrin·co·nar tr. *(en un rincón)* to put in a corner; *(acorralar)* to corner; *(abandonar)* to neglect —reflex. to withdraw.

a·rris·ca·mien·to m. daring, boldness.

a·rris·car §70 AMER. tr. to turn up, fold up —reflex. to dress up.

a·rrit·mia f. lack of rhythm; MED. arrhythmia.

a·rro·ba·do, a adj. enraptured.

a·rro·ba·mien·to m. ecstasy, rapture.

a·rro·bar tr. to enrapture —reflex. *(extasiarse)* to be enraptured.

a·rro·ce·ro, a I. adj. rice **II.** m.f. rice grower.

a·rro·di·llar tr. to make (someone) kneel —reflex. to kneel (down).

a·rro·gan·cia f. arrogance.

a·rro·gan·te adj. arrogant.

a·rro·gar §47 tr. *(atribuir)* to arrogate; *(adoptar)* to adopt —reflex. to arrogate to oneself.

a·rro·ja·do, a adj. *(atrevido)* bold; *(resuelto)* resolute.

a·rro·jar tr. to hurl, fling; *(emitir)* to emit; *(vomitar)* to throw up; COM. to show —reflex. to throw *or* hurl oneself; *(resolverse)* to rush ♦ **a. sobre** to rush at, attack.

a·rro·jo m. *(atrevimiento)* boldness; *(resolución)* resoluteness.

a·rro·lla·dor, ·ra adj. overwhelming.

a·rro·llar tr. *(envolver)* to roll up; *(llevar)* to sweep *or* carry away <*el agua arrolla la arena* the water sweeps away the sand>; *(atropellar)* to trample; *(derrotar)* to crush.

a·rro·par tr. *(cubrir)* to wrap with clothes; *(acostar)* to tuck in (to bed) —reflex. *(cubrirse)* to wrap up *or* clothe oneself; *(acostarse)* to tuck oneself in.

a·rro·rró/ú m. AMER., COLL. lullaby.

a·rros·trar tr. & reflex. to face (up to).

a·rro·yo m. brook; *(cuneta)* gutter.

a·rroz m. rice ♦ **a. con leche** rice pudding.

a·rro·zal m. rice field *or* paddy.

a·rru·ga f. *(en la piel)* wrinkle, line; *(en la ropa)* wrinkle, crease; GEOL. ruga, fold.

a·rru·ga·do, a adj. wrinkled.

a·rru·gar §47 tr. *(fruncir)* to wrinkle; *(hacer arrugas)* to wrinkle, crease; *(papel)* to crumple ♦ **a. el entrecejo** to frown —reflex. to wrinkle, become wrinkled; *(plegarse)* to become wrinkled *or* creased; *(apañuscarse)* to become crumpled (up).

a·rrui·nar tr. to ruin; FIG. to destroy —reflex. to fall into ruin.

a·rru·lla·dor, ·ra adj. soothing.
a·rru·llar tr. to coo; *(adormecer)* to lull *or* sing to sleep; *(enamorar)* to woo.
a·rru·llo m. ORNITH. cooing; MUS. lullaby.
a·rru·ma·co m. *(abrazo)* caress; *(zalamería)* flattery ♦ pl. endearments ♦ **andar con a.** to flatter.
a·rrum·bar tr. *(desechar)* to cast *or* put aside; *(arrinconar)* to neglect.
a·rru·rruz m. arrowroot.
ar·se·nal m. *(astillero)* shipyard; MIL. arsenal; *(depósito)* storehouse.
ar·sé·ni·co m. arsenic.
ar·te m. *or* f. art; *(habilidad)* art, skill ♦ **bellas artes** fine arts ♦ **con a.** skillfully, cleverly ● **no tener ni a. ni parte** to have nothing to do with ● **por amor al a.** for free ♦ **por a. de magia** as if by magic.
ar·te·fac·to m. *(aparato)* appliance; ARCHEOL. artifact.
ar·te·ria f. artery.
ar·te·rial adj. arterial.
ar·te·rios·cle·ro·sis f. arteriosclerosis.
ar·te·ro, a adj. cunning, sly.
ar·te·sa·na·do m. *(artesanos)* craftsmen; *(arte)* artisanship.
ar·te·sa·nal adj. artisan, pertaining to craftsmen *or* artisans.
ar·te·sa·ní·a f. *(habilidad)* craftsmanship; *(producto)* crafts.
ar·te·sa·no, a m.f. artisan, craftsman —f. craftswoman.
ar·te·sia·no, a adj. artesian.
ár·ti·co, a adj. & m. Arctic.
ar·ti·cu·la·ción f. ANAT., MECH. joint; *(pronunciación)* enunciation ♦ **a. esférica** ball-and-socket joint ● **a. giratoria** swivel joint.
ar·ti·cu·la·do, a I. adj. articulate II. m. articles.
ar·ti·cu·lar¹ adj. ANAT. articular, of the joints.
ar·ti·cu·lar² tr. *(pronunciar)* to enunciate; *(dividir)* to divide into articles; MECH. to join.
ar·tí·cu·lo m. article; *(cosa)* item, thing; *(escrito)* essay; *(en un diccionario)* entry; GRAM. article; ANAT. joint; LAW section ♦ **a. de fondo** JOURN. editorial ● **a. de primera necesidad** basic commodity ♦ pl. goods ● **a. de consumo** consumer goods ● **a. de tocador** toiletries.
ar·tí·fi·ce m.f. artisan; FIG. architect.
ar·ti·fi·cial adj. artificial.
ar·ti·fi·cia·li·dad f. artificiality.
ar·ti·fi·cio m. *(habilidad)* ability; *(aparato)* device; *(ardid)* trick.
ar·ti·fi·cio·so, a adj. ingenious; FIG. cunning.
ar·ti·lle·rí·a f. artillery.
ar·ti·lle·ro m. artillery soldier.
ar·ti·lu·gio m. *(aparato)* contraption; *(trampa)* gimmick.
ar·ti·ma·ña f. *(trampa)* trick; *(astucia)* cunning.
ar·tis·ta m.f. artist; *(actor, actriz)* actor, actress ♦ **a. invitado** guest artist.
ar·tís·ti·co, a adj. artistic.
ar·trí·ti·co, a adj. & m.f. arthritic.
ar·tri·tis f. MED. arthritis.
ar·ve·ja f. *(algarroba)* (spring) vetch, tare; AMER. green pea.
ar·zo·bis·po m. archbishop.
as m. ace.
a·sa f. handle ♦ **en asas** akimbo.
a·sa·do m. *(carne)* roasted meat; AMER. barbecued meat; *(comida)* cookout, barbecue.

a·sa·dor m. *(varilla)* spit; *(aparato)* grill.
a·sa·la·ria·do, a I. adj. salaried II. m.f. salaried worker.
a·sa·la·riar tr. to set a salary for.
a·sal·ta·dor, ·ra/tan·te m.f. assailant.
a·sal·tar tr. *(atacar)* to assault; *(sobrevenir)* to overtake.
a·sal·to m. *(ataque)* assault; *(fiesta)* surprise party; *(en el boxeo)* round; *(en la esgrima)* bout.
a·sam·ble·a f. *(reunión)* meeting; *(congreso)* conference.
a·sam·ble·ís·ta m.f. member of an assembly.
a·sar tr. to roast ♦ **a. al horno** to bake ● **a. a la parrilla** to broil —reflex. FIG. to roast.
as·cen·den·cia f. ancestry.
as·cen·den·te I. adj. ascending, upward II. m. ASTROL. ascendant.
as·cen·der §50 intr. to rise; *(de categoría)* to be promoted ♦ **a. a** to amount to, reach —tr. to promote.
as·cen·dien·te I. adj. ascending II. m.f. ancestor —m. influence.
as·cen·sión f. ascension, rise.
as·cen·so m. *(adelanto)* promotion; *(subida)* ascent, rise.
as·cen·sor m. elevator, lift (G.B.) ♦ **a. de carga** freight elevator.
as·cen·so·ris·ta m.f. elevator operator.
as·ce·ta m.f. ascetic.
as·cé·ti·co, a I. adj. ascetic II. f. asceticism.
as·cien·da, do see **ascender.**
as·co m. disgust, revulsion ♦ **dar a.** to sicken *or* disgust ● **estar hecho un a.** COLL. to be filthy ● **ser un a.** COLL. to be disgusting *or* worthless.
as·cua f. ember ♦ **estar en ascuas** COLL. to be on edge.
a·se·a·do, a adj. *(limpio)* clean; *(ordenado)* neat, tidy.
a·se·ar tr. *(lavar)* to wash; *(limpiar)* to clean; *(ordenar)* to tidy (up) —reflex. *(lavarse)* to wash (up); *(limpiarse)* to clean (up); *(ordenarse)* to tidy (up).
a·se·char tr. to trap, snare.
a·se·diar tr. *(sitiar)* to besiege; *(importunar)* to pester.
a·se·dio m. siege.
a·se·gu·ra·do, a I. adj. insured II. m.f. insured (person), policyholder.
a·se·gu·ra·dor, ·ra I. adj. insuring, assuring II. m. insurance company —m.f. insurance agent.
a·se·gu·rar tr. *(afirmar)* to secure; *(garantizar)* to guarantee; *(tranquilizar)* to assure; COM. to insure —reflex. *(cerciorarse)* to make sure; COM. to take out insurance.
a·se·me·jar tr. *(hacer semejante)* to make alike *or* similar; *(comparar)* to compare —reflex. to resemble.
a·sen·ta·de·ras f.pl. COLL. behind, buttocks.
a·sen·ta·do, a adj. *(juicioso)* judicious; *(estable)* stable.
a·sen·tar §49 tr. *(anotar)* to record; *(fundar)* to found; *(colocar)* to place; *(afirmar)* to affirm; *(aplanar)* to level; COM. to enter; MEX. to sadden; ARG. to iron —intr. to suit —reflex. *(establecerse)* to establish oneself; *(las aves)* to perch; *(los líquidos)* to settle; ARCHIT. to settle.
a·sen·ti·mien·to m. consent, assent.
a·sen·tir §65 intr. to assent, agree ♦ **a. con la cabeza** to nod (one's approval).

a·se·o m. *(limpieza)* cleanliness; *(orden)* neatness, tidiness.

a·se·qui·ble adj. *(accesible)* accessible; *(posible)* feasible; *(comprensible)* understandable.

a·ser·ción f. assertion, affirmation.

a·se·rra·de·ro m. sawmill.

a·se·rra·do, a I. adj. serrated **II.** m. sawing.

a·se·rrar §49 tr. to saw.

a·se·rrín m. sawdust.

a·se·si·nar tr. to murder; POL. to assassinate.

a·se·si·na·to m. murder; POL. assassination.

a·se·si·no, a I. adj. murderous **II.** m.f. killer, murderer; POL. assassin.

a·se·sor, ·ra I. adj. advising, advisory **II.** m.f. adviser, counselor.

a·se·so·ra·mien·to m. *(acción)* advising; *(consejo)* advice.

a·se·so·rar tr. to advise —reflex. to seek advice.

a·se·so·rí·a f. consultant's office.

a·ses·tar tr. *(arma)* to aim; *(balazo)* to fire; *(golpe)* to deal.

a·se·ve·ra·ción f. asseveration, assertion.

a·se·ve·rar tr. to asseverate, assert.

a·se·ve·ra·ti·vo, a adj. assertive, affirmative.

a·se·xua·do, a/xual adj. asexual.

as·fal·ta·do, a I. adj. paved **II.** m. asphalt.

as·fal·tar tr. to asphalt.

as·fal·to m. asphalt.

as·fi·xia f. asphyxia, suffocation.

as·fi·xiar tr. to asphyxiate —reflex. to suffocate.

as·ga, go see **asir.**

a·sí I. adv. *(de esta manera)* so, this way; *(de esa manera)* that way, like that; *(tanto)* so, in such a way • **a. a.** so-so, fair • **a. como** as soon as • **a. de (grande)** so (big) • **a. no más** just like that • **a. sea** so be it • **a. y todo** even so, just the same • **o algo a.** or thereabouts, or something like that • **y a.** thus, and so • **y a. sucesivamente** and so on, and so forth **II.** conj. *(en consecuencia)* therefore, thus; *(aunque)* even if, even though • **a. pues** therefore, and so **III.** adj. such.

a·si·de·ro m. *(asa)* handle; ARG. basis.

a·si·dui·dad f. assiduousness.

a·si·duo, a adj. *(persistente)* assiduous; *(frecuente)* frequent.

a·sien·ta, te, to see **asentar** or **asentir.**

a·sien·to m. seat; *(silla)* chair; *(sitio)* site; *(poso)* sediment; *(empacho)* indigestion; *(trasero)* behind; *(estabilidad)* stability; ARCHIT. settling; COM. entry.

a·sie·rre, rre see **aserrar.**

a·sig·na·ción f. *(distribución)* allotment; *(cita)* appointment; *(salario)* salary.

a·sig·nar tr. *(señalar)* to assign; *(nombrar)* to appoint.

a·sig·na·tu·ra f. subject, course (in school) • **aprobar una a.** to pass a course.

a·si·lar tr. *(albergar)* to place in an asylum; *(refugiar)* to give shelter; POL. to give political asylum —reflex. *(albergarse)* to enter an asylum; *(refugiarse)* to take refuge; POL. to seek political asylum.

a·si·lo m. asylum; *(establecimiento)* home; *(refugio)* shelter • **a. de ancianos** old folks' home • **a. de huérfanos** orphanage • **a. de locos** insane asylum • **a. de pobres** poorhouse • **dar a.** to shelter.

a·si·mé·tri·co, a adj. asymmetric.

a·si·mi·la·ción f. assimilation.

a·si·mi·lar tr. to assimilate —reflex. to be similar.

a·si·mis·mo adj. *(igualmente)* likewise, in like manner; *(también)* also, too.

a·sin·tie·ra, tió see **asentir.**

a·sir §08 tr. & intr. to grasp —reflex. • **a. de** to avail oneself of.

a·sis·ten·cia f. *(concurrencia)* attendance; *(ayuda)* aid; MEX. parlor • **a. pública** AMER. health clinic.

a·sis·ten·cial adj. assisting, relief.

a·sis·ten·te, a I. adj. assisting **II.** m.f. *(ayudante)* assistant —m. MIL. aide.

a·sis·tir intr. to attend —tr. *(acompañar)* to accompany; *(ayudar)* to aid; *(cuidar)* to nurse.

as·ma f. asthma.

as·má·ti·co, a adj. & m.f. asthmatic.

as·na·da f. COLL. stupidity.

as·no m. donkey; FIG. jackass.

a·so·cia·ción f. association • **a. gremial** trade union • **a. sindical** labor union.

a·so·cia·do, a I. adj. associated **II.** m.f. associate.

a·so·ciar tr. *(ligar)* to connect; *(combinar)* to combine —reflex. to become partners • **a. a** *or* **con** to join.

a·so·la·dor, ·ra adj. ravaging.

a·so·lar¹ tr. AGR. to scorch, parch.

a·so·lar² §19 tr. to ravage —reflex. CHEM. to settle.

a·so·le·a·mien·to m. sunstroke.

a·so·le·ar tr. to put out in the sun —reflex. *(tomar el sol)* to sun oneself; *(tostarse)* to become tanned; *(sofocarse)* to suffer heat suffocation.

a·so·ma·da f. *(aparición)* brief appearance; *(atalaya)* vantage point.

a·so·mar intr. to appear —tr. to show —reflex. *(mostrarse)* to show oneself, appear; *(una ventana)* to look *or* lean out.

a·som·bra·dor, ·ra adj. amazing, astonishing.

a·som·brar tr. *(sorprender)* to amaze, astonish; *(oscurecer)* to darken, make darker (colors) —reflex. to be amazed *or* astonished.

a·som·bro m. *(sorpresa)* amazement; *(maravilla)* marvel.

a·som·bro·so, a adj. amazing, astonishing.

a·so·mo m. *(mirada)* look; *(señal)* hint • **ni un a. de** not the least bit of • **ni por a.** no way.

a·so·nan·cia f. POET., RHET. assonance; PHONET. consonance.

as·pa f. *(cruz)* X-shaped cross; *(devanadera)* spool; *(de molinos)* blade.

as·par tr. *(hilo)* to reel; *(crucificar)* to crucify.

as·pa·ven·tar §49 tr. to frighten, scare.

as·pa·ven·te·ro/to·so, a adj. effusive, theatrical.

as·pa·vien·tar·se reflex. C. AMER. to become frightened *or* alarmed.

as·pa·vien·to m. exaggerated behavior, theatricality • **hacer aspavientos** to make a fuss.

as·pec·to m. aspect.

as·pe·re·za f. *(escabrosidad)* ruggedness; *(brusquedad)* gruffness.

ás·pe·ro, a adj. *(rugoso)* rough; *(escabroso)* rugged; *(brusco)* gruff.

as·per·sión f. sprinkling • **sistema de a. automática** (automatic) sprinkling system.

as·pi·ra·ción f. PHYSIOL. inhalation; *(anhelo)* aspiration; *(succión)* suction; PHONET. aspiration.

as·pi·ra·do, a adj. PHONET. aspirated.

as·pi·ra·dor, ·ra I. adj. aspirating; MECH. sucking **II.** m. MECH., MED. aspirator; MECH. suction pump —f. vacuum cleaner.

as·pi·ran·te m.f. candidate.

as·pi·rar tr. to inhale; MECH. *(atraer)* to suck, draw in; PHONET. *(pronunciar)* to aspirate **♦ a. a** to aspire to.

as·pi·ri·na f. aspirin.

as·que·ar tr. to disgust —intr. to be disgusting.

as·que·ro·si·dad f. *(suciedad)* filth; *(vileza)* vileness.

as·que·ro·so, a adj. *(repugnante)* repulsive; *(sucio)* filthy.

as·ta f. *(lanza)* spear; *(de lanza)* shaft; *(de bandera)* flagpole; *(mango)* handle; *(cuerno)* horn, antler **♦ a media a.** at half-staff.

as·te·ris·co m. asterisk.

as·te·roi·de I. m. asteroid **II.** adj. asteroidal.

as·tig·má·ti·co, a adj. astigmatic.

as·tig·ma·tis·mo m. astigmatism.

as·ti·lla f. splinter **♦ hacer astillas** to splinter.

as·ti·llar tr. to chip, splinter.

as·ti·lle·ro m. MARIT. shipyard; COM. lumberyard.

as·tra·cán m. astrakhan, astrachan.

as·trin·gen·cia f. astringency.

as·trin·gen·te adj. & m. astringent.

as·trin·gir §32 tr. to astringe, contract.

as·tro m. star.

as·tro·fí·si·co, a I. adj. astrophysical **II.** m.f. astrophysicist —f. astrophysics.

as·tro·lo·gí·a f. astrology.

as·tro·ló·gi·co, a adj. astrological.

as·tró·lo·go, a I. m.f. astrologist **II.** adj. astrological.

as·tro·nau·ta m.f. astronaut, cosmonaut.

as·tro·náu·ti·ca f. astronautics.

as·tro·na·ve f. spaceship, spacecraft.

as·tro·no·mí·a f. astronomy.

as·tro·nó·mi·co, a adj. astronomic; FIG. astronomical.

as·tró·no·mo, a m.f. astronomer.

as·tu·cia f. *(listeza)* astuteness; *(ardid)* trick.

as·tu·to, a adj. *(listo)* astute, clever; *(mañoso)* crafty, shrewd.

a·sue·le, lo see **asolar²**.

a·sue·to m. holiday **♦ día de a.** day off, holiday.

a·su·mir tr. to assume, take on.

a·sun·ción f. assumption.

a·sun·tar intr. DOM. REP. to pay attention; C. AMER. to investigate, pry.

a·sun·to m. *(tópico)* topic; *(tema)* subject matter; *(argumento)* plot; COLL. *(amorío)* love affair **♦ a. pendiente** unresolved matter **♦ el a. es que . . .** the fact is that . . . **• ir al a.** to get down to business **♦ pl.** business **• tener muchos a.** entre manos to have many matters to deal with.

a·sus·ta·di·zo, a adj. easily frightened, skittish.

a·sus·tar tr. to frighten, scare —reflex. to be frightened or scared *(de, por, con* by).

a·ta·ba·ca·do, a adj. tobacco-colored.

a·ta·be m. pipe vent.

a·ta·blar tr. AGR. to level.

a·ta·ca·dor, ·ra/can·te I. adj. attacking, assaulting **II.** m.f. attacker.

a·ta·ca·du·ra f./**mien·to** m. fastening.

a·ta·car §70 tr. to attack; *(abrochar)* to fasten; *(criticar)* to criticize; *(iniciar)* to start work on; ARM. to pack or tamp down; CHEM. to corrode.

a·ta·de·ras f.pl. COLL. garters.

a·ta·de·ro m. tie, fastener; *(aro)* loop.

a·ta·do, a I. adj. timid **II.** m. *(manojo)* bundle; ARG. cigarette pack.

a·ta·du·ra f. *(acción)* tying; *(cuerda)* cord; *(traba)* restriction.

a·ta·ja·da f. AMER., SPORT. catch.

a·ta·jar tr. *(detener)* to intercept; *(impedir)* to halt; *(interrumpir)* to interrupt, cut off; *(contener)* to stop; AMER. *(tomar)* to catch (in mid-air) **♦ a. un golpe** AMER. to parry a blow —intr. to take a short cut.

a·ta·jo m. short cut.

a·ta·la·ya f. *(torre)* observation tower; *(altura)* vantage point —m. guard.

a·ta·ñer §68 intr. to concern, pertain.

a·ta·que m. attack **♦ a. aéreo** air raid.

a·tar tr. to tie, fasten **♦ a. cabos** to put two and two together.

a·tar·de·cer §17 **I.** intr. to get dark **II.** m. late afternoon, dusk **♦ al a.** at dusk.

a·ta·re·ar tr. to assign work to —reflex. to busy or occupy oneself.

a·ta·ru·gar §47 tr. *(asegurar)* to pin; *(tapar)* to plug —reflex. COLL. to stuff oneself.

a·ta·sa·jar tr. to jerk (beef).

a·tas·ca·de·ro m. bog; FIG. stumbling block.

a·tas·ca·mien·to m. obstruction; FIG. obstacle.

a·tas·car §70 tr. *(obstruir)* to clog; *(impedir)* to hamper —reflex. *(estancarse)* to get stuck or clogged.

a·tas·co m. obstruction; FIG. obstacle.

a·ta·úd m. coffin, casket.

a·ta·viar §30 tr. to adorn, deck out.

a·tá·vi·co, a adj. atavistic.

a·ta·ví·o m. *(adorno)* decoration; *(vestido)* attire **♦ pl.** finery, trappings.

a·ta·vis·mo m. atavism, intermittent heredity.

a·ta·xia f. ataxia, ataxy.

a·te·mo·ri·zar §04 tr. to frighten —reflex. to be frightened *(de, por* by).

a·tem·pe·ra·ción f. tempering.

a·tem·pe·rar tr. *(moderar)* to temper; *(adecuar)* to adjust.

a·te·na·ce·ar/azar §04 tr. to torture by tearing off the flesh with pincers; FIG. to torture.

a·ten·ción f. attention **♦ llamar la a.** *(atraer)* to catch the eye; *(reprender)* to reprimand **• prestar a.** to pay attention **♦ pl.** courtesies.

a·ten·der §50 tr. *(hacer caso de)* to pay attention to; *(tener en cuenta)* keep in mind; *(cuidar)* to take care of; *(obedecer)* to heed; COM. to wait on —intr. to pay attention.

a·te·ne·o m. athenaeum.

a·te·ner·se §69 reflex. **♦ a. a** *(adherirse a)* to rely on; *(sujetarse)* to abide by **• no saber a qué a.** FIG. not to know which way to turn.

a·ten·ta·do m. *(crimen)* crime; *(ataque)* attempt.

a·ten·tar §49 tr. to attempt to commit —intr. to make an attempt.

a·ten·to, a I. see **atender II.** adj. *(observador)* attentive; *(cortés)* considerate **♦ a. a** in view of.

a·te·nua·ción f. attenuation.

a·te·nuan·te adj. attenuating; LAW extenuating.

a·te·nuar §67 tr. to attenuate; LAW to extenuate.

a·te·o, a I. adj. atheistic **II.** m.f. atheist.

a·ter·cio·pe·la·do, a adj. velvety.

a·te·ri·do, a adj. numb with cold.

a·te·rir·se §38 reflex. to be numb with cold.

a·te·rra·dor, ·ra adj. terrifying.
a·te·rrar¹ §49 tr. *(echar por tierra)* to knock down; *(derribar)* to destroy, demolish —intr. AVIA. to land; MARIT. to stand inshore.
a·te·rrar² tr. to terrify.
a·te·rri·za·je m. landing ♦ **a. a ciegas** blind landing • **a. forzoso** emergency landing.
a·te·rri·zar §04 intr. to land.
a·te·rro·ri·za·dor, ·ra adj. terrifying.
a·te·rro·ri·zar §04 tr. to terrorize.
a·te·so·ra·mien·to m. hoarding.
a·te·so·rar tr. to store up; FIG. to possess.
a·tes·ta·ción f. affidavit, deposition.
a·tes·ta·do, a adj. full to the rim.
a·tes·ta·du·ra f./**mien·to** m. cramming.
a·tes·tar¹ §49 tr. to stuff.
a·tes·tar² tr. to attest, witness.
a·tes·ti·gua·ción f./**mien·to** m. attestation.
a·tes·ti·guar §10 tr. to attest.
a·te·za·do, a adj. *(bronceado)* suntanned; *(negro)* black.
a·te·zar §04 tr. & reflex. to tan.
a·ti·bo·rra·mien·to m. cramming.
a·ti·bo·rrar tr. to cram —reflex. COLL. to stuff oneself.
á·ti·co, a I. adj. HIST., LIT. Attic **II.** m.f. HIST. *(persona)* Attic —m. *(idioma)* Attic; ARCHIT. attic.
a·tien·da, do see atender.
a·tie·ne·se see atenerse.
a·tien·te, to see atentar.
a·tie·sar tr. to stiffen, harden.
a·ties·te, to see atestar¹.
a·ti·gra·do, a adj. tiger-striped.
a·til·da·do, a adj. neat.
a·til·da·du·ra f./**mien·to** m. neatness.
a·til·dar tr. to spruce up.
a·ti·nar tr. *(encontrar)* to find; *(acertar)* to hit upon ♦ **a. a** to manage to, succeed in.
a·ti·ran·tar tr. to make taut.
a·tis·bar tr. to watch.
a·tis·bo m. *(acecho)* watching; *(indicio)* glimmer.
a·ti·za·dor m. poker (tool).
a·ti·zar §04 tr. *(el fuego)* to poke; *(avivar)* to arouse; COLL. *(pegar)* to strike.
a·ti·zo·nar tr. *(un muro)* to bond; *(un madero)* to embed.
at·las m.inv. atlas.
at·le·ta m.f. athlete.
at·lé·ti·co, a adj. athletic.
at·mós·fe·ra f. atmosphere.
at·mos·fé·ri·co, a adj. atmospheric.
a·to·char tr. *(de esparto)* to fill with esparto; *(rellenar)* to stuff.
a·to·ci·nar tr. *(un cerdo)* to cut up; *(tocino)* to make into bacon; COLL. *(asesinar)* to murder.
a·to·lla·de·ro m. bog; FIG. obstruction ♦ **estar en un a.** to be in a fix or jam.
a·to·llar intr. to get stuck in the mud —reflex. COLL. to be stuck in a situation.
a·to·lon·dra·do, a adj. *(impulsivo)* reckless; *(turbado)* bewildered.
a·to·lon·dra·mien·to m. *(irreflexión)* recklessness; *(aturdimiento)* bewilderment.
a·to·lon·drar tr. to bewilder —reflex. to be bewildered.
a·tó·mi·co, a adj. atomic.
a·to·mis·ta m.f. PHILOS. atomist.
a·to·mi·za·dor m. atomizer, sprayer.
a·to·mi·zar §04 tr. to atomize, pulverize.

á·to·mo m. atom; FIG. iota ♦ **á. fisionado** split atom.
a·to·nal adj. atonal.
a·to·na·li·dad f. atonality, tonelessness.
a·to·ní·a f. atony.
a·tó·ni·to, a adj. astonished, amazed.
á·to·no, a adj. atonic.
a·ton·ta·mien·to m. *(embrutecimiento)* stupefaction; *(aturdimiento)* confusion.
a·ton·tar tr. *(embrutecer)* to stun; *(aturdir)* to confuse.
a·to·ra·mien·to m. obstruction, blockage.
a·to·rar tr. to clog —reflex. to choke.
a·tor·men·ta·dor, ·ra adj. *(afligente)* tormenting; *(preocupante)* worrisome.
a·tor·men·tar tr. to torment; *(torturar)* to torture —reflex. to worry.
a·tor·ni·llar tr. to screw in or on.
a·to·ro m. blockage, obstruction.
a·to·rran·te m. R.P., COLL. bum.
a·tor·to·lar tr. COLL. to confuse —reflex. ARG. to fall in love.
a·to·si·ga·dor, ·ra adj. poisonous, toxic.
a·to·si·ga·mien·to m. poisoning; FIG. pressing.
a·to·si·gar §47 tr. to poison; FIG. to press —reflex. to get flustered.
a·tó·xi·co, a adj. nontoxic.
a·tra·bi·lis f.inv. black bile; FIG. bad temper.
a·tra·ca·de·ro m. pier, dock.
a·tra·car §70 tr. *(asaltar)* to hold up; COLL. *(hartar)* to stuff; MARIT. to bring alongside —intr. MARIT. to dock —reflex. to stuff oneself.
a·trac·ción f. attraction ♦ **sentir a. por** to feel attracted to.
a·tra·co m. holdup, robbery.
a·tra·cón m. COLL. *(comida)* big feed; AMER. brawl.
a·trac·ti·vo, a I. adj. attractive **II.** m. *(encanto)* charm; *(aliciente)* attraction.
a·tra·er §72 tr. to attract.
a·tra·gan·ta·mien·to m. choking, gagging.
a·tra·gan·tar·se reflex. COLL. to get tongue-tied ♦ **a. con** to choke on.
a·trai·ga, go see atraer.
a·trai·llar tr. to leash; FIG. to hold in check.
a·trai·mien·to m. attraction.
a·tra·je·ra, jo see atraer.
a·tran·car §70 tr. *(cerrar)* to bolt; *(obstruir)* to block —reflex. MEX. to be stubborn.
a·tran·co/que m. obstruction; FIG. jam.
a·tra·pa·mos·cas f.inv. Venus's-flytrap.
a·tra·par tr. COLL. *(apresar)* to catch; *(conseguir)* to land; *(engañar)* to take in.
a·tra·que m. MARIT. mooring; ASTRONAUT. docking, link-up; ARM. packing.
a·trás adv. back, behind; *(antes)* back, ago ♦ **¡a.!** get back! • **dar marcha a.** AUTO. to back up • **ir hacia a.** to go backward.
a·tra·sa·do, a adj. *(reloj)* slow; *(persona)* late; *(cuenta)* in arrears; *(revista)* back; *(país)* underdeveloped ♦ **a. de noticias** behind the times.
a·tra·sar tr. *(retardar)* to delay; *(reloj)* to set back —intr. to be slow —reflex. to be late.
a·tra·so m. delay; *(retraso)* tardiness ♦ pl. arrears ♦ **a. mental** mental retardation ♦ pl. arrears.
a·tra·ve·sa·do, a adj. *(bizco)* cross-eyed; *(confuso)* incongruous; ZOOL. crossbred.
a·tra·ve·sar §49 tr. *(pasar)* to cross (over); *(poner oblicuo)* to put or lay across; *(traspasar)* to

pierce —reflex. *(obstruir)* to block; *(reñir)* to quarrel.

a·tra·yen·do see **atraer.**

a·tra·yen·te adj. attractive.

a·tre·guar §10 tr. to grant (a truce).

a·tre·ver·se reflex. to dare ♦ **a. a** to dare to • **a. con** *or* **contra** *(descararse)* to be disrespectful to; *(retar)* to take on.

a·tre·vi·do, a I. see **atreverse** II. adj. *(osado)* bold; *(descarado)* impudent III. m.f. *(temerario)* bold person; *(caradura)* insolent person.

a·tre·vi·mien·to m. *(osadía)* boldness; *(insolencia)* rudeness.

a·tri·bu·ción f. attribution; *(función)* duty ♦ pl. authority.

a·tri·bui·ble adj. attributable.

a·tri·buir §18 tr. *(otorgar)* to credit; *(imputar)* to grant —reflex. to take credit for.

a·tri·bu·lar tr. to distress, afflict —reflex. to become distressed.

a·tri·bu·ti·vo, a adj. attributive.

a·tri·bu·to m. attribute; *(símbolo)* symbol; GRAM., LOG. *(predicado)* predicate.

a·tri·bu·ya, ye·ra, yo, yó see **atribuir.**

a·tril m. lectern.

a·trin·che·rar tr. to surround with trenches —reflex. to entrench oneself, dig in.

a·trio m. *(patio)* atrium; *(andén)* portico; *(entrada)* vestibule.

a·tri·to, a adj. THEOL. repentant.

a·tro·ci·dad f. atrocity; FIG. enormity.

a·tro·fia f. atrophy.

a·tro·fia·do, a adj. atrophied, atrophic.

a·tro·fiar tr. & reflex. to atrophy.

a·tro·na·do, a adj. hasty, reckless.

a·tro·na·dor, ·ra adj. deafening.

a·tro·nar §19 tr. *(asordar)* to deafen; *(aturdir)* to stun.

a·tro·pe·lla·do, a adj. hasty, hurried.

a·tro·pe·lla·dor, ·ra I. adj. trampling II. m.f. trampler.

a·tro·pe·lla·mien·to m. var. of **atropello.**

a·tro·pe·llar tr. *(pisotear)* to trample (on); *(derribar)* to run over; *(agraviar)* to bully; *(hacer precipitadamente)* to do hurriedly, rush through; *(agobiar)* to overwhelm, oppress —reflex. to act hastily.

a·tro·pe·llo m. assault; FIG. abuse.

a·troz adj. atrocious; FIG. enormous.

a·true·ne see **atronar.**

a·tuen·do m. attire.

a·tu·far tr. to annoy —reflex. *(oler mal)* to smell bad; *(enfadarse)* to get angry.

a·tún m. tuna (fish), tunny (G.B.).

a·tur·di·do, a adj. *(estupefacto)* stunned; *(turbado)* confused.

a·tur·di·mien·to m. *(choque)* shock; *(turbación)* confusion.

a·tur·dir tr. *(atontar)* to stun; *(turbar)* to confuse.

a·tur·que·sa·do, a adj. turquoise (blue).

a·tu·rru·llar tr. COLL. to baffle —reflex. to become flustered.

a·tu·sar tr. *(recortar)* to trim; *(alisar)* to slick back —reflex. FIG. to spruce up.

a·tu·vie·ra, vo see **atenerse**

au·da·cia f. audacity.

au·daz I. adj. audacious II. m.f. audacious *or* bold person.

au·di·ción f. *(facultad)* hearing; *(programa)* program; THEAT. audition.

au·dien·cia f. audience.

au·dí·fo·no m. *(aparato)* hearing aid; *(auricular)* earphone.

au·dió·me·tro m. audiometer.

au·dio·vi·sual adj. audio-visual.

au·di·ti·vo, a adj. auditive, auditory.

au·di·tor, ·ra m.f. counselor; COM. auditor.

au·di·to·rí·a f. ACC. *(cargo)* auditorship; *(oficio)* auditing; LAW *(cargo)* office of judge advocate; *(tribunal)* judge advocate's court.

au·di·to·rio, a m. *(público)* audience; *(sala)* auditorium.

au·ge m. *(apogeo)* peak; COM. boom; ASTRON. apogee.

au·gu·rar tr. to augur, predict.

au·gu·rio m. augury, omen.

au·gus·to, a adj. august.

au·la f. classroom, lecture hall.

au·lla·dor, ·ra I. adj. howling II. m. ZOOL. howler monkey.

au·llar intr. to howl, wail.

au·lli·do *or* **a·ú·llo** m. howl, wail ♦ **dar aullidos** to howl, wail.

au·men·tar tr. to increase; OPT. to magnify; PHOTOG. to enlarge; RAD. to amplify; *(salario)* to raise —intr. to increase.

au·men·ta·ti·vo, a adj. & m. augmentative.

au·men·to m. increase; OPT. magnification; PHOTOG. enlargement; RAD. amplification; *(de sueldo)* raise ♦ **ir en a.** to be on the increase.

aun adv. even ♦ **a. así** even so • **a. cuando** although, even though.

a·ún adv. still, yet ♦ **a. no** not yet • **más a.** furthermore.

au·nar tr. & reflex. to join, unite.

aun·que conj. *(si bien)* although, even though; *(a pesar de)* even if ♦ **a. más** no matter how much.

au·ra f. aura; *(brisa)* gentle breeze.

áu·re·o, a adj. *(de oro)* gold; *(dorado)* golden.

au·re·o·la f. RELIG. halo; ASTRON. aureole.

au·re·o·la·do, a adj. haloed.

au·re·o·lar tr. to halo; FIG. to exalt.

au·rí·cu·la f. auricle.

au·ri·cu·lar I. adj. auricular II. m. TELEC. earpiece ♦ pl. earphones.

au·rí·fe·ro, a adj. auriferous, gold-bearing.

au·ro·ra f. dawn; FIG. beginning; BOT. sagebrush ♦ **a. austral** southern lights • **a. boreal** northern lights.

aus·cul·ta·ción f. auscultation.

aus·cul·tar tr. to auscultate, diagnose by sound.

au·sen·cia f. absence ♦ **brillar uno por su a.** to be conspicuous by one's absence.

au·sen·tar tr. to send away —reflex. *(alejarse)* to leave.

au·sen·te I. adj. absent; FIG. absent-minded II. m.f. absentee.

au·sen·tis·mo m. absenteeism.

aus·pi·ciar tr. AMER. to sponsor.

aus·pi·cio m. auspice ♦ pl. auspices.

aus·pi·cio·so, a adj. AMER. auspicious.

aus·te·ri·dad f. austerity.

aus·te·ro, a adj. austere.

aus·tral adj. austral, southern.

au·tar·quí·a f. autarchy, autarky.

au·tár·qui·co, a adj. autarchic, autarkic.

au·ten·ti·ca·ción f. authentication.

au·tén·ti·ca·men·te adv. authentically.

au·ten·ti·car §70 tr. to authenticate.

au·ten·ti·ci·dad f. authenticity, genuineness.

au·tén·ti·co, a adj. authentic, genuine.

au·tis·ta adj. autistic.

au·to¹ m. LAW judicial decree *or* ruling; THEAT. short play ♦ pl. LAW case file.

auto² m. COLL. car, auto.

au·to·ad·he·si·vo, a adj. self-adhesive.

au·to·bio·gra·fí·a f. autobiography.

au·to·bio·grá·fi·co, a adj. autobiographical.

au·to·bús m. bus.

au·to·ca·mión m. truck.

au·to·car m. bus, motorcoach.

au·to·cla·ve f. autoclave.

au·to·cra·cia f. autocracy.

au·tó·cra·ta m.f. autocrat.

au·to·crá·ti·co, a adj. autocratic.

au·to·crí·ti·ca f. self-criticism.

au·tóc·to·no, a adj. & m.f. native.

au·to·des·truc·ción f. self-destruction.

au·to·de·ter·mi·na·ción f. self-determination.

au·to·di·dac·to, a adj. & m.f. self-taught (person).

au·tó·dro·mo m. automobile racetrack.

au·to·en·cen·di·do m. self-ignition.

au·to·fe·cun·da·ción f. BOT. self-fertilization.

au·tó·ge·no, a adj. autogenous.

au·to·gi·ro m. autogiro, autogyro.

au·tó·gra·fo, a I. adj. autographic. **II.** m. autograph.

au·to·in·duc·ción f. self-induction.

au·to·ma·ción f. automation.

au·tó·ma·ta m. automaton; FIG. robot.

au·to·má·ti·co, a I. adj. automatic **II.** m. (*corchete*) snap.

au·to·ma·tis·mo m. automatism.

au·to·ma·ti·za·ción f. automatization.

au·to·ma·ti·zar §04 tr. to automate.

au·to·me·di·car·se §70 reflex. to self-medicate.

au·to·mo·tor, triz adj. automotive.

au·to·mó·vil I. adj. self-propelled **II.** m. automobile, car ♦ **a. de carreras** racing car.

au·to·mo·vi·lis·mo m. motoring; (*industria*) automobile industry ♦ **a. deportivo** car racing.

au·to·mo·vi·lis·ta m.f. driver, motorist.

au·to·mo·vi·lís·ti·co, a adj. automobile.

au·to·no·mí·a f. autonomy.

au·tó·no·mo, a adj. autonomous.

au·to·pis·ta f. expressway, superhighway.

au·to·pro·pul·sa·do, a adj. self-propelled.

au·to·pro·pul·sión f. self-propulsion.

au·top·sia f. autopsy.

au·tor, ·ra m.f. author; (*escritor*) writer; (*originador*) creator; LAW perpetrator —f. authoress.

au·to·ri·dad f. authority; (*oficial*) official; (*experto*) expert ♦ **con a.** authoritatively.

au·to·ri·ta·rio, a adj. (*dictatorial*) authoritarian; (*imperioso*) imperious.

au·to·ri·za·ción f. authorization.

au·to·ri·za·do, a adj. (*digno de respeto*) authoritative; (*oficial*) authorized.

au·to·ri·zar §04 tr. to authorize; (*dar permiso*) to permit; (*legalizar*) to legalize.

au·to·rre·gu·la·ción f. self-regulation.

au·to·rre·tra·to m. self-portrait.

au·to·ser·vi·cio m. self-service.

au·to·stop m. hitchhiking ♦ **hacer a.** to hitchhike.

au·to·su·fi·cien·cia f. self-sufficiency.

au·to·su·ges·tión f. self-suggestion.

au·to·su·ges·tio·nar·se reflex. to induce in one's own thought.

au·xi·lia·dor, ·ra I. adj. helping **II.** m.f. helper.

au·xi·liar¹ I. adj. auxiliary **II.** m.f. (*subalterno*) assistant; (*maestro*) assistant teacher —m. GRAM. auxiliary.

au·xi·liar² tr. to assist, aid.

au·xi·lio m. assistance, aid ♦ **primeros auxilios** first aid.

a·val m. COM. endorsement; (*garantía*) guarantee ♦ **por a.** as a guarantee.

a·va·lan·cha f. avalanche.

a·va·lar tr. COM. to endorse; (*garantizar*) to be the guarantor of.

a·va·lo·rar tr. to appraise; FIG. to encourage.

a·va·luar §67 tr. to appraise.

a·va·lú·o m. appraisal, valuation.

a·van·ce¹ m. advance; COM. balance sheet; MECH. feed; CUBA vomit; MEX. looting.

a·van·ce² m. preview.

a·van·za·do, a adj. advanced.

a·van·zar §04 tr. to advance; CUBA to vomit; MEX. to loot —intr. & reflex. to advance.

a·van·zo m. (*balance*) balance sheet; (*presupuesto*) estimate.

a·va·ri·cia f. avarice, greed.

a·va·ri·cio·so/rien·to, a I. adj. (*tacaño*) avaricious, miserly; (*codicioso*) greedy **II.** m.f. (*tacaño*) miser; (*codicioso*) greedy person.

a·va·ro, a I. adj. (*tacaño*) miserly; (*codicioso*) greedy **II.** m.f. (*tacaño*) miser; (*codicioso*) greedy person.

a·va·sa·lla·dor, ·ra I. adj. subjugating **II.** m.f. subjugator.

a·va·sa·lla·mien·to m. subjugation.

a·va·sa·llar tr. to subjugate.

a·ve f. bird ♦ **a. cantora** songbird • **a. de corral** barnyard fowl • **a. de paso** wanderer • **a. de rapiña** bird of prey.

a·ve·cin·dar tr. to domicile —reflex. to settle.

a·ve·jen·tar tr. & reflex. to age prematurely.

a·ve·ji·gar §47 tr. to blister.

a·ve·lla·no, a I. adj. hazel **II.** m. hazel (tree) —f. hazelnut.

a·ve·ma·rí·a f. (*oración*) Hail Mary; (*del rosario*) small rosary bead ♦ **en un a.** COLL. in a flash.

¡A·ve Ma·rí·a! interj. good heavens!

a·ve·na f. oat, oats.

a·ve·nen·cia f. (*acuerdo*) agreement; (*arreglo*) compromise.

a·ve·ni·ble adj. reconcilable.

a·ve·ni·do, a I. adj. ♦ **bien a.** in agreement • **mal a.** in disagreement **II.** f. (*calle*) avenue; (*desbordamiento*) flood.

a·ve·ni·mien·to m. reconciliation.

a·ve·nir §76 tr. to reconcile, conciliate —intr. to happen, occur —reflex. (*entenderse*) to come to an agreement; (*armonizar*) to go together.

a·ven·ta·ja·do, a adj. (*notable*) outstanding; (*ventajoso*) advantageous.

a·ven·ta·jar tr. (*superar*) to surpass; (*ganar*) to beat; (*llevar ventaja*) to be ahead of.

a·ven·ta·mien·to m. winnowing.

a·ven·tar §49 tr. (*echar al aire*) to cast to the winds; to winnow (grain); CUBA, MEX., AGR. to dry in the sun.

a·ven·tu·ra f. adventure; (*riesgo*) risk.

a·ven·tu·ra·do, a adj. adventurous.

a·ven·tu·rar tr. (*arriesgar*) to risk; (*proponer*) to venture —reflex. to take a risk.

a·ven·tu·re·ro, a I. adj. adventurous **II.** m. adventurer —f. adventuress.

a·ver·gon·zar §09 tr. to shame —reflex. to be ashamed (*de* to, *por* of).

a·ve·rí·a f. (daño) damage; (rotura) breakdown.
a·ve·ria·do, a adj. (estropeado) damaged; (echado a perder) spoiled; (roto) broken.
a·ve·riar §30 tr. (estropear) to damage; (echar a perder) to spoil; (romper) to break —reflex. (estropearse) to become damaged; (arruinarse) to spoil; (descomponerse) to break (down).
a·ve·ri·gua·ción f. (investigación) investigation; (verificación) verification.
a·ve·ri·guar §10 tr. (comprobar) to ascertain; (investigar) to investigate; (verificar) to verify.
a·ve·rru·ga·do, a adj. warty.
a·ve·rru·gar·se §47 reflex. to become warty.
a·ver·sión f. aversion ♦ **cobrar** or **coger una a.** to develop an aversion to.
a·ves·truz m. ostrich.
a·via·ción f. aviation; MIL. air force.
a·via·dor, ·ra m. pilot, aviator —f. pilot, aviatrix.
a·ví·co·la adj. poultry-breeding.
a·vi·cul·tor, ·ra m.f. chicken farmer.
a·vi·cul·tu·ra f. poultry breeding.
a·vi·dez f. (ansia) avidity; (codicia) greed ♦ **con a.** (ansiosamente) eagerly; (avariciosamente) greedily.
á·vi·do, a adj. (ansioso) avid; (codicioso) greedy.
a·vien·te, to see **aventar**.
a·vie·so, a adj. twisted; FIG. perverse.
a·vi·na·gra·do, a adj. sour.
a·vi·na·grar tr. to make sour —reflex. to turn sour; FIG. to become sour.
a·vi·nie·ra, no see **avenir**.
a·ví·o m. (provisiones) provisions; AMER. loan ♦ pl. equipment, materials • **a. de pesca** fishing tackle.
a·vión m. airplane, plane ♦ **a. de caza** fighter plane • **a. de bombardeo** bomber • **a. a chorro** or **de reacción** jet plane • **por a.** by air mail.
a·vio·ne·ta f. light airplane.
a·vi·sar tr. (informar) to inform; (advertir) to warn.
a·vi·so m. (notificación) notice; (advertencia) warning; (anuncio) advertisement; MARIT. dispatch boat ♦ **estar sobre a.** to be on the alert.
a·vis·pa f. wasp.
a·vis·pa·do, a adj. COLL. clever.
a·vis·par tr. to whip —reflex. COLL. to become quick-witted.
a·vis·pe·ro m. (panal) honeycomb; (nido) wasps' nest ♦ **meterse en un a.** to get into a big mess.
a·vis·pón m. hornet.
a·vis·tar tr. to sight.
a·vi·tua·lla·mien·to m. provisioning.
a·vi·tua·llar tr. to provision, supply with food.
a·vi·va·dor, ·ra I. adj. livening, reviving **II.** m. ARCHIT. quirk; CARP. rabbet plane.
a·vi·va·mien·to m. (animación) enlivening; (de colores) brightening; (renacimiento) revival; (de un fuego) stoking.
a·vi·var tr. (animar) to spur on; (colores) to brighten; (un fuego) to stoke; (encender) to arouse —intr. & reflex. to revive, liven up.
a·vi·zor, ·ra I. adj. watchful ♦ **estar ojo a.** to keep one's eyes open **II.** m.f. watcher.
a·vi·zo·rar tr. to watch, spy on.
a·xi(a)l adj. axial, axal.
a·xi·la f. BOT. axil; ANAT. axilla, armpit.
a·xio·ma m. axiom.
a·xio·má·ti·co, a adj. axiomatic.

¡ay! I. interj. (dolor) ow!, ouch!; (aflicción) oh dear!, alas!; (admiración) oh!, wow! ♦ **¡a. de mí!** woe is me! **II.** m. sigh, moan.
a·yer I. adv. yesterday; (en el pasado) formerly, in the past ♦ **a. no más** only yesterday • **de a. a hoy** recently **II.** m. yesterday, past.
a·yo, a m.f. tutor —f. governess.
a·yu·da f. (auxilio) help, aid; (dinero) financial aid; (jeringa) syringe; (lavativa) enema; EDUC. partial scholarship; EQUIT. spur ♦ **a. de cámara** valet.
a·yu·dan·te, a m.f. assistant, aide; MIL. adjutant ♦ **a. de campo** aide-de-camp.
a·yu·dan·tí·a f. assistantship; MIL. adjutancy.
a·yu·dar tr. to help, aid ♦ **a. a** to help to.
a·yu·nar intr. to fast.
a·yu·no, a I. adj. fasting; FIG. uninformed ♦ **en a.** or **ayunas** (sin comer) fasting; (sin desayunar) before breakfast; (sin saber) in the dark, all at sea • **quedarse en ayunas** FIG. to be completely in the dark **II.** m. fast, fasting.
a·yun·ta·mien·to m. (reunión) meeting; (corporación) city council; (edificio) city hall; (coito) sexual intercourse.
a·za·ba·che m. MIN. jet; ORNITH. titmouse.
a·za·da f. hoe.
a·za·dón m. large hoe.
a·za·do·nar tr. to hoe.
a·za·fai·fa f. jujube.
a·za·fa·ta f. AVIA. stewardess; (criada) lady-in-waiting.
a·za·frán m. saffron.
a·za·har f. orange, lemon or citron blossom.
a·zar m. (casualidad) chance; (desgracia) misfortune ♦ **al a.** at random • **por a.** by chance.
a·za·ran·dar tr. to strain, sieve.
a·za·ro·so, a adj. (arriesgado) risky; (desgraciado) unlucky.
á·zi·mo adj. unleavened.
a·zo·ga·do, a adj. silvered.
a·zo·gar §47 tr. to silver —reflex to get mercury poisoning; (inquietarse) to be restless.
a·zo·gue m. quicksilver.
a·zo·ra·mien·to m. (sobresalto) alarm; (turbación) fluster.
a·zo·ran·te adj. (sobresaltante) alarming; (desconcertante) confusing.
a·zo·rar tr. (sobresaltar) to alarm; (confundir) to confuse —reflex. (sobresaltarse) to be alarmed or startled; (confundirse) to become confused or bewildered.
a·zo·rra·do, a adj. foxy.
a·zo·ta·do, a adj. multicolored, motley.
a·zo·tai·na f. COLL. flogging.
a·zo·ta·mien·to m. flogging.
a·zo·tar tr. to flog; FIG. to beat upon.
a·zo·ta·zo m. (whip)lash; COLL. spank, swat.
a·zo·te m. (látigo) whip; (golpe) lash; (zurra) spanking; (embate) beating.
a·zo·te·a f. (tejado) terraced roof; COLL. (cabeza) head.
a·zo·ti·na f. COLL. drubbing, thrashing.
a·zú·car m. or f. sugar ♦ **a. candi** rock candy • **a. de caña** cane sugar • **a. en terrones** lump sugar • **a. en polvo** powdered sugar • **a. moreno** or **negro** brown sugar.
a·zu·ca·ra·do, a adj. sweet.
a·zu·ca·rar tr. (endulzar) to sugar-coat; COLL. (suavizar) to sweeten —reflex. (almibarar) to become sugary; AMER. (cristalizar) to become crystallized.

a·zu·ca·re·ro, a I. adj. sugar II. f. *(recipiente)* sugar bowl; *(fábrica)* sugar factory.
a·zu·ce·na f. white *or* Madonna lily.
a·zu·fai·fa f. jujube.
a·zu·fra·do, a I. adj. sulfurous; *(color)* sulfur-colored II. m. sulfurization.
a·zu·frar tr. *(impregnar)* to sulfur; *(sahumar)* to fumigate with sulfur.
a·zu·fre m. sulfur, sulphur.
a·zul I. adj. blue II. m. *(color)* blue; *(azulete)* bluing ♦ **a. celeste** sky blue • **a. marino** navy blue • **a. turquí** indigo.
a·zu·la·do, a adj. bluish.
a·zu·lar tr. to blue, dye *or* color blue.
a·zu·le·jo m. *(baldosa)* glazed tile.
a·zu·li·no, a adj. bluish.
a·zu·zar §04 tr. to set the dogs on; FIG. to stir.

B

b, B f. second letter of the Spanish alphabet.
ba·ba f. spittle ♦ **caérsele a uno la b.** to drool • **echar b.** to drool.
ba·bar·se tr. to dribble.
ba·ba·za f. slime; ZOOL. slug.
ba·be·ar intr. to drool.
ba·bel m.f. COLL. babel.
ba·be·ra f. beaver of a helmet; *(babero)* bib.
ba·be·ro m. bib; *(guardapolvos)* dust cover.
ba·bie·ca COLL. adj. & m.f. simple (person).
ba·bor m. port.
ba·bo·se·ar intr. & tr. to drool (over).
ba·bo·se·o m. dribbling.
ba·bo·so, a I. adj. drooling; FIG. mushy; C. AMER. foolish II. m.f. drooler; FIG. immature person —f. ZOOL. slug.
ba·bu·cha f. slipper ♦ **a b.** ARG. piggyback.
ba·ca·la·o m. codfish ♦ **cortar el b.** COLL. to be in charge.
ba·cán m. AMER. *(amante)* sugar daddy; R.P. *(holgazán)* loafer.
ba·ca·nal f. orgy.
ba·can·te f. FIG. loud drunken woman.
ba·ca·rr(r)á m. baccarat.
ba·ce·ta f. widow (cards).
ba·che m. pothole; AER. air pocket; FIG. rough spot.
ba·chi·ller m.f. student ready for admission into an advanced university program.
ba·chi·lle·rar tr. to confer a bachelor's degree on —reflex. to be graduated as a bachelor.
ba·chi·lle·ra·to m. studies which enable a student to enter an advanced university program.
ba·ci·lo m. bacillus.
ba·cín m. *(orinal grande)* large chamber pot; *(de mendigo)* beggar's bowl.
ba·ci·ne·te m. *(armadura)* basinet (helmet); *(soldado)* cuirassier; ANAT. pelvis.
ba·ci·ni·ca/lla f. *(de mendigo)* beggar's bowl; *(orinal)* chamber pot.
bac·te·ria f.inv. bacterium.
bac·te·rio·lo·gí·a f. bacteriology.
bac·te·rio·ló·gi·co, a adj. bacteriological.
bac·te·rió·lo·go, a m.f. bacteriologist.
bá·cu·lo m. *(cayado)* staff; FIG. *(apoyo)* support; *(alivio)* relief.
ba·da·jo m. bell clapper; FIG. chatterbox.
ba·de·a f. *(cosa)* tasteless thing; *(fruta)* insipid melon or cucumber; *(persona)* dull person.
ba·du·la·que adj. & m. foolish (person).

ba·du·la·que·ar intr. S. AMER. *(engañar)* to cheat; *(ser terco)* to be stubborn.
ba·ga·je m. MIL. equipment; *(acémila)* beast of burden; *(caudal)* stock of knowledge; S. AMER. luggage.
ba·ga·te·la f. trifle.
ba·ga·zo m. bagasse; C. AMER. creep.
ba·gre m. catfish; S. AMER. hag.
¡bah! interj. bah!
ba·hí·a f. bay.
bai·la·dor, ·ra I. adj. dancing II. m.f. dancer.
bai·lar intr. to dance; *(girar)* to spin (tops); *(retozar)* to romp ♦ **b. al son que tocan** FIG. to adapt to the circumstances —tr. to dance.
bai·la·rín, i·na I. adj. dancing II. m.f. dancer —f. ballerina.
bai·le[1] m. dance; THEAT. ballet ♦ **b. de máscaras** *or* **disfraces** costume *or* masked ball.
bai·le[2] m. ARCH. alderman.
bai·lí·a f. bailiwick.
bai·lon·go m. AMER. public *or* village dance.
bai·lo·te·ar intr. *(bailar mucho)* to dance a lot; *(bailar sin esmero)* to dance clumsily.
bai·lo·te·o m. dancing about.
bai·vel m. bevel *or* miter square.
ba·ja f. *(disminución)* drop; MIL. loss; COM. rebate ♦ **dar de b.** to expel; MIL. to discharge • **darse de b.** to drop out • **estar en b.** *or* **ir de b.** to lose value.
ba·já m. pasha.
ba·ja·da f. drop; *(camino)* sloped path ♦ **b. de aguas** downspout.
ba·ja·mar f. low tide.
ba·jan·te f. AMER. low tide.
ba·jar intr. to descend; *(apearse)* to get off; *(disminuir)* to drop —tr. to lower; *(llevar abajo)* to bring *or* take down; *(ir abajo)* to go down; *(disminuir)* to lower; *(inclinar)* to bow; *(apear)* to help down; *(humillar)* to humble —reflex. to go down; *(apearse)* to get down *or* off; *(agacharse)* to bend down.
ba·je·za f. lowliness; *(villanía)* baseness ♦ **b. de ánimo** timidity.
ba·jí·o m. *(banco de arena)* sandbank; *(terreno bajo)* low-lying ground.
ba·jis·ta m.f. bear (in stock market).
ba·jo I. m. *(tierra)* lowland; *(bajío)* shoal; *(voz)* bass; *(violoncelo)* cello ♦ pl. *(piso)* ground floor; *(enaguas)* underskirt; *(barrio)* slums II. adv. *(abajo)* below; *(en voz baja)* low ♦ **por lo b.** secretly III. prep. under ♦ **b. llave** under lock and key • **b. palabra** on parole • **b. pena de** under penalty of.
ba·jo, a adj. *(poco elevado)* low; *(de estatura)* short; *(inclinado)* downcast; *(poco vivo)* pale *(sonido)* low; *(vulgar)* vulgar; *(abyecto)* abject; *(humilde)* humble; *(barato)* cheap ♦ **b. de ley** METAL. base • **b. relieve** ARTS bas-relief.
ba·jón[1] m. MUS. bassoon.
ba·jón[2] m. drop.
ba·jo·nis·ta m.f. bassoonist.
ba·la f. *(proyectil)* bullet; *(de cañón)* cannonball; *(de carabina)* shot; *(fardo)* bale ♦ **b. fría** spent bullet • **b. perdida** stray bullet • **como una b.** FIG., COLL. like a shot.
ba·la·da f. ballad(e).
ba·la·dí adj. [pl. **-íes**] trivial.
ba·la·dro m. *(grito)* shout; *(chillido)* shriek.
ba·la·drón, o·na I. adj. boasting II. m.f. braggart.
ba·la·dro·na·da f. boast.
ba·la·dro·ne·ar intr. to boast, brag.

bá·la·go m. *(de cereal)* grain stalk; *(de jabón)* soapsuds.

ba·la·lai·ca f. balalaika.

ba·lan·ce m. *(vacilación)* vacillation; *(resultado)* balance; COM. balance ◆ **b. comercial** balance of trade ◆ **b. pendiente** balance due.

ba·lan·ce·ar intr. to rock; FIG. to vacillate, waver —tr. to balance —reflex. to rock.

ba·lan·ce·o m. rocking.

ba·lan·cín m. *(contrapeso)* acrobat's balancing pole; *(volante)* minting mill; *(juguete)* seesaw; *(mecedora)* rocking chair ◆ pl. MARIT. sheets.

ba·lan·dra f. MARIT. sloop.

ba·lan·drán m. monk's cassock.

ba·lan·dro m. small sloop.

bá·la·no *or* **ba·la·no** m. glans penis.

ba·lan·za f. scales; FIG. comparison; AMER. acrobat's balancing pole ◆ **b. comercial** *or* **mercantil** ECON. balance of trade.

ba·lar intr. to bleat.

ba·las·tar tr. to ballast.

ba·las·to m. ballast.

ba·laus·tra·da f. balustrade.

ba·laus·trar tr. to build a balustrade on.

ba·la·zo m. *(golpe)* shot; *(herida)* bullet wound.

bal·bo·a PAN., FIN. balboa.

bal·bu·ce·ar intr. var. of **balbucir**.

bal·bu·ce·o m. stammering.

bal·bu·cien·te adj. stammering.

bal·bu·cir §38 intr. to stammer.

bal·cón m. balcony; FIG. vantage *or* observation point.

bal·dar tr. *(lisiar)* to cripple; *(en los naipes)* to trump; *(molestar)* to inconvenience —reflex. *(lisiarse)* to become crippled; COLL. *(cansarse)* to become exhausted.

bal·de¹ m. pail ◆ **como un b. de agua fría** like a ton of bricks.

bal·de² adv. ◆ **de b.** *(gratuitamente)* free; *(sin motivo)* without reason ◆ **en b.** in vain ◆ **estar de b.** to be in excess.

bal·de·ar tr. *(regar)* to wash down; *(achicar)* to bail out.

bal·dí·o, a I. adj. AGR. uncultivated; *(vano)* useless; *(vagabundo)* vagrant II. m. uncultivated land.

bal·do·sa f. floor tile.

ba·le·ar tr. AMER. to shoot (at); C. AMER. to swindle —reflex. to shoot at one another.

ba·le·ro m. bullet mold; AMER. cup and ball.

ba·li·do m. bleating.

ba·lín m. pellet ◆ pl. buckshot.

ba·lís·ti·co, a I. adj. ballistic II. f. ballistics.

ba·li·za f. MARIT. buoy; AVIA. beacon.

ba·li·zar §04 tr. to mark with buoys.

ba·lle·na f. whale; *(de un corsé)* stay.

ba·lle·na·to m. whale calf.

ba·lle·ne·ro, a I. adj. whaling II. m. whaler.

ba·lles·ta f. crossbow; MECH. spring.

ba·lles·te·ar tr. to shoot (with a crossbow).

ba·lles·te·ra f. loophole for crossbows.

ba·lles·te·rí·a f. *(deporte)* archery; *(ballesteros)* crossbowmen.

ba·lles·te·ro m. crossbowman.

ba·lles·ti·lla f. small whiffletree.

ba·llet m. [pl. **s**] ballet.

bal·ne·a·rio, a I. adj. bathing II. m. bathing resort; *(medicinal)* spa.

ba·lom·pié m. soccer.

ba·lón m. *(pelota)* football; *(fardo)* bale; *(recipiente)* glass flask; *(globo)* balloon.

ba·lon·ces·to m. basketball.

ba·lon·ma·no m. handball.

ba·lon·vo·le·a m. volleyball.

ba·lo·ta f. ballot.

ba·lo·ta·je m. AMER. balloting.

bal·sa f. *(charca)* pool; *(embarcación)* raft; BOT. balsa ◆ **b. de aceite** tranquil place.

bal·sá·mi·co, a adj. balsamic.

bál·sa·mo m. balsam.

bal·se·ro m. ferryman.

ba·luar·te m. bulwark.

bam·ba·le·ar intr. to sway.

bam·ba·li·na f. THEAT. top curtain ◆ **tras bambalinas** FIG. behind the scenes.

bam·bo·le·ar intr. & reflex. to wobble.

bam·bo·le·o m. wobble.

bam·bo·lla f. COLL. ostentation.

bam·bo·lle·ro, a adj. COLL. showy.

bam·bú m. [pl. **-úes**] bamboo.

ba·nal adj. banal.

ba·na·na f. /no m. banana.

ba·na·nal/nar m. banana grove *or* plantation.

ba·na·ne·ro, a adj. & m. banana (tree).

ban·ca f. *(asiento)* bench; *(puesto)* stall; COM. banking; *(juego)* baccarat ◆ **hacer saltar la b.** to break the bank • **tener b.** R.P. to have influence.

ban·ca·da f. *(asiento)* stone bench; *(mesa)* large table.

ban·ca·rio, a adj. bank.

ban·ca·rro·ta f. bankruptcy.

ban·co m. bench; *(caballete)* workbench; COM. bank; MAS. row of bricks; MARIT. bank; *(cardumen)* school ◆ **b. de ahorros** savings bank • **b. de arena** sandbar • **b. de datos** data bank • **b. de liquidación** clearing house • **b. de nieve** snowbank • **b. de pruebas** TECH. testing bench.

ban·da¹ f. *(faja)* band; *(cinta)* ribbon; *(lado)* side ◆ **b. sonora** *or* **de sonido** soundtrack • **b. transportadora** conveyor belt • **cerrarse en b.** FIG. to stick to one's guns.

ban·da² f. MIL. band; *(pandilla)* gang; *(partido)* faction; *(de aves)* flock; MUS. band.

ban·da·da f. *(grupo)* group; *(de aves)* flock; *(de peces)* school.

ban·da·zo m. lurch (of a boat); *(paseo)* stroll; *(tumbo)* fall.

ban·de·ja f. tray.

ban·de·ra f. *(pabellón)* flag; *(estandarte)* banner ◆ **a banderas desplegadas** openly • **b. de parlamento** *or* **de paz** white flag • **con banderas desplegadas** with flying colors • **de b.** COLL. terrific • **jurar la b.** to pledge allegiance.

ban·de·ri·lla f. TAUR. banderilla; AMER. swindle.

ban·de·rín m. pennant; *(soldado)* infantry guide.

ban·de·ri·zar §04 tr. to divide into bands.

ban·de·ro·la f. pennant.

ban·di·da·je m. banditry.

ban·di·do m. bandit; COLL. rascal.

ban·do m. *(edicto)* edict; *(facción)* faction; *(de peces)* school; *(de aves)* flock ◆ pl. marriage banns.

ban·do·le·ra f. bandoleer.

ban·do·le·ris·mo m. banditry.

ban·do·le·ro m. bandit.

ban·do·ne·ón m. concertina.

ban·jo m. banjo.

ban·que·ro m. banker.

ban·que·ta f. stool; *(para los pies)* footstool; MIL. banquette.

ban·que·te m. banquet.
ban·qui·llo m. stool; *(para los pies)* footstool; *(del acusado)* defendant's seat.
ba·ña·de·ra f. AMER. bathtub.
ba·ña·do m. AMER. swamp.
ba·ña·dor, ·ra I. adj. bathing **II.** m.f. AMER. bather —m. *(traje de baño)* bathing suit.
ba·ñar tr. to bathe; *(sumergir)* to immerse; *(cubrir)* to coat; *(tocar)* to lap; *(llenar)* to flood —reflex. to bathe.
ba·ñe·ra f. bathtub.
ba·ñe·ro m. bathhouse owner.
ba·ñis·ta m.f. swimmer.
ba·ño m. *(ducha)* bath; *(bañera)* bathtub; *(cuarto de baño)* bathroom; *(capa)* coat ♦ **b. de María** CUL. double boiler ♦ pl spa.
bap·tis·te·rio m. baptistry.
ba·que·li·ta f. bakelite.
ba·que·ta f. MIL. ramrod; *(castigo)* gauntlet.
ba·que·ta·zo m. blow with a ramrod; COLL. fall.
ba·que·te·a·do, a adj. *(endurecido)* hardened; *(experimentado)* experienced.
ba·que·te·ar tr. *(ejercitar)* to exercise; *(tratar mal)* to mistreat; *(castigar)* to force to run the gauntlet; FIG. to harass.
ba·que·te·o m. *(molestia)* burden; *(cansancio)* exhaustion.
ba·quia·no, a adj. & m.f. S. AMER. expert.
bar¹ m. barroom.
bar² m. PHYS. bar.
ba·ra·hún·da f. uproar.
ba·ra·ja f. *(naipes)* deck (of cards); AMER. playing card ♦ **entrarse en b.** to give up • **jugar con dos barajas** to double-deal.
ba·ra·jar tr. *(los naipes)* to shuffle; *(mezclar)* to jumble; *(cifras)* to juggle —intr. to fight, quarrel —reflex. to get mixed up.
ba·ran·da f. banister; *(de billar)* cushion.
ba·ran·di·lla f. banister, handrail; *(balaustrada)* railing.
ba·ra·te·ar tr. to sell at a discount, sell cheap.
ba·ra·ti·ja f. trinket, bauble ♦ pl. junk.
ba·ra·ti·llo m. *(mercancías)* secondhand goods; *(tienda)* junk shop; *(venta)* bargain sale.
ba·ra·to, a I. adj. & adv. cheap(ly), inexpensive(ly) ♦ **de b.** for free, gratis **II.** m. bargain sale —f. *(trueque)* barter; COL., MEX. bargain sale; CHILE, PERU cockroach.
ba·ra·ún·da f. var. of **barahúnda**.
bar·ba f. *(barbilla)* chin; *(pelo)* beard; ORNITH. wattle, gill; BOT. beard ♦ **barbas de chivo** goatee • **en las barbas de uno** under one's nose • **hacer la b.** to shave, give a shave to; FIG. *(adular)* to flatter, fawn over; *(fastidiar)* to annoy, pester • **mentir por la b.** to tell a barefaced lie ♦ pl. whiskers.
bar·ba·co·a f. barbecue; AMER. makeshift cot.
bar·bar intr. to grow a beard.
bar·bá·ri·co, a adj. barbaric, barbarian.
bar·ba·ri·dad f. barbarity; *(necedad)* foolish act, nonsense; COLL. an enormous amount ♦ **¡qué b.!** how awful!
bar·ba·rie f. barbarousness, barbarity.
bar·ba·ris·mo m. barbarism.
bar·ba·ri·zar §04 tr. to make barbarous —intr. to talk nonsense.
bár·ba·ro, a I. adj. barbaric, barbarous; *(temerario)* bold, reckless; *(inculto)* barbarian; COLL. *(espléndido)* tremendous, terrific; *(grande)* huge **II.** m.f. barbarian.
bar·be·rí·a f. barbershop.

bar·be·ro, a m. barber.
bar·bi·lla f. chin; ICHTH. barb, barbel; CARP. tenon, rabbet.
bar·bi·tú·ri·co, a adj. & m. barbituric (acid).
bar·bo·tar/te·ar tr. & intr. to mutter, mumble.
bar·bo·te·o m. murmuring.
bar·bu·do, a adj. heavily bearded.
bar·bu·lia f. COLL. jabbering, chatter.
bar·bu·llar intr. COLL. to jabber, chatter.
bar·bu·llón, o·na I. adj. jabbering, chattering **II.** m.f. jabberer, chatterer.
bar·ca f. small boat ♦ **b. de pasaje** ferryboat.
bar·ca·da f. *(carga)* boatload; *(viaje)* crossing.
bar·ca·za f. launch.
bar·cia f. chaff.
bar·ci·no, a adj. roan, brindled.
bar·co m. boat, ship; *(barranco)* shallow ravine ♦ **b. de carga** freighter • **como b. sin timón** FIG. aimlessly.
bar·da f. bard, armor for a horse; METEOROL. thundercloud.
bar·da·gue·ra f. willow.
ba·rio m. barium.
ba·rí·to·no m. baritone.
bar·lo·ven·te·ar intr. *(navegar)* to tack to windward; *(vagabundear)* to wander, meander.
bar·lo·ven·to m. windward.
bar·niz m. varnish, lacquer; *(maquillaje)* make-up, cosmetics; FIG. veneer, thin coat.
bar·ni·za·do m. varnish(ing), lacquer(ing).
bar·ni·zar §04 tr. to varnish, lacquer.
ba·ro·mé·tri·co, a adj. barometric.
ba·ró·me·tro m. barometer.
ba·rón m. baron.
ba·ro·ne·sa f. baroness.
bar·que·ar tr. & intr. to go across *or* about in a boat.
bar·que·ro m. boatman; ENTOM. water bug.
bar·qui·lla f. small boat.
bar·qui·llo m. cone.
bar·quín m. large bellows.
bar·qui·na·zo m. COLL. bump, jolt; *(vuelco)* rollover, roll.
ba·rra f. bar; *(barandilla)* railing; *(mostrador)* counter, bar; *(de arena)* sandbar, sandbank; MECH. rod, lever; AMER. public, spectators ♦ **b. de labios** lipstick • **barras paralelas** SPORT. parallel bars • **sin pararse en barras** to stop at nothing.
ba·rra·bás m. [pl. **-ases**] scoundrel, rascal.
ba·rra·ba·sa·da f. COLL. dirty *or* mean trick.
ba·rra·ca f. hut, cabin; AMER. warehouse.
ba·rra·cón m. stall, booth.
ba·rra·cu·da f. barracuda.
ba·rran·co m./ca f. ravine, gorge; FIG. *(obstáculo)* obstacle, difficulty.
ba·rran·cón m. gully, ravine.
ba·rran·co·so, a adj. full of ravines.
ba·rra·que·ro, a m.f. builder of a cottage; AMER. warehouse owner.
ba·rre·ar tr. *(fortificar)* to barricade, close (up); *(barretear)* to bar, fasten with bars.
ba·rre·de·ra f. street sweeper.
ba·rre·de·ro, a I. adj. dragging, sweeping **II.** f. street sweeper.
ba·rre·dor, ·ra I. adj. sweeping **II.** m.f. sweeper ♦ **b. eléctrica** vacuum cleaner.
ba·rre·du·ra f. sweeping ♦ pl. refuse, residue.
ba·rre·na f. *(instrumento)* drill, gimlet; *(barra)* (drill) bit; AVIA. spin <*b. picada* tailspin>.
ba·rre·nar tr. MECH. to drill, bore; MARIT. to scuttle; FIG. *(desbaratar)* to foil, undermine;

LAW to violate, infringe.

ba·rren·de·ro, a m.f. street sweeper.

ba·rre·ne·ro m. driller, borer.

ba·rre·no m. *(instrumento)* large drill, auger; *(agujero)* bore, drill hole; MIN. blasting hole.

ba·rrer tr. to sweep; *(rozar)* to graze, touch lightly —intr. to sweep ♦ **b. con todo** COLL. to make a clean sweep • **b. hacia adentro** to look out for number one.

ba·rre·ra[1] f. barrier; FIG. obstacle, hindrance ♦ **b. de peaje** tollgate.

ba·rre·ra[2] f. *(sitio)* clay pit; *(alacena)* crockery cupboard.

ba·rria·da f. neighborhood, district.

ba·rrial m. *(gredal)* clay pit; AMER. *(barrizal)* bog.

ba·rri·ca f. medium-sized barrel *or* cask.

ba·rri·ca·da f. barricade, barrier.

ba·rri·do, a m. sweep, sweeping —f. S. AMER. sweep, police raid.

ba·rri·ga f. abdomen, stomach; COLL. paunch, belly; *(de una vasija, pared)* bulge ♦ **rascarse la b.** COLL. to twiddle one's thumbs.

ba·rri·gón, o·na/gu·do, a adj. COLL. potbellied.

ba·rril m. *(tonel)* barrel, keg; *(jarro)* jug.

ba·rri·llo m. blackhead, pimple.

ba·rrio n. neighborhood ♦ **barrios bajos** slums • **el otro b.** COLL. the other world.

ba·rris·ta m.f. gymnast on the horizontal bars.

ba·rro m. *(lodo)* mud; *(arcilla)* clay; *(vaso)* earthenware vessel; *(granillo)* blackhead.

ba·rro·co, a adj. baroque; *(extravagante)* ornate, elaborate.

ba·rro·te m. *(barra)* heavy bar, rail; *(sostén)* rung; CARP. crosspiece.

ba·rrun·tar tr. to suspect, guess.

ba·rrun·te/to m. *(sospecha)* feeling, suspicion; *(indicio)* sign, clue.

bar·to·la ♦ a la b. without a care in the world, nonchalantly ♦ **echarse a la b.** to let oneself go.

bár·tu·los m.pl. household goods, belongings; MECH. equipment, gear.

ba·ru·llo m. COLL. racket, rowdiness.

ba·sa f. base; FIG. basis, foundation.

ba·sal·to m. basalt.

ba·sa·men·to m. base of a column.

ba·sar tr. to build on a base; FIG. to base, support —reflex. to be based.

bas·ca f. nausea, queasiness.

bás·cu·la f. TECH. bascule; *(balanza)* platform scale, balance.

ba·se f. base; FIG. *(fundamento)* basis, foundation ♦ **a b. de** with • **b. imponible** tax base • **en b. a** on the basis of.

bá·si·co, a adj. basic.

ba·sí·li·co, a I. f. basilica II. adj. basilic.

ba·si·lis·co m. basilisk ♦ **estar hecho un b.** COLL. to be furious or enraged.

bas·ta f. see **basto, a.**

bas·tan·te I. adj. enough, sufficient II. adv. enough, sufficiently; *(muy)* rather, quite.

bas·tar intr. to suffice ♦ **¡basta!** that's enough of that! —reflex. to be self-sufficient.

bas·tar·de·ar intr. to degenerate, decline —tr. to bastardize, adulterate.

bas·tar·dí·a f. bastardy, illegitimacy; FIG. nasty remark or trick.

bas·tar·di·llo, a adj. & f. italic(s).

bas·tar·do, a I. m.f. bastard; BOT., ZOOL. crossbreed, hybrid —m. ZOOL. boa II. adj. bastard, illegitimate; BOT., ZOOL. hybrid.

bas·te m. basting, tacking.

bas·te·ar tr. SEW. to baste, tack.

bas·ti·dor m. *(armazón)* frame, framework; THEAT. flat, wing; AUTO. chassis ♦ **entre bastidores** FIG. behind the scenes; THEAT. off-stage.

bas·ti·lla f. hem.

bas·tión m. bastion.

bas·to, a I. adj. coarse, rough **II.** m. *(albarda)* packsaddle —f. SEW. basting, tacking.

bas·tón m. cane, walking stick; *(vara)* truncheon, staff; FIG. authority, command.

bas·to·na·da f./**na·zo** m. blow with a cane.

bas·to·ne·ar tr. to cane, beat with a stick.

bas·to·ne·ra f. umbrella stand.

ba·su·ra f. *(desperdicio)* garbage, trash; *(estiércol)* dung, horse manure.

ba·su·ral m. AMER. (garbage) dump.

ba·su·re·ar tr. ARG., COLL. to sling mud on.

ba·su·re·ro m. garbage collector; *(cubo)* garbage or trash can; *(basural)* dump.

ba·ta f. housecoat; *(de trabajo)* frock, smock.

ba·ta·ca·zo m. bump, thud.

ba·ta·ho·la f. COLL. rumpus, ruckus.

ba·ta·lla f. battle ♦ **b. campal** pitched battle • **dar** or **librar b.** to do battle • **de b.** ordinary, everyday.

ba·ta·lla·dor, ·ra I. adj. battling, fighting **II.** m. battler, fighter.

ba·ta·llar intr. to battle, fight; *(disputar)* to dispute, argue; *(vacilar)* to vacillate.

ba·ta·llón m. battalion.

ba·ta·ta f. sweet potato, yam

ba·ta·ta·zo m. AMER. lucky shot, fluke ♦ **dar b.** *(ganar los caballos)* to win by an upset; *(tener chiripa)* to make a lucky shot.

ba·te m. SPORT. bat; CUBA. busybody.

ba·te·a f. *(bandeja)* wicker tray; *(artesilla)* deep trough; MARIT. scow, punt; RAIL. flatcar.

ba·te·a·dor, ·ra m.f. SPORT. batter, hitter.

ba·te·ar tr. SPORT. to bat, hit.

ba·te·rí·a f. battery; *(bombardeo)* battering; THEAT. footlights; MUS. drums, percussion ♦ **b. de cocina** kitchen utensils.

ba·ti·do, a I. adj. beaten, well-trodden **II.** m. *(acción)* beating; CUL. batter; *(bebida)* shake <**b. de leche** milkshake> —f. *(cacería)* beat, beating; *(registro)* search; *(de policía)* police raid.

ba·ti·dor, ·ra I. adj. beating **II.** m. beater; MIL. scout —f. AMER. mixing bowl.

ba·tien·te I. adj. beating **II.** m. CONSTR. *(marco)* jamb; *(de puerta)* leaf.

ba·ti·fon·do m. ARG. rumpus, uproar.

ba·tin·tín m. gong.

ba·tir tr. to beat, hit; *(derribar)* to demolish, knock down; *(martillar)* to hammer; *(revolver)* to beat, mix; *(agitar)* to beat, flap; *(peinar)* to comb, tease; *(registrar)* to scour, search; *(vencer)* to beat, defeat; *(superar)* to beat, outdo; NUMIS. to mint; AMER. to tattle ♦ **b. el vuelo** FIG. to scram, beat it • **b. palmas** to clap hands • **b. tiendas** MIL. to break camp —intr. to beat violently, pound —reflex. to fight ♦ **b. en retirada** to beat a retreat.

ba·tis·ca·fo m. bathyscaph.

ba·tis·ta f. batiste, fine cambric.

ba·to·lo·gí·a f. RHET. needless repetition.

ba·tra·cio, a adj. & m. batrachian.

ba·tu·que·ar tr. AMER. to shake, shake up.

ba·tu·ta f. MUS. baton ♦ **llevar la b.** COLL. to be the boss.

ba·úl m. trunk; *(cofre)* coffer, chest.

bau·tis·mal adj. baptismal.
bau·tis·mo m. baptism, christening; *(iniciación)* baptism, initiation.
bau·tis·ta m.f. baptizer; RELIG. Baptist.
bau·tis·te·rio m. baptistry, baptistery.
bau·ti·zar §04 tr. to baptize, christen; *(nombrar)* to name, call; *(apodar)* to nickname; *(mezclar con agua)* to water (down), dilute.
bau·ti·zo m. baptism, christening.
bau·xi·ta f. bauxite.
ba·yo, a adj. & m. bay.
ba·yo·ne·ta f. bayonet; AMER. yucca.
ba·zar m. bazaar, marketplace.
ba·zo, a I. adj. yellowish-brown II. m. ANAT. spleen —f. *(en los naipes)* trick (in cards); *(oportunidad)* stroke of luck ♦ **meter b.** COLL. to butt in.
ba·zo·fia f. *(sobras)* leftovers, table scraps; *(comida)* slop, swill; *(suciedad)* filth, rubbish.
ba·zu·ca m. bazooka.
be·a·gle m. beagle.
be·a·te·rí·a f. sanctimoniousness, false piety.
be·a·ti·fi·ca·ción f. beatification.
be·a·ti·fi·car §70 tr. to beatify, bless.
be·a·tí·fi·co, a adj. beatific, beatifical.
be·a·ti·tud f. beatitude; *(alegría)* bliss.
be·a·to, a I. adj. *(feliz)* blissful; *(beatificado)* beatified; *(piadoso)* pious; *(santurrón)* prudish II. m.f. *(religioso)* lay brother *or* sister; *(piadoso)* devout person; *(santurrón)* prude.
be·bé m. *(nene)* baby; SL. babe, doll.
be·be·de·ro, a I. adj. drinkable, potable II. m. watering place *or* trough; *(de aves)* birdbath; *(pico de vasija)* lip, spout.
be·be·dor, ·ra I. adj. drinking II. m.f. drinker; *(borracho)* heavy drinker, boozer.
be·ber tr. to drink; *(absorber)* to drink in, imbibe ♦ **b. a sorbos** to sip ♦ **b. a tragos** to gulp (down) ♦ **b. los vientos por** to long for —intr. to drink booze ♦ **b. como una cuba** *or* **esponja** to drink like a fish.
be·bi·do, a I. adj. tipsy, drunk II. f. drink, beverage; *(vicio)* drink, drinking.
be·ca f. *(embozo)* sash, hood; *(colegiatura)* grant, scholarship; *(pensión)* room and board.
be·ca·rio, a m.f. scholarship student, fellow.
be·ce·rro, a m. yearling bull ♦ **b. marino** ZOOL. seal • **b. de oro** golden calf —f. ZOOL. yearling calf; BOT. snapdragon.
be·cha·mel f. white *or* béchamel sauce.
be·cua·dro m. MUS. natural sign.
be·del m. EDUC. proctor.
be·go·nia f. begonia.
béis·bol m. baseball.
be·ju·co m. rattan.
bel·dad f. beauty.
be·lén m. crèche, nativity scene; *(confusión)* confusion, bedlam ♦ **meterse en belenes** COLL. to get mixed up in trouble.
be·li·cis·mo m. warmongering, militarism.
be·li·cis·ta adj. & m.f. militarist(ic).
bé·li·co, a adj. bellicose, warlike.
be·li·co·si·dad f. bellicosity.
be·li·co·so, a adj. bellicose.
be·li·ge·ran·cia f. belligerency.
be·li·ge·ran·te adj. & m. belligerent.
be·lio m. bel.
be·lla·co, a I. adj. *(astuto)* sly, cunning; *(pícaro)* knavish, roguish II. m.f. rascal, rogue.
be·lla·que·rí·a f. *(astucia)* slyness, cunning; *(maldad)* roguishness; *(trampa)* sly trick.
be·lle·za f. beauty.

be·llo, a adj. beautiful, lovely; *(bueno)* fine, noble ♦ **bellas artes** fine arts.
be·llo·ta f. acorn; *(clavel)* carnation bud; *(borla)* tassel, pompom.
bem·ba f./**bo** m. AMER. muzzle, snout.
bem·bón, o·na/bu·do, a adj. AMER., DEROG. thick-lipped.
be·mol m. & adj. MUS. flat.
ben·ci·na f. benzin(e).
ben·de·cir §11 tr. to bless; *(consagrar)* to consecrate; *(alabar)* to praise, extol; *(agradecer)* to bless, thank.
ben·di·ción f. blessing; RELIG. benediction ♦ **b. de la mesa** grace • **bendiciones nupciales** wedding ceremony • **echar la b. a** to give one's blessing to.
ben·di·ga, go, jera, jo see bendecir.
ben·di·to, a I. see bendecir II. adj. *(santo)* holy, blessed; *(dichoso)* fortunate, lucky; *(tonto)* simple, simple-minded ♦ **como el pan b.** like hot cakes III. m.f. *(santo)* saint; *(bonachón)* good soul; *(tonto)* simpleton —m. *(oración)* prayer; AMER. Benedictine.
be·ne·dic·ti·no, a adj. & m.f. Benedictine.
be·ne·fac·tor m. benefactor.
be·ne·fi·cen·cia f. benevolence; *(asistencia)* welfare, public assistance.
be·ne·fi·cia·do, a m.f. beneficiary.
be·ne·fi·ciar tr. *(mejorar)* to benefit; AGR. to cultivate; MIN. to develop *or* work; *(tratar)* to smelt, treat; COM. to sell at a discount; AMER. to slaughter —intr. to be of benefit —reflex. to profit *(de* by, from).
be·ne·fi·cia·rio, a m.f. beneficiary ♦ **b. de cheque** COM. payee ♦ **b. de patente** COM. patentee.
be·ne·fi·cio m. benefit, advantage; *(ganancia)* profit, gain; AGR. cultivation; MIN. working; *(tratamiento)* smelting, treatment; THEAT. benefit (performance); RELIG. benefice; AMER. slaughter; C. AMER. processing plant, refinery ♦ **a b. de** for the benefit of • **no tener oficio ni b.** to be without means.
be·ne·fi·cio·so, a adj. beneficial.
be·né·fi·co, a adj. *(caritativo)* beneficent, charitable; *(provechoso)* beneficial.
be·ne·mé·ri·to, a adj. meritorious, worthy.
be·ne·plá·ci·to m. approval, consent.
be·ne·vo·len·cia f. benevolence, kindness.
be·né·vo·lo, a adj. benevolent, kind.
be·nig·no, a adj. benign.
ben·ja·mín m. baby of the family.
ben·juí m. benzoin, benjamin.
ben·zo·a·to m. benzoate.
be·o·dez f. drunkenness.
be·o·do, a adj. & m.f. drunk.
ber·be·re·cho m. cockle.
be·ren·je·na f. eggplant.
ber·ga·mo·ta f. bergamot.
ber·gan·te m. COLL. scoundrel, rascal.
ber·gan·tín m. brig.
be·ri·lio m. beryllium.
ber·ke·lio m. berkelium.
ber·lin·ga f. SP. clothesline pole.
ber·me·jo, a adj. bright red.
ber·me·llón m. vermilion.
ber·mu·da f. Bermuda grass ♦ pl. Bermuda shorts.
be·rra f. watercress.
be·rre·ar intr. *(balar)* to bleat; *(gritar)* to howl.
be·rre·o m. temper tantrum, rage.
be·rri·do m. *(balido)* bleat; *(chillido)* shriek.

be·rrin·che m. COLL. rage, tantrum.
be·rro m. watercress.
be·rrue·co m. granite rock.
ber·za f. cabbage.
be·sar tr. to kiss; (rozar) to graze, touch —reflex. to kiss one another.
be·so m. kiss; (roce) brush, glance.
bes·tia I. f. beast, animal —m.f. COLL. (bruto) beast, brute; (imbécil) idiot, blockhead ♦ **b. de albarda** pack animal ♦ **b. de carga** beast of burden II. adj. stupid, ignorant.
bes·tia·je m. beasts of burden.
bes·tial adj. bestial, beastly; COLL. (magnífico) fabulous; (enorme) gigantic.
bes·tia·li·dad f. beastliness, bestiality; (estupidez) stupidity, foolishness; (gran cantidad) a lot ♦ **¡qué b.!** how awful!
bes·tia·li·zar §04 tr. to bestialize, brutalize —reflex. to become bestialized.
be·su·ca·dor, ·ra COLL. I. adj. fond of kissing II. m.f. kisser.
be·su·car §70 tr. var. of besuquear.
be·su·cón, o·na adj. & m.f. var. of besucador.
be·su·go m. sea bream; FIG., COLL. (idiota) idiot, twerp.
be·su·que·ar tr. COLL. to smooch, lavish kisses.
be·su·que·o m. COLL. smooching.
be·ta·rra·ga/ta f. beet.
be·tún m. shoe polish.
be·tu·nar/ne·ar tr. CUBA, ECUAD. (pulir) to shine, polish; (asfaltar) to tar, asphalt.
bian·gu·lar adj. biangular.
bia·tó·mi·co, a adj. diatomic.
bi·be·rón m. baby bottle.
bi·blia f. bible ♦ **B.** Bible.
bí·bli·co, a adj. Biblical, biblical.
bi·bliό·fi·lo, a m.f. bibliophile, booklover.
bi·blio·gra·fí·a f. bibliography.
bi·blio·grá·fi·co, a adj. bibliographic(al).
bi·bliό·gra·fo, a m.f. bibliographer.
bi·blio·lo·gí·a f. bibliology.
bi·blio·te·ca f. library; AMER. bookcase.
bi·blio·te·ca·rio, a m.f. librarian.
bi·car·bo·na·ta·do, a adj. bicarbonate.
bi·car·bo·na·to m. bicarbonate ♦ **b. de sodio** or **de sosa** bicarbonate of soda; CUL. baking soda.
bi·cé·fa·lo, a adj. bicephalic, bicephalous.
bi·cen·te·na·rio m. bicentennial, bicentenary.
bí·ceps m.inv. biceps.
bi·cho m. bug, insect; (animal) beast, animal; (toro) bull; (fenómeno) freak, odd person ♦ **todo b. viviente** COLL. everyone.
bi·ci f. COLL. bike.
bi·ci·cle·ta f. bicycle.
bi·ci·clo m. velocipede.
bi·co·ca f. trifle, trinket; (ganga) bargain.
bi·co·lor adj. bicolor, two-tone.
bi·cón·ca·vo, a adj. biconcave.
bi·con·ve·xo, a adj. biconvex.
bi·cro·má·ti·co, a adj. dichromatic, two-color.
bi·cús·pi·de adj. bicuspid.
bi·dé m. bidet.
bi·dón m. large can, drum.
bie·la f. connecting rod, pitman.
bien I. m. good, goodness; (provecho) good, benefit ♦ **en b. de** for the good of • **hacer (el) b.** to do good ♦ pl. property, goods • **b. dotales** dowry • **b. gananciales** community property • **b. inmuebles** or **raíces** real estate • **b. muebles** chattels, personal property • **b. patri-**

moniales capital assets • **b. relictos** estate, inheritance II. adv. well; (justamente) right, correctly; (con éxito) successfully; (de buena gana) willingly, readily; (sin dificultad) easily; (bastante) quite, very; (sí) okay ♦ **de b. en mejor** better and better • **más b.** rather • **no b.** just as, as soon as • **o b.** or else, otherwise • **por b.** willingly • **pues b.** then, well now • **y b.** well then III. adj. well-to-do.
bie·nal adj. & f. biennial.
bie·na·ven·tu·ra·do, a adj. & m.f. (afortunado) fortunate, lucky (person); (inocente) simple, naive (person); RELIG. blessed (person).
bie·na·ven·tu·ran·za f. happiness, well-being.
bie·nes·tar m. well-being, comfort.
bien·ha·bla·do, a adj. well-spoken, courteous.
bien·he·chor, ·ra I. adj. beneficent, beneficial II. m. benefactor —f. benefactress.
bie·nin·ten·cio·na·do, a adj. & m.f. well-meaning (person).
bie·nio m. biennium.
bien·ve·ni·da f. safe arrival; (salutación) welcome, greeting.
biés m. bias.
bi·fe m. AMER. steak, beefsteak; R.P. slap.
bi·fo·cal adj. bifocal.
bi·for·me adj. biform.
bif·tec m. [pl. s] steak, beefsteak.
bi·fur·ca·ción f. bifurcation, branch; (de un camino) fork; (en ferrocarriles) junction.
bi·fur·ca·do, a adj. forked, bifurcate.
bi·fur·car·se §70 reflex. to bifurcate, branch (off); (dividirse un camino) to fork.
bi·ga·mia f. bigamy.
bí·ga·mo, a I. adj. bigamous II. m.f. bigamist.
bi·ga·rra·do, a adj. multicolored, motley.
bi·gor·nia f. two-beaked anvil.
bi·go·te m. mustache; MIN. slag tap ♦ pl. whiskers • **tener b.** or **ser hombre de b.** COLL. to be firm or stern.
bi·go·te·ra f. mustache cover; FIG. mustache (after drinking).
bi·go·tu·do, a adj. mustached, mustachioed.
bi·gu·dí m. hair curler.
bi·la·bia·do, a adj. bilabiate.
bi·la·bial adj. & f. bilabial.
bi·la·te·ral adj. bilateral.
bi·liar or **bi·lia·rio, a** adj. biliary.
bi·lin·güe adj. bilingual.
bi·lio·so, a adj. bilious.
bi·lis f.inv. bile ♦ **descargar la b.** to vent one's spleen • **exaltársele a uno la b.** to get angry.
bi·llar m. (juego) billiards; (mesa) billiard table; (lugar) billiard room ♦ **b. automático** or **romano** pinball • **b. ruso** snooker.
bi·lle·te m. ticket; (de lotería) lottery ticket; (papel moneda) bill; (carta) note, short letter.
bi·lle·te·ra f./ro m. wallet, billfold.
bi·llón m. [10^{12}] trillion (U.S.), billion (G.B.).
bi·llo·né·si·mo, a adj. & m. trillionth (U.S.), billionth (G.B.).
bi·lo·bu·la·do, a adj. bilobate.
bi·lo·ca·ción f. bilocation.
bi·men·sual adj. bimonthly, twice a month.
bi·mes·tral adj. bimonthly, bimestrial.
bi·mes·tre adj. & m. bimonthly (payment).
bi·me·ta·lis·mo m. bimetallism.
bi·mo·tor adj. & m. twin-engine (plane).
bi·na·dor, ·ra m.f. plower.
bi·na·rio, a adj. binary.
bi·no·cu·lar adj. binocular.

bi·nó·cu·lo m. pince-nez.
bi·no·mio m. binomial.
bio·di·ná·mi·ca f. biodynamics.
bio·fí·si·ca f. biophysics.
bio·gra·fí·a f. biography.
bio·gra·fiar §30 tr. to write a biography of.
bio·grá·fi·co, a adj. biographic(al).
bió·gra·fo, a m.f. biographer.
bio·lo·gí·a f. biology.
bio·ló·gi·co, a adj. biologic(al).
bió·lo·go, a m.f. biologist.
biom·bo m. folding screen.
bio·me·cá·ni·ca f. biomechanics.
biop·sia f. biopsy.
bio·quí·mi·co, a I. adj. biochemical **II.** m.f. biochemist —f. biochemistry.
bios·fe·ra f. biosphere.
bió·xi·do m. dioxide.
bi·par·ti·dis·mo m. two-party system.
bi·par·ti·dis·ta adj. bipartisan, two-party.
bi·par·ti·to/do, a adj. bipartite.
bí·pe·de/do, a adj. & m. biped.
bi·pla·no m. AVIA. biplane.
bir·lar tr. (derribar) to kill or knock down with one blow; (robar) to steal, swipe.
bir·lo·cha f. kite (toy).
bi·rre·te m. RELIG. biretta; (bonete) cap.
bis adv. bis, again.
bi·sa·bue·lo, a m.f. great-grandparent.
bi·sa·gra f. hinge.
bi·se·car §70 tr. to bisect.
bi·sec·tor, triz I. adj. bisecting **II.** f. bisector.
bi·sel m. bevel, beveled edge.
bi·se·la·do m. beveling.
bi·se·lar tr. to bevel.
bi·se·ma·nal adj. biweekly, semiweekly.
bi·se·xual adj. & m.f. bisexual.
bi·sies·to adj. & m. leap (year).
bi·sí·la·bo/si·lá·bi·co, a adj. bisyllabic.
bis·mu·to m. bismuth.
bis·nie·to, a m.f. great-grandchild.
bi·son·te m. bison.
bi·so·ña·da/ñe·rrí·a f. blunder.
bi·so·ñé m. toupee, hairpiece.
bi·so·ño, a adj. & m.f. inexperienced (person).
bis·té/tec m. beefsteak.
bi·su·te·rí·a f. costume jewelry, paste.
bi·tá·co·ra f. binnacle.
bi·tio m. bit.
bi·tu·mi·no·so, a adj. bituminous.
bi·va·len·te adj. bivalent.
bi·zan·ti·no, a I. adj. Byzantine; FIG. intricate; decadent **II.** m.f. Byzantine.
bi·za·rrí·a f. (valor) bravery, courage; (generosidad) generosity, magnanimity.
bi·za·rro, a adj. (valiente) brave, gallant; (generoso) generous, magnanimous.
bi·za·za f. saddlebag.
biz·car §70 intr. to squint, be cross-eyed —tr. to wink at.
biz·co, a adj. & m.f. cross-eyed (person) ♦ **dejar a uno b.** to dumbfound, flabbergast.
biz·co·cho m. sponge cake; MARIT. hardtack; CERAM. bisque, biscuit.
biz·ma f. MED. poultice.
biz·nie·to, a m. var. of **bisnieto.**
biz·que·ar intr. COLL. to squint.
biz·que·ra f. strabismus.
blan·ca f. MUS. half note ♦ **estar sin b.** COLL. to be broke.
blan·co, a I. adj. white; (claro) fair, light; (cobarde) yellow, chicken ♦ **más b. que el papel**
as white as a sheet **II.** m.f. white (person); (cobarde) coward, chicken —m. white; (tiro) target; (centro) center; (espacio) blank space, blank; (fin) goal, aim ♦ **calentar al b.** to make white-hot ♦ **dar en el b.** to hit the nail on the head • **pasar una noche en b.** to spend a sleepless night • **quedarse en b.** to draw a blank.
blan·cu·ra f./ cor m. whiteness.
blan·cuz·co, a adj. whitish.
blan·dir tr. to brandish, wave —intr. to quiver, shake.
blan·do, a adj. soft; (tierno) tender; (fláccido) flabby; (amable) gentle, kind; (cobarde) cowardly ♦ **b. de carácter** weak-willed.
blan·du·ra f. softness; (ternura) tenderness; (flaccidez) flabbiness; (amabilidad) gentleness, kindness; (cobardía) cowardice, weakness; (lisonja) flattery; (emplasto) poultice, plaster.
blan·que·a·do m. (acción) whitening; (encalado) whitewashing; (decoloración) bleaching.
blan·que·a·dor, ·ra I. adj. whitening **II.** m. or f. whitener; (cal) whitewash; (líquido) bleach.
blan·que·a·du·ra f. var. of **blanqueo.**
blan·que·ar tr. to whiten; (dar cal) to whitewash; (lavar) to bleach (clothes) —intr. to turn white or whitish.
blan·que·ci·no, a adj. whitish.
blan·que·o m. whitening; (encalado) whitewashing; (decoloración) bleaching.
blas·fe·mar intr. to blaspheme.
blas·fe·mia f. blasphemy.
blas·fe·mo, a I. adj. blasphemous **II.** m.f. blasphemer.
bla·són m. heraldry; (escudo) coat of arms, escutcheon; (honor) honor, glory.
bla·so·nar tr. to emblazon —intr. to boast.
bla·so·ne·rí·a f. braggadocio, boasting.
ble·do m. ♦ **no importarle un b.** not to give a darn or hoot about • **no valer un b.** not to be worth two cents.
blin·da·do, a armored, armor-plated.
blin·da·je m. armor, armor plate.
blin·dar tr. to armor, cover with armor plate.
bloc m. writing pad or tablet.
blo·que m. block; (grupo) bloc, coalition; (papel) pad, notepad.
blo·que·ar tr. MIL. to blockade; (impedir) to block, obstruct; (frenar) to brake; (obstruir) to jam, block; COM. to freeze (assets).
blo·que·o m. MIL. blockade; (obstáculo) block, obstacle; COM. freeze.
blu·sa f. blouse.
blu·són m. long blouse, smock.
bo·a f. ZOOL. boa (constrictor) —m. (adorno) boa.
bo·ar·di·lla f. attic, garret.
bo·a·to m. show, ostentation.
bo·ba·da f. foolish act or remark.
bo·ba·li·cón, o·na adj. & m.f. silly (person).
bo·be·ar intr. to do or say silly things.
bo·be·ra/rí·a f. foolish act or remark.
bo·bi·na f. spool, reel; SEW. bobbin; ELEC. coil.
bo·bo, a I. adj. (tonto) silly, foolish; (cándido) gullible, naive **II.** m.f. (tonto) idiot, fool —m. (gracioso) clown, jester.
bo·ca f. mouth; ZOOL. pincer; GEOG. mouth; FIG. entrance, opening; (persona) mouth, person; (filo) cutting edge; (sabor) flavor, bouquet (wine) ♦ **a b. de costal** freely, abundantly • **a b. de jarro** FIG. pointblank, at close range • **andar de b. en b.** FIG. to be the subject of

gossip • **b. abajo, arriba** face down, up • **b. de agua** or **de riego** hydrant • **b. de dragón** BOT. snapdragon • **b. de fuego** firearm • **buscar a uno la b.** to draw someone out, pump someone • **¡cállate la b.!** COLL. be quiet! shut up! • **no decir esta b. es mía** COLL. not to open one's mouth • **quedarse con la b. abierta** to be astonished or amazed.

bo·ca·ca·lle f. intersection.

bo·ca·cha f. bigmouth, blabbermouth.

bo·ca·di·llo m. *(comida ligera)* snack, tidbit; *(emparedado)* sandwich.

bo·ca·do m. mouthful, bite; EQUIT. bridle, bit ♦ **b. de Adán** Adam's apple • **b. de cardenal** choice morsel • **b. sin hueso** COLL. cushy job.

bo·ca·ja·rro adv. ♦ **a b.** *(a quemarropa)* point-blank; *(de improviso)* unexpectedly.

bo·ca·lla·ve f. keyhole.

bo·ca·man·ga f. cuff, wristband.

bo·ca·na·da f. swallow, swig; *(de humo)* puff; *(de aire)* gust, rush; *(de gente)* throng.

bo·ca·za m.f. COLL. bigmouth, blabbermouth.

bo·ce·lar tr. to emboss.

bo·ce·tar tr. to sketch, draft.

bo·ce·to m. sketch, draft.

bo·cha f. wooden ball.

bo·char tr. AMER. to reject, rebuff; ARG. to fail, flunk.

bo·che m. hole in the ground; COLL. *(repulsa)* rebuff, slight.

bo·chin·che m. COLL. uproar, commotion; *(taberna)* dive, low-class bar.

bo·chin·che·ar intr. AMER. to cause an uproar.

bo·chin·che·ro, a adj. & m.f. COLL. rowdy.

bo·chor·no m. *(vergüenza)* embarrassment, shame; *(sonrojo)* flush, blush; *(calor)* suffocating heat.

bo·chor·no·so, a adj. shameful, embarrassing; *(sofocante)* suffocating, stifling.

bo·ci·na f. horn; MARIT. foghorn; MUS. trumpet, horn; *(megáfono)* megaphone; *(caracol)* conch shell; TELEC. mouthpiece.

bo·ci·nar intr. to play a horn.

bo·ci·na·zo m. COLL. honk, toot.

bo·cio m. goiter.

bo·da f. wedding, marriage ♦ **bodas de Camacho** feast, banquet.

bo·de·ga f. wine cellar; *(despensa)* pantry; MARIT. hold; AGR. granary; *(taberna)* tavern, bar; *(depósito)* warehouse; AMER. grocery store.

bo·de·gón m. COLL. cheap restaurant, dive; *(taberna)* tavern, bar; ARTS still life.

bo·de·gue·ro, a m.f. keeper of a wine cellar; AMER. grocer

bo·drio m. AMER., COLL. muddle, confusion.

bo·fe m. lung ♦ **echar los bofes** to break one's back • **ser un b.** to be a bore.

bo·fe·ta·da f. slap; *(afrenta)* insult.

bo·ga f. rowing; *(moda)* fashion, vogue —m.f. *(bogador)* rower.

bo·gar §47 tr. & intr. to row; *(navegar)* to sail.

bo·he·mio, a adj. & m.f. bohemian.

bo·hí·o m. AMER. hut, shack.

boi·co·te·ar tr. to boycott.

boi·co·te·o m. boycott, boycotting.

boi·na f. beret, cap.

boi·te f. nightclub.

boj or **bo·je** m. box tree, boxwood.

bo·la f. ball; *(canica)* marble; *(betún)* shoe polish; *(mentira)* lie, fib; CHILE kite; CUBA rumor, gossip; MEX. *(tumulto)* tumult, uproar ♦ **b. del mundo** globe • **b. de nieve** snowball •

dejar rodar la b. to let (something) ride, let things take their course • **no dar pie con b.** to miss the mark.

bo·la·da f. stroke, billiard shot; AMER. opportunity, lucky break; *(mentira)* lie, fib.

bo·la·zo m. blow with a ball; *(mentira)* lie, fib; ARG. *(disparate)* silly or foolish remark ♦ **de b.** hurriedly, carelessly.

bo·le·a·do·ras f.pl. R.P. bolas.

bo·le·ar tr. AMER. to entangle, entrap —intr. *(jugar)* to play (billiards) for fun; COLL. *(mentir)* to fib, lie —reflex. AMER. ro rear and fall, roll over (horses); *(ruborizarse)* to get flustered; R.P. *(tropezar)* to stumble, falter.

bo·le·o m. bowling; *(sitio)* bowling alley.

bo·le·ro, a I. adj. *(truhán)* truant; *(mentiroso)* lying, fibbing **II.** m.f. *(novillero)* truant; *(mentiroso)* liar, fibber —m. MUS. bolero —f. bowling alley.

bo·le·ta f. admission ticket; MIL. billet; *(vale)* voucher; AMER. ballot.

bo·le·te·rí·a f. AMER. ticket office, box office.

bo·le·te·ro, a m.f. AMER. ticket seller.

bo·le·tín m. bulletin; *(billete)* ticket.

bo·le·to m. AMER. ticket.

bo·li·che m. *(bolín)* jack; *(juego)* bowling, ninepins; AMER., COLL. *(almacén)* small store; *(taberna)* dive, cheap restaurant.

bó·li·do m. fireball, meteorite; FIG. bullet.

bo·lí·gra·fo m. ballpoint pen.

bo·li·llo m. bobbin ♦ pl. S. AMER. drumsticks.

bo·lí·var VEN., FIN. bolivar.

bo·llo m. bun, roll; *(hueco)* dent; *(plegado)* fold, crease; *(chichón)* lump, bump; *(lío)* fuss, to-do ♦ **armar un b.** to kick up a fuss.

bo·llón m. *(clavo)* boss, stud; *(pendiente)* button earring, stud.

bo·llo·na·do, a adj. studded, embossed.

bo·lo m. *(palo)* pin, ninepin; *(tonto)* dunce, dummy; ARCHIT. newel post ♦ pl. bowling, ninepins • **echar a rodar los b.** COLL. to stir up trouble.

bol·sa f. *(saco)* sack, bag; *(bolso)* purse, pocketbook; ANAT. pocket, sac; MIN. pocket, lode; FIN. stock market; FIG. wealth, money; SPORT. purse, prize money ♦ **aflojar la b.** COLL. to loosen the pursestrings • **b. alcista, bajista** FIN. bull, bear market • **b. de comercio** commodity exchange • **b. negra** black market • **hacer bolsas** to bag, sag.

bol·si·llo m. pocket; *(dinero)* purse, money.

bol·sis·ta m.f. stockbroker; AMER. pickpocket.

bol·so m. purse, pocketbook.

bol·són m. large purse or handbag; AMER. school bag.

bom·ba f. MIL. bomb, shell; TECH. pump; *(sorpresa)* bombshell, stunning news; AMER. *(mentira)* lie, fib; *(borrachera)* drinking bout ♦ **a prueba de bombas** bombproof • **b. aspirante** suction pump • **b. de mano** TECH. hand pump; MIL. grenade • **caer como una b.** to hit like a bombshell • **estar echando bombas** COLL. to be boiling hot • **estar en b.** AMER. to be drunk • **pasarlo b.** to have a ball.

bom·ba·cha(s) f.(pl.) R.P. baggy trousers.

bom·bar·de·ar tr. to bombard, bomb.

bom·bar·de·o m. bombardment, bombing ♦ **b. en picado** dive bombing.

bom·bar·de·ro, a I. m. *(avión)* bomber; *(soldado)* bombardier **II.** adj. bombing.

bom·bar·di·no m. saxhorn.

bom·ba·sí m. bombazine, fustian.

bom·bás·ti·co, a adj. bombastic.
bom·ba·zo m. bomb explosion; *(daño)* damage.
bom·be·ar tr. to bomb, shell; *(sacar)* to pump; *(abombar)* to make convex; *(dar bombo a)* to make a fuss over.
bom·be·ro m. fireman, firefighter.
bom·bi·lla f. light bulb; MARIT. lantern.
bom·bín m. COLL. bowler, derby; *(inflador)* bicycle pump.
bom·bo, a I. adj. COLL. *(atónito)* dazed, dumbfounded; *(tibio)* lukewarm II. m. *(tambor)* bass drum; *(músico)* bass drummer; *(barco)* barge; *(publicidad)* fanfare, buildup ♦ **dar b. a** COLL. to make a fuss over.
bom·bón m. bonbon, chocolate; COLL. *(persona)* gem, peach.
bom·bo·ne·ra f. COLL. cute place, cozy cottage.
bo·na·chón, o·na adj. & m.f. COLL. *(bueno)* good-natured (person); *(crédulo)* gullible (person).
bo·nan·za f. bonanza ♦ **ir en b.** to be fortunate.
bon·dad f. goodness, kindness ♦ **tener la b. de** to be so kind as to.
bon·da·do·so, a adj. good, kind.
bo·ne·te m. bonnet, cap; RELIG. biretta; *(dulcera)* candy dish; *(fortificación)* bonnet.
bo·ne·te·rí·a f. AMER. notions shop.
bo·nia·to m. sweet potato.
bo·ni·fi·ca·ción f. improvement; *(rebaja)* discount, reduction.
bo·ni·fi·car §70 tr. to improve, ameliorate; *(rebajar)* to discount, reduce the price of.
bo·ni·to, a I. adj. *(lindo)* pretty, nice-looking; *(bueno)* good, satisfactory II. m. tuna.
bo·no m. *(vale)* voucher, certificate; COM. *(fianza)* bond.
bo·que·a·da f. gasp.
bo·que·ar intr. *(jadear)* to gasp; *(morirse)* to be at death's door —tr. to mouth, utter.
bo·que·ra f. sluice; MED. lip sore, mouth ulcer.
bo·que·rón m. large aperture or hole; *(bocaza)* big mouth.
bo·que·te m. narrow entrance; *(agujero)* hole.
bo·quia·bier·to, a adj. open-mouthed, gaping; *(atónito)* amazed, astonished.
bo·qui·lla f. MUS. mouthpiece; *(del cigarrillo)* cigarette holder; *(filtro)* filter tip; *(mechero)* nozzle; *(de pantalones)* pant leg opening.
bo·ra·ci·ta f. boracite.
bo·ra·to m. borate.
bó·rax m. borax.
bor·bo·llar/lle·ar intr. to bubble, boil; *(tartamudear)* to stutter, stammer.
bor·bo·lle·o m. bubbling, boiling.
bor·bo·tar/te·ar intr. to boil, bubble.
bor·bo·te·o m. boiling, bubbling.
bor·bo·tón m. boiling, bubbling.
bor·da f. MARIT. gunwale; *(choza)* hut, cabin.
bor·da·do m. embroidery, embroidering.
bor·da·dor, ·ra m.f. embroiderer.
bor·dar tr. to embroider; FIG. to embellish.
bor·de m. border, edge; *(canto)* brim, rim; MARIT. board, side.
bor·de·ar tr. to border; *(ir por el borde)* to skirt, go around; *(aproximarse)* to approach.
bor·di·llo m. curb.
bor·do m. MARIT. board, shipboard; *(bordada)* tack.
bor·dón m. *(bastón)* staff; *(estribillo)* refrain;

(frase repetida) pet phrase; *(guía)* helping hand, guide.
bo·re·al adj. boreal, northern.
bor·go·ña m. Burgundy (wine).
bó·ri·co adj. boric.
bor·la f. *(hebras)* tassel; *(de polvera)* powder puff.
bor·lar·se reflex. AMER. to get one's doctorate.
bor·ne m. point, tip; ELEC. terminal.
bor·ne·ar tr. to twist, bend; *(guiñar)* to squint one's eyes —reflex. to warp, become warped.
bor·ne·o m. twisting, bending; *(del cuerpo)* swinging, twisting.
bo·ro m. boron.
bo·rra f. *(del café)* coffee grounds; *(sedimento)* dregs; *(relleno)* flock, stuffing.
bo·rra·che·ar intr. COLL. to booze.
bo·rra·che·ra f. *(ebriedad)* drunkenness; *(parranda)* binge, spree; *(exaltación)* ecstasy, exultation.
bo·rra·chín m. COLL. drunkard, sot.
bo·rra·cho, a I. adj. *(ebrio)* drunk; *(alcoholizado)* drunken, alcoholic; *(morado)* violet, purple; *(de ron)* rum-soaked; *(dominado)* blind, wild ♦ **b. como una cuba** COLL. drunk as a skunk II. m.f. drunken person; *(alcohólico)* drunkard, alcoholic.
bo·rra·dor m. *(escrito)* rough draft; *(papel)* scratch pad; COM. daybook; *(de borrar)* eraser.
bo·rra·du·ra f. erasure, deletion.
bo·rra·jo m. ember, cinder.
bo·rrar tr. to erase.
bo·rras·ca f. *(tempestad)* storm, tempest; *(riesgo)* hazard, danger.
bo·rras·co·so, a adj. *(tempestuoso)* stormy, tempestuous; *(desordenado)* rowdy.
bo·rre·ga·da f. flock (of lambs).
bo·rre·go, a m.f. lamb; FIG. simpleton, fool.
bo·rri·ca f. she-ass; FIG. stupid woman.
bo·rri·ca·da f. donkey ride; *(necedad)* foolish remark or act.
bo·rri·co m. ass, donkey; *(de carpintero)* sawhorse; *(idiota)* ass, dimwit.
bo·rri·que·te m. sawhorse.
bo·rro m. yearling lamb.
bo·rrón m. *(mancha)* ink blot, smudge; *(borrador)* rough draft; FIG. blemish ♦ **b. y cuenta nueva** FIG., COLL. clean slate ♦ pl. jottings, scribbling.
bo·rro·ne·ar tr. *(escribir)* to scribble, scrawl; *(esbozar)* to outline.
bo·rro·si·dad f. blurriness, fuzziness.
bo·rro·so, a adj. blurred, fuzzy.
bos·ca·je m. thicket, copse; *(pintura)* landscape.
bos·co·so, a adj. wooded, woody.
bós·fo·ro m. strait.
bos·que m. woods, forest; FIG. confusion.
bos·que·jar tr. to sketch, outline.
bos·que·jo m. sketch, outline, draft.
bos·ta f. manure.
bos·te·zar §04 intr. to yawn.
bos·te·zo m. yawn.
bo·ta f. boot; *(odre)* wineskin; *(tonel)* wooden cask ♦ **estar con las botas puestas** to be ready to go • **ponerse las botas** to strike it rich.
bo·ta·do, a AMER. I. adj. *(expulsado)* fired, kicked out; *(barato)* cheap II. m.f. foundling.
bo·tá·ni·co, a I. adj. botanical II. m.f. botanist —f. botany.
bo·ta·nis·ta m.f. botanist.
bo·tar tr. to fling, hurl; COLL. *(despedir)* to dis-

miss, fire; MARIT. to turn; *(lanzar al agua)* to launch; AMER. *(tirar)* to throw away; *(malgastar)* to waste, squander —intr. to bounce.

bo·ta·ra·te m. *(tonto)* fool, idiot; AMER. spendthrift, squanderer.

bo·ta·va·ra f. gaffsail.

bo·te m. *(golpe)* thrust, blow; *(brinco)* prance, caper; *(rebote)* bounce; *(pote)* pot, jar; *(lata)* tin can; *(barco)* rowboat ♦ **de b. y voleo** immediately, instantly • **de b. en b.** full, jammed.

bo·te·lla f. bottle.

bo·ti·ca f. pharmacy, drugstore.

bo·ti·ca·rio, a m.f. pharmacist, druggist.

bo·ti·ja f. earthenware jar; C. AMER. buried treasure ♦ **estar hecho una b.** to be very fat.

bo·ti·jo m. earthenware jug; *(persona gorda)* chubby person.

bo·tín[1] m. *(bota)* ankle boot, half boot.

bo·tín[2] m. *(presa)* booty, spoils.

bo·ti·ne·rí·a f. boot *or* shoe store.

bo·ti·ne·ro, a m.f. *(persona que hace botines)* bootmaker, cobbler; *(vendedor)* boot seller.

bo·ti·quín m. medicine chest *or* cabinet; *(estuche)* first-aid kit.

bo·tón m. button; *(llamador)* doorbell, buzzer; BOT. bud ♦ **al b.** AMER. in vain • **b. de arranque** AUTO. starter • **b. de oro** BOT. buttercup.

bo·to·na·du·ra f. buttons, set of buttons.

bo·to·nes m.pl. bellboy, bellhop.

bo·tu·lis·mo m. botulism.

bó·ve·da f. vault; *(techo)* dome, cupola; *(cripta)* crypt; *(caverna)* cave, cavern ♦ **b. celeste** firmament, heavens • **b. palatina** palate, roof of the mouth.

bo·vi·no, a adj. bovine.

bo·xe·a·dor m. boxer.

bo·xe·ar intr. to box.

bo·xe·o m. boxing.

bo·ya f. buoy.

bo·yar intr. to float, to buoy.

bo·zal **I.** m. muzzle; AMER. halter, headstall —m.f. *(idiota)* simpleton, fool; *(novato)* novice **II.** adj. *(tonto)* ignorant; *(novato)* raw, green; *(salvaje)* wild, untamed.

bo·zo m. down, fuzz (on upper lip); *(boca)* mouth; *(cabestro)* halter.

bra·ce·ar intr. to flail one's arms; *(nadar)* to swim; *(esforzarse)* to struggle, strive.

bra·ce·o m. waving of the arms; *(natación)* stroke.

bra·ce·ro, a **I.** adj. throwing **II.** m. laborer, worker.

bra·co, a adj. & m.f. pug-nosed (person).

bra·ga f. *(cuerda)* sling, rope; *(pañal)* diapers; *(calzón femenino)* panties.

bra·ga·do, a adj. resolute, firm.

bra·ga·du·ra f. crotch.

bra·ga·zas m.inv. henpecked husband.

bra·gue·ro m. MED. truss.

bra·gue·ta f. fly (of pants).

bra·mar intr. to roar, bellow; FIG. to howl.

bra·mi·do m. roar, bellow.

bran·ca·da f. trammel net.

bran·dal m. backstay.

bran·quia f. branchia, gill.

bra·quial adj. brachial, of the arm.

bra·sa f. live *or* hot coal.

bras·ca f. fettling.

bra·se·ro m. brazier.

bra·sil m. brazilwood.

bra·va·ta f. *(reto)* dare, threat; *(jactancia)* boast, brag.

bra·ve·ar intr. *(jactarse)* to boast, bluster; *(aplaudir)* to cheer, shout bravo!

bra·ví·o, a **I.** adj. *(feroz)* wild, untamed; *(silvestre)* wild, uncultivated; *(rústico)* uncouth, coarse **II.** m. fierceness, ferocity.

bra·vo, a adj. brave, valiant; *(excelente)* excellent, great; *(feroz)* ferocious, wild; *(áspero)* craggy, rugged; *(valentón)* boastful, swaggering; *(enojado)* angry, furious ♦ **¡b.!** bravo!, well done!

bra·vu·cón, o·na adj. & m.f. boastful (person).

bra·vu·co·ne·ar intr. to boast, swagger.

bra·vu·ra f. bravery, courage; *(fiereza)* fierceness, ferocity; *(bravata)* bluster, bravado.

bra·za f. MARIT. fathom; *(modo de nadar)* breaststroke.

bra·za·da f. extension of the arms; AMER. fathom ♦ **b. de espaldas** backstroke • **b. de pecho** breaststroke.

bra·zal m. armband.

bra·za·le·te m. bracelet.

bra·zo m. arm; ZOOL. foreleg; *(de balanza)* arm, crosspiece; *(fuerza)* power, strength ♦ **a b. partido** *(sin armas)* bare-fisted; FIG. fast and furiously • **asidos** *or* **cogidos del b.** arm in arm ♦ pl. *(jornaleros)* hands, laborers; *(valedores)* backers, supporters.

bre·a f. tar, pitch; *(lienzo)* tarpaulin ♦ **b. seca** rosin.

bre·ar tr. COLL. *(maltratar)* to abuse, ill-treat; *(chasquear)* to make fun of, tease ♦ **b. de golpes** to beat up.

bre·ba·je m. unpalatable concoction *or* brew.

bre·cha f. MIL. breach; *(abertura)* gap, opening; FIG. impression.

bré·col m./**co·les** m.pl. broccoli.

bre·ga f. *(pelea)* fight, scrap; *(trabajo)* hard work, task; *(burla)* practical joke, trick.

bre·gar §47 intr. *(pelear)* to fight, scrap; *(trabajar)* to toil, slave away; *(esforzarse)* to struggle, fight.

bren·ca f. sluice post.

bre·ñal m. brambly, rugged ground.

bre·te m. *(grillete)* shackle, fetter; *(aprieto)* jam, tight spot; BOT. betel.

bre·va f. *(higo)* early fig; *(ventaja)* windfall, piece of luck.

bre·ve adj. brief, short ♦ **en b.** *(pronto)* shortly, soon; *(con brevedad)* in brief.

bre·ve·dad f. briefness, brevity.

bre·via·rio m. breviary; *(compendio)* compendium, abstract.

bri·bón, o·na adj. & m.f. *(perezoso)* lazy (person); *(pícaro)* roguish (person).

bri·bo·na·da f. roguishness.

bri·bo·ne·ar intr. *(holgazanear)* to loaf, bum around; *(hacer bribonadas)* to play tricks.

bri·da f. bridle ♦ **a toda b.** at full gallop; FIG. at full speed.

bridge m. bridge; DENT. bridge, bridgework.

bri·ga·da f. brigade; *(división)* squad, unit; *(de bestias)* team, train; *(de máquinas)* fleet; *(equipo)* gang, team.

bri·ga·dier m. brigadier general.

bri·llan·te adj. brilliant.

bri·llan·tez f. brilliance, brightness.

bri·llan·ti·na f. brilliantine.

bri·llar intr. to shine.

bri·llo m. *(lustre)* brilliance, shine; *(gloria)* distinction, glory ♦ **dar** *or* **sacar b.** to shine, polish.

brin·car §70 intr. to jump, leap about; *(retozar)*

to frolic, gambol; *(enfadarse)* to get angry, flare up —tr. to bounce.
brin·co m. jump, hop ♦ **en** *or* **de un b.** in a jiffy.
brin·dar intr. to toast, drink a toast —tr. *(ofrecer)* to offer; *(convidar)* to invite —reflex. to offer, volunteer.
brin·dis m. toast.
brí·o m. strength, vigor; *(garbo)* grace, charm.
brio·so, a adj. *(energético)* vigorous; *(determinado)* determined, resolute; *(animoso)* fiery, spirited; *(garboso)* graceful, charming.
bri·que·ta f. charcoal briquette.
bri·sa f. breeze, light wind; AGR. bagasse.
briz·na f. bit, piece.
bro·ca f. SEW. reel; MECH. drill, bit.
bro·ca·do, a adj. & m. brocade.
bro·ce·o m. AMER. depletion (of a mine).
bro·cha f. paintbrush; *(de afeitar)* shaving brush; *(dado)* loaded die.
bro·cha·da f. brush stroke.
bro·cha·zo m. brush stroke.
bro·che m. clasp, hook and eye; *(prendedor)* brooch; AMER. paper clip ♦ **b. de oro** crowning glory ♦ pl. AMER. cuff links.
bro·che·ta f. brochette, skewer.
bró·cu·li m. broccoli.
bro·ma f. joke, prank; *(diversión)* fun, jest ♦ **b. pesada** practical joke, prank • **gastar** *or* **hacer una b. a** to play a joke on • **ni en b.** not on your life.
bro·ma·to m. bromate.
bro·me·ar intr. to joke, jest.
bro·mis·ta I. adj. joking **II.** m.f. joker.
bro·mo m. CHEM. bromine; BOT. brome grass.
bro·mu·ro m. bromide.
bron·ca f. see **bronco, a.**
bron·ce m. bronze.
bron·ce·a·do, a I. adj. *(color)* bronze, bronze-colored; *(tostado)* tanned, bronzed **II.** m. bronzing; *(piel tostada)* suntan.
bron·ce·ar tr. to bronze; *(piel)* to tan, suntan —reflex. to get a tan, suntan.
bron·co, a I. adj. *(tosco)* rough, coarse; *(desapacible)* harsh, gruff **II.** f. row, quarrel ♦ **armar b.** to kick up a rumpus, start a row.
bron·co·neu·mo·ní·a f. bronchopneumonia.
bron·que·dad/ra f. *(tosquedad)* coarseness, roughness; *(aspereza)* harshness, gruffness.
bron·quial adj. bronchial.
bron·quio m. bronchus, bronchial tube.
bron·quio·lo m. bronchiole.
bron·qui·tis f. bronchitis.
bro·quel m. buckler, small shield; *(amparo)* shield, protection.
bro·que·lar·se reflex. to shield oneself.
bro·que·ta f. brochette, skewer.
bro·ta·du·ra f. sprouting, budding.
bro·tar intr. to bud, sprout; *(agua)* to spring, flow; *(estallar)* to break out, spring up —tr. BOT. to sprout.
bro·te m. bud, sprout; *(estallido)* outbreak, rash; *(comienzo)* origin, germ.
bru·ces ♦ **a** *or* **de b.** adv. face down, on one's face • **caer de b.** to fall flat on one's face.
bru·ja f. witch, sorceress.
bru·je·rí·a f. witchcraft, sorcery.
bru·jo m. *(adivino)* sorcerer, wizard; *(de una tribu)* witch doctor, medicine man.
brú·ju·la f. compass; *(norma)* standard, norm.
bru·lo·te m. fire ship; AMER. *(palabrota)* swear word; *(escrito)* satiric article.

bru·ma f. fog, mist.
bru·mo m. refined wax, pure wax.
bru·mo·so, a adj. foggy, misty.
bru·no, a adj. dark-colored, black.
bru·ñi·do, a I. m. burnishing, polishing; *(brillo)* shine, gloss **II.** adj. burnished, polished.
bru·ñi·du·ra f. polishing, burnishing.
bru·ñir §12 tr. to burnish, polish; AMER. to annoy, pester —reflex. to put on make-up.
brus·co, a adj. brusque.
brus·que·dad f. brusqueness.
bru·tal I. adj. brutal; *(formidable)* terrific, tremendous **II.** m. brute, beast.
bru·ta·li·dad f. brutality; *(incapacidad)* stupidity, foolishness; *(gran cantidad)* loads, slew.
bru·ta·li·zar §04 tr. to brutalize, maltreat —reflex. to be brutalized.
bru·te·za f. brutishness, boorishness.
bru·to, a I. adj. brutish, boorish; *(necio)* stupid, ignorant; *(diamante)* rough, uncut; *(enorme)* huge, enormous; COM. gross **II.** m. *(persona)* brute; *(animal)* beast, animal.
bru·za f. scrubbing brush.
bu m. bogeyman.
bu·ba f. pustule, small tumor.
bu·bón m. large tumor or swelling.
bu·bó·ni·co, a adj. bubonic.
bu·cal adj. buccal, oral.
bú·ca·ro m. *(arcilla)* fragrant clay; *(botijo)* clay water jug; *(florero)* ceramic flower vase.
bu·ce·ar intr. to swim under water; *(oficio)* to work as a diver; *(explorar)* to delve into.
bu·ce·o m. *(natación)* underwater swimming; *(exploración)* exploration, searching.
bu·che m. ORNITH. crop, craw; ZOOL. maw; *(porción)* mouthful, swallow; *(pliegue)* sag, pucker; *(estómago)* belly, gut; *(pecho)* chest, bosom.
bu·cle m. ringlet, curl; AVIA. spin, loop.
bu·có·li·co, a adj. & f. bucolic *or* pastoral (poem).
bu·dín m. pudding.
buen adj. contr. of **bueno.**
bue·na·ven·tu·ra f. *(suerte)* good fortune, luck; *(adivinación)* fortune.
bue·no, a I. adj. good; *(bondadoso)* kind, benevolent; *(útil)* fit, appropriate; *(sano)* well, healthy; *(agradable)* nice, polite; *(grande)* considerable, goodly; *(bonachón)* innocent, naive ♦ **a** *or* **por las buenas** willingly • **a la b. de Dios** carelessly, any old way • **buenas noches, tardes** good night, afternoon • **buenos días** morning • **de buenas a primeras** all of a sudden • **estar de buenas** to be in a good mood **II.** adv. all right, okay **III.** f. good.
buey m. ox, bullock ♦ **trabajar como un b.** COLL. to work like a dog.
bú·fa·lo, a m.f. *(buey salvaje)* buffalo; *(bisonte)* bison.
bu·fan·da f. scarf, muffler.
bu·far intr. *(resoplar)* to snort; *(enojarse)* to snort, puff.
bu·fe·te m. *(escritorio)* writing desk *or* table; *(despacho)* lawyer's office; *(clientela)* lawyer's clientele, practice.
bu·fi·do m. bellow, snort.
bu·fo, a I. adj. comic, farcical **II.** m. clown, buffoon.
bu·fón, o·na adj. & m. buffoon(ish).
bu·fo·na·da/ne·rí·a f. buffoonery; *(sarcasmo)* sarcastic joke *or* remark.
bu·fo·ni·zar §04 intr. to joke, jest.

bu·har·da/di·lla f. *(ventana)* dormer; *(desván)* attic, garret.
bú·ho m. horned owl; *(recluso)* hermit.
bu·ho·ne·ro m. peddler, hawker.
bui·tre m. vulture.
bu·je m. axle box, bushing.
bu·jí·a f. *(vela)* candle; *(candelero)* candlestick; PHYS. candle, candlepower; ELEC. spark plug.
bu·la f. metal seal, bulla; RELIG. papal bull.
bul·bo m. bulb.
bul(l)·dog m. bulldog.
bu·le·var m. boulevard.
bu·li·mia f. bulimia.
bu·lla f. *(ruido)* noise, racket; *(muchedumbre)* crowd, mob; *(prisa)* bustling, rush; AMER. argument, row.
bu·lli·cio m. bustle, hubbub.
bu·lli·cio·so, a adj. *(animado)* bustling; *(alborotador)* riotous, tumultuous.
bu·llir §13 intr. to boil; *(moverse)* to bustle about; ZOOL. to swarm —tr. to move —reflex. to budge, stir
bul·to m. *(tamaño)* bulk, size; *(forma)* form, shape; *(fardo)* package, bundle; MED. swelling, lump; ARTS bust, statue; AMER. briefcase, satchel ♦ **a b.** broadly; COM. wholesale • **de b.** important • **escurrir el b.** to duck, dodge • **hacer b.** to take up space.
bu·me·rán/ang m. boomerang.
bu·ñue·lo m. fried dough, fritter; COLL. mess, bungle.
bu·que m. ship, vessel; *(casco)* hull ♦ **b. almirante** flagship • **b. tanque** tanker • **b. velero** *or* **de vela** sailboat, sailing ship.
bu·qué m. bouquet.
bur·bu·ja f. bubble.
bur·bu·je·ar intr. to bubble.
bur·del I. adj. lustful, licentious II. m. brothel.
bur·de·os adj. maroon, deep red.
bur·do, a adj. coarse, rough.
bur·gués, e·sa adj. & m.f. bourgeois.
bur·gue·sí·a f. bourgeoisie, middle class.
bu·ril m. burin, graver.
bu·ri·lar tr. to engrave.
bur·la f. *(mofa)* jeer, taunt; *(chanza)* joke, jest; *(engaño)* trick, hoax ♦ **de burlas** in fun, for fun • **hacer b. de** to make fun of, mock.
bur·lar tr. to make fun of; *(frustrar)* to frustrate, thwart —reflex. to make fun, joke ♦ **b. de** to make fun of, ridicule.
bur·les·co, a adj. burlesque.
bur·le·te m. weather stripping.
bur·lón, o·na I. adj. jeering, joking II. m.f. *(mofador)* jeerer, mocker; *(bromista)* joker, jokester.
bu·ro·cra·cia f. bureaucracy.
bu·ró·cra·ta m.f. bureaucrat.
bu·ro·crá·ti·co, a adj. bureaucratic.
bu·rra f. she-ass, jenny; COLL. *(ignorante)* stupid woman, dunce; *(trabajadora)* hard worker, slave.
bu·rre·ro m. donkey driver.
bu·rro m. donkey, jackass; *(caballete)* sawhorse, sawbuck; *(rueda)* cogwheel; *(borrico)* ass, dunce ♦ **b. de carga** COLL. hard worker, drudge.
bur·sá·til adj. stock, stock market.
bu·ru·jo m. *(bulto)* lump; *(nudo)* tangle, knot.
bus·ca f. search ♦ **ir en** *or* **a la b. de** to go in search of.
bus·ca·pié m. feeler, insinuation.
bus·ca·piés m.inv. firecracker, squib.

bus·car §70 tr. to search *or* look for, seek; COLL. *(provocar)* to provoke —reflex. ♦ **buscársela** *(ingeniarse)* to get by, manage; *(provocar)* to look for trouble.
bus·ca·vi·das m.f.inv. *(entremetido)* snoop, busybody; *(ambicioso)* go-getter.
bu·si·lis m.inv. *(clave)* crux of a matter; *(dificultad)* hitch, snag.
bús·que·da f. search.
bus·to m. ANAT. chest, bust; SCULP. bust.
bu·ta·ca f. armchair, easy chair; THEAT. orchestra *or* box seat.
bu·ta·no m. butane.
bu·ti·le·no m. butylene.
bu·zo m. (deep-sea) diver.
bu·zón m. mailbox, letter box; *(conducto)* sluice, canal; *(tapón)* stopper, plug.

C

c, C f. third letter of the Spanish alphabet.
ca·bal adj. *(exacto)* precise, fair; *(completo)* complete ♦ FIG. **no estar en sus cabales** not to be in one's right mind.
cá·ba·la f. RELIG. cabala.
ca·bal·gar §47 intr. to ride horseback.
ca·ba·lla f. mackerel.
ca·ba·lla·da f. herd of horses; AMER. asinine remark *or* action.
ca·ba·lle·res·co adj. knightly; FIG. gentlemanly.
ca·ba·lle·rí·a f. *(animal)* mount, steed; MIL. cavalry.
ca·ba·lle·ri·za f. stable; *(criados)* stablehands.
ca·ba·lle·ri·zo m. stableman.
ca·ba·lle·ro, a I. m. *(noble)* nobleman; *(persona condecorada)* knight; *(señor)* gentleman; *(como cortesía)* sir ♦ **armar c.** to knight • **c. andante** knight-errant II. adj. riding.
ca·ba·lle·ro·si·dad f. gentlemanliness.
ca·ba·lle·te m. *(soporte)* sawhorse; *(trípode)* easel; AGR. ridge; ANAT. bridge (of the nose).
ca·ba·lli·to m. pony; *(juguete)* hobbyhorse ♦ **c. del diablo** dragonfly • **c. de mar** sea horse.
ca·ba·llo m. horse; *(en ajedrez)* knight; COLL. *(bestia)* beast; CARP. sawhorse ♦ **a c.** on horseback • **a c. de** astride • **c. de batalla** FIG. forte • **c. de carga** packhorse • **c. de carrera** racehorse • **c. de fuerza** MECH. horsepower • **c. de montar** *or* **de silla** saddle horse • **c. de tiro** draft horse • **c. hora** MECH. horsepower-hour • **como c. desbocado** hastily • **montar a c.** to go horseback riding ♦ pl. horsepower.
ca·ba·ña f. hut, cabin.
ca·ba·ret m. night club, cabaret.
ca·be·ce·ar intr. *(el caballo)* to toss the head; *(negar)* to shake one's head; *(de sueño)* to nod (sleepily); AVIA., MARIT. to pitch —tr. SPORT. to head (a ball).
ca·be·ce·ra f. *(lugar principal)* head <la c. de la mesa the head of the table>; *(de una cama)* headboard ♦ **médico de c.** attending physician.
ca·be·ci·lla m. ringleader.
ca·be·lle·ra f. head of hair; ASTRON. tail (of a comet).
ca·be·llo m. hair ♦ **asirse de un c.** FIG., COLL. to grasp at straws ♦ pl. hair • **ponérsele a uno los c. de punta** COLL. to make one's hair stand on end • **traer (una cosa) por los c.** COLL. to be irrelevant.

ca·ber §14 intr. *(tener lugar)* to fit; *(corresponder)* to fall to; *(ser posible)* to be possible ♦ **cabe decir** one might say • **no cabe duda** there is no doubt • **no cabe más** FIG. that's the limit • **no c. en sí** to be beside oneself • **no c. un alfiler** to be full • **¡no me cabe en la cabeza!** it's beyond me!

ca·bes·tri·llo m. MED. sling.

ca·bes·tro m. halter.

ca·be·za f. head; *(cráneo)* skull; *(jefe)* chief; *(juicio)* judgment; *(capital)* seat ♦ **a la c. de** *(delante)* at the head of; *(en control)* in charge of • **alzar** *o* **levantar la c.** COLL. to get back on one's feet • **doblar la c.** COLL. to give in • **c. de ajo** garlic bulb • **c. de chorlito** COLL. featherbrain • **c. de partido** POL. district seat • **c. de puente** MIL. bridgehead • **c. de turco** COLL. scapegoat • **de la c. de uno** of one's own invention • **estar metido de c. con** to be head over heels in love with • **hacer c.** to lead • **írsele de la c.** to go out of one's mind • **írsele la c.** COLL. to feel dizzy • **jugarse la c.** COLL. to risk one's life • **meterse de c. en** COLL. to plunge into • **metérsele en la c.** COLL. to take it into one's head • **pasarle a uno por la c.** COLL. to occur to one • **romperse la c.** COLL. to rack one's brains • **sentar la c.** COLL. to settle down • **subirse a la c.** to go to one's head • **tocado de la c.** COLL. touched in the head.

ca·be·za·da f. *(con la cabeza)* butt; *(en la cabeza)* blow to the head; *(inclinación)* nod.

ca·be·za·zo m. *(golpe)* butt; SPORT. header.

ca·be·zón, o·na adj. COLL. *(terco)* pigheaded; *(cabezudo)* bigheaded.

ca·be·zo·ta m.f. COLL. mule.

ca·be·zu·do, a adj. bigheaded; FIG. pigheaded.

ca·bi·da f. *(capacidad)* room, capacity; *(alcance)* extent ♦ **tener c. en** FIG. to have a place in.

ca·bil·do m. town council.

ca·bi·na f. booth; MARIT. cabin; AVIA. cockpit; AUTO. cab; CINEM. projection booth.

ca·biz·ba·jo, a adj. crestfallen, downhearted.

ca·ble m. cable ♦ **c. aéreo** overhead cable • **c. de remolque** towline.

ca·ble·gra·fiar §30 tr. & intr. to cable.

ca·ble·gra·ma m. cable, cablegram.

ca·ble·vi·sión f. cable television.

ca·bo m. end; *(pedazo)* stub, bit; *(mango)* handle; GEOG. cape; MARIT. cable; MIL. corporal ♦ **al c. de** at the end of • **al fin y al c.** after all • **atar cabos** to put two and two together • **dar c. a** to put the finishing touches on • **de c. a rabo** COLL. from start to finish • **llevar a c.** to carry out.

ca·bo·ta·je m. COM. coastal trading.

ca·bra f. goat ♦ **c. montés** mountain goat • **estar loco como una c.** to be crazy as a loon • **la c. siempre tira al monte** a leopard never changes its spots.

ca·bre·ro, a I. m.f. goatherd II. adj. R.P., COLL. hot-tempered.

ca·bri·lle·ar intr. to form whitecaps.

ca·brio·la f. *(salto)* jump; *(voltereta)* somersault.

ca·brio·lar intr. *(saltar)* to jump; *(voltear)* to tumble.

ca·brio·lé m. *(carruaje)* cabriolet; *(coche)* convertible.

ca·bri·ti·lla f. lambskin, kid.

ca·bri·to m. kid, young goat.

ca·brón m. goat; SL. *(cornudo)* cuckold; *(cre-*

tino) bastard.

ca·bro·na·da f. COLL. dirty *or* nasty trick.

ca·bru·no, a adj. of goats, goatlike.

ca·bu·jón/chón m. *(piedra)* cabochon.

ca·ca·hue·te m. peanut.

ca·ca·o m. cacao; CUL. cocoa.

ca·ca·re·a·dor, ·ra adj. cackling; FIG. boasting.

ca·ca·re·ar intr. to cackle —tr. FIG. to boast.

ca·ca·re·o m. cackling; FIG. boasting.

ca·ca·tú·a f. cockatoo.

ca·ce·rí·a f. *(caza)* hunting; *(partida)* hunting party; *(animales)* game bagged ♦ **ir de c.** to go hunting.

ca·ce·ro·la f. casserole, pot.

ca·cha f. *(de mango)* handle plate; AMER. *(engaño)* trick, deceit.

ca·cha·da f. R.P. joke.

ca·cha·lo·te m. sperm whale.

ca·char tr. *(astillar)* to chip; *(aserrar)* to split; R.P. *(burlar)* to tease; *(agarrar)* to nab; *(sorprender)* to catch; *(robar)* to rob, steal.

ca·cha·rre·ro, a m.f. pottery vendor.

ca·cha·rro m. *(vasija)* crock; *(pedazo)* shard; COLL. *(trasto)* piece of junk; *(máquina)* wreck; *(coche)* jalopy; AMER. jail, prison ♦ pl. *(trastos)* junk; *(utensilios)* tools.

ca·cha·za f. *(lentitud)* sluggishness; *(aguardiente)* cheap rum.

ca·cha·zu·do, a I. adj. sluggish **II.** m.f. slowpoke.

ca·che·ar tr. to search, frisk.

ca·che·mi·ra f./**mir** m. cashmere.

ca·che·ta·da f. AMER. slap.

ca·che·te m. *(mejilla)* cheek; *(cachetada)* slap.

ca·che·te·ar tr. AMER. to slap.

ca·che·ti·na f. fist fight.

ca·che·tu·do, a adj. chubby-cheeked, plumpcheeked.

ca·chi·po·rra f. club, bludgeon.

ca·chi·po·rra·zo m. blow with a club.

ca·chi·va·che m. piece of junk; FIG. good-fornothing ♦ pl. COLL. *(utensilios)* pots and pans; *(cacharros)* junk.

ca·cho m. *(pedazo)* piece; AMER. *(cuerno)* horn; R.P. *(plátanos)* bunch of bananas ♦ **un c.** SL. a bit.

ca·chon·de·ar·se reflex. COLL. ♦ **c. de** to tease.

ca·chon·de·o m. COLL. teasing.

ca·chon·dez f. *(celo)* heat; *(lujuria)* lust.

ca·chon·do, a adj. *(en celo)* in heat; *(libidinoso)* lustful.

ca·cho·rro, a m.f. *(perro)* puppy; *(de otros mamíferos)* cub.

ca·chu·che·ar tr. *(mimar)* to spoil; *(adular)* to flatter.

ca·chue·la f. *(guisado)* stew; *(rápido)* rapids.

ca·ci·que m. *(indio)* Indian chief; COLL. *(jefe)* political boss; *(déspota)* tyrant.

ca·ci·que·ar intr. COLL. to boss people around.

ca·co m. *(ladrón)* burglar; *(cobarde)* chicken.

ca·co·fo·ní·a f. cacophony.

cac·to/tus m. cactus.

ca·cu·men m. COLL. acumen, astuteness.

ca·da adj. each, every ♦ **c. cual** *or* **uno** each one, everyone • **¿c. cuánto?** how often? • **c. vez más** more and more • **c. vez menos** less and less • **c. vez peor** worse and worse • **c. vez que** whenever.

ca·dal·so m. *(tablado)* platform; *(horca)* gallows.

ca·dá·ver m. corpse, cadaver.
ca·da·vé·ri·co, a adj. cadaverous; FIG. deathly pale.
ca·de·na f. chain ♦ **c. de emisoras** network • **c. de fabricación** *or* **de montaje** assembly line • **c. de montañas** mountain range • **c. perpetua** life imprisonment • **reacción en c.** chain reaction.
ca·den·cia f. cadence, rhythm.
ca·de·ne·ro m. SURV. chainman; AMER. *(caballo)* workhorse.
ca·de·ni·lla f. small ornamental chain.
ca·de·ra f. hip, hip joint.
ca·de·te m. MIL. cadet.
cad·mio m. cadmium.
ca·du·car §70 intr. *(expirar)* to lapse, expire; LAW to be invalid.
ca·du·ci·dad f. caducity.
ca·du·co, a adj. *(extinguido)* lapsed, expired; LAW canceled; *(senil)* senile, decrepit.
ca·er §15 intr. to fall; *(de rodillas)* to drop; *(derrumbarse)* to fall down, collapse; *(el cabello, telas)* to hang down; *(mala fortuna)* to befall; *(buena fortuna)* to get, receive; *(los precios, intereses)* to drop; *(el sol)* to set; *(morir)* to die; *(comprender)* to see ♦ **al c. la noche** at nightfall • **c. bien** *(prenda)* to suit; *(persona)* to make a good impression on; *(alimento)* to agree with • **c. de pie** to land on one's feet • **c. de plano** to fall flat • **c. en** to fall on *or* into • **c. de espaldas** to fall on one's back; FIG. to be stunned • **c. enfermo** *or* **en cama** to fall ill • **c. en gracia** to make a good impression on • **c. en la cuenta** to realize • **c. mal** *(prenda)* to fit poorly; *(persona)* to displease; *(alimento)* to upset one's stomach • **c. parado** COLL. to be a nuisance • **c. por su propio peso** to be self-evident • **estar al c.** to be about to arrive —reflex. to fall; *(de las manos)* to drop <*se me cayó el libro* I dropped the book>; *(cabello)* to fall out • **c. de espaldas** to fall on one's back; FIG. to be stunned • **c. de sí mismo** to be obvious • **caérsele el alma a los pies** COLL. to become disheartened • **c. muerto** to drop dead • **c. redondo** to collapse • **no tener dónde c. muerto** to be destitute —tr. ♦ **c.** to knock down.
ca·fé m. coffee; *(establecimiento)* café, coffee shop; S. AMER., COLL. scolding ♦ **c. negro** *or* **solo** black coffee • **c. tostado** roasted coffee.
ca·fe·í·na f. caffeine.
ca·fe·tal m. coffee plantation.
ca·fe·ta·le·ro, a I. adj. coffee II. m. coffee grower.
ca·fe·te·rí·a f. coffee shop, café.
ca·fe·te·ro, a I. adj. coffee II. m.f. *(comerciante)* coffee merchant; *(dueño)* café owner —f. CUL. coffeepot ♦ **c. de filtro** percolator.
ca·fe·tín m. small café.
ca·í·do, a I. see **caer** II. adj. weak; FIG. downhearted ♦ **andar de capa c.** COLL. to suffer a setback • **c. del cielo** out of the blue • **c. de un nido** naive • **c. en desuso** obsolete, outmoded III. f. fall, falling; *(tumbo)* tumble; *(declive)* slope; *(de tela)* hang; *(de temperatura, precios)* drop; *(ruina)* downfall; GEOL. dip ♦ **a la c. de la tarde** at dusk.
cai·ga, go see **caer.**
cai·mán m. alligator.
cai·rel m. *(peluca)* hairpiece; *(fleco)* fringe.
ca·ja f. box; *(de madera)* chest; *(ataúd)* coffin; *(ventanilla)* cashier's window; *(tambor)* drum; *(armazón)* cabinet; ARM. gun stock; ARCHIT.

shaft; PRINT. type case; THEAT. wings ♦ **c. chica** COM. petty cash • **c. de ahorros** savings bank • **c. de cambios** *or* **velocidades** AUTO. transmission • **c. de colores** paint box • **c. de conexiones** ELEC. junction box • **c. de fusibles** ELEC. fuse box • **c. de herramientas** toolbox • **c. de hierro** AMER. safe • **c. de jubilaciones** pension fund • **c. de música** music box • **c. de reclutamiento** MIL. recruiting office • **c. de seguridad** safe-deposit box • **c. de sorpresa** jack-in-the-box • **c. efectivo** COM. cash on hand • **c. fuerte** safe • **c. registradora** cash register • **c. torácica** chest • **echar a alguien con cajas destempladas** COLL. to send someone packing.
ca·je·ro m. teller, cashier.
ca·je·ti·lla f. *(paquete)* pack —m. R.P., COLL. dandy.
ca·jis·ta m.f. PRINT. typesetter, compositor.
ca·jón m. *(caja grande)* case; *(gaveta)* drawer; S. AMER. *(ataúd)* coffin ♦ **de c.** COLL. customary.
ca·jo·ne·rí·a f. set of drawers.
cal f. MIN. lime ♦ **c. apagada** slaked lime • **c. viva** quicklime.
ca·la f. GEOG. cove; *(trozo)* sample; BOT. calla lily.
ca·la·ba·za f. squash; COLL. *(tonto)* blockhead ♦ **dar calabazas a** COLL. to jilt.
ca·la·bo·zo m. *(cárcel)* underground prison; *(celda)* jail cell.
ca·la·do m. SEW. drawnwork; MARIT. depth.
ca·la·dor m. MECH. driller; AMER. *(sonda)* probe.
ca·la·fa·te·ar tr. to caulk.
ca·la·mar m. squid.
ca·lam·bre m. cramp.
ca·la·mi·dad f. *(desastre)* misfortune; COLL. *(persona)* disgrace.
ca·la·mi·to·so, a adj. calamitous.
ca·lan·drar tr. to calender (paper, cloth).
ca·lan·dria f. ORNITH. type of lark; MECH., TEX. calender.
ca·la·ña f. nature, character.
ca·lar tr. *(mojar)* to drench; *(penetrar)* to penetrate; COLL. *(descubrir)* to see through; *(cortar)* to cut a sample of; MARIT. to draw; MIL. to fix, aim (weapons); R.P. to stare at —reflex. *(mojarse)* to get drenched; *(ponerse)* to put on ♦ **c. hasta los huesos** to get soaked to the skin.
ca·la·ve·ra f. skull —m. reveler.
ca·la·ve·ra·da f. reckless escapade, tomfoolery.
ca·la·ve·re·ar intr. to have a wild time.
cal·ca·ñal/ñar m. heel, heel bone.
cal·car §70 tr. to trace; FIG. to copy.
cal·cá·re·o, a adj. calcareous, limy.
cal·ce m. *(llanta)* steel rim *or* tire; *(cuña)* wedge.
cal·ce·ta f. knee-high sock *or* stocking ♦ **hacer c.** to knit (socks).
cal·ce·tín m. sock.
cal·ci·fi·ca·ción f. calcification.
cal·ci·fi·car §70 tr. to calcify.
cal·ci·nar tr. to calcine; FIG. to burn.
cal·cio m. calcium.
cal·co m. tracing; FIG. copy.
cal·co·ma·ní·a f. decal, transfer.
cal·cu·la·ble adj. calculable.
cal·cu·la·dor, ·ra I. f. *(máquina de calcular)* calculator; *(electrónica)* computer ♦ **c. electrónica** computer —m.f. calculator II. adj. calculating.
cal·cu·lar tr. *(computar)* to calculate; *(proyec-*

tar) to estimate.

cal·cu·lis·ta m.f. calculator, planner.

cál·cu·lo m. *(proceso)* calculation; *(suposición)* estimate; MED. stone, calculus; MATH. calculus ♦ **c. biliar** MED. gallstone • **c. mental** mental arithmetic • **c. renal** MED. kidney stone • **obrar con mucho c.** to act shrewdly.

cal·de·ar tr. to heat *or* warm (up); FIG. to enliven.

cal·de·ra f. caldron; MECH. boiler; MIN. sump ♦ **c. de vapor** steam boiler.

cal·de·ro m. small caldron.

cal·de·rón m. large caldron; *(párrafo)* paragraph mark; MUS. pause sign.

cal·do m. *(consomé)* broth; *(jugo)* juice ♦ **c. de cultivo** BIOL. culture medium • **hacer a uno el c. gordo** to play into someone's hands.

ca·le·fac·ción f. heat, heating.

ca·le·fac·tor m. heater.

ca·len·da·rio m. calendar; *(programa)* schedule ♦ **c. judicial** court calendar.

ca·lén·du·la f. calendula, pot marigold.

ca·len·ta·dor, ·ra I. adj. heating, warming II. m. heater; *(para agua)* water heater; *(de cama)* bed warmer.

ca·len·tar §49 tr. to warm *or* heat (up); *(azotar)* to beat, thrash ♦ **c. al blanco** to make white-hot • **c. al rojo** to make red-hot • **c. las orejas a** COLL. *(chismear)* to gossip • **c. la sangre a** to make (someone's) blood boil • **c. la silla** FIG. to overstay one's welcome —reflex. to warm oneself up; ZOOL. to be in heat; COLL. *(alterarse)* to get excited; AMER. to get angry.

ca·len·tu·ra f. fever.

ca·len·tu·rien·to, a adj. feverish.

ca·le·ra f. *(cantera)* limestone quarry; *(horno)* limekiln.

ca·le·sa f. calash, calèche (light carriage).

ca·li·bra·ción f. calibration.

ca·li·bra·dor m. calibrator, calipers.

ca·li·brar tr. *(medir)* to gauge; *(graduar)* to calibrate.

ca·li·bre m. ARM. caliber; TECH. *(tubo)* diameter; *(alambre)* thickness; *(importancia)* importance.

ca·li·can·to m. stone masonry.

ca·li·có m. calico.

ca·li·dad f. quality; *(clase)* class; *(capacidad)* position; *(índole)* nature ♦ **a c. de que** on the condition that • **en c. de** as.

cá·li·do, a adj. warm.

ca·l(e)i·dos·co·pio m. kaleidoscope.

ca·lien·ta·piés m. foot warmer.

ca·lien·ta·pla·tos m. plate warmer, hot plate.

ca·lien·te adj. hot; FIG. *(acalorado)* angry ♦ **c. de cascos** hot-tempered • **estar c.** *(animal)* to be in heat.

ca·li·fa m. caliph.

ca·li·fi·ca·ción f. *(clasificación)* classification; *(nota)* grade.

ca·li·fi·ca·do, a adj. *(capaz)* qualified; *(eminente)* eminent; *(probado)* proven.

ca·li·fi·ca·dor, ·ra I. adj. examining II. m.f. assessor; *(clasificador)* classifier.

ca·li·fi·car §70 tr. *(clasificar)* to classify; *(dar una nota a)* to grade; *(tratar)* to call <*me calificó de estúpido* she called me stupid>.

ca·li·fi·ca·ti·vo, a I. adj. qualifying II. m. qualifier.

ca·li·for·nio m. californium.

ca·li·gra·fí·a f. calligraphy.

ca·lí·gra·fo, a m.f. calligrapher ♦ **c. perito**

handwriting expert.

ca·lis·te·nia f. calisthenics.

cá·liz m. chalice; POET. cup; BOT. calyx.

ca·li·zo, a I. adj. calcareous, limy II. f. limestone.

ca·lla·do, a I. adj. *(silencioso)* silent; *(reservado)* reserved II. f. silence.

ca·llar intr. to be or become silent —tr. *(silenciar)* to silence; *(guardar secreto)* to keep secret; *(no mencionar)* not to mention —reflex. *(guardar silencio)* to be quiet or silent; *(guardarse callado)* to keep quiet ♦ **¡cállate!** be quiet! • **¡cállate la boca!** COLL. shut up!

ca·lle f. street ♦ **echar a la c.** COLL. to throw out of the house • **echarse a la c.** COLL. to take to the streets • **poner en la c.** to put out on the street.

ca·lle·je·ar intr. to wander or walk the streets.

ca·lle·je·o m. roaming about.

ca·lle·je·ro, a adj. fond of wandering the streets ♦ **perro c.** stray dog.

ca·lle·jón m. alley ♦ **c. sin salida** blind alley; FIG. deadlock.

ca·llo m. corn ♦ pl. tripe.

ca·llo·si·dad f. callosity, callus.

cal·man·te I. adj. calming; MED. sedative II. m. sedative.

cal·mar tr. to soothe, calm (down) —intr. to calm (down), abate —reflex. to calm down.

cal·mo, a I. adj. calm II. f. *(tranquilidad)* calm; *(serenidad)* calmness; COLL. *(pachorra)* sluggishness ♦ **con c.** calmly • **en c.** calm; COM. in a slack period • **perder la c.** to lose one's composure.

ca·ló m. gypsy dialect.

ca·lo·frí·o m. chill, shiver.

ca·lor m. warmth, heat; *(pasión)* ardor; *(de la batalla)* thick ♦ **dar c. a** to encourage • **entrar en c.** to get warm • **hacer c.** *(tiempo)* to be hot or warm • **tener c.** *(persona)* to be hot or warm.

ca·lo·rí·a f. calorie.

ca·lo·rí·fe·ro, a I. adj. heat-producing II. m. heater ♦ **c. de aire** air heater.

ca·lo·rí·fu·go, a adj. heat-resistant.

ca·lo·rí·me·tro m. calorimeter.

cal·lum·nia f. calumny, slander.

ca·lum·nia·dor, ·ra I. adj. slanderous II. m.f. slanderer.

ca·lum·niar tr. to calumniate, slander.

ca·lu·ro·so, a adj. warm, hot; FIG. warm, enthusiastic.

cal·va·rio m. calvary; RELIG. Calvary.

cal·vez/vi·cie f. baldness.

cal·vo, a I. adj. bald ♦ **quedarse c.** to go bald II. m.f. bald person —f. bald spot.

cal·za f. *(cuña)* wedge; COLL. *(media)* stocking ♦ pl. breeches.

cal·za·da f. highway, road.

cal·za·do m. footwear ♦ **tienda de c.** shoe store.

cal·za·dor m. shoehorn.

cal·zar §04 tr. to put shoes on; *(poner calces)* to wedge; COLL. *(comprender)* to grasp, understand ♦ **¿qué número calza?** what size do you take? —reflex. to put on shoes.

cal·zón m. *(pantalones)* pants, trousers; R.P. panties; MEX. chaps ♦ **a c. quitado** COLL. boldly • pl. pants, trousers • **tener bien puestos los c.** COLL. to be quite a man.

cal·zon·ci·llos m.pl. underwear, shorts.

ca·ma f. bed; *(armazón)* bedstead; *(guarida)* lair; *(de paja)* straw bed; CUL. layer ♦ **caer en**

c. to fall ill • **c. gemela** twin bed • **c. matrimonial** double bed • **guardar c.** or **estar en c.** to stay in bed.

ca·ma·da f. ZOOL. litter; ORNITH. brood; (capa) layer.

ca·ma·fe·o m. cameo.

ca·ma·le·ón m. chameleon.

ca·man·du·le·ar intr. R.P., COLL. to be hypocritical, intrigue.

ca·man·du·le·ro, a R.P., COLL. **I.** adj. sly, cunning **II.** m.f. hypocrite.

cá·ma·ra f. (sala) hall; (junta) chamber; AGR. granary; AUTO. inner tube; POL. house; MARIT. cabin; ARM. chamber; PHOTOG. camera • **c. cinematográfica** movie camera • **c. de compensación** COM. clearing house • **c. de oxígeno** oxygen tent • **c. de televisión** television or video camera • **c. frigorífica** cold storage chamber • **c. lenta** slow motion • **c. mortuoria** funeral chamber.

ca·ma·ra·da m.f. comrade.

ca·ma·ra·de·rí·a f. camaraderie, comradeship.

ca·ma·re·ro, a m.f. waiter, waitress; MARIT. steward, stewardess.

ca·ma·ri·lla f. clique, coterie.

ca·ma·rín m. RELIG. niche; THEAT. dressing room.

ca·ma·rón m. shrimp, prawn.

ca·ma·ro·te m. MARIT. cabin, berth.

ca·mas·tro m. COLL. makeshift bed; MIL. cot.

cam·ba·la·che m. COLL. (trueque) swap; R.P. secondhand store.

cam·ba·la·che·ar tr. COLL. to swap, trade.

cam·ba·la·che·ro, a I. adj. swapping, trading **II.** m.f. swapper, trader; R.P. owner of a secondhand store.

cam·bia·ble adj. (que se puede alterar) changeable; (por otra cosa) exchangeable.

cam·bia·di·zo, a adj. changeable, variable.

cam·bia·dor, ·ra m.f. moneychanger —m. CHILE, MEX., RAIL. switchman • **c. automático** or **de discos** record changer.

cam·biar tr. to change; (alterar) to alter; (reemplazar) to replace; (trocar) to exchange; COM. to exchange, change —intr. to change; METEOROL. to shift • **c. de casa** to move • **c. de color** to change color • **c. de dueño** to change hands • **c. de parecer** to change one's mind • **c. de ropa** to change clothes —reflex. to change.

cam·bia·ví·a m. RAIL. switch; AMER. switchman.

cam·bio m. change; (alteración) alteration; (trueque) exchange; COM. (tipo de cambio) rate of exchange; RAIL. switch; AUTO. transmission • **a c. de** in exchange for • **a la primera de c.** COLL. before you know it • **c. automático** AUTO. automatic transmission • **c. de marchas** or **velocidades** AUTO. gearshift • **casa de c.** foreign exchange office • **en c.** (en vez de) instead; (por otra parte) on the other hand.

cam·bis·ta m.f. moneychanger, broker —m. R.P. switchman.

ca·me·lar tr. COLL. (halagar) to flatter; (enamorar) to woo; (engañar) to deceive; MEX. to watch.

ca·me·le·ar tr. COLL. to deceive.

ca·me·le·o m. COLL. flattery, wheedling.

ca·me·lia f. camellia.

ca·me·lo m. camel.

ca·me·lo m. COLL. wooing • **dar c. a** to tease.

ca·me·ri·no m. THEAT. dressing room.

ca·me·ro, a adj. (de camas) double.

ca·mi·lla f. MED. stretcher.

ca·mi·lle·ro m. stretcher-bearer.

ca·mi·nar intr. to walk; (viajar) to travel; FIG. to move along • **c. derecho** to behave properly —tr. to walk.

ca·mi·na·ta f. walk, hike.

ca·mi·no m. road; (senda) path, trail; (vía) route; (viaje) trip; FIG. means • **abrir c.** to make way • **allanar el c.** COLL. to smooth the way • **a medio c.** halfway • **c. a** towards • **c. trillado** FIG. beaten path • **en c.** on the way • **en c. de** FIG. on the way to • **ponerse en c.** to get started • **por buen c.** FIG. on the right track.

ca·mión m. truck, lorry (G.B.); MEX. bus • **c. de bomberos** fire engine • **c. de mudanzas** moving van.

ca·mio·ne·ro, a m.f. truck driver.

ca·mio·ne·ta f. van.

ca·mi·sa f. shirt; (envoltura) jacket; MECH. casing • **c. de dormir** nightshirt • **c. de fuerza** straitjacket • **dejar sin c.** COLL. to leave penniless • **en mangas de c.** in shirtsleeves • **perder hasta la c.** COLL. to lose the shirt off one's back.

ca·mi·se·ta f. T-shirt; (ropa interior) undershirt; SPORT. jersey.

ca·mi·so·la f. camisole.

ca·mi·són m. nightgown.

ca·mo·mi·la f. camomile, chamomile.

ca·mo·rra f. COLL. squabble • **armar c.** to pick a fight • **buscar c.** to go looking for trouble.

ca·mo·rre·ar intr. COLL. to squabble, quarrel.

ca·mo·rris·ta adj. & m.f. quarrelsome (person).

ca·mo·te AMER. m. (batata) sweet potato; COLL. (enamoramiento) infatuation • **tener un c.** AMER. to be infatuated.

cam·pa·men·to m. camp • **c. de verano** summer camp.

cam·pa·na f. bell; R.P. lookout • **tañer** or **tocar las campanas** to ring the bells.

cam·pa·na·da f. stroke, ring (of a bell).

cam·pa·na·rio m. bell tower, belfry.

cam·pa·ne·ar intr. to ring the bells; R.P. (mirar) to be the lookout.

cam·pa·ni·lla f. (campana) hand bell; (timbre) doorbell; ANAT. uvula; BOT. bellflower.

cam·pan·te adj. unruffled, relaxed.

cam·pa·ña f. plain; MIL., POL. campaign; AMER. countryside • **hacer c.** to campaign • **tienda de c.** tent.

cam·pe·cha·no, a adj. COLL. good-natured.

cam·pe·ón, o·na m.f. champion.

cam·pe·o·na·to m. championship.

cam·pe·si·na·do m. peasantry.

cam·pe·si·no, a I. adj. rustic **II.** m.f. peasant.

cam·pes·tre adj. rural.

cam·pi·ña f. large field.

cam·po m. country, countryside; (plantío) field; MIL., SPORT. field • **a c. traviesa** cross-country • **casa de c.** country house • **c. de batalla** battlefield • **c. de deportes** athletic field • **c. de juego** playground • **c. de tiro** firing range • **c. magnético** PHYS. magnetic field • **c. petrolífero** oil field • **c. raso** open country • **c. visual** field of vision • **dar c. a** FIG. to give ground to • **trabajo de c.** field work.

cam·po·san·to m. cemetery, graveyard.

ca·mu·fla·je m. camouflage.

ca·mu·flar tr. to camouflage.

can m. (perro) dog; (gatillo) trigger.

ca·na f. see **cano, a.**
ca·nal m. canal; *(estrecho)* strait, channel; *(de puerto)* navigation channel; *(tubo)* pipe, conduit, tube; ANAT. tract; ARCHIT. gutter; RAD., TELEV. channel.
ca·na·le·ta f. conduit; R.P. gutter.
ca·na·li·za·ción f. canalization; TECH. piping; ELEC. wiring.
ca·na·li·zar §04 tr. *(abrir canales)* to canalize; *(controlar aguas)* to channel; *(por tuberías)* to pipe; FIG. to channel.
ca·na·lla COLL. m. scoundrel —f. riffraff.
ca·na·lla·da f. dirty trick.
ca·na·lles·co, a adj. low, despicable.
ca·na·lón m. gutter, drainpipe.
ca·na·pé m. *(sofá)* sofa; CUL. canapé.
ca·nas·ta f. basket; *(naipes)* canasta.
ca·nas·ti·lla f. *(canasta pequeña)* small basket; *(de bebé)* layette; AMER. trousseau.
ca·nas·to m. basket.
can·cel m. *(puerta)* storm door; *(mampara)* partition.
can·ce·la f. iron gate.
can·ce·lar tr. to cancel; *(saldar)* to pay off; FIG. to wipe out.
cán·cer m. cancer.
can·cer·be·ro m. severe doorman.
can·ce·ró·lo·go, a m.f. cancer specialist.
can·ce·ro·so, a adj. cancerous.
can·cha f. *(campo)* field; *(de tenis)* court ♦ **dar c. a** ARG., CHILE, C. RICA to give the advantage to • **estar uno en su c.** R.P., COLL. to be in one's element • **tener c.** R.P., COLL. to be experienced.
can·che·ro, a I.m.f. R.P. expert; AMER. groundskeeper II. adj. R.P. expert, skilled.
can·ci·ller m. chancellor.
can·ci·lle·rí·a f. chancellery.
can·ción f. song ♦ **c. de cuna** lullaby.
can·cio·ne·ro m. MUS. songbook.
can·cio·nis·ta m.f. *(compositor)* songwriter; *(cantante)* singer.
can·cro m. MED. cancer; BOT. canker.
can·da·do m. padlock.
can·de·al I. adj. ♦ **pan c.** white bread II. m. ARG., CHILE, PERU hot beverage made with cognac, milk and eggs.
can·de·la f. *(vela)* candle; COLL. *(lumbre)* heat; *(fire)* light.
can·de·la·bro m. candelabrum; ARG. cactus.
can·de·la·ria f. Candlemas; BOT. great mullein.
can·de·le·ro m. candlestick; *(velón)* oil lamp; MARIT. stanchion ♦ **estar en el c.** to be at the top.
can·den·te adj. *(incandescente)* white-hot; *(ardiente)* burning; FIG. *(cargado)* charged; *(grave)* burning, important.
can·di·da·to, a m.f. candidate.
can·di·da·tu·ra f. candidacy.
can·di·dez f. candor; FIG. naiveté.
cán·di·do, a adj. candid; FIG. naive.
can·dil m. oil lamp.
can·di·le·ja f. oil reservoir ♦ pl. footlights.
can·dom·be m. AMER. dance of South American blacks.
can·dor m. candor; *(ingenuidad)* naiveté.
can·do·ro·so, a adj. candid; *(ingenuo)* naive.
ca·ne·ar intr. to grow gray-haired.
ca·ne·la f. cinnamon.
ca·ne·lón m. *(cañería)* roof gutter; *(carámbano)* icicle; *(labor)* tubular braid.

ca·ne·lo·nes m.pl. cannelloni (pasta).
ca·ne·sú m. *(de camisa)* yoke; *(de vestido)* bodice.
can·gre·jo m. crab ♦ **c. de mar** crab • **c. de río** crayfish.
can·gre·na f. var. of **gangrena.**
can·gu·ro m. kangaroo.
ca·ní·bal I. adj. cannibalistic II. m.f. cannibal.
ca·ni·ca f. marble ♦ pl. (game of) marbles.
ca·ni·cie f. grayness (of hair).
ca·ní·cu·la f. dog days, midsummer heat.
ca·ni·lla f. ANAT. shinbone; *(carrillo)* spool; AMER. *(del agua)* tap; MEX., FIG. *(fuerza)* strength; AMER., COLL. *(pierna)* skinny leg.
ca·ní·lli·ta m. S. AMER. newspaper boy.
ca·ni·no, a adj. & m. canine.
can·je m. exchange, trade.
can·je·a·ble adj. exchangeable.
can·je·ar tr. to exchange, trade.
ca·no, a I. adj. gray-haired; FIG. old II. f. *(cabello)* white or gray hair; AMER., COLL. jail ♦ **echar una c. al aire** to have fun ♦ pl. gray hair(s).
ca·no·a f. canoe; *(bote)* rowboat.
ca·non m. canon.
ca·nó·ni·co, a adj. canonical, canonic.
ca·nó·ni·go m. canon, prebendary.
ca·no·ni·za·ción f. canonization.
ca·no·ni·zar §04 tr. to canonize.
ca·no·ro, a adj. melodious ♦ **ave c.** songbird.
ca·no·so, a adj. gray-haired.
can·sa·do, a *(fatigado)* tired; *(agotado)* worn-out ♦ **a las cansadas** R.P. after much delay.
can·san·cio m. tiredness ♦ **muerto de c.** dog-tired.
can·sar tr. to tire, make tired; *(aburrir)* to bore; *(fastidiar)* to annoy ♦ **c. la vista** to strain one's eyes —reflex. to become or get tired —intr. to be tiring; *(aburrir)* to be boring.
can·tan·te I. adj. singing ♦ **llevar la voz c.** to be in charge II. m.f. singer, vocalist.
can·tar[1] m. song, folk song ♦ **eso es otro c.** COLL. that's another story.
can·tar[2] tr. & intr. to sing; FIG. to confess ♦ **en menos de lo que canta un gallo** COLL. in a jiffy.
cán·ta·ro m. jug ♦ **llover a cántaros** COLL. to rain cats and dogs.
can·te·ra f. quarry, pit.
can·te·ro m. *(pedrero)* stonemason; R.P. flowerbed.
cán·ti·co m. canticle; FIG. song.
can·ti·dad f. quantity; *(suma)* sum.
can·ti·le·na f. MUS. cantilena; FIG. same old story.
can·tim·plo·ra f. canteen.
can·ti·na f. canteen; AMER. saloon.
can·ti·ne·la f. var. of **cantilena.**
can·ti·ne·ro, a m.f. AMER. saloonkeeper.
can·to[1] m. *(canción)* song; *(arte)* singing; *(monótono)* chant; *(poema)* heroic poem.
can·to[2] m. *(extremo)* edge; *(borde)* border; *(de cuchillo)* blunt edge; *(de un libro)* front edge; *(guijarro)* pebble ♦ **c. rodado** boulder • **de c.** *(de lado)* on end, on edge; *(grueso)* thick.
can·tor, ·ra I. adj. singing II. m.f. singer.
can·tu·rre·ar/rriar intr. COLL. to sing softly.
cá·nu·la f. small reed; MED. cannula.
ca·nu·to m. tube.
ca·ña f. reed; *(de azúcar)* cane; *(tallo)* stalk; *(de una bota)* leg; ANAT. long bone; ZOOL. shank; ARCHIT. shaft of a column ♦ **c. de pes-**

car fishing rod • **c. dulce** sugar cane.

ca·ña·da f. ravine; AMER. stream.

ca·ña·dón m. AMER. *(barranca)* ravine; *(arroyo profundo)* deep stream.

ca·ñal m. cane thicket.

ca·ña·ma·zo m. canvas.

ca·ña·miel f. sugar cane.

ca·ña·mo m. hemp.

ca·ña·ve·ra f. reed-grass.

ca·ña·ve·ral m. cane thicket; *(plantación)* sugar-cane plantation.

ca·ñe·rí·a f. *(tubo)* pipe; *(tubería)* pipeline.

ca·ñe·ro m. sugarcane vendor.

ca·ño m. *(tubo)* pipe; *(albañal)* sewer; MARIT. narrow channel; MIN. gallery.

ca·ñón m. MIL. cannon; ARM. barrel; GEOG. canyon, gorge; *(de chimenea)* flue ♦ **c. antiaéreo** antiaircraft gun • **c. antitanque** antitank gun.

ca·ño·na·zo m. *(tiro)* cannon shot; COLL. *(noticia)* bombshell; SPORT. shot.

ca·ño·ne·ar tr. to cannonade, shell.

ca·ño·ne·o m. cannonade, shelling.

ca·ño·ne·ro, a adj. armed with cannons.

ca·ñu·ti·llo m. bead.

ca·o·ba f. mahogany.

ca·os m. chaos.

ca·ó·ti·co, a adj. chaotic.

ca·pa f. *(manto)* cape; *(de pintura)* coat; *(cubierta)* covering; GEOL. layer; ZOOL. coat ♦ **a c. y espada** through thick and thin • **andar** *or* **ir de c. caída** COLL. *(decaer)* to be in rough shape; *(estar triste)* to be depressed.

ca·pa·che·ro m. porter.

ca·pa·ci·dad f. capacity; *(espacio)* room; *(talento)* ability; LAW capacity ♦ **c. adquisitiva** purchasing power • **c. de ganancia** earning power.

ca·pa·ci·tar tr. *(instruir)* to train; *(calificar)* to qualify; *(autorizar)* to empower —reflex. to become qualified.

ca·par tr. to castrate.

ca·pa·ra·zón m. shell, carapace.

ca·pa·taz m. foreman.

ca·paz adj. capable.

cap·cio·so, a adj. deceitful ♦ **pregunta c.** tricky question.

ca·pe·ar tr. COLL. *(engañar)* to fool; *(eludir)* to dodge; MARIT. to weather.

ca·pe·llán m. chaplain.

ca·pe·ru·za f. *(gorro)* hood; *(de pluma)* cap.

ca·pi·cú·a f. palindrome.

ca·pi·lar adj. & m. capillary.

ca·pi·la·ri·dad f. capillarity.

ca·pi·lla f. chapel; *(camarilla)* clan; TECH. hood ♦ **c. ardiente** funeral chapel • **estar en c.** to be on tenterhooks.

ca·pi·llo m. *(de niño)* baby bonnet; *(de bautizo)* baptismal cape; *(del calzado)* toe lining; *(capullo)* silk cocoon.

ca·pi·ro·ta·zo m. fillip, flick (with a finger).

ca·pi·ro·te m. hood ♦ **tonto de c.** fool.

ca·pi·ru·cho m. COLL. hood, cap.

ca·pi·tal I. adj. capital; *(esencial)* vital *<de importancia c.* of vital importance>* II. m. capital; *(el que produce intereses)* principal ♦ **c. activo** working capital • **c. circulante** working capital • **c. de inversión** investment capital • **c. disponible** available funds • **c. en giro** operating capital • **c. fijo** fixed capital • **c. líquido** net worth • **c. social** capital stock —f. capital, capital city.

ca·pi·ta·li·no, a I. adj. of the capital II. m.f native *or* inhabitant of the capital.

ca·pi·ta·lis·ta I. adj. capitalist, capitalistic II. m.f. capitalist.

ca·pi·ta·li·za·ción f. capitalization.

ca·pi·ta·li·zar §04 tr. to capitalize; *(interés)* to compound.

ca·pi·tán, a·na m. captain; FIG. leader ♦ **c. de corbeta** lieutenant commander • **c. de fragata** commander —m.f. SPORT. team captain.

ca·pi·ta·ne·ar tr. to captain; FIG. to command.

ca·pi·ta·ní·a f. *(cargo)* captainship; *(de tropas)* company.

ca·pi·tel m. capital (of a column).

ca·pi·to·lio m. capitol.

ca·pi·tu·la·ción f. capitulation.

ca·pi·tu·lar intr. to capitulate.

ca·pí·tu·lo m. chapter; *(reunión)* assembly; ANAT., BOT. capitulum.

ca·pó m. AUTO. hood, bonnet (G.B.).

ca·pón I. adj. castrated II. m. capon; R.P. castrated sheep.

ca·po·ral m. foreman; FIG. boss.

ca·po·ta f. *(de mujer)* bonnet; *(de coche)* hood, bonnet (G.B.); *(capa corta)* short cape; AUTO. folding top of a convertible.

ca·po·tar intr. to turn over, roll over.

ca·po·te m. cape ♦ **c. de montar** riding cape • **c. de monte** poncho.

ca·pri·cho m. whim; *(antojo)* fancy; MUS. caprice ♦ **tener c. por** to fancy.

ca·pri·cho·so, a adj. whimsical; *(inconstante)* fickle.

cáp·su·la f. capsule; ARM. cartridge shell.

cap·tar tr. *(atraer)* to attract, win; *(aprehender)* to grasp.

cap·tu·ra f. capture, apprehension.

cap·tu·rar tr. to capture, apprehend.

ca·pu·cha f. hood; PRINT. circumflex accent.

ca·pu·chi·no, a adj. & m.f. RELIG. Capuchin.

ca·pu·llo m. *(brote)* bud; *(de larva)* cocoon; *(de bellota)* cup ♦ **c. de rosa** rosebud.

ca·qui m. BOT. kaki; *(tela y color)* khaki.

ca·ra I. f. face; *(semblante)* look; *(superficie)* surface; *(frente)* front; *(aspecto)* appearance; COLL. *(descaro)* nerve; GEOM. plane; *(anverso)* heads ♦ **asomar la c.** to show one's face • **caérsele la c. de vergüenza** COLL. to blush with shame • **c. a c.** face to face • **c. de pascua** COLL. happy face • **c. de pocos amigos** COLL. unfriendly face • **c. de viernes** COLL. long face • **c. dura** nerve, cheek • **c. o cruz** heads or tails • **cruzar la c. a** to slap • **dar c. a** to face • **dar la c.** to face the consequences • **de dos caras** two-faced • **echar la c. o cruz** to toss a coin • **echar en c.** to reproach • **hacer c. a** to confront • **sacar la c. por** COLL. to stick up for • **saltar a la c.** FIG. to hit the eye immediately • **tener c. de** COLL. to look like • **tener c. para** COLL. to have the nerve to II. adv. ♦ **c. a** *or* **de c.** facing.

ca·ra·be·la f. caravel.

ca·ra·bi·na f. carbine.

ca·ra·col m. snail; *(concha)* conch; *(espiral)* spiral; *(rizo)* curl; ANAT. cochlea ♦ **¡caracoles!** my goodness! • **escalera de c.** spiral staircase.

ca·ra·co·la f. conch.

ca·rác·ter m. character; *(índole)* nature; *(rasgo)* trait; *(capacidad)* capacity; *(de letra)* handwriting; *(estilo)* style; *(entereza)* moral character ♦ **c. de imprenta** typeface.

ca·rac·te·rís·ti·co, a I. adj. characteristic

II. m. THEAT. character actor —f. *(rasgo)* characteristic; THEAT. character actress; MATH. characteristic; ARG. telephone exchange.
ca·rac·te·ri·za·do, a adj. distinguished.
ca·rac·te·ri·za·dor, ·ra adj. distinguishing.
ca·rac·te·ri·zar §04 tr. to characterize; THEAT. to portray (a role) expressively —reflex. to be characterized; THEAT. to make up.
ca·ra·cú m. AMER. bone marrow.
ca·ra·cul m. karakul.
ca·ra·du·ra adj. & m.f. shameless (person).
¡ca·ram·ba! interj. *(asombro)* good heavens!; *(enfado)* damn it!
ca·rám·ba·no m. icicle.
ca·ram·bo·la f. carom (in billiards); COLL. *(doble resultado)* killing two birds with one stone; *(casualidad)* chance.
ca·ra·me·li·zar §04 tr. *(bañar)* to cover with caramel; *(convertir)* to caramelize.
ca·ra·me·lo m. caramel; *(dulce)* candy.
ca·ran·cho m. AMER. carrion hawk.
ca·rá·tu·la f. *(careta)* mask; AMER. title page.
ca·ra·va·na f. caravan.
¡ca·ray! interj. damn!
car·bo·hi·dra·to m. carbohydrate.
car·bón m. coal; *(de leña)* charcoal; *(lápiz)* carbon pencil; *(papel)* carbon (paper); ELEC. carbon ♦ **c. animal** boneblack • **negro como el c.** black as the ace of spades.
car·bo·nar tr. to char, make into charcoal —reflex. to become carbonized *or* charred.
car·bo·na·to m. carbonate.
car·bon·ci·llo m. ARTS charcoal pencil; *(carbonilla)* small coal.
car·bo·ne·rí·a f. coal shop.
car·bo·ne·ro, a I. adj. charcoal II. m. coal supplier; MARIT. coal ship —f. *(pila de leña)* charcoal pile; *(depósito)* coal bin.
car·bo·ní·fe·ro, a adj. & m. carboniferous.
car·bo·ni·lla f. coal dust; *(de la locomotora)* soot; ARG. charcoal pencil.
car·bo·ni·zar §04 tr. to carbonize, char.
car·bo·no m. carbon.
car·bo·run·do m. carborundum.
car·bun·clo m. MIN. carbuncle.
car·bún·cu·lo m. carbuncle, ruby.
car·bu·ra·dor m. carburetor.
car·bu·ran·te I. m. fuel II. adj. containing a hydrocarbon.
car·bu·rar tr. to carburize —intr. COLL. to run, go.
car·bu·ro m. carbide.
car·ca·ja·da f. loud laughter ♦ **reír a carcajadas** to split one's sides laughing.
car·ca·mán m. MARIT. old ship; AMER. pretentious person; CUBA low-class foreigner.
car·ca·za f. quiver.
cár·cel f. *(prisión)* jail; TECH. clamp.
car·ce·le·ro, a I. adj. jail II. m.f. jailer II. adj. jail.
car·ci·no·ma f. carcinoma, cancer.
car·co·mer tr. to eat away, gnaw —reflex. to rot, decay.
car·da·dor, ·ra m.f. TEX. carder —f. carding machine.
car·dán m. cardan *or* universal joint.
car·dar tr. TEX. to card, comb.
car·de·nal m. cardinal; COLL. *(mancha)* bruise.
cár·de·no, a adj. purple.
car·dia·co/dí·a·co, a I. adj. cardiac II. m.f. cardiac ♦ **ataque c.** heart attack.
car·di·nal adj. cardinal.

car·dió·gra·fo, a m.f. cardiologist —m. electrocardiograph.
car·dio·gra·ma m. electrocardiogram.
car·dio·lo·gí·a f. cardiology.
car·dió·lo·go, a m.f. cardiologist.
car·do m. thistle.
car·du·me(n) m. school (of fish).
ca·re·ar tr. *(confrontar)* to bring face to face; *(cotejar)* to compare.
ca·re·cer §17 intr. ♦ **c. de** to lack.
ca·ren·cia f. lack; MED. deficiency.
ca·ren·te adj. lacking (in), devoid of.
ca·re·o m. *(confrontación)* confrontation; *(cotejo)* comparison.
ca·re·ro, a adj. expensive (a shopkeeper).
ca·res·tí·a f. scarcity; COM. high prices ♦ **c. de la vida** high cost of living.
ca·re·ta f. mask ♦ **c. antigás** gas mask • **quitarle a uno la c.** to unmask someone.
ca·rey m. sea turtle; *(caparazón)* tortoiseshell.
car·ga f. load; *(acción)* loading; *(flete)* cargo; *(peso)* burden; *(obligación)* duty; *(responsabilidad)* onus; *(impuesto)* tax, duty; MIL. attack; *(de armas)* charge; ELEC. charge ♦ **c. bruta** gross tonnage • **c. personal** personal obligation • **c. útil** payload • **llevar la c. de** to be responsible for • **tomar c.** to take on cargo • **volver a la c.** to persist.
car·ga·de·ro m. loading platform.
car·ga·do, a I. adj. laden; *(sabor)* strong; *(atmósfera)* heavy; ELEC. charged ♦ **c. de años** old, ancient • **c. de espaldas** round-shouldered II. f. MEX. loading; R.P. practical joke.
car·ga·men·to m. load, cargo.
car·gan·te adj. tiresome, burdensome.
car·gar §47 tr. to load; *(llenar)* to fill; *(imputar)* to ascribe; *(con obligaciones)* to burden; *(con impuestos)* to impose; COLL. *(importunar)* to pester; ELEC., MIL. to charge; COM. to debit; AMER. to carry ♦ **c. la mano a** FIG. *(exigir mucho)* to be exacting; *(apremiar)* to press • **c. en cuenta** COM. to charge to one's account —intr. to load; ARCHIT. to rest ♦ **c. con** to carry; FIG. to shoulder —reflex. COLL. *(molestarse)* to become annoyed; METEOROL. to become cloudy ♦ **c. de** to have a lot of • **c. de años** old, getting along (in years).
car·go m. *(peso)* load; *(dignidad)* position; *(dirección)* direction; *(obligación)* obligation; *(acusación)* charge; COM. debit ♦ **a c. de** in charge of • **c. de conciencia** remorse • **hacer c. a uno de** to hold someone responsible for • **hacerse c. de** to take charge of.
car·go·se·ar tr. AMER. to pester, bother.
car·go·so, a adj. AMER. bothersome, tiresome.
car·gue·ro, a I. adj. freight II. m. MARIT. freighter.
ca·ria·con·te·ci·do, a adj. COLL. glum.
ca·ria·do, a adj. decayed.
ca·riar tr. & reflex. to decay.
ca·ri·be m. ICHTH. caribe, piranha.
ca·ri·ca·tu·ra f. caricature.
ca·ri·ca·tu·rar tr. to caricature.
ca·ri·ca·tu·ris·ta m.f. caricaturist.
ca·ri·ca·tu·ri·zar §04 tr. to caricature.
ca·ri·cia f. caress ♦ **hacer caricias a** to caress.
ca·ri·dad f. charity ♦ **¡por c.!** for pity's sake! • **la c. bien entendida empieza por casa** charity begins at home.
ca·ries f.inv. MED. caries, decay.
ca·ri·lla f. page, side.
ca·ri·llón m. carillon.

ca·ri·ño m. *(afecto)* affection; *(amor)* love; *(caricia)* caress; *(esmero)* care ♦ **sentir c. por** *or* **tener c. a** to be fond of • **tomar c. a** to take a liking to ♦ pl. love (in a letter).
ca·ri·ño·so, a adj. affectionate, loving.
ca·ris·ma m. charisma.
ca·ris·má·ti·co, a adj. charismatic.
ca·ri·ta·ti·vo, a adj. charitable.
ca·riz m. COLL. prospects, outlook.
car·me·li·ta I. adj. Carmelite; AMER. brown II. m.f. Carmelite —f. nasturtium flower.
car·me·sí [pl. **-íes**] adj. & m. crimson.
car·mín I. adj. crimson II. m. *(color)* crimson; *(tinta)* carmine; *(rosal)* mallow rose ♦ **c. de labios** lipstick.
car·na·da f. *(cebo)* bait; *(trampa)* trap, snare.
car·nal adj. carnal; *(sensual)* lustful; *(hermano)* full.
car·na·li·dad f. carnality, lust.
car·na·val m. carnival.
car·ne f. flesh; CUL. meat; BOT. pulp ♦ **c. asada al horno** roast (of meat) • **c. asada a la parrilla** broiled meat • **c. de carnero** mutton • **c. de cerdo** *or* **de puerco** pork • **c. de cordero** *or* **de oveja** lamb • **c. de gallina** COLL. goose bumps • **c. de ternera** veal • **c. de vaca** beef • **c. picada** chopped meat • **en c. viva** raw • **ser c. y uña** to be very close.
car·ne·ar tr. AMER. to slaughter.
car·ne·ro m. sheep; *(macho)* ram; CUL. mutton; R.P. scab.
car·net/né m. [pl. **-nés**] card.
car·ni·ce·rí·a f. butcher shop; FIG. carnage.
car·ni·ce·ro, a I. adj. *(carnívoro)* carnivorous; *(cruel)* savage II. m.f. butcher.
car·ní·vo·ro, a I. adj. carnivorous II. m. carnivore.
car·no·so/nu·do, a adj. meaty.
ca·ro, a I. adj. *(costoso)* expensive; *(amado)* dear II. adv. at a high price.
ca·ro·ti·na f. carotene.
ca·ro·zo m. stone, pit.
car·pa[1] f. carp ♦ **c. dorada** goldfish.
car·pa[2] f. AMER. *(tienda)* tent; *(toldo)* awning.
car·pe·ta f. *(cubierta)* folder; *(tapete)* table cover.
car·pin·cho m. AMER., ZOOL. capybara.
car·pin·te·rí·a f. *(oficio)* carpentry; *(taller)* carpenter shop.
car·pin·te·ro m. carpenter; ORNITH. woodpecker.
ca·rras·pe·ar intr. to clear one's throat.
ca·rras·pe·o m./**pe·ra** f. hoarseness.
ca·rre·ra f. *(espacio recorrido)* run; *(competencia)* race; *(pista)* racetrack; *(profesión)* career; *(hilera)* row; ARCHIT. beam; MUS. run ♦ **a la c.** running • **c. a pie** footrace • **c. de armamentos** MIL. arms race • **c. de fondo** long-distance race • **c. de obstáculos** steeplechase • **c. de relevos** relay race ♦ pl. races.
ca·rre·ris·ta m.f. racing fan.
ca·rre·ta f. wagon ♦ **c. de bueyes** oxcart • **c. de mano** wheelbarrow • **andar como una c.** to go at a snail's pace.
ca·rre·te m. *(bobina)* bobbin; *(de la caña de pescar)* reel.
ca·rre·te·ar tr. to cart; AER. to taxi —intr. AER. to taxi.
ca·rre·tel m. AMER. spool.
ca·rre·te·ra f. highway, road ♦ **c. de circunvalación** bypass • **c. de cuatro vías** four-lane highway • **c. de vía libre** expressway.

ca·rre·ti·lla f. *(carro pequeño)* cart; *(de una rueda)* wheelbarrow; *(del niño)* baby walker; R.P. jaw.
ca·rri·co·che m. *(carro cubierto)* covered wagon; DEROG. decrepit car, jalopy.
ca·rril m. *(surco)* groove; AGR. furrow; *(de tránsito)* lane; RAIL. rail ♦ **c. americano** trail • **c. conductor** contact rail • **c. de cambio** *or* **de aguja** switch rail.
ca·rri·llo m. jowl; *(garrucha)* pulley ♦ **comer a dos carrillos** to stuff oneself.
ca·rro m. *(vehículo)* cart; AMER. *(automóvil)* car; *(contenido)* cartload; *(de máquina)* carriage; MIL. tank ♦ **c. alegórico** parade float • **c. blindado** armored car • **c. de asalto** MIL. heavy tank.
ca·rro·ce·rí·a f. AUTO. body.
ca·rro·ma·to m. covered wagon.
ca·rro·ño, a I. adj. rotten **II.** f. carrion; FIG. trash.
ca·rro·za f. carriage; *(de desfile)* float; AMER. hearse.
ca·rrua·je m. carriage.
ca·rru·sel m. carousel, merry-go-round.
car·ta f. letter; *(naipe)* playing card; *(de derechos)* charter; *(documento)* document; *(mapa)* map ♦ **a c. cabal** in every respect • **a la c.** à la carte • **c. aérea** airmail letter • **c. blanca** carte blanche • **c. de porte** COM. bill of lading • **echar una c. al correo** to mail a letter • **poner las cartas sobre la mesa** to put one's cards on the table • **tomar cartas** COLL. to intervene.
car·ta·pa·cio m. *(cuaderno)* notebook; AMER. portfolio.
car·te·ar·se reflex. to write to each other.
car·tel m. poster; FIN. cartel ♦ **prohibido fijar carteles** post no bills.
car·te·le·ra f. billboard; *(de un periódico)* entertainment section.
car·te·o m. exchange of letters.
cár·ter m. MECH. casing ♦ **c. del cigüeñal** crankcase • **c. de engranajes** gearbox.
car·te·ra f. *(de hombre)* wallet; *(de mujer)* pocketbook; *(portadocumentos)* briefcase; *(de bolsillo)* pocket flap; *(ministerio)* cabinet post; COM., FIN. portfolio ♦ **tener en c.** to be planning.
car·te·ris·ta m. pickpocket.
car·te·ro m. mailman, postman.
car·tí·la·go m. cartilage.
car·ti·lla f. *(abecedario)* primer; *(folleto)* booklet.
car·to·gra·fí·a f. cartography, mapmaking.
car·tó·gra·fo, a m.f. cartographer, mapmaker.
car·to·man·cia f. cartomancy.
car·tón m. *(papel)* cardboard; *(caja)* cardboard box; *(de cigarrillos)* carton; *(boceto)* sketch; *(de un libro)* board ♦ **c. piedra** papier-mâché • **c. yeso** plasterboard.
car·tu·che·ra f. cartridge box.
car·tu·cho m. MIL. cartridge; *(cono)* paper cone; *(bolsa)* paper bag • **c. de dinamita** dynamite stick • **c. de fogueo** blank cartridge • **quemar el último c.** to play one's last card.
car·tu·li·na f. pasteboard, fine cardboard.
ca·sa f. house; *(residencia)* home; *(nobleza)* house; *(establecimiento)* firm ♦ **caérsele la c. encima** COLL. to be overwhelmed • **c. de altos** R.P. multistory building • **c. de beneficencia** *or* **de caridad** poorhouse • **c. de citas** house of assignment • **c. de cuna** foundling home • **c. de departamentos** S. AMER. apartment house •

c. de empeños pawnshop • **c. de expósitos** orphanage • **c. de la moneda** mint • **c. editorial** publishing house • **c. matriz** headquarters • **c. mortuoria** funeral home • **como Pedro por su c.** COLL. right at home • **echar la c. por la ventana** COLL. to go all out • **empezar la c. por el tejado** to put the cart before the horse • **en c.** at home, in • **estar de c.** to be casually dressed • **estar fuera de c.** to be out • **sentirse como en la c. de uno** to feel at home.

ca·sa·ca f. dress coat.

ca·sa·de·ro, a adj. of marrying age.

ca·sa·do, a I. adj. married • **recién casados** newlyweds II. m. PRINT. imposition.

ca·sa·mien·to m. marriage, wedding ♦ **c. a la fuerza** shotgun wedding.

ca·sar intr. to marry —tr. to marry (off); PRINT. to impose —reflex. to get married • **c. con** to get married to • **c. en segundas nupcias** to remarry • **c. por interés** to marry for money • **c. por detrás de la iglesia** to live together • **c. por poderes** to marry by proxy • **no c. con nadie** COLL. to maintain one's independence.

cas·ca·bel m. small bell • **poner el c. al gato** to bell the cat, stick one's neck out • **ser alegre como un c.** to be as happy as a lark • **serpiente de c.** rattlesnake.

cas·ca·be·le·ar intr. to jingle, tinkle.

cas·ca·do, a adj. I. cracked; COLL. decrepit II. f. waterfall.

cas·ca·jo m. (guijo) gravel; (nuez) nut; (trasto) rubbish; (fragmento) shard ♦ **estar hecho un c.** COLL. to be a wreck.

cas·ca·nue·ces m.inv. nutcracker.

cas·car §70 tr. (quebrar) to crack; COLL. (pegar) to beat —intr. COLL. to kick the bucket —reflex. to crack.

cás·ca·ra f. shell; (de fruta) skin; (de queso, fruta) rind; (de cereal) husk.

cas·ca·ri·lla I. f. (de cacao) cacao-leaf tea; (de metal) foil; AMER. quick-tempered person II. adj. AMER. quick-tempered.

cas·ca·rón m. (cáscara) thick peel or rind; (de huevo) eggshell ♦ **no haber salido aún del c.** to be inexperienced.

cas·ca·rra·bias m.f.inv. COLL. grouch.

cas·co m. MIL. helmet; (tonel) barrel; MARIT. hull; ZOOL. hoof; MECH. casing; COLL. (head) skull; (de sombrero) crown; (fragmento) shard ♦ **c. de buzo** diver's helmet ♦ pl. **ligero de c.** COLL. (persona) scatterbrained; (mujer) easy.

cas·co·te m. rubble, debris.

ca·se·río m. (pueblo) hamlet; (cortijo) country house or estate.

ca·se·ro, a I. adj. (de la casa) domestic; (de la familia) family <una reunión c. a family gathering>; (hecho en casa) homemade; (hogareño) home-loving ♦ **cocina c.** home cooking II. m.f. (dueño) owner, landlord; (administrador) caretaker —f. landlady.

ca·se·rón m. COLL. large dilapidated house.

ca·se·ta f. (casa) cottage; (casilla) booth.

ca·se·te m. or f. cassette, tape cartridge.

ca·si adv. almost, nearly ♦ **c. c.** COLL. very nearly • **c. nada** next to nothing • **c. nunca** hardly ever.

ca·si·lla f. (casa pequeña) cabin; (caseta) watchman's hut; (del mercado) stall; AMER. post-office box • **c. telefónica** AMER. telephone booth ♦ pl. **sacar a uno de sus c.** COLL. to infuriate • **salir uno de sus c.** COLL. to lose one's temper, fly off the handle.

ca·si·lle·ro m. filing cabinet with pigeonholes.

ca·si·no m. casino.

ca·so m. case; (acontecimiento) event; (circunstancia) circumstance ♦ **c. fortuito** unexpected event; LAW act of God • **c. perdido** lost cause • **el c. es que** that fact is that • **en c. de** in the event of • **en c. de que** in case • **en el mejor de los casos** at best • **en el peor de los casos** at worst • **en todo c.** in any case • **en último c.** as a last resort • **hablar al c.** to speak to the question • **hacer** or **venir al c.** COLL. to be relevant • **hacer c. a** to heed • **hacer c. de** to pay attention to • **hacer c. omiso de** to ignore • **no hacer** or **venir al c.** COLL. to be beside the point • **poner por c.** to take as an example • **verse en el c. de** to be compelled to.

ca·són m./**so·na** f. large house, mansion.

cas·pa f. dandruff.

¡cás·pi·ta! interj. COLL. gosh!, holy cow!

cas·que·te m. MIL. helmet; RELIG. skullcap; (de mujer) toque; MECH. cap ♦ **c. glaciar** ice cap.

cas·qui·va·no, a adj. COLL. featherbrained.

cas·set·te m. or f. cassette.

cas·ta·ña f. see **castaño, a.**

cas·ta·ña·zo m. COLL. punch, sock.

cas·ta·ñe·ta f. (chasquido) snap of the fingers; (instrumento) castanet.

cas·ta·ñe·te·ar tr. to play on the castanets; (los dedos) to snap —intr. to chatter.

cas·ta·ñe·te·o m. (de las castañuelas) clacking; (de los dedos) snapping; (de los dientes) chattering.

cas·ta·ño, a I. adj. chestnut, brown II. m. chestnut ♦ **pasar algo de c. obscuro** COLL. to go too far —f. BOT. chestnut; (puñetazo) punch • **c. del Brasil** or **de Pará** Brazil nut • **sacar las castañas del fuego** COLL. to have to face the music on behalf of someone else.

cas·ta·ñue·la f. castanet ♦ **estar como unas castañuelas** COLL. to be in a jolly mood.

cas·te·lla·ni·zar §04 tr. to make Spanish.

cas·te·lla·no m. Spanish; (señor) lord of a castle.

cas·ti·dad f. chastity.

cas·ti·gar §47 tr. to punish; (mortificar) to discipline; SPORT. to penalize.

cas·ti·go m. punishment; (mortificación) self-denial; SPORT. penalty ♦ **levantar el c.** to withdraw the sentence or penalty.

cas·ti·llo m. castle; MARIT. forecastle ♦ **c. de naipes** house of cards.

cas·ti·zo, a I. adj. (verdadero) genuine; (típico) typical; LIT. pure II. m.f. AMER. quadroon (offspring of a mestizo and a Spaniard).

cas·to, a I. adj. chaste II. f. (de personas) lineage; (de la sociedad) caste; ZOOL. breed ♦ **de c.** (animales) purebred; (personas) of breeding; (auténtico) genuine • **le viene de c.** it runs in the family.

cas·tor m. beaver.

cas·tra or **cas·tra·ción** f. castration.

cas·tra·do, a I. adj. castrated II. m. (hombre) eunuch; (caballo) gelding.

cas·trar tr. to castrate.

cas·tren·se adj. military.

ca·sual adj. chance, coincidental.

ca·sua·li·dad f. chance ♦ **dar la c. que** to just so happen that • **de c.** by chance • **por c.** by any chance.

ca·sual·men·te adv. by chance or accident.

ca·su·lla f. chasuble.
ca·ta·clis·mo m. cataclysm; FIG. upheaval.
ca·ta·cum·bas f.pl. catacombs.
ca·ta·dor, ·ra m.f. taster, sampler.
ca·ta·le·jo m. spyglass, small telescope.
ca·ta·lép·ti·co, a adj. & m.f. cataleptic.
ca·tá·li·sis f.inv. catalysis.
ca·ta·li·za·dor m. catalyst.
ca·ta·lo·ga·dor, ·ra I. adj. cataloguing **II.** m.f. cataloguer.
ca·ta·lo·gar §47 tr. to catalogue, list.
ca·tá·lo·go m. catalogue.
ca·ta·plas·ma f. poultice; FIG. bore.
¡ca·ta·plum!/plún! interj. crash!, bang!
ca·ta·pul·tar tr. to catapult.
ca·tar tr. to sample, taste
ca·ta·ra·ta f. waterfall; MED. cataract ♦ **las cataratas del Niágara** Niagara Falls.
ca·ta·rro m. cold, catarrh.
ca·tar·sis f.inv. catharsis.
ca·tár·ti·co, a adj. cathartic.
ca·tas·tro m. cadaster, official land register.
ca·tás·tro·fe f. catastrophe.
ca·tas·tró·fi·co, a adj. catastrophic.
ca·te·cis·mo m. catechism (book).
cá·te·dra f. (rango) professorship; (asiento) professor's chair; (aula) classroom; (asignatura) subject.
ca·te·dral f. cathedral.
ca·te·drá·ti·co m. university professor.
ca·te·go·rí·a f. category; (clase) type; FIG. standing ♦ **de c.** important ♦ **de primera c.** first-rate ♦ **de segunda c.** second-rate.
ca·te·gó·ri·co, a adj. categorical.
ca·te·que·sis f./**quis·mo** m. catechism.
ca·te·qui·zar §04 tr. to catechize; FIG. to convince.
ca·ter·va f. band, gang
ca·té·ter m. catheter.
ca·te·to m. leg of a right triangle.
ca·tin·ga f. AMER. foul smell, body odor.
ca·tó·li·co, a adj. & m.f. Catholic ♦ **no ser muy c.** to be or look suspicious.
ca·to·li·zar §04 tr. to catholicize.
ca·tor·ce adj. & m. fourteen(th).
ca·tre m. cot ♦ **c. de tijera** folding canvas cot.
cau·ce m. (lecho) riverbed; (acequia) ditch.
cau·cho m. (goma) rubber; (planta) rubber plant or tree.
cau·ción f. (precaución) caution; (advertencia) warning; (fianza) bail ♦ **bajo c.** on bail.
cau·dal I. adj. ZOOL. caudal; (caudaloso) carrying a lot of water **II.** m. (riqueza) wealth; (de agua) volume; (abundancia) abundance.
cau·da·lo·so, a adj. (río) deep; (persona) wealthy.
cau·di·llo m. leader; AMER. political boss.
cau·sa f. cause; (motivo) reason; LAW lawsuit ♦ **a or por c. de** because of.
cau·sal I. adj. causative **II.** f. reason.
cau·sa·li·dad f. causation; (origen) cause.
cau·san·te I. adj. causative **II.** m.f. originator; LAW person from whom a right is derived.
cau·sar tr. to cause; (provocar) to provoke.
cau·sa·ti·vo, a adj. causative.
caus·ti·ci·dad f. causticity; FIG. sarcasm.
cáus·ti·co, a adj. caustic; FIG. scathing.
cau·ta·men·te adv. cautiously.
cau·te·la f. caution.
cau·te·lo·so, a adj. cautious.
cau·te·rio m. (cauterización) cauterization; (instrumento) cauterizer.
cau·te·ri·za·dor, ·ra I. adj. cauterizing **II.** m.f. cauterizer.
cau·te·ri·zar §04 tr. to cauterize.
cau·ti·van·te adj. captivating.
cau·ti·var tr. (aprisionar) to capture; FIG. (interés, atención) to capture; (fascinar) to captivate.
cau·ti·ve·rio m./**vi·dad** f. captivity.
cau·ti·vo, a adj. & m.f. captive.
cau·to, a adj. cautious.
ca·va·dor, ·ra m.f. digger.
ca·var tr. to dig —intr. to delve into.
ca·ver·na f. cavern, cave; MED. cavity.
ca·ver·no·so, a adj. cavernous; FIG. deep, low.
ca·vial/viar m. caviar.
ca·vi·dad f. cavity.
ca·vi·la·ción f. pondering, rumination.
ca·vi·lar intr. to ponder, ruminate.
ca·vi·lo·so, a adj. COLL. mistrustful.
ca·ye·ra, yó see **caer**.
ca·yo m. MARIT. key, islet.
ca·za f. (cacería) hunt; (animales) game ♦ **andar or ir a c. de** COLL. to be on the lookout for ♦ **dar c.** to give chase ♦ **dar c. a** to hunt down ♦ **ir de c.** to go hunting —m. AVIA. fighter plane, fighter.
ca·za·be m. AMER., CUL. cassava bread.
ca·za·dor, ·ra I. adj. hunting; ZOOL. predatory **II.** m. hunter, huntsman ♦ **c. de alforja or de pieles** trapper ♦ **c. de cabezas** head-hunter —f. (mujer) hunter, huntress; (chaqueta) hunting jacket.
ca·zar §04 tr. to hunt; (coger) to catch; (conseguir) to land ♦ **c. al vuelo** COLL. to catch on quickly.
ca·zo m. CUL. (cucharón) ladle; (cacerola) saucepan; CARP. gluepot.
ca·zo·le·ta f. ARTIL. pan (of a musket); (de espada) hand guard; (de pipa) bowl.
ca·zón m. dogfish, small shark.
ca·zue·la f. casserole; (guisado) stew; THEAT. gallery.
ca·zu·rro, a adj. & m.f. reserved (person).
ce·ba·de·ra f. nose bag; MARIT. spritsail.
ce·ba·do, a I. adj. AMER., ZOOL. fattened **II.** f. BOT. barley ♦ **c. perlada** pearl barley.
ce·bar tr. (engordar) to fatten; (un fuego) to stoke; (un anzuelo) to bait; (fomentar) to fuel; ARM. to prime; MECH. to start up; R.P. to brew (maté) —reflex. (excitarse) to become excited; (entregarse) to devote oneself.
ce·bi·che m. AMER. marinated raw fish.
ce·bo m. (alimento) feed; (detonador) charge; (del anzuelo) bait; (aliciente) enticement; ARM. primer.
ce·bo·lla f. onion; (bulbo) bulb.
ce·bo·lle·ta f. BOT. chive.
ce·bo·lli·no m. (sementera) onion seed; BOT., CUL. chive(s).
ce·bra f. zebra.
ce·bú m. [pl. **-úes**] zebu, Asiatic ox.
ce·ca f. royal mint.
ce·ce·ar intr. to lisp.
ce·ce·o m. lisp.
ce·ci·na f. cured meat; ARG. jerky, charqui.
ce·ci·nar tr. to cure (meat).
ce·da·zo m. sieve ♦ **pasar por c.** to sift.
ce·der tr. to cede; (transferir) to transfer; SPORT. to pass —intr. to cede; (rendirse) to yield, give in or up; (disminuirse) to abate.
ce·di·lla f. cedilla.
ce·dro m. cedar.

cé·du·la f. document ♦ **c. de identidad** identification card *or* papers.

cé·fi·ro m. zephyr.

ce·gar §52 tr. to blind; *(tapar)* to clog —reflex. FIG. to be blinded.

ce·ga·to, a COLL. adj. & m.f. nearsighted (person).

ce·gue·dad/ra f. blindness.

ce·ja f. eyebrow; *(saliente)* projection; *(borde)* border; METEOROL. cloud cover; MUS. bridge ♦ **fruncir las cejas** to frown • **meterse algo entre c. y c.** COLL. to get something into one's head.

ce·jar intr. to back up; FIG. to slacken.

ce·la·da f. ambush; FIG. trap.

ce·la·dor, ·ra I. adj. watchful, vigilant II. m.f. *(en la escuela)* monitor; *(de prisión)* guard.

ce·lar tr. to comply with ♦ **c. por** *or* **sobre** to watch out for.

cel·da f. cell.

ce·le·bra·ción f. celebration; *(aclamación)* praise.

ce·le·bran·te adj. I. celebrating II. m. celebrant.

ce·le·brar tr. to celebrate; *(alabar)* to praise; *(venerar)* to venerate; *(una reunión)* to hold; *(un acuerdo)* to reach —reflex. *(cumpleaños)* to be *or* fall on; *(una reunión)* to take place.

cé·le·bre adj. celebrated, famous.

ce·le·bri·dad f. celebrity.

ce·le·ri·dad f. speed ♦ **con toda c.** as quickly as possible.

ce·les·te I. adj. sky-blue ♦ **cuerpo c.** heavenly body II. m. sky blue.

ce·les·tial adj. heavenly.

ce·les·ti·na f. procuress, madam.

ce·li·ba·to m. celibacy.

cé·li·be adj. & m.f. celibate.

ce·llis·ca f. sleet (storm).

ce·lo m. *(cuidado)* diligence; *(entusiasmo)* zeal; *(envidia)* jealousy ♦ **estar en c.** to be in heat ♦ pl. jealousy • **dar c.** to make jealous • **tener c.** to be jealous.

ce·lo·fán m. cellophane.

ce·lo·sí·a f. *(ventana)* lattice window; *(enrejado)* latticework.

ce·lo·so, a adj. *(con celos)* jealous; *(suspicaz)* suspicious; *(consciente)* zealous.

cé·lu·la f. cell.

ce·lu·li·tis f. cellulitis.

ce·lu·loi·de m. celluloid.

ce·lu·lo·so, a I. adj. cellulous, cellular II. f. cellulose.

ce·men·te·rio m. cemetery.

ce·men·to m. cement; *(hormigón)* concrete ♦ **c. armado** reinforced concrete.

ce·na f. dinner, supper ♦ **la santa** *or* **última C.** the Last Supper.

ce·na·gal m. swamp.

ce·nar intr. to have dinner *or* supper —tr. to have for dinner *or* supper.

cen·ce·rre·ar intr. *(sonar)* to clang bells; COLL. *(tocar mal)* to play out of tune; *(chirriar)* to squeak.

cen·ce·rro m. cowbell, bell.

ce·ni·ce·ro m. ashtray.

ce·ni·cien·to, a adj. ashen, ash-gray.

ce·nit m. zenith.

ce·ni·zo, a I. adj. ashen II. m. BOT. goosefoot; *(persona)* jinx ♦ **tener el c.** COLL. to have bad luck, be jinxed —f. *(polvo)* ash, ashes; *(restos)* ashes.

cen·so m. census; *(lista)* roll; *(arrendamiento)* rental ♦ **levantar el c.** to take a census.

cen·sor m. censor.

cen·su·ra f. censure; *(de expresión, arte)* censorship.

cen·su·rar tr. to censor; *(criticar)* to criticize.

cen·tau·ro m. centaur.

cen·ta·vo, a I. adj. hundredth II. m. AMER. cent.

cen·te·lla f. *(rayo)* flash; *(chispa)* spark.

cen·te·lle·an·te adj. sparkling.

cen·te·lle·ar/llar intr. *(fulgurar)* to sparkle; *(destellar)* to twinkle; *(chispear)* to flicker.

cen·te·na f. (one) hundred.

cen·te·nar m. (one) hundred ♦ **a centenares** by the hundreds.

cen·te·na·rio, a I. adj. *(viejo)* centenarian; *(aniversario)* centennial II. m.f. centenarian —m. centennial.

cen·te·no m. rye.

cen·té·si·mo, a I. adj. hundredth II. m. hundredth; PAN., URUG. centesimo (coin).

cen·tí·gra·do, a adj. centigrade.

cen·ti·gra·mo m. centigram.

cen·ti·li·tro m. centiliter.

cen·tí·me·tro m. centimeter.

cén·ti·mo, a I. adj. hundredth II. m. cent.

cen·ti·ne·la m.f. sentinel, sentry; FIG. lookout.

cen·to·lla f. spider crab.

cen·tra·do, a adj. centered; FIG. balanced.

cen·tral I. adj. central II. f. *(oficina)* headquarters ♦ **c. de correos** main post office.

cen·tra·li·za·ción f. centralization.

cen·tra·li·zar §04 tr. to centralize —reflex. to be *or* become centralized.

cen·trar tr. to center; *(determinar)* to find the center of; *(enfocar)* to focus; FIG. to aim.

cén·tri·co, a adj. central, centric.

cen·tri·fu·gar §47 tr. to centrifuge.

cen·trí·fu·go, a adj. centrifugal.

cen·trí·pe·to, a adj. centripetal.

cen·tro m. center; *(medio)* middle; *(núcleo)* core; *(ciudad)* downtown ♦ **c. comercial** shopping center • **c. de mesa** centerpiece • **c. turístico** tourist center

cén·tu·plo, a adj. & m. hundredfold.

ce·ñir §59 tr. *(atar)* to bind; *(ropa)* to be tight on; *(abreviar)* to condense —reflex. *(moderarse)* to limit oneself; *(ajustarse)* to adjust.

ce·ño m. frown ♦ **arrugar** *or* **fruncir el c.** to frown.

ce·pa f. *(tronco)* stump; *(de la vid)* rootstalk; *(vid)* vine ♦ **de buena c.** of good stock • **de pura c.** genuine.

ce·pi·llar tr. *(limpiar)* to brush; CARP. to plane.

ce·pi·llo m. brush; CARP. plane ♦ **c. de dientes** toothbrush • **c. para el pelo** hairbrush • **c. para el suelo** scrub brush • **c. para las uñas** nailbrush.

ce·po m. *(rama)* bough; *(del reo)* pillory ♦ **caer en el c.** to fall into the trap.

ce·ra f. wax; *(de los oídos)* earwax; *(de lustrar)* polish.

ce·rá·mi·co, a I. adj. ceramic II. f. ceramics.

cer·ba·ta·na f. blowpipe, blowgun.

cer·ca I. adv. nearby, close by ♦ **c. de** *(cercano a)* near, close to; *(alrededor de)* about • **de c.** closely II. f. fence ♦ **c. alambrada** wire fence • **c. viva** hedge.

cer·ca·do m. *(huerto)* garden; *(valla)* fence.

cer·ca·ní·a f. nearness, proximity ♦ pl. outskirts.

cer·ca·no, a adj. *(próximo)* close; *(vecino)*

neighboring; FIG. impending.

cer·car §70 tr. *(con cerco)* to fence in; *(rodear)* to surround; MIL. to besiege.

cer·ce·nar tr. *(cortar)* to cut; *(disminuir)* to cut down.

cer·cio·rar tr. to assure —reflex. to make sure.

cer·co m. *(círculo)* circle; *(borde)* edge; *(seto)* hedge; *(cercado)* enclosure; *(de un tonel)* hoop; TECH. rim; MIL. siege; ASTRON. corona.

cer·da f. bristle; ZOOL. sow.

cer·da·da f. COLL. dirty *or* lousy trick.

cer·do m. pig ♦ **carne de c.** pork.

ce·re·al adj. & m. cereal ♦ pl. cereals, grain.

ce·re·be·lo m. cerebellum.

ce·re·bro m. brain; FIG. brains.

ce·re·mo·nia f. ceremony; *(cumplido)* affected compliment ♦ **con c.** ceremoniously.

ce·re·mo·nial adj. & m. ceremonial.

ce·re·mo·nio·so, a adj. ceremonious.

ce·re·za f. cherry (fruit).

ce·re·zo m. cherry (tree).

ce·ri·lla f. *(vela)* wax taper; *(fósforo)* match; *(de los oídos)* earwax.

ce·rio m. cerium.

cer·ner §50 tr. to sift, sieve; FIG. to scan —reflex. FIG. to loom.

cer·ni·do m. *(acción)* sifting; *(harina)* sifted flour.

cer·ni·dor m. sieve.

cer·nir §25 tr. to sift, sieve.

ce·ro m. zero ♦ **ser un c. a la izquierda** COLL. to be totally useless.

ce·ro·te m. *(de zapatero)* cobbler's wax; COLL. *(miedo)* fear.

cer·qui·llo m. tonsure.

ce·rra·du·ra f. lock.

ce·rra·do, a adj. closed; *(nublado)* overcast; *(espeso)* thick; R.P. stubborn ♦ **a puerta c.** behind closed doors ♦ **c. de mollera** AMER., COLL. dense.

ce·rra·je·rí·a f. *(oficio)* locksmith's trade; *(taller)* locksmith shop.

ce·rra·je·ro m. locksmith.

ce·rrar §49 tr. to close (up), shut; *(con cerrojo)* to bolt; *(cercar)* to enclose; *(paquete, abertura)* to seal (up); *(negocio, fábrica)* to close down; *(llave, canilla)* to turn off; *(camino, acceso)* to block up; *(debate, polémica)* to conclude; *(cuenta bancaria)* to close out ♦ **c. con llave** to lock ♦ **c. los oídos a** to turn a deaf ear to ♦ **c. los ojos** to die ♦ **c. los puños** to clench one's fists —intr. to close, shut; *(la noche)* to fall —reflex. to close, shut; *(insistir)* to persist; MED. to close up; METEOROL. to cloud over.

ce·rra·zón f. *(cielo)* dark *or* overcast sky; *(torpeza)* denseness.

ce·rro m. hill; ZOOL. *(cuello)* neck; *(espinazo)* backbone.

ce·rro·jo m. bolt, latch.

cer·ta·men m. contest, competition.

cer·te·ro, a adj. accurate, skillful.

cer·te·za/ti·dum·bre f. certainty, certitude.

cer·ti·fi·ca·ción f. certification; *(certificado)* certificate.

cer·ti·fi·ca·do, a I. adj. certified; *(cartas)* registered II. m. certificate ♦ **c. de acciones** COM. stock certificate ♦ **c. de defunción** death certificate.

cer·ti·fi·car §70 tr. *(verificar)* to certify; *(cartas)* to register.

cer·ti·tud f. certainty, certitude.

ce·ru·men m. earwax.

cer·ve·ce·rí·a f. *(fábrica)* brewery; *(taberna)* bar, pub.

cer·ve·za f. beer, ale ♦ **c. de barril** draft beer ♦ **c. negra** dark beer.

cer·vi·cal adj. cervical.

cer·viz f. cervix, nape (of the neck) ♦ **de dura c.** stubborn, headstrong ♦ **doblar** *or* **bajar la c.** to humble oneself.

ce·sa·ción f. cessation, discontinuance.

ce·san·te adj. & m.f. unemployed (person) ♦ **dejar c.** to dismiss.

ce·san·tí·a f. suspension; *(desempleo)* unemployment.

ce·sar intr. to end, stop ♦ **sin c.** unceasingly.

ce·sá·re·a adj. & f. Caesarean section.

ce·se m. *(suspensión)* cessation; *(revocación)* dismissal ♦ **c. de fuego** *or* **de hostilidades** cease-fire.

ce·sio m. cesium.

ce·sión f. cession.

ce·sio·na·rio, a m.f. cessionary, transferee.

ce·sio·nis·ta m.f. transferor, assignor.

cés·ped m. *(prado)* lawn, grass; *(gallón)* sod; SPORT. field.

ces·ta f. basket; *(cestada)* basketful; *(cochecillo)* wicker cart; *(pala)* jai alai racket; *(baloncesto)* basket ♦ **c. de costura** sewing basket ♦ **c. para papeles** wastepaper basket.

ces·to m. basket ♦ **c. de** *or* **para papeles** wastepaper basket.

ce·tá·ce·o, a adj. & m. cetacean.

ce·tri·no, a adj. sallow, olive.

ce·tro m. scepter; RELIG. staff.

cha·ba·ca·ne·ar intr. AMER. to behave in a coarse *or* crude way.

cha·ba·ca·ne·rí·a f. *(falta de gusto)* tastelessness; *(grosería)* crude thing.

cha·ba·ca·no, a adj. *(sin gusto)* tasteless; *(grosero)* crude; *(mal hecho)* shoddy.

cha·cal m. jackal.

cha·ca·re·ro, a m.f. AMER. farmer, peasant —f. R.P. peasant dance.

cha·co·ta f. *(bulla)* merriment, fun; *(burla)* ridicule, making fun ♦ **estar de ch.** to be in a joking mood ♦ **hacer ch. de** to ridicule ♦ **tomar a ch.** *(burlarse de)* to make fun of; *(tomar a broma)* to take as a joke.

cha·co·te·ar intr. to kid.

cha·co·te·o m. joking, kidding.

cha·co·te·ro, a m.f. kidder.

cha·cra f. AMER. farm.

chá·cha·ra f. COLL. chatter ♦ **estar de ch.** to make small talk.

cha·cha·re·ar intr. COLL. *(charlar)* to chatter.

cha·fa·lo·ní·a f. scrap silver *or* gold.

chai·ra f. shoemaker's knife.

cha·já m. ARG. crested screamer.

chal m. shawl.

cha·la f. AMER. corn husk *or* shuck.

cha·lán, a·na I. adj. horse-trading II. m.f. *(comerciante)* horse dealer *or* trader —m. AMER. horse trainer —f. barge, flat-bottomed boat.

cha·lar tr. to drive mad *or* crazy —reflex. to fall head over heels in love.

cha·le·co m. vest ♦ **ch. de fuerza** AMER. straitjacket ♦ **ch. salvavidas** life jacket.

cha·let m. [pl. **s**] chalet; *(de playa)* beach house; *(de lujo)* villa.

cha·li·na f. *(corbata)* cravat; AMER. *(chal)* narrow shawl.

cha·lo·te m. shallot.

cha·lu·pa f. boat; AMER. small canoe.

cha·ma·co, a m.f. CARIB., MEX. kid.
cham·be·lán m. chamberlain.
cham·ber·go m. AMER. broad-brimmed soft hat.
cham·be·ro, a m.f. MEX. itinerant worker.
cham·bón, o·na COLL. I. adj. clumsy II. m.f. bungler.
cham·bo·na·da f. AMER. bungle.
cham·bo·ne·ar intr. AMER. to bungle.
cha·mi·za f. BOT. chamiso; (*leña*) brushwood.
cha·mi·zar §04 tr. AMER. to thatch (with chamiso).
cha·mi·zo m. (*leño quemado*) half-burnt log; (*choza*) thatched hut; COLL. (*garito*) joint.
cha·mo·rro, a adj. shorn, clipped.
cham·pán/pa·ña m. champagne.
cham·pi·ñón m. mushroom, champignon.
cham·pú m. [pl. (e)s] shampoo.
cham·pu·rra·do m. AMER. hodgepodge, mess.
cham·pu·rrar tr. COLL. to mix (drinks).
cham·pu·rro m. COLL. mixed drink.
cha·mu·llar intr. AMER., SL. to talk, speak.
cha·mus·car §70 tr. (*quemar*) to scorch; MEX. to sell cheaply —reflex. (*quemarse*) to get singed *or* scorched.
cha·mus·qui·na f. (*acción*) scorching; (*riña*) quarrel ♦ **oler a ch.** to look like trouble.
chan·ca·do·ra f. AMER., MIN. crusher, grinder.
chan·car §70 tr. AMER. to crush, grind.
chan·ce m. chance.
chan·ce·ar intr. & reflex. to joke.
chan·ci·ller m. var. of **canciller.**
chan·ci·lle·rí·a f. chancery.
chan·cle·ta m.f. COLL. good-for-nothing —f. (*zapatilla*) slipper; AMER., COLL. baby girl ♦ **largar la ch.** COLL. to let one's hair down.
chan·cle·ta·zo m. blow with a slipper.
chan·cle·te·ar intr. to drag around (in slippers).
chan·cle·te·o m. shuffle of slippers.
chan·clo m. (*zueco*) clog; (*zapato*) galosh.
chan·cro m. chancre.
chan·cha·da f. AMER., COLL. dirty trick; (*porquería*) mess.
chan·cho, a I. adj. AMER. dirty, filthy II. m. pig, hog ♦ **hacerse un ch. rengo** AMER. to pretend not to notice • **quedar como ch.** AMER. to let someone down • **ser como chanchos** AMER. to be close friends —f. AMER. sow.
chan·chu·lle·ro, a m.f. COLL. crook, swindler.
chan·chu·llo m. COLL. crooked deal ♦ pl. **andar en ch.** to be involved in swindles.
chan·ga·dor m. ARG., BOL. porter.
chan·gar §47 intr. (*picholear*) to do odd jobs; ARG., BOL. to work as a porter.
chan·go, a I. adj. CARIB., MEX. playful II. m.f. CARIB., MEX. (*bromista*) prankster; MEX. youngster —m. R.P. youngster.
chan·ta·je m. blackmail.
chan·ta·jis·ta m.f. blackmailer.
chan·tar tr. (*clavar*) to drive in; COLL. (*cantárselas*) to tell to someone's face.
chan·ti·llí m. whipped cream.
chan·za f. joke, jest ♦ **de** *or* **en ch.** in fun • **estar de ch.** to be joking ♦ pl. **entre ch. y veras** half in fun and half in earnest • **gastar ch.** to crack jokes.
cha·pa f. (*de metal, madera*) sheet; AMER., AUTO. license plate ♦ **ch. de estarcir** stencil • **ch. metálica** sheet metal.
cha·pa·do, a adj. (*de metal*) plated; (*de ma-*

dera) veneered ♦ **ch. a la antigua** old-fashioned.
cha·pa·le·ar intr. to splash.
cha·pa·le·o m. splash; (*acción*) splashing.
cha·pa·po·te m. asphalt.
cha·par tr. (*con metal*) to plate; (*con madera*) to veneer; (*encajar*) to come out with; AMER., SL. (*agarrar*) to grasp; (*apresar*) to catch.
cha·pa·rral m. thicket, chaparral.
cha·pa·rro, a I. adj. short and thick II. m. dwarf *or* scrub oak; (*persona*) short and chubby man; MEX. (*niño*) kid.
cha·pa·rrón m. downpour; FIG. shower.
cha·pe·ar tr. (*con metal*) to plate; (*con madera*) to veneer; AMER. to clear (the land).
cha·pis·ta m. sheet-metal worker; AUTO. body repairman.
cha·po·dar tr. to prune; FIG. to trim.
cha·po·te·ar tr. to dampen —intr. to splash.
cha·po·te·o m. splash.
cha·pu·ce·ar tr. COLL. (*chafallar*) to botch, bungle; MEX. (*engañar*) to deceive.
cha·pu·ce·rí·a f. COLL. sloppy job.
cha·pu·ce·ro, a I. COLL. adj. sloppy II. m.f. careless worker.
cha·puz m. (*obra*) odd job; (*acción*) ducking; (*chapucería*) botched job.
cha·pu·za f. COLL. botched job.
cha·pu·zón m. dive ♦ **darse un ch.** to go for a swim.
cha·qué/quet m. morning coat.
cha·que·ta f. jacket ♦ **ch. de fumar** smoking jacket • **ch. salvavidas** life jacket.
cha·que·ti·lla f. short jacket, bolero.
cha·que·tón m. overcoat.
cha·ra·da f. charade.
cha·ra·mus·ca f. MEX. candy twist; AMER. (*leña*) brushwood; CUBA, P. RICO noise.
cha·ran·ga f. brass band.
cha·ran·go m. AMER. small five-stringed Andean guitar.
cha·ra·pe m. MEX. spicy fermented beverage.
char·ca f. pond, pool.
char·co m. puddle, pool.
char·la f. (*conversación*) chat; (*conferencia*) talk.
char·la·dor, ·ra I. adj. talkative II. m.f. chatterbox.
char·lar intr. COLL. (*parlotear*) to chatter; (*hablar*) to chat.
char·la·tán, a·na I. adj. (*parlanchín*) talkative; (*chismoso*) gossipy II. m.f. (*parlanchín*) chatterbox; (*murmurador*) gossip; (*curandero*) quack.
char·la·ta·ne·ar intr. to chatter.
char·la·ta·ne·rí·a f. talkativeness.
char·lis·ta m.f. lecturer.
char·io·te·ar intr. COLL. to chatter.
cha·rol m. (*barniz*) lacquer; (*cuero*) patent leather; AMER. (*bandeja*) tray.
cha·ro·la·do, a adj. (*barnizado*) varnished; (*lustroso*) shiny.
cha·ro·lar tr. to lacquer.
char·que m. ARG., MEX. jerky.
char·que·ar tr. AMER. to dry, cure.
char·qui m. AMER. jerky.
cha·rre·te·ra f. epaulet(te).
cha·rro, a I. adj. (*tosco*) unsophisticated; COLL. (*de mal gusto*) gaudy; AMER. (*diestro*) skilled in horsemanship; MEX. (*pintoresco*) picturesque II. m. MEX. cowboy.
cha·rrú·a f. small tugboat.

¡chas! interj. pow!, wham!
chas·ca f. kindling.
chas·car §70 intr. (la madera) to crack; (la lengua) to click —tr. to crunch.
chas·co m. (burla) trick; (decepción) disappointment.
cha·sis m.inv. chassis.
chas·que·ar[1] tr. (burlarse) to play a joke on; (decepcionar) to disappoint.
chas·que·ar[2] tr. (látigo) to crack; (dedos) to snap —intr. to crackle.
chas·qui m. AMER. (mensajero) messenger; (correo) mail.
chas·qui·do m. crack, snap.
cha·ta·rra f. scrap iron.
cha·ta·rre·rí·a f. junk yard.
cha·to, a I. adj. (de nariz) flat-nosed; (la nariz) flat; (bajo) low; (llano) shallow; AMER., COLL. ordinary ♦ **dejar ch.** AMER. to defeat; MEX. to swindle ♦ **quedarse ch.** AMER. to fail II. m. (querido) darling; (vaso) small wine glass —f. (embarcación) barge; (bacín) bedpan; AMER. (carro) flatcar; COLL. (querida) darling.
cha·tu·ra f. flatness.
¡chau! interj. AMER. goodbye, ciao.
chau·cha f. S. AMER. (patata) new potato; (dinero) money; ARG. (judía) string bean.
chau·vi·nis·ta I. adj. chauvinistic II. m.f. chauvinist.
cha·val, ·la I. adj. young II. m. youngster —f. young girl.
cha·ve·ta f. (clavija) key; COLL. (chiflado) nut ♦ **perder la ch.** COLL. to go off one's rocker.
¡che! interj. AMER. hey!, listen!
che·lo I. m. cello II. adj. MEX. blond.
che·que m. check, cheque (G.B.) ♦ **ch. de viajero** travelers check.
che·que·ar tr. AMER. (inspeccionar) to check, inspect; (cotejar) to compare; MED. to give a checkup to.
che·que·o m. AMER. check; MED. checkup.
che·que·ra f./ro m. checkbook.
chi·bo·lo m. AMER. swelling, bump.
chic adj. chic, stylish.
chi·ca·na f. AMER. chicanery, trickery.
chi·ca·ne·ar intr. AMER. to engage in chicanery.
chi·ca·no, a adj. & m.f. Chicano, Mexican-American.
chi·cle m. (de mascar) chewing gum; (gomorresina) chicle; MEX. (suciedad) filth.
chi·co, a I. adj. small, little II. m. boy —f. girl; (criada) maid.
chi·co·ria f. chicory.
chi·co·ta·zo m. AMER. whiplash.
chi·co·te m. AMER. whip; MARIT. end of a rope; COLL. (cigarro) cigar.
chi·cha f. (bebida) chicha; COLL. (carne) meat ♦ **estar ch.** MEX. to be pleasant or amusing.
chí·cha·ro m. pea; COL., COLL. bad cigar.
chi·cha·rra f. cicada; COLL. (persona) chatterbox; SP. nuisance ♦ **hablar como una ch.** to be a real chatterbox.
chi·cha·rre·ro m. hot place, oven.
chi·cha·rro m. ICHTH. horse mackerel; (chicharrón) fried pork rind.
chi·cha·rrón m. (cerdo) crisp pork rind; FIG. overcooked or burned food; COLL. (persona) very tanned person.
chi·che I. m. AMER. (persona) elegant person; (lugar) well-decorated place; ARG. (juguete) toy; ARG., CHILE (alhaja) trinket, bauble;

MEX. (nodriza) wet nurse II. adj. C. AMER. easy, comfortable.
chi·chón m. bump (on the head).
chi·cho·ne·ar intr. S. AMER., COLL. to make or play jokes.
chi·cho·ta f. AMER. bump; (legumbre) chickpea.
chi·fla f. (acción) whistling; (silbato) whistle; (cuchillo) paring knife; MEX. bad mood.
chi·fla·do, a adj. COLL. (loco) nuts; (enamorado) in love.
chi·fla·du·ra f. COLL. (locura) craziness; (silbido) whistling.
chi·flar intr. to whistle; MEX., ORNITH. to sing —tr. to boo —reflex. (volverse loco) to go crazy; (enamorarse) to fall in love; COLL. (gustar) to be crazy about.
chi·fle m. (silbato) whistle; (reclamo) bird call; (para la pólvora) powder horn.
chi·fli·do m. whistle.
chi·hua·hua m. chihuahua.
chi·le m. AMER. pepper, chili; C. AMER. (patraña) hoax.
chi·lla·do m. CARP. roof made of laths and shingles.
chi·lla·dor, ·ra I. adj. screaming, shrieking II. m.f. screamer.
chi·llar intr. (gritar) to shriek; (chirriar) to squeak; (destacarse) to be loud —reflex. AMER. to take offense.
chi·lli·do m. (grito) shriek; (chirrido) squeak.
chi·llón, o·na I. adj. COLL. (gritón) shrieking; (estridente) loud II. m.f. screamer.
chi·me·ne·a f. chimney; (hogar) fireplace, hearth; INDUS. smokestack; MARIT. stack ♦ **caerle a uno una cosa por la ch.** COLL. to receive a windfall ♦ **ch. de aire** air shaft.
chim·pan·cé m. chimpanzee.
chi·na f. see chino, a.
chi·nam·pa f. MEX. floating garden near Mexico City.
chin·char tr. (molestar) to pester; (causar molestia) to bother —reflex. to get upset.
chin·che f. bedbug; (clavito) thumbtack ♦ **morir como chinches** to drop like flies —m.f. COLL. boring person.
chin·che·ta f. thumbtack.
chin·chi·lla f. chinchilla.
chin·cho·rro m. (red) sweep net; (bote de remos) dinghy; MEX. small herd.
chin·chu·do, a adj. ARG. hot-tempered.
chi·ne·la f. (babucha) slipper; (chanclo) clog.
chin·ga f. AMER. (barato) fee paid by gamblers; ZOOL. skunk; C. AMER. cigar butt.
chin·gar §47 tr. C. RICA to cut the tail off of; MEX., SALV. to harass —reflex. AMER. (fracasar) to be a flop.
chin·go, a adj. AMER. (corto) ill-fitting; (desnudo) without a stitch; (rabón) tailless; C. AMER. (mocho) blunt.
chi·no, a I. adj. AMER. of mixed ancestry; MEX. kinky, curly II. m.f. AMER. (mestizo) person of mixed ancestry; (niño) kid; (criado) servant; (cariño) honey; (campesino) peasant ♦ **trabajar como un ch.** COLL. to work like a slave —f. (india) Indian woman; (sirvienta) maid; (niñera) nanny; (tejido) Chinese silk.
chi·que·ro m. (pocilga) pigsty; TAUR. bullpen.
chi·qui·lín m. AMER., COLL. small boy.
chi·qui·lla·da f. childish act.
chi·qui·llo, a I. adj. small II. m.f. child.
chi·qui·tín, i·na I. adj. tiny II. m.f. tot.

chi·qui·to, a I. adj. tiny II. m.f. *(niño)* child —m. R.P. ♦ **esperar un ch.** COLL. to wait just a minute.

chi·ri·bi·ta f. spark ♦ pl. spots before the eyes • **echar ch.** COLL. to be fuming.

chi·ri·bi·til m. *(desván)* garret, attic; COLL. *(cuarto)* tiny room.

chi·ri·go·ta f. COLL. joke, quip.

chi·ri·go·te·ar intr. COLL. to joke, banter.

chi·ri·go·te·ro, a I. adj. joking, bantering II. m.f. joker.

chi·rim·bo·lo m. COLL. gadget ♦ pl. COLL. gear.

chi·ri·mo·ya f. cherimoya.

chi·ri·mo·yo m. cherimoya tree.

chi·ri·pa f. stroke of luck ♦ **de** or **por ch.** COLL. by a fluke.

chi·ri·pá m. R.P. gaucho's trousers.

chir·lar intr. COLL. to chatter, jabber.

chir·le I. adj. COLL. tasteless II. m. dung.

chir·lo m. *(herida)* gash (on face); *(cicatriz)* scar.

chi·ro·la f. AMER. *(moneda)* coin of little value; *(cárcel)* slammer.

chi·rre·ar intr. var. of **chirriar**.

chi·rria·dor, ·ra/rrian·te adj. *(un gozne)* creaking; *(al freír)* sizzling; *(un pájaro)* chirping; COLL. *(una voz)* shrill.

chi·rriar §30 intr. *(rechinar)* to squeak; *(al freír)* to sizzle; ORNITH. to screech; COLL. *(cantar)* to sing out of tune.

chi·rri·do m. *(ruido)* screeching; *(grito)* shriek; *(al freír)* sizzle.

¡chis! interj. sh!, hush!

chis·ca·rra f. soft crumbly limestone.

chis·cón m. SL. garret, closet (small room).

chis·chás m. clash (of swords).

chis·ga·ra·bís m. COLL. busybody, meddler.

chis·gue·te m. COLL. *(trago)* swig, drink; *(chorro)* jet, spurt; AMER., BOT. rubber tree.

chis·mar intr. var. of **chismear**.

chis·me m. *(murmuración)* gossip; COLL. *(baratija)* trinket.

chis·me·ar intr. to gossip.

chis·me·rí·a f. gossip.

chis·me·ro, a I. adj. gossiping, tattling II. m.f. gossipmonger.

chis·mo·gra·fí·a f. COLL. *(afición)* fondness for gossip; *(cuento)* gossiping.

chis·mo·rre·ar intr. to gossip.

chis·mo·so, a I. adj. gossipy II. m.f. gossipmonger.

chis·pa I. f. *(chiribita)* spark; *(relámpago)* flash; *(poquito)* little bit; *(de lluvia)* sprinkle; *(viveza)* wit; COLL. *(borrachera)* drunkenness ♦ **ser una ch.** or **tener mucha ch.** to be a live wire ♦ pl. **dar ch.** to be bright • **echar ch.** to fume (with anger) • **ni ch.** not the least bit II. adj. MEX. amusing, funny.

chis·par tr. MEX. to take out —reflex. COLL. to get drunk or tipsy.

chis·pa·zo m. spark.

chis·pe·ar intr. *(destellar)* to spark; *(relucir)* to sparkle; *(lloviznar)* to drizzle; *(brillar)* to be brilliant —reflex. AMER. to get tipsy.

chis·po·rro·te·ar intr. to spark, crackle.

chis·po·rro·te·o m. COLL. *(del aceite)* sizzling; *(de la leña)* crackling.

¡chist! interj. sh!, hush!

chis·tar intr. to speak ♦ **sin ch.** COLL. without a word.

chis·te m. *(cuento)* joke; *(prank)* broma ♦ **caer en el ch.** COLL. to get the joke • **ch. verde** dirty or off-color joke • **dar en el ch.** to guess the trouble • **hacer ch. de** to make a joke of.

chis·te·ra f. *(de pescador)* fisherman's basket; COLL. *(sombrero)* top hat.

chis·ti·do m. whistle.

chis·to·so, a adj. funny.

chi·ta f. ANAT. anklebone; *(juego)* game of throwing stones at an upright bone ♦ **a la ch. callando** on the quiet or sly • **dar en la ch.** to hit the nail on the head.

chi·tar intr. var. of **chistar**.

¡chi·to! interj. hush!, sh!

¡chi·tón! interj. COLL. hush!, quiet!

chi·va f. AMER. *(barba)* goatee; C. AMER. *(manta)* blanket ♦ pl. MEX. odds and ends.

chi·var tr. COLL. *(fastidiar)* to annoy; *(delatar)* to denounce —reflex. COLL. to get annoyed.

chi·va·te·o m. COLL. *(delación)* informing; AMER. *(gritería)* shouting.

chi·va·to, a m.f. ZOOL. kid; COLL. *(delator)* informer, stool pigeon.

chi·vo, a m.f. ZOOL. kid ♦ **ch. expiatorio** scapegoat.

cho·can·te adj. *(desagradable)* offensive; MEX. annoying.

cho·car §70 intr. *(topar)* to crash; *(pelear)* to clash; *(disgustar)* to offend ♦ **ch. los cinco** COLL. to shake hands • **ch. de frente** to hit head on.

cho·ca·rre·ar intr. to tell dirty jokes.

cho·ca·rre·rí·a f. dirty joke.

cho·ca·rre·ro, a I. adj. coarse II. m.f. teller of dirty jokes.

cho·clo m. *(chanclo)* clog; AMER. *(maíz)* ear of corn; *(carga)* burden; PERU *(conjunto)* bunch, group; ARG. *(dificultad)* difficulty ♦ **meter el ch.** MEX. to make a mistake.

cho·co I. m. small cuttlefish; CHILE, PERU spaniel; AMER. disabled person; AUTO. brake shoe II. adj. AMER. disabled.

cho·co·la·te I. adj. chocolate II. m. chocolate; *(bebida)* hot chocolate, cocoa.

cho·co·la·te·rí·a f. *(fábrica)* chocolate factory; *(tienda)* chocolate shop.

cho·co·la·te·ro, a I. m.f. *(fabricante)* chocolate maker; *(vendedor)* chocolate seller II. adj. fond of chocolate.

cho·cha·per·diz f. woodcock.

cho·che·ar/char intr. to be senile.

cho·che·ra/chez f. *(senilidad)* senility; COLL. *(admiración)* fondness, doting.

cho·cho, a adj. *(caduco)* senile; COLL. *(lelo)* doting.

chó·fer or **cho·fer** m. chauffeur.

cho·lo, a adj. & m.f. half-breed, mestizo.

chom·ba/pa f. jersey, sweater.

chon·go m. GUAT. curl, lock (of hair); MEX. *(moño)* bun, chignon; *(dulce)* sweet, dessert; COLL. *(broma)* joke; PERU *(querido)* darling.

cho·po m. black poplar; COLL. *(fusil)* rifle, gun.

cho·que m. *(colisión)* collision; *(impacto)* impact; *(pelea)* clash; *(disputa)* dispute; ELEC., MED. shock ♦ **ch. de frente** head-on collision.

cho·ri·ce·rí·a f. sausage shop.

cho·ri·ce·ro, a m.f. *(fabricante)* sausage maker; *(vendedor)* sausage seller; SP. frontier dweller.

cho·ri·zo m. sausage.

chor·li·to m. plover; *(tonto)* scatterbrain.

cho·rre·a·du·ra f. *(chorrea)* dripping; *(mancha)* stain.

cho·rre·ar intr. *(fluir)* to gush; *(gotear)* to

trickle —tr. *(derramar)* to pour; R.P. to steal —reflex. to steal.

cho·rre·ra f. *(canal)* gully; *(serie)* string.

cho·rro m. *(de líquido)* spout; *(de luz)* flood; R.P., COLL. thief ♦ **pl. a ch.** abundantly • **llover a ch.** to rain cats and dogs • **salir a ch.** to gush out.

cho·ta·ca·bras m.pl. nightjar, goatsucker.

cho·tis m. schottische (dance).

cho·to m. *(cabrito)* kid; *(ternero)* calf.

cho·va f. chough, jackdaw.

cho·za f. hut, shack.

chu·bas·co m. *(lluvia)* downpour; *(contratiempo)* setback.

chú·ca·ro, a adj. AMER. *(salvaje)* wild; *(huraño)* shy.

chu·ce·ar tr. AMER. to wound with a pike *or* lance.

chu·che·ar intr. *(cazar)* to trap, snare; *(cuchichear)* to whisper.

chu·che·rí·a f. trinket.

chu·cho, a m. COLL. *(perro)* dog; AMER. *(escalofrío)* shivers; ARG. *(susto)* fright —f. body odor.

chue·co, a adj. *(patizambo)* bowlegged; *(torcido)* crooked.

chu·la·da f. *(acción)* coarse action; COLL. *(gracia)* self-assurance; *(jactancia)* showing off.

chu·le·ar tr. MEX. to court, flirt with; COLL. to play a joke on —reflex. *(burlarse)* to make fun of, tease; COLL. *(presumir)* to show off.

chu·le·rí·a f. COLL. wit, verve.

chu·le·ta f. *(carne)* cutlet; COLL. *(de estudiantes)* cheat sheet, crib.

chu·lo, a I. adj. *(picaresco)* roguish; *(chulesco)* showy; *(descarado)* impudent **II.** m.f. SP. lower-class Madrilenian —m. *(rufián)* rascal; *(alcahuete)* pimp.

chum·bar tr. R.P. to bark.

chu·ño m. AMER. potato starch.

chu·pa·ci·rios m.inv. COLL. sanctimonious person.

chu·pa·do, a I. adj. COLL. emaciated; ARG., CHILE, CUBA drunk **II.** f. sucking.

chu·pa·dor, ·ra I. adj. sucking **II.** m. *(chupete)* pacifier; *(de biberón)* nipple —m.f. boozer.

chu·par tr. to suck; *(absorber)* to soak up; AMER. *(fumar)* to smoke; COLL. *(extraer)* to bleed —intr. to suck; AMER. *(beber)* to drink —reflex. to become emaciated, waste away ♦ **ch. el dedo** COLL. to be naive • **ch. los dedos** COLL. to lick one's fingers • **¡chúpate esa!** COLL. take that!

chu·pa·tin·tas m.inv. COLL. pencil-pusher.

chu·pe·te m. *(de niños)* pacifier; *(de mamadera)* nipple; AMER. *(dulce)* lollipop.

chu·pe·te·ar intr. to suck, take little licks.

chu·pón, o·na I. adj. sucking **II.** m.f leech —m. COLL. *(beso)* hickey; MIN. piston, plunger; AMER. *(biberón)* baby bottle; *(chupete)* pacifier; *(de mamadera)* nipple.

chur·dón m. raspberry jam.

chu·rras·co m. AMER. grilled *or* broiled steak.

chu·rras·que·ar intr. AMER. to have a barbecue.

chu·rre m. *(pringue)* thick grease *or* fat; COLL. *(suciedad)* filth.

chu·rre·ro, a m.f. *(fabricante)* fritter maker; *(vendedor)* fritter seller.

chu·rre·te m. stain.

chu·rrien·to, a adj. grimy.

chu·rro, a I. adj. coarse **II.** m. CUL. fritter; COLL. *(chapuza)* botch.

chu·rru·lle·ro, a adj. & m.f. talkative (person).

chu·rrus·car·se §70 reflex. to start to burn.

chu·rrus·co m. burnt toast.

chu·rum·bel m. COLL. kid, youngster.

chu·ru·mo m. COLL. juice.

chus·ca·da f. joke, witticism.

chus·ma f. *(galeotes)* crew of galley slaves; *(gentuza)* riffraff; COLL. *(multitud)* crowd.

chu·zo m. *(bastón)* stick; AMER. *(látigo)* horsewhip; *(aguijada)* goad; *(pica)* pike.

cia·nu·ro m. cyanide.

ciá·ti·co, a I. adj. sciatic **II.** f. sciatica, lumbago.

ci·be·li·na f. sable.

ci·ber·né·ti·ca f. cybernetics.

cí·bo·lo m. bison.

ci·ca·triz f. scar.

ci·ca·tri·za·ción f. healing.

ci·ca·tri·zar §04 tr. & intr. to heal.

ci·ce·ro·ne m. guide, cicerone.

cí·cli·co, a adj. cyclical, cyclic.

ci·clis·ta I. adj. cycling, cycle **II.** m.f. cyclist.

ci·clo m. cycle.

ci·clo·mo·tor m. moped, motorbike.

ci·clón m. cyclone ♦ **entrar como un c.** to burst in.

ci·cu·ta f. hemlock.

cid m. FIG. brave *or* valiant man.

cie·go, a adj. & m.f. blind (person) ♦ **c. como un topo** blind as a bat • **quedar c.** to go blind ♦ **pl. a c.** blindly; FIG. *(sin reflexión)* thoughtlessly, carelessly • **andar a c.** to grope one's way.

cie·go, gue see cegar.

cie·lo m. sky; *(atmósfera)* atmosphere; *(paraíso)* heaven; *(la providencia)* Heaven; COLL. *(querido)* darling ♦ **a c. abierto** *or* **raso** in the open air • **caído** *or* **llovido del c.** COLL. heavensent • **cerrarse el c.** to cloud up • **c. raso** ceiling • **escupir al c.** to spit into the wind • **venirse el c. abajo** COLL. to rain cats and dogs ♦ **pl. ¡c.!** good heavens! • **poner por los c.** to praise to the skies.

ciem·piés m.inv. centipede.

cien adj. contr. of **ciento**.

cié·na·ga f. swamp, marsh.

cien·cia f. science; *(erudición)* knowledge; *(habilidad)* skill ♦ **a** *or* **de c. cierta** for certain.

cie·no m. muck.

cien·tí·fi·co, a I. adj. scientific **II.** m.f. scientist.

cien·to adj. & m. one hundred, a hundred ♦ **c. por c.** one hundred per cent • **por c.** per cent.

cier·na, no see **cerner** *or* **cernir**.

cier·ne m. ♦ **en c.** in blossom; FIG. just beginning.

cie·rre m. *(acción)* closing; *(clausura)* shut down; *(cremallera)* zipper; JOURN. deadline ♦ **c. de cremallera** zipper • **c. patronal** R.P. lockout • **c. relámpago** zipper.

cie·rre, rro see **cerrar**.

cier·to, a I. adj. certain; *(determinado)* definite; *(verdadero)* true; *(alguno)* some **II.** adv. certainly ♦ **de c.** certainly • **estar en lo c.** to be right • **lo c. es que** the fact is that • **por c.** *(a propósito)* incidentally; *(ciertamente)* certainly • **por c. que** of course.

cier·vo m. deer, stag.

ci·fra f. *(número)* digit; *(cantidad)* quantity; *(total)* sum (total); *(clave)* cipher; *(monograma)* monogram; *(síntesis)* synthesis.

ci·frar tr. to encode ♦ **c. en** FIG. to place in.

ci·ga·rra f. cicada.
ci·ga·rre·ra f. cigar box *or* case.
ci·ga·rre·rí·a f. AMER. tobacco *or* smoke shop.
ci·ga·rri·llo m. cigarette.
ci·ga·rro m. cigar.
ci·go·to m. zygote, fertilized egg.
ci·güe·ña f. stork.
ci·güe·ñal m. winch; *(de motor)* crankshaft.
ci·lan·tro m. coriander.
ci·lin·drar tr. *(comprimir)* to calender; *(carreteras)* to steamroller.
ci·lín·dri·co, a adj. cylindrical, cylindric.
ci·lin·dro m. cylinder; *(rodillo)* roller.
ci·ma f. *(cumbre)* summit; FIG. pinnacle.
cim·ba·le·ro/lis·ta m. cymbalist.
cím·ba·los m.pl. cymbals.
cim·brar/bre·ar tr. & intr. to vibrate.
ci·men·tar §49 tr. CONSTR. to lay the foundation of; *(afirmar)* to consolidate; METAL. to refine.
ci·mien·to m. CONSTR. foundation; FIG. basis ♦ **echar los cimientos** to lay the foundation.
ci·mi·ta·rra f. scimitar.
cinc m. zinc.
cin·cel m. chisel.
cin·ce·lar tr. to chisel, carve (with a chisel).
cin·cha f. girth, cinch ♦ **a revienta cinchas** *(de mala gana)* unwillingly; *(rápido)* at breakneck speed.
cín·char tr. EQUIT. to girth, cinch.
cin·cho m. *(faja)* belt; *(zuncho)* metal hoop; *(de rueda)* iron rim; ARCHIT. projecting rib of an arch; AMER. girth.
cin·co I. adj. five; *(quinto)* fifth ♦ **las c.** five o'clock **II.** m. five; *(guitarra)* five-string guitar; *(moneda)* five-cent piece ♦ **estar sin un c.** to be broke.
cin·cuen·ta I. adj. fifty; *(quincuagésimo)* fiftieth **II.** m. fifty.
cin·cuen·ta·vo, a adj. & m.f. fiftieth.
cin·cuen·te·na·rio m. fiftieth anniversary.
cin·cuen·te·na f. group of fifty.
cin·cuen·tón, o·na adj. & m.f. fifty-year-old (person).
ci·ne m. cinema; PHOTOG., TECH. cinematography; COLL. *(espectáculo)* movies; *(teatro)* movie theater ♦ **c. de estreno** first-run movie theater • **c. mudo** silent films • **c. parlante** *or* **sonoro** talking pictures.
ci·ne·as·ta m.f. *(director)* filmmaker; *(productor)* film producer.
ci·ne·ma·sco·pe m. cinemascope.
ci·ne·ma·te·ca f. film library *or* archive.
ci·ne·ma·to·gra·fí·a f. cinematography.
ci·ne·ma·to·gra·fiar §30 tr. to film, shoot.
ci·ne·ma·to·grá·fi·co, a adj. cinematographic.
ci·ne·ma·tó·gra·fo m. *(proyector)* (film) projector; *(teatro)* movie theater.
ci·né·ti·co, a I. adj. kinetic **II.** f. kinetics.
cín·ga·ro, a adj. & m.f. gypsy.
cí·ni·co, a I. adj. cynical **II.** m.f. cynic.
ci·nis·mo m. cynicism.
cin·ta f. ribbon; *(película)* film ♦ **c. adhesiva** adhesive tape • **c. de freno** brake lining • **c. de medir** measuring tape • **c. de teletipo** ticker tape • **c. magnetofónica** recording tape • **c. métrica** tape measure • **c. transportadora** conveyor belt.
cin·ti·lar tr. to sparkle, twinkle.
cin·to m. *(ceñidor)* belt; *(cintura)* waist.
cin·tu·ra f. waist, waistline ♦ **c. pelviana** pelvic girdle.

cin·tu·rón m. belt ♦ **apretarse el c.** to tighten one's belt • **c. de castidad** chastity belt • **c. de seguridad** seat *or* safety belt • **c. salvavidas** life preserver.
ci·ña, ño, ñera, ñó see **ceñir.**
ci·prés m. cypress.
cir·cen·se adj. circus.
cir·co m. circus; GEOL. cirque.
cir·cón m. zircon.
cir·co·nio m. zirconium.
cir·cui·to m. circuit; *(circunferencia)* circumference; *(de carreteras)* network ♦ **corto c.** short circuit.
cir·cu·la·ción f. circulation; *(transmisión)* dissemination; *(tráfico)* traffic ♦ **poner en c.** to put into circulation.
cir·cu·lar[1] **I.** adj. circular **II.** f. circular, flier.
cir·cu·lar[2] intr. & tr. to circulate.
cir·cu·la·to·rio, a adj. ANAT. circulatory; AUTO. traffic.
cír·cu·lo m. circle; *(circunferencia)* circumference ♦ **c. vicioso** vicious circle, circular argument.
cir·cun·ci·dar tr. to circumcise.
cir·cun·ci·sión f. circumcision.
cir·cun·dar tr. to surround, encircle.
cir·cun·fe·ren·cia f. circumference.
cir·cun·fle·jo, a adj. & m. circumflex.
cir·cun·lo·cu·ción f. /**lo·quio** m. circumlocution.
cir·cun·na·ve·ga·ción f. circumnavigation.
cir·cuns·cri·bir §80 tr. to circumscribe —reflex. to restrict *or* limit oneself.
cir·cuns·pec·ción f. circumspection; *(prudencia)* caution, prudence.
cir·cuns·pec·to, a adj. circumspect.
cir·cuns·tan·cia f. circumstance ♦ **en las circunstancias actuales** under the present circumstances.
cir·cuns·tan·cial adj. circumstantial; GRAM. adverbial.
cir·cun·va·la·ción f. MIL. circumvallation ♦ **línea de c.** AUTO. loop.
cir·cun·va·lar tr. to surround, encircle.
cir·cun·vo·lu·ción f. circumvolution ♦ **c. cerebral** cerebral convolution.
ci·rio m. church candle.
ci·rro m. cirrus; MED. scirrhus (tumor).
ci·rro·sis f. cirrhosis.
ci·rue·la f. plum; *(pasa)* prune ♦ **c. pasa** prune.
ci·rue·lo m. plum tree.
ci·ru·gí·a f. surgery ♦ **c. plástica** *or* **estética** plastic *or* cosmetic surgery • **c. mayor** major surgery • **c. menor** minor surgery.
ci·ru·ja·no, a m.f. surgeon.
ci·sión f. incision.
cis·ma m. schism; *(discordia)* discord.
cis·ne m. swan; R.P. powder puff.
cis·ter·na f. cistern, reservoir.
cis·ti·tis f. cystitis.
ci·su·ra f. scission, fissure.
ci·ta f. *(entrevista)* appointment, meeting; *(con novio, amigo)* date; *(referencia)* quote ♦ **darse c.** to set up a meeting *or* date with someone.
ci·ta·ción f. subpoena ♦ **c. de remate** notice of public sale.
ci·tar tr. *(convocar)* to make an appointment *or* date with; *(referirse)* to cite; LAW to summon.
cí·ta·ra f. zither, zithern.
ci·to·lo·gí·a f. cytology.
ci·to·plas·ma m. cytoplasm.

cí·tri·co, a I. adj. citric; BOT. citrus II. m.pl. citrus fruits.
ciu·dad f. city.
ciu·da·da·ní·a f. (derecho) citizenship; (población) citizenry.
ciu·da·da·no, a I. adj. civic, city II. m.f. citizen.
ciu·da·de·la f. citadel, fortress.
cí·vi·co, a adj. civic.
ci·vil I. adj. civil II. m.f. civilian.
ci·vi·li·dad f. civility.
ci·vi·li·za·ción f. civilization.
ci·vi·li·za·do, a adj. civilized, refined.
ci·vi·li·zar §04 tr. to civilize —reflex. to become civilized.
ci·vis·mo m. civic-mindedness.
ci·za·ña f. BOT. (bearded) darnel; (vicio) evil; (disensión) discord ♦ **meter** or **sembrar c.** to cause trouble.
ci·za·ñar tr. to cause or make trouble for.
ci·za·ñe·ro, a I. adj. troublemaking II. m.f. troublemaker.
cla·mar intr. to clamor, FIG. to demand —tr. to cry out for.
cla·mor m. clamor, outcry.
cla·mo·re·ar intr. & tr. to cry out (for).
cla·mo·re·o m. clamoring.
cla·mo·ro·so, a adj. clamorous ♦ **éxito c.** resounding success.
clan m. clan.
clan·des·ti·no, a adj. clandestine.
cla·ra f. see **claro, a.**
cla·ra·bo·ya f. skylight.
cla·re·ar tr. & intr. to dawn ♦ **al c. el día** at the break of dawn.
cla·re·cer §17 intr. to dawn.
cla·re·te adj. & m. claret (wine).
cla·ri·dad f. clarity; (luz) brightness; (nitidez) clearness ♦ **con c.** clearly.
cla·ri·fi·ca·ción f. clarification.
cla·ri·fi·car §70 tr. to clarify.
cla·rín m. clarion; (músico) trumpet player.
cla·ri·ne·te m. clarinet; (músico) clarinetist.
cla·ri·ne·tis·ta m.f. clarinetist.
cla·ri·vi·den·cia f. clairvoyance.
cla·ri·vi·den·te adj. clairvoyant.
cla·ro, a I. adj. clear; (luminoso) bright; (despejado) cloudless; (cristalino) transparent; (aguado) thin; (obvio) obvious; (inteligible) intelligible; (sin ambages) straightforward ♦ **a las claras** openly • **c. como el agua** as plain as the nose on your face II. adv. plainly ♦ **¡c.!** or **¡c. que sí!** of course!, sure! III. m. (abertura) gap; (espacio) clearing ♦ **c. de luna** moonlight ♦ **poner** or **sacar en c.** to clarify, explain —f. white (of egg).
cla·ros·cu·ro m. chiaroscuro.
cla·se f. class; (lección) lesson; (aula) classroom ♦ **c. turista** coach • **de c.** of distinction • **toda c. de** all kinds of.
cla·si·cis·ta adj. & m.f. classicist.
clá·si·co, a I. adj. classic, classical; (notable) outstanding II. m.f. (autor) classic author; (clasicista) classicist.
cla·si·fi·ca·ción f. classification.
cla·si·fi·car §70 tr. to classify; (archivar) to file —reflex. SPORT. to qualify.
clau·di·ca·ción f. backing down.
clau·di·car §70 intr. to back down.
claus·tro m. cloister; EDUC. faculty ♦ **c. materno** womb.
claus·tro·fo·bia f. claustrophobia.
cláu·su·la f. clause ♦ **c. absoluta** GRAM. (latín)

ablative absolute; (inglés) absolute construction • **c. simple** simple sentence.
clau·su·ra f. (abadía) cloister; (estado) monastic life; (conclusión) closing ceremony; AMER. (cierre) closing; EDUC. commencement.
clau·su·rar tr. (terminar) to bring to a close; (cerrar) to close, shut.
cla·va·do, a adj. (con claves) nail-studded; (en punto) sharp, on the dot.
cla·var tr. to nail; (hincar) to thrust, drive; FIG. (fijar) to fix or rivet on; COLL. (engañar) to cheat.
cla·ve I. f. (cifra) code; (esencia) key; ARCHIT. keystone; MUS. clef ♦ **c. de do** tenor or alto clef • **c. de fa** base clef • **c. de sol** treble clef —m. clavichord II. adj. key.
cla·ve·cín m. harpsichord.
cla·vel m. carnation.
cla·ve·te·ar tr. to stud.
cla·vi·cém·ba·lo m. harpsichord.
cla·vi·cor·dio m. clavichord.
cla·ví·cu·la f. clavicle, collarbone.
cla·vi·ja f. (clavo) peg, pin; CARP. peg, dowel; ELEC. plug; MUS. peg ♦ **ajustarle** or **apretarle a uno las clavijas** COLL. to put the screws on or to someone.
cla·vo m. nail; BOT. clove; R.P. (mercadería) white elephant; (perjuicio) nasty business ♦ **dar en el c.** COLL. to hit the nail on the head.
cle·men·cia f. clemency.
clep·to·ma·ní·a f. kleptomania.
clep·tó·ma·no, a adj. & m.f. kleptomaniac.
clé·ri·go m. clergyman.
cle·ro m. clergy.
cli·ché m. cliché; PRINT. (plancha) cliché, (stereotype) plate; (negativo) negative.
clien·te m.f. COM. client, customer; DENT., MED. patient; LAW client.
clien·te·la f. COM. customers, clientele; DENT., MED. practice, patients; LAW clients.
cli·ma m. climate; FIG. atmosphere.
cli·má·ti·co, a adj. climatic.
cli·ma·ti·za·ción f. air conditioning.
cli·ma·ti·zar §04 tr. to air-condition.
clí·max m.inv. climax.
clí·ni·co, a I. adj. clinical II. m. clinician —f. private hospital.
clip m. (sujetapapeles) paper clip; (aro) earring.
clí·per m. AVIA., MARIT. clipper.
cli·sé m. see **cliché.**
clí·to·ris m. clitoris.
clo·a·ca f. sewer.
clo·car §73 intr. to cluck, cackle.
clon m. clone.
clo·que·ar intr. to cluck, cackle.
clo·que·ra f. brooding, broodiness.
clo·ra·to m. chlorate.
clor·hi·dra·to m. hydrochloride.
clor·hí·dri·co, a adj. hydrochloric.
cló·ri·co, a adj. chloric.
clo·ro m. chlorine.
clo·ro·fi·la f. chlorophyll.
clo·ro·for·mo m. chloroform.
clo·ru·ro m. chloride.
club m. [pl. (e)s] club.
clue·co, a I. adj. broody; COLL. (decrépito) feeble II. f. brooder.
clue·que see **clocar.**
co·ac·ción f. coercion; LAW duress.
co·ac·cio·nar tr. to coerce.
co·a·cre·e·dor, ·ra m.f. joint creditor.
co·a·cu·sa·do, a m.f. codefendant.

co·ad·qui·ri·dor, ·ra m.f. LAW joint purchaser.
co·ad·yu·var tr. & intr. to help.
co·a·gen·te m.f. coagent.
co·a·gu·la·dor, ·ra adj. coagulant, coagulative.
co·a·gu·lan·te adj. coagulating, coagulative.
co·a·gu·lar tr. & reflex. to coagulate; *(leche)* to curdle.
co·á·gu·lo m. clot; *(leche)* curd.
co·a·li·ción f. coalition.
co·ar·ta·da f. alibi ◆ **presentar una c.** to provide an alibi.
co·ar·tar tr. to hinder.
co·au·tor, ·ra m.f. co-author.
co·a·xial adj. coaxial.
co·bal·to m. cobalt.
co·bar·de I. adj. cowardly II. m.f. coward.
co·bar·dí·a f. cowardice, cowardliness.
co·ber·ti·zo m. *(protección)* shelter; *(barraca)* shed; *(cochera)* garage.
co·ber·tor m. *(colcha)* bedspread; *(de plumas)* comforter; *(manta)* blanket.
co·ber·tu·ra f. cover, covering.
co·bi·ja f. *(cubierta)* cover, covering; *(teja)* ridge tile; ORNITH. covert; AMER. blanket; MEX. *(chal)* short shawl, wrap.
co·bi·jar tr. to cover (up); FIG. to harbor.
co·bra f. cobra.
co·bra·dor, ·ra m.f. *(recaudador)* bill or tax collector; *(perro)* retriever.
co·bran·za f. collection; *(recuperación)* trerieval; *(de un cheque)* cashing; *(pago)* payment.
co·brar tr. *(recibir)* to collect; *(recuperar)* to retrieve; *(precios)* to charge; *(un cheque)* to cash ◆ **c. afecto** *or* **cariño a** to take a liking to • **c. ánimo** to take heart • **c. fama de** to get a reputation for being • **c. fuerza** to gather strength • **c. valor** to muster courage —reflex. to recoup one's losses.
co·bre m. copper; MUS. brass instrument; AMER. cent ◆ **quedarse sin un c.** to be broke.
co·bri·zo, a adj. copper, copper-colored.
co·bro m. collection, collecting; *(de un cheque)* cashing ◆ **c. a la entrega** collect on delivery • **presentar al c.** to present for cashing.
co·ca f. coca; PHARM. cocaine.
co·ca·í·na f. cocaine.
coc·ción f. cooking; *(hervor)* boiling; *(en un horno)* baking.
cóc·cix m.inv. coccyx.
co·ce·ar intr. to kick.
co·cer §71 tr. to cook; *(hervir)* to boil; *(en un horno)* to bake —intr. *(hervir)* to boil; *(fermentar)* to ferment.
co·che m. *(carruaje)* carriage; *(automóvil)* car ◆ **c. blindado** armored car • **c. cama** sleeper, sleeping car • **c. comedor** dining car • **c. de alquiler** *(taxi)* taxi, cab; *(alquilado)* rental car • **c. de carreras** sports car • **c. fúnebre** hearse.
co·che·ra f. garage.
co·che·ro m. coachman.
co·chi·na·da/ne·rí·a f. COLL. *(suciedad)* dirt, filth; *(palabra)* dirty word; *(acto)* dirty trick ◆ pl. **decir c.** to use foul language.
co·chi·ne·ar intr. COLL. to act like a pig.
co·chi·ni·llo m. piglet, suckling pig.
co·chi·no, a I. m.f. pig; COLL. *(persona)* swine II. adj. *(sucio)* filthy; COLL. *(ruin)* rotten.
co·chi·tril m. COLL. pigsty.
co·cien·te m. quotient.
co·ci·mien·to m. cooking; *(al horno)* baking; *(de hierbas)* medicinal extraction.

co·ci·na f. *(cuarto)* kitchen; *(aparato)* stove, range; *(estilo)* cuisine ◆ **de c.** kitchen.
co·ci·nar tr. & intr. to cook.
co·ci·ne·ro, a m.f. cook, chef.
co·co m. coconut; COLL. *(cabeza)* noggin.
co·co·dri·lo m. crocodile.
co·co·ro·có m. cock-a-doodle-doo.
co·co·tal m. coconut grove.
co·co·te·ro m. coconut palm.
cóc·tel m. *(bebida)* cocktaïl; *(reunión)* cocktail party.
coc·te·le·ra f. cocktail shaker.
co·da f. coda.
co·da·zo m. jab, poke (with one's elbow) ◆ **dar un c.** to jab ◆ pl. **abrirse paso a c.** to elbow one's way through.
co·de·ar intr. to elbow —reflex. COLL. to rub elbows with.
co·de·í·na f. codeine.
co·de·ra f. elbow patch.
co·deu·dor, ·ra m.f. codebtor, joint debtor.
có·di·ce m. codex, manuscript.
co·di·cia f. *(avaricia)* greed; *(envidia)* envy; FIG. thirst.
co·di·ciar tr. to covet, desire.
co·di·cio·so, a adj. & m.f. greedy (person) ◆ **ser c. de** to covet.
co·di·fi·ca·ción f. encoding; LAW codification.
co·di·fi·ca·dor, ·ra I. adj. codifying II. m.f. codifier.
co·di·fi·car §70 tr. to encode; LAW to codify.
có·di·go m. code ◆ **c. de edificación** building code • **c. de leyes** legal code • **c. fiscal** tax code • **c. postal** zip code.
co·do m. elbow; FIG. bend ◆ **alzar** *or* **empinar el c.** to have a lot to drink • **c. con c.** neck and neck ◆ pl. **hablar por los c.** to be a chatterbox.
co·e·fi·cien·te adj. & m. coefficient.
co·er·ción f. coercion.
co·er·ci·ti·vo, a adj. coercive, restrictive.
co·e·tá·ne·o, a adj. & m.f. contemporary.
co·e·xis·ten·cia f. coexistence.
co·e·xis·ten·te adj. coexistent.
co·e·xis·tir intr. to coexist.
co·fia f. *(red)* hair net; *(gorro)* bonnet.
co·fra·de m.f. member.
co·fra·dí·a f. *(de hombres)* brotherhood; *(de mujeres)* sisterhood; *(gremio)* guild.
co·fre m. *(arca)* chest; *(caja)* box.
co·ger §34 tr. to grab, grasp; *(recoger)* to gather up; *(apresar)* to capture; *(ocupar)* to take up; *(absorber)* to absorb; *(alcanzar)* to catch up with; *(encontrar)* to find; *(sorprender)* to catch by surprise; *(enfermedad)* to catch; *(entender)* to understand.
co·gi·do m. SEW. pleat, fold.
cog·na·do, a m.f. cognate.
cog·ni·ción f. cognition.
cog·nos·ci·ti·vo, a adj. cognitive.
co·go·llo m. heart (of vegetables).
co·go·te m. back of the neck ◆ **tieso de c.** arrogant.
co·go·tu·do, a AMER., COLL. m.f. & adj. *(rico)* wealthy *or* influential (person); *(orgulloso)* arrogant (person).
co·ha·bi·tar intr. to live together, cohabit.
co·he·cho m. bribe, bribery.
co·he·ren·cia f. coherence; PHYS. cohesion.
co·he·ren·te adj. coherent.
co·he·sión f. cohesion.
co·he·si·vo, a adj. cohesive.
co·he·te m. rocket ◆ **al c.** ARG., BOL., COLL. in

vain • **c. balístico** ballistic missile • **c. de seña-les** flare • **salir como un c.** COLL. to be off like a shot.

co·hi·bi·ción f. inhibition.

co·hi·bir tr. (*inhibir*) to inhibit; (*desasosegar*) to make uneasy —reflex. to be *or* feel inhibited.

co·hor·te f. cohort.

coi·ma f. AMER. bribe, payola.

co·in·ci·den·cia f. coincidence.

co·in·ci·den·te adj. coincidental, coincident.

co·in·ci·dir intr. to coincide; (*concordar*) to agree.

co·in·qui·li·no, a m.f. joint tenant.

coi·to m. coitus, sexual intercourse.

co·je·ar intr. to limp; (*una mesa*) to wobble.

co·je·ra f. limp, lameness.

co·jín m. cushion.

co·ji·ne·te m. small cushion; RAIL. socket; MECH. bearing; PRINT. roller clamp • **c. de bo-las** ball bearing • pl. COL., MEX., VEN. saddlebags.

co·jo, a I. adj. (*tullido*) crippled; (*un mueble*) wobbly • **no ser c. ni manco** COLL. to be all there **II.** m.f. cripple.

col f. cabbage • **c. de Bruselas** Brussels sprouts.

co·la¹ f. tail; (*de vestido*) train; (*fila*) queue; (*parte final*) rear • **a la c.** last • **c. de caballo** BOT. horsetail; (*pelo*) ponytail • **hacer c.** to line up • **piano de c.** grand piano • **tener** *or* **traer c.** to have serious consequences.

co·la² f. glue, gum • **eso no pega ni con c.** COLL. that's nonsense.

co·la·bo·ra·ción f. collaboration.

co·la·bo·ra·cio·nis·ta m.f. collaborationist.

co·la·bo·ra·dor, ·ra I. adj. (*cooperador*) collaborating; LIT. contributing **II.** m.f. (*cooperador*) collaborator; LIT. contributor.

co·la·bo·rar intr. to collaborate; LIT. to contribute.

co·la·ción f. (*merienda*) snack; RELIG. collation • **sacar** *or* **traer a c.** to bring up.

co·la·da f. (*blanqueo*) whitening; (*cañada*) cattle trail; METAL. tap (on a furnace).

co·la·de·ro m. (*cedazo*) strainer; (*camino*) narrow trail; (*examen*) lenient examination.

co·la·do, a adj. cast • **hierro c.** cast iron.

co·la·dor m. strainer; RELIG. collator.

co·lap·so m. collapse • **c. nervioso** nervous breakdown.

co·lar §19 tr. to strain; (*blanquear*) to bleach; COLL. to pass *or* foist (off); METAL. to cast —intr. to squeeze through —reflex. to sneak in.

co·la·te·ral adj. & m.f. collateral.

col·cha f. bedspread.

col·cha·do, a I. adj. quilted **II.** m. quilting.

col·chón m. mattress • **c. de aire** air cushion • **c. de muelles** spring mattress • **c. de plumas** feather bed.

col·cho·ne·ro, a I. adj. SEW. tufting **II.** m.f. (*fabricante*) mattress manufacturer; (*vendedor*) mattress seller.

col·cho·ne·ta f. light mattress.

co·le·a·da f. flick (of the tail); (*de un perro*) wag (of the tail).

co·lec·ción f. collection; LIT. anthology.

co·lec·cio·na·dor, ·ra m.f. collector.

co·lec·cio·nar tr. to collect.

co·lec·cio·nis·ta m.f. collector.

co·lec·ta f. collection.

co·lec·tar tr. to collect.

co·lec·ti·vi·dad f. community.

co·lec·ti·vis·ta I. adj. collectivistic **II.** m.f. collectivist.

co·lec·ti·vi·za·ción f. collectivization.

co·lec·ti·vo, a I. adj. collective; (*mutuo*) joint **II.** m. GRAM. collective (noun); ARG., BOL., PERU small bus.

co·lec·tor m. collector • **c. de aceite** AUTO. drip pan.

co·le·ga m. colleague, associate.

co·le·gia·do, a adj. collegiate.

co·le·gial adj. school.

co·le·gial, ·la m.f. schoolboy, schoolgirl.

co·le·gio m. (*primario*) elementary school; (*secundario*) high school; (*asociación*) college, association <*c. de abogados* bar association> • **c. de internos** boarding school • **c. de párvulos** nursery school • **c. electoral** electoral college.

co·le·gir §57 tr. to infer, gather.

co·le·óp·te·ro I. adj. coleopteral **II.** m. coleopteran.

có·le·ra f. choler; FIG. anger • **dar c.** to infuriate • **descargar la c. en** to vent one's anger on • **montar en c.** to get angry —m. MED. cholera.

co·lé·ri·co, a I. adj. suffering from cholera; FIG. choleric, irascible **II.** m.f. cholera patient; FIG. irascible person.

co·les·te·rol m./**ri·na** f. cholesterol.

co·le·ta f. (*pelo*) pigtail; FIG., COLL. (*adición escrita*) postscript; AMER. (*lona*) coarse canvas.

co·le·ta·zo m. blow with the tail; AUTO. sway.

co·le·to m. jerkin • **decir para su c.** to say to oneself.

col·ga·do, a adj. let down • **dejar c. a** to let down.

col·ga·jo m. (*jirón*) tatter; (*racimo*) bunch.

col·gan·te I. adj. hanging • **puente c.** suspension bridge **II.** m. pendant.

col·gar §16 tr. to hang (up); (*adornar*) to drape with hangings; (*reprobar*) to flunk • **c. los hábitos** to give up the cloth; FIG. to give up an action *or* profession —intr. to hang; (*caer*) to hang down.

co·li·brí m. [pl. **-íes**] hummingbird.

có·li·co, a I. adj. colonic **II.** m. colic.

co·li·flor f. cauliflower.

co·li·gar·se §47 reflex. to ally, unite.

co·li·ge, ja, jo see **colegir.**

co·li·lla f. cigarette butt.

co·li·na f. hill.

co·lin·dan·te adj. adjacent, adjoining.

co·lin·dar intr. to be adjacent, adjoin.

co·li·ne·al adj. collinear.

co·li·rio m. collyrium, eyewash.

co·li·se·o m. coliseum, colosseum.

co·li·sión f. collision; FIG. conflict.

co·li·tis f. colitis, colonitis.

co·lla I. adj. BOL. Andean; ARG. Bolivian **II.** m.f. BOL. inhabitant of the Andean plateau; ARG. Bolivian.

co·lla·do m. (*cerro*) hill; (*entre montañas*) mountain pass.

co·llar m. (*adorno*) necklace; (*cadena*) chain; (*de animal*) collar; MECH. ring, collar; ORNITH., ZOOL. collar, ruff.

co·lla·rín m. (*collar*) small collar; RELIG. collar.

col·ma·do, a I. adj. (*lleno*) full, filled; (*cucharada*) heaping **II.** m. (*café*) café; (*almacén*) grocery store.

col·mar tr. (*llenar*) to fill (up), fill to the brim;

FIG. to shower; *(satisfacer)* to fulfill, satisfy ♦ **¡eso colma la medida!** that's the last straw!

col·me·na f. beehive, hive.

col·me·nar m. apiary.

col·me·ne·ro, a m.f. beekeeper, apiarist —m. honey bear.

col·mi·llo m. canine tooth, eyetooth; ZOOL. *(del elefante)* tusk; *(del perro)* fang ♦ pl. **enseñar los c.** COLL. to show one's teeth.

col·mo m. *(exceso)* overflow; *(cumbre)* height; *(límite)* limit ♦ **para c. de desgracias** to make matters worse.

co·lo·ca·ción f. *(acción)* placing; *(lugar)* place; *(empleo)* position.

co·lo·car §70 tr. to place, position; *(dinero)* to invest.

co·lo·fón m. colophon.

co·lo·fo·nia f. rosin.

co·loi·dal/de·o, a adj. colloidal.

co·loi·de m. colloid.

co·lom·bó·fi·lo, a I. adj. pigeon-breeding II. m.f. pigeon breeder.

co·lon m. ANAT. colon.

co·lón m. C. RICA, SALV., FIN. colon.

co·lo·nia f. colony; *(perfume)* cologne ♦ **c. penitenciaria** prison camp.

co·lo·nial adj. colonial.

co·lo·nia·lis·ta adj. & m.f. colonialist.

co·lo·ni·za·ción f. colonization.

co·lo·ni·za·dor, ·ra I. adj. colonizing, settling II. m.f. colonizer, settler.

co·lo·ni·zar §04 tr. to colonize, settle.

co·lo·no m. settler; AGR. tenant farmer.

co·lo·quio m. *(conversación)* talk; *(conferencia)* seminar.

co·lor m. color; *(colorante)* tint; *(aspecto)* aspect ♦ **a c.** in color • **c. elemental** primary color • **c. firme** fast color • **c. vivo** bright color • **de c.** colored • **mudar de c.** COLL. *(sonrojarse)* to blush; *(palidecer)* to turn pale • **subido de c.** off-color • **ver las cosas de c. de rosa** COLL. to see things through rose-colored glasses ♦ pl. **ponerse de mil c.** COLL. to flush.

co·lo·ra·ción f. coloring ♦ **c. defensiva** BIOL. protective markings.

co·lo·ra·do, a I. adj. *(que tiene color)* colored; *(rojizo)* red, reddish ♦ **ponerse c.** to blush II. m. red.

co·lo·ra·do·te, a adj. COLL. ruddy, red-faced.

co·lo·ran·te I. adj. coloring II. m. colorant.

co·lo·rar tr. *(dar color)* to color; *(teñir)* to dye; *(pintar)* to paint.

co·lo·re·ar tr. *(dar color)* to color —intr. to turn red.

co·lo·re·te m. rouge.

co·lo·ri·do m. *(acción)* coloring; *(colores)* coloration; *(color)* color; FIG. style.

co·lo·rín·che m. R.P. gaudy combination of colors.

co·lo·sal adj. colossal.

co·lo·so m. *(estatua)* colossus; *(gigante)* giant.

co·lum·na f. column, pillar ♦ **c. de dirección** AUTO. steering column • **c. vertebral** spine, spinal column.

co·lum·na·ta f. colonnade.

co·lum·nis·ta m.f. columnist.

co·lum·piar tr. to swing —reflex. *(mecerse)* to swing; COLL. *(contonearse)* to sway.

co·lum·pio m. swing.

co·lu·sión f. collusion.

co·lu·to·rio m. mouthwash, gargle.

co·ma[1] f. comma ♦ **sin faltar una c.** in the minutest detail.

co·ma[2] m. coma.

co·ma·dre f. godmother; *(relación)* mother of the child (in relation to the godmother); *(partera)* midwife.

co·ma·dre·ar intr. COLL. to gossip.

co·ma·dre·ja f. weasel; ARG. opossum.

co·ma·dro·na f. midwife.

co·man·dan·cia f. *(grado)* command; *(distrito)* district; *(edificio)* headquarters.

co·man·dan·te m. commanding officer; *(grado)* major ♦ **c. de armas** commandant • **c. de barco** commander • **c. en jefe** *or* **general** commander-in-chief.

co·man·dar tr. MIL. to command, lead.

co·man·di·ta f. ♦ **sociedad en c.** silent partnership.

co·man·di·ta·rio, a COM. I. adj. silent II. m.f. silent partner.

co·man·do m. MIL. commando; *(mando)* command; TECH. control ♦ **c. a distancia** remote control.

co·mar·ca f. region, district.

co·mar·car §70 intr. to border on, adjoin —tr. to plant trees in straight lines.

co·ma·to·so, a adj. comatose.

com·ba f. see **comba, a.**

com·ba·du·ra f. bending, curving.

com·bar tr. & reflex. *(encorvar)* to bend, curve; *(alabear)* to warp.

com·ba·te m. combat; FIG. conflict; SPORT. contest ♦ **c. naval** naval *or* sea battle • **c. nulo** draw • **fuera de c.** out of action • **ganar por fuera de c.** SPORT. to win by a knockout.

com·ba·tien·te I. adj. fighting II. m. combatant, fighter; MIL. soldier.

com·ba·tir intr. to battle —tr. *(luchar contra)* to fight; *(acometer)* to attack; *(impugnar)* to oppose; FIG. to beat upon —reflex. to fight, struggle.

com·ba·ti·vo, a adj. combative.

com·bi·na·ción f. combination; *(prenda)* slip; *(plan)* plan; CHEM. compound; RAIL. connection; MATH. permutation.

com·bi·na·do m. stereo; CHEM. compound.

com·bi·nar tr. to combine; *(arreglar)* to work out <**c. ideas** to work out ideas> —reflex. to combine.

com·bo, a I. adj. bent, curved II. m. *(asiento)* stand on which wine casks are placed; ARG., CHILE *(martilla)* sledge hammer; CHILE *(puñetazo)* punch, blow —f. *(convexidad)* bend, curve; *(alabeo)* warp; *(juego y cuerda)* skipping rope.

com·bus·ti·ble I. adj. combustible II. m. fuel.

com·bus·tión f. combustion.

co·me·de·ro m. *(recipiente)* feeding trough; *(lugar)* manger.

co·me·dia f. comedy; *(obra)* play; *(edificio)* theater; *(fingimiento)* farce ♦ **c. de capa y espada** cloak-and-dagger play • **c. de costumbres** comedy of manners • **c. en un acto** one-act play • **hacer la c.** COLL. to pretend.

co·me·dian·te, a m. *(cómico)* actor —f. (comic) actress —m.f. COLL. hypocrite.

co·me·di·do, a adj. *(cortés)* courteous; *(reservado)* reserved; S. AMER. obliging.

co·me·dir·se §48 reflex. to restrain oneself.

co·me·dor, ·ra I. adj. gluttonous II. m.f. big eater —m. *(cuarto)* dining room; *(muebles)* dining room suite ♦ **coche c.** dining car.

co·men·da·dor m. knight commander.

co·men·da·do·ra f. mother superior.

co·men·sal m.f. mealtime companion.

co·men·ta·dor, ra m.f. commentator.

co·men·tar tr. to comment on.

co·men·ta·rio m. commentary ♦ **sin c.** no comment ♦ pl. *(memorias históricas)* commentaries, historical memoirs; *(chisme)* gossip.

co·men·ta·ris·ta m.f. commentator.

co·men·zar §29 tr. & intr. to begin, start ♦ **c. a** to begin to • **c. con** to begin with • **c. por** to begin with *or* by.

co·mer tr. to eat; *(roer)* to corrode; *(consumir)* to consume; *(en los juegos)* to take (a piece in chess or checkers) ♦ **sin comerlo ni beberlo** COLL. without having had anything to do with it —intr. to eat ♦ **c. y callar** COLL. beggars can't be choosers • **dar de c.** to feed • **ser de buen c.** COLL. to have a healthy appetite • **tener qué c.** to have enough to live on —reflex. to eat up <*me lo comí todo* I ate it all up>; *(disipar)* to squander; *(pasar)* to skip over.

co·mer·cial I. adj. commercial, business ♦ **centro c.** shopping center **II.** m. AMER. commercial, advertisement.

co·mer·cia·li·za·ción f. commercialization.

co·mer·cia·li·zar §04 tr. to commercialize.

co·mer·cian·te m.f. merchant —m. businessman, shopkeeper —f. businesswoman ♦ **c. al por mayor** wholesaler • **c. al por menor** retailer.

co·mer·ciar intr. to trade, deal.

co·mer·cio m. *(negocio)* business; *(tienda)* store ♦ **c. exterior** foreign trade • **c. interior** domestic trade.

co·mes·ti·ble I. adj. edible **II.** m. foodstuff ♦ pl. groceries.

co·me·ta m. comet —f. *(juguete)* kite.

co·me·ter tr. *(encargar)* to charge with; *(un crimen)* to commit; *(un error)* to make.

co·me·ti·do m. assignment.

co·me·zón f. itch.

co·mi·ble adj. COLL. edible.

co·mi·cas·tro m. second-rate actor.

co·mi·ci·dad f. comedy, humor.

co·mi·cio m. elections.

có·mi·co, a I. adj. comical, funny **II.** m. comic actor —f. comic actress.

co·mi·da f. *(almuerzo, cena)* food, meal; *(almuerzo)* lunch.

co·mi·di·lla f. COLL. talk.

co·mi·do, a adj. fed, having eaten ♦ **c. de gusanos** worm-eaten • **c. y bebido** COLL. supported, kept • **estar c.** to have eaten • **sin haberlo c. ni bebido** for no apparent reason.

co·mien·ce, zo see **comenzar.**

co·mien·zo m. beginning, start; MED. onset ♦ **al c.** at first • **dar c.** to begin, start.

co·mi·llas f.pl. quotation marks ♦ **abrir, cerrar c.** to open, close quotation marks • **entre c.** in quotes.

co·mi·lón, o·na I. adj. gluttonous **II.** m.f. glutton —f. COLL. feast, spread ♦ **darse una c.** to have a feast.

co·mi·no m. cumin ♦ **no importarle a uno un c.** COLL. not to give a damn about • **no valer un c.** COLL. to be worthless.

co·mi·sar tr. to seize, confiscate.

co·mi·sa·rí·a f.**/·ria·to** m. *(cargo)* commissariat; *(oficina)* office of a commissioner; AMER. police station.

co·mi·sa·rio m. commissioner.

co·mi·sión f. commission; *(encargo)* assignment ♦ **a c.** on a commission basis • **c. mixta** joint committee • **c. permanente** standing committee • **c. planificadora** planning board.

co·mi·sio·na·do, a I. adj. commissioned, authorized **II.** m.f. *(comisario)* commissioner; FIN., POL. committee or board member.

co·mi·sio·nar tr. to commission, authorize.

co·mi·sio·nis·ta m.f. COM. commission merchant.

co·mi·so m. *(confiscación)* confiscation; *(objeto)* confiscated goods.

co·mi·su·ra f. ANAT. commissure, corner.

co·mi·té m. committee.

co·mi·ti·va f. retinue, party ♦ **c. fúnebre** funeral procession.

co·mo I. adv. *(lo mismo que)* as; *(de tal modo)* like; *(en calidad de)* as, in the capacity of; *(casi)* about, approximately; *(según)* as ♦ **c. quiera que** no matter how • **c. sea** one way or the other **II.** conj. *(puesto que)* as, since; *(si)* if; *(así que)* as, like *(por ejemplo)* such as, like • **así c.** as soon as • **c. que** as if • **c. quien dice** so to speak • **c. si** as if • **hacer c. si** to pretend.

có·mo adv. *(en qué condiciones)* how; *(por qué)* why, how come ♦ **¿a c.?** how much? • **¡c. no!** AMER. of course!

có·mo·da f. chest of drawers, bureau.

có·mo·da·men·te adv. *(confortablemente)* comfortably; *(convenientemente)* conveniently.

co·mo·di·dad f. *(confort)* comfortableness; *(conveniencia)* convenience; *(ventaja)* advantage ♦ pl. comforts.

co·mo·dín m. AMER. comfort lover; *(naipes)* wild card.

có·mo·do, a adj. *(confortable)* comfortable; *(útil)* convenient.

co·mo·do·ro m. commodore.

co·mo·quie·ra adv. anyway, anyhow.

com·pac·tar tr. to compact, compress.

com·pac·to, a adj. *(apretado)* compact; *(denso)* tight.

com·pa·de·cer §17 tr. & reflex. to sympathize (with), feel sorry (for).

com·pa·dre m. godfather; *(relación)* father of the child (in relation to the godfather); COLL. pal.

com·pa·dre·ar intr. *(ser amigos)* to be friends; R.P., COLL. *(jactarse)* to brag.

com·pa·gi·na·ción f. *(ordenamiento)* arranging, putting in order; PRINT. page make-up.

com·pa·gi·na·dor, ·ra m.f. PRINT. pager; *(ordenador)* arranger.

com·pa·gi·nar tr. *(arreglar)* to put in order; *(acordar)* to agree; PRINT. to make up —reflex. to be compatible.

com·pa·ñe·ris·mo m. camaraderie.

com·pa·ñe·ro, a m.f. companion; *(colega)* colleague; *(de una pareja)* mate ♦ **c. de armas** comrade in arms • **c. de clase** classmate • **c. de colegio** schoolmate • **c. de cuarto** roommate • **c. de trabajo** fellow worker • **c. de viaje** traveling companion.

com·pa·ñí·a f. company ♦ **c. anónima** stock company • **c. comanditaria** silent partnership • **c. de seguros** insurance company • **c. tenedora** holding company • **hacer c. a alguien** to keep someone company.

com·pa·ra·ción f. comparison; LIT. simile ♦ **en c. con** in comparison with *or* to • **sin c.** beyond comparison.

com·pa·rar tr. *(relacionar)* to compare; *(cotejar)* to collate, check.

com·pa·ra·ti·vo, a adj. & m. comparative.

com·pa·re·cen·cia f. LAW appearance ♦ **orden de c.** summons.

com·pa·re·cer §17 intr. LAW to appear.

com·pa·re·cien·te m.f. LAW person appearing.

com·pa·ren·do m. summons, subpoena.

com·par·sa m.f. THEAT. extra —f. THEAT. chorus; *(banda)* masquerade.

com·par·ti·m(i)en·to m. *(división)* division; *(departamento)* compartment ♦ **c. estanco** watertight compartment.

com·par·tir tr. *(repartir)* to divide (up); *(participar)* to share.

com·pás m. MATH. compass, compasses; MARIT. compass; MUS. *(ritmo)* rhythm; *(unidad métrica)* measure ♦ **al c. de** in step with • **c. binario** MUS. double time • **fuera de c.** out of step • **llevar el c.** MUS. to keep time • **perder el c.** MUS. to lose the beat.

com·pa·sión f. compassion, pity ♦ **¡por c.!** for pity's sake! • **sin c.** merciless • **tener c. de** to feel sorry for.

com·pa·si·vo, a adj. compassionate.

com·pa·ti·ble adj. compatible.

com·pa·trio·ta m.f. compatriot.

com·pe·ler tr. to compel, force.

com·pen·diar tr. to summarize, abridge.

com·pen·dio m. summary, abridgment.

com·pe·ne·tra·ción f. *(interpenetración)* interpenetration; *(afinidad)* mutual understanding.

com·pe·ne·trar·se reflex. to interpenetrate; *(tener afinidad)* to understand each other.

com·pen·sa·ción f. compensation; LAW recompense, redress ♦ **en c.** in exchange *or* return.

com·pen·sa·dor, ·ra I. adj. compensating, compensatory II. m. compensator (pendulum).

com·pen·sar tr. to compensate; *(recompensar)* to indemnify.

com·pen·sa·to·rio, a adj. compensatory.

com·pe·ten·cia f. competition; *(rivalidad)* rivalry; *(incumbencia)* responsibility; *(aptitud)* competence; *(campo)* field <*no es de mi c.* it's outside my field>; LAW jurisdiction ♦ **hacer la c. a** to compete with *or* against.

com·pe·ten·te adj. *(adecuado)* suitable; *(apto)* competent; LAW competent.

com·pe·ter intr. *(pertenecer)* to be one's business *or* concern; *(incumbir)* to be up to someone.

com·pe·ti·ción f. competition; *(rivalidad)* rivalry.

com·pe·ti·dor, ·ra I. adj. competing, rival II. m.f. competitor.

com·pe·tir §48 intr. *(contender)* to compete; *(igualar)* to be on a par.

com·pe·ti·ti·vo, a adj. competitive.

com·pi·la·ción f. compilation.

com·pi·la·dor, ·ra I. adj. compiling II. m.f. compiler.

com·pi·lar tr. to compile.

com·pin·che m.f. COLL. pal, chum; *(cómplice)* accomplice.

com·pi·ta, to, tiera, tió see **competir.**

com·pla·cen·cia f. complacency; *(tolerancia)* tolerance.

com·pla·cer §51 tr. to please, gratify —reflex. ♦ **c. en** *or* **de** to delight in, take pleasure in.

com·pla·ci·do, a adj. satisfied, content ♦ **c. de sí** self-satisfied.

com·pla·cien·te adj. *(satisfecho)* satisfied; *(obsequio·so)* complaisant.

com·ple·ji·dad f. complexity.

com·ple·jo, a I. adj. *(complicado)* complex, complicated; GRAM. complex; MATH. compound II. m. INDUS., PSYCH. complex.

com·ple·men·tar tr. & reflex. to complement (each other).

com·ple·men·ta·rio, a adj. complementary.

com·ple·men·to m. complement; GRAM. object.

com·ple·tar tr. to complete; *(acabar)* to finish.

com·ple·to, a adj. complete; *(acabado)* finished; *(lleno)* full ♦ **por c.** completely.

com·ple·xión f. constitution.

com·pli·ca·ción f. complication.

com·pli·ca·do, a adj. complicated; *(intricado)* complex; FIG. difficult.

com·pli·car §70 tr. to complicate; *(embrollar)* to entangle —reflex. to become complicated; *(embrollarse)* to become involved.

cóm·pli·ce m.f. accomplice.

com·plot m. plot; *(intriga)* scheme.

com·plo·tar intr. to plot, conspire.

com·po·nen·te adj. & m. component.

com·po·ner §54 tr. to compose; *(reparar)* to fix; *(adornar)* to decorate; *(reconciliar)* to reconcile; *(arreglar)* to arrange; COLL. *(calmar)* to settle; S. AMER., MED. to set (bones) —intr. to compose —reflex. to be composed *or* made up (de of); *(calmarse)* to compose oneself ♦ **componérselas** COLL. to fend for oneself.

com·pon·ga, go see **componer.**

com·por·ta·mien·to m. behavior, conduct.

com·por·tar tr. to entail —reflex. to behave ♦ **c. mal** to misbehave.

com·po·si·ción f. composition ♦ **hacer c. de lugar** to size up the situation.

com·po·si·tor, ·ra m.f. MUS. composer; PRINT. compositor.

com·pos·tu·ra f. *(reparación)* repair; *(aseo)* neatness; *(decoro)* decorum; *(calma)* composure ♦ **en c.** under repair.

com·po·ta f. compote, stewed fruit.

com·po·te·ra f. compote bowl *or* dish.

com·pra f. *(acción)* purchasing; *(adquisición)* purchase ♦ **c. al contado** cash purchase • **c. a plazos** credit purchase ♦ pl. **hacer c.** to shop • **ir de c.** to go shopping.

com·pra·dor, ·ra I. adj. purchasing II. m.f. *(adquiridor)* purchaser; *(cliente)* customer.

com·prar tr. to buy, purchase; *(sobornar)* to bribe ♦ **c. al contado** to pay cash for • **c. al por mayor** to buy wholesale • **c. al por menor** to purchase at retail • **c. a plazos** *or* **fiado** to buy on credit.

com·pra·ven·ta f. buying and selling ♦ **boleto de c.** purchase and sale agreement.

com·pren·de·dor, ·ra adj. understanding.

com·pren·der tr. to understand; *(contener)* to include.

com·pren·si·ble adj. comprehensible.

com·pren·sión f. understanding.

com·pren·si·vo, a adj. comprehensive.

com·pre·sa f. compress ♦ **c. fría** cold pack.

com·pre·si·ble adj. compressible.

com·pre·sión f. compression; GRAM. syneresis.

compre·so, a see **comprimir.**

com·pre·sor, ·ra I. adj. compressing, compressive II. m. MECH. compressor.

com·pri·mi·do, a I. adj. compressed; FIG. repressed II. m. tablet, pill.

com·pri·mir tr. to compress; FIG. to repress.
com·pro·ba·ción f. (verificación) verification; (prueba) proof.
com·pro·ban·te m. proof; COM. voucher ♦ **c. de venta** sales slip.
com·pro·bar §19 tr. (cotejar) to check; (verificar) to verify.
com·pro·ba·to·rio, a adj. confirming.
com·pro·me·te·dor, ra adj. compromising.
com·pro·me·ter tr. (poner en peligro) to endanger; (poner en apuros) to compromise; (la salud) to impair; (obligar) to oblige —reflex. (obligarse) to commit oneself; (ponerse en peligro) to compromise oneself; (novios) to get engaged ♦ **c. a** to undertake to.
com·pro·me·ti·do, a adj. (envuelto) implicated; (embarazoso) compromising; (escritor) committed; (busy) tied up.
com·pro·mi·so m. (obligación) obligation; (apuro) jam; (convenio) agreement; (novios) engagement ♦ **sin c.** without obligation.
com·prue·be, bo see **comprobar.**
com·puer·ta f. (esclusa) floodgate; (puerta) hatch.
com·pues·to, a I. see **componer II.** adj. compound; (arreglado) decked out; (mesurado) calm **III.** m. compound, composite.
com·pul·sar tr. LAW to compare.
com·pul·sión f. LAW compulsion, duress.
com·pun·ción f. compunction, remorse.
com·pun·gir §32 tr. to move to compunction —reflex. to feel compunction ♦ **c. por** to grieve at.
com·pu·sie·ra, so see **componer.**
com·pu·ta·ción f. computation, calculation.
com·pu·ta·dor m./**do·ra** f. computer.
com·pu·tar tr. to compute, calculate.
com·pu·ta·ri·zar/te·ri·zar §04 tr. to computerize.
cóm·pu·to m. computation, calculation.
co·mul·gar §47 tr. to administer communion to —intr. to take communion; FIG. to commune.
co·mún I. adj. common; (usual) customary, usual; (compartido) shared, joint; (vulgar) common, vulgar; FIN. common, public ♦ **por lo c.** commonly, generally **II.** m. general public or population ♦ **el c. de las gentes** most people.
co·mu·na f. commune; AMER. municipality.
co·mu·nal adj. communal.
co·mu·ni·ca·ble adj. (transmisible) communicable; (sociable) sociable.
co·mu·ni·ca·ción f. communication; TELEC. connection ♦ **estar en c. con** to be in touch with.
co·mu·ni·ca·do m. communiqué ♦ **c. de prensa** press release.
co·mu·ni·car §70 tr. to communicate; (transmitir) to transmit; (propagar) to spread —intr. (tener paso) to adjoin; (tratar) to communicate —reflex. to communicate; (tener paso) to be connected.
co·mu·ni·ca·ti·vo, a adj. communicative.
co·mu·ni·dad f. community.
co·mu·nión f. communion; (comunicación) fellowship; (sacramento) (Holy) Communion.
co·mu·nis·ta m.f. communist.
co·mún·men·te adv. commonly, generally; (usualmente) usually.
con prep. with; (a pesar de) in spite of, despite; (hacia) to, towards ♦ **c. ira** in anger • **c.**

que so then • **c. tal (de) que** provided that • **c. todo** nevertheless.
co·na·to m. attempt.
con·ca·de·nar tr. to link (up), concatenate.
con·ca·te·na·ción f. concatenation.
con·ca·vi·dad f. (calidad) hollowness; (hueco) hollow.
cón·ca·vo, a adj. concave, hollow.
con·ce·bi·ble adj. conceivable, imaginable.
con·ce·bir §48 tr. (imaginar) to imagine; (comprender) to understand; (engendrar) to conceive —intr. to conceive.
con·ce·der tr. (otorgar) to grant; (admitir) to concede.
con·ce·jal, ·la m.f. (town) councilor —m. councilman —f. councilwoman.
con·cen·tra·ción f. concentration.
con·cen·tra·do, a adj. (centrado) centered; (condensado) concentrated.
con·cen·trar tr. & reflex. to concentrate.
con·cén·tri·co, a adj. concentric.
con·cep·ción f. conception.
con·cep·to m. concept; (idea) idea; (juicio) opinion ♦ **bajo ningún c.** under no circumstances • **en** or **por c. de** as, by way of • **tener buen c. de** or **tener en buen c. a** to think highly of.
con·cep·tual adj. conceptual.
con·cep·tuar §67 tr. to consider, judge.
con·cer·nien·te adj. concerning, regarding ♦ **en lo c. a** as for, with regard to.
con·cer·nir §25 tr. to concern, be pertinent to —intr. to be pertinent or related.
con·cer·tar §49 tr. (coordinar) to arrange, coordinate —intr. to agree.
con·cer·tis·ta m.f. concert performer, soloist.
con·ce·sión f. concession.
con·ce·sio·na·rio, a I. adj. concessionary **II.** m.f. concessionaire, licensee.
con·cha f. ZOOL. shell; (molusco) shellfish, mollusk; (carey) tortoise shell.
con·cha·bar tr. (unir) to join; (mezclar) to mix; AMER. to hire on —reflex. COLL. to band together.
con·ci·ba, bo, biera, bió see **concebir.**
con·cien·cia f. conscience; (integridad) conscientiousness; (conocimiento) consciousness ♦ **a c.** conscientiously • **en c.** in good conscience or faith • **remorderle a uno la c.** to have a guilty conscience • **sin c.** unscrupulous • **tener** or **tomar c.** to be or become aware of.
con·cien·zu·do, a adj. conscientious.
con·cier·na, ne see **concernir.**
con·cier·te, to see **concertar.**
con·cier·to m. concert; (ajuste) agreement; MUS. harmony; (obra) concerto.
con·ci·lia·ble adj. conciliable, reconcilable.
con·ci·liá·bu·lo m. secret meeting.
con·ci·lia·ción f. conciliation, reconciliation.
con·ci·lia·dor, ra adj. conciliatory.
con·ci·liar tr. to conciliate, reconcile ♦ **c. el sueño** to get to sleep —reflex. to win, gain.
con·ci·lia·ti·vo/to·rio, a adj. conciliatory.
con·ci·lio m. council.
con·ci·so, a adj. concise, succinct.
con·ciu·da·da·no, a m.f. fellow citizen.
cón·cla·ve or **con·cla·ve** m. conclave.
con·cluir §18 tr. to conclude, finish; (deducir) to deduce; LAW to sum up —intr. to finish, end ♦ **c. con** or **en** to end with or in • **c. por** to end up —reflex. to finish, end.
con·clu·sión f. conclusion, end; (deducción)

deduction; *(decisión)* decision; LAW summary ♦ **en c.** in conclusion, finally • **llegar a una c.** to come to a conclusion.
con·clu·si·vo, a adj. conclusive, final.
con·clu·ya, yo, yera, yó see **concluir.**
con·clu·yen·te adj. conclusive, decisive.
con·co·mi·tan·cia f. concomitance.
con·co·mi·tan·te adj. concomitant.
con·cor·dan·cia f. agreement; MUS. harmony.
con·cor·dar §19 tr. to bring into agreement; GRAM. to make agree —intr. to agree.
con·cor·de adj. in accord, in agreement.
con·cor·dia f. *(armonía)* concord; *(ajuste)* agreement.
con·cre·tar tr. *(resumir)* to summarize; *(precisar)* to specify —reflex. to limit *or* confine oneself; *(tomar forma)* to take shape.
con·cre·ti·zar §04 tr. to materialize.
con·cre·to, a I. adj. concrete; *(definido)* specific, definite ♦ **en c.** in short **II.** m. AMER. concrete.
con·cu·bi·na f. concubine.
con·cu·bi·na·to m. common-law marriage.
con·cuer·de, do see **concordar.**
con·cu·ña·do, a m. husband of one's sister-in-law —f. wife of one's brother-in-law.
con·cu·pis·cen·cia f. *(lascivia)* concupiscence; *(codicia)* greed.
con·cu·pis·cen·te adj. *(lascivo)* concupiscent; *(avaro)* greedy.
con·cu·rren·cia f. audience, crowd; *(simultaneidad)* concurrence.
con·cu·rren·te I. adj. *(coincidente)* coinciding; *(presente)* in attendance **II.** m.f. person in attendance.
con·cu·rri·do, a adj. *(animado)* busy, crowded; *(popular)* well-attended; *(frecuentado)* frequented.
con·cu·rrir intr. *(convenir)* to concur, agree; *(converger)* to converge; *(presenciar)* to attend; *(coincidir)* to coincide; *(contribuir)* to contribute ♦ **c. en** to agree *or* concur with.
con·cur·san·te m.f. competitor, contestant.
con·cur·so m. competition, contest ♦ **c. hípico** horse show • **fuera de c.** out of the running.
con·da·do m. *(dignidad)* earldom; *(territorio)* county.
con·de m. count, earl.
con·de·co·ra·ción f. *(insignia)* medal; *(ceremonia)* award ceremony.
con·de·co·rar tr. to decorate, award.
con·de·na f. *(juicio)* sentence; *(declaración)* conviction; *(extensión)* term ♦ **c. condicional** suspended sentence • **c. perpetua** life sentence • **cumplir una c.** to serve a sentence.
con·de·na·do, a I. adj. *(culpable)* convicted; *(réprobo)* reprobate **II.** m.f. *(prisionero)* convict; *(réprobo)* reprobate; COLL. *(desgraciado)* wretch.
con·de·nar tr. *(castigar)* to condemn, sentence; *(declarar culpable)* to convict; *(reprobar)* to censure; *(desaprobar)* to disapprove of; *(cerrar)* to board up.
con·de·na·to·rio, a adj. LAW condemnatory.
con·den·sa·ble adj. condensable.
con·den·sa·ción f. condensation.
con·den·sa·dor, ra I. adj. condensing **II.** m. condenser.
con·den·sar tr. *(reducir)* to condense; *(abreviar)* to shorten.
con·de·sa f. countess.
con·des·cen·den·cia f. acquiescence.

con·des·cen·der §50 intr. to acquiesce ♦ **c. a** to be gracious enough to.
con·des·cen·dien·te adj. agreeable, obliging.
con·di·ción f. condition; *(estado)* state; *(clase)* status; *(cláusula)* stipulation; *(calidad)* capacity ♦ **a c. de que** on the condition that ♦ pl. *(aptitud)* talent; *(circunstancias)* circumstances • **c. convenidas** COM. terms agreed upon • **c. de pago** COM. terms of payment • **c. de vida** living conditions • **estar en c. de** to be fit for • **poner en c.** to get ready • **sin c.** unconditionally.
con·di·cio·na·do, a adj. *(acondicionado)* conditioned; *(condicional)* conditional ♦ **c. a** dependent upon.
con·di·cio·nal adj. conditional.
con·di·cio·nar intr. to agree —tr. ♦ **c. a** to make (something) conditional on.
con·di·men·tar tr. to season, flavor.
con·di·men·to m. condiment, seasoning.
con·dis·cí·pu·lo, a m.f. classmate.
con·do·len·cia f. condolence, sympathy.
con·do·ler·se §78 reflex. to sympathize *(de, por* with).
con·do·mi·nio m. condominium.
con·dón m. condom.
con·do·na·ción f. *(acción)* pardoning; *(resultado)* pardon.
cón·dor m. condor.
con·duc·ción f. *(transporte)* transportation; *(cañería)* piping; AUTO. driving; PHYS. conduction.
con·du·cen·te adj. conducive.
con·du·cir §22 tr. *(guiar)* to lead; *(dirigir)* to manage; *(llevar)* to transport; AUTO. to drive —intr. to lead; AUTO. to drive —reflex. to conduct oneself.
con·duc·ta f. conduct ♦ **mala c.** misconduct.
con·duc·ti·vo, a adj. conductive.
con·duc·to m. conduit; ANAT. duct ♦ **por c. de** by means of, through • **por c. regular** through regular channels.
con·duc·tor, ra I. adj. conducting; PHYS. conductive **II.** m.f. AUTO. driver; PHYS. conductor.
con·due·la, lo see **condolerse.**
con·due·ño, a m.f. joint owner, co-owner.
con·du·je·ra, jo, zca, zco see **conducir.**
co·nec·tar tr. to connect; *(acoplar)* to hook up; *(enchufar)* to plug in; *(relacionar)* to put in touch with.
co·ne·ja f. doe rabbit ♦ **ser una c.** COLL. to have a lot of children.
co·ne·je·ro, a m.f. *(criador)* rabbit breeder; *(vendedor)* rabbit seller —f. rabbit burrow.
co·ne·ji·llo m. bunny ♦ **c. de Indias** guinea pig.
co·ne·jo m. rabbit.
co·ne·xión f. connection.
co·ne·xo, a adj. connected, related.
con·fa·bu·la·ción f. plot, conspiracy.
con·fa·bu·la·dor, ra m.f. schemer, plotter.
con·fa·bu·lar tr. to discuss —reflex. to plot.
con·fec·ción f. *(fabricación)* manufacture; *(ropa hecha)* ready-to-wear clothing.
con·fec·cio·nar tr. to make, manufacture.
con·fe·de·ra·ción f. confederation; *(liga)* league.
con·fe·de·ra·do, a I. adj. confederated, allied **II.** m.f. confederate, ally.
con·fe·de·rar tr. & reflex. to confederate.
con·fe·ren·cia f. conference; *(discusión)* discussion; *(discurso)* lecture ♦ **c. de prensa** press

conference • **c. de alto nivel** summit conference.

con·fe·ren·cian·te m.f. lecturer, speaker.

con·fe·ren·ciar intr. to confer.

con·fe·ren·cis·ta m.f. lecturer, speaker.

con·fe·rir §65 tr. to confer, bestow.

con·fe·sar §49 tr. to confess; *(admitir)* to admit; *(proclamar)* to proclaim ♦ **c. de plano** to make a clean breast of —reflex. to confess.

con·fe·sión f. confession; *(admisión)* admission; *(del reo)* testimony.

con·fe·sor m. confessor.

con·fia·do, a adj. *(en sí mismo)* confident; *(en los demás)* trusting; *(crédulo)* gullible.

con·fian·za f. confidence; *(seguridad)* self-confidence; *(familiaridad)* closeness ♦ **con toda c.** in all confidence • **de c.** *(confiable)* reliable; *(íntimo)* close • **defraudar la c. de alguien** to let someone down • **en c.** confidentially • **tener c. con alguien** to be on close terms with someone • **tratar a alguien con c.** to treat someone informally.

con·fian·zu·do, a adj. COLL. bold, fresh.

con·fiar §30 intr. to trust, feel confident; *(contar con)* to count on ♦ **c. a la memoria** to commit to memory —tr. *(encargar)* to entrust; *(un secreto)* to confide —reflex. to trust, have faith.

con·fi·den·cia f. *(confianza)* confidence; *(secreto)* secret.

con·fi·den·cial adj. confidential.

con·fi·den·te m.f. *(consejero)* confidant; *(informante)* informant —m. *(canapé)* love seat.

con·fie·ra, ro see **conferir**.

con·fie·se, so see **confesar**.

con·fi·gu·rar tr. to shape, form.

con·fín I. adj. bordering II. m. border ♦ pl. confines.

con·fi·na·mien·to m. confinement; *(destierro)* exile.

con·fi·nar intr. to border —tr. *(encarcelar)* to confine; *(desterrar)* to exile.

con·fi·rie·ra, rió see **conferir**.

con·fir·ma·ción f. confirmation.

con·fir·mar tr. to confirm; *(corroborar)* to endorse.

con·fis·ca·ción f. confiscation, appropriation.

con·fis·car §70 tr. to confiscate, appropriate.

con·fi·ta·do, a adj. candied, sugar-coated.

con·fi·tar tr. to candy.

con·fi·te m. candy, sweet.

con·fi·te·rí·a f. candy shop; AMER. tearoom, café.

con·fi·tu·ra f. confiture, preserve.

con·fla·gra·ción f. conflagration.

con·flic·ti·vo, a adj. conflicting.

con·flic·to m. conflict; *(lucha)* struggle; *(choque)* clash; *(apuro)* quandary; *(angustia)* agony.

con·fluen·cia f. confluence.

con·fluir §18 intr. to converge.

con·for·mar tr. *(adaptar)* to conform, adapt; *(dar forma)* to shape, fashion —intr. to agree *(con, en* with, on); *(satisfacer)* to please —reflex. to resign oneself.

con·for·me I. adj. ♦ **c. a** consistent with • **c. con** resigned to • **c. en** in agreement on II. adv. as soon as ♦ **c. a** in accordance with III. m. approval.

con·for·mi·dad f. *(concordancia)* agreement; *(asentimiento)* consent; *(resignación)* resignation ♦ **de c.** in agreement.

con·for·mis·ta adj. & m.f. conformist.

con·fort m. comfort.

con·for·ta·ble adj. comfortable.

con·for·tan·te adj. comforting, consoling.

con·for·tar tr. *(consolar)* to console; *(dar vigor)* to invigorate; *(animar)* to cheer.

con·fra·ter·ni·dad f. fraternity, fellowship.

con·fra·ter·ni·zar §04 intr. to fraternize.

con·fron·ta·ción f. confrontation; *(comparación)* comparison.

con·fron·tar tr. to confront; *(comparar)* to compare.

con·fun·di·do, a adj. confused.

con·fun·dir tr. to confuse; *(desordenar)* to mix up; *(desconcertar)* to perplex —reflex. *(mezclarse)* to be mixed up; *(en una multitud)* to mingle; *(equivocarse)* to get mixed up; *(turbarse)* to be confused or perplexed.

con·fu·sa·men·te adv. *(con turbación)* confusedly; *(en desorden)* in confusion or disorder.

con·fu·sión f. confusion.

con·fu·so, a adj. *(mezclado)* mixed up; *(no claro)* unclear; *(desconcertado)* perplexed.

con·ga f. AMER., MUS. conga.

con·ge·la·ble adj. *(que se puede congelar)* freezable; *(que se puede cuajar)* congealable.

con·ge·la·ción f. freezing, congealing.

con·ge·la·dor m. freezer.

con·ge·la·mien·to m. var. of **congelación**.

con·ge·lar tr. to freeze —reflex. to become frozen.

con·gé·ne·re m. fellow.

con·ge·nial adj. congenial.

con·ge·niar intr. to be compatible, get along.

con·gé·ni·to, a adj. congenital.

con·ges·tión f. congestion ♦ **c. cerebral** stroke • **c. pulmonar** pneumonia.

con·ges·tio·nar tr. to congest —reflex. to become or be congested.

con·glo·me·ra·ción f. conglomeration.

con·glo·me·ra·do, a I. adj. conglomerate II. m. conglomerate; FIG. conglomeration.

con·glo·me·rar tr. & reflex. to conglomerate.

con·go·ja f. *(angustia)* anguish; *(pena)* grief.

con·go·jar tr. to distress, cause anguish.

con·gra·ciar tr. to win over —reflex. to ingratiate oneself.

con·gra·tu·la·ción f. congratulation.

con·gra·tu·lar tr. to congratulate.

con·gra·tu·la·to·rio, a adj. congratulatory.

con·gre·ga·ción f. congregation.

con·gre·gar §47 tr. & reflex. to congregate.

con·gre·sal/sis·ta m.f. AMER. congressman/woman, delegate.

con·gre·so m. *(reunión)* congress, meeting; POL. Congress (of the United States).

con·grio m. conger eel.

con·gruen·cia f. congruity; MATH. congruence.

con·gruen·te f. fitting; MATH. congruent.

có·ni·co, a adj. conic, conical.

co·ní·fe·ro, a I. adj. coniferous II. f. conifer.

co·ni·for·me adj. coniform, cone-shaped.

con·je·tu·ra f. conjecture, guess.

con·je·tu·rar tr. to conjecture, guess.

con·ju·ga·ción f. conjugation.

con·ju·gar §47 tr. to combine; GRAM. to conjugate.

con·jun·ción f. conjunction.

con·jun·ta·men·te adv. jointly, together.

con·jun·ti·vi·tis f. conjunctivitis.

con·jun·ti·vo, a I. adj. conjunctive II. f. ANAT. conjunctiva.

con·jun·to m. (totalidad) whole; (agregado) collection; (vestido) outfit; (de muebles) suite (of furniture); MECH. unit; MUS. band ♦ **c. motriz** ARG. power plant • **en c.** altogether.

con·ju·rar tr. (exorcizar) to exorcise; (alejar) to ward off —intr. & reflex. to conspire.

con·ju·ro m. exorcism; (sortilegio) spell.

con·me·mo·ra·ción f. commemoration.

con·me·mo·rar tr. to commemorate, celebrate.

con·me·mo·ra·ti·vo, a adj. commemorative.

con·men·su·rar tr. to make commensurate.

con·mi·go pron. with me ♦ **c. mismo** with myself.

con·mi·na·ción f. threat, menace.

con·mi·nar tr. to threaten, menace.

con·mi·se·ra·ción f. commiseration.

con·mi·se·rar·se reflex. to commiserate.

con·mo·ción f. commotion; (sacudimiento) shock; (tumulto) upheaval ♦ **c. cerebral** concussion.

con·mo·ve·dor, ·ra adj. moving, touching.

con·mo·ver §78 tr. (emocionar) to move, touch; (sacudir) to shake —reflex. to be moved or touched.

con·mu·ta·ble adj. commutable.

con·mu·ta·ción f. commutation.

con·mu·tar tr. to trade; LAW to commute.

con·no·ta·ción f. connotation.

con·no·tar tr. to connote, imply.

con·nu·bio m. matrimony, marriage.

co·no m. cone.

co·no·ce·dor, ·ra I. adj. knowledgeable, informed II. m.f. connoisseur.

co·no·cer §17 tr. to know; (tener contacto) to meet; (reconocer) to recognize ♦ **c. de nombre** to know by name • **c. de vista** to know by sight —intr. ♦ **c. de** to know about.

co·no·ci·ble adj. knowable.

co·no·ci·do, a I. adj. well-known, famous II. m.f. acquaintance.

co·no·ci·mien·to m. knowledge; (entendimiento) understanding; MED. consciousness ♦ **con c. de causa** with full knowledge of the facts • **c. de embarque** COM. bill of lading • **perder el c.** to lose consciousness • **poner en c. de** to inform, notify.

con·que conj. (and) so.

con·quis·ta f. conquest.

con·quis·ta·ble adj. (que se puede conquistar) conquerable; (fácil de conseguir) attainable.

con·quis·ta·dor, ·ra I. adj. conquering II. m.f. conqueror; FIG. Don Juan.

con·quis·tar tr. to conquer; (conseguir) to win; (cautivar) to win over.

con·sa·bi·do, a adj. (tradicional) usual; (muy conocido) well-known.

con·sa·gra·ción f. consecration.

con·sa·gra·do, a adj. (sagrado) consecrated; (dedicado) devoted; (confirmado) time-honored.

con·sa·grar tr. RELIG. to consecrate; (dedicar) to devote; (confirmar) to establish —reflex. (dedicarse) to devote or dedicate oneself (a to); (adquirir fama) to establish oneself.

con·sa·gra·to·rio, a adj. consecratory, consecrative.

con·san·guí·ne·o, a I. adj. consanguineous II. m.f. blood relation.

con·san·gui·ni·dad f. blood relationship.

cons·cien·cia f. var. of **conciencia**.

cons·cien·te adj. (enterado) aware; MED. conscious; (responsable) conscientious.

cons·cien·te·men·te adv. knowingly.

cons·crip·ción f. AMER. conscription.

cons·crip·to m. AMER. conscript, draftee.

con·se·cuen·cia f. consequence; (deducción) deduction; (resultado) outcome ♦ **a** or **como c. de** as a result or consequence of • **de c.** of consequence or importance • **en c.** accordingly • **por c.** consequently, therefore • **sacar en c.** to conclude • **traer como c.** to result in.

con·se·cuen·te adj. & m. consequent.

con·se·cuen·te·men·te adv. consequently, therefore.

con·se·cu·ti·vo, a adj. consecutive.

con·se·guir §64 tr. (obtener) to obtain; (llegar a hacer) to attain; (lograr) to manage.

con·se·je·ro, a m.f. (guía) counselor; (de un consejo) councilor.

con·se·jo m. advice; POL. council ♦ **c. de guerra** court-martial • **c. de ministros** cabinet.

con·sen·so m. consensus.

con·sen·ti·do, a adj. spoiled, pampered.

con·sen·ti·mien·to m. consent.

con·sen·tir §65 tr. (autorizar) to consent; (permitir) to allow; (mimar) to spoil, pamper; (soportar) to bear ♦ **c. a** or **con** to be indulgent with.

con·ser·je m. (custodio) concierge; (portero) porter.

con·ser·je·rí·a f. concierge's office; (de un hotel) reception desk.

con·ser·va f. (confitura) preserve; (alimentos) preserved food ♦ **conservas alimenticias** canned goods • **en c.** canned.

con·ser·va·ción f. conservation; (cuidado) up-keep.

con·ser·va·dor, ·ra I. adj. (preservativo) conserving; POL. conservative; (prudente) prudent II. m.f. POL. conservative; (oficio) conservator.

con·ser·var tr. to conserve; (preservar) preserve; (guardar) to keep; (cuidar) to keep up; (mantener) to keep; CUL. to can —reflex. (permanecer) to survive; (cuidarse) to take care of oneself; (guardar para sí) to keep for oneself; CUL. to keep, stay fresh.

con·ser·va·to·rio, a I. adj. conservatory, preservative II. m. conservatory.

con·si·de·ra·ble adj. considerable; (poderoso) powerful; (importante) important.

con·si·de·ra·ción f. consideration; (atención) attention; (importancia) importance; (respeto) regard ♦ **bajo** or **en c.** under consideration • **de c.** considerable • **en c. a** considering in consideration of • **por c.** out of consideration • **tomar en c.** to take into consideration.

con·si·de·ra·do, a adj. (respetuoso) considerate; (respetado) respected.

con·si·de·ran·do m. LAW whereas.

con·si·de·rar tr. to consider; (reflexionar) to take into consideration; (estimar) to regard —reflex. to be considered; (a sí mismo) to consider oneself.

con·sien·ta, te see **consentir**.

con·si·ga, go see **conseguir**.

con·sig·na f. (órdenes) orders; (slogan) watchword; (depósito) checkroom.

con·sig·na·ción f. COM. consignment; FIN. (depósito) deposit.

con·sig·na·dor m.f. consignor.

con·sig·nar tr. to consign; *(depositar)* to deposit; *(citar)* to note down; *(asignar)* to allocate.

con·sig·na·to·rio m. COM. consignee; LAW assignee.

con·si·go pron. with him, her, them, you ♦ **c. mismo** with himself, oneself, yourself • **c. misma** with herself, yourself • **c. mismos** *or* **mismas** with themselves, yourselves.

con·si·guien·te adj. consequent, resulting ♦ **por c.** consequently, therefore.

con·si·guie·ra, guió see **conseguir**.

con·sin·tie·ra, tió see **consentir**.

con·sis·ten·cia f. consistency; *(estabilidad)* stability; *(coherencia)* coherence ♦ **sin c.** insubstantial; CUL. thin.

con·sis·ten·te adj. consistent.

con·sis·tir intr. to consist *(en* of, in).

con·so·la f. console table.

con·so·la·ción f. consolation.

con·so·lar §19 tr. & reflex. to console (oneself).

con·so·li·da·ción f. consolidation.

con·so·li·dar tr. to consolidate; *(asegurar)* to strengthen —reflex. to consolidate.

con·so·mé m. consommé.

con·so·nan·cia f. consonance.

con·so·nan·te adj. & f. consonant.

con·sor·cio m. consortium; *(de circunstancias)* conjunction.

con·sor·te m.f. consort ♦ pl. LAW joint litigants.

cons·pi·cuo, a adj. famous, eminent.

cons·pi·ra·ción f. conspiracy.

cons·pi·ra·dor, ·ra m.f. conspirator.

cons·pi·rar intr. to conspire.

cons·tan·cia f. constancy; *(perseverancia)* perseverance; *(evidencia)* record; AMER. proof.

cons·tan·te **I.** adj. constant; *(perseverante)* persevering **II.** f. constant.

cons·tar intr. *(ser cierto)* to be clear *or* evident; *(quedar registrado)* to be on record; *(consistir)* to consist *(de* of) ♦ **hacer c.** to point out • **hacer c. por escrito** to put on record • **que conste que** let it be clearly known that.

cons·ta·tar tr. to verify, confirm.

cons·te·la·ción f. constellation.

cons·ter·na·ción f. consternation.

cons·ter·nar tr. to consternate —reflex. to be dismayed.

cons·ti·pa·do m. cold, head cold.

cons·ti·par tr. to give a cold to —reflex. to catch a cold.

cons·ti·tu·ción f. constitution; *(composición)* composition.

cons·ti·tuir §18 tr. to constitute; *(ser)* to be; *(establecer)* to establish —reflex. to be established ♦ **c. en** to assume the position of • **c. en fiador de** to answer for • **c. prisionero** to give oneself up.

cons·ti·tu·ti·vo, a/yen·te adj. & m. component.

cons·tre·ñi·mien·to m. compulsion.

cons·tre·ñir §59 tr. *(compeler)* to compel; *(apretar)* to constrict; *(estreñir)* to constipate.

cons·tric·ción f. constriction.

cons·tric·ti·vo, a adj. constraining.

cons·tri·ña, ñera, ño, ñó see **constreñir**.

cons·truc·ción f. construction; *(edificio)* building ♦ **c. de buques** shipbuilding • **en** *or* **en vías de c.** under construction.

cons·truc·ti·vo, a adj. constructive.

cons·truc·tor, ·ra **I.** adj. construction **II.** m.f. constructor ♦ **c. naval** shipbuilder.

cons·truir §18 tr. to construct, build; *(fabricar)* to manufacture.

con·sue·gro, a m.f. father/mother-in-law of one's son *or* daughter (in relation to oneself).

con·sue·le, lo see **consolar**.

con·sue·lo m. *(alivio)* consolation, solace; *(alegría)* joy, delight ♦ **sin c.** inconsolable.

con·sue·tu·di·na·rio, a adj. *(habitual)* customary; *(empedernido)* confirmed.

cón·sul m. consul ♦ **c. general** consul general.

con·su·la·do m. consulate.

con·sul·ta f. consultation; *(opinión)* opinion, advice ♦ **c. a domicilio** house call.

con·sul·tar intr. to consult (with), get advice (from) ♦ **c. con la almohada** to sleep on it —tr. to consult; *(verificar)* to check; *(discutir)* to discuss.

con·sul·tor, ·ra **I.** adj. advisory **II.** m. advisor.

con·sul·to·rio m. *(oficina)* office; MED. doctor's office.

con·su·ma·ción f. consummation; *(fin)* end.

con·su·ma·do, a adj. consummate ♦ **hecho c.** accomplished fact.

con·su·mar tr. to consummate.

con·su·mi·ción f. consumption; *(bebida)* drink ♦ **c. mínima** cover charge.

con·su·mi·do, a adj. thin, emaciated.

con·su·mi·dor, ·ra **I.** adj. consuming **II.** m.f. consumer.

con·su·mir tr. to consume; *(gastar)* use up; *(destruir)* to destroy; *(malgastar)* to waste; *(evaporar)* to evaporate; *(afligir)* to consume —reflex. to be consumed *or* used (up); *(destruirse)* to be destroyed; *(malgastarse)* to waste away; *(evaporarse)* to evaporate; *(afligirse)* to be consumed.

con·su·mo m. consumption ♦ **bienes de c.** consumer goods.

con·ta·bi·li·dad f. *(teneduría de libros)* bookkeeping; *(profesión)* accountancy.

con·ta·bi·li·zar §04 tr. COM. to enter, record.

con·ta·ble **I.** adj. countable, computable; *(relatable)* relatable **II.** m.f. accountant.

con·tac·to m. contact ♦ **lentes** *or* **lentillas de c.** contact lenses • **ponerse en c.** to get in touch.

con·ta·do, a adj. rare ♦ **al c.** (in) cash.

con·ta·dor, ·ra **I.** adj. counting **II.** m.f. *(de libros)* accountant; *(administrador)* auditor —m. *(aparato)* counting device; TECH. meter ♦ **c. público nacional** certified public accountant.

con·ta·du·rí·a f. *(estudio)* accounting; *(oficio)* accountancy; *(oficina)* accounting office.

con·ta·giar tr. MED. to contaminate; FIG. to corrupt —reflex. MED. to become infected; FIG. to become corrupt.

con·ta·gio m. MED. contagion; FIG. contamination.

con·ta·gio·so, a adj. MED. contagious; FIG. catching.

con·ta·mi·na·ción f. contamination; *(corrupción)* corruption; *(del aire, agua)* pollution.

con·ta·mi·nar tr. to contaminate; *(aire, agua)* to pollute; *(corromper)* to corrupt —reflex. to be contaminated; *(corromperse)* to be corrupted.

con·tan·te adj. ♦ **dinero c. y sonante** cash.

con·tar §19 tr. to count (up); *(referir)* to tell —intr. to count ♦ **c. con** *(confiar)* to count *or*

rely on; *(tener en cuenta)* to figure on • ¿qué cuentas? what's up?
con·tem·pla·ción f. contemplation.
con·tem·plar tr. & intr. to contemplate.
con·tem·po·ra·nei·dad f. contemporaneity.
con·tem·po·rá·ne·o, a adj. & m.f. contemporary.
con·tem·po·ri·za·ción f. compromise.
con·tem·po·ri·zar §04 intr. to compromise.
con·tén see **contener.**
con·ten·ción f. containment; *(contienda)* competition; LAW dispute.
con·ten·cio·so, a adj. contentious.
con·ten·der §50 intr. to contend; *(competir)* to compete; *(disputar)* to dispute.
con·ten·dien·te I. adj. contending, opposing II. m.f. contender, competitor.
con·te·ner §69 tr. to contain; *(impedir)* to hold back —reflex. to contain *or* control oneself.
con·te·ni·do, a I. adj. contained, controlled II. m. content(s).
con·ten·ta·di·zo, a adj. easily satisfied.
con·ten·tar tr. to content —reflex. to be content.
con·ten·to, a I. adj. *(alegre)* happy, pleased; *(satisfecho)* satisfied, content II. m. *(alegría)* happiness; *(satisfacción)* contentment.
con·tes·ta·ción f. answer.
con·tes·tar tr. to answer; LAW. to corroborate —intr. to answer.
con·tex·to m. context.
con·tien·da f. *(pelea)* battle; *(disputa)* argument; *(competencia)* contest.
con·tien·da, do see **contender.**
con·tie·ne see **contener.**
con·ti·go pron. with you ♦ **c. mismo** with yourself.
con·ti·guo, a adj. contiguous, adjacent.
con·ti·nen·cia f. continence, abstinence.
con·ti·nen·te adj. & m. continent.
con·tin·gen·cia f. contingency.
con·tin·gen·te adj. & m. contingent.
con·ti·nua·ción f. continuation; *(prolongación)* continuance ♦ **a c.** next, following.
con·ti·nuar §67 tr. to continue (on) —intr. to continue, go on.
con·ti·nuo, a I. adj. continuous; *(constante)* constant ♦ **de c.** continually II. m. continuum III. adv. continually.
con·to·ne·ar·se reflex. to sway one's hips.
con·to·ne·o m. swaying of the hips.
con·tor·cer·se §71 reflex. to contort oneself.
con·tor·ción f. contortion.
con·tor·no m. contour, outline; *(perímetro)* perimeter ♦ pl. surroundings.
con·tor·sión f. contortion; *(mueca)* grimace.
con·tor·sio·nis·ta m.f. contortionist.
con·tra I. prep. against ♦ **c. viento y marea** against all odds • **en c. de** against II. m. con —f. ♦ **llevar la c.** to oppose • **hacerle** *or* **llevarle la c. (a alguien)** to contradict (someone).
con·tra·al·mi·ran·te m. MARIT. rear admiral.
con·tra·a·ta·que m. counterattack.
con·tra·ban·de·ar intr. to smuggle.
con·tra·ban·dis·ta m.f. smuggler.
con·tra·ban·do m. *(mercancía)* contraband; *(acción)* smuggling.
con·trac·ción f. contraction.
con·tra·cep·ción f. contraception.
con·tra·cep·ti·vo, a adj. & m. contraceptive.
con·tra·cha·pa·do, a adj. & m. plywood.

con·trac·tual adj. contractual.
con·tra·cul·tu·ra f. counterculture.
con·tra·de·cir §11 tr. to contradict —reflex. to contradict oneself.
con·tra·dic·ción f. contradiction.
con·tra·dic·to·rio, a adj. contradictory.
con·tra·er §72 tr. to contract; *(reducir)* to shorten; *(deudas)* to incur; *(enfermedad)* to catch; *(vicio)* to pick up ♦ **c. la frente** to wrinkle one's brow • **c. matrimonio** to get married.
con·tra·es·pio·na·je m. counterespionage.
con·tra·faz f. reverse, other side.
con·tra·he·cho, a adj. deformed, hunchbacked.
con·trai·ga, go see **contraer.**
con·tra·in·di·ca·ción f. contraindication.
con·tra·in·di·car §70 tr. to contraindicate.
con·tra·je·ra, jo see **contraer.**
con·tral·mi·ran·te m. var. of **contraalmirante.**
con·tra·lor m. comptroller, inspector.
con·tra·ma·es·tre m. *(en un taller)* foreman; MARIT. boatswain.
con·tra·ma·no adv. ♦ **a c.** the wrong way.
con·tra·mar·cha f. countermarch; AUTO. reverse.
con·tra·o·fen·si·va f. counteroffensive.
con·tra·par·ti·da f. COM. cross entry.
con·tra·pe·lo adv. ♦ **a c.** against the grain; FIG. contrary to normal practice.
con·tra·pe·sar tr. to counterbalance.
con·tra·pe·so m. counterbalance.
con·tra·po·ner §54 tr. *(oponer)* to oppose; *(comparar)* to contrast —reflex. to set oneself against.
con·tra·po·si·ción f. *(oposición)* opposition; *(comparación)* comparison; *(contraste)* contrast.
con·tra·pro·du·cen·te adj. counterproductive.
con·tra·pro·po·si·ción f. counterproposal.
con·tra·pues·to, a see **contraponer.**
con·tra·pun·to m. counterpoint.
con·tra·pu·sie·ra, so see **contraponer.**
con·tra·ria f. see **contrario, a.**
con·tra·riar §30 tr. *(oponer)* to oppose; *(contradecir)* to contradict; *(enfadar)* to vex.
con·tra·rie·dad f. *(obstáculo)* obstacle; *(desazón)* annoyance; *(contratiempo)* setback; *(percance)* mishap.
con·tra·rio, a I. adj. opposite; *(adverso)* adverse ♦ **al c.** to the contrary • **al c. de** contrary to • **por el c.** on the contrary • **todo lo c.** quite the opposite II. m.f. opponent, adversary —f. ♦ **llevar la c.** COLL. to contradict.
con·tra·rres·tar tr. to offset; *(resistir)* to resist.
con·tra·rre·vo·lu·ción f. counterrevolution.
con·tra·sen·ti·do m. *(contradicción)* contradiction; *(disparate)* absurdity.
con·tra·se·ña f. password ♦ **c. de salida** readmission ticket.
con·tras·tar intr. to contrast —tr. to verify; METAL. to assay and hallmark.
con·tras·te m. contrast; *(oposición)* opposition; METAL. *(control)* assay; *(marcador)* assayer ♦ **en c. con** in contrast to • **hacer c. con** to contrast to *or* with • **por c.** in contrast.
con·tra·tar tr. to contract for; *(emplear)* to hire.
con·tra·tiem·po m. setback; MUS. syncopation.
con·tra·tis·ta m.f. contractor ♦ **c. de obras** building contractor.
con·tra·to m. contract ♦ **c. colectivo de trabajo** labor contract • **c. de administración** manage-

ment contract • **c. de locación** lease • **c. de compraventa** purchase agreement • **c. de fideicomiso** deed of trust • **c. de palabra** verbal contract • **c. de prenda** collateral contract • **c. de trabajo** employment contract • **c. matrimonial** marriage contract.

con·tra·ven·ción f. contravention.

con·tra·ve·nir §76 intr. LAW to contravene.

con·tra·ven·ta·na f. *(puertaventana)* storm window; *(postigo)* shutter.

con·tra·ven·tor, ·ra I. adj. violating **II.** m.f. violator.

con·tri·bu·ción f. contribution; *(impuesto)* tax ♦ **c. territorial** land tax • **c. urbana** property *or* real estate tax.

con·tri·bui·dor, ·ra I. adj. contributory, contributing **II.** m.f. contributor.

con·tri·buir §18 tr. & intr. to contribute.

con·tri·bu·yen·te I. adj. *(que contribuye)* contributing; *(que paga impuestos)* taxpaying **II.** m.f. *(que contribuye)* contributor; *(que paga impuestos)* taxpayer.

con·tri·ción f. contrition, repentance.

con·trin·can·te m. rival, opponent.

con·tri·to, a adj. contrite, repentant.

con·trol m. control; *(inspección)* inspection; *(comprobación)* check; *(lugar)* checkpoint; *(examen)* examination; COM. audit ♦ **c. de frontera** border checkpoint • **c. de la natalidad** birth control • **c. sobre sí mismo** self-control.

con·tro·lar tr. to control; *(inspeccionar)* to inspect; *(comprobar)* to check; COM. to audit.

con·tro·ver·sia f. controversy, dispute.

con·tro·ver·ti·ble adj. controvertible.

con·tu·maz adj. obstinate; LAW in default ♦ **condenar por c.** to convict by default.

con·tun·den·te adj. overwhelming.

con·tu·sión f. bruise, contusion.

con·tu·so, a adj. & m.f. bruised (person).

con·tu·vie·ra, vo see **contener.**

con·va·le·cen·cia f. convalescence.

con·va·le·cer §17 intr. to convalesce.

con·va·le·cien·te adj. & m.f. convalescent (patient).

con·va·li·dar tr. to confirm, ratify.

con·ven·cer §75 tr. to convince —reflex. to be *or* become convinced.

con·ven·ci·ble adj. convincible.

con·ven·ci·mien·to m. conviction.

con·ven·ción f. convention.

con·ven·drá, dría, ga, go see **convenir.**

con·ve·ni·ble adj. *(dócil)* easy-going; *(precio)* fair.

con·ve·ni·do adv. agreed.

con·ve·nien·cia f. *(provecho)* advantage; *(comodidad)* convenience ♦ **ser de la c. de uno** to be convenient for someone.

con·ve·nien·te adj. convenient; *(oportuno)* suitable; *(aconsejable)* advisable; *(provechoso)* advantageous ♦ **creer** or **juzgar c.** to think or see fit.

con·ve·nio m. agreement; *(pacto)* pact; COM. settlement ♦ **c. comercial** trade agreement • **llegar a un c.** to reach an agreement.

con·ve·nir §76 intr. *(acordar)* to concur; *(corresponder)* to be fitting; *(venir bien)* to suit; *(ser aconsejable)* to be advisable.

con·ven·ti·lle·ro, a m.f. R.P. gossip, meddler.

con·ven·ti·llo m. AMER. tenement house.

con·ven·to m. convent; *(monasterio)* monastery.

con·ver·gen·cia f. convergence.

con·ver·gen·te adj. convergent, converging.

con·ver·ger §34/gir §32 intr. to converge; *(concurrir)* to concur.

con·ver·sa f. COLL. talk, chat.

con·ver·sa·ción f. conversation ♦ **cambiar de c.** to change the subject • **dar c.** to make conversation • **dirigir la c. a uno** to address someone • **trabar c.** to strike up a conversation.

con·ver·sa·dor, ·ra adj. & m.f. talkative (person).

con·ver·sar intr. to converse, talk.

con·ver·sión f. conversion.

con·ver·ti·ble I. adj. convertible, changeable **II.** m. AUTO. convertible.

con·ver·ti·dor m. ELEC., METAL. converter.

con·ver·tir §65 tr. *(cambiar)* to change, turn; *(persuadir)* to convert; COM., FIN. to exchange —reflex. to convert, be converted ♦ **c. en** to turn into.

con·ve·xo, a adj. convex.

con·vic·ción f. conviction.

con·vic·to, a I. see **convencer II.** adj. convicted **III.** m.f. convict.

con·vi·da·do, a m.f. guest.

con·vi·dar tr. to invite ♦ **c. a uno con** to treat someone to.

con·vie·ne see **convenir.**

con·vier·ta, to see **convertir.**

con·vin·cen·te adj. convincing.

con·vi·nie·ra, no see **convenir.**

con·vir·tie·ra, tió see **convertir.**

con·vi·te m. *(invitación)* invitation; *(banquete)* banquet, feast.

con·vi·ven·cia f. living together; *(coexistencia)* coexistence.

con·vi·vir intr. to live together.

con·vo·ca·ción f. convocation.

con·vo·car §70 tr. to convoke, summon.

con·vo·ca·to·ria f. summons, notice.

con·voy m. convoy; *(escolta)* escort; *(vinagreras)* cruet; *(tren)* train; *(séquito)* retinue.

con·vul·sión f. convulsion; *(trastorno)* upheaval; *(temblor)* tremor.

con·vul·sio·nar tr. to convulse; FIG. to agitate.

con·vul·si·vo, a adj. convulsive ♦ **tos c.** whooping cough.

con·yu·gal adj. conjugal, connubial.

cón·yu·ge m.f. spouse ♦ pl. husband and wife.

co·ñac m. [pl. **s**] cognac, brandy.

co·o·pe·ra·ción f. cooperation.

co·o·pe·rar intr. to cooperate.

co·o·pe·ra·ti·vo, a adj. & f. cooperative.

co·or·de·na·da f. MATH. coordinate.

co·or·di·na·ción f. coordination.

co·or·di·na·dor, ·ra I. adj. coordinating **II.** m.f. coordinator.

co·or·di·nar tr. to coordinate.

co·pa f. glass, goblet; *(contenido)* glassful; *(trago)* drink; *(de árbol)* treetop; *(de sombrero)* crown; SPORT. cup ♦ **tomarse una c.** to have a drink *or* cocktail.

co·par tr. *(en un juego)* to cover *or* wager (the bank); POL. to win, sweep (an election).

co·par·ti·ci·pe m.f. copartner.

co·pe·te m. *(mechón)* tuft (of hair); ZOOL. forelock; ORNITH. crest; *(cima)* summit, top ♦ **de alto c.** high-class • **tener mucho c.** to be arrogant.

co·pe·tín m. AMER., COLL. drink, cocktail.

co·pia f. copy; *(duplicado)* duplicate; *(imagen)* image; *(imitación)* imitation; ARTS reproduction; CINEM., PHOTOG. print ♦ **c. fotostática** photostat • **sacar una c.** to make a copy.

co·pia·dor, ·ra I. adj. copying **II.** m.f. copyist —m. COM. letter book —f. photocopier.

co·piar tr. to copy; *(hacer una copia)* to make a copy of; *(apuntar)* to copy down.

co·pi·lo·to m. copilot.

co·pio·si·dad f. copiousness, abundance.

co·pio·so, a adj. copious, abundant.

co·pla f. *(canción)* ballad; *(estrofa)* stanza ♦ pl. COLL. verses, poetry.

co·po m. *(de nieve)* snowflake; TEX. *(mechón)* bundle (of flax) ♦ **c. de algodón** cotton ball.

co·po·se·sión f. co-ownership.

co·pro·duc·ción f. coproduction.

co·pro·pie·dad f. joint ownership.

co·pro·pie·ta·rio, a m.f. co-owner.

có·pu·la f. *(unión)* coupling; *(coito)* copulation; GRAM. copula.

co·pu·la·ti·vo, a adj. copulative.

co·que·te·ar intr. to flirt.

co·que·te·o m. flirtation.

co·que·te·rí·a f. flirtatiousness.

co·que·to, a I. adj. *(agradable)* charming; *(mujer)* flirtatious **II.** f. flirt.

co·que·tón, o·na COLL. adj. *(agradable)* charming; *(mujer)* flirtatious.

co·ra·je m. *(valor)* courage; *(ira)* anger ♦ **dar c. a** to make angry.

co·ral[1] m. coral —f. coral snake.

co·ral[2] **I.** adj. choral **II.** m. chorale.

co·ra·za f. *(armadura)* cuirass; FIG. armor; ZOOL. shell.

co·ra·zón m. heart; *(valor)* spirit; *(amor)* love ♦ **blando de c.** softhearted • **con el c. en la mano** frankly, openly • **de c.** sincerely • **duro de c.** hardhearted • **encogérsele a uno el c.** to be moved with pity • **helársele a uno el c.** to be stunned • **no caberle al c. en el pecho** to be bursting (with joy) • **no tener c.** to be heartless • **ojos que no ven, c. que no siente** out of sight, out of mind.

co·ra·zo·na·da f. *(impulso)* impulse; *(presentimiento)* premonition.

cor·ba·ta f. tie, necktie ♦ **con c.** wearing a tie • **c. de lazo** bow tie.

cor·cel m. steed, charger.

cor·che·a f. eighth note, quaver (G.B.) ♦ **doble c.** sixteenth note, semiquaver (G.B.).

cor·che·te m. *(broche)* hook and eye, clasp; *(macho del broche)* hook (of clasp); PRINT. *(llave)* bracket.

cor·cho m. cork; *(de la pesca)* float ♦ **sacar el c.** to uncork.

¡cór·cho·lis! interj. good heavens!, gracious!

cor·co·ve·ar intr. to buck; FIG. to grumble.

cor·del m. cord, thin rope.

cor·de·ro m. lamb; *(piel)* lambskin.

cor·dial I. adj. *(afectuoso)* cordial, warm; *(reconfortante)* tonic ♦ **saludos cordiales** cordially yours **II.** m. tonic.

cor·dia·li·dad f. cordiality, warmth.

cor·di·lle·ra f. chain of mountains, cordillera.

cor·di·lle·ra·no, a adj. & m.f. Andean.

cór·do·ba f. NIC., FIN. cordoba.

cor·dón m. *(cuerda)* cord; *(cinta)* cordon, braid; ANAT., ELEC. CORD.

cor·don·ci·llo m. *(de tela)* rib; *(de una moneda)* milling.

cor·du·ra f. prudence, wisdom.

co·re·o·gra·fí·a f. choreography.

co·re·ó·gra·fo m. choreographer.

co·ris·ta m.f. MUS. chorus singer; RELIG. chorister; THEAT. member of the chorus.

cor·na·da f. *(golpe)* butt (with a horn); *(herida)* goring ♦ **dar una c.** to gore.

cor·na·men·ta f. horns; *(de ciervo)* antlers.

cór·ne·a f. cornea.

cor·ne·ta f. bugle; *(de caza)* hunting horn; MIL. cornet —m. bugler.

cor·ne·tín m. cornet; *(persona)* cornetist; MIL. bugle.

cor·ni·sa f. cornice.

cor·no m. horn.

cor·nu·co·pia f. cornucopia.

cor·nu·do, a I. adj. horned; COLL. cuckolded ♦ **tras c., apaleado** COLL. adding insult to injury **II.** m. COLL. cuckold.

co·ro m. chorus, choir ♦ **a c.** in unison.

co·ro·la f. BOT. corolla.

co·ro·la·rio m. corollary.

co·ro·na f. crown; *(de laureles)* wreath; *(aureola)* halo; ARCHIT., ASTRON. corona ♦ **ceñirse la c.** to assume the crown *or* throne.

co·ro·na·ción f. crowning, coronation.

co·ro·nar tr. to crown; *(en ajedrez)* to queen.

co·ro·nel m. colonel.

co·ro·ni·lla f. crown ♦ **estar hasta la c.** COLL. to be fed up.

cor·pa(n)·chón m. COLL. big *or* bulky body.

cor·pi·ño m. *(jubón)* sleeveless bodice; R.P. bra, brassiere.

cor·po·ra·ción f. corporation.

cor·po·rei·dad f. corporeity, corporeality.

cor·pó·re·o, a adj. *(material)* corporeal; *(corporal)* corporal.

cor·pu·len·cia f. corpulence.

cor·pús·cu·lo m. corpuscle.

co·rral m. corral; *(redil)* pen.

co·rra·lón m. *(de animales)* large corral; *(de madera)* lumberyard.

co·rre·a f. *(de cuero)* strap; *(cinturón)* belt; TECH. belt.

co·rre·a·je m. straps, belts.

co·rre·a·zo m. blow with a leather strap.

co·rrec·ción f. *(modificación)* adjustment; *(urbanidad)* propriety ♦ **c. de pruebas** proofreading.

co·rrec·cio·nal I. adj. corrective **II.** m. reformatory, prison.

co·rrec·to, a I. see **corregir II.** adj. correct.

co·rrec·tor, ·ra I. adj. corrective **II.** m.f. corrector; PRINT. proofreader.

co·rre·de·ra f. *(carril)* track; *(de molino)* upper millstone; MECH. slide valve.

co·rre·di·zo, a adj. *(puerta)* sliding; *(nudo)* slip.

co·rre·dor, ·ra I. adj. running **II.** m.f. runner —m. *(pasillo)* corridor; *(galería)* gallery; COM. agent ♦ **c. de apuestas** bookmaker • **c. de cambios** stockbroker • **c. de seguros** insurance agent.

co·rre·gir §57 tr. *(enmendar)* to correct; *(castigar)* to chastise; PRINT. to proofread —reflex. to mend one's ways.

co·rre·la·ción f. correlation.

co·rre·la·cio·nar tr. to correlate, relate.

co·rre·la·ti·vo, a adj. & m. correlative.

co·rre·li·gio·na·rio, a m.f. FIG. colleague.

co·rren·ta·da f. AMER. strong current.

co·rre·o m. mail; *(mensajero)* messenger; *(buzón)* mailbox; *(oficina)* post office ♦ **a vuelta de c.** by return mail • **c. aéreo** air mail • **c. certificado** registered mail • **echar al c.** to

mail • **por c.** by mail ♦ pl. *(servicio)* mail service; *(oficina)* post office.
co·rrer intr. to run; *(en una carrera)* to race; *(aguas)* to flow; *(viento)* to blow; *(camino)* to run; *(horas)* to pass; *(la moneda)* to be valid; *(rumor)* to circulate ♦ **a todo c.** at full speed • **c. a** to hurry to • **c. con** to be responsible for • **c. la voz** to be said • **c. por cuenta de** *or* **a cargo de** to be the responsibility of —tr. to race; *(riesgo)* to run; *(mundo)* to cover; *(persona)* to chase; *(muebles)* to move; *(balanza)* to tip; *(cortinas)* to draw; *(cerrojo)* to slide; *(nudo)* to slip; *(aventuras)* to meet with; AMER. to throw (someone) out ♦ **correrla** COLL. to live it up —reflex. *(deslizarse)* to slide; *(moverse)* to slide over.
co·rre·rí·a f. excursion; MIL. foray.
co·rres·pon·den·cia f. *(relación)* relationship; *(conformidad)* agreement; *(cartas)* correspondence, mail.
co·rres·pon·der intr. *(ser igual a)* to correspond, match; *(tener proporción con)* to fit *or* go with; *(reciprocar)* to return; *(incumbir)* to fall to; *(tocar)* to be one's turn to; *(pertenecer)* to belong; *(ser la proporción)* to be the share of —reflex. *(escribir)* to correspond; *(amarse)* to love each other.
co·rres·pon·dien·te **I.** adj. corresponding **II.** m.f. correspondent.
co·rres·pon·sal adj. & m.f. correspondent.
co·rre·ta·je m. *(oficio)* brokerage; *(comisión)* broker's fee.
co·rre·te·ar intr. *(vagar)* to wander the streets; *(retozar)* to frolic —tr. *(perseguir)* to chase; C. AMER. *(despedir)* to dismiss.
co·rre·ve(i)·di·le m.f. COLL. gossipmonger.
co·rri·da f. race, run ♦ **c. de toros** bullfight • **dar una c.** to make a dash • **de c.** quickly • **en una c.** in a flash.
co·rri·do, a **I.** adj. *(excedido)* full; *(consecutivo)* straight; *(experimentado)* worldly ♦ **de c.** *(con fluidez)* fluently; *(rápido)* quickly **II.** m. ballad.
co·rrien·te **I.** adj. *(que corre)* running; *(actual)* current; *(sabido)* well-known; *(usual)* usual; *(ordinario)* ordinary; *(moderno)* up-to-date ♦ **al c.** up-to-date • **poner al c.** to bring up-to-date • **tener al c.** to keep informed **II.** f. current; FIG. trend *<una nueva c. a new trend>* ♦ **c. alterna** alternating current • **c. continua** *or* **directa** direct current • **dejarse llevar por la c.** *or* **ir con la c.** to go along with the crowd • **llevarle** *or* **seguirle la c. (a alguien)** to humor (someone).
co·rrien·te·men·te adv. *(actualmente)* currently; *(comúnmente)* usually.
co·rri·ja, jo see **corregir**.
co·rri·llo m. small circle *or* group, clique.
co·rro m. *(de personas)* circle of talkers; *(espacio)* ring.
co·rro·bo·ra·ción f. corroboration.
co·rro·bo·rar tr. to corroborate.
co·rro·bo·ra·ti·vo, a adj. corroborative.
co·rro·er §61 tr. *(carcomer)* to corrode; GEOL. to erode; FIG. to eat away at.
co·rrom·per tr. to corrupt; *(pervertir)* to pervert; *(seducir)* to seduce; *(sobornar)* to bribe; *(pudrir)* to decay —reflex. *(pervertirse)* to become corrupt; *(degenerar)* to degenerate.
co·rro·sión f. corrosion.
co·rro·si·vo, a adj. corrosive.
co·rro·ya, yera, yó see **corroer**.
co·rrup·ción f. corruption.

co·rrup·ti·ble adj. corruptible.
co·rrup·to, a **I.** see **corromper** **II.** adj. corrupt, corrupted.
co·rrup·tor, ·ra **I.** adj. corrupting **II.** m.f. corrupter.
cor·sa·rio m. corsair.
cor·sé m. corset, corselet.
cor·ta·cés·ped m. lawnmower.
cor·ta·cir·cui·tos m.inv. circuit breaker.
cor·ta·co·rrien·te m. current breaker, switch.
cor·ta·do, a **I.** adj. *(estilo)* disjointed; COLL. *(sin palabras)* speechless; AMER. *(sin dinero)* broke **II.** m. coffee with milk —f. AMER. cut, gash.
cor·ta·dor, ·ra **I.** adj. cutting **II.** m. *(el que corta)* cutter; *(carnicero)* butcher —f. cutter.
cor·ta·du·ra f. *(acción)* cutting; *(incisión)* cut; GEOG. mountain pass ♦ pl. scraps.
cor·tan·te adj. cutting, sharp.
cor·ta·pa·pel/pe·les m. letter opener.
cor·ta·plu·mas m.inv. pocketknife.
cor·tar tr. to cut; *(recortar)* to trim; *(carne, aves)* to carve; *(en porciones)* to cut up; *(separar)* to cut off; *(un árbol)* to cut down, fell; *(con un molde)* to cut out; *(atravesar)* to cut through; *(diluir)* to dilute; *(omitir)* to cut out; *(suspender)* to discontinue; *(interrumpir)* to cut off; *(acortar)* to cut short, criticize; R.P. *(ahorrar camino)* to cut (through *or* across) ♦ **c. por la mitad** to cut in half —intr. to cut; *(el frío)* to be cutting ♦ **c. por lo sano** to take drastic measures —reflex. *(turbarse)* to become flustered; *(la piel)* to chap; *(la leche)* to curdle.
cor·ta·ú·ñas m.inv. nail clipper.
cor·te¹ m. *(acción)* cutting; *(filo)* *(cutting)* edge; SEW. cutting (out); *(de tela)* length; *(estilo)* cut; TECH. section ♦ **c. de pelo** haircut • **c. y confección** dressmaking • **darse c.** COLL. to put on airs.
cor·te² f. *(residencia)* (royal) court; *(comitiva)* retinue; AMER. court of law ♦ **hacer la c. a** to court.
cor·te·jar tr. *(galantear)* to woo; *(halagar)* to court.
cor·te·jo m. *(galanteo)* courting; *(séquito)* entourage ♦ **c. fúnebre** funeral cortege.
cor·tés adj. courteous, polite.
cor·te·sa·no, a **I.** adj. courtly **II.** m. courtier —f. courtesan.
cor·te·sí·a f. courtesy; *(galantería)* charm.
cor·te·za f. *(de árbol)* bark; *(de fruta)* peel; *(del pan)* crust; *(de queso, tocino)* rind; ANAT., BOT. cortex.
cor·ti·jo m. farm, grange.
cor·ti·na f. curtain; FIG. screen ♦ **c. de fuego** barrage of fire • **c. de hierro** Iron Curtain.
cor·to, a adj. short; *(breve)* brief; *(escaso)* short; *(tímido)* shy ♦ **a la c. o a la larga** sooner or later • **c. de vista** shortsighted • **ni c. ni perezoso** without thinking twice • **quedarse c.** to fall short.
cor·to·cir·cui·to m. short circuit.
cor·va·du·ra f. curvature; ARCHIT. curve.
cor·var tr. to curve, bend.
co·sa f. thing; *(algo)* something; *(en negaciones)* anything; *(asunto)* business ♦ **como c. tuya** as if it came from you • **como quien no quiere la c.** COLL. offhandedly • **como si tal c.** COLL. as if such a thing had never happened • **c. del otro mundo** COLL. extraordinary thing • **c. de ver** something worth seeing • **c. nunca vista** COLL. something unheard of • **cosas de la vida**

ups and downs • **c. seria** serious matter • **ni c. que lo parezca** nor anything of the kind • **no es gran c.** it's nothing great • **no hay tal c.** there's no such thing • **no sea c. que** lest • **¿qué c.?** COLL. what did you say?

cos·co·rrón m. knock on the head.

co·se·cha f. harvest; *(temporada)* harvest time; FIG. crop ♦ **de su propia c.** of one's own invention.

co·se·cha·do·ra f. combine.

co·se·char tr. to harvest; *(frutas, flores)* to pick —intr. to harvest.

co·se·no m. cosine.

co·ser tr. to sew ♦ **c. a puñaladas** to stab repeatedly —intr. to sew.

cos·mé·ti·co, a adj. & m. cosmetic.

cós·mi·co, a adj. cosmic.

cos·mo·gó·ni·co, a adj. cosmogonic.

cos·mo·gra·fí·a f. cosmography.

cos·mo·lo·gí·a f. cosmology.

cos·mo·ló·gi·co, a adj. cosmological.

cos·mo·nau·ta m.f. cosmonaut, astronaut.

cos·mo·po·li·ta adj. & m.f. cosmopolitan (person).

cos·mos m.inv. cosmos, universe.

cos·qui·llas f.pl. ticklishness ♦ **hacer c.** to tickle • **tener c.** to be ticklish.

cos·qui·lle·ar tr. to tickle.

cos·ta f. *(costo)* cost; *(orilla)* shore ♦ **a c. ajena** at someone else's expense • **a c. de** at the expense of • **a toda c.** at all costs ♦ pl. LAW fees, costs.

cos·ta·do m. side; MIL. flank ♦ **de c.** sideways • **por los cuatro costados** through and through • **tenderse de c.** to lie on one's side.

cos·tal m. sack ♦ **ser harina de otro c.** COLL. to be another story.

cos·ta·ne·ro, a adj. coastal; *(inclinado)* sloping.

cos·tar §19 intr. to cost; FIG. *(ser difícil)* to find it difficult to ♦ **c. barato** to be cheap *or* inexpensive • **c. caro** to be expensive • **c. trabajo** to take a lot to • **c. un ojo de la cara** COLL. to cost a fortune • **cueste lo que cueste** at all costs.

cos·te m. cost.

cos·te·ar tr. to finance; MARIT. to coast —reflex. R.P. to arrive with difficulty.

cos·te·ro, a I. adj. coastal II. f. *(cuesta)* slope; *(costa)* shore; MARIT. fishing season.

cos·ti·lla f. ANAT. rib; *(chuleta)* cutlet, chop; *(de una silla)* rung; *(de un barril)* stave ♦ pl. COLL. back • **a las c. de** at the expense of.

cos·ti·llar m. ribs.

cos·to m. cost ♦ **al c.** at cost • **c. de la vida** cost of living • **c. efectivo** actual cost.

cos·to·so, a adj. *(caro)* costly; *(grave)* grievous.

cos·tra f. crust; MED. scab.

cos·tum·bre f. custom; *(hábito)* habit; *(práctica)* practice ♦ **de c.** *(usual)* usual; *(usualmente)* usually • **novela de costumbres** novel of manners • **por c.** out of habit • **tener por c.** to be in the habit of.

cos·tu·ra f. needlework; *(unión)* seam; MARIT. seam, splice; MED. scar ♦ **alta c.** high fashion • **sin c.** seamless.

cos·tu·re·ra f. seamstress.

cos·tu·re·ro m. sewing basket.

co·ta f. coat of arms ♦ **c. de malla** coat of mail.

co·te·jar tr. to compare.

co·te·jo m. comparison.

co·te·rrá·ne·o, a adj. of the same country *or* region.

co·ti·dia·no, a adj. daily, everyday.

co·ti·le·dón m. cotyledon, seed leaf.

co·ti·llo m. head (of a hammer).

co·ti·llón m. cotillion (dance).

co·ti·za·ción f. COM. quotation.

co·ti·zar §04 tr. COM. to quote; *(valorar)* to price.

co·to m. *(terreno)* reserved area; *(mojón)* boundary marker; *(población)* small village in an estate ♦ **c. de caza** game preserve • **poner c.** **a** to put a stop to.

co·to·rra f. *(loro)* parakeet; *(urraca)* magpie; COLL. chatterbox.

co·to·rre·ar intr. COLL. to chatter, babble.

co·to·rre·o m. COLL. chatter, babbling.

co·tu·fa f. Jerusalem artichoke.

co·va·cha f. *(cueva)* small cave; AMER. *(vivienda)* shack.

co·xis m.inv. coccyx.

co·yo·te m. coyote.

co·yun·tu·ra f. ANAT. joint; *(oportunidad)* chance; *(circunstancias)* circumstance.

coz f. kick; ARM., recoil ♦ **dar** *or* **pegar coces** to kick.

cra·ne·al/a·no, a adj. cranial.

crá·ne·o m. cranium, skull.

cra·so, a adj. crass, gross.

crá·ter m. crater.

cre·a·ción f. creation.

cre·a·dor, ·ra I. adj. creative II. m.f. creator.

cre·ar tr. to create; *(fundar)* to found; *(establecer)* to establish; *(inventar)* to invent.

cre·cer §17 intr. to grow; *(aumentar)* to increase; *(la luna)* to wax; *(un río)* to swell ♦ **c. como la cizaña** to grow like weeds • **dejarse c. la barba** to grow a beard.

cre·ces f.pl. ♦ **con c.** amply.

cre·ci·do, a I. adj. *(grande)* large; *(adulto)* grown ♦ **estar c.** *(un río)* to be in flood II. f. spate.

cre·cien·te I. adj. *(que crece)* growing; *(que aumenta)* increasing; *(la luna)* crescent II. m. HER. crescent —f. *(luna)* crescent moon; *(marea)* flood tide.

cre·ci·mien·to m. *(acción)* growth; *(aumento)* increase; *(de la luna)* waxing; *(de un río)* swelling.

cre·den·cial I. adj. accrediting II. f. credential.

cré·di·to m. *(aceptación)* credence; *(reputación)* reputation; COM. credit ♦ **dar** *or* **dar c.** **a** to give *or* extend credit to • **a c.** on credit.

cre·do m. creed; *(doctrina)* credo.

cré·du·lo, a adj. credulous, gullible.

cre·en·cia f. *(convicción)* belief; *(fe)* faith.

cre·er §43 tr. to believe; *(imaginar)* to think; *(estimar)* to consider ♦ **c. a ciencia cierta** to be convinced of • **c. a pie juntillas** to believe blindly • **c. que sí** to think so • **según creo** to the best of my knowledge • **¡ya lo creo!** COLL. I should say so! —intr. to believe ♦ **ver es c.** seeing is believing —reflex. to consider *or* regard oneself ♦ **¿qué se cree?** who does he think he is?

cre·í·ble adj. credible, believable.

cre·í·do, a I. see **creer** II. adj. *(confiado)* credulous; *(vanidoso)* conceited.

cre·ma f. cream; *(natillas)* custard; *(cosmética)* cold cream; *(lo mejor)* cream of the crop ♦ **c.**

batida whipped cream • **c. de afeitar** shaving cream.

cre·ma·ción f. cremation.

cre·ma·lle·ra f. MECH. toothed bar; *(cierre)* zipper.

cre·ma·to·rio, a adj. & m. crematory.

cre·mo·so, a adj. creamy.

cren·cha f. *(raya)* part (of hair); *(parte)* each side of parted hair.

cre·o·so·ta f. creosote.

cre·pé m. *(tela fina)* crepe, crêpe; *(caucho)* crepe rubber.

cre·pi·tar intr. to crackle.

cre·pus·cu·lar adj. twilight.

cre·pús·cu·lo m. twilight.

cres·po, a adj. *(cabello)* kinky; *(hoja)* curly.

cres·ta f. crest; *(copete)* tuft; *(cima)* summit ♦ **c. de gallo** cockscomb • **alzar** or **levantar la c.** COLL. to show arrogance • **dar en la c. a uno** COLL. to cut someone down to size.

cre·ta f. chalk.

cre·tá·ce·o, a adj. cretaceous.

cre·ti·nis·mo m. cretinism.

cre·ti·no, a I. adj. cretinous; FIG. stupid II. m.f. cretin.

cre·yen·te I. adj. believing II. m.f. believer.

cre·ye·ra, yó see **creer.**

crí·a f. raising; *(animal)* offspring; *(camada)* litter.

cria·de·ro, a m. BOT. nursery; ZOOL. breeding place ♦ **c. de ostras** oyster bed.

cria·di·lla f. testicle (of an animal).

cria·do, a I. adj. bred, brought up II. m. servant —f. maid.

cria·dor, ·ra m.f. breeder.

crian·za f. nurturing; ZOOL. raising; *(lactancia)* lactation; *(cortesía)* manners ♦ **dar c.** to bring up.

criar §30 tr. *(nutrir)* to nurse; *(animales)* to raise; *(niños)* to bring up ♦ **c. carnes** COLL. to put on weight —intr. to reproduce, have young —reflex. to be brought up; *(crecer)* to grow.

cria·tu·ra f. *(niño)* infant; *(cosa creada)* creature.

cri·ba f. screen, sieve.

cri·bar tr. to sift, screen.

cric m. MECH. jack.

cri·men m. crime; FIG. shame.

cri·mi·nal adj. & m.f. criminal.

cri·mi·na·li·dad f. *(calidad)* criminality; *(índice)* crime rate.

cri·mi·na·lis·ta m.f. criminologist; *(abogado)* criminal lawyer.

cri·mi·no·lo·gí·a f. criminology.

cri·mi·nó·lo·go m. criminologist.

crin f. horsehair.

crí·o m. COLL. *(de pecho)* infant; *(niño)* kid.

crio·llo, a adj. & m.f. native.

crip·ta f. crypt.

cri·sá·li·da f. chrysalis, pupa.

cri·san·te·mo m./ma f. chrysanthemum.

cri·sis f.inv. crisis; *(escasez)* shortage ♦ **c. ministerial** cabinet crisis • **c. nerviosa** nervous breakdown • **hacer c.** to reach crisis point.

cris·ma f. COLL. head ♦ **romperle la c. a alguien** COLL. to bash in someone's head.

cri·sol m. crucible.

cris·par tr. ANAT. to contract; FIG. to irritate —reflex. ANAT. to twitch; FIG. to become irritated.

cris·tal m. crystal; *(vidrio)* glass; *(hoja de vidrio)* pane of glass; *(espejo)* mirror ♦ **c. ahumado** smoked glass • **c. de roca** rock crystal •

c. hilado fiber glass • **c. inastillable** splinter-proof glass • **c. irrompible** shatterproof glass • **c. tallado** cut glass • **de c.** glass.

cris·ta·le·rí·a f. glasswork(s); *(tienda)* crystal shop; *(juego)* crystal service; *(objetos)* glassware.

cris·ta·li·no, a I. adj. *(de cristal)* crystalline; *(diáfano)* crystal clear II. m. crystalline lens.

cris·ta·li·zar §04 tr., intr. & reflex. to crystallize.

cris·tian·dad f. Christendom.

cris·tia·nis·mo m. Christianity.

cris·tia·ni·zar §04 tr. to convert to Christianity.

cris·tia·no, a I. adj. Christian II. m.f. Christian; COLL. *(español)* plain Spanish; *(alguien)* living soul.

Cris·to m. Christ.

cri·te·rio m. *(regla)* criterion; *(juicio)* judgment; *(opinión)* opinion.

cri·ti·car §70 tr. to criticize; *(murmurar)* to gossip about.

crí·ti·co, a I. adj. critical; *(crucial)* crucial II. m.f. critic, reviewer —f. criticism; *(reseña)* review; *(murmuración)* gossip.

cri·ti·cón, o·na I. adj. faultfinding II. m.f. faultfinder.

cro·ar intr. to croak.

cro·chet m. crochet.

cro·ma·do m. chromium plating, chroming.

cro·mar tr. to chrome.

cro·má·ti·co, a adj. chromatic.

cro·mo·so·ma m. chromosome.

cró·ni·co, a I. adj. chronic; *(inveterado)* inveterate II. f. *(historia)* chronicle; *(artículo)* article.

cro·nis·ta m.f. *(historiador)* chronicler; *(periodista)* reporter.

cro·nó·gra·fo m. *(persona)* chronologist; *(aparato)* chronograph.

cro·no·lo·gí·a f. chronology.

cro·no·ló·gi·co, a adj. chronologic, chronological.

cro·no·me·trar tr. to time with a chronometer.

cro·nó·me·tro m. chronometer.

cro·que·ta f. CUL. croquette.

cro·quis m.inv. sketch.

crou·pier m.f. croupier.

cru·ce m. *(acción)* crossing; *(punto)* intersection; RAIL. crossing; BIOL. crossbreeding; *(híbrido)* cross, hybrid ♦ **c. a nivel** grade or level crossing • **c. de peatones** pedestrian crossing.

cru·ce·ro m. cruise; ARCHIT. transept; PRINT. crossbar (of a chase).

cru·cial adj. crucial.

cru·ci·fi·car §70 tr. to crucify.

cru·ci·fi·jo m. crucifix.

cru·ci·fi·xión f. crucifixion.

cru·ci·gra·ma m. crossword puzzle.

cru·de·za f. *(estado)* rawness; *(rudeza)* harshness ♦ **con c.** harshly.

cru·do, a I. adj. raw; *(verde)* green; *(amarillento)* yellowish; *(seda)* raw; *(petróleo)* crude; *(clima)* harsh; FIG. cruel II. m. crude oil.

cruel adj. cruel; *(despiadado)* merciless; *(fiero)* savage; *(severo)* severe.

cruel·dad f. cruelty; *(inhumanidad)* inhumanity; *(ferocidad)* savagery; *(severidad)* severity.

cruen·to, a adj. bloody.

cru·ji·do m. *(de hoja, tela)* rustling; *(de puerta)* creaking; *(de dientes)* rattling; *(de huesos)* cracking.

cru·jir intr. *(hoja, tela)* to rustle; *(puerta, madera)* to creak; *(dientes)* to rattle, chatter; *(huesos)* to crack; *(grava)* to crunch.
crus·tá·ce·o, a adj. & m. crustacean.
cruz f. cross; *(reverso)* tails; FIG. cross; PRINT. dagger; MARIT. crown ♦ **en c.** cross-shaped.
cru·za·do, a I. adj. crossed; BIOL., ZOOL. hybrid II. m. crusader —f. HIST. Crusade; FIG. crusade.
cru·za·mien·to m. *(acción)* crossing; *(animales)* crossbreeding.
cru·zar §04 tr. to cross ♦ **cruzarle a uno la cara** FIG. to slap someone across the face —reflex. to cross one another <*las líneas se cruzan* the lines cross one another>; *(pasarse)* to pass ♦ **c. de brazos** to do nothing.
cua·der·no m. notebook.
cua·dra f. stable; *(de casas)* block.
cua·dra·di·llo m. *(regla)* ruler; *(de camisa)* gusset.
cua·dra·do, a adj. & m. square.
cua·dra·ge·na·rio, a adj. & m.f. quadragenarian.
cua·dra·gé·si·mo, a adj. & m. fortieth.
cua·dran·gu·lar adj. quadrangular.
cua·drán·gu·lo, a I. adj. quadrangular II. m. quadrangle.
cua·dran·te m. MARIT., MATH. quadrant; *(reloj)* sundial; *(de reloj)* face.
cua·drar tr. to square —intr. *(conformar)* to square, agree; COM. to balance —reflex. MIL. to stand at attention.
cua·drí·cu·la f. grid.
cua·dri·cu·lar[1] adj. squared.
cua·dri·cu·lar[2] tr. to divide into squares, square (paper).
cua·drie·nio m. quadrennium.
cua·dril m. *(hueso)* hipbone; *(anca)* rump.
cua·dri·lá·te·ro, a adj. & m. quadrilateral.
cua·dri·lla f. *(de obreros)* crew; *(de malhechores)* gang; *(baile)* quadrille; TAUR. team assisting a bullfighter.
cua·dri·pli·car §70 tr. to quadruplicate.
cua·dro m. square; ARTS painting; *(descripción)* description; *(espectáculo)* spectacle; THEAT. scene; *(conjunto de oficiales)* cadre; SPORT. team ♦ **a cuadros** checkered • **c. al óleo** oil painting • **c. vivo** tableau vivant • **en c.** square.
cua·drú·ma·no, a I. adj. quadrumanous II. m.f. quadrumane.
cua·drú·pe·do, a I. adj. quadrupedal II. m.f. quadruped.
cuá·dru·ple adj. quadruple, fourfold.
cua·dru·pli·car §70 tr. & intr. to quadruple.
cuá·dru·plo, a adj. & m. quadruple.
cua·ja·do, a I. adj. ♦ **c. de** full of II. f. curd (of milk).
cua·jar tr. to coagulate, congeal; *(leche)* to curdle; *(adornar)* to cover —intr. COLL. *(tener éxito)* to turn out well —reflex. to coagulate, congeal; *(leche)* to curdle.
cua·jo m. rennet ♦ **de c.** by the roots.
cual I. rel. pron. ♦ **al c.** *(persona)* to whom; *(cosa)* to which • **cada c.** each one, every one • **con lo c.** whereupon, upon which • **del c.** of which • **el c.** *(persona)* who; *(cosa)* which • **por lo c.** whereby, because of which II. adv. like, as ♦ **c. . . . tal** like . . . like • **c. si** as if • **quedarse tal c.** COLL. to be cool as a cucumber.
cuál I. adj. which II. rel. pron. which (one) III. indef. pron. some IV. adv. how.

cua·les·quier see **cualquier.**
cua·les·quie·ra see **cualquiera.**
cua·li·dad f. quality, characteristic.
cua·li·fi·car §70 tr. to qualify, characterize.
cua·li·ta·ti·vo, a adj. qualitative.
cual·quier adj. [pl. **cuales-**] contr. of **cualquiera** used before nouns.
cual·quie·ra [pl. **cuales-**] I. adj. (just) any, any ordinary II. indef. pron. any(one), anybody ♦ **un (hombre) c.** a nobody III. rel. pron. *(persona)* whoever; *(cosa)* whatever; *(nadie)* nobody.
cuan adv. as.
cuán adv. how.
cuan·do I. adv. when, since ♦ **c. más** *or* **mucho** at the most • **c. menos** at least • **de c. en c.** from time to time II. conj. when; *(aunque)* although, even if; *(puesto que)* since; *(si)* if ♦ **aun c.** even though, although • **c. no** if not, otherwise • **c. quiera** whenever III. prep. *(durante)* at the time of; as <*c. niño* as a child>.
cuán·do adv. when.
cuan·tí·a f. *(cantidad)* amount; *(importancia)* importance.
cuan·ti·más adv. COLL. all the more.
cuan·tio·so, a adj. *(grande)* large; *(abundante)* abundant; *(numeroso)* numerous.
cuan·ti·ta·ti·vo, a adj. quantitative.
cuan·to[1] m. quantum.
cuan·to[2] I. adv. *(todo lo que)* as much as; *(todo el tiempo que)* as long as ♦ **c. antes** as soon as possible • **c. más** even more so • **en c.** as soon as • **en c. a** as to, as for • **por c.** insofar as, inasmuch as II. adj. & pron. see **cuanto, a.**
cuán·to I. adv. how ♦ **¡c. me alegro!** how happy I am! • **¡c. cuesta la carne!** how expensive beef is! • **¡c. dura esta película!** how long this movie is! II. adj. & pron. see **cuánto, a.**
cuan·to, a I. adj. as much as ♦ **c. más . . . (tanto) más** the more . . . the more • **c. menos** the less • **cuantos** as many • **unos cuantos** a few, some II. pron. all that, everything, as much as ♦ **unos cuantos** some, a few.
cuán·to, a I. adj. how much ♦ **¿cada c. tiempo?** how often? • **cuántos, cuántas** how many II. pron. how much ♦ **¿a cuántos estamos hoy?** what is today's date? • **¿c. cuesta . . . ?** how much is . . . ? • **cuántos, cuántas** how many.
cua·ren·ta adj. & m. forty; *(cuadragésimo)* fortieth ♦ **cantarle las c. a alguien** COLL. to give someone a piece of one's mind.
cua·ren·ta·vo, a adj. fortieth.
cua·ren·te·na f. *(conjunto)* group of forty; MED. quarantine; COLL. *(aislamiento)* isolation.
cua·ren·tón, o·na adj. & m.f. forty-year-old.
cua·res·ma f. Lent.
cuar·ta f. *(medida)* span (of the hand); ASTRON. quadrant ♦ **andar de la c. al pértigo** R.P., COLL. to live from hand to mouth.
cuar·te·ar tr. *(dividir)* to quarter; *(descuartizar)* to cut up; *(fragmentar)* to crack —reflex. to crack.
cuar·tel m. MIL. barracks ♦ **c. de bomberos** firehouse • **no dar c. a** to show no mercy to • **sin c.** merciless.
cuar·to, a I. adj. fourth II. m. *(habitación)* room; *(cantidad)* fourth, quarter ♦ **c. creciente** first quarter (of the moon) • **c. de baño** bathroom • **c. de dormir** bedroom • **c. de estar** living room • **c. delantero** forequarter • **c. menguante** third quarter (of the moon) • **c.**

trasero hindquarter • **c. y comida** room and board.

cuar·zo m. quartz.

cua·si adv. almost, quasi.

cua·te, a AMER. **I.** adj. *(gemelo)* twin; *(semejante)* similar, alike **II.** m.f. *(gemelo)* twin; *(amigo)* buddy, pal.

cua·tre·re·ar tr. R.P. to steal, rustle (cattle).

cua·tre·ro, a I. adj. *(de caballos)* pertaining to horse thievery; *(de vacas)* cattle-rustling; MEX., COLL. joking **II.** m.f. *(de caballos)* horse thief; AMER. *(de vacas)* cattle rustler; MEX., COLL. joker.

cua·tri·lli·zo, a m.f. quadruplet.

cua·tri·mo·tor m. four-engine plane.

cua·tro I. adj. four; *(cuarto)* fourth ♦ **las c.** four o'clock • **c. gatos locos** COLL. a mere handful of people **II.** m. four; S. AMER. four-string guitar ♦ **más de c.** COLL. quite a few.

cua·tro·cien·tos, as adj. & m. four hundred.

cu·ba f. *(tonel)* cask; *(tina)* vat ♦ **beber como una c.** COLL. to drink like a fish • **estar hecho una c.** COLL. to be plastered.

cu·be·ta f. *(cubo)* bucket; *(tina)* small vat; CHEM., PHOTOG. tray.

cú·bi·co, a adj. GEOM. cubic; MATH. cube (root).

cu·bier·to, a I. see **cubrir II.** m. *(de mesa)* table setting; *(abrigo)* shelter; *(comida)* meal (at a fixed price) ♦ **a c. de** under the protection of • **bajo c.** under cover • **poner los cubiertos** to set the table • **ponerse a c.** to take cover —f. *(cobertura)* cover; *(sobre)* envelope; *(envoltura)* wrapping; MARIT. deck; AUTO. tire.

cu·bil m. lair, den.

cu·bi·le·te m. *(vaso)* tumbler; *(de dados)* dicebox; *(molde)* mold.

cu·bis·ta adj. & m.f. ARTS cubist.

cú·bi·to m. ulna, cubitus.

cu·bo m. cube; *(balde)* bucket; *(tina)* vat; *(de rueda)* hub; *(estanque)* millpond ♦ **a cubos** abundantly • **elevar al c.** MATH. to cube.

cu·bre·ca·de·na m. bicycle chainguard.

cu·bre·ca·ma m. bedcover, bedspread.

cu·brir §80 tr. to cover (up); *(proteger)* to protect; *(esconder)* to conceal; *(con honores, atenciones)* to shower —reflex. *(ponerse ropa)* to cover oneself; *(protegerse)* to protect oneself; COM. to cover a debt.

cu·ca·ra·cha f. cockroach.

cu·cha·ra f. spoon; *(cucharada)* spoonful; TECH. scoop ♦ **c. de albañil** trowel • **c. de postre** dessert spoon • **c. sopera** soupspoon • **meter la c.** COLL. to meddle.

cu·cha·ra·da f. spoonful.

cu·cha·rón m. *(cazo)* ladle; TECH. scoop.

cu·che·ta f. AMER. cabin, berth.

cu·chi·che·ar intr. to whisper.

cu·chi·che·o m. whisper, whispering.

cu·chi·lla f. *(cuchillo)* knife; *(hoja)* blade; *(de afeitar)* razor blade.

cu·chi·lla·da f./zo m. *(golpe)* stab; *(herida)* stab wound.

cu·chi·lle·rí·a f. cutler's shop.

cu·chi·llo m. knife ♦ **c. de cocina** kitchen knife • **pasar a c.** COLL. to kill.

cu·chi·tril m. COLL. pigsty.

cu·cli·llas adv. ♦ **en c.** squatting, crouching • **ponerse** or **sentarse en c.** to squat, crouch.

cu·co, a I. adj. COLL. *(bonito)* cute; *(astuto)* crafty **II.** m.f. clever person —m. ENTOM. caterpillar; ORNITH. cuckoo; *(fantasma)* ghost.

cu·cú m. cuckoo (call of the cuckoo).

cue·ce see **cocer.**

cue·le, lo see **colar.**

cuel·ga, gue see **colgar.**

cue·llo m. neck; *(tira de tela)* collar; BOT. stalk ♦ **alargar el c.** to stretch or crane one's neck • **c. alto** turtleneck • **c. de palomita** wing collar • **c. de pico** V-neck • **c. duro** stiff collar • **c. postizo** detachable collar.

cuen·ca f. ANAT. eye socket; GEOG. valley.

cuen·co m. earthenware bowl.

cuen·ta f. *(de restaurante)* check; *(cálculo)* calculation; *(acción de contar)* counting; *(bolita)* bead; COM. account; *(explicación)* account; *(cargo)* responsibility ♦ **abonar en c.** to credit an account • **a c.** on account • **caer en la c.** COLL. to realize • **cargar en c.** to debit an account • **c. acreedora** credit account • **c. bancaria** or **de banco** bank account • **c. corriente** checking account • **c. de ahorros** savings account • **c. de gastos** expense account • **dar c. de** *(contar)* to give an account of; COLL. *(gastar)* to use up • **darse c. de** to realize • **más de la c.** too much • **perder la c. de** to lose track of • **por c. de** on behalf of • **por su propia c.** for oneself • **por c. y riesgo de uno** at one's own risk • **tener en c.** to bear in mind • **tomar en c.** to take into account • **trabajar por su c.** to be self-employed ♦ pl. accounts • **a fin de c.** in the final analysis • **ajustar c.** COLL. to settle up • **en resumidas c.** in short • **llevar las c.** to keep the books • **pedir c. a** to call to account • **rendir c. de** to give an account of.

cuen·ta·go·tas m.inv. dropper, eyedropper ♦ **dar con c.** to give something bit by little.

cuen·ta·ki·ló·me·tros m.inv. odometer.

cuen·ta·rre·vo·lu·cio·nes m.inv. tachometer.

cuen·te, to see **contar.**

cuen·te·ro, a I. adj. gossip **II.** m.f. gossipmonger.

cuen·tis·ta m.f. LIT. short-story writer; COLL. *(chismoso)* gossipmonger.

cuen·to m. story, tale; LIT. short story; *(chisme)* gossip; *(embuste)* hoax ♦ **c. de hadas** fairy tale • **c. del tío** con game • **c. de nunca acabar** endless story • **c. de viejas** COLL. old wives' tale • **¡puro c.!** all lies! • **traer a c.** COLL. to bring up • **venir a c.** to be to the point • **vivir del c.** COLL. to live by one's wits.

cuer·da f. *(cordón)* cord, string; *(del reloj)* watch spring; MUS. string ♦ **aflojar la c.** COLL. to ease up • **andar en la c. floja** COLL. to walk a tightrope • **bajo c.** underhandedly • **c. floja** tightrope • **dar c. a uno** COLL. to get someone started on a topic • **dar c. a un reloj** to wind a watch • **c. vocales** ANAT. vocal cords.

cuer·do, a adj. & m.f. sane, sensible (person).

cue·re·ar tr. AMER. *(desollar)* to skin; R.P. *(criticar)* to slander.

cuer·no m. horn ♦ **c. de la abundancia** horn of plenty • **¡vete al c.!** go to hell! • ♦ pl. **¡c.!** MEX. fat chance! • **poner los c. a** to cuckold.

cue·ro m. *(piel)* hide; *(de zapatos)* leather; *(odre)* wineskin ♦ **c. cabelludo** scalp • **c. charolado** patent leather • **en cueros** naked.

cuer·pe·ar intr. AMER.to dodge.

cuer·po m. body; *(torso)* torso; *(figura)* figure; *(largo)* length; *(cadáver)* corpse; *(corpiño)* bodice; *(espesor)* thickness; *(parte)* component; GEOM. three-dimensional figure ♦ **a c. de rey** like a king • **c. a c.** hand-to-hand (combat)

• **c. celeste** heavenly body • **c. de baile** dance company • **c. del delito** LAW corpus delicti • **c. diplomático** diplomatic corps • **dar con el c. en la tierra** to fall down • **dar c. a** to thicken • **de c. entero** full-length; FIG. real, true • **estar de c. presente** to lie in state • **ir de c.** COLL. to relieve oneself • **tomar c.** to take shape.

cuer·vo m. crow, raven.

cues·ta f. slope, hill ♦ **a cuestas** on one's shoulders; FIG. upon oneself • **c. abajo** downhill • **c. arriba** uphill • **hacérsele c. arriba** COLL. to find it hard to.

cues·ta, te see **costar.**

cues·tión f. (asunto) question, matter <es una c. de fe it is a matter of faith>; (duda) dispute ♦ **en c. de** in the matter of.

cues·tio·na·ble adj. questionable, debatable.

cues·tio·nar tr. to discuss, debate.

cues·tio·na·rio m. (encuesta) questionnaire; (examen) test questions.

cue·va f. cave ♦ **c. de ladrones** COLL. den of thieves.

cueza, zo see **cocer.**

cui·da·do m. care; (cautela) caution; (miedo) concern ♦ **con c.** (con esmero) carefully; (con cautela) cautiously • **¡c.!** be careful!, watch out! • **c. con** beware of • **perder c.** not to worry • **poner c. en** to take care in • **sin c.** carelessly • **tener c.** to be careful.

cui·da·dor, ·ra I. adj. caretaking II. m.f. caretaker.

cui·da·do·so, a adj. (cauteloso) careful; (atento) attentive.

cui·dar tr. & intr. ♦ **c. de** to take care of —reflex. to take care of oneself ♦ **c. de** (preocuparse) to care about; (protegerse) to be careful about.

cui·ta f. grief.

cu·lan·tro m. coriander.

cu·la·ta f. (del caballo) croup; (del arma) butt; (del cañón) breech ♦ **salir el tiro por la c.** to backfire.

cu·la·ta·zo m. (golpe) blow with a gun butt; ARM. recoil.

cu·le·bra f. snake.

cu·le·bri·lla f. MED. ringworm.

cu·li·na·rio, a adj. culinary.

cul·mi·na·ción f. culmination.

cul·mi·nan·te adj. culminating.

cul·mi·nar intr. to culminate.

cul·pa f. blame, guilt; (falta) fault ♦ **por c. de** through the fault of • **echar la c. a uno** to blame someone • **tener la c.** to be to blame, be guilty.

cul·pa·bi·li·dad f. guilt.

cul·pa·ble I. adj. guilty; (acusado) accused ♦ **confesarse c.** to plead guilty • **declarar c.** to find guilty II. m.f. (reo) culprit; (acusado) accused (party).

cul·pa·do, a I. adj. guilty; (acusado) accused II. m.f. (reo) culprit; (acusado) accused (party).

cul·par tr. (acusar) to accuse; (censurar) to criticize.

cul·ti·va·ción f. cultivation.

cul·ti·va·dor, ·ra I. adj. cultivating II. m.f. cultivator.

cul·ti·var tr. to cultivate; (arar) to farm; (plantar) to grow; BIOL. to culture.

cul·ti·vo m. (labor) cultivation; (cosecha) crop; BIOL. culture ♦ **caldo de c.** culture fluid.

cul·to, a I. adj. (civilizado) cultured; (instruido)

learned II. m. (secta) cult, religion; (homenaje) worship; (rito) ritual ♦ **rendir c. a** (venerar) to worship; (homenajear) to pay tribute to.

cul·tu·ra f. culture; (educación) refinement.

cul·tu·ral adj. cultural.

cum·bre m. summit; FIG. pinnacle.

cum·ple·a·ños m.inv. birthday.

cum·pli·do, a I. adj. (completo) complete; (perfecto) perfect; (cortés) courteous II. m. (cortesía) polite gesture; (piropo) compliment.

cum·pli·dor, ·ra I. adj. trustworthy, reliable II. m.f. reliable person.

cum·pli·men·tar tr. (felicitar) to congratulate; (visitar) to pay one's respects to; (ejecutar) to carry out.

cum·pli·mien·to m. fulfillment; (cortesía) polite gesture.

cum·plir tr. (llevar a cabo) to carry out; (la palabra) to keep; (los años) to be; (la ley) to obey; (una condena) to serve —intr. ♦ **c. con** (promesa) to fulfill; (obligaciones) to fulfill one's obligations • **por c.** as a formality —reflex. (realizarse) to be fulfilled; COM. to fall due.

cú·mu·lo m. pile; (nube) cumulus.

cu·na f. (cama) cradle; (origen) stock; (lugar de nacimiento) birthplace ♦ **canción de c.** lullaby.

cun·dir intr. (extenderse) to spread; (inflar) to expand ♦ **cunde la voz que** rumor has it that.

cu·nei·for·me adj. cuneiform; BOT. cuneate.

cu·ne·ta f. (de un foso) ditch; (de una calle) gutter.

cu·ña f. wedge; ANAT. tarsal bone; PRINT. quoin ♦ **meter c.** to sow discord • **tener cuñas** R.P. to have pull or influence.

cu·ña·do, a m.f. brother/sister-in-law.

cu·ño m. (troquel) die; (impresión) impression; FIG. mark ♦ **de nuevo c.** new.

cuo·ta f. (parte) quota, share; (pago) fee, dues ♦ **c. de admisión** admission fee.

cu·pé m. coupé.

cu·pie·ra, po see **caber.**

cu·plé m. popular song, variety song.

cu·po m. quota.

cu·pón m. coupon.

cú·pu·la f. dome, cupola.

cu·ra¹ m. RELIG. priest.

cu·ra² f. (curación) cure; (apósito) dressing ♦ **no tener c.** COLL. to be incorrigible.

cu·ra·ble adj. curable.

cu·ra·ción f. cure, treatment.

cu·ra·do, a adj. (endurecido) inured; (curtido) tanned ♦ **estoy c. de espanto** nothing can shock me anymore.

cu·ran·de·ro, a m.f. quack.

cu·rar intr. ♦ **c. de** MED. to recover from —tr. MED. (sanar) to cure; (tratar) to treat; FIG. to soothe; (cueros) to tan; (madera) to season; (carnes) to cure ♦ **c. al humo** to smoke —reflex. (recobrarse) to get well; (sanarse) to heal.

cu·ra·re m. curare.

cu·ra·ti·vo, a adj. & f. curative.

cur·da COLL. m. (persona) drunk —f. (borrachera) drunkenness ♦ **agarrarse una c.** COLL. to get drunk.

cu·ria f. (tribunal) court; LAW bar.

cu·rio m. curium.

cu·rio·se·ar intr. to snoop, pry.

cu·rio·si·dad f. curiosity; (cosa curiosa) curio.

cu·rio·so, a I. adj. curious; (limpio) neat; (cui-

dadoso) careful; *(excepcional)* odd **II.** m.f. curious person; *(entremetido)* busybody.

cu·rri·cu·lum vi·tae m. resumé.

cur·sar tr. *(estudiar)* to study; *(dar curso a)* to attend to.

cur·si adj. *(presumido)* pretentious; *(de mal gusto)* tasteless.

cur·si·le·rí·a s. pretentiousness, snobbery.

cur·si·llo m. *(curso)* short course; *(conferencias)* series of lectures.

cur·si·vo, a I. adj. cursive; PRINT. italic **II.** f. cursive script; PRINT. italics.

cur·so m. course; FIN. circulation ♦ **c. acelerado** crash course • **c. por correspondencia** correspondence course • **dar libre c. a** to give free rein to • **en c.** under way • **tener c. legal** to be legal tender.

cur·ti·do m. tanning ♦ pl. tanned leather.

cur·ti·dor m. tanner.

cur·tiem·bre m. *(proceso)* tanning; *(factory)* tannery.

cur·ti·mien·to m. tanning.

cur·tir tr. *(adobar)* to tan; *(acostumbrar)* to inure —reflex. *(por la intemperie)* to become weather-beaten; *(acostumbrarse)* to become inured.

cur·va f. curve; *(recodo)* curve, bend ♦ **c. cerrada** sharp curve.

cur·va·do, a adj. curved, bent.

cur·var tr. to curve, bend.

cur·va·tu·ra f. *(recodo)* curvature; *(acción)* curving.

cur·ve·ar intr. to curve.

cur·vi·lí·ne·o, a adj. curvilinear.

cur·vo, a adj. curved, bent.

cús·pi·de f. summit; FIG. pinnacle; ANAT., BOT. cusp.

cus·to·dia f. *(vigilia)* custody; *(cuidado)* care; *(persona)* custodian.

cus·to·diar tr. *(cuidar)* to take care of; *(vigilar)* to watch over; *(proteger)* to protect.

cus·to·dio adj. & m. guardian.

cu·tá·ne·o, a adj. cutaneous, skin.

cu·tí·cu·la f. cuticle.

cu·tis m.inv. skin, complexion.

cu·yo, a rel. pron. whose; *(personas)* of whom; *(cosas)* of which.

D

d, D f. fourth letter of the Spanish alphabet.

da·ble adj. possible, feasible.

dac·ti·lo·gra·fí·a f. typewriting, typing.

dac·ti·ló·gra·fo m.f. typist.

dá·di·va f. present, gift.

da·di·vo·si·dad f. generosity, liberality.

da·di·vo·so, a adj. generous, lavish.

da·do, a I. adj. given **II.** m. die ♦ **correr el d.** COLL. to be in luck ♦ pl. dice • **cargar los d.** to load the dice.

da·dor, ·ra I. adj. giving **II.** m.f. donor.

da·ga f. dagger; AMER. machete.

da·gue·rro·ti·po m. daguerreotype.

da·lia f. dahlia.

dal·to·nis·mo m. colorblindness.

da·ma f. lady; *(de la reina)* lady-in-waiting; *(manceba)* mistress, concubine; *(actriz)* actress; *(en damas)* king; *(en ajedrez, naipes)* queen ♦ **d. de honor** maid of honor ♦ pl. checkers, draughts (G.B.)

da·ma·jua·na f. demijohn.

da·mas·co m. damask.

da·mi·se·la f. damsel; *(cortesana)* courtesan.

dam·ni·fi·ca·do, a I. adj. damaged, harmed; **II.** m.f. victim.

dam·ni·fi·car §70 tr. to damage, harm.

dan·ta f. *(anta)* elk; *(tapir)* tapir.

dan·za f. dance; COLL. shady business deal; *(riña)* quarrel ♦ **andar** or **estar en la d.** COLL. to be mixed up in a shady deal • **d. de figuras** square dance.

dan·za·dor, ·ra I. adj. dancing **II.** m.f. dancer.

dan·zan·te I. adj. dancing **II.** m.f. dancer; *(estafador)* hustler; *(cabeza de chorlito)* scatterbrain; *(entremetido)* busybody.

dan·zar §04 tr. to dance —intr. *(bailar)* to dance; *(temblar)* to dance, bob up and down; COLL. *(entremeterse)* to get mixed up or involved.

dan·za·rín, i·na m.f. dancer.

da·ña·do, a adj. evil, wicked; *(perjudicado)* damaged.

da·ñar tr. to damage, harm —reflex. to become damaged; *(echarse a perder)* to spoil, go bad.

da·ñi·no, a adj. damaging, harmful.

da·ño m. damage, harm ♦ **hacer d.** *(doler)* to hurt; *(perjudicar)* to harm, injure.

dar §20 tr. to give; *(conferir)* to grant; *(proponer)* to propose, offer; *(sacrificar)* to give up; *(repartir)* to deal; *(producir)* to produce, bear; *(soltar)* to give off, emit; *(propinar)* to deal *<el ladrón le dio un tremendo golpe* the thief dealt him a tremendous blow>; *(imponer)* to impose; *(sonar)* to strike *<el reloj dio las dos* the clock struck two>; THEAT. to show; *(aplicar)* to apply, put on; *(comunicar)* to express, convey ♦ **d. a conocer** to make known • **d. a luz** to give birth; FIG. to publish, print • **d. aviso** to give notice • **d. cabezadas** to nod, doze • **d. como** *(considerar)* to regard, consider; *(producir)* to produce • **d. cuenta de** to report on, account for • **d. cuerda a** to wind (clocks); FIG. *(alargar)* to prolong; *(animar)* to encourage, get (someone) started • **d. de lado** to shun, ignore • **d. diente con diente** to shiver • **d. el pésame** to express condolences • **d. el sí** to assent • **d. en cara** to reproach, scold • **d. en prenda** *(prometer)* to pledge; *(empeñar)* to hock, pawn • **d. fe** to certify • **d. fiado** COM. to give credit • **d. fianza** to post bail, bail out • **d. fin a** to complete, finish • **d. frente a** to face, be facing • **darle ganas de** to feel like, have a mind to • **d. gusto** to please, make happy • **d. la bienvenida** to welcome • **d. la casualidad que** to just so happen that • **d. la lata** COLL. to pester • **d. la razón a** to agree with, support • **d. las espaldas** to turn one's back on • **d. los buenos días** to greet, say good morning • **d. margen** to afford an opportunity • **d. muerte a** to kill • **d. pábulo a** FIG. to feed, foster • **d. palmadas** *(aplaudir)* to applaud, clap hands; *(pegar)* to spank • **d. por** to consider, regard • **d. prestado** to lend • **d. punto final** to conclude • **d. un abrazo** to hug • **d. una vuelta, paseo** to take a stroll, walk • **no d. un bledo** COLL. not to give a hoot —intr. *(tener vista de)* to overlook, face; *(ocurrir)* to arise, occur; *(sobrevenir)* to come over, set in ♦ **¡dale!** COLL. *(¡apúrate!)* hurry up!; *(¡adelante!)* keep it up! • **d. con** *(encontrar)* to find, hit on; *(encontrarse)* to meet, run into;

(chocar) to hit, bang • **d. de** to fall on • **d. en** *(caer)* to fall; *(empeñarse)* to be bent on; *(acertar)* to catch on to, get • **d. en el clavo** FIG. to hit the nail on the head • **d. igual** *or* **lo mismo** to be all the same • **darle por** to take it into one's head • **d. sobre** to look out on • **d. tras** to chase, pursue —reflex. to give oneself up, surrender; *(suceder)* to arise, occur; *(dedicarse)* to devote oneself; *(tomar el hábito de)* to take to, give in to • **d. a conocer** to introduce oneself • **d. a entender** to make oneself understood; *(ser evidente)* to become evident *or* clear • **d. con** *or* **contra** to hit, bump against • **d. cuenta de** to realize • **dárselas de** to consider oneself, to act like • **d. las manos** *or* **la mano** to shake hands • **dársele a uno** to care about • **dársele bien** to be lucky • **d. por** to consider oneself • **d. prisa** to hurry • **d. tono** to put on airs.

dar·do m. dart, arrow; FIG. cutting remark, barb.

dár·se·na f. inner harbor, dock.

da·ta f. date; COM. data, items.

da·tar tr. to date; COM. to enter, credit —intr. to date, begin • **d. de** to date from.

da·ti·vo, a adj. & m. dative.

da·to m. fact, datum; *(documento)* document • pl. data, information.

de prep. *(posesión)* of, -'s, -s'; *(asunto)* of, about, on; *(contenido)* of; *(origen)* from, according to; *(distancia)* from; *(manera)* in, with, on, as; *(hora)* in, at, by, from; *(causa)* from, with, out of, if; *(comparación)* than, of, in.

dé see **dar**.

de·am·bu·lar intr. to wander *or* roam around.

de·án m. RELIG. dean.

de·ba·jo adv. underneath, below • **d. de** underneath, below • **por d.** underneath, below.

de·ba·te m. debate, discussion.

de·ba·tir tr. to debate, discuss; *(combatir)* to fight, struggle.

de·be m. COM. debit.

de·ber[1] tr. to owe; *(hay que)* to ought to • **d. de** to be probable —reflex. to be due to.

de·ber[2] m. duty, obligation; *(faena)* chore; *(deuda)* debt • pl. AMER. homework.

de·bi·da·men·te adv. properly, duly.

de·bi·do, a adj. due; *(apropiado)* proper, fitting.

dé·bil I. adj. weak; *(marchito)* faint, faded II. m.f. weakling.

de·bi·li·dad f. weakness.

de·bi·li·ta·ción f. debilitation.

de·bi·li·tar tr. & reflex. to weaken.

dé·bi·to m. *(deuda)* debt; COM. debit.

de·but m. debut, opening.

de·bu·tan·te I. adj. beginning II. m.f. beginner, newcomer —f. debutante.

de·bu·tar intr. to begin; THEAT. to debut.

dé·ca·da f. decade.

de·ca·den·cia f. decadence, decline.

de·ca·den·te adj. & m.f. decadent.

de·ca·er §15 intr. to decline, fall.

de·caí·do, a I. see **decaer** II. adj. *(débil)* weak, run-down; *(deprimido)* depressed, discouraged.

de·cai·mien·to m. *(decadencia)* decadence, decline; *(debilidad)* weakness, feebleness; *(desaliento)* discouragement, dejection.

de·ca·no m.f. EDUC. dean; *(viejo)* doyen.

de·can·ta·ción f. decanting, pouring off.

de·can·tar tr. to decant, pour off; *(engrande-*

cer) to exaggerate, aggrandize.

de·ca·pi·tar tr. to decapitate, behead.

de·cat·lón m. decathlon.

de·ca·ye·ra, yó see **decaer**.

de·ce·na f. group of ten; MUS. tenth.

de·cen·cia f. decency.

de·cen·te adj. decent.

de·cep·ción f. deception; *(desengaño)* disenchantment, disappointment.

de·cep·cio·nar tr. to disenchant, disappoint.

de·ce·so m. decease, death.

de·cha·do m. model, perfect example; SEW. sampler.

de·ci·bel/be·lio m. decibel.

de·ci·di·do, a adj. determined, resolute.

de·ci·dir tr. to decide, resolve; *(persuadir)* to persuade, convince —intr. to decide —reflex. to decide, make up one's mind.

de·ci·mal adj. & m. decimal.

de·cí·me·tro m. decimeter.

dé·ci·mo, a adj. & m. tenth.

de·ci·moc·ta·vo, a adj. eighteenth.

de·ci·mo·cuar·to, a adj. fourteenth.

de·ci·mo·no·no/no·ve·no, a adj. nineteenth.

de·ci·mo·quin·to, a adj. fifteenth.

de·ci·mo·sép·ti·mo, a adj. seventeenth.

de·ci·mo·sex·to, a adj. sixteenth.

de·ci·mo·ter·ce·ro, a adj. thirteenth.

de·cir[1] m. *(refrán)* saying; *(ocurrencia)* witty remark; *(suposición)* figure of speech.

de·cir[2] §21 tr. to say; *(relatar, divulgar)* to tell; *(hablar)* to talk, speak; *(ordenar)* to tell, order; *(mostrar)* to show, reveal; *(nombrar)* to call, name • **como quien dice** *or* **como si dijéramos** COLL. so to speak • **d. entre** *or* **para sí** to say to oneself • **d. por d.** to talk for the sake of talking • **¡diga!** hello! • **el qué dirán** what people may say • **es d.** that is (to say) • **¡no me digas!** you don't say!, really! • **querer d.** to mean • **según el d. general** by all accounts.

de·ci·sión f. decision; *(firmeza)* determination, resoluteness; *(sentencia)* verdict, ruling.

de·ci·si·vo, a adj. decisive, conclusive.

de·cla·mar tr. & intr. to declaim, recite.

de·cla·ra·ción f. declaration, statement; LAW deposition, evidence; *(de cartas)* bid, call.

de·cla·ra·da·men·te adv. manifestly, openly.

de·cla·ran·te I. adj. declaring II. m.f. LAW declarant, witness.

de·cla·rar tr. to declare; *(en los juegos de cartas)* to bid, declare; LAW to find, pronounce —intr. to declare; LAW to testify, give evidence —reflex. to declare oneself.

de·cli·na·ción f. decline; GRAM. declension; ASTRON. declination.

de·cli·nar intr. to decline; *(ir hacia su fin)* to wane, draw to a close —tr. to decline, refuse; GRAM. to decline.

de·cli·ve m. slope, incline; *(decadencia)* decadence, decline.

de·co·lo·ra·ción f. discoloration, fading; *(del pelo)* bleaching.

de·co·lo·ran·te m. decolorant.

de·co·lo·rar tr. to discolor, fade.

de·co·mi·sar tr. to confiscate, seize.

de·co·mi·so m. confiscation, seizure.

de·co·ra·ción f. decoration; THEAT. scenery.

de·co·ra·do m. THEAT. scenery, set; *(acción)* decoration.

de·co·ra·dor, ·ra I. adj. decorative, ornamental II. m.f. decorator.

de·co·rar tr. to decorate; *(memorizar)* to

memorize, learn by heart.

de·co·ra·ti·vo, a adj. decorative, ornamental.

de·co·ro m. respect, honor; *(recato)* decorum, propriety.

de·co·ro·so, a adj. decorous, decent; *(digno)* respectable, honorable.

de·cre·cer §17 intr. to decrease, diminish.

de·cre·ci·mien·to m. decrease, diminution.

de·cré·pi·to, a adj. decrepit, aged.

de·cre·pi·tud f. decrepitude, old age.

de·cre·tar tr. to decree, order.

de·cre·to m. decree, order.

de·dal m. thimble.

de·di·ca·ción f. dedication.

de·di·car §70 tr. & reflex. to dedicate (oneself).

de·di·ca·to·rio, a I. adj. dedicatory, dedicative **II.** f. dedication, inscription.

de·di·llo m. little finger, pinky ♦ **al d.** COLL. perfectly, thoroughly • **saber al d.** to know by heart.

de·do m. *(de la mano)* finger; *(del pie)* toe; *(porción)* bit, smidgen ♦ **a dos dedos de** FIG., COLL. within an inch of • **cogerse los dedos** to get caught • **chuparse los dedos** to smack one's lips • **d. anular** ring finger • **d. cordial** or **del corazón** middle finger • **d. índice** index finger, forefinger • **d. meñique** little finger, pinky • **d. pulgar** or **gordo** *(de la mano)* thumb; *(del pie)* big toe • **morderse los dedos** to bite one's nails; COLL. *(arrepentirse)* to regret.

de·duc·ción f. deduction; LOG. inference.

de·du·cir §22 tr. to deduce, conclude; *(rebajar)* to deduct, subtract.

de·duc·ti·vo, a adj. deductive.

de·fal·car §70 tr. *(rebajar)* to deduct; *(robar)* to embezzle.

de·fe·ca·ción f. defecation.

de·fe·car §70 tr. & intr. to defecate.

de·fec·ción f. defection, desertion.

de·fec·ti·vo, a adj. defective.

de·fec·to m. defect, flaw; *(falta)* absence, lack ♦ **en d. de** in the absence of, for want of.

de·fec·tuo·so, a adj. defective, faulty.

de·fen·der §50 tr. to defend —intr. & reflex. to defend or protect oneself; *(arreglárselas)* to manage, get by.

de·fen·di·do, a I. adj. defended **II.** m.f. LAW defendant.

de·fen·sa f. defense ♦ **d. propia** or **legítima** self-defense.

de·fen·si·vo, a I. adj. defensive **II.** m. defense, safeguard —f. defensive.

de·fen·sor, o·ra I. adj. defending, protecting **II.** m.f. defender, protector —m. LAW defense counsel.

de·fe·ren·cia f. deference.

de·fe·rir §65 intr. to defer —tr. to refer, delegate.

de·fi·cien·cia f. deficiency, lack.

de·fi·cien·te adj. deficient, lacking; *(defectuoso)* defective, poor.

dé·fi·cit m. [pl. **s**] COM. deficit; FIG. *(carencia)* shortage, lack.

de·fien·da, do see **defender.**

de·fie·ra, ro see **deferir.**

de·fi·ni·ción f. definition; *(determinación)* determination, decision.

de·fi·ni·do, a I. adj. defined; GRAM. definite **II.** m. definition.

de·fi·nir tr. to define; *(determinar)* to determine, decide.

de·fi·ni·ti·vo, a adj. definitive, final ♦ **en defi-**

ni·ti·va *(por fin)* once and for all, finally; *(de verdad)* really, exactly; *(en resumen)* in short.

de·fi·rie·ra, rió see **deferir.**

de·for·ma·ción f. deformation; RAD. distortion; MECH. strain; *(alabeo)* warp.

de·for·mar tr. to deform —reflex. to be or become deformed.

de·for·me adj. deformed, misshapen.

de·for·mi·dad f. deformity.

de·frau·da·ción f. fraud, cheating; *(decepción)* disappointment.

de·frau·dar tr. to defraud, cheat; *(decepcionar)* to disappoint; *(frustrar)* to dash, thwart (hopes); *(turbar)* to disturb, spoil.

de·fun·ción f. demise, death.

de·ge·ne·ra·ción f. degeneration; *(de moral)* degeneracy.

de·ge·ne·ra·do, a adj. & m.f. degenerate.

de·ge·ne·rar intr. to degenerate; *(perder mérito)* to decline, decay.

de·go·lla·de·ro m. throat, windpipe; *(del vestido)* neckline; *(matadero)* slaughterhouse; *(cadalso)* scaffold, block.

de·go·llar §19 tr. *(guillotinar)* to cut or slit the throat of; *(decapitar)* to behead, decapitate; *(masacrar)* to massacre, slaughter; *(destruir)* to destroy, ruin; COLL. *(aburrir)* to bore to death.

de·gra·da·ción f. degradation, debasement.

de·gra·dan·te adj. degrading, debasing.

de·gra·dar tr. & reflex. to degrade or debase (oneself).

de·güe·lle, llo see **degollar.**

de·güe·llo m. throat-cutting; *(decapitación)* beheading, decapitation; *(matanza)* massacre, slaughter ♦ **entrar a d.** to massacre • **tirar a d.** to harm.

de·gus·ta·ción f. tasting, sampling.

dei·dad f. deity, divinity.

dei·fi·car §70 tr. to deify; *(ensalzar)* to glorify.

de·ja·dez f. carelessness, negligence; *(desaliño)* slovenliness, untidiness; *(pereza)* laziness.

de·ja·do, a adj. careless, negligent; *(desaliñado)* slovenly, untidy; *(perezoso)* lazy; *(deprimido)* depressed, dejected.

de·jar tr. to leave; *(consentir)* to let, allow; *(producir)* to yield, produce; *(desamparar)* to abandon, desert; *(nombrar)* to name, designate; *(cesar)* to stop, quit; *(prestar)* to lend, loan ♦ **¡deja!** or **¡déjalo!** never mind! • **d. caer** to drop, let go of • **d. el paso libre** to let pass • **d. en blanco** to leave blank • **d. fresco a** COLL. to baffle, perplex • **d. mal** to let down • **d. plantado** COLL. to leave in the lurch, stand up —intr. ♦ **d. de** to stop, leave off • **d. de existir** to die • **no d. de** not to neglect to, not to fail to —reflex. *(descuidarse)* to let oneself go, become sloppy; *(abandonarse)* to give oneself up to, abandon oneself to; *(permitirse)* to allow oneself to be ♦ **d. caer** *(caerse)* to fall, flop; COLL. *(insinuar)* to drop a hint, insinuate; *(presentarse)* to drop in unexpectedly • **d. de** to stop • **d. decir** to let slip, let out • **d. de rodeos** to stop beating around the bush, come to the point • **d. llevar** to get carried away with • **d. ver** *(aparecer)* to show; *(presentarse)* to show up.

de·jo m. *(dejación)* abandonment, relinquishment; *(fin)* end, termination; *(acento)* accent, lilt; *(inflexión)* drop (in voice); *(gusto)* aftertaste; *(flojedad)* neglect, indolence; FIG. aftertaste.

del contr. of **de** and **el.**

de·lan·tal m. *(sin peto)* apron; *(con peto)* pin-

85

afore.

de·lan·te adv. *(con prioridad)* in front, ahead; *(enfrente)* facing, opposite ♦ **d. de** in front of.

de·lan·te·ro, a I. adj. front, fore **II.** m. *(de un vestido)* front; SPORT. forward —f. *(frente)* front, front part; *(ventaja)* advantage, lead ♦ **coger** *or* **tomar la d.** to take the lead • **llevar la d.** to lead, be in the lead ♦ pl. overalls.

de·la·tar tr. to denounce, inform on; *(revelar)* to reveal, expose.

de·le·ga·ción f. delegation; *(cargo y oficina)* office; *(sucursal)* branch.

de·le·ga·do, a I. adj. delegated **II.** m.f. delegate, representative.

de·le·gar §47 tr. to delegate.

de·lei·ta·ble adj. delightful, enjoyable.

de·lei·tar tr. to delight, please —reflex. ♦ **d. con** *or* **en** to take pleasure in, delight in.

de·lei·te m. delight, pleasure.

de·le·tre·ar tr. *(pronunciar)* to spell (out) FIG. *(descifrar)* to decipher, interpret.

de·le·tre·o m. spelling; *(desciframiento)* deciphering.

de·lez·na·ble adj. *(que se rompe fácilmente)* crumbly; *(resbaladizo)* slippery; *(quebradizo)* brittle, fragile; FIG. frail, weak.

del·fín m. dolphin; *(príncipe)* dauphin.

del·ga·do, a adj. *(esbelto)* slender, slim; *(flaco)* thin; *(tenue)* tenuous, delicate; *(agudo)* sharp, clever ♦ **hilar d.** COLL. to split hairs • **ponerse d.** to lose weight **II.** m.pl. flanks (of animals).

de·li·be·ra·do, a adj. deliberate, intentional.

de·li·be·rar intr. to deliberate, ponder —tr. to decide, resolve.

de·li·ca·de·za f. delicacy; *(discreción)* tactfulness, discretion; *(debilidad)* weakness, frailty ♦ **tener la d. de** to be thoughtful enough to.

de·li·ca·do, a adj. delicate; *(difícil)* difficult, delicate; *(exigente)* demanding, exacting; *(quebradizo)* fragile, delicate; *(enfermizo)* frail, delicate.

de·li·cia f. delight, pleasure.

de·li·cio·so, a adj. *(agradable)* delightful; *(sabroso)* delicious.

de·li·mi·tar tr. to delimit.

de·lin·ca, co see **delinquir**.

de·lin·cuen·cia f. delinquency.

de·lin·cuen·te adj. & m.f. delinquent.

de·li·ne·a·m(i)en·to m. delineation.

de·li·ne·ar tr. to delineate, outline.

de·lin·quir §23 intr. to break the law.

de·li·ran·te adj. delirious.

de·li·rar intr. to be delirious; *(decir tonterías)* to rave, talk nonsense.

de·li·rio m. delirium; *(manía)* mania, frenzy; *(disparate)* raving ♦ **d. de grandeza** delusions of grandeur • **tener d. por** to be crazy about.

de·li·to m. offense, crime ♦ **d. de mayor cuantía** felony • **d. de menor cuantía** misdemeanor.

del·ta m. delta.

de·ma·cra·do, a adj. emaciated, wasted away.

de·ma·crar·se reflex. to become emaciated.

de·ma·go·gia f. demagogy, demagoguery.

de·ma·gó·gi·co, a adj. demagogic.

de·ma·go·go, a m. demagogue.

de·man·da f. demand; *(petición)* appeal, request; *(limosna)* alms; *(pregunta)* question, inquiry; *(empresa)* enterprise; *(empeño)* perseverance; COM. demand; *(pedido)* order; ELEC. load; LAW *(escrito)* writ; *(acción)* lawsuit, action; THEAT. call ♦ **demandas y respuestas** haggling • **ir en d. de** to go in search of • **salir uno a la d.** to defend.

de·man·da·do, a m.f. defendant.

de·man·dan·te m.f. plaintiff.

de·man·dar tr. *(pedir)* to request, ask for; LAW to sue, file suit against.

de·mar·car §70 tr. to demarcate, delimit.

de·más I. adj. other, rest of the ♦ **lo d.** the rest • **por d.** *(en demasía)* excessively, too much; *(inútilmente)* in vain • **por lo d.** otherwise, other than that • **todo lo d.** everything else • **y d.** etcetera, and so on; *(y los otros)* and the others **II.** adv. moreover, besides.

de·ma·sí·a f. excess, surplus; *(abuso)* disregard, abuse; *(insolencia)* insolence, audacity ♦ **en d.** excessively.

de·ma·sia·do, a I. adj. too much *or* many, excessive **II.** adv. too, too much.

de·men·cia f. madness, insanity; MED. dementia.

de·men·te I. adj. insane, demented **II.** m.f. insane person, lunatic.

de·mo·cra·cia f. democracy.

de·mó·cra·ta I. adj. democratic **II.** m.f. democrat.

de·mo·crá·ti·co, a adj. democratic.

de·mo·cra·ti·zar §04 tr. to make democratic.

de·mo·grá·fi·co, a adj. demographic.

de·mo·le·dor, ·ra I. adj. demolishing, destructive; *(arruinador)* devastating **II.** m.f. demolisher, wrecker.

de·mo·ler §78 tr. to demolish, destroy.

de·mo·li·ción f. demolition, destruction.

de·mo·nio m. *(diablo)* demon, devil; *(genio)* evil spirit; COLL. *(travieso)* rascal, mischievous person ♦ **como el d.** like the devil, like hell • **¡que me lleve el d!** I'll be damned! • pl. **¿cómo d.?** how in the hell . . . ? • **¡d.!** hell!, damn! • **de mil d.** *or* **todos los d.** a hell of a.

de·mo·ra f. delay, wait.

de·mo·rar tr. to delay, hold up —intr. to linger, stay —reflex. to take a long time, delay.

de·mos·tra·ción f. demonstration; *(ostentación)* show, display; *(prueba)* proof.

de·mos·trar §19 tr. to demonstrate, show.

de·mos·tra·ti·vo, a adj. & m. demonstrative.

de·mu·dar tr. to change, turn pale —reflex. to change, turn pale; *(alterarse)* to become upset suddenly.

de·mue·la, lo see **demoler**.

de·mues·tre, tro see **demostrar**.

de·ne·gar §52 tr. *(rechazar)* to refuse, reject; *(negar)* to deny.

de·nie·go, gue see **denegar**.

de·ni·gra·ción f. denigration, disparagement.

de·ni·gra·dor, ·ra/gran·te I. adj. denigrating, disparaging **II.** m.f. denigrator, disparager.

de·ni·grar tr. *(desacreditar)* to denigrate, disparage; *(injuriar)* to insult.

de·no·da·do, a adj. bold, intrepid.

de·no·mi·na·ción f. denomination.

de·no·mi·na·dor, ·ra I. adj. denominating, denominative **II.** m.f. denominator.

de·no·mi·nar tr. to denominate, name.

de·nos·tar §19 tr. to abuse, insult.

de·no·tar tr. to denote.

den·si·dad f. density.

den·so, a adj. dense, thick; *(sólido)* heavy, solid; *(oscuro)* dark, black.

den·ta·do, a I. adj. dentate, toothed **II.** m. perforation —f. AMER. bite.

den·ta·du·ra f. (set of) teeth.

den·tal adj. dental.

den·tar §49 tr. to tooth, put teeth in; *(endentecer)* to serrate.

den·te·lla·do, a I. adj. dentate, toothed **II.** f. *(movimiento)* snap of the jaws; *(mordisco)* bite; *(señal)* tooth mark.

den·te·llar intr. to chatter (teeth).

den·te·lle·ar tr. to nibble, bite.

den·te·ra f. *(envidia)* envy, jealousy; *(deseo intenso)* vehement desire, longing ♦ **dar a alguien d.** *(incomodar)* to set someone's teeth on edge; *(dar envidia)* to make someone jealous.

den·tí·fri·co m. toothpaste.

den·tis·ta m.f. dentist.

den·tro adv. inside, within; *(de un edificio)* inside, indoors ♦ **d. de poco** shortly, soon • **de** *or* **desde d.** from (the) inside • **por d.** inwardly, (on the) inside.

de·nue·do m. bravery, courage.

de·nues·te, to see **denostar.**

de·nues·to m. insult, affront.

de·nun·cia f. accusation, denunciation; *(declaración)* declaration, report.

de·nun·cia·dor, ·ra/cian·te I. adj. denouncing **II.** m.f. denouncer.

de·nun·ciar tr. to accuse, denounce; *(pronosticar)* to foretell, prophesy; *(declarar)* to declare, announce; *(indicar)* to indicate, reveal; *(delatar)* to denounce, censure.

de·pa·rar tr. to supply, provide.

de·par·ta·men·to m. department, section; *(distrito)* province, district; *(compartimiento)* compartment; *(piso)* apartment, flat (G.B.).

de·par·tir intr. to talk, converse.

de·pen·den·cia f. dependence, reliance; *(parentesco)* relationship, kinship; *(amistad)* friendship, relationship; *(sucursal)* branch (office); *(negocio)* business, agency; *(empleados)* employees, subordinates ♦ pl. accessories.

de·pen·der intr. to depend (de *on*).

de·pen·dien·te, a I. adj. dependent, subordinate **II.** m.f. *(empleado)* employee; *(de tienda)* clerk, salesperson.

de·pi·la·ción f. depilation.

de·pi·lar tr. to depilate, remove hair from.

de·plo·rar tr. to deplore, lament.

de·po·ner §54 tr. *(apartar)* to lay *or* put aside; *(privar)* to depose; LAW to testify, provide testimony for; *(bajar)* to lower, bring *or* take down —intr. *(defecar)* to defecate, move the bowels; *(dar testimonio)* to testify, make a deposition.

de·por·ta·ción f. deportation.

de·por·tar tr. to deport, exile.

de·por·te m. sport.

de·por·tis·ta I. adj. sporting, sporty; COLL. *(aficionado)* fond of sports **II.** m.f. sports fan, sportsman/woman.

de·por·ti·vo, a adj. sporting, sports; *(aficionado)* sportive, fond of sports.

de·po·si·ción f. deposition; LAW deposition, testimony; PHYSIOL. bowel movement.

de·po·si·tan·te I. adj. depositing **II.** m.f. depositor.

de·po·si·tar tr. to deposit; *(encomendar)* to place —reflex. to settle.

de·po·si·ta·rio, a m.f. depositary, trustee —m. *(cajero)* cashier; *(tesorero)* treasurer.

de·pó·si·to m. deposit; *(almacén)* warehouse, storehouse; *(cisterna)* cistern, tank; *(desembolso inicial)* deposit, down payment; CHEM., GEOL., MIN. deposit; MIL. depot, dump.

de·pra·va·ción f. corruption, depravity; *(alteración)* alteration.

de·pra·va·do, a I. adj. depraved, corrupted **II.** m.f. depraved person, degenerate.

de·pra·var tr. to deprave, corrupt; *(echar a perder)* to harm, damage.

de·pre·car §70 tr. to beg, implore.

de·pre·ca·to·rio, a adj. imploring.

de·pre·cia·ción f. depreciation.

de·pre·ciar tr. to depreciate.

de·pre·dar tr. to plunder, pillage.

de·pre·sión f. depression; *(humillación)* humiliation, embarrassment.

de·pre·si·vo, a adj. MED. depressive; *(deprimente)* depressing.

de·pri·men·te adj. depressing.

de·pri·mi·do, a adj. depressed.

de·pri·mir tr. to depress; *(humillar)* to humiliate, embarrass —reflex. to get depressed.

de·pu·ra·ción f. depuration, purification; POL. purge, purging.

de·pu·rar tr. to depurate, purify; POL. to purge.

de·pu·sie·ra, so see **deponer.**

de·re·chis·ta adj. & m.f. rightist.

de·re·cho, a I. adj. right; right-hand <*el margen* **d.** the right-hand margin>; *(vertical)* upright, erect; *(recto)* straight, even; AMER. lucky, fortunate ♦ **a derechas** right, properly **II.** f. *(lado derecho)* right side, right-hand side; *(diestra)* right hand; POL. right, right wing ♦ **a la d.** to *or* on the right • **¡d.!** MIL. right face! —m. right, authority; *(privilegio)* right, privilege; *(conjunto de leyes)* law; *(justicia)* justice; *(estudio)* law ♦ **de d.** LAW de jure, by right • **d. consuetudinario** common law • **d. de paso** right of way • **d. escrito** *or* **positivo** statute law • **d. mercantil** business law • **d. penal** criminal law • **hecho y d.** complete, full • **tener d. a** to have a right to ♦ pl. *(impuestos)* duties, taxes; *(honorarios)* fees, charges • **d. de autor** royalties • **d. de entrada** import duties • **hacer valer sus d.** to exercise one's rights **III.** adv. straight, right; COLL. right, honestly ♦ **todo d.** straight ahead.

de·ri·va f. drift, deviation ♦ **ir a la d.** to drift.

de·ri·va·ción f. derivation; ELEC. *(pérdida)* loss of current; *(circuito)* by-pass, shunt.

de·ri·va·do, a I. adj. derived, derivative **II.** m. derivative —f. MATH. derivative.

de·ri·var tr. to derive; *(dirigir)* to lead, direct —intr. to derive, be derived; AVIA., MARIT. to drift, go off course —reflex. to be derived *or* come from.

der·ma·to·lo·gí·a f. dermatology.

der·ma·tó·lo·go, a m.f. dermatologist.

der·mis f. derma, dermis.

de·ro·ga·ción f. LAW derogation, repeal; *(disminución)* decrease, deterioration.

de·ro·gar §47 tr. LAW to derogate, repeal; *(destruir)* to destroy, abolish.

de·rra·ma·mien·to m. spilling; *(rebosamiento)* overflowing; *(dispersión)* dispersion, scattering; *(despilfarro)* squandering, wasting ♦ **d. de sangre** bloodshed, spilling of blood.

de·rra·mar tr. *(verter)* to spill, pour out; *(sangre)* to spill, shed; *(lágrimas)* to shed; *(dispersar)* to scatter, spread; *(diseminar)* to spread, make known; *(impuestos)* to apportion (taxes) —reflex. to overflow, spill over.

de·rra·me m. *(derramamiento)* spilling, pouring out; *(sangre)* spilling, shedding; *(lágrimas)* shedding; *(dispersión)* scattering, spreading;

(diseminación) spreading, dissemination; *(pérdida)* leakage, waste; *(rebosamiento)* overflow; *(declive)* slope, incline ♦ **d. cerebral** cerebral hemorrhage • **d. sinovial** MED. water on the knee.

de·rre·dor m. periphery, circumference ♦ **al** or **en d.** around ♦ **por todo el d.** all around.

de·rre·tir §48 tr. to liquefy, dissolve; *(hielo)* to melt, thaw; *(consumir)* to squander, waste —reflex. COLL. *(enamorarse)* to fall madly in love; *(inquietarse)* to worry, fret; *(impacientarse)* to be impatient.

de·rri·bar tr. to knock down; *(subvertir)* to overthrow, topple; MIL. to shoot down; *(humillar)* to humiliate, prostrate —reflex. to fall to the ground.

de·rri·ta, to, tiera, tió see **derretir**.

de·rro·car §70 tr. *(despeñar)* to hurl or throw down; *(arruinar)* to demolish, knock down; *(subvertir)* to oust, overthrow.

de·rro·cha·dor, ·ra I. adj. wasteful, squandering **II.** m.f. spendthrift, squanderer.

de·rro·char tr. to squander, waste.

de·rro·che m. squandering, waste.

de·rro·ta f. MIL. defeat, rout; *(camino)* route, path; MARIT. ship's course, tack; *(desorden)* disorder, shambles.

de·rro·tar tr. to defeat, beat; *(arruinar)* to ruin, spoil; *(echar a perder)* to waste, squander —reflex. MARIT. to drift or be driven off course.

de·rro·te·ro m. *(rumbo)* course, tack; *(modo de obrar)* course, plan of action; *(tesoro)* hidden or buried treasure.

de·rro·tis·ta adj. & m.f. defeatist.

de·rruir §18 tr. to knock down, demolish.

de·rrum·ba·mien·to m. *(caída)* plunge, headlong fall; *(demolición)* demolition; *(desplome)* collapse, falling down; *(ruina)* collapse, fall; *(derrocamiento)* overthrow; MIN. cave-in ♦ **d. de tierra** landslide.

de·rrum·bar tr. *(despeñar)* to hurl or cast down; *(demoler)* to knock down, demolish —reflex. *(caerse)* to collapse, fall; *(tirarse)* to throw oneself headfirst; MIN. to cave in, collapse; AMER. to fail.

de·rrum·be·bo m. *(despeñadero)* precipice, cliff; *(socavón)* cave-in; *(de tierra)* landslide; *(demolición)* demolition, knocking down; *(desplome)* falling down, collapse.

de·rru·ya, yera, yo, yó see **derruir**.

de·sa·bo·to·nar tr. to unbutton, undo —intr. BOT. to blossom, bloom —reflex. to come unbuttoned.

de·sa·bri·do, a adj. *(de poco sabor)* tasteless, insipid; *(de mal sabor)* bad-tasting, unsavory; METEOROL. inclement, unpleasant; FIG. gruff, surly.

de·sa·bri·gar §47 tr. to uncover; *(quitar la ropa)* to undress; *(desamparar)* to deprive of shelter or protection.

de·sa·bro·char tr. to undo, unfasten; FIG. to open, uncover —reflex. to undo or unfasten one's clothing; *(confiarse)* to unburden oneself, confide.

de·sa·ca·tar tr. to show disrespect for —reflex. to behave disrespectfully.

de·sa·ca·to m. disrespect, irreverence; LAW contempt.

de·sa·cer·ta·do, a adj. mistaken, misguided.

de·sa·cier·to m. error, mistake.

de·sa·co·mo·dar tr. to inconvenience, bother; *(despedir)* to discharge, dismiss —reflex. to lose one's job.

de·sa·co·plar tr. to uncouple, disconnect.

de·sa·cor·de adj. discordant.

de·sa·cos·tum·bra·do, a adj. unusual, uncommon.

de·sa·cos·tum·brar tr. & reflex. to break (oneself) of the habit (of).

de·sa·cre·di·ta·do, a adj. discredited, disgraced.

de·sa·cre·di·tar tr. to discredit, disgrace.

de·sac·ti·var tr. to deactivate.

de·sa·cuer·do m. disagreement, discord; *(error)* error, mistake; *(olvido)* forgetfulness, loss of memory.

de·sa·fia·dor, ·ra I. adj. defying, challenging **II.** m.f. challenger.

de·sa·fiar §30 tr. to challenge, dare; *(competir)* to oppose, compete with.

de·sa·fi·lar tr. to blunt, dull.

de·sa·fi·nar intr. MUS. to be out of tune; *(tocar)* to play out of tune; *(cantar)* to sing out of tune; COLL. to speak out of turn —reflex. MUS. to get out of tune.

de·sa·fí·o m. *(reto)* challenge, defiance; *(duelo)* duel; *(competencia)* competition, rivalry.

de·sa·fo·ra·do, a adj. huge; *(sin límite)* boundless; *(contra fuero)* illegal, unlawful.

de·sa·fo·rar §19 tr. to violate (a person's) rights —reflex. to lose control, fly off the handle.

de·sa·for·tu·na·do, a adj. unfortunate.

de·sa·fue·ro m. infringement; *(abuso)* outrage, excess.

de·sa·gra·da·ble adj. disagreeable.

de·sa·gra·dar tr. to displease, offend.

de·sa·gra·de·cer §17 tr. to be ungrateful.

de·sa·gra·de·ci·do, a adj. & m.f. ungrateful (person).

de·sa·gra·do m. displeasure, discontent ♦ **con d.** ungraciously, reluctantly.

de·sa·gra·vio m. compensation, amends ♦ **en d. de** in amends for.

de·sa·gua·de·ro m. drain, outlet.

de·sa·guar §10 tr. to drain, empty of water; *(malgastar)* to waste, squander —intr. to empty or flow into the sea —reflex. *(vomitar)* to vomit; *(defecar)* to defecate.

de·sa·güe m. *(avenamiento)* draining, drainage; *(desaguadero)* drain, outlet.

de·sa·ho·ga·do, a adj. *(descarado)* brazen, fresh; *(despejado)* clear, open; *(espacioso)* roomy, spacious; *(acomodado)* relaxing, easy.

de·sa·ho·gar §47 tr. *(aliviar)* to alleviate, ease; *(dar rienda suelta)* to vent, give rein to —reflex. *(dar rienda suelta)* to let off steam; *(confiarse)* to confide; *(descansar)* to relax, take it easy; *(recobrarse)* to recover, feel better; *(desempeñarse)* to extricate oneself from difficulty.

de·sa·ho·go m. *(alivio)* relief, alleviation; *(descanso)* rest, respite; *(expansión)* space, room; *(libertad)* freedom; *(comodidad)* comfort, ease; *(descaro)* impudence; *(salida)* outlet.

de·sa·hu·ciar tr. *(quitar toda esperanza)* to remove all hope from; *(desesperar)* to lose hope for; *(un inquilino)* to evict.

de·sai·rar tr. to reject, rebuff; *(desestimar)* to underestimate.

de·sai·re m. *(falta de gracia)* gracelessness, lack of charm; *(desprecio)* slight, snub; *(rechazo)* rebuff.

de·sa·jus·tar tr. to disturb, put out of order; *(estropear)* to spoil, upset —reflex. to go *wrong, get out of order; (compromiso)* to break.

de·sa·jus·te m. *(mal ajuste)* maladjustment; *(avería)* breakdown, failure; *(ruptura)* breaking.

de·sa·len·tar §49 tr. to leave breathless, put out of breath; *(desanimar)* to discourage, dishearten —reflex. to become discouraged *or* disheartened.

de·sa·lien·to m. discouragement.

de·sa·li·ña·do, a adj. *(desaseado)* slovenly, untidy; *(descuidado)* careless, neglectful.

de·sa·li·ñar tr. to disarrange, make untidy; *(arrugar)* to crease —reflex. to become disarranged *or* untidy.

de·sa·li·ño m. *(descompostura)* slovenliness, untidiness; *(descuido)* carelessness, neglect.

de·sal·ma·do, a adj. heartless, cruel.

de·sa·lo·jar tr. *(sacar)* to remove, expel; *(desplazar)* to dislodge, displace; *(abandonar)* to abandon, evacuate —intr. to leave.

de·sa·lo·jo m. removal, expulsion; *(desplazamiento)* dislodgement, displacement; *(abandonamiento)* abandonment, evacuation.

de·sal·qui·lar tr. *(dejar de tener alquilado)* to stop renting; *(mudarse)* to vacate —reflex. to become vacant.

de·sa·mor m. indifference, lack of affection; *(antipatía)* enmity, dislike.

de·sam·pa·rar tr. to forsake, abandon.

de·sam·pa·ro m. helplessness, abandonment.

de·san·dar §05 tr. to retrace (one's steps), go back.

de·san·grar tr. to bleed; *(vaciar)* to drain, empty; *(empobrecer)* to impoverish, bleed dry —reflex. to bleed profusely; *(morir)* to bleed to death.

de·sa·ni·ma·do, a adj. downhearted, discouraged; *(poco animado)* dull, lifeless.

de·sa·ni·mar tr. to discourage, depress —reflex. to become discouraged *or* depressed.

de·sá·ni·mo m. discouragement, dejection.

de·sa·nu·dar/ñu·dar tr. to untie, unknot; *(desenmarañar)* to straighten out, clarify.

de·sa·pa·ci·ble adj. unpleasant, disagreeable.

de·sa·pa·re·cer §17 tr. to make disappear, cause to vanish —intr. & reflex. to disappear, vanish; *(disipar)* to wear off.

de·sa·pa·ri·ción f. disappearance, vanishing.

de·sa·pa·sio·na·do, a adj. dispassionate.

de·sa·pe·gar §47 tr. to unstick; *(desaficionar)* to estrange, alienate —reflex. to come unstuck; *(desaficionarse)* to become estranged *or* alienated.

de·sa·pe·go m. indifference, estrangement; *(imparcialidad)* impartiality.

de·sa·per·ci·bi·do, a adj. unprepared, unready; *(inadvertido)* unnoticed, unseen.

de·sa·pli·ca·do, a I. adj. lazy, idle **II.** m.f. lazybones, idler.

de·sa·pre·ciar tr. to underestimate.

de·sa·pren·si·vo, a adj. unscrupulous.

de·sa·pro·ba·ción f. disapproval.

de·sa·pro·bar §19 tr. to disapprove (of).

de·sa·pro·ve·char tr. to waste, misuse —intr. to lose ground, go backwards.

de·sa·prue·be, bo see **desaprobar.**

de·sar·ma·do, a adj. *(desprovisto)* unarmed; *(desmontado)* in pieces, dismantled.

de·sar·mar tr. *(desmontar)* to take apart, dismantle; *(templar)* to calm, appease; *(encantar)* to disarm, charm —intr. & reflex. to disarm; *(desmontar)* to fall apart *or* to

pieces.

de·sar·me m. disarmament; *(desmontaje)* dismantling.

de·sa·rrai·ga·do, a adj. uprooted, rootless.

de·sa·rrai·gar §47 tr. to uproot, dig up; *(extirpar)* to extirpate, eradicate; *(desterrar)* to banish, expel —reflex. to become uprooted.

de·sa·rrai·go m. uprooting; *(extirpación)* extirpation, eradication; *(destierro)* banishment, expulsion.

de·sa·rre·gla·do, a adj. untidy, disorderly; *(roto)* out of order, broken (down).

de·sa·rre·glar tr. to make untidy, mess (up); *(estropear)* to spoil, upset; *(quebrar)* to put out of order, break —reflex. to become untidy *or* messy; *(quebrar)* to get out of order, break (down).

de·sa·rre·glo m. untidiness, disorder; *(de un mecanismo)* breakdown, trouble.

de·sa·rro·lla·do, a adj. developed.

de·sa·rro·llar tr. *(deshacer)* to unroll, unfold; *(extender)* to develop, expand; *(explicar)* to expound, elaborate —reflex. *(deshacerse)* to unroll, unfold; *(extenderse)* to develop, expand; *(tener lugar)* to take place.

de·sa·rro·llo m. *(despliegue)* unrolling, unfolding; *(extensión)* development, expansion; *(explicación)* exposition, elaboration; *(de los sucesos)* development, course.

de·sa·rru·gar §47 tr. to unwrinkle, smooth the wrinkles from —reflex. to become unwrinkled.

de·sar·ti·cu·lar tr. to dislocate, throw out of joint; *(desmontar)* to disassemble, take apart —reflex. to become dislocated *or* out of joint.

de·sa·se·a·do, a adj. & m.f. *(sucio)* dirty (person); *(desarreglado)* messy (person).

de·sa·se·ar tr. *(ensuciar)* to dirty, soil; *(poner en desorden)* to mess up, disorder.

de·sa·se·o m. *(suciedad)* dirtiness, uncleanliness; *(desarreglo)* untidiness, messiness.

de·sa·sir §08 tr. to release, let go —reflex. to yield, give up.

de·sa·so·ciar tr. to dissociate, separate.

de·sa·so·se·gar §52 tr. to make uneasy, disturb —reflex. to become uneasy *or* disturbed.

de·sa·so·sie·go m. uneasiness, restlessness.

de·sas·tre m. disaster, catastrophe.

de·sas·tro·so, a adj. disastrous, catastrophic.

de·sa·tar tr. to untie, undo; *(soltar)* to unleash, let go; *(aclarar)* to unravel, solve —reflex. to come untied *or* undone; *(soltarse)* to break away *or* loose; *(hablar)* to chatter, babble; *(descomedirse)* to be rude, let oneself go; *(perder el encogimiento)* to loosen up ♦ **d. de** to get out of, rid oneself of.

de·sa·tas·car §70 tr. to pull out of the mud; *(desatrancar)* to clear, unblock; *(ayudar)* to get someone out of a jam —reflex. to get out of the mud.

de·sa·ten·der §50 tr. *(no hacer caso)* to neglect; *(no prestar atención)* to ignore, disregard.

de·sa·ten·to, a I. adj. inattentive; *(descortés)* discourteous, impolite **II.** m.f. impolite person.

de·sa·ti·na·do, a I. adj. foolish, silly; *(imprudente)* rash, reckless **II.** m.f. fool.

de·sa·ti·nar tr. to exasperate, bewilder; *(atolondrar)* to make lose one's head —intr. *(cometer desaciertos)* to make blunders; *(disparatar)* to rave, talk nonsense.

de·sa·ti·no m. nonsense, foolishness; *(acción)* silly *or* foolish act.

de·sa·tran·car §70 tr. *(la puerta)* to unbar, un-bolt; *(desatrampar)* to clear, unblock.

de·sau·to·ri·za·do, a adj. unauthorized.

de·sau·to·ri·zar §04 tr. to deprive of authority; *(desmentir)* to deny; *(prohibir)* to prohibit.

de·sa·ve·nen·cia f. discord, enmity.

de·sa·ve·nir §76 tr. to cause discord between —reflex. to disagree, quarrel.

de·sa·yu·nar intr. to have breakfast, breakfast —reflex. to have breakfast, breakfast; FIG. to receive the first news of —tr. to breakfast on, have for breakfast.

de·sa·yu·no m. breakfast.

de·sa·zón f. tastelessness, insipidity; *(disgusto)* annoyance, irritation; *(desasosiego)* anxiety, uneasiness; MED. upset, discomfort.

des·ban·car §70 tr. to break the bank; FIG. to supplant, replace.

des·ban·dar·se reflex. to disband; *(dispersarse)* to disperse, scatter.

des·ba·ra·jus·te m. confusion, disorder.

des·ba·ra·ta·do, a I. adj. *(desordenado)* wild, unruly; *(roto)* wrecked, broken down **II.** m.f. ruin, wreck; COLL. libertine, debauchee.

des·ba·ra·tar tr. to ruin, wreck; *(malgastar)* to squander, waste; *(estorbar)* to hinder, frustrate; MECH. to break, put out of order; MIL. to rout, throw into confusion —intr. to talk *or* act wildly —reflex. to talk *or* act wildly; MECH. to break down, fall apart.

des·bo·ca·do, a I. adj. *(roto)* chipped; *(mellado)* nicked, damaged; *(malhablado)* foulmouthed; S. AMER. overflowing **II.** m.f. COLL. foul mouth.

des·bo·ca·mien·to m. bolting (of a horse); *(injurias)* insults, abuse.

des·bo·car §70 tr. *(astillar)* to chip; *(mellar)* to nick —intr. *(dirigir a)* to lead *or* open into; *(desembocar)* to flow *or* empty into —reflex. EQUIT. to bolt, run away; *(injuriar)* to start to swear.

des·bor·da·mien·to m. *(inundación)* overflowing, running over; *(de cólera)* outburst.

des·bor·dar intr. *(derramarse)* to overflow, run over; *(rebosar)* to burst *or* brim with —reflex. *(derramarse)* to overflow, run over; *(rebosar)* to burst *or* brim with; *(desmandarse)* to lose one's self-control —tr. to pass, go beyond.

des·bro·zar §04 tr. to clear of rubbish *or* undergrowth.

des·bro·zo m. clearing away of rubbish *or* undergrowth; *(basura)* rubbish; *(maleza)* undergrowth.

des·ca·be·lla·do, a adj. wild, crazy.

des·ca·be·zar §04 tr. *(decapitar)* to behead, decapitate; *(desmochar)* to top, cut the top of; *(vencer)* to get over the worst of, surmount ♦ **d. el sueño** to take a nap, doze —intr. to abut, border on —reflex. COLL. to rack one's brains.

des·ca·fei·na·do, a adj. & m. decaffeinated (coffee).

des·ca·la·bra·do, a I. adj. wounded in the head; *(que pierde)* losing, unsuccessful **II.** m.f. loser.

des·ca·la·brar tr. to injure, wound; COLL. to damage, harm —reflex. to injure one's head.

des·ca·la·bro m. setback, misfortune; MIL. defeat.

des·ca·li·fi·ca·ción f. disqualification; *(descrédito)* discredit.

des·ca·li·fi·car §70 tr. to disqualify.

des·cal·zar §04 tr. to take off; *(quitar un calzo)* to remove a wedge *or* block from; *(socavar)* to dig under, undermine —reflex. to take off shoes; *(un caballo)* to lose a shoe.

des·cal·zo, a adj. barefoot(ed), shoeless; *(pobre)* destitute, poor.

des·cam·pa·do, a I. adj. open, clear **II.** m. open field ♦ **en d.** in the open country.

des·cam·par intr. to clear up (weather).

des·can·sa·do, a adj. *(tranquilo)* restful, tranquil; *(refrescado)* rested, relaxed.

des·can·sar intr. to rest, take a rest; *(calmarse)* to relax; *(reposar)* to repose, lie down; *(fiarse)* to rely on; *(basarse)* to be based on; *(apoyarse)* to rest *or* lean on; *(yacer)* to lie, rest —tr. to rest, give rest to; *(ayudar)* to help, aid; *(apoyar)* to rest *or* lean (something) on —reflex. to rest, take a rest ♦ **d. en** to rely on, have trust in.

des·can·so m. rest, repose; *(alivio)* relief; *(período)* break; *(licencia)* leave; SPORT. half time; THEAT. intermission; ARCHIT. landing.

des·ca·po·ta·ble adj. & m. convertible.

des·ca·ra·do, a adj. & m.f. shameless (person).

des·car·ga f. unloading; ARM. discharge, firing; ELEC. discharge.

des·car·ga·de·ro m. pier, unloading dock.

des·car·gar §47 tr. to unload; *(disparar)* to discharge, shoot; *(extraer la carga de)* to unload, disarm; ELEC. to discharge; *(golpear)* to deal; *(liberar)* to release, free; *(aliviar)* to ease, relieve; *(absolver)* to acquit, clear —intr. to flow, empty —reflex. *(dimitir)* to resign, quit; *(eximirse)* to unburden oneself; *(exonerarse)* to clear oneself.

des·car·go m. unloading; COM. entry; *(excusa)* excuse; *(dispensa)* release.

des·ca·ri·ñar·se reflex. to lose one's affection *or* love for.

des·car·nar tr. DENT. to scrape flesh from; *(desmoronar)* to wear *or* eat away; *(desapegar)* to disembody —reflex. to wear away, be eaten away.

des·ca·ro m. shamelessness, brazenness.

des·ca·rriar §30 tr. to misdirect, send the wrong way; *(un animal)* to separate from the herd; *(apartar de la razón)* to lead astray —reflex. *(desviarse)* to stray, get lost; *(apartarse de la razón)* to err, go astray.

des·ca·rri·la·mien·to m. RAIL. derailment; *(descarrío)* act of going astray.

des·ca·rri·lar intr. to be derailed, jump the track; *(una persona)* to get off the track.

des·car·tar tr. to discard, put aside —reflex. to discard ♦ **d. de** to excuse oneself from.

des·car·te m. discard; *(excusa)* excuse.

des·cas·ca·rar tr. & reflex. to peel.

des·cas·ca·ri·llar tr. to peel, husk.

des·cen·den·cia f. *(hijos)* descendants, offspring; *(linaje)* descent, origin.

des·cen·der §50 intr. to descend, go down; *(proceder)* to descend *or* be descended from; *(un líquido)* to run *or* flow down; *(de nivel)* to drop, fall; *(derivar)* to derive *or* come from —tr. *(bajar)* to descend, go down; *(bajar una cosa)* to lower, bring down.

des·cen·dien·te I. adj. descending **II.** m.f. descendant, offspring.

des·cen·so m. descent, going down; *(de nivel)* fall, drop; *(degradación)* demotion; *(decaimiento)* drop, decline.

des·cen·tra·do, a adj. off-center.

des·cen·tra·li·za·ción f. decentralization.

des·cen·trar tr. to put off center, uncenter

—reflex. to become off center.

des·ce·rra·jar tr. to force, break open; *(descargar)* to fire, discharge.

des·cha·ve·ta·do, a adj. AMER. crazy, loony.

des·cien·da, do see **descender.**

des·ci·frar tr. to decipher; *(con clave)* to decode; *(aclarar)* to make out.

des·co·ca·do, a adj. & m.f. brazen, forward (person).

des·co·car §70 reflex. to be impudent *or* brazen.

des·co·di·fi·car §70 tr. to decode.

des·col·gar §16 tr. *(quitar)* to take down; *(bajar)* to lower, let down; *(teléfono)* to pick up —reflex. *(caer)* to come *or* fall down; *(bajarse)* to climb *or* come down; *(presentarse)* to show up, drop in ♦ **d. con** to come up with.

des·co·llar §19 intr. to stand out, be outstanding.

des·co·lo·rar tr. to discolor; *(desteñir)* to fade; *(blanquear)* to bleach —reflex. to be discolored; *(desteñirse)* to become faded; *(quedar blanco)* to be bleached; *(el pelo)* to bleach.

des·co·lo·ri·do, a adj. discolored; *(pálido)* pallid, colorless; *(desteñido)* faded; *(blanqueado)* whitened, bleached.

des·co·lo·rir §38 tr. to fade, discolor.

des·com·pa·sar tr. to go too far —reflex. to be rude, be impolite.

des·com·po·ner §54 tr. *(desordenar)* to disarrange, mess up; *(podrir)* to decompose, cause to rot; MECH. to break, put out of order; *(trastornar)* to upset, disturb —reflex. *(corromperse)* to rot, decompose; MECH. to break down; *(indisponerse)* to feel sick; *(irritarse)* to become disturbed, get upset.

des·com·po·si·ción f. decomposition, decay; *(desarreglo)* disorder, disarrangement.

des·com·pos·tu·ra f. disorder, disarrangement; *(deseaseo)* slovenliness, messiness; *(descaro)* impudence, rudeness; MECH. breakdown.

des·com·pre·sión f. decompression.

des·com·pri·mir tr. to decompress.

des·com·pues·to, a I. see **descomponer II.** adj. decomposed, rotten; *(desarreglado)* slovenly, messy; MECH. out of order, broken; *(perturbado)* upset; *(descarado)* impudent, rude; S. AMER. tipsy.

des·com·pu·sie·ra, so see **descomponer.**

des·co·mu·nal adj. *(enorme)* enormous, huge; *(extraordinario)* extraordinary.

des·co·mu·nal·men·te adv. excessively.

des·con·cer·tan·te adj. disconcerting.

des·con·cer·tar §49 tr. to disconcert, upset; *(descomponer)* to put out of order; *(desordenar)* to disarrange, disrupt; MED. to dislocate —reflex. to be disconcerted; *(descomponer)* to get out of order; *(desavenirse)* to fall out, disagree; *(descomedirse)* to go off the deep end; MED. to become dislocated.

des·co·nec·tar tr. to disconnect —reflex. to become disconnected.

des·con·fia·do, a adj. & m.f. distrustful, suspicious (person).

des·con·fian·za f. distrust, mistrust.

des·con·fiar §30 intr. to distrust, mistrust.

des·con·ge·lar tr. *(deshelar)* to thaw; *(la nevera)* to defrost; COM. to unfreeze.

des·con·ges·tio·nar tr. to clear.

des·co·no·cer §17 tr. not to know; *(no recordar)* not to remember; *(no reconocer)* not to recognize; *(negar)* to deny, disavow; *(desentenderse)* to pretend not to know, ignore.

des·co·no·ci·do, a I. adj. unknown; *(desagradecido)* ungrateful; *(muy cambiado)* unrecognizable; *(extraño)* strange, unfamiliar **II.** m.f. *(extraño)* stranger; *(recién llegado)* newcomer.

des·co·no·ci·mien·to m. ignorance; *(despreocupación)* disregard; *(ingratitud)* ingratitude; *(olvido)* forgetfulness.

des·con·si·de·ra·ción f. thoughtlessness.

des·con·si·de·ra·do, a adj. & m.f. inconsiderate, thoughtless (person).

des·con·so·la·do, a adj. disconsolate, sad; *(el estómago)* empty, starved.

des·con·so·lar §19 tr. to distress, grieve —reflex. to lose heart, become distressed.

des·con·sue·lo m. grief, distress; *(del estómago)* empty feeling.

des·con·ta·mi·nar tr. to decontaminate.

des·con·tar §19 tr. *(quitar)* to deduct, take away; *(rebajar)* to disregard, discount; *(dar por cierto)* to take for granted, assume; COM. to discount.

des·con·ten·tar tr. to discontent, displease —reflex. to become discontented *or* displeased.

des·con·ten·to, a I. adj. discontented, dissatisfied **II.** m. discontent, dissatisfaction.

des·co·ra·zo·nar tr. to tear out the heart of; FIG. to discourage, dishearten —reflex. to lose heart, become discouraged.

des·cor·char tr. to uncork.

des·co·rrer tr. to run back over (ground already covered); *(cortinas)* to draw back, open —intr. & reflex. to flow.

des·cor·tés adj. & m.f. discourteous, rude (person).

des·cor·te·sí·a f. discourtesy, rudeness.

des·cor·te·zar §04 tr. to strip the bark from, decorticate; *(el pan)* to remove the crust from; *(la fruta)* to peel; *(desbastar)* to refine, knock the rough edges off.

des·co·ser tr. SEW. to unstitch, rip —reflex. SEW. to come unstitched, rip ♦ **no d. los labios** to keep one's lips sealed.

des·co·si·do, a adj. SEW. unstitched, ripped; *(indiscreto)* indiscreet, talkative; *(desordenado)* disorderly, chaotic; *(excesivo)* immoderate, excessive.

des·co·te m. low-cut neckline, décolletage.

des·co·yun·tar tr. MED. to dislocate; FIG. to bother, annoy —reflex. MED. to become dislocated.

des·cré·di·to m. discredit, disrepute.

des·cre·í·do, a I. adj. disbelieving, incredulous **II.** m.f. disbeliever; RELIG. nonbeliever, infidel.

des·cri·bir §80 tr. to describe; *(trazar)* to trace, describe.

des·crip·ción f. description.

des·cri(p)·to, a see **describir.**

des·cuar·ti·zar §04 tr. to quarter, cut up.

des·cu·bier·to, a I. see **descubrir II.** adj. uncovered, exposed; *(yermo)* bare, barren; *(sin sombrero)* bareheaded, without a hat ♦ **a d.** uncovered; COM. unbacked ● **al d.** COM. short; FIG. openly, in the open ● **estar en d.** COM. to be overdrawn; FIG. to be at a loss for words ● **girar en d.** COM. overdraw **III.** m. COM. deficit, shortage.

des·cu·bri·dor, ·ra I. adj. discovering, exploring **II.** m.f. *(explorador)* discoverer, explorer —m. MIL. scout.

des·cu·bri·mien·to m. discovery; *(revelación)* disclosure, revelation.

des·cu·brir §80 tr. to discover; (*revelar*) to reveal, uncover; (*alcanzar a ver*) to be able to see, make out; (*enterarse*) to find out; MIL. to reconnoiter —reflex. (*el sombrero*) to take off or remove one's hat; (*dejarse ver*) to reveal oneself, show oneself.

des·cuel·go, gue see **descolgar**.

des·cue·lle, llo see **descollar**.

des·cuen·te, to see **descontar**.

des·cuen·to m. discount, reduction; (*acción de descontar*) deduction.

des·cue·rar tr. AMER. to skin, flay; (*criticar*) to criticize, tear apart.

des·cui·da·do, a I. adj. (*negligente*) careless; (*desaliñado*) untidy, slovenly; (*desprevenido*) unprepared, off guard; (*abandonado*) neglected, abandoned; (*despreocupado*) carefree, easygoing **II.** m.f. (*negligente*) careless person; (*desaliñado*) sloppy person, slob.

des·cui·dar tr. (*libertar*) to relieve, free of an obligation; (*no cuidar*) to neglect, forget; (*distraer*) to distract —intr. to be careless —reflex. to be careless; (*desaliñarse*) to neglect oneself, not take care of oneself.

des·cui·do m. carelessness, negligence; (*olvido*) forgetfulness; (*desaliño*) untidiness, slovenliness; (*desatención*) slight, oversight; (*falta*) error, mistake ♦ **al d.** nonchalantly, casually ♦ **en un d.** AMER. when least expected.

des·de prep. from, since ♦ **d. hace** for <*no le hemos visto d. hace un año* we have not seen him for a year> ♦ **d. luego** of course ♦ **d. que** since ♦ **d. ya** AMER. right now.

des·de·cir §11 intr. ♦ **d. de** not to live up to, to fall short of; (*venir a menos*) to degenerate, decline —reflex. ♦ **d. de** to retract, withdraw.

des·dén m. disdain, scorn ♦ **al d.** nonchalantly.

des·de·ña·ble adj. despicable, contemptible.

des·de·ñar tr. to disdain, scorn —reflex. to be disdainful ♦ **d. de** not to deign to.

des·di·bu·jar·se reflex. to become blurred.

des·di·ce see **desdecir**.

des·di·cha f. (*desgracia*) misfortune; (*pobreza*) poverty, misery ♦ **por d.** unfortunately.

des·di·cha·do, a I. adj. (*desgraciado*) unfortunate, pitiful; (*infeliz*) unhappy, wretched **II.** m.f. wretch.

des·di·ga, go, jera, jo see **desdecir**.

des·do·bla·mien·to m. (*extensión*) unfolding, spreading out; (*fraccionamiento*) splitting, breaking down; (*aclaración*) explanation, elucidation ♦ **d. de la personalidad** split personality.

des·do·blar tr. (*extender*) to unfold, spread out; (*separar*) to split, break down.

de·se·ar tr. to wish, desire.

de·se·car §70 tr. to dry, desiccate; (*volver insensible*) to dry up, harden.

de·se·char tr. (*rechazar*) to reject, decline; (*renunciar*) to refuse, turn down; (*apartar*) to cast aside, get rid of; (*menospreciar*) to underrate, undervalue; (*despreciar*) to scorn.

de·se·cho m. residue; (*desperdicio*) waste, rubbish; (*lo peor*) scum, dregs; (*metal*) scrap; (*desprecio*) scorn, contempt.

de·sem·ba·lar tr. to unpack.

de·sem·ba·ra·za·do, a adj. free, clear; (*desenvuelto*) free and easy.

de·sem·ba·ra·zar §04 tr. to clear, rid of obstacles; AMER. to give birth to —reflex. to free oneself, get rid (of).

de·sem·bar·ca·de·ro m. pier, wharf.

de·sem·bar·car §70 tr. to disembark, unload —intr. to disembark, go ashore.

de·sem·bar·co m. landing, disembarkation; MIL. landing; (*escalera*) landing.

de·sem·bar·gar §47 tr. to clear, remove obstacles from.

de·sem·bar·que m. (*de mercancías*) debarkation, unloading; (*de pasajeros*) disembarkation, landing.

de·sem·bo·ca·du·ra f. outlet.

de·sem·bo·car §70 intr. (*río*) to flow, run; (*calle*) to lead to, run.

de·sem·bol·sar tr. to take out of a purse or bag; (*pagar*) to disburse, pay.

de·sem·bol·so m. (*pago*) disbursement, payment; (*gasto*) expenditure, outlay.

de·sem·bo·zar §04 tr. & reflex. to unmask (oneself).

de·sem·bra·gar §47 tr. MECH. to disengage (gears).

de·sem·bria·gar §47 tr. to sober up.

de·sem·bro·llar tr. to unravel, untangle.

de·sem·bu·char tr. ORNITH. to disgorge; COLL. (*revelar*) tell, reveal.

de·sem·pa·car §70 tr. to unpack, unwrap.

de·sem·pa·cho m. ease, self-confidence.

de·sem·pa·ñar tr. (*un cristal*) to clean, polish; (*un niño*) to unswaddle.

de·sem·pa·pe·lar tr. to remove paper from; (*desenvolver*) to unwrap.

de·sem·pa·que m. unpacking.

de·sem·pa·que·tar tr. to unpack, unwrap.

de·sem·pa·tar tr. to break a tie between.

de·sem·pe·ñar tr. (*rescatar*) to recover, redeem; (*pagar*) to get out of debt; (*cumplir*) to fulfill, carry out; (*sacar de apuro*) to get (someone) out of trouble; THEAT. to play (a part) —reflex. (*pagar*) to get oneself out of debt; (*sacarse de apuro*) to get oneself out of trouble.

de·sem·pe·ño m. (*rescate*) redemption, redeeming; (*de deudas*) freeing from debt; (*cumplimiento*) fulfillment; THEAT. performance.

de·sem·ple·a·do, a adj. & m.f. unemployed (person).

de·sem·ple·o m. unemployment.

de·sen·ca·de·na·mien·to m. unchaining; (*de sucesos*) unfolding.

de·sen·ca·de·nar tr. to unchain, unfetter; (*liberar*) to free, unleash; (*incitar*) to start, incite —reflex. to break loose; (*sucesos*) to unfold.

de·sen·ca·jar tr. MED. to dislocate; (*desconectar*) to disconnect; (*sacar*) to remove, take out —reflex. to become distorted or contorted; (*deshacerse*) to fall apart, become disconnected.

de·sen·ca·mi·nar tr. to lead astray, misdirect.

de·sen·can·tar tr. to disenchant, disillusion.

de·sen·can·to m. disenchantment.

de·sen·ce·rrar §49 tr. (*sacar del encierro*) to free (from confinement); (*abrir*) to open, unlock; (*descubrir*) to bring to light, reveal.

de·sen·chu·far tr. to unplug, disconnect.

de·sen·cla·vi·jar tr. to disconnect, loosen.

de·sen·co·ger §34 tr. (*extender*) to stretch or spread out; (*desdoblar*) to unfold —reflex. to come out of one's shell.

de·sen·co·le·ri·zar §04 tr. to calm, pacify.

de·sen·co·nar tr. MED. to relieve the inflammation of; (*desahogar*) to soothe, pacify —reflex. to calm down, cool off.

de·sen·co·no m. MED. relief of inflammation; *(apaciguamiento)* calming, pacification.

de·sen·fa·da·do, a adj. *(desenvuelto)* confident, self-assured; *(despreocupado)* carefree, uninhibited; *(espacioso)* spacious, ample.

de·sen·fa·dar tr. to soothe, pacify —reflex. to calm down, cool off.

de·sen·fa·do m. *(desenvoltura)* confidence, self-assurance; *(facilidad)* ease, naturalness.

de·sen·fre·nar tr. to unbridle —reflex. to surrender oneself, give oneself over; *(las pasiones)* to break loose, be unleashed; *(una tempestad)* to break, burst.

de·sen·fre·no m. wantonness, licentiousness.

de·sen·fun·dar tr. to unsheath.

de·sen·ga·ña·do, a adj. disillusioned.

de·sen·ga·ñar tr. to disillusion —reflex. to become disillusioned.

de·sen·gan·char tr. to unhook, unfasten; *(caballerías)* to unhitch, unharness.

de·sen·ga·ño m. disillusionment; *(comprensión)* enlightenment.

de·sen·gra·nar tr. MECH. to disengage.

de·sen·gra·sar tr. to remove the grease from —intr. *(enflaquecer)* to lose weight, grow slim; *(variar el trabajo)* to change jobs.

de·sen·la·ce m. untying, unfastening; LIT. denouement, ending; *(resultado)* result, outcome.

de·sen·la·zar §04 tr. to unfasten, untie; *(resolver)* to clear up, resolve; LIT. to unravel —reflex. to become untied or loose; LIT. to reach a dénouement.

de·sen·ma·ra·ñar tr. to untangle, unravel.

de·sen·mas·ca·rar tr. *(quitar la máscara)* to unmask; *(descubrir)* to reveal, expose.

de·sen·mu·de·cer §17 tr. & intr. to rid (oneself) of a speech impediment; *(hablar)* to break a long silence.

de·se·no·jo m. calm, calmness (after anger).

de·sen·re·dar tr. to disentangle, unravel; *(poner en orden)* to put in order, straighten out —reflex. to extricate oneself.

de·sen·re·do m. disentangling, disentanglement; *(aclaración)* putting in order, straightening out; LIT. dénouement, ending.

de·sen·ro·llar tr. to unroll, unwind.

de·sen·sam·blar tr. to disassemble.

de·sen·si·bi·li·zar §04 tr. to desensitize.

de·sen·si·llar tr. to unsaddle.

de·sen·ta·blar tr. *(desarreglar)* to disarrange, disturb; *(deshacer)* to break up.

de·sen·ten·der·se §50 reflex. to feign ignorance, pretend not to know ♦ **d. de** to take no part in, have nothing to do with.

de·sen·te·rrar §49 tr. to unearth, dig up; COLL. to dig up, recall.

de·sen·to·nar tr. to humiliate, humble —intr. MUS. to be out of tune; FIG. to clash, not to match —reflex. to be rude or insolent.

de·sen·to·no m. MUS. dissonance; FIG. rude or insolent tone of voice.

de·sen·tra·ñar tr. to eviscerate, disembowel; *(solucionar)* to get to the bottom of —reflex. to give one's all.

de·sen·tu·me·cer §17 tr. to rid of numbness.

de·sen·vai·nar tr. *(un sable)* to draw, unsheathe; *(las uñas)* to bare (claws); COLL. *(sacar a relucir)* to uncover, expose.

de·sen·vol·tu·ra f. *(confianza)* naturalness, confidence; *(elocuencia)* eloquence, facility; *(desvergüenza)* forwardness, brazenness.

de·sen·vol·ver §78 tr. to unroll, unwrap; *(explicar)* to develop, expand; *(aclarar)* to unravel, disentangle —reflex. to come unrolled or unwrapped; *(desempacharse)* to become self-assured; *(desenredarse)* to get oneself out of trouble.

de·sen·vol·vi·mien·to m. unrolling, unwrapping; *(explicación)* development, expansion; *(desenredo)* way out, escape.

de·sen·vuel·to, a I. see **desenvolver II.** adj. *(confiado)* natural, confident; *(elocuente)* eloquent, fluent; *(desvergonzado)* forward, brazen.

de·se·o m. desire, wish.

de·se·o·so, a adj. desirous, anxious.

de·se·qui·li·bra·do, a adj. & m.f. unbalanced (person).

de·se·qui·li·brar tr. to throw off balance —reflex. to lose one's balance; *(dementarse)* to become mentally unbalanced.

de·se·qui·li·brio m. lack of equilibrium, imbalance; *(de la mente)* derangement.

de·ser·ción f. desertion, abandonment; MIL. desertion.

de·ser·tar tr., intr. & reflex. to desert.

de·sér·ti·co, a adj. desert-like, barren; *(sin habitantes)* deserted, unpopulated.

de·ser·tor, ·ra m.f. deserter.

de·ses·pe·ra·ción f. despair, desperation; *(cólera)* anger, exasperation.

de·ses·pe·ra·do, a adj. & m.f. hopeless, desperate (person) ♦ **a la d.** in desperation, as a last hope.

de·ses·pe·ran·te adj. *(que impacienta)* exasperating, infuriating; *(descorazonador)* discouraging, causing despair.

de·ses·pe·ran·za f. despair, hopelessness.

de·ses·pe·ran·zar §04 tr. to deprive of hope, discourage —intr. & reflex. to despair, lose hope.

de·ses·pe·rar tr. to drive to despair, discourage; *(irritar)* to exasperate —intr. & reflex. to lose hope, despair.

de·ses·ti·mar tr. to hold in low esteem.

des·fa·cha·ta·do, a adj. cheeky, insolent.

des·fa·cha·tez f. cheek, nerve.

des·fal·car §70 tr. to remove part of; *(robar)* to embezzle, defalcate.

des·fal·co m. embezzlement, defalcation.

des·fa·lle·cer §17 tr. to weaken, debilitate —intr. to weaken; *(desmayarse)* to faint, pass out.

des·fa·lle·ci·do, a adj. faint, dizzy.

des·fa·lle·ci·mien·to m. weakness, debilitation; MED. fainting, swooning.

des·fa·sa·do, a adj. out of phase.

des·fa·vo·ra·ble adj. unfavorable, adverse.

des·fa·vo·re·cer §17 tr. to disfavor; *(oponer)* to oppose, contradict.

des·fi·gu·ra·ción f./m**i**en·to m. disfiguring, disfigurement; *(objeto)* defacement; *(hecho)* distortion, misrepresentation; *(disfraz)* disguise, camouflage.

des·fi·gu·rar tr. *(afear)* to disfigure, mar; *(deformar)* to deform, misshape; *(disfrazar)* to disguise, camouflage; *(desvirtuar)* to distort, misrepresent —reflex. to be disfigured.

des·fi·la·de·ro m. defile, narrow pass.

des·fi·lar intr. to parade, march.

des·fi·le m. march, procession; MIL. parade.

des·flo·ra·ción f./m**i**en·to m. deflowering.

des·flo·rar tr. to strip the flowers from; *(ajar)* to tarnish, spoil; *(desvirgar)* to deflower.

des·fo·gar §47 tr. to vent; *(apagar)* to slake;

(soltar) to vent, give vent to —reflex. to vent one's anger, let off steam.

des·fo·gue m. *(agujero)* vent; *(desahogo)* letting off steam, venting.

des·fon·dar tr. to knock the bottom out of —reflex. to have the bottom fall out; *(agotarse)* to wear oneself out, exhaust oneself.

des·for·mar tr. to deform, disfigure.

des·ga·jar tr. to rip or tear off —reflex. to come or break off.

des·ga·na f. lack of appetite; *(renuencia)* reluctance, unwillingness.

des·ga·na·do, a adj. without appetite, not hungry; *(sin entusiasmo)* indifferent, unenthusiastic.

des·ga·nar tr. to take away (a person's) desire or interest —reflex. to lose one's appetite; FIG. *(cansarse)* to get bored, lose interest.

des·ga·no m. var. of **desgana**.

des·ga·ñi·tar·se reflex. to scream loudly.

des·gar·ba·do, a adj. awkward, ungainly.

des·ga·rra·do, a adj. torn, ripped; COLL. impudent, shameless.

des·ga·rra·dor, ·ra adj. *(que da miedo)* bloodcurdling; AMER. heartbreaking, heartrending.

des·ga·rra·mien·to m. ripping, tearing.

des·ga·rrar tr. to rip, tear; *(expectorar)* to spit, expectorate —reflex. to rip, tear; *(apartarse)* to break away, go off by oneself.

des·gas·tar tr. to wear away or down; *(debilitar)* to weaken —reflex. *(perder fuerza)* to become weak or feeble; *(agotarse)* to wear oneself out.

des·gas·te m. erosion; *(daño)* damage, wear; *(debilitación)* weakening, debilitation.

des·glo·se m. breakdown; CINEM. cutting, editing.

des·gra·cia f. misfortune, adversity; *(accidente)* mishap, setback; *(pérdida de favor)* disgrace, disfavor; *(desagrado)* displeasure; *(falta de gracia)* gracelessness, clumsiness ♦ **por d.** unfortunately.

des·gra·cia·da·men·te adv. unfortunately.

des·gra·cia·do, a adj. & m.f. unfortunate, unlucky (person); *(infeliz)* unhappy (person); *(desagradable)* unpleasant, disagreeable (person); *(sinvergüenza)* wretched, despicable (person).

des·gra·ciar tr. to displease, annoy; *(estropear)* to ruin, spoil; AMER. *(seducir)* to seduce —reflex. *(perder favor)* to lose favor; *(estropearse)* to be ruined or spoiled; *(malograrse)* to fail, fall through.

des·gra·na·dor, ·ra I. adj. threshing, shelling II. m.f. thresher, sheller —f. threshing machine.

des·gra·nar tr. to thresh, shell.

des·gra·sar tr. to remove grease from.

des·gra·var tr. *(rebajar)* to reduce taxes or duties; *(eximir)* to exempt from taxes or duties; *(aligerar)* to lighten.

des·gre·ñar tr. to dishevel, tousle —reflex. to become disheveled or tousled; *(reñir)* to have a heated argument.

des·guar·ne·cer §17 tr. to remove the trimmings; *(desarmar)* to dismantle.

des·ha·bi·ta·do, a adj. uninhabited.

des·ha·bi·tar tr. to vacate, leave; *(despoblar)* to depopulate, leave without inhabitants.

des·ha·bi·tuar §67 tr. & reflex. to break of a habit.

des·ha·cer §40 tr. to undo; *(destruir)* to destroy, ruin; *(desgastar)* to wear out; *(dividir)* to

cut up; *(desarmar)* to take apart; *(disolver)* to melt, dissolve; *(desconcertar)* to break —reflex. *(descomponerse)* to fall apart, break; *(disolverse)* to melt, dissolve; *(desaparecer)* to vanish, disappear; *(inquietarse)* to go to pieces, get worked up; *(desvivirse)* to go out of one's way; *(extenuarse)* to become weak ♦ **d. de** to get rid of ♦ **d. en** to dissolve into.

des·he·cho, a I. see **deshacer** II. adj. undone; *(cansado)* tired, worn out.

des·he·lar §49 tr. & reflex. to melt, thaw.

des·he·re·da·do, a adj. & m.f. disinherited (person); *(pobre)* poor, underprivileged (person).

des·he·re·dar tr. to disinherit.

des·he·rrar §49 tr. to unshackle, unchain —reflex. to free oneself from shackles or chains; *(un caballo)* to lose a shoe.

des·hi·cie·ra, hice see **deshacer**.

des·hi·dra·ta·ción f. dehydration.

des·hi·dra·tar tr. to dehydrate —reflex. to become dehydrated.

des·hie·le see **deshelar**.

des·hie·lo m. thawing, defrosting.

des·hie·rre, rro see **desherrar**.

des·hi·la·char tr. to ravel, remove threads from —reflex. to fray, become frayed.

des·hi·lar tr. to undo, unravel; FIG. to cut to ribbons or pieces —intr. to get or grow thin —reflex. to become frayed.

des·hil·va·na·do, a adj. disjointed, disconnected.

des·hil·va·nar tr. to remove tacking or basting from.

des·hin·char tr. to reduce the swelling of; *(un balón)* to deflate; *(la cólera)* to give vent to —reflex. to go down; COLL. to be taken down a peg or two.

des·hi·zo see **deshacer**.

des·ho·ja·du·ra f./**mien·to** m. defoliation.

des·ho·jar tr. to defoliate —reflex. to lose leaves.

des·ho·je m. falling of leaves.

des·ho·lli·na·dor, ·ra I. adj. nosy, inquisitive II. m.f. *(persona que deshollina)* chimney sweep; *(escudriñador)* busybody, snoop.

des·ho·lli·nar tr. to sweep chimneys; *(escudriñar)* to scrutinize, examine closely.

des·ho·nes·ti·dad f. dishonesty; *(indecencia)* indecency, impropriety.

des·ho·nes·to, a adj. dishonest; *(indecente)* indecent, improper.

des·ho·nor m. dishonor; *(afrenta)* insult.

des·hon·ra f. dishonor.

des·hon·rar tr. to dishonor, disgrace; *(afrentar)* to insult, affront.

des·hon·ro·so, a adj. dishonorable.

des·ho·ra f. inconvenient time.

des·hue·sar tr. *(carne)* to debone; *(fruta)* to remove the pit from.

des·hu·ma·ni·za·ción f. dehumanization.

des·hu·ma·ni·zar §04 tr. to dehumanize.

des·hu·me·de·cer §17 tr. & reflex. to dry out.

de·si·dia f. negligence, carelessness; *(pereza)* laziness, indolence.

de·sier·to, a I. adj. deserted, uninhabited; *(desolado)* desolate, bleak II. m. desert.

de·sig·na·ción f. designation.

de·sig·nar tr. to design, plan; *(nombrar)* to designate, appoint; *(señalar)* to point out; *(fijar)* to decide on, fix.

de·sig·nio m. design, plan.

de·si·gual adj. unequal; *(quebrado)* uneven; *(diferente)* different; *(injusto)* unfair, inequitable; *(arduo)* arduous, difficult; *(inconstante)* changeable, inconstant.

de·si·gual·dad f. inequality, disparity; *(aspereza)* roughness, ruggedness; *(inconstancia)* inconstancy, changeableness.

de·si·lu·sión f. disillusionment.

de·si·lu·sio·nar tr. to disillusion —reflex. to become disillusioned.

de·si·man·tar tr. to demagnetize.

de·sin·cor·po·rar tr. to dissolve, break up.

de·sin·fec·ción f. disinfection.

de·sin·fec·tan·te adj. & m. disinfectant.

de·sin·fec·tar tr. to disinfect.

de·sin·fla·mar tr. to reduce inflammation in.

de·sin·flar tr. to deflate, let air out of —reflex. to deflate, collapse; COLL. to lose one's nerve.

de·sin·te·gra·ción f. disintegration.

de·sin·te·grar tr. *(disociar)* to disintegrate, break up; PHYS. to split.

de·sin·te·rés m. unselfishness.

de·sin·te·re·sa·do, a adj. disinterested, impartial; *(generoso)* altruistic, unselfish.

de·sin·te·re·sar·se reflex. to lose interest, take no interest in.

de·sin·to·xi·ca·ción f. detoxification.

de·sin·to·xi·car §70 intr. to detoxify.

de·sis·tir intr. to desist; *(de un derecho)* to waive.

des·jui·cia·do, a adj. injudicious.

des·jun·tar tr. & reflex. to separate, divide.

des·la·bo·nar tr. to unlink, disconnect the links of; *(desconcertar)* to upset; *(deshacer)* to ruin, destroy —reflex. to come apart, become disconnected; *(deshacerse)* to fail, fall apart; *(apartarse)* to break away, withdraw.

des·la·zar §04 tr. to unlace, untie.

des·le·al I. adj. disloyal, traitorous II. m.f. traitor.

des·le·al·tad f. disloyalty, treachery.

des·le·ír §58 tr. to dissolve, liquefy; *(un discurso)* to dilute, weaken —reflex. to dissolve.

des·len·gua·do, a adj. *(grosero)* foul-mouthed, coarse; *(descarado)* rude, insolent.

des·len·guar §10 tr. to remove the tongue from —reflex. *(descararse)* to be insolent; *(hablar groseramente)* to use foul language, swear.

des·li·a, lío, liera, lió see **desleír.**

des·liar §30 tr. *(desatar)* to untie, undo; *(desenvolver)* to unwrap.

des·li·gar §47 tr. *(desatar)* to untie, unfasten; *(desenredar)* to untangle, unravel; *(dispensar)* to dispense, administer; *(absolver)* to absolve, exonerate; MUS. to pick —reflex. *(desatarse)* to become untied or unfastened; *(librarse)* to extricate oneself, break away.

des·lin·dar tr. to delimit, mark the boundaries of; *(aclarar)* to clarify, elucidate.

des·liz m. slip.

des·li·za·mien·to m. *(desliz)* slipping, sliding ♦ **d. de tierra** landslide.

des·li·zar §04 tr. to slip, slide; *(decir por descuido)* to let slip —intr. to slide, slip —reflex. to slide, slip; *(sobre el agua)* to glide; *(escaparse)* to slip away, escape; COLL. *(caerse)* to slip; *(meter la pata)* to slip up.

des·lo·mar tr. to break the back of; *(cansar)* to exhaust, wear out —reflex. to exhaust oneself, wear oneself out.

des·lu·ci·do, a adj. *(sin brillo)* tarnished, dull; *(sin vida)* lackluster, mediocre.

des·lu·cir §44 tr. *(estropear)* to spoil, ruin; *(quitar el brillo a)* to dull, tarnish; *(desacreditar)* to discredit —reflex. *(perder el brillo)* to become dull or tarnished; *(desacreditarse)* to become discredited.

des·lum·bra·dor, ·ra/bran·te adj. *(brillante)* dazzling, brilliant; *(asombrante)* overwhelming.

des·lum·bra·mien·to m. *(ceguera)* dazzling, dazzle; *(confusión)* confusion, bewilderment.

des·lum·brar tr. *(cegar)* to dazzle, blind; *(confundir)* to overwhelm, bewilder.

des·lus·tre m. *(falta de brillo)* dullness, lack of shine; *(empañadura)* tarnishing, dulling; *(deshonra)* dishonor, disgrace.

des·ma·de·jar tr. to weaken, enervate.

des·ma·le·zar §04 tr. AMER. to weed.

des·mán m. *(ultraje)* outrage, abuse; *(desgracia)* misfortune, mishap; ZOOL. muskrat.

des·man·da·do, a adj. disobedient.

des·man·dar tr. I. to countermand, rescind II. reflex. to go too far, get out of hand.

des·ma·no adv. ♦ **a d.** out of reach.

des·man·te·la·do, a adj. dismantled, disassembled; *(mal cuidado)* dilapidated, run-down.

des·man·te·lar tr. *(derribar)* to knock down, dismantle; *(una casa)* to vacate, abandon.

des·ma·ña f./ño m. clumsiness, awkwardness.

des·ma·ña·do, a adj. & m.f. clumsy (person).

des·ma·ra·ñar tr. to disentangle, unravel.

des·ma·ya·do, a adj. unconscious; *(un color)* dull, wan; *(desanimado)* discouraged, disheartened; *(agotado)* weak, worn-out.

des·ma·yar tr. to make faint, cause to faint —intr. to lose heart, be discouraged —reflex. to faint, swoon.

des·ma·yo m. *(síncope)* faint, swoon; *(estado)* unconsciousness; *(desánimo)* depression, downheartedness; BOT. weeping willow.

des·me·di·do, a adj. *(excesivo)* excessive, immoderate; *(sin límite)* boundless, limitless.

des·me·dro m. decline, deterioration.

des·me·jo·rar tr. to impair, damage —intr. & reflex. to deteriorate, get worse.

des·mem·bra·ción f./mien·to m. dismemberment; *(división)* division, breaking up.

des·mem·brar tr. to dismember.

des·me·mo·ria·do, a adj. & m.f. forgetful, absent-minded (person).

des·me·mo·riar·se reflex. to become forgetful, lose one's memory.

des·men·ti·da f. *(negación)* denial; *(contradicción)* contradiction.

des·men·tir §65 tr. to contradict; *(refutar)* to refute, disprove; *(proceder contrariamente)* to go against —intr. to deviate, go out of line —reflex. to contradict oneself.

des·me·nu·zar §04 tr. to crumble, break into pieces; *(examinar)* to examine closely, scrutinize.

des·me·re·cer §17 tr. to be unworthy or undeserving of —intr. *(decaer)* to deteriorate; *(ser inferior)* to be inferior, compare unfavorably.

des·me·re·ci·mien·to m. demerit, unworthiness.

des·me·su·ra·do, a adj. *(desmedido)* excessive, inordinate; *(sin límite)* boundless, limitless; *(insolente)* insolent, impudent.

des·me·su·rar tr. *(desordenar)* to put in disorder; *(descomponer)* to disturb, upset —reflex. to go too far, forget oneself.

des·mien·ta, to see **desmentir.**

des·mi·gar §47 tr. to crumble (bread).

des·mi·ne·ra·li·za·ción f. demineralization.
des·min·tie·ra, tió see **desmentir**.
des·mo·char tr. *(un árbol)* to top; *(una obra)* to cut.
des·mol·dar tr. to unmold.
des·mon·ta·ble I. adj. detachable **II.** m. tire iron.
des·mon·tar tr. to dismantle, disassemble; *(bajar)* to dismount; *(árboles)* to fell, cut down; *(terreno)* to level; *(arma de fuego)* to uncock —intr. & reflex. to dismount.
des·mo·ra·li·za·ción f. demoralization.
des·mo·ra·li·za·dor, ·ra I. adj. demoralizing **II.** m.f. demoralizer.
des·mo·ra·li·zar §04 tr. to demoralize; *(corromper)* to corrupt —reflex. to become demoralized; *(corromperse)* to become corrupt *or* depraved.
des·mo·ro·na·mien·to m. decay, crumbling.
des·mo·ro·nar tr. to wear away, erode —reflex. to crumble, fall to pieces.
des·mo·ta·dor, ·ra m.f. burler —f. cotton gin.
des·mo·tar tr. to burl.
des·mo·vi·li·za·ción f. demobilization.
des·mo·vi·li·zar §04 tr. to demobilize.
des·na·ta·do·ra f. cream separator, skimmer.
des·na·tar tr. to skim the cream off; *(sacar lo mejor)* to take the cream *or* the best of.
des·na·tu·ra·li·za·do, a adj. denaturalized; *(corrompido)* perverted, corrupted; *(malo)* cruel, unnatural; CHEM. denatured.
des·na·tu·ra·li·zar §04 tr. to denaturalize; *(corromper)* to pervert, corrupt; CHEM. to denature —reflex. to become denaturalized.
des·ni·vel m. unevenness; *(depresión)* depression, drop; *(diferencia)* difference, disparity.
des·ni·ve·lar tr. to make uneven; *(desequilibrar)* to throw out of balance, unbalance; *(una balanza)* to tip, tilt.
des·nu·car §70 tr. to break the neck of —reflex. to break one's neck.
des·nu·dar tr. to strip, undress; *(descubrir)* to lay bare, uncover; ARM. to bare, draw; *(en el juego)* to fleece, clean out ♦ **d. un santo para vestir a otro** COLL. to rob Peter to pay Paul —reflex. to get undressed, strip ♦ **d. de** to free *or* rid oneself of.
des·nu·dez f. nudity, nakedness.
des·nu·dis·ta adj. & m.f. nudist.
des·nu·do, a I. adj. undressed; *(en cueros)* naked, nude; *(despojado)* stripped, bare; *(pobre)* dispossessed, destitute; *(patente)* clear, naked ♦ **d. de** devoid of, lacking **II.** m. ARTS nude.
des·nu·tri·ción f. malnutrition.
de·so·be·de·cer §17 tr. to disobey.
de·so·be·dien·cia f. disobedience.
de·so·be·dien·te adj. & m.f. disobedient (person).
de·so·cu·pa·ción f. *(desempleo)* unemployment; *(ociosidad)* idleness.
de·so·cu·pa·do, a I. adj. unemployed; *(sitio)* vacant **II.** m.f. *(ocioso)* idler; *(sin empleo)* unemployed person.
de·so·cu·par tr. *(una casa)* to vacate, move out of; *(una vasija)* to empty —reflex. to leave, quit.
de·so·do·ran·te I. adj. deodorizing **II.** m. deodorant.
de·so·do·ri·zar §04 tr. to deodorize.
de·so·ír §45 tr. to ignore, pay no attention to.

de·so·la·ción f. desolation.
de·so·lar §19 tr. to desolate —reflex. to be grieved, be distressed.
de·so·llar §19 tr. to skin, flay; *(dañar)* to harm, injure; *(hacer pagar mucho)* to skin, fleece; *(criticar)* to flay, criticize; *(murmurar de)* to slander.
de·sor·bi·tar tr. to exaggerate, carry to extremes —reflex. *(los ojos)* to bulge; *(descomedirse)* to go to extremes, lose one's sense of proportion.
de·sor·den m. disorder, disarray; *(lío)* muddle, mess; *(conducta)* disorderliness, unruliness; MED. upset, disorder; *(exceso)* excess, license.
de·sor·de·na·do, a adj. disorderly; *(falta de aseo)* slovenly, untidy; *(excesivo)* excessive, inordinate; *(conducta)* unruly, wild.
de·sor·de·nar tr. to disorder; *(causar confusión)* to throw into confusion; *(desasear)* to make untidy *or* messy —reflex. to become disorderly; *(salirse de la regla)* to get out of order *or* out of control.
de·sor·ga·ni·za·ción f. disorganization.
de·sor·ga·ni·zar §04 tr. to disorganize.
de·so·rien·ta·ción f. disorientation.
de·so·rien·tar tr. to disorient; *(confundir)* to confuse —reflex. to be disoriented; *(confundirse)* to become confused.
de·so·vi·llar tr. to unravel; *(dar ánimo)* to encourage.
de·so·ye·ra, yó see **desoír**.
des·pa·bi·la·do, a adj. *(despierto)* alert, wideawake; *(listo)* clever, sharp.
des·pa·bi·la·dor m. candle snuffer.
des·pa·bi·lar tr. *(apagar)* to snuff; *(robar)* to steal, pinch; *(avivar)* to liven up, stimulate; *(malgastar)* to squander; *(despachar)* to finish quickly; *(matar)* to kill, snuff out —reflex. *(despertarse)* to wake up; *(avivarse)* to liven up; AMER. to leave, disappear.
des·pa·chan·te m. ARG. clerk, employee.
des·pa·char tr. to complete, conclude; *(resolver)* to resolve, settle; *(enviar)* to dispatch, send; *(despedir)* to fire, dismiss; *(vender)* to sell; *(expedir)* to expedite, hurry along; COLL. *(acabar con)* to polish *or* knock off; *(matar)* to kill, knock off —intr. *(darse prisa)* to hurry up; *(hablar)* to speak one's mind; COM. to do business —reflex. AMER. *(darse prisa)* to hurry up ♦ **d. de** to get rid of.
des·pa·cho m. *(envío)* dispatch, sending; *(oficina)* office, bureau; *(estudio)* study, office; *(tienda)* store, shop; *(venta)* sale; *(comunicación)* dispatch, message; *(resolución)* efficiency; *(cédula)* commission ♦ **tener buen d.** to be efficient.
des·pa·chu·rrar tr. *(aplastar)* to crush, squash; *(una cuenta)* to confuse, mix up; *(una persona)* to silence, squelch.
des·pa·cio I. adv. slow, slowly; *(poco a poco)* little by little, gradually; AMER. in a low voice, quietly **II.** interj. easy does it!, take it easy!
des·pam·pa·nan·te adj. COLL. astounding, stunning.
des·pan·zu·rrar/chu·rrar tr. COLL. to rip open the belly of, disembowel.
des·pa·re·jo, a adj. *(dispar)* odd; *(sin alineación)* not matching; *(no parejo)* uneven.
des·par·pa·jo m. *(desenvoltura)* ease, confidence; *(descaro)* pertness, freshness.
des·pa·rra·mar tr. to spread; *(derramar)* to

spill, splash; *(malgastar)* to squander —reflex. to scatter, spread; *(divertirse)* to let one's hair down.

des·pa·ta·rrar tr. to astonish, flabbergast —reflex. *(abrirse de piernas)* to open one's legs wide; *(caerse)* to fall with legs apart; *(aturdirse)* to be astonished *or* flabbergasted.

des·pa·vo·ri·do, a adj. terrified, afraid.

des·pa·vo·rir §38 intr. & reflex. to be terrified.

des·pe·char tr. *(enojar)* to anger; *(causar disgusto a)* to displease, disgust; *(irritar)* to vex, peeve; *(destetar)* to wean —reflex. to become angry.

des·pe·cho m. *(ira)* spite, wrath; *(descontento)* displeasure, disgust; *(desesperación)* despair, dejection ♦ **a d. de** in spite of, in defiance of • **por d.** out of spite.

des·pec·ti·vo, a adj. disparaging, pejorative.

des·pe·da·za·mien·to m. breaking *or* tearing to pieces; *(ruina)* ruin, destruction.

des·pe·da·zar §04 tr. to break *or* tear to pieces —reflex. *(caerse)* to fall *or* break into pieces; *(arruinarse)* to be ruined, be destroyed.

des·pe·di·da f. *(adiós)* good-bye, farewell; *(despacho)* dismissal, firing.

des·pe·dir §48 tr. *(soltar)* to throw (out), eject; *(decir adiós)* to say good-bye; *(despachar)* to dismiss, fire; *(deshacerse de)* to get rid of, throw out; *(emitir)* to emit, give off —reflex. to say good-bye *(de* to).

des·pe·ga·ble adj. detachable.

des·pe·gar §47 tr. to unstick, unglue; *(separar)* to detach, separate; *(quitar)* to remove, take off —intr. AVIA. to take off —reflex. to become unstuck *or* unglued; *(separarse)* to become detached *or* separated; *(desapegarse)* to grow indifferent.

des·pe·gue m. takeoff.

des·pei·nar tr. to disarrange the hair of.

des·pe·ja·do, a adj. confident, sure of oneself; *(listo)* clever, bright; METEOROL. clear, cloudless; *(sin impedimento)* clear, open; *(espacioso)* spacious, wide.

des·pe·jar tr. to clear; *(quitar)* to get rid of, remove; *(aclarar)* to clear up, sort out —reflex. to become self-confident; METEOROL. to clear up; *(divertirse)* to enjoy oneself; MED. to go down.

des·pe·lle·jar tr. *(desollar)* to skin, flay; *(criticar)* to flay, criticize.

des·pe·lu·zar §04 tr. *(desmelenar)* to dishevel, muss; *(erizar)* to make (someone's hair) stand on end —reflex. to be frightened.

des·pen·sa f. *(lugar)* larder, pantry; *(provisiones)* provisions, supplies; *(oficio)* stewardship.

des·pe·ña·de·ro, a I. adj. steep, precipitous **II.** m. precipice, cliff; *(peligro)* danger, risk.

des·pe·ñar tr. to hurl, throw —reflex. *(precipitarse)* to hurl *or* throw oneself; *(entregarse)* to give oneself up.

des·pe·pi·tar tr. to remove pits *or* seeds from —reflex. to shout, rant; *(proceder descomedidamente)* to act rashly, forget oneself ♦ **d. por algo** to be dying for something.

des·per·di·cia·do, a adj. wasted, squandered.

des·per·di·ciar tr. to waste, squander; *(no aprovecharse de)* not to take advantage of, miss.

des·per·di·cio m. waste, squandering; *(residuo)* waste, remains.

des·per·di·gar §47 tr. to scatter, disperse —reflex. to become scattered *or* dispersed.

des·pe·re·zar·se §04 reflex. to stretch.

des·pe·re·zo m. stretching, stretch; *(despertamiento)* waking up, shaking off sleep.

des·per·fec·to m. flaw, blemish; *(deterioro)* wear and tear.

des·per·ta·dor, ·ra I. adj. awakening, arousing **II.** m.f. alarm clock; *(aviso)* warning.

des·per·tar §49 tr. to wake up, awaken; *(resucitar)* to revive, resuscitate; *(suscitar)* to awaken, revive; *(excitar)* to whet, excite —intr. to wake up, awaken; *(ser más listo)* to wise up —reflex. to wake up, awaken.

des·pia·da·do, a adj. pitiless, merciless.

des·pi·da, do, diera, dió see **despedir**.

des·pi·do m. dismissal, firing.

des·pier·to, a I. see **despertar II.** adj. awake; *(despabilado)* alert, wide-awake; *(listo)* clever, sharp.

des·pil·fa·rra·dor, ·ra adj. & m.f. spendthrift.

des·pil·fa·rrar tr. to squander, waste —reflex. to squander a fortune.

des·pil·fa·rro m. waste, extravagance; *(destrozo)* spoiling, ruining.

des·pio·jar tr. *(espulgar)* to delouse; COLL. *(sacar de miseria)* to free from poverty.

des·pis·ta·do, a adj. & m.f. absent-minded (person).

des·pis·tar tr. to lead astray —reflex. to be disoriented, lose one's bearings.

des·pis·te m. confusion, bewilderment.

des·plan·te m. arrogant remark *or* action.

des·pla·za·mien·to m. displacement; *(traslado)* moving, shifting.

des·pla·zar §04 tr. to displace; *(trasladar)* to move, shift.

des·ple·gar §52 tr. to unfold, spread out; *(aclarar)* to explain, unfold; *(mostrar)* to display, show —reflex. to unfold, spread out.

des·plie·gue m. unfolding, spreading out; *(muestra)* display, show.

des·plo·mar tr. to put *or* throw out of a plumb —reflex. *(inclinarse)* to lean, get out of plumb; *(caerse)* to fall down, collapse; *(desmayarse)* to faint, collapse; ECON. to plummet, drop.

des·plo·me m. *(inclinación)* leaning, getting out of plumb; *(caída)* collapse, fall; ARCHIT. overhang; *(desmayo)* fainting, collapsing.

des·plu·mar tr. to pluck, remove the feathers from; COLL. to fleece, skin.

des·po·bla·do m. wilderness.

des·po·blar §19 tr. to depopulate; *(despojar)* to clear, strip; *(devastar)* to lay waste, ravage —reflex. to become depopulated *or* deserted.

des·po·jar tr. to deprive, dispossess; *(quitar)* to strip; *(robar)* to rob —reflex. *(desnudarse)* to undress, strip; *(renunciar)* to give up, relinquish.

des·po·jo m. depriving, dispossession; *(botín)* loot, plunder; ZOOL. offal; ORNITH. giblets; *(víctima)* prey, victim ♦ pl. scrap, usable rubble; *(restos mortales)* remains, corpse; *(sobras)* leftovers • **d. de hierro** scrap iron.

des·po·sa·do, a I. adj. newly wed; *(aprisionado)* handcuffed **II.** m.f. newlywed; *(aprisionado)* person in handcuffs.

des·po·sar tr. to marry, perform a marriage ceremony for —reflex. *(contraer esponsales)* to get engaged; *(contraer matrimonio)* to marry, wed.

des·po·se·er §43 tr. to dispossess, divest —reflex. to renounce, give up.

des·po·sei·mien·to m. dispossession.

dés·po·ta m.f. despot, tyrant.

des·pó·ti·co, a adj. despotic, tyrannical.
des·po·tri·car §70 intr. to rant, rave.
des·pre·cia·ble adj. abject, despicable.
des·pre·ciar tr. to disdain, look down on; *(desairar)* to slight, snub —reflex. to disdain, not to deign.
des·pre·cia·ti·vo, a adj. scornful.
des·pre·cio m. disdain, scorn; *(desaire)* slight, snub.
des·pren·der tr. to unfasten, detach; *(soltar)* to loosen; *(emitir)* to emit, give off —reflex. to come undone, become detached; *(ser emitido)* to issue, emanate; *(proceder)* to be inferred, follow; MED. to be detached ♦ **d. de** to give up, part with.
des·pren·di·do, a adj. detached, loose; *(generoso)* generous, unselfish; *(desinteresado)* disinterested, detached; MED. detached.
des·pren·di·mien·to m. detachment; *(emisión)* emission, release; *(caída de tierra)* landslide; *(generosidad)* generosity, largesse; *(desapego)* disinterest, detachment; MED. detachment.
des·pre·o·cu·pa·ción f. nonchalance; *(imparcialidad)* impartiality, open-mindedness; *(falta de conformidad)* unconventionality; *(descuido)* carelessness, negligence.
des·pre·o·cu·pa·do, a adj. unconcerned, nonchalant; *(imparcial)* impartial, open-minded; *(descuidado)* untidy, sloppy; *(que no conforma)* unconventional.
des·pre·o·cu·par·se reflex. to stop worrying; *(descuidarse)* to become negligent *or* careless ♦ **d. de** *(olvidarse de)* to forget, neglect; *(no hacer caso de)* not to care about, to disregard.
des·pres·ti·giar tr. to ruin (someone's) reputation; *(desacreditar)* to discredit, disparage —reflex. to lose one's prestige.
des·pres·ti·gio m. loss of prestige.
des·pre·ve·ni·do, a adj. unprepared, off guard.
des·pro·por·ción f. disproportion.
des·pro·por·cio·nar tr. to disproportion.
des·pue·ble, blo see despoblar.
des·pués adv. *(más tarde)* afterward, later; *(entonces)* next, then ♦ **d. de (que)** after.
des·pun·tar tr. to break off *or* dull the point of; MARIT. to sail around, round —intr. *(el día)* to begin, break; *(manifestar agudeza)* to show wit *or* intelligence; *(sobresalir)* to excel, stand out; BOT. to bud, sprout —reflex. to break its point.
des·qui·cia·dor, ·ra adj. unhinging; *(que turba)* disturbing, disruptive.
des·qui·cia·mien·to m. unhinging; *(perturbación)* perturbation, mental unrest; *(trastorno)* disturbance, disruption.
des·qui·ciar tr. to unhinge; *(desconectar)* to loosen, disconnect; *(descomponer)* to unsettle, undermine; *(quitar la confianza)* to unseat —reflex. to come unhinged; *(desconectarse)* to come loose, become disconnected; *(descomponerse)* to become unsettled; *(trastornarse)* to become upset.
des·qui·tar tr. to compensate —reflex. ♦ **d. de** *(resarcirse de)* to recoup, win back; *(tomar satisfacción)* to get even with.
des·qui·te m. *(de pérdida)* recovery, recouping; *(compensación)* compensation, restitution; *(venganza)* revenge, retaliation.
des·ta·ca·men·to m. MIL. detachment, detail; *(lugar)* post, station.
des·ta·car §70 tr. to emphasize, highlight; MIL. to detail, assign —intr. to stand out, be out-

standing —reflex. to stand out, be outstanding; *(aventajarse)* to break away, draw ahead.
des·ta·jo m. *(trabajo)* piecework; *(tarea)* job, stint ♦ **a d.** by the piece; AMER., COLL. at a guess, roughly • **hablar a d.** to chatter, talk excessively.
des·ta·par tr. to open, uncover; *(una botella)* to uncork, uncap; *(descubrir)* to reveal, discover —reflex. to show one's true colors; *(desahogarse)* to unburden oneself, open one's heart; *(desnudarse)* to take off one's clothes.
des·ta·pe m. uncovering, revealing; *(desnudo)* nude.
des·ta·po·nar tr. to unplug, unstop; *(una botella)* to uncork.
des·tar·ta·la·do, a adj. ramshackle, dilapidated.
des·te·char tr. to remove the roof from.
des·te·jer tr. to unweave, unravel; *(desbaratar)* to upset, disrupt.
des·te·llar tr. to flash —intr. to flash; *(centellar)* to sparkle, glitter.
des·te·llo m. flash (of light); *(centelleo)* sparkle, glitter ♦ pl. signs, indications.
des·tem·pla·do, a adj. immoderate, intemperate; *(desigual)* uneven, irregular; METAL. untempered; MUS. out of tune; MED. irregular; *(indispuesto)* indisposed, feverish.
des·tem·plan·za f. intemperance, lack of moderation; *(inclemencia)* inclemency, harshness; MED. irregularity; *(desazón)* indisposition.
des·tem·plar tr. to disturb the order of; *(poner en infusión)* to steep, infuse; METAL. to untemper; MUS. to put out of tune —reflex. *(descomponerse)* to get upset *or* worked up; METAL. to lose temper; MUS. to get out of tune; MED. to have a slight fever; *(el pulso)* to become irregular; AMER. to have one's teeth on edge.
des·te·ñir §59 tr. & intr. to fade, discolor.
des·ter·ni·llar·se reflex. to tear a cartilage ♦ **d. de risa** to split one's sides laughing.
des·te·rrar §49 tr. to exile, banish —reflex. to go into exile.
des·te·tar tr. to wean —reflex. to be weaned; *(deshabituarse)* to break a habit.
des·tiem·po adv. ♦ **a d.** inopportunely.
des·tie·rre, rro see desterrar.
des·tie·rro m. exile, banishment; *(lugar apartado)* remote place.
des·ti·la·ción f. distillation, filtration.
des·ti·lar tr. to distill; *(filtrar)* to filter; *(exudar)* to exude, ooze —intr. *(gotear)* to drip, trickle; *(exudar)* to exude, ooze.
des·ti·le·rí·a f. distillery.
des·ti·na·ción f. destination.
des·ti·nar tr. to destine, intend; *(asignar)* to assign, appoint; *(mandar)* to send; COM. to allot, earmark —reflex. to intend to go into.
des·ti·na·ta·rio, a m.f. *(de una carta)* addressee; *(de un giro)* payee.
des·ti·no m. destiny, fate; *(destinación)* destination; *(empleo)* job, position; *(uso)* use, function ♦ **con d.** a bound for.
des·ti·ña, ñera, ño, ñó see desteñir.
des·ti·tu·ción f. dismissal.
des·ti·tuir §18 tr. *(revocar)* to dismiss; *(privar)* to deprive.
des·tor·ni·lla·dor m. screwdriver.
des·tor·ni·llar tr. to unscrew —reflex. to come unscrewed; *(perder el juicio)* to go crazy.
des·tra·bar tr. to untie, unfetter; *(desprender)* to separate, disconnect.

des·tren·zar §04 tr. to unbraid, unplait.
des·tre·za f. skill, dexterity.
des·tri·par tr. to gut, disembowel; *(sacar lo interior)* to remove the stuffing from; *(despachurrar)* to crush, squash.
des·tri·zar §04 tr. *(hacer trizas)* to tear into strips; *(desmenuzar)* to crumble, shred —reflex. to be heartbroken, overcome with grief.
des·tro·na·mien·to m. dethronement; *(derrocamiento)* overthrow.
des·tro·nar tr. to dethrone; *(desposeer)* to overthrow, bring down.
des·tron·car §70 tr. to cut down, fell; *(interrumpir)* to cut off, interrupt; *(descoyuntar)* to dislocate; *(mutilar)* to maim, mutilate; *(cansar)* to exhaust, tire out; *(arruinar)* to ruin.
des·tro·za·dor, ·ra I. adj. destructive II. m.f. destroyer, wrecker.
des·tro·zar §04 tr. to smash, break into pieces; *(arruinar)* to destroy, ruin; *(estropear)* to spoil, shatter —reflex. to smash, break into pieces.
des·tro·zo m. *(daño)* damage; *(destrucción)* destruction, ruin; MIL. defeat.
des·truc·ción f. destruction.
des·truc·ti·vo, a adj. destructive.
des·truc·tor, ·ra I. adj. destructive II. m.f. destructive person —m. MARIT. destroyer.
des·truir §18 tr. to destroy, ruin; *(malgastar)* to squander, waste; *(deshacer)* to shatter, dash.
de·sue·le, lo see **desolar.**
de·sue·lle, llo see **desollar.**
de·su·nir tr. to disunite, separate; *(enemistar)* to cause discord; TECH. to disconnect, disengage —reflex. to separate, break apart.
de·su·sa·do, a adj. *(fuera de uso)* obsolete, out of date; *(poco usado)* uncommon, rare.
de·su·sar tr. to stop using —reflex. to become obsolete.
de·su·so m. disuse, obsolescence.
des·vá·li·do, a adj. & m.f. needy, destitute (person).
des·va·li·jar tr. to rob, plunder.
des·va·lo·rar tr. to depreciate; *(una moneda)* to devalue, devaluate; *(despreciar)* to disdain.
des·va·lo·ri·za·ción f. depreciation; *(de una moneda)* devaluation.
des·va·lo·ri·zar §04 tr. to devalue —reflex. to depreciate, lose value.
des·va·lua·ción f. devaluation, depreciation.
des·ván m. attic, garret.
des·va·ne·cer §17 tr. to make vanish or disappear; *(envanecer)* to make vain or presumptuous; *(hacer desmayar)* to make dizzy; *(disipar)* to remove, dispel —reflex. to vanish, disappear; *(envanecerse)* to become vain; *(evaporarse)* to evaporate; *(desmayarse)* to become dizzy, faint.
des·va·ne·ci·mien·to m. disappearance; *(desmayo)* dizziness, faintness; *(evaporación)* evaporation; *(altanería)* arrogance, haughtiness.
des·va·riar §30 intr. to be delirious.
des·va·rí·o m. delirium, madness; *(disparate)* raving, nonsense; *(capricho)* whim; *(monstruosidad)* monstrosity.
des·ve·lar tr. to keep awake —reflex. to stay awake, go without sleep; *(dedicarse)* to devote or dedicate oneself ✦ **d. por** to be watchful for, take great care over.
des·ve·lo m. sleeplessness, insomnia; *(esfuerzo)* effort; *(esmero)* watchfulness, care; *(devoción)* devotion, dedication ✦ pl. trouble.
des·ven·ci·jar tr. *(aflojar)* to loosen, weaken;

(estropear) to ruin; *(romper)* to break; *(agotar)* to exhaust —reflex. *(romperse)* to break, come apart; COLL. *(estar agotado)* to be exhausted; MED. to rupture oneself.
des·ven·ta·ja f. disadvantage, drawback.
des·ven·ta·jo·so, a adj. disadvantageous.
des·ven·tu·ra f. misfortune, bad luck.
des·ver·gon·za·do, a adj. & m.f. impudent, shameless (person).
des·ver·güen·za f. shamelessness, brazenness; *(insolencia)* insolence.
des·ves·tir §48 tr. & reflex. to undress.
des·via·ción f. *(rodeo)* detour, diversion; *(de un golpe)* deflection; *(de una norma)* deviation, departure.
des·viar §30 tr. *(extraviar)* to divert, deflect; *(disuadir)* to dissuade —reflex. to turn off; *(perder la ruta)* to go off course; *(mudar de dirección)* to change direction; *(hacer un rodeo)* to take a detour; *(apartarse)* to deviate.
des·vin·cu·lar tr. to separate from, break ties with —reflex. ✦ **d. de** or **con** to break contact with, dissociate oneself from.
des·ví·o m. *(rodeo)* detour, diversion; *(desapego)* indifference, coolness; *(desagrado)* aversion, displeasure; PHYS. deviation, deflection; RAIL. siding.
des·vir·gar §47 tr. to deflower.
des·vir·tuar §67 tr. *(echar a perder)* to spoil, impair —reflex. to spoil, go bad.
des·vis·ta, to, tiera, tió see **desvestir.**
des·vi·vir·se reflex. *(mostrar interés)* to be eager, show a great desire; *(estar enamorado)* to be madly in love; *(esforzarse)* to strive, do one's utmost; *(dedicarse)* to dedicate or devote oneself.
de·ta·lla·da·men·te adv. in detail.
de·ta·llar tr. to detail, relate in detail; *(especificar)* to specify, itemize; COM. to sell retail.
de·ta·lle m. detail; *(gesto)* gesture, kind thought.
de·ta·llis·ta I. adj. retail II. m.f. COM. retailer; *(considerado)* thoughtful person.
de·tec·tar tr. to detect.
de·tec·ti·ve m. detective.
de·tec·tor, ·ra I. m. detector II. adj. detecting.
de·tén see **detener.**
de·ten·ción f. stopping, halting; *(estado)* stoppage, standstill; *(retraso)* delay; *(arresto)* arrest; *(prisión)* detention; *(cuidado)* care, thoroughness.
de·te·ner §69 tr. to stop, halt; *(retrasar)* to delay, detain; *(arrestar)* to arrest; *(retener)* to keep, retain —reflex. to stop; *(retardarse)* to linger, tarry.
de·te·ni·do, a I. adj. *(cuidadoso)* thorough, close; *(tímido)* timid, fainthearted; *(escaso)* sparing; *(preso)* detained, in custody II. m.f. person under arrest.
de·te·ni·mien·to m. var. of **detención.**
de·ter·gen·te adj. & m. detergent.
de·te·rio·ra·ción f. deterioration; *(daño)* damage, harm; *(con el uso)* wear and tear.
de·te·rio·rar tr. to deteriorate; *(estropear)* to damage, spoil; *(desgastar)* to wear (out) —reflex. *(dañarse)* to damage, harm; *(desgastarse)* to wear out.
de·te·rio·ro m. deterioration; *(daño)* harm, damage.
de·ter·mi·na·ción f. *(decisión)* decision; *(resolución)* determination, resolve.
de·ter·mi·na·do, a adj. determined, resolute;

(preciso) specific, particular.

de·ter·mi·nar tr. to determine; *(convencer)* to convince, decide; *(fijar)* to specify, fix; *(causar)* to cause, bring about; *(distinguir)* to distinguish, discern; *(estipular)* to stipulate, specify —reflex. to decide, make up one's mind.

de·ter·mi·nis·ta I. adj. deterministic II. m.f. determinist.

de·tes·ta·ble adj. detestable, hateful.

de·tes·tar tr. to detest, hate.

de·tie·ne see **detener.**

de·to·na·ción f. detonation, explosion; *(ruido)* report, blast.

de·to·na·dor m. detonator.

de·to·nan·te I. adj. detonating, explosive II. m. explosive.

de·to·nar intr. to detonate, explode.

de·trac·ción f. denigration, disparagement; *(retiro)* withdrawal.

de·trac·tar tr. to denigrate, disparage.

de·trac·tor, ·ra I. adj. detracting, defamatory II. m.f. detractor, defamer.

de·trás adv. behind ♦ **d. de** behind, in back of • **por d.** behind one's back.

de·tri·men·to m. detriment, damage.

de·tu·vie·ra, vo see **detener.**

deu·da f. debt.

deu·do, a m.f. relative.

deu·dor, ·ra I. adj. debit; *(que debe)* indebted II. m.f. debtor.

de·va·lua·ción f. devaluation.

de·va·luar §67 tr. to devaluate.

de·va·nar tr. to reel, wind.

de·vas·ta·ción f. devastation.

de·vas·tar tr. to devastate, destroy.

de·ve·lar tr. to reveal.

de·ven·gar §47 tr. to be owed; *(interés)* to earn.

de·ve·nir §76 intr. *(suceder)* to happen, come about; *(llegar a ser)* to become, evolve into.

de·vo·ción f. devotion; *(piedad)* devoutness, piety; *(afición)* affection, attachment.

de·vo·lu·ción f. return; *(restauración)* restoration; COM. refund.

de·vol·ver §78 tr. to return, give back; *(corresponder)* to return; *(restaurar)* to restore; *(vomitar)* to throw up, vomit; COM. to refund —reflex. AMER. to return.

de·vo·rar tr. to devour, eat up; *(disipar)* to squander, waste; *(arruinar)* to ruin, destroy.

de·vo·to, a I. adj. devout, pious; *(venerable)* venerable, revered; *(aficionado)* devoted, attached II. m.f. devout person; *(aficionado)* devotee, enthusiast.

de·vuel·va, vo see **devolver.**

dex·te·ri·dad f. dexterity, skillfulness.

dex·tro·sa f. dextrose.

di see **dar** or **decir**[2].

dí·a m. day; *(tiempo de claridad)* daytime, daylight; *(tiempo)* weather ♦ **de d.** per day, a day; *(al corriente)* up to date • **al otro d.** on the following day, the next day • **d.** by day • **d. de fiesta** holiday • **d. entre semana** weekday • **d. señalado** red-letter day • **hoy (en) d.** nowadays, these days • **todo el santo d.** all day long, all the livelong day ♦ pl. ¡**buenos d.!** good morning • **de d.** old • **ocho d.** a week • **quince d.** two weeks, fortnight • **todos los d.** every day, daily.

dia·bé·ti·co, a adj. & m.f. diabetic.

dia·blo m. devil, demon; *(travieso)* scamp, devil; *(requetefeo)* monster, ugly person ♦ **al d. or**

como el d. COLL. like the devil, a hell of a lot • **darse al d.** to get angry • ¡**diablo(s)!** COLL. wow! • ¡**qué diablos!** what the hell!

dia·blu·ra f. deviltry, prank.

dia·bó·li·co, a adj. diabolical, devilish.

dia·co·ni·sa f. deaconess.

diá·co·no m. deacon.

dia·de·ma f. diadem, crown.

diá·fa·no, a adj. diaphanous, transparent.

dia·frag·ma m. diaphragm.

diag·no·sis f. diagnosis.

diag·nos·ti·car §70 tr. to diagnose.

diag·nós·ti·co, a I. adj. diagnostic II. m. diagnosis.

dia·go·nal adj. & f. diagonal.

dia·gra·ma m. diagram.

dia·léc·ti·co, a I. adj. dialectical II. m.f. dialectician —f. dialectics.

dia·lec·to m. dialect.

diá·lo·go m. dialogue.

dia·man·te m. diamond.

dia·man·ti·no, a adj. diamantine.

dia·me·tral adj. diametric, diametrical.

diá·me·tro m. diameter.

dia·pa·són m. diapason, tuning fork.

dia·po·si·ti·va f. slide, transparency.

dia·ria·men·te adv. daily, every day.

dia·rio, a I. adj. daily II. m. daily (paper); *(relación)* diary, journal; *(gasto)* daily expenses; COM. journal, daybook III. adv. daily ♦ **a d.** daily, every day • **de d.** *(diariamente)* daily, every day; *(ordinario)* everyday.

dia·rre·a f. diarrhea.

di·bu·jan·te I. adj. drawing, sketching II. m. drawer, sketcher; *(de dibujos animados)* cartoonist; TECH. draftsman.

di·bu·jar tr. to draw, sketch; *(describir)* to describe, depict —reflex. *(delinearse)* to be outlined, stand out; *(aparecer)* to appear.

di·bu·jo m. drawing, sketch; *(descripción)* description, depiction ♦ pl. **d. animados** cartoons.

dic·ción f. diction.

dic·cio·na·rio m. dictionary.

di·ce see **decir**[2].

di·cha f. *(felicidad)* happiness; *(suerte)* good fortune ♦ **a o por d.** fortunately, happily.

di·cha·ra·che·ro, a COLL. I. adj. *(gracioso)* witty, racy; *(hablador)* talkative II. m.f. *(gracioso)* joker; *(hablador)* chatterbox.

di·cho, a I. see **decir**[2] II. adj. said, aforementioned ♦ **d. y hecho** no sooner said than done • ¡**haberlo d.!** you should have said so! • **mejor d.** rather, more accurately III. m. *(refrán)* saying, proverb; *(ocurrencia)* witticism, witty remark; COLL. *(expresión insultante)* insulting remark; LAW statement, deposition ♦ **d. de las gentes** gossip, talk ♦ pl. marriage vows.

di·cho·so, a adj. *(feliz)* happy, contented; *(afortunado)* lucky, fortunate; COLL. *(enfadoso)* blasted.

di·ciem·bre m. December.

di·co·to·mí·a f. dichotomy.

dic·ta·do m. title; *(acción)* dictation ♦ pl. dictates.

dic·ta·dor m. dictator.

dic·ta·du·ra f. dictatorship.

dic·tá·fo·no m. dictaphone.

dic·ta·men m. *(juicio)* opinion, judgment; *(consejo)* advice; *(informe)* report.

dic·ta·mi·nar intr. to express an opinion.

dic·tar tr. to dictate; *(sentencia)* to pronounce,

pass; *(inspirar)* to dictate, direct; AMER. *(una conferencia)* to give, deliver; AMER. *(una clase)* to give, teach.

di·dác·ti·co, a I. adj. didactic, pedagogical II. f. didactics.

die·ci·nue·ve adj. & m. nineteen(th).

die·cio·cho adj. & m. eighteen(th).

die·ci·séis adj. & m. sixteen(th).

die·ci·sie·te adj. & m. seventeen(th).

dien·te m. tooth; ZOOL. fang; *(de una rueda)* cog; *(de una sierra)* tooth; *(de un tenedor)* prong; BOT. clove ♦ **aguzarse** *or* **afilarse los dientes** to whet one's appetite • **dar d. con d.** to chatter (teeth) • **d. de león** dandelion • **dientes postizos** false teeth • **estar a d.** to be famished *or* ravenous ♦ **hablar entre dientes** to mumble, mutter.

die·ra, ron see **dar.**

dies·tro, a I. adj. deft, dexterous; *(derecho)* right; *(astuto)* shrewd, astute II. right hand ♦ **a d. y siniestra** all over, right and left.

die·ta f. diet.

die·té·ti·co, a I. adj. dietetic, dietary II. m.f. dietician —f. dietetics.

diez I. adj. ten; *(décimo)* tenth ♦ **las d.** ten o'clock II. m. ten ♦ **d. y var.** of **dieci-.**

diez·mar tr. to decimate.

diez·mo m. tithe.

di·fa·ma·ción f. defamation.

di·fa·mar tr. to defame, slander.

di·fe·ren·cia f. difference ♦ **a d. de** unlike, in contrast to • **hacer d. entre** to make *or* draw a distinction between.

di·fe·ren·cia·ción f. differentiation.

di·fe·ren·ciar tr. to differentiate, distinguish; *(variar)* to vary, change —intr. to differ, disagree —reflex. to distinguish oneself; *(ser diferente)* to differ, be different.

di·fe·ren·te I. adj. different ♦ **diferentes** various, several II. adv. differently.

di·fe·rir §65 tr. to defer, postpone —intr. to differ, be different.

di·fí·cil adj. difficult.

di·fí·cil·men·te adv. difficultly, with difficulty.

di·fi·cul·tad f. difficulty, obstacle; *(objeción)* objection, doubt.

di·fi·cul·tar tr. to make difficult, complicate.

di·fi·cul·to·so, a adj. difficult; *(feo)* ugly, unpleasant.

di·fi·den·cia f. mistrust, diffidence.

di·fie·ra, ro, firiera, firió see **diferir.**

dif·te·ria f. diphtheria.

di·fun·dir tr. to diffuse; *(derramar)* to spread, scatter; *(divulgar)* to divulge, make known; *(diseminar)* to disseminate, propagate —reflex. to spread, be diffused.

di·fun·to, a I. adj. deceased, dead II. m.f. dead person; *(cadáver)* corpse, cadaver.

di·fu·sión f. diffusion; *(radio)* broadcasting.

di·fu·so, a I. see **difundir** II. adj. diffuse, wordy; *(ancho)* wide, extended; *(vago)* vague, hazy.

di·fu·sor, ·ra I. adj. diffusing II. f. broadcasting station.

di·ga, go see **decir².**

di·ge·rir §65 tr. to digest; *(sufrir)* to suffer, endure.

di·ges·tión f. digestion.

dí·gi·to m. digit.

dig·nar·se reflex. to deign, condescend.

dig·na·ta·rio m. dignitary.

dig·ni·dad f. dignity; *(cargo)* post, rank.

dig·no, a adj. *(merecedor)* worthy; *(apropiado)* proper, fitting; *(mesurado)* dignified.

di·gre·sión f. digression, deviation.

di·je m. *(adorno)* trinket, charm; COLL. *(persona)* jewel, gem ♦ pl. boasting, bravado.

di·je, jo, jera, jeron see **decir².**

di·la·ción f. delay, delaying.

di·la·pi·dar tr. to waste, squander.

di·la·ta·ción f. dilation, expansion; *(desahogo)* serenity, calmness.

di·la·tar tr. to dilate, expand; *(retrasar)* to postpone, delay; *(propagar)* to spread —reflex. to dilate, expand; *(propagarse)* to extend, stretch.

di·la·to·ria I. f. delay II. adj. dilatory.

di·lec·to, a adj. beloved, loved.

di·le·ma m. dilemma.

di·le(t)·tan·te m.f. dilettante.

di·li·gen·cia f. diligence, care; *(prisa)* speed, briskness; *(recado)* errand, task; LAW proceeding.

di·li·gen·ciar tr. to take the necessary steps to obtain.

di·li·gen·te adj. diligent; *(rápido)* speedy, quick.

di·lu·ci·da·ción f. elucidation, explanation.

di·lu·ci·dar tr. to elucidate, explain.

di·luir §18 tr. to dilute; *(disolver)* to dissolve; *(debilitar)* to water down, weaken.

di·lu·viar intr. to pour down, rain hard.

di·lu·vio m. flood.

di·men·sión f. dimension.

di·mi·nu·ción f. diminution, lessening.

di·mi·nuir §18 tr. to diminish, lessen.

di·mi·nu·ti·vo, a adj. & m. diminutive.

di·mi·nu·to, a adj. diminutive, little.

di·mi·sión f. resignation (from office).

di·mi·ten·te I. adj. resigning II. m.f. resigner.

di·mi·tir intr. & tr. to resign, relinquish.

di·mos see **dar.**

di·ná·mi·co, a I. adj. dynamic II. f. dynamics.

di·na·mis·mo m. dynamism.

di·na·mi·ta f. dynamite.

di·na·mi·tar tr. to dynamite, blast.

di·na·mo *or* **dí·na·mo** f. dynamo.

di·nas·tí·a f. dynasty.

di·ne·ra·da f./ral m. fortune.

di·ne·ro m. money; *(caudal)* wealth, fortune ♦ **d. al contado** *or* **al contante** ready cash • **d. suelto** loose change.

di·no·sau·rio m. dinosaur.

din·tel m. lintel.

dio see **dar.**

dios m. god ♦ **D.** God • **D. mediante** God willing • **¡D. mío!** my God!, oh my! • **por D.** for God's sake • **¡válgame D.!** goodness gracious!

dio·sa f. goddess.

di·plo·ma m. diploma, certificate.

di·plo·ma·cia f. diplomacy.

di·plo·ma·do, a I. adj. having a diploma II. m.f. graduate.

di·plo·mar tr. & reflex. to graduate.

di·plo·má·ti·co, a I. adj. diplomatic II. m.f. diplomat —f. diplomacy.

dip·só·ma·no, a adj. & m.f. dipsomaniac.

dip·ton·go m. diphthong.

di·pu·ta·do, a m.f. delegate, representative.

di·que m. dike, sea wall; *(restricción)* check, restriction ♦ **d. de carena** *or* **seco** dry dock • **d. de contención** dam.

di·rá, ría see **decir².**

di·rec·ción f. direction; *(junta)* board of directors, executive board; *(cargo)* directorship, managership; *(señas)* address; AUTO., TECH. steering ♦ **d. general** headquarters, head office.

di·rec·ti·vo, a I. adj. directing II. m.f. director —f. *(orden)* directive, instruction; *(junta)* board of directors.

di·rec·to, a I. adj. direct; *(derecho)* straight II. f. AUTO. high gear.

di·rec·tor, ·ra I. adj. directing II. m.f. director, manager; *(de escuela)* principal, headmaster; MUS. conductor.

di·rec·to·rio, a I. adj. directory II. m. *(instrucción)* manual, directory; *(junta)* directorate.

di·ri·gen·te m.f. leader, director.

di·ri·gir §32 tr. to direct; *(administrar)* to manage; *(una carta)* to address; *(guiar)* to guide; *(dedicar)* to dedicate; AUTO. to drive, steer; MUS. to conduct; CINEM., THEAT. to direct —reflex. to go, make one's way; *(hablar)* to address, speak.

dis·cer·ni·mien·to m. discernment.

dis·cer·nir §25 tr. to discern, distinguish.

dis·ci·pli·na f. discipline; *(doctrina)* doctrine; *(azote)* whip.

dis·ci·pli·nar tr. to discipline; *(enseñar)* to teach, instruct; *(azotar)* to whip, scourge —reflex. to discipline oneself.

dis·cí·pu·lo, a m.f. disciple, follower; *(alumno)* student, pupil.

dis·co m. disk, disc; *(para escuchar)* record; *(para el tránsito)* traffic signal; SPORT. discus; COMPUT. diskette ♦ **d. rayado** COLL. broken record.

dís·co·lo, a adj. wayward, intractable.

dis·con·for·me adj. disagreeing, differing.

dis·con·for·mi·dad f. difference.

dis·con·ti·nuar §67 tr. to discontinue.

dis·con·ti·nui·dad f. discontinuity.

dis·cor·dan·cia f. discordance, disagreement.

dis·cor·dar §19 intr. to differ, disagree; MUS. to be out of tune or dissonant.

dis·cor·de adj. disagreeing, discordant; MUS. discordant, dissonant.

dis·cor·dia f. discord, disagreement.

dis·co·te·ca f. record collection; *(salón de baile)* discotheque.

dis·cre·ción f. discretion, tact; *(astucia)* wisdom, shrewdness.

dis·cre·pan·cia f. discrepancy; *(desacuerdo)* disagreement, dissent.

dis·cre·par intr. to differ, disagree.

dis·cre·to, a adj. discreet; *(ingenioso)* witty, clever; MATH., MED., PHYS. discrete.

dis·cri·mi·nar tr. to discriminate.

dis·cuer·de, do see **discordar.**

dis·cul·pa f. *(por una ofensa)* apology; *(excusa)* excuse.

dis·cul·par tr. to excuse, pardon —reflex. to apologize *(con* to, de, por for).

dis·cu·rrir intr. to roam, wander; *(reflexionar)* to reflect, ponder; *(hablar)* to speak, discourse; *(fluir)* to flow, run; *(el tiempo)* to pass —tr. to invent, think up.

dis·cur·sar/se·ar intr. to discourse or lecture on.

dis·cur·so m. speech, discourse; *(facultad)* reasoning, ratiocination; *(transcurso)* passage, course.

dis·cu·sión f. discussion; *(disputa)* dispute, argument.

dis·cu·ti·ble adj. debatable, disputable.

dis·cu·tir tr. to discuss, debate —intr. *(debatir)* to discuss, talk about; *(disputar)* to argue.

di·se·car §70 tr. to dissect; *(conservar)* to stuff, mount.

di·sec·ción f. dissection.

di·se·mi·na·ción f. dissemination, spreading.

di·se·mi·nar tr. to disseminate, spread —reflex. to become disseminated, spread.

di·sen·sión f. dissension, strife.

di·sen·te·rí·a f. dysentery.

di·sen·tir §65 intr. to dissent, differ.

di·se·ñar tr. to design; *(dibujar)* to draw, sketch.

di·se·ño m. design; *(dibujo)* drawing, sketch.

di·ser·ta·ción f. dissertation, discourse.

di·ser·tar intr. to discourse, expound.

dis·fraz m. disguise; *(máscara)* mask; *(pretexto)* pretext, excuse.

dis·fra·zar §04 tr. & reflex. to disguise (oneself).

dis·fru·tar tr. *(gozar)* to enjoy; *(aprovechar)* to make the most of —intr. to enjoy.

dis·fru·te m. *(gozo)* enjoyment; *(provecho)* benefit; *(uso)* use.

dis·gus·ta·do, a adj. annoyed, displeased.

dis·gus·tar tr. to annoy, displease —reflex. *(desagradarse)* to be annoyed or displeased; *(desazonarse)* to fall out.

dis·gus·to m. *(desagrado)* annoyance, displeasure; *(contienda)* quarrel, disagreement ♦ **a d.** unwillingly.

di·si·den·cia f. dissidence, disagreement.

di·si·den·te adj. & m.f. dissident.

di·si·dir intr. to dissent.

di·sien·ta, to see **disentir.**

di·sí·mil adj. dissimilar, unlike.

di·si·mu·la·ción f. *(simulación)* dissimulation, dissembling; *(encubrimiento)* concealment, hiding; *(tolerancia)* tolerance.

di·si·mu·la·do, a I. adj. *(simulado)* dissimulating, dissembling; *(encubierto)* concealed, hidden II. m.f. dissimulator, dissembler ♦ **hacerse el d.** to act dumb, feign ignorance.

di·si·mu·lar tr. to dissimulate, dissemble; *(encubrir)* to conceal, hide; *(fingir)* to feign, pretend; *(tolerar)* to tolerate, overlook —intr. to dissimulate, dissemble.

di·si·mu·lo m. var. of **disimulación.**

di·sin·tie·ra, tió see **disentir.**

di·si·pa·ción f. dissipation; *(derroche)* squandering, wasting.

di·si·pa·do, a I. adj. dissipated; *(libertino)* dissolute; *(derrochador)* wasteful II. m.f. *(libertino)* dissolute person; *(derrochador)* squanderer, wasteful person.

di·si·par tr. to dissipate; *(derrochar)* to squander, waste; *(una duda)* to dispel —reflex. *(desaparecer)* to disappear, vanish; *(dispersarse)* to disperse, scatter.

dis·lo·ca·ción f. dislocation.

dis·lo·car §70 tr. & reflex. to dislocate.

dis·mi·nu·ción f. diminution.

dis·mi·nuir §18 tr., intr. & reflex. to diminish.

di·so·cia·ción f. dissociation, separation.

di·so·ciar tr. & reflex. to dissociate (oneself).

di·so·lu·ción f. dissolution; *(libertinaje)* dissoluteness, dissipation; *(ruptura)* breakup; COM. liquidation; CHEM. solution.

di·so·lu·to, a adj. & m.f. dissolute (person).

di·sol·ver §78 tr. to dissolve; *(dispersar)* to break up; *(anular)* to annul; COM. to liquidate —reflex. to dissolve.

di·so·nan·cia f. MUS. dissonance.
dis·par adj. unequal; *(diferente)* different.
dis·pa·ra·dor, **·ra** m.f. shooter, firer —m. trigger; PHOTOG. shutter release.
dis·pa·rar tr. to fire, shoot; *(echar)* to throw, hurl; SPORT. to shoot —intr. to fire, shoot; *(disparatar)* to act foolishly —reflex. ARM. to go off; *(enfurecerse)* to lose one's patience; AMER. *(irse corriendo)* to rush *or* dash off.
dis·pa·ra·ta·do, a adj. absurd, nonsensical; COLL. excessive, enormous.
dis·pa·ra·tar intr. to talk *or* act foolishly.
dis·pa·ra·te m. absurd *or* nonsensical thing; COLL. enormous amount ♦ pl. nonsense.
dis·pa·ri·dad f. disparity, dissimilarity.
dis·pa·ro m. firing, shooting; *(tiro)* shot; MECH. release, trip.
dis·pen·sar tr. to dispense, give out; *(eximir)* to exempt; *(perdonar)* to forgive, excuse —reflex. to excuse oneself.
dis·pen·sa·rio m. dispensary, clinic ♦ **d. de alimentos** soup kitchen.
dis·pep·sia f. dyspepsia, indigestion.
dis·per·sar tr. & reflex. to disperse, scatter; *(dividir)* to divide.
dis·per·sión f. dispersion, dispersal.
dis·pli·cen·cia f. indifference, coolness.
dis·pli·cen·te adj. disagreeable, unpleasant; *(indiferente)* indifferent, cool.
dis·po·ner §54 tr. *(colocar)* to arrange, place; *(preparar)* to prepare, get ready; *(ordenar)* to order —intr. ♦ **d. de** *(poseer)* to have, have at one's disposal; *(utilizar)* to make use of; *(deshacerse de)* to dispose of —reflex. to prepare, get ready; *(prepararse a morir)* to prepare to die, make one's will.
dis·po·ni·bi·li·dad f. availability.
dis·po·ni·ble adj. available, on hand.
dis·po·si·ción f. disposition; *(posesión)* disposal; *(aptitud)* aptitude, talent; LAW *(precepto)* provision; *(orden)* decree, order ♦ **estar en d. de** to be ready to, be in a position to • **última d.** last will and testament ♦ pl. measures.
dis·po·si·ti·vo, a I. adj. dispositive II. m. device, mechanism.
dis·pues·to, a I. see **disponer** II. adj. good-looking, elegant; *(hábil)* clever, capable ♦ **bien d.** well-disposed; *(saludable)* well, not sick • **estar d. a** to be prepared *or* willing to • **estar poco d. a** to be reluctant to • **mal d.** ill-disposed; *(enfermo)* ill, indisposed.
dis·pu·sie·ra, so see **disponer**.
dis·pu·ta f. dispute.
dis·pu·ta·ble adj. disputable, debatable.
dis·pu·tar tr. to dispute —intr. to argue, quarrel —reflex. to be disputed.
dis·qui·si·ción f. disquisition.
dis·tan·cia f. distance; *(diferencia)* difference ♦ **a (la) d.** at *or* from a distance • **a larga d.** long-distance.
dis·tan·ciar tr. to separate, space out; *(alejar)* to place at a distance; *(dejar atrás)* to outdistance —reflex. to become separated; *(enajenarse)* to become estranged, drift away.
dis·tan·te adj. distant.
dis·tar intr. to be a certain distance from; *(diferenciarse)* to be different *or* far from.
dis·te see **dar**.
dis·ten·der §50 tr. to distend —intr. to become distended.
dis·tin·ción f. distinction; *(trato)* respect, deference; *(claridad)* distinctness ♦ **a d. de** as distinct from, in contrast to.
dis·tin·gui·do, a adj. distinguished.
dis·tin·guir §26 tr. to distinguish; *(preferir)* to favor, show preference for; *(honrar)* to pay tribute to, honor —intr. to distinguish, discriminate —reflex. *(ser distinto)* to be distinguished, differ; *(sobresalir)* to distinguish oneself, excel.
dis·tin·ti·vo, a I. adj. distinctive II. m. badge, emblem; FIG. distinguishing mark.
dis·tin·to, a adj. distinct.
dis·tor·sio·nar tr. to distort.
dis·trac·ción f. distraction; *(libertinaje)* dissoluteness; *(error)* slip, oversight; FIN. embezzlement, misappropriation.
dis·tra·er §72 tr. to distract; *(descaminar)* to lead astray; *(entretener)* to amuse, entertain; FIN. to embezzle, misappropriate —intr. to be entertaining —reflex. *(entretenerse)* to amuse oneself; *(descuidarse)* to be distracted.
dis·tra·í·do, a I. see **distraer** II. adj. *(divertido)* amusing, entertaining; *(desatento)* inattentive, absent-minded; *(libertino)* dissolute, libertine.
dis·trai·ga, go see **distraer**.
dis·trai·mien·to m. var. of **distracción**.
dis·tra·je·ra, jo see **distraer**.
dis·tri·bu·ción f. distribution.
dis·tri·bui·dor, ·ra I. adj. distributing, distributive II. m.f. distributor —m. AUTO., TELEC. distributor ♦ **d. automático** vending machine.
dis·tri·buir §18 tr. to distribute.
dis·tri·to m. district, zone.
dis·tur·bar tr. to disturb.
dis·tur·bio m. disturbance, trouble.
di·sua·dir tr. to dissuade, discourage.
di·sua·sión f. dissuasion.
di·suel·to, ta, va, vo see **disolver**.
dis·yun·ti·vo, a adj. & f. disjunctive.
diu·ré·ti·co, a adj. & m. diuretic.
diur·no adj. & m. diurnal.
di·va·ga·ción f. digression, rambling.
di·va·gar §47 intr. *(errar)* to digress, ramble; *(vagar)* to wander, roam.
di·ván m. divan, couch.
di·ver·gen·cia f. divergence.
di·ver·gir §32 intr. to diverge, differ.
di·ver·si·dad f. diversity.
di·ver·si·fi·ca·ción f. diversification.
di·ver·si·fi·car §70 tr. to diversify.
di·ver·sión f. diversion.
di·ver·so, a adj. diverse ♦ pl. several, various.
di·ver·ti·do, a adj. amusing, entertaining; AMER. drunk.
di·ver·tir §65 tr. *(entretener)* to amuse, entertain; *(distraer)* to divert, distract —reflex. to amuse oneself, have a good time; *(distraerse)* to be distracted.
di·vi·den·do m. dividend.
di·vi·dir tr. to divide —reflex. to divide; *(separarse)* to separate.
di·vier·ta, to see **divertir**.
di·vi·na·to·rio, a adj. divinatory.
di·vi·ni·dad f. divinity; *(belleza)* beauty.
di·vi·no, a adj. divine.
di·vir·tie·ra, tió see **divertir**.
di·vi·sa f. emblem, insignia; COM. currency.
di·vi·sar tr. to discern, make out.
di·vi·sor, ·ra I. adj. dividing II. m. divider; MATH. divisor, denominator.

di·vi·so·rio, a I. adj. dividing; *(divisivo)* divisive II. f. dividing line; GEOL. divide.

di·vo, a m.f. opera star —f. FIG. prima donna.

di·vor·cia·do, a I. adj. divorced II. m. divorcé —f. divorcée.

di·vor·ciar tr. to divorce; *(separar)* to separate, divide —reflex. to divorce, get divorced.

di·vor·cio m. divorce; *(separación)* separation, division.

di·vul·ga·ción f. *(revelación)* disclosure, revelation; *(popularización)* popularization.

di·vul·gar §47 tr. to divulge, disclose; *(popularizar)* to popularize —reflex. to be divulged.

do m. MUS. do, C; COLL. supreme effort.

do·bla·di·llo m. hem.

do·bla·du·ra f. fold, crease.

do·blar tr. to double; *(encorvar)* to bend; to turn, round *<d. la esquina* to turn the corner>; CINEM. to dub —intr. to toll, ring; THEAT. to double, stand in —reflex. *(plegarse)* to fold; *(encorvarse)* to double over; *(ceder)* to yield, give in.

do·ble I. adj. double; *(grueso)* thick, heavy; *(disimulado)* two-faced II. m. double; *(pliegue)* fold, crease; *(toque)* death knell; *(copia)* copy, reproduction; COM. margin ♦ **al d.** doubly —m.f. double, stand-in III. adv. doubly.

do·ble·gar §47 tr. to fold, crease; *(curvar)* to bend, flex; *(blandir)* to brandish; *(hacer ceder)* to force someone to give in —reflex. to fold, crease; *(encorvarse)* to bend, flex; *(ceder)* to yield, give in.

do·ble·men·te adv. doubly; *(maliciosamente)* falsely, deceitfully.

do·blez m.f. duplicity, two-facedness —m. *(pliegue)* fold, crease; *(dobladillo)* hem.

do·ce I. adj. twelve; *(duodécimo)* twelfth ♦ **las d.** twelve o'clock II. m. twelve.

do·ce·na f. dozen.

do·cen·te adj. teaching, educational.

dó·cil adj. docile; *(dúctil)* ductile.

doc·to, a adj. & m.f. learned (person).

doc·tor, ·ra m.f. doctor; *(maestro)* teacher, professor; COLL. doctor, physician.

doc·to·ra·do m. doctorate.

doc·to·rar tr. to confer a doctor's degree —reflex. to get a doctor's degree.

doc·tri·na f. doctrine, teaching; *(conocimiento)* knowledge, learning.

doc·tri·na·rio, a adj. & m.f. doctrinaire.

do·cu·men·ta·ción f. documentation.

do·cu·men·ta·do, a adj. documented; *(informado)* well-informed, well-read.

do·cu·men·tal adj. & m. documentary.

do·cu·men·tar tr. to document; *(educar)* to educate —reflex. to research, investigate.

do·cu·men·to m. document; *(prueba)* proof, evidence ♦ **d. a la vista** sight bill, draft • **d. justificativo** voucher, certificate.

do·gal m. *(de caballo)* halter; *(para ahorcar)* noose, hangman's rope ♦ **estar con el d. al cuello** *or* **a la garganta** COLL. to be in a tight spot.

dog·ma m. dogma.

dog·má·ti·co, a I. adj. dogmatic II. m.f. dogmatist —f. dogmatics.

do·go, a m.f. bulldog.

dó·lar m. dollar.

do·len·cia f. illness, ailment.

do·ler §78 intr. to hurt —reflex. *(arrepentirse)* to repent; *(sentir)* to regret; *(compadecerse)* to sympathize, be sorry; *(quejarse)* to complain.

do·lo m. fraud.

do·lor m. pain, ache; *(congoja)* sorrow, distress; *(arrepentimiento)* repentance, regret.

do·lo·ri·do, a adj. sore, aching; *(desconsolado)* pained, distressed.

do·lo·ro·so, a adj. *(lastimoso)* pitiful, distressing; *(sensible)* painful.

do·ma f. taming.

do·ma·dor, ·ra m.f. *(de fieras)* tamer, trainer; *(de caballos)* horsebreaker, broncobuster.

do·mar tr. to tame, domesticate; *(vencer)* to subdue, master.

do·mes·ti·car §70 tr. to tame, domesticate; *(vencer)* to subdue, conquer; *(educar)* to educate, refine.

do·més·ti·co, a I. adj. domestic II. m.f. domestic, household servant.

do·mi·ci·liar tr. to domicile, establish in a residence —reflex. to settle, take up residence ♦ **¿en dónde se domicilia usted?** where do you live?

do·mi·ci·lio m. domicile, residence ♦ **adquirir** *or* **elegir d.** to settle, take up residence • **d. social** head office, corporate headquarters.

do·mi·na·ción f. domination; *(señorío)* rule, dominion; MIL. high ground.

do·mi·na·dor, ·ra I. adj. dominating; *(avasallador)* domineering, overbearing II. m.f. dominator; *(avasallador)* domineering person.

do·mi·nan·te I. adj. dominant; *(avasallador)* domineering, overbearing II. f. dominant.

do·mi·nar tr. to dominate; *(someter)* to subdue, control; *(saber a fondo)* to know well, master —intr. to dominate, stand out —reflex. to control *or* restrain oneself.

do·min·go m. Sunday.

do·mi·nio m. dominion, power; *(superioridad)* dominance, supremacy; *(maestría)* mastery, command; *(tierra)* domain, dominion.

do·mi·nó m. dominoes.

don¹ m. *(regalo)* gift, present; *(gracia)* gift, talent, knack ♦ **d. de acertar** *or* **errar** knack for doing the right *or* wrong thing • **d. de gentes** personal charm.

don² m. Don (title of respect used before a man's first name).

do·na·ción f. donation, contribution; *(regalo)* gift, present.

do·nai·re m. *(gracia)* grace, gentility; *(agudeza)* witticism, quip.

do·nar tr. to donate, give.

do·na·ti·vo m. donation, gift.

don·cel I. m. young nobleman II. adj. mellow, mild.

don·ce·lla f. maiden, young maid; *(criada)* maid, housemaid.

don·de I. adv. where ♦ **d. no** otherwise • **en d.** in which • **por d.** whereby II. prep. S. AMER. to *or* at the house of.

dón·de adv. where ♦ **¿a d.?** where? • **¿de d.?** from where? • **¿por d.?** why?

don·de·quie·ra adv. anywhere ♦ **d. que** wherever • **por d.** everywhere, all over the place.

do·no·so, a adj. *(gracioso)* witty, funny; *(elegante)* elegant, poised.

do·no·su·ra f. *(gracia)* grace, gentility; *(agudeza)* witticism, quip.

do·ña f. Mrs., Madame.

do·quier/quie·ra adv. var. of **dondequiera**.

do·ra·do, a I. adj. golden; *(cubierto de oro)* gilt, gilded II. m. gilding.

do·ra·dor, ·ra m.f. gilder.

do·rar tr. to gild, cover with gold; METAL. to

gold-plate; *(paliar)* to palliate, minimize —reflex. to become golded *or* gilded.

dor·mi·lón, o·na I. adj. sleepy **II.** m.f. sleepyhead —f. easy sleep.

dor·mir §27 intr. to sleep; *(pernoctar)* to spend the night; *(sosegarse)* to grow calm, subside ♦ **d. de un tirón** *or* **a pierna suelta** to sleep soundly —reflex. to fall asleep; MARIT. to heel, list ♦ **d. en los laureles** to rest on one's laurels —tr. to put to sleep ♦ **d. la mona** to sleep it off • **d. la siesta** to take a nap.

dor·mi·tar intr. to doze, snooze.

dor·mi·to·rio m. bedroom; *(residencia)* dormitory.

dor·so m. back.

dos I. adj. two; *(segundo)* second ♦ **las d.** two o'clock **II.** m. two; *(naipe)* deuce ♦ **cada d. por tres** frequently ♦ **en un d. por tres** in a jiffy • **los** *or* **las d.** both.

dos·cien·tos, as adj. & m. two hundred.

do·si·fi·ca·ción f. dosage.

do·si·fi·car §70 tr. to dose, give in doses.

do·sis f. dose; FIG. portion, quantity.

do·ta·ción f. endowment, bequest; *(dote)* dowry; MARIT. crew; *(personal)* personnel.

do·tar tr. to endow, provide; *(bodas)* to give a dowry; *(testamento)* to bequeath, leave; *(personal)* to man, staff.

do·te m. *or* f. dowry —f. endowment; *(habilidad)* talent, ability.

doy see **dar**.

do·za·vo, a adj. & m.f. twelfth.

drac·ma m.f. FIN. drachma; *(peso)* dram.

dra·ga f. dredge.

dra·gar §47 tr. to dredge, drag.

dra·gón m. dragon; BOT. snapdragon; MIL. dragoon.

dra·ma m. drama.

dra·má·ti·co, a I. adj. dramatic **II.** m.f. dramatist, playwright —m. actor —f. *(actriz)* actress; *(arte dramático)* drama.

dra·ma·ti·zar §04 tr. to dramatize.

dra·ma·tur·gia f. dramaturgy, dramatic art.

dra·ma·tur·go, a m.f. playwright, dramatist.

drás·ti·co, a adj. drastic.

dre·na·je m. drainage.

dre·nar tr. to drain.

dro·ga f. drug; *(embuste)* fib, lie; *(trampa)* trick; *(molestia)* nuisance; AMER. bad debt.

dro·ga·dic·ción f. drug addiction.

dro·ga·dic·to, a m.f. drug addict.

dro·ga·do, a I. adj. drugged, doped **II.** m.f. drug addict —m. drugging, doping.

dro·gar §47 tr. to drug, dope.

dro·gue·rí·a f. drugstore, pharmacy; *(comercio)* drug trade.

dro·me·da·rio m. dromedary.

dua·li·dad f. duality.

du·bi·ta·ti·vo, a adj. doubtful.

du·ca·do m. dukedom; NUMIS. ducat.

du·cha f. *(baño)* shower; MED. douche, irrigation.

du·char tr. & reflex. to shower; MED. to douche.

du·cho, a adj. skillful, expert.

dúc·til adj. ductile; FIG. pliant, docile.

du·da f. doubt, uncertainty ♦ **no cabe** *or* **no hay d.** (there is) no doubt ♦ **poner en d.** to question, doubt • **sin sombra de d.** beyond the shadow of a doubt.

du·dar tr. to doubt, question —intr. to doubt; *(vacilar)* to vacillate, waver.

du·do·so, a adj. doubtful, uncertain; *(sospechoso)* dubious; *(vacilante)* hesitant, wavering.

due·la, lo see **doler**.

due·lo¹ m. duel.

due·lo² m. *(dolor)* grief, sorrow; *(luto)* mourning, bereavement; *(los afligidos)* mourners ♦ **estar de d.** to be in mourning • **sin d.** unrestrainedly ♦ pl. troubles.

duen·de m. goblin, ghost; FIG. enchanting quality, magic; TEX. gold *or* silver cloth.

due·ña f. owner; *(ama)* lady of the house; *(señora)* lady, matron.

due·ño m. owner; *(amo)* master of a house) ♦ **ser d. de sí mismo** to have self-control.

duer·ma, mo see **dormir**.

dul·ce I. adj. sweet; *(dúctil)* soft, ductile; *(agua)* fresh **II.** m. candy, sweet **III.** adv. gently, softly.

dul·ce·ro, a I. adj. fond of sweets, sweet-toothed **II.** m.f. confectioner —f. candy dish.

dul·zu·ra f. sweetness; *(mansedumbre)* mildness, gentleness; *(verbal)* endearment, sweet nothing.

du·na f. dune.

dú·o m. duet, duo.

duo·dé·ci·mo, a adj. & m. twelfth.

du·plex m. duplex, split-level (apartment).

du·pli·ca·ción f. duplication, doubling.

du·pli·ca·do m. copy, duplicate.

du·pli·ca·dor, ·ra I. adj. duplicating, copying; *(que dobla)* doubling **II.** m. copier, copying machine.

du·pli·car §70 tr. to duplicate, copy; *(doblar)* to double.

du·plo, a adj. & m. double, twofold.

du·que m. duke.

du·que·sa f. duchess.

du·ra·ción f. duration.

du·ra·de·ro, a adj. durable, lasting.

du·ran·te prep. during.

du·rar intr. to last, endure; *(quedar)* to remain.

du·raz·ne·ro m. peach tree.

du·raz·no m. peach.

du·re·za f. hardness; *(fuerza)* strength, toughness; *(dificultad)* difficulty; *(severidad)* severity, harshness; *(obstinación)* obstinacy, stub-borness; *(indiferencia)* indifference.

dur·mien·te I. adj. asleep, sleeping; *(inactivo)* dormant, inactive **II.** m.f. sleeper —m. RAIL. sleeper, crosstie; CARP. girder, rafter.

dur·mie·ra, mió see **dormir**.

du·ro, a I. adj. hard; *(fuerte)* tough, strong; *(resistente)* resistent, resilient; *(cruel)* callous, cruel; *(obstinado)* stubborn, obstinate; *(terco)* mean, stingy; *(áspero)* harsh ♦ **a duras penas** with difficulty **II.** adv. hard.

E

e, E f. fifth letter of the Spanish alphabet.

e conj. and.

e·ba·nis·ta m. cabinetmaker, woodworker.

é·ba·no m. ebony.

e·brie·dad f. inebriation, intoxication.

e·brio, a I. adj. inebriated, drunk **II.** m.f. drunk, drunkard.

e·bu·lli·ción f. boiling; *(efervescencia)* ebullience.

e·char tr. *(arrojar)* to throw, cast, toss; *(expulsar)* to throw out, expel; *(destituir)* to dismiss, fire; (*desechar*) to throw out *or* away; (*derramar*) to shed; (*emitir*) to emit, give off; (*verter*) to pour; (*añadir*) to add, put in; BOT. to sprout, begin to grow; (*los dientes*) to cut; (*tomar*) to take; (*aplicar*) to put on, apply; (*imponer*) to impose, give; (*condenar*) to condemn, sentence; (*las cartas*) to deal; (*apostar*) to wager, gamble; (*llave*) to turn; (*cerrojo*) to shoot; (*publicar*) to publish, issue; (*representar*) to put on, present; (*pronunciar*) to give, deliver; (*presentar*) to bring, present; (*conjeturar*) to attribute, guess to be; (*adquirir*) to develop, get; ZOOL. to mate, couple ♦ **e. a perder** (*arruinar*) to spoil, ruin; (*pervertir*) to corrupt; (*malograr*) to waste • **e. a pique** to sink • **e. de menos a** to miss; (*descuidar*) to neglect • **e. de ver** to notice, observe • **echarla de** to pose as, pretend to be • **e. mano a** to grab, get a hold of • **e. suertes** to draw lots • **e. tierra a** FIG. to hush *or* cover up —intr. to grow, sprout ♦ **e. a** to begin, start; (*romper*) to burst out • **e. por** (*una carrera*) to choose, go into; (*ir*) to go —reflex. to throw oneself; (*tenderse*) to lie down, stretch out ♦ **e. a** to begin, start • **echárselas de** to pose as, pretend to be • **e. una siesta** to take a nap.

e·char·pe m. stole, shawl.

e·cléc·ti·co, a adj. & m.f. eclectic.

e·cle·siás·ti·co, a adj. & m. ecclesiastic.

e·clip·sar tr. to eclipse —reflex. to be eclipsed; (*desaparecer*) to disappear, vanish.

e·clip·se m. eclipse.

e·co m. echo; (*noticia*) news; (*acogida*) response, reception ♦ **hacerse e. de** to repeat, spread • **tener e.** to catch on, be popular.

e·co·lo·gí·a f. ecology.

e·co·no·mí·a f. economy; (*ciencia*) economics; (*parsimonia*) thrift, frugality; (*escasez*) scantiness, scarcity; (*miseria*) poverty, want ♦ **e. doméstica** home economics • **hacer economías** to economize, save.

e·co·nó·mi·co, a adj. economic; (*ahorrador*) economical.

e·co·no·mis·ta m.f. economist.

e·co·no·mi·zar §04 tr. to economize on.

e·co·sis·te·ma m. ecosystem.

e·cua·ción f. equation.

e·cua·dor m. equator.

e·cuá·ni·me adj. even-tempered, levelheaded; (*imparcial*) impartial.

e·cua·ni·mi·dad f. equanimity, levelheadedness; (*imparcialidad*) impartiality.

e·cua·to·rial adj. equatorial.

e·cues·tre adj. equestrian.

e·cu·mé·ni·co, a adj. ecumenical, universal.

e·cu·me·nis·mo m. ecumenism.

ec·ze·ma m. eczema.

e·dad f. age; (*período*) time; (*época*) era, epoch ♦ **e. crítica** menopause, change of life • **E. Media** Middle Ages • **e. viril** prime of life • **mayor de e.** of age • **menor de e.** underage • **¿qué e. tienes?** how old are you?

e·di·ción f. publication; (*conjunto de libros o periódicos*) edition; (*conjunto de revistas*) issue ♦ **segunda e.** COLL. spitting image, carbon copy.

e·dic·to m. edict, proclamation.

e·di·fi·car §70 tr. to build, construct; (*establecer*) to establish, form; (*mejorar*) to edify, enlighten.

e·di·fi·cio m. building, edifice; FIG. structure, fabric.

e·di·tar tr. to publish.

e·di·tor, ·ra I. adj. publishing II. m.f. publisher; (*redactor*) editor.

e·di·to·rial I. adj. publishing II. m. editorial —f. publishing house.

e·du·ca·ción f. education, training.

e·du·ca·do, a adj. educated, trained; (*cortés*) well-mannered, polite.

e·du·car §70 tr. to educate, teach; (*criar*) to raise, bring up; (*desarrollar*) to develop, train.

e·fe·bo m. youth, adolescent.

e·fec·ti·va·men·te adv. (*en realidad*) really, in fact; (*por supuesto*) indeed, certainly.

e·fec·ti·vi·dad f. effectiveness; MIL. nominal rank.

e·fec·ti·vo, a I. adj. effective; (*verdadero*) real, actual; (*permanente*) permanent II. m. (*dinero*) (hard) cash; (*número total*) total number.

e·fec·to m. effect, result; (*fin*) end, purpose; (*impresión*) impression, impact; (*rotación*) spin; COM. commercial paper ♦ **a efectos de** for the purpose of • **con** *or* **en e.** (*efectivamente*) in effect, in fact; (*en conclusión*) indeed, precisely • **dar e.** to produce sound effects • **efectos de resultado** *or* **de residuo** COMPUT. output • **e. útil** MECH. output • **hacer e.** to have an effect • **llevar a** *or* **poner en e.** to put into effect, implement • **surtir e.** to have the desired effect, work • **tener e.** (*efectuarse*) to take effect; (*ocurrir*) to take place ♦ pl. effects, property; (*mercancía*) goods, merchandise; FIN. bills, securities.

e·fec·tuar §67 tr. to effect, bring about —reflex. to take effect.

e·fer·ves·cen·cia f. effervescence; FIG. excitement, vivacity.

e·fi·ca·cia f. efficacy, effectiveness.

e·fi·caz adj. efficacious, effective.

e·fi·cien·cia f. efficiency.

e·fi·cien·te adj. efficient, effective.

e·fi·gie f. effigy.

e·fí·me·ro, a adj. ephemeral.

e·flu·vio m. effluvium; FIG. vibration, aura.

e·fu·sión f. effusion; FIG. effusiveness, intensity.

e·fu·si·vo, a adj. effusive.

é·gi·da f. aegis, protection.

e·go m. ego, the self.

e·go·cén·tri·co, a adj. egocentric.

e·go·ís·ta adj. & m.f. egoistic (person).

e·go·la·trí·a f. self-worship, narcissism.

e·go·tis·ta I. adj. egotistic, egotistical II. m.f. egotist.

e·gre·sa·do, a AMER. adj. & m.f. graduate.

e·gre·sar intr. AMER. to graduate.

¡eh! interj. hey!; (*para confirmar*) all right?, okay?

e·je m. axis; FIG. crux, main point; MECH., TECH. shaft, axle.

e·je·cu·ción f. execution, realization; CRIMIN. execution; MUS. performance, rendition.

e·je·cu·tar tr. to execute, carry out; CRIMIN. to execute, put to death; MUS. to perform, play.

e·je·cu·ti·vo, a adj. & m. executive.

e·je·cu·tor, ·ra I. adj. executing; MUS. performing II. m.f. executor ♦ **e. de la justicia** executioner • **e. testamentaria** executrix • **e. testamentario** executor.

e·jem·plar I. adj. exemplary II. m. example; PRINT. copy; (*número*) number, issue; (*precedente*) precedent; SCI. specimen ♦ **e. de regalo** complimentary copy • **sin e.** unprecedented, unique.

e·jem·pli·fi·car §70 tr. to exemplify, illustrate.

e·jem·plo m. example ♦ **dar e.** to set an example • **por e.** for example, for instance • **sin e.** unprecedented.

e·jer·cer §75 tr. to exercise; *(desempeñar)* to practice —intr. to be in practice, practice a profession.

e·jer·ci·cio m. exercise; *(desempeño)* practice; *(tarea)* exercise, drill; *(prueba)* examination; MIL. exercise, drill; POL. tenure ♦ **e. económico** fiscal year.

e·jer·ci·tar tr. *(desempeñar)* to practice; *(adiestrar)* to train, drill —reflex. to train, drill.

e·jér·ci·to m. MIL. army; FIG. army, flock.

el I. def. art. the II. pron. the one ♦ **el que** the one that; *(él)* he who.

él pron. [pl. **ellos**] he; him *<para él for him>*; it *<tomó el lápiz y escribió con él she took the pencil and wrote with it>* ♦ **de él** his • **él mismo** he himself ♦ pl. they, them • **de ellos** theirs • **ellos mismos** they themselves.

e·la·bo·rar tr. *(fabricar)* to manufacture, produce; *(crear)* to make, create; *(labrar)* to work; *(preparar)* to prepare, work out.

e·lan m. elan, zest.

e·las·ti·ci·dad f. elasticity; FIG. flexibility.

e·lás·ti·co, a I. adj. elastic; *(flexible)* flexible II. m. elastic, elastic band ♦ pl. suspenders —f. AMER. undershirt, T-shirt.

e·lec·ción f. election; *(selección)* selection, choice.

e·lec·to, a adj. & m.f. elect, chosen (person).

e·lec·tor, ·ra I. adj. electing II. m.f. elector, voter.

e·lec·to·ra·do m. electorate.

e·lec·tri·ci·dad f. electricity.

e·lec·tri·cis·ta I. adj. electrical II. m.f. electrician.

e·léc·tri·co, a adj. electric(al); FIG. lightning-fast.

e·lec·tri·fi·car §70 tr. to electrify.

e·lec·tri·zan·te adj. electrifying.

e·lec·tri·zar §04 tr. to electrify.

e·lec·tro·car·dio·gra·ma m. electrocardiogram.

e·lec·tro·cu·ción f. electrocution.

e·lec·tro·cu·tar tr. to electrocute.

e·lec·tro·en·ce·fa·lo·gra·ma m. electroencephalogram.

e·lec·troi·mán m. electromagnet.

e·lec·tro·mag·ne·tis·mo m. electromagnetism.

e·lec·tro·mo·tor, ra I. adj. electromotive II. m. electromotor.

e·lec·trón m. electron.

e·lec·tró·ni·co, a I. adj. electronic II. f. electronics.

e·lec·tro·tec·nia f. electrical engineering.

e·le·fan·te m. elephant.

e·le·gan·cia f. elegance, polish.

e·le·gan·te adj. elegant.

e·le·gí·a f. elegy.

e·le·gir §57 tr. to choose, select; POL. to elect.

e·le·men·tal adj. elemental; *(obvio)* elementary, obvious; *(fundamental)* fundamental, essential.

e·le·men·to m. element; *(miembro)* member; ELEC. cell; AMER. dimwit, blockhead ♦ pl. rudiments, basic principles; *(recursos)* resources, means; *(condiciones atmosféricas)* elements.

e·len·co m. THEAT. company, cast.

e·le·va·ción f. elevation; *(construcción)* erection, building; FIG. promotion; *(enajenamiento)* rapture, ecstasy; MATH. raising.

e·le·va·do, a adj. tall, high; *(sublime)* elevated, lofty.

e·le·va·dor m. AMER. elevator.

e·le·va·mien·to m. var. of **elevación**.

e·le·var tr. to elevate; *(ennoblecer)* to ennoble; MATH. to raise.

e·li·gie·ra, gió, ja, jo see **elegir**.

e·li·mi·nar tr. to eliminate.

e·li·mi·na·to·rio, a I. adj. eliminatory II. f. SPORT. preliminary, preliminary round.

e·lip·se f. ellipse.

e·lip·sis f. ellipsis.

e·líp·ti·co, a adj. elliptic(al).

e·li·tis·ta adj. elitist.

e·li·xir m. elixir.

e·lla pron. she; her *<para e. for her>*; it *<tomó la gorra y se fue con e.* he picked up his cap and left with it> ♦ **de e.** hers ♦ **e. misma** she herself ♦ pl. they, them • **de e.** theirs • **e. mismas** they themselves.

e·llo pron. it.

e·llos, e·llas pron. see **él, ella.**

e·lo·cu·ción f. elocution.

e·lo·cuen·cia f. eloquence.

e·lo·cuen·te adj. eloquent.

e·lo·giar tr. to eulogize, praise.

e·lo·gio m. eulogy, praise.

e·lu·ci·dar tr. to elucidate, explain.

e·lu·dir tr. to elude, avoid.

e·lu·si·vo, a adj. elusive, evasive.

e·ma·na·ción f. emanation, efflux.

e·ma·nar intr. to emanate, flow.

e·man·ci·pa·ción f. emancipation, liberation.

e·man·ci·par tr. to emancipate, liberate —reflex. to become emancipated *or* liberated.

e·mas·cu·lar tr. to emasculate, castrate.

em·ba·dur·nar tr. to smear, daub.

em·ba·ja·da f. embassy; *(cargo)* ambassadorship; COLL. impertinent proposition.

em·ba·ja·dor, ·ra m.f. ambassador.

em·ba·la·dor m. packer.

em·ba·la·je m. packing, crating; *(materia)* packing material.

em·ba·lar tr. to pack, crate; *(acelerar)* to rev —intr. to race, sprint —reflex. AUTO. to rev; FIG. to be carried away.

em·bal·do·sa·do m. tiling; *(suelo)* tiled floor.

em·bal·do·sar tr. to tile.

em·bal·sa·mar tr. to embalm; *(perfumar)* to perfume, scent.

em·bal·sar tr. to dam up, dam —reflex. to be dammed up.

em·bal·se m. dam.

em·ban·de·rar tr. to decorate with flags.

em·ba·ra·za·da·men·te adv. with embarrassment; *(con dificultad)* with difficulty.

em·ba·ra·za·do, a I. adj. *(preñado)* pregnant; *(molesto)* troubled, bothered II. f. pregnant woman, expectant mother.

em·ba·ra·zar §04 tr. to hinder, impede; *(preñar)* to impregnate, make pregnant; *(molestar)* to bother, embarrass —reflex. to be hindered; *(preñarse)* to become pregnant.

em·ba·ra·zo m. *(preñez)* pregnancy; *(dificultad)* difficulty; *(timidez)* embarrassment.

em·ba·ra·zo·so, a adj. troublesome.

em·bar·ca·ción f. boat, vessel; *(embarco)* embarkation; *(viaje)* voyage.

em·bar·ca·de·ro m. landing stage, pier;

(muelle) wharf, dock; AMER. loading platform.

em·bar·car §70 tr. to embark; *(poner a bordo)* to load, ship aboard; *(incluir)* to involve; AMER. to deceive —reflex. to embark; *(enredarse)* to get involved in, engage in.

em·bar·co m. embarkation.

em·bar·gar §47 tr. *(estorbar)* to impede, hamper; LAW to lay an embargo on, distrain; FIG. to overcome.

em·bar·go m. MARIT. embargo; LAW seizure, distraint; MED. indigestion ♦ sin e. however, nevertheless.

em·bar·ni·zar §04 tr. to varnish.

em·bar·que m. loading, shipment.

em·ba·rrar tr. to splash with mud; *(manchar)* to stain; AMER. to annoy, irritate —reflex. to become covered with mud.

em·ba·ru·llar tr. COLL. *(mezclar)* to muddle, mix up; *(chapucear)* to bungle, botch.

em·bas·tar tr. *(un colchón)* to quilt; *(hilvanar)* to baste, tack.

em·ba·te m. dashing, pounding; *(viento)* sea breeze; *(acometida)* sudden attack.

em·bau·ca·dor, ·ra I. adj. deceiving, swindling II. m.f. deceiver, swindler.

em·bau·car §70 tr. to deceive, swindle.

em·be·ber tr. to absorb, soak up; *(empapar)* to soak, wet; *(contener)* to contain, enclose; *(ropa)* to take in —intr. to shrink —reflex. to be absorbed or engrossed.

em·be·le·sar tr. to enthrall, fascinate —reflex. to be enthralled or fascinated.

em·be·le·so m. delight, enchantment.

em·be·lle·ce·dor, ·ra I. adj. beautifying, embellishing II. m. AUTO. hubcap.

em·be·lle·cer §17 tr. to beautify, embellish.

em·bes·ti·da f. attack, onslaught.

em·bes·tir §48 tr. & intr. to attack.

em·be·tu·nar tr. to polish; *(asfaltar)* to cover with pitch or tar.

em·blan·de·cer §17 tr. & intr. to soften.

em·blan·que·cer §17 tr. to whiten, bleach —reflex. to become whitened or bleached.

em·ble·ma m. emblem, symbol.

em·bo·bar tr. to stupefy, fascinate —reflex. to be stupefied or fascinated.

em·bo·ca·du·ra f. MUS. mouthpiece; *(del caballo)* bit; *(desembocadura)* mouth (of a river); *(sabor)* taste.

em·bo·car §70 tr. to put in the mouth; *(engañar)* to make someone swallow; COLL. *(engullir)* to gorge, gulp down; *(comenzar)* to begin, undertake —reflex. to enter, go into.

em·bo·chin·char tr. AMER. to raise a ruckus.

em·bo·lia f. embolism, clot.

ém·bo·lo m. piston.

em·bol·sar tr. to pocket, collect.

em·bo·que m. passage through a narrow place; COLL. trick, hoax.

em·bo·rra·char tr. to intoxicate; *(adormecer)* to make drowsy —reflex. to get drunk.

em·bo·rras·car §70 tr. to irritate, annoy —reflex. to become stormy; *(irritarse)* to become irritated or annoyed; *(fracasar)* to fail, go wrong.

em·bo·rro·nar tr. to cover with smudges or blots; *(escribir)* to scribble.

em·bos·ca·da f. ambush.

em·bos·car §70 tr. to ambush —reflex. to ambush, lie in ambush; COLL. to find an easy way out.

em·bo·ta·du·ra f. bluntness, dullness.

em·bo·ta·mien·to m. blunting, dulling.

em·bo·tar tr. to blunt, dull —reflex. to become blunt or dull.

em·bo·te·lla·mien·to m. bottling; *(de la circulación)* traffic jam, bottleneck.

em·bo·te·llar tr. to bottle; *(obstruir)* to jam, block; *(memorizar)* to learn by heart, memorize.

em·bra·gar §47 tr. to connect, engage.

em·bra·gue m. AUTO. clutch.

em·bra·ve·cer §17 tr. to irritate, infuriate —intr. to flourish, thrive —reflex. to become irritated; *(el mar)* to become choppy.

em·bre·ar tr. to cover with tar or pitch.

em·bria·ga·dor, ·ra/gan·te adj. intoxicating.

em·bria·gar §47 tr. to intoxicate —reflex. to get drunk.

em·bria·guez f. intoxication.

em·brión m. embryo.

em·bro·lla·dor, ·ra I. adj. confusing, embroiling II. m.f. troublemaker.

em·bro·llar tr. to confuse, embroil.

em·bro·llo m. confusion, tangle; *(embuste)* trick, fraud.

em·bro·llón, o·na I. adj. confusing, embroiling II. m.f. troublemaker.

em·bro·mar tr. *(burlarse de)* to make fun of, tease; *(engañar)* to cheat, hoodwink; AMER. *(fastidiar)* to annoy —reflex. AMER. to get annoyed.

em·bru·jar tr. to bewitch, cast a spell on.

em·bru·jo m. spell, charm.

em·bru·te·cer §04 tr. to brutalize.

em·bu·char tr. COLL. *(tragar)* to gulp down, wolf down; *(hacer creer)* to try to make (someone) swallow (something).

em·bu·do m. funnel; *(trampa)* trick, fraud.

em·bus·te m. hoax, fraud; *(mentira)* lie, fib.

em·bus·te·ro, a I. adj. lying, deceitful II. m.f. liar, cheat.

em·bu·ti·do m. inlay, marquetry; CUL. sausage.

em·bu·tir tr. to stuff, cram; *(taracear)* to inlay; *(tragar)* to swallow —reflex. COLL. to stuff oneself, gorge.

e·mer·gen·cia f. *(surgimiento)* emergence; *(accidente)* emergency.

e·mer·ger §34 intr. to emerge.

e·mi·gra·do, a m.f. emigrant, émigré.

e·mi·gran·te I. adj. emigrating, migrating II. m.f. emigrant, émigré.

e·mi·grar intr. to emigrate; ZOOL. to migrate.

e·mi·nen·cia f. eminence.

e·mi·nen·te adj. *(elevado)* high, lofty; *(distinguido)* eminent, distinguished.

e·mi·sa·rio, a m.f. emissary, secret agent.

e·mi·sión f. emission; TELEC. transmission, broadcast; COM. issuance, issue.

e·mi·sor, ·ra I. adj. emitting; TELEC. broadcasting; COM. issuing II. m.f. issuer; TELEC. *(aparato)* transmitter; *(estación)* broadcasting station.

e·mi·tir tr. to emit, throw off; *(poner en circulación)* to issue; *(expresar)* to utter, express —intr. to broadcast, transmit.

e·mo·ción f. emotion, feeling.

e·mo·cio·na·do, a adj. *(conmovido)* moved, touched; *(perturbado)* upset, distressed.

e·mo·cio·nan·te adj. moving, thrilling.

e·mo·cio·nar tr. to move, affect —reflex. to be moved or affected.

e·mo·lu·men·to m. emolument, wage.

e·mo·ti·vo, a adj. emotive, emotional.

em·pa·car §70 tr. to pack, bale; AMER. to annoy, anger —intr. to pack —reflex. to be stubborn; (turbarse) to be flustered.

em·pa·char tr. to give indigestion to; (estorbar) to obstruct, hinder; (hacer pasar un apuro) to embarrass —reflex. to have indigestion.

em·pa·cho m. indigestion; (apuro) embarrassment, shame.

em·pa·dro·na·mien·to m. census.

em·pa·dro·nar tr. to take a census of.

em·pa·la·gar §47 tr. to cloy, sicken; (fastidiar) to annoy, tire —intr. to be boring, be tiresome —reflex. to be annoyed (with), be tired (of).

em·pa·la·go m. surfeit, excess; (molestia) annoyance, irritation.

em·pa·la·go·so, a I. adj. cloying, sickening; (fastidioso) annoying, tiresome. II. m.f. pest, nuisance.

em·pa·li·za·da f. MIL. palisade, stockade.

em·pa·li·zar §04 tr. MIL. to palisade, stockade.

em·pal·mar tr. (unir) to connect, join; CARP. to join; PHOTOG. to splice; (combinar) to link (up), combine —intr. & reflex. to meet, join; RAIL. to connect, join ♦ **e. con** to follow.

em·pal·me m. join, joint; RAIL., AUTO. junction; PHOTOG. SPLICE.

em·pa·na·do, a I. adj. CUL. breaded II. f. CUL. turnover.

em·pa·nar tr. to bread.

em·pa·ñar tr. (con pañales) to diaper, swaddle; (obscurecer) to blur, mist; (manchar) to tarnish, blemish.

em·pa·par tr. to soak; (absorber) to absorb, soak up —reflex. to get soaked; (imbuirse) to become inspired; (ahitarse) to stuff oneself, gorge oneself.

em·pa·pe·la·do m. papering, lining; (papel) wrapping or lining paper.

em·pa·pe·lar tr. (envolver en papel) to wrap in paper; (forrar) to paper, line with paper; (cubrir paredes) to wallpaper.

em·pa·que·tar tr. to pack, wrap; (muchas personas) to stuff, pack; (emperejilar) to dress up.

em·pa·re·da·do, a I. adj. imprisoned, confined; (retirado) reclusive II. m.f. prisoner, captive; (hermitaño) recluse, hermit —m. sandwich.

em·pa·re·jar tr. to match, pair (off); (poner a nivel) to (make) level, level off —intr. (alcanzar) to catch up, draw abreast; (ser pareja) to match —reflex. to form pairs, pair off.

em·pa·ren·tar §49 intr. to become related by marriage.

em·pas·tar tr. to cover with paste; BKB. to bind; DENT. to fill.

em·pas·te m. DENT. (tooth) filling; BKB. bookbinding.

em·pa·tar tr. (igualar) to tie, equal; (estorbar) to impede, hold up; AMER. to couple, join —intr. to tie, be equal —reflex. to result in a tie or draw ♦ **empatársela a uno** (igualarle) to be a match for someone.

em·pa·te m. tie, draw; AMER. (estorbo) obstacle, impediment; (unión) joint, connection.

em·pe·ci·na·do, a adj. stubborn, obstinate.

em·pe·ci·na·mien·to m. stubbornness, obstinacy.

em·pe·ci·nar tr. to be stubborn or obstinate.

em·pe·der·ni·do, a adj. hardhearted, insensitive; (inveterado) hardened, inveterate.

em·pe·dra·do, a I. adj. dappled, spotted

II. m. cobblestones.

em·pe·drar §49 tr. to pave (with stones); (cubrir) to strew, scatter.

em·pei·ne m. (del vientre) groin; (del pie) instep; MED. impetigo.

em·pe·llar or **em·pe·ller** §28 tr. to push, shove.

em·pe·llón m. push, shove ♦ **a empellones** roughly, violently.

em·pe·lo·tar tr. COLL. to wrap up —reflex. (reñir) to get into a row, quarrel ♦ **e. con** or **por** AMER., COLL. to fall madly in love with.

em·pe·ñar tr. to pawn; (obligar) to oblige, compel; MIL. to engage in, begin; (enredar) to embroil, involve —reflex. (entramparse) to go into debt; (insistir) to insist, persist ♦ **e. en** to be bent on or determined to ♦ **e. por** or **con** to intercede or mediate on behalf of.

em·pe·ño m. pawn, pledge; (deudor) debtor; (constancia) insistence, tenacity; (protector) patron, supporter ♦ **poner** or **tomar e. en** to take great pains in ♦ **tener e.** to be eager.

em·pe·o·rar tr. to make worse —intr. & reflex. to worsen, deteriorate.

em·pe·que·ñe·cer §17 tr. to diminish, make small; (desprestigiar) to belittle, disparage.

em·pe·ra·dor m. emperor.

em·pe·ra·triz f. empress.

em·pe·ri·ji·lar/ri·fo·llar tr. COLL. to dress up, doll up —reflex. to get all dressed up.

em·pe·ro conj. but, however.

em·pe·rrar·se reflex. (encolerizarse) to flare up, lose one's temper; (obstinarse) to be dead set, be determined.

em·pe·zar §29 tr. & intr. to begin (a to, por by) ♦ **al e.** at the beginning or start ● **para e.** to begin with, first.

em·pie·zo see empezar.

em·pi·na·do, a adj. very high, lofty; FIG. proud, haughty.

em·pi·nar tr. to stand (up), set straight; (elevar) to raise, lift ♦ **e. el codo** COLL. to drink heavily —reflex. (un caballo) to rear; (una persona) to stand on tiptoe; (una estructura) to tower.

em·pí·ri·co, a I. adj. empirical II. m.f. empiricist.

em·pi·za·rrar tr. to cover or roof with slate.

em·plas·tar tr. to plaster; (maquillar) apply cosmetics to; (detener) to hamper, hold up —reflex. (ensuciarse) to become smeared or covered; (maquillarse) to make up.

em·plas·to m. plaster, poultice; COLL. (enfermizo) weakling, sickly person.

em·pla·zar §04 tr. to call together, convene; LAW to summon to appear in court.

em·ple·a·do, a m.f. employee.

em·ple·a·dor, ·ra I. adj. employing II. m.f. employer.

em·ple·ar tr. to employ; (invertir) to invest —reflex. to get a job, become employed ♦ **empleársele bien a uno** to get what one deserves, get one's just deserts.

em·ple·o m. job, occupation; (uso) use, utilization; MIL. rank, position; (inversión) investment.

em·plo·mar tr. to cover or line with lead; (poner sellos) to seal with lead; (diente) to fill.

em·plu·mar tr. to feather; (castigar) to tar and feather —intr. ORNITH. to fledge, grow feathers; AMER. to flee, take flight.

em·po·bre·cer §17 tr. to impoverish —intr. & reflex. to become poor or impoverished.

em·po·bre·ci·do, a adj. impoverished.

em·po·bre·ci·mien·to m. impoverishment.

em·po·llar tr. to hatch, brood; (*estudiar mucho*) to bone up on; (*meditar*) to brood or dwell on —intr. to breed, brood; (*estudiar mucho*) to grind, cram.

em·pol·var tr. to powder; (*ensuciar*) to cover with dust —reflex. to powder (oneself); (*ensuciarse*) to get dusty.

em·pon·zo·ñar tr. to poison.

em·por·car §73 tr. to soil, dirty —reflex. to become soiled or dirty.

em·po·rio m. emporium, market; (*lugar famoso*) capital, center; AMER. department store.

em·po·trar tr. to embed.

em·pren·de·dor, ·ra adj. enterprising.

em·pren·der tr. to begin, set about ♦ **emprenderla con** to quarrel or wrangle with.

em·pre·sa f. enterprise, undertaking; (*sociedad*) company, firm; (*dirección*) management; (*lema*) emblem, legend.

em·pre·sa·rial adj. managerial, management.

em·pre·sa·rio, a m.f. manager, director; THEAT. impresario.

em·prés·ti·to m. loan.

em·puer·que, co see **emporcar**.

em·pu·jar tr. to push; (*despedir*) to oust; (*hacer presión*) to pressure.

em·pu·je m. push, shove; (*presión*) pressure; (*energía*) energy, drive.

em·pu·jón m. push, shove ♦ **a empujones** roughly, brusquely.

em·pu·ña·du·ra f. (*de espada*) hilt; (*de paraguas*) handle; COLL. beginning of a story.

em·pu·ñar tr. to seize, grasp.

e·mu·la·ción f. emulation.

e·mu·lar tr. to emulate, rival.

e·mul·sión f. emulsion.

en prep. (*location*) in, into, at, on, upon; (*time*) in, at, as soon as; (*manner*) in, by, at, for, if, into.

e·na·guas f.pl. petticoat, underskirt.

e·na·je·na·ble adj. alienable.

e·na·je·na·ción f. alienation; (*distracción*) distraction, absent-mindedness ♦ **e. mental** madness.

e·na·je·nar tr. to alienate; (*turbar*) to drive crazy, drive to distraction —reflex. to become alienated or estranged.

e·nal·te·ce·dor, ·ra adj. extolling, praising.

e·nal·te·cer §17 tr. to extol, praise.

e·na·mo·ra·di·zo, a adj. easily infatuated.

e·na·mo·ra·do, a I. adj. enamored, in love (of with, of); (*enamoradizo*) easily infatuated, always falling in love **II.** m.f. lover.

e·na·mo·ra·mien·to m. falling in love.

e·na·mo·rar tr. to enamor, inspire love; (*cortejar*) to court, woo —reflex. to fall in love (*de* with); (*aficionarse*) to become enamored (*de* of).

e·na·no, a I. adj. small, minute **II.** m.f. dwarf.

e·nar·bo·lar tr. to raise, hoist —reflex. to rear up; (*enfadarse*) to be angry.

e·nar·car §70 tr. to bend, arch; (*barriles*) to hoop ♦ **e. las cejas** to raise one's eyebrows —reflex. to bend, arch.

e·nar·de·ce·dor, ·ra adj. fiery, inflammatory.

e·nar·de·cer §17 tr. to ignite, set aflame —reflex. to be ignited.

e·na·re·nar tr. to cover with sand —reflex. MARIT. to run aground.

en·ca·bes·trar tr. to put a halter on; (*atraer*) to attract, seduce.

en·ca·be·za·mien·to m. (*titular*) caption, headline; (*de una carta*) heading; (*registro*) census list or register; (*impuestos*) tax roll.

en·ca·be·zar §04 tr. to head; (*registrar*) to register, enroll —reflex. to agree, come to terms.

en·ca·bri·tar·se reflex. (*un caballo*) to rear up; (*un vehículo*) to pitch upwards; COLL. to get angry.

en·ca·de·na·ción/na·du·ra f./**na·mien·to** m. enchainment; (*eslabón*) connection.

en·ca·de·nar tr. to chain; (*conectar*) to connect, link.

en·ca·jar tr. to fit, insert; (*ajustar*) to force; COLL. (*engañar*) to pass off; (*golpe*) to deal, land —intr. to fit (well) —reflex. to squeeze in.

en·ca·je m. lace; (*inserción*) insertion, inserting; (*unión*) joining, fitting; TECH. inlay.

en·ca·jo·nar tr. to box, crate; (*estrechar*) to squeeze in.

en·ca·lar tr. to whitewash.

en·ca·lla·de·ro m. shoal, sandbank; (*atascadero*) obstruction, stumbling block.

en·ca·llar intr. MARIT. to run aground; FIG. to founder, bog down.

en·ca·lle·cer §17 intr. & reflex. to develop corns, become callused; FIG. to harden, become callous.

en·ca·lle·ci·do, a adj. hardened, calloused.

en·ca·mar·se reflex. COLL. to stay in bed.

en·ca·mi·nar tr. to direct, guide —reflex. to make for, set out for.

en·ca·mi·sar tr. to put a shirt on; (*enfundar*) to put a cover on; (*envolver*) to wrap; MECH. to reline.

en·ca·mo·ta·do, a adj. AMER. in love.

en·ca·mo·tar·se reflex. AMER. to fall in love.

en·ca·na·lar tr. to channel through pipes.

en·ca·na·li·zar §04 tr. var. of **encanalar**.

en·can·di·la·do, a adj. COLL. erect, tall.

en·can·di·lar tr. (*deslumbrar*) to dazzle; (*avivar la lumbre*) to stir, rake; (*excitar*) to kindle, excite —reflex. to light up.

en·ca·ne·cer §17 intr. & reflex. to go gray; FIG. to age, grow old; (*ponerse mohoso*) to become moldy —tr. to age.

en·can·ta·ción f. var. of **encantamiento**.

en·can·ta·do, a adj. delighted, charmed; (*distraído*) absent-minded, distracted; (*casa*) haunted.

en·can·ta·dor, ·ra I. adj. enchanting, charming **II.** m.f. charmer —m. magician, sorcerer —f. sorceress.

en·can·ta·mien·to m. enchantment; (*hechizo*) bewitchment, spell.

en·can·tar tr. to enchant, charm; (*hechizar*) to bewitch, cast a spell on.

en·can·to m. enchantment, bewitchment; (*magia*) magic ♦ pl. charms.

en·ca·ño·nar tr. to channel, pipe; (*apuntar*) to take aim at; (*encanillar*) to wind on a spool or bobbin.

en·ca·po·ta·do, a adj. overcast, cloudy.

en·ca·po·tar tr. to cloak —reflex. (*poner rostro ceñudo*) to frown; (*nublarse*) to become cloudy or overcast.

en·ca·pri·char·se reflex. to take it into one's head, take a fancy (*por, con* to).

en·ca·pu·char tr. to hood, cover with a hood.

en·ca·ra·mar tr. (*levantar*) to lift, raise; (*a un puesto elevado*) to elevate, promote; (*elogiar*) to extol, praise —reflex. to climb up; AMER. to blush.

en·ca·rar intr. & reflex. to face, confront —tr. *(apuntar)* to take aim at; *(confrontar)* to confront, face.

en·car·ce·lar tr. to incarcerate, imprison; CARP. to clamp.

en·ca·re·cer §17 tr. to raise the price of; *(elogiar)* to extol, praise; *(recomendar)* to recommend, urge —intr. & reflex. to become more expensive.

en·ca·re·ci·da·men·te adv. earnestly.

en·car·ga·do, a I. adj. in charge II. m.f. person in charge ✦ **e. de negocios** chargé d'affaires.

en·car·gar §47 tr. to entrust, put in charge; *(pedir)* to advise, recommend; *(ordenar)* to order, request —reflex. to take charge or responsibility.

en·car·go m. *(recado)* errand, task; *(trabajo)* assignment, job; *(empleo)* post ✦ **hecho de e.** made to order.

en·ca·ri·ñar tr. to make fond of, endear —reflex. to become fond *(con* of).

en·car·na·ción f. incarnation.

en·car·na·do, a I. adj. *(de color de carne)* flesh-colored; *(colorado)* red; *(personificado)* incarnate II. m. flesh color; *(rojo)* red.

en·car·nar intr. to become incarnate; *(cicatrizar)* to heal, close up; *(herir)* to penetrate the flesh or skin; FIG. to make a lasting impression —tr. to personify, embody —reflex. to mix, join.

en·car·ni·za·do, a adj. *(ensangrentado)* bloodshot; *(sangriento)* bloody; *(intenso)* fierce.

en·car·ni·za·mien·to m. bloodthirstiness.

en·car·ni·zar §04 tr. to make cruel, brutalize —reflex. *(encrudecerse)* to become cruel or brutal; *(pelear)* to fight fiercely.

en·ca·rri·l(l)ar tr. to direct, guide; *(colocar sobre rieles)* to put on tracks; *(dar buena orientación)* to put on the right track.

en·cas·co·tar tr. to fill with debris or rubble.

en·ca·si·llar tr. to pigeonhole; *(clasificar)* to classify, class.

en·cas·que·tar tr. to pull on, put on; *(meter en la cabeza)* to put into someone's head —reflex. to pull on; *(obstinarse)* to take it into one's head.

en·cau·sar tr. to prosecute, sue.

en·cau·zar §04 tr. to channel, direct.

en·ce·fa·li·tis f. encephalitis.

en·ce·fa·lo·gra·ma m. encephalogram.

en·cel·dar tr. to put in a cell, incarcerate.

en·cen·de·dor m. lighter.

en·cen·der §50 tr. to light; *(pegar fuego)* to ignite; *(incendiar)* to set on fire; *(luz)* to turn on; *(excitar)* to arouse, excite; *(causar)* to spark, start —reflex. to light; *(incendiarse)* to catch on fire; *(excitarse)* to get excited; *(estallar)* to break out; *(ruborizarse)* to blush.

en·cen·di·do, a I. adj. lit, switched on; *(hecho ascua)* red, red-hot; *(inflamado)* inflamed, red II. m. AUTO. ignition.

en·ce·ra·do, a I. adj. wax-colored; *(pulido)* waxed, polished II. m. wax; *(pizarra)* blackboard; *(tela)* oilcloth, oilskin; MARIT. tarpaulin.

en·ce·ra·dor, ra m.f. floor polisher or waxer.

en·ce·rar tr. to wax, polish —intr. & reflex. to turn yellow, ripen.

en·ce·rrar §49 tr. to enclose, confine; *(incluir)* to hold, contain; *(implicar)* to involve, entail

—reflex. to go into seclusion.

en·cha·pa·do m. veneer, overlay; *(acción)* veneering, plating.

en·cha·par tr. to veneer, overlay.

en·char·car §70 tr. to flood —reflex. to become flooded, become swamped; *(encenagarse)* to wallow.

en·chi·la·da f. enchilada.

en·chi·la·do, a adj. AMER. seasoned with chili; *(rojo)* (bright) red, vermillion.

en·chi·var·se reflex. AMER. to fly into a rage.

en·chu·far tr. ELEC. to connect, plug in; *(acoplar tubos)* to fit together, couple; COM. to combine, merge; *(ejercer influencia)* to pull strings for —reflex. to land a job through connections.

en·chu·fe m. ELEC., TECH. connection; *(hembra)* socket; *(macho)* plug; COLL. *(puesto)* cushy job, sinecure; *(relaciones)* contacts, pull.

en·cí·a f. gum, gingiva.

en·cí·cli·ca f. encyclical (letter).

en·ci·clo·pe·dia f. encyclop(a)edia.

en·cien·da, do see **encender**.

en·cie·rre, rro see **encerrar**.

en·cie·rro m. *(acción)* shutting, closing; *(recinto)* enclosure; *(clausura)* seclusion; *(retiro)* retirement.

en·ci·ma adv. *(sobre)* on top; *(además)* in addition, besides ✦ **e. de** above ✦ **por e.** superficially ✦ **por e. de** in spite of.

en·cin·ta adj. pregnant, with child.

en·cin·tar tr. to beribbon, adorn with ribbon.

en·claus·trar tr. to put in a cloister; *(esconder)* to hide, conceal.

en·cla·var tr. CARP. to nail (down); *(traspasar)* to pierce, transfix; *(ubicar)* to locate, situate; *(engañar)* to trick, dupe.

en·cla·ve m. enclave.

en·clen·que adj. & m.f. weak, sickly (person).

en·co·co·rar tr. COLL. to annoy, vex —reflex. to be annoyed or vexed.

en·co·frar tr. to plank, timber.

en·co·ger §34 tr. to contract, draw in; *(reducir)* to shrink, make smaller —intr. & reflex. to contract; *(reducirse)* to shrink, become smaller ✦ **e. de hombros** to shrug one's shoulders.

en·co·gi·do, a adj. & m.f. *(tímido)* shy or bashful (person); *(pusilánime)* faint-hearted or cowardly (person).

en·co·ja, jo see **encoger**.

en·co·lar tr. to glue, stick.

en·co·le·ri·zar §04 tr. to anger, enrage —reflex. to become angry or enraged.

en·co·men·dar §49 tr. to entrust, commend —reflex. to entrust or commend oneself; *(enviar recuerdos)* to send one's regards.

en·co·miar tr. to praise, extol.

en·co·mien·da f. *(encargo)* commission, task; *(recomendación)* praise, commendation; *(amparo)* care, protection; AMER. postal parcel or package ✦ pl. regards, compliments.

en·co·mien·de, do see **encomendar**.

en·co·mio m. encomium, praise.

en·co·nar tr. MED. to inflame, irritate; *(enfadar)* to anger, irritate —reflex. MED. to become inflamed or irritated; *(enfadarse)* to become angry or irritated.

en·co·no m. rancor, ill will; MED. inflammation.

en·con·trar §19 tr. to find; *(topar)* to meet,

encounter —intr. to meet —reflex. to meet; (chocar) to clash, differ; (enemistarse) to have a falling out, become enemies; (estar) to be, be located; (sentirse) to find oneself ♦ **e. con** (hallar) to find, run across; (topar) to meet, run into.

en·con·trón/tro·na·zo m. crash, collision; (riña) quarrel, dispute.

en·co·pe·tar tr. to raise high —reflex. to put on airs, be conceited.

en·cor·do·nar tr. to bind with cord.

en·co·rra·lar tr. to corral, pen.

en·cor·ti·nar tr. to provide with curtains.

en·cor·va·du·ra f./**mien·to** m. bend, curve.

en·cor·var tr. to bend, curve —reflex. to stoop, bend down; (inclinarse) to lean toward, be partial to.

en·cos·trar tr. to cover with a crust —intr. & reflex. to form a crust.

en·cres·par tr. to curl; (erizar) to make (one's hair) stand on end —reflex. to curl; (erizarse) to stand on end; (enredarse) to become complicated; (enardecerse) to become agitated.

en·cru·ci·ja·da f. crossroads, intersection; (emboscada) ambush, snare.

en·cua·der·na·ción f. bookbinding; (taller) bindery.

en·cua·der·na·dor, ·ra m.f. bookbinder.

en·cua·der·nar tr. to bind.

en·cua·drar tr. to frame; (encajar) to fit in, insert; (rodear) to surround, enclose.

en·cu·bier·to, a I. see encubrir **II.** adj. hidden, concealed.

en·cu·bri·dor, ·ra m.f. accessory after the fact.

en·cu·brir §80 tr. to hide, conceal; (amparar un criminal) to harbor.

en·cuen·tre, tro see encontrar.

en·cuen·tro m. meeting, encounter; (choque) crash, collision; (oposición) clash, conflict; (hallazgo) find, discovery; SPORT. match, game; ARCHIT. joint ♦ **salir al e. de** (recibir) to go out to meet; (oponer) to oppose, confront.

en·cues·ta f. investigation, inquiry; (sondeo) survey, poll.

en·cum·bra·do, a adj. high, lofty.

en·cum·brar tr. to raise, lift; FIG. to exalt, honor —reflex. to put on airs, become haughty; (elevarse mucho) to tower, rise.

en·cur·de·lar·se reflex. COLL. to get drunk.

en·cur·ti·do m. pickled fruit or vegetable.

en·cur·tir tr. to pickle, preserve.

en·de adv. ♦ **por e.** therefore, consequently.

en·de·ble adj. weak, flimsy.

en·dé·mi·co, a adj. endemic.

en·de·mo·nia·do, a I. adj. possessed; FIG. devilish, fiendish **II.** m.f. person possessed.

en·den·te·cer §17 intr. to teethe, cut teeth.

en·de·re·zar §04 tr. to straighten; (poner vertical) to set or stand up straight; (encaminar) to direct, guide; (enmendar) to correct, rectify —intr. to go straight to —reflex. to become straight; (ponerse vertical) to stand up straight.

en·deu·dar·se reflex. to fall into debt, become indebted.

en·dia·bla·do, a adj. devilish, diabolical; (feísimo) hideous, repulsive.

en·di·bia f. endive.

en·dil·gar §47 tr. COLL. to send off, dispatch; (encajar) to foist or palm off.

en·dio·sar tr. to deify —reflex. to become vain; (enajenarse) to become preoccupied.

en·do·min·gar·se §47 reflex. to dress up.

en·do·sa·ble adj. endorsable.

en·do·san·te m.f. endorser.

en·do·sar tr. to endorse; (encajar) to palm off.

en·do·so m. endorsement.

en·do·ve·no·so, a adj. intravenous.

en·dul·zar §04 tr. to sweeten; (suavizar) to soften, ease.

en·du·re·cer §17 tr. to harden; (robustecer) to toughen (up), make hardy —reflex. to harden; (robustecerse) to become tough or hardy; (encruelecerse) to become hardhearted or cruel.

e·ne·bro m. juniper.

e·ne·mi·go, a m.f. enemy, adversary —f. enmity.

e·ne·mis·tad f. animosity, enmity.

e·ne·mis·tar tr. to antagonize —reflex. to become enemies.

e·ner·gí·a f. energy; (vigor) vitality, vigor; (eficacia) efficacy, effectiveness; (ánimo) spirit.

e·nér·gi·co, a adj. energetic.

e·ne·ro m. January.

e·ner·va·ción f./**mien·to** m. enervation.

e·ner·var tr. to enervate, weaken.

e·né·si·mo, a adj. nth, umpteenth.

en·fa·da·di·zo, a adj. touchy, irritable.

en·fa·dar tr. to anger, annoy —reflex. to get angry or annoyed.

en·fa·do m. annoyance, anger.

en·fa·jar tr. to girdle.

en·fan·gar §47 tr. to cover with mud —reflex. (ensuciarse) to become muddy; COLL. to get involved in dirty business.

en·far·dar tr. to pack, bale.

én·fa·sis m. emphasis.

en·fá·ti·co, a adj. emphatic.

en·fer·mar intr. to get sick, become sick —tr. to make ill; (debilitar) to weaken.

en·fer·me·dad f. illness, sickness.

en·fer·me·rí·a f. infirmary.

en·fer·me·ro, a m.f. nurse.

en·fer·mi·zo, a adj. sickly, unhealthy.

en·fer·mo, a adj. & m.f. sick (person).

en·fer·vo·ri·zar §04 tr. to enliven, enthuse; (animar) to encourage.

en·fie·re·cer·se §17 reflex. to become furious.

en·fi·lar tr. to line up, put in line; (enhebrar) to thread, string; (apuntar) to direct, point; (seguir) to go down or along.

en·fi·se·ma m. emphysema.

en·fla·que·cer §17 tr. to make thin; (debilitar) to weaken, debilitate —intr. to grow thin, lose weight; (desanimarse) to weaken, lose heart.

en·fo·car §70 tr. to focus.

en·fo·que m. focus.

en·fren·tar tr. to bring or put face to face —intr. to face —reflex. to confront, face.

en·fren·te adv. facing, opposite; (delante) in front.

en·fria·mien·to m. cooling; MED. chill, cold.

en·friar §30 tr. to cool; COLL. to kill —intr. to cool, become cold —reflex. to be cold; (contraer un catarro) to catch a cold.

en·fun·dar tr. to put in a case, to sheathe.

en·fu·re·cer §17 tr. to madden, infuriate —reflex. to become furious, lose one's temper.

en·fu·re·ci·mien·to m. rage, fury.

en·ga·la·nar tr. to adorn, decorate; (vestir) to dress up, deck out —reflex. to adorn oneself, deck oneself out.

en·ga·llar·se reflex. to put on airs.

en·gan·char tr. to hook; (comprometer) to wheedle, persuade; MIL. to enlist, recruit

—reflex. to get caught *or* hooked up; MIL. to enlist.

en·gan·che m. *(acción)* hook (up); *(gancho)* hook; *(acoplamiento)* coupling; MIL. enlistment, recruitment.

en·ga·ña·bo·bos m.f.inv. COLL. cheat, swindler —m. fraud, swindle.

en·ga·ña·di·zo, a adj. gullible, credulous.

en·ga·ña·dor, ·ra I. adj. deceiving, deceptive **II.** m.f. deceiver, trickster.

en·ga·ñar tr. to deceive, trick; *(distraer)* to ward *or* stave off; *(pasar)* to kill, while away —intr. to be deceptive *or* misleading —reflex. to deceive oneself; *(equivocarse)* to be mistaken *or* wrong.

en·ga·ñi·f(l)a f. COLL. trick, swindle.

en·ga·ño m. *(equivocación)* error, mistake; *(trampa)* deception, trick; *(estafa)* swindle, fraud.

en·ga·ño·so, a adj. *(burlador)* deceiving, tricking; *(deshonesto)* dishonest, deceitful; *(mentiroso)* misleading, wrong.

en·gar·ce m. stringing, threading; *(encadenamiento)* linking, joining; JEWEL. setting.

en·gar·zar §04 tr. to string, thread; *(engastar)* to set, mount; *(rizar)* to curl; *(encadenar)* to link, join.

en·gas·ta·dor, ·ra I adj. setting **II.** m.f. setter, mounter.

en·gas·tar tr. JEWEL. to set, mount.

en·gas·te m. setting, mounting.

en·ga·tu·sa·dor, ·ra COLL. **I.** adj. coaxing, cajoling **II.** m.f. wheedler.

en·ga·tu·sar tr. COLL. to cajole, coax.

en·gen·drar tr. to engender.

en·gen·dro m. fetus; *(monstruo)* monster, freak.

en·glo·bar tr. to include, comprise.

en·go·la·do, a adj. presumptuous, arrogant.

en·go·lle·ta·do, a adj. COLL. conceited, proud.

en·go·lle·tar·se reflex. to become conceited.

en·go·lo·si·nar tr. to entice, tempt —reflex. to develop a taste (for), take a liking (to).

en·go·ma·do, a adj. gummy, gluey.

en·go·mar tr. to glue, gum.

en·go·mi·nar tr. to put on hair cream.

en·gor·dar tr. to fatten —intr. to get fat; *(hacerse rico)* to get rich.

en·gor·de m. fattening.

en·go·rro m. obstacle, impediment.

en·go·rro·so, a adj. annoying, troublesome.

en·goz·nar tr. to hinge.

en·gra·na·je m. MECH. gear; *(acción)* engaging, meshing; COLL. connection, link.

en·gra·nar intr. MECH. to mesh, engage; *(enlazar)* to connect, link.

en·gran·de·cer §17 tr. to augment, increase; *(alabar)* to laud, praise; *(elevar)* to enhance, heighten; *(exagerar)* to exaggerate —reflex. to become exalted; *(elevarse)* to rise, be promoted.

en·gra·pa·do·ra f. stapler.

en·gra·par tr. to clamp, cramp.

en·gra·sa·do m. lubrication, lubricant.

en·gra·sa·dor, ·ra I. adj. greasing, lubricating **II.** m. grease gun.

en·gra·sar tr. to grease; *(aceitar)* to oil; *(fertilizar)* to spread with manure.

en·gra·se/sa·mien·to m. lubrication, lubricant.

en·gre·í·do, a adj. conceited, arrogant; AMER. spoiled.

en·grei·mien·to m. pride, haughtiness.

en·gre·ír §58 tr. to make vain *or* conceited; AMER. *(mimar)* to spoil, pamper —reflex. to become vain *or* conceited.

en·gri·llar tr. to put in irons, shackle; *(sujetar)* to bring under control, subdue.

en·gro·sar §19 tr. to make thick, thicken; *(aumentar)* to increase, swell —intr. to get fat, put on weight; *(crecer)* to grow.

en·gru·do m. paste.

en·guir·nal·dar tr. to decorate with garlands.

en·gu·llir §13 tr. to gulp down, gobble.

en·ha·ci·nar tr. to pile, heap.

en·ha·ri·nar tr. to flour, coat with flour.

en·he·bi·llar tr. to put a buckle on.

en·he·brar tr. to thread, string; FIG. to link, connect.

en·hes·tar §49 tr. to raise, lift; *(poner derecho)* to erect, set upright —reflex. to be raised *or* lifted; *(ponerse derecho)* to stand upright.

en·hies·to, a I. see **enhestar II.** adj. upright, erect.

en·hi·lar tr. to string, thread; *(ordenar)* to order, arrange; *(dirigir)* to direct, guide —intr. to set out for, make for.

en·ho·ra·bue·na I. f. congratulations **II.** adv. luckily, fortunately; *(con mucho gusto)* welcome, with pleasure.

en·hor·nar tr. to put in an oven.

e·nig·ma m. enigma, riddle.

e·nig·má·ti·co, a adj. enigmatic(al).

en·ja·bo·nar tr. to soap, wash with soap; *(adular)* to soft-soap, flatter; *(reprender)* to scold, reprimand.

en·ja·e·zar §04 tr. to harness, saddle.

en·jam·brar tr. to (collect into a) hive —intr. to swarm; FIG. to multiply, abound.

en·jam·bre m. swarm; FIG. crowd, throng.

en·jau·lar tr. to cage, put in a cage; *(encarcelar)* to jail.

en·jo·yar tr. to adorn *or* set with jewels; *(embellecer)* to embellish, beautify.

en·jua·ga·dien·tes m. COLL. mouthwash.

en·jua·gar §47 tr. & reflex. to rinse.

en·jua·gue/ga·to·rio m. rinse, rinsing water; *(recipiente)* washbowl, rinsing cup; *(estratagema)* scheme, plot.

en·ju·ga·ma·nos m.inv. AMER. towel.

en·ju·gar §47 tr. to dry; *(cancelar)* to wipe out, settle —reflex. to wipe dry; *(adelgazarse)* to grow thin *or* lean.

en·jui·cia·mien·to m. judgment, judging; *(proceso)* trial, prosecution; *(pleito)* lawsuit.

en·jui·ciar tr. *(juzgar)* to judge, examine; *(instruir una causa)* to institute legal proceedings against; *(sujetar a juicio)* to indict, prosecute.

en·jun·dia f. grease, fat; *(substancia)* essence, substance; *(vigor)* strength, vitality; *(carácter)* character, personality.

en·ju·to, a I. adj. dry; *(delgado)* skinny, lean **II.** m.pl. *(tascos)* brushwood, kindling; *(tapas)* snacks, tidbits.

en·la·ce m. connection, link; *(casamiento)* marriage, matrimony; *(parentesco)* tie, bond; *(intermediario)* intermediary, liaison; *(empalme de vías)* junction, crossing.

en·la·dri·lla·do m. brick pavement.

en·la·dri·llar tr. to pave with bricks.

en·la·na·do, a adj. covered with wool.

en·lar·dar tr. to lard, baste.

en·la·tar tr. to can, put in cans.

en·la·za·dor, ·ra I. adj. linking, connective **II.** m.f. binder, connector.

en·la·zar §04 tr. to lace, interlace; *(trabar)* to link, connect; *(agarrar)* to lasso, rope —intr. RAIL. to connect —reflex. to become connected; *(casarse)* to marry, get married; *(contraer parentesco)* to become related by marriage.

en·le·jiar §30 tr. to bleach, steep in lye.

en·llan·tar tr. to rim or shoe.

en·lo·da·du·ra f./**mien·to** m. muddying.

en·lo·dar tr. to muddy; FIG. to besmirch, stain —reflex. to become muddy.

en·lo·que·ce·dor, ·ra adj. maddening.

en·lo·que·cer §17 tr. to drive mad or insane; *(excitar)* to excite, drive crazy —intr. & reflex. to go insane or crazy; *(trastornarse)* to get excited, go crazy.

en·lo·que·ci·mien·to m. madness, insanity.

en·lo·sa·do m. tiled floor.

en·lo·sa·dor m. tiler, tile layer.

en·lo·sar tr. to tile, pave with tiles.

en·lo·zar §04 tr. AMER. to coat with enamel.

en·lu·ci·do, a I. adj. plastered **II.** m. plaster, coat of plaster.

en·lu·ci·dor m. *(de paredes)* plasterer; *(de metales)* polisher.

en·lu·cir §44 tr. to plaster.

en·lu·ta·do, a adj. in mourning.

en·lu·tar tr. *(cubrir de luto)* to put in mourning; *(poner de luto)* to bereave, sadden; *(obscurecer)* to darken, make gloomy —reflex. to go into mourning; *(obscurecerse)* to get dark or gloomy.

en·ma·de·ra·do/mien·to m. timbering.

en·ma·de·rar tr. to plank, timber.

en·ma·le·cer·se §17/**zar·se** §04 reflex. AMER. to become overgrown with weeds.

en·man·gar §47 tr. to put a handle or haft on.

en·man·tar tr. to cover with a blanket —reflex. to become melancholy or sad.

en·ma·ra·ña·mien·to m. tangle, confusion.

en·ma·ra·ñar tr. to entangle, snarl; *(confundir)* to muddle, confuse —reflex. to become tangled; *(confundirse)* to become muddled, METEOROL. to become cloudy or overcast.

en·ma·rar·se reflex. to sail the high seas.

en·mar·car §70 tr. to frame.

en·ma·ri·dar intr. & reflex. to marry, take a husband.

en·ma·ri·lle·cer·se §17 reflex. to turn yellow.

en·ma·ro·mar tr. to tie with a rope, rope.

en·mas·ca·ra·do, a m.f. masked person.

en·mas·ca·rar tr. to mask; *(disfrazar)* to conceal, disguise —reflex. to put on a mask.

en·ma·si·llar tr. to putty, caulk.

en·men·da·ble adj. amendable, rectifiable.

en·men·da·ción f. correction, amendment.

en·men·dar §49 tr. to correct, amend; *(resarcir)* to make amends for, compensate —reflex. to mend one's ways.

en·mien·da f. amendment; *(reparo)* reparation, compensation.

en·mien·de, do see enmendar.

en·mo·he·cer §17 tr. & reflex. to make moldy; *(metales)* to rust.

en·mo·he·ci·mien·to m. molding, mildewing; *(de metales)* rusting.

en·mor·da·zar §04 tr. to gag, muzzle.

en·mu·de·cer §17 tr. to silence, hush —intr. to be silent, keep quiet.

en·mu·gre·cer §17/**grar** §04 tr. to soil, dirty —re-

flex. to become soiled or dirty.

en·ne·gre·cer §17 tr. to blacken; *(obscurecer)* to darken —reflex. to turn black; *(obscurecerse)* to darken.

en·ne·gre·ci·mien·to m. blackening, darkening.

en·no·ble·cer §17 tr. to ennoble.

e·no·ja·di·zo, a adj. quick-tempered, touchy.

e·no·jar tr. to anger, make angry —reflex. to become angry.

e·no·jo m. anger; *(molestia)* bother, annoyance.

e·no·jo·so, a adj. bothersome, annoying.

e·no·lo·gí·a f. oenology

e·nó·lo·go, a I. adj. oenological **II.** m.f. oenologist.

e·nor·gu·lle·cer §17 tr. to make proud, fill with pride —reflex. to be proud, pride oneself.

e·nor·me adj. enormous, huge.

e·nor·me·men·te adv. enormously, extremely.

e·nor·mi·dad f. enormity, hugeness.

en·qui·ciar tr. to hang.

en·rai·zar §06 intr. to take root.

en·ra·le·cer §17 intr. to get thin.

en·ra·ma·da f. bower, arbor.

en·ra·mar tr. to embower, interweave; *(adornar)* to decorate with branches —intr. to put out branches.

en·ran·ciar tr. & reflex. to spoil.

en·ra·re·cer §17 tr. *(el aire)* to thin, rarefy; *(hacer escaso)* to make rare or scarce —intr. & reflex. to become rare or scarce.

en·ra·re·ci·mien·to m. thinning, rarefying; *(escasez)* scarcity.

en·ra·sar tr. CONSTR. to level, make flush; *(allanar)* to smooth, plane —intr. to be at the same level.

en·re·da·de·ra I. adj. climbing, trailing **II.** f. climbing plant, creeper.

en·re·da·dor, ·ra I. adj. gossip **II.** m.f. gossip, busybody.

en·re·dar tr. *(atrapar)* to net; *(tender)* to lay, set; *(enmarañar)* to tangle up, snarl; *(enemistar)* to cause trouble between; *(embrollar)* to complicate, confuse; *(comprometer)* to involve, embroil —intr. to get into mischief, cause trouble —reflex. to get tangled up, become snarled; *(complicarse)* to become complicated or confused; *(comprometerse)* to become involved, COLL. *(amancebarse)* to get involved, have an affair.

en·re·do m. *(maraña)* tangle, snarl; *(engaño)* deceit; *(lío)* mess, muddle; *(trama)* plot ♦ pl. COLL. things, stuff.

en·re·ja·do m. railings; *(celosía)* latticework, trellis.

en·re·jar tr. to surround with railings; *(una ventana)* to put latticework on; *(apilar tablas)* to lay crosswise.

en·re·ve·sa·do, a adj. intricate, complicated; *(travieso)* mischievous, unruly.

en·rie·lar tr. METAL. to make into ingots or bars; *(echar en la rielera)* to cast into ingot molds; AMER. *(poner rieles)* to put rails on; *(encarrilar)* to put on rails.

en·ri·que·cer §17 tr. to enrich, make wealthy; *(adornar)* to adorn, embellish —intr. & reflex. to get rich, become wealthy.

en·ris·car §70 tr. to raise, lift.

en·ris·trar¹ tr. to string.

en·ris·trar² tr. *(ir derecho hacia)* to go straight toward; *(acertar una cosa difícil)* to overcome.

en·ro·je·cer §17 tr. *(con fuego)* to make red-hot; *(dar color rojo)* to redden, make red —intr. to blush, turn red —reflex. *(por fuego)* to turn red-hot; *(ponerse rojo)* to redden, turn red; *(ruborizarse)* to blush, turn red.

en·ro·je·ci·mien·to m. reddening, blush.

en·ro·lar tr. to sign up, recruit.

en·ro·llar tr. to roll or wind up; *(enredar)* to entangle, involve —reflex. to be rolled or wound up; COLL. to get involved.

en·ron·que·cer §17 tr. make hoarse —reflex. to become hoarse.

en·ro·ñar tr. & reflex. to rust.

en·ros·ca·du·ra f. coil, twist.

en·ros·car §70 tr. to coil, twist; *(atornillar)* to screw in.

en·ru·lar tr. AMER. to curl.

en·sa·la·da f. CUL. salad; FIG. hodgepodge.

en·sa·la·de·ra f. salad bowl.

en·sal·mis·ta m.f. quack, charlatan.

en·sa·lo·brar·se reflex. to become salty.

en·sal·za·mien·to m. praise, exaltation.

en·sal·zar §04 tr. to exalt, glorify.

en·sam·bla·dor m. joiner.

en·sam·bla·du·ra f./**bla·je/ble** m. CARP. joint, connection.

en·sam·blar tr. to join, connect.

en·san·cha·mien·to m. expansion, extension.

en·san·char tr. to widen, expand; *(extender)* to stretch, extend —intr. & reflex. *(envanecerse)* to get puffed up or conceited; *(engrandecerse)* to expand, broaden.

en·san·che m. extension, expansion; *(barrio nuevo)* suburban development.

en·san·gren·tar §49 tr. *(manchar)* to stain with blood; *(derramar)* to shed blood —reflex. *(mancharse)* to become blood-stained; *(encolerizarse)* to fly into a rage, become furious.

en·sa·ña·mien·to m. cruelty, brutality.

en·sa·ñar tr. to enrage, infuriate —reflex. to be cruel or merciless.

en·sar·tar tr. to string, thread; *(atravesar)* to run through, pierce; *(decir tonterías)* to rattle off —reflex. AMER. to get stuck with.

en·sa·ya·dor, ·ra m.f. assayer.

en·sa·yar tr. to test, try out; THEAT. to rehearse, practice; *(adiestrar)* to train, teach; *(intentar)* to try or attempt —reflex. to practice, rehearse.

en·sa·yis·ta m.f. essayist.

en·sa·yo m. test, trial; *(ejercicio)* exercise, practice; *(intento)* attempt; LIT. essay; METAL. assay, assaying; THEAT. rehearsal.

en·se·gui·da or **en seguida** adv. immediately, at once.

en·se·na·da f. cove, inlet.

en·se·ña f. badge, emblem.

en·se·ñan·za f. *(arte)* teaching; *(instrucción)* training; *(educación)* education; *(lección)* lesson; RELIG. doctrine, teaching.

en·se·ñar tr. to teach; *(indicar)* to indicate, point out; *(mostrar)* to show —reflex. to accustom oneself to, get used to.

en·se·ño·re·ar·se reflex. to take over, take possession.

en·se·res m.pl. equipment, accouterments ♦ **e. domésticos** household goods.

en·si·llar tr. to saddle, put a saddle on.

en·si·mis·ma·do, a adj. pensive, absorbed in thought; AMER. *(engreído)* conceited, vain.

en·si·mis·ma·mien·to m. pensiveness, absorption; AMER. *(engreimiento)* conceit, vanity.

en·si·mis·mar·se reflex. to be or become absorbed in thought; AMER. *(engreírse)* to become conceited or vain.

en·so·ber·be·cer §17 tr. to make proud or arrogant —reflex. to become proud or arrogant; MARIT. to become rough.

en·som·bre·cer §17 tr. to darken; *(eclipsar)* to overshadow, eclipse —reflex. to darken, get dark; *(entristecerse)* to become sad.

en·so·par tr. *(empapar)* to soak, drench; *(el pan)* to dip, dunk —reflex. to get soaked.

en·sor·de·ce·dor, ·ra adj. deafening.

en·sor·de·cer §17 tr. to make deaf, deafen; *(amortiguar)* to muffle —intr. to go or become deaf; *(enmudecer)* to pretend not to hear.

en·sor·de·ci·mien·to m. deafness.

en·sor·ti·jar tr. *(rizar)* to curl, put curls into; *(enrollar)* to coil —reflex. to become curly.

en·su·ciar tr. to dirty, soil; *(estropear)* to make a mess of, mess up; *(desacreditar)* to stain, besmirch —reflex. to become dirty or soiled; *(desacreditar)* to discredit oneself ♦ **e. por dinero** to accept or take bribes.

en·sue·ño m. dream; *(fantasía)* fantasy, illusion.

en·ta·bla·do m. floor, flooring.

en·ta·blar tr. to board (up); *(empezar)* to begin, start; MED. to splint, put in a splint; LAW to bring, file ♦ **e. amistad** to become friends —intr. AMER. to tie, draw —reflex. to begin, start.

en·ta·bli·llar tr. to splint, put in a splint.

en·ta·llar tr. to carve, sculpture; *(grabar)* to engrave; CARP. to notch, groove; SEW. to tailor, adjust —intr. to fit well.

en·ta·pi·zar §04 tr. *(paredes)* to tapestry, hang with tapestries; *(muebles)* to upholster; *(cubrir)* to grow over, cover.

en·ta·ri·ma·do m. parquet, parquetry.

en·ta·ri·mar tr. to parquet.

en·te m. entity, being; *(sujeto)* character; COM. firm, company ♦ **e. de razón** imaginary being • **e. de ficción** fictional character.

en·ten·de·de·ras f.pl. brains, intelligence.

en·ten·de·dor, ·ra I. adj. expert; *(listo)* clever, sharp II. m.f. one who understands; *(experto)* expert.

en·ten·der §50 I. tr. to understand, comprehend; *(creer)* to believe, think; *(querer)* to mean, intend —intr. ♦ **e. en** or **de** *(tener aptitud)* to be good at; *(ocuparse)* to deal with; *(tener autoridad)* to be in charge of ♦ **dar a e.** to insinuate, hint at • **e. mal** to misunderstand —reflex. to be understood; *(interpretarse)* to be meant; *(comprenderse a sí mismo)* to understand oneself; *(tener motivo)* to have one's reasons; *(ponerse de acuerdo)* to come to an agreement; *(llevarse bien)* to get along; *(tener relaciones amorosas)* to have an affair II. m. opinion.

en·ten·di·do, a I. adj. expert, informed; *(inteligente)* intelligent, smart ♦ **no darse por e.** to pretend not to understand II. m.f. expert, connoisseur.

en·ten·di·mien·to m. understanding, comprehension; *(juicio)* judgment, sense; *(inteligencia)* intelligence, intelligence.

en·te·ra·do, a adj. *(informado)* informed, aware; *(bien informado)* well-informed ♦ **darse por e. de** to be well aware of • **estar e.** to be informed, know.

en·te·rar tr. *(informar)* to inform, make aware;

AMER. to pay; S. AMER. to complete, make up —reflex. to find out, become aware.

en·te·re·za f. (cualidad) integrity, uprightness; (fortaleza) fortitude; (severidad) strictness.

en·te·ri·zo, a adj. entire, whole.

en·ter·ne·ce·dor, ·ra adj. touching, moving.

en·ter·ne·cer §17 tr. to soften, make tender; (conmover) to touch, move —reflex. (conmoverse) to be touched or moved; (ceder) to relent.

en·te·ro, a I. adj. entire, complete; (robusto) robust, healthy; (justo) just, fair; (firme) steadfast, resolute; MATH. whole, integral ♦ **por e.** entirely, completely **II.** m. integer, whole number; FIN. point; AMER. payment.

en·te·rrar §49 tr. to bury; (clavar) to sink or drive in; (sobrevivir) to outlive, survive —reflex. to withdraw, bury oneself.

en·ti·biar tr. to make lukewarm; (templar) to temper, moderate —reflex. to become lukewarm; (moderar) to relax, cool down.

en·ti·dad f. entity; (organización) organization; COM. company, concern.

en·tien·da, do see entender.

en·tie·rre, rro see enterrar.

en·tie·rro m. burial, interment; (funerales) funeral; (sepulcro) tomb, grave.

en·tin·ta·do m. inking.

en·tin·tar tr. PRINT. to ink; (teñir) to dye, tint.

en·tol·dar tr. to put an awning over; (tapizar) to cover with a tapestry —reflex. to put on airs; METEOROL. to become overcast, cloud over.

en·to·mo·lo·gí·a f. entomology.

en·to·mó·lo·go m. f. entomologist.

en·to·na·ción f. intonation; (arrogancia) arrogance, conceit.

en·to·nar tr. (cantar) to sing in tune; (dar cierto tono) to modulate; (empezar a cantar) to intone —intr. (cantar) to sing in tune; (empezar a cantar) to intone; (armonizar) to harmonize; PAINT. to match (colors) —reflex. to be arrogant, put on airs.

en·ton·ces adv. (en aquel momento) then, at that time; (en tal caso) then, in that case ♦ **desde e.** since then, from then on • **en aquel e. or por e.** around that time, at that time • **hasta e.** till then.

en·tor·nar tr. to half-close, leave ajar.

en·tor·no m. environment.

en·tor·pe·cer §17 tr. to make torpid or slow; (embrutecer) to dull, deaden; (obstaculizar) to hamper, obstruct.

en·tra·da f. entry, entrance; (vestíbulo) vestibule, entrance hall; (ingreso) admission; (privilegio) admittance, entrée; (billete) admission ticket; (taquilla) gate, receipts; (desembolso) deposit, down payment; COM. entry; CUL. entrée; MECH. intake; COMPUT., ELEC., input; MIL. invasion, encroachment ♦ **de e.** right away, from the start • **tener e.** to be welcome ♦ pl. FIN. income, receipts.

en·tra·ma·do m. framework.

en·tra·mar tr. to build a frame for.

en·tram·par tr. to trap, snare; (engañar) to deceive, trick; (enredar) to entangle, make a mess of; (gravar con deudas) to burden with debts —reflex. COLL. to get into debt.

en·tran·te adj. (próximo) next, coming; (nuevo) new, incoming; ARCHIT. recessed.

en·tra·ña f. entrails, innards; (esencia) core, essence; (centro) center, middle; (voluntad)

will; (genio) disposition, nature ♦ pl. bowels, innermost part ♦ **arrancar las e. a alguien** to break someone's heart • **dar hasta las e.** to give one's all • **sin e.** heartless, pitiless.

en·tra·ña·ble adj. intimate, close; (querido) beloved, dear.

en·tra·ñar tr. (enterrar) to bury deep; (llevar en sí) to carry within; (acarrear) to entail —reflex. to become deeply attached.

en·trar intr. to enter, come in; (ser admitido) to be admitted; (ingresar) to join; (encajar) to go, fit; (desaguar) to flow; (formar parte de) to enter, be part; (ser contado) to be included or counted; (emplearse) to go, be used; (empezar) to begin, come in; (atacar) to attack, charge ♦ **e. a** to begin to • **e. en** to enter, go in; (abrazar) to take up, adopt • **no entrarle a uno** (desagradar) to dislike; (no comprender) to be unable to get —tr. (meter) to bring or put inside; (introducir) to introduce, bring in; (invadir) to invade, attack; (influir) to influence, get at —reflex. to get in, sneak in.

en·tre prep. between; (en el número de) among, amongst; (en) in <e. paréntesis in parentheses>; to <pensé e. mí I thought to myself> ♦ **de e.** out of, from among • **e. tanto** meanwhile • **por e.** through.

en·tre·a·bier·to, a I. see entreabrir **II.** adj. half-open, ajar.

en·tre·a·brir §80 tr. to open halfway, set ajar —reflex. to be open halfway, be ajar.

en·tre·ac·to m. intermission, entr'acte.

en·tre·ca·no, a adj. graying.

en·tre·ca·var tr. to dig shallowly.

en·tre·ce·jo m. ANAT. space between the eyebrows; (ceño) frown ♦ **arrugar or fruncir el e.** to frown.

en·tre·ce·rrar §49 tr. to half-close, leave ajar.

en·tre·co·mi·llar tr. to put in quotation marks.

en·tre·cor·tar tr. to cut into, cut partially; (interrumpir) to interrupt, cut off.

en·tre·cru·za·do, a adj. interwoven.

en·tre·cru·zar §04 tr. to intercross, interweave —reflex. to be intercrossed, be interwoven.

en·tre·di·cho m. prohibition, interdiction; RELIG. interdict; ♦ **estar en e.** to be in question.

en·tre·dós m. dresser, low cupboard; SEW. insert, panel.

en·tre·fi·no, a adj. of medium quality.

en·tre·ga f. delivery; (rendición) handing over.

en·tre·gar §47 tr. (dar) to deliver; (poner en manos) to hand over or in; (traicionar) to betray —reflex. (rendirse) to surrender, submit; (abandonarse) to abandon oneself (a to).

en·tre·la·zar §04 tr. to interlace, interweave.

en·tre·me·dias adv. (entre dos cosas) in between, halfway; (mientras tanto) in the meantime, meanwhile ♦ **e. de** between, among.

en·tre·més¹ m. appetizer; hors d'oeuvre.

en·tre·més² m. THEAT. entr'acte, short play.

en·tre·me·ter tr. to insert, put or place in between —reflex. (injerirse) to meddle, interfere; (una conversación) to interrupt, butt in.

en·tre·me·ti·do, a I. adj. meddlesome, interfering **II.** m.f. meddler, busybody.

en·tre·mez·clar tr. to intermingle.

en·tre·na·dor, ·ra m.f. trainer, coach.

en·tre·na·mien·to m. training, coaching.

en·tre·nar tr. & reflex. to train.

en·tre·o·ír §45 tr. to half-hear, hear partially.

en·tre·pier·na(s) f.(pl.) crotch.

en·tre·pi·so m. mezzanine.

en·tre·sa·car §70 tr. to pick out, select.
en·tre·sue·lo m. mezzanine.
en·tre·ta·llar tr. to engrave, carve; *(detener)* to hinder, impede —reflex. to fit together.
en·tre·tan·to I. adv. meanwhile, in the meantime **II.** m. meantime, meanwhile.
en·tre·te·cho m. AMER. attic, loft.
en·tre·te·jer tr. to interweave, interlace.
en·tre·te·la f. SEW. interlining.
en·tre·te·lar tr. to interline.
en·tre·te·ner §69 tr. to entertain, amuse; *(ocupar)* to occupy, keep busy; *(detener)* to detain, delay —reflex. *(detenerse)* to dally, dawdle; *(divertirse)* to be entertained *or* amused.
en·tre·te·ni·do, a adj. amusing, entertaining.
en·tre·te·ni·mien·to m. amusement, entertainment; *(detenimiento)* detainment, delay.
en·tre·tiem·po m. between-season.
en·tre·tie·ne, tuviera, tuvo see **entretener**.
en·tre·ver §77 tr. to half-see, see partially; *(adivinar)* to guess, surmise.
en·tre·ve·rar tr. to intermingle, mix.
en·tre·ve·ro m. confusion, jumble.
en·tre·ví, vimos see **entrever**.
en·tre·vis·ta f. meeting, conference; JOURN. interview.
en·tre·vis·ta·dor, ra m.f. interviewer.
en·tre·vis·tar tr. to interview —reflex. to hold an interview *or* a meeting.
en·tri·pa·do, a I. adj. intestinal **II.** m. COLL. gnawing resentment.
en·tris·te·cer §17 tr. to sadden, grieve —reflex. to become sad *or* grieved.
en·tro·me·ter tr. & reflex. var. of **entremeter**.
en·trom·par·se reflex. COLL. to get drunk *or* intoxicated; AMER. to get angry.
en·tro·ni·zar §04 tr. to enthrone, put on the throne; *(ensalzar)* to revere, praise.
en·tu·ba·ción f./**mien·to** m. tubing.
en·tu·bar tr. to tube, insert a tube in.
en·tuer·to m. wrong, injustice.
en·tu·me·cer §17 tr. to (make) numb —reflex. to go *or* become numb; *(hincharse)* to swell.
en·tu·me·ci·mien·to m. numbness, torpor; *(crecida)* swelling, rise.
en·tur·biar tr. to cloud —reflex. to become clouded *or* cloudy.
en·tu·sias·mar tr. to enthuse —reflex. to become enthusiastic.
en·tu·sias·mo m. enthusiasm.
en·tu·sias·ta I. adj. enthusiastic **II.** m.f. enthusiast.
e·nu·me·ra·ción f. enumeration.
e·nu·me·rar tr. to enumerate.
e·nun·cia·ción f. enunciation, declaration.
e·nun·cia·do m. enunciation, statement.
e·nun·ciar tr. to enunciate, express clearly.
en·vai·nar tr. to sheathe; *(envolver)* to enclose.
en·va·len·to·nar tr. to encourage, embolden —reflex. to become bold.
en·va·ne·cer §17 tr. make vain *or* conceited —reflex. to become vain *or* conceited.
en·va·sa·dor, ra m.f. packer; *(embotellador)* bottler —m. large funnel.
en·va·sar tr. to pack, package; *(embotellar)* to bottle; *(beber)* to drink to excess; *(apuñalar)* to stab.
en·va·se m. packing, packaging; *(paquete)* package; *(botella)* bottle.
en·ve·je·cer §17 tr. to age, make old —intr. & reflex. to grow old, age.
en·ve·je·ci·mien·to m. aging, age.

en·ve·ne·nar tr. to poison.
en·ver·ga·du·ra f. wingspan, wingspread; FIG. importance, significance.
en·ver·gar §47 tr. to fasten.
en·vés m. other side, back.
en·ve·sa·do, a adj. showing the opposite side.
en·via·do m. envoy.
en·viar §30 tr. to send, dispatch; *(transmitir)* to convey, transmit ♦ **e. a uno a pasear** *or* **a paseo** COLL. to send someone packing.
en·vi·ciar tr. to corrupt, pervert —reflex. *(aficionarse)* to become addicted *(con, en* to); *(corromperse)* to become corrupt *or* perverted.
en·vi·dia f. envy.
en·vi·diar tr. to envy, be envious of.
en·vi·dio·so, a adj. & m.f. envious (person).
en·vi·le·cer §17 tr. & reflex. to degrade (oneself).
en·vi·le·ci·mien·to m. degradation.
en·ví·o m. sending, dispatch; *(transmisión)* conveyance, transmission; *(paquete)* package, parcel; *(dinero)* remittance; *(mercancías)* shipment, consignment.
en·vión m. push, shove.
en·vi·te m. bet; *(empujón)* push, shove; *(ofrecimiento)* offering ♦ **al primer e.** right off (the bat), from the outset *or* start.
en·viu·dar intr. to be widowed.
en·vol·to·rio m. bundle; *(cubierta)* wrapper.
en·vol·tu·ra f. cover, covering.
en·vol·ven·te adj. enveloping.
en·vol·ver §78 tr. *(cubrir)* to envelop, cover; *(empaquetar)* to pack, bundle up; *(vestir)* to swaddle; *(arrollar)* to wind; MIL. to surround; FIG. to involve, mix up; *(ocultar)* to enshroud —reflex. *(cubrirse)* to be covered; *(complicarse)* to become involved *or* mixed up; *(amancebarse)* to have an affair; *(luchar)* to fight.
en·vuel·to, a I. see **envolver II.** f.pl. swaddling clothes.
en·vuel·va, vo see **envolver**.
en·ye·sar tr. to plaster; MED. to set in plaster.
en·yu·gar §47/**yun·tar** tr. to yoke.
en·zar·zar §04 tr. to cover with brambles; *(malquistar)* to entangle, embroil —reflex. to get caught *or* entangled.
en·zi·ma f. enzyme.
e·ón m. eon.
¡e·pa! interj. AMER. *(¡hola!)* hey!, hello!; *(¡ea!)* come on!; *(¡cuidado!)* whoa!
e·pi·cen·tro m. epicenter.
é·pi·co, a adj. epic.
e·pi·cú·re·o, a adj. & m.f. epicurean.
e·pi·de·mia f. epidemic.
e·pi·dé·mi·co, a adj. epidemic.
e·pi·de·mio·lo·gí·a f. epidemiology.
e·pi·dér·mi·co, a adj. epidermal, epidermic.
e·pi·der·mis f.inv. epidermis, outer skin.
e·pi·glo·tis f.inv. epiglottis.
e·pí·gra·fe m. epigraph.
e·pi·lep·sia f. epilepsy.
e·pi·lép·ti·co, a adj. & m.f. epileptic.
e·pí·lo·go m. epilogue; *(resumen)* summary, compendium.
e·pis·co·pa·do m. episcopate.
e·pi·so·dio m. episode.
e·pis·te·mo·lo·gí·a f. epistemology.
e·pís·to·la f. epistle.
e·pi·ta·fio m. epitaph.
e·pi·te·lio m. epithelium.
e·pí·te·to m. epithet.
e·pí·to·me m. epitome, summary.

é·po·ca f. epoch, era; *(período)* time, period; GEOL. age ♦ **en aquella é.** at that time • **formar** *or* **hacer é.** to make history.

e·pó·ni·mo, a I. adj. eponymous, eponymic **II.** m. eponym.

e·po·pe·ya f. epic poem, epic.

e·qui·dad f. equity.

e·qui·dis·tan·cia f. equidistance.

e·qui·dis·tan·te adj. equidistant.

e·qui·lá·te·ro, a adj. equilateral.

e·qui·li·bra·do, a adj. *(ecuánime)* stable, well-balanced; *(sensato)* sensible, reasonable.

e·qui·li·brar tr. & reflex. to balance.

e·qui·li·brio m. equilibrium.

e·qui·li·bris·mo m. acrobatics; *(del volatinero)* tightrope walking.

e·qui·li·bris·ta m.f. acrobat; *(volatinero)* tightrope walker, funambulist.

e·qui·no, a adj. equine, horse.

e·qui·noc·cio m. equinox.

e·qui·pa·je m. luggage, baggage; MARIT. crew.

e·qui·par tr. to equip, outfit.

e·qui·pa·ra·ble adj. comparable *(con* to, with).

e·qui·pa·ra·ción f. comparison, comparing.

e·qui·pa·rar tr. to compare.

e·qui·po m. *(acción)* equipping, outfitting; *(equipamiento)* equipment, gear; SPORT. team; *(de trabajadores)* shift, crew ♦ **e. de primeros auxilios** first-aid kit.

e·qui·ta·ción f. riding, equitation.

e·qui·ta·ti·vo, a adj. equitable, fair.

e·qui·va·len·cia f. equivalence, equivalency.

e·qui·va·len·te adj. & m. equivalent.

e·qui·va·ler §74 intr. to be equivalent, equal.

e·qui·vo·ca·ción f. error, mistake.

e·qui·vo·ca·da·men·te adv. mistakenly.

e·qui·vo·ca·do, a adj. wrong, mistaken.

e·qui·vo·car §70 tr. to mistake —intr. to equivocate, lie —reflex. to be mistaken.

e·quí·vo·co, a I. adj. equivocal **II.** m. ambiguity; *(malentendido)* misunderstanding.

e·ra[1] f. era, age; *(período)* period, time.

e·ra[2] see **ser**[2].

e·ra·rio m. treasury.

er·bio m. erbium.

e·rec·ción f. erection.

e·rec·to, a adj. erect.

e·re·mi·ta m. hermit, eremite.

e·res see **ser**[2].

er·go conj. ergo, therefore.

er·gui·mien·to m. erection, raising up.

er·guir §31 tr. to raise, lift up —reflex. to straighten up; *(envanecerse)* to become vain *or* conceited.

e·rial adj. & m. untilled, uncultivated (land).

e·ri·gir §32 tr. to erect, build; *(fundar)* to found, establish —reflex. to set, establish oneself.

e·ri·za·do, a adj. bristly, spiky.

e·ri·zar §04 tr. to make stand on end, set on end —reflex. to stand on end.

e·ri·zo m. ZOOL. hedgehog; BOT. burr.

er·mi·ta·ño, a m.f. hermit —m. hermit crab.

e·ro·ga·ción f. distribution; AMER. donation.

e·ró·ge·no, a adj. erogenous.

e·ro·sión f. erosion.

e·ró·ti·co, a adj. erotic.

e·ro·tis·mo m. eroticism, erotism.

e·rra·bun·do, a adj. wandering, roving.

e·rra·di·ca·ción f. eradication.

e·rra·di·car §70 tr. to eradicate, root out; *(descuajar)* to uproot, tear up by the roots.

e·rra·do, a adj. wrong, mistaken.

e·rran·te adj. errant, wandering.

e·rrar §33 tr. *(no acertar)* to miss; *(faltar)* to fail (someone) —intr. *(vagar)* to wander, roam; *(equivocarse)* to be mistaken, make a mistake —reflex. to be mistaken, make a mistake.

e·rra·ta f. erratum.

e·rró·ne·o, a adj. erroneous, mistaken.

e·rror m. error, mistake.

e·ruc·tar intr. to burp, belch.

e·ruc·to m. burp, belch.

e·ru·di·ción f. erudition, learning.

e·ru·di·to, a adj. & m.f. erudite.

e·rup·ción f. eruption.

es see **ser**[2].

e·sa adj. see **ese, esa**.

é·sa pron. see **ése, ésa**.

es·bel·tez f. slenderness, svelteness.

es·bel·to, a adj. slender, svelte.

es·bo·zar §04 tr. to sketch, outline.

es·bo·zo m. sketch, outline.

es·ca·be·char tr. to pickle, marinate.

es·ca·be·che m. *(adobo)* marinade; *(pescado)* marinated fish salad; *(tinte)* hair dye.

es·ca·bel m. *(asiento)* stool, small seat; *(para los pies)* footstool.

es·ca·bro·so, a adj. *(desigual)* rough, rugged; *(áspero)* harsh, cruel; *(atrevido)* dirty, smutty.

es·ca·bu·llir·se §13 reflex. to escape.

es·ca·fan·dra f./**dro** m. diver's *or* diving suit.

es·ca·la f. scale; *(escalera de mano)* ladder, stepladder; *(gama)* range; MARIT. port of call; MIL. register, list; MUS. scale ♦ **e. móvil** sliding scale • **hacer e.** MARIT. to put in, call.

es·ca·la·fón m. list.

es·ca·lar tr. to scale, climb; *(robar)* to break in *or* into, burgle —intr. to rise, climb (by dubious means); MIL., POL. to escalate.

es·cal·da·du·ra f. scald, scalding.

es·cal·dar tr. to scald, burn; *(abrasar)* to make red hot —reflex. to chafe, become chafed.

es·ca·le·ra f. stairs, staircase; *(escalerilla)* ladder; *(de naipes)* straight ♦ **e. de caracol** winding staircase • **e. de mano** stepladder • **e. mecánica** *or* **automática** escalator.

es·ca·le·ri·lla f. stepladder; *(de naipes)* series of three cards; MARIT. gangway.

es·cal·far tr. to poach.

es·ca·li·na·ta f. flight of steps.

es·ca·lo·frí·o m. *(de miedo)* shiver, shudder; *(de fiebre)* chill, shiver.

es·ca·lón m. step, stair ♦ **en escalones** unevenly.

es·ca·lo·nar tr. *(colocar)* to space out; *(horas)* to stagger; AGR. to terrace.

es·ca·lo·pe m. cutlet, scaloppini.

es·cal·par tr. to scalp.

es·cal·pe·lo m. scalpel.

es·ca·ma f. scale.

es·ca·ma·du·ra f. scaling.

es·ca·mar tr. to scale.

es·ca·mo·so, a adj. scaly.

es·ca·mo·te·a·dor, ·ra I. adj. conjuring **II.** m.f. conjurer, magician; COLL. *(ladrón)* thief.

es·ca·mo·te·ar tr. to make disappear *or* vanish (by sleight of hand); COLL. *(robar)* to filch, steal; *(evitar)* to avoid, evade.

es·cam·pa·da f. clear spell.

es·cam·pa·do, a adj. clear, open.

es·cam·par tr. & intr. to clear (up).

es·can·ciar tr. to serve, pour —intr. to drink wine.

es·can·da·li·zar §04 tr. to scandalize, shock —intr. to make a fuss —reflex. to be shocked.

es·cán·da·lo m. scandal; (*alboroto*) uproar, ruckus ♦ armar un e. to make a scene.

es·can·da·lo·so, a adj. scandalous, shocking; (*alborotoso*) noisy, uproarious.

es·can·dio m. CHEM. scandium.

es·ca·pa·da f. (*huida*) escape, flight; (*aventura*) escapade.

es·ca·par intr. & reflex. to escape ♦ escaparse por un pelo COLL. to have a close call.

es·ca·pa·ra·te m. shop *or* display window; AMER. (*ropero*) wardrobe, closet.

es·ca·pa·to·ria f. escape, flight; COLL. (*pretexto*) excuse, pretext.

es·ca·pe m. escape, flight; (*de un reloj*) escapement; AUTO. exhaust (pipe).

es·ca·ra·ba·jo m. scarab, black beetle ♦ pl. COLL. scribbles, scrawls.

es·ca·ra·mu·za f. (*combate*) skirmish; (*argumento*) quarrel, dispute.

es·car·ba·dien·tes m.inv. toothpick.

es·car·bar tr. (*rascar*) to scrape, scratch; (*los dientes*) to pick; (*atizar*) to rake, poke; (*averiguar*) to poke around, investigate.

es·car·ce·os m.pl. wanderings, ramblings ♦ e. amorosos flirtation.

es·car·cha f. frost.

es·car·char intr. to become frosted —tr. to frost.

es·car·da f. weeding hoe.

es·car·dar tr. to weed (out).

es·ca·ri·fi·car §70 tr. to scarify.

es·car·la·ta adj. & f. scarlet.

es·car·la·ti·na f. scarlet fever.

es·car·me·nar tr. (*peinar*) to comb; (*castigar*) to punish, castigate; (*estafar*) to swindle little by little.

es·car·men·tar §49 tr. to chastise, teach a lesson to —intr. to learn one's lesson.

es·car·mien·to m. (*aviso*) warning, lesson; (*castigo*) punishment.

es·car·ne·cer §17 tr. to ridicule, mock.

es·car·nio m. ridicule, mocking.

es·ca·ro·la f. escarole.

es·car·pa·do, a adj. (*pendiente*) steep, sheer; (*escabroso*) craggy, rugged.

es·car·par tr. to rasp, scrape.

es·car·pe m. scarp, escarpment.

es·car·pia f. hook.

es·car·pín m. pump.

es·ca·sa·men·te adv. scarcely, just.

es·ca·se·ar tr. to skimp, give sparingly —intr. to become *or* be scarce.

es·ca·sez f. scarcity, lack; (*mezquindad*) stinginess; (*pobreza*) poverty, need.

es·ca·so, a adj. scarce, limited; (*mezquino*) miserly, stingy; (*falto*) scanty, insufficient.

es·ca·ti·mar tr. to skimp on, spare.

es·ca·to·lo·gí·a f. eschatology; (*de excrementos*) scatology.

es·ca·to·ló·gi·co, a adj. eschatological; (*excrementicio*) scatological.

es·ce·na f. scene; THEAT. stage; (*arte dramático*) theater, dramatic art ♦ poner en e. to stage, present.

es·ce·na·rio m. stage, scene.

es·ce·ni·fi·car §70 tr. to stage, dramatize.

es·ce·no·gra·fí·a f. scenery.

es·ce·nó·gra·fo, a m.f. set designer.

es·cép·ti·co, a I. adj. skeptical II. m.f. skeptic.

es·cin·dir tr. to divide, split —reflex. to split.

es·ci·sión f. division, split; MED. excision.

es·cla·re·cer §17 tr. to illuminate, light up; (*elucidar*) to clarify, elucidate; (*ennoblecer*) to ennoble —intr. to dawn.

es·cla·vis·ta adj. pro-slavery.

es·cla·vi·tud f. slavery.

es·cla·vi·zar §04 tr. to enslave.

es·cla·vo, a I. adj. enslaved II. m.f. slave —f. bracelet, bangle.

es·cle·ro·sis f.inv. sclerosis.

es·clu·sa f. lock, sluice; (*compuerta*) floodgate.

es·co·ba f. broom.

es·co·bar tr. to sweep.

es·co·bi·lla f. brush, small broom.

es·co·bi·llar tr. AMER. to brush.

es·co·bi·na f. sawdust; (*de metal*) filings.

es·co·cer §71 intr. to sting, smart —reflex. become chafed *or* irritated; (*sentirse*) to be hurt.

es·co·fi·na f. coarse file, rasp.

es·co·ger §34 tr. to choose, select.

es·co·gi·do, a adj. select, choice; (*elegido*) chosen, selected.

es·co·lar I. adj. scholastic, school II. m.f. pupil, student.

es·co·la·ri·dad f. education, schooling.

es·co·lás·ti·co, a adj. scholastic.

es·col·ta f. escort.

es·col·tar tr. to escort.

es·co·llar intr. to run aground.

es·co·lle·ra f. jetty, breakwater.

es·co·llo m. reef, rock; FIG. stumbling block.

es·com·brar tr. to sweep, clear.

es·com·bro m. rubble, debris; MIN. slag.

es·con·der tr. & reflex. to hide, conceal.

es·con·di·da·men·te adv. secretly, covertly.

es·con·di·das f.pl. ♦ a e. secretly, covertly.

es·con·di·te m. hiding place; (*juego*) hide-and-seek.

es·con·dri·jo m. hiding place.

es·co·pe·ta f. shotgun, rifle.

es·co·pe·ta·zo m. gunshot (wound); (*noticia*) bad news, blow.

es·co·rar tr. MARIT. to list, heel; CONSTR. to shore *or* prop up —intr. & reflex. to list, heel.

es·cor·bu·to m. scurvy.

es·cor·char tr. to skin, flay.

es·co·ria f. scoria.

es·co·rial m. slag dump.

es·cor·pión m. scorpion.

es·co·tar tr. to cut, trim; (*sacar agua*) to drain water from; (*partir un gasto*) to go Dutch.

es·co·te m. neck, neckline ♦ ir *or* pagar a e. to go Dutch.

es·co·ti·lla f. hatch(way).

es·co·zor m. smarting; (*pena*) grief, sorrow.

es·cri·ba·ní·a f. notary public's position *or* office; (*oficio de secretario*) clerkship; (*escritorio*) writing desk; (*recado de escribir*) writing materials.

es·cri·ba·no m. notary public; (*secretario*) clerk, secretary.

es·cri·bien·te m.f. amanuensis, clerk.

es·cri·bir §80 tr. & intr. to write ♦ e. a máquina to type —reflex. to write to each other, correspond; (*deletrearse*) to be spelled; (*inscribirse*) to enroll, enlist.

es·cri·to, a I. see escribir II. adj. written ♦ e. a

mano handwritten • **e. a máquina** typed, typewritten **III.** m. document, writing ♦ **por e.** in writing.

es·cri·tor, ·ra m.f. writer.

es·cri·to·rio m. desk; *(despacho)* office, study.

es·cri·tu·ra f. writing; *(sistema de signos)* script; LAW document, instrument; *(contrato)* indenture, deed.

es·cri·tu·rar tr. to notarize, execute by deed; THEAT. to book, sign.

es·cro·to m. scrotum.

es·crú·pu·lo m. scruple.

es·cru·pu·lo·si·dad f. scrupulousness.

es·cru·pu·lo·so, a adj. & m.f. scrupulous (person).

es·cru·tar tr. to scrutinize, examine.

es·cru·ti·nio m. scrutiny, examination.

es·cru·ti·ña·dor, ·ra m.f. scrutinizer.

es·cua·dra f. triangle; CARP. carpenter's square; *(grapa)* angle iron; MIL. squad, squadron.

es·cua·dri·lla f. squadron.

es·cua·drón m. cavalry squadron.

es·cuá·li·do, a adj. squalid, filthy.

es·cu·cha f. listening; RELIG. chaperone ♦ **estar a la e.** *or* **en e.** to be listening —m. night scout.

es·cu·char tr. to listen to —reflex. to like to hear oneself talk.

es·cu·dar tr. & reflex. to shield, protect (oneself).

es·cu·de·rí·a f. *(servicio)* position of a page *or* squire; AUTO. fleet.

es·cu·de·ro m. squire, page; *(hidalgo)* nobleman.

es·cu·di·lla f. wide bowl.

es·cu·do m. shield; *(insignia)* escutcheon.

es·cu·dri·ña·mien·to m. scrutiny.

es·cu·dri·ñar tr. to scrutinize, examine.

es·cue·la f. school ♦ **e. de artes y oficios** trade *or* technical school • **e. de párvulos** kindergarten • **tener buena e.** to be well-trained *or* schooled.

es·cuer·zo m. toad.

es·cue·to, a adj. concise, direct; *(libre)* free, unencumbered.

es·cue·za, zo see escocer.

es·cul·pir tr. to sculpt, carve; *(grabar)* to engrave.

es·cul·tor, ·ra m.f. sculptor —f. sculptress.

es·cul·tu·ra f. sculpture, carving.

es·cul·tu·ral adj. sculptural.

es·cu·pi·de·ra f. spittoon, cuspidor; AMER. *(orinal)* urinal.

es·cu·pir tr. to spit; COLL. *(pagar)* to cough up, fork over *or* out; *(confesar)* to spill, give —intr. to spit.

es·cu·rre·pla·tos m.inv. dish rack.

es·cu·rri·de·ro m. drainboard, draining rack; MIN. drainpipe.

es·cu·rri·di·zo, a adj. slippery.

es·cu·rri·dor m. colander.

es·cu·rrir tr. to drain; *(hacer que chorree)* to wring (out) —intr. to drip, trickle; *(deslizar)* to slip, slide —reflex. to drain, to drip; *(deslizar)* to slip, slide; *(escapar)* to slip out, escape; COLL. *(equivocarse)* to slip up.

e·se, e·sa adj. [pl. **esos, esas**] that ♦ pl. those.

é·se, é·sa pron. [pl. **ésos, ésas**] that one; *(el primero)* the former; *(allí)* there, your town ♦ pl. those.

e·sen·cia f. essence ♦ **quinta e.** quintessence.

e·sen·cial adj. essential.

es·fe·ra f. sphere; *(del reloj)* dial, face.

es·fé·ri·co, a I. adj. spherical **II.** m. ball.

es·fe·ro·grá·fi·ca f. ARG. ball-point pen.

es·fin·ge f. sphinx.

es·fín·ter m. sphincter.

es·for·za·do, a adj. brave, courageous.

es·for·zar §37 tr. to strengthen; *(dar ánimo)* to encourage —reflex. to strive.

es·fuer·zo m. effort, exertion; *(valor)* courage, bravery; *(ánimo)* spirit, heart.

es·fu·mar tr. to stump; *(suavizar)* to tone down, soften —reflex. to disappear, vanish.

es·gri·ma f. fencing.

es·gri·mir tr. to wield, brandish; *(servirse de)* to use, make use of —intr. to fence.

es·gri·mis·ta m.f. fencer.

es·guin·ce m. *(regate)* dodge, swerve; *(gesto de desdén)* frown, grimace; MED. sprain, twist.

es·la·bón m. link; *(hierro)* steel.

es·la·bo·nar tr. to link —reflex. to be linked.

es·lo·ra f. length (of a ship).

es·mal·tar tr. to enamel; *(hermosear)* to embellish, adorn.

es·mal·te m. enamel; *(labor)* enameling, enamel work; *(color azul)* smalt, cobalt blue ♦ **e. de** *or* **para uñas** nail polish.

es·me·ra·do, a adj. careful, meticulous.

es·me·ral·da f. emerald.

es·me·rar tr. to polish, brighten —reflex. to be painstaking, take great care.

es·me·ril m. emery.

es·me·ri·la·dor, ·ra m.f. polisher.

es·me·ri·lar tr. to polish with emery.

es·me·ro m. extreme care, meticulousness.

es·mi·rria·do, a adj. COLL. skinny, thin.

es·mo·quin m. dinner jacket, tuxedo.

es·nob m.f. snob.

e·so pron. that ♦ **a e. de** about, around • **e. es** that's it • **e. mismo** exactly, the same • **por e.** therefore, that's why.

e·só·fa·go m. esophagus.

e·sos see ese.

é·sos see é·se.

e·so·té·ri·co, a adj. esoteric.

es·pa·cia·dor m. space bar, spacer.

es·pa·cial adj. spatial; *(del espacio)* space.

es·pa·ciar tr. to space *or* spread out —reflex. *(dilatarse)* to expatiate, go on at length; *(solazarse)* to relax.

es·pa·cio m. space.

es·pa·cio·sa·men·te adv. slowly, deliberately.

es·pa·cio·so, a adj. spacious, roomy; *(lento)* slow, deliberate.

es·pa·da f. sword; *(espadachín)* swordsman; *(naipe)* spade ♦ **de capa y e.** cloak-and-dagger • **entre la e. y la pared** between a rock and a hard place.

es·pa·da·chín m. skilled swordsman; *(bravucón)* swashbuckler.

es·pa·dín m. dress *or* ceremonial sword.

es·pa·gue·ti m. spaghetti.

es·pal·da f. back ♦ **dar** *or* **volver la e.** to turn one's back ♦ pl. back • **a e. de alguien** behind someone's back • **de e.** from behind • **tener buenas e.** to be very patient.

es·pal·dar m. back (of a chair); *(enrejado)* trellis, espalier.

es·pal·da·ra·zo m. blow *or* slap on the back; FIG. *(apoyo)* support, backing.

es·pan·ta·da f. *(huida)* flight, escape; *(miedo)*

sudden scare *or* fright.

es·pan·ta·di·zo, a adj. jumpy, skittish.

es·pan·ta·jo m. scarecrow; *(persona fea)* sight, fright.

es·pan·ta·pá·ja·ros m.inv. scarecrow.

es·pan·tar tr. to frighten, scare —reflex. to be frightened *or* scared.

es·pan·to m. fright, scare; *(fantasma)* ghost, phantom.

es·pan·to·so, a adj. frightening, terrifying.

es·pa·ra·dra·po m. adhesive tape.

es·par·ci·do, a adj. scattered, strewn; *(alegre)* merry, cheerful.

es·par·cir §35 tr. to scatter, spread —reflex. to scatter, be scattered; *(descansarse)* to relax, take it easy.

es·pá·rra·go m. asparagus.

es·par·te·ña f. espadrille.

es·par·to m. esparto.

es·pas·mo m. spasm.

es·pas·mó·di·co, a adj. spasmodic.

es·pá·tu·la f. CUL. spatula; ORNITH. spoonbill.

es·pe·cia f. spice.

es·pe·cial adj. special ♦ **en e.** especially.

es·pe·cia·li·dad f. specialty.

es·pe·cia·lis·ta adj. & m.f. specialist.

es·pe·cia·li·za·ción f. specialization.

es·pe·cia·li·za·do, a adj. specialized.

es·pe·cia·li·zar §04 tr., intr. & reflex. to specialize.

es·pe·cial·men·te adv. especially, specially.

es·pe·cie f. species; *(tipo)* type, kind; *(asunto)* matter, affair; *(noticia)* bit of news; *(pretexto)* pretext.

es·pe·ci·fi·ca·ción f. specification.

es·pe·ci·fi·car §70 tr. to specify.

es·pe·ci·fi·ci·dad f. specificity.

es·pe·cí·fi·co, a adj. & m. specific.

es·pé·ci·men m. [pl. **-címenes**] specimen.

es·pe·cio·so, a adj. specious; *(hermoso)* beautiful, perfect.

es·pec·ta·cu·lar adj. spectacular.

es·pec·tá·cu·lo m. spectacle.

es·pec·ta·dor, ·ra m.f. spectator, onlooker ♦ pl. audience, public.

es·pec·tral adj. spectral; *(fantasmal)* ghostly.

es·pec·tro m. PHYS. spectrum; *(fantasma)* ghost, spook; *(horror)* specter, horror.

es·pe·cu·la·ción f. speculation.

es·pe·cu·la·dor, ·ra m.f. speculator.

es·pe·cu·lar tr. to examine, inspect; *(conjeturar)* to speculate —intr. to speculate in.

es·pe·cu·la·ti·vo, a adj. speculative.

es·pe·jis·mo/je·o m. mirage.

es·pe·jo m. mirror; *(modelo)* model, example.

es·pe·luz·nan·te adj. COLL. hair-raising.

es·pe·luz·nar tr. to ruffle, muss; *(pelo)* to make stand on end —reflex. to become ruffled *or* mussed; *(pelo)* to stand on end.

es·pe·ra f. wait; LAW respite.

es·pe·ran·za f. hope.

es·pe·ran·zar §04 tr. to make hopeful.

es·pe·rar tr. *(tener esperanza)* to hope (for); *(aguardar)* to wait for, await; *(confiar en)* to expect ♦ **e. en** to trust, put one's faith in —intr. to wait.

es·per·ma f. sperm, semen.

es·per·ma·to·zoi·de m. spermatozoid.

es·per·pen·to m. COLL. *(espanto)* fright, sight; *(desatino)* absurdity, nonsense.

es·pe·sar tr. to thicken —reflex. to grow *or* become thicker.

es·pe·so, a adj. thick; *(sucio)* dirty, unkempt.

es·pe·sor m. thickness; *(densidad)* density.

es·pe·tar tr. CUL. to skewer, spit; *(atravesar)* to pierce, run through —reflex. *(ponerse tenso)* to become serious *or* solemn; COLL. *(asegurarse)* to establish oneself.

es·pí·a m.f. spy —f. MARIT. warping, warp.

es·piar §30 tr. to spy on —intr. to spy; MARIT. to warp.

es·pi·char tr. to prick —intr. COLL. to kick the bucket, die.

es·pi·ga f. BOT. spike, ear; CARP. tenon; *(clavija)* peg, pin.

es·pi·ga·do, a adj. spiky.

es·pi·gar §47 tr. to glean; CARP. to tenon, dovetail —reflex. to grow *or* shoot up.

es·pi·gón m. point; *(mazorca)* ear (of corn); MARIT. breakwater, jetty.

es·pi·na f. thorn; *(de pez)* fishbone; ANAT. spine, backbone; *(pesar)* grief, sorrow ♦ **dar mala e.** to cause suspicion • **estar en espinas** to be on pins and needles.

es·pi·na·ca f. spinach.

es·pi·nar tr. to prick; FIG. to hurt, offend.

es·pi·na·zo m. ANAT. spine, backbone; ARCHIT. keystone.

es·pi·nel m. boulter, trotline.

es·pi·ni·lla f. shinbone; *(granillo)* blackhead.

es·pi·no m. hawthorn, thornbush.

es·pi·no·so, a adj. thorny, spiny; *(arduo)* difficult, sticky.

es·pio·na·je m. espionage, spying.

es·pi·ra·ción f. exhalation, expiration.

es·pi·ral I. adj. spiral, winding II. m. balance spring, hairspring; MED. coil —f. spiral.

es·pi·rar tr. to exhale, breathe out; *(exudar)* to give off, exude —intr. to exhale, breathe out.

es·pi·ri·tis·ta I. adj. spiritualistic, spiritistic II. m.f. spiritualist, spiritist.

es·pi·ri·to·so, a adj. spirited, lively; *(alcohólico)* spirituous, alcoholic.

es·pí·ri·tu m. spirit; *(alma)* soul; *(mente)* intelligence, wit ♦ **exhalar el e.** to die, give up the ghost • **e. de cuerpo** esprit de corps.

es·pi·ri·tual adj. & m. spiritual.

es·pi·ri·tua·li·dad f. spirituality.

es·pi·ri·tua·lis·ta I. adj. spiritualistic II. m.f. spiritualist.

es·pi·ta f. tap, spigot; *(bebedor)* drunkard, boozer.

es·pi·tar tr. to tap, put a spigot on.

es·plen·den·te adj. shining, resplendent.

es·plén·di·do, a adj. splendid; *(generoso)* generous; *(resplandeciente)* resplendent.

es·plen·dor m. splendor.

es·plen·do·ro·so, a adj. resplendent.

es·plín m. melancholy, depression.

es·po·le·ar tr. EQUIT. to spur, prod with a spur; FIG. to incite, urge.

es·po·le·o m. spurring.

es·po·le·ta f. ARM. fuse; ORNITH. wishbone.

es·po·lón m. spur; ZOOL. fetlock; MARIT. cutwater; ARCHIT. buttress; MED chilblain.

es·pol·vo·re·ar tr. to dust (off).

es·pon·ja f. sponge ♦ **beber como una e.** COLL. to drink like a fish • **tirar** *or* **arrojar la e.** to throw in the towel, give up.

es·pon·jar tr. to make spongy *or* fluffy —reflex. to become spongy; *(envanecerse)* to put on airs; COLL. *(rebozar)* to glow with health.

es·pon·je·ar intr. to snoop, pry.

es·pon·jo·so, a adj. spongy.

es·pon·sa·les m.pl. betrothal, engagement.
es·pon·ta·nei·dad f. spontaneity.
es·pon·tá·ne·o, a adj. spontaneous.
es·po·ra f. spore.
es·po·rá·di·co, a adj. sporadic.
es·po·sa f. wife, spouse ♦ pl. handcuffs.
es·po·sa·do, a adj. var. of **desposado, a.**
es·po·sar tr. to handcuff, put handcuffs on.
es·po·so m. husband, spouse.
es·pue·la f. spur.
es·pul·gar §47 tr. to delouse; (examinar) to scrutinize, examine closely.
es·pu·ma f. foam; (de un líquido) froth, spume; (de jabón) lather; (desechos) scum ♦ **crecer como e.** or **la e.** COLL. to shoot up, spread like wildfire • **e. de caucho** foam rubber.
es·pu·ma·de·ra f. skimmer.
es·pu·ma·je·ar intr. to foam at the mouth.
es·pu·man·te adj. foaming, frothing; (vino) sparkling.
es·pu·mar tr. to skim, remove foam from —intr. to foam, froth.
es·pu·ma·ra·jo m. foam, froth.
es·pu·mo·so, a adj. frothy, foamy.
es·pu·rio, a adj. spurious.
es·pu·tar tr. to spit, expectorate.
es·pu·to m. spit, spittle.
es·que·la f. note, short letter; (aviso) notice.
es·que·lé·ti·co, a adj. skeletal.
es·que·le·to m. skeleton.
es·que·ma m. scheme, outline.
es·que·má·ti·co, a adj. schematic.
es·que·ma·ti·zar §04 tr. to schematize.
es·quí m. [pl. -s] ski; (deporte) skiing.
es·quia·dor, ·ra m.f. skier.
es·quiar §30 intr. to ski.
es·qui·la f. shearing, fleecing.
es·qui·lar tr. to shear, fleece.
es·quil·mar tr. to harvest, gather; (empobrecer) to impoverish; FIG. to exhaust.
es·qui·na f. corner ♦ **a la vuel·ta de la e.** just around the corner • **doblar la e.** (dar una vuelta) to turn the corner; AMER., FIG. to die, kick the bucket • **hacer e.** to be on the corner.
es·qui·na·do, a adj. cornered, angular.
es·qui·nar tr. (formar esquina) to form a corner with; (poner en esquina) to put in a corner; (poner a mal) to set against, estrange —intr. to form a corner (with) —reflex. ♦ **e. con** to quarrel with.
es·qui·na·zo m. COLL. corner; ARG., CHILE serenade ♦ **dar e. a alguien** COLL. to give someone the slip.
es·quir·la f. splinter.
es·qui·var tr. to avoid, evade; (rehusar) to shun, reflex. to withdraw, shy away.
es·qui·vez f. coldness, disdain.
es·qui·vo, a adj. cold, disdainful.
es·qui·zo·fre·nia f. schizophrenia.
es·qui·zo·fré·ni·co, a adj. & m.f. schizophrenic.
es·ta see **este, a.**
és·ta see **este, a.**
es·ta·ba see **estar.**
es·ta·bi·li·dad f. stability.
es·ta·bi·li·zar §04 tr. to stabilize, make stable.
es·ta·ble adj. stable.
es·ta·ble·ce·dor, ·ra I. adj. establishing, founding II. m.f. establisher, founder.
es·ta·ble·cer §17 tr. to establish, found; (decretar) to decree, ordain —reflex. to establish oneself.
es·ta·ble·ci·mien·to m. establishment.
es·ta·blo m. stable.
es·ta·ca f. stake, post; (garrote) club, cudgel; BOT. cutting; CARP. spike, nail.
es·ta·ca·da f. picket fence; MIL. stockade, palisade ♦ **dejar a alguien en la e.** COLL. to leave someone in the lurch • **quedar en la e.** COLL. to be defeated or beaten.
es·ta·car §70 tr. (atar) to tie to a stake or post; (señalar) to stake out; AMER. to fasten down with stakes —reflex. to freeze, stand stock-still.
es·ta·ción f. (estado) position; (tiempo) season; RAIL., TELEC. station.
es·ta·cio·na·mien·to m. stationing, positioning; AUTO. parking place or space.
es·ta·cio·nar tr. to station, place; AUTO. to park —reflex. to remain stationary; (colocarse) to station oneself.
es·ta·cio·na·rio, a adj. stationary.
es·ta·da/dí·a f. stay, stop.
es·ta·dio m. stadium; (fase) phase, stage.
es·ta·dis·ta m. statesman; (estadístico) statistician.
es·ta·dís·ti·co, a I. adj. statistical II. m. statistician —f. statistics; (dato) statistics.
es·ta·do m. state; (condición) condition; (calidad) status; (jerarquía) rank, grade; estate <el cuarto e. the fourth estate>; (resumen) statement, report; MIL. post, garrison ♦ **e. civil** marital status • **e. mayor** general staff.
es·ta·fa f. swindle, hoax.
es·ta·fa·dor, ·ra m.f. swindler, crook.
es·ta·far tr. to swindle, cheat.
es·ta·fe·ta f. mail, post; (casa de correo) post office; DIPL. diplomatic pouch.
es·ta·fi·lo·co·co m. staphylococcus.
es·ta·la f. port of call; (establo) stable.
es·ta·lac·ti·ta f. stalactite.
es·ta·lag·mi·ta f. stalagmite.
es·ta·llar intr. to burst, explode; (sobrevenir) to break out.
es·ta·lli·do/llo m. (explosión) explosion; ARM. report; FIG. outbreak, outburst.
es·tam·bre m. TEX. worsted yarn; BOT. stamen.
es·tam·pa f. (imagen) print; (huella) track, mark; (aspecto) aspect, appearance.
es·tam·pa·do, a I. adj. TEX. stamped II. m. printing, engraving.
es·tam·pa·dor m. printer, engraver.
es·tam·par tr. to print, stamp; (grabar) to emboss, engrave; (dejar huella) to leave a mark; COLL. (arrojar) to throw, hurl.
es·tam·pi·da f. explosion, bang; AMER. stampede.
es·tam·pi·do m. explosion, bang.
es·tam·pi·lla f. stamp, seal; AMER. postage stamp.
es·tam·pi·llar tr. to stamp, mark with a stamp.
es·tan·car §70 tr. to dam up, stem; COM. to monopolize —reflex. to stagnate, become stagnant; (detenerse) to come to a standstill.
es·tan·cia f. (mansión) country house, estate; (estadía) stay; AMER. ranch, farm.
es·tan·cie·ro m. AMER. rancher, farmer.
es·tan·dar·te m. standard, banner.
es·tan·que m. (charca) pond, pool; (depósito) tank, reservoir.
es·tan·te I. adj. (existente) extant; (permanente) fixed II. m. shelving, shelves.

es·tan·te·rí·a f. shelving, shelves.
es·ta·ñar tr. to tin, plate with tin.
es·ta·ño m. tin.
es·ta·qui·lla f. wooden peg.
es·ta·qui·llar tr. to peg, fasten with pegs.
es·tar §36 intr. to be ✦ **¿a cuántos estamos?** or **¿a qué estamos?** what is the date? • **¿cómo estás?** how are you? • **está bien** or **bien está** okay, all right • **e. a** to sell at, cost • **e. al caer** to be about to happen • **e. bien** *(convenir)* to be suitable or fitting; *(gozar de buena salud)* to be well or healthy • **e. de más** to be superfluous • **e. en** *(entender)* to understand; *(consistir en)* to depend on, lie in • **e. en sí** to know what one is doing • **e. mal** *(no convenir)* to be unsuitable or inappropriate; *(padecer de mala salud)* to be ill • **e. para** *(gustar)* to be in the mood for; to be about to <*estamos para salir* we are about to leave> • **e. por** *(favorecer)* to be for, be in favor of; to be about to <*e. por terminarlo* to be about to finish it>; *(quedar)* to remain to be; *(tener ganas)* to have a mind to, be inclined to.
es·tar·cir §35 tr. to stencil.
es·ta·tal adj. state, of the state.
es·tá·ti·co, a I. adj. static II. f. static; MECH. statics.
es·ta·tua f. statue; COLL. *(persona)* cold fish.
es·ta·tua·rio, a adj. & m.f. statuary.
es·ta·tuir §18 tr. to establish, enact; *(demostrar)* to demonstrate, prove.
es·ta·tu·ra f. stature.
es·ta·tu·to m. *(ley)* statute, law; *(regla)* rule.
es·te m. east.
es·te, a adj. [pl. **estos, -tas**] this ✦ pl. these.
és·te, a pron. [pl. **éstos, -tas**] this one; *(el segundo)* the latter; *(aquí)* here, this town ✦ pl. these.
es·té see **estar.**
es·te·la f. AVIA. trail; MARIT. wake.
es·te·lar adj. stellar.
es·te·no·gra·fí·a f. stenography, shorthand.
es·te·nó·gra·fo, a m.f. stenographer.
es·ten·tó·re·o, a adj. stentorian, loud.
es·te·pa f. steppe.
es·te·ra f. matting.
es·ter·co·lar[1] m. dung heap, manure pile.
es·ter·co·lar[2] tr. to manure, fertilize.
es·té·re·o adj. & f. stereo.
es·te·re·o·fo·ní·a f. stereophony, stereo.
es·te·re·o·fó·ni·co, a adj. stereophonic, stereo.
es·te·re·o·ti·par tr. to stereotype.
es·te·re·o·tí·pi·co, a adj. stereotypical.
es·te·re·o·ti·po m. stereotype.
es·té·ril adj. sterile, infertile; *(árido)* barren.
es·te·ri·li·dad f. sterility.
es·te·ri·li·za·ción f. sterilization.
es·te·ri·li·zar §04 tr. to sterilize.
es·ter·li·na adj. sterling.
es·ter·nón m. sternum, breastbone.
es·te·ro m. estuary; AMER. *(pantano)* marsh, swamp; AMER. *(charca)* puddle, pool.
es·ter·tor m. death rattle; MED. stertor.
es·te·ta m. aesthete.
es·té·ti·co, a I. adj. aesthetic II. m. aesthetic, aesthete —f. aesthetics.
es·te·tos·co·pio m. stethoscope.
es·te·va·do, a adj. & m.f. bowlegged (person).
es·ti·ba·dor m. stevedore.
es·ti·bar tr. to pack tightly, compress; MARIT. to stow.
es·tiér·col m. dung, manure.
es·tig·ma m. stigma ✦ pl. RELIG. stigmata.

es·tig·ma·ti·zar §04 tr. to stigmatize, brand; FIG. to censure, reproach.
es·ti·lar intr. & reflex. *(usar)* to be customary, be the custom; *(estar de moda)* to be in fashion —tr. to draw up.
es·ti·le·te m. stylus, style; *(puñal)* stiletto; MED. probe, stylet.
es·ti·lis·ta m.f. stylist.
es·ti·lís·ti·co, a I. adj. stylistic II. f. stylistics.
es·ti·li·zar §04 tr. to stylize.
es·ti·lo m. style ✦ **por el e.** like that.
es·ti·lo·grá·fi·co, a I. adj. stylographic II. f. fountain pen, stylograph.
es·ti·ma f. esteem, respect.
es·ti·ma·ble adj. estimable; *(valioso)* worthy of esteem, admirable.
es·ti·ma·ción f. esteem, respect; COM. appraisal, valuation.
es·ti·ma·dor, ·ra I. adj. appreciative II. m. COM. appraiser.
es·ti·mar tr. to esteem, hold in esteem; COM. to estimate, appraise; *(juzgar)* to consider, deem —reflex. to be esteemed.
es·ti·mu·lan·te I. adj. stimulating II. m. stimulant.
es·ti·mu·lar tr. to stimulate; *(aguijonear)* to prod, push; *(incitar)* to incite, urge on.
es·tí·mu·lo m. stimulus.
es·tí·o m. summer.
es·ti·pen·dio m. stipend, remuneration.
es·ti·pu·lar tr. to stipulate.
es·ti·ra·do, a adj. stretched; *(vanidoso)* pompous, haughty; *(tacaño)* stingy, tight.
es·ti·rar tr. to stretch; *(extender)* to extend ✦ **e. la pata** COLL. to die, kick the bucket —reflex. to stretch oneself.
es·ti·rón m. yank, tug ✦ **dar un e.** to shoot up.
es·tir·pe f. stock, lineage; LAW heirs.
es·ti·val adj. summer, estival.
es·to pron. this; *(asunto)* this business or matter ✦ **por e.** for this reason.
es·to·ca·da f. thrust, stab; *(herida)* stab wound.
es·to·fa f. TEX. brocade; FIG. class, quality.
es·to·fa·do, a I. adj. stewed; *(acolchado)* quilted II. m. stew; *(acolchadura)* quilting.
es·to·far tr. to stew.
es·toi·co, a adj. & m.f. stoic.
es·to·la f. stole.
es·tó·ma·go m. stomach.
es·to·pa f. *(fibra)* tow; *(tela)* burlap; MARIT. oakum ✦ **e. de acero** steel wool.
es·to·que·ar tr. to kill or wound with a sword.
es·tor·bar tr. to obstruct, block; *(dificultar)* to hinder, hamper.
es·tor·bo m. obstruction, obstacle; *(dificultad)* hindrance; *(molestia)* bother, annoyance.
es·tor·nu·dar intr. to sneeze.
es·tor·nu·do m. sneeze.
es·tos see **este, a.**
és·tos see **éste, a.**
es·toy see **estar.**
es·tra·do m. dais; *(sala)* drawing room.
es·tra·fa·la·rio, a COLL. I. adj. outlandish, bizarre; *(desaliñado)* slovenly II. m.f. eccentric.
es·tra·go m. destruction, devastation.
es·tra·gón m. tarragon.
es·tram·bó·ti·co, a adj. COLL. outlandish.
es·tran·gu·la·ción f. strangulation.
es·tran·gu·la·do, a adj. strangled.
es·tran·gu·la·dor, ·ra I. adj. strangulating II. m.f. strangler —m. AUTO. choke.

es·tran·gu·lar tr. to strangle, strangulate; MECH. to choke.

es·tra·ta·ge·ma f. stratagem.

es·tra·te·ga m.f. strategist.

es·tra·te·gia f. strategy.

es·tra·té·gi·co, a I. adj. strategic II. m.f. strategist.

es·tra·ti·fi·car §70 tr. & reflex. to stratify.

es·tra·to m. stratum; METEOROL. stratus.

es·tra·tos·fe·ra f. stratosphere.

es·tra·za f. rag ◆ **papel de e.** brown wrapping paper.

es·tre·cha·mien·to m. narrowing, tightening.

es·tre·char tr. (reducir) to narrow; (apretar) to tighten; (sisar) to take in; (abrazar) to hug; (obligar) to compel ◆ **e. la brecha** to close the gap • **e. la mano a** to shake hands with —reflex. to narrow; (apretarse) to tighten, become tight; (ceñirse) to squeeze together; (reducir gastos) to economize; (amistarse) to become close or intimate.

es·tre·chez f. narrowness; (aprieto) bind, jam; (amistad) closeness, intimacy; (pobreza) poverty, need; (austeridad) austerity.

es·tre·cho, a I. adj. narrow; (apretado) tight; (tacaño) stingy, mean; (íntimo) close, intimate; (rígido) rigid, severe; (limitado) narrow-minded II. m. strait, channel.

es·tre·lla f. star; (asterisco) asterisk ◆ **e. de mar** starfish.

es·tre·lla·do, a adj. star-shaped; (con estrellas) starry ◆ **huevos estrellados** fried eggs.

es·tre·llar tr. to cover with stars; COLL. (romper) to smash, shatter —reflex. to become starry; COLL. (romperse) to smash, crash.

es·tre·lla·to m. stardom.

es·tre·me·ce·dor, ra adj. frightening.

es·tre·me·cer §17 tr. to shake —reflex. to shake, tremble.

es·tre·me·ci·mien·to m. shake, shudder; (de frío) shiver, shivering.

es·tre·nar tr. to use or wear for the first time; (representar) to première, open —reflex. to première, debut.

es·tre·no m. opening, debut; (representación) première.

es·tre·nuo, a adj. strenuous.

es·tre·ñi·do, a adj. constipated; FIG. stingy.

es·tre·ñi·mien·to m. constipation.

es·tre·ñir §59 tr. to constipate —reflex. to be or get constipated.

es·tré·pi·to m. uproar, din.

es·tre·pi·to·so, a adj. noisy, deafening.

es·trep·to·co·co m. streptococcus.

es·trep·to·mi·ci·na f. streptomycin.

es·trí·a f. ARCHIT. fluting, stria; (ranura) groove.

es·tria·do, a adj. striated, fluted.

es·triar §30 tr. ARCHIT. to striate, flute; (hacer ranuras) to groove —reflex. to be grooved.

es·tri·bar intr. to rest, lie on; (fundarse) to be based, rest.

es·tri·bi·llo m. POET. refrain; MUS. chorus.

es·tri·bo m. stirrup; (de carruaje) footboard; TECH. bracket, brace; GEOG. spur ◆ **perder los estribos** to lose one's head.

es·tri·bor m. starboard.

es·tric·ni·na f. strychnine.

es·tric·to, a adj. strict.

es·tri·den·cia f. stridence, shrillness.

es·tri·den·te adj. strident, shrill.

es·tri·ña, ño, ñera, ñó see **estreñir.**

es·tro·fa f. strophe, stanza.

es·tron·cio m. strontium.

es·tro·pa·jo m. dishcloth, rag.

es·tro·pe·ar tr. to damage, ruin; (dañar) to hurt, injure; (maltratar) to mistreat, mishandle.

es·tro·pi·cio m. COLL. uproar, clatter.

es·truc·tu·ra f. structure.

es·truc·tu·ra·ción f. construction.

es·truc·tu·ral adj. structural.

es·truc·tu·rar tr. to structure, construct.

es·truen·do m. clamor, uproar.

es·truen·do·so, a adj. clamorous, noisy.

es·tru·jar tr. to squeeze, crush.

es·tru·jón m. squeezing, pressing.

es·tua·rio m. estuary.

es·tu·che m. case, box; (vaina) sheath; (conjunto) set of instruments.

es·tu·co m. stucco.

es·tu·dian·ta·do m. student body, pupils.

es·tu·dian·te m. student, pupil.

es·tu·dian·til adj. student.

es·tu·diar tr. & intr. to study.

es·tu·dio m. study; (cuarto) study, studio.

es·tu·dio·so, a adj. & m.f. studious (person).

es·tu·fa f. stove, heater; (invernáculo) hothouse, greenhouse; (sauna) steam room.

es·tu·pe·fac·ción f. stupefaction.

es·tu·pe·fa·cien·te I. adj. stupefying, astonishing; PHARM. narcotic, stupefacient II. m. narcotic, stupefacient.

es·tu·pe·fac·to, a adj. stupefied, astonished.

es·tu·pen·do, a adj. stupendous, tremendous.

es·tu·pi·dez f. stupidity, idiocy.

es·tú·pi·do, a I. adj. stupid, dumb II. m.f. idiot, dumbbell.

es·tu·por m. MED. stupor, torpor; FIG. stupefaction, astonishment.

es·tu·rión m. sturgeon.

es·tu·vie·ra, vo see **estar.**

es·vás·ti·ca f. swastika.

e·ta·pa f. phase, stage; MIL. field ration.

et·cé·te·ra adv. et cetera.

é·ter m. ether.

e·té·re·o, a adj. ethereal.

e·ter·ni·dad f. eternity.

e·ter·ni·zar §04 tr. to perpetuate; (hacer durar) to prolong indefinitely —reflex. to be everlasting or eternal; FIG. to drag on.

e·ter·no, a adj. eternal.

é·ti·co, a I. adj. ethical, moral II. m.f. moralist —f. ethics.

e·ti·lo m. ethyl.

e·ti·mo·lo·gí·a f. etymology.

e·ti·mo·ló·gi·co, a adj. etymological.

e·ti·mó·lo·go, a m.f. etymologist.

e·ti·que·ta f. etiquette, ceremony; (rótulo) tag, label ◆ **de e.** formal.

e·ti·que·tar tr. to label, pigeonhole.

ét·ni·co, a adj. ethnic.

et·no·ci·dio m. genocide.

et·nó·lo·go m.f. ethnologist.

eu·ca·lip·to m. eucalyptus.

eu·ca·ris·tí·a f. Eucharist.

eu·ca·rís·ti·co, a adj. Eucharistic.

eu·fe·mis·mo m. euphemism.

eu·fo·ria f. euphoria.

eu·fó·ri·co, a adj. euphoric, jubilant.

eu·nu·co m. eunuch.

eu·ro·pio m. europium.

eu·ta·na·sia f. euthanasia.

e·va·cua·ción f. evacuation.

e·va·cuar tr. to evacuate.

e·va·cua·ti·vo, a I. adj. evacuating; *(purgativo)* evacuant, purgative II. m. purgative.

e·va·cua·to·rio, a I. adj. evacuating; *(purgativo)* evacuant, purgative II. m. evacuation site; *(retrete)* public lavatory, rest room.

e·va·dir tr. to evade, avoid —reflex. to escape, sneak away.

e·va·luar §67 tr. to evaluate, assess.

e·va·nes·cen·te adj. evanescent, vanishing.

e·van·gé·li·co, a adj. evangelical.

e·van·ge·lio m. gospel.

e·van·ge·lis·ta m. evangelist.

e·van·ge·li·zar §04 tr. to evangelize.

e·va·po·ra·ción f. evaporation.

e·va·po·rar tr. & reflex. to evaporate.

e·va·po·ri·zar §04 tr. to vaporize, evaporate.

e·va·sión f. escape; *(evasiva)* evasion.

e·va·si·vo, a I. adj. evasive II. f. evasion.

e·va·sor, ·ra adj. evading, eluding.

e·ven·to m. chance event, contingency.

e·ven·tual adj. unexpected, incidental.

e·ven·tual·men·te adv. by chance, unexpectedly; *(posiblemente)* possibly, perhaps.

e·vic·ción f. eviction, dispossession.

e·vi·den·cia f. certainty, obviousness; AMER. proof, evidence.

e·vi·den·ciar tr. *(probar)* to prove, demonstrate; *(hacer patente)* to make evident or clear.

e·vi·den·te adj. evident, clear.

e·vi·tar tr. to avoid.

e·vo·ca·dor, ·ra adj. evocative.

e·vo·car §70 tr. to evoke; *(invocar)* to invoke.

e·vo·ca·ti·vo, a adj. evocative.

e·vo·lu·ción f. evolution.

e·vo·lu·cio·nar intr. to evolve.

e·vo·lu·ti·vo, a adj. evolutionary, evolutional.

ex·a·brup·to m. abrupt or sharp remark.

e·xa·cer·bar tr. to exacerbate, aggravate.

e·xac·ti·tud f. exactitude, exactness; *(puntualidad)* punctuality.

e·xac·to, a adj. exact, precise; *(puntual)* punctual.

e·xa·ge·ra·ción f. exaggeration.

e·xa·ge·ra·do, a adj. exaggerated.

e·xa·ge·rar tr. to exaggerate.

e·xá·go·no m. hexagon.

e·xal·ta·ción f. exaltation; *(aumento del espíritu)* exhilaration, over-excitement.

e·xal·ta·do, a I. adj. exalted; *(sobreexcitado)* over-excited, hotheaded II. m.f. hothead.

e·xal·tar tr. to exalt, glorify —reflex. to get worked up.

e·xa·men m. examination, test; *(interrogación)* interrogation.

e·xa·mi·na·dor, ·ra m.f. examiner.

e·xa·mi·nar tr. to examine —reflex. to take an exam.

e·xan·güe adj. exsanguine, bloodless; *(aniquilado)* weak, exhausted; *(muerto)* dead.

e·xá·ni·me adj. inanimate, lifeless; *(debilitado)* weak, faint.

e·xas·pe·ra·ción f. exasperation.

e·xas·pe·rar tr. to exasperate —reflex. to become exasperated.

ex·ca·va·ción f. excavation.

ex·ca·var tr. to excavate, dig.

ex·ce·den·te I. adj. excessive; *(sobrante)* excess, surplus II. m. excess, surplus.

ex·ce·der tr. to exceed, surpass —reflex. to exceed oneself; *(sobrepasarse)* to go too far.

ex·ce·len·cia f. excellence.

ex·ce·len·te adj. excellent.

ex·cel·so, a adj. sublime, lofty.

ex·cen·tri·ci·dad f. eccentricity.

ex·cén·tri·co, a adj. eccentric.

ex·cep·ción f. exception ♦ a or con e. de except for.

ex·cep·cio·nal adj. exceptional.

ex·cep·to prep. except, excepting.

ex·cep·tuar §67 tr. to exclude, exempt —reflex. to be excluded or exempted.

ex·ce·si·vo, a adj. excessive.

ex·ce·so m. excess; COM. surplus ♦ en e. to excess, too much.

ex·ci·sión f. excision.

ex·ci·ta·bi·li·dad f. excitability.

ex·ci·ta·ble adj. excitable.

ex·ci·ta·ción f. excitement; BIOL. excitation.

ex·ci·tan·te I. adj. stimulating II. m. stimulant.

ex·ci·tar tr. to excite —reflex. to become excited.

ex·cla·ma·ción f. exclamation; *(signo ortográfico)* exclamation point.

ex·cla·mar intr. to exclaim.

ex·cla·ma·ti·vo/to·rio, a adj. exclamatory.

ex·cluir §18 tr. to exclude; *(expulsar)* to throw out, expel.

ex·clu·sión f. exclusion.

ex·clu·si·ve adv. exclusively; *(no incluyendo)* exclusive of, not including.

ex·clu·si·vo, a I. adj. exclusive II. f. *(repulsa)* rejection; *(privilegio)* exclusive or sole right.

ex·clu·ya, yo, yera, yó see excluir.

ex·com·ba·tien·te adj. & m.f. veteran.

ex·co·mul·ga·do, a adj. excommunicant.

ex·co·mul·gar tr. to excommunicate.

ex·co·mu·nión f. excommunication.

ex·co·riar tr. to excoriate, chafe.

ex·cre·ción f. excretion.

ex·cre·men·to m. excrement.

ex·cre·tar intr. to excrete.

ex·cul·par tr. to exculpate, exonerate.

ex·cur·sión f. excursion.

ex·cur·sio·nis·ta m.f. excursionist, sightseer.

ex·cu·sa f. excuse ♦ a e. secretly.

ex·cu·sa·do, a I. adj. exempt; *(reservado)* reserved, private; *(inútil)* unnecessary, superfluous II. m. toilet.

ex·cu·sar tr. to excuse; *(evitar)* to avoid, prevent; *(exentar)* to exempt —reflex. to excuse oneself ♦ e. de to refuse.

e·xe·cra·ción f. execration.

e·xe·crar tr. to execrate.

e·xé·ge·sis f. exegesis.

e·xe·ge·ta m.f. exegete.

e·xen·ción f. exemption.

e·xen·tar tr. to exempt, excuse —reflex. to exempt oneself.

e·xen·to, a I. see eximir and exentar II. adj. exempt, free; *(descubierto)* clear, unobstructed.

e·xe·quias f.pl. funeral rites, obsequies.

ex·ha·la·ción f. exhalation; *(vapor)* fumes, vapor; *(estrella)* shooting star; *(centella)* flash of lightning.

ex·ha·lar tr. to exhale; *(suspiros)* to breathe —reflex. *(respirar)* to breathe hard; *(correr)* to hurry, run.

ex·haus·ti·vo, a adj. exhaustive.

ex·haus·to, a adj. exhausted.

ex·hi·bi·ción f. exhibition, exhibit.

ex·hi·bi·cio·nis·ta m.f. exhibitionist.

ex·hi·bir tr. to exhibit, display —reflex. to show up, to show oneself.

ex·hor·ta·ción f. exhortation.
ex·hor·tar tr. to exhort.
ex·hu·mar tr. to exhume, disinter.
e·xi·gen·cia f. exigency, demand.
e·xi·gen·te adj. & m.f. demanding (person).
e·xi·gir §32 tr. to exact; *(requerir)* to demand, require.
e·xi·l(i)a·do, a I. adj. exiled, in exile II. m.f. exile.
e·xi·l(i)ar tr. to exile, banish —reflex. to be exiled *or* banished.
e·xi·lio m. exile, banishment.
e·xi·mio, a adj. *(distinguido)* distinguished, eminent; *(excelente)* select, choice.
e·xi·mir tr. to free, exempt —reflex. to excuse oneself.
e·xis·ten·cia f. existence ♦ pl. stock, goods.
e·xis·ten·cial adj. existential.
e·xis·ten·cia·lis·ta adj. & m.f. existentialist.
e·xis·ten·te adj. existent; COM. in stock.
e·xis·tir intr. to exist, be in existence.
é·xi·to m. success; *(resultado)* result, outcome ♦ **é. rotundo** huge success, hit • **tener é.** to be successful.
e·xi·to·so, a adj. AMER. successful.
é·xo·do m. exodus.
e·xo·ne·rar tr. to exonerate; *(despedir)* to dismiss ♦ **e. el vientre** to have a bowel movement.
e·xor·bi·tan·cia f. exorbitance, excess.
e·xor·bi·tan·te adj. exorbitant, excessive.
e·xor·cis·ta m. exorcist.
e·xor·ci·zar §04 tr. to exorcise.
e·xo·ti·ci·dad/quez f. exoticism.
e·xó·ti·co, a adj. exotic.
e·xo·tis·mo m. exoticism.
ex·pan·dir tr. to expand, spread.
ex·pan·sión f. expansion; *(recreo)* relaxation, recreation; *(franqueza)* expansiveness.
ex·pan·sio·nis·ta adj. & m.f. expansionist.
ex·pan·si·vo, a adj. expandable, expansible; *(franco)* open, expansive.
ex·pa·tria·ción f. expatriation.
ex·pa·triar §30 tr. to expatriate, banish —reflex. to go into exile; *(emigrar)* to emigrate.
ex·pec·ta·ción f. expectation.
ex·pec·ta·ti·vo, a I. adj. expectant, hopeful II. f. expectation, anticipation.
ex·pec·to·ra·ción f. expectoration.
ex·pec·to·ran·te adj. & m. expectorant.
ex·pec·to·rar tr. & intr. to expectorate.
ex·pe·di·ción f. expedition; *(prontitud)* speed, dispatch; COM. shipping, shipment.
ex·pe·di·cio·na·rio, a I. adj. expeditionary II. m.f. member of an expedition; *(expedidor)* sender.
ex·pe·di·dor, ·ra m.f. sender, shipper —m. dispenser.
ex·pe·dien·te I. adj. expedient II. m. expedient; *(archivo)* file, dossier, record; LAW proceedings.
ex·pe·dir §48 tr. *(enviar)* to send, ship; *(despachar)* to expedite, dispatch; *(dictar)* to issue.
ex·pe·di·tar tr. S. AMER. to expedite, dispatch.
ex·pe·di·ti·vo, a adj. expeditious.
ex·pe·di·to, a adj. ready, free; *(una vía)* clear.
ex·pe·ler tr. to expel, eject.
ex·pen·de·dor, ·ra I. adj. spending II. m.f. dealer, retailer; THEAT. ticket agent.
ex·pen·der tr. to expend, spend; *(hacer circular)* to circulate; *(vender al por menor)* to retail, sell.
ex·pen·dio m. expense, outlay; AMER. *(tienda)* store, shop; *(venta al por menor)* retailing.
ex·pen·sas f.pl. expenses, costs.
ex·pe·rien·cia f. experience; CHEM., PHYS. experiment.
ex·pe·ri·men·ta·ción f. experimentation.
ex·pe·ri·men·ta·do, a adj. experienced.
ex·pe·ri·men·tal adj. experimental.
ex·pe·ri·men·tar tr. to try out, test; *(sentir en sí)* to experience, undergo.
ex·pe·ri·men·to m. experiment, experimentation.
ex·per·to adj. & m. expert.
ex·pia·ción f. expiation, atonement.
ex·piar §30 tr. to atone for, expiate.
ex·pia·ti·vo, a adj. expiative, expiatory.
ex·pia·to·rio, a adj. expiatory.
ex·pi·ra·ción f. expiration.
ex·pi·rar intr. to expire.
ex·pla·na·da f. esplanade.
ex·pla·yar tr. to extend, spread out —reflex. *(dilatarse)* to expatiate, speak at length; *(divertirse)* to relax, unwind; *(confiarse)* to confide *(a, con in)*.
ex·ple·ti·vo, a adj. expletive.
ex·pli·ca·ción f. explanation.
ex·pli·car §70 tr. to explain; *(exponer)* to expound; *(enseñar)* to teach —reflex. to explain oneself; *(comprender)* to understand.
ex·pli·ca·ti·vo, a adj. explanatory.
ex·plí·ci·to, a adj. explicit.
ex·plo·ra·ción f. exploration.
ex·plo·ra·dor, ·ra I. adj. exploring, exploratory II. m.f. explorer —m. boy scout.
ex·plo·rar tr. & intr. to explore.
ex·plo·sión f. explosion.
ex·plo·si·vo, a adj. & m.f. explosive.
ex·plo·ta·ción f. exploitation; *(operación)* running; *(cultivo)* cultivation.
ex·plo·tar tr. to exploit; *(operar)* to run, operate; *(una mina)* to work; *(cultivar)* to cultivate —intr. to go off, explode.
ex·po·nen·cial adj. & f. exponential.
ex·po·nen·te I. adj. explaining, expounding II. m.f. exponent —m. MATH. exponent; *(ejemplo)* example <un magnífico e. a magnificent example>; AMER. model, best <e. de calidad the best in quality>.
ex·po·ner §54 tr. to expose; *(explicar)* to propound, explain; *(exhibir)* to exhibit; *(abandonar)* to abandon; —reflex. to expose oneself.
ex·por·ta·ción f. exportation, exporting; *(mercancías)* exports; *(artículo)* export (item).
ex·por·ta·dor, ·ra I. adj. exporting II. m.f. exporter.
ex·por·tar tr. & intr. to export.
ex·po·si·ción f. exhibition, show; *(explicación)* explanation; *(orientación)* exposure.
ex·pó·si·to, a I. adj. abandoned II. m.f. foundling.
ex·po·si·tor, ·ra I. adj. expository II. m.f. exponent; *(en una exposición)* exhibitor.
ex·pre·sa·do, a adj. above-mentioned.
ex·pre·sa·men·te adv. *(claramente)* clearly, explicitly; *(de propósito)* expressly, specifically.
ex·pre·sar tr. & reflex. to express (oneself).
ex·pre·sión f. expression.
ex·pre·si·vo, a adj. expressive.
ex·pre·so, a I. see **expresar** II. adj. express III. m. *(tren)* express train; *(correo)* express mail.
ex·pri·mi·dor m. squeezer, juicer.
ex·pri·mir tr. to squeeze.

ex·pro·piar tr. to expropriate.
ex·pues·to, a I. see **exponer** II. adj. dangerous, hazardous.
ex·pul·sar tr. to expel, drive out.
ex·pul·sión f. ejection, expulsion.
ex·pur·gar §47 tr. (purificar) to purge, purify; (un libro) to expurgate.
ex·pu·sie·ra, so see **exponer**.
ex·qui·si·tez f. exquisiteness.
ex·qui·si·to, a adj. exquisite.
ex·ta·siar·se §30 reflex. to become ecstatic.
éx·ta·sis f.inv. ecstasy, rapture.
ex·tá·ti·co, a adj. (arrebatado) ecstatic, enraptured; (profundo) deep, profound.
ex·tem·po·ra·nei·dad f. inopportuneness.
ex·tem·po·rá·ne·o, a adj. inopportune.
ex·ten·der §50 tr. to extend, enlarge; (desdoblar) to spread out, spread; (despachar) to draw up, issue —reflex. to stretch, extend; (dilatarse) to speak at length; (propagarse) to spread.
ex·ten·sa·men·te adv. extensively.
ex·ten·si·ble adj. extensible, extendible.
ex·ten·sión f. extension; (amplitud) expanse, stretch; (dimensión) extent, size.
ex·ten·si·vo, a adj. (flexible) extendible, extensible; (grande) extensive, wide; (por extensión) extended.
ex·ten·so, a I. see **extender** II. adj. extensive, ample, vast ♦ **por e.** at length, in (great) detail.
ex·te·nua·do, a adj. debilitated, weakened.
ex·te·nuar §67 tr. to debilitate, weaken.
ex·te·rior I. adj. exterior, outer; (extranjero) foreign II. m. exterior, outside; (apariencia) personal appearance.
ex·te·rio·ri·dad f. exteriority; (apariencia) outward appearance ♦ pl. pomp, show.
ex·te·rio·ri·zar §04 tr. to express, externalize.
ex·ter·mi·na·ción f. var. of **exterminio**.
ex·ter·mi·na·dor, ·ra m.f. exterminator.
ex·ter·mi·nar tr. to exterminate.
ex·ter·mi·nio m. extermination.
ex·ter·no, a I. adj. external, outward II. m.f. day school pupil.
ex·tien·da, de see **extender**.
ex·tin·ción f. extinction.
ex·tin·gui·ble adj. extinguishable.
ex·tin·guir §26 tr. to extinguish —reflex. (apagarse) to fade, go out; (desaparecerse) to become extinct, die out.
ex·tin·to, a I. see **extinguir** II. adj. extinguished; (desaparecido) extinct.
ex·tir·par tr. to extirpate.
ex·tor·sión f. extortion; (molestia) harm, trouble.
ex·tor·sio·na·dor, ·ra m.f. extortioner, extortionist.
ex·tor·sio·nar tr. to extort.
ex·tra I. adj. extra II. prep. ♦ **e. de** COLL. besides, in additon to III. m.f. CINEM., THEAT. extra —m. (gaje) extra, gratuity; (gasto) extra charge or expense; (comida) seconds.
ex·trac·ción f. extraction.
ex·trac·tar tr. to abstract, summarize.
ex·trac·to m. extract; (compendio) summary.
ex·trac·tor, ·ra m.f. extractor.
ex·tra·di·ción f. extradition.
ex·tra·er §72 tr. to extract.
ex·tra·li·mi·tar·se reflex. to overstep one's power or authority.
ex·tran·je·ro, a I. adj. alien, foreign II. m.f.

foreigner, alien —m. abroad.
ex·tra·ñar tr. (desterrar) to banish, exile; (privar) to estrange; (sentir la novedad) to find strange, not to be used to; AMER. to miss —reflex. to be surprised or astonished.
ex·tra·ño, a I. adj. (extranjero) foreign, alien; (raro) strange, odd; (que no tiene que ver) extraneous II. m.f. foreigner.
ex·tra·o·fi·cial adj. unofficial, nonofficial.
ex·tra·or·di·na·rio, a I. adj. extraordinary; (extraño) strange, odd II. m. (correo urgente) special delivery; (periódico) special edition; (remuneración) bonus.
ex·tra·po·lar tr. to extrapolate.
ex·tra·te·rre·no, a/rres·tre adj. & m.f. extraterrestrial.
ex·tra·va·gan·cia f. extravagance.
ex·tra·va·gan·te I. adj. extravagant II. m.f. eccentric.
ex·tra·ver·ti·do, a I. adj. extroverted, outgoing II. m.f. extrovert, outgoing person.
ex·tra·via·do, a adj. (apartado) out-of-the-way; (perdido) lost, missing.
ex·tra·viar §30 tr. (desviar) to lead astray, misguide; (perder) to misplace, lose —reflex. to get lost.
ex·tra·ví·o m. (pérdida del camino) going astray, losing one's way; (pérdida) misplacement, loss.
ex·tre·mar tr. to carry to an extreme —reflex. to take great pains, exert oneself to the utmost.
ex·tre·ma·un·ción f. extreme unction.
ex·tre·mi·dad f. (punta) end, tip; (parte extrema) extremity ♦ pl. extremities.
ex·tre·mis·ta adj. & m.f. extremist.
ex·tre·mo, a I. adj. (último) last, ultimate; (intenso) extreme, greatest, utmost; (distante) far, farthest II. m. extreme.
ex·tro·ver·sión f. extroversion, extraversion.
ex·tro·ver·ti·do, a I. adj. extroverted, extraverted II. m.f. extrovert, extravert.
e·xu·be·ran·cia f. exuberance, abundance.
e·xu·be·ran·te adj. exuberant, abundant.
e·xu·dar tr. & intr. to exude.
e·xul·tar intr. to exult, rejoice.
e·ya·cu·la·ción f. ejaculation.
e·ya·cu·lar tr. to ejaculate.

F

f, F f. sixth letter of the Spanish alphabet.
fá·bri·ca f. factory, works; (fabricación) manufacture; (edificio) building, construction; (invención) fabrication.
fa·bri·ca·ción f. manufacture; (construcción) construction ♦ **f. en serie** mass production.
fa·bri·can·te m.f. (manufacturador) manufacturer; (dueño) factory owner.
fa·bri·car §70 tr. to manufacture, make; (construir) to build, construct; (inventar) to fabricate, invent; (labrar) to work.
fa·bril adj. manufacturing.
fá·bu·la f. fable; (invención) lie, fiction; (objeto de burla) laughingstock; (habladuría) gossip, talk.
fa·bu·lo·sa·men·te adv. fabulously, extremely; (fingidamente) falsely.
fa·bu·lo·so, a adj. fabled, imaginary; (extraordinario) fabulous.
fac·ción f. faction, party; (rasgo) feature, facial feature; MIL. combat, battle ♦ **f. de guardia**

guard duty.

fa·ce·ta f. facet; FIG. facet, aspect.

fa·cha f. look, appearance ♦ **f. a f.** face to face • **estar hecho una f.** to look a mess or sight.

fa·cha·da f. façade; (dimensión) frontage; (portada) title page ♦ **con f. a** facing • **hacer f. con** or **a** to be opposite, face.

fá·cil I. adj. easy; (probable) likely, probable; (dócil) easygoing; (liviana) loose, of easy virtue II. adv. easily.

fa·ci·li·dad f. facility, ease; (oportunidad) opportunity, chance ♦ **tener f. de** to be apt to • **tener f. para** to have a gift or an aptitude for ♦ pl. terms.

fa·ci·li·tar tr. to facilitate, make easy; (proporcionar) to supply, furnish.

fa·ci·ne·ro·so, a adj. & m.f. criminal, delinquent; (malévolo) wicked (person).

fac·sí·mil/le m. facsimile.

fac·ti·ble adj. feasible, practicable.

fac·tor m. factor; COM. factor, agent.

fac·to·rí·a f. colonial trading post; AMER. plant, factory; ECUAD., PERU foundry, ironworks.

fac·tu·ra f. making; COM. invoice, bill.

fac·tu·ra·ción f. billing, invoicing.

fac·tu·rar tr. to invoice, bill.

fa·cul·tad f. faculty; (virtud) gift, advantage; (derecho) power, right; (licencia) license, permission; EDUC. school, college, faculty.

fa·cul·tar tr. to authorize, empower.

fa·cul·ta·ti·vo, a I. adj. facultative; (profesional) professional; MED. medical II. m. MED. physician, doctor.

fa·e·na f. manual labor; (quehacer) task, chore; (trabajo mental) mental task; COLL. (trastada) dirty trick ♦ **estar en plena f.** to be hard at work.

fai·sán m. pheasant.

fa·ja f. strip, belt; (corsé) girdle, corset; (tira de papel) wrapper; AMER. belt, waistband.

fa·ja·du·ra f. banding, belting; AMER. attack, beating.

fa·jar tr. to band, belt; (vendar) to bandage, swathe; (envolver) to wrap; AMER. to attack, assault —reflex. AMER. to set out to do something ♦ **f. con** or **a** to attack, fall on.

fa·ji·na f. AGR. shock, rick of sheaves; (leña) kindling; MIL. call to quarters, taps.

fa·jo m. bundle, sheaf; (de billetes) wad, roll; AMER. shot, swig.

fa·la·cia f. deception, deceitfulness; (error) fallacy.

fa·lan·ge f. phalanx; MIL. army, troops.

fa·lan·gis·ta adj. & m.f. Falangist.

fa·laz adj. deceitful, deceptive.

fal·da f. skirt; (ala de sombrero) brim, flap; (de un monte) foot; (regazo) lap ♦ pl. COLL. ladies, skirts • **aficionado a las f.** womanizer.

fal·de·ar tr. to skirt, go around.

fal·de·ro, a adj. skirt; lap <perro f. lap dog> ♦ **hombre f.** lady's man • **niño** or **niña f.** mama's boy or girl.

fal·dón m. tail; (saya) skirt; EQUIT. flap, skirt.

fa·li·ble adj. fallible.

fá·li·co, a adj. phallic.

fa·lla f. see **fallo, a.**

fa·llar tr. to fail, disappoint —intr. to fail; (perder resistencia) to give way ♦ **sin f.** without fail.

fa·lle·cer §17 intr. (morir) to die, expire; (faltar) to run out, end.

fa·lle·ci·mien·to m. death, demise.

fa·lli·do, a adj. unsuccessful; COM. bankrupt.

fa·llir intr. to run out, end.

fa·llo, a I. adj. void, lacking a suit (in cards) II. m. (sentencia) ruling, judgment; (decisión) decision; (falta) error, fault ♦ **tener fallos de memoria** to have lapses in one's memory —f. defect, fault; GEOG., MIN. fault; AMER. fault, failure.

fa·lo m. phallus, penis.

fal·se·ar tr. to falsify; (contrahacer) to fake, counterfeit; (cerradura) to pick; ARCHIT. to bevel —intr. (flaquear) to sag, become weak; (torcerse) to bend, warp.

fal·se·dad f. falseness; (hipocresía) hypocrisy; (mentira) falsehood, lie.

fal·se·te m. (corcho) plug, bung; (puerta) small door; MUS. falsetto.

fal·si·fi·car §70 tr. to falsify; (copiar) to counterfeit, forge; CHEM. to adulterate.

fal·so, a I. adj. false; (erróneo) fallacious; (engañoso) deceitful, false; (falsificado) counterfeit, fake; (inexacto) inexact, inaccurate; (fingido) fake, phony II. m. reinforcement, patch ♦ **dar un paso en f.** to trip, stumble • **de** or **en f.** falsely.

fal·ta f. lack, shortage; (ausencia) absence; (defecto) defect, flaw; (infracción) misdemeanor; (culpa) fault; (abuso) breach; (error) error, mistake ♦ **a f. de** for lack of, for want of • **hacer f.** (faltar) to be lacking, need; (ser necesario) to be necessary; to miss <me haces f. I miss you> • **sin f.** without fail.

fal·tar intr. (hacer falta) to lack, need; (carecer de) to be lacking; (estar ausente) to be missing; (no acudir a) to be absent, miss; (no responder) to fail to function; (morir) to die; (fallar) to fail in; (no cumplir) to fail to keep, break; (ofender) to insult ♦ **f. mucho para** to be a long way off • **f. ... para** to be ... to <faltan diez minutos para las ocho it is ten minutes to eight> • **f. poco para** not to be long before • **f. por** to remain to be.

fal·to, a adj. lacking, wanting; (escaso) short; (mezquino) poor, wretched.

fa·ma f. fame; (reputación) reputation ♦ **es f. que** it is rumored or reported that.

fa·mé·li·co, a adj. starving, famished.

fa·mi·lia f. family ♦ **venir de f.** to run in the family.

fa·mi·liar I. adj. (relativo a la familia) familial, family; (llano) casual; (conocido) familiar; (corriente) colloquial, familiar II. m. family or household member; (amigo íntimo) intimate friend.

fa·mi·lia·ri·zar §04 tr. & reflex. to familiarize (oneself).

fa·mo·so, a adj. famous; COLL. excellent.

fá·mu·la f. COLL. maid, servant.

fa·ná·ti·co, a I. adj. fanatic(al) II. m.f. fanatic; (entusiasta) fan.

fa·na·tis·mo m. fanaticism.

fa·na·ti·zar §04 tr. to fanaticize.

fan·dan·go m. fandango; COLL. row, uproar.

fan·fa·rre·ar intr. var. of **fanfarronear.**

fan·fa·rria f. COLL. bragging; MUS. fanfare.

fan·fa·rrón, o·na I. adj. COLL. bragging; (presumido) flashy, showy II. m.f. COLL. braggart.

fan·fa·rro·na·da f. bragging.

fan·fa·rro·ne·ar intr. to brag.

fan·fa·rro·ne·rí·a f. bragging.

fan·gal/gar m. quagmire, mudhole.

fan·go m. mud, mire.
fan·go·si·dad f. muddiness.
fan·go·so, a adj. muddy, miry.
fan·ta·se·ar intr. to daydream, dream.
fan·ta·sí·a f. fantasy ♦ **de f.** fancy.
fan·ta·sio·so, a adj. COLL. conceited, vain.
fan·tas·ma m. ghost, apparition; (visión) vision, illusion; (persona seria) stuffed shirt —f. scarecrow.
fan·tas·ma·gó·ri·co, a adj. phantasmagoric.
fan·tás·ti·co, a adj. fantastic.
fan·to·cha·da f. ridiculous action.
fan·to·che m. puppet, marionette; COLL. boastful nincompoop.
fa·rán·du·la f. theater, show business; (compañía) troupe.
fa·ran·du·le·ar intr. COLL. to boast, brag.
fa·ran·du·le·ro, a I. m.f. THEAT. wandering player; (trapacero) swindler **II.** adj. swindling.
fa·ra·ón m. Pharaoh, pharaoh.
far·do m. large bundle or parcel.
far·fu·llar COLL. tr. to jabber, gabble; FIG. (chapucear) to do hastily —intr. to jabber, gabble.
fa·ri·ná·ce·o, a adj. farinaceous.
fa·rin·ge f. pharynx.
fa·ri·se·o m. Pharisee, pharisee.
far·ma·céu·ti·co, a I. adj. pharmaceutical **II.** m.f. pharmacist, druggist.
far·ma·cia f. pharmacy.
far·ma·co·lo·gí·a f. pharmacology.
far·ma·co·pe·a f. pharmacopoeia.
fa·ro m. (torre) lighthouse; (señal) beacon; AUTO. headlight; FIG. guiding light.
fa·rol m. (linterna) lantern; (luz pública) street lamp; (luz) light; (fachendoso) show-off.
fa·ro·la f. (farol) streetlight, street lamp; (faro) beacon.
fa·ro·le·ar intr. COLL. to boast, brag.
fa·ro·le·rí·a f. COLL. boastfulness.
fa·ro·le·ro, a I. adj. boastful, bragging **II.** m.f. braggart; (el que cuida de los faroles) lamplighter.
fa·rra f. AMER. binge, spree.
fa·rre·ar intr. AMER. to go on a binge, carouse.
fa·rre·ro, a/rris·ta AMER. **I.** adj. carousing, reveling **II.** m.f. carouser, reveler.
far·sa f. farce; (compañía) company of actors; FIG. farce, sham.
far·san·te, a I. m.f. comic actor, farceur —m. fake, charlatan **II.** adj. COLL. fraud, fake.
far·se·ar intr. AMER. to fool around.
far·sis·ta m.f. writer of farces, farceur.
fas·cí·cu·lo m. fascicle.
fas·ci·na·ción f. fascination.
fas·ci·nan·te adj. fascinating.
fas·ci·nar tr. to fascinate; (engañar) to deceive.
fas·cis·ta adj. & m.f. fascist, Fascist.
fa·se f. phase; TECH. stage.
fas·ti·diar tr. (molestar) to annoy; (cansar) to tire, bore —reflex. to get annoyed.
fas·ti·dio m. (molestia) annoyance, bother; (repugnancia) repugnance; (aburrimiento) boredom.
fas·ti·dio·so, a adj. (molesto) annoying, bothersome; (cargante) tiresome, tedious.
fas·to, a I. adj. auspicious, happy **II.** m. pomp, splendor.
fas·tuo·si·dad f. pomp, splendor.
fas·t(u)o·so, a adj. lavish, splendid.

fa·tal adj. fatal; (funesto) mournful, unfortunate.
fa·ta·li·dad f. (destino) fate, destiny; (desgracia) misfortune, calamity.
fa·ta·lis·ta I. adj. fatalistic **II.** m.f. fatalist.
fa·tal·men·te adv. (desdichadamente) unfortunately, unhappily; (inevitablemente) fatefully, inevitably; (muy mal) wretchedly.
fa·tí·di·co, a adj. fatidic, prophetic.
fa·ti·ga f. fatigue; (respiración) shortness of breath ♦ **dar f.** to trouble, annoy • **f. visual** eyestrain ♦ pl. (dificultades) difficulties; (penas) sorrows.
fa·ti·gar §47 tr. to fatigue; (molestar) to annoy —reflex. to get tired.
fa·ti·go·so, a adj. fatigued, tired; (que cansa) fatiguing, tiring; COLL. (cargante) bothersome, annoying.
fa·tui·dad f. fatuity; (tontería) fatuous remark or act; (presunción) conceit, vanity.
fa·tuo, a I. adj. fatuous; (presumido) conceited, vain **II.** m.f. fool, fatuous person; (presumido) vain person.
fau·ces f.pl. fauces, gullet ♦ **las f. de la muerte** the jaws of death.
fau·na f. fauna, animal life.
faus·to, a I. adj. fortunate, lucky **II.** m. luxury, splendor.
fa·vor m. favor; (amparo) protection ♦ **a f. de** in favor of, in behalf of • **a f. de la noche** under cover of darkness • **de f.** complimentary, free • **en f. de** in favor of • **por f.** please.
fa·vo·ra·ble adj. favorable.
fa·vo·re·cer §17 tr. to favor, support; AMER. to protect —reflex. to help one another ♦ **f. de** to avail oneself of.
fa·vo·ri·tis·mo m. favoritism, partiality.
fa·vo·ri·to, a adj. & m.f. favorite.
faz f. face; NUMIS. obverse ♦ **a la f. de** in front of.
fe f. faith; (creencia) credence; (confianza) trust, confidence; (palabra de honor) word of honor; (documento) certificate ♦ **a buena fe** undoubtedly, doubtless • **a** or **de fe** truly • **dar fe a** to confirm, certify • **fe de erratas** errata • **fe pública** legal authority • **hacer fe** to be sufficient proof.
fe·al·dad f. ugliness; (torpeza) turpitude, foulness.
fe·bre·ro m. February.
fe·cal adj. fecal.
fe·cha f. date; (día) day; (momento actual) now, the present ♦ **con** or **de f. de** dated • **hasta la f.** so far, to date.
fe·cha·dor m. date stamp; AMER. (matasellos) postmark.
fe·char tr. to date.
fe·cho, a adj. done, executed (used in legal documents).
fe·cho·rí·a f. misdeed, misdemeanor.
fé·cu·la f. starch.
fe·cun·dar tr. to make fertile; (engendrar) to fertilize, fecundate.
fe·cun·di·dad f. fecundity; FIG. fruitfulness.
fe·cun·di·zar §04 tr. (hacer fecundo) to make fertile; (engendrar) to fertilize.
fe·cun·do, a adj. fecund; FIG. abundant, rich.
fe·de·ral adj. & m.f. federal.
fe·de·ra·lis·ta adj. & m.f. federalist.
fe·de·rar tr. & reflex. to federate, confederate.
fe·ha·cien·te adj. authentic, reliable.
fe·li·ci·dad f. felicity, happiness; (suerte feliz)

good luck ♦ pl. *(enhorabuena)* congratulations; *(deseos amistosos)* best or warm wishes.

fe·li·ci·ta·ción f. congratulation(s).

fe·li·ci·tar tr. to congratulate; *(desear bien)* to wish well —reflex. to congratulate oneself; *(contentarse)* to be happy.

fe·li·grés, e·sa m.f. parishioner.

fe·li·gre·sí·a f. parish, parishioners.

fe·li·no, a adj. & m. feline.

fe·liz adj. happy; *(acertado)* felicitous, apt; *(oportuno)* lucky.

fe·lo·ní·a f. treachery, perfidy.

fel·pa f. TEX. plush; COLL. *(zurra)* beating, thrashing; *(represión)* telling off, scolding.

fel·pa·do, a adj. plush.

fel·par tr. to cover with plush.

fel·po m. mat, rug.

fel·po·so, a adj. plush, velvety.

fel·pu·do, a I. adj. plush, velvety **II.** m. mat, rug.

fe·me·ni·no, a adj. & m. feminine.

fe·mi·n(e)i·dad f. femininity.

fe·mi·nis·ta adj. & m.f. feminist.

fé·mur m. femur, thighbone.

fe·ne·cer §17 tr. to finish, settle —intr. *(morir)* to die, pass away; *(acabarse)* to come to an end, conclude.

fé·ni·co, a adj. phenic, carbolic.

fé·nix f.inv. phoenix.

fe·no·bar·bi·tal m. phenobarbital.

fe·nol m. phenol.

fe·no·me·nal adj. phenomenal.

fe·nó·me·no m. phenomenon; *(monstruo)* freak, monster.

fe·o, a I. adj. ugly ♦ **dejar f.** to slight, hurt ♦ **más f. que Picio** as ugly as sin **II.** adv. AMER. nasty, awful **III.** m. COLL. *(desaire)* insult, slight; *(fealdad)* ugliness.

fé·re·tro m. *(ataúd)* coffin; *(andas)* bier.

fe·ria f. *(mercado)* market; *(exposición)* fair; *(día de fiesta)* holiday.

fe·ria·do, a adj. ♦ **día f.** holiday.

fe·rian·te I. adj. fair-going **II.** m.f. fairgoer; *(comerciante)* trader, exhibitor.

fe·ri·no, a adj. fierce, ferocious ♦ **tos f.** whooping cough.

fer·men·tar tr. & intr. to ferment.

fer·men·to m. ferment; BIOCHEM. enzyme; CUL. leaven(ing).

fer·mio m. fermium.

fe·ro·ci·dad f. ferocity.

fe·roz adj. *(cruel)* ferocious, fierce; COLL. *(tremendo)* tremendous, terrible.

fe·rrar §49 tr. to plate or trim with iron.

fé·rre·o, a adj. iron.

fe·rre·te·rí·a f. ironworks, foundry; *(comercio)* hardware store; *(quincalla)* hardware.

fe·rre·te·ro, a m.f. hardware dealer.

fe·rro·ca·rril m. railroad, railway.

fe·rro·via·rio, a adj. & m.f. railroad (employee).

fér·til adj. fertile ♦ **f. de** or **en** abundant or rich in.

fer·ti·li·dad f. fertility; *(abundancia)* abundance.

fer·ti·li·zan·te I. adj. fertilizing **II.** m. fertilizer.

fer·ti·li·zar §04 tr. to fertilize.

fer·vien·te adj. fervent, fervid.

fer·vor m. fervor.

fer·vo·ro·so, a adj. fervent, fervid.

fes·te·jar tr. to entertain; *(celebrar)* to celebrate; *(galantear)* to court, woo; MEX. to beat, thrash.

fes·te·jo m. entertainment, feast; *(galanteo)* courting, wooing; AMER. celebration, party.

fes·tín m. banquet, feast.

fes·ti·val m. festival.

fes·ti·vi·dad f. festivity; *(día)* feast or holy day.

fes·ti·vo, a adj. festive; *(agudo)* witty, humorous.

fes·tón m. festoon.

fes·to·ne·ar/nar tr. to festoon.

fe·tal adj. fetal.

fe·ti·che m. fetish.

fe·ti·chis·ta adj. & m.f. fetishist(ic).

fe·ti·dez f. fetidness, stench.

fé·ti·do, a adj. fetid, foul-smelling.

fe·to m. fetus.

fe·ú·c(h)o, a adj. COLL. ugly, hideous.

feu·dal adj. feudal, feudalistic.

feu·do m. *(territorio)* feud, fee; *(tributo)* tribute, tithe; *(vasallaje)* vassalage, fealty.

fez m. fez.

fia·ble adj. reliable, dependable.

fia·do, a adj. trusting ♦ **al f.** on credit.

fia·dor, ·ra m.f. guarantor; LAW bailsman, bailer —m. *(presilla)* fastener; TECH. catch.

fiam·bre I. adj. CUL. (served) cold; COLL. *(sin novedad)* old, stale ♦ **estar hecho f.** COLL. to kick the bucket, drop dead **II.** m. cold cut; AMER., COLL. boring party.

fiam·bre·rí·a f. S. AMER. delicatessen.

fian·za f. guaranty; *(depósito)* security, deposit; *(fiador)* guarantor.

fiar §30 tr. to guaranty; *(vender)* to sell on credit; *(confiar)* to entrust —intr. & reflex. to trust *(de, a* in).

fias·co m. fiasco, failure.

fi·bra f. fiber; *(de madera)* grain; *(vigor)* vigor, energy; MIN. vein; TEX. staple.

fi·bro·ce·men·to m. asbestos cement.

fi·bro·ma m. fibroma.

fi·bro·so, a adj. fibrous.

fic·ción f. fiction.

fi·cha f. *(en los juegos)* counter, chip; *(dominó)* domino; *(disco de metal)* token; *(tarjeta)* index card —m. AMER. rogue, rascal.

fi·char tr. to keep on an index card; *(en bares, restaurantes)* to keep a tab; *(en fábricas)* to punch in or out; *(en dominó)* to play; COLL. *(cuidarse de)* to keep tabs on.

fi·che·ro m. file (cabinet); COMPUT. file.

fic·ti·cio, a adj. fictitious.

fi·de·dig·no, a adj. trustworthy, reliable.

fi·dei·co·mi·sa·rio, a adj. & m.f. fiduciary.

fi·de·li·dad f. fidelity; *(exactitud)* exactness, accuracy.

fi·de·o m. noodle; COLL. *(persona delgada)* skinny person, rail.

fi·du·cia·rio, a adj. & m.f. fiduciary.

fie·bre f. fever ♦ **tener f.** to run a fever.

fiel I. adj. faithful, loyal; *(exacto)* exact, accurate; *(honrado)* honest, trustworthy; *(religioso)* faithful **II.** m. *(oficial)* public inspector; *(aguja)* needle, pointer; *(clavillo)* pin (of scissors).

fiel·tro m. felt; *(sombrero)* felt hat.

fie·re·za f. *(crueldad)* fierceness, ferocity; *(deformidad)* ugliness, deformity.

fie·ro, a I. adj. fierce, ferocious; *(grande)* enormous, huge **II.** m. bluff, threat ♦ **echar fieros** to bluster, make threats —f. *(bestia)* wild animal or beast; *(persona irritada)* hothead, ornery person; *(persona cruel)* beast, brute ♦ **ser una f. para** to be a fiend for.

fie·rre, rro see **ferrar.**

fie·rro AMER. m. brand, mark ♦ pl. tools.

fies·ta f. party, celebration; *(feriado)* holiday; RELIG. feast, holy day ♦ **aguar la f.** COLL. to spoil the fun • **hacer f.** to take a holiday • **no estar para fiestas** to be in no mood for joking • **se acabó la f.** COLL. the party's over.

fi·gu·ra f. figure; *(cara)* face, countenance; *(actor)* character; *(naipe)* face card; *(mudanza)* figure, step; MUS. note.

fi·gu·ra·ble adj. imaginable, conceivable.

fi·gu·ra·ción f. figuration; *(idea)* idea, invention.

fi·gu·ra·do, a adj. figurative.

fi·gu·ran·te, a m.f. THEAT. extra, walk-on; FIG. supernumerary.

fi·gu·rar tr. to represent, depict; *(fingir)* to feign, simulate —intr. to figure, take part —reflex. to imagine, figure ♦ **¡figúrate!** just imagine!

fi·gu·ra·ti·vo, a adj. figurative.

fi·gu·rín m. fashion plate ♦ pl. fashion magazines.

fi·ja f. see **fijo, a.**

fi·ja·ción f. fixing, fixation.

fi·ja·dor, ·ra I. adj. fixing, fixative **II.** m. CONST. pointer; *(para el pelo)* hair spray; PHOTOG. fixative.

fi·ja·men·te adv. firmly; *(atentamente)* fixedly, steadfastly.

fi·jar tr. to fix, fasten; *(establecer)* to establish ♦ **f. los ojos** *(mirar)* to stare; COLL. *(morir)* to die —reflex. to settle, become fixed; *(atender)* to pay attention ♦ **¡fíjate!** just imagine!

fi·je·za f. firmness, steadfastness ♦ **mirar con f.** to stare at, look at fixedly.

fi·jo, a I. adj. fixed; *(permanente)* permanent; *(estable)* stable, steady; *(de colores)* fast, indelible ♦ **de f.** certainly, surely **II.** m. fixed salary —f. *(bisagra)* large hinge; CONSTR. trowel; AMER. *(cosa segura)* sure thing.

fi·la f. *(hilera)* file; *(cola)* line, queue; *(línea)* row, line; COLL. dislike, aversion; SL. *(rostro)* face; MIL. rank ♦ **alistarse en filas** to sign up, enlist • **en filas** on active duty *or* service.

fi·la·men·to m. filament.

fi·lan·tro·pí·a f. philanthropy.

fi·lán·tro·po, a m.f. philanthropist.

fi·lar·mo·ní·a f. love of music.

fi·lar·mó·ni·co, a adj. & m.f. philharmonic.

fi·la·te·lis·ta m.f. philatelist, stamp collector.

fi·le·te m. CUL. fillet; TECH. thread.

fi·le·te·ar tr. CUL. to fillet; TECH. to thread.

fi·lia·ción f. filiation; *(señas personales)* description.

fi·lial I. adj. filial; COM. subsidiary, branch **II.** f. COM. branch (office); *(subdivisión)* subsidiary.

fi·li·bus·te·ro m. filibuster.

fi·li·gra·na f. filigree; PRINT. watermark.

fi·li·lí m. [pl. **-íes.**] COLL. fineness, delicacy.

fi·lí·pi·ca f. philippic, invective.

fi·lis·te·o, a adj. & m.f. Philistine —m. giant, big man.

film *or* **fil·me** m. film, movie.

fil·mar tr. to film, shoot.

fíl·mi·co, a adj. film, movie.

fi·lo m. *(cutting edge)* C. AMER., MEX. hunger ♦ **al f. de la medianoche** at the stroke of midnight • **dar f.** *or* **un f.** *(afilar)* to sharpen; *(inci-*

tar) to incite, excite • **por f.** exactly.

fi·lo·lo·gí·a f. philology.

fi·ló·lo·go, a m.f. philologist, philologer.

fi·lón m. MIN. vein, lode; FIG. gold mine.

fi·lo·so, a adj. AMER. sharp, sharp-edged.

fi·lo·so·fal adj. • **piedra f.** philosopher's stone.

fi·lo·so·far intr. to philosophize.

fi·lo·so·fí·a f. philosophy.

fi·ló·so·fo, a I. adj. philosophic(al) **II.** m.f. philosopher.

fil·tra·ción f. filtration.

fil·tran·te adj. filtering.

fil·trar tr. & intr. to filter —reflex. *(pasarse)* to filter, pass through; *(disminuirse)* to disappear, dwindle.

fil·tro m. filter; *(bebedizo)* love potion, philter.

fin m. end; *(meta)* aim, end ♦ **a f. de** in order to • **a f. de cuentas** in the final analysis • **a f. de que** so that • **a fines de** at the end of • **al f.** at last, finally • **al f. y al cabo** after all, when all is said and done • **dar f. a** to finish off • **en f.** *(finalmente)* finally; *(en resumen)* in brief, in short • **f. de semana** weekend • **poner f. a** to finish, put an end to • **por f.** finally, at last • **sin f.** endless • **un sin f.** no end.

fi·na·do, a m.f. deceased, dead person.

fi·nal I. adj. final, last **II.** m. *(fin)* end, ending; MUS. finale —f. SPORT. final ♦ **al f.** in *or* at the end.

fi·na·li·dad f. purpose, objective.

fi·na·lis·ta m.f. finalist.

fi·na·li·za·ción f. conclusion, finish.

fi·na·li·zar §04 tr. to finish, conclude —intr. to (come to an) end.

fi·nan·cia·ción f./**mien·to** m. financing.

fi·nan·ciar tr. to finance.

fi·nan·cie·ro, a I. adj. financial **II.** m.f. financier.

fi·nan·zas f.pl. finance(s).

fin·ca f. property, real estate; AMER. farm.

fin·car §70 tr. & intr. to acquire property *or* real estate; *(establecerse)* to settle, get established; AMER. to rest, lie —reflex. to acquire property.

fi·ne·za f. fineness; *(cortesía)* courtesy, politeness; *(amabilidad)* kindness, affection; *(regalo)* gift, present.

fin·gi·do, a I. adj. false, feigned **II.** m.f. feigner, dissembler.

fin·gi·mien·to m. feigning, pretense.

fin·gir §32 tr. to pretend, feign.

fi·ni·qui·tar tr. to close, settle; *(concluir)* to conclude, finish; *(matar)* to bump off, rub out.

fi·ni·to, a adj. finite.

fi·no, a adj. fine; *(precioso)* precious; *(puro)* pure; *(cortés)* refined, elegant; *(delicado)* delicate; *(astuto)* astute, shrewd.

fi·nu·ra f. fineness; *(urbanidad)* refinement, politeness; *(sutileza)* subtlety, delicacy.

fiord *or* **fior·do** m. fjord, fiord.

fir·ma f. signature; *(acción)* signing; COM. firm, company ♦ **f. en blanco** carte blanche.

fir·ma·men·to m. firmament, heavens.

fir·man·te I. adj. signatory **II.** m.f. signer.

fir·mar tr. & reflex. to sign.

fir·me I. adj. firm; *(constante)* steadfast, staunch ♦ **de f.** hard • **en f.** final, definitive • **mantenerse** *or* **ponerse f.** to stand firm **II.** m. foundation, bed **III.** adv. firmly, steadily.

fir·me·za f. firmness.

fi·ru·le·tes m.pl. AMER. ornaments.

fis·cal I. adj. fiscal **II.** m. *(tesorero)* treasurer;

(abogado) district attorney, public prosecutor (G.B.); *(entremetido)* busybody, snooper.

fis·ca·li·zar §04 tr. *(controlar)* to supervise, oversee; *(investigar)* to investigate, inspect; *(curiosear)* to pry into, snoop.

fis·co m. public treasury, exchequer (G.B.).

fis·gar §47 tr. to spear, harpoon; *(husmear)* to pry into, snoop on —intr. & reflex. to make fun of.

fis·gón, o·na COLL. m.f. *(curioso)* snooper; *(burlador)* tease, mocker.

fis·go·ne·ar tr. COLL. to snoop, pry.

fí·si·co, a I. adj. physical **II.** m.f. *(persona)* physicist —m. physique, appearance —f. physics.

fi·sio·lo·gí·a f. physiology.

fi·sió·lo·go, a m.f. physiologist.

fi·sión f. fission.

fi·sio·te·ra·pia f. physiotherapy.

fi·s(i)o·no·mí·a f. physiognomy.

fís·tu·la f. fistula.

fi·su·ra f. fissure.

fla(c)·ci·dez f. flaccidity, flabbiness.

flá(c)·ci·do, a adj. flaccid, flabby.

fla·co, a I. adj. thin, lean; *(sin fuerza)* weak, feeble **II.** m. FIG. weak spot, weakness.

fla·ge·la·ción f. flagellation.

fla·ge·la·do, a adj. flagellate.

fla·ge·lar tr. to flagellate.

fla·ge·lo m. whip, scourge.

fla·gran·te adj. flagrant ♦ **en f. (delito)** in the act, red-handed.

fla·man·te adj. brilliant, bright; *(nuevo)* brand-new, like new.

fla·me·ar intr. *(llamear)* to blaze, flame; *(ondear)* to flap, flutter.

fla·men·co, a I. adj. flamenco; *(achulado)* cocky; C. AMER., MEX. skinny **II.** m. *(cuchillo)* dagger, sheath knife; ORNITH. flamingo.

flan m. flan, caramel custard.

flan·co m. side, flank; MIL. flank.

flan·que·ar tr. to flank.

fla·que·ar intr. to weaken.

fla·que·za f. thinness, leanness; *(debilidad)* weakness; *(fragilidad)* frailty.

fla·to m. flatus, gas; AMER. melancholy.

fla·tu·len·cia f. flatulence.

flau·ta f. flute ♦ **entre pitos y flautas** one thing or another ♦ **¡la gran f.!** AMER., COLL. my God! —m. flautist, flutist.

flau·tín m. piccolo.

flau·tis·ta m.f. flautist, flutist.

fle·bi·tis f. phlebitis.

fle·bo·to·mí·a f. phlebotomy, bloodletting.

fle·co m. *(adorno)* fringe; *(borde desgastado)* frayed edge; *(flequillo)* bangs.

fle·cha f. arrow.

fle·char tr. *(el arco)* to draw; *(asaetear)* to shoot *or* kill with an arrow; *(enamorar)* to infatuate, make a hit with.

fle·cha·zo m. *(disparo)* arrow shot *or* wound; COLL. *(amor)* love at first sight.

fle·je m. iron band or strip.

fle·ma f. phlegm.

fle·má·ti·co, a adj. phlegmatic(al).

fle·qui·llo m. bangs.

fle·tar tr. *(alquilar)* to charter; *(embarcar)* to load; AMER. to hire, rent.

fle·te m. *(alquiler)* charter fee; *(carga)* freight, cargo; AMER. freightage; *(precio de transporte)* freightage; AMER. *(caballo)* spirited horse.

fle·xi·bi·li·dad f. flexibility.

fle·xi·ble I. adj. flexible **II.** m. electric cord.

fle·xión f. flexion; GRAM. inflection.

fle·xor, ·ra adj. & m. flexor.

flir·te·ar intr. to flirt.

flir·te·o m. flirtation, flirting.

flo·je·ar intr. *(obrar con flojedad)* to slacken, idle; *(flaquear)* to weaken.

flo·je·dad f. *(flaqueza)* weakness, debility; *(pereza)* laziness, carelessness.

flo·je·ra f. laziness, carelessness.

flo·jo, a I. adj. *(suelto)* loose, slack; *(fláccido)* limp, flabby; *(débil)* weak; *(holgazán)* lazy, shiftless **II.** m.f. idler, loafer.

flor f. flower; blossom, bloom <*en f.* in bloom>; *(frescura)* bloom, prime; *(piropo)* compliment; *(de la piel)* grain ♦ **a f. de** on the surface of, level with • **f. de lis** jacobean lily; HER. fleur-de-lis • **f. y nata** the cream of the crop.

flo·ra f. flora.

flo·re·ar tr. to flower, decorate with flowers; *(cerner)* to sift —intr. to brandish a sword; COLL. *(echar flores)* to pay compliments; *(escoger lo mejor)* to pick the best.

flo·re·cer §17 intr. to flower, bloom; *(prosperar)* to thrive, flourish —reflex. to become moldy.

flo·re·ci·do, a adj. moldy.

flo·re·cien·te adj. flowering, blooming; *(próspero)* thriving, prosperous.

flo·re·ci·mien·to m. flowering.

flo·re·o m. chatter, small talk; *(dicho frívolo)* quip, jest; *(en esgrima)* flourish; MUS. arpeggio.

flo·re·rí·a f. flower *or* florist's shop.

flo·re·ro, a I. adj. joking, jesting **II.** m.f. florist —m. (flower) vase.

flo·res·cen·cia f. CHEM. efflorescence; BOT. florescence.

flo·res·ta f. *(bosque)* wood, forest; *(antología)* anthology.

flo·re·te I. adj. superfine **II.** m. foil.

flo·ri·cul·tor, ·ra m.f. floriculturist.

flo·ri·cul·tu·ra f. floriculture.

flo·ri·do, a adj. flowery; *(escogido)* choice, select.

flo·ris·ta m.f. florist.

flo·ta f. *(buques)* fleet; *(aviones)* squadron.

flo·ta·ción f. flotation, floating.

flo·ta·dor, ·ra I. adj. floating, buoyant **II.** m. float; MARIT. outrigger.

flo·tan·te adj. floating, buoyant.

flo·tar intr. to float.

flo·te m. ♦ **a f.** afloat.

flo·ti·lla f. flotilla.

fluc·tua·ción f. fluctuation.

fluc·tuan·te adj. fluctuating.

fluc·tuar §67 intr. to fluctuate; *(ondear)* to bob, undulate; *(estar en peligro)* to be in danger, be at risk; *(dudar)* to vacillate, waver.

fluen·cia f. *(acción)* stream, flow; *(fuente)* source, spring.

flui·dez f. fluidity.

flui·do, a I. adj. fluid; *(inseguro)* in flux **II.** m. fluid; ELEC. current.

fluir §18 intr. to flow; *(brotar)* to gush, stream.

flu·jo m. flow, flux; FIG. flood, stream ♦ **f. de risa** fit of laughter • **f. de sangre** hemorrhage • **f. de vientre** diarrhea • **f. y reflujo** ebb and flow.

flú·or m. fluorine.

fluo·res·cen·te adj. fluorescent.

fluo·ri·za·ción f. fluoridation.

fluo·ros·co·pio m. fluoroscope.
fluo·ru·ro m. fluoride.
flu·vial adj. fluvial, river.
flux m.inv. flush ♦ **estar a f. de todo** AMER. to have nothing • **hacer f.** AMER. to squander everything.
flu·ya, ya, yera, yó see **fluir**.
flu·yen·te adj. flowing.
fo·bia f. phobia.
fo·ca f. seal.
fo·cal adj. focal.
fo·co m. focus; *(fuente)* source; *(reflector)* spotlight.
fo·fo, a adj. soft, spongy.
fo·ga·ta f. bonfire.
fo·gón m. *(cocina)* stove, range; *(de caldera)* firebox; AMER. bonfire.
fo·go·na·zo m. powder flash.
fo·go·ne·ro m. stoker, fireman.
fo·go·si·dad f. fire, spirit.
fo·go·so, a adj. fiery, spirited.
fo·ja f. leaf, sheet (of paper).
fo·lia·ción f. foliation.
fo·liar I. tr. PRINT. to foliate, number **II.** adj. BOT. foliar.
fo·lí·cu·lo m. follicle.
fo·lio m. page, leaf; PRINT. running head *or* title ♦ **de a f.** COLL. very big, huge.
folk·lo·re m. folklore.
folk·ló·ri·co, a adj. folk(loric); *(pintoresco)* picturesque, quaint.
fo·lla·je m. foliage; *(adorno)* tasteless decoration; *(palabrería)* verbiage.
fo·lle·tín m. serial.
fo·lle·ti·nes·co, a adj. serial; *(melodramático)* melodramatic.
fo·lle·to m. pamphlet, brochure.
fo·men·tar tr. *(calentar)* to warm, incubate; *(instigar)* to foment, stir up; *(promover)* to promote, foster.
fo·men·to m. *(calor)* warmth; *(pábulo)* fuel; *(auxilio)* promotion, development.
fon·da f. *(posada)* inn; *(restaurante)* restaurant; AMER. tavern, bar; CHILE refreshment stand.
fon·da·ble adj. fit for anchoring.
fon·de·a·de·ro m. anchorage.
fon·de·a·do, a adj. AMER. rich, wealthy.
fon·de·ar tr. to sound, fathom; *(examinar)* investigate, probe —intr. to anchor, drop anchor —reflex. AMER. to get rich.
fon·di·llo m. rear (end), butt ♦ pl. seat of the pants.
fon·do m. *(base)* bottom; *(hondura)* depth, bed; *(parte más lejos)* rear, back; *(campo)* ground, background; *(colección)* collection; *(residuo)* residue; *(índole)* character, nature; *(lo principal)* essence, bottom; *(reserva)* store, reservoir ♦ **a f.** completely, thoroughly • **bajos fondos** scum, dregs • **dar f.** to drop anchor • **de f.** main, leading • **echar a f.** to sink • **en f.** abreast • **irse a f.** to sink, founder • **sin f.** bottomless ♦ pl. funds, capital • **estar con f.** to have money • **f. disponibles** ready cash.
fo·ne·ma m. phoneme.
fo·né·ti·co, a I. adj. phonetic **II.** f. phonetics.
fo·ne·tis·ta m.f. phonetician, phoneticist.
fó·ni·co, a adj. phonic.
fo·no·grá·fi·co, a adj. phonographic.
fo·nó·gra·fo m. phonograph, record player.
fo·ra·ji·do, a adj. & m.f. fugitive, outlaw.

fo·rá·ne·o, a adj. foreign, alien.
fo·ras·te·ro, a I. adj. foreign, alien **II.** m.f. stranger, outsider.
for·ce·jar/je·ar intr. to struggle, resist.
for·ce·je·o/jo m. struggle, struggling.
fór·ceps m.inv. forceps.
fo·ren·se adj. forensic.
fo·res·ta·ción f. (re)forestation.
fo·res·tal adj. forest(al).
for·ja f. forge; *(fragua)* forge, hammer; *(ferrería)* ironworks, foundry; *(argamasa)* mortar.
for·ja·du·ra f./**mien·to** m. forging.
for·jar tr. to forge, hammer; *(fabricar)* to make, form; *(inventar)* to invent, make up —reflex. to forge; AMER. to make a bundle.
for·ma f. form; *(dimensiones)* shape; *(silueta)* figure, outline; *(molde)* mold, pattern; *(formato)* format; *(documento)* form, questionnaire; *(manera)* way, method ♦ **de f. que** so that, in such a way that • **en debida f.** in due form, duly • **formas sociales** manners, social conventions • **guardar las formas** to keep up appearances • **hacer f.** to line up.
for·ma·ción f. formation; *(educación)* upbringing, training.
for·ma·do, a adj. formed, shaped.
for·mal adj. formal.
for·mal·de·hí·do m. formaldehyde.
for·ma·li·dad f. formality.
for·ma·lis·mo m. formalism.
for·ma·li·zar §04 tr. to formalize —reflex. to take offense.
for·mar tr. to form; *(moldear)* to shape; *(criar)* to bring up, rear —intr. MIL. to fall in —reflex. to take form; *(desarrollarse)* to develop.
for·ma·ti·vo, a adj. formative.
for·ma·to m. format; *(tamaño)* size.
for·mi·da·ble adj. formidable.
for·món m. firmer chisel.
fór·mu·la f. formula; MED. prescription; CUL. recipe; *(expresión)* formality ♦ **por f.** as a matter of form.
for·mu·lar I. tr. to formulate **II.** adj. formulaic.
for·mu·la·rio I. m. formulary **II.** adj. formulistic.
for·ni·ca·ción f. fornication.
for·ni·car §70 intr. to fornicate.
for·ni·do, a adj. robust, strong.
fo·ro m. forum; LAW court, tribunal; *(profesión)* bar, legal profession.
fo·rra·je m. forage, fodder; *(fárrago)* hodgepodge, mess.
fo·rra·je·ar tr. & intr. to forage.
fo·rrar tr. *(coser)* to line; *(cubrir)* to cover —reflex. AMER., COLL. *(enriquecerse)* to get rich; *(atiborrarse)* to stuff oneself.
fo·rro m. lining; *(cubierta)* cover, covering; MARIT. sheathing; TECH. liner, lining.
for·ta·le·ce·dor, ·ra adj. fortifying.
for·ta·le·cer §17 tr. to fortify.
for·ta·le·ci·mien·to m. *(acción)* fortifying, strengthening; *(defensas)* fortifications, defenses.
for·ta·le·za f. *(vigor)* strength, vigor; *(virtud)* fortitude; *(fortín)* fortress, stronghold.
for·ti·fi·ca·ción f. fortification.
for·ti·fi·can·te I. adj. fortifying **II.** m. tonic.
for·ti·fi·car §70 tr. to fortify.
for·tín m. *(fuerte)* small, fort; *(refugio)* bunker.
for·tui·to, a adj. fortuitous, chance.
for·tu·na f. fortune; *(borrasca)* storm, tempest

◆ **por** f. fortunately • **probar** f. to try one's luck.

fo·rún·cu·lo m. boil, furuncle.

for·za·da·men·te adv. by force, forcibly.

for·za·do, a I. adj. forced **II.** m. convict.

for·zar §37 tr. to force; *(capturar)* to take by force; *(violar)* to rape; *(obligar)* to force, compel.

for·zo·sa·men·te adv. by force, forcibly; *(ineludiblemente)* unavoidably, inevitably.

for·zo·so, a adj. unavoidable, inevitable.

for·zu·do, a adj. strong, robust.

fo·sa f. *(sepultura)* grave, tomb; ANAT. fossa ◆ **f. séptica** septic tank • **fosas nasales** nostrils.

fos·fa·to m. phosphate.

fos·fo·res·cen·cia f. phosphorescence.

fos·fo·res·cen·te adj. phosphorescent.

fós·fo·ro m. phosphorus; *(cerilla)* match.

fó·sil I. m. fossil **II.** adj. fossil, fossilized; COLL. *(antiguo)* old, outdated.

fo·si·li·za·ción f. fossilization.

fo·si·li·zar·se §04 reflex. to fossilize.

fo·so m. pit, ditch; THEAT. pit; MIL. moat, trench.

fo·to f. photo, picture ◆ **sacar fotos** to take *or* snap pictures.

fo·to·com·po·si·ción f. photocomposition, phototypesetting.

fo·to·co·pia f. photocopy.

fo·to·co·piar tr. to photocopy.

fo·to·gé·ni·co, a adj. photogenic.

fo·to·gra·ba·do m. photoengraving.

fo·to·gra·bar tr. to photoengrave.

fo·to·gra·fí·a f. photography; *(retrato)* photograph, picture; *(taller)* photography studio.

fo·to·gra·fiar §30 tr. to photograph.

fo·to·grá·fi·co, a adj. photographic.

fo·tó·gra·fo, a m.f. photographer.

fo·to·me·trí·a f. photometry.

fo·tó·me·tro m. photometer.

fo·tón m. photon.

fo·to·sen·si·ble adj. photosensitive.

fo·to·sín·te·sis f. photosynthesis.

fo·to·tro·pis·mo m. phototropism.

frac m. [pl. **s** *or* **-ques**] tails, formal coat.

fra·ca·sa·do, a I. adj. failed, unsuccessful **II.** m.f. failure, unsuccessful person.

fra·ca·sar intr. to fail.

fra·ca·so m. failure.

frac·ción f. fraction.

frac·cio·na·mien·to m. *(división)* division, breaking (into parts); MATH. fractionization; CHEM. fractionation.

frac·cio·nar tr. to divide, break (into parts); MATH. to fractionize; CHEM. to fractionate.

frac·tu·ra f. fracture, break.

frac·tu·rar tr. to fracture, break.

fra·gan·cia f. fragrance, perfume; *(fama)* good reputation.

fra·gan·te adj. fragrant, perfumed; *(flagrante)* flagrant.

fra·ga·ta f. MARIT. frigate; ORNITH. frigate bird.

frá·gil adj. fragile; *(fugaz)* perishable, fleeting.

frag·men·tar tr. to fragment.

frag·men·ta·rio, a adj. fragmentary.

frag·men·to m. fragment; *(trozo)* passage, excerpt.

fra·gor m. din, uproar.

fra·go·ro·so, a adj. roaring, thunderous.

fra·go·so, a adj. rough, rugged; *(ruidoso)* thunderous.

fra·gua f. forge, smithy.

fra·gua·do m. setting, hardening.

fra·guar §10 tr. *(hierro)* to forge; *(inventar)* to plan, plot —intr. to set, harden.

frai·le m. friar, monk.

fram·bue·sa f. raspberry.

fram·bue·so m. raspberry bush.

fran·ca·che·la f. COLL. *(comilona)* feast, spread; *(parranda)* spree, binge.

fran·cio m. francium.

fran·cis·ca·no/co, a adj. & m.f. Franciscan.

fran·co, a I. adj. *(sincero)* frank; *(liberal)* generous; *(desembarazado)* open, clear; *(exento)* exempt, free ◆ **f. de porte** postpaid **II.** m. FIN. franc.

fra·ne·la f. TEX. flannel; AMER. undershirt.

fran·ja f. fringe, border; *(banda)* strip, band.

fran·je·ar tr. to fringe, trim.

fran·que·ar tr. *(eximir)* to exempt; *(conceder)* to grant; *(desembarazar)* to clear, open; *(pagar el porte)* to frank; *(liberar)* to free, enfranchise; *(atravesar)* to cross, pass through —reflex. *(acceder)* to yield, give in; *(confiar)* to confide.

fran·que·o m. *(de correo)* franking; *(sellos)* postage.

fran·que·za f. frankness, candor; *(exención)* freedom, exemption; *(generosidad)* generosity.

fran·qui·cia f. exemption ◆ **f. postal** frank, franking privilege.

fra·que m. var. of **frac.**

fras·co m. small bottle; *(redoma)* flask, vial; ARM. powder flask.

fra·se f. sentence, phrase ◆ **f. hecha** set expression.

fra·se·ar tr. to phrase.

fra·se·o m. phrasing.

fra·se·o·lo·gí·a f. phraseology; *(estilo)* phrasing, style.

fra·ter·nal adj. brotherly, fraternal.

fra·ter·nal·men·te adv. fraternally.

fra·ter·ni·dad f. brotherhood, fraternity.

fra·ter·ni·zar §04 intr. to fraternize.

fra·ter·no, a adj. fraternal.

fra·tri·ci·da I. adj. fratricidal **II.** m.f. fratricide.

fra·tri·ci·dio m. fratricide.

frau·de m. fraud.

frau·du·len·to, a adj. fraudulent.

fray m. Fra, Brother.

fra·za·da f. blanket.

fre·cuen·cia f. frequency.

fre·cuen·tar tr. to frequent.

fre·cuen·te adj. frequent; *(común)* habitual.

fre·ga·de·ro m. kitchen sink.

fre·ga·do, a I. m. scrubbing, scouring; COLL. *(enredo)* mess, tangle **II.** adj. AMER. stubborn, obstinate.

fre·ga·du·ra f. **/mien·to** m. var. of **fregado.**

fre·gar §52 tr. to scour, scrub; *(lavar)* to wash; AMER., COLL. *(molestar)* to annoy, bother —reflex. AMER. to become annoyed.

fre·gón, o·na I. adj. AMER. bothersome, annoying **II.** m.f. AMER. pest, annoyance —f. scullery maid.

frei·du·ra f. **/mien·to** m. frying.

fre·ír §58 tr. CUL. to fry; *(fastidiar)* to pester, annoy; AMER., COLL. *(matar a tiros)* to kill, shoot —reflex. COLL. to be excited ◆ **f. de calor** to be boiling hot.

fre·nar tr. *(caballo)* to bridle; *(vehículo)* to brake, apply the brake to; *(hábito, vicio)* to curb, check.

fre·na·zo m. sudden braking.

fre·ne·sí m. [pl. **-íes**] *(delirio)* frenzy.
fre·né·ti·co, a adj. frenetic, frenzied; *(colérico)* mad, furious.
fre·ni·llo m. muzzle, bridle ♦ **no tener f. en la lengua** to speak one's mind.
fre·no m. EQUIT. bit; MECH. brake; *(obstáculo)* obstacle, check ♦ **tascar** or **morder el f.** COLL. to champ at the bit.
fren·te f. forehead, brow; *(rostro)* face, countenance; *(cabeza)* head ♦ **arrugar la f.** to knit one's brow • **f. a f.** face to face —m. front; *(fachada)* face, façade; *(anverso)* obverse; MIL., METEOROL. front ♦ **al** or **en f.** in front, opposite • **al f. de** at the head of, in charge of • **de f.** resolutely, without hesitation • **f. a** facing, opposite • **hacer f.** to face, confront.
fre·sa adj. & f. strawberry.
fres·co, a I. adj. cool; *(nuevo)* fresh; *(descarado)* fresh, cheeky, impudent ♦ **estar** or **quedar f.** COLL. to fail, be disappointed • **¡que f.!** what a nerve! **II.** m. cool, coolness; *(aire)* fresh air; ARTS fresco; AMER. cool drink ♦ **al f.** in the open air, in the fresh air —f. fresh air; COLL. *(dicho desagradable)* biting or blunt remark.
fres·cor m. freshness, coolness.
fres·cu·ra f. freshness, coolness; *(chanza)* fresh remark; *(serenidad)* serenity, equanimity; *(descuido)* coolness.
freu·dia·no, a adj. & m.f. Freudian.
frial·dad f. coldness, frigidity; *(indiferencia)* indifference; *(falta de animación)* dullness; MED. frigidity, impotence; *(necedad)* nonsense, foolishness.
frí·a·men·te adv. coldly, coolly; *(sin gracia)* dully, colorlessly.
fri·ca·ti·vo, a adj. & f. fricative.
fric·ción f. friction; *(masaje)* massage, rubdown.
fric·cio·nar tr. to rub; *(dar masajes)* to massage.
frie·ga f. *(fricción)* massage, rubdown; AMER., COLL. *(fastidio)* bother, annoyance.
frie·go, gue see **fregar.**
frie·ra, frió see **freír.**
fri·gi·dai·re m. refrigerator.
fri·gi·dez f. frigidity.
frí·gi·do, a adj. frigid.
fri·go·rí·fi·co, a I. adj. refrigerator, refrigerating **II.** m. refrigerator; *(establecimiento industrial)* cold-storage plant; *(cámara)* locker, cold-storage room.
frí·jol or **fri·jol** m. bean.
frí·o, a I. adj. cold; *(sin gracia)* graceless, insipid **II.** m. cold, coldness; *(bebida)* cool drink ♦ **coger f.** to catch a cold • **hacer f.** to be cold *<hace mucho f. hoy* it is very cold today> • **tener f.** to be cold *<tengo f.* I am cold> ♦ pl. AMER. malaria; *(helados)* frozen treats.
frio·len·to, a adj. sensitive to the cold.
frio·le·ro, a I. adj. sensitive to the cold **II.** f. trifle, bauble; FIG. a mere, only.
fri·sa f. frieze.
fri·sar tr. to rub —intr. to be compatible, get along (with) ♦ **f. con** or **en** to be close to, border on.
fri·so m. frieze.
fri·ta·da f. fried dish, fry.
fri·to, a I. see **freír II.** adj. fried **III.** m. fried food.
fri·tu·ra f. fried food.
fri·vo·li·dad f. frivolity, frivolousness.

frí·vo·lo, a adj. frivolous.
fron·da f. /**de** m. frond; *(hoja)* leaf, shoot ♦ pl. foliage, leaves.
fron·do·so, a adj. frondose, leafy.
fron·tal adj. frontal.
fron·te·ri·zo, a adj. *(contiguo)* border, frontier; *(de enfrente)* facing, opposite.
fron·te·ro, a I. adj. facing, opposite **II.** m. MIL. border commander —f. border, frontier; ARCHIT. façade.
fron·tis·pi·cio m. frontispiece.
fron·tón m. SPORT. *(pared)* front wall of a handball court; *(cancha)* handball court; ARCHIT. pediment, gable.
fro·ta·du·ra f./**mien·to** m. rubbing, rub.
fro·tar tr. to rub —reflex. to rub (together).
fro·te m. rub, rubbing.
fruc·tí·fe·ro, a adj. fructiferous.
fruc·ti·fi·car §70 intr. to bear or produce fruit; *(producir utilidad)* to be fruitful.
fruc·tuo·so, a adj. fruitful, productive.
fru·frú m. frou-frou.
fru·gal adj. frugal.
fru·ga·li·dad f. frugality, frugalness.
frui·ción f. fruition, enjoyment.
frun·ce/ci·do m. gather, shirr.
frun·cir §35 tr. SEW. to gather, shirr; *(los labios)* to purse; *(la frente)* to frown, knit one's brow; *(reducir)* to contract, reduce.
frus·le·rí·a f. trifle, trinket.
frus·tra·ción f. frustration.
frus·tra·do, a adj. frustrated, thwarted; *(malogrado)* failed.
frus·trar tr. to frustrate, thwart —reflex. *(fracasar)* to fail; *(privarse)* to be frustrated.
fru·ta f. fruit; COLL. *(resultado)* fruit, result.
fru·tal I. adj. fruit **II.** m. fruit tree.
fru·te·rí·a f. fruit store or stand.
fru·te·ro, a I. adj. fruit **II.** m.f. fruit seller or merchant —m. fruit bowl or plate.
fru·ti·lla f. rosary bead.
fru·to m. fruit.
fu·ci·lar intr. to sparkle, flash.
fue see **ser²** or **ir.**
fue·go m. fire; *(llama)* flame, heat; *(hogar)* hearth, home; *(fósforo)* light *<¿tienes f.?* do you have a light?>; *(ardor)* heat, passion; *(faro)* beacon; MIL. fire, discharge; MED. rash ♦ **a f. lento** slowly, little by little; CUL. on a low flame • **entre dos fuegos** between a rock and a hard place • **¡f.!** fire!, shoot! • **f. fatuo** ignis fatuus, jack-o'-lantern • **fuegos artificiales** fireworks • **hacer f.** to fire, shoot • **pegar f.** to set on fire • **romper el f.** to open fire.
fue·lle m. *(implemento)* bellows; *(frunce)* pucker, gather; *(chismoso)* tattletale, gossip.
fuen·te f. *(manantial)* spring; *(aparato)* fountain, water fountain; *(pila)* font; *(plato)* platter, serving dish; *(cabecera)* source, headwater; *(origen)* source, origin ♦ **beber en buenas fuentes** to be well-informed.
fue·ra adv. outside, out ♦ **¡f.!** get out! • **f. de** outside of; *(además de)* besides, except for • **f. de que** aside from the fact that • **f. de sí** beside oneself • **por f.** on the outside.
fue·ra see **ser²** or **ir.**
fue·ro m. jurisdiction, power; *(cuerpo de leyes)* code; *(privilegio)* privilege, exemption ♦ pl. COLL. arrogance, pride.
fuer·te I. adj. strong; *(fortificado)* fortified; *(intenso)* powerful, forceful; loud *<un grito f.* a loud shout> **II.** m. fort, fortress; *(talento)*

forte, strong point **III.** adv. hard; *(en voz alta)* loudly.

fuer·te·men·te adv. hard; *(en voz alta)* loudly.

fuer·za f. force, strength; *(violencia)* force, coercion; *(poder)* power ♦ **a f. de** by dint of • **a la f.** *or* **por f.** by force, forcibly; *(forzosamente)* perforce, necessarily • **a f. viva** by sheer force • **es f.** it is necessary to, one must • **f. mayor** act of God, force majeure.

fu·ga f. flight, escape; *(ardor)* ardor, impetuosity; *(escape)* leak, leakage; MUS. fugue ♦ **darse a la f.** *or* **ponerse en f.** to flee, take (to) flight.

fu·ga·ci·dad f. fugacity, brevity.

fu·gar·se §47 reflex. to flee, run away; *(salirse)* leak (out).

fu·gaz adj. fleeting, brief; ASTRON. shooting.

fu·gi·ti·vo, a adj. & m.f. fugitive.

fui, fuimos, fuiste see **ser²** *or* **ir.**

fu·la·no, a m.f. so-and-so.

ful·gir §32 intr. to shine, sparkle.

ful·gor m. brilliance, radiance.

ful·gu·rar intr. to flash brilliantly.

fu·lle·rí·a f. *(en cartas)* cheating; *(astucia)* astuteness, guile.

fu·lle·ro, a I. adj. crooked, dishonest; COLL. *(astuto)* sharp, wily **II.** m.f. cardsharp, cheat; *(astuto)* sharpie.

ful·mi·nar tr. *(un rayo)* to strike (and kill) by lightning; *(hacer morir bruscamente)* to strike down *or* dead; *(arrojar)* to throw, hurl; FIG. to thunder.

fu·ma·da f. puff (of smoke).

fu·ma·dor, ·ra I. adj. smoking **II.** m.f. smoker.

fu·mar intr. & tr. to smoke —reflex. COLL. *(malgastar)* to squander; *(faltar)* to skip, cut <*f. la clase* to cut class>.

fu·mi·ga·dor, ·ra m.f. fumigator.

fu·mi·gar §47 tr. to fumigate.

fun·ción f. function; *(empleo)* position; THEAT. show, performance.

fun·cio·nal adj. functional, operative.

fun·cio·na·li·dad f. functionality.

fun·cio·na·mien·to m. functioning, operating.

fun·cio·nar intr. to work, run.

fun·cio·na·rio, a m.f. civil servant, official.

fun·da f. cover, case.

fun·da·ción f. foundation.

fun·da·dor, ·ra I. adj. founding **II.** m.f. founder.

fun·da·men·tal adj. fundamental.

fun·da·men·tar tr. to lay the foundations of; *(basar)* to base.

fun·da·men·to m. foundation; *(razón)* reason, ground.

fun·dar tr. to build, raise; *(instituir)* to found, establish; *(apoyar)* to base, rest —reflex. FIG. to be founded *or* based.

fun·di·ción f. melting, smelting; *(fábrica)* foundry, smeltery; *(hierro)* cast iron.

fun·dir tr. METAL. to melt, smelt; *(moldear)* to cast, mold; *(bombilla)* to burn out —reflex. to merge, fuse; AMER. to go bankrupt.

fú·ne·bre adj. funereal.

fu·ne·ral adj. & m. funeral.

fu·né·re·o, a adj. funeral.

fu·nes·to, a adj. unfortunate, regrettable; *(fatal)* ill-fated.

fun·gi·ci·da I. adj. fungicidal **II.** m. fungicide.

fu·ni·cu·lar I. adj. funicular **II.** m. cable car.

fu·ñi·que adj. & m.f. awkward, clumsy (person).

fur·gón f. *(carro)* van, wagon; RAIL. boxcar.

fur·go·ne·ta f. van, truck.

fu·ria f. fury.

fu·ri·bun·do, a adj. enraged, furious.

fu·rio·sa·men·te adv. furiously, frantically.

fu·rio·so, a adj. furious; *(grande)* tremendous.

fu·ror m. fury, rage.

fur·ti·vo, a adj. furtive, stealthy.

fu·rún·cu·lo m. boil, furuncle.

fu·se·la·je m. fuselage.

fu·si·ble I. adj. fusible **II.** m. fuse.

fu·sil m. rifle, gun.

fu·si·la·mien·to m. shooting, execution.

fu·si·lar tr. to shoot; COLL. *(plagiar)* to plagiarize.

fu·sión f. melting, fusion; COM. merger.

fu·sio·nar intr. to merge.

fus·te m. shaft; *(importancia)* importance, consequence.

fus·ti·ga·dor, ·ra I. adj. whipping; *(censurador)* censuring **II.** m.f. whipper; *(censurador)* censurer.

fus·ti·gar §47 tr. to whip, lash; *(criticar)* to censure, reprimand.

fút·bol *or* **fut·bol** m. soccer, football (G.B.) ♦ **f. americano** football.

fut·bo·lis·ta m.f. soccer player, footballer (G.B.).

fú·til adj. trivial, insignificant.

fu·ti·li·dad f. triviality, insignificance.

fu·tu·ris·ta adj. & m.f. futurist.

fu·tu·ro, a I. adj. future **II.** m. future; COLL. *(novio)* fiancé, intended; COLL. *(novia)* fiancée, intended.

G

g, G f. seventh letter of the Spanish alphabet.

ga·ba·cho, a I. adj. DEROG. French **II.** m.f. DEROG. French person.

ga·bán m. overcoat, topcoat.

ga·bar·di·na f. gabardine; *(sobretodo)* raincoat.

ga·ba·zo m. bagasse.

ga·bi·ne·te m. *(cuarto)* study, office; *(de una mujer)* boudoir; *(laboratorio)* laboratory; POL. cabinet.

ga·ce·la f. gazelle.

ga·ce·ta f. gazette, journal; *(chismoso)* gossip, gossipmonger.

ga·ce·ti·lla f. *(noticia breve)* short news item; *(columna de chismes)* gossip column; *(chismoso)* gossipmonger.

ga·chí f. [pl. **s**] SL. girl, chick.

ga·cho, a I. adj. *(inclinado)* bowed, bent; *(flojo)* drooping, floppy ♦ **a gachas** on all fours **II.** m. AMER. slouch hat —f. mush, paste ♦ pl. porridge • **hacerse unas g.** COLL. to get mushy.

ga·do·li·nio m. gadolinium.

ga·fas f.pl.inv. (eye)glasses.

ga·fe m. COLL. jinx.

ga·fo, a I. adj. claw-handed **II.** f. *(gancho)* hook; *(grapa)* clamp.

ga·gá adj. doting, foolish.

gai·ta f. MUS. bagpipe; *(organillo)* hurdy-gurdy; COLL. *(pescuezo)* neck.

gai·te·ro, a I. adj. flamboyant, gaudy **II.** m.f. bagpiper.

ga·je m. salary ♦ pl. salary, wages • **g. del oficio** occupational hazard.
ga·jo m. *(rama)* branch; *(racimo)* bunch; *(división)* section; *(punta)* prong, tine; AMER. curl.
ga·la f. *(vestido)* full dress; *(gracia)* elegance; CUBA, MEX. tip ♦ **hacer g. de** *or* **tener a g.** to show off ♦ pl. *(adornos)* finery, trappings; *(regalos)* wedding gifts *or* presents.
ga·lác·ti·co, a adj. galactic.
ga·lán m. handsome man; *(pretendiente)* beau, suitor; THEAT. leading man.
ga·la·na·men·te adv. *(con gala)* smartly; *(elegantemente)* elegantly.
ga·lan·ce·te m. handsome young man.
ga·la·ní·a f. elegance.
ga·la·no, a adj. *(bien vestido)* spruce, smart; *(elegante)* elegant.
ga·lan·te adj. gallant; *(amatorio)* flirtatious.
ga·lan·te·a·dor, ·ra I. adj. flirtatious **II.** m. gallant, flirt.
ga·lan·te·ar tr. *(cortejar)* to woo, court; *(coquetear)* to flirt with.
ga·lan·te·o m. *(cortejo)* courting; *(coqueteo)* flirting.
ga·lan·te·rí·a f. gallantry; *(gracia)* grace, elegance; *(liberalidad)* generosity.
ga·la·nu·ra f. elegance.
ga·lá·pa·go m. ZOOL. sea turtle; METAL. ingot; EQUIT. English saddle.
ga·lar·dón m. reward.
ga·lar·do·nar tr. to reward.
ga·la·xia f. galaxy.
ga·le·na f. MIN. galena.
ga·le·no m. COLL. doctor.
ga·le·ón m. galleon.
ga·le·o·te m. galley slave.
ga·le·ra f. galley; *(carro)* covered wagon; *(cárcel)* women's prison; *(sala)* hospital ward.
ga·le·ra·da f. *(carga)* wagonload; PRINT. galley (proof).
ga·le·rí·a f. gallery.
gal·go, a m.f. greyhound.
gal·gue·ar intr. AMER. to be starved.
ga·li·llo m. uvula.
ga·li·ma·tí·as m.inv. gibberish, nonsense.
ga·lio m. gallium.
ga·llar·de·ar intr. to act with ease and grace.
ga·llar·de·te m. streamer, pennant.
ga·llar·dí·a f. *(bizarría)* elegance, grace; *(valor)* gallantry, bravery.
ga·llar·do, a adj. *(airoso)* elegant, graceful; *(valiente)* brave, valiant.
ga·lle·ar intr. *(gritar)* to shout; *(sobresalir)* to stand out, excel.
ga·lle·ta f. *(bizcocho de mar)* sea biscuit, hardtack; *(bizcocho)* biscuit, cracker; COLL. *(bofetada)* slap ♦ **colgar** *or* **dar la g. a alguien** AMER. to fire, dismiss someone.
ga·lli·na f. hen, chicken —m.f. FIG. chicken, coward ♦ **como g. en corral ajeno** COLL. like a fish out of water • **g. ciega** blindman's buff.
ga·lli·ná·ce·o, a adj. gallinaceous.
ga·lli·ne·rí·a f. *(tienda)* poultry shop; *(bandada)* flock of hens; *(cobardía)* cowardice.
ga·lli·ne·ro m. *(jaula)* chicken coop, henhouse; *(sitio ruidoso)* madhouse; THEAT. top balcony.
ga·lli·to m. *(fanfarrón)* braggart, showoff; *(persona importante)* somebody, celebrity.
ga·llo m. ORNITH. cock, rooster; *(nota falsa)* false note; *(jefe)* boss, chief; AMER. *(valiente)* cocky person; *(carro)* fire engine; *(serenata)* serenade; *(objeto de segunda mano)* secondhand

object ♦ **g. de pelea** gamecock, fighting cock • **tener mucho g.** to be cocky.
ga·llón m. lawn, turf.
ga·lo·cha f. wooden *or* iron clog.
ga·lón m. *(de líquidos)* gallon; *(cinta)* braid, galloon; MIL. stripe.
ga·lo·ne·ar tr. SEW. to trim with braid.
ga·lo·pan·te adj. galloping.
ga·lo·par/pe·ar intr. to gallop.
ga·lo·pe m. gallop ♦ **a g. tendido** at full gallop • **ir de g.** to gallop, go at a gallop.
gal·pón m. AMER. large shed.
gal·vá·ni·co, a adj. galvanic.
gal·va·ni·za·ción f. galvanization.
gal·va·ni·za·do, a I. adj. galvanized **II.** m. galvanization.
gal·va·ni·zar §04 tr. to galvanize.
ga·ma f. gamut.
ga·ma·da adj. ♦ **cruz g.** swastika.
gam·ba f. prawn.
gam·ba·do, a adj. bowlegged.
gam·bar·se reflex. AMER. to become bowlegged.
gam·be·ta f. AMER. caper, prance.
gam·be·te·ar intr. to caper, prance.
ga·me·to m. gamete.
gam·ma f. gamma.
ga·mu·za f. chamois.
ga·na f. *(deseo)* desire, longing; *(apetito)* appetite ♦ **darle ganas** *or* **darle la g. de** to feel like • **de buena, mala g.** willingly, unwillingly • **de g.** energetically, eagerly ♦ pl. **con g.** heartily • **tener g. de** to want to, feel like • **sin g.** unwillingly.
ga·na·de·rí·a f. *(ganado)* cattle, livestock; *(raza)* breed, strain.
ga·na·de·ro, a I. adj. cattle **II.** m.f. cattle rancher, cattleman.
ga·na·do m. livestock, stock; AMER. cattle.
ga·na·dor, ·ra I. adj. winning, victorious **II.** m.f. *(el que gana)* winner; *(asalariado)* wage earner.
ga·nan·cia f. profit, gain.
ga·nan·cial adj. profit, pertaining to profit.
ga·nar tr. *(lograr)* to gain; *(llevarse)* to win, get; *(recibir)* to earn, make; *(triunfar)* to win; *(vencer)* to beat, defeat; *(aventajar)* to surpass; *(captar)* to win over; *(merecer)* to earn, merit; *(alcanzar)* to reach, arrive at —intr. to earn; *(mejorar)* to improve, advance —reflex. ♦ **g. la vida** to earn one's living.
gan·chi·llo m. *(horquilla)* hairpin; *(aguja)* crochet needle; *(labor)* crochet.
gan·cho m. *(garfio)* hook; *(cayado)* crook, staff; *(puñetazo)* hook; COLL. *(timador)* cajoler; *(rufián)* pimp; *(atractivo)* charm, allure; AMER. hairpin ♦ **echar el g.** to hook, snare.
gan·dul, ·la I. adj. COLL. lazy, shiftless **II.** m.f. COLL. loafer, good-for-nothing.
gan·du·le·ar intr. to loaf, idle.
gan·du·le·rí·a f. laziness.
gan·ga f. bargain, steal.
gan·glio m. ganglion.
gan·go·si·dad f. nasality (of voice).
gan·go·so, a adj. nasal, twangy.
gan·gre·na f. gangrene.
gan·gre·nar·se reflex. to become gangrenous.
gan·gue·ar intr. to speak nasally.
gan·gue·o m. nasal tone, twang.
ga·no·so, a adj. desirous, anxious.
gan·sa·da f. COLL. nonsense.
gan·se·ar intr. COLL. to do *or* say silly things.

gan·so, a m. gander —f. goose —m.f. *(torpe)* dummy; *(rústico)* bumpkin.
gan·zú·a f. *(instrumento)* picklock; *(ladrón)* picklock, thief.
ga·ño·te m. COLL. throat, gullet ♦ **de g.** COLL. free, gratis.
ga·ra·ba·te·ar intr. *(echar un garabato)* to hook; *(escribir)* to scribble; *(tergiversar)* to beat around the bush —tr. to scribble.
ga·ra·ba·to m. *(gancho)* hook, grapple; *(escarabajos)* scribble; COLL. *(gracia)* sex appeal, attractiveness.
ga·ra·je m. garage.
ga·ran·te I. adj. responsible II. m.f. guarantor.
ga·ran·tí·a f. guarantee; *(fianza)* security, deposit.
ga·ran·tir §38 tr. *(asegurar)* to guarantee; *(preservar)* to protect, defend.
ga·ran·ti·zar §04 tr. to guarantee.
ga·ra·pi·ña f. frozen state.
ga·ra·pi·ñar tr. *(helar)* to freeze; *(bañar)* to sugar-coat.
ga·ra·tu·sa f. compliment.
gar·ban·zo m. chickpea ♦ **g. negro** COLL. black sheep.
gar·be·ar intr. *(fanfarronear)* to swagger; *(robar)* to rob —tr. *(robar)* to steal —reflex. COLL. *(arreglárselas)* to manage, get by; *(pasearse)* to go for a walk.
gar·bi·llar tr. AGR. to sieve.
gar·bi·llo m. sieve.
gar·bo m. *(gallardía)* elegance, grace; *(generosidad)* generosity.
gar·bo·so, a adj. *(airoso)* elegant, graceful; *(generoso)* generous.
gar·de·nia f. gardenia.
gar·du·ño, a m.f. COLL. thief, pickpocket.
ga·re·te m. ♦ **ir(se) al g.** to drift.
gar·fa f. claw.
gar·fe·ar intr. to hook, grab with a hook.
gar·fio m. grappling iron, grapple.
gar·ga·je·ar intr. to spit.
gar·ga·jo m. phlegm, spit.
gar·gan·ta f. throat; *(del pie)* instep; *(desfiladero)* gorge.
gar·gan·te·ar intr. to warble, trill.
gar·gan·ti·lla f. necklace, choker.
gár·ga·ra f. gargling ♦ pl. AMER. gargle.
gar·ga·ris·mo m. gargling; *(líquido)* gargle.
gar·ga·ri·zar §04 intr. to gargle.
gár·gol m. groove.
gár·go·la f. gargoyle.
gar·gue·ro/güe·ro m. windpipe, trachea.
ga·ri·ta f. *(de centinela)* sentry box; *(portería)* porter's office; *(retrete)* lavatory.
ga·ri·te·ro m. gambler.
ga·ri·to m. *(local)* gambling house; *(ganancia)* gambling profits.
gar·lar intr. COLL. to chatter, gab.
gar·li·to m. *(de pesca)* fish trap; COLL. *(trampa)* trap, snare.
gar·lo·pa f. jack plane.
gar·na·cha f. judge's robe *or* gown.
gar·nu·cho m. MEX. rap, fillip.
ga·rra f. claw, talon; MARIT. hook; AMER. *(fuerza)* bite, kick ♦ **caer en las garras de alguien** to fall into someone's clutches • **como una g.** AMER. very thin • **echar la g.** to lay one's hands on ♦ pl. AMER. tatters, rags.
ga·rra·fa f. carafe, decanter.
ga·rra·fal adj. COLL. huge, enormous.

ga·rra·fón m. demijohn.
ga·rra·pa·ta f. tick, mite; *(caballo)* nag.
ga·rra·pa·te·ar intr. to scribble, scrawl.
ga·rra·pa·to m. scribble, scrawl.
ga·rra·pi·ñar intr. to grab, snatch.
ga·rro·cha f. TAUR. lance, goad; SPORT. pole.
ga·rrón m. talon, claw.
ga·rro·ta·zo m. blow.
ga·rro·te m. *(palo)* club; *(tormento)* garrote; MEX. brake ♦ **dar g.** to garrote.
ga·rro·te·ar tr. AMER. to club.
ga·rro·ti·llo m. croup.
ga·rru·cha f. pulley.
ga·rru·lar intr. to chatter, prattle.
ga·rru·le·rí·a f. chatter, prattle.
gá·rru·lo, a adj. *(cantor)* noisy, chirping; *(hablador)* garrulous, talkative.
ga·rú·a/ru·ja f. AMER. drizzle, fine rain.
ga·ruar §67 intr. AMER. to drizzle.
ga·ru·fa f. ARG., SL. spree, binge.
ga·ru·fe·ar intr. ARG., SL. to go on a spree.
gar·zo, a I. adj. blue II. f. heron.
gas m. gas.
ga·sa f. gauze; *(de luto)* crepe.
ga·se·ar tr. *(hacer gaseoso)* to carbonate; *(asfixiar)* to gas, asphyxiate.
ga·se·o·so, a I. adj. gaseous II. f. carbonated beverage.
ga·si·fi·ca·ción f. gasification.
ga·si·fi·ca·dor m. gasifier.
ga·si·fi·car §70 tr. to gasify.
ga·so·duc·to m. gas pipeline.
gas oil *or* **ga·soil/só·le·o** m. gas *or* diesel oil.
ga·so·li·na f. gasoline, gas.
ga·so·li·ne·ra f. *(lancha)* motorboat; *(tienda)* gas station.
gas·ta·do, a adj. *(debilitado)* worn-out, exhausted; *(usado)* worn, threadbare; *(trillado)* hackneyed, worn-out.
gas·ta·dor, ·ra I. adj. spendthrift II. m.f. *(derrochador)* spendthrift; *(prisionero)* convict —m. MIL. sapper.
gas·tar tr. *(pagar)* to spend; *(consumir)* to consume, exhaust; *(echar a perder)* to wear out; *(malgastar)* to waste, squander; *(llevar)* to sport, wear ♦ **gastarlas** COLL. to behave, act —intr. to spend —reflex. *(consumirse)* to be used up, run out; *(deteriorarse)* to wear out; *(debilitarse)* to wear oneself out.
gas·to m. *(desembolso)* expenditure, expense; *(consumo)* use, consumption; *(deterioro)* wear and tear ♦ **hacer el g. de la conversación** COLL. to do all the talking.
gás·tri·co, a adj. gastric.
gas·tri·tis f. gastritis.
gas·tro·en·te·ri·tis f. gastroenteritis.
gas·tro·in·tes·ti·nal adj. gastrointestinal.
gas·tro·no·mí·a f. gastronomy.
gas·tro·nó·mi·co, a adj. gastronomic(al).
gas·tró·no·mo, a m.f. gastronome, gourmet.
ga·ta f. see **gato, a.**
ga·te·ar intr. to crawl, walk on all fours; *(trepar)* to climb (trees) —tr. *(arañar)* to scratch, claw; *(robar)* to swipe, steal.
ga·ti·llo m. ARM. *(percusor)* hammer, firing pin; *(disparador)* trigger; *(ratero)* petty thief.
ga·to, a m. cat, tomcat; *(gancho)* clamp, vice; *(cric)* jack; COLL. *(portamonedas)* moneybags; COLL. *(ladrón)* sneak thief; *(hombre astuto)* fox, slyboots ♦ **buscarle tres pies al g.** to complicate matters unnecessarily • **dar g. por liebre** COLL. to swindle, pull the wool over someone's

eyes —f. cat, tabby; MEX. maid ♦ **a gatas** on all fours.
ga·tu·no, a adj. feline, catlike.
gau·cha·da f. AMER., COLL. clever trick.
gau·cho, a adj. gaucho.
gau·ches·co, a adj. gaucho.
gau·cho, a adj. & m. gaucho.
ga·ve·ta f. drawer.
ga·vi·lán m. sparrow hawk; (escritura) flourish (in penmanship); (pluma) nib.
ga·vi·lla f. (cereales) sheaf of grain; (sarmientos) bundle of vines; (gente) gang, band.
ga·vi·lle·ro m. stack or row of sheaves.
ga·vio·ta f. seagull, gull.
ga·za·pa f. COLL. lie, fib.
ga·za·pa·tón m. COLL. blunder.
ga·za·pe·ra f. (madriguera) rabbit warren; COLL. (pandilla) shady gang; (riña) brawl, scuffle.
ga·za·pi·na f. (pandilla) gang; (riña) fight, brawl.
ga·za·po m. young rabbit; COLL. (hombre astuto) sly fox; COLL. (disparate) slip of the tongue or pen.
ga·za·pón m. gambling house.
gaz·mo·ña·da/ñe·rí·a f. prudishness, priggishness.
gaz·mo·ñe·ro/ño, a I. adj. prudish, priggish **I.** m.f. prig, prude.
gaz·ná·pi·ro, a I. adj. simple-minded, dull-witted **II.** m.f. numbskull, dunce.
gaz·na·ta·da f. blow to the throat; AMER. slap.
gaz·na·te m. (garguero) throat, windpipe; (fruta de sartén) fritter.
gaz·pa·cho m. gazpacho.
géi·ser m. geyser.
ge·la·ti·na f. gelatin.
ge·la·ti·no·so, a adj. gelatinous.
gé·li·do, a adj. gelid, icy.
ge·ma f. gem; BOT. bud, gemma.
ge·me·bun·do, a adj. groaning loudly.
ge·me·lo, a I. adj. twin **II.** m.f. twin ♦ m.pl. (anteojos) binoculars, field glasses; (de camisa) cuff links ♦ **g. de teatro** opera glasses.
ge·mi·do m. moan, groan.
ge·mir §48 intr. (quejarse) to moan, groan; (aullar) to howl, wail.
gen or **ge·ne** m. [pl. **-es**] gene.
gen·dar·me m. gendarme, policeman.
gen·dar·me·rí·a f. gendarmerie.
ge·ne·a·lo·gí·a f. genealogy.
ge·ne·a·ló·gi·co, a adj. genealogical.
ge·ne·ra·ción f. generation.
ge·ne·ra·dor, ·ra I. adj. generating, engendering **II.** m.f. generator, engenderer —m. ELEC., MECH. generator —f. generatrix.
ge·ne·ral I. ♦ adj. general ♦ **en g.** or **por lo g.** generally, in general **II.** m. general ♦ **g. de brigada** brigadier general ● **g. de división** major general ● **g. en jefe** commander in chief.
ge·ne·ra·la·to m. generalship.
ge·ne·ra·li·dad f. generality; (el mayor número) majority.
ge·ne·ra·lí·si·mo m. generalissimo.
ge·ne·ra·li·za·ción f. generalization; (extensión) expansion.
ge·ne·ra·li·zar §04 tr. to generalize; (ampliar) to widen, expand.
ge·ne·rar tr. to generate, produce.
ge·ne·ra·ti·vo, a adj. generative.
ge·ne·ra·triz f. GEOM. generatrix; ELEC., MECH. generator.
ge·né·ri·ca·men·te adv. generically.

ge·né·ri·co, a adj. generic.
gé·ne·ro m. type, kind; (manera) manner, style; COM. commodity; TEX. fabric, material; BIOL. genus; GRAM. gender; ARTS, LIT. genre ♦ **g. humano** humankind.
ge·ne·ro·si·dad f. generosity.
ge·ne·ro·so, a adj. generous; (ilustre) highborn; (excelente) excellent, fine.
gé·ne·sis f.inv. origin, beginning.
ge·né·ti·co, a I. adj. genetic **II.** f. genetics.
ge·nial adj. brilliant, inspired; COLL. (agradable) genial, pleasant; (característica) typical.
ge·nia·li·dad f. (rareza) peculiarity, trait; (obra) brilliant or inspired work.
ge·nia·zo m. COLL. bad or violent temper.
ge·nio m. (carácter) temperament, disposition; (talento) genius; (deidad pagana) genius, spirit ♦ **de mal g.** bad-tempered.
ge·ni·tal adj. & m. genital ♦ pl. genitals, genitalia.
ge·ni·ti·vo, a m. genitive.
ge·ni·tor, ·ra I. adj. engendering, reproductive **II.** m. procreator, reproducer.
ge·no·ci·dio m. genocide.
ge·no·ti·po m. genotype.
gen·te f. people; (nación) nation, folk; COLL. (facción) clan, gang; (familia) family, folks; MIL. troops; AMER. decent folk ♦ **g. baja** common people ● **g. bien** upper class ● **g. de paz** friend ● **g. de trato** tradespeople ● **g. menuda** COLL. kids, small fry.
gen·til I. adj. RELIG. gentile; (gracioso) genteel, polite; (notable) remarkable, excellent **II.** m.f. RELIG. gentile.
gen·ti·le·za f. (gracia) genteelness; (cortesía) courtesy; (amabilidad) kindness; (bizarría) stylishness.
gen·til·hom·bre m. [pl. **-tileshombres**] handsome young man; HIST. gentleman-in-waiting.
gen·ti·li·cio, a I. adj. national; (relativo al linaje) hereditary **II.** m. GRAM. word indicating origin.
gen·ti·li·dad f./**lis·mo** m. RELIG. Gentile religion; (personas) (the) Gentiles.
gen·tí·o m. crowd, mob.
gen·tu·za f. riffraff, rabble.
ge·nu·fle·xión f. genuflection.
ge·nui·no, a adj. genuine.
ge·o·cén·tri·co, a adj. geocentric.
ge·o·da f. geode.
ge·o·fí·si·co, a I. adj. geophysical **II.** m.f. geophysicist —f. geophysics.
ge·o·gra·fí·a f. geography.
ge·o·grá·fi·co, a adj. geographic(al).
ge·ó·gra·fo, a m.f. geographer.
ge·o·lo·gí·a f. geology.
ge·o·ló·gi·co, a adj. geologic(al).
ge·ó·lo·go, a m.f. geologist.
ge·ó·me·tra m.f. geometrician, geometer.
ge·o·me·trí·a f. geometry.
ge·o·mé·tri·co, a adj. geometric(al); (exacto) exact, precise.
ge·o·po·lí·ti·co, a I. adj. geopolitical **II.** f. geopolitics.
ge·ra·nio m. geranium.
ge·ren·cia f. (gestión) management; (cargo) managership, directorship; (oficina) manager's or director's office.
ge·ren·te m.f. manager, director.
ge·ria·tra m.f. geriatrician, geriatrist.
ge·riá·tri·co, a adj. geriatric.
ger·ma·nes·co, a adj. slang.

ger·ma·ní·a f. slang of gypsies and thieves.
ger·ma·nio m. germanium.
ger·men m. germ.
ger·mi·ci·da I. adj. germicidal **II.** m. germicide, germ killer.
ger·mi·na·ción f. germination.
ger·mi·nar intr. to germinate.
ge·ron·to·lo·gí·a f. gerontology.
ge·ron·tó·lo·go, a m.f. gerontologist.
ge·run·dio m. GRAM. (del español) present participle; (del latín) gerund.
ges·ta f. exploits, heroic deeds.
ges·ta·ción f. gestation.
ges·tar tr. to gestate, carry —reflex. to develop, grow.
ges·te·ar intr. (hacer muecas) to grimace, make faces; (hacer ademanes) to gesture, gesticulate.
ges·ti·cu·la·ción f. (mueca) grimace, face; (ademán) gesture, gesticulation.
ges·ti·cu·la·dor, ·ra adj. (que hace muecas) grimacing; (que hace ademanes) gesturing.
ges·ti·cu·lar intr. (hacer muecas) to grimace, make faces; (hacer ademanes) to gesture, gesticulate.
ges·tión f. (dirección) administration, management; (trámite) step, measure; (cuasicontrato) agreement.
ges·tio·nar tr. to take steps or measures to obtain.
ges·to m. (expresión) look, facial expression; (mueca) grimace, face; (ademán) gesture, gesticulation ♦ **estar de buen, mal g.** to be in a good, bad mood • **hacer gestos** (hacer muecas) to make faces, grimace; (hacer ademanes) to gesture, gesticulate.
ges·tor, ·ra I. adj. managing **II.** m.f. manager, administrator.
géy·ser m. geyser.
gi·ba f. (corcova) hump, hunch; (molestia) nuisance.
gi·bar tr. (corcovar) to bend, curve; COLL. (molestar) to annoy.
gi·bón m. gibbon.
gi·bo·so, a adj. & m.f. hunchback(ed).
gi·gan·ta f. giantess; BOT. sunflower.
gi·gan·te I. adj. giant, gigantic **II.** m. giant.
gi·gan·tes·co, a adj. gigantic, huge.
gi·gan·tez f. gigantic size.
gí·go·lo m. gigolo.
gi·ma, mo, miera, mió see gemir.
gim·na·sia f. gymnastics ♦ **g. sueca** calisthenics.
gim·na·sio m. gymnasium, gym; (escuela) high or secondary school.
gim·nas·ta m.f. gymnast.
gim·nás·ti·ca f. var. of **gimnasia**.
gi·mo·te·a·dor, ·ra I. adj. whining **II.** m.f. whiner.
gi·mo·te·ar intr. COLL. to whine.
gi·mo·te·o m. COLL. whine, whining.
gi·ne·bra f. (bebida) gin; (juego) gin (rummy); (ruido) din, uproar; (confusión) confusion, bedlam.
gi·ne·co·lo·gí·a f. gynecology.
gi·ne·có·lo·go, a m.f. gynecologist.
gin·gi·vi·tis f. gingivitis.
gi·ra f. trip, outing.
gi·ra·dis·cos m.inv. (tocadiscos) record player, phonograph; (plato) turntable.
gi·ra·do m.f. COM. drawee.
gi·ra·dor, ·ra m.f. drawer, one who draws money on an account.

gi·ral·da f. weather vane, weathercock.
gi·rar intr. (dar vueltas) to revolve, rotate; (moverse alrededor de un eje) to gyrate; (torcer) to turn, veer; (negociar) to do business; (enviar) to wire; COM. to draw ♦ **g. en descubierto** to overdraw —tr. (rodar) to rotate, turn; COM. to draw.
gi·ra·sol m. BOT. sunflower; FIG. social climber, sycophant.
gi·ra·to·rio, a adj. turning, rotating.
gi·ro m. (rotación) revolution, rotation; (vuelta) turn; (aspecto) turn; (frase) turn of phrase, expression; COM. draft; (negocio) business, line of business ♦ **andar de mal g.** to be in a bad way • **g. a la vista** sight draft • **g. en descubierto** overdraft • **g. postal** money order.
gi·ro·a·vión m. gyroplane.
gi·ros·co·pio m. gyroscope, gyro.
gis m. (tiza) chalk; COL. slate pencil.
gi·ta·ne·ar intr. to wheedle, cajole.
gi·ta·ne·rí·a f. (reunión) band of gypsies; (adulación) wheedling, cajolery.
gi·ta·nes·co, a adj. gypsy, gypsy-like.
gi·ta·no, a I. adj. gypsy; (adulador) wheedling, cajoling; (socaliñero) sly, crafty **II.** m.f. gypsy.
gla·cia·ción f. glaciation.
gla·cial adj. glacial; (helado) icy, frozen; FIG. icy, cold.
gla·ciar I. m. glacier **II.** adj. glacial.
gla·dia·dor/tor m. gladiator.
gla·dí·o·lo/dio·lo m. gladiolus.
glan·de m. glans penis.
glán·du·la f. gland.
glan·du·lar adj. glandular.
gla·se·a·do, a adj. glazed, glossy.
gla·se·ar tr. to glaze.
glau·co·ma m. glaucoma.
gli·ce·ri·na f. glycerine, glycerol.
gli·ci·na f. BOT. wisteria; CHEM. glycine.
gli·col m. glycol.
glo·bal adj. global; COM. total.
glo·bal·men·te adv. as a whole.
glo·bo m. globe; (Tierra) Earth; (de goma) balloon ♦ **en g.** as a whole • **g. ocular** or **del ojo** eyeball • **g. sonda** sounding balloon.
glo·bu·lar adj. globular.
glo·bu·li·na f. globulin.
gló·bu·lo m. globule; ANAT. corpuscle.
glo·gló m. gurgle, gurgling.
glo·ria f. glory; (honor) fame, renown; (esplendor) splendor, greatness; (cielo) heaven ♦ **a g.** heavenly, divinely • **estar en la g.** or **en su g.** to be in seventh heaven • **ganar la g.** to go to heaven.
glo·riar §30 tr. to glorify —reflex. (preciarse) to boast; (complacerse mucho) to glory (in).
glo·rie·ta f. plaza, square; (cenador) bower, arbor.
glo·ri·fi·ca·ción f. glorification.
glo·ri·fi·ca·dor, ·ra I. adj. glorifying **II.** m.f. glorifier.
glo·ri·fi·car §70 tr. to glorify, praise —reflex. to glory.
glo·rio·so, a adj. glorious; (bendito) blessed; (vanidoso) boastful, conceited.
glo·sa f. gloss.
glo·sa·dor, ·ra I. adj. glossing **II.** m.f. commentator, glossarist.
glo·sar tr. to gloss; (comentar) to comment; (interpretar mal) to gloss, criticize.
glo·sa·rio m. glossary.
glo·se m. glossing, annotating.

glo·tis f. glottis.
glo·tón, o·na I. adj. gluttonous II. m.f. glutton.
glo·to·ne·ar intr. to eat gluttonously.
glo·to·ne·rí·a f. gluttony.
glu·ce·mia f. glycemia.
glu·co·sa f. glucose.
glu·glú m. *(del agua)* gurgle; *(del pavo)* gobble, gobbling.
glu·glu·te·ar intr. to gobble.
glu·ten m. gluten.
glu·ti·no·so, a adj. glutinous, sticky.
gno·mo m. gnome.
gnós·ti·co, a adj. & m.f. gnostic.
gnu m. gnu.
go·ber·na·ción f. government ♦ **Ministerio de la G.** Ministry of the Interior.
go·ber·na·dor I. adj. governing II. m. governor.
go·ber·nan·ta f. ARG. governess.
go·ber·nan·te I. adj. ruling, governing II. m.f. ruler, leader; COLL. *(pez gordo)* big shot.
go·ber·nar §49 tr. to govern; *(dirigir)* to control; *(conducir)* to steer —intr. MARIT. to steer.
go·bier·no m. government; *(oficio y duración)* governorship; *(edificio)* governor's house; MARIT. *(timón)* rudder; *(manejo)* steering, navigability ♦ **g. de la casa** housekeeping • **servir de g.** to serve as a guide.
go·ce m. enjoyment, pleasure.
go·fo, a adj. crude, ignorant.
gol m. [pl. **(e)s**] goal ♦ **marcar** or **meter un g.** to make or score a goal.
go·la f. *(garganta)* gullet, throat; *(adorno)* gorget, ruff.
go·le·a·da f. high score.
go·le·a·dor, ·ra m.f. goal scorer.
go·le·ar tr. to score many goals against —intr. to score.
go·le·ta f. schooner.
golf m. golf.
gol·fo, a m.f. urchin —m. gulf <*el G. de México* the Gulf of Mexico>; bay <*el G. de Vizcaya* the Bay of Biscay>.
go·li·lla f. collar, ruff; ORNITH. ruff; TECH. pipe collar or flange.
go·lle·te m. *(cuello)* throat, neck; *(de una botella)* bottleneck.
go·lon·dri·na f. swallow.
go·lon·dri·no m. ORNITH. male swallow; *(vagabundo)* vagrant, bum; MIL. deserter.
go·lo·sa·men·te adv. eagerly, with relish.
go·lo·si·na f. *(manjar agradable)* delicacy; *(deseo)* longing, craving; *(gula)* gluttony; *(chuchería)* trifle, frivolity.
go·lo·si·nar/ne·ar intr. to nibble on sweets.
go·lo·so, a I. m.f. sweet-toothed person II. adj. *(glotón)* sweet-toothed; *(deseoso)* gluttonous; *(apetitoso)* appetizing, tempting.
gol·pa·zo m./da f. heavy or hard blow.
gol·pe m. blow, hit <*el policía le dio un g.* the policeman dealt him a blow>; *(sacudida)* bump; *(latido)* heartbeat; *(explosión)* gust, blast; *(multitud)* crowd, throng; *(desgracia)* blow, shock; *(pestillo)* spring lock; *(sorpresa)* surprise; *(gracia)* wit, wittiness; SEW. pocket flap ♦ **a golpes** in fits and starts, sporadically • **al g.** AMER. instantly • **de g.** suddenly • **de g. y porrazo** hastily, hurriedly • **de un g.** at one fell swoop • **g. de estado** coup d'état • **g. de fortuna** or **de suerte** stroke of luck • **g. de gra-cia** coup de grâce, death blow • **g. de mano** coup de main, sudden attack • **g. de vista** glance, look • **g. en vano** miss • **no dar g.** not to do a lick of work.
gol·pe·a·du·ra f./**pe·o** m. beating.
gol·pe·ar tr. & intr. to beat, strike.
gol·pe·te·ar tr. to pound, pummel.
gol·pi·za f. ECUAD., MEX. beating, thrashing.
go·ma f. *(savia)* gum; *(caucho)* rubber; *(pegamento)* glue; *(elástico)* rubber band ♦ **g. arábiga** gum arabic • **g. de borrar** eraser • **g. de mascar** chewing gum • **g. laca** shellac.
go·mal m. AMER. rubber plantation.
go·me·ro, a I. adj. rubber, gum II. m. AMER. rubber tree; *(productor)* rubber planter; *(obrero)* rubber-plantation worker.
go·mi·na f. hair cream or dressing.
go·mo·si·dad f. gumminess, adhesiveness.
go·mo·so, a I. adj. gummy; C. AMER. hungover II. m. fop, dandy.
gó·na·da f. gonad.
gón·do·la f. gondola.
gon·do·le·ro m. gondolier.
gong or **gon·go** m. gong.
go·no·co·co m. gonococcus.
go·no·rre·a f. gonorrhea.
gor·di(n)·flón, o·na COLL. I. adj. chubby, tubby II. m.f. fatty, tub.
gor·do, a I. adj. *(obeso)* fat, plump; *(abultado)* big; *(graso)* fatty, greasy; *(grueso)* thick coarse; hard <*agua g.* hard water>; *(importante)* important II. m.f. fat person —m. *(sebo)* fat, suet; *(premio)* first prize.
gor·du·ra f. *(grasa)* fat, grease; *(corpulencia)* obesity, fatness.
gor·go·jo m. *(insecto)* weevil; *(persona)* midget.
gor·go·ri·tos m.pl. COLL. trills.
gor·go·te·ar intr. to gurgle, burble.
gor·go·te·o m. gurgling, gurgle.
go·ri·la m. gorilla.
gor·jal m. priest's collar.
gor·je·a·dor, ·ra/je·an·te adj. warbling.
gor·je·ar intr. to warble, trill —reflex. COLL. to gurgle.
gor·je·o m. *(quiebro)* warble, trill; *(habla de niños)* gurgling.
go·rra f. *(sombrero)* cap; *(de bebé)* (baby) bonnet ♦ **pasar la g.** to pass the hat —m. sponger, freeloader ♦ **andar** or **vivir de g.** COLL. to sponge, freeload • **de g.** COLL. at another's expense.
go·rre·ar intr. AMER. to freeload.
go·rrín m. piglet, suckling pig.
go·rri·ne·ra f. pigpen, pigsty.
go·rri·ne·rí·a f. *(porquería)* filth, dirtiness; COLL. *(acción grosera)* dirty trick.
go·rri·no, a I. m.f. ZOOL. piglet, suckling pig; FIG. pig, slovenly person II. adj. filthy.
go·rrión m. ORNITH. sparrow; AMER. hummingbird.
go·rro m. *(sombrero)* cap; *(de niños)* bonnet.
go·rrón, o·na I. adj. sponging, freeloading; AMER. *(egoísta)* selfish, greedy II. m.f. sponger, freeloader.
go·rro·ne·ar intr. to sponge, freeload.
go·rro·ne·rí·a f. *(acción)* sponging, freeloading; AMER. *(avaricia)* selfishness, greediness.
go·ta f. drop; MED. gout; ARCHIT. gutta ♦ **g. a g.** bit by bit, little by little • **sudar la g. gorda** COLL. to sweat blood.
go·te·ar intr. to drip, trickle.

go·te·o m. dripping, trickling.
go·te·ra f. *(gotas de agua)* leak; *(señal de agua)* water mark; *(cenefa)* valance ♦ pl. aches and pains; AMER. outskirts, environs.
go·te·ro m. AMER. eyedropper.
go·te·rón m. large raindrops.
gó·ti·co, a adj. & m.f. Gothic.
go·zar §04 tr. *(poseer)* to have, enjoy —intr. *(disfrutar)* to enjoy, take pleasure in —reflex. to rejoice.
goz·ne m. hinge.
go·zo m. joy, pleasure.
go·zo·so, a adj. joyful.
gra·ba·ción f. recording ♦ **g. en cinta** tape recording.
gra·ba·do m. *(arte, obra)* engraving; *(ilustración)* print, illustration ♦ **g. al agua fuerte** etching • **g. en madera** woodcut.
gra·ba·dor, ·ra m.f. engraver —f. tape recorder.
gra·bar tr. ARTS to engrave; *(registrar sonidos)* to record, tape; *(fijar)* to engrave, imprint.
gra·ce·jo m. wit, humor.
gra·cia f. *(donaire)* charm, grace; *(beneficio)* favor, kindness; *(perdón)* pardon; *(buen trato)* good graces; RELIG. grace; *(agudeza)* witty remark, joke ♦ **caer de la g.** to fall out of favor • **caer en g.** to please, find favor • **de g.** free, gratis • **en g. a** for the sake of *or* benefit of • **hacer g.** *(agradar)* to please; *(divertir)* to amuse, strike as funny ♦ **tener g.** to be funny ♦ pl. thank you, thanks • **dar g.** to give thanks • **g. a** thanks to, owing to • **g. a Dios** thank God.
gra·cia·ble adj. *(afable)* affable, good-natured; *(fácil de conceder)* easily granted.
grá·cil adj. slender, thin.
gra·cio·sa·men·te adv. *(con gracia)* gracefully; *(de balde)* gratuitously, free.
gra·cio·so, a I. adj. *(encantador)* charming, graceful; *(divertido)* amusing, funny; *(gratuito)* free, gratis II. m.f. gracioso, clown; THEAT. fool.
gra·da f. *(peldaño)* step, stair; *(asientos)* tier ♦ pl. AMER. atrium.
gra·da·ción f. gradation.
gra·da·do, a adj. stepped, with steps.
gra·de·rí·a f./o m. *(gradas)* tiers, rows (of seats); *(escalera)* flight of steps.
gra·do m. *(calidad)* grade, quality; *(nivel)* degree; *(fase)* stage, step; *(peldaño)* step, stair; *(título académico)* degree, academic title; *(clase)* class, grade; MIL. rank ♦ **de buen, mal g.** willingly, unwillingly • **de g. en g.** by degrees, gradually • **en alto g.** to a high degree • **en sumo g.** to the highest degree.
gra·dua·ción f. graduation; *(proporción de alcohol)* alcoholic strength; MIL. rank, grade.
gra·dua·do, a I. adj. graduated II. m.f. graduate.
gra·dual adj. gradual.
gra·dual·men·te adv. gradually, by degrees.
gra·duar §67 tr. *(evaluar)* to gauge; *(dividir en grados)* to graduate; EDUC. to graduate, confer a degree on —reflex. to graduate.
grá·fi·co, a I. adj. graphic II. m. *o* f. graph, chart.
gra·fi·to m. graphite.
gra·fo·lo·gí·a f. graphology.
gra·ge·a f. *(confite)* Jordan almond; *(píldora)* sugar-coated pill.
gra·jo m. rook, crow; AMER. body odor.

gra·ma·ti·cal adj. grammatical.
gra·má·ti·co, a I. adj. grammatical II. m.f. grammarian —f. grammar.
gra·mo m. gram, gramme (G.B.).
gra·mó·fo·no m. gramophone, phonograph.
gran adj. contr. of **grande**.
gra·na f. *(acción)* seeding; *(época)* seeding time; *(semilla)* seed; *(insecto)* cochineal; *(color)* scarlet ♦ **dar g.** to go to seed.
gra·na·da f. see **granado, a.**
gra·na·de·ro m. grenadier.
gra·na·di·lla f. *(planta y flor)* passionflower; *(fruto)* passion fruit.
gra·na·di·no, a m. pomegranate flower —f. *(jarabe)* grenadine; TEX. grenadine.
gra·na·do, a I. adj. *(notable)* distinguished, notable; *(experto)* expert ♦ **lo más g.** de the cream *or* pick of II. m. pomegranate (tree) —f. BOT. pomegranate (fruit); MIL. grenade; ARTIL. shell ♦ **g. de mano** hand grenade • **g. de mortero** mortar shell.
gra·nar intr. to go to seed.
gra·na·te adj. & m. garnet.
gran·de I. adj. *(enorme)* large, big; *(considerable)* great; *(grandioso)* grand, impressive; *(eminente)* great, eminent ♦ **en g.** on a grand scale II. m. Spanish grandee.
gran·de·men·te adv. *(muy bien)* grandly, very well; *(en extremo)* extremely, greatly.
gran·de·za f. *(tamaño)* size; *(magnitud)* bigness, largeness; *(nobleza)* greatness, grandeur; *(dignidad)* grandeeship.
gran·di·lo·cuen·cia f. grandiloquence.
gran·di·lo·cuen·te/cuo, a adj. grandiloquent.
gran·dio·si·dad f. grandeur, magnificence.
gran·dio·so, a adj. grand, magnificent.
gran·dor m. size, magnitude.
gran·do·te, a adj. COLL. very big, huge.
gra·ne·a·do, a adj. *(granulado)* granulated, ground; *(punteado)* stippled; MIL. heavy, continuous <*fuego g.* heavy fire>.
gra·nel m. ♦ **a g.** *(sin envase)* in bulk, loose; *(abundantemente)* in abundance.
gra·ne·ro m. granary.
gra·ní·ti·co, a adj. granitic, granite.
gra·ni·to m. granite; MED. small pimple.
gra·ni·za·da f. *(copia de granizo)* hailstorm; *(multitud)* shower, torrent.
gra·ni·za·do m. iced drink.
gra·ni·zar §04 intr. to hail; FIG. to rain, shower.
gra·ni·zo m. hail; FIG. hail, torrent.
gran·ja f. *(hacienda)* farm, grange; *(quinta)* country house; *(lechería)* dairy.
gran·je·ar tr. *(conquistar)* to win over, capture —reflex. to gain, win.
gran·je·ro a m.f. farmer.
gra·no m. *(semilla)* grain, seed; *(fruto)* grain, cereal; *(partícula)* grain, particle; MED. pimple; *(medida de peso)* grain; *(de la piel)* grain ♦ **ir al g.** COLL. to get down to brass tacks.
gra·no·so, a adj. granular, grainy.
gra·nu·ja f. loose grapes —m. COLL. ragamuffin, street urchin.
gra·nu·ja·da f. rascality, deviltry.
gra·nu·lar adj. granular, grainy; *(granujiento)* pimply.
grá·nu·lo m. *(grano)* small grain, granule; *(pildorilla)* small pill.
gra·pa f. *(para los papeles)* staple; *(para la madera)* clip, clamp.
gra·sien·to, a adj. greasy.

gra·so, a I. adj. fatty, greasy **II.** m. fattiness, greasiness —f. *(sebo)* fat, grease; *(suciedad)* grease, grime; *(grasilla)* pounce ♦ **g. de ballena** blubber ♦ pl. METAL. slag.

gra·so·so, a adj. greasy, oily.

gra·ta·men·te adv. *(de manera grata)* pleasingly; *(con agrado)* with pleasure; AMER. gratefully.

gra·ti·fi·ca·ción f. *(recompensa)* reward, recompense; *(propina)* tip, gratuity; S. AMER. gratification.

gra·ti·fi·car §70 tr. *(recompensar)* to reward; *(dar una propina)* to tip; *(satisfacer)* to gratify.

gra·tis adv. gratis, free.

gra·ti·tud f. gratitude.

gra·to, a adj. *(placentero)* pleasing; *(gratis)* free, gratis; AMER. grateful.

gra·tui·to, a adj. *(gratis)* free (of charge); *(arbitrario)* gratuitous.

gra·va f. gravel.

gra·va·men m. *(carga)* burden, obligation; *(impuesto)* tax; LAW encumbrance.

gra·var tr. *(cargar)* to burden, encumber; *(exigir un impuesto)* to levy, impose.

gra·ve adj. *(serio)* grave, serious; *(importante)* important; *(bajo)* deep, low; *(pesado)* weighty, heavy.

gra·ve·dad f. *(seriedad)* gravity, seriousness; *(importancia)* importance; PHYS. gravity; *(peso)* weight.

gra·ve·mente adv. *(con formalidad)* seriously; *(de manera grave)* gravely.

grá·vi·do, a adj. pregnant.

gra·vi·ta·ción f. gravitation.

gra·vi·tar intr. to gravitate ♦ **g. sobre** to be a burden to, weigh on.

gra·vi·ta·to·rio, a/cio·nal adj. gravitational.

gra·vo·so, a adj. *(oneroso)* onerous, burdensome; *(costoso)* costly, expensive.

graz·nar intr. *(chillar)* to squawk; *(cacarear)* to quack; *(el cuervo)* to caw.

graz·ni·do m. *(chillido)* squawk; *(del cuervo)* caw; *(del pato)* quack; *(del ganso)* cackle.

gre·dal I. adj. clayey **II.** m. clay pit.

gre·ga·rio, a adj. gregarious; *(servil)* servile, slavish.

gre·mial I. adj. union, trade-union; HIST. guild **II.** m. union member; HIST. guildsman.

gre·mio m. *(sindicato)* union, trade union; *(asociación)* association, society; HIST. guild.

gre·ña f. *(cabellera)* shock *or* mop of hair; *(maraña)* entanglement ♦ **andar a la g.** COLL. to quarrel, squabble

gre·ñu·do, a adj. disheveled, unkempt.

gres·ca f. *(jaleo)* uproar, hubbub; *(riña)* quarrel, row.

grey f. *(rebaño)* flock, herd; *(raza)* people, nation; *(fieles)* congregation, flock.

grial m. Grail.

grie·ta f. crack, crevice; MED. chap.

grie·tar·se/te·ar·se reflex. *(agrietarse)* to crack; MED. to get chapped.

gri·fo, a I. adj. *(crespo)* curly, kinky; PRINT. italic; AMER. *(intoxicado por la marijuana)* stoned, high **II.** m. *(caño)* tap, spigot; MYTH. griffin, griffon —f. COLL. marijuana.

gri·fón m. *(grifo)* large faucet *or* spigot; *(perro)* griffon.

gri·lla f. female cricket; S. AMER. annoyance, bother.

gri·lle·te m. fetter, shackle.

gri·llo m. cricket; FIG. *(obstáculo)* obstacle,

hindrance ♦ pl. fetters, shackles.

gri·ma f. annoyance, disgust ♦ **dar g.** to grate on someone's nerves, annoy.

grin·go, a I. adj. *(extranjero)* foreign; *(norteamericano)* Yankee; S. AMER. blond, fair **II.** m.f. *(extranjero)* foreigner; *(norteamericano)* Yankee; S. AMER. blond, fair-haired person —m. COLL. gibberish.

gri·pe f. grippe, flu.

gris I. adj. *(color)* gray; *(triste)* dull, gloomy **II.** m. gray ♦ **hacer g.** COLL. to be brisk.

gri·sá·ce·o, a adj. grayish.

grí·se·o, a adj. gray.

gri·ta f. outcry, shouting ♦ **dar g. a** COLL. to boo at, hoot at.

gri·tar intr. *(dar gritos)* to shout, scream; *(abuchear)* to jeer, boo —tr. to jeer at, boo.

gri·te·rí·a f./o m. din, uproar.

gri·to m. *(alarido)* shout, scream; *(clamor)* outcry, clamor; ZOOL. cry, call ♦ **dar gritos** to shout, scream • **el último g.** the latest craze • **poner g. en el cielo** COLL. to raise the roof.

gri·tón, o·na adj. COLL. noisy, loud-mouthed.

gro·se·lla f. currant ♦ **g. silvestre** gooseberry.

gro·se·ra·men·te adv. *(con descortesía)* rudely; *(con ignorancia)* crudely, stupidly; *(con indecencia)* coarsely, indelicately.

gro·se·rí·a f. *(tosquedad)* coarseness, roughness; *(rusticidad)* ignorance, stupidity; *(indecencia)* vulgarity; *(descortesía)* rudeness.

gro·se·ro, a I. adj. *(basto)* coarse, crude; *(descortés)* rude; *(rústico)* rustic, unpolished; *(craso)* gross **II.** m. boor.

gro·sor m. thickness.

gros·so mo·do adv. roughly, approximately.

gro·tes·co, a adj. grotesque.

grú·a f. *(máquina)* crane, derrick; *(camión de auxilio)* wrecker, tow truck.

grue·so, a I. adj. *(corpulento)* stout, fat; *(grande)* big, bulky; *(en grano)* coarse; *(de grosor)* thick **II.** m. *(espesor)* thickness; *(parte principal)* bulk ♦ **en g.** COM. in bulk, gross —f. gross (twelve dozen).

gru·lla f. ORNITH. crane.

gru·me·te m. cabin boy.

gru·mo m. *(de líquido)* lump; *(de sangre)* clot; *(de leche)* curd; *(de uvas)* bunch, cluster.

gru·mo·so, a adj. *(de líquido)* lumpy; *(de sangre)* clotty; *(de leche)* curdy; *(de uvas)* clustered.

gru·ñi·do m. *(de un cerdo)* grunt; *(de un perro)* growl; *(de una persona)* grumble, grunt.

gru·ñir §12 intr. *(un cerdo)* to grunt; *(un perro)* to growl; *(refunfuñar)* to grumble; *(chirriar)* to creak.

gru·ñón, o·na COLL. **I.** adj. grouchy, grumpy **II.** m.f. grouch, grump.

gru·pa f. rump (of a horse).

gru·po m. group.

gru·ta f. grotto, cavern.

gua·ba f. guava.

gua·ca f. AMER. *(sepultura)* Indian tomb; *(tesoro)* hidden treasure; *(hucha)* money box.

gua·ca·mol/mo·le m. C. AMER., MEX. guacamole.

gua·co I. m. BOT. guaco; ORNITH. currasow **II.** adj. AMER. harelipped.

gua·cho, a I. adj. S. AMER. orphaned; CHILE, PERU *(desparejo)* unmatched, odd (sock) **II.** m. *(pollo)* chick, baby bird; S. AMER. orphan, foundling.

gua·da·ña f. scythe.

gua·da·ñar tr. to scythe, mow.
gua·gua f. (cosa baladí) trifle, triviality; S. AMER. (nene) baby, infant; CARIB. (autobús) bus ♦ **de g.** free, gratis.
gua·ji·ro, a I. adj. AMER. rustic, boorish **II.** m.f. peasant.
gual·dra·pa f. (cobertura) caparison, horse trappings; COLL. (guiñapo) tatter, rag.
gua·no m. guano, fertilizer; CUBA palm tree; AMER. money, cash.
guan·te m. glove ♦ **arrojar el g.** to throw down the gauntlet • **echar el g. a** COLL. to grab, nab • **echar un g.** COLL. to pass the hat • **recoger el g.** to accept a challenge ♦ pl. tip.
guan·te·ar tr. AMER. to slap.
guan·te·le·te m. gauntlet.
guan·te·ro, a m.f. glover, glove maker —f. glove compartment.
gua·pe·ar intr. COLL. (ser valiente) to bluster; (vestirse) to show off; AMER. (fanfarronear) to brag, boast.
gua·pe·tón, o·na adj. COLL. (lindo) very attractive; (animoso) brave, bold; (ostentoso) flashy.
gua·pe·za f. COLL. (bizarría) boldness, daring; (ostentación) flashiness.
gua·po, a I. adj. (lindo) good-looking, attractive; (ostentoso) flashy; COLL. (animoso) brave, daring **II.** m. (pendenciero) bully; COLL. (galán) ladies' man.
gua·que·ro, a m.f. AMER. hunter of buried treasure.
gua·ra·cha f. CUBA, P. RICO (diversión) merrymaking, revelry; AMER. (bulla) noise, hubbub.
gua·ra·che m. MEX. huarache, sandal.
gua·ran·go, a adj. R.P. boorish, ill-mannered; S. AMER. dirty, filthy.
gua·ran·gue·ar intr. R.P. to behave boorishly.
gua·ra·ní m. PAR., FIN. guarani.
gua·ra·pón m. AMER. broad-brimmed hat.
guar·da m.f. guard, custodian —f. (tutela) custody, guardianship; (cumplimiento) observance; (de la llave) ward; (hoja de papel) endpaper, flyleaf —m. ARG. bus driver.
guar·da·ba·rre·ra m.f. gatekeeper.
guar·da·ba·rros m.pl. fender, mudguard.
guar·da·bos·que m. forest ranger, forester.
guar·da·bri·sa m. windshield.
guar·da·ca·de·na m. bicycle chain guard.
guar·da·cos·tas m.inv. coast guard cutter.
guar·da·es·pal·das m.inv. bodyguard.
guar·da·fan·go m. AMER. var. of **guardabarros.**
guar·da·fre·nos m.inv. brakeman.
guar·da·gu·jas m.inv. switchman.
guar·da·me·ta m. goalkeeper, goalie.
guar·da·mon·te m. ARM. trigger guard; (capote) riding cape or cloak.
guar·da·pol·vo m. (cubierta) dust cover; (vestido) duster.
guar·da·pun·tas m.inv. pencil cap.
guar·dar tr. (vigilar) to guard, watch over; (proteger) to protect; (animales) to keep, tend; (cumplir) to keep; (conservar) to save, put away ♦ **g. cama** to be confined to bed • **g. silencio** to keep quiet —intr. ♦ **¡guarda!** COLL. watch out!, look out! —reflex. (reservarse) to keep; (protegerse) to be on one's guard ♦ **g. de** to guard against.
guar·da·rro·pa m. (cuarto) cloakroom, checkroom; (ropas) wardrobe —m.f. cloakroom attendant.
guar·de·rí·a f. (empleo) guardship; (local) daycare center, nursery.
guar·dia f. (tropas) guard; (defensa) defense, protection ♦ **en g.** on guard • **g. municipal** city police force —m. (centinela) guard, guardsman; (policía) policeman.
guar·dián, a·na m.f. guardian, custodian; (vigilante) watchman.
guar·di·lla f. attic, garret.
gua·re·cer §17 tr. to shelter, protect —reflex. to hide, take refuge.
gua·ri·da f. (de animales) lair, den; (refugio) shelter, refuge; (querencia) haunt, hangout; (escondite) hideout.
gua·ris·mo m. number, figure.
guar·ne·cer §17 tr. (adornar) to trim, border; (proveer) to supply, provide; JEWEL. to set; MIL. to garrison; MAS. to plaster; CUL. to garnish.
guar·ni·ción f. (adorno) trim, border; JEWEL. setting; MIL. garrison; CUL. garnish.
gua·sa·da f. ARG. vulgarism, coarse word.
guas·ca f. CHILE, PERU whip.
guas·ca·zo m. AMER. lash.
gua·se·rí·a f. ARG., CHILE coarseness.
gua·so, a I. m.f. AMER. farmer, peasant —f. COLL. (pesadez) slowness, dullness; (burla) joke, jest **II.** adj. AMER. crude, coarse.
guau m. bow wow.
gua·ya·ba f. BOT. guava; (jalea) guava jelly.
gua·ya·be·ro, a AMER. **I.** adj. lying **II.** m.f. liar —f. lightweight shirt.
gua·ya·bo m. guava.
gu·ber·na·men·tal adj. governmental.
gu·ber·na·ti·vo, a adj. governmental.
gue·rra f. (combate) war; (ciencia) warfare ♦ **dar g.** COLL. to give no peace to • **hacer la g.** to wage war • **Primera, Segunda Guerra Mundial** First, Second World War.
gue·rre·a·dor, ra I. adj. warring, fighting **II.** m.f. warrior, fighter.
gue·rre·ar intr. (luchar) to war, fight; (resistir) to oppose, resist.
gue·rre·ro, a I. adj. (que guerrea) warring, fighting; (travieso) mischievous **II.** m. warrior, fighter —f. MIL. tunic.
gue·rri·lla f. MIL. guerrilla warfare; (partida) band of guerrillas.
gue·rri·lle·ar intr. to wage guerrilla warfare.
gue·rri·lle·ro m. guerrilla.
guí·a m.f. guide; (consejero) adviser; (director) director, leader —f. (faro) guide; (poste) guidepost; (libro) guide, directory; (manillas) handlebars; BOT. leader, guide shoot; MECH. guide ♦ pl. reins.
guiar §30 tr. to guide, lead; (conducir) to drive.
gui·ja·rro m. pebble.
gui·llo·ti·na f. guillotine.
gui·llo·ti·nar tr. to guillotine.
guin·che or **güin·che** m. AMER. winch, hoist.
guin·da f. sour cherry.
guin·dar tr. (colgar) to hang high, hoist; (obtener) to get, land; (ahorcar) to hang.
guin·di·lla f. red pepper.
gui·ña·da f. wink.
gui·ñar tr. to wink.
gui·ño m. wink ♦ **hacer guiños** to wink.
guión m. (bandera) banner, standard; CINEM., THEAT. script; GRAM. hyphen.
guio·nis·ta m.f. scriptwriter.
güi·ro m. AMER. gourd, calabash.

gui·sa f. manner, way ♦ **a g. de** as, like.
gui·sa·do m. stew.
gui·san·te m. pea.
gui·sar tr. *(cocinar)* to cook; *(estofar)* to stew; *(arreglar)* to arrange.
gui·so m. *(estofado)* stew; *(plato)* cooked dish.
gui·ta f. *(cuerda)* twine; SL. *(dinero)* bucks.
gui·ta·rra f. guitar.
gui·ta·rre·ar intr. to play the guitar.
gui·ta·rris·ta m.f. guitarist, guitar player.
gui·ta·rrón m. large guitar; *(pícaro)* sly rascal, scoundrel.
gu·la f. gluttony.
gul·den m. FIN. gulden, guilder.
gu·rí, i·sa m.f. ARG. Indian child.
gu·rru·mi·no, a I. adj. sickly, puny **II.** m. henpecked husband —f. COLL. uxoriousness.
gu·sa·ne·ar intr. to swarm, teem.
gu·sa·ni·llo m. ZOOL. small worm.
gu·sa·no m. worm; ENTOM. caterpillar.
gus·tar tr. *(probar)* to taste, sample; *(experimentar)* to test, try —intr. to like; *(agradar)* to please, be pleasing (to).
gus·ta·zo m. COLL. great pleasure *or* delight.
gus·ti·llo m. aftertaste.
gus·to m. taste; *(sabor)* flavor; *(placer)* pleasure; *(capricho)* whim, fancy ♦ **a g.** comfortable; *(a voluntad)* at will; CUL. to taste • **con mucho g.** with pleasure • **dar g. a** to please, gratify • **tener el g. de** to have the pleasure of • **tomar g. a** to take a liking to.
gus·to·sa·men·te adv. with pleasure
gus·to·so, a adj. *(sabroso)* tasty, savory; *(con placer)* pleased, glad; *(agradable)* pleasant, agreeable.

H

h, H f. eighth letter of the Spanish alphabet.
ha, has, han see **haber²**.
ha·ba f. *(planta)* fava bean; *(fruto, semilla)* bean ♦ **en todas partes se cuecen h.** COLL. it's the same all over the world.
ha·ber¹ m. COM. credit ♦ **tener uno en su h.** to have to one's credit ♦ pl. assets, property.
ha·ber² §39 aux. to have ♦ **h. de** to have to, must —impers. ♦ **hay** *ago* ... **habidos y por h.** past, present and future • **hay** there is, there are • **hay que** it is necessary • **no hay de qué** don't mention it, you're welcome • **¿qué hay?** what's up?, what's happening? • **¿qué hay de nuevo?** what's new? • **todo lo habido y por h.** everything imaginable —tr. *(poseer)* to have; *(alcanzar)* to get one's hands on; *(capturar)* to catch —reflex. ♦ **habérselas con alguien** to have it out with someone.
há·bil adj. *(capaz)* capable; *(diestro)* skillful.
ha·bi·li·dad f. *(capacidad)* capability; *(ingeniosidad)* skill.
ha·bi·li·tar tr. *(permitir)* to enable; *(preparar)* to equip; COM. to finance.
ha·bi·ta·ble adj. inhabitable.
ha·bi·ta·ción f. *(cuarto)* room; *(domicilio)* dwelling; *(aposento)* room; BOT., ZOOL. habitat.
ha·bi·tan·te m.f. inhabitant.
ha·bi·tar tr. to inhabit, live in.
há·bi·to m. *(costumbre)* habit; RELIG. habit ♦ **colgar el h.** RELIG. to give up the cloth • **tomar el h.** RELIG. *(monjas)* to take the veil; *(sacerdotes)* to take holy orders ♦ pl. RELIG. vestments.

ha·bi·tual adj. habitual.
ha·bi·tuar §67 tr. to habituate —reflex. to become accustomed (to).
ha·bla f. *(facultad)* speech; *(idioma)* language ♦ **al h.** in contact • **perder el h.** *or* **quedarse sin h.** to be speechless • **quitar el h. a** to stop speaking to.
ha·bla·do, a I. adj. spoken **II.** f. MEX. gossip ♦ **bien h.** well-spoken • **cine h.** talking pictures • **mal h.** foul-mouthed.
ha·bla·dor, ·ra I. adj. *(que habla mucho)* talkative; *(chismoso)* gossipy **II.** m.f. *(charlatán)* chatterbox; *(chismoso)* gossip; MEX. boaster.
ha·bla·du·rí·a f. *(charla)* chatter; *(rumor)* rumor; *(chisme)* gossip.
ha·blan·chín, ina COLL. **I.** adj. *(parlanchín)* talkative; *(chismoso)* gossipy **II.** m.f. *(charlatán)* chatterbox; *(chismoso)* gossip.
ha·blar intr. to speak, talk ♦ **h. alto** to speak loudly • **h. a tontas y a locas** to talk through one's hat • **h. bajo** to speak softly • **h. bien de** to speak well of • **h. claro** to speak frankly • **h. como un loro** to chatter • **h. de** to talk about • **h. en plata** to speak clearly • **h. entre dientes** to mumble • **h. mal de** to speak ill of • **h. por** to speak for • **h. por h.** to talk for talking's sake • **h. por los codos** to talk a blue streak • **¡eso es h.!** COLL. now you're talking! • **eso es puro h.** COLL. that's baloney! • **¡ni h.!** out of the question! —tr. to speak; *(decir)* to talk; *(dar a entender)* to speak of ♦ **hablarlo todo** to tell all —reflex. to speak to one another.
ha·brá, bría see **haber²**.
ha·cer §40 tr. to make; *(efectuar)* to do; *(formar)* to form; *(componer)* to compose; *(causar)* to cause; *(obligar)* to force; *(representar)* to play the part of; *(igualar)* to equal; *(suponer)* to assume to be ♦ **h. agua** MARIT. to leak • **h. alarde** to boast • **h. cara** *or* **frente a** to face • **h. caso de** *or* **a** to pay attention to • **h. cola** to stand in line • **h. conocer** to make known • **h. daño** to hurt • **h. estimación** to estimate • **h. falta** *(faltar)* to be needed; *(echar de menos)* to be missed • **h. fe** to testify • **h. juego** to match • **h. la barba** to shave • **h. la guerra** to wage war • **h. mofa de** to mock • **h. pedazos** to smash • **h. presente** to notify • **h. recados** to run errands • **h. saber** to let know • **h. sombra** to cast a shadow • **h. un milagro** to work a miracle • **h. una apuesta** to place a bet • **h. una maleta** to pack a suitcase • **h. una pregunta** to ask a question • **h. una visita** to pay a visit • **h. una de las suyas** to be up to one's old tricks —intr. to matter, be relevant ♦ **h. de** to serve as —impers. ♦ **desde hace** for • **hace frío** it is cold • **hace mucho** long ago • **hace poco** a little while ago • **hace tanto tiempo** so long ago —reflex. *(volverse)* to grow, become; *(convertirse)* to turn into; *(aumentarse)* to grow; *(proveerse)* to provide oneself; *(acostumbrarse)* to get used to ♦ **h. atrás** to move back • **h. a un lado** to step aside • **h. con** to make off with • **h. la vida** to earn one's living • **hacérsele a uno** to strike, seem.
ha·cha f. *(herramienta)* ax, axe; *(del toro)* bull's horn ♦ **de h. y tiza** tough • **h. de armas** battle-ax • **ser un h.** to be an ace.
ha·che f. ♦ **llámele h.** call it what you like (it's all the same).
ha·che·ro m. lumberjack.
ha·chís m. hashish.
ha·chón m. *(tea)* large torch; *(brasero)* cresset.

ha·cia prep. toward; *(alrededor de)* about, around ♦ **h. abajo** downward • **h. acá** here, this way • **h. adelante** forward • **h. arriba** upward • **h. atrás** backward.

ha·cien·da f. *(finca)* ranch; *(fortuna)* fortune; AMER. livestock.

ha·ci·na f. stack, pile.

ha·ci·nar tr. to stack, pile.

ha·da f. fairy ♦ **cuento de hadas** fairy tale.

ha·do m. destiny, fate.

ha·ga, go see **hacer.**

ha·la·gar §47 tr. *(lisonjear)* to flatter; *(mostrar afecto)* to show affection for; *(agradar)* to please; *(adular)* to cajole.

ha·la·go m. *(lisonja)* flattery; *(adulación)* cajolery.

ha·la·güe·ño, a adj. *(lisonjero)* flattering; *(alentador)* promising; *(agradable)* pleasing; *(atractivo)* attractive.

ha·lar tr. *(tirar)* to pull toward oneself; MARIT. to tow —intr. MARIT. to pull.

hal·cón m. falcon, hawk.

hal·co·ne·rí·a f. falconry, hawking.

hal·co·ne·ro m. falconer, hawker.

hal·da f. *(falda)* skirt; *(harpillera)* burlap.

há·li·to m. *(aliento)* breath; *(vapor)* vapor; POET. *(viento suave)* gentle breeze.

ha·llar tr. *(por casualidad)* to come across; *(encontrar)* to find; *(averiguar)* to find out; *(notar)* to note; *(descubrir)* to discover —reflex. *(encontrarse)* to be, find oneself; *(estar)* to be ♦ **h. uno en todo** to have one's hand in everything • **no h.** to feel out of place.

ha·llaz·go m. *(acción)* discovery; *(objeto)* good find.

ha·ma·ca f. *(cama)* hammock; *(vehículo)* palanquin; AMER. swing.

ham·bre f. hunger; *(de una nación)* famine; *(deseo)* longing ♦ **h. canina** ravenous hunger • **matar el h.** to stave off hunger • **morir** or **morirse de h.** to be starving • **tener h.** to be hungry.

ham·brien·to, a I. adj. *(famélico)* starved; *(con hambre)* hungry; *(deseoso)* longing II. m.f. starving or hungry person.

ham·bur·gue·sa f. hamburger.

ha·mo m. fishhook.

ham·pa f. underworld.

ham·pón I. adj. tough II. m. thug.

ha·rá, ría see **hacer.**

ha·ra·gán, a·na I. adj. lazy, idle II. m.f. loafer.

ha·ra·ga·ne·ar intr. to be idle, loaf.

ha·ra·pien·to, a adj. tattered.

ha·ra·po m. *(andrajo)* tatter; *(aguardiente)* weak or inferior alcohol, rotgut.

ha·ra·po·so, a adj. tattered.

ha·rén m. harem.

ha·ri·na f. *(trigo molido)* flour; *(cereal molido)* meal; *(polvo)* powder ♦ **h. de hueso** bone meal • **ser h. de otro costal** COLL. to be a horse of a different color.

ha·ri·ne·ro, a I. adj. flour II. m. *(persona)* flour dealer; *(receptáculo)* flour bin.

ha·ri·no·so, a adj. *(que tiene harina)* floury; *(farinácea)* farinaceous.

har·ne·ro m. sieve.

har·pi·lle·ra f. burlap.

har·tar tr. *(saciar el apetito)* to stuff; *(satisfacer)* to satisfy; *(fastidiar)* to annoy; *(aburrir)* to bore; *(cansar)* to tire.

har·taz·go m. fill ♦ **darse un h. de** *(comer mucho)* to eat one's fill of; FIG. to have had one's fill of.

har·to, a I. adj. *(saciado)* satiated; *(cansado)* fed up II. adv. *(bastante)* enough; *(muy)* very.

har·tu·ra f. *(hartazgo)* bellyful, fill; POET. *(abundancia)* wealth; *(logro)* fulfillment.

has·ta I. prep. until; up to, as far as ♦ **h. la vista** or **h. luego** see you, so long • **h. mañana** see you tomorrow • **h. que** until II. adv. even.

has·tiar §30 tr. *(cansar)* to tire; *(asquear)* to sicken; *(fastidiar)* to annoy.

has·tí·o m. *(repugnancia)* repugnance; *(fastidio)* annoyance; *(tedio)* boredom.

ha·to m. *(de ganado)* herd; *(cabaña)* pastor's hut; *(banda)* gang; *(montón)* bunch.

ha·to m. everyday clothes, belongings ♦ **liar uno el h.** COLL. to pack one's things.

hay, haya see **haber.**

haz m. *(fardo)* bundle; *(de leña)* fagot; PHYS. pencil (of light rays) ♦ pl. **haces de rectas** MATH. pencil of lines.

haz f. *(cara)* countenance; *(de tela)* right side.

haz see **hacer.**

ha·za f. plot of arable land.

ha·za·ña f. feat, exploit.

ha·za·ño·so, a adj. *(heroico)* heroic; *(valiente)* gallant.

haz·me·rre·ír m. COLL. laughingstock.

he adv. lo, behold ♦ **h. allí** there is or are • **h. aquí** here is or are • **helo aquí** here it is.

he see **haber.**

he·bi·lla f. buckle, clasp.

he·bra f. *(hilo)* thread; *(fibra)* fiber; *(filamento)* filament; *(veta)* grain; FIG. thread ♦ **de una h.** CHILE all at once, in one breath • **pegar la h.** to strike up a conversation.

he·chi·ce·rí·a f. *(brujería)* witchcraft; *(hechizo)* spell.

he·chi·ce·ro, a I. adj. *(bewitching)* II. m. *(brujo)* sorcerer; *(encantador)* charmer —f. *(bruja)* sorceress; *(encantadora)* charmer.

he·chi·zar §04 tr. *(encantar)* to bewitch; *(cautivar)* to charm.

he·chi·zo m. *(sortilegio)* spell; *(encanto)* charm; *(persona)* charmer.

he·cho, a I. see **hacer** II. adj. *(perfecto)* complete; *(terminado)* finished; *(acostumbrado)* used to; *(proporcionado)* proportioned; *(maduro)* mature; *(semejante a)* like; *(cocido)* done; *(ropa)* ready-made ♦ **h. y derecho** in every respect III. m. *(acto)* act, action; *(hazaña)* deed; *(suceso)* event; *(realidad)* fact; *(asunto)* point ♦ **a lo h., pecho** let's make the best of it now • **de h.** *(en realidad)* as a matter of fact; LAW de facto • **h. consumado** fait accompli.

he·chu·ra f. *(fabricación)* making; *(criatura)* creature; *(forma)* form; *(forma del cuerpo)* shape; *(confección)* workmanship.

he·der §50 intr. *(apestar)* to stink; *(enfadar)* to annoy.

he·dion·dez f. *(hedor)* stink; *(cosa hedionda)* foul-smelling thing.

he·dion·do, a adj. *(maloliente)* stinking, smelling; *(repugnante)* sickening; *(obsceno)* obscene; *(molesto)* annoying.

he·dor m. stench, stink.

he·ge·mo·ní·a f. hegemony.

he·la·de·rí·a f. ice-cream parlor.

he·la·de·ro, a m.f. ice-cream street vendor.

he·la·do, a I. adj. frozen; *(muy frío)* freezing, icy; *(atónito)* dumfounded; *(desdeñoso)* cold, frosty II. m. *(manjar)* ice cream; *(sorbete)* sherbet —f. frost.

he·la·dor, ·ra I. adj. freezing **II.** f. ice cream machine.

he·lar §49 tr. *(congelar)* to freeze; *(dejar pasmado)* to dumfound; *(desanimar)* to discourage —reflex. to freeze ♦ **se me heló la sangre** my blood curdled.

hé·li·ce f. helix; AVIA. propeller; ZOOL. snail.

he·li·cóp·te·ro m. helicopter.

he·lio m. helium.

he·li·puer·to m. heliport.

he·ma·to·lo·gí·a f. hematology.

hem·bra f. *(mujer)* woman; *(animal)* female; *(cola de caballo)* thin horse tail; BOT. female plant; SEW. *(corchete)* eye; MECH. female; ELEC. *(enchufe)* socket; *(tornillo)* nut; *(cerradura)* strike; *(molde)* hollow mold ♦ **h. de cerrojo** or **pestillo** strike plate • **h. del timón** gudgeon.

he·mi·ci·clo m. *(semicírculo)* semicircle; ARCHIT. hemicycle.

he·mis·fe·rio m. hemisphere ♦ **h. austral** southern hemisphere • **h. boreal** northern hemisphere • **h. cerebral** or **del cerebro** cerebral hemisphere • **h. occidental** western hemisphere.

he·mo·fi·lia f. hemophilia.

he·mo·fí·li·co, a I. adj. hemophilic **II.** m.f. hemophiliac.

he·mo·glo·bi·na f. hemoglobin.

he·mo·rra·gia f. hemorrhage ♦ **h. nasal** nosebleed.

he·mo·rroi·de f. hemorrhoid ♦ pl. hemorrhoids, piles.

he·mos see **haber²**.

he·nal m. hayloft.

hen·chi·mien·to m. *(henchidura)* filling; *(madera)* wood used to fill holes; *(suelo)* rough floor.

hen·chir §48 tr. to fill —reflex. to stuff oneself.

hen·der §50 tr. *(cortar)* to split; *(un fluido)* to cut through; *(abrirse paso)* to make one's way through.

hen·di·du·ra f. crack.

hen·di·mien·to m. cracking.

he·nil m. hayloft.

he·no m. hay ♦ **h. blanco** velvet grass.

he·ñir §59 tr. to knead.

he·pa·ti·tis f. hepatitis.

hep·tá·go·no, a I. adj. heptagonal **II.** m. heptagon.

he·rál·di·co, a I. adj. heraldic **II.** m.f. herald —f. heraldry.

her·bá·ce·o, a adj. herbaceous.

her·ba·rio, a I. adj. herbal **II.** m. *(experto)* herbalist; *(colección)* herbarium; *(libro)* herbal; ZOOL. rumen.

her·be·cer §17 intr. to begin to grow.

her·bí·vo·ro, a I. adj. herbivorous **II.** m. herbivore.

her·bo·la·rio, a I. adj. COLL. mad **II.** m. *(comerciante)* herbalist; *(tienda)* herbalist's shop —m.f. COLL. crazy person.

her·bo·so, a adj. herbaceous.

her·cú·le·o, a adj. Herculean; FIG. herculean.

he·re·dad f. country estate or property ♦ **h. residual** or **residuaria** residual estate.

he·re·dar tr. *(recibir)* to inherit; LAW *(dar)* to bequeath.

he·re·de·ro, a I. adj. inheriting ♦ **príncipe h.** crown prince **II.** m.f. inheritor —m. heir —f. heiress ♦ **h. forzoso** heir apparent • **h. legal** heir at law • **instituir h.** or **por h. a** to appoint as one's heir.

he·re·di·ta·rio, a adj. hereditary; FIG. ancestral.

he·re·je m.f. heretic; FIG. rascal.

he·re·jí·a f. heresy; *(insulto)* insult.

he·ren·cia f. *(patrimonio)* inheritance; *(tradición)* heritage; BIOL. heredity ♦ **h. yacente** LAW unclaimed estate.

he·ré·ti·co, a adj. heretical.

he·ri·do, a I. adj. *(lesionado)* wounded; *(ofendido)* offended **II.** m.f. *(persona herida)* wounded or injured person —m. ♦ **los heridos** the wounded —f. *(lesión)* wound; *(ofensa)* offense; *(tormento)* torment ♦ **h. contusa** contusion • **renovar la h.** to reopen an old wound • **tocar en la h.** to touch a sore spot.

he·rir §65 tr. *(lesionar)* to wound; *(hacer doler)* to hurt; *(ofender)* to offend; *(el sol)* to shine on; *(tañer)* to pluck.

her·ma·fro·di·ta I. adj. hermaphroditic **II.** m.f. hermaphrodite.

her·ma·na f. see **hermano, a.**

her·ma·nar tr. *(juntar)* to join; *(fraternizar)* to treat as a brother —reflex. to be united.

her·ma·nas·tro, a m.f. stepbrother/sister.

her·man·dad f. *(fraternidad)* brotherhood; *(de hermanas)* sisterhood; *(semejanza)* likeness; *(amistad)* close friendship; *(liga)* league.

her·ma·no, a m. brother ♦ **h. carnal** blood brother • **h. de leche** foster brother • **h. gemelo** twin brother • **h. lego** lay brother • **h. mayor** older or oldest brother • **h. menor** younger or youngest brother • **h. político** brother-in-law • **hermanos siameses** Siamese twins • **medio h.** half brother • **primo h.** first cousin —f. sister ♦ **h. gemela** twin sister • **h. lega** lay sister • **h. mayor** older or oldest sister • **h. menor** younger or youngest sister • **h. política** sister-in-law • **prima h.** first cousin —m.f. twin, mate.

her·mé·ti·co, a adj. *(cerrado)* airtight; *(incomprensible)* impenetrable.

her·mo·se·ar tr. to beautify —intr. to show off one's beauty.

her·mo·so, a adj. *(bello)* beautiful; *(niño)* healthy; *(tiempo)* fine.

her·mo·su·ra f. *(belleza)* beauty; *(mujer)* beauty, beautiful woman.

her·nia f. hernia.

hé·ro·e m. hero; *(protagonista)* main character; *(semidiós)* demigod.

he·roi·co, a adj. heroic.

he·ro·í·na f. heroine; PHARM. heroin.

he·roís·mo m. heroism; *(hazaña)* heroic deed.

her·pes m. or f.pl. herpes.

he·rra·dor m. blacksmith.

he·rra·du·ra f. *(hierro)* horseshoe; *(resguardo)* hoof guard; ZOOL. horseshoe bat ♦ **mostrar las herraduras** to take to one's heels.

he·rra·je m. hardware.

he·rra·mien·ta f. *(instrumento)* tool; *(conjunto de instrumentos)* tools, set of tools; *(dentadura)* grinders, choppers; *(arma)* weapon ♦ **h. cortante** or **de corte** cutting tool.

he·rrar §49 tr. *(caballos)* to fit with horseshoes; *(ganado)* to brand; *(guarnecer)* to trim with iron or metal.

he·rre·rí·a f. *(fábrica)* foundry; *(taller)* blacksmith's shop; *(oficio)* blacksmithing.

he·rre·ro m. blacksmith.

he·rrín m. rust.

he·rrum·brar tr. to rust.

he·rrum·bre f. *(orín)* rust; *(sabor)* iron taste; BOT. rust, mildew.
he·rrum·bro·so, a adj. rusty, rusted.
her·vi·de·ro m. boiling; *(manantial)* bubbling spring; *(muchedumbre)* swarm.
her·vi·dor m. *(utensilio)* kettle; TECH. heating tube *or* chamber.
her·vir §65 intr. to boil; MARIT. to become rough ♦ **h. a fuego lento** to simmer • **h. de** *or* **en** to seethe with; *(pasión)* to be consumed with.
her·vor m. boiling; *(fogosidad)* ardor ♦ **levantar el h.** to come to a boil • **h. de la sangre** skin rash.
her·vo·ro·so, a adj. *(hirviente)* boiling; *(fogoso)* ardent.
he·si·ta·ción f. hesitation.
he·si·tar intr. to hesitate.
he·te·ro·do·xia f. heterodoxy.
he·te·ro·gé·ne·o, a adj. heterogeneous; *(diferente)* dissimilar.
he·te·ro·se·xual adj. & m.f. heterosexual.
hé·ti·co, a I. adj. MED. consumptive; FIG. emaciated **II.** m.f. MED. consumptive.
he·xá·go·no, a I. adj. hexagonal **II.** m. hexagon.
hez f. *(de licor)* sediment; FIG. scum ♦ pl. feces.
hia·to m. hiatus.
hi·ber·na·ción f. hibernation.
hi·ber·nar intr. to hibernate.
hi·bis·co m. hibiscus.
hí·bri·do, a adj. & m.f. hybrid.
hi·cie·ra, ce see **hacer.**
hi·dal·go, a I. adj. *(noble)* noble; *(generoso)* magnanimous **II.** m.f. noble.
hi·dal·guez/guí·a f. *(nobleza)* nobility; *(generosidad)* generosity.
hi·dra f. *(pólipo)* hydra; *(culebra)* poisonous aquatic snake; *(peligro)* recurring danger.
hi·dra·ta·ción f. hydration.
hi·dra·tar tr. to hydrate.
hi·dra·to m. hydrate ♦ **h. amónico** ammonium hydroxide • **h. de calcio** calcium hydrate • **h. de carbono** carbohydrate.
hi·dráu·li·ca f. hydraulics.
hí·dri·co, a adj. hydric; MED. water.
hi·dro·a·vión m. hydroplane.
hi·dro·car·bu·ro m. hydrocarbon.
hi·dro·ce·fa·lia f. hydrocephaly.
hi·dro·e·léc·tri·co, a adj. hydroelectric.
hi·dro·fo·bia f. hydrophobia.
hi·dro·ge·nar tr. to hydrogenate.
hi·dró·ge·no m. hydrogen.
hi·dró·li·sis f. hydrolysis.
hi·dró·me·tro m. hydrometer.
hi·dro·pla·no m. MARIT. hydrofoil; AVIA. seaplane.
hi·dros·fe·ra f. hydrosphere.
hi·dro·tec·nia f. hydraulic engineering.
hi·dro·te·ra·pia f. hydrotherapy.
hi·dro·ter·mal adj. hydrothermal.
hi·dró·xi·do m. hydroxide.
hie·dra f. ivy.
hiel f. bile; FIG. bitterness ♦ **echar la h.** COLL. to sweat blood • pl. sorrows.
hie·le, lo see **helar.**
hie·lo m. ice; *(frialdad)* coldness ♦ **estar hecho un h.** to be freezing cold • **ser más frío que el h.** *or* **ser como un pedazo de h.** to be cold as ice.
hie·ma·ción f. wintering; BOT. winter blooming.

hie·na f. hyena.
hie·ra, ro see **herir.**
hie·rá·ti·co, a adj. RELIG. hieratic; FIG. solemn.
hier·ba f. *(pasto)* grass; *(medicinal)* herb; COLL. *(droga)* grass ♦ **h. mate** *or* **del Paraguay** maté • **mala h.** weed; FIG. troublemaker ♦ pl. *(pastos)* pasture • **h. marinas** algae • **y otras h.** and so forth.
hier·ba·bue·na f. mint.
hie·rre, rro see **herrar.**
hie·rro m. iron; *(marca)* brand; *(punta)* iron tip; *(arma)* weapon ♦ **h. colado** *or* **fundido** cast iron • **h. dulce** soft iron • **h. forjado** wrought iron • **h. galvanizado** galvanized iron ♦ pl. shackles.
hier·va, vo see **hervir.**
hi·ga f. *(amuleto)* fist-shaped amulet; *(gesto)* nose-thumbing; *(desprecio)* mockery ♦ **dar una h. a alguien** to thumb one's nose at • **no dar dos higas por** not to give a damn about.
hí·ga·do m. liver ♦ pl. COLL. guts • **echar los h.** COLL. to break one's back • **hasta los h.** COLL. with heart and soul.
hi·gié·ni·co, a adj. hygienic.
hi·go m. fig ♦ **de higos a brevas** once in a blue moon • **h. de tuna** prickly pear • **no dársele a uno un h. de** COLL. not to care a fig about.
hi·gue·ra f. fig tree ♦ **estar en la h.** COLL. to be in another world • **h. chumba** *or* **de Indias** *or* **de pala** prickly pear • **h. infernal** castor-oil plant.
hi·jas·tro, a m.f. stepchild, stepson/daughter.
hi·jo, a m. son; *(obra)* brain child; *(en nombres)* junior ♦ **h. de vecino** COLL. every mother's son • **h. de su padre** his father's son • **h. político** son-in-law —f. *(niña)* daughter ♦ **h. de su madre** her mother's daughter • **h. política** daughter-in-law —m.f. *(niño)* child; *(nativo)* native; *(descendiente)* descendant; *(querido)* dear ♦ **h. adoptivo** adopted child • **h. bastardo** *or* **natural** illegitimate child • **h. de familia** minor • **h. de la cuna** foundling • **h. leche** foster child ♦ pl. children; *(descendientes)* descendants.
hi·jue·la f. *(añadido)* widening strip *or* gore; *(colchón)* small mattress; *(acequia)* small irrigation ditch; *(camino)* branch; *(correo)* rural postal service; RELIG. pall; LAW schedule; *(bienes)* estate; BOT. palm seed.
hi·la f. *(fila)* line, row; *(acción)* spinning; *(tripa delgada)* gut thread ♦ **a la h.** single file • **h. de agua** irrigation ditch ♦ pl. lint (for dressing wounds).
hi·la·cha f./o m. raveled thread.
hi·la·cho·so, a adj. frayed.
hi·la·da f. *(hilera)* row; ARCHIT. course.
hi·la·do m. *(acción)* spinning; *(hilo)* thread.
hi·la·dor, ·ra m.f. spinner.
hi·lan·de·rí·a f. *(arte)* spinning; *(fábrica)* spinning mill.
hi·lar tr. to spin; FIG. to ponder ♦ **h. delgado** *or* **muy fino** COLL. to split hairs.
hi·la·ran·te adj. hilarious, uproarious.
hi·la·ri·dad f. hilarity.
hi·le·ra f. *(línea recta)* row, file; *(hilo)* thread; METAL. drawplate; ARCHIT. ridgepole ♦ pl. spinneret.
hí·le·ro m. eddy, current.
hi·lo m. *(hebra)* thread; *(filamento)* filament; *(alambre)* fine wire; *(tejido)* linen; *(filo)* edge; *(colgajo)* bunch; ZOOL. hilum; *(de sangre)*

trickle; *(de conversación)* thread ♦ **a h.** uninterruptedly • **al h.** SEW. along the thread; *(nervioso)* on edge • **colgar de un h.** to hang by a thread • **cortar el h.** to interrupt • **de h.** straight, directly • **h. de bramante** twine • **h. de cajas** *or* **de monjas** fine thread • **h. de gallinero** chicken wire • **h. de la vida** course of life • **h. de perlas** string of pearls • **h. de tierra** ELEC. ground wire • **tener el alma en un h.** to have one's heart in one's throat.

hil·ván m. basting, tacking.

hil·va·nar tr. to baste, tack; COLL. *(hacer con prisa)* to throw together; *(enlazar)* to coordinate.

hi·men m. hymen.

him·na·rio m. hymnal, hymnbook.

him·no m. hymn ♦ **h. nacional** national anthem.

hin m. whinny, neigh.

hin·ca·du·ra f. sinking, driving.

hin·ca·pié m. planting one's feet ♦ **hacer h.** en COLL. to insist on, stress.

hin·car §70 tr. *(clavar)* to sink, drive (in); *(apoyar)* to brace, plant (against) ♦ **h. el pico** COLL. to kick the bucket —reflex. to sink into ♦ **h. de rodillas** to kneel down.

hin·cha f. COLL. hatred, enmity ♦ **tener h.** a **alguien** to have *or* hold a grudge against someone —m. COLL. fan, supporter.

hin·cha, cho see **henchir.**

hin·cha·do, a I. adj. *(inflado)* inflated, blown up; *(lleno)* full, filled up; MED. swollen; *(vanidoso)* conceited; *(pomposo)* pompous II. f. ♦ **la h.** COLL. the fans.

hin·char tr. *(aumentar)* to swell; *(inflar)* to blow up; *(exagerar)* to exaggerate; MED. to swell —reflex. MED. to swell; *(comer)* to fill *or* stuff oneself; *(envanecerse)* to become conceited ♦ **h. las narices** COLL. to get one's dander up.

hin·cha·zón f. MED. swelling; *(vanidad)* conceit; *(pomposidad)* pomposity.

hin·co m. post, stake.

hin·cón m. mooring post; *(mojón)* marker.

hi·no·jo¹ m. fennel.

hi·no·jo² m. knee ♦ **de hinojos** on one's knees, kneeling.

hi·ña, ño, ñera, ñó see **heñir.**

hi·par intr. *(tener hipo)* to have the hiccups; *(los perros)* to pant; *(fatigarse)* to wear *or* tire oneself out; *(gimotear)* to whimper ♦ **h. por** to long *or* yearn to.

hi·pér·bo·la f. GEOM. hyperbola.

hi·pér·bo·le f. RHET. hyperbole.

hi·per·bó·li·co, a adj. hyperbolic(al).

hi·per·crí·ti·co, a I. adj. hypercritical II. m.f. hypercritic, severe critic.

hi·per·gli·ce·mia/·glu·ce·mia f. hyperglycemia.

hi·per·me·tro·pí·a f. hypermetropy, farsightedness.

hi·per·sen·si·ble adj. hypersensitive.

hi·per·ten·sión f. hypertension, high blood pressure.

hi·per·ten·so, a adj. hypertensive.

hi·per·ter·mia f. hyperthermia.

hi·per·ven·ti·la·ción f. hyperventilation.

hí·pi·co, a adj. horse, equine ♦ **concurso h.** horse show.

hi·pi·do m. whimper, whine.

hi·pis·mo m. horse racing.

hip·no·sis f. hypnosis.

hip·no·te·ra·pia f. hypnotherapy.

hip·nó·ti·co, a adj. & m. hypnotic.

hip·no·tis·mo m. hypnotism.

hip·no·ti·zar §04 tr. to hypnotize.

hi·po m. hiccup; *(ansia)* yearning, longing; *(odio)* grudge, aversion ♦ **quitar el h.** COLL. to astonish • **tener h.** to have (the) hiccups.

hi·po·cen·tro m. hypocenter.

hi·po·con·drí·a f. hypochondria.

hi·po·con·dria·co/drí·a·co, a adj. & m.f. hypochondriac.

hi·po·cre·sí·a f. hypocrisy.

hi·pó·cri·ta I. adj. hypocritical II. m.f. hypocrite.

hi·po·dér·mi·co, a adj. hypodermic.

hi·pó·dro·mo m. racetrack.

hi·po·gli·ce·mia/glu·ce·mia f. hypoglycemia.

hi·po·pó·ta·mo m. hippopotamus.

hi·po·tá·la·mo m. hypothalamus.

hi·po·te·ca f. mortgage.

hi·po·te·car §70 tr. to mortgage; *(comprometer)* to compromise.

hi·po·ten·sión f. hypotension, low blood pressure.

hi·po·te·nu·sa f. hypotenuse.

hi·po·ter·mia f. hypothermia.

hi·pó·te·sis f. hypothesis.

hi·po·té·ti·co, a adj. hypothetical.

hi·rien·te adj. *(arma)* cutting; *(mordaz)* offensive, cutting.

hi·rie·ra, rió see **herir.**

hir·su·to, a adj. *(peludo)* hirsute, hairy; *(erizado)* coarse, bristly; *(brusco)* gruff.

hir·vien·te adj. boiling.

hir·vie·ra, VIÓ see **hervir.**

his·pa·no·ha·blan·te adj. & m.f. Spanish-speaking (person), Hispanophone.

his·te·rec·to·mí·a f. hysterectomy.

his·te·ria f. hysteria.

his·té·ri·co, a I. adj. *(uterino)* uterine; *(alterado)* hysteric(al) II. m. *(histerismo)* hysteria —m.f. hysteric, hysterical person.

his·to·ria f. history; *(cuento)* story, tale; *(chisme)* gossip ♦ **dejarse de historias** to get to the point • **h. antigua** ancient history • **pasar a la h.** COLL. to be past history.

his·to·ria·do, a adj. ornate; ARTS storied.

his·to·ria·dor, ·ra m.f. historian.

his·to·rial I. adj. historic, historical II. m. *(archivo)* file, dossier; *(reseña personal)* résumé, curriculum vitae.

his·to·riar tr. *(contar)* to tell the story of; *(escribir)* to chronicle.

his·tó·ri·co, a adj. historic(al).

his·to·rie·ta f. story, anecdote ♦ pl. **h. ilustradas** *or* **cómicas** comic strips.

his·trión, io·ni·sa m.f. *(actor)* actor; *(bufón)* clown; *(prestidigitador)* juggler.

his·trio·nis·mo m. *(oficio)* acting; *(mundo teatral)* theater world; *(teatralidad)* histrionics.

hi·to, a I. adj. *(inmediato)* adjoining; *(fijo)* fixed II. m. *(señal de límite)* boundary marker; *(señal de distancia)* milestone; *(juego)* quoits; *(blanco)* bull's-eye, target ♦ **a h.** firmly • **dar en el h.** to hit the nail on the head • **mirar de h. en h.** to stare at.

hi·zo see **hacer.**

ho·ci·car §70 tr. *(escarbar)* to nuzzle; COLL. *(besuquear)* to smooch —intr. *(golpearse)* to hit one's face (against); COLL. *(tropezar)* to run into (difficulties); COLL. *(darse por vencido)* to give up; MARIT. to pitch.

ho·ci·co m. ZOOL. muzzle, snout; COLL. *(boca)* mouth; *(labios)* kisser; *(gesto)* sour face ♦ **caer de hocicos** COLL. to fall flat on one's face • **dar de hocicos** COLL. to hit one's face (against something) • **estar de hocicos** SL. to be teed off • **meter el h. en todo** COLL. to stick one's nose into everything • **poner h.** COLL. to put on a sour face.

ho·ci·no m. *(angostura)* narrows; *(en una quebrada)* dale.

hoc·key m. hockey ♦ **h. sobre hielo** ice hockey.

ho·ga·ño adv. COLL. *(hoy en día)* these days, nowadays; *(en este año)* this year.

ho·gar m. *(de una chimenea)* hearth, fireplace; *(hoguera)* bonfire; *(casa)* home; *(vida familiar)* home or family life.

ho·ga·re·ño, a adj. home-loving, domestic.

ho·ga·za f. *(pan grande)* large loaf of bread; *(pan grueso)* coarse bread.

ho·gue·ra f. bonfire.

ho·ja f. leaf; *(pétalo)* petal; *(de papel)* sheet, leaf; *(lámina de metal)* sheet, foil; *(folio)* leaf, page; *(documento)* sheet, form; *(cuchilla)* blade; *(de una puerta)* leaf; *(de ventana)* pane, sheet (of glass); *(de tierra)* strip of fallow land; *(espada)* sword; *(periódico)* newspaper, sheet ♦ **de h. perenne** evergreen • **h. de aluminio** aluminum foil • **h. de estaño** tinfoil • **h. de lata** tin plate • **h. de parra** fig leaf • **h. de ruta** COM. waybill • **h. de servicios** service record • **h. suelta** leaflet • **volver la h.** *(hojear)* to turn the page; *(cambiar de tema)* to change the subject; *(empezar nueva vida)* to turn over a new leaf.

ho·ja·la·ta f. tin plate.

ho·ja·la·te·ro m. tinsmith.

ho·jal·dre m.f. puff pastry.

ho·ja·ras·ca f. *(hojas secas)* dead or fallen leaves; *(frondosidad)* excessive foliage; *(cosas inútiles)* rubbish.

ho·je·ar tr. *(trashojar)* to skim or leaf (through) —intr. METAL. to peel, flake; *(susurrar)* to rustle.

ho·jo·so adj. leafy.

ho·jue·la f. *(hoja pequeña)* small leaf; *(masa frita)* pancake; *(de aceituna)* pressed olive skin; *(de metal)* metal leaf or foil; BOT. leaflet, foliole.

¡ho·la! interj. hello!, hi!

hol·ga·do, a adj. *(ancho)* big, loose; *(que vive con bienestar)* comfortable, well-off.

hol·gan·za f. *(descanso)* rest, leisure; *(ociosidad)* idleness; *(placer)* pleasure.

hol·gar §16 intr. *(descansar)* to relax; *(estar ocioso)* to be idle; *(estar alegre)* to be happy or glad; *(ser inútil)* to be unnecessary; *(no ajustar)* to be too big ♦ **huelga decir que** needless to say • **¡huelgan los comentarios!** no comment! —reflex. *(divertirse)* to have a good time; *(alegrarse)* to be pleased.

hol·ga·zán, a·na I. adj. lazy II. m.f. loafer.

hol·ga·za·ne·ar intr. to loaf, be idle.

hol·ga·za·ne·rí·a f. laziness.

hol·go·rio m. COLL. boisterous merrymaking.

hol·gu·ra f. *(regocijo)* enjoyment; *(anchura)* fullness; *(bienestar)* comfort, affluence; MECH. play.

ho·lla·du·ra f. treading, trampling.

ho·llar §19 tr. *(pisar)* to tread or trample (on); *(humillar)* to trample on, humiliate.

ho·lle·jo m. skin, peel.

ho·llín m. soot.

ho·lli·nien·to, a adj. sooty.

ho·lo·caus·to m. *(sacrificio)* holocaust, burnt offering; *(víctima)* sacrifice, victim.

ho·lo·gra·fí·a f. holography.

ho·ló·gra·fo, a I. m. holograph II. adj. holographic.

ho·lo·gra·ma m. hologram.

hom·bra·da f. manly action.

hom·bre m. man; *(humanidad)* man, mankind; COLL. *(esposo)* husband, man ♦ **de h. a h.** man-to-man • **¡h.!** what a surprise!, my goodness! • **¡h. al agua!** man overboard! • **h. de bien** honorable man • **h. de estado** statesman • **h. de letras** scholar • **h. del momento** man of the hour • **h. de mar** seaman, sailor • **h. de mundo** man of experience • **h. de negocios** businessman • **h. de paja** straw man, front • **h. de palabra** man of his word • **h. de pelo en pecho** COLL. real man • **h. de pro** or **de provecho** worthy man • **h. rana** frogman • **pobre h.** wretch, poor devil • **ser muy h.** to be a real man.

hom·bre·ar[1] intr. COLL. *(echárselas de hombre)* to act in a manly way; *(querer igualarse)* to strive to equal; MEX. to work in masculine occupations (said of women) —reflex. to strive to equal.

hom·bre·ar[2] intr. to push with the shoulders.

hom·bre·ra f. shoulder pad; ARM. shoulder plate; *(adorno)* epaulet, epaulette.

hom·brí·a f. manliness ♦ **h. de bien** integrity, honesty.

hom·bri·llo m. yoke.

hom·bro m. shoulder ♦ **a hombros** piggyback • **arrimar el h.** COLL. *(trabajar)* to put one's shoulder to the wheel; *(ayudar)* to lend a hand • **echar el h.** to shoulder, take on • **encogerse de hombros** to shrug • **mirar a uno por encima del h.** to look down on someone • **sobre los hombros** on one's shoulders.

hom·bru·no, a adj. COLL. manly, masculine.

ho·me·na·je m. homage.

ho·me·na·je·a·do, a m.f. person to whom homage is paid.

ho·me·na·je·ar tr. to pay homage to.

ho·mi·ci·da I. adj. homicidal, murderous II. m.f. homicide, murderer.

ho·mi·ci·dio m. homicide.

ho·mi·lí·a f. homily.

ho·mo·fi·lia f. homophilia.

ho·mó·ga·mo, a adj. homogamous.

ho·mo·ge·nei·dad f. homogeneity.

ho·mo·ge·nei·za·ción f. homogenization.

ho·mo·ge·nei·zar §04 tr. to homogenize.

ho·mo·gé·ne·o, a adj. homogeneous.

ho·mo·ni·mia f. homonymy.

ho·mó·ni·mo, a I. adj. homonymous II. m. homonym —m. or f. namesake.

ho·mo·se·xual adj. & m.f. homosexual.

ho·mo·se·xua·li·dad f. homosexuality.

hon·da·men·te adv. *(con hondura)* deeply; *(profundamente)* deeply, profoundly.

hon·da·zo m. shot from a sling.

hon·do, a I. adj. *(profundo)* deep; *(bajo)* low; *(intenso)* intense; *(recóndito)* innermost **II.** m. bottom ♦ **de h.** deep, in depth —f. sling, slingshot.

hon·dón m. *(fondo)* bottom; *(valle)* glen; *(ojo de aguja)* eye.

hon·do·na·da f. ravine, gorge.

hon·du·ra f. depth, profundity ♦ pl. **meterse en h.** to get in over one's depth.

ho·nes·ti·dad f. *(honradez)* honesty; *(decencia)* decency; *(pudor)* modesty.

ho·nes·to, a adj. *(honrado)* honest; *(decente)* decent; *(pudoroso)* modest; *(razonable)* reasonable.

hon·go m. BOT. mushroom; MED. fungus; *(sombrero)* derby, bowler (hat) ♦ **h. marino** sea anemone ♦ **h. yesguero** tinder fungus.

ho·nor m. *(virtud)* honor; *(recato)* virtue; *(buena reputación)* (good) reputation, prestige; *(celebridad)* fame, glory ♦ **hacer h. a** to honor • **hacer los honores a** to do justice to.

ho·no·ra·ble adj. honorable.

ho·no·ra·rio, a I. adj. honorary II. m. honorarium ♦ pl. fees, emoluments.

ho·no·rí·fi·co, a adj. *(que da honor)* honorific; *(no oficial)* honorary, honorific.

hon·ra f. *(dignidad propia)* honor, self-respect; *(buena fama)* reputation; *(pudor)* virtue ♦ pl. last respects.

hon·ra·dez f. honesty, integrity.

hon·ra·do, a adj. honest, honorable.

hon·ra·dor, ·ra I. adj. honoring II. m.f. honorer.

hon·rar tr. to honor, respect.

hon·ro·so, a adj. *(que da honra)* honorable; *(decente)* decent.

ho·pe·ar intr. *(menear la cola)* to wag the tail; *(corretear)* to run *or* chase around.

ho·po I. m. *(cola)* bushy tail; *(copete)* tuft *or* shock of hair; *(tupé)* toupee II. interj. COLL. get out!, scram!

ho·ra I. f. hour; *(momento)* time ♦ **a buena h.** in good time, opportunely • **a la h.** on time, punctually • **a primera h.** first thing in the morning • **¿a qué h.?** at what time?, when? • **a todas horas** at all hours • **a última h.** at the last minute; *(por la noche)* last thing at night • **dar h.** to make an appointment • **dar la h.** to strike • **de última h.** last-minute • **en h. buena** fortunately • **en h. mala** unfortunately • **h. de comer** mealtime • **h. legal** standard time • **h. punta** rush hour; ELEC. peak hour • **la última h.** death • **pedir h.** to request an appointment • **poner en h.** to set • **por h.** per hour, by the hour • **¿qué h. es?** what time is it? ♦ pl. RELIG. book of hours • **h. canónicas** canonical hours • **h. de oficina** office *or* business hours • **h. extraordinarias** overtime • **h. libres** free time • **por h.** by the hours • **tener las h. contadas** to be at death's door II. adv. now.

ho·ra·dar tr. to drill, bore.

ho·ra·do m. *(agujero)* bore *or* drill hole; *(caverna)* grotto.

ho·ra·rio, a I. adj. hourly II. m. *(mano del reloj)* hour hand; RAIL. schedule, timetable.

hor·ca f. *(aparato de suplicio)* gallows; AGR. pitchfork; *(ristra)* string.

hor·ca·ja·das adv. ♦ **a h. astride**, straddling.

hor·cón m. *(horca)* pitchfork; *(apoyo)* forked pole supporting tree branches; AMER. wooden column supporting ceiling beams.

ho·ri·zon·tal adj. & f. horizontal.

ho·ri·zon·te m. horizon.

hor·ma f. *(forma)* form, mold; *(de zapatero)* (shoemaker's) last; *(para zapatos)* shoetree; *(de sombrero)* hat block; CONSTR. dry wall ♦ **hallar la h. de su zapato** to get what's coming to one.

hor·mi·ga f. ant ♦ **ser una h.** to be industrious *or* hard-working.

hor·mi·gón m. concrete ♦ **h. armado** reinforced concrete • **h. hidráulico** hydraulic lime

mortar • **h. precomprimido** *or* **pretensado** prestressed concrete.

hor·mi·go·ne·ra f. cement *or* concrete mixer.

hor·mi·gue·ar intr. *(sentir hormigueo)* to tingle; *(bullir)* to teem.

hor·mi·gue·o m. *(multitud)* swarm, throng; *(sensación)* tingling.

hor·mi·gue·ro m. ENTOM. anthill; ORNITH. wryneck; FIG. hub of activity.

hor·mi·gui·lla f. COLL. *(picazón)* tingling sensation; *(remordimiento)* remorse.

hor·mi·gui·llo m. VET. founder; *(de personas)* human chain; *(picazón)* tingling sensation ♦ **parecer tener h.** COLL. to have ants in one's pants.

hor·mi·gui·ta f. COLL. industrious *or* diligent person.

hor·mo·na f. hormone.

hor·na·chue·la f. hut, hovel.

hor·na·da f. CUL. batch (of baked goods); FIG. group (of people).

hor·na·gue·ro, a I. adj. *(amplio)* ample, wide; MIN. coal-bearing II. f. coal.

hor·ne·ar intr. & tr. to bake.

hor·ne·ro, a m.f. baker.

hor·ni·lla f. ORNITH. pigeonhole.

hor·ni·llo m. *(cocina)* stove; MIN. blasthole; MIL. fougasse ♦ **h. de atanor** athanor.

hor·no m. oven; TECH. furnace; CERAM. kiln ♦ **h. reverbero** TECH. reverberatory furnace • **no está el h. para bollos** COLL. the time is not ripe.

ho·rós·co·po m. horoscope.

hor·que·ta f. AGR. pitchfork; *(del árbol)* fork; AMER. fork (in a road).

hor·qui·lla f. AGR. pitchfork; *(sostén)* forked stake; *(del cabello)* hairpin, hair clip; *(de una bicicleta)* fork.

ho·rren·do, a adj. horrendous.

ho·rri·ble adj. horrible.

ho·rri·dez f. horridness.

hó·rri·do, a adj. horrid.

ho·rri·fi·car §70 tr. to horrify.

ho·rrí·fi·co, a adj. horrific.

ho·rri·pi·lan·te adj. hair-raising, terrifying.

ho·rri·pi·lar tr. *(erizar)* to make one's hair stand on end, give one the creeps; *(horrorizar)* to terrify.

ho·rror m. horror; *(temor)* terror; *(repulsión)* revulsion; *(atrocidad)* atrocity; COLL. *(cantidad)* tons, loads.

ho·rro·ri·zar §04 tr. to horrify —reflex. to be horrified.

ho·rro·ro·so, a adj. *(horrible)* horrible; COLL. *(feo)* hideous; *(muy malo)* terrible.

ho·rru·ra f. filth, dirt ♦ pl. MIN. scoria, slag.

hor·ta·li·za f. vegetable.

hor·te·la·no, a I. adj. *(del jardín)* (of the) garden; *(del huerto)* (of the) orchard II. m. *(jardinero)* gardener; ORNITH. ortolan.

hor·ten·se adj. *(del jardín)* (of the) garden; *(del huerto)* (of the) orchard.

hor·ten·sia f. hydrangea.

hor·ti·co·la adj. horticultural.

hor·ti·cul·tor, ·ra m.f. horticulturist.

hor·ti·cul·tu·ra f. horticulture.

hos·co, a adj. *(obscuro)* gloomy; *(moreno)* dark-skinned; *(áspero)* gruff.

hos·pe·da·je m. lodging.

hos·pe·dar tr. to lodge, put up —reflex. to lodge *or* stay (at).

hos·pe·de·rí·a f. *(hotel)* inn, hostel; *(hospedaje)*

lodging; RELIG. hospice.
hos·pe·de·ro, a m.f. innkeeper.
hos·pi·cio m. (para pobres) poorhouse; (para huérfanos) orphanage; RELIG. hospice.
hos·pi·tal m. hospital ♦ **h. de sangre** MIL. field hospital.
hos·pi·ta·la·rio, a adj. (cordial) hospitable; (acogedor) inviting; RELIG. of the Hospitalers.
hos·pi·ta·li·cio, a adj. hospitable.
hos·pi·ta·li·dad f. (cordialidad) hospitality; (permanencia) hospital stay.
hos·pi·ta·li·za·ción f. hospitalization.
hos·pi·ta·li·zar §04 tr. to hospitalize.
hos·que·dad f. (obscuridad) gloominess; (de la piel) darkness; (aspereza) gruffness.
hos·te·le·rí·a f. (profesión) hotel management; (industria) hotel trade or business.
hos·te·le·ro, a m.f. innkeeper.
hos·te·rí·a f. inn, hostel.
hos·tia f. (sacrificio) sacrifice; RELIG. wafer; SL. (golpe) punch ♦ **darle una h. a alguien** COLL. to give someone a beating.
hos·ti·ga·mien·to m. (azotamiento) whipping; (acosamiento) harassment.
hos·ti·gar §47 tr. (azotar) to whip; (acosar) to harass; (incitar) to urge, press.
hos·til adj. hostile.
hos·ti·li·dad f. hostility ♦ pl. hostilities, fighting ♦ **romper las h.** MIL. to begin or commence hostilities.
hos·ti·li·zar §04 tr. to antagonize; MIL. to harass.
ho·tel m. (hostería) hotel; (casa) house, villa.
ho·te·le·ro, a I. adj. hotel **II.** m.f. (dueño) hotelkeeper, hotel owner; (encargado) hotel manager.
hoy adv. (en este día) today; (en el tiempo presente) nowadays ♦ **de h. a mañana** at any moment • **de** or **desde h. en adelante** from now on, from this day forward • **h. (en) día** nowadays • **h. mismo** this very day • **h. por h.** at the present time • **por h.** for now, for the time being.
ho·ya f. (hoyo) pit, hole; (sepultura) grave; (remolino) eddy; (valle) dale.
ho·yar tr. to dig holes.
ho·yo m. (cavidad) hole; (sepultura) grave; MED. pockmark; SPORT. hole.
ho·yue·lo m. (en las mejillas) dimple; (en la barbilla) cleft; (en la garganta) depression.
hoz f. sickle.
hu·bie·ra, bo see **haber²**.
hu·cha f. (alcancía) piggy bank; (arca) chest; (ahorros) savings.
hue·co, a I. adj. (vacío) hollow; (retumbante) deep; (mullido) spongy; (vacuo) vacuous; (vano) vain **II.** m. (cavidad) hollow; (agujero) hole; (espacio) space; COLL. (vacante) vacancy; (vacío) gap, void; ARCHIT. opening ♦ **h. de ascensor** elevator shaft.
hue·la, lo see **oler**.
huel·ga f. (paro) strike; AGR. fallow ♦ **declararse en h.** to go on strike • **h. de brazos caídos** sit-down strike • **h. de hambre** hunger strike • **h. intermitente** slowdown • **h. patronal** lockout • **h. por solidaridad** sympathy strike.
huel·go, gue see **holgar**.
huel·go m. (aliento) breath; (anchura) room, space; MECH. play.
huel·guis·ta m.f. striker, striking worker.
hue·lla f. (del pie) footprint; (de un animal) track, print; (vestigio) trace, mark; (del escalón)

tread; FIG. footstep ♦ **h. digital** or **dactilar** fingerprint.
hue·llo m. (camino) track; (pisada) tread, step; (del casco) sole.
huér·fa·no, a I. adj. (sin padres) orphan(ed); (sin amparo) defenseless; (sin hijos) childless ♦ **h. de** without, devoid of **II.** m.f. orphan.
huer·ta f. (sembrado) large vegetable garden; (de árboles) orchard; SP. (regadío) irrigated land.
huer·to m. (jardín) vegetable garden; (de árboles) orchard.
hue·sa f. grave.
hue·so m. ANAT. bone; BOT. pit, stone; (cosa difícil) drudgery; (lo inútil) piece of junk; (persona desagradable) pain in the neck; C. AMER., MEX. (empleo oficial) government job ♦ **dar** or **tropezar en un h.** to hit a snag • **de buen h.** lucky • **estar en los huesos** to be nothing but skin and bones • **h. colorado** MEX. northerly wind • **h. de la alegría** funny bone • **h. de la suerte** wishbone • **h. duro de roer** hard nut to crack • **h. palomo** coccyx • **la sin h.** COLL. tongue • **meterse a h. de puerco** MEX. to swagger, show off • **no dejar a uno h. salvo** to rake over the coals • **soltar la sin h.** COLL. to shoot off one's mouth • **tener los huesos molidos** COLL. to be dead tired.
hue·so·so, a adj. bony, osseous.
hués·ped, a m.f. (invitado) guest; BIOL. host —m. (invitante) host —f. (invitante) hostess.
hues·te f. (ejército) army, troop; (partidarios) followers.
hue·su·do, a adj. bony.
hue·va f. roe.
hue·vo m. egg ♦ **h. duro** hard-boiled egg • **h. escalfado** poached egg • **h. estrellado** or **frito** fried egg • **h. pasado por agua** soft-boiled egg • **huevos revueltos** scrambled eggs.
hui·do, a I. adj. (fugitivo) fugitive, fleeing; (reservado) withdrawn **II.** f. (fuga) escape; (pretexto) pretext; EQUIT. bolt.
hui·llón, o·na AMER. **I.** adj. cowardly **II.** m.f. coward.
huir §18 intr. (escapar) to escape, run away; (evitar) to avoid, flee from; (alejarse) to slip away —reflex. to escape, run away —tr. to avoid, shun.
hu·le m. (caucho) rubber; (tela) oilcloth.
hu·lla f. coal ♦ **h. blanca** water power, hydraulic power.
hu·ma·nar tr. to humanize —reflex. to become human; RELIG. to become man (God).
hu·ma·ni·dad f. humanity; (género) mankind; (bondad) humaneness; COLL. (corpulencia) corpulence ♦ pl. humanities.
hu·ma·nis·ta I. m.f. humanist **II.** adj. humanistic.
hu·ma·ni·ta·rio, a adj. humanitarian.
hu·ma·ni·zar §04 tr. to humanize —reflex. to become more human, soften.
hu·ma·no, a I. adj. human; (benévolo) humane **II.** m. human (being).
hu·ma·re·da f./ma·zo m. dense smoke.
hu·me·an·te adj. (que humea) smoking, smoky; (que echa vapor) steaming.
hu·me·ar intr. (echar humo) to smoke; (echar vapor) to steam; (permanecer) to smolder; (presumir) to become conceited —tr. AMER. to fumigate.
hu·me·dad f. humidity; (calidad de húmedo) dampness, moisture.

hu·me·de·ce·dor m. humidifier.
hu·me·de·cer §17 tr. to humidify; *(mojar)* to dampen, moisten —reflex. to become damp *or* moist.
hú·me·do, a adj. humid; *(mojado)* damp, moist.
hu·me·ra f. COLL. drunkenness.
hu·me·ro m. chimney, smokestack.
hú·me·ro m. humerus.
hu·mil·dad f. *(virtud)* humility, humbleness; *(de cuna)* lowliness (of birth); *(acción)* humble act.
hu·mil·de adj. *(sumiso)* humble, meek; *(bajo)* humble, lowly; *(de poco monto)* modest.
hu·mi·lla·ción f. humiliation.
hu·mi·llan·te adj. humiliating.
hu·mi·llar tr. *(rebajar)* to humble; *(avergonzar)* humiliate; *(bajar la frente)* to bow (one's head) —reflex. to humble oneself.
hu·mi·llo m. pride.
hu·mo m. *(gas)* smoke; *(vapor)* steam ♦ **a h. de pajas** lightly, without thinking • **echar h.** to smoke • **hacerse h.** to vanish into thin air ♦ pl. airs • **bajarle los h. a uno** to put someone in his place • **tener muchos h.** to put on airs.
hu·mor m. humor; *(talante)* mood, humor; *(agudeza)* humor, wit.
hu·mo·ra·do, a I. adj. ♦ **bien, mal h.** good/bad-humored **II.** f. *(chiste)* joke; *(capricho)* whim, fancy.
hu·mo·ris·mo m. humor, wit.
hu·mo·ris·ta I. adj. humorous **II.** m.f. humorist.
hu·mo·rís·ti·co, a adj. humorous.
hu·mo·so, a adj. *(lleno de humo)* smoky; *(que echa humo)* smoking.
hun·di·do, a adj. *(sumido)* sunken; *(de ojos)* sunken, deep-set; *(mejillas)* hollow, sunken.
hun·di·mien·to m. *(naufragio)* sinking; *(derrumbe)* cave-in; *(ruina)* ruin, collapse.
hun·dir tr. *(sumergir)* to sink; *(confundir)* to confuse; *(arruinar)* to ruin; *(derrotar)* to defeat; *(clavar)* to plunge —reflex. *(sumergirse)* to sink; *(caer)* to fall down, collapse.
hu·ra·cán m. hurricane.
hu·ra·ño, a adj. unsociable.
hur·ga·dor, ra I. adj. poking **II.** m. poker.
hur·gar §47 tr. *(atizar)* to poke, stir; *(revolver)* to poke *or* rummage around in.
hur·gón m. poker.
hur·go·ne·ar tr. *(atizar)* to poke, stir; *(tirar estocadas)* to jab at.
hur·gui·llas m.f. busybody.
hu·rón, o·na m. ferret —m.f. COLL. *(curioso)* snoop; *(persona huraña)* unsociable person.
hu·ro·ne·ar tr. *(cazar)* to ferret, hunt with a ferret; COLL. *(curiosear)* to snoop, pry.
hu·ro·ne·ra f. ferret hole.
hu·rra·ca f. ORNITH. magpie; COLL. *(charlatán)* chatterbox.
hur·ta·di·llas adv. ♦ **a h.** secretly, furtively.
hur·tar tr. *(robar)* to steal, thieve; *(dar de menos)* to shortchange; *(plagiar)* to plagiarize.
hur·to m. *(robo)* theft, robbery; *(cosa hurtada)* stolen object.
hu·si·llo m. *(tornillo)* screw, worm; *(desaguadero)* drain, drainage canal.
hus·me·a·dor, ra I. adj. snooping, prying **II.** m.f. snoop.
hus·me·ar tr. *(olfatear)* to scent, smell out; *(indagar)* to snoop, pry —intr. *(oler mal)* to stink, smell; *(curiosear)* to snoop, pry.

hus·me·o m. *(olfateo)* smelling; *(fisgoneo)* snooping, prying.
hu·so m. SEW., TEX. spindle; MECH. drum; AER. fuselage ♦ **h. horario** time zone.
hu·ya, yo, yera, yó see **huir**.

I

i, I f. [pl. **íes**] ninth letter of the Spanish alphabet ♦ **poner los puntos sobre las íes** COLL. to dot the i's.
i·ba see **ir**.
i·bis f.inv. ibis.
i·co·no m. icon.
i·co·no·clas·ta adj. & m.f. iconoclast.
i·co·no·gra·fí·a f. iconography.
ic·te·ri·cia f. jaundice.
ic·tio·lo·gí·a f. ichthyology.
ic·tió·lo·go m. ichthyologist.
i·da f. see **ido, a**.
i·de·a f. idea; *(concepto)* concept; *(noción)* notion; *(imagen)* image, picture; *(ingenio)* imagination ♦ **cambiar de i.** to change one's mind • **darle a uno la i.** to get it into one's head • **hacerse** *or* **metérsele a uno una i. en la cabeza** COLL. to get an idea into one's head • **¡ni i.!** COLL. search me! • **no puedes tener i.** you can't imagine • **tener i. de** to intend to.
i·de·al I. adj. ideal; *(perfecto)* perfect **II.** m. ideal ♦ **lo i.** the perfect thing.
i·de·a·lis·ta adj. & m.f. idealist.
i·de·a·li·zar §04 tr. to idealize.
i·de·ar tr. *(concebir)* to think up, plan; *(inventar)* to invent, design.
i·dén·ti·co, a adj. identical.
i·den·ti·dad f. identity.
i·den·ti·fi·ca·ble adj. identifiable.
i·den·ti·fi·car §70 tr. to identify —reflex. to identify (oneself) with, be identified with.
i·de·o·lo·gí·a f. ideology.
i·de·o·ló·gi·co, a adj. ideological.
i·dí·li·co, a adj. idyllic.
i·di·lio m. idyll.
i·dio·ma m. language, tongue.
i·dio·má·ti·co, a adj. idiomatic.
i·dio·sin·cra·sia f. idiosyncrasy.
i·dio·sin·crá·si·co, a adj. idiosyncratic.
i·dio·ta I. adj. foolish, idiotic **II.** m.f. idiot, imbecile.
i·dio·tez f. idiocy.
i·do, a I. see **ir II.** adj. COLL. *(chiflado)* nuts, crazy ♦ **estar i.** COLL. to be distracted **III.** f. *(acción)* going; *(viaje)* trip ♦ **i. y vuelta** round trip • **idas y venidas** comings and goings.
i·dó·la·tra I. adj. idolatrous, idolizing **II.** m.f. idolater, idolizer.
i·do·la·trar tr. to idolize.
i·do·la·trí·a f. idolatry.
í·do·lo m. idol.
i·do·nei·dad f. *(aptitud)* aptitude, capacity; *(conveniencia)* suitability, fitness.
i·dó·ne·o, a adj. *(apto)* capable, apt; *(conveniente)* suitable, fit.
i·gle·sia f. church ♦ **i. parroquial** parish church.
íg·ne·o, a adj. igneous.
ig·ni·ción f. ignition.
ig·no·mi·nia f. ignominy.
ig·no·mi·nio·so, a adj. ignominious.
ig·no·ran·cia f. ignorance.

ig·no·ran·te I. adj. *(sin educación)* ignorant, uneducated; *(que ignora)* uninformed, unaware **II.** m.f. ignoramus.

ig·no·rar tr. to be ignorant of, not to know.

ig·no·to, a adj. unknown, undiscovered.

i·gual I. adj. equal; *(semejante)* similar, alike; *(mismo)* like; *(parejo)* even, level ♦ **darle a uno i.** to be the same to one • **ir iguales** to be even • **ser i. a** *(ser lo mismo)* to be the same as; *(igualar)* to equal • **todo me es i.** it's all the same to me **II.** m. MATH. equal sign —m.f. equal ♦ **al i. que** just like • **de i. a i.** as an equal • **i. que** the same as • **no tener i.** to have no equal, be unrivaled • **sin i.** unparalleled, unequaled.

i·gua·la·dor, ·ra I. adj. equalizing, leveling **II.** m.f. equalizer, leveler.

i·gua·la·mien·to m. equalization.

i·gua·lar tr. *(hacer igual)* to equalize, make equal; *(allanar)* to smooth; *(juzgar igual)* to consider equal, equate; *(comparar)* to compare; SPORT. to tie —intr. & reflex. *(ser iguales)* to be equal; SPORT. to be tied ♦ **i. a** or **con** to be equal to, be the equal of.

i·gual·dad f. equality; *(semejanza)* similarity, likeness; *(uniformidad)* evenness ♦ **en i. de condiciones** on an equal basis, on equal terms.

i·gua·li·ta·rio, a adj. & m.f. egalitarian.

i·gual·men·te adv. equally; *(también)* also, too; *(en la misma manera)* the same in, the same way.

i·gua·na m. iguana.

i·ja·da f. *(de un animal)* flank; *(del hombre)* side; *(dolor)* colic, pain in the side.

i·la·ción f. *(deducción)* inference; *(de ideas)* connectedness, cohesiveness.

i·le·gal adj. illegal.

i·le·ga·li·dad f. illegality.

i·le·gi·ble adj. illegible.

i·le·gi·ti·mi·dad f. illegitimacy.

i·le·gí·ti·mo, a adj. illegitimate.

i·le·so, a adj. unhurt, unscathed.

i·le·tra·do, a adj. & m.f. illiterate.

i·lí·ci·to, a adj. illicit.

i·ló·gi·co, a adj. illogical.

i·lu·mi·na·ción f. illumination; *(alumbrado)* lighting; *(espiritual)* enlightenment.

i·lu·mi·na·do, a I. adj. *(alumbrado)* lit (up), illuminated; *(realizado)* enlightened **II.** m.f. *(hereje)* illuminist; *(visionario)* visionary ♦ **los iluminados** the Illuminati.

i·lu·mi·na·dor, ·ra I. adj. illuminating, illuminative **II.** m.f. illuminator of a manuscript.

i·lu·mi·nar tr. to illuminate; *(alumbrar)* to light; *(espiritualmente)* to enlighten.

i·lu·sión f. illusion; *(esperanza)* hope ♦ **hacerse la i. de que** to imagine that • **hacerse ilusiones de** to cherish hopes of • **tener i. por** to look forward to.

i·lu·sio·nar tr. *(forjar esperanzas)* to build up (someone's) hopes; *(engañar)* to deceive —reflex. to have hopes (of).

i·lu·sio·nis·ta m.f. illusionist, magician.

i·lu·so, a I. adj. deluded **II.** m.f. dreamer.

i·lu·so·rio, a adj. illusory, false.

i·lus·tra·ción f. illustration; *(grabado)* picture ♦ **la I.** the Enlightenment.

i·lus·tra·do, a I. adj. *(persona)* learned, erudite; *(libro)* illustrated **II.** m.f. erudite person.

i·lus·tra·dor, ·ra I. adj. illustrative **II.** m.f. illustrator.

i·lus·trar tr. to illustrate; *(aclarar)* to eluci-

date; *(instruir)* to instruct, enlighten.

i·lus·tra·ti·vo, a adj. illustrative.

i·lus·tre adj. illustrious, distinguished.

i·ma·gen f. image ♦ **i. fantasma** TELEV. double image, ghost • **ser la i. viva de** to be the living image of.

i·ma·gi·na·ble adj. imaginable.

i·ma·gi·na·ción f. imagination ♦ **dejarse llevar por la i.** to let the imagination run away with one • **pasar por la i.** to occur, cross one's mind.

i·ma·gi·nar tr. to imagine; *(inventar)* to invent; *(suponer)* to suppose, presume —reflex. to imagine.

i·ma·gi·na·rio, a adj. imaginary.

i·ma·gi·na·ti·vo, a adj. imaginative.

i·mán[1] m. RELIG. imam.

i·mán[2] m. magnet; FIG. magnetism.

i·ma·nar/man·tar tr. to magnetize.

im·bé·cil adj. & m.f. imbecile.

im·be·ci·li·dad f. imbecility.

im·bo·rra·ble adj. indelible.

im·buir §18 tr. to imbue.

i·mi·ta·ble adj. imitable.

i·mi·ta·ción f. imitation.

i·mi·ta·dor, ·ra m.f. imitator, mimic.

i·mi·tar tr. to imitate, mimic.

i·mi·ta·ti·vo, a adj. imitative.

im·pa·cien·cia f. impatience.

im·pa·cien·tar tr. to make (someone) lose patience —reflex. to lose one's patience.

im·pa·cien·te adj. impatient, restless.

im·pac·to m. impact; *(choque)* shock; *(repercusión)* repercussion.

im·pal·pa·ble adj. impalpable.

im·par adj. odd, uneven.

im·pa·ra·ble adj. unstoppable.

im·par·cial adj. impartial.

im·par·cia·li·dad f. impartiality.

im·par·tir tr. to grant, concede.

im·pa·si·bi·li·dad f. impassiveness.

im·pa·si·ble adj. impassive.

im·pa·vi·dez f. fearlessness, courage.

im·pá·vi·do, a adj. fearless, dauntless.

im·pe·ca·ble adj. impeccable.

im·pe·di·do, a adj. & m.f. disabled (person).

im·pe·di·men·to m. impediment.

im·pe·dir §48 tr. to prevent, obstruct.

im·pe·ler tr. to impel.

im·pe·ne·tra·ble adj. impenetrable.

im·pe·ni·ten·te I. adj. confirmed, inveterate **II.** m.f. stubborn or intractable person.

im·pen·sa·ble adj. unthinkable, unimaginable.

im·pen·sa·do, a adj. unexpected, fortuitous.

im·pe·ran·te adj. ruling, dominant.

im·pe·rar tr. to rule, reign.

im·pe·ra·ti·vo, a adj. & m. imperative ♦ **imperativos económicos** economic considerations.

im·per·cep·ti·ble adj. imperceptible.

im·per·di·ble m. safety pin.

im·per·do·na·ble adj. inexcusable.

im·pe·re·ce·de·ro, a adj. *(duradero)* indestructible; *(inmortal)* immortal.

im·per·fec·ción f. imperfection.

im·per·fec·to, a adj. imperfect.

im·pe·rial adj. imperial.

im·pe·ri·cia f. *(torpeza)* unskillfulness; *(incapacidad)* inexperience.

im·pe·rio m. empire; *(autoridad)* authority; *(duración)* reign.

im·pe·rio·si·dad f. imperiousness.

im·pe·rio·so, a adj. *(autoritario)* imperious, overbearing; *(imperativo)* imperative, urgent.

im·per·me·a·bi·li·dad f. impermeability.
im·per·me·a·bi·li·zar §04 tr. to (make) water-proof.
im·per·me·a·ble I. adj. impermeable, water-proof **II.** m. raincoat, mackintosh.
im·per·mu·ta·ble adj. unexchangeable.
im·per·so·nal adj. impersonal.
im·per·té·rri·to, a adj. intrepid, dauntless.
im·per·ti·nen·cia f. impertinence.
im·per·ti·nen·te I. adj. impertinent; *(insolente)* insolent; *(molesto)* meddlesome **II.** m. ♦ pl. lorgnette, opera glasses.
im·per·tur·ba·ble adj. imperturbable.
im·pé·ti·go m. impetigo.
im·pe·tra·ción f. impetration; *(súplica)* beseeching.
im·pe·trar tr. to impetrate; *(obtener)* to obtain by entreaty; *(suplicar)* to beseech.
ím·pe·tu m. impetus; *(violencia)* violence; *(energía)* energy; *(fogosidad)* impetuosity.
im·pe·tuo·si·dad f. *(ímpetu)* impetus; *(violencia)* violence; *(fogosidad)* impetuosity.
im·pe·tuo·so, a adj. *(violento)* violent; *(fogoso)* impetuous, impulsive.
im·pi·da, do, diera, dió see **impedir.**
im·pie·dad f. impiety.
im·pí·o, a I. adj. impious **II.** m.f. infidel.
im·pla·ca·ble adj. implacable.
im·plan·ta·ción f. implantation; *(introducción)* introduction.
im·plan·tar tr. to implant; *(introducir)* to introduce.
im·pli·ca·ción f. implication; *(complicidad)* complicity; *(consecuencia)* consequence.
im·pli·can·te adj. implicating.
im·pli·car §70 tr. to implicate; *(significar)* to imply, mean —reflex. to become involved.
im·plí·ci·to, a adj. implicit.
im·plo·rar tr. to implore.
im·pon·de·ra·ble adj. & m. imponderable.
im·po·nen·te adj. *(grandioso)* imposing; COLL. *(atractivo)* good-looking.
im·po·ner §54 tr. *(ordenar)* to impose; *(informar)* to inform; *(infundir)* to inspire, instill —reflex. *(ser impuesto)* to be imposed on or upon; *(ser necesario)* to be necessary; *(obligarse)* to take on ♦ **i. a** to dominate.
im·po·ni·ble adj. taxable, subject to tax.
im·po·pu·lar adj. unpopular.
im·por·ta·ción f. importation, importing; *(bienes importados)* imported goods.
im·por·ta·dor, ·ra I. adj. importing **II.** m.f. importer.
im·por·tan·cia f. importance; *(valor)* significance; *(autoridad)* authority; *(influencia)* influence ♦ **darse i.** to put on airs.
im·por·tan·te adj. important ♦ **lo i.** the most important thing.
im·por·tar intr. to be important, matter —tr. *(valer)* to cost, be worth; *(introducir en un país)* to import; *(llevar consigo)* to entail.
im·por·te m. amount, cost.
im·por·tu·nar tr. to importune.
im·por·tu·ni·dad f. importunity.
im·por·tu·no, a adj. inopportune.
im·po·si·bi·li·dad f. impossibility.
im·po·si·bi·li·ta·do, a adj. *(tullido)* disabled, crippled; *(impedido)* prevented.
im·po·si·bi·li·tar tr. *(prevenir)* to make impossible; *(impedir)* to prevent.
im·po·si·ble I. adj. impossible; *(inservible)* useless; *(intratable)* intractable, difficult; *(la-*

mentable) lamentable; AMER. dirty, filthy **II.** m. impossible ♦ **hacer lo i.** to do the impossible, do the utmost.
im·po·si·ción f. imposition.
im·pos·tor, ·ra I. adj. slanderous **II.** m. impostor, slanderer.
im·pos·tu·ra f. *(engaño)* imposture; *(calumnia)* slander.
im·po·ten·cia f. impotence.
im·po·ten·te adj. & m. impotent (man).
im·prac·ti·ca·ble adj. *(irrealizable)* impracticable, unfeasible; *(intransitable)* impassable.
im·pre·ca·ción f. imprecation, curse.
im·pre·car §70 tr. to imprecate, curse.
im·pre·ci·sión f. lack of precision, inexactness.
im·pre·ci·so, a adj. imprecise.
im·preg·na·ción f. impregnation.
im·preg·nar tr. to impregnate.
im·pre·me·di·ta·do, a adj. unpremeditated.
im·pren·ta f. *(arte)* printing; *(establecimiento)* printing house.
im·pres·cin·di·ble adj. indispensable.
im·pre·sión f. impression; *(edición)* printing; *(obra)* edition ♦ **i. digital** or **dactilar** fingerprint • **tener la i. de** or **que** to have the impression that.
im·pre·sio·na·ble adj. impressionable.
im·pre·sio·nan·te adj. impressive.
im·pre·sio·nar tr. to make an impression on, impress; *(conmover)* to move, touch —reflex. to be moved.
im·pre·sio·nis·ta adj. & m.f. impressionist.
im·pre·so, a I. see **imprimir II.** adj. printed **III.** m. leaflet.
im·pre·sor, ·ra m.f. printer, owner of a printing house —f. *(maquina)* printer.
im·pre·vi·si·ble adj. unpredictable.
im·pre·vi·sión f. lack of foresight.
im·pre·vis·to, a I. adj. unforeseen, unexpected **II.** m. ♦ pl. incidental expenses.
im·pri·mir §80 tr. *(reproducir)* to print; *(estampar)* to stamp, imprint; *(dejar una huella)* to imprint; *(transmitir)* to impart.
im·pro·ba·bi·li·dad f. improbability.
im·pro·ba·ble adj. improbable.
ím·pro·bo, a adj. *(sin probidad)* dishonest; *(muy duro)* arduous.
im·pro·ce·den·te adj. *(inadecuado)* inappropriate; LAW irrelevant.
im·pro·duc·ti·vo, a adj. unproductive.
im·pro·pie·dad f. impropriety.
im·pro·pio, a adj. *(inadecuado)* inappropriate; *(no exacto)* incorrect; MATH. improper.
im·pro·vi·sa·ción f. improvisation.
im·pro·vi·sa·do, a adj. *(de cosas)* makeshift, improvised; *(de un discurso)* impromptu, extemporaneous; MUS. improvised.
im·pro·vi·sar tr. to improvise; RHET. to extemporize.
im·pro·vi·so, a adj. unexpected ♦ **al** or **de i.** unexpectedly, suddenly.
im·pru·den·cia f. imprudence.
im·pru·den·te adj. & m.f. imprudent (person).
im·pu·den·cia f. impudence.
im·pú·di·co, a adj. & m.f. shameless (person).
im·pu·dor m. *(desvergüenza)* shamelessness; *(falta de pudor)* impudicity.
im·pues·to, a I. see **imponer II.** m. tax, duty ♦ **i. a las rentas** income tax • **i. a las ventas** sales tax • **i. de herencias** inheritance tax • **i. adicional** ARG. surtax • **i. de aduanas** customs duty • **i. inmobiliario** real-estate tax • **i.**

sobre bienes property tax.
im·pug·na·ble adj. impugnable.
im·pug·na·ción f. refutation, contradiction.
im·pug·nar tr. to refute, impugn.
im·pul·sar tr. to impel, drive.
im·pul·sión f. impulsion, impulse.
im·pul·si·vi·dad f. impulsiveness.
im·pul·si·vo, a adj. & m.f. impulsive (person).
im·pul·so m. impulse.
im·pul·sor, ·ra I. adj. impelling, driving
II. m.f. (*fuerza*) driving force; (*instigador*) instigator.
im·pu·ne adj. unpunished.
im·pu·ni·dad f. impunity.
im·pu·re·za f. impurity.
im·pu·ro, a adj. impure.
im·pu·sie·ra, so see **imponer**.
im·pu·ta·ble adj. imputable.
im·pu·ta·ción f. imputation, charge.
im·pu·tar tr. (*atribuir*) to impute, charge with;
COM. (*asignar*) to assign.
i·na·bor·da·ble adj. unapproachable.
i·na·bro·ga·ble adj. irrevocable.
i·na·ca·ba·ble adj. interminable, endless.
i·na·ca·ba·do, a adj. unfinished.
i·nac·ce·si·ble adj. inaccessible.
i·nac·ción f. inaction.
i·na·cep·ta·ble adj. unacceptable.
i·na·cos·tum·bra·do, a adj. unaccustomed.
i·nac·ti·vi·dad f. inactivity.
i·nac·ti·vo, a adj. inactive.
i·na·dap·ta·ble adj. unadaptable.
i·na·de·cua·do, a adj. unsuitable, inadequate.
i·nad·mi·si·ble adj. inadmissible.
i·nad·ver·ten·cia f. inadvertence, carelessness.
i·nad·ver·ti·do, a adj. (*sin cuidado*) careless;
(*no advertido*) unnoticed.
i·na·go·ta·ble adj. inexhaustible, endless.
i·na·guan·ta·ble adj. unbearable, insufferable.
i·na·lám·bri·co, a adj. wireless.
i·nal·can·za·ble adj. unreachable.
i·nal·te·ra·ble adj. unalterable.
i·na·ne adj. inane.
i·na·ni·dad f. inanity.
i·na·ni·ma·do, a adj. inanimate, lifeless.
i·na·pa·ga·ble adj. inextinguishable.
i·na·pla·za·ble adj. unpostponable.
i·na·pli·ca·ble adj. inapplicable.
i·na·pre·cia·ble adj. (*inestimable*) invaluable;
(*imperceptible*) imperceptible.
i·na·pro·pia·do, a adj. inappropriate.
i·nar·ti·cu·la·do, a adj. inarticulate.
i·na·ta·ca·ble adj. impregnable, unassailable.
i·na·ten·ción f. inattention.
i·na·ten·to, a adj. unattentive.
i·nau·di·to, a adj. (*no oído*) unheard-of; (*extraordinario*) unprecedented; (*monstruoso*) outrageous.
i·nau·gu·ra·ción f. inauguration, opening.
i·nau·gu·rar tr. to inaugurate, open.
in·cal·cu·la·ble adj. incalculable.
in·ca·li·fi·ca·ble adj. indescribable.
in·can·des·cen·cia f. incandescence.
in·can·des·cen·te adj. incandescent.
in·can·sa·ble adj. untiring, indefatigable.
in·ca·pa·ci·dad f. incapacity.
in·ca·pa·ci·ta·do, a adj. incapacitated.
in·ca·pa·ci·tar tr. to incapacitate.
in·ca·paz adj. incapable, unable; (*incompetente*) incompetent; LAW incapacitated.
in·cau·ta·ción f. seizure, confiscation.

in·cau·tar·se reflex. to seize, confiscate.
in·cau·to, a adj. (*imprudente*) incautious, unwary; (*inocente*) gullible, naive.
in·cen·diar tr. to set on fire, set fire to —reflex. to catch fire.
in·cen·dia·rio, a adj. & m.f. incendiary.
in·cen·dio m. fire.
in·cen·sa·rio m. incense vessel.
in·cen·ti·vo m. incentive.
in·cer·ti·dum·bre f. uncertainty, doubt.
in·ce·sa·ble/san·te adj. incessant.
in·ces·to m. incest.
in·ces·tuo·so, a adj. incestuous.
in·ci·den·cia f. (*incidente*) incident, occurrence; PHYS. incidence.
in·ci·den·tal adj. (*incidente*) incidental; (*en paréntesis*) parenthetical.
in·ci·den·te adj. & m. incident.
in·ci·dir intr. to fall upon, strike ♦ **i. en un error** to fall into error ♦ **i. sobre** to influence.
in·cien·so m. incense.
in·cier·to, a adj. uncertain, doubtful.
in·ci·ne·ra·ción f. incineration, cremation.
in·ci·ne·rar tr. to incinerate, cremate.
in·ci·pien·te adj. incipient.
in·ci·sión f. incision.
in·ci·si·vo, a adj. cutting, incisive ♦ **diente i.** incisor.
in·ci·so m. article.
in·ci·tar tr. to incite, instigate.
in·ci·vil adj. uncivil, rude.
in·ci·vi·li·dad f. incivility, rudeness.
in·cle·men·cia f. inclemency.
in·cle·men·te adj. inclement.
in·cli·na·ción f. inclination; (*del cuerpo*) bowing; (*pendiente*) slope, slant; (*tendencia*) inclination.
in·cli·nar tr. (*la cabeza*) to bow, lower; (*torcer*) to slant, tilt; (*persuadir*) to persuade —intr. to resemble, take after —reflex. (*doblarse*) to bow; (*desviar*) to slant, slope; (*parecerse*) to resemble, take after; (*estar dispuesto*) to be or feel inclined.
in·cluir §18 tr. to include; (*encerrar*) to enclose; (*contener*) to contain; (*comprender*) to comprise.
in·clu·sión f. inclusion ♦ **con i. de** including.
in·clu·si·ve adv. inclusive, included.
in·clu·si·vo, a adj. inclusive, including.
in·clu·so, a I. see **incluir** II. adv. (*inclusivamente*) inclusively; (*aun más*) even <i. le avisé I even warned him>.
in·clu·ya, yo, yera, yó see **incluir**.
in·co·bra·ble adj. irrecoverable, uncollectable.
in·cóg·ni·to, a I. adj. unknown ♦ **de i.** incognito II. m. incognito —f. MATH. unknown quantity; (*misterio*) question.
in·co·he·ren·cia f. incoherence.
in·co·he·ren·te adj. incoherent.
in·co·lo·ro, a adj. (*sin color*) colorless; (*sin brillo*) dull.
in·có·lu·me adj. unharmed, unscathed.
in·com·bus·ti·ble adj. incombustible, fireproof.
in·co·mes·ti·ble adj. inedible.
in·co·mi·ble adj. COLL. inedible.
in·co·mo·dar tr. to inconvenience, bother —reflex. to become angry.
in·co·mo·do m./di·dad f. (*falta de comodidad*) discomfort; (*molestia*) inconvenience.
in·có·mo·do, a I. adj. uncomfortable, awkward II. m. discomfort, inconvenience.

in·com·pa·ra·ble adj. incomparable.
in·com·pa·ti·ble adj. incompatible.
in·com·pe·ten·te adj. incompetent.
in·com·ple·to, a adj. incomplete, unfinished.
in·com·pren·si·ble adj. incomprehensible.
in·co·mu·ni·ca·ble adj. incommunicable.
in·co·mu·ni·ca·do, a adj. *(aislado)* isolated, cut off; CRIMIN. incommunicado.
in·con·ce·bi·ble adj. inconceivable.
in·con·ci·lia·ble adj. irreconcilable.
in·con·clu·so, a adj. inconclusive.
in·con·di·cio·nal adj. unconditional.
in·co·ne·xo, a adj. disconnected, unconnected.
in·con·fe·sa·ble adj. unspeakable.
in·con·fun·di·ble adj. unmistakable.
in·con·gruen·cia f. incongruity.
in·con·gruen·te adj. incongruous.
in·con·men·su·ra·ble adj. *(inmensurable)* incommensurable; *(enorme)* enormous.
in·cons·cien·cia f. *(pérdida del conocimiento)* unconsciousness; *(irreflexión)* thoughtlessness.
in·cons·cien·te I. adj. *(sin conocimiento)* unconscious; *(sin consciencia)* unconscious, unaware; *(irreflexivo)* thoughtless II. m. unconscious.
in·con·se·cuen·te adj. inconsistent.
in·con·si·de·ra·do, a I. adj. *(no considerado)* inconsiderate; *(atolondrado)* rash II. m.f. inconsiderate person.
in·con·sis·ten·cia f. inconsistency.
in·con·sis·ten·te adj. inconsistent.
in·con·so·la·ble adj. inconsolable.
in·cons·tan·cia f. changeableness, fickleness.
in·cons·tan·te adj. & m.f. fickle (person).
in·cons·ti·tu·cio·nal adj. unconstitutional.
in·con·ta·ble adj. *(innumerable)* countless; *(que no puede narrarse)* unrepeatable.
in·con·te·ni·ble adj. irrepressible.
in·con·tes·ta·do, a adj. uncontested.
in·con·ti·nen·cia f. incontinence.
in·con·ti·nen·te adj. incontinent.
in·con·tro·la·ble adj. uncontrollable.
in·con·tro·ver·ti·ble adj. incontrovertible.
in·con·ven·ci·ble adj. steadfast, unshakable.
in·con·ve·nien·cia f. inconvenience; *(incomodidad)* discomfort; *(grosería)* crude remark.
in·con·ve·nien·te I. adj. inconvenient; *(inapropiado)* inappropriate; *(grosero)* crude II. m. *(obstáculo)* obstacle; *(objeción)* objection; *(desventaja)* drawback ◆ **tener i.** to mind, object.
in·con·ver·ti·ble adj. inconvertible.
in·cor·po·ra·ción f. incorporation.
in·cor·po·ral adj. incorporeal.
in·cor·po·rar tr. to incorporate —reflex. *(sentarse)* to sit up; *(formar parte)* to join ◆ **i. a las filas** to join the ranks.
in·cor·pó·re·o, a adj. incorporeal.
in·co·rrec·to, a adj. incorrect.
in·co·rre·gi·ble adj. incorrigible.
in·co·rrup·ti·ble adj. incorruptible.
in·co·rrup·to, a adj. incorrupt; *(virgen)* virginal.
in·cre·du·li·dad f. incredulity.
in·cré·du·lo, a I. adj. incredulous; RELIG. unbelieving II. m.f. RELIG. unbeliever.
in·cre·í·ble adj. incredible, unbelievable.
in·cre·men·tar tr. to increase, augment.
in·cre·men·to m. increment, increase.
in·cre·pa·ción f. severe rebuke *or* reproach.
in·cre·par tr. to rebuke, reprimand.
in·cri·mi·na·ción f. incrimination.
in·cri·mi·nar tr. to incriminate.

in·crus·ta·ción f. incrustation; ARTS inlaying.
in·crus·tar tr. GEOL. to encrust; ARTS to inlay —reflex. to become encrusted *or* embedded.
in·cu·ba·ción f. incubation.
in·cu·ba·dor, ·ra I. adj. incubating II. f. incubator.
in·cu·bar tr. & intr. to incubate.
in·cues·tio·na·ble adj. unquestionable.
in·cul·car §70 tr. to inculcate.
in·cul·to, a adj. uncultured, uneducated.
in·cum·ben·cia f. incumbency.
in·cum·bir §38 intr. to be of concern to.
in·cu·ra·ble I. adj. incurable II. m.f. incurably ill person.
in·cu·rrir intr. ◆ **i. en** to commit, incur.
in·cur·sión f. incursion, raid.
in·da·ga·ción f. investigation, inquiry.
in·da·gar §47 tr. to investigate, inquire into.
in·da·ga·to·rio, a adj. investigatory.
in·de·bi·do, a adj. *(ilegal)* illegal; *(desconsiderado)* improper.
in·de·cen·cia f. *(falta de decencia)* indecency; *(acto)* indecent action.
in·de·cen·te adj. indecent.
in·de·ci·ble adj. unspeakable.
in·de·ci·sión f. indecision.
in·de·ci·so, a adj. *(irresoluto)* undecided; *(incierto)* indecisive.
in·de·co·ro·so, a adj. indecorous.
in·de·fen·so, a adj. *(sin defensa)* defenseless; *(desamparado)* helpless.
in·de·fi·ni·do, a adj. *(no definido)* undefined; *(indeterminado)* indefinite; GRAM. indefinite.
in·de·le·ble adj. indelible.
in·dem·ne adj. uninjured, unhurt.
in·dem·ni·dad f. indemnity.
in·dem·ni·za·ción f. indemnity.
in·dem·ni·zar §04 tr. to indemnify.
in·de·pen·den·cia f. independence.
in·de·pen·dien·te I. adj & m.f. independent II. adv. independently.
in·de·pen·di·zar §04 tr. to free, liberate —reflex. to become independent.
in·des·ci·fra·ble adj. undecipherable; FIG. impenetrable.
in·des·crip·ti·ble adj. indescribable.
in·de·se·a·ble adj. & m.f. undesirable.
in·des·truc·ti·ble adj. indestructible.
in·de·ter·mi·na·ble adj. undeterminable.
in·de·ter·mi·na·do, a adj. indeterminate; GRAM. indefinite.
in·di·ca·ción f. indication; *(señal)* sign; *(sugerencia)* suggestion; *(señas)* directions; *(instrucción)* direction; *(observación)* remark.
in·di·ca·do, a adj. *(adecuado)* suitable; *(aconsejado)* recommended.
in·di·ca·dor, ·ra I. adj. indicating II. m. indicator ◆ **i. de carretera** road sign.
in·di·car §70 tr. to indicate; *(mostrar)* to show; *(sugerir)* to suggest.
in·di·ca·ti·vo, a adj. & m. indicative.
ín·di·ce I. m. *(general)* table of contents; *(alfabético)* index; *(de biblioteca)* catalogue; *(indicio)* index; *(coeficiente)* rate; *(cifra)* index; *(dedo)* index finger II. adj. index.
in·di·cio m. indication, sign ◆ pl. clues.
in·di·fe·ren·cia f. indifference.
in·di·fe·ren·te adj. indifferent.
in·dí·ge·na adj. & m.f. native.
in·di·gen·cia f. indigence.
in·di·gen·te I. adj. indigent II. m. ◆ **los indigentes** the poor, the needy.

in·di·ges·tar tr. to cause indigestion —reflex. *(tener indigestión)* to have indigestion; COLL. *(no agradar)* to dislike.

in·di·ges·tión f. indigestion.

in·dig·na·ción f. indignation.

in·dig·nar tr. to anger, infuriate —reflex. to become indignant.

in·dig·ni·dad f. *(carácter)* unworthiness; *(afrenta)* indignity.

in·dig·no, a adj. *(sin mérito)* unworthy; *(vil)* despicable.

ín·di·go m. indigo.

in·di·rec·to, a I. adj. indirect **II.** f. hint ♦ lanzar *or* soltar *or* tirar una i. COLL. to hint at.

in·dis·ci·pli·na·do, a adj. undisciplined.

in·dis·cre·ción f. indiscretion.

in·dis·cre·to, a adj. & m.f. indiscreet (person).

in·dis·cu·ti·ble adj. indisputable.

in·dis·pen·sa·ble adj. indispensable.

in·dis·po·ner §54 tr. to set against —reflex. *(enfermarse)* to become indisposed; *(malquistarse)* to fall out.

in·dis·po·si·ción f. indisposition.

in·dis·pues·to, a adj. indisposed.

in·dis·pu·sie·ra, so see **indisponer.**

in·dis·pu·ta·ble adj. indisputable.

in·dis·tin·gui·ble adj. indistinguishable.

in·dis·tin·to, a adj. indistinct.

in·di·vi·dual adj. individual; *(habitación)* single.

in·di·vi·dua·li·dad f. individuality.

in·di·vi·dua·lis·ta I. adj. individualistic **II.** m.f. individualist.

in·di·vi·dua·li·zar §04 tr. to individualize.

in·di·vi·duo, a I. adj. individual **II.** m. individual; *(de una sociedad)* member.

in·di·vi·si·bi·li·dad f. indivisibility.

in·di·vi·si·ble adj. indivisible.

in·dó·cil adj. indocile, unruly.

in·do·ci·li·dad f. indocility, unruliness.

in·do·cu·men·ta·do, a I. adj. undocumented **II.** m.f. person without identification papers.

ín·do·le f. *(naturaleza)* nature; *(tipo)* type.

in·do·len·cia f. indolence.

in·do·len·te I. adj. indolent **II.** m.f. idler.

in·do·lo·ro, a adj. indolent, painless.

in·do·ma·ble adj. *(animal)* untamable; *(caballo)* unbreakable; *(persona)* uncontrollable; *(pasión, valor)* indomitable.

in·dó·mi·to, a adj. *(no domado)* untamed; *(no domesticable)* untamable; *(persona)* unruly; *(carácter)* indomitable.

in·duc·ción f. induction.

in·du·cir §22 tr. *(llevar)* to induce, lead; *(deducir)* to induce, infer.

in·duc·ti·vo, a adj. inductive.

in·du·da·ble adj. indubitable, certain.

in·du·je·ra, jo see **inducir.**

in·dul·gen·cia f. indulgence.

in·dul·gen·te adj. indulgent.

in·dul·tar tr. *(perdonar)* to pardon; *(exonerar)* to exempt; LAW to grant amnesty.

in·dul·to m. *(perdón)* pardon; *(exoneración)* exemption.

in·du·men·ta·ria f. clothing, garments.

in·dus·tria f. industry.

in·dus·trial I. adj. industrial **II.** m. industrialist.

in·dus·tria·li·zar §04 tr. to industrialize —reflex. to become industrialized.

in·dus·trio·so, a adj. industrious.

i·né·di·to, a adj. unpublished.

i·ne·fa·ble adj. ineffable.

i·ne·fi·ca·cia f. inefficacy.

i·ne·fi·caz adj. ineffective, inefficacious.

i·ne·lu·di·ble adj. inescapable.

i·nep·ti·tud f. ineptitude.

i·nep·to, a adj. & m.f. inept (person).

i·ne·quí·vo·co, a adj. unequivocal.

i·ner·cia f. inertia.

i·ner·te adj. inert.

i·nes·cru·ta·ble adj. inscrutable.

i·nes·cu·dri·ña·ble adj. inscrutable.

i·nes·pe·ra·do, a adj. unexpected.

i·nes·ta·bi·li·dad f. instability.

i·nes·ta·ble adj. unstable.

i·nes·ti·ma·ble adj. inestimable.

i·ne·vi·ta·ble adj. inevitable.

i·ne·xac·to, a adj. inexact, inaccurate.

i·ne·xcu·sa·ble adj. inexcusable.

i·ne·xis·ten·te adj. inexistent, nonexistent.

i·ne·xo·ra·ble adj. inexorable.

i·ne·xper·to, a adj. & m.f. inexperienced (person).

i·ne·xpli·ca·ble adj. inexplicable.

i·ne·xplo·ra·do, a adj. unexplored.

i·ne·xpug·na·ble adj. *(invencible)* impregnable; *(irreductible)* unshakable.

i·ne·xtin·gui·ble adj. *(que no se apaga)* inextinguishable; *(que no se aplaca)* unquenchable; *(inagotable)* perpetual.

i·ne·xtri·ca·ble adj. inextricable.

in·fa·li·bi·li·dad f. infallibility.

in·fa·li·ble adj. *(inequívoco)* infallible; *(inevitable)* inevitable.

in·fa·man·te adj. defamatory, slanderous.

in·fa·mar tr. to defame, slander.

in·fa·me adj. infamous; *(odioso)* thankless; *(vil)* vile **II.** m.f. infamous person.

in·fa·mia f. infamy.

in·fan·cia f. infancy.

in·fan·ta f. *(niña)* infant; *(del rey)* infanta.

in·fan·te m. *(niño)* infant; *(del rey)* infante; MIL. infantryman.

in·fan·te·rí·a f. infantry ♦ i. de marina marines.

in·fan·ti·ci·da I. adj. infanticidal **II.** m.f. infanticide.

in·fan·ti·ci·dio m. infanticide.

in·fan·til adj. infantile; FIG. childish.

in·far·to m. infarct, infarction.

in·fa·ti·ga·ble adj. indefatigable, untiring.

in·fa·tua·ción f. conceit.

in·fa·tuar §67 tr. to make conceited —reflex. to become conceited.

in·faus·to, a adj. unfortunate.

in·fec·ción f. infection.

in·fec·cio·so, a adj. infectious.

in·fec·tar tr. to infect —reflex. to become infected.

in·fe·cun·do, a adj. infecund, sterile.

in·fe·li·ci·dad f. unhappiness.

in·fe·liz I. adj. *(desgraciado)* unfortunate; *(miserable)* wretched; COLL. *(bondadoso)* good-hearted **II.** m.f. *(pobre diablo)* poor devil; COLL. *(persona bondadosa)* good-hearted person.

in·fe·ren·cia f. inference.

in·fe·rior I. adj. *(de abajo)* lower; *(menor)* inferior; *(menos)* less **II.** m. inferior.

in·fe·rio·ri·dad f. inferiority.

in·fe·rir §65 tr. *(deducir)* to infer, deduce; *(ocasionar)* to cause, inflict.

in·fer·nal adj. infernal.

in·fes·ta·ción f. infestation.
in·fes·tar tr. to infest.
in·fi·de·li·dad f. infidelity.
in·fiel I. adj. *(falto de fidelidad)* unfaithful; *(desleal)* disloyal II. m.f. RELIG. infidel.
in·fie·ra, ró see **inferir**.
in·fier·no m. hell; FIG. madhouse ♦ **en el quinto i.** COLL. (out) in the boondocks.
in·fil·tra·ción f. infiltration.
in·fil·trar tr. & reflex. to infiltrate.
ín·fi·mo, a adj. *(muy bajo)* least, lowest; *(peor)* worst.
in·fi·ni·dad f. infinity; *(cantidad)* a lot ♦ **una i. de personas** countless people.
in·fi·ni·te·si·mal adj. infinitesimal.
in·fi·ni·ti·vo, a adj. & m. GRAM. infinitive.
in·fi·ni·to, a I. adj. infinite II. m. infinite; MATH., PHYS. infinity III. adv. ♦ **a lo i.** ad infinitum.
in·fla·ción f. inflation.
in·fla·cio·na·rio, a adj. inflationary.
in·fla·dor m. air pump, inflater.
in·fla·ma·ble adj. inflammable.
in·fla·ma·ción f. inflammation.
in·fla·mar tr. *(encender)* to set on fire; *(enardecer las pasiones)* to inflame —reflex. *(encenderse)* to catch fire; *(enardecerse)* to become aroused.
in·fla·ma·to·rio, a adj. inflammatory.
in·flar tr. to inflate —reflex. to become conceited *or* puffed up.
in·fle·xi·ble adj. inflexible, rigid.
in·fli·gir §32 tr. to inflict.
in·fluen·cia f. influence.
in·fluen·ciar tr. AMER. to influence.
in·fluen·za f. influenza, flu.
in·fluir §18 intr. to have influence.
in·flu·jo m. influence.
in·flu·yen·te adj. influential.
in·for·ma·ción f. information; *(datos)* data.
in·for·mal adj. informal; *(de poco fiar)* unreliable.
in·for·ma·li·dad f. informality; *(falta de seriedad)* irresponsibility.
in·for·mar tr. *(comunicar)* to inform; PHILOS. to form —reflex. to find out.
in·for·má·ti·ca f. data processing.
in·for·ma·ti·vo, a adj. informative.
in·for·me¹ adj. shapeless, formless.
in·for·me² m. report, piece of information.
in·for·tu·na·do, a adj. & m.f. unfortunate (person).
in·for·tu·nio m. misfortune, bad luck.
in·frac·ción f. infraction, transgression.
in·frac·tor, ·ra I. adj. transgressing II. m.f. transgressor.
in·fra·es·truc·tu·ra f. infrastructure.
in·fran·que·a·ble adj. insurmountable.
in·fra·rro·jo, a adj. infrared.
in·fre·cuen·te adj. infrequent.
in·frin·gir §32 tr. to infringe, violate.
in·fruc·tí·fe·ro, a adj. unfruitful, unprofitable.
in·fruc·tuo·so, a adj. fruitless, useless.
in·fun·da·do, a adj. unfounded, groundless.
in·fun·dio m. COLL. lie, false story.
in·fun·dio·so, a adj. lying, mendacious.
in·fun·dir tr. to instill, arouse.
in·fu·sión f. infusion.
in·ge·niar tr. to devise —reflex. to manage *(para* to) ♦ **ingeniárselas** to manage.
in·ge·nie·rí·a f. engineering.
in·ge·nie·ro m. engineer ♦ **i. agrónomo** agron-

omist.
in·ge·nio m. *(habilidad)* ingenuity; *(talento)* talent; *(agudeza)* wit; *(de azúcar)* sugar mill ♦ **afilar** *or* **aguzar el i.** to sharpen one's wits.
in·ge·nio·si·dad f. ingenuity.
in·ge·nio·so, a adj. ingenious.
in·ge·nuo, a adj. & m.f. naive (person).
in·ge·rir §65 tr. to ingest.
in·ges·tión f. ingestion.
in·gle f. groin.
in·gra·ti·tud f. ingratitude, ungratefulness.
in·gra·to, a adj. *(desagradecido)* ungrateful; *(que no satisface)* thankless, unrewarding.
in·gre·dien·te m. ingredient.
in·gre·sar intr. *(entrar)* to enter; *(hacerse miembro)* to become a member of —tr. to deposit.
in·gre·so m. *(acción)* entrance; *(entrada)* entryway; *(de dinero)* income ♦ pl. earnings.
in·há·bil adj. *(incapaz)* unskillful; *(inadecuado)* unfit.
in·ha·bi·li·dad f. *(falta de maña)* unskillfulness; *(ineptitud)* incompetence; *(impedimento)*; handicap.
in·ha·bi·li·tar tr. to disqualify.
in·ha·bi·ta·ble adj. uninhabitable.
in·ha·bi·ta·do, a adj. uninhabited, deserted.
in·ha·lar tr. to inhale.
in·he·ren·te adj. inherent.
in·hi·bi·ción f. inhibition.
in·hi·bir tr. to inhibit —reflex. to withdraw.
in·hos·pi·ta·la·rio, a adj. inhospitable.
in·hu·ma·ni·dad f. inhumanity, cruelty.
in·hu·ma·no, a adj. inhuman, cruel.
i·ni·cia·ción f. initiation.
i·ni·cia·do, a I. adj. initiated II. m.f. initiate.
i·ni·cia·dor, ·ra I. adj. initiating II. m.f. initiator.
i·ni·cial adj. & f. initial.
i·ni·ciar tr. to initiate; *(admitir)* to introduce.
i·ni·cia·ti·va f. initiative.
i·ni·cio m. beginning.
i·ni·cuo, a adj. iniquitous, wicked.
i·ni·gua·la·do, a adj. unequaled.
i·ni·ma·gi·na·ble adj. unimaginable.
i·ni·mi·ta·ble adj. inimitable.
i·nin·te·li·gi·ble adj. unintelligible.
i·ni·qui·dad f. iniquity.
in·je·ren·cia f. interference.
in·je·rir §65 tr. to insert —reflex. to interfere.
in·jer·tar tr. to graft, implant.
in·jer·to m. graft, transplant.
in·ju·ria f. *(insulto)* insult; *(daño)* injury.
in·ju·riar tr. *(ofender)* to insult; *(dañar)* to injure.
in·ju·rio·so, a adj. injurious.
in·jus·ti·cia f. injustice.
in·jus·ti·fi·ca·ble adj. unjustifiable.
in·jus·to, a adj. unjust.
in·ma·cu·la·do, a adj. spotless, immaculate.
in·ma·du·rez f. immaturity.
in·ma·du·ro, a adj. *(fruta)* unripe, green; *(persona)* immature.
in·me·dia·ción f. immediacy ♦ pl. environs.
in·me·dia·to, a adj. next to, adjoining ♦ **de i.** immediately, at once.
in·me·mo·rial adj. immemorial.
in·men·si·dad f. immensity, vastness.
in·men·so, a adj. immense.
in·men·su·ra·ble adj. immeasurable.
in·me·re·ci·do, a adj. unmerited, undeserved.
in·mer·sión f. immersion.

in·mi·gra·ción f. immigration.
in·mi·gran·te adj. & m.f. immigrant.
in·mi·grar intr. to immigrate.
in·mi·gra·to·rio, a adj. immigrant.
in·mi·nen·cia f. imminence, imminency.
in·mi·nen·te adj. imminent.
in·mis·cuir §18 tr. to mix —reflex. to meddle, interfere.
in·mo·bi·lia·rio, a adj. real estate.
in·mo·de·ra·do, a adj. immoderate, excessive.
in·mo·des·to, a adj. immodest.
in·mo·la·ción f. immolation.
in·mo·lar tr. & reflex. to immolate (oneself).
in·mo·ral adj. immoral.
in·mo·ra·li·dad f. immorality.
in·mor·tal adj. immortal.
in·mor·ta·li·dad f. immortality.
in·mor·ta·li·zar §04 tr. to immortalize.
in·mo·vi·ble adj. immovable.
in·mó·vil adj. immobile.
in·mo·vi·li·dad f. immobility.
in·mo·vi·li·za·ción f. immobilization.
in·mo·vi·li·zar §04 tr. to immobilize; COM. to tie up capital.
in·mue·ble I. adj. ♦ **bienes inmuebles** real estate **II.** m. building.
in·mun·di·cia f. filth, dirt.
in·mun·do, a adj. dirty, filthy.
in·mu·ni·dad f. immunity.
in·mu·ni·za·ción f. immunization.
in·mu·ni·zar §04 tr. to immunize.
in·mu·no·lo·gí·a f. immunology.
in·mu·ta·bi·li·dad f. immutability.
in·mu·ta·ble adj. immutable.
in·mu·tar tr. to change —reflex. to lose one's composure.
in·na·to, a adj. innate.
in·ne·ce·sa·rio, a adj. unnecessary.
in·ne·ga·ble adj. undeniable.
in·no·ble adj. ignoble.
in·no·va·ción f. innovation.
in·no·va·dor, ·ra I. adj. innovative **II.** m.f. innovator.
in·no·var tr. to innovate.
in·nu·me·ra·ble adj. innumerable.
i·no·cen·cia f. innocence.
i·no·cen·te adj. & m.f. innocent ♦ **día de los i.** April Fools' Day.
i·no·cu·la·ción f. inoculation.
i·no·cu·lar tr. to inoculate.
i·no·cuo, a adj. innocuous.
i·no·do·ro, a I. adj. odorless **II.** m. toilet.
i·nol·vi·da·ble adj. unforgettable.
i·no·pe·ra·ble adj. inoperable.
i·no·por·tu·no, a adj. inopportune.
i·nor·gá·ni·co, a adj. inorganic.
i·no·xi·da·ble adj. rustproof ♦ **acero i.** stainless steel.
in·que·bran·ta·ble adj. unbreakable.
in·quie·tan·te adj. disquieting, disturbing.
in·quie·tar tr. (perturbar) to disturb; (alarmar) to alarm —reflex. to worry.
in·quie·to, a adj. (intranquilo) restless; (desasosegado) worried, anxious.
in·quie·tud f. (agitación) restlessness; (aprensión) uneasiness.
in·qui·li·na·to m. (alquiler) leasing; (derecho) tenancy.
in·qui·li·no, a m.f. tenant.
in·qui·na f. animosity, dislike ♦ **tenerle i. a alguien** to hold a grudge against.
in·qui·rir §02 tr. to investigate, probe.

in·qui·si·ción f. inquisition; HIST. Inquisition.
in·qui·si·dor, ·ra I. adj. inquisitive **II.** m.f. inquirer —m. HIST. Inquisitor.
in·qui·si·ti·vo, a adj. inquisitive.
in·sa·cia·ble adj. insatiable.
in·sa·lu·bre adj. insalubrious.
in·sa·no, a adj. (demente) insane; (insalubre) unhealthy.
in·sa·tis·fac·ción f. dissatisfaction.
in·sa·tis·fac·to·rio, a adj. unsatisfactory.
in·sa·tis·fe·cho, a adj. (no satisfecho) unsatisfied; (desilusionado) dissatisfied.
ins·cri·bir §80 tr. (grabar) to engrave; (matricular) to register; (anotar) to record —reflex. to register, enroll.
ins·crip·ción f. (acción) inscribing; (epígrafe) inscription; (anotación) record; (matriculación) enrollment.
in·sec·ti·ci·da I. adj. insecticidal **II.** m. insecticide.
in·sec·to m. insect.
in·se·gu·ri·dad f. insecurity.
in·se·gu·ro, a adj. insecure.
in·se·mi·na·ción f. insemination.
in·sen·sa·tez f. (estupidez) stupidity; (dicho) foolish remark.
in·sen·sa·to, a I. adj. foolish, senseless **II.** m.f. fool, dolt.
in·sen·si·ble adj. (que no siente) insensible; (sin compasión) unfeeling; (imperceptible) imperceptible; (inconsciente) unconscious.
in·se·pa·ra·ble adj. inseparable.
in·ser·ción f. insertion.
in·ser·tar tr. to insert.
in·si·dia f. malice.
in·si·dio·so, a adj. insidious.
in·sig·ne adj. famous, illustrious.
in·sig·nia f. badge, emblem.
in·sig·ni·fi·can·te adj. insignificant.
in·sin·ce·ri·dad f. insincerity.
in·sin·ce·ro, a adj. insincere.
in·si·nua·ción f. insinuation.
in·si·nuar §67 tr. to insinuate —reflex. to ingratiate oneself.
in·sí·pi·do, a adj. tasteless; FIG. dull.
in·sis·ten·cia f. insistence.
in·sis·ten·te adj. insistent.
in·sis·tir intr. to insist (en on).
in·so·bor·na·ble adj. incorruptible.
in·so·cia·ble adj. unsociable.
in·so·la·ción f. sunstroke, overexposure.
in·so·lar tr. to expose to the sun —reflex. to get sunstroke.
in·so·len·cia f. insolence.
in·so·len·te adj. insolent.
in·só·li·to, a adj. unusual, uncommon.
in·so·lu·ble adj. insoluble.
in·sol·ven·te adj. & m.f. insolvent.
in·som·nio m. insomnia, sleeplessness.
in·son·da·ble adj. unfathomable.
in·so·por·ta·ble adj. unbearable, intolerable.
in·sos·te·ni·ble adj. untenable.
ins·pec·ción f. inspection, examination.
ins·pec·cio·nar tr. to inspect, examine.
ins·pec·tor, ·ra m.f. inspector.
ins·pi·ra·ción f. inspiration; (de aire) inhalation.
ins·pi·rar tr. to inhale; (infundir sentimientos) to inspire —reflex. to be inspired (en by).
ins·ta·la·ción f. installation; (equipo) equipment ♦ **i. sanitaria** plumbing.
ins·ta·la·dor, ·ra m.f. installer, fitter.

ins·ta·lar tr. to install —reflex. to establish oneself.

ins·tan·cia f. instance ♦ **a i. de** at the request of • **en última i.** as a final resort.

ins·tan·tá·ne·o, a adj. instantaneous.

ins·tan·te m. instant, moment ♦ **a cada i.** constantly • **al i.** immediately.

ins·tar tr. to urge, press —intr. to be urgent.

ins·tau·ra·ción f. establishment.

ins·tau·rar tr. to establish.

ins·ti·ga·ción f. instigation.

ins·ti·gar §47 tr. to incite.

ins·ti·lar tr. to instill.

ins·tin·ti·vo, a adj. instinctive.

ins·tin·to m. instinct ♦ **por i.** by instinct.

ins·ti·tu·ción f. institution.

ins·ti·tu·cio·nal adj. institutional.

ins·ti·tu·cio·na·li·zar §04 tr. to institutionalize.

ins·ti·tuir §18 tr. to institute.

ins·ti·tu·to m. institute; *(escuela)* school.

ins·truc·ción f. instruction; *(enseñanza)* teaching; *(educación)* education; *(conocimiento)* learning; MIL. drill ♦ pl. directions.

ins·truc·ti·vo, a adj. instructive.

ins·truc·tor, ·ra m.f. instructor.

ins·truir §18 tr. to instruct, teach.

ins·tru·men·ta·ción f. arrangement.

ins·tru·men·tal I. adj. instrumental **II.** m. instruments.

ins·tru·men·tar tr. to orchestrate, arrange.

ins·tru·men·to m. instrument.

ins·tru·ya, tú, yera, yó see **instruir**.

in·su·bor·di·na·ción f. insubordination.

in·su·bor·di·na·do, a I. adj. insubordinate **II.** m.f. rebel.

in·su·bor·di·nar tr. to incite to rebellion —reflex. to rebel.

in·subs·tan·cial adj. *(sin substancia)* insubstantial; *(vacío)* shallow.

in·su·fi·cien·cia f. insufficiency; MED. failure.

in·su·fi·cien·te adj. insufficient.

in·su·li·na f. insulin.

in·sul·so, a adj. *(sin sabor)* tasteless; *(soso)* dull.

in·sul·tan·te adj. insulting.

in·sul·tar tr. to insult.

in·sul·to m. insult.

in·su·pe·ra·ble adj. insurmountable.

in·sur·gen·te adj. & m.f. insurgent.

in·su·rrec·ción f. insurrection.

in·su·rrec·to, a I. adj. insurgent **II.** m.f. rebel.

in·tac·to, a adj. intact.

in·ta·cha·ble adj. irreproachable, stainless.

in·tan·gi·ble adj. intangible.

in·te·gra·ción f. integration.

in·te·gra·dor, ·ra I. adj. integrating **II.** m.f. integrator.

in·te·gral adj. & f. integral.

in·te·grar tr. *(componer)* to make up, compose; *(hacer entrar)* to integrate; MATH. to integrate ♦ **estar integrado por** to be composed of.

in·te·gri·dad f. integrity.

ín·te·gro, a adj. *(entero)* whole, complete; *(honrado)* honest, upright.

in·te·lec·to m. intellect.

in·te·lec·tual adj. & m.f. intellectual.

in·te·lec·tua·li·zar §04 intr. to intellectualize.

in·te·li·gen·cia f. intelligence; *(comprensión)* understanding; *(habilidad)* ability.

in·te·li·gen·te adj. & m.f. intelligent (person).

in·te·li·gi·ble adj. intelligible.

in·tem·pe·ran·cia f. intemperance.

in·tem·pe·ran·te adj. intemperate.

in·tem·pe·rie f. bad weather ♦ **a la i.** outdoors.

in·tem·pes·ti·vo, a adj. inopportune, ill-timed.

in·ten·ción f. intention; *(voluntad)* wish ♦ **con i.** intentionally • **segunda i.** underhandedness • **tener malas intenciones** to be up to no good.

in·ten·cio·nal adj. intentional.

in·ten·si·dad f. intensity, strength.

in·ten·si·fi·ca·ción f. intensification.

in·ten·si·fi·car §70 tr. to intensify.

in·ten·si·vo, a adj. intensive.

in·ten·so, a adj. intense.

in·ten·tar tr. *(tener intención)* to intend, plan; *(ensayar)* to try, attempt.

in·ten·to m. *(propósito)* intent; *(tentativa)* attempt.

in·te·rac·ción f. interaction.

in·ter·ca·lar tr. to intercalate.

in·ter·cam·bia·ble adj. interchangeable.

in·ter·cam·biar tr. to interchange, exchange.

in·ter·cam·bio m. interchange, exchange.

in·ter·ce·der tr. to intercede.

in·ter·cep·tar tr. *(detener)* to intercept; *(obstruir)* to block; *(un teléfono)* to wiretap.

in·ter·ce·sión f. intercession.

in·ter·dic·ción f. prohibition, interdiction.

in·te·rés m. interest ♦ **devengar i.** to bear interest • **i. acumulado** accrued interest • **i. propio** self-interest • **sentir** or **tener i. en** to be interested in • **tipo de i.** rate of interest ♦ pl. possessions, interest • **i. creados** vested interests.

in·te·re·sa·do, a I. adj. *(que tiene interés)* interested; *(guiado por el interés)* selfish **II.** m.f. interested person or party.

in·te·re·san·te adj. interesting.

in·te·re·sar tr. *(inspirar interés)* to interest, arouse interest in; MED. to afflict —intr. to be of interest —reflex. to be or become interested *(en, por* in).

in·ter·fe·ren·cia f. interference.

in·ter·fe·rir §65 intr. to interfere.

ín·te·rin m. interim, meantime.

in·te·ri·no, a I. adj. *(provisorio)* interim; *(sustituto)* acting **II.** m.f. substitute.

in·te·rior I. adj. *(interno)* interior, inner; *(nacional)* domestic, internal; *(íntimo)* inner, innermost **II.** m. *(parte interna)* interior, inside; *(alma)* heart, soul; GEOG. interior.

in·ter·jec·ción f. interjection.

in·ter·lo·cu·tor, ·ra m.f. interlocutor.

in·ter·me·diar tr. to mediate.

in·ter·me·dia·rio, a I. adj. intermediate **II.** m. intermediary.

in·ter·me·dio, a I. adj. intermediate **II.** m. *(intervalo)* interval; THEAT. intermission.

in·ter·mi·na·ble adj. interminable.

in·ter·mi·ten·cia f. intermittence.

in·ter·mi·ten·te adj. intermittent.

in·ter·na·ción f. *(en hospital)* hospitalization; *(encerramiento)* confinement.

in·ter·na·cio·nal adj. international.

in·ter·na·cio·na·li·zar §04 tr. to internationalize.

in·ter·na·do, a I. adj. institutionalized **II.** m. boarding school.

in·ter·nar tr. *(hospitalizar)* to hospitalize; *(trasladar)* to send inland; *(encerrar)* to confine —reflex. to penetrate.

in·ter·no, a I. adj. *(de adentro)* internal; *(interior)* interior, inside; *(estudiante)* boarding

II. m.f. *(alumno)* boarding student; *(médico)* internist.

in·ter·pe·la·ción f. appeal, plea.

in·ter·pe·lar tr. *(a un oficial)* to question formally; *(rogar)* to plead.

in·ter·po·lar tr. to interpolate.

in·ter·po·ner §54 tr. to interpose; LAW to lodge *or* file —reflex. *(intervenir)* to intervene; *(estorbar)* to get in the way of.

in·ter·pre·ta·ción f. interpretation ♦ **mala i.** misinterpretation.

in·ter·pre·tar tr. to interpret; MUS. to perform; THEAT. to play.

in·ter·pre·ta·ti·vo, a adj. interpretative.

in·tér·pre·te m.f. *(traductor)* interpreter; *(actor)* actor; *(cantante)* singer.

in·ter·pu·sie·ra, so see **interponer.**

in·te·rro·ga·ción f. interrogation; *(pregunta)* question; GRAM. question mark.

in·te·rro·ga·dor, ra m.f. interrogator.

in·te·rro·gan·te I. adj. interrogating ♦ **punto i.** GRAM. question mark **II.** m.f. *(pregunta)* question; *(incógnita)* unanswered question.

in·te·rro·gar §47 tr. to interrogate, question.

in·te·rro·ga·ti·vo, a adj. & m. interrogative.

in·te·rro·ga·to·rio m. interrogation.

in·te·rrum·pir tr. to interrupt; *(obstruir)* to block, obstruct.

in·te·rrup·ción f. interruption.

in·te·rrup·tor m. switch; *(de circuito)* circuit breaker.

in·ter·sec·ción f. intersection.

in·ters·ti·cio m. interstice.

in·ter·va·lo m. interval ♦ **a intervalos** at intervals, intermittently.

in·ter·ven·ción f. *(mediación)* intervention, mediation; *(participación)* participation; *(de cuentas)* auditing, audit ♦ **i. quirúrgica** surgical procedure, operation.

in·ter·ve·nir §76 intr. *(participar)* to participate, take part; *(interceder)* to mediate; *(interponerse)* to intervene —tr. *(las cuentas)* to audit; *(la comunicación)* to wiretap; SURG. to operate on.

in·tes·ti·nal adj. intestinal.

in·tes·ti·no, a I. adj. internal **II.** m. intestine ♦ **i. ciego** caecum • **i. delgado** small intestine • **i. grueso** large intestine.

in·ti·ma(·ción) f. *(conminación)* ultimatum; *(indicio)* intimation; LAW notice.

in·ti·mar tr. *(hacer saber)* to make known; *(mandar)* to order —intr. to become friendly.

in·ti·mi·da·ción f. intimidation.

in·ti·mi·dad f. *(amistad)* close friendship; *(vida privada)* privacy; *(cercanía)* intimacy, closeness ♦ **en la i.** privately • **en la i. de** in the privacy of.

in·ti·mi·dar tr. to intimidate.

ín·ti·mo, a I. adj *(interior)* intimate, innermost; *(esencial)* essential; *(estrecho)* intimate, close; *(privado)* private **II.** m.f. intimate *or* close friend.

in·to·ca·ble adj. untouchable.

in·to·le·ra·ble adj. intolerable.

in·to·xi·ca·ción f. intoxication.

in·to·xi·car §70 tr. to intoxicate.

in·tran·qui·li·dad f. uneasiness.

in·tran·qui·lo, a adj. uneasy.

in·trans·cen·den·te adj. insignificant.

in·tran·si·gen·cia f. intransigence.

in·tran·si·gen·te adj. & m.f. intransigent.

in·tran·si·ta·ble adj. impassable.

in·tran·si·ti·vo, a adj. intransitive.

in·tra·ta·ble adj. *(incontrolable)* unmanageable; *(insociable)* unsociable; *(grosero)* rude.

in·tra·ve·no·so, a adj. intravenous.

in·tre·pi·dez f. intrepidness.

in·tré·pi·do, a adj. intrepid.

in·tri·ga f. intrigue.

in·tri·gar §47 intr. & tr. to intrigue.

in·trin·ca·do, a adj. *(complicado)* intricate; *(denso)* dense.

in·trín·se·co, a adj. intrinsic.

in·tro·duc·ción f. introduction; *(inserción)* insertion; *(prefacio)* preface; *(preámbulo)* preamble; MUS. overture.

in·tro·du·cir §22 tr. *(dar entrada)* to show *(en into)*; *(meter)* to put in *or* into, stick in; *(insertar)* to insert; *(presentar)* to introduce —reflex. to enter, get in.

in·tro·duc·ti·vo, a adj. introductory.

in·tros·pec·ción f. introspection.

in·tros·pec·ti·vo, a adj. introspective.

in·tro·ver·ti·do, a I. adj. introverted **II.** m.f. introvert.

in·tru·sión f. intrusion.

in·tru·so, a I. adj. intrusive **II.** m.f. intruder.

in·tui·ción f. intuition.

in·tuir §18 tr. to intuit, sense.

in·tui·ti·vo, a adj. intuitive.

i·nun·da·ción f. flood.

i·nun·dar tr. to flood.

i·nu·si·ta·do, a adj. unusual, uncommon.

i·nu·sual adj. unusual, uncommon.

i·nú·til I. adj. *(inservible)* useless; *(vano)* vain, fruitless **II.** m.f. good-for-nothing.

i·nu·ti·li·zar §04 tr. *(arruinar)* to destroy; *(inhabilitar)* to make unusable.

in·va·dir tr. to invade.

in·va·li·da·ción f. invalidation.

in·va·li·dar tr. to invalidate.

in·va·li·dez f. invalidity.

in·vá·li·do, a I. adj. invalid, disabled; *(nulo)* invalid, null **II.** m.f. invalid, disabled person.

in·va·ria·ble adj. invariable.

in·va·sión f. invasion.

in·va·sor, ra I. adj. invading **II.** m.f. invader.

in·ven·ci·ble adj. invincible.

in·ven·ción f. invention.

in·ven·tar tr. to invent; *(forjar)* to fabricate, make up.

in·ven·ta·riar §30 tr. to inventory.

in·ven·ta·rio f. inventory.

in·ven·ti·vo, a I. adj. inventive **II.** f. inventiveness.

in·ven·to m. invention; *(creación)* creation; *(engaño)* fabrication; COLL. *(mentira)* lie.

in·ven·tor, ra I. adj. inventive **II.** m.f. inventor.

in·ver·na·de·ro m. *(invernáculo)* greenhouse; *(para el ganado)* winter pasture.

in·ver·nar §49 intr. *(pasar el invierno)* to winter; ZOOL. to hibernate.

in·ve·ro·sí·mil adj. *(improbable)* improbable, unlikely; *(increíble)* unbelievable.

in·ver·sión f. inversion; FIN. investment.

in·ver·sio·nis·ta m.f. investor.

in·ver·so, a adj. inverse, inverted ♦ **a la i.** the opposite way.

in·ver·te·bra·do, a adj. & m. invertebrate.

in·ver·tir §65 tr. to invert; COM., FIN. to invest; *(tiempo)* to spend time.

in·ves·ti·du·ra f. investiture.

in·ves·ti·ga·ción f. investigation; *(estudio)* research.

in·ves·ti·ga·dor, ·ra I. adj. investigative; *(que experimenta)* researching II. m.f. investigator; *(científico)* researcher.

in·ves·ti·gar §47 tr. to investigate; *(estudiar)* to research, study.

in·ves·tir §48 tr. to invest, confer (on).

in·ve·te·ra·do, a adj. inveterate.

in·vier·no m. winter.

in·vier·ta, to see **invertir**.

in·vio·la·ble adj. inviolable.

in·vir·tie·ra, tió see **invertir**.

in·vi·si·ble adj. invisible.

in·vi·ta·ción f. invitation.

in·vi·ta·do, a m.f. guest.

in·vi·tar tr. to invite.

in·vo·ca·ción f. invocation.

in·vo·car §70 tr. to invoke.

in·vo·lu·crar tr. to involve, implicate.

in·vo·lun·ta·rio, a adj. involuntary.

in·vul·ne·ra·ble adj. invulnerable.

in·yec·ción f. injection.

in·yec·tar tr. to inject.

ion m. ion.

ir §41 intr. to go; *(moverse)* to move; *(caminar)* to walk; *(viajar)* to travel; *(dirigirse)* to lead; *(extenderse)* to extend; *(proceder)* to proceed; *(quedar bien)* to suit, become; *(apostar)* to be at stake, ride ♦ **¿cómo le va?** how is it going? • **¿cómo va el asunto?** how is the matter going? • **i. a** *(estar a punto de)* to be about to, to be going to <*voy a comer en casa* I am going to eat at home> • **i. adelante** to progress, go forward • **i. de caza** to go hunting • **i. de compras** to go shopping • **i. de mal en peor** to go from bad to worse • **i. de paseo** to go for a walk • **i. de viaje** to go on a trip • **i. por** to go for, fetch • **¡vaya!** *(sorpresa)* you don't say!, is that so!; what a <*¡vaya memoria!*> what a memory!> —reflex. *(partir)* to go away, leave; *(deslizarse)* to slip; *(morirse)* to die ♦ **i. abajo** to topple, collapse • **i. a pique** MARIT. to sink • **vámonos** let's go • **vete a saber** there's no telling.

i·ra f. *(cólera)* anger; *(furia)* fury ♦ **llenarse de i.** to become angry.

i·ra·cun·do, a adj. irate, angered.

i·ras·ci·ble adj. irascible.

ir·go, gue, guiera, guió see **erguir**.

i·ri·dis·cen·te adj. iridescent.

i·ris m. iris; MIN. noble opal ♦ **arco i.** rainbow.

i·ro·ní·a f. irony.

i·ró·ni·co, a adj. ironic(al).

i·rra·cio·nal adj. irrational.

i·rra·diar tr. to irradiate.

i·rra·zo·na·ble adj. absurd, ridiculous.

i·rre·al adj. unreal.

i·rre·a·li·dad f. unreality.

i·rre·ba·ti·ble adj. irrefutable, indisputable.

i·rre·con·ci·lia·ble adj. irreconcilable.

i·rre·fu·ta·ble adj. irrefutable.

i·rre·gu·lar adj. irregular.

i·rre·gu·la·ri·dad f. irregularity.

i·rre·le·van·te adj. irrelevant.

i·rre·pa·ra·ble adj. irreparable.

i·rre·pri·mi·ble adj. irrepressible.

i·rre·pro·cha·ble adj. irreproachable, faultless.

i·rre·sis·ti·ble adj. irresistible.

i·rre·so·lu·to, a adj. & m.f. irresolute (person).

i·rres·pe·tuo·so, a adj. & m.f. disrespectful (person).

i·rres·pon·sa·bi·li·dad f. irresponsibility.

i·rres·pon·sa·ble adj. & m.f. irresponsible.

i·rre·ve·ren·cia f. irreverence.

i·rre·ve·ren·te adj. & m.f. irreverent (person).

i·rre·ver·si·ble adj. irreversible.

i·rre·vo·ca·ble adj. irrevocable.

i·rri·ga·ción f. irrigation.

i·rri·gar §47 tr. to irrigate.

i·rri·so·rio, a adj. *(risible)* laughable; *(bajo)* ridiculously low.

i·rri·ta·ble adj. irritable.

i·rri·ta·ción f. irritation.

i·rri·tan·te adj. irritant.

i·rri·tar tr. to irritate.

i·rrum·pir intr. to burst *(en into)*.

i·rrup·ción f. *(acometida)* bursting *or* rushing into; *(invasión)* invasion.

is·la f. island.

is·lá·mi·co, a adj. Islamic.

is·le·ta f. *(isla pequeña)* isle, islet; *(acera)* traffic island.

i·só·to·po m. isotope.

ist·mo m. isthmus.

i·tá·li·co, a adj. italic ♦ **letra i.** italics.

i·ti·ne·ra·rio, a adj. & m. itinerary.

iz·quier·dis·ta adj. & m.f. leftist.

iz·quier·do, a I. adj. left II. f. *(mano)* left hand; *(lado)* left ♦ **a la i.** *(dirección)* left, to the left; *(sitio)* on the left • **de la i.** on the left • **la i.** POL. the left *or* Left • **por la i.** on the left.

J

j, J f. tenth letter of the Spanish alphabet.

ja·ba·lí m. [pl. **-íes**] wild boar.

ja·ba·li·na¹ f. ZOOL. wild sow.

ja·ba·li·na² f. javelin.

ja·bón m. soap ♦ **dar un j. a** R.P., COLL. to frighten • **j. de afeitar** shaving soap • **j. de tocador** *or* **de olor** toilet soap • **j. en polvo** soap powder • **tener j.** R.P., COLL. to be afraid.

ja·bo·na·do, a m. *(jabonadura)* soaping; *(ropa)* wash —f. AMER. soaping.

ja·bo·na·du·ra f. soaping.

ja·bo·nar tr. *(la ropa, el cuerpo)* to wash; *(la barba)* to lather.

ja·bon·ci·llo m. *(jabón)* bar of soap; BOT. soapberry.

ja·bo·ne·ro, a I. adj. soap II. m.f. soapmaker —f. soap dish.

ja·bo·no·so, a adj. soapy.

ja·ca f. pony, small horse.

ja·ca·ran·do·so, a adj. COLL. merry, lively.

ja·ca·re·ro, a/ris·ta adj. merry, lively.

já·ce·na f. girder, main beam.

ja·cin·to m. BOT. hyacinth; MIN. zircon ♦ **j. occidental** topaz • **j. oriental** ruby.

jaco m. *(jamelgo)* hack, nag; *(cota)* short-sleeved coat of mail.

jac·tan·cia f. *(alardeo)* boast; *(arrogancia)* arrogance.

jac·tan·cio·so, a adj. boastful, arrogant.

jac·tar·se reflex. to boast *(de about)*.

ja·da f. hoe, spade.

ja·de m. jade.

ja·de·ar intr. to pant, gasp.

ja·diar tr. to hoe, dig with a spade.

ja·ez m. *(arreo)* harness; DEROG. *(carácter)* ilk, sort.

ja·guar m. jaguar.

ja·guay m. AMER. watering trough.

ja·güey m. AMER. pond.

ja·lar tr. COLL. *(tirar)* to pull; C. AMER. to make love to; COL., VEN. to do, perform —intr. AMER. to leave.

jal·be·gar §47 tr. to whitewash.

ja·le·a f. jelly ♦ **hacerse** *or* **volverse una j.** to go sweet (on).

ja·le·a·dor, ·ra I. adj. cheering II. m.f. cheerer.

ja·le·ar tr. *(animar)* to encourage; *(incitar)* to urge on; AMER. to pester.

ja·le·o m. *(animación)* clapping and cheering; *(incitación)* urging; *(baile)* popular Andalusian dance; COLL. *(tumulto)* fuss, uproar ♦ **armar un j.** to kick up a fuss • **estar de j.** to have a good time.

jal·ma f. packsaddle.

ja·lón[1] m. *(hito)* milestone; *(estaca)* stake.

ja·lón[2] m. AMER., COLL. *(tirón)* pull; *(trecho)* stretch, distance.

ja·lo·nar tr. *(con jalones)* to stake out; *(marcar)* to mark.

ja·más adv. *(nunca)* never; *(alguna vez)* ever ♦ **j. de los jamases** never ever • **nunca j.** never again • **para siempre j.** for ever and ever.

jam·ba f. jamb.

jam·ba·je m. *(de una puerta)* door frame; *(de una ventana)* window frame.

ja·mel·go m. nag, hack.

jam·ón m. ham ♦ **j. ahumado** smoked ham • **j. serrano** cured ham.

ja·mo·na COLL. I. adj. plump II. f. buxom (middle-aged) woman ♦ **una mujer j.** a good-looking woman.

jan·ga·da f. *(armadía)* float; *(de árboles)* log-jam.

ja·que[1] m. check ♦ **dar j.** to check • **dar j. y mate** to checkmate • **j. mate** checkmate • **tener en j.** *(amenazar)* to keep in check; *(hostigar)* to pester.

ja·que[2] m. COLL. braggart.

ja·que·ar tr. *(en ajedrez)* to check; *(hostigar)* to pester.

ja·que·ca f. *(migraña)* migraine headache; COLL. *(molestia)* pain in the neck.

ja·que·tón m. man-eating shark.

ja·ra f. BOT. rockrose; *(arma)* dart.

ja·ra·be m. syrup ♦ **dar j.** to butter up • **estar hecho un j.** to go sweet on • **j. de pico** COLL. lip service • **j. para la tos** cough syrup • **j. tapatío** hat dance.

ja·ra·na f. *(alboroto)* fuss, uproar; AMER. *(chanza)* joke ♦ **andar** *or* **ir de j.** to carouse • **estar de j.** to live it up.

ja·ra·ne·ar intr. *(divertirse)* to have a good time; AMER. *(chancear)* to joke.

ja·ra·ne·ro, ·a I. adj. fun-loving II. m.f. ca-rouser.

jar·ca f. acacia.

jar·cia(s) f.(pl.) rigging, ropes.

jar·dín m. garden ♦ **j. de la infancia** kindergarten.

jar·di·ne·ra f. *(para flores)* flower stand *or* box; *(que cuida un jardín)* gardener.

jar·di·ne·rí·a f. gardening.

jar·di·ne·ro m. gardener.

ja·re·ta f. *(dobladillo)* hem; MARIT. cable.

ja·rra f. *(vasija)* jug, pitcher; *(de cerveza)* mug, beer mug ♦ **de** *or* **en jarra(s)** with arms akimbo.

ja·rre·tar tr. *(enervar)* to enervate; *(quitar las fuerzas)* to weaken.

ja·rre·te m. back of the knee; *(de un animal)* hock.

ja·rre·te·ra f. *(liga)* garter; *(orden militar)* Order of the Garter.

ja·rro m. pitcher, jug ♦ **echar un j. de agua fría a** COLL. to throw cold water on.

ja·rrón m. urn, vase.

jas·pe m. MIN. jasper; *(mármol)* veined marble.

jas·pe·ar tr. to marble, speckle.

ja·to a, m.f. calf.

jau·la f. cage; *(embalaje)* crate; *(para niños)* playpen; MIN. cage.

jau·rí·a f. pack (of animals).

jaz·mín m. jasmine ♦ **j. del Cabo** gardenia.

je·be m. alum; AMER., BOT. rubber plant.

je·fa f. boss, chief.

je·fa·tu·ra f. *(dirección)* management; *(oficina)* headquarters.

je·fe m. *(superior)* boss; *(gerente)* manager; *(líder)* leader; *(cabeza)* head ♦ **comandante en j.** commander-in-chief • **j. de escuadra** rear admiral • **j. de estación** stationmaster • **j. de estado mayor** chief of staff • **j. de redacción** editor-in-chief • **j. de taller** foreman.

je·me·que m. COLL. whine.

je·mi·que·ar intr. CHILE to whimper, whine.

jen·gi·bre m. ginger.

je·rar·ca m. hierarch, high official.

je·rar·quí·a f. hierarchy, rank.

je·rár·qui·co, a adj. hierarchic(al).

jer·bo m. jerboa, mouse.

je·re·mi·a·da f. jeremiad, lamentation.

je·re·mí·as m.f. whiner, complainer.

je·rez m. sherry.

jer·ga[1] f. *(tela)* coarse woolen cloth; *(colchón)* straw mattress; AMER. saddle blanket.

jer·ga[2] f. *(jerigonza)* jargon; *(galimatías)* gibberish.

jer·gón m. straw mattress.

je·ri·be·que m. *(mueca)* grimace; *(guiño)* wink.

je·ri·gon·za f. *(jerga)* jargon, slang; *(galimatías)* gibberish.

je·rin·ga f. syringe; AMER., COLL. *(molestia)* nuisance ♦ **j. de engrase** grease gun.

je·rin·ga·dor, ·ra COLL. I. adj. irksome, annoying II. m.f. pest.

je·rin·gar §47 tr. *(inyectar)* to inject; COLL. *(fastidiar)* to pester.

je·rin·ga·zo m. injection.

je·rin·gón, o·na adj. AMER. annoying.

je·rin·guear tr. AMER. to annoy, pester.

je·rin·gui·lla f. small syringe; BOT. mock orange.

je·ro·glí·fi·co, a I. adj. hieroglyphic II. m. hieroglyph.

je·ta f. *(hocico)* snout; *(labios)* thick lips; COLL. *(cara)* mug ♦ **poner j.** COLL. to make a face.

je·tu·do, a adj. thick-lipped.

ji·bia f. cuttlefish.

ji·fia f. swordfish.

jil·gue·ro m. goldfinch, linnet.

ji·li·po·lla·da/llez f. SL. *(acción)* stupid thing to do; *(dicho)* stupid thing to say ♦ **esos son jilipolleces** that's a lot of bull • **¡qué j.!** how stupid can you get!

ji·mio, a adj. & m.f. simian.

jin·da(·ma) f. COLL. fear, fright.

ji·ne·ta[1] f. ZOOL. genet.

ji·ne·ta[2] f. *(lanza corta)* short lance; *(hombrera)* epaulette; *(que cabalga)* horsewoman.

ji·ne·te m. *(cabalgador)* horseman; MIL. cavalryman; *(caballo)* thoroughbred horse.

ji·ne·te·ar intr. to ride on horseback —tr. AMER. to break in (horses).

jin·glar intr. to swing, rock.

jin·jol m. jujube.

ji·par intr. AMER., COLL. (*hipar*) to hiccup; (*jadear*) to pant.

ji·pi·do m. AMER., COLL. hiccup, hiccough.

ji·pi·ja·pa m. straw hat, Panama hat.

ji·qui·le·te m. indigo plant.

ji·ra f. (*tira*) strip; (*jirón*) shred; (*excursión*) excursion.

ji·ra·fa f. giraffe; (*del micrófono*) boom.

ji·rón m. (*pedazo*) shred, piece; (*ropa*) facing; (*estandarte*) pennant ♦ **hacer jirones** to tear to shreds.

ji·ro·na·do, a adj. torn, tattered.

jo·co·se·rio, a adj. tragicomic.

jo·co·si·dad f. (*gracia*) humor, wit; (*divertimiento*) fun; (*chiste*) joke.

jo·co·so, a adj. humorous, amusing.

jo·cun·di·dad f. jocundity, cheerfulness.

jo·cun·do, a adj. jocund, cheerful.

jo·fai·na f. washbasin, washbowl.

jol·go·rio m. merriment, fun ♦ **ir** *or* **estar de j.** COLL. to have a good time.

jo·pe·o m. stroll, walk.

jo·po m. tuft.

jor·na·da f. (*viaje*) journey, trip; (*día de trabajo*) workday; PRINT. day's print run ♦ **de media j.** part-time.

jor·nal m. (*sueldo*) day's wage; (*día de trabajo*) workday ♦ **a j.** by the day • **j. mínimo** minimum wage.

jor·na·le·ro m.f. day laborer.

jo·ro·ba f. (*giba*) hump; COLL. (*molestia*) nuisance.

jo·ro·ba·do, a I. adj. hunchbacked II. m.f. hunchback.

jo·ro·bar tr. COLL. to bother, pester.

jo·ro·be·ta f. COLL. hunchback.

jo·rrar tr. to tow, haul (a net).

jo·rro m. dragnet.

jo·ta[1] f. iota, bit ♦ **no decir ni j.** COLL. not to say a word • **no entender ni j.** COLL. not to understand at all • **sin faltar una j.** without missing a thing.

jo·ta[2] f. Spanish dance and its music.

jo·ta[3] f. AMER. sandal.

jo·ven I. adj. young, youthful II. m.f. young person, youth.

jo·vial adj. jovial, cheerful.

jo·via·li·dad f. joviality.

jo·ya f. (*alhaja*) jewel; (*objeto de adorno*) piece of jewelry; FIG. gem ♦ pl. jewelry • **j. de fantasía** costume jewelry.

jo·yel m. small jewel.

jo·ye·ra f. jewelry box.

jo·ye·rí·a f. jewelry trade *or* business; (*tienda*) jewelry store.

jo·ye·ro, a m.f. jeweler, jeweller (G.B.) —m. (*caja*) jewelry box; AMER. goldsmith.

ju·bi·la·ción f. (*retiro*) retirement; (*rental*) pension.

ju·bi·la·do, a adj. & m.f. retired (person).

jubilar[1] adj. jubilee.

jubilar[2] tr. (*pensionar*) to retire; COLL. (*desechar*) to discard —reflex. to retire.

ju·bi·le·o m. (*aniversario*) jubilee; (*idas y venidas*) comings and goings ♦ **por j.** once in a lifetime.

jú·bi·lo m. jubilation, joy.

ju·bi·lo·so, a adj. jubilant, joyful.

ju·dai·co, a adj. Judaic, Jewish.

ju·das m. (*traidor*) traitor; (*muñeco de paja*) effigy of Judas burnt during Holy Week.

ju·dí·a f. see **judío, a.**

ju·di·ca·tu·ra f. (*cargo*) judicature; (*mandato*) judge's term of office; (*conjunto de jueces*) judiciary.

ju·di·cial adj. judicial, juridical.

ju·di·cia·rio, a adj. judicial.

ju·dí·o, a I. adj. Jewish II. m.f. Jew —f. Jew, Jewess; BOT. bean ♦ **j. blanca** haricot bean • **j. escarlata** kidney bean.

jue·go m. (*recreo*) play, game; (*deporte*) sport; (*en tenis*) game; (*broma*) jest; (*vicio*) gambling; (*en naipes*) hand; MECH. play, slack; (*de loza, cristal*) set; (*de muebles*) set, suite; (*intención*) game, scheme ♦ **a j.** matching • **en j.** in play, at stake • **hacer doble j.** to be two-faced • **hacer j.** to match • **hacer j. de ojos** to flirt • **hacerle el j.** (*ceder la ventaja*) to play into someone's hands; (*cooperar*) to play along with someone • **¡hagan j.!** place your bets! • **j. de azar** *or* **de suerte** game of chance • **j. de billar** billiards • **j. de bolas** ball bearing • **j. de damas** checkers • **j. de ingenio** guessing game • **j. de manos** sleight of hand • **j. de niños** child's play • **j. de palabras** pun, play on words • **j. limpio, sucio** fair, foul play • **poner en j.** to put into play • **verle el j.** to know someone's game *or* intentions ♦ pl. **j. malabares** juggling.

jue·go, gue see **jugar.**

juer·ga f. COLL. fun ♦ **ir de j.** to live it up.

juer·gue·ar·se reflex. COLL. to have a good time.

juer·guis·ta COLL. I. adj. carousing II. m.f. carouser.

jue·ves m.inv. Thursday ♦ **J. Santo** Holy Thursday.

juez m.f. judge; (*árbitro*) arbitrator; (*en los deportes*) referee ♦ **j. arbitrador** arbitrator • **j. de apelaciones** judge of the court of appeals • **j. de línea** SPORT. linesman • **j. de paz** justice of the peace.

ju·ga·da f. play, move ♦ **hacer una mala j.** to play a dirty trick.

ju·ga·dor, ra m.f. (*en los juegos*) player; (*en el azar*) gambler.

ju·gar §42 intr. (*divertirse*) to play, cavort; (*en el azar*) to gamble; (*hacer una jugada*) to make a play; (*en las damas, ajedrez*) to make a move ♦ **j. a** to play • **j. con dos barajas** to be two-faced • **j. sucio** to play dirty —tr. to play; (*apostar*) to wager; (*una carta*) to wield; (*hacer juego*) to match; (*tomar parte*) to take part, participate —reflex. to risk ♦ **j. el todo por el todo** to risk everything.

ju·ga·rre·ta f. COLL. dirty trick.

ju·glar I. adj. (*de trovadores*) of minstrels; (*chistoso*) comical II. m. (*trovador*) troubadour; (*bufón*) buffoon.

ju·go m. (*zumo*) juice; CUL. gravy; (*lo esencial*) essence; PHYSIOL. juice.

ju·go·si·dad f. juiciness.

ju·go·so, a adj. (*lleno de jugo*) juicy; FIG. substantial.

ju·gue·te m. (*de un niño*) toy; (*chanza*) joke, jest; THEAT. skit, short play; FIG. toy, plaything ♦ **de j.** toy.

ju·gue·te·ar intr. (*divertirse*) to play, cavort; (*jugar*) to toy.

ju·gue·te·rí·a f. toy store.

ju·gue·tón, o·na adj. playful, frisky.

jui·cio m. judgment; *(discernimiento)* discernment; *(opinión)* opinion; *(razonamiento)* reason; *(sentido común)* common sense; *(cordura)* good sense; LAW *(pleito)* trial; *(sentencia)* verdict ♦ **asentar el j.** to come to one's senses • **Día del J.** Judgment Day • **estar en su j.** to be of sound mind • **estar fuera de j.** to be out of one's mind • **j. final** Last Judgment • **perder el j.** to lose one's mind • **poner en tela de j.** to call into question.

jui·cio·so, a adj. judicious, wise.

ju·le·pe m. *(poción)* julep; *(naipes)* a card game; COLL. *(reprimenda)* tongue-lashing; AMER. scare, fright.

ju·lio¹ m. July.

ju·lio² m. PHYS. joule.

ju·mar·se reflex. AMER., COLL. to get drunk.

ju·men·to, a m.f. ass, donkey; FIG. stupid person.

ju·me·ra f. AMER., COLL. drunk, drunken spree.

jun·cia f. sedge ♦ **vender j.** to brag, boast.

jun·co¹ m. BOT. rush; *(bastón)* cane ♦ **j. de Indias** rattan • **j. florido** flowering rush • **j. oloroso** camel grass.

jun·co² m. MARIT. Chinese junk.

ju·nio m. June.

ju·nior m. *(el menor)* junior; RELIG. novice priest.

ju·ní·pe·ro m. juniper; COL. idiot, fool.

jun·que·ra f. rush, bulrush.

jun·qui·llo m. *(flor)* jonquil; *(junco de Indias)* rattan; *(moldura)* rounded molding.

jun·ta f. see **junto, a.**

jun·tar tr. *(unir)* to join; *(reunir)* to assemble; *(dinero)* to amass; *(entornar)* to half-close —reflex. *(reunirse)* to gather; *(asociarse)* to get together; *(copular)* to mate, copulate; AMER. to live together.

jun·to, a I. adj. *(unido)* united, joined; *(cercano)* close **II.** adv. together, at the same time ♦ **j. a** close to, near • **j. con** along with, together with • **todo j.** at the same time, all together **III.** f. *(de personas)* board, junta; *(reunión)* meeting, session; *(unión)* union, junction; CONSTR. joint, scarf; TECH. gasket, washer; MARIT. seam; AMER. junction (of two rivers) ♦ **j. administrativa** administrative council • **j. cardánica** or **universal** universal joint • **j. de educación, sanidad** board of education, health • **j. directiva** board of directors • **j. esférica** ball joint • **j. militar** military junta.

jun·tu·ra f. *(punto de unión)* juncture; ANAT., TECH. joint.

ju·ra f. *(juramento)* oath; *(ceremonia)* swearing in.

ju·ra·do, a I. adj. sworn, under oath **II.** m. *(tribunal)* jury; *(miembro del tribunal)* juror; *(de una competición)* panel of judges.

ju·ra·men·ta·do, a adj. sworn, under oath.

ju·ra·men·tar tr. to swear in, put under oath —reflex. to be sworn in, take an oath.

ju·ra·men·to m. *(jura)* oath; *(ofensa)* curse, swearword ♦ **bajo j.** under oath • **j. falso** perjury • **j. hipocrático** Hippocratic oath • **prestar j.** to take an oath • **soltar j.** to curse • **tomar j.** to swear in.

ju·rar tr. *(prestar juramento)* to swear, take an oath; *(prometer)* to swear, pledge (allegiance) —intr. *(blasfemar)* to swear, curse —reflex. ♦ **j. en falso** to commit perjury —reflex. ♦ **jurársela a uno** to have it in for someone.

ju·rel m. saurel, jack mackerel.

ju·ri·di·ci·dad f. lawfulness.

ju·rí·di·co, a adj. juridical.

ju·ris·con·sul·to m. jurist, legal expert.

ju·ris·dic·ción f. jurisdiction ♦ **traslado de j.** change of venue.

ju·ris·dic·cio·nal adj. jurisdictional.

ju·ris·pe·ri·cia f. jurisprudence.

ju·ris·pe·ri·to, a m.f. legal expert, jurist.

ju·ris·pru·den·cia f. jurisprudence; *(precedentes)* case law, legislation.

ju·ris·ta m.f. *(abogado)* jurist, lawyer; *(pensionado)* pensioner; *(dueño)* one who has the right of ownership.

ju·ro m. *(derecho)* right of ownership; *(renta)* pension.

jus·ta f. see **justo, a.**

jus·ta·men·te adv. *(con justicia)* justly, fairly; *(precisamente)* exactly, precisely.

jus·ti·cia f. justice; *(equidad)* fairness; *(castigo)* retribution; *(castigo de muerte)* execution; *(policía)* law, police ♦ **de j.** justly, duly • **tomarse la j. por las manos** to take the law into one's own hands.

jus·ti·ciar tr. *(ajusticiar)* to execute; *(condenar)* to condemn.

jus·ti·cie·ro, a I. adj. *(justo)* just, fair; *(riguroso)* strict, severe **II.**m.f. just *or* righteous person.

jus·ti·fi·ca·ble adj. justifiable.

jus·ti·fi·ca·ción f. justification; *(prueba)* proof, evidence.

jus·ti·fi·ca·dor, ·ra I. adj. justifying **II.** m. justification bar.

jus·ti·fi·can·te I. adj. justifying **II.** m. voucher.

jus·ti·fi·car §70 tr. to justify; *(defender)* to defend —reflex. *(explicarse)* to justify *or* explain oneself; *(probar la inocencia)* to prove one's innocence.

jus·ti·fi·ca·ti·vo, a adj. justifying.

jus·ti·pre·ciar tr. to appraise, estimate.

jus·ti·pre·cio m. appraisal, estimate.

jus·to, a I. adj. just, fair; *(legítimo)* justified, legitimate; *(honrado)* righteous, upright; *(exacto)* exact, precise; *(apretado)* tight **II.** m.f. just person —f. *(torneo)* joust; FIG. *(competencia)* contest **III.** adv. *(con justicia)* justly; *(exactamente)* exactly; *(frugalmente)* sparingly.

ju·ve·níl adj. young, youthful.

ju·ven·tud f. *(edad)* youth; *(vigor juvenil)* youthfulness ♦ **la j.** *(los jóvenes)* the youth.

juz·ga·do m. *(tribunal)* court, tribunal; *(judicatura)* judicature.

juz·ga·dor, ·ra I. adj. judging **II.**m.f. judge.

juz·gar §47 tr. to judge; *(arbitrar)* to pass judgment on; *(considerar)* to consider; *(estimar)* to assess ♦ **a j. por** judging by *or* from • **j. mal** to misjudge.

K

k, K f. eleventh letter of the Spanish alphabet.

ka·ki adj. & m. khaki.

kan m. khan.

kan·gu·ro m. kangaroo.

ka·ra·te m. karate.

ke·ro·se·ne/sén m. AMER. kerosene.

ki·lo m. kilo, kilogram.

ki·lo·ci·clo m. kilocycle.

ki·lo·gra·mo m. kilogram.
ki·lo·li·tro m. kiloliter.
ki·ló·me·tro m. kilometer.
ki·lo·tón m. kiloton.
ki·lo·va·tio m. kilowatt.
ki·ne·si·te·ra·peu·ta m. masseur —f. masseuse.
ki·ne·si·te·ra·pia f. kinesitherapy, massage.
kirsch m. kirsch, cherry brandy.
ki·wi m. kiwi.
kla·xon m. horn.
ko·a·la m. koala.
ko·pek m. kopeck.
krip·tón m. krypton.

L

l, L f. twelfth letter of the Spanish alphabet.
la¹ I. def. art. the ♦ **la que** the one that, the one who II. pron. her <*la miré* I looked at her>; it <*buscó la cinta y finalmente la encontró* she looked for the ribbon and finally found it>; you <*no la vi a usted en la fiesta, Ana* I didn't see you at the party, Ann>.
la² MUS. la.
la·be·rin·to m. labyrinth.
la·bia f. COLL. eloquence ♦ **tener mucha l.** to have the gift of gab.
la·bio m. lip; *(borde)* lip, rim; *(órgano del habla)* lip, mouth ♦ **sellar los labios** to keep one's lips sealed • **l. leporino** harelip.
la·bor f. *(trabajo)* work; *(faena)* task, job; *(labranza)* farm work; *(bordado)* embroidery ♦ pl. **l. de aguja** needlework • **l. domésticas** household chores.
la·bo·ra·ble adj. work, working.
la·bo·ral adj. *(del trabajo)* labor; *(técnico)* technical.
la·bo·rar tr. *(trabajar)* to work; *(cultivar)* to cultivate; *(arar)* to plow —intr. to scheme.
la·bo·ra·to·rio m. laboratory.
la·bo·re·ar tr. to work —intr. MARIT. to reeve.
la·bo·rio·so, a adj. *(trabajador)* industrious; *(penoso)* arduous.
la·bra·do, a I. adj. *(forjado)* wrought; *(tallado)* carved; *(repujado)* tooled; *(cultivado)* cultivated; *(arado)* plowed; *(bordado)* embroidered II. m. *(campo)* cultivated *or* tilled land; *(de metales)* working; *(de madera, piedra)* carving; *(de cuero)* tooling; *(cultivo)* tilling; *(arada)* plowing; *(bordado)* embroidery.
la·bra·dor, ·ra I. adj. farm, farming II. m.f. *(agricultor)* farmer; *(arador)* plowman; *(campesino)* peasant.
la·bran·za f. *(cultivo)* farming; *(hacienda)* farm; *(tierra)* farmland.
la·brar tr. *(trabajar)* to work; *(metales)* to work; *(tallar)* to carve; *(cuero)* to tool; *(cultivar)* to cultivate; *(arar)* to plow; *(bordar)* to embroider; *(causar)* to bring about; *(edificar)* to build —intr. to work.
la·brie·go, a m.f. farm hand *or* worker.
la·ca f. *(resina)* lac; *(pintura)* lacquer, shellac; *(barniz)* lacquer; *(objeto)* lacquered object; *(pelo)* hair spray ♦ **l. de uñas** nail polish.
la·ca·yo m. *(criado)* lackey, valet; *(mozo de espuelas)* groom, attendant.
la·ce·ar tr. *(adornar)* to trim with bows; R.P. to whip with a lasso.
la·ce·ra·ción f. laceration.

la·ce·rar tr. to lacerate; *(dañar)* to injure.
la·ce·ria f. *(pobreza)* misery, want; *(trabajo penoso)* drudgery, toil.
la·cio, a adj. *(cabello)* straight; *(marchito)* wilted; *(flojo)* limp.
la·có·ni·co, a adj. laconic.
la·cra f. *(señal)* scar; *(defecto)* blemish.
la·crar tr. to seal with wax.
la·cre I. m. sealing wax II. adj. red.
la·cri·mó·ge·no, a adj. tear-producing ♦ **gas l.** tear gas.
la·cri·mo·so, a adj. *(que tiene lágrimas)* tearful; *(triste)* sorrowful.
lac·ta·ción f. nursing.
lac·tan·cia f. lactation.
lac·tan·te I. adj. nursing, suckling II. m.f. nursing infant.
lac·tar tr. & intr. to nurse, suckle.
lác·te·o, a adj. milky ♦ **Vía L.** Milky Way.
lác·ti·co, a adj. lactic.
lac·to·sa f. lactose.
la·de·ar tr. to bend, tilt —reflex. to lean, tilt.
la·de·o m. slope, inclination.
la·de·ra f. slope.
la·di·lla f. crab louse ♦ **pegarse a alguien como una l.** COLL. to stick to someone like a leech.
la·di·no, a adj. astute.
la·do m. side; *(sitio)* room; *(aspecto)* aspect; *(camino)* way; *(protección)* protection; MIL. flank; SPORT. end ♦ **al l.** near, close at hand • **al l. de** beside, next to • **a un l.** aside • **dar de l. a alguien** to give someone the cold shoulder • **dejar a un l.** to leave aside • **de l. a l.** from side to side • **echar a un l.** to cast aside • **hacerse a un l.** to get out of the way • **l. a l.** side by side • **l. débil** *or* **flaco** weak spot • **mirar de l.** to look sideways at • **poner a un l.** to put aside • **ponerse del l. de** to side with • **por el l. de** toward, in the direction of • **por otro l.** on the other hand • **por un l.** on the one hand.
la·drar intr. to bark; FIG. to growl, snarl.
la·dri·do m. bark.
la·dri·llo m. brick; *(azulejo)* tile ♦ **es un l.** it's *or* he's a bore • **l. crudo** adobe.
la·drón, o·na adj. thieving II. m.f. thief, robber ♦ **l. de corazones** COLL. lady-killer.
la·dro·ne·ra f. *(refugio)* den of thieves; *(de agua)* sluice gate; *(robo)* theft, robbery; *(alcancía)* money box.
la·dro·ne·rí·a f. thievery, theft.
la·dron·zue·lo, a m.f. petty thief.
la·ga·ña f. rheum.
la·gar·ta f. female lizard; ENTOM. gypsy moth; COLL. *(mujer)* crafty woman.
la·gar·ti·ja f. small lizard.
la·gar·ti·jo m. small lizard; MEX. sharp dresser.
la·gar·to m. lizard; COLL. *(hombre astuto)* sly devil; AMER. alligator.
la·gar·to·na f. COLL. crafty woman.
la·go m. lake.
lá·gri·ma f. tear; FIG. drop ♦ **llorar a l. viva** to cry one's heart out ♦ pl. sorrows, troubles • **beberse las l.** to hold back one's tears • **deshacerse en l.** to burst into tears • **enjugarse las l.** to dry one's eyes *or* tears • **l. de cocodrilo** crocodile tears • **ser el paño de l. (de alguien)** to be someone's consolation.
la·gri·me·ar intr. *(ojos)* to water, tear; *(persona)* to cry, weep.
la·gri·mo·so, a adj. *(ojos)* watery, teary; *(lacrimoso)* tearful.

la·gu·na f. lagoon; *(texto)* hiatus; *(falta)* gap.
lai·ca·do m. laity.
lai·cal adj. lay, laical.
lai·co, a adj. lay, laical.
la·ja f. stone slab; MARIT. reef.
la·ma[1] f. *(cieno)* mud; BOT. algae; *(tela)* (silver *or* gold) lamé; AMER. slime.
la·ma[2] m.f. lama.
lam·ber tr. AMER. *(lamer)* to lick; *(adular)* to fawn on, suck up to.
la·me·du·ra f. lick, licking.
la·men·ta·ble adj. lamentable.
la·men·ta·ción f. lamentation.
la·men·tar tr. *(sentir)* to regret, be sorry for; *(llorar)* to bemoan —reflex. to grieve, lament.
la·men·to m. lament.
la·men·to·so, a adj. plaintive, mournful.
la·mer tr. *(con la lengua)* to lick; *(tocar suavemente)* to lap.
la·me·ta·da f./**zo** m. AMER. licking, lick.
la·mi·do, a I. m.f. licking II. adj. *(flaco)* thin and pale; *(relamido)* polished, finely finished.
lá·mi·na f. *(plancha)* lamina, plate; PRINT. engraved plate; *(estampa)* print.
la·mi·na·ción f. lamination.
la·mi·na·do, a I. adj. laminated ♦ **hierro l.** sheet metal II. m. lamination.
la·mi·nar I. adj. laminar, laminal II. tr. to laminate.
lám·pa·ra f. lamp; RAD., TELEV. valve, tube ♦ **l. de alcohol** spirit lamp • **l. de arco** arc lamp • **l. de incandescencia** incandescent lamp • **l. de seguridad** safety lamp • **l. de soldar** blowtorch • **l. de techo** ceiling lamp • **l. fluorescente** fluorescent lamp • **l. neón** neon light.
lam·pa·ri·lla f. *(lámpara pequeña)* small lamp; *(que se enciende de noche)* night-light.
lam·pa·rón m. *(aceite)* grease spot *or* stain; MED. scrofula; VET. glanders.
lam·pi·ño, a adj. *(sin barba)* beardless; *(con poco vello)* hairless.
la·na f. wool; MEX., COLL. *(dinero)* dough, bread; AMER. *(mentira)* lie ♦ **cardarle a alguien la l.** COLL. to tell someone off • **de l.** wool, woolen • **ir por l. y salir trasquilado** to get more than one bargained for • **l. de acero** steel wool • **l. de vidrio** glass wool.
la·na·do, a adj. woolly, fleecy.
lan·ce m. *(acontecimiento)* event, occurrence; *(trance)* predicament; *(jugada)* move; *(riña)* quarrel, argument ♦ **l. apretado** COLL. tight spot, jam • **l. de honor** duel.
lan·ce·ar tr. to lance.
lan·ce·ro m. lancer ♦ pl. lancers (dance).
lan·ce·ta f. lancet.
lan·cha f. *(embarcación)* boat; *(piedra)* stone slab ♦ **l. motora** motorboat • **l. salvavidas** lifeboat • **l. torpedera** torpedo boat.
lan·char m. flagstone quarry.
lan·che·ro m. boatman, ferryman.
lan·chón m. barge.
lan·da f. moor, heath.
la·ne·ro, a I. adj. woolen II. m. *(negociante)* wool dealer; *(almacén)* wool warehouse.
lan·gos·ta f. ENTOM. locust; ZOOL. lobster.
lan·gos·ti·no/tín m. crayfish.
lan·gui·de·cer §17 intr. to languish.
lan·gui·dez f. *(flaqueza)* weakness, feebleness; *(falta de energía)* listlessness, lethargy.
lán·gui·do, a adj. languid.
lan·guor m. languor.
la·ni·lla f. *(pelillo)* nap; *(tejido)* flannel.

la·no·li·na f. lanolin.
la·no·so, a adj. woolly.
lan·za I. f. lance, spear; *(soldado)* lancer ♦ **correr lanzas** to joust • **estar con la l. en ristre** to be ready for action • **romper lanzas por** to defend, fight for II. adj. MEX. crafty, deceptive.
lan·za·bom·bas m.inv. *(de trinchera)* trench mortar; *(de aviones)* bomb release.
lan·za·co·he·tes m.inv. rocket launcher.
lan·za·da f. *(golpe)* lance thrust; *(herida)* lance wound.
lan·za·lla·mas m.inv. flame thrower.
lan·za·mien·to m. throw, throwing ♦ **l. de abastecimientos** airdrop • **l. del disco** discus throwing • **l. de un barco** launching of a ship.
lan·zar §04 tr. *(arrojar)* to throw, hurl; *(dardos, flechas)* to shoot, fire; *(un proyectil)* to launch; *(una bomba)* to drop; *(aves)* to release; COLL. *(vomitar)* to vomit, throw up; *(brotar)* to put forth; *(decir)* to let loose, let out; *(insultos)* to hurl; *(dar a conocer)* to launch; *(despojar)* to dispossess; *(desalojar)* to evict; SPORT. to throw —reflex. *(arrojarse)* to throw *or* hurl oneself; *(saltar)* to jump; *(apresurarse)* to rush, attack ♦ **l. a** to launch into, embark upon.
lan·za·tor·pe·dos m.inv. MIL. torpedo tube.
la·pi·ce·ro m. *(instrumento)* mechanical pencil; *(lápiz)* pencil; ARG., PERU penholder.
lá·pi·da f. tombstone.
la·pi·dar tr. *(matar)* to stone to death; AMER. to carve gems.
la·pi·da·rio, a I. adj. *(de las piedras preciosas)* lapidary; *(muy conciso)* concise, succinct ♦ **frase l.** memorable phrase II. m. lapidary.
lá·piz m. *(grafito)* graphite, lead; *(instrumento)* pencil ♦ **l. de color** colored pencil • **l. de labios** lipstick.
lap·so, a m. *(de tiempo)* lapse, interval; *(error)* lapse, slip.
lap·sus m. lapsus, slip ♦ **l. cálami** slip of the pen • **l. linguae** slip of the tongue.
la·que·ar tr. to lacquer, varnish.
lar·dar/de·ar tr. to baste, lard.
lar·do m. lard, animal fat.
lar·ga·men·te adv. *(con extensión)* at length; FIG. generously, liberally.
lar·gar §47 tr. *(aflojar)* to slacken; *(soltar)* to release, let go; *(despedir)* to fire, dismiss; *(tirar)* to throw, hurl; *(expulsar)* to throw out, expel; COLL. *(decir)* to let out, let fly <*l. una palabrota* to let fly an obscenity>; *(una bofetada)* to deal —reflex. COLL. *(marcharse)* to beat it, scram; *(comenzar)* to begin to.
lar·go, a I. adj. long; *(extenso)* lengthy; *(alto)* tall; *(abundante)* abundant; MARIT. loose, slack ♦ **a la l.** *(con el tiempo)* in the long run; *(poco a poco)* little by little • **a lo l.** lengthwise; *(por)* along; *(a través)* throughout • **de l.** in formal dress • **l. de manos** heavy-handed • **largos años** many years • **l. y tendido** COLL. at length II. m. length; MUS. largo ♦ **de l.** long <*la piscina tiene quince pies de l.* the pool is fifteen feet long> • **pasar de l.** *(no parar)* to pass by; *(no hacer caso de)* to ignore III. interj. get out! ♦ **¡l. de aquí!** get out of here!
lar·gor m. length.
lar·go·ru·to/gu·cho, a adj. lanky.
lar·gue·a·do, a adj. striped.
lar·gue·za f. *(liberalidad)* largesse; *(largura)* length.
lar·gui·ru·cho, a adj. lanky.

lar·gu·ra f. length.
la·rin·ge f. larynx.
la·rin·gi·tis f. laryngitis.
lar·va f. [pl. **-vae**] larva.
lar·val adj. larval.
las f. def. art. the **II.** pron. them.
las·ci·via f. lasciviousness.
las·ci·vo, a adj. & m.f. lascivious (person).
lá·ser m. laser ♦ **rayo l.** laser beam.
la·si·tud f. lassitude.
la·so, a adj. (cansado) tired, weary; (flojo) weak, languid; (sin torcer) limp.
lás·ti·ma f. (sentimiento) pity, compassion; (cosa) pity, shame ♦ **dar l.** to be pitiful • **es una l. que** it's a shame that • **¡qué l.!** what a shame! • **tener l. de** to feel sorry for.
las·ti·ma·du·ra f. (daño) injury; (herida) wound.
las·ti·mar tr. (dañar) to injure, hurt; (agraviar) to hurt, offend —reflex. to hurt or injure oneself.
las·ti·me·ro, a adj. sad, pitiful.
las·ti·mo·so, a adj. pitiful, deplorable.
las·tra f. flagstone, stone slab.
las·tre m. AER., MARIT. ballast; FIG. dead weight, burden.
la·ta f. (hoja de lata) tin plate; (envase) tin can, can; (madero) small log; (para tejas) roof lath; AMER., COLL. (persona) pest, nuisance ♦ **dar la l.** COLL. to annoy • **¡qué l.!** what a nuisance!
la·ta·zo m. COLL. bore.
la·te·ar tr. AMER., COLL. to bore, bend (someone's) ear.
la·ten·te adj. latent.
la·te·ral adj. lateral, side.
la·ti·do m. (del corazón) beat, beating; (dolor) throb, throbbing.
la·tien·te adj. (pulso) beating; (herida) throbbing.
la·ti·ga·zo m. (golpe) whiplash; (chasquido) whip-cracking ♦ **dar latigazos a** to whip, flog • **darse un l.** COLL. to have a snort.
lá·ti·go m. (azote) whip; COL., ECUAD., PERU whiplash ♦ **l. de montar** riding crop.
la·ti·guer·ar intr. (el látigo) to crack the whip; AMER. to flog, whip.
la·tir intr. (el corazón) to beat; (una herida) to throb; MEX. to have an inkling or a hunch.
la·ti·tud f. (ancho) width, breadth; (extensión) extent, scope; GEOG. latitude; (libertad) freedom, latitude.
la·ti·tu·di·nal adj. latitudinal.
la·to, a adj. broad, wide.
la·tón m. brass ♦ **l. de aluminio** aluminum brass • **l. en hojas** or **planchas** sheet brass.
la·to·ne·rí·a f. slipworks.
la·to·ne·ro m. brassworker.
la·to·so, a adj. COLL. annoying, bothersome.
la·tro·ci·nio m. robbery, theft.
la·úd m. MUS. lute; MARIT. catboat; ZOOL. striped turtle.
lau·da·ble adj. laudable.
lau·dar tr. to rule, render a verdict on.
lau·da·to·rio, a I. adj. laudatory **II.** f. eulogy.
lau·de f. tombstone.
lau·do m. ruling, verdict.
lau·re·a·do, a adj. & m.f. laureate.
lau·re·ar tr. (coronar) to crown with laurel; (premiar) to honor, reward.
lau·re·dal m. laurel grove.
lau·rel m. laurel, bay ♦ pl. laurels, honors •

dormirse en los l. to rest on one's laurels.
láu·re·o, a adj. laurel.
lau·ré·o·la/la·re·o·la f. (corona) laurel wreath or crown; (aureola) halo, aureola.
la·va f. lava.
la·va·ble adj. washable.
la·va·bo m. (lavamanos) wash basin; (cuarto) bathroom.
la·va·ca·ras m.f.inv. COLL. toady, bootlicker.
la·va·co·ches m.inv. car washer.
la·va·da f. washing.
la·va·de·ro m. (lavandería) laundry; (de un río) washing place; MIN. placer.
la·va·do m. (acción) washing, wash; MED. lavage; PAINT. wash ♦ **l. de cabeza** COLL. reprimand • **l. de cerebro** brainwashing • **l. en seco** dry cleaning.
la·va·dor, ·ra I. adj. washing **II.** m.f. (persona) washer —m. PHOTOG. washer; ARM. ramrod —f. (máquina) washing machine, washer; (mujer) laundress ♦ **l. de platos** dishwasher.
la·va·du·ra f. (acción) washing, wash; (lavazas) dishwater, dirty water.
la·va·ma·nos m.inv. washbasin, washbowl.
la·van·da f. lavender.
la·van·de·ra f. washerwoman, laundrywoman.
la·van·de·rí·a f. laundry, laundromat.
la·van·de·ro m. laundryman, launderer.
la·va·o·jos m.inv. eyecup.
la·va·pla·tos m.inv. dishwasher.
la·var tr. (limpiar) to wash; (purificar) to wipe away, clean; PAINT. to paint in water colors; MAS. to whitewash; MIN. to wash ♦ **l. el cerebro** to brainwash —reflex. to wash (oneself) ♦ **l. las manos de** to wash one's hands of.
la·va·ti·va f. (líquido) enema; (aparato) enema bag; COLL. (molestia) nuisance.
la·xar tr. to loosen, slacken.
la·xa·ti·vo, a adj. & m. laxative.
la·xo, a adj. (flojo) loose, slack; (relajado) lax.
la·ya¹ f. AGR. spade.
la·ya² f. breed, kind ♦ **eso es de otra l.** that's a horse of a different color.
la·yar tr. to spade (up), dig with a spade.
la·za·da f. (nudo) bowknot; (lazo) lasso.
la·zar §04 tr. to lasso, rope.
la·za·ri·llo m. person who guides the blind.
la·za·ri·no, a I. adj. leprous **II.** m.f. leper.
lá·za·ro m. (pobre) ragged beggar; (leproso) leper.
la·za·ro·so, a I. adj. leprous **II.** m.f. leper.
la·zo m. (nudo) knot; (para animales) lasso; (cordel) lashing rope; (trampa) snare, trap; (asechanza) trap; (vínculo) bond, tie ♦ **l. corredizo** slipknot.
le pron. him <la niña le siguió the little girl followed him>; you <no le vi a usted I didn't see you>; to him, to her, to it, to you <le dimos un regalo we gave a present to him>; for him, for her, for it, for you <le compré una cámara I bought a camera for her>; from him, from her, from it, from you <el gobierno le quitó la tierra the government took his land from him>.
le·al adj. loyal, faithful ♦ **a mi l. saber y entender** to the best of my knowledge.
le·al·tad f. loyalty, fidelity.
lec·ción f. lesson; (discurso) lecture; (capítulo) lesson, chapter; (lectura) reading ♦ **dar a uno una l.** to teach someone a lesson.
le·cha·da f. (de paredes) whitewash; (argamasa) mortar, grout; (papel) pulp; (emulsión)

emulsion ♦ **l. de cal** milk of lime.

le·char tr. AMER. to milk; C. AMER., MEX. to whitewash.

le·che f. milk; BOT. milky sap ♦ **dientes de l.** milk teeth • **l. desnatada** skim milk • **l. de vaca** cow's milk • **l. en polvo** powdered milk.

le·che·rí·a f. *(tienda)* dairy store; AMER. dairy farm.

le·che·ro, a l. adj. *(lechoso)* milky; *(que tiene leche)* milk, dairy **II.** f. *(vendedora)* milkmaid, dairymaid; *(recipiente)* milk can; *(jarra)* milk jug; AMER. *(vaca)* milk cow —m. milkman.

le·che·rón m. *(vasija)* milk pail; *(tela)* flannel wrap.

le·chi·ga·da f. *(nidada)* brood; *(cría)* litter.

le·cho m. bed; *(capa)* layer; ARCHIT. base; GEOL. bed, layer ♦ **abandonar el l.** to get out of bed • **l. de roca** bedrock.

le·chón m. *(cochinillo)* suckling pig; *(cerdo)* hog; *(persona)* pig, slob.

le·cho·so, a l. adj. milky **II.** m. papaya tree —f. papaya.

le·chu·ga f. lettuce; *(cuello)* ruff ♦ **como una l.** fresh as a daisy • **fresco como una l.** cool as a cucumber • **l. romana** romaine lettuce.

le·chu·za f. owl; COLL. *(mujer)* hag.

lec·ti·vo, a adj. school ♦ **año l.** school year • **día l.** school day.

lec·tor, ·ra l. adj. reading **II.** m.f. reader.

lec·tu·ra f. *(acción)* reading; *(cosa leída)* reading matter; PRINT. pica ♦ **ser una persona de mucha l.** to be well-read.

le·er §43 tr. to read ♦ **l. pruebas de imprenta** to proofread —intr. to read ♦ **l. a primera vista** MUS. to sight-read.

le·ga·ción f. legation.

le·ga·do m. legacy.

le·ga·jo m. file, dossier.

le·gal adj. legal.

le·ga·li·dad f. legality.

le·ga·lis·ta l. adj. legalistic **II.** m.f. legalist.

le·ga·li·za·ción f. legalization; *(validación)* authentication, validation.

le·ga·li·zar §04 tr. to legalize; *(certificar)* to authenticate, validate.

le·gar §47 tr. *(dejar)* to leave, bequeathe; *(enviar)* to delegate; *(transmitir)* to bequeathe, hand down.

le·ga·ta·rio, a m.f. legatee, heir ♦ **l. universal** general legatee.

le·gen·da·rio, a l. adj. legendary, fabled **II.** m. book of legends.

le·gi·ble adj. legible.

le·gión f. legion; *(multitud)* legion, multitude ♦ **la L. Extranjera** the Foreign Legion.

le·gio·na·rio, a l. adj. legionary **II.** m. legionary, legionnaire.

le·gis·la·ción f. legislation.

le·gis·la·dor, ·ra l. adj. legislative **II.** m.f. legislator, lawmaker.

le·gis·lar intr. to legislate.

le·gis·la·ti·vo, a adj. legislative.

le·gis·la·tu·ra f. legislature.

le·gis·ta m. *(experto)* legist; *(profesor)* law professor; *(estudiante)* law student; *(abogado)* lawyer ♦ **médico l.** AMER. medical forensic expert.

le·gi·ti·mar tr. *(certificar)* to legitimize; *(un hijo)* to make legitimate.

le·gi·ti·mi·dad f. legitimacy; *(autenticidad)* authenticity.

le·gí·ti·mo, a adj. legitimate; *(cierto)* genuine;

(auténtico) real, authentic; *(válido)* valid.

le·go, a l. adj. *(seglar)* lay, secular; *(sin instrucción)* ignorant, uninformed; *(analfabeto)* illiterate ♦ **ser l. en** to know nothing about **II.** m. layman; RELIG. lay brother.

le·gua f. league ♦ **a la l.** far away, miles away • **se ve a la l.** you can see it a mile away.

le·gum·bre f. legume.

le·í·ble adj. legible, readable.

le·í·do, a l. see **leer II.** adj. well-read **III.** f. reading.

le·ja·ní·a f. *(distancia)* distance; *(paraje)* distant or remote place.

le·ja·no, a adj. distant, remote.

le·jí·a f. *(agua alcalina)* lye; *(detergente)* bleach; COLL. *(reprimenda)* scolding.

le·jos adv. far (away) ♦ **a lo l.** in the distance, far away • **de l.** from afar, from a distance • **desde l.** from afar, from a distance • **ir l.** to go too far, go a long way • **l. de** *(a gran distancia)* far from, a long way from; *(en lugar de)* far from • **más l.** further, farther.

le·lo, a l. adj. silly, foolish **II.** m.f. dolt, ninny ♦ **estar l. por** to be head over heels in love with • **quedarse l.** to be stunned.

le·ma m. motto; LIT. theme; LOG. lemma.

lem·pi·ra m. HOND., FIN. lempira.

len·ce·rí·a f. *(ropa blanca)* underwear; *(géneros)* linen goods; *(comercio)* linen trade.

len·gua f. tongue; *(idioma)* language; *(badajo)* bell clapper; CUL. tongue ♦ **buscarle a uno la l.** COLL. to pick a fight with someone • **estar con la l. fuera** to have one's tongue hanging out • **hablar en lenguas** RELIG. to speak in tongues • **írsele a uno la l.** COLL. to talk too much, run off at the mouth • **l. de víbora** COLL. backbiter, gossip • **l. de fuego** tongue of fire, flame • **l. de tierra** promontory, tongue of land • **l. franca** lingua franca • **l. materna** mother tongue, native language • **ligero de l.** indiscreet • **mala l.** backbiter, gossip • **morderse la l.** to bite one's tongue • **sacar la l. a** to stick one's tongue out at • **tirar de la l.** to make someone talk • **trabársele a uno la l.** to become tongue-tied.

len·gua·do m. sole, flounder.

len·gua·je m. language, speech ♦ **l. cifrado** or **convenido** code language.

len·gua·raz adj. *(bilingüe)* bilingual; *(deslenguado)* foul-mouthed, vulgar; *(hablador)* talkative, garrulous.

len·guaz adj. garrulous.

len·güe·ta f. *(lengua pequeña)* small tongue; *(de zapato)* tongue; ANAT. epiglottis; *(de una balanza)* pointer, needle; MUS. reed; CARP. tongue ♦ **ensambladura de ranura y l.** tongue-and-groove joint.

le·ni·ti·vo, a l. adj. lenitive, soothing **II.** m. lenitive, palliative.

len·te m. or f. lens ♦ **l. de aumento** magnifying glass • **l. de contacto** contact lens • **l. electrónico** electron lens • **l. telegráfico** telephoto lens ♦ pl. eyeglasses, spectacles.

len·te·ja f. lentil.

len·te·jue·la f. sequin.

len·ti·lla f. contact lens.

len·ti·tud f. slowness.

len·to, a l. adj. slow; *(tardo)* slow; MED. viscous **II.** adv. MUS. lento.

le·ña f. *(madera)* firewood; COLL. *(paliza)* beating ♦ **echar l. al fuego** to add fuel to the fire • **llevar l. al monte** to carry coals to Newcastle.

le·ña·dor, ·ra m.f. woodcutter.

le·ña·zo m. COLL. *(garrotazo)* clubbing, cudgeling; AMER. *(golpe)* blow, wallop.

le·ñe·ra f. woodshed.

le·ño m. *(trozo de árbol)* log; *(madera)* wood; POET. ship ♦ **dormir como un l.** COLL. to sleep like a log.

le·ño·so, a adj. woody.

le·ón m. lion; AMER. puma ♦ **ponerse como un l.** to get furious.

le·o·na f. lioness.

le·o·na·do, a adj. reddish-brown, tawny.

le·o·ne·ro, a I. adj. AMER. rowdy, disorderly **II.** m. MEX. place where brawls occur; COLL. *(tablajero)* gambler —m.f. lionkeeper —f. *(jaula)* lion cage; COLL. *(casa de juego)* gambling den; *(cuarto desarreglado)* messy room.

le·o·ni·no, a adj. leonine.

le·o·par·do m. leopard.

le·o·tar·do m. leotard.

le·po·ri·no, a adj. leporine ♦ **labio l.** harelip.

le·pra f. leprosy.

le·pro·so, a I. adj. leprous **II.** m.f. leper.

ler·do, a I. adj. sluggish **II.** m.f. dullwitted person.

les pron. to them, to you *‹déles el libro* give the book to them*›*; for them, for you *‹quiero comprarles unos zapatos* I want to buy shoes for you*›*; from them, from you *‹les quitaron la oportunidad* they took the opportunity away from you*›*.

les·bia·na/bia adj. & f. lesbian.

le·sión f. lesion, injury.

le·sio·na·do, a I. adj. *(herido)* injured, wounded; *(dañado)* damaged, hurt **II.** m. ♦ **los lesionados** the wounded.

le·sio·nar tr. *(herir)* to wound, injure; *(dañar)* to damage —reflex. to get hurt, get injured.

les·na f. awl.

le·so, a adj. *(agraviado)* injured, wronged; *(perturbado)* perturbed; AMER. silly, stupid ♦ **l. majestad** lese majesty.

le·tal adj. lethal.

le·ta·ní·a f. litany.

le·tár·gi·co, a adj. lethargic.

le·tar·go m. lethargy.

le·tra f. letter; *(modo de escribir)* handwriting, writing; *(sentido)* letter, literal meaning; MUS. lyrics, words; COM. draft, bill of exchange ♦ **a la l.** to the letter, literally ♦ **l. a la vista** at sight, on sight • **l. a la vista** sight draft • **l. bastardilla** italics • **l. de cambio** bill of exchange • **l. de imprenta** type • **l. de mano** handwriting • **l. de molde** printed letter • **l. gótica** black letter • **l. magnética** laser printing • **l. mayúscula** capital letter • **l. minúscula** lower-case letter • **l. negrilla** boldface type ♦ pl. letters, learning • **bellas l.** belles-lettres, literature • **l. humanas** humanities • **l. sagradas** Scriptures • **primeras l.** primary schooling.

le·tra·do, a I. adj. learned, educated **II.** m. attorney, lawyer.

le·tre·ro m. *(señal)* sign; *(etiqueta)* label.

le·tri·na f. latrine, privy.

leu·ce·mia f. leukemia.

leu·dar tr. to leaven, add yeast to.

le·va f. MARIT. weighing anchor, sailing; MIL. levy, conscription; MECH. *(palanca)* lever; *(álabe)* vane; *(rueda)* cam.

le·va·di·zo, a adj. which can be raised ♦ **puente l.** drawbridge.

le·va·du·ra f. *(fermento)* yeast; CARP. sawed-off plank; *(germen)* germ ♦ **l. de cerveza** brewer's yeast • **l. en polvo** baking powder.

le·van·ta·dor, ·ra I. adj. raising, lifting **II.** m.f. lifter.

le·van·ta·mien·to m. *(acción)* raising, lifting; *(motín)* uprising ♦ **l. topográfico** (land) survey.

le·van·tar tr. *(alzar)* to raise, lift; *(elevar)* to lift up; *(enderezar)* to straighten up; *(quitar)* to remove; *(construir)* to raise, erect; *(establecer)* to found, set up; *(producir)* to raise; *(la caza)* to flush out; *(mudar)* to move; *(prohibición, embargo)* to raise, lift; *(los ánimos, la voz)* to raise; *(acusación)* to bring; *(el ancla)* to weigh; *(campamento)* to break ♦ **l. cabeza** to improve one's condition in life —reflex. *(elevarse)* to rise; *(ponerse de pie)* to stand up; *(de la cama)* to get out of bed; *(sobresalir)* to stand out; *(sublevarse)* to rebel; METEOROL. to rise ♦ **l. con** to make off with.

le·var tr. MARIT. to weigh.

le·ve adj. *(ligero)* light; *(de poca importancia)* slight, trivial.

le·vi·ta·ción f. levitation.

lé·xi·co, a I. adj. lexical **II.** m. *(diccionario)* dictionary, lexicon; *(de un escritor)* vocabulary, lexicon.

le·xi·co·gra·fí·a f. lexicography.

le·xi·có·gra·fo, a m.f. lexicographer.

le·xi·co·lo·gí·a f. lexicology.

ley f. *(estatuto)* law, statute; *(código)* law, body of laws; *(regla)* rule, regulation; *(acto)* act, bill; *(religión)* law; *(norma)* standard; METAL. fineness ♦ **al margen de la l.** outside the law • **a toda l.** strictly • **de buena l.** sterling, excellent • **de mala l.** crooked, disreputable • **l. de prescripción** statute of limitations • **l. de quiebras** bankruptcy law • **l. humana** social law • **l. no escrita** unwritten law.

le·yen·da f. *(fábula)* legend, myth; *(de una moneda)* inscription; *(texto)* legend, caption.

le·ye·ra, yó see **leer.**

lez·na f. awl.

liar §30 tr. *(atar)* to tie, bind; *(envolver)* to wrap (up); *(un cigarrillo)* to roll; COLL. *(engañar)* to take in, fool; *(mezclar)* to mix up in ♦ **liarlas** COLL. *(huir)* to beat it, scram; *(morir)* to kick the bucket —reflex. *(amancebarse)* to live together; *(mezclarse)* to be mixed up in ♦ **l. a palos** to come to blows • **liárselas** COLL. *(huir)* to beat it, scram; *(morir)* to kick the bucket.

li·ba·ción f. libation.

li·bar tr. *(los insectos)* to suck; *(echar)* to pour; *(degustar)* to taste, sip.

li·be·lis·ta m. *(de escritos satíricos)* lampoonist; LAW libeler.

li·be·lo m. *(escrito satírico)* lampoon; *(infamatorio)* libel; LAW petition.

li·bé·lu·la f. dragonfly.

li·be·ra·ción f. liberation; *(del enemigo)* deliverance ♦ **l. condicional** parole.

li·be·ra·dor, ·ra I. adj. liberating **II.** m.f. liberator.

li·be·ral I. adj. liberal; *(generoso)* generous; *(progresista)* progressive **II.** m.f. liberal.

li·be·ra·li·dad f. liberality.

li·be·ra·li·zar §04 tr. to liberalize.

li·be·rar tr. *(librar)* to free, liberate; *(de una deuda)* to release, discharge —reflex. to be released or discharged.

li·ber·tad f. liberty, freedom; *(independencia)* independence; *(exención)* exemption; *(franqueza)* openness; *(derecho)* right, liberty ♦ **en l.**

freely • **l. condicional** probation • **l. de comercio** free trade • **l. de conciencia** freedom of worship • **l. de imprenta** or **de prensa** freedom of the press • **l. de palabra** freedom of speech • **l. provisional** parole • **poner en l.** to free, set free ♦ pl. (*inmunidades*) rights; (*maneras*) liberties • **tomarse l.** to take liberties.

li·ber·ta·dor, ·ra I. adj. liberating **II.** m.f. liberator.

li·ber·tar tr. to free, liberate; (*salvar*) to save, deliver; (*eximir*) to exempt, release.

li·ber·ta·rio, a adj. & m.f. libertarian.

li·ber·ti·na·je m. libertinism.

li·ber·ti·no, a adj. & m.f. libertine.

li·bi·di·no·so, a adj. libidinous.

li·bi·do m. libido.

li·bra f. pound ♦ **l. carnicera** kilogram • **l. esterlina** pound sterling.

li·brar tr. (*salvar*) to free, deliver; COM. to draw; (*eximir*) to exempt, release; (*batalla, duelo*) to wage ♦ **¡Dios me libre!** heaven forbid! —reflex. to avoid, escape.

li·bre adj. free; (*independiente*) independent; (*soltero*) single, unmarried; (*desembarazado*) clear, open; (*vacante*) free, unoccupied; (*sin trabas*) free, unrestrained; (*atrevido*) bold; (*exento*) free, exempt; (*en la natación*) freestyle ♦ **l. albedrío** free will • **l. cambio** free trade • **l. de** free from • **l. de derechos** duty-free.

li·brea f. livery, uniform.

li·bre·cam·bio m. free trade or exchange.

li·bre·pen·sa·dor, ·ra I. adj. freethinking **II.** m.f. freethinker.

li·bre·pen·sa·mien·to m. freethinking, free thought.

li·bre·rí·a f. (*tienda*) bookstore, bookshop; (*comercio*) book trade; (*oficio*) booksellers, book dealers; (*armario*) bookcase, bookshelf; (*biblioteca*) library.

li·bre·ro m. (*vendedor*) bookseller, book dealer; (*armario*) bookcase, bookshelf.

li·bre·ta f. (*cuaderno*) notebook; (*agenda*) calendar, appointment book ♦ **l. de ahorros** savings book, passbook • **l. de cheques** checkbook • **l. de direcciones** address book.

li·bre·tis·ta m.f. librettist.

li·bro m. book; (*registro*) register; MUS. libretto ♦ **examinar los libros** COM. to audit • **l. nuevo** COLL. to turn over a new leaf • **l. borrador** blotter, daily record • **l. copiador** letter book • **l. de asiento** or **de cuentas** account book • **l. de caja** cashbook • **l. de horas** Book of Hours • **l. de texto** textbook • **l. diario** journal, daybook • **l. mayor** ledger • **l. en rústica** paperback • **libros sagrados** Scriptures.

li·cen·cia f. license; (*permiso*) permission; (*documento*) license, permit; EDUC. licentiate degree; MIL. discharge ♦ **l. absoluta** discharge • **l. por enfermedad** sick leave.

li·cen·cia·do, a I. adj. exempted **II.** m.f. (*graduado*) university graduate, bachelor; COLL. (*estudiante*) student; AMER. lawyer —m. discharged soldier.

li·cen·ciar tr. MIL. to discharge; (*dar permiso*) to license, permit; (*despedir*) to dismiss, discharge; EDUC. to graduate —reflex. to graduate.

li·cen·cia·mien·to m. MIL. discharge; EDUC. graduation.

li·cen·cia·tu·ra f. (*título*) bachelor's degree; (*acto*) graduation; (*estudios*) degree program.

li·cen·cio·so, a adj. licentious.

li·ce·o m. (*sociedad*) lyceum; AMER. (*escuela*) grammar or high school.

li·ci·ta·ción f. bid, tender.

li·ci·ta·dor m. bidder.

li·ci·tar tr. (*ofrecer precio*) to bid for or on; AMER. to auction.

lí·ci·to, a adj. licit.

li·cor m. liquor, spirits; (*cordial*) liqueur, cordial.

li·cua·do·ra f. mixer, blender.

li·cuar §67 tr. to liquefy; METAL. to liquate.

lid f. fight ♦ **en buena l.** in a fair fight.

lí·der m. leader, chief.

li·de·ra·to/raz·go m. leadership.

li·dia f. fight, battle ♦ **toro de l.** fighting bull.

li·dia·dor, ·ra m.f. (*luchador*) fighter, combatant —m. bullfighter.

li·diar tr. (*torear*) to fight —intr. (*luchar*) to fight, battle; (*oponerse a uno*) to oppose, face; (*contender*) to struggle, contend; (*soportar*) to put up with.

lie·bre f. hare; FIG. coward ♦ **levantar la l.** COLL. to spill the beans • **l. corrida** MEX. whore • **dar gato por l.** to swindle.

lien·zo m. (*tela*) linen, canvas; PAINT. canvas; ARCHIT. façade.

li·ga f. (*de medias*) garter; (*venda*) band; (*materia viscosa*) birdlime; (*aleación*) alloy; (*confederación*) alliance, league; SPORT. league; (*mezcla*) compound, mixture ♦ **hacer buena** or **mala l. con** to get along well or badly with.

li·ga·ción f. (*acción*) tying, binding; (*enlace*) bond, union; (*liga*) compound, mixture.

li·ga·du·ra f. (*acción*) tying, binding; (*atadura*) tie, bond; (*traba*) impediment; MED. (*torniquete*) tourniquet; (*de una vena*) ligature; MUS. tie, ligature.

li·ga·men·to m. tying, binding; ANAT. ligament.

li·gar §47 tr. (*atar*) to tie, bind; (*unir*) to join, link; (*obligar*) to bind, commit; METAL. to alloy; MUS. to slur —intr. AMER. (*entenderse*) to get along well; (*tener suerte*) to be lucky —reflex. to unite.

li·ga·zón f. bond, connection.

li·ge·re·za f. (*liviandad*) lightness; (*rapidez*) quickness, swiftness; (*agilidad*) agility, nimbleness; (*acción irreflexiva*) indiscretion.

li·ge·ro, a I. adj. (*leve*) light; (*rápido*) quick, swift; (*ágil*) agile, nimble; (*insignificante*) unimportant, insignificant; (*digerible*) light; (*tenue*) light; (*inconstante*) fickle ♦ **l. de cascos** COLL. featherbrained, empty-headed • **l. de dedos** or **de manos** light-fingered • **l. de pies** fleet-footed, quick **II.** adv. lightly, swiftly ♦ **a la l.** (*de prisa*) quickly; (*sin reflexión*) without much thought.

lig·ni·to m. lignite, brown coal.

lig·no·so, a adj. woody.

li·ja I. f. (*pez*) dogfish; (*papel*) sandpaper ♦ **darse l.** AMER. to put on airs **II.** adj. MEX., P. RICO shrewd, sharp.

li·ja·do·ra f. sander, sanding machine.

li·jar tr. to sand, sandpaper.

li·la f. & adj. lilac.

li·ma¹ m. (*fruto*) lime; (*limero*) lime tree.

li·ma² f. file ♦ **comer como una l.** to eat like a horse • **l. para las uñas** nail file.

li·ma·du·ra f. filing.

li·mar tr. (*desbastar*) to file down; (*pulir*) to polish, refine; (*cercenar*) to pare, trim ♦ **l. asperezas** to smooth over disputes.

li·ma·tón m. *(herramienta)* rasp; AMER. roof beam.

lim·bo m. THEOL. limbo; ASTRON., BOT. limb ♦ **estar en l.** to be in a daze.

li·mi·ta·ción f. limitation, limit.

li·mi·ta·do, a adj. limited; *(poco inteligente)* limited, slow-witted; *(pequeño)* small.

li·mi·tar tr. to limit; *(delimitar)* to delimit; *(restringir)* to restrict; *(acortar)* to reduce —intr. to be bounded —reflex. to limit oneself.

lí·mi·te m. limit; *(frontera)* boundary ♦ **fecha l.** deadline • **l. de elasticidad** ENGIN. elastic limit • **precio l.** final price.

li·mo m. mud, slime.

li·món m. *(fruto)* lemon; *(árbol)* lemon tree; AMER. *(de escalera)* string, shaft ♦ **refresco de l.** lemonade.

li·mo·na·do, a I. adj. lemon-colored II. f. lemonade ♦ **l. purgante** citrate of magnesia • **ni chicha ni l.** neither fish nor fowl.

li·mo·nar m. lemon grove.

li·mo·ne·ro, a m.f. lemon seller —m. lemon tree.

li·mo·si·dad f. *(cieno)* muddiness; DENT. tartar.

li·mo·si·na f. limousine.

li·mos·na f. charity, alms.

li·mos·ne·ar intr. to beg.

li·mos·ne·ro, a I. adj. charitable, generous II. m.f. *(recolector)* almoner; AMER. beggar —f. alms bag or box.

li·mo·so, a adj. muddy, slimy.

lim·pia f. *(limpieza)* cleaning; COLL. *(trago)* drink, shot; *(limpiabotas)* bootblack.

lim·pia·bo·tas m.inv. shoe shiner, bootblack.

lim·pia·chi·me·ne·as m.inv. chimney sweep.

lim·pia·dor, ·ra I. adj. cleaning II. m.f. cleaner —f. cleaning woman or lady.

lim·pia·du·ra f. cleaning.

lim·pia·pa·ra·bri·sas m.inv. windshield wiper.

lim·piar tr. *(quitar lo sucio)* to clean, cleanse; *(purificar)* to clear, exonerate; *(desembarazar)* to clear, rid; COLL. *(robar)* to swipe; *(ganar)* to clean up; MEX. to beat, whip.

lím·pi·do, a adj. limpid.

lim·pie·za f. *(calidad)* cleanliness; *(acción)* cleaning, cleansing; *(precisión)* neatness, accuracy ♦ **l. de corazón** honesty, rectitude • **l. en seco** dry cleaning.

lim·pio, a I. adj. *(sin mancha)* clean, spotless; *(sin mezcla)* pure; *(cantidad)* net; *(exento)* free, clear; *(aseado)* neat, tidy; *(que ha perdido en el juego)* clean; COLL. *(sin dinero)* cleaned out, broke ♦ **en l.** free and clear, net • **quedar l.** COLL. to be broke, be cleaned out II. adv. fair ♦ **poner en l.** to make a clean copy • **quedar en l.** to become clear • **sacar algo en l.** to understand, get a clear idea (of).

li·na·je m. *(familia)* lineage, ancestry; *(clase)* kind, genre.

li·na·za f. flaxseed, linseed ♦ **aceite de l.** linseed oil.

lin·ce I. m. lynx; FIG. shrewd person II. adj. sharp.

lin·char tr. to lynch.

lin·dan·te adj. bordering, adjacent.

lin·dar intr. to border (on), be adjacent (to).

lin·de m.f. boundary, limit.

lin·de·ro, a I. adj. bordering II. m. edge, border.

lin·do, a I. adj. pretty, lovely; *(perfecto)* perfect, exquisite II. m. COLL. *(hombre presu-*

mido) showoff III. adv. R.P. prettily, nicely ♦ **de lo l.** much, a lot.

lí·ne·a f. line; *(ascendencia)* lineage; *(límite)* limit, boundary; *(silueta)* figure, outline ♦ **en toda la l.** all along the line, completely • **estar en l.** AMER. to be slim, in shape • **guardar la l.** to keep one's figure • **l. aérea** airline • **l. de agua** or **de flotación** water line • **l. de conducta** or **l. política** policy • **l. de fuego** firing line • **l. de montaje** assembly line • **l. de partido** party line • **l. de puntos** dotted line • **l. de tiro** line of fire • **l. equinoccial** equator • **l. férrea** railway • **l. telegráfica** telegraph line.

li·ne·al adj. linear.

li·ne·a·m(i)en·to m. lineament, contour.

li·ne·ar¹ adj. linear.

li·ne·ar² tr. *(tirar líneas)* to draw lines; *(bosquejar)* to outline, sketch.

lin·fa f. lymph.

lin·fá·ti·co, a I. adj. lymphatic II. m.f. person suffering from lymphatism.

lin·go·te m. ingot ♦ **lingotes de oro** gold bullion.

lin·güis·ta m.f. linguist.

lin·güís·ti·co, a I. adj. linguistic II. f. linguistics.

li·ni·men·to m. liniment.

li·no m. *(planta)* flax; *(tela)* linen; *(de vela)* canvas, sailcloth; ARG., P. RICO flaxseed, linseed.

li·nó·le·o/leum m. linoleum.

lin·tel m. lintel.

lin·ter·na f. *(luz)* lantern; *(de bolsillo)* flashlight; *(lámpara)* lamp, light; MECH. lantern wheel or pinion.

lí·o m. *(bulto)* bundle, package; COLL. *(embrollo)* jam, mess ♦ **armar un l.** COLL. to make a fuss or racket • **hacerse un l.** COLL. to get into a jam or fix.

lí·pi·do m. lipid.

li·po·so·lu·ble adj. fat-soluble.

li·que·fac·ción f. liquefaction.

li·quen m. lichen.

li·qui·da·ción f. *(un negocio)* liquidation; *(cuenta)* settlement; *(venta)* liquidation, clearance sale.

li·qui·dar tr. *(hacer líquido)* to liquefy; *(vender)* to sell off, liquidate; *(pagar)* to settle, clear; *(poner fin)* to resolve; AMER., COLL. *(matar)* to eliminate.

li·qui·dez f. liquidity.

lí·qui·do, a I. adj. liquid; *(sin gravamen)* net ♦ **dinero l.** ready cash II. m. liquid, fluid; COM. net amount ♦ **l. imponible** taxable income.

li·ra f. MUS. lyre; FIN. lira.

lí·ri·co, a adj. lyric(al).

li·rio m. lily ♦ **l. blanco** white or Madonna lily • **l. de agua** calla lily • **l. del valle** lily of the valley.

li·ris·mo m. lyricism.

li·rón m. dormouse ♦ **dormir como un l.** to sleep like a log.

li·siar tr. to cripple, disable.

li·so, a adj. *(parejo)* smooth, even; *(llano)* flat; *(sin labrar)* plain, unadorned ♦ **l. y llano** simple, straightforward.

li·son·ja f. flattery.

li·son·je·a·dor, ·ra I. adj. flattering II. m.f. flatterer.

li·son·je·ar tr. *(adular)* to flatter; *(deleitar)* to delight, please.

li·son·je·ro, a I. adj. *(que lisonjea)* flattering; *(agradable)* pleasing, gratifying **II.** m.f. flatterer.

lis·ta f. *(enumeración)* list; *(de personas)* roll; *(recuento)* roll call; *(tira)* strip; *(raya)* stripe ♦ **l. de comidas** menu • **l. de correos** general delivery • **l. negra** blacklist • **pasar l.** to call roll.

lis·ta·do, a adj. striped.

lis·te·za f. smartness, alertness.

lis·to, a adj. *(hábil)* skillful; *(inteligente)* smart, clever; *(preparado)* ready; *(sagaz)* shrewd ♦ **andar l.** to be careful *or* cautious • **¿estás l.?** are you ready? • **pasarse de l.** to be too clever for one's own good.

lis·tón m. *(cinta)* ribbon; ARCHIT. listel, fillet; CARP. lath, cleat.

li·su·ra f. *(igualdad)* smoothness, evenness; *(sinceridad)* sincerity, candor; AMER. *(atrevimiento)* boldness, impudence.

li·te·ra f. *(vehículo)* litter; *(en tren)* berth, bunk.

li·te·ral adj. literal.

li·te·ra·rio, a adj. literary.

li·te·ra·to, a I. adj. well-read, erudite **II.** m.f. man *or* woman of letters.

li·te·ra·tu·ra f. literature.

li·ti·ga·ción f. litigation.

li·ti·gan·te adj. & m.f. litigant.

li·ti·g(i)ar tr. to litigate —intr. to contend, dispute.

li·ti·gio m. lawsuit, litigation; *(contienda)* dispute.

li·ti·gio·so, a adj. litigious.

li·tio m. lithium.

li·to·gra·fí·a f. *(arte)* lithography; *(imagen)* lithograph.

li·to·gra·fiar §30 tr. to lithograph.

li·tó·gra·fo m. lithographer.

li·to·ral adj. & m. littoral, coast.

li·tro m. liter.

li·tur·gia f. liturgy.

li·túr·gi·co, a adj. liturgical.

li·via·no, a adj. *(ligero)* light; *(inconstante)* fickle, faithless; *(de poca importancia)* slight, trivial.

li·vi·dez f. lividity, lividness.

lí·vi·do, a adj. livid.

lla·ga f. *(herida)* wound, sore; *(úlcera)* ulcer, sore; *(daño)* wound, injury ♦ **poner el dedo en la ll.** to touch on a sore spot.

lla·gar §47 tr. to wound, injure.

lla·ma¹ f. flame; FIG. flame, passion ♦ **en llamas** in flames, aflame.

lla·ma² f. ZOOL. llama.

lla·ma·da f. call, calling; *(de timbre)* ring; *(de puerta)* knock; *(telefónica)* telephone call; *(seña)* reference mark; *(ademán)* gesture, signal; *(atracción)* call, lure; MEX. cowardice ♦ **ll. al orden** call to order • **ll. de socorro** distress signal.

lla·ma·dor, ·ra m.f. caller —m. *(aldaba)* door knocker; *(timbre)* doorbell.

lla·ma·mien·to m. calling; *(convocación)* call, summons; RELIG. calling, vocation.

lla·mar tr. *(dar voces)* to call; *(convocar)* to call, summon; *(telefonear)* to call, telephone; *(apellidar)* to call; *(nombrar)* to call; *(atraer)* to attract; *(suplicar)* to call upon, appeal to ♦ **ll. al orden** to call to order • **ll. a voces** to shout • **ll. por teléfono** to telephone, phone —intr. *(hacer sonar un timbre)* to ring a doorbell; *(to-*

car a la puerta) to knock at the door; *(por teléfono)* to call, telephone ♦ **¿quién llama?** who is it? —reflex. to be called *or* named <¿*cómo se llama?* what's your name?>.

lla·ma·ra·da f. *(fuego)* flare; *(bochorno)* flush; *(arrebato)* outburst.

lla·ma·ti·vo, a adj. showy, flashy.

lla·me·an·te adj. flaming, blazing.

lla·me·ar intr. to flame, blaze.

lla·ne·za f. simplicity.

lla·no, a I. adj. *(liso)* flat, even; *(sencillo)* natural, simple; *(claro)* clear, evident; *(corriente)* clear, open; *(simple)* simple, plain ♦ **de ll.** plainly, clearly **II.** m. GEOG. plain —f. MAS. trowel, float; *(de papel)* side; *(llanura)* plain.

llan·ta f. *(de una rueda)* rim; AMER. tire.

llan·to m. crying, weeping.

lla·nu·ra f. *(lisura)* evenness; *(planicie)* plain.

lla·ve f. key; *(grifo)* tap, faucet; ELEC. switch; MECH. wrench; *(corchete)* bracket; MUS. clef; *(en lucha libre)* lock ♦ **ama de llaves** housekeeper • **bajo ll.** under lock and key • **echar ll.** to lock • **la ll. del éxito** the key to success • **ll. de bola** *or* **de flotador** ball cock • **ll. de paso** water valve • **ll. inglesa** monkey wrench.

lla·ve·ro m. key ring.

lle·ga·da f. arrival; SPORT. finish.

lle·gar §47 intr. *(venir)* to arrive, come; *(durar)* to reach, last; *(alcanzar)* to reach, extend <*la falda le llega hasta las rodillas* the skirt reaches her knees>; *(ascender)* to amount, come <*la cuenta llegó a quinientos pesos* the bill came to five hundred pesos>; *(suceder)* to arrive, come <*llegó el momento de la verdad* the moment of truth arrived> ♦ **ll. a** *(destino)* to arrive at, reach; *(acuerdo)* to reach; *(lograr)* to manage to <*llegó a controlar la situación* he managed to control the situation> • **ll. a las manos** COLL. to come to blows • **ll. a saber** to find out • **ll. a ser** to become —reflex. *(acercarse)* to move closer, come near; *(ir)* to stop by.

lle·nar tr. to fill up <*llene el vaso de vino* fill the glass with wine>; *(ocupar)* to fill, occupy <*él llena el puesto de la persona que se fue* he is filling the position of the person who left>; *(cumplir)* to fulfill, meet <*ll. las condiciones del contrato* to meet the conditions of the contract>; *(formulario)* to fill out; *(satisfacer)* to satisfy <*su explicación no me llena* his explanation does not satisfy me>; *(colmar)* to heap <*ll. de insultos a* to heap insults on> —intr. ASTRON. to be full —reflex. to fill up, be filled <*la sala se llenaba de gente* the room was filling up with people>; COLL. *(hartarse)* to stuff oneself, gorge; COLL. *(irritarse)* to be fed up.

lle·no, a I. adj. *(ocupado)* full, filled; *(redondo)* full ♦ **de ll.** fully, completely • **ll. de** full of, filled with **II.** m. THEAT. full house.

lle·var tr. *(transportar)* to carry, take <*le llevó flores al hospital* he took flowers to her in the hospital>; *(vestir)* to wear <*lleva medias negras* he is wearing black socks>; *(traer)* to carry, have <*no llevo dinero conmigo* I have no money with me>; *(conducir)* to take, lead <*este camino te llevará a Barcelona* this road will take you to Barcelona>; *(vivir)* to lead <*ll. una vida de perros* to lead a dog's life>; *(encargarse de)* to manage, run <*ella lleva las cuentas de la casa* she manages the household accounts>; *(tolerar)* to endure, put up with; *(cobrar)* to charge;

(arrancar) to tear off, sever *<la metralla le llevó la pierna* the shrapnel severed his leg>; *(pasar)* to have spent, have spent *<llevo cinco noches sin dormir* I have spent five nights without sleep>; *(ser mayor)* to be older *<mi hermana me lleva tres años* my sister is three years older than I>; MATH. to carry ♦ **II. a cabo** to carry out • **II. adelante** to go ahead *or* forward with • **llevarla hecha** COLL. to have it all figured out • **II. la peor parte** to get the worst of it • **II. las de perder** COLL. to be on the losing end —intr. to lead *<la carretera lleva a la ciudad* the highway leads to the city> —reflex. *(sacar)* to take away, carry off *<se llevó el premio gordo* she carried off the first prize>; *(robar)* to take *<se llevó el dinero del banco* he took the money from the bank>; *(conseguir)* to get *<se llevó lo que quería* he got what he wanted> ♦ **II. bien, mal** to get along well, badly.

llo·rar intr. *(derramar lágrimas)* to cry, weep; *(los ojos)* to water, run ♦ **II. a lágrima viva** to cry one's heart out —tr. *(lamentar)* to mourn; *(sentir mucho)* to regret, bemoan.

llo·ri·que·ar intr. to whine, whimper.

llo·ri·que·o m. whining, whimpering.

llo·ro m. crying, weeping.

llo·rón, o·na I. adj. crying, weeping ♦ **sauce II.** weeping willow **II.** m.f. *(llorador)* weeper; *(lloraduelos)* crybaby.

llo·ro·so, a adj. *(que ha llorado)* tearful; *(triste)* sad, sorrowful.

llo·ver §78 intr. to rain; FIG. to rain, shower ♦ **como llovido del cielo** unexpectedly • **II. a cántaros** *or* **a mares** to rain cats and dogs, rain buckets • **llueva o no** rain or shine.

llo·viz·na f. drizzle.

llo·viz·nar intr. to drizzle.

llue·va, ve see **llover.**

llu·via f. *(acción)* rain, raining; *(agua)* rain; *(cantidad)* rainfall; *(abundancia)* shower ♦ **II. atómica** fallout.

llu·vio·so, a adj. rainy, wet.

lo I. def. art. the ... thing, the ... part *<lo mejor* the best part>; how *<no puedo creer lo rico que es* I cannot believe how rich he is> ♦ **lo de** the matter of, the business of *<¿y lo de vender la casa?* and the matter of selling the house'> • **lo que** what, which *<no revelarán lo que les dijiste* they will not reveal what you told them> • **lo que es** as to, as for **II.** pron. it *<no lo creo* I don't believe it>; him *<lo vi* I saw him>; [not translated] *<¿eres estudiante? no, no lo soy* are you a student? no, I am not>.

lo·a f. praise ♦ **cantar l.** *or* **hacer l. de** to sing the praises of.

lo·a·ble adj. laudable, praiseworthy.

lo·ar tr. to praise, laud.

lo·ba f. female wolf; *(vestido)* (ecclesiastical or academic) robe, gown.

lo·bo¹ m. wolf; ICHTH. loach; AMER., ZOOL. coyote ♦ **l. de mar** old salt, sea dog • **l. marino** seal.

lo·bo² m. BOT. lobe.

ló·bre·go, a adj. *(obscuro)* dark, somber; *(triste)* sad, gloomy.

lo·bre·guez f. darkness, obscurity.

ló·bu·lo m. lobe, lobule.

lo·ca·ción f. rental, leasing.

lo·cal I. adj. local **II.** m. *(edificio)* premises; *(lugar)* locale, site.

lo·ca·li·dad f. *(población)* district, locality; *(local)* locale, site; THEAT. *(asiento)* seat; *(billete)* ticket.

lo·ca·li·zar §04 tr. *(limitar a un punto)* to localize; *(encontrar)* to locate, find.

lo·ca·ta·rio, a m.f. tenant, lessee.

lo·ce·rí·a f. AMER. pottery shop, china shop.

lo·ción f. lotion.

lo·co, a I. adj. *(demente)* mad, crazy; *(imprudente)* crazy, reckless; *(extraordinario)* extraordinary, unbelievable ♦ **andar** *or* **volverse l.** to go mad, go crazy • **a tontas y a locas** COLL. without rhyme or reason • **como l.** like crazy, like mad • **estar l. de** *or* **por** to be crazy about • **estar l. de atar** *or* **de remate** COLL. to be stark raving mad • **estar l. de contento** COLL. to be wild with joy **II.** m.f. *(demente)* madman/woman, lunatic ♦ **cada l. con su tema** everyone has his own ax to grind • **hacerse el l.** COLL. to play dumb • **l. rematado** COLL. raving lunatic.

lo·co·mo·ción f. locomotion.

lo·co·mo·tor, triz adj. locomotor, locomotive.

lo·co·mo·to·ra f. locomotive.

lo·cua·ci·dad f. loquacity.

lo·cuaz adj. loquacious.

lo·cu·ción f. *(modo de hablar)* locution, expression; GRAM. phrase.

lo·cu·ra f. madness, insanity; FIG. folly, lunacy ♦ **gastar una l.** to spend a fortune • **hacer locuras** to commit follies.

lo·cu·tor, ra m.f. radio announcer.

lo·do m. *(barro)* mud, sludge; MIN. sludge ♦ **arrastrar por el l.** to drag through the mud.

lo·ga·rit·mo m. logarithm.

lo·gia f. lodge.

ló·gi·cial m. COMPUT. software.

ló·gi·co, a I. adj. logical **II.** m.f. logician —f. logic.

lo·gís·ti·ca I. f. MIL. logistics; PHILOS. symbolic logic **II.** adj. logistic(al).

lo·grar tr. *(obtener)* to get, obtain; *(realizar)* to achieve ♦ **dar (algo) por logrado** to take (something) for granted —reflex. to succeed, be successful.

lo·gro m. *(éxito)* success, achievement; *(lucro)* profit, gain; *(usura)* usury.

lo·ma f. hillock, knoll.

lom·briz f. worm, earthworm ♦ **l. solitaria** tapeworm.

lo·mo m. ANAT., CUL. loin; ZOOL. back; *(de un libro)* spine; *(de un cuchillo)* back ♦ **pasar la mano por el l.** COLL. to pat on the back.

lon·che m. AMER. lunch.

lon·ga·ni·za f. pork sausage.

lon·ge·vi·dad f. longevity.

lon·ge·vo, a adj. long-lived.

lon·gi·tud f. *(dimensión)* length; GEOG. longitude ♦ **l. de onda** wavelength.

lon·gi·tu·di·nal adj. longitudinal.

lon·ja f. *(tira)* slice; COM. *(edificio)* marketplace, exchange; ARCHIT. porch, portico; R.P. leather strap.

lo·or m. praise.

lo·que·ar intr. to act like a crazy person; *(alborotar)* to frolic, romp.

lo·que·ra f. *(jaula)* padded cell; AMER. madness, insanity.

lo·que·rí·a f. AMER. insane asylum.

lo·que·ro m. asylum guard *or* attendant.

lo·ro m. parrot; COLL. hag.

los I. def. art. the **II.** pron. them.

lo·sa f. slab, stone ♦ **l. sepulcral** tombstone.

lo·sar tr. to tile.

lo·te m. *(parte)* lot, share; COM. *(grupo de obje-*

tos) lot.
lo·te·ar tr. to divide into lots *or* shares.
lo·te·rí·a f. *(juego público)* lottery, raffle; *(juego casero)* bingo; *(cosa incierta)* gamble.
lo·za f. *(barro vidriado)* glazed pottery; *(platos)* china.
lo·za·ní·a f. *(de las plantas)* lushness; *(salud)* healthiness; *(orgullo)* pride, haughtiness.
lo·za·no, a adj. *(frondoso)* leafy, luxuriant; *(robusto)* robust, vigorous.
lu·bri·ca·ción f. lubrication.
lu·bri·can·te I. adj. lubricating **II.** m. lubricant.
lu·bri·(fi)·car §70 tr. to lubricate.
lu·ce·ro m. *(astro)* bright star; *(planeta)* Venus; *(de un animal)* white star ♦ **l. del alba** morning star ♦ **l. de la tarde** evening star ♦ pl. POET. the eyes.
lu·cha f. *(conflicto)* struggle, conflict; SPORT. wrestling ♦ **l. de clases** class struggle.
lu·cha·dor, ·ra m.f. fighter; SPORT. wrestler.
lu·char intr. *(pelear)* to fight, struggle; *(disputar)* to argue, quarrel; SPORT. to wrestle.
lu·ci·dez f. lucidity.
lú·ci·do, a adj. *(brillante)* bright, shining; *(inteligente)* brilliant, intelligent.
lu·cien·te adj. shining, brilliant.
lu·ciér·na·ga f. glowworm, firefly.
lu·ci·(l)(o m. tomb, sarcophagous.
lu·ci·mien·to m. *(brillo)* brilliance, luster; *(éxito)* success, triumph.
lu·cir §44 intr. *(brillar)* to shine; *(distinguirse)* to shine, excel; *(tener apariencia)* to show —tr. *(alardear)* to show off, display; *(iluminar)* to illuminate, light up —reflex. *(vestir bien)* to dress up; *(salir bien)* to come out with flying colors; *(distinguirse)* to shine, distinguish oneself.
lu·crar tr. to win, profit.
lu·cra·ti·vo, a adj. lucrative.
lu·cro m. profit, gain.
lu·cu·bra·ción f. lucubration.
lue·go I. adv. *(después)* then, afterward; *(más tarde)* later, later on; *(pronto)* soon ♦ **desde l.** of course, naturally ♦ **hasta l.** so long, until later • **l. de** after • **l. que** as soon as • **tan l. como** as soon as **II.** conj. therefore.
lu·gar m. *(sitio)* place; *(espacio)* room, space; *(pueblo)* town, village; *(puesto)* position ♦ **en l. de** instead of • **en primer l.** in the first place, first • **no ha l.** LAW petition denied • **tener l.** to take place, happen.
lu·ga·re·ño, a I. adj. of a village **II.** m.f. villager.
lu·gar·te·nen·cia f. lieutenancy.
lu·gar·te·nien·te m. lieutenant.
lú·gu·bre adj. lugubrious.
lu·jo m. luxury ♦ **artículos de l.** luxury goods • **de l.** de luxe • **vivir en l. asiático** to live like a king.
lu·jo·so, a adj. luxurious.
lu·ju·ria f. *(lascivia)* lust, lechery; *(exceso)* excess.
lu·ju·rian·te adj. lush, luxurious.
lu·ju·rio·so, a adj. lustful, lascivious.
lum·ba·go m. lumbago.
lum·bar adj. lumbar.
lum·bre f. *(luz)* light; *(fuego)* fire; *(fósforo, encendedor)* light ♦ **dar l.** to give (someone) a light.
lum·bre·ra f. *(cuerpo luminoso)* light, luminary; *(en un techo)* skylight; MECH. port, vent; CARP.

mouth (of a plane); MARIT. porthole; *(persona)* luminary; MEX. box (in a bullring).
lu·mi·na·ria f. RELIG. altar lamp ♦ pl. *(decorative)* lights.
lu·mi·nis·cen·cia/nes·cen·cia f. luminescence.
lu·mi·nis·cen·te/nes·cen·te adj. luminescent.
lu·mi·no·si·dad f. luminosity.
lu·mi·no·so, a adj. *(que despide luz)* luminous; *(excelente)* bright, brilliant.
lu·na f. moon; *(vidrio)* plate glass; *(espejo)* mirror; *(lente)* lens; *(capricho)* notion, wild idea ♦ **estar de buena, mala l.** to be in a good, bad mood • **estar en la l.** to be daydreaming • **l. creciente** crescent moon • **l. de miel** honeymoon • **l. llena** full moon • **l. menguante** waning moon • **l. nueva** new moon • **media l.** half moon; AMER. *(pastry)* croissant.
lu·nar[1] m. *(de la piel)* mole, beauty mark; *(defecto)* flaw ♦ **vestido de lunares** polka-dot dress.
lu·nar[2] adj. lunar.
lu·ná·ti·co, a adj. & m.f. lunatic.
lu·nes m. Monday.
lu·ne·ta f. *(de anteojos)* lens; THEAT. orchestra seat; ARCHIT. *(bocateja)* front tile (of roof); *(bovedilla)* lunette.
lú·nu·la f. half-moon of fingernails; GEOM. arc.
lu·pa f. magnifying glass, loupe.
lu·pa·nar m. brothel.
lu·pi·no, a I. adj. lupine, wolf-like **II.** m. BOT. lupine.
lú·pu·lo m. hops.
lus·tra·bo·tas m.inv. AMER. shoe shiner.
lus·trar tr. *(limpiar)* to polish, shine; *(purificar)* to lustrate, purify.
lus·tre m. *(brillo)* luster, shine; *(esplendor)* splendor, glory; *(betún)* shoe polish.
lus·tro·so, a adj. lustrous, shiny.
lu·to m. mourning ♦ **ponerse de l.** to go into mourning.
luz f. *(claridad)* light; *(lámpara)* light, lamp; *(día)* day, daylight; *(guía)* guiding light; ARCHIT. window; LIGHT; PAINT. lighting ♦ **a primera l.** at daybreak • **a todas luces** clearly, from every angle • **dar a l.** PHYSIOL. to give birth; *(publicar)* to publish, print • **l. de Bengala** Bengal light, sparkler • **l. de tráfico** traffic light • **sacar a l.** *(revelar)* to bring to light; *(publicar)* to bring out, publish • **salir a l.** *(publicarse)* to come out, publish; *(descubrirse)* to come to light ♦ pl. enlightenment, learning • **corto de l.** COLL. not very bright.

M

m, M f. thirteenth letter of the Spanish alphabet.
ma·ca·bro, a adj. macabre, funereal.
ma·ca·dam m. [pl. **s**] macadam.
ma·ca·rrón m. macaroon ♦ pl. macaroni.
ma·ce·ra·ción f./**mien·to** m. maceration; FIG. mortification.
ma·ce·rar tr. to macerate.
ma·ce·ta[1] f. *(mango)* handle; *(martillo)* stonemason's hammer; AMER. mallet.
ma·ce·ta[2] f. flowerpot.
ma·ce·te·ro m. flowerpot stand.
ma·cha·ca f. *(instrumento)* crusher, pounder —m.f. *(persona pesada)* bore, boring person.
ma·cha·ca·dor, ·ra I. adj. crushing, pounding

II. m.f. *(que machaca)* crusher, pounder —f. *(máquina)* crusher, crushing machine.

ma·cha·car §70 tr. to crush, pound —intr. *(importunar)* to bother, pester; *(insistir)* to insist, go on about ♦ **m. en hierro frío** to bang one's head against a wall.

ma·cha·cón, o·na I. adj. insistent, tiresome **II.** m.f. bore, pest.

ma·cha·da f. *(hato)* flock of billy goats; COLL. *(necedad)* stupidity, foolish remark; *(hombrada)* manly action.

ma·cha·do m. hatchet.

ma·cha·que·o m. *(trituración)* crushing, pounding; *(insistencia)* insistence.

ma·che·ta·zo m. blow with a machete.

ma·che·te m. machete.

ma·che·te·ar tr. *(herir)* to wound with a machete; *(talar)* to cut down with a machete.

ma·che·te·ro m. *(desmontador)* cutter, clearer (of a path); *(de caña)* cane-cutter.

ma·chi·hem·bra·do m. tongue and groove.

ma·chi·na f. *(grúa grande)* crane, derrick; *(martinete)* pile driver.

ma·cho¹ I. adj. male; *(fuerte)* strong, tough; *(viril)* manly, virile **II.** m. *(animal)* male; *(mulo)* mule; MECH. pin, peg; ELEC. plug; COLL. *(fuerte)* he-man ♦ **m. cabrío** billy goat.

ma·cho² m. *(mazo)* sledgehammer; *(banco de yunque)* anvil block; *(yunque)* square anvil.

ma·chón, o·na I. m. abutment, pilaster **II.** adj. AMER. mannish woman.

ma·cho·te m. COLL. virile man, he-man ♦ **dárselas de m.** to act like a he-man.

ma·chu·ca·du·ra f. *(golpe)* pounding, beating; *(magullamiento)* bruising, bruise.

ma·chu·car §70 tr. *(golpear)* to pound, beat; *(magullar)* to bruise.

ma·ci·len·to, a adj. emaciated, lean.

ma·ci·zo, a I. adj. *(fuerte)* strong, solid; *(sin hueco)* solid; *(fundado)* well-founded, solid **II.** m. *(masa)* mass; ARCHIT. section of a wall (between two bays); GEOG., GEOL. massif; *(de edificios)* block; *(de plantas)* flowerbed.

ma·co·na f. large basket.

ma·cro·bió·ti·co, a I. adj. macrobiotic **II.** f. macrobiotics.

ma·cro·cos·mo m. macrocosm.

ma·cro·e·co·no·mí·a f. macroeconomics.

ma·cro·mo·lé·cu·la f. macromolecule.

má·cu·la f. *(mancha)* stain, spot; COLL. *(engaño)* deception, trick; ASTRON. macula.

ma·cu·to m. alms basket.

ma·de·ja f. skein; *(de pelo)* mop (of hair) ♦ **enredar** or **enredarse la m.** to get complicated.

ma·de·ra f. wood; *(de construcción)* timber, lumber; ZOOL. horny part of a hoof ♦ **de m.** wooden, of wood ♦ **m. flotante** driftwood ♦ **m. fósil** lignite ♦ **m. laminada** or **contrachapada** plywood ♦ **tocar m.** to knock on wood.

ma·de·ra·da f. raft, float.

ma·de·ra·je f./men m. wooden framework.

ma·de·re·rí·a f. lumberyard.

ma·de·re·ro, a I. adj. lumber, timber **II.** m. *(comerciante)* lumber or timber dealer; *(carpintero)* carpenter.

ma·de·ro m. log, length of timber.

ma·dras·tra f. stepmother.

ma·dre f. mother; *(matrona)* matron; *(cauce)* riverbed; *(acequia)* main irrigation ditch; *(causa)* cause ♦ **¡m. mía!** my goodness! ♦ **m. patria** mother country, old country ♦ **m. política** mother-in-law ♦ **m. soltera** unwed mother

♦ **salirse de m.** to overflow.

ma·dre·per·la f. pearl oyster; *(nácar)* mother-of-pearl.

ma·dre·sel·va f. honeysuckle.

ma·dri·gue·ra f. *(cuevecilla)* burrow, hole; *(cubil)* den; *(escondrijo)* hideout, lair.

ma·dri·na f. *(de bautismo)* godmother; *(de boda)* bridesmaid; *(protectora)* protectress, patroness; *(yegua)* lead mare.

ma·dru·ga·da f. *(amanecer)* dawn; *(levantada)* early rising ♦ **a las dos de la m.** at two o'clock in the morning ♦ **de m.** at daybreak, very early.

ma·dru·ga·dor, ·ra I. adj. early-rising **II.** m.f. early riser.

ma·dru·gar §47 intr. *(levantarse temprano)* to get up early; *(ganar tiempo)* to anticipate, be ahead ♦ **a quien madruga, Dios le ayuda** the early bird catches the worm —tr. ARG., MEX., SL. to get the better of (someone).

ma·dru·gón, o·na I. adj. early-rising **II.** m. ♦ **darse un m.** to get up very early.

ma·du·ra·ción f. maturation, ripening.

ma·du·ra·dor, ·ra adj. maturing, ripening.

ma·du·rar tr. AGR. to ripen, mature; *(problema)* to think out, work out; MED. to induce suppuration; *(persona)* to mature —intr. AGR. to ripen, mature; *(persona)* to mature; MED. to maturate, suppurate.

ma·du·rez f. AGR. ripeness; *(sabiduría)* sound judgment; *(edad adulta)* maturity.

ma·du·ro, a adj. AGR. ripe; *(juicioso)* wise; *(entrado en años)* mature; MED. ripe.

ma·es·tra f. see **maestro, a.**

ma·es·tran·za f. MIL. *(almacén)* armory; *(talleres)* arsenal; *(operarios)* arsenal workers.

ma·es·tre m. master.

ma·es·trí·a f. *(habilidad)* mastery, skill; *(título avanzado)* Master's degree; *(título de maestro)* teaching degree.

ma·es·tro, a I. adj. *(perfecto)* master; *(principal)* main, principal **II.** m. *(profesor)* teacher; *(perito)* expert, master; *(artesano)* master; EDUC. master; MUS. maestro ♦ **m. de capilla** choirmaster ♦ **m. de cocina** chef ♦ **m. de escuela** schoolmaster ♦ **m. de obras** master builder —f. *(profesora)* teacher, schoolmistress; *(listón)* guide line.

ma·gan·ce·rí·a f. deception, trickery.

ma·ga·ña f. trick, cunning stratagem.

ma·gia f. magic ♦ **como por arte de m.** as if by magic.

má·gi·co, a I. adj. *(de la magia)* magic(al); *(maravilloso)* marvellous, amazing **II.** f. magic.

ma·gín m. COLL. imagination, mind.

ma·gis·te·rio m. *(profesión)* teaching profession; *(conjunto)* teaching staff.

ma·gis·tra·do m. magistrate.

ma·gis·tral adj. *(del maestro)* magisterial, imposing; *(excelente)* skillful, masterful.

ma·gis·tra·tu·ra f. magistracy, magistrature.

mag·na·ni·mi·dad f. magnanimity.

mag·ná·ni·mo, a adj. magnanimous.

mag·na·te m. magnate.

mag·ne·sia f. magnesia.

mag·ne·sio m. magnesium.

mag·né·ti·co, a adj. magnetic.

mag·ne·tis·mo m. magnetism.

mag·ne·ti·zar §04 tr. to magnetize; *(hipnotizar)* to hypnotize, mesmerize.

mag·ne·to·fó·ni·co, a adj. magnetic ♦ **cinta m.** magnetic tape.

mag·ne·tó·fo·no/to·fón m. tape recorder.

mag·ni·fi·ca·dor, ·ra adj. magnifying.
mag·ni·fi·car §70 tr. *(engrandecer)* to magnify, exaggerate; *(ensalzar)* to exalt, glorify; OPT. to magnify, enlarge.
mag·ni·fi·cen·cia f. *(opulencia)* magnificence; *(generosidad)* generosity.
mag·ni·fi·cen·te adj. magnificent.
mag·ní·fi·co, a adj. *(hermoso)* magnificent, beautiful; *(excelente)* excellent; *(generoso)* generous.
mag·ni·tud f. *(tamaño)* magnitude, size; *(importancia)* importance, order; ASTRON. magnitude; MATH. quantity.
mag·no, a adj. great, grand.
mag·no·lia f. magnolia.
ma·go, a I. adj. magic, magical ♦ **los Reyes Magos** the Magi **II.** m. *(hechicero)* magician, wizard; *(sacerdote)* magus, sage.
ma·gro, a I. adj. lean, thin **II.** m. lean pork.
ma·gu·lla·du·ra f./**mien·to** m. bruise, contusion.
ma·gu·llar tr. to bruise, batter.
ma·gu·llón m. AMER. bruise.
mai·ce·na f. cornstarch.
mai·ti·nes m.pl. matins ♦ **llamar** *or* **tocar a m.** to call *or* ring to matins.
ma·íz m. [pl. **-íces**] corn, maize (G.B.) ♦ **rose·tas de m.** popcorn.
mai·zal m. cornfield.
ma·ja f. see **majo, a.**
ma·ja·da f. *(redil)* sheepfold; *(estiércol)* manure, dung; ARG., CHILE flock of sheep.
ma·ja·de·rí·a f. nonsense, stupid act *or* remark.
ma·ja·de·ro, a I. adj. silly, foolish **II.** m.f. silly person, fool.
ma·ja·do m. mash, pulp.
ma·ja·du·ra f. mashing, pounding.
ma·jal m. shoal, school (of fish).
ma·jar tr. to mash, pound; COLL. *(molestar)* to annoy, bother; *(azotar)* to beat, flog.
ma·jes·tad f. *(poder)* majesty, sovereignty; *(grandeza)* grandeur, stateliness ♦ **Su M.** Your Majesty.
ma·jes·tuo·si·dad f. majesty, grandeur.
ma·jes·tuo·so, a adj. majestic, grand.
ma·jo, a SP. **I.** adj. *(vistoso)* flashy, showy; *(bonito)* pretty, attractive; *(simpático)* nice, sweet; *(elegante)* smart, well-dressed **II.** m. gay blade, cocky youth —f. *(majadera)* pestle; SP. flashy young woman.
mal¹ I. adj. see **malo, a II.** m. *(vicio)* evil; *(daño)* damage, harm; *(desgracia)* misfortune; *(enfermedad)* illness, disease ♦ **echar a m.** to scorn, despise • **hacer m.** to harm, hurt • **m. de mar** seasickness • **m. de montaña** altitude sickness • **m. de ojo** evil eye • **¡m. haya!** damn! • **tomar a m.** to be offended, take offense.
mal² adv. *(pobremente)* badly, poorly; *(desacertadamente)* wrongly, incorrectly; *(difícilmente)* hardly <m. puedo ayudarte I can hardly help you> ♦ **de m. en peor** from bad to worse • **menos m.** just as well • **si m. no recuerdo** if I remember correctly.
ma·la·bar m. ♦ **hacer juegos malabares** to juggle.
ma·la·ba·ris·ta m. juggler.
ma·la·ca·te m. *(cabrestante)* winch; AMER. spindle.
ma·la·con·se·ja·do, a adj. ill-advised.
ma·la·cos·tum·bra·do, a adj. having bad habits; *(mal criado)* ill-bred, ill-mannered; *(mimado)* spoiled.

ma·la·cos·tum·brar·se reflex. to get into bad habits.
ma·la·crian·za f. AMER. bad manners.
ma·la·gra·de·ci·do, a adj. AMER. ungrateful, unappreciative.
ma·lan·dan·za f. misfortune, calamity.
ma·lan·drín, i·na I. adj. wicked, evil **II.** m.f. rascal, scoundrel.
ma·la·pa·ta f. COLL. bad luck —m.f. unlucky person.
ma·lar I. adj. malar, cheek **II.** m. malar.
ma·la·ria f. malaria.
ma·la·san·gre adj. mean *or* evil-minded.
ma·la·ve·ni·do, a adj. incompatible.
ma·la·ven·tu·ra f. misfortune, adversity.
ma·la·ven·tu·ra·do, a I. adj. ill-fated, unfortunate **II.** m.f. unfortunate person, poor soul.
ma·la·ven·tu·ran·za f. misfortune, ill fortune.
mal·ba·ra·ta·dor, ·ra I. adj. *(que malvende)* underselling; *(malgastador)* squandering **II.** m.f. *(que malvende)* underseller; *(malgastador)* squanderer, spendthrift.
mal·ba·ra·tar tr. *(malvender)* to undersell; *(malgastar)* to squander.
mal·ca·sa·do, a adj. *(infiel)* unfaithful, adulterous; *(casado con persona de condición inferior)* married to someone below one's station.
mal·ca·sar tr. *(ser incompatibles)* to mismatch; *(casar con persona de condición inferior)* to marry below one's station —reflex. to be mismarried *or* mismatched.
mal·co·mer intr. to eat poorly.
mal·co·mi·do, a adj. malnourished, underfed.
mal·con·si·de·ra·do, a adj. inconsiderate.
mal·con·ten·to, a I. adj. *(disgustado)* discontented, unhappy; *(rebelde)* malcontent, rebellious **II.** m.f. malcontent.
mal·cria·dez/·de·za f. AMER. bad manners, lack of breeding.
mal·cria·do, a adj. spoiled, ill-bred.
mal·criar §30 tr. to spoil, pamper.
mal·dad f. *(carácter de malo)* wickedness, evil; *(acto)* evil act ♦ **cometer maldades** to do evil *or* wrong.
mal·de·ci·do, a adj. & m.f. evil, wicked (person).
mal·de·cir §11 tr. *(echar una maldición)* to curse, damn; *(calumniar)* to slander; *(renegar de)* to curse —intr. to curse.
mal·di·cien·te I. adj. slandering, defaming **II.** m.f. *(calumniador)* slanderer; *(detractor)* detractor; *(persona que maldice)* curser.
mal·di·ción I. f. curse, damnation **II.** interj. damn!, damnation!
mal·di·ga, o, jera, jo see **maldecir.**
mal·dis·pues·to, a adj. *(de mala gana)* reluctant; *(enfermo)* indisposed.
mal·di·to, a adj. *(desagradable)* damned, lousy <esta m. lluvia this damned rain>; *(de mal carácter)* bad, wicked; THEOL. damned, condemned ♦ **¡m. lo que me importa!** damned if I care!
ma·le·a·bi·li·dad f. malleability.
ma·le·a·ble adj. malleable.
ma·le·an·te I. adj. *(que pervierte)* vicious, corrupting; *(perverso)* perverse; *(maligno)* malicious, wicked **II.** m.f. crook, evildoer.
ma·le·ar tr. *(estropear)* to spoil, ruin; *(pervertir)* to pervert, corrupt —reflex. *(estropearse)* to be ruined; *(pervertirse)* to be perverted *or* corrupted.
ma·le·cón m. sea wall, dike.

ma·le·di·cen·cia f. slander.

ma·le·du·ca·do, a adj. bad-mannered.

ma·le·fi·cen·cia f. maleficence, evil.

ma·le·fi·cen·te adj. maleficent.

ma·le·fi·cio m. spell, curse.

ma·lé·fi·co, a adj. *(dañino)* maleficent, evil; *(que hace maleficios)* spell-casting, bewitching.

ma·len·ten·di·do m. misunderstanding.

ma·les·tar m. *(del cuerpo)* malaise, indisposition; *(inquietud)* malaise, uneasiness.

ma·le·ta f. suitcase, valise ♦ **hacer la m.** to pack one's bag —m. COLL. bungler, incompetent.

ma·le·te·ro m. station porter; AUTO. trunk.

ma·le·tín m. small suitcase.

ma·le·tón m. AMER. hunchback, humpback.

ma·le·tu·do, a adj. AMER. hunchbacked.

ma·le·vo·len·cia f. malevolence.

ma·lé·vo·lo, a adj. & m.f. malevolent (person).

ma·le·za f. *(hierbas)* weeds; *(zarzales)* underbrush.

mal·for·ma·ción f. malformation.

mal·gas·ta·dor, ra adj. & m.f. spendthrift.

mal·gas·tar tr. to waste, misspend.

mal·ha·bla·do, a adj. foul-mouthed, vulgar.

mal·ha·da·do, a adj. wretched, unfortunate.

mal·ha·ya adj. AMER., COLL. damned, cursed ♦ **¡m. sea!** damn it!

mal·he·chor, ra I. adj. evil, doing evil **II.** m.f. wrongdoer, evildoer.

mal·he·rir §65 tr. to wound *or* injure badly.

mal·hu·mor m. bad temper.

mal·hu·mo·ra·do, a adj. bad-tempered.

mal·hu·mo·rar tr. to annoy, irritate.

ma·li·cia f. *(perversidad)* malice, wickedness; *(disimulo)* slyness, cunning; *(travesura)* mischievousness, naughtiness; COLL. *(sospecha)* suspicion.

ma·li·ciar·se reflex. to be suspicious ♦ **algo me malicio en ese lío** there's something fishy about this business.

ma·li·cio·so, a I. adj. malicious; *(astuto)* sly, cunning **II.** f. malicious person.

ma·lig·ni·dad f. malignancy.

ma·lig·no, a adj. malignant.

ma·lin·ten·cio·na·do, a adj. & m.f. ill-intentioned person.

ma·lla f. *(de red)* mesh, netting; *(de armadura)* mail, chain mail; AMER. *(traje de baño)* swimsuit, bathing trunks.

ma·llo m. *(mazo)* mallet, maul; *(juego y terreno)* mall, pall mall.

mal·man·da·do, a adj. disobedient.

mal·mi·ra·do, a adj. disliked, disfavored.

ma·lo, a I. adj. bad; *(pobre)* poor; *(perverso)* evil; *(dañino)* harmful; *(desagradable)* unpleasant, nasty *‹pasamos un mal rato* we had an unpleasant time›; *(enfermo)* sick, ill; *(travieso)* naughty; *(nocivo)* noxious *‹un mal olor* a noxious odor›; COLL. *(malicioso)* mean, malicious ♦ **a la m.** AMER. by force • **a (las) malas** on bad terms • **de m. gana** reluctantly ♦ **de malas** *(con desgracia)* unlucky, out of luck *‹estar de malas* to be out of luck›; *(con mala intención)* with bad intentions; COLL. *(molesto)* upset, out of sorts *‹hoy estoy de malas* I am out of sorts today› • **lo m. es que** the trouble is . . . • **ponerse m.** to become sick • **por las malas** by force **II.** m. ♦ **el m.** the bad guy, the villain.

ma·lo·gra·do, a adj. frustrated, abortive.

ma·lo·grar tr. to waste, lose; *(estropear)* to spoil, ruin —reflex. *(fracasar)* to fail, come to nothing; *(morir prematuramente)* to come to an untimely end.

ma·lo·gro m. *(fracaso)* failure; *(fin)* untimely end.

ma·lo·lien·te adj. smelly, foul-smelling.

ma·lón m. AMER. surprise Indian attack.

mal·pa·rar tr. *(maltratar)* to hurt, harm; *(dañar)* to damage.

mal·pa·rir intr. to miscarry, have a miscarriage.

mal·par·to m. miscarriage.

mal·pen·sa·do, a adj. & m.f. evil-minded *or* malicious (person).

mal·que·rer §55 tr. to bear ill will toward, dislike.

mal·quis·tar tr. to alienate, estrange.

mal·quis·to, a adj. disliked, unpopular.

mal·sa·no, a adj. unhealthy.

mal·so·nan·te adj. *(que suena mal)* ill-sounding, harsh; *(indecente)* nasty, offensive.

mal·su·fri·do, a adj. impatient.

mal·ta f. malt; *(grano tostado)* toasted grain; R.P. black beer.

mal·te·ar tr. to malt.

mal·tra·ta·mien·to m. mistreatment.

mal·tra·tar tr. to maltreat, mistreat.

mal·tra·to m. var. of **maltratamiento.**

mal·tre·cho, a adj. damaged, battered.

mal·va I. f. mallow; MEX., COLL. marijuana, weed —m. *(color)* mauve, light violet ♦ **m. arbórea** *or* **loca** *or* **rósea** rose mallow, hollyhock **II.** adj. mauve, light violet.

mal·va·do, a I. adj. evil, wicked **II.** m.f. evildoer, wicked person.

mal·ven·der tr. to sell at a loss, sell off cheap.

mal·ver·sa·ción f. embezzlement.

mal·ver·sa·dor, ra I. adj. embezzling **II.** m.f. embezzler.

mal·ver·sar tr. to embezzle.

mal·vi·vir intr. to live badly.

ma·ma f. mamma, mammary gland; COLL. *(madre)* mama, mommy.

ma·má f. COLL. mama, mommy.

ma·ma·ca·llos m.inv. COLL. fool, sucker.

ma·ma·de·ra f. AMER. *(biberón)* baby bottle; *(tetina de biberón)* rubber nipple.

ma·ma·do, a I. adj. COLL. drunk, sloshed **II.** f. COLL. *(acción)* nursing, sucking; *(cantidad de leche tomada)* amount of milk that a child takes in sucking *or* nursing ♦ **agarrarse una m.** ARG., COLL. to get drunk.

ma·man·tón, o·na adj. suckling.

ma·mar tr. *(chupar)* to suckle, nurse; FIG. *(aprender)* to learn (from childhood) —intr. to suck, nurse —reflex. AMER., COLL. to get drunk *or* smashed ♦ **m. el dedo** COLL. to let oneself be sucked in, be fooled.

ma·ma·rio, a adj. mammary.

ma·ma·rra·cha·da f./**cho** m. COLL. *(cuadro malo)* junk, bad painting; *(basura)* junk, rubbish; *(idiota)* fool, idiot; *(sandez)* stupidity, idiocy.

ma·me·lón m. nipple.

ma·mí·fe·ro I. adj. mammalian **II.** m. mammal, mammalian.

ma·mi·la f. *(de la hembra)* woman's breast around the nipple; *(del hombre)* nipple.

ma·món, o·na I. adj. unweaned, still nursing **II.** m.f. *(bebé que mama todavía)* unweaned baby, baby who still nurses —m. BOT. shoot, sucker.

ma·mo·tre·to m. *(libro de apuntes)* notebook, memo book; COLL. *(legajo grueso)* thick bundle of papers; *(libraco)* large, bulky book; AMER. *(armatoste)* monstrosity.

mam·pa·ra f. *(cancel)* movable room divider *or* partition; *(biombo)* screen.

mam·po·rro m. COLL. bump (on the head).

ma·mu·jar tr. to nurse intermittently.

ma·mu·llar tr. *(comer o masticar)* to suck in; COLL. *(mascullar)* to mumble, mutter.

ma·ná m. manna.

ma·na·da f. *(hato)* flock, herd; *(de lobos)* pack; COLL. *(banda)* gang, bunch ♦ **a manadas** COLL. in droves *or* crowds.

ma·na·de·ro, a I. adj. flowing, running II. m. *(manantial)* spring, source; *(pastor)* shepherd.

ma·nan·te adj. flowing, running.

ma·nan·tial I. adj. spring, running II. m. *(fontanal)* spring, source; *(origen)* source, origin.

ma·nan·tí·o, a adj. flowing, running.

ma·nar tr. & intr. to run or flow *(de* from).

ma·na·tí [pl. **-íes**] m. manatee, sea cow; *(piel)* manatee hide.

ma·na·za f. large *or* hefty hand.

ma·na·zas I. adj. clumsy, all thumbs II. m.f. inv. clumsy person.

man·ca·mien·to m. disabling.

man·car §70 tr. to maim, disable.

man·ca·rrón, o·na I. adj. worn-out II. m. AMER. nag, worn-out horse.

man·ce·ba f. mistress, concubine.

man·ce·bí·a f. brothel, whorehouse.

man·ce·bo m. *(joven)* young man, youth; *(soltero)* bachelor, single man.

man·ce·ra f. plow handle.

man·cha f. stain, spot; *(borrón)* blot, smudge; FIG. stain, blot ♦ **m. solar** sunspot ♦ **sin m.** unblemished.

man·char tr. *(hacer manchas)* to stain, spot; *(ensuciar)* to soil, dirty; FIG. to soil, stain; PAINT. to daub —reflex. *(hacerse manchas)* to become stained *or* spotted; *(ensuciarse)* to get dirty, become soiled.

man·chón m. *(mancha grande)* large spot *or* stain; AGR. patch of thick vegetation.

man·ci·lla f. stain, blemish.

man·ci·llar tr. to stain, blemish.

man·ci·par tr. to enslave.

man·co, a I. adj. *(de una mano)* one-handed; *(de un brazo)* one-armed; *(sin el uso de un miembro)* maimed, disabled; POET. halting ♦ **no ser manco** COLL. to be important, count II. m.f. *(persona con una mano)* one-handed person; *(persona con un brazo)* one-armed person; *(persona sin el uso de un miembro)* person with a disabled extremity.

man·co·mu·nar tr. *(unir)* to unite, join; *(combinar)* to combine, pool; LAW to make jointly liable —reflex. to unite, join together.

man·co·mu·ni·dad f. *(asociación)* association, union; *(comunidad)* community.

man·cor·nar §19 tr. *(derribar los cuernos)* to hold down by the horns; *(atar los cuernos)* to tie together by the horns.

man·cuer·na f. ♦ pl. MEX. cufflinks.

man·da f. legacy, bequest.

man·da·de·ro, a m.f. messenger, errand boy *or* girl.

man·da·do m. *(orden)* order; *(encargo)* task, assignment; *(recado)* errand.

man·da·más m.inv. COLL. honcho, big shot.

man·da·mien·to m. *(orden)* order, command; BIBL. commandment; LAW writ ♦ **m. de arresto** *or* **de detención** arrest warrant • **m. de em-**

bargo writ of attachment.

man·dar tr. *(ordenar)* to order, command; *(enviar)* to send; *(legar)* to leave, bequeath ♦ **m. a volar** MEX., COLL. to kiss off, get rid of • **m. al otro barrio** COLL. to kill, knock off • **m. a paseo** COLL. to send packing —intr. to be in command, be in charge ♦ **¿mande?** MEX. pardon me?, come again?

man·da·ri·na f. mandarin orange, tangerine.

man·da·ta·rio m. agent, mandatary ♦ **el primer m.** the president.

man·da·to m. *(orden)* order, command; *(encargo)* charge, trust; DIPL., POL. mandate; *(contrato)* power of attorney ♦ **m. jurídico** court order, injunction.

man·dí·bu·la f. jaw, mandible ♦ **reír a m. batiente** to laugh one's head off.

man·dil m. *(delantal)* apron, pinafore; *(bayeta)* cloth for grooming horses; *(red)* fine-meshed fishing net; AMER. *(manta de caballo)* horse blanket.

man·di·lón m. COLL. coward, weakling.

man·dio·ca f. cassava, manioc; *(tapioca)* tapioca.

man·do m. *(autoridad)* authority, power; *(dirección)* command, leadership; POL. term of office; MECH. control ♦ **entregar el m.** to hand over command • **estar al m.** to be in command • **m. doble** MECH. dual control; AUTO. dual drive • **tablero de mandos** instrument panel.

man·do·lín m./**li·na** f. mandolin.

man·dón, o·na adj. & m.f. bossy (person).

man·dra·cho m. gambling house.

man·dria I. adj. *(cobarde)* cowardly, timid; *(inútil)* useless, worthless II. m.f. *(cobarde)* coward; *(necio)* fool, useless person.

man·dril m. mandrill.

man·du·car §70 tr. & intr. COLL. to eat, chow down.

ma·ne·a f. hobble, shackle.

ma·ne·ar tr. to hobble.

ma·ne·ci·lla f. *(del reloj)* hand; *(broche)* clasp; PRINT. index (mark); *(palanquilla)* small lever.

ma·ne·ja·ble adj. manageable.

ma·ne·jar tr. *(situación)* to handle; *(empresa)* to run, manage; *(caballo)* to handle; *(automóvil)* to drive —reflex. *(moverse)* to get *or* move around; *(comportarse)* to behave —intr. AMER. to drive.

ma·ne·jo m. *(uso)* handling; *(funcionamiento)* running, operation; *(dirección)* handling, management; *(maquinación)* machination, trick; EQUIT. horsemanship; *(de auto)* driving ♦ **instrucciones de m.** directions.

ma·ne·ra f. manner; *(modo)* manner, way; *(tipo)* type; *(estilo)* style ♦ **a (la) m.** de like, in the manner of • **de alguna m.** somehow, in some way • **de cualquier m.** anyhow, any old way • **de la misma m.** similarly, in the same way • **de mala m.** badly, rudely • **de m. que** so, so that • **de ninguna m.** by no means, in no way • **de otra m.** otherwise • **de tal m.** in such a way • **de todas maneras** at any rate, anyway • **en gran m.** in large measure, greatly • **m. de ser** personality, the way one is • **m. de ver** outlook, point of view • **¡qué m. de . . .!** what a way to . . .! • **sobre m.** exceedingly.

man·ga f. sleeve; *(manguera)* hose; *(red)* tubular fishing net; *(tromba de agua)* waterspout; *(colador)* strainer; MARIT. beam, breadth ♦ **en mangas de camisa** in shirt sleeves • **sin mangas** sleeveless.

man·ga·ne·so m. manganese.

man·ga·ni·lla f. trick, ruse.

man·gar §47 tr. COLL. (*robar*) to steal, swipe; AMER. (*pedir*) to mooch, sponge.

man·go[1] m. handle, haft.

man·go[2] m. mango (tree and fruit).

man·gón m. second-hand dealer; AMER. corral; COL. pastureland.

man·go·ne·ar intr. (*entremeterse*) to meddle, pry; COLL. (*mandar*) to boss people about, take charge; AMER. to profit by illicit means; MEX. to steal.

man·go·ne·ro, a adj. COLL. meddlesome.

man·gos·ta f. mongoose.

man·gue·ar tr. AMER. (*caza*) to flush, startle; (*ganado*) to drive into a gangway.

man·gue·ra f. (*de riego*) hose, garden hose; MARIT. pump hose.

man·gue·ro m. (*bombero*) fireman; (*tabla*) board for ironing sleeves; MEX. mango.

man·gue·ta f. (*enema*) enema; ARCHIT. beam, tie; (*palanca*) lever; (*de retrete*) U-tube.

man·gui·ta f. case, cover.

man·gui·te·ro m. furrier.

man·gui·to m. (*de piel*) muff; (*mangote*) oversleeve; (*manopla*) glove; TECH. sleeve, bushing.

ma·ní m. [pl. **-níes**] peanut.

ma·ní·a f. (*locura*) mania; (*capricho*) craze, fad; (*costumbre*) habit; COLL. (*tirria*) dislike, aversion ♦ **m. persecutoria** persecution mania *or* complex ♦ **tenerle m. a alguien** COLL. to dislike someone.

ma·nia·bier·to, a adj. & m.f. generous (person).

ma·ní·a·co, a adj. & m.f. maniac.

ma·nia·tar tr. to manacle, handcuff.

ma·niá·ti·co, a I. adj. maniacal **II.** m.f. maniac.

ma·ni·co·mio m. insane asylum.

ma·ni·cor·to, a COLL. **I.** adj. stingy, tightfisted **II.** m.f. skinflint, miser.

ma·ni·cu·ro, a m.f. (*persona*) manicurist —f. (*cuidado*) manicure.

ma·ni·do, a adj. trite, hackneyed.

ma·ni·fes·ta·ción f. manifestation.

ma·ni·fes·tan·te m.f. demonstrator.

ma·ni·fes·tar §49 tr. (*expresar*) to manifest, express; (*anunciar*) to show, reveal —intr. to demonstrate —reflex. to reveal oneself.

ma·ni·fies·to, a I. adj. manifest, obvious **II.** m. manifest.

ma·ni·gue·ta f. handle, haft.

ma·ni·ja f. (*mango*) handle; (*abrazadera*) clamp.

ma·ni·lar·go, a adj. (*de manos largas*) longhanded; COLL. (*generoso*) generous, openhanded; AMER. (*ladrón*) light-fingered.

ma·ni·lla f. (*pulsera*) bracelet; (*manija*) handle; (*grillete*) handcuff, manacle.

ma·ni·llar m. handlebars (of a bicycle).

ma·nio·bra f. (*acto*) handling, operation; (*artificio*) maneuver, stratagem; MIL. maneuver; MARIT. (*arte*) seamanship; (*aparejos*) rigging, gear ♦ pl. MARIT., MIL. maneuvers; RAIL. shunting ♦ **estar de m.** to be on maneuvers.

ma·nio·brar intr. & tr. to maneuver.

ma·ni·pu·la·ción f. manipulation; COM. handling.

ma·ni·pu·la·dor, ·ra I. adj. manipulating **II.** m.f. manipulator —m. TELEC. telegraph key.

ma·ni·pu·lar tr. to manipulate; (*manejar*) to handle; COM. to manage; (*mercancías*) to handle.

ma·ni·pu·le·o m. COLL. manipulation.

ma·ni·quí m. [pl. **-íes**] mannequin.

ma·nir tr. (*ablandar*) to age; (*sobar*) to knead —reflex. to become gamy.

ma·ni·rro·to, a adj. & m.f. spendthrift.

ma·ni·tas m. inv. handyman.

ma·ni·va·cí·o, a COLL. empty-handed.

ma·ni·ve·la f. crank.

man·jar m. (*alimento*) food; (*plato*) dish.

ma·no[1] f. hand; (*pata*) forefoot, front paw; (*trompa del elefante*) elephant's trunk; CUL. foot, trotter; (*del reloj*) hand; (*almirez*) pestle, pounder; (*capa*) coat; (*lado*) side <*el río está a m. izquierda* the river is on the left side>; (*lance*) hand, round <*echar una m. de dominó* to play a round of dominoes>; (*el primero a jugar*) lead <*yo soy m.* I am the lead>; (*ayuda*) hand, help ♦ **a la m.** on hand, at hand • **alzar la m. a** to raise one's hand to, threaten • **a m.** by hand <*escrito a m.* written by hand>; (*cerca*) at hand, on hand • **a m. armada** armed, by force • **a manos llenas** generously, openly • **bajo m.** underhandedly, secretly • **buena m.** skill, dexterity • **cargar la m.** to be heavy-handed • **coger a alguien con las manos en la masa** COLL. to catch someone red-handed, catch in the act • **con el corazón en la m.** straight from the heart • **con las manos vacías** empty-handed • **dar la m. a** to shake hands with • **dar la última m. a** to put the finishing touches on • **darse las manos** (*unirse*) to join hands, unite; (*saludarse*) to shake hands • **dar una m. a** to lend a hand to • **dejar de la m. to** abandon • **de m.** hand <*equipaje de m.* hand luggage> • **de m. a m.** from hand to hand • **de primera m.** firsthand • **de segunda m.** secondhand • **echar m. de** to make use of • **estrechar la m. a** to shake hands with • **hacer lo que está en sus manos** to do everything within one's power • **hecho a m.** handmade • **imponer las manos** RELIG. to lay on hands • **a m.** (*juntos*) hand in hand, jointly; (*sin ventaja*) even • **m. de obra** labor • **m. derecha** *or* **diestra** right-hand man • **¡manos a la obra!** let's get to work! • **¡manos arriba!** hands up! • **meter m. en** COLL. to interfere, butt in • **pedir la m. a** to ask for someone's hand • **tener algo entre manos** to be working on something • **traer algo entre manos** to be involved *or* mixed up in something • **untar la m. a alguien** to grease someone's palm • **venir a m.** to be convenient • **venir** *or* **llegar a las manos** to come to blows.

ma·no[2] m. AMER., MEX., COLL. friend, pal.

ma·no·jo m. (*haz*) bundle, bunch; (*puñado*) handful ♦ **a manojos** abundantly.

ma·no·se·ar tr. to handle, touch.

man·se·dum·bre f. (*suavidad*) gentleness, mildness; (*de un animal*) tameness.

man·sión f. residence.

man·so, a I. adj. (*suave*) gentle, mild; (*domesticado*) tame **II.** m. bellwether (of a flock).

man·ta f. (*frazada*) blanket; (*para caballos*) horse blanket; (*mantón*) shawl; COLL. (*paliza*) beating, drubbing; AMER. (*poncho*) poncho; COL., MEX. (*algodón*) coarse cotton cloth; AMER., ICHTH. manta ray.

man·te·ca f. (*grasa*) grease, fat; (*de cerdo*) lard; (*de vaca*) butter ♦ **como m.** soft, smooth.

man·te·cón m. COLL. milksop, mollycoddle.

man·te·co·so, a adj. buttery.

man·tel m. *(de la mesa)* tablecloth; *(del altar)* altar cloth.

man·te·le·rí·a f. table linen.

man·te·ne·dor m. president (of a tournament) ♦ **m. de familia** breadwinner.

man·te·nen·cia f. *(acto)* maintenance; *(sostenimiento)* support; *(sustento)* sustenance, food.

man·te·ner §69 tr. *(alimentar)* to feed; *(sustentar)* to maintain, support; *(sostener)* to support, hold up; *(conservar)* to maintain, keep; *(continuar)* to maintain, keep up; *(afirmar)* to affirm ♦ **m. a distancia** *or* **a raya** to keep at a distance ● **m. en buen uso** to keep in good condition —reflex. *(alimentarse)* to feed oneself; *(sustentarse)* to maintain *or* support oneself; *(perseverar)* to remain *or* stand firm; *(permanecer)* to remain, keep oneself ♦ **m. a distancia** to keep one's distance ● **m. en sus trece** COLL. to stick to one's guns ● **m. firme** to hold one's ground.

man·te·ni·mien·to m. *(mantenencia)* maintenance; *(sostenimiento)* support; *(sustento)* sustenance, food.

man·te·que·rí·a f. creamery, dairy.

man·te·que·ro, a I. m. *(persona)* dairyman; *(vasija)* butter dish —f. *(persona)* dairymaid, dairy vendor; *(máquina)* butter churn; *(vasija)* butter dish **II.** adj. butter, of butter.

man·te·qui·lla f. *(de vaca)* butter; *(con azúcar)* butter cream.

man·te·qui·lle·ra f. AMER. butter dish.

man·tie·ne see **mantener.**

man·ti·lla f. mantilla; *(de un niño)* swaddling clothes; *(del caballo)* saddlecloth; PRINT. blanket.

man·to m. *(capa)* cloak, mantle; *(mantilla)* long mantilla; *(vestidura)* robe; *(de la chimenea)* mantel; FIG. cloak, cover; ZOOL. mantle; MIN. layer, stratum; MEX., BOT. bellflower.

man·tón m. shawl.

man·tu·vie·ra, vo see **mantener.**

ma·nual adj. & m. manual.

ma·nu·brio m. TECH. crank; *(manija)* handle; *(de bicicleta)* handlebars.

ma·nu·fac·tu·ra f. *(fábrica)* factory; *(artículo)* manufactured article; *(fabricación)* manufacture.

ma·nu·fac·tu·rar tr. to manufacture.

ma·nu·fac·tu·re·ro, a adj. manufacturing.

ma·nu·mi·sión f. manumission, emancipation.

ma·nus·cri·to, a I. adj. handwritten **II.** m. manuscript.

ma·nu·ten·ción f. *(acción)* maintenance; *(conservación)* conservation.

man·za·na f. apple; *(cuadra)* block; *(de espada)* pommel.

man·za·nal m. *(huerto)* apple orchard; *(árbol)* apple tree.

man·za·nar m. apple orchard.

man·za·ni·lla f. chamomile; *(infusión)* chamomile tea; *(aceituna)* olive; *(jerez)* manzanilla.

man·za·no m. apple tree.

ma·ña f. *(habilidad)* skill, dexterity; *(astucia)* craftiness, guile; *(hábito)* bad habit ♦ **darse m. para** to manage to ● **más vale m. que fuerza** brain is better than brawn ● **tener m. para** to have a knack for.

ma·ña·na I. f. morning ♦ **a la m. siguiente** the next morning ● **ayer por la m.** yesterday morning ● **de** *or* **en** *or* **por la m.** in the morning ● **de la noche a la m.** overnight ● **(muy) de m.** very early (in the morning) —m. tomorrow, future

II. adv. *(el próximo día)* tomorrow; *(en el futuro)* in the future ♦ **a partir de m.** starting tomorrow, as of tomorrow ● **hasta m.** see you tomorrow ● **m. por la m.** tomorrow morning ● **pasado m.** the day after tomorrow.

ma·ñe·ar tr. to manage *or* handle cleverly —intr. to be artful *or* crafty.

ma·ñe·ro, a adj. *(astuto)* clever, shrewd; R.P. *(mañoso)* hard to manage.

ma·ño·so, a adj. *(hábil)* skillful; *(astuto)* cunning; *(con malas mañas)* hard to manage.

ma·pa m. map, chart ♦ **desaparecer del m.** to vanish from the face of the earth ● **m. mudo** blank *or* skeleton map ● **no estar en el m.** COLL. to be out of this world.

ma·pa·che/chín m. raccoon.

ma·pa·mun·di m. map of the world.

ma·que·ar tr. *(poner laca)* to lacquer; MEX. to varnish —reflex. COLL. to dress up.

ma·qui·lla·je m. *(acción)* making up (of one's face); *(cosmético)* makeup, cosmetics.

ma·qui·llar tr. to make up (one's face), apply cosmetics to.

má·qui·na f. *(aparato)* machine; *(motor)* engine; *(locomotora)* locomotive, engine; LIT., THEAT. machine, deus ex machina ♦ **a toda m.** at full speed ● **hecho a m.** machine-made ● **m. de escribir** typewriter ● **m. de lavar** washing machine ● **m. herramienta** machine tool ● **m. neumática** air pump ● **m. registradora** S. AMER. cash register.

ma·qui·na·ción f. machination, plotting.

ma·qui·na·dor, ·ra I. adj. plotting, scheming **II.** m.f. plotter, schemer.

ma·qui·nal adj. mechanical.

ma·qui·nar tr. to plot, scheme.

ma·qui·na·ria f. *(conjunto)* machinery; *(mecanismo)* mechanism.

ma·qui·ni·lla f. small machine *or* device ♦ **m. de afeitar** *or* **de seguridad** safety razor ● **m. para cortar el pelo** hair clippers.

ma·qui·nis·mo m. mechanization; PHILOS. mechanism.

ma·qui·nis·ta m. machinist; RAIL. engineer, engine driver; THEAT. stagehand.

mar m. *or* f. sea; *(marejada)* tide, swell; FIG. sea, flood ♦ **alta m.** high seas ● **correr a mares** to stream, flow ● **hablar de la m.** to speak of the impossible ● **hacerse a la m.** to put out to sea ● **la m. de** *(muchos)* loads of, lots of <*la m. de trabajo* loads of work>; *(muy)* very <*él es la m. de tonto* he is very foolish> ● **llover a mares** to rain cats and dogs ● **m. agitado** *or* **picado** choppy sea ● **m. bravo** rough seas ● **m. de fondo** ground swell.

ma·ra·ña f. *(maleza)* thicket; BOT. kermes oak; *(enredo)* tangle, mess.

ma·ras·mo m. MED. marasmus; *(apatía)* apathy; *(estancación)* stagnation, paralysis.

ma·ra·tón m. marathon.

ma·ra·vi·lla f. *(fenómeno)* wonder, marvel; *(asombro)* wonder, astonishment; *(caléndula)* marigold ♦ **a las mil maravillas** wonderfully, excellently ● **a m.** marvellously ● **hacer maravillas** to work wonders ● **venirle a uno de m.** to be just what the doctor ordered.

ma·ra·vi·llar tr. to amaze, astonish —reflex. to marvel, be amazed *(con, de* at, by).

ma·ra·vi·llo·so, a adj. marvelous, wonderful.

mar·be·te m. *(etiqueta)* label, tag; *(orilla)* border, edge.

mar·ca f. *(señal)* mark; *(de ganadería)* brand;

(tipo) make, brand *<¿de qué m. es su auto?* what make is your car?>; *(estampa)* stamp; COM. trademark; *(medidor)* measuring stick, rule; *(medida)* standard (size); *(cicatriz)* scar; SPORT. mark, record; MARIT. seamark; GEOG. march, frontier ♦ **de m.** excellent, outstanding • **de m. mayor** high quality, first-class • **m. de agua** watermark • **m. de fábrica** trademark • **m. registrada** (registered) trademark.

mar·ca·do I. adj. marked, notable **II.** m. marking.

mar·ca·dor, ·ra I. adj. marking **II.** m.f. *(que marca)* marker; *(lápiz)* marker, marking pen —m. *(de bordado)* embroidery sampler; *(de herrero)* blacksmith's hammer; PRINT. feeder operator; SPORT. scoreboard.

mar·ca·pa·so(s) m. pacemaker.

mar·car §70 tr. *(poner marca)* to mark; *(herrar)* to brand; *(estampillar)* to stamp; *(la ropa)* to label; *(anotar)* to observe, note; *(indicar)* to say, indicate *<la balanza marca tres kilos* the scale indicates three kilos>; *(aplicar)* to assign, destine; *(subrayar)* to mark, underline; *(poner el precio)* to mark, price; *(el pelo)* to set; *(un número de teléfono)* to dial; PRINT. to feed; SPORT. to score ♦ **m. el compás** MUS. to keep time • **m. el paso** MIL. to mark time.

mar·cha f. *(movimiento)* march, movement; *(velocidad)* speed, velocity; *(salida)* departure; *(progresión)* march *<la m. del tiempo* the march of time>; *(curso)* course, progress; *(funcionamiento)* operation, running ♦ **a toda m.** at full speed • **dar m. atrás** to go into reverse • **estar en m.** *(comenzar)* to be underway; *(funcionar)* to be running *or* working • **m. atrás** AUTO. reverse • **m. forzada** MIL. forced march • **m. fúnebre** funeral march • **poner en m.** to start • **ponerse en m.** to start off • **sobre la m.** on the double.

mar·chan·te, a m.f. *(vendedor)* merchant, dealer; *(cliente)* customer, patron.

mar·char intr. *(ir)* to go; *(andar)* to walk; *(moverse)* to move, go; *(funcionar)* to run, work; *(progresar)* to go, proceed *<todo marcha bien* everything is going well>; MIL. to march —reflex. to go (away), leave.

mar·chi·tar tr. *(secar)* to wilt; *(debilitar)* to debilitate, weaken —reflex. *(secarse)* to wilt; *(debilitarse)* to become weak, languish.

mar·chi·to, a adj. wilted.

mar·cho·so, a adj. COLL. cheerful, merry.

mar·cial adj. martial; *(militar)* military *<porte m.* military bearing>.

mar·co m. *(cerco)* frame; FIN. mark (monetary unit); *(peso)* mark (unit of weight); *(patrón)* standard; *(estructura)* framework *<dentro del m. del pensamiento hegeliano* within the framework of Hegelian thought>.

ma·re·a f. tide; *(viento)* sea breeze; FIG. flood ♦ **contra viento y m.** against all odds • **m. alta** high tide • **m. baja** low tide • **m. creciente** rising tide • **m. menguante** low tide.

ma·re·a·do, a adj. *(malo)* sick; *(en el mar)* seasick; *(bebido)* drunk; *(aturdido)* dizzy.

ma·re·a·mien·to m. seasickness.

ma·re·ar tr. to navigate, sail; *(fastidiar)* to annoy, bother —reflex. *(tener náuseas)* to become nauseated; *(en barcos)* to become seasick; *(malograrse)* to become damaged.

ma·re·ja·da f. *(del mar)* swell, turbulence; *(agitación)* agitation, ferment.

ma·re·o m. *(náusea)* sickness, nausea; *(en bar-*

cos) seasickness; *(en vehículos)* motion sickness.

mar·fil m. ivory ♦ **m. vegetal** ivory nut.

mar·ga·ri·na f. margarine.

mar·ga·ri·ta f. BOT. daisy; *(perla)* margarite, pearl; ZOOL. periwinkle ♦ **echar margaritas a los cerdos** to throw pearls before swine.

mar·gen m. *(borde)* margin, border; *(nota)* marginal note; *(amplitud)* leeway, margin *<me dejaron m. en mis trabajos* they gave me leeway in my work>; COM. margin ♦ **al m.** *(de papel)* in the margin; *(afuera)* on the fringe *<vive al m. de la sociedad* he lives on the fringe of society> • **dar m. para** to give occasion for, give an opportunity for • **m. de ganancias** COM. profit margin —f. bank.

mar·gi·nal adj. marginal.

mar·gi·nar tr. *(dejar márgenes)* to marginate, leave a margin on; *(poner notas)* to make marginal notes on; *(apartar)* to leave out.

ma·ri·ca m. COLL., DEROG. gay man, sissy.

ma·ri·cas·ta·ña f. ♦ **en tiempos de M.** in days of yore, in the olden days.

ma·ri·cón m. SL., DEROG. *(homosexual)* gay man; *(pesado)* jerk.

ma·ri·dar intr. *(casar)* to marry, wed; *(vivir juntos)* to live together —tr. to join, unite.

ma·ri·do m. husband, spouse.

ma·ri·gua·na/hua·na/jua·na f. marijuana.

ma·ri·ma·cho m. COLL. mannish woman.

ma·rim·ba f. *(tambor)* drum; AMER. *(tímpano)* kettledrum; *(xilófono)* marimba, xylophone.

ma·ri·na f. see **marino, a.**

ma·ri·nar tr. to marinate; MARIT. to man.

ma·ri·ne·rí·a f. *(profesión)* seafaring, sailoring; *(tripulación)* ship's crew, seamen.

ma·ri·ne·ro, a I. adj. *(gobernable)* seaworthy; *(marino)* marine, sea; *(marinesco)* sailor, of sailors **II.** m. sailor, mariner ♦ **m. de agua dulce** landlubber —f. *(blusa)* middy blouse, sailor top; CHILE, ECUAD., PERU marinera (folk dance).

ma·ri·no, a I. adj. marine, sea ♦ **azul m.** navy blue **II.** m. sailor, mariner —f. *(costa)* coast; *(náutica)* navigation, seamanship; MIL. navy ♦ **Infantería de M.** Marine Corps • **m. de guerra** navy • **m. mercante** merchant marine.

ma·rio·ne·ta f. marionette, puppet.

ma·ri·po·sa I. f. butterfly; TECH. *(llave)* butterfly valve; *(tuerca)* butterfly *or* wing nut; *(lamparilla)* night light —m. DEROG. fairy, queer **II.** adj. SPORT. butterfly.

ma·ri·po·se·ar intr. *(ser inconstante)* to be fickle *or* capricious; *(dar vueltas)* to hover *or* flit about.

ma·ri·qui·ta f. ENTOM. *(coleóptero)* ladybug; *(hemíptero)* firebug; ORNITH. parakeet —m. COLL., DEROG. sissy, pansy.

ma·ris·cal m. marshal ♦ **m. de campo** field marshal.

ma·ris·co m. shellfish, crustacean.

ma·ris·ma f. salt marsh.

ma·ri·tal adj. marital.

ma·rí·ti·mo, a adj. maritime, sea ♦ **por vía m.** by sea.

mar·mi·ta f. pot, saucepan.

mar·mi·tón m. kitchen helper.

már·mol m. marble ♦ **de m.** hardhearted, cold.

mar·mo·le·rí·a f. *(conjunto)* marblework; *(obra)* marble; *(taller)* workshop, studio.

mar·mó·re·o, a adj. marble, marmoreal.

mar·mo·ta f. marmot; FIG. sleepyhead ♦ **dor-**

mir como una m. to sleep like a log.
ma·ro·me·ro, a m.f. AMER. tightrope walker.
mar·qués m. marquis.
mar·que·sa f. (persona) marquise, marchioness; AMER. (sillón) armchair, easy chair.
mar·que·si·na f. marquee, canopy.
mar·que·te·rí·a f. (taracea) marquetry, inlaid work; (ebanistería) cabinet work.
ma·rra·na·da/ne·rí·a f. COLL. (mala pasada) dirty or rotten trick; (suciedad) filth, filthiness.
ma·rra·no, a I. adj. dirty, filthy II. m. ZOOL. pig, hog; COLL. (sucio) pig, slob; (canalla) swine —f. ZOOL. sow; DEROG. (mujer) slut; TECH. axle (of a water wheel).
ma·rrar intr. (errar) to miss (a shot); (fallar) to fail; (desviarse) to go astray or wrong.
ma·rro m. (juego de niños) tag; (con bolos) ninepins; (ladeo) dodge, swerve; (falta) slip, error; MEX. mallet.
ma·rrón I. adj. brown II. m. (color) brown; (castaña) candied chestnut.
ma·rru·lla/lle·rí·a f. coaxing, wheedling.
ma·rru·lle·ro, a I. adj. conniving II.m.f. conniver, flatterer.
mar·so·p(l)a f. porpoise.
mar·su·pial adj. & m. marsupial.
mar·ta f. pine marten ♦ **m. cebellina** ZOOL. sable.
mar·tes m. Tuesday ♦ **m. de carnaval** or **carnestolendas** RELIG. Shrove Tuesday.
mar·ti·lla·da f. hammer blow.
mar·ti·llar tr. to hammer.
mar·ti·lla·zo m. hard blow of a hammer.
mar·ti·lle·ro m. AMER. auctioneer.
mar·ti·llo m. hammer; (mallo) gavel <m. de subastador auctioneer's gavel>; ICHTH. hammerhead (shark); (establecimiento) auction house; ANAT. malleus, hammer; MUS. tuning hammer; ♦ **m. de fragua** or **m. pilón** MECH. drop hammer • **m. neumático** pneumatic drill.
mar·tín pes·ca·dor m. kingfisher.
mar·ti·ne·te[1] m. heron.
mar·ti·ne·te[2] m. (de piano) hammer; (mazo) drop hammer; (de estacas) pile driver ♦ **m. a vapor** steam hammer • **m. de fragua** trip hammer.
már·tir m.f. martyr.
mar·ti·rio m. martyrdom.
mar·ti·ri·zar §04 tr. (hacer sufrir martirio) to martyr, martyrize; (atormentar) to torment.
mar·zo m. March.
mas conj. but <no lo vi, m. lo escuché I didn't see it, but I heard it>.
más I. adv. more <m. importante more important>; most <la alumna m. inteligente the most intelligent student>; longer <durar m. to last longer>; rather <m. quiero morir I would rather die> ♦ **a lo m.** at most, at the most • **a m.** besides, in addition • **a m. de** besides, in addition to • **a m. no poder** as much as possible or as can be • **a m. y mejor** a lot, really <llovía a m. y mejor it was really raining> • **con el que m.** as much as anyone • **de m.** too much, extra • **en lo m. mínimo** in the slightest • **m.** more • **estar de m.** to be superfluous or unnecessary • **m. allá** further • **m. bien** rather • **m. de more** than • **m. que** more than <yo sé m. que él I know more than he>; (sino) but, except <nadie puede hacerlo m. que Carlos no one can do it except Charles> • **ni m. ni menos** no more, no less • **no m.** only, no more • **no m. que** only • **por m. que** no matter how much •

¿qué m. da? what difference does it make? •
sin m. ni m. without further ado II. m. plus sign ♦ **el m. y el menos** the pros and the cons •
tener sus m. y sus menos COLL. to have good points and bad points III. prep. plus <cinco m. ocho son trece five plus eight is thirteen>.
ma·sa f. mass; (volumen) volume, bulk; (cuerpo compacto) lump <una m. de arcilla a lump of clay>; (el pueblo) people, masses; (pasta) dough; ELEC. ground; MAS. mortar ♦ **con las manos en la m.** in the act, redhanded • **en m.** (todos juntos) all together, en masse; (en gran escala) mass <protesta en m. mass protest> • **m. atómica** atomic mass • **m. de aire** air mass • **producción en m.** mass production.
ma·sa·crar tr. to massacre.
ma·sa·cre m. massacre.
ma·sa·je m. massage.
ma·sa·jis·ta m. masseur —f. masseuse.
mas·car §70 tr. (masticar) to chew; COLL. (mascullar) to mumble.
más·ca·ra f. (careta) mask; (traje) disguise, costume; (pretexto) mask, pretense —m.f. (persona) masker, masquerader ♦ **baile de máscaras** masquerade, masked ball • **m. antigás** gas mask • **m. de oxígeno** oxygen mask • **quitarse la m.** to drop one's pretenses.
mas·ca·ra·da f. (fiesta) masquerade, masked ball; (desfile) masked parade; (cosa falsa) masquerade, charade.
mas·ca·rón m. sculpted head or face ♦ **m. de proa** MARIT. figurehead.
mas·co·ta f. mascot.
mas·cu·li·ni·dad f. masculinity.
mas·cu·li·no, a I. adj. male; (propio de los hombres) masculine, manly; GRAM. masculine II. m. GRAM. masculine (gender).
mas·cu·llar tr. COLL. to mumble, mutter.
ma·si·lla f. putty.
ma·si·vo, a adj. (grande) massive; mass <comunicación m. mass communication>.
ma·so·quis·ta adj. & m.f. masochist.
mas·ti·car §70 tr. (triturar) to chew, masticate; (rumiar) to ponder over, ruminate.
más·til m. mast; (palo) pole; (de una pluma) quill ♦ **m. totémico** totem pole.
mas·tín m. mastiff ♦ **m. danés** Great Dane.
más·ti·que m. mastic.
mas·toi·des adj. & f.inv. mastoid.
mas·tur·ba·ción f. masturbation.
mas·tur·bar tr. & reflex. to masturbate.
ma·ta f. (arbusto) bush, shrub; (pie de una planta) sprig, tuft; (grupo de árboles) orchard, grove ♦ **m. de pelo** head of hair.
ma·ta·can·de·las m.inv. candle snuffer.
ma·ta·de·ro m. (de ganado) slaughterhouse; COLL. (trabajo) drudgery, chore.
ma·ta·dor, ·ra I. adj. (que mata) killing; COLL. (penoso) killing, deadly II. m.f. (asesino) killer, murderer —m. (en naipes) trump card; TAUR. bullfighter, matador.
ma·ta·fue·go m. fire extinguisher.
má·ta·las ca·llan·do m.f.c. COLL. sly dog, wolf in sheep's clothing.
ma·ta·mos·cas m.inv. fly swatter.
ma·tan·za f. (acción) killing, slaughtering; (de personas) massacre; (de animales) slaughtering, butchering.
ma·tar tr. to kill; (animales) to butcher, slaughter; (apagar) to put out, extinguish <m. el fuego to put out the fire>; (cal) to slake; (en naipes) to beat, top; (arruinar) to ruin, break

<*m. un proyecto* to ruin a project> ♦ **estar a m. con** to be at loggerheads with • **matarlas callando** to be a sly dog —reflex. (*quitarse la vida*) to kill oneself; to be killed <*su hijo se mató en un accidente* his son was killed in an accident>; FIG. to kill oneself —intr. to kill.

ma·ta·ri·fe m. butcher, slaughterer.

ma·ta·rra·tas m.inv. (*raticida*) rat poison; COLL. rotgut, firewater.

ma·ta·sa·nos m. COLL. quack (doctor).

ma·ta·se·llar tr. to cancel, postmark.

ma·ta·se·llos m.inv. (*instrumento*) canceller; (*marca*) postmark, cancellation.

ma·te[1] adj. (*sin brillo*) matte; (*apagado*) dull.

ma·te[2] m. checkmate, mate ♦ **dar jaque m.** to checkmate.

ma·te[3] m. AMER., BOT. (*arbusto*) maté tree; (*calabaza*) maté gourd; (*bebida*) maté; COLL. (*cabeza*) noodle ♦ **yerba m.** maté (tea).

ma·te·má·ti·co, a I. adj. mathematical II. m.f. mathematician —f. mathematics ♦ pl. mathematics.

ma·te·ria f. matter; (*material*) material, substance; EDUC. subject ♦ **en m. de** as regards, in the matter of • **entrar en m.** to come to the point, get down to business • **índice de materias** table of contents • **m. colorante** dyestuff • **m. de estado** POL. affair of state • **m. gris** gray matter • **m. prima** raw material.

ma·te·rial I. adj. material; (*corpóreo*) physical; (*materialista*) materialistic II. m. (*aparato*) materials, equipment; (*substancia*) material, substance <*hecho de buen m.* made of good material>; (*ingrediente*) ingredient.

ma·te·ria·li·dad f. materiality; (*apariencia*) outward appearance.

ma·te·ria·lis·ta I. adj. materialistic II. m.f. materialist.

ma·ter·nal adj. maternal.

ma·ter·ni·dad f. (*estado*) maternity; (*establecimiento*) maternity hospital.

ma·ter·no, a adj. (*maternal*) maternal, motherly; maternal <*abuelo m.* maternal grandfather>; (*nativo*) mother, native <*lengua m.* native language>.

ma·ti·nal adj. morning, matinal.

ma·tiz m. (*de color*) shade, tint; (*aspecto*) shade, nuance.

ma·ti·zar §04 tr. (*combinar*) to match, harmonize; (*teñir*) to tint, shade; (*variar*) to vary <*m. la voz* to vary one's tone of voice>.

ma·tón m. COLL. bully.

ma·to·rral m. (*maleza*) brushwood, scrub; (*soto*) thicket.

ma·tra·ca·la·da f. crowd, mob.

ma·tre·ro, a I. adj. cunning, shrewd II. m. AMER. bandit.

ma·triar·ca·do m. matriarchy.

ma·triar·cal adj. matriarchal.

ma·tri·ci·dio m. matricide.

ma·trí·cu·la f. (*lista*) register, list; (*inscripción*) registration, matriculation; (*gente matriculada*) roll; AUTO. registration.

ma·tri·cu·la·ción f. registration.

ma·tri·cu·lar tr. & reflex. to register, matriculate.

ma·tri·mo·nial adj. matrimonial.

ma·tri·mo·niar intr. to marry, get married.

ma·tri·mo·nio m. (*casamiento*) marriage, matrimony; COLL. (*marido y mujer*) married couple ♦ **contraer m.** to marry • **fuera del m.** out of wedlock • **m. civil** civil marriage • **m. por pode·**

res marriage by proxy • **partida de m.** marriage certificate.

ma·triz I. f. womb, uterus; (*molde*) mold, die; (*tuerca*) nut; MATH., MIN. matrix II. adj. original ♦ **casa m.** headquarters, main office.

ma·tro·na f. (*madre de familia*) matron; (*partera*) midwife; (*encargada*) matron.

ma·tro·nal adj. matronly.

ma·tu·te m. (*acción*) smuggling; (*contrabando*) contraband, smuggled goods.

ma·tu·te·ar intr. to smuggle.

mau·la m.f. swindler, cheat.

mau·llar intr. to meow, mew.

mau·lli·do/ú·llo m. (*voz*) meow, mew; (*acción*) meowing, mewing.

mau·so·le·o m. mausoleum.

má·xi·ma·men·te adv. principally, chiefly.

má·xi·me adv. principally, all the more.

má·xi·mo, a I. adj. maximum, greatest <*m. común divisor* greatest common denominator>; highest <*el punto m.* the highest point>; greatest <*el pensador m. de su tiempo* the greatest thinker of his time> II. m. maximum ♦ **al m.** to the maximum • **como m.** at the most • **hacer el m.** to do one's utmost —f. (*aforismo*) maxim; (*temperatura*) maximum temperature.

ma·yo m. May.

ma·yó·li·ca f. majolica ware.

ma·yo·ne·sa f. mayonnaise.

ma·yor I. adj. (*más grande*) bigger, larger <*la m. parte* the larger part>; (*importante*) greater; (*el más importante*) greatest <*el problema m.* the greatest problem>; (*de más edad*) older, elder <*mi hermano m.* my older brother>; elderly <*un señor m.* an elderly gentleman>; (*el más viejo*) oldest, eldest; (*adulto*) adult; (*principal*) main <*calle m.* main street>; RELIG. high <*misa m.* high mass>; MUS. major ♦ **al por m.** COM. wholesale • **caza m.** big game hunting • **estado m.** MIL. staff • **m. de edad** of age II. m. MIL. major; (*jefe*) chief ♦ pl. elders, ancestors.

ma·yo·raz·go m. (*derecho*) right of primogeniture; (*herencia*) estate inherited by primogeniture; (*heredero*) inheritor of an entailed estate; (*hijo primogénito*) first-born son; COLL. (*primogenitura*) seniority.

ma·yor·do·mí·a f. (*cargo*) stewardship; (*oficina*) majordomo's office.

ma·yor·do·mo m. majordomo.

ma·yo·rí·a f. majority ♦ **en la m. de los casos** in most cases • **en su m.** in the main • **m. absoluta** absolute majority • **m. de edad** legal age.

ma·yo·ri·dad f. majority, adult age.

ma·yo·ris·ta I. adj. wholesale II. m. wholesaler.

ma·yús·cu·lo, a I. adj. (*letra*) capital; (*importante*) important, prominent; COLL. (*grande*) enormous, tremendous II. f. capital letter.

ma·za f. (*arma*) mace; (*utensilio para machacar*) mallet; (*martinete*) drop hammer, pile driver.

ma·za·co·te m. COLL. (*plato*) lumpy mess <*el flan se ha hecho un m.* the pudding is a lumpy mess>; (*obra artística fea*) monstrosity.

ma·za·mo·rra f. cornmeal mush.

ma·za·pán m. marzipan.

maz·mo·rra f. dungeon.

ma·zo m. (*martillo*) mallet; (*manojo*) bunch.

ma·zor·ca f. ear, cob (of corn).

me pron. me <*me vieron en el jardín* they saw me in the garden>; me, to me <*dame la llave* give me the key>; me, for me <*ella me compró* *un regalo* she bought a present for me>; from me <*me quitó el pañuelo* he took the handkerchief from me>; myself <*me miré en el espejo* I looked at myself in the mirror>.

me·cá·ni·co, a I. adj. *(de la mecánica)* mechanical, machine-operated; *(automático)* automatic, machine-like II. m. *(maquinista)* mechanic; *(chófer)* driver —f. *(ciencia)* mechanics; *(mecanismo)* mechanism.

me·ca·nis·mo m. *(aparato)* mechanism, working parts; *(estructura)* structure, workings.

me·ca·ni·zar §04 tr. to mechanize.

me·ca·no·gra·fí·a f. typing, typewriting.

me·ca·no·gra·fiar §30 tr. to type.

me·ca·nó·gra·fo, a m.f. typist.

me·ce·de·ro m. stirrer, swizzle stick.

me·ce·do·ra f. rocking chair, rocker.

me·ce·nas m.inv. patron (of the arts).

me·cer §75 tr. *(acunar)* to rock; *(columpiar)* to swing; *(balancear)* to move to and fro, sway; *(agitar)* to shake —reflex. to rock < *m. en una mecedora* to rock in a rocking chair>; *(columpiarse)* to swing; *(balancearse)* to move to and fro.

me·cha f. *(de lámpara)* wick; *(espoleta)* fuse; *(para encender)* match; *(mechón)* lock; MED., SURG. tent; AMER. *(del taladro)* drill bit ♦ **a toda m.** at full speed • **aguantar la m.** to grin and bear it.

me·char tr. to stuff.

me·che·ra f. shoplifter.

me·che·ro m. *(boquilla)* burner, jet <*m. de gas* gas burner>; *(encendedor)* lighter, cigarette lighter; *(canutillo)* wick, holder; *(del candelero)* candle socket.

me·chón m. *(de pelo)* lock, tuft; *(de lana)* tuft.

me·da·lla f. medal; *(joya)* medallion ♦ **el reverso de la m.** the other side of the coin.

me·da·llis·ta m.f. medalist.

me·da·llón m. *(medalla grande)* medallion; *(joya)* locket.

mé·da·no or **me·da·no** m. *(duna)* dune, sand dune; *(banco de arena)* sandbank.

me·dia f. *(de mujer)* stocking; *(de hombre)* sock; *(tiempo)* half past <*las dos y media* half past two>.

me·dia·ción f. mediation, arbitration.

me·dia·do, a adj. half full ♦ **a mediados de** halfway through, in the middle of.

me·dia·dor, ·ra I. adj. mediating II. m.f. mediator.

me·dia·ne·ro, a I. adj. *(que está en medio)* dividing; *(mediador)* mediating II. m.f. *(intercesor)* mediator —f. adjoining wall.

me·dia·no, a adj. *(regular)* average, medium; COLL. *(mediocre)* mediocre, poor II. f. GEOM. median.

me·dia·no·che f. midnight.

me·dian·te I. adj. interceding II. adv. through, by means of ♦ **Dios m.** God willing.

me·diar intr. *(llegar a la mitad)* to get halfway; *(estar en medio)* to be in the middle; *(interponerse)* to intercede, come between; *(transcurrir)* to elapse, go by.

me·di·ca·ción f. *(tratamiento)* medication, medical treatment; *(medicamentos)* medication, medicines.

me·di·ca·men·to m. medicine, medicament.

me·di·car §70 tr. to medicate.

me·di·cas·tro m. quack, medicaster.

me·di·ci·na f. *(ciencia)* medicine, art of healing; *(medicamento)* medicine, medication ♦

doctor en m. doctor of medicine.

me·di·ci·nal adj. medicinal.

me·di·ci·nar tr. to treat (with medicine), give medicine to.

me·di·ción f. measurement, measuring.

mé·di·co, a I. adj. medical II. m.f. doctor, physician ♦ **m. de cabecera** family doctor • **m. de consulta** consulting physician • **m. general** general practitioner.

me·di·da f. measure, measurement <*m. para líquidos* liquid measure>; *(medición)* measuring, measurement; *(recipiente)* measure, measuring device; *(norma)* standard, gauge <*todo depende de la m. en que se juzgue* it all depends on the standard by which one judges>; *(proporción)* proportion, degree <*me pagan a m. de mi trabajo* they pay me in porportion to my work>; *(prevención)* measure, step <*tomó medidas para evitar más problemas* he took steps to avoid further problems>; *(prudencia)* measure, moderation; POET. measure, meter ♦ **a m. que** as, while • **en la m. en que** insofar as • **en menor m.** to a lesser extent • **hecho a la m.** made-to-order • **pasarse de la m.** to carry things too far • **sin m.** immoderately, in excess.

me·di·dor, ·ra I. adj. measuring II. m.f. *(persona)* measurer —m. AMER. *(contador)* meter.

me·die·val adj. medieval.

me·dio, a I. adj. *(tres horas y m.* three and a half hours>; *(mediano)* middle, medium <*una persona de talla m.* a person of medium height>; *(central)* middle, midway <*el punto m.* the midway point>; *(regular)* average <*el español m.* the average Spaniard>; MATH. average, mean ♦ **m. hermana** half sister • **m. hermano** half brother • **m. luna** half-moon • **m. pasaje** half fare II. m. *(centro)* middle, center; *(ambiente)* environment, medium; *(medida)* measure, step <*procedió adoptando los medios necesarios* he proceeded, taking the necessary measures>; *(medium)* medium, spiritualist; *(moderación)* middle ground; MATH. half; BIOL. medium; LOG. middle term; SPORT. halfback ♦ **de m. a m.** *(en el centro)* in the middle; *(completamente)* completely, entirely • **de por m.** in between • **en m. de** *(en la mitad)* in the middle; *(sin embargo)* notwithstanding; *(entre tanto)* in the midst of <*en m. de todo eso logró salir bien* in the midst of all that, he managed to come out all right> • **estar de por m.** *(mediar)* to intervene, mediate; *(involucrarse)* to be in the middle, be involved • **m. ambiente** environment • **meterse de por m.** or **en m.** to intervene • **por m. de** by means of • **por todos los medios** by all means, at all costs • **quitar de en m.** to get rid of, do away with • **quitarse de en m.** to get out of the way III. adv. half, partially <*m. terminado* half finished> ♦ **a m.** half <*a m. vestir* half-dressed> • **a medias** halfway <*no lo reparó sino a medias* he just repaired it halfway>; *(no del todo)* half <*dormido a medias* half asleep>.

me·dio·cre adj. mediocre.

me·dio·cri·dad f. mediocrity.

me·dio·dí·a m. midday, noon.

me·dir §48 tr. to measure; *(comparar)* to compare; *(moderar)* to weigh <*mide sus palabras cuidadosamente* he weighs his words carefully> —reflex. to be moderate, act with restraint.

me·di·ta·bun·do, a adj. meditative, thoughtful.

me·di·ta·ción f. meditation.

me·di·tar tr. & intr. to meditate.

me·di·ta·ti·vo, a adj. meditative.

mé·dium m.inv. medium.

me·drar intr. *(crecer)* to grow, thrive; *(mejorar)* to improve; *(prosperar)* to prosper.

me·dro·so, a I. adj. fearful, timorous **II.** m.f. coward.

me·du·la *or* **mé·du·la** f. medulla, marrow; BOT. medulla, pith; *(esencia)* essence ♦ **hasta la m.** to the core • **m. espinal** spinal cord • **m. ósea** bone marrow.

me·du·sa f. medusa, jellyfish.

me·gá·fo·no m. megaphone.

me·ga·lo·ma·ní·a f. megalomania.

me·ga·ló·ma·no, a I. adj. megalomaniacal **II.** m.f. megalomaniac.

me·ga·tón m. megaton.

me·ji·lla f. cheek.

me·ji·llón m. mussel.

me·jor I. adj. *(superior)* better <este coche es m. que el otro this car is better than the other>; best <el m. estudiante de la clase the best student in the class> ♦ **lo m. posible** as well as possible **II.** adv. *(más bien)* better <ella escribe m. que él she writes better than he does>; *(antes)* rather <m. morirme que perder la honra I would rather die than lose my honor> ♦ **a lo m.** maybe, perhaps • **en el m. de los casos** at best • **m. dicho** rather, more specifically • **m. que m.** all the better, so much the better • **tanto m.** better still, so much the better.

me·jo·ra f. *(adelanto)* improvement, betterment; *(aumento)* increase.

me·jo·ra·mien·to m. improvement.

me·jo·rar tr. *(poner mejor)* to improve, make better; *(aumentar)* to raise ♦ **mejorando lo presente** present company excepted —intr. & reflex. *(ponerse mejor)* to improve, get better; *(el tiempo)* to clear up.

me·jo·rí·a f. *(mejora)* improvement, betterment; *(convalecencia)* improvement.

me·lan·co·lí·a f. *(tristeza)* melancholy, sadness; MED. melancholia.

me·lan·có·li·co, a adj. & m.f. melancholy (person).

me·la·za f. molasses.

mel·co·cha f. taffy.

me·le·na f. *(cabello)* long hair, mop (of hair); *(de león)* mane.

me·le·ro I. m. honey vendor **II.** adj. honey.

me·lí·fluo, a adj. mellifluous.

me·lin·dre·rí·a f. affectation, fussiness.

me·lin·dro·so/dre·ro, a adj. & m.f. affected *or* fussy (person).

me·lla f. *(abolladura)* dent; *(en un filo)* nick, notch; *(en la porcelana)* chip; *(hueco)* gap, hole ♦ **hacer m. a** to have an effect upon, impress ♦ **hacer m. en** to harm.

me·llar tr. *(metal)* to dent; *(un filo)* to nick, notch; *(porcelana)* to chip; *(menoscabar)* to harm —intr. *(superficie)* to become dented *or* chipped; *(dañarse)* to be harmed *or* injured.

me·lli·zo, a m.f. & adj. twin.

me·lo·co·tón m. *(fruto)* peach; *(árbol)* peach tree.

me·lo·co·to·ne·ro m. peach tree.

me·lo·dí·a f. *(canto)* melody, tune; *(calidad)* melody, melodiousness.

me·ló·di·co, a adj. melodic, tuneful.

me·lo·dio·so, a adj. melodious, tuneful.

me·lo·dra·ma m. melodrama.

me·lo·dra·má·ti·co, a adj. melodramatic(al).

me·lón m. melon; FIG. idiot, fool.

me·lo·so, a adj. *(dulce)* sweet, honeyed; *(suave)* smooth; FIG. sweet, gentle.

me·lo·te m. molasses; SP. honey preserves.

mem·bra·na f. membrane.

mem·bre·te m. *(del remitente)* letterhead; *(del destinatario)* addressee's name and address.

mem·bri·llo m. *(árbol)* quince tree; *(fruta)* quince; *(dulce)* quince jam *or* jelly.

mem·bru·do, a adj. robust, muscular.

me·mo·ra·ble adj. memorable.

me·mo·rán·dum m. [pl. **pl. inv.** *or* **-da**] *(nota)* memorandum, memo; *(libreta)* memo book.

me·mo·rar tr. to remember, recall.

me·mo·ria f. memory; *(recuerdo)* memory, remembrance; COM. *(informe)* financial report *or* statement ♦ **borrar de la m.** to forget completely • **conservar la m. de** to remember • **de m.** by heart • **digno de m.** memorable • **en m. de** in memory of • **falta de m.** forgetfulness • **hacer m. de** to remember • **irse de la m.** to slip one's mind • **traer a la m. de uno** to remind one • **venir a la m.** to come to mind ♦ pl. *(libro)* memoirs.

me·mo·rial m. *(libreta)* memo book, notebook; *(petición)* memorial, petition; *(publicación)* publication, bulletin.

me·mo·ri·za·ción f. memorization, memorizing.

me·mo·ri·zar §04 tr. to memorize, learn by heart.

men·ción f. mention ♦ **hacer m. de** to make mention of, mention • **m. honorífica** honorable mention.

men·cio·nar tr. to mention ♦ **sin m.** not to mention.

men·da·ci·dad f. *(hábito)* mendacity; *(mentira)* lie.

men·daz I. adj. mendacious, lying **II.** m.f. liar.

men·di·can·te adj. & m.f. mendicant.

men·di·gar §47 tr. to beg (for) —intr. to beg.

men·di·go, a m.f. beggar, mendicant.

men·dru·go m. crust, crumb.

me·ne·ar tr. & reflex. *(mover)* to move; *(agitar)* to shake, wag; *(oscilar)* to sway, swing.

me·ne·o m. *(movimiento)* movement; *(agitación)* shake; *(oscilación)* sway, swing.

me·nes·ter m. *(falta)* need, want; *(ocupación)* occupation ♦ **haber** *or* **tener m. de** to need *or* want • **ser m. que** to be necessary that.

men·gua f. *(disminución)* diminution, decrease; *(falta)* lack; *(pobreza)* poverty; *(descrédito)* discredit, disgrace.

men·gua·do, a I. adj. *(disminuido)* diminished, decreased; *(cobarde)* cowardly, timid **II.** m. drop stitch.

men·guan·te I. adj. *(que disminuye)* diminishing, decreasing; ASTRON. waning; MARIT. ebb **II.** m. *(disminución)* diminution, decrease; AS-TRON. waning; MARIT. ebb; *(decadencia)* decline, decadence ♦ **cuarto m.** last quarter (of the moon).

men·guar §10 intr. *(disminuir)* to diminish, decrease; ASTRON. to wane; MARIT. to ebb; *(en tejido)* to decrease; *(declinar)* to decline, go downhill —tr. *(disminuir)* to diminish, decrease; *(velocidad)* to reduce; *(peso, responsabilidad)* to lessen, diminish; *(menoscabar)* to detract from <esto no mengua en nada su fama this in no way detracts from his reputation>.

me·nin·gi·tis f. meningitis.

me·no·pau·sia f. menopause.

me·nor I. adj. less, lesser <*de m. importancia* of lesser importance>; least <*no tengo la m. idea* I don't have the least idea>; *(más joven)* younger <*mi hermano m.* my younger brother>; *(el más joven)* youngest; COLL. *(más pequeño)* smaller; *(el más pequeño)* smallest; MUS., RELIG. minor ♦ **al por m.** COM. retail • **m. de edad** minor, under age **II.** m. minor, juvenile ♦ **tribunal de menores** juvenile court.

me·no·rí·a f. *(subordinación)* subordination; *(edad)* minority (of age).

me·no·ris·ta m. AMER. retailer, retail dealer.

me·nos I. adv. less <*ella tiene m. dinero que él* she has less money than he>; least <*Paco es el m. listo de la clase* Frank is the least clever boy in the class>; fewer <*había m. de cincuenta personas en la reunión* there were fewer than fifty people at the meeting> ♦ **al m.** at least • **a m. que** unless • **cada vez m.** less and less • **cuanto m. . . . m.** the less . . . the less • **de m.** short <*dos kilos de m.* two kilograms short> • **echar a alguien de m.** to miss someone • **más o m.** more or less • **lo m.** the least • **m. de** less than <*m. de cien dólares* less than one hundred dollars> • **m. que** less than • **ni más ni m.** exactly • **no ser para m.** to be no wonder, little wonder that • **por lo m.** at least • **ser lo de m.** to be the least important thing • **tener a m.** to consider it beneath oneself • **venir a m.** to decline, come down in the world **II.** m. minus sign **III.** conj. but, except <*todo m. eso* all but that> **IV.** prep. minus <*quince m. siete son ocho* fifteen minus seven is eight>.

me·nos·ca·bar tr. to damage, impair.

me·nos·ca·bo m. *(mengua)* diminishing, lessening; *(daño)* damage; *(descrédito)* damage ♦ **con m. de** to the detriment of.

me·nos·pre·cia·ble adj. despicable, contemptible.

me·nos·pre·ciar tr. *(despreciar)* to despise, scorn; *(subestimar)* to underestimate, underrate.

me·nos·pre·cia·ti·vo, a adj. disdainful, contemptuous.

me·nos·pre·cio m. *(desprecio)* contempt, scorn; *(subestimación)* underestimation, underrating; *(falta de respeto)* disrespect ♦ **hacer m. de** to make light of, scoff at.

men·sa·je m. message ♦ **m. en clave** coded message.

men·sa·je·ro, a adj. & m.f. messenger.

mens·trua·ción f. menstruation.

mens·trual adj. menstrual.

mens·truar §67 intr. to menstruate.

men·sual adj. monthly.

men·sua·li·dad f. *(salario)* monthly wage; *(pago)* monthly installment.

men·su·ra f. measure, measurement.

men·su·ra·ble adj. mensurable, measurable.

men·su·ra·dor, ra I. adj. measuring **II.** measurer, meter.

men·su·rar tr. to measure.

men·ta f. mint.

men·ta·do, a adj. famous, renowned.

men·tal adj. mental.

men·ta·li·dad f. mentality, mind ♦ **m. abierta** open mind.

men·tar §49 tr. to name, mention.

men·te f. *(potencia intelectual)* mind, intellect; *(inteligencia)* intelligence; *(pensamiento)* mind <*tener en la m.* to have in mind>; *(propósito)* mind, intention <*tener en m.* to have in mind (to do)>.

men·te·ca·to, a I. adj. silly, foolish **II.** m.f. fool, simpleton.

men·tir §65 intr. to lie, tell lies.

men·ti·ra f. *(falsedad)* lie, falsehood; *(manchita blanca)* white spot (on a fingernail) ♦ **¡m.!** that's a lie! • **m. inocente** or **piadosa** white lie • **parece m.** it seems unbelievable.

men·ti·rón m. whopping lie, whopper.

men·ti·ro·so, a I. adj. lying **II.** m.f. liar.

men·tol m. menthol.

men·to·la·do, a adj. mentholated.

men·tor m. mentor.

me·nú m. menu, bill of fare.

me·nu·de·o m. *(repetición)* frequent repetition; *(venta al por menor)* retail ♦ **vender al m.** to sell retail.

me·nu·do, a I. adj. *(pequeño)* small, little; *(sin importancia)* small, insignificant <*problemas menudos* small problems>; *(fino)* fine <*lluvia m.* fine rain>; *(irónico)* fine <*¡en m. lío estamos!* a fine mess we're in!> ♦ **a m.** often, frequently • **por m.** in detail, minutely **II.** m. *(moneda)* loose change ♦ pl. innards; *(de las reses)* offal; *(de las aves)* giblets.

me·ñi·que I. adj. *(del dedo)* little, baby; *(pequeño)* tiny **II.** m. little finger, pinkie.

me·o·llo m. *(médula)* marrow; *(seso)* brain, gray matter; *(inteligencia)* brains.

me·que·tre·fe m. COLL. jackanapes.

mer·ca·chi·fle m. *(buhonero)* peddler, hawker; *(comerciante)* small-time merchant; DEROG. *(avaro)* shark, money grubber.

mer·ca·de·o m. marketing.

mer·ca·de·rí·a f. var. of **mercancía.**

mer·ca·do m. *(feria)* market; *(sitio)* marketplace ♦ **acaparar el m. de** to corner the market • **m. de cambios** foreign exchange market • **m. de valores** stock market • **m. exterior** foreign market • **m. interior** or **nacional** domestic market.

mer·ca·do·tec·nia f. marketing (research).

mer·can·cí·a f. *(artículo)* piece of merchandise, article; *(existencias)* merchandise, goods.

mer·can·te adj. & m. merchant.

mer·can·til adj. mercantile, commercial ♦ **derecho m.** commercial law • **sociedad m.** trading company.

mer·car §70 tr. to purchase, buy.

mer·ced f. *(beneficio)* gift, favor; RELIG. mercy; ARCH. *(título)* grace, worship ♦ **a la m. de** at the mercy of • **m. a** thanks to • **tenga la m. de** please be so kind as.

mer·ce·na·rio, a adj. & m. mercenary.

mer·ce·rí·a f. notions shop.

mer·cu·rial adj. mercurial.

mer·cu·rio m. mercury.

mer·cu·ro·cro·mo m. mercurochrome.

me·re·ce·dor, ra adj. worthy, deserving ♦ **m. de confianza** trustworthy.

me·re·cer §17 tr. *(ser digno de)* to deserve, be worthy of; *(lograr)* to earn, get ♦ **m. la pena** to be worthwhile, be worth the trouble —reflex. to be deserving or worthy.

me·re·ci·do m. just deserts, due <*llevar su m.* to get one's just deserts>.

me·re·ci·mien·to m. merit, worth.

me·ren·dar §49 tr. to snack on —intr. to have a snack.

me·ren·gue m. meringue; R.P. COLL. mess.

me·re·triz f. prostitute, whore.

me·ri·dia·no, a adj. & m. meridian.

me·rien·da f. snack.

me·rien·de, do see **merendar.**

mé·ri·to m. (virtud) merit; (valor) worth, value ♦ **de m.** of merit, notable • **hacer méritos para** to strive to be deserving of.

me·ri·to·rio, a I. adj. meritorious **II.** m. unpaid trainee.

mer·lu·za f. hake.

mer·mar tr. & intr. to decrease, diminish.

mer·me·la·da f. marmalade.

me·ro m. ICHTH. grouper.

me·ro, a adj. (puro) mere, pure; MEX. (verdadero) real ♦ **ser el m. malo** to be wickedness itself.

me·ro·de·a·dor, ·ra I. adj. marauding **II.** m.f. marauder.

me·ro·de·ar intr. to maraud, plunder.

mes m. (período del año) month; (sueldo) monthly salary <cobrar el m. to draw one's monthly salary>; COLL. (menstruo) menstruation ♦ **al** or **por m.** by the month.

me·sa f. (mueble) table; (junta) board, council <m. electoral electoral board>; GEOG. meseta, plateau; JEWEL. facet, face; (comida) fare, food ♦ **de m.** table <vino de mesa table wine> • **levantar** or **alzar la m.** to clear the table • **m. de noche** night table, nightstand • **m. de operaciones** operating table • **m. de tijera** or **de doblar** card table, folding table • **poner la m.** to set the table.

me·se·ro, a MEX. m. (camarero) waiter —f. (camarera) waitress.

me·se·ta f. (de escalera) landing; GEOG. plateau.

me·siá·ni·co, a adj. messianic.

me·són m. inn, tavern.

me·so·ne·ro, a m.f. innkeeper.

mes·ti·zo, a I. adj. of mixed parentage **II.** m.f. mestizo (of white and Indian parentage).

me·su·ra f. moderation, restraint.

me·su·ra·do, a adj. moderate, circumspect.

me·ta f. (fin) goal, objective; (de carrera) finish; (guardameta) goalkeeper.

me·ta·bó·li·co, a adj. metabolic.

me·ta·bo·lis·mo m. metabolism.

me·ta·fí·si·co, a I. adj. metaphysical **II.** m. metaphysician —f. metaphysics.

me·tá·fo·ra f. metaphor.

me·ta·fó·ri·co, a adj. metaphoric(al).

me·tal m. metal; (latón) brass; (calidad) nature, quality; (timbre) tone, ring ♦ **m. blanco** nickel • **m. de imprenta** type metal • **m. en láminas** sheet metal.

me·tá·li·co, a I. adj. metallic **II.** m. cash, currency.

me·ta·li·zar §04 tr. to metalize —reflex. to become metalized.

me·ta·lur·gia f. metallurgy.

me·ta·lúr·gi·co, a I. adj. metallurgical **II.** m. metallurgist, metalworker.

me·ta·lur·gis·ta m. metallurgist, metalworker.

me·ta·mór·fi·co, a adj. GEOL. metamorphic.

me·ta·mor·fo·sis/mór·fo·sis f. inv. BIOL. metamorphosis; (transformación) transformation.

me·ta·no m. methane.

me·te·ó·ri·co, a adj. meteoric.

me·te·o·ri·to m. meteorite.

me·te·o·ro/té·o·ro m. meteor.

me·te·o·ro·lo·gía f. meteorology.

me·te·o·ro·lo·gis·ta/ró·lo·go, a m.f. meteorologist.

me·ter tr. (introducir) to put in, insert <ella metió el dinero en el bolsillo she put the money in her pocket>; (promover) to start, cause <m. enredos to start trouble>; (causar) to make <m. ruido to make noise>; (implicar) to involve, get into <metió a su hermano en el negocio he got his brother into the business>; (apretar) to squeeze into, squash together; (apostar) to stake, wager; COLL. (golpe) to give, deal; SEW. to take in ♦ **m. de contrabando** to smuggle in • **m. en vereda** COLL. to bring into line —reflex. (entrar) to get into, enter <se metieron en el coche they got into the car>; (entrometerse) to intervene, butt in; (enredarse) to get mixed up in ♦ **m. a** (empezar) to start; (hacerse) to set oneself up as • **m. con** to provoke, annoy • **m. de** AMER. to become • **m. en sí mismo** to withdraw into one's shell • **m. en todo** to meddle.

me·ti·cu·lo·so, a adj. meticulous.

me·ti·do, a I. see **meter II.** adj. (abundante) full; (interesado) involved; AMER. meddlesome ♦ **m. en sí** withdrawn **III.** m.f. AMER. meddler.

me·ti·lo m. methyl.

me·tó·di·co, a adj. methodical.

mé·to·do m. method, technique ♦ **con m.** methodically.

me·to·do·lo·gía f. methodology.

me·tra·je m. footage, length (of a film) ♦ **corto m.** short (film) • **largo m.** full-length or feature film.

me·tra·lle·ta f. submachine gun, tommy gun.

mé·tri·co, a I. adj. metric; POET. metrical ♦ **cinta m.** tape measure **II.** f. metrics.

me·tro[1] m. (medida) meter, metre (G.B.); (regla) ruler ♦ **m. cuadrado** square meter • **m. cúbico** cubic meter.

me·tro[2] m. abbr. of **metropolitano.**

me·tró·po·li f. (capital) capital; (nación) metropolis.

me·tro·po·li·ta·no, a I. adj. metropolitan **II.** m. subway, underground (G.B.).

mez·ca·li·na f. mescaline.

mez·cla f. (acción) mixing; (combinación) mixture, combination; (de personas) mixture, assortment; (tejido) tweed; CONST. mortar.

mez·cla·dor, ·ra I. adj. mixing, blending **II.** m.f. (persona) mixer —f. (máquina) mixing machine; CONST. cement mixer.

mez·cla·du·ra f./**mien·to** m. mixture, blend.

mez·clar tr. (unir) to mix, blend; (reunir) to mix, mingle; (desordenar) to mix up; (en naipes) to shuffle —reflex. (unirse) to mix, blend; (reunirse) to mix, mingle; (meterse) to become involved or mixed up.

mez·co·lan·za f. COLL. hodgepodge, jumble.

mez·quin·dad f. (avaricia) stinginess, miserliness; (acción tacaña) ill turn, act of meanness.

mez·qui·no, a I. adj. (pobre) poor, wretched; (avaro) stingy, miserly; (miserable) petty, small; (pequeño) small, tiny **II.** m. MEX. wart.

mez·qui·ta f. mosque.

mí pron. [pl. **used after prepositions**] me <lo compró para mí he bought it for me> ♦ **me toca a mí** it's my turn • **¿(y) a mí qué?** so what?

mi, mis adj. my <mis hermanas my sisters>.

miau m. meow.

mi·co m. mico, long-tailed monkey.

mi·cro·bio m. microbe.

mi·cro·bio·lo·gía f. microbiology.

mi·cro·bús m. microbus, minibus.

mi·cro·cir·cui·to m. microcircuit.
mi·cro·ci·ru·gí·a f. microsurgery.
mi·cro·com·pu·ta·dor m./**do·ra** f. microcomputer.
mi·cro·cós·mi·co, a adj. microcosmic.
mi·cro·cos·mo(s) m. microcosm.
mi·cro·e·co·no·mí·a f. microeconomics.
mi·cro·fi·cha f. microfiche.
mi·cro·fil·m(e) m. microfilm.
mi·cró·fo·no m. microphone.
mi·cro·on·das f.pl. microwaves.
mi·cro·or·de·na·dor m. microcomputer.
mi·cro·pla·que·ta f. microchip.
mi·cros·có·pi·co, a adj. microscopic.
mi·cros·co·pio m. microscope ♦ **m. electró-nico** electron microscope.
mi·da, di·da, diera, dió see **medir.**
mie·do m. (temor) fear, dread; (aprensión) apprehension ♦ **dar m. a** to frighten • **meterle m. a** to frighten • **morirse de m.** to be scared to death • **que da** or **mete m.** frightening, fearsome • **tener m.** to be afraid • **tener m. a** or **de** to be afraid of, fear • **tener m. (de) que** to be afraid that.
mie·do·so, a I. adj. fearful, cowardly II. m. coward.
miel f. honey; (jarabe) molasses; (dulzura) honey, sweetness ♦ **no hay m. sin hiel** every rose has a thorn • **m. de caña** molasses • **panal de m.** honeycomb.
miel·ga f. alfalfa.
miem·bro m. member; ANAT. (extremidad) member, limb; (pene) penis ♦ **m. viril** penis • **m. vitalicio** life member.
mien·ta, to see **mentir.**
mien·tras I. adv. ♦ **m. más** the more <m. más consigue más quiere the more he gets, the more he wants> • **m. tanto** meanwhile, in the meantime II. conj. (pero) while, whereas <mi casa es pequeña m. la tuya es grande my house is small whereas yours is large>; (durante) while, as long as <m. la huelga duraba while the strike lasted> ♦ **m. que** while.
miér·co·les m. inv. Wednesday ♦ **m. de ceniza** RELIG. Ash Wednesday ♦ **¡m.!** AMER., COLL. shoot!, darn it!
mies f. (cereal) grain; (tiempo de la siega) harvest time ♦ pl. grain fields.
mi·ga f. (pedacito) bit, scrap; (del pan) crumb; (substancia) substance, pith ♦ **hacer buenas, malas migas con** to get along well, badly with.
mi·ga·ja f. (del pan) crumb; (pedacito) scrap, bit ♦ **m. de pan** bread crumb ♦ pl. scraps.
mi·gra·ción f. migration.
mi·gra·ña f. migraine (headache).
mi·gra·to·rio, a adj. migratory.
mil I. adj. thousand; (milésimo) thousandth; (muchos) thousand, countless <m. veces a thousand times> ♦ **a las m. y quinientas** at the last minute • **m. millones** billion, milliard (G.B.) II. m. a thousand, one thousand.
mi·la·gro m. miracle ♦ **hacer milagros** to work wonders • **vivir de m.** COLL. to be or stay alive by a miracle.
mi·la·gro·so, a adj. miraculous.
mi·le·nio m. millennium.
mi·lé·si·mo, a adj. & m. thousandth.
mi·li f. COLL. military service.
mi·li·cia f. (arte militar) art of war; (tropa) military, soldiery; (de ciudadanos) militia; (servicio militar) military service ♦ **m. nacional** national guard.

mi·li·cia·no, a I. adj. military II. m. militiaman.
mi·li·gra·mo m. milligram.
mi·li·li·tro m. milliliter.
mi·lí·me·tro m. millimeter.
mi·li·tan·te I. adj. militant II. m.f. militant, activist.
mi·li·tar[1] I. adj. military II. m. soldier ♦ **los militares** the military.
mi·li·tar[2] intr. (como soldado) to serve; (en un partido) to be active ♦ **m. en favor de** to lend support to.
mi·li·ta·ri·zar §04 tr. to militarize.
mi·lla f. (medida inglesa) mile; MARIT. mile, nautical mile ♦ **m. náutica** nautical mile.
mi·llar m. (conjunto de mil) thousand <un m. de hombres a thousand men> ♦ pl. thousands, scores • **a m.** by the thousands.
mi·llón m. million ♦ **tener millones** COLL. to be a millionaire.
mi·llo·na·rio, a adj. & m.f. millionaire.
mil·piés m.inv. millipede.
mi·mar tr. (acariciar) to caress, fondle; (consentir) to pamper, spoil.
mim·bre m. (arbusto) osier; (tallo) wicker.
mi·me·o·gra·fí·a f. (acción) mimeographing; (copia) mimeograph.
mi·me·o·gra·fiar §30 tr. to mimeograph.
mi·me·ó·gra·fo m. mimeograph (machine).
mí·mi·co, a I. adj. mimic, imitative II. f. THEAT. mime; (imitación) imitation, mimicry.
mi·mo m. THEAT. mime; (caricia) caressing, fondling ♦ **hacerle mimos a alguien** to pamper or indulge someone.
mi·mo·so, a adj. pampered, spoiled.
mi·na f. mine; (galería) underground passage; FIG. mine, storehouse; (de lápiz) pencil lead; AMER. mistress.
mi·na·dor, ·ra I. adj. mining II. m. (ingeniero) mining engineer; (obrero) miner; MIL. miner, sapper; MARIT. minelayer.
mi·nar tr. to mine; (debilitar) to undermine, destroy <m. la salud to undermine one's health>.
mi·na·re·te m. minaret.
mi·ne·ral adj. & m. mineral.
mi·ne·ra·lo·gí·a f. mineralogy.
mi·ne·ra·ló·gi·co, a adj. mineralogical.
mi·ne·ra·lo·gis·ta m. mineralogist.
mi·ne·rí·a f. (trabajo) mining; (minas) mines; (mineros) miners.
mi·ne·ro, a I. adj. mining II. m. (trabajador) miner; (propietario) mine owner.
min·gi·to·rio m. urinal.
min·go m. object ball (in billiards).
mi·nia·tu·ra f. miniature.
mi·nia·tu·ris·ta m.f. miniaturist.
mi·ni·com·pu·ta·dor m./**do·ra** f. minicomputer.
mi·ni·fal·da f. miniskirt.
mi·ni·fun·dio m. small farm.
mi·ni·mi·zar §04 tr. to minimize.
mí·ni·mo, a I. adj. (pequeño) minimum, least; (minucioso) minute, minimal II. m. (límite inferior) minimum; METEOROL. low pressure zone ♦ **al m.** or **a lo más m.** to a minimum • **como m.** at least, at the very least • **en lo más m.** in the slightest • **m. común múltiplo** lowest common multiple • **m. vital** subsistence income —f. MUS. half note, minim; METEOROL. minimum temperature.
mi·nis·te·rial adj. ministerial.
mi·nis·te·rio m. ministry; (cuerpo de ministros) cabinet ♦ **M. de Agricultura** Department of

Agriculture • **M. de Comercio** Department of Commerce • **M. de Hacienda** Treasury Department • **M. de Guerra** Defense Department • **M. de Trabajo** Department of Labor • **M. de Marina** Department of the Navy • **M. de Relaciones Exteriores** State Department.

mi·nis·trar tr. to hold office.

mi·nis·tro m.f. minister ♦ **M. de Agricultura** Secretary of Agriculture • **M. de Comercio** Secretary of Commerce • **M. de Hacienda** Secretary of the Treasury • **M. de Guerra** Defense Secretary • **M. de Marina** Secretary of the Navy • **M. de Relaciones Exteriores** Secretary of State • **primer m.** POL. prime minister.

mi·no·ra·ción f. diminution, reduction.

mi·no·rar tr. to diminish, reduce.

mi·no·rí·a/rí·dad f. minority.

mi·no·ris·ta I. adj. retail **II.** m.f. retailer.

mi·no·ri·ta·rio, a I. adj. minority **II.** m.f. member of a minority.

min·tie·ra, tió see **mentir**.

mi·nu·cia f. small thing, trifle.

mi·nu·cio·so, a adj. thorough, minute.

mi·nús·cu·lo, a I. adj. *(muy pequeño)* minuscule, tiny; *(insignificante)* insignificant ♦ **letra m.** small *or* lowercase letter **II.** f. small *or* lowercase letter.

mi·nu·ta f. *(borrador)* rough draft; *(acta)* minutes, record; *(nota)* note, memorandum; *(cuenta)* lawyer's bill; *(de una comida)* menu, bill of fare.

mi·nu·te·ro m. minute hand.

mi·nu·to m. minute ♦ **al m.** at once.

mí·o, a I. adj. mine *<estos libros son míos* these books are mine>; of mine *<un amigo m.* a friend of mine>; my *<¡Dios m.!* my God!>; *(querido)* my dear *<madre m.* my dear mother>* **II.** pron. mine *<¿dónde está el m.?* where is mine?> ♦ **ésta es la m.** COLL. this is my big chance • **lo m.** my affair, my business • **los míos** my people, my folks.

mio·pe I. adj. myopic, nearsighted **II.** m.f. myope, myopic person.

mio·pí·a f. myopia, nearsightedness.

mi·ra f. ARM., TECH. sight; *(intención)* aim, intention ♦ **con miras a** with an eye to, with a view to • **estar a la m. de** COLL. to be on the lookout for • **poner la m. en** to aim to, aspire to.

mi·ra·do, a I. adj. *(circunspecto)* cautious, circumspect; regarded *<mal m.* ill-regarded> **II.** f. *(acción)* look, glance; *(apariencia)* look, expression ♦ **echar una m.** to cast a glance at • **m. fija** stare • **m. perdida** distant look.

mi·ra·dor, ·ra I. adj. looking, watching **II.** m.f. *(observador)* observer, spectator —m. *(balcón)* balcony, terrace.

mi·rar tr. *(ver)* to look at; *(observar)* to watch, observe; *(contemplar)* to gaze at; *(reflexionar)* to think about, consider ♦ **m. bien** *or* **con buenos ojos** to look with favor on, approve of • **m. de arriba abajo** to look up and down • **m. de hito en hito** to stare at • **m. de reojo** to look askance at • **m. de soslayo** to look sideways at • **m. mal** *or* **con malos ojos** to disapprove of • **m. por** to look out for, look after *<sólo miran por sus intereses* they only look out for their own interests>; to look out (of) *<miraban por la ventana* they were looking out the window> • **m. por encima** to glance at, look over • **m. por encima del hombro** to look down on —intr. *(ver)* to look; *(observar)* to watch; *(dar a)* to

look out on, overlook *<el balcón mira a la plaza* the balcony overlooks the plaza> ♦ **¡mira!** *(como advertencia)* watch out!, be careful!; *(como amenaza)* look here! • **mire** well, let me say this —reflex. to look at oneself *<me miré en el espejo* I looked at myself in the mirror>; to look at one another *<se miraban con amor* they looked at one another lovingly> ♦ **m. unos a otros** FIG. to look at each other helplessly.

mi·ra·sol m. sunflower.

mi·rí·a·da f. myriad.

mi·ri·lla f. *(para observar)* peephole; SURV. target, sight.

mir·lo m. blackbird.

mi·rón, o·na adj. & m.f. nosy *or* inquisitive (person).

mi·sa f. Mass ♦ **decir m.** to say *or* celebrate Mass • **m. de difuntos** *or* **de requiem** Requiem Mass • **m. de gallo** Midnight Mass • **m. mayor** High Mass • **m. rezada** Low Mass.

mi·sán·tro·po m. misanthrope.

mis·ce·lá·ne·o, a I. adj. miscellaneous **II.** f. miscellany.

mi·se·ra·ble I. adj. *(pobre)* poor, wretched; *(tacaño)* stingy, miserly; *(lastimoso)* miserable, pitiful; *(despreciable)* despicable, vile ♦ **¡m. de mí!** woe is me! **II.** m.f. *(pobre)* wretch, unfortunate person; *(tacaño)* miser, skinflint; *(canalla)* cad, scoundrel.

mi·se·ria f. *(infortunio)* misery, suffering; *(pobreza)* poverty; *(avaricia)* stinginess, miserliness; COLL. *(cosa pequeña)* pittance ♦ **estar en la m.** to be down and out.

mi·se·ri·cor·dia f. mercy, compassion.

mi·se·ri·cor·dio·so, a adj. & m.f. compassionate *or* merciful (person).

mí·se·ro, a adj. wretched, unfortunate.

mi·sil m. missile.

mi·sión f. mission.

mi·sio·nal adj. missionary.

mi·sio·ne·ro, a adj. & m.f. missionary.

mi·si·va f. missive, letter.

mis·mo, a adj. *(idéntico)* same *<leí el m. libro* I read the same book>; *(exacto)* very *<en ese m. momento* at that very moment> ♦ **ahora m.** right now • **así m.** *(de esta manera)* in the same way, likewise; *(también)* also • **lo m.** the same thing • **por lo m.** for that reason, for that very reason • **yo m.** I myself.

mi·so·gi·nia f. misogyny.

mis·te·rio m. mystery.

mis·te·rio·so, a adj. mysterious.

mis·ti·cis·mo m. mysticism.

mís·ti·co, a I. adj. mystic(al) **II.** m.f. mystic —f. mystical theology.

mis·ti·fi·car §70 tr. to mystify, trick.

mis·tu·ra f. mixture.

mi·tad f. *(una de dos partes)* half *<la m. de la población* half of the population>; *(medio)* middle *<durante la m. de la película* during the middle of the movie> ♦ **a** *or* **en la m. de** in the middle of • **mi cara m.** COLL. my better half • **por la m.** in half, in two.

mí·ti·co, a adj. mythic(al).

mi·ti·ga·ción f. mitigation.

mi·ti·ga·dor, ·ra/gan·te I. adj. mitigating **II.** m.f. mitigator.

mi·ti·gar §47 tr. to mitigate.

mi·tin m. [pl. **mí·ti·nes**] meeting, rally.

mi·to m. *(relato)* myth; *(leyenda)* myth, legend.

mi·to·lo·gí·a f. mythology.

mi·to·lo·gis·ta/tó·lo·go m. mythologist.

mi·tón m. mitt.

mi·tra f. *(toca de obispo)* miter; *(obispado)* bishopric; *(arzobispado)* archbishopric.

mix·to, a I. adj. *(mezclado)* mixed; *(mestizo)* of mixed race **II.** m. explosive compound.

mix·tu·ra f. *(mezcla)* mixture; PHARM. compound, mixture.

mix·tu·rar tr. to mix.

mne·mo·tec·nia/téc·ni·ca f. mnemonics.

mne·mo·téc·ni·co, a adj. mnemonic.

mo·bi·lia·rio, a I. adj. movable **II.** m. furniture, furnishings.

mo·bla·je m. furniture, furnishings.

mo·blar §19 tr. to furnish.

mo·ca·sín m. moccasin.

mo·ce·dad f. youth.

mo·char tr. to hack *or* lop off.

mo·cha·zo m. blow with a rifle butt.

mo·chi·la f. *(de caminante)* pack, knapsack; *(de cazador)* game bag; MIL. ration.

mo·cho, a I. adj. *(sin punta)* blunt; *(sin cuernos)* hornless; COLL. *(pelado)* shorn, cropped **II.** m. *(mango)* handle; *(culata)* stock, butt.

mo·ción f. motion.

mo·co m. mucus; COLL. snot ♦ **limpiarse los mocos** COLL. to blow one's nose ♦ **llorar a m. tendido** COLL. to cry like a baby.

mo·co·so, a I. adj. snotty, bratty **II.** m.f. snotty kid, brat.

mo·da f. style, fashion ♦ **a la m.** *or* **de m.** fashionable, in fashion ♦ **estar** *or* **ser de m.** to be in fashion ♦ **fuera de m.** out of fashion ♦ **pasado de m.** old-fashioned ♦ **pasarse de m.** to go out of fashion ♦ **ponerse de m.** to come into fashion ♦ **ser la última m.** to be the latest fashion.

mo·dal I. adj. modal **II.** m.pl. manners, behavior.

mo·da·li·dad f. modality, nature.

mo·de·lar tr. to model —reflex. to model oneself after someone, emulate.

mo·de·lo I. m. model —m.f. fashion model ♦ **desfile de modelos** fashion show • **m. a escala** scale model **II.** adj. model, exemplary.

mo·de·ra·ción f. moderation.

mo·de·ra·do, a adj. & m.f. moderate.

mo·de·ra·dor, ·ra I. adj. moderating **II.** m.f. moderator —m. PHYS. moderator.

mo·de·rar tr. *(templar)* to moderate, regulate; *(contener)* contain, restrain —reflex. to contain *or* restrain oneself.

mo·der·nis·ta I. adj. modernist, modernistic **II.** m.f. modernist.

mo·der·ni·za·ción f. modernization.

mo·der·ni·zar §04 tr. to modernize.

mo·der·no, a I. adj. modern **II.** m.f. modern ♦ **a la moderna** *or* **a lo moderno** in the modern manner *or* fashion.

mo·des·tia f. modesty.

mo·des·to, a adj. & m.f. modest (person).

mó·di·co, a adj. moderate, reasonable.

mo·di·fi·ca·ción f. modification.

mo·di·fi·ca·dor, ·ra I. adj. modifying **II.** m.f. modifier.

mo·di·fi·car §70 tr. to modify —reflex. to change, become modified.

mo·dis·mo m. idiom, idiomatic expression.

mo·dis·ta m.f. dressmaker, modiste.

mo·dis·te·rí·a f. dress shop.

mo·do m. *(manera)* manner, way; GRAM. mood; MUS. mode ♦ **a mi m.** in my own way • **del mismo m.** in the same way • **de m. que** so that

• **de ningún m.** by no means • **de todos modos** at any rate, in any case • **en cierto m.** to a certain extent • **m. de ser** character, way of being ♦ pl. manners.

mo·do·rra f. drowsiness, heaviness.

mo·do·so, a adj. well-behaved, well-mannered.

mo·du·la·ción f. modulation ♦ **m. de amplitud** RAD. amplitude modulation, AM • **m. de frecuencia** RAD. frequency modulation, FM.

mo·du·la·dor, ·ra I. adj. modulating **II.** m.f. modulator.

mo·du·lar tr. & intr. to modulate.

mó·du·lo m. ARCHIT. module; PHYS. modulus; MUS. modulation ♦ **m. lunar** lunar module.

mo·fa f. mockery, ridicule ♦ **hacer m. de** to mock, ridicule.

mo·far intr. & reflex. to mock, ridicule ♦ **mofarse de** to mock, ridicule.

mo·he·cer §17 tr. *(hacer mohoso)* to make moldy; *(aherrumbrar)* to make rusty —reflex. *(hacerse mohoso)* to mildew; *(aherrumbrarse)* to rust.

mo·hín m. grimace, face ♦ **hacer mohines** to grimace, make faces.

mo·hí·no, a I. adj. *(triste)* sad, melancholy; *(enfadado)* ill-humored, sulky **II.** —m. ORNITH. blue magpie —f. *(enojo)* anger, displeasure; *(melancolía)* sadness, melancholy.

mo·ho m. *(hongo)* mold, mildew; *(herrumbre)* rust, corrosion; *(desidia)* laziness, indolence ♦ **criar m.** to get moldy.

mo·ho·so, a adj. *(lleno de hongos)* moldy, mildewed; *(herrumbroso)* rusty, corroded.

mo·ja·dor, ·ra I. adj. wetting **II.** m.f. wetter —m. PRINT. moistening tank; *(esponja)* sponge.

mo·jar tr. *(humedecer)* to wet, make wet; *(empapar)* to drench, soak; *(pan)* to dip <mojar el pan en aceite to dip the bread in oil> —reflex. to get wet.

mo·ja·se·llos m.inv. moistener, sponge (for stamps).

mo·je m. gravy, juice.

mo·ji·gan·ga f. *(fiesta de máscaras)* masquerade, costume party; THEAT. farce, comedy; *(burla)* mockery, joke.

mo·ji·ga·te·rí·a f. *(hipocresía)* hypocrisy, dissimulation; *(santurronería)* sanctimoniousness.

mo·ji·ga·to, a I. adj. *(hipócrita)* hypocritical; *(santurrón)* sanctimonious **II.** m.f. *(hipócrita)* hypocrite; *(santurrón)* sanctimonious person.

mo·jón m. *(de término)* boundary marker; *(de guía)* road marker.

mo·jo·nar tr. to set up boundary markers around.

mo·jo·ne·ro m. appraiser, assessor.

mo·lar adj. & m. molar.

mol·de m. mold; *(forma)* pattern, model; *(persona ejemplar)* model; PRINT. form ready for printing ♦ **de m.** fitting, opportune • **letra de m.** print • **venir de m.** *or* **venir como de m.** to be just what one needs.

mol·de·a·do m. molding, casting.

mol·de·ar tr. *(sacar el molde)* to mold, shape; *(vaciar)* to cast.

mo·lé·cu·la f. molecule.

mo·le·cu·lar adj. molecular.

mo·le·dor, ·ra I. adj. grinding **II.** m. grinder.

mo·ler §78 tr. *(trigo)* to grind, mill; *(caña)* to press; *(cansar)* to exhaust, drain; *(destruir)* to beat up, cream ♦ **m. a golpes** *or* **palos** to beat to a pulp.

mo·les·tar tr. (*fastidiar*) to bother, annoy; (*interrumpir*) to disturb, disrupt; (*causar dolor*) to bother, trouble —reflex. to bother, take the trouble ♦ **no se moleste** don't bother.

mo·les·tia f. (*fastidio*) bother, annoyance; (*incomodidad*) inconvenience, trouble; (*malestar*) discomfort ♦ **si no es m.** if it isn't too much trouble.

mo·les·to, a adj. (*fastidioso*) bothersome, annoying; (*enojado*) bothered, annoyed; (*incómodo*) uncomfortable, awkward; (*inconveniente*) inconvenient, troublesome.

mo·li·do, a adj. (*aplastado*) ground, milled; (*derrengado*) beat, worn-out.

mo·lien·da f. (*acción*) grinding, milling; (*molino*) mill; (*temporada*) milling season.

mo·li·fi·car §70 tr. to mollify, soften.

mo·li·mien·to m. grinding, milling.

mo·li·ne·ro, a I. adj. milling II. m. miller, grinder.

mo·li·ne·te m. (*ventilador*) ventilating fan; (*juguete de papel*) pinwheel.

mo·li·ni·llo m. (*para moler*) mill, grinder; (*para batir*) whisk, beater.

mo·li·no m. mill ♦ **m. de viento** windmill ♦ **molinos de viento** imaginary enemies.

mo·llar adj. soft, tender.

mo·lle·ra f. (*cráneo*) crown (of the head); (*fontanela*) fontanelle; (*seso*) brains, ability ♦ **cerrado de m.** COLL. stupid.

mo·lus·co m. mollusk.

mo·men·tá·ne·o, a adj. momentary.

mo·men·to m. moment; (*ocasión*) occasion, time ♦ **a cada m.** continually, at every instant • **a partir de este m.** from this moment (on) • **al m.** immediately, at once • **de m.** at present, for the moment • **de un m. a otro** any moment, from one minute to the next • **dentro de un m.** in a moment • **desde este m.** from this moment (on) • **¡m.!** just a minute! • **momentos después** moments later.

mo·mi·fi·car §70 tr. to mummify —reflex. to become mummified.

mo·mio, a I. adj. lean, thin II. m. cushy job —f. mummy ♦ **estar hecho una m.** to be all skin and bones.

mo·mo m. funny face.

mo·na f. (*hembra*) female monkey; COLL. (*mimo*) mimic; (*borrachera*) drunkenness; MEX. coward ♦ **coger** or **pillar una m.** COLL. to get loaded or plastered • **dormir la m.** COLL. to sleep it off.

mo·na·cal adj. monastic.

mo·na·da f. (*gesto*) monkey or funny face; (*cosa o persona graciosa*) pretty or lovely thing.

mo·na·gui·llo m. acolyte, altar boy.

mo·nar·ca m. monarch, sovereign.

mo·nar·quí·a f. monarchy.

mo·nár·qui·co, a I. adj. monarchic(al) II. m.f. monarchist.

mo·nas·te·rio m. monastery.

mo·nás·ti·co, a adj. monastic(al).

mon·da f. (*limpieza*) cleaning; (*poda*) pruning, trimming; (*peladura*) peeling, skinning; (*parte podada*) trimmings; (*parte pelada*) peelings, peels.

mon·da·dien·tes m.inv. toothpick.

mon·da·dor, ·ra I. adj. (*podador*) pruning, trimming; (*que pela*) peeling II. m.f. (*podador*) pruner, trimmer; (*pelador*) peeler.

mon·da·du·ra f. (*poda*) pruning, trimming; (*peladura*) peeling; (*parte podada*) trimmings;

(*parte pelada*) peelings.

mon·dar tr. (*fruta*) to peel, skin; (*nueces*) to shell; (*podar*) to prune, trim.

mo·ne·da f. coin; FIN. mint; COLL. (*caudal*) wealth, money ♦ **acuñar m.** to mint money • **m. corriente** currency • **pagar con la misma m.** to give someone a taste of his own medicine.

mo·ne·de·ro m. change purse.

mo·ne·rí·a f. (*monada*) cute or amusing thing; (*gesto*) funny or monkey face; (*tontería*) silliness, foolishness.

mo·ne·ta·rio, a I. adj. monetary II. m. coin collection.

mo·ne·ti·zar §04 tr. (*amonedar*) to mint coin; (*dar curso legal*) to monetize.

mon·gó·li·co, a adj. & m.f. MED. mongoloid.

mon·go·lis·mo m. mongolism, Down's syndrome.

mo·nín, i·na adj. COLL. cute, pretty.

mo·ni·tor m. (*admonitor*) monitor, adviser; (*entrenador*) trainer; COMPUT. monitor.

mon·ja f. nun; MEX. round sweet bread.

mon·je m. (*fraile*) monk; (*solitario*) recluse.

mo·no, a I. adj. COLL. cute, darling II. m. monkey, ape; (*imitador*) mimic, ape; (*traje*) coveralls.

mo·nó·cu·lo, a m. (*lente*) monocle; (*vendaje*) eye patch.

mo·no·ga·mia f. monogamy.

mo·nó·ga·mo, a adj. monogamous.

mo·no·gra·fí·a f. monograph.

mo·no·gra·ma m. monogram.

mo·no·lin·güe adj. monolingual.

mo·no·li·to m. monolith.

mo·no·lo·gar §47 intr. to soliloquize.

mo·nó·lo·go m. monologue, soliloquy.

mo·no·pla·no m. monoplane.

mo·no·po·lio m. monopoly.

mo·no·po·li·zar §04 tr. to monopolize.

mo·no·to·ní·a f. monotony.

mo·nó·to·no, a adj. monotonous.

mons·truo m. monster.

mons·truo·si·dad f. monstrosity.

mons·truo·so, a adj. monstrous.

mon·ta f. (*acción*) mounting; (*suma*) sum, total ♦ **de poca m.** of no account, insignificant.

mon·ta·car·gas m.inv. freight elevator.

mon·ta·do, a I. adj. (*que va a caballo*) mounted; (*caballo*) saddled; (*máquina*) assembled; THEAT. staged II. m. assembly.

mon·ta·je m. assembly, installation; CINEM. montage ♦ **cadena de m.** assembly line.

mon·tan·te m. (*de una armazón*) upright, strut; (*ventana*) transom; (*listón*) mullion.

mon·ta·ña f. mountain; FIG. mountain, heap ♦ **hacer de todo una m.** to make a mountain out of a molehill • **m. rusa** rollercoaster ♦ pl. highlands.

mon·ta·ñe·ro, a m.f. mountaineer, mountain climber.

mon·ta·ñés, e·sa I. adj. mountain, highland II. m.f. mountain dweller, highlander.

mon·ta·ño·so, a adj. mountainous.

mon·ta·pla·tos m.inv. dumbwaiter.

mon·tar intr. (*subir*) to mount, get on; (*subir a caballo*) to mount a horse; (*cabalgar*) to ride (horseback); (*alcanzar*) to reach ♦ **m. a caballo** to ride horseback • **m. en** to ride <*m. en bicicleta* to ride a bicycle> • **m. en cólera** to get angry —tr. (*subir*) to mount <*m. un caballo* to mount a horse>; (*valer*) to mount or amount to <*sus cuentas montaron mil dólares* his bills mounted to one thousand dollars>; *(armar)* to assemble, set up; *(establecer)* to set up <m. un negocio to set up a business>; CINEM. to edit; THEAT. to produce; JEWEL. to set; *(acoplar)* to mount.

mon·te m. *(montaña)* mount, mountain; *(bosque)* forest, woodland; COLL. *(establecimiento)* pawnshop; *(juego de naipes)* monte ✦ **m. alto** forest, woodland (with tall trees) • **m. bajo** brush, brushwood.

mon·te pí·o m. pawnshop.

mon·tés adj. wild, undomesticated.

mon·tí·cu·lo m. knoll, hillock.

mon·to m. amount, total.

mon·tón m. *(acopio)* pile, heap; COLL. *(mucho)* heaps, lots ✦ **a montones** by the truckload ✦ **del m.** COLL. ordinary, average • **ser del m.** COLL. to be one of the herd.

mon·tu·ra f. *(cabalgadura)* mount; *(silla)* saddle, mount; *(de una máquina)* assembly, installation; JEWEL. setting.

mo·nu·men·tal adj. monumental, huge.

mo·nu·men·to m. monument.

mon·zón m.f. monsoon.

mo·ño m. *(de la mujer)* bun, chignon; *(lazo)* bow, knot; ORNITH. crest.

mo·que·ar intr. to snivel, have a runny nose.

mo·ra·do, a I. adj. purple, violet **II.** m. purple —f. *(casa)* house, dwelling; *(estancia)* stay, sojourn.

mo·ra·dor, ·ra I. adj. living, residing **II.** m.f. tenant, resident.

mo·ral I. adj. moral **II.** f. *(ética)* morals, ethics; *(ánimo)* morale, spirits.

mo·ra·le·ja f. moral.

mo·ra·li·dad f. morality; *(moraleja)* moral.

mo·ra·li·zar §04 tr. & intr. to moralize.

mo·rar intr. to live, reside.

mo·ra·to·ria f. moratorium.

mor·bi·dez f. softness, delicateness.

mór·bi·do, a adj. soft, delicate; MED. morbid.

mor·bi·li·dad/di·dad f. morbidity.

mor·bo·si·dad f. morbidity, disease.

mor·bo·so, a adj. *(no sano)* morbid; *(enfermo)* sick, diseased.

mor·ci·lla f. CUL. blood pudding or sausage; THEAT., coll. ad lib, improvisation ✦ **¡que te den m.!** COLL. take a walk!, get lost!

mor·da·ci·dad f. mordacity.

mor·daz adj. *(corrosivo)* corrosive, mordant; *(picante)* burning, pungent; *(punzante)* biting, mordant.

mor·da·za f. *(silencio)* gag; TECH. clamp.

mor·de·du·ra f. bite.

mor·der §78 tr. to bite; *(mordiscar)* to nibble (at); *(asir)* to bite, grip; ARTS, PRINT. to etch —intr. to bite.

mor·dien·te I. adj. mordant, biting **II.** m. *(agua fuerte)* caustic acid; *(de tintorero)* color fixative.

mor·dis·car §70/que·ar tr. to nibble (at).

mor·dis·co m. nibble, bite ✦ **dar** or **pegar un m.** to take a bite (of).

mo·re·no, a I. adj. *(pardo)* brown; *(tostado)* brown-skinned, dark-skinned; *(pelo)* brown, brunet; AMER., COLL. *(mulato)* mulatto **II.** m.f. *(negro)* Black, Negro; *(de pelo castaño)* brunet, brunette; AMER. *(mulato)* mulatto.

mor·fi·na f. morphine.

mor·fo·lo·gí·a f. morphology.

mor·gue f. morgue.

mo·ri·bun·do, a adj. moribund, dying

II. m.f. dying person.

mo·rir §27 intr. to die; *(extinguirse)* to die, go out; *(desaparecer)* to die, die out ✦ **m. ahogado** to drown • **m. ahorcado** to be hanged • **m. de frío** to freeze to death • **m. de risa** to die laughing • **m. fusilado** to be shot —reflex. *(fallecer)* to die; *(extinguirse)* to die, go out ✦ **m. de aburrimiento** to be bored to death • **m. de ganas** to be dying to • **m. por** *(estar loco por)* to be crazy about; *(querer)* to be dying to <me muero por ir a Francia I am dying to go to France>.

mo·ro·si·dad f. *(lentitud)* slowness; *(demora)* delay, lateness; *(falta de actividad)* inactivity.

mo·ro·so, a adj. *(lento)* slow; *(perezoso)* lazy; *(tardío)* tardy; *(en el pago)* in arrears, delinquent.

mo·rro m. snout, nose.

mo·rru·do, a adj. *(que tiene hocico)* snouted; *(que tiene labios gruesos)* thick-lipped; R.P. brawny.

mor·sa f. walrus.

mor·se m. Morse code.

mor·ta·ja f. shroud.

mor·tal I. adj. mortal; FIG. dreadful, awful **II.** m. man, mortal.

mor·ta·li·dad f. mortality.

mor·tan·dad f. death toll, mortality.

mor·te·ci·no, a adj. dying, fading.

mor·te·ro m. mortar.

mor·tí·fe·ro, a adj. fatal, lethal.

mor·ti·fi·ca·ción f. mortification; FIG. annoyance.

mor·ti·fi·ca·dor, ·ra adj. mortifying.

mor·ti·fi·can·te adj. mortifying.

mor·ti·fi·car §70 tr. to mortify, FIG. to annoy.

mor·tuo·rio, a I. adj. mortuary, funereal **II.** m. funeral.

mos·ca f. fly; *(cebo)* fly (for fishing); COLL. *(dinero)* dough, bread; COLL. *(persona)* pest, pain in the neck ✦ **aflojar** or **soltar la m.** COLL. to fork it out or over, cough it up • **cazar moscas** COLL. to waste time • **m. muerta** COLL. hypocrite • **no matar una m.** not to hurt a fly • **papar moscas** to daydream • **peso m.** lightweight • **por si las moscas** just in case —m. MEX. stowaway, tramp.

mos·ca·tel m. muscatel.

mos·que·ar tr. *(ahuyentar moscas)* to swat; *(responder)* to answer back (with a fresh remark) —intr. MEX. to travel as a tramp, stow away.

mos·que·ro m. *(trampa)* flytrap; AMER. swarm of flies.

mos·que·te m. musket.

mos·qui·te·ro m. mosquito net.

mos·qui·to m. mosquito; *(mosca pequeña)* gnat, midge.

mos·ta·za f. mustard; *(mostacilla)* bird shot.

mos·to m. *(zumo)* must; COLL. *(vino)* wine.

mos·tra·dor, ·ra I. adj. demonstrative **II.** m.f. demonstrator —m. counter, table top.

mos·trar §19 tr. *(enseñar)* to show; *(explicar)* to demonstrate, show; *(indicar)* to point out; *(expresar)* to show, express —reflex. *(darse a conocer)* to show oneself or prove to be <se muestra buen profesor he shows himself to be a good professor>; *(aparecer)* to show oneself, appear.

mos·tren·co, a I. adj. ownerless <bienes mostrencos ownerless property> **II.** m.f. COLL. *(persona ruda)* dolt; *(persona torpe)* dim-witted person.

mo·te¹ m. *(enigma)* riddle; *(divisa)* motto; *(apodo)* nickname ♦ **poner m. a alguien** to nickname someone.

mo·te² m. AMER. stewed corn.

mo·tel m. motel.

mo·tín m. insurrection, riot.

mo·ti·va·ción f. motivation.

mo·ti·var tr. *(causar)* to motivate, cause; *(explicar)* to explain; *(justificar)* justify.

mo·ti·vo m. *(causa)* motive, cause; MUS. theme; ART. motif ♦ **bajo ningún m.** under no circumstances • **con mayor m.** even more so • **dar m.** to give cause • **no ser m. para** to be no reason to *or* for • **sin m.** without reason.

mo·to f. COLL. cycle, motorcycle.

mo·to·ci·cle·ta f. motorcycle.

mo·to·ci·clis·ta I. adj. motorcycle II. m.f. motorcyclist.

mo·to·náu·ti·ca I. adj. motorboat II. f. motorboating.

mo·to·na·ve f. motorboat, motor ship.

mo·tor, ·ra I. adj. motor II. m. motor engine ♦ **m. auxiliar** booster (engine) • **m. de arranque** starter • **m. de cilindro en V** V-engine • **m. de cohete** rocket engine • **m. de combustión interna** *or* **de explosión** internal combustion engine • **m. de reacción** *or* **de chorro** jet engine • **m. de vapor** steam engine • **m. diesel** diesel (engine) • **m. fuera de borda** outboard motor.

mo·to·ris·ta m.f. *(motociclista)* motorcyclist; *(de automóvil)* motorist.

mo·to·ri·zar §04 tr. to motorize.

mo·ve·di·zo, a adj. *(que se mueve)* moving, shifting; *(inconstante)* fickle, changeable ♦ **arenas movedizas** quicksand.

mo·ver §78 tr. to move; *(agitar)* to move about, stir; *(la cabeza)* to shake; MECH. to drive, power; *(inducir)* to induce, move; *(incitar)* to incite, provoke; *(conmover)* to excite, stir ♦ **m. a** to move to <m. a compasión to move to pity> —intr. ARCHIT. to spring; AGR. to sprout, bud —reflex. to move.

mo·vi·ble adj. movable.

mo·vi·do, a adj. *(persona)* active, lively; *(mar)* choppy, rough; *(fotografía)* fuzzy, blurry.

mó·vil I. adj. *(que puede moverse)* mobile, movable; *(inestable)* unstable, variable II. m. *(motivo)* motive, reason; PHYS. moving body; ARTS mobile.

mo·vi·li·dad f. mobility.

mo·vi·li·za·ción f. mobilization.

mo·vi·li·zar §04 tr. to mobilize.

mo·vi·mien·to m. *(acción)* movement, motion; *(efecto)* move, movement; *(actividad)* activity, movement; *(sentimiento)* feeling; MECH. motion; MIL., MUS. movement; COM. activity ♦ **m. perpetuo** perpetual motion • **m. sísmico** earth tremor ♦ **poner en m.** to put in motion.

mo·zo, a I. adj. young II. m. *(camarero)* waiter; *(tentemozo)* prop, shore ♦ **buen m.** AMER. handsome • **m. de caballos** stable boy, groom • **m. de cordel** *or* **de cuerda** porter —f. girl ♦ **buena m.** AMER. good-looking.

mo·zue·lo, a m.f. *(muchacho)* lad; *(muchacha)* girl.

mu·cha·cha·da f. AMER. group of youngsters.

mu·cha·cho, a m.f. *(niño)* child, youngster; COLL. *(adolescente)* youth, kid —m. *(chico)* boy; *(mozo)* houseboy, servant —f. *(chica)* girl; *(moza)* maid, servant.

mu·che·dum·bre f. multitude, crowd.

mu·cho, a I. adj. *(abundante)* much, a lot of <m. agua a lot of water>; very <hace m. frío it is very cold> ♦ pl. many, a lot of <muchos problemas many problems> II. pron. a lot <¿tienes dinero? no, pero mi amiga tiene m. do you have any money? no, but my friend has a lot> ♦ pl. many <muchos vinieron tarde many came late> III. adv. a lot, much <ellos trabajan m. they work a lot>; much <m. después much later>; *(largo tiempo)* for a long time <hace m. que viven en Portugal they have lived in Portugal for a long time> ♦ **ni m. menos** not by a long shot, far from it • **por m. que** however much, no matter how much • **tener en m.** to hold in high regard, think a lot of.

mu·ci·la·go/ci·la·go m. mucilage.

mu·co·si·dad f. mucosity.

mu·co·so, a adj. & f. mucous (membrane).

mu·cus m. mucus.

mu·da f. *(de ropa)* change of clothing; *(de plumas)* molting, molt; *(tiempo)* molting season.

mu·da·ble adj. *(cambiable)* changeable; *(inconstante)* inconstant, fickle.

mu·dan·za f. *(cambio)* change; *(traslado)* move, moving; *(figura de baile)* figure; *(inconstancia)* inconstancy, fickleness ♦ **estar de m.** to be moving.

mu·dar tr. *(cambiar)* to change; *(trasladar)* to move; ORNITH., ZOOL. to molt, shed ♦ **m. de idea** *or* **de opinión** to change one's mind —reflex. *(cambiarse)* to change; *(trasladarse)* to move.

mu·dez f. dumbness, muteness.

mu·do, a I. adj. *(que no puede hablar)* mute, dumb; *(silencioso)* silent, mute; GRAM. silent II. m.f. dumb *or* mute person.

mue·bla·je m. furniture.

mue·ble I. adj. movable II. m. piece of furniture ♦ pl. furniture.

mue·ble, blo see **moblar.**

mue·ble·rí·a f. furniture store.

mue·ca f. face, grimace ♦ **hacer muecas** to make faces.

mue·la f. *(de molino)* millstone; *(de afilar)* grindstone, whetstone; ANAT. molar ♦ **m. de juicio** wisdom tooth.

mue·la, lo see **moler.**

mue·lle¹ I. adj. *(blando)* soft, tender; *(elástico)* elastic, springy II. m. spring.

mue·lle² m. pier, dock; RAIL. loading platform.

mue·ra, re see **morir.**

muer·da, do see **morder.**

muér·da·go m. mistletoe.

muer·te f. death; *(homicidio)* murder, homicide ♦ **a m.** to the death <un duelo a m. a duel to the death>; *(implacablemente)* to the death, relentlessly <odiar a m. to hate relentlessly> • **de mala m.** COLL. crummy, lousy • **de m.** seriously, fatally <enfermo de m. fatally ill> • **hasta la m.** until death.

muer·to, a I. see **morir** II. adj. dead; *(apagado)* lifeless; *(marchito)* faded; *(cansado)* exhausted ♦ **más m. que vivo** half-dead • **m. de** dying of <estoy m. de sed I am dying of thirst> • **no tener dónde caerse m.** COLL. to be penniless III. m.f. *(difunto)* dead person; *(cadáver)* corpse ♦ **cargar con el m.** COLL. to be left holding the bag • **echarle el m. a** COLL. to put the blame on • **hacerse el m.** COLL. to play possum, play dead • **los muertos** the dead.

mues·tra¹ f. *(ejemplo)* sample, specimen; *(señal)* sign, indication <una m. de buena fe an

indication of good faith>; (*modelo*) model, guide ✦ **dar muestras de** to show signs of.

mues·tra² f. show, exhibition.

mues·tre, tro see mostrar.

mue·va, ve see mover.

mu·gir §32 intr. (*las vacas*) to moo; (*los toros*) to bellow; (*bramar*) to roar, howl.

mu·gre f. filth, grime.

mu·grien·to, a adj. filthy, grimy.

mu·gue·te m. lily of the valley.

mu·jer f. (*hembra*) woman; (*esposa*) wife ✦ **m. de la limpieza** cleaning woman • **m. de su casa** housewife, homemaker • **m. de la vida** *or* **de mal vivir** prostitute.

mu·je·rie·go, a adj. womanizing, philandering ✦ **ser un m.** to be a womanizer *or* ladies' man.

mu·la f. female mule ✦ **ser una m.** to be stubborn as a mule.

mu·la·to, a I. adj. (*de raza mixta*) mulatto; (*de color moreno*) dark, dark-skinned **II.** m.f. (*persona*) mulatto —m. AMER., MIN. dark silver ore.

mu·le·ro m. muleteer.

mu·le·ta f. (*para andar*) crutch; (*sostén*) crutch, support.

mu·lli·do, a I. adj. fluffy, soft **II.** m. stuffing, filling.

mu·llir §13 tr. (*esponjar*) to fluff (up); (*la tierra*) to loosen.

mu·lo m. mule; FIG. brute, beast.

mul·ta f. fine; AUTO. parking ticket.

mul·tar tr. to fine.

mul·ti·co·lor adj. multicolor.

mul·ti·co·pis·ta f. duplicating machine, copier.

mul·ti·mi·llo·na·rio, a adj. & m.f. multimillionaire.

mul·ti·na·cio·nal adj. multinational.

múl·ti·ple adj. multiple.

mul·ti·pli·ca·ción f. multiplication.

mul·ti·pli·car §70 tr. & reflex. to multiply.

mul·ti·pli·ci·dad f. muliplicity.

mul·ti·pro·ce·sa·dor adj. & m. COMPUT. multiprocessor.

mul·ti·tud f. multitude.

mul·ti·tu·di·na·rio, a adj. multitudinous.

mun·da·nal adj. worldly, mundane.

mun·da·no, a adj. (*del mundo*) worldly, mundane; (*que mundanea*) worldly-minded.

mun·dial I. adj. (*del mundo*) world <*guerra m.* world war>; (*universal*) worldwide, universal **II.** m. world championship <*m. de fútbol* world soccer championship>.

mun·do m. (*universo*) world; (*tierra*) earth; (*género humano*) world, society; (*agrupación*) world <*el m. de las artes* the art world> ✦ **correr el m.** to travel far and wide • **desde que el m. es m.** since time began • **echar al m.** to bring into the world, bring forth • **echarse al m.** to enter the life of prostitution • **irse al otro m.** to pass away • **medio m.** COLL. crowd of people, multitude • **no ser del otro m.** COLL. to be no big deal • **tener m.** to know one's way around • **todo el m.** everyone, everybody • **venir al m.** to come into the world, be born • **ver m.** to travel, see the world.

mu·ni·ción f. (*pertrechos*) ammunition, munitions; (*bastimentos*) provisions, rations.

mu·ni·cio·nar tr. (*con armas*) to munition, supply with munitions; (*con bastimentos*) to provision, provide with food *or* rations.

mu·ni·ci·pal adj. municipal.

mu·ni·ci·pa·li·dad f. municipality.

mu·ni·ci·pio m. (*ayuntamiento*) town council,

municipality; (*pueblo*) township, district.

mu·ni·fi·cen·cia f. munificence, generosity.

mu·ni·fi·cen·te adj. munificent, generous.

mu·ñe·ca f. wrist; (*juguete*) doll; (*maniquí*) mannequin; COLL. (*presumida*) conceited girl; (*muchacha bonita*) doll, pretty girl ✦ **m. de trapo** rag doll.

mu·ñe·co m. (*juguete*) doll; (*marioneta*) puppet.

mu·ñón m. stump.

mu·ral I. adj. & m. mural.

mu·ra·lis·ta I. adj. mural **II.** m.f. muralist.

mu·ra·lla f. wall, rampart.

mur·cié·la·go m. bat.

mu·rie·ra, rió see morir.

mur·mu·llo m. (*ruido sordo*) murmur, murmuring; (*de la gente*) murmur; (*del agua*) babbling, gurgle; (*del viento*) sighing, sigh; (*de las hojas*) rustling, rustle; (*queja*) grumble, complaint.

mur·mu·ra·ción f. gossip.

mur·mu·ra·dor, ·ra I. adj. (*murmurante*) murmuring; (*chismoso*) gossiping **II.** m.f. gossip.

mur·mu·rar intr. to murmur; (*hablar quedo*) to whisper; (*agua*) to babble, gurgle; (*viento*) to sigh; (*hojas*) to rustle; (*quejar*) to grumble; COLL. (*chismear*) to gossip.

mu·ro m. (*pared*) wall; (*muralla*) rampart.

mu·sa f. muse ✦ **las musas** the liberal arts.

mus·cu·lar adj. muscular.

mus·cu·la·tu·ra f. musculature.

mús·cu·lo m. muscle.

mus·cu·lo·so, a adj. muscular.

mu·se·o m. museum ✦ **m. de cera** wax museum.

mus·go m. moss.

mu·si·cal adj. & m. musical.

mú·si·co, a I. adj. musical **II.** m.f. (*instrumentista*) musician —f. (*arte*) music; (*papel*) sheet music; (*obra musical*) musical composition ✦ **irse con la m. a otra parte** COLL. to take one's troubles elsewhere • **m. de cámara** chamber music • **m. de fondo** background music • **m. y letra** words and music • **poner m. a** to set music to, set to music.

mu·si·co·lo·gí·a f. musicology.

mu·si·có·lo·go, a m.f. musicologist.

mu·si·tar tr. (*susurrar*) to whisper; (*murmurar*) to mumble, mutter.

mus·lo m. thigh; (*de pollo*) drumstick, leg.

mus·tiar·se reflex. to wither, become withered.

mus·tio, a adj. (*triste*) sad, gloomy; (*marchito*) withered, wilted; MEX. hypocritical.

mu·ta·bi·li·dad f. mutability.

mu·ta·ble adj. mutable.

mu·ta·ción f. mutation.

mu·ti·la·ción f. mutilation.

mu·ti·la·do, a I. adj. mutilated; (*inválido*) disabled **II.** m.f. disabled person, cripple ✦ **m. de guerra** disabled veteran.

mu·ti·lar tr. to mutilate; (*destruir*) to deface; (*acortar*) to cut up.

mu·tual I. adj. mutual **II.** f. mutual benefit society.

mu·tua·li·dad f. (*calidad*) mutuality; (*corporación*) mutual benefit society.

mu·tuo, a I. adj. mutual **II.** m. FIN., LAW loan, mutuum.

muy adv. very, quite <*m. alto* very tall>; greatly, quite <*estoy m. satisfecho* I am quite satisifed>; (*demasiado*) too <*ella es m. joven para ocupar ese puesto* she is too young to occupy that post>; quite a, very much a <*él es m.*

hombre he is quite a man> ♦ **m. de noche** late at night • **m. señor mío** Dear Sir ♦ **ser m. de** to be just like <*eso es m. de ella* that is just like her> ♦ **ser m. de su casa** COLL. to be a homebody.

N

n, N f. fourteenth letter of the Spanish alphabet.
na·bo m. *(planta)* turnip; ARCHIT. *(bolo)* newel, newel post; *(eje)* central pillar; MARIT. mast.
ná·car m. nacre, mother-of-pearl.
na·ca·ri·no/cá·re·o, a adj. nacreous.
na·cer §17 intr. *(venir al mundo)* to be born; *(salir del huevo)* to be hatched; *(germinar)* to sprout, begin to grow; *(florecer)* to bud, blossom; *(los astros)* to rise; *(brotar)* to rise, start to flow; *(provenir)* to stem or originate from <*el vicio nace de la ociosidad* vice stems from idleness>; *(originar)* to originate, be conceived ♦ **al n.** at birth • **n. de pie** COLL. to be born lucky • **n. para** to be born to <*nació para cantar* he was born to sing> ♦ **volver a n.** COLL. to have a narrow escape.
na·ci·do, a I. adj. born ♦ **bien n.** well-born, well-bred • **mal n.** ill-bred, mean • **recién n.** newborn II. m. human being ♦ **ningún n.** nobody • **todos los nacidos** everybody.
na·cien·te I. adj. *(que nace)* nascent; *(inicial)* incipient, initial; *(reciente)* recent, growing <*la n. curiosidad* the growing curiosity>; rising <*el sol n.* the rising sun> II. m. Orient, East.
na·ci·mien·to m. birth; *(de pájaros)* hatching; *(de ríos)* source; *(manantial)* spring; *(linaje)* descent, origin; *(natividad)* crèche, Nativity scene ♦ **dar n. a** to give rise to • **de n.** from birth ♦ **por n.** by birth.
na·ción f. nation; *(pueblo)* country, people.
na·cio·nal adj. national, domestic.
na·cio·na·li·dad f. nationality, citizenship ♦ **doble n.** dual citizenship.
na·cio·na·lis·ta adj. & m.f. nationalist.
na·cio·na·li·za·ción f. *(expropiación)* nationalization, expropriation; *(naturalización)* naturalization.
na·cio·na·li·zar §04 tr. *(convertir en nacional)* to nationalize; *(naturalizar)* to naturalize —reflex. to become naturalized.
na·da I. pron. nothing, not anything <*no he visto n.* I have not seen anything> ♦ **antes de n.** first, before anything else • **de n.** you're welcome • **n. de** no, none <*n. de quejas* no complaints> • **n. de eso** none of that, not at all • **n. menos** no less, nothing less • **ni n.** COLL. or anything <*no iré ni n.* I will not go or anything> • **no es n.** it's nothing • **no hay n. como** there is nothing like • **por n. del mundo** not for all the world II. adv. in no way, not at all <*no es n. extraño* it's not at all strange> III. f. *(inexistencia)* nothingness, nothing; *(cosa mínima)* the slightest thing <*una n. le hace llorar* the slightest thing makes him cry>.
na·da·dor, ·ra I. adj. swimming II. m.f. swimmer.
na·dar intr. to swim ♦ **n. de espalda** or **de pecho** to do the backstroke or breaststroke • **n. en** to have an abundance of • **n. entre dos aguas** to sit on the fence, be undecided.
na·de·rí·a f. insignificant thing, trifle.
na·die I. pron. nobody, no one II. m. a no-

body ♦ **no ser n.** to be a nobody • **un don n.** a nobody, an unimportant person.
naf·ta f. naphtha; AMER. gasoline.
naf·ta·li·na f. naphthalene; COLL. *(contra la polilla)* mothballs.
nai·pe m. card, playing card ♦ **barajar los naipes** to shuffle the cards • **castillo de n.** house of cards ♦ pl. deck (of cards).
nal·ga f. buttock ♦ pl. bottom, behind.
na·na f. COLL. *(abuela)* granny; *(arrullo)* lullaby; AMER. *(niñera)* nanny.
na·ran·ja I. f. orange —m. orange (color) ♦ **media n.** COLL. better half • **n. de ombligo** navel orange • **n. tangerina, mandarina** tangerine, mandarin orange II. adj. orange.
na·ran·ja·da f. orangeade.
na·ran·jal m. orange grove.
na·ran·je·ro, a I. adj. orange II.m.f. *(vendedor)* orange seller; *(cultivador)* orange grower.
na·ran·jo m. orange tree.
nar·ci·sis·ta I. adj. narcissistic II. m.f. narcissist.
nar·có·ti·co, a adj. & m. narcotic.
nar·co·ti·zan·te adj. & m.f. narcotic.
nar·co·ti·zar §04 tr. to narcotize, drug.
nar·co·tra·fi·can·te m. drug dealer.
nar·do m. nard, spikenard.
na·ri·gu·do, a adj. large-nosed.
na·riz f. nose; *(cada orificio)* nostril; *(olfato)* sense of smell; MECH. socket (of a bolt) ♦ **estar hasta las narices** to have had it up to here, be fed up • **fruncir** or **torcer la n.** COLL. to turn one's nose up at • **meter las narices en** COLL. to interfere, stick one's nose into • **n. aguileña** aquiline nose • **n. chata** pug nose • **n. respingada** or **respingona** snub nose • **no ver más allá de las narices** COLL. not to see past one's nose • **sonarse la n.** to blow one's nose • **tener de las narices** COLL. to lead around by the nose.
na·rra·ción f. *(narrativa)* narrative, account; *(acción)* narration.
na·rra·dor, ·ra I. adj. narrative II. m.f. narrator.
na·rrar tr. to narrate, relate.
na·rra·ti·vo, a I. adj. narrative II. f. *(narración)* narrative, account; *(habilidad)* narrative skill.
nar·val m. narwhal.
na·sal adj. & f. nasal.
na·ta f. *(crema)* cream; *(capa)* skim; *(lo mejor)* (the) cream, (the) best; AMER. *(de metal)* scum.
na·ta·ción f. swimming.
na·tal adj. *(relativo al nacimiento)* natal, pertaining to birth; *(nativo)* native <*ciudad n.* native city>.
na·ta·li·cio adj. & m. birthday.
na·ta·li·dad f. natality, birthrate.
na·ta·to·rio, a I. adj. swimming, bathing II. m. swimming pool.
na·ti·llas f.pl. custard.
Na·ti·vi·dad f. *(Navidad)* Christmas; *(retablo)* Nativity scene, crèche.
na·ti·vo, a I. adj. *(indígena)* native, indigenous; *(natural)* innate, inborn; MIN. native, pure II.m.f. native.
na·to, a adj. born, natural <*él es un criminal n.* he is a born criminal>.
na·tu·ra f. nature ♦ **contra n.** unnatural.
na·tu·ral adj. natural; *(nativo)* native, indigenous; *(innato)* innate, native; *(ilegítimo)* illegitimate <*hijo n.* illegitimate son>; MUS.

natural ♦ **al n.** naturally, without adornment **II.** m.f. native.

na·tu·ra·le·za f. nature ♦ **contra la n.** against nature, unnatural • **n. muerta** still life • **por n.** by nature, naturally.

na·tu·ra·li·dad f. naturalness.

na·tu·ra·li·za·ción f. naturalization.

na·tu·ra·li·zar §04 tr. (*nacionalizar*) to naturalize, nationalize; (*aclimatar*) to acclimate, adapt —reflex. to be naturalized *or* nationalized.

nau·fra·gar §47 intr. MARIT. to be shipwrecked; FIG. to fail, flounder.

nau·fra·gio m. MARIT. shipwreck; FIG. failure.

náu·fra·go, a adj. & m.f. shipwrecked (person).

náu·se·a f. nausea; (*repugnancia*) disgust ♦ **dar náuseas** to disgust, nauseate • **sentir náuseas** to feel sick.

nau·se·a·bun·do, a/se·ante adj. nauseating, sickening.

nau·se·ar intr. to feel sick, feel nauseous.

náu·ti·co, a I. adj. nautical, maritime ♦ **club n.** yacht club • **deportes náuticos** water sports **II.** f. navigation.

na·va·ja f. (*cortaplumas*) jackknife, penknife; ZOOL. razor clam ♦ **n. de afeitar** razor • **n. de resorte** switchblade.

na·val adj. naval, maritime.

na·ve f. ship, vessel; ARCHIT. nave ♦ **n. aérea** airship • **n. de guerra** battleship • **n. espacial** spaceship ♦ **quemar las naves** to burn one's bridges.

na·ve·ga·ble adj. navigable.

na·ve·ga·ción f. navigation, sailing ♦ **n. aérea** aerial navigation • **n. costera** coastal navigation • **n. fluvial** river navigation.

na·ve·gar §47 intr. (*viajar*) to travel by boat, sail; MEX. to tolerate, bear —tr. to navigate, steer.

Na·vi·dad f. Christmas, Nativity ♦ **¡Feliz N.!** Merry Christmas!

na·vie·ro, a I. adj. shipping <*compañía n.* shipping company> **II.** m.f. ship owner.

na·ví·o m. ship, vessel.

ne·bli·na f. mist, fog.

ne·bli·no·so, a adj. misty, foggy.

ne·bu·lo·si·dad f. (*bruma*) cloudiness, haziness; FIG. vagueness.

ne·bu·lo·so, a adj. (*sombrío*) cloudy, nebulous; (*difícil de entender*) hazy, vague; ASTRON. nebular.

ne·ce·dad f. foolishness, nonsense.

ne·ce·sa·rio, a adj. necessary; (*esencial*) essential.

ne·ce·ser m. (*de tocador*) toilet case, dressing case; (*estuche*) kit.

ne·ce·si·dad f. necessity, need; (*pobreza*) need, poverty; (*menester*) jam, tight spot ♦ **de n.** necessarily, by necessity • **en caso de n.** if necessary • **n. extrema** extreme need, dire straits • **por n.** out of necessity.

ne·ce·si·ta·do, a I. adj. (*pobre*) needy, poor; (*falto*) in need, lacking **II.** m.f. needy person.

ne·ce·si·tar tr. (*hacer falta*) to need, want; (*requerir*) to require, necessitate; (*deber*) to have to, need to <*necesitamos escribirlo* we have to write it> —intr. ♦ **n. de** to need, be in need of.

ne·cio, a I. adj. (*tonto*) ignorant, foolish; (*terco*) stubborn, obstinate; ARG., P. RICO touchy **II.** m.f. fool ♦ **a necias** foolishly.

ne·cro·fi·lia f. necrophilia.

ne·cro·lo·gí·a f. necrology, obituary.

ne·cro·man·cia f. necromancy, black magic.

néc·tar m. nectar.

nec·ta·ri·na f. nectarine.

ne·fas·to, a adj. ominous, unlucky.

ne·frí·ti·co, a adj. nephritic, renal.

ne·fri·tis f. nephritis.

ne·ga·ble adj. deniable, refutable.

ne·ga·ción f. (*negativa*) negation, denial; (*denegación*) refusal; GRAM. negative (particle).

ne·gar §52 tr. to deny; (*contradecir*) to deny, refute; (*rehusar*) to refuse; (*prohibir*) to prohibit, forbid; (*repudiar*) to disclaim, disavow —reflex. (*rehusar*) to refuse; (*privarse*) to deny oneself.

ne·ga·ti·vi·dad f. negativity, negativeness.

ne·ga·ti·vo, a I. adj. negative **II.** m. PHOTOG. negative —f. (*negación*) negation, denial; (*rechazo*) refusal, denial.

ne·gli·gé m. negligee.

ne·gli·gen·cia f. (*irresponsabilidad*) negligence, carelessness; (*descuido*) neglect, disregard.

ne·gli·gen·te adj. & m.f. negligent (person).

ne·go·cia·ble adj. negotiable.

ne·go·cia·ción f. (*acción*) negotiation; (*negocio*) business deal, transaction.

ne·go·cia·do m. (*departamento*) department, office; (*negocio*) business deal, transaction; (*negocio ilícito*) shady deal.

ne·go·cia·dor, ·ra I. adj. negotiating **II.** m.f. negotiator.

ne·go·cian·te m.f. (*comerciante*) merchant, dealer; (*de negocios*) businessman/woman.

ne·go·ciar intr. (*tratar*) to negotiate, discuss; (*comerciar*) to deal, do business (*con, en,* in) —tr. to negotiate.

ne·go·cio m. (*comercio*) business, business concern; (*trabajo*) job, occupation; (*transacción*) transaction, deal; (*utilidad*) profit, return; (*asunto*) affair, concern; R.P. shop, store ♦ **negocios** business <*hombre de negocios* businessman> • **encargado de negocios** chargé d'affaires • **n. redondo** profitable deal • **n. sucio** shady deal.

ne·gri·lla f. PRINT. boldface (type).

ne·gro, a I. adj. black; (*oscuro*) dark, black ♦ **n. como boca de lobo** pitch-black • **pasarlas negras** COLL. to have a hard time • **poner a alguien n.** to anger someone • **ponerse n.** (*enojarse*) to get angry; (*broncearse*) to get a tan • **ver todo n.** to be pessimistic **II.** m.f. (*persona*) Black, Negro; AMER. (*querido*) dear, darling —m. (*color*) black ♦ **en blanco y n.** in black and white • **n. de humo** lampblack —f. MUS. quarter note.

ne·gru·ra f. blackness, darkness.

ne·gruz·co, a adj. blackish, dark.

né·me·sis f. nemesis.

ne·ne, a m.f. COLL. (*bebé*) baby, infant; (*querido*) dear, darling.

ne·nú·far m. water lily.

ne·o·clá·si·co, a I. adj. neoclassic(al) **II.** m.f. neoclassicist.

ne·ó·fi·to, a m.f. neophyte, novice.

ne·o·lí·ti·co, a I. adj. neolithic **II.** m.f. neolith.

ne·o·lo·gis·mo m. neologism.

ne·ón m. neon.

ne·o·na·to m. newborn baby.

ne·po·tis·mo m. nepotism.

ner·vio m. nerve; (*tendón*) tendon, sinew; BOT. rib, vein ♦ pl. **crisparle los n. a alguien** to get on someone's nerves • **tener los n. de punta** to

be on edge.
ner·vio·si·dad f. nervousness, agitation.
ner·vio·so, a adj. nervous; nerve <*célula n.* nerve cell> ♦ **ponerse n.** to get nervous.
ner·vo·si·dad f. nervousness.
ne·to, a adj. (*claro*) pure, simple; net <*precio n.* net price>.
neu·má·ti·co, a I. adj. pneumatic II. m. tire ♦ **n. de repuesto** spare tire.
neu·mo·ní·a f. pneumonia.
neu·ral·gia f. neuralgia.
neu·ro·ci·ru·ja·no, a m.f. neurosurgeon.
neu·ro·ci·ru·gí·a f. neurosurgery.
neu·ro·lo·gí·a f. neurology.
neu·ro·ló·gi·co, a adj. neurological.
neu·ró·lo·go, a m.f. neurologist.
neu·ro·na f. neuron(e).
neu·ro·sis f.inv. neurosis.
neu·ró·ti·co, a adj. & m.f. neurotic.
neu·to·nio m. newton.
neu·tral adj. & m.f. neutral.
neu·tra·li·dad f. neutrality.
neu·tra·li·za·ción f. neutralization.
neu·tra·li·zan·te I. adj. neutralizing II. m.f. neutralizer.
neu·tra·li·zar §04 tr. to neutralize —reflex. to be neutralized.
neu·tro, a I. adj. (*indiferente*) neutral; BIOL. neuter, sexless; GRAM. (*género*) neuter; (*verbos*) intransitive; CHEM., ELEC. neutral II. m. GRAM. neuter.
neu·trón m. neutron.
ne·va·do, a I. adj. snowy, snow-covered; FIG. snow-white II. f. snowfall.
ne·var §49 intr. to snow —tr. to whiten, make white.
ne·ve·ra f. refrigerator, icebox.
ne·vis·ca f. light snowfall, snow flurry.
ne·vis·car §70 tr. to snow lightly.
ne·xo m. nexus, link ♦ **sin n.** unrelated.
ni conj. neither, nor <*no tomo ni fumo* I neither drink nor smoke>; not even <*ni (siquiera)me hablaron* they did not even speak to me> ♦ **ni que** not even if.
ni·cho m. (*en la pared*) niche, recess; (*tumba*) tomb, vault.
ni·co·ti·na f. nicotine.
ni·da·da f. (*de huevos*) nestful (of eggs); (*de pájaros*) brood.
ni·dal m. (*nido*) nest; (*huevo*) nest egg; (*lugar frecuentado*) hangout, haunt.
ni·do m. nest; (*morada*) abode, home; (*guarida*) den, lair; (*centro*) center, hotbed <*n. de discordias* a hotbed of controversy ♦ **caerse del n.** COLL. to be extremely gullible ♦ **patearle el n.** a R.P. to pull the rug out from under.
nie·bla f. (*bruma*) fog, mist; (*nube*) cloud.
nie·go, gue see **negar.**
nie·to, a m.f. grandchild, grandson/daughter ♦ pl. grandchildren.
nie·va see **nevar.**
nie·ve f. snow; (*blancura*) whiteness ♦ **a punto de n.** stiff.
ni·gro·man·cia f. necromancy, black magic.
ni·gro·man·te m.f. necromancer.
ni·hi·lis·ta I. adj. nihilistic II. m.f. nihilist.
ni·lón m. nylon.
nim·bo m. (*aureola*) halo; METEOROL. nimbus.
ni·mie·dad f. trifle, trivial detail.
ni·mio, a adj. trivial, insignificant.
nin·fa f. nymph; ZOOL. nymph, pupa.
nin·fe·a f. water lily.

nin·fo m. COLL. fop, dandy.
nin·fó·ma·na f. nymphomaniac.
nin·fo·ma·ní·a f. nymphomania.
nin·gún adj. contr. of **ninguno.**
nin·gu·no, a I. adj. none, no, not any <*no tengo n. opinión* I have no opinion> ♦ **de n. manera** *or* **de ningún modo** in no way, by no means ♦ **en n. parte** nowhere II. pron. none, not any <*no quiero n. de ellos* I do not want any of them>; (*nadie*) no one, nobody.
ni·ña f. see **niño, a.**
ni·ñe·rí·a f. childish act; FIG. trifle.
ni·ñe·ro, a I. adj. fond of children II. f. nursemaid, babysitter.
ni·ñez f. (*infancia*) childhood; (*principio*) infancy, beginning.
ni·ño, a I. adj. (*joven*) young, childlike; (*impulsivo*) immature, childish; (*inexperto*) inexperienced II. m.f. (*muchacho*) child; S. AMER. master (used by servants); CHILE scoundrel —m. boy ♦ **de n.** as a child ♦ **desde n.** from childhood ♦ **n. explorador** Boy Scout ♦ **n. prodigio** child prodigy ♦ pl. children —f. (*muchacha*) girl; (*del ojo*) pupil (of the eye).
ní·quel m. nickel; AMER. coin.
ni·que·lar tr. to nickel, nickel-plate.
ni·ti·dez f. (*claridad*) clarity; (*de fotos*) sharpness.
ní·ti·do, a adj. (*claro*) clear; (*de fotos*) sharp.
ni·tra·to m. nitrate ♦ **n. de potasio** potassium nitrate ♦ **n. de sodio** sodium nitrate.
ní·tri·co, a adj. nitric.
ni·tri·to m. nitrite.
ni·tró·ge·no m. nitrogen.
ni·tro·gli·ce·ri·na f. nitroglycerin.
ni·vel m. (*altura*) level, height; (*grado*) level, standard <*n. cultural* cultural level> ♦ **a n.** level ♦ **de alto n.** high-level ♦ **n. de agua** water level ♦ **n. de vida** standard of living ♦ **n. del mar** sea level ♦ **paso a n.** railroad crossing.
ni·ve·lar tr. (*igualar*) to make level; SURV. to survey, grade; (*equilibrar*) to balance.
no I. adv. no <*¿puedes verlo? no* can you see it? no>; not <*ni. vengo* I am not coming>; not <*no intervención* nonintervention> ♦ **¿a qué no?** COLL. do you want to bet? ♦ **¿cómo no?** of course, why not? ♦ **no bien** no sooner ♦ **no más** no more, only; AMER., COLL. feel free to <*continúe no más* feel free to continue> ♦ **no obstante** nevertheless, notwithstanding ♦ **no sea que** in case, lest II. m. no <*un no definitivo* a definite no>.
no·ble I. adj. (*aristocrático*) noble, aristocratic; (*elevado*) noble, honorable II. m.f. nobleman/woman.
no·ble·za f. (*aristocracia*) nobility, aristocracy; (*honradez*) nobleness, gentility.
no·che f. (*anochecer*) night, evening; (*oscuridad*) darkness ♦ **a primera n.** at nightfall, just after dark ♦ **buenas noches** good evening, good night ♦ **cerrar la n.** to become completely dark ♦ **de la n. a la mañana** suddenly, overnight ♦ **de n.** (*por la noche*) at night; evening, night <*traje de n.* evening gown> ♦ **hacer n.** to spend the night ♦ **esta n.** tonight ♦ **hacerse de n.** to grow dark ♦ **n. cerrada** dark night ♦ **por la n.** at night.
no·ción f. notion, idea.
no·ci·vi·dad f. noxiousness, harmfulness.
no·ci·vo, a adj. noxious, harmful.
noc·tám·bu·lo, a I. adj. night-wandering II. m.f. night owl.

noc·tur·nal adj. nocturnal.

noc·tur·no, a I. adj. nocturnal, nightly; *(triste)* sad, melancholy **II.** m. RELIG. nocturn; MUS. nocturne.

no·dri·za f. wet nurse.

nó·du·lo m. nodule.

no·gal m. walnut.

nó·ma·da/de I. adj. nomadic **II.** m.f. nomad.

nom·bra·do, a adj. *(célebre)* renowned, famous; *(sobredicho)* aforementioned.

nom·bra·mien·to m. *(acción)* naming; *(nominación)* nomination, appointment.

nom·brar tr. *(llamar)* to name, mention by name; *(nominar)* to nominate, appoint.

nom·bre m. name; GRAM. *(renombre)* name, reputation ♦ **de n.** by name; in name only <*presidente de n.* president in name only> • **en n. de** in the name of, by the authority of • **no tener n.** to be unspeakable <*su conducta no tiene n.* his conduct is unspeakable> • **n. artístico** stage name; LIT. pen name • **n. común** or **apelativo** common noun • **n. y apellido** full name • **poner n. a** to name • **sin n.** nameless.

no·men·cla·tu·ra f. nomenclature.

no·me·ol·vi·des f.inv. forget-me-not.

nó·mi·na f. *(lista)* list, roll; COM. payroll.

no·mi·na·ción f. nomination, appointment.

no·mi·na·dor, ·ra I. adj. nominating **II.** m.f. nominator.

no·mi·nal adj. nominal, titular; COM. face <*valor n.* face value>; GRAM. nominal, substantival.

no·mi·nar tr. to nominate, appoint.

no·mi·na·ti·vo, a I. adj. personal GRAM. nominative **II.** m. nominative case.

non I. adj. odd, uneven **II.** m. MATH. odd number ♦ pl. repeated denial.

no·na·da f. trifle, nothing much.

no·na·ge·na·rio/gé·si·mo, a adj. & m.f. nonagenarian.

no·na·gé·si·mo, a adj. & m. ninetieth.

no·no, a I. adj. ninth **II.** m. *(noveno)* ninth; R.P., COLL. grandpa —f. grandma.

no·que·ar tr. SPORT. to knock out.

nor·des·te or **no·res·te** m. northeast.

no·ria f. water wheel.

nor·ma f. *(modelo)* norm; *(regla)* rule.

nor·mal I. adj. normal, standard ♦ **escuela n.** teachers training school **II.** f. GEOM. perpendicular.

nor·ma·li·dad f. normality, normalcy.

nor·ma·lis·ta m.f. student teacher.

nor·ma·li·za·ción f. normalization; INDUS. standardization.

nor·ma·li·zar §04 tr. to normalize; INDUS. to standardize.

nor·ma·ti·vo, a adj. normative.

no·ro·es·te m. northwest.

nor·te m. north; *(guía)* guide, lodestar.

nor·te·ño, a I. adj. northern **II.** m.f. northerner.

nór·ti·co, a adj. northern, northerly.

nos pron. us <*ellos n. vieron* they saw us>; us, to us, for us, from us <*él n. vendió la casa* he sold the house to us>; one another, each other <*n. queremos* we love each other>; ourselves <*n. estamos mirando en el espejo* we are looking at ourselves in the mirror>.

no·so·tros, as pron. we <*n. lo hicimos* we did it>; us, ourselves <*no es para n.* it is not for us>.

nos·tal·gia f. nostalgia, homesickness.

nos·tál·gi·co, a adj. nostalgic, homesick.

no·ta f. *(comentario)* note, observation; *(apostilla)* note, notation; *(reparo)* notice, heed; *(calificación)* grade, mark; MUS. note ♦ **dar la n.** to stand out • **de mala n.** with a bad reputation • **de n.** of note, famous • **forzar la n.** to go too far • **n. falsa** wrong note.

no·ta·ble adj. *(apreciable)* notable, noteworthy; *(superior)* outstanding, striking.

no·ta·ción f. *(anotación)* note, annotation; ARTS, MATH. notation.

no·tar tr. *(indicar)* to note, point out; *(observar)* to notice, observe —reflex. to see, notice <*se nota la diferencia* one can see the difference>.

no·ta·rio, a m. notary, notary public.

no·ti·cia f. news item, piece of news ♦ pl. news • **n. de última hora** the latest news.

no·ti·cia·rio m. RAD. newscast; CINEM. newsreel.

no·ti·cie·ro, a I. adj. news **II.** m. news report.

no·ti·cio·so, a I. adj. informed, well-informed **II.** m. AMER. news report.

no·ti·fi·ca·ción f. notification, notice.

no·ti·fi·car §70 tr. to notify, inform.

no·to·rie·dad f. *(reputación)* notoriety; *(fama)* fame, renown.

no·to·rio, a adj. notorious, well-known.

no·va·to, a COLL. **I.** adj. beginning **II.** m.f. beginner, novice.

no·ve·cien·tos, as adj. & m. nine hundred.

no·ve·dad f. *(calidad de nuevo)* newness; *(innovación)* novelty, innovation; *(cambio)* change; *(noticia)* recent event ♦ **no hay n.** nothing is new • **sin n.** *(nada nuevo)* as usual, no change; *(bien)* safely, well.

no·ve·do·so, a adj. novel, new.

no·vel adj. new, inexperienced.

no·ve·la f. novel ♦ **n. policíaca** detective story.

no·ve·les·co, a adj. novelesque.

no·ve·lis·ta m.f. novelist.

no·ve·no, a adj. & m. ninth —f. RELIG. novena.

no·ven·ta I. adj. ninety; *(nonagésimo)* ninetieth **II.** m. ninety.

no·ven·ta·vo, a adj. & m. ninetieth.

no·ven·tón, o·na adj. & m.f. nonagenarian.

no·via f. see **novio, a.**

no·viaz·go m. *(relaciones amorosas)* courtship; *(compromiso)* engagement, betrothal.

no·vi·cia·do m. novitiate.

no·vi·cio, a I. adj. beginning, new **II.** m.f. novice; *(aprendiz)* beginner, apprentice.

no·viem·bre m. November.

no·vi·llo, a m. young bull —f. heifer, young cow.

no·vio, a m. *(amigo)* boyfriend; *(prometido)* fiancé; *(recién casado)* groom ♦ pl. *(casados)* newlyweds; *(prometidos)* engaged couple —f. *(amiga)* girlfriend; *(prometida)* fiancée; *(recién casada)* bride.

nu·ba·rrón m. large black cloud.

nu·be f. cloud; *(sombra)* shadow; *(multitud)* swarm, multitude; *(en los ojos)* cloud, film; JEWEL. flaw ♦ **estar en las nubes** to have one's head in the clouds • **n. de lluvia** rain cloud • **por las nubes** sky-high.

nú·bil adj. nubile, marriageable.

nu·bi·li·dad f. nubility.

nu·bla·do, a adj. cloudy, overcast.

nu·blar tr. to cloud, darken —reflex. to become cloudy or overcast.

nu·bo·si·dad f. cloudiness.
nu·bo·so, a adj. cloudy, overcast.
nu·ca f. nape (of the neck).
nu·cle·ar adj. nuclear.
nu·clei·co, a adj. nucleic.
nú·cle·o m. nucleus; ELEC. core; BOT. kernel, pit; *(esencial)* core, essence.
nu·cle·ón m. nucleon.
nu·di·llo m. knuckle.
nu·dis·ta m.f. nudist.
nu·do m. *(lazo)* knot; ANAT. node, lump; BOT., MARIT. knot; *(lazo)* bond, tie; *(enredo)* crux, core <*el n. de la trama* the crux of the plot> ♦ **n. corredizo** slipknot, noose • **n. gordiano** Gordian knot • **tener un n. en la garganta** to have a lump in one's throat.
nu·do·so, a adj. knotty, knotted.
nue·ra f. daughter-in-law.
nues·tro, a I. adj. our, of ours <*n. coche* our car> **II.** pron. ours, of ours <*el n. es rojo* ours is red> ♦ **los nuestros** our people, our side.
nue·ve I. adj. nine; *(noveno)* ninth ♦ **las n.** nine o'clock **II.** m. nine.
nue·vo, a I. adj. new; *(otro)* new, another <*compró un n. libro* she bought a new book> ♦ **de n.** again • **N. Mundo** New World • **N. Testamento** New Testament • **¿qué hay de n.?** what's new? **II.** f. news, tidings.
nuez f. nut; *(del nogal)* walnut; ANAT. Adam's apple; MUS. nut ♦ **n. moscada** *or* **de especie** nutmeg.
nu·li·dad f. nullity; *(incapacidad)* inability, incompetence; *(inutilidad)* worthlessness; COLL. *(persona)* useless person.
nu·lo, a adj. null, void; *(sin mérito)* useless, worthless ♦ **n. y sin valor** null and void.
nu·me·ra·ción f. numeration, numbering; *(números)* numbers, numerals ♦ **n. arábiga, romana** Arabic, Roman numerals.
nu·me·ra·dor m. numerator.
nu·me·ral adj. numeral.
nu·me·rar tr. *(foliar)* to number; *(contar)* to count, enumerate.
nu·me·ra·rio, a I. adj. numerary **II.** m. cash, currency.
nu·mé·ri·co, a adj. numerical.
nú·me·ro m. number; *(signo)* numeral; *(ejemplar)* issue, copy; *(medida)* size; THEAT. number, act ♦ **n. arábigo** Arabic numeral • **n. atrasado** back issue • **n. cardinal** cardinal number • **n. complejo** compound number • **n. dígito** digit • **n. entero** whole number • **n. extraordinario** special edition *or* issue • **n. fraccionario** *or* **quebrado** fraction • **n. impar** odd number • **n. ordinal** ordinal number • **n. par** even number • **n. primo** prime number • **n. redondo** round number • **n. romano** Roman numeral • **n. uno** the best, the first • **sin n.** countless, numberless.
nu·me·ro·so, a adj. numerous.
nu·mis·má·ti·co, a I. adj. numismatic **II.** m.f. numismatist —f. numismatics.
nun·ca adv. never, not ever ♦ **más que n.** more than ever • **n. jamás** *or* **n. más** never again.
nup·cial adj. nuptial.
nup·cias f.pl. nuptials, wedding.
nu·tria f. otter.
nu·tri·cio, a adj. nutritious.
nu·tri·ción f. nutrition.
nu·tri·do, a adj. *(alimentado)* nourished, fed <*bien n.* well-fed>; *(abundante)* large, abun-

dant <*una concurrencia muy n.* a large crowd>.
nu·tri·mien·to m. nourishment.
nu·trir tr. *(alimentar)* to nourish, feed; *(fortalecer)* to nurture, strengthen.
nu·tri·ti·vo, a adj. nutritious, nutritive.

Ñ

ñ, Ñ f. fifteenth letter of the Spanish alphabet.
ña·me m. yam.
ñan·dú m. American ostrich.
ña·pa f. AMER. bonus, extra ♦ **de ñ.** AMER. to boot, into the bargain.
ña·que m. odds and ends.
ña·to, a adj. AMER. snub-nosed.
ñe·que I. m. AMER. strength, vigor; C. AMER., MEX. slap, blow **II.** adj. AMER. strong, vigorous ♦ **hombre de ñ.** COLL. he-man.
ño·ñe·rí·a *or* **ño·ñez** f. foolishness, simplemindedness.
ño·ño, a adj. & m.f. COLL. *(apocado)* bashful (person); *(soso)* dull (person).
ño·que/qui m. AMER. gnocchi.
ñor·bo m. ARG., ECUAD., PERU passionflower.
ñu·do m. ARCH. knot ♦ **al ñ.** R.P. in vain.

O

o, O f. sixteenth letter of the Spanish alphabet.
o conj. or <*blanco o negro* black or white>; either <*lo harás o de buen grado o por la fuerza* you will do it, either willingly or unwillingly> ♦ **o sea** that is to say.
o·a·sis m.inv. oasis.
ob·ce·ca·da·men·te adv. blindly.
ob·ce·car §70 tr. to obfuscate, blind.
o·be·de·cer §17 tr. to obey —intr. to obey ♦ **o. a** *(responder a)* to respond to <*esta enfermedad obedece al tratamiento* this illness responds to treatment>; *(deberse a)* to be due to, arise from <*su ausencia obedece a varias circunstancias* his absence is due to a number of circumstances>.
o·be·dien·cia f. obedience.
o·be·dien·te adj. obedient.
o·be·lis·co m. obelisk.
o·ber·tu·ra f. overture.
o·be·si·dad f. obesity.
o·be·so, a adj. obese.
ó·bi·ce m. obstacle, impediment.
o·bis·po m. bishop.
ob·je·ción f. objection ♦ **hacer** *or* **levantar una o.** to object, raise an objection.
ob·je·ta·ble adj. objectionable.
ob·je·tar tr. to object to, raise objections to ♦ **no tener nada que o.** to have no objection *or* objections.
ob·je·ti·var tr. to objectify.
ob·je·ti·vi·dad f. objectivity.
ob·je·ti·vis·mo m. objectivism.
ob·je·ti·vo, a adj. & m. objective.
ob·je·to m. object; *(tema)* subject, theme; *(fin)* aim; GRAM. object ♦ **carecer de o.** to be useless • **con o. de** in order to • **¿con qué o.?** to what end? • **ser o. de** to be the object of • **tener por o.** to be one's aim.

o·ble·a f. wafer; PHARM. capsule.
o·bli·cuo, a adj. *(inclinado)* oblique, slanting; ANAT., GEOM. oblique.
o·bli·ga·ción f. obligation; *(responsabilidad)* responsibility; *(deber)* duty; FIN. bond ♦ **o. colectiva** joint obligation • **o. implícita** implied obligation ♦ pl. family obligations • **faltar a sus o.** to fail in one's duties.
o·bli·gar §47 tr. *(imponer)* to oblige, obligate; *(compeler)* to force, compel; *(favorecer)* to oblige, favor <*nos obligó con su presencia* he favored us with his presence> —reflex. to obligate oneself.
o·bli·ga·to·rie·dad f. compulsoriness.
o·bli·ga·to·rio, a adj. obligatory, compulsory.
o·blon·go, a adj. oblong.
o·bo·e m. MUS. oboe; *(músico)* oboist.
o·bra f. work; *(acto)* act <*una o. de misericordia* an act of mercy>; *(labor)* workmanship, labor; *(construcción)* construction site ♦ **de o.** in deed • **¡manos a la o.!** let's get to work! • **o. de caridad** charitable deed • **o. maestra** masterpiece • **obras públicas** public works • **por o. de** thanks to.
o·brar tr. to work —intr. to act, proceed ♦ **o. en** to be in <*la carta obra en manos de Juan* the letter is in John's hands>.
o·bre·ro, a I. adj. working <*clase o.* working class> ♦ **sindicato o.** labor union II. m.f. *(trabajador)* worker; *(jornalero)* laborer ♦ **o. portuario** dockworker.
obs·ce·ni·dad f. obscenity.
obs·ce·no, a adj. obscene.
obs·cu·ro, a adj. var. of **oscuro, a.**
obs·cu·ri·dad f. var. of **oscuridad.**
ob·se·quiar tr. *(regalos)* to give as a gift; *(agasajar)* to entertain.
ob·se·quio m. *(regalo)* gift, present; *(agasajo)* attention, kindness ♦ **deshacerse en obsequios (con alguien)** to lavish attention (on someone) • **en o.** in honor of, for the sake of.
ob·se·quio·so, a adj. *(cortés)* obliging, attentive; *(servil)* obsequious, deferential; MEX. fond of giving gifts.
ob·ser·va·ción f. observation; *(nota aclaratoria)* observation, explanatory note or remark; *(objeción)* objection ♦ **en** or **bajo o.** under observation • **hacer una o.** to make a remark.
ob·ser·va·dor, ·ra I. adj. observant, observing II. m.f. observer ♦ **o. de pájaros** birdwatcher.
ob·ser·van·cia f. observance.
ob·ser·var tr. to observe; *(cumplir)* to obey; *(espiar)* to watch; *(notar)* to notice; *(comentar)* to remark.
ob·ser·va·to·rio m. observatory.
ob·se·sión f. obsession.
ob·se·sio·nan·te adj. obsessive.
ob·se·sio·nar tr. to obsess.
ob·se·si·vo, a adj. obsessive.
ob·se·so, a adj. & m.f. obsessive.
ob·so·le·to, a adj. obsolete.
obs·ta·cu·li·zar §04 tr. to obstruct, hinder.
obs·tá·cu·lo m. obstacle ♦ **carrera de obstáculos** steeplechase, obstacle course • **poner obstáculos** *(impedir)* to obstruct, hinder; *(objetar)* to object.
obs·tan·te adj. obstructing ♦ **no o.** nevertheless, however.
obs·tar intr. *(impedir)* to obstruct, hinder; *(oponerse una cosa a otra)* to stand in the way of.
obs·té·tri·co, a adj. obstetric(al).

obs·ti·na·ción f. obstinacy.
obs·ti·na·do, a adj. obstinate.
obs·ti·nar·se reflex. to be or become obstinate.
obs·truc·ción f. obstruction.
obs·truc·cio·nis·ta I. m.f. obstructionist II. adj. obstructionist(ic).
obs·truir §18 tr. to obstruct.
ob·ten·ción f. obtaining.
ob·te·ner §69 tr. *(conseguir)* to obtain, get; *(conservar)* to have, keep.
ob·tu·ra·dor, a I. adj. obturating, plugging II. m. *(tapón)* plug, stopper; PHOTOG. shutter ♦ **o. de plano** focal plane shutter.
ob·tu·rar tr. to obturate, stop up.
ob·tu·so, a adj. obtuse.
ob·tu·vie·ra, vo see **obtener.**
ob·viar tr. to obviate, prevent —intr. to stand in the way.
ob·vio, a adj. obvious.
o·ca·sión f. occasion; *(oportunidad)* opportunity; *(motivo)* reason, cause; *(tiempo)* time <*en aquella o.* at that time>; *(circunstancia)* circumstance; AMER. bargain ♦ **aprovechar una o.** to take advantage of an opportunity • **con o. de** on the occasion of • **de o.** *(de segunda mano)* secondhand; *(de precio reducido)* bargain • **dar o. a** to give rise to • **en cierta o.** once, on a certain occasion • **en la primera o.** at the first opportunity • **en ocasiones** sometimes.
o·ca·sio·nal adj. occasional; *(fortuito)* chance.
o·ca·sio·nar tr. *(causar)* to occasion, cause; *(provocar)* to stir up, provoke.
o·ca·so m. *(del sol)* sunset, sundown; *(de un astro)* setting; *(occidente)* occident, west; *(decadencia)* decline.
oc·ci·den·tal adj. western, occidental II. m.f. westerner, occidental.
oc·ci·den·te m. west, occident.
oc·ci·pi·tal adj. & m. occipital (bone).
o·cé·a·no m. ocean; FIG. ocean, sea.
o·ce·a·no·gra·fí·a f. oceanography.
o·ce·a·no·grá·fi·co, a adj. oceanographic.
o·chen·ta adj. & m. eighty.
o·chen·ta·vo, a adj. & m. eightieth.
o·chen·tón, o·na adj. & m.f. COLL. octogenarian.
o·cho I. adj. eight; *(octavo)* eighth ♦ **las o.** eight o'clock • **o. días** a week II. m. eight.
o·cho·cien·tos, as adj. & m. eight hundred.
o·cio m. *(inactividad)* idleness, inactivity; *(tiempo libre)* leisure, free time.
o·cio·si·dad f. idleness ♦ **la o. es la madre de todos los vicios** idleness is the root of all evil.
o·cio·so, a I. adj. idle II. m.f. idler, loafer.
o·cre m. ocher, ochre.
oc·ta·vo, a adj. & m. eighth —f. MUS. octave.
oc·te·to m. octet.
oc·to·ge·na·rio, a adj. & m.f. octogenarian.
oc·to·gé·si·mo, a adj. & m. eightieth.
oc·to·go·nal adj. octagonal.
oc·tó·go·no, a I. adj. octagonal II. m. octagon.
oc·tu·bre m. October.
o·cu·lar I. adj. ocular, pertaining to the eye II. m. eyepiece, ocular.
o·cu·lis·ta m.f. oculist.
o·cul·ta·men·te adv. stealthily, secretly.
o·cul·tar tr. *(esconder)* to hide, conceal *(de from)*; *(callar)* to hush, silence; *(disfrazar)* to disguise.
o·cul·tis·mo m. occultism.
o·cul·to, a adj. *(escondido)* hidden, concealed;

(sobrenatural) occult ♦ **en o.** secretly.

o·cu·pa·ción f. occupation; *(empleo)* profession, trade; *(trabajo)* daily activities *or* routine.

o·cu·pa·do, a adj. *(teléfono, línea)* engaged, busy; *(ciudad, territorio)* occupied; *(seat)* taken <¿está o. este asiento? is this seat taken?>.

o·cu·pan·te I. adj. occupying **II.** m.f. occupant.

o·cu·par tr. *(apoderarse)* to occupy, take possession of; *(llenar)* to occupy, fill; *(habitar)* to occupy, live in; to hold, fill <ocupó el puesto de ministro he held the post of minister>; *(emplear)* to employ, give work to; *(encargar)* to occupy, keep busy —reflex. *(emplearse)* to occupy oneself; *(interesarse)* to concern oneself; *(atender a)* to attend, pay attention *(de)* to.

o·cu·rren·cia f. *(ocasión)* occurrence, event; *(chiste)* witticism ♦ **¡qué o.!** what a thought! • **tener ocurrencias** to be witty.

o·cu·rren·te adj. witty, funny.

o·cu·rrir intr. *(suceder)* to occur, happen; *(acudir)* to go to, show up for ♦ **¿qué ocurre?** what's the matter? —reflex. to occur to, strike <se me ocurrió que estaba en peligro it occured to me that I was in danger>.

o·da f. ode.

o·da·lis·ca f. odalisque.

o·diar tr. to hate, loathe.

o·dio m. hatred, loathing.

o·dio·so, a adj. odious.

o·di·se·a f. odyssey.

o·don·to·lo·gí·a f. odontology, dentistry.

o·don·tó·lo·go, a m.f. odontologist, dentist.

o·dre m. wineskin.

o·es·te m. west.

o·fen·der tr. *(injuriar)* to offend, insult; *(dañar)* to hurt, injure —intr. to be offensive —reflex. to take offense.

o·fen·sa f. offense.

o·fen·si·vo, a adj. & f. offensive.

o·fen·sor, ·ra I. adj. offending **II.** m.f. offender.

o·fer·ta f. *(propuesta)* offer, proposal; COM. bid, tender ♦ **o. en firme** firm offer • **o. y demanda** supply and demand.

o·fer·tar tr. to tender; AMER. to offer.

o·fi·cial I. adj. official **II.** m. *(funcionario)* official, officer; *(obrero)* skilled worker; MIL. officer ♦ **o. de guardia** officer of the watch • **o. del día** officer of the day • **o. mayor** chief clerk • **primer o.** MARIT. first mate.

o·fi·cia·li·dad f. officer corps, officers; *(carácter oficial)* official character.

o·fi·cia·li·zar §04 tr. to make official.

o·fi·cian·te m. officiant.

o·fi·ciar tr. RELIG. to celebrate; *(comunicar)* to communicate officially —intr. RELIG. to officiate ♦ **o. de** to act as.

o·fi·ci·na f. office; *(de farmacia)* laboratory ♦ **horas de o.** business hours • **o. de colocación** employment agency.

o·fi·ci·nis·ta m.f. clerk, office worker.

o·fi·cio m. *(ocupación)* labor, work; *(empleo)* office, post; *(artesanía)* trade, craft; *(función)* function, role; *(comunicación)* communiqué, official notice; RELIG. office, service ♦ **artes y oficios** arts and crafts • **buenos oficios** good offices • **de o.** *(oficialmente)* ex officio, officially; *(de profesión)* by trade • **gajes del o.** occupational hazards • **Santo O.** Holy Office, Inquisition.

o·fi·cio·sa·men·te adj. *(con diligencia)* dili-

gently; *(con complacencia)* obligingly; *(con entremetimiento)* officiously.

o·fi·cio·so, a adj. *(laborioso)* hard-working, diligent; *(solícito)* solicitous, obliging; *(importuno)* officious, meddlesome.

o·fre·cer §17 tr. to offer; COM. to offer, bid; RELIG. to offer up, dedicate —reflex. to offer oneself, volunteer.

o·fre·ci·mien·to m. offer, offering.

o·fren·da f. offering, gift.

o·fren·dar tr. to make an offering.

of·tal·mo·lo·gí·a f. ophthalmology.

of·tal·mó·lo·go m. ophthalmologist.

o·fus·ca·ción f./**mien·to** m. *(acción)* blinding, dazzling; *(confusión)* confusion, bewilderment.

o·fus·car §70 tr. *(cegar)* to blind, dazzle; *(confundir)* to confuse, bewilder.

o·gro m. ogre.

¡oh! interj. oh!

oh·mio *or* **ohm** m. ohm.

o·í·do m. *(sentido)* hearing, sense of hearing; ANAT. ear <o. interno inner ear>; MUS. ear <ella tiene buen o. she has a good ear> ♦ **abrir los oídos** to listen attentively • **aguzar el o.** to prick up one's ears • **al o.** confidentially • **caer en oídos sordos** to fall on deaf ears • **cerrar los oídos a** to turn a deaf ear to • **dar oídos a** *(escuchar)* to listen to; *(dar crédito a)* to believe, credit • **de o.** by ear • **duro de o.** hard of hearing • **prestar oídos a** to lend an ear to • **ser todo oídos** to be all ears.

o·ír §45 tr. *(escuchar)* to hear; *(atender)* to listen to, pay attention to; *(entender)* to understand; *(asistir)* to attend ♦ **o. bien** to listen well • **o. hablar de** to hear about • **¡oye!** *or* **¡oiga!** *(para llamar la atención)* listen!; *(para reprender)* look here!

o·jal m. *(en la ropa)* buttonhole; *(agujero)* hole.

¡o·ja·lá! interj. would to God!, I hope that.

o·je·a·da f. glance, glimpse.

o·je·ar tr. *(mirar)* to eye, look at; *(aojar)* to cast the evil eye on.

o·je·ra f. dark circle *or* ring (under the eyes).

o·je·ri·za f. animosity, grudge.

o·je·ro·so/ru·do, a adj. having dark circles under the eyes, haggard.

o·je·te m. SEW. eyelet, drawstring hole.

o·jo m. eye; *(agujero)* hole <o. de la cerradura keyhole>; *(de un puente)* span, arch; *(malla)* mesh; *(atención)* attention <pon o. en lo que haces pay attention to what you are doing>; *(aptitud)* eye <el tiene buen o. he has a good eye> ♦ **abrir los ojos** to be on the alert, keep one's eyes open • **a o.** *or* **a o. de buen cubero** roughly, by a rough estimate • **a ojos cerrados** blindly, with one's eyes closed • **a ojos vistas** visibly, openly • **cerrar los ojos** COLL. *(dormir)* to sleep; *(morir)* to die • **clavar los ojos en** to stare at • **comerse con los ojos** COLL. to devour with one's eyes • **con mucho o.** very carefully • **costar un o. de la cara** COLL. to cost an arm and a leg • **cuatro ojos** four-eyes • **dichosos los ojos que te ven** COLL. you're a sight for sore eyes • **echar un o. a** to have one's eye on • **en un abrir y cerrar de ojos** COLL. in the twinkling of an eye • **írsele los ojos por** *or* **tras** not to be able to keep one's eyes off of • **mirar con buenos, malos ojos** to look favorably, unfavorably on • **¡mucho o.!** be careful! • **no pegar o.** not to sleep a wink • **no quitar los ojos de** not to take one's eyes off of • **¡ojo!** look out!, watch out! • **o. avizor** eagle eye • **o.**

de buey (*ventana*) bull's eye; MARIT. porthole • **o. de la tempestad** eye of the storm • **o. de vidrio** glass eye • **o. morado** black eye • **o. por o.** an eye for an eye • **ojos rasgados** slanted eyes • **ojos reventones** or **saltones** popeyes, bulging eyes • **tener entre ojos** to have a grudge against.

o·jo·ta f. AMER. sandal.

o·la f. wave ♦ **o. de frío** cold spell.

o·le·a·da f. (*embate de ola*) beating of waves; (*movimiento*) wave, surge <*una o. de gente* a surge of people>; (*cantidad*) wave, large number <*una o. de protestas* a wave of protests>.

o·le·a·gi·no·so, a adj. oily, oleaginous.

o·le·a·je m. (*olas*) surf, waves; (*marejada*) swell.

ó·le·o m. oil ♦ **pintura al ó.** oil painting.

o·le·o·duc·to m. oil pipeline.

o·le·o·mar·ga·ri·na f. oleomargarine.

o·ler §46 tr. (*olfatear*) to smell; (*averiguar*) to smell out, uncover; (*inquirir*) to nose or pry into —intr. (*tener olor*) to smell; (*parecer*) to smell of or like ♦ **no o. bien** to smell fishy.

ol·fa·te·ar tr. (*oler*) to sniff; COLL. (*descubrir*) to get wind of; (*curiosear*) to pry into.

ol·fa·to m. (*sentido*) sense of smell; (*intuición*) intuition; (*instinto*) instinct ♦ **tener o. para los negocios** to have a good nose for business.

ol·fa·to·rio, a adj. olfactory.

o·li·gar·ca m. oligarch.

o·li·gar·quí·a f. oligarchy.

o·li·gár·qui·co, a adj. oligarchic.

o·lim·pia·da/pí·a·da f. Olympic games.

o·lím·pi·co, a adj. Olympian, Olympic ♦ **juegos olímpicos** Olympic games.

o·li·va adj. & f. olive.

o·li·var m. olive grove.

o·li·va·re·ro, a adj. olive-growing <*región o.* olive-growing region>; olive <*industria o.* olive industry>.

o·li·vo m. olive tree; (*color*) olive.

o·lla f. (*vasija*) pot, kettle; (*cocido*) stew ♦ **o. de presión** pressure cooker.

ol·mo m. elm (tree) ♦ **pedir peras al o.** to ask for the moon.

o·ló·gra·fo, a I. adj. holographic **II.** m. holograph.

o·lor m. (*sensación*) smell; (*perfume*) smell, odor ♦ **tener o. a** to smell of.

o·lo·ro·so, a adj. perfumed, fragrant.

ol·vi·da·di·zo, a adj. (*desmemoriado*) forgetful, absent-minded; (*ingrato*) ungrateful ♦ **hacerse el o.** to pretend to forget.

ol·vi·da·do, a adj. (*desconocido*) forgotten; (*olvidadizo*) forgetful, absent-minded; (*ingrato*) ungrateful.

ol·vi·dar tr. & reflex. (*no recordar*) to forget; (*dejar*) to leave (behind) <*me olvidé los libros* I left the books behind>; (*omitir*) to leave out or off <*olvidaron incluir su nombre en el registro* they left his name off the register>; (*descuidar*) to neglect ♦ **olvidarse de** to forget to.

ol·vi·do m. (*desmemoria*) forgetfulness; (*estado*) oblivion <*los planes cayeron en el o.* the plans fell into oblivion> ♦ **echar al** or **en o.** to forget • **enterrar en el o.** to cast into oblivion.

om·bli·go m. navel.

om·bli·gue·ro m. bellyband (for infants).

o·mi·sión f. omission.

o·mi·so, a adj. neglectful, careless.

o·mi·tir tr. to omit.

óm·ni·bus m. omnibus, bus.

om·ni·po·ten·cia f. omnipotence.

om·ni·po·ten·te adj. omnipotent.

om·ni·sa·pien·te adj. omniscient.

o·mó·pla·to m. shoulder blade.

o·na·nis·mo m. onanism.

on·ce I. adj. eleven; (*undécimo*) eleventh ♦ **las o.** eleven o'clock **II.** m. eleven.

on·ce·no, a adj. eleventh.

on·co·lo·gí·a f. oncology.

on·da f. wave ♦ **estar en la o.** COLL. to be with it.

on·de·a·do, a adj. wavy.

on·de·ar intr. (*agua*) to ripple; (*ondular*) to wave, flutter.

on·du·la·ción f. (*movimiento*) undulation; (*sinuosidad*) winding; (*del cabello*) wave.

on·du·la·do, a adj. wavy.

on·du·lar tr. to wave —intr. to undulate.

o·ne·ro·so, a adj. onerous.

ó·nix f. onyx.

o·no·más·ti·co, a adj. onomastic ♦ **fiesta** or **día o.** saint's day.

o·no·ma·to·pe·ya f. onomatopoeia.

o·no·ma·to·pé·yi·co, a adj. onomatopoeic.

on·za f. ounce.

on·za·vo adj. & m. eleventh.

o·pa AMER. **I.** adj. stupid, foolish **II.** m.f. COLL. fool, dolt.

o·pa·ci·dad f. opacity, opaqueness.

o·pa·co, a adj. opaque.

ó·pa·lo m. opal.

op·ción f. option, choice.

op·cio·nal adj. optional.

ó·pe·ra f. opera ♦ **o. bufa** comic opera.

o·pe·ra·ción f. operation; FIN. transaction ♦ **o. cesárea** Caesarean section.

o·pe·ra·dor, ·ra I. adj. operating **II.** m.f. MECH. operator —m. CINEM. cameraman.

o·pe·ran·te adj. operating, working <*capital o.* working capital>.

o·pe·rar intr. to operate; COM. to deal, do business —tr. to operate on.

o·pe·ra·rio, a m.f. operator, worker.

o·pe·ra·ti·vo, a adj. operative.

o·pi·nar intr. (*formar opinión*) to think, have an opinion; (*expresar la opinión*) to express an opinion ♦ **o. en** or **sobre** to give an opinion on.

o·pi·nión f. opinion.

o·pio m. opium.

o·pió·ma·no m. opium addict.

o·pí·pa·ro, a adj. sumptuous, magnificent.

o·po·ner §54 tr. (*contraponer*) to set up or put against; (*poner enfrente*) to oppose, put opposite —reflex. (*objetar*) to oppose, object to; (*ser contrario*) to be in opposition to, be contrary <*sus ideas nunca se oponen a las mías* his ideas are never contrary to mine>.

o·por·to m. port (wine).

o·por·tu·na·men·te adv. opportunely, conveniently.

o·por·tu·ni·dad f. (*ocasión*) opportunity, chance; (*de una medida*) appropriateness.

o·por·tu·nis·ta adj. & m.f. opportunist.

o·por·tu·no, a I. adj. (*conveniente*) opportune, timely; (*apropiado*) suitable, fitting; (*ocurrente*) witty **II.** m.f. witty person.

o·po·si·ción f. opposition.

o·po·si·tor, ·ra m.f. opponent.

o·pre·sión f. oppression ♦ **o. del pecho** tightness in the chest.

o·pre·si·vo, a adj. oppressive.

o·pre·so, a I. see **oprimir II.** adj. oppressed.

o·pre·sor, ·ra I. adj. oppressive, tyrannical **II.** m.f. oppressor, tyrant.

o·pri·mi·do, a adj. oppressed ♦ **tener el corazón o.** to be sick at heart.

o·pri·mir tr. *(tiranizar)* to oppress, tyrannize; *(apretar)* to press, squeeze.

o·pro·biar tr. to vilify, defame.

o·pro·bio m. shame, disgrace.

o·pro·bio·so, a adj. shameful, disgraceful.

op·tar tr. to choose, select.

op·ta·ti·vo, a I. adj. *(facultativo)* optional; GRAM. optative **II.** m. GRAM. optative.

óp·ti·co, a I. adj. optical **II.** m. optician —f. PHYS. optics.

op·ti·mis·ta I. adj. optimistic **II.** m.f. optimist.

óp·ti·mo, a adj. optimal, best.

op·tó·me·tra m.f. optometrist.

op·to·me·trí·a f. optometry.

o·pues·to, a I. see **oponer II.** adj. *(enfrente)* opposite; *(contrario)* opposing, contrary.

o·pu·len·cia f. opulence.

o·pu·len·to, a adj. opulent.

o·pu·sie·ra, so see **oponer.**

o·ra conj. *(ahora)* now <o. de este lado, o. del otro lado now this way, now the other way>; *(o bien)* either <o. de día, o. de noche either by day or by night>.

o·ra·ción f. *(discurso)* speech, oration; RELIG. prayer; GRAM. *(frase)* sentence; *(cláusula)* clause ♦ **o. adjetiva** adjectival clause ♦ **o. adverbial** adverbial clause ♦ **o. compuesta** or **coordinada** compound or complex sentence ♦ **o. sustantiva** noun clause.

o·rá·cu·lo m. oracle.

o·ra·dor, ·ra m.f. orator.

o·ral adj. oral.

o·ran·gu·tán m. orangutan.

o·rar intr. *(hablar)* to speak, make a speech; *(rezar)* to pray.

o·ra·to·rio, a I. adj. oratory, oratorical **II.** m. *(capilla)* oratory, chapel; MUS. oratorio —f. oratory, rhetoric.

or·be m. *(esfera)* orb, sphere; *(mundo)* world.

ór·bi·ta f. orbit; *(esfera)* sphere, field.

or·den m. *(disposición)* order <o. cronológico chronological order>; *(sistema)* method, system; *(paz)* order, peace <el o. público public order>; *(categoría)* nature, character <asuntos de o. filosófico matters of a philosophical nature>; ARCHIT., BIOL. order ♦ **de primer o.** of the first order, first-rate ♦ **en o.** in order ♦ **llamar al o.** to call to order ♦ **o. de antigüedad** seniority ♦ **o. del día** agenda ♦ **poner en o.** to put in order ♦ **por o.** in its turn —f. order ♦ **a la o. de** at the order of ♦ **a sus órdenes** at your service ♦ **o. de arresto** arrest warrant ♦ **o. del día** MIL. order of the day ♦ **o. de registro** search warrant ♦ **o. judicial** court order.

or·de·na·ción f. *(orden)* arrangement; *(acción)* ordering, arranging; RELIG. ordination.

or·de·na·da f. ordinate.

or·de·na·do, a adj. orderly, methodical.

or·de·na·dor, ·ra I. adj. ordering, arranging **II.** m. or f. computer.

or·de·nan·za f. regulation, ordinance —m. MIL. orderly; *(empleado)* messenger.

or·de·nar tr. *(organizar)* to order, put in order; *(arreglar)* to arrange; *(mandar)* to order, command; *(dirigir)* to direct; RELIG. to ordain —reflex. RELIG. to be ordained.

or·de·ña·dor, ·ra I. adj. milking **II.** m.f.

milker —f. milking machine.

or·de·ñar tr. to milk.

or·di·nal adj. ordinal.

or·di·na·riez f. COLL. vulgarity, commonness.

or·di·na·rio, a adj. *(común)* ordinary, common; *(inculto)* coarse, uncouth; *(mediocre)* ordinary, mediocre; *(diario)* daily.

o·re·ar tr. to air, ventilate —reflex. to get some air, take a walk.

o·re·ja f. ear; *(parte lateral)* flap; *(asa)* handle; MECH. lug, flange ♦ **aguzar las orejas** to prick up one's ears ♦ **con las orejas caídas** or **gachas** crestfallen ♦ **mojarle la o. a alguien** —tr. COLL. to pick a fight with someone.

o·re·je·ra f. *(de gorra)* earflap; *(de arado)* moldboard.

o·re·jón m. *(fruta)* dried peach half; HIST. Inca nobleman.

or·fa·na·to m. orphanage.

or·fan·dad f. *(estado de huérfano)* orphanhood; *(privación)* abandonment.

or·fe·bre m. goldsmith or silversmith.

or·fe·bre·rí·a f. *(arte)* gold or silver work; *(taller)* gold or silver workshop.

or·fe·li·na·to m. orphanage.

or·gá·ni·co, a adj. organic.

or·ga·ni·llo m. barrel organ, hurdy-gurdy.

or·ga·nis·mo m. organism; *(organización)* organization, institution.

or·ga·nis·ta m.f. organist.

or·ga·ni·za·ción f. organization.

or·ga·ni·za·dor, ·ra I. adj. organizing **II.** m.f. organizer.

or·ga·ni·zar §04 tr. to organize —reflex. to be organized.

ór·ga·no m. organ; *(medio)* medium, agency; *(periódico)* journal.

or·gas·mo m. orgasm.

or·gí·a f. orgy.

or·gia·co/giás·ti·co, a adj. orgiastic.

or·gu·llo m. *(arrogancia)* arrogance, conceit; *(sentimiento legítimo)* pride ♦ **no caber en sí de o.** to be bursting with pride.

or·gu·llo·so, a I. adj. *(que tiene orgullo)* proud; *(engreído)* conceited, arrogant **II.** m.f. proud person.

o·rien·ta·ción f. orientation; *(colocación)* positioning; *(consejo)* guidance, direction.

o·rien·tal I. adj. oriental, eastern **II.** m.f. oriental.

o·rien·tar tr. *(colocar)* to position <o. un cañón to position a cannon>; *(un edificio)* to orient, orientate; *(encaminar)* to guide.

o·rien·te m. east, orient.

o·ri·fi·cio m. orifice, opening.

o·ri·gen m. origin; *(principio)* source; *(linaje)* birth <de o. noble of noble birth>; *(causa)* cause ♦ **dar o. a** to give rise to ♦ **en su o.** originally.

o·ri·gi·nal I. adj. original; *(primero)* first; *(nuevo)* new, novel <un concepto o. a novel concept>; *(inventivo)* inventive; *(raro)* odd, singular; *(auténtico)* authentic **II.** m. original; *(manuscrito)* manuscript.

o·ri·gi·na·li·dad f. *(novedad)* originality, novelty; *(carácter excéntrico)* eccentricity.

o·ri·gi·nar tr. & reflex. to originate.

o·ri·gi·na·ria·men·te adv. originally.

o·ri·gi·na·rio, a adj. coming or arising *(de* from).

o·ri·lla f. *(borde)* border, edge; *(del mar)* shore; *(de un río)* bank ♦ **a la o.** or **a orillas de** by,

beside <*a orillas del mar* by the seashore>.
o·ri·llar tr. *(poner orilla)* to border, edge; *(guarnecer)* to trim, decorate.
o·rín[1] m. rust.
o·rín[2] m. urine.
o·ri·na f./**nes** m.inv. urine.
o·ri·nal m. urinal.
o·ri·nar intr. to urinate —reflex. to wet oneself, wet one's pants.
o·riun·do, a adj. native ✦ **ser o. de** to come from, be native to.
or·la f. border; COST. fringe, trimming; HER. orle.
or·lar tr. to border, edge.
or·na·men·tal adj. ornamental.
or·na·men·tar tr. to ornament, adorn.
or·na·men·to m. *(adorno)* ornament, adornment; ARCHIT. ornamentation, molding.
or·nar tr. to bedeck, embellish.
or·ni·to·lo·gí·a f. ornithology.
or·ni·tó·lo·go m.f. ornithologist.
o·ro m. gold; *(moneda)* gold coin; *(riqueza)* wealth, riches ✦ **comprar a peso de o.** to buy dearly, pay a fortune for ✦ **chapado de o.** gold-plated ✦ **de o.** gold, golden ✦ **o. batido** gold leaf ✦ **o. en barras** gold bars, bullion ✦ **o. en polvo** gold dust ✦ **o. negro** black gold, oil ✦ pl. suit in Spanish deck of cards.
o·ron·do, a adj. COLL. *(hinchado)* puffed up, self-satisfied; *(una vasija)* pot-bellied.
o·ro·pel m. tinsel.
or·ques·ta f. orchestra.
or·ques·ta·ción f. orchestration.
or·ques·tal adj. orchestral.
or·ques·tar tr. to orchestrate.
or·quí·de·a f. orchid.
or·ti·ga f. nettle.
or·to·don·cia f. orthodontia.
or·to·don·tis·ta I. adj. orthodontic II. m.f. orthodontist.
or·to·do·xo, a adj. orthodox.
or·to·gra·fí·a f. orthography.
or·to·grá·fi·co, a adj. orthographic.
or·to·pé·di·co, a I. adj. orthopedic II. m.f. orthopedist.
or·to·pe·dis·ta m.f. orthopedist.
o·ru·ga f. ENTOM. caterpillar; AUTO. caterpillar tread.
o·ru·jo m. marc, residue (of pressed grapes).
or·zue·lo m. sty.
os pron. you <*os vi en el museo* I saw you in the museum>; to you <*os dieron la oportunidad de discutirlo* they gave you the opportunity to discuss it>; you, for you <*os buscaba un asiento* he was looking for a seat for you>; from you <*os robaron un coche* they stole a car from you>; yourselves <*vosotros os laváis* you wash yourselves>; each other <*vosotros os amáis* you love each other>.
o·sa·dí·a f. boldness, audacity.
o·sa·do, a adj. bold, daring.
o·sa·men·ta f. *(conjunto de huesos)* bones; *(esqueleto)* skeleton.
o·sar intr. to dare.
os·ci·la·ción f. oscillation; *(balanceo)* swing, swinging movement; *(vacilación)* vacillation, wavering.
os·ci·la·dor m. oscillator.
os·ci·lar intr. to oscillate; *(balancearse)* to swing, move back and forth; *(fluctuar)* to fluctuate, vary; *(vacilar)* to vacillate, waver.
os·ci·la·to·rio, a adj. oscillatory.
ós·cu·lo m. kiss.

os·cu·re·cer §17 tr. *(volver oscuro)* to obscure, darken; *(volver poco inteligible)* to obscure, conceal; *(eclipsar)* to overshadow, eclipse; *(debilitar el brillo)* to tarnish, dim; PAINT. to shade, shadow —intr. to be getting dark —reflex. *(ponerse oscuro)* to darken, grow dark; *(nublarse)* to become cloudy or overcast.
os·cu·re·ci·mien·to m. darkening.
os·cu·ri·dad f. *(sombra)* darkness; *(imprecisión)* obscurity, haziness; *(incertidumbre)* uncertainty.
os·cu·ro, a adj. *(sin luz)* dark; *(desconocido)* obscure <*un poeta o.* an obscure poet>; *(negro)* dark; *(sombrío)* gloomy; *(confuso)* hazy, unclear; *(incierto)* uncertain; *(nebuloso)* cloudy, overcast ✦ **a oscuras** in the dark ✦ **hacer o.** to become dark ✦ **o. como boca de lobo** pitch-black, pitch-dark ✦ **quedarse a oscuras** to be left in the dark.
ó·se·o, a adj. osseous, bony.
o·si·fi·car·se §70 reflex. to ossify.
os·mio m. osmium.
ós·mo·sis or **os·mo·sis** f. osmosis.
o·so m. bear ✦ **o. gris** grizzly bear.
os·ten·si·ble adj. ostensible.
os·ten·si·vo, a adj. ostensive.
os·ten·ta·ción f. ostentation.
os·ten·tar tr. *(mostrar)* to show; *(hacer gala)* to flaunt, make a show of.
os·ten·to·so, a adj. showy, grandiose.
os·te·ó·lo·go, a m.f. osteologist.
os·te·o·pa·tí·a f. osteopathy.
os·tra f. oyster.
os·tra·cis·mo m. ostracism.
o·te·ar tr. *(desde lugar alto)* to scan, survey; *(escudriñar)* to watch, observe.
o·ti·tis f. otitis, inflammation of the ear.
o·to·ñal adj. autumnal.
o·to·ño m. autumn, fall.
o·tor·ga·dor, ·ra I. adj. granting II. m.f. grantor.
o·tor·gar §47 tr. *(consentir)* to grant, give; LAW to execute, draw up.
o·to·rri·no·la·rin·go·lo·gí·a f. otorhinolaryngology.
o·tro, a I. adj. *(distinto)* other, another <*¿quieres o. taza de café?* do you want another cup of coffee?>; *(igual)* another <*ella es o. María Callas* she is another Maria Callas> ✦ **o. cosa** something else ✦ **o. vez** again ✦ **por o. parte** on the other hand II. pron. another one <*no tengo o.* I do not have another one> ✦ **¡o.!** THEAT. encore! ✦ **unos a otros** each other, one another ✦ pl. others.
o·va·ción f. ovation.
o·va·cio·nar tr. to give an ovation to.
o·val or **o·va·la·do, a** adj. oval.
ó·va·lo m. oval.
o·vá·ri·co adj. ovarian.
o·va·rio m. ovary.
o·ve·ja f. ewe, female sheep ✦ **o. descarriada** lost sheep.
o·ve·je·ro, a I. m. shepherd —f. shepherdess II. adj. ✦ **perro o.** sheepdog.
o·ver·tu·ra f. overture.
o·vi·llar tr. to roll or wind —reflex. to roll or curl up.
o·vi·llo m. *(de hilo)* ball; *(cosa enredada)* tangle, snarl ✦ **hacerse un o.** COLL. *(acurrucarse)* to curl up; *(embrollarse)* to get tangled up.
o·vi·no, a adj. ovine, of sheep.
o·ví·pa·ro, a I. adj. oviparous II. m.f. ovip-

arous animal.

ov·ni m. UFO, unidentified flying object.

o·vu·la·ción f. ovulation.

o·vu·lar I. adj. ovular **II.** intr. to ovulate.

ó·vu·lo m. ovule.

o·xi·da·ción f. oxidation.

o·xi·dar tr. & reflex. to oxidize, rust.

ó·xi·do m. oxide.

o·xi·ge·na·do, a adj. oxygenated ♦ **agua o.** hydrogen peroxide.

o·xi·ge·nar tr. to oxygenate —reflex. to breathe fresh air.

o·xí·ge·no m. oxygen.

o·yen·te I. adj. hearing, listening **II.** m.f. *(persona que oye)* hearer, listener; EDUC. auditor ♦ **los oyentes** the audience.

o·ye·ra, yó see **oír.**

o·zo·no m. ozone.

P

p, P f. seventeenth letter of the Spanish alphabet.

pa·be·llón m. *(bandera)* flag, banner; *(tienda de campaña)* bell tent; *(dosel)* bed canopy; *(edificio)* pavilion; MARIT. registration; ANAT. outer ear ♦ **arriar el p.** to lower the flag ♦ **p. de caza** shooting box.

pa·bi·lo m. candle wick.

pá·bu·lo m. *(alimento)* food, pabulum; *(sustento)* support, encouragement ♦ **dar p. a** to encourage.

pa·cer §17 intr. to graze.

pa·chón m. COLL. dull fellow.

pa·cho·rra f. AMER., COLL. slowness, sluggishness.

pa·cien·cia f. patience ♦ **acabársele** or **agotársele a uno la p.** to lose one's patience • **armarse de p.** to arm oneself with patience • **perder la p.** to lose one's temper.

pa·cien·te adj. & mf. patient.

pa·ci·fi·ca·ción f. pacification.

pa·ci·fi·ca·dor, ·ra I. adj. pacifying **II.** m.f. pacifier, peacemaker.

pa·ci·fi·car §70 tr. to pacify —reflex. to calm down.

pa·cí·fi·co, a adj. peaceful, pacific.

pa·ci·fis·ta adj. & m.f. pacifist.

pa·co·ti·lla f. ♦ **de p.** shoddy, junky.

pac·tar tr. to agree to or upon —intr. to come to an agreement, make a pact ♦ **p. con el diablo** to sell one's soul to the devil.

pac·to m. pact, agreement.

pa·de·cer §17 tr. *(sufrir)* to suffer *(de from)*; *(soportar)* to endure, bear; *(ser víctima)* to be the victim of <*padece una equivocación* he is the victim of an error> —intr. *(sufrir)* to suffer; *(recibir daño)* to be damaged ♦ **p. del corazón** to have heart trouble.

pa·de·ci·mien·to m. *(sufrimiento)* suffering; *(enfermedad)* ailment, illness.

pa·dras·tro m. stepfather; *(pellejo)* hangnail.

pa·dre I. m. father; FIG. father, creator; RELIG. father, priest ♦ **p. espiritual** confessor • **P. Eterno** Heavenly Father • **P. Nuestro** Lord's Prayer • **p. político** father-in-law • **Santo P.** RELIG. Holy Father ♦ pl. parents **II.** adj. COLL. terrific, tremendous.

pa·dre·nues·tro m. Lord's Prayer, Our Father ♦ **en un p.** COLL. in the wink of an eye.

pa·dri·llo m. AMER. sire, stallion.

pa·dri·no m. *(de niño)* godfather; *(de boda)* best man; *(de desafío)* second; *(patrocinador)* sponsor ♦ pl. godparents.

pa·drón m. *(censo)* census, register; *(columna)* memorial column or pillar; AMER. sire, stallion.

¡paf! interj. bang!, thud!

pa·ga f. *(acción)* payment; *(sueldo)* wages ♦ **buena p.** good pay.

pa·ga·de·ro, a adj. payable, due ♦ **p. a la vista, entrega** payable on sight, delivery.

pa·ga·do, a adj. ♦ **p. de sí mismo** self-satisfied.

pa·ga·no, a adj. & m.f. pagan.

pa·gar §47 tr. to pay; *(recompensar)* to repay <*p. un favor* to repay a favor> ♦ **p. a crédito** or **a plazos** to pay in installments • **p. con la misma moneda** to give (someone) a taste of their own medicine • **pagarla(s)** to pay for it • **p. por adelantado** to pay in advance —intr. to pay.

pa·ga·ré m. promissory note, IOU.

pá·gi·na f. page.

pa·gi·nar tr. to paginate, number the pages of.

pa·go¹ adj. COLL. paid ♦ **estar p.** to be even.

pa·go² m. *(entrega)* payment; *(recompensa)* repayment, recompense.

pa·ís m. *(territorio)* country, nation; *(región)* region, territory.

pai·sa·je m. landscape.

pai·sa·jis·ta I. adj. landscape **II.** m.f. landscape painter.

pai·sa·no, a I. adj. of the same country or region **II.** m.f. *(campesino)* peasant; *(compatriota)* fellow countryman/woman.

pa·ja f. straw; *(lo desechable)* deadwood, chaff; *(cosa sin substancia)* rubbish; *(para beber)* (drinking) straw.

pa·jar m. straw loft, barn.

pa·ja·re·ar intr. *(cazar)* to hunt birds; *(holgazanear)* to loaf about.

pa·ja·re·ra f. bird cage.

pa·ja·re·rí·a f. bird shop.

pa·ja·re·ro, a I. adj. bird **II.** m. *(vendedor)* bird seller; *(cazador)* bird catcher.

pá·ja·ro m. bird ♦ **matar dos pájaros de un tiro** COLL. to kill two birds with one stone • **p. carpintero** woodpecker • **tener la cabeza llena de pájaros** COLL. to be a featherbrain.

pa·ja·rra·co m. *(pájaro)* large ugly bird; COLL. *(pillo)* clever bastard.

pa·je m. HIST. page.

pa·la f. *(herramienta)* shovel, spade; *(contenido)* shovelful; *(parte plana)* blade; *(del remo)* blade; *(del curtidor)* fleshing knife; *(de bisagra)* leaf; *(de la hélice)* (propeller) blade ♦ **p. mecánica** power shovel.

pa·la·bra f. word; *(facultad)* speech; *(elocuencia)* eloquence; *(promesa)* word, promise ♦ **bajo p.** on one's word of honor • **cogerle la p. a alguien** to take someone at his word • **conceder** or **dar la p. a** to give the floor to • **correr la p.** to pass the word • **cruzar p.** to talk, converse • **cumplir** or **mantener su p. uno** to keep one's word • **decir** or **tener la última p.** to have the last word • **dejar a alguien con la p. en la boca** to turn one's back on someone who is speaking • **de p.** orally • **dirigir la p. a** to address, speak to • **empeñar la p.** to pledge one's word • **en dos** or **en pocas palabras** in brief • **en una p.** in a word, in short • **faltar a su p.** to go back on one's word • **medir uno sus palabras** to weigh one's words • **no decir**

p. not to say a word • **no tener p.** to be unreliable • **¡p.!** on my word of honor! • **p. de honor** word of honor • **p. de matrimonio** promise of marriage • **p. por p.** word for word, verbatim • **palabras mayores** strong language • **pedir la p.** to ask for the floor • **quedarse sin palabras** to be left speechless • **quitarle a alguien la p. de la boca** to take the words right out of someone's mouth • **tomar la p.** to take the floor.

pa·la·bre·o m. chatter.

pa·la·bre·rí·a f. *lo* m. COLL. idle chatter.

pa·la·bro·ta f. COLL. swearword, dirty word ♦ **decir palabrotas** to swear.

pa·la·ce·te m. elegant house.

pa·la·cie·go, a adj. *(magnífico)* palatial, magnificent; *(del palacio)* court, palace.

pa·la·cio m. palace ♦ **p. de justicia** courthouse.

pa·la·da f. shovelful.

pa·la·dar m. *(de la boca)* palate, roof of the mouth; *(gusto)* taste.

pa·la·de·ar tr. to savor, relish.

pa·la·dín m. paladin; FIG. champion.

pa·la·dio m. palladium.

pa·la·frén m. palfrey.

pa·la·fre·ne·ro m. groom, equerry.

pa·lan·ca f. lever; *(utensilio)* crowbar; *(palo)* shaft, pole; COLL. *(influencia)* pull, influence ♦ **p. de cambio** gearshift • **p. del timón** rudder bar.

pa·lan·ga·na f. washbasin.

pa·lan·quín m. palanquin.

pa·la·tal adj. & f. palatal.

pal·co m. THEAT. box.

pa·le·ar tr. to shovel.

pa·len·que m. hitching post.

pa·le·o·lí·ti·co, a adj. & m. Paleolithic.

pa·le·on·to·lo·gí·a f. paleontology.

pa·le·on·tó·lo·go, a m.f. paleontologist.

pa·le·o·zoi·co, a adj. & m. Paleozoic.

pa·les·tra f. *(lugar de lucha)* palestra, gymnasium; *(campo)* arena ♦ **salir a la p.** to enter the fray or the arena.

pa·le·ta f. *(pala pequeña)* small shovel or spade; *(del pintor)* palette; *(del albañil)* trowel; ANAT. shoulder blade; MECH. *(álabe)* paddle (of water wheel); *(de la hélice)* blade; *(diente)* front tooth.

pa·le·ti·lla f. shoulder blade.

pa·le·tó m. coat, greatcoat.

pa·lia·ti·vo, a adj. & m. palliative.

pa·li·de·cer §17 intr. *(ponerse pálido)* to turn pale, grow pale; *(descolorarse)* to fade.

pa·li·dez f. paleness, pallor.

pá·li·do, a adj. *(descolorido)* pale, pallid; FIG. pallid, lackluster.

pa·li·du·cho, a adj. COLL. pale.

pa·li·llo m. *(palito)* small stick; *(para agujas)* knitting-needle holder; *(mondadientes)* toothpick; *(de tambor)* drumstick.

pa·li·to m. small stick ♦ **pisar el p.** AMER., COLL. to fall into the trap.

pa·li·za f. beating, thrashing.

pa·llar[1] intr. to sing improvised songs —tr. MIN. to sort.

pa·llar[2] m. *(alubia)* lima or butter bean; *(judía)* haricot bean.

pal·ma f. *(de la mano)* palm; *(palmera)* palm (tree); *(hoja)* palm leaf; *(victoria)* victory, triumph; VET. palm (of a hoof) ♦ **llevarse la p.** to carry the day • pl. applause • **andar en p.** to be applauded • **batir p.** to applaud.

pal·ma·do, a I. adj. *(de forma de palma)* palmate, palm-shaped; *(ligado)* webbed **II.** f. *(golpe)* slap, pat; *(ruido)* hand clap ♦ **dar palmadas** to clap one's hands.

pal·mar[1] **I.** adj. ANAT. palmar **II.** m. palm grove.

pal·mar[2] intr. COLL. to die, kick the bucket.

pal·me·a·do, a adj. *(de forma de palma)* palmate, palm-shaped; *(ligado)* webbed.

pal·me·ar intr. *(batir palmas)* to clap, applaud —tr. R.P. to pat, slap.

pal·me·ra f. palm tree.

pal·mí·pe·do, a adj. & m. webfooted (animal).

pal·mi·to m. palm heart.

pal·mo m. span, palm ♦ **crecer a palmos** to shoot up • **dejar a alguien con un p. de narices** to let someone down • **p. a p.** little by little, inch by inch.

pal·mo·te·ar intr. to applaud.

pa·lo m. *(vara)* stick, pole; *(mango)* stick, handle <p. de escoba broomstick>; MARIT. mast, spar; *(golpe)* hit, whack ♦ **dar de palos** to whack • **de tal p., tal astilla** like father, like son • **de p.** wooden • **p. ensebado** AMER. greased pole • **p. mayor** mainmast • **p. santo** lignum vitae • **palos de golf** golf clubs.

pa·lo·ma f. dove, pigeon ♦ **p. buchona** pouter pigeon • **p. mensajera** homing pigeon.

pa·lo·mar m. dovecote, pigeon loft.

pa·lo·me·ta f. *(pez)* saurel, yellow jack; *(tuerca)* wing or butterfly nut.

pa·lo·mi·lla f. *(de graneros)* grain moth; *(de caballerías)* back, fore-rump; *(tuerca)* wing or butterfly nut; *(sostén)* wall bracket.

pa·lo·mi·ta f. popcorn.

pa·lo·mo m. *(macho)* cock pigeon; *(paloma torcaz)* ring-necked dove.

pa·lo·te m. MUS. drumstick; *(trazo)* pothook.

pal·pa·ble adj. palpable.

pal·par tr. *(tocar)* to touch, feel; *(experimentar)* to appreciate —reflex. to be felt, be perceptible.

pal·pi·ta·ción f. palpitation.

pal·pi·tan·te adj. palpitating; FIG. burning.

pal·pi·tar intr. *(temblar)* to palpitate, throb; *(latir)* to beat; *(emocionarse)* to quiver, be aflutter (with emotion); *(manifestar)* to throb <en su verso palpita la emoción his poetry throbs with emotion>.

pál·pi·to m. COLL. hunch, presentiment.

pal·ta f. AMER. avocado.

pa·lu·dis·mo m. malaria.

pa·lur·do, a I. adj. boorish **II.** m.f. boor.

pam·pa f. pampa, plain.

pám·pa·no m. *(pimpollo)* tendril, vine shoot; *(hoja)* vine leaf; ICHTH. salp.

pam·pe·ro, a I. adj. of or from the pampas **II.** m.f. AMER. pampero (inhabitant).

pam·pli·na f. COLL. *(tontería)* nonsense; *(insignificancia)* trifle.

pam·pli·na·da f. COLL. nonsense.

pan m. bread; *(pieza)* loaf of bread <un p. grande a big loaf of bread>; *(masa)* dough; cake <un p. de jabón a cake of soap>; *(sustento)* bread, food; METAL. leaf, foil ♦ **a p. y agua** on bread and water • **contigo p. y cebolla** COLL. for better or for worse • **ganarse el p.** to earn a living • **p. de maíz** cornbread • **p. fermentado** leavened bread • **p. integral** whole-wheat bread • **ser más bueno que el p.** to be kindness itself • **ser p. comido** COLL. to be a cinch.

pa·na f. corduroy.

pa·na·ce·a f. panacea.
pa·na·de·rí·a f. bakery.
pa·na·de·ro, a m.f. baker.
pa·nal m. honeycomb.
pa·na·má m. Panama hat.
pa·na·me·ri·ca·no, a adj. Pan-American.
pa·na·te·la f. long thin sponge cake.
pán·cre·as m.inv. pancreas.
pan·cre·á·ti·co, a adj. pancreatic.
pan·cro·má·ti·co, a adj. panchromatic.
pan·cho, a COLL. **I.** adj. calm, unruffled ♦ **quedarse tan p.** to keep one's cool **II.** m. R.P. hot dog.
pan·da m. panda.
pan·de·ar intr. & reflex. *(la madera)* to warp; *(la pared)* to bulge.
pan·de·mo·nio/mó·nium m. pandemonium.
pan·de·re·ta f. tambourine.
pan·de·ro m. tambourine.
pan·de·re·te·ar intr. to play the tambourine.
pan·di·lla f. gang, band.
pan·di·lle·ro/llis·ta m. member of a gang.
pa·ne·ci·llo m. roll, bun.
pa·ne·gí·ri·co, a **I.** adj. panegyrical **II.** m. panegyric.
pa·nel m. panel ♦ pl. paneling.
pa·ne·ra f. breadbasket.
pán·fi·lo, a adj. *(cachazudo)* slow; *(bobo)* foolish.
pan·fle·to m. pamphlet.
pa·nia·gua·do m. favorite, protégé.
pá·ni·co, a adj. & m. panic.
pa·ni·zo m. *(mijo)* millet; *(maíz)* corn, maize.
pa·no·plia f. panoply.
pa·no·ra·ma m. panorama.
pa·no·rá·mi·co, a adj. panoramic.
pan·que·que m. AMER. pancake.
pan·ta·lla f. *(de lámpara)* lamp shade; *(de hogar)* fire screen; *(telón)* movie screen; *(de radar)* screen; *(de cine)* film <*las estrellas de la p.* film stars>; *(protección)* shield.
pan·ta·lón m./**lo·nes** m.pl. *(de hombre)* trousers, pants; *(de mujer)* slacks ♦ **llevar los pantalones** COLL. to wear the pants in the family • **p. corto** shorts • **p. vaquero** jeans.
pan·ta·lo·ne·ra f. trouser maker.
pan·ta·nal m. marsh, bog.
pan·ta·no m. marsh; FIG. difficulty.
pan·ta·no·so, a adj. boggy, marshy.
pan·te·ís·ta **I.** adj. pantheistic **II.** m.f. pantheist.
pan·te·ón m. pantheon.
pan·te·ra f. panther.
pan·tó·gra·fo m. pantograph.
pan·to·mi·ma f. pantomime.
pan·to·rri·lla f. calf.
pan·tu·fla f. slipper.
pan·za f. COLL. *(barriga)* belly, paunch; ZOOL. rumen; *(de vasija)* belly.
pan·za·da f. push given with the belly ♦ **darse una p.** to gorge oneself on.
pan·za·zo m. ♦ **darse un p.** to do a bellyflop.
pan·zón, a/on·a/zu·do, a adj. paunchy.
pa·ñal m. diaper ♦ **dejar en pañales a alguien** COLL. to leave someone standing • **estar en pañales** *(ser niño)* to be in diapers; *(ser novato)* to be wet behind the ears.
pa·ño m. *(tela)* cloth; *(de lana)* woolen cloth; *(tapiz)* drapery; *(ancho)* panel; *(trapo)* rag ♦ **p. de lágrimas** shoulder to cry on • **paños menores** underwear.
pa·ño·le·ta f. scarf, fichu.

pa·ño·lón m. shawl.
pa·ñue·lo m. handkerchief; *(pañoleta)* scarf ♦ **p. de bolsillo** pocket handkerchief.
pa·pa¹ m. Pope ♦ **ser más papista que el p.** to be more Catholic than the Pope.
pa·pa² f. AMER. potato ♦ **p. dulce** sweet potato • **no saber ni p. de** COLL. not to know a thing about ♦ pl. COLL. *(comida)* food, grub; *(puches)* pap, mush.
pa·pá m. papa, daddy ♦ **P. Noel** Father Christmas.
pa·pa·da f. double chin.
pa·pa·ga·yo m. parrot.
pa·pal **I.** adj. papal **II.** m. AMER. potato field.
pa·pa·lo·te/pe·lo·te m. C. AMER., MEX. kite.
pa·pa·mos·cas m.inv. COLL. simpleton, fool.
pa·pa·na·tas m.inv. COLL. fool.
pa·par tr. ♦ **p. moscas** to gape.
pa·pa·ya f. papaya.
pa·pel m. paper; *(hoja)* piece of paper; *(documento)* document; *(función)* role; THEAT. role ♦ **hacer buen p.** to do well • **hacer el p. de** to act as • **hacer mal p.** to do poorly • **p. cuadriculado** graph paper • **p. de arroz** rice paper • **p. de calcar** tracing paper • **p. de cartas** stationery • **p. de estraza** brown wrapping paper • **p. de lija** sandpaper • **p. de seda** tissue paper • **p. encerado** wax paper • **p. higiénico** toilet paper • **p. moneda** paper money • **p. para escribir** writing paper • **p. rayado** lined paper • **p. secante** blotting paper ♦ pl. *(documentos)* papers, documents; *(identificación)* identification papers.
pa·pe·le·o m. FIG. red tape, paper work.
pa·pe·le·ro, a **I.** adj. paper **II.** m.f. *(fabricante)* paper manufacturer; *(vendedor)* stationer.
pa·pe·le·ta f. *(cédula)* card; *(cucurucho)* paper cone or bag; *(de voto)* ballot paper ♦ **p. de empeño** pawn ticket.
pa·pe·lón m. ♦ **hacer un p.** to make a fool of oneself.
pa·pe·ra f. goiter ♦ pl. mumps.
pa·pi m. COLL. daddy, pop.
pa·pi·la f. papilla.
pa·pi·lla f. pap, soft food ♦ **estar hecho p.** COLL. to be exhausted or beat • **hacer p. a** COLL. to make mincemeat of.
pa·pi·ro m. papyrus.
pa·pis·ta adj. & m.f. papist.
pa·que·bo·te m. packet boat, packet.
pa·que·te **I.** m. *(bulto)* package; *(caja)* pack, packet <*un p. de cigarillos* a pack of cigarettes>; *(paquebote)* packet boat, packet; COLL. *(mentira)* lie **II.** adj. AMER. smart, elegant.
pa·que·te·rí·a f. elegance, chic.
pa·qui·der·mo m. pachyderm.
par **I.** adj. *(igual)* equal; MATH. even; ZOOL. paired **II.** m. *(dos)* couple <*un p. de huevos* a couple of eggs>; pair <*un p. de pantalones* a pair of pants>; *(yunta)* pair, team; *(dignidad)* peer; MATH. even number; ARCHIT. rafter ♦ **a la p.** *(igualmente)* on a par, equally; *(a un tiempo)* at the same time; COM. at par ♦ **al p. de** on the same level as • **a pares** or **en pares** in pairs, by twos • **de p. en p.** wide <*abierto de p. en p.* wide open> • **sin p.** without peer or equal.
pa·ra prep. *(movimiento)* towards, for; *(destino, fin)* for, to, in order to; *(duración, tiempo)* for, by, about to, on the point of, to, for; *(comparación)* for, to, considering; *(en provecho de)* for; *(no se traduce)* <*crema p. afeitar* shaving cream> **• p.**

con toward • **p. concluir** in conclusion • **p. que** so that, in order that • **¿p. qué?** why *<¿p. qué has venido?* why have you come?>; for what *<¿p. qué sirve esa manija?* what is this handle for?> • **p. siempre** forever.

pa·ra·bién m. congratulations.

pa·rá·bo·la f. *(cuento)* parable; GEOM. parabola.

pa·ra·bri·sas m.inv. windshield, windscreen (G.B.).

pa·ra·ca·í·das f.inv. parachute.

pa·ra·cai·dis·ta m.f. *(aficionado)* parachutist; MIL. paratrooper.

pa·ra·cho·ques m.inv. bumper, fender.

pa·ra·da f. see **parado, a.**

pa·ra·de·ro m. *(sitio)* whereabouts; *(destino)* destination ♦ **averiguar el p. de** to locate • **ignorar el p. de algo, alguien** not to know where something, someone is.

pa·ra·dig·ma m. paradigm.

pa·ra·di·sia·co/sí·a·co, a adj. heavenly.

pa·ra·do, a I. adj. *(inmóvil)* stationary; *(detenido)* stopped; *(inactivo)* idle; *(sin empleo)* unemployed; AMER. standing ♦ **salir bien, mal p.** to come off well, badly **II.** f. *(acto)* stop; *(suspensión)* halt; *(sitio)* stop *<p. de autobús* bus stop>; MIL. parade ♦ **p. de taxis** taxi *or* cab stand • **p. en firme** *or* **en seco** dead stop.

pa·ra·do·ja f. paradox.

pa·ra·dó·ji·co, a adj. paradoxical.

pa·ra·dor m. inn, roadhouse.

pa·ra·fi·na f. paraffin.

pa·ra·fi·nar tr. to paraffin, treat with paraffin.

pa·ra·fra·se·ar tr. to paraphrase.

pa·ra·fra·sis f.inv. paraphrase.

pa·ra·guas m.inv. umbrella.

pa·ra·güe·rí·a f. umbrella shop.

pa·ra·güe·ro, a m.f. umbrella maker *or* seller —m. umbrella stand.

pa·ra·í·so m. paradise; THEAT. top balcony.

pa·ra·je m. *(lugar)* spot; *(región)* area.

pa·ra·le·lo, a I. adj. parallel **II.** m. GEOG. parallel; *(comparación)* parallel, comparison ♦ **correr p.** to run parallel to • **establecer un p.** to draw a parallel between, compare —f. *(línea)* parallel line ♦ pl. SPORT. parallel bars.

pa·ra·le·lo·gra·mo m. parallelogram.

pa·ra·li·sis f.inv. paralysis ♦ **p. cerebral** cerebral palsy • **p. infantil** poliomyelitis.

pa·ra·lí·ti·co, a adj. & m.f. paralytic.

pa·ra·li·za·ción f. immobilization, paralyzation; COM. *(estancamiento)* stagnation.

pa·ra·li·zar §04 tr. *(causar parálisis)* to paralyze; FIG. *(estorbar)* to impede, stop —reflex. to become paralyzed.

pa·ra·mé·di·co, a adj. paramedical.

pa·rá·me·tro m. parameter.

pá·ra·mo m. high barren plain.

pa·ran·gón m. comparison, parallel ♦ **sin p.** matchless.

pa·ra·no·ia f. paranoia.

pa·ra·noi·co, a adj. & m.f. paranoid.

pa·ra·pe·tar·se reflex. MIL. to defend oneself with parapets; FIG. to protect oneself.

pa·ra·pe·to m. parapet.

pa·ra·plé·ji·co, a adj. & m.f. paraplegic.

pa·ra·psi·co·lo·gí·a f. parapsychology.

pa·rar intr. *(cesar)* to stop, halt; COLL. *(terminar)* to end up *<¿adónde vas a p. con esos preparativos?* where are you going to end up with all those preparations?>; *(alojarse)* to lodge, stay; *(caer)* to end up, land *<la carta paró en manos*

de su hija the letter ended up in the hands of his daughter> ♦ **ir a p.** to end up • **p. en** to end up, result in • **p. en seco** to stop dead • **sin p.** ceaselessly, nonstop —tr. *(detener)* to stop, halt; *(impedir)* to check; *(prevenir)* to forestall ♦ **p. la oreja** AMER. to prick up one's ears —reflex. *(detenerse)* to stop; COLL. *(beneficiarse)* to prosper; AMER. to stand up ♦ **p. a** to stop, pause *<p. a pensar* to stop to think>.

pa·ra·rra·yos m. lightning rod.

pa·ra·sí·ti·co, a adj. parasitic.

pa·rá·si·to, a I. adj. parasitic **II.** m. parasite.

pa·ra·sol m. parasol.

par·ce·la f. parcel, plot.

par·ce·lar tr. to divide into plots, parcel.

par·che m. *(emplasto)* plaster; *(remiendo)* patch; *(de tambor)* drumhead.

par·cial I. adj. partial **II.** m. *(partidario)* partisan, follower; *(examen)* periodic exam.

par·cia·li·dad f. partiality; *(prejuicio)* bias.

par·co, a adj. *(corto)* sparing *<p. en el hablar* sparing in words>; *(frugal)* frugal, economical; *(moderado)* moderate.

¡par·diez! interj. COLL. good God!, by Jove!

par·do, a I. adj. *(moreno)* brown; *(oscuro)* dark **II.** m.f. AMER. mulatto.

par·dus·co, a adj. brownish.

pa·re·ar tr. to match, pair.

pa·re·cer¹ m. *(opinión)* opinion, view; *(aspecto)* appearance ♦ **al p.** apparently • **cambiar de p.** to change one's mind • **ser del p. que** to be of the opinion that.

pa·re·cer² §17 intr. *(dar la impresión)* to seem; *(querer)* to like *<si te parece, saldremos inmediatamente* if you like, we will leave immediately>; *(semejarse)* to resemble, seem like; *(tener cierto aspecto)* to look, appear ♦ **al p.** apparently • **así parece** so it seems • **p. mentira** to be hard to believe —reflex. to look alike • **p. a** to resemble, look like.

pa·re·ci·do, a I. adj. similar ♦ **bien p.** good-looking • **ser p. a** to resemble, be like **II.** m. similarity.

pa·red f. wall ♦ **darse contra la p.** to knock one's head against the wall • **p. por medio** next door.

pa·re·dón m. large thick wall.

pa·re·jo, a I. adj. *(igual)* alike, equal; *(liso)* even, smooth; *(llano)* flat, level ♦ **ir parejos** *(cosas, personas)* to be equal; *(caballos)* to go neck and neck **II.** f. *(par)* pair; *(hombre y mujer)* couple; *(dos compañeros)* pair, couple; *(de baile)* dancing partner; *(de juego)* partner in card games ♦ **por parejas** two by two, in pairs.

pa·ren·te·la f. relations, relatives.

pa·ren·tes·co m. *(vínculo)* kinship; *(lazo)* tie.

pa·rén·te·sis m.inv. parenthesis; *(frase)* parenthetical statement; *(interrupción)* break, interruption ♦ **entre p.** in parentheses • **sea dicho entre p.** incidentally.

pa·ria m.f. pariah.

pa·ri·dad f. parity.

pa·rien·te, a m.f. relative, relation ♦ **p. consanguíneo** blood relation.

pa·rie·tal adj. & m. parietal (bone).

pa·ri·hue·las f.pl. stretcher.

pa·rir intr. & tr. to give birth (to).

pa·ri·ta·rio, a adj. joint.

par·la·men·ta·rio, a/ris·ta I. adj. parliamentary **II.** m.f. member of parliament.

par·la·men·to m. *(asamblea)* parliament; *(discurso)* address; THEAT. long speech.

par·lan·chín, i·na I. adj. talkative, chattering **II.** m.f. chatterbox.

par·lan·te adj. speaking, talking.

par·lar intr. to chatter.

par·lo·te·ar intr. COLL. to chatter.

par·lo·te·o m. COLL. chatter.

pa·ro m. (suspensión) stoppage, standstill; (desempleo) unemployment ♦ **p. forzoso** layoff • **p. laboral** strike.

pa·ro·dia f. parody.

pa·ro·diar tr. to parody.

pa·ro·dis·ta m.f. parodist.

pa·ró·ni·mo, a I. adj. paronymous **II.** m. paronym.

pa·ro·xis·mo m. paroxysm.

par·pa·de·ar intr. (párpados) to blink; (luz) to flicker; (estrellas) to twinkle.

par·pa·de·o m. (ojos) blink; (luz) flicker; (estrellas) twinkle.

pár·pa·do m. eyelid.

par·que m. park; (estacionamiento) parking lot ♦ **p. de atracciones** amusement park.

par·qué m. parquet.

par·que·ar tr. AMER. to park.

par·que·o m. AMER. (acción) parking; (lugar) parking lot.

par·que·dad f. (prudencia) economy; (templanza) moderation.

par·quí·me·tro m. parking meter.

pa·rra f. grapevine ♦ **hoja de p.** fig leaf (on statue).

pá·rra·fo m. paragraph ♦ **echar un p.** COLL. to have a chat • **hacer p. aparte** COLL. to change the subject.

pa·rral m. (lugar) vineyard; (parra con armazón) vine arbor.

pa·rran·da f. COLL. party, spree ♦ **andar** or **estar de p.** to be out for a good time.

pa·rran·de·ar intr. COLL. to go out partying.

pa·rran·dis·ta m.f. COLL. reveler.

pa·rri·ci·da m.f. parricide.

pa·rri·ci·dio m. parricide.

pa·rri·lla f. grill; (rejilla) grating; (restaurant) steak house.

pa·rri·lla·da f. dish of grilled fish or seafood; R.P. dish of grilled meats.

pá·rro·co I. m. parish priest **II.** adj. parish.

pa·rro·quia f. (territorio) parish; (habitantes) parishioners; (iglesia) parish church.

pa·rro·quial adj. parochial, parish.

pa·rro·quia·no, a I. adj. parochial, parish **II.** m.f. (feligrés) parishioner; (cliente) customer.

par·si·mo·nia f. (templanza) moderation; (calma) calm.

par·si·mo·nio·so, a adj. (sobrio) parsimonious; (tranquilo) unhurried.

par·te f. part; (porción) portion; (cantidad asignada) share; (sitio) place, spot; (lado) side; (facción) side; COM., LAW party; THEAT. role ♦ **a esta p.** ago, past <de un mes a esta p. a month ago> • **de p. de** (a nombre de) in the name of, on behalf of; (en favor de) on the side of; (por orden de) at the command of • **¿de p. de quién?** who's calling? • **en alguna p.** somewhere • **en cualquier p.** anywhere • **en gran p.** for the most part • **en ninguna p.** nowhere • **en p. partly** • **en** or **por todas partes** everywhere • **hacer su p.** to do one's share • **la mayor p.** the majority • **llevar la mejor p.** to have the upper hand • **no ser p. de** to have nothing to do with • **p. actora** LAW plaintiff • **p. de la**

oración GRAM. part of speech • **p. por p.** bit by bit • **poner de su p.** to do what one can • **ponerse de p. de** to side with • **por la mayor p.** for the most part • **por mi p.** as far as I am concerned • **por otra p.** on the other hand • **partes** step by step • **tener** or **tomar p. en** to take part in, participate in —m. (escrito) note; (despacho) dispatch, message; (informe) report ♦ **dar p.** to report • **dar p. a** to notify, inform.

par·te·no·gé·ne·sis f. parthenogenesis.

par·te·ra f. midwife.

par·te·ro m. male midwife.

par·ti·ción f. division, partition.

par·ti·ci·pa·ción f. participation; (contribución) contribution; (de lotería) share in a lottery ticket; COM. (acción) share, interest ♦ **p. de boda** wedding invitation • **p. en las utilidades** profit sharing.

par·ti·ci·pan·te I. adj. participating, sharing **II.** m.f. (que toma parte) participant; SPORT. competitor.

par·ti·ci·par tr. to inform —intr. (tomar parte) to participate, take part; (compartir) to share.

par·ti·ci·pe I. adj. participating **II.** m.f. (colaborador) participant; (interesado) interested party ♦ **hacer a alguien p. de** to inform someone of.

par·ti·ci·pio m. participle.

par·tí·cu·la f. particle.

par·ti·cu·lar I. adj. (privado) private; (individual) individual, personal; (especial) particular, special <un talento p. a special talent> **II.** m.f. (individuo) individual, private person; (asunto) matter, point ♦ **nada de p.** nothing special.

par·ti·cu·la·ri·dad f. peculiarity.

par·ti·cu·la·ri·zar §04 tr. (especificar) to specify; (detallar) to detail —reflex. to stand out.

par·ti·cu·lar·men·te adv. particularly.

par·ti·da·rio, a adj. & m.f. partisan.

par·ti·dis·ta I. adj. party **II.** m.f. partisan.

par·ti·do, a I. adj. divided **II.** m. (bando) (political) party; (provecho) profit, advantage; (distrito) district; SPORT. game ♦ **sacar p. de** to benefit from • **tomar p.** (decidir) to decide; (ponerse de parte) to take sides —f. (salida) departure; (expedición) party, group; (mano de juego) hand, round; COM. (artículo) entry, item; (porción) lot, batch ♦ **p. de defunción** death certificate • **p. de matrimonio** marriage certificate • **p. simple** COM. single entry.

par·tir tr. (dividir) to divide, split; to crack <p. nueces to crack nuts>; (romper) to break, split open; (repartir) to share —intr. to leave ♦ **a p. de** as of, starting from.

par·ti·ti·vo, a adj. partitive.

par·ti·tu·ra f. score.

par·to m. childbirth, delivery.

par·tu·rien·ta f. woman in labor.

par·va f. unthreshed grain; FIG. heap, pile.

pár·vu·lo, a m.f. small child, tot.

pa·sa f. see **paso, a**.

pa·sa·di·zo m. (pasillo) passage; (callejón) alley.

pa·sa·do, a I. adj. past, gone by <en años pasados in past years>; (anterior) last <el mes p. last month>; GRAM. past, preterit; CUL. (podrido) spoiled; (poco fresco) stale; (muy cocido) overdone ♦ **p. de moda** old-fashioned • **p. la una** after one (o'clock) • **p. mañana** day after tomorrow **II.** m. past ♦ **lo p.** let bygones be bygones —f. (acto) passage, passing; SEW. stitch ♦ **de p.** (de paso) on the way; (ligera-

mente) cursorily • **mala p.** dirty trick.

pa·sa·dor, ·ra I. adj. passing II. m. *(barra)* bolt; *(chaveta)* cotter (pin); *(de pelo)* hairpin.

pa·sa·je m. passage; *(billete)* ticket; *(pasajeros)* passengers; *(paso público)* passageway.

pa·sa·je·ro, a I. adj. passing, fleeting II. m.f. passenger, traveler.

pa·sa·ma·no m. handrail.

pa·sa·mon·ta·ñas m.pl. balaclava (hat).

pa·sa·por·te m. passport.

pa·sar tr. *(alcanzar)* to pass, hand; *(atravesar)* to cross; *(ir más allá)* to go beyond <p. los límites to go beyond the limits>; COLL. *(contrabandear)* to smuggle; *(poner en circulación)* to circulate; *(transferir)* to transfer; *(introducir)* to insert; *(colar)* to filter; *(disfrutar)* to spend, pass <pasamos el verano en la playa we spent the summer at the beach>; *(sufrir)* to suffer, undergo <hemos pasado muchas desgracias we have undergone many misfortunes>; *(desecar)* to dry in the sun; *(aprobar)* to pass <p. un examen to pass a test> ✦ **p. en limpio** to make a clear copy • **p. la noche en blanco** to spend a sleepless night • **p. las de Caín** to go through hell • **p. lista** to call roll • **pasarla bien, mal** to have a good, bad time • **p. por las armas** to execute • **p. por alto** to omit —intr. *(transcurrir)* to go by; *(entrar)* to come in; *(ocurrir)* to happen, occur <¿qué pasó? what happened?>; *(durar)* to last; *(cesar)* to pass, be over; *(conceder)* to yield, pass; *(transferirse)* to be handed down ✦ **hacerse p. por** to pass oneself off as • **ir pasándola** to get along • **p. a** to proceed to • **p. a mejor vida** to go on to the great beyond • **p. a ser** to become • **p. de** *(exceder)* to exceed, surpass; *(edad)* to be over • **p. de moda** to go out of fashion • **p. por** *(simular ser)* to pretend to be; *(detenerse)* to stop by; *(padecer)* to go through, undergo • **p. por encima** to go over someone's head • **p. sin** to do *or* go without —reflex. *(cambiar de partido)* to go over; *(olvidarse)* to forget; *(deslizar)* to run <se pasó la mano por la frente she ran her hand across her brow>; *(excederse)* to go too far; *(echarse a perder)* to go bad; *(estar muy cocido)* to be overcooked ✦ **p. de** to be too • **p. de la raya** to go too far • **p. la gran vida** to live it up.

pa·sa·re·la f. *(puentecillo)* footbridge; MARIT. gangway; THEAT. catwalk.

pa·sa·tiem·po m. pastime.

Pas·cua f. *(de resurrección)* Easter; *(Navidad)* Christmas; *(Epifanía)* Epiphany; *(Pentecostés)* Pentecost; *(fiesta judía)* Passover ✦ **dar las pascuas** to wish (someone) a Merry Christmas • **estar como unas pascuas** COLL. to be happy as a lark • **P. florida** RELIG. Easter • **santas pascuas** COLL. that's all there is to it ✦ pl. Christmastide.

pa·se m. pass.

pa·se·ar intr. *(andar)* to go for a walk; *(a caballo)* to ride (on a horse); *(en coche)* to go for a ride; *(en bicicleta)* to go for a bicycle ride —tr. to take for a walk.

pa·se·o m. *(caminata)* stroll; *(a caballo, coche)* ride; *(excursión)* outing; *(avenida)* avenue; TAUR. parade (of toreadors before the bullfight) ✦ **dar un p.** *(andar)* to go for a walk; *(en coche)* to go for a ride • **echar** *or* **mandar a p.** to send (someone) packing • **ir de p.** *(andar)* to walk; *(viajar)* to go on a trip • **¡vete a p.!** take a walk!

pa·si·llo m. corridor.

pa·sión f. passion.

pa·sio·nal adj. passionate, emotional ✦ **crimen p.** crime of passion.

pa·si·vo, a I. adj. passive II. m. COM. liabilities.

pas·ma·do, a adj. COLL. *(atónito)* astounded, astonished; *(helado)* frozen.

pas·mar tr. *(enfriar)* to freeze, chill; *(dejar atónito)* to stun; *(asombrar)* to astound —reflex. *(enfriarse)* to freeze; *(atontarse)* to be stunned; *(asombrarse)* to be astounded.

pas·mo m. *(enfriamiento)* chill; *(asombro)* astonishment.

pas·mo·so, a adj. astonishing, amazing.

pa·so m. step; *(marcha)* walk; EQUIT. gait; *(distancia)* pace; *(acción)* passing, passage; *(camino)* passage; GEOG. pass; MARIT. strait; *(pisada)* footstep; *(en el baile)* step ✦ **abrir p. a** to make way for • **a buen p.** quickly • **a cada p.** at every turn • **a dos pasos** at a short distance • **a ese p.** at that rate • **aflojar el p.** to slow down • **a grandes pasos** by leaps and bounds • **apretar el p.** to go faster • **al p. que** *(al mismo tiempo)* while; at the rate that <al p. que vas, nunca vas a terminar at the rate that you are going, you will never finish> • **a p. de tortuga** at a snail's pace • **a p. lento** slowly • **a pocos pasos** at a short distance • **ceder el p.** to step aside • **cerrar el p.** to block the way • **cortar el p.** to cut off • **de p.** in passing • **marcar el p.** to keep time • **p. a nivel** grade crossing • **p. a p.** little by little • **p. por p.** step by step • **salir del p.** to get out of a jam • **salirle al p.** *(salir al encuentro)* to intercept; *(confrontar)* to confront • **seguirle los pasos a alguien** to tail someone • **volver sobre sus pasos** to retrace one's steps.

pa·so, a I. adj. dried (fruit) ✦ **ciruela pasa** prune • **uvas pasas** raisins II. f. raisin • **estar** *or* **quedarse hecho una p.** COLL. to become all dried and wrinkled • **p. de Corinto** currant.

pas·quín m. rag, scandal sheet.

pas·ta f. *(masa)* paste; PAINT. impasto ✦ **p. de dientes** toothpaste • **tener p. de** to have the makings of ✦ pl. noodles, pasta.

pas·tar tr. to take to pasture —intr. to graze.

pas·tel m. CUL. *(dulce)* cake; *(de carne, queso)* pie; PAINT. pastel; COLL. *(ardid)* scheme, game ✦ pl. pastry.

pas·te·le·rí·a f. *(sitio)* pastry shop; *(oficio)* pastry-making.

pas·te·le·ro, a m.f. pastry cook.

pas·te(u)·ri·zar §04 tr. to pasteurize.

pas·te(u)·ri·za·ción f. pasteurization.

pas·ti·lla f. *(de jabón)* bar, cake; *(medicinal)* lozenge, drop; *(de menta)* mint.

pas·ti·zal m. pasture, grazing land.

pas·to m. *(hierba)* grass; *(sitio)* pasture; *(comida)* feed, fodder; FIG. food, fuel.

pas·tor, ·ra m. *(ovejero)* shepherd; *(prelado)* pastor —f. shepherdess.

pas·to·ral I. adj. pastoral II. f. MUS. pastorale.

pas·to·re·ar tr. to take to pasture.

pas·to·so, a adj. *(blando)* doughy; *(voz)* mellow; *(lengua)* coated.

pa·ta f. ZOOL. *(pie)* paw, foot; *(pierna)* leg; COLL. *(pierna humana)* leg; *(base)* leg <las patas de la mesa the legs of the table>; ORNITH. female duck ✦ **a cuatro patas** on all fours • **a p.** COLL. on foot • **estirar la p.** COLL. to kick the bucket • **meter la p.** COLL. to put one's foot in it • **p. de gallo** crowfoot; *(arruga)* crow's-foot

• **p. de palo** wooden leg • **patas arriba** COLL. *(boca arriba)* upside-down; *(en desorden)* topsy-turvy • **salir** *or* **ser p.** *or* **patas** to end in a draw *or* a tie • **tener mala p.** COLL. to be unlucky.

pa·ta·da f. kick ♦ **a patadas** COLL. in abundance • **dar la p. a alguien** COLL. to give someone the boot • **darle a alguien una p.** to kick someone • **echar a alguien a patadas** to kick someone out.

pa·ta·le·ar intr. *(dar patadas)* to kick; *(pisar)* to stamp.

pa·ta·le·ta f. COLL. tantrum, fit.

pa·tán m. COLL. lout, boor.

pa·ta·ta f. potato ♦ **patatas fritas** French fries.

pa·ta·tín pa·ta·tán interj. ♦ **que p.** COLL. this and that.

pa·ta·tús m. COLL. fainting spell.

pa·te·ar tr. COLL. to kick —intr. COLL. *(dar patadas)* to stamp one's feet <p. de rabia to stamp with rage>; AMER., COLL. *(andar mucho)* to chase all over the place; *(cocear)* to kick.

pa·ten·tar tr. to patent, register.

pa·ten·te I. adj. patent, obvious ♦ **hacer p.** to make evident **II.** f. *(permiso)* warrant; *(licencia)* licence; *(de invención)* patent ♦ **p. de navegación** certificate of registration.

pa·ter·nal adj. paternal.

pa·ter·ni·dad f. paternity; FIG. authorship.

pa·ter·no, a adj. paternal.

pa·té·ti·co, a adj. pathetic.

pa·tí·bu·lo m. scaffold, gallows.

pa·ti·llas f.pl. sideburns.

pa·ti·llu·do, a adj. having long and heavy sideburns.

pa·tín m. skate; AVIA. skid ♦ **p. de hielo** ice skate • **p. de ruedas** roller skate.

pá·ti·na f. patina.

pa·ti·na·dor, ·ra I. adj. skating **II.** m.f. skater.

pa·ti·na·je m. skating ♦ **p. artístico** figure skating • **p. sobre hielo** ice skating • **p. sobre ruedas** roller skating.

pa·ti·nar intr. *(con patines)* to skate; *(un vehículo)* to skid; *(resbalar voluntariamente)* to slide; *(resbalar sin querer)* to slip; *(meter la pata)* to slip up —tr. to give a patina to.

pa·ti·na·zo m. skid.

pa·tio m. patio, courtyard ♦ **p. de escuela** schoolyard.

pa·ti·tie·so, a adj. *(paralizado)* stiff-legged; *(aturdido)* paralyzed ♦ **dejar p.** to dumbfound.

pa·ti·zam·bo, a adj. & m.f. knock-kneed (person).

pa·to m. *(ave)* duck; *(pato macho)* drake; AMER. *(bacineta)* bedpan; COLL. *(pelmazo)* bore, drip ♦ **estar hecho un p.** to be soaked to the skin • **pagar el p.** COLL. to take the rap • **p. flojel** eider duck • **p. real** *or* **silvestre** mallard, wild duck.

pa·tó·ge·no, a I. adj. pathogenic **II.** m. pathogen.

pa·to·lo·gí·a f. pathology.

pa·tó·lo·go, a m.f. pathologist.

pa·tón, o·na adj. COLL. big-footed.

pa·to·ta f. R.P. street gang.

pa·to·te·ro m. R.P. COLL. member of a street gang.

pa·tra·ña f. COLL. hoax.

pa·triar·ca m. patriarch.

pa·triar·cal adj. patriarchal.

pa·tri·cio, a adj. & m.f. patrician.

pa·tri·mo·nio m. patrimony, heritage.

pa·trio, a I. adj. *(de la patria)* native; *(del padre)* paternal **II.** f. homeland, native land ♦ **madre p.** motherland.

pa·trio·ta m.f. patriot.

pa·trio·te·rí·a f. exaggerated patriotism.

pa·trio·te·ro, a I. adj. COLL. excessively patriotic **II.** m.f. jingoist.

pa·trió·ti·co, a adj. patriotic.

pa·tro·ci·na·dor, ·ra I. adj. sponsoring **II.** m.f. sponsor, patron.

pa·tro·ci·nar tr. to sponsor, patronize.

pa·trón, o·na m.f. RELIG. patron saint —m. *(amo)* master, boss; MARIT. skipper, captain; *(modelo)* pattern; *(unidad)* standard ♦ **cortado por el mismo p.** cut of the same cloth.

pa·tro·nal adj. employers', management.

pa·tro·na·to m. *(protección)* patronage, sponsorship; *(organización)* board, council ♦ **p. de las artes** arts council.

pa·tro·no, a m.f. *(jefe)* boss; *(empresario)* employer; *(santo)* patron saint —m. *(dueño)* landlord; *(señor)* lord —f. *(casera)* landlady; *(señora)* lady.

pa·tru·lla f. squad, patrol.

pa·tru·llar intr. & tr. to patrol.

pa·tru·lle·ro, a I. adj. patrol **II.** m. *(coche)* patrol car; *(buque)* patrol boat; *(avión)* patrol plane.

pa·tu·do, a adj. COLL. big-footed.

pau·la·ti·na·men·te adv. gradually.

pau·la·ti·no, a adj. gradual.

pau·pé·rri·mo, a adj. very poor.

pau·sa f. *(interrupción)* pause, break; *(lentitud)* slowness, calm; MUS. rest ♦ **con p.** slowly.

pau·sa·do, a I. adj. slow **II.** adv. slowly.

pau·ta f. *(regla)* rule, guide; *(rayas)* guidelines ♦ **dar la p.** to set the example.

pa·va¹ f. turkey hen.

pa·va² f. *(fuelle)* furnace bellows; R.P. teapot.

pa·va·da f. stupidity, foolishness.

pa·vi·men·ta·ción f. paving.

pa·vi·men·tar tr. *(piso)* to floor; *(calle)* to pave.

pa·vi·men·to m. pavement.

pa·vo, a I. adj. foolish **II.** m. turkey; *(hombre soso)* fool ♦ **edad del p.** awkward age • **p. real** peacock.

pa·vo·na·do, a I. adj. dark blue **II.** m. METAL. bluing, browning.

pa·vo·ne·ar intr. & reflex. to show off.

pa·vor m. fright, terror.

pa·vo·ro·so, a adj. frightening, terrifying.

pa·vu·ra f. fright, terror.

pa·ya·da f. R.P. improvisation by singing gauchos.

pa·ya·dor m. R.P. singing gaucho.

pa·yar intr. R.P. *(cantar)* to improvise songs; *(contar cuentos)* to tell stories.

pa·ya·sa·da f. buffoonery ♦ **hacer payasadas** to fool around.

pa·ya·se·ar intr. AMER. to clown around.

pa·ya·so m. clown, buffoon.

paz f. peace; *(tratado)* peace treaty; *(tranquilidad)* peacefulness, tranquility ♦ **dejar en p.** to leave alone • **estar en p.** to be at peace; FIG. to be even • **hacer las paces** to make peace • **poner p. entre** to make peace between.

paz·gua·te·rí·a f. foolishness.

paz·gua·to, a I. adj. foolish **II.** m.f. fool.

pe·a·je m. toll.

pe·al m. *(pie)* foot (of a stocking); *(pial)* lasso.

pe·a·tón m. pedestrian.

pe·a·to·nal adj. pedestrian.
pe·be·te, a m.f. R.P. kid, child.
pe·be·te·ro m. incense burner.
pe·ca f. freckle.
pe·ca·do m. sin ♦ **siete pecados capitales** seven deadly sins.
pe·ca·dor, ·ra I. adj. sinful, **II.** m.f. sinner.
pe·ca·mi·no·so, a adj. sinful.
pe·car §47 intr. to sin; *(faltar)* to transgress.
pe·ca·rí or **pé·ca·rí** m. peccary.
pe·ce·ra f. fishbowl, aquarium.
pe·cha·dor m. AMER., COLL. sponger.
pe·char tr. *(pagar tributo)* to pay; *(asumir)* to shoulder; AMER., COLL. *(dinero)* to hit for a loan; *(empujar)* to shove (with the chest).
pe·cha·zo m. R.P. touch for a loan.
pe·che·ro, a m. bib —f. shirt front.
pe·cho m. chest; *(busto)* breast; *(seno)* bosom, breast; ORNITH. breast ♦ **abrir el p.** to unbosom oneself • **dar el p.** to suckle, nurse • **de p.** nursing • **hombre de pelo en p.** he-man • **poner el p. a** to face • **tomar a p.** to take to heart.
pe·chu·ga f. *(del ave)* breast; *(de persona)* chest, breast.
pe·cí·o·lo/cio·lo m. petiole.
pé·co·ra f. head of sheep.
pe·co·so, a adj. freckled.
pec·ti·na f. pectin.
pec·to·ral I. adj. pectoral **II.** m. pectoral; *(cruz)* pectoral cross.
pe·cu·liar adj. peculiar.
pe·cu·lia·ri·dad f. peculiarity.
pe·cu·lio m. LAW peculium; FIG. one's own or personal money.
pe·cu·nia f. COLL. money.
pe·cu·nia·rio, a adj. pecuniary, financial.
pe·da·go·gí·a f. pedagogy.
pe·da·go·go m. pedagogue.
pe·dal m. *(de pie)* (foot) pedal, treadle; MUS. pedal; *(nota)* sustained note ♦ **p. de embrague** clutch pedal • **p. de freno** brake pedal.
pe·da·le·ar intr. to pedal.
pe·da·le·o m. pedaling.
pe·dan·te I. adj. pedantic **II.** m.f. pedant.
pe·dan·te·rí·a f./**tis·mo** m. pedantry.
pe·da·zo m. piece ♦ **a pedazos** in pieces or bits • **caerse a pedazos** COLL. *(deshacerse)* to fall to pieces; *(estar cansadísimo)* to be dead tired • **hacer pedazos** *(romper)* to smash into pieces; *(desgarrar)* to tear into pieces • **p. de bruto** COLL. blockhead • **ser un p. de pan** COLL. to be an angel.
pe·de·ras·ta m. pederast.
pe·de·ras·tia f. pederasty.
pe·der·nal m. flint.
pe·des·tal m. pedestal; FIG. foundation.
pe·des·tre adj. pedestrian.
pe·dí·a·tra/dia·tra m.f. pediatrician.
pe·dia·trí·a f. pediatrics.
pe·dí·cu·lo m. peduncle.
pe·di·cu·ro, a m.f. podiatrist.
pe·di·do m. *(encargo)* order; *(petición)* request ♦ **a p. de** at the request of • **a p. del público** by public demand • **hacer un p.** to place an order • **p. en firme** firm order.
pe·di·gre·e/grí m. pedigree.
pe·di·güe·ño, a I. adj. persistent, pestering **II.** m.f. pest, nuisance.
pe·dir §48 tr. *(rogar)* to ask, request; to ask for <le pedí diez dólares I asked him for ten dollars>; *(demandar)* to demand; *(mendigar)* to beg; to order <pidió una taza de café he ordered a cup of coffee>; COM. to ask ♦ **a p. de boca** to one's heart's content • **p. disculpas** to apologize • **p. prestado** to borrow.
pe·dra·da f. blow with a stone ♦ **matar a pedradas** to stone to death • **pegar una p. a alguien** to throw a stone at someone.
pe·dre·gal m. rocky terrain.
pe·dre·go·so, a adj. rocky.
pe·dre·rí·a f. precious stones, gems.
pe·dre·ro m. stonecutter.
pe·dris·ca f. *(granizo)* hail; *(granizada)* hailstorm.
pe·drus·co m. COLL. rough or uncut stone.
pe·dún·cu·lo m. peduncle.
pe·ga f. *(acción)* sticking; *(dificultad)* snag.
pe·ga·da f. COLL. stroke of luck.
pe·ga·di·zo, a adj. *(que se pega)* adhesive; *(que se contagia)* catching; *(que capta la atención)* catchy.
pe·ga·du·ra f. *(acción)* sticking; *(unión)* adhesion.
pe·ga·jo·si·dad f. stickiness.
pe·ga·jo·so, a adj. *(pegadizo)* adhesive; *(contagioso)* catching; COLL. *(meloso)* cloying; *(excesivamente meloso)* gooey.
pe·ga·mien·to m. sticking, gluing.
pe·ga·pe·ga f. AMER. birdlime.
pe·gar §47 tr. *(engomar)* to glue; *(arrimar)* to move closer <p. el sofá a la pared to move the sofa closer to the wall>; *(unir)* to fasten; *(botón)* to sew on; *(golpear)* to hit; to give <p. un grito to give a yell> ♦ **no p. un ojo** not to sleep a wink • **p. fuego a** to set fire to • **p. un salto** to jump • **p. un susto** to frighten • **p. un tiro** to shoot —intr. *(adherir)* to adhere; *(golpear)* to hit; *(armonizar)* to go together; MED. to be catching —reflex. *(unirse)* to adhere; CUL. *(quemarse)* to stick to the pan; to pick up <el vicio de fumar se le pegó de mí she picked up the vice of smoking from me> ♦ **p. un tiro** to shoot oneself.
pe·go·te m. *(cosa pegajosa)* gooey mess; *(guisado)* thick stew.
pei·na·da f. COLL. combing ♦ **darse una p.** to comb one's hair.
pei·na·do m. hair style, coiffure.
pei·na·dor, ·ra m.f. hairdresser —f. woolcombing machine.
pei·nar tr. *(el cabello)* to comb; *(lana)* to card ♦ **p. canas** COLL. to be old —reflex. to comb one's hair.
pei·ne m. *(para el pelo)* comb; *(para la lana)* card ♦ **pasarse el p.** to comb one's hair.
pei·ne·ta f. ornamental comb.
pe·la·do, a I. adj. *(calvo)* bald; *(con el pelo cortado)* shorn; *(frutos)* peeled; *(desplumado)* plucked; *(sin carne)* bare; *(desnudo)* barren; *(pobre)* broke **II.** m. *(corte de pelo)* haircut; *(esquileo)* shearing; *(pobre)* pauper —f. *(cabeza)* bald head; *(corte de pelo)* crew cut.
pe·la·du·ra f. peeling.
pe·la·ga·tos m.inv. COLL. poor devil.
pe·la·gra f. pellagra.
pe·lam·bre m. *(pieles)* hides; *(pelo)* matted hair.
pe·lar tr. *(cortar el pelo)* to cut; *(mondar)* to peel; *(desplumar)* to pluck; *(quitar la piel)* to strip; COLL. *(despojar)* to clean out; *(despellejar)* to tear down • **p. la pava** COLL. to court.
pel·da·ño m. rung.

pe·le·a f. fight ♦ **p. de gallos** cockfight.
pe·le·a·dor, ·ra adj. (que pela) fighting; (propenso a pelear) quarrelsome.
pe·le·ar intr. to fight; (disputar) to quarrel; (batallar) to battle.
pe·le·le m. (muñeco) rag doll; COLL. (tonto) nincompoop; (traje) child's pajamas.
pe·le·te·rí·a f. (oficio) fur trade; (tienda) fur shop; (pieles finas) furs.
pe·le·te·ro m. (fabricante) fur maker; (vendedor) furrier.
pe·lia·gu·do, a adj. COLL. difficult, tricky.
pe·lí·ca·no m. pelican.
pe·lí·cu·la f. (piel) skin; (telilla) film; PHOTOG. film; CINEM. motion picture ♦ **de p.** COLL. extraordinary • **p. del oeste** western • **p. en colores** film in color; PHOTOG. color film • **p. hablada** talking picture • **p. muda** silent movie.
pe·li·grar intr. to be in danger.
pe·li·gro m. danger ♦ **correr el p. de** to run the risk of • **correr p.** or **estar en p.** to be in danger • **poner en p.** to endanger.
pe·li·gro·so, a adj. dangerous.
pe·li·llo m. (pelo corto) short hair; COLL. (nadería) trifle.
pe·li·rro·jo, a I. adj. red-haired, redheaded II. m.f. redhead.
pe·lla f. (masa redonda) round mass; BOT. head (of cauliflower); (de cerdo) raw lard.
pe·lle·jo m. (de animal) hide; (de fruta) peel; (piel) skin; (odre) wineskin ♦ **estar en el p. de otro** FIG. to be in another's shoes • **jugarse el p.** to risk one's neck • **no tener más que el p.** to be as thin as a rail • **quitarle el p. a alguien** COLL. to criticize • **salvar el p.** to save one's skin.
pe·lliz·car §70 tr. (apretar) to pinch; (comer un poco) to nibble.
pe·lliz·co m. (acción) pinch; (pizca) small portion.
pe·llón m. sheepskin.
pel·ma·zo m. (cosa aplastada) flattened mass; (en el estómago) lump; COLL. (persona) bore.
pe·lo m. (cabello) hair; (de la barba) whisker; (de cepillo) bristle; ZOOL. (de animal) fur, coat; BOT., ORNITH. down; (filamento) strand; TECH. hairspring; (del tejido) nap; JEWEL. flaw ♦ **agarrarse a un p.** to grasp at straws • **al p.** COLL. perfectly • **a p.** with the grain • **contra p.** against the grain • **estar hasta los pelos** COLL. to be fed up • **hombre de p. en pecho** he-man • **no tener pelos en la lengua** COLL. not to mince words • **p. de camello** camel hair • **ponérsele a uno los pelos de punta** COLL. to make one's hair stand on end • **por los pelos** or **por un p.** by the skin of one's teeth • **tomar a alguien el p.** COLL. to pull someone's leg • **traído por los pelos** farfetched • **venir al p.** COLL. (ser perfecto) to be just right; (ser oportuno) to come in handy.
pe·lo·ta f. ball; (juego) ball game ♦ **p. vasca** jai alai.
pe·lo·ta·ri m.f. pelota or jai alai player.
pe·lo·te·ar intr. (jugar) to kick a ball around; (lanzar) to toss back and forth; (reñir) to quarrel, argue.
pe·lo·te·ra f. COLL. brawl, scuffle.
pe·lo·tón m. squad.
pel·tre m. pewter.
pe·lu·ca f. wig.
pe·lu·che f. plush.

pe·lu·do, a I. adj. hairy, shaggy II. m. (felpudo) thick mat; ARG., ZOOL. armadillo.
pe·lu·que·rí·a f. (para hombres) barber shop; (para mujeres) beauty shop or parlor.
pe·lu·que·ro, a m.f. (para hombres) barber; (para hombres y mujeres) hairdresser.
pe·lu·quín m. (peluca) small wig; (bisoñé) toupee.
pe·lu·sa f. (de plantas) down; (de telas) fuzz.
pel·vis f.inv. pelvis.
pe·na f. (castigo) punishment; (aflicción) sorrow; (dolor) pain ♦ **a duras penas** with great difficulty • **a penas** hardly, scarcely • **bajo** or **so p. de** under penalty of • **dar p.** to grieve • **p. de muerte** death penalty • **¡qué p.!** what a shame! • **valer la p.** to be worthwhile.
pe·na·cho m. (copete) crest; (adorno) plume.
pe·na·do, a I. adj. grieved II. m.f. convict.
pe·nal I. adj. penal II. m. prison.
pe·na·li·dad f. (pena) hardship; LAW penalty.
pe·na·li·zar §04 tr. to penalize.
pe·nar tr. to punish —intr. to suffer.
pen·co m. COLL. hack, nag.
pen·de·ja·da f. SL. (tontería) stupidity; (cobardía) cowardliness.
pen·de·jo, a SL. I. adj. (cobarde) cowardly; (tonto) stupid II. m.f. (cobarde) coward; AMER. (tonto) jerk —m. (pelo) pubic hair.
pen·den·ciar intr. to quarrel.
pen·den·cie·ro, a I. adj. quarrelsome II. m.f. troublemaker.
pen·der intr. (colgar) to hang; (cernerse) to hover; (estar pendiente) to be pending.
pen·dien·te I. adj. (colgante) hanging; (sin solucionar) pending II. m. (arete) earring; (colgante) pendant —f. (cuesta) slope; (del tejado) pitch.
pen·dón m. (bandera) banner; (estandarte) standard.
pén·du·lo, a I. adj. hanging II. m. pendulum.
pe·ne m. penis.
pe·ne·tra·ble adj. penetrable.
pe·ne·tra·ción f. penetration; (sagacidad) insight.
pe·ne·tran·te adj. (que penetra) penetrating; (inteligencia) acute; (voz, mirada) piercing; (frío) biting.
pe·ne·trar tr. to penetrate; (empapar) to permeate; (afectar) to pierce —intr. to penetrate, enter —reflex. (comprender) to fathom; (empaparse) to steep oneself (de in).
pe·ni·ci·li·na f. penicillin.
pe·nín·su·la f. peninsula.
pe·nin·su·lar I. adj. peninsular II. m.f. inhabitant of a peninsula.
pe·ni·que m. penny.
pe·ni·ten·cia f. (sentimiento) penitence; (castigo) penance ♦ **hacer p.** to do penance.
pe·ni·ten·cia·rí·a f. penitentiary.
pe·ni·ten·cia·rio, a adj. & m. penitentiary.
pe·ni·ten·te adj. & m.f. penitent.
pe·no·so, a adj. (difícil) arduous; (triste) sad.
pen·sa·do, a adj. ♦ **bien p.** (bien reflexionado) well thought-out; (con pensamientos favorables) well-intentioned • **el día menos p.** when least expected • **mal p.** (mal reflexionado) poorly thought-out; (con pensamientos malos) evil-minded • **tener p.** to have in mind
pen·sa·dor, ·ra I. adj. thinking II. m. thinker ♦ **libre p.** freethinker.
pen·sa·mien·to¹ m. thought; (idea) idea; (sentencia) maxim ♦ **no pasarle por el p.** not to

cross one's mind.

pen·sa·mien·to² m. BOT. pansy.

pen·san·te adj. thinking.

pen·sar §49 tr. *(considerar)* to think about, consider; *(creer)* to think, believe; *(planear)* to intend ♦ **pensándolo mejor** or **bien** on second thought —intr. to think ♦ **p. en** or **sobre** to think about • **p. entre sí** or **para sí** to think to oneself *¿qué piensas de . . . ?* what is your opinion about . . . ? ♦ **sin p.** without thinking.

pen·sa·ti·vo, a adj. pensive.

pen·sión f. *(en un hotel)* room and board; *(de retiro)* pension, annuity; *(de estudios)* grant; *(casa)* boarding house.

pen·sio·na·do, a I. adj. pensioned II. m.f. pensioner —m. boarding school.

pen·sio·nar tr. to pension.

pen·sio·nis·ta m.f. *(retirado)* pensioner; *(en hotel)* boarder.

pen·tá·go·no, a I. adj. pentagonal II. m. pentagon.

pen·ta·gra·ma m. MUS. stave, staff.

pen·to·tal m. pentothal.

pe·núl·ti·mo, a adj. & m.f. penultimate.

pe·num·bra f. shadow; PHYS. penumbra.

pe·nu·ria f. penury, want.

pe·ña f. *(roca)* boulder; *(círculo)* circle.

pe·ñas·co m. large rock, crag.

pe·ñas·co·so, a adj. rocky.

pe·ñón m. craggy rock ♦ **p. de Gibraltar** Rock of Gibraltar.

pe·ón m. AMER. farmhand, peon; *(jornalero)* unskilled laborer; *(en ajedrez)* pawn; *(en damas)* man; MIL. infantryman.

pe·o·na·da f./**je** m. gang of laborers.

pe·or I. adj. worse *<éste es p. que el otro* this one is worse than the other>; worst *<soy el p. jugador* I am the worst player> ♦ **cada vez p.** worse and worse • **y lo que es p.** and what's worse II. adv. worse ♦ **p. que p.** or **tanto p.** worse still III. m.f. worse *<soy el p. de los dos* I am the worse of the two>; worst *<ella es la p. de las bailarinas* she is the worst of the dancers> ♦ **en el p. de los casos** if worst comes to worst • **lo p.** the worst thing.

pe·pa f. AMER. pip, seed.

pe·pi·no m. cucumber ♦ **no importar un p.** COLL. not to matter a whit.

pe·pi·ta f. pip, seed; VET. pip; MIN. nugget.

pép·ti·co, a adj. peptic.

pe·que·ñez f. *(calidad)* smallness, littleness; *(menudencia)* trifle ♦ **p. de miras** narrow-mindedness.

pe·que·ñín, i·na I. adj. teeny, tiny II. m.f. child, tot.

pe·que·ño, a I. adj. small; *(corto)* short; *(joven)* young II. m.f. child ♦ **de p.** as a child.

pe·que·ñue·lo, a I. adj. tiny, teeny II. m.f. little child, tot ♦ **los pequeñuelos** the little ones.

pe·ra f. *(fruta)* pear; *(barba)* goatee ♦ **pedir peras al olmo** COLL. to ask for the moon.

pe·ral m. pear tree.

per·cal m. percale.

per·can·ce m. mishap.

per·ca·tar intr. to notice —reflex. to become aware.

per·cep·ción f. *(de dinero)* receiving; *(sensación)* perception.

per·cep·ti·vo, a adj. perceptive.

per·cha f. *(madero)* pole, prop; *(perchero)* clothes rack; *(de colgar)* hanger, coat hanger.

per·che·ro m. clothes rack.

per·ci·bir tr. *(distinguir)* to perceive, sense; *(cobrar)* to collect, receive.

per·cu·dir tr. to tarnish, dull —reflex. to become stained.

per·cu·sión f. percussion.

per·cu·tir intr. to percuss, strike.

per·cu·tor m. firing pin.

per·de·dor, ·ra I. adj. losing II. m.f. loser.

per·der §50 tr. to lose; *(desperdiciar)* to miss; *(arruinar)* to spoil ♦ **echar a p.** to spoil • **p. de vista** to lose sight of • **p. el juicio** to lose one's mind • **p. la vista** to lose one's eyesight —intr. to lose; *(desteñirse)* to fade —reflex. to lose, mislay; *(desorientarse)* to get lost; *(dejar de ser útil)* to go to waste; *(arruinarse)* to go astray ♦ **p. de vista** to disappear.

per·di·ción f. *(ruina)* ruin; RELIG. damnation.

pér·di·da f. *(privación)* loss, waste; *(daño)* damage, harm ♦ **pérdidas y ganancias** profit and loss.

per·di·da·men·te adv. madly.

per·di·do, a I. adj. *(extraviado)* lost, lost; *(bala)* stray; *(rematado)* confirmed *<un borracho p.* a confirmed drunkard>; *(incorregible)* dissolute ♦ **estar p. por** to be madly in love with II. m. libertine.

per·di·gón m. partridge; ARM. small shot.

per·di·gue·ro m. pointer.

per·diz f. partridge.

per·dón m. pardon, forgiveness ♦ **¡p.!** sorry!

per·do·nar tr. *(disculpar)* to pardon, forgive; *(la vida)* to spare; *(renunciar)* to forego.

per·du·ra·ble adj. *(eterno)* eternal, everlasting; *(duradero)* durable, lasting.

per·du·rar intr. to last.

pe·re·ce·de·ro, a adj. perishable.

pe·re·cer §17 intr. to perish, die.

pe·re·ci·mien·to m. demise.

pe·re·gri·na·ción f./**je** m. pilgrimage.

pe·re·gri·nar intr. *(andar)* to journey; *(a un santuario)* to make a pilgrimage.

pe·re·gri·no, a I. adj. *(que viaja)* traveling; *(en una peregrinación)* on a pilgrimage; ORNITH. migratory II. m.f. pilgrim.

pe·re·jil m. parsley.

pe·ren·ga·no m. m.f. so-and-so.

pe·ren·ne adj. perennial.

pe·ren·to·ria·men·te adv. peremptorily.

pe·ren·to·rie·dad f. peremptoriness.

pe·ren·to·rio, a adj. *(terminante)* peremptory; *(apremiante)* urgent.

pe·re·za f. *(holgazanería)* laziness; *(lentitud)* slowness.

pe·re·zo·so, a I. adj. *(holgazán)* lazy; *(pesado)* slow II. m. ZOOL. sloth.

per·fec·ción f. perfection ♦ **a la p.** to perfection.

per·fec·cio·na·mien·to m. *(perfección)* perfection; *(mejora)* improvement.

per·fec·cio·nar tr. *(hacer perfecto)* to make perfect; *(mejorar)* to improve.

per·fec·cio·nis·ta adj. & m.f. perfectionist.

per·fec·ta·men·te adv. perfectly ♦ **¡p.!** right!

per·fec·to, a adj. perfect.

per·fi·dia f. perfidy.

pér·fi·do, a I. adj. unfaithful II. m.f. traitor.

per·fil m. profile; *(contorno)* outline; *(sección)* cross section ♦ **de p.** in profile • **de medio p.** three-quarter.

per·fi·la·do, a adj. *(rostro)* long and thin; *(nariz)* perfect.

per·fi·lar tr. PAINT. to profile; *(pulir)* to polish

—reflex. *(colocarse de perfil)* to show one's profile; *(tomar forma)* to take shape.

per·fo·ra·ción f. perforation; MIN. drilling.

per·fo·ra·do m. perforation.

per·fo·ra·dor, ·a I. adj. perforating; MIN. drilling II. f. *(para papeles)* punch; MIN. drill.

per·fo·rar tr. to perforate; MIN. to drill.

per·fu·mar tr. to perfume.

per·fu·me m. perfume; *(aroma)* fragrance.

per·fu·me·ría f. perfumery.

per·fu·me·ro, a/mis·ta m.f. perfumer.

per·ga·mi·no m. *(papel)* parchment; *(diploma)* diploma; *(documento)* manuscript.

pér·go·la f. pergola.

pe·ri·car·dio m. pericardium.

pe·ri·car·pio m. pericarp.

pe·ri·cia f. skill, expertise.

pe·ri·co m. parakeet.

pe·ri·fe·ria f. periphery.

pe·ri·fo·llo m. BOT. chervil; COLL. ornaments.

pe·ri·lla f. *(adorno)* pear-shaped ornament; *(barbilla)* goatee; *(tirador)* knob, handle ♦ **ve·nir de perillas** COLL. to come in handy.

pe·rí·me·tro m. perimeter.

pe·rió·di·ca·men·te adv. periodically.

pe·rió·di·co, a I. adj. periodic(al) II. m. newspaper.

pe·rio·dis·mo m. journalism.

pe·rio·dis·ta m.f. journalist.

pe·rí·o·do/río·do m. period; GEOL. age.

pe·ri·pa·té·ti·co, a adj. Aristotelian; COLL. *(ridículo)* ridiculous.

pe·ri·pe·cia f. vicissitude.

pe·rís·to·le f. peristalsis.

pe·ri·que·te m. ♦ **en un p.** COLL. in a jiffy.

pe·ri·qui·to m. parakeet.

pe·ris·co·pio m. periscope.

pe·ris·ti·lo m. peristyle.

pe·ri·to, a adj. & m.f. expert.

pe·ri·to·ne·o m. peritoneum.

per·ju·di·car §70 tr. *(dañar)* to damage; *(estropear)* to harm.

per·ju·di·cial adj. harmful, detrimental.

per·jui·cio m. *(material)* damage; *(moral)* injury; FIN. loss.

per·ju·rar intr. to commit perjury.

per·ju·rio m. perjury.

per·ju·ro, a I. adj. perjured II. m.f. perjurer.

per·la f. pearl; FIG. treasure ♦ **de perlas** perfectly ♦ **p. de cultivo** cultured pearl ♦ **venir de perlas** to come at the right moment.

per·la·do, a adj. pearl-colored, pearly.

per·ma·ne·cer §17 intr. to stay, remain.

per·ma·nen·cia f. *(duración)* permanence; *(estancia)* stay.

per·ma·nen·te I. adj. permanent II. f. permanent wave.

per·mi·si·ble adj. permissible.

per·mi·si·vo, a adj. permissive.

per·mi·so m. *(autorización)* permission; *(documento)* permit; MIL. leave ♦ **con (su) p.** *(perdóneme)* excuse me; *(con su autorización)* with your permission ♦ **p. de conducir** driver's license.

per·mi·ti·do, a adj. permitted, allowed.

per·mi·tir tr. *(autorizar)* to permit, let; *(tolerar)* to allow, tolerate ♦ **permítame** allow me ♦ **si lo permite el tiempo** weather permitting —reflex. to be permitted *or* allowed ♦ **no se permite fumar** no smoking.

per·mu·ta/ción f. exchange; MATH. permutation.

per·mu·tar tr. to exchange; MATH. to permute.

per·ne·ra f. pant leg.

per·ni·cio·so, a adj. pernicious.

per·nil m. *(de animal)* haunch and thigh; *(de cerdo)* ham.

per·no m. bolt, pin.

per·noc·tar intr. to spend the night.

pe·ro I. conj. but <*es bonita p. antipática* she is pretty but disagreeable>; yet <*gana mucho dinero p. nunca tiene un centavo* he earns a lot of money yet he is always broke> II. m. ♦ **no hay p. que valga** COLL. there are no buts about it ♦ **poner peros** COLL. to raise objections.

pe·ro·gru·lla·da f. COLL. trite remark.

pe·ro·né m. fibula.

pe·ro·rar intr. to perorate, make a speech.

pe·ro·ra·ta f. long-winded speech.

pe·ró·xi·do m. peroxide.

per·pen·di·cu·lar adj. & f. perpendicular.

per·pe·tra·ción f. perpetration.

per·pe·tra·dor, ·a I. adj. perpetrating II. m.f. perpetrator.

per·pe·trar tr. to perpetrate.

per·pe·tua·ción f. perpetuation.

per·pe·tua·men·te adv. perpetually.

per·pe·tuar §67 tr. to perpetuate —reflex. to be perpetuated.

per·pe·tui·dad f. perpetuity.

per·pe·tuo, a adj. perpetual ♦ **cadena p.** life imprisonment.

per·ple·ji·dad f. perplexity.

per·ple·jo, a adj. perplexed.

pe·rre·ra f. *(lugar)* dog kennel; *(carro)* dog-catcher's wagon.

pe·rre·rí·a f. *(jauría)* pack of dogs; *(mala acción)* dirty trick.

pe·rro, a I. m.f. dog; FIG. dirty dog ♦ **¡a otro p. con ese hueso!** COLL. tell it to the Marines! ♦ **p. cobrador** retriever ♦ **p. de aguas** *or de lanas* poodle ♦ **p. dogo** *or* **de presa** bulldog ♦ **p. faldero** lap dog ♦ **p. galgo** greyhound ♦ **p. lebrel** whippet ♦ **p. lobo** wolfhound ♦ **p. mastín** mastiff ♦ **p. ovejero** sheep dog ♦ **p. sabueso** bloodhound ♦ **una vida de perros** a lousy life —f. bitch; COLL. *(moneda)* five- *or* ten-cent piece II. adj. lousy, rotten.

pe·rru·no, a adj. canine, of dogs.

per·se·cu·ción f. *(tormento)* persecution; *(seguimiento)* pursuit, chase.

per·se·gui·dor, ·a I. adj. *(que atormenta)* persecuting; *(que sigue)* chasing II. m.f. *(que atormenta)* persecutor; *(que sigue)* pursuer.

per·se·guir §64 tr. *(seguir)* to pursue, chase; *(acosar)* to persecute; *(atormentar)* to torment; *(molestar)* to pester.

per·se·ve·ran·cia f. perseverance.

per·se·ve·ran·te adj. persevering.

per·se·ve·rar intr. to persevere.

per·sia·na f. blind.

per·si·ga, go see perseguir.

per·sig·nar tr. to cross.

per·si·guie·ra, guió see perseguir.

per·sis·ten·cia f. persistence.

per·sis·ten·te adj. persistent.

per·sis·tir intr. to persist.

per·so·na f. person ♦ **p. jurídica** LAW legal entity ♦ **por p.** per person, each ♦ **tercera p.** GRAM. third person; *(mediador)* third party ♦ pl. people.

per·so·na·je m. celebrity; LIT. character.

per·so·nal I. adj. personal II. m. personnel ♦ **p. de tierra** ground crew.

per·so·na·li·dad f. personality; *(personaje)* public figure.

per·so·na·li·zar §04 tr. to personalize; GRAM. to make personal.

per·so·ni·fi·ca·ción f. personification.

per·so·ni·fi·car §70 tr. to personify.

pers·pec·ti·va f. perspective; *(vista)* view; *(contingencia)* outlook; *(apariencia)* appearance.

pers·pi·ca·cia/ci·dad f. perspicacity.

pers·pi·caz adj. *(agudo)* sharp, keen; *(sagaz)* shrewd, perspicacious.

per·sua·dir tr. *(a hacer)* to persuade; *(a creer)* to convince —reflex. to be persuaded *or* convinced.

per·sua·sión f. persuasion.

per·sua·si·vo, a adj. persuasive.

per·te·ne·cer §17 intr. *(ser de)* to belong, be; *(ser parte)* to belong <el anillo pertenece a la colección real the ring belongs to the royal collection>; *(concernir)* to pertain (a to).

per·te·ne·cien·te adj. pertaining (a to).

per·te·nen·cia f. *(derecho)* ownership; *(posesión)* belonging.

pér·ti·ga f. pole ♦ **salto de p.** pole vault.

pér·ti·go m. shaft.

per·ti·naz adj. obstinate, tenacious.

per·ti·nen·cia f. pertinence, relevance.

per·ti·nen·te adj. pertinent, relevant.

per·tre·char tr. MIL. to supply, equip; *(disponer)* to prepare —reflex. ♦ **p. de** *or* **con** to supply oneself with.

per·tre·chos m.pl. *(víveres)* supplies; *(instrumentos)* equipment.

per·tur·ba·ción f. disturbance.

per·tur·ba·dor, ra I. adj. disturbing II. m.f. disturber.

per·tur·bar tr. *(trastornar)* to disturb; *(desasegar)* to perturb.

pe·rú m. ♦ **valer un p.** to be worth a fortune.

per·ver·si·dad f. perversity.

per·ver·sión f. perversion.

per·ver·so, a adj. & m. wicked (person).

per·ver·ti·do, a I. adj. perverted II. m.f. pervert.

per·ver·tir §65 tr. to pervert —reflex. to become perverted.

pe·sa f. weight ♦ pl. dumbbells, weights.

pe·sa·car·tas m.inv. letter scale.

pe·sa·da f. quantity weighed at one time.

pe·sa·dez f. *(calidad)* heaviness; *(molestia)* nuisance.

pe·sa·di·lla f. nightmare.

pe·sa·do, a adj. *(que pesa)* heavy; *(sueño)* deep; *(corazón)* heavy; *(tiempo)* oppressive; *(aburrido)* boring; *(molesto)* annoying; *(fatigante)* tedious; *(difícil)* tough; *(ofensivo)* offensive; *(obeso)* obese.

pe·sa·dum·bre f. *(pesadez)* heaviness; *(pesar)* grief.

pé·sa·me m. condolence ♦ **dar el p.** to express condolences.

pe·sar¹ m. *(pena)* sorrow; *(arrepentimiento)* regret ♦ **a p. de** in spite of, despite ♦ **a p. de uno** against one's will ♦ **a p. de todo** in spite of everything.

pe·sar² tr. *(determinar el peso)* to weigh; to weigh down <me pesa el fardo the bundle is weighing me down>; *(examinar)* to weigh, consider; *(agobiar)* to sadden —intr. *(tener peso)* to weigh; *(ser pesado)* to weigh a lot; *(ser importante)* to carry weight ♦ **pese a quien le**

pese say what they will.

pe·sa·ro·so, a adj. *(arrepentido)* sorry; *(triste)* sad.

pes·ca f. *(acción)* fishing; *(lo pescado)* catch ♦ **p. de alta mar** deep-sea fishing.

pes·ca·de·rí·a f. fish market.

pes·ca·de·ro, a m.f. fishmonger.

pes·ca·di·lla f. whiting.

pes·ca·do m. fish (out of water).

pes·ca·dor m. fisherman.

pes·can·te m. *(de los cocheros)* coachman's seat; CONSTR. jib; MARIT. davit.

pes·car §70 tr. *(coger peces)* to fish (for); *(lograr)* to land <p. un marido to land a husband>; *(sorprender)* to catch.

pes·cue·zo m. *(de animal)* neck; *(de persona)* scruff of the neck.

pe·se·bre f. manger.

pe·se·ta f. FIN. peseta.

pe·si·mis·ta I. adj. pessimistic II. m.f. pessimist.

pé·si·mo, a adj. very bad, terrible.

pe·so m. weight; FIN. peso; *(pesa)* counterweight; *(carga)* burden; SPORT. shot <lanzamiento del p. shot-put> ♦ **caerse de su propio p.** COLL. to be self-evident ♦ **levantamiento de pesos** weightlifting ♦ **levantar en p.** to lift up ♦ **p. bruto** gross weight ♦ **p. específico** density ♦ **p. gallo** bantamweight ♦ **p. liviano** lightweight ♦ **p. medio** middleweight ♦ **p. mosca** flyweight ♦ **p. pesado** heavyweight ♦ **p. semimedio** welterweight ♦ **quitarle a alguien un p. de encima** to take a load off someone's mind.

pes·pun·tar/te·ar tr. to backstitch.

pes·pun·te m. backstitch.

pes·que·ro, a adj. fishing.

pes·qui·sa f. *(averiguación)* investigation —m. ARG., ECUAD. secret police.

pes·ta·ña f. eyelash; *(de una rueda)* rim; *(borde)* edge; SEW. fringe ♦ **no pegar p.** not to sleep a wink ♦ **quemarse las pestañas** COLL. to burn the midnight oil.

pes·ta·ñe·ar intr. to blink, wink.

pes·ta·ñe·o m. blinking, winking.

pes·te f. plague; *(olor)* stench; *(molestia)* nuisance ♦ **huir de alguien como de la p.** to avoid someone like the plague ♦ pl. offensive words ♦ **echar p.** to complain bitterly.

pes·ti·len·cia f. *(peste)* pestilence, plague; *(olor)* stench, stink.

pes·ti·llo m. bolt (of a lock).

pes·to·so, a adj. foul.

pe·ta·ca f. *(bolsa)* tobacco pouch; *(estuche)* cigarette case; *(baúl)* leather trunk.

pé·ta·lo m. petal.

pe·tar·do m. MIL. petard; *(cohete)* firecracker.

pe·ta·te m. *(estera)* sleeping mat; *(de ropa)* bundle.

pe·ti·ción f. petition; LAW claim ♦ **a p. de** at the request of.

pe·ti·cio·nar tr. to petition.

pe·ti·cio·na·rio, a/nan·te I. adj. petitioning II. m.f. petitioner.

pe·ti·me·tre m. fop.

pe·ti·so, a AMER. I. adj. short II. m. small horse.

pe·ti·to·rio, a I. adj. petitionary II. m. petition.

pé·tre·o, a adj. rocky.

pe·tri·fi·car §70 tr. to petrify —reflex. to become petrified.

pe·tro·dó·la·res m.pl. petrodollars.

pe·tró·le·o m. petroleum, oil ♦ **p. bruto** or **crudo** crude oil • **p. combustible** fuel oil.
pe·tro·le·ro, a I. adj. oil, petroleum II. m. oil tanker.
pe·tro·lí·fe·ro, a adj. oil-bearing.
pe·tro·quí·mi·ca f. petrochemistry.
pe·tro·quí·mi·co, a adj. petrochemical.
pe·tu·lan·cia f. arrogance.
pe·tu·lan·te adj. arrogant.
pe·tu·nia f. petunia.
pe·yo·ra·ti·vo, a adj. pejorative.
pe·yo·te m. peyote.
pez¹ m. fish ♦ **estar como el p. en el agua** COLL. to feel completely at home • **p. espada** swordfish • **p. gordo** COLL. big shot.
pez² f. pitch, tar.
pe·zón m. *(de la teta)* nipple; *(extremo)* point.
pe·zo·ne·ra f. *(de eje)* linchpin; *(de mujeres)* nipple shield.
pe·zu·ña f. (cloven) hoof.
¡pf! interj. hah!
pia·do·so, a adj. *(que compadece)* compassionate; *(devoto)* pious.
pia·nis·ta m.f. pianist.
pia·no I. m. piano ♦ **p. de cola** grand piano • **p. de media cola** baby grand • **p. vertical** upright piano II. adv. softly.
pia·no·for·te m. pianoforte, piano.
piar §30 intr. to cheep, chirp.
pi·be, a m.f. R.P. COLL. kid.
pi·ca·de·ro m. *(para caballos)* ring; MARIT. boat skid or which.
pi·ca·di·llo m. chopped meat ♦ **hacer p.** to make mincemeat of.
pi·ca·do, a I. adj. *(perforado)* perforated; COLL. *(ofendido)* ticked off II. m. *(acción)* perforating; MUS. staccato; AVIA. nose dive.
pi·ca·dor m. *(de caballos)* horsebreaker; TAUR. picador.
pi·ca·du·ra f. bite.
pi·ca·flor m. hummingbird; AMER. flirt.
pi·ca·ma·de·ros m.inv. woodpecker.
pi·ca·na f. R.P. goad.
pi·ca·ne·ar tr. R.P. to goad.
pi·can·te adj. spicy; *(arriesgado)* risqué.
pi·ca·plei·tos m.inv. COLL. shyster.
pi·ca·por·te m. *(barrita)* latch; *(llave)* latchkey; *(aldaba)* doorknocker.
pi·car §70 tr. *(punzar)* to prick; *(agujerear)* to perforate; *(punch <p. los billetes* to punch tickets>; TAUR. to goad; *(espolear)* to spur; *(morder)* to bite; ICHTH. to bite; ORNITH. to peck (at); *(comer)* to nibble; *(quemar)* to burn, sting; *(cortar)* to mince; *(estimular)* to arouse, pique; *(enojar)* to pique, vex; PAINT. to stipple —intr. *(escocer)* to itch; *(morder)* to sting; *(calentar)* to be hot; AVIA., ORNITH. to dive; ICHTH. to bite —reflex. *(agujerearse)* to become moth-eaten; *(echarse a perder)* to rot; *(avinagrarse)* to turn sour; MARIT. to become choppy; *(irritarse)* to get annoyed.
pi·car·dí·a f. *(acción baja)* dirty trick; *(travesura)* mischief.
pi·ca·res·co, a adj. mischievous; LIT. picaresque.
pi·ca·ro, a I. adj. *(astuto)* sly; *(malicioso)* wicked; *(en sentido cariñoso)* impish II. m.f. *(bribón)* scoundrel; *(astuto)* sly person; *(en sentido cariñoso)* rascal —m. LIT. rogue.
pi·ca·rón, o·na I. adj. COLL. mischievous II. m.f. COLL. rascal.
pi·ca·zón f. itch, itching.

pi·chón m. *(paloma)* young pigeon; COLL. *(nombre cariñoso)* honey; AMER. novice.
pi·co m. *(de aves)* beak; *(punta)* tip; *(de vasija)* spout; *(herramienta)* pick; *(cima)* peak ♦ **callar** or **cerrar el p.** COLL. to shut one's trap • **tener mucho p.** COLL. to gab a lot • **y p.** odd <*veinte dólares y p.* twenty-odd dollars>; a little after <*son las ocho y p.* it is a little after eight>.
pi·cor m. itching.
pi·co·ta·da f./**zo** m. peck.
pi·co·te·ar tr. *(con el pico)* to peck; *(comer)* to nibble, peck (at).
pic·tó·ri·co, a adj. pictorial.
pi·da, do, diera, dió see pedir.
pie m. foot; *(base)* base, stand; *(sedimento)* sediment; *(tronco)* trunk; *(tallo)* stalk ♦ **al p. de la letra** to the letter • **a p.** on foot • **a p. firme** steadfastly • **a p. juntillas** steadfastly • **caer de p.** to land on one's feet • **con pies de plomo** *(lentamente)* slowly; *(con prudencia)* cautiously • **dar p. a** to give rise to • **de p.** upright • **de pies a cabeza** from head to foot • **en p. de guerra** ready for war • **entrar con buen p.** to get off to a good start • **estar con el p. en el estribo** to be about to leave • **estar con un p. en la sepultura** to have one foot in the grave • **hacer p.** *(hallar fondo)* to touch bottom; *(estar seguro)* to be on a firm footing • **levantarse con el p. izquierdo** COLL. to get up on the wrong side of the bed • **nacer de p.** COLL. to be born lucky • **no dar p. con bola** COLL. to do nothing right • **no tener pies ni cabeza** to make no sense whatsoever • **perder p.** to slip • **p. de atleta** athlete's foot • **pies planos** flatfeet • **poner pies en polvorosa** COLL. to run away • **ponerse de p.** to stand up.
pie·dad f. *(devoción)* piety; *(lástima)* pity.
pie·dra f. *(peña)* stone, rock; *(granizo)* hailstone ♦ **p. de afilar** grindstone • **p. de amolar** whetstone • **p. angular** cornerstone • **p. caliza** limestone • **p. de chispa** flint • **p. de molino** millstone • **p. filosofal** philosophers' stone • **p. fundamental** keystone • **p. pómez** pumice stone • **p. preciosa** precious stone.
piel f. skin; ZOOL. *(sin pelo)* skin, hide; *(con pelo)* fur, pelt; *(cuero)* leather; BOT. peel ♦ **p. de cabra** goat-skin • **p. de cerdo** pigskin • **p. de gallina** goose pimples • **ser de la p. del diablo** COLL. to be a little devil.
pien·se, so see pensar¹.
pien·so m. fodder.
pier·da, do see perder.
pier·na f. leg; R.P. player (in a card game) ♦ **dormir a p. suelta** COLL. to sleep like a log.
pie·za f. piece; *(de maquinaria)* part; *(moneda)* coin; *(de tela)* bolt; *(habitación)* room; *(animal)* head; *(ficha)* man ♦ **de una p.** *(sólido)* solid; *(honesto)* honest • **dejar de una p.** COLL. to leave speechless • **p. de repuesto** spare part • **quedarse de una p.** COLL. to be left speechless.
pi·fia f. *(en billar)* miscue; COLL. *(error)* slip.
pi·fiar intr. & tr. *(en billar)* to miscue; COLL. *(chapucear)* to bungle; AMER. to mock.
pig·men·ta·ción f. pigmentation.
pig·men·tar tr. to pigment.
pig·men·to m. pigment.
pig·me·o adj. & m.f. pygmy.
pi·ja·ma m. pajamas.
pi·la f. *(recipiente)* basin; *(de cocina)* sink;

(fuente) fountain; *(montón)* pile; *(de bautismo)* baptismal font; *(de agua bendita)* holy water font; ELEC. battery, cell ♦ **nombre de p.** Christian name • **p. atómica** atomic reactor.

pi·lar m. *(columna)* pillar, column; *(de puente)* pier.

pil·cha f. R.P. piece of clothing.

píl·do·ra f. pill ♦ **dorar la p.** COLL. to sugarcoat the pill.

pi·le·ta f. *(pila)* sink; AMER. *(piscina)* swimming pool.

pi·llar tr. *(robar)* to plunder; *(coger)* to catch.

pi·lle·rí·a f. prank, trick.

pi·lle·te/llín m. COLL. rascal.

pi·llo, a COLL. I. adj. mischievous II. m.f. scoundrel.

pi·llue·lo, a I. adj. mischievous II. m.f. rascal.

pi·lón¹ m. *(pila)* basin, trough; *(mortero)* pounding mortar; *(pan de azúcar)* sugarloaf; *(pesa móvil)* movable weight.

pi·lón² m. ARCHIT. pylon.

pi·lo·tar/te·ar tr. to pilot; *(conducir)* to drive.

pi·lo·te m. stake.

pi·lo·to I. m. pilot; *(navegante)* navigator; *(segundo de un buque)* first mate; *(guía)* guide; *(llama)* pilot light ♦ **p. automático** automatic pilot • **p. de pruebas** test pilot • **p. de puerto** harbor pilot • **p. práctico** coastal pilot II. adj. pilot, model.

pil·tra·fa f. *(carne)* gristly meat; *(persona)* wretch.

pi·men·tón m. paprika.

pi·mien·ta f. pepper.

pi·mien·to m. BOT. pepper; *(pimentón)* paprika ♦ **p. chile** chili pepper • **p. morrón** sweet pepper.

pim·pan·te adj. *(bien vestido)* elegant, spruce; *(garboso)* graceful, poised.

pim·po·llo m. *(capullo)* rosebud; *(vástago)* shoot —m.f. COLL. attractive youth.

pi·na·co·te·ca f. art gallery.

pi·ná·cu·lo m. pinnacle.

pi·nar m. pine grove.

pin·cel m. brush.

pin·ce·la·da f./zo m. brush stroke ♦ **dar la última p.** a to put the last touches on.

pin·cha·du·ra f. puncture.

pin·char tr. to puncture; FIG. to annoy ♦ **ni pincha ni corta** COLL. he has little say.

pin·cha·zo m. puncture.

pin·che I. m. *(de cocina)* kitchen boy; AMER. *(de oficina)* clerk II. adj. MEX., COLL. miserable, lousy.

pin·cho m. *(aguijón)* prickle, thorn; *(de aduanero)* sampling stick; *(de sombrero)* hatpin.

pin·ga·jo m. COLL. tatter, rag.

pin·go m. COLL. *(pingajo)* tatter; *(pendón)* bum, good-for-nothing; R.P. fast horse.

pin·güe adj. *(graso)* greasy; *(grande)* huge.

pin·güi·no m. penguin.

pi·ni·to m. first step.

pi·no m. pine *(tree)* ♦ **p. albar** Scotch pine.

pin·ta f. see **pinto, a.**

pin·ta·do, a I. adj. spotted, mottled ♦ **como p.** just right • **no poder ver (a alguien) ni p.** COLL. not to be able to stand (someone) • **venir como p.** to suit to a tee.

pin·tar tr. to paint; *(describir)* to depict —intr. to paint —reflex. to put on make-up.

pin·ta·rra·jar/je·ar COLL. tr. to paint amateurishly —reflex. to put on heavy make-up.

pin·to, a I. adj. speckled II. f. *(mancha)* spot; COLL. *(aspecto)* look; *(medida)* pint ♦ **tener p. de** COLL. to look like.

pin·tón, o·na adj. *(de frutas)* ripening; *(de ladrillos)* half-baked; R.P., COLL. *(elegante)* sharp.

pin·tor, ·ra m.f. painter ♦ **p. de brocha gorda** house painter; FIG. bad painter.

pin·to·res·co, a adj. picturesque.

pin·tu·ra f. *(arte)* painting; *(cuadro)* painting, picture; *(color)* paint; *(descripción)* portrayal ♦ **p. a la acuarela** water color • **p. al fresco** fresco painting • **p. al óleo** oil painting • **p. al pastel** pastel *(drawing).*

pin·za f. *(de langosta)* claw; SEW. dart ♦ pl. *(tenacillas)* tweezers; *(tenazas)* tongs.

pi·ña f. *(del pino)* pine cone; *(ananás)* pineapple; COLL. *(puñetazo)* blow ♦ **darse piñas** AMER., COLL. to come to blows.

pi·ñón¹ m. *(simiente)* pine nut; *(arbusto)* nut pine.

pi·ñón² m. MECH. pinion (wheel).

pí·o, a I. adj. *(devoto)* pious; *(compasivo)* compassionate II. m. chirping ♦ **no decir ni p.** COLL. not to say a word.

pio·jo m. louse ♦ **p. resucitado** COLL. upstart.

pio·jo·so, a adj. *(lleno de piojos)* lousy; *(sucio)* dirty; *(miserable)* stingy.

pio·la f. string, cord.

pio·ne·ro, a m.f. & adj. pioneer.

pio·rre·a f. pyorrhea.

pi·pa¹ f. *(tonel)* barrel; *(para fumar)* pipe.

pi·pa² f. pip, seed.

pi·per·mín m. peppermint.

pi·pe·ta f. pipette.

pi·pí m. COLL. wee-wee ♦ **hacer p.** COLL. to make wee-wee.

pi·piar §30 intr. to chirp.

pi·pón, o·na adj. AMER. *(lleno)* full; *(barrigón)* paunchy.

pi·que¹ m. resentment.

pi·que² m. ♦ **echar a p.** to sink; FIG. to ruin • **irse a p.** to sink; FIG. to be ruined.

pi·qué m. piqué.

pi·que·ta f. pick.

pi·que·te m. picket, squad.

pi·ra·gua f. pirogue.

pi·ra·mi·dal adj. pyramidal.

pi·rá·mi·de f. pyramid.

pi·ra·ña f. AMER. piranha.

pi·rar·se reflex. COLL. to take off, leave.

pi·ra·ta m. & adj. pirate ♦ **p. aéreo** hijacker.

pi·ra·te·rí·a f. *(de barcos)* piracy; *(robo)* theft ♦ **p. aérea** hijacking.

pi·ri·ta f. pyrites.

pi·ró·ma·no, a I. adj. pyromaniacal II. m.f. pyromaniac.

pi·ro·pe·ar tr. COLL. to pay flirtatious compliments to.

pi·ro·po m. *(requiebro)* flattering remark; *(granate)* garnet ♦ **decir piropos** to pay flirtatious compliments *(a* to).

pi·ro·tec·nia f. pyrotechnics, pyrotechny.

pi·ro·téc·ni·co, a I. adj. pyrotechnic(al) II. m. pyrotechnist.

pí·rri·co, a adj. Pyrrhic.

pi·rue·ta f. pirouette.

pi·ru·lí m. [pl. **-ís**] lollipop.

pis m. COLL. wee-wee ♦ **hacer p.** to pee.

pi·sa·da f. *(acción)* step; *(huella)* footprint.

pi·sa·pa·pe·les m.inv. paperweight.

pi·sar tr. *(andar)* to step *or* walk on; *(frutas)* to press; (tierra) to pack down; ORNITH. to copulate with; (cubrir) to cover.

pi·sa·ú·vas m.inv. grape treader.

pis·ci·cul·tu·ra f. pisciculture.

pis·ci·na f. (para nadar) swimming pool; (para peces) fishpond.

pis·co·la·bis m.inv. COLL. snack.

pi·so m. (suelo) ground; (de una habitación) floor; (pavimento) pavement; (planta) floor, story; (apartamento) apartment, flat (G.B.) ♦ **p. bajo** ground floor • **primer p.** second floor, first floor (G.B.).

pi·són m. rammer, tamper.

pi·so·ne·ar tr. to ram down, tamp.

pi·so·te·ar tr. (pisar) to trample; (maltratar) to abuse.

pi·so·tón m. ♦ **dar un p.** to step on someone's foot.

pis·ta f. (huella) trail; (de carrera) racetrack; (de bailar) dance floor; (del circo) ring; (de aterrizaje) runway; (indicio) clue; (camino) trail ♦ **estar sobre la p.** to be on the trail or track.

pis·ta·cho m. pistachio (nut).

pis·ti·lo m. pistil.

pis·to·la f. (arma) pistol; (para pintar) paint sprayer ♦ **p. ametralladora** submachine gun • **p. de engrase** grease gun.

pis·to·le·ro m. COLL. gunman.

pis·to·le·ta·zo m. pistol shot.

pis·tón m. piston; AMER. cornet.

pi·ta f. BOT. agave; TEX. pita.

pi·ta·da f. whistle; AMER. puff, drag.

pi·tan·za f. (reparto) ration; (alimento) daily bread.

pi·tar intr. (tocar el pito) to blow a whistle; S. AMER. (fumar) to smoke ♦ **salir pitando** to go off like a shot —tr. (silbar) to hiss at; S. AMER. (fumar) to smoke.

pi·te·cán·tro·po m. pithecanthropus.

pi·ti·do m. whistling.

pi·ti·lle·ra f. cigarette case.

pi·ti·llo m. cigarette.

pi·to m. whistle ♦ **no darle** or **importarle a uno un p.** COLL. not to give a damn • **no tocar p. en** to have nothing to do with • **no valer un p.** to be worthless.

pi·tón¹ m. ZOOL. python.

pi·tón² m. (cuerno) horn; (pitorro) spout; (del árbol) shoot; AMER. nozzle.

pi·to·ni·sa f. pythoness.

pi·tui·ta·rio, a adj. pituitary.

pi·vo·te m. pivot.

pi·ya·ma m. var. of **pijama**.

pi·za·rra f. (troca) slate; (pizarrón) blackboard.

pi·za·rrín m. slate pencil.

pi·za·rrón m. AMER. blackboard.

piz·ca f. pinch ♦ **ni p.** COLL. not (at all).

piz·pe·re·ta/piz·pi·re·ta adj. COLL. lively.

pla·ca f. plaque; (chapa) plate; (insignia) badge; (disco) record; ELEC., PHOTOG. plate; COMPUT. chip ♦ **p. de matrícula** license plate.

pla·ce·bo m. placebo.

plá·ce·me m. congratulations.

pla·cen·ta f. placenta.

pla·cen·te·ro, a adj. pleasant.

pla·cer¹ m. (deleite) pleasure; (diversión) delight; (voluntad) desire.

pla·cer² §51 tr. to please <me place hacerlo it pleases me to do it>.

pla·ci·dez f. placidness, placidity.

plá·ci·do, a adj. (quieto) placid; (grato) pleasant.

pla·ga f. plague; BOT. blight.

pla·gar §47 tr. to plague —reflex. to become infested with.

pla·giar tr. to plagiarize.

pla·gia·rio, a I. adj. plagiarizing II. m.f. plagiarist.

pla·gio m. plagiarism.

plan m. plan; (esquema) scheme; (proyecto) project; (programa) program ♦ **p. de estudios** curriculum, course of study.

pla·na f. (página) page, side; PRINT. page; MAS. trowel ♦ **de primera p.** front page.

plan·cha f. (lámina) sheet; (utensilio) iron <p. a vapor steam iron>; COLL. (error) blooper; PRINT. plate ♦ **a la p.** grilled • **hacer la p.** to float on one's back.

plan·cha·do, a m. (acción) ironing; (ropa) ironing, clothes to be ironed —f. (puentecillo) gangplank; AMER., COLL. (metedura de pata) blunder.

plan·cha·dor, ·ra m.f. presser.

plan·char tr. to iron.

plan·cha·zo m. COLL. blunder.

pla·ne·a·ción f./**mien·to** m. planning.

pla·ne·a·dor m. glider.

pla·ne·ar tr. to plan —intr. AER. to glide.

pla·ne·ta m. planet.

pla·ne·ta·rio, a I. adj. planetary II. m. planetarium.

pla·ne·toi·de m. planetoid.

pla·ni·cie f. plain.

pla·ni·fi·ca·ción f. planning.

pla·ni·fi·ca·dor, ·ra I. adj. planning II. m.f. planner.

pla·ni·fi·car §70 tr. to plan.

pla·ni·lla f. AMER. (lista) list; (cuadro) table; (formulario) form.

pla·no, a I. adj. (llano) level, even; (liso) smooth; (chato) flat II. m. plane; (superficie) surface; (diagrama) diagram; (mapa) map, chart; (de una espada) flat ♦ **caer de p.** to fall flat • **de p.** plainly • **levantar un p.** TOP. to make a survey • **primer p.** CINEM. (foto) close-up; (área) foreground.

plan·ta f. plant; (del pie) sole; (diseño) floor plan; (piso) floor; (proyecto) plan, project ♦ **p. baja** ground floor, first floor • **primera p.** second floor, first floor (G.B.).

plan·ta·ción f. (acción) planting; (explotación) plantation.

plan·ta·do, a adj. planted ♦ **bien p.** COLL. good-looking • **dejar (a alguien) p.** to stand (someone) up.

plan·tar tr. to plant, sow; (colocar) to put; COLL. (un golpe) to land; (abandonar) to leave —reflex. (resistir) to stand firm; COLL. (pararse) to balk <el caballo se plantó frente al arroyo the horse balked at the stream>; (en naipes) to stand pat.

plan·te·a·mien·to m. (exposición) exposition; (propuesta) proposal; (establecimiento) establishment; (enfoque) focus.

plan·te·ar tr. (exponer) to expound; (empezar) to start; (planear) to outline; (establecer) to establish; (proponer) to propose.

plan·tel m. (conjunto) group; (criadero) nursery, seedbed.

plan·te·o m. var. of **planteamiento**.

plan·ti·lla f. (suela) insole; TECH. (patrón) template; (de una llanta) rim.

plan·tón m. (pimpollo) seedling; (estaca) cutting ♦ **estar de p.** COLL. to be standing around a long time • **dar un p.** to keep (someone) waiting.

pla·ñi·de·ro, a adj. plaintive.

pla·ñi·do m. moan, lament.

pla·ñir §12 intr. to lament.

pla·que·ta f. blood platelet.

plas·ma m. plasma.

plas·mar tr. to shape, mold.

plás·ti·co, a adj. & m. plastic —f. plastic arts.

plas·ti·fi·ca·ción f./**do** m. shellacking.

plas·ti·fi·car §70 tr. to shellac.

pla·ta f. silver; (moneda) silver (coin); AMER. money.

pla·ta·for·ma f. platform; FIG. (trampolín) stepping stone; (vagón) open wagon ♦ **p. continental** continental shelf ♦ **p. de lanzamiento** launching pad.

pla·tal m. AMER., COLL. fortune.

plá·ta·no m. (de banano) banana; (de sombra) plane tree; BOT., CUL. plantain.

pla·te·a f. orchestra seat or section.

pla·te·a·do, a I. adj. (bañado) silver-plated; (de color) silvery; MEX. wealthy **II.** m. silver plating.

pla·te·ar tr. to silver-plate.

pla·te·rí·a f. (arte) silversmithing; (tienda) silversmith's shop.

pla·te·ro m. silversmith.

plá·ti·ca f. chat, talk.

pla·ti·car §70 intr. to chat, talk (sobre over, about).

pla·ti·llo m. (plato pequeño) saucer; (balanza) tray; MUS. cymbal ♦ **p. volador** flying saucer.

pla·ti·na f. PRINT. (mesa) imposing table; (de prensa) platen; TECH. plate (of air pump); (microscopio) slide.

pla·ti·nar tr. to platinize; (hair) to bleach.

pla·ti·no m. platinum.

pla·to m. plate, dish; (contenido) plateful, dish; (comida) dish; course <p. **fuerte** main course>; (de la balanza) pan; MECH. plate ♦ **pagar los platos rotos** COLL. to pay the consequences.

pla·tó·ni·co, a adj. platonic.

pla·tu·do, a adj. AMER., COLL. rich, wealthy.

plau·si·ble adj. plausible.

pla·ya f. beach ♦ **p. de estacionamiento** AMER. parking lot.

pla·ye·ro, a adj. beach <sombrero **p.** beach hat>.

pla·za f. (lugar público) plaza, square; (mercado) marketplace; (sitio) place; (empleo) position ♦ **p. de toros** bullring.

pla·zo m. (término) term, period; (pago) installment ♦ **a corto p.** short-term • **a largo p.** long-term • **comprar a plazos** to buy on credit • **en breve p.** within a short time • **vender a plazos** to sell on credit.

pla·zo·le·ta f. small square.

ple·a·mar f. high tide or water.

ple·be f. (multitud) masses; DEROG. riffraff.

ple·be·yo, a adj. & m.f. plebeian.

ple·bis·ci·to m. plebiscite.

ple·ga·ble adj. folding, collapsible.

ple·ga·de·ra f. paperknife; PRINT. folder.

ple·ga·di·zo, a adj. (que se dobla) folding; (fácil de doblar) foldable, easy to fold.

ple·ga·do m.f. (acción) folding; (pliegue) fold.

ple·ga·mien·to m. fold.

ple·gar §52 tr. (hacer pliegues) to pleat; (doblar) to fold —reflex. (doblarse) to bend, fold; (someterse) to yield; (adherirse) to join.

ple·ga·ria f. prayer.

plei·te·ar intr. to litigate.

plei·te·sí·a f. homage, tribute ♦ **rendir p.** to pay homage.

plei·to m. LAW lawsuit; (disputa) quarrel ♦ **entablar p.** to bring suit • **ganar el p.** to obtain a favorable judgment • **poner p.** to sue.

ple·na·mar f. var. of **pleamar.**

ple·na·rio, a adj. plenary.

ple·ni·lu·nio m. full moon.

ple·ni·po·ten·cia f. unlimited powers.

ple·ni·po·ten·cia·rio, a adj. & m.f. plenipotentiary.

ple·ni·tud f. fullness; FIG. prime.

ple·no, a I. adj. full ♦ **en p.** right in the middle of <en p. **calle** right in the middle of the street> • **en p. día** in broad daylight **II.** m. joint session.

plé·to·ra f. plethora.

pleu·re·sí·a f. pleurisy.

ple·xo m. plexus ♦ **p. solar** solar plexus.

plie·go m. (papel doblado) folded sheet of paper; (hoja de papel) sheet of paper; (documento cerrado) sealed document; PRINT. signature ♦ **p. de condiciones** specifications.

plie·go, gue see **plegar.**

plie·gue m. fold; SEW. pleat.

pli·sa·do m. (acción) pleating; (efecto) pleat.

pli·sar tr. to pleat.

plo·ma·da f. plumb (line); MARIT. plumb or sounding line; (perdigonada) shot with pellets.

plo·me·rí·a f. (techo) lead roofing; AMER. (oficio) plumbing.

plo·me·ro m. AMER. plumber.

plo·mi·zo, a adj. leaden.

plo·mo, a I. adj. leaden **II.** m. lead; COLL. (bala) bullet; (persona) bore ♦ **a p.** plumb.

plu·ma f. feather; (conjunto de plumas) feather, down <una almohada de plumas a down pillow>; (para escribir) quill; (estilográfica) pen; (adorno) plume ♦ AMER. **p. fuente** or **estilográfica** fountain pen.

plu·ma·da f. pen stroke.

plu·ma·fuen·te f. AMER. fountain pen.

plu·ma·je m. (plumas) plumage; (adorno) plume.

plu·ma·zo m. pen stroke ♦ **de un p.** with one stroke of the pen.

plu·me·ro m. (para polvo) feather duster; (penacho) plume.

plu·mi·lla f. nib.

plu·món m. (pluma) down; (colchón) feather mattress.

plu·ral adj. & m. plural.

plu·ra·li·dad f. plurality.

plu·ra·li·zar §04 tr. to pluralize.

plus·cuam·per·fec·to m. pluperfect.

plus·va·lí·a f. appreciation.

plu·to·cra·cia f. plutocracy.

plu·tó·cra·ta m.f. plutocrat.

plu·to·nio m. plutonium.

plu·vial adj. pluvial, rain.

po·bla·ción f. population; (lugar) locality; (ciudad) city; (pueblo) town.

po·bla·do m. (habitantes) population; (ciudad) city; (pueblo) town.

po·bla·dor, ·ra m.f. resident, inhabitant.

po·blar §19 tr. to populate; AGR. to plant —reflex. to become populated; (llenarse) to become crowded (de with).

po·bre I. adj. poor; (necesitado) needy; (desprovisto) lacking (de, en in); (humilde) humble;

FIG. unfortunate ♦ **más p. que una rata** COLL. as poor as a church mouse **II.** m. beggar, pauper ♦ **los pobres** the poor.

po·bre·men·te adv. *(con pobreza)* poorly, indigently; *(con escasez)* poorly, inadequately.

po·bre·tón, o·na I. adj. wretched **II.** m.f. wretch.

po·bre·za f. poverty; *(indigencia)* indigence; *(escasez)* lack.

po·ce·ro m. well digger.

po·cil·ga f. pigsty.

po·ci·llo m. cup.

pó·ci·ma f. *(cocimiento medicinal)* potion; *(bebida)* concoction.

po·ción f. potion.

po·co, a I. adj. little ♦ **p. tiempo** short while *or* time • **ser p. cosa** to be unimportant ♦ pl. few, not many • **pocas veces** not very often, rarely **II.** m. little ♦ **dentro de p.** in a short while, soon • **otro p.** a little more • **tener en p.** to have a low opinion *(a of)* • **un p. de** a little, some <*tiene un p. de dinero* he has a little money> ♦ pl. <*p. saben la respuesta* few know the answer> **III.** adv. *(con escasez)* little, not much <*habló p. durante la clase* he spoke little during the class>; *(en corta duración)* not long, a short while <*tardó p. en terminar* he did not take long to finish>; *(no muy)* not very ♦ **a p. de** shortly after <*a p. de comer fuimos al cine* shortly after eating, we went to the movies> • **falta p. para** it will not be long before <*falta p. para comer* it will not be long before we eat> • **hace p.** a short time ago • **p. a p.** little by little • **p. después** a little after • **p. más o menos** more or less • **por p.** almost.

po·da f. *(acción)* pruning; *(tiempo)* pruning season.

po·da·de·ra f. AGR. pruning shears.

po·da·dor, ra I. adj. pruning **II.** m.f. pruner.

po·dar tr. to prune.

po·den·co, a adj. & m.f. spaniel (dog).

po·der¹ m. power; *(autoridad)* authority; *(vigor)* might; *(fuerza física)* strength; *(capacidad)* capacity; *(posesión)* hands <*tengo en mi p. su carta del once de mayo* I have in my hands your letter of the eleventh of May>; MIL. strength; POL. government; LAW power of attorney ♦ **dar p. a** to empower • **p. adquisitivo** purchasing power • **p. ejecutivo** the executive • **p. judicial** the judiciary • **p. legislativo** the legislative branch • **por poderes** by proxy.

po·der² §53 tr. *(lograr)* to be able to <*podremos salir a las ocho* we will be able to leave at eight o'clock>; can <*¿puedes acompañarme?* can you come with me?> —intr. to be able, can <*me gustaría ayudarte pero no puedo* I would like to help you but I am not able to>; to be possible, may <*puede que llueva mañana* it may rain tomorrow> ♦ **a más no p.** to the utmost • **no p. con** *(no lograr)* not to be able to handle; *(no soportar)* not to be able to stand • **no p. más** *(estar fatigado)* to be exhausted; *(estar harto)* to be fed up • **no p. menos que** not to be able to help but • **no p. valerse por sí mismo** to be helpless • **no puede ser** that is not possible • **puede ser** maybe • **¿se puede?** may I?

po·de·rí·o m. power.

po·de·ro·so, a adj. *(fuerte)* powerful; *(rico)* wealthy; *(eficaz)* effective.

po·dí·a·tra/dia·tra m. AMER. podiatrist.

po·drá, dría see poder².

po·dre·dum·bre f. putrefaction.

po·dri·do, a adj. rotten ♦ **estar p. en plata** AMER., COLL. to be rolling in money.

po·drir tr. & reflex. to rot, putrefy.

po·e·ma m. poem.

po·e·sí·a f. poetry; *(poema)* poem.

po·e·ta m. poet.

po·é·ti·co, a I. adj. poetic **II.** f. poetics.

po·e·ti·sa f. poetess.

po·lai·na f. legging.

po·lar adj. polar; ELEC. pole.

po·la·ri·za·ción f. polarization.

po·la·ri·zar §04 tr. to polarize —intr. to become polarized.

po·le·a f. pulley.

po·lé·mi·co, a I. adj. polemic(al) **II.** f. *(arte)* polemics; *(controversia)* polemic.

po·le·mi·zar §04 intr. to argue *(sobre* about).

po·len m. pollen.

po·li m. SL. cop —f. cops <*¡la p.!* the cops!>.

po·li·cí·a f. police —m. policeman.

po·li·cia·co/cí·a·co, a adj. *(de policía)* police; detective <*novela p.* detective novel>.

po·li·cial I. adj. *(de policía)* police; *(de detective)* detective **II.** m. AMER. policeman.

po·li·clí·ni·ca f. polyclinic.

po·li·cro·mí·a f. polychromy.

po·lie·dro m. polyhedron.

po·li·fo·ní·a f. polyphony.

po·li·ga·mia f. polygamy.

po·lí·glo·to/lí·go·to, a adj. & m.f. polyglot.

po·lí·go·no m. polygon.

po·li·lla f. moth.

po·lí·me·ro m. polymer.

po·li·ni·za·ción f. pollination.

po·li·no·mio m. polynomial.

po·lio/mie·li·tis) f. polio, poliomyelitis.

pó·li·po m. polyp.

po·li·téc·ni·co, a adj. polytechnic.

po·lí·ti·cas·tro m. DEROG. politician.

po·lí·ti·co, a I. adj. political; *(de parentesco)* -in-law <*hermana p.* sister-in-law> **II.** m.f. politician —f. politics; *(modo de obrar)* policy <*p. monetaria* monetary policy>.

po·li·ti·que·ar intr. COLL. to talk politics.

po·li·ti·que·ro, a m.f. political maneuverer.

po·li·ti·zar §04 tr. to politicize.

po·liu·re·ta·no m. polyurethane.

po·li·va·len·te adj. polyvalent.

pó·li·za f. *(de seguros)* insurance policy; *(contrato)* contract; *(sello)* stamp.

po·li·zón m. stowaway.

po·lla f. young hen.

po·lle·ra f. henouse; AMER. skirt.

po·lle·rí·a f. poultry shop.

po·lle·ro m. poulterer.

po·llo m. *(cría)* chick; CUL. chicken; SL. *(gargajo)* spit.

po·lo¹ m. pole ♦ **p. antártico** *or* **austral** South Pole • **p. ártico** *or* **boreal** North Pole • **ser el p. opuesto de** to be the opposite of.

po·lo² m. pole • **p. acuático** water polo.

pol·trón, o·na I. adj. lazy **II.** f. easy chair.

po·lu·ción f. pollution.

pol·va·re·da f. *(nube)* cloud of dust; *(alboroto)* rumpus.

pol·ve·ra f. compact.

pol·vo m. *(tierra)* dust; *(substancia pulverizada)* powder; *(porción)* pinch ♦ **en. p.** powdered • **estar hecho p.** COLL. *(exhausto)* to be exhausted; *(desmoralizado)* to be overwhelmed • **hacer morder el p. a alguien** to defeat • **hacer**

p. COLL. (romper) to smash; (aniquilar) to annihilate ♦ pl. cosmetic powder.

pól·vo·ra f. powder ♦ **ser una p.** to be a whip.

pol·vo·rien·to, a adj. dusty.

pol·vo·rín m. (explosivo) fine gunpowder; (lugar) powder magazine.

po·ma·da f. pomade.

po·me·lo m. (fruta) grapefruit; (árbol) grapefruit tree.

pó·mez adj. ♦ **piedra p.** pumice stone.

po·mo m. pome; (para licores) flagon; (para perfumes) perfume bottle.

pom·pa f. pomp; (ostentación) display; (procesión) procession; (burbuja) bubble ♦ **pompas fúnebres** funeral.

pom·po·si·dad f. (esplendor) pomp; (arrogancia) pomposity.

pom·po·so, a adj. (espléndido) magnificent; (arrogante) pompous.

pó·mu·lo m. (hueso) cheekbone; (mejilla) cheek.

pon see **poner.**

pon·cha·da f. AMER., COLL. large quantity.

pon·che m. punch.

pon·che·ra f. punch bowl.

pon·cho m. poncho.

pon·de·ra·ble adj. ponderable; (digno de ponderación) worthy of consideration.

pon·de·ra·ción f. (examinación) consideration; (peso) weighing; (equilibrio) balance.

pon·de·ra·do, a adj. prudent, careful.

pon·de·rar tr. (alabar) to praise; (examinar) to ponder; (pesar) to weigh.

pon·drá, dría see **poner.**

po·ne·dor, ·ra adj. egg-laying.

po·ner §54 tr. (colocar) to put, place <¿dónde pusiste la tijera? where did you put the scissors?>; (disponer) to set <María puso la mesa Mary set the table>; (escribir) to write; (instalar) to set up <p. casa to set up house>; (suponer) to suppose <pongamos que esto es así let's suppose that this is so>; (tardar) to take; (dejar) to leave <lo pongo en tus manos I leave it in your hands>; (asignar) to assign <le pusimos a hacer las decoraciones> he assigned him to do the decorations>; (nombrar) to name <le pusieron el apodo de Paco they gave him the nickname of Frank>; ORNITH. to lay; THEAT. to put on; (apostar) to put, stake; (contribuir) to contribute; (imponer) to levy; (exponer) to put <sin darme cuenta puse a Tomás en una situación peligrosa without realizing it I put Thomas in a dangerous situation>; (insultar) to insult <¡cómo lo pusieron! how they insulted him!>; (causar) to put <eso lo pondrá de mal humor that will put him in a bad mood>; (enviar) to send <me puso un telegrama she sent me a telegram> ♦ **p. al corriente** or **al día** to bring up to date ♦ **p. aparte** or **a un lado** to put aside ♦ **p. de la parte de uno** to do what one can ♦ **p. en claro** to make clear ♦ **p. en duda** to call into question ♦ **p. en movimiento** to set in motion ♦ **p. en práctica** to put into practice ♦ **p. en ridículo** to ridicule ♦ **p. en venta** to put up for sale ♦ **p. fin a** to put a stop to ♦ **p. manos a la obra** to get to work ♦ **p. miedo** to frighten ♦ **p. por encima** to prefer ♦ **p. por escrito** to put in writing ♦ **p. por las nubes** to praise to the skies —intr. ORNITH. to lay —reflex. (colocarse) to put or place oneself; (vestirse) to put on <se puso el sombrero he put on his hat>; (arriesgarse) to put oneself <p. en peligro to put oneself in danger>; ASTRON. to set; (hacerse) to become <se pusieron furiosos they became furious>; (dedicarse) to apply oneself ♦ **p. a** to begin to ♦ **p. al corriente** to bring oneself up to date ♦ **p. bien** to get well ♦ **p. colorado** to blush ♦ **p. de acuerdo** to reach an agreement ♦ **p. de pie** to stand up ♦ **p. en camino** to set out.

po·nien·te m. (occidente) west; (viento) west wind.

pon·ti·fi·cal adj. pontifical.

pon·ti·fi·car §70 intr. to pontificate.

pon·tí·fi·ce m. RELIG. pontiff ♦ **Sumo P.** Sovereign Pontiff.

pon·tón m. (barco chato) pontoon; (puente) pontoon bridge.

pon·zo·ña f. venom.

pon·zo·ño·so, a adj. poisonous.

po·pa f. stern ♦ **a p.** MARIT. astern, abaft ♦ **viento en p.** FIG. smoothly, well.

po·pu·la·cho m. populace.

po·pu·lar adj. (del pueblo) of the people, people's; (grato al pueblo) popular, well-liked; (coloquial) colloquial; (música) folk.

po·pu·la·ri·dad f. popularity.

po·pu·la·ri·zar §04 tr. to popularize —reflex. to become popular.

po·pu·rrí m. potpourri.

po·que·dad f. (escasez) scantiness, paucity; (timidez) timidity.

pó·quer m. poker.

por prep. (sitio) by, on, along, through, around, over, towards, through; (tiempo) for, around, about, in, at, not yet, still to be; (agente) by, via; (causa, motivo) because of, out of, on account of, on behalf of, for, for the sake of, in order to; (modo) by, by means of, in, after, as, for; (distributiva) for, in exchange for, per, a, by, times; (concesión) however, no matter how ♦ **p. acá** or **aquí** around here ♦ **p. ahí** or **allí** around there ♦ **p. ahora** for the time being ♦ **p. casualidad** perchance ♦ **p. causa de** because of ♦ **p. ciento** per cent ♦ **p. cierto** indeed ♦ **p. completo** completely ♦ **p. consiguiente** therefore ♦ **p. correo** by mail ♦ **p. cuenta de uno** (sin ayuda) by oneself; (sin requerimiento) of one's own accord ♦ **p. desgracia** unfortunately ♦ **¡p. Dios!** for Heaven's sake! ♦ **p. entre** between, among ♦ **p. eso** therefore ♦ **p. lo bajo** softly ♦ **p. lo menos** at least ♦ **p. lo tanto** therefore ♦ **p. medio de** through ♦ **p. otra parte** or **p. lo demás** on the other hand ♦ **¿p. qué?** why? ♦ **p. regla general** as a general rule ♦ **p. si acaso** in case ♦ **p. sí mismo** by oneself ♦ **p. sobre** above ♦ **p. supuesto** of course ♦ **p. todos lados** everywhere ♦ **p. valor de** in the amount of.

por·ce·la·na f. porcelain; (vajilla) china; (esmalte) porcelain enamel; (color) porcelain blue.

por·cen·ta·je m. percentage.

por·cen·tual adj. percentage.

por·che m. porch.

por·ci·no, a I. adj. (del puerco) porcine, pig **II.** m. small pig.

por·ción f. portion; (parte) part; (cuota) share.

por·dio·se·ar intr. to beg.

por·dio·se·ro, a m.f. beggar.

por·fí·a f. stubbornness.

por·fia·do, a adj. & m.f. stubborn (person).

por·fiar §30 intr. (disputar) to argue stubbornly; (insistir) to persist.

por·me·nor m. detail, particular.
por·no·gra·fí·a f. pornography.
por·no·grá·fi·co, a adj. pornographic.
po·ro m. interstice; BIOL. pore.
po·ro·si·dad f. porosity.
po·ro·so, a adj. porous.
po·ro·to m. AMER. bean.
por·que conj. *(por causa de que)* because *<trabajo p. quiero comer* I work because I want to eat>; *(para que)* in order that, so that ♦ **p. sí** just because.
por·qué m. reason *(de* for), cause.
por·que·rí·a f. *(suciedad)* filth; *(basura)* garbage; *(grosería)* vulgarity; *(jugarreta)* dirty trick; *(cosa de poco valor)* junk.
por·que·ri·za f. pigsty.
po·rra f. *(clava)* club; *(de herrero)* sledgehammer; COLL. *(cabellera)* long hair.
po·rra·zo m. *(golpe)* blow; *(choque)* bump ♦ **pegarse un p. contra algo** to bump into something.
po·rro m. leek.
por·ta·a·vio·nes m.inv. aircraft carrier.
por·ta·ban·de·ra f. flag holder.
por·ta·bom·bas m.inv. bomb carrier.
por·ta·da f. ARCHIT. facade; PRINT. *(frontispicio)* title page; *(tapa)* cover.
por·ta·dor, ·ra I. adj. bearing **II.** m.f. carrier.
por·ta·e·qui·pa·jes m.inv. *(baúl)* trunk (of a car); *(rejilla)* luggage rack.
por·ta·es·tan·dar·te m. standard-bearer.
por·ta·fo·lio m. briefcase.
por·tal m. *(zaguán)* entrance hall; *(porche)* porch.
por·ta·lám·pa·ras m.inv. socket.
por·ta·li·bros m.inv. book straps.
por·ta·plu·mas m.inv. penholder.
por·tar tr. to carry, bear —reflex. to behave.
por·ta·rre·tra·tos m.inv. picture frame.
por·tá·til adj. portable.
por·ta·voz m.f. spokesman/woman.
por·ta·zo m. slam ♦ **dar un p. a alguien** to slam the door in someone's face.
por·te m. *(acción)* transporting; *(costo)* transport charge; *(presencia)* demeanor.
por·ten·to m. marvel.
por·ten·to·so, a adj. marvelous.
por·te·ño, a I. adj. of Buenos Aires **II.** m.f. native of Buenos Aires.
por·te·rí·a f. *(oficina)* concierge's office; SPORT. goal.
por·te·ro, a m.f. *(conserje)* concierge; *(de vivienda)* janitor; SPORT. goalkeeper.
pór·ti·co m. portico.
por·ti·lla f. *(paso)* gate; MARIT. porthole.
por·ti·llo m. *(de muro)* opening; *(puerta)* gate; *(paso angosto)* pass.
por·tón m. *(puerta grande)* large door; *(del zaguán)* vestibule door.
por·tua·rio, a adj. port, harbor.
por·ve·nir m. future.
pos adv. ♦ **en p. de** in pursuit of.
po·sa·da f. *(mesón)* inn; *(hogar)* home; *(hospedaje)* shelter.
po·sa·de·ras f.pl. buttocks.
po·sa·de·ro, a m.f. innkeeper.
po·sar intr. *(hospedarse)* to lodge; *(descansar)* to rest; *(las aves)* to perch; PAINT., PHOTOG. to pose —reflex. *(las aves)* to perch; AVIA. to land —tr. to put.
pos·da·ta f. postscript.
po·se f. pose.

po·se·e·dor, ·ra I. adj. who possesses **II.** m.f. *(dueño)* owner; holder *<el p. de una marca mundial* the holder of a world record> ♦ **p. de acciones** stockholder.
po·se·er §43 tr. to possess; *(tener)* to have *<ella posee una buena biblioteca* she has a good library>; to hold *<posee el record mundial* he holds the world record>.
po·se·í·do, a I. adj. possessed *(de* by) **II.** m.f. possessed person.
po·se·sión f. possession; *(propiedad)* property; AMER. property, estate ♦ pl. possessions, personal property.
po·se·sio·nar tr. to give possession of —reflex. to take possession of, take over.
po·se·si·vo, a adj. & m. possessive.
po·se·so, a adj. & m.f. possessed (person).
po·se·sor, ·ra adj. & m.f. var. of **poseedor, ra.**
po·se·ye·ra, yó see **poseer.**
pos·fe·cha f. postdate.
pos·gue·rra f. postwar period.
po·si·bi·li·dad f. possibility ♦ pl. chances.
po·si·bi·li·tar tr. to make possible.
po·si·ble adj. possible ♦ **de ser p.** if possible • **dentro de** *or* **en lo p.** as far as possible • **hacer p.** to make possible • **hacer (todo) lo p.** to do everything possible • **lo antes p.** as soon as possible.
po·si·ción f. position; *(postura)* posture; *(condición social)* status.
po·si·ti·vis·ta adj. & m.f. positivist.
po·si·ti·vo, a I. adj. positive **II.** m. PHOTOG. print; GRAM. positive.
po·so m. *(sedimento)* sediment; *(de café)* coffee grounds.
po·so·lo·gí·a f. dosage.
pos·po·ner §54 *(poner detrás)* to put behind; *(diferir)* to postpone.
pos·ta f. *(de caballos)* relay; *(lugar)* staging post; *(tajada)* slice.
pos·tal I. adj. postal ♦ **giro p.** money order **II.** f. postcard.
post·da·ta f. var. of **posdata.**
pos·te m. post ♦ **p. indicador** signpost.
pos·ter·ga·ción f. postponement.
pos·ter·gar §47 *(aplazar)* to postpone; *(en un empleo)* to pass over.
pos·te·ri·dad f. posterity.
pos·te·ri·or adj. *(ulterior)* subsequent *(a* to), later; *(trasero)* rear, back.
pos·te·rio·ri·dad f. posteriority ♦ **con p.** later *(a* than), subsequently *(a* to).
pos·te·rior·men·te adv. later (on).
post·gue·rra f. var. of **posguerra.**
pos·ti·go m. *(puerta falsa)* hidden door; *(contraventana)* shutter; *(de ciudad)* side gate.
pos·ti·zo, a I. adj. false *<dentadura p.* false teeth>; artificial *<brazo p.* artificial arm>; *(de quitapón)* detachable **II.** m. hair piece.
pos·to·pe·ra·to·rio, a adj. postoperative.
pos·tor m. bidder ♦ **mejor p.** highest bidder.
pos·trar tr. *(humillar)* to humiliate; *(debilitar)* to debilitate —reflex. *(arrodillarse)* to kneel down; *(debilitarse)* to become debilitated.
pos·tre m. dessert ♦ **a la p.** in the end.
pos·tre·mo, a adj. last, final.
pos·trer adj. contr. of **postrero.**
pos·tre·ro, a adj. last, final
pos·tri·me·rí·a f. last years, final stages.
pos·tu·la·do m. postulate.
pos·tu·lan·te, a m.f. applicant.
pos·tu·lar tr. to ask for, seek.

pós·tu·mo, a adj. posthumous.
pos·tu·ra f. posture; (*posición*) position; (*actitud*) attitude; (*opinión*) stand; (*de huevos*) laying of eggs.
po·ta·ble adj. potable.
po·ta·je m. (*guiso*) stew; (*bebida*) brew.
po·ta·sio m. potassium.
po·te m. pot, jar.
po·ten·cia f. (*poder*) power; (*fuerza*) potency, strength; (*nación*) power <una p. mundial a world power>; ARM. range; PHILOS. potential ♦ **segunda p.** square • **tercera p.** cube.
po·ten·ta·do m. (*soberano*) potentate; (*rico*) tycoon.
po·ten·te adj. (*poderoso*) powerful; (*que engendra*) potent, virile; (*grande*) big, mighty.
po·tes·tad f. power, authority ♦ **patria p.** parental authority.
po·to m. S. AMER., COLL. buttocks.
po·tra f. young mare.
po·tran·ca f. young mare.
po·tre·ar tr. to romp, frolic.
po·tre·ro m. (*dehesa*) pasture; R.P. playground (in a vacant lot).
po·tri·llo m. colt.
po·tro m. colt; SPORT. horse; (*de tormento*) rack.
po·zo m. (*de agua*) well; (*en un río*) deep pool; (*hoyo*) pit; MARIT. bilge; FIG. mine, source ♦ **p. de petróleo** oil well • **p. negro** cesspool.
prac·ti·can·te, a I. adj. practicing II. m.f. (*que ejerce*) practitioner; (*aprendiz*) medical intern.
prac·ti·car §70 tr. to practice; (*hacer*) to perform, carry out.
prác·ti·co, a I. adj. practical; (*conveniente*) useful; (*diestro*) experienced II. m. MARIT. pilot —f. practice; (*experiencia*) experience ♦ **en la p.** in practice • **poner en p.** to put into practice.
pra·de·ra f. meadow.
pra·do m. (*campo*) meadow; (*paseo*) promenade.
prag·má·ti·co, a adj. pragmatic.
pre·ám·bu·lo m. (*prólogo*) preamble; (*rodeo*) digression.
pre·ca·rio, a adj. precarious.
pre·cau·ción f. precaution; (*prudencia*) caution ♦ **por p.** as a precaution.
pre·ca·ver tr. to take precautions against —reflex. to take precautions ♦ **p. contra** to forestall • **p. de** to guard against.
pre·ca·vi·do, a adj. cautious.
pre·ce·den·te I. adj. preceding II. m. precedent ♦ **sentar un p.** to set a precedent.
pre·ce·der tr. to precede.
pre·cep·to m. precept.
pre·cep·tor, ·ra m.f. preceptor, tutor; (*profesor*) teacher —f. governess.
pre·ces f.pl. RELIG. prayers.
pre·cia·do, a adj. (*de valor*) precious; (*estimado*) prized.
pre·ciar·se reflex. to brag, boast ♦ **p. de** to consider or think oneself.
pre·cin·ta f. (*en un paquete*) strap; (*en las aduanas*) official stamp or seal.
pre·cin·ta·do, a I. adj. sealed II. m. sealing.
pre·cin·tar tr. (*un paquete*) to bind, strap; (*sellar*) to seal, stamp.
pre·cin·to m. (*de un paquete*) strapping; (*acción*) sealing; (*ligadura*) strap.
pre·cio m. (*valor pecuniario*) price, cost; (*valor*) value, worth <es una obra de gran p. it is a work

of great worth>; (*sacrificio*) price, cost ♦ **al p. de** at the cost of • **no tener p.** to be priceless • **p. al contado** cash price • **p. de cierre** closing price • **p. de compra** purchase price • **p. de factura** invoice price • **p. de lista** list price • **p. de venta** selling price.
pre·cio·si·dad f. (*objeto*) beauty; (*persona*) jewel.
pre·cio·so, a adj. (*de valor*) precious, valuable; (*lindo*) lovely.
pre·cio·su·ra f. AMER., COLL. beauty.
pre·ci·pi·cio m. precipice, cliff.
pre·ci·pi·ta·ción f. precipitation ♦ **con p.** hastily • **p. radiactiva** (radioactive) fallout.
pre·ci·pi·ta·do, a adj. & m. precipitate.
pre·ci·pi·tar tr. (*lanzar*) to hurl; (*apresurar*) to hasten; CHEM. to precipitate —reflex. (*darse prisa*) to hurry; (*lanzarse*) to rush headlong.
pre·ci·sa·men·te adv. (*justamente*) precisely; (*especialmente*) specially.
pre·ci·sar tr. (*explicar*) to explain; (*fijar*) to set; (*necesitar*) to need —reflex. to be necessary or needed.
pre·ci·sión f. precision.
pre·ci·so, a adj. (*necesario*) necessary; (*fijo*) precise; (*exacto*) exact; (*claro*) distinct ♦ **cuando sea p.** when necessary • **tener tiempo p. para** to have just enough time for.
pre·ci·ta·do, a adj. abovementioned.
pre·cla·ro, a adj. illustrious.
pre·co·ci·dad f. precocity.
pre·cog·ni·ción f. precognition.
pre·co·lom·bi(a)·no, a adj. pre-Columbian.
pre·con·ce·bi·do, a adj. preconceived.
pre·con·ce·bir §48 tr. to preconceive.
pre·co·ni·zar §04 tr. to recommend.
pre·coz adj. precocious.
pre·cur·sor, ·ra I. adj. precursory II. m.f. precursor.
pre·de·ce·sor, ·ra m.f. predecessor.
pre·de·cir §11 tr. to predict.
pre·des·ti·na·ción f. predestination.
pre·des·ti·nar tr. to predestine.
pre·de·ter·mi·nar tr. to predetermine.
pré·di·ca f. sermon.
pre·di·ca·ción f. (*acción*) preaching; (*sermón*) sermon.
pre·di·ca·do m. GRAM., LOG. predicate.
pre·di·ca·dor, ·ra I. adj. preaching II. m. preacher.
pre·di·car §70 tr. to preach —intr. to preach ♦ **p. con el ejemplo** to set an example.
pre·dic·ción f. prediction.
pre·di·cho, a adj. aforesaid.
pre·di·lec·ción f. predilection.
pre·di·lec·to, a adj. favorite.
pre·dio m. property.
pre·dis·po·ner §54 tr. to predispose ♦ **p. contra** to prejudice against.
pre·dis·po·si·ción f. predisposition.
pre·do·mi·nan·te adj. predominant.
pre·do·mi·nar intr. to prevail.
pre·do·mi·nio m. predominance.
pre·e·mi·nen·te adj. pre-eminent.
pre·es·co·lar adj. preschool.
pre·es·ta·ble·ci·do, a adj. pre-established.
pre·fa·bri·ca·do, a adj. prefabricated.
pre·fa·bri·car §70 tr. to prefabricate.
pre·fa·cio m. preface.
pre·fec·to m. prefect.
pre·fec·tu·ra f. prefecture.
pre·fe·ren·cia f. preference.

pre·fe·ren·te adj. *(principal)* preferential; *(preferible)* preferable.
pre·fe·ren·te·men·te adv. preferably.
pre·fe·ri·ble adj. preferable.
pre·fe·ri·do, a adj. preferred.
pre·fe·rir §65 tr. to prefer.
pre·fi·jar tr. to prearrange.
pre·fi·jo m. prefix; TELEC. area code.
pre·fi·rie·ra, rió see **preferir.**
pre·gón m. street vendor's shout.
pre·go·nar tr. *(publicar)* to proclaim; *(un vendedor)* to hawk; *(revelar)* to divulge.
pre·go·ne·ro, a m.f. *(anunciador)* announcer; *(vendedor)* hawker, peddler —m. *(oficial)* town crier.
pre·gun·ta f. question ♦ **hacer una p.** to ask a question.
pre·gun·tar tr. *(una pregunta)* to ask; *(interrogar)* to question ♦ **p. por** *(noticias)* to inquire about; *(persona)* to ask for —reflex. to wonder.
pre·gun·tón, o·na adj. & m.f. COLL. nosy *or* inquisitive (person).
pre·his·to·ria f. prehistory.
pre·his·tó·ri·co, a adj. prehistoric.
pre·jui·cio m. prejudice.
pre·juz·gar §47 tr. to prejudge.
pre·la·do m. prelate.
pre·li·mi·nar adj. & m. preliminary.
pre·lu·dio m. prelude.
pre·ma·tu·ro, a adj. premature.
pre·me·di·ta·ción f. premeditation.
pre·me·di·ta·da·men·te adv. deliberately.
pre·me·di·ta·do, a adj. premeditated.
pre·me·di·tar tr. to premeditate.
pre·miar tr. *(recompensar)* to reward; *(en certamen)* to award a prize to.
pre·mio m. *(recompensa)* reward; *(en certamen)* prize; FIN. premium ♦ **p. en efectivo** cash prize • **p. gordo** COLL. jackpot.
pre·mi·sa f. premise.
pre·mo·ni·ción f. premonition.
pre·mo·ni·to·rio, a adj. premonitory.
pre·mu·ra f. urgency.
pre·na·tal adj. prenatal.
pren·da f. *(garantía)* guaranty; *(de vestir)* article of clothing; *(señal)* token ♦ **en p.** as security • **en p. de** as token of • **no soltar p.** to be very discreet • **p. interior** undergarment.
pren·dar tr. to pawn —reflex. to become fond.
pren·de·dor m. *(broche)* clasp; JEWEL. pin.
pren·der tr. *(asir)* to grasp; *(aprehender)* to apprehend; *(encarcelar)* to put in prison; *(clavar)* to fasten; AMER. *(con fuego)* to light; *(un aparato)* to turn *or* switch on ♦ **p. con alfileres** to pin • **p. fuego a** to set fire to —intr. *(planta)* to take root; *(fuego)* to catch fire; *(vacuna)* to take (effect).
pren·sa f. press; *(imprenta)* printing press.
pren·sar tr. to press.
pren·sil adj. prehensile.
pre·nup·cial adj. prenuptial.
pre·ña·do, a adj. pregnant.
pre·ñar tr. to impregnate.
pre·ñez f. pregnancy.
pre·o·cu·pa·ción f. preoccupation; *(inquietud)* anxiety.
pre·o·cu·pa·do, a adj. preoccupied; *(inquieto)* worried.
pre·o·cu·par tr. to preoccupy; *(inquietar)* to worry —reflex. *(inquietarse)* to worry (con, de,

por about); *(cuidarse)* to take care.
pre·pa·ra·ción f. preparation.
pre·pa·ra·dor, ·ra m.f. SPORT. trainer, coach.
pre·pa·rar tr. & reflex. to prepare (oneself).
pre·pon·de·ran·cia f. preponderance.
pre·pon·de·ran·te adj. preponderant.
pre·po·si·ción f. preposition.
pre·po·si·cio·nal adj. prepositional.
pre·po·ten·cia f. prepotency.
pre·po·ten·te adj. prepotent.
pre·pu·cio m. prepuce.
pre·rro·ga·ti·va f. prerogative.
pre·sa f. *(acción)* capture; *(cosa apresada)* catch; *(en la caza)* prey; *(víctima)* victim; *(conducto)* ditch; *(porción)* morsel; ZOOL. fang ♦ **hacer p.** to capture.
pre·sa·giar tr. to presage.
pre·sa·gio m. *(señal)* omen; *(adivinación)* premonition.
pres·bí·te·ro m. presbyter, priest.
pres·cin·den·cia f. AMER. omission ♦ **con p. de** without.
pres·cin·di·ble adj. nonessential.
pres·cin·dir intr. *(ignorar)* to ignore; *(privarse)* to do without ♦ **prescindiendo de** regardless of.
pres·cri·bir §80 tr. & intr. to prescribe.
pres·crip·ción f. prescription.
pre·se·lec·ción f. preselection.
pre·sen·cia f. presence; *(figura)* appearance ♦ **hacer acto de p.** to put in an appearance • **p. de ánimo** presence of mind.
pre·sen·cial adj. ♦ **testigo p.** eyewitness.
pre·sen·ciar tr. to witness.
pre·sen·ta·ción f. presentation; *(exhibición)* exhibition.
pre·sen·tar tr. to present; *(mostrar)* to show; *(exhibir)* to display; *(dar)* to give; *(proponer)* to nominate; *(introducir)* to introduce; LAW to bring —reflex. *(mostrarse)* to present oneself; *(venir)* to show up <el alumno se presentó al terminar la clase the student showed up as the class ended>; *(aparecer)* to present itself, appear; *(dar el nombre)* to introduce oneself.
pre·sen·te I. adj. present; *(actual)* current ♦ **hacer p.** *(declarar)* to state; *(notificar)* to notify • **tener p.** to keep in mind **II.** m. *(regalo)* present, gift; GRAM. present (tense) ♦ **al p.** at present • **hasta el p.** up to the present • **la p.** this letter • **los presentes** those present **III.** interj. present, here.
pre·sen·ti·mien·to m. premonition.
pre·sen·tir §65 tr. to have a premonition of.
pre·ser·va·ción f. preservation.
pre·ser·var tr. to preserve.
pre·ser·va·ti·vo, a I. adj. preservative **II.** m. *(remedio)* preservative; *(anticonceptivo)* prophylactic, condom.
pre·si·den·cia f. *(de nación)* presidency; *(de reunión)* chairmanship; *(silla)* chair; *(oficina)* president's office.
pre·si·den·cial adj. presidential.
pre·si·den·ta f. (woman) president; *(de reunión)* chairwoman.
pre·si·den·te m. president; *(de reunión)* chairman; *(del parlamento)* speaker; *(de tribunal)* presiding judge.
pre·si·dia·rio m. convict.
pre·si·dio m. prison.
pre·si·dir tr. *(dirigir)* to preside over; *(predominar)* to dominate.
pre·si·lla f. *(lazo)* loop; *(para papeles)* paper

clip.
pre·sión f. pressure ♦ **olla a p.** pressure cooker • **p. arterial** blood pressure.
pre·sio·nar tr. *(apretar)* to press; *(hacer presión)* to put pressure on.
pre·so, a I. see **prender II.** adj. under arrest **III.** m.f. prisoner.
pres·ta·ción f. services ♦ **p. de juramento** swearing-in.
pres·ta·do adj. *(dado)* lent; *(tomado)* borrowed ♦ **dar p.** to lend • **de p.** as a loan • **pedir** or **tomar p.** to borrow.
pres·ta·dor, ·ra I. adj. lending **II.** m.f. lender.
pres·ta·men·te adv. quickly.
pres·ta·mis·ta m.f. moneylender.
prés·ta·mo m. *(acción de dar)* lending; *(acción de recibir)* borrowing; *(empréstito)* loan ♦ **p. a plazo fijo** COM. time loan.
pres·tar tr. to lend ♦ **p. atención** to pay attention • **p. auxilio** or **ayuda** to help, assist • **p. juramento** to take the oath • **p. oídos** to lend an ear —reflex. *(consentir)* to consent; *(ser apto para)* to lend itself *(a, para* to); *(ofrecerse)* to offer.
pres·te·za f. promptness.
pres·ti·di·gi·ta·ción f. prestidigitation.
pres·ti·di·gi·ta·dor, ·ra m.f. prestidigitator.
pres·ti·giar tr. to lend prestige to.
pres·ti·gio m. prestige.
pres·ti·gio·so, a adj. prestigious.
pres·to, a I. adj. prompt; MUS. presto **II.** adv. promptly.
pre·su·mi·ble adj. presumable.
pre·su·mi·do, a adj. & m.f. presumptuous or conceited (person).
pre·su·mir tr. to presume —intr. ♦ **p. de** to think oneself.
pre·sun·ción f. *(vanidad)* presumptuousness; *(suposición)* presumption; LAW presumption.
pre·sun·ta·men·te adv. presumably.
pre·sun·to, a I. see **presumir II.** adj. presumed.
pre·sun·tuo·so, a adj. & m.f. presumptuous or conceited (person).
pre·su·po·ner §54 tr. to presuppose.
pre·su·po·si·ción f. presupposition.
pre·su·pues·tar tr. to budget.
pre·su·pues·ta·rio, a adj. budgetary.
pre·su·pues·to, a I. see **presuponer II.** m. budget estimate ♦ **equilibrar el p.** to balance the budget.
pre·su·ri·zar §04 tr. to pressurize.
pre·su·ro·so, a adj. *(rápido)* quick; *(con prisa)* in a hurry.
pre·ten·cio·so, a adj. pretentious.
pre·ten·der tr. *(buscar)* to seek; *(intentar)* to try, attempt; *(a una mujer)* to court; *(afirmar)* to claim.
pre·ten·dien·te, a I. adj. *(que reclama derecho)* seeking; *(al trono)* pretending to; *(a una mujer)* courting **II.** m.f. *(reclamante)* claimant; *(a un puesto)* candidate; *(al trono)* claimant —m. suitor.
pre·ten·sión f. *(aspiración)* desire; *(derecho)* claim; AMER. *(vanidad)* pretentiousness ♦ **sin pretensiones** unpretentious • **tener la p. de** to think one is going to.
pre·ten·sio·so, a adj. pretentious.
pre·té·ri·to, a adj. & m. past.
pre·tex·tar tr. to allege.
pre·tex·to m. pretext.
pre·va·le·cer §17 intr. *(sobresalir)* to prevail;

BOT. to take root.
pre·va·le·cien·te adj. prevailing.
pre·va·ler §74 intr. to prevail.
pre·ven·ción f. prevention; *(apresto)* preparedness; *(precaución)* precautionary measure; *(providencia)* foresight.
pre·ve·ni·do, a adj. *(preparado)* prepared; *(advertido)* forewarned; *(precavido)* prudent.
pre·ve·nir §76 tr. *(preparar)* to prepare; *(prever)* to foresee; *(impedir)* to prevent; *(avisar)* to forewarn ♦ **p. de** to provide with —reflex. *(disponerse)* to prepare oneself; *(tomar precauciones)* to take precautions.
pre·ven·ti·vo, a adj. preventive.
pre·ver §77 tr. to foresee.
pre·via·men·te adv. previously.
pre·vio, a adj. *(anterior)* previous, former; *(preparatorio)* preliminary, prior <*p. aviso* prior notice>; *(a condición de)* subject to <*p. acuerdo de las partes interesadas* subject to the agreement of the interested parties>; *(después)* after, upon <*p. pago* after or upon payment>.
pre·vi·si·ble adj. foreseeable.
pre·vi·sión f. *(clarividencia)* foresight; *(prudencia)* precaution ♦ **p. social** social security.
pre·vi·sor, ·ra adj. & m.f. cautious or prudent (person).
pre·vis·to, a I. see **prever II.** adj. *(anticipado)* foreseen; *(estipulado)* provided <*p. por la ley* provided by law>.
prez m. honor, glory.
prie·to, a adj. dark.
pri·ma¹ f. *(indemnización)* insurance premium; *(recompensa)* premium; MUS. treble.
pri·ma² f. see **primo, a.**
pri·ma·cí·a f. superiority.
pri·ma·do m. RELIG. primate.
pri·ma·rio, a adj. primary; *(primero)* first.
pri·ma·te m. primate.
pri·ma·ve·ra f. *(estación)* spring; *(época)* springtime; *(de la vida)* prime.
pri·ma·ve·ral adj. spring(like).
pri·mer adj. contr. of **primero.**
pri·me·ra·men·te adv. first, in the first place.
pri·me·ro, a I. adj. first; front <*la p. página* the front page>; *(mejor)* best <*ella es la p. alumna de la clase* she is the best student in the class>; *(fundamental)* basic <*las primeras necesidades* the basic needs>; *(anterior)* former ♦ **a p. vista** at first sight • **de buenas a primeras** all at once • **de primera** first-class • **en primer lugar** first of all • **primer actor** leading man • **p. actriz** leading lady **II.** m.f. first <*Pedro fue el p. en llegar* Peter was the first to arrive>; *(el mejor)* best —f. AUTO. first gear **III.** adv. first; *(más bien)* first, sooner <*p. morir que pedir ayuda* sooner dead than ask for help>.
pri·mi·cia f. exclusive news.
pri·mi·ti·vo, a adj. & m.f. primitive.
pri·mo, a I. adj. first; MATH. prime **II.** m.f. cousin • **p. hermano** or **carnal** first cousin.
pri·mo·gé·ni·to, a adj. & m.f. first-born.
pri·mor m. *(finura)* delicacy; *(cosa exquisita)* exquisite thing.
pri·mor·dial adj. primordial.
pri·mo·ro·so, a adj. beautiful, exquisite.
prin·ce·sa f. princess.
prin·ci·pa·do m. *(título)* princedom; *(territorio)* principality.
prin·ci·pal I. adj. principal; *(más importante)* main; *(esencial)* essential; GRAM. main (clause) ♦ **lo p.** the main thing **II.** m. FIN. principal.

prín·ci·pe I. adj. first **II.** m. prince ♦ **p. consorte** prince consort • **p. heredero** crown prince.

prin·ci·pes·co, a adj. princely.

prin·ci·pian·te, a I. adj. beginning **II.** m.f. beginner, novice.

prin·ci·piar tr. to begin.

prin·ci·pio m. (comienzo) beginning; (fundamento) principle; (causa primitiva) source ♦ **a p.** or **principios de** at the beginning of • **al p.** at first, in or at the beginning • **dar p. a** to start off • **del p. al fin** or **desde el p. hasta el fin** from beginning to end • **en un p.** at the beginning • **por p.** on principle • **sin principios** unprincipled • **tener por p.** to make a point of.

prin·gar §47 tr. (ensuciar) to get grease on; (empapar) to dip in fat.

prin·go·so, a adj. greasy.

prin·gue m.f. grease; FIG. filth.

prio·ri·dad f. priority.

pri·sa f. (apuro) haste; (velocidad) speed; (urgencia) urgency ♦ **a** or **de p.** quickly • **a toda p.** as quickly as possible • **andar** or **estar de p.** to be in a hurry • **dar** or **meter p. a alguien** to rush someone • **darse p.** to hasten, hurry (up) • **tener p.** to be in a hurry (por, en to).

pri·sión f. prison; (de afecto) bond, tie ♦ **p. preventiva** LAW preventive custody.

pri·sio·ne·ro, a m.f. prisoner.

pris·ma m. prism.

pris·má·ti·co, a I. adj. prismatic **II.** m.pl. binoculars.

prís·ti·no, a adj. pristine.

pri·va·ción f. (acción) deprivation; (falta) lack.

pri·va·do, a I. adj. private ♦ **p. de** without, bereft of • **vida p.** privacy **II.** m. protégé.

pri·var tr. (despojar) to deprive; (prohibir) to forbid —reflex. to abstain (de from).

pri·va·ti·za·ción f. privatization.

pri·va·ti·zar §04 tr. to privatize.

pri·vi·le·giar tr. to favor.

pri·vi·le·gio m. privilege.

pro m.f. profit, benefit ♦ **en p. de** in favor of • **el p. y el contra** pro and con.

pro·a f. prow, bow.

pro·ba·bi·li·dad f. probability ♦ **probabilidades de vida** life expectancy.

pro·ba·ble adj. probable; (demostrable) provable.

pro·ba·dor, ·ra I. adj. proving **II.** m. fitting room.

pro·bar §19 tr. (ensayar) to test; (confirmar) to prove; (ropa) to try on; (comida) to taste ♦ **p. ventura** to try one's luck —intr. to try ♦ **p. de todo** to take a taste of everything —reflex. to try on.

pro·be·ta f. test tube.

pro·bi·dad f. probity, integrity.

pro·ble·ma m. problem.

pro·ble·má·ti·co, a I. adj. problematic(al). **II.** f. issues.

pro·bo, a adj. upright.

pro·ca·ci·dad f. indecency.

pro·caz adj. (insolente) insolent; (indecente) indecent.

pro·ce·den·cia f. (origen) origin; (punto de salida) point of departure; (de conducta) properness.

pro·ce·den·te adj. (que procede) (coming) from; LAW admissible.

pro·ce·der¹ m. conduct.

pro·ce·der² intr. (originarse) to originate in; (ejecutar) to go on (to); (ir con orden) to proceed; (portarse) to behave; (continuar) to go on or ahead with; (ser apropiado) to be fitting or appropriate.

pro·ce·di·mien·to m. (método) procedure; (proceso) process; LAW proceedings.

pró·cer adj. & m. eminent or illustrious (person).

pro·ce·sa·do, a m.f defendant.

pro·ce·sa·mien·to m. LAW prosecution; COMPUT. processing ♦ **p. de datos** data processing.

pro·ce·sar tr. LAW to prosecute; COMPUT. to process.

pro·ce·sión f. procession ♦ **la p. va por dentro** COLL. still waters run deep.

pro·ce·so m. process; (transcurso) course; LAW (causa) trial; (autos) proceedings.

pro·cla·ma·ción f. proclamation.

pro·cla·mar tr. & reflex. to proclaim (oneself).

pro·cli·ve adj. inclined (a to).

pro·cre·a·ción f. procreation.

pro·cre·ar tr. to procreate.

pro·cu·ra·dor, ·ra I. adj. procuring **II.** m.f. (apoderado) proxy; (abogado) attorney.

pro·cu·rar tr. (intentar) to endeavor; (obtener) to obtain —reflex. to obtain.

pro·di·gar §47 tr. to lavish —reflex. to go out of one's way.

pro·di·gio m. (persona) prodigy; (fenómeno) wonder.

pro·di·gio·so, a adj. marvelous.

pró·di·go, a adj. (malgastador) prodigal, wasteful; (muy generoso) generous.

pro·duc·ción f. production; (producto) product ♦ **p. en serie** mass production.

pro·du·cir §22 tr. to produce; (engendrar) to bear; (elaborar) to manufacture; (ocasionar) to cause; FIN. to yield ♦ **p. en serie** to mass-produce —reflex. to take place.

pro·duc·ti·vi·dad f. productivity.

pro·duc·ti·vo, a adj. productive; (lucrativo) lucrative.

pro·duc·to, a m. product; COM. (beneficio) profit; (ingresos) proceeds ♦ **p. derivado** byproduct • **productos de consumo** consumer goods.

pro·duc·tor, ·ra I. adj. productive, producing **II.** m.f. producer.

pro·du·je·ra, jo see **producir**.

pro·e·za f. feat.

pro·fa·na·ción f. desecration.

pro·fa·nar tr. (maltratar) to desecrate; (deshonrar) to disgrace.

pro·fa·no, a I. adj. profane; (irreverente) irreverent; (no iniciado) uninitiated **II.** m.f. layman/woman.

pro·fe·cí·a f. prophecy.

pro·fe·rir §65 tr. to utter.

pro·fe·sar tr. (ejercer) to practice; (enseñar) to teach; (creer) to believe in; (declarar) to profess; (afecto) to feel —intr. to take vows.

pro·fe·sión f. profession ♦ **de p.** by trade.

pro·fe·sio·nal adj. & m.f. professional.

pro·fe·sor, ·ra m.f. (de escuela) teacher; (de universidad) professor ♦ **p. auxiliar** assistant professor • **p. suplente** substitute teacher.

pro·fe·so·ra·do m. (cargo) teaching position; (cuerpo docente) faculty.

pro·fe·ta m. prophet.

pro·fe·ti·sa f. prophetess.

pro·fe·ti·zar §04 tr. to prophesy.

pro·fie·ra, ro see **proferir**.

pro·fi·lác·ti·co, a **I.** adj. prophylactic **II.** m. condom —f. prophylaxis.
pro·fi·la·xis f. prophylaxis.
pro·fi·rie·ra, rió see **proferir.**
pró·fu·go, a adj. & m.f. fugitive.
pro·fun·di·dad f. profundity, depth ♦ **de p.** deep, in depth.
pro·fun·di·zar §04 tr. *(cavar)* to make deeper; *(estudiar)* to delve into —intr. to go deeply into a subject.
pro·fun·do, a **I.** adj. *(hondo)* deep; *(intenso)* profound; *(difícil)* difficult; *(penetrante)* deep; *(sincero)* heartfelt **II.** m. depth.
pro·fu·sión f. profusion.
pro·fu·so, a adj. profuse.
pro·ge·nie f. progeny.
pro·ge·ni·tor m. progenitor ♦ pl. *(antepasados)* ancestors; *(padres)* parents.
pro·gra·ma m. program ♦ **p. de estudios** curriculum • **p. doble** CINEM. double feature.
pro·gra·ma·ción f. programming.
pro·gra·ma·dor, ·ra **I.** adj. programming **II.** m.f. programmer.
pro·gra·mar tr. *(planificar)* to plan; COMPUT. to program.
pro·gre·sar intr. to progress.
pro·gre·sión f. progression.
pro·gre·sis·ta adj. & m.f. progressive.
pro·gre·si·vo, a adj. progressive.
pro·gre·so m. progress.
pro·hi·bi·ción f. prohibition.
pro·hi·bi·do, a adj. prohibited, forbidden ♦ **p. estacionar** no parking • **p. la entrada** no admittance.
pro·hi·bir tr. to prohibit, forbid ♦ **p. a alguien hacer algo** to prohibit someone from doing something, forbid someone to do something • **se prohibe fumar** no smoking.
pro·hi·bi·ti·vo/to·rio, a adj. prohibitive.
pró·ji·mo m. *(otra persona)* fellow man; *(humanidad)* mankind; COLL. *(sujeto)* fellow.
pro·le f. progeny.
pro·le·ta·ria·do m. proletariat.
pro·le·ta·rio, a adj. & m.f. proletarian.
pro·li·fe·ra·ción f. proliferation.
pro·li·fe·rar intr. to proliferate.
pro·lí·fi·co, a adj. prolific.
pro·li·jo, a adj. *(pesado)* long-winded; *(meticuloso)* meticulous.
pró·lo·go m. prologue.
pro·lon·ga·ción f. prolongation; *(parte)* continuation.
pro·lon·ga·da·men·te adv. at great length.
pro·lon·ga·do, a adj. prolonged.
pro·lon·ga·mien·to m. var. of **prolongación.**
pro·lon·gar §47 tr. *(continuar)* to prolong; *(alargar)* to lengthen —reflex. *(extenderse)* to extend; *(durar más tiempo)* to last longer.
pro·me·diar tr. *(sacar el promedio)* to average; *(dividir en dos)* to divide in half —intr. to be halfway through ♦ **al p. el mes** halfway through the month.
pro·me·dio m. average; *(mitad)* middle ♦ **por p.** on average.
pro·me·sa f. promise; RELIG. vow ♦ **cumplir (con) una p.** to keep a promise • **faltar a una p.** to break a promise.
pro·me·te·dor, ·ra adj. promising.
pro·me·ter tr. to promise ♦ **p. el oro y el moro** to promise the moon and stars —intr. to be promising —reflex. *(esperar)* to expect; *(apalabrar)* to become engaged.

pro·me·ti·do, a m. fiancé —f. fiancée.
pro·mi·nen·cia f. prominence.
pro·mi·nen·te adj. prominent.
pro·mis·cui·dad f. promiscuity.
pro·mis·cuo, a adj. promiscuous.
pro·mi·so·rio, a adj. promising.
pro·mo·ción f. promotion; EDUC. graduating class.
pro·mo·cio·nar tr. to promote.
pro·mon·to·rio m. promontory; *(pila)* heap.
pro·mo·tor, ·ra **I.** adj. *(que promociona)* promoting; *(instigador)* instigating **II.** m.f. *(que promociona)* promoter; *(instigador)* instigator.
pro·mo·ve·dor, ·ra **I.** adj. *(que promociona)* promoting; *(instigador)* instigating **II.** m.f. *(que promociona)* promoter; *(instigador)* instigator.
pro·mo·ver §78 tr. to promote; *(fomentar)* to foster; *(provocar)* to cause.
pro·mul·ga·ción f. promulgation.
pro·mul·gar §47 tr. to promulgate; *(proclamar)* to proclaim.
pro·no, a adj. prone.
pro·nom·bre m. pronoun.
pro·no·mi·nal adj. pronominal.
pro·nos·ti·car §70 tr. to prognosticate, predict.
pro·nós·ti·co m. *(predicción)* prediction; *(señal)* omen ♦ **p. del tiempo** weather forecast.
pron·ti·tud f. *(velocidad)* speed; *(diligencia)* promptness; *(ingenio)* sharpness (of mind).
pron·to, a **I.** adj. *(veloz)* quick; *(diligente)* prompt; *(preparado)* ready ♦ **p. a** quick to <*p. a enfadarse* quick to anger> **II.** adv. *(velozmente)* quickly; *(diligentemente)* promptly; *(en seguida)* at once; *(dentro de poco)* soon; *(temprano)* early ♦ **de p.** suddenly • **lo más p. posible** as soon as possible • **por lo p.** for the moment • **tan p. como** as soon as.
pron·tua·rio m. dossier; AMER., CRIMIN. record, file.
pro·nun·cia·ción f. pronunciation.
pro·nun·cia·mien·to m. *(golpe de estado)* military coup; LAW pronouncement.
pro·nun·ciar tr. to pronounce; *(decir)* to utter; *(discurso)* to deliver —reflex. *(sublevarse)* to rebel; *(sentencia)* to pass; *(declararse)* to declare oneself.
pro·pa·ga·ción f. propagation.
pro·pa·gan·da f. propaganda; *(publicidad)* advertising ♦ **hacer p.** to advertise.
pro·pa·gan·dís·ti·co, a adj. propagandistic.
pro·pa·gar §47 tr. & reflex. to propagate; FIG. to spread.
pro·pa·lar tr. to divulge.
pro·pa·sar tr. to go beyond —reflex. to go too far.
pro·pen·der intr. to tend *(a* to, toward).
pro·pen·sión f. propensity; MED. predisposition.
pro·pen·so, a adj. prone *(a* to).
pro·pia·men·te adv. *(con propiedad)* properly; *(realmente)* exactly ♦ **p. dicho** strictly speaking.
pro·pi·ciar tr. AMER. to sponsor.
pro·pi·cio, a adj. propitious.
pro·pie·dad f. property; *(posesión)* ownership; *(heredad)* estate <*es dueño de una gran p.* he's the owner of a great estate>; *(exactitud)* accuracy; *(conveniencia)* appropriateness <*la p. de una palabra* the appropriateness of a word> ♦ **hablar con p.** to speak correctly • **p. horizontal** cooperative property • **p. inmobiliaria** real es-

tate • **p. intelectual** copyright.
pro·pie·ta·rio, a I. adj. proprietary II. m. owner, proprietor —f. owner, proprietress.
pro·pi·na f. tip, gratuity.
pro·pi·nar tr. COLL. to give <p. una paliza to give a beating>.
pro·pio, a adj. own <mató a su p. padre he killed his own father>; (original) own, very <ésas son sus propias palabras those are her very words>; (natural) own, natural <su p. pelo his own hair>; (mismo) -self <el p. interesado debe asistir a la reunión the interested party himself must attend the meeting>; (conveniente) proper, suitable <no es p. para este caso it is not suitable for this case>; (característico) typical, characteristic <eso es p. de ella that is typical of her>; GRAM., MATH. proper.
pro·po·ne·dor, ·ra/nen·te I. adj. proposing II. m.f. proponent.
pro·po·ner §54 tr. (sugerir) to propose; (exponer) to propound; (plantear) to pose; (presentar) to propose, nominate <lo propuse para la vacante I proposed him for the vacant post>; (opinar) to move <propongo que se aplace la sesión I move that the meeting be postponed> —reflex. to intend to do.
pro·por·ción f. proportion; (tamaño) size ♦ **en p. a** in proportion to • **guardar p. con** to be in proportion with ♦ pl. proportions, dimensions.
pro·por·cio·na·do, a adj. (con proporción) proportionate; (adecuado) commensurate.
pro·por·cio·nal adj. proportional.
pro·por·cio·nar tr. (distribuir) to apportion; (suministrar) to provide —reflex. to get, obtain.
pro·po·si·ción f. proposition; (propuesta) proposal; (moción) motion; GRAM. clause.
pro·pó·si·to m. (intención) intention; (objetivo) purpose ♦ **a p.** (por cierto) by the way; (adrede) deliberately • **a p. de** apropos of • **con el p. de** in order to • **con este p.** to this end.
pro·pues·ta f. (proposición) proposition; (oferta) proposal; COM. bid.
pro·pug·nar tr. to advocate.
pro·pul·sar tr. to propel.
pro·pul·sión f. propulsion ♦ **p. a chorro** jet propulsion • **p. delantera** front wheel drive.
pro·pul·sor, ·ra I. adj. propellant II. m. propeller.
pro·pu·sie·ra, so see **proponer.**
pro·rra·ta f. share.
pro·rra·te·ar tr. to prorate.
pró·rro·ga f. extension.
pro·rro·gar §47 tr. to extend.
pro·rrum·pir intr. to burst (en into).
pro·sa f. prose.
pro·sai·co, a adj. prosaic.
pro·sa·pia f. lineage.
pros·ce·nio m. proscenium.
pros·cri·bir §80 tr. (desterrar) to exile; (prohibir) to proscribe.
pros·crip·ción f. (destierro) exile; (prohibición) proscription.
pro·se·cu·ción f. continuation.
pro·se·guir §64 tr. & intr. (seguir) to pursue; (continuar) to carry on with.
pro·se·li·tis·ta adj. proselytizing.
pros·pec·to m. prospectus, brochure.
pros·pe·rar intr. to prosper.
pros·pe·ri·dad f. prosperity.
prós·pe·ro, a adj. prosperous.
prós·ta·ta f. prostate (gland).

pros·ter·nar·se reflex. to prostrate oneself.
pros·tí·bu·lo m. brothel.
pros·ti·tu·ción f. prostitution.
pros·ti·tuir §18 tr. & reflex. to prostitute (oneself).
pros·ti·tu·ta f. prostitute.
pro·ta·go·nis·ta m.f. protagonist —m. hero —f. heroine.
pro·ta·go·ni·zar §04 tr. to star in.
pro·tec·ción f. protection.
pro·tec·cio·nis·ta adj. & m.f. protectionist.
pro·tec·tor, ·ra I. adj. (defensor) protective; (patrocinador) supporting II. m.f. (defensor) protector; (patrocinador) patron. —f. patroness.
pro·tec·to·ra·do m. protectorate.
pro·te·ger §34 tr. to protect.
pro·te·gi·do, a m. protégé —f. protégée.
pro·te·í·na f. protein.
pró·te·sis f. MED. prosthesis; GRAM. prothesis.
pro·tes·ta f. protest; LAW protestation.
pro·tes·tan·te adj. & m.f. RELIG. Protestant.
pro·tes·tar tr. (asegurar) to affirm; (la fe) to profess; COM. to protest —intr. to protest.
pro·tes·to m. COM. protest.
pro·to·co·lo m. (registro) record book; (de un congreso) minutes; DIPL. protocol.
pro·tón m. proton.
pro·to·plas·ma m. protoplasm.
pro·to·ti·po m. prototype.
pro·to·zo·a·rio/zo·o m. protozoan.
pro·tu·be·ran·cia f. protuberance.
pro·ve·cho m. (beneficio) benefit; (ganancia) profit; (adelantamiento) advancement ♦ **¡buen p.!** COLL. enjoy your meal! • **en p. de** to the benefit of • **en p. propio** to one's own advantage • **sacar p. de** (beneficiarse) to benefit from; (aprovecharse) to take advantage of.
pro·ve·cho·so, a adj. (beneficioso) profitable; (bueno) good; (ventajoso) advantageous.
pro·ve·e·dor, ·ra m.f. supplier.
pro·ve·er §43 tr. (suministrar) to provide (de with); (conferir) to grant.
pro·ve·nien·te adj. proceeding (de from).
pro·ve·nir §76 intr. (proceder) to proceed (de from); (originarse) to come (en from).
pro·ver·bial adj. proverbial.
pro·ver·bio m. proverb.
pro·ve·ye·ra, yó see **proveer.**
pro·vi·den·cia f. (disposición) provision; LAW ruling ♦ **P.** RELIG. Providence • **tomar providencias** to take measures.
pro·vi·den·cial adj. providential.
pro·vin·cia f. province.
pro·vin·cia·no, a adj. & m.f. provincial.
pro·vi·sión f. provision; (surtido) supply; (medida) measure; FIN. funds, cover ♦ **p. de fondos** FIN. funds ♦ pl. supplies.
pro·vi·sio·nal adj. temporary.
pro·vi·so·rio, a adj. AMER. temporary.
pro·vo·ca·ción f. provocation; (insulto) insult; (desafío) challenge.
pro·vo·ca·dor, ·ra I. adj. (irritante) provoking; (sensual) provocative II. m.f. provoker.
pro·vo·car §70 tr. (incitar) to provoke; (irritar) to annoy; (motivar) to move; (despertar) to rouse; (causar) to cause.
pro·vo·ca·ti·vo, a adj. inviting, tempting.
pro·xe·ne·ta m. procurer, pimp —f. procuress.
pró·xi·ma·men·te adv. soon, before long.

pro·xi·mi·dad f. proximity.
pró·xi·mo, a adj. *(cercano)* near; *(siguiente)* next *<el año p.* next year*>* ♦ **p. a** *(al lado de)* near to; *(a punto de)* about to.
pro·yec·ción f. projection; CINEM. screening.
pro·yec·tar tr. *(lanzar)* to hurl; *(planear)* to plan; *(sombra)* to cast; ARCHIT., TECH. to design; CINEM., GEOM. to project.
pro·yec·til m. projectile, missile ♦ **p. antiaéreo** antiaircraft missile • **p. balístico intercontinental** intercontinental ballistic missile • **p. de avión a tierra** air-to-surface missile • **p. dirigido** *or* **teledirigido** guided missile.
pro·yec·to m. *(plan)* plan; *(boceto)* design; *(bosquejo)* draft ♦ **en p.** in the planning stages • **p. experimental** pilot project • **p. de ley** bill.
pro·yec·tor m. *(reflector)* searchlight; CINEM. projector; OPT. condenser; THEAT. spotlight ♦ **p. cinematográfico** movie projector.
pru·den·cia f. prudence.
pru·den·te adj. prudent.
prue·ba f. *(razón)* proof, evidence; *(indicio)* sign; *(ensayo)* sample; *(examen)* test; *(dificultad)* ordeal; MATH., PRINT. proof; CHEM., TECH. test; PHOTOG. proof, print; SEW. fitting; COM. trial *<a p.* on trial*>* ♦ **a p. de agua** waterproof • **a p. de aire** airtight • **a p. de balas** bulletproof • **poner a p.** to put to the test.
prue·be, bo see probar.
pseu·do adj. pseudo.
psi·co·a·ná·li·sis m. *or* f. psychoanalysis.
psi·co·a·na·lis·ta m.f. psychoanalyst.
psi·co·a·na·li·zar §04 tr. to psychoanalyze.
psi·co·dé·li·co, a adj. psychedelic.
psi·co·lo·gí·a f. psychology.
psi·có·lo·go, a m.f. psychologist.
psi·có·pa·ta m.f. psychopath.
psi·co·pa·tí·a f. psychopathy.
psi·co·sis f.inv. psychosis.
psi·co·te·ra·peu·ta m.f. psychotherapist.
psi·co·te·ra·pia f. psychotherapy.
psi·que/quis f. psyche.
psi·quí·a·tra/quia·tra m.f. psychiatrist.
psi·quia·trí·a f. psychiatry.
psí·qui·co, a adj. psychic.
pso·ria·sis f. psoriasis.
pú·a f. *(punta)* sharp point; BOT. thorn; AGR. graft; ZOOL. quill; *(de fonógrafo)* needle; *(espolón)* spur; COLL. *(persona)* cunning person.
pu·ber·tad f. puberty.
pu·bis m.inv. *(vientre)* pubic region; *(hueso)* pubis (bone).
pu·bli·ca·ción f. publication.
pu·bli·car §70 tr. *(proclamar)* to proclaim; *(editar)* to publish.
pu·bli·ci·dad f. publicity; *(anuncio)* advertisement ♦ **agencia de p.** advertising agency.
pú·bli·co, a I. adj. public; *(patente)* known *<es p. que* it is known that*>*; *(del pueblo)* common *<el bien p.* the common good*>* **II.** m. public; *(auditorio)* audience; *(espectadores)* spectators; *(lectores)* readers; TELEV. viewers.
pu·che·ro m. CUL. stew; COLL. *(alimento diario)* daily bread; COLL. *(gesto)* pout ♦ **ganarse el p.** COLL. to earn one's daily bread • **hacer pucheros** COLL. to pout.
pu·cho m. COLL. *(colilla)* cigarette stub; *(poco)* trifle, bit; *(sobrante)* leftover.
pú·di·co, a adj. modest.
pu·dien·te adj. & m.f. rich *or* wealthy (person).
pu·die·ra, do see poder².

pu·dor m. *(recato)* shyness; *(vergüenza)* shame ♦ **sin p.** shameless(ly).
pu·do·ro·so, a adj. shy.
pu·dri·ción f. putrefaction, rot.
pu·drir tr. *(descomponer)* to rot; COLL. *(molestar)* to annoy —reflex. *(descomponerse)* to rot; COLL. *(molestarse)* to be annoyed ♦ **¡ahí te pudras!** COLL. to hell with you! —intr. to rot.
pue·ble, blo see poblar.
pue·blo m. *(población)* town; *(habitantes)* population; *(nación)* people, nation; *(gente común)* (the) common *or* working people.
pue·da, do see poder².
puen·te m. bridge ♦ **p. aéreo** airlift • **p. colgante** suspension bridge • **p. levadizo** drawbridge.
puer·co, a I. adj. *(sucio)* filthy; *(bajo)* contemptible; *(asqueroso)* disgusting **II.** m. ZOOL. pig, hog; COLL. *(hombre)* pig, swine ♦ **echar margaritas a los puercos** COLL. to throw pearls before swine —f. ZOOL. sow.
pue·ril adj. childish.
pue·ri·li·dad f. *(calidad)* childishness; *(bagatela)* trifle.
pue·rro m. leek.
puer·ta f. door; *(armazón)* gate; *(entrada)* doorway; *(camino)* gateway *<la virtud es p. de la felicidad* virtue is the gateway to happiness*>* ♦ **a p. cerrada** behind closed doors • **dar a alguien con la p. en las narices** to slam the door in someone's face • **de p. en p.** from door to door • **echar las puertas abajo** to knock the door down • **p. corrediza** sliding door • **p. giratoria** revolving door • **p. trasera** back door • **p. de vidrio** glass door.
puer·to m. port, harbor; *(ciudad)* port, seaport ♦ **p. de escala** port of call.
pues I. conj. since, as *<cómpralo, p. a tí te gusta* buy it, since you like it*>* **II.** adv. *(en tal caso)* well, all right *<¿no quieres escucharme? ¡p. te arrepentirás!* you don't want to listen to me? well, you'll regret it!*>*; *(partícula continuativa)* then *<repito, p., que hace bien* I repeat, then, that he's doing the right thing*>* ♦ **p. bien** well then • **¡p. claro!** of course! • **¿p. qué?** so what? • **sí p.** yes, of course.
pues·to, a I. see poner **II.** adj. dressed *<bien p.* well dressed*>* **III.** m. *(sitio)* place; *(de venta)* stall; *(cargo)* position; MIL. post ♦ **p. que** since, as —f. ASTRON. setting; ORNITH. laying ♦ **p. del sol** sunset • **p. en escena** staging • **p. en marcha** start.
¡puf! interj. ugh!, yecch!
pú·gil m. *(gladiador)* pugilist; SPORT. boxer.
pu·gi·lis·ta m. boxer.
pug·na f. *(lucha)* battle; *(oposición)* conflict ♦ **estar en p. con** to clash with.
pug·nar intr. to struggle *(por)* to.
pug·naz adj. pugnacious, aggressive.
pu·ja f. *(esfuerzo)* struggle; *(acción de licitar)* bidding.
pu·jan·te adj. strong.
pu·jan·za f. strength.
pu·jar tr. to raise (a bid) —intr. to struggle *(por, para)* to.
pul·cri·tud f. *(esmero)* neatness; *(cuidado)* care.
pul·cro, a adj. neat.
pul·ga f. flea ♦ **tener malas pulgas** COLL. to be touchy.
pul·ga·da f. inch.

pul·gar adj. & m. thumb.
pu·li·do, a adj. *(metal)* polished; *(pulcro)* neat; *(refinado)* refined.
pu·li·dor, ·ra I. adj. polishing **II.** m. polisher.
pu·lir tr. *(bruñir)* to polish; *(alisar)* to smooth; FIG. to put the finishing touches on; *(perfeccionar)* to polish; *(civilizar)* to refine.
pu·lla f. *(palabra grosera)* obscenity; *(chanza)* gibe; *(crítica mordaz)* cutting remark.
pul·món m. lung.
pul·mo·nar adj. pulmonary.
pul·mo·ní·a f. pneumonia.
pul·pa f. pulp.
púl·pi·to m. pulpit.
pul·po m. octopus.
pul·po·so, a adj. fleshy.
pul·sa·dor, ·ra I. adj. pulsating **II.** m. buzzer.
pul·sar tr. *(tocar)* to play; *(apretar)* to push; *(sondear)* to sound out —intr. to beat.
pul·se·ar intr. to arm-wrestle.
pul·se·ra f. bracelet; *(de reloj)* watch band.
pul·so m. *(latido)* pulse; *(muñeca)* wrist; *(seguridad)* steady hand; *(cuidado)* caution.
pu·lu·lar intr. to swarm.
pul·ve·ri·za·dor m. pulverizer; *(para pintar)* paint sprayer; *(de perfume)* atomizer.
pul·ve·ri·zar §04 tr. *(reducir a polvo)* to pulverize; *(perfume)* to spray; FIG. to smash.
¡pum! interj. bang!, boom!
pu·ma m. puma, American panther.
pun·do·nor m. honor.
pu·ni·ti·vo, a adj. punitive.
pun·ta f. point; *(extremidad)* tip; *(cima)* top; *(colilla)* stub; *(clavo)* small nail; ZOOL. *(asta)* horn ♦ **de p. a cabo** from one end to the other • **de p. en blanco** COLL. to the nines • **estar hasta la p. de los pelos** COLL. to be fed up • **hacer p.** to go first • **poner los nervios de p.** to put someone's nerves on edge • **p. de lanza** spearhead • **sacar p. a** to sharpen.
pun·ta·da f. SEW. stitch; *(dolor)* sharp pain.
pun·tal m. *(madero)* brace; *(elemento principal)* foundation.
pun·ta·pié m. kick *<dar un p. to kick>* ♦ **echar a puntapiés** to kick out.
pun·te·rí·a f. aim ♦ **afinar la p.** to aim carefully • **dirigir la p.** en or **hacia** to aim at • **tener buena p.** to be a good shot.
pun·te·ro, a I. adj. leading **II.** m. *(vara)* pointer; *(punzón)* metal punch —f. *(de media)* toe patch; *(de calzado)* toecap.
pun·tia·gu·do, a adj. sharp, pointed.
pun·ti·lla f. *(tachuela)* tack; *(encaje)* lace trim; *(puñal)* dagger; CARP. tracing point.
pun·ti·llo·so, a adj. punctilious.
pun·to m. point; *(señal pequeña)* dot; *(sitio)* spot; *(momento)* moment; *(asunto)* matter; *(cuestión)* question; GRAM.; *(sobre letra)* dot; *(de oración)* period, full stop (G.B.); SEW. *(puntada)* stitch *<p. por encima* overcast stitch>; *(malla)* mesh; SURG. stitch ♦ **al p.** at once • **a p.** just in time • **a p. de** about to • **de p.** knitted • **dos puntos** colon • **en p.** on the dot, sharp *<llegaron a las dos en p.* they arrived at two on the dot> • **estar a p. de** to be on the verge of • **hasta cierto p.** up to a point • **poner p. final a** to put a stop to • **p. atrás** SEW. backstitch • **p. culminante** climax • **p. de apoyo** fulcrum • **p. de arranque** starting point • **p. de congelación** freezing point • **p. de vista** point of view, viewpoint • **p. final** period • **p. muerto**

dead center; AUTO. neutral; FIG. stalemate • **p. por p.** in detail • **puntos suspensivos** suspension points • **p. y aparte** new paragraph • **p. y coma** semicolon • **subir de p.** COLL. to heat up *<la conversación estaba subiendo de p.* the conversation was heating up> • **¡y p.!** COLL. and that's all!
pun·tua·ción f. punctuation; *(calificación)* grade.
pun·tual adj. prompt.
pun·tua·li·zar §04 tr. *(concretar)* to finalize; *(referir detalladamente)* to describe in detail.
pun·tual·men·te adv. promptly
pun·za·da f. *(dolor agudo)* stabbing pain; *(herida)* stab; *(de conciencia)* pang.
pun·zan·te adj. sharp.
pun·zar §04 tr. to prick; FIG. to torment.
pun·zón m. *(instrumento)* punch; *(para estampar)* stamp.
pu·ña·do m. handful.
pu·ñal m. dagger.
pu·ña·la·da f. stab; FIG. stab of pain ♦ **coser a puñaladas** COLL. to cut someone to pieces.
pu·ñe·ta·zo m. punch ♦ **a p.** with one's fists • **dar a alguien de p.** to punch someone.
pu·ño m. fist; SEW. cuff ♦ **apretar los puños** to clench one's fists • **de propio p.** or **de p. y letra de uno** by one's own hand.
pu·pi·lo, a m.f. student (at a boarding school) ♦ **medio p.** student who eats lunch at school —f. ANAT. pupil.
pu·pi·tre m. writing desk.
pu·ra·men·te adv. purely.
pu·ré m. CUL. purée.
pu·re·za f. purity.
pur·ga f. *(medicina)* purgative; *(eliminación)* purge.
pur·ga·ción f. *(acción)* purging; *(purificación)* purification; *(expiación)* atonement.
pur·gan·te adj. & m. laxative.
pur·gar §47 tr. *(eliminar)* to purge; *(limpiar)* to cleanse; *(purificar)* to purify; *(a un enfermo)* to purge; *(expiar)* to atone; MECH. to drain or vent; POL. to purge —reflex. to take a purgative.
pur·ga·to·rio m. Purgatory; FIG. purgatory.
pu·ri·fi·ca·ción f. purification.
pu·ri·fi·car §70 tr. *(volver puro)* to purify; *(limpiar)* to cleanse —intr. to become purified.
pu·ris·ta adj. & m.f. purist.
pu·ri·ta·no, a I. adj. Puritan; *(estricto)* puritan(ical) **II.** m.f. Puritan; *(estricto)* puritan.
pu·ro, a I. adj. pure; *(no aguado)* unadulterated *<vino p.* unadulterated wine>; *(casto)* chaste; *(incorrupto)* disinterested; *(mero)* mere *<por p. casualidad* by mere chance>; *(simple)* absolute *<la p. verdad* the absolute truth>; *(sin agua, soda)* straight ♦ **de p.** out of sheer *<de p. cansado* out of sheer tiredness> **II.** m. cigar.
púr·pu·ra f. *(color)* purple; *(colorante)* purple dye; MED. purpura.
pur·pú·re·o, a adj. purple.
pus m. pus.
pu·sie·ra, so see **poner.**
pu·si·lá·ni·me adj. pusillanimous.
pús·tu·la f. pustule.
pu·ta·ti·vo, a adj. putative.
pu·tre·fac·ción f. rotting.
pu·tre·fac·to, a adj. rotten.

Q

q, Q f. eighteenth letter of the Spanish alphabet.
quan·tum m. [pl. **-ta**] quantum.
que I. rel. pron. that, which <*el coche q. compraron es azul* the car that they bought is blue>; who <*los niños, que jugaban afuera, no vieron nada* the children, who were playing outside, saw nothing>; whom <*los amigos con q. cuento* the friends on whom I am relying> ♦ **el q.** he who, the one who or that ♦ **la q.** she who, the one who or that ♦ **las q.** or **los q.** those who, the ones who or that ♦ **lo q.** which <*murió joven, lo q. no le permitió alcanzar fama* he died young, which did not allow him to achieve fame>; what <*no entiendo lo q. dices* I don't understand what you're saying> **II.** conj. that <*me escribieron q. venían* they wrote to me that they were coming>; than <*yo sé más q. tú* I know more than you>; (*porque*) because, since; that <*habla tan rápido q. no lo comprendemos* he speaks so fast that we do not understand him>; (*si*) whether <*q. quiera, q. no quiera, lo tiene que hacer* whether he wants to or not, he has to do it>; that <*te pido q. salgas* I ask that you leave>; and <*uno habla q. habla pero ella nunca escucha* one talks and talks but she never listens>; [not translated] <*hay mucho q. hacer* there is a lot to do> ♦ **a q.** I bet that ♦ **yo q. tú** if I were you.
qué I. adj. which <*¿q. libros necesitan ustedes?* which books do you need?>; what <*¡q. tiempo hace!* what nice weather we're having!> **II.** pron. what <*¿q. quieres?* what do you want?> **III.** adv. how <*¡q. precioso!* how lovely!> ♦ **¡a mí q.!** so what! ♦ **no hay de q.** you're welcome, don't mention it ♦ **¿para q.?** what for? ♦ **¿por q.?** why? ♦ **q. de** how many <*¡q. de desgracias sufrieron!* how many misfortunes they suffered!>; ♦ **¿q. hay?** or **¿q. tal?** how goes it? ♦ **¿q. pasa?** what's the matter? ♦ **¡q. va!** nonsense!, come on! ♦ **un no sé qué** a certain something ♦ **¿y q.?** so what?
que·bra·cho m. quebracho.
que·bra·da f. (*desfiladero*) ravine; (*hendedura*) crack, gap; AMER. stream.
que·bra·di·zo, a adj. brittle, fragile.
que·bra·do, a I. adj. (*roto*) broken; (*en quiebra*) bankrupt; GEOG. rough; MED. herniated **II.** m.f. (*en quiebra*) bankrupt person; MED. person with a hernia —m. MATH. fraction.
que·bra·du·ra f. (*grieta*) crack; (*rotura*) fracture; MED. (*hernia*) rupture; (*fractura*) fracture.
que·bra·jar tr. to crack.
que·bran·ta·dor, ·ra I. adj. (*rompedor*) breaking; (*machacador*) crushing, smashing **II.** m. crushing machine.
que·bran·ta·mien·to m. (*rompimiento*) breaking; (*hendimiento*) cracking; (*acción*) crushing; (*debilitación*) weakening, deterioration; (*violación*) violation.
que·bran·tar tr. (*romper*) to break; (*hender*) to crack; (*machacar*) to crush; (*forzar*) to force, break <*q. la voluntad de alguien* to break someone's will>; (*debilitar*) to weaken; (*la ley*) to break ♦ **q. la salud** to ruin one's health —reflex. (*romperse*) to break; (*henderse*) to crack.
que·bran·to m. (*debilitación*) weakening; (*pérdida*) loss; (*aflicción*) sorrow.
que·brar §49 tr. (*romper*) to break <*q. un vaso*

to break a glass>; (*torcer*) to twist; (*interrumpir*) to interrupt —intr. to break off or up <*q. con el novio* to break up with one's boyfriend>; COM. to go bankrupt —reflex. (*romperse*) to be broken; (*hacerse una hernia*) to get a hernia.
que·da f. curfew ♦ **toque de q.** curfew bell or signal.
que·da·men·te adv. calmly, softly.
que·dar intr. (*permanecer*) to remain, stay <*el hombre quedó atrás* the man stayed behind>; (*estar*) to be <*el teatro queda muy lejos* the theater is very far away>; (*restar*) to be left <*me quedan cinco dólares* I have five dollars left>; (*acabar*) to be, end up <*quedamos conformes* we are in agreement>; MATH. to leave ♦ **¿en qué quedamos?** what have we decided? ♦ **q. bien** (*salir bien*) to come out well; FIG. to look good <*ese vestido te queda bien* that dress looks good on you> ♦ **q. en** to agree ♦ **q. mal** to come out badly ♦ **q. por** to remain to be <*el contrato queda por firmar* the contract remains to be signed> —reflex. (*permanecer*) to stay; (*estar*) to be <*se quedó perplejo* he was perplexed>; to become <*q. sordo* to become deaf> ♦ **q. con** to keep ♦ **q. sin** to run out of ♦ **q. para vestir santos** COLL. to be an old maid.
que·do, a I. adj. still, calm **II.** adv. low, softly.
que·ha·ce·res m.pl. chores.
que·ja f. (*lamento*) moan, groan; (*resentimiento*) grudge; LAW complaint.
que·jar·se reflex. (*gemir*) to moan; (*lamentarse*) to whine, complain (*de* about).
que·ji·do m. moan, groan ♦ **dar quejidos** to groan.
que·jón, o·na adj. whining.
que·jo·so, a adj. annoyed, complaining.
que·jum·bro·so, a adj. grumbling, complaining.
que·ma f. (*accion*) burning; (*incendio*) fire.
que·ma·de·ro m. incinerator.
que·ma·do, a adj. burned, burnt; (*resentido*) resentful; (*agotado*) burned out ♦ **q. por el sol** sunburned.
que·ma·dor, ·ra I. adj. burning; (*incendiario*) incendiary **II.** m.f. (*incendiario*) arsonist, incendiary —m. burner <*q. de gas* gas burner>.
que·ma·du·ra f. burn.
que·mar tr. (*arder*) to burn; (*incendiar*) to set on fire; (*consumir con fuego*) to burn (up); (*destruir con fuego*) to burn (down); (*chamuscar*) to scorch; (*escaldar*) to scald; (*calentar mucho*) to heat up; (*plantas*) to blight; (*picar*) to sting; (*malbaratar*) to sell cheaply; (*fusible*) to blow ♦ **q. balas** to fire shots ♦ **q. las naves** to burn one's bridges behind one —intr. (*arder*) to burn; (*estar muy caliente*) to be burning hot —reflex. (*arderse*) to burn, be or get burned; to burn oneself <*se quemó con la plancha* she burned herself on the iron>; (*consumir con fuego*) to burn (up); (*destruirse*) to burn (down); (*sentir calor*) to feel hot; (*plantas*) to be blighted; (*broncearse*) to get a tan; (*fusible*) to blow; COLL. (*estar cerca de encontrar*) to be warm or hot (in a game) ♦ **q. con** or **por algo** to get annoyed over or by something ♦ **q. las pestañas** COLL. to burn the midnight oil.
que·ma·rro·pa adv. ♦ **a q.** at pointblank range.
que·ma·zón f. (*quema*) burning; (*calor*) intense heat; COLL. (*comezón*) itching.
que·na f. AMER. Peruvian reed flute.
que·re·lla f. (*queja*) complaint, lament; (*dis-

puta) dispute, quarrel; LAW complaint.

que·re·llan·te I. adj. complaining **II.** m.f. plaintiff.

que·ren·cia f. COLL. home, nest.

que·ren·cio·so, a adj. homing.

que·ren·dón, o·na I. adj. AMER. loving, affectionate **II.** m.f. COLL. darling, sweetheart.

que·rer¹ m. love, affection.

que·rer² §55 tr. *(desear)* to want *<¿quieres otra taza de té?* do you want another cup of tea?>; *(amar)* to love; *(resolver)* to want *<quiero subir a la cima* I want to climb to the top>; *(requerir)* to require **• como quien no quiere la cosa** offhandedly, casually **• como quiera que sea** in whatever way **• cuando quiera** at any time **• no q.** to refuse **• ¿qué más quieres?** COLL. what more do you want? **• q. decir** to mean **• q. es poder** where there's a will, there's a way **• q. más** to prefer **• quiera que no** like it or not **• sin q.** *(sin intención)* unintentionally; *(por acaso)* by chance —intr. to look as if it is going to *<quiere nevar* it looks as if it is going to snow>.

que·ri·do, a I. adj. dear, beloved **II.** f. *(amante)* lover —m.f. COLL. darling, dear.

que·rrá, rría see querer².

que·ru·bín m. cherubim.

que·sa·di·lla f. CUL. *(pastel)* cheesecake; AMER. cornmeal pie filled with cheese.

que·se·rí·a f. cheese store.

que·so m. cheese ♦ **q. de nata** cream cheese.

quet·zal m. ORNITH. quetzal; GUAT., FIN. quetzal.

qui·cio m. pivot hole ♦ **estar fuera de q.** COLL. to be beside oneself ♦ **sacar de q.** COLL. to exasperate.

quid m. gist, crux.

quie·bra f. *(rotura)* break; *(en la tierra)* crack; *(pérdida)* loss; COM. bankruptcy.

quie·bre, bro see quebrar.

quien pron. [pl. **es**] who *<los jefes, quienes estaban ausentes, tenían la información necesaria* the managers, who were absent, had the necessary information>; whom *<la chica de q. hablo se llama Isabel* the girl of whom I am speaking is named Elizabeth>; whoever, he *or* she who *<q. mal anda mal acaba* whoever lies down with dogs gets up with fleas>.

quién pron. [pl. **es**] who *<¿q. es ese chico?* who is that boy?>; whom *<no sé de q. hablas* I do not know of whom you are speaking> ♦ **de q.** *or* **de quiénes** whose *<¿de q. es ese libro?* whose book is that?>.

quien·quie·ra pron. [pl. **quienesquiera**] whoever, whomever *<q. que sea* whoever it is>.

quie·ra, ro see querer².

quie·to, a adj. *(inmóvil)* still; *(sosegado)* quiet.

quie·tud f. *(inmovilidad)* motionlessness; *(sosiego)* calm, tranquillity.

qui·ja·da f. jawbone, jaw.

qui·jo·ta·da f. quixotism, quixotic action.

qui·jo·tes·co, a adj. quixotic.

qui·la·te m. carat; FIG. value.

qui·lla f. keel; ORNITH. breastbone, keel ♦ **dar de q.** MARIT. to keel (over).

qui·lo m. kilo, kilogram.

qui·lom·bo m. R.P., SL. brothel.

qui·me·ra f. chimera; *(ilusión)* illusion.

qui·mé·ri·co, a adj. chimerical.

quí·mi·ca f. chemistry ♦ **q. analítica** analytic chemistry **• q. atómica** atomic chemistry **• q. biológica** biochemistry.

quí·mi·co, a I. adj. chemical ♦ **producto** *or* **sustancia q.** chemical (substance) **II.** m.f. chemist.

qui·mio·te·ra·pia f. chemotherapy.

qui·mo·no m. kimono.

qui·na f. BOT. cinchona bark; MED. quinine ♦ **más malo que la q.** COLL. terrible, horrible **• tragar q.** SL. to put up with a lot.

quin·ca·lla f. hardware.

quin·ca·lle·rí·a f. hardware store.

quin·ce I. adj. fifteen; *(decimoquinto)* fifteenth ♦ **q. días** fortnight **II.** m. fifteen ♦ **dar q. y raya a** to get the better of, be superior to.

quin·ce·na f. *(quince días)* fortnight, fifteen days; *(paga)* fortnightly pay.

quin·ce·nal adj. biweekly, semimonthly.

quin·ce·nal·men·te adv. every two weeks.

quin·cua·ge·na·rio, a I. adj. *(de cincuenta unidades)* having fifty parts; *(de cincuenta años)* fifty years old **II.** m.f. quinquagenarian.

quin·cua·gé·si·mo, a adj. & m. fiftieth.

qui·nie·las f.pl. betting against the bank (on football and other games), quinella.

qui·nien·tos, as adj. & m. five hundred.

qui·ni·na f. quinine.

quin·que·nal adj. five-year.

quin·que·nio m. five-year period.

quin·ta f. see quinto, a.

quin·ta·e·sen·cia f. quintessence.

quin·tal m. quintal, hundredweight ♦ **q. métrico** 100 kilograms.

quin·tar tr. *(sacar uno de cada cinco)* to take one out of every five; MIL. to draft.

quin·te·to m. quintet.

quin·ti·lli·zos, as m.f.pl. quintuplets.

quin·to, a I. adj. fifth **II.** m. fifth —f. *(casa)* country house; MIL. draft; MUS. fifth.

quín·tu·plo, a I. adj. quintuple, fivefold **II.** m. quintuple.

quin·za·vo, a adj & m. fifteenth.

quios·co m. kiosk ♦ **q. de música** bandstand **• q. de refrescos** refreshment stand **• q. de periódicos** newsstand.

qui·qui·ri·quí m. cock-a-doodle-do.

qui·ró·fa·no m. operating room.

qui·ro·man·cia f. palmistry.

quir·quin·cho m. AMER., ZOOL. armadillo.

qui·rúr·gi·co, a adj. surgical.

qui·sie·ra, so see querer².

quis·qui·llo·so, a adj. & m.f. *(melindroso)* finicky (person); *(susceptible)* touchy (person).

quis·te m. cyst.

qui·ta f. acquittance, release (from a debt) ♦ **de q. y pon** detachable.

qui·ta·es·mal·te m. nail polish remover.

qui·ta·man·chas m. *or* f.inv. stain remover.

qui·ta·nie·ves m.inv. snowplow.

qui·tar tr. *(apartar)* to take away; *(hurtar)* to rob of; *(restar)* to subtract; *(abrogar)* to repeal; *(prohibir)* to forbid; *(impedir)* to hinder; *(librar)* to free from; *(privar)* to deprive of ♦ **q. la mesa** to clear the table **• quitarle a uno las palabras de la boca** to take the words out of one's mouth **• sin q. ni poner** verbatim —reflex. to take off *<se quitó la chaqueta* he took off his jacket>; *(mancha)* to come out ♦ **q. de encima** to get rid of **• q. de en medio** to get out of the way **• q. el sombrero** to take one's hat off.

qui·ta·sol m. parasol.

qui·zá(s) adv. maybe, perhaps.

quó·rum m. quorum.

R

r, R f. nineteenth letter of the Spanish alphabet.

ra·ba·di·lla f. tailbone; COLL. rump.

rá·ba·no m. radish ♦ **me importa un r.** COLL. I couldn't care less.

ra·bí m. [pl. **-íes**] rabbi.

ra·bia f. rabies; FIG. fury ♦ **cogerle r. a alguien** to get furious with someone • **dar r.** to infuriate.

ra·biar intr. to have rabies; FIG. to be furious ♦ **a r.** rabid <*un aficionado de béisbol a r.* a rabid baseball fan> • **que rabia** COLL. like mad *or* crazy • **r. de hambre** to be dying of hunger • **r. por algo** to be dying for something.

ra·bi·cor·to, a adj. short-tailed.

ra·bie·ta f. COLL. tantrum.

ra·bi·llo m. *(cola)* small tail; *(para pantalones)* strap; *(de una hoja)* leaf stalk; *(de una fruta)* stem.

ra·bi·no m. rabbi.

ra·bio·so, a adj. rabid; FIG. furious; COLL. *(un color)* garish.

ra·bo m. tail; *(ángulo)* corner <*mirar con el r. del ojo* to look out of the corner of one's eye>; BOT. stem ♦ **salir con el r. entre las piernas** COLL. to leave with one's tail between the legs.

ra·bón, o·na I. adj. *(rabicorto)* short-tailed; *(sin rabo)* tailless II. f. ♦ **hacer la r.** COLL. to play hooky.

ra·bo·ne·ar intr. COLL. to play hooky.

ra·cha f. *(viento)* gust; *(suerte)* run (of luck) ♦ **a rachas** by fits and starts.

ra·cial adj. racial.

ra·ci·mar AGR. tr. to pick the remaining grapes from —reflex. to form clusters.

ra·ci·mo m. raceme; FIG. cluster.

ra·cio·ci·nio m. *(razón)* reason; *(razonamiento)* reasoning.

ra·ción f. ration; RELIG. prebend ♦ **poner a media r.** to put on short rations.

ra·cio·nal I. adj. rational II. m. breastplate.

ra·cio·na·lis·ta adj. & m.f. rationalist.

ra·cio·na·li·zar §04 tr. to rationalize.

ra·cio·na·mien·to m. rationing.

ra·cio·nar tr. to ration.

ra·cis·ta adj. & m.f. racist.

ra·da f. bay.

ra·dar m. radar ♦ **r. acústico** sound radar.

ra·dia·ción f. radiation.

ra·diac·ti·vi·dad f. radioactivity.

ra·diac·ti·vo, a adj. radioactive.

ra·dia·dor m. radiator.

ra·dial adj. radial; R.P. radio <*locutor r.* radio announcer>.

ra·dian·te adj. radiant.

ra·diar intr. to radiate; RAD. to broadcast.

ra·di·ca·ción f. taking root.

ra·di·cal adj. & m.f. radical.

ra·di·car §70 intr. *(arraigar)* to take root; *(estar)* to be located; *(habitar)* to reside —reflex. *(arraigarse)* to take root; *(domiciliarse)* to establish oneself.

ra·dio¹ m. radius; *(rayo)* spoke.

ra·dio² m. radium.

ra·dio³ m. *or* f. radio.

ra·dio·ac·ti·vi·dad f. var. of **radiactividad**.

ra·dio·ac·ti·vo, a adj. var. of **radiactivo, a.**

ra·dio·a·fi·cio·na·do, a m.f. ham radio operator.

ra·dio·di·fun·dir tr. & intr. to broadcast.

ra·dio·di·fu·sión/e·mi·sión f. broadcasting.

ra·dio·di·fu·so·ra/e·mi·so·ra f. (broadcasting) station.

ra·dio·es·cu·cha m.f. radio listener.

ra·dio·gra·fí·a f. *(técnica)* radiography; *(imagen)* x-ray.

ra·dio·gra·fiar §30 tr. to x-ray.

ra·dio·gra·ma m. radiogram.

ra·dio·lo·gí·a f. radiology.

ra·dio·lo·go, a m.f. radiologist.

ra·dio·na·ve·ga·ción f. radio navigation.

ra·dio·rre·cep·tor m. receiver.

ra·dios·co·pia f. radioscopy.

ra·dio·te·le·fo·ní·a f. radiotelephony.

ra·dio·te·lé·gra·fo m. radiotelegraph.

ra·dio·te·ra·pia f. radiotherapy.

ra·dio·trans·mi·sor m. radio transmitter.

ra·dio·yen·te m.f. radio listener.

ra·e·du·ra f. scrapings.

ra·er §56 tr. *(raspar)* to scrape; COLL. *(la ropa)* to wear out.

rá·fa·ga f. *(de viento)* gust (of wind); *(de ametralladora)* burst.

raid m. raid.

ra·í·do, a adj. worn.

rai·ga, go see **raer.**

rai·gam·bre f. roots; FIG. stability; *(tradición)* tradition.

ra·íz f. root; FIG. root, origin ♦ **a r. de** as a result of • **bienes raíces** real estate • **de r.** completely • **echar raíces** to take root; *(instalarse)* to settle (down) • **r. cuadrada** square root.

ra·ja f. *(hendidura)* crack; *(de madero)* splinter; *(de fruta)* slice.

ra·já m. [pl. **-aes**] rajah.

ra·ja·do, a adj. cracked.

ra·ja·du·ra f. crack.

ra·jar tr. *(dividir)* to slice; *(hender)* to crack; R.P. COLL. to fire —reflex. *(henderse)* to crack; COLL. *(acobardarse)* to chicken out; C. AMER. to spend lavishly; R.P., CARIB. to rush off.

ra·le·ar intr. *(una tela)* to become worn; AGR. to yield thin bunches of grapes; *(una persona)* to reveal one's true nature.

ra·lla·dor m. grater.

ra·llar tr. to grate; COLL. *(molestar)* to grate on.

ra·lo, a adj. thin.

ra·ma f. branch; PRINT. chase ♦ **andarse por las ramas** COLL. to digress • **en r.** raw.

ra·ma·da f. grove.

ra·ma·je m. branches.

ra·mal m. *(cabo)* strand; *(ronzal)* halter; *(de escalera)* flight; *(ramificación)* branch.

ra·ma·la·zo m. *(de viento)* gust; *(señal)* welt ♦ **un r. de enojo** a burst of anger.

ram·bla f. boulevard; AMER. promenade.

ra·me·ra f. prostitute.

ra·mi·fi·ca·ción f. ramification.

ra·mi·fi·car·se §70 reflex. to branch off *or* out.

ra·mi·lle·te m. *(conjunto)* cluster; *(de flores)* bouquet.

ra·mo m. *(ramillete)* bouquet; *(rama pequeña)* small branch; *(rama cortada)* cut branch; *(subdivisión)* branch ♦ **Domingo de Ramos** Palm Sunday.

ra·mo·ne·ar tr. *(los árboles)* to prune; *(los animales)* to graze.

ram·pa f. ramp ♦ **r. de lanzamiento** ASTRONAUT. launching pad.

ra·na f. frog ♦ **no ser r.** COLL. to be nobody's fool • **r. de zarzal** tree frog • **r. mugidora** bullfrog.

ran·che·rí·a f. settlement.

ran·che·ro m. *(cocinero)* camp cook; *(dueño)* rancher.

ran·cho m. AMER. *(choza)* hut; *(granja)* farm; *(comida)* mess; *(campamento)* camp; R.P. straw hat ♦ **alborotar el r.** COLL. to make room • **hacer r. aparte** to go one's own way.

ran·ciar tr. to make rancid —reflex. to turn rancid.

ran·ci·dez/cie·dad f. rancidity.

ran·cio, a adj. *(comida)* rancid; *(anticuado)* old-fashioned.

ran·go m. rank; AMER. pomp.

ra·nu·ra f. groove.

ra·pa·ce·rí·a f. childish prank.

ra·pa·ci·dad f. rapacity.

ra·pa·du·ra f./**mien·to** m. *(afeitada)* shave; *(de pelo)* haircut.

ra·pa·piés m.inv. firecracker.

ra·pa·pol·vo m. COLL. scolding.

ra·par tr. *(la barba)* to shave; *(el pelo)* to crop; COLL. *(hurtar)* to snatch.

ra·paz, a I. m.f. youngster II. adj. rapacious.

ra·pe m. *(afeitada)* quick shave; COLL. *(reprensión)* scolding ♦ **al r.** close-cropped.

ra·pé adj. & m. powdered (tobacco).

ra·pi·dez f. speed.

rá·pi·do, a I. adj. quick II. m. *(tren)* express train; *(en un río)* rapids III. adv. quickly.

ra·pi·ña f. robbery ♦ **ave de r.** bird of prey.

ra·po·sa f. vixen.

rap·so·dia f. rhapsody.

rap·tar tr. to abduct.

rap·to m. *(arrebato)* burst; *(delito)* kidnaping; *(éxtasis)* rapture; MED. faint.

rap·tor, ra I. adj. kidnaping II. m.f. kidnaper.

ra·que·ta f. racket; *(para nieve)* snowshoe; *(en casinos)* croupier's rake.

ra·quí·de·o, a adj. rachidian.

ra·quí·ti·co, a adj. & m.f. rachitic (person).

ra·qui·tis·mo m./**tis** f. rickets.

ra·ra·men·te adv. rarely.

ra·re·za f. rarity; *(cosa rara)* rare thing.

ra·ro, a adj. rare; *(extraño)* odd; *(insigne)* notable ♦ **rara vez** rarely.

ras m. ♦ **a r. de** level with.

ra·san·te I. adj. (just) touching ♦ **tiro r.** low-angle fire • **vuelo r.** low-level flight II. f. slope.

ra·sar tr. to brush.

ras·ca·cie·los m.inv. skyscraper.

ras·ca·du·ra f. *(acción)* scratching; *(rasguño)* scratch.

ras·ca·mo·ño m. hairpin.

ras·car §70 tr. *(con la uña)* to scratch; *(raspar)* to scrape —reflex. to scratch oneself.

ras·ca·zón f. itch.

ra·se·ro m. leveler.

ras·ga·do, a I. adj. *(desgarrado)* torn; *(ojos)* almond-shaped II. m. tear.

ras·ga·du·ra f. tear.

ras·gar §47 tr. to tear.

ras·go m. *(trazo)* stroke; *(carácter)* trait, feature ♦ **a grandes rasgos** in broad strokes ♦ pl. features.

ras·gón m. tear.

ras·gue·ar tr. to strum.

ras·gue·o m. strumming.

ras·gu·ñar tr. to scratch.

ras·gu·ño m. scratch.

ra·so, a I. adj. *(llano)* flat; *(el cielo)* clear; *(hasta el borde)* level; MIL. private <*soldado r.* private soldier> ♦ **al r.** in the open air • **cielo r.** ceiling II. m. satin.

ras·pa f. *(de pescado)* spine; AGR. bear; AMER., COLL. reprimand.

ras·pa·dor m. scraper.

ras·pa·du·ra f. scraping; COLL. *(rapadura)* shave.

ras·pan·te adj. *(vino)* sharp; *(abrasivo)* abrasive.

ras·par tr. *(raer)* to scrape (off); *(rasar)* to graze.

ras·pón m. AMER. *(reprimenda)* scolding; *(desolladura)* scratch ♦ **de r.** in passing.

ras·qui·ña f. AMER. itch.

ras·tra f. *(señal)* trail; *(ristra)* string of dried fruit; AGR. hoe; MARIT. dredge ♦ **a rastras** dragging.

ras·tre·a·dor, ·ra I. adj. tracking II. m. tracker ♦ **r. de minas** MIL. mine sweeper.

ras·tre·ar tr. *(seguir el rastro)* to trail; *(pescar)* to trawl; *(indagar)* to inquire into; MARIT. to dredge.

ras·tre·o m. *(seguimiento)* tracking; *(pesca)* trawling; MARIT. dragging; AGR. raking.

ras·tre·ro, a adj. *(arrastrándose)* trailing; *(bajo)* vile ♦ **perro r.** tracker.

ras·tri·llar tr. TEX. to comb; AGR. to rake.

ras·tri·llo m. rake; TEX. comb.

ras·tro m. *(pista)* trail; *(señal)* trace.

ras·tro·jar tr. to clear of stubble.

ras·tro·jo m. *(residuo)* stubble; *(campo segado)* stubble field.

ra·su·rar tr. *(afeitar)* to shave; *(raer)* to scrape.

ra·ta f. rat ♦ **más pobre que una r.** COLL. as poor as a church mouse.

ra·te·ar tr. to pilfer —intr. to creep.

ra·te·rí·a f. pilfering.

ra·te·ro, a I. adj. *(ladrón)* thieving; *(bajo)* base II. m.f. thief.

ra·ti·fi·ca·ción f. ratification.

ra·ti·fi·car §70 tr. to ratify.

ra·ti·fi·ca·to·rio, a adj. ratifying.

ra·to m. while ♦ **a cada r.** all the time • **al poco r.** shortly after • **de r. en r.** from time to time • **un buen r.** quite some time.

ra·tón m. ZOOL., COMPUT. mouse ♦ **r. de biblioteca** bookworm.

ra·to·ne·ro, a I. adj. mouselike ♦ **perro r.** ratter (dog) II. f. *(trampa)* mousetrap; *(agujero)* mousehole.

rau·dal m. torrent; FIG. abundance.

rau·do, a adj. swift.

ra·vio·les m.pl. ravioli.

ra·ya[1] f. *(lista)* stripe; *(línea)* line; *(veta)* streak; *(arañazo)* scratch; *(en el pelo)* part; *(pliegue)* crease; *(límite)* limit; *(punto)* point; GRAM., TELEC. dash; PHYS. line; SPORT. line, mark; AMER. hopscotch; MEX. pay ♦ **a rayas** striped • **hacerse la r.** to part one's hair • **mantener a r. (a alguien)** COLL. to keep (someone) in his place • **pasarse de la r.** COLL. to go too far • **tener a r.** to keep at bay.

ra·ya[2] f. ICHTH. ray.

ra·ya·no, a adj. adjacent ♦ **r. en** bordering on.

ra·yar tr. to draw lines on —intr. *(lindar)* to be next to; *(amanecer)* to dawn; *(aparecer)* to appear; *(arañar)* to scratch; *(aproximar)* to be approaching; *(sobresalir)* to stand out ♦ **al r. el alba** at the crack of dawn • **r. a gran altura** to excel —reflex. to get scratched.

ra·yo m. ray; *(de rueda)* spoke; *(descarga)* thunderbolt; *(infortunio)* blow; *(dolor)* flash of pain; *(persona)* fast worker; *(relámpago)* flash of lightning ♦ **echar rayos y centellas** to be furious • **r. del radio** radio beam.

ra·yón m. rayon.

ra·yue·la f. pitch and toss; AMER. hopscotch.

ra·za f. race; *(de animales)* breed ♦ **de pura r.** *(caballos)* thoroughbred; *(perros)* pedigreed.

ra·zón f. reason; *(recado)* message; *(cómputo)* rate; MATH. ratio, proportion ♦ **asistirle a uno la r.** to be in the right • **con mayor r.** with all the more reason • **con r.** with good reason • **dar la r. a alguien** to side with someone • **entrar en r.** to come to one's senses • **meter a alguien en r.** to talk sense into someone • **perder la r.** to go out of one's mind • **r. social** business name • **tener r.** to be right.

ra·zo·na·ble adj. reasonable.

ra·zo·na·da·men·te adv. rationally.

ra·zo·na·do, a adj. reasoned.

ra·zo·nar intr. *(pensar)* to reason; *(hablar)* to speak —tr. to give reasons for.

re m. re, D.

re·ac·ción f. reaction ♦ **avión de r.** jet plane • **r. en cadena** chain reaction.

re·ac·cio·nar intr. to react.

re·ac·cio·na·rio, a adj. & m.f. reactionary.

re·a·cio, a adj. stubborn.

re·ac·ti·va·ción f. reactivation; ECON. recovery.

re·ac·ti·var tr. to reactivate.

re·ac·tor m. jet engine; PHYS. reactor.

re·a·dap·ta·ción f. readaptation.

re·a·dap·tar tr. to readapt.

re·a·fir·mar tr. to reaffirm.

re·a·jus·tar tr. to readjust.

re·a·jus·te m. readjustment.

re·al¹ adj. real.

re·al² I. adj. royal; FIG. fine II. m. *(moneda)* real; MIL. army camp ♦ **no tener un r.** COLL. not to have a penny.

re·al·ce m. *(lustre)* luster; PAINT. highlight; *(adorno)* embossment ♦ **poner de r.** to highlight.

re·a·le·za f. royalty.

re·a·li·dad f. reality ♦ **en r.** actually.

re·a·lis·ta I. adj. realistic; *(monárquico)* royalist II. m.f. *(realidad)* realist; *(monárquico)* royalist.

re·a·li·za·ble adj. attainable.

re·a·li·za·ción f. *(ejecución)* execution; *(cumplimiento)* fulfillment; CINEM. production.

re·a·li·za·dor, ·ra I. adj. fulfilling II. m.f. CINEM. producer.

re·a·li·zar §04 tr. *(cumplir)* to realize; *(ejecutar)* to accomplish; COM. to sell —reflex. to come true.

re·al·zar §04 tr. to enhance.

re·a·ni·mar tr. to revive —reflex. to recover.

re·a·nu·da·ción f. resumption.

re·a·nu·dar tr. to resume —reflex. to begin again.

re·a·pa·re·cer §17 intr. to reappear.

re·a·pa·ri·ción f. reappearance.

re·a·su·mir tr. to resume.

re·a·vi·var tr. to revive.

re·ba·ja f. *(acción)* reduction; *(descuento)* discount.

re·ba·jar tr. *(reducir)* to reduce; *(bajar)* to lower; *(humillar)* to humiliate —reflex. to degrade oneself ♦ **r. a** to stoop to.

re·bal·sa f. puddle.

re·bal·sar tr. & intr. *(estancarse)* to form a pool; *(rebosar)* to overflow.

re·bal·se m. *(piscina)* pool; *(presa)* dam.

re·ba·na·da f. slice.

re·ba·nar tr. to slice.

re·ba·ño m. herd.

re·ba·sar tr. to surpass —intr. to overflow.

re·ba·tir tr. *(argumento)* refute; *(ataque)* to ward off; *(tentación)* to resist.

re·be·lar·se reflex. to rebel.

re·bel·de I. adj. rebellious; MED. resistant; LAW in default II. m.f. rebel; LAW defaulter.

re·bel·dí·a f. rebelliousness; LAW default.

re·be·lión f. rebellion.

re·ben·ca·zo m. lash (of a whip).

re·ben·que m. AMER. whip.

re·bién adv. COLL. extremely well.

re·bor·de m. border.

re·bo·san·te adj. ♦ **r. de** bursting with.

re·bo·sar intr. & reflex. to overflow *(de* with).

re·bo·tar intr. *(pelota)* to bounce; *(bala)* to ricochet.

re·bo·te m. rebound ♦ **de r.** on the rebound.

re·bo·zo m. shawl.

re·bu·jar tr. to tuck in.

re·bus·ca f. *(acción)* hunt; *(fruto)* gleanings.

re·bus·ca·do, a adj. pedantic.

re·buz·nar intr. to bray.

re·buz·no m. braying.

re·ca·bar tr. to request.

re·ca·do m. *(mensaje)* message; *(mandado)* errand; AMER., EQUIT. riding gear ♦ **mandar r.** to send word.

re·ca·er §15 intr. to relapse ♦ **r. en** to fall to.

re·ca·í·da f. relapse.

re·ca·lar tr. to saturate —intr. MARIT. to sight land; S. AMER. to arrive.

re·cal·car §70 tr. *(apretar)* to squeeze (in); *(insistir)* to stress —reflex. to sprain.

re·cal·ci·tran·te adj. recalcitrant.

re·ca·len·ta·mien·to m. reheating.

re·ca·len·tar §49 tr. *(volver a calentar)* to reheat; *(calentar demasiado)* to overheat.

re·ca·ma·do m. relief embroidery.

re·ca·mar tr. to do relief embroidery on.

re·cá·ma·ra f. dressing room; ARTIL. gun breech; MEX. bedroom.

re·cam·bio m. *(acción)* changing again; *(pieza)* spare part.

re·ca·pa·ci·tar tr. to reconsider.

re·ca·pi·tu·la·ción m. recapitulation.

re·ca·pi·tu·lar tr. to recapitulate.

re·car·ga·do, a adj. overloaded; FIG. overdone.

re·car·gar §47 tr. to reload; *(aumentar)* to increase; *(sobrecargar)* to overload; *(abrumar)* to overburden; *(adornar)* to overdecorate; *(cobrar más)* to charge extra; *(cobrar demasiado)* to overcharge; TECH. to recharge.

re·car·go m. surcharge.

re·ca·ta·do, a adj. *(cauteloso)* reserved; *(tímido)* shy; *(pudoroso)* modest.

re·ca·tar tr. to cover up —reflex. *(mostrar recelo)* to behave prudently.

re·ca·to m. *(cautela)* caution; *(modestia)* modesty.

re·cau·chu·tar tr. AMER. to retread.

re·cau·da·ción f. *(cobranza)* collection; *(cantidad)* receipts.

re·cau·da·dor m. tax collector.

re·cau·dar tr. to collect.
re·cau·do m. caution ♦ **poner a buen r.** to place in safekeeping.
re·ca·ye·ra, yó see **recaer**.
re·ce·lar tr. to suspect.
re·ce·lo m. suspicion.
re·ce·lo·so, a adj. suspicious.
re·cep·ción f. reception; *(admisión)* admission; *(reunión)* party; *(en un hotel)* front desk.
re·cep·cio·nis·ta m.f. receptionist.
re·cep·tá·cu·lo m. receptacle.
re·cep·ti·vi·dad f. receptivity.
re·cep·ti·vo, a adj. receptive.
re·cep·tor, ·ra I. adj. receiving **II.** m. receiver.
re·ce·sión f. recession.
re·ce·so m. *(separación)* withdrawal; AMER. adjournment.
re·ce·ta f. MED. prescription; CUL. recipe; FIG. formula.
re·ce·tar tr. to prescribe.
re·ce·ta·rio m. prescription book.
re·cha·za·mien·to m. rejection; *(negativa)* refusal; *(del enemigo)* repelling.
re·cha·zar §04 tr. to reject; *(declinar)* to refuse; *(repeler)* to repel; *(tentación)* to resist; *(negar)* to deny.
re·cha·zo m. rejection.
re·chi·fla f. *(abucheo)* hissing; *(burla)* derision.
re·chi·flar tr. to hiss.
re·chi·nar intr. *(hacer ruido)* to grate; *(los dientes)* to grind.
re·chon·cho, a adj. COLL. chubby.
re·chu·pe·te COLL. ♦ **de r.** *(fantástico)* terrific; *(delicioso)* scrumptious.
re·ci·bi·dor, ·ra I. adj. receiving **II.** m.f. receiver —m. *(entrance)* hall.
re·ci·bi·mien·to m. reception; *(vestíbulo)* *(entrance)* hall.
re·ci·bir tr. & intr. to receive —reflex. ♦ **r. de** to graduate as.
re·ci·bo m. receipt; *(sala)* reception room ♦ **acusar r. de** to acknowledge receipt of.
re·ci·cla·je m. *(persona)* retraining; *(cosa)* recycling.
re·ci·clar tr. to recycle —reflex. to be retrained.
re·cién adv. recently ♦ **r. nacido** newborn.
re·cien·te adj. recent; *(moderno)* modern.
re·cien·te·men·te adv. recently.
re·cin·to m. place.
re·cio, a adj. *(vigoroso)* strong; *(abultado)* bulky; *(tiempo)* severe; *(lluvia)* heavy; *(veloz)* swift ♦ **en lo más r. de** in the thick of.
re·ci·pien·te I. adj. receiving **II.** m. container.
re·ci·pro·ca·men·te adv. reciprocally.
re·ci·pro·car §70 tr. to reciprocate.
re·ci·pro·ci·dad f. reciprocity.
re·cí·pro·co, a adj. reciprocal.
re·ci·ta·do m. recitative.
re·ci·ta·dor, ·ra I. adj. reciting **II.** m.f. reciter.
re·ci·tal m. MUS. recital; LIT. reading.
re·ci·tar tr. to recite.
re·cla·ma·ción f. *(petición)* claim; *(protesta)* complaint.
re·cla·ma·dor, ·ra I. adj. claiming <*parte r.* claiming party> **II.** m.f. claimant.
re·cla·mar tr. *(pedir)* to claim; *(exigir)* to demand; LAW to summon —intr. to protest.
re·cla·mo m. *(llamada)* birdcall; *(instrumento)* decoy whistle; *(reclamación)* claim; COM. advertisement; PRINT. catchword.
re·cli·nar tr. to lean *or* rest on —reflex. to

recline.
re·cli·na·to·rio m. kneeling-stool.
re·cluir §18 tr. *(encerrar)* to seclude; *(encarcelar)* to imprison —reflex. to shut oneself in.
re·clu·sión f. *(encierro)* seclusion; *(prisión)* imprisonment.
re·clu·so, a I. see **recluir II.** adj. *(encerrado)* secluded; *(preso)* imprisoned **III.** m.f. prisoner.
re·clu·ta f. recruitment —m. recruit.
re·clu·ta·mien·to m. recruitment.
re·clu·tar tr. to recruit.
re·clu·ya, yo, yera, yó see **recluir**.
re·co·brar tr. & reflex. to recover.
re·co·bro m. recovery.
re·co·dar intr. & reflex. to lean one's elbows (on).
re·co·do m. bend.
re·co·ge·dor, ·ra I. adj. collecting **II.** m.f. collector —m. AGR. gleaner.
re·co·ger §34 tr. *(volver a coger)* to pick up; *(juntar)* to gather; *(coleccionar)* to save; *(dar asilo)* to shelter; *(encerrar)* to lock up; AGR. to harvest; MARIT., SEW. to take in —reflex. to withdraw ♦ **r. las mangas** to roll up one's sleeves.
re·co·gi·do, a I. adj. *(apartado)* withdrawn; *(pequeño)* small; *(tranquilo)* quiet, tranquil **II.** f. gathering.
re·co·gi·mien·to m. *(acción)* collecting; *(retiro)* retirement; *(ensimismamiento)* withdrawal.
re·co·lec·ción f. *(acción)* collection; *(resumen)* summary; AGR. harvest; RELIG. spiritual absorption.
re·co·lec·tar tr. to gather.
re·co·lec·tor, ·ra m.f. *(de cosechas)* harvester; *(recaudador)* collector.
re·co·men·da·ble adj. recommendable.
re·co·men·da·ción f. recommendation.
re·co·men·da·do, a m. protégé —f. protégée.
re·co·men·dar §49 tr. to recommend.
re·com·pen·sa f. reward.
re·com·pen·sar tr. *(premiar)* to recompense; *(compensar)* to compensate.
re·con·ci·lia·ble adj. reconcilable.
re·con·ci·lia·ción f. reconciliation.
re·con·ci·liar tr. & reflex. to reconcile.
re·cón·di·to, a adj. recondite, hidden.
re·con·for·tar tr. to comfort; MED. to fortify.
re·co·no·cer §17 tr. to recognize; *(identificar)* to identify; *(agradecer)* to appreciate; *(examinar)* to examine; MIL. to reconnoiter; SURV. to survey ♦ **r. la evidencia** to bow to the evidence —reflex. to be clear *or* apparent; *(confesar)* to confess <*r. culpable* to admit one's guilt>.
re·co·no·ci·da·men·te adv. *(con gratitud)* gratefully; *(evidentemente)* clearly.
re·co·no·ci·do, a adj. *(agradecido)* grateful; *(aceptado)* recognized; *(confesado)* acknowledged.
re·co·no·ci·mien·to m. *(identificación)* recognition; *(confesión)* acknowledgement; *(gratitud)* gratitude; *(examinación)* examination; MIL. reconnaissance ♦ **en r. de** in gratitude for.
re·con·quis·tar tr. to recover.
re·con·si·de·rar tr. to reconsider.
re·cons·ti·tuir §18 tr. to reconstitute.
re·cons·ti·tu·yen·te I. adj. reconstituent **II.** m. tonic.
re·cons·truc·ción f. reconstruction; CONSTR. rebuilding.
re·cons·truir §18 tr. to reconstruct; CONSTR. to

rebuild.

re·con·tar §19 tr. to recount.

re·co·pi·la·ción f. compilation.

re·co·pi·la·dor m. compiler.

re·co·pi·lar tr. to compile.

ré·cord m. & adj. inv. record <*una cosecha r.* a record crop>.

re·cor·da·ción f. memory.

re·cor·dar §19 tr. to remember; (*avisar*) to remind; (*evocar*) to remind of —intr. to remember; (*contar recuerdos*) to reminisce; (*despertar*) to wake up —reflex. to be remembered ♦ **r. que** to remind oneself that.

re·co·rrer tr. (*viajar*) to travel; (*mirar*) to look over ♦ **r. el mundo** to see the world.

re·co·rri·do m. (*viaje*) journey; (*trayecto*) path; (*de cartero, recadero*) route.

re·cor·tar tr. (*cortar*) to trim; (*reducir*) to reduce; ARTS to cut out —reflex. to stand out.

re·cor·te m. (*acción*) trimming; (*de periódico*) newspaper clipping; (*de pelo*) trim.

re·cos·tar §19 tr. to lean (on) —reflex. (*reclinarse*) to recline; (*acostarse*) to lie down ♦ **r. en** or **sobre** to lean on.

re·co·va f. poultry market; AMER. market.

re·co·ve·co m. nook ♦ pl. recesses • **sin r.** frank, open.

re·cre·a·ción f. recreation.

re·cre·ar tr. (*divertir*) to entertain; (*crear de nuevo*) to re-create —reflex. to enjoy.

re·cre·a·ti·vo, a adj. (*divertido*) entertaining; recreational <*terapia r.* recreational therapy>.

re·cre·o m. (*acción*) recreation; (*en escuela*) recess ♦ **de r.** pleasure <*barco de r.* pleasure boat>.

re·cri·mi·na·ción f. recrimination.

re·cri·mi·nar intr. & reflex. to recriminate (each other).

re·cru·de·cer §17 intr. & reflex. to worsen.

re·cru·de·ci·mien·to m. worsening.

rec·ta f. see **recto, a.**

rec·tán·gu·lo I. adj. rectangular II. m. rectangle.

rec·ti·fi·ca·ción f. rectification.

rec·ti·fi·car §70 tr. (*enderezar*) to straighten; (*corregir*) to rectify; CHEM., ELEC., MATH. to rectify; MECH. to resurface.

rec·ti·tud f. straightness; FIG. honesty.

rec·to, a I. adj. (*derecho*) straight; (*honrado*) honest; FIG. sound; GEOM. right II. m. ANAT. rectum; PRINT. recto —f. GEOM. straight line ♦ **r. final** home stretch III. adv. straight.

rec·tor, ·ra I. adj. ruling II. m.f. (*de colegio*) principal —m. (*cura*) parish priest; (*de universidad*) president.

re·cua·dro m. ARCHIT. panel; PRINT. box.

re·cu·brir tr. to cover.

re·cuen·te, to see **recontar.**

re·cuen·to m. (*segunda enumeración*) recount; (*enumeración*) count.

re·cuer·de, do see **recordar.**

re·cuer·do m. (*memoria*) memory; (*regalo*) souvenir ♦ pl. regards.

re·cues·te, to see **recostar.**

re·cu·la·da f. backward movement; (*de vehículo*) backing (up); ARM. recoil; COLL. (*acción de ceder*) backing down.

re·cu·lar intr. to back up; ARM. to recoil; COLL. (*ceder*) to retreat.

re·cu·pe·ra·ble adj. recoverable.

re·cu·pe·ra·ción f. recovery.

re·cu·pe·rar tr. (*recobrar*) to recover; (*fuerzas*, *sentido*) to regain consciousness; (*reconquistar*) to win back; (*una pérdida*) to recoup; (*el tiempo*) to make up for; TECH. to reclaim —reflex. to recover.

re·cu·rren·te I. adj. recurrent II. m.f. LAW appellant.

re·cu·rrir intr. (*acudir*) to turn or appeal (to); (*volver*) to return or revert (to).

re·cur·so m. (*acción*) recourse; (*medio*) means; resource <*recursos naturales* natural resources>.

re·cu·sa·ción f. rejection; LAW challenge.

re·cu·sar tr. to reject, refuse; LAW to challenge.

red f. net; (*malla*) mesh; (*redecilla*) hairnet; (*de tiendas*) chain; (*conspiración*) network; RAIL., TELEC. network ♦ **caer en la r.** to fall into a trap • **tender las redes** to cast one's net.

re·dac·ción f. (*escritura*) writing; (*oficina*) editorial office; (*personal*) editorial staff.

re·dac·tar tr. to draft.

re·dac·tor, ·ra I. adj. writing II. m.f. (*escritor*) writer; (*revisor*) editor ♦ **r. jefe** editor in chief.

re·da·da f. (*de pescados*) catch; (*de la policía*) roundup, dragnet.

re·de·ci·lla f. (*tejido*) mesh; (*para el pelo*) hairnet; (*bolsa*) string bag.

re·de·dor m. surroundings ♦ **al r.** around.

re·den·ción f. redemption.

re·den·tor, ·ra I. adj. redeeming II. m.f. redeemer.

re·dil m. fold.

re·di·mir tr. to redeem; (*de obligación*) to exempt.

ré·di·to m. interest.

re·di·tua·ble adj. interest-yielding.

re·di·tuar §67 tr. to yield.

re·do·bla·do, a adj. stocky; MECH. reinforced ♦ **paso r.** MIL. double time.

re·do·blar tr. (*intensificar*) to intensify; (*doblar*) to fold —intr. to roll.

re·do·ble m. (*redoblamiento*) redoubling; (*de tambor*) roll.

re·don·da f. see **redondo, a.**

re·don·de·a·do, a adj. round.

re·don·de·ar tr. to make round; MATH. to round off —reflex. to become round.

re·don·del m. COLL. circle; TAUR. arena.

re·don·dez f. roundness.

re·don·do, a I. adj. round ♦ **caer (en) r.** to collapse • **en r.** around • **girar en r.** COLL. to turn around • **salir r. (a alguien)** to go well (for someone) II. f. region; MUS. whole note ♦ **a la r.** around.

re·duc·ción f. reduction; (*sumisión*) subjecting.

re·du·ci·do, a adj. reduced; (*estrecho*) narrow; (*pequeño*) small, limited.

re·du·ci·mien·to m. var. of **reducción.**

re·du·cir §22 tr. to reduce; (*sujetar*) to subjugate —reflex. to be reduced; (*venir a ser*) to boil down (*a* to).

re·duc·tor, ·ra I. adj. reducing II. m. CHEM., ELEC. reducer.

re·du·je·ra, jo see **reducir.**

re·dun·dan·cia f. redundancy.

re·dun·dan·te adj. redundant.

re·dun·dar intr. (*rebosar*) to overflow; (*resultar*) to redound (*en* to).

re·e·le·gir §54 tr. to re-elect.

re·em·bol·sa·ble adj. reimbursable.

re·em·bol·sar tr. to reimburse.

re·em·bol·so m. reimbursement ♦ **enviar con-**

tra r. to send C.O.D.

re·em·pla·zan·te I. adj. replacing II. m.f. replacement.

re·em·pla·zar §04 tr. to replace.

re·em·pla·zo m. replacement.

re·en·car·na·ción f. reincarnation.

re·en·car·nar intr. to reincarnate —reflex. to be reincarnated.

re·en·cuen·tro m. ♦ **tener un r.** to meet again.

re·en·gan·char tr. & reflex. to re-enlist.

re·es·truc·tu·ra·ción f. restructuring.

re·es·truc·tu·rar tr. to restructure.

re·fac·ción f. (colación) snack; (reparación) renovation.

re·fac·cio·nar tr. AMER. to renovate.

re·fa·jo m. underskirt.

re·fec·to·rio m. refectory.

re·fe·ren·cia f. reference.

re·fe·ren·te adj. referring (a to).

re·fe·rir §65 tr. to refer; (contar) to relate, tell —reflex. to refer (a to).

re·fi·lón adv. ♦ **de r.** obliquely; (de pasada) in passing.

re·fi·na·do, a adj. refined.

re·fi·na·mien·to m. refinement.

re·fi·nar tr. to refine —reflex. to become refined.

re·fi·ne·rí·a f. refinery.

re·fi·rie·ra, rió see referir.

re·flec·tor, ·ra I. adj. reflecting II. m. OPT. reflector; (proyector) spotlight; MIL. searchlight.

re·fle·jar tr. to reflect —reflex. to be reflected.

re·fle·jo, a I. adj. PHYS. reflected; PHYSIOL. reflex II. m. reflection; PHYSIOL. reflex; (brillo) gleam.

re·fle·xión f. reflection.

re·fle·xio·nar intr. & tr. to reflect (en, sobre on).

re·fle·xi·vo, a adj. reflective; GRAM. reflexive.

re·flo·re·cer §17 intr. to bloom again.

re·flu·jo m. ebb.

re·fo·res·ta·ción f. AMER. reforestation.

re·for·ma f. reform; (modificación) alteration.

re·for·ma·do, a adj. reformed; (modificado) altered.

re·for·mar tr. to reform; (mejorar) to improve; (restaurar) to renovate; (modificar) to alter —reflex. to reform.

re·for·ma·to·rio, a adj. & m. reformatory.

re·for·mis·ta adj. & m.f. reformist.

re·for·za·do, a adj. reinforced.

re·for·zar §37 tr. to reinforce; FIG. to encourage.

re·frac·ción f. refraction.

re·frac·tar tr. to refract.

re·frán m. saying ♦ **como dice** or **según reza el r.** as the saying goes.

re·fre·gar §52 tr. (frotar) to scrub; COLL. (reprochar) to throw back at.

re·fre·nar tr. to restrain.

re·fren·dar tr. (firmar) to endorse; (pasaporte) to stamp.

re·fren·da·rio m. countersigner.

re·fres·can·te adj. refreshing.

re·fres·car §70 tr. to refresh —intr. & reflex. to become cool; (tomar fuerzas) to refresh (oneself).

re·fres·co m. (alimento) refreshment; (bebida) soft drink.

re·frie·ga f. skirmish, scuffle.

re·frie·go, gue see refregar.

re·fri·ge·ra·ción f. refrigeration; (de aire) air conditioning ♦ **r. por agua** water-cooling.

re·fri·ge·ra·dor, ·ra I. adj. refrigerating II. m. or f. refrigerator.

re·fri·ge·ran·te I. adj. refrigerating II. m. cooling bath.

re·fri·ge·rar tr. to refrigerate.

re·fri·ge·rio m. snack.

re·fri·to, a I. adj. refried II. m. COLL. rehash.

re·fuer·zo m. reinforcement; (sostén) support.

re·fu·gia·do, a adj. & m.f. refugee.

re·fu·giar tr. to give refuge —reflex. to take refuge.

re·fu·gio m. refuge ♦ **r. antiaéreo** air-raid shelter.

re·ful·gen·te adj. refulgent.

re·ful·gir §32 intr. to shine brightly.

re·fun·fu·ña·dor, ·ra I. adj. grumbling, whining II. m.f. grumbler.

re·fun·fu·ñar intr. to grumble.

re·fun·fu·ño m. grumble.

re·fun·fu·ñón, o·na I. adj. grumbling II. m.f. grumbler.

re·fu·ta·ción f. rebuttal.

re·fu·tar tr. to rebut.

re·ga·de·ra f. watering can.

re·ga·dí·o, a I. adj. irrigable II. m. irrigated land.

re·ga·la·do, a adj. (delicado) dainty; (con comodidades) easy; (barato) dirt-cheap.

re·ga·lar tr. (dar) to give (as a present); (donar) to give away; (halagar) to flatter —reflex. to indulge oneself.

re·ga·lí·a f. (derecho real) royal privilege; (excepción) privilege; (sueldo) bonus; (de autor) royalties.

re·ga·liz m./li·za f. licorice.

re·ga·lo m. (obsequio) present, gift; (placer) joy, pleasure; (comodidad) comfort, ease.

re·ga·lón, o·na adj. COLL. spoiled.

re·ga·ña·dien·tes ♦ **a r.** COLL. grudgingly.

re·ga·ñar intr. (reñir) to quarrel, argue; (refunfuñar) to grumble —tr. COLL. to scold.

re·ga·ño m. scolding.

re·ga·ñón, o·na I. adj. grumbling II. m.f. grumbler.

re·gar §52 tr. to water; (esparcir) to strew; (con lágrimas) to bathe; (con bebida) to wash down.

re·ga·ta f. regatta.

re·ga·te·a·dor, ·ra AMER. I. adj. haggling II. m.f. haggler.

re·ga·te·ar tr. (negociar) to bargain for; (vender) to retail —intr. (negociar) to bargain; (poner dificultades) to be difficult.

re·ga·te·o m. haggling.

re·ga·zo m. lap.

re·ge·ne·ra·ción f. regeneration.

re·ge·ne·ra·dor, ·ra I. adj. regenerating, regenerative II. m.f. regenerator.

re·ge·ne·rar tr. to regenerate.

re·gen·tar/te·ar tr. to direct.

re·gen·te m.f. regent —m. RELIG. director of studies; (gerente) manager.

ré·gi·men m. regime; (sistema) system; (reglas) regulations; MED. diet.

re·gi·men·tar §49 tr. to regiment.

re·gi·mien·to m. government; MIL. regiment.

re·gio, a adj. regal; FIG. magnificent.

re·gión f. region.

re·gio·nal adj. regional.

re·gio·na·lis·mo m. regionalism.

re·gir §57 tr. (gobernar) to govern; (manejar)

to run; LAW to govern; GRAM. to take —intr. to apply —reflex. ♦ **r. por** to be guided by.

re·gis·tra·dor, ·ra I. adj. *(que inspecciona)* examining; *(que registra)* registering ♦ **caja r.** cash register **II.** m.f. *(que inspecciona)* examiner; *(que registra)* register —f. cash register.

re·gis·trar tr. *(inspeccionar)* to examine; *(en un registro)* to register; *(rebuscar)* to search; *(anotar)* to note —intr. to search —reflex. to register; *(ocurrir)* to happen.

re·gis·tro m. *(acción)* registration; *(inspección)* examination; *(búsqueda)* search; *(libro)* register; *(oficina)* registry; *(asiento)* entry; *(padrón)* census list; *(género de voces)* register ♦ **tocar todos los registros** COLL. to use all possible means • **r. de la propiedad** real estate registry.

re·gla f. *(para trazar)* ruler; *(norma)* rule; *(modelo)* model; *(instrucciones)* instructions; *(menstruación)* period ♦ **en r.** by the book • **poner algo en r.** to put *or* set something straight • **r. de cálculo** slide rule.

re·gla·men·ta·ción f. *(acción)* regulation; *(regla)* rule.

re·gla·men·tar tr. to regulate.

re·gla·men·ta·rio, a adj. prescribed.

re·gla·men·to m. *(reglas)* rules.

re·glar tr. *(rayar)* to rule; *(regular)* to regulate —reflex. to be guided (*por* by).

re·go·ci·jar tr. to delight —reflex. to be delighted.

re·go·ci·jo m. joy.

re·go·de·ar·se reflex. COLL. *(deleitarse)* to take pleasure in; *(bromear)* to joke.

re·go·de·o m. pleasure.

re·gor·de·te, a adj. COLL. plump.

re·gre·sar tr., intr. & reflex. AMER. to return.

re·gre·sión f. regression.

re·gre·si·vo, a adj. regressive.

re·gre·so m. return ♦ **estar de r.** to be back.

re·güe·ro m. *(chorro)* stream; AGR. irrigation ditch; *(señal)* trail; *(de sangre)* trickle.

re·gu·la·ción f. regulation; *(control)* control.

re·gu·la·do, a adj. *(regular)* according to rule; *(ajustado)* regulated; *(controlado)* controlled.

re·gu·la·dor, ·ra I. adj. regulating **II.** m. regulator; RAD. control knob.

re·gu·lar[1] **I.** adj. regular; *(aceptable)* fairly good; *(mediano)* average; GRAM. regular ♦ **por lo r.** as a rule **II.** adv. ♦ **estar r.** COLL. to be so-so.

re·gu·lar[2] tr. *(ajustar)* to regulate; *(controlar)* to control; *(ordenar)* to order.

re·gu·la·ri·dad f. regularity ♦ **con r.** regularly.

re·gu·la·ri·zar §04 tr. to regularize.

re·gu·lar·men·te adv. regularly; *(medianamente)* fairly well.

re·gur·gi·ta·ción f. regurgitation.

re·gur·gi·tar intr. to regurgitate.

re·ha·bi·li·ta·ción f. rehabilitation; *(reinstalación)* reinstatement.

re·ha·bi·li·tar tr. to rehabilitate; *(en un puesto)* to reinstate.

re·ha·cer §40 tr. *(hacer)* to redo; *(elaborar)* to remake.

re·hén m. hostage.

re·hi·lar tr. to twist too hard —intr. to whiz.

re·hi·le·te m. *(flechilla)* dart; TAUR. banderilla.

re·ho·gar §47 tr. to brown.

re·huir §18 tr. to avoid —reflex. to flee *or* shrink from.

re·hu·sar tr. to refuse.

re·hu·ya, yo, yera, yó see **rehuir.**

re·im·pri·mir §80 tr. to reprint.

rei·na f. queen.

rei·na·do m. reign.

rei·nan·te adj. ruling; FIG. prevailing.

rei·nar tr. to reign.

re·in·ci·den·cia f. relapse; CRIMIN. recidivism.

re·in·ci·den·te I. adj. *(que recae)* relapsing; CRIMIN. recidivous **II.** m.f. recidivist.

re·in·ci·dir intr. to relapse.

re·in·cor·po·ra·ción f. reincorporation.

re·in·cor·po·rar tr. to reincorporate.

re·in·gre·sar intr. to re-enter.

rei·no m. kingdom

re·ins·ta·la·ción f. reinstallation; *(en un puesto)* reinstatement.

re·ins·ta·lar tr. to reinstall; *(en un puesto)* to reinstate.

re·in·te·gra·ción f. reintegration; *(reembolso)* refund.

re·in·te·grar tr. *(restablecer)* to reintegrate; *(reembolsar)* to refund —reflex. *(recibir reembolso)* to be reimbursed; *(volver)* to rejoin.

re·in·te·gro m. *(restablecimiento)* reintegration; *(reembolso)* reimbursement; *(pólizas)* fiscal stamps.

re·ír §58 intr. to laugh; *(los ojos)* to sparkle ♦ **r. a carcajadas** to laugh out loud • **r. de** to laugh at —tr. to laugh at —reflex. to laugh; *(burlarse de)* to laugh at.

rei·te·ra·ción f. reiteration.

rei·te·rar tr. to reiterate.

rei·te·ra·ti·vo, a adj. reiterative.

rei·vin·di·ca·ción f. LAW recovery; *(vindicación)* vindication.

rei·vin·di·car §70 tr. LAW to recover; *(vindicar)* to vindicate.

re·ja f. *(del arado)* plowshare; *(de ventana)* grating ♦ **estar entre rejas** to be behind bars.

re·ji·lla f. grille; *(de una silla)* wickerwork; *(de un horno)* fire grate; RAIL. luggage rack.

re·jun·tar tr. to gather.

re·ju·ve·ne·cer §58 tr., intr. & reflex. to rejuvenate.

re·ju·ve·ne·ci·mien·to m. rejuvenation.

re·la·ción f. relation; *(conexión)* connection; *(relato)* account; *(informe)* report; *(lista)* list; MATH. ratio ♦ **con** *or* **en r. a** in relation to • **guardar r. con** to bear relation with ♦ pl. *(cortejo)* courtship; *(conocidos)* acquaintances • **estar en buenas r. con** to be on good terms with • **mantener r. con** to be in touch with • **tener buenas r. con** to be well-connected.

re·la·cio·na·do, a adj. related *(con* to, with).

re·la·cio·nar tr. to relate —reflex. to be related; *(hacer amistades)* to make friends.

re·la·ja·ción f. relaxation; *(aflojamiento)* loosening; *(moral)* laxity.

re·la·ja·do, a adj. relaxed; *(aflojado)* loose; AMER. *(depravado)* depraved.

re·la·ja·mien·to m. var. of **relajación.**

re·la·jar tr. *(mente, cuerpo)* to relax; *(aflojar)* to loosen; *(la tensión)* to ease; *(divertir)* to amuse —reflex. to relax; *(viciarse)* to let oneself go.

re·la·jo m. AMER. COLL. *(desorden)* commotion; *(depravación)* debauchery.

re·la·mer tr. to lick —reflex. to lick one's lips.

re·la·mi·do, a adj. affected.

re·lám·pa·go m. lightning; FIG. flash.

re·lam·pa·gue·ar intr. to flash with lightning; FIG. to sparkle.

re·lam·pa·gue·o m. lightning.

re·lap·so, a I. adj. relapsed **II.** m.f. backslider.

re·la·ta·dor, ·ra m.f. narrator.
re·la·tar tr. to narrate.
re·la·ti·vi·dad f. relativity.
re·la·ti·vo, a adj. & m. GRAM. relative ♦ **en lo r. a** with regard to.
re·la·to m. narration; (*informe*) account; (*cuento*) story.
re·la·tor, ·ra I. adj. narrating II. m.f. (*de cuentos*) narrator; (*de expedientes*) court reporter.
re·le·er §43 tr. to reread.
re·le·gar §47 tr. to relegate ♦ **r. al olvido una cosa** to cast something into oblivion.
re·le·van·te adj. outstanding.
re·le·var tr. (*exonerar*) to relieve (*de* of, from); (*absolver*) to pardon; (*exaltar*) to praise; (*reemplazar*) to relieve (*de* from); PAINT. to paint in relief —reflex. to take turns.
re·le·vo m. (*acto*) change of the guard; (*soldado*) relief; SPORT. relay.
re·li·ca·rio m. reliquary; (*medallón*) locket.
re·lie·ve m. ART., GEOG. relief; (*estampado*) embossing; (*renombre*) prominence ♦ **poner en r.** to emphasize.
re·li·gión f. religion.
re·li·gio·si·dad f. religiosity.
re·li·gio·so, a I. adj. religious II. m. monk —f. nun.
re·lin·char intr. to neigh.
re·lin·cho m. neigh; FIG. whoop.
re·li·quia f. relic ♦ **r. de familia** family heirloom.
re·lla·nar tr. to level again —reflex. to stretch out in one's chair.
re·lla·no m. landing.
re·lle·nar tr. (*llenar*) to refill; (*llenar completamente*) to fill up; CUL. to stuff; SEW. to pad.
re·lle·no, a I. adj. stuffed II. m. stuffing; SEW. padding.
re·loj m. (*de pared*) clock; (*de pulsera*) watch ♦ **como un r.** like clockwork ♦ **r. de caja** grandfather's clock • **r. de sol** sundial • **r. despertador** alarm clock.
re·lo·je·rí·a f. (*arte*) watchmaking, clockmaking; (*taller*) watch *or* clock factory; (*tienda*) jewelry store.
re·lo·je·ro, a m.f. watchmaker.
re·lu·cien·te adj. shining.
re·lu·cir §44 intr. to shine ♦ **sacar a r.** (*mencionar*) to bring up; (*poner en relieve*) to bring out • **salir a r.** to come to light.
re·lum·bran·te adj. dazzling.
re·lum·brar intr. to dazzle.
re·ma·char tr. (*roblonar*) to rivet; (*machacar*) to clinch; FIG. to drive home.
re·ma·che m. (*de clavo*) clinching; (*roblón*) rivet.
re·ma·llar tr. to mend.
re·ma·nen·te m. remnant; COM. surplus.
re·man·gar §47 tr. to roll *or* tuck up.
re·man·so m. backwater.
re·mar intr. to row.
re·ma·ta·do, a adj. utter; LAW convicted.
re·ma·ta·dor, ·ra m. goal scorer —m.f. R.P. auctioneer.
re·ma·tar tr. (*acabar*) to finish (off); (*agotar*) to use up; (*matar*) to kill off; (*subastar*) to auction (off); ARCHIT. to top; SPORT. to shoot, kick (a goal) —intr. to end.
re·ma·te m. (*fin*) conclusion; (*toque final*) finishing touch; (*subasta*) auction; SPORT. shot ♦ **como r.** to top it all (off) • **de r.** utter.
re·me·dar tr. (*imitar*) to imitate; (*burlarse*) to

mimic.
re·me·dia·ble adj. remediable ♦ **fácilmente r.** easy to remedy.
re·me·diar tr. to remedy; (*ayudar*) to assist; (*librar*) to save; (*evitar*) to prevent.
re·me·dio m. remedy; (*ayuda*) relief ♦ **como último r.** as a last resort • **no haber (más) r.** to be unavoidable • **no tener más r.** to have no alternative (*que* but) • **no tener r.** to be hopeless.
re·me·do m. imitation; (*parodia*) travesty.
re·mem·bran·za f. remembrance.
re·me·mo·ra·ción f. remembrance.
re·me·mo·rar tr. to remember.
re·men·dar §49 tr. (*reparar*) to mend; SEW. to darn; (*corregir*) to correct.
re·men·dón, o·na m.f. mender; (*zapatero*) cobbler.
re·me·ro, a m.f. rower.
re·me·sa f. (*de dinero*) remittance; (*de mercancías*) consignment.
re·me·sar tr. (*dinero*) to remit; (*mercancías*) to consign.
re·mien·de, do see remendar.
re·mien·do m. (*acción*) mending; (*enmienda*) correction; SEW. patch.
re·mil·ga·do, a adj. affected.
re·mil·gar·se §47 reflex. to behave affectedly.
re·mil·go m. affectation.
re·mi·nis·cen·cia f. reminiscence.
re·mi·sión f. (*envío*) remittance; (*entrega*) delivery; (*perdón*) pardon; MED. remission.
re·mi·so, a adj. remiss.
re·mi·ten·te I. adj. remitting II. m.f. sender.
re·mi·tir tr. (*enviar*) to send; (*dinero*) to remit; (*perdonar*) to forgive; (*demorar*) to put off; (*ceder*) to diminish; (*al juicio de otro*) to leave to (someone's) judgment; (*referir*) to refer; COM. to ship —intr. to diminish —reflex. to refer (*a* to).
re·mo m. (*grande*) oar; (*pequeño*) paddle; SPORT rowing.
re·mo·jo m. soaking ♦ **poner en r.** to soak.
re·mo·la·cha f. beet.
re·mol·ca·dor, ·ra I. adj. towing II. m. AUTO. tow truck; MARIT. tugboat.
re·mol·car §70 tr. to tow.
re·mo·li·ne·ar tr. & intr. to whirl.
re·mo·li·no m. (*de agua*) whirlpool; (*de aire*) whirlwind; (*de pelo*) cowlick.
re·mo·lón, o·na I. adj. lazy II. m.f. loafer.
re·mo·lo·ne·ar intr. COLL. to loaf.
re·mol·que m. (*acción*) towing; (*vehículo que remolca*) tow truck; (*vehículo remolcado*) towed vehicle ♦ **a r.** in tow.
re·mon·tar tr. (*calzado*) to repair; (*un río*) to go up; (*superar*) to surmount; (*elevar*) to raise; (*encumbrar*) to honor —reflex. (*volar*) to soar; (*hasta el origen*) to go back (*a* to).
ré·mo·ra f. remora.
re·mor·der §78 tr. to bite, gnaw; FIG. to trouble ♦ **r. la conciencia** to weigh on one's conscience —reflex. to show.
re·mor·di·mien·to m. remorse.
re·mo·to, a adj. remote.
re·mo·ver §78 tr. (*mover*) to move; (*quitar*) to remove; (*destituir*) to dismiss; (*mezclar*) to stir; (*recuerdos*) to revive —reflex. to shake.
re·mo·zar §04 tr. to rejuvenate; FIG. to bring up to date —reflex. to be rejuvenated.
rem·pu·jón m. COLL. var. of empujón.
re·muer·da, do see remorder.

re·mue·va, vo see **remover.**
re·mu·ne·ra·ción f. remuneration.
re·mu·ne·rar tr. to remunerate.
re·mu·ne·ra·ti·vo, a adj. remunerative.
re·na·cen·tis·ta I. adj. Renaissance II. m.f. expert on the Renaissance.
re·na·cer §17 intr. *(nacer de nuevo)* to be reborn; *(recobrar fuerzas)* to recover; *(reaparecer)* to reappear.
re·na·ci·mien·to m. revival ♦ **R.** Renaissance.
re·na·cua·jo m. tadpole; FIG. shrimp.
re·nal adj. renal.
ren·ci·lla f. quarrel.
ren·cor m. rancor ♦ **guardar r. a alguien** to hold a grudge against someone.
ren·co·ro·so, a adj. resentful.
ren·di·ción f. *(entrega)* surrender; *(utilidad)* yield.
ren·di·do, a adj. *(obsequioso)* obsequious; *(sumiso)* submissive; *(cansado)* exhausted.
ren·di·ja f. crack.
ren·di·mien·to m. *(cansancio)* exhaustion; *(sumisión)* submissiveness; *(obsequiosidad)* obsequiousness; *(producto)* yield; *(funcionamiento)* performance.
ren·dir §48 tr. *(vencer)* to defeat; *(sujetar)* to dominate; *(entregar)* to surrender; *(restituir)* to give back; *(producir)* to yield; *(dar fruto)* to bear; *(cansar)* to tire out; *(las armas)* to lay down ♦ **r. cuentas de** to give an account of • **r. culto a** *(venerar)* to worship; *(homenajear)* to pay tribute to • **r. examen** to take an examination • **r. homenaje a** to pay homage to —intr. *(dar utilidad)* to yield; AMER. *(durar mucho)* to last longer than usual —reflex. *(someterse)* to surrender; *(entregarse)* to yield <r. a la fuerza to yield to force>; *(cansarse)* to exhaust oneself.
re·ne·ga·do, a adj. & m.f. *(apóstata)* apostate; COLL. *(de mal carácter)* gruff (person).
re·ne·gar §52 tr. to deny strongly —intr. RELIG. to apostasize; *(blasfemar)* to swear; COLL. *(quejarse)* to grumble ♦ **r. de** to renounce.
re·ne·gri·do, a adj. black.
ren·glón m. *(línea)* line (of words); *(partida)* item ♦ **a r. seguido** COLL. right after.
ren·go, a adj. & m.f. lame (person).
ren·gue·ar intr. AMER. to limp.
re·nie·gue, go see **renegar.**
re·no m. reindeer.
re·nom·bra·do, a adj. renowned.
re·nom·bre m. renown.
re·no·va·ción f. *(extensión)* renewal; *(restauración)* renovation.
re·no·var §19 tr. *(extender)* to renew; *(reemplazar)* to replace; *(restaurar)* to renovate.
ren·ta f. *(ingresos)* income; *(ganancia)* profit; *(interés)* interest; *(alquiler)* rent; *(anual)* annuity; *(deuda pública)* national debt ♦ **r. bruta** gross income.
ren·ta·ble adj. profitable.
ren·tar tr. *(producir renta)* to yield; AMER. *(alquilar)* to rent.
ren·tis·ta m.f. *(accionista)* bondholder; *(rico)* wealthy person.
re·nuen·cia f. reluctance.
re·nuen·te adj. reluctant.
re·nue·ve, vo see **renovar.**
re·nun·cia f. *(abandono)* renunciation; *(a un puesto)* resignation.
re·nun·cia·ción f./**mien·to** m. renunciation.
re·nun·ciar tr. *(abandonar)* to renounce; *(a un*

puesto) to resign; *(no aceptar)* to reject.
re·nun·cio m. COLL. lie.
re·ñi·de·ro m. pit ♦ **r. de gallos** cockpit.
re·ñi·do, a adj. *(enemistado)* at odds; *(difícil)* hard-fought ♦ **r. con** contrary to.
re·ñi·dor, ·ra adj. quarrelsome.
re·ñir §59 intr. to quarrel ♦ **r. en buena lid** to have a fair fight • **r. por** to fight for *or* over —tr. *(regañar)* to scold; *(llevar a cabo)* to wage.
re·o, a m.f. defendant.
re·o·jo adv. ♦ **mirar de r.** to look out of the corner of one's eye.
re·or·ga·ni·za·ción f. reorganization.
re·or·ga·ni·zar §04 tr. to reorganize.
re·pan·chi·gar·se/ti·gar·se §47 reflex. COLL. to stretch *or* sprawl out.
re·pa·ra·ción f. *(compostura)* repair.
re·pa·ra·dor, ·ra I. adj. restorative II. m.f. *(que compone)* repairer; *(reparón)* faultfinder —m. repairman.
re·pa·rar tr. *(componer)* to repair; *(notar)* to notice; *(desagraviar)* to make amends for; *(remediar)* to redress; *(restablecer)* to restore —intr. to stop ♦ **no r. en nada** to stop at nothing.
re·pa·ro m. *(objeción)* objection; *(duda)* misgiving; *(defensa)* protection ♦ **no andar con reparos** not to hesitate.
re·par·ti·dor, ·ra I. adj. distributing II. m.f. *(que reparte)* distributor; *(entregador)* deliverer ♦ **r. de periódicos** newspaper boy.
re·par·ti·ja f. AMER., COLL. var. of **reparto.**
re·par·tir tr. *(dividir)* to divide; *(distribuir)* to distribute; *(entregar)* to deliver; *(esparcir)* to spread out.
re·par·to m. *(distribución)* distribution; *(entrega)* delivery; CINEM., THEAT. cast.
re·pa·sa·dor m. AMER. dishcloth.
re·pa·sar tr. *(pasar)* to pass (by) again; *(examinar)* to review; *(hojear)* to glance over; *(explicar, hacer)* to go over again —intr. to pass (by) again.
re·pa·so m. review ♦ **dar un r. a** to look over *or* through.
re·pa·tria·ción f. repatriation.
re·pa·tria·do, a I. adj. repatriated II. m.f. repatriate.
re·pa·triar §30 tr. & reflex. to repatriate (oneself).
re·pe·cho m. short steep incline ♦ **a r.** uphill.
re·pe·len·te adj. repellent.
re·pe·ler tr. to repel; *(rechazar)* to reject.
re·pen·te m. start ♦ **de r.** suddenly.
re·pen·ti·no, a adj. sudden.
re·per·cu·sión f. repercussion.
re·per·cu·tir intr. *(rebotar)* to rebound; *(resonar)* to reverberate ♦ **r. en** to have repercussions on.
re·per·to·rio m. repertory, repertoire.
re·pe·ti·ción f. repetition; *(mecanismo)* repeater.
re·pe·tir §48 tr. to repeat; *(comer más)* to have a second helping of; *(recitar)* to recite —intr. to repeat —reflex. to repeat itself *or* oneself.
re·pe·ti·ti·vo, a adj. repetitive.
re·pi·car §70 intr. to ring out.
re·pi·que·te·ar intr. *(las campanas)* to ring; *(tambor)* to beat; *(golpear)* to drum.
re·pi·que·te·o m. *(de campanas)* lively ringing; *(de lluvia)* pitter-patter; *(con los dedos)* tap-

ping.
re·pi·sa f. shelf.
re·pi·ta, to, tiera, tió see **repetir**.
re·plan·tar tr. to replant.
re·plan·te·ar tr. *(exponer)* to restate; ARCHIT. to lay out a ground plan of.
re·ple·gar §52 tr. to fold over; AER. to retract —reflex. MIL. to retreat.
re·ple·to, a adj. full ♦ **r. de** packed with.
ré·pli·ca f. *(contestación)* retort; *(copia)* replica; LAW replication.
re·pli·car §70 intr. to retort.
re·plie·go, gue see **replegar**.
re·po·bla·ción f. repopulation.
re·po·blar §19 tr. to repopulate.
re·po·llo m. cabbage.
re·po·ner §54 tr. *(poner)* to put back; *(reemplazar)* to replace; *(replicar)* to reply; THEAT. to revive —reflex. *(recuperarse)* to recover; *(serenarse)* to calm down.
re·por·ta·je m. *(artículo)* report; *(de noticias)* news coverage; *(entrevista)* interview.
re·por·tar tr. to bring —reflex. to control oneself.
re·por·te m. *(chisme)* gossip; *(noticia)* news.
re·por·te·ro, a I. adj. reporting II. m.f. reporter.
re·po·sa·piés m.inv. footrest.
re·po·sar intr. *(descansar)* to rest; *(yacer)* to lie.
re·po·si·ción f. *(acción)* replenishment; THEAT. revival.
re·po·so m. repose.
re·pos·te·rí·a f. *(tienda)* pastry shop; *(oficio)* confectionery.
re·pos·te·ro m.f. confectioner.
re·pren·der tr. to reprimand.
re·pren·sión f. reprimand.
re·pre·sa f. dam.
re·pre·sa·lia f. reprisal.
re·pre·sar tr. to dam.
re·pre·sen·ta·ción f. representation; THEAT. performance.
re·pre·sen·tan·te I. adj. representing II. m.f. representative.
re·pre·sen·tar tr. to represent; *(volver a presentar)* to present again; *(aparentar)* to appear to be; THEAT. to perform —intr. to picture.
re·pre·sen·ta·ti·vo, a adj. representative.
re·pre·sión f. repression.
re·pre·si·vo, a adj. repressive.
re·pre·sor, ·ra I. adj. repressing II. m.f. repressor.
re·pri·men·da f. reprimand.
re·pri·mir tr. & reflex. to repress (oneself).
re·pro·bar §19 tr. *(desaprobar)* to disapprove; *(en exámenes)* to fail.
ré·pro·bo, a adj. & m.f. reprobate.
re·pro·char tr. to reproach.
re·pro·che m. reproach.
re·pro·duc·ción f. reproduction.
re·pro·du·cir §22 tr. & reflex. to reproduce.
re·pro·duc·tor, ·ra I. adj. *(que copia)* reproducing; BIOL. reproductive; ZOOL. breeding II. m.f. reproducer; ZOOL. breeder.
re·prue·be, bo see **reprobar**.
rep·tar intr. to crawl.
rep·til I. adj. reptilian II. m. reptile.
re·pú·bli·ca f. republic.
re·pu·bli·ca·no, a adj. & m.f. republican.
re·pu·dia·ción f. repudiation.
re·pu·diar tr. to repudiate; LAW to renounce.

re·pu·dio m. repudiation.
re·pu·drir tr. & reflex. to rot away; FIG. to eat one's heart out.
re·pues·to, a I. see **reponer** II. adj. MED. recovered III. m. *(reserva)* supply; *(pieza)* spare (part) ♦ **de r.** spare.
re·pug·nan·cia f. repugnance.
re·pug·nan·te adj. repugnant.
re·pug·nar intr. to detest <*las arañas me repugnan* I detest spiders>.
re·pu·jar tr. to do repoussé on.
re·pul·gar §47 tr. to hem.
re·pul·sar tr. to reject.
re·pul·sión f. repulsion.
re·pul·si·vo, a adj. repulsive.
re·pun·tar tr. to turn.
re·pun·te m. turning.
re·pu·ta·ción f. reputation.
re·pu·tar tr. to deem.
re·que·brar §49 tr. *(volver a quebrar)* to break again; *(lisonjear)* to flatter.
re·que·mar tr. to burn.
re·que·ri·mien·to m. requirement; LAW summons; *(demanda)* request.
re·que·rir §65 tr. *(necesitar)* to require; *(intimar)* to order; *(solicitar)* to request ♦ **r. (de amores)** to woo.
re·que·són m. *(queso)* cottage *or* pot cheese; *(cuajada)* curd.
re·que·te·bién adv. COLL. wonderfully.
re·quie·bro m. flattery.
ré·quiem m. requiem.
re·quie·ra, ro, quiriera, quirió see **requerir**.
re·qui·sa f. *(revista)* inspection; MIL. requisition; AMER. search.
re·qui·sar tr. to requisition; AMER. to search.
re·qui·si·ción f. requisition.
re·qui·si·to m. requirement.
res f. animal ♦ **r. vacuna** head of cattle.
re·sa·bi·do, a adj. well-known.
re·sa·bio m. *(sabor)* unpleasant aftertaste; *(vicio)* bad habit.
re·sa·ca f. MARIT. undertow; COM. redraft.
re·sa·la·do, a adj. COLL. charming.
re·sa·lir §63 intr. to jut out.
re·sal·tar intr. to jut out; FIG. to stand out ♦ **hacer r.** to stress.
re·sar·ci·ble adj. indemnifiable.
re·sar·cir §35 tr. to indemnify —reflex. to make up (de *for*).
res·ba·la·di·zo, a adj. slippery.
res·ba·lar intr. to slip; AUTO to skid.
res·ba·lón m. slip; AUTO. skid.
res·ba·lo·so, a adj. slippery.
res·ca·ta·dor, ·ra I. adj. rescuing II. m.f. rescuer.
res·ca·tar tr. *(recobrar)* to recover; *(cautivos)* to ransom; *(salvar)* to rescue.
res·ca·te m. *(acción)* rescue; *(recobro)* recovery; *(dinero)* ransom money.
res·cin·dir tr. to rescind.
res·ci·sión f. rescission.
res·col·do m. embers.
re·se·car §70 tr. & reflex. to dry out.
re·sen·ti·do, a adj. resentful.
re·sen·ti·mien·to m. resentment.
re·sen·tir·se §65 reflex. *(sentir los efectos)* to feel the effects; *(debilitarse)* to be impaired; FIG. to feel hurt ♦ **r. por** to take offense at.
re·se·ña f. MIL. inspection; *(descripción)* outline; *(relación)* account; *(análisis)* review.
re·se·ñar tr. MIL. to inspect; *(describir)* to de-

scribe; *(analizar)* to review.
re·se·ro m. AMER. herdsman.
re·ser·va f. reserve; *(provisión)* stock; *(reservación, excepción)* reservation; *(discreción)* discretion; COM., MIL. reserve ♦ **a r. de** except for • **a r. de que** unless • **sin r.** openly.
re·ser·va·ción f. reservation.
re·ser·va·do, a I. adj. reserved; *(discreto)* discreet; *(confidencial)* confidential II. m. reserved room *or* area.
re·ser·var tr. to reserve; *(guardar)* to save; *(encubrir)* to conceal; *(no comunicar)* to withhold; *(dilatar)* to put off; *(dispensar)* to exempt —reflex. to save one's strength *or* oneself.
re·ser·vis·ta I. adj. reserve II. m. reservist.
res·fria·do m. cold.
res·friar §30 tr. *(enfriar)* to cool; *(moderar)* to temper —intr. to cool —reflex. to catch a cold.
res·guar·dar tr. & reflex. to protect (oneself).
res·guar·do m. *(protección)* protection; *(documento)* safeguard.
re·si·den·cia f. residence.
re·si·den·cial adj. residential.
re·si·den·te adj. & m.f. resident.
re·si·dir intr. to reside.
re·si·duo m. residue ♦ pl. waste.
re·sien·ta, to see **resentirse**.
re·sig·na·ción f. resignation.
re·sig·nar tr. & reflex. to resign (oneself).
re·si·na f. resin.
re·sin·tie·ra, tió see **resentirse**.
re·sis·ten·cia f. resistance; *(aguante)* endurance ♦ **oponer r.** to resist • **r. de tensión** tensile strength.
re·sis·ten·te adj. resistant; BOT. hardy.
re·sis·tir intr. to resist; *(durar)* to endure —tr. to resist; *(aguantar)* to bear —reflex. to resist; *(luchar)* to fight; *(negarse)* to refuse (*a* to).
re·so·llar §19 intr. to breathe heavily; FIG. to show signs of life ♦ **sin r.** COLL. without a word.
res·ma f. ream.
re·so·lu·ción f. resolution; *(decisión)* decision; *(solución)* solution.
re·so·lu·to, a adj. resolute.
re·sol·ver §78 tr. to resolve; *(solucionar)* to solve; *(resumir)* to sum up; CHEM. to dissolve —reflex. to resolve; *(ser solucionado)* to resolve itself ♦ **r. por** to decide in favor of —intr. to decide.
re·so·nan·cia f. resonance; FIG. repercussion ♦ **tener r.** to cause a stir.
re·so·nan·te adj. resounding.
re·so·nar §19 intr. to resound; FIG. to have repercussions.
re·so·plar intr. to puff.
re·so·pli·do/plo m. puffing.
re·sor·te m. spring ♦ pl. **tocar los r.** to pull the strings.
res·pal·dar¹ m. back of a chair.
res·pal·dar² tr. *(apuntar)* to endorse; *(garantizar)* to back —reflex. to lean back; *(basarse)* to base oneself (*en* on).
res·pal·do m. *(de silla)* back; *(garantía)* backing.
res·pec·ti·vo, a adj. respective.
res·pec·to m. respect ♦ **al r.** about the matter • **r. a** *or* **de** with respect to.
res·pe·tar tr. to respect.
res·pe·to m. respect ♦ **faltar al r.** to be disrespectful.

res·pe·tuo·so, a adj. respectful.
res·pin·gar §47 intr. to balk.
res·pin·go m. start; COLL. *(movimiento)* gesture of impatience.
res·pi·ra·ción f. respiration.
res·pi·ra·de·ro m. *(abertura)* vent; *(cañería)* ventilation shaft; *(descanso)* rest.
res·pi·ra·dor m. *(máquina)* respirator; ANAT. respiratory muscle.
res·pi·rar intr. to breathe; FIG. to breathe a sigh of relief ♦ **no dejar r. a alguien** not to give someone a moment's peace • **no r.** COLL. not to breathe a word —tr. to breathe (in); FIG. to exude <*r. honradez* to exude honesty>.
res·pi·ro m. *(respiración)* respiration; *(descanso)* rest, respite; FIG. break.
res·plan·de·cer §17 intr. to shine.
res·plan·de·cien·te adj. resplendent.
res·plan·dor/de·ci·mien·to m. brightness; *(de llamas)* glow; *(brillo)* shine; *(esplendor)* splendor.
res·pon·der tr. to answer —intr. *(contestar)* to answer; *(corresponder)* to return; *(replicar)* to answer back; *(resultar)* to perform <*la máquina nueva responde bien* the new machine performs well>; *(reaccionar)* to respond ♦ **r. a una descripción** to fit a description • **r. a una necesidad** to meet a need • **r. a una obligación** to honor an obligation • **r. por** to be responsible for.
res·pon·sa·bi·li·dad f. responsibility ♦ **r. limitada** limited liability.
res·pon·sa·bi·li·zar §04 tr. to make responsible —reflex. to take the responsibility.
res·pon·sa·ble adj. responsible; LAW liable ♦ **hacerse r. de** to assume responsibility for.
res·pon·so m. RELIG. prayer for the dead.
res·pues·ta f. answer.
res·que·bra·(ja·)du·ra f./**·ja·mien·to** m. crack.
res·que·bra·jar tr. & reflex. to crack.
res·que·brar §49 intr. to crack.
res·que·mor m. *(resentimiento)* resentment; *(remordimiento)* remorse.
res·qui·cio m. crack; FIG. glimmer <*un r. de esperanza* a glimmer of hope>.
res·ta f. subtraction.
res·ta·ble·cer §17 tr. to reestablish —reflex. to recover.
res·ta·ble·ci·mien·to m. reestablishment, restoration; MED. recovery.
res·ta·llar intr. to crack.
res·tan·te I. adj. remaining II. m. remainder.
res·tar tr. MATH. to subtract; *(quitar)* to take away —intr. to remain; MATH. to subtract.
res·tau·ra·ción f. restoration.
res·tau·ra·dor, ·ra I. adj. restoring I. m.f. restorer.
res·tau·ran·te m. restaurant.
res·tau·rar tr. to restore.
res·ti·tu·ción f. restitution.
res·ti·tuir §18 tr. to restore —reflex. to come back.
res·to m. remainder; COM. balance ♦ pl. leftovers • **r. mortales** mortal remains.
res·to·rán m. restaurant.
res·tre·gar §52 tr. to rub.
res·tric·ción f. restriction.
res·tric·ti·vo, a adj. restrictive.
res·trin·gir §32 tr. to restrict; MED. to contract —reflex. to cut down on.
res·tri·ñir §12 tr. *(astringir)* to constrict; *(estreñir)* to constipate.

re·su·ci·tar tr. to resuscitate; FIG. to revive —intr. to be resuscitated.

re·sue·lle, llo see **resollar.**

re·sue·llo m. breathing ♦ **perder el r.** to be out of breath.

re·suel·to, a I. see **resolver II.** adj. determined.

re·suel·va, vo see **resolver.**

re·sue·ne see **resonar.**

re·sul·ta f. result, consequence ♦ **de resultas** as a result of.

re·sul·ta·do m. result; (consecuencia) outcome; MATH. answer ♦ **dar r.** to produce results.

re·sul·tar intr. to turn out to be <si resulta posible, te acompañaremos if it turns out to be possible, we'll go with you>; (salir) to turn out <la investigación no resultó como pronosticaban the investigation didn't turn out as they predicted>; (funcionar) to work (out); (encontrar) to find <ella me resulta muy simpática I find her very nice> ♦ **estar resultando** to be beginning <este tema me está resultando aburrido ya this topic is beginning to bore me> • **r. de** to result or stem from • **r. que** to turn out that.

re·su·men m. summary ♦ **en r.** in short.

re·su·mi·da·men·te adv. briefly.

re·su·mi·de·ro m. AMER. sewer.

re·su·mir tr. to summarize; (acortar) to shorten —reflex. to be summed up ♦ **r. en** to boil down to.

re·sur·gi·mien·to m. resurgence.

re·sur·gir §32 intr. to reappear.

re·su·rrec·ción f. resurrection.

re·ta·dor, ·ra I. adj. challenging **II.** m.f. challenger.

re·ta·guar·dia f. rear.

re·ta·hí·la f. string.

re·tar tr. (desafiar) to challenge; (censurar) to scold.

re·tar·dar tr. to delay.

re·tar·do m. delay.

re·ta·zo m. (de tela) remnant; (de discurso) fragment.

re·te·ner §69 tr. to retain; (deducir) to withhold.

re·te·ni·mien·to m. retention.

re·ten·ti·vo, a I. adj. retentive **II.** f. memory.

re·ti·cen·cia f. reticence.

re·ti·cen·te adj. reticent.

re·ti·cu·lar adj. reticular.

re·tí·cu·lo m. BIOL. reticulum; OPT. reticle.

re·ti·na f. retina.

re·ti·ni·tis f. retinitis.

re·tin·to, a adj. dark brown.

re·ti·ra·da f. retreat ♦ **emprender una r.** to beat a retreat.

re·ti·ra·do, a I. adj. secluded; (jubilado) retired **II.** m.f. retired person.

re·ti·rar tr. (remover) to remove; (separar) to move away; (de circulación) to withdraw; (quitar) to take away; (retractar) to retract; (jubilar) to retire; DIPL. to recall; FIN. to withdraw —reflex. (apartarse) to withdraw; (irse para atrás) to move back; (jubilarse) to retire; MIL. to retreat ♦ **r. a dormir** to go to bed.

re·ti·ro m. (retirada) withdrawal; (lugar) retreat; (jubilación) retirement; (pensión) pension; RELIG. retreat.

re·to m. challenge.

re·to·ba·do, a adj. AMER. stubborn.

re·to·bar AMER. tr. to wrap in leather —reflex.

to become irritated.

re·to·car §70 tr. PHOTOG. to touch up; SEW. to alter; FIG. to put the finishing touch on.

re·to·mar tr. to take back.

re·to·ñar intr. to sprout; FIG. to reappear.

re·to·ño m. sprout.

re·to·que m. PHOTOG. retouching; SEW. alteration.

re·tor·cer §71 tr. to twist; (los bigotes) to twirl; (interpretar mal) to misinterpret, twist —reflex. to twist; (de dolor) to writhe.

re·tor·ci·do, a adj. twisted.

re·tor·ci·jón m. var. of **retortijón.**

re·tor·ci·mien·to m. (torsión) twisting; (contorsión) writhing.

re·tó·ri·co, a I. adj. rhetorical **II.** m. rhetorician —f. rhetoric.

re·tor·nar tr. to return, give back —intr. to return, go back.

re·tor·no m. return; (trueque) exchange.

re·tor·ti·jón m. twisting ♦ **r. de tripas** stomach cramps.

re·to·zar §04 intr. to frolic.

re·to·zo m. frolic.

re·to·zón, o·na adj. frolicsome.

re·trac·tar tr. & reflex. to retract.

re·trác·til adj. retractable.

re·tra·er §72 tr. to dissuade; LAW to redeem —reflex. (refugiarse) to take refuge; (retirarse) to retreat.

re·traí·do, a adj. (solitario) reclusive; (poco comunicativo) withdrawn.

re·trai·mien·to m. seclusion.

re·tran·ca f. breeching.

re·trans·mi·tir tr. to retransmit; (difundir) to rebroadcast; TELEC. to relay.

re·tra·sa·do, a adj. (tardío) late; (persona) retarded; (país) backward.

re·tra·sar tr. (demorar) to delay; (aplazar) to postpone; (un reloj) to set back —intr. to lag, fall behind; (un reloj) to be slow —reflex. to be late or delayed.

re·tra·so m. delay; (subdesarrollo) backwardness ♦ **con r.** late.

re·tra·tar tr. PAINT. to paint a portrait of; (describir) to depict; PHOTOG. to photograph —reflex. PAINT. to have one's portrait painted; PHOTOG. to have one's photograph taken; (reflejarse) to be reflected.

re·tra·tis·ta m.f. PAINT. portrait painter; PHOTOG. photographer.

re·tra·to m. PAINT. portrait; (descripción) trait, description; AMER. photograph.

re·tre·ta f. MIL. retreat; AMER. (retahíla) series, string; MUS. open-air band concert.

re·tre·te m. toilet.

re·tri·bu·ción f. retribution.

re·tri·buir §18 tr. (pagar) to pay; (recompensar) to reward; AMER. to reciprocate.

re·tro·ac·ti·vi·dad f. retroactivity.

re·tro·ac·ti·vo, a adj. retroactive.

re·tro·ce·der intr. (volver atrás) to go back; (un paso) to step back; (nivel) to recede; MIL. to withdraw.

re·tro·ce·so m. (regresión) retrocession; ARM. recoil; MIL. withdrawal; MECH. return.

re·tró·gra·do, a I. adj. retrogressive; ASTRON. retrograde; POL. reactionary **II.** m.f. reactionary.

re·tro·pro·pul·sión f. jet propulsion.

re·tros·pec·ción f. retrospection.

re·tros·pec·ti·vo, a adj. & f. retrospective.

re·tro·tra·er §72 tr. to antedate.
re·tro·vi·sor m. rearview mirror.
re·tru·car §70 intr. R.P., COLL. to retort.
re·trué·ca·no m. play on words.
re·tum·bar intr. to resound.
re·ú·ma or **reu·ma** m. var. of **reumatismo**.
reu·má·ti·co, a adj. & m.f. rheumatic.
reu·ma·tis·mo m. rheumatism.
reu·nión f. (de negocios) meeting; (de ex-alum-nos) reunion; (fiesta) party.
reu·nir §60 tr. (juntar) to unite; (agrupar) to gather; (requisitos) to fulfill; (fondos) to collect; MIL. to assemble —reflex. (juntarse) to unite; (en una reunión) to meet.
re·vá·li·da f. revalidation; (examen) final examination; (certificado) certificate.
re·va·li·da·ción f. revalidation; (renovación) renewal.
re·va·li·dar tr. to revalidate; (renovar) to renew.
re·va·lo·ri·za·ción f. revaluation.
re·va·lo·ri·zar §04 tr. to revalue.
re·van·cha f. revenge.
re·ve·la·ción f. revelation.
re·ve·la·do m. PHOTOG. developing.
re·ve·la·dor, ·ra I. adj. revealing **II.** m. PHOTOG. developer.
re·ve·lar tr. to reveal; PHOTOG. to develop.
re·ven·de·dor, ·ra I. adj. reselling **II.** m.f. (que revende) reseller; (detallista) retailer ♦ **r. de entradas** ticket scalper.
re·ven·der tr. to resell; COM. to retail.
re·ven·ta f. resale.
re·ven·tar §49 intr. var. (globo) to burst; (neumático) to blow; (olas) to break; COLL. (morir) to kick the bucket ♦ **r. de cansancio** to be exhausted ♦ **r. de envidia** to be bursting with envy —tr. to burst; (aplastar) to smash; (causar) to exhaust; (causar daño) to wreck; COLL. (molestar) to annoy —reflex. to burst; (cansarse) to exhaust oneself.
re·ven·tón m. burst; (de neumático) flat tire.
re·ver §77 tr. to review; LAW to retry.
re·ver·be·ra·ción f. reverberation.
re·ver·be·ran·te adj. reverberating.
re·ver·be·rar intr. to reverberate.
re·ve·ren·cia f. reverence; (saludo) bow ♦ **ha·cer una r.** to bow.
re·ve·ren·ciar tr. to revere.
re·ve·ren·dí·si·mo, a adj. Most Reverend.
re·ve·ren·do, a adj. reverend; COLL. huge.
re·ve·ren·te adj. respectful.
re·ver·so, a adj. & m. reverse.
re·ver·tir §65 intr. to revert.
re·vés m. (envés) back; (desgracia) setback ♦ **al r.** (al contrario) backwards; (con lo de dentro fuera) inside out ♦ **al r. de** contrary to.
re·ve·sa·do, a adj. intricate.
re·ves·ti·mien·to m. covering.
re·ves·tir §48 tr. to cover; FIG. to take on.
re·vien·te, to see **reventar**.
re·vier·ta, to, virtiera, virtió see **revertir**.
re·vi·sar tr. to check.
re·vi·sión f. revision.
re·vi·sio·nis·ta adj. & m.f. revisionist.
re·vi·sor, ·ra I. adj. revising, checking **II.** m.f. inspector ♦ **r. de cuentas** auditor.
re·vis·ta f. (periódico) magazine; (revisión) review; THEAT. revue ♦ **pasar r.** to review ● **r. literaria** literary review.
re·vis·ta, to see **revestir**.
re·vis·te·ro, a m.f.c. (persona) reviewer; (mueble)

magazine rack.
re·vis·tie·ra, tió see **revestir**.
re·vi·ta·li·zar §04 tr. to revitalize.
re·vi·vi·fi·car §70 tr. to revive.
re·vi·vir intr. to revive.
re·vo·ca·ción f. revocation; DIPL. recall.
re·vo·ca·dor m. plasterer.
re·vo·car §70 tr. (anular) to repeal; (destituir) to dismiss; CONSTR. to plaster.
re·vol·car §73 tr. to knock down —reflex. (en el suelo) to roll; (en el fango) to wallow.
re·vol·cón m. COLL. fall.
re·vo·lo·te·ar intr. to flutter.
re·vo·lo·te·o m. fluttering.
re·vol·ti·jo/llo m. jumble ♦ **r. de huevos** scrambled eggs.
re·vol·to·so, a I. adj. troublemaking **II.** m.f. troublemaker; (rebelde) rebel.
re·vo·lu·ción f. revolution.
re·vo·lu·cio·nar tr. to revolutionize.
re·vo·lu·cio·na·rio, a adj. & m.f. revolutionary.
re·vol·ver §78 tr. (mezclar) to mix; (líquidos) to stir; (agitar) to shake; (desordenar) to mix up; (producir náuseas) to turn —reflex. (dar vueltas) to turn around; (revolcarse) to roll; (retorcerse) to writhe ♦ **r. contra alguien** to turn against someone.
re·vól·ver m. revolver.
re·vo·que m. plaster.
re·vuel·co m. (en el suelo) roll; (en el fango) wallowing.
re·vue·lo m. (revoloteo) fluttering; (turbación) commotion ♦ **de r.** in passing.
re·vuel·ta f. revolt; (riña) quarrel.
re·vuel·to, a I. adj. (en desorden) jumbled; (inquieto) turbulent; (travieso) mischievous; (enrevesado) complicated ♦ **huevos revueltos** scrambled eggs.
rey m. king ♦ **a cuerpo de r.** like a king ● **día de Reyes** Epiphany.
re·yer·ta f. quarrel.
re·za·gar §47 tr. (dejar atrás) to leave behind; (aplazar) to put off —reflex. to lag behind.
re·zar §04 tr. to say —intr. to pray. ♦ **según reza el refrán** as the saying goes.
re·zo m. prayer.
re·zon·ga·dor, ·ra I. adj. grumbling **II.** m.f. grumbler.
re·zon·gar §47 intr. to grumble.
re·zu·mar tr., intr. & reflex. to ooze.
rí·a, río see **reír**.
ria·cho/chue·lo m. stream.
ri·be·ra f. shore.
ri·be·re·ño/ra·no, a I. adj. the shore, riparian **II.** shore dweller.
ri·be·te m. (borde) trimming; (a un cuento) embellishment.
ri·be·te·a·do I. adj. trimmed **II.** m. trimming.
ri·be·te·ar tr. to trim.
ri·ca·cho, a/chón, o·na m.f. COLL. moneybags.
ri·ca·men·te adv. richly.
ri·ci·no m. castor-oil plant ♦ **aceite de r.** castor oil.
ri·co, a I. adj. rich; (acaudalado) wealthy; (fértil) fertile; (abundante) abundant; (magnífico) luxurious; (sabroso) delicious; COLL. (simpático) adorable ♦ **hacerse r.** to get rich **II.** m.f. rich person ♦ **los ricos** the rich.
ric·tus m. rictus ♦ **r. de dolor** wince of pain.
ri·cu·ra f. tastiness; FIG. cutie.
ri·di·cu·lez f. absurdity; (insignificancia) trifle.

ri·di·cu·li·zar §04 tr. to ridicule.
ri·dí·cu·lo, a I. adj. ridiculous **II.** m. ridiculous situation ♦ **hacer el r.** to make a fool of oneself • **poner en r.** to make a fool of.
rie·go m. irrigation ♦ **boca de r.** hydrant.
rie·go, gue see **regar.**
riel m. rail ♦ **andar sobre rieles** to go like clockwork.
rien·da f. rein; (sujeción) restraint ♦ **a r. suelta** (con velocidad) at full speed; (sin sujeción) without restraint.
rie·ra, rió see **reír.**
ries·go m. risk.
ri·fa f. raffle.
ri·far tr. to raffle.
ri·fle m. rifle.
ri·gi·dez f. rigidity.
rí·gi·do, a adj. stiff.
ri·gie·ra, gió see **regir.**
ri·gor m. rigor ♦ **de r.** de rigueur.
ri·gu·ro·so, a adj. rigorous.
ri·ja, o see **regir.**
ri·ma f. rhyme ♦ pl. poems.
ri·mar intr. & tr. to rhyme.
rim·bom·ban·cia f. bombast.
rim·bom·ban·te adj. resounding, echoing; (pomposo) bombastic; (ostentoso) showy.
rí·mel m. mascara.
rin·cón m. corner.
rin·co·ne·ra f. corner furniture.
rin·da, do, diera, dió see **rendir.**
ri·no·ce·ron·te m. rhinoceros.
ri·ña f. quarrel.
ri·ña, ño, ñera, ñó see **reñir.**
ri·ñón m. kidney ♦ **costar un r.** COLL. to cost a fortune ♦ pl. lower back.
rí·o m. river; FIG. flood ♦ **r. abajo** downstream.
ri·que·za f. (abundancia) wealth; (opulencia) opulence; (fecundidad) richness ♦ pl. riches • **r. naturales** natural resources.
ri·sa f. laugh <una r. ahogada a stifled laugh>; laughter <no hizo caso de la r. de los estudiantes he took no notice of the students' laughter>; laugh, joke <la explicación que dio fue una r. the explanation he gave was a laugh>; (hazmerreír) laughingstock ♦ **desternillarse o reventar de r.** to burst with laughter • **contener la r.** to keep a straight face • **dar r. a alguien** to make someone laugh • **¡qué r.!** how funny! • **tener un ataque de r.** to have a fit of laughter • **tomar a r.** to take as a joke.
ris·co m. cliff.
ri·si·ble adj. laughable.
ri·so·ta·da f. guffaw.
ris·tra f. string <r. de ajos string of garlic>.
ri·sue·ño, a adj. smiling; (agradable) pleasant; (favorable) bright.
rít·mi·co, a adj. rhythmic.
rit·mo m. rhythm.
ri·to m. rite, ceremony.
ri·tual adj. & m. ritual.
ri·val adj. & m.f. rival.
ri·va·li·dad f. rivalry.
ri·va·li·zar §04 intr. to rival.
ri·za·do m. curling.
ri·zar §04 tr. (pelo) to curl; (olas) to ripple —reflex. (pelo) to curl (up); (mar) to become choppy.
ri·zo m. (mechón) ringlet; TEX. ribbed velvet.
ró·ba·lo or ro·ba·lo m. ICHTH. bass.
ro·bar tr. to rob; (saquear) to burgle; (la voluntad) to steal (away).

ro·ble m. oak; FIG. pillar of strength.
ro·blón m. (clavo) rivet; (teja) ridge of tiles.
ro·bo m. robbery; (en naipes) draw.
ro·bus·te·cer §17 tr. to strengthen.
ro·bus·to, a adj. robust.
ro·ca f. rock.
ro·ce m. (acción) rubbing; (toque) touch; (trato frecuente) close contact; (fricción) animosity.
ro·cia·dor m. sprayer.
ro·cia·du·ra f./**mien·to** m. sprinkling.
ro·ciar §30 intr. to fall (dew) —tr. (mojar) to sprinkle; (arrojar) to scatter.
ro·cín m. (asno) donkey; (caballo bajo) workhorse.
ro·cí·o m. dew; (llovizna) sprinkle.
ro·co·so, a adj. rocky.
ro·da·ba·llo m. turbot, flounder.
ro·da·do, a R.P. vehicle.
ro·da·ja f. (de metal) disc; (de fruta) slice.
ro·da·je m. (conjunto de ruedas) wheels; (impuesto) vehicle tax; CINEM. filming.
ro·da·mien·to m. bearing.
ro·dar §19 intr. (girar) to roll; (funcionar) to run; (moverse con ruedas) to run (on wheels); (caer dando vueltas) to tumble (down); (vagar) to roam; CINEM. to shoot —tr. (hacer rodar) to roll; CINEM. to shoot.
ro·de·ar intr. to go around; (ir por el camino más largo) to go by a roundabout way; (hablar con rodeos) to beat around the bush —tr. to surround; (dar la vuelta) to go around; AMER. to round up —reflex. ♦ **r. de** to surround oneself with.
ro·de·o m. (acción) surrounding; (camino indirecto) roundabout way; (fiesta) rodeo; (de ganado) roundup; (circunloquio) circumlocution; (subterfugio) subterfuge ♦ **andar con rodeos** to beat around the bush.
ro·de·te m. bun.
ro·di·lla f. knee ♦ **de rodillas** on one's knees.
ro·di·lla·da f./**zo** m. blow with the knee.
ro·di·lle·ra f. knee guard.
ro·di·llo m. roller; CUL. rolling pin.
ro·e·dor, ·ra I. adj. gnawing **II.** m. rodent.
ro·ent·gen/ge·nio m. roentgen.
ro·er §61 tr. to gnaw; (molestar) to worry; (gastar) to erode.
ro·gar §16 tr. to beg —intr. to pray ♦ **hacerse de r.** to play hard to get.
ro·ji·zo, a adj. reddish.
ro·jo, a I. adj. (colorado) red; (mejillas) ruddy ♦ **mal r.** VET. swine fever • **ponerse r.** to blush • **ponerse r. de ira** to become furious **II.** m.f. red, revolutionary —m. (color) red ♦ **al r.** red-hot • **estar al r. vivo** to be heated or tense.
rol·da·na f. pulley wheel.
ro·lli·zo, a I. adj. (redondo) round; (grueso) chubby, plump **II.** m. round log.
ro·llo m. roll <un r. de cinta adhesiva a roll of adhesive tape>; (de escritura) scroll; (de cuerda) coil; MECH., TECH. roller; CUL. rolling pin ♦ **en r.** rolled (up) • **soltar el r.** COLL. to go on and on.
ro·ma·na f. steelyard.
ro·man·ce I. adj. Romance (language) **II.** m. (lengua moderna) Romance language; (castellano) Spanish (language); LIT. ballad; POET. romance ♦ **en buen r.** in clear language.
ro·man·ce·ro, a m.f. writer of romances —m. collection of romances.
ro·ma·no, a adj. Roman ♦ **número r.** Roman numeral.

ro·mán·ti·co, a adj. & m.f. romantic.
rom·bo m. rhombus.
ro·me·rí·a f. *(peregrinación)* pilgrimage; *(fiesta)* festival.
ro·me·ro m. rosemary.
ro·mo, a adj. GEOM. obtuse; ANAT. snub-nosed.
rom·pe·ca·be·zas m.inv. jigsaw puzzle; FIG. riddle.
rom·pe·de·ro, a adj. fragile.
rom·pe·hie·los m.inv. icebreaker.
rom·pe·nue·ces m.inv. nutcracker.
rom·pe·o·las m.inv. breakwater.
rom·per §80 tr. to break; *(en pedazos)* to tear or rip (up); *(surcar)* to plow; *(iniciar)* to begin; *(cancelar)* to break off; AGR. to plow; MIL. to break through ♦ **r. el paso** to break step • **r. filas** to fall out • **r. la cara** *or* **las narices a alguien** to smash someone's face in • **r. la marcha** to lead the way —intr. to break ♦ **r. a** to begin suddenly to <rompió a cantar she began suddenly to sing> • **r. con** to break up with • **r. en** to burst into —reflex. *(quebrarse)* to break; *(descomponerse)* to break (down); *(separarse en pedazos)* to tear; *(partirse)* to snap; MED. to fracture ♦ **r. el alma** to break one's neck • **r. la cabeza** to rack one's brains.
rom·pi·mien·to m. break; *(de noviazgo)* breakup.
ron m. rum.
ron·ca·dor, ·ra I. adj. snoring **II.** m.f. *(persona)* snorer.
ron·car §70 intr. to snore.
ron·cha f. *(herida)* welt; *(cardenal)* bruise.
ron·co, a adj. *(afónico)* hoarse; *(áspero)* harsh.
ron·da f. *(de músicos)* street serenaders; AMER. *(de gente)* circle.
ron·da·na f. gasket; AMER. pulley wheel.
ron·dar intr. *(vigilar)* to patrol; *(dar una serenata)* to serenade; *(vagar)* to prowl around —tr. *(dar vueltas)* to hover around; *(galantear)* to court; *(asediar)* to besiege.
ron·que·ar intr. to speak hoarsely.
ron·que·ra/quez f. hoarseness.
ron·qui·do m. snore; FIG. roar.
ron·ro·ne·ar intr. to purr.
ro·ña f. *(sarna)* rash; *(mugre)* filth; COLL. *(tacañería)* stinginess.
ro·ño·so, a adj. *(sarnoso)* scabby; *(sucio)* filthy; *(tacaño)* stingy.
ro·pa f. clothes, clothing ♦ **a quema r.** *(de cerca)* pointblank; *(de improviso)* suddenly • **r. de cama** bed linen • **r. interior** underwear • **r. sucia** laundry.
ro·pa·je m. vestments.
ro·pe·ro m. closet.
ro·sa I. f. rose; *(color)* pink; ARCHIT. rose window; JEWEL. rose-cut diamond ♦ **verlo todo de color de r.** to see everything through rose-colored glasses **II.** adj. pink.
ro·sá·ce·o, a adj. rosy.
ro·sa·do, a I. adj. *(color)* pink; *(vino)* rosé **II.** m. rosé.
ro·sal m. rosebush; AMER. rose garden.
ro·sa·le·da/ra f. rose garden.
ro·sa·rio m. rosary; FIG. string.
ros·bif m. roast beef.
ros·ca f. *(círculo)* ring, circle; *(espiral)* thread; CUL. ring; R.P. *(discusión)* argument ♦ **hacer la r. a alguien** COLL. to flatter someone.
ros·car §70 tr. to thread.
ros·tro m. face.
ro·ta·ción f. rotation.

ro·ta·ti·vo, a I. adj. revolving **II.** f. MECH. rotary press —m. newspaper.
ro·ta·to·rio, a adj. rotating.
ro·to, a I. see **romper II.** adj. *(dañado)* broken; *(quebrado)* smashed; torn, ripped <una página r. a torn page>.
ro·ton·da f. rotunda.
ro·tor m. rotor.
ro·to·so, a adj. AMER. tattered.
ró·tu·la f. kneecap; MECH. rounded joint.
ro·tu·la·do m. label.
ro·tu·la·dor, ·ra I. adj. labeling **II.** m.f. labeling device.
ro·tu·lo m. label ♦ pl. CINEM. subtitles.
ro·tun·do, a adj. *(sonoro)* resounding; *(definitivo)* categorical.
ro·tu·ra f. break; *(en papel, tela)* tear.
ro·tu·ra·dor, ·ra I. adj. plowing **II.** m.f. plower —f. plow.
ro·tu·rar tr. to plow.
ro·za·gan·te adj. splendid.
ro·za·mien·to m. rubbing; FIG. friction.
ro·zar §04 tr. *(frotar)* to rub; *(raer)* to scrape; *(tocar)* to brush against; *(volar a ras de)* to skim; *(rayar en)* to border on; MED. to chafe —intr. to touch lightly —reflex. to rub *(con against)*.
roz·nar intr. to bray.
roz·ni·do m. braying noise.
ru·bé·o·la f. rubella.
ru·bí m. [pl. **-íes**] ruby.
ru·bi·cun·do, a adj. ruddy.
ru·bio, a I. adj. blond(e) **II.** m. blond —f. blonde.
ru·blo m. ruble.
ru·bor m. blush; *(vergüenza)* embarrassment ♦ **sentir r.** to be embarrassed.
ru·bo·ri·zar·se §04 reflex. to blush.
ru·bo·ro·so, a adj. red in the face.
rú·bri·ca f. rubric; *(firma)* signature flourish.
ru·bri·car §70 tr. *(firmar y sellar)* to sign and seal; *(con iniciales)* to initial.
ru·bro m. title; ACC. item.
ru·da f. BOT. rue.
ru·de·za f. *(tosquedad)* roughness; *(falta de pulimento)* rudeness.
ru·di·men·ta·rio, a adj. rudimentary.
ru·di·men·to m. rudiment.
ru·do, a adj. *(tosco)* rough; *(sin pulimento)* rude; *(arte)* crude; *(tiempo)* severe.
rue·ca f. distaff.
rue·da f. wheel; *(de un mueble)* roller; *(rodaja)* slice; *(corro)* ring (of people); *(suplicio)* rack ♦ **hacer r.** to make a circle • **ir sobre ruedas** to go smoothly • **r. de presos** lineup • **r. dentada** cogwheel.
rue·de, do see **rodar.**
rue·do m. *(borde)* edge; *(circunferencia)* circumference; *(dobladillo)* hem; TAUR. bullring ♦ **dar la vuelta al r.** TAUR. to go around the bullring receiving applause • **echarse al r.** to enter the fray.
rue·ga, go see **rogar.**
rue·go m. request.
ru·fián m. *(chulo)* pimp; *(granuja)* ruffian.
ru·gi·do m. roar.
ru·gi·dor, a/gien·te adj. roaring.
ru·gir §32 intr. to roar; FIG. to howl.
ru·go·so, a adj. wrinkled.
rui·do m. noise; *(alboroto)* din; FIG. stir ♦ **hacer r.** to create a stir • **mucho r. y pocas**

nueces much ado about nothing • **sin r.** silently.

rui·do·so, a adj. noisy, loud; FIG. smashing.

ruin adj. (*despreciable*) despicable; (*avaro*) stingy; (*animales*) mean; (*miserable*) poor; (*raquítico*) puny.

rui·na f. (*destrucción*) ruin; (*hundimiento*) downfall ♦ **estar hecho una r.** to be a wreck.

rui·no·so, a adj. dilapidated.

rui·se·ñor m. nightingale.

ru·le·ta f. roulette.

ru·lo m. (*cilindro*) roller; R.P. (*de pelo*) ringlet.

rum·ba f. rumba.

rum·be·ar intr. AMER. to head (*para, hacia* for).

rum·bo m. direction; AER., MARIT. course ♦ **con r. a** bound for • **ir con r. a** to be heading for • **perder el r.** to lose one's bearings • **tomar buen r.** to take a turn for the better.

ru·mian·te adj. & m. ruminant.

ru·miar tr. to ruminate; FIG. to grumble.

ru·mor m. murmur; (*de árboles*) rustle; (*chismes*) rumor.

ru·mo·re·ar·se/rar·se reflex. to be rumored.

rup·tu·ra f. (*acción*) breaking; MED. fracture; (*de relaciones*) breakup.

ru·ral I. adj. rural II. m.f. AMER. peasant.

rús·ti·co, a I. adj. rustic, rural; (*grosero*) rough, gross ♦ **a la o en r.** paperback (book edition) II. m.f. peasant, hick.

ru·ta f. route.

ru·ti·lan·te adj. brilliant.

ru·ti·lar intr. to shine.

ru·ti·na f. routine.

ru·ti·na·rio, a adj. routine.

S

s, S f. twentieth letter of the Spanish alphabet.

sá·ba·do m. Saturday; RELIG. Sabbath ♦ **S. de Gloria** or **Santo** Easter Saturday.

sa·ba·na f. AMER. savannah.

sá·ba·na f. bed sheet ♦ **pegársele a uno las sábanas** COLL. to oversleep.

sa·ban·di·ja f. bug; FIG. louse.

sa·be·lo·to·do m.f. COLL. know-it-all.

sa·ber[1] m. learning, knowledge ♦ **según mi leal s. y entender** to the best of my knowledge.

sa·ber[2] §62 tr. to know <*ella sabe lo que ocurrió* she knows what happened>; (*tener habilidad*) to know how <*¿sabes cocinar?* do you know how to cook?>; to learn <*supe la noticia demasiado tarde* I learned the news too late> ♦ **hacer s.** to inform • **no s. dónde meterse** COLL. not to know where to hide • **¿qué sé yo?** how should I know? • **que yo sepa** as far as I know • **s. de buena tinta** to have on good authority • **s. de memoria** to know by heart • **sin saberlo yo** without my knowledge • **un no sé qué** a certain something • **véte a s.** your guess is as good as mine —intr. to know; (*acostumbrar*) to be in the habit of <*él sabe llegar temprano* he is in the habit of arriving early> ♦ **a s.** namely • **no se sabe** nobody knows • **¿quién sabe?** who knows? • **s. a** to taste like; FIG. to smack of • **s. de** (*conocer*) to know about, be familiar with; to hear from <*hace mucho tiempo que no sabemos de José* we have not heard from Joe in a long time> —reflex. to be known ♦ **sabérselo todo** to know it all.

sa·bi·do, a adj. (*conocido*) known; COLL. (*docto*) learned.

sa·bi·du·rí·a f. (*prudencia*) wisdom; (*conocimiento*) knowledge ♦ **s. popular** folk wisdom.

sa·bien·das adv. ♦ **a s.** knowingly.

sa·bi·hon·do, a COLL. adj. & m.f. know-it-all.

sa·bio, a I. adj. (*prudente*) wise; (*instruido*) learned II. m.f. (*persona prudente*) wise person; (*instruido*) learned person.

sa·bla·zo m. (*golpe*) saber blow; (*herida*) saber wound; COLL. sponging ♦ **dar un s. a alguien** COLL. to sponge money off someone.

sa·ble m. saber.

sa·ble·ar intr. COLL. to sponge.

sa·bor m. (*gusto*) taste, flavor; (*carácter*) flavor, color ♦ **con s. a limón** lemon-flavored • **sin s.** tasteless • **tener s. a** to taste of.

sa·bo·re·ar tr. (*notar el sabor*) to taste; (*apreciar*) to relish.

sa·bo·ta·je m. sabotage.

sa·bo·te·a·dor, ·ra I. adj. sabotaging II. m.f. saboteur.

sa·bo·te·ar tr. to sabotage.

sa·brá, bría see **saber**[2].

sa·bro·su·ra f. AMER. delicious or tasty thing.

sa·bro·so, a adj. (*delicioso*) tasty; (*agradable*) delightful; (*picante*) racy.

sa·bue·so m. bloodhound.

sa·ca·bo·ca·dos m.inv. punch.

sa·ca·bo·tas m.inv. bootjack.

sa·ca·cla·vos m.inv. nail puller or claw.

sa·ca·cor·chos m.inv. corkscrew.

sa·ca·man·chas m. or f.inv. stain remover.

sa·ca·pun·tas m.inv. pencil sharpener.

sa·car §70 tr. to take out <*sacó su cartera del bolsillo* he took his wallet out of his pocket>; (*quitar*) to remove <*s. una mancha* to remove a stain>; (*arrancar*) to pull out; (*un arma*) to draw; (*de un apuro*) to bail out; (*información*) to get out; (*deducir*) to take it <*de tu expresión saco que estás preocupado* from your expression I take it that you are worried>; (*resolver*) to figure out; (*conseguir*) to get; (*ganar*) to win; (*elegir*) to elect; (*moda, estilo*) to come out with; (*publicar*) to publish; (*restar*) to subtract; (*fotografiar*) to take <*quiero s. una foto del grupo* I want to take a picture of the group>; (*apuntar*) to take <*s. apuntes* to take notes>; (*citar*) to quote (*de* from); SPORT. to serve; CHEM. to extract ♦ **s. a bailar** to ask to dance • **s. adelante** (*lograr*) to carry out; (*criar*) to bring up • **s. a luz** (*revelar*) to bring to light; (*publicar*) to publish • **s. a relucir** to bring up • **s. de quicio** or **de sí** to infuriate • **s. el jugo** COLL. to bleed dry • **s. en claro** to figure out • **s. la cara por** COLL. to stand for • **s. en claro** or **en limpo** to understand • **s. provecho de** to benefit from • **s. sangre** to bleed • **s. una copia** to make a copy • **s. ventaja** to take advantage —reflex. to take off.

sa·ca·ri·na f. saccharin.

sa·cer·do·cio m. priesthood.

sa·cer·do·te m. priest ♦ **sumo s.** high priest.

sa·cer·do·ti·sa f. priestess.

sa·ciar tr. to satiate ♦ **s. la sed** to quench one's thirst —reflex. to be satiated.

sa·co m. (*bolsa*) bag; AMER. (*chaqueta*) jacket; ANAT. sac ♦ **no echar en s. roto** COLL. to keep in mind, not to forget • **s. de dormir** sleeping bag • **s. de huesos** COLL. bag of bones.

sa·cra·men·to m. sacrament ♦ **recibir los sacramentos** to receive the last rites.

sa·cri·fi·car §70 tr. to sacrifice; *(animales)* to slaughter —reflex. to sacrifice oneself.
sa·cri·fi·cio m. sacrifice; *(de animales)* slaughter.
sa·cri·le·gio m. sacrilege.
sa·crí·le·go, a adj. & m.f. sacrilegious (person).
sa·cris·tán m. sacristan.
sa·cro, a I. adj. *(sagrado)* sacred; ANAT. sacral **II.** m. ANAT. sacrum.
sa·cro·san·to, a adj. sacrosanct.
sa·cu·di·da f. *(acción)* shake; *(tirón)* tug; *(sismo)* tremor; *(de explosión)* blast; *(emoción)* jolt ♦ **s. eléctrica** electric shock.
sa·cu·dir tr. *(agitar)* to shake; *(quitar el polvo)* to dust; *(tirar)* to tug; *(golpear)* to beat; *(un ala)* to flap; *(alterar)* to jolt —reflex. *(agitarse)* to shake; *(la ropa)* to shake *or* brush off.
sa·cu·dón m. AMER. var. of **sacudida.**
sá·di·co, a I. adj. sadistic **II.** m.f. sadist.
sa·do·ma·so·quis·ta I. adj. sadomasochistic **II.** m.f. sadomasochist.
sa·e·ta f. *(flecha)* dart; *(del reloj)* hand; *(copla)* short song sung in religious ceremonies.
sa·ga f. saga.
sa·ga·ci·dad f. sagacity.
sa·gaz adj. sagacious, astute.
sa·gra·do, a adj. sacred.
sa·hu·ma·dor m. incense burner.
sa·hu·mar tr. to perfume with incense.
sa·hu·me·rio m. *(humo)* aromatic smoke; *(materia)* incense.
sai·ne·te m. one-act farce.
sa·í·no m. peccary.
sa·ke m. sake.
sal[1] f. salt; *(gracia)* charm; *(agudeza)* wit ♦ **echar s. a** to salt • **la s. de la vida** the spice of life • **s. de mesa** table salt • **sales aromáticas** smelling salts • **sales de baño** bath salts.
sal[2] see **salir.**
sa·la f. living room; *(cuarto grande)* large room; *(teatro)* house; MED. hospital ward ♦ **s. de clase** classroom • **s. de conferencias** lecture hall • **s. de espectáculos** theater, hall • **s. de espera** waiting room • **s. de estar** living room • **s. de máquinas** engine room • **s. de partos** delivery room.
sa·la·do, a adj. salt, salty *<agua s.* salt water>; salty, salted *<un plato muy s.* a highly salted dish>; *(gracioso)* witty, amusing; R.P. *(caro)* expensive.
sa·la·man·dra f. salamander.
sa·la·me m. AMER. salami.
sa·lar tr. to salt; *(curar)* to cure.
sa·la·rial adj. wage *<aumento s.* wage increase>.
sa·la·rio m. wage ♦ **s. vital** living wage • **s. a destajo** piece rate • **s. por hora** hourly wage.
sa·laz adj. salacious.
sal·chi·cha f. pork sausage.
sal·chi·che·rí·a f. sausage shop.
sal·chi·chón m. sausage.
sal·dar tr. COM. *(liquidar)* to pay off; *(vender)* to remainder.
sal·do m. COM. *(liquidación)* payment; *(cifra)* balance; *(mercancías)* remnants ♦ **s. acreedor** *or* **a favor** credit balance • **s. deudor** debit balance • **s. disponible** available balance.
sal·drá, dría see **salir.**
sa·le·ro m. *(de mesa)* saltshaker; *(gracia)* wit.
sa·le·ro·so, a adj. COLL. witty.
sal·ga, go see **salir.**
sa·li·da f. *(acción)* departure; *(abertura)* exit;

(escapatoria) way out; *(solución)* solution; *(ocurrencia)* witty remark; COM. *(venta)* sale; *(posibilidad de venta)* market; ACC. entry; ELEC., MECH. outlet ♦ **dar s. a** to vent • **s. del sol** sunrise • **tener s.** COM. to sell well.
sa·lien·te I. adj. *(que sobresale)* projecting; *(prominente)* salient; *(el sol)* rising **II.** f. projection.
sa·li·ne·ra f. salt mine *or* pit.
sa·li·no, a I. adj. saline **II.** f. salt mine *or* pit.
sa·lir §63 intr. to leave *<salimos de la casa a las tres* we left the house at three o'clock>; to go out *<no es prudente s. por la noche solo* it is not wise to go out alone at night>; *(partir)* to leave *(para* for); *(librarse)* to get out; *(aparecer)* to come out; *(el sol)* to rise; *(flor, fruto)* to come up *(de* from); *(idea, concepto)* to emerge; *(mancha)* to come out; *(libro)* to come out; *(oportunidad)* to come *or* turn up *<cuando salga la oportunidad* when the opportunity comes up>; *(costar)* to cost; *(cálculo)* to work out; *(en el juego)* to lead; *(ir a parar)* to lead *<esta calle sale a la plaza* this street leads to the plaza>; *(parecerse)* to take after; *(ser elegido)* to be elected ♦ **salga lo que salga** COLL. come what may ♦ **s. adelante** to get ahead • **s. bien, mal** to turn out well, badly • **s. con** to come out with *<él salió con una observación importante* he came out with an important observation>; to go out with, date *<Juan sale con Anita ahora* John is dating Anita now> • **s. del paso** to get out of a jam • **s. pitando** COLL. *(correr)* to run out quickly; *(enfadarse)* to blow up —reflex. *(derramarse)* to leak; *(rebosar)* to boil over ♦ **s. con la suya** to get one's own way • **s. de la regla** to break the rule • **s. de madre** to overflow • **s. del tema** to digress.
sa·li·tral m. saltpeter bed *or* deposit.
sa·li·tre m. saltpeter.
sa·li·tro·so, a adj. saltpetrous.
sa·li·va f. saliva, spit ♦ **gastar s. en balde** COLL. to waste one's breath.
sa·li·va·de·ra f. AMER. spittoon.
sa·li·val/var adj. salivary.
sa·li·var intr. to salivate; *(escupir)* to spit.
sa·li·va·zo m. COLL. spit, spittle.
sa·li·ve·ras f.pl. knobs on a horse's bit.
sal·mo m. psalm.
sal·món m. salmon.
sal·mue·ra f. brine.
sa·lo·bre adj. briny.
sa·lón m. *(sala grande)* hall *<s. de conferencias* lecture hall>; *(para visitas)* drawing room; *(exposición)* exhibition; *(tertulia)* salon ♦ **s. de actos** *or* **sesiones** assembly hall • **s. de baile** ballroom • **s. de belleza** beauty parlor • **s. de té** tearoom • **s. de ventas** salesroom.
sal·pi·ca·du·ra f. *(acción)* splashing; *(salpicón)* splash.
sal·pi·car §70 tr. *(con un líquido)* to splash; *(rociar)* to sprinkle; *(motear)* to fleck.
sal·pi·cón m. *(carne picada)* cold hash; COLL. *(cosa picada)* shredded *or* minced item; *(salpicadura)* splash.
sal·pi·men·tar §49 tr. to season; FIG. to spice.
sal·pu·lli·do m. var. of **sarpullido.**
sal·sa f. sauce, gravy ♦ **en su propia s.** in one's element • **s. rusa** Russian dressing.
sal·se·ra f. gravy boat.
sal·se·ro m. CHILE salt vendor.
sal·si·fí m. [pl. **-íes**] BOT. goat's beard.
sal·ta·dor, ·ra I. adj. jumping **II.** m.f. jumper

♦ **s. de pértiga** or **con garrocha** pole vaulter.
sal·ta·mon·tes m.inv. grasshopper.
sal·tar intr. *(brincar)* to jump *(de* with); *(levantarse)* to jump up; *(dar saltitos)* to hop; *(lanzarse)* to jump *(a* into); *(rebotar)* to bounce; *(desprenderse)* to come off; *(salir con ímpetu)* to bound; *(enfadarse)* to blow up ♦ **s. a la vista** or **a los ojos** to be self-evident • **s. sobre** to pounce on —tr. *(atravesar)* to jump over; *(omitir)* to skip over.
sal·ta·rre·gla f. bevel square.
sal·te·a·do, a adj. sautéed.
sal·te·ar tr. *(robar)* to hold up; *(hacer algo con interrupciones)* to skip; *(sofreír)* to sauté.
sal·tim·ban·qui m. COLL. *(charlatán)* charlatan; *(acróbata)* acrobat; *(malabarista)* juggler.
sal·to m. *(brinco)* jump; *(obstáculo)* hurdle; *(despeñadero)* ravine; *(juego)* leapfrog; *(ascenso)* promotion, jump; SPORT. jump <*s. de altura* high jump> ♦ **a s. de mata** COLL. from hand to mouth • **a saltos** by leaps and bounds • **en un s.** in a jiffy • **s. de cama** negligée • **s. de la carpa** jackknife dive • **s. de pértiga** or **con garrocha** pole vault.
sa·lu·bre adj. healthful.
sa·lud I. f. health; *(bienestar)* welfare, well-being ♦ **beber a la s. de** to drink to the health of • **estar bien, mal de s.** to be in good, bad health II. interj. COLL. *(al estornudar)* (God) bless you!; *(brindis)* cheers!
sa·lu·da·ble adj. *(sano)* healthy; *(provechoso)* beneficial.
sa·lu·dar tr. *(mostrar cortesía)* to greet; *(honrar)* to salute; MARIT. to dip the flag to ♦ **Le saluda atentamente** Yours faithfully or truly.
sa·lu·do m. *(cortesía)* greeting; *(inclinación)* bow; MIL. salute ♦ pl. regards.
sa·lu·ta·ción f. greeting.
sal·va f. see **salvo, a.**
sal·va·ción f. salvation.
sal·va·da f. AMER., COLL. good fortune or luck.
sal·va·guar·dar tr. to safeguard.
sal·va·guar·dia f. *(salvoconducto)* safe-conduct; *(protección)* safeguard.
sal·va·ja·da f. savagery.
sal·va·je I. adj. *(silvestre)* wild; *(no domesticado)* wild, untamed; *(feroz)* savage; *(rudo)* rude; *(primitivo)* uncivilized II. m.f. *(bárbaro)* savage; COLL. *(bruto)* boor.
sal·va·men·to m. rescue; RELIG. salvation.
sal·var tr. *(librar)* to save; *(resolver)* to overcome; *(evitar)* to avoid; *(recorrer)* to cover; RELIG. to save ♦ **salvando a los presentes** present company excluded • **salvar las apariencias** to save face —reflex. to escape ♦ **¡sálvese quien pueda!** every man for himself! • **s. por los pelos** COLL. to escape by the skin of one's teeth.
sal·va·vi·das I. m.inv. *(artefacto)* life preserver; *(bote)* lifeboat —m.f. *(bañero)* lifeguard II. adj. lifesaving.
sal·ve·dad f. *(condición)* proviso; *(excepción)* exception; *(reserva)* reservation.
sal·via f. sage.
sal·vo, a I. adj. safe ♦ **a s.** safe (and sound) • **a s. de** safe from • **poner a s.** to save • **ponerse a s.** to reach safety II. adv. except (for), save • **s. que** unless III. f. MIL. salvo ♦ **s. de aplausos** round of applause.
sal·vo·con·duc·to m. safe-conduct.
san adj. contr. of **santo.**
sa·na·lo·to·do m. cure-all.
sa·na·men·te adv. *(con sanidad)* wholesomely;

(sinceramente) sincerely.
sa·nar tr. to heal —intr. *(enfermedad)* to recover *(from* illness); *(herida)* to heal.
sa·na·to·rio m. sanatorium; *(hospital)* hospital.
san·ción f. *(ratificación)* ratification; *(pena)* punishment; *(aprobación)* sanction.
san·cio·nar tr. *(ratificar)* to sanction; *(autorizar)* to sanction; *(castigar)* to punish.
san·co·char tr. to parboil.
san·co·cho m. AMER. stew containing parboiled meat, yucca and bananas; FIG. mishmash.
san·da·lia f. sandal.
sán·da·lo m. sandalwood.
san·dez f. nonsense.
san·dí·a f. watermelon.
san·dun·gue·ro, a adj. COLL. witty, charming.
sa·ne·a·mien·to m. *(mejora)* improvement; *(limpieza)* sanitation; *(corrección)* righting.
sa·ne·ar tr. *(mejorar)* to improve; *(limpiar)* to sanitize; *(corregir)* to right; LAW to indemnify.
san·fa·són m. ♦ **a la s.** AMER., COLL. carelessly.
san·grar tr. to bleed; *(un terreno)* to drain; *(un árbol)* to tap; PRINT. to indent —intr. to bleed.
san·gre f. blood; *(linaje)* lineage ♦ **a s. fría** in cold blood • **chupar la s. a alguien** COLL. to be a bloodsucker • **de s. caliente** warm-blooded • **de s. fría** cold-blooded • **echar s.** to bleed • **llevar en la s.** to have in one's blood • **no llegar la s. al río** COLL. not to be a serious matter • **pura s.** thoroughbred.
san·grí·a f. *(extracción)* bloodletting; *(de líquidos)* draining; *(bebida)* sangria; PRINT. indentation; *(gasto)* bleeding.
san·grien·ta·men·te adv. cruelly.
san·grien·to, a adj. *(que echa sangre)* bloody; *(manchado de sangre)* blood-stained; *(sanguinario)* bloodthirsty; *(cruel)* cruel.
san·gui·jue·la f. leech.
san·gui·na·rio, a adj. bloodthirsty, cruel.
san·guí·ne·o, a adj. blood <*grupo s.* blood group>.
san·gui·no·len·to, a adj. *(manchado)* blood-stained; *(inflamado)* bloodshot.
sa·ni·dad f. health, healthiness ♦ **s. pública** board of health.
sa·ni·ta·rio, a adj. sanitary.
sa·no, a adj. *(de salud)* healthy; *(saludable)* healthful; *(provechoso)* wholesome; *(en condición)* sound; *(sin daño)* unharmed; *(sin vicio)* wholesome; *(entero)* whole ♦ **cortar por lo s.** to take drastic measures • **s. y salvo** safe and sound.
san·se·a·ca·bó adv. COLL. that's the end of it <*no voy y s.* I'm not going and that's the end of it>.
san·tia·mén m. COLL. jiffy.
san·ti·dad f. sanctity ♦ **Su S.** His Holiness.
san·ti·fi·car §70 tr. *(hacer santo)* to sanctify; *(consagrar)* to consecrate; *(venerar)* to revere.
san·ti·guar §10 tr. to make the sign of the cross on —reflex. to cross oneself.
san·tí·si·mo, a I. adj. most holy II. m. Holy Sacrament.
san·to, a I. adj. holy; *(bendito)* blessed; COLL. blessed <*esperamos todo el s. día* we waited the whole blessed day> ♦ **S. Padre** Holy Father II. m.f. saint —m. *(imagen)* image of a saint; *(festividad)* saint's day ♦ **¿a s. de qué?** what on earth for? • **dar el s. y seña** to give the

password • **desnudar a un s. para vestir a otro** to rob Peter to pay Paul • **no ser s. de su devoción** to not be keen on.

san·tua·rio m. sanctuary; *(intimidad)* privacy.

san·tu·rrón/lón, o·na adj. & m.f. sanctimonious *or* hypocritical (person).

sa·ña f. fury.

sa·pien·cia f. wisdom.

sa·pien·te adj. wise.

sa·po m. toad ♦ **echar sapos y culebras** COLL. to swear.

sa·que m. *(tenis)* serve; *(fútbol)* kickoff; *(raya)* service line.

sa·que·ar tr. to plunder.

sa·que·o m. plundering.

sa·ram·pión m. measles.

sa·ra·o m. soirée, evening party.

sar·cas·mo m. sarcasm.

sar·cás·ti·co, a adj. sarcastic.

sar·có·fa·go m. sarcophagus.

sar·di·na f. sardine ♦ **como s. en lata** COLL. packed like sardines.

sar·dó·ni·co, a adj. sardonic.

sar·ga f. TEX. serge; PAINT. painted wall fabric.

sar·ga·zo m. sargasso.

sar·gen·te·ar tr. to command as a sergeant; FIG. to boss —intr. to be bossy.

sar·gen·to m. sergeant.

sa·ri·lla f. marjoram.

sar·na f. scabies; VET. mange ♦ **más viejo que la s.** COLL. as old as the hills.

sar·no·so, a **I.** adj. scabby; VET. mangy **II.** m.f. person suffering from scabies.

sar·pu·lli·do m. rash.

sa·rro m. crust; DENT. tartar.

sar·ta f. string.

sar·tén f. frying pan; *(sartenada)* panful ♦ **tener la s. por el mango** COLL. to have the upper hand.

sa·sa·frás m. sassafras.

sas·tre m. tailor; THEAT. costumer ♦ **traje s.** woman's tailored suit.

sas·tre·rí·a f. tailor's (shop).

sa·tá·ni·co, a adj. BIBL. Satanic; FIG. satanic.

sa·té·li·te adj. m. satellite.

sa·tén/tín m. satin.

sa·ti·na·do, a **I.** adj. satiny ♦ **papel s.** glossy *or* coated paper **II.** m. *(acción)* calendering; *(brillo)* gloss.

sa·ti·nar tr. PRINT., TEX. to calender.

sá·ti·ra f. satire.

sa·tí·ri·co, a **I.** adj. satiric(al) **II.** m.f. satirist.

sa·ti·ri·zar §04 tr. & intr. to satirize.

sá·ti·ro m. satyr.

sa·tis·fac·ción f. satisfaction ♦ **a s.** satisfactorily • **a s. de** to the satisfaction of • **pedir s.** to demand satisfaction.

sa·tis·fa·cer §40 tr. to satisfy; *(pagar)* to pay; *(cumplir)* to meet *<s. los requisitos* to meet the requirements>* —reflex. to satisfy oneself.

sa·tis·fac·to·rio, a adj. satisfactory.

sa·tis·fe·cho, a **I.** see **satisfacer II.** adj. satisfied ♦ **darse por s. con** to be satisfied *or* content with • **estar** *or* **quedar s.** to be full or sated.

sa·tis·fi·cie·ra, ce, zo see **satisfacer**.

sa·tu·ra·ción f. saturation.

sa·tu·ra·do, a adj. saturated.

sa·tu·rar tr. to saturate.

sau·ce m. willow ♦ **s. llorón** weeping willow.

sau·da·de f. nostalgia.

sau·zal m. willow grove.

sa·via f. sap.

sa·xó·fo·no/fón m. saxophone.

sa·ya f. *(falda)* skirt; *(enaguas)* petticoat.

sa·yo m. *(casaca)* cassock; *(túnica)* tunic.

sa·zón f. season *<fruta en s.* fruit in season>; *(condimento)* seasoning ♦ **a la s.** at that time.

sa·zo·na·do, a adj. seasoned, flavorful.

sa·zo·nar tr. *(dar sabor)* to season; *(madurar)* to ripen —intr. & reflex. to ripen.

se reflex. pron. oneself, himself, herself, yourself, itself, themselves, yourselves *<las chicas se están mirando en el espejo* the girls are looking at themselves in the mirror>; to oneself, to himself, to herself, to yourself, to itself, to themselves, to yourselves *<ese viejo se habla a sí mismo* that old man talks to himself>; [to indicate the owner of the direct object of a verb] *<Juan se puso el sombrero* John put on his hat>; [to provide reflex. form to verbs not reflex. in meaning] *<mi tío se murió* my uncle died>; *(uno a otro)* each other, one another *<mis padres se aman* my parents love each other>; to each other, to one another *<ellos se mandaron regalos* they sent presents to one another> —indef. pron. one, they, people *<se dice que la economía mejorará* they say that the economy will improve> —aux. pron. [to give passive meaning to active verbs] *<se venden libros aquí* books are sold here> —pers. pron. [used instead of **le** *or* **les** before **lo, la, los** *or* **las**] to him, to her, to you, to it, to them *<Ana se lo dijo a él* Ann said it to him>; for him, for her, for you, for it, for them *<se la voy a comprar a usted* I am going to buy it for you>; from him, from her, from you, from it, from them *<él se lo robó a ellos* he stole it from them>.

sé see **saber²** *or* **ser²**.

se·bá·ce·o, a adj. sebaceous.

se·bo m. *(para velas)* tallow; *(grasa)* grease; *(gordura)* fat.

se·bo·rre·a f. seborrhea.

se·ca f. see **seco, a.**

se·ca·de·ro m. drying room.

se·ca·dor m. hair dryer.

se·ca·do·ra f. clothes dryer.

se·ca·men·te adv. dryly.

se·can·te **I.** adj. *(que seca)* drying; GEOM. secant; *(fastidioso)* annoying **II.** f. GEOM. secant —m. blotting paper.

se·car §70 tr. to dry; *(fastidiar)* to annoy, bother —reflex. to dry (out) *<la ropa se secó en unas horas* the clothes dried in a few hours>; to dry oneself, dry off; *(ríos y fuentes)* to dry up, run dry; BOT. to wither.

sec·ción f. section; *(división)* department *<s. de niños* children's department> ♦ **s. transversal** cross section.

sec·cio·nar tr. to section.

se·ce·sión f. secession.

se·ce·sio·nis·ta adj. & m.f. secessionist.

se·co, a **I.** adj. dry; *(desecado)* dried; *(corto y brusco)* sharp *<un golpe s.* a sharp blow>; *(poco cariñoso)* undemonstrative; *(ronco)* harsh; *(desabrido)* laconic ♦ **a secas** curtly • **dejar a alguien s.** COLL. to kill instantly *<lo atropelló el tren y lo dejó s.* the train hit him and killed him instantly>; *(dejar atónito)* to stun • **en s.** COLL. *(bruscamente)* suddenly; *(sin causa)* without cause *or* reason; *(sin medios)* without resources • **limpiar en s.** to dry-clean

II. f. drought.
se·co·ya f. sequoia.
se·cre·ción f. secretion.
se·cre·ta·men·te adv. secretly.
se·cre·ta·ria f. secretary.
se·cre·ta·rí·a f. *(cargo)* secretaryship; *(oficina)* secretary's office; *(oficina administrativa)* secretariat ♦ **S. de Estado** State Department.
se·cre·ta·ria·do m. *(oficina)* secretariat; *(cargo)* secretaryship.
se·cre·ta·rio m. secretary ♦ **s. municipal** *or* **de ayuntamiento** town clerk.
se·cre·te·ar intr. COLL. to whisper.
se·cre·te·o m. whispering.
se·cre·ter m. writing desk.
se·cre·to, a I. m. secret; *(reserva)* secrecy <*s. profesional* professional secrecy; MUS. sound-board ♦ **en s.** secretly • **guardar un s.** to keep a secret • **s. a voces** COLL. open secret • **s. de Estado** state secret • **s. de confesión** RELIG. seal of confession **II.** adj. secret; *(invisible)* hidden; *(confidencial)* confidential; *(reservado)* secretive.
sec·ta f. sect.
sec·ta·rio, a adj. & m.f. sectarian.
sec·tor m. sector.
sec·to·rial adj. sectorial.
se·cuaz m.f. *(subalterno)* henchman; *(partidario)* partisan.
se·cue·la f. consequence.
se·cuen·cia f. sequence.
se·cues·tra·dor, ·ra I. adj. *(de personas)* kidnapping; *(de vehículos)* hijacking **II.** m.f. *(de personas)* kidnapper; *(de vehículos)* hijacker.
se·cues·trar tr. *(personas)* to kidnap; *(vehículos)* to hijack.
se·cues·tro m. *(de personas)* kidnapping; *(de vehículos)* hijacking.
se·cu·lar adj. secular.
se·cu·la·ris·mo m. secularism.
se·cu·la·ri·zar §04 tr. to secularize.
se·cun·dar tr. to second.
se·cun·da·rio, a adj. & m. secondary.
sed f. thirst.
se·da f. silk ♦ **como una s.** *(suave)* as smooth as silk; *(dócil)* as gentle as a lamb.
se·dal m. fishing line; SURG. seton.
se·dan·te adj. & m. sedative.
se·dar tr. to soothe; MED. to sedate.
se·da·ti·vo, a adj. & m. sedative.
se·de f. *(del gobierno)* seat; *(de organización)* headquarters ♦ **Santa S.** Holy See.
se·den·ta·rio, a adj. sedentary.
se·de·rí·a f. *(negocios)* silk trade; *(tienda)* silk shop.
se·di·ción f. sedition.
se·dien·to, a adj. *(con sed)* thirsty; *(árido)* dry; *(deseoso)* desirous.
se·di·men·to m. sediment.
se·do·so, a adj. silky.
se·duc·ción f. seduction; *(atractivo)* allure.
se·du·cir §22 tr. to seduce; *(cautivar)* to captivate.
se·duc·ti·vo, a/tor, ·ra I. adj. *(que seduce)* seductive; *(fascinante)* captivating **II.** m.f. *(que seduce)* seducer; *(que encanta)* charmer.
se·ga·dor, ·ra I. adj. mowing **II.** m.f. harvester —f. *(máquina)* harvester, combine.
se·gar §52 tr. *(la mies)* to harvest; *(la hierba)* to mow; FIG. to cut off.
se·glar I. adj. secular **II.** m.f. layman/woman.
seg·men·ta·ción f. segmentation.

seg·men·to m. segment.
se·gre·ga·ción f. segregation.
se·gre·ga·cio·nis·ta adj. & m.f. segregationist.
se·gre·gar §47 tr. to segregate; MED. to secrete.
se·gui·da·men·te adv. *(sin interrupción)* continuously; *(después)* next.
se·gui·do, a I. adj. *(continuo)* continuous; *(consecutivo)* consecutive **II.** adv. AMER. often ♦ **en seguida** immediately, at once
se·gui·dor, ·ra I. adj. following **II.** m.f. follower.
se·guir §64 tr. to follow; *(venir después)* to come after <*el reinado de Juan Carlos siguió a la dictadura de Franco* the reign of Juan Carlos came after Franco's dictatorship>; *(continuar)* to keep *or* go on; *(ir en pos)* to pursue; *(perseguir)* to chase; *(espiar)* to watch closely; *(observar)* to watch <*s. los acontecimientos mundiales* to watch world events>; *(prestar atención)* to pay attention (to); *(emular)* to emulate; *(estudiar)* to study <*sigo medicina* I study medicine> —intr. *(continuar)* to continue; *(estar de salud)* to feel <¿*cómo sigue el enfermo hoy?* how is the patient feeling today?>.
se·gún I. prep. according to <*s. este informe* according to this report> **II.** adv. *(como)* depending on <*s. como te comportes te llevaré al cine* depending on how you behave I'll take you to the movies>; according to <*el Evangelio s. San Mateo* the Gospel according to Saint Matthew> ♦ **s. y conforme** *(de igual manera)* exactly as; *(de acuerdo a las circunstancias)* depending on the circumstances.
se·gun·de·ro m. second hand.
se·gun·do, a I. adj. second <*febrero es el s. mes del año* February is the second month of the year>; *(otro)* another <*él es un s. Mozart* he is another Mozart> ♦ **de s. clase** second-class • **de s. mano** secondhand • **s. enseñanza** secondary education • **s. intención** double meaning **II.** m. second; *(subjefe)* second-in-command; *(asistente)* assistant —f. AUTO. second gear.
se·gur *(hacha)* ax; *(hoz)* sickle.
se·gu·ra·men·te adv. *(ciertamente)* certainly; *(probablemente)* probably.
se·gu·ri·dad f. security, safety ♦ **con toda s.** with absolute certainty • **de s.** safety <*cinturón de s.* safety belt> • **tener la s. de que** to be certain that.
se·gu·ro, a I. adj. *(protegido)* safe; *(cierto)* certain; *(confiado)* sure; *(confiable)* trustworthy; *(firme)* stable **II.** m. *(aseguración)* insurance; *(dispositivo)* safety catch ♦ **s. contra accidentes** accident insurance • **s. de vida** life insurance **III.** adv. certainly, for sure.
seis I. adj. six; *(sexto)* sixth ♦ **las s.** six o'clock **II.** m. six.
seis·cien·tos, tas adj. & m. six hundred.
se·lec·ción f. selection.
se·lec·cio·nar tr. to select.
se·lec·ti·vo, a adj. selective.
se·lec·to, a adj. select.
se·llar tr. *(imprimir)* to stamp; *(cerrar)* to seal, close; FIG. to conclude.
se·llo m. stamp; *(de documento)* seal; PHARM. cachet ♦ **s. de correo** *or* **s. postal** postage stamp • **s. fiscal** LAW revenue stamp.
sel·va f. *(bosque)* woods; *(jungla)* jungle.
sel·vá·ti·co, a adj. forest.
se·má·fo·ro m. semaphore.

se·ma·na f. week; (*salario*) weekly pay ♦ **entre s.** during the week • **s. laboral** working week.
se·ma·nal adj. weekly.
se·ma·nal·men·te adv. weekly.
se·ma·na·rio, a I. adj. weekly II. m. weekly publication.
se·mán·ti·co, a I. adj. semantic II. f. semantics.
sem·blan·te m. (*rostro*) face; (*apariencia*) appearance ♦ **estar de mal s.** to look ill.
sem·blan·za f. biographical sketch *or* profile.
sem·bra·dí·o/do m. sown field *or* land.
sem·bra·dor, ·ra I. adj. sowing II. m.f. (*persona*) sower —f. (*máquina*) seed drill.
sem·brar §49 tr. to sow; (*esparcir*) to scatter.
se·me·jan·te I. adj. (*similar*) similar; (*tal*) such, like that <*nunca he visto hombre s.* I have never seen such a man> II. m.f. fellow man.
se·me·jan·za f. similarity; RHET. simile ♦ **a s. de** as.
se·me·jar intr. & reflex. to resemble (one another) ♦ **s. a** to look like.
se·men m. semen, sperm; BOT. seed.
se·men·tar §49 tr. to seed.
se·men·te·ra f. (*tierra*) sown field; (*temporada*), seedtime, sowing time.
se·mes·tral adj. semiannual, biannual.
se·mes·tre m. six months, semester; COM. half-yearly payment.
se·mia·ca·ba·do, a adj. half-finished.
se·miau·to·má·ti·co, a adj. semiautomatic.
se·mi·cir·cu·lar adj. semicircular.
se·mi·cír·cu·lo m. semicircle.
se·mi·cor·che·a f. sixteenth note, semiquaver (G.B.).
se·mi·des·nu·do adj. half-naked.
se·mi·diós m. demigod.
se·mi·fi·na·lis·ta adj. & m.f. semifinalist.
se·mi·lla f. seed.
se·mi·lle·ro m. (*plantación*) seed bed; (*vivero*) nursery; FIG. breeding ground.
se·mi·nal adj. seminal.
se·mi·na·rio m. seminary.
se·mi·na·ris·ta m. seminarian.
se·mi·pe·sa·do adj. & m. light heavyweight.
se·mi·pre·cio·so, a adj. semiprecious.
se·mí·ti·co, a adj. Semitic.
se·mi·to·no m. half tone.
sé·mo·la f. semolina.
sem·pi·ter·no, a adj. everlasting.
se·na·do m. senate.
se·na·dor m. senator.
sen·ci·lla·men·te adv. simply, plainly.
sen·ci·llez f. (*simplicidad*) simplicity; (*ingenuidad*) innocence.
sen·ci·llo, a I. (*fácil*) easy; (*sin adorno*) plain; CHEM., PHYS. simple; (*ingenuo*) innocent II. m. AMER. change.
sen·da f./**de·ro** m. path; FIG. road.
sen·dos, as adj. each <*los niños recibieron s. regalos* the children each received a present>.
se·nec·tud f. old age.
se·nil adj. senile.
se·no m. (*hueco*) hollow; (*regazo*) bosom; (*pecho*) breast; (*cavidad*) cavity <*senos nasales* sinus cavities>; (*matriz*) womb; FIG. bosom; MATH. sine; ARCHIT. spandrel; MARIT. inlet.
sen·sa·ción f. sensation; (*impresión*) feeling.
sen·sa·cio·nal adj. sensational.
sen·sa·cio·na·lis·ta adj. sensational(istic).
sen·sa·tez f. good sense.
sen·sa·to adj. & adj. sensible.

sen·si·bi·li·dad f. (*facultad*) sensibility; (*emotividad*) sensitivity, sensitiveness; (*susceptibilidad*) sensitivity.
sen·si·bi·li·zar §04 tr. to sensitize.
sen·si·ble adj. (*que percibe*) sentient; (*sentimental*) sentimental; (*impresionable*) sensitive; (*susceptible*) sensitive.
sen·si·ble·rí·a f. sentimentality.
sen·si·ble·ro, a adj. overly sentimental.
sen·si·ti·vo, a adj. (*sensible*) sensitive; (*capaz de sentir*) sentient; (*sensorial*) sense <*órgano s.* sense organ>.
sen·so·rio, a/rial adj. sensorial.
sen·sual adj. (*sensitivo*) sensuous; (*lujurioso*) sensual.
sen·sua·li·dad f. sensuality.
sen·ta·do, a I. adj. seated; (*establecido*) settled; (*juicioso*) judicious ♦ **dar por s.** to take for granted II. f. sitting.
sen·tar §49 tr. to sit; (*establecer*) to set <*s. precedente* to set a precedent> —intr. (*la comida*) to agree with; (*la ropa*) to fit; (*favorecer*) to become <*esos aires no se sientan bien* those airs do not become you> —reflex. to sit (down).
sen·ten·cia f. (*juicio*) sentence; (*decisión*) ruling; (*refrán*) maxim ♦ **pronunciar la s.** to pass sentence • **cumplir la s.** to serve one's sentence • **s. de muerte** death sentence.
sen·ten·ciar tr. (*juzgar*) to pass judgment; (*condenar*) to sentence.
sen·ten·cio·so, a adj. (*conceptuoso*) sententious; (*grave*) grave.
sen·ti·do, a I. adj. (*sincero*) heartfelt <*un s. pésame* heartfelt condolences>; (*quisquilloso*) touchy II. m. sense; (*interpretación*) interpretation; (*conciencia*) consciousness <*recobrar el s.* to regain consciousness>; (*dirección*) direction ♦ **aguzar el s.** COLL. to prick up one's ears • **con todos los cinco sentidos** heart and soul • **doble s.** double meaning • **en el s. de que** to the effect that • **no tener s.** not to make sense • **poner los cinco sentidos** to give one's all to • **sin s.** (*insensato*) meaningless; (*inconsciente*) unconscious • **tener s.** to make sense.
sen·ti·men·tal adj. sentimental.
sen·ti·mien·to m. (*emoción*) sentiment; (*pesar*) sorrow.
sen·tir¹ m. (*sentimiento*) feeling; (*opinión*) opinion.
sen·tir² §65 tr. to feel <*siento el calor del sol en la cara* I feel the heat of the sun on my face>; (*experimentar*) to experience; (*oír*) to hear; (*lamentar*) to regret; (*opinar*) to think <*siempre dice lo que siente* he always says what he thinks>; (*presentir*) to sense; (*apreciar*) to appreciate ♦ **lo siento** I'm sorry —intr. to feel —reflex. to feel; AMER. (*ofenderse*) to take offense ♦ **s. a sus anchas** to feel at ease • **s. como en (su) casa** to feel at home.
se·ña f. (*indicio*) sign; (*señal*) signal <*los dos niños tenían u s. secreta* the two children had a secret signal>; (*marca*) mark; MIL. password ♦ **dar señas de** to show signs of • **hablar por señas** to communicate by gestures • **hacer señas** to signal • **s. personales** description.
se·ñal f. (*marca*) sign; (*mojón*) landmark; (*seña*) reminder; (*para libros*) bookmark; (*vestigio*) trace; (*prodigio*) mark of distinction; (*aviso*) signal <*s. de peligro* danger signal>; (*síntoma*) symptom; COM. deposit ♦ **dar señales de vida** to show signs of life • **en s. de** as a sign of • **ni s.** not a trace.

se·ña·la·do, a adj. *(notable)* outstanding; *(fijado)* appointed.

se·ña·lar tr. *(poner señal)* to put a mark or sign on; *(indicar)* to point (at); *(determinar)* to determine, set *<pronto señalaremos el día para la fiesta* soon we will set the day for the party>; *(hacer señal)* to signal; *(nombrar)* to appoint; AMER. *(ganado)* to brand.

se·ña·li·za·ción f. *(colocación)* posting of signs; *(señales)* road or railway signs.

se·ña·li·zar §04 tr. to place signposts.

se·ñe·ro, a adj. *(solitario)* solitary; *(único)* extraordinary.

se·ñor, a I. adj. COLL. hell of a *<me dio una s. bofetada* he dealt me a hell of a blow> **II.** m. Mister, Mr. *<vi al s. Márquez en el mercado* I saw Mr. Márquez in the market>; sir *<siéntese, s.* sit down, sir>; *(dueño)* master *<el s. de la casa* the master of the house>; *(noble)* lord; *(caballero)* gentleman ♦ **el S.** RELIG. the Lord • **muy s. mío** Dear Sir • **¡S.!** COLL. Good Lord! —f. Mistress, Mrs. *<aquí viene la s. Martínez* here comes Mrs. Martínez>; madam *<buenas tardes, s.* good afternoon, madam>; *(dueña, noble)* lady; *(esposa)* wife ♦ **muy s. mía** Dear Madam • **Nuestra S.** RELIG. Our Lady.

se·ño·rial adj. *(propio de señor)* of a lord; *(majestuoso)* majestic.

se·ño·río m. *(dominio)* dominion; *(territorio)* domain; *(título)* lordship; *(propiedad)* estate; *(dignidad)* solemnity.

se·ño·ri·ta f. *(joven)* young lady; *(antes del apellido)* Miss.

se·ño·ri·to m. *(joven)* young man; COLL. *(amo)* master; DEROG. *(ocioso)* rich kid.

se·ño·rón, ona I. adj. lordly **II.** m. great gentleman —f. great lady.

se·ñue·lo m. *(para aves)* decoy; *(cebo)* bait; *(trampa)* trap.

se·pa see **saber²**.

sé·pa·lo m. sepal.

se·pa·ra·ción f. separation.

se·pa·ra·da·men·te adv. separately.

se·pa·ra·do, a I. adj. separate, separated ♦ **por s.** *(separadamente)* separately; *(correos)* under separate cover **II.** m.f. separated man/woman.

se·pa·rar tr. to separate; *(partir)* to divide; *(boxeadores)* to break; *(despedir)* to dismiss —reflex. to separate.

se·pa·ra·tis·ta adj. & m.f. separatist.

se·pe·lio m. burial.

se·pia f. sepia.

sep·ten·trio·nal adj. northern(ly).

sep·te·to m. septet.

sép·ti·co, a adj. septic.

sep·tiem·bre m. September.

sép·ti·mo, a adj. & m. seventh —f. MUS. seventh.

sep·tin·gen·té·si·mo, a adj. & m. sevenhundredth.

sep·tua·ge·na·rio, a adj. & m.f. septuagenarian.

sep·tua·gé·si·mo, a adj. & m. seventieth.

se·pul·cral adj. sepulchral; *(lúgubre)* gloomy.

se·pul·cro m. sepulcher.

se·pul·tar tr. to bury.

se·pul·to, a adj. buried.

se·pul·tu·ra f. *(entierro)* burial; *(tumba)* grave ♦ **dar s. a** to bury • **estar con un pie en la s.** to have one foot in the grave.

se·pul·tu·re·ro m. gravedigger.

se·que·dad f. dryness.

se·quí·a f. drought.

sé·qui·to m. entourage.

ser¹ m. *(ente)* being; *(esencia)* essence ♦ **s. humano** human being • **s. vivo** living creature.

ser² §66 aux. to be *<el Nuevo Mundo fue descubierto por Colón en 1492* the New World was discovered by Columbus in 1492> —intr. to be ♦ **a or de no s. por** if it were not for • **a no s. que** unless • **así sea** so be it • **¡cómo es eso!** what do you mean by that! • **de no s. así** otherwise • **érase que se era** once upon a time • **es de** it is to be *<es de esperar* it is to be hoped>; *(valer)* to be worth *<es de verse* it is worth seeing> • **no es para menos** COLL. rightly so • **no sea que** lest • **o sea or esto es** that is to say • **o sea que** in other words • **sea como sea** one way or the other • **sea lo que sea** be that as it may • **s. de** *(pertenecer)* to belong to *<este libro es de Marta* this book belongs to Martha>; to be made of *<la cadena es de oro* the chain is made of gold>; *(tener origen)* to be or come from *<mi madre era de Inglaterra* my mother was from England>; *(formar parte)* to be or come from *<el profesor es de la Universidad de Madrid* the professor is from the University of Madrid>; *(suceder)* to become of *<¿qué será de nosotros?* what will become of us?>; *(corresponder)* to be unique or suitable for *<su conducta no es la de un profesional* his conduct is not suitable for a professional> • **s. de lo que es** COLL. to be what it is • **siendo que** since • **ya sea . . . ya sea** either . . . or.

se·ra·fín m. angel.

se·re·nar tr. *(calmar)* to calm; *(apaciguar)* to soothe —reflex. to grow calm.

se·re·na·ta f. serenade ♦ **dar la s.** COLL. to pester.

se·re·ni·dad f. serenity.

se·re·no, a I. adj. calm **II.** m. *(rocío)* evening dew; *(guarda)* night watchman ♦ **al s.** in the night air.

se·rial adj. & m. serial.

se·ria·men·te adv. seriously.

se·rie f. series ♦ **fabricar or producir en s.** to mass-produce • **fuera de s.** COLL. out of sight.

se·rie·dad f. seriousness; *(comportamiento)* dependability.

se·ri·gra·fí·a f. silk-screening.

se·rio, a adj. serious; *(grave)* grave; *(concienzudo)* earnest; *(sombrío)* solemn; *(severo)* stern; *(confiable)* reliable ♦ **en s.** *(gravemente)* seriously; *(sinceramente)* truly • **hablar en s.** to be serious • **tomar en s.** to take seriously.

ser·món m. sermon.

ser·mo·ne·ar tr. to lecture.

ser·pien·te f. snake ♦ **s. de cascabel** rattlesnake.

se·rra·do, a adj. *(cortado)* sawed; *(con dientes)* serrated.

se·rra·ní·a f. mountains.

se·rra·no, a I. adj. *(que habita)* mountain-dwelling; *(de las sierras)* mountain **II.** m.f. highlander.

se·rrar §49 tr. to saw.

se·rre·rí·a f. sawmill.

se·rru·cho m. saw.

ser·vi·ble adj. useful.

ser·vi·cial adj. obliging.

ser·vi·cio m. service; *(criados)* help; *(utilidad)* usefulness; *(orinal)* urinal; *(retrete)* bathroom ♦ **al s. de** in the service of • **prestar un s.** to perform a service.

ser·vi·dor, ·ra m.f. servant ♦ **s. de usted** at your service • **su seguro s.** yours truly.
ser·vi·dum·bre f. *(esclavitud)* slavery; *(conjunto)* staff of servants.
ser·vil adj. servile.
ser·vi·lle·ta f. napkin.
ser·vi·lle·te·ro m. napkin ring.
ser·vir §48 intr. to serve ♦ **no s. para nada** to be useless • **s. de** *(hacer el papel de)* to act or serve as <*s. de guía* to act as a guide>; *(valer)* to be of use • **s. para** to be of use —tr. to serve; *(a un cliente)* to wait on —reflex. *(valerse)* to make use of ♦ **sírvase** please.
ser·vo·fre·no m. power brake.
ser·vo·mo·tor m. servomotor.
sé·sa·mo m. sesame.
se·se·ar intr. to lisp.
se·sen·ta I. adj. sixty; *(sexagésimo)* sixtieth II. m. sixty.
se·sen·ta·vo, a adj. & m. sixtieth.
se·sen·tón, o·na adj. & m.f. COLL. sexagenarian.
se·se·o m. lisp.
ses·gar §47 tr. *(inclinar)* to slant; SEW. *(cortar)* to cut on the bias.
ses·go m. slant; SEW. bias ♦ **al s.** obliquely; SEW. on the bias • **tomar un mal s.** COLL. to take a turn for the worse.
se·sión f. session, meeting ♦ **levantar la s.** to adjourn the meeting • **s. espiritista** seance.
se·sio·nar intr. to hold a meeting.
se·so m. brain; FIG. sense ♦ **perder el s.** to lose one's mind, go crazy ♦ pl. brains • **devanarse los s.** to rack one's brains.
se·su·do, a adj. wise.
se·te·cien·tos, as adj. & m. seven hundred.
se·ten·ta I. adj. seventy; *(septuagésimo)* seventieth II. m. seventy.
se·ten·ta·vo, a adj. & m. seventieth.
se·ten·tón, o·na COLL. adj. & m.f. septuagenarian.
se·tiem·bre m. September.
se·to m. fence ♦ **s. vivo** hedge.
seu·dó·ni·mo, a LIT. I. adj. pseudonymous II. m. pseudonym.
se·ve·ra·men·te adv. severely; *(con rigor)* rigorously; *(inexorablemente)* relentlessly; *(rígidamente)* strictly; *(gravemente)* gravely; *(duramente)* harshly.
se·ve·ri·dad f. severity; *(rigor)* rigor; *(inexorabilidad)* relentlessness; *(rigidez)* strictness; *(gravedad)* graveness; *(dureza)* harshness.
se·ve·ro, a adj. severe; *(rigoroso)* rigorous; *(inexorable)* unyielding; *(rígido)* strict; *(grave)* grave; *(duro)* harsh.
se·xa·ge·na·rio, a adj. & m.f. sexagenarian.
se·xa·gé·si·mo, a adj. & m. sixtieth.
se·xis·ta adj. & m.f. sexist.
se·xo m. sex; *(órganos)* genitals ♦ **el bello s.** the fair sex.
sex·tan·te m. sextant.
sex·te·to m. sextet.
sex·to, a adj. & m. sixth.
se·xua·do, a adj. sexed.
se·xual adj. sexual.
se·xua·li·dad f. sexuality.
si¹ m. MUS. ti.
si² conj. if; whether <*no sabemos si está casado o no* we do not know whether he is married or not> ♦ **como si** as if • **por si acaso** just in case • **si bien** although • **si no** if not, otherwise.
sí¹ pron. oneself, himself, herself, yourself, it-

self, themselves, yourselves ♦ **dar de sí** to give of oneself • **de por sí** or **en sí** in itself • **de sí** in itself • **fuera de sí** beside oneself • **para sí** to oneself • **sí mismo** oneself <*Mateo piensa sólo en sí mismo* Matthew thinks only of himself>.
sí² adv. yes; *(en votación)* aye; *(ciertamente)* certainly <*ellos sí vendrán* they will certainly come>; so <*creo que sí* I think so> II. m. yes <*un sí categórico* a categorical yes>; *(consentimiento)* consent, permission <*conseguimos el sí del maestro* we got the teacher's permission> ♦ **dar el sí** to say yes.
si·ba·ri·ta I. adj. sybaritic II. m.f. sybarite.
si·ba·rí·ti·co, a adj. sybaritic.
si·bi·la f. sibyl.
si·bi·lan·te adj. & m.f. sibilant.
si·co·a·ná·li·sis m. var. of **psicoanálisis.**
si·co·lo·gí·a f. var. of **psicología.**
si·có·lo·go, a adj. & m. var. of **psicólogo, a.**
si·co·mo·ro m. sycamore.
si·co·sis f. var. of **psicosis.**
si·co·te·ra·pia f. var. of **psicoterapia.**
SIDA m. AIDS.
si·de·ral/dé·re·o adj. astral.
si·de·rur·gia f. iron and steel industry.
si·de·rúr·gi·co, a adj. iron and steel <*industria s.* iron and steel industry>.
si·dra f. alcoholic cider.
sie·ga f. *(acción)* harvesting; *(temporada, cosecha)* harvest.
siem·bra f. *(acción)* sowing; *(temporada)* sowing season; *(sembrado)* sown land.
siem·bre, bro see **sembrar.**
siem·pre adv. always ♦ **como s.** as always • **de s.** usual • **para** or **por s.** forever • **s. jamás** forever and ever • **s. lo mismo** always the same • **s. que** *(cada vez)* every time <*s. que entro en la casa, me quito los zapatos* every time I enter the house, I take off my shoes>; *(a condición de)* provided that • **s. y cuando** provided that.
sien f. temple.
sien·ta, te, to see **sentir²** or **sentar.**
sie·rra f. *(instrumento)* saw; ICHTH. sawfish; GEOL. mountain range ♦ **s. de cinta** band saw • **s. de mano** handsaw.
sier·vo, a m.f. *(esclavo)* slave; *(esclavo feudal)* serf; *(servidor)* servant.
sies·ta f. afternoon nap ♦ **dormir** or **echar la s.** to take a nap after lunch.
sie·te I. adj. seven; *(séptimo)* seventh ♦ **las s.** seven o'clock II. m. seven.
sí·fi·lis f. syphilis.
si·fi·lí·ti·co, a adj. & m.f. syphilitic.
si·fón m. *(tubería)* U-bend; *(para líquidos)* siphon; COLL. *(agua gaseosa)* soda water.
si·ga, go see **seguir.**
si·gi·lo m. secrecy; *(discreción)* discretion.
si·gi·lo·so, a adj. *(secreto)* secretive; *(prudente)* discreet.
si·gla f. acronym.
si·glo m. century; *(época)* age <*el s. del átomo* the atomic age>; FIG. ages ♦ **en** or **por los siglos de los siglos** forever and ever • **S. de las Luces** the Enlightenment • **S. de Oro** Golden Age.
sig·ni·fi·ca·ción f. *(significado)* meaning; *(importancia)* significance.
sig·ni·fi·ca·do, a I. adj. significant II. m. meaning.
sig·ni·fi·can·te adj. significant.
sig·ni·fi·car §70 tr. *(querer decir)* to mean; *(hacer saber)* to indicate; *(representar)* to signify

—reflex. to distinguish oneself (*como* as).

sig·ni·fi·ca·ti·vo, a adj. significant.

sig·no m. sign; (*de puntuación*) mark; (*destino*) fate ♦ **s. de admiración** exclamation point • **s. de interrogación** question mark • **s. diacrítico** diacritical mark • **s. de igual** equal sign • **s. de más** plus sign • **s. de menos** minus sign.

si·guien·te adj. following, next.

si·guie·ra, guió see seguir.

sí·la·ba f. syllable.

si·la·be·ar intr. to syllable.

si·la·be·o m. syllabication.

sil·ba f. booing.

sil·bar intr. to whistle; (*una bala*) to whizz; (*chiflar*) to boo.

sil·ba·ti·na f. AMER. booing.

sil·ba·to m. whistle.

sil·bi·do m. (*silbo*) whistle; (*de culebra*) hissing; (*de bala*) whizzing; MED. wheeze ♦ **s. de oídos** ringing in the ears • **dar un s.** to whistle.

si·len·cia·dor m. silencer; AUTO. muffler, silencer (G.B.).

si·len·ciar tr. (*guardar en silencio*) to keep silent about; (*ahogar*) to muffle; (*ocultar*) to hush up; (*hacer callar*) to silence.

si·len·cio m. silence; MUS. rest ♦ **guardar s.** to keep silent.

si·len·cio·so, a adj. quiet, silent.

si·li·co·na f. silicone.

si·lla f. (*asiento*) chair; (*para montar*) saddle ♦ **s. de ruedas** wheelchair.

si·lle·rí·a f. (*conjunto*) set of chairs; RELIG. choir stalls; (*taller*) chair shop; (*tienda*) chair store.

si·llín m. (*de bicicleta*) seat; (*silla ligera*) light riding cycle.

si·llón m. armchair ♦ **s. giratorio** swivel chair.

si·lo m. silo.

si·lo·gis·mo m. syllogism.

si·lo·gís·ti·co, a adj. syllogistic.

si·lue·ta f. outline.

sil·ves·tre adj. wild.

sil·vi·cul·tor m. forester.

si·ma f. chasm.

sim·bio·sis f. symbiosis.

sim·bió·ti·co, a adj. symbiotic.

sim·bó·li·co, a adj. symbolic(al).

sim·bo·li·zar §04 tr. to symbolize.

sím·bo·lo m. symbol ♦ **s. de prestigio** status symbol.

si·me·trí·a f. symmetry.

si·mé·tri·co, a adj. symmetric(al).

si·mien·te f. seed.

si·mil adj. similar.

si·mi·lar adj. similar.

si·mi·li·tud f. similarity.

si·mio, a m.f. simian.

sim·pa·tí·a f. (*afecto*) affection; (*afinidad*) affinity; (*amabilidad*) congeniality ♦ **ganarse la s. de** to win the affection of • **tener s. a** or **por** to like • **tomarle s. a** to take a liking to.

sim·pá·ti·co, a I. adj. pleasant II. m. ♦ **gran s.** sympathetic nervous system.

sim·pa·ti·zan·te I. adj. sympathizing II. m.f. sympathizer.

sim·pa·ti·zar §04 intr. to get along (together) <*no simpatizan para nada* they don't get along at all>.

sim·ple I. adj. simple; (*fácil*) easy; (*sin adornos*) plain; (*modesto*) modest; (*tonto*) simple-minded II. m.f. simpleton; MED. simple.

sim·ple·za f. (*necedad*) simpleness; (*ingenuidad*) simplicity ♦ pl. foolish remarks.

sim·pli·ci·dad f. simplicity.

sim·pli·fi·ca·ción f. simplification.

sim·pli·fi·car §70 tr. to simplify.

sim·plón, o·na/plo·te COLL. I. adj. simple II. m.f. simpleton.

sim·po·sio/sium m. symposium.

si·mu·la·ción f. pretense.

si·mu·la·cro m. pretense; MIL. war games.

si·mu·la·dor, ·ra I. adj. simulating II. m.f. simulator.

si·mu·lar tr. to feign.

si·mul·tá·ne·o, a adj. simultaneous.

sin prep. without <*salió s. abrigo* he went out without a coat>; (*fuera de*) not including <*nos cobraron cien dólares s. los gastos de envío* they charged us one hundred dollars, not including the postage>; without <*salieron s. advertirnos* they went out without telling us>; un- <*dejaron mucho s. hacer* they left much undone>; -less <*me quedé s. un centavo* I was left penniless> ♦ **s. embargo** however, nevertheless • **s. que** without <*robaron el banco s. que la policía los capturara* they robbed the bank without being caught by the police>.

si·na·go·ga f. synagogue.

sin·ce·ri·dad f. sincerity ♦ **con toda s.** in all sincerity.

sin·ce·ro, a adj. sincere.

sín·co·pa f. GRAM. syncope; MUS. syncopation.

sin·co·pa·do, a adj. syncopated.

sín·co·pe m. GRAM., MED. syncope ♦ **s. cardíaco** heart attack.

sin·cro·ní·a f. synchrony.

sin·cro·ni·za·ción f. synchronization.

sin·cro·ni·zar §04 tr. to synchronize —intr. RAD. to tune in.

sin·di·cal adj. trade-union <*movimiento s.* trade-union movement>.

sin·di·ca·lis·ta I. adj. trade-union II. m.f. trade unionist.

sin·di·ca·li·za·ción f. unionization.

sin·di·ca·li·zar §04 tr. to unionize —reflex. (*formar*) to form a labor union; (*unirse*) to join a labor union.

sin·di·car §70 tr. (*un sindicato*) to unionize; (*acusar*) to accuse.

sin·di·ca·to m. labor or trade union.

sín·di·co m. LAW trustee; (*de una quiebra*) receiver.

sín·dro·me m. syndrome ♦ **s. de inmunodeficiencia adquirida** acquired immune deficiency syndrome.

si·ne·cu·ra f. sinecure.

si·ner·gí·a f. synergy.

sin·fín m. endless number or quantity <*hizo un s. de sugerencias* she made an endless number of suggestions>.

sin·fo·ní·a f. symphony.

sin·fó·ni·co, a adj. symphonic, symphony <*orquesta s.* symphony orchestra>.

sin·gu·lar I. adj. single; (*excepcional*) unique; (*peculiar*) peculiar II. m. GRAM. singular ♦ **en s.** in particular.

sin·gu·la·ri·dad f. singularity; (*carácter excepcional*) uniqueness; (*peculiaridad*) peculiarity.

sin·gu·la·ri·zar §04 tr. (*distinguir*) to distinguish; GRAM. to make singular —reflex. to distinguish oneself (*por* by).

sin·hue·so f. COLL. tongue ♦ **soltar la s.** COLL. to shoot off one's mouth.

si·nies·tro, a I. adj. (*izquierdo*) left, left-hand; (*perverso*) wicked; (*funesto*) fateful II. m. disaster.

sin·nú·me·ro m. countless or endless number <*un s. de invitados* a countless number of guests>.

si·no[1] m. fate.

si·no[2] conj. but <*no llegué el martes s. el jueves* I did not arrive on Tuesday but on Thursday>; (excepto) except <*nadie lo sabía s. Pedro* no one knew it except Peter> ♦ **no sólo . . . s.** not only . . . but also <*no sólo es rico s. generoso* he is not only rich but also generous>.

si·no·ni·mia f. synonymy.

si·nó·ni·mo, a I. adj. synonymous **II.** m. synonym.

si·nop·sis f.inv. synopsis.

si·nóp·ti·co, a adj. synoptic(al).

sin·ra·zón f. injustice.

sin·sa·bor m. (disgusto) discontent; (pena) grief.

sin·tác·ti·co, a adj. syntactic.

sin·ta·xis f. syntax.

sín·te·sis f.inv. synthesis.

sin·té·ti·co, a adj. synthetic.

sin·te·ti·za·dor m. synthesizer.

sin·te·ti·zar §04 tr. to synthesize.

sin·tie·ra, tió see **sentir**[2].

sín·to·ma m. symptom.

sin·to·má·ti·co, a adj. symptomatic.

sin·to·ní·a f. tuning (in).

sin·to·ni·za·dor m. tuner.

sin·to·ni·zar §04 tr. to tune (in) ♦ **s. con** to be tuned to.

si·nuo·si·dad f. sinuosity.

si·nuo·so, a adj. sinuous; FIG. devious.

sin·ver·güen·za adj. & m.f. COLL. shameless or brazen (person).

sin·ver·güen·za·da f. AMER. COLL. dirty trick.

si·qui·a·tra/qui·a·tra m.f. psychiatrist.

si·quia·trí·a f. psychiatry.

sí·qui·co, a adj. psychic.

si·quie·ra I. conj. even though, if only **II.** adv. at least <*espéreme diez minutos s.* wait for me for ten minutes at least> ♦ **ni s.** not even.

si·re·na f. siren; MYTH. mermaid ♦ **s. de niebla** foghorn.

sir·va, vo see **servir**.

sir·vien·ta f. maid.

sir·vien·te m. servant.

sir·vie·ra, vió see **servir**.

si·sa f. armhole.

si·se·ar tr. & intr. to boo.

sís·mi·co, a adj. seismic.

sis·mo m. earthquake.

sis·mó·gra·fo m. seismograph.

sis·te·ma m. system ♦ **con s.** systematically • **s. métrico (decimal)** metric system • **s. nervioso** nervous system.

sis·te·má·ti·co, a I. adj. systematic **II.** f. systematics.

sis·te·ma·ti·za·ción f. systematization.

sis·te·ma·ti·zar §04 tr. to systematize.

sís·to·le f. systole.

si·tial m. seat of honor.

si·tiar tr. MIL. to lay siege; (rodear) to surround.

si·tio m. (localidad) site; (lugar) place <*el libro no está en su s.* the book is not in its place>; MIL. siege.

si·to, a adj. situated.

si·tua·ción f. situation; (estado) position.

si·tuar §67 tr. to place.

smo·king m. tuxedo.

snob I. adj. snobbish **II.** m.f. snob.

so[1] m. COLL. you ♦ **¡s. tonto!** you idiot!

so[2] prep. under ♦ **s. pena de muerte** under penalty of death.

so·a·sar tr. to roast lightly, brown.

so·ba·co m. armpit.

so·ba·que·ra f. (refuerzo) armhole reinforcement; (resguardo) underarm shield.

so·ba·qui·na f. underarm odor.

so·bar tr. (la masa) to knead; (las pieles) to full; (zurrar) to thrash; (toquetear) to fondle; AMER. (adular) to flatter.

so·be·o m. strap.

so·be·ra·ní·a f. sovereignty.

so·be·ra·no, a adj. & m.f. sovereign.

so·ber·bio, a I. adj. (orgulloso) arrogant; (magnífico) superb **II.** f. arrogance.

so·bón, o·na adj. & m.f. COLL. mushy or overly fond (person).

so·bor·nar tr. to bribe.

so·bor·no m. bribery.

so·bra f. excess ♦ **de s.** superfluous • **estar de s.** to be one too many ♦ pl. leftovers.

so·bra·da·men·te adv. only too well.

so·bra·do, a adj. plenty of.

so·bran·te I. adj. (que sobra) remaining; (excesivo) surplus **II.** m. surplus.

so·brar tr. to surpass —intr. (estar de más) to be more than enough; (quedar) to remain; (ser inútil) to be superfluous.

so·bre[1] m. envelope.

so·bre[2] prep. (encima) above, over <*los pájaros volaban s. los verdes campos* birds flew over the green fields>; (en) on, on top of <*ella puso el mantel s. la mesa* she put the tablecloth on the table>; (superior a) above, over <*el rango de capitán está s. el de teniente* the rank of captain is above that of lieutenant>; (acerca de) about, on <*escribí s. los problemas* I wrote about the problems>; (más o menos) about <*vendremos s. las dos* we will come at about two o'clock>; (además) on top of, over <*me dieron cincuenta dólares s. lo acordado* they gave me fifty dollars over what was agreed upon>; (tras) on top of, upon <*insulto s. insulto* one insult on top of another>; (en prenda de) on, against <*un préstamo s. la finca* a loan on the farm>; on <*un impuesto s. la mercancía importada* a tax on imported goods>; (de) in, out of <*seis s. cien* six out of one hundred> ♦ **dar s.** to face • **s. manera** exceedingly • **s. todo** especially.

so·bre·a·bun·dan·cia f. superabundance.

so·bre·a·bun·dan·te adj. superabundant.

so·bre·a·bun·dar intr. to be overabundant ♦ **s. en** to superabound in.

so·bre·a·li·men·tar tr. to overfeed.

so·bre·car·ga f. overload.

so·bre·car·gar §47 tr. to overload; FIG. to overburden.

so·bre·ce·jo/ño m. frown.

so·bre·co·ger §34 tr. to scare —reflex. to be scared.

so·bre·co·si·do m./**cos·tu·ra** f. whipstitch.

so·bre·cu·bier·ta f. cover; (de un libro) dust jacket.

so·bre·cue·llo m. overcollar.

so·bre·di·cho, a adj. above-mentioned.

so·bre·dien·te m. snaggletooth.

so·bre·en·ten·der §50 tr. & reflex. var. of **sobrentender**.

so·bre·en·ten·di·do, a adj. understood.

so·bre·ex·ci·ta·ción f. overexcitement.

so·bre·ex·ci·tar tr. to overexcite.
so·bre·fal·da f. overskirt.
so·bre·hue·so m. bony tumor.
so·bre·hu·ma·no, a adj. superhuman.
so·bre·lle·nar tr. to overfill.
so·bre·lle·var tr. to bear.
so·bre·ma·ne·ra adv. exceedingly.
so·bre·me·sa f. after-dinner conversation ♦ **de s.** after-dinner.
so·bre·na·tu·ral adj. supernatural.
so·bre·nom·bre m. nickname.
so·bren·ten·der §50 tr. to understand —reflex. to be understood.
so·bre·pa·sar intr. to surpass.
so·bre·pe·so m. overload.
so·bre·po·ner §54 tr. to superimpose —reflex. (*controlarse*) to control oneself; (*vencer*) to triumph.
so·bre·pre·cio m. surcharge.
so·bre·pues·to, a tr. I. see **sobreponer** II. adj. (*puesto encima*) superimposed; SEW. appliqué III. m. SEW. appliqué.
so·bre·sa·lien·te I. adj. outstanding II. m. highest mark.
so·bre·sa·lir §63 intr. (*resaltar*) to project; (*sobrepujar*) to be outstanding.
so·bre·sal·tar tr. to startle —reflex. to be startled (*con, por* by, at).
so·bre·sal·to m. fright.
so·bres·cri·to m. address.
so·bres·drú·ju·lo, a I. adj. accented on the syllable preceding the antepenult II. f. word accented on the syllable preceding the antepenult.
so·bre·sei·mien·to m. LAW stay (of proceedings) ♦ **s. definitivo** dismissal.
so·bres·ti·mar tr. to overestimate.
so·bre·suel·do m. bonus.
so·bre·to·do m. overcoat.
so·bre·ve·nir §76 intr. to occur unexpectedly.
so·bre·vi·vien·te I. adj. surviving II. m.f. survivor.
so·bre·vi·vir intr. to survive.
so·brie·dad f. moderation.
so·bri·no, a m. nephew —f. niece.
so·brio, a adj. (*sin beber*) sober; (*conservador*) moderate.
so·ca·rrar tr. to scorch.
so·ca·rrón, o·na adj. & m.f. sarcastic (person).
so·ca·rro·ne·rí·a f. sarcasm.
so·ca·var tr. to excavate; FIG. to undermine.
so·ca·vón m. (*mina*) tunnel; (*hundimiento*) cave-in.
so·cia·bi·li·dad f. friendliness.
so·cia·ble adj. sociable.
so·cial adj. social.
so·cia·lis·ta adj. & m.f. socialist.
so·cia·li·za·ción f. socialization.
so·cia·li·zar §04 tr. to socialize.
so·cie·dad f. society; COM. corporation ♦ **formar s.** to associate • **s. anónima** corporation • **s. en comandita** limited partnership • **s. cooperativa** cooperative partnership • **s. de control** holding company • **s. de crédito** credit union • **s. de responsabilidad limitada** limited-liability company • **s. gremial** trade union • **s. mercantil** trading company • **s. regular colectiva** general partnership, copartnership.
so·cio, a m.f. (*asociado*) member; (*accionista*) business associate; COLL. (*amigo*) pal ♦ **s. capitalista** financial partner • **s. comanditario** silent partner • **s. honorario** honorary member.

so·cio·e·co·nó·mi·co, a adj. socioeconomic.
so·cio·lo·gí·a f. sociology.
so·cio·ló·gi·co, a adj. sociological.
so·ció·lo·go, a m.f. sociologist.
so·co·rrer tr. to aid.
so·co·rro I. m. (*apoyo*) aid; MIL. (*tropas*) relief; (*provisiones*) supplies ♦ **puesto de s.** first-aid station • **señal de s.** distress signal II. interj. help!
so·dio m. sodium.
so·do·mí·a f. sodomy.
so·do·mi·ta I. adj. sodomitical II. m.f. sodomite.
so·ez adj. vulgar.
so·fá m. sofa.
so·fis·ma m. sophism.
so·fis·ta I. adj. sophistic II. m.f. sophist.
so·fis·ti·ca·ción f. sophistication.
so·fis·ti·ca·do, a adj. sophisticated.
so·fo·ca·ción f. suffocation; FIG. embarrassment.
so·fo·ca·dor, ·ra/can·te adj. suffocating.
so·fo·car §70 tr. (*asfixiar*) to suffocate; (*un fuego*) to put out; (*una rebelión*) to suppress; (*avergonzar*) to embarrass —reflex. to suffocate; FIG. to get embarrassed.
so·fo·co m. suffocation; (*ahogo*) choking sensation ♦ **pasar un s.** to suffer an embarrassment.
so·fo·cón m. COLL. annoyance ♦ **darle un s. (a uno)** COLL. to have a fit.
so·fre·ír §58 tr. to fry lightly.
so·fri·to I. see **sofreír** II. m. lightly-fried dish.
so·ga f. rope ♦ **dar s. a alguien** COLL. to excite someone • **con la s. al cuello** COLL. with the knife at one's throat.
so·ja f. soya, soybean.
so·juz·gar §47 tr. to subjugate.
sol[1] m. sun; (*luz*) sun, sunlight; PERU., FIN. sol ♦ **al ponerse el s.** at sunset • **al salir el s.** at sunrise • **arrimarse al s. que más calienta** COLL. to know on which side one's bread is buttered • **de s. a s.** from sunrise to sunset • **hacer s.** to be sunny • **no dejar ni a s. ni a sombra** to give someone no peace • **tomar el s.** to sunbathe.
sol[2] m. MUS. sol.
so·la·men·te adv. only.
so·la·no m. east wind.
so·la·pa f. (*de sobre*) flap; (*de chaqueta*) lapel.
so·la·pa·do, a adj. underhanded.
so·la·par SEW. to put lapels on; (*traslapar*) to overlap; FIG. to conceal —intr. to overlap.
so·lar[1] adj. solar.
so·lar[2] m. (*terreno*) lot; (*bajo construcción*) building site; (*casa*) ancestral home.
so·la·rie·go, a adj. (*del patrimonio*) ancestral; (*noble*) noble.
so·la·rium/rio m. solarium.
so·laz m. (*descanso*) relaxation; (*consuelo*) solace.
so·la·zar §04 tr. & reflex. to amuse (oneself).
so·la·zo m. COLL. scorching sunshine.
sol·da·do m. soldier ♦ **s. raso** private • **s. de caballería** cavalryman • **s. de infantería** infantryman • **s. de marina** marine.
sol·da·dor m. (*obrero*) solderer; (*soplete*) blow torch.
sol·da·du·ra f. (*acción*) soldering; (*material*) solder; (*compostura*) repair ♦ **s. autógena** welding • **s. por arco** arc welding.
sol·dar §19 tr. to solder —reflex. (*pegarse*) to

join together; *(huesos)* to knit.

so·le·a·do adj. sunny.

so·le·ar tr. to expose to the sun —reflex. to sun oneself.

so·le·cis·mo m. solecism.

so·le·dad f. *(aislamiento)* solitude; *(sentirse solo)* loneliness; *(lugar)* solitary place.

so·lem·ne adj. solemn.

so·lem·ni·dad f. solemnity.

so·ler §78 intr. *(acostumbrar)* to be in the habit of <*Miguel suele levantarse temprano* Michael is in the habit of getting up early>; *(ser frecuente)* to tend to <*suele llover mucho en Londres* it tends to rain a lot in London>; *(equivalentes adverbiales)* usually, often <*yo suelo levantarme tarde* I usually get up late>; <*suele nevar mucho aquí* it often snows a lot here>.

so·le·ra f. *(soporte)* crossbeam; *(piedra)* plinth; *(del molino)* lower millstone; *(del horno)* floor.

so·le·van·tar tr. to lift; FIG. to stir up.

sol·fa f. MUS. musical notation ♦ **poner en s.** COLL. to ridicule.

sol·fe·ar tr. to sing sol-fa.

sol·fe·o m. solfeggio.

so·li·ci·ta·ción f. request.

so·li·ci·tan·te I. adj. petitioning II. m.f. petitioner.

so·li·ci·tar tr. *(pedir)* to request; *(gestionar)* to apply for; *(atraer)* to attract.

so·lí·ci·to, a adj. solicitous.

so·li·ci·tud f. *(cuidado)* solicitude; *(petición)* request; *(instancia)* petition; *(gestión)* application ♦ **a s.** on request ♦ **a s. de** at the request of ♦ **presentar una s.** to submit an application.

so·li·da·ri·dad f. solidarity ♦ **por s. con** in solidarity with.

so·li·da·rio, a adj. *(en común)* joint; *(obligatorio)* mutually binding; TECH. integral.

so·li·da·ri·zar·se §04 reflex. to join together.

so·li·dez f. solidity; *(fuerza)* strength.

so·li·di·fi·ca·ción f. solidification.

so·li·di·fi·car §70 tr. & reflex. to solidify.

só·li·do, a I. adj. solid; *(fuerte)* strong II. m. solid.

so·li·lo·quio m. soliloquy.

so·lis·ta m.f. soloist.

so·li·ta·rio, a I. adj. *(solo)* lone; *(desierto)* solitary II. m.f. *(ermitaño)* recluse —m. *(diamante, juego)* solitaire —f. ZOOL. hermit crab —f. ZOOL. tapeworm.

so·li·vian·tar tr. *(excitar)* to stir up; *(irritar)* to irritate; *(preocupar)* to worry.

so·li·viar tr. to lift.

so·llo·zar §04 intr. to sob.

so·llo·zo m. sob ♦ **estallar** *or* **prorrumpir en sollozos** to burst into sobs.

so·lo, a I. adj. *(sin compañía)* alone; *(único)* sole; *(aislado)* lonely ♦ **a solas** alone II. m. MUS. solo.

só·lo adv. only.

so·lo·mi·llo m. sirloin.

sols·ti·cio m. solstice.

sol·tar §19 tr. *(aflojar)* to loosen; *(desasir)* to let go of <*suelta mi brazo* let go of my arm>; *(liberar)* to free; *(irrumpir)* to let out <*el prisionero soltaba gritos de terror* the prisoner let out cries of terror>; *(decir)* to blurt out; *(en tejidos)* to drop —reflex. *(adquirir soltura)* to become proficient; *(volverse desenvuelto)* to loosen up; COLL. *(empezar)* to begin.

sol·te·rí·a f. bachelorhood.

sol·te·ro, a I. adj. single II. m. bachelor —f. unmarried woman.

sol·te·rón, o·na I. adj. old and unmarried II. m. confirmed bachelor —f. spinster; COLL. old maid.

sol·tu·ra f. *(aflojamiento)* looseness; *(seguridad)* confidence; *(agilidad)* agility; *(al hablar)* fluency; *(descaro)* brazenness ♦ **con s.** confidently.

so·lu·ble adj. CHEM. soluble; *(que se puede resolver)* solvable.

so·lu·ción f. solution; *(desenlace)* ending.

so·lu·cio·nar tr. to solve.

sol·ven·cia f. solvency; FIN. settlement; *(fiabilidad)* reliability ♦ **s. moral** character.

sol·ven·tar tr. *(pagar)* to settle; *(costear)* to finance; *(resolver)* to resolve.

sol·ven·te I. adj. *(libre de deudas)* solvent; *(responsable)* reliable II. m. solvent.

so·má·ti·co, a adj. somatic.

so·ma·ti·za·ción f. somatization.

so·ma·ti·zar §04 intr. to somatize.

som·bra f. *(obscuridad)* darkness; *(área)* shade; *(imagen)* shadow <*la s. del molino* the shadow of the windmill>; *(penumbra)* shade <*a la s. del manzano* in the shade of the apple tree>; *(espectro)* ghost; *(confusión)* confusion ♦ **dar s.** to cast a shadow • **poner a la s.** COLL. to put in jail.

som·brar tr. to shade.

som·bre·a·dor m. eye shadow.

som·bre·ar tr. *(poner sombra)* to shade; *(dar sombra)* to throw shadow on.

som·bre·re·ra f. *(para señoras)* milliner; *(para hombres)* hat maker; *(caja)* hatbox.

som·bre·re·rí·a f. *(señoras)* milliner's (shop); *(hombres)* hatter's (shop).

som·bre·re·ro m. *(para señoras)* milliner; *(para hombres)* hat maker.

som·bre·ro m. hat; BOT., MECH. cap ♦ **s. de copa** top hat • **s. hongo** derby, bowler (G.B.).

som·bri·lla f. parasol.

som·brí·o, a adj. *(lugar)* gloomy; *(persona)* sullen.

so·me·ra·men·te adv. superficially.

so·me·ro, a adj. *(sin profundidad)* shallow; *(superficial)* superficial; *(breve)* brief.

so·me·ter tr. *(subyugar)* to subjugate; *(subordinar)* to subordinate; *(entregar)* to submit; to subject *or* put to <*lo sometieron a una prueba científica* they subjected it to a scientific test> ♦ **s. a prueba** to test • **s. a tratamiento** to put under treatment • **s. algo a una autoridad** to refer something to an authority —reflex. *(rendirse)* to surrender; to undergo <*s. a una operación* to undergo an operation>.

so·me·ti·mien·to m. submission.

som·ní·fe·ro, a I. adj. sleep-inducing II. m. sleeping pill.

som·no·len·cia f. somnolence.

so·mos see **ser²**.

son¹ m. COLL. tune ♦ **¿a s. de qué?** for what reason? • **en s. de** as <*en s. de broma* as a joke> • **sin ton ni s.** COLL. without rhyme or reason.

son² see **ser²**.

so·na·do, a adj. *(muy divulgado)* talked-about; SL. *(chiflado)* crazy.

so·na·je·ro m. rattle.

so·nám·bu·lo, a I. adj. sleep II. m.f. sleepwalker.

so·nar¹ m. TECH. sonar.

so·nar² §19 intr. *(producir sonido)* to sound;

(tintinear) to ring; *(parecer)* to sound like <*esto me suena a tontería* this sounds like foolishness to me>; *(el reloj)* to strike; *(recordar)* to ring a bell <*ese nombre no me suena* that name does not ring a bell with me>; PHONET. to be pronounced ♦ **como suena** literally —tr. *(hacer que suene)* to sound; *(tocar)* to play; *(repicar)* to ring; *(la nariz)* to blow —reflex. to blow.

son·da f. *(sondeo)* sounding; *(instrumento)* sounding line *or* lead; ASTRONAUT. probe <*s. espacial* space probe>; MED. probe; TECH. drill ♦ **s. acústica** sound finder.

son·de·ar/dar tr. to sound; MED. to probe; TECH. to drill; *(explorar)* to explore, inquire into; *(averiguar)* to sound out.

son·de·o m. sounding; MED. probing; TECH. drilling; *(encuesta)* poll.

so·ne·to m. sonnet.

so·ni·do m. sound; MED. murmur.

so·no·ri·dad f. sonority.

so·no·ro, a adj. *(sonido)* sound; *(resonante)* sonorous.

son·re·ír §58 intr. to smile; FIG. to smile on <*la fortuna le sonríe* luck smiles on him> —reflex. to smile.

son·rien·te adj. smiling.

son·ri·sa f. smile.

son·ro·jar·se reflex. to blush.

son·ro·jo m. blush.

son·ro·sar tr. to turn pink.

son·sa·car §70 tr. to wheedle.

son·sa·ear intr. AMER. to fool around.

son·so, a AMER., COLL. I. adj. silly II. m.f. fool.

son·so·ne·te m. singsong.

so·ña·do, a adj. dream, of one's dreams.

so·ña·dor, ·ra I. adj. dreamy II. m.f. dreamer.

so·ñar §19 tr. & intr. to dream ♦ **¡ni soñarlo!** not on your life! • **s. con** to dream of *or* about • **s. con los angelitos** COLL. to have sweet dreams • **s. despierto** to daydream.

so·ño·len·cia f. somnolence.

so·ño·lien·to, a adj. sleepy.

so·pa f. soup; *(pan mojado)* sop ♦ **estar** *or* **quedar hecho una s.** COLL. to be soaking wet.

so·pa·pe·ar tr. to slap.

so·pa·po m. slap.

so·pe·ro, a I. adj. soup <*plato s.* soup plate *or* bowl> II. m. soup plate *or* bowl —f. soup tureen.

so·pe·sar tr. to weigh.

so·pe·tón m. slap ♦ **de s.** suddenly.

so·pla·do, a m. glassblowing.

so·pla·dor, ·ra I. adj. blowing II. m. glass blower.

so·plar intr. to blow —tr. *(mover el viento)* to blow (away) <*el viento sopla la hojarasca en el otoño* the wind blows the dead leaves during the fall>; *(velas)* to blow out; *(globos)* to blow up; COLL. *(apuntar)* to prompt; *(hurtar)* to swipe.

so·ple·te m. blowtorch ♦ **s. de arena** sandblast • **s. oxiacetilénico** oxyacetylene torch.

so·plo m. blow; FIG. instant.

so·plón, o·na I. adj. COLL. squealing II. m.f. COLL. stool pigeon.

so·pon·cio m. COLL. faint.

so·por m. MED. sopor; FIG. sleepiness.

so·po·rí·fe·ro/fi·co, a I. adj. sleep-inducing; FIG. boring II. m. sleeping pill.

so·por·ta·ble adj. bearable.

so·por·tar tr. *(sostener)* to support; *(sufrir)* to bear.

so·por·te m. *(sostén)* support; *(base)* stand.

so·pra·no m.f. soprano.

sor f. RELIG. sister.

sor·ber tr. *(beber)* to sip; *(absorber)* to absorb.

sor·be·te m. sherbet.

sor·bo m. sip <*un s. de vino* a sip of wine>; *(trago)* swallow, gulp.

sor·de·ra f. deafness.

sor·di·dez f. *(suciedad)* squalor; *(vileza)* sordidness.

sór·di·do, a adj. *(sucio)* squalid; *(vil)* sordid.

sor·di·na f. MUS. damper.

sor·do, a I. adj. deaf; *(silencioso)* silent; *(apagado)* muffled; FIG. indifferent; GRAM. voiceless ♦ **a sordas** silently • **quedarse s.** to go deaf • **s. como una tapia** stone deaf II. m.f. *(persona)* deaf person; GRAM. surd ♦ **hacerse el s.** to pretend not to hear.

sor·do·mu·do, a adj. & m.f. deaf-mute.

sor·go m. sorghum.

sor·na f. sarcasm.

so·ro·char·se reflex. AMER., MED. to get mountain sickness.

so·ro·che m. AMER. mountain sickness.

sor·pren·den·te adj. *(admirable)* surprising; *(raro)* unusual.

sor·pren·der tr. *(coger desprevenido)* to take by surprise; *(asombrar)* to surprise; *(descubrir)* to discover —reflex. to be surprised *or* amazed.

sor·pre·sa f. surprise; *(asombro)* amazement ♦ **coger de s.** to take by surprise.

sor·pre·si·vo, a adj. unexpected.

sor·te·ar tr. *(echar a suertes)* to draw lots for; *(rifar)* to raffle; *(evitar)* to avoid.

sor·te·o m. *(acción)* drawing; *(rifa)* raffle ♦ **por s.** by lot.

sor·ti·ja f. *(anillo)* ring; *(de pelo)* ringlet.

sor·ti·le·gio m. *(hechicería)* witchcraft; *(hechizo)* spell ♦ **echar un s. a** to cast a spell on.

so·sa f. BOT. saltwort; CHEM. soda ♦ **s. cáustica** caustic soda.

so·se·ga·do, a adj. quiet, peaceful.

so·se·gar §52 tr. & intr. to calm (down) —reflex. to calm down.

so·sie·go m. tranquility, quiet.

sos·la·yar tr. *(poner al soslayo)* to put on a slant; *(evitar)* to sidestep.

sos·la·yo, a I. adj. slanted II. adv. ♦ **al** *or* **de s.** *(oblicuamente)* on a slant; *(de lado)* sideways; *(de pasada)* in passing • **mirar de s.** to look out of the corner of one's eye (at); *(desaprobar)* to look askance (at).

so·so, a adj. *(de poco sabor)* tasteless; *(sin sal)* unsalted; *(zonzo)* dull.

sos·pe·cha f. suspicion.

sos·pe·char tr. to suspect —intr. to be suspicious.

sos·pe·cho·so, a adj. & m.f. suspicious (person).

sos·tén[1] see **sostener**.

sos·tén[2] m. *(acción)* sustenance; *(apoyo)* support; *(prenda)* bra ♦ **s. de familia** breadwinner.

sos·ten·drá, dría see **sostener**.

sos·te·ne·dor, ·ra I. adj. supporting II. m.f. supporter.

sos·te·ner §69 tr. *(sustentar)* to support; *(sujetar)* to hold (up); *(mantener)* to keep up; *(defender)* to uphold; *(apoyar)* to back —reflex. *(mantenerse parado)* to hold oneself up; *(mantenerse)* to support oneself; *(continuar)* to continue.

sos·te·ni·do, a I. adj. *(continuo)* sustained; MUS. sharp **II.** m. MUS. sharp.

sos·te·ni·mien·to m. *(apoyo)* support; *(mantenimiento)* maintenance; *(sustento)* sustenance.

sos·tie·ne, tuviera, tuvo see **sostener.**

so·ta·na f. soutane.

só·ta·no m. basement.

so·ta·ven·to m. MARIT. leeward **♦ a s.** to leeward.

so·to m. *(arboleda)* grove; *(matorral)* thicket.

soy see **ser².**

Sr. m. [abbr. of **Señor**] Mr.

Sra. f. [abbr. of **Señora**] Mrs.

stan·dard adj. & m. standard **♦ s. de vida** standard of living.

su, sus adj. one's, his, her, your, its, their.

sua·ve adj. soft; *(liso)* smooth; *(dulce)* sweet; *(tranquilo)* gentle.

sua·vi·dad f. softness; *(lisura)* smoothness; *(dulzura)* sweetness; *(tranquilidad)* gentleness.

sua·vi·za·dor, ·ra I. adj. softening **II.** m. razor strop.

sua·vi·zar §04 tr. to soften; *(hacer plano)* to smooth; *(moderar)* to temper —reflex. to soften; *(volver plano)* to become smooth; *(moderarse)* to be tempered.

su·ba f. R.P. rise.

su·ba·cuá·ti·co, a adj. underwater.

su·bal·ter·no, a adj. & m.f. subordinate.

su·ba·rren·da·mien·to m. sublease.

su·ba·rren·dar §49 tr. to sublet.

su·ba·rrien·do m. *(contrato)* sublease; *(precio)* sublease rent.

su·bas·ta f. auction **♦ en s.** for auction • **sacar a s.** to put up for auction • **vender en s.** to auction off.

su·bas·tar tr. to auction.

sub·co·mi·sión f. subcommittee.

sub·cons·cien·cia f. subconscious mind.

sub·cons·cien·te I. adj. subconscious **II.** m. subconscious mind.

sub·cu·tá·ne·o, a adj. subcutaneous.

sub·de·sa·rro·lla·do, a adj. underdeveloped.

sub·di·rec·tor, ·ra m.f. assistant manager.

súb·di·to, a I. adj. subject **II.** m.f. *(de un monarca)* subject; *(ciudadano)* citizen.

sub·di·vi·dir tr. & reflex. to subdivide.

sub·di·vi·sión f. subdivision.

su·bes·ti·mar tr. to underestimate.

sub·go·ber·na·dor, ·ra m.f. lieutenant governor.

su·bi·ba·ja m. seesaw.

su·bi·do, a I. adj. *(fuerte)* deep <*rojo s.* deep red>; *(elevado)* high f. *(ascensión)* climb; *(aumento)* increase; *(cuesta)* hill.

su·bir tr. *(escalar)* to climb, go up <*subí la cuesta* I climbed the hill>; *(llevar arriba)* to take *or* carry up; *(levantar, extender)* to raise; *(aumentar)* to raise —intr. *(elevarse)* to rise <*el humo subía* the smoke was rising>; *(ascender)* to go up; *(montar)* to get on *or* into <*sube al coche* get into the car>; *(cabalgar)* to mount; *(crecer)* to rise; *(alcanzar)* to come *or* amount to <*la cuenta sube a cincuenta dólares* the bill comes to fifty dollars>; *(aumentar)* to rise <*los precios han subido* prices have risen>; *(en un empleo)* to be promoted; *(agravarse)* to get worse <*le subió la fiebre* his fever got worse>; MUS. to raise the pitch **♦ s. al trono** to ascend the throne • **s. de punto** to increase • **s. de tono** *(sonido)* to get louder; *(conversación)*

to become heated —reflex. *(ascender)* to go up; *(montar)* to get on *or* into <*el niño se subió al tren* the little boy got on the train> **♦ subír·sele a uno a la cabeza** to go to one's head.

sú·bi·ta·men·te adv. suddenly.

sú·bi·to, a I. adj. *(imprevisto)* sudden; *(precipitado)* hasty **♦ de s.** suddenly, all of a sudden **II.** adv. suddenly.

sub·je·fe m. assistant manager.

sub·je·ti·vi·dad f. subjectivity.

sub·je·ti·vo, a adj. & m. subjective.

sub·jun·ti·vo, a adj. & m. subjunctive.

su·ble·va·ción f./mien·to m. uprising.

su·ble·var tr. *(agitar)* to incite to rebellion; *(enojar)* to annoy —reflex. to revolt.

su·bli·ma·ción f. sublimation.

su·bli·mar tr. to sublimate —reflex. to be sublimated.

su·bli·me adj. sublime.

sub·ma·ri·no, a adj. & m. submarine.

su·bo·fi·cial adj. MIL. non-commissioned *or* warrant officer; MARIT. petty officer.

su·bor·di·na·ción f. subordination.

su·bor·di·na·do, a adj. & m.f. subordinate.

su·bor·di·nar tr. to subordinate —intr. to become subordinate.

sub·pro·duc·to m. by-product.

su·bra·ya·do m. underlining.

su·bra·yar tr. *(señalar)* to underline; *(poner énfasis)* to emphasize.

su·brep·ti·cio, a adj. surreptitious.

su·bro·gar §47 tr. LAW to subrogate.

sub·sa·nar tr. to correct.

subs·cri·bir §80 tr. *(documento)* to sign; *(idea, moción)* to subscribe to; COM. to underwrite —reflex. to subscribe *(a* to).

subs·crip·ción f. subscription.

subs·crip·tor, ·ra m.f. subscriber.

sub·se·cre·ta·rí·a f. *(oficio)* undersecretaryship; *(oficina)* undersecretary's office.

sub·se·cre·ta·rio, a m.f. *(en una oficina)* assistant secretary; *(de un ministro)* undersecretary.

sub·se·cuen·te adj. subsequent.

sub·si·diar tr. to subsidize.

sub·si·dia·rio, a adj. subsidiary; LAW ancillary.

sub·si·dio m. *(subvención)* subsidy; *(ayuda)* aid.

sub·si·guien·te adj. subsequent.

sub·sis·ten·cia f. *(vida)* subsistence; *(provisión)* sustenance.

sub·sis·ten·te adj. subsistent.

sub·sis·tir intr. *(vivir)* to subsist; *(permanecer)* to remain.

subs·tan·cia f. substance; *(materia)* matter; *(esencia)* essence; *(jugo)* extract; *(juicio)* sense.

subs·tan·cia·ción f. substantiation.

subs·tan·cial adj. substantial.

subs·tan·cial·men·te adv. *(en substancia)* substantially; *(esencialmente)* essentially.

subs·tan·ciar tr. to substantiate.

subs·tan·cio·so, a adj. substantial.

subs·tan·ti·va·ción f. substantivation.

subs·tan·ti·var tr. to substantivate.

subs·tan·ti·vo, a I. adj. substantive **II.** m. noun.

subs·ti·tu·ción f. substitution.

subs·ti·tuir §18 tr. to substitute.

subs·ti·tu·ti·vo, a adj. & m. substitute.

subs·ti·tu·to, a m.f. replacement; THEAT. understudy.

subs·trac·ción f. *(acción)* taking away; *(deduc-*

ción) deduction; *(robo)* theft; MATH. subtraction.

subs·tra·en·do m. subtrahend.

subs·tra·er §72 tr. *(quitar)* to take away; *(deducir)* to deduce; *(robar)* to steal; MATH. to subtract —reflex. to avoid.

subs·tra·to m. substratum; PHILOS. essence.

sub·sue·lo m. basement; GEOL. subsoil.

sub·te m. R.P., COLL. subway.

sub·te·nien·te m. second lieutenant.

sub·ter·fu·gio m. subterfuge.

sub·te·rrá·ne·o, a I. adj. underground II. m. *(lugar)* underground place; AMER. *(tren)* subway.

sub·tí·tu·lo m. subtitle.

su·bur·ba·no, a I. adj. suburban II. m.f. suburbanite.

su·bur·bio m. *(arrabal)* suburb; *(barrio pobre)* slum.

sub·ven·ción f. subsidy.

sub·ven·cio·nar tr. to subsidize.

sub·ver·sión f. *(acción)* subversion; *(revolución)* revolution.

sub·ver·si·vo, a adj. subversive.

sub·ya·cen·te adj. underlying.

sub·yu·ga·dor, ·ra I. adj. subjugating; FIG. captivating II. m.f. subjugator; FIG. captivator.

sub·yu·gar §47 tr. to subjugate; FIG. to captivate.

suc·ción f. suction.

su·ce·dá·ne·o, a adj. & m. substitute.

su·ce·der intr. *(reemplazar)* to succeed; *(ocurrir)* to occur —reflex. to follow one another.

su·ce·di·do m. COLL. event.

su·ce·sión f. succession; *(herederos)* heirs; *(herencia)* inheritance.

su·ce·si·va·men·te adv. successively ♦ **y así s.** and so on.

su·ce·si·vo, a adj. consecutive ♦ **en lo s.** in the future.

su·ce·so m. event; *(transcurso)* course; *(resultado)* outcome.

su·ce·sor, ·ra I. adj. succeeding II. m.f. successor; *(heredero)* heir.

su·cie·dad f. *(mugre)* dirt; *(inmundicia)* filth.

su·cin·to, a adj. succinct.

su·cio, a adj. *(no limpio)* dirty; *(asqueroso)* filthy; *(vil)* vile; *(deshonesto)* indecent.

su·cre m. ECUAD., FIN. sucre.

su·cu·len·cia f. succulence.

su·cu·len·to, a adj. succulent.

su·cum·bir intr. to succumb.

su·cur·sal I. adj. branch II. f. *(oficina)* branch (office); *(de empresa)* subsidiary.

sud m. south.

su·dar intr. to sweat; FIG. to work hard —tr. *(empapar en sudor)* to sweat; FIG. to work hard for; BOT. to ooze ♦ **s. la gota gorda** COLL. to be dripping with sweat; FIG. to work hard.

su·da·rio m. shroud.

su·des·ta·da f. R.P. rainy southeast wind.

su·des·te m. southeast.

su·do·es·te m. southwest.

su·dor m. sweat ♦ **con el s. de la frente** by the sweat of one's brow.

su·do·rí·fe·ro/fi·co, a I. adj. sudoriferous II. m. sudorific.

su·do·ro·so, a adj. sweaty.

sue·gra f. mother-in-law.

sue·gro m. father-in-law ♦ pl. in-laws.

sue·la f. sole; *(cuero)* tanned leather; TECH. washer ♦ **media s.** half sole • **un pícaro de siete suelas** COLL. an out-and-out rascal.

sue·la, lo see **soler**.

suel·de, do see **soldar**.

suel·do m. salary ♦ **a s.** on a salary.

sue·lo m. *(tierra)* ground; *(terreno)* soil; *(territorio)* land; *(piso)* floor; *(pavimento)* pavement; *(tierra)* earth, world ♦ **estar por los suelos** COLL. to be dirt cheap • **s. natal** homeland • **venir** or **venirse al s.** to fall down, collapse; FIG. to fail.

suel·te, to see **soltar**.

suel·to, a I. adj. loose; *(desatado)* untied; *(que no hace juego)* odd; *(ágil)* nimble; *(atrevido)* daring ♦ **s. de lengua** *(charlatán)* loose-tongued; *(insolente)* sharp-tongued • **venderse s.** *(por peso)* to be sold in bulk; *(por separado)* to be sold singly II. m. *(artículo)* insert; *(dinero)* loose change.

sue·ne, no see **sonar²**.

sue·ñe, ño see **soñar**.

sue·ño m. *(acto)* sleep; *(representación)* dream; *(adormecimiento)* drowsiness; *(ilusión)* dream; *(encanto)* dream <este bebé es un s. this baby is a dream> ♦ **caerse de s.** to be falling asleep on one's feet • **dar s.** to make sleepy • **echar un s.** to take a nap • **entre sueños** while half asleep • **ni en** or **por sueños** not even in one's dreams • **no poder conciliar el s.** not to be able to sleep • **perder el s. por algo** to lose sleep over something • **quitar el s.** to keep awake • **s. dorado** life's dream • **s. hecho realidad** dream come true • **s. pesado** heavy sleep • **tener el s. liviano** to be a light sleeper • **tener s.** to be sleepy.

sue·ro m. serum; *(de la leche)* whey.

suer·te f. *(destino)* fate; *(fortuna)* luck; *(condición)* lot <mejorar la s. del pueblo to improve the lot of the people>; *(género)* kind ♦ **buena s.** good luck • **caerle** or **tocarle a uno en s.** to fall to one's lot • **dar** or **traer s.** to bring luck • **de otra s.** otherwise • **de s. que** in a way that • **echar suertes** to draw lots • **estar de mala s.** to be out of luck • **estar de s.** to be in luck • **la s. está echada** the die is cast • **por s.** *(por casualidad)* by chance; *(por fortuna)* luckily • **s. negra** very bad luck • **tener s.** to be lucky.

sué·ter m. sweater.

su·fi·cien·cia f. *(aptitud)* competence; COLL. *(presunción)* smugness.

su·fi·cien·te adj. *(bastante)* sufficient; *(presumido)* pedantic.

su·fi·jo m. suffix.

su·fra·gar §47 tr. to pay (for) —intr. AMER. to vote.

su·fra·gio m. *(derecho)* suffrage; *(voto)* vote.

su·fra·gis·ta POL. m.f. suffragist —f. suffragette.

su·fri·do, a adj. patient.

su·fri·mien·to m. suffering.

su·frir tr. *(padecer)* to suffer; *(experimentar)* to undergo; *(soportar)* to endure —intr. *(padecer)* to suffer; *(preocuparse)* to worry ♦ **s. de** to suffer from.

su·ge·ren·cia f. suggestion.

su·ge·rir §65 tr. to suggest.

su·ges·tión f. suggestion.

su·ges·tio·nar tr. *(influenciar)* to influence; *(hipnotizar)* to hypnotize.

su·ges·ti·vo, a adj. *(sugerente)* suggestive; *(interesante)* appealing.

su·gie·ra, ro, riera, rió see **sugerir**.

sui·ci·da I. adj. suicidal II. m.f. suicide.

sui·ci·dar·se reflex. to commit suicide.

sui·ci·dio m. suicide.

su·je·ción f. *(dominación)* subjection; *(ligadura)* fastening ◆ **con s. a** subject to.

su·je·ta·dor, ·ra I. adj. fastening II. m.f. *(objeto que sujeta)* fastener; *(horquilla)* clip —m. *(sostén)* bra.

su·je·ta·li·bros m.inv. bookend.

su·je·ta·pa·pe·les m.inv. paper clip *or* clamp.

su·je·tar tr. *(fijar)* to fasten; *(agarrar)* to grasp; *(dominar)* to subject ◆ **s. con clavos** to nail down • **s. con grapas** to staple —reflex. *(someterse)* to subject oneself; *(agarrarse)* to hang *or* hold on; *(ajustarse)* to conform.

su·je·to, a I. see **sujetar** II. adj. *(susceptible)* subject *(a* to); *(fijado)* fastened III. m. subject; COLL. *(tipo)* individual.

sul·fa·to m. sulfate, sulphate.

sul·fu·ro m. sulfide.

sul·tán, ·a·na m. sultan —f. sultana.

su·ma f. sum; MATH. *(adición)* addition; *(cantidad)* amount of money; FIG. summary ◆ **en s.** in short.

su·ma·men·te adv. extremely.

su·man·do m. addend.

su·mar tr. *(resumir)* to add (up); *(totalizar)* to add up to —reflex. to join (in) ◆ **s. a** *(añadirse a)* to be added to; *(agregarse a)* to join; *(adherirse a)* to adhere to.

su·ma·ria·men·te adv. summarily.

su·ma·rio, a I. adj. brief; LAW summary II. m. summary; LAW indictment.

su·mer·gi·ble adj. & m. submersible.

su·mer·gir §32 tr. to submerge; FIG. plunge —reflex. to dive, submerge ◆ **s. en** to become immersed *or* absorbed in.

su·mi·de·ro m. drain.

su·mi·nis·tra·dor, ·ra m.f. supplier.

su·mi·nis·trar tr. to supply.

su·mi·nis·tro m. supply ◆ **s. a domicilio** home delivery.

su·mir tr. to sink, submerge —reflex. *(hundirse)* to sink; *(en duda, depresión)* to become immersed.

su·mi·sión f. *(acción)* submission; *(carácter)* submissiveness; *(obediencia)* obedience.

su·mi·so, a adj. *(sometido)* submissive; *(obediente)* obedient.

su·mo, a adj. greatest; FIG. enormous ◆ **a lo sumo** at (the) most • **de sumo** completely.

sun·tua·rio, a adj. luxury.

sun·tuo·si·dad f. sumptuousness.

sun·tuo·so, a adj. sumptuous.

su·pe·di·tar tr. to subordinate ◆ **estar supeditado a** to depend on.

su·pe·ra·bun·dan·te adj. superabundant.

su·pe·ra·bun·dar intr. to superabound.

su·pe·ra·ción f. *(de dificultad)* overcoming; *(de uno mismo)* self-improvement.

su·pe·rar tr. *(sobrepujar)* to surpass; *(dificultades)* to overcome; *(adversario)* to beat ◆ **estar superado** to be over *or* finished —reflex. to improve oneself.

su·pe·rá·vit m. [pl. inv. *or* **s**] surplus.

su·per·che·rí·a f. deceit.

su·per·do·ta·do, a adj. & m.f. exceptionally gifted (child).

su·pe·res·truc·tu·ra f. superstructure.

su·per·fi·cial adj. superficial; FIG. shallow.

su·per·fi·cie f. surface; GEOM. area ◆ **salir a la s.** to (come to the) surface.

su·per·fi·no, a adj. extra fine.

su·per·fluo, a adj. superfluous.

su·per·hom·bre m. superman.

su·pe·rin·ten·den·te m.f. superintendent.

su·pe·rior I. m. superior II. adj. *(de más altura)* upper <*pisos superiores* upper floors>; *(más alto)* higher <*enseñanza s.* higher education>; *(mejor)* better; *(excelente)* superior.

su·pe·rio·ra f. mother superior.

su·pe·rio·ri·dad f. *(calidad)* superiority; *(autoridad)* higher authority.

su·per·la·ti·vo, a adj. & m. superlative.

su·per·mer·ca·do m. supermarket.

su·per·nu·me·ra·rio, a adj. & m.f. supernumerary.

su·per·po·bla·ción f. overpopulation.

su·per·po·bla·do, a adj. overpopulated.

su·per·po·ner §54 tr. *(poner encima de)* to superimpose; *(anteponer)* to place above *or* before.

su·per·po·ten·cia f. superpower.

su·per·pro·duc·ción f. overproduction.

su·per·só·ni·co, a adj. supersonic.

su·pers·ti·ción f. superstition.

su·pers·ti·cio·so, a adj. superstitious.

su·per·vi·sar tr. to supervise.

su·per·vi·sión f. supervision.

su·per·vi·sor, ·ra I. adj. supervisory II. m.f. supervisor.

su·per·vi·ven·cia f. survival.

su·pie·ra, po see **saber**[2].

su·pi·no, a I. adj. supine ◆ **ignorancia s.** crass ignorance II. m. supine.

su·plan·tar tr. to supplant.

su·ple·men·tal/ta·rio, a adj. supplemental, supplementary.

su·ple·men·to m. supplement; RAIL., THEAT. supplementary *or* extra charge.

su·plen·cia f. replacement.

su·plen·te I. adj. *(que suple)* substitute; SPORT. reserve II. m.f. replacement; SPORT. reserve player; THEAT. understudy.

sú·pli·ca f. *(ruego)* plea; *(petición)* request.

su·pli·can·te I. adj. *(que ruega)* pleading; *(que pide)* petitioning II. m.f. supplicant.

su·pli·car §70 tr. to implore.

su·pli·cio m. *(tortura)* torture; *(castigo corporal)* corporal punishment; *(dolor)* suffering.

su·plir tr. *(compensar)* to make up for; *(reemplazar)* to replace.

su·pón, pondrá, dría see **suponer**[2].

su·po·ner[1] m. COLL. supposition.

su·po·ner[2] §54 tr. *(presumir)* to suppose; *(imaginar)* to imagine; *(traer consigo)* to entail <*el proyecto supone grandes gastos* the project entails a considerable outlay> ◆ **ser de s.** to be possible *or* likely.

su·pon·ga, go see **suponer**[2].

su·po·si·ción f. supposition; *(conjetura)* assumption.

su·po·si·to·rio m. suppository.

su·pra·rre·nal adj. suprarenal.

su·pre·ma·cí·a f. supremacy.

su·pre·mo, a adj. supreme; *(definitivo)* final.

su·pre·sión f. elimination.

su·pri·mir tr. to eliminate.

su·pues·to, a I. see **suponer**[2] II. adj. *(fingido)* assumed <*nombre s.* assumed name>; *(que se supone)* supposed; *(imaginario)* imaginary; *(hipotético)* hypothetical ◆ **dar por s.** to take for granted • **por s.** of course III. m. supposition ◆ **en el s. de que** supposing that.

su·pu·rar intr. to suppurate.

su·pu·sie·ra, so see **suponer²**.
sur m. south.
sur·car §70 tr. AGR. to plow; MARIT. to cut *or* plow through.
sur·co m. *(en la tierra)* trench; *(en el rostro)* wrinkle.
sur·gir §32 intr. *(surtir)* to shoot up; *(aparecer)* to arise.
sur·me·na·je m. mental strain *or* fatigue.
su·rre·a·lis·ta I. adj. surrealistic II. m.f. surrealist.
sur·ti·do, a I. adj. assorted II. m. selection.
sur·ti·dor, ·ra I. adj. supplying II. m. *(proveedor)* supplier; *(chorro)* spout; *(fuente)* fountain ♦ **s. de gasolina** filling station.
sur·tir tr. to supply ♦ **s. efecto** to have the desired effect —intr. to gush.
sus·cep·ti·bi·li·dad f. susceptibility, sensitivity.
sus·cep·ti·ble/ti·vo, a adj. susceptible; *(quisquilloso)* sensitive.
sus·ci·tar tr. to stir up.
sus·cri·bir §80 tr. & reflex. var. of **subscribir**.
sus·crip·ción f. var. of **subscripción**.
sus·crip·tor, ·ra m.f. var. of **subscriptor, a**.
su·so·di·cho, a adj. abovementioned.
sus·pen·der tr. to suspend; *(colgar)* to hang; *(interrumpir)* to interrupt; *(reprobar)* to fail; LAW to adjourn.
sus·pen·sión f. suspension; LAW adjournment ♦ **s. de hostilidades** cease-fire • **s. de garantías** suspension of constitutional rights.
sus·pen·si·vo, a adj. suspensive ♦ **puntos suspensivos** ellipsis.
sus·pen·so, a I. see **suspender** II. m. EDUC. failing mark ♦ **de s.** suspense *<una película de s.* a suspense movie>* • **en s.** pending • **mantener en s.** to keep guessing.
sus·pen·so·res m.pl. AMER. suspenders.
sus·pen·so·rio, a I. adj. suspensory II. m. MED. truss; SPORT. athletic supporter.
sus·pi·ca·cia f. distrust.
sus·pi·caz adj. distrustful.
sus·pi·rar intr. to sigh ♦ **s. por** to long for.
sus·pi·ro m. sigh ♦ **dar** *or* **exhalar el último s.** to breathe one's last.
sus·tan·cia f. var. of **substancia**.
sus·tan·ti·vo, a adj. & m. var. of **substantivo**.
sus·ten·ta·mien·to m./**ción** f. *(alimento)* sustenance; *(base)* support; AER. lift.
sus·ten·tar tr. *(alimentar)* to sustain; *(apoyar)* to support; *(afirmar)* to uphold —reflex. *(alimentarse)* to nourish oneself; *(mantenerse)* to support oneself ♦ **s. con** *or* **de** to feed on.
sus·ten·to m. *(alimento)* sustenance; *(apoyo)* support; *(medios)* livelihood ♦ **ganarse el s.** to earn one's living.
sus·ti·tu·ción f. var. of **substitución**.
sus·ti·tuir §18 tr. var. of **substituir**.
sus·ti·tu·to, a adj. & m.f. var. of **substituto, a**.
sus·to m. *(miedo)* scare; *(preocupación)* dread ♦ **caerse del s.** COLL. to be frightened to death • **darse** *or* **pegarse un s.** COLL. to get a scare • **dar un s. a alguien** to frighten someone.
sus·trac·ción f. var. of **substracción**.
sus·tra·er §72 tr. var. of **substraer**.
su·su·rran·te adj. *(que susurra)* whispering; *(follaje)* rustling.
su·su·rrar intr. *(murmurar)* to whisper; *(el agua)* to murmur; *(hojas)* to rustle —reflex. to be rumored.
su·su·rro m. *(murmullo)* whisper; *(de hojas)* rustling.
su·til adj. subtle; *(perspicaz)* sharp.
su·ti·le·za/li·dad f. subtlety; *(agudeza)* sharpness.
su·tu·ra f. suture.
su·tu·rar tr. to suture.
su·yo, a I. adj. his, her, your, their *<la casa s. elegantísima; la nuestra es bastante fea* their house is very elegant; ours is rather ugly>; of his, of hers, of yours, of theirs *<ese amigo s.* that friend of yours>* II. pron. his, hers, yours, theirs *<estos libros son suyos* these books are yours>* ♦ **hacer de las suyas** COLL. to be up to one's old tricks • **ir a lo s.** to look after one's own interest • **lo s.** one's share • **los suyos** one's friends *or* family • **salirse con la s.** COLL. to get one's way.
svás·ti·ca f. swastika.

T

t, T f. twenty-first letter of the Spanish alphabet.
ta·ba f. ANAT. anklebone ♦ pl. knucklebones.
ta·ba·cal m. tobacco field.
ta·ba·ca·le·ro, a I. adj. tobacco II. m.f. *(cultivador)* tobacco grower *or* dealer.
ta·ba·co m. tobacco.
tá·ba·no m. gadfly.
ta·ba·que·rí·a f. tobacco store.
ta·ba·que·ro, a I. adj. tobacco II. m.f. tobacco processor *or* dealer —f. tobacco box *or* pouch.
ta·ber·na f. tavern.
ta·ber·ná·cu·lo m. tabernacle.
ta·ber·ne·ro, a m.f. bartender.
ta·bi·que m. partition ♦ **t. nasal** nasal bone.
ta·bla f. *(de madera)* board; *(de mármol)* slab; *(índice)* index; *(lista)* table; *(faja de tierra)* strip of land; PAINT., SEW. panel ♦ **hacer t. rasa de** to disregard • **t. de lavar** washboard • **t. de planchar** ironing board • **t. de salvación** last resort • **t. rasa** tabula rasa ♦ pl. *(empate)* tie; THEAT. boards.
ta·bla·do m. *(tablas)* floorboards; *(plataforma)* wooden platform; THEAT. stage; CRIMIN. execution scaffold.
ta·bla·o m. SP. stage of flamenco nightclub.
ta·ble·a·do, a I. adj. pleated II. m. pleats.
ta·ble·ar tr. CARP. to divide wood into planks; SEW. to divide into pleats.
ta·ble·ro m. *(tabla)* board; *(en el juego)* board *<t. de ajedrez* chessboard>; *(pizarra)* blackboard; ELEC. switchboard ♦ **poner** *or* **traer al t.** to risk, stake • **t. contador** abacus • **t. de dibujo** drawing board • **t. de instrumentos** instrument panel; AUTO. dashboard.
ta·ble·ta f. tablet.
ta·ble·te·o m. machine-gun fire.
ta·bli·lla f. *(para anuncios)* bulletin board; *(en billar)* cushion between side pockets; MED. splint.
ta·blón m. thick plank.
ta·bú adj. & m. [pl. **-úes**] taboo.
ta·bu·la·dor m.f. tabulator.
ta·bu·re·te m. stool.
ta·ca·ñe·ar intr. COLL. to be stingy.
ta·ca·ñe·rí·a f. stinginess.
ta·ca·ño, a I. adj. stingy II. m.f. miser.
ta·ca·zo m. blow (with a billiard cue).
ta·cha¹ f. flaw ♦ **sin t.** upright.

ta·cha² f. large tack.
ta·cha·du·ra f. erasure.
ta·char tr. to cross out ♦ **t. de** to accuse of.
ta·cho m. AMER. can ♦ **irse al t.** R.P., COLL. to fail ♦ **t. de basura** AMER. garbage can.
ta·cho·nar tr. to stud.
ta·chue·la f. tack.
tá·ci·to, a adj. tacit.
ta·ci·tur·no, a adj. taciturn.
ta·co m. (cuña) wedge; (en billar) billiard cue; (canuto) blowpipe; (de papel) pad; (de billetes) book of tickets; ARM. wad; (baqueta) ramrod; (atasco) obstruction; MEX. taco.
ta·cón m. heel.
ta·co·na·zo m. blow with the heel.
ta·co·ne·ar intr. to tap one's heels.
tác·ti·co, a I. adj. tactical II. m.f. tactician —f. tactics.
tác·til adj. tactile.
tac·to m. (sentido) (sense of) touch; (acción) touching; (delicadeza) tact ♦ **al t.** to the touch.
ta·cua·ra f. ARG., BOT. kind of bamboo.
ta·fe·tán m. taffeta.
ta·fi·le·te m. morocco leather.
ta·húr, u·ra m.f. cardsharp.
tai·ma·do, a adj. & m.f. cunning or crafty (person).
ta·ja·da f. slice ♦ **sacar t.** to benefit or profit (de from).
ta·jan·te adj. sharp; FIG. categorical.
ta·jar tr. to slice.
ta·jo m. (corte) cut; (con la espada) slash.
tal I. adj. such (a) <nunca he visto t. cosa I have never seen such a thing>; (cierto) certain <un t. José Gómez te llamó a certain Joseph Gómez called you> ♦ **como si t. cosa** as if there were nothing to it ♦ **t. cual** such as <te lo venderé t. cual es I will sell it to you such as it is> ♦ **t. vez** perhaps, maybe II. pron. such a thing <yo no haría t. I would not do such a thing>; (alguno) some, someone ♦ **fulano de t.** so-and-so ♦ **t. para cual** COLL. two of a kind III. adv. thus, so ♦ **con t. que** provided that ♦ **¿qué t.?** COLL. how goes it?
ta·la f. (de árboles) felling; (destrucción) destruction, ruin.
ta·la·bar·te·rí·a f. saddlery.
ta·la·bar·te·ro m. saddler.
ta·la·dor, ·ra I. adj. cutting II. m.f. cutter.
ta·la·dra·dor, ·ra I. adj. drilling II. m.f. (persona) driller —f. (máquina) drill.
ta·la·drar tr. to drill ♦ **t. los oídos** to pierce the ears.
ta·la·dro m. (taladradora) drill; (barrena) gimlet; (agujero) drill hole; ENTOM. shipworm.
tá·la·mo m. nuptial bed; ANAT., BOT. thalamus.
ta·lán m. ding dong.
ta·lan·te m. (humor) mood; (voluntad) will ♦ **hacer algo de buen t.** to do something willingly ♦ **hacer algo de mal t.** to do something unwillingly.
ta·lar tr. (un árbol) to fell, cut down; (destruir) to destroy.
tal·co m. talc; PHARM. talcum powder.
ta·le·ga f. (saco) sack; (dinero) wealth.
ta·len·to m. talent.
ta·len·to·so/tu·do, a adj. talented.
ta·lión m. talion ♦ **ley del t.** principle of an eye for an eye.
ta·lis·mán m. talisman.
ta·lla f. (estatura) height; (medida) size; (escultura) wood carving ♦ **tener t. para** to be cut

out for.
ta·lla·do, a I. adj. (madera) carved; (metal) engraved; JEWEL. cut ♦ **bien t.** well-built II. m. (en madera) carving; (en metal) engraving; JEWEL. cutting.
ta·lla·dor m. engraver.
ta·llar tr. (madera) to carve; (en metal) to engrave; JEWEL. to cut; ARTS to sculpt.
ta·lla·rín m. noodle.
ta·lle m. (de mujer) figure; (de hombre) physique; (cintura) waist; SEW. bodice.
ta·ller m. (de obreros) shop; (de artistas) studio ♦ **t. de reparaciones** AUTO. body shop.
ta·llo m. stem.
tal·mud m. Talmud.
tal·mú·di·co, a adj. Talmudic.
ta·lón m. heel; (moldura) talon; (de cubierta) rim; (comprobante) receipt; (de cheque) stub ♦ **pisarle a alguien los talones** FIG. to be at someone's heels.
ta·lo·na·rio m. (de recibos) receipt book; (de cheques) checkbook.
ta·lo·ne·ra f. heel piece.
ta·mal m. AMER., CUL. tamale.
ta·man·go m. R.P., COLL. shoe.
ta·ma·ño, a I. adj. (tan grande) so large or big, such a large or big <nunca podremos reembolsar t. deuda we can never repay such a large debt>; (muy grande) very big or wide <abrir tamaños ojos to open one's eyes wide>; (igual) such (a) II. m. (dimensión) size; (volumen) volume ♦ **del t. de** as large as ♦ **t. natural** life-size.
ta·ma·rin·do m. tamarind.
tam·ba·le·an·te adj. staggering.
tam·ba·le·ar intr. to stagger.
tam·bién adv. (además) also, too; (asimismo) likewise.
tam·bo m. R.P. dairy farm.
tam·bor m. drum; (persona) drummer; ANAT. eardrum; TECH. cylinder; SEW. embroidery frame; (del revólver) cylinder ♦ **a t. batiente** FIG. triumphantly.
tam·bo·ra f. drum.
tam·bo·re·te m. MARIT. cap.
tam·bo·ril m. small drum.
tam·bo·ri·le·ar intr. (el tamboril) to beat; (con los dedos) to tap.
tam·bo·ri·le·o m. beating (of a drum).
tam·bo·ri·le·ro, a m.f. drummer.
ta·miz m. sieve.
ta·mi·zar §04 tr. (con tamiz) to sift; (luz) to filter; FIG. to screen.
tam·po·co adv. neither, nor.
tam·pón m. ink pad; PHARM. tampon.
tam·tam m. tom-tom.
tan adv. so, as <no soy t. alto como Enrique I am not as tall as Henry> ♦ **t. pronto como** as soon as ♦ **t. siquiera** at least ♦ **t. sólo** only.
tan·da f. (turno) turn; (de trabajadores) shift; (capa) layer <una t. de ladrillos a layer of bricks>; COLL. (gran cantidad) bunch.
tan·gen·te adj. & f. tangent ♦ **irse** or **salir por la t.** to go off on a tangent.
tan·gi·ble adj. tangible.
tan·go m. tango.
tan·gue·ar intr. to tango.
ta·ni·no m. tannin.
tan·que m. tank; (barco) tanker.
tan·te·ar tr. (calcular) to do a rough calculation of; (medir) to gauge; (considerar) to consider carefully; (explorar) to test; (sondear) to sound

out; *(bosquejar)* to sketch —intr. to feel one's way.

tan·te·o m. rough calculation ♦ **al t.** roughly.

tan·to, a I. adj. so much, so many *<jamás he visto t. dinero* I have never seen so much money>* II. pron. that *<a t. arrastra la codicia* that is what greed leads to>* ♦ **las tantas** wee hours • **por (lo) t.** therefore • **t. como** or **cuanto** as much as III. m. *(cantidad)* certain amount; *(en deportes)* point ♦ **a tantos de** on a certain date in *<a tantos de junio* on a certain date in June>* • **en** or **entre t.** in the meantime • **no ser para t.** not to be so bad • **otro t.** the same thing • **t. por ciento** per cent • **y tantos** and some, odd *<mil y tantos* a thousand odd>* IV. adv. *(de tal modo)* so much *<comí t.* I ate so much>; so long *<tardaron t.* it took them so long>; *(hasta tal grado)* to such an extent ♦ **t. como** as much as • **t. más** all the more • **t. mejor** all the better • **t. que** so much that.

ta·ñer §68 tr. *(instrumento)* to play; *(campana)* to toll.

ta·ñi·do m. tolling.

ta·pa f. *(de olla)* lid; *(de libro)* cover; *(bocado)* hors d'oeuvre ♦ **levantarse la t. de los sesos** COLL. to blow someone's brains out.

ta·pa·do m. coat.

ta·par tr. *(cubrir)* to cover (up); *(cerrar)* to plug up; *(ocultar)* to block; FIG. to conceal —reflex. to cover oneself up.

ta·pa·rra·bo m. loincloth.

ta·pe·te m. *(alfombra)* small rug or carpet; *(de mesa)* table runner ♦ **estar sobre el t.** to be under discussion • **poner sobre el t.** to bring up for discussion.

ta·pia f. *(pared de tierra)* mud or adobe wall; *(cerca)* (adjoining) wall ♦ **más sordo que una t.** COLL. deaf as a post.

ta·pial m. (adjoining) wall.

ta·piar tr. to wall in.

ta·pi·ce·rí·a f. *(de tapices)* tapestry-making; *(de muebles)* upholstery; *(tienda)* upholsterer's shop.

ta·pi·ce·ro, a m.f. *(de tapices)* tapestry maker; *(de muebles)* upholsterer.

ta·pio·ca f. tapioca.

ta·pir m. tapir.

ta·piz m. tapestry.

ta·pi·zar §04 tr. *(adornar)* to hang with tapestries; *(muebles)* to upholster; *(el suelo)* to carpet.

ta·pón m. *(de botellas)* cork; *(de tonel)* plug; SURG. tampon ♦ **t. de desagüe** drain plug.

ta·po·nar tr. *(un agujero)* to plug; SURG. to tampon.

ta·po·na·zo m. pop (of a cork).

ta·pu·jo m. ♦ **andar con tapujos** COLL. to be full of secrecy.

ta·que·ra f. rack (for billiard cues).

ta·qui·gra·fí·a f. stenography.

ta·qui·gra·fiar §30 tr. to write in shorthand.

ta·qui·gra·fo, a m.f. stenographer.

ta·qui·lla f. THEAT. *(ventanilla)* box office; *(cantidad)* receipts ♦ **hacer t.** to be a box-office hit.

ta·qui·lle·ro, a I. m.f. ticket agent II. adj. ♦ **éxito t.** box-office hit.

ta·ra¹ f. *(peso)* tare; *(defecto)* defect ♦ **tener una t.** COLL. to be an idiot.

ta·ra² f. tally stick.

ta·ra·do, a adj. & m.f. AMER., COLL. idiot.

ta·ram·ba·na m.f. scatterbrain.

ta·rán·tu·la f. tarantula.

ta·ra·re·ar tr. to hum.

ta·ra·re·o m. humming.

ta·ras·ca·da f. bite.

ta·ras·car §70 tr. to bite.

tar·dan·za f. delay.

tar·dar intr. *(demorarse)* to delay *<no tardes en avisarnos* don't delay in informing us>; *(durar)* to take *<el tren tardó tres horas en llegar* the train took three hours to arrive>; *(tomar tiempo)* to take a long time *<él tardó en contestar* he took a long time to answer>; *(llegar tarde)* to be late ♦ **a más t.** at the latest.

tar·de I. f. afternoon, (early) evening ♦ **buenas tardes** good afternoon II. adv. *(a hora avanzada)* late *<nos acostamos t.* we went to bed late>; *(fuera de tiempo)* too late *<el médico llegó t.* the doctor arrived too late>* ♦ **a la caída de la t.** at dusk • **hacerse t.** to get late • **lo más t.** at the latest • **más vale t. que nunca** better late than never • **por** or **en la t.** in the afternoon • **t. o temprano** sooner or later.

tar·dí·o, a adj. late; *(lento)* slow.

ta·re·a f. task ♦ **t. escolar** homework.

ta·ri·fa f. *(tasa)* tariff; *(precio)* fare; *(tabla)* price list.

ta·ri·far tr. to apply a tariff or rate to.

ta·ri·ma f. movable platform.

tar·je·ta f. card *<t. de identidad* identity card>* ♦ **t. de crédito** credit card • **t. de visita** calling card • **t. perforada** punch card • **t. postal** post card.

tar·je·te·ro m. card case.

tar·quín m. mud.

tar·ra·ja f. MECH. diestock.

ta·rro m. *(vasija)* jar; *(de lata)* tin can ♦ **tener t.** SL. to be lucky.

tar·so m. tarsus.

tar·ta f. pie.

tar·ta·mu·de·ar intr. to stammer.

tar·ta·mu·de·o m./**dez** f. stammering.

tar·ta·mu·do, a I. adj. stammering II. m.f. stammerer.

tar·tán m. tartan.

tár·ta·ro, a adj. & m. tartar.

tar·te·ra f. baking pan.

ta·ru·go m. *(clavija)* wooden peg; *(taco)* wooden block; FIG. blockhead.

ta·sa f. rate ♦ **t. aduanera** customs duty.

ta·sa·ción f. appraisal.

ta·sa·dor, ·ra I. adj. appraising II. m.f. appraiser.

ta·sa·jear tr. AMER., CUL. to jerk.

ta·sa·jo m. jerky.

ta·sar tr. *(poner precio)* to set the price of; *(valorar)* to appraise.

tas·ca f. SL. dive, joint.

tas·car §70 tr. to chomp ♦ **t. el freno** FIG. to chomp at the bit.

ta·ta m. AMER., COLL. daddy.

ta·ta·ra·bue·lo, a m. great-great-grandfather —f. great-great-grandmother ♦ pl. great-great-grandparents.

ta·ta·ra·nie·to, a m. great-great-grandson —f. great-great-granddaughter ♦ pl. great-great-grandchildren.

ta·tua·je m. tattoo.

ta·tuar §67 tr. to tattoo.

tau·ri·no, a adj. taurine.

tau·ro·ma·quia f. bullfighting.

tau·to·lo·gí·a f. tautology.

ta·xi m. taxi.

ta·xi·der·mia f. taxidermy.

ta·xí·me·tro m. *(reloj)* meter; *(vehículo)* taxi.

ta·xis·ta m.f. taxi driver.

ta·xo·no·mí·a f. taxonomy.

ta·za f. cup; *(contenido)* cupful; *(de fuente)* basin; *(de retrete)* bowl.

ta·zón m. large cup.

te pron. you <*te quiero* I love you>; you, to you <*te mandaron una carta* they sent a letter to you>; you, for you <*te compré un regalo* I bought a present for you>; from you <*no le dejes quitarte la pelota* don't let him take the ball from you>; yourself <*cálmate* calm yourself>.

té m. tea ♦ **t. del Paraguay** maté.

te·a f. torch.

te·a·tral adj. theatrical.

te·a·tra·li·dad f. theatricality.

te·a·tro m. theater.

te·cha·do m. *(techo)* roof; *(cobertizo)* shed ♦ **bajo t.** indoors.

te·cha·dor m. roofer.

te·char tr. to roof.

te·cho m. *(tejado)* roof; *(parte interior)* ceiling; AVIA. ceiling ♦ **no tener t.** not to have a roof over one's head.

te·cla f. key ♦ **dar en la t.** COLL. to hit the nail on the head.

te·cla·do m. keyboard.

te·cle·a·do m. fingering.

te·cle·ar intr. *(las teclas)* to finger a keyboard; COLL. *(los dedos)* to drum with the fingers; *(el piano)* to play the piano; FIG. to be doing poorly.

te·cle·o m. drumming with the fingers.

téc·ni·co, a I. adj. technical **II.** m.f. *(especialista)* technician; *(ingeniero)* engineer ♦ **t. agrícola** agronomist • **t. electricista** electrical engineer —f. *(método, habilidad)* technique; *(tecnología)* technology; *(ingeniería)* engineering ♦ **t. electrónica** electronics.

tec·no·cra·cia f. technocracy.

tec·no·lo·gí·a f. technology.

tec·no·ló·gi·co, a adj. technological.

te·dio m. tedium.

te·dio·so, a adj. tedious.

te·gu·men·to m. tegument.

te·ja f. *(mosaico)* tile; *(de techo)* slate.

te·ja·do m. roof ♦ **empezar la casa por el t.** to put the cart before the horse.

te·jar¹ m. brick or tile factory.

te·jar² tr. to tile.

te·je·dor, ·ra I. adj. weaving **II.** m.f. weaver —m. weaverbird —f. AMER. weaving machine.

te·je·ma·ne·je m. COLL. intrigue.

te·jer intr. *(con telar)* to weave; *(hacer punto)* to knit.

te·ji·do m. *(tela)* fabric; *(textura)* weave; ANAT., BIOL. tissue ♦ **t. de alambre** wire mesh • **t. de punto** jersey.

te·jo m. *(para jugar)* chip; *(juego)* quoits; *(de metal)* metal disk; MEX., TECH. step bearing; BOT. yew tree.

te·jón¹ m. ZOOL. badger.

te·jón² m. gold ingot or disk.

te·la f. *(paño)* fabric; *(membrana)* membrane; *(nata)* film; *(de araña)* web; ANAT. film; BOT. skin; ARTS *(lienzo)* canvas; *(pintura)* painting ♦ **poner en t. de juicio** to call into question • **t. adhesiva** adhesive tape • **t. aislante** electrical tape • **t. metálica** wire netting.

te·lar m. TEX. loom; *(de puerta)* frame; BKB. sewing press ♦ **en el t.** in the making.

te·la·ra·ña f. spider web ♦ pl. **tener t. en los ojos** COLL. to have blinders on.

te·le·co·mu·ni·ca·ción f. telecommunication.

te·le·di·fun·dir tr. to telecast.

te·le·di·fu·sión f. telecast.

te·le·di·ri·gi·do, a adj. remote-controlled.

te·le·di·ri·gir §32 tr. to guide by remote control.

te·le·fo·na·zo m. COLL. phone call.

te·le·fo·ne·ar tr. to phone.

te·le·fo·ní·a f. telephony.

te·le·fó·ni·ca·men·te adv. by phone.

te·le·fó·ni·co, a adj. phone ♦ **cabina t.** phone booth • **guía t.** telephone directory.

te·le·fo·nis·ta m.f. telephone operator.

te·lé·fo·no m. telephone.

te·le·fo·to m. telephoto.

te·le·fo·to·gra·fí·a f. telephotography.

te·le·gra·fí·a f. telegraphy.

te·le·gra·fiar §30 tr. to telegraph.

te·le·grá·fi·co, a adj. telegraphic.

te·le·gra·fis·ta m.f. telegrapher.

te·lé·gra·fo m. telegraph.

te·le·gra·ma m. telegram.

te·le·guia·do, a adj. remote-controlled.

te·le·im·pre·sor m. teleprinter.

te·le·man·do m. remote control.

te·le·me·trí·a f. telemetry.

te·le·ob·je·ti·vo m. telephoto lens.

te·le·pa·tí·a f. telepathy.

te·le·pá·ti·co, a adj. telepathic.

te·les·có·pi·co, a adj. telescopic.

te·les·co·pio m. telescope.

te·les·pec·ta·dor, ·ra m.f. television viewer.

te·le·ti·po m. teletype.

te·le·vi·den·te m.f. television viewer.

te·le·vi·sar tr. to televise.

te·le·vi·sión f. television.

te·le·vi·sor m. television (set).

te·lex m. telex.

te·lón m. THEAT. curtain; MEX. riddle ♦ **t. de boca** drop curtain • **t. de fondo** backdrop.

te·lú·ri·co, a adj. telluric.

te·lu·rio m. tellurium.

te·ma m. *(asunto)* subject; *(escrito)* composition; *(idea fija)* obsession; MUS. theme.

te·ma·rio m. agenda.

te·má·ti·co, a II. adj. *(del tema)* thematic; *(terco)* obstinate **II.** f. subject.

tem·bla·de·ra f. *(acción)* trembling fit; *(vasija)* thin two-handled cup.

tem·blar §49 intr. *(temblequear)* to tremble; *(tener miedo)* to be afraid ♦ **t. de frío** to shiver with cold • **t. de miedo** to quiver with fear.

tem·ble·que m. *(persona)* trembler; *(terremoto)* earthquake.

tem·ble·que·ar intr. to tremble.

tem·blor m. tremor; AMER. earthquake ♦ **t. de tierra** earthquake.

tem·blo·(ro·)so, a adj. shaking.

te·mer tr. & intr. to fear ♦ **t. a** to be afraid of • **t. por** to fear for.

te·me·ra·rio, a adj. reckless.

te·me·ri·dad f. temerity.

te·me·ro·so, a adj. *(temible)* frightening; *(tímido)* timid.

te·mi·ble adj. frightful.

te·mor m. *(miedo)* fear; *(presunción)* foreboding.

tém·pa·no m. *(de hielo)* iceberg; *(tapa de tonel)* barrel head.

tem·pe·ra·men·tal adj. temperamental.

tem·pe·ra·men·to m. *(naturaleza)* temperament; *(temperie)* weather.

tem·pe·ran·cia f. temperance.

tem·pe·rar tr. *(calmar)* to calm; *(moderar)* to temper.

tem·pe·ra·tu·ra f. temperature.

tem·pes·tad f. storm ♦ **t. en un vaso de agua** tempest in a teapot.

tem·pes·tuo·so, a adj. stormy.

tem·pla·do, a adj. *(moderado)* moderate; *(tibio)* lukewarm; *(el clima)* mild.

tem·plan·za f. *(sobriedad)* temperance; *(moderación)* moderation; *(del clima)* mildness.

tem·plar tr. *(moderar)* to temper; *(la temperatura)* to make lukewarm; METAL. to temper; MUS. to tune; *(mitigar)* to mitigate; *(apaciguar)* to appease —intr. to warm up.

tem·ple m. *(de metales)* temper; *(índole)* nature; *(disposición)* mood <estar de buen t. to be in a good mood>; *(valentía)* courage.

tem·plo m. temple.

tem·po·ra·da f. *(del año)* season; *(período)* period ♦ **de fuera de t.** off-season ♦ **por temporadas** off and on • **t. baja** off season.

tem·po·ral I. adj. *(pasajero)* temporary; *(secular)* temporal **II.** m. *(tempestad)* storm; *(lluvia persistente)* rainy spell.

tem·po·rá·ne·o/ra·rio, a adj. temporary.

tem·pra·ne·ro, a adj. early ♦ **ser t.** to be an early riser.

tem·pra·no, a adj. & adv. early.

ten see **tener.**

te·na·ci·dad f. tenacity.

te·naz adj. tenacious.

te·na·za(s) f.(pl.) *(herramienta)* pliers; ZOOL. pincers; *(del fuego)* tongs; MED. forceps ♦ **t. de rizar** curling iron.

ten·de·de·ro m. clothesline.

ten·den·cia f. *(propensión)* tendency; *(de moda, mercado)* trend.

ten·den·cio·so, a adj. tendentious.

ten·der §50 tr. *(extender)* to spread (out); *(alargar)* to stretch out <me tendió la mano he stretched out his hand to me>; *(ropa)* to hang out; *(cable)* to lay; *(puente)* to build —intr. to tend *(a* to) —reflex. to lie down.

ten·de·ro, a m.f. shopkeeper.

ten·di·do, a I. adj. *(extendido)* stretched *or* spread out; EQUIT. full **II.** m. *(acción)* spreading; *(ropa)* load of wash.

ten·dien·te adj. AMER. tending.

ten·dón m. tendon.

ten·drá, dría see **tener.**

te·ne·bro·so, a adj. *(sombrío)* dark; *(secreto)* shady; *(oscuro)* obscure.

te·ne·dor, ·ra m.f. *(poseedor)* owner; COM. bearer —m. fork ♦ **t. de acciones** stockholder • **t. de libros** bookkeeper.

te·ne·du·rí·a f. bookkeeping.

te·nen·cia f. possession.

te·ner §69 tr. to have; *(poseer)* to possess; *(asir)* to take hold of <ten el cable take hold of the rope>; *(contener)* to contain; *(mantener)* to maintain; *(considerar)* to consider <tuvo a menos trabajar en tal cosa she considered it beneath her to work on anything like that>; to be <tiene sesenta años de edad he is sixty years of age>; *(cumplir)* to keep, fulfill ♦ **no t. sobre qué caerse muerto** not to have a cent to one's name • **t. a bien** to see fit to • **t. calor, frío** to be hot, cold • **t. celos** to be jealous • **t. cuidado** to be careful • **t. en cuenta** to take into account • **t. en mucho** to esteem • **t. en poco** to think little of • **t. éxito** to succeed • **t. ganas de** to feel like • **t. hambre, sed** to be hungry, thirsty • **t. la bondad de** to be kind enough to • **t. la culpa** to be to blame • **t. lugar** to take place • **t. miedo** to be afraid • **t. mucho de** to resemble • **t. por** to think <lo tengo por sabio I consider him wise> • **t. presente** to bear in mind • **t. prisa** to be in a hurry • **t. que** to have to <tenemos que hacerlo we have to do it> • **t. que ver con** to have to do with • **t. razón** to be right • **t. sueño** to be sleepy • **t. suerte** to be lucky —m/f. MUS. tenor. to be well-off —reflex. to steady oneself ♦ **t. de pie** to stand up • **t. por** to consider oneself.

te·nia f. tapeworm.

te·nien·te m. lieutenant; *(sustituto)* substitute, deputy.

te·nis m. tennis ♦ **t. de mesa** Ping-Pong.

te·nis·ta m.f. tennis player.

te·nor[1] m. tenor; tone ♦ **a t. de** in accordance with.

te·nor[2] m. MUS. tenor.

te·no·rio m. Don Juan.

ten·sar tr. to stretch.

ten·sión f. tension; *(emocional)* stress ♦ **t. arterial** blood pressure.

ten·so, a adj. *(tirante)* tense; *(nervios, situación)* strained; *(emocionalmente)* stressed.

ten·sor, ·ra I. adj. tensile **II.** m. *(aparato)* tightener; TECH. turnbuckle.

ten·ta·ción f. temptation.

ten·tá·cu·lo m. tentacle.

ten·ta·dor, ·ra I. adj. tempting **II.** m. tempter.

ten·tar §49 tr. *(palpar)* to grope; *(seducir)* to tempt; *(intentar)* to try.

ten·ta·ti·vo, a I. adj. tentative **II.** f. attempt ♦ **t. de delito** LAW attempted crime.

te·nue adj. *(delgado)* thin; *(luz)* soft.

te·ñir §59 tr. to dye; PAINT. to darken; FIG. to imbue.

te·o·cra·cia f. theocracy.

te·o·lo·gí·a f. theology.

te·ó·lo·go, a m.f. theologian.

te·o·re·ma m. theorem.

te·o·ré·ti·co, a adj. theoretical.

te·o·rí·a f. theory.

te·ó·ri·co, a I. adj. theoretical **II.** m.f. theoretician.

te·o·ri·zar §04 tr. to theorize.

te·o·so·fí·a f. theosophy.

te·ó·so·fo, a m.f. theosophist.

te·qui·la f. tequila.

te·ra·peu·ta m.f. therapist.

te·ra·péu·ti·co, a I. adj. therapeutic **II.** f. therapy.

te·ra·pia f. therapy.

ter·cer adj. contr. of **tercero.**

ter·cer·mun·dis·ta adj. third-worldist.

ter·ce·ro, a I. adj. third <ella vive en la t. casa a la derecha she lives in the third house on the right> **II.** m. *(mediador)* mediator; LAW third party —f. MUS. third; AUTO. third gear.

ter·ce·to m. POET. tercet; MUS. trio.

ter·cia·do, a adj. *(azúcar)* brown; *(atravesado)* crosswise.

ter·ciar tr. to place diagonally across —intr. *(interponerse)* to mediate; *(participar)* to take part <t. en una conversación to take part in a conversation>; *(completar)* to fill in.

ter·cio, a adj. & m. third.

ter·cio·pe·lo m. velvet.

ter·co, a adj. stubborn.
ter·gi·ver·sa·ción f. distortion.
ter·gi·ver·sar tr. to distort.
ter·mal adj. thermal.
ter·mas f.pl. hot baths or springs.
ter·mi·na·ción f. ending.
ter·mi·nal I. adj. terminal **II.** m. ELEC. terminal —f. (estación) terminal.
ter·mi·nan·te adj. definite.
ter·mi·nar tr. (poner término) to end; (acabar) to complete —intr. (tener término) to come to an end ♦ **t. de** (acabar de) to have just; (concluir) to finish <terminamos de comer we finished eating> • **t. en** to end up in • **t. por** to end up <terminó por marcharse enfadado he ended up going away angry> —reflx. to come to an end.
tér·mi·no m. (conclusión) end; (palabra, tiempo) term; (límite) boundary; LOG., MATH. term ♦ **dar t. a** to finish off • **en buenos términos con** on good terms with • **en último t.** in the last analysis • **llevar a t.** to carry out • **poner t. a** to put an end to • **por t. medio** on the average • **t. medio** MATH. average; (compromiso) middle ground.
ter·mi·no·lo·gí·a f. terminology.
ter·mi·ta m. termite.
ter·mo m. thermos (bottle).
ter·mo·di·ná·mi·ca f. thermodynamics.
ter·mo·e·léc·tri·co, a adj. thermoelectric.
ter·mó·me·tro m. thermometer.
ter·mo·nu·cle·ar adj. thermonuclear.
ter·mo·rre·gu·la·dor m. thermostat.
ter·mos·ta·to m. thermostat.
ter·na f. (lista) list of three candidates; (en dados) pair of three.
ter·ne·ra f. (animal) female calf; (carne) veal.
ter·ne·ro m. male calf.
ter·no m. (tres) set of three; (vestido) three-piece suit; (en lotería) set of three numbers.
ter·nu·ra f. tenderness.
ter·que·dad f. stubbornness.
te·rra·co·ta f. terra cotta.
te·rra·mi·ci·na f. terramycin.
te·rra·plén m. embankment.
te·rra·ple·nar tr. (llenar) to fill up with earth; (hacer terraplén) to embank.
te·rrá·que·o, a adj. terrestrial ♦ **globo t.** the earth.
te·rra·te·nien·te m. landowner.
te·rra·za f. (balcón) terrace; (azotea) roof terrace; (de un café) veranda.
te·rre·mo·to m. earthquake.
te·rre·nal adj. earthly.
te·rre·no, a I. adj. (terrestre) earthly; (terrenal) worldly **II.** m. (tierra) land; (campo) piece of land; (suelo) ground; GEOL. terrain; SPORT. field ♦ **preparar el t.** to pave the way • **reconocer el t.** to get the lay of the land • **t. conocido** familiar territory.
te·rres·tre adj. terrestrial.
te·rri·ble adj. terrible.
te·rrí·co·la m.f. earthling.
te·rri·to·rial adj. territorial.
te·rri·to·rio m. territory; (comarca) zone.
te·rrón m. (de tierra) clod; (de azúcar) lump.
te·rror m. terror.
te·rro·rí·fi·co, a adj. terrifying.
te·rro·ris·ta adj. & m.f. terrorist.
te·rru·ño m. (tierra) land; (país) native land.
ter·so, a adj. (limpio) clear; (estilo) smooth.
ter·tu·lia f. (reunión) social gathering; THEAT.

upper gallery ♦ **t. literaria** literary circle.
te·sis f.inv. thesis; (opinión) theory.
te·si·tu·ra f. tessitura; (actitud) frame of mind.
te·són m. tenacity.
te·so·ne·ro, a adj. tenacious.
te·so·re·rí·a f. treasury.
te·so·re·ro, a m.f. COM. treasurer —m. RELIG. custodian.
te·so·ro m. (dinero) treasure; (fondos públicos) treasury; FIG. gem.
tes·ta f. head.
tes·ta·dor, ra m.f. testator.
tes·ta·fe·rro m. figurehead.
tes·ta·men·ta·rio, a I. adj. testamentary **II.** m. executor —f. executrix.
tes·ta·men·to m. will ♦ **Antiguo T.** Old Testament • **Nuevo T.** New Testament.
tes·tar intr. to make a will.
tes·ta·ru·do, a adj. & m.f. stubborn (person).
tes·te m. testicle.
tes·tí·cu·lo m. testicle.
tes·ti·fi·car §70 tr. to testify (to).
tes·ti·go m.f. witness ♦ **t. de cargo** witness for the prosecution • **t. de descargo** witness for the defense • **t. ocular** eyewitness —m. FIG. proof.
tes·ti·mo·niar tr. to testify (to).
tes·ti·mo·nio m. testimony; (atestación) affidavit; FIG. token ♦ **falso t.** perjury.
tes·tuz m. (frente) forehead; (nuca) nape.
te·ta f. (pecho) breast; (de vaca) udder; (pezón) nipple ♦ **dar la t. a** to nurse • **niño de t.** nursing infant • **quitar la t. a** to wean.
té·ta·no(s) m. tetanus.
te·te·ra f. teapot.
te·ti·lla f. (de mamíferos) teat; (de biberón) nipple.
te·tra·e·dro m. tetrahedron.
té·tri·co, a adj. gloomy.
tex·til adj. & m. textile.
tex·to m. (contenido) text; (libro) textbook.
tex·tual adj. textual.
tex·tu·ra f. texture.
tez f. complexion.
ti pron. you <lo compré para ti I bought it for you>; yourself <hazlo para ti do it for yourself>.
tí·a f. aunt; COLL. (mujer cualquiera) dame ♦ **cuéntaselo a tu t.** COLL. tell it to the marines • **no hay tu t.** COLL. no use • **t. abuela** great-aunt.
tia·ra f. tiara.
ti·bia f. tibia.
ti·bio, a adj. lukewarm.
ti·bu·rón m. shark.
tic m. tic.
tic·tac or **tic tac** m. ticking.
tiem·ble, blo see **temblar.**
tiem·po m. time; (época) times <en t. de Napoleón in the times of Napoleon>; (ocasión) moment; (estación) season; METEOROL. weather ♦ **al mismo t.** at the same time • **al t. que** just as • **andando el t.** in the course of time • **a su t.** in due time • **a t.** in or on time • **cargarse el t.** to become overcast • **con t.** (por adelantado) in advance; (en el momento oportuno) in good time • **dar t. al t.** to bide one's time • **de algún t. a esta parte** for some time now • **de t. en t.** from time to time • **en los buenos tiempos** in the good old days • **en t. de Maricastaña** COLL. in olden times • **fuera de t.** at the wrong time • **ganar t.** to save time • **perder el t.** to

waste time • **t. atrás** some time ago.

tien·da f. dress shop ♦ **ir de tiendas** to go shopping • **t. de campaña** tent • **t. de modas** boutique.

tien·da, do see tender.

tie·ne see tener.

tien·ta f. ♦ **a tientas** gropingly • **andar a tientas** to feel one's way.

tien·te, to see tentar.

tien·to m. (tacto) touch; (palo de ciego) blindman's cane; (balancín) balancing pole; (pulso) steady hand; (prudencia) caution; (correa) leather strip ♦ **con t.** cautiously.

tier·no, a adj. (afectuoso) loving; (blando) soft; tender <carne t. tender meat>.

tie·rra f. (superficie) land <viajar por t. to travel by land>; (suelo) ground; (patria) country; (comarca) region; (campo) land <t. de cultivo arable land>; ELEC. ground ♦ **caer a t.** to fall down • **dar en t. con** to knock down • **poner t. de por medio** to make oneself scarce • **T.** Earth • **t. adentro** inland • **t. de nadie** FIG., no man's land • **venir(se) a t.** to collapse.

tie·so, a adj. (rígido) stiff; (estirado) arrogant.

ties·to m. (pedazo) piece of earthenware; (maceta) flowerpot; (vasija) bowl.

ti·foi·de·o, a I. adj. typhoid **II.** f. typhoid fever.

ti·fón m. typhoon.

ti·fus m. typhus.

ti·gre m. tiger ♦ **t. americano** jaguar.

ti·gre·sa f. tigress.

ti·gri·llo m. AMER. wildcat.

ti·je·ra(s) f.(pl.) (instrumento) scissors; (zanja) drainage ditch ♦ **cortado por la misma t.** cut from the same cloth.

ti·je·re·ta f. BOT. tendril; ENTOM. earwig; ORNITH. scissortail.

ti·je·re·ta·da f./**zo** m. snip.

ti·je·re·te·ar tr. to snip —intr. COLL. to butt in.

ti·je·re·te·o m. (acción) snipping; (ruido) snip-snip.

til·dar tr. (poner acento) to put a tilde on; (llamar) to call <t. a alguien de necio to call someone a fool>.

til·de m. (sobre la ñ) tilde; (acento) accent; (tacha) flaw —f. iota.

ti·lin·go, a adj. & m.f. COLL. silly (person).

ti·lo m. linden.

ti·ma·dor, ra m.f. cheat.

ti·mar tr. to cheat.

tim·ba f. COLL. (partida) hand of cards; (garito) gambling den.

tim·bal m. kettledrum; CUL. meat pie.

tim·ba·le·ro, a m.f. kettledrummer.

tim·bra·do, a adj. stamped.

tim·brar tr. to stamp.

tim·bra·zo m. loud ringing.

tim·bre m. (sello) stamp; (sello oficial) tax stamp; (aparato) buzzer; (sonido) ring; (sonoridad) timbre.

ti·mi·dez f. timidity.

tí·mi·do, a adj. timid.

ti·mo¹ m. thymus.

ti·mo² m. swindle.

ti·món m. MARIT. rudder; AVIA. control stick; AGR. plow beam; (pértigo) whippletree; FIG. helm ♦ **manejar el t.** to be at the helm.

ti·mo·ne·ar tr. & intr. to steer.

ti·mo·nel m. helmsman.

ti·mo·ra·to, a adj. shy.

tím·pa·no m. MUS. kettledrum; ANAT. eardrum.

ti·na or **ti·na·ja** f. (vasija) large earthen vat; (cubo) vat; (baño) bathtub.

tin·gla·do m. (cobertizo) shed; (tablado) platform; (enredo) ruse.

ti·nie·blas f.pl. darkness; FIG. ignorance.

ti·no m. (puntería) good aim; (juicio) good judgment ♦ **sacar de t.** to drive crazy • **sin t.** recklessly.

tin·ta f. ink; (color) dye ♦ **media t.** ARTS halftone • **saber de buena t.** COLL. to have it on good authority • **sudar t.** COLL. to sweat blood • **t. china** India ink • **t. simpática** invisible ink ♦ pl. colors • **a medias t.** vaguely • **cargar** or **recargar las t.** to exaggerate.

tin·te m. (acción) dyeing; (colorante) dye; (color) tint; FIG. tinge.

tin·te·ro m. inkwell; PRINT. ink fountain ♦ **quedársele a uno en el t. una cosa** COLL. to slip one's mind.

tin·tín/ti·(li·)ne·o m. (de vasos) clinking; (de campanilla) jingling.

tin·ti·nar/ne·ar intr. (vasos) to clink; (campanilla) to jingle.

tin·to, a I. see teñir **II.** adj. dark-red **III.** m. red wine.

tin·to·re·rí·a f. dry cleaner's shop.

tin·to·re·ro, a m.f. (que tiñe) dyer; (que limpia) dry cleaner.

tin·tu·ra f. dye; PHARM. tincture.

ti·ña f. MED. ringworm; COLL. (miseria) squalor, poverty; (mezquindad) stinginess.

ti·ña, ño, ñera, ñó see teñir.

ti·ño·so, a I. adj. scabby; FIG. stingy **II.** m.f. MED. person suffering from ringworm; FIG. miser.

tí·o m. (pariente) uncle; COLL. (persona cualquiera) fellow ♦ **t. abuelo** great-uncle ♦ pl. aunt and uncle.

tio·vi·vo m. merry-go-round.

ti·pa f. AMER., DEROG. trollop.

tí·pi·co, a adj. typical.

ti·pi·fi·car §70 tr. to typify.

ti·ple m. MUS. (voz) soprano; (instrumento) treble guitar; MARIT. single-piece mast —m.f. MUS. soprano.

ti·po m. (clase) kind; (modelo) type; (figura) figure; DEROG. character; (persona) guy <¿quién es ese t.? who is that guy?>; PRINT. type; COM. rate <t. de interés interest rate>.

ti·po·gra·fí·a f. typography.

ti·pó·gra·fo, a m.f. typesetter.

ti·ra f. strip.

ti·ra·bo·tas m.inv. bootjack.

ti·ra·bu·zón m. (sacacorchos) corkscrew; (bucle) ringlet.

ti·ra·da f. (lanzamiento) throw; (distancia) distance; (serie) series; (edición) edition ♦ **de una t.** at one stretch.

ti·ra·do, a adj. dirt-cheap.

ti·ra·dor, ra m. (de pistola) shot; (de cajón) knob; (de campanilla) bellpull, catapult ♦ pl. suspenders —f. shot.

ti·ra·lí·ne·as m.inv. ruling pen.

ti·ra·ní·a f. tyranny.

ti·ra·ni·zar §04 tr. to tyrannize.

ti·ra·no, a I. adj. tyrannical **II.** m.f. tyrant.

ti·ran·te I. adj. (tenso) tight; (relaciones) strained **II.** m. (correa) strap; ARCHIT. tie beam; TECH. brace ♦ pl. suspenders.

ti·ran·tez f. tightness; FIG. strain.

ti·rar tr. (arrojar) to throw; (desechar) to throw

away; *(derribar)* to knock down; *(estirar)* to stretch; *(disparar)* to fire; *(trazar)* to draw <*t. paralelas* to draw parallel lines>; *(dar)* to give <*le tiré una patada* I gave him a kick>; *(imprimir)* to print; *(malgastar)* to waste ♦ **t. a alguien de la lengua** to draw someone out ♦ **tirarla de** to boast of being <*tirarla de sabio* to boast of being wise> —intr. *(atraer)* to attract <*el imán tira del metal* the magnet attracts metal>; *(traer hacia sí)* to pull; *(producir corriente)* to draw <*esta chimenea no tira bien* this chimney does not draw well>; *(torcer)* to turn, go <*t. hacia la izquierda* to turn towards the left>; *(durar)* to last <*los zapatos no tirarán otro año* his shoes will not last another year>; *(aspirar)* to aspire; *(atraer el ánimo)* to have an appeal; *(asemejarse)* to take after <*ella tira a su madre* she takes after her mother>; *(parecerse)* to have a touch of <*este color tira a rojo* this color has a touch of red>; COLL. *(funcionar)* to run <*el coche tira bien* the car runs well> ♦ **ir tirando** COLL. to manage • **t. de** to pull • **tira y afloja** give-and-take —reflex. *(arrojarse)* to throw *or* hurl oneself; *(tenderse)* to lie down.

ti·ri·lla f. neckband.

ti·ri·tar intr. to shiver.

ti·ro m. *(lanzada)* throw; *(disparo)* shot; *(campo)* shooting range *or* gallery; *(de tela)* length; *(caballos)* team *or* (of horses); *(de chimenea)* draft; *(de escalera)* flight ♦ **a t. de** within reach *or* range of • **a t. limpio** *or* **a tiros** with gunfire • **darse** *or* **pegarse un t.** to shoot oneself • **ni a tiros** COLL. not by a long shot • **salirle a uno el t. por la culata** to backfire • **t. al blanco** target practice.

ti·roi·des adj. & m. thyroid.

ti·rón m. *(acción)* pull; *(estirón)* yank; COLL. *(distancia)* distance ♦ **de un t.** in one stretch.

ti·ro·te·ar tr. to snipe *or* fire at —reflex. to exchange fire.

ti·ro·te·o m. shooting.

ti·rria f. COLL. dislike.

ti·sa·na f. infusion.

tí·si·co, a adj. & m.f. consumptive.

ti·sis f. tuberculosis.

ti·sú m. gold *or* silver lamé.

tí·te·re m. puppet ♦ **no dejar t. con cabeza** COLL. to leave nothing standing ♦ pl. puppet show.

ti·ti·lar intr. *(temblar)* to quiver; *(una estrella)* to twinkle.

ti·ti·le·o m. *(temblor)* quivering; *(de estrella)* twinkling.

ti·ti·ri·tar intr. to tremble.

ti·ti·ri·te·ro, a m.f. puppeteer.

ti·tu·be·ar intr. *(oscilar)* to stagger; *(vacilar)* to hesitate.

ti·tu·be·o m. *(al andar)* staggering; *(vacilación)* hesitation.

ti·tu·la·do, a adj. *(libro)* entitled; *(persona)* titled.

ti·tu·lar[1] **I.** adj. *(que tiene título)* titular; regular <*el profesor t.* the regular professor> **II.** m. PRINT. headline —m.f. holder (of a passport, office).

ti·tu·lar[2] tr. to entitle —intr. to receive a title —reflex. EDUC. to receive one's degree.

tí·tu·lo m. title; *(encabezado)* heading; *(diploma)* degree ♦ **a t. de** by way of.

ti·za f. chalk.

tiz·nar tr. to smudge; FIG. to stain.

tiz·ne m. *or* f. soot.

ti·zo·ne·ar intr. to poke.

to·a·lla f. towel.

to·a·lle·ro m. towel rack.

to·bi·lle·ra f. ankle support.

to·bi·llo m. ankle.

to·bo·gán m. *(para niños)* slide; *(para mercancías)* chute; *(para la nieve)* sled.

to·ca f. *(sombrero)* hat; *(de religiosa)* wimple.

to·ca·dis·cos m.inv. record player.

to·ca·do, a I. adj. COLL. touched **II.** m. *(peinado)* hairdo; *(sombrero)* hat.

to·ca·dor m. *(mueble)* dressing table; *(cuarto)* dressing room ♦ **artículos de t.** toiletries.

to·can·te adj. ♦ **t. a** concerning.

to·car §70 tr. to touch; *(palpar)* to feel <*lo toqué con el dedo* I felt it with my finger>; *(manosear)* to handle; *(hacer sonar)* to sound; *(tañer)* to ring; MUS. to play; *(aludir)* to touch on ♦ **t. fondo** to hit bottom • **t. la diana** MIL. to play reveille —intr. *(corresponder)* to be up to, fall to <*me toca a mí darle la noticia* it is up to me to give him the news>; to be one's turn <*¿a quién le toca?* whose turn is it?>; *(recibir)* to get <*le toca la mitad* he gets half>; *(caer en suerte)* to win <*le tocó el premio gordo* he won the grand prize>; *(llegar el momento)* to be time <*ahora toca pagar* now it is time to pay> ♦ **t. a rebato** to sound the alarm • **t. a su fin** to come to an end • **t. de cerca** to hit home.

to·ca·yo, a m.f. namesake.

to·ci·no m. salt pork.

to·da·ví·a adv. still <*t. están durmiendo* they are still sleeping>; *(sin embargo)* nevertheless; *(aún)* even <*él es t. más inteligente que ella* he is even more intelligent than she> ♦ **t. no** not yet.

to·do, a I. adj. all <*se comió t. el pan* he ate all the bread>; *(cada)* each, every <*t. delito merece castigo* every crime deserves punishment>; all <*este jardín es t. hierbas* this garden is all weeds>; whole, entire <*t. el universo* the whole universe> ♦ **t. el mundo** everybody **II.** m. whole <*el t. es mayor que sus partes* the whole is greater than its parts>; all, everything <*t. está listo* everything is ready> ♦ **ante t.** first of all • **así y t.** for all that • **con t.** still • **del t.** entirely • **sobre t.** above all ♦ pl. everybody, everyone **III.** adv. all

to·do·po·de·ro·so, a adj. almighty ♦ **El T.** the Almighty.

to·ga f. *(de los romanos)* toga; *(de los magistrados)* robe.

tol·do m. awning.

to·le m. COLL. uproar.

to·le·ran·cia f. tolerance.

to·le·ran·te adj. tolerant.

to·le·rar tr. to tolerate; *(condescender)* to be tolerant of; *(permitir)* to allow.

to·lon·drón, o·na I. adj. scatterbrained **II.** m.f. *(persona)* scatterbrain; *(chichón)* bump ♦ **a tolondrones** COLL. by fits and starts.

to·ma f. *(acción)* taking; *(captura)* capture; *(dosis)* dose; *(entrada)* intake; CINEM. take ♦ **t. de conciencia** awareness • **t. de corriente** ELEC. plug • **t. de posesión** *(investidura)* inauguration; MIL. occupation • **t. y daca** give-and-take.

to·ma·dor, ·ra I. adj. AMER. drinking **II.** m.f. AMER. *(bebedor)* drinker; COM. drawee.

to·ma·du·ra f. *(toma)* taking; MIL. capture ♦ **t. de pelo** practical joke.

to·mar tr. to take; *(capturar)* to capture;

(comer) to have <tomé el desayuno a las siete I had breakfast at seven o'clock>; *(beber)* to have <¿quieres t. una cerveza conmigo? do you want to have a beer with me?>; *(agarrar)* to take up <t. la pluma to take up one's pen>; *(cobrar)* to gather <t. fuerzas to gather strength>; *(robar)* to steal; *(escoger)* to pick <tome uno de estos naipes pick one of these cards>; *(considerar)* to mistake <lo tomé por el jefe I mistook him for the boss>; *(adquirir)* to acquire <t. malas costumbres to acquire bad habits>; *(imitar)* to adopt <tomó los modales de su hermana mayor she adopted the manners of her older sister>; *(alquilar)* to rent; *(contratar)* to hire; *(padecer)* to catch <t. frío to catch cold> ♦ **t. a bien, mal** to take well, badly • **t. a pecho** to take to heart • **t. asiento** to take a seat • **t. conciencia** to become aware • **t. el fresco** to take the air • **t. el pelo a alguien** to pull someone's leg • **t. en broma** to take as a joke • **t. en cuenta** to take into account • **t. las de Villadiego** COLL. to beat it • **t. parte** to participate • **t. partido** to take sides • **t. prestado** to borrow —intr. to go <tomamos por la izquierda we went to the left> ♦ **¡tomal!** really!

to·ma·te m. tomato ♦ **ponerse como un t.** to become red as a beet.

tóm·bo·la f. charity raffle.

to·mi·llo m. thyme.

to·mo m. tome.

ton m. ♦ **sin t. ni son** without rhyme or reason.

to·na·da f. *(canción)* tune; AMER. regional accent.

to·na·li·dad f. tonality.

to·nel m. barrel.

to·ne·la·da f. ton.

to·ne·la·je m. tonnage.

tó·ni·co, a adj. & m.f. tonic ♦ **dar la t.** to set the tone.

to·ni·fi·ca·dor, ·ra/can·te adj. strengthening.

to·ni·fi·car §70 tr. to tone.

to·ni·na f. ICHTH. tuna; ZOOL. dolphin.

to·no m. tone ♦ **a t.** in tune • **bajar el t.** to tone down • **dar el t.** to set the tone • **darse t.** to put on airs • **fuera de t.** out of place • **subir el t.** *(acalorarse)* to become heated; *(gritar)* to get louder.

ton·su·rar tr. *(un clérigo)* to tonsure; *(el pelo)* to cut; *(la lana)* to shear.

ton·te·ar intr. to act foolishly.

ton·te·rí·a/dad/ra f. *(cualidad)* foolishness; *(acción)* foolish action; *(dicho)* stupid remark; *(nadería)* trifle ♦ **decir tonterías** to talk nonsense.

ton·to, a I. adj. foolish ♦ **a tontas y a locas** COLL. any which way **II.** m.f. *(necio)* fool; *(payaso)* clown ♦ **hacerse el t.** to play the fool • **t. de capirote** COLL. total fool.

to·pa·cio m. topaz.

to·par tr. *(chocar)* to bump (into); *(encontrar)* to run into —intr. to butt ♦ **t. con** or **contra** to bump into.

to·pe I. m. *(extremo)* butt; *(para sostener)* catch ♦ **estar hasta los topes** *(estar lleno)* to be filled to the brim; *(estar harto)* to be fed up **II.** adj. top <precio t. top price>.

to·pe·tar/te·ar tr. *(animales)* to butt; COLL. *(chocar)* to bump —intr. to bump (into).

to·pe·ta·zo m. bump (with the head).

tó·pi·co m. topic; MED. local application.

to·po m. ZOOL. mole; COLL. *(persona)* clumsy person.

to·po·gra·fí·a f. topography.

to·pó·gra·fo, a m.f. topographer.

to·que m. touch; *(de campana)* chime; *(de sirena)* blast; *(de tambor)* beat; *(golpe)* tap ♦ **dar el último t. a** to give the finishing touch to • **t. de diana** MIL. reveille • **t. de queda** curfew.

to·que·tear tr. to handle.

to·que·te·o m. handling.

to·rá·ci·co, a adj. thoracic.

tó·rax m. thorax.

tor·be·lli·no m. *(viento)* whirlwind; *(agua)* vortex; FIG. lively.

tor·ce·du·ra f. *(acción)* twisting; *(efecto)* twist; MED. sprain.

tor·cer §71 tr. to twist; *(doblar)* to bend; *(la cara)* to contort; MED. to sprain —intr. to turn ♦ **no dar el brazo a t.** to stand firm —reflex. *(estar torcido)* to be twisted; *(doblarse)* to be bent.

tor·ci·do, a adj. *(no recto)* crooked; *(doblado)* bent.

tor·ci·jón m. stomach cramp.

tor·do I. m. *(caballo)* dapple-gray horse; ORNITH. thrush **II.** adj. dapple-gray.

to·re·a·dor m. toreador.

to·re·ar tr. to fight —intr. to fight bulls.

to·re·o m. bullfighting.

to·re·ro, a I. adj. of bullfighting **II.** m. bull-fighter.

tor·men·ta f. storm; FIG. turmoil.

tor·men·to m. torment.

tor·men·to·so, a adj. stormy.

tor·na·do m. tornado.

tor·nar tr. *(devolver)* to return; *(mudar)* to turn <la sangre tornó el agua roja the blood turned the water red> —intr. to return —reflex. to become.

tor·na·sol m. BOT. sunflower; CHEM. litmus.

tor·na·so·la·do, a adj. iridescent.

tor·ne·ar tr. to turn.

tor·ne·o m. tournament.

tor·ne·ro, a m.f. lathe operator.

tor·ni·llo m. screw ♦ **apretar a alguien los tornillos** to put the screws on someone • **faltarle un t.** to have a loose screw.

tor·ni·que·te m. tourniquet.

tor·no m. lathe; *(elevador)* winch; *(giratorio)* revolving dumbwaiter ♦ **en t. a** around • **t. de alfarero** potter's wheel.

to·ro m. bull ♦ **echar a alguien el t.** COLL. to give someone a piece of one's mind • **t. de lidia** fighting bull ♦ pl. bullfight.

to·ron·ja f. grapefruit.

tor·pe adj. *(desmañado)* clumsy; *(necio)* stupid.

tor·pe·de·ar tr. to torpedo.

tor·pe·do m. torpedo fish; MIL. torpedo ♦ **t. de fondo** ground torpedo • **t. flotante** submarine mine.

tor·pe·za f. *(cualidad)* clumsiness; *(necedad)* stupidity ♦ **cometer una t.** to make a blunder.

tor·por m. torpor.

tor·rar tr. to roast.

to·rre f. tower; *(de ajedrez)* castle; *(de petróleo)* oil derrick; MARIT. turret ♦ **t. de vigía** observation tower; MARIT. crow's nest.

to·rre·ja f. French toast.

to·rren·cial adj. torrential.

to·rren·te m. *(de agua)* torrent; *(de sangre)* bloodstream; FIG. avalanche.

to·rre·ón m. large fortified tower.

tó·rri·do, a adj. torrid.

tor·sión f. torsion ♦ **momento de t.** torque.

tor·so m. torso.

tor·ta f. cake; COLL. *(bofetada)* slap; PRINT. font; MEX. sandwich ♦ **ni t.** COLL. not a thing.

tor·ta·zo m. COLL. blow.

tor·te·ra f. baking pan.

tor·tí·co·li(s) m. stiff neck.

tor·ti·lla f. CUL. omelet; AMER. tortilla ♦ **hacer t. a** COLL. to flatten • **volverse la t.** COLL. to turn the tables.

tór·to·la f. turtledove.

tor·tu·ga f. turtle.

tor·tuo·so, a adj. tortuous; FIG. devious.

tor·tu·ra f. torture.

tor·tu·rar tr. to torture.

tor·vo, a adj. grim.

tos f. cough, coughing ♦ **acceso de t.** coughing fit • **t. convulsiva** whooping cough.

tos·co, a adj. *(basto)* crude; *(una persona)* coarse.

to·ser intr. to cough.

tos·que·dad f. coarseness.

tos·ta·do, a I. adj. *(pan)* toasted; *(café)* roasted; FIG. tanned II. m. *(de pan)* toasting; *(de café)* roasting —f. toast.

tos·ta·dor, ·ra m.f. toaster.

tos·tar §19 tr. *(pan)* to toast; *(café)* roast; *(calentar mucho)* to scorch; *(la piel)* to tan —reflex. to become tanned.

tos·tón m. crouton; *(cosa demasiado asada)* burned *or* scorched thing; *(cochinillo)* roast suckling pig; MEX. silver coin ♦ pl. CARIB., CUL. fried plantain chips.

to·tal I. adj. & m. total II. adv. so <*t. que se fue* so, he left>.

to·ta·li·dad f. totality.

to·ta·li·ta·rio, a adj. & m.f. totalitarian.

to·ta·li·zar §04 tr. to total.

tó·tem m. [pl. **es** *or* **totems**] totem.

to·to·ra f. AMER. cattail.

to·xe·mia f. toxemia.

to·xi·ci·dad f. toxicity.

tó·xi·co, a I. adj. toxic II. m. poison.

to·xi·có·lo·go, a m.f. toxicologist.

to·xi·có·ma·no, a I. m.f. drug addict II. adj. addicted to drugs.

to·xi·na f. toxin.

to·zu·do, a adj. stubborn.

tra·ba f. *(liga)* tie; *(para caballos)* hobble; *(para puertas)* bolt; *(estorbo)* obstacle ♦ **poner tra·bas a** to put obstacles in the way of.

tra·ba·ja·do, a adj. *(cansado)* worn-out; *(elaborado)* elaborate.

tra·ba·ja·dor, ·ra I. adj. hard-working II. m.f. worker.

tra·ba·jar intr. to work ♦ **hacer t. el dinero** to make one's money work • **poner a t.** to put to work • **ponerse a t.** to get to work • **t. de** to work as —tr. to work; AGR. to till.

tra·ba·jo m. work; *(labor)* labor <*t. manual* manual labor>; *(tarea)* job; *(esfuerzo)* trouble <*tomarse el t. de* to take the trouble to> ♦ **costar t.** to be hard • **t. a destajo** piecework • **trabajos forzados** hard labor.

tra·ba·jo·so, a adj. demanding.

tra·ba·len·guas m.inv. tongue twister.

tra·bar tr. *(unir)* to join; *(atar)* to fasten; *(asegurar)* to bolt; *(echar trabas a)* to hobble; *(una sierra)* to set; *(empezar)* to start up <*t. una conversación* to start up a conversation> ♦ **t. amistad** to strike up a friendship —intr. *(espesar)* to thicken; *(agarrar)* to take hold —reflex. *(atascarse)* to jam; *(enredarse)* to get

tangled up ♦ **t. a golpes** to come to blows • **trabársele a uno la lengua** to get tongue-tied.

tra·bi·lla f. *(del pantalón)* foot strap; *(de cintura)* half belt; *(punto)* dropped stitch.

tra·bu·car §70 tr. to mix up.

tra·bu·co m. blunderbuss.

trac·ción f. traction ♦ **t. delantera** front-wheel drive.

trac·to m. *(de tiempo)* interval; MED., RELIG. tract.

trac·tor m. tractor ♦ **t. oruga** caterpillar tractor.

tra·di·ción f. tradition.

tra·di·cio·nal adj. traditional.

tra·duc·ción f. translation.

tra·du·cir §22 tr. *(una lengua)* to translate; *(expresar)* to express.

tra·duc·tor, ·ra I. adj. translating II. m.f. translator.

tra·er §72 tr. to bring <*traiga los libros a la clase* bring your books to class>; *(llevar)* to wear <*traía un sombrero nuevo* he was wearing a new hat>; *(atraer)* to attract; *(causar)* to bring about <*esto trae muchos problemas* this brings about many problems>; *(alegar)* to adduce <*t. ejemplos* to adduce examples>; *(publicar)* to carry <*este periódico traía un artículo sobre el escándalo* this newspaper carried an article about the scandal> ♦ **t. a mal** *(maltratar)* to abuse; *(molestar)* to pester • **t. al mundo** to bring into the world • **t. cola** *(tener consecuencias)* to have serious consequences; *(venir acompañado)* to bring along with • **t. consigo** to entail • **t. entre manos** to be up to.

tra·fi·can·te I. adj. dealing II. m.f. dealer.

tra·fi·car §70 intr. to deal *(en, con* in).

trá·fi·co m. traffic.

tra·ga·dor, ·ra I. adj. *(que traga)* swallowing; *(glotón)* gluttonous II. m.f. *(persona que traga)* swallower; *(glotón)* glutton.

tra·gal·da·bas m.f.inv. COLL. glutton.

tra·ga·le·guas m.f.inv. person who walks a lot.

tra·ga·luz m. skylight.

tra·ga·pe·rras adj. COLL. coin-operated.

tra·gar §47 intr. to swallow —tr. *(ingerir)* to swallow; *(comer)* to devour; *(hundirse)* to swallow up <*el mar se tragó el barco* the sea swallowed up the boat>; *(aceptar)* to believe; *(soportar)* to stomach <*no trago a ese chico* I cannot stomach that boy>; *(consumir)* to eat up.

tra·ge·dia f. tragedy.

trá·gi·co, a I. adj. tragic II. m.f. tragedian.

tra·gi·co·me·dia f. tragicomedy.

tra·gi·có·mi·co, a adj. tragicomic.

tra·go m. *(bebida)* drink; *(porción)* gulp ♦ **de un t.** in one shot • **pasar un t. amargo** to have a bad time of it.

trai·ción f. treason.

trai·cio·nar tr. to betray.

trai·cio·ne·ro, a I. adj. traitorous II. m.f. traitor.

trai·dor, ·ra I. adj. traitorous II. m.f. traitor.

trai·ga, go see **traer.**

tra·í·lla f. leash.

tra·je m. *(vestido)* dress; *(conjunto)* suit; THEAT. costume ♦ **t. de baño** bathing suit • **t. de luces** bullfighter's costume.

tra·je·a·do, a adj. dressed.

tra·je·ar tr. to dress.

tra·je·ra, jo see **traer.**

tra·jín m. *(trabajo)* work; COLL. *(ajetreo)* hustle

and bustle.

tra·ji·nar tr. to carry —intr. COLL. to bustle about.

tra·ma f. *(de un tejido)* weft; *(intriga)* scheme; *(de novela)* plot; *(en fotograbado)* line screen.

tra·ma·dor, ·ra I. adj. weaving **II.** m.f. weaver.

tra·mar tr. *(un tejido)* to weave; COLL. *(maquinar)* to scheme.

tra·mi·ta·ción f. *(de un asunto)* transaction; *(trámites)* procedures.

tra·mi·tar tr. *(un asunto)* to negotiate; *(tomar medidas)* to take the necessary steps.

trá·mi·te m. procedure ♦ pl. formalities.

tra·mo m. *(de terreno)* stretch; *(de una escalera)* flight.

tra·mo·ya f. THEAT. stage machinery; *(enredo)* plot.

tra·mo·yis·ta m.f. THEAT. stagehand; COLL. *(tramposo)* swindler.

tram·pa f. *(cepo)* trap; *(puerta)* trap door; *(ardid)* trick ♦ **caer en la t.** to fall into a trap ♦ **hacer trampas** to cheat.

tram·pe·ar intr. COLL. *(con dinero)* to cheat; *(vivir de su ingenio)* to live by one's wits —tr. COLL. to trick, deceive.

tram·po·lín m. *(del gimnasta)* trampoline; *(del nadador)* diving board; FIG. springboard.

tram·po·so, a adj. **I.** COLL. cheating **II.** m.f. *(engañador)* swindler; *(en naipes)* cardsharp.

tran·ca f. *(garrote)* cudgel; *(de puerta)* crossbar; AMER. gate ♦ **agarrarse una t.** COLL. to get loaded.

tran·ca·da f. stride ♦ **en dos trancadas** COLL. in a jiffy.

tran·car §70 tr. to bar.

tran·ca·zo m. *(garrotazo)* blow with a stick; COLL. *(gripe)* flu.

tran·ce m. *(crisis)* crisis; *(apuro)* tight spot; *(del médium)* trance ♦ **a todo t.** at all costs ♦ **en t. de muerte** on the point of death.

tran·co m. *(paso largo)* stride; *(umbral)* threshold; AMER. gallop ♦ **en dos trancos** COLL. in a jiffy.

tran·que·ra f. *(estacada)* stockade; AMER. gate.

tran·qui·li·dad f. tranquility.

tran·qui·li·zan·te I. adj. tranquilizing **II.** m. tranquilizer.

tran·qui·li·zar §04 tr. to quiet —reflex. to be quieted.

tran·qui·lo, a adj. tranquil ♦ **¡déjame t.!** leave me alone!

tran·sac·ción f. COM. transaction; *(acuerdo)* settlement.

tran·sar intr. AMER. to compromise.

tran·sat·lán·ti·co, a I. adj. transatlantic **II.** m. ocean liner.

trans·bor·da·dor m. ferry ♦ **t. espacial** space shuttle.

trans·bor·dar tr. to transfer, transship.

trans·bor·do m. transfer, transshipment.

trans·cen·den·cia f. transcendence.

trans·cen·den·tal adj. transcendental.

trans·cen·den·te adj. transcendent(al).

trans·cen·der §50 tr. to transcend.

trans·con·ti·nen·tal adj. transcontinental.

trans·cri·bir §80 tr. to transcribe.

trans·crip·ción f. transcription.

trans·cu·rrir intr. to elapse.

trans·cur·so m. course *<en el t. de un mes in the course of a month>*.

tran·se·ún·te I. adj. passing, transient **II.** m.f. *(que pasa)* passerby; *(que reside transitoria-*

mente) transient.

tran·se·xual adj. & m.f. transsexual.

trans·fe·ren·cia f. transfer(ence).

trans·fe·rir §65 tr. *(trasladar)* to transfer; *(aplazar)* to postpone.

trans·fi·gu·ra·ción f. transfiguration.

trans·for·ma·ción f. transformation.

trans·for·ma·dor, ·ra I. adj. transforming **II.** m.f. transformer —m. ELEC. transformer.

trans·for·mar tr. *(cambiar)* to transform; *(mejorar)* to improve; SPORT. to convert —reflex. to undergo a transformation.

tráns·fu·ga m.f./go m. *(fugitivo)* fugitive; *(desertor)* deserter.

trans·fun·dir tr. to transfuse.

trans·fu·sión f. transfusion.

trans·gre·dir §38 tr. to transgress.

trans·gre·sión f. transgression.

trans·gre·sor, ·ra I. adj. transgressing **II.** m.f. transgressor.

tran·si·ción f. transition.

tran·si·do, a adj. overcome.

tran·si·gen·te adj. accommodating.

tran·si·gir §32 intr. to compromise.

tran·sis·tor m. transistor.

tran·si·ta·ble adj. passable.

tran·si·tar intr. *(pasar)* to go; *(viajar)* to travel.

tran·si·ti·vo, a adj. transitive.

trán·si·to m. *(paso)* transit; *(tráfico)* traffic; *(lugar de parada)* stop ♦ **de mucho t.** busy *<una calle de mucho t. a busy street>* ♦ **de t.** in transit.

tran·si·to·rio, a adj. temporary.

trans·la·ción f. translation.

trans·li·te·ra·ción f. transliteration.

trans·lú·ci·do, a adj. translucent.

trans·lu·cir·se §44 reflex. *(ser translúcido)* to be translucid; *(ser evidente)* to be evident.

trans·mi·gra·ción f. transmigration.

trans·mi·grar intr. to transmigrate.

trans·mi·sión f. *(acción)* transmission; RAD., TELEV. broadcast ♦ **t. delantera** AUTO. frontwheel drive ♦ **t. del pensamiento** telepathy.

trans·mi·sor, ·ra I. adj. transmitting **II.** m. ELEC. transmitter.

trans·mi·tir tr. *(comunicar)* to transmit; RAD., TELEV. to broadcast.

trans·mu·ta·ción f. transmutation.

trans·mu·tar tr. to transmute —reflex. to be transmuted.

trans·o·ce·á·ni·co, a adj. transoceanic.

trans·pa·ren·cia f. *(cualidad)* transparence; PHOTOG. slide.

trans·pa·ren·tar·se reflex. *(verse)* to show through; *(ser transparente)* to be transparent; *(ser evidente)* to be obvious.

trans·pa·ren·te I. adj. *(un objeto)* transparent; *(evidente)* obvious **II.** m. shade.

trans·pi·ra·ción f. perspiration.

trans·pi·rar intr. *(sudar)* to perspire; *(rezumarse)* to leak out.

trans·plan·tar tr. to transplant.

trans·po·ner §54 tr. *(mudar de sitio)* to move; *(trasplantar)* to transplant; *(intercambiar)* to transpose; *(desaparecer)* to disappear around *<los agresores transpusieron la esquina the assailants disappeared around the corner>*.

trans·por·ta·ción f. transportation, transport.

trans·por·ta·dor, ·ra I. adj. transporting **II.** m.f. transporter —m. MATH. protractor; MECH. conveyor.

trans·por·tar tr. *(llevar)* to transport; MUS. to

transpose —reflex. FIG. to get carried away.
trans·por·te m. transportation; COM. transport; *(embarcación)* transport ship.
trans·por·tis·ta m.f. carrier.
trans·po·si·ción f. transposition.
trans·pu·sie·ra, so see **transponer.**
trans·va·sar tr. to decant.
trans·ver·sal I. adj. *(que atraviesa)* transverse; *(pariente)* collateral II. m.f. collateral relative —f. side street.
trans·ver·so, a adj. & m. transverse (muscle).
tran·ví·a m. streetcar.
tran·via·rio, a I. adj. streetcar <red t. streetcar system> II. m. *(empleado)* streetcar worker; *(conductor)* streetcar driver.
tra·pe·ar tr. AMER. to mop.
tra·pe·cio m. GEOM. trapezoid; *(de gimnasia)* trapeze; ANAT. *(músculo)* trapezius; *(hueso)* trapezium.
tra·pe·cis·ta m.f. trapeze artist.
tra·pe·rí·a f. *(trapos)* rags; *(tienda)* old clothing store.
tra·pe·ro, a m.f. ragpicker.
tra·pe·zoi·de m. trapezoid; ANAT. trapezium.
tra·pi·che m. *(de aceituna)* olive press; *(de azúcar)* sugar mill; AMER. *(ingenio)* sugar plantation; *(de mineral)* grinding machine.
tra·pien·to, a adj. ragged.
tra·pi·son·da f. COLL. *(jaleo)* racket; *(enredo)* scheme.
tra·po m. rag; MARIT. sails; TAUR. muleta ♦ **a todo t.** under full sail • **poner a alguien como un t.** COLL. to rake someone over the coals • **sacar los trapos a relucir** COLL. to wash one's dirty linen in public ♦ pl. clothing.
trá·que·a *or* **tra·que·ar·te·ria** f. trachea.
tra·que·(te·)ar intr. *(un cohete)* to go off; *(hacer ruido)* to clatter, rattle; *(agitarse)* to shake, jolt —tr. *(agitar)* to shake; COLL. *(manosear)* to handle.
tra·que·te·o m. AMER. *(ruido)* bang; *(movimiento)* shaking.
tras prep. *(después de)* after <día t. día day after day>; *(detrás de)* behind <caminaban t. un carretón they walked behind a wagon>; *(además)* in addition <t. de ser rico, es guapo in addition to being rich, he is good-looking>; *(en busca de)* in search of.
tra·sat·lán·ti·co, a adj. transatlantic.
tras·cen·den·cia f. PHILOS. transcendence; *(importancia)* significance.
tras·cen·den·tal adj. PHILOS. transcendental; *(que se extiende)* far-reaching; *(importante)* very significant.
tras·cen·den·te adj. transcendent.
tras·cen·der §50 intr. *(divulgarse)* to become known; *(extenderse)* to extend; *(oler)* to smell.
tras·co·rral m. backyard.
tra·se·char tr. to lie in wait for.
tra·se·gar §52 tr. *(trastornar)* to mix up; *(un líquido)* to decant; COLL. *(beber mucho)* to guzzle.
tra·se·ro, a I. adj. back II. m. ANAT. behind; ZOOL. rump —f. back.
tras·fon·do m. background.
tras·ho·jar tr. to leaf through.
tra·sie·go m. decanting.
tra·sie·go, gue see **trasegar.**
tras·la·ción f. *(transporte)* moving; *(traducción)* translation; RHET. metaphor; MECH., PHYS. translation.

tras·la·dar tr. *(mover)* to move; *(a un empleado)* to transfer; *(aplazar)* to postpone; *(traducir)* to translate; *(copiar)* to transcribe —reflex. to change residence.
tras·la·do m. *(copia)* copy <fiel t. true copy>; *(de un empleado)* transfer; *(de residencia)* change of residence; LAW notification ♦ **dar t.** to send a copy.
tras·luz m. *(luz)* light seen through a transparent body; *(luz reflejada)* reflected light ♦ **al t.** against the light.
tras·ma·no m. ♦ **a t.** *(del alcance)* out of reach; *(lugar)* out of the way.
tras·mun·do m. the other world.
tras·no·cha·do, a adj. *(macilento)* haggard; *(trillado)* trite.
tras·no·cha·dor, ·ra I. adj. staying up late II. m.f. night owl.
tras·no·char intr. to stay up all night.
tras·pa·pe·lar tr. to misplace —reflex. to get lost.
tras·pa·pe·la·do, a adj. misplaced.
tras·pa·sar tr. *(perforar)* to pierce; *(atravesar)* to cross <t. el río to cross the river>; *(transferir)* to transfer; *(violar)* to break; FIG. to pierce <t. el corazón de dolor to pierce someone's heart with pain> —reflex. to go too far.
tras·pa·so m. *(cesión)* transfer; *(venta)* sale; *(lo traspasado)* transferred property; *(precio)* transfer fee.
tras·pié m. stumble ♦ **dar traspiés** to stumble.
tras·plan·tar tr. to transplant —reflex. to uproot oneself.
tras·plan·te m. *(acción)* transplanting; *(injerto)* transplant.
tras·pun·te m. prompter.
tras·qui·la·dor, ·ra m.f. shearer.
tras·qui·lar tr. *(el pelo)* to clip; *(el ganado)* to shear.
tras·ta·bi·llar intr. to stagger.
tras·ta·bi·llón m. slip.
tras·ta·da f. COLL. dirty trick.
tras·ta·zo m. COLL. whack.
tras·te m. MUS. fret; *(chisme)* thingamajig, whatnot; SP. wine-taster's glass; AMER., COLL. behind ♦ **dar al t. con** COLL. to spoil • **ir al t.** COLL. to fall through.
tras·te·ar intr. to move furniture —tr. TAUR. to tease (a bull) with a red cape; MUS. to strum.
tras·tien·da f. stock room.
tras·to m. *(mueble)* old piece of furniture; *(utensilio)* utensil <trastos de cocina kitchen utensils>; *(cosa inútil)* piece of junk; THEAT. flat, piece of scenery ♦ **tirarse los trastos a la cabeza** COLL. to have a terrible fight ♦ pl. gear.
tras·to·car §70 tr. to twist —reflex. to go mad.
tras·tor·nar tr. *(derribar)* to turn upside down; *(perturbar)* to disrupt; *(inquietar)* to worry; *(enloquecer)* to drive mad ♦ **trastornarle la mente a alguien** to drive someone mad —reflex. to go mad.
tras·tor·no m. upset.
tras·tra·bi·llar intr. to stagger.
tras·tro·car §73 tr. to twist.
tra·sun·tar tr. *(copiar)* to copy; *(compendiar)* to summarize.
tra·ta f. slave trade ♦ **t. de blancas** white slavery.
tra·ta·ble adj. sociable.
tra·ta·do m. *(obra)* treatise; *(entre gobiernos)*

treaty; *(entre compañías)* agreement.

tra·ta·mien·to m. treatment; *(título)* form of address; TECH. process ♦ **dar t. de** to address as • **t. de la información** COMPUT. data processing.

tra·tan·te m.f. dealer.

tra·tar tr. to treat *<no me trates mal* do not treat me badly>; *(manejar)* to handle *<hay que t. este asunto con cuidado* it is necessary to handle this matter carefully>; *(dar el tratamiento de)* to address as *<le traté de doña* I addressed her as Madame>; *(comerciar)* to manage *<t. la venta del negocio* to manage the sale of the business>; CHEM. to process; MED. to treat —intr. ♦ **t. con** to have dealings with • **t. de** *(discutir)* to be about *<este artículo trata de la economía* this article is about the economy>; *(procurar)* to try to *<traté de salir temprano* I tried to leave early> —reflex. to treat each other ♦ **t. de** to be a question of *<se trata de encontrar una solución* it is a question of finding a solution>.

tra·to m. treatment *<t. especial* preferential treatment>; *(título)* form of address; *(relaciones)* dealings; *(negocio)* trade; *(convenio)* agreement ♦ **¡t. hecho!** COLL. it's a deal!

trau·ma m. trauma.

trau·má·ti·co, a adj. traumatic.

trau·ma·ti·zar §04 tr. to traumatize.

tra·vés m. *(inclinación)* slant; *(torcimiento)* bend; SEW. bias ♦ **a** *or* **al t.** through • **de t.** crosswise.

tra·ve·sa·ño m. *(barra)* crossbeam; *(almohada)* bolster.

tra·ve·sí·a f. *(camino)* crossroad; *(de una carretera)* part of a highway that goes through a town; *(distancia)* distance across; *(viaje)* crossing; *(viento)* crosswind.

tra·ves·tí·ti·do m. transvestite.

tra·ves·su·ra f. mischief.

tra·vie·so, a adj. mischievous ♦ **a campo tra-viesa** cross-country.

tra·yec·to m. *(distancia)* distance; *(recorrido)* way.

tra·yec·to·ria f. trajectory.

tra·za f. *(diseño)* design; *(plan)* plan; *(aspecto)* appearance; GEOM. trace ♦ **darse trazas para** to find a way to.

tra·za·do, a I. adj. ♦ **bien t.** good-looking • **mal t.** unattractive II. m. *(diseño)* design; *(plan)* plan; *(bosquejo)* sketch.

tra·zar §04 tr. *(diseñar)* to design; *(bosquejar)* to outline; *(discurrir)* to draw up; *(describir)* to depict.

tra·zo m. *(línea)* line *<t. rectilíneo* straight line>; *(diseño)* design; *(de una letra)* stroke ♦ **al t.** drawn in outline.

tra·zu·mar·se reflex. to seep.

tré·bol m. BOT. clover; ARCHIT. trefoil ♦ pl. clubs.

tre·ce I. adj. thirteen; *(decimotercero)* thirteenth II. m. thirteen ♦ **mantenerse** *or* **seguir en sus treces** COLL. to stick to one's guns.

tre·cho m. *(distancia)* stretch; *(de tiempo)* spell ♦ **a trechos** *(en ciertas partes)* in places, in parts; *(con interrupción)* in stages • **de t. en t.** *(distancia)* at intervals; *(tiempo)* every now and then.

tre·fi·lar tr. to make into wire.

tre·gua f. truce; *(descanso)* rest; *(pausa)* lull ♦ **no dar t.** never to let up.

trein·ta I. adj. thirty; *(trigésimo)* thirtieth

II. m. thirty.

trein·ta·vo, a adj. & m. thirtieth ♦ **trein·te·na** f. *(treinta unidades)* thirty; *(treintava parte)* thirtieth part.

tre·me·bun·do, a adj. dreadful.

tre·men·do, a adj. *(horrendo)* horrible; *(digno de respeto)* tremendous; COLL. *(grandísimo)* tremendous, terrible *<un disparate t.* a terrible blunder> ♦ **tomarlo a la t.** COLL. to make a big fuss.

tre·men·ti·na f. turpentine ♦ **esencia de t.** oil of turpentine.

tre·mo·lar tr. *(enarbolar)* to hoist; *(agitar)* to wave.

tre·mo·li·na f. rustling; FIG. racket ♦ **armar la t.** COLL. to kick up a rumpus.

tré·mo·lo m. tremolo.

tre·mor m. tremor.

tré·mu·lo, a adj. *(tembloroso)* trembling; *(voz)* quivering; *(luz)* flickering.

tren m. *(ferrocarril)* train; *(instrumentos)* gear, equipment *<t. de dragado* dredging gear>; MIL. convoy; MEX., URUG. streetcar ♦ **t. de aterri-zaje** landing gear • **t. de vida** way of life • **t. directo** *or* **expreso** express train • **vivir a todo t.** COLL. to live in style.

tren·ci·lla f. braid.

tren·ci·llar tr. to trim with braid.

tren·ci·llo m. gold *or* silver hatband.

tren·za f. braid.

tren·za·do m. braid.

tren·zar §04 tr. to braid.

tre·pa·na·ción f. trephination.

tre·pa·nar tr. to trephine.

tré·pa·no m. SURG. trephine; *(perforadora)* drill.

tre·par[1] intr. to climb.

tre·par[2] tr. *(taladrar)* to drill; SEW. to trim, edge —reflex. to lean backwards.

tre·pi·da·ción f. trepidation.

tre·pi·dar intr. to vibrate.

tres I. adj. three; *(tercero)* third ♦ **las t.** three o'clock II. m. three.

tres·cien·tos, as adj. & m. three hundred.

tres cuar·tos m. three-quarter-length coat.

tre·si·llo m. *(naipes)* ombre; *(muebles)* three-piece suite; *(sortija)* ring with three stones; MUS. triplet.

tres·piés m.inv. *(trébede)* trivet; *(trípode)* tripod.

tre·ta f. *(ardid)* trick; SPORT. feint.

tre·za·vo, a adj. & m. thirteenth.

trí·a·da f. triad.

trian·gu·lar adj. triangular.

trián·gu·lo I. adj. triangular II. m. triangle ♦ **t. rectángulo** right triangle.

tri·bal adj. tribal.

tri·bu f. tribe.

tri·bu·la·ción f. tribulation.

tri·bu·na f. *(de un orador)* rostrum; SPORT. bleachers.

tri·bu·nal m. *(lugar)* court; *(magistrados)* bench; *(jueces de exámenes)* board of examiners ♦ **t. de menores** juvenile court.

tri·bu·no m. HIST. tribune; *(orador)* orator.

tri·bu·ta·ble adj. taxable.

tri·bu·tar tr. to pay.

tri·bu·ta·rio, a I. adj. *(de los impuestos)* tax *<régimen t.* tax system>; *(un río)* tributary II. m.f. *(que paga impuestos)* taxpayer; *(que paga tributo)* tributary.

tri·bu·to m. *(impuesto)* tax; *(respeto)* tribute.

tri·cen·te·na·rio m. tricentennial.
tri·cen·té·si·mo, a adj. & m. three-hundredth.
tri·ceps adj. & m.inv. triceps.
tri·ci·clo m. tricycle.
tri·co·lor adj. tricolor.
tri·cor·nio I. adj. three-cornered. **II.** m. three-cornered hat.
tri·cot m. tricot.
tri·cús·pi·de adj. & f. tricuspid.
tri·den·te I. adj. tridentate **II.** m. trident.
tri·di·men·sio·nal adj. three-dimensional.
trie·dro, a I. adj. trihedral **II.** m. trihedron.
trie·nal adj. triennial.
trie·nio m. triennium.
tri·ful·ca f. COLL. rumpus <*armar una t.* to kick up a rumpus>.
tri·fur·car·se §70 reflex. to divide into three.
tri·gal m. wheat field.
tri·ga·za adj. wheat <*paja t.* wheat chaff>.
tri·gé·si·mo, a adj. & m. thirtieth.
tri·go m. wheat ♦ **no ser t. limpio** COLL. to be dishonest • **t. candeal** white wheat • **t. sarraceno** buckwheat.
tri·go·no·me·tría f. trigonometry.
tri·gue·ño, a adj. *(tez)* olive-skinned; *(pelo)* dark blond.
tri·gue·ro, a I. adj. wheat <*campo t.* wheat field> **II.** m. wheat sieve.
tri·la·te·ral adj. trilateral.
tri·lá·te·ro, a adj. trilateral.
tri·lin·güe adj. trilingual.
tri·lla f. *(trillo)* thresher; *(acción)* threshing; ICHTH. gurnard.
tri·lla·de·ra f. thresher.
tri·lla·do, a adj. *(muy común)* trite; *(camino)* beaten.
tri·lla·dor, ·ra I. adj. threshing **II.** f. threshing machine ♦ **t. segadora** combine.
tri·llar tr. to thresh; COLL. *(emplear mucho)* to use frequently; *(maltratar)* to beat.
tri·lli·zo, a I. adj. triple **II.** m.f. triplet.
tri·llo m. thresher; AMER. path, lane.
tri·llón m. [10¹⁸] one million trillion (U.S.), trillion (G.B.).
tri·lo·gía f. trilogy.
tri·mes·tral adj. quarterly.
tri·mes·tral·men·te adv. quarterly.
tri·mes·tre I. adj. trimestral **II.** m. *(tres meses)* quarter; *(pago)* quarterly payment; *(revista)* quarterly.
tri·nar intr. MUS. to trill; ORNITH. to warble; COLL. *(enojarse)* to fume.
trin·ca f. triad; MARIT. cable.
trin·car §70 tr. to smash.
trin·cha·dor, ·ra I. adj. carving **II.** carver, slicer —m. *(cuchillo)* carving knife; MEX. carving board.
trin·chan·te I. adj. carving **II.** m. *(persona)* carver; *(tenedor)* carving fork.
trin·char tr. to carve.
trin·che·ra f. MIL. trench; RAIL. cutting; *(abrigo)* trench coat; MEX. sharp instrument ♦ **guerra de trincheras** trench warfare.
trin·che·te m. shoemaker's knife.
tri·ne·o m. sleigh.
tri·ni·ta·ria f. wild pansy.
tri·no, a m. trill.
tri·no·mio m. trinomial.
trin·que·te m. MARIT. *(palo)* foremast; *(vela)* foresail; SPORT. covered pelota court; MECH. pawl.
trí·o m. trio.

tri·pa f. intestine; *(de una vasija)* belly; *(de cigarro)* tobacco filling ♦ **echar las tripas** COLL. to retch, vomit • **hacer de tripas corazón** COLL. to pluck up one's courage • **tener malas tripas** to be hardhearted ♦ pl. *(panza)* guts; BOT. core; FIG. innards.
tri·par·ti·to, a adj. tripartite.
tri·pi·ca·llos m.pl. tripe (stew).
tri·ple adj. & m. triple.
tri·pli·ca·ción f. triplication.
tri·pli·ca·do m. triplicate ♦ **por t.** in triplicate.
tri·pli·car §70 tr. to triplicate.
tri·plo, a adj. & m. triple.
trí·po·de I. m.f. tripod **II.** adj. three-legged.
tri·pón, o·na COLL. adj. & m.f. pot-bellied (person).
tríp·ti·co m. triptych.
trip·ton·go m. triphthong.
tri·pu·do, a adj. & m.f. pot-bellied (person).
tri·pu·la·ción f. AVIA., MARIT. crew ♦ **t. de tierra** AVIA. ground crew.
tri·pu·lan·te m.f. crew member.
tri·pu·lar tr. AVIA., MARIT. to man.
tri·qui·no·sis f. trichinosis.
tri·qui·ñue·la f. COLL. trick, ruse ♦ **andar con triquiñuelas** to have tricks up one's sleeve.
tri·qui·tra·que m. *(de un tren)* clickety-clack; *(cohete)* firecracker ♦ **a cada t.** at every step.
tris m. *(ruido)* crack; *(instante)* jiffy ♦ **estar en un t. de** COLL. to be within an inch of.
tris·ca f. *(ruido)* crack; *(jaleo)* racket.
tris·car §70 intr. *(patear)* to stamp; *(retozar)* to frolic.
tris·te adj. sad; *(melancólico)* melancholy; *(deplorable)* miserable <*una vida t.* a miserable life>; *(insuficiente)* measly.
tris·te·za f. sadness; *(dolor)* sorrow.
tris·tón, o·na adj. melancholy.
tri·tón m. newt.
tri·tu·ra·ción f. crushing.
tri·tu·rar tr. TECH. to triturate; *(moler)* to crush; *(mascar)* to chew; *(una persona)* to beat up; *(un argumento)* to demolish.
triun·fa·dor, ·ra I. adj. triumphant **II.** m.f. winner.
triun·fal adj. triumphal; *(brillante)* triumphant <*una acogida t.* a triumphant reception>.
triun·fan·te adj. triumphant.
triun·far intr. to win; FIG. to succeed.
triun·fo m. triumph; FIG. success.
triun·vi·ra·to m. triumvirate.
tri·va·len·te adj. trivalent.
tri·vial adj. trivial.
tri·via·li·dad f. triviality.
tri·za f. piece ♦ **hacer trizas** to tear to pieces.
tro·car §73 tr. *(cambiar)* to barter; *(confundir)* to mix up —reflex. to change.
tro·ce·ar tr. to divide into pieces.
tro·ce·o m. cutting up.
tro·cha f. *(atajo)* shortcut; *(camino)* path; AMER., RAIL. gauge.
tro·che·mo·che adv. ♦ **a t.** or **a troche y moche** COLL. helter-skelter.
tro·cla or **tró·co·la** f. pulley.
tro·fe·o m. *(objeto)* trophy; *(despojos)* spoils (of war); *(victoria)* triumph.
tro·glo·di·ta I. adj. *(de cavernas)* troglodytic; *(bárbaro)* barbarous; *(comilón)* gluttonous **II.** m.f. *(habitante de cavernas)* troglodyte; *(bruto)* brute; *(comilón)* glutton.
troi·ca f. troika.
tro·le m. trolley.

tro·le·bús m. trolley bus.
tro·le·ro, a COLL. I. adj. lying II. m.f. liar.
trom·ba f. waterspout ♦ **como una t.** FIG. violently.
trom·bón m. (*instrumento*) trombone; (*músico*) trombonist ♦ **t. de pistones** valve trombone • **t. de varas** slide trombone.
trom·bo·sis f. thrombosis.
trom·pa f. MUS. horn; ZOOL. trunk; ENTOM. proboscis ♦ **t. de caza** hunting horn • **t. de Falopio** Fallopian tube —m. MUS. horn player.
trom·pa·da f. COLL. (*golpe*) punch; (*encontrón*) bump.
trom·paz·o m. punch ♦ **darse un t. con la pared** to bump into the wall.
trom·pe·ar tr. AMER. to punch.
trom·pe·ta f. trumpet —m.f. (*persona*) trumpeter; COLL. (*persona despreciable*) rascal.
trom·pe·ta·zo m. trumpet blast.
trom·pe·te·ro m. (*tocador*) trumpeter; (*fabricante*) trumpet maker; ICHTH. trumpet fish.
trom·pe·ti·lla f. (*para oír*) ear trumpet; (*cigarro*) cheroot.
trom·pe·tis·ta m.f. trumpeter.
trom·pi·car §70 intr. to trip.
trom·pi·cón m. (*tropezón*) trip; AMER., COLL. (*mojicón*) punch in the nose ♦ **a trompicones** by fits and starts.
trom·pis m.inv. COLL. punch.
trom·po m. top.
trom·pón m. (*juguete*) large spinning top; (*golpe*) blow.
trom·pu·do, a adj. AMER. thick-lipped.
tro·na·da f. thunderstorm.
tro·na·dor, ·ra I. adj. (*que truena*) thundering; (*un cohete*) detonating II. f. MEX. begonia.
tro·nan·te adj. thundering.
tro·nar §19 intr. to thunder; COLL. (*arruinarse*) to go broke ♦ **estar que truena** COLL. to be in a rage ♦ **por lo que pueda** COLL. just in case.
tron·cal adj. trunk.
tron·car §70 tr. to truncate.
tron·cha f. AMER. (*tajada*) chunk, slice; COLL. (*ganga*) cushy job.
tron·char tr. (*un árbol*) to fell; (*romper*) to split ♦ **troncharse de risa** COLL. to split one's sides laughing.
tron·co m. trunk; GEOM. frustum; (*caballos*) team (of horses); COLL. (*torpe*) dimwit, blockhead ♦ **dormir como un t.** COLL. to sleep like a log • **t. de cono** truncated cone.
tro·ne·ra f. MIL. loophole; MARIT. porthole; (*en billar*) pocket.
tro·ni·do m. (*de trueno*) thunderclap; (*de cañón*) roar.
tro·no m. throne; RELIG. tabernacle.
tron·zar §04 tr. to cut up.
tro·pa f. (*muchedumbre*) crowd; MIL. (*ejército*) army; AMER. (*ganado*) herd ♦ pl. troops • **t. de asalto** storm troops.
tro·pel m. confusion ♦ **en t.** in a mad rush.
tro·pe·lí·a f. (*prisa*) rush; (*ultraje*) abuse; (*violencia*) violence.
tro·pe·zar §29 intr. (*dar un traspié*) to stumble; (*encontrar un estorbo*) to trip; (*cometer un error*) to slip up ♦ **t. con** COLL. to bump into.
tro·pe·zón m. (*traspiés*) stumble; (*obstáculo*) stumbling block; (*desliz*) slip ♦ **a tropezones** COLL. by fits and starts.
tro·pi·cal adj. tropical.
tró·pi·co, a m. tropic ♦ **t. de Cáncer, Capricor-**

nio Tropic of Cancer, Capricorn.
tro·pie·zo m. (*obstáculo*) stumbling block; (*traspiés*) stumble; (*desliz*) slip.
tro·pis·mo m. tropism.
tro·po m. trope.
tro·pos·fe·ra f. troposphere.
tro·quel m. (*stamping*) die.
tro·que·lar tr. to mint.
tro·ta·ca·lles m.f.inv. COLL. gadabout.
tro·ta·da f. trot.
tro·ta·dor, ·ra adj. trotting.
tro·ta·mun·dos m.f.inv. globetrotter.
tro·tar intr. to trot; FIG. to run around.
tro·te m. (*andar*) trot; COLL. (*actividad*) bustle; (*apuro*) chore ♦ **al t.** (*trotando*) trotting; (*de prisa*) quickly • **de** or **para todo t.** COLL. for everyday use.
tro·tón, o·na I. adj. trotting II. m. trotter.
tro·va f. ballad.
tro·va·dor, ·ra I. adj. versifying II. m. (*poeta*) poet; HIST. troubador —f. poetess.
tro·va·do·res·co, a adj. troubador <*canción t.* troubador song>.
tro·var intr. to write verses or poetry.
tro·za f. (*de madera*) log; MARIT. parrel truck.
tro·zar §04 tr. (*hacer pedazos*) to cut into pieces; (*un árbol*) to cut into logs.
tro·zo m. (*pedazo*) piece; (*de madera, queso*) chunk; (*de una obra*) excerpt.
tru·cha f. ICHTH. trout; MECH. derrick.
tru·co m. trick; (*juego de naipes*) card game ♦ **cogerle el t. a algo** COLL. to get the hang of something.
tru·cu·len·cia f. truculence.
tru·cu·len·to, a adj. (*cruel*) ferocious; (*atroz*) atrocious.
true·co, que see **trocar**.
true·ne, no see **tronar**.
true·no m. thunder; (*de un arma*) shot.
true·que m. barter.
tru·fa¹ f. lie.
tru·fa² f. truffle.
tru·far¹ intr. to lie.
tru·far² tr. to stuff with truffles.
tru·hán, a·na I. adj. crooked II. m.f. scoundrel.
tru·ha·ne·ar intr. to cheat.
trun·ca·do, a adj. truncated.
trun·ca·mien·to m. truncation.
trun·car §70 tr. (*cortar*) to truncate; (*dejar incompleto*) to leave unfinished.
trun·co, a adj. (*truncado*) truncated; AMER. incomplete.
tse-tsé f. tsetse fly.
tú pron. you, thou ♦ **¡más eres tú!** COLL. look who's talking! • **tratar de tú** to address as *tú*.
tu, tus adj. your <*tu amigo* your friend>.
tu·ba f. tuba.
tu·ber·cu·li·na f. tuberculin.
tu·bér·cu·lo m. BOT. tuber; MED. tubercle.
tu·ber·cu·lo·sis f. tuberculosis.
tu·ber·cu·lo·so, a adj. BOT. tuberous; MED. tubercular II. m.f. MED. tuberculosis sufferer.
tu·be·rí·a f. (*serie*) pipes; (*tubo*) pipe; (*instalación*) plumbing; (*fábrica*) pipe factory.
tu·be·ro·so, a adj. tuberous.
tu·bo m. tube; ANAT., ZOOL. canal <*t. digestivo* alimentary canal> ♦ **t. de desagüe** drainpipe • **t. de escape** exhaust pipe • **t. lanzallamas** flame thrower • **t. lanzatorpedos** torpedo tube.
tu·bu·la·do, a adj. tubular.
tu·bu·lar adj. tubular.

tu·cán m. toucan.

tu·co m. R.P. (salsa) tomato sauce; ORNITH. owl.

tuer·ca f. MECH. nut ♦ **t. de alas** or **de mariposa** wing nut.

tuer·ce see **torcer**.

tue·ro m. (leño grueso) thick log; (leña) firewood.

tuer·to, a I. adj. (torcido) crooked; (que no ve) one-eyed **II.** m.f. one-eyed person —m. wrong.

tuer·za, zo see **torcer**.

tues·te see **tostar**.

tues·te, to see **tostar**.

tué·ta·no m. marrow ♦ pl. **estar enamorado hasta los t.** COLL. to be head over heels in love • **hasta los t.** through and through.

tu·fo m. fume; FIG. stench.

tu·gu·rio m. (habitación) hole, dump; (casucha) shack; (bar) dive, joint.

tul m. tulle.

tu·li·pa f. (pantalla) tulip-shaped lampshade; BOT. small tulip.

tu·li·pán m. tulip.

tu·lli·do, a adj. crippled.

tu·llir §13 tr. to cripple —reflex. to become crippled.

tum·ba f. (sepulcro) tomb; (voltereta) somersault; (caída) fall.

tum·bar tr. (derribar) to knock down; COLL. (atontar) to knock out <tanto alcohol nos tumbó so much alcohol knocked us out> —intr. (caer) to fall over; MARIT. to keel over, capsize —reflex. to lie down.

tum·bo m. (caída) fall; (sacudida) jolt ♦ **dar tumbos** to jolt.

tum·bón, o·na I. adj. COLL. lazy **II.** m.f. COLL. lazy person —f. deck chair.

tu·me·fac·to, a adj. swollen.

tu·mes·cen·cia f. tumescence.

tu·mes·cen·te adj. tumescent.

tu·mor m. tumor <t. cerebral brain tumor>.

tú·mu·lo m. (sepulcro) burial mound; (catafalco) catafalque; (sepultura) tomb.

tu·mul·to m. tumult.

tu·mul·tuo·so, a adj. tumultuous.

tu·na f. prickly pear.

tu·nal m. (niguera) prickly pear; (sitio) prickly pear grove.

tu·nan·ta COLL. **I.** adj. cunning **II.** f. hussy.

tu·nan·te I. adj. crooked **II.** m.f. rascal.

tu·nan·te·ar intr. to be a crook or rascal.

tu·nan·te·rí·a f. (acción) dirty trick; (cualidad) crookedness.

tun·da f. (del paño) shearing; COLL. (azotaina) beating.

tun·de·ar tr. to beat.

tun·di·dor, ·ra I. adj. shearing **II.** m.f. shearer —f. shearing machine.

tun·di·du·ra f. shearing.

tun·dir tr. (el paño) to shear; COLL. (golpear) to beat.

tun·dra f. tundra.

tú·nel m. tunnel <t. aerodinámico wind tunnel>.

tu·ne·rí·a f. roguishness.

tungs·te·no m. tungsten.

tú·ni·ca f. tunic.

tu·pé m. (pelo) toupee; COLL. (descaro) gall.

tu·pi·do, a adj. (espeso) thick, dense; (paño) tightly-woven; COLL. (torpe) thickheaded.

tu·pir tr. (apretar) to pack tightly; (una tela) to weave closely.

tur·ba¹ f. mob.

tur·ba² f. peat.

tur·ba·ción f. (emoción) upset; (desorden) confusion.

tur·ba·dor, ·ra I. adj. disturbing **II.** m.f. disturber.

tur·ba·mul·ta f. COLL. mob.

tur·ban·te m. turban.

tur·bar tr. (perturbar) to upset; (desconcertar) to embarrass —reflex. to be upset.

túr·bi·do, a adj. muddy.

tur·bie·dad f. (de líquidos) muddiness; (oscuridad) opaqueness.

tur·bi·na f. turbine.

tur·bio, a I. adj. (un líquido) muddy; (un negocio) shady; (agitado) turbulent <un período t. a turbulent period>; (vista) blurred; (oscuro) confused **II.** m.pl. sediment.

tur·bión m. shower; FIG. torrent.

tur·bo·hé·li·ce/pro·pul·sor m. turboprop.

tur·bo·rre·ac·tor m. turbojet.

tur·bu·len·cia f. turbulence.

tur·bu·len·to, a adj. turbulent.

túr·gi·do, a or **tur·gen·te** adj. turgid.

tu·ris·ta m.f. tourist.

tu·rís·ti·co, a adj. tourist.

tur·nar intr. & reflex. to take turns.

tur·nio, a adj. & m.f. cross-eyed (person).

tur·no m. (vez) turn; (de obreros) shift ♦ **de t.** on duty • **por t.** in turn • **por turnos** by turns • **trabajar por turnos** to work shifts • **t. de día** or **de noche** day or night shift.

tur·que·sa f. turquoise.

tur·quí [pl. -íes]/**qui·no, a** adj. indigo.

tu·rrón m. nougat.

tu·ru·la·to, a adj. COLL. stunned.

tu·rum·bón m. COLL. bump on the head.

tu·sa f. AMER. (del maíz) cornhusk; (cigarro) cigar rolled in a cornhusk; (del caballo) mane.

tu·sar tr. AMER., COLL. to trim.

tu·te·ar tr. to address as **tú**.

tu·te·la f. (de personas) guardianship; (de territorios) trusteeship; (protección) protection; (dirección) guidance ♦ **territorio bajo t.** trust territory.

tu·te·lar adj. protective.

tu·te·o m. addressing as **tú**.

tu·tor, ·ra m.f. guardian.

tu·to·rí·a f. guardianship.

tu·vie·ra, vo see **tener**.

tu·yo, a I. adj. yours <¿es t. el coche? is the car yours?>; of yours <un pariente t. a relative of yours> **II.** pron. yours <¿quién tiene el t.? who has yours?> ♦ **lo t.** your affair • **los tuyos** your people.

U

u, U f. twenty-second letter of the Spanish alphabet.

u conj. var. of **o** used before (h)o.

u·bé·rri·mo, a adj. (tierra) very fertile; (vegetación) luxuriant.

u·bi·ca·ción f. (sitio) location; (acción) placing.

u·bi·car §70 tr. AMER. to locate —reflex. to be located; (encontrar trabajo) to get hired.

u·bi·cuo, a adj. ubiquitous.

u·bre f. udder.

Ud., Uds. pron. abbrev. of **usted, ustedes.**

¡uf! interj. *(cansancio)* whew!; *(repugnancia)* ugh!

u·fa·nar·se reflex. to boast.

u·fa·no, a adj. *(orgulloso)* proud; *(satisfecho)* pleased.

u·jier m. doorkeeper.

úl·ce·ra f. ulcer.

ul·ce·ra·ción f. ulceration.

ul·ce·rar tr. & reflex. to ulcerate.

ul·ce·ro·so, a adj. ulcerous.

ul·te·rior adj. *(más allá)* ulterior; *(que ocurre después)* subsequent.

ul·te·rior·men·te adv. subsequently.

úl·ti·ma·men·te adv. *(por último)* ultimately; *(recientemente)* lately.

ul·ti·mar tr. *(acabar)* to conclude; AMER., COLL. to finish off.

ul·ti·má·tum m. ultimatum.

úl·ti·mo, a adj. *(final)* last <la ú. partida de la temporada the last game of the season>; *(de dos)* latter; *(más reciente)* latest, most recent; *(remoto)* farthest; *(mejor)* finest; *(de abajo)* bottom; *(de arriba)* top; *(de atrás)* back; FIG. *(definitivo)* last <como ú. remedio as a last resort>; COM. lowest ♦ **a últimos de** at or towards the end of (a month) • **el ú. grito (de la moda)** the latest craze • **estar a lo ú. de** to be nearly at the end of • **estar en las últimas** COLL. *(estar moribundo)* to be on one's last legs; *(estar en la miseria)* to be down and out • **llegar el ú.** to arrive last • **por ú.** lastly.

ul·tra I. adv. besides II. m.f. extremist.

ul·tra·de·re·cha f. far right.

ul·tra·de·re·chis·ta adj. & m.f. far rightist.

ul·tra·jan·te adj. offensive, outrageous.

ul·tra·jar tr. to insult, outrage.

ul·tra·je m. insult, outrage.

ul·tra·mar m. overseas country.

ul·tra·ma·ri·no, a I. adj. overseas II. m.pl. *(comestibles)* imported foods; *(tienda)* grocery store.

ul·tra·mo·der·no, a adj. ultramodern.

ul·tran·za adj. ♦ **a u.** *(a muerte)* to the death; *(resueltamente)* determinedly.

ul·tra·rro·jo, a adj. ultrared.

ul·tra·só·ni·co, a adj. ultrasonic.

ul·tra·so·ni·do m. ultrasound.

ul·tra·tum·ba f. otherworld.

ul·tra·vio·le·ta adj. ultraviolet.

u·lu·lar intr. to howl.

um·bi·li·cal adj. umbilical.

um·bral m. threshold.

um·brí·o, a I. adj. shady II. f. shade.

um·bro·so, a adj. shady.

un contr. of **uno.**

u·ná·ni·me adj. unanimous.

u·na·ni·mi·dad f. unanimity ♦ **por u.** unanimously.

un·ción f. unction; RELIG. extreme unction.

un·cir §35 tr. to yoke.

un·dé·ci·mo, a adj. & m. eleventh.

un·du·lan·te adj. undulating.

un·du·lar intr. to undulate.

un·gir §32 tr. to anoint.

un·güen·to m. ointment.

u·ni·ce·lu·lar adj. unicellular.

u·ni·ci·dad f. uniqueness.

ú·ni·co, a I. adj. *(solo)* only; *(extraordinario)* unique II. m.f. only one <es el ú. que me queda it's the only one I have left> ♦ **lo ú.** only thing <¡lo ú. que faltaba! that's the only thing that was missing!>.

u·ni·cor·nio m. unicorn.

u·ni·dad f. *(acuerdo)* unity; *(armonía)* harmony; *(cada uno)* each (one) <valen veinte pesos la u. they cost twenty pesos each>; MATH., MIL., TECH. unit ♦ **u. monetaria** monetary unit.

u·ni·do, a adj. *(juntos)* united; *(que se quieren)* close.

u·ni·fi·car §70 tr. to unify.

u·ni·for·mar tr. to make uniform.

u·ni·for·me I. adj. *(igual)* uniform; *(terreno)* level; *(ritmo)* steady; *(sin variedad)* plain <estilo u. plain style> II. m. uniform.

u·ni·for·mi·dad f. uniformity.

u·ni·gé·ni·to, a I. adj. only <hijo u. only child> II. m. RELIG. Son of God.

u·ni·la·te·ral adj. unilateral.

u·nión f. union; *(armonía)* unity; *(conexión)* joint.

u·nir tr. *(juntar)* to unite; *(combinar)* to join (together); *(casar)* to unite (by marriage); *(mezclarse)* to mix; *(aliar)* to combine <u. la teoría con la experiencia práctica to combine theory with practical experience>; COM. to merge; MECH., TECH. to join —reflex. *(juntarse)* to join; *(casarse)* to marry; *(mezclarse)* to mix; COM. to merge ♦ **u. a** to join • **u. en matrimonio** to be united in marriage.

u·ni·se·xo adj. unisex.

u·ní·so·no, a I. adj. in unison II. m. unison ♦ **al u.** in unison.

u·ni·ta·rio, a I. adj. unified; RELIG. Unitarian II. m.f. RELIG. Unitarian.

u·ni·ver·sal adj. universal; *(del mundo)* world <historia u. world history>.

u·ni·ver·sa·li·dad f. universality.

u·ni·ver·sa·li·zar §04 tr. to universalize.

u·ni·ver·si·dad f. university.

u·ni·ver·si·ta·rio, a I. adj. university II. m.f. university student.

u·ni·ver·so m. universe.

u·no, a I. m. one II. adj. one ♦ **la u.** one o'clock • **u. que otro** a few <unos estudiantes some students>; ♦ pl. some, a few <unos veinte kilómetros de aquí approximately <unos veinte kilómetros de aquí about twenty kilometers from here> III. indef. pron. one <u. de mis amigos one of my friends>; one, you <u. no puede escaparse de aquí you cannot escape from here>; *(alguien)* somebody <u. lo hizo somebody did it> ♦ **cada u.** each one, every one • **de u. en u.** one by one • **u. a otro** or **con otro** each other, one another <se miraron u. a otro they looked at each other> • **u. a** or **por u.** one at a time • **u. y otro** both • **u. tras otro** one after another ♦ pl. **u. a otros** one another • **u. cuantos** a few, some IV. indef. art. a, an <necesito u. pluma I need a pen>.

un·tar tr. *(engrasar)* to grease; *(manchar)* to smear; to spread <u. el pan con mermelada to spread bread with jam>; MED. to rub ♦ **u. la mano a alguien** COLL. to grease someone's palm.

un·to m. *(materia grasa)* grease; *(del animal)* fat ♦ **u. de México** COLL. bribe.

un·tuo·si·dad f. greasiness.

un·tuo·so, a adj. greasy.

un·tu·ra f. *(acción)* greasing; *(sustancia)* ointment.

u·ña f. *(de la mano)* fingernail; *(del pie)* toenail; *(garra)* claw; *(pezuña)* hoof; *(garfio)* claw; *(gancho)* hook ♦ **comerse las uñas** to

bite one's nails • **sacar las uñas** COLL. to show one's claws • **ser u. y carne** to be inseparable.
¡u·pa! interj. upsy-daisy! ♦ **a u.** in arms.
u·ra·nio m. uranium.
ur·ba·ni·dad f. urbanity.
ur·ba·nis·ta m.f. city planner.
ur·ba·nís·ti·co, a adj. *(de la ciudad)* urban; *(del urbanismo)* city-planning.
ur·ba·ni·za·ción f. *(urbanismo)* urbanization, city planning; *(desarrollo)* development.
ur·ba·ni·zar §04 tr. *(civilizar)* to civilize; *(un terreno)* to develop ♦ **zona sin u.** undeveloped area.
ur·ba·no, a adj. *(de la ciudad)* urban; *(cortés)* urbane.
ur·be f. large city.
ur·di·dor, ·ra TEX. I. adj. warping II. m.f. warper.
ur·dim·bre f. TEX. warping; FIG. scheming.
ur·dir tr. TEX. to warp; FIG. to scheme.
u·re·a f. urea.
u·ré·ter m. ureter.
u·re·tra f. urethra.
ur·gen·cia f. urgency ♦ **con u.** urgently ♦ **cura de u.** first aid.
ur·gen·te adj. urgent.
ur·gir §32 intr. to be urgent.
u·ri·na·rio, a I. adj. urinary II. m. urinal.
ur·na f. *(vasija)* urn; *(arca)* glass case ♦ **acudir** *or* **ir a las urnas** to go to the polls.
u·ró·lo·go, a m.f. urologist.
u·rra·ca f. magpie.
ur·ti·ca·ria f. hives.
u·sa·do, a adj. *(deteriorado)* worn-out; *(de segunda mano)* secondhand.
u·san·za f. custom.
u·sar tr. *(emplear)* to use; *(llevar ropa)* to wear ♦ **sin u.** unused —intr. *(soler)* to be accustomed (to) <*uso nadar todos los días* I'm accustomed to swimming every day>; *(emplear)* to use, make use of <*u. de artimaña* to use trickery> ♦ **u. mal de** to misuse —reflex. *(estar de moda)* to be the custom *or* the fashion; *(estar en uso)* to be used.
u·so m. *(empleo)* use <*el u. de fibras sintéticas* the use of synthetic fibers>; *(goce)* exercise <*el u. del privilegio hereditario* the exercise of hereditary privilege>; *(moda)* fashion; *(costumbre)* custom; *(desgaste)* wear and tear ♦ **al u. de** in the style of ♦ **deteriorado con el u.** well-used ♦ **estar fuera de u.** to be obsolete ♦ **hacer mal u. de** to misuse ♦ **hacer u. de** to use ♦ **hacer u. de la palabra** to speak ♦ **para todo u.** all-purpose ♦ **ser de u.** *(emplearse)* to be used; *(llevarse)* to be worn ♦ **u. de razón** power of reason.
us·ted pron. you ♦ **de u.** yours • **hablar** *or* **tratar de u.** to use the polite form of address ♦ pl. you, all of you.
u·sual adj. usual.
u·sua·rio, a I. adj. usufructuary <*derechos usuarios* usufructuary rights> II. m.f. user.
u·su·fruc·to m. usufruct.
u·su·ra f. usury.
u·su·re·ro, a I. adj. usurious II. m.f. usurer.
u·sur·pa·ción f. usurpation.
u·sur·pa·dor, ·ra I. adj. usurping II. m.f. usurper.
u·sur·par tr. to usurp.
u·ten·si·lio m. utensil.
u·te·ri·no, a adj. uterine.

ú·te·ro m. uterus.
ú·til I. adj. *(que sirve)* useful; *(apto)* fit II. m. tool, utensil ♦ pl. implements • **ú. de pesca** fishing tackle.
u·ti·li·dad f. *(cualidad)* usefulness; *(provecho)* profit ♦ **u. bruta** gross profit ♦ pl. profits • **u. de capital** capital gains • **u. impositivas** taxable profits • **u. líquidas** net profits.
u·ti·li·zar §04 tr. to utilize.
u·to·pí·a f. utopia.
u·tó·pi·co, a adj. & m.f. utopian.
u·va f. grape ♦ **estar hecho una u.** COLL. to be drunk as a skunk • **u. pasa** raisin.
ú·vu·la f. uvula.
u·xo·ri·ci·da I. adj. uxoricidal II. m. uxoricide.
¡uy! interj. *(sorpresa)* oh!; *(dolor)* ouch!

V

v, V f. twenty-third letter of the Spanish alphabet ♦ **v. doble** double-u, w.
va·ca f. cow; CUL. beef; *(cuero)* cowhide, leather; *(dinero)* gambling pool ♦ **v. de San Antón** ladybug • **v. lechera** milk cow • **v. marina** manatee, sea cow • **vacas gordas** years of plenty.
va·ca·ción f. vacation ♦ **estar de vacaciones** to be on vacation.
va·can·te I. adj. vacant II. f. vacancy.
va·cia·de·ro m. dump.
va·cia·do m. *(de metales)* casting; *(figura)* cast.
va·ciar §30 tr. *(dejar vacío)* to empty <*v. una caja* to empty a box>; *(verter)* to drain <*v. una botella* to drain a bottle>; *(fundir)* to cast; *(sacar filo)* to sharpen; *(ahuecar)* to hollow out —intr. to empty —reflex. to empty.
va·ci·la·ción f. hesitation ♦ **sin v.** unhesitatingly.
va·ci·lan·te adj. *(persona)* hesitating; *(luz)* flickering.
va·ci·lar intr. *(moverse)* to sway; *(la luz)* to flicker; *(dudar)* to hesitate; MEX. to go on a spree ♦ **sin v.** unhesitatingly.
va·cí·o, a I. adj. *(desocupado)* vacant; *(hueco)* hollow; *(falto)* devoid <*una cabeza v. de ideas* a mind devoid of ideas> II. m. *(cavidad)* emptiness; *(hueco)* hollow; *(espacio)* empty space; *(falta)* void <*su muerte ha dejado un gran v.* his death has left a great void>; PHYS. vacuum ♦ **envasado al v.** vacuum-packed ♦ **hacer el v. a alguien** COLL. to give someone the cold shoulder.
va·cui·dad f. vacuity.
va·cu·na·ción f. vaccination.
va·cu·nar tr. to vaccinate.
va·cu·no, a adj. bovine ♦ **ganado v.** cattle.
va·cuo, a adj. vacuous.
va·de·ar tr. *(un río)* to ford; *(a pie)* to wade across; *(una dificultad)* to overcome.
va·do m. *(de un río)* ford; *(recurso)* remedy.
va·ga·bun·de·ar intr. to wander.
va·ga·bun·do, a adj. & m.f. vagabond.
va·ga·men·te adv. vaguely.
va·gan·cia f. *(delito)* vagrancy; *(ociosidad)* idleness.
va·gar §47 intr. *(errar)* to wander; *(andar ocioso)* to be idle.
va·gi·do m. cry.
va·gi·na f. vagina.
va·go, a I. adj. *(indeterminado)* vague; *(holga-*

zán) lazy; *(vagabundo)* vagrant **II.** m. *(holga-zán)* loafer; *(vagabundo)* vagrant; ANAT. vagus nerve.

va·gón m. RAIL. car, coach; *(para mercancías)* truck, van ♦ **v. cama** sleeping car • **v. de carga** freight car • **v. de equipajes** baggage car • **v. de pasajeros** passenger car • **v. de primera** first-class car • **v. restaurante** dining car.

va·go·ne·ta f. small wagon *or* cart.

va·gue·ar intr. to wander.

va·gue·dad f. *(cualidad)* vagueness; *(expresión vaga)* vague remark.

va·hí·do m. dizzy spell.

va·ho m. steam.

vai·na **I.** f. *(envoltura)* sheath; BOT. pod; MA-RIT. casing; AMER., COLL. *(molestia)* nuisance **II.** adj. AMER., COLL. annoying.

vai·ni·lla f. vanilla; SEW. hemstitch.

vai·vén m. *(oscilación)* oscillation; *(balanceo)* swaying; *(fluctuación)* fluctuation.

va·ji·lla f. tableware ♦ **lavar la v.** to wash the dishes • **v. de plata** silverware • **v. de porce-lana** china.

val·drá, dría see **valer.**

va·le m. *(pagaré)* voucher; *(recibo)* receipt.

va·le·de·ro, a adj. valid.

va·len·cia f. valence.

va·len·tí·a f. *(valor)* bravery; *(ánimo)* boldness.

va·len·tón, o·na **I.** adj. boastful **II.** m.f. brag-gart.

va·len·to·na(·da) f. boast.

va·ler §74 **I.** intr. *(tener valor)* to be worth; *(te-ner mérito)* to be of value; *(ser válido)* to be valid *<esta moneda no vale* this coin is not valid>; *(tener autoridad)* to have authority *<el supervisor no vale para esto* the supervisor does not have authority in this matter>; *(servir)* to be useful, be of use *<no le valdrán todas sus pa-lancas* all of his connections will be of no use to him> ♦ **más vale** it is better —tr. *(tener un valor de)* to be worth *<el reloj vale cien dólares* the watch is worth a hundred dollars>; *(costar)* to be *<¿cuánto vale?* how much is it?>; *(repre-sentar)* to be worth *<una blanca vale dos negras* a half note is worth two quarter notes>; *(produ-cir)* to yield *<esa inversión le valió cien mil pesos* that investment yielded him a hundred thou-sand pesos>; *(causar)* to cause *<nuestra con-ducta nos valió muchos disgustos* our conduct caused us a lot of trouble> ♦ **hacer v. sus dere-chos** to assert one's rights • **v. la pena** to be worthwhile • **v. lo que pesa en oro** to be worth its weight in gold —reflex. to manage for one-self ♦ **v. de** to make use of **II.** m. worth.

va·le·ro·so, a adj. courageous.

va·le·tu·di·na·rio, a adj. & m.f. sickly (person).

val·ga, go see **valer.**

va·lí·a f. worth.

va·li·da·ción f. validation.

va·li·dar tr. to validate.

va·li·dez f. validity.

vá·li·do, a adj. valid.

va·lien·te **I.** adj. *(valeroso)* brave; *(osado)* bold; COLL. *(irón.)* fine *<¡v. amigo eres tú!* a fine friend you are!> ♦ **¡v. frío!** it's freezing! **II.** m. *(valeroso)* brave man; *(valentón)* braggart.

va·li·ja f. *(maleta)* suitcase; *(saco de correo)* mailbag ♦ **v. diplomática** diplomatic pouch.

va·lio·so, a adj. valuable.

va·lla f. *(cerca)* fence; *(obstáculo)* obstacle; SPORT. hurdle.

va·llar tr. to fence in.

va·lle m. *(entre montañas)* valley; *(de un río)* river basin ♦ **v. de lágrimas** vale of tears.

va·lor m. *(cualidad)* worth; *(precio)* price *<el v. de la propiedad* the price of the property>; *(im-portancia)* importance; *(osadía)* nerve *<tener el v. de negarlo* to have the nerve to deny it>; *(coraje)* valor; MATH., MUS. value ♦ **dar v. a** to attach importance to • **de v.** valuable • **sin v.** worthless • **v. adquisitivo** purchasing power • **v. comercial** market value • **v. nominal** COM. face value ♦ pl. COM. securities • **v. inmuebles** real estate.

va·lo·ra·ción f. appraisal.

va·lo·rar tr. *(dar mérito)* to appreciate; *(valuar)* to appraise; *(aumentar el valor)* to increase the value of.

va·lo·ri·za·ción f. appraisal.

va·lo·ri·zar §04 tr. *(evaluar)* to appraise; *(au-mentar el valor)* to raise the value of.

vals m. waltz.

va·lua·ción f. appraisal.

va·luar §67 tr. to appraise, value.

vál·vu·la f. valve; RAD. tube.

va·mos, van see **ir.**

vam·pi·re·sa f. vamp.

vam·pi·ro m. vampire.

va·na·glo·ria f. pride.

va·na·glo·riar·se reflex. to boast.

va·na·glo·rio·so, a adj. & m.f. boastful (per-son).

va·na·men·te adv. *(inútilmente)* vainly; *(con vanidad)* presumptuously; *(tontamente)* fool-ishly.

van·da·lis·mo m. vandalism.

van·guar·dia f. MIL. vanguard; ARTS, LIT. avant-garde ♦ **ir a la v.** to be in the forefront.

van·guar·dis·ta adj. & m.f. avant-garde (art-ist).

va·ni·dad f. *(cualidad)* vanity; *(ostentación)* os-tentation; *(orgullo)* conceit.

va·ni·do·so, a adj. & m.f. vain *or* conceited (person).

va·no, a **I.** adj. *(inútil)* vain; *(frívolo)* frivo-lous; *(vanidoso)* conceited ♦ **en v.** in vain, vainly **II.** m. ARCHIT. window.

va·por m. *(gas)* steam; *(vaho)* vapor; *(buque)* steamship ♦ **al v.** CUL. steamed • **v. de ruedas** paddle steamer.

va·po·ri·za·dor m. vaporizer.

va·po·ri·zar §04 tr. to vaporize.

va·po·ro·so, a adj. *(que despide vapores)* vapor-ous; *(tejido)* sheer.

va·pu·le·ar tr. to thrash.

va·que·ro, a **I.** adj. pertaining to cowhands ♦ **pantalón v.** jeans **II.** m. cowboy.

va·que·ta f. cowhide.

va·ra f. *(palo)* stick; *(rama)* rod; *(bastón)* staff; BOT. stalk; *(medida)* linear measurement (.84 meters); *(de trombón)* slide; TAUR. *(pica)* pike; *(garrochazo)* thrust with a pike.

va·ra·de·ro m. dry dock.

va·ra·du·ra f. running aground.

va·rar MARIT. tr. to beach —intr. to run aground.

va·ra·zo m. *(golpe)* blow with a stick; TAUR. thrust with a lance.

va·re·a·dor, ra m.f. *(de árboles)* beater; *(del ganado)* cowhand.

va·re·ar tr. *(derribar)* to knock down; *(dar golpes)* to cudgel; TAUR. to jab with the lance.

va·ria·ble adj. & f. MATH. variable.

va·ria·ción f. variation.

va·ria·do, a adj. varied.

va·rian·te I. adj. varying II. f. variant.

va·riar §30 tr. & intr. to vary.

va·ri·ce f. varicose vein.

va·ri·ce·la f. chicken pox.

va·rie·dad f. variety ♦ pl. *(cosas diversas)* miscellany; THEAT. variety show.

va·ri·lla f. *(vara)* rod; *(de un paraguas)* rib; *(de corsé)* stay; MEX. peddler's wares ♦ **v. de pistón** piston rod • **v. mágica** magic wand.

va·rio, a I. adj. *(que varía)* varied; *(cambiadizo)* varying, changeable ♦ pl. several II. m.f. ♦ pl. several <*varios piensan que sí* several think so>.

va·rón m. *(hombre)* male; *(niño)* boy <*tienen dos hijas y un v.* they have two girls and one boy> ♦ **santo v.** COLL. plain simple man.

va·ro·nil adj. *(masculino)* virile; *(dicho de mujer)* mannish.

va·sa·lla·je m. servitude.

va·sa·llo, a I. adj. subordinate II. m.f. HIST. vassal; *(súbdito)* subject.

vas·cu·lar adj. vascular.

va·sec·to·mí·a f. vasectomy.

va·se·li·na f. Vaseline (trademark).

va·si·ja f. container.

va·so m. glass; *(jarrón)* vase; ZOOL. hoof; ANAT., BOT. vessel.

vás·ta·go m. BOT. shoot; *(hijo)* offspring; MECH. rod ♦ **v. de válvula** *or* **de distribución** valve rod *or* stem.

vas·to, a adj. vast.

va·ti·ci·na·dor, ·ra I. adj. prophesying II. m.f. prophet.

va·ti·ci·nar tr. to predict.

va·ti·ci·nio m. prediction.

va·tio m. watt.

va·tio-ho·ra m. watt-hour.

va·ya see **ir.**

ve see **ir** *or* **ver**[2].

ve·a, veo see **ver**[2].

ve·ci·nal adj. local.

ve·cin·dad f. *(cualidad)* nearness; *(vecindario)* neighbors; *(cercanías)* vicinity ♦ **casa de v.** apartment building.

ve·cin·da·rio m. neighborhood.

ve·ci·no, a I. adj. *(próximo)* next ♦ **v. a** *or* **de** near II. m.f. neighbor ♦ **cualquier hijo de v.** COLL. anybody.

ve·da f. *(prohibición)* prohibition; HUNT. closed season.

ve·da·do, a I. adj. prohibited II. m. game preserve.

ve·dar tr. *(prohibir)* to prohibit; *(impedir)* to prevent.

ve·e·dor, ·ra I. adj. prying II. m.f. busybody —m. supervisor.

ve·ge·ta·ción f. vegetation.

ve·ge·tal I. adj. vegetable ♦ **reino v.** plant kingdom II. m. vegetable; *(planta)* plant.

ve·ge·tar intr. to vegetate.

ve·ge·ta·ria·no, a adj. & m.f. vegetarian.

ve·ge·ta·ti·vo, a adj. vegetative.

ve·he·men·cia f. vehemence.

ve·he·men·te adj. vehement.

ve·hí·cu·lo m. vehicle; MED. carrier.

ve·í·a see **ver**[2].

vein·ta·vo, a adj. & m. twentieth.

vein·te I. adj. twenty; *(vigésimo)* twentieth II. m. twenty.

vein·te·na f. score.

vein·ti·dós adj. & m. twenty-two.

vein·ti·tan·tos, as adj. *(cantidad)* twenty or so;

(del mes) around the twentieth.

vein·ti·ún adj. contr. of **veintiuno.**

vein·tiu·no, a I. adj. twenty-one; *(vigésimo primero)* twenty-first II. m. twenty-one.

ve·ja·ción f. vexation.

ve·ja·men m. *(molestia)* vexation; *(insulto)* affront; *(represión satírica)* derision.

ve·jar tr. to vex.

ve·jes·to·rio m. DEROG. *(persona)* old fool; *(cosa)* old wreck.

ve·je·te COLL. I. adj. old II. m. old man.

ve·jez f. old age.

ve·ji·ga f. ANAT. bladder; *(en la piel)* blister ♦ **v. de la bilis** gall bladder • **v. natatoria** swim bladder.

ve·la[1] f. *(vigilia)* vigil; *(trabajo)* night shift; *(luz)* candle <*v. de cera* wax candle>; MEX. reprimand ♦ **en v.** awake • **estar a dos velas** FIG. to be broke • **no darle a alguien v. en un entierro** FIG. not to give someone a say in the matter.

ve·la[2] f. MARIT. sail ♦ **a toda v.** under full sail • **barco de v.** sailboat • **buque de v.** sailing ship • **hacerse a la v.** to set sail • **v. de cuchillo** staysail • **v. mayor** mainsail.

ve·la·da f. evening ♦ **quedarse de v.** to spend the evening.

ve·la·do, a adj. *(oculto)* veiled; *(voz)* muffled; *(imagen)* blurred.

ve·la·dor, ·ra I. adj watching II. m.f. *(persona que vela)* vigil-keeper —m. *(mesita)* night table; R.P. bedside lamp; MEX. glass lampshade.

ve·la·me(n) m. sails.

ve·lar tr. *(vigilar)* to keep watch over; *(cuidar)* to sit up with <*v. a un niño enfermo* to sit up with a sick child>; *(cubrir)* to cover with a veil; *(esconder)* to hide —intr. *(no dormir)* to stay awake; *(trabajar)* to work late; RELIG. to keep vigil ♦ **v. por** to care for, look after —reflex. PHOTOG. to blur.

ve·la·to·rio m. wake.

ve·lei·dad f. *(deseo vano)* whim; *(inconstancia)* fickleness.

ve·lei·do·so, a adj. fickle.

ve·le·ro, a I. adj. swift-sailing II. m.f. *(de velas para buques)* sailmaker; *(de velas de cera)* candlemaker —m. sailboat.

ve·le·ta f. weather vane —m.f. COLL. weathercock.

ve·llo m. *(pelo)* hair; *(pelusilla)* fuzz.

ve·llo·ci·no m. fleece.

ve·llón m. *(lana)* fleece; *(piel)* sheepskin; *(mechón)* tuft of wool.

ve·llu·do, a I. adj. hairy II. m. TEX. velveteen.

ve·lo m. veil; *(humeral)* humeral veil ♦ **correr** *or* **echar un v. sobre algo** to hush something up • **tomar el v.** to take the veil • **v. del paladar** soft palate.

ve·lo·ci·dad f. velocity; AUTO. gear ♦ **exceso de v.** speeding • **v. de ascensión** AER. climbing speed • **v. límite** speed limit • **v. máxima** top speed.

ve·lo·cí·me·tro m. speedometer.

ve·ló·dro·mo m. velodrome.

ve·lo·rio m. wake; R.P. dull party.

ve·loz adj. swift.

ve·lu·do m. plush.

ven see **venir.**

ve·na f. vein; *(inspiración)* inspiration ♦ **darle a uno la v.** to feel like doing something crazy • **estar en v.** to be in the mood.

ve·na·blo m. javelin.

ve·na·do m. stag; CUL. venison ♦ **pintar el v.** MEX. to play hooky.

ven·ce·de·ro, a adj. COM. payable.

ven·ce·dor, ·ra I. adj. *(conquistador)* conquering; *(victorioso)* winning **II.** m.f. *(conquistador)* conqueror; *(ganador)* winner.

ven·cer §75 tr. *(conquistar)* to conquer; *(derrotar)* to defeat; *(aventajar)* to surpass; *(superar)* to overcome; to be overcome <le venció el sueño he was overcome by sleep>; to control, master <v. las pasiones to control one's emotions> —intr. *(ganar)* to win; COM. *(cumplirse un plazo)* to expire; *(una deuda)* to fall due —reflex. *(combarse)* to bend; *(romperse)* to collapse.

ven·ci·do, a I. adj. *(derrotado)* defeated; COM. *(una deuda)* due; *(cumplido)* expired **II.** m.f. loser —f. ♦ **a la tercera va la v.** *(exhortando)* the third time is the charm; *(amenazando)* three strikes and you're out.

ven·ci·mien·to m. *(victoria)* victory; *(derrota)* defeat; *(torcimiento)* bending; *(al romperse)* collapse; COM. *(término)* expiration; *(de una deuda)* maturity.

ven·da f. bandage; *(de cabeza)* headband ♦ **te ner una v. en los ojos** to be blindfolded.

ven·da·je m. bandage.

ven·dar tr. to bandage ♦ **v. los ojos** to blindfold.

ven·da·val m. gale.

ven·de·dor, ·ra I. adj. selling **II.** m.f. *(persona que vende)* seller; *(de tienda)* salesperson ♦ **v. ambulante** peddler.

ven·der tr. to sell; *(hacer comercio)* to market; *(sacrificar)* to sell (out); *(traicionar)* to betray ♦ **v. al contado** to sell for cash • **v. al por mayor** to sell wholesale • **v. al por menor** to sell retail • **v. a plazos** to sell on installment • **v. caro** to be expensive —reflex. to sell, be sold <las manzanas se venden por docena apples are sold by the dozen>; *(dejarse sobornar)* to sell oneself ♦ **se vende** for sale.

ven·di·mia f. *(cosecha)* grape harvest; *(año)* vintage.

ven·di·mia·dor, ·ra m.f. grape picker.

ven·drá, dría see **venir**.

ve·ne·no m. *(toxina)* poison; FIG. venom.

ve·ne·no·so, a adj. poisonous.

ve·ne·ra·ble adj. venerable.

ve·ne·ra·ción f. veneration.

ve·ne·rar tr. to venerate.

ve·né·re·o, a adj. & m. venereal (disease).

ven·ga, go see **venir**.

ven·ga·dor, ·ra I. adj. avenging **II.** m.f. avenger.

ven·gan·za f. vengeance.

ven·gar §47 tr. & reflex. to avenge (oneself) ♦ **v. de alguien** to take revenge on someone.

ven·ga·ti·vo, a adj. vindictive.

ve·nia f. *(perdón)* forgiveness; *(permiso)* permission; AMER., MIL. salute.

ve·ni·da f. *(llegada)* arrival; *(regreso)* return.

ve·ni·de·ro, a adj. coming, upcoming.

ve·nir §76 intr. to come; *(llegar)* to arrive; *(ropa)* to fit <esta chaqueta ya no me viene this jacket no longer fits me>; *(tener)* to get <me vino un dolor de cabeza I got a headache>; *(inferirse)* to follow <esta conclusión viene de tal postura this conclusion follows from such a posture>; *(presentarse)* to occur <la idea me vino inesperadamente the idea occurred to me unexpectedly>; *(producirse)* to grow <el trigo

viene bien en esta región wheat grows well in this region>; *(suceder)* to end up <vino a morir he ended up dying>; *(resultar)* to end up <vine a ser lo mismo it ends up being all the same>; *(repetir)* to have been <vengo diciéndolo desde hace cinco meses I have been saying so for five months> ♦ **que viene** next <el año que viene next year> • **v. a la memoria** to come to mind • **v. al caso** to be relevant • **v. al mundo** to come into the world • **v. al pelo** COLL. to come in the nick of time • **venga lo que venga** come what may • **venirle ancho a uno** to be too big for one • **ver v.** to see it coming —reflex. ♦ **v. abajo** or **por tierra** or **al suelo** to collapse, fall down.

ven·ta f. sale ♦ **servicio de v.** sales department • **v. al contado** cash sale • **v. a crédito** credit sale • **v. al por mayor** wholesale • **v. al por menor** retail.

ven·ta·ja f. *(superioridad)* advantage; *(en una carrera)* lead; *(provecho)* benefit ♦ **llevar v. a** to have the lead over • **sacar v. a** to be ahead of • **sacar v. de** to profit from.

ven·ta·jo·so, a adj. advantageous.

ven·ta·na f. window; ANAT. nostril ♦ **echar** or **tirar por la v.** to squander.

ven·ta·nal m. large window.

ven·ta·ni·lla f. *(de vehículo)* window; *(portilla)* porthole; *(taquilla)* box office.

ven·ta·rrón m. COLL. gale.

ven·ti·la·ción f. ventilation.

ven·ti·la·dor m. fan.

ven·ti·lar tr. *(un lugar)* to air out; *(discutir)* to air; *(hacer público)* to make public —reflex. COLL. to get some fresh air.

ven·tis·ca f. blizzard.

ven·tis·car §70 intr. to snow heavily.

ven·tis·que·ro m. *(ventisca)* blizzard; *(de un monte)* snowcap.

ven·to·le·ra f. gust of wind ♦ **darle a uno la v. de hacer algo** COLL. to take it into one's head to do something.

ven·to·se·ar intr. to break wind.

ven·to·si·dad f. gas.

ven·to·so, a I. adj. windy **II.** f. MED. cupping glass; ZOOL. sucker; *(abertura)* air hole.

ven·tre·ra f. *(faja)* bellyband; *(armadura)* stomach plate (of armor); *(del caballo)* cinch.

ven·tri·cu·lar adj. ventricular.

ven·trí·cu·lo m. ventricle.

ven·trí·lo·cuo, a m.f. ventriloquist.

ven·tri·lo·quia f. ventriloquism.

ven·tro·so/tru·do, a adj. paunchy.

ven·tu·ra f. *(felicidad)* happiness; *(suerte)* luck ♦ **a la (buena) v.** with no set plan • **decir la buena v. a alguien** to tell someone's fortune • **por v. as** luck would have it • **probar v.** to try one's luck.

ven·tu·ro·so, a adj. fortunate.

ver¹ m. *(apariencia)* appearance; *(opinión)* opinion <a mi v. in my opinion>.

ver² §77 tr. to see; *(mirar)* to look at; *(televisión, películas)* to watch; *(visitar)* to visit; *(averiguar)* to look and see <vea usted si está Pedro look and see if Peter is here>; *(examinar)* to examine <veamos este párrafo let's examine this paragraph>; *(observar)* to observe ♦ **a** or **hasta más v.** so long • **a v.** let's see • **estar** or **quedar en veremos** AMER. to be a long way off • **tener que v. con** to have to do with • **veremos** we'll see • **v. venir** to see it coming —reflex. *(ser visto)* to be seen; *(ser obvio)* to be obvious or clear; *(mirarse)* to see oneself <v. en el espejo to see oneself in the mirror>; *(hallarse)* to find oneself <me veo pobre y sin amigos I find myself poor and without friends>; *(visitarse)* to see one another; *(encontrarse)* to meet <v. con los amigos to meet with friends> ♦ **estar por v.** to remain to be seen ♦ **véase** se (in references) • **vérselas con** COLL. to have to deal with • **vérselas negras** COLL. to be in a jam.

ve·ra f. edge ♦ **a la v. de** next to.

ve·ra·ci·dad f. veracity.

ve·ra·ne·an·te m.f. summer resident.

ve·ra·ne·ar intr. to spend the summer.

ve·ra·ne·o m. vacationing ♦ **ir de v.** to go on vacation • **lugar de v.** summer resort.

ve·ra·nie·go, a adj. *(del verano)* summer; *(ligero)* light.

ve·ra·no m. summer.

ve·ras f.pl. *(verdad)* truth; *(seriedad)* earnestness ♦ **de v.** really.

ve·raz adj. truthful.

ver·ba f. loquaciousness.

ver·bal adj. verbal.

ver·be·na f. verbena, vervain; *(fiesta)* festival held on the eve of a saint's day.

ver·bi·gra·cia *or* **ver·bi·grá·tia** adv. for example, for instance.

ver·bo m. GRAM. verb; RELIG. Word.

ver·bo·rre·a f. COLL. verbosity.

ver·bo·si·dad f. verbosity.

ver·bo·so, a adj. verbose.

ver·dad f. truth <decir la v. to tell the truth>; *(veracidad)* truthfulness ♦ **a decir v.** *or* **a la v.** to be honest • **de v.** *(de veras)* truly; *(verdadero)* real <él es un héroe de v. he is a real hero> • **¿de v.?** really? • **la pura v.** the plain truth • **¿no es v.?** isn't that so? • **¿v.?** is that so?

ver·da·de·ro, a adj. *(real)* true; *(auténtico)* genuine; *(veraz)* truthful.

ver·de I. adj. green; unseasoned <leña v. unseasoned wood>; *(inmaduro)* unripe; *(obsceno)* dirty; *(libertino)* dirty <un viejo v. a dirty old man> ♦ **poner v. a uno** to tell someone off • **v. de envidia** green with envy II. m. *(color)* green; *(verdor)* verdure; *(hierba)* grass; *(follaje)* foliage; *(alcacer)* fresh fodder; R.P. maté ♦ **v. esmeralda** emerald green • **v. mar** sea green • **v. oliva** olive green.

ver·de·mar I. adj. sea-green II. m. sea green.

ver·dín m. *(de las plantas)* fresh green; *(musgo)* moss.

ver·dor m. verdancy.

ver·do·so, a adj. greenish.

ver·du·go m. BOT. twig; *(de justicia)* executioner; *(de ladrillos)* layer of bricks.

ver·du·gón m. *(roncha)* welt; BOT. shoot.

ver·du·le·rí·a f. grocery store.

ver·du·le·ro, a m.f. greengrocer.

ver·du·ra f. *(verdor)* greenness; *(legumbre)* vegetable; *(follaje)* greenery.

ver·dus·co, a adj. dark greenish.

ve·re·da f. *(senda)* trail; AMER. sidewalk ♦ **entrar en v.** to fall in line.

ve·re·dic·to m. verdict.

ver·ga f. ANAT. penis; *(de ballesta)* steel bow; MARIT. yard.

ver·ga·jo m. pizzle.

ver·gel m. orchard.

ver·gon·zan·te adj. shamefaced.

ver·gon·zo·so, a I. adj. *(ignominioso)* shameful; *(tímido)* shy II. m.f. shy person.

ver·güen·za f. *(bochorno)* shame; *(desconcierto)* embarrassment; *(timidez)* shyness; *(oprobio)* disgrace <él es la v. de su familia he is the disgrace of his family> ♦ **darle v. a uno** to be ashamed <me da v. decírtelo I am ashamed to tell you> • **no tener v.** to be shameless • **perder la v.** to lose all sense of shame • **¡que v.!** what a disgrace! • **sin v.** shameless(ly) • **tener v.** to be ashamed.

ve·ri·cue·to m. rugged path.

ve·rí·di·co, a adj. true.

ve·ri·fi·ca·ción f. verification.

ve·ri·fi·ca·dor, ·ra I. adj. checking II. m.f. checker.

ve·ri·fi·car §70 tr. *(la verdad)* to verify; *(una máquina)* to check; *(realizar)* to carry out —reflex. *(tener lugar)* to take place; *(una predicción)* to come true.

ve·ris·mo m. verism.

ver·ja f. *(de cerca)* railings; *(de ventana)* grating.

ver·me m. intestinal worm.

ver·mi·ci·da I. adj. vermicidal II. m. vermicide.

ver·mí·fu·go, a I. adj. vermifugal II. m. vermifuge.

ver·mut/mú m. *(aperitivo)* vermouth —f. AMER., CINEM., THEAT. matinée.

ver·ná·cu·lo, a adj. vernacular.

ver·nal adj. vernal.

ve·ró·ni·ca f. BOT. veronica, speedwell; TAUR. pass with the cape.

ve·ro·sí·mil adj. probable.

ve·ro·si·mi·li·tud f. probability.

ve·rru·ga f. wart.

ver·sa·do, a adj. versed.

ver·sar intr. ♦ **v. sobre** to deal with.

ver·sá·til adj. versatile; FIG. changeable.

ver·sa·ti·li·dad f. fickleness.

ver·sí·cu·lo m. versicle.

ver·si·fi·car §70 intr. & tr. to versify.

ver·sión f. version.

ver·so¹ m. verse; *(versículo)* versicle ♦ **echar versos** MEX. to gab.

ver·so² m. PRINT. verso.

vér·te·bra f. vertebra.

ver·te·bra·do, a adj. & m. vertebrate.

ver·te·bral adj. vertebral.

ver·te·de·ro m. *(desaguadero)* drain; *(de basura)* garbage dump.

ver·te·dor, ·ra I. adj. emptying II. m. *(canal)* drain; MARIT. bailer.

ver·ter §50 tr. *(derramar)* to spill; *(lágrimas, sangre)* to shed; *(vaciar)* to empty out; *(volcar)* to turn upside down; *(traducir)* to translate —intr. to flow.

ver·ti·cal adj. & f. vertical.

ver·ti·ca·li·dad f. verticality.

vér·ti·ce m. apex.

ver·tien·te I. adj. flowing II. f. *(declive)* slope; *(manantial)* spring.

ver·ti·gi·no·si·dad f. vertiginousness.

ver·ti·gi·no·so, a adj. vertiginous.

vér·ti·go m. vertigo; *(arrebato)* frenzy ♦ **tener v.** to feel dizzy.

ve·sí·cu·la f. vesicle ♦ **v. biliar** gall bladder.

ve·si·cu·lar adj. vesicular.

ves·per·ti·no, a adj. evening.

ves·tal adj. & f. vestal.

ves·tí·bu·lo m. *(antesala)* vestibule; *(en un hotel, teatro)* lobby.

ves·ti·do m. *(de mujer)* dress; *(de hombre)* suit ♦ **v. de noche** evening gown.

ves·ti·du·ra f. *(prenda de vestir)* garment; *(ropa)* clothes ♦ pl. RELIG. vestments.

ves·ti·gio m. vestige.

ves·ti·men·ta f. clothes.

ves·tir §48 tr. to dress <*vistieron a la novia* they dressed the bride>; *(llevar)* to wear <*vestía un traje rosado* she was wearing a pink suit>; *(cubrir)* to cover <*v. una puerta de acero* to cover a door with steel>; *(proveer con ropa)* to clothe <*v. a los pobres* to clothe the poor>; *(hacer ropa)* to dress <*este sastre viste a mis hermanos* this tailor dresses my brothers>; FIG. to dress up ♦ **quedarse para v. santos** COLL. to be an old maid —intr. *(ir vestido)* to dress <*ellos visten bien* they dress well>; *(lucir)* to look good <*la seda viste mucho* silk looks very good> ♦ **v. de** to wear <*él viste de uniforme* he wears a uniform> —reflex. *(ataviarse)* to get dressed; *(ir vestido)* to dress <*v. a la moda* to dress fashionably>; *(cubrirse)* to be covered <*el campo se viste de flores* the field is covered with flowers>.

ves·tua·rio m. wardrobe; *(cuarto)* dressing room; SPORT. locker room.

ve·ta f. *(de madera)* grain; MIN. vein.

ve·tar tr. to veto.

ve·te·a·do, a adj. streaked.

ve·te·ar tr. to streak.

ve·te·ra·ní·a f. *(larga experiencia)* long experience; *(antigüedad)* seniority.

ve·te·ra·no, a adj. & m.f. veteran.

ve·te·ri·na·rio, a I. adj. veterinary **II.** m.f. veterinarian —f. veterinary medicine.

ve·to m. veto ♦ **poner el v. a** to veto.

ves·tus·to, a adj. decrepit.

vez f. time <*te lo dije cuatro veces* I told you four times>; *(ocasión)* time <*hay veces que conviene no hablar* there are times when it is best not to talk>; *(turno)* turn <*la v. que me tocó no estuve aquí* when it was my turn, I was not here> ♦ **a la v.** at the same time • **a la v. que** while • **alguna que otra v.** once in a while • **algunas veces** sometimes • **a su v.** in turn • **a veces** at times • **cada v.** every time • **cada v. más** more and more • **cada v. menos** less and less • **cada v. que** whenever • **de una v.** all at once • **de una v. por todas** once and for all • **de v. en cuando** from time to time • **dos veces** twice • **en v. de** instead of • **érase una v.** once upon a time • **hacer las veces de** to stand in for • **muchas veces** often • **otra v.** again • **pocas** or **raras veces** rarely • **por enésima v.** COLL. for the umpteenth time • **repetidas veces** repeatedly • **tal v.** perhaps • **una que otra v.** once in a while • **una v.** once • **una v. que** as soon as.

vi, vimos see ver².

ví·a¹ prep. via <*vamos v. Quito* we are going via Quito>.

ví·a² f. *(camino)* road; *(ruta)* route <*v. terrestre* land route>; RAIL. *(carril)* track; ANAT. tract; CHEM. process; LAW proceedings ♦ **en vías de** in the process of • **por v. oral** orally • **v. aérea** airway; *(correo)* airmail • **V. Crucis** Way of the Cross; FIG. ordeal • **v. de comunicación** channel of communication • **v. férrea** railroad • **v. fluvial** waterway • **V. Láctea** Milky Way • **v. marítima** seaway.

via·ble adj. viable.

via·duc·to m. viaduct.

via·jan·te adj. & m. traveling (salesman).

via·jar intr. to travel.

via·je m. trip <*¡buen v.!* bon voyage! • **de un v.** AMER. all at once • **ir de v.** to go on a trip • **v. de ida y vuelta** round trip ♦ pl. travel.

via·je·ro, a I. adj. traveling **II.** m.f. traveler.

vial adj. road, traffic.

via·li·dad f. highway administration.

vian·da f. food.

viá·ti·co m. *(dietas)* per diem; RELIG. viaticum.

ví·bo·ra f. viper.

vi·bra·ción f. vibration.

vi·brar —intr. *(sacudirse)* to vibrate; *(sentirse conmovido)* to be moved.

vi·ca·rí·a f. *(oficio y territorio)* vicariate; *(residencia)* vicarage.

vi·ca·rio, a I. adj. deputy **II.** m. vicar.

vi·ce·al·mi·ran·te m. vice admiral.

vi·ce·can·ci·ller m. vice chancellor.

vi·ce·cón·sul m. vice consul.

vi·ce·ge·ren·te m. assistant manager.

vi·ce·go·ber·na·dor, ·ra m.f. lieutenant governor.

vi·ce·pre·si·den·cia f. *(en un país)* vice-presidency; *(en reunión)* vice-chairmanship.

vi·ce·pre·si·den·te m.f. *(en un país)* vice president; *(en reunión)* vice chairman.

vi·ce·ver·sa adv. vice versa.

vi·ciar tr. *(contaminar)* to pollute; *(pervertir)* to corrupt; *(adulterar)* to adulterate; *(falsificar)* to falsify; *(anular)* to invalidate —reflex. *(contaminarse)* to become polluted; *(entregarse al vicio)* to become corrupt.

vi·cio m. *(perversión)* vice; *(mala costumbre)* bad habit ♦ **de v.** without reason.

vi·cio·so, a I. adj. *(incorrecto)* incorrect; *(depravado)* depraved **II.** m.f. *(persona depravada)* depraved person; *(toxicómano)* drug addict.

vi·ci·si·tud f. vicissitude.

víc·ti·ma f. victim.

vic·to·re·ar tr. to cheer.

vic·to·ria f. victory; *(éxito)* success; *(coche)* victoria.

vic·to·ria·no, a adj. & m.f. HIST. Victorian.

vic·to·rio·so, a I. adj. victorious **II.** m.f. victor.

vi·cu·ña f. vicuña.

vid f. grapevine.

vi·da f. life; *(duración)* lifetime; *(sustento)* living <*ganarse la v.* to earn one's living>; *(modo de vivir)* way of life; *(biografía)* life story; *(viveza)* liveliness ♦ **así es la v.** such is life • **buscarse la v.** COLL. to hustle • **dar mala v. a** to mistreat • **darse buena v.** to lead the good life • **echarse a la v.** to become a prostitute • **en la v.** never • **entre la v. y la muerte** at death's door • **escapar con v.** to come out alive • **la otra v.** the hereafter • **pasar a mejor v.** to pass away • **quitarse la v.** to take one's life • **v. mía** COLL. my dear • **v. y milagros** COLL. life history • **vivir la v.** to lead the good life.

vi·den·te m.f. clairvoyant.

vi·de·o m. video.

vi·de·o·ca·se·te m. or f. videocassette.

vi·de·o·cin·ta f. videotape.

vi·de·o·dis·co m. videodisc/disk.

vi·do·rra f. COLL. life of ease.

vi·dria·do, a I. adj. glazed **II.** m. *(barniz)* glaze; *(loza)* glazed earthenware.

vi·driar tr. to apply a glaze to —intr. to become glazed.

vi·drie·ra f. window.

vi·drie·ro, a m.f. glazier.

vi·drio m. glass; R.P. window-pane ♦ **v. tallado** cut glass.

vi·drio·so, a adj. (quebradizo) fragile; (suelo) slippery; (delicado) tricky; (ojos) glassy.

vie·jo, a I. adj. old II. m. old man ♦ pl. old folks —f. old woman.

vie·ne see **venir**.

vien·to m. wind; (cuerda) guide rope; MUS. wind <instrumentos de v. wind instruments> ♦ **a los cuatro vientos** to the four winds • **contra v. y marea** against all odds • **hacer v.** to be windy • **ir v. en popa** to go smoothly or well.

vien·tre m. (abdomen) belly; (matriz) womb; (intestino) bowels <evacuar el v. to move one's bowels>; FIG. belly ♦ **bajo v.** lower abdomen.

vier·nes m.inv. Friday ♦ **V. Santo** Good Friday.

vier·ta, te see **verter**.

vi·ga f. (madero) beam; (de metal) girder ♦ **v. transversal** crossbeam.

vi·gen·cia f. force <en v. in force>.

vi·gen·te adj. in force.

vi·gé·si·mo, a adj. & m. twentieth.

vi·gí·a m. MARIT. lookout —f. watchtower; MARIT. reef.

vi·gi·lan·cia f. vigilance.

vi·gi·lan·te I. adj. vigilant II. m. (guarda) watchman; AMER. policeman.

vi·gi·lar tr. to watch over.

vi·gi·lia f. (vela) vigil; (falta de sueño) sleeplessness; (víspera) eve ♦ **día de v.** day of abstinence.

vi·gor m. vigor; (de una ley) force, effect <entrar en v. to go into force>.

vi·go·ri·zar §04 tr. to invigorate.

vi·go·ro·so, a adj. vigorous.

vi·hue·la f. guitar.

vil adj. & m.f. base, despicable (person).

vi·le·za f. (cualidad) vileness; (acción) contemptible action.

vi·li·pen·diar tr. to vilify.

vi·li·pen·dio m. vilification.

vi·lla f. (pueblo) village; (casa) villa.

vi·llan·ci·co m. Christmas carol.

vi·lla·ní·a f. despicable act.

vi·lla·no, a I. adj. (que no es noble) common; (paisano) peasant; (grosero) coarse, rude; (vil) base II. m.f. (paisano) commoner; (persona mala) villain.

vi·lo adv. ♦ **en v.** up in the air.

vi·na·gre m. vinegar ♦ **cara de v.** COLL. sourpuss.

vi·na·gre·ra f. vinegar bottle ♦ pl. cruet.

vi·na·gre·ta f. vinaigrette.

vi·na·te·rí·a f. wine shop.

vi·na·te·ro, a adj. & m.f. wine (merchant).

vin·cha f. headband.

vin·cu·la·ción f. link.

vin·cu·lar tr. (enlazar) to link; LAW to entail.

vín·cu·lo m. link; LAW entailment.

vin·di·ca·ción f. (venganza) revenge; (defensa) vindication.

vin·di·car §70 tr. (vengar) to avenge; (defender) to vindicate; LAW to claim, recover.

vin·dic·ta f. revenge.

vi·ní·co·la I. adj. wine-making II. m. winemaker.

vi·ni·cul·tor, ra m.f. grape grower.

vi·ni·cul·tu·ra f. viniculture.

vi·nie·ra, no see **venir**.

vi·ní·li·co, a adj. of vinyl.

vi·ni·lo m. vinyl.

vi·no m. wine ♦ **bautizar el v.** COLL. to water the wine • **v. añejo** vintage wine • **v. de Jerez** sherry • **v. de mesa** table wine • **v. de Oporto** port wine • **v. tinto** red wine.

vi·ña f. vineyard.

vi·ña·te·ro, a AMER. I. adj. grape-growing II. m.f. grape grower.

vi·ñe·do m. vineyard.

vi·ñe·ta f. vignette.

vio·la f. viola —m.f. violist.

vio·lá·ce·o, a adj. violet.

vio·la·ción f. violation; (de mujer) rape; (profanación) desecration.

vio·la·dor, ra m.f. violator —m. rapist.

vio·lar tr. (las leyes) to violate; (a una mujer) to rape; (cosas sagradas) to desecrate.

vio·len·cia f. (fuerza) violence; (violación) rape; (turbación) embarrassment.

vio·len·tar tr. (forzar) to force; (entrar por fuerza) to break into; (torcer) to distort; (atropellar) to infuriate.

vio·len·to, a adj. violent; (intenso) intense <una discusión v. an intense discussion>; (molesto) embarrassing <es v. que me traten así it is embarrassing to be treated like this>.

vio·le·ta f. & adj. violet.

vio·lín m. violin —m.f. violinist.

vio·li·nis·ta m.f. violinist.

vio·lón m. (instrumento) double bass, bass viol; (persona) double bass player.

vio·lon·c(h)e·lo m. cello.

vi·pe·ri·no, a adj. venomous.

vi·ra·da f. turn; MARIT. tack.

vi·ra·je m. (acción) veering; (giro) turn; MARIT. tack; (cambio) turning point; PHOTOG. toning.

vi·rar tr. MARIT. (de rumbo) to turn; (el cabrestante) to wind; PHOTOG. to tone —intr. to swerve.

vir·gen adj. & f. virgin.

vir·gi·nal/ne·o, a adj. virginal.

vir·gi·ni·dad f. virginity.

vir·go m. (virginidad) virginity; ANAT. hymen.

vír·gu·la f. (vara) small rod; PRINT. virgule; BACT. cholera bacillus.

vi·ril adj. virile.

vi·ri·li·dad f. virility.

vir·tual adj. virtual.

vir·tud f. (cualidad) virtue; (eficacia) ability ♦ **en v. de** by virtue of.

vir·tuo·si·dad f./**sis·mo** m. virtuosity.

vir·tuo·so, a I. adj. virtuous II. m.f. virtuoso.

vi·rue·la f. (enfermedad) smallpox; (cicatriz) pockmark.

vi·ru·len·to, a adj. virulent.

vi·rus m.inv. virus.

vi·ru·ta f. shavings.

vi·sa f. AMER. visa.

vi·sar tr. (pasaporte) to visa; (documento) to endorse; ARTIL., SURV. to sight.

vís·ce·ra f. organ ♦ pl. viscera.

vis·co·si·dad f. viscosity.

vis·co·so, a adj. viscous.

vi·se·ra f. visor.

vi·si·bi·li·dad f. visibility.

vi·si·ble adj. visible; COLL. (decente) decent.

vi·si·llo m. window curtain.

vi·sión f. vision; (vista) eyesight ♦ **quedarse como quien ve visiones** COLL. to look as though one has seen a ghost • **ver visiones** COLL. to see things.

vi·sio·na·rio, a adj. & m.f. visionary.

vi·sir m. vizir.

vi·si·ta f. *(acción)* visit; *(persona)* visitor ♦ **hacer una v.** *or* **ir de v.** to pay a visit • **v. de cortesía** *or* **de cumplido** courtesy call • **v. de médico** COLL. brief visit.

vi·si·tar tr. & reflex. to visit (one another).

vis·lum·brar tr. to glimpse.

vis·lum·bre f. glimmer.

vi·so m. *(reflejo)* sheen; *(destello)* gleam; *(forro)* colored undergarment; *(apariencia)* appearance <*tener v. de verdad* to have the appearance of truth>; FIG. veneer.

vi·són m. mink.

vi·sor m. PHOTOG. viewfinder; ARTIL. sight.

vís·pe·ra f. eve ♦ **en v. de** on the eve of ♦ pl. RELIG. vespers.

vis·ta, to, tiera, tió see **vestir.**

vis·ta·zo m. glance ♦ **dar un v. a** to take a glance at.

vis·to, a I. see **ver² II.** adj. ♦ **bien v.** proper • **es** *or* **está v.** it is commonly accepted • **mal v.** improper • **nunca v.** unheard-of • **por lo v.** apparently • LAW whereas • **v. bueno** O.K. • **v. que** see **III.** f. *(visión)* sight; eyesight <*él tiene buena v.* he has good eyesight>; *(panorama)* view; *(cuadro)* scene; *(mirada)* eyes <*dirigió la v. a la pantalla* he turned his eyes toward the screen>; *(vistazo)* look, glance; LAW hearing ♦ **aguzar la v.** to keep one's eyes open • **a la v.** COM. at sight • **a la v. de todos** publicly • **alzar la v.** to look up • **apartar la v.** to look away; *(ser evidente)* to be obvious; *(estar al acecho)* to turn a blind eye to the screen>; *(estar al acecho)* to keep an eye on • **hacer la v. gorda** COLL. to turn a blind eye • **hasta la v.** so long • **medir con la v.** to size up • **no perder de v. a** not to lose sight of • **perder de v.** to lose sight of • **perderse de v.** to disappear • **saltar a la v.** to hit the eye • **v. cansada** tired eyes • **v. de águila** *or* **de lince** hawk eye • **v. doble** MED. double vision • **volver la v. atrás** to look back — m. customs inspector.

vis·to·so, a adj. colorful.

vi·sual I. adj. visual **II.** f. line of vision.

vi·sua·li·za·ción f. AMER. visualization.

vi·sua·li·zar §04 tr. AMER. to visualize.

vi·tal adj. vital.

vi·ta·li·cio, a adj. life <*miembro v.* life member>.

vi·ta·li·dad f. vitality.

vi·ta·li·zar §04 tr. to vitalize.

vi·ta·mi·na f. vitamin.

vi·te·la f. vellum.

vi·ti·vi·ní·co·la I. adj. vine-growing **II.** m.f. vine grower.

vi·to·re·ar tr. to cheer.

vi·tral m. stained-glass window.

ví·tre·o, a adj. vitreous.

vi·tri·fi·car §70 tr. & reflex. to vitrify.

vi·tri·na f. *(caja)* display case; *(de tienda)* window.

vi·trió·li·co, a adj. vitriolic.

vi·tua·llar tr. to provision.

vi·tua·llas f.pl. provisions.

vi·tu·pe·ra·dor, ·ra I. vituperative **II.** m.f. vi-

tuperator, scold.

vi·tu·pe·rar tr. to vituperate.

vi·tu·pe·rio m. *(insulto)* insult; *(censura)* vituperation.

viu·dez f. *(de viudo)* widowhood; *(de viuda)* widowhood.

viu·do, a I. adj. widowed **II.** m. widower —f. *(mujer)* widow; BOT. mourning bride.

vi·vac m. [pl. **-ques**] MIL. bivouac.

vi·va·ci·dad f. *(en las acciones)* vivacity; *(del espíritu)* sharpness; *(de color)* vividness.

vi·va·ra·cho, a adj. COLL. lively.

vi·vaz adj. quick-witted; BOT. perennial.

vi·ven·cia f. (personal) experience.

ví·ve·res m.pl. provisions.

vi·ve·ro m. BOT. nursery; *(de peces)* fish hatchery; *(de moluscos)* farm.

vi·ve·za f. *(vivacidad)* liveliness; *(prontitud)* quickness; *(agudeza)* sharpness; *(brillo)* vividness.

ví·vi·do, a adj. vivid.

vi·vi·dor, ·ra m.f. COLL. sponger.

vi·vien·da f. *(lugar)* housing <*escasez de v.* housing shortage>; *(morada)* dwelling; *(casa)* house.

vi·vien·te adj. living.

vi·vi·fi·ca·dor, ·ra/can·te adj. vivifying.

vi·vi·fi·car §70 tr. to vivify.

vi·vir¹ m. life ♦ **de mal v.** disreputable.

vi·vir² intr. to live ♦ **¿quién vive?** MIL. who goes there? • **saber v.** to know how to live • **¡viva!** hurrah! • **al día** to live from hand to mouth • **v. a lo grande** to live it up • **v. de** to live on *or* off <*ella vive de sus rentas* she lives off her investments> • **v. del aire** to live on next to nothing —tr. to live; *(experimentar)* to go through.

vi·vi·sec·ción f. vivisection.

vi·vo, a I. adj. *(con vida)* alive; *(intenso)* deep; *(brillante)* vivid; *(listo)* sharp; *(astuto)* sly; MED. raw <*carne v.* raw skin> ♦ **al rojo v.** red-hot • **en v.** TELEC. live **II.** m. *(borde)* edge; SEW. piping; VET. mange; COLL. *(hombre listo)* wise guy ♦ **los vivos** the living.

viz·ca·cha f. viscacha.

viz·con·de m. viscount.

viz·con·de·sa f. viscountess.

vo·ca·blo m. term.

vo·ca·bu·la·rio m. vocabulary.

vo·ca·bu·lis·ta m.f. lexicographer.

vo·ca·ción f. vocation.

vo·ca·cio·nal adj. vocational.

vo·cal I. adj. vocal **II.** m.f. *(en una junta)* board or committee member —f. vowel.

vo·ca·lis·ta m.f. vocalist.

vo·ca·li·za·ción f. vocalization.

vo·ca·li·zar §04 intr. to vocalize.

vo·ce·a·dor, ·ra *(vocinglero)* loud *or* vociferous person —m. *(pregonero)* town crier; MEX. street hawker.

vo·ce·ar intr. & tr. to shout.

vo·ce·o m. shouting.

vo·ce·rí·a f./o m. *(gritería)* shouting; *(clamor)* uproar.

vo·ce·ro, a mf. spokesman/woman.

vo·ci·fe·ra·dor, ·ra I. adj. vociferous **II.** m.f. vociferator.

vo·ci·fe·rar intr. & tr. to shout.

vo·la·da f. short flight.

vo·lan·do adv. COLL. in a flash.

vo·lan·te I. adj. flying II. m. MECH. flywheel; AUTO. steering wheel; (del reloj) balance wheel; (papel) flier; (juego) badminton.

vo·lan·tín, i·na I. adj. flying II. m. (para pescar) fishing line with several hooks; S. AMER. (cometa) small kite.

vo·lar §19 intr. to fly; (irse volando) to fly away; (desaparecer) to disappear; (divulgarse) to spread quickly —tr. to blow up.

vo·lá·til adj. (que vuela) flying; CHEM. volatile.

vo·la·tín m. acrobatic stunt.

vo·la·ti·ne·ro, a m.f. tightrope walker.

vol·cán m. volcano.

vol·cá·ni·co, a adj. volcanic.

vol·car §73 tr. (verter) to dump; (persuadir) to make (someone) change his mind —intr. to overturn —reflex. (derribarse) to tip over; (entregarse) to do one's utmost.

vo·le·ar tr. SPORT. to volley; AGR. to scatter.

vo·le·o m. SPORT. volley ♦ **del primer** or **de un v.** COLL. quickly • **sembrar a v.** AGR. to scatter (seed).

vo·li·ción f. volition.

vol·tai·co, a adj. voltaic <arco v. voltaic arc>.

vol·ta·je m. voltage.

vol·tá·me·tro m. voltammeter.

vol·te·ar tr. (volcar) to turn over; (dar la vuelta a) to turn around; (poner al revés) to turn upside down; (derribar) to knock down or over —intr. to tumble.

vol·te·re·ta f. somersault.

vol·tí·me·tro m. voltmeter.

vol·tio m. volt.

vo·lu·ble adj. voluble; FIG. fickle.

vo·lu·men m. volume; (cuerpo) bulk ♦ **a todo v.** loud.

vo·lu·mi·no·so, a adj. voluminous.

vo·lun·tad f. (facultad) will; (firmeza) will power <faltarle la v. de hacerlo to lack the will power to do it>; (intención) intention; (deseo) wish ♦ **a v.** at will • **buena, mala v.** good, ill will • **fuerza de v.** will power • **ganar la v. de alguien** to win someone over • **última v.** last will and testament.

vo·lun·ta·rio, a I. adj. voluntary II. m.f. volunteer.

vo·lun·ta·rio·so, a adj. (caprichoso) willful; (deseoso) willing.

vo·lup·tuo·si·dad f. voluptuousness.

vo·lup·tuo·so, a adj. voluptuous.

vol·ver §78 tr. to turn <v. la hoja to turn the page>; (dar vuelta) to turn around; to turn over <v. el colchón to turn over the mattress>; to turn inside out <v. los calcetines to turn socks inside out>; (dirigir) to turn <volvió los ojos hacia la puerta she turned her eyes toward the door>; to return <¿volviste el libro al estante? did you return the book to the shelf?>; (corresponder) to repay; (restablecer) to restore; (dar) to give back ♦ **v. la cara** to turn around • **v. la espalda a alguien** to turn one's back on someone • **v. loco a alguien** COLL. to drive someone crazy —intr. (regresar) to return <volvimos a casa muy tarde we returned home very late>; (reanudar) to get back • **v. a to . . . again** <volví a empezar I began again> • **v. en sí** to come to —reflex. (darse vuelta) to turn around; (hacerse) to become <v. religioso to become religious> ♦ **v. atrás** (desdecirse) to back down; (no cumplir) to back out • **v. contra** to turn against or on • **v. loco** to go crazy.

vo·mi·tar tr. to vomit; (decir) to spew; (un se-

creto) to spill —intr. to vomit.

vo·mi·ti·vo, a adj. & m. vomitive.

vó·mi·to m. (acción) vomiting; (resultado) vomit.

vo·ra·ci·dad f. voracity.

vo·rá·gi·ne f. whirlpool.

vo·ra·gi·no·so, a adj. turbulent.

vo·raz adj. voracious.

vór·ti·ce m. (torbellino) vortex; (de ciclón) center of a cyclone.

vos pron. you, thou, ye; S. AMER. you.

vo·se·ar tr. to address as vos.

vo·se·o m. use of vos in addressing someone.

vo·so·tros, as pron. you, yourselves <entre v. among yourselves>.

vo·ta·ción f. (acción) voting; (voto) vote.

vo·tan·te I. adj. voting II. m.f. voter.

vo·tar intr. (en elección) to vote; RELIG. to make a vow —tr. to vote.

vo·ti·vo, a adj. votive.

vo·to m. vote <depositar un v. to cast a vote>; vow <v. de castidad vow of chastity>; (deseo) wish ♦ **hacer votos por** to sincerely hope for.

voz f. voice; (vocablo) term; (rumor) rumor <se corrió la v. the rumor got around>; (opinión) opinion <v. pública public opinion> ♦ **alzar** or **levantar la v.** to raise one's voice • **a media v.** in a low voice • **a una v.** unanimously • **a voces** shouting • **a v. en cuello** at the top of one's voice • **dar voces** to shout • **en v. alta** in a loud voice • **llevar la v. cantante** to call the shots • **pedir a voces** to cry out for • **tener v.** to have a say • **tener v. ronca** to be hoarse.

vo·za·rrón m. booming voice.

vuel·co m. overturning ♦ **darle un v. el corazón** COLL. to skip a beat • **dar un v.** (un coche) to overturn; (un barco) to capsize.

vuel·co, que see volcar.

vue·le, lo see volar.

vue·lo m. (acción) flight; (plumas) flight feathers; SEW. (de falda) flare; (adorno) ruffle ♦ **al v.** COLL. immediately • **de alto v.** big-time • **levantar el v.** (echar a volar) to take flight; (imaginarse) to let one's imagination go; (engreírse) to become arrogant • **v. espacial** space flight.

vuel·to, a I. see volver II. f. (giro) turn; (revolución) revolution; (curvatura) curve <v. cerrada sharp curve>; (regreso) return <te veré a la v. I will see you upon my return>; (revés) reverse; (repetición) recurrence; SPORT. lap; SEW. facing; (bóveda) vault; MUS. ritornello ♦ **agarrarle a alguien** or **algo la v.** COLL. to find out what makes someone or something tick • **a la v.** (al volver) on the way back; (al revés) on the other side; (cerca) around the corner • **a la v. de la esquina** around the corner • **a v. de correo** by return mail • **darle vueltas a** to turn over in one's mind • **dar vueltas** to go around in circles • **dar** or **darse una v.** (pasear) to take a walk; (en auto) to go for a ride • **dar vueltas** (girar) to go around; (torcer) to twist and turn <la carretera da muchas vueltas the highway twists and turns a great deal> • **de ida y v.** round-trip • **déjate de vueltas** COLL. stop beating around the bush • **estar de v.** (volver) to be back; COLL. (saber) to have been there and back • **media v.** MIL. about-face • **no tener v. de hoja** COLL. to be undeniable • **poner a alguien de v. y media** COLL. to let someone have it —m. AMER. change <quédese con el v. keep the change>.

vuel·va, ve see **volver**.
vues·tro, a poss. adj. *(su)* your; *(suyo)* (of) yours *<uno de vuestros parientes* a relative of yours> ♦ **los vuestros** or **las vuestras** yours.
vul·ca·ni·zar §04 tr. to vulcanize.
vul·gar adj. *(común)* common; *(grosero)* vulgar.
vul·ga·ri·dad f. vulgarity.
vul·ga·ris·mo m. vulgarism.
vul·ga·ri·zar §04 tr. *(hacer vulgar)* to vulgarize; *(hacer asequible)* to popularize.
vul·gar·men·te adv. *(groseramente)* coarsely; *(comúnmente)* commonly.
vul·go m. masses.
vul·ne·ra·bi·li·dad f. vulnerability.
vul·ne·ra·ble adj. vulnerable.
vul·ne·rar tr. *(herir)* to wound; *(la ley)* to violate.
vul·va f. vulva.

W

w, W f. letter which, although not a part of the Spanish alphabet, is used in the spelling of words of foreign origin.
wat m. watt.
wel·ter m. welterweight.
whis·ky m. whiskey.

X

x, X f. twenty-fourth letter of the Spanish alphabet.
xe·no·fo·bia f. xenophobia.
xe·nó·fo·bo, a I. adj. xenophobic II. m.f. xenophobe.
xe·ro·gra·fí·a f. xerography.
xe·ro·gra·fiar §30 tr. to Xerox.
xe·ro·grá·fi·co, a adj. xerographic.
xi·ló·fo·no m. xylophone.
xi·lo·gra·fí·a f. *(arte)* xylography; *(impresión)* xylograph.

Y

y, Y f. twenty-fifth letter of the Spanish alphabet.
y conj. and ♦ **¿y bien?** and then? • **y eso que** even though • **¿y qué?** so what?
ya I. adv. *(finalmente)* already *<ya hemos terminado* we have already finished>; *(ahora)* now *<ya es famoso* now he is famous>; *(pronto)* soon; *(en seguida)* right away; *(por último)* now *<ya es hora de tomar una decisión* now it is time to make a decision> ♦ **ya lo creo** of course • **ya no** no longer • **ya que** since II. conj. now, at times *<demuestra su talento ya en las artes, ya en las ciencias* she demonstrates her talent at times in the arts, at times in the sciences> III. interj. I see!
yac m. yak.
ya·ca·ré m. AMER. alligator.
ya·cen·te I. adj. lying II. m. MIN. floor of a vein.
ya·cer §79 intr. *(estar tendido)* to lie; *(estar)* to be.

ya·cien·te adj. & m. var. of **yacente**.
ya·ci·mien·to m. GEOL. deposit ♦ **y. petrolífero** oil field.
ya·guar m. jaguar.
yám·bi·co, a adj. iambic.
yam·bo m. POET. iamb.
yan·qui adj. & m.f. Yankee.
ya·pa f. AMER. *(adehala)* bonus; MEX. gratuity.
yar·da f. yard.
ya·te m. yacht.
ye·gua f. mare.
ye·gua·da f. herd of horses; C. AMER. blunder.
ye·gua·ri·zo, a I. adj. equine II. m. R.P. stud.
ye·güe·rí·a f. herd of horses.
ye·ís·mo m. pronunciation of Spanish *ll* as *y*.
yel·mo m. helmet.
ye·ma f. *(del huevo)* yolk; BOT. bud ♦ **y. del dedo** finger tip.
yen m. FIN. yen.
yer·ba f. grass; S. AMER. maté.
yer·bal m. R.P. field of maté.
yer·ba·te·ro, a I. adj. AMER. of maté II. m.f. *(curandero)* quack; *(vendedor)* maté seller.
yer·go, gue see **erguir**.
yer·mar tr. to strip.
yer·mo, a I. adj. barren II. m. desert.
yer·no m. son-in-law.
ye·rra f. AMER. cattle branding.
ye·rre, rro see **errar**.
ye·rro m. *(falta)* fault; *(pecado)* sin; *(error)* error.
yer·to, a adj. ♦ **y. de frío** frozen stiff.
ye·se·ro, a I. adj. plaster II. m. plasterer.
ye·so m. GEOL. gypsum; ARTS, CONSTR. plaster; *(vaciado)* plaster cast.
yo I. pron. I *<yo lo hice* I did it> ♦ **soy yo** it's I or me • **yo mismo** I myself II. m. ego.
yo·da·do, a adj. iodized.
yo·da·to m. iodate.
yo·do m. iodine.
yo·du·ro m. iodide.
yo·ga m. yoga.
yo·g(h)i m. yogi.
yo·gur(t) m. yogurt.
yo·yo m. yo-yo.
yu·ca f. *(mandioca)* manioc; *(izote)* yucca.
yu·cal m. yucca field.
yu·do m. judo.
yu·ga·da f. *(tierra)* day's plowing; *(de bueyes)* yoke (of oxen).
yu·go m. *(arreo)* yoke; *(opresión)* oppression; *(carga pesada)* burden; MARIT. transom.
yu·gu·lar adj. & f. jugular.
yun·que m. anvil; ANAT. incus.
yun·ta f. yoke (of oxen).
yu·te m. jute.
yux·ta·po·ner §54 tr. to juxtapose.
yux·ta·po·si·ción f. juxtaposition.
yu·yal m. AMER. weed patch.
yu·yo m. AMER. weed.
yu·yu·ba f. jujube.

Z

z, Z f. twenty-sixth letter of the Spanish alphabet.
za·fa·do, a adj. & m.f. R.P. brazen (person).
za·far tr. MARIT. *(un cabo)* to untie; *(una vela)* to unbend —reflex. *(de peligro)* to escape *(de* from); *(de compromiso)* to get out of; *(de persona)*

to get rid of; *(una correa)* to come off; AMER, ANAT. to become dislocated.

za·fa·rran·cho m. MARIT. clearing the decks; COLL. *(trastorno)* havoc ♦ **z. de combate** clearing for action.

za·fio, a adj. crude.

za·fi·ro m. sapphire.

za·fra¹ f. jar.

za·fra² f. *(cosecha)* sugar cane harvest; *(fabricación)* sugar-making; *(temporada)* sugar cane harvest season.

za·ga f. *(parte)* rear; SPORT. defense ♦ **a la z.** behind • **no irle uno en z. a otro** to be just as good as another —m. *(en el juego)* last player.

za·guán m. front hall, vestibule.

za·gue·ro a I. adj. *(trasero)* rear; *(que va en zaga)* lagging behind II. m. *(en fútbol)* defense; *(en pelota)* backstop.

za·he·rir §65 tr. *(criticar)* to criticize; *(ridiculizar)* to mock.

za·hon·dar tr. to dig —intr. to sink.

zai·no, a adj. *(caballo)* pure chestnut; *(ganado)* pure black.

za·la·me·rí·a f. flattery.

za·la·me·ro, a I. adj. flattering II. m.f. flatterer.

za·ma·rra f. *(chaqueta)* sheepskin jacket; *(piel)* sheepskin.

za·ma·rre·ar tr. *(sacudir)* to shake; *(maltratar)* to push around.

za·ma·rre·o m. *(sacudimiento)* shaking; *(trato malo)* rough treatment.

za·ma·rro m. *(chaqueta)* sheepskin jacket; *(piel)* sheepskin; FIG., COLL. *(hombre tosco)* boor.

zam·bar·do m. luck.

zam·bo, a adj. & m.f. bowlegged (person).

zam·bom·ba f. zambomba (drum-like folk instrument) ♦ **¡z.!** wow!

zam·bom·bo m. COLL. boor.

zam·bra f. *(fiesta morisca)* Moorish festival; *(baile gitano)* Andalusian gypsy dance.

zam·bu·lli·da f. *(en agua)* plunge; *(en esgrima)* thrust ♦ **darse una z.** to take a dip.

zam·bu·llir §13 tr. to plunge —reflex. *(en el agua)* to dive; *(esconderse)* to hide, duck out of sight.

zam·bu·llo m. AMER. waste barrel.

zam·pa·li·mos·nas m.f.inv. COLL. bum.

zam·par tr. *(esconder)* to hide quickly; *(comer)* to gobble.

zam·pa·tor·tas m.f.inv. COLL. *(persona glotona)* pig; *(torpe)* blockhead.

zam·po·ña f. reed flute.

zam·pu·zar §04 tr. to hide quickly.

za·na·ho·ria f. carrot; R.P., FIG. nitwit.

zan·ca f. bird's leg; COLL. *(pierna)* long thin leg; *(de escalera)* stringboard.

zan·ca·da f. stride ♦ **en dos zancadas** COLL. in a jiffy.

zan·ca·di·lla f. *(caída)* tripping; COLL. *(engaño)* trick; *(trampa)* trap ♦ **hacerle una z. a alguien** to trip someone.

zan·ca·je·ar intr. to rush *or* dash around.

zan·ca·jo m. *(hueso)* heel bone; *(talón)* heel.

zan·ca·jo·so, a adj. bowlegged.

zan·co m. stilt.

zan·cón, o·na adj. COLL. long-legged.

zan·cu·do, a I. adj. long-legged; ORNITH. wading II. f.pl. wading birds —m. AMER. mosquito.

zan·ga·na·da f. COLL. stupid remark.

zan·gan·don·go/dun·go m. COLL. *(holgazán)*

lazybones; *(desmañado)* clumsy ox.

zan·ga·ne·ar intr. COLL. to loaf (around).

zan·ga·ne·rí·a f. loafing (around).

zán·ga·no f. ENTOM. drone; COLL. *(holgazán)* parasite.

zan·go·lo·te·ar COLL. tr. to jiggle —intr. to fidget —reflex. to rattle.

zan·go·lo·te·o m. COLL. rattling.

zan·guan·go, a COLL. I. adj. lazy, idle II. m.f. malingering, faking illness.

zan·ja f. ditch, trench ♦ **z. de desagüe** drainage ditch.

zan·jar tr. to dig a ditch around, trench.

zan·jón m. large ditch.

zan·que·ar intr. to walk a lot.

za·pa f. spade.

za·pa·dor m. sapper.

za·pa·llo m. AMER. pumpkin.

za·pa·pi·co m. pickax.

za·par intr. to sap, mine.

za·pa·rras·tro·so, a I. adj. COLL. ragged, shabby II. m.f. bum, tramp.

za·pa·ta f. *(calzado)* half boot; MECH. shoe; *(arandela)* washer.

za·pa·ta·zo m. *(golpe)* blow with a shoe; MARIT. sail-flapping ♦ pl. **dar z.** to stamp one's feet.

za·pa·te·a·do m. heel-tapping dance.

za·pa·te·a·dor, ra I. adj. tap dancing II. m.f. tap dancer.

za·pa·te·ar tr. *(golpear)* to hit with the shoe; *(bailar)* to tap-dance —intr. *(bailar)* to tap one's feet.

za·pa·te·o m. *(acción)* tapping; *(baile)* tap dancing.

za·pa·te·rí·a f. *(taller)* shoemaker's shop; *(tienda)* shoe store.

za·pa·te·ro, a I. adj. underdone, undercooked (vegetables) II. m.f. *(fabricación)* shoemaker; *(venta)* shoe seller; *(remendón)* cobbler ♦ **z., a tus zapatos** mind your own business.

za·pa·ti·lla f. *(pantufla)* slipper; *(de baile)* dancing shoe.

za·pa·to m. shoe ♦ **saber uno dónde le aprieta el z.** to know what is best for oneself.

za·pa·tu·do, a adj. *(zapatos)* wearing clodhoppers; *(pezuña)* thick-hoofed.

za·po·tal m. sapodilla grove.

za·po·te m. sapodilla tree *or* fruit.

za·po·te·ro m. sapodilla tree.

za·qui·za·mí m. [pl. **-íes**] *(desván)* attic; *(cuarto)* hole.

zar m. czar.

za·ra·ban·da f. sarabande.

za·ra·ga·ta f. COLL. ruckus.

za·ran·da f. sieve.

za·ran·da·ja f. COLL. trifles.

za·ran·dar/de·ar tr. *(cribar)* to sift; *(sacudir)* to shake —reflex. to be on the go.

za·ran·de·o m. *(criba)* sifting; *(colador)* straining; *(sacudida)* shaking; *(prisa)* bustle.

za·ra·za f. chintz.

zar·ci·llo m. *(pendiente)* earring; BOT. tendril.

zar·co, a adj. light blue.

za·ri·güe·ya f. opossum.

za·ri·na f. czarina.

za·ris·ta m.f. czarist.

zar·pa f. claw.

zar·pa·da f. clawing.

zar·par tr. to weigh —intr. to set sail.

zar·pa·zo m. lash of a paw.

za·rra·pas·tro·so, a I. adj. ragged, shabby II. m.f. bum, tramp.

zar·za f. bramble.
zar·zal m. bramble patch.
zar·za·mo·ra f. blackberry.
zar·za·pa·rri·lla f. sarsaparilla.
zar·zo·so, a adj. prickly, thorny.
zar·zue·la f. MUS., THEAT. Spanish comedy *or* operetta; SP., CUL. rice and seafood dish.
¡zas! interj. bang!
ze·nit m. zenith.
zi·go·to m. zygote.
zig·zag m. zigzag.
zig·za·gue·ar intr. to zigzag.
zig·za·gue·o m. zigzagging.
zinc m. zinc.
zín·ga·ro, a adj. & m.f. gypsy.
zó·ca·lo m. *(de edificio)* socle; *(pedestal)* plinth; *(de pared)* skirting board; GEOL. shelf; MEX. public square.
zo·dia·cal adj. zodiacal.
zo·dia·co/dí·a·co m. zodiac.
zo·na f. zone; *(distrito)* district.
zo·nal adj. zonal.
zon·ce·ra f. nonsense.
zo·ni·fi·ca·ción f. zoning.
zo·ni·fi·car §70 tr. to zone.
zon·zo, a COLL. I. adj. foolish II. m.f. fool.
zo·o m. zoo.
zo·o·gra·fí·a f. zoography.
zo·o·lo·gí·a f. zoology.
zo·o·ló·gi·co, a adj. zoological ♦ **jardín z.** zoo.
zo·ó·lo·go, a m.f. zoologist.
zoom m. zoom lens.
zo·pen·co, a COLL. I. adj. dumb, dopey II. m.f. dummy, dope.
zo·pi·lo·te m. buzzard.
zo·pi·sa f. tar, pitch.
zo·po, a adj. & m.f. deformed (person).
zo·que·te m. *(de madera)* chunk of wood; *(de pan)* hunk of bread; *(tonto)* dummy.
zo·rra f. fox; *(hembra)* vixen; *(astuta)* sly fox;

COLL. *(prostituta)* whore; *(carro)* dray; MEX., COLL. *(borrachera)* drunkenness.
zo·rre·rí·a f. COLL. cunning.
zo·rri·llo/no m. AMER. skunk.
zo·rro m. fox; COLL. *(astuto)* sly fox ♦ **hacerse el z.** to play dumb.
zo·rru·no, a adj. foxlike.
zor·zal m. thrush.
zo·zo·bra f. *(hundimiento)* capsizing, sinking; METEOROL. dangerous weather; *(inquietud)* anxiety.
zo·zo·brar intr. to capsize, sink; FIG. to fail.
zue·co m. clog.
zu·ma·que m. sumac.
zum·ba f. bullroarer.
zum·bar intr. *(un insecto)* to buzz; *(los oídos)* to ring.
zum·bi·do m. *(de insecto)* buzzing; *(de los oídos)* ringing.
zum·bón, o·na I. adj. teasing II. m.f. joker.
zu·mo m. juice.
zu·mo·so, a adj. juicy.
zun·char tr. to fasten with a metal strap.
zun·cho m. metal strap.
zur·ci·do m. darn.
zur·cir §35 tr. to darn ♦ **¡anda y que te zurzan!** COLL. go jump in the lake!
zur·do, a I. adj. left-handed II. m.f. left-handed person ♦ **no ser z.** to be agile and clever.
zu·rra f. tanning; FIG. thrashing.
zu·rra·pa f. dregs.
zu·rrar tr. to tan; FIG. to give a beating.
zu·rri·do m. *(golpe)* whack; *(ruido)* harsh noise.
zu·rrón m. *(bolsa)* leather bag; BOT. husk; MED. amniotic sac.
zu·rro·na f. COLL. loose woman.
zu·ru·llo m. round lump of soft material.
zu·ta·no, a COLL. m. what's-his-name —f. what's-her-name —m.f. so-and-so.

Inglés/Español

A

a, A (ā) s. primera letra del alfabeto inglés; MÚS. la *m* ♦ **from A to Z** de cabo a rabo.

a (ə, ā), **an** (ən, ăn) art. indef. un <*a book* un libro>; *(per)* a, por, cada, el <*twice an hour* dos veces por hora>.

a·back (ə-băk′) adv. ♦ **to be taken a.** quedar desconcertado • **to take a.** desconcertar.

a·ban·don (ə-băn′dən) I. tr. abandonar; *(to desert)* desertar, dejar ♦ **to a. oneself to** entregarse a II. s. abandono, desenfreno.

a·ban·doned (:dənd) adj. abandonado, desierto.

a·base (ə-bās′) tr. rebajar, humillar.

a·bash (ə-băsh′) tr. avergonzar.

a·bate (ə-bāt′) intr. menguar, amainar.

ab·bess (ăb′ĭs) s. abadesa.

ab·bey (ăb′ē) s. abadía, convento.

ab·bot (ăb′ət) s. abad *m*.

ab·bre·vi·ate (ə-brē′vē-āt′) tr. abreviar, resumir.

ab·bre·vi·a·tion (-′-ā′shən) s. *(shortening)* abreviación *f*; *(shortened form)* abreviatura.

ab·di·cate (ăb′dĭ-kāt′) tr. & intr. abdicar.

ab·do·men (ăb′də-mən) s. abdomen *m*, vientre *m*.

ab·duct (ăb-dŭkt′) tr. secuestrar, raptar.

ab·duc·tion (ăb-dŭk′shən) s. rapto, secuestro.

ab·duc·tor (:tər) s. *(kidnapper)* raptor *m*, secuestrador *m*; ANAT. abductor *m*.

a·bed (ə-bĕd′) adv. en cama, acostado.

ab·er·rant (ă-bĕr′ənt) adj. aberrante.

ab·er·ra·tion (ăb′ə-rā′shən) s. aberración *f*.

a·bet (əbĕt′) tr. **-tt-** incitar, instigar (a cometer un delito) ♦ **to aid and a.** ser cómplice de.

a·bey·ance (ə-bā′əns) s. ♦ **in a.** en suspenso.

ab·hor (ăb-hôr′) tr. **-rr-** aborrecer, detestar.

ab·hor·rence (:əns) s. aborrecimiento, odio.

a·bide (ə-bīd′) tr. **-d** *o* **abode** tolerar, soportar —intr. permanecer, continuar ♦ **to a. by** cumplir con, acatar.

a·bid·ing (ə-bī′dĭng) adj. constante, duradero.

a·bil·i·ty (ə-bĭl′ĭ-tē) s. *(skill)* capacidad *f*, habilidad *f*; *(talent)* aptitud *f*; *(power)* facultad *f*.

ab·ject (ăb′jĕkt′) adj. abyecto, vil.

ab·jure (ăb-jŏŏr′) tr. abjurar.

a·blaze (ə-blāz′) adj. ardiente, encendido.

a·ble (ā′bəl) adj. **-er, -est** capaz, hábil ♦ **to be a. to** poder, ser capaz (de).

a·ble-bod·ied (:bŏd′ēd) adj. sano, fuerte.

ab·lu·tion (ə-blōō′shən) s. ablución *f* ♦ pl. FAM. lavabo.

a·bly (ā′blē) adv. hábilmente, diestramente.

ab·nor·mal (ăb-nôr′məl) adj. anormal.

ab·nor·mal·i·ty (-′-măl′ĭ-tē) s. anormalidad *f*.

a·board (ə-bôrd′) adv. & prep. a bordo (de) ♦ **all a.!** ¡pasajeros al tren!

a·bode (ə-bōd′) I. cf. **abide** II. s. morada.

a·bol·ish (ə-bŏl′ĭsh) tr. abolir, eliminar.

ab·o·li·tion (ăb′ə-lĭsh′ən) s. abolición *f*.

A-bomb (ā′bŏm′) s. bomba atómica.

a·bom·i·nate (ə-bŏm′ə-nāt′) tr. abominar, detestar.

ab·o·rig·i·ne (ăb′ə-rĭj′ə-nē) s. aborigen *mf*, indígena *mf*.

a·bort (ə-bôrt′) tr. & intr. abortar.

a·bor·tion (ə-bôr′shən) s. aborto.

a·bor·tion·ist (:shə-nĭst) s. abortista *mf*.

a·bor·tive (:tĭv) adj. MED. abortivo; FIG. fracasado, frustrado.

a·bound (ə-bound′) intr. abundar.

a·bout (ə-bout′) I. prep. *(concerning)* acerca de, sobre; *(with regard to)* con respecto a; *(approximately)* a eso de, alrededor de <*a. ten o'clock* alrededor de las diez>; *(all around)* acá y allá, a la redonda ♦ **how a. that!** ¡qué te parece! • **how a. you?** ¿y tú? • **to be a. to** estar a punto de II. adv. aproximadamente, casi; *(all around)* aquí y allá, por todas partes ♦ **all a.** por todas partes • **to be up and a.** estar levantado (de la cama).

a·bout-face (:fās′) s. media vuelta.

a·bove (ə-bŭv′) I. adv. en lo alto, encima; *(in a text)* más arriba ♦ **a. all** sobre todo • **from a.** desde lo alto II. prep. *(over)* sobre, por encima de; *(greater than)* superior a ♦ **a. and beyond** mucho más allá de III. adj. precitado, antedicho IV. s. ♦ **the a.** lo dicho, lo anterior.

a·bove·board (:bôrd′) adj. franco, abierto.

a·bove-men·tioned (:mĕn′shənd) adj. anteriormente citado, de referencia.

a·bra·sion (ə-brā′zhən) s. abrasión *f*.

a·bra·sive (:sĭv) adj. & s. abrasivo.

a·breast (ə-brĕst′) adv. en una línea ♦ **to keep a. of** mantenerse al corriente de • **two a.** de dos en fondo.

a·bridge (ə-brĭj′) tr. abreviar, condensar.

a·bridg(e)·ment (:mənt) s. abreviación *f*, condensación *f*; *(synopsis)* compendio, resumen *m*.

a·broad (ə-brôd′) adv. en el extranjero; *(out and about)* fuera de casa ♦ **to go a.** ir al extranjero.

ab·ro·gate (ăb′rə-gāt′) tr. abrogar, revocar.

a·brupt (ə-brŭpt′) adj. *(curt)* abrupto, brusco; *(sudden)* inesperado, repentino; *(steep)* escarpado.

ab·scess (ăb′sĕs′) s. absceso.

ab·scond (ăb-skŏnd′) intr. largarse.

ab·sence (ăb′səns) s. ausencia, falta.

ab·sent I. adj. (ăb′sənt) ausente; *(lacking)* que falta; *(distracted)* abstraído II. tr. (ăb-sĕnt′) ♦ **to a. oneself from** ausentarse de.

ab·sen·tee (ăb′sən-tē′) s. ausente *mf*.

ab·sen·tee·ism (:′ĭz′əm) s. absentismo.

ab·sent-mind·ed (ăb′sənt-mīn′dĭd) adj. distraído.

ab·sinth(e) (ăb′sĭnth′) s. licor *m* de ajenjo.

ab·so·lute (ăb′sə-lōōt′) adj. absoluto; *(unconditional)* total; *(monarchy)* autocrático.

ab·so·lut·ist (:lōō′tĭst) s. & adj. absolutista *mf.*

ab·solve (ab-zŏlv′) tr. absolver; *(of obligation)* eximir; *(of guilt)* exculpar.

ab·sorb (ab-sôrb′) tr. absorber; *(to muffle)* amortiguar, FIG. ocupar (tiempo).

ab·sorbed (ab-sôrbd′) adj. absorto, abstraído.

ab·sorb·ent (ab-sòr′bənt) adj. & s. absorbente *m.*

ab·sorp·tion (ab-sôrp′shən) s. absorción *f*; FIG. concentración *f*, ensimismamiento.

ab·stain (ăb-stān′) intr. abstenerse *(from* de).

ab·sti·nence (ăb′stə-nəns) s. abstinencia.

ab·sti·nent (:nənt) adj. abstemio.

ab·stract (ăb-străkt′) I. adj. abstracto II. s. (′′) sumario, resumen *m* ♦ **In the a.** en abstracto III. tr. extraer, quitar.

ab·stract·ed (ăb-străk′tĭd) adj. ensimismado.

ab·strac·tion (:shən) s. abstracción; *f*; *(idea)* idea abstracta; *(distraction)* distracción *f.*

ab·struse (ăb-strōōs′) adj. abstruso.

ab·surd (ab-sûrd′) adj. absurdo, ridículo.

ab·surd·i·ty (ab-sûr′dĭ-tē) s. ridiculez *f.*

a·bun·dance (ə-bŭn′dəns) s. abundancia.

a·bun·dant (:dənt) adj. abundante.

a·buse I. tr. (ə-byōoz′) abusar de; *(to hurt)* maltratar; *(to berate)* insultar II. s. (ə-byōōs′) abuso; *(injury)* maltrato; *(sexually)* violación *f*; *(insult)* insulto.

a·bu·sive (ə-byōō′sĭv) adj. *(abusing)* abusivo; *(insulting)* injurioso, insultante.

a·but (ə-bŭt′) tr. -**tt-** lindar con.

a·bys·mal (ə-bĭz′məl) adj. malísimo, pésimo.

a·byss (ə-bĭs′) s. abismo; FIG. infierno.

ac·a·de·mi·a (ăk′ə-dē′mē-ə) s. el mundo académico.

ac·a·dem·ic (:dēm′ĭk) I. adj. académico, universitario; *(speculative)* teórico II. s. catedrático.

ac·a·de·mi·cian (ə-dĕ-mĭsh′ən) s. académico.

a·cad·e·my (ə-kăd′ə-mē) s. academia.

ac·cede (ăk-sēd′) intr. ♦ **to a.** to consentir en, acceder a; *(the throne, office)* subir a, ascender a.

ac·cel·er·ate (ăk-sĕl′ə-rāt′) tr. acelerar, apresurar —intr. apresurarse, darse prisa.

ac·cel·er·a·tor (:rā′tər) s. acelerador *m.*

ac·cent (ăk′sĕnt′) I. s. acento; POÉT. énfasis *m* ♦ **written a.** acento ortográfico II. tr. acentuar.

ac·cen·tu·ate (ăk-sĕn′chōō-āt′) tr. acentuar.

ac·cept (ăk-sĕpt′) tr. aceptar; *(to admit)* admitir, dar acogida a.

ac·cept·a·ble (ăk-sĕp′tə-bəl) adj. aceptable, admisible.

ac·cep·tance (:təns) s. aceptación *f*; *(reception)* (buena) acogida; *(approval)* aprobación *f.*

ac·cept·ed (:tĭd) adj. aceptado; *(widely used)* corriente, normal.

ac·cess (ăk′sĕs′) s. acceso, entrada.

ac·ces·si·ble (:-bəl) adj. accesible.

ac·ces·sion (ăk-sĕsh′ən) s. accesión *f*, ascenso; *(addition)* ampliación *f*, expansión *f*; *(outburst)* arrebato.

ac·ces·so·ry (ăk-sĕs′ə-rē) I. s. accesorio; DER. cómplice *mf* II. adj. accesorio, adjunto.

ac·ci·dent (ăk′sĭ-dənt) s. *(mishap)* accidente *m*; *(chance)* casualidad *f* ♦ **by a.** por casualidad.

ac·ci·den·tal·ly (′-dĕn′tl-ē) adv. *(by chance)* por casualidad; *(unintentionally)* sin querer.

ac·claim (ə-klām′) I. tr. aclamar, ovacionar II. s. aclamación *f*, ovación *f.*

ac·cla·ma·tion (ăk′lə-mā′shən) s. aclamación *f*, aprobación *f* unánime.

ac·cli·mate (ăk′lə-māt′) tr. & intr. aclimatar(se).

ac·cli·ma·tion (′-mā′shən) s. aclimatación *f.*

ac·cli·ma·tize (ə-klī′mə-tīz′) tr. aclimatar.

ac·co·lade (ăk′ə-lād′) s. aprobación *f*, elogio.

ac·com·mo·date (ə-kŏm′ə-dāt′) tr. *(to oblige)* hacer un favor a, complacer; *(to hold)* dar cabida a —intr. adaptarse.

ac·com·mo·dat·ing (:dā′tĭng) adj. *(obliging)* solícito, servicial; *(adaptable)* acomodadizo.

ac·com·mo·da·tion (′-dā′shən) s. acomodación *f*; *(convenience)* favor *m*, servicio ♦ pl. alojamiento.

ac·com·pa·ni·ment (ə-kŭm′pə-nē-mənt) s. acompañamiento.

ac·com·pa·ny (ə-kŭm′pə-nē) tr. & intr. acompañar(se).

ac·com·plice (ə-kŏm′plĭs) s. cómplice *mf.*

ac·com·plish (ə-kŏm′plĭsh) tr. lograr, realizar.

ac·com·plished (:plĭsht) adj. *(completed)* consumado, realizado; *(skilled)* competente.

ac·com·plish·ment (:plĭsh-mənt) s. *(completion)* realización *f*, logro; *(skill)* pericia, consumación *f.*

ac·cord (ə-kôrd′) I. tr. conceder, otorgar —intr. avenirse, concordar II. s. acuerdo, convenio ♦ **In a. with** de acuerdo con ♦ **of one's own a.** de propia voluntad.

ac·cor·dance (ə-kôr′dns) s. acuerdo *f*, conformidad *f* ♦ **In a. with** de conformidad con.

ac·cord·ing·ly (:dĭng-lē) adv. *(in keeping with)* en conformidad; *(consequently)* por consiguiente.

according to prep. conforme a, según.

ac·cor·di·on (ə-kôr′dē-ən) s. acordeón *m.*

ac·cost (ə-kôst′) tr. abordar, dirigirse a.

ac·count (ə-kount′) I. s. *(report)* relato, informe *m*; *(explanation)* explicación *f*, motivo; COM. cuenta ♦ **by all accounts** según el decir *o* la opinión general ♦ **charge a.** cuenta corriente ♦ **joint a.** cuenta indistinta ♦ **of no a.** de poca monta ♦ **on a. of** a causa de, por ♦ **on no a.** de ninguna manera ♦ **to give an a. of (oneself)** dar buena cuenta de (sí) ♦ **to take into a.** tomar en cuenta ♦ pl. COM. estado de cuenta II. intr. ♦ **to a. for** dar razón de.

ac·count·a·ble (ə-koun′tə-bəl) adj. responsable *(for* por); *(explicable)* justificable.

ac·count·ant (:tənt) s. contador *m*, contable *mf.*

ac·count·ing (:tĭng) s. contabilidad *f.*

ac·cou·ter·ment (ə-kōō′tər-mənt) s. equipaje *m*, atavío ♦ pl. adornos, atavío.

ac·cred·it (ə-krĕd′ĭt) tr. acreditar, reconocer.

ac·cred·i·ta·tion (′-ĭ-tā′shən) s. EDUC. autorización *f*; DIPL. acreditación *f.*

ac·cred·it·ed (′-tĭd) adj. autorizado, reconocido.

ac·crue (ə-krōō′) intr. acumularse ♦ **to a. from** resultar de.

ac·cul·tur·ate (ə-kŭl′chə-rāt′) intr. adaptarse por asimilación cultural.

ac·cu·mu·late (ə-kyōōm′yə-lāt′) tr. & intr. acumular(se), amontonar(se).

ac·cu·mu·la·tion (′-lā′shən) s. acumulación *f.*

ac·cu·ra·cy (ăk′yər-ə-sē) s. exactitud *f*, precisión *f.*

ac·cu·rate (ăk′yər-ĭt) adj. exacto, preciso.

ac·curs·ed (ə-kûr′sĭd) adj. odioso, infausto.

ac·cu·sa·tion (ăk′yə-zā′shən) s. acusación *f.*

ac·cuse (ə-kyōōz′) tr. acusar.

ac·cused (ə-kyōōzd′) adj. acusado ♦ **the a.** el

acusado, el inculpado.

ac·cus·er (ə-kyōō'zər) s. acusador *m*.

ac·cus·tom (ə-kŭs'təm) tr. acostumbrar.

ac·cus·tomed (:təmd) adj. acostumbrado, habitual ♦ **a. to** acostumbrado a.

ace (ās) s. as *m* ♦ **a. in the hole** FAM. as de reserva.

a·cer·bi·ty (ə-sûr'bĭ-tē) s. acerbidad *f*, acritud *f*; FIG. aspereza.

ac·e·tate (ăs'ĭ-tāt') s. acetato.

a·ce·tic (ə-sē'tĭk) adj. acético.

a·cet·y·lene (ə-sĕt'l-ēn') s. acetileno ♦ **a. torch** soplete oxiacetilénico.

ache (āk) I. intr. doler ♦ **to a. for** anhelar, ansiar II. s. dolor *m*.

a·chieve (ə-chēv') tr. llevar a cabo, lograr.

a·chieve·ment (:mənt) s. *(act)* ejecución *f*, realización *f*; *(accomplishment)* logro, hazaña.

a·chiev·er (ə-chē'vər) s. ganador *m*.

ac·id (ăs'ĭd) I. s. ácido; JER. LSD ♦ **a. test** prueba decisiva II. adj. ácido; *(sour)* agrio; FIG. mordaz, punzante.

ac·id-fast (:făst') adj. a prueba de ácidos.

a·cid·ic (ə-sĭd'ĭk) adj. ácido.

a·cid·i·fy (:ə-fī') tr. & intr. acidificar(se).

a·cid·i·ty (:ĭ-tē) s. acidez *f*.

a·cid·u·lous (ə-sĭj'ə-ləs) adj. acídulo, cáustico.

ac·knowl·edge (ăk-nŏl'ĭj) tr. *(to admit)* admitir, confesar; *(to recognize)* reconocer; *(a gift)* agradecer ♦ **to a. receipt of** acusar recibo de.

ac·knowl·edged (:ĭjd) adj. reconocido.

ac·knowl·edg(e)·ment (:ĭj-mənt) s. *(confession)* admisión *f*; *(recognition)* reconocimiento; *(receipt)* acuse *m* de recibo.

ac·me (ăk'mē) s. cumbre *f*, cima.

ac·ne (ăk'nē) s. acné *m*.

ac·o·lyte (ăk'ə-līt') s. acólito, monaguillo.

a·corn (ā'kôrn') s. bellota.

a·cous·tic/ti·cal (ə-kōō'stĭk) adj. acústico ♦ **acoustic nerve** nervio auditivo ♦ **acoustics** s.sg. acústica.

ac·quaint (ə-kwānt') tr. familiarizar, poner al corriente ♦ **to be acquainted** conocerse • **to be acquainted with** conocer, estar al corriente de.

ac·quain·tance (ə-kwān'təns) s. *(knowledge)* conocimiento; *(person)* conocido.

ac·qui·esce (ăk'wē-ĕs') intr. consentir, asentir.

ac·qui·es·cence (:əns) s. aquiescencia.

ac·quire (ə-kwīr') tr. adquirir, obtener ♦ **acquired immune deficiency syndrome** síndrome de inmunodeficiencia adquirida.

ac·qui·si·tion (ăk'wĭ-zĭsh'ən) s. adquisición *f*.

ac·quis·i·tive (ə-kwĭz'ĭ-tĭv) adj. codicioso.

ac·quit (ə-kwĭt') tr. **-tt-** absolver, exculpar ♦ **to a. oneself** portarse, conducirse.

ac·quit·tal (:l) s. absolución *f*, descargo.

a·cre (ā'kər) s. acre *m*.

ac·rid (ăk'rĭd) adj. acre, cáustico.

ac·ri·mo·ny (ăk'rə-mō'nē) s. acrimonia.

ac·ro·bat (ăk'rə-băt') s. acróbata *mf*.

ac·ro·bat·ic ('-'ĭk) adj. acrobático ♦ **acrobatics** s.sg. *o* pl. acrobacia.

ac·ro·nym (ăk'rə-nĭm') s. siglas.

a·cross (ə-krôs') I. prep. *(through)* por, a través de; *(on the other side of)* al *o* en el otro lado de II. adv. *(on the other side)* a través, del otro lado; *(crosswise)* transversalmente, en cruz ♦ **to be ten feet a.** tener diez pies de ancho • **to come** *o* **run a.** encontrarse con • **to go a.** atravesar, cruzar.

a·cross-the-board (-'thə-bôrd') adj. general, para todos.

a·cros·tic (ə-krô'stĭk) s. acróstico.

a·cryl·ic (ə-krĭl'ĭk) adj. acrílico.

act (ăkt) I. intr. actuar, hacer algo; *(to behave)* conducirse, comportarse; *(to perform)* hacer un papel, actuar ♦ **to a. like** *o* **as if** hacer como que • **to a. on** *o* **upon** influir en, obrar sobre • **to a. up** portarse mal —tr. representar, hacer el papel de II. s. *(action)* acto, hecho; *(deed)* acción *f*; *(performance)* número; TEAT. acto; *(pretense)* simulación *f*, fingimiento; *(a law)* ley *f*, decreto ♦ **to catch in the a.** coger con las manos en la masa • **to put on an a.** simular, fingir.

act·ing (ăk'tĭng) I. adj. interino, suplente II. s. TEAT. actuación *f*.

ac·tion (ăk'shən) s. acción *f*; *(act)* acto, hecho; *(motion)* operación *f*, movimiento; *(activity)* actividad *f*; *(effect)* influencia, efecto; MIL. batalla, acción *f* de guerra ♦ **to put out of a.** destrozar, inutilizar • **to take a.** tomar medidas ♦ pl. conducta.

ac·ti·vate (ăk'tə-vāt') tr. activar, agitar.

ac·tive (ăk'tĭv) adj. activo, en movimiento; *(energetic)* enérgico, vigoroso ♦ **a. duty** MIL. servicio activo • **to take an a. interest in** interesarse vivamente por.

ac·tiv·ist (ăk'tə-vĭst) adj. & s. activista *mf*.

ac·tiv·i·ty (ăk-tĭv'ĭ-tē) s. actividad *f*.

ac·tor (ăk'tər) s. actor *m*.

ac·tress (ăk'trĭs) s. actriz *f*.

ac·tu·al (ăk'chōō-əl) adj. real, verdadero.

ac·tu·al·i·ty ('-ăl'ĭ-tē) s. realidad *f*.

ac·tu·al·ly ('-ə-lē) adv. en realidad.

ac·tu·ar·y (ăk'chōō-ĕr'ē) s. actuario de seguros.

ac·tu·ate (ăk'chōō-āt') tr. activar, impulsar.

a·cu·men (ə-kyōō'mən) s. perspicacia, ingenio.

ac·u·punc·ture (ăk'yə-pŭngk'chər) s. acupuntura.

a·cute (ə-kyōōt') adj. agudo; *(sensitive)* sagaz, perspicaz; *(critical)* grave.

ad (ăd) s. FAM. anuncio, publicidad *f*.

ad·age (ăd'ĭj) s. adagio, proverbio.

ad·a·mant (ăd'ə-mənt) adj. inexorable, inflexible.

ad·a·man·tine ('-măn'tēn') adj. inflexible.

Ad·am's apple (ăd'əmz) s. nuez *f* de la garganta.

a·dapt (ə-dăpt') tr. & intr. adaptar(se), acomodar(se).

a·dapt·a·ble (ə-dăp'tə-bəl) adj. adaptable, acomodable.

ad·ap·ta·tion (ăd'əp-tā'shən) s. adaptación *f*.

a·dapt·er/·tor (ə-dăp'tər) s. adaptador *m*.

add (ăd) tr. añadir, agregar; MAT. sumar ♦ **adding machine** sumadora • **to a. up** sumar • **to a. up to** FAM. venir a ser, equivaler a —intr. aumentar, acrecentar; MAT. sumar ♦ **to a. up** FAM. tener sentido.

ad·dend (ăd'ĕnd') s. sumando.

ad·den·dum (ə-dĕn'dəm) s. [pl. **-da**] addenda *m*, apéndice *m*.

ad·der (ăd'ər) s. víbora, culebra.

ad·dict I. tr. (ə-dĭkt') ♦ **addicted to** *(drugs)* adicto a; FAM. dedicado a, entregado a II. s. (ăd'ĭkt) adicto; FAM. fanático.

ad·dic·tion (ə-dĭk'shən) s. vicio; FAM. afición *f*.

ad·dic·tive (:tĭv) adj. que forma hábito.

ad·di·tion (ə-dĭsh'ən) s. adición *f*; MAT. suma ♦ **in a.** además, también.

ad·di·tion·al (:ə-nəl) adj. adicional.

ad·di·tive (ăd'ĭ-tĭv) adj. & s. aditivo.

ad·dle (ăd'l) tr. enturbiar, confundir.

ad·dress I. s. (ə-drĕs', ăd'rĕs') *(postal)* direc-

ción *f*, señas; *(lecture)* discurso, alocución *f* ♦
home a. (dirección de) domicilio **II.** tr. (ə-
drĕs′) *(a person)* dirigirse a, dirigir la palabra a;
(a group) dar un discurso a; *(letter)* dirigir, poner las señas a ♦ **to a.** oneself to aplicarse a • **to
a.** someone as dar a alguien el tratamiento de.
ad·dress·ee (ăd′rĕ-sē′) s. destinatario.
a·dept (ə-dĕpt′) adj. perito.
ad·e·qua·cy (ăd′ĭ-kwə-sē) s. suficiencia.
ad·e·quate (ăd′ĭ-kwĭt) adj. adecuado.
ad·here (ăd-hîr′) intr. *(to stick)* pegarse; *(to be
loyal)* adherirse; *(to follow)* ceñirse.
ad·her·ence (:əns) s. adherencia; *(devotion)*
adhesión *f.*
ad·he·sion (ăd-hē′zhən) s. adhesión *f.*
ad·he·sive (:sĭv) **I.** adj. adhesivo, pegajoso ♦ **a.
tape** cinta adhesiva **II.** s. adhesivo.
ad·ja·cent (ə-jā′sənt) adj. adyacente, contiguo.
ad·jec·tive (ăj′ĭk-tĭv) s. adjetivo.
ad·join (ə-join′) tr. estar contiguo a, lindar con.
ad·join·ing (ə-joi′nĭng) adj. contiguo.
ad·journ (ə-jûrn′) tr. suspender, levantar (una
sesión) —intr. *(a meeting)* aplazarse; *(to move)*
cambiarse, trasladarse (to a).
ad·journ·ment (:mənt) s. *(closing)* suspensión
f, clausura; *(transfer)* traslación *f.*
ad·judge (ə-jŭj′) tr. DER. considerar.
ad·ju·di·cate (ə-jōō′dĭ-kāt′) tr. juzgar, fallar.
ad·junct (ăj′ŭngkt′) adj. & s. adjunto.
ad·just (ə-jŭst′) tr. *(to fit)* ajustar; *(to fix)* arreglar; *(to adapt)* adaptar; COM. liquidar, ajustar
(reclamo) —intr. ajustarse.
ad·just·a·ble (ə-jŭs′tə-bəl) adj. ajustable.
ad·just·er/·tor (:tər) s. MEC. regulador *m*; COM.
ajustador *m*, liquidador *m* (de reclamos).
ad·just·ment (ə-jŭst′mənt) s. ajuste *m*; *(fixing)*
arreglo; COM. liquidación *f* (de una cuenta).
ad·ju·tant (ăj′ə-tnt) s. ayudante *m.*
ad lib (ăd lĭb′) adv. de manera improvisada.
ad·min·is·ter (ăd-mĭn′ĭ-stər) tr. administrar;
(to manage) dirigir, manejar ♦ **to a. an oath to**
tomar juramento a • **to a. to** ayudar, cuidar (de
una persona).
ad·min·is·trate (:strāt′) tr. administrar.
ad·min·is·tra·tion (-′-strā′shən) s. administración *f*, manejo; POL. dirección *f*, gobierno ♦ **the
A.** el gobierno.
ad·min·is·tra·tor (-′-strā′tər) s. administrador
m.
ad·mi·ra·ble (ăd′mər-ə-bəl) adj. admirable.
ad·mi·ral (ăd′mər-əl) s. almirante *m.*
ad·mi·ra·tion (ăd′mə-rā′shən) s. admiración *f.*
ad·mire (ăd-mīr′) tr. admirar.
ad·mir·er (:ər) s. admirador *m*; *(suitor)* enamorado.
ad·mis·si·ble (ăd-mĭs′ə-bəl) adj. admisible,
aceptable.
ad·mis·sion (ăd-mĭsh′ən) s. admisión *f*; *(fee)*
entrada; *(acceptance)* ingreso (al foro, universidad); *(confession)* admisión, concesión *f.*
ad·mit (ăd-mĭt′) tr. -**tt**- *(to let in)* admitir, dar
entrada a; *(to confess)* confesar, reconocer; *(to
concede)* conceder —intr. dar entrada a ♦ **to a.
of** permitir, dejar lugar a.
ad·mit·tance (:ns) s. *(admission)* admisión *f*;
(permission to enter) acceso, entrada.
ad·mix·ture (ăd-mĭks′chər) s. mixtura, mezcla.
ad·mon·ish (ăd-mŏn′ĭsh) tr. *(to reprove)* amonestar; *(to caution)* advertir.
ad·mo·ni·tion (ăd′mə-nĭsh′ən) s. *(reproof)* admonición *f*; *(warning)* advertencia.
a·do (ə-dōō′) s. bulla, alboroto.

ad·o·les·cence (ăd′l-ĕs′əns) s. adolescencia.
ad·o·les·cent (:ənt) s. & adj. adolescente *mf.*
a·dopt (ə-dŏpt′) tr. adoptar.
a·dopt·ed (ə-dŏp′tĭd) adj. *(a child)* adoptivo;
(assumed) adoptado.
a·dop·tion (:shən) s. adopción *f.*
a·dop·tive (:tĭv) adj. adoptivo.
a·dor·a·ble (ə-dôr′ə-bəl) adj. adorable.
ad·o·ra·tion (ăd′ə-rā′shən) s. adoración *f.*
a·dore (ə-dôr′) tr. adorar.
a·dorn (ə-dôrn′) tr. adornar, decorar.
a·dorn·ment (:mənt) s. adorno, decoración *f.*
ad·re·nal (ə-drē′nəl) adj. adrenal, suprarrenal.
a·dren·a·line (ə-drĕn′ə-lĭn) s. adrenalina.
a·drift (ə-drĭft′) adv. & adj. a la deriva.
a·droit (ə-droit′) adj. diestro, hábil.
ad·u·la·tion (ăj′ə-lā′shən) s. adulación *f.*
a·dult (ə-dŭlt′, ăd′ŭlt′) s. adulto ♦ pl. mayores.
a·dul·ter·ate (ə-dŭl′tə-rāt′) tr. adulterar.
a·dul·ter·er (:tər-ər) s. adúltero.
a·dul·ter·ess (:ĭs) s. adúltera.
a·dul·ter·ous (:əs) adj. adúltero.
a·dul·ter·y (ə-dŭl′tə-rē) s. adulterio.
a·dult·hood (ə-dŭlt′hŏŏd′) s. edad adulta.
ad·vance (ăd-văns′) **I.** tr. avanzar, adelantar;
(to propose) proponer, presentar; *(to further)*
fomentar, promover; *(to hasten)* adelantar; *(to
lend)* anticipar —intr. avanzar; *(to improve)*
hacer progresos; *(to rise)* elevarse, subir (valor,
posición) **II.** s. avance *m*, adelanto; *(progress)*
progreso; *(rise)* alza, aumento (de valor); *(loan)*
anticipo ♦ pl. propuesta amorosa **III.** adj. adelantado, anticipado ♦ **a. guard** avanzada, vanguardia • **in a.** por anticipado, de antemano.
ad·vanced (ăd-vănst′) adj. *(in level, degree)*
avanzado, superior; *(in time, ability)* adelantado.
ad·vance·ment (ăd-văns′mənt) s. avance *m*;
(improvement) adelanto; *(development)* progreso; *(promotion)* ascenso.
ad·van·tage (ăd-văn′tĭj) s. ventaja; *(gain)* provecho, partido ♦ **to one's a.** para ventaja propio • **to take a. of** *(to make use of)* aprovechar,
valerse de; *(to exploit)* abusarse de.
ad·van·ta·geous (-′-tā′jəs) adj. ventajoso.
ad·vent (ăd′vĕnt′) s. advenimiento, llegada.
ad·ven·ture (ăd-vĕn′chər) **I.** s. aventura ♦ **a.
story** historia de aventuras **II.** tr. & intr. aven-
turar(se), arriesgar(se).
ad·ven·tur·er (:ər) s. aventurero.
ad·ven·tur·ous (:əs) adj. aventurero, emprendedor.
ad·verb (ăd′vûrb′) s. adverbio.
ad·ver·sar·y (ăd′vər-sĕr′ē) s. adversario.
ad·verse (ăd-vûrs′, ′′) adj. adverso, desfavorable.
ad·ver·si·ty (ăd-vûr′sĭ-tē) s. adversidad *f.*
ad·ver·tise (ăd′vər-tīz′) tr. anunciar ♦ **to a. for**
buscar por medio de avisos —intr. poner un
anuncio, hacer publicidad.
ad·ver·tise·ment (:mənt, ăd-vûr′tĭs-) s. anuncio, publicidad *f.*
ad·ver·tis·er (ăd′vər-tī′zər) s. anunciante *mf.*
ad·ver·tis·ing (:zĭng) s. publicidad *f*, propaganda.
ad·vice (ăd-vīs′) s. consejo ♦ **to take a.** seguir
el consejo.
ad·vis·a·ble (ăd-vī′zə-bəl) adj. prudente.
ad·vise (ăd-vīz′) tr. *(to counsel)* dar consejo a,
aconsejar; *(to suggest)* recomendar, sugerir; *(to
notify)* notificar.
ad·vise·ment (:mənt) s. deliberación *f* ♦ **to**

take under a. someter a consideración.
ad·vis·er/·sor (ăd-vī′zər) s. consejero, asesor *m.*
ad·vi·so·ry (:zə-rē) I. adj. consultivo, asesor II. s. aviso de precaución.
ad·vo·ca·cy (ăd′və-kə-sē) s. apoyo, promoción *f* (de una causa o idea).
ad·vo·cate (ăd′və-kāt′) I. tr. abogar por (causa, idea) II. s. (:kăt′, kĭt′) defensor *m*, partidario; G.B. abogado.
adz(e) (ădz) s. azuela.
ae·gis (ē′jĭs) s. ♦ **under the a. of** bajo el patrocinio de.
aer·ate (âr′āt′) tr. gasear (un líquido); oxigenar (la sangre); *(to air)* airear.
aer·i·al (âr′ē-əl) I. adj. aéreo, de aire II. s. antena.
aer·ie (âr′ē, îr′ē) s. aguilera.
aer·o·bic (â-rō′bĭk) adj. aeróbico.
aer·o·dy·nam·ic (âr′ō-dī-năm′ĭk) adj. aerodinámico ♦ **aerodynamics** s.sg. aerodinámica.
aer·o·naut (âr′ə-nôt′) s. aeronauta *mf.*
aer·o·nau·tic/ti·cal (:nô′tĭk) adj. aeronáutico ♦ **aeronautics** s.sg. aeronáutica.
aer·o·sol (âr′ə-sôl′) s. aerosol *m* ♦ **a. bomb** bomba de aerosol, vaporizador.
aer·o·space (âr′ō-spās′) adj. aeroespacial.
aes·thete (ĕs′thēt′) s. esteta *mf.*
aes·thet·ic (ĕs-thĕt′ĭk) adj. estético ♦ **aesthetics** s.sg. estética.
a·far (ə-fär′) adv. ♦ **from a.** de lejos.
af·fa·ble (ăf′ə-bəl) adj. afable, amable.
af·fair (ə-fâr′) s. *(business)* asunto; *(event)* incidente *m*; *(liaison)* amorío; *(gathering)* acontecimiento social ♦ **world affairs** situación mundial ♦ **pl.** asuntos personales.
af·fect¹ (ə-fĕkt′) tr. *(to influence)* afectar, influir en; *(to move)* afectar, conmover.
af·fect² tr. *(to feign)* fingir, simular.
af·fec·ta·tion (ăf′ĕk-tā′shən) s. afectación *f.*
af·fect·ed¹ (ə-fĕk′tĭd) adj. *(influenced)* afectado; *(moved)* conmovido, impresionado.
af·fect·ed² adj. *(mannered)* afectado, amanerado.
af·fect·ing (:tĭng) adj. sensible, conmovedor.
af·fec·tion (:shən) s. afecto, cariño.
af·fec·tion·ate (:shə-nĭt) adj. afectuoso, cariñoso.
af·fi·da·vit (ăf′ĭ-dā′vĭt) s. afidávit *m.*
af·fil·i·ate (ə-fĭl′ē-āt′) I. tr. & intr. afiliar(se), asociar(se) *(with a)* II. s. (:ĭt) socio, asociado.
af·fil·i·a·tion (-′ā′shən) s. afiliación *f.*
af·firm (ə-fûrm′) tr. afirmar, aseverar.
af·fir·ma·tive (ə-fûr′mə-tĭv) I. adj. afirmativo II. s. afirmativa.
af·fix (ə-fĭks′) tr. *(to attach)* pegar, adherir; *(to append)* agregar, añadir; *(a signature)* poner.
af·flict (ə-flĭkt′) tr. afligir, acongojar ♦ **to be afflicted with** padecer de, sufrir de.
af·flic·tion (ə-flĭk′shən) s. aflicción *f.*
af·flu·ence (ăf′lōō-əns) s. riqueza, opulencia.
af·flu·ent (:ənt) adj. rico, opulento.
af·ford (ə-fôrd′) tr. *(monetarily)* tener con qué comprar; *(to spare)* poder disponer de; *(to risk)* afrontar; *(to provide)* proporcionar, dar.
af·ford·a·ble (ə-fôr′də-bəl) adj. que se puede comprar o dar.
af·front (ə-frŭnt′) I. tr. afrentar, insultar II. s. afrenta, insulto.
a·field (ə-fēld′) adv. ♦ **far a.** muy lejos.
a·fire (ə-fīr′) adj. & adv. ardiendo, en llamas.

a·flame (ə-flām′) adj. & adv. en llamas.
a·float (ə-flōt′) adj. & adv. *(floating)* a flote, flotando; *(at sea)* a bordo; COM. en circulación, corriente.
a·foot (ə-fŏŏt′) adj. & adv. a pie; FIG. en marcha.
a·fore·said (ə-fôr′sĕd′) adj. antedicho.
a·fore·thought (:thôt′) adj. ♦ **with malice a.** con premeditación.
a·foul (ə-foul′) adv. ♦ **to run a. of** enredarse con, meterse en líos con.
a·fraid (ə-frād′) adj. asustado, atemorizado ♦ **to be a. (of)** tener miedo (de *o* a) • **to be a. that** temer que.
a·fresh (ə-frĕsh′) adv. de nuevo, otra vez.
aft (ăft) adj. & adv. a, en, *o* hacia popa.
af·ter (ăf′tər) I. prep. *(in place, order)* después de, detrás de; *(in time)* después de; *(following)* tras <*day a. day* día tras día>; *(in pursuit of)* en pos, tras; *(at the end of)* al cabo de ♦ **a. all** al fin y al cabo • **to be a. someone** perseguir a alguien II. conj. después (de) que III. adv. *(afterward)* después; *(behind)* atrás.
af·ter·birth (:bûrth′) s. secundinas, placenta.
af·ter·bur·ner (:bûr′nər) s. quemador *m* auxiliar.
af·ter·ef·fect (:ĭ-fĕkt′) s. consecuencia.
af·ter·im·age (:ĭm′ĭj) s. imagen consecutiva *o* accidental.
af·ter·life (:līf′) s. vida venidera.
af·ter·math (:măth′) s. consecuencias, resultados.
af·ter·noon (:nōōn′) s. tarde *f* ♦ **good a.!** ¡buenas tardes!
af·ter·taste (:tāst′) s. *(taste)* dejo, resabio; FIG. sabor *m*, impresión *f.*
af·ter·ward(s) (:wərd[z]) adv. después, luego.
af·ter·world (:wûrld′) s. el otro mundo.
a·gain (ə-gĕn′) adv. otra vez, de nuevo ♦ **a. and a.** una y otra vez • **and then a.** por otra parte • **as much a.** otro tanto más • **never a.** nunca más • **now and a.** de vez en cuando.
a·gainst (ə-gĕnst′) prep. *(touching)* contra; *(in opposition to)* en contra de, contra; *(in contrast to)* en contraste con, sobre; *(as a defense from)* como protección contra.
a·gape (ə-gāp′) adv. & adj. boquiabierto.
ag·ate (ăg′ĭt) s. ágata.
age (āj) I. s. edad *f*; *(era)* época, era ♦ **a. of consent** edad núbil • **middle a.** edad mediana • **of a.** mayor de edad • **old a.** vejez, senectud • **to come of a.** llegar a la mayoría de edad • **under a.** menor de edad II. tr. & intr. envejecer(se), madurar(se); *(wine)* añejar.
ag·ed (āj′ĭd) adj. *(old)* envejecido, anciano; (ājd) *(of the age of)* de la edad de, de.
age·less (āj′lĭs) adj. eternamente joven.
age·long (āj′lông′) adj. eterno, de siempre.
a·gen·cy (ā′jən-sē) s. *(a means)* medio, acción *f*; *(business)* agencia; POL. ministerio, dependencia gubernamental.
a·gen·da (ə-jĕn′də) s. agenda, temario.
a·gent (ā′jənt) s. *(person)* agente *mf*, representante *mf*; *(means)* instrumento, medio; CHEM. agente *m*, factor *m.*
age-old (āj′ōld′) adj. antiquísimo.
ag·glu·ti·na·tion (ə-glōōt′n-ā′shən) s. aglutinación *f.*
ag·gran·dize (ə-grăn′dīz′) tr. agrandar, engrandecer.
ag·gra·vate (ăg′rə-vāt′) tr. *(to worsen)* agravar, empeorar; *(to annoy)* irritar, exasperar ♦ **aggra-**

vated assault asalto con intención de crimen.

ag·gra·va·tion ('-vā'shən) s. *(worsening)* agravación *f*; *(annoyance)* irritación *f*.

ag·gre·gate (ăg'rĭ-gĭt) I. adj. & s. agregado ♦ **in the a.** en total II. tr. (:gāt') agregar, unir.

ag·gress (ə-grĕs') intr. agredir.

ag·gres·sion (ə-grĕsh'ən) s. agresión *f*.

ag·gres·sive (ə-grĕs'ĭv) adj. *(hostile)* agresivo, ofensivo; *(assertive)* emprendedor, dinámico.

ag·gres·sor (:ər) s. agresor *m*.

ag·grieve (ə-grēv') tr. apenar, afligir.

a·ghast (ə-găst') adj. espantado, horrorizado.

ag·ile (ăj'əl, ăj'īl') adj. ágil, ligero.

a·gil·i·ty (ə-jĭl'ĭ-tē) s. agilidad *f*, ligereza.

ag·ing (ā'jĭng) s. añejamiento.

ag·i·tate (ăj'ĭ-tāt') tr. *(physically)* agitar; *(to upset)* inquietar —intr. agitar.

ag·i·tat·ed (:tĭd) adj. agitado, inquieto.

ag·i·ta·tion ('-'shən) s. agitación *f*, perturbación *f*.

ag·i·ta·tor ('-'tər) s. agitador *m*.

a·glow (ə-glō') adj. resplandeciente ♦ **a. with** radiante de.

ag·nos·tic (ăg-nŏs'tĭk) s. & adj. agnóstico.

a·go (ə-gō') adj. & adv. hace <*two years a.* hace dos años> ♦ **how long a.?** ¿cuánto tiempo hace?

a·gog (ə-gŏg') adj. ansioso, anhelante.

ag·o·nize (ăg'ə-nīz') intr. hacer grandes esfuerzos ♦ **to a. over** atormentarse por (una duda, decisión).

ag·o·ny (:nē) s. *(pain)* dolor *m*, tortura; *(anguish)* angustia, tormento.

a·grar·i·an (ə-grâr'ē-ən) adj. agrario.

a·gree (ə-grē') intr. *(to consent)* consentir, acceder a; *(to concur)* estar de acuerdo, coincidir; *(to match)* corresponder a, concordar; GRAM. concordar ♦ **don't you a.?** ¿no le parece? • **to a. on** avenirse a, ponerse de acuerdo con • **to a. that** quedar en • **to a. with one** sentarle bien.

a·gree·a·ble (:ə-bəl) adj. *(pleasant)* agradable; *(willing to agree)* complaciente.

a·greed (ə-grēd') adj. convenido, entendido.

a·gree·ment (ə-grē'mənt) s. *(accord)* concordancia, conformidad *f*; *(contract)* acuerdo, pacto ♦ **in a. with** de acuerdo con • **to enter into an a.** firmar un contrato.

ag·ri·cul·tur·al (ăg'rĭ-kŭl'chər-əl) adj. agrícola.

ag·ri·cul·ture (ăg'rĭ-kŭl'chər) s. agricultura.

ag·ri·cul·tur·ist ('-'-ĭst) s. agrónomo.

a·gron·o·mist (ə-grŏn'ə-mĭst) s. agrónomo.

a·gron·o·my (:mē) s. agronomía.

a·ground (ə-ground') adv. & adj. varado, encallado ♦ **to run a.** encallar.

a·head (ə-hĕd') adv. *(at or to the front)* delante, al frente, adelante; *(in advance)* por adelantado ♦ **a. of** antes que • **go a.!** ¡adelante! • **to be a. of** llevar ventaja a • **to get a.** progresar, adelantar.

a·hoy (ə-hoi') interj. ♦ **ship a.!** ¡barco a la vista!

aid (ād) I. tr. & intr. ayudar, auxiliar II. s. ayuda, auxilio ♦ **first a.** primeros auxilios.

aide (ād) s. asistente *mf*, ayudante *mf*.

aide-de-camp (ād'dĭ-kămp') s. [pl. **aides-**] ayudante *m* de campo, edecán *m*.

AIDS (ādz) s. SIDA.

ail (āl) intr. estar enfermo —tr. afligir, doler.

ail·ing (ā'lĭng) s. enfermizo, achacoso.

ail·ment (āl'mənt) s. dolencia, enfermedad *f*.

aim (ām) I. tr. apuntar —intr. *(a weapon)* apuntar; *(to aspire)* aspirar, proponerse II. s. *(of a weapon)* puntería, apunte *m*; *(goal)* obje-

tivo, meta ♦ **to take a. at** apuntar a.

aim·less (:lĭs) adj. sin objeto, a la deriva.

ain't (ānt) FAM. contr. de **am not, is not, are not, has not,** y **have not.**

air (âr) I. s. aire *m*; *(aura)* apariencia, aspecto ♦ **a. brake** freno neumático • **a. conditioner** acondicionador de aire • **a. conditioning** aire acondicionado • **a. force** fuerza aérea • **a. freight** carga aérea, flete por avión • **a. letter** carta aérea • **a. mattress** colchón de aire • **to be on the a.** RAD., TELEV. estar emitiéndose (un programa) • **to clear the a.** aclarar las cosas • **up in the a.** incierto, no resuelto ♦ pl. aires, afectación • **to put on a.** darse aires II. tr. *(to expose to air)* orear, ventilar; FIG. hacer público, divulgar.

air·borne (âr'bôrn') adj. *(by aircraft)* aerotransportado; *(flying)* volando, en el aire; *(pollen, seeds)* llevado por el aire.

air·brush *o* **air brush** (âr'brŭsh') s. aerógrafo.

air·con·di·tion (âr'kən-dĭsh'ən) tr. acondicionar el aire, climatizar.

air·cool (âr'kōōl') tr. enfriar por aire.

air·craft (âr'krăft') s.inv. nave aérea ♦ **a. carrier** portaaviones.

air·drome (âr'drōm') s. aeródromo.

air·fare (âr'fâr') s. tarifa aérea.

air·field (âr'fēld') s. campo de aviación.

air·i·ly (âr'ə-lē) adv. ligeramente, alegremente.

air·ing (âr'ĭng) s. *(exposure to air)* ventilación *f*, oreo; FIG. ventilación (de ideas, opiniones).

air·less (âr'lĭs) adj. sin aire, sofocante.

air·lift (âr'lĭft') I. s. puente aéreo II. tr. transportar por vía aérea.

air·line (âr'līn') s. aerolínea.

air·lin·er (âr'lī'nər) s. avión *m* de pasajeros.

air·mail (âr'māl') s. ♦ **by a.** por vía aérea.

air·man (âr'mən) s. [pl. **-men**] MIL. soldado de la fuerza aérea; *(aviator)* aviador *m*.

air·plane (âr'plān') s. avión *m*, aeroplano.

air·port (âr'pôrt') s. aeropuerto, aeródromo.

air·sick (âr'sĭk') adj. mareado (en avión).

air·space (âr'spās') s. espacio aéreo.

air·strip (âr'strĭp') s. pista de aterrizaje.

air·tight (âr'tīt') adj. hermético.

air·wor·thy (âr'wûr'*th*ē) adj. en condiciones de vuelo.

air·y (âr'ē) adj. **-i-** *(breezy)* bien ventilado; *(delicate)* diáfano, ligero; *(light-hearted)* alegre; *(casual)* despreocupado.

aisle (īl) s. pasillo; *(of church)* nave *f*.

a·jar (ə-jär') adv. & adj. entreabierto.

a·kim·bo (ə-kĭm'bō) adj. & adv. en jarras.

a·kin (ə-kĭn') adj. ♦ **a. to** parecido a.

al·a·bas·ter (ăl'ə-băs'tər) s. alabastro.

a·lac·ri·ty (ə-lăk'rĭ-tē) s. presteza, prontitud *f*.

a·larm (ə-lärm') I. s. *(fear)* alarma, temor *m*; *(device)* señal *f* de alarma; MIL. rebato ♦ **a. clock** (reloj) despertador II. tr. *(to frighten)* alarmar; *(to warn)* dar la alarma.

a·larm·ing (ə-lär'mĭng) adj. alarmante.

a·larm·ist (:mĭst) s. alarmista *mf*.

a·las (ə-lăs') interj. ¡ay!, ¡ay de mí!

al·ba·tross (ăl'bə-trôs') s. [pl. inv. *o* **es**] albatros *m*; FIG. pena, sufrimiento.

al·be·it (ôl-bē'ĭt) conj. aunque, si bien.

al·bi·no (ăl-bī'nō) s. albino.

al·bum (ăl'bəm) s. álbum *m*; *(record)* elepé *m*.

al·che·mist (ăl'kə-mĭst) s. alquimista *mf*.

al·che·my (:mē) s. alquimia.

al·co·hol (ăl'kə-hôl') s. alcohol *m*.

al·co·hol·ic ('-hô'lĭk) I. adj. alcohólico II. s.

bebedor alcoholizado.
al·co·hol·ism (′-′liz′ əm) s. alcoholismo.
al·cove (ăl′kōv′) s. trasalcoba.
al·de·hyde (ăl′də-hīd′) s. aldehído.
al·der (ôl′dər) s. aliso.
al·der·man (ôl′dər-mən) s. [pl. **-men**] concejal *m.*
ale (āl) s. ale *f.*
a·lem·bic (ə-lĕm′bĭk) s. alambique *m.*
a·lert (ə-lûrt′) **I.** adj. alerta **II.** s. alarma ♦ **to be on the a.** estar sobre aviso **III.** tr. *(to warn)* alertar; *(to inform)* poner sobre aviso.
al·fal·fa (ăl-făl′fə) s. alfalfa, mielga.
al·gae (ăl′jē) s.pl. algas.
al·ge·bra (ăl′jə-brə) s. álgebra.
al·ge·bra·ic (′-brā′ĭk) adj. algebraico.
al·go·rithm (ăl′gə-rĭth′əm) s. algoritmia, algoritmo.
a·li·as (ā′lē-əs) **I.** s. alias *m*, seudónimo **II.** adv. alias, conocido por.
al·i·bi (ăl′ə-bī′) **I.** s. DER. coartada, alibí *m*; FAM. excusa **II.** intr. FAM. excusarse.
a·li·en (ā′lē-ən) **I.** adj. *(foreign)* extranjero; *(unfamiliar)* ajeno, extraño ♦ **a. to** contrario a **II.** s. *(foreigner)* extranjero; CIENC. FIC. ser *m* de otro planeta.
al·ien·ate (āl′yə-nāt′) tr. alienar, enajenar; DER. enajenar, traspasar.
al·ien·a·tion (′-nā′shən) s. alienación *f.*
a·light[1] (ə-līt′) intr. **-ed** *o* **alit** *(to perch)* posarse; *(to dismount)* bajar, apearse.
a·light[2] adj. iluminado.
a·lign (ə-līn′) tr. & intr. alinear(se) ♦ **to a. oneself with** ponerse del lado de.
a·lign·ment (:mənt) s. *(in a line)* alineación *f*; POL. alineamiento.
a·like (ə-līk′) **I.** adj. semejante, parecido **II.** adv. igualmente, de la misma manera.
al·i·men·ta·ry (ăl′ə-mĕn′tə-rē) adj. alimental, alimentario ♦ **a. canal** tubo digestivo.
al·i·mo·ny (ăl′ə-mō′nē) s. pensión *f* (por divorcio o separación).
a·line (ə-līn′) tr. alinear, poner en línea.
a·lit (ə-lĭt′) cf. **alight**[1].
a·live (ə-līv′) adj. vivo ♦ **a. to** sensible a • **a. with** rebosante de • **to be a. and kicking** estar vivito y coleando • **to come a.** FIG. cobrar vida.
al·ka·li (ăl′kə-lī′) s. [pl. **(e)s**] álcali *m.*
al·ka·line (:līn, :līn′) adj. alcalino.
al·ka·loid (:loid′) s. alcaloide *m.*
al·kyl (ăl′kəl) s. alcohilo, alquilo.
all (ôl) **I.** adj. todo ♦ **and a. that** y otras cosas por el estilo ♦ **of a. things!** ¡imagínate! **II.** pron. todo(s), todo el mundo ♦ **above a.** sobre todo • **after a.** al fin y al cabo • **a. in a.** en resumen • **not at a.** nada, en absoluto; *(you're welcome)* no hay de qué **III.** s. todo ♦ **that's a.** eso es todo, nada más **IV.** adv. *(completely)* completamente; *(exclusively)* solamente; *(apiece)* por (cada) bando ♦ *a score of five a.* cinco puntos por bando> ♦ **a. along** siempre, desde el principio • **a. around** por todas partes • **a. at once** de repente, de golpe • **a. but** casi • **a. of a sudden** de repente • **a. over** *(finished)* terminado; *(everywhere)* por todas partes • **a. right** *(satisfactory)* satisfactorio, bueno; *(uninjured)* ileso, sin daño; *(very well)* muy bien; *(yes)* sí • **a. the better, worse** tanto mejor, peor • **a. too** demasiado, muy.
all-a·round (ôl′ə-round′) adj. *(comprehensive)* completo; *(versatile)* versátil.
al·lay (ə-lā′) tr. calmar, aquietar.
al·le·ga·tion (ăl′ĭ-gā′shən) s. alegación *f*; DER. alegato.
al·lege (ə-lĕj′) tr. *(to declare)* alegar; *(to assert)* sostener, pretender.
al·leged (ə-lĕjd′) adj. alegado, supuesto.
al·le·giance (ə-lē′jəns) s. lealtad *f.*
al·le·gor·ic/i·cal (ăl′ĭ-gôr′ĭk) adj. alegórico.
al·le·go·ry (ăl′ĭ-gôr′ē) s. alegoría.
al·ler·gen (ăl′ər-jən) s. alérgeno.
al·ler·gic (ə-lûr′jĭk) adj. alérgico.
al·ler·gist (ăl′ər-jĭst) s. alergista *mf.*
al·ler·gy (:jē) s. alergia.
al·le·vi·ate (ə-lē′vē-āt′) tr. aliviar.
al·le·vi·a·tion (-′-ā′shən) s. alivio.
al·ley (ăl′ē) s. *(street)* callejón *m*, callejuela; *(in bowling)* pista ♦ **blind a.** callejón sin salida • **bowling a.** bolera • **up one's a.** lo de uno.
al·li·ance (ə-lī′əns) s. alianza, unión *f.*
al·lied (ə-līd′, ăl′īd′) adj. aliado.
al·li·ga·tor (ăl′ĭ-gā′tər) s. caimán *m.*
al·lit·er·a·tion (ə-lĭt′ə-rā′shən) s. aliteración *f.*
al·lo·cate (ăl′ə-kāt′) tr. destinar, asignar.
al·lo·ca·tion (′-kā′shən) s. asignación *f*, reparto.
al·lot (ə-lŏt′) tr. **-tt-** *(to apportion)* asignar, distribuir; *(to allocate)* destinar.
al·lot·ment (:mənt) s. *(act)* distribución *f*; *(object, quantity)* lote *m*, porción *f.*
all-out (ôl′out′) adj. extremo, máximo.
al·low (ə-lou′) tr. *(to permit)* dejar, permitir; *(to give)* conceder, dar; *(to set aside)* dar, poner aparte; *(to admit)* confesar, admitir; *(to discount)* deducir, descontar ♦ **a. me** permítame • **to a. for** tener en cuenta, tomar en consideración • **to a. oneself** darse el gusto de.
al·low·a·ble (ə-bəl) adj. permisible.
al·low·ance (:əns) s. *(permission)* permiso; *(rebate)* rebaja; *(money)* dinero de bolsillo (que se da a los niños) ♦ **to make a. for** tener en cuenta, tomar en consideración.
al·loy **I.** s. (ăl′oi) aleación *f* **II.** tr. (ə-loi′) alear.
all-pur·pose (ôl′pûr′pəs) adj. de uso múltiple.
all-right (ôl′rīt′) adj. JER. bueno, excelente.
all·spice (ôl′spīs′) s. pimienta de Jamaica.
all-star (ôl′stär′) adj. de primeras figuras.
all-time (ôl′tīm′) adj. nunca visto *o* alcanzado.
al·lude (ə-lōōd′) intr. aludir, referirse.
al·lure (ə-lōōr′) **I.** tr. atraer, fascinar **II.** s. atracción *f*, fascinación *f.*
al·lu·sion (ə-lōō′zhən) s. alusión *f.*
al·lu·vi·al (ə-lōō′vē-əl) adj. aluvial, de aluvión.
al·ly **I.** tr. & intr. (ə-lī′) unir(se), aliar(se) **II.** s. (ăl′ī′) aliado.
al·ma mat·er (äl′mə mä′tər) s. la universidad donde uno se ha recibido.
al·ma·nac (ôl′mə-năk′) s. almanaque *m.*
al·might·y (ôl-mī′tē) adj. todopoderoso.
al·mond (ä′mənd) s. *(tree)* almendro; *(nut)* almendra.
al·most (ôl′mōst′, -′) adv. casi, por poco.
alms (ämz) s.pl. limosna, caridad *f.*
al·oe (ăl′ō) s. áloe *m*, alcíbar *m.*
a·loft (ə-lôft′) adv. *(in the air)* en el aire; *(in flight)* en vuelo; MARÍT. en la arboladura.
a·lone (ə-lōn′) **I.** adj. solo; *(with nothing added)* solamente, en sí mismo ♦ **let a.** sin mencionar, mucho menos • **to leave** *o* **let a.** no molestar, dejar en paz • **to stand a.** ser único **II.** adv. *(only)* sólo, solamente ♦ *(by oneself)* a solas.
a·long (ə-lông′) **I.** adv. *(in line with)* a lo largo de; *(forward)* adelante; *(with one)* consigo ♦ **all**

a. desde el principio • **a. about** FAM. a eso de • **a. with** punto con • **to get a. with someone** llevarse bien con alguien • **to go a. with** JER. aceptar, estar conforme con (idea, plan) II. prep. a lo largo de, por.

a·long·side (:sīd′) adv. & prep. a lo largo (de), junto (a); MARÍT. al costado (de).

a·loof (ə-lōōf′) I. adj. distante, reservado II. adv. a distancia (de los otros), aparte ♦ **to keep a.** from mantenerse apartado de.

a·loud (ə-loud′) adv. en voz alta.

al·pha (ăl′fə) s. alfa ♦ **a. ray** rayo alfa.

al·pha·bet (ăl′fə-bĕt′) s. alfabeto, abecedario.

al·pha·bet·ic/i·cal (′-′ĭk) adj. alfabético.

al·pha·bet·ize (ăl′fə-bĭ-tīz′) tr. alfabetizar.

al·pha·nu·mer·ic (′-nōō-mĕr′ĭk) adj. alfanumérico.

al·pine (ăl′pīn′) adj. alpino.

al·read·y (ôl-rĕd′ē) adv. ya.

al·so (ôl′sō) adv. también, además.

al·tar (ôl′tər) s. altar m ♦ **a. boy** monaguillo.

al·tar·piece (:pēs′) s. retablo.

al·ter (ôl′tər) tr. alterar, cambiar; COST. arreglar —intr. cambiarse, transformarse.

al·ter·a·tion (ôl′tə-rā′shən) s. alteración f; COST. arreglo.

al·ter·cate (ôl′tər-kāt′) intr. altercar, disputar.

al·ter·ca·tion (′-kā′shən) s. altercado, disputa.

al·ter·nate (ôl′tər-nāt′) I. tr. & intr. alternar II. adj. (:nĭt) (substitute) sustituto, alterno; (every other) alterno III. s. (:nĭt) sustituto, suplente mf.

al·ter·nate·ly (:nĭt-lē) adv. alternativamente, por turno.

al·ter·na·tive (ôl-tûr′nə-tĭv) I. s. alternativa II. adj. alternativo.

al·ter·na·tor (ôl′tər-nā′tər) s. alternador m.

al·though (ôl-thō′) conj. aunque, si bien.

al·tim·e·ter (ăl-tĭm′ĭ-tər) s. altímetro.

al·ti·tude (ăl′tĭ-tōōd′) s. altitud f, altura ♦ **a. sickness** mal de altura, puna.

al·to (ăl′tō) adj. & s. contralto.

al·to·geth·er (ôl′tə-gĕth′ər) adv. (entirely) enteramente, del todo; (all told) en total ♦ **in the a.** FAM. en cueros.

al·tru·is·tic (ăl′trōō-ĭs′tĭk) adj. altruista.

al·um (ăl′əm) s. alumbre m.

a·lu·mi·num (ə-lōō′mə-nəm) s. aluminio.

a·lum·na (ə-lŭm′nə) s. [pl. -nae] graduada.

a·lum·nus (:nəs) s. [pl. -ni] graduado.

al·ways (ôl′wāz) adv. siempre; (forever) para siempre.

am (ăm, əm) primera persona sing. de be.

a·mal·gam (ə-măl′gəm) s. QUÍM. amalgama, aleación f; (mixture) mezcla.

a·mal·ga·mate (:gə-māt′) tr. & intr. QUÍM. amalgamar(se); COM. unir(se).

am·a·ryl·lis (ăm′ə-rĭl′ĭs) s. amarilis f.

a·mass (ə-măs′) tr. acumular, amontonar.

am·a·teur (ăm′ə-tûr′, -ə-chōōr′) I. s. (nonprofessional) amateur mf; (unskillful person) chapucero II. adj. amateur.

am·a·to·ry (ăm′ə-tôr′ē) adj. amoroso, amatorio.

a·maze (ə-māz′) tr. asombrar, sorprender.

a·mazed (ə-māzd′) adj. asombrado.

a·maze·ment (ə-māz′mənt) s. asombro.

a·maz·ing (ə-mā′zĭng) adj. (astonishing) asombroso; (surprising) sorprendente; (marvelous) maravilloso.

am·bas·sa·dor (ăm-băs′ə-dər) s. embajador m ♦ **a. at large** embajador viajero.

am·ber (ăm′bər) I. s. ámbar m II. adj. ambarino.

am·bi·ance (ăm′bē-əns) s. ambiente m.

am·bi·dex·trous (ăm′bĭ-dĕk′strəs) adj. ambidextro.

am·bi·ent (ăm′bē-ənt) adj. ambiente.

am·bi·gu·i·ty (ăm′bĭ-gyōō′ĭ-tē) s. ambigüedad f.

am·big·u·ous (ăm-bĭg′yōō-əs) adj. ambiguo.

am·bi·tion (ăm-bĭsh′ən) s. ambición f, afán m.

am·bi·tious (:əs) adj. ambicioso; (grand) grandioso.

am·biv·a·lence (ăm-bĭv′ə-ləns) s. ambivalencia.

am·biv·a·lent (:lənt) adj. ambivalente.

am·ble (ăm′bəl) intr. deambular.

am·bu·lance (ăm′byə-ləns) s. ambulancia.

am·bu·la·to·ry (:lə-tôr′ē) adj. ambulatorio.

am·bush (ăm′bōōsh′) I. s. emboscada, celada II. tr. emboscar, tender una celada a.

a·me·lio·rate (ə-mēl′yə-rāt′) tr. & intr. mejorar(se), aliviar(se).

a·me·lio·ra·tion (′-′-rā′shən) s. mejora, alivio.

a·men (ā-mĕn′, ä-mĕn′) interj. amén.

a·me·na·ble (ə-mē′nə-bəl) adj. receptivo ♦ **to be a.** to estar dispuesto a.

a·mend (ə-mĕnd′) tr. (to correct) corregir, rectificar; (to revise) enmendar.

a·mend·ment (:mənt) s. (correction) corrección f; (alteration) enmienda.

a·mends (ə-mĕndz′) s.pl. ♦ **to make a. for** dar satisfacción por.

a·men·i·ty (ə-mĕn′ĭ-tē) s. amenidad f, afabilidad f ♦ pl. (civilities) modales, cortesías; (comforts) comodidades.

A·mer·i·can (ə-mĕr′ĭ-kən) adj. americano; (of U.S.A.) norteamericano.

A·mer·i·can·ism (:kə-nĭz′əm) s. americanismo.

A·mer·i·can·ize (:nīz′) tr. americanizar.

am·e·thyst (ăm′ə-thĭst) s. amatista.

a·mi·a·ble (ā′mē-ə-bəl) adj. amable, afable.

am·i·ca·ble (ăm′ĭ-kə-bəl) adj. amigable.

a·mid(st) (ə-mĭd[st]′) prep. en medio de, entre.

a·mi·no acid (ə-mē′nō) s. aminoácido.

a·miss (ə-mĭs′) I. adj. fuera de orden II. adv. ♦ **to go a.** salir mal • **to take a.** tomar a mal.

am·i·ty (ăm′ĭ-tē) s. amistad f, concordia.

am·me·ter (ăm′mē′tər) s. amperímetro.

am·mo (ăm′ō) s. munición f.

am·mo·nia (ə-mōn′yə) s. (gas) amoníaco; (cleanser) agua amoniacal.

am·mo·ni·um (ə-mō′nē-əm) s. amonio.

am·mu·ni·tion (ăm′yə-nĭsh′ən) s. municiones f.

am·ne·sia (ăm-nē′zhə) s. amnesia.

am·ne·si·ac (:zē-ăk′) s. & adj. amnésico.

am·nes·ty (ăm′nĭ-stē) I. s. amnistía, indulto II. tr. indultar.

a·moe·ba (ə-mē′bə) s. [pl. s o -bae] ameba.

a·moe·bic (:bĭk) adj. ♦ **a. dysentery** amebiasis.

a·mong(st) (ə-mŭng[st]′) prep. entre, en medio de.

a·mor·al (ā-môr′əl) adj. amoral.

am·o·rous (ăm′ər-əs) adj. amativo.

a·mor·phous (ə-môr′fəs) adj. amorfo, informe.

am·or·tize (ăm′ər-tīz′) tr. amortizar.

a·mount (ə-mount′) I. s. cantidad f, monto II. intr. ♦ **to a. to** (to come to) subir a, ascender a; (to be equivalent to) ser igual a, (venir a) ser lo mismo que.

am·per·age (ăm′pər-ĭj) s. amperaje m.

am·pere (ăm′pîr′) s. amperio.

am·phet·a·mine (ăm-fĕt′ə-mēn′) s. anfetamina.

303

am·phib·i·an (ăm-fĭb′ē-ən) adj. & s. anfibio.
am·phib·i·ous (:ē-əs) adj. anfibio.
am·phi·the·a·ter (ăm′fə-thē′ə-tər) s. anfiteatro.
am·ple (ăm′pəl) adj. **-er, -est** *(large)* extenso, amplio; *(generous)* generoso; *(adequate)* suficiente.
am·pli·fi·er (ăm′plə-fī′ər) s. amplificador *m.*
am·pli·fy (ăm′plə-fī′) tr. ELECTRÓN. amplificar; *(an idea)* desarrollar.
am·pli·tude (ăm′plĭ-tōōd′) s. amplitud *f* ♦ **a. modulation** modulación de amplitud.
am·ply (ăm′plē) adv. ampliamente.
am·pu·tate (ăm′pyə-tāt′) tr. amputar.
am·pu·ta·tion (′-tā′shən) s. amputación *f.*
am·pu·tee (:tē′) s. amputado.
a·muck (ə-mŭk′) adv. ♦ **to run a.** abandonarse a la furia, volverse loco.
am·u·let (ăm′yə-lĭt) s. amuleto, talismán *m.*
a·muse (ə-myōōz′) tr. entretener, divertir ♦ **to a. oneself** divertirse, entretenerse.
a·muse·ment (:mənt) s. *(pastime)* entretenimiento; *(laughter)* risa.
a·mus·ing (ə-myōō′zĭng) adj. entretenido, divertido.
am·yl (ăm′əl) s. amilo.
an (ən, ăn) cf. **a.**
a·nach·ro·nism (ə-năk′rə-nĭz′əm) s. anacronismo.
a·nach·ro·nis·tic (′-nĭs′tĭk) adj. anacrónico.
an·a·gram (ăn′ə-grăm′) s. anagrama *m.*
a·nal (ā′nəl) adj. anal.
an·al·ge·sic (ăn′əl-jē′zĭk) s. & adj. analgésico.
an·a·log computer (ăn′ə-lôg′) s. computadora analógica.
a·nal·o·gous (ə-năl′ə-gəs) adj. análogo.
a·nal·o·gy (ə-năl′ə-jē) s. *(correspondence)* analogía, semejanza; *(correlation)* correlación *f.*
a·nal·y·sis (ə-năl′ĭ-sĭs) s. [pl. **-ses**] análisis *m*; PSIC. psicoanálisis *m.*
an·a·lyst (ăn′ə-lĭst) s. analista *mf.*
an·a·lyt·ic/i·cal (′-lĭt′ĭk) adj. analítico.
an·a·lyze (ăn′ə-līz′) tr. analizar; PSIC. psicoanalizar.
an·ar·chic/chi·cal (ăn-är′kĭk) adj. anárquico.
an·ar·chist (ăn′ər-kĭst) s. anarquista *mf.*
an·ar·chy (:kē) s. anarquía.
a·nath·e·ma (ə-năth′ə-mə) s. anatema *m.*
a·nath·e·ma·tize (:tīz′) tr. anatematizar.
an·a·tom·ic/i·cal (ăn′ə-tŏm′ĭk) adj. anatómico.
a·nat·o·mist (ə-năt′ə-mĭst) s. anatomista *mf.*
a·nat·o·mize (:mīz′) tr. anatomizar.
a·nat·o·my (:mē) s. anatomía; FIG. análisis *m* (de obra, crimen); *(body)* cuerpo humano.
an·ces·tor (ăn′sĕs′tər) s. antepasado.
an·ces·tral (′-trəl) adj. ancestral.
an·ces·try (′′ trē) s. linaje *m*, abolengo.
an·chor (ăng′kər) I. s. ancla, áncora; FIG. soporte *m*; TELEV. locutor *m*, anunciador *m* ♦ **at a.** anclado ♦ **to cast a.** echar anclas ♦ **to weigh a.** levar anclas, zarpar II. intr. anclar, fondear —tr. sujetar, asegurar.
an·chor·age (:ĭj) s. ancladero, fondeadero.
an·chor·man (:măn′) s. [pl. **-men**] locutor *m*, anunciador *m.*
an·cho·vy (ăn′chō′vē) s. [pl. inv. o **-vies**] anchoa.
an·cient (ăn′shənt) I. adj. antiguo, vetusto II. s. anciano ♦ pl. (los) antiguos.
an·cil·lar·y (ăn′sə-lĕr′ē) adj. auxiliar.
and (ənd, ănd) conj. y, e ♦ **try a. come** trata de venir ♦ **go a. see** anda a ver.

and·i·ron (ănd′ī′ərn) s. morillo.
an·droid (ăn′droid′) s. androide *m*, robot *m.*
an·ec·do·tal (ăn′ĭk-dōt′l) adj. anecdótico.
an·ec·dote (ăn′ĭk-dōt′) s. anécdota.
a·ne·mi·a (ə-nē′mē-ə) s. anemia.
a·ne·mic (:mĭk) adj. anémico.
an·e·mom·e·ter (ăn′ə-mŏm′ĭ-tər) s. anemómetro.
a·nem·o·ne (ə-něm′ə-nē) s. anémona.
an·es·the·sia (ăn′ĭs-thē′zhə) s. anestesia.
an·es·the·si·ol·o·gy (:thē′zē-ŏl′ə-jē) s. anestesiología.
an·es·thet·ic (:thĕt′ĭk) s. & adj. anestésico.
a·nes·the·tist (ə-nĕs′thĭ-tĭst) s. anestesista *mf.*
a·nes·the·tize (:tīz′) tr. anestesiar.
an·eu·rysm (ăn′yə-rĭz′əm) s. aneurisma *m.*
a·new (ə-nōō′) adv. nuevamente, de nuevo.
an·gel (ān′jəl) s. ángel *m.*
an·gel·ic/i·cal (ăn-jĕl′ĭk) adj. angélico, angelical.
an·ger (ăng′gər) I. s. ira, enojo II. tr. & intr. airar(se), enojar(se).
an·gle[1] (ăng′gəl) intr. pescar con caña ♦ **to a.** for FIG. ir a la pesca de.
an·gle[2] I. s. ángulo; *(corner)* esquina, codo; *(point of view)* ángulo, punto de vista; *(scheme)* ardid *m* ♦ **at an a.** en ángulo • **at right angles** en ángulo recto II. tr. & intr. mover(se) en ángulo.
an·gler (:glər) s. pescador *m* (de caña).
an·gle·worm (:wûrm′) s. lombriz *f.*
An·gli·can (ăng′glĭ-kən) adj. & s. anglicano.
An·gli·cize (:sīz′) tr. anglicanizar.
an·gling (ăng′glĭng) s. pesca con caña.
An·glo-Sax·on (ăng′glō-săk′sən) adj. & s. anglosajón *m.*
an·gri·ly (ăng′grə-lē) adv. con enojo, con ira.
an·gry (ăng′grē) adj. **-i-** enojado, enfadado; *(sky)* amenazador; MED. enconado ♦ **to be a. at** *o* **about (something)** estar enojado por (algo) • **to make (someone) a.** enojar (a alguien).
angst (ăngkst) s. angustia, ansiedad *f.*
an·guish (ăng′gwĭsh) I. s. angustia, congoja II. tr. & intr. angustiar(se), acongojar(se).
an·guished (:gwĭsht) adj. angustiado, acongojado.
an·hy·drous (ăn-hī′drəs) adj. anhidro.
an·i·lin(e) (ăn′ə-lĭn) s. anilina ♦ **a. dye** color de anilina.
an·i·ma (ăn′ə-mə) s. alma, espíritu *m.*
an·i·mal (ăn′ə-məl) adj. & s. animal *m.*
an·i·mal·cule (′-măl′kyōōl) s. animáculo.
an·i·mal·is·tic (:mə-lĭs′tĭk) adj. como o de animal.
an·i·mate (ăn′ə-māt′) I. tr. animar II. adj. (:mĭt) animado, viviente.
an·i·mat·ed (:mā′tĭd) adj. animado, vivaz ♦ **a. cartoon** dibujos animados.
an·i·ma·tion (′-′shən) s. animación *f*, vivacidad *f* ♦ **suspended a.** muerte aparente.
an·i·mism (ăn′ə-mĭz′əm) s. animismo.
an·i·mos·i·ty (ăn′ə-mŏs′ĭ-tē) s. animosidad *f.*
an·i·mus (′-məs) s. animosidad *f.*
an·i·on (ăn′ī′ən) s. anión *m*, ion negativo.
an·ise (ăn′ĭs) s. anís *m.*
an·i·sette (ăn′ĭ-sĕt′) s. anisete *m.*
an·kle (ăng′kəl) s. tobillo.
an·kle·bone (:bōn′) s. hueso del tobillo, taba.
an·klet (ăng′klĭt) s. *(ornament)* ajorca para el tobillo; *(socks)* media tobillera.
an·nals (ăn′əlz) s.pl. anales *m.*
an·neal (ə-nēl′) tr. recocer (cristal, metales).

an·ne·lid (ăn'ə-lĭd) adj. & s. anélido.
an·nex I. tr. (ə-nĕks') anexar, anexionar II. s. (ăn'ĕks') anexo.
an·nex·a·tion (ăn'ĭk-sā'shən) s. anexión f.
an·ni·hi·late (ə-nī'ə-lāt') tr. aniquilar.
an·ni·hi·la·tion (-'-lā'shən) s. aniquilación f.
an·ni·ver·sa·ry (ăn'ə-vûr'sə-rē) s. aniversario.
an·no·tate (ăn'ə-tāt') tr. anotar.
an·no·ta·tion ('-tā'shən) s. anotación f, nota.
an·nounce (ə-nouns') tr. anunciar, declarar.
an·nounce·ment (:mənt) s. anuncio, declaración f.
an·nounc·er (ə-noun'sər) s. anunciador m, locutor m.
an·noy (ə-noi') tr. molestar, fastidiar.
an·noy·ance (:əns) s. molestia, fastidio.
an·noy·ing (:ĭng) adj. molesto, irritante.
an·nu·al (ăn'yōō-əl) I. adj. anual II. s. (year-book) anuario; BOT. planta anual.
an·nu·al·ly (:ə-lē) adv. anualmente, cada año.
an·nu·i·ty (ə-nōō'ĭ-tē) s. (payment) anualidad f; (income for life) renta vitalicia.
an·nul (ə-nŭl') tr. **-ll-** (to nullify) anular, invalidar; (to cancel) cancelar.
an·nul·ment (:mənt) s. (invalidation) anulación f, invalidación f; (cancellation) cancelación f.
an·ode (ăn'ōd') s. ánodo.
an·o·dyne (ăn'ə-dīn') adj. & s. anodino.
a·noint (ə-noint') tr. untar; RELIG. ungir.
a·nom·a·lous (ə-nŏm'ə-ləs) adj. anómalo.
a·nom·a·ly (:lē) s. anomalía.
an·o·nym·i·ty (ăn'ə-nĭm'ĭ-tē) s. anonimato.
a·non·y·mous (ə-nŏn'ə-məs) adj. anónimo.
a·noph·e·les (ə-nŏf'ə-lēz') s. anofeles m.
an·oth·er (ə-nŭth'ər) I. adj. otro; (different) (otro) distinto; (additional) más ♦ **a. one** otro más • **a. time** otro día • **without a. word** sin más palabras II. pron. otro ♦ **one a.** uno(s) a otro(s).
an·swer (ăn'sər) I. s. respuesta, contestación f; (solution) solución f, resultado; (reason) explicación f, razón f ♦ **to know all the answers** saberlo todo II. intr. dar contestación, responder; (to suffice) servir; (to match) corresponder (to a) ♦ **answering machine** contestador automático (de teléfono) • **to a. back** replicar con insolencia —tr. responder a, contestar a; (correctly) resolver, solucionar (problema, enigma) ♦ **to a. for** ser responsable por • **to a. the telephone** contestar el teléfono.
an·swer·a·ble (ə-bəl) adj. responsable (for por).
ant (ănt) s. hormiga.
ant·ac·id (ănt-ăs'ĭd) adj. & s. antiácido.
an·tag·o·nism (ăn-tăg'ə-nĭz'əm) s. antagonismo, rivalidad f.
an·tag·o·nis·tic (-'-nĭs'tĭk) adj. antagónico.
an·tag·o·nize ('-nīz') tr. provocar la hostilidad de.
an·te (ăn'tē) s. apuesta inicial (en póker).
ant·eat·er (ănt'ē'tər) s. oso hormiguero.
an·te·cede (ăn'tĭ-sēd') tr. & intr. anteceder (a).
an·te·ce·dent (:nt) adj. & s. antecedente m.
an·te·date (ăn'tĭ-dāt') tr. preceder (en tiempo); (a document) antedatar.
an·te·di·lu·vi·an ('-də-lōō'vē-ən) adj. antediluviano; FIG. anticuado.
an·te·lope (ăn'tl-ōp') s. [pl. inv. o **s**] antílope m.
an·ten·na (ăn-tĕn'ə) s. ZOOL. [pl. **-nae**] antena; RAD. [pl. **-nas**] antena.
an·te·room (ăn'tē-rōōm') s. antesala.

an·them (ăn'thəm) s. (hymn) himno <national a. himno nacional>; RELIG. antífona.
an·ther (ăn'thər) s. antera, borlilla.
ant·hill (ănt'hĭl') s. hormiguero.
an·thol·o·gize (ăn-thŏl'ə-jīz') tr. compilar.
an·thol·o·gy (:jē) s. antología.
an·thra·cite (ăn'thrə-sīt') s. antracita.
an·thrax (ăn'thrăks') s. ántrax m.
an·thro·po·cen·tric (ăn'thrə-pə-sĕn'trĭk) adj. antropocéntrico.
an·thro·pol·o·gist (:pŏl'ə-jĭst) s. antropólogo.
an·thro·pol·o·gy (:pŏl'ə-jē) s. antropología.
an·ti·a·bor·tion (ăn'tē-ə-bôr'shən) adj. que se opone al aborto.
an·ti·air·craft (:âr'krăft') adj. antiaéreo.
an·ti·bal·lis·tic (:bə-lĭs'tĭk) adj. antibalístico.
an·ti·bi·ot·ic (:bī-ŏt'ĭk) s. & adj. antibiótico.
an·ti·bod·y (ăn'tĭ-bŏd'ē) s. anticuerpo.
an·tics (ăn'tĭks) s.pl. travesuras.
an·ti·christ (ăn'tĭ-krīst') s. anticristo.
an·tic·i·pate (ăn-tĭs'ə-pāt') tr. (to foresee) anticipar, prever; (to expect) esperar, contar con; (with pleasure) gozar de antemano; (to forestall) adelantarse, anticiparse a.
an·tic·i·pa·tion (-'-pā'shən) s. (act) anticipación f; (expectation) expectación f, esperanza; (eagerness) ilusión f.
an·ti·cli·mac·tic (ăn'tē-klī-măk'tĭk) adj. decepcionante.
an·ti·cli·max (:klī'măks') s. anticlímax m, decepción f.
an·ti·com·mu·nist (:kŏm'yə-nĭst) s. & adj. anticomunista mf.
an·ti·dote (ăn'tĭ-dōt') s. antídoto.
an·ti·freeze (:frēz') s. anticongelante m.
an·ti·gen (:jən) s. antígeno.
an·ti·he·ro (:hîr'ō) s. [pl. **es**] protagonista m que es todo lo contrario del héroe clásico.
an·ti·his·ta·mine (ăn'tē-hĭs'tə-mēn') s. antihistamínico.
an·ti·ma·lar·i·al (:mə-lâr'ē-əl) I. adj. antipalúdico II. s. droga antipalúdica.
an·ti·mat·ter (ăn'tĭ-măt'ər) s. antimateria.
an·ti·mo·ny (ăn'tə-mō'nē) s. antimonio.
an·tip·a·thy (ăn-tĭp'ə-thē) s. antipatía.
an·ti·per·spi·rant (ăn'tē-pûr'spər-ənt) adj. & s. antisudoral m, desodorante m.
an·tip·o·des (ăn-tĭp'ə-dēz') s.pl. antípodas f.
an·ti·quar·i·an (ăn'tĭ-kwâr'ē-ən) s. anticuario.
an·ti·quat·ed ('-kwā'tĭd) adj. anticuado.
an·tique (ăn-tēk') I. adj. (ancient) antiguo; (old) viejo, anticuado; (furniture) de época II. s. antigüedad f, antigualla.
an·tiq·ui·ty (ăn-tĭk'wĭ-tē) s. antigüedad f.
an·ti·rust (ăn'tē-rŭst') adj. & s. antioxidante m.
an·ti·Sem·ite (:sĕm'īt') s. antisemita mf.
an·ti·Se·mit·ic (:sə-mĭt'ĭk) adj. antisemítico.
an·ti·sep·tic (ăn'tĭ-sĕp'tĭk) adj. & s. antiséptico.
an·ti·se·rum ('-sîr'əm) s. [pl. **s** o **-ra**] antisuero.
an·ti·slav·er·y (ăn'tē-slā'və-rē) adj. en contra de la esclavitud, antiesclavista.
an·ti·so·cial (:sō'shəl) adj. antisocial.
an·ti·tank (:tăngk') adj. antitanque.
an·ti·ter·ror·ism (:tĕr'ə-rĭz'əm) s. antiterrorismo.
an·ti·theft device (:thĕft') s. dispositivo antirrobo.
an·tith·e·sis (ăn-tĭth'ĭ-sĭs) s. [pl. **-ses**] antítesis f, contraste m.
an·ti·thet·i·cal (ăn'tĭ-thĕt'ĭ-kəl) adj. antitético.
an·ti·tox·in (ăn'tē-tŏk'sĭn) s. antitoxina.

an·ti·trust (:trŭst´) adj. antimonopolio.
an·ti·ven·in (:vĕn´ən) s. contraveneno.
ant·ler (ănt´lər) s. asta, mogote m.
an·to·nym (ăn´tə-nĭm´) s. antónimo.
a·nus (ā´nəs) s. ano.
an·vil (ăn´vĭl) s. yunque m.
anx·i·e·ty (ăng-zī´ĭ-tē) s. ansiedad f, ansia;
PSIC. angustia.
anx·ious (ăngk´shəs) adj. (worried) ansioso, inquieto; (eager) deseoso, anhelante.
an·y (ĕn´ē) I. adj. (no matter which) cualquier <a. book cualquier libro>; (some) algún <do you have a. doubt? ¿tienes alguna duda?>; (negative) algún, ningún <there isn't a. reason no hay ninguna razón>; (every) cualquiera, todo <we must avoid a. contact debemos evitar todo contacto> ♦ a. minute pronto • at a. cost a toda costa • at a. rate o in a. case de todos modos II. pron. alguno, cualquiera; (negative) ninguno • if a. si los hay III. adv. algo, de algún modo <do you feel a. better? ¿te sientes algo mejor?>; (negative) nada, para nada <I don't feel a. better no me siento nada mejor> ♦ a. longer más tiempo, todavía.
an·y·bod·y (:bŏd´ē) pron. cualquiera, quienquiera, cualquier persona <a. could do it cualquiera podría hacerlo>; (interrogative) alguien, alguno <did you see a.? ¿viste a alguien?>; (negative) ninguno, nadie <I didn't see a. no vi a nadie>.
an·y·how (:hou´) adv. (even so) de todas maneras, de todos modos; (carelessly) de cualquier manera.
an·y·more (´-môr´) adv. (negative) nunca más, ya más, ya no <I don't run a. ya no corro más>; (interrogative) aún, todavía <do you run a.? ¿corres todavía?>.
an·y·one (´-wŭn´) cf. anybody.
an·y·place (:plās´) cf. anywhere.
an·y·thing (:thĭng´) pron. (interrogative) algo, alguna cosa <are you doing a. now? ¿estás haciendo algo ahora?>; (negative) nada, ninguna cosa <I can't see a. no veo nada>; (affirmative) cualquier cosa, todo lo que <take a. you like toma todo lo que quieras> ♦ a. else? ¿algo más?, ¿alguna otra cosa? • like a. FAM. a más no poder.
an·y·time (:tīm´) adv. a cualquier hora, en cualquier momento.
an·y·way (:wā´) adv. (in any case) de cualquier manera, de cualquier modo; (even so) lo mismo, de todos modos.
an·y·where (:hwâr´) adv. (affirmative) dondequiera, a o en cualquier sitio o parte; (negative) en, a, o por ninguna parte o ningún lado; (interrogative) en algún lugar, en alguna parte ♦ a. from FAM. entre <you can save a. from five to ten dollars puedes ahorrar entre cinco y diez dólares>.
A-OK o **A-o·kay** (ā´ō-kā´) adj. & adv. perfecto, excelente.
a·pace (ə-pās´) adv. rápidamente, velozmente.
a·part (ə-pärt´) adv. aparte, a distancia ♦ a. from aparte de, con la excepción de • to come a. desprenderse, desunirse • to fall a. descomponerse; FIG. venirse abajo • to keep a. apartar, separar • to take a. desarmar, desmontar • to tear a. despedazar, destrozar • to tell a. distinguir, diferenciar • to stand a. mantenerse apartado; FIG. distinguirse • to set a. reservar, poner a un lado.
a·part·ment (ə-pärt´mənt) s. (residence) departamento, apartamento; (room) cuarto ♦ a. house casa o edificio de departamentos.
ap·a·thet·ic (ăp´ə-thĕt´ĭk) adj. apático.
ap·a·thy (´-thē) s. apatía.
ape (āp) I. s. mono; FIG. imitamonos mf II. tr. imitar, remedar.
a·pé·ri·tif (ä´pĕr´ĭ-tēf´) s. aperitivo.
ap·er·ture (ăp´ər-chər) s. abertura.
a·pex (ā´pĕks´) s. [pl. es o -pices] ápice m; FIG. cima, cumbre m.
a·pha·sia (ə-fā´zhə) s. afasia.
a·phid (ā´fĭd) s. pulgón m.
aph·o·rism (ăf´ə-rĭz´əm) s. aforismo, refrán m.
aph·ro·dis·i·ac (ăf´rə-dīz´ē-ăk´) adj. & s. afrodisíaco.
a·pi·ar·y (ā´pē-ĕr´ē) s. abejar m, colmenar m.
a·piece (ə-pēs´) adv. por cabeza, cada uno.
a·plomb (ə-plŏm´) s. aplomo.
a·poc·a·lypse (ə-pŏk´ə-lĭps´) s. revelación f.
a·poc·a·lyp·tic (-´-lĭp´tĭk) adj. apocalíptico.
a·poc·ry·phal (ə-pŏk´rə-fəl) adj. apócrifo.
ap·o·gee (ăp´ə-jē) s. apogeo.
a·po·lit·i·cal (ā´pə-lĭt´ĭ-kəl) adj. apolítico.
a·po·lo·get·ic (ə-pŏl´ə-jĕt´ĭk) adj. lleno de disculpas.
a·po·lo·get·i·cal·ly (:ĭ-kə-lē) adv. disculpándose.
a·pol·o·gist (ə-pŏl´ə-jĭst) s. apologista mf.
a·pol·o·gize (:jīz´) intr. disculparse (for por, de) (to con).
a·pol·o·gy (:jē) s. (for an offense) disculpa; (formal defense) apología ♦ to make an a. disculparse.
ap·o·plec·tic (ăp´ə-plĕk´tĭk) adj. apoplético.
a·pos·tate (ə-pŏs´tāt´) s. apóstata mf.
a·pos·tle (ə-pŏs´əl) s. apóstol mf.
ap·os·tol·ic (ăp´ə-stŏl´ĭk) adj. apostólico.
a·pos·tro·phe (ə-pŏs´trə-fē) s. GRAM. apóstrofo; RET. apóstrofe m.
a·poth·e·car·y (ə-pŏth´ĭ-kĕr´ē) s. boticario.
a·poth·e·o·sis (ə-pŏth´ē-ō´sĭs) s. [pl. -ses] apoteosis f.
ap·pall (ə-pôl´) tr. pasmar, horrorizar.
ap·pall·ing (ə-pô´lĭng) adj. pasmoso, horrendo.
ap·pa·ra·tus (ăp´ə-rā´təs, -răt´əs) s. [pl. inv. o es] aparato; (mechanism) mecanismo.
ap·par·el (ə-păr´əl) s. ropa, indumentaria.
ap·par·ent (ə-păr´ənt) adj. (seeming) aparente; (perceptible) evidente, claro.
ap·par·ent·ly (:lē) adv. (seemingly) aparentemente, por lo visto; (obviously) evidentemente.
ap·pa·ri·tion (ăp´ə-rĭsh´ən) s. aparición f.
ap·peal (ə-pēl´) I. s. (plea) súplica; (a call for) llamada; (petition) petición f, instancia; (charm) atracción f, encanto; DER. apelación f, recurso ♦ without a. DER. sin recurso, inapelable II. intr. ♦ to a. to suplicar a; DER. recurrir a, apelar a; (to be attractive) tener atractivo para —tr. llevar a un tribunal superior.
ap·peal·ing (ə-pē´lĭng) adj. atrayente.
ap·pear (ə-pîr´) intr. (to come into view) aparecer, asomarse; (to seem) parecer; (to present oneself) presentarse; (on the stage) actuar; (in court) comparecer; (in print) publicarse.
ap·pear·ance (:əns) s. (act) aparición f; (looks) aspecto, apariencia; (pretense) pretensión f, simulación f ♦ to make an a. hacer acto de presencia ♦ pl. apariencias, exterioridad.
ap·pease (ə-pēz´) tr. apaciguar, aplacar.
ap·pease·ment (:mənt) s. apaciguamiento.
ap·pel·lant (ə-pĕl´ənt) I. adj. de apelación II. s. apelante mf.

ap·pel·late (:īt) adj. de apelación.
ap·pel·la·tion (ăp'ə-lā'shən) s. nombre m.
ap·pend (ə-pĕnd') tr. anexar, adjuntar.
ap·pend·age (ə-pĕn'dĭj) s. apéndice m.
ap·pen·dec·to·my (ăp'ən-dĕk'tə-mē) s. apendectomía.
ap·pen·di·ci·tis (ə-pĕn'dĭ-sī'tĭs) s. apendicitis f.
ap·pen·dix (ə-pĕn'dĭks) s. [pl. **es** o **-dices**] apéndice m.
ap·pe·tite (ăp'ĭ-tīt') s. apetito, apetencia.
ap·pe·tiz·er (:tī'zər) s. aperitivo.
ap·pe·tiz·ing (:zĭng) adj. apetitoso, gustoso.
ap·plaud (ə-plôd') tr. & intr. aplaudir.
ap·plause (ə-plôz') s. aplauso.
ap·ple (ăp'əl) s. manzana ♦ **a. tree** manzano.
ap·ple·sauce (:sôs') s. compota de manzana.
ap·pli·ance (ə-plī'əns) s. artefacto, aparato ♦ **household a.** aparato electrodoméstico.
ap·pli·cant (ăp'lĭ-kənt) s. aspirante mf.
ap·pli·ca·tion ('-kā'shən) s. (act) aplicación f; (relevance) correspondencia, pertinencia; (diligence) esmero; (request) solicitación f; (form) solicitud f, aplicación.
ap·pli·ca·tor ('-kā'tər) s. aplicador m.
ap·pli·qué (ăp'lĭ-kā') s. aplicación, aplicación f.
ap·ply (ə-plī') tr. (to put on) aplicar; (to use) emplear, usar (to para) ♦ **to a. oneself** to aplicarse a —intr. ser pertinente o aplicable ♦ **to a. for** solicitar (empleo, admisión).
ap·point (ə-point') tr. (to designate) nombrar, designar; (a date) fijar, determinar.
ap·point·ed (ə-poin'tĭd) adj. nombrado, designado.
ap·point·ee (-'tē') s. persona designada.
ap·point·ment (ə-point'mənt) s. (act) nombramiento, designación f; (post) puesto, cargo; (date) cita, compromiso.
ap·por·tion (ə-pôr'shən) tr. prorratear.
ap·prais·al (ə-prā'zəl) s. tasación f.
ap·praise (ə-prāz') tr. evaluar, tasar.
ap·pre·cia·ble (ə-prē'shə-bəl) adj. perceptible, sensible.
ap·pre·cia·bly (:blē) adv. sensiblemente.
ap·pre·ci·ate (ə-prē'shē-āt') tr. (to recognize) darse cuenta de, reconocer; (to value) apreciar, estimar; (to be grateful for) agradecer —intr. valorizarse, subir de precio o valor.
ap·pre·ci·a·tion ('-ā'shən) s. (recognition) apreciación f, reconocimiento; (gratitude) gratitud f; COM. valorización f.
ap·pre·cia·tive (ə-prē'shə-tĭv) adj. apreciador, agradecido.
ap·pre·hend (ăp'rĭ-hĕnd') tr. (to arrest) aprehender, arrestar; (to understand) comprender.
ap·pre·hen·sion (:hĕn'shən) s. (dread) aprensión f; (arrest) aprehensión f; (understanding) comprensión f.
ap·pre·hen·sive (:sĭv) adj. aprensivo.
ap·pren·tice (ə-prĕn'tĭs) **I.** s. aprendiz m **II.** tr. poner de aprendiz.
ap·pren·tice·ship (:shĭp') s. aprendizaje m.
ap·prise (ə-prīz') tr. informar, notificar.
ap·proach (ə-prōch') **I.** intr. aproximarse, acercarse —tr. aproximarse a, acercarse a; (to make overtures to) abordar; (to take up) abordar, emprender (tarea, asunto) **II.** s. (act) acercamiento; (access) acceso, vía de entrada; (overture) proposición f, propuesta; (method) método, enfoque m (de un asunto, situación).
ap·proach·ing (ə-prō'chĭng) adj. (upcoming) venidero, próximo; (nearing) que se acerca.
ap·pro·ba·tion (ăp'rə-bā'shən) s. aprobación f.

ap·pro·pri·ate (ə-prō'prē-ĭt) **I.** adj. apropiado, adecuado **II.** tr. (:āt') (to set apart) destinar, consignar; (to seize) apropiarse de.
ap·pro·pri·a·tion (-'-ā'shən) s. (act) apropiación f; (allocation) asignación f.
ap·prov·al (ə-prōō'vəl) s. aprobación f, sanción f ♦ **on a.** a prueba.
ap·prove (ə-prōōv') tr. (to endorse) aprobar, consentir; (to ratify) sancionar, ratificar —intr. dar su aprobación, aprobar.
ap·prox·i·mate (ə-prŏk'sə-mĭt) **I.** adj. aproximado **II.** tr. & intr. (:māt') aproximar(se), acercar(se).
ap·prox·i·ma·tion (-'-mā'shən) s. aproximación f.
ap·pur·te·nance (ə-pûr'tn-əns) s. accesorio.
a·pri·cot (ăp'rĭ-kŏt', ā'prĭ-) s. albaricoque m.
A·pril (ā'prəl) s. abril m.
a·pron (ā'prən) s. delantal m; AVIA. pista (delante de los hangares) ♦ **to be tied to (a mother's) a. strings** estar cosido a las faldas de (la madre).
ap·ro·pos (ăp'rə-pō') **I.** adj. adecuado, oportuno **II.** adv. & prep. a propósito (de).
apse (ăps) s. ábside m.
apt (ăpt) adj. (suitable) apropiado, acertado; (inclined) propenso; (bright) apto, listo.
ap·ti·tude (ăp'tĭ-tōōd') s. aptitud f, capacidad f.
aq·ua·ma·rine (ăk'wə-mə-rēn') s. (color) aguamarina.
aq·ua·plane (ăk'wə-plān') s. acuaplano.
a·quar·i·um (ə-kwâr'ē-əm) s. [pl. **s** o **-ia**] acuario.
a·quat·ic (ə-kwŏt'ĭk) adj. acuático, acuátil.
aq·ua·tint (ăk'wə-tĭnt') s. (process) acuatinta; (etching) grabado al acuatinta.
aq·ue·duct (ăk'wĭ-dŭkt') s. acueducto.
a·que·ous (ā'kwē-əs) adj. acuoso, ácueo.
aq·ui·fer (ăk'wə-fər) s. roca acuífera.
aq·ui·line (ăk'wə-lĭn') adj. aguileño, aquilino.
ar·a·besque (ăr'ə-bĕsk') s. arabesco.
Ar·a·bic numeral (ăr'ə-bĭk) s. número arábigo.
ar·a·ble (ăr'ə-bəl) adj. arable, cultivable.
a·rach·nid (ə-răk'nĭd) s. arácnido.
ar·bi·ter (ăr'bĭ-tər) s. árbitro.
ar·bi·trar·y (:trĕr'ē) adj. arbitrario.
ar·bi·trate (:trāt') tr. & intr. arbitrar.
ar·bi·tra·tion ('-trā'shən) s. arbitraje m.
ar·bi·tra·tor ('-trā'tər) s. arbitrador m, árbitro.
ar·bor (ăr'bər) s. enramada, pérgola.
ar·bo·re·al (ăr-bôr'ē-əl) adj. arbóreo.
ar·bor·vi·tae (ăr'bər-vī'tē) s. árbol m de la vida.
arc (ărk) **I.** s. arco ♦ **a. lamp** lámpara de arco • **electric a.** arco voltaico **II.** intr. **-c(k)-** formar arco.
ar·cade (ăr-kād') s. arcada; (roofed passageway) galería.
ar·cane (ăr-kān') adj. arcano.
arch¹ (ărch) **I.** s. arco **II.** tr. (to bend) enarcar, arquear; (to span) atravesar —intr. arquearse.
arch² (ărch) adj. (principal) principal; (mischievous) astuto, pícaro.
ar·chae·o·log·i·cal (ăr'kē-ə-lŏj'ĭ-kəl) adj. arqueológico.
ar·chae·ol·o·gist (:öl'ə-jĭst) s. arqueólogo.
ar·chae·ol·o·gy (:jē) s. arqueología.
ar·cha·ic (ăr-kā'ĭk) adj. arcaico.
arch·an·gel (ărk'ān'jəl) s. arcángel m.
arch·bish·op (ărch-bĭsh'əp) s. arzobispo.
arched (ărcht) adj. arqueado, enarcado.
arch·en·e·my (ărch-ĕn'ə-mē) s. enemigo acé-

rrimo, el mayor enemigo.

arch·er (är′chər) s. arquero (de arco y flecha).

arch·er·y (är′chə-rē) s. tiro de arco y flecha.

ar·che·type (är′kĭ-tīp′) s. arquetipo, prototipo.

ar·chi·pel·a·go (är′kə-pĕl′ə-gō′) s. [pl. **(e)s**] archipiélago.

ar·chi·tect (är′kĭ-tĕkt′) s. arquitecto.

ar·chi·tec·tur·al (′-tĕk′chər-əl) adj. arquitectónico.

ar·chi·tec·ture (är′kĭ-tĕk′chər) s. arquitectura.

ar·chive (är′kīv′) s. archivo.

ar·chi·vist (är′kə-vĭst) s. archivista mf.

arch·priest (ärch-prēst′) s. arcipreste m.

arch·way (ärch′wā′) s. arcada, arco.

arc·tic (ärk′tĭk, är′tĭk) adj. frígido, glacial.

ar·dent (är′dnt) adj. ardiente, vehemente.

ar·dor (är′dər) s. ardor m, pasión f.

ar·du·ous (är′jōō-əs) adj. arduo, penoso.

are (är) segunda persona sing. y pl. de **be**.

ar·e·a (âr′ē-ə) s. área; (region) zona, región f ♦ **a. code** prefijo telefónico.

a·re·na (ə-rē′nə) s. (circus ring) arena, pista; (auditorium) estadio; FIG. área, campo.

aren't (ärnt, är′ənt) contr. de **are not**.

ar·gon (är′gŏn′) argón m, argo.

ar·got (är′gō, ′-gət) s. argot m.

ar·gu·a·ble (är′gyōō-ə-bəl) adj. discutible, disputable.

ar·gue (är′gyōō) tr. (to debate) argüir, presentar; (to maintain) razonar, argumentar; (to persuade) persuadir, convencer —intr. (to debate) argumentar, argüir (en favor o en contra de algo); (to quarrel) disputar, discutir.

ar·gu·ment (är′gyə-mənt) s. (debate) discusión f, debate m; (quarrel) pelea, disputa; (contention) razonamiento, argumento.

ar·gu·men·ta·tion (′-mĕn-tā′shən) s. (act) argumentación f; (debate) debate m.

ar·gu·men·ta·tive (′-′tə-tĭv) adj. discutidor.

a·ri·a (ä′rē-ə) s. aria.

ar·id (är′ĭd) adj. árido, seco.

a·rid·i·ty (ə-rĭd′ĭ-tē) s. aridez f, sequedad f.

a·right (ə-rīt′) adv. correctamente, rectamente.

a·rise (ə-rīz′) intr. arose, -n (to get up) levantarse, ponerse en pie; (to ascend) ascender, elevarse; (to originate) surgir, originarse.

ar·is·toc·ra·cy (är′ĭ-stŏk′rə-sē) s. aristocracia.

a·ris·to·crat (ə-rĭs′tə-krăt′) s. aristócrata mf.

a·ris·to·crat·ic (′-′ĭk) adj. aristocrático.

Ar·is·to·te·lian (är′ĭ-stə-tē′lē-ən) adj. aristotélico.

a·rith·me·tic (ə-rĭth′mĭ-tĭk) s. aritmética.

ar·ith·met·ic/i·cal (är′ĭth-mĕt′ĭk) adj. aritmético.

ark (ärk) s. arca, barcaza.

arm¹ (ärm) s. ANAT. brazo ♦ **a. in a.** tomados del brazo • **to keep at a.'s length** mantener a distancia prudencial.

arm² I. s. MIL. arma ♦ **arms race** carrera de armamentos • **to be up in arms** alzarse en armas; FIG. poner el grito en el cielo • **to bear arms** llevar las armas • **to lay down one's arms** rendir las armas II. tr. armar.

ar·ma·ment (är′mə-mənt) s. armamento ♦ pl. armas, armamento.

ar·ma·ture (är′mə-chŏor′) s. armadura.

arm·band (ärm′bänd′) s. brazalete m, brazal m.

arm·chair (:chär′) s. sillón m, butaca ♦ **a. politician** político de café.

armed (ärmd) adj. armado ♦ **a. forces** fuerzas armadas.

arm·ful (ärm′fŏol′) s. brazada.

ar·mi·stice (är′mĭ-stĭs) s. armisticio, tregua.

ar·moire (ärm-wär′) s. armario, ropero.

ar·mor (är′mər) I. s. armadura; (metal plating) blindaje m ♦ **a. plate** plancha de blindaje, coraza II. tr. blindar, acorazar.

ar·mor·clad (:klăd′) adj. acorazado, blindado.

ar·mored (är′mərd) adj. acorazado, blindado.

ar·mor·y (är′mə-rē) s. (arsenal) armería, arsenal m; (factory) fábrica de armas.

arm·pit (ärm′pĭt′) s. axila.

ar·my (är′mē) s. ejército; FIG. multitud f.

a·ro·ma (ə-rō′mə) s. aroma m, fragancia.

ar·o·mat·ic (är′ə-măt′ĭk) adj. aromático.

a·rose (ə-rōz′) cf. **arise**.

a·round (ə-round′) I. adv. (in all directions) por todos lados, en derredor; (in a circle) alrededor; (here and there) por aquí, por allá; (in circumference) de circunferencia ♦ **all a.** por todos lados • **the other way a.** al contrario, al revés • **to get a.** (person) viajar, ir a lugares; (news) divulgarse, propalarse • **to have been a.** tener experiencia, haber corrido mundo II. prep. (about) cerca de, alrededor de; (encircling) alrededor de; (here and there) por todos lados, en torno de ♦ **a. the corner** a la vuelta de la esquina.

a·round-the-clock (′-thə-klŏk′) adj. continuamente.

a·rous·al (ə-rou′zəl) s. despertar m.

a·rouse (ə-rouz′) tr. (to awaken) despertar; (to stir up) estimular, incitar.

ar·peg·gi·o (är-pĕj′ē-ō) s. arpegio.

ar·raign (ə-rān′) tr. (before a court) citar, hacer comparecer; (to charge) denunciar, acusar.

ar·raign·ment (:mənt) s. DER. acusación f.

ar·range (ə-rānj′) tr. (to order) arreglar, ordenar; (to settle upon) fijar, señalar (fechas, convenios); (to plan) preparar; MÚS. arreglar —intr. acordar, convenir en.

ar·range·ment (:mənt) s. arreglo; (order) disposición f; (agreement) convenio ♦ pl. planes, medidas.

ar·rant (är′ənt) adj. notorio, consumado.

ar·ray (ə-rā′) I. tr. (to arrange) arreglar, disponer; (to adorn) adornar (con lujo); MIL. formar II. s. (impressive display) conjunto sorprenante; (attire) vestimenta lujosa; MIL. orden m de batalla.

ar·rears (ə-rîrz′) s.pl. ♦ **to be in a.** estar atrasado en pagos de deuda.

ar·rest (ə-rĕst′) I. tr. (to halt) detener, parar; (to seize) arrestar, detener; (to engage) cautivar II. s. arresto, detención f ♦ **under a.** detenido.

ar·rest·ing (ə-rĕs′tĭng) adj. llamativo, impresionante.

ar·ri·val (ə-rī′vəl) s. llegada, arribo.

ar·rive (ə-rīv′) intr. llegar; (by boat) arribar; FAM. tener éxito, llegar ♦ **to a. at** llegar a (conclusión, objetivo).

ar·ro·gance (är′ə-gəns) s. arrogancia, altivez f.

ar·ro·gant (:gənt) adj. arrogante, altivo.

ar·row (är′ō) s. flecha.

ar·row·head (:hĕd′) s. punta de flecha.

ar·row·root (:rōot′) s. arrurruz m.

ar·se·nal (är′sə-nəl) s. arsenal m.

ar·se·nic (är′sə-nĭk) s. & adj. arsénico.

ar·son (är′sən) s. incendio premeditado.

ar·son·ist (är′sə-nĭst) s. incendiario.

art (ärt) s. arte m; (skill) destreza, técnica ♦ **fine arts** bellas artes.

ar·ter·y (är′tə-rē) s. arteria.

art·ful (ärt′fəl) adj. (skillful) ingenioso, diestro;

(clever) artificioso; *(deceitful)* mañoso.
ar·thrit·ic (är-thrĭt'ĭk) adj. & s. artrítico.
ar·thri·tis (är-thrī'tĭs) s. artritis *f.*
ar·ti·choke (är'tĭ-chōk') s. alcachofa.
ar·ti·cle (är'tĭ-kəl) s. artículo; *(of a document)* cláusula ♦ **a. of clothing** prenda de vestir • **articles and conditions** COM. pliego de condiciones • **articles of incorporation** COM. estatutos de una sociedad anónima.
ar·tic·u·late (är-tĭk'yə-lĭt) **I.** adj. *(speaking)* que habla; *(distinct)* articulado; *(well-expressed)* inteligible, claro; BIOL. articulado **II.** tr. (:lāt') *(to enunciate)* articular, enunciar; *(to form a joint)* articular.
ar·ti·fact (är'tə-făkt') s. artefacto.
ar·ti·fice (är'tə-fĭs) s. artificio; *(trickery)* engaño.
ar·ti·fi·cial ('-fĭsh'əl) adj. artificial.
ar·til·ler·y (är-tĭl'ə-rē) s. artillería.
ar·ti·san (är'tĭ-zən) s. artesano, artífice *mf.*
art·ist (är'tĭst) s. artista *mf.*
ar·tis·tic (är-tĭs'tĭk) adj. artístico.
art·ist·ry (är'tĭ-strē) s. arte *mf,* talento artístico.
art·less (ärt'lĭs) adj. *(naive)* sencillo, ingenuo; *(natural)* natural; *(crude)* desmañado, torpe.
Ar·y·an (âr'ē-ən) adj. & s. ario.
as (ăz, əz) **I.** adv. *(equally)* así de, tan; *(for example)* (tal) como ♦ **as . . . as** tan . . . como <*as strong as an ox* tan fuerte como un buey> • **as far as I'm concerned** en cuanto a mí respecta • **as far as I know** que yo sepa **II.** conj. *(to the same degree)* igual que, como <*sweet as sugar* dulce como el azúcar>; *(while)* mientras; *(because)* ya que, porque ♦ **as from** a partir de • **as if** como si • **as it** si como para • **as yet** hasta ahora **III.** prep. como ♦ **as a rule** por regla general • **as for** en cuanto a **IV.** pron. *(which)* que <*do the same things as I do* haz las mismas cosas que yo hago>; *(a fact that)* como <*she is very careful, as her work shows* ella es muy cuidadosa, como lo demuestra su trabajo>.
as·bes·tos (ăs-bĕs'təs) s. asbesto, amianto ♦ **a. cement** fibrocemento.
as·cend (ə-sĕnd') intr. *(to rise)* elevarse, remontarse; *(to slope upward)* ascender, subir —tr. *(to climb)* subir (escalera, montaña); *(the throne)* subir a, ascender a.
as·cen·dance/dence (ə-sĕn'dəns) s. ascendiente m, predominio.
as·cen·dant/dent (:dənt) adj. ascendiente.
as·cend·ing (:dĭng) adj. ascendente.
as·cen·sion (:shən) s. ascensión *f.*
as·cent (ə-sĕnt') s. *(act)* subida, ascensión *f; (in rank)* ascenso; *(upward slope)* cuesta.
as·cer·tain (ăs'ər-tān') tr. determinar.
as·cet·ic (ə-sĕt'ĭk) **I.** s. asceta *mf* **II.** adj. ascético.
as·cot (ăs'kət) s. corbata (a la inglesa).
as·cribe (ə-skrīb') tr. atribuir, imputar.
a·sep·tic (ə-sĕp'tĭk) adj. aséptico.
ash[1] (ăsh) s. *(from fire)* ceniza.
ash[2] s. BOT. fresno.
a·shamed (ə-shāmd') adj. avergonzado ♦ **to be a.** tener vergüenza.
ash·en (ăsh'ən) adj. pálido, ceniciento.
a·shore (ə-shôr') adv. a o en tierra ♦ **to go a.** bajar a tierra, desembarcar.
ash·tray (ăsh'trā') s. cenicero.
a·side (ə-sīd') **I.** adv. *(to one side)* al lado, a un

lado <*step a.* hágase a un lado>; *(apart)* de lado, aparte <*joking a.* bromas aparte> ♦ **a. from** a no ser por **II.** s. TEAT. aparte *m; (digression)* digresión *f.*
as·i·nine (ăs'ə-nīn') adj. estúpido, necio.
ask (ăsk) tr. preguntar <*he asked me my age* me preguntó mi edad>; *(to request)* solicitar, pedir; *(to demand)* exigir; *(to invite)* invitar ♦ **to a. a favor** pedir un favor • **to a. a question** hacer una pregunta —intr. preguntar *(about, after por)* ♦ **to a. for** pedir • **to a. for it** FAM. buscársela • **to be had for the asking** basta pedirlo para conseguirlo.
a·skance (ə-skăns') adv. *(sidewise)* de reojo, de soslayo; *(with suspicion)* con recelo.
a·skew (ə-skyōō') **I.** adj. ladeado, torcido **II.** adv. oblicuamente, sesgadamente.
a·sleep (ə-slēp') adj. dormido; *(inactive)* inactivo; *(numb)* adormecido ♦ **to fall a.** dormirse, quedarse dormido.
asp (ăsp) s. áspid *m,* áspide *m.*
as·par·a·gus (ə-spăr'ə-gəs) s. espárrago.
as·pect (ăs'pĕkt') s. aspecto.
as·pen (ăs'pən) s. álamo temblón.
as·per·i·ty (ă-spĕr'ĭ-tē) s. aspereza.
as·per·sion (ə-spûr'zhən) s. calumnia.
as·phalt (ăs'fôlt') **I.** s. asfalto **II.** tr. asfaltar.
as·phyx·i·ate (ăs-fĭk'sē-āt) tr. & intr. asfixiar(se), sofocar(se).
as·phyx·i·a·tion (-'-ā'shən) s. asfixia.
as·pic (ăs'pĭk) s. gelatina (de carne o tomate).
as·pi·rant (ăs'pər-ənt) s. aspirante *mf.*
as·pi·rate (ăs'pə-rāt') **I.** tr. aspirar **II.** s. (:pər-ĭt) aspiración *f.*
as·pi·ra·tion (ăs'pə-rā'shən) s. aspiración *f.*
as·pire (ə-spīr') intr. aspirar, ambicionar.
as·pi·rin (ăs'pər-ĭn) s. aspirina.
ass (ăs) s. asno, burro; *(fool)* tonto, imbécil *mf.*
as·sail (ə-sāl') tr. asaltar, atacar.
as·sail·ant (ə-sā'lənt) s. asaltante *mf.*
as·sas·sin (ə-săs'ĭn) s. asesino.
as·sas·si·nate (:ə-nāt') tr. asesinar.
as·sas·si·na·tion (-'-nā'shən) s. asesinato.
as·sault (ə-sôlt') **I.** s. asalto, ataque *m* ♦ **a. and battery** asalto y agresión **II.** tr. & intr. asaltar, atacar.
as·say **I.** s. (ăs'ā') ensaye *m* **II.** tr. (ă-sā') ensayar (metales o aleación).
as·sem·ble (ə-sĕm'bəl) tr. *(to gather)* congregar, reunir; MEC. armar, montar —intr. congregarse, reunirse.
as·sem·bly (:blē) s. *(meeting)* asamblea, congreso; MEC. montaje *m;* MIL. asamblea ♦ **a. language** lenguaje ensamblador • **a. line** línea de montaje.
as·sent (ə-sĕnt') **I.** intr. asentir, convenir **II.** s. asentimiento, aprobación *f.*
as·sert (ə-sûrt') tr. *(to declare)* asertar, afirmar; *(one's right)* mantener, hacer valer ♦ **to a. oneself** imponerse, hacer valer uno sus derechos.
as·ser·tion (ə-sûr'shən) s. aserción *f.*
as·ser·tive (:tĭv) adj. agresivo.
as·sess (ə-sĕs') tr. *(to appraise)* avaluar, tasar *(at en); (to levy)* gravar, multar; *(to evaluate)* evaluar, juzgar.
as·sess·ment (:mənt) s. *(appraisal)* avaluación *f,* tasación *f; (amount assessed)* tasa.
as·ses·sor (:ər) s. tasador *m* (de impuestos).
as·set (ăs'ĕt') s. *(item)* posesión *f,* bien *m; (advantage)* ventaja ♦ **assets** pl. bienes, activo.
as·sid·u·ous (ə-sĭj'ōō-əs) adj. asiduo.
as·sign (ə-sīn') tr. asignar; *(a task)* señalar; *(to*

ascribe) indicar; DER. transferir, traspasar.

as·sig·na·tion (ăs'ĭg-nā'shən) s. asignación *f*; *(date)* cita *(amorosa)*.

as·sign·ment (ə-sīn'mənt) s. *(act)* asignación *f*; *(task)* tarea, deber *m*; *(position)* puesto.

as·sim·i·late (ə-sīm'ə-lāt') tr. & intr. asimilar(se).

as·sim·i·la·tion (-'-lā'shən) s. asimilación *f*.

as·sist (ə-sīst') I. tr. & intr. asistir, auxiliar II. s. ayuda, auxilio.

as·sis·tance (ə-sīs'təns) s. asistencia, ayuda ♦ **to be of a. to** ayudar a.

as·sis·tant (:tənt) s. & adj. ayudante *mf*, auxiliar *m*.

as·so·ci·ate (ə-sō'shē-āt', -sē-) I. tr. & intr. asociar(se) ♦ **to a. with someone** juntarse *o* tratarse con alguien II. s. (:ĭt) *(partner)* socio, consocio; *(companion)* compañero III. adj. (:ĭt) asociado, adjunto.

as·so·ci·a·tion (-'-ā'shən) s. asociación *f*.

as·so·nance (ăs'ə-nəns) s. asonancia.

as·sort (ə-sôrt') tr. clasificar, ordenar.

as·sort·ed (ə-sôr'tĭd) adj. surtido, variado.

as·sort·ment (ə-sôrt'mənt) s. surtido, colección variada.

as·suage (ə-swāj') tr. *(to ease)* aliviar, mitigar; *(to satisfy)* satisfacer, saciar.

as·sum·able (ə-sōō'mə-bəl) adj. asumible.

as·sume (ə-sōōm') tr. asumir; *(to arrogate)* arrogarse (un derecho); *(to feign)* fingir, simular; *(to presume)* presumir, suponer.

as·sumed (ə-sōōmd') adj. *(feigned)* simulado, fingido; *(taken for granted)* supuesto, presunto.

as·sum·ing (ə-sōō'mĭng) adj. pretensioso.

as·sump·tion (ə-sŭmp'shən) s. *(act)* asunción *f*; *(supposition)* suposición *f*.

as·sur·ance (ə-shŏŏr'əns) s. *(guarantee)* garantía, promesa; *(certainty)* certeza, seguridad *f*; *(self-confidence)* aplomo.

as·sure (ə-shŏŏr') tr. asegurar; *(to reassure)* tranquilizar; *(to ensure)* garantizar.

as·sured (ə-shŏŏrd') adj. *(sure)* seguro, cierto; *(self-confident)* seguro (de sí mismo).

as·ter·isk (ăs'tə-rĭsk') s. asterisco.

a·stern (ə-stûrn') adv. a *o* de popa.

as·ter·oid (ăs'tə-roid') s. asteroide *m*.

asth·ma (ăz'mə) s. asma.

asth·mat·ic (ăz-măt'ĭk) adj. & s. asmático.

as·tig·mat·ic (ăs'tĭg-măt'ĭk) adj. astigmático.

a·stir (ə-stûr') adj. *(moving about)* activo, en movimiento; *(out of bed)* levantado.

a·ston·ish (ə-stŏn'ĭsh) tr. asombrar.

a·ston·ish·ing (:ĭ-shĭng) adj. asombroso.

a·ston·ish·ment (:ĭsh-mənt) s. asombro.

a·stound (ə-stound') tr. maravillar, asombrar.

a·stray (ə-strā') adv. por mal camino ♦ **to go a.** extraviarse • **to lead a.** descarriar.

a·stride (ə-strīd') adv. & prep. a horcajadas (sobre).

as·trin·gent (ə-strĭn'jənt) I. adj. MED. astringente; *(harsh)* áspero II. s. astringente *m*.

as·trol·o·ger (ə-strŏl'ə-jər) s. astrólogo.

as·tro·log·i·cal (ăs'trə-lŏj'ĭk) adj. astrológico.

as·trol·o·gy (ə-strŏl'ə-jē) s. astrología.

as·tro·naut (ăs'trə-nôt') s. astronauta *mf*.

as·tron·o·mer (ə-strŏn'ə-mər) s. astrónomo.

as·tro·nom·i·cal (ăs'trə-nŏm'ĭk) adj. astronómico.

as·tron·o·my (ə-strŏn'ə-mē) s. astronomía.

as·tro·phys·ics (ăs'trō-fĭz'ĭks) s.sg. astrofísica.

as·tute (ə-stōōt') adj. astuto, sagaz.

a·sun·der (ə-sŭn'dər) adv. en pedazos, en dos.

a·sy·lum (ə-sī'ləm) s. asilo.

a·sym·me·try (ā-sĭm'ĭ-trē) s. asimetría.

at (ăt, ət) prep. en <*at right angles* en ángulo recto>; a <*at noon* al mediodía>; por <*to be angry at something* estar enfadado por algo>; de <*don't laugh at me!* ¡no te rías de mí!>; en casa de <*I'll be at Roberto's* estaré en casa de Roberto>.

at·a·vism (ăt'ə-vĭz'əm) s. atavismo.

at·a·vis·tic ('-vĭs'tĭk) adj. atávico.

ate (āt) cf. **eat.**

a·the·ism (ā'thē-ĭz'əm) s. ateísmo.

a·the·ist (:ĭst) s. ateo.

ath·lete (ăth'lēt') s. atleta *mf* ♦ **a.'s foot** pie de atleta.

ath·let·ic (ăth-lĕt'ĭk) adj. atlético ♦ **athletics** s.sg. *o* pl. atletismo.

a·thwart (ə-thwôrt') I. adv. de través II. prep. a través de.

at·las (ăt'ləs) s. atlas *m*.

at·mos·phere (ăt'mə-sfîr') s. atmósfera.

at·mos·pher·ic ('-'ĭk) adj. atmosférico.

a·toll (ăt'ôl', ā'tôl') s. atolón *m*.

at·om (ăt'əm) s. átomo ♦ **a. bomb** bomba atómica.

a·tom·ic (ə-tŏm'ĭk) adj. atómico.

at·om·ize (ăt'ə-mīz') tr. atomizar.

at·om·iz·er (:mī'zər) s. atomizador *m*.

a·ton·al (ā-tō'nəl) adj. atonal.

a·tone (ə-tōn') intr. dar reparación *(for* por), expiar.

a·tone·ment (:mənt) s. expiación *f*, reparación *f*.

a·top (ə-tŏp') adv. & prep. encima (de).

a·tri·um (ā'trē-əm) s. [pl. **s** *o* **-ia**] atrio.

a·tro·cious (ə-trō'shəs) adj. atroz, abominable.

a·troc·i·ty (ə-trŏs'ĭ-tē) s. atrocidad *f*.

at·ro·phy (ăt'rə-fē) I. s. atrofia II. tr. & intr. atrofiar(se).

at·tach (ə-tăch') tr. *(to fasten)* ligar, sujetar; *(to bond)* unir, pegar; *(to ascribe)* dar, atribuir (importancia, significado); DER. incautarse de.

at·ta·ché (ăt'ə-shā') s. agregado ♦ **a. case** portafolio, maletín.

at·tached (ə-tăcht') adj. *(fastened)* adherido, adjunto ♦ **a. to** *(fond of)* encariñado con, apegado a.

at·tach·ment (ə-tăch'mənt) s. *(act)* unión *f*; *(extra part)* accesorio; *(affection)* afición *f*; MEC. acoplamiento; DER. incautación *f*.

at·tack (ə-tăk') I. tr. atacar, agredir; FIG. acometer (tarea, problema) —intr. ir al ataque II. s. ataque *m*, agresión *f*.

at·tack·er (:ər) s. agresor *m*, asaltante *mf*.

at·tain (ə-tān') tr. *(to accomplish)* lograr, conseguir; *(to arrive at)* llegar a, alcanzar.

at·tain·a·ble (ə-tā'nə-bəl) adj. lograble, alcanzable.

at·tain·der (ə-tān'dər) s. proscripción *f*, muerte civil *f*.

at·tain·ment (:mənt) s. logro, realización *f*.

at·tempt (ə-tĕmpt') I. tr. intentar, tratar de II. s. *(try)* intento, prueba; *(attack)* atentado.

at·tend (ə-tĕnd') tr. *(to go to)* atender, asistir a; *(to accompany)* acompañar; *(to wait upon)* asistir, servir; *(to take care of)* atender, cuidar ♦ **to a. to** prestar atención a.

at·ten·dance (ə-tĕn'dəns) s. asistencia, concurrencia.

at·ten·dant (:dənt) I. s. asistente *m*, mozo II. adj. concomitante, concurrente.

at·ten·tion (ə-tĕn'shən) s. atención f; *(attentiveness)* cuidado ♦ **a.!** MIL. ¡firmes! • **to pay a. (to)** prestar atención (a) ♦ pl. cortesías, atenciones.
at·ten·tive (:tĭv) adj. atento.
at·ten·u·ate (ə-tĕn'yōō-āt') tr. & intr. atenuar(se), disminuir(se).
at·test (ə-tĕst') tr. atestiguar —intr. ♦ **to a. to** dar fe de.
at·tes·ta·tion (ăt'ĕ-stā'shən) s. atestación f.
at·tic (ăt'ĭk) s. desván m, guardilla.
at·tire (ə-tīr') I. tr. ataviar, vestir II. s. atavío, vestido.
at·ti·tude (ăt'ĭ-tōōd') s. actitud f.
at·tor·ney (ə-tûr'nē) s. abogado, apoderado ♦ **a. general** fiscal o procurador general.
at·tract (ə-trăkt') tr. & intr. atraer.
at·trac·tion (ə-trăk'shən) s. atracción f; *(allure)* atractivo.
at·trac·tive (:tĭv) adj. atractivo, atrayente.
at·trib·ute (ə-trĭb'yōōt) I. tr. atribuir II. s. (ăt'rə-byōōt') atributo.
at·tri·tion (ə-trĭsh'ən) s. reducción f (en el número del personal por retiro, renuncia, etc.).
at·tune (ə-tōōn') tr. adaptar, armonizar.
a·typ·i·cal (ā-tĭp'ĭ-kəl) adj. anormal, irregular.
au·burn (ô'bərn) adj. castaño.
auc·tion (ôk'shən) I. s. subasta, remate m II. tr. subastar, rematar.
auc·tion·eer (ôk'shə-nîr') s. subastador m.
au·da·cious (ô-dā'shəs) adj. *(bold)* audaz; *(insolent)* atrevido, descarado.
au·dac·i·ty (ô-dăs'ĭ-tē) s. *(boldness)* audacia; *(insolence)* atrevimiento, descaro.
au·di·ble (ô'də-bəl) adj. audible, oíble.
au·di·ence (ô'dē-əns) s. *(public)* auditorio, público; *(formal hearing)* audiencia.
au·di·o (ô'dē-ō') I. adj. de frecuencia audible ♦ **a. frequency** audiofrecuencia II. TELEV. transmisión f o recepción f del sonido.
au·di·o·vi·su·al (:vĭzh'ōō-əl) adj. audiovisual ♦ **a. aids** material audiovisual
au·dit (ô'dĭt) I. s. intervención f (de cuentas) II. tr. intervenir.
au·di·tion (ô-dĭsh'ən) I. s. audición f II. tr. dar audición a —intr. actuar en una audición.
au·di·tive (ô'dĭ-tĭv) adj. auditivo.
au·di·tor (:tər) s. COM. auditor m, interventor m; EDUC. alumno libre.
au·di·to·ri·um (ô'dĭ-tôr'ē-əm) s. auditorio.
au·di·to·ry (ô'dĭ-tôr'ē) adj. auditorio, auditivo.
au·ger (ô'gər) s. barrena.
aught (ôt) s. cero.
aug·ment (ôg-mĕnt') tr. & intr. aumentar(se).
aug·men·ta·tion (ôg'mĕn-tā'shən) s. aumento.
au·gur (ô'gər) I. s. adivino II. tr. & intr. augurar ♦ **to a. ill, well** ser de mal, bien agüero.
au·gu·ry (ô'gyə-rē) s. augurio.
au·gust (ô-gŭst') adj. augusto.
Au·gust (ô'gəst) s. agosto.
aunt (ănt, änt) s. tía.
au·ra (ôr'ə) s. aura.
au·ral (ôr'əl) adj. auricular.
au·ri·cle (ôr'ĭ-kəl) s. aurícula.
aus·pice (ô'spĭs) s. auspicio ♦ **under the auspices of** bajo los auspicios de.
aus·pi·cious (ô-spĭsh'əs) adj. propicio, favorable.
aus·tere (ô-stîr') adj. austero.
aus·ter·i·ty (ô-stĕr'ĭ-tē) s. austeridad f.
au·then·tic (ô-thĕn'tĭk) adj. auténtico.
au·then·ti·cate (:tĭ-kāt') tr. autenticar.
au·then·tic·i·ty ('-tĭs'ĭ-tē) s. autenticidad f.

au·thor (ô'thər) I. s. autor m II. tr. escribir.
au·thor·i·tar·i·an (ə-thôr'ĭ-târ'ē-ən) adj. & s. autoritario.
au·thor·i·tar·i·an·ism (:ə-nĭz'əm) s. autoritarismo.
au·thor·i·ta·tive (ə-thôr'ĭ-tā'tĭv) adj. *(official)* autorizado; *(imperious)* autoritario.
au·thor·i·ty (:ĭ-tē) s. autoridad f ♦ **on good a.** de buena tinta.
au·thor·i·za·tion (ô'thər-ĭ-zā'shən) s. autorización f, permiso.
au·thor·ize (ô'thə-rīz') tr. autorizar.
au·thor·ized (:rīzd) adj. autorizado.
au·thor·ship (ô'thər-shĭp') s. paternidad literaria.
au·tism (ô'tĭz'əm) s. autismo.
au·to (ô'tō) s. FAM. automóvil m, auto.
au·to·bi·o·graph·ic/i·cal (ô'tō-bī'ə-grăf'ĭk) adj. autobiográfico.
au·to·bi·og·ra·phy ('--ŏg'rə-fē) s. autobiografía.
au·toc·ra·cy (ô-tŏk'rə-sē) s. autocracia.
au·to·crat (ô'tə-krăt') s. autócrata mf.
au·to·crat·ic ('-'ĭk) adj. autocrático.
au·to·di·dact (ô'tō-dī'dăkt) s. autodidacto.
au·to·graph (ô'tə-grăf') I. s. autógrafo II. tr. autografiar.
au·to·im·mune (ô'tō-ĭ-myōōn') adj. autoinmune.
au·to·load·ing (:lō'dĭng) adj. semiautomático.
au·to·mate (ô'tə-māt') tr. automatizar.
au·to·mat·ic ('-măt'ĭk) I. adj. automático ♦ **a. rifle** fusil ametrallador II. s. arma automática.
au·to·ma·tion (:mā'shən) s. automación f, automatización f.
au·tom·a·tize (ô-tŏm'ə-tīz') tr. automatizar.
au·tom·a·ton (:tən) s. [pl. **s** o **-ta**] autómata mf.
au·to·mo·bile (ô'tə-mō-bēl') s. automóvil m.
au·to·mo·tive ('-'tĭv) adj. automotor, automotriz; *(industry)* automovilístico.
au·ton·o·mous (ô-tŏn'ə-məs) adj. autónomo.
au·ton·o·my (:mē) s. autonomía.
au·top·sy (ô'tŏp'sē) s. autopsia.
au·tumn (ô'təm) s. otoño.
au·tum·nal (ô-tŭm'nəl) adj. otoñal, de otoño.
aux·il·ia·ry (ôg-zĭl'yə-rē) I. adj. auxiliar II. s. *(assistant)* auxiliar mf, asistente mf; *(group)* grupo auxiliar.
a·vail (ə-vāl') I. tr. beneficiar ♦ **to a. oneself of** aprovecharse de, valerse de II. s. ♦ **of** o **to no a.** en vano.
a·vail·a·bil·i·ty (ə-vā'lə-bĭl'ĭ-tē) s. disponibilidad f.
a·vail·a·ble ('-'bəl) adj. *(obtainable)* obtenible; *(at hand)* disponible ♦ **to make a. to** poner a la disposición de.
av·a·lanche (ăv'ə-lănch') s. avalancha.
a·vant-garde (ä'vänt-gärd') adj. & s. (de) vanguardia.
av·a·rice (ăv'ər-ĭs) s. avaricia, codicia.
av·a·ri·cious (ăv'ə-rĭsh'əs) adj. avaricioso.
a·venge (ə-vĕnj') tr. & intr. vengar(se).
a·veng·er (ə-vĕn'jər) s. vengador m.
av·e·nue (ăv'ə-nōō') s. avenida; FIG. medios, camino.
a·ver (ə-vûr') tr. **-rr-** afirmar, declarar.
av·er·age (ăv'ər-ĭj) I. s. promedio, término medio ♦ **on the a.** por término medio, como promedio II. adj. *(de término)* medio <**a. cost** costo medio>; *(ordinary)* regular III. tr. *(to compute)* calcular el promedio de; *(to obtain)* alcanzar un promedio de; *(to prorate)* prorra-

tear.

a·verse (ə-vûrs') adj. opuesto, contrario ♦ **to be a. to** oponerse a.

a·ver·sion (ə-vûr'zhən) s. aversión f.

a·vert (ə-vûrt') tr. *(to turn away)* desviar, apartar (mirada); *(to prevent)* prevenir (peligro).

a·vi·ar·y (ā'vē-ĕr'ē) s. pajarera.

a·vi·a·tion (ā'vē-ā'shən) s. aviación f.

a·vi·a·tor ('-'tər) s. aviador m.

av·id (ăv'ĭd) adj. ávido; *(ardent)* entusiasta.

a·vid·i·ty (ə-vĭd'ĭ-tē) s. avidez f.

av·o·ca·do (ăv'ə-kä'dō) s. aguacate m, palta.

av·o·ca·tion (ăv'ō-kā'shən) s. pasatiempo.

a·void (ə-void') tr. evitar.

a·void·a·ble (ə-voi'də-bəl) adj. evitable.

a·void·ance (ə-void'ns) s. evitación f.

a·vow (ə-vou') tr. reconocer, confesar.

a·vowed (ə-voud') adj. reconocido, declarado.

a·vun·cu·lar (ə-vŭng'kyə-lər) adj. avuncular.

a·wait (ə-wāt') tr. & intr. esperar, aguardar.

a·wake (ə-wāk') I. tr. & intr. **awoke, -d** despertar(se) II. adj. despierto.

a·wak·en (ə-wā'kən) tr. & intr. despertar(se).

a·wak·en·ing (:kə-nĭng) s. despertar m.

a·ward (ə-wôrd') I. tr. *(to bestow)* premiar; *(legally)* adjudicar II. s. *(prize)* premio, recompensa; *(decision)* decisión f, fallo.

a·ware (ə-wâr') adj. consciente, percatado ♦ **to be a. of** o **that** tener conciencia de o que • **to become a. of** enterarse de.

a·ware·ness (:nĭs) s. conciencia, conocimiento.

a·wash (ə-wŏsh') adj. & adv. inundado.

a·way (ə-wā') I. adv. lejos de, a <*a house two miles a. from here* una casa a dos millas de aquí>; *(continuously)* sin parar <*to fire a.* disparar sin parar>; *(aside)* en el sentido opuesto ♦ **far a.** lejos • **right a.** inmediatamente II. adj. *(absent)* ausente, fuera <*she's a from home* está fuera de la casa>; *(at a distance)* distante, lejano.

awe (ô) I. s. temor m o admiración f reverente ♦ **to stand in a.** of temer a, admirar a II. tr. infundir temor o admiración reverente.

a·weigh (ə-wā') adj. pendiente (ancla) ♦ **anchors a.!** ¡levanten anclas!

awe·some (ô'səm) adj. pasmoso, asombroso.

awe·struck/strick·en (ô'strŭk'/strĭk'ən) adj. pasmado, asombrado.

aw·ful (ô'fəl) adj. *(terrible)* pavoroso; *(atrocious)* atroz, horrible; *(great)* enorme, tremendo.

aw·ful·ly (ô'fə-lē) adv. *(atrociously)* horriblemente, muy mal; *(very)* muchísimo, muy.

a·while (ə-hwīl') adv. un rato, algún tiempo.

awk·ward (ôk'wərd) adj. *(clumsy)* torpe, desmañado; *(embarrassing)* embarazoso; *(situation)* delicado, difícil; *(shape)* inconveniente, difícil de manejar.

awk·ward·ness (:nĭs) s. *(clumsiness)* torpeza; *(embarrassment)* desconcierto.

awl (ôl) s. lezna, punzón m.

awn·ing (ô'nĭng) s. toldo.

a·woke (ə-wōk') cf. **awake**.

a·wry (ə-rī') adv. de soslayo ♦ **to go a.** salir mal.

ax(e) (ăks) I. s. hacha ♦ **to get the a.** JER. ser despedido • **to have an a. to grind** FAM. tener intereses personales II. tr. cortar (con hacha).

ax·i·om (ăk'sē-əm) s. axioma.

ax·i·o·mat·ic/i·cal ('-ō-măt'ĭk) adj. axiomático.

ax·is (ăk'sĭs) s. [pl. **axes**] eje m.

ax·le (ăk'səl) s. eje m, árbol m.

a·ya·tol·lah (ī'ə-tō'lə) s. RELIG. líder religioso islámico de la secta chiíta.

ay(e) (ī) I. s. [pl. **es**] voto a favor ♦ **the ayes** los que votan a favor II. adv. sí.

az·ure (ăzh'ər) adj. & s. azul m celeste.

B

b, B (bē) s. segunda letra del alfabeto inglés; MÚS. si m.

baa (bă, bä) I. intr. balar II. s. balido.

bab·ble (băb'əl) I. intr. *(to prattle)* barbotar; *(to chatter)* parlotear; *(a brook)* murmurar, susurrar II. s. *(prattle)* barboteo; *(chatter)* parloteo; *(murmur)* murmullo.

babe (bāb) s. bebé m; JER. *(girl)* bebé, monada.

ba·boon (bă-bōōn') s. babuino.

ba·by (bā'bē) I. s. *(infant)* bebé m, nene m; *(childish person)* niño; JER. *(girl)* bebé, monada ♦ **b. brother, sister** hermanito, hermanita • **b. carriage** cochecito de niños • **b. talk** balbuceo II. tr. mimar, consentir.

ba·by·hood (:hōōd') s. *(primera)* infancia, niñez f.

ba·by·ish (:ĭsh) adj. infantil, de niño.

ba·by·sit (:sĭt') intr. & tr., **-sat, -tting** cuidar niños.

bac·cha·nal (băk'ə-năl') s. bacanal f.

bach·e·lor (băch'ə-lər) s. soltero; EDUC. *(degree)* bachillerato; *(graduate)* bachiller m.

bach·e·lor·hood (:hōōd') s. soltería.

bach·e·lor's-but·ton (băch'ə-lərz-bŭt'n) s. aciano.

ba·cil·lus (bə-sĭl'əs) s. [pl. **-li**] bacilo.

back (băk) I. s. *(person)* espalda; *(animal)* lomo, espinazo; *(reverse side)* envés m, revés m; *(coin, check)* dorso, reverso; *(chair)* respaldo; *(room, house)* fondo; DEP. defensa, zaga ♦ **b. to b.** uno detrás del otro • **behind someone's b.** a espaldas de alguien • **on one's b.** postrado, en cama • **with one's b. to the wall** entre la espada y la pared II. adv. atrás, hacia atrás ♦ **as far b. as** ya en • **b. and forth** de acá para allá • **in b. of** detrás de, tras de • **to be b.** estar de vuelta • **to go** o **come b.** volver, regresar • **to go b. on one's word** desdecirse, faltar a una promesa • **years b.** años atrás, hace años III. adj. *(in the rear)* de atrás, posterior; *(remote)* lejano; *(overdue)* atrasado ♦ **b. door, stairs** puerta, escalera de servicio • **b. talk** impertinencia(s) • **b. yard** traspatio • **to take a b. seat** pasar al segundo plano IV. tr. mover hacia atrás; *(vehicle)* dar marcha atrás a; *(to support)* respaldar, apoyar ♦ **b. up** *(vehicle)* dar marcha atrás; *(drain)* atascar(se); *(to support)* respaldar; *(to justify)* justificar con pruebas; *(to guarantee)* respaldar (fondos) —intr. moverse hacia atrás, retroceder ♦ **b. away** alejarse retrocediendo • **to b. down** ceder, echarse atrás • **to b. out** retractarse, volverse atrás • **to b. up** o **off** retroceder.

back·ache ('āk') s. dolor m de espalda.

back·bit·ing (:bī'tĭng) s. calumnia, murmuración f.

back·bone (:bōn') s. *(spine)* espinazo, columna vertebral; FIG. carácter m, firmeza.

back·break·ing (:brā'kĭng) adj. agobiador.

back·date (:dāt') tr. antedatar.

back·drop (:drŏp') s. telón m de fondo.

back·er (:ər) s. patrocinador m, promotor m.

back·fire (:fīr') I. s. petardeo II. intr. AUTO. petardear; *(scheme)* salir al revés.

back·gam·mon (:găm'ən) s. chaquete m.

back·ground (:ground') s. fondo, trasfondo; *(of events)* antecedentes m; *(experience)* experiencia.

back·hand (:hănd') adv. & s. (de) revés m.

back·hand·ed (:hăn'dĭd) adj. ambiguo.

back·ing (:ĭng) s. respaldo (moral, económico).

back·lash (:lăsh') s. *(motion)* contragolpe m, sacudida; *(reaction)* reacción f.

back·log (:lôg') s. acumulación f (de trabajo, pedidos).

back·pack (:păk') s. mochila.

back·rest (:rĕst') s. respaldo (de un asiento).

back·side (:sīd') s. FAM. trasero, nalgas.

back·slide (:slīd') intr. **-slid, slid(den)** reincidir (en el pecado, delito).

back·space (:spās') intr. hacer retroceder (el carro de una máquina de escribir).

back·stage (:stāj') adv. entre bastidores.

back·stair(s) (:stâr[z]') adj. furtivo.

back·stitch (:stĭch') I. s. pespunte m II. tr. pespuntear.

back·stop (:stŏp') s. red o valla para retener la pelota.

back·stretch (:strĕch') s. pista opuesta a la recta final.

back·stroke (:strōk') s. *(backhand)* revés m; *(in swimming)* brazada de espalda.

back·track (:trăk') intr. desandar.

back·up (:ŭp') I. s. *(reserve)* reserva; *(substitute)* suplente mf; *(support)* respaldo; *(clog)* atascamiento; MÚS. acompañamiento II. adj. suplente, de reserva.

back·ward (:wərd) I. adv. o **-wards** hacia o para atrás <to look b. mirar para atrás>; de espaldas <to fall b. caerse de espaldas>; al revés, al contrario <they do everything b. lo hacen todo al revés> ♦ **to know backwards and forwards** saberse al dedillo II. adj. hacia atrás <a b. look una mirada hacia atrás>; *(motion)* de retroceso; *(reverse)* al revés, inverso; *(unprogressive)* atrasado (país, época).

back·ward·ness (:wərd-nĭs) s. atraso, retraso.

back·wa·ter (:wô'tər) s. *(water)* agua estancada; *(place)* lugar atrasado.

back·woods (:wŏŏdz') s.pl. monte m, selva.

ba·con (bā'kən) s. tocino ♦ **to bring home the b.** FAM. ganar el pan.

bac·te·ri·a (băk-tîr'ē-ə) cf. **bacterium.**

bac·te·ri·al (:ē-əl) adj. bacteriano.

bac·te·ri·cide (:ĭ-sīd') s. bactericida m.

bac·te·ri·um (:ē-əm) s. [pl. **-ria**] bacteria.

bad (băd) worse, worst I. adj. malo; *(shoddy)* inferior; *(defective)* defectuoso; *(check)* sin fondos; *(naughty)* desobediente; *(harmful)* perjudicial; *(severe)* fuerte <a b. cold un catarro fuerte>; *(rotten)* podrido ♦ **from b. to worse** de mal en peor • **not b.** FAM. no está mal • **to feel b.** *(ill)* sentirse mal; *(sad)* estar triste • **to feel b. about** sentir, lamentar • **to go b.** echarse a perder • **too b.!** ¡qué lástima!, ¡mala suerte! II. s. lo malo III. adv. FAM. mucho <it hurts b. me duele mucho> ♦ **to be b. off** FAM. estar mal.

bade (băd, bād) cf. **bid.**

badge (băj) s. distintivo, insignia.

badg·er (băj'ər) I. s. tejón m II. tr. importunar, molestar.

bad·lands (băd'lăndz') s.pl. pedregal m.

bad·ly (:lē) adv. mal; *(very much)* mucho, con urgencia; *(seriously)* gravemente, de gravedad ♦ **to take something b.** tomar a mal algo.

bad·min·ton (băd'mĭn'tən) s. volante m.

bad·mouth (băd'mouth') tr. JER. hablar pestes de, poner por los suelos.

bad-tem·pered (:tĕm'pərd) adj. *(character)* de mal genio; *(mood)* malhumorado.

baf·fle (băf'əl) I. tr. *(to bewilder)* confundir, desconcertar; *(to foil)* eludir II. s. deflector m.

baf·fle·ment (:mənt) s. confusión f.

baf·fling (băf'lĭng) adj. desconcertante.

bag (băg) I. s. bolsa, saco; *(purse)* bolso, cartera; *(suitcase)* valija, maletín m; DEP. caza ♦ **b. and baggage** totalmente • **in the b.** JER. en el bolsillo, seguro ♦ es equipaje II. tr. **-gg-** meter en una bolsa; *(to hunt)* cazar; FAM. *(to capture)* coger, pescar —intr. formar bolsas, abultarse.

bag·gage (:ĭj) s. equipaje m, maletas; MIL. bagaje m.

bag·gy (:ē) adj. **-i-** bombacho.

bag·man (:mən) s. [pl. **-men**] JER. recaudador m (de dinero mal habido).

bag·pipe (:pīp') s. gaita.

bail¹ (bāl) I. s. fianza, caución f ♦ **out on b.** en libertad bajo fianza ♦ **to go b. for** dar fianza por II. tr. dar fianza o caución por ♦ **to b. out** sacar de apuros.

bail² tr. & intr. MARÍT. achicar (agua) ♦ **to b. out** saltar (en paracaídas).

bail·ee (bā-lē') s. DER. depositario.

bail·iff (bā'lĭf) s. alguacil m.

bail·i·wick (bā'lə-wĭk') s. alguacilazgo.

bail·or (bā'lər) s. fiador m, fianza.

bail·out (bāl'out') s. rescate financiero.

bails·man (bālz'mən) s. [pl. **-men**] fiador m, fianza.

bait (bāt) s. cebo, carnada ♦ **to take the b.** tragarse el anzuelo II. tr. poner el cebo en (anzuelo, trampa); *(to torment)* atormentar.

baize (bāz) s. bayeta.

bake (bāk) I. tr. cocer al horno —intr. cocerse II. s. cocción f (al horno).

bak·er (bā'kər) s. panadero.

bak·er·y (bā'kə-rē) s. panadería.

bak·ing (bā'kĭng) s. cocción f ♦ **b. powder** levadura en polvo • **b. soda** bicarbonato de sodio.

bal·ance (băl'əns) I. s. *(scale)* balanza; *(equilibrium)* equilibrio; TEN. *(equality)* balance m; *(difference)* saldo; FAM. *(remainder)* resto; *(sanity)* juicio ♦ **b. due** saldo deudor • **b. sheet** balance • **b. wheel** volante compensador • **off b.** *(unstable)* en desequilibrio; *(off guard)* desprevenido • **to be in the b.** estar en la balanza • **to strike a b.** encontrar el término medio • **to throw off b.** desconcertar II. tr. *(to bring into equilibrium)* balancear, equilibrar; *(to counterbalance)* compensar, contrarrestar; TEN. equilibrar ♦ **to b. the books** pasar balance —intr. equilibrarse; *(to sway)* balancearse; TEN. cuadrar.

bal·anced (:ənst) adj. balanceado, equilibrado.

bal·co·ny (băl'kə-nē) s. balcón m; TEAT. galería, paraíso.

bald (bôld) adj. calvo; *(blunt)* categórico, sin rodeos ♦ **to go b.** quedarse calvo.

bald-faced (:fāst') adj. descarado.

bald·ness (:nĭs) s. calvicie f.

bale (bāl) I. s. bala, fardo II. tr. embalar, enfardar.

ba·leen (bə-lēn') s. barba de ballena.

bale·ful (bāl'fəl) adj. maléfico, funesto.
balk (bôk) I. intr. *(to stop)* plantarse; *(to refuse)* oponerse *(at* a) —tr. impedir, frustrar II. s. obstáculo, impedimento.
balk·y (bô'kē) adj. **-i-** reacio.
ball¹ (bôl) I. s. bola; DEP. pelota, balón m; *(cannonball)* bala de cañón ♦ **b. bearing** cojinete de bolas • **to be on the b.** JER. estar atento • **to play b.** FAM. cooperar II. tr. ♦ **to b. (something) up** enredar, embrollar (algo).
ball² s. baile m de etiqueta ♦ **to have a b.** JER. divertirse mucho, pasarla muy bien.
bal·lad (bāl'əd) s. balada.
ball-and-sock·et joint (bôl'ən-sŏk'ĭt) s. articulación f de rótula.
bal·last (bāl'əst) s. *(weight)* lastre m; *(gravel)* balasto.
bal·le·ri·na (bāl'ə-rē'nə) s. bailarina (de ballet).
bal·let (bă-lā') s. ballet m.
bal·lis·tic (bə-lĭs'tĭk) adj. balístico ♦ **ballistics** s.sg. balística.
bal·loon (bə-lōōn') I. s. globo II. intr. *(to swell)* hincharse, inflarse; *(to increase)* aumentar rápidamente.
bal·lot (bāl'ət) I. s. *(paper)* papeleta (electoral); *(voting)* votación f; *(electoral ticket)* candidaturas ♦ **b. box** urna electoral II. intr. votar.
ball·park *o* **ball park** (bôl'pärk) s. estadio ♦ **in the b.** FAM. aproximado.
ball-point pen (:point') s. bolígrafo.
ball·room (:rōōm') s. salón *m* de baile.
bal·ly·hoo (bāl'ē-hōō') s. FAM. bombo, propaganda exagerada.
balm (bäm) s. bálsamo.
balm·y (bä'mē) adj. **-i-** *(weather)* agradable, suave; JER. *(silly)* chiflado, tocado.
ba·lo·ney (bə-lō'nē) s. FAM. *(bologna)* salchicha de Bolonia; *(nonsense)* disparates m.
bal·sa (bôl'sə) s. balsa.
bal·sam (bôl'səm) s. *(ointment)* bálsamo; *(tree)* abeto balsámico.
bal·us·ter (bāl'ə-stər) s. balaustre m.
bal·us·trade (:strād') s. balaustrada.
bam·boo (băm-bōō') s. *(tree)* bambú m; *(stem)* caña (de bambú).
bam·boo·zle (băm-bōō'zəl) tr. FAM. embaucar.
ban (băn) I. tr. **-nn-** prohibir, proscribir II. s. prohibición f, proscripción f.
ba·nal (bə-năl', bā'nəl) adj. banal, trivial.
ba·nan·a (bə-năn'ə) s. plátano, banana ♦ **b. tree** plátano, banano ♦ pl. JER. chiflado.
band¹ (bănd) I. s. banda, faja; *(of paper)* tira; *(stripe)* franja, lista; JOY. anillo (de boda); *(on hat, dress)* cinta II. tr. fajar, atar.
band² I. s. banda; *(gang)* cuadrilla; MÚS. *(military)* banda; *(jazz)* orquesta; *(rock)* conjunto II. tr. & intr. ♦ **to b. together** agrupar(se), juntar(se).
band·age (băn-dĭj) I. s. venda II. tr. vendar.
ban·dan·(n)a (băn-dăn'ə) s. pañuelo grande.
ban·dit (băn'dĭt) s. bandido, bandolero.
ban·do·leer/lier (băn'də-lîr') s. bandolera.
band·stand (bănd'stănd') s. quiosco de orquesta.
band·wag·on (:wăg'ən) s. ♦ **to get** *o* **jump on the b.** FAM. arrimarse al que lleva la batuta.
ban·dy (băn'dē) tr. *(to toss)* pasarse, tirar (de un lado a otro); *(words)* intercambiar.
ban·dy-leg·ged (:lĕg'ĭd) s. patizambo.
bane (bān) s. ♦ **to be the b. of someone's existence** hacerle la vida imposible a alguien.
bane·ful ('fəl) s. pernicioso, nocivo.

bang (băng) I. s. *(explosion)* estallido; *(loud slam)* golpe m, golpetazo; JER. *(thrill)* emoción f, excitación f II. tr. *(to bump, pound)* golpear; *(to slam)* cerrar de un golpetazo ♦ **to b. up** estropear —intr. *(to explode)* detonar; *(to make a loud noise)* dar un golpetazo; *(to crash)* chocar *(into* con) III. adv. exactamente IV. interj. *(shot)* ¡pum!; *(blow)* ¡zas!
bangs (băngz) s.pl. cerquillo, flequillo.
ban·gle (băng'gəl) s. esclava, ajorca.
bang-up (băng'ŭp') adj. JER. excelente.
ban·ish (băn'ĭsh) tr. *(to exile)* exiliar, desterrar; *(to cast out)* echar fuera, ahuyentar.
ban·ish·ment (:mənt) s. *(exile)* exilio, destierro; *(ban)* proscripción f.
ban·is·ter (băn'ĭ-stər) s. barandilla, baranda.
ban·jo (băn'jō) s. [pl. **(e)s**] banjo.
bank¹ (băngk) I. s. *(of a river)* ribera, orilla; *(hillside)* loma; *(of snow)* montón m; AVIA. inclinación f lateral ♦ pl. MARÍT. bajío, banco (de arena) II. tr. *(a fire)* cubrir; *(a road)* peraltar; AVIA. inclinar —intr. AVIA. inclinarse.
bank² I. s. COM. banco; *(in gambling)* banca ♦ **b. account** cuenta bancaria • **b. note** billete de banco II. tr. depositar en un banco —intr. COM. tener cuenta ♦ **to b. on** contar con, confiar en.
bank³ s. *(row)* hilera, fila.
bank·book ('bŏŏk') s. libreta de banco.
bank·er (băng'kər) s. banquero.
bank·ing (:kĭng) s. *(occupation)* banca; *(bank business)* operaciones bancarias.
bank·roll (băngk'rōl') FAM. I. s. dinero en el banco, fondos II. tr. costear, financiar.
bank·rupt (:rəpt) I. adj. COM. insolvente; *(ruined)* arruinado; *(lacking)* falto, carente ♦ **to go b.** declararse en quiebra, quebrar II. tr. hacer quebrar, arruinar.
bank·rupt·cy (:sē) s. quiebra, bancarrota.
ban·ner (băn'ər) I. s. bandera, estandarte m; PERIOD. titular m a toda plana II. adj. sobresaliente.
banns (bănz) s.pl. amonestaciones f.
ban·quet (băng'kwĭt) I. s. banquete m II. tr. & intr. banquetear.
ban·ter (băn'tər) I. s. broma, burla II. intr. burlar, bromear.
bap·tism (băp'tĭz'əm) s. bautismo.
bap·tist (:tĭst) s. bautista mf.
bap·tis·ter·y/try (:tĭ-strē) s. baptisterio.
bap·tize (tīz') tr. bautizar.
bar (bär) I. s. barra; *(of gold)* lingote m; *(lever)* palanca; *(of a prison)* barrote m; *(of soap)* pastilla; *(of chocolate)* tableta; *(obstacle)* obstáculo; *(tavern)* bar m; *(counter)* mostrador m; MARÍT. banco (de arena, grava); DER. *(tribunal)* tribunal m; *(legal profession)* abogacía; MÚS. compás m ♦ **behind bars** entre rejas II. tr. **-rr-** *(to fasten)* cerrar con barras; *(to obstruct)* obstruir; *(to exclude)* excluir; *(to prohibit)* prohibir III. prep. ♦ **b. none** sin excepción.
barb (bärb) s. púa; *(cutting remark)* observación f mordaz.
bar·bar·i·an (bär-bâr'ē-ən) s. & adj. bárbaro.
bar·bar·ic (:băr'ĭk) adj. bárbaro.
bar·ba·rism ('bə-rĭz'əm) s. barbarie f.
bar·bar·i·ty (bär'ī-tē) s. barbaridad f.
bar·ba·rous ('bər-əs) adj. bárbaro.
bar·be·cue (bär'bĭ-kyōō') I. s. barbacoa, parrillada II. tr. asar a la parrilla.
barbed (bärbd) adj. con púas; *(cutting)* mordaz ♦ **b. wire** alambre de púas.

bar·bell (bär'bĕl') s. barra con pesas, haltera.
bar·ber (bär'bər) I. s. barbero, peluquero II. tr. *(to shave)* afeitar; *(to cut hair)* cortar el pelo.
bar·ber·shop (:shŏp') s. barbería, peluquería.
bar·bi·tu·rate (bär-bĭch'ər-ĭt) s. barbitúrico.
bard (bärd) s. poeta *m*, bardo.
bare (bâr) I. adj. desnudo; *(head)* descubierto; *(feet)* descalzo; *(undisguised)* descubierto, a la vista; *(empty)* desprovisto, vacío; *(plain)* puro, sencillo; *(mere)* mínimo ♦ **to lay b.** revelar, poner al descubierto II. tr. desnudar; *(to reveal)* revelar, descubrir.
bare·back ('bäk') adv. & adj. a o en pelo.
bare·faced (:fäst') adj. descarado.
bare·foot(·ed) (:fŏot'[ĭd]) adv. & adj. descalzo.
bare·hand·ed (:hăn'dĭd) adj. & adv. sin guantes; *(without tools)* sólo con las manos; *(unarmed)* desarmado.
bare·head·ed (:hĕd'ĭd) adj. & adv. con la cabeza descubierta.
bare·ly (bâr'lē) adv. apenas.
bar·gain (bär'gən) I. s. *(deal)* pacto, convenio; *(good buy)* ganga ♦ **into the b.** por añadidura • **to strike a b.** llegar a un acuerdo II. intr. *(to negotiate)* negociar, pactar; *(to haggle)* regatear ♦ **to b. for** o **on** esperar —tr. trocar, cambiar.
bar·gain·ing (:gə-nĭng) s. *(haggling)* regateo; *(negotiation)* negociación *f*.
barge (bärj) I. s. barcaza, gabarra II. intr. ♦ **to b. in** entremeterse • **to b. into** irrumpir en.
bar·i·tone (bär'ĭ-tōn') s. barítono.
bar·i·um (bär'ē-əm) s. bario.
bark¹ (bärk) I. s. ladrido ♦ **his b. is worse than his bite** perro que ladra no muerde II. tr. & intr. ladrar ♦ **to b. up the wrong tree** equivocarse.
bark² s. BOT. corteza.
bar·keep(·er) (bär'kēp'[ər]) s. barman *m*.
bar·ley (bär'lē) s. cebada.
bar·maid (bär'mād') s. camarera, cantinera.
barn (bärn) s. *(for grain)* granero; *(for livestock)* establo.
bar·na·cle (bär'nə-kəl) s. percebe *m*.
barn·yard (bärn'yärd') adj. & s. (de) corral *m*.
ba·rom·e·ter (bə-rŏm'ĭ-tər) s. barómetro.
bar·o·met·ric/·cal (bär'ə-mĕt'rĭk) adj. barométrico.
bar·on (băr'ən) s. barón *m*.
bar·on·ess (:ə-nĭs) s. baronesa.
ba·roque (bə-rōk') adj. & s. barroco.
bar·racks (băr'əks) s.pl. cuartel *m*, barraca.
bar·rage (bə-räzh') s. MIL. bombardeo, cortina de fuego; FIG. *(burst)* andanada.
bar·rel (băr'əl) I. s. barril *m*, tonel *m*; *(of a gun)* cañón *m*; MAQ. cubo, tambor *m* ♦ **to be a b. of fun** ser divertidísimo • **to be over a b.** estar con el agua al cuello II. tr. entonelar, embarrilar —intr. JER. ir a gran velocidad.
bar·ren (băr'ən) I. adj. *(sterile)* estéril, infecundo; *(land)* yermo; *(unproductive)* infructuoso, vano II. s. ♦ **pl. tierras** yerma, páramo.
bar·rette (bə-rĕt') s. pasador *m*.
bar·ri·cade (băr'ĭ-kād') I. s. barricada, barrera II. tr. levantar barricadas.
bar·ri·er (băr'ē-ər) s. barrera, valla.
bar·ring (bär'ĭng) prep. salvo, excepto.
bar·ris·ter (băr'ĭ-stər) s. G.B. abogado.
bar·room (bär'rōm') s. bar *m*.
bar·row (băr'ō) s. carretilla.
bar·tend·er (bär'tĕn'dər) s. camarero, barman *m*.

bar·ter (bär'tər) I. intr. & tr. trocar, cambiar II. s. trueque *m*, cambio.
bas·al (bā'səl) adj. fundamental, básico.
ba·salt (bə-sôlt') s. basalto.
base¹ (bās) I. s. base *f*; ARQ. basa ♦ **to be off b.** estar equivocado II. adj. de la base III. tr. ♦ **to b. (up)on** basar en o sobre.
base² adj. *(vile)* ruin; *(lowly)* bajo; *(metal)* inferior, de baja ley.
base·ball ('bôl') s. béisbol *m*; *(ball)* pelota.
base·board (:bôrd') s. zócalo.
base·born (:bôrn') adj. *(of birth)* de humilde cuna; *(contemptible)* bajo, despreciable.
base·less (:lĭs) adj. infundado.
base·ment (:mənt) s. sótano.
ba·ses (bā'sēz') cf. **basis**.
bash (băsh) FAM. I. tr. golpear *(blow)* golpazo, porrazo; *(party)* fiesta, parranda.
bash·ful (băsh'fəl) adj. tímido, encogido.
ba·sic (bā'sĭk) I. adj. básico II. s. base *f*.
ba·sic·i·ty (bā-sĭs'ĭ-tē) s. basicidad *f*.
bas·il (băz'əl, bā'zəl) s. albahaca.
ba·sil·i·ca (bə-sĭl'ĭ-kə) s. basílica.
ba·sin (bā'sĭn) s. palangana, jofaina; *(washbowl)* pila, pileta; GEOG. cuenca.
ba·sis (bā'sĭs) s. [pl. **-ses**] base *f*, fundamento ♦ **on the b. of** en base a.
bask (băsk) intr. gozar, complacerse.
bas·ket (băs'kĭt) s. cesta, canasta.
bas·ket·ball (:bôl') s. baloncesto; *(ball)* pelota.
bas·ket·ry (băs'kĭ-trē) s. cestería.
bas·ket·weave (:kĭt-wēv') s. tejido esterilla.
bas·re·lief (bä'rĭ-lēf') s. bajo relieve.
bass¹ (băs) s. [pl. inv. o **es**] ICT. róbalo.
bass² (bās) s. *(voice)* bajo; *(instrument)* contrabajo ♦ **b. clef** clave de fa • **b. drum** bombo.
bas·si·net (băs'ə-nĕt') s. cuna.
bas·soon (bə-sōōn') s. fagot *m*, bajón *m*.
bas·tard (băs'tərd) I. s. bastardo; JER. *(scoundrel)* canalla II. adj. ilegítimo; *(spurious)* espurio.
baste (bāst) tr. *(to sew)* hilvanar; CUL. lardear.
bas·tion (băs'chən) s. baluarte *m*.
bat (băt) I. s. DEP. bate *m*; ZOOL. murciélago ♦ **right off the b.** FAM. inmediatamente ♦ **to go to b. for** FAM. sacar la cara por II. tr. -tt- golpear; DEP. batear ♦ **not to b. an eye** no pestañear • **to b. around** FAM. discutir mucho.
batch (băch) s. CUL. hornada; *(lot)* partida, lote *m*; *(group)* grupo, tanda.
bate (bāt) tr. moderar, disminuir.
bat·ed (bā'tĭd) adj. ♦ **with b. breath** con aliento entrecortado o pasmado.
bath (băth) s. baño; *(bathroom)* cuarto de baño ♦ **pl. casa de baños.**
bathe (bāth) intr. bañarse —tr. *(to wet)* bañar; *(to wash)* lavar; *(to flood)* inundar.
bath·ing suit (bā'thĭng) s. traje *m* de baño.
bath·robe (băth'rōb') s. bata, albornoz *m*.
bath·room (:rōōm') s. cuarto de baño.
bath·tub (:tŭb') s. bañera.
ba·tiste (bə-tēst') s. batista.
ba·ton (bə-tŏn') s. batuta.
bat·tal·ion (bə-tăl'yən) s. batallón *m*.
bat·ter¹ (băt'ər) tr. *(to beat)* golpear, apalear; *(to damage)* deteriorar, estropear.
bat·ter² s. CUL. pasta; DEP. bateador *m*.
bat·ter·ing-ram (:ĭng-răm') s. ariete *m*.
bat·ter·y (băt'ə-rē) s. ELEC., MIL. batería; *(dry cell)* pila; *(storage)* acumulador *m*; DER. asalto.

bat·tle (băt'l) I. s. MIL. batalla, combate *m*; FIG. lucha II. intr. & tr. combatir, luchar.

bat·tle-ax(e) (:ăks') s. hacha (de combate).

bat·tle·field (:fēld') s. campo de batalla.

bat·tle·ground (:ground') s. campo de batalla.

bat·tle·ship (:shĭp') s. acorazado.

bat·ty (băt'ē) adj. -l- JER. chiflado.

bau·ble (bô'bəl) s. chuchería, baratija.

baud (bôd) s. baudio.

baux·ite (bôk'sīt') s. bauxita.

bawd (bôd) s. ramera.

bawd·y (bô'dē) adj. -l- obsceno.

bawd·y·house (:hous') s. burdel *m*.

bawl (bôl) intr. (to cry) llorar; (to shout) gritar —tr. gritar, vociferar ♦ **to b. out** regañar.

bay¹ (bā) s. GEOG. bahía.

bay² s. ARQ. intercolumnio; (compartment) compartimento ♦ **b. window** ventana salediza.

bay³ adj. & s. (horse, color) bayo.

bay⁴ I. s. aullido ♦ **to keep at b.** mantener a raya II. intr. & tr. ladrar (a), aullar (a).

bay⁵ s. BOT. laurel *m*.

bay·o·net (bā'ə-nĕt') s. bayoneta.

ba·za(a)r (bə-zär') s. bazar *m*.

ba·zoo·ka (bə-zōo'kə) s. bazuca *m*.

be (bē) intr. I. (inherent quality, time, possession, passive voice) ser <ice is cold el hielo es frío> <what time is it? ¿qué hora es?> <is it yours? es tuyo?> <it was done yesterday fué hecho ayer> <it is possible es posible> II. (location, impermanence) estar <where are you? ¿dónde estás?> <my coffee is cold mi café está frío> III. (age, physical sensation) tener; (weather) haber, hacer; (reaction) quedarse <she was speechless se quedó sin palabras> ♦ **as it were** por decirlo • **be that as it may** sea como fuere • **so be it** así sea • **there is** o **are** hay • **to be** to tener que, deber <you are to leave tonight tienes que o debes partir esta noche>.

beach (bēch) I. s. playa II. tr. varar.

beach·head ('hĕd') s. cabeza de playa.

bea·con (bē'kən) s. (lighthouse) faro; (signal fire) almenara; AVIA. (light) baliza; (radio) radiofaro; (signal) faro, guía *m*.

bead (bēd) I. s. (ornament) cuenta, abalorio; (drop) gota ♦ **to draw a b. on** apuntar a ♦ pl. JOY. collar; RELIG. rosario II. intr. formarse en gotas.

bead·y (bē'dē) adj. -l- ♦ **b. eyes** ojos pequeños y brillantes.

beak (bēk) s. pico.

beak·er (bē'kər) s. vaso de precipitación.

beam (bēm) I. s. (of light) haz *m*, rayo; ARQ. viga; MARÍT. manga; RAD. onda dirigida ♦ **to be on the b.** FAM. estar sobre la pista II. tr. emitir, dirigir —intr. (to shine) destellar, irradiar; (to smile) sonreír radiantemente.

bean (bēn) s. habichuela, judía, frijol *m*; (seed) haba; (of coffee) grano; JER. (head) coco ♦ **to spill the beans** FAM. descubrir el pastel II. tr. JER. pegar en el coco.

bean·bag ('băg') s. bolsita con frijoles secos usado para los niños para jugar.

bean·pole (:pōl') s. JER. persona larguirucha.

bean·stalk (:stôk') s. tallo de la planta de frijoles.

bear¹ (bâr) tr. bore, born(e) (to support) sostener; (to carry, display) llevar; (a grudge) guardar; (oneself) conducirse; (to endure) aguantar; (to give birth to) dar a luz; (to yield) producir, dar ♦ **to b. in mind** tener en cuenta • **to b. mention** merecer

mencionarse • **to b. off** llevarse • **to b. out** corroborar • **to b. with** tener paciencia con —intr. (to produce) producir, rendir; (to pressure) pesar; (to go) mantenerse sobre <b. right manténgase sobre la derecha ♦ **to b. on** o **upon** relacionarse con • **to b. up** resistir • **to bring to b.** aplicar, utilizar.

bear² s. oso. FIN. bajista *mf*.

bear·a·ble ('ə-bəl) adj. soportable.

beard (bîrd) s. barba.

beard·ed (bîr'dĭd) adj. barbudo.

bear·er (bâr'ər) s. (carrier) porteador *m*; (of message, check) portador *m*.

bear·ing (:ĭng) s. (poise) porte *m*; MEC. cojinete *m*; AER., MARÍT. rumbo ♦ **to have a b. on** tener relación con ♦ pl. orientación • **to get one's b.** orientarse.

beast (bēst) s. bestia, bruto ♦ **b. of burden** bestia de carga.

beast·ly (:lē) I. adj. -l- bestial, brutal II. adv. G.B. sumamente.

beat (bēt) I. tr. **beat, beat(en)** (to hit) golpear; (to flog) pegar, aporrear; (to pound, flap, stir) batir; (to defeat) vencer, derrotar; (to surpass) superar a; JER. (to perplex) confundir, dejar perplejo; MÚS. (a drum) tocar; (rhythm) marcar, llevar ♦ **b. it!** ¡lárgate! • **off the beaten path** fuera de lo común • **to b. back** o **off** repeler • **to b. down** derribar —intr. (to hit) golpear, caer con violencia; (to throb) latir, pulsar; (drums) redoblar ♦ **to b. around the bush** andarse con rodeos • **to b. down on** azotar (el sol) II. s. (throb) latido, pulsación *f*; (tempo) compás *m*, ritmo; (route) ronda III. adj. FAM. rendido, deslomado.

beat·er (bē'tər) s. batidor *m*.

be·a·tif·ic (bē'ə-tĭf'ĭk) adj. beatífico.

be·at·i·fy (bē-ăt'ə-fī') tr. beatificar.

beat·ing (bē'tĭng) s. (thrashing) paliza; (defeat) derrota; (of the heart) latido.

be·at·i·tude (bē-ăt'ĭ-tōōd') s. beatitud *f*.

beau (bō) s. [pl. s o -x] (suitor) pretendiente *m*; (dandy) galán *m*.

beau·ti·cian (byōō-tĭsh'ən) s. cosmetólogo.

beau·ti·ful (byōō'tə-fəl) adj. bello, hermoso.

beau·ti·ful·ly (:fə-lē) adv. (attractively) bellamente; (very well) espléndidamente.

beau·ti·fy (:fī') tr. embellecer.

beau·ty (byōō'tē) s. belleza, hermosura ♦ (person, thing) belleza ♦ **b. parlor** o **salon** salón de belleza • **that was a (real) b.!** ¡que golpe más bueno!

bea·ver (bē'vər) s. castor *m*.

be·cause (bĭ-kôz', -kŭz') conj. porque ♦ **b. of** a causa de, por.

beck (bĕk) s. ♦ **at someone's b. and call** al servicio de alguien.

beck·on (bĕk'ən) tr. & intr. (to summon) hacer señas; (to entice) atraer, llamar.

be·come (bĭ-kŭm') intr. **-came, -come** (to turn into) llegar a ser, convertirse en; (angry, etc.) hacerse, ponerse, volverse ♦ **b. of** ser, hacerse <what has b. of George? ¿qué se ha hecho de Jorge?> —tr. quedar o sentar bien.

be·com·ing (:ĭng) adj. (suitable) apropiado, conveniente; (attractive) que sienta bien.

bed (bĕd) I. s. cama, lecho; (lodging) alojamiento; (of flowers) macizo ♦ **b. and board** pensión completa • **to go to b.** acostarse II. intr. -dd- ♦ **to b. down** acostarse.

be·daz·zle (bĭ-dăz'əl) tr. deslumbrar.

bed·bug (bĕd'bŭg') s. chinche *f*.

bed·cham·ber (:chăm′bər) s. alcoba.
bed·clothes (:klōthz′) s.pl. ropa de cama.
bed·ding (:ĭng) s. ropa de cama.
be·dev·il (bĭ-dĕv′əl) tr. fastidiar, dificultar.
bed·fel·low (bĕd′fĕl′ō) s. *(bedmate)* compañero de cama; *(associate)* socio.
bed·lam (bĕd′ləm) s. algarabía, alboroto.
bed·pan (bĕd′păn′) s. orinal *m*, chata.
bed·post (:pōst′) s. pilar *m* de cama.
bed·rid·den (:rĭd′n) adj. postrado en cama.
bed·roll (:rōl′) s. lecho portátil que se enrolla.
bed·room (:rōōm′) s. dormitorio, alcoba.
bed·side (:sīd′) adj. & s. (de) cabecera.
bed·sore (:sôr′) s. úlcera por decúbito.
bed·spread (:sprĕd′) s. cubrecama *m*, colcha.
bed·spring (:sprĭng′) s. colchon *m* de muelles.
bed·stead (:stĕd′) s. armadura de la cama.
bed·time (:tīm′) s. hora de acostarse.
bed-wet·ting (:wĕt′ĭng) s. enuresis nocturna.
bee (bē) s. abeja; FAM. *(contest)* concurso.
beech (bēch) s. haya.
beef (bēf) I. s. [pl. **-ves**] carne *f* de res; JER. *(complaint)* [pl. **s**] queja **a to have a b.** quejarse II. intr. JER. quejarse —tr. ♦ **to b. up** JER. reforzar.
beef·steak (′stāk′) s. bistec *m*, biftec *m*.
beef·y (bē′fē) adj. **-i-** fornido, musculoso.
bee·hive (bē′hīv′) s. colmena.
bee·keep·ing (bē′kē′pĭng) s. apicultura.
bee·line (bē′lĭn′) s. línea recta.
been (bĭn) part. p. de **be.**
beep (bēp) I. s. sonido agudo II. intr. & tr. sonar con sonido agudo.
beep·er (bē′pər) s. dispositivo de llamada.
beer (bĭr) s. cerveza ♦ **dark, light b.** cerveza negra, dorada.
bees·wax (bēz′wăks′) s. cera.
beet (bēt) s. remolacha.
bee·tle (bēt′l) s. escarabajo.
be·fall (bĭ-fôl′) tr. **-fell, -en** acontecer a.
be·fit·ting (bĭ-fĭt′ĭng) adj. propio, conveniente.
be·fore (bĭ-fôr′) I. adv. *(earlier)* antes; *(in the past)* anteriormente, ya una vez ♦ **to go b.** ir delante (de) II. prep. *(in time)* antes de o que; *(in space)* delante de; *(in front of)* ante III. conj. *(in advance)* antes de que; *(rather than)* antes que.
be·fore·hand (:hănd′) adv. *(earlier)* antes; *(in anticipation)* de antemano.
be·friend (bĭ-frĕnd′) tr. entablar amistad con.
be·fud·dle (bĭ-fŭd′l) tr. confundir.
beg (bĕg) tr. & intr. **-gg-** *(for charity)* mendigar, pedir (limosna); *(to entreat)* suplicar, rogar ♦ **to b. for mercy** implorar clemencia ♦ **to b. pardon** pedir perdón ♦ **to b. off** disculparse
be·gan (bĭ-găn′) cf. **begin.**
be·get (bĭ-gĕt′) tr. **-got, -got(ten)** engendrar.
beg·gar (bĕg′ər) s. mendigo, pobre *mf.*
beg·gar·ly (:lē) adj. mísero, pobre.
beg·gar·y (bĕg′ə-rē) s. miseria, penuria.
be·gin (bĭ-gĭn′) tr. & intr. **-gan, -gun, -nn-** empezar, comenzar ♦ **to b. by** empezar por ♦ **to b. with** para empezar.
be·gin·ner (:ər) s. principiante *mf*, novato.
be·gin·ning (:ĭng) s. comienzo, principio; *(source)* origen *m* ♦ **b. with** a partir de.
be·gone (bĭ-gôn′) interj. ¡fuera!
be·grudge (bĭ-grŭj′) tr. *(to envy)* envidiar; *(to give reluctantly)* dar de mala gana.
be·guile (bĭ-gīl′) tr. encantar, seducir.
be·gun (bĕ-gŭn′) cf. **begin.**
be·half (bĭ-hăf′) s. ♦ **in b. of** de para, a favor de •

on b. of en nombre de.
be·have (bĭ-hāv′) tr. & intr. portarse, comportarse; *(properly)* portarse bien; *(machine)* funcionar.
be·hav·ior (:yər) s. comportamiento, conducta.
be·head (bĭ-hĕd′) tr. decapitar, descabezar.
be·hind (bĭ-hīnd′) I. adv. *(in back)* atrás, detrás; *(late)* atrasado; *(slow)* con retraso II. prep. *(in back of)* detrás de; *(in a prior place)* atrás; *(underlying)* detrás de; *(in support of)* detrás ♦ **b. schedule** atrasado III. s. FAM. trasero, nalgas.
be·hold (bĭ-hōld′) tr. **-held** mirar, contemplar —interj. ¡mirad!, he aquí.
be·hold·en (bĭ-hōl′dən) adj. obligado *(to con).*
be·hoove (bĭ-hōōv′) tr. convenir.
beige (bāzh) s. & adj. beige *m.*
be·ing (bē′ĭng) s. existencia; *(entity, essence)* ser *m* ♦ **human b.** ser humano • **to bring into b.** realizar, crear.
be·la·bor (bĭ-lā′bər) tr. *(to scold)* regañar; *(to harp on)* machacar.
be·lat·ed (bĭ-lā′tĭd) adj. atrasado, tardío.
belch (bĕlch) I. intr. & tr. eructar; FIG. arrojar, vomitar II. s. eructo.
be·lea·guer (bĭ-lē′gər) tr. asediar, acosar.
bel·fry (bĕl′frē) s. campanario.
be·lie (bĭ-lī′) tr. **-lying** desmentir, contradecir.
be·lief (bĭ-lēf′) s. creencia, fe *f*; *(conviction)* convicción *f*, opinión *f*; *(confidence)* confianza.
be·liev·a·ble (bĭ-lē′və-bəl) adj. creíble.
be·lieve (bĭ-lēv′) tr. & intr. creer —intr. creer; *(to trust)* confiar; *(to support)* ser partidario (in de) ♦ **to make b.** fingir.
be·liev·er (bĭ-lē′vər) s. creyente *mf.*
be·lit·tle (bĭ-lĭt′l) tr. menospreciar.
bell (bĕl) I. s. campana; *(of a door)* timbre *m*; *(of animals)* cencerro; *(of collar)* cascabel *m* ♦ **b. jar** campana de cristal • **to ring a b.** FIG. sonarle a uno II. tr. ♦ **to b. the cat** poner el cascabel al gato.
bell-bot·tom (′bŏt′əm) adj. acampanado.
bell·boy (:boi′) s. botones *m*, paje *m.*
belle (bĕl) s. belleza, mujer bella.
bell·flow·er (bĕl′flou′ər) s. campanilla.
bell·hop (:hŏp′) s. botones *m*, paje *m.*
bel·li·cose (bĕl′ĭ-kōs′) adj. belicoso, agresivo.
bel·lig·er·ence/·cy (bə-lĭj′ər-əns) s. beligerancia, hostilidad *f.*
bel·lig·er·ent (:ənt) adj. & s. beligerante *mf.*
bel·low (bĕl′ō) I. intr. bramar, rugir —tr. vociferar II. s. bramido, rugido.
bel·lows (bĕl′ōz) s. fuelle *m*, barquín *m.*
bel·ly (bĕl′ē) s. vientre *m*; *(stomach)* estómago; FAM. *(paunch)* panza, barriga ♦ **b. flop** panzazo • **b. laugh** carcajada II. intr. & tr. inflar(se), hinchar(se).
bel·ly·ache (:āk′) I. s. *(pain)* dolor *m* de barriga; JER. *(gripe)* queja II. intr. JER. quejarse.
bel·ly·but·ton (:bŭt′n) s. FAM. ombligo.
bel·ly·ful (:fōōl′) s. FAM. panzada, hartazgo.
be·long (bĭ-lông′) intr. *(to have a place)* deber estar, corresponder; *(to fit into a group)* estar en su ambiente ♦ **to b. to** *(as property)* pertenecer a, ser de; *(as a member)* ser miembro de; *(as part of)* corresponder a.
be·long·ings (:ĭngz) s.pl. efectos personales.
be·lov·ed (bĭ-lŭv′ĭd) adj. & s. querido.
be·low (bĭ-lō′) I. adv. abajo; *(in a text)* más abajo II. prep. *(por)* debajo de; *(on a scale)* bajo <b. zero bajo cero>.
belt (bĕlt) I. s. cinturón *m*, cinto; *(region)*

zona, faja; JER. *(punch)* golpe *m*; *(of whiskey)* trago; TEC. *(band)* correa ♦ **seat** *or* **safety b.** cinturón de seguridad • **to hit below the b.** golpear bajo II. tr. *(clothing)* ceñir; JER. *(to punch)* golpear, asestar un golpe ♦ **to b. out** cantar (con voz chillona).

be·moan (bĭ-mōn′) tr. lamentar.

be·muse (bĭ-myōōz′) tr. dejar perplejo.

bench (bĕnch) s. *(seat, workbench)* banco; DER. *(office of the judge)* judicatura; *(court)* tribunal *m*; G.B. *(in Parliament)* escaño ♦ **b. warrant** DER. auto de detención.

bend (bĕnd) I. tr. **bent** *(the head)* inclinar; *(the knee)* doblar; *(one's back)* encorvar; *(to curve)* doblar, plegar; *(to subdue)* doblegar —intr. *(to curve)* doblarse, curvarse; *(to swerve)* desviarse, torcer ♦ **to b. back** doblarse hacia atrás • **to b. down** *o* **over** encorvarse • **to b. over backwards** hacer el mayor esfuerzo posible II. s. *(curve)* curva; *(turn)* vuelta, recodo ♦ pl. parálisis que afecta a los buceadores.

bend·er (bĕn′dər) s. FAM. borrachera, juerga.

be·neath (bĭ-nēth′) I. prep. *(below)* (por) debajo de; *(under)* bajo; *(unworthy)* indigno de II. adv. *(below)* abajo; *(underneath)* debajo.

ben·e·dic·tion (bĕn′ĭ-dĭk′shən) s. bendición *f.*

ben·e·fac·tor (bĕn′ə-făk′tər) s. benefactor.

ben·e·fac·tress (:trĭs) s. benefactora.

ben·e·fice (bĕn′ə-fĭs) s. beneficio.

be·nef·i·cent (bə-nĕf′ĭ-sənt) adj. benéfico.

ben·e·fi·cial (bĕn′ə-fĭsh′əl) adj. provechoso.

ben·e·fi·ci·ar·y (:ē-ĕr′ē) s. beneficiario.

ben·e·fit (bĕn′ə-fĭt) I. s. *(profit)* beneficio, provecho; *(advantage)* ventaja; *(fund-raiser)* beneficio ♦ **for the b. of** en beneficio de • **to give someone the b.** of the doubt no juzgar a alguien por anticipado ♦ pl. asistencia II. tr. beneficiar —intr. ♦ **to b. by** *o* **from** sacar provecho de.

be·nev·o·lence (bə-nĕv′ə-ləns) s. benevolencia; *(kindly act)* acto de caridad.

be·nev·o·lent (:lənt) adj. benévolo; *(philanthropic)* benéfico.

be·night·ed (bĭ-nī′tĭd) adj. ignorante.

be·nign (bĭ-nīn′) adj. benigno.

bent (bĕnt) I. cf. **bend** II. adj. *(crooked)* doblado, torcido; *(determined)* empeñado III. s. inclinación *f*, tendencia.

be·numb (bĭ-nŭm′) tr. entumecer; *(to stupefy)* entorpecer.

ben·zene (bĕn′zēn′) s. benceno.

be·queath (bĭ-kwēth′, -kwēth′) tr. legar.

be·quest (bĭ-kwĕst′) s. legado.

be·rate (bĭ-rāt′) tr. reprender, regañar.

be·reaved (bĭ-rēvd′) adj. afligido (por la muerte) ♦ **the b.** los deudos del difunto.

be·reave·ment (bĭ-rēv′mənt) s. *(grief)* luto, duelo; *(loss)* pérdida (de un ser querido).

be·reft (bĭ-rĕft′) adj. privado *(of* de).

be·ret (bə-rā′) s. boina.

ber·ry (bĕr′ē) s. baya.

ber·serk (bər-sûrk′) adj. frenético, loco ♦ **to go b.** volverse loco.

berth (bûrth) s. *(on a train)* litera; MARÍT. *(cabin)* camarote *m*; *(at a wharf)* atracadero; *(employment)* puesto ♦ **to give a wide b. to** evitar.

be·ryl·li·um (bə-rĭl′ē-əm) s. berilio.

be·seech (bĭ-sēch′) tr. **-ed** *o* **-sought** suplicar, implorar.

be·set (bĭ-sĕt′) tr. **-set, -tting** *(to harass)* asediar, acosar; *(to surround)* rodear.

be·side (bĭ-sīd′) prep. junto a, al lado de ♦ **to be b. oneself** estar fuera de sí • **to be b. the point** no venir al caso.

be·sides (bĭ-sīdz′) I. adv. *(in addition)* además, también; *(moreover)* además; *(otherwise)* por otro lado, aparte de eso II. prep. *(in addition to)* además de; *(except)* aparte de, fuera de.

be·siege (bĭ-sēj′) tr. MIL. sitiar; *(to hem in)* rodear; *(to harass)* asediar, abrumar ♦ **to be besieged with** *(calls, requests)* haber recibido un torrente de *(llamadas, peticiones).*

be·smirch (bĭ-smûrch′) tr. ensuciar, manchar.

be·speak (bĭ-spēk′) tr. **-spoke, -spoke(n)** indicar, revelar.

best (bĕst) [superl. de **good**] I. adj. mejor; *(favorite)* favorito <*my b. friend* mi amigo favorito> ♦ **b. man** padrino (de una boda) • **b. seller** libro de gran éxito • **to know what is b. for one** saber lo que más le conviene a uno II. adv. mejor; *(most)* más <*which do you like b.?* ¿cuál te gusta más?> III. s. el mejor, lo mejor ♦ **at b.** a lo más • **to do one's b.** hacer lo mejor que uno puede • **to make the b. of it** salir de un mal negocio lo mejor posible • **to the b. of my recollection** que yo recuerde IV. tr. vencer, ganar.

bes·tial (bĕs′chəl) adj. bestial.

bes·ti·al·i·ty (′chē-ăl′ĭ-tē) s. bestialidad *f.*

be·stir (bĭ-stûr′) tr. ♦ **to b. oneself** rebullirse.

be·stow (bĭ-stō′) tr. otorgar, conceder.

be·stow·al (:əl) s. otorgamiento.

be·strewn (bĭ-strōōn′) adj. salpicado *(with* de).

bet (bĕt) I. s. apuesta ♦ **to be a sure b.** ser cosa segura II. tr. **bet(ted), -tting** apostar ♦ **I b....** FAM. a que..., seguro que... —intr. *(to wager)* apostar; *(to gamble)* jugar ♦ **I b.!** FAM. ¡ya lo creo! • **you b.!** FAM. ¡claro!

be·to·ken (bĭ-tō′kən) tr. indicar, presagiar.

be·tray (bĭ-trā′) tr. traicionar; *(to inform on)* delatar; *(a secret)* revelar.

be·tray·al (:əl) s. traición *f*, delación *f*; *(of a secret)* revelación *f.*

be·troth (bĭ-trōth′) tr. ♦ **to become betrothed** desposarse.

be·troth·al (bĭ-trō′thəl) s. compromiso matrimonial.

be·trothed (bĭ-trōthd′) s. prometido, novio.

bet·ter (bĕt′ər) [comp. de **good**] I. adj. mejor; *(preferable)* más apropiado, preferible ♦ **the b. part of** la mayor parte de • **to be b.** to valer más, ser mejor II. adv. mejor ♦ **all the b.** *o* **so much the b.** tanto mejor • **b. and b.** cada vez mejor • **b. late than never** más vale tarde que nunca • **b. off** en mejores condiciones • **had b.** más vale que <*we had b. go* más vale que nos vayamos> • **to get b.** mejorar III. tr. & intr. mejorar(se) IV. s. el mejor ♦ **for b. or worse** en la fortuna como en la desventura • **to get the b. of** superar, vencer ♦ pl. superiores.

bet·ter·ment (:mənt) s. mejora, mejoramiento.

bet·tor (bĕt′ər) s. apostador *m*, apostante *mf.*

be·tween (bĭ-twēn′) I. prep. entre ♦ **b. now and then** de aquí a entonces • **b. you and me** entre nosotros II. adv. en medio, de por medio ♦ **far b.** a grandes intervalos • **in b.** mientras tanto.

be·twixt (bĭ-twĭkst′) adv. ♦ **b. and between** entre una cosa y otra.

bev·el (bĕv′əl) I. s. bisel *m* II. tr. biselar.

bev·eled (:əld) adj. biselado.

bev·er·age (bĕv′ər-ĭj) s. bebida.

bev·y (bĕv′ē) s. *(of birds)* bandada; *(of people)* grupo.

be·wail (bĭ-wāl') tr. lamentar.
be·ware (bĭ-wâr') I. tr. & intr. tener cuidado (con) ♦ **b. of** cuidado con II. interj. ¡cuidado!
be·wil·der (bĭ-wĭl'dər) tr. aturdir, dejar perplejo.
be·wil·der·ment (:mənt) s. aturdimiento.
be·witch (bĭ-wĭch') tr. hechizar.
be·witch·ment (:mənt) s. hechizo.
be·yond (bĭ-yŏnd') I. prep. (greater than) más allá, fuera de; (after) después de ♦ **b. belief** increíble • **b. dispute** incontestable • **b. (a) doubt** fuera de duda • **b. help** sin remedio • **it's b. me** no alcanzo a comprender II. adv. más lejos, más allá.
bi·an·nu·al (bī-ăn'yōō-əl) adj. semestral.
bi·as (bī'əs) I. s. (tendency) inclinación f; (prejudice) prejuicio; (partiality) preferencia; COST. bies m II. tr. predisponer, influenciar ♦ **to be biased** ser parcial.
bib (bĭb) s. babero; (of an apron) peto.
Bi·ble (bī'bəl) s. Biblia ♦ **b.** biblia.
Bib·li·cal o **bib·li·cal** (bĭb'lĭ-kəl) adj. bíblico.
bib·li·og·ra·pher (bĭb'lē-ŏg'rə-fər) s. bibliógrafo.
bib·li·og·ra·phy (:fē) s. bibliografía.
bib·li·o·phile (bĭb'lē-ə-fīl') s. bibliófilo.
bi·car·bon·ate (bī-kär'bə-nāt') s. bicarbonato ♦ **b. of soda** bicarbonato de sosa.
bi·cen·ten·ni·al (bī'sĕn-tĕn'ē-əl) adj. & s. bicentario.
bi·ceps (bī'sĕps') s. [pl. inv. o **es**] bíceps m.
bick·er (bĭk'ər) intr. reñir, disputar.
bi·cy·cle (bī'sĭk'əl) I. s. bicicleta II. intr. montar or ir en bicicleta.
bi·cy·clist (:lĭst) s. ciclista mf.
bid (bĭd) I. tr. **bid** o **bade**, **bid(den)**, **-dd-** (to order) ordenar, mandar; (to offer) licitar; (in cards) declarar ♦ **to b. farewell** o **good-bye to** decir adiós a —intr. hacer una oferta II. s. (offer) licitación f, oferta; (in cards) declaración f; (effort) tentativa.
bid·der (:ər) s. postor m.
bid·ding (:ĭng) s. (command) orden f; (at an auction) oferta; (in cards) declaración f.
bid·dy (bĭd'ē) s. gallina; JER. vieja chacharera.
bide (bīd) tr. **-d** o **bode**, **-d** ♦ **to b. one's time** aguardar el momento oportuno.
bi·en·ni·al (bī-ĕn'ē-əl) adj. bienal.
bier (bîr) s. féretro.
bi·fo·cal (bī-fō'kəl) I. adj. bifocal II. s. ♦ **b.** anteojos bifocales.
bi·fur·cate (bī'fər-kāt') intr. bifurcarse.
bi·fur·ca·tion ('-kā'shən) s. bifurcación f.
big (bĭg) **-gg-** I. adj. gran, grande; (great in intensity) fuerte; (older) mayor <my b. brother mi hermano mayor>; (important) importante, de gran significado ♦ **b. shot** o **wheel** pez gordo II. adv. ♦ **to be b. on** FAM. ser entusiasta de • **to make it b.** tener gran éxito • **to talk b.** jactarse.
big·a·mist (bĭg'ə-mĭst) s. bígamo.
big·a·my (:mē) s. bigamia.
big-heart·ed (bĭg'här'tĭd) adj. generoso.
big·ness (:nĭs) s. grandor m, grandeza.
big·ot (bĭg'ət) s. intolerante mf.
big·ot·ed (:ə-tĭd) adj. intolerante.
big·ot·ry (:trē) s. intolerancia.
big-time (bĭg'tīm') adj. JER. de los grandes.
big·wig (:wĭg') s. FAM. pez gordo.
bike (bīk) I. s. (bicycle) bici f; (motorcycle) moto f II. intr. montar en bici, manejar una moto.

bik·er (bī'kər) s. motociclista mf.
bi·lat·er·al (bī-lăt'ər-əl) adj. bilateral.
bile (bīl) s. (fluid) bilis f; (ill temper) mal genio.
bilge (bĭlj) s. MARÍT. sentina; JER. (nonsense) disparates m ♦ **b. water** agua de sentina.
bi·lin·gual (bī-lĭng'gwəl) adj. bilingüe.
bil·ious (bĭl'yəs) adj. bilioso.
bilk (bĭlk) tr. estafar, defraudar.
bill¹ (bĭl) I. s. (invoice) cuenta, factura; (poster) cartel m; (bank note) billete m; POL. proyecto de ley ♦ **b. of exchange** letra de cambio • **b. of fare** carta, menú • **b. of lading** conocimiento de embarque • **b. of rights** declaración de derechos • **b. of sale** boleto de compra y venta • **to fill the b.** FAM. satisfacer todos los requisitos • **to foot the b.** FAM. correr con los gastos II. tr. (a customer) pasar la cuenta a; (expenses, goods) facturar; (to promote) anunciar, promocionar.
bill² (bĭl) s. (beak) pico; (visor) visera.
bill·board ('bôrd') s. cartelera.
bil·let (bĭl'ĭt) MIL. I. s. alojamiento II. tr. alojar.
bill·fold (bĭl'fōld') s. billetera, cartera.
bil·liards (bĭl'yərdz) s.sg. billar m.
bill·ing (bĭl'ĭng) s. publicidad f ♦ pl. facturación.
bil·lion (bĭl'yən) s. E.U. [10^9] mil millones m; G.B. [10^{12}] billón m.
bil·lion·aire (:yə-nâr') s. & adj. billonario.
bil·low (bĭl'ō) I. s. oleada, ola II. intr. (sea) ondular; (sails) hincharse.
bil·low·y (:ē) adj. ondulante.
bil·ly (bĭl'ē) ♦ **b. club** porra, bastón (de policía) • **b. goat** macho cabrío.
bi·month·ly (bī-mŭnth'lē) adj. & adv. bimestral(mente).
bin (bĭn) s. (box) cajón m; (container) recipiente m, compartimiento.
bi·na·ry (bī'nə-rē) adj. binario.
bind (bīnd) I. tr. **bound** (to tie) amarrar, atar; (to restrain) ceñir; (a wound) vendar; (morally, legally) obligar, comprometer a; (by sentiment) ligar, vincular; (a contract) ratificar; (a book) encuadernar, empastar; (sheaves) agavillar; (to constipate) estreñir ♦ **to be bound up with** estar ligado o relacionado con • **to b. over** poner bajo fianza —intr. (to be tight) apretar; (a mix) aglutinarse; (a contract) tener fuerza obligatoria II. s. ♦ **to be in a b.** estar en un aprieto o un apuro.
bind·er (bīn'dər) s. IMPR. encuadernador m; (fastener) atadura; (notebook cover) carpeta; (payment) garantía; (contract) contrato provisional.
bind·er·y (:də-rē) s. taller m de encuadernación.
bind·ing (:ĭng) I. s. IMPR. encuadernación f; COST. ribete m II. adj. (tight) apretado; DER. obligatorio; (promise) que compromete a uno.
binge (bĭnj) s. JER. parranda ♦ **to go on a (shopping, eating) b.** darse un banquete (comprando, comiendo).
bin·oc·u·lar (bə-nŏk'yə-lər) I. adj. binocular II. s. ♦ pl. gemelos, prismáticos.
bi·no·mi·al (bī-nō'mē-əl) adj. & s. binomio.
bi·o·chem·i·cal (bī'ō-kĕm'ĭ-kəl) adj. bioquímico.
bi·o·chem·ist (:ĭst) adj. bioquímico.
bi·o·chem·is·try (:ĭ-strē) s. bioquímica.
bi·o·feed·back (bī'ō-fēd'băk') s. biorreacción f.

bi·og·ra·pher (bī-ŏg′rə-fər) s. biógrafo.
bi·o·graph·ic/i·cal (bī′ə-grăf′ĭk) adj. biográfico.
bi·og·ra·phy (bī-ŏg′rə-fē) s. biografía.
bi·o·log·ic/i·cal (bī′ə-lŏj′ĭk) adj. biológico.
bi·ol·o·gist (bī-ŏl′ə-jĭst) s. biólogo.
bi·ol·o·gy (:jē) s. biología.
bi·on·ics (bī-ŏn′ĭks) s.sg. biónica.
bi·o·phys·ics (bī′ō-fĭz′ĭks) s.sg. biofísica.
bi·op·sy (bī′ŏp′sē) s. biopsia.
bi·o·rhythm (bī′ō-rĭth′əm) s. ritmo biológico.
bi·o·sci·ence (′sī′əns) s. ciencia natural.
bi·par·ti·san (bī-pär′tĭ-zən) adj. bipartidista.
bi·par·tite (:tīt′) adj. bipartito.
bi·ped (bī′pĕd′) s. & adj. bípedo.
bi·plane (bī′plān′) s. biplano.
bi·ra·cial (bī-rā′shəl) adj. de dos razas.
birch (bûrch) s. abedul *m*.
bird (bûrd) I. s. pájaro; *(large)* ave *f*; *(game)* caza de pluma ♦ **birds of a feather** lobos de la misma camada • **for the birds** cosa de bobos • **odd b.** bicho raro II. intr. observar pájaros.
bird·cage (′kāj′) s. jaula.
bird·call (:kôl′) s. canto; *(device)* reclamo.
bird·house (:hous′) s. pajarera, aviario.
bird·lime (:īm′) s. liga.
bird's-eye (bûrdz′ī′) adj. ♦ **b. view** vista panorámica.
birth (bûrth) s. nacimiento; *(ancestry)* linaje *m*; MED. parto ♦ **b. control** control de la natalidad • **by b.** de nacimiento • **to give b. to** dar a luz a.
birth·day (′dā′) s. cumpleaños ♦ **on one's (15th, 25th) b.** al cumplir los (15, 25) años.
birth·mark (:märk′) s. lunar *m*.
birth·place (:plās′) s. lugar *m* de nacimiento.
birth·rate (:rāt′) s. índice *m* de natalidad.
birth·right (:rīt′) s. derechos de nacimiento.
bis·cuit (bĭs′kĭt) s. bizcocho; G.B. galletita.
bi·sect (bī-sĕkt′) tr. bisecar.
bi·sec·tion (bī-sĕk′shən) s. bisección *f*.
bi·sex·u·al (bī-sĕk′shōō-əl) adj. & s. bisexual *mf*.
bish·op (bĭsh′əp) s. obispo; *(in chess)* alfil *m*.
bis·muth (bĭz′məth) s. bismuto.
bi·son (bī′sən) s. bisonte *m*.
bit¹ (bĭt) s. *(piece)* pedacito, trocito; *(amount)* poco <a b. larger un poco más grande>; *(moment)* ratito ♦ **a good b.** bastante • **a little b.** un poquito • **b. by b.** poco a poco • **b. part** papel secundario • **bits and pieces** cosas sueltas • **not a b.** en absoluto • **the whole b.** FAM. todo • **to blow to bits** hacer pedazos o añicos • **to do one's b.** poner de la parte de uno.
bit² s. *(drill)* broca, barrena; *(of a bridle)* freno, bocado.
bit³ s. COMPUT. bit *m*, bitio.
bitch (bĭch) I. s. *(dog)* perra; JER. *(shrew)* zorra, arpía; *(complaint)* queja II. intr. JER. quejarse.
bitch·y (′ē) adj. -**i**- rencoroso.
bite (bīt) I. tr. & intr. **bit, bit(ten)** morder; *(insects, snakes, fish)* picar; *(to cut into)* cortar ♦ **to b.** off arrancar de un mordisco • **to b. the bullet** apretar los dientes y aguantar • **to b. the dust** morder el polvo II. s. mordisco, dentellada; *(wound)* mordedura; *(sting)* picada; *(in fishing)* picada; *(mouthful)* mordisco, bocado ♦ **to have a b. to eat** FAM. tomar un piscolabis • **to have b.** ser incisivo o penetrante.
bit·ing (bī′tĭng) adj. *(wind)* cortante; *(incisive)*

penetrante; *(sarcastic)* mordaz.
bit·ter (bĭt′ər) I. adj. **-er, -est** amargo; *(wind, cold)* cortante, penetrante; *(hard to accept)* duro; *(fierce)* encarnizado, implacable; *(resentful)* resentido, amargado ♦ **to the b. end** hasta vencer o morir II. s. ♦ pl. bíter *m*.
bit·ter·ness (:nĭs) s. amargura; *(fierceness)* encarnizamiento; *(resentment)* rencor *m*.
bit·ter·sweet (:swēt′) adj. agridulce.
bi·tu·men (bī-tōō′mən) s. betún *m*.
bi·tu·mi·nous (:mə-nəs) adj. bituminoso.
bi·va·lent (bī-vā′lənt) adj. bivalente.
bi·valve (bī′vălv′) s. & adj. bivalvo.
bi·week·ly (bī-wēk′lē) adj. quincenal.
bi·zarre (bī-zär′) adj. extravagante, extraño.
blab (blăb) I. tr. **-bb-** soltar, descubrir (secreto) —intr. *(to tell secrets)* descubrir el pastel; *(to chatter)* cotorrear II. s. charloteo, cotorreo.
blab·ber (:ər) I. intr. cotorrear II. s. cotorreo.
blab·ber·mouth (:mouth′) s. JER. cotorra.
black (blăk) I. s. negro ♦ **B. o b.** *(person)* negro • **in b. and white** por escrito • **to be in the b.** estar haciendo ganancias • **to wear b.** estar de luto II. adj. negro; *(gloomy)* sombrío; *(wicked)* malvado; *(sullen)* hosco ♦ **B. o b.** *(Negroid)* negro • **b. box** AVIA. registrador de vuelo • **b. eye** ojo a la funerala • **b. market** mercado negro, estraperlo III. tr. ♦ **to b. out** MIL. apagar las luces; MED. perder el conocimiento.
black-and-blue (′ən-blōō′) adj. FAM. amoratado.
black·ball (′bôl′) I. s. bola negra II. tr. dar o echar bola negra.
black·ber·ry (:bĕr′ē) s. zarzamora.
black·bird (:bûrd′) s. mirlo.
black·board (:bôrd′) s. pizarra, pizarrón *m*.
black·en (:ən) tr. ennegrecer; *(to defame)* mancillar, difamar —intr. ennegrecerse.
black·head (:hĕd′) s. espinilla, grano.
black·jack (:jăk′) s. *(bludgeon)* cachiporra; *(game)* veintiuna.
black·list (:lĭst′) I. s. lista negra II. tr. poner en la lista negra.
black·mail (:māl′) I. s. chantaje *m* II. tr. chantajear.
black·mail·er (:mā′lər) s. chantajista *mf*.
black·out (:out′) s. *(of a city)* apagón *m*; MED. desmayo, pérdida de la memoria; *(of news)* supresión *f*.
black·smith (:smĭth′) s. herrero.
black·top (:tŏp′) s. asfalto.
blad·der (blăd′ər) s. vejiga.
blade (blād) s. hoja; *(of a razor, skate)* cuchilla; *(of an oar)* pala; *(of a propeller, fan)* aleta; *(of grass)* brizna; *(young man)* galán *m*.
blahs (blăz) s.pl. JER. ♦ **to get the b.** desanimarse.
blame (blām) I. tr. ♦ **to be to b. for** tener la culpa de • **to b. on** echar la culpa a II. s. culpa ♦ **to put the b.** on echar la culpa a.
blame·less (′lĭs) adj. libre de culpa.
blame·wor·thy (:wûr′the) adj. **-i**- censurable, culpable.
bland (blănd) adj. *(mild)* suave; *(dull)* insulso.
blan·dish·ment (blăn′dĭsh-mənt) s. lisonja.
blank (blăngk) I. adj. *(paper, tape)* en blanco; *(wall)* liso; *(look)* vago; *(mind)* vacío ♦ **b. check** cheque en blanco; FIG. carta blanca • **to go b.** quedarse en blanco II. s. *(space)* blanco, vacío; *(form)* formulario (en blanco); *(car-*

tridge) cartucho de fogueo ♦ **to draw a b.** no saber qué decir o contestar **III.** tr. ♦ **to b. out** borrar.

blan·ket (blăng′kĭt) **I.** s. manta, frazada; FIG. manto, capa ♦ **wet b.** aguafiestas **II.** adj. general, comprensivo **III.** tr. tapar, cubrir.

blare (blâr) **I.** intr. resonar —tr. proclamar, pregonar **II.** s. estruendo.

blar·ney (blär′nē) s. FAM. labia.

bla·sé (blä-zā′) adj. hastiado, indiferente.

blas·pheme (blăs-fēm′) tr. & intr. blasfemar (contra).

blas·phe·mous (′fə-məs) adj. blasfemo.

blas·phe·my (:mē) s. blasfemia.

blast (blăst) **I.** s. *(gust)* ráfaga; *(explosion)* explosión *f*; *(explosive)* carga explosiva; *(shock)* onda de choque; MÚS. toque *m*, soplido ♦ **b. furnace** alto horno • **(at) full b.** a todo vapor • **to have a b.** JER. pasarla muy bien **II.** tr. *(to blow up)* volar; *(hopes)* acabar con; *(a hole)* abrir, perforar (con barrenos); FAM. *(to criticize)* criticar ♦ **to b. away** disparar repetidamente • **to b. off** despegar.

blast·ed (blăs′tĭd) adj. FAM. condenado, maldito.

blast·off o **blast-off** (blăst′ôf′) s. lanzamiento.

bla·tant (blāt′nt) adj. patente, evidente.

blath·er (blăth′ər) **I.** intr. decir disparates **II.** s. disparates *m.*

blaze[1] (blāz) **I.** s. llamarada; *(glare)* resplandor *m*; *(fire)* fuego, hoguera; *(outburst)* arranque *m* **II.** intr. arder ♦ **blazing with (lights, colors)** resplandeciente de (luces, colores) • **to b. away** disparar continuamente.

blaze[2] (blāz) **I.** s. *(white spot)* lucero; *(trail mark)* marca **II.** tr. ♦ **to b. a trail** abrir un camino.

blaz·er (blā′zər) s. chaqueta deportiva.

bla·zon·ry (blā′zən-rē) s. blasón *m.*

bleach (blēch) **I.** tr. blanquear; *(clothes)* colar; *(hair)* de(s)colorar —intr. de(s)colorarse **II.** s. de(s)colorante *m*; *(for clothes)* lejía.

bleach·ers (blē′chərz) s.pl. gradas.

bleak (blēk) adj. desolado, frío; *(dreary)* sombrío; *(prospect)* poco prometedor.

blear (blîr) tr. nublar.

blear·y (′ē) adj. **-i-** *(eyes)* nublado; *(exhausted)* agotado, exhausto.

bleat (blēt) **I.** s. balido **II.** intr. balar.

bleed (blēd) intr. **bled** sangrar, perder sangre; BOT. exudar, perder savia; *(colors)* correrse ♦ **to b. to death** morir desangrado —tr. desangrar a, sacar sangre a; *(liquids)* sangrar; JER. *(to extort)* desplumar a ♦ **to b. white** o **dry** FAM. chuparle la sangre a.

bleep (blēp) tr. & s. (hacer un) sonido electrónico agudo.

blem·ish (blĕm′ĭsh) **I.** tr. manchar, mancillar **II.** s. mancha; *(flaw)* tacha.

blend (blĕnd) **I.** tr. **-ed** o **blent** *(to mix)* mezclar; *(to harmonize)* armonizar —intr. *(to mix)* mezclarse, entremezclarse; *(to harmonize)* armonizar, hacer juego **II.** s. mezcla.

blend·er (blĕn′dər) s. licuadora, batidora.

bless (blĕs) tr. **-ed** o **blest** bendecir ♦ **b. my soul!** o **me!** ¡válgame Dios! • **to b. with** dotar de.

bless·ed (′ĭd) adj. bendito, santo ♦ **b. event** feliz acontecimiento • **not a b. thing** FAM. nada en absoluto.

bless·ing (:ĭng) s. bendición *f*; *(benefit)* ventaja; *(approval)* aprobación *f.*

blew (blo͞o) cf. **blow**[1].

blight (blīt) **I.** s. BOT. añublo; *(decay)* ruina, decadencia **II.** tr. arruinar, destruir.

blimp (blĭmp) s. dirigible no rígido.

blind (blīnd) **I.** adj. ciego; *(hidden)* escondido; *(street)* sin salida ♦ **b. as a bat** ciego como un topo • **b. in one eye** tuerto • **b. date, navigation** cita, navegación a ciegas • **b. spot** ángulo muerto; FIG. punto flaco • **b. with** ciego de • **to turn a b. eye** hacer la vista gorda **II.** s. persiana **III.** adv. a ciegas ♦ **b. drunk** borracho como una cuba **IV.** tr. cegar; *(to dazzle)* deslumbrar.

blind·ers (blīn′dərz) s.pl. anteojeras.

blind·fold (blīnd′fōld′) **I.** tr. vendar los ojos a **II.** s. venda.

blind·ing (:ĭng) adj. cegador, deslumbrante.

blind·ly (:ē) adv. ciegamente, a ciegas.

blind·ness (:nĭs) s. ceguera.

blink (blĭngk) **I.** intr. parpadear, pestañear; *(signal)* brillar intermitentemente; *(to back down)* ceder, echarse atrás —tr. abrir y cerrar ♦ **to b. an eye** hacer la vista gorda • **without blinking an eye** sin pestañear **II.** s. parpadeo, pestañeo ♦ **on the b.** JER. descompuesto.

blink·er (blĭng′kər) s. intermitente *m* ♦ pl. anteojeras.

blink·ing (:kĭng) adj. *(flickering)* parpadeante; *(intermittent)* intermitente; G.B., JER. maldito.

blip (blĭp) s. ELECTRÓN. cresta de eco.

bliss (blĭs) s. dicha, felicidad *f.*

bliss·ful (′fəl) adj. dichoso, feliz.

blis·ter (blĭs′tər) **I.** s. ampolla; BOT. verruga **II.** tr. & intr. ampollar(se).

blis·ter·ing (:ĭng) adj. *(hot)* abrasador; *(harsh)* feroz (palabras); *(fast-paced)* forzado.

blithe (blīth) adj. alegre, despreocupado.

blitz (blĭts) s. MIL. ataque relámpago.

bliz·zard (blĭz′ərd) s. ventisca; FIG. torrente *m.*

bloat (blōt) tr. & intr. hinchar(se), inflar(se).

blob (blŏb) s. masa informe; *(of color)* mancha.

bloc (blŏk) s. bloque *m.*

block (blŏk) **I.** s. bloque *m*; *(chunk)* trozo; *(for chopping)* tajo; *(hat mold)* horma; *(chock)* calza; *(toy)* tarugo; *(pulley)* polea; *(of a city)* cuadra, manzana; *(street)* calle *f*, cuadra; *(obstacle)* obstrucción *f*, obstáculo; JER. *(head)* coco, cabeza; DEP., MED., PSICOL. bloqueo, obstrucción ♦ **b. and tackle** aparejo de poleas **II.** tr. *(to obstruct)* bloquear, obstruir (tráfico, avance); *(a wheel)* calzar; MED., PSICOL. obstruir, interrumpir.

block·ade (blŏk-kād′) **I.** s. bloqueo **II.** tr. bloquear.

block·age (blŏk′ĭj) s. obstrucción *f.*

block·bust·er (:bŭs′tər) s. éxito rotundo.

block·head (:hĕd′) s. FAM. zoquete *m.*

bloke (blōk) s. G.B., FAM. tipo, fulano.

blond (blŏnd) s. & adj. rubio.

blonde (blŏnd) s. & adj. rubia.

blood (blŭd) **I.** s. sangre *f*; *(bloodshed)* derrame *m* de sangre; *(lineage)* linaje *m*; *(kinship)* parentesco ♦ **b. bath** matanza • **b. count** recuento globular • **b. relation** consanguíneo • **b. test** análisis de sangre • **b. type** tipo sanguíneo.

blood·cur·dling (′kûrd′lĭng) adj. espeluznante.

blood·hound (:hound′) s. sabueso.

blood·less (:lĭs) adj. exangüe; *(coup)* sin derramamiento de sangre.

blood·shed (:shĕd′) s. derramamiento de

sangre.
blood·shot (:shŏt′) adj. inyectado de sangre.
blood·stain (:stān′) **I.** s. mancha de sangre **II.** tr. ensangrentar.
blood·stream (:strēm′) s. corriente sanguínea.
blood·thirst·y (:thûr′stē) adj. sanguinario.
blood·y (:ē) **I.** adj. -i- sangriento; G.B., JER. maldito, infame **II.** adv. G.B., JER. muy **III.** tr. ensangrentar.
bloom (blōōm) **I.** s. flor f; (flowering) florecimiento; (vigor) lozanía ♦ **in b.** en flor **II.** intr. florecer.
bloom·ers (blōō′mərz) s.pl. calzón bombacho.
bloop·er (blōō′pər) s. FAM. metida de pata.
blos·som (blŏs′əm) **I.** s. flor f; (flowering) florecimiento ♦ **in b.** en flor **II.** intr. florecer.
blot (blŏt) **I.** s. mancha, borrón m **II.** tr. -tt- manchar; (ink) secar ♦ **blotting paper** papel secante • **b. out** borrar.
blotch (blŏch) **I.** s. mancha, manchón m **II.** tr. & intr. cubrir(se) de manchas.
blot·ter (blŏt′ər) s. (paper) secante m; (register) registro.
blouse (blous) s. blusa; (smock) blusón m; MIL. guerrera.
blow¹ (blō) **I.** intr. **blew, -n** soplar; (a horn) sonar; (a whale) respolar; (a fuse) quemarse; (to pant) resollar; (to burst) explotar ♦ **to b. in** FAM. llegar inesperadamente • **to b. out** (tire) estallar, reventarse; (fuse) fundirse, quemarse • **to b. over** (storm) pasar; (scandal) olvidarse • **to b. up** (to explode) explotar; (with anger) encolerizarse —tr. soplar; (instrument) tocar; (smoke) echar; (the nose) sonar; (a fuse) fundir; (to waste) malgastar; FAM. (to leave town) irse, largarse de ♦ **to b. away** llevarse • **to b. down** derribar • **to b. off steam** desahogarse emocionalmente • **to b. out** soplar, apagar • **to b. over** derribar; FIG. sorprender • **to b. up** (to destroy) volar, hacer saltar; (to inflate) inflar; FOTOG. ampliar **II.** s. soplido, soplo; (storm) tormenta.
blow² s. golpe m; (setback) revés m ♦ **to come to blows** agarrarse a puñetazos.
blow-by-blow (′bī′) adj. detallado.
blow-dry·er (:drī′ ər) s. secador m de cabello.
blow·gun (:gŭn′) s. cerbatana.
blow·hard (:härd′) s. JER. fanfarrón m.
blow·hole (:hōl′) s. respiradero.
blown (blōn) cf. **blow¹**.
blow·out (:out′) s. AUTO. reventón m, pinchazo; JER. (bash) gran festín m, comilona.
blow·torch (:tôrch′) s. soplete m.
blow·up (:ŭp′) s. explosión f; (of temper) estallido; FOTOG. ampliación f.
blub·ber (blŭb′ər) **I.** intr. lloriquear, gimotear —tr. decir llorando **II.** s. grasa de ballena; (body fat) grasa, gordura.
bludg·eon (blŭj′ən) **I.** s. cachiporra, maza **II.** tr. aporrear.
blue (blōō) **I.** s. azul m ♦ **out of the b.** de repente ♦ pl. melancolía; MÚS. jazz melancólico **II.** adj. azul; (gloomy) triston, melancólico ♦ **b. chip** acción selecta • **b. jay** arrendajo • **b. jeans** pantalones vaqueros.
blue·bell (′bĕl′) s. campanilla.
blue·bot·tle (:bŏt′l) s. moscarda, mosca azul.
blue-col·lar (:kŏl′ər) adj. de obreros.
blue-pen·cil (:pĕn′səl) tr. corregir, revisar.
blue·print (:prĭnt′) s. cianotipo, anteproyecto; FIG. proyecto detallado.
blue·stock·ing (:stŏk′ĭng) s. marisabidilla.

bluff¹ (blŭf) **I.** tr. (to fool) engañar —intr. farolear, aparentar **II.** s. engaño, farol m ♦ **to call someone's b.** desenmascarar.
bluff² s. (cliff) acantilado; (river bank) ribera escarpada.
bluff·er (′ər) s. fanfarrón m, farolero.
blu·ing (blōō′ĭng) s. añil m, azulete m.
blun·der (blŭn′dər) **I.** s. error craso, metida de pata **II.** intr. (to move) andar a tropezones; (to err) cometer un error craso.
blunt (blŭnt) **I.** adj. desafilado; (frank) franco, brusco **II.** tr. desafilar, embotar.
blur (blûr) **I.** tr. -rr- empañar, nublar —intr. oscurecerse, ponerse borroso **II.** s. borrón m, manchón m.
blurb (blûrb) s. propaganda.
blur·ry (blûr′ē) adj. -i- confuso, borroso.
blurt (blûrt) tr. ♦ **to b. out** dejar escapar, decir impulsivamente.
blush (blŭsh) **I.** intr. ruborizarse, sonrojarse ♦ **to b. at** avergonzarse de **II.** s. rubor m, sonrojo.
blus·ter (blŭs′tər) **I.** intr. (wind) bramar; (to boast) echar bravatas **II.** s. fanfarronada.
boar (bôr) s. (hog) verraco; (wild pig) jabalí m.
board (bôrd) **I.** s. madero, tabla; (for games) tablero; (table) mesa; (meals) pensión f; (council) junta, consejo ♦ **above b.** honesto, sin reservas • **b. of directors** directorio • **b. of trade** junta de comercio • **on b.** a bordo ♦ pl. TEAT. tablas, escenario **II.** tr. embarcar(se) en ♦ **to b. up** tapar con tablas —intr. hospedarse con comida.
board·er (bôr′dər) s. pensionista mf.
board·ing·house (:dĭng-hous′) s. pensión f.
board·walk (bôrd′wôk′) s. paseo entablado.
boast (bōst) **I.** intr. jactarse, alardear ♦ **to be nothing to b. about** no ser cosa para jactarse —tr. ostentar **II.** s. jactancia, alarde m.
boast·ful (′fəl) adj. jactancioso.
boast·ing (bō′stĭng) s. jactancia, vanagloria.
boat (bōt) s. (small craft) bote m, barca; (ship) barco, buque m ♦ **to be in the same b.** estar en la misma situación.
boat·ing (bō′tĭng) s. paseo en bote.
boat·man (:mən) s. [pl. -men] lanchero.
boat·swain (bō′sən) s. contramaestre m.
bob¹ (bŏb) **I.** s. (dip) sacudida; CARP. plomo, peso **II.** intr. -bb- balancearse (esp. en el agua).
bob² s.inv. G.B., JER. chelín m.
bob·ber (′ər) s. flotador m (de pescador).
bob·bin (bŏb′ĭn) s. bobina, carrete m.
bob·ble (bŏb′əl) tr. dejar caer (una pelota).
bob·by (bŏb′ē) s. G.B., FAM. policía mf ♦ **b. pin** horquilla • **b. socks** o **sox** tobilleras.
bob·cat (bŏb′kăt′) s. gato montés, lince m.
bob·tail (′tāl′) s. cola cortada.
bode¹ (bōd) tr. presagiar ♦ **to b. well, ill** ser de buen, mal agüero.
bode² cf. **bide**.
bod·ice (bŏd′ĭs) s. cuerpo, corpiño.
bod·i·ly (bŏd′l-ē) **I.** adj. corporal **II.** adv. (physically) corporalmente; (as a whole) en pleno.
bod·ing (bō′dĭng) adj. presagioso, ominoso.
bod·y (bŏd′ē) s. cuerpo; (trunk) torso; (corpse) cadáver m; (organization) organismo; (group) grupo, conjunto; (of water) masa; AVIA. fuselaje m; AUTO. carrocería ♦ **b. and soul** completamente, con toda el alma **II.** tr. ♦

to b. forth representar, simbolizar (idea, concepto).

bod·y·guard (:gärd') s. guardaespaldas *m*.

bog (bôg) **I.** s. pantano, ciénaga **II.** tr. & intr. **-gg- ♦ to b. down** empantanar(se), atascar(se).

bog·ey·man (bŏg'ē-mān') s. [pl. -men] FAM. cuco, coco.

bog·gle (bŏg'əl) tr. & intr. sobresaltar(se) ♦ it **boggles the mind** es de volverse loco.

bo·gus (bō'gəs) adj. falso, fraudulento.

boil¹ (boil) **I.** intr. hervir; *(to cook)* cocer; FIG. bullir ♦ **to b. down (to)** reducirse (a) • **to b. over** *(pot)* rebosar (al hervir); *(person)* enfurecerse —tr. hacer hervir; *(to cook)* cocer, herventar; *(an egg)* pasar por agua **II.** s. hervor *m* ♦ **to bring to a b.** calentar hasta que hierva • **to come to a b.** comenzar a hervir.

boil² s. MED. furúnculo, divieso.

boil·er (boi'lər) s. caldera.

boil·ing (:ĭng) **I.** adj. hirviente **II.** s. ebullición *f* ♦ **b. point** FÍS. punto de ebullición; FAM. límite de la paciencia.

bois·ter·ous (boi'stər-əs) adj. bullicioso, alborotado.

bold (bōld) adj. *(fearless)* intrépido; *(daring)* audaz; *(impudent)* descarado ♦ **in b. face** en letra negrilla.

boll (bōl) s. vaina, cápsula.

bo·lo·gna (bə-lō'nē) s. salchicha de Bolonia.

bol·ster (bōl'stər) **I.** s. cabezal *m* **II.** tr. *(to strengthen)* reforzar, apoyar; *(to hearten)* animar.

bolt (bōlt) **I.** s. MEC. tornillo, perno; *(lock)* cerrojo, pestillo; *(of cloth)* rollo; *(dash)* salto brusco *o* rápido; *(thunderbolt)* rayo ♦ **a b. from the blue** suceso inesperado • **b. and nut** perno y tuerca • **to make a b. for** precipitarse hacia **II.** tr. *(to lock)* echar el cerrojo a, cerrar con pestillo; *(to fasten)* sujetar con tornillos *o* pernos; *(to gulp)* engullir —intr. *(to dash off)* fugarse; *(a horse)* desbocarse ♦ **to b. off** fugarse, huir • **to b. out** salir de repente.

bomb (bŏm) **I.** s. bomba; JER. *(failure)* fracaso, fiasco ♦ **b. shelter** refugio contra bombardeos **II.** tr. bombardear —intr. arrojar bombas; JER. *(to fail)* fracasar.

bom·bard (-bärd') tr. *(to bomb)* bombardear; *(to harass)* abrumar, acosar.

bom·bar·dier (' bər-dîr') s. bombardero.

bom·bard·ment (-bärd'mənt) s. bombardeo.

bom·bast ('băst') s. discurso grandilocuente.

bomb·er (:ər) s. bombardero.

bomb·ing (:ĭng) s. bombardeo.

bomb·proof (:prōōf') adj. a prueba de bombas.

bomb·shell (:shĕl') s. MIL., FIG. bomba.

bomb·sight (:sīt') s. visor *m* de bombardeo.

bo·na fide (bō'nə fīd') adj. auténtico.

bond (bŏnd) **I.** s. lazo, atadura; DER. fianza, garantía; FIN. bono, obligación *f*; QUÍM. enlace *m* ♦ **in b.** en depósito, afianzado ♦ pl. cadenas **II.** tr. unir; DER. afianzar, dar fianza a; —intr. unirse, pegarse.

bond·age (bŏn'dĭj) s. esclavitud *f*.

bond·ed (bŏn'dĭd) adj. depositado bajo fianza.

bond·hold·er (bŏnd'hōl'dər) s. obligacionista *mf*.

bond·ser·vant (:sûr'vənt) s. esclavo, siervo.

bonds·man (bŏndz'mən) s. [pl. -men] DER. fiador *m*; *(bondservant)* esclavo.

bone (bōn) **I.** s. hueso; *(of fish)* espina ♦ **b. of contention** manzana de la discordia • **to make no bones of** *o* **about** no andarse con rodeos • **to the b.** FIG. al máximo, completamente **II.** tr. deshuesar; *(fish)* quitar las espinas a —intr. ♦ **to b. up on** JER. estudiar duro.

bone-dry (drī') adj. completamente seco.

bon·er (bō'nər) s. FAM. metedura de pata.

bon·fire (bŏn'fīr') s. fogata, hoguera.

bon·net (bŏn'ĭt) s. *(hat)* gorra, cofia; MEC. sombrerete *m*; G.B., AUTO. capó.

bo·nus (bō'nəs) s. plus *m*, sobresueldo.

bon·y (bō'nē) adj. -i- óseo; *(thin)* esquelético, flaco; *(fish)* espinoso.

boo (bōō) **I.** s. abucheo, rechifla **II.** interj. ¡bú! **III.** intr. & tr. abuchear (a), rechiflar (a).

boob (bōōb) s. FAM. *(fool)* bobalicón *m*; JER. *(breast)* teta.

boo-boo (bōō'bōō) s. JER. *(blunder)* metida de pata; *(injury)* nana, pupa.

boo·by (:bē) s. FAM. bobalicón *m*; JER. teta ♦ **b. prize** premio al peor • **b. trap** engañabobos.

book (bŏŏk) **I.** s. libro; *(notebook)* libreta; *(register)* registro ♦ **to go by the b.** proceder según las reglas • **to throw the b. at someone** JER. castigar severamente **II.** tr. *(a suspect)* asentar, registrar; *(to reserve)* reservar, hacer reservación de; *(to hire)* contratar (artistas) ♦ **to be booked up** *(hotel, restaurant)* estar completo; *(person)* tener otro compromiso.

book·bind·ing (' bīn'dĭng) s. encuadernación *f*.

book·case (:kās') s. estantería para libros.

book·end (:ĕnd') s. sujetalibros *m*.

book·ie (:ē) s. FAM. corredor *m* (de apuestas).

book·ing (:ĭng) s. *(engagement)* contratación *f*; *(reservation)* reservación *f*, reserva.

book·ish (:ĭsh) adj. libresco.

book·keep·er (:kē'pər) s. tenedor *m* de libros.

book·keep·ing (:kē'pĭng) s. teneduría de libros, contabilidad *f*.

book·let (:lĭt) s. folleto.

book·plate (:plāt') s. ex libris *m*.

book·sell·er (:sĕl'ər) s. librero.

book·shelf (:shĕlf') s. [pl. -ves] estante *m* para libros.

book·store (:stôr') s. librería.

book·worm (:wûrm') s. *(larva)* polilla (que roe los libros); FIG. ratón *m* de biblioteca.

boom¹ (bōōm) **I.** s. *(sound)* estampido, trueno; COM. auge *m* **II.** intr. *(to thunder)* tronar, retumbar; COM. estar en auge.

boom² s. MARÍT. botalón *m*; MEC. pescante *m* (de grúa); CINEM. jirafa (de micrófono).

boo·mer·ang (bōō'mə-răng') **I.** s. bumerang *m* **II.** intr. ser contraproducente.

boon (bōōn) s. bendición *f*, dicha.

boon·docks (bōōn'dŏks') s.pl. JER. los quintos infiernos.

boon·dog·gle (bōōn'dô'gəl) s. FAM. trabajo pagado innecesario.

boor (bŏŏr) s. patán *m*.

boor·ish ('ĭsh) adj. tosco, rudo.

boost (bōōst) **I.** tr. *(to lift)* alzar, levantar; *(to increase)* aumentar **II.** s. *(push)* impulso; *(increase)* aumento.

boost·er (bōō'stər) s. promotor *m* ♦ **b. rocket** cohete acelerador • **b. shot** inyección de refuerzo.

boot (bōōt) s. bota; G.B. *(trunk)* portaequipajes *m* ♦ **to b.** FAM. además • **to get the b.** FAM. ser despedido del empleo **II.** tr. *(to kick)* patear; JER. *(to fire)* despedir.

booth (bōōth) s. *(compartment)* cabina; *(stand)*

puesto, quiosco.

boot·leg (bo͞ot′lĕg′) I. tr. & intr. **-gg-** contrabandear II. adj. & s. (de) contrabando.

boot·leg·ger (′lĕg′ər) s. contrabandista *mf.*

boot·lick·er (′lĭk′ər) s. adulón *m.*

boot·strap (′străp′) s. tirante *m* ♦ **by one's bootstraps** por sí mismo.

boo·ty (bo͞o′tē) s. botín *m.*

booze (bo͞oz) FAM. I. s. bebida alcohólica II. intr. beber.

bop (bŏp) FAM. I. tr. **-pp-** golpear II. s. golpe *m.*

bor·der (bôr′dər) I. s. *(boundary)* frontera; *(edge)* borde *m,* orilla II. tr. *(to edge)* bordear; *(to adjoin)* lindar con —intr. ♦ **to b. on** lindar con; *(caliber)* calibre *m.*

bor·der·line (:līn′) I. s. frontera II. adj. dudoso.

bore¹ (bôr) I. tr. & intr. *(to drill)* taladrar, barrenar II. s. *(hole)* agujero; *(diameter)* diámetro interior; *(caliber)* calibre *m.*

bore² I. tr. *(to weary)* aburrir, cansar II. s. *(person)* pesado, pelmazo; *(thing)* pesadez *f.*

bore³ cf. **bear¹**.

bore·dom (′dəm) s. aburrimiento.

bo·ric (bôr′ĭk) adj. bórico.

bor·ing (bôr′ĭng) adj. aburrido, pesado.

born (bôrn) I. cf. **bear¹** ♦ **to be b.** nacer; *(to originate)* originarse II. adj. nato ♦ **a b. fool** un tonto de nacimiento • **a b. liar** un mentiroso innato.

born-a·gain (′ə-gĕn′) adj. renacido.

borne (bôrn) cf. **bear¹**.

bo·ron (bôr′ŏn′) s. boro.

bor·ough (bûr′ō) s. municipio.

bor·row (bŏr′ō) tr. *(a loan)* tomar prestado; *(to use)* apropiarse (de) —intr. tomar un préstamo.

bor·row·er (:ər) s. prestatario.

bo's'n *o* **bos'n** (bō′sən) var. de **boatswain**.

bos·om (bo͞oz′əm) s. pecho; FIG. seno ♦ **b. buddy** FAM. amigo del alma.

boss (bôs) I. s. *(supervisor)* supervisor *m,* capataz *m; (leader)* jefe *m,* cacique *m* II. tr. dirigir, mandar.

boss·y (bô′sē) adj. **-i-** mandón.

bo·tan·ic/i·cal (bə-tăn′ĭk) adj. botánico.

bo·ta·nist (bŏt′n-ĭst) s. botánico.

bo·ta·ny (:ē) s. botánica.

botch (bŏch) I. tr. chapucear II. s. chapucería.

both (bōth) I. pron. & adj. ambos, los dos ♦ **of us, you** nosotros, vosotros dos • **to have it b. ways** sacar ventaja de una manera u otra II. conj. . . . y . . . además *<he is b. strong and healthy* él es fuerte y sano además>.

both·er (bŏth′ər) I. tr. & intr. molestar(se) *(about, with, por)* II. s. molestia, fastidio.

both·er·some (:səm) adj. molesto, fastidioso.

bot·tle (bŏt′l) I. s. botella; *(baby's)* biberón *m* ♦ **to hit the b.** JER. beber II. tr. embotellar, envasar ♦ **to b. up** reprimir.

bot·tle·neck (:nĕk′) s. cuello; FIG. embotellamiento.

bot·tom (bŏt′əm) s. fondo; *(of a list)* final *m; (foot)* pie *m; (of sea, river)* lecho; *(essence)* meollo, base *f;* FAM. *(buttocks)* trasero ♦ **b. dollar** precio más bajo • **b. line** FIN. balance; FIG. quid.

bot·tom·less (:lĭs) adj. sin fondo.

bot·u·lism (bŏch′ə-lĭz′əm) s. botulismo.

bough (bou) s. rama.

bought (bôt) cf. **buy**.

bouil·lon (bo͞ol′yŏn′) s. caldo.

boul·der (bōl′dər) s. canto rodado.

boul·e·vard (bo͞ol′ə-värd′) s. bulevar *m.*

bounce (bouns) I. intr. rebotar; *(to jump)* saltar, dar brincos; FAM. *(a check)* ser rechazado ♦ **to b. back** recuperarse —tr. hacer rebotar; JER. *(to expel)* echar; *(to fire)* despedir II. s. *(leap)* salto, brinco; *(rebound)* rebote *m; (springiness)* elasticidad *f.*

bounc·er (bouns′ər) s. JER. persona encargada de echar a los alborotadores.

bounc·ing (:sĭng) adj. robusto, fuerte.

bounc·y (:sē) adj. **-i-** vivo, exuberante.

bound¹ (bound) I. intr. saltar, dar brincos II. s. *(leap)* salto, brinco; *(bounce)* rebote *m.*

bound² I. cf. **bind** II. adj. *(tied)* atado, amarrado; *(certain)* seguro; *(obliged)* obligado; IMPR. encuadernado ♦ **b. up in** entregado a • **b. up with** estrechamente relacionado con • **it is b. to happen** tiene forzosamente que ocurrir.

bound³ adj. ♦ **b. for** con destino a.

bound·a·ry (boun′də-rē) s. límite *m,* frontera.

bound·less (bound′lĭs) adj. ilimitado, infinito.

bounds (boundz) s.pl. límite *m* ♦ **out of b.** DEP. fuera de la cancha; *(behavior)* fuera de los límites; *(prohibited)* prohibido.

boun·ti·ful (boun′tə-fəl) adj. generoso.

boun·ty (boun′tē) s. *(generosity)* generosidad *f; (gift)* regalo; *(reward)* recompensa.

bou·quet (bō-kā′, bo͞o-) s. *(of flowers)* ramillete *m; (of wine)* buqué *m.*

bour·geois (bo͞or-zhwä′) s. & adj. burgués *m.*

bour·geoi·sie (′-zē′) s. burguesía.

bout (bout) s. *(contest)* combate *m; (spell)* ataque *m* (de una enfermedad).

bou·tique (bo͞o-tēk′) s. tienda pequeña de artículos de moda.

bo·vine (bō′vīn′) adj. & s. bovino.

bow¹ (bou) s. MARÍT. proa.

bow² (bou) I. intr. *(to stoop)* inclinarse, doblegarse; *(to nod)* saludar; *(in obeisance)* inclinarse, hacer una reverencia; *(to submit)* someterse ♦ **to b. out** retirarse, renunciar —tr. *(the head, body)* inclinar; *(the knee)* doblar II. s. *(obeisance)* reverencia; *(greeting)* saludo.

bow³ (bō) s. ARM., MÚS. arco; *(knot)* lazo; *(curve)* arco, curva ♦ **b. tie** corbata de lazo.

bow·el (bou′əl) s. intestino ♦ pl. entrañas.

bowl¹ (bōl) s. *(dish)* fuente *f,* cuenco; *(cup)* tazón *m; (washbasin)* jofaina; *(toilet)* taza; DEP. estadio.

bowl² intr. DEP. jugar a los bolos —tr. lanzar, tirar (la bola) ♦ **b. over** derribar; FIG. pasmar.

bow·leg·ged (bō′lĕg′ĭd) adj. estevado.

bowl·er¹ (bō′lər) s. jugador *m* de bolos.

bowl·er² s. *(hat)* sombrero hongo, bombín *m.*

bowl·ing (bō′lĭng) s. bolos ♦ **b. alley** bolera.

box¹ (bŏks) I. s. caja; *(large)* cajón *m; (small)* estuche *m; (pigeonhole)* casilla; *(printed)* casilla, cuadro; TEAT. palco; *(in newspaper)* recuadro ♦ **b. office** taquilla, boletería • **b. spring** colchón de resortes II. tr. ♦ **to b. in** encerrar • **to b. up** encajonar, empaquetar.

box² I. s. *(blow)* bofetada, cachete *m* II. tr. abofetear; DEP. boxear —intr. boxear.

box·car (′kär′) s. F.C. furgón *m.*

box·er (bŏk′sər) s. boxeador *m,* púgil *m.*

box·ing (:sĭng) s. boxeo ♦ **b. glove** guante de boxeo.

box·wood (bŏks′wo͝od′) s. boj *m.*

boy (boi) I. s. niño; *(youth, servant)* muchacho

II. interj. ¡chico!, ¡hombre!

boy·cott (boi'kŏt') **I.** tr. boicotear **II.** s. boicoteo, boicot *m*.

boy·friend (boi'frĕnd') s. FAM. novio.

boy·hood (:hŏŏd') s. niñez *f*, infancia.

bra (brä) s. sostén *m*, corpiño.

brace (brās) **I.** s. *(support)* refuerzo, puntal *m*; TEC. tirante *m*; MED. braguero; IMPR. corchete *m* ♦ pl. ODONT. aparato de ortodoncia **II.** tr. *(to support)* asegurar, reforzar; *(to hold steady)* asegurar; *(to invigorate)* vigorizar ♦ to b. oneself for prepararse para (golpe, noticia) ♦ to b. up cobrar ánimo.

brace·let (brās'lĭt) s. brazalete *m*, pulsera.

brac·ing (brā'sĭng) adj. fortificante, vigorizante.

brack·et (brăk'ĭt) **I.** s. *(support)* soporte *m*, escuadra; *(shelf)* repisa; *(category)* categoría, grupo; IMPR. corchete *m* **II.** tr. agrupar, clasificar.

brack·ish (brăk'ĭsh) adj. salino, salobre.

bract (brăkt) s. bráctea.

brad (brăd) s. puntilla, clavito.

brag (brăg) **I.** tr. & intr. **-gg-** jactarse (de) **II.** s. jactancia, alarde *m*.

brag·gart ('ərt) s. & adj. fanfarrón *m*.

braid (brād) **I.** tr. *(to plait)* trenzar; COST. galonear **II.** s. *(plait)* trenza; *(trim)* galón *m*.

brain (brān) **I.** s. cerebro ♦ **b. child** FAM. invento, creación ♦ pl. CUL. sesos; *(intelligence)* cabeza ♦ to rack one's b. devanarse los sesos **II.** tr. JER. romper la crisma a.

brain·storm ('stôrm') s. idea genial.

brain·wash (:wŏsh') tr. lavar el cerebro.

brain·y (brā'nē) adj. **-i-** FAM. inteligente, listo.

braise (brāz) tr. dorar a fuego lento en cazuela tapada.

brake (brāk) **I.** s. freno ♦ **b. drum** tambor de freno **II.** tr. frenar —intr. aplicar el freno.

bram·ble (brăm'bəl) s. zarzamora.

bran (brăn) s. salvado, afrecho.

branch (brănch) **I.** s. rama; *(division)* ramo, rama; *(of a river)* brazo; F.C. ramal *m* ♦ **b. office** sucursal **II.** intr. *(trees)* echar ramas; *(to spread out)* ramificarse; *(to split)* bifurcarse ♦ **to b. out** extender las actividades.

brand (brănd) **I.** s. COM. marca (de fábrica); *(style)* modo, manera; *(type)* clase *f*; *(on cattle)* marca (de hierro); *(firebrand)* tizón *m* **II.** tr. *(cattle)* marcar, herrar; *(to stigmatize)* calificar de, tildar de.

brand·ing (brăn'dĭng) s. herradero, hierra ♦ **b. iron** hierro de marcar.

bran·dish (brăn'dĭsh) tr. blandir, esgrimir.

brand-new (brănd'nŏŏ') adj. flamante.

bran·dy (brăn'dē) s. coñac *m*, aguardiente *m*.

brash (brăsh) adj. *(rash)* impetuoso; *(impudent)* descarado, insolente.

brass (brăs) s. latón *m*; FAM. *(gall)* descaro ♦ **b. hat** MIL., JER. oficial de estado mayor • **b. knuckles** manopla ♦ pl. MÚS. cobres.

bras·siere (brə-zîr') s. sostén *m*, corpiño.

brass·y (brăs'ē) adj. **-i-** *(sound)* metálico; FAM. *(impudent)* descarado.

brat (brăt) s. niño malcriado, mocoso.

bra·va·do (brə-vä'dō) s. [pl. **(e)s**] bravata.

brave (brāv) **I.** adj. valiente, bravo **II.** s. guerrero indio **III.** tr. *(to face)* afrontar; *(to defy)* desafiar.

brav·er·y (brā'və-rē) s. valentía, valor *m*.

brawl (brôl) **I.** s. pelea **II.** intr. pelear.

brawn (brôn) s. fuerza muscular.

brawn·y (brô'nē) adj. **-i-** musculoso.

bray (brā) **I.** s. rebuzno **II.** intr. rebuznar.

bra·zen (brā'zən) adj. descarado.

bra·zier (brā'zhər) s. brasero.

breach (brēch) **I.** s. *(of law)* violación *f*; *(of promise)* incumplimiento; *(of relations)* ruptura; MIL. brecha **II.** tr. MIL. abrir brecha en; DER. violar.

bread (brĕd) **I.** s. pan *m*; JER. *(money)* plata, pasta ♦ **b. and butter** FAM. pan de cada día **II.** tr. CUL. empanar.

bread·bas·ket (brĕd'băs'kĭt) s. panera; *(region)* granero.

bread·board (:bôrd') s. tabla para cortar pan.

breadth (brĕdth) s. *(width)* anchura; *(scope)* extensión *f*; *(openness)* liberalidad *f*.

bread·win·ner (brĕd'wĭn'ər) s. sostén *m* de la familia.

break (brāk) **I.** tr. broke, broken romper; *(crack)* quebrar, fracturar; *(to damage)* estropear, descomponer; *(a law)* infringir, violar; *(spirit, will)* quebrantar; *(a horse)* domar; *(a blow, fall)* amortiguar, parar; *(a bill)* cambiar; *(a record)* batir; *(a code)* descifrar; ELEC. interrumpir, cortar ♦ **to b. down** *(to analyze)* detallar, analizar ♦ *(to destroy)* derrumbar • **to b. in** *(shoes)* amoldar; *(machine)* ajustar • **to b. off** *(to detach)* romper, separar; *(relations)* romper; *(talks)* suspender • **to b. one's back** romperse el alma • **to b. oneself of** una costumbre • **to b. open** abrir forzando, forzar • **to b. someone's heart** partirle el corazón a alguien • **to b. up** *(to crumble)* desmenuzar; *(to put an end to)* acabar, terminar; *(to upset)* quebrantar, apesadumbrar; *(with laughter)* hacer morir de risa • **to b. (up) with** romper con (una relación) —intr. *(to shatter)* romperse; *(to come apart)* partirse; *(to become unusable)* estropearse, descomponerse; *(fever)* bajar; *(day)* apuntar, rayar; *(the heart)* partirse, romperse; *(the voice)* fallar; *(news)* revelarse; DEP. separarse (los púgiles) ♦ **to b. away** *(to withdraw)* separarse; *(to escape)* escaparse; *(to start suddenly)* arrancar • **to b. down** *(to malfunction)* averiarse, descomponerse; *(physically)* debilitarse; *(emotionally)* abatirse, sufrir un colapso • **to b. even** salir sin ganar o perder • **to b. in** *(to enter)* entrar forzadamente (con intención de robar); *(to interrupt)* interrumpir • **to b. into** *(to enter)* entrar forzadamente en; *(tears, laughter)* echarse a • **to b. loose** *(to come off)* soltarse, desprenderse; *(to escape)* escaparse • **to b. off** *(to come off)* soltarse, desprenderse; *(to stop)* detenerse • **to b. out** *(to escape)* escaparse; *(to erupt)* estallar; MED. salirle a uno (sarpullido, manchas) • **to b. through** atravesar, abrirse paso • **to b. up** *(to end)* acabarse, terminarse (partido, reunión); *(to split up)* separarse (una relación); *(to scatter)* dispersarse, levantarse **II.** s. *(act)* ruptura, rompimiento; *(fracture)* fractura; *(crack)* grieta, raja; *(gap)* abertura; *(change)* cambio, interrupción *f*; *(pause)* intervalo, pausa; *(sudden dash)* salida, arrancada; *(escape)* fuga, evasión *f*; ELEC. interrupción, corte *m* ♦ **at the b. of day** al amanecer • **lucky b.** coyuntura feliz ♦ **to give someone a b.** dar una oportunidad a alguien • **to take a b.** descansar • **without a b.** sin parar.

break·a·ble (brā'kə-bəl) **I.** adj. rompible, frágil **II.** s. ♦ pl. objetos frágiles.

break·age (:kĭj) s. rotura; *(loss)* daños de rotura.

break·down (brāk'doun') s. MEC. avería; *(fail-*

ure) fracaso; MED. colapso, depresión *f; (of costs)* desglose *m;* QUÍM. descomposición *f.*

break·er (brā'kər) s. ELEC. interruptor automático; *(wave)* cachón *m.*

break·fast (brĕk'fəst) **I.** s. desayuno **II.** intr. desayunar, tomar el desayuno.

break·in (brāk'ĭn') s. *(illegal entry)* entrada forzada; *(testing)* periodo de prueba.

break·neck (:nĕk') adj. ♦ **at b. speed** a mata caballo.

break·through (:thrōō') s. MIL. ruptura; *(achievement)* adelanto, progreso.

break·up (:ŭp') s. *(separation)* separación *f; (of marriage, firm)* disolución *f*, desintegración *f.*

break·wa·ter (:wô'tər) s. rompeolas *m.*

breast (brĕst) s. pecho; *(of a woman)* pecho, seno; *(of a fowl)* pechuga ♦ **b. stroke** brazada de pecho.

breast·bone ('bōn') s. esternón *m.*

breast-feed (:fēd') tr. **-fed** amamantar.

breath (brĕth) s. respiración *f*, aliento; *(of an animal)* hálito; *(of air)* soplo ♦ **in one b.** de un tirón • **in the same b.** al mismo tiempo • **out of b.** sin aliento • **short of b.** corto de resuello • **to catch one's b.** recobrar el aliento • **under one's b.** en voz baja • **to waste one's b.** gastar saliva en balde.

breathe (brēth) intr. respirar; *(to blow)* soplar suavemente —tr. respirar; *(to impart)* infundir; *(to whisper)* susurrar, decir ♦ **to b. in** inhalar, aspirar • **to b. one's last** exhalar el último suspiro • **to b. out** exhalar.

breath·er (brē'thər) s. FAM. respiro, pausa.

breath·ing (:thĭng) s. respiración *f* ♦ **b. space** respiro, pausa.

breath·less (brĕth'lĭs) adj. sin aliento; *(panting)* jadeante; *(amazed)* sin resuello, pasmado.

breath·tak·ing (:tā'kĭng) adj. impresionante.

breath·y (:ē) adj. **-i-** velado (voz).

breech (brēch) s. ANAT. trasero; ARM. recámara ♦ pl. (brĭch'ĭz) calzones; FAM. pantalones.

breech·cloth (:klôth') s. taparrabo.

breed (brēd) **I.** tr. **bred** *(to engender)* engendrar; *(to raise, bring up)* criar —intr. procrear, reproducirse **II.** s. *(strain)* raza; *(type)* casta, especie *f.*

breed·er (brē'dər) s. criador *m.*

breed·ing (:dĭng) s. crianza, educación *f.*

breeze (brēz) **I.** s. brisa; FAM. *(easy task)* paseo, papa **II.** intr. ♦ **to b. in** entrar alegremente • **to b. through** pasar como si tal cosa.

breez·y (brē'zē) adj. **-i-** *(windy)* ventoso; *(casual)* despreocupado.

brev·i·ty (brĕv'ĭ-tē) s. brevedad *f.*

brew (brōō) **I.** tr. *(beer)* fabricar; *(tea)* preparar, hacer —intr. *(to loom)* amenazar **II.** s. *(beverage)* infusión *f*; FAM. *(beer)* cerveza; *(concoction)* brebaje *m*, mezcla.

brew·er ('ər) s. cervecero.

brew·er·y (:ə-rē) s. cervecería.

bri·ar (brī'ər) s. brezo, zarza.

bribe (brīb) **I.** s. soborno ♦ **to take bribes** dejarse sobornar **II.** tr. sobornar.

brib·er·y (brī'bə-rē) s. soborno.

bric-a-brac (brĭk'ə-brăk') s. baratijas.

brick (brĭk) **I.** s. ladrillo **II.** tr. ♦ **to b. up** tapiar con ladrillos.

brick·bat ('băt') s. crítica cortante, pulla.

brick·lay·er (:lā'ər) s. albañil *m.*

bri·dal (brīd'l) **I.** s. boda, casamiento **II.** adj. nupcial ♦ **b. gown** traje de boda.

bride (brīd) s. novia, desposada.

bride·groom ('grōōm') s. novio, desposado.

brides·maid (brīdz'mād') s. dama de honor.

bridge (brĭj) **I.** s. puente *m; (of the nose)* caballete *m* ♦ **to burn one's bridges** quemar las naves **II.** tr. *(to build)* tender un puente sobre; *(to span)* extenderse a través de.

bri·dle (brīd'l) **I.** s. brida ♦ **b. path** camino de herradura **II.** tr. *(a horse)* embridar; *(passions)* refrenar, dominar —intr. picarse *(at por).*

brief (brēf) **I.** adj. *(in time)* breve; *(in length)* corto; *(succinct)* conciso **II.** s. *(summary)* sumario, resumen *m;* DER. escrito ♦ **in b.** en resumen ♦ pl. calzoncillos **III.** tr. informar; *(to give instructions)* dar instrucciones.

brief·case ('kās') s. portafolio, cartera.

brief·ing (brē'fĭng) s. reunión *f* de información.

brig (brĭg) s. MIL., FAM. calabozo.

bri·gade (brĭ-gād') s. brigada.

brig·a·dier (brĭg'ə-dîr') s. general *m* de brigada.

brig·and (brĭg'ənd) s. bandido, bandolero.

brig·an·tine (brĭg'ən-tēn') s. bergantín *m.*

bright (brīt) **I.** adj. *(shining)* brillante, resplandeciente; *(color)* subido; *(smart)* inteligente, despierto; *(happy)* alegre **II.** s. ♦ pl. AUTO. luces altas *o* de carretera.

bright·en ('n) tr. & intr. *(with light)* aclarar(se), iluminar(se); *(with joy)* alegrar(se), animar(se).

bright·ness (:nĭs) s. *(quality)* claridad *f*, brillantez *f; (degree)* minosidad *f.*

bril·liance/·cy (brĭl'yəns) s. brillo.

bril·liant (brĭl'yənt) adj. *(shining)* brillante; *(inventive)* genial; *(splendid)* magnífico.

brim (brĭm) **I.** s. *(of a cup)* borde *m; (of a hat)* ala **II.** intr. **-mm-** estar lleno hasta el tope ♦ **to b. over** desbordarse.

brim·ful ('fŏŏl) adj. lleno hasta el tope.

brine (brīn) s. CUL. salmuera; *(sea)* mar *mf.*

bring (brĭng) tr. **brought** traer; *(to carry)* llevar; *(to persuade)* convencer; *(a price)* rendir; *(charges)* formular ♦ **to b. about** *(to effect)* efectuar, realizar; *(to cause)* causar, provocar • **to b. around** *(to revive)* revivir; *(to persuade)* convencer • **to b. back** *(to return)* devolver; *(a memory)* hacer recordar, traer a (la mente) • *(to cause to return)* traer de vuelta • **to b. before** encomendar a, someter a • **to b. down** *(to lower)* bajar; *(to overthrow)* derribar • **to b. forth** *(to bear)* producir (frutos); *(to reveal)* poner de manifiesto • **to b. in** *(to harvest)* recoger; *(money)* rendir, producir; DER. *(a verdict)* pronunciar • **to b. off** conseguir, lograr hacer • **to b. on** ocasionar, causar • **to b. oneself** to resignarse a • **to b. out** *(a product)* presentar; *(to highlight)* hacer resaltar; *(to reveal)* revelar, mostrar • **to b. up** *(children)* criar, educar; *(a topic)* plantear, traer a colación • **to b. upon oneself** buscarse, acarrearse.

brink (brĭngk) s. borde *m*, margen *f* ♦ **on the b. of** a punto de.

brink·man·ship ('mən-shĭp') s. política arriesgada.

bri·quet(te) (brĭ-kĕt') s. briqueta.

brisk (brĭsk) adj. *(energetic)* enérgico, vigoroso; *(invigorating)* estimulante.

bris·ket (brĭs'kĭt) s. falda (de una res).

bris·tle (brĭs'əl) **I.** s. cerda **II.** intr. ♦ **to b. with** estar lleno *o* erizado de.

britch·es (brĭch'ĭz) s.pl. FAM. pantalones *m* ♦ **too big for one's b.** FAM. arrogante, engreído.

brit·tle (brĭt'l) **I.** adj. **-er, -est** quebradizo, frá-

gil **II.** s. caramelo de nueces.
broach (brōch) **I.** s. broche *m* **II.** tr. *(a subject)* abordar, sacar a colación; *(a cask)* espitar.
broad (brôd) **I.** adj. *(wide)* ancho; *(spacious)* extenso, amplio; *(general)* general; *(obvious)* evidente, claro; *(tolerant)* liberal, de miras amplias; *(accent)* marcado ♦ **b. jump** salto de longitud • **in b. daylight** en pleno día **II.** s. JER. *(woman)* mina, fulana **III.** adv. plenamente, completamente.
broad·cast (brôd′kăst′) **I.** tr. **-cast(ed)** RAD. emitir, radiar; TELEV. transmitir, televisar; *(to make known)* difundir, divulgar; AGR. sembrar a voleo —intr. RAD. emitir, radiar un programa; TELEV. transmitir, televisar un programa **II.** s. *(act)* transmisión *f*, emisión *f*; *(program)* programa *m*.
broad·cast·er (:kăs′tər) s. locutor *m*.
broad·cast·ing (:tĭng) s. radiodifusión *f*; TE-LEV. transmisión *f*, difusión *f*.
broad·cloth (:klôth′) s. paño fino.
broad·en (:n) tr. & intr. ensanchar(se).
broad-mind·ed (:mīn′dĭd) adj. tolerante, comprensivo.
broad·side (:sīd′) **I.** s. MARÍT. costado; MIL., FIG. andanada; IMPR. pliego suelto **II.** adv. de costado.
bro·cade (brō-kād′) s. brocado.
broc·co·li (brŏk′ə-lē) s. brécol *m*, brócoli *m*.
bro·chure (brō-shŏŏr′) s. folleto.
brogue (brōg) s. *(shoe)* zapato grueso; *(accent)* acento irlandés.
broil (broil) tr. asar a la parrilla —intr. asarse, achicharrarse.
broil·er (broi′lər) s. parrilla; *(chicken)* pollo para asar.
broke (brōk) **I.** cf. **break II.** adj. JER. pelado.
bro·ken (brō′kən) **I.** cf. **break II.** adj. roto, quebrado; *(out of order)* descompuesto; *(language)* chapurreado; *(health, law)* quebrantado; *(line)* quebrado; *(ground)* accidentado; *(spirit)* sumiso; *(heart)* destrozado.
bro·ken-down (:doun′) adj. decrépito.
bro·ken·heart·ed (:här′tĭd) adj. con el corazón destrozado.
bro·ker (brō′kər) s. agente *mf*, corredor *m* de bolsa.
bro·ker·age (:ĭj) s. corretaje *m*.
bro·mide (brō′mīd′) s. QUÍM. bromuro; *(platitude)* trivialidad *f*.
bro·mine (brō′mēn′) s. bromo.
bron·chi·al (brŏng′kē-əl) adj. bronquial ♦ **b. tube** bronquio.
bron·chi·tis (-kī′tĭs) s. bronquitis *f*.
bron·co (brŏng′kō) s. mustango, potro cerril.
bronze (brŏnz) **I.** s. bronce *m* **II.** adj. de bronce; *(color)* bronceado **III.** tr. broncear.
brooch (brōch, brōōch) s. broche *m*.
brood (brōōd) **I.** s. ORNIT. nidada; *(children)* progenie *f*, prole *f* **II.** tr. empollar —intr. empollar; *(to ponder)* cavilar **III.** adj. de cría.
brook[1] (brŏŏk) s. arroyo.
brook[2] tr. tolerar, aguantar.
broom (brŏŏm) s. escoba; BOT. retama.
broom·stick (′stĭk′) s. palo de escoba.
broth (brôth) s. caldo.
broth·el (brŏth′əl) s. burdel *m*, lupanar *m*.
broth·er (brŭth′ər) s. hermano; *(fellow member)* compañero; RELIG. hermano.
broth·er·hood (:hŏŏd′) s. hermandad *f*, fraternidad *f*; *(guild)* gremio.

broth·er-in-law (:ĭn-lô′) s. [pl. **brothers-**] cuñado, hermano político.
broth·er·ly (:lē) adj. fraternal, fraterno.
brought (brôt) cf. **bring.**
brow (brou) *(eyebrow)* ceja; *(forehead)* frente *f*.
brow·beat (′bĕt′) tr. **-beat, -en** intimidar.
brown (broun) **I.** s. marrón *m*, castaño **II.** adj. marrón; *(hair)* castaño; *(skin, sugar)* moreno **III.** tr. & intr. CUL. dorar(se).
brown·ie (brou′nē) s. bizcocho de chocolate.
brown·out (broun′out′) s. apagón *m* parcial.
browse (brouz) intr. *(shop)* curiosear; *(book)* hojear un libro; *(to graze)* pacer.
bruise (brōōz) **I.** s. *(skin)* magulladura, contusión *f*; *(fruit)* daño **II.** tr. magullar, contusionar; *(fruit)* dañar; *(feelings)* herir —intr. magullarse, dañarse.
brunch (brŭnch) s. combinación de desayuno y almuerzo.
bru·net (brōō-nĕt′) adj. & s. moreno ♦ **brunette** morena.
brunt (brŭnt) s. fuerza, impacto (de ataque, crítica) ♦ **to bear the b. of** llevar el peso de.
brush[1] (brŭsh) **I.** s. cepillo; *(paintbrush)* brocha; *(of an artist)* pincel *m*; *(brushing)* cepillado; *(encounter)* encuentro **II.** tr. cepillar; *(to sweep)* quitar, barrer *(off* de); *(to graze)* rozar al pasar ♦ **to b. off** o **aside** hacer caso omiso de • **to b. up** repasar, retocar ♦ **to b. up on** refrescar los conocimientos de —intr. pasar rozando.
brush[2] s. maleza.
brush-off (′ôf′) s. FAM. despedida brusca.
brush·wood (:wŏŏd′) s. maleza.
brusque o **brusk** (brŭsk) adj. brusco.
bru·tal (brŏōt′l) adj. brutal, bestial.
bru·tal·i·ty (-tăl′ĭ-tē) s. brutalidad *f*.
bru·tal·ize (brōōt′l-īz′) tr. brutalizar.
brute (brōōt) **I.** s. *(animal)* bestia; *(person)* bestia *mf*, bruto **II.** adj. *(instinctive)* bruto; *(cruel)* brutal.
bub·ble (bŭb′əl) **I.** s. burbuja; *(of soap)* pompa ♦ **b. gum** chicle de globo • **to blow bubbles** hacer pompas de jabón • **to burst someone's b.** desengañar a alguien **II.** intr. burbujear ♦ **to b. over with** rebosar de.
bub·bly (:lē) adj. **-i-** efervescente.
bu·bon·ic plague (bŏō-bŏn′ĭk) s. peste bubónica.
buc·ca·neer (bŭk′ə-nîr′) s. bucanero.
buck[1] (bŭk) **I.** s. ZOOL. macho; *(deer)* ciervo; FAM. *(youth)* joven despabilado **II.** intr. *(horse)* botar, corcovear; *(to balk)* resistirse ♦ **to b. up** FAM. animarse —tr. *(to unseat)* derribar; *(to oppose)* oponerse.
buck[2] s. JER. dólar *m*.
buck·a·roo/er·oo (bŭk′ə-rōō′) s. vaquero.
buck·et (bŭk′ĭt) s. cubo, balde *m* ♦ **to kick the b.** FAM. estirar la pata.
buck·le[1] (bŭk′əl) **I.** s. *(fastener)* hebilla **II.** tr. & intr. abrochar(se) ♦ **to b. down** to dedicarse con empeño a.
buck·le[2] **I.** tr. & intr. *(to bend)* combar(se) **II.** s. comba.
buck·shot (bŭk′shŏt′) s. perdigón *m*, posta.
buck·skin (:skĭn′) s. ante *m*.
buck·tooth (:tōōth′) s. [pl. **-teeth**] diente *m* saliente.
buck·wheat (:hwēt′) s. trigo sarraceno.
bud (bŭd) **I.** s. *(shoot)* brote *m*; *(flower)* capullo ♦ **in the b.** en cierne(s) • **to nip in the b.** cortar de raíz **II.** intr. **-dd-** *(plant)* echar brotes o

capullos; *(flower)* brotar; *(to show promise)* estar en cierne.

bud·dy (bŭd'ē) s. FAM. amigo, compadre *m*.

budge (bŭj) tr. & intr. *(object)* mover(se) un poco; *(person)* (hacer) ceder.

budg·et (bŭj'ĭt) I. s. presupuesto II. tr. presupuestar.

budg·et·ar·y (:ĭ-tĕr'ē) adj. presupuestario.

buff¹ (bŭf) I. s. *(leather)* cuero, ante *m* ◆ **in the b.** en cueros II. adj. de color del ante III. tr. pulir.

buff² s. FAM. entusiasta *mf*, aficionado.

buf·fa·lo (bŭf'ə-lō') I. s. [pl. inv. *o* **es**] búfalo, bisonte *m* II. tr. JER. intimidar, confundir.

buff·er (bŭf'ər) s. *(shock absorber)* amortiguador *m*; *(intercessor)* intercesor *m*; *(for polishing)* pulidor *m* ◆ **b. state** estado tapón.

buf·fet¹ (bə-fā') s. *(sideboard)* aparador *m*; *(restaurant)* cantina, buffet *m*.

buf·fet² (bŭf'ĭt) I. s. bofetada II. tr. abofetear.

buf·foon (bə-fōōn') s. bufón *m*, payaso.

buf·foon·er·y (bə-fōō'nə-rē) s. bufonada, payasada.

bug (bŭg) I. s. insecto, bicho; FAM. *(germ)* microbio; *(defect)* defecto, falla (en un sistema); JER. *(enthusiast)* entusiasta *mf*; *(microphone)* micrófono oculto II. tr. **-gg-** JER. *(to pester)* fastidiar, importunar; *(a room, phone)* instalar un micrófono oculto en.

bug·gy (bŭg'ē) s. *(horse-drawn)* calesa; *(baby carriage)* coche *m* de niño.

bug·house (bŭg'hous') s. JER. manicomio.

bu·gle (byōō'gəl) s. clarín *m*, corneta.

build (bĭld) I. tr. **built** construir, edificar; *(monuments)* erigir; *(fire)* preparar; *(to make)* hacer; *(to assemble)* armar ◆ **to b. up** *(theory)* elaborar; *(collection)* hacer, reunir; *(reputation)* crear; *(sales)* aumentar; *(health)* fortalecer —intr. ◆ **to b. up** *(to increase)* aumentar; *(to intensify)* intensificarse, ir en aumento II. s. talle *m*, figura.

build·er (bĭl'dər) s. constructor *m*, contratista *mf*.

build·ing (:dĭng) s. edificio, casa.

build-up (bĭld'ŭp') s. aumento; MIL. *(of troops)* concentración *f*; FAM. *(publicity)* publicidad *f* ◆ **arms b.** incremento bélico.

built-in (bĭlt'ĭn') adj. *(closet)* empotrado; *(as integral part)* que es parte integral.

built-up (:ŭp') adj. urbanizado.

bulb (bŭlb) s. BOT. bulbo; *(lamp)* bombilla.

bul·bous (bŭl'bəs) adj. protuberante.

bulge (bŭlj) I. s. protuberancia, bulto; *(in wall)* pandeo II. intr. & tr. hinchar(se), abultar.

bulg·ing (bŭl'jĭng) adj. *(swollen)* hinchado; *(protuberant)* saltón.

bulk (bŭlk) I. s. volumen *m*, tamaño; *(largest part)* grueso ◆ **in b.** *(loose)* a granel, suelto; *(in large amounts)* en grandes cantidades II. intr. ◆ **to b. large** ser importante.

bulk·head (:hĕd') s. MARÍT. mamparo.

bulk·y (bŭl'kē) adj. **-i-** *(massive)* voluminoso; *(unwieldy)* pesado.

bull¹ (bŏŏl) I. s. toro; *(elephant, seal)* macho; FIN. alcista *mf*; JER. *(nonsense)* tontería ◆ **b. session** FAM. tertulia ◆ **to shoot the b.** JER. charlar, parlotear II. tr. ◆ **to b. one's way** abrirse paso III. adj. macho ◆ **b. market** mercado en alza ◆ **b. neck** cuello de toro.

bull² s. RELIG. bula.

bull·dog ('dôg') s. buldog *m*, dogo.

bull·doze ('dōz') tr. nivelar *o* excavar con una excavadora.

bull·doz·er (:dōz'zər) s. excavadora.

bul·let (bŏŏl'ĭt) s. bala.

bul·le·tin (bŏŏl'ĭ-tn) s. *(periodical)* boletín *m*; *(report)* comunicado ◆ **b. board** tablero de anuncios.

bul·let·proof (bŏŏl'ĭt-prōōf') adj. a prueba de balas.

bull·fight (bŏŏl'fīt') s. corrida de toros.

bull·fight·er (:fī'tər) s. torero.

bull·frog (:frôg') s. rana toro.

bull·head·ed (:hĕd'ĭd) adj. testarudo, terco.

bull·horn (:hôrn') s. megáfono eléctrico.

bul·lion (bŏŏl'yən) s. oro *o* plata en lingotes.

bull·ish (bŏŏl'ĭsh) adj. FIN. en alza.

bul·lock (:ək) s. buey *m*.

bull·ring (:rĭng') s. plaza de toros.

bull's-eye (bŏŏlz'ī') s. *(target)* blanco; *(shot)* acierto ◆ **to hit the b.** dar en el blanco.

bull·whip (bŏŏl'hwĭp') s. látigo (de cuero).

bul·ly (bŏŏl'ē) I. s. matón *m*, abusador *m* II. tr. intimidar, amedrentar —intr. abusar.

bul·rush (bŏŏl'rŭsh') s. espadaña.

bul·wark (bŏŏl'wərk) s. baluarte *m*.

bum (bŭm) I. s. *(hobo)* vagabundo; *(loafer)* vago, holgazán *m*; FAM. *(buttocks)* trasero II. tr. & intr. **-mm-** gorronear, sablear ◆ **to b. around** vagar III. adj. FAM. *(worthless)* sin valor, inútil; *(sore)* dolorido.

bum·ble (bŭm'bəl) intr. obrar con torpeza.

bum·ble·bee (bŭm'bəl-bē') s. abejorro.

bump (bŭmp) I. tr. *(to collide with)* topar, chocar contra; *(to knock against)* golpear contra; *(to displace)* desplazar; FAM. *(to oust)* quitar el puesto ◆ **to b. into** tropezarse con • **to b. off** JER. matar, despachar —intr. chocar contra, *(to jolt)* moverse a sacudidas II. s. *(collision)* choque *m*, topetón *m*; *(swelling)* hinchazón *f*, chichón *m*; *(in a road)* bache *m*.

bump·er (bŭm'pər) s. parachoques *m*.

bump·kin (bŭmp'kĭn) s. patán *m*, palurdo.

bump·y (bŭm'pē) adj. **-i-** *(uneven)* desigual, accidentado; *(jolty)* agitado, sacudido.

bun (bŭn) s. CUL. bollo, panecillo; *(hair)* moño.

bunch (bŭnch) I. s. *(of grapes)* racimo; *(of flowers)* ramillete *m*; *(handful)* montón *m*, puñado; FAM. *(of people)* grupo II. tr. & intr. agrupar(se), juntar(se).

bun·dle (bŭn'dl) I. s. bulto, fardo; *(papers)* fajo; *(tied)* atado; JER. *(money)* montón *m* de dinero II. tr. *(to tie)* atar; *(to wrap)* envolver; *(to dress warmly)* arropar bien —intr. ◆ **to b. up** arroparse, abrigarse.

bun·gle (bŭng'gəl) I. tr. & intr. chapucear II. s. chapucería.

bun·ion (bŭn'yən) s. juanete *m*.

bunk¹ (bŭngk) I. s. *(bed)* litera II. intr. dormir en una litera.

bunk² s. JER. *(nonsense)* tontería, sandez *f*.

bun·ny (bŭn'ē) s. FAM. conejo, conejito.

bunt·ing (bŭn'tĭng) s. tela para banderas.

buoy (bōō'ē, boi) I. s. *(buoyancy)* boya ◆ **life b.** salvavidas II. tr. MARÍT. aboyar; *(to keep afloat)* mantener a flote; FIG. *(to hearten)* animar, alentar.

buoy·an·cy (boi'an-sē) s. *(capacity)* flotabilidad *f*; *(cheerfulness)* optimismo.

buoy·ant (:ənt) adj. boyante; *(animated)* animado; *(cheerful)* optimista.

bur (bûr) s. erizo, parte espinosa.

bur·den (bûr'dn) I. s. carga ♦ **the b. of proof** la carga de la prueba II. tr. *(to load)* cargar; *(to oppress)* agobiar.

bu·reau (byŏŏr'ō) s. [pl. **s** o **-x**] *(dresser)* tocador *m*; POL. departamento; *(business)* agencia; G.B. *(desk)* escritorio.

bu·reauc·ra·cy (byŏŏ-rŏk'rə-sē) s. burocracia.

bu·reau·crat (byŏŏr'ə-krăt') s. burócrata *mf.*

bur·geon (bûr'jən) intr. crecer, florecer.

burg·er (bûr'gər) s. FAM. hamburguesa.

burgh·er (bûr'gər) s. burgués *m.*

bur·glar (bûr'glər) s. ladrón *m* ♦ **b. alarm** alarma antirrobo.

bur·glar·ize (:glə-rīz') tr. robar (casa, tienda).

bur·gla·ry (:rē) s. robo con allanamiento de morada.

bur·i·al (bĕr'ē-əl) s. entierro ♦ **b. ground** cementerio, camposanto.

bur·lap (bûr'lăp') s. arpillera.

bur·lesque (bər-lĕsk') I. s. *(parody)* parodia; *(vaudeville)* espectáculo de variedades II. tr. parodiar III. adj. burlesco.

bur·ly (bûr'lē) adj. **-i-** fuerte, robusto.

burn (bûrn) I. tr. **-ed** o **-t** quemar; *(a building)* incendiar; *(to expend)* gastar (dinero, energías) ♦ **to b. down** incendiar • **to b. into** grabar en • **to b. oneself out** JER. agotarse, gastarse (uno) • **to b. the candle at both ends** vivir una vida agitada • **to b. to a crisp** achicharrar • **to b. the ground** reducir a cenizas • **to b. up** *(to consume)* consumir; FAM. *(to enrage)* enfurecer, indignar • **to get burned** FAM. estar embaucado —intr. quemarse, arder; *(building)* consumirse; *(light bulb)* estar encendido; *(with fever)* arder; *(with passion)* consumirse; *(food)* quemarse ♦ **to b. down** quemarse por completo • **to b. out** *(fire)* apagarse; *(fuse, bulb)* quemarse, fundirse • **to b. up** *(in flames)* quemarse o consumirse completamente; *(with anger)* enfurecerse, indignarse • **to b. up with** arder de II. s. *(injury)* quemadura; *(sunburn)* quemadura de sol.

burn·er (bûr'nər) s. quemador *m*, mechero.

burn·ing (:nĭng) adj. *(hot)* ardiente, abrasador; *(passionate)* ardiente; *(urgent)* urgente.

bur·nish (bûr'nĭsh) I. tr. pulir, bruñir II. s. brillo, lustre *m.*

bur·noose (bər-nŏŏs') s. albornoz *m.*

burn·out (bûrn'out') s. *(failure)* extinción *f*; *(exhaustion)* agotamiento.

burp (bûrp) I. s. eructo II. intr. eructar —tr. hacer eructar (a un niño).

burr (bûr) s. *(tool)* taladro; *(roughness)* rebaba; BOT. erizo, parte espinosa.

bur·row (bûr'ō) I. s. madriguera II. intr. *(to dig)* hacer una madriguera; *(to hide)* amadrigarse —tr. cavar, excavar.

bur·sar (bûr'sər) s. tesorero.

burst (bûrst) I. intr. **burst** *(to break open)* estallar, reventarse; *(to explode)* explotar; *(to be full)* rebosar (with de) ♦ **to b. in** *(to interrupt)* interrumpir; *(to enter)* irrumpir en • **to b. into bloom** brotar • **to b. into flame(s)** estallar en llamas • **to b. open** abrirse violentamente • **to b. out** *(to exclaim)* exclamar; *(to emerge)* surgir; *(to bloom)* brotar; *(crying, laughing)* echarse a —tr. *(to shatter)* reventar; *(to force open)* romper • **to b. into** *(a room)* irrumpir en; *(tears, laughter)* desatarse en • **to b. with** rebosar de II. s. reventón *m*, explosión *f*; *(of laugh-*

ter) estallido; *(of gunfire)* ráfaga; *(of energy)* explosión; *(of anger)* arranque *m*; *(of applause)* salva.

bur·y (bĕr'ē) tr. enterrar; *(to inter, conceal)* sepultar ♦ **to b. oneself** sumergirse, sepultarse.

bus (bŭs) I. s. [pl. **es** o **-ses**] autobús *m*, ómnibus *m* II. tr. **-s-** o **-ss-** transportar en autobús.

bus·boy (bŭs'boi') s. ayudante *m* de camarero.

bush (bŏŏsh) s. *(shrub)* arbusto; *(thicket)* maleza; *(land)* matorral *m.*

bushed (bŏŏsht) adj. FAM. agotado, hecho polvo.

bush·el (bŏŏsh'əl) s. medida de áridos (35,24 litros); FAM. *(great deal)* montón *m.*

bush·whack (bŏŏsh'hwăk') intr. abrirse paso en la maleza —tr. tender una emboscada.

bush·y (:ē) adj. **-i-** *(land)* breñoso, lleno de arbustos; *(hair)* tupido, espeso.

bus·i·ly (bĭz'ə-lē) adv. diligentemente.

busi·ness (bĭz'nĭs) s. *(establishment)* comercio, negocio; *(firm)* firma, empresa; *(commerce)* negocios; *(matter, concern)* asunto ♦ **b. school** escuela de comercio • **that's none of your b.** eso no es cosa tuya • **to mean b.** no andar con juegos.

busi·ness·like (:līk') adj. metódico, serio.

busi·ness·man (:măn') s. [pl. **-women**] hombre *m* de negocios, comerciante *m.*

busi·ness·wom·an (:wŏŏm'ən) s. [pl. **-women**] mujer *f* de negocios, comerciante *f.*

bust¹ (bŭst) s. ARTE., ANAT. busto.

bust² FAM. I. tr. *(to break)* romper; *(to damage)* descomponer; *(to punch)* pegar; *(to arrest)* arrestar —intr. romperse, descomponerse II. s. *(flop)* chasco, fracaso; COM. quiebra; ECON. época de depresión económica; *(punch)* puñetazo; *(arrest)* arresto; *(raid)* redada, batida.

bus·tle (bŭs'əl) I. intr. apresurarse II. s. bullicio, animación *f.*

bus·y (bĭz'ē) I. adj. **-i-** *(person)* atareado, ocupado; *(place)* animado, concurrido; *(telephone)* ocupado ♦ **b. signal** señal de ocupado II. tr. & intr. mantener(se) ocupado.

bus·y·bod·y (:bŏd'ē) s. entremetido.

but (bŭt, bət) I. conj. *(on the other hand)* pero, mas; *(rather)* sino; *(nevertheless)* no obstante, sin embargo; *(except)* excepto ♦ **b. then** pero por otra parte • **cannot (help) b.** no poder menos que • **none b.** solamente II. adv. nada más que, solamente ♦ **all b.** casi • **to do nothing b.** no hacer más que III. prep. menos, excepto ♦ **b. for** a no ser por IV. s. pero.

bu·tane (byŏŏ'tān') s. butano.

butch·er (bŏŏch'ər) I. s. carnicero ♦ **b. shop** carnicería II. tr. *(animals)* matar; *(to murder)* asesinar; FAM. *(to botch)* chapucear.

butch·er·y (:ə-rē) s. *(carnage)* matanza; *(botch)* chapucería.

but·ler (bŭt'lər) s. mayordomo.

butt¹ (bŭt) I. tr. & intr. topar, dar un topetazo ♦ **to b. in(to)** FAM. entremeterse en II. s. topetazo.

butt² *(to attach)* empalmar; *(to abut)* colindar —intr. estar empalmado.

butt³ s. *(object of ridicule)* hazmerreír *m.*

butt⁴ s. *(of a rifle)* culata; *(cigarette end)* colilla; JER. *(cigarette)* rubio, pitillo; FAM. *(buttocks)* trasero.

but·ter (bŭt'ər) I. s. mantequilla II. tr. untar con mantequilla ♦ **to b. up** adular, lisonjear.

but·ter·cup (:kŭp') s. botón *m* de oro.

but·ter·fat (:făt′) s. grasa *o* nata de la leche.
but·ter·fin·gers (:fĭng′gərz) s. FAM. persona torpe.
but·ter·fly (:flī′) s. mariposa ♦ **to have butterflies in one's stomach** tener cosquillas en el estómago.
but·ter·milk (:mĭlk′) s. suero de la leche.
but·ter·scotch (:skŏch′) s. caramelo.
but·tock (bŭt′ək) s. nalga ♦ pl. trasero.
but·ton (bŭt′n) **I.** s. botón *m*; *(switch)* botón, pulsador *m*; *(badge)* insignia, distintivo ♦ **on the b.** FAM. correcto, exacto **II.** tr. & intr. abotonar(se), abrochar(se).
but·ton·hole (:hōl′) **I.** s. ojal *m* **II.** tr. retener (a alguien y obligarlo a escuchar).
but·tress (bŭt′rĭs) **I.** s. ARQ. contrafuerte *m*; *(support)* apoyo, sostén *m* **II.** tr. reforzar, apoyar.
bux·om (bŭk′səm) adj. rollizo, frescachón.
🠖**buy** (bī) **I.** tr. **bought** comprar, adquirir; FAM. *(to bribe)* sobornar; FAM. *(to believe)* creer, aceptar ♦ **to b. into** comprar cantidades importantes de acciones de (una empresa) • **to b. off** sobornar • **to b. out** COM. comprar la parte de • **to b. up** acaparar —intr. hacer compras **II.** s. *(purchase)* compra; FAM. *(bargain)* ganga ♦ **a good b.** ganga.
buy·er (bī′ər) s. comprador *m*.
buzz (bŭz) **I.** intr. *(insect, motor)* zumbar; *(room)* llenarse de charla; *(buzzer)* sonar; *(to ring)* tocar el timbre ♦ **to b. around** *o* **about** jetrearse • **b. off!** FAM. ¡lárgate! —tr. hacer zumbar; FAM. *(to fly)* volar muy cerca de; *(with a buzzer)* llamar con un timbre; FAM. *(to telephone)* telefonear, dar un telefonazo **II.** s. *(drone)* zumbido; *(murmur)* murmullo; FAM. *(telephone call)* telefonazo ♦ **b. saw** sierra circular.
buz·zard (bŭz′ərd) s. buitre *m*.
buzz·er (bŭz′ər) s. timbre *m*.
by (bī) **I.** prep. *(agent, measure, route)* por <*made by* hecho por> <*by the dozen* por do­cena> <*by mail* por correo>; *(origin, time)* de <*by birth* de nacimiento> <*by night* de noche>; *(next to)* junto a, cerca de <*by the bed* junto a la cama>; *(according to)* según, de acuerdo con <*by the rules* de acuerdo con las reglas>; *(not later than)* para <*by noon* para el mediodía>; *(after)* a <*day by day* día a día ♦ **by the day** de paso, a propósito • **by the way** de paso, entre paréntesis • **by this time** *(hour)* a esta hora; *(point)* a estas alturas **II.** adv. *(nearby)* cerca, al lado de; *(aside)* a un lado, aparte ♦ **by and by** *(soon)* pronto; *(after a while)* más tarde • **by and large** en términos generales • **by then** para entonces.
by-and-by (bī′ən-bī′) s. ♦ **in the b.** en el futuro.
bye (bī) s. ♦ **by the b.** incidentalmente.
bye(-bye) (bī[-bī]) interj. FAM. ¡adiós!, ¡chau!
by·gone (bī′gôn′) **I.** adj. pasado **II.** s. ♦ **to let bygones be bygones** olvidar lo pasado.
by·law (bī′lô′) s. *(of an organization)* reglamento; *(of a city)* ordenanza municipal.
by-line (bī′līn′) s. PERIOD. renglón *m* con el nombre del autor.
by-pass *o* **by·pass** (bī′păs′) **I.** s. *(road)* carretera de circunvalación; ELEC. derivación *f* ♦ **coronary b.** desviación coronaria **II.** tr. evitar, pasar por alto.
by-prod·uct (bī′prŏd′əkt) s. INDUS. subproducto, derivado; *(side effect)* efecto secundario.
by·road (bī′rōd′) s. carretera secundaria.

by·stand·er (bī′stăn′dər) s. espectador *m*, circunstante *mf*.
byte (bīt) s. byte *m*, octeto.
by·way (bī′wā′) s. carretera secundaria.
by·word (bī′wûrd′) s. *(proverb)* refrán *m*; *(synonymn)* sinónimo.

C

c, C (sē) s. tercera letra del alfabeto inglés; MÚS. do.
cab (kăb) s. taxi *m*; *(of vehicle)* cabina.
ca·bal (kə-băl′) s. *(plot)* cábala, intriga; *(conspirators)* camarilla.
cab·a·la (kăb′ə-lə, kə-bä′-) s. cábala.
cab·a·ret (kăb′ ə-rā′) s. cabaret *m*.
cab·bage (kăb′ĭj) s. col *f*, berza.
cab·by/bie (kăb′ē) s. FAM. taxista *mf*.
cab·driv·er (:drī′vər) s. taxista *mf*.
cab·in (kăb′ĭn) s. *(house)* barraca, choza; *(of ship)* camarote *m*; *(of plane)* cabina ♦ **c. cruiser** yate de recreo.
cab·i·net (kăb′ə-nĭt) s. armario; POL. consejo *o* gabinete *m* de ministros.
cab·i·net·mak·er (:mā′kər) s. ebanista *mf*.
cab·i·net·work (:wûrk′) s. ebanistería.
ca·ble (kā′bəl) **I.** s. cable *m*; *(cablegram)* cablegrama *m*; TELEV. televisión *f* por cable ♦ **c. car** funicular **II.** tr. & intr. cablegrafiar.
ca·ble·gram (:grăm′) s. cablegrama *m*.
ca·ble·vi·sion (:vĭzh′ən) s. televisión *f* por cable.
ca·boo·dle (kə-bōōd′l) s. FAM. ♦ **the whole c.** el montón entero.
ca·boose (kə-bōōs′) s. furgón *m* de cola.
cab·stand (kăb′stănd′) s. parada de taxis.
ca·ca·o (kə-kā′ō) s. cacao.
cache (kăsh) **I.** s. *(place)* escondrijo; *(goods)* reserva escondida **II.** tr. guardar en un escondrijo.
ca·chet (kă-shā′) s. sello.
cack·le (kăk′əl) **I.** intr. *(hen)* cacarear; *(to laugh)* reírse estridentemente **II.** s. *(of hens)* cacareo; *(laughter)* risa estridente.
ca·coph·o·ny (kə-kŏf′ə-nē) s. cacofonía.
cac·tus (kăk′təs) s. [pl. **es** *o* **-ti**] cactus *m*, cacto.
cad (kăd) s. desvergonzado, sinvergüenza *m*.
ca·dav·er (kə-dăv′ər) s. cadáver *m*.
ca·dav·er·ous (:əs) adj. cadavérico.
cad·die (kăd′ē) **I.** s. caddy *m* **II.** intr. **-dying** (servir de) caddy.
cad·dy (kăd′ē) s. cajita para el té.
ca·dence/·cy (kād′ns) s. cadencia.
ca·det (kə-dĕt′) s. cadete *m*.
cadge (kăj) tr. & intr. FAM. gorronear.
cad·mi·um (kăd′mē-əm) s. cadmio.
ca·dre (kăd′rē) s. cuadro.
ca·du·ce·us (kə-dōō′sē-əs) s. [pl. **-cei**] caduceo.
Cae·sar·e·an section (sĭ-zâr′ē-ən) s. operación cesárea.
ca·fé/te (kă-fā′) s. café *m*.
caf·e·te·ri·a (kăf′ĭ-tîr′ē-ə) s. cafetería.
caf·fein(e) (kă-fēn′) s. cafeína.
caf·tan (kăf′tăn′) s. túnica.
cage (kāj) **I.** s. jaula **II.** tr. enjaular.
cag·(e)y (kā′jē) adj. **-i-** astuto.
ca·hoots (kə-hōōts′) s.pl. FAM. ♦ **to be in c. with** estar en connivencia con.
cai·man (kā′mən) s. caimán *m*.

cairn (kârn) s. montón *m* de piedras.
cais·son (kā′sŏn′) s. CONSTR. cajón hidráulico; MARIT. camello; MIL. cajón de municiones.
ca·jole (kə-jōl′) tr. engatusar.
cake (kāk) **I.** s. pastel *m*; *(sponge)* bizcocho; *(pancake)* torta; *(of soap)* pastilla ♦ **to take the c.** FAM. ser el colmo **II.** tr. & intr. endurecer(se).
cal·a·bash (kăl′ə-băsh′) s. *(vine)* calabaza; *(tree)* güira; *(bowl)* totumo.
cal·a·boose (kăl′ə-bōos′) s. JER. calabozo.
cal·a·mine (kăl′ə-mīn′) s. calamina.
ca·lam·i·ty (kə-lăm′ĭ-tē) s. calamidad *f.*
cal·ci·fy (kăl′sə-fī′) tr. & intr. calcificar(se).
cal·ci·mine (kăl′sə-mīn′) s. encalado.
cal·ci·um (kăl′sē-əm) s. calcio.
cal·cu·late (kăl′kyə-lāt′) tr. calcular —intr. hacer cálculos; *(to guess)* suponer ♦ **to c. on** FAM. contar con.
cal·cu·lat·ed (:lā′tĭd) adj. deliberado, intencional.
cal·cu·lat·ing (:tĭng) adj. calculador.
cal·cu·la·tion (′-shən) s. cálculo.
cal·cu·la·tor (′-′tər) s. calculadora.
cal·cu·lus (kăl′kyə-ləs) s. [pl. **es** o **-li**] cálculo.
cal·dron (kôl′drən) s. caldera.
cal·en·dar (kăl′ən-dər) s. calendario; *(schedule)* agenda.
calf¹ (kăf) s. [pl. **-ves**] *(of cow)* becerro, ternero; *(of whale, elephant)* cría.
calf² s. [pl. **-ves**] ANAT. pantorrilla.
calf·skin (′skĭn′) s. piel *f* de becerro.
cal·i·ber (kăl′ə-bər) s. calibre *m.*
cal·i·brate (:brāt′) tr. calibrar.
cal·i·co (kăl′ĭ-kō′) s. [pl. **(e)s**] calicó.
cal·i·per(s) (kăl′ə-pər[z]) s. calibrador *m* ♦ **vernier c.** calibrador micrométrico.
ca·liph (kā′lĭf) s. califa *m.*
ca·liph·ate (kā′lĭ-fāt′) s. califato.
cal·is·then·ics (kăl′ĭs-thĕn′ĭks) s. calistenia.
ca·lix (kā′lĭks) s. [pl. **-ces**] cáliz *m.*
call (kôl) **I.** tr. llamar; *(a meeting)* convocar; *(to telephone)* telefonear, llamar a; *(birds)* reclamar a; *(to consider)* considerar, juzgar *<I c. that fair* lo considero razonable>; *(to label)* calificar (de); *(a strike)* declarar; *(to predict)* predecir ♦ **to c. back** volver a llamar **to** TEL. volver a llamar ♦ **to c. down** FAM. *(to scold)* regañar, reñir; *(to invoke)* invocar ♦ **to c. forth** hacer surgir ♦ **to c. in** *(to summon)* hacer venir, llamar; COM. *(a debt, loan)* pedir el reembolso de ♦ **to c. into play** hacer entrar en juego ♦ **to c. off** *(to cancel)* cancelar; *(to halt)* parar, suspender ♦ **to c. oneself** llamarse ♦ **to c. out** *(to mobilize)* convocar a la acción; *(to shout)* llamar ♦ **to c. together** convocar, reunir ♦ **to c. to account** pedir cuentas ♦ **to c. to mind** evocar, traer a la memoria ♦ **to c. to order** llamar al orden ♦ **to c. (one's) attention to** hacer notar o reparar en ♦ **to c. up** llamar a, telefonear; MIL. llamar a las armas —intr. *(to telephone)* hacer una llamada (telefónica), llamar; *(to visit)* hacer una visita; *(to yell)* llamar, gritar; ORNIT., ZOOL. reclamarse ♦ **to c. again** venir otra vez **to c. at** MARIT. hacer escala en ♦ **to c. back** volver a llamar por teléfono ♦ **to c. for** requerir, necesitar ♦ **to c. on** o **upon** *(to visit)* visitar a, ir a ver a; *(to appeal)* recurrir a; *(God)* invocar ♦ **to c. out** exclamar, gritar **II.** s. llamada; ORNIT., ZOOL. reclamo, canto; *(of bugle)* toque *m*; *(short visit)* visita; *(summons, appeal)* llamamiento; COM. *(demand)* demanda, pedido ♦ **c.**

button botón de llamada • **c. girl** FAM. prostituta • **on c.** de guardia • **port of c.** puerto de escala • **to pay a c. on** hacer visita a • **within c.** al alcance de la voz.
call·er (kô′lər) s. visita, visitante *mf.*
cal·lig·ra·pher (kə-lĭg′rə-fər) s. calígrafo.
cal·lig·ra·phy (:fē) s. caligrafía.
call·ing (kô′lĭng) s. vocación *f* ♦ **c. card** tarjeta de visita.
cal·li·o·pe (kə-lī′ə-pē) s. órgano de vapor.
cal·lous (kăl′əs) **I.** adj. insensible, duro de corazón **II.** intr. *(skin)* encallecerse; hacerse insensible.
cal·low (kăl′ō) adj. **-er, -est** *(person)* inmaturo.
call-up (kôl′ŭp′) s. MIL. llamada a filas.
cal·lus (kăl′əs) **I.** s. [pl. **es**] callo **II.** intr. encallecerse.
calm (käm) **I.** adj. sereno, tranquilo **II.** s. calma **III.** tr. & intr. aplacar(se), calmar(se).
calm·ness (′nĭs) s. tranquilidad *f.*
ca·lor·ic (kə-lôr′ĭk) adj. & s. calórico.
cal·o·rie (kăl′ə-rē) s. caloría.
ca·lum·ni·ate (kə-lŭm′nē-āt′) tr. calumniar.
cal·um·ny (kăl′əm-nē) s. calumnia.
cal·va·ry (kăl′və-rē) s. calvario.
calve (kăv) intr. parir (la vaca).
calves (kăvz) cf. **calf¹·².**
ca·lyx (kā′lĭks) s. [pl. **es** o **-ces**] cáliz *m.*
cam (kăm) s. leva.
ca·ma·ra·der·ie (kä′mə-rä′də-rē) s. compañerismo, camaradería.
cam·ber (kăm′bər) s. *(of road)* peralte *m*; AUTO. inclinación *f.*
cam·bi·um (kăm′bē-əm) s. cambium *m.*
came (kām) cf. **come.**
cam·el (kăm′əl) s. camello.
ca·mel·lia (kə-mēl′yə) s. camelia.
cam·e·o (kăm′ē-ō′) s. camafeo.
cam·er·a (kăm′ər-ə) s. FOTOG. cámara, máquina; CINEM. cámara ♦ **in c.** DER. en sesión secreta.
cam·er·a·man (:măn′) s. [pl. **-men**] cameraman *m.*
cam·i·sole (kăm′ĭ-sōl′) s. cubrecorsé *m.*
cam·ou·flage (kăm′ə-fläzh′) **I.** s. camuflaje *m* **II.** tr. & intr. camuflar.
camp (kămp) **I.** s. campo; *(encampment)* campamento **II.** intr. & tr. acampar.
cam·paign (kăm-pān′) intr. & s. (hacer una) campaña.
cam·pa·ni·le (kăm′pə-nē′lē) s. [pl. **s** o **-li**] campanil *m*, campanario.
camp·er (kăm′pər) s. AUTO. campista *mf*; caravana.
camp·fire (kămp′fīr′) s. hoguera de campamento.
camp·ground (:ground′) s. camping *m.*
cam·phor (kăm′fər) s. alcanfor *m.*
camp·ing (kăm′pĭng) s. camping *m.*
camp·site (:sīt′) s. camping *m.*
cam·pus (kăm′pəs) s. [pl. **es**] ciudad universitaria.
cam·shaft (kăm′shăft′) s. árbol *m* de levas.
can¹ (kăn, kən) aux. [pret. **could**] *(to be able to)* poder; *(to know how to)* saber *<he c. cook* él sabe cocinar>.
can² (kăn) **I.** s. *(tin)* lata; *(for trash)* tacho, cubo; JER. *(jail)* chirona; *(toilet)* retrete *m*; *(buttocks)* nalgas ♦ **c. opener** abrelatas **II.** tr. **-nn-** *(food)* enlatar; JER. *(to fire)* despedir ♦ **c. it l** JER. ¡a callar!, ¡basta!
ca·nal (kə-năl′) s. canal *m.*

ca·nard (kə-närd′) s. bulo, patraña.
ca·nar·y (kə-nâr′ē) s. canario.
can·cel (kăn′səl) I. tr. anular, cancelar; *(to cross out)* tachar; *(a stamp)* matar; *(to offset)* contrarrestar II. s. cancelación *f*, anulación *f*.
can·cel·la·tion (′sə-lā′shən) s. cancelación *f*; *(of stamp)* matasellos *m*.
can·cer (kăn′sər) s. cáncer *m*.
can·cer·ous (:əs) adj. canceroso.
can·de·la·brum (kăn′dl-ä′brəm) s. [pl. **s** *o* **-ra**] candelabro.
can·des·cent (kăn-dĕs′ənt) adj. candente.
can·did (kăn′dĭd) adj. *(frank)* franco; *(not posed)* espontáneo.
can·di·da·cy (kăn′dĭ-də-sē) s. candidatura.
can·di·date (kăn′dĭ-dāt′) s. candidato.
can·died (kăn′dēd) adj. escarchado.
can·dle (kăn′dl) s. vela, bujía; *(in church)* cirio ♦ **not to hold a c.** to no llegar ni a la suela del zapato de.
can·dle·hold·er (:hōl′dər) s. candelero.
can·dle·light (:līt′) s. luz *f* de una vela.
can·dle·pow·er (:pou′ər) s. candela.
can·dle·stick (:stĭk′) s. candelero.
can·dor (kăn′dər) s. franqueza.
can·dy (kăn′dē) I. s. caramelo ♦ **c. store** confitería II. tr. & intr. escarchar(se).
cane (kān) I. s. *(stick)* bastón *m*; *(switch)* vara; *(plant)* caña; *(wicker)* mimbre *m*; *(sugar cane)* caña de azúcar II. tr. golpear con una vara.
cane·brake (′brāk′) s. cañaveral *m*.
ca·nine (kā′nīn′) I. adj. canino II. s. *(animal)* animal canino; *(tooth)* diente canino.
can·is·ter (kăn′ĭ-stər) s. lata.
can·ker (sore) (kăng′kər) s. úlcera en la boca.
can·ker·ous (:əs) adj. ulceroso.
can·na·bis (kăn′ə-bĭs) s. cáñamo índico.
canned (kănd) adj. enlatado; FAM. *(taped)* grabado.
can·ner·y (kăn′ə-rē) s. fábrica de conservas.
can·ni·bal (kăn′ə-bəl) s. caníbal *m*, antropófago.
can·ni·bal·ism (:bə-lĭz′əm) s. canibalismo.
can·ni·bal·is·tic (′-lĭs′tĭk) adj. caníbal.
can·ni·bal·ize (′-līz′) tr. recuperar las piezas servibles de (avión, tanque).
can·ning (kăn′ĭng) s. conservería.
can·non (kăn′ən) [pl. inv. *o* **s**] cañón *m*.
can·non·ade (′-nād′) I. tr. & intr. cañonear II. s. cañoneo.
can·non·ball (′ən-bôl′) s. bala de cañón.
can·non·eer (′ə-nîr′) s. artillero.
can·not (kăn′ŏt′, kə-nŏt′) negación de **can¹**.
can·ny (kăn′ē) adj. **-i-** astuto.
ca·noe (kə-nōō′) intr. **-oeing** & s. (ir en) canoa.
can·on (kăn′ən) s. *(church law)* canon *m*; *(priest)* canónigo.
ca·non·ic/i·cal (kə-nŏn′ĭk) adj. RELIG. canónico; FIG. ortodoxo.
can·on·ize (kăn′ə-nīz′) tr. canonizar.
can·o·py (kăn′ə-pē) s. dosel *m*; *(of leaves, stars)* bóveda.
cant¹ (kănt) I. s. inclinación *f* II. tr. inclinar.
cant² s. *(whine)* quejido; *(insincere talk)* hipocresía; *(jargon)* jerga.
can't (kănt) contr. de **cannot**.
can·ta·loup(e) (kăn′tl-ōp′) s. cantalupo.
can·tan·ker·ous (kăn-tăng′kər-əs) adj. FAM. malhumorado, pendenciero.
can·teen (kăn-tēn′) s. *(store, cafeteria)* cantina; *(flask)* cantimplora.

can·ter (kăn′tər) intr. & s. (ir a) medio galope.
can·ti·cle (kăn′tĭ-kəl) s. cántico.
can·ti·le·ver (kăn′tl-ē′vər) tr. & s. (construir con una) ménsula.
can·ton (kăn′tən) s. cantón *m*.
can·tor (kăn′tər) s. solista *m* (de una sinagoga).
can·vas (kăn′vəs) s. lona; *(painting)* lienzo; *(sails)* velamen *m*.
can·vass (kăn′vəs) I. tr. & intr. *(to solicit)* solicitar (votos); *(to poll)* hacer una encuesta (de); *(to examine)* examinar II. s. *(of votes)* solicitación *f*; *(survey)* encuesta; *(examination)* examen *m*.
can·yon (kăn′yən) s. cañón *m*.
cap (kăp) I. s. *(hat)* gorro, gorra; *(academic)* birrete *m*; *(cover)* tapa; *(limit)* tope *m*; ARM. cápsula, pistón *m* ♦ **c. gun** pistola de fulminante II. tr. **-pp-** *(to cover)* cubrir, poner una gorra; *(to complete)* terminar ♦ **to c. off** culminar.
ca·pa·bil·i·ty (kā′pə-bĭl′ĭ-tē) s. capacidad *f*.
ca·pa·ble (kā′pə-bəl) adj. capaz.
ca·pa·cious (kə-pā′shəs) adj. espacioso.
ca·pac·i·tor (kə-păs′ĭ-tər) s. condensador *m*.
ca·pac·i·ty (kə-păs′ĭ-tē) s. capacidad *f*; *(production)* rendimiento máximo ♦ **in the c. of** en calidad de ♦ **to fill to c.** llenar completamente.
ca·par·i·son (kə-păr′ĭ-sən) s. caparazón *m*.
cape¹ (kāp) s. GEOG. cabo.
cape² s. *(garment)* capa.
ca·per¹ (kā′pər) I. s. *(leap)* cabriola; *(prank)* travesura; JER. *(plot)* conspiración criminal *f* ♦ **to cut a c.** hacer cabriolas II. intr. brincar.
ca·per² s. CUL. alcaparra.
cap·il·lar·y (kăp′ə-lĕr′ē) s. & adj. (vaso) capilar.
cap·i·tal¹ (kăp′ĭ-tl) I. s. *(city)* capital *f*; *(assets, wealth)* capital *m*; IMPR. *(letter)* mayúscula ♦ **c. assets** activo fijo ♦ **c. gain** ganancias sobre el capital ♦ **c. punishment** pena capital *o* de muerte II. adj. *(foremost)* capital; *(excellent)* excelente; *(involving death)* capital; IMPR. mayúscula.
cap·i·tal² s. ARQ. capitel *m*.
cap·i·tal·ism (:ĭz′əm) s. capitalismo.
cap·i·tal·ist (:ĭst) s. capitalista *mf*.
cap·i·tal·is·tic (′-ĭs′tĭk) adj. capitalista.
cap·i·tal·i·za·tion (:ĭ-zā′shən) s. ECON. capitalización *f*; IMPR. uso de letras mayúsculas.
cap·i·tal·ize (′--īz′) tr. FIN. capitalizar; IMPR. escribir con mayúscula —intr. ♦ **to c. on** aprovechar, sacar provecho de.
cap·i·tal·ly (:ē) adv. admirablemente.
cap·i·tol (kăp′ĭ-tl) s. capitolio.
ca·pit·u·late (kə-pĭch′ə-lāt′) intr. capitular.
ca·pon (kā′pŏn′) s. capón *m*.
ca·price (kə-prēs′) s. capricho, antojo.
ca·pri·cious (kə-prĭsh′əs) adj. caprichoso.
cap·size (kăp′sīz′) tr. & intr. (hacer) volcar.
cap·stan (kăp′stən) s. *(hoist)* cabrestante *m*; *(of tape recorder)* espiga.
cap·sule (kăp′səl, -sōōl) s. cápsula; *(summary)* resumen *m* breve.
cap·tain (kăp′tən) I. s. capitán *m* II. tr. capitanear.
cap·tion (kăp′shən) I. s. *(of picture)* pie *m*, leyenda; CINEM. subtítulo; *(heading)* encabezamiento II. tr. *(to title)* encabezar; *(a picture)* poner una leyenda.
cap·tious (kăp′shəs) adj. *(carping)* criticón; *(deceptive)* engañoso.
cap·ti·vate (kăp′tĭ-vāt′) tr. cautivar, fascinar.
cap·ti·va·tion (′-vā′shən) s. encanto.

cap·tive (kăp′tĭv) **I.** s. cautivo **II.** adj. *(confined)* cautivo; *(charmed)* cautivado.
cap·tiv·i·ty (-′ĭ-tē) s. cautividad *f*, cautiverio.
cap·tor (kăp′tər) s. capturador *m*.
cap·ture (:chər) **I.** tr. capturar; *(a prize)* ganar **II.** s. captura.
car (kär) s. AUTO. coche *m*, carro; F.C. coche *m*, vagón *m*; *(tramcar)* tranvía *m*.
ca·rafe (kə-răf′) s. garrafa.
car·a·mel (kăr′ə-məl) s. *(candy)* caramelo; *(burnt sugar)* azúcar quemado.
car·a·pace (kăr′ə-pās′) s. caparazón *m*.
car·at (kăr′ət) s. quilate *m*.
car·a·van (kăr′ə-văn′) s. caravana.
car·a·vel (kăr′ə-věl′) s. carabela.
car·a·way seed (kăr′ə-wā′) s. carvi *m*.
car·bide (kär′bīd′) s. carburo.
car·bine (kär′bīn′) s. carabina.
car·bi·neer (′bə-nîr′) s. carabinero.
car·bo·hy·drate (kär′bō-hī′drāt′) s. carbohidrato.
car·bon (kär′bən) s. QUÍM. carbono; *(paper)* papel *m* carbón; *(copy)* copia ♦ **c. copy** copia al carbón • **c. dioxide** bióxido de carbono • **c. paper** papel carbón.
car·bon·ate (:bə-nāt′) tr. carbonatar ♦ **carbonated water** gaseosa.
car·bon·if·er·ous (:nĭf′ər-əs) adj. carbonífero.
car·bun·cle (kär′bŭng′kəl) s. carbunco.
car·bu·re·tion (kär′bə-rā′shən) s. carburación *f*.
car·bu·re·tor (′-′tər) s. carburador *m*.
car·bu·ret·tor (kär′bə-rět′ər) G.B. var. de **carburetor**.
car·cass (kär′kəs) s. res muerta, cadáver *m*; FAM. *(body)* cuerpo.
car·cin·o·gen (kär-sĭn′ə-jən) s. agente cancerígeno.
car·cin·o·gen·ic (kär′sə-nə-jěn′ĭk) adj. cancerígeno.
card¹ (kärd) **I.** s. *(playing)* naipe *m*, carta; *(greeting)* tarjeta; *(post)* (tarjeta) postal *f*; *(index)* ficha; *(ID)* carnet *m*; FAM. *(jokester)* bromista *mf* ♦ **c. catalog** fichero • **pl.** naipes • **house of cards** castillo de naipes • **it's in the c.** está escrito • **to hold all the c.** tener todos los triunfos en la mano • **to play one's c.** maniobrar bien **II.** tr. FAM. comprobar la edad de.
card² TEJ. **I.** s. carda **II.** tr. cardar.
card·board (′bôrd′) s. cartón *m*.
car·di·ac (kär′dē-ăk′) adj. cardiaco, cardíaco.
car·di·gan (kär′dĭ-gən) s. chaqueta de punto.
car·di·nal (kär′dn-əl) **I.** adj. cardinal; *(red)* purpúreo **II.** s. ORNIT., RELIG. cardenal *m*; *(red)* púrpura.
car·di·o·gram (kär′dē-ə-grăm′) s. cardiograma *m*.
car·di·ol·o·gy (′-ŏl′ə-jē) s. cardiología.
card·sharp (kärd′shärp′) s. fullero, tahúr *m*.
care (kâr) **I.** s. *(worry)* inquietud *f*, preocupación *f*; *(grief)* pena; *(charge)* cargo <*in my c.* a mi cargo>; *(caution)* cuidado <*I don't c.* con cuidado>; *(custody)* custodia; *(close attention)* esmero ♦ **(in) c. of** para entregar a • **to take c. (not to)** tener cuidado (de que no) • **to take c. of** *(person)* cuidar de; *(thing)* (pre)ocuparse de; *(expenses)* correr con • **to take c. of itself** resolverse por sí mismo • **under (someone's) c.** a cargo de (alguien) **II.** intr. *(to be concerned)* preocuparse; *(to mind)* importar <*I don't c.* no me importa> ♦ **I couldn't c. less** FAM. me importa un pito • **to c. for** *(to look after)* cuidar;

(to love, want) querer • **to c. to** tener ganas de, querer.
ca·reen (kə-rēn′) intr. dar bandazos —tr. inclinar (un bote).
ca·reer (kə-rîr′) **I.** s. carrera, profesión *f*; *(course)* curso (de la vida) **II.** intr. precipitarse.
care·free (kâr′frē′) adj. despreocupado.
care·ful (:fəl) adj. *(cautious)* cauteloso, prudente; *(thorough)* cuidadoso ♦ **to be c.** tener cuidado.
care·less (:lĭs) adj. *(negligent)* descuidado; *(unconcerned)* indiferente; *(offhand)* espontáneo.
ca·ress (kə-rěs′) **I.** s. caricia **II.** tr. acariciar.
care·tak·er (kâr′tā′kər) s. guardián *m*; *(of a residence)* portero.
care·worn (:wôrn′) adj. agobiado.
car·fare (kär′fâr′) s. precio de trayecto.
car·go (kär′gō) s. [pl. **(e)s**] carga, cargamento.
car·i·ca·ture (kär′ĭ-kə-chŏŏr′) **I.** s. caricatura **II.** tr. caricaturizar.
car·il·lon (kär′ə-lŏn′) s. carillón *m*.
car·mine (kär′mĭn) s. & adj. carmín *m*.
car·nage (kär′nĭj) s. carnicería, matanza.
car·nal (kär′nəl) adj. carnal.
car·na·tion (kär-nā′shən) s. clavel *m*.
car·ni·val (kär′nə-vəl) s. *(season)* carnaval *m*; *(fair)* feria, parque *m* de atracciones.
car·ni·vore (kär′nə-vôr′) s. carnívoro.
car·niv·o·rous (-nĭv′ər-əs) adj. carnívoro.
car·ob bean (kär′əb) s. algarroba.
car·ol (kär′əl) **I.** s. villancico **II.** tr. & intr. cantar (villancicos).
car·om (kär′əm) s. & intr. (hacer) carambola.
ca·rous·al (kə-rou′zəl) s. jarana, juerga.
ca·rouse (kə-rouz′) intr. andar de jarana.
car·ou·sel (kär′ə-sěl′) s. carrusel *m*, tiovivo.
carp¹ (kärp) intr. quejarse ♦ **to c. at** criticar.
carp² s. ICT. carpa.
car·pen·ter (kär′pən-tər) s. carpintero.
car·pen·try (:trē) s. carpintería.
car·pet (kär′pĭt) **I.** s. alfombra ♦ **to be on the c.** estar recibiendo una regañina **II.** tr. alfombrar.
car·pet·bag (:băg′) s. maleta hecha de alfombra.
carp·ing (kär′pĭng) adj. criticón.
car·port (kär′pôrt′) s. cobertizo para automóviles.
car·rel (kär′əl) s. cubículo de estudio.
car·riage (kär′ĭj) s. carruaje *m*, coche *m*; *(posture)* porte *m*; MEC. carro; COM. transporte *m*; G.B., F.C. vagón *m* ♦ **baby c.** cochecito de niños.
car·ri·er (kär′ē-ər) s. portador *m*, transportador *m*; COM. transportista *mf* ♦ **c. pigeon** paloma mensajera.
car·ri·on (kär′ē-ən) s. carroña.
car·rot (kär′ət) s. zanahoria.
car·ry (kär′ē) **I.** tr. llevar; *(a disease)* transmitir; *(merchandise)* tener surtido de; *(a penalty)* llevar aparejado, acarrear; *(an election)* ganar; *(a motion)* aprobar; *(to extend)* prolongar, extender; *(to impel)* mover, impulsar; *(to contain)* contener; *(to print)* publicar; *(to broadcast)* transmitir; MAT. llevarse ♦ **to be carried away (by)** estar entusiasmado (con) • **to c. along** arrastrar • **to c. forward** TEN. llevar, transportar a (columna, cuenta) • **to c. off** *(prize)* llevarse; *(plan)* realizar, llevar a cabo • **to c. on** *(conversation)* mantener, sostener; *(business)* dirigir, asumir el manejo • **to c. out** realizar, llevar a cabo • **to c. over** TEN. pasar a otra columna *o* página • **to c. something too far** lle-

var algo al exceso • **to c. through** *(to complete)* completar, llevar a cabo; *(to sustain)* sostener • **to c. weight** ser de peso *o* influencia —intr. *(motion, proposal)* ganar, aprobarse; *(to extend)* llegar, extenderse; *(sound)* oírse; *(voice)* proyectarse ♦ **c. on!** ¡siga!, ¡continúe! • **to c. on** *(to continue)* seguir, continuar; *(to misbehave)* portarse mal • **to c. over** conservarse (del pasado) **II.** s. *(portage)* transporte m; *(range)* alcance m.

car·ry·all (:ôl') s. maletín m.

car·ry·o·ver (:ō'vər) s. remanente m.

car·sick (kär'sĭk') adj. mareado.

cart (kärt) **I.** s. carro; *(handcart)* carretilla **II.** tr. acarrear; *(to lug)* arrastrar ♦ **to c. away** *o* **off** llevar.

cart·age (kär'tĭj) s. acarreo, porte m.

carte blanche (kärt blänch') s. carta blanca.

car·tel (kär-tĕl') s. cártel m.

car·ti·lage (kär'tl-ĭj) s. cartílago.

cart·load (kärt'lōd') s. carretada.

car·tog·ra·pher (kär-tŏg'rə-fər) s. cartógrafo.

car·tog·ra·phy (:fē) s. cartografía.

car·ton (kär'tn) s. caja de cartón.

car·toon (kär-tōn') s. *(political)* caricatura; *(comic)* tira, historieta; *(film)* dibujos animados.

car·toon·ist (:tō'nĭst) s. caricaturista mf.

car·tridge (kär'trĭj) s. cartucho; *(phonograph pickup)* fonocaptor m; *(cassette)* casete m; *(ink refill)* repuesto ♦ **c. belt** cartuchera.

cart·wheel (kärt'hwēl') s. voltereta lateral.

cart·wright (:rīt') s. carretero.

carve (kärv) tr. CUL. trinchar; ARTE. *(to sculpt)* tallar, cincelar; *(to engrave)* grabar ♦ **to c. out** labrar —intr. trinchar carne.

carv·ing (kär'vĭng) s. talla, escultura.

cas·cade (kă-skād') **I.** s. cascada; FIG. chorro, torrente m **II.** intr. caer en forma de cascada.

case¹ (kās) s. *(instance)* caso; *(example)* ejemplo; *(matter)* cuestión f <a c. of honor una cuestión de honor>; *(argument)* argumento; MED., GRAM. caso; DER. causa, pleito ♦ **a c. in point** un caso pertinente • **c. history** hoja *o* historia clínica • **in any c.** en todo caso • **in no c.** de ningún modo • **in that c.** en tal caso • **it is not a c. of** no se trata de • **that being the c.** si ése es el caso • **to bring a c. against** poner un pleito a • **to make one's c.** probar la tesis de uno • **to put** *o* **state one's c.** presentar uno los argumentos • **to rest one's c.** terminar uno el alegato **II.** tr. JER. estudiar, campanear.

case² **I.** s. *(box)* caja; *(outer covering)* estuche m; *(slipcover)* funda; ARQ. *(frame)* bastidor m, marco **II.** tr. empacar, embalar.

case·ment ('mənt) s. *(frame)* marco de ventana; *(window)* ventana batiente.

case·work (:wûrk') s. estudio de los antecedentes personales *o* familiares.

cash (kăsh) **I.** s. efectivo ♦ **c. register** caja registradora • **to pay (in) c.** pagar al contado **II.** tr. hacer efectivo, cobrar ♦ **to c. in** convertir en efectivo • **to c. in on** sacar partido de.

cash·book ('bŏŏk') s. libro de caja.

cash·box (:bŏks') s. caja.

cash·ew (kăsh'ōō) s. anacardo.

cash·ier (kă-shîr') s. cajero ♦ **c.'s check** cheque de caja.

cash·mere (kăzh'mîr') s. cachemira.

cas·ing (kā'sĭng) s. cubierta, envoltura.

ca·si·no (kə-sē'nō) s. casino.

cask (kăsk) s. barril m, tonel m.

cas·ket (kăs'kĭt) s. ataúd m; *(box)* estuche m.

cas·sa·va (kə-sä'və) s. mandioca; *(flour, bread)* cazabe m.

cas·se·role (kăs'ə-rōl') s. cazuela, cacerola.

cas·sette (kə-sĕt') s. *(film)* cartucho; *(tape)* casete mf.

cas·sock (kăs'ək) s. sotana.

cast (kăst) **I.** tr. **cast** *(to hurl)* tirar, arrojar; *(anchor)* echar; *(vote)* echar, depositar; *(glance)* volver, dirigir; *(light, shadow)* proyectar; *(dice)* tirar; CINEM. *(roles)* repartir; *(actor)* asignar una parte a; METAL. *(to mold)* moldear ♦ **to c. aside** *o* **away** desechar, descartar • **to c. doubt (up)on** poner en duda • **to c. down** *(eyes)* bajar; *(spirits)* desanimar • **to c. light on** esclarecer • **to c. off** desechar • **to c. out** echar fuera, arrojar —intr. ♦ **to c. about (for)** buscar • **to c. off** MARÍT. desamarrar; COST. terminar una vuelta **II.** s. tirada, lanzamiento; *(of dice)* tirada; *(of color)* tinte m; *(appearance)* apariencia; *(tendency)* tendencia; MED. enyesadura; CINEM., TEAT. reparto ♦ **c. iron** hierro fundido.

cas·ta·nets (kăs'tə-nĕts') s.pl. castañuelas.

cast·a·way (kăst'ə-wā') adj. & s. náufrago.

caste (kăst) s. casta.

cast·er (kăs'tər) s. *(wheel)* ruedecilla; *(stand)* convoy, vinagrera.

cas·ti·gate (kăs'tĭ-gāt') tr. castigar, reprobar.

cast·ing (kăs'tĭng) s. METAL. pieza fundida; TEAT. reparto.

cast-i·ron (kăst'ī'ərn) adj. de hierro fundido; *(tough)* férreo.

cas·tle (kăs'əl) **I.** s. castillo; *(in chess)* torre f, roque m **II.** tr. & intr. enrocar (al rey).

cast-off (kăst'ôf') adj. desechado.

cas·tor oil (kăs'tər) s. aceite m de ricino.

cas·trate (kăs'trāt') tr. castrar, capar.

cas·tra·tion (kă-strā'shən) s. castración f.

ca·su·al (kăzh'ōō-əl) adj. *(accidental)* casual; *(occasional)* que ocurre de vez en cuando; *(indifferent)* despreocupado; *(informal)* informal; *(superficial)* superficial.

ca·su·al·ly (:ē) adv. *(by chance)* casualmente; *(by the by)* de paso; *(informally)* informalmente.

ca·su·al·ty (:tē) s. *(accident)* accidente m; *(victim)* accidentado, víctima; MIL. baja.

ca·su·ist·ry (kăzh'ōō-ĭ-strē) s. casuística.

cat (kăt) s. gato; JER. *(guy)* tipo ♦ **to let the c. out of the bag** revelar un secreto.

ca·tab·o·lism (kə-tăb'ə-lĭz'əm) s. catabolismo.

cat·a·clysm (kăt'ə-klĭz'əm) s. cataclismo.

cat·a·combs (kăt'ə-kōmz') s.pl. catacumbas.

cat·a·log(ue) (kăt'l-ôg') **I.** s. catálogo **II.** tr. catalogar —intr. hacer un catálogo.

cat·a·lyst (kăt'l-ĭst) s. catalizador m.

cat·a·lyt·ic (-ĭt'ĭk) adj. catalítico.

cat·a·lyze ('-īz') tr. catalizar.

cat·a·pult (kăt'ə-pŭlt') **I.** s. catapulta **II.** tr. catapultar.

cat·a·ract (kăt'ə-răkt') s. catarata.

ca·tarrh (kə-tär') s. catarro.

ca·tas·tro·phe (kə-tăs'trə-fē) s. catástrofe f.

cat·a·stroph·ic (kăt'ə-strŏf'ĭk) adj. catastrófico.

cat·a·ton·ic (kăt'ə-tŏn'ĭk) adj. catatónico.

cat·call (kăt'kôl') s. silbido, silbatina.

catch (kăch, kĕch) **I.** tr. **caught** *(with the hands)* coger, agarrar; *(to capture)* prender, capturar; *(animals)* atrapar, cazar; *(fish)* pescar; *(bus, train)* alcanzar, tomar; *(to snag, hook)* engancharse *(on* en); *(to pinch)* agarrarse *(in* con); *(an illness)* coger, contraer; *(to surprise)* coger desprevenido, sorprender; *(to warning)* entender, captar; FAM. *(to take in)* (ir a) ver (película, espectáculo) ♦ **to c. hold of** agarrarse a, asirse a • **to c. it** FAM. ganarse una paliza o reprimenda • **to c. oneself** *(to check oneself)* contenerse; *(to realize)* darse cuenta • **to c. up** ponerse al corriente en cuanto a • **to c. up with** alcanzar —intr. *(to become fastened, hooked)* engancharse; *(to snag)* enredarse; *(to hold)* agarrar, engancharse; *(to catch fire)* prender fuego, encenderse ♦ **to c. on** *(to understand)* comprender; *(to become aware)* caer en la cuenta; *(a fad)* hacerse o volverse muy popular • **to c. up** ponerse al día o al corriente **II.** s. *(act)* cogida; *(lock)* cerradura; *(in hunting)* presa; *(in fishing)* pesca; *(capture)* captura; FAM. *(hitch)* truco, trampa; *(good match)* buen partido.

catch•er (kăch′ər) s. DEP. receptor m.

catch•ing (:ĭng) adj. contagioso.

catch•word (:wûrd′) s. lema m, slogan m.

catch•y (:ē) adj. -i- *(easy to remember)* pegadizo; *(tricky)* capcioso.

cat•e•chism (kăt′ĭ-kĭz′əm) s. catecismo.

cat•e•chist (:kĭst) s. catequista mf.

cat•e•chize (:kĭz′) tr. catequizar.

cat•e•gor•ic/i•cal (kăt′ə-gôr′ĭk) adj. categórico.

cat•e•go•rize (′-gə-rīz′) tr. clasificar.

cat•e•go•ry (:gôr′ē) s. categoría.

ca•ter (kā′tər) intr. abastecer de comida o servicios ♦ **to c. to** intentar satisfacer los deseos de.

cat•er-cor•ner(ed) (kăt′ər-kôr′nər[d]) adj. & adv. (en) diagonal.

ca•ter•er (kā′tər-ər) s. encargado de banquetes.

ca•ter•ing (:ĭng) s. servicio de banquetes.

cat•er•pil•lar (kăt′ər-pĭl′ər) s. oruga.

cat•er•waul (kăt′ər-wôl′) intr. *(to meow)* maullar; *(to screech)* chillar.

cat•fish (kăt′fĭsh′) s. [pl. inv. o **es**] siluro, bagre m.

cat•gut (:gŭt′) s. cuerda de tripa.

ca•thar•sis (kə-thär′sĭs) s. [pl. **-ses**] catarsis f.

ca•the•dral (kə-thē′drəl) s. catedral f.

cath•e•ter (kăth′ĭ-tər) s. catéter m.

cath•ode (kăth′ōd′) s. cátodo ♦ **c. ray** rayo catódico.

cath•o•lic (kăth′ə-lĭk) **I.** adj. general, universal ♦ **C.** católico **II.** s. ♦ **C.** católico.

cat•kin (kăt′kĭn′) s. amento.

cat•nap (kăt′năp′) s. & intr. **-pp-** (echar una) siesta corta.

cat•nip (:nĭp′) s. nébeda.

cat-o′-nine-tails (′ə-nīn′tālz′) s. látigo de nueve colas.

cat•sup (kăt′səp, kăch′əp) var. de **ketchup**.

cat•tail (kăt′tāl′) s. anea, espadaña.

cat•tle (kăt′l) s. ganado vacuno.

cat•tle•man (:măn′) s. [pl. **-men**] ganadero.

cat•ty (kăt′ē) adj. -i- malicioso.

cat•walk (:wôk′) s. pasadizo, pasarela.

cau•cus (kô′kəs) **I.** s. [pl. **es** o **-ses**] reunión f electoral **II.** intr. celebrar reunión electoral.

caught (kôt) cf. **catch**.

cau•li•flow•er (kô′lĭ-flou′ər) s. coliflor f.

caulk (kôk) tr. calafatear.

cau•sa•tion (kô-zā′shən) s. causalidad f.

caus•a•tive (kô′zə-tĭv) adj. causativo.

cause (kôz) **I.** s. causa; *(reason)* motivo, razón f **II.** tr. causar, provocar.

cause•way (:wā′) s. carretera elevada.

caus•tic (kô′stĭk) adj. & s. cáustico.

cau•ter•ize (kô′tə-rīz′) tr. cauterizar.

cau•tion (kô′shən) **I.** s. cautela, precaución f; *(warning)* advertencia **II.** tr. advertir, amonestar.

cau•tion•ar•y (kô′shə-nĕr′ē) adj. *(preventive)* preventivo; *(exemplary)* aleccionador.

cau•tious (kô′shəs) adj. cauteloso, precavido.

cav•al•cade (kăv′əl-kād′) s. cabalgata.

cav•a•lier (kăv′ə-lîr′) **I.** s. caballero **II.** adj. arrogante.

cav•al•ry (kăv′əl-rē) s. caballería.

cav•al•ry•man (:mən) s. [pl. **-men**] soldado de caballería.

cave (kāv) **I.** s. cueva ♦ **c. dweller** o **man** cavernícola, troglodita **II.** intr. ♦ **to c. in** *(to collapse)* derrumbarse; *(to yield)* ceder.

cave-in (′ĭn′) s. hundimiento, socavón m.

cav•ern (kăv′ərn) s. caverna.

cav•ern•ous (:ər-nəs) adj. cavernoso.

cav•i•ty (kăv′ĭ-tē) s. cavidad f; ODONT. caries f.

ca•vort (kə-vôrt′) intr. cabriolar, juguetear.

caw (kô) **I.** s. graznido **II.** intr. graznar.

cay (kē, kā) s. cayo.

cay•enne pepper (kī-ĕn′) s. pimienta del ají.

cease (sēs) **I.** tr. *(to stop)* dejar de; *(to discontinue)* suspender ♦ **c. fire!** MIL. ¡alto el fuego! —intr. cesar **II.** s. cese m ♦ **without c.** incesantemente.

cease-fire (′fīr′) s. suspensión f de fuego.

cease•less (:lĭs) adj. incesante, continuo.

ce•dar (sē′dər) s. cedro.

cede (sēd) tr. ceder.

ceil•ing (sē′lĭng) s. cielo raso, techo; AER. techo; *(limit)* tope m.

cel•e•brant (sĕl′ə-brənt) s. celebrante mf.

cel•e•brate (:brāt′) tr. celebrar; *(an occasion)* festejar, conmemorar —intr. festejarse.

cel•e•brat•ed (:brā′tĭd) adj. célebre, famoso.

cel•e•bra•tion (′-′shən) s. celebración f.

ce•leb•ri•ty (sə-lĕb′rĭ-tē) s. celebridad f.

cel•er•y (sĕl′ə-rē) s. apio.

ce•les•tial (sə-lĕs′chəl) adj. *(of the sky)* celeste; *(divine)* celestial.

cel•i•ba•cy (sĕl′ə-bə-sē) s. celibato.

cel•i•bate (:bĭt) adj. & s. célibe mf.

cell (sĕl) s. *(room)* celda; BIOL., ELEC., POL. célula.

cel•lar (sĕl′ər) s. sótano; *(of wines)* bodega.

cel•lo (chĕl′ō) s. violoncelo.

cel•lo•phane (sĕl′ə-fān′) s. celofán m.

cel•lu•lar (sĕl′yə-lər) adj. celular.

cel•lu•loid (:loid′) s. celuloide m.

cel•lu•lose (:lōs′) s. celulosa.

ce•ment (sĭ-mĕnt′) **I.** s. cemento; *(glue)* pegamento ♦ **c. mixer** hormigonera **II.** tr. unir con cemento; *(to glue)* pegar; FIG. *(to strengthen)* cimentar.

cem•e•ter•y (sĕm′ĭ-tĕr′ē) s. cementerio.

cen•ser (sĕn′sər) s. incensario.

cen•sor (sĕn′sər) **I.** s. censor m **II.** tr. censurar.

cen•so•ri•ous (sĕn-sôr′ē-əs) adj. censurador.

cen•sor•ship (sĕn′sər-shĭp′) s. censura.

cen•sure (sĕn′shər) **I.** s. censura **II.** tr. censurar.

cen•sus (sĕn′səs) s. censo.

cent (sĕnt) s. centavo, céntimo.

cen•taur (sĕn′tôr′) s. centauro.

cen•ten•ni•al (sĕn-tĕn′ē-əl) adj. & s. centenario.

cen•ter (sĕn′tər) **I.** s. centro **II.** tr. centrar; *(to concentrate)* concentrar —intr. concentrarse ♦ **to c. on** centrarse en.

cen·ter·piece (:pēs′) s. centro de mesa; FIG. foco principal.
cen·ti·grade (sĕn′tĭ-grād′) adj. centígrado.
cen·ti·gram (:grăm′) s. centigramo.
cen·ti·li·ter (:lē′tər) s. centilitro.
cen·ti·me·ter (:mē′tər) s. centímetro.
cen·ti·pede (:pēd′) s. ciempiés m.
cen·tral (sĕn′trəl) adj. central.
cen·tral·ize (:trə-līz′) tr. & intr. centralizar(se).
cen·tre (sĕn′tər) G.B. var. de **center.**
cen·tric (:trĭk) adj. céntrico, central.
cen·trif·u·gal (-trĭf′yə-gəl) adj. centrífugo.
cen·tri·fuge (′trə-fyōoj′) s. centrifugadora.
cen·trip·e·tal (-trĭp′ĭ-tl) adj. centrípeto.
cen·trist (′trĭst) s. centrista mf.
cen·tu·ry (sĕn′chə-rē) s. siglo ♦ **c. plant** ma-
guey.
ce·phal·ic (sə-făl′ĭk) adj. cefálico.
ce·ram·ic (sə-răm′ĭk) s. (clay) arcilla, barro;
(porcelain) porcelana ♦ **ceramics** sg. cerámica.
ce·re·al (sîr′ē-əl) s. cereal m.
cer·e·bral (sĕr′ə-brəl, sə-rē′-) adj. cerebral.
cer·e·brum (:brəm) s. [pl. **s** o **-ra**] cerebro.
cer·e·mo·ni·al (sĕr′ə-mō′nē-əl) adj. & s. ceremonial m.
cer·e·mo·ni·ous (:əs) adj. ceremonioso.
cer·e·mo·ny (sĕr′ə-mō′nē) s. ceremonia.
cer·tain (sûr′tn) adj. (definite) cierto; (sure) seguro; (some) algunos, ciertos ♦ **for c.** por
cierto ♦ **to make c.** asegurarse.
cer·tain·ly (:lē) adv. (surely) cierto; (of course)
por supuesto; (without fail) seguro.
cer·tain·ty (:tē) s. certeza; (fact) cosa segura.
cer·ti·fi·a·ble (sûr′tə-fī′ə-bəl) adj. certificable.
cer·tif·i·cate (sər-tĭf′ĭ-kĭt) s. certificado, partida.
cer·ti·fi·ca·tion (sûr′tə-fĭ-kā′shən) s. certifica-
ción f; (document) certificado.
cer·ti·fied (′-fīd′) adj. certificado ♦ **c. public
accountant** contador público titulado.
cer·ti·fy (sûr′tə-fī′) tr. & intr. certificar.
cer·ti·tude (:tōōd′) s. certidumbre f, certeza.
cer·vix (sûr′vĭks) s. [pl. **es** o **-ces**] (neck) cerviz
f; (of the uterus) cuello del útero.
ce·si·um (sē′zē-əm) s. cesio.
ces·sa·tion (sĕ-sā′shən) s. cesación f, cese m.
ces·sion (sĕsh′ən) s. cesión f.
cess·pool (sĕs′pōōl′) s. pozo negro; FIG. cloaca, sentina.
ce·ta·ce·an (sī-tā′shən) adj. & s. cetáceo.
chafe (chāf) tr. (to rub) rozar; (to annoy) irritar; (to warm) frotar —intr. rozarse ♦ **to c.** at
enfadarse por.
chaff (chăf) I. s. AGR. ahechaduras; (trifle)
paja; (banter) chanza II. tr. zumbar, chasquear.
cha·grin (shə-grĭn′) I. s. desilusión f, desazón f
II. tr. desilusionar.
chain (chān) I. s. cadena ♦ **c. gang** cadena de
presidiarios • **c. mail** cota de mallas • **c. reaction** reacción en cadena • **c. saw** sierra de
cadena • **c. store** sucursal de una cadena de
tiendas II. tr. encadenar.
chain-smoke (:smōk′) intr. & tr. fumar un
cigarrillo tras otro.
chair (châr) I. s. silla; (chairman) presidente
m; EDUC. cátedra ♦ **c. lift** telesilla II. tr. presidir.
chair·man (′mən) s. [pl. **-men**] presidente m.
chair·man·ship (:mən-shĭp′) s. presidencia.
chair·per·son (:pûr′sən) s. presidente m, presi-
denta.

chair·wom·an (:wŏŏm′ən) s. [pl. **-women**] pre-
sidenta.
chal·ced·o·ny (kăl-sĕd′n-ē) s. calcedonia.
cha·let (shă-lā′) s. chalet m.
chal·ice (chăl′ĭs) s. cáliz m.
chalk (chôk) I. s. MIN. creta; (marker) tiza
II. tr. marcar, escribir (con tiza) ♦ **to c. up**
apuntarse (tanto, victoria).
chalk·board (′bôrd′) s. pizarrón m, pizarra.
chal·lenge (chăl′ənj) I. s. desafío, reto; MIL.
quién vive m; DER. recusación f II. tr. desafiar,
retar; (to contest) disputar; MIL. dar el quién
vive; DER. recusar.
chal·leng·er (′ən-jər) s. desafiador m, retador
m.
chal·leng·ing (:jĭng) adj. arduo, difícil.
cham·ber (chām′bər) s. cámara ♦ **c. pot** orinal
♦ pl. despacho (de un juez).
cham·ber·lain (:lən) s. chambelán m.
cham·ber·maid (:mād′) s. camarera, criada.
cha·me·leon (kə-mēl′yən) s. camaleón m.
cham·ois (shăm′ē) s.inv. gamuza.
cham·o·mile (kăm′ə-mīl′) s. manzanilla.
champ (chămp) s. FAM. campeón m.
cham·pagne (shăm-pān′) s. champaña m.
cham·pi·on (chăm′pē-ən) I. s. campeón m
II. tr. abogar por.
cham·pi·on·ship (:shĭp′) s. campeonato.
chance (chăns) I. s. casualidad f; (luck) suerte
f; (opportunity) oportunidad f <give me a c. to
go déme la oportunidad de >; (possibility)
posibilidad f; (risk) riesgo <to take a c. correr
un riesgo> ♦ **by any c.** por casualidad • **to
stand a c.** tener una posibilidad II. intr. suceder, acaecer —tr. arriesgar ♦ **to c. on** o **upon**
encontrarse con III. adj. casual, fortuito.
chan·cel (chăn′səl) s. antealtar m.
chan·cel·ler·y (:sə-lə-rē) s. cancillería.
chan·cel·lor (:lər) s. POL. canciller m; EDUC.
rector m.
chanc·y (chăn′sē) adj. **-i-** arriesgado.
chan·de·lier (shăn′də-lîr′) s. araña.
change (chānj) I. tr. & intr. cambiar (de);
(clothes, color) mudar (de); (to transform) con-
vertir(se) ♦ **to c. over** turnarse • **to c. over** cambiar II. s. (act) cambio; (substitution)
substitución f, relevo; (of clothing) muda;
(money) cambio, vuelto; (coins) suelto ♦ **a c.
for the better** un cambio beneficioso • **c. of
heart** arrepentimiento • **for a c.** para variar •
keep the c. quédese con el vuelto.
change·a·ble (chān′jə-bəl) adj. cambiable; (inconstant) variable.
change·ling (chānj′lĭng) s. niño cambiado por
otro.
change·o·ver (:ō′vər) s. cambio.
chang·er (chān′jər) s. (device) cambiador m;
FIN. cambiante mf, cambista mf.
chan·nel (chăn′əl) I. s. canal m; (riverbed)
cauce m; (groove) ranura II. tr. canalizar.
chant (chănt) I. s. canto; (psalm) cántico, sal-
modia II. tr. & intr. cantar, salmodiar.
chan·ti·cleer (chăn′tĭ-klîr′) s. gallo.
cha·os (kā′ŏs′) s. caos m.
cha·ot·ic (kā-ŏt′ĭk) adj. caótico.
chap¹ (chăp) tr. & intr. **-pp-** paspar(se).
chap² s. FAM. (fellow) tipo, muchacho.
chap·el (chăp′əl) s. capilla.
chap·er·on(e) (shăp′ə-rōn′) I. s. carabina
II. tr. hacer de carabina con.
chap·lain (chăp′lĭn) s. capellán m.
chaps (chăps, shăps) s.pl. zahones m.

chap·ter (chăp′tər) s. capítulo; *(of a club)* sección *f.*

char (chär) tr. & intr. **-rr-** *(to scorch)* chamuscar(se); *(to reduce to coal)* carbonizar(se).

char·ac·ter (kăr′ək-tər) s. carácter *m*; LIT. *(role)* personaje *m*, papel *m*; FAM. *(guy)* tipo ♦ **in c.** característico.

char·ac·ter·is·tic (′-tə-rĭs′tĭk) I. adj. característico II. s. característica.

char·ac·ter·ize (′--rīz′) tr. caracterizar.

cha·rade (shə-rād′) s. charada.

char·coal (chär′kōl′) s. carbón *m* vegetal *o* de leña; DIB. carboncillo.

chard (chärd) s. acelga.

charge (chärj) I. tr. *(to entrust)* encargar, encomendar; DER. *(to instruct)* instruir; *(to accuse)* acusar; COM. *(a price)* pedir, cobrar; *(on credit)* cargar; *(to saturate)* impregnar; MIL. *(to attack)* atacar, acometer; ELEC. cargar —intr. atacar, ir a la carga; COM. cobrar II. s. *(management)* cargo, dirección *f; (accusation)* acusación *f; (burden)* carga, peso; *(cost)* costo, precio; *(tax)* impuesto; *(attack)* carga; ARM., ELEC. carga ♦ **in c. of** encargado de ♦ **to appear on a c. of** DER. comparecer acusado de ♦ **to be in c.** ser el encargado ♦ **to bring charges against** DER. hacer acusaciones contra ♦ **to reverse the charges** TEL. llamar a cobro revertido ♦ **to take c.** asumir el mando ♦ **to take c. of** encargarse de, hacerse cargo de.

char·gé d'af·faires (shär-zhā′ də-fâr′) s. [pl. **chargés**] encargado de negocios.

charg·er (chär′jər) s. caballo de batalla.

char·i·ot (chăr′ē-ət) s. carro de batalla.

cha·ris·ma (kə-rĭz′mə) s. carisma *m.*

char·i·ta·ble (chăr′ĭ-tə-bəl) adj. caritativo.

char·i·ty (chăr′ĭ-tē) s. caridad *f*, beneficencia; *(institution)* beneficencia.

char·la·tan (shär′lə-tn) s. charlatán *m.*

charm (chärm) I. s. encanto; *(amulet)* amuleto ♦ **like a c.** como por encanto II. tr. encantar; *(to beguile)* seducir; *(to bewitch)* embrujar.

charm·er (chär′mər) s. encantador *m.*

charm·ing (:mĭng) adj. encantador.

chart (chärt) I. s. MARÍT. carta de navegación II. tr. trazar.

char·ter (chär′tər) I. s. POL. carta; *(of organization)* estatutos; *(lease)* fletamento ♦ **c. flight** vuelo fletado • **c. member** socio fundador II. tr. establecer los estatutos de; *(to rent)* fletar.

char·ter·house (:hous′) s. cartuja.

char·wom·an (chär′wŏom′ən) s. [pl. **-women**] G.B. criada, empleada de limpieza.

char·y (châr′ē) adj. **-i-** parco.

chase¹ (chās) I. tr. perseguir *(after* a) ♦ **to c. away** *o* **off** ahuyentar • **to c. out** echar fuera —intr. ir corriendo II. s. persecución *f* ♦ **the c.** *(sport)* la cacería; *(quarry)* caza, presa.

chase² I. s. *(groove)* ranura, estría II. tr. acanalar.

chasm (kăz′əm) s. abismo.

chas·sis (chăs′ē, chās′ē) s.inv. chasis *m.*

chaste (chāst) adj. casto.

chas·ten (chā′sən) tr. castigar, disciplinar.

chas·tise (chăs-tīz′) tr. castigar.

chas·ti·ty (chăs′tĭ-tē) s. castidad *f.*

chat (chăt) I. intr. **-tt-** charlar, platicar II. s. charla, plática.

chat·tel (chăt′l) s. bien *m* mueble.

chat·ter (chăt′ər) I. intr. parlotear, chacharear; *(teeth)* castañetear II. s. parloteo, cháchara.

chat·ter·box (:bŏks′) s. parlanchín *m.*

chat·ty (chăt′ē) adj. **-i-** parlanchín.

chauf·feur (shō′fər, shō-fûr′) I. s. chofer *o* chófer *m* II. tr. conducir.

chau·vin·ist (shō′və-nĭst) s. chauvinista *mf.*

chau·vin·is·tic (′-nĭs′tĭk) adj. chauvinista.

cheap (chēp) I. adj. barato; *(inferior)* de mala calidad; *(tawdry)* charro; *(stingy)* tacaño ♦ **dirt c.** baratísimo • **to feel c.** sentirse rebajado II. adv. barato.

cheap·en (chē′pən) tr. & intr. rebajar(se), degradar(se).

cheap·ly (chēp′lē) adv. barato, a bajo precio ♦ **c. made** de baja calidad.

cheap·ness (:nĭs) s. bajo precio; *(quality)* mala calidad; *(stinginess)* tacañería.

cheap·skate (:skāt′) s. JER. tacaño.

cheat (chēt) I. tr. *(to swindle)* defraudar, estafar; *(to deceive)* engañar —intr. hacer trampa; *(on exam)* copiar II. s. *(swindler)* tramposo; *(trick)* trampa; *(swindle)* estafa.

cheat·er (chē′tər) s. tramposo.

cheat·ing (:tĭng) I. adj. tramposo, fraudulento II. s. trampa.

check (chĕk) I. s. *(halt)* parada, detención *f; (restraint)* freno, impedimento; *(verification)* comprobación *f*, chequeo; *(mark)* marca, señal *f; (ticket)* talón *m; (bill)* cuenta (de restaurante); *(bank draft)* cheque *m; (pattern)* cuadros; *(square)* cuadro; *(in chess)* jaque *m* ♦ **c. list** lista de control • **to keep** *o* **to hold in c.** tener a raya, tener controlado II. interj. ¡jaque! III. tr. *(to halt)* detener; *(to restrain)* refrenar, contener; *(an emotion)* reprimir; *(to test)* examinar, controlar; *(to verify)* verificar; *(hat, coat)* depositar; *(luggage)* facturar; *(in chess)* dar jaque a ♦ **c. it out!** JER. ¡mire esto! • **to c. against** chequear, cotejar • **to c. off** marcar (uno por uno), chequear • **to c. out** FAM. comprobar • **to c. up on** comprobar, verificar • **to c. with** consultar con —intr. *(to halt)* detenerse; *(to agree)* concordar (listas, cifras) ♦ **to c. in (to)** registrarse (en un hotel) • **to c. out (of)** pagar la cuenta y marcharse (de un hotel).

check·book (′bŏok′) s. chequera, talonario.

check·er (:ər) s. *(examiner)* verificador *m; (cashier)* cajero; *(in the game)* pieza del juego de damas ♦ pl. damas.

check·er·board (:bŏrd′) s. tablero de damas.

check·ered (chĕk′ərd) adj. *(design)* cuadriculado, a cuadros; FIG. *(uneven)* con altibajos.

check·mate (:māt′) I. tr. dar jaque y mate II. s. jaque y mate *m.*

check·out (:out′) s. *(exit)* salida (de hotel, supermercado); *(inspection)* inspección *f.*

check·point (:point′) s. lugar *m* de inspección.

check·room (:rŏom′) s. guardarropa *m; (for luggage)* consigna.

check·up (:ŭp′) s. chequeo, reconocimiento médico general.

cheek (chēk) s. mejilla; *(impudence)* descaro ♦ **c. by jowl** codo con codo.

cheek·bone (′bōn′) s. pómulo.

cheek·y (chē′kē) adj. **-i-** descarado, caradura.

cheep (chēp) I. s. piada II. tr. & intr. piar.

cheer (chîr) I. tr. *(to gladden)* animar, alegrar; *(to encourage)* alentar; *(to shout)* vitorear, ovacionar ♦ **to c. on** animar, alentar • **to c. up** alegrar, animar —intr. aplaudir ♦ **c. up!** ¡ánimo! • **to c. up** alegrarse II. s. alegría, ánimo; *(shout)* viva, hurra ♦ pl. **c.!** ¡salud!

cheer·ful (′fəl) adj. alegre.

cheer·i·ly (:ə-lē) adv. alegremente.
cheer·lead·er (:lē'dər) s. persona que dirige los vivas en una encuesta deportiva.
cheer·less (:lĭs) adj. triste.
cheer·y (:ē) adj. -i- alegre.
cheese (chēz) s. queso.
cheese·cake ('kāk') s. quesadilla.
cheese·cloth (:klôth') s. estopilla.
chees·y (chē'zē) adj. -i- caseoso; *(cheap)* vulgar, de pacotilla.
chef (shĕf) s. cocinero, jefe *m* de cocina.
chem·i·cal (kĕm'ĭ-kəl) I. adj. químico II. s. sustancia química.
che·mise (shə-mēz') s. camisa (de mujer).
chem·ist (kĕm'ĭst) s. químico; G.B. *(pharmacist)* farmacéutico.
chem·is·try (kĕm'ĭ-strē) s. química.
che·mo·ther·a·py (kē'mō-thĕr'ə-pē) s. quimioterapia.
cheque (chĕk) s. G.B. cheque *m*.
cher·ish (chĕr'ĭsh) tr. *(to hold dear)* querer, estimar; *(thoughts, ideas)* abrigar.
cher·ry (chĕr'ē) I. s. cereza ♦ **c. tree** cerezo II. adj. de color rojo cereza.
cher·ub (chĕr'əb) s. [pl. -im] querubín *m*.
che·ru·bic (chə-rō̄'bĭk) adj. querúbico.
chess (chĕs) s. ajedrez *m* ♦ **c. player** ajedrecista.
chess·board ('bôrd') s. tablero de ajedrez.
chess·man (:măn') s. [pl. -men] trebejo.
chest (chĕst) s. pecho; *(box)* cofre *m*, arca *m*; *(dresser)* cómoda.
chest·nut (chĕs'nət) I. s. *(nut)* castaña; *(horse)* zaino; *(joke)* chiste gastado ♦ **c. tree** castaño II. adj. castaño, marrón.
chew (chō̄) I. tr. & intr. masticar, mascar ♦ **to c. out** regañar, reprender ♦ **to c. over** rumiar, meditar ♦ **to c. the fat** charlar, parlotear II. s. mascada (esp. de tabaco).
chew·ing ('ĭng) s. masticación *f* ♦ **c. gum** chicle, goma de mascar.
chew·y (ē) adj. -i- *(meat)* fibroso, duro; *(sweets)* que se pega a los dientes.
chic (shēk) s. & adj. chic *m*.
chi·ca·ner·y (shĭ-kā'nə-rē) s. trapacería.
chick (chĭk) s. polluelo; JER. *(girl)* chavala.
chick·en (chĭk'ən) I. s. gallina, pollo ♦ **c. pox** varicela II. adj. FAM. miedoso, cobarde III. intr. ♦ **to c. out** acobardarse.
chick·en-heart·ed (:här'tĭd) adj. cobarde.
chick·pea (chĭk'pē') s. garbanzo.
chic·o·ry (chĭk'ə-rē) s. achicoria.
chide (chīd) tr. -d *o* chid regañar, reprender.
chief (chēf) I. s. jefe *m* ♦ **c. executive** primer mandatario ♦ **c. justice** presidente del tribunal ♦ **c. of staff** jefe del estado mayor II. adj. principal.
chief·ly ('lē) adv. principalmente.
chief·tain (:tən) s. cacique *m*, caudillo.
chif·fon (shĭ-fŏn') s. chifón *m*, gasa.
chig·ger (chĭg'ər) s. pique *m*, nigua.
child (chīld) s. [pl. -ren] niño; *(offspring)* hijo; FIG. *(product)* fruto, producto ♦ **c.'s play** juego de niños ♦ **with c.** embarazada.
child·bear·ing ('bâr'ĭng) s. maternidad *f*.
child·birth (:bûrth') s. parto, alumbramiento.
child·hood (:hŏŏd') s. niñez *f*, infancia.
child·ish (chīl'dĭsh) adj. infantil, pueril.
child·less (chīld'lĭs) adj. sin hijos.
child·like (:līk') adj. infantil.
chil·dren (chĭl'drən) cf. **child**.
chil·i (chĭl'ē) s. chile *m*, ají *m*.

chill (chĭl) I. s. *(coolness)* frío; *(shiver)* escalofrío; *(damper)* enfriamiento ♦ **to catch a c.** resfriarse ♦ **to take the c. off** calentar II. adj. frío III. tr. *(to cool)* enfriar; *(food)* refrigerar.
chill·er ('ər) s. historia escalofriante.
chill·ing (:ĭng) adj. *(cold)* frío; *(frightening)* escalofriante; *(discouraging)* frío.
chill·y (:ē) adj. -i- frío.
chime (chīm) I. s. carillón *m*; *(sound)* repique *m* ♦ pl. carillón II. intr. repicar, sonar ♦ **to c. in** intervenir (en una conversación) —tr. dar (la hora).
chi·me·ra (kĭ-mîr'ə) s. quimera.
chim·ney (chĭm'nē) s. chimenea; *(of a lamp)* tubo de vidrio ♦ **c. sweep** deshollinador.
chim·ney·piece (:pēs') s. repisa de una chimenea.
chimp (chĭmp) s. FAM. chimpancé *m*.
chim·pan·zee (chĭm'păn-zē') s. chimpancé *m*.
chin (chĭn) I. s. barbilla, mentón *m* ♦ **c. up!** ¡ánimo! ♦ **to keep one's c. up** no desanimarse II. tr. -nn- ♦ **to c. oneself** hacer flexiones en la barra tocándola con la barbilla.
chi·na (chī'nə) s. china, porcelana; *(crockery)* loza.
chink[1] (chĭngk) s. *(crack)* grieta, rajadura.
chink[2] I. s. *(metallic sound)* tintín *m* II. tr. & intr. tintinear.
chintz (chĭnts) s. zaraza.
chintz·y (chĭnt'sē) adj. -i- FAM. de oropel.
chip (chĭp) I. s. pedacito, trozo; *(splinter)* astilla; *(of stone)* lasca; *(in china)* desportilladura; *(in gambling)* ficha; ELECTRÓN. placa ♦ **a c. off the old block** de tal palo, tal astilla ♦ **in the chips** JER. forrado de dinero ♦ **the chips are down** JER. la suerte está echada ♦ **to have a c. on one's shoulder** estar resentido ♦ pl. patatas fritas II. tr. -pp- *(to splinter)* hacer astillas; *(to chop)* picar; *(to chisel)* cincelar ♦ **to c. off** desportillar —intr. *(china)* desportillarse; *(wood)* astillarse ♦ **to c. in** contribuir.
chip·munk (chĭp'mŭngk') s. ardilla listada.
chip·per (chĭp'ər) adj. FAM. animado, jovial.
chi·ro·prac·tor (kī'rə-prăk'tər) s. quiropráctico.
chirp (chûrp) I. s. *(bird)* gorjeo; *(cricket)* chirrido II. intr. *(bird)* gorjear; *(cricket)* chirriar.
chis·el (chĭz'əl) I. s. cincel *m* II. tr. cincelar; FAM. *(to cheat)* estafar.
chis·el·er (:ə-lər) s. cincelador *m*; FAM. *(swindler)* estafador *m*.
chit (chĭt) s. vale *m*, cuenta.
chit-chat (chĭt'chăt') s. charla, cháchara.
chiv·al·rous (shĭv'əl-rəs) adj. caballeresco.
chiv·al·ry (:rē) s. caballerosidad *f*.
chive (chīv) s. cebollino.
chlo·ride (klôr'īd') s. cloruro.
chlo·ri·nate (:ə-nāt') tr. tratar con cloro.
chlo·rine (klôr'ēn') s. cloro.
chlo·ro·form (:ə-fôrm') I. s. cloroformo II. tr. cloroformizar.
chlo·ro·phyl(l) (:fĭl') s. clorofila.
chock (chŏk) s. calza, cuña II. tr. calzar.
chock-full (fŏŏl') adj. repleto, colmado.
choc·o·late (chŏk'lĭt) adj. & s. (de) chocolate *m*.
choice (chois) I. s. elección *f*, selección *f*; *(option)* opción *f*; *(assortment)* surtido; *(alternative)* alternativa ♦ **by c.** por gusto ♦ **to have no c.** no tener alternativa ♦ **to make a c.** escoger, elegir II. adj. escogido, superior.
choir (kwīr) s. coro.

choir·boy ('boi') s. niño de coro.
choke (chōk) **I.** tr. *(to strangle)* estrangular, ahogar; *(to suffocate)* sofocar; *(food)* atragantar; *(to clog)* atorar, atascar; AUTO. estrangular ♦ **to c. back** contener, ahogar • **to c. down** tragar con asco • **to c. off** cortar *o* terminar abruptamente • **to c. up** obstruir, atascar —intr. sofocarse, ahogarse; *(on food)* atragantarse; *(to clog)* atorarse ♦ **to c. up** FAM. emocionarse **II.** s. sofocación *f*, ahogo; AUTO. estrangulador *m*.
chok·er (chō'kər) s. gargantilla.
chol·er (kŏl'ər) s. ira, cólera.
chol·er·a (kŏl'ər-ə) s. MED. cólera *m*.
chol·er·ic (kŏl'ə-rĭk) adj. colérico.
cho·les·ter·ol (kə-lĕs'tə-rôl') s. colesterol *m*.
chomp (chŏmp) tr. & intr. ronzar.
choose (chōz) tr. **chose, chosen** elegir, escoger; *(to prefer)* preferir —intr. ♦ **to do as one chooses** hacer lo que quiere.
choos·ing (chō'zĭng) s. elección *f*, selección *f*.
choos·y (:zē) adj. **-i-** FAM. quisquilloso.
chop (chŏp) **I.** tr. **-pp-** cortar; *(to mince)* picar ♦ **to c. down** talar • **to c. up** cortar en trozos **II.** s. corte *m*, tajo; CUL. chuleta.
chop·per (:ər) s. FAM. helicóptero ♦ pl. JER. dientes (postizos).
chop·ping block (:ĭng) s. tajo.
chop·py (:ē) adj. **-i-** picado, agitado.
chops (chŏps) s.pl. quijada ♦ **to lick one's c.** relamerse.
chop·sticks (chŏp'stĭks') s.pl. palillos chinos.
cho·ral (kôr'əl) adj. & s. coral *f*.
chord (kôrd) s. MÚS. acorde *m*; GEOM. cuerda *f*.
chore (chôr) s. quehacer *m*, faena.
cho·re·o·graph (kôr'ē-ə-grăf') tr. hacer la coreografía de.
cho·re·og·ra·pher ('-ŏg'rə-fər) s. coreógrafo.
cho·re·og·ra·phy (:fē) s. coreografía.
cho·ris·ter (kôr'ĭ-stər) s. corista *mf*.
chor·tle (chôr'tl) **I.** intr. reír entre dientes **II.** s. risa ahogada.
cho·rus (kôr'əs) s. [pl. **es**] coro; *(refrain)* estribillo ♦ **c. girl** corista • **in c.** al unísono.
chose (chōz) cf. **choose.**
cho·sen (chō'zən) **I.** cf. **choose II.** adj. & s. elegido, escogido.
chow (chou) **I.** s. FAM. comida **II.** intr. ♦ **to c. down** comer.
chow·der (chou'dər) s. sopa de pescado.
chris·ten (krĭs'ən) tr. bautizar.
Chris·ten·dom (:dəm) s. cristiandad *f*.
chris·ten·ing (:ĭng) s. bautismo, bautizo.
Chris·tian (krĭs'chən) adj. & s. cristiano ♦ **C. name** nombre de pila.
Chris·ti·an·i·ty (chē-ăn'ĭ-tē) s. cristianismo; *(Christendom)* cristiandad *f*.
Chris·tian·ize ('chə-nīz') tr. cristianizar.
Christ·mas (krĭs'məs) s. Navidad *f*.
chro·mat·ic (krō-măt'ĭk) adj. cromático.
chrome (krōm) s. cromo.
chro·mi·um (krō'mē-əm) s. cromo.
chro·mo·some (krō'mə-sōm') s. cromosoma *m*.
chron·ic (krŏn'ĭk) adj. crónico.
chron·i·cle (krŏn'ĭ-kəl) **I.** s. crónica **II.** tr. hacer la crónica de.
chron·o·log·i·c/i·cal (krŏn'ə-lŏj'ĭk) adj. cronológico.
chro·nol·o·gy (krə-nŏl'ə-jē) s. cronología.
chro·nom·e·ter (krə-nŏm'ĭ-tər) s. cronómetro.
chrys·a·lis (krĭs'ə-lĭs) s. crisálida.

chry·san·the·mum (krĭ-săn'thə-məm) s. crisantemo.
chub·by (chŭb'ē) adj. **-i-** rechoncho.
chuck[1] (chŭk) **I.** tr. *(to pat)* hacer la mamola ♦ **to c. out** tirar, botar **II.** s. *(pat)* mamola; MEC. mandril *m*.
chuck[2] s. CUL. paletilla.
chuck·hole (chŭk'hōl') s. FAM. bache *m*.
chuck·le (chŭk'əl) **I.** intr. reírse entre dientes **II.** s. risita, risa ahogada.
chug (chŭg) **I.** s. traqueteo **II.** intr. **-gg-** traquetear.
chum (chŭm) s. compañero, compinche *m*.
chum·my (:ē) adj. **-i-** amistoso.
chunk (chŭngk) s. pedazo, trozo; *(amount)* cantidad *f* grande.
chunk·y (chŭng'kē) adj. **-i-** corto y grueso; *(in chunks)* en pedazos.
church (chûrch) s. iglesia.
church·go·er (:gō'ər) s. devoto (que va a misa regularmente).
church·man (:mən) s. [pl. **-men**] clérigo.
church·yard (:yärd') s. camposanto.
churl (chûrl) s. patán *m*.
churl·ish (chûr'lĭsh) adj. maleducado.
churn (chûrn) **I.** s. mantequera **II.** tr. CUL. hacer (mantequilla); *(to shake)* agitar, revolver ♦ **to c. out** producir en profusión —intr. agitarse, revolverse.
chute (shōōt) s. *(ramp)* rampa, tobogán *m*; *(conduit)* conducto; PARA.caídas *m*.
ci·ca·da (sĭ-kā'də) s. [pl. **s** *o* **-ae**] cigarra.
ci·der (sī'dər) s. sidra.
ci·gar (sĭ-gär') s. cigarro, puro.
cig·a·ret(te) (sĭg'ə-rĕt') s. cigarrillo.
cil·i·um (sĭl'ē-əm) s. [pl. **-ia**] cilio.
cinch (sĭnch) **I.** s. EQUIT. cincha; FAM. *(snap)* cosa fácil **II.** tr. EQUIT. cinchar; FAM. *(to make certain)* asegurar.
cin·der (sĭn'dər) s. carbonilla ♦ pl. cenizas.
cin·e·ma (sĭn'ə-mə) s. cine *m*.
cin·e·mat·ic ('-măt'ĭk) adj. fílmico.
cin·e·ma·tog·ra·phy (:mə-tŏg'rə-fē) s. cinematografía.
cin·na·mon (sĭn'ə-mən) s. canela.
ci·pher (sī'fər) **I.** s. *(code)* cifra; *(zero)* cero **II.** intr. hacer un cálculo —tr. cifrar.
cir·cle (sûr'kəl) **I.** s. círculo; *(orbit)* órbita; *(turn)* vuelta ♦ **to come full c.** volver al punto de partida • **to go around in circles** estar en un círculo vicioso **II.** tr. *(to enclose)* cercar, rodear; *(to draw)* hacer un círculo alrededor de; *(to revolve around)* girar alrededor de —intr. dar vueltas.
cir·cuit (sûr'kĭt) **I.** s. circuito ♦ **c. breaker** cortacircuitos • **c. court** tribunal de distrito **II.** intr. & tr. dar la vuelta (a).
cir·cu·i·tous (sər-kyōō'ĭ-təs) adj. indirecto.
cir·cuit·ry (sûr'kĭ-trē) s. sistema *m* de circuitos.
cir·cu·lar (sûr'kyə-lər) adj. & s. circular *f*.
cir·cu·late (:lāt') tr. & intr. circular.
cir·cu·lat·ing (:lā'tĭng) adj. circulante.
cir·cu·la·tion ('-'shən) s. circulación *f*.
cir·cum·cise (sûr'kəm-sīz') tr. circuncidar.
cir·cum·cised (:sīzd') adj. circunciso.
cir·cum·fer·ence (sər-kŭm'fər-əns) s. circunferencia.
cir·cum·flex (sûr'kəm-flĕks') s. acento circunflejo.
cir·cum·lo·cu·tion (sûr'kəm-lō-kyōō'shən) s. circunlocución *f*, circunloquio.
cir·cum·nav·i·gate (:năv'ĭ-gāt') tr. circunnave-

gar.

cir·cum·scribe ('-skrīb') tr. circunscribir.

cir·cum·spect (:spĕkt') adj. circunspecto.

cir·cum·stance (sûr'kəm-stăns') s. circunstancia; *(ceremony)* ceremonia ◆ pl. situación, posición • **under no c.** de ninguna manera.

cir·cum·stan·tial (' -stăn'shəl) adj. circunstancial ◆ **c. evidence** pruebas indirectas.

cir·cum·vent (:vĕnt') tr. evitar.

cir·cus (sûr'kəs) s. circo.

cir·rho·sis (sĭ-rō'sĭs) s. cirrosis *f.*

cir·rus (sĭr'əs) s. [pl. **-ri**] cirro.

cis·tern (sĭs'tərn) s. cisterna, aljibe *m.*

cit·a·del (sĭt'ə-dəl) s. ciudadela.

ci·ta·tion (sī-tā'shən) s. *(quote)* cita; DER. citación *f.*; MIL. mención *f.*

cite (sīt) tr. *(to quote)* citar; DER. citar; MIL. mencionar.

cit·i·fied (sĭt'ĭ-fīd') adj. urbanizado.

cit·i·zen (sĭt'ĭ-zən) s. ciudadano.

cit·i·zen·ry (:rē) s. ciudadanos.

cit·i·zen·ship (:shĭp') s. ciudadanía.

cit·ric (sĭt'rĭk) adj. cítrico.

cit·ron (:rən) s. cidra.

cit·rus (:rəs) adj. cítrico ◆ **c. fruits** agrios.

cit·y (sĭt'ē) s. ciudad *f* ◆ **c. hall** ayuntamiento.

civ·et (sĭv'ĭt) s. civeta.

civ·ic (sĭv'ĭk) adj. cívico ◆ **civics** s.sg. estudio del gobierno civil.

civ·il (sĭv'əl) adj. civil ◆ **c. liberty** libertad ciudadana • **c. servant** empleado público • **c. service** administración pública.

ci·vil·ian (sĭ-vĭl'yən) adj. & s. civil *m,* (de) paisano.

ci·vil·i·ty (:ĭ-tē) s. urbanidad *f,* civilidad *f.*

civ·i·li·za·tion (sĭv'ə-lĭ-zā'shən) s. civilización *f.*

civ·i·lize (sĭv'ə-līz') tr. civilizar.

clack (klăk) I. intr. castañetear II. s. castañeteo.

clad (klăd) cf. **clothe.**

claim (klām) I. tr. *(to demand)* reclamar; *(to state)* afirmar; *(to deserve)* merecer II. s. *(demand)* reclamación *f; (assertion)* afirmación *f; (right)* derecho, título; MIN. concesión *f;* DER. demanda.

claim·ant (klā'mənt) s. DER. demandante *mf; (to a position)* pretendiente *mf.*

clair·voy·ance (klâr-voi'əns) s. clarividencia.

clair·voy·ant (:ənt) adj. & s. clarividente *mf.*

clam (klăm) I. s. almeja II. intr. **-mm-** pescar almejas ◆ **c. up** callarse como un muerto.

clam·ber (klăm'bər) intr. subir gateando.

clam·my (klăm'ē) adj. **-i-** frío y húmedo.

clam·or (klăm'ər) I. s. clamor *m* II. tr. & intr. clamar.

clam·or·ous (:əs) adj. clamoroso.

clamp (klămp) I. s. TEC. grapa, abrazadera; CARP. cárcel *f* II. tr. sujetar con abrazadera; FIG. agarrar firmemente ◆ **to c. down on** FAM. *(person)* apretar las clavijas a; *(expression)* reprimir.

clan (klăn) s. clan *m.*

clan·des·tine (klăn-dĕs'tĭn) adj. clandestino.

clang (klăng) intr. & s. (sonar con) sonido metálico.

clan·gor (:ər) s. estruendo.

clank (klăngk) I. s. ruido metálico II. intr. hacer un ruido metálico.

clan·nish (klăn'ĭsh) adj. exclusivo.

clans·man (klănz'mən) s. [pl. **-men**] miembro de un clan.

clap (klăp) I. intr. **-pp-** dar palmadas; *(objects)*

golpearse ◆ **to c. shut** cerrarse de golpe —tr. aplaudir; *(to tap)* dar una palmada a ◆ **to c. together** FAM. improvisar II. s. aplauso; *(tap)* palmada; *(bang)* estampido.

clap·per (:ər) s. badajo.

clap·ping ('ĭng) s. aplausos; *(in time)* palmadas.

clap·trap (:trăp') s. charlatanería, palabrería.

claque (klăk) s. claque *f.*

clar·et (klăr'ĭt) s. clarete *m.*

clar·i·fi·ca·tion (klăr'ə-fĭ-kā'shən) s. aclaración *f.*

clar·i·fy (klăr'ə-fī') tr. & intr. aclarar(se).

clar·i·net (klăr'ə-nĕt') s. clarinete *m.*

clar·i·on (klăr'ē-ən) adj. estentóreo, sonoro.

clar·i·ty (klăr'ĭ-tē) s. claridad *f.*

clash (klăsh) I. intr. *(to collide)* chocar, entrechocarse; *(to conflict)* chocar, estar en conflicto II. s. *(noise)* estruendo; *(collision)* choque *m; (conflict)* desacuerdo.

clasp (klăsp) I. s. *(device)* cierre *m,* broche *m; (hug)* abrazo; *(of the hands)* apretón *m* ◆ **c. knife** navaja de muelle II. tr. *(to hook)* abrochar, enganchar; *(to hug)* abrazar; *(to clutch)* agarrar; *(the hand)* apretar.

class (klăs) I. s. clase *f* ◆ **c. of 1988** promoción de 1988 II. tr. clasificar.

class-con·scious ('kŏn'shəs) adj. con conciencia de clase social.

clas·sic (klăs'ĭk) adj. & s. clásico.

clas·si·cal (:ĭ-kəl) adj. clásico.

clas·si·cism (:sĭz'əm) s. clasicismo.

clas·si·cist (:sĭst) s. clasicista *mf.*

clas·si·fi·ca·tion ('-fĭ-kā'shən) s. clasificación *f.*

clas·si·fied (klăs'ə-fīd') adj. clasificado; *(secret)* secreto.

clas·si·fy (klăs'ə-fī') tr. clasificar; *(to restrict)* restringir.

class·mate (klăs'māt') s. compañero de clase.

class·room (:rōōm') s. aula, sala de clase.

class·y (klăs'ē) adj. **-i-** JER. elegante.

clat·ter (klăt'ər) I. intr. traquetear II. s. traqueteo; *(din)* estruendo.

clause (klôz) s. cláusula *f;* GRAM. oración *f.*

claus·tro·pho·bi·a (klô'strə-fō'bē-ə) s. claustrofobia.

clav·i·chord (klăv'ĭ-kôrd') s. clavicordio.

clav·i·cle (klăv'ĭ-kəl) s. clavícula.

claw (klô) I. s. garra; *(of cat)* uña; *(of crab)* tenaza, pinza ◆ **c. hammer** martillo sacaclavos II. tr. & intr. arañar.

clay (klā) s. arcilla.

clean (klēn) I. adj. limpio; *(pure)* puro; *(total)* completo, radical; JER. *(innocent)* inocente (de sospechas) ◆ **c. as a whistle** limpio como una patena ◆ **to make a c. breast of it** confesar de plano II. adv. limpiamente; FAM. *(entirely)* completamente ◆ **to come c.** confesarlo todo III. tr. limpiar; CUL. *(meat)* quitar la grasa a; *(vegetables)* pelar; *(fish)* escamar y abrir ◆ **to c. out** *(to empty out)* vaciar; *(to use up)* agotar; FAM. *(to leave penniless)* sacarle hasta el último centavo a ◆ **to c. up** acabar con (un asunto) —intr. limpiar(se) ◆ **to c. house** FIG. poner las cosas en orden • **to c. up** FAM. ganarse una fortuna.

clean-cut ('kŭt') adj. *(sharp)* nítido, definido; *(wholesome)* sano.

clean·er (klē'nər) s. limpiador *m,* quitamanchas *m* ◆ **c.'s** tintorería.

clean·ing (:nĭng) s. limpieza.

clean·li·ness (klĕn′lē-nĭs) s. limpieza, aseo.
cleanse (klĕnz) tr. limpiar, purificar.
cleans·er (klĕn′zər) s. limpiador *m.*
clean-shav·en (klĕn′shā′vən) adj. bien afeitado.
clean-up (:ŭp′) s. limpieza general *o* a fondo.
clear (klîr) I. adj. claro; *(sky, view)* despejado; *(air, water)* transparente; *(evident)* evidente; *(conscience)* limpio, tranquilo; *(net)* neto, en limpio ♦ **as c. as day** más claro que el agua ♦ **as c. as mud** nada claro • **c. of** libre de • **c. profit** beneficio neto ♦ **to make oneself c.** explicar claramente II. adv. claro, con claridad ♦ **to stand c.** mantenerse aparte III. tr. *(to make clear)* aclarar; *(to unobstruct)* despejar; *(a path, way)* abrir; *(the table)* levantar; *(to remove)* quitar; *(to pass over)* salvar; *(to pass by)* pasar sin rozar; *(the throat)* aclararse; *(conscience)* descargar, aliviar; *(to exonerate)* limpiar; *(to acquit)* absolver; *(to approve)* aprobar; *(a profit)* ganar; *(a check)* compensar; *(debt)* liquidar; *(customs)* sacar de la aduana ♦ **to c. away** quitar • **to c. off** despejar • **to c. out** *(to empty)* vaciar; *(to clean)* limpiar • **to c. up** *(doubt)* disipar; *(mystery)* aclarar —intr. *(to become clear)* aclararse; *(sky)* despejarse; *(crowd)* dispersarse; *(impurities)* limpiarse ♦ **to c. out** irse, largarse • **to c. through** pasar por, ser aprobado por • **to c. up** despejarse IV. s. ♦ **in the c.** fuera de sospecha.
clear·ance (′əns) s. *(removal)* despejo; *(sale)* liquidación *f,* saldo; *(leeway)* espacio, margen *m; (permission)* permiso; *(by customs)* despacho; *(of a check)* compensación *f.*
clear-cut (:kŭt′) adj. claro.
clear·ing (:ĭng) s. claro.
clear·ing-house (:hous′) s. oficina de compensación.
clear·ly (klîr′lē) adv. claramente; *(evidently)* evidentemente; *(of course)* por supuesto.
clear-sight·ed (:sī′tĭd) adj. perspicaz.
cleat (klēt) s. MARÍT. cornamusa; *(on shoes)* clavo, tapón *m.*
cleav·age (klē′vĭj) s. hendidura, división *f.*
cleave (klēv) tr. & intr. **-d** *o* **cleft** partir(se), hender(se).
cleav·er (klē′vər) s. cuchillo (de carnicero).
clef (klĕf) s. clave *f.*
cleft (klĕft) I. cf. **cleave** II. adj. hendido, partido ♦ **c. palate** fisura palatina III. s. fisura.
clem·en·cy (klĕm′ən-sē) s. clemencia.
clench (klĕnch) I. tr. apretar II. s. apretón *m.*
cler·gy (klûr′jē) s. clero.
cler·gy·man (:mən) s. [pl. **-men**] clérigo.
cler·ic (klĕr′ĭk) s. clérigo.
cler·i·cal (′ĭ-kəl) adj. de oficina; RELIG. clerical.
clerk (klûrk) s. *(in office)* oficinista *mf; (in store)* dependiente *mf;* DER. escribano, amanuense *mf.*
clev·er (klĕv′ər) adj. **-er, -est** *(bright)* listo, inteligente; *(witty)* ingenioso; *(skillful)* hábil.
clev·er·ness (:nĭs) s. *(skill)* habilidad *f; (intelligence)* inteligencia.
cli·ché (klē-shā′) s. cliché *m,* clisé *m.*
click (klĭk) I. s. chasquido, ruido seco II. intr. chasquear; JER. *(to succeed)* salir bien —tr. *(tongue)* chasquear; *(heels)* taconear.
cli·ent (klī′ənt) s. cliente *mf.*
cli·en·tele (klī′ən-tĕl′) s. clientela.
cliff (klĭf) s. acantilado, precipicio.
cli·mac·tic (klī-măk′tĭk) adj. culminante.
cli·mate (klī′mĭt) s. clima *m.*

cli·mat·ic (-măt′ĭk) s. climático.
cli·max (klī′măks′) I. s. culminación *f;* LIT., RET. clímax *m* II. intr. culminar.
climb (klīm) I. tr. & intr. subir; *(to scale)* escalar, trepar ♦ **to c. down** descender, bajar II. s. subida, ascenso.
climb·er (klī′mər) s. alpinista *mf.*
climb·ing (:mĭng) I. adj. trepador II. s. alpinismo.
clinch (klĭnch) I. tr. *(a nail)* remachar; *(to secure)* afianzar; *(a deal)* decidir, concluir; *(a title)* ganar —intr. luchar cuerpo a cuerpo (en boxeo) II. s. lucha cuerpo a cuerpo (en boxeo).
cling (klĭng) intr. **clung** *(to hold fast)* asirse, agarrarse; *(to stick)* pegarse; *(to persist in)* aferrarse.
clin·ic (klĭn′ĭk) s. clínica.
clin·i·cal (:ĭ-kəl) adj. clínico.
cli·ni·cian (klĭ-nĭsh′ən) s. clínico.
clink (klĭngk) I. tr. & intr. tintinear II. s. tintín *m,* tintineo.
clink·er (klĭng′kər) s. *(residue)* escoria; *(mistake)* error *m.*
clip¹ (klĭp) I. tr. **-pp-** cortar, recortar; *(to trim)* podar; *(to shear)* esquilar (ovejas); FAM. *(to hit)* pegar; *(to overcharge)* estafar ♦ **c. along** ir a buen paso II. s. FAM. *(blow)* golpe *m; (pace)* paso rápido.
clip² I. s. *(fastener)* sujetador *m; (for paper)* sujetapapeles *m; (for hair)* horquilla; *(of rifle)* cargador *m* II. tr. **-pp-** sujetar.
clip·board (′bôrd′) s. tablilla con sujetapapeles.
clip·per (:ər) s. *(shears)* tijeras; *(for sheep)* esquiladora; MARÍT. clíper *m* ♦ pl. tijeras • **nail c.** cortaúñas.
clip·ping (:ĭng) s. recorte *m.*
clique (klĕk, klĭk) s. pandilla, camarilla.
cloak (klōk) I. s. capa, manto II. tr. encubrir.
cloak-and-dag·ger (′ən-dăg′ər) adj. de capa y espada.
cloak·room (′rōōm′) s. guardarropa *m.*
clob·ber (klŏb′ər) tr. JER. *(to hit)* golpear; *(to defeat)* dar una paliza.
clock (klŏk) I. s. reloj *m* (de pie, de mesa); *(chronometer)* cronómetro III. tr. cronometrar.
clock·wise (′wīz′) adv. & adj. en el sentido de las agujas del reloj.
clock·work (:wûrk′) s. mecanismo de relojería ♦ **like c.** como un reloj.
clod (klŏd) s. *(of dirt)* terrón *m; (dolt)* bobo.
clog (klŏg) I. s. *(blockage)* obstrucción *f,* atasco; *(shoe)* zueco II. tr. & intr. **-gg-** obstruir(se), atascar(se).
clois·ter (kloi′stər) I. s. claustro; *(monastery)* monasterio, convento II. tr. enclaustrar.
clomp (klŏmp) intr. andar pesada y ruidosamente.
clone (klōn) I. s. clon *m* II. tr. & intr. reproducir(se) asexualmente.
close I. adj. (klōs) cercano; *(relationship)* íntimo; *(similar)* parecido; *(contest)* reñido; *(resemblance)* casi igual; *(copy)* fiel, exacto; *(rigorous)* minucioso; *(attention)* total; *(enclosed)* encerrado; *(tight-fitting)* ajustado; *(stuffy)* mal ventilado; *(confining)* estrecho; *(strict)* estricto ♦ **a c. resemblance** un gran parecido • **at c. range** a quemarropa, de cerca • **c. call** FAM. escape difícil • **c. combat** MIL. combate cuerpo a cuerpo • **c. quarters** lugar estrecho II. tr. (klōz) cerrar; *(letter)* concluir; *(session)* levantar; *(gap, distance)* acortar ♦ **to**

c. down cerrar definitivamente • **to c. in** rodear, cercar • **to c. out** *(account)* cerrar; *(product)* liquidar • **to c. up** *(shop)* cerrar; *(opening)* tapar • **to c. up shop** cesar toda actividad —intr. cerrarse; *(shop)* cerrar; *(story, show)* terminarse, concluirse; *(to agree)* ponerse de acuerdo • **to c. down** clausurarse, cerrarse definitivamente • **to c. in** *(to surround)* rodear; *(to draw near)* acercarse • **to c. up** *(shop)* cerrar; *(wound)* cerrarse, cicatrizarse III. s. (klōz) final *m*, conclusión *f* • **at the c. of the day** a la caída de la tarde • **to bring to a c.** terminar IV. adv. (klōs) cerca • **c. at hand** a mano • **c. by** muy cerca • **c. to** muy cerca de, junto a • **c. together** muy juntos • **to come c.** acercarse.

closed (klōzd) adj. cerrado; *(finished)* concluido; *(season)* vedado; *(restricted)* reservado; *(mind)* estrecho.

closed-cir·cuit television (:sûr′kĭt) s. televisión *f* en circuito cerrado.

close·down (klōz′doun′) s. cierre *m*.

close·ly (klōs′lē) adv. (de) cerca; *(intimately)* estrechamente; *(exactly)* con fidelidad; *(attentively)* atentamente.

close·ness (:nĭs) s. cercanía, proximidad *f*; *(intimacy)* intimidad *f*.

close-out (klōz′out′) s. liquidación *f*.

clos·et (klŏz′ĭt) s. armario, ropero.

close-up (klōs′ŭp′) s. primer plano.

clos·ing (klō′zĭng) s. cierre *m* • **c. remarks** observaciones finales • **in c.** para concluir.

clot (klŏt) I. s. coágulo II. intr. **-tt-** coagularse, cuajarse.

cloth (klôth) s. [pl. **s**] tela, paño; *(strip)* trapo • **the c.** el clero.

clothe (klōth) tr. **-d** o **clad** vestir, arropar.

clothes (klōthz) s.pl. ropa, vestimenta.

clothes·line (′līn′) s. cuerda para tender ropa.

clothes·pin (:pĭn′) s. pinza para tender ropa.

cloth·ing (klō′thĭng) s. ropa, indumentaria.

cloud (kloud) I. s. nube *f*; *(shadow)* sombra • **on c. nine** FAM. contentísimo • **under a c.** bajo sospecha II. tr. & intr. nublar(se), anublar(se) • **to c. over** o **up** nublarse.

cloud·burst (′bûrst′) s. aguacero.

cloud·y (klou′dē) adj. **-i-** *(overcast)* nublado; *(vague)* nebuloso; *(liquid)* turbio.

clout (klout) I. s. *(blow)* bofetada; FAM. *(influence)* poder *m* II. tr. abofetear.

clove (klōv) s. *(spice)* clavo de especia; *(of garlic)* diente *m*.

clo·ven hoof (klō′vən) s. pezuña hendida.

clo·ver (klō′vər) s. trébol *m* • **to be in c.** vivir como un rey.

clo·ver·leaf (:lēf′) s. cruce *m* en trébol.

clown (kloun) I. s. payaso II. intr. payasear.

cloy·ing (kloi′ĭng) adj. empalagoso.

club (klŭb) I. s. *(cudgel)* porra; *(golf)* palo; *(in cards)* trébol *m*, basto; *(association)* club *m* • **c. car** F.C. coche salón II. tr. **-bb-** aporrear.

club·foot (′fŏŏt′) s. pie *m* deforme.

club·house (:hous′) s. club *m*.

cluck (klŭk) I. s. *(sound)* cloqueo; FAM. *(dolt)* estúpido, tonto II. intr. cloquear.

clue (klōō) I. s. pista, indicio; *(in puzzle)* indicación *f* • **I haven't a c.** no tengo ni idea II. tr. **-(e)ing** • **to c. in** poner al tanto de la situación.

clump (klŭmp) I. s. *(lump)* masa; *(trees)* grupo II. intr. andar con pisadas fuertes —tr. agrupar.

clum·sy (klŭm′zē) adj. **-i-** *(awkward)* torpe; *(unwieldy)* incómodo; *(unrefined)* crudo.

clung (klŭng) cf. **cling.**

clunk (klŭngk) s. sonido sordo.

clus·ter (klŭs′tər) I. s. grupo; *(bunch)* racimo, ramo II. tr. & intr. agrupar(se), arracimar(se).

clutch (klŭch) I. tr. agarrar, asir —intr. • **to c. at** agarrarse a II. s. *(grasp)* apretón *m*; MEC. embrague *m* • **in the c.** en situación crítica • pl. FIG. garras.

clut·ter (klŭt′ər) I. s. desorden *m* II. tr. esparcir desordenadamente.

coach (kōch) I. s. *(carriage)* coche *m*, carruaje *m*; *(bus)* ómnibus *m*; F.C. vagón *m* de pasajeros; AVIA. clase económica; *(trainer)* entrenador *m*; *(tutor)* maestro particular II. tr. & intr. *(to tutor)* dar lecciones suplementarias; *(to train)* entrenar.

coach·man (′mən) s. [pl. **-men**] cochero.

co·ag·u·late (kō-ăg′yə-lāt′) tr. & intr. coagular(se).

coal (kōl) s. carbón *m*, hulla; *(ember)* ascua • **c. tar** alquitrán de hulla • **hard c.** antracita, hulla seca • **soft c.** carbón bituminoso.

co·a·lesce (kō′ə-lĕs′) intr. unirse.

coal·field (kōl′fēld′) s. cuenca carbonífera.

co·a·li·tion (kō′ə-lĭsh′ən) s. coalición *f*.

coarse (kôrs) adj. *(inferior)* basto; *(uncouth)* vulgar; *(rough)* áspero, tosco; *(grainy)* granular.

coars·en (kôr′sən) intr. volverse tosco o vulgar —tr. vulgarizar.

coarse·ness (kôrs′nĭs) s. *(of manners)* grosería; *(texture)* aspereza.

coast (kōst) I. s. costa • **c. guard** guardacostas • **the c. is clear** no hay moros en la costa II. intr. *(to slide)* deslizarse; *(bicycle, car)* rodar sin impulso.

coast·al (kō′stəl) adj. costero.

coast·er (kō′stər) s. *(sled)* trineo; *(mat)* posavasos.

coast·line (kōst′līn′) s. costa, litoral *m*.

coat (kōt) I. s. *(overcoat)* abrigo; *(jacket)* saco, chaqueta; *(of animal)* piel *f*, pelo; *(paint)* mano *f*, capa; *(coating)* baño • **c. of arms** escudo de armas • **c. of mail** cota de malla II. tr. *(to cover)* revestir; *(to paint)* dar una mano o capa; *(to plate)* bañar.

coat·ed (kō′tĭd) adj. cubierto, bañado.

coat·ing (kō′tĭng) s. *(layer)* capa, mano *f*; *(gold, silver)* baño, revestimiento.

coat·tail (kōt′tāl′) s. faldón *m* • **on someone's coattails** a base del éxito de otra persona.

coax (kōks) tr. engatusar.

coax·ing (kōk′sĭng) I. s. engatusamiento II. adj. engatusador.

cob (kŏb) s. elote *m*, mazorca.

co·balt (kō′bôlt′) s. cobalto.

cob·bler (kŏb′lər) s. zapatero; *(pie)* tarta de fruta.

cob·ble·stone (kŏb′əl-stōn′) s. piedra redonda • **c. pavement** empedrado.

co·bra (kō′brə) s. cobra.

cob·web (kŏb′wĕb′) s. telaraña.

co·ca (kō′kə) s. coca.

co·caine (kō-kān′) s. cocaína.

coc·cyx (kŏk′sĭks) s. [pl. **-yges**] cóccix *m*.

cock (kŏk) I. s. *(rooster)* gallo; *(male bird)* macho; *(faucet)* grifo, llave *f*; ARM. *(hammer)* martillo II. tr. ARM. amartillar; *(a hat)* inclinar (hacia arriba); *(fist, ears)* alzar, levantar.

cock·ade (kŏ-kād′) s. escarapela.

cock·a·ma·mie (kŏk′ə-mā′mē) adj. JER. absurdo.

cock-and-bull story (kŏk′ən-bŏŏl′) s. FAM. patraña, cuento increíble.

cock·a·too (kŏk′ə-tōō′) s. cacatúa.

cock·er·el (kŏk′ər-əl) s. gallo joven.

cock·eyed (kŏk′īd′) adj. OFTAL. bizco; JER. (crooked) oblicuo, torcido; (foolish) absurdo.

cock·fight (kŏk′fīt′) s. pelea de gallos.

cock·i·ness (kŏk′ē-nĭs) s. presunción f.

cock·le (kŏk′əl) s. berberecho ♦ **the cockles of one's heart** las entretelas del corazón.

cock·ney (kŏk′nē) s. lenguaje m o habitante mf de los barrios bajos de Londres.

cock·pit (kŏk′pĭt′) s. (arena) cancha; AVIA. cabina.

cock·roach (kŏk′rōch′) s. cucaracha.

cocks·comb (kŏks′kōm′) s. ZOOL. cresta de gallo; (fop) petimetre m, fatuo.

cock·sure (kŏk′shŏŏr′) adj. demasiado seguro.

cock·tail (kŏk′tāl′) s. cóctel m.

cock·y (kŏk′ē) adj. -i- FAM. presumido, engreído.

co·coa (kō′kō) s. cacao.

co·co(a)·nut (kō′kə-nət) s. coco ♦ **c. palm** cocotero.

co·coon (kə-kōōn′) s. capullo.

cod (kŏd) s. [pl. inv. o s] bacalao.

cod·dle (kŏd′l) tr. (to cook) cocer a fuego lento; (to pamper) mimar, consentir.

code (kōd) I. s. código; (cipher) clave f, cifra ♦ **Morse c.** alfabeto Morse II. tr. codificar; (a message) cifrar.

co·de·fend·ant (kō′dĭ-fĕn′dənt) s. coacusado.

co·deine (kō′dēn′) s. codeína.

cod·ger (kŏj′ər) s. FAM. vejete m.

cod·fish (kŏd′fĭsh′) s. [pl. inv. o es] bacalao.

cod·i·fy (kŏd′ə-fī′, kō′də-) tr. codificar.

co·di·rec·tion (kō′dĭ-rĕk′shən) s. codirección f.

cod-liv·er oil (kŏd′lĭv′ər) aceite m de hígado de bacalao.

co·ed (kō′ĕd′) I. s. FAM. I. s. alumna de una universidad mixta II. adj. coeducacional.

co·ed·u·ca·tion (kō-ĕj′ə-kā′shən) s. coeducación f, enseñanza mixta.

co·ed·u·ca·tion·al (:shə-nəl) adj. coeducacional.

co·ef·fi·cient (kō′ə-fĭsh′ənt) s. coeficiente m.

co·erce (kō-ûrs′) tr. coaccionar, obligar.

co·er·cion (kō-ûr′zhən) s. coacción f; DER. (restraint) coerción f.

co·e·val (kō-ē′vəl) adj. & s. coetáneo.

co·ex·ist (kō′ĭg-zĭst′) intr. coexistir.

co·ex·is·tence (:zĭs′təns) s. coexistencia.

co·ex·ten·sive (kō′ĭk-stĕn′sĭv) adj. coextenso.

cof·fee (kô′fē) s. café m ♦ **c. shop** café, cafetería • **c. table** mesa de café o de centro.

cof·fee·pot (:pŏt′) s. cafetera.

cof·fer (kô′fər) s. cofre m ♦ pl. fondos.

cof·fin (kô′fĭn) s. ataúd m.

cog (kŏg) s. MEC. diente m.

co·gent (kō′jənt) adj. profundamente pensado.

cog·i·tate (kŏj′ĭ-tāt′) intr. & tr. reflexionar.

co·gnac (kōn′yăk′) s. coñac m.

cog·nate (kŏg′nāt′) adj. & s. (palabra) afín.

cog·ni·tion (kŏg-nĭsh′ən) s. (faculty) cognición f; (knowledge) percepción f.

cog·ni·zance (kŏg′nĭ-zəns) s. conocimiento ♦ **to take c. of** tener en cuenta.

cog·ni·zant (:zənt) adj. enterado, informado ♦ **to be c. of** saber.

cog·wheel (kŏg′hwēl′) s. rueda dentada.

co·hab·it (kō-hăb′ĭt) intr. cohabitar.

co·here (kō-hîr′) intr. (objects) adherirse;

(thoughts) tener coherencia, ser coherente.

co·her·ence/·cy (:əns) s. coherencia.

co·her·ent (:ənt) adj. coherente.

co·he·sion (kō-hē′zhən) s. cohesión f.

co·he·sive (:sĭv) adj. cohesivo.

co·hort (kō′hôrt′) s. FAM. socio, compañero.

coif·fure (kwä-fyŏŏr′) s. tocado, peinado.

coil (koil) I. s. rollo; (single) anillo, vuelta; (of pipe) serpentín m; ELEC. bobina II. tr. & intr. enrollar(se), enroscar(se).

coin (koin) I. s. moneda II. tr. (to mint) acuñar; (phrase, word) inventar.

co·in·cide (kō′ĭn-sīd′) intr. coincidir.

co·in·ci·dence (kō-ĭn′sĭ-dəns) s. (identicalness) coincidencia; (chance) casualidad f.

co·in·ci·den·tal (′-dĕn′təl) adj. (identical) coincidente; (accidental) casual, fortuito.

co·i·tus (kō′ĭ-təs) s. coito.

coke[1] (kōk) s. MIN. coque m.

coke[2] s. JER. cocaína.

co·la (kō′lə) s. cola (nuez, bebida).

col·an·der (kŭl′ən-dər) s. colador m.

cold (kōld) I. adj. frío; (impassive) impasible; (fact, truth) mero, sencillo; FAM. (unconscious) sin conocimiento; (unprepared) sin preparación ♦ **c. comfort** poco consuelo • **c. cream** crema para el cutis • **c. cuts** fiambres • **c. feet** JER. miedo • **c. shoulder** FAM. indiferencia, frialdad • **c. snap** o **spell** ola de frío • **c. sore** afta (labial) • **in c. blood** a sangre fría • **to be c.** (object) estar frío; (person) tener frío; (weather) hacer frío II. adv. (totally) completamente; (unprepared) sin preparación, en seco ♦ **to know c.** saber al dedillo III. s. frío; MED. catarro, resfriado ♦ **out in the c.** en la estacada • **to catch a c.** resfriarse.

cold-blood·ed (′blŭd′ĭd) adj. impasible; (murder) a sangre fría; ZOOL. de sangre fría.

cold-heart·ed (:här′tĭd) adj. insensible.

cold·ness (:nĭs) s. frío, frialdad f.

cole (kōl) s. colza, col f.

col·ic (kŏl′ĭk) s. cólico.

col·i·se·um (kŏl′ĭ-sē′əm) s. coliseo.

co·li·tis (kō-lī′tĭs) s. colitis f.

col·lab·o·rate (kə-lăb′ə-rāt′) intr. colaborar.

col·lab·o·ra·tion (′-rā′shən) s. colaboración f; (treason) colaboracionismo.

col·lab·o·ra·tion·ist (:shə-nĭst) s. colaboracionista mf.

col·lab·o·ra·tive (′-′tĭv) adj. cooperativo.

col·lab·o·ra·tor (:tər) s. colaborador m; (traitor) colaboracionista mf.

col·lage (kə-läzh′) s. collage m, montaje m.

col·lapse (kə-lăps′) I. intr. caerse, derrumbarse; (person) desplomarse; (business) fracasar; (to fold) plegarse —tr. plegar II. s. caída, derrumbe f; (business) fracaso; MED. colapso.

col·laps·i·ble/a·ble (kə-lăp′sə-bəl) adj. plegable.

col·lar (kŏl′ər) I. s. cuello; JOY., MEC. collar m; (harness) collera II. tr. (an animal) poner collar a; FAM. (to nab) agarrar, detener.

col·lar·bone (:bōn′) s. clavícula.

col·late (kə-lāt′, kō′lāt′) tr. (texts) colacionar; (pages) ordenar.

col·lat·er·al (kə-lăt′ər-əl) I. adj. colateral; (evidence) corroborante; FIN. con garantía de pago II. s. prenda, hipoteca.

col·league (kŏl′ēg′) s. colega mf.

col·lect (kə-lĕkt′) I. tr. (to gather) juntar, reunir; (as hobby) coleccionar; (payments) recau-

dar ♦ **to c. oneself** controlarse —intr.
juntarse, acumularse **II.** adj. & adv. *(telephone call)* de cobro revertido.

col·lect·ed (kə-lĕk′tĭd) adj. recogido, sosegado ♦ **c. works** obras completas.

col·lec·tion (:shən) s. colección f; *(heap)* acumulación f; *(of money)* cobro; *(donation)* colecta.

col·lec·tive (:tĭv) **I.** adj. colectivo ♦ **c. farm** granja cooperativa **II.** s. cooperativa.

col·lec·tiv·ist (:tə-vĭst) s. colectivista mf.

col·lec·tiv·ize (:tə-vīz′) tr. colectivizar.

col·lec·tor (:tər) s. colector m; *(of taxes)* recaudador m; *(of bills)* cobrador m; *(as hobby)* coleccionista mf.

col·lege (kŏl′ĭj) s. universidad f; *(department)* facultad f; RELIG. colegio.

col·le·gian (kə-lē′jən) s. estudiante mf universitario.

col·le·giate (:jĭt) adj. universitario.

col·lide (kə-līd′) intr. chocar.

col·lie (kŏl′ē) s. perro pastor escocés.

col·lier (kŏl′yər) s. G.B. minero de carbón.

col·li·sion (kə-lĭzh′ən) s. choque m.

col·loid (kŏl′oid′) s. & adj. coloide m.

col·lo·qui·al (kə-lō′kwē-əl) adj. familiar.

col·lo·qui·al·ism (:ə-lĭz′əm) s. estilo o expresión f familiar.

col·lo·qui·um (:əm) s. [pl. s o -ia] coloquio.

col·lo·quy (kŏl′ə-kwē) s. coloquio.

col·lude (kə-lōōd′) intr. confabularse.

col·lu·sion (kə-lōō′zhən) s. confabulación f.

co·logne (kə-lōn′) s. colonia (perfume).

co·lon¹ (kō′lən) s. GRAM. dos puntos.

co·lon² s. [pl. s o -la] ANAT. colon m.

colo·nel (kûr′nəl) s. coronel m.

co·lo·ni·al (kə-lō′nē-əl) **I.** adj. *(of a colony)* colonial; *(colonizing)* colonizador **II.** s. colono.

co·lo·ni·al·ist (:ə-lĭst) s. & adj. colonialista mf.

col·o·nist (kŏl′ə-nĭst) s. *(colonizer)* colonizador m; *(inhabitant)* colono.

col·o·nize (:nīz′) tr. colonizar.

col·o·niz·er (:nī′zər) s. colonizador m.

col·on·nade (kŏl′ə-nād′) s. columnata.

col·o·ny (kŏl′ə-nē) s. colonia.

col·or (kŭl′ər) **I.** s. color m; ARTE., MÚS. colorido ♦ **c. guard** escolta de bandera • **c. line** FIG. barrera racial • **c. photography** cromofotografía • **c. television** televisión en color • **in c.** en colores • **in full c.** a todo color • **off c.** verde • **to change c.** mudar de color • **to lose c.** palidecer ♦ pl. *(flag)* bandera, estandarte; *(of school)* insignia; *(character)* carácter m • **with flying c.** con mucho éxito **II.** tr. colorear; *(to paint)* pintar; *(to dye)* teñir; *(to distort)* alterar, embellecer; *(to influence)* influir en —intr. sonrojarse, ruborizarse.

col·or·a·tion (′ə-rā′shən) s. coloración f.

col·or·blind (′ər-blīnd′) adj. MED. daltoniano; FIG. insensible a distinciones raciales.

col·ored (:ərd) **I.** adj. coloreado, de color; *(person)* de color **II.** s. persona de color.

col·or·fast (:ər-făst′) adj. de color fijo.

col·or·ful (:fəl) adj. *(vivid)* de gran colorido; *(picturesque)* pintoresco.

col·or·ing (:ĭng) s. *(coloration)* coloración f; *(dye)* colorante m.

col·or·less (:lĭs) adj. incoloro.

co·los·sal (kə-lōs′əl) adj. colosal.

co·los·sus (:əs) s. [pl. es o -si] coloso.

co·los·to·my (kə-lōs′tə-mē) s. colostomía.

col·our (kŭl′ər) G.B. var. de **color.**

colt (kōlt) s. potro.

col·umn (kŏl′əm) s. columna.

col·um·nist (:nĭst) s. columnista mf.

co·ma (kō′mə) s. coma m.

co·ma·tose (:tōs′) adj. comatoso.

comb (kōm) **I.** s. peine m; ORNIT. *(crest)* cresta; *(honeycomb)* panal m **II.** tr. peinar; *(to search)* registrar (detalladamente) ♦ **to c. one's hair** peinarse.

com·bat I. tr. (kəm-băt′, kŏm′băt′) pelear contra, dar batalla; FIG. combatir, resistir **II.** s. (kŏm′băt′) combate m.

com·bat·ant (kəm-băt′nt) s. combatiente m.

com·bat·ive (:ĭv) adj. combativo.

com·bi·na·tion (kŏm′bə-nā′shən) s. combinación f; *(mix)* mezcla.

com·bine I. tr. & intr. (kəm-bīn′) combinar(se); *(to mix)* mezclar **II.** s. (kŏm′bīn′) AGR. segadora; *(association)* asociación f.

com·bo (kŏm′bō) s. conjunto.

com·bus·ti·ble (kəm-bŭs′tə-bəl) adj. & s. combustible m.

com·bus·tion (:chən) s. combustión f.

come (kŭm) **I.** intr. **came, come** venir; *(to arrive at, extend to)* llegar; *(to amount to)* ascender a ♦ **c. what may** pase lo que pase • **to c. about** suceder, ocurrir; MARÍT. virar • **to c. across** *(to find)* encontrarse con; *(to be understood)* ser comprendido • **to c. after** *(to follow)* seguir; *(to pursue)* venir en busca de • **to c. along** *(to accompany)* acompañar; *(to progress)* progresar • **to c. around** *(to visit)* hacer una visita; *(to revive)* volver en sí • **to c.** atacar • **to c. away** irse, retirarse • **to c. back** volver • **to c. before** preceder; DER. comparecer ante (juez, tribunal) • **to c. between** interponerse entre • **to c. by** *(to visit)* hacer una visita; *(to obtain)* obtener, lograr • **to c. down** bajar; *(to collapse)* derrumbarse; *(to fall)* caer(se) • **to c. down on** *(to collapse)* caer encima; *(to reproach)* reprochar • **to c. down to** reducirse a • **to c. down with** FAM. caer enfermo con • **to c. in** *(to enter)* entrar; *(in a race)* llegar; *(to figure into)* figurar, entrar • **to c. in for** FAM. recibir • **to c. into** heredar • **to c. of** resultar de, suceder por • **to c. off** *(to detach)* soltarse, separarse; *(to acquit oneself)* salir (bien, mal); *(to happen)* tener lugar • **to c. on** TEAT. salir a escena; *(to present oneself)* presentarse (as como) • **to c. on to** FAM. tirarse a • **to c. out** salir; *(to detach)* desprenderse; *(to appear)* asomar; *(book)* publicarse; *(to result)* resultar (bien, mal); *(for or against)* declararse; *(stain)* quitarse; *(truth)* salir a la luz, revelarse; *(to bloom)* florecer • **to c. out with** *(to announce)* revelar, publicar; *(a product)* salir con, ofrecer; FAM. *(to say)* saltar con, soltar (comentario, maldición) • **to c. over** *(to happen to)* sobrevenir, invadir; FAM. *(to visit)* venir • **to c. through** *(to do what is wanted)* cumplir; *(to be apparent)* manifestarse; *(to endure)* pasar por, salir de • **to c. through with** JER. cumplir con • **to c. to** *(to revive)* recobrar los sentidos, volver en sí; *(to amount to)* reducirse a • **to c. to one** ocurrírsele • **to c. under** *(a category)* figurar entre; *(to be subject to)* caer bajo, estar sometido a (poder, influencia) • **to c. up** subir; *(to arise)* presentarse, surgir; *(to be mentioned)* ser mencionado • **to c. up against** tropezar o dar con • **to c. up to** *(in quality)* estar a la altura de; *(in height)* llegar hasta; *(to approach)* acercarse a • **to c. up with** *(to produce)* producir; *(to propose)* sugerir, proponer • **to c.**

within entrar *o* estar dentro de • **when it comes to** cuando se trata de **II.** interj. ¡venga!, ¡ven! ♦ **c. again?** ¿cómo? • **c. in!** ¡adelante!, ¡pase! • **c. off it!** FAM. ¡no me vengas con eso! • **c. now!** ¡vamos!, ¡no es para tanto! • **c. on!** FAM. *(hurry up!)* ¡date prisa!, ¡apúrate!; *(you're kidding!)* ¡no me digas!

come·back ('băk') s. réplica, respuesta ingeniosa ♦ **to make a c.** restablecerse, reaparecer.

co·me·di·an (kə-mē'dē-ən) s. *(entertainer)* cómico; *(actor)* comediante *m.*

co·me·di·enne (-'-ěn') s. *(entertainer)* cómica; *(actress)* comediante.

come·down (kŭm'doun') s. *(in status)* bajón *m,* pérdida de rango; *(disappointment)* revés *m.*

com·e·dy (kŏm'ĭ-dē) s. comedia.

come·ly (kŭm'lē) adj. -i- atractivo.

come-on (:ŏn') s. aliciente *m,* incentivo.

com·er (:ər) s. *(arrival)* persona que llega; FAM. *(rising star)* persona prometedora.

com·et (kŏm'ĭt) s. cometa *m.*

come·up·pance (kŭm-ŭp'əns) s. FAM. castigo merecido.

com·fort (kŭm'fərt) **I.** tr. confortar, consolar; *(to relieve)* aliviar **II.** s. *(well-being)* confort *m;* *(relief)* alivio; *(consolation)* consuelo; *(ease)* comodidad *f* ♦ **c. station** excusado público • **to be a c.** ser un consuelo.

com·fort·a·ble (:fər-tə-bəl) adj. *(easy)* confortable, cómodo; FAM. *(sufficient)* adecuado.

com·fort·er (:tər) s. *(person)* consolador *m;* *(quilt)* edredón *m.*

com·fy (kŭm'fē) adj. -i- FAM. cómodo.

com·ic (kŏm'ĭk) adj. & s. cómico ♦ **c. book** revista de historietas ilustradas • **c. strip** tira cómica.

com·i·cal (:ĭ-kəl) adj. cómico.

com·ing (kŭm'ĭng) **I.** adj. venidero **II.** s. venida, llegada ♦ **comings and goings** idas y venidas.

com·ma (kŏm'ə) s. GRAM. coma.

com·mand (kə-mănd') **I.** tr. mandar; *(to give orders)* ordenar; *(to rule)* regir; *(to have available)* disponer de, poseer; *(to deserve)* infundir; *(to overlook)* dominar —intr. mandar, dar órdenes **II.** s. mando; *(order)* orden *f;* *(mastery)* dominio; MIL. *(jurisdiction)* comando ♦ **at one's c.** a la disposición de uno • **c. headquarters** centro de comando • **c. post** puesto de mando • **to be in c. of** estar al mando de • **under the c. of** al mando de.

com·man·dant (kŏm'ən-dănt') s. comandante *m.*

com·man·deer (:dîr') tr. *(to confiscate)* confiscar; FAM. *(to seize)* apoderarse de.

com·mand·er (kə-măn'dər) s. jefe *m;* MARÍT. capitán *m* de fragata; MIL. comandante *m.*

com·mand·ing (:dĭng) adj. que está al mando; *(impressive)* imponente; *(position)* dominante.

com·mand·ment (kə-mănd'mənt) s. orden *f;* RELIG. mandamiento.

com·man·do (kə-măn'dō) s. [pl. **(e)s**] comando.

com·mem·o·rate (kə-mĕm'ə-rāt') tr. conmemorar.

com·mence (kə-mĕns') tr. & intr. comenzar.

com·mence·ment (:mənt) s. comienzo, principio; EDUC. ceremonia de entrega de diplomas.

com·mend (kə-mĕnd') tr. *(to praise)* elogiar, alabar; *(to recommend)* recomendar; *(to entrust)* encomendar.

com·mend·a·ble (kə-mĕn'də-bəl) adj. loable.

com·men·da·tion (kŏm'ən-dā'shən) s. *(praise)* elogio; *(recommendation)* recomendación *f;* *(citation)* mención *f.*

com·men·su·rate (kə-mĕn'sər-ĭt) adj. proporcionado.

com·ment (kŏm'ĕnt') **I.** s. comentario; *(remark)* observación *f* **II.** intr. comentar, observar.

com·men·tar·y (:ən-tĕr'ē) s. comentario.

com·men·tate (:tāt') tr. & intr. comentar.

com·men·ta·tor (:tā'tər) s. locutor *m.*

com·merce (kŏm'ərs) s. comercio.

com·mer·cial (kə-mûr'shəl) **I.** adj. comercial **II.** s. anuncio.

com·mer·cial·ism (:shə-lĭz'əm) s. comercialismo.

com·mer·cial·ize (:līz') tr. comercializar.

com·mie (kŏm'ē) s. FAM. rojo, comunista *mf.*

com·min·gle (kə-mĭng'gəl) intr. mezclarse.

com·mis·er·ate (kə-mĭz'ə-rāt') intr. compadecerse *(with* de).

com·mis·sar (kŏm'ĭ-sär') s. comisario.

com·mis·sar·i·at ('-sär'ē-ĭt) s. intendencia militar.

com·mis·sar·y ('-sĕr'ē) s. economato.

com·mis·sion (kə-mĭsh'ən) **I.** s. comisión *f;* MIL. nombramiento ♦ **out of c.** fuera de servicio; *(broken)* descompuesto • **to put out of c.** *(to ruin)* inutilizar; FAM. *(to sideline)* poner fuera de combate, acabar con • **to work on c.** trabajar a comisión **II.** tr. MIL. nombrar; *(to order)* encargar, mandar a hacer; *(ship)* poner en servicio.

com·mis·sion·er (:ə-nər) s. miembro de una comisión; *(official)* comisario.

com·mit (kə-mĭt') tr. -**tt**- cometer; *(to entrust)* encomendar; *(to jail)* encarcelar; *(to institutionalize)* internar; *(to dispose of)* entregar ♦ **to c. oneself** comprometerse • **to c. to paper** *o* **writing** consignar por escrito.

com·mit·ment (:mənt) s. *(pledge)* compromiso; *(institutionalization)* internamiento, reclusión *f;* *(obligation)* obligación *f.*

com·mit·tal (:l) s. *(confinement)* confinamiento, reclusión *f;* *(pledging)* obligación *f.*

com·mit·tee (kə-mĭt'ē) s. comité *m,* comisión *f.*

com·mode (kə-mōd') s. *(bureau)* cómoda; *(washbowl)* palanganero; *(toilet)* retrete *m.*

com·mo·di·ous (kə-mō'dē-əs) adj. espacioso, amplio.

com·mod·i·ty (kə-mŏd'ĭ-tē) s. mercancía.

com·mo·dore (kŏm'ə-dôr') s. comodoro.

com·mon (kŏm'ən) **I.** adj. común, **-er, -est** común; *(public)* público; *(widespread)* general; *(frequent)* usual, frecuente; *(quality)* mediocre, inferior ♦ **c. cold** resfriado, catarro • **c. fraction** fracción ordinaria • **c. ground** tema de interés mutuo • **c. law** derecho consuetudinario • **c. sense** sentido común • **c. stock** acciones ordinarias **II.** s. ejido, campo comunal ♦ **Commons** G.B. Cámara de los Comunes.

com·mon·er (:ə-nər) s. plebeyo.

com·mon-law marriage (:ən-lô') s. matrimonio consensual.

com·mon·place (:plās') **I.** adj. común, ordinario **II.** s. lugar *m* común.

com·mon·wealth (:wĕlth') s. *(people)* comunidad *f;* *(state)* república.

com·mo·tion (kə-mō'shən) s. tumulto, alboroto.

com·mu·nal (kə-myōo'nəl) adj. comunal.

com·mune¹ (kə-myōōn') intr. comunicarse, comulgar.

com·mune² (kŏm'yōōn') s. POL. comuna; *(community)* vivienda colectiva.

com·mu·ni·ca·ble (kə-myōō'nĭ-kə-bəl) adj. comunicable; *(contagious)* contagioso.

com·mu·ni·cant (:kənt) s. RELIG. comulgante *m*; *(communicator)* comunicante *m*.

com·mu·ni·cate (:kāt') tr. & intr. comunicar(se).

com·mu·ni·ca·tion (-'-kā'shən) s. comunicación *f*.

com·mu·ni·ca·tive (-'-'-tĭv) adj. comunicativo.

com·mu·ni·ca·tor (:kā'tər) s. comunicante *mf*.

com·mun·ion (kə-myōōn'yən) s. comunión *f*.

com·mu·ni·qué (kə-myōō'nĭ-kā') s. comunicado oficial.

com·mu·nism (kŏm'yə-nĭz'əm) s. comunismo.

com·mu·nist (:nĭst) s. & adj. comunista *mf*.

com·mu·nis·tic ('-nĭs'tĭk) adj. comunista.

com·mu·ni·ty (kə-myōō'nĭ-tē) s. comunidad *f*; *(local inhabitants)* vecindario.

com·mu·nize (kŏm'yə-nīz') tr. convertir en propiedad comunal.

com·mu·ta·tion (kŏm'yə-tā'shən) s. conmutación *f* ♦ **c. ticket** billete de abono.

com·mu·ta·tive (kə-myōō'tə-tĭv) adj. conmutativo.

com·mute (kə-myōōt') I. tr. conmutar —intr. viajar diariamente al lugar en que se trabaja II. s. viaje diario.

com·mut·er (kə-myōō'tər) s. persona que viaja diariamente (esp. al trabajo).

com·pact¹ I. adj. (kəm-păkt', kŏm'păkt') compacto; *(concise)* conciso II. tr. (kəm-păkt') comprimir III. s. (kŏm'păkt') polvera; AUTO. automóvil compacto.

com·pact² (kŏm'păkt') s. pacto, convenio.

com·pan·ion (kəm-păn'yən) s. compañero.

com·pan·ion·a·ble (:yə-nə-bəl) adj. sociable.

com·pan·ion·ship (:yən-shĭp') s. compañerismo.

com·pan·ion·way (:wā') s. escalera de cámara.

com·pa·ny (kŭm'pə-nē) s. compañía; *(group)* grupo; *(guests)* invitado(s) ♦ **to keep c. with** asociarse con • **to keep someone c.** hacerle compañía a alguien • **to part c.** separarse.

com·pa·ra·ble (kŏm'pər-ə-bəl, kəm-păr'-) adj. comparable.

com·par·a·tive (kəm-păr'ə-tĭv) I. adj. comparativo; *(relative)* relativo ♦ **c. literature** literatura comparada II. s. comparativo.

com·pare (kəm-pâr') I. tr. & intr. (poderse) comparar ♦ **as compared with** comparado con II. s. ♦ **beyond c.** incomparable.

com·par·i·son (:ĭ-sən) s. comparación *f* ♦ **by c.** en comparación.

com·part·ment (kəm-pärt'mənt) s. compartimiento.

com·pass (kŭm'pəs) I. s. *(magnetic)* brújula, compás *m*; *(perimeter)* perímetro; *(scope)* alcance *m* ♦ **c.** o pl. GEOM. compás II. tr. circundar, rodear.

com·pas·sion (kəm-păsh'ən) s. compasión *f*.

com·pas·sion·ate (:ə-nĭt) adj. compasivo.

com·pat·i·ble (kəm-păt'ə-bəl) adj. compatible.

com·pa·tri·ot (kəm-pā'trē-ət) s. compatriota *mf*.

com·pel (kəm-pĕl') tr. **-ll-** compeler, obligar; *(respect, belief)* imponer.

com·pel·ling (:ĭng) adj. obligatorio; *(evidence)* incontestable; *(need)* apremiante.

com·pen·di·um (kəm-pĕn'dē-əm) [pl. **s** o **-ia**] s. compendio.

com·pen·sate (kŏm'pən-sāt') tr. compensar; COM. indemnizar —intr. ♦ **to c.** for compensar.

com·pen·sa·tion ('-sā'shən) s. compensación *f*; COM. indemnización *f*.

com·pete (kəm-pēt') intr. competir ♦ **to c. in** concursar o tomar parte en.

com·pe·tence (kŏm'pĭ-tns) s. competencia.

com·pe·tent (:tnt) adj. competente.

com·pe·ti·tion ('-tĭsh'ən) s. competencia ♦ **the c.** nuestros competidores.

com·pet·i·tive (kəm-pĕt'ĭ-tĭv) adj. competitivo; *(person)* competidor; *(spirit)* de competencia.

com·pet·i·tor (:tər) s. competidor *m*.

com·pi·la·tion (kŏm'pə-lā'shən) s. compilación *f*, recopilación *f*.

com·pile (kəm-pīl') tr. compilar, recopilar.

com·pla·cen·cy/·cence (kəm-plā'sən-sē/-səns) s. *(gratification)* complacencia; *(smugness)* satisfacción *f* de sí mismo.

com·pla·cent (:sənt) adj. pagado de sí mismo.

com·plain (kəm-plān') intr. quejarse *(about* de).

com·plain·ant (:plā'nənt) s. demandante *mf*.

com·plaint (:plānt') s. queja; *(protest)* reclamación *f*; DER. querella, demanda.

com·plai·sant (kəm-plā'sənt) adj. complaciente.

com·ple·ment (kŏm'plə-mənt) I. s. complemento II. tr. complementar.

com·ple·men·ta·ry ('-mĕn'tə-rē) adj. complementario.

com·plete (kəm-plēt') I. adj. completo; *(thorough)* total; *(utter)* verdadero II. tr. completar, llevar a cabo; *(a form)* llenar; *(to conclude)* terminar.

com·ple·tion (-plē'shən) s. terminación *f* ♦ **to be near c.** estar al terminarse.

com·plex I. adj. (kəm-plĕks', kŏm'plĕks') *(composite)* compuesto; *(intricate)* intrincado, complejo II. s. (kŏm'plĕks') complejo.

com·plex·ion (kəm-plĕk'shən) s. *(skin)* tez *f*; *(character)* aspecto, carácter *m*.

com·pli·ance (kəm-plī'əns) s. *(with an order)* acatamiento; *(acquiescence)* conformidad *f* ♦ **in c. with** conforme a.

com·pli·ant (:ənt) adj. obediente, dócil.

com·pli·cate (kŏm'plĭ-kāt') tr. complicar.

com·pli·cat·ed (:kā'tĭd) adj. complicado.

com·pli·ca·tion ('-kā'shən) s. complicación *f*.

com·plic·i·ty (kəm-plĭs'ĭ-tē) s. complicidad *f*.

com·pli·ment (kŏm'plə-mənt) I. s. *(praise)* elogio; *(honor)* honor *m*; *(flattery)* piropo ♦ **to pay a c.** elogiar • **to take it as a c. that** ser un honor para uno que ♦ pl. saludos • **with the c. of** obsequio de II. tr. elogiar, felicitar.

com·pli·men·ta·ry ('-mĕn'tə-rē) adj. elogioso, halagador; *(free)* de favor.

com·ply (kəm-plī') intr. *(with an order)* acatar, obedecer; *(with a request)* acceder.

com·po·nent (kəm-pō'nənt) I. s. componente *m*, elemento II. adj. componente; *(system)* de elementos.

com·port·ment (kəm-pôrt'mənt) s. comportamiento, conducta.

com·pose (kəm-pōz') tr. & intr. componer ♦ **to be composed of** estar integrado por • **to c. oneself** tranquilizarse.

com·posed (:pōzd') adj. sosegado, tranquilo.

com·pos·er (:pō'zər) s. compositor *m*.

com·pos·ite (:pŏz'ĭt) adj. & s. compuesto.

com·po·si·tion (kŏm′pə-zĭsh′ən) s. composición *f.*

com·po·sure (kəm-pō′zhər) s. serenidad *f.*

com·pound¹ (kŏm′pound′) I. adj. compuesto ♦ **c. fracture** MED. fractura complicada II. s. compuesto; GRAM. palabra compuesta III. tr. (kəm-pound′) *(to combine)* mezclar, combinar; *(interest)* calcular cumulativamente; *(to add to)* agravar.

com·pound² s. *(buildings)* conglomerado encerrado de residencias.

com·pre·hend (kŏm′prĭ-hĕnd′) tr. comprender.

com·pre·hen·si·ble (:hĕn′sə-bəl) adj. comprensible.

com·pre·hen·sion (:shən) s. comprensión *f.*

com·pre·hen·sive (:sĭv) adj. *(broad)* amplio, general; *(overall)* de conjunto; *(knowledge)* comprensivo; *(charge)* total; *(insurance)* a todo riesgo.

com·press I. tr. (kəm-prĕs′) comprimir; *(to shorten)* condensar II. s. (kŏm′prĕs′) compresa.

com·pressed (kəm-prĕst′) adj. comprimido.

com·pres·sion (:prĕsh′ən) s. compresión *f.*

com·prise (kəm-prīz′) tr. *(to include)* comprender, incluir; *(to consist of)* constar de.

com·pro·mise (kŏm′prə-mīz′) I. s. compromiso, acuerdo; *(concession)* concesión *f* II. tr. *(to settle)* componer; *(to endanger)* comprometer —intr. hacer concesiones.

com·pro·mis·ing (:mī′zĭng) adj. *(accommodating)* transigente; *(detrimental)* comprometedor.

com·pul·sion (kəm-pŭl′shən) s. compulsión *f*; *(impulse)* impulso ♦ **to feel a c.** to sentirse obligado o impelido ♦ **under c.** a la fuerza.

com·pul·sive (:sĭv) adj. *(desire)* incontrolable; *(person)* obsesivo.

com·pul·so·ry (:sə-rē) adj. *(coercive)* compulsorio; *(required)* obligatorio.

com·punc·tion (kəm-pŭngk′shən) s. compunción *f* ♦ **without c.** sin escrúpulo.

com·pu·ta·tion (kŏm′pyōō-tā′shən) s. cálculo.

com·pute (kəm-pyōōt′) tr. computar, calcular.

com·put·er (:pyōō′tər) s. computadora, ordenador *m* ♦ **c. language** lenguaje de máquina.

com·put·er·ize (:tə-rīz′) tr. *(data)* computarizar; *(office)* instalar computadoras en ♦ **to be computerized** hacerse por computadoras.

com·rade (kŏm′răd′) s. camarada *mf.*

con¹ (kŏn) adv. & s. contra *m.*

con² JER. I. s. tr. **-nn-** estafar, engañar II. s. estafa ♦ **c. game** estafa • **c. man** estafador.

con·cat·e·nate (kən-kăt′n-āt′) tr. concadenar.

con·cave (kŏn-kāv′) adj. cóncavo.

con·ceal (kən-sēl′) tr. ocultar; *(a crime)* encubrir.

con·ceal·ment (:mənt) s. ocultación *f*; *(of a crime)* encubrimiento.

con·cede (kən-sēd′) tr. conceder —intr. hacer una concesión.

con·ceit (kən-sēt′) s. vanidad *f*, presunción *f*; *(metaphor)* concepto.

con·ceit·ed (:sē′tĭd) adj. vanidoso, engreído.

con·ceiv·a·ble (kən-sē′və-bəl) adj. concebible.

con·ceive (kən-sēv′) tr. & intr. concebir.

con·cen·trate (kŏn′sən-trāt′) I. tr. & intr. concentrar(se) II. s. concentrado.

con·cen·tra·tion (′-trā′shən) s. concentración *f* ♦ **c. camp** campo de concentración.

con·cen·tric (kən-sĕn′trĭk) adj. concéntrico.

con·cept (kŏn′sĕpt′) s. concepto.

con·cep·tion (kən-sĕp′shən) s. concepción *f*; *(plan)* proyecto; *(idea)* concepto, idea.

con·cep·tu·al (:chōō-əl) adj. conceptual.

con·cern (kən-sûrn′) I. tr. *(to be about)* tratar de; *(to affect)* concernir a; *(to trouble)* preocupar ♦ **as concerns** en lo que concierne a • **to c. oneself with** ocuparse de, interesarse por • **those concerned** los interesados • **to whom it may c.** a quien corresponda II. s. *(affair)* asunto; *(interest)* interés *m*; *(worry)* preocupación *f* ♦ **to be of no c.** carecer de importancia.

con·cerned (:sûrnd′) adj. *(interested)* interesado; *(worried)* preocupado.

con·cern·ing (:sûr′nĭng) prep. referente a.

con·cert I. s. (kŏn′sûrt′) concierto ♦ **in c. with** de concierto con II. tr. & intr. (kən-sûrt′) concertar(se).

con·cert·ed (kən-sûr′tĭd) adj. conjunto.

con·cer·to (kən-chĕr′tō) s. [pl. **s** o **-ti**] concierto.

con·ces·sion (kən-sĕsh′ən) s. concesión *f.*

con·ces·sion·aire (′-ə-nâr′) s. concesionario.

conch (kŏngk, kŏnch) s. [pl. **(e)s**] caracol marino; *(shell)* caracola.

con·cil·i·ate (kən-sĭl′ē-āt′) tr. conciliar.

con·cil·i·a·tor (:ā′tər) s. mediador *m.*

con·cise (kən-sīs′) adj. conciso, sucinto.

con·clude (kən-klōōd′) tr. & intr. concluir.

con·clu·sion (:klōō′zhən) s. conclusión *f* ♦ **to bring to a c.** concluir.

con·clu·sive (:sĭv) adj. concluyente, decisivo.

con·coct (kən-kŏkt′) tr. *(food)* confeccionar, preparar; *(to invent)* fabricar.

con·coc·tion (:kŏk′shən) s. confección *f*; *(brew)* brebaje *m*; *(lie)* fabricación *f.*

con·cord (kŏn′kôrd′) s. concordia; *(treaty)* tratado.

con·course (kŏn′kôrs′) s. *(throng)* multitud *f*; *(for passengers)* salón *m*, vestíbulo.

con·crete (kŏn-krēt′) I. adj. concreto; CONSTR. (′′) de concreto o hormigón II. s. (′′) concreto, hormigón *m.*

con·cu·bine (kŏng′kyə-bīn′) s. concubina.

con·cu·pis·cent (kŏn-kyōō′pĭ-sənt) adj. concupiscente.

con·cur (kən-kûr′) intr. **-rr-** *(to agree)* convenir; *(to coincide)* concurrir, coincidir.

con·cur·rence (:əns) s. *(agreement)* acuerdo; *(coincidence)* concurrencia, coincidencia

con·cur·rent (:ənt) adj. concurrente.

con·cus·sion (kən-kŭsh′ən) s. *(shock)* concusión *f*; *(injury)* conmoción *f* cerebral.

con·demn (kən-dĕm′) tr. condenar; *(a building)* declarar inhabitable.

con·dem·na·ble (:nə-bəl) adj. condenable.

con·den·sa·tion (kŏn′dən-sā′shən) s. condensación *f*; LIT. versión condensada.

con·dense (kən-dĕns′) tr. & intr. condensar(se).

con·dens·er (:dĕn′sər) s. condensador *m.*

con·de·scend (kŏn′dĭ-sĕnd′) intr. dignarse.

con·de·scend·ing (:sĕn′dĭng) adj. condescendiente.

con·de·scen·sion (:shən) s. condescendencia.

con·di·ment (kŏn′də-mənt) s. condimento.

con·di·tion (kən-dĭsh′ən) I. s. condición *f*; *(health)* estado de salud ♦ **on c. that** a condición que • **on one c.** con una condición • **to be in no c. to** no estar en condiciones de • **to keep in c.** mantenerse en forma II. tr. *(to qualify, train)* condicionar; *(to make fit)* poner en condiciones; *(by exercising)* poner en forma; *(to adapt)* acostumbrar.

con·di·tion·al (:ə-nəl) adj. condicional ♦ **to be c. on** depender de.

con·di·tion·er (:nər) s. acondicionador *m.*

con·di·tion·ing (:nĭng) s. acondicionamiento.

con·do·lence (kən-dō′ləns) s. condolencia ♦ **to offer condolences to** dar el pésame a.

con·dom (kŏn′dəm) s. preservativo.

con·do·min·i·um (kŏn′də-mĭn′ē-əm) s. condominio.

con·done (kən-dōn′) tr. condonar.

con·dor (kŏn′dôr′) s. cóndor *m.*

con·du·cive (kən-dōō′sĭv) adj. ♦ **c. to** conducente a.

con·duct I. tr. (kən-dŭkt′) *(to direct)* dirigir (negocio, orquesta); *(to carry out)* llevar a cabo, hacer; *(a tour)* servir de guía a; FIS. conducir ♦ **to c. oneself** conducirse II. s. (kŏn′dŭkt′) *(behavior)* conducta, comportamiento; *(management)* dirección *f.*

con·duc·tor (kən-dŭk′tər) s. *(train, bus)* conductor *m*, cobrador *m*; MÚS. director *m*; FIS. conductor.

con·duit (kŏn′dĭt, :dōō-ĭt) s. conducto.

cone (kōn) s. cono; CUL. barquillo, cucurucho.

con·fect (kən-fĕkt′) tr. confeccionar.

con·fec·tion (:fĕk′shən) s. confección *f*; *(sweet)* confitura.

con·fec·tion·er (:shə-nər) s. confitero.

con·fed·er·a·cy (kən-fĕd′ər-ə-sē) s. confederación *f*; *(conspiracy)* complot *m.*

con·fed·er·ate I. adj. & s. (:ər-ĭt) confederado II. tr. & intr. (:ə-rāt′) confederar(se).

con·fer (kən-fûr′) tr. & intr. **-rr-** conferir.

con·fer·ence (kŏn′fər-əns) s. *(assembly)* conferencia, congreso; *(meeting)* reunión *f.*

con·fer·ral (kən-fûr′əl) s. concesión *f.*

con·fess (kən-fĕs′) tr. confesar —intr. confesar; RELIG. confesarse.

con·fessed (:fĕst′) adj. declarado.

con·fes·sion (:fĕsh′ən) s. confesión *f.*

con·fes·sion·al (:ə-nəl) I. adj. confesional II. s. confesionario.

con·fes·sor (kən-fĕs′ər) s. *(priest)* confesor *m*; *(sinner)* penitente *mf.*

con·fet·ti (kən-fĕt′ē) s.pl. confeti *m.*

con·fi·dant (kŏn′fĭ-dänt′) s. confidente *mf.*

con·fide (kən-fīd′) tr. & intr. confiar.

con·fi·dence (kŏn′fĭ-dəns) s. confianza; *(secret)* confidencia ♦ **c. man** estafador • **to place one's c. in** confiar en • **to take someone into one's c.** confiarse a alguien.

con·fi·dent (:dənt) s. *(certain)* seguro; *(self-assured)* confiado; *(manner)* de confianza.

con·fi·den·tial (′-dĕn′shəl) adj. confidencial, privado.

con·fi·den·ti·al·i·ty (′-′ shē-ăl′ĭ-tē) s. carácter confidencial *o* privado.

con·fid·ing (kən-fī′dĭng) adj. confiado.

con·fig·u·ra·tion (kən-fĭg′yə-rā′shən) s. configuración *f.*

con·fine (kən-fīn′) I. tr. *(person)* confinar, recluir; *(answer)* limitar ♦ **to be confined to bed** tener que guardar cama II. s. (kŏn′fīn′) ♦ pl. confines.

con·fine·ment (:mənt) s. *(seclusion)* confinamiento, reclusión *f*; *(restriction)* limitación *f*; *(lying-in)* parto ♦ **in solitary c.** incomunicado.

con·firm (kən-fûrm′) tr. confirmar; POL. ratificar.

con·firmed (:fûrmd′) adj. confirmado; POL. ra-

tificado; *(inveterate)* habitual.

con·fis·cate (kŏn′fĭ-skāt′) tr. confiscar.

con·fla·gra·tion (kŏn′flə-grā′shən) s. conflagración *f.*

con·flict I. s. (kŏn′flĭkt′) conflicto ♦ **to be in c. with** estar en pugna con • **to come into c.** chocar II. intr. (kən-flĭkt′) contradecirse.

con·flict·ing (kən-flĭk′tĭng) adj. contradictorio.

con·flu·ence (kŏn′flōō-əns) s. confluencia.

con·form (kən-fôrm′) intr. conformarse, concordar; *(to standards, rules)* ajustarse —tr. ajustar.

con·form·ist (:fôr′mĭst) s. conformista *mf.*

con·for·mi·ty (:mĭ-tē) s. conformidad *f* ♦ **in c. with** conforme a.

con·found (kən-found′) tr. confundir ♦ **c. it!** ¡maldito sea!

con·front (kən-frŭnt′) tr. *(to face)* enfrentar, hacer frente a; *(to encounter)* encontrar; *(dangers)* arrostrar.

con·fuse (kən-fyōōz′) tr. confundir.

con·fused (:fyōōzd′) adj. *(bewildered)* confundido, desconcertado; *(disordered)* confuso.

con·fus·ing (:fyōō′zĭng) adj. confuso.

con·fu·sion (:zhən) s. confusión *f* ♦ **to be in c.** *(person)* estar confundido; *(things)* estar en desorden.

con·fute (kən-fyōōt′) tr. confutar, refutar.

con·geal (kən-jēl′) tr. & intr. *(to freeze)* congelar(se); *(to coagulate)* coagular(se).

con·gen·ial (kən-jēn′yəl) adj. *(kindred)* afín; *(sociable)* simpático; *(suitable)* agradable.

con·gen·i·tal (kən-jĕn′ĭ-tl) adj. congénito.

con·ger eel (kŏng′gər) s. congrio.

con·gest (kən-jĕst′) tr. & intr. congestionar(se).

con·gest·ed (:jĕs′tĭd) adj. *(by traffic)* congestionado; *(area)* superpoblado; *(chest, nose)* constipado.

con·ges·tion (:chən) s. congestión *f.*

con·glom·er·ate (kən-glŏm′ə-rāt′) I. tr. & intr. conglomerar(se) II. s. & adj. (:ər-ĭt) conglomerado.

con·glom·er·a·tion (′-′-rā′shən) s. conglomeración *f.*

con·grat·u·late (kən-grăch′ə-lāt′) tr. felicitar ♦ **to c. oneself** congratularse.

con·grat·u·la·tion (′-′-lā′shən) s. felicitación *f*, congratulación *f* ♦ **congratulations!** ¡felicidades!, ¡enhorabuena!

con·grat·u·la·to·ry (′-′-lə-tôr′ē) adj. de felicitación.

con·gre·gate (kŏng′grĭ-gāt′) intr. & tr. congregar(se).

con·gre·ga·tion (′-gā′shən) s. congregación *f*, reunión *f*; RELIG. *(worshipers)* feligreses *m*; *(order)* congregación.

con·gress (kŏng′grĭs) s. congreso.

con·gres·sion·al (kən-grĕsh′ə-nəl) adj. del congreso.

con·gress·man (kŏng′grĭs-mən) s. [pl. **-men**] E.U. diputado de la Cámara de Representantes.

con·gress·wom·an (:wŏm′ən) s. [pl. **-women**] E.U. diputada de la Cámara de Representantes.

con·gru·ous (kŏng′grōō-əs) adj. congruente.

con·ic/·i·cal (kŏn′ĭk) adj. cónico.

con·i·fer (kŏn′ə-fər) s. conífera.

co·nif·er·ous (kə-nĭf′ər-əs) adj. conífero.

con·jec·tur·al (kən-jĕk′chər-əl) adj. conjetural.

con·jec·ture (:chər) I. s. conjetura II. tr. conjeturar —intr. hacer conjeturas.

con·ju·gal (kŏn′jə-gəl) adj. conyugal.

con·ju·gate (kŏn′jə-gāt′) I. tr. & intr. conjugar(se) II. adj. (:gĭt) conjugado.

con·ju·ga·tion (′-gā′shən) s. conjugación f.

con·junc·tion (kən-jŭngk′shən) s. conjunción f ♦ **in c. with** conjuntamente con.

con·junc·ti·vi·tis (-′tə-vī′tĭs) s. conjuntivitis f.

con·junc·ture (-′chər) s. coyuntura.

con·jure (kŏn′jər) tr. ♦ **to c. up** (a spirit) invocar; (by magic) hacer aparecer por arte de magia; (to evoke) evocar —intr. hacer juegos de manos.

con·jur·er/·or (:ər) s. mago.

conk (kŏngk) tr. FAM. golpear en el coco —intr. ♦ **to c. out** (machine) romperse; (person) caerse redondo.

con·nect (kə-nĕkt′) tr. (to join) conectar, unir; (to associate) vincular, relacionar; TEL. poner en comunicación; ELEC. conectar —intr. unirse; (rooms) comunicarse; (buses, trains) hacer combinación.

con·nect·ed (kə-nĕk′tĭd) adj. conectado; (socially) relacionado, enchufado.

con·nec·tion (:shən) s. conexión f; (association) vínculo, relación f; (social) enchufe m, relación; (buses, trains) combinación f ♦ **in c. with** en relación con.

con·nec·tive (:tĭv) adj. conectivo.

con·nec·tor/·er (:tər) s. MEC. conectador m; ELEC. hilo de conexión.

con·ning tower (kŏn′ĭng) s. torre f (de mando).

con·nive (kə-nīv′) intr. intrigar, conspirar.

con·niv·ing (kə-nī′vĭng) adj. confabulador m.

con·nois·seur (kŏn′ə-sûr′) s. conocedor m.

con·no·ta·tion (:tā′shən) s. connotación f.

con·note (kə-nōt′) tr. connotar.

con·quer (kŏng′kər) tr. conquistar; (enemy, disease) vencer —intr. vencer, triunfar.

con·quer·or (:ər) s. conquistador m, vencedor m.

con·quest (kŏng′kwĕst′) s. conquista.

con·science (kŏn′shəns) s. conciencia ♦ **in all c.** en conciencia • **to have something on one's c.** tener un cargo de conciencia.

conscience-strick·en (:strĭk′ən) adj. arrepentido, con remordimientos de conciencia.

con·sci·en·tious (kŏn′shē-ĕn′shəs) adj. concienzudo ♦ **c. objector** objetor de conciencia.

con·scious (kŏn′shəs) adj. consciente; (intentional) deliberado ♦ **to become c.** volver en sí • **to become c. of** darse cuenta de.

con·scious·ness (:nĭs) s. (awareness) conciencia; FISIOL. conocimiento.

con·script MIL. I. tr. (kən-skrĭpt′) reclutar, alistar II. s. (kŏn′skrĭpt′) recluta m, conscripto.

con·scrip·tion (kən-skrĭp′shən) s. conscripción f, reclutamiento.

con·se·crate (kŏn′sĭ-krāt′) tr. consagrar.

con·sec·u·tive (kən-sĕk′yə-tĭv) adj. consecutivo.

con·sen·sus (kən-sĕn′səs) s. consenso ♦ **c. of opinion** opinión o consenso general.

con·sent (kən-sĕnt′) I. intr. consentir II. s. consentimiento.

con·se·quence (kŏn′sĭ-kwĕns′) s. consecuencia; (importance) importancia ♦ **in c.** por consiguiente.

con·se·quent (:kwĕnt′) adj. consiguiente.

con·se·quen·tial (′-kwĕn′shəl) adj. consiguiente; (significant) de consecuencia.

con·se·quent·ly (′-kwĕnt′lē) adv. por consiguiente.

guiente.

con·ser·va·tion (kŏn′sər-vā′shən) s. conservación f.

con·ser·va·tism (kən-sûr′və-tĭz′əm) s. conservadurismo.

con·ser·va·tive (:tĭv) I. adj. (traditional) conservador; (moderate) moderado; (cautious) prudente II. s. conservador m.

con·ser·va·tor (:tər) s. DER. tutor m.

con·ser·va·to·ry (:tôr′ē) s. (for plants) invernadero; (school) conservatorio.

con·serve (kən-sûrv′) tr. conservar.

con·sid·er (kən-sĭd′ər) tr. & intr. considerar ♦ **all things considered** considerando todos los puntos • **to c. oneself** considerarse.

con·sid·er·a·ble (:ə-bəl) adj. considerable.

con·sid·er·ate (:ĭt) adj. considerado, atento.

con·sid·er·a·tion (kən-sĭd′ə-rā′shən) s. consideración f; (payment) retribución f ♦ **after due c.** después de un detenido examen • **in c. of** en reconocimiento de • **out of c. for** por respeto a • **under c.** en consideración.

con·sid·er·ing (-′ər-ĭng) I. prep. considerando II. adv. FAM. después de todo.

con·sign (kən-sīn′) tr. consignar.

con·sign·ee (:sī′nē′) s. consignatario.

con·sign·ment (:sīn′mənt) s. consignación f.

con·sig·nor (:sī′nôr′) s. consignador m.

con·sist (kən-sĭst′) intr. consistir (of, in en).

con·sis·ten·cy (:sĭs′tən-sē) s. (agreement) coherencia, acuerdo; (texture) consistencia.

con·sis·tent (:tənt) adj. (in agreement) coherente, de acuerdo; (uniform) consistente.

con·so·la·tion (kŏn′sə-lā′shən) s. consolación f, consuelo.

con·sole¹ (kən-sōl′) tr. consolar.

con·sole² (kŏn′sōl′) s. (cabinet) gabinete m (de radio o televisor); TEC. tablero de mando.

con·sol·i·date (kən-sōl′ĭ-dāt′) tr. & intr. consolidar(se); (to merge) fusionar(se).

con·so·nant (kŏn′sə-nənt) adj. & s. consonante f.

con·sort I. s. (kŏn′sôrt′) consorte mf II. tr. & intr. (kən-sôrt′) asociar(se), juntar(se).

con·sor·ti·um (kən-sôr′shē-əm) s. [pl. -ia] consorcio.

con·spic·u·ous (kən-spĭk′yŏŏ-əs) adj. (noticeable) destacado, evidente; (remarkable) conspicuo ♦ **to be c.** destacar(se) • **to be c. by one's absence** brillar uno por su ausencia.

con·spir·a·cy (kən-spĭr′ə-sē) s. conspiración f.

con·spir·a·tor (:tər) s. conspirador m.

con·spire (kən-spīr′) intr. conspirar.

con·sta·ble (kŏn′stə-bəl) s. (peace officer) alguacil m; G.B. policía m.

con·stab·u·lar·y (kən-stăb′yə-lĕr′ē) s. policía f.

con·stan·cy (kŏn′stən-sē) s. constancia; (faithfulness) lealtad f.

con·stant (kŏn′stənt) I. adj. constante; (faithful) leal; (changeless) invariable II. s. constante f.

con·stel·la·tion (kŏn′stə-lā′shən) s. constelación f.

con·ster·na·tion (kŏn′stər-nā′shən) s. consternación f.

con·sti·pate (kŏn′stə-pāt′) tr. estreñir.

con·sti·pa·tion (′-pā′shən) s. estreñimiento.

con·stit·u·en·cy (kən-stĭch′ŏŏ-ən-sē) s. (voters) electorado; (district) distrito electoral.

con·stit·u·ent (:ənt) I. adj. constituyente; (electoral) electoral II. s. componente m; (voter) elector m.

con·sti·tute (kŏn'stĭ-tōōt') tr. constituir.

con·sti·tu·tion ('-tōō'shən) s. constitución f.

con·sti·tu·tion·al (:shə-nəl) adj. constitucional.

con·strain (kən-strān') tr. *(to oblige)* constreñir, compeler; *(to restrict)* restringir.

con·straint (:strānt') s. *(coercion)* constreñimiento; *(restriction)* limitación f; *(embarrassment)* molestia.

con·strict (kən-strĭkt') tr. & intr. estrechar(se), encoger(se); *(to compress)* comprimir(se).

con·struct (kən-strŭkt') tr. construir.

con·struc·tion (:strŭk'shən) s. construcción f; *(structure)* estructura; *(interpretation)* interpretación f ♦ **c.** en construcción.

con·struc·tive (:tĭv) adj. constructivo.

con·strue (kən-strōō') tr. interpretar.

con·sul (kŏn'səl) s. cónsul m.

con·su·late (:sə-lĭt) s. consulado m.

con·sult (kən-sŭlt') tr. & intr. consultar.

con·sult·ant (:sŭl'tənt) s. consultor m.

con·sum·a·ble (kən-sōō'mə-bəl) I. adj. consumible ♦ **c. resources** recursos de consumo II. s. artículo de consumo.

con·sume (kən-sōōm') tr. consumir; *(food)* tragar; *(time, effort)* tomar ♦ **to be consumed with** consumirse de.

con·sum·er (:sōō'mər) s. consumidor m ♦ **c. goods** bienes de consumo.

con·sum·er·ism (:mə-rĭz'əm) s. movimiento de protección al consumidor.

con·sum·mate I. tr. (kŏn'sə-māt') consumar II. adj. (:mət, kən-sŭm'ĭt) consumado.

con·sum·ma·tion (kŏn'sə-mā'shən) s. consumación f; *(of a goal)* culminación f.

con·sump·tion (kən-sŭmp'shən) s. consumo; MED. consunción f.

con·sump·tive (:tĭv) I. adj. consuntivo; MED. tísico II. s. tísico.

con·tact (kŏn'tăkt') I. s. contacto; *(connection)* relación f ♦ **c. lens** lente de contacto • **to come, get in c. with** entrar, ponerse en contacto con II. tr. ponerse en contacto con III. adj. de contacto.

con·ta·gion (kən-tā'jən) s. contagio.

con·ta·gious (:jəs) adj. contagioso.

con·tain (kən-tān') tr. contener ♦ **to c. oneself** contenerse.

con·tain·er (:tā'nər) s. recipiente m, envase m; COM. contenedor m ♦ **c. ship** buque de carga (en contenedores).

con·tain·er·ize (:nə-rīz') tr. embalar en contenedor.

con·tain·ment (kən-tān'mənt) s. contención f.

con·tam·i·nant (kən-tăm'ə-nənt) s. contaminador m, contaminante m.

con·tam·i·nate (:nāt') tr. contaminar.

con·tem·plate (kŏn'təm-plāt') tr. contemplar; *(to intend)* pensar, proyectar.

con·tem·pla·tion ('-plā'shən) s. contemplación f; *(intention)* intención f, perspectiva.

con·tem·po·ra·ne·ous (kən-tĕm'pə-rā'nē-əs) adj. contemporáneo.

con·tem·po·rar·y (-'-rĕr'ē) adj. & s. contemporáneo, coetáneo.

con·tempt (kən-tĕmpt') s. desprecio, desdén m; DER. desacato ♦ **beneath c.** despreciable • **to hold in c.** despreciar.

con·temp·ti·ble (:tĕmp'tə-bəl) adj. despreciable.

con·temp·tu·ous (:chōō-əs) adj. despreciativo.

con·tend (kən-tĕnd') intr. contender —tr.

mantener, sostener.

con·tend·er (:tĕn'dər) s. contendiente mf.

con·tent¹ (kŏn'tĕnt') s. contenido; *(meaning)* significado ♦ pl. contenido, materia.

con·tent² (kən-tĕnt') I. adj. contento, satisfecho ♦ **to be c. with** conformarse con II. tr. contentar; satisfacer III. s. satisfacción f.

con·tent·ed (:tĕn'tĭd) adj. contento, satisfecho.

con·ten·tion (kən-tĕn'shən) s. *(conflict)* disputa; *(rivalry)* competencia; *(assertion)* argumento.

con·tent·ment (kən-tĕnt'mənt) s. satisfacción f.

con·test I. s. (kŏn'tĕst') *(struggle)* contienda; *(competition)* competencia, concurso II. tr. (kən-tĕst') cuestionar, impugnar —intr. contender.

con·tes·tant (kən-tĕs'tənt) s. *(rival)* contendiente mf; *(participant)* concursante mf.

con·text (kŏn'tĕkst') s. contexto.

con·tig·u·ous (kən-tĭg'yōō-əs) adj. contiguo.

con·ti·nence (kŏn'tə-nəns) s. continencia.

con·ti·nent (:nənt) adj. & s. continente m.

con·ti·nen·tal (kŏn'tə-nĕn'tl) adj. continental ♦ **C.** europeo • **c. breakfast** desayuno completo.

con·tin·gen·cy (kən-tĭn'jən-sē) s. contingencia.

con·tin·gent (:jənt) I. adj. contingente, eventual ♦ **to be c. on** depender de II. s. contingente m.

con·tin·u·al (kən-tĭn'yōō-əl) adj. continuo.

con·tin·u·a·tion (-'-ā'shən) s. continuación f.

con·tin·ue (kən-tĭn'yōō) intr. continuar, seguir; *(to last)* prolongarse, durar ♦ **to be continued** continuará —tr. continuar; *(to prolong)* prolongar; DER. *(to postpone)* aplazar.

con·ti·nu·i·ty (kŏn'tə-nōō'ĭ-tē) s. continuidad f.

con·tin·u·ous (kən-tĭn'yōō-əs) adj. continuo.

con·tin·u·um (:əm) s. [pl. **a** o **-ua**] continuo.

con·tort (kən-tôrt') tr. torcer, retorcer —intr. desfigurarse (el rostro).

con·tor·tion (:tôr'shən) s. contorsión f.

con·tour (kŏn'tōōr') s. contorno; TOP. curva de nivel.

con·tra·band (kŏn'trə-bănd') adj. & s. (de) contrabando.

con·tra·bass (:bās') s. contrabajo.

con·tra·cep·tion ('-sĕp'shən) s. contracepción f.

con·tra·cep·tive (:tĭv) adj. & s. anticonceptivo.

con·tract I. s. (kŏn'trăkt') contrato II. tr. (kən-trăkt') *(to agree to)* contratar; *(to acquire)* contraer; *(to shrink)* contraer, encoger —intr. contraerse, encogerse.

con·trac·tion (kən-trăk'shən) s. contracción f.

con·trac·tor (kŏn'trăk'tər) s. contratista mf.

con·tra·dict (kŏn'trə-dĭkt') tr. contradecir ♦ **to c. oneself** contradecirse.

con·tra·dic·tion (:dĭk'shən) s. contradicción f.

con·trail (kŏn'trāl') s. estela de condensación.

con·trap·tion (kən-trăp'shən) s. artefacto.

con·tra·pun·tal (kŏn'trə-pŭn'tl) adj. de contrapunto.

con·tra·ri·e·ty (:rī'ə-tē) s. contrariedad f.

con·trar·y (kŏn'trĕr'ē) I. adj. contrario; *(ornery)* terco II. s. lo contrario, lo opuesto ♦ **on** o **to the c.** al o por el contrario • **quite the c.!** ¡todo lo contrario! III. adv. ♦ **c. to** en contra de.

con·trast I. tr. & intr. (kən-trăst') (hacer) contrastar II. s. (kŏn'trăst') contraste m ♦ **in c.** por contraste • **in c. to** a diferencia de.

con·tra·vene (kŏn'trə-vēn') tr. contravenir.

con·trib·ute (kən-trĭb′yŏot) tr. contribuir; *(an article)* escribir *(to para)*; *(information)* aportar —intr. contribuir; PERIOD. colaborar.

con·tri·bu·tion (kŏn′trĭ-byŏo′shən) s. contribución *f.*

con·trib·u·tor (kən-trĭb′yə-tər) s. contribuidor *m*, colaborador *m.*

con·trite (kən-trīt′, kŏn′trīt′) adj. contrito.

con·tri·tion (kən-trĭsh′ən) s. contrición *f.*

con·tri·vance (kən-trī′vəns) s. invento.

con·trive (kən-trīv′) tr. inventar, idear ♦ **to c.** to conseguir (hacer algo).

con·trived (:trīvd′) adj. artificial.

con·trol (kən-trōl′) I. tr. -ll- controlar, dirigir; *(to regulate)* regular; *(passions)* dominar ♦ **to c. oneself** dominarse II. s. control *m*; *(restraint)* dominio ♦ **out of** o **beyond c.** fuera de control • **to be in c.** tener el mando ♦ **to get out of c.** desmandarse ♦ pl. mandos, controles.

con·trol·la·ble (:trō′lə-bəl) adj. controlable.

con·trol·ler (:lər) s. MEC. regulador *m*, control *m*; AVIA. controlador *m*; POL. interventor *m.*

con·trol·ling (:lĭng) adj. predominante, determinante ♦ **c. interest** mayoría de acciones.

con·tro·ver·sial (kŏn′trə-vûr′shəl) adj. polémico, discutible.

con·tro·ver·sy (′-′sē) s. controversia, polémica.

con·tu·sion (kən-tŏo′zhən) s. contusión *f.*

co·nun·drum (kə-nŭn′drəm) s. enigma *m.*

con·va·lesce (kŏn′və-lĕs′) intr. convalecer.

con·va·les·cence (:əns) s. convalecencia.

con·vec·tion (kən-vĕk′shən) s. convección *f.*

con·vene (kən-vēn′) intr. reunirse —tr. convocar.

con·ven·ience (kən-vēn′yəns) s. *(suitability)* conveniencia; *(comfort)* comodidad *f*; *(device)* dispositivo útil; G.B. *(toilet)* baño ♦ **at your c.** cuando guste • **at your earliest c.** tan pronto como le sea posible.

con·ven·ient (:yənt) adj. *(suitable)* conveniente; *(handy)* útil; *(comfortable)* cómodo.

con·vent (kŏn′vənt) s. convento.

con·ven·tion (kən-vĕn′shən) s. convención *f*; *(custom)* costumbre *f*, regla convencional.

con·ven·tion·al (:shə-nəl) adj. convencional; *(accepted)* corriente; *(war, weapons)* clásico.

con·ven·tion·al·i·ty (′-′năl′ĭ-tē) s. convencionalismo.

con·ven·tion·eer (:nîr′) s. convencionista *mf.*

con·verge (kən-vûrj′) intr. converger.

con·ver·sant (kən-vûr′sənt) adj. ♦ **c. with** versado en.

con·ver·sa·tion (kŏn′vər-sā′shən) s. conversación *f* ♦ **to make c.** dar conversación, platicar.

con·ver·sa·tion·al (:shə-nəl) adj. *(tone)* familiar; *(method)* de conversación.

con·verse¹ (kən-vûrs′) intr. conversar.

con·verse² (kŏn′vûrs′) adj. & s. (lo) opuesto, (lo) contrario.

con·verse·ly (kən-vûrs′lē) adv. a la inversa.

con·ver·sion (kən-vûr′zhən) s. conversión *f.*

con·vert I. tr. & intr. (kən-vûrt′) convertir(se) II. s. (kŏn′vûrt) converso.

con·vert·er/·tor (kən-vûr′tər) s. convertidor *m.*

con·vert·i·ble (:tə-bəl) I. adj. convertible II. s. AUTO. descapotable *m.*

con·vex (kŏn′vĕks′, kən-vĕks′) adj. convexo.

con·vey (kən-vā′) tr. *(to carry)* transportar, llevar; *(to transmit)* transmitir; *(a meaning)* comunicar, dar a entender.

con·vey·ance (:əns) s. transporte *m*; *(vehicle)* vehículo; DER. *(transfer)* cesión *f*, traspaso.

con·vey·er/or (:ər) s. transportador *m*; *(belt)* cinta transportadora.

con·vict I. tr. (kən-vĭkt′) declarar culpable, condenar II. s. (kŏn′vĭkt′) convicto.

con·vic·tion (kən-vĭk′shən) s. convicción *f*; DER. condena ♦ **to carry c.** ser convincente.

con·vince (kən-vĭns′) tr. convencer.

con·viv·i·al (kən-vĭv′ē-əl) adj. *(sociable)* sociable; *(festive)* jovial, festivo.

con·vo·ca·tion (kŏn′və-kā′shən) s. convocación *f*; *(assembly)* asamblea.

con·voke (kən-vōk′) tr. convocar.

con·vo·lut·ed (kŏn′və-lŏo′tĭd) adj. *(coiled)* enrollado; *(intricate)* intrincado, complicado.

con·vo·lu·tion (:shən) s. enrollamiento.

con·voy (kŏn′voi′) I. tr. convoyar II. s. convoy *m.*

con·vulse (kən-vŭls′) tr. convulsionar ♦ **to be convulsed with laughter** estar muerto de risa —intr. padecer convulsiones.

con·vul·sion (:vŭl′shən) s. convulsión *f*; *(laughter)* ataque *m* de risa.

coo (kŏo) I. s. arrullo II. intr. arrullar.

cook (kŏok) I. tr. cocinar, guisar; TEC. cocer ♦ **to c. up** FAM. inventar —intr. *(food)* cocinarse; *(chef)* cocinar ♦ **what's cooking?** FAM. ¿qué pasa? II. s. cocinero.

cook·book (′bŏok′) s. libro de cocina.

cook·ie (:ē) var. de **cooky.**

cook·ing (:ĭng) adj. & s. (de) cocina.

cook·out (:out′) s. comida cocinada al aire libre.

cook·y (:ē) s. galletita, bizcochito.

cool (kŏol) I. adj. fresco; *(calm)* tranquilo; *(unenthusiastic)* frío; JER. *(excellent)* fenomenal ♦ **a c. (million)** la friolera de (un millón de dólares) • **as c. as a cucumber** más fresco que una lechuga • **to keep c.** no perder la calma • **to play it c.** tomarlo con calma II. tr. & intr. refrescar(se), enfriar(se); *(passions)* entibiar(se) ♦ **c. it!** JER. ¡cálmate! • **to c. off** o **down** *(to get colder)* refrescarse; *(to calm down)* calmarse III. s. fresco, frescor *m* ♦ **to keep, lose one's c.** conservar, perder la serenidad.

cool·ant (kŏo′lənt) s. líquido refrigerante.

cool·er (:lər) s. enfriador *m.*

coo·lie (kŏo′lē) s. culi *m.*

cool·ing (kŏo′lĭng) adj. refrescante.

cool·ly (kŏol′lē) adv. *(coldly)* friamente, con frialdad; *(calmly)* tranquilamente.

cool·ness (:nĭs) s. frescor *m*, fresco; *(calmness)* calma; *(lack of enthusiasm)* frialdad *f.*

coon (kŏon) s. FAM. mapache *m.*

coop (kŏop) I. s. gallinero ♦ **to fly the c.** fugarse, escaparse II. tr. ♦ **to c. up** enjaular.

co-op (kŏ′ŏp′) s. FAM. cooperativa.

coo·per (kŏo′pər) s. barrilero, cubero.

co·op·er·ate (kŏ-ŏp′ə-rāt′) intr. cooperar.

co·op·er·a·tive (:ər-ə-tĭv′) I. adj. *(joint)* cooperativo; *(helpful)* servicial II. s. cooperativa.

co·or·di·nate (kŏ-ôr′dn-ĭt) I. s. coordenada II. adj. coordinado; *(equal)* igual, semejante III. tr. & intr. (:āt′) coordinar(se).

co·or·di·na·tor (:ā′tər) s. coordinador *m.*

cop (kŏp) I. s. FAM. policía *m* II. tr. -pp- JER. robar ♦ **to c. out** echarse atrás.

co·part·ner (kŏ-pärt′nər) s. consocio.

cope (kŏp) intr. FAM. *(to strive)* arreglárselas *(with para)*; *(to face up)* hacer frente *(with a).*

cop·i·er (kŏp′ē-ər) s. copiadora.

co·pi·lot (kŏ′pī′lət) s. copiloto.

cop·ing (kŏ′pĭng) s. albardilla.

co·pi·ous (kō′pē-əs) adj. copioso, abundante.
co-plain·tiff (kō-plān′tĭf) s. codemandante *mf.*
cop-out (kŏp′out′) s. JER. rendición *f*, resignación *f*.
cop·per¹ (kŏp′ər) I. s. cobre *m* II. adj. (de) cobre; *(color)* cobrizo.
cop·per² s. JER. policía *m.*
cop·per·y (:ē) adj. cobrizo.
copse (kŏps) s. bosquecillo, soto.
cop·ter (kŏp′tər) s. FAM. helicóptero.
cop·u·late (kŏp′yə-lāt′) intr. copularse.
cop·u·la·tion (:lā′shən) s. cópula.
cop·y (kŏp′ē) I. s. copia; *(book, magazine)* ejemplar *m*; IMPR. original *m*, material *m* ♦ **c. editor** redactor *s.* ♦ **to make a c.** of copiar, sacar una copia de II. tr. copiar, sacar en limpio; *(to imitate)* imitar —intr. hacer una copia; *(to cheat)* copiar (en un examen).
cop·y·cat (:kăt′) s. FAM. imitador *m.*
cop·y-ed·it (:ĕd′ĭt) tr. corregir (manuscrito).
cop·y·right (:rīt′) I. s. propiedad literaria II. tr. registrar como propiedad literaria.
cop·y·writ·er (:rī′tər) s. redactor *m* de textos publicitarios.
co·quette (kō-kĕt′) s. coqueta.
cor·al (kôr′əl) adj. & s. (de) coral *m.*
cord (kôrd) s. cuerda; ELEC. cordón *m*; TEJ. pana ♦ pl. FAM. pantalones de pana.
cor·dial (kôr′jəl) I. adj. amable II. s. cordial *m.*
cor·dial·i·ty (kôr-jăl′ĭ-tē) s. amabilidad *f.*
cord·less (kôrd′lĭs) adj. a baterías, a pilas.
cor·don (kôr′dn) I. s. cordón *m* II. tr. ♦ **to c. off** acordonar.
cor·do·van (kôr′də-vən) s. cordobán *m.*
cor·du·roy (kôr′də-roi′) s. pana ♦ pl. pantalones de pana.
core (kôr) I. s. *(essence)* corazón *m*, médula; *(center)* núcleo, foco; *(of fruit)* corazón; *(of reactor)* núcleo; COMPUT. nucleo magnético ♦ **to the c.** hasta la médula II. tr. quitar el corazón de.
co·re·spon·dent (kō′rĭ-spŏn′dənt) s. cómplice *m* del demandado en un divorcio.
co·ri·an·der (kôr′ē-ăn′dər) s. cilantro.
cork (kôrk) I. s. corcho ♦ **to blow one's c.** FAM. explotar, enojarse II. tr. encorchar.
cork·er (kôr′kər) s. FAM. mentira grande.
cork·screw (kôrk′skrōō′) s. tirabuzón *m*, sacacorchos *m.*
cor·mo·rant (kôr′mər-ənt) s. cuervo marino.
corn¹ (kôrn) s. maíz *m*; JER. *(sentimentality)* sensiblería; G.B. *(wheat)* trigo ♦ **c. flakes** copos de maíz ♦ **c. on the cob** maíz en la mazorca.
corn² s. MED. callo, callosidad *f.*
corn·ball (:bôl′) adj. JER. demasiado obvio.
corn·cob (:kŏb′) s. mazorca.
corn·crib (:krĭb′) s. granero.
cor·ne·a (kôr′nē-ə) s. córnea.
corned beef (kôrnd) s. carne *f* en conserva.
cor·ner (kôr′nər) I. s. esquina; *(inside)* rincón *m*; *(of eye)* rabillo; *(of mouth)* comisura; *(predicament)* aprieto, apuro; *(spot, region)* rincón; COM. monopolio ♦ **out of the c.** of one's eye con el rabillo del ojo • **the four corners of the earth** las cinco partes del mundo • **to cut corners** hacer economías • **to drive someone into a c.** acorralar a alguien • **to turn the c.** doblar la esquina; *(to improve)* pasar el punto crítico II. tr. *(to trap)* arrinconar, acorralar; COM. monopolizar, acaparar.

cor·nered (:nərd) adj. arrinconado.
cor·ner·stone (:nər-stōn′) s. piedra angular.
cor·net s. (kôr-nĕt′) cornetín *m.*
cor·nice (kôr′nĭs) s. cornisa.
corn·meal (kôrn′mēl′) s. harina de maíz.
corn·stalk (:stôk′) s. tallo del maíz.
corn·starch (:stärch′) s. maicena.
corn·y (kôr′nē) adj. **-i-** *(mawkish)* sensiblero; *(joke)* demasiado obvio.
co·rol·la (kə-rŏl′ə, -rō′lə) s. corola.
cor·ol·lar·y (kôr′ə-lĕr′ē) I. s. corolario II. adj. consecuente.
cor·o·nar·y (kôr′ə-nĕr′ē) adj. & s. coronario.
cor·o·na·tion (kôr′ə-nā′shən) s. coronación *f.*
cor·o·ner (kôr′ə-nər) s. pesquisidor *m* (que investiga la causa de un fallecimiento).
cor·o·net (kôr′ə-nĕt′) s. corona, diadema.
cor·po·ral¹ (kôr′pər-əl) adj. corporal ♦ **c. punishment** castigo corporal.
cor·po·ral² s. MIL. cabo.
cor·po·rate (kôr′pər-ĭt) adj. corporativo; *(joint)* colectivo.
cor·po·ra·tion (′pə-rā′shən) s. corporación *f*, sociedad anónima.
cor·po·re·al (kôr-pôr′ē-əl) adj. corpóreo.
corps (kôr) s.inv. cuerpo.
corpse (kôrps) s. cadáver *m.*
cor·pu·lence (kôr′pyə-ləns) s. corpulencia.
cor·pu·lent (:lənt) adj. corpulento.
cor·pus (kôr′pəs) s. [pl. **-pora**] cuerpo.
cor·pus·cle (kôr′pə-səl) s. corpúsculo.
cor·ral (kə-răl′) I. s. corral *m* II. tr. **-ll-** acorralar; FAM. *(to seize)* capturar.
cor·rect (kə-rĕkt′) I. tr. corregir; *(to remedy)* remediar; *(to adjust)* ajustar —intr. hacer correcciones o ajustes ♦ **to stand corrected** confesar que uno se equivocó II. adj. correcto ♦ **to be c.** tener razón.
cor·rec·tion (kə-rĕk′shən) s. corrección *f*; *(punishment)* castigo; *(adjustment)* ajuste *m.*
cor·rec·tive (:tĭv) adj. correctivo.
cor·rect·ness (kə-rĕkt′nĭs) s. *(propriety)* corrección *f*; *(accuracy)* exactitud *f.*
cor·re·late (kôr′ə-lāt′) I. tr. correlacionar —intr. estar en correlación II. adj. & s. correlativo.
cor·rel·a·tive (kə-rĕl′ə-tĭv) adj. & s. correlativo.
cor·re·spond (kôr′ĭ-spŏnd′) intr. corresponder; *(to write)* escribirse.
cor·re·spon·dence (:spŏn′dəns) s. correspondencia ♦ **c. course** curso por correspondencia.
cor·re·spon·dent (:dənt) I. s. correspondiente *mf*; PERIOD. corresponsal *mf* II. adj. correspondiente.
cor·re·spond·ing (:dĭng) adj. correspondiente.
cor·ri·dor (kôr′ĭ-dər) s. pasillo, corredor *m.*
cor·rob·o·rate (kə-rŏb′ə-rāt′) tr. corroborar.
cor·rode (kə-rōd′) tr. & intr. corroer(se).
cor·ro·sion (kə-rō′zhən) s. corrosión *f.*
cor·ro·sive (:sĭv) I. adj. corrosivo II. sustancia corrosiva.
cor·ru·gate (kôr′ə-gāt′) tr. & intr. estriar(se).
cor·ru·gat·ed (:gā′tĭd) adj. *(cardboard)* estriado; *(metal)* acanalado.
cor·rupt (kə-rŭpt′) I. adj. corrompido; *(dishonest)* corrupto II. tr. & intr. corromper(se).
cor·rupt·ing (kə-rŭp′tĭng) adj. corruptor.
cor·rup·tion (:shən) s. corrupción *f.*
cor·sage (kôr-säzh′) s. ramillete *m.*
cor·sair (kôr′sâr′) s. corsario.
cor·set (kôr′sĭt) s. corsé *m.*
cor·tege (kôr-tĕzh′) s. cortejo, séquito.

cor·tex (kôr′těks′) s. [pl. **es** o **-ices**] corteza.
cor·ti·sone (kôr′tĭ-sōn′) s. cortisona.
co·run·dum (kə-rŭn′dəm) s. corindón m.
cor·vette (kôr-vět′) s. corbeta.
co·sign (kō′sīn′) tr. firmar junto con otro; FIN. *(to endorse)* avalar.
co·sig·na·to·ry (kō-sĭg′nə-tôr′ē) s. cosignatario.
co·sign·er (kō′sī′nər) s. cosignatario.
cos·met·ic (kŏz-mět′ĭk) s. & adj. cosmético.
cos·mic (kŏz′mĭk) adj. cósmico.
cos·mol·o·gy (kŏz-mŏl′ə-jē) s. cosmología.
cos·mo·naut (kŏz′mə-nôt′) s. cosmonauta mf.
cos·mo·pol·i·tan (kŏz′mə-pŏl′ĭ-tn) adj. & s. cosmopolita mf.
cos·mop·o·lite (-mŏp′ə-līt′) s. cosmopolita mf.
cos·mos (kŏz′məs) s. cosmos m.
cost (kôst) I. s. costo, coste m; *(in time, effort)* costa ♦ **at all costs** o **at any c.** cueste lo que cueste • **at c.** a precio de costo • **at the c. of** a costa de ♦ pl. gastos; *(risks)* riesgos II. intr. **cost** costar.
co·star o **co-star** (kō′stär′) I. s. actor m de uno de los papeles estelares II. intr. **-rr-** ♦ **co-starring** con.
cost·ly (kôst′lē) adj. **-i-** caro; *(entailing loss)* costoso.
cost-plus (:plŭs′) s. costo de producción más una utilidad fija.
cos·tume (kŏs′tōōm′) I. s. *(dress)* traje m; *(disguise)* máscara, disfraz m ♦ **c. ball** baile de disfraces ♦ pl. TEAT. vestuario II. tr. vestir, disfrazar.
cos·tum·er (:tōō′mər) sastre m de teatro.
co·sy (kō′zē) var. de **cozy.**
cot (kŏt) s. catre m.
cote (kōt) s. redil m.
co·ten·ant (kō-těn′ənt) s. coinquilino.
co·ter·ie (kō′tə-rē) s. tertulia, camarilla.
co·ter·mi·nous (kō-tûr′mə-nəs) adj. limítrofe.
co·til·lion (kō-tĭl′yən) s. cotillón m.
cot·tage (kŏt′ĭj) s. casa de campo, chalet m ♦ **c. cheese** requesón, cuajada.
cot·ter pin (kŏt′ər) s. pasador m de chaveta.
cot·ton (kŏt′n) I. s. algodón m ♦ **c. gin** desmotadora • **c. wool** G.B. algodón absorbente II. intr. ♦ **c. to** FAM. sentirse atraído por.
cot·ton·seed (:sēd′) s. [pl. inv. o **s**] semilla de algodón.
cot·ton·tail (:tāl′) s. liebre f de cola blanca.
cot·ton·wood (:wŏŏd′) s. álamo de Virginia.
couch (kouch) I. s. sofá m II. tr. expresar, formular.
cou·gar (kōō′gər) s. puma m.
cough (kôf) I. intr. toser —tr. ♦ **to c. up** escupir; JER. *(money)* soltar II. s. tos f ♦ **c. drop** pastilla para la tos.
could (kŏŏd) cf. **can[1].**
coun·cil (koun′səl) s. consejo, junta; RELIG. concilio ♦ **city c.** concejo municipal.
coun·cil·man (:mən) s. [pl. **-men**] concejal m.
coun·cil·(l)or (koun′sə-lər) s. consejero.
coun·sel (koun′səl) I. s. *(advice)* consejo; *(consultation)* consulta; *(attorney)* abogado ♦ **c. for the defense** abogado defensor • **to keep one's own c.** guardar secreto • **to take c.** consultar II. tr. aconsejar —intr. consultar.
coun·sel·(l)or (:sə-lər) s. *(adviser)* consejero; *(lawyer)* abogado.
count[1] (kount) I. tr. contar; *(to deem)* considerar ♦ **to c. against** pesar contra • **to c. for** valer por • **to c. in** incluir • **to c. on** contar con

• **to c. out** excluir • **to c. up** contar —intr. contar; *(to matter)* tener importancia, valer ♦ **to c. down** contar hacia atrás II. s. *(act)* cuenta; *(number)* cómputo, cálculo ♦ **to keep, lose c. of** llevar, perder la cuenta de.
count[2] s. *(nobleman)* conde m.
count·down (′doun′) s. cuenta atrás.
coun·te·nance (koun′tə-nəns) I. s. semblante m, cara ♦ **to be out of c.** estar desconcertado • **to give c. to** sancionar II. tr. sancionar, aprobar.
coun·ter[1] (koun′tər) I. adj. & s. (lo) contrario, (lo) opuesto II. tr. *(a blow)* contrarrestar; *(to oppose)* oponerse a; *(to respond)* contestar III. adv. de modo contrario ♦ **to go** o **run c. to** ir en contra de.
coun·ter[2] s. mostrador m; *(of a kitchen)* tablero; *(chip, token)* ficha ♦ **over the c.** FIN. mediante un corredor de bolsa; *(drugs)* sin receta • **under the c.** por debajo del tapete.
coun·ter·act (′-ăkt′) tr. contrarrestar.
coun·ter·at·tack I. s. (′-ə-tăk′) contraataque m II. intr. & tr. (′-ə-tăk′) contraatacar.
coun·ter·bal·ance I. s. (′-băl′əns) contrapeso II. tr. (′-′-) contrapesar.
coun·ter·claim (′-klām′) s. contrademanda.
coun·ter·clock·wise (′-klŏk′wīz′) adv. & adj. en sentido contrario a las agujas del reloj.
coun·ter·cul·ture (′-kŭl′chər) s. contracultura.
coun·ter·es·pi·o·nage (′-ěs′pē-ə-näzh′) s. contraespionaje m.
coun·ter·feit (koun′tər-fĭt′) I. tr. falsificar, contrahacer; *(to feign)* fingir II. adj. contrahecho, falso; *(feigned)* fingido III. s. falsificación f, imitación f; *(money)* moneda falsa.
coun·ter·feit·er (:ər) s. falsificador m.
coun·ter·in·tel·li·gence (koun′tər-ĭn-tĕl′ə-jəns) s. contraespionaje m.
coun·ter·mand (:mănd′) tr. contramandar.
coun·ter·mea·sure (′-mězh′ər) s. contramedida.
coun·ter·of·fen·sive (:ə-fĕn′sĭv) s. contraofensiva.
coun·ter·pane (:pān′) s. colcha.
coun·ter·part (:pärt′) s. complemento.
coun·ter·plot (:plŏt′) s. contracomplot m.
coun·ter·point (:point′) s. contrapunto.
coun·ter·poise (:poiz′) I. s. contrapeso; *(equilibrium)* equilibrio II. tr. contrabalancear.
coun·ter·pro·duc·tive (′-prə-dŭk′tĭv) adj. contraproducente.
coun·ter·ref·or·ma·tion (:rĕf′ər-mā′shən) s. contrarreforma.
coun·ter·rev·o·lu·tion (:rĕv′ə-lōō′shən) s. contrarrevolución f.
coun·ter·sign (:sīn′) I. tr. refrendar II. s. refrendata; *(password)* contraseña.
coun·ter·sig·na·ture (:-sĭg′nə-chər) s. refrendata, aval m.
coun·ter·spy (′-spī′) s. contraespía mf.
coun·ter·weight (:wāt′) s. contrapeso.
count·ess (koun′tĭs) s. condesa.
count·ing (koun′tĭng) s. cuenta, contaje m.
count·ing·house (:hous′) s. oficina de contabilidad.
count·less (kount′lĭs) adj. incontable.
coun·try (kŭn′trē) s. país m; *(rural area)* campo; *(homeland)* patria ♦ **c. house** casa de campo, quinta.
coun·try·man (:mən) s. [pl. **-men**] compatriota mf.
coun·try·side (:sīd′) s. campo, paisaje m.

coun·try·wom·an (:wŏŏm'ən) s. [pl. **-women**] compatriota.

coun·ty (koun'tē) s. condado, distrito ♦ **c. seat** cabeza de distrito.

coup (kōō) s. golpe maestro; *(coup d'état)* golpe (de estado) ♦ **c. de grâce** golpe de gracia.

coup d'é·tat (kōō' dā-tä') s. golpe *m* de estado.

coupe/·pé (kōōp/kōō-pā') s. cupé *m*.

cou·ple (kŭp'əl) I. s. par *m*; *(of people)* pareja; *(several)* unos cuantos II. tr. juntar; TEC. acoplar —intr. juntarse; *(to mate)* acoplarse.

cou·pler (:lər) s. acoplador *m*; F.C. empalme *m*.

cou·plet (kŭp'lĭt) s. pareado.

cou·pon (kōō'pŏn') s. cupón *m*.

cour·age (kûr'ĭj) s. coraje *m*, valor *m* ♦ **to take c.** animarse.

cou·ra·geous (kə-rā'jəs) adj. valiente.

cou·ri·er (kŏŏr'ē-ər) s. correo, cosario.

course (kôrs) I. s. *(flow, path)* curso; *(duration)* transcurso; *(route)* rumbo; *(policy)* línea de conducta; *(of a meal)* plato; *(of studies)* programa *m*; *(subject)* curso; *(racetrack)* pista; *(in golf)* campo; *(of bricks)* hilada ♦ **c. of action** línea de acción • **in due c.** a su debido tiempo • **of c.** por supuesto, claro • **of c. not** por supuesto que no, claro que no • **to change c.** cambiar de rumbo • **to take** *o* **run its c.** seguir a su curso II. intr. correr.

court (kôrt) I. s. corte *f*; *(tribunal)* tribunal *m*; *(session)* audiencia; DEP. cancha ♦ **c. jester** bufón de la corte • **c. order** orden judicial • **to pay c. to** cortejar • **to settle out of c.** llegar a un arreglo • **to take to c.** llevar a los tribunales II. tr. *(to curry favor)* cortejar; *(to woo)* enamorar; *(to seek)* buscar; *(to invite)* ir en busca de —intr. hacer la corte.

cour·te·ous (kûr'tē-əs) adj. cortés, atento.

cour·te·san (kôr'tĭ-zən) s. cortesana.

cour·te·sy (kûr'tĭ-sē) s. cortesía ♦ **c. of** de parte de • **out of c.** por cortesía • **to do someone the c. of** tener la amabilidad de.

court·house (kôrt'hous') s. palacio de justicia.

court·i·er (kôr'tē-ər) s. cortesano.

court·ly (kôrt'lē) adj. -i- cortés.

court-mar·tial (:mär'shəl) s. [pl. **courts-**] consejo de guerra.

court·room (:rōōm') s. sala de justicia.

court·ship (:shĭp') s. corte *f*; *(period)* noviazgo.

court·yard (:yärd') s. patio.

cous·in (kŭz'ĭn) s. primo ♦ **first, second c.** primo hermano, segundo.

cove (kōv) s. abra, cala.

cov·en (kŭv'ən) s. reunión *f* de brujas.

cov·e·nant (kŭv'ə-nənt) s. convenio, pacto.

cov·er (kŭv'ər) I. tr. cubrir; *(to coat)* revestir; *(with a lid)* tapar; *(a book, chair)* forrar; *(a subject)* tratar; *(to clothe)* tapar; *(to encompass)* abarcar; *(to conceal)* ocultar; *(to insure)* asegurar ♦ **covered wagon** carromato • **to c. over** cubrir por completo • **to c. up** disimular, encubrir —intr. cubrir ♦ **to c. for** *(to substitute)* cubrir el puesto; *(to shield)* encubrir, servir de pantalla • **to c. up** cubrirse, abrigarse II. s. cubierta; *(lid)* tapa; *(slipcover, case)* funda, forro; *(jacket)* forro; *(of a magazine)* portada; *(bedspread)* sobrecama; *(pretense)* pretexto; *(shelter)* refugio; *(protection)* amparo; *(hiding place)* escondite *m*; *(table setting)* cubierto ♦ **c. charge** precio del cubierto • **c. girl** modelo fotográfica • **c. letter** carta adjunta *o* explicato-

ria • **to break c.** salir del escondite • **to take c.** refugiarse, ponerse a cubierto • **under c.** cubiertamente, clandestinamente • **under separate c.** por separado, aparte ♦ pl. ropa de cama.

cov·er·age (:ĭj) s. *(of a topic)* tratamiento; *(news)* reportaje *m*; *(insurance)* riesgos incluidos, protección *f*.

cov·er·alls (ôlz') s.pl. mono.

cov·er·ing (:ĭng) s. cubierta; *(wrapping)* envoltura; *(clothing)* ropa; *(layer)* capa.

cov·ert (kŭv'ərt, kō-vûrt') adj. secreto, clandestino.

cov·er-up *o* **cov·er·up** (kŭv'ər-ŭp') s. encubrimiento, ocultamiento.

cov·et (kŭv'ĭt) tr. codiciar.

cov·et·ous (:ĭ-təs) adj. codicioso.

cov·ey (kŭv'ē) s. nidada.

cow¹ (kou) s. vaca; *(whale, elephant)* hembra.

cow² tr. intimidar, atemorizar.

cow·ard (kou'ərd) s. cobarde *mf*.

cow·ard·ice (:ər-dĭs) s. cobardía.

cow·ard·ly (:ərd-lē) I. adj. cobarde II. adv. cobardemente.

cow·bell (kou'bĕl') s. cencerro.

cow·boy (:boi') s. vaquero.

cow·er (kou'ər) intr. encogerse de miedo.

cow·girl (kou'gûrl') s. vaquera.

cow·herd (:hûrd') s. vaquero.

cow·hide (:hīd') s. cuero (de vaca).

cowl (koul) s. capucha; AVIA. capota.

cow·lick (kou'lĭk') s. mechón *m* (de pelo).

cow·man (:mən) s. [pl. **-men**] ganadero.

co·work·er (kō'wûr'kər) s. compañero de trabajo.

cow·poke (kou'pōk') s. FAM. vaquero.

cow·pox (:pŏks') s. VET. vacuna.

cow·punch·er (:pŭn'chər) s. FAM. vaquero.

cow·ry/rie (kou'rē) s. cauri *m*.

cox·comb (kŏks'kōm') s. petimetre *m*.

coy (koi) adj. remilgado, evasivo.

coy·o·te (kī-ō'tē, kī'ōt') s. coyote *m*.

co·zi·ness (kō'zē-nĭs) s. *(comfort)* comodidad *f*; *(privacy)* intimidad *f*.

co·zy (kō'zē) I. adj. -i- cómodo, calentito ♦ **to play it c.** JER. actuar con cautela II. intr. ♦ **to c. up to** FAM. arrimarse a.

crab¹ (krăb) I. s. cangrejo; *(louse)* ladilla ♦ **c. apple** manzana silvestre II. intr. **-bb-** pescar cangrejos; *(to move)* moverse oblicuamente.

crab² I. s. refunfuñón *m*, cascarrabias *mf* II. intr. **-bb-** FAM. refunfuñar.

crab·by (:ē) adj. -i- de malas pulgas.

crab·grass (:grăs') s. garranchuelo.

crack (krăk) I. intr. *(to break)* romperse; *(whip)* restallar; *(to snap)* chasquear; *(bones, knuckles)* crujir; *(to split)* rajarse, agrietarse; *(to splinter)* astillarse; *(the voice)* cascarse; FAM. *(to give in)* ceder, quebrarse; *(to go mad)* chiflarse ♦ **to c. down** tomar medidas represivas • **to c. up** *(to wreck)* estrellarse; *(mentally)* chiflarse; *(to laugh)* morirse de risa • **to get cracking** FAM. poner manos a la obra —tr. *(to break)* romper; *(a whip)* chasquear; *(to pop)* hacer crujir; *(to split)* rajar, agrietar; *(to splinter)* astillar; *(to break open)* partir; *(a safe)* forzar; *(eggs, nuts)* cascar; *(to solve)* solucionar; *(a code)* descifrar; FAM. *(a joke)* contar ♦ **to c. open** abrir un poquito (ventana, puerta) • **to c. up** *(to wreck)* estrellar; *(with laughter)* hacer morir de risa II. s. *(snap)* chasquido; *(of a whip)* restallido; *(of the knuckles)* crujido; *(of a* *gun)* estallido; *(split)* rajadura, grieta; *(slit)* rendija; *(blow)* golpe *m,* porrazo; *(chance)* oportunidad *f; (joke)* salida, chiste *m; (gibe)* pulla ♦ **at the c. of dawn** al romper el alba • **to fall through the cracks** ser pasado por alto • **to take a c. at** probar, intentar **III.** adj. experto; *(marksman)* certero.

crack·down *(:doun')* s. medidas represivas.
cracked (krăkt) adj. FAM. chiflado, loco.
crack·er (krăk'ər) s. galleta.
crack·er·jack *(:jăk')* adj. JER. maravilloso.
crack·le (krăk'əl) **I.** intr. crepitar, crujir —tr. hacer crujir **II.** s. crepitación *f,* chisporroteo; *(rustle)* crujido.
crack·pot (krăk'pŏt') s. chiflado, excéntrico.
crack·up (:ŭp') s. *(plane)* choque *m; (plane)* caída; *(mental)* colapso.
cra·dle (krăd'l) **I.** s. cuna; *(of a phone)* horquilla, gancho ♦ **to rob the c.** FAM. salir *o* casarse con una persona muy joven **II.** tr. mecer en los brazos; *(to support)* sostener.
craft (krăft) s. habilidad *f,* arte *m; (guile)* astucia; *(trade)* oficio; *(boat)* embarcación *f; (airplane)* avión *m.*
crafts·man (krăfts'mən) s. [pl. **-men**] artesano.
crafts·man·ship *(:shĭp')* s. artesanía; *(skill)* arte *m,* destreza.
craft·y (krăf'tē) adj. **-i-** hábil, astuto.
crag (krăg) s. risco, peñasco.
crag·gy (:ē) adj. **-i-** peñascoso.
cram (krăm) tr. **-mm-** *(to force)* meter a la fuerza; *(to stuff)* abarrotar, rellenar; *(with food)* atiborrarse de —intr. FAM. estudiar a última hora.
cramp¹ (krămp) MED. **I.** s. calambre *m* ♦ pl. retortijones **II.** intr. ♦ **to c. up** acalambrarse.
cramp² **I.** s. TEC. grapa, cárcel *f; (limitation)* restricción *f* **II.** tr. engrapar; *(to restrict)* restringir ♦ **to c. one's style** JER. cortar los vuelos a uno.
cramped (krămpt) adj. apretado, apiñado; *(financially)* incómodo; *(illegible)* ilegible.
cran·ber·ry (krăn'bĕr'ē) s. arándano.
crane (krān) **I.** s. ORNIT. grulla; TEC. grúa **II.** tr. estirar (el cuello).
cra·ni·um (krā'nē-əm) s. [pl. **s** *o* **-ia**] cráneo.
crank (krăngk) **I.** s. manivela; FAM. *(grouch)* cascarrabias *mf; (eccentric)* chiflado **II.** tr. arrancar (un motor) dando vueltas a la manivela ♦ **to c. out** producir como si fuera una máquina • **to c. up** echar a andar.
crank·case ('kās') s. cárter *m* del cigüeñal *m.*
crank·shaft (:shăft') s. cigüeñal *m.*
crank·y (:kē) adj. **-i-** *(irritable)* quisquilloso; *(odd)* estrafalario.
cran·ny (krăn'ē) s. grieta.
crape (krāp) s. crespón *m,* crepé *m.*
craps (krăps) s.pl. dados ♦ **to shoot c.** jugar a los dados.
crash (krăsh) **I.** intr. estrellarse, chocar; *(to break)* hacerse pedazos; *(to resound)* retumbar; *(to fail)* quebrar, fracasar; JER. *(to sleep)* irse a dormir ♦ **to c. through** irrumpir en —tr. estrellar, hacer pedazos; FAM. *(a party)* zamparse en **II.** s. *(noise)* estrépito; *(collision)* choque *m,* colisión *f;* AVIA. caída; COM. *(failure)* ruina, quiebra ♦ **c. helmet** casco protector **III.** adj. *(course, diet)* intensivo; AVIA. de emergencia.
crash-land ('lănd') intr. hacer un aterrizaje forzoso.
crass (krăs) adj. craso, burdo.

crate (krāt) **I.** s. cajón *m* **II.** tr. encajonar.
cra·ter (krā'tər) s. cráter *m.*
cra·vat (krə-văt') s. corbata.
crave (krāv) tr. ansiar, morirse por.
cra·ven (krā'vən) adj. & s. cobarde *mf.*
crav·ing (krā'vĭng) s. anhelo, antojo.
craw (krô) s. buche *m.*
crawl (krôl) **I.** intr. arrastrarse, reptar; *(baby)* gatear; *(traffic)* avanzar a paso de tortuga; *(skin)* erizarse; DEP. nadar estilo crol ♦ **to be crawling with** hervir de • **to c. up** trepar **II.** s. gateado; DEP. crol *m* ♦ **at a c.** a paso de tortuga.
cray·fish (krā'fĭsh') s. [pl. inv. *o* **es**] astaco.
cray·on (krā'ŏn') s. & tr. (dibujar al) pastel *m.*
craze (krāz) **I.** tr. enloquecer, volver loco **II.** s. moda.
crazed (krāzd) adj. loco, enloquecido.
cra·zy (krā'zē) adj. **-i-** loco; *(foolish)* de locos, disparatado ♦ **to be c. about** *(person)* estar loco por; *(fad)* estar loco con • **to go c.** volverse loco.
creak (krēk) **I.** intr. crujir, chirriar **II.** s. crujido, chirrido.
creak·y (krē'kē) adj. **-i-** que cruje, chirriante; *(dilapidated)* desvencijado.
cream (krēm) **I.** s. crema ♦ **c. cheese** queso crema • **c. of tartar** cremor tártaro • **c. puff** pastelito de crema • **c. sauce** salsa bechamel • **the c. of the crop** la flor y nata • **whipped c.** (crema) chantillí **II.** tr. batir; JER. *(to defeat)* hacer polvo, aplastar.
cream·y (krē'mē) adj. **-i-** cremoso.
crease (krēs) **I.** s. pliegue *m; (of trousers)* filo, raya; *(wrinkle)* arruga **II.** tr. plegar; *(to press)* hacer el filo a —intr. arrugarse.
cre·ate (krē-āt') tr. crear; *(to cause)* producir.
cre·a·tion (:ā'shən) s. creación *f.*
cre·a·tive (:tĭv) adj. creador, imaginativo ♦ **c. writing** composición literaria.
cre·a·tiv·i·ty ('-ĭtē) s. originalidad *f.*
cre·a·tor (krē-ā'tər) s. creador *m.*
cre·a·ture (krē'chər) s. criatura; *(being)* ente *m,* ser *m; (animal)* bestia, bicho.
crèche (krĕsh) s. nacimiento; G.B. *(nursery)* guardería.
cre·dence (krēd'ns) s. crédito, fe *f.*
cre·den·tial (krĭ-dĕn'shəl) s. credencial *f.*
cred·i·ble (krĕd'ə-bəl) adj. creíble.
cred·it (krĕd'ĭt) **I.** s. crédito; *(merit)* mérito; *(recognition)* reconocimiento; *(praise)* encomio; TEN. haber *m* ♦ **c. card, line** tarjeta, límite de crédito • **on c.** a crédito • **to give c.** COM. dar crédito; *(to praise, name)* reconocer (el mérito, a autor) • **to take c. for** atribuirse el mérito de ♦ pl. títulos de crédito **II.** tr. dar crédito a, creer; *(to recognize)* otorgar reconocimiento; *(to attribute)* atribuir; COM. abonar en cuenta.
cred·it·a·ble (:ĭ-tə-bəl) adj. encomiable, loable.
cred·i·tor (:tər) s. acreedor *m.*
cred·u·lous (krĕj'ə-ləs) adj. crédulo.
creed (krēd) s. credo.
creek (krēk) s. riachuelo, arroyo ♦ **up the c.** FAM. en apuros.
creel (krēl) s. nasa.
creep (krēp) **I.** intr. **crept** arrastrarse, deslizarse; *(to crawl)* gatear; *(cautiously)* avanzar con cautela; *(slowly)* ir a paso de tortuga; BOT. trepar ♦ **to c. by** pasar lentamente • **to c. up on someone** acercarse a alguien sigilosamente • **to make one's flesh c.** hacer ponérsele la piel de gallina **II.** s. *(crawl)* gateado; *(pace)* paso

lento; JER. *(jerk)* desgraciado, cretino ♦ pl. FAM. escalofrío, pavor.

creep·er (krē'pər) s. enredadera.

creep·y (:pē) adj. **-i-** FAM. horripilante, espeluznante.

cre·mate (krē'māt') tr. incinerar.

cre·ma·tion (krĭ-mā'shən) s. cremación *f.*

cre·ma·to·ri·um (krē'mə-tôr'ē-əm) s. [pl. **s** o **-ia**] crematorio.

cre·o·sote (krē'ə-sōt') s. creosota.

crepe *o* **crêpe** (krāp) s. *(fabric)* crespón *m,* crepé *m; (rubber)* crepé; CUL. panqueque *m* ♦ **c. paper** papel crepé.

crept (krĕpt) cf. **creep.**

cres·cent (krĕs'ənt) I. s. medialuna; *(semicircle)* semicírculo II. adj. creciente.

crest (krĕst) I. s. cresta; *(on a helmet)* penacho, cimera; HER. timbre *m* II. tr. llegar hasta la cumbre de.

crest·fall·en (:fô'lən) adj. alicaído, abatido.

cre·tin (krēt'n) s. cretino.

cre·vasse (krĭ-văs') s. fisura (esp. de glaciar).

crev·ice (krĕv'ĭs) s. grieta, rajadura.

crew (krōō) s. AVIA., MARÍT. tripulación *f;* MIL. dotación *f; (of workers)* equipo; *(staff)* personal *m* ♦ **c. cut** pelado al cepillo.

crib (krĭb) I. s. cuna; *(corncrib)* granero; FAM. *(plagiarism)* plagio ♦ **c. sheet** FAM. chuleta II. tr. **-bb-** FAM. plagiar —intr. usar una chuleta.

crick (krĭk) s. ♦ **c. in the neck** torticolis *f.*

crick·et¹ (krĭk'ĭt) s. ENTOM. grillo.

crick·et² s. DEP. críquet *m* ♦ **it's not c.** FAM. no es jugar limpio.

cri·er (krī'ər) s. pregonero.

crime (krīm) s. crimen *m* ♦ **c. rate** criminalidad.

crim·i·nal (krĭm'ə-nəl) adj. & s. criminal *mf* ♦ **c. record** antecedentes penales.

crim·i·nol·o·gist ('-nŏl'ə-jĭst) s. criminalista *mf.*

crimp (krĭmp) I. tr. *(cloth)* plisar; *(hair)* rizar, encrespar II. s. pliegue *m,* rizo ♦ **to put a c. in** poner trabas a.

crim·son (krĭm'zən) I. adj. & s. carmesí *m* II. tr. teñir de carmesí —intr. sonrojarse.

cringe (krĭnj) intr. encogerse, acobardarse.

crin·kle (krĭng'kəl) I. tr. & intr. arrugar(se) II. s. arruga.

crin·o·line (krĭn'ə-lĭn) s. crinolina.

crip·ple (krĭp'əl) I. s. lisiado, cojo II. tr. lisiar, tullir; FIG. inutilizar, estropear.

cri·sis (krī'sĭs) s. [pl. **-ses**] crisis *f.*

crisp (krĭsp) I. adj. *(crunchy)* tostado, crujiente; *(fresh)* fresco; *(bracing)* vivificante; *(precise)* preciso, claro II. s. ♦ **to burn** *o* **fry to a c.** achicharrar(se) ♦ pl. G.B. papas fritas.

crisp·y (krĭs'pē) adj. **-i-** tostado, crujiente.

criss·cross (krĭs'krôs') I. tr. & intr. entrecruzar(se) II. s. entrecruzamiento III. adj. entrecruzado IV. adv. en cruz.

cri·te·ri·on (krī-tîr'ē-ən) s. [pl. **s** o **-ia**] criterio.

crit·ic (krĭt'ĭk) s. crítico.

crit·i·cal ('ĭ-kəl) adj. crítico; *(carping)* criticón ♦ **in c. condition** grave • **to be c. of** criticar.

crit·i·cal·ly (:kə-lē) adv. gravemente.

crit·i·cism (:sĭz'əm) s. crítica.

crit·i·cize (:sīz') tr. & intr. criticar.

cri·tique (krĭ-tēk') s. crítica.

crit·ter (krĭt'ər) s. FAM. bicho, animal *m.*

croak (krōk) I. s. *(of frog)* croar *m; (of crow)* graznido II. intr. *(frog)* croar, cantar; *(crow)*

graznar; JER. *(to die)* estirar la pata.

cro·chet (krō-shā') tr. & s. (tejer a) ganchillo.

crock (krŏk) s. vasija de barro.

crocked (krŏkt) adj. JER. hecho una uva.

crock·er·y (krŏk'ə-rē) s. vajilla de barro, loza.

croc·o·dile (krŏk'ə-dīl') s. cocodrilo.

cro·cus (krō'kəs) s. [pl. **es** *o* **-ci**] azafrán *m.*

croft (krŏft) s. G.B. finca en arrendamiento.

crone (krōn) s. arpía.

cro·ny (krō'nē) s. compinche *mf,* amigote *m.*

crook (krŏŏk) I. s. *(staff)* báculo; *(curve)* ángulo; *(of river, path)* recodo; FAM. *(thief)* tramposo, ladrón *m* II. tr. & intr. doblar(se).

crook·ed (:ĭd) adj. *(road, thief)* torcido; *(nose)* corvo; *(back)* encorvado.

croon (krōōn) I. intr. canturrear; *(pop singer)* cantar de modo sentimental II. s. canturreo.

croon·er (krōō'nər) s. cantante *mf* sentimental.

crop (krŏp) I. s. cosecha; *(variety)* cultivo; *(haircut)* pelado corto; *(whip)* fusta; ORNIT. buche *m* II. tr. **-pp-** *(to trim)* cortar, recortar; *(hair)* cortar muy corto; *(ears)* desmochar ♦ **to c. up** surgir.

cross (krôs) I. s. cruz *f; (mixture)* mezcla; *(crossbreed)* híbrido II. tr. cruzar; *(one's arms)* cruzarse de; *(to oppose)* contrariar ♦ **to c. off** *o* **out** tachar • **to c. oneself** santiguarse • **to c. over** atravesar —intr. *(to intersect, breed)* cruzarse; *(to go across)* cruzar, atravesar III. adj. *(intersecting)* transversal; *(angry)* de mal humor; *(reciprocal)* recíproco ♦ **c. hair** retículo • **c. section** sección transversal; FIG. muestra representativa • **c. street** (calle) transversal • **to get c.** enfadarse.

cross·bar ('bär') s. travesaño; *(of door)* tranca.

cross·beam (:bēm') s. traviesa.

cross·bow (:bō') s. ballesta.

cross·breed (:brēd') I. tr. & intr. **-bred** cruzar(se) II. s. híbrido.

cross·coun·try (:kŭn'trē) adj. a campo traviesa; *(flight, drive)* a través del país.

cross·cur·rent (:kûr'ənt) s. contracorriente *f.*

cross·ex·am·i·na·tion ('ĭg-zăm'ə-nā'shən) s. repregunta, interrogatorio.

cross·ex·am·ine ('-'ĭn) tr. repreguntar, interrogar.

cross·eyed (krôs'īd') adj. bizco.

cross·fer·til·i·za·tion ('fûr'tl-ī-zā'shən) s. fecundación cruzada.

cross·fire (fîr') s. fuego cruzado.

cross·ing (krô'sĭng) s. cruce *m; (ford)* vado; F.C. paso a nivel.

cross·piece (krôs'pēs') s. travesaño.

cross·pol·li·na·tion ('pŏl'ə-nā'shən) s. polinización cruzada.

cross·pur·pose ('pûr'pəs) s. ♦ **to be at cross-purposes** no entenderse.

cross·ques·tion ('kwĕs'chən) I. tr. repreguntar, interrogar II. s. repregunta, interrogación *f.*

cross·ref·er·ence (:rĕf'ər-əns) s. remisión *f.*

cross·road (:rōd') s. vía transversal *f* ♦ pl. encrucijada.

cross-stitch (:stĭch') s. punto cruzado.

cross·talk (:tôk') s. interferencias.

cross·tie (:tī') s. traviesa.

cross·walk (:wôk') s. paso de peatones.

cross·wind (:wĭnd') s. viento de costado.

cross·wise/ways (:wīz'/wāz') adv. al través.

cross·word puzzle (:wûrd') s. crucigrama *m.*

crotch (krŏch) s. *(of tree)* horquilla; ANAT. entrepiernas.

crotch·et·y (krŏch′ĭ-tē) adj. caprichoso.
crouch (krouch) intr. agacharse, acuclillarse.
croup¹ (krōōp) s. MED. crup m, garrotillo.
croup² s. grupa (del caballo).
crow¹ (krō) s. cuervo ♦ **as the c. flies** en línea recta • **to eat c.** FAM. besar la correa.
crow² I. intr. -ed o crew cantar, cacarear ♦ **to c. over** jactarse de II. s. canto, cacareo.
crow·bar (′bär′) s. pata de cabra, palanca.
crowd (kroud) I. s. multitud f, muchedumbre f; (mob) gentío; (spectators) público; (clique) gente f ♦ **to follow the c.** hacer lo que todos • **to rise above the c.** destacarse II. intr. apiñarse, amontonarse ♦ **to c. into** atestar, apiñarse dentro —tr. apiñar, amontonar; (to fill) atestar, llenar ♦ **to c. out** empujar.
crowd·ed (krou′dĭd) adj. lleno, concurrido; (cramped) apiñado.
crown (kroun) I. s. corona; (of a hat, tree) copa; (summit, honor) cima; (achievement) coronación f ♦ **c. prince** príncipe heredero II. tr. coronar; (to top off) rematar; FAM. (to hit) dar un cocotazo a ♦ **to c. it all** para rematar.
crown·ing (krou′nĭng) s. coronación f.
crow's-feet (krōz′fēt′) s.pl. patas de gallo.
crow's-nest (:nēst′) s. cofa de vigía.
cru·cial (krōō′shəl) adj. crucial, decisivo.
cru·ci·ble (krōō′sə-bəl) s. crisol m.
cru·ci·fix (krōō′sə-fĭks′) s. crucifijo.
cru·ci·fix·ion (′-fĭk′shən) s. crucifixión f.
cru·ci·fy (′-fī′) tr. crucificar.
crude (krōōd) I. adj. (vulgar) ordinario, grosero; (rough) tosco, basto; (raw) crudo, bruto II. s. (petróleo) crudo.
crude·ness (:nĭs) o **cru·di·ty** (krōō′dĭ-tē) s. (vulgarity) grosería; (roughness) tosquedad f, bastedad f.
cru·el (krōō′əl) adj. -er, -est cruel, despiadado.
cru·el·ty (:tē) s. crueldad f.
cru·et (krōō′ĭt) s. vinagrera, aceitera.
cruise (krōōz) I. intr. (to sail) navegar; (as a tourist) hacer un crucero; (car) circular; (to patrol) patrullar ♦ **to c. for** clamar. circular en busca de —tr. (ship) cruzar; (car) circular o patrullar por II. s. crucero.
cruis·er (krōō′zər) s. (warship) crucero; (motorboat) yate m con camarotes; (police car) patrullero.
crumb (krŭm) s. miga, migaja.
crum·ble (krŭm′bəl) tr. & intr. desmigajar(se); FIG. desmoronar(se).
crum·my o **crumb·y** (krŭm′ē) adj. -i- (miserable) malísimo; (cheap) de mala muerte.
crum·pet (krŭm′pĭt) s. G.B. panecillo blando.
crum·ple (krŭm′pəl) tr. & intr. (to crush) arrugar(se), estrujar(se); (to collapse) derribar(se).
crunch (krŭnch) I. tr. triturar —intr. crujir II. s. crujido; FAM. (crisis) aprieto, crisis f; (shortage) escasez f.
crunch·y (krŭn′chē) adj. crujiente.
cru·sade (krōō-sād′) s. & intr. (hacer una) cruzada.
cru·sad·er (:′sā′dər) s. cruzado.
crush (krŭsh) I. tr. (to squash) aplastar; (to squeeze) exprimir; (to crumple) estrujar; (to hug forcefully) apretar; (to grind) triturar, moler; (enemy, revolt) aplastar; (to overwhelm) agobiar II. s. aplastamiento; (crowd) multitud f; (infatuation) enamoramiento ♦ **to have a c. on someone** FAM. perder la chaveta por alguien.

crust (krŭst) I. s. (bread, pie) corteza; (coating, scab) costra; (layer) capa II. tr. & intr. encostrar(se).
crus·ta·cean (krŭ-stā′shən) s. & adj. crustáceo.
crust·y (krŭs′tē) adj. -i- de corteza dura; (surface) costroso; (surly) áspero, brusco.
crutch (krŭch) s. muleta; FIG. sostén m.
crux (krŭks) s. [pl. es o -ces] punto crítico; (of an argument) quid m.
cry (krī) I. intr. llorar; (to shout) gritar; (animals) aullar ♦ **to c. for** clamar por • **to c. for joy** llorar de alegría • **to c. out** exclamar, gritar • **to c. over** lamentarse por —tr. gritar, decir a gritos; (in public) pregonar ♦ **to c. down** menospreciar • **to c. forgiveness** implorar perdón II. s. grito; (weeping) llanto; (entreaty) petición f; (peddler's call) pregón m ♦ **a far c. from** muy distante de • **in full c.** en plena persecución • **to have a good c.** llorar a lágrima viva.
cry·ba·by (′bā′bē) s. llorón m.
crypt (krĭpt) s. cripta.
cryp·tic (krĭp′tĭk) adj. enigmático, misterioso.
cryp·to·gram (′tə-grăm′) s. criptograma m.
cryp·tog·ra·phy (-tŏg′rə-fē) s. criptografía.
crys·tal (krĭs′təl) I. s. cristal m ♦ **c. ball** bola de cristal • **c. clear** claro como el agua II. adj. de cristal; (transparent) cristalino.
crys·tal·line (′tə-lĭn) adj. cristalino.
crys·tal·lize (:līz′) tr. & intr. cristalizar(se).
crys·tal·log·ra·phy (′-lŏg′rə-fē) s. cristalografía.
cub (kŭb) s. cachorro; (novice) novato.
cub·by·hole (kŭb′ē-hōl′) s. (room) cuchitril m; (cupboard) armario pequeño.
cube (kyōōb) I. s. cubo ♦ **c. root** raíz cúbica • **sugar c.** terrón de azúcar II. tr. MAT. cubicar; (to cut) picar en cubos.
cu·bic (kyōō′bĭk) adj. cúbico.
cu·bi·cle (′bĭ-kəl) s. compartimiento.
cub·ist (′bĭst) s. cubista mf.
cuck·old (kŭk′əld) I. s. cornudo II. tr. poner los cuernos a.
cuck·oo (kōō′kōō) I. s. (bird) cuco, cuclillo; (call) cucú m II. adj. loco, chiflado.
cu·cum·ber (kyōō′kŭm′bər) s. pepino.
cud (kŭd) s. bolo alimenticio ♦ **to chew the c.** rumiar.
cud·dle (kŭd′l) I. tr. & intr. abrazar(se), acurrucar(se) II. s. abrazo.
cud·dly (:lē) adj. -i- mimoso.
cudg·el (kŭj′əl) s. garrote m, bastón m ♦ **take up the cudgels for** salir en defensa de.
cue¹ (kyōō) s. (billiard stick) taco ♦ **c. ball** mingo, bola blanca.
cue² I. s. TEAT. pie m, señal f ♦ **to take one's c. from** guiarse por II. tr. dar el pie o la señal a.
cuff¹ (kŭf) s. (shirt) puño; (pant) bajos, vuelta ♦ **c. links** gemelos, yugos • **off the c.** FAM. de improviso ♦ pl. esposas.
cuff² I. tr. abofetear II. s. bofetada.
cui·rass (kwĭ-răs′) s. coraza.
cui·sine (kwĭ-zēn′) s. cocina, arte culinario.
cu·li·nar·y (kyōō′lə-nĕr′ē, kŭl′ə-) adj. culinario.
cull (kŭl) tr. entresacar, seleccionar ♦ **to c. out** sacar, separar.
cul·mi·nate (kŭl′mə-nāt′) intr. culminar.
cul·pa·ble (kŭl′pə-bəl) adj. culpable.
cul·prit (kŭl′prĭt) s. culpable mf.
cult (kŭlt) s. culto; (sect) secta.
cult·ist (kŭl′tĭst) s. fanático, devoto.
cul·ti·vate (kŭl′tə-vāt′) tr. cultivar.

cul·ti·va·tion ('-vă'shən) s. cultivo; *(refinement)* cultura, refinamiento.

cul·ti·va·tor ('-'tər) s. cultivador *m.*

cul·tur·al (kŭl'chər-əl) adj. cultural.

cul·ture (kŭl'chər) s. cultura; AGR., BIOL. cultivo.

cul·tured (:chərd) adj. *(person)* culto; *(pearl)* de cultivo.

cul·vert (kŭl'vərt) s. alcantarilla.

cum·ber (kŭm'bər) tr. agobiar, embarazar.

cum·ber·some (:səm) adj. embarazoso, incómodo.

cum·in (kŭm'ĭn) s. comino.

cum·mer·bund (kŭm'ər-bŭnd') s. faja.

cu·mu·late (kyōōm'yə-lāt') tr. & intr. cumular(se), acumular(se).

cu·mu·la·tive (:lā'tĭv, -lə-tĭv) adj. acumulativo.

cu·mu·lus (ləs) s. [pl. **-li**] cúmulo.

cun·ning (kŭn'ĭng) I. adj. *(crafty)* astuto, taimado; *(masterful)* hábil, ingenioso; *(cute)* mono, precioso II. s. astucia, habilidad *f.*

cup (kŭp) I. s. taza; *(trophy)* copa; *(chalice)* cáliz *m; (hollow)* hoyo **♦ that's not my c. of tea** eso no es de mi gusto • **in one's cups** FAM. borracho, bebido II. tr. **-pp-** ahuecar.

cup·board (kŭb'ərd) s. *(cabinet)* aparador *m; (closet)* alacena.

cup·cake (kŭp'kāk') s. bizcochito redondo.

cup·ful (:fōōl') s. taza.

cu·pid·i·ty (kyōō-pĭd'ĭ-tē) s. codicia, avaricia.

cu·po·la (kyōō'pə-lə) s. cúpula.

cu·pric (kōō'prĭk) adj. cúprico.

cur (kûr) s. perro cruzado; *(person)* canalla *m.*

cur·a·ble (kyōōr'ə-bəl) adj. curable.

cu·ras·sow (kōōr'ə-sō') s. guaco.

cu·rate (kyōōr'ĭt) s. cura *m.*

cu·ra·tor (kyōō-rā'tər) s. conservador *m.*

curb (kûrb) I. s. *(of a street)* bordillo; *(restraint)* freno; *(of bridle)* barbada II. tr. refrenar.

curb·stone ('stōn') s. bordillo.

curd (kûrd) s. cuajada, requesón *m.*

cur·dle (kûr'dl) tr. & intr. cuajar(se) **♦ to c. one's blood** helarle la sangre a uno.

cure (kyōōr) I. s. cura; *(remedy)* remedio II. tr. & intr. curar(se).

cure·all (:ôl') s. curalotodo, panacea.

cu·ret·tage (kyōōr'ĭ-täzh') s. raspado.

cur·few (kûr'fyōō) s. (toque *m* de) queda.

cu·ri·o (kyōōr'ē-ō') s. curiosidad *f*, baratija.

cu·ri·os·i·ty (kyōōr'ē-ŏs'ĭ-tē) s. curiosidad.

cu·ri·ous (kyōōr'ē-əs) adj. curioso **♦ to be c. to** tener deseos de.

curl (kûrl) I. tr. & intr. *(to twist)* rizar(se), ensortijar(se); *(to coil)* enrollar(se); *(the lips)* fruncir(se); *(smoke)* formar volutas **♦ to c. up** hacerse un ovillo, acurrucarse II. s. riza, crespo; *(of smoke)* voluta.

curl·er (kûr'lər) s. bigudí *m.*

curl·i·cue (:lĭ-kyōō') s. rasgo, plumada.

curl·y (:lē) adj. **-i-** rizado, crespo.

cur·mudg·eon (kər-mŭj'ən) s. cascarrabias *mf.*

cur·rant (kûr'ənt) s. grosella; *(raisin)* pasa de Corinto.

cur·ren·cy (kûr'ən-sē) s. *(money)* moneda, dinero (corriente); *(use)* vigencia, boga **♦ foreign c.** divisas, moneda extranjera.

cur·rent (kûr'ənt) I. adj. *(present-day)* actual; *(in progress)* corriente, en curso; *(edition)* último; *(accepted)* corriente; *(in use)* en boga **♦ c. events** actualidades • **c. liabilities** pasivo exigible II. s. corriente *f* **♦ alternating, direct c.**

corriente alterna, continua.

cur·rent·ly (:lē) adv. *(now)* actualmente; *(commonly)* corrientemente.

cur·ric·u·lum (kə-rĭk'yə-ləm) s. [pl. **s** *o* **-la**] programa *m* de estudios **♦ c. vitae** historial profesional.

cur·ry¹ (kûr'ē) tr. *(a horse)* almohazar; *(hides)* zurrar **♦ to c. favor with** congraciarse con.

cur·ry² s. CUL. (salsa de) cari *m.*

curse (kûrs) I. s. maldición *f; (scourge)* desgracia, calamidad *f; (obscenity)* mala palabra, grosería II. tr. **-d** *o* **curst** maldecir; *(to afflict)* desgraciar, afligir; *(to swear at)* insultar a **♦ to be cursed with** tener la desgracia de —intr. decir malas palabras **♦ to c. at** insultar a.

curs·ed (kûr'sĭd, kûrst) adj. maldito.

cur·sive (kûr'sĭv) adj. cursiva.

cur·sor (kûr'sər) s. cursor *m.*

cur·so·ry (kûr'sə-rē) adj. superficial, rápido.

curt (kûrt) adj. brusco, seco.

cur·tail (kər-tāl') tr. cortar, reducir.

cur·tain (kûr'tn) I. s. cortina; TEAT. telón *m* **♦ c. call** llamada a escena • **c. time** hora de subir el telón • **to draw the c.** over *o* on correr un velo sobre • **to raise the c. on** poner al descubierto **♦ pl.** JER. fin II. tr. velar, encubrir **♦ to c. off** separar con cortinas.

curt·sy (kûrt'sē) s. & intr. (hacer una) reverencia.

cur·va·ceous (kûr-vā'shəs) adj. voluptuoso.

cur·va·ture (kûr'və-chōōr') s. curvatura; *(of the spine)* encorvamiento.

curve (kûrv) I. s. curva II. intr. curvear; *(surface)* doblarse —tr. encorvar; *(to bend)* doblar.

curved (kûrvd) adj. curvo, curvado; *(bent)* doblado.

cush·ion (kōōsh'ən) I. s. cojín *m*, almohadilla; FIG. amortiguador *m*, resguardo II. tr. *(to pad)* acolchar; *(a blow)* amortiguar.

cush·y (kōōsh'ē) adj. **-i-** JER. fácil, cómodo.

cusp (kŭsp) s. cúspide *f; (of moon)* cuerno.

cus·pid (kŭs'pĭd) s. diente canino, colmillo.

cus·pi·dor (kŭs'pĭ-dôr') s. escupidera.

cuss (kŭs) FAM. I. intr. decir palabrotas —tr. maldecir **♦ to c. out** insultar a II. s. palabrota; *(person)* majadero.

cus·tard (kŭs'tərd) s. natilla **♦ caramel c.** flan.

cus·to·di·an (kŭ-stō'dē-ən) s. custodio, guardián *m; (janitor)* conserje *m.*

cus·to·dy (kŭs'tə-dē) s. custodia; *(detention)* detención *f* **♦ to be in c.** estar detenido • **to take into c.** detener, arrestar.

cus·tom (kŭs'təm) s. costumbre *f; (patronage)* clientela **♦ pl.** aduana • **to go through c.** pasar la aduana II. adj. hecho a la medida.

cus·tom·ar·i·ly ('tə-mâr'ə-lē) adv. acostumbradamente; *(ordinarily)* normalmente.

cus·tom·ar·y ('-mĕr'ē) adj. acostumbrado, de costumbre **♦ to be c.** ser costumbre.

cus·tom·er (:mər) s. cliente *mf.*

cus·tom·house (kŭs'təm-hous') s. aduana.

cus·tom·ize (kŭs'tə-mīz') tr. preparar a gusto del comprador.

cus·tom-made (kŭs'təm-mād') adj. hecho a gusto del comprador.

cut (kŭt) I. tr. **cut** cortar; *(to divide)* dividir, repartir; *(to omit)* omitir, excluir; *(to harvest)* segar; *(to fell)* talar; *(to carve)* tallar; *(hole)* practicar, abrir; *(teeth)* echar; *(the size of)* reducir, acortar; *(time)* abreviar; *(prices)* rebajar; *(grease)* disolver; *(to hurt feelings)* lastimar, herir; *(to shut off)* parar; *(a record)* grabar; *(to quit)* dejarse de, acabar con; FAM. *(classes)* fumarse, faltar a ♦ **c. it out!** ¡basta ya! • **to c. back** *(to trim)* recortar; *(to reduce)* reducir, disminuir • **to c. down** *(a tree)* talar; JER. *(to kill)* matar • **to c. off** *(to sever)* cortar; *(to shut off)* parar; *(to block)* aislar, bloquear; *(a view)* tapar; *(to disinherit)* desheredar • **to c. out** *(to remove)* cortar; *(designs)* recortar; *(to delete)* suprimir; *(to quit)* dejar de • **to c. to the bone** reducir al mínimo • **to c. up** cortar en pedazos, partir —intr. cortar; *(a substance)* cortarse; *(to turn sharply)* virar, doblar ♦ **to be c. out for** estar hecho para • **to c. across** cortar por; *(categories)* derribar • **to c. back (on)** hacer reducciones (en) • **to c. both ways** tener doble filo • **to c. down on** reducir(se), aminorar • **to c. in** *(a line of people)* colarse; *(to interrupt)* interrumpir • **to c. loose** JER. hablar *o* actuar sin cuidarse • **to c. up** hacer diabluras II. s. corte *m*; *(notch)* muesca; *(reduction)* reducción *f*; *(discount)* rebaja; FAM. *(share)* tajada, parte *f*; JOY. talla; IMPR. grabada; CINEM. corte, interrupción *f* ♦ **a c. above** un poco mejor que.

cut-and-dried (kŭt'ən-drīd') adj. rutinario.

cu·ta·ne·ous (kyŏo-tā'nē-əs) adj. cutáneo.

cut·back (kŭt'băk') s. reducción *f*.

cute (kyŏot) adj. *(pretty)* mono; *(contrived)* afectado ♦ **to get c. with** hacerse el listo con.

cu·ti·cle (kyŏo'tĭ-kəl) s. cutícula.

cut·ie (kyŏo'tē) s. JER. monada.

cut·lass (kŭt'ləs) s. sable *m*.

cut·ler (:lər) s. cuchillero.

cut·ler·y (:lə-rē) s. cubiertos.

cut·let (kŭt'lĭt) s. chuleta.

cut·off (kŭt'ôf') s. *(limit)* límite *m*; *(short cut)* atajo; *(device)* cierre *m*, obturador *m*.

cut-rate ('rāt') adj. rebajado, de descuento.

cut·ter ('ər) s. cortador *m*; MARÍT. cúter *m* ♦ **coast guard c.** guardacostas.

cut·throat (:thrōt') I. s. degollador *m*, asesino II. adj. *(cruel)* cruel, sanguinario; *(competition)* implacable.

cut·ting (:ĭng) I. s. *(clipping)* recorte *m*; AGR. rampollo II. adj. cortante; *(remark)* mordaz.

cut·tle·fish (kŭt'l-fĭsh') s. [pl. inv. *o* **es**] jibia.

cy·a·nide (sī'ə-nīd') cianuro.

cy·ber·net·ics (sī'bər-nĕt'ĭks) s.sg. cibernética.

cy·cla·mate (sī'klə-māt') s. ciclamato.

cy·cle (sī'kəl) I. s. ciclo; *(bike)* bici *f*, moto *f* II. intr. ocurrir cíclicamente; *(to go)* ir en bicicleta *o* motocicleta.

cy·clic/cli·cal (sīk'lĭk) adj. cíclico.

cy·clist (sī'klĭst) s. *(bicycle)* ciclista *mf*; *(motorcycle)* motociclista *mf*.

cy·clone (sī'klōn') s. ciclón *m*.

cy·clo·tron (sī'klə-trŏn') s. ciclotrón *m*.

cyg·net (sĭg'nĭt) s. pichón *m* de cisne.

cyl·in·der (sĭl'ən-dər) s. cilindro.

cy·lin·dri·cal (sə-lĭn'drĭ-kəl) adj. cilíndrico.

cym·bal (sĭm'bəl) s. címbalo, platillo.

cyn·ic (sĭn'ĭk) s. & adj. cínico.

cyn·i·cal (:ĭ-kəl) adj. cínico.

cyn·i·cism (:sĭz'əm) s. cinismo.

cy·no·sure (sī'nə-shŏor') s. centro de atracción.

cy·press (sī'prəs) s. ciprés *m*.

cyst (sĭst) s. quiste *m*.

cys·tic (sĭs'tĭk) adj. enquistado.

cys·ti·tis (sĭ-stī'tĭs) s. cistitis *f*.

cy·to·plasm (sī'tə-plăz'əm) s. citoplasma *m*.

czar (zär) s. zar *m*.

czar·e·vitch ('ə-vĭch') s. zarevitz *m*.

cza·ri·na (zä-rē'nə) s. zarina.

D

d, D (dē) s. cuarta letra del alfabeto inglés; MÚS. re *m*.

dab (dăb) I. tr. **-bb-** dar toques a, retocar suavemente II. s. *(bit)* pizca; *(pat, tap)* golpe ligero.

dab·ble (dăb'əl) tr. salpicar —intr. *(to splash)* chapotear; *(as amateur)* interesarse superficialmente *(in, at* por).

dab·bler (:lər) s. diletante *mf*.

dachs·hund (däks'hŏont') s. perro salchicha.

dad (dăd) s. FAM. papá *m*.

dad·dy ('ē) s. FAM. papacito, papito.

daf·fo·dil (dăf'ə-dĭl') s. narciso.

daf·fy (dăf'ē) adj. **-i-** FAM. chalado, chiflado.

dag·ger (dăg'ər) s. daga, puñal *m*; IMPR. obelisco ♦ **to look daggers at** apuñalar con la mirada.

da·guerre·o·type (də-gâr'ə-tīp') s. daguerrotipo.

dahl·ia (dăl'yə) s. dalia.

dai·ly (dā'lē) I. adj. & s. diario II. adv. diariamente, cada día.

dain·ty (dān'tē) adj. **-i-** exquisito, delicado; *(affected)* remilgado.

dair·y (dâr'ē) s. lechería ♦ **d. cattle** vacas lecheras • **d. farm** granja lechera.

dair·y·man (:mən) s. [pl. **-men**] lechero.

da·is (dā'ĭs) s. tarima, estrado.

dai·sy (dā'zē) s. margarita.

dale (dāl) s. valle *m*.

dal·li·ance (dăl'ē-əns) s. *(dawdling)* gandulería; *(flirtation)* coqueteo.

dal·ly (dăl'ē) tr. *(to flirt)* coquetear; *(to waste time)* gandulear.

dam[1] (dăm) I. s. *(barrier)* presa; *(reservoir)* embalse *m* II. tr. **-mm-** embalsar, represar.

dam[2] s. madre *f* (de cuadrúpedos).

dam·age (dăm'ĭj) I. s. daño; *(mechanical)* avería; FIG. perjuicio ♦ pl. daños y perjuicios II. tr. & intr. dañar(se), estropear(se).

dam·ask (dăm'əsk) s. damasco.

dame (dām) s. dama; JER. hembra.

damn (dăm) I. tr. condenar; *(to swear at)* maldecir II. interj. ♦ **d. (it)!** ¡maldito sea!, ¡maldición! III. s. ♦ **I don't give a d.** no me importa un comino • **it's not worth a d.** no vale un comino IV. adj. maldito V. adv. muy.

dam·na·tion (-nā'shən) I. s. condenación *f* II. interj. ¡maldición!

damned (dămd) I. adj. **-er, -est** condenado, maldito; FAM. *(huge)* tremendo II. adv. FAM. muy, sumamente III. s. ♦ **the d.** los condenados.

damp (dămp) I. adj. húmedo II. s. humedad *f*; *(gas)* mofeta III. tr. humedecer; *(a fire)* apagar; *(to discourage)* desanimar.

damp·en (dăm'pən) tr. humedecer; *(spirit, zeal)* deprimir, disminuir —intr. humedecerse.

damp·er (dăm'pər) s. TEC. compuerta de tiro; FÍS. amortiguador *m*; MÚS. sordina ♦ **to put a d. on** desanimar, apagar *(entusiasmo, ánimo)*.

damp·ness (dămp'nĭs) s. humedad *f*.

dam·sel (dăm′zəl) s. damisela.
dance (dăns) I. tr. & intr. bailar II. s. baile *m*.
danc·er (dăn′sər) s. bailador *m*; *(ballet)* bailarín *m*.
danc·ing (:sĭng) adj. & s. (de) baile *m*.
dan·de·li·on (dăn′dl-ī′ən) s. diente *m* de león.
dan·der (dăn′dər) s. FAM. cólera ♦ **to get someone's d. up** hacer que alguien rabie.
dan·dle (dăn′dl) tr. mecer.
dan·druff (dăn′drəf) s. caspa.
dan·dy (dăn′dē) I. s. dandi *m*, petimetre *m* II. adj. **-i-** FAM. excelente.
dan·ger (dān′jər) s. peligro.
dan·ger·ous (:əs) adj. peligroso.
dan·gle (dăng′gəl) tr. & intr. colgar(se), balancear(se) en el aire.
dank (dăngk) adj. malsano y húmedo.
dap·per (dăp′ər) adj. atildado, apuesto.
dap·ple (dăp′əl) I. tr. motear II. adj. moteado.
dare (dâr) I. tr. osar, atreverse —tr. *(to face)* arrostrar; *(to challenge)* retar, desafiar ♦ **I d. say** me parece probable II. s. desafío, reto.
dare·dev·il (′dĕv′əl) adj. & s. atrevido.
dar·ing (:ĭng) I. adj. temerario, audaz II. s. audacia, atrevimiento.
dark (därk) I. adj. oscuro; *(skin)* moreno, morocho; *(sky)* amenazador; *(dismal)* triste; *(evil)* siniestro; *(unknown)* misterioso; *(ignorant)* ignorante ♦ **Dark Ages** Alta Edad Media • **d. horse** candidato con un apoyo inesperado II. s. oscuridad *f*; *(nightfall)* anochecer *m*, noche *f* ♦ **to be in the d.** no estar informado.
dark·en (där′kən) tr. & intr. oscurecer(se); *(to sadden)* entristecer(se).
dark·ness (därk′nĭs) s. oscuridad *f*.
dark·room (:rōōm′) s. cuarto oscuro.
dar·ling (där′lĭng) I. s. querido, amado; *(favorite)* predilecto II. adj. querido, amado; FAM. *(charming)* encantador.
darn¹ (därn) COST. I. tr. zurcir —intr. hacer zurcidos II. s. zurcido.
darn² I. interj. ¡maldición! II. adj. maldito III. adv. FAM. muy.
darned (därnd) I. adj. maldito II. adv. muy.
darn·ing (där′nĭng) s. COST. zurcido.
dart (därt) I. intr. correr, lanzarse —tr. lanzar, arrojar II. s. dardo; *(movement)* movimiento rápido; COST. *(tuck)* pinza.
dash (dăsh) I. tr. *(to smash)* estrellar, romper; *(to hurl)* tirar; *(to splash)* salpicar; *(to spoil)* arruinar, frustrar ♦ **to d. off** hacer rápidamente —intr. correr, lanzarse ♦ **to d. in, out** entrar, salir corriendo II. s. *(bit)* pizca; *(rush)* prisa; *(race)* carrera corta; *(verve)* brío; IMPR. raya; AUTO. salpicadero ♦ **at a d.** de un golpe • **to make a d. at, for** precipitarse sobre, hacia • **to make a d. for it** echarse a correr, huir.
dash·board (′bôrd′) s. tablero de instrumentos, salpicadero.
dash·ing (:ĭng) adj. gallardo.
das·tard·ly (dăs′tərd-lē) adj. vil, ruin.
da·ta (dā′tə, dăt′ə) s.pl. *o* sg. información *f*, datos ♦ **d. bank** base *o* banco de datos • **d. processing** procesamiento de datos • **d. processor** ordenador, computadora.
da·ta·base (:bās′) s. base *f* de datos.
date¹ (dāt) I. s. fecha; *(epoch)* época; *(appointment)* cita, compromiso; *(companion)* acompañante *mf* ♦ **d. line** meridiano de cambio de fecha • **to d.** hasta la fecha II. tr. & intr. fechar; *(socially)* salir (con) ♦ **to d. back to** remontar(se) a • **to d. from** datar de.

date² s. *(fruit)* dátil *m* ♦ **d. palm** datilero.
dat·ed (dā′tĭd) adj. fechado; *(out-of-date)* pasado de moda, anticuado.
date·line (dāt′līn′) s. fecha y lugar *m* de origen.
da·tum (dā′təm, dăt′əm) s. [pl. **-ta**] dato.
daub (dôb) I. tr. revestir, embadurnar —intr. pintarrajear II. s. revestimiento, capa.
daugh·ter (dô′tər) s. hija.
daugh·ter-in-law (:ĭn-lô′) s. [pl. **daughters-**] nuera, hija política.
daunt (dônt) tr. intimidar; *(to dishearten)* desanimar.
daunt·less (′lĭs) adj. intrépido.
dau·phin (dô′fĭn) s. delfín *m*.
dav·en·port (dăv′ən-pôrt′) s. sofá *m* grande.
daw·dle (dôd′l) intr. andar despacio, demorarse —tr. ♦ **to d. away** perder, malgastar.
dawn (dôn) I. s. amanecer *m*, alba; FIG. albor *m* II. intr. amanecer ♦ **it dawned on me** caí en la cuenta.
day (dā) s. día *m*; *(workday)* jornada; *(epoch)* época ♦ **d. bed** sofá cama • **d. care** cuidado de niños durante el día • **day-care center** guardería • **d. in, d. out** día tras día • **d. laborer** jornalero, peón • **d. off** día franco • **d. school** externado • **from d. to d.** de un día para otro • **the d. after** al día siguiente • **the d. before...** la víspera de... • **these days** hoy en día • **to call it a d.** dar por acabado, retirarse • **to carry the d.** triunfar, llevarse la palma • **to have had one's d.** haber pasado de moda.
day·book (dā′bŏŏk′) s. diario.
day·break (dā′brāk′) s. amanecer *m*, alba.
day·dream (dā′drēm′) I. s. ensueño II. intr. **ed** *o* **-t** soñar despierto.
day·light (dā′līt′) s. luz *f* del día; *(dawn)* amanecer *m*; *(daytime)* día *m* ♦ **to scare the daylights out of** FAM. asustar mucho • **to see d.** llegar a comprender.
day·light-sav·ing (′-sā′vĭng) hora de verano.
day·long (dā′lông′) adj. & adv. (que dura) todo el día.
day·time (dā′tīm′) s. día *m*.
day-to-day (dā′tə-dā′) adj. *(daily)* cotidiano; *(a day at a time)* al día.
daze (dāz) I. tr. *(to stun)* aturdir; *(to dazzle)* deslumbrar II. s. aturdimiento.
daz·zle (dăz′əl) I. tr. deslumbrar II. s. deslumbramiento.
daz·zling (:lĭng) adj. deslumbrante.
dea·con (dē′kən) s. diácono.
dea·con·ess (dē′kə-nĭs) s. diaconisa.
de·ac·ti·vate (dē-ăk′tə-vāt′) tr. desactivar.
dead (dĕd) I. adj. muerto; *(numb)* insensible; *(motionless)* estancado; *(dull)* triste, aburrido; *(sounds)* sordo; *(a ball)* sin rebote; *(utter)* completo, absoluto; *(exact)* exacto, certero; DEP. fuera de juego; ELEC. sin corriente; *(battery)* descargado ♦ **d. center, weight** punto, peso muerto • **d. end** callejón sin salida • **d. letter** carta no reclamada • **d. reckoning** estima II. s. muerto ♦ **the d.** los muertos • **the d. of night, winter** plena noche, pleno invierno III. adv. *(absolutely)* completamente, absolutamente; *(exactly)* exactamente, justo.
dead·beat (′bĕt′) s. JER. gorrón *m*, holgazán *m*.
dead·en (:n) tr. amortiguar.
dead-end (:ĕnd′) adj. sin salida; FIG. sin porvenir.
dead·line (:līn′) s. fecha tope, plazo.
dead·lock (:lŏk′) I. s. estancamiento II. tr. & intr. estancar(se).

dead·ly (:lē) I. adj. -i- *(lethal)* mortífero; *(implacable)* mortal; *(destructive)* devastador; *(aim)* certero; *(sin)* capital; FAM. *(dull)* pesado extremadamente. II. adv. extremadamente.
dead·pan (:pǎn') JER. I. s. cara impasible II. adj. & adv. (de forma) impasible.
dead·wood (:wŏŏd') s. rama muerta; FIG. persona o cosa inútil.
deaf (děf) adj. sordo.
deaf-and-dumb ('ən-dǔm') s. & adj. sordomudo.
deaf·en ('ən) tr. ensordecer.
deaf·en·ing (:ə-nĭng) adj. ensordecedor.
deaf-mute (:myŏŏt') s. & adj. sordomudo.
deaf·ness (:nĭs) s. sordera.
deal (dēl) I. tr. dealt *(to apportion)* repartir, distribuir; *(a blow)* asestar; *(cards)* dar, repartir —intr. comerciar *(in en)* ◆ **to d. with** COM. tratar con; *(a situation)* enfrentarse con; *(to manage)* dirigir; *(to treat)* tratar de o sobre; *(to handle)* ocuparse de, encargarse de; *(to punish)* castigar II. s. *(agreement)* arreglo, convenio; *(in cards)* reparto; FAM. *(dealings)* trato ◆ **a good o great d.** mucho • **big d.!** ¡gran cosa! • **it's a d.!** ¡trato hecho! • **to make a big d. out of nothing** FAM. hacer un escándalo por nada.
deal·er (dē'lər) s. negociante mf, traficante mf; *(in cards)* banquero.
deal·er·ship (:shĭp') s. negocio.
deal·ings (dē'lĭngz) s.pl. *(business)* negocios; *(relations)* trato.
dean (dēn) s. EDUC. decano; RELIG. deán m.
dear (dîr) I. adj. querido; *(esteemed)* estimado; *(precious)* valioso; *(costly)* caro ◆ **D. Sir** Muy o Estimado señor mío II. adv. caro III. s. querido.
dear·ly (:lē) adv. *(costly)* caro; *(fondly)* con cariño; *(very much)* mucho.
dearth (dûrth) s. escasez f.
dear·y (dîr'ē) s. FAM. querido.
death (děth) s. muerte f ◆ **d. certificate** partida de defunción • **d. mask** mascarilla • **d. penalty** pena de muerte • **d. rate** índice de mortalidad • **d. warrant** orden de ejecución • **to be bored to d.** repetir hasta el aburrimiento • **to put to d.** ejecutar.
death·bed ('běd') s. lecho de muerte.
death·less (:lĭs) adj. inmortal.
death·ly (:lē) I. adj. cadavérico, sepulcral II. adv. mortalmente, muy.
death's-head (děths'hěd') s. calavera.
death·trap (děth'trǎp') s. construcción f o situación peligrosa.
death·watch (:wŏch') s. velatorio.
de·ba·cle (dĭ-bä'kəl) s. desastre m, fracaso.
de·bar (dē-bär') tr. -rr- excluir, prohibir.
de·bark (dĭ-bärk') tr. & intr. desembarcar.
de·bar·ka·tion (dē'bär-kā'shən) s. *(of people)* desembarco; *(of cargo)* desembarque m.
de·base (dĭ-bās') tr. *(to devalue)* desvalorizar; *(to degrade)* degradar, rebajar.
de·bat·a·ble (dĭ-bā'tə-bəl) adj. discutible.
de·bate (dĭ-bāt') I. tr. & intr. discutir, debatir II. s. discusión f, debate m.
de·bat·er (dĭ-bā'tər) s. polemista mf.
de·bauch (dĭ-bôch') tr. corromper, pervertir.
de·bauch·er·y (dĭ-bôch'ə-rē) s. libertinaje m.
de·bil·i·tate (dĭ-bĭl'ĭ-tāt') tr. debilitar.
deb·it (děb'ĭt) I. s. débito, debe m ◆ **d. balance** saldo deudor II. tr. cargar en cuenta.
deb·o·nair (děb'ə-nâr') adj. alegre, garboso.
de·brief (dē-brēf') tr. someter a un interrogatorio (después de cumplida una misión).
de·bris o **dé·bris** (də-brē', dā-) s. escombros m, desechos m; GEOL. detrito.
debt (dět) s. deuda ◆ **to be in someone's d.** estar en deuda con alguien • **to get** o **run into d.** contraer deudas.
debt·or (:ər) s. deudor m.
de·bug (dē-bǔg') tr. -gg- anular un dispositivo electrónico secreto; COMPUT. suprimir errores en, corregir.
de·but o **dé·but** (dā-byŏŏ') I. s. estreno, debut m II. intr. FAM. debutar.
de·bu·tante o **dé·bu·tante** (děb'yŏŏ-tänt') s. debutante f.
dec·ade (děk'ād') s. decenio, década.
de·ca·dence (děk'ə-dns) s. decadencia.
de·ca·dent (:dnt) adj. & s. decadente mf.
de·cal (dē'kǎl', dĭ-kǎl') s. calcomanía.
dec·a·me·ter (děk'ə-mē'tər) s. decámetro.
de·camp (dĭ-kǎmp') intr. FAM. largarse; MIL. decampar.
de·cant (dĭ-kǎnt') tr. decantar.
de·cant·er (dĭ-kǎn'tər) s. garrafa, jarra.
de·cap·i·tate (dĭ-kǎp'ĭ-tāt') tr. decapitar.
de·cath·lon (dĭ-kǎth'lən) s. decatlón m.
de·cay (dĭ-kā') I. intr. pudrirse, descomponerse; *(a tooth)* cariarse; FIS. desintegrarse; *(to get worse)* decaer II. s. descomposición f; *(of a tooth)* caries f; FIS. desintegración f; *(of morals)* decadencia.
de·cease (dĭ-sēs') I. intr. morir, fallecer II. s. muerte f, fallecimiento.
de·ceased (dĭ-sēst') adj. & s. difunto.
de·ce·dent (dĭ-sēd'nt) s. difunto.
de·ceit (dĭ-sēt') s. engaño, fraude m.
de·ceit·ful (:fəl) adj. engañoso.
de·ceive (dĭ-sēv') tr. & intr. engañar.
de·ceiv·er (dĭ-sē'vər) s. embustero.
de·cel·er·ate (dē-sěl'ə-rāt') tr. disminuir la velocidad de —intr. decelerar.
De·cem·ber (dĭ-sěm'bər) s. diciembre m.
de·cen·cy (dē'sən-sē) s. decencia, decoro.
de·cent (dē'sənt) adj. decente; *(kind)* bueno; FAM. *(dressed)* vestido.
de·cen·tral·ize (dē-sěn'trə-līz') tr. descentralizar.
de·cep·tion (dĭ-sěp'shən) s. engaño, fraude m.
de·cep·tive (:tĭv) adj. engañoso.
de·ci·bel (děs'ə-běl') s. decibel m, decibelio.
de·cide (dĭ-sīd') tr. & intr. decidir ◆ **to d. (up) on** optar por.
de·cid·ed (dĭ-sī'dĭd) adj. *(resolute)* decidido; *(definite)* claro, indudable.
de·cid·u·ous (dĭ-sĭj'ŏŏ-əs) adj. caduco.
dec·i·mal (děs'ə-məl) s. & adj. decimal m ◆ **d. point** coma.
dec·i·mate (:māt') tr. diezmar.
dec·i·me·ter (:mē'tər) s. decímetro.
de·ci·pher (dĭ-sī'fər) tr. descifrar.
de·ci·sion (dĭ-sĭzh'ən) s. decisión f.
de·ci·sive (dĭ-sī'sĭv) adj. decisivo.
de·ci·sive·ness (:nĭs) s. firmeza, decisión f.
deck¹ (děk) s. cubierta; *(of cards)* baraja ◆ **d. hand** marinero de cubierta • **to clear the d.** prepararse para la acción II. tr. tumbar.
deck² tr. adornar, engalanar ◆ **to d. oneself out** emperifollarse.
de·claim (dĭ-klām') tr. & intr. declamar.
dec·la·ra·tion (děk'lə-rā'shən) s. declaración f.
de·clar·a·tive (dĭ-klǎr'ə-tĭv) adj. declaratorio.
de·clare (dĭ-klâr') tr. declarar —intr. hacer una declaración ◆ **to d. against, for** pronun-

ciarse en contra, a favor de.

de·clas·si·fy (dē-klās'ə-fī') tr. anular la clasificación confidencial de.

de·clen·sion (dĭ-klĕn'shən) s. declinación f.

de·cline (dĭ-klīn') I. intr. *(to refuse)* rehusar, negarse; *(to slope)* inclinarse; *(to deteriorate)* deteriorarse; *(health)* decaer; *(prices)* bajar —tr. rehusar, rechazar; GRAM. declinar II. s. *(decrease)* disminución f; *(deterioration)* deterioro, declive m; *(of prices)* descenso.

de·clin·ing (dĭ-klī'nĭng) adj. declinante.

de·cliv·i·ty (dĭ-klĭv'ĭ-tē) s. declive m.

de·code (dē-kōd') tr. descifrar, descodificar.

de·cod·er (dē-kō'dər) s. descifrador m.

dé·colle·tage (dā'kŏl-täzh') s. escote m.

de·col·o·nize (dē-kŏl'ə-nīz') tr. descolonizar.

de·com·pose (dē'kəm-pōz') tr. & intr. *(into parts)* descomponer(se); *(to rot)* pudrir(se).

de·com·po·si·tion (dē-kŏm'pə-zĭsh'ən) s. descomposición f, putrefacción f.

de·com·press (dē'kəm-prĕs') tr. descomprimir.

de·com·pres·sor (:ər) s. descompresor m.

de·con·ges·tant (dē'kən-jĕs'tənt) s. descongestionante m.

de·con·tam·i·nate (dē'kən-tăm'ə-nāt') tr. descontaminar.

de·con·trol (dē'kən-trōl') I. tr. -ll- librar de control (gubernamental) II. s. anulación f del control.

dé·cor o **de·cor** (dā'kôr') s. decoración f.

dec·o·rate (dĕk'ə-rāt') tr. decorar; *(with medals)* condecorar.

dec·o·ra·tion ('-rā'shən) s. decoración f; *(medal)* condecoración f.

dec·o·ra·tive (dĕk'ər-ə-tĭv) adj. decorativo.

dec·o·ra·tor (:ə-rā'tər) s. decorador m.

dec·o·rous (:ər-əs) adj. decoroso.

de·co·rum (dĭ-kôr'əm) s. decoro.

de·coy I. s. (dē'koi') señuelo II. tr. (dĭ-koi') atraer con señuelo.

de·crease I. intr. & tr. (dĭ-krēs') disminuir, reducir II. s. (dē'krēs') disminución f.

de·creas·ing (dĭ-krē'sĭng) adj. decreciente.

de·cree (dĭ-krē') I. s. decreto II. tr. decretar.

de·crep·it (dĭ-krĕp'ĭt) adj. decrépito.

de·crim·i·nal·ize (dē-krĭm'ə-nə-līz') tr. legalizar.

de·cry (dĭ-krī') tr. despreciar, criticar.

ded·i·cate (dĕd'ĭ-kāt') tr. dedicar.

ded·i·ca·tion ('-kā'shən) s. dedicación f; *(inscription)* dedicatoria f.

de·duce (dĭ-dōōs') tr. deducir, inferir.

de·duct (dĭ-dŭkt') tr. restar, substraer.

de·duct·i·ble (dĭ-dŭk'tə-bəl) adj. deducible.

de·duc·tion (:shən) s. deducción f.

de·duc·tive (:tĭv) adj. deductivo.

deed (dēd) I. s. *(act)* acto; *(action)* hecho; *(feat)* proeza; DER. *(title)* escritura f (de propiedad) II. tr. traspasar por escritura.

deem (dēm) tr. considerar, juzgar.

deep (dēp) I. adj. profundo; *(measuring)* de profundidad; *(thick)* de espesor; *(distant)* distante; *(shrewd)* astuto; *(in thought)* absorto; *(colors)* subido; MÚS. bajo, grave ♦ **d. down** en el fondo • **d. in debt** cargado de deudas • **to go off the d. end** ponerse histérico II. adv. profundamente, en lo más hondo ♦ **d. into the night** hasta muy entrada la noche III. s. profundidad f; *(of night, winter)* lo más profundo; POÉT. el mar.

deep·en (dē'pən) tr. & intr. ahondar(se).

deep-fry (dēp'frī') tr. freír (por inmersión en aceite).

deep-sea (:sē') adj. de mar profundo.

deep-seat·ed (:sē'tĭd) adj. profundamente arraigado.

deep-set (:sĕt') adj. hundidos (los ojos).

deer (dîr) s.inv. ciervo, venado.

deer·skin ('skĭn) s. gamuza.

de·es·ca·late (dē-ĕs'kə-lāt') tr. disminuir.

de·face (dĭ-fās') tr. desfigurar, mutilar.

de·fam·a·to·ry (dĭ-făm'ə-tôr'ē) adj. difamatorio.

de·fame (dĭ-fām') tr. difamar, calumniar.

de·fault (dĭ-fôlt') I. s. incumplimiento; DER. contumacia ♦ **to win by d.** ganar por abandono II. intr. dejar de cumplir, faltar a un compromiso; DER. estar en rebeldía; DEP. dejar de presentarse.

de·feat (dĭ-fēt') I. tr. *(to beat)* derrotar, vencer; *(to thwart)* frustrar II. s. *(loss)* derrota; *(failure)* fracaso; *(frustration)* frustración f.

de·feat·ist (dĭ-fē'tĭst) s. derrotista mf.

def·e·cate (dĕf'ĭ-kāt') intr. defecar.

de·fect I. s. (dē'fĕkt') defecto, desperfecto II. intr. (dĭ-fĕkt') desertar.

de·fec·tion (dĭ-fĕk'shən) s. defección f.

de·fec·tive (:tĭv) adj. *(faulty)* defectuoso; *(subnormal)* deficiente; GRAM. defectivo.

de·fec·tor (:tər) s. desertor m.

de·fend (dĭ-fĕnd') tr. defender; *(to justify)* justificar; *(a theory)* sostener —intr. hacer una defensa.

de·fen·dant (dĭ-fĕn'dənt) s. acusado, demandado.

de·fend·er (:dər) s. defensor m.

de·fend·ing (:dĭng) adj. defensor.

de·fense (dĭ-fĕns') s. defensa.

de·fense·less (:lĭs) adj. indefenso.

de·fen·sive (dĭ-fĕn'sĭv) adj. defensivo.

de·fer (dĭ-fûr') tr. -rr- aplazar, postergar; MIL. otorgar una prórroga a —intr. deferir.

def·er·ence (dĕf'ər-əns) s. deferencia.

def·er·en·tial ('-rĕn'shəl) adj. deferente.

de·fer·ment (dĭ-fûr'mənt) s. aplazamiento; MIL. prórroga.

de·fer·ra·ble (:ə-bəl) adj. diferible, aplazable.

de·fer·ral (:əl) var. de **deferment**.

de·fi·ance (dĭ-fī'əns) s. desafío, reto.

de·fi·ant (:ənt) adj. provocador, desafiante.

de·fi·cient (dĭ-fĭsh'ənt) adj. deficiente, carente ♦ **to be d.** in carecer de.

def·i·cit (dĕf'ĭ-sĭt) s. déficit f ♦ **d. spending** gasto deficitario.

de·file (dĭ-fīl') tr. *(to dirty)* ensuciar, contaminar; *(to desecrate)* profanar; *(to rape)* violar.

de·fine (dĭ-fīn') tr. definir.

def·i·nite (dĕf'ə-nĭt) adj. definido; *(certain)* definitivo; *(explicit)* claro, explícito.

def·i·nite·ly (:lē) I. adv. definitivamente II. interj. ¡por supuesto!, ¡desde luego!

def·i·ni·tion (dĕf'ə-nĭsh'ən) s. definición f; *(of power, authority)* limitación f.

de·fin·i·tive (dĭ-fĭn'ĭ-tĭv) adj. definitivo.

de·flate (dĭ-flāt') tr. desinflar; *(pride)* rebajar; *(currency)* desvalorizar —intr. desinflarse.

de·fla·tion (dĭ-flā'shən) s. desinflamiento; *(of currency)* deflación f.

de·flect (dĭ-flĕkt') tr. & intr. desviar(se).

de·flow·er (dē-flou'ər) tr. desflorar.

de·fo·li·ant (dē-fō'lē-ənt) s. defoliante m.

de·fo·li·ate (:āt') tr. & intr. deshojar(se).

de·for·est (dē-fôr'ĭst) tr. desmontar.

de·form (dĭ-fôrm′) tr. & intr. deformar(se).
de·formed (dĭ-fôrmd′) adj. deforme, desfigurado.
de·for·mi·ty (dĭ-fôr′mĭ-tē) s. deformidad *f.*
de·fraud (dĭ-frôd′) tr. defraudar.
de·fray (dĭ-frā′) tr. sufragar, costear.
de·fray·al (:əl) s. subvención de gastos *f.*
de·frock (dē-frŏk′) tr. expulsar de una orden religiosa.
de·frost (dē-frôst′) tr. & intr. descongelar(se).
de·frost·er (dē-frô′stər) s. descongelador *m.*
deft (dĕft) adj. hábil, diestro.
deft·ness (:nĭs) s. habilidad *f,* destreza.
de·funct (dĭ-fŭngkt′) adj. difunto.
de·fuse (dē-fyōōz′) tr. quitar la espoleta a; *(hostility)* templar, minorar.
de·fy (dĭ-fī′) tr. desafiar; *(to resist)* resistir.
de·gen·er·a·cy (dĭ-jĕn′ər-ə-sē) s. degeneración *f.*
de·gen·er·ate (:ər-ĭt) I. adj. & s. degenerado II. intr. (:ə-rāt′) degenerar.
de·gen·er·a·tive (:ər-ə-tĭv) adj. degenerativo.
de·grade (dĭ-grād′) tr. degradar.
de·grad·ing (dĭ-grā′dĭng) adj. degradante.
de·gree (dĭ-grē′) s. grado; EDUC. título ♦ **by degrees** gradualmente, poco a poco • **doctor's d.** doctorado • **to a certain d.** hasta cierto punto • **to take a d. in** licenciarse en.
de·hu·man·ize (dē-hyōō′mə-nīz′) tr. deshumanizar.
de·hu·mid·i·fy (dē′hyōō-mĭd′ə-fī′) tr. deshumedecer.
de·hy·drate (dē-hī′drāt′) tr. deshidratar.
de·ice (dē-īs′) tr. deshelar.
de·i·cide (dē′ĭ-sīd′) s. deicidio; *(killer)* deicida *mf.*
de·i·fy (dē′ə-fī′) tr. deificar.
deign (dān) tr. & intr. dignarse (a).
de·ism (dē′ĭz′əm) s. deísmo.
de·i·ty (dē′ĭ-tē) s. deidad *f* ♦ **D.** Dios.
de·ject (dĭ-jĕkt′) tr. desanimar.
de·ject·ed (dĭ-jĕk′tĭd) adj. desanimado.
de·jec·tion (:shən) s. depresión *f.*
de·lay (dĭ-lā′) I. tr. *(to postpone)* postergar; *(to make late)* retrasar, demorar; *(to stall)* entretener —intr. demorarse, tardar II. s. demora, retraso; *(postponement)* postergación *f* ♦ **a five minute d.** cinco minutos de atraso.
de·lec·ta·ble (dĭ-lĕk′tə-bəl) adj. delicioso.
del·e·gate I. s. (dĕl′ĭ-gĭt) delegado, diputado II. tr. (:gāt′) delegar.
de·lete (dĭ-lēt′) tr. tachar, suprimir.
del·e·te·ri·ous (dĕl′ĭ-tîr′ē-əs) adj. deletéreo.
de·le·tion (dĭ-lē′shən) s. tachadura, supresión *f.*
de·lib·er·ate I. adj. (dĭ-lĭb′ər-ĭt) deliberado, a propósito; *(slow)* pausado II. intr. & tr. (:ə-rāt′) deliberar.
de·lib·er·a·tion (dĭ-lĭb′ə-rā′shən) s. deliberación *f; (slowness)* lentitud *f.*
del·i·ca·cy (dĕl′ĭ-kə-sē) s. delicadeza; *(fine food)* manjar *m,* gollería.
del·i·cate (dĕl′ĭ-kĭt) adj. delicado.
del·i·ca·tes·sen (dĕl′ĭ-kə-tĕs′ən) s. fiambrería.
de·li·cious (dĭ-lĭsh′əs) adj. delicioso.
de·light (dĭ-līt′) I. s. deleite *m; (person, thing)* encanto II. tr. deleitar, encantar —intr. ♦ **to d. in** deleitarse con *o* en.
de·light·ed (dĭ-lī′tĭd) adj. encantado.
de·light·ful (dĭ-līt′fəl) adj. delicioso, encantador.
de·lin·e·ate (dĭ-lĭn′ē-āt′) tr. delinear; *(to depict)* describir, pintar.

de·lin·quen·cy (dĭ-lĭng′kwən-sē) s. delincuencia.
de·lin·quent (:kwənt) I. adj. delincuente; *(in payment)* moroso II. s. delincuente *mf.*
del·i·quesce (dĕl′ĭ-kwĕs′) intr. licuarse.
de·lir·i·ous (dĭ-lîr′ē-əs) adj. delirante.
de·lir·i·um (:əm) s. delirio, desvarío.
de·liv·er (dĭ-lĭv′ər) tr. *(to free)* liberar; *(to hand over)* entregar; *(mail)* repartir; *(a blow, speech)* dar; *(missile)* lanzar; *(baby)* asistir al parto de ♦ **to d. oneself of an opinion** opinar —intr. cumplir *(on con); (to give birth)* alumbrar ♦ **we d.** entregamos a domicilio.
de·liv·er·ance (:əns) s. liberación *f.*
de·liv·er·er (:ər) s. liberador *m.*
de·liv·er·y (dĭ-lĭv′ə-rē) s. entrega; *(release)* liberación *f; (birth)* parto; *(style)* elocución *f.*
de·liv·er·y·man (:măn′) s. [pl. **-men**] repartidor *m.*
dell (dĕl) s. valle pequeño.
de·louse (dē-lous′) tr. despiojar, espulgar.
del·phin·i·um (dĕl-fĭn′ē-əm) s. delfinio.
de·lude (dĭ-lōōd′) tr. engañar, despistar.
del·uge (dĕl′yōōj) I. tr. inundar II. s. inundación *f,* diluvio.
de·lu·sion (dĭ-lōō′zhən) s. engaño, ilusión *f;* MED. delirio.
de·lu·sive (:sĭv) adj. ilusorio, falso.
de luxe *o* **de·luxe** (dĭ-lŭks′) adj. de lujo, lujoso.
delve (dĕlv) intr. indagar, hurgar.
dem·a·gog·ic (dĕm′ə-gŏj′ĭk) adj. demagógico.
dem·a·gogue (dĕm′ə-gôg′) s. demagogo.
dem·a·gogu·er·y (:gŏ′gə-rē) s. demagogia.
de·mand (dĭ-mănd′) I. tr. *(to ask for)* demandar; *(to claim, require)* reclamar, exigir II. s. *(request)* solicitud *f; (claim)* reclamación *f; (requirement)* necesidad *f;* COM. demanda ♦ **d. deposit** depósito a la vista ♦ **on d.** COM. a la vista; *(by request)* a petición • **to be in d.** ser popular.
de·mand·ing (dĭ-măn′dĭng) adj. exigente.
de·mar·cate (dĭ-mär′kāt′) tr. demarcar.
de·mean (dĭ-mēn′) tr. rebajar ♦ **to d. oneself** rebajarse.
de·mean·or (dĭ-mē′nər) s. comportamiento.
de·ment·ed (dĭ-mĕn′tĭd) adj. demente, loco.
de·mer·it (dĭ-mĕr′ĭt) s. desmerecimiento.
dem·i·god (dĕm′ē-gŏd′) s. semidiós *m.*
dem·i·john (:jŏn′) s. damajuana, garrafón *m.*
de·mil·i·ta·rize (dē-mĭl′ĭ-tə-rīz′) tr. desmilitarizar.
de·mise (dĭ-mīz′) s. fallecimiento, defunción *f;* DER. traspaso (de bienes).
dem·i·tasse (dĕm′ē-tăs′) s. tacita de café.
de·mo·bil·ize (dē-mō′bə-līz′) tr. desmovilizar.
de·moc·ra·cy (dĭ-mŏk′rə-sē) s. democracia.
dem·o·crat (dĕm′ə-krăt′) s. demócrata *mf.*
dem·o·crat·ic ('-′ĭk) adj. democrático.
de·moc·ra·tize (dĭ-mŏk′rə-tīz′) tr. democratizar.
dem·o·graph·ic (dĕm′ə-grăf′ĭk) adj. demográfico ♦ **demographics** s.pl. datos demográficos.
de·mog·ra·phy (dĭ-mŏg′rə-fē) s. demografía.
de·mol·ish (dĭ-mŏl′ĭsh) tr. demoler, derribar.
dem·o·li·tion (dĕm′ə-lĭsh′ən) s. demolición *f.*
de·mon (dē′mən) s. demonio.
de·mon·ic (dĭ-mŏn′ĭk) adj. demoníaco.
dem·on·strate (dĕm′ən-strāt′) tr. demostrar —intr. protestar, manifestarse.
dem·on·stra·tion ('-strā′shən) s. demostración *f; (rally)* manifestación *f.*
de·mon·stra·tive (dĭ-mŏn′strə-tĭv) adj. demos-

trativo; *(expressive)* expresivo, efusivo.

dem·on·stra·tor (dĕm′ən-strā′tər) s. *(sample)* modelo de muestra; *(person)* manifestante *mf.*

de·mor·al·ize (dĭ-môr′ə-līz′) tr. desmoralizar.

de·mote (dĭ-mōt′) tr. degradar.

de·mo·tion (dĭ-mō′shən) s. degradación *f.*

de·mur (dĭ-mûr′) intr. **-rr-** hacer objeciones.

de·mure (dĭ-myŏŏr′) adj. **-er, -est** recatado.

den (dĕn) s. *(lair)* cubil *m; (study)* estudio.

de·na·ture (dē-nā′chər) tr. desnaturalizar.

de·ni·al (dĭ-nī′əl) s. negativa; *(disavowal)* repudio; DER. denegación *f.*

den·i·grate (dĕn′ĭ-grāt′) tr. denigrar.

den·im (dĕn′ĭm) s. dril *m* de algodón ♦ pl. vaqueros.

den·i·zen (dĕn′ĭ-zən) s. habitante *mf.*

de·nom·i·na·tion (dĭ-nŏm′ə-nā′shən) s. denominación *f; (sect)* secta, creencia.

de·nom·i·na·tion·al (:shə-nəl) adj. sectario.

de·nom·i·na·tor (-′-′tər) s. denominador *m.*

de·note (dĭ-nōt′) tr. denotar.

dé·noue·ment (dā′nŏŏ-mä′) s. desenlace *m.*

de·nounce (dĭ-nouns′) tr. denunciar.

dense (dĕns) adj. denso; FAM. estúpido.

den·si·ty (dĕn′sĭ-tē) s. densidad *f;* FAM. estupidez *f.*

dent (dĕnt) **I.** s. abolladura, mella **II.** tr. & intr. abollar(se), mellar(se).

den·tal (dĕn′tl) adj. dental ♦ **d. plate** dentadura postiza.

den·ti·frice (:tə-frĭs) s. dentífrico.

den·tist (dĕn′tĭst) s. dentista *mf.*

den·tist·ry (:tĭ-strē) s. odontología.

den·ture (:chər) s. dentadura postiza.

de·nude (dĭ-nŏŏd′) tr. desnudar, despojar.

de·nun·ci·a·tion (dĭ-nŭn′sē-ā′shən) s. denuncia; *(criticism)* censura, crítica.

de·ny (dĭ-nī′) tr. negar; *(to withhold)* rehusar; *(to repudiate)* repudiar ♦ **to d. oneself** privarse de.

de·o·dor·ant (dē-ō′dər-ənt) s. desodorante *m.*

de·o·dor·ize (:də-rīz′) tr. desodorizar.

de·part (dĭ-pärt′) intr. marcharse, irse; *(train, bus)* salir ♦ **to d. from** apartarse de —tr. partir de.

de·part·ed (dĭ-pär′tĭd) adj. & s. difunto.

de·part·ment (dĭ-pärt′mənt) s. departamento; POL. ministerio ♦ **d. store** gran almacén.

de·par·ture (dĭ-pär′chər) s. partida, salida; *(deviation)* desviación *f.*

de·pend (dĭ-pĕnd′) intr. ♦ **to d. (up)on** *(as a dependent, consequence)* depender de; *(to trust)* confiar en, fiar; *(to count on)* contar con • **you can d. on it!** ¡puedes estar seguro!

de·pend·a·bil·i·ty (dĭ-pĕn′də-bĭl′ĭ-tē) s. *(person)* seriedad *f; (machine)* seguridad *f* de funcionamiento.

de·pend·a·ble (-′-bəl) adj. *(trustworthy)* (digno de confianza; *(reliable)* seguro.

de·pend·ence/ance (dĭ-pĕn′dəns) s. dependencia *(on, upon* de); *(trust)* confianza *(on, upon* en).

de·pend·ent/ant (:dənt) **I.** adj. ♦ **d. (up)on** dependiente de, *(upon)* basarse a cargo.

de·per·son·al·ize (dē-pûr′sə-nə-līz′) tr. despersonalizar.

de·pict (dĭ-pĭkt′) tr. representar, pintar.

de·pil·a·to·ry (dĭ-pĭl′ə-tôr′ē) **I.** adj. depilatorio **II.** s. crema depilatoria.

de·plane (dē-plān′) intr. bajar del avión.

de·plete (dĭ-plēt′) tr. agotar, reducir.

de·ple·tion (dĭ-plē′shən) tr. agotamiento.

de·plor·a·ble (dĭ-plôr′ə-bəl) adj. deplorable.

de·plore (dĭ-plôr′) tr. deplorar, desaprobar.

de·ploy (dĭ-ploi′) tr. & intr. desplegar(se).

de·ploy·ment (:mənt) s. despliegue *m.*

de·po·nent (dĭ-pō′nənt) s. declarante *mf.*

de·pop·u·late (dē-pŏp′yə-lāt′) tr. despoblar.

de·port (dĭ-pôrt′) tr. deportar, expulsar.

de·port·ee (dē′pôr-tē′) s. deportado.

de·port·ment (dĭ-pôrt′mənt) s. conducta.

de·pose (dĭ-pōz′) tr. deponer.

de·pos·it (dĭ-pŏz′ĭt) **I.** tr. depositar; COM. *(down payment)* dar de señal o de entrada **II.** s. depósito; *(down payment)* señal *f,* entrada.

dep·o·si·tion (dĕp′ə-zĭsh′ən) s. POL. deposición *f;* DER. declaración *f.*

de·pos·i·tor (dĭ-pŏz′ĭ-tər) s. cuentacorrentista *mf.*

de·pos·i·to·ry (:tôr′ē) s. depositaría, almacén *m.*

de·pot (dē′pō) s. *(bus, train)* estación *f; (warehouse)* almacén *m,* depósito.

de·prave (dĭ-prāv′) tr. depravar, pervertir.

de·prav·i·ty (dĭ-prăv′ĭ-tē) s. depravación *f.*

dep·re·cate (dĕp′rĭ-kāt′) tr. desaprobar.

de·pre·ci·ate (dĭ-prē′shē-āt′) tr. *(to devalue)* depreciar, desvalorar; *(to belittle)* despreciar —intr. depreciarse.

de·pre·ci·a·tion (-′-ā′shən) s. depreciación *f,* desvalorización *f.*

dep·re·da·tion (dĕp′rĭ-dā′shən) s. depredación *f,* pillaje *m.*

de·press (dĭ-prĕs′) tr. *(to dispirit)* deprimir, desanimar; *(to press down)* presionar; *(prices)* bajar.

de·pres·sant (:ənt) s. sedante *m.*

de·pressed (dĭ-prĕst′) adj. deprimido; ECON. *(period)* de depresión; *(economy)* deprimido.

de·press·ing (dĭ-prĕs′ĭng) adj. deprimente.

de·pres·sion (dĭ-prĕsh′ən) s. *(a hollow)* cavidad *f,* hueco; ECON., MED. depresión *f.*

de·pres·sur·ize (dē-prĕsh′ə-rīz′) tr. descomprimir.

dep·ri·va·tion (dĕp′rə-vā′shən) s. privación *f.*

de·prive (dĭ-prīv′) tr. privar.

de·prived (dĭ-prīvd′) adj. pobre, necesitado.

depth (dĕpth) s. profundidad *f; (most intense part)* lo más profundo; *(color)* intensidad *f* ♦ **d. charge** carga de profundidad ♦ **in d.** a fondo ♦ pl. lo más hondo, FIG. lo más recóndito.

dep·u·tize (dĕp′yə-tīz′) tr. diputar, delegar.

dep·u·ty (:tē) s. *(delegate)* delegado; *(assistant)* asistente *m; (legislator)* diputado.

de·rail (dē-rāl′) tr. & intr. (hacer) descarrilar.

de·range (dĭ-rānj′) tr. *(to disturb)* perturbar, desordenar; *(to make insane)* enloquecer.

de·ranged (dĭ-rānjd′) adj. loco, trastornado.

de·range·ment (dĭ-rānj′mənt) s. desorden *m,* desarreglo; MED. trastorno (mental).

der·by (dûr′bē) s. *(race)* carrera; *(hat)* sombrero hongo.

de·reg·u·late (dē-rĕg′yə-lāt′) tr. quitar las reglamentaciones de.

der·e·lict (dĕr′ə-lĭkt′) **I.** s. *(person)* vago; *(ship)* derrelicto **II.** adj. *(remiss)* remiso; *(property)* abandonado.

de·ride (dĭ-rīd′) tr. burlarse de, mofarse de.

de·ri·sion (dĭ-rĭzh′ən) s. burla, mofa.

de·ri·sive/so·ry (dĭ-rī′sĭv/sə-rē) adj. *(mocking)* burlón, mofador; *(ridiculous)* irrisorio.

de·rive (dĭ-rīv′) tr. & intr. derivar *(from* de).

der·ma·tol·o·gy (dûr′mə-tŏl′ə-jē) s. dermatología.

der·o·ga·tion (dĕr′ə-gā′shən) s. *(disparagement)* menosprecio; DER. derogación *f.*

de·rog·a·to·ry/tive (dĭ-rŏg′ə-tôr′ē/tĭv) adj. *(disparaging)* despectivo; DER. derogatorio.

der·rick (dĕr′ĭk) s. *(crane)* grúa; *(of oil well)* torre *f* de perforación.

der·ring-do (dĕr′ĭng-dōo′) s. intrepidez *f.*

der·vish (dûr′vĭsh) s. derviche *m.*

de·sal·i·nate (dē-săl′ə-nāt′) tr. desalar.

de·scend (dĭ-sĕnd′) intr. descender; *(inheritance)* transmitirse por herencia ♦ **to d. on** o **upon** caer encima de —tr. descender, bajar.

de·scen·dant (dĭ-sĕn′dənt) s. descendiente *mf.*

de·scent (dĭ-sĕnt′) s. descenso; *(slope)* declive *m; (lineage)* descendencia; MIL. embestida.

de·scribe (dĭ-skrīb′) tr. describir.

de·scrip·tion (dĭ-skrĭp′shən) s. descripción *f* ♦ **of every d.** de toda clase.

de·scrip·tive (:tĭv) adj. descriptivo.

de·scry (dĭ-skrī′) tr. divisar, descubrir.

des·e·crate (dĕs′ĭ-krāt′) tr. profanar.

de·seg·re·gate (dē-sĕg′rĭ-gāt′) intr. & tr. eliminar la segregación racial (en).

de·sen·si·tize (dē-sĕn′sĭ-tīz′) tr. desensibilizar.

des·ert[1] (dĕz′ərt) s. desierto ♦ **d. heat** calor desértico.

de·sert[2] (dĭ-zûrt′) s. ♦ pl. *(one's due)* merecido.

de·sert[3] (dĭ-zûrt′) tr. abandonar; MIL. desertar de —intr. desertar.

de·sert·er (dĭ-zûr′tər) s. desertor *m.*

de·ser·tion (:shən) s. deserción *f.*

de·serve (dĭ-zûrv′) tr. & intr. merecer(se).

de·serv·ing (dĭ-zûr′vĭng) adj. digno, meritorio.

des·ic·cate (dĕs′ĭ-kāt′) tr. & intr. desecar(se).

de·sign (dĭ-zīn′) I. tr. *(to invent)* idear; *(a plan)* diseñar; *(pattern)* dibujar; *(to intend)* proyectar —intr. hacer diseños II. s. diseño; ARTE. dibujo; ARQ. plano; *(intention)* propósito ♦ **by d.** intencionalmente • **to have designs on** poner las miras en.

des·ig·nate (dĕz′ĭg-nāt′) I. tr. designar; *(to characterize)* describir II (:nĭt) adj. designado.

de·sign·er (dĭ-zī′nər) s. diseñador *m.*

de·sir·a·ble (dĭ-zīr′ə-bəl) adj. deseable.

de·sire (dĭ-zīr′) I. tr. desear II. s. deseo.

de·sir·ous (:əs) adj. deseoso.

de·sist (dĭ-zĭst′) intr. dejar de hacer algo.

desk (dĕsk) s. escritorio; *(at school)* pupitre *m; (in hotel)* recepción *f; (counter, booth)* mesa.

des·o·late I. adj. (dĕs′ə-lĭt) desolado II. tr. (:lāt′) *(to distress)* desconsolar.

de·spair (dĭ-spâr′) I. s. desesperación *f* II. intr. desesperar(se).

des·per·a·do (dĕs′pə-rä′dō) s. [pl. **(e)s**] forajido, bandolero.

des·per·ate (dĕs′pər-ĭt) adj. desesperado; *(grave)* crítico; *(urgent)* apremiante.

des·per·a·tion (′pə-rā′shən) s. desesperación *f.*

des·pi·ca·ble (dĕs′pĭk′ə-bəl) adj. odioso, vil.

de·spise (dĭ-spīz′) tr. despreciar.

de·spite (dĭ-spīt′) prep. a pesar de, no obstante.

de·spoil (dĭ-spoil′) tr. expoliar, saquear.

de·spon·dence/·cy (dĭ-spŏn′dəns) s. desánimo.

de·spon·dent (:dənt) adj. desanimado.

des·pot (dĕs′pət) s. déspota *mf.*

des·pot·ic (dĕ-spŏt′ĭk) adj. despótico.

des·pot·ism (dĕs′pə-tĭz′əm) s. despotismo.

des·sert (dĭ-zûrt′) s. CUL. postre *m.*

de·sta·bi·lize (dē-stā′bə-līz′) tr. desestabilizar.

des·ti·na·tion (dĕs′tə-nā′shən) s. destino.

des·tine (dĕs′tĭn) tr. destinar ♦ **destined for** con destino a.

des·ti·ny (dĕs′tə-nē) s. destino, sino.

des·ti·tute (dĕs′tĭ-tōot′) adj. indigente.

des·ti·tu·tion (′-tōo′shən) s. miseria.

de·stroy (dĭ-stroi′) tr. destruir.

de·stroy·er (:ər) s. destructor *m.*

de·struct (dĭ-strŭkt′) s. destrucción deliberada de un vehículo espacial.

de·struc·tion (dĭ-strŭk′shən) s. destrucción *f.*

de·struc·tive (:tĭv) adj. destructivo, destructor ♦ **d. of** o **to** perjudicial para.

des·ul·to·ry (dĕs′əl-tôr′ē) adj. sin entusiasmo.

de·tach (dĭ-tăch′) tr. separar, desprender.

de·tach·a·ble (:ə-bəl) adj. desmontable.

de·tached (dĭ-tăcht′) adj. separado; *(aloof)* indiferente, despreocupado.

de·tach·ment (dĭ-tăch′mənt) s. separación *f; (impartiality)* objetividad *f; (aloofness)* indiferencia; MIL. destacamento.

de·tail (dĭ-tāl′, dē′tāl′) I. s. detalle *m*, pormenor *m*; MIL. destacamento II. tr. detallar.

detailed (dĭ-tāld′, dē′tāld′) adj. detallado, minucioso.

de·tain (dĭ-tān′) tr. *(to delay)* retardar, demorar; *(in custody)* detener.

de·tect (dĭ-tĕkt′) tr. percibir, detectar.

de·tec·tion (dĭ-tĕk′shən) s. descubrimiento.

de·tec·tive (dĭ-tĕk′tĭv) s. detective *mf* ♦ **d. story** novela policial.

de·tec·tor (:tər) s. detector *m.*

dé·tente (dā-tänt′) s. distensión *f.*

de·ten·tion (dĭ-tĕn′shən) s. detención *f.*

de·ter (dĭ-tûr′) tr. **-rr-** impedir.

de·ter·gent (dĭ-tûr′jənt) s. detergente *m.*

de·te·ri·o·rate (dĭ-tîr′ē-ə-rāt′) intr. empeorar, degenerar.

de·ter·mi·nant (dĭ-tûr′mə-nənt) adj. & s. determinante *m.*

de·ter·mi·nate (:nĭt) adj. definitivo.

de·ter·mi·na·tion (-′-nā′shən) s. determinación *f; (resolve)* resolución *f;* DER. *(ruling)* decisión *f.*

de·ter·mine (dĭ-tûr′mĭn) tr. determinar —intr. decidir.

de·ter·mined (:mĭnd) adj. determinado.

de·ter·min·ing (:mĭ-nĭng) adj. decisivo.

de·ter·rence (:əns) s. disuasión *f.*

de·ter·rent (:ənt) I. s. agente disuasivo; MIL. fuerza de disuasión II. adj. impeditivo; MIL. de disuasión.

de·test (dĭ-tĕst′) tr. detestar, aborrecer.

de·throne (dē-thrōn′) tr. destronar.

det·o·nate (dĕt′n-āt′) tr. & intr. (hacer) detonar.

det·o·na·tor (:ā′tər) s. detonador *m.*

de·tour (dē′tŏŏr′) I. s. desvío II. s. & intr. & tr. desviar(se).

de·tox·i·fi·ca·tion (dē-tŏk′sə-fĭ-kā′shən) s. desintoxicación *f.*

de·tract (dĭ-trăkt′) intr. ♦ **to d. from** disminuir.

de·trac·tion (dĭ-trăk′shən) s. disminución *f.*

de·train (dē-trān′) intr. bajar de un tren.

det·ri·ment (dĕt′rə-mənt) s. detrimento.

det·ri·men·tal (′-mĕn′tl) adj. perjudicial.

deuce (dōos) s. dos *m.*

deu·te·ri·um (dōo-tîr′ē-əm) s. deuterio.

de·val·u·ate/val·ue (dē-văl′yōo-āt′/văl′yoo) tr. devaluar, desvalorizar.

dev·as·tate (dĕv′ə-stāt′) tr. devastar, asolar; *(to overwhelm)* abrumar.

dev·as·tat·ing (:stā′tĭng) adj. devastador.

dev·as·ta·tion ('-'shən) s. devastación f.
de·vel·op (dĭ-vĕl'əp) tr. desarrollar; *(the body)* fortalecer; *(an ability)* formar; *(land)* urbanizar; *(taste)* adquirir; *(habit, disease)* contraer; FOTOG. revelar —intr. desarrollarse; *(to advance)* progresar; *(to be disclosed)* descubrirse, revelarse.
de·vel·op·er (:ə-pər) s. urbanizador m; FOTOG. revelador m.
de·vel·op·ing (:pĭng) adj. en (vías de) desarrollo.
de·vel·op·ment (dĭ-vĕl'əp-mənt) s. desarrollo; *(event)* suceso, FOTOG. revelado.
de·vi·ance (dē'vē-əns) s. desviación f.
de·vi·ant (:ənt) adj. & s. pervertido.
de·vi·ate (dē'vē-āt') intr. desviarse.
de·vi·a·tion ('-ā'shən) s. desviación f; *(from the truth)* alejamiento.
de·vice (dĭ-vīs') s. *(scheme)* ardid m; *(mechanism)* dispositivo, aparato; LIT. recurso.
dev·il (dĕv'əl) s. diablo ♦ **a d. of (something)** (algo) del diablo ♦ **d.'s advocate** abogado del diablo • **to give the d. his due** dar a cada uno lo suyo.
dev·il·ish (:ə-lĭsh) I. adj. diabólico, malvado; *(mischievous)* travieso.
dev·il·try/ry (:əl-trē/rē) s. diablura.
de·vi·ous (dē'vē-əs) adj. tortuoso.
de·vise (dĭ-vīz') tr. *(to conceive)* idear, concebir; *(to contrive)* trazar, tramar.
de·vi·tal·ize (dē-vīt'l-īz') tr. debilitar.
de·void (dĭ-void') adj. desprovisto, carente.
de·volve (dĭ-vŏlv') tr. transferir, delegar.
de·vote (dĭ-vōt') tr. dedicar, consagrar.
de·vot·ed (dĭ-vō'tĭd) adj. *(loving)* afectuoso; *(dedicated)* devoto; *(ardent)* fervoroso.
dev·o·tee (dĕv'ə-tē') s. devoto.
de·vo·tion (dĭ-vō'shən) s. devoción f ♦ pl. oraciones, rezos.
de·vo·tion·al (:shə-nəl) I. adj. devoto II. s. oficio religioso breve.
de·vour (dĭ-vour') tr. devorar, engullir.
de·vour·ing (dĭ-vou'rĭng) adj. devorador.
de·vout (dĭ-vout') adj. **-er, -est** *(pious)* devoto; *(earnest)* fervoroso.
de·vout·ness (:nĭs) s. devoción f, piedad f.
dew (dōō) s. rocío ♦ **d. point** punto de condensación.
dew·drop ('drŏp') s. gota de rocío.
dew·y (:ē) adj. rociado; FIG. puro, fresco.
dex·ter·i·ty (dĕk-stĕr'ĭ-tē) s. destreza.
dex·ter·ous (dĕk'tər-əs) adj. diestro, hábil.
dex·trose (dĕk'strōs') s. dextrosa.
di·a·be·tes (dī'ə-bē'tĭs) s. diabetes f.
di·a·bet·ic (:bĕt'ĭk) adj. & s. diabético.
di·a·bol·ic/i·cal (dī'ə-bŏl'ĭk) adj. diabólico.
di·a·crit·ic (dī'ə-krĭt'ĭk) s. signo diacrítico.
di·a·dem (dī'ə-dĕm') s. diadema.
di·ag·nose (dī'əg-nōs') tr. diagnosticar.
di·ag·no·sis (:nō'sĭs) s. [pl. **-ses**] diagnóstico.
di·ag·nos·tic (:nŏs'tĭk) adj. diagnóstico.
di·ag·o·nal (dī-ăg'ə-nəl) adj. & s. diagonal f.
di·a·gram (dī'ə-grăm') I. s. diagrama m II. tr. **-mm-** representar con un diagrama.
di·al (dī'əl) I. s. *(scale, clock)* esfera, cuadrante m; RAD., TELEV. dial m, botón m selector; TEL. disco ♦ **d. tone** TEL. tono para marcar II. tr. RAD., TELEV. sintonizar; TEL. marcar (un número).
di·a·lect (dī'ə-lĕkt') s. dialecto.
di·a·lec·tic (dī'ə-lĕk'tĭk) I. s. dialéctica II. adj. /**ti·cal** dialéctico.

di·a·lec·tics (:tĭks) s.sg. dialéctica.
di·a·log(ue) (dī'ə-lôg') s. diálogo.
di·al·y·sis (dī-ăl'ĭ-sĭs) s. diálisis f.
di·am·e·ter (dī-ăm'ĭ-tər) s. diámetro.
di·a·met·ric/ri·cal (dī'ə-mĕt'rĭk) adj. diametral, del diámetro; *(contrary)* opuesto.
di·a·mond (dī'ə-mənd) s. diamante m; *(shape)* rombo ♦ **d. ring** sortija de diamantes.
di·a·per (dī'pər) I. s. pañal m II. tr. poner el pañal a.
di·aph·a·nous (dī-ăf'ə-nəs) adj. diáfano.
di·a·phragm (dī'ə-frăm') s. diafragma m.
di·a·rist (dī'ə-rĭst) s. diarista mf.
di·ar·rh(o)e·a (dī'ə-rē'ə) s. diarrea.
di·a·ry (dī'ə-rē) s. diario.
di·as·to·le (dī-ăs'tə-lē) s. diástole f.
di·a·tribe (dī'ə-trīb') s. diatriba.
dice (dīs) I. s.pl. [sg. **die**] dados II. tr. picar en cubitos.
di·chot·o·my (dī-kŏt'ə-mē) s. dicotomía.
dick (dĭk) s. JER. sabueso, detective m.
dick·ens (dĭk'ənz) s. diablo, demonio.
dick·er (dĭk'ər) intr. ♦ **to d. (over)** regatear.
dic·tate I. tr. (dĭk'tāt', -') *(letter)* dictar; *(policy)* imponer —intr. mandar II. s. ('') mandato ♦ pl. dictados.
dic·ta·tion (dĭk-tā'shən) s. dictado.
dic·ta·tor (dĭk'tā'tər) s. dictador m.
dic·ta·tor·ship ('-'shĭp) s. dictadura.
dic·tion (dĭk'shən) s. dicción f.
dic·tion·ar·y (dĭk'shə-nĕr'ē) s. diccionario.
dic·tum (dĭk'təm) s. [pl. **s** o **-ta**] dictamen m.
did (dĭd) cf. **do.**
di·dac·tic/ti·cal (dī-dăk'tĭk) adj. didáctico.
didn't (dĭd'nt) contr. de **did not.**
die¹ (dī) intr. **dy·ing** morir; *(to lose force)* apagarse, disminuir; *(to become extinct)* extinguirse, desaparecer.
die² s. [pl. **s**] MAQ. cuño, troquel m; [pl. **dice**] *(for gambling)* dado ♦ **the d. is cast** la suerte está echada.
die·hard (dī'härd') s. testarudo.
die·sel engine (dē'zəl) s. motor diesel.
di·et¹ (dī'ĭt) s. & intr. (estar a) dieta.
di·et² s. POL. dieta.
di·e·tar·y (dī'ĭ-tĕr'ē) adj. dietético.
di·et·er (:tər) s. persona que hace dieta.
di·e·tet·ic (dī'ĭ-tĕt'ĭk) adj. dietético.
di·e·ti·tian/cian (:tĭsh'ən) s. dietista mf.
dif·fer (dĭf'ər) intr. disentir, no estar de acuerdo ♦ **to d. from** diferir con, ser diferente de.
dif·fer·ence (:əns) s. diferencia ♦ **it makes no d.** da lo mismo • **what d. does it make?** ¿qué más da? • **what's the d.?** ¿qué importa?
dif·fer·ent (:ənt) adj. diferente, distinto.
dif·fer·en·ti·ate (dĭf'ə-rĕn'shē-āt') tr. & intr. diferenciar(se), distinguir(se).
dif·fi·cult (dĭf'ĭ-kəlt) adj. difícil.
dif·fi·cul·ty (:kəl-tē) s. dificultad f ♦ pl. apuros.
dif·fi·dent (dĭf'ĭ-dnt) adj. tímido.
dif·frac·tion (dĭ-frăk'shən) s. difracción f.
dif·fuse I. tr. & intr. (dĭ-fyōōz') difundir(se) II. adj. (dĭ-fyōōs') difuso.
dig (dĭg) I. tr. **dug, -gging** cavar, excavar; *(well, tunnel)* hacer, abrir; MIN. extraer, sacar; JER. *(to understand)* comprender; *(to like)* gustar ♦ **to d. in(to)** hincar, hundir en • **to d. out** *(hole)* excavar; *(object)* extraer; *(facts)* sacar • **to d. up** *(object)* extraer, desenterrar; *(facts)* descubrir —intr. cavar ♦ **to d. for** buscar • **to d. in** *(to entrench oneself)* atrincherarse; FAM. *(to eat)* atacar II. s. *(prod)* golpe m; *(with the*

elbow) codazo; *(gibe)* pulla, indirecta; ARQUEOL. excavación *f* ♦ pl. G.B., FAM. *(lodgings)* alojamiento.

di·gest I. tr. & intr. (dĭ-jĕst′, dī-) digerir(se) II. s. (dī′jĕst′) compendio, sinopsis *f.*

di·gest·i·ble (dĭ-jĕs′tə-bəl, dī-) adj. digestible.

di·ges·tion (:chən) s. digestión *f.*

di·ges·tive (:tĭv) adj. & s. digestivo.

dig·ger (dĭg′ər) s. *(person)* cavador m; *(tool)* azadón m; *(machine)* excavadora.

dig·ging (:ĭng) s. excavación *f.*

digit (dĭj′ĭt) s. ANAT. dedo; MAT. dígito.

dig·i·tal (:ĭ-tl) adj. digital ♦ **d. clock** reloj numérico.

dig·i·tal·is (dĭj′ĭ-tăl′ĭs) s. digitalina.

dig·ni·fied (dĭg′nə-fīd′) adj. digno, decoroso.

dig·ni·fy (:fī′) tr. dignificar.

dig·ni·tar·y (dĭg′nĭ-tĕr′ē) s. dignatario.

dig·ni·ty (dĭg′nĭ-tē) s. dignidad *f.*

di·gress (dĭ-grĕs′, dī-) intr. divagar.

di·gres·sive (:ĭv) adj. digresivo, inconexo.

dike (dīk) s. dique m, represa.

di·lap·i·dat·ed (dĭ-lăp′ĭ-dā′tĭd) adj. desvencijado.

di·late (dī-lāt′) tr. & intr. dilatar(se).

di·la·tion (dī-lā′shən) s. dilatación *f.*

dil·a·to·ry (dĭl′ə-tôr′ē) adj. dilatorio.

di·lem·ma (dĭ-lĕm′ə, dī-) s. dilema m.

dil·et·tante (dĭl′ĭ-tänt′) s. diletante *mf.*

dil·i·gence (dĭl′ə-jəns) s. diligencia.

dil·i·gent (dĭl′ə-jənt) adj. diligente.

dill (dĭl) s. eneldo.

dil·ly (dĭl′ē) s. FAM. joya, perla.

dil·ly-dal·ly (:dăl′ē) intr. perder el tiempo.

di·lute (dī-lōōt′, dī-) I. tr. diluir, desleir II. adj. diluido.

dim (dĭm) **-mm-** I. adj. *(dark)* oscuro; *(lights)* bajo, débil; *(outline)* borroso; *(vision)* turbio; *(memory)* vago; *(person)* de pocas luces ♦ **to take a d. view of** ver de modo poco favorable II. tr. *(room)* oscurecer; *(lights)* bajar —intr. oscurecerse; *(lights)* perder intensidad; *(outline, memory)* borrarse.

dime (dīm) s. E.U. moneda de diez centavos ♦ **d. store** tienda de baratijas.

di·men·sion (dĭ-mĕn′shən, dī-) s. dimensión *f.*

di·min·ish (dĭ-mĭn′ĭsh) tr. & intr. disminuir.

dim·i·nu·tion (dĭm′ə-nōō′shən) s. disminución *f.*

di·min·u·tive (dĭ-mĭn′yə-tĭv) I. adj. *(tiny)* diminuto; GRAM. diminutivo II. s. diminutivo.

dim·ple (dĭm′pəl) s. hoyuelo.

dim·wit (dĭm′wĭt′) s. JER. mentecato.

din (dĭn) s. estrépito; *(of a crowd)* clamoreo.

dine (dīn) intr. comer; *(in the evening)* cenar.

din·er (dī′nər) s. comensal *mf*; F.C. vagón m restaurante; *(restaurant)* restaurante m popular.

di·nette (dī-nĕt′) s. comedor pequeño.

ding-dong (dĭng′dông′) s. talán talán m.

din·ghy (dĭng′ē) s. bote m (de remo).

din·gy (dĭn′jē) adj. -i- sórdido, sucio.

dining (dī′nĭng) adj. ♦ **d. car** vagón restaurante • **d. hall** refectorio • **d. room** comedor.

din·ky (dĭng′kē) adj. -i- FAM. diminuto.

din·ner (dĭn′ər) s. cena; *(at noon)* comida (principal); *(formal)* banquete m ♦ **d. jacket** smoking.

di·no·saur (dī′nə-sôr′) s. dinosaurio.

dint (dĭnt) s. ♦ **by d. of** a fuerza de.

di·o·cese (dī′ə-sĭs) s. diócesis *f.*

di·ode (dī′ōd′) s. diodo.

di·ox·ide (dī-ŏk′sīd′) s. dióxido.

dip (dĭp) I. tr. **-pp-** *(to dunk)* bañar, mojar; *(to immerse)* sumergir, meter; *(to scoop)* sacar; *(to lower)* inclinar, bajar —intr. *(to plunge)* sumergirse; *(prices, road)* bajar; *(out of sight)* hundirse; AVIA. bajar en picado ♦ **to d. into** *(a subject)* meterse en; *(a book)* hojear; *(savings)* echar mano a II. s. *(immersion)* inmersión *f*; *(swim)* chapuzón m; *(liquid)* baño; *(slope, drop)* bajada; *(of magnetic needle)* inclinación *f*; *(hollow)* depresión *f*; *(in a road)* badén m; CUL. salsa; AVIA. bajón m ♦ **to take a d.** darse un chapuzón.

diph·the·ri·a (dĭf-thĭr′ē-ə, dĭp-) s. difteria.

diph·thong (dĭf′thông′, dĭp′-) s. diptongo.

di·plo·ma (dĭ-plō′mə) s. diploma m.

di·plo·ma·cy (dĭ-plō′mə-sē) s. diplomacia.

dip·lo·mat (dĭp′lə-măt′) s. diplomático.

dip·lo·mat·ic (′-′ĭk) adj. diplomático.

di·pole (dī′pōl′) s. dipolo.

dip·per (dĭp′ər) s. cazo, cucharón m.

dip·stick (:stĭk′) s. indicador m de nivel.

dire (dīr) adj. terrible, espantoso; *(extreme)* extremo ♦ **to be in d. need of** necesitar urgentemente.

di·rect (dĭ-rĕkt′, dī-) I. tr. dirigir; *(to order)* ordenar ♦ **to d. one's attention to** fijarse en II. adj. directo; *(candid)* franco ♦ **the d. opposite** exactamente lo contrario III. adv. directamente.

di·rec·tion (dĭ-rĕk′shən, dī-) s. dirección *f*; *(order)* orden *f* ♦ pl. instrucciones.

di·rec·tive (:tĭv) s. directriz *f.*

di·rect·ly (dĭ-rĕkt′lē, dī-) adv. directamente; *(immediately)* inmediatamente.

di·rec·tor (dĭ-rĕk′tər, dī-) s. director m.

di·rec·tor·ship (:shĭp′) s. dirección *f.*

di·rec·tor·ate (:ĭt) s. directorio.

di·rec·to·ry (dĭ-rĕk′tə-rē) s. guía telefónica ♦ **d. assistance** información telefónica.

dirge (dûrj) s. endecha, canto fúnebre.

dirt (dûrt) s. tierra; *(grime)* mugre *f*; *(filth)* suciedad; *(gossip)* chisme m; *(smut)* porquería ♦ **to treat like d.** tratar como un trapo.

dirt-cheap (′chēp′) adj. & adv. FAM. baratísimo, tirado.

dirt·y (dûr′tē) I. adj. -i- sucio; *(joke)* verde; *(language)* grosero; *(weather)* malo ♦ **d. language** groserías • **d. trick** mala jugada • **d. word** taco • **d. work** trabajo pesado o desagradable • **to give a d. look** mirar con mala cara II. tr. & intr. ensuciar(se), manchar(se).

dis·a·bil·i·ty (dĭs′ə-bĭl′ĭ-tē) s. incapacidad *f*; *(handicap)* invalidez *f*, inhabilidad *f.*

dis·a·ble (dĭs-ā′bəl) tr. incapacitar; *(to cripple)* lisiar.

dis·a·bled (:bəld) adj. incapacitado; *(crippled)* lisiado, inválido; *(vehicle)* averiado.

dis·a·buse (dĭs′ə-byōōz′) tr. desengañar.

dis·ad·van·tage (dĭs′əd-văn′tĭj) s. desventaja, inconveniente ♦ **to be, put at a d.** estar, poner en situación desventajosa • **to the d. of** en detrimento de.

dis·ad·van·taged (:tĭjd) adj. desvalido.

dis·ad·van·ta·geous (dĭs-ăd′vən-tā′jəs) adj. desventajoso, desfavorable.

dis·af·fect (dĭs′ə-fĕkt′) tr. indisponer.

dis·af·fect·ed (:fĕk′tĭd) adj. desafecto.

dis·af·fec·tion (:shən) s. desafección *f.*

dis·a·gree (dĭs′ə-grē′) intr. no estar de acuerdo, estar en desacuerdo; *(food)* sentar mal; *(to quarrel)* reñir.

dis·a·gree·a·ble (:ə-bəl) adj. desagradable.
dis·a·gree·ment (:mənt) s. desacuerdo; *(quarrel)* riña.
dis·al·low (dĭs′ə-lou′) tr. prohibir; DEP. anular.
dis·ap·pear (dĭs′ə-pîr′) intr. desaparecer.
dis·ap·pear·ance (:əns) s. desaparición *f.*
dis·ap·point (dĭs′ə-point′) tr. decepcionar, desilusionar; *(to fail to please)* defraudar.
dis·ap·point·ed (:poin′tĭd) adj. decepcionado; *(a lover)* desengañado.
dis·ap·point·ing (:tĭng) adj. decepcionante.
dis·ap·point·ment (dĭs′ə-point′mənt) s. desilusión *f*, decepción *f*; *(in love)* desengaño.
dis·ap·prov·al (dĭs′ə-prō̌′vəl) s. desaprobación *f.*
dis·ap·prove (dĭs′ə-prō̌v′) tr. desaprobar —intr. ♦ **to d. of** no gustarle a uno.
dis·arm (dĭs-ärm′) tr. & intr. desarmar(se).
dis·ar·ma·ment (:är′mə-mənt) s. desarme *m.*
dis·arm·ing (dĭs-är′mĭng) adj. cautivante.
dis·ar·range (dĭs′ə-rānj′) tr. desarreglar.
dis·ar·ray (dĭs′ə-rā′) I. s. desarreglo, desorden *m*; *(clothing)* desaliño II. tr. desarreglar.
dis·as·sem·ble (dĭs′ə-sĕm′bəl) tr. desmontar.
dis·as·so·ci·ate (dĭs′ə-sō′shē-āt′) tr. disociar.
dis·as·ter (dĭ-zăs′tər) s. desastre *m.*
dis·as·trous (:trəs) adj. desastroso.
dis·a·vow (dĭs′ə-vou′) tr. desconocer.
dis·a·vow·al (:əl) s. negación *f*, repudio.
dis·band (dĭs-bănd′) tr. & intr. dispersar(se).
dis·bar (dĭs-bär′) tr. **-rr-** excluir del foro.
dis·bar·ment (:mənt) s. exclusión *f* del foro.
dis·be·lief (dĭs′bĭ-lēf′) s. incredulidad *f.*
dis·be·lieve (:lēv′) tr. no creer —intr. ser incrédulo.
dis·burse (dĭs-bûrs′) tr. desembolsar.
dis·burse·ment (:mənt) s. desembolso.
disc (dĭsk) s. disco ♦ **d. jockey** animador.
dis·card I. tr. (dĭs-kärd′) descartar; *(clothing, books)* desechar —intr. descartarse II. s. (″) descarte *m.*
dis·cern (dĭ-sûrn′) tr. discernir; *(to perceive)* percibir —intr. hacer distinciones.
dis·cern·ing (dĭ-sûr′nĭng) adj. perspicaz.
dis·cern·ment (dĭ-sûrn′mənt) s. discernimiento.
dis·charge I. tr. (dĭs-chärj′) descargar; *(soldiers)* licenciar; *(patients)* dar de alta; *(employees)* despedir; *(pus)* arrojar; *(duty)* desempeñar, ejecutar; *(promise)* cumplir (con); *(debt)* saldar; *(prisoner)* librar —intr. *(river, pipe)* descargar; ELEC. descargarse II. s. (″) descarga; *(emission)* escape *m*; *(secretion)* secreción *f*; *(flow)* flujo; *(of duty)* desempeño; *(from hospital)* alta; *(of soldiers)* licenciamiento.
dis·ci·ple (dĭ-sī′pəl) s. discípulo.
dis·ci·pli·nar·y (dĭs′ə-plə-nĕr′ē) adj. disciplinario.
dis·ci·pline (dĭs′ə-plĭn) I. s. disciplina; *(punishment)* castigo II. tr. disciplinar; *(to punish)* castigar.
dis·claim (dĭs-klām′) tr. desconocer, denegar.
dis·claim·er (dĭs-klā′mər) s. denegación *f*, repudio.
dis·close (dĭ-sklōz′) tr. divulgar, revelar.
dis·clo·sure (dĭ-sklō′zhər) s. divulgación *f.*
dis·co (dĭs′kō′) s. (baile *m* de) discoteca.
dis·col·or (dĭs-kŭl′ər) tr. descolorar, desteñir.
dis·com·bob·u·late (dĭs′kəm-bŏb′yə-lāt′) tr. FAM. confundir, trastornar.
dis·com·fit (dĭs-kŭm′fĭt) tr. *(to thwart)* frustrar;

(to disconcert) desconcertar.
dis·com·fi·ture (:fĭ-chŏr′) s. frustración *f.*
dis·com·fort (dĭs-kŭm′fərt) I. s. molestia, malestar *m* II. tr. molestar.
dis·com·pose (dĭs′kəm-pōz′) tr. perturbar.
dis·com·po·sure (:pō′zhər) s. agitación *f.*
dis·con·cert (dĭs′kən-sûrt′) tr. desconcertar.
dis·con·nect (dĭs′kə-nĕkt′) tr. separar; ELEC., TEL. desconectar.
dis·con·nect·ed (:nĕk′tĭd) adj. desconectado; *(unrelated)* sin relación; *(illogical)* inconexo.
dis·con·so·late (dĭs-kŏn′sə-lĭt) adj. desconsolado.
dis·con·tent (dĭs′kən-tĕnt′) adj. & s. descontento.
dis·con·tent·ed (:tĕn′tĭd) adj. descontento.
dis·con·tin·ue (dĭs′kən-tĭn′yōō) tr. discontinuar, suspender.
dis·con·tin·u·ous (:əs) adj. discontinuo.
dis·cord (dĭs′kôrd′) s. discordia; MÚS. disonancia.
dis·cor·dant (dĭ-skôr′dnt) adj. discorde.
dis·co·theque/thèque (dĭs′kə-tĕk′) s. discoteca.
dis·count (dĭs′kount′) I. tr. descontar II. s. descuento, rebaja ♦ **d. rate** tasa de descuento • **d. store** tienda de rebajas.
dis·cour·age (dĭ-skûr′ĭj) tr. desanimar, desalentar; *(to hinder)* no fomentar, impedir ♦ **to d. from** disuadir *o* recomendar que no.
dis·cour·age·ment (:ĭj-mənt) s. desaliento, desánimo.
dis·cour·ag·ing (:ə-jĭng) adj. desalentador.
dis·course I. s. (dĭs′kôrs′) discurso; *(conversation)* plática II. intr. (dĭ-skôrs′) conversar ♦ **to d. on** disertar sobre.
dis·cour·te·ous (dĭs-kûr′tē-əs) adj. descortés.
dis·cov·er (dĭ-skŭv′ər) tr. descubrir; *(to realize)* darse cuenta de.
dis·cov·er·er (:ər) s. descubridor *m.*
dis·cov·er·y (dĭ-skŭv′ə-rē) s. descubrimiento.
dis·cred·it (dĭs-krĕd′ĭt) I. tr. *(to disbelieve)* no dar crédito a; *(to disparage)* desprestigiar, desacreditar II. s. desprestigio, descrédito ♦ **to be a d. to** deshonrar a • **to be to the d. of** ir en descrédito de.
dis·creet (dĭ-skrēt′) adj. discreto.
dis·crep·an·cy (dĭ-skrĕp′ən-sē) s. discrepancia.
dis·crete (dĭ-skrēt′) adj. separado, inconexo.
dis·cre·tion (dĭ-skrĕsh′ən) s. discreción *f* ♦ **at the d. of** a juicio de, según el deseo de.
dis·cre·tion·ar·y (:ə-nĕr′ē) adj. discrecional.
dis·crim·i·nate (dĭ-skrĭm′ə-nāt′) intr. & tr. discriminar *(against* en contra de; *from* de).
dis·crim·i·nat·ing (:nā′tĭng) adj. discerniente.
dis·crim·i·na·tion (-′-nā′shən) s. *(prejudice)* discriminación *f*; *(perception)* discernimiento; *(distinction)* distinción *f.*
dis·crim·i·na·to·ry (-′-nə-tôr′ē) adj. *(biased)* discriminatorio; *(selective)* exigente.
dis·cur·sive (dĭ-skûr′sĭv) adj. digresivo.
dis·cus (dĭs′kəs) s. disco.
dis·cuss (dĭ-skŭs′) tr. *(to talk over)* hablar de *o* sobre; *(formally)* discutir, tratar.
dis·cus·sion (dĭ-skŭsh′ən) s. *(conversation)* discusión *f* ♦ **to be under d.** estar en discusión.
dis·dain (dĭs-dān′) I. tr. desdeñar, menospreciar ♦ **to d. to** no dignarse a II. s. desdén *m*, menosprecio.
dis·dain·ful (:fəl) adj. desdeñoso.
dis·ease (dĭ-zēz′) s. enfermedad *f.*

dis·eased (dǐ-zēzd') adj. enfermo.
dis·em·bark (dǐs'ĕm-bärk') tr. & intr. desembarcar.
dis·em·bod·ied (dǐs'ĕm-bŏd'ēd) adj. incorpóreo.
dis·em·bod·y (:ē) tr. separar del cuerpo.
dis·em·bow·el (dǐs'ĕm-bou'əl) tr. desentrañar.
dis·en·chant (dǐs'ĕn-tăng'gəl) tr. desencantar.
dis·en·chant·ment (:mənt) s. desencanto.
dis·en·cum·ber (dǐs'ĕn-kŭm'bər) tr. librar.
dis·en·fran·chise (dǐs'ĕn-frăn'chīz') tr. privar de derechos civiles.
dis·en·gage (dǐs'ĕn-gāj') tr. & intr. *(to uncouple)* desenganchar(se); *(gears)* desengranar(se); MIL. retirar(se); AUTO. desembragar(se).
dis·en·gaged (:gājd') adj. *(free)* desembarazado, libre; AUTO. desembragado.
dis·en·tan·gle (dǐs'ĕn-tăng'gəl) tr. & intr. desenredar(se), desenmarañar(se).
dis·e·qui·lib·ri·um (dǐs-ē'kwə-lǐb'rē-əm) s. desequilibrio.
dis·fa·vor (dǐs-fā'vər) I. s. desaprobación *f* ♦ **to fall into d.** caer en desgracia II. tr. desfavorecer, desaprobar.
dis·fig·ure (dǐs-fǐg'yər) tr. desfigurar, afear.
dis·fran·chise (dǐs-frăn'chīz') tr. privar de derechos civiles.
dis·gorge (dǐs-gôrj') tr. vomitar.
dis·grace (dǐs-grās') I. s. deshonra; *(ignominy)* ignominia II. tr. deshonrar.
dis·grace·ful (:fəl) adj. vergonzoso.
dis·grun·tled (dǐs-grŭn'tld) adj. disgustado.
dis·guise (dǐs-gīz') I. s. disfraz *m* II. tr. disfrazar.
dis·gust (dǐs-gŭst') tr. repugnar, asquear II. s. repugnancia.
dis·gust·ed (:gŭs'tǐd) adj. asqueado, repugnado.
dis·gust·ing (:tǐng) adj. repugnante, asqueroso.
dish (dǐsh) I. s. plato; RAD., TELEV. disco (de antena) II. tr. ♦ **to d. out** *(food)* servir; *(advice, abuse)* repartir, dar.
dis·har·mo·ny (dǐs-här'mə-nē) s. discordia.
dis·heart·en (dǐs-här'tn) tr. desanimar, desalentar.
di·shev·el(l)ed (dǐ-shĕv'əld) adj. desaliñado.
dis·hon·est (dǐs-ŏn'ǐst) adj. deshonesto, deshonrado; *(dealings)* fraudulento.
dis·hon·es·ty (:ǐ-stē) s. falta de honradez; *(fraud)* fraude *m*.
dis·hon·or (:ər) I. s. deshonra; *(shame)* vergüenza II. tr. deshonrar; COM. rechazar.
dis·hon·or·a·ble (:ə-bəl) adj. deshonroso.
dish·rag (dǐsh'răg') s. trapo de fregar.
dish·wash·er (:wŏsh'ər) s. lavaplatos *m*.
dis·il·lu·sion (dǐs'ǐ-lōō'zhən) I. tr. desilusionar II. s. desilusión *f*.
dis·il·lu·sion·ment (:mənt) s. desilusión *f*.
dis·in·cen·tive (dǐs'ǐn-sĕn'tǐv) s. falta de incentivo.
dis·in·clined (dǐs'ǐn-klīnd') adj. maldispuesto.
dis·in·fect (dǐs'ǐn-fĕkt') tr. desinfectar.
dis·in·fec·tant (:fĕk'tənt) s. & adj. desinfectante *m*.
dis·in·for·ma·tion (dǐs-ǐn'fər-mā'shən) s. información incorrecta (para despistar).
dis·in·gen·u·ous (dǐs'ǐn-jĕn'yōō-əs) adj. insincero, falso.
dis·in·her·it (dǐs'ǐn-hĕr'ǐt) tr. desheredar.
dis·in·te·grate (dǐs-ǐn'tǐ-grāt') tr. & intr. desintegrar(se).

dis·in·ter (dǐs'ǐn-tûr') tr. **-rr-** desenterrar.
dis·in·ter·est (dǐs-ǐn'tər-ǐst) s. desinterés *m*.
dis·in·ter·est·ed (:trǐ-stǐd) adj. *(impartial)* desinteresado; *(indifferent)* indiferente.
dis·in·vest·ment (dǐs'ǐn-vĕst'mənt) s. disminución *f* del capital invertido.
dis·join (dǐs-join') tr. desunir, separar.
dis·joint·ed (dǐs-join'tǐd) adj. desarticulado; *(incoherent)* incoherente, inconexo.
dis·junc·tion (dǐs-jŭngk'shən) s. disyunción *f*.
disk (dǐsk) s. disco ♦ **d. jockey** animador.
disk·ette (dǐ-skĕt') s. disco, diskette *m*.
dis·lik(e)·a·ble (dǐs-lī'kə-bəl) adj. antipático.
dis·like (dǐs-līk') I. tr. tener aversión a, no gustarle a uno II. s. antipatía, aversión *f*.
dis·lo·cate (‘-kā'shən) s. dislocación *f*.
dis·lo·ca·tion (‘-kā'shən) s. dislocación *f*.
dis·lodge (dǐs-lŏj') tr. desalojar, echar fuera.
dis·loy·al (dǐs-loi'əl) adj. desleal.
dis·loy·al·ty (:tē) s. deslealtad *f*.
dis·mal (dǐz'məl) adj. triste, deprimente.
dis·man·tle (dǐs-măn'tl) tr. *(to tear down)* desmantelar; *(to disassemble)* desarmar.
dis·may (dǐs-mā') I. tr. *(to upset)* consternar; *(to dishearten)* desalentar II. s. consternación *f*, desaliento.
dis·mem·ber (dǐs-mĕm'bər) tr. desmembrar.
dis·miss (dǐs-mǐs') tr. dar permiso para salir; *(employee)* despedir; *(officials)* destituir; *(doubt)* alejar; *(claim)* desestimar.
dis·miss·al (:əl) s. *(employee)* despido; *(official)* destitución *f*; *(idea)* abandono; DER. desestimación *f*.
dis·mount (dǐs-mount') tr. & intr. desmontar(se).
dis·o·be·di·ent (dǐs'ə-bē'dē-ənt) adj. desobediente.
dis·o·bey (dǐs'ə-bā') tr. & intr. desobedecer.
dis·or·der (dǐs-ôr'dər) I. s. desorden *m*; MED. trastorno II. tr. desordenar; MED. trastornar.
dis·or·der·ly (:lē) adj. desordenado; *(unruly)* alborotador ♦ **d. conduct** conducta escandalosa.
dis·or·gan·ize (dǐs-ôr'gə-nīz') tr. desorganizar.
dis·o·ri·ent (dǐs-ôr'ē-ĕnt') tr. desorientar.
dis·own (dǐs-ōn') tr. repudiar.
dis·par·age (dǐ-spăr'ǐj) tr. menospreciar.
dis·par·ag·ing (:ǐ-jǐng) adj. menospreciativo.
dis·pa·rate (dǐs'pər-ǐt) adj. dispar, desigual.
dis·par·i·ty (dǐ-spăr'ǐ-tē) s. disparidad *f*.
dis·pas·sion·ate (dǐs-păsh'ə-nǐt) adj. desapasionado; *(unbiased)* imparcial.
dis·patch (dǐ-spăch') I. tr. despachar II. s. despacho; *(speed)* diligencia.
dis·pel (dǐ-spĕl') tr. **-ll-** disipar.
dis·pen·sa·ble (dǐ-spĕn'sə-bəl) adj. prescindible.
dis·pen·sa·ry (dǐ-spĕn'sə-rē) s. dispensario.
dis·pen·sa·tion (dǐs'pən-sā'shən) s. reparto, distribución *f*; *(exemption)* dispensa.
dis·pense (dǐ-spĕns') tr. dispensar.
dis·per·sal (dǐ-spûr'səl) s. dispersión *f*.
dis·perse (dǐ-spûrs') tr. & intr. dispersar(se).
di·spir·it·ed (dǐ-spǐr'ǐ-tǐd) adj. desalentado.
dis·place (dǐs-plās') tr. desplazar; *(to supplant)* substituir, suplantar ♦ **displaced person** persona expatriada.
dis·place·ment (:mənt) s. desplazamiento; *(substitution)* reemplazo, sustitución *f*.
dis·play (dǐ-splā') I. tr. exhibir, mostrar; *(to show off)* ostentar; *(to unfurl)* desplegar II. s.

exhibición f; (show) despliegue m; (ostentation) ostentación f; COMPUT. representación f visual.

dis·please (dĭs-plēz′) tr. & intr. desagradar.

dis·pleas·ing (:plē′zĭng) adj. desagradable.

dis·pleas·ure (:plĕzh′ər) s. desagrado.

dis·pos·a·ble (dĭ-spō′zə-bəl) adj. (available) disponible; (discardable) desechable.

dis·pos·al (:zəl) s. disposición f; (of waste) eliminación f; (sale) venta ♦ at your d. a su disposición.

dis·pose (dĭ-spōz′) tr. disponer; (to incline) volver propenso a ♦ to d. of (property, business) despachar; (waste) eliminar, desechar.

dis·posed (dĭ-spōzd′) adj. dispuesto.

dis·po·si·tion (dĭs′pə-zĭsh′ən) s. disposición f; (tendency) predisposición f.

dis·pos·sess (dĭs′pə-zĕs′) tr. desposeer.

dis·proof (dĭs-prōōf′) s. refutación f.

dis·pro·por·tion·ate (dĭs′prə-pôr′shə-nĭt) adj. desproporcionado.

dis·prove (dĭs-prōōv′) tr. refutar.

dis·pu·tant (dĭ-spyōōt′nt) s. disputador m.

dis·pute (dĭ-spyōōt′) I. tr. disputar; (to doubt) cuestionar; (in court) litigar, contender —intr. disputar, discutir; (to quarrel) pelear II. s. (debate) disputa; (conflict) conflicto; (quarrel) pelea.

dis·qual·i·fi·ca·tion (dĭs-kwŏl′ə-fĭ-kā′shən) s. descalificación f; (unfitness) incapacidad f.

dis·qual·i·fy (dĭs-kwŏl′ə-fī′) tr. descalificar; (to render unfit) incapacitar.

dis·qui·et (dĭs-kwī′ĭt) I. tr. inquietar II. s. inquietud f.

dis·re·gard (dĭs′rĭ-gärd′) I. tr. no hacer caso de, desatender II. s. desatención f, negligencia.

dis·re·pair (dĭs′rĭ-pâr′) s. mal estado, falta de arreglo ♦ to fall into d. (machinery) descomponerse; (a house) caer en ruina.

dis·rep·u·ta·ble (dĭs-rĕp′yə-tə-bəl) adj. de mala fama, desacreditado.

dis·re·pute (dĭs′rĭ-pyōōt′) s. mala fama, descrédito ♦ to bring (fall) into d. desprestigiar(se).

dis·re·spect (dĭs′rĭ-spĕkt′) I. s. falta de respeto, descortesía II. tr. faltar el respeto.

dis·re·spect·ful (:fəl) adj. irrespetuoso.

dis·robe (dĭs-rōb′) tr. & intr. desvestir(se).

dis·rupt (dĭs-rŭpt′) tr. (to upset) perturbar; (to interrupt) interrumpir; (to rupture) romper.

dis·rup·tion (dĭs-rŭp′shən) s. (upset) perturbación f; (interruption) interrupción f; (rupture) rompimiento.

dis·rup·tive (:tĭv) adj. (upsetting) perturbador; (interfering) interruptor, obstructor.

dis·sat·is·fac·tion (dĭs-săt′ĭs-făk′shən) s. insatisfacción f, descontento.

dis·sat·is·fy (dĭs-săt′ĭs-fī′) tr. no contentar.

dis·sect (dĭ-sĕkt′, dī-) tr. disecar.

dis·sec·tion (dĭ-sĕk′shən, dī-) s. disección f.

dis·sem·ble (dĭ-sĕm′bəl) tr. & intr. disimular.

dis·sem·i·nate (dĭ-sĕm′ə-nāt′) tr. & intr. diseminar(se).

dis·sen·sion (dĭ-sĕn′shən) s. disensión f.

dis·sent (dĭ-sĕnt′) I. intr. disentir II. s. disensión f; RELIG. disidencia.

dis·sent·er (dĭ-sĕn′tər) s. disidente mf.

dis·ser·ta·tion (dĭs′ər-tā′shən) s. (discourse) disertación f; (thesis) tesis f.

dis·ser·vice (dĭs-sûr′vĭs) s. perjuicio, daño.

dis·si·dent (dĭs′ĭ-dnt) adj. & s. disidente mf.

dis·sim·i·lar (dĭ-sĭm′ə-lər) adj. disímil.

dis·sim·u·late (:yə-lāt′) tr. & intr. disimular.

dis·si·pate (dĭs′ə-pāt′) tr. & intr. disipar(se).

dis·si·pat·ed (:pā′tĭd) adj. disipado.

dis·so·ci·ate (dĭ-sō′shē-āt′) tr. disociar ♦ to d. oneself from disociarse de.

dis·so·lute (dĭs′ə-lōōt′) adj. disoluto, disipado.

dis·so·lu·tion (′-lōō′shən) s. disolución f.

dis·solve (dĭ-zŏlv′) tr. & intr. disolver(se) ♦ to d. in tears deshacerse en lágrimas.

dis·so·nant (dĭs′ə-nənt) adj. disonante.

dis·suade (dĭ-swād′) tr. disuadir.

dis·taff (dĭs′tăf′) s. (staff) rueca; (women) las mujeres ♦ d. side línea femenina.

dis·tance (dĭs′təns) I. s. distancia; (range) alcance m; (stretch) trecho, tirada; (coolness) frialdad f, reserva ♦ a good d. away bastante lejos • at o from a d. a (la) distancia • in the d. a lo lejos • to keep one's d. guardar las distancias • within walking d. suficientemente cerca como para ir andando II. tr. alejar, distanciar.

dis·tant (dĭs′tənt) adj. distante, alejado; (in relationship) lejano; (aloof) reservado, frío.

dis·taste (dĭs-tāst′) s. aversión f.

dis·taste·ful (:fəl) adj. desagradable.

dis·tem·per (dĭs-tĕm′pər) s. moquillo.

dis·tend (dĭ-stĕnd′) tr. & intr. (to expand) distender(se); (to swell) hinchar(se).

dis·ten·sion/sion (dĭ-stĕn′shən) s. (expansion) distensión f; (swelling) hinchazón f.

dis·till (dĭ-stĭl′) tr. & intr. destilar.

dis·til·late (dĭs′tə-lāt′) s. destilado.

dis·till·er·y (dĭ-stĭl′ə-rē) s. destilería.

dis·tinct (dĭ-stĭngkt′) adj. distinto; (clear) claro; (unquestionable) marcado, indudable.

dis·tinc·tion (dĭ-stĭngk′shən) s. distinción f ♦ to gain d. distinguirse • with d. con mérito.

dis·tinc·tive (:tĭv) adj. distintivo.

dis·tin·guish (dĭ-stĭng′gwĭsh) tr. & intr. distinguir ♦ to d. oneself distinguirse, descollar.

dis·tin·guish·a·ble (:gwĭ-shə-bəl) adj. distinguible.

dis·tin·guished (:gwĭsht) adj. distinguido.

dis·tort (dĭ-stôrt′) tr. (to contort) distorsionar; (to misrepresent) tergiversar, alterar.

dis·tor·tion (dĭ-stôr′shən) s. distorsión f; (misrepresentation) tergiversación f, alteración f.

dis·tract (dĭ-străkt′) tr. distraer; (to bewilder) aturdir, turbar.

dis·trac·tion (dĭ-străk′shən) s. distracción f; (frenzy) frenesí m.

dis·traught (dĭ-strôt′) adj. (worried) aturdido, turbado; (crazed) desequilibrado.

dis·tress (dĭ-strĕs′) I. s. (suffering) aflicción f, pena; (anxiety) ansiedad f; (need) apuro; (danger) peligro II. tr. afligir.

dis·tressed (dĭ-strĕst′) adj. afligido, angustiado; (in danger) en peligro; (poor) en apuros.

dis·trib·ute (dĭ-strĭb′yōōt) tr. distribuir.

dis·tri·bu·tion (dĭs′trə-byōō′shən) s. distribución f, reparto.

dis·trib·u·tor (dĭ-strĭb′yə-tər) s. distribuidor m.

dis·trict (dĭs′trĭkt) s. región f, comarca; (of a city) zona, barrio; POL. distrito, partido ♦ d. attorney fiscal • d. court tribunal federal.

dis·trust (dĭs-trŭst′) I. s. desconfianza, recelo II. tr. desconfiar de, sospechar.

dis·trust·ful (:fəl) adj. desconfiado.

dis·turb (dĭ-stûrb′) tr. (to alter) perturbar; (to upset) turbar, trastornar; (to interrupt) interrumpir; (to bother) molestar; (to disarrange) desordenar; PSIC. desequilibrar ♦ do not d. no molestar.

dis·tur·bance (dĭ-stûr′bəns) s. perturbación f; (worry) trastorno; (interruption) interrupción f; *(bother)* molestia; *(disorder)* desorden m; *(riot)* disturbio; PSIC. desequilibrio.

dis·u·ni·ty (dĭs-yōō′nĭ-tē) s. desunión f.

dis·use (dĭs-yōōs′) s. desuso.

ditch (dĭch) I. s. *(trench)* zanja; *(irrigation)* acequia; *(drainage)* canal m; *(of a road)* cuneta II. tr. cavar zanjas en; FAM. *(to discard)* abandonar.

dith·er (dĭth′ər) s. nerviosismo, agitación f.

dit·to (dĭt′ō) I. s. ídem m; *(copy)* copia, duplicado II. adv. ídem III. tr. sacar un duplicado de.

dit·ty (dĭt′ē) s. cancioncita.

di·van (dĭ-văn′) s. diván m.

dive (dīv) I. intr. **-d** o **dove, -d** *(headfirst)* zambullirse (de cabeza); DEP. saltar; *(submarine)* sumergirse; *(scuba)* bucear; *(airplane)* bajar en picado; *(to plummet)* caer a plomo; FIG. lanzarse, meterse de lleno II. s. *(headfirst)* zambullida; DEP. salto; *(plane)* picado; *(submarine)* sumersión f; *(drop)* caída, baja; JER. *(bar)* garito.

dive-bomb (′bŏm′) tr. bombardear en picada.

div·er (dī′vər) s. DEP. saltador m (de trampolín); *(underwater)* buzo, buceador m.

di·verge (dĭ-vûrj′, dī-) intr. divergir.

di·ver·gent (dĭ-vûr′jənt, dī-) adj. divergente.

di·vers (dī′vərz) adj. diversos, varios.

di·verse (dĭ-vûrs′, dī-) adj. diverso; *(varied)* variado.

di·ver·si·fy (dĭ-vûr′sə-fī′, dī-) tr. & intr. diversificar(se).

di·ver·sion (dĭ-vûr′zhən, dī-) s. diversión f; *(detour)* desviación f.

di·ver·si·ty (:sĭ-tē) s. diversidad f, variedad f.

di·vert (dĭ-vûrt′, dī-) tr. divertir; *(to turn aside)* desviar.

di·vest (dĭ-vĕst′, dī-) tr. despojar, desposeer.

di·ves·ti·ture (dĭ-vĕs′tĭ-chər) s. despojo, desposeimiento.

di·vide (dĭ-vīd′) I. tr. & intr. dividir(se) ♦ **to d. up** *(to apportion)* repartir; *(to separate)* dividir(se) II. s. divisoria.

di·vid·ed (dĭ-vī′dĭd) adj. dividido; BOT. seccionado ♦ **d. highway** carretera con barrera divisoria.

div·i·dend (dĭv′ĭ-dĕnd′) s. dividendo.

di·vid·er (dĭ-vī′dər) s. divisor m; *(partition)* separación f ♦ pl. compás de punta seca.

div·i·na·tion (dĭv′ə-nā′shən) s. adivinación f.

di·vine¹ (dĭ-vīn′) I. adj. **-er, -est** divino II. s. clérigo.

di·vine² tr. & intr. adivinar.

div·ing (dī′vĭng) s. DEP. salto; *(scuba)* buceo ♦ **d. board** trampolín • **d. suit** escafandra.

di·vin·i·ty (dĭ-vĭn′ĭ-tē) s. divinidad f; *(theology)* teología ♦ **D.** Dios.

di·vi·sion (dĭ-vĭzh′ən) s. división f; *(section)* sección f, departamento.

di·vi·sive (dĭ-vī′sĭv) adj. divisivo.

di·vi·sor (dĭ-vī′zər) s. divisor m.

di·vorce (dĭ-vôrs′) I. s. divorcio II. tr. *(things, couple)* divorciar; *(a spouse)* divorciarse de.

di·vor·cée (dĭ-vor′sā′, :sē′) s. divorciado ♦ **divorcée** divorciada.

di·vulge (dĭ-vŭlj′) tr. divulgar.

diz·zi·ness (dĭz′ē-nĭs) s. vertigo, mareo.

diz·zy (dĭz′ē) I. adj. **-i-** *(giddy)* mareado; *(bewildered)* aturdido; *(speed, height)* vertiginoso; FAM. *(foolish)* bobo II. tr. marear, dar vértigo.

do (dōō) I. tr. **did, done** hacer; *(one's duty)* cumplir con; *(to wash)* limpiar; *(dishes)* fregar;

(one's hair, nails) arreglarse; *(justice, homage)* rendir, tributar; *(to work as)* dedicarse a; *(to prepare)* preparar; *(to cook)* cocinar; *(to work on)* trabajar en; *(to tour)* recorrer; *(to decorate)* decorar; JER. *(drugs)* tomar, usar ♦ **to do again** volver a hacer, hacer de nuevo • **to do away with** *(to eliminate)* eliminar; *(to abolish)* abolir; FAM. *(to kill)* matar • **to do for** servir de, hacer el papel de • **to do in** JER. *(to kill)* liquidar; *(to ruin)* arruinar; *(to exhaust)* agotar, cansar • **to do over** *(to do again)* volver a hacer; FAM. *(to redecorate)* redecorar • **to do up** *(laces)* atarse; *(buttons)* abrocharse; FAM. *(to do with style)* hacer con estilo • **to do with** *(to get along on)* conformarse con; *(to find desirable)* venirle a uno (muy) bien • **what can I do for you?** ¿en qué puedo servirle? —intr. *(to behave)* conducirse, comportarse; *(to perform)* obrar, actuar; *(to get along)* andar, irle a uno; *(to feel)* encontrarse, sentirse; *(to serve the purpose)* servir ♦ **how do you do?** ¿cómo está usted? • **nothing doing!** JER. ¡nada de eso!, ¡ni hablar! • **that will do!** ¡basta ya! • **that will never do** o **that won't do** *(it is improper)* eso no se hace; *(it is unsuitable)* eso no conviene • **to be doing badly** irle mal • **to do or die** vencer o morir —aux. *(interrogative)* <do you think it's funny? ¿crees que eso es gracioso?>; *(negative)* <I don't know no sé>; *(emphatic)* <do behave pórtate bien>; *(substitute)* <do you understand me? Yes, I do ¿me entiendes? sí> II. s. [pl. **s** o **-'s**] *(party)* fiesta; *(hairdo)* peinado ♦ **the do's and don'ts** lo que se debe y lo que no se debe hacer.

doc·ile (dŏs′əl, :īl′) adj. dócil.

dock¹ (dŏk) I. s. *(wharf)* muelle m, embarcadero; *(for trucks, trains)* andén m II. tr. & intr. *(ship)* (hacer) atracar al muelle; *(spacecraft)* acoplar(se).

dock² tr. VET. cercenar (la cola); *(to deduct)* descontar (de un salario).

dock³ s. *(in court)* banquillo del acusado.

dock·et (dŏk′ĭt) s. *(agenda)* agenda; DER. sumario de causas.

dock·hand (dŏk′hănd′) s. estibador m.

dock·work·er (:wûr′kər) s. estibador m.

dock·yard (:yärd′) s. astillero.

doc·tor (dŏk′tər) s. médico, doctor m; EDUC. doctor II. tr. *(to treat)* tratar, atender; *(to repair)* remendar; *(to falsify)* adulterar.

doc·tor·ate (:ĭt) s. doctorado.

doc·tri·naire (dŏk′trə-nâr′) s. & adj. doctrinario.

doc·trine (dŏk′trĭn) s. doctrina.

doc·u·ment (dŏk′yə-mənt) I. s. documento II. tr. documentar, probar con documentos.

doc·u·men·ta·ry (′-mĕn′tə-rē) adj. & s. documental m.

dod·der·ing (dŏd′ər-ĭng) adj. senil.

dodge (dŏj) I. tr. esquivar; *(by cunning)* evadir, eludir —intr. echarse a un lado II. s. regate m.

doe (dō) s. [pl. inv. o **s**] gama.

does (dŭz) tercera persona sg. de **do.**

doe·skin (dō′skĭn′) s. piel f de gamo, ante m.

doff (dŏf) tr. quitarse.

dog (dôg) I. s. perro; *(scoundrel)* canalla mf; FAM. *(fellow)* tipo; *(fiasco)* bomba, desastre m ♦ **d. days** canícula ♦ pl. JER. pies m, patas II. tr. **-gg-** perseguir, seguir.

dog·catch·er (′kăch′ər) s. lacero.

doge (dōj) s. dux m.

dog-eat-dog (dôg′ĕt-dôg′) adj. atrozmente

competitivo.
dog·fight ('fīt') s. combate aéreo reñido.
dog·ged (dô'gĭd) adj. terco, obstinado.
dog·ger·el (dô'gər-əl) s. coplas de ciego.
dog·gone (dôg'gôn') s. FAM. maldito.
dog·gy/ie (dô'gē) s. FAM. perrito.
dog·house (dôg'hous') s. caseta de perro ♦ **in the d.** JER. en desgracia.
do·gie (dô'gē) s. becerro sin madre.
dog·ma (dôg'mə) s. dogma m.
dog·mat·ic (-măt'ĭk) adj. dogmático.
dog·ma·tist (-mə-tĭst) s. dogmatizador m.
do·good·er (dōō'gōōd'ər) s. FAM. bienhechor m.
dog·trot (dôg'trŏt') s. trote m suave, trote lento.
dog·wood ('wōōd') s. cornejo, sanguiñuelo.
doi·ly (doi'lē) s. tapete m.
do·ing (dōō'ĭng) s. (act) hecho, obra; (effort) esfuerzo ♦ pl. fiestas, actividades.
do-it-your·self (dōō'ĭt-yər-sĕlf') adj. FAM. diseñado para ser hecho por uno mismo.
dol·drums (dōl'drəmz') s.pl. (inactivity) estancamiento; (listlessness) decaimiento; MARÍT. calmas ecuatoriales.
dole (dōl) I. s. limosna; G.B. (welfare) subsidio de paro ♦ **to be on the d.** estar acogido al paro II. tr. dar limosna ♦ **to d. out** repartir, distribuir.
dole·ful (dōl'fəl) adj. triste.
doll (dōl) I. s. muñeca II. intr. & tr. ♦ **to d. (oneself) up** JER. emperifollar(se).
dol·lar (dŏl'ər) s. dólar m ♦ **to bet one's bottom d.** JER. apostarse la cabeza.
dol·ly (dŏl'ē) I. s. (toy) muñeca; (platform) carretilla; CINEM. travelín m, plataforma rodante II. intr. ♦ **to d. in** acercarse la cámara.
dol·phin (dŏl'fĭn) s. ZOOL. delfín m; ICT. dorado.
dolt (dōlt) s. tonto, idiota mf.
do·main (dō-mān') s. dominio; FIG. campo.
dome (dōm) s. cúpula, domo.
do·mes·tic (də-měs'tĭk) I. adj. doméstico; (home-loving) casero; ECON. (not foreign) nacional, del país ♦ **d. science** economía doméstica II. s. doméstico.
do·mes·ti·cate (-tī-kāt') tr. (animal) domesticar, amansar; (person) volver casero.
do·mes·tic·i·ty (dō'mĕ-stĭs'ī-tē) s. (of animals) domesticidad f; (home life) vida casera.
dom·i·cile (dŏm'ĭ-sīl', dŏ'mĭ-) I. s. domicilio II. tr. domiciliar —intr. residir.
dom·i·nance (dŏm'ə-nəns) s. dominación f.
dom·i·nant (-nənt) adj. & s. dominante f.
dom·i·nate (-nāt') tr. & intr. dominar.
dom·i·neer ('-nîr') tr. & intr. tiranizar.
do·min·ion (də-mĭn'yən) s. dominio.
dom·i·no (dŏm'ə-nō') s. [pl. (e)s] (mask) dominó; (game piece) ficha ♦ pl. (game) dominó.
don¹ (dŏn) s. (Spanish gentleman) hidalgo; G.B. (head) catedrático ♦ **D.** don, señor.
don² tr. (clothes) ponerse; (air) asumir.
do·nate (dō'nāt') tr. donar.
do·na·tion (dō-nā'shən) s. donación f; (gift) donativo.
done (dŭn) I. cf. **do** II. adj. terminado, hecho; CUL. cocido, hecho ♦ **d.!** ¡trato hecho! • **d. for** FAM. vencido • **well d.!** ¡muy bien!
don·key (dông'kē) s. burro, asno.
do·nor (dō'nər) s. donador m, donante mf.
do-no·thing (dōō'nŭth'ĭng) I. adj. que no hace nada II. s. perezoso, persona sin iniciativa.

don't (dōnt) contr. de **do not.**
doo·dle (dōōd'l) FAM. I. intr. hacer garabatos (distraídamente) II. s. garabato.
doom (dōōm) I. s. (sentence) condena; (ruin) ruina, perdición f; (death) muerte f II. tr. condenar.
doom·say·er ('sā'ər) s. pesimista mf.
dooms·day (dōōmz'dā') s. día m del juicio final.
door (dôr) s. puerta; AUTO. portezuela; (doorway) entrada ♦ **to knock the d. down** echar la puerta abajo • **to lay at the d. of** echar la culpa a • **to lie at one's d.** recaer sobre uno.
door·bell ('bĕl') s. timbre m.
door·keep·er (:kē'pər) s. portero.
door·knob (:nŏb') s. perilla.
door·man (:măn') s. [pl. **-men**] portero.
door·mat (:măt') s. felpudo, estera.
door·nail (:nāl') s. clavo de puerta ♦ **dead as a d.** completamente muerto.
door·step (:stĕp') s. escalón m de la puerta ♦ **at one's d.** cerca de uno.
door-to-door (dôr'tə-dôr') adj. de puerta en puerta; (salesman) que vende a domicilio.
door·way (dôr'wā') s. puerta, entrada.
dope (dōp) I. s. (varnish) barniz m; FAM. (narcotic) narcótico, droga; JER. (dolt) tonto; (information) datos II. tr. FAM. drogar ♦ **to d. out** calcular, deducir.
dop·(e)y (dō'pē) adj. **-i-** JER. (drugged) drogado; (lethargic) atontado, aletargado; (stupid) tonto.
dorm (dôrm) s. FAM. (room) dormitorio; (building) residencia para estudiantes.
dor·mant (dôr'mənt) adj. durmiente; ZOOL. en estado letárgico; BOT. en estado latente.
dor·mer (dôr'mər) s. buharda, buhardilla.
dor·mi·to·ry (dôr'mĭ-tôr'ē) s. (room) dormitorio; (building) residencia.
dor·mouse (dôr'mous') s. lirón m.
dor·ry (dôr'ē) s. esquife f de fondo plano.
dos·age (dō'sĭj) s. dosificación f; (amount) dosis f.
dose (dōs) I. s. dosis f II. tr. medicinar.
dos·si·er (dŏs'ē-ā') s. expediente m.
dot (dŏt) I. s. punto ♦ **on the d.** FAM. (on time) a la hora; (exactly) exactamente m; (o'clock) en punto II. tr. **-tt-** poner el punto a; (to scatter) salpicar ♦ **dotted line** línea de puntos.
dot·age (dō'tĭj) s. chochez f.
dote (dōt) intr. chochear ♦ **to d. on** adorar.
dot·ty (dŏt'ē) adj. **-i-** chiflado.
dou·ble (dŭb'əl) I. adj. doble; (folded) doblado ♦ **d. agent** espía doble • **d. bass** contrabajo • **d. chin** papada • **d. entry** partida doble • **d. take** reacción tardía • **d. talk** lenguaje ambiguo • **d. time** (wage) paga doble; MIL. paso ligero; MÚS. compás binario II. s. doble m; MAT. duplo ♦ **on the d.** FAM. con toda rapidez; MIL. a paso ligero III. tr. doblar; (to repeat) redoblar —intr. doblarse, duplicarse ♦ **to d. as** servir como • **to d. back** volver uno sobre sus pasos • **to d. for** sustituir a • **to d. up** (from pain) doblarse en dos; (to share) compartir la misma habitación o cama • **to d. up with laughter** desternillarse de risa IV. adv. doble, doblemente; (two together) dos juntos ♦ **d. or nothing** doble o nada.
dou·ble-bar·reled ('-băr'əld) adj. ARM. de dos cañones; FIG. de doble efecto.
dou·ble-breast·ed (:brĕs'tĭd) adj. cruzado.
dou·ble-check (:chĕk') tr. & intr. verificar por

double-cross | drape

segunda vez.

dou·ble-cross (:krôs') JER. **I.** tr. traicionar (a un cómplice) **II.** s. traición *f.*

dou·ble-deal·er (:dē'lər) s. embustero.

dou·ble-deck·er (:dĕk'ər) s. *(bus)* omnibus *m* de dos pisos; *(sandwich)* emparedado doble.

dou·ble-dig·it (:dĭj'ĭt) adj. de dos dígitos.

dou·ble-edged (:ĕjd') adj. de doble filo.

dou·ble-joint·ed (:join'tĭd) adj. de articulaciones dobles.

dou·ble-park (:pärk') tr. & intr. estacionar en doble fila.

dou·ble-quick (:kwĭk') adj. rapidísimo.

dou·ble-space (:spās') intr. & tr. escribir a máquina con doble espacio.

dou·blet (dŭb'lĭt) s. *(pair)* pareja; *(jacket)* jubón *m;* GRAM. *(word)* doblete *m.*

dou·bloon (dŭ-blōōn') s. doblón *m.*

dou·bly (dŭb'lē) adv. doblemente.

doubt (dout) **I.** tr. dudar; *(to distrust)* desconfiar de —intr. dudar **II.** s. duda ♦ beyond d. fuera de duda • **in d.** dudoso • **no d.** sin duda.

doubt·er (dou'tər) s. escéptico.

doubt·ful (dout'fəl) adj. dudoso.

doubt·less (:lĭs) **I.** adj. seguro **II.** adv. *(certainly)* sin duda; *(probably)* probablemente.

douche (dōōsh) **I.** s. ducha **II.** tr. & intr. duchar(se).

dough (dō) s. masa, pasta; JER. *(money)* plata.

dough·nut (dō'nət) s. buñuelo.

dour (dŏŏr, dour) adj. *(stern)* severo; *(sullen)* hosco.

douse (dous) tr. *(to immerse)* sumergir; *(to drench)* empapar; *(to extinguish)* extinguir.

dove[1] (dŭv) s. paloma; FIG. pacifista *mf.*

dove[2] (dōv) cf. **dive.**

dove·tail (dŭv'tāl') s. cola de milano.

dow·a·ger (dou'ə-jər) s. *(widow)* viuda con viudedad; *(elderly woman)* señora mayor.

dow·dy (dou'dē) adj. -i- desaliñado.

dow·el (dou'əl) s. clavija.

dow·er (dou'ər) s. viudedad *f.*

down[1] (doun) **I.** adv. *(downward)* (hacia) abajo; *(on the ground)* en tierra; *(in writing)* por escrito; COM. *(in advance)* como adelanto ♦ **d. and out** sin real, pobrísimo • **d. below** abajo • **d. with...!** ¡abajo...! **II.** adj. *(descending)* que va hacia abajo; *(depressed)* deprimido; COM. inicial, a cuenta ♦ **to be d. on** tenerle inquina a • **to be d. with** estar enfermo con **III.** prep. abajo ♦ **d. the centuries** a través de los siglos • **d. the road** más abajo **IV.** s. descenso, caída **V.** tr. *(food)* tragar, engullir; *(liquids)* vaciar de un trago; *(an airplane)* derribar.

down[2] s. *(feathers)* plumón *m;* *(hair, fibers)* pelusa, vello.

down·cast ('kăst') adj. *(depressed)* abatido, desalentado; *(eyes)* hacia abajo.

down·er (dou'nər) s. JER. *(pill)* tranquilizante *m;* *(experience)* experiencia que deprime.

down·fall (doun'fôl') s. ruina, caída.

down·grade (:grād') **I.** s. bajada, pendiente *f* **II.** tr. disminuir (de categoría, importancia).

down·heart·ed (:här'tĭd) adj. abatido.

down·hill (:hĭl') adv. cuesta abajo ♦ **to go d.** deteriorarse; *(health)* debilitarse, decaer.

down·play (:plā') tr. minimizar.

down·pour (:pôr') s. chaparrón *m,* aguacero.

down·right (:rīt') **I.** adj. *(complete)* absoluto, completo; *(forthright)* categórico **II.** adv. completamente, categóricamente.

down·stage (:stāj') adv. & s. (hacia el) proscenio.

down·stairs (:stârz') **I.** adv. & adj. *(lower floor)* en *o* del piso de abajo; *(main floor)* en *o* de la planta baja ♦ **to go d.** bajar (de un piso a otro) **II.** s.pl. planta baja.

down·stream (:strēm') adv. agua *o* río abajo.

down-to-earth ('tə-ûrth') adj. práctico.

down·town ('toun') **I.** adv. & s. (hacia *o* en el) centro de una ciudad **II.** adj. del centro.

down·trod·den (:trŏd'n) adj. pisoteado.

down·turn (:tûrn') s. baja, bajón *m.*

down·ward (:wərd) **I.** adv. *o* **-wards** hacia abajo **II.** adj. descendente.

down·wind (:wĭnd') adv. & adj. de *o* a sotavento, a favor del viento.

dow·ry (dou'rē) s. dote *f.*

doze (dōz) **I.** intr. dormitar ♦ **to d. off** dormirse, echar una cabezada **II.** s. sueño ligero.

doz·en (dŭz'ən) **I.** s.inv. docena ♦ **dozens of** miles de **II.** adj. docena de.

drab (drăb) adj. -bb- *(brownish)* pardusco; *(dull)* ordinario, monótono.

draft (drăft) **I.** s. corriente *f* de aire; *(of a chimney)* tiro; *(sketch)* bosquejo; *(written)* borrador *m,* versión *f;* *(gulp)* trago; MIL. conscripción *f,* quinta; MARÍT. calada; COM. giro ♦ **d. board** junta de reclutamiento • **on d.** de barril **II.** tr. *(a bill)* hacer un anteproyecto de; *(a writing)* hacer un borrador de; *(a speech, plan)* redactar; MIL. quintar, reclutar **III.** adj. *(horse)* de tiro; *(beer)* de barril.

draft·ee (drăf-tē') s. recluta *m,* conscripto.

drafts·man (drăfts'mən) s. [pl. **-men**] dibujante *m,* diseñador *m.*

drag (drăg) **I.** tr. -gg- arrastrar; *(river, lake)* dragar; *(to bring forcibly)* llevar de los pelos ♦ **to d. along** arrastrar • **to d. out** *(to extract)* sacar; *(to prolong)* alargar interminablemente —intr. *(to trail)* arrastrar(se); *(to pass slowly)* hacerse interminable; JER. *(on a cigarette)* dar una pitada ♦ **to d. on** hacerse interminable **II.** s. *(act)* arrastre *m;* *(hindrance)* estorbo; AER. resistencia al avance; JER. *(bore)* pesado; *(puff)* chupada, pitada ♦ **in d.** vestido de mujer (un hombre, o viceversa) • **main d.** JER. calle principal.

drag·net (drăg'nĕt') s. *(net)* red barredera; *(roundup)* pesquisa.

drag·on (drăg'ən) s. dragón *m.*

drag·on·fly (:flī') s. libélula.

dra·goon (drə-gōōn') **I.** s. dragón *m* **II.** tr. coaccionar.

drain (drān) **I.** tr. drenar, desaguar; *(to drink)* beber; *(to empty)* vaciar; *(to exhaust)* agotar —intr. desaguarse, vaciarse **II.** s. desagüe *m,* desaguadero; FIG. desgaste *m* ♦ **down the d.** por la ventana.

drain·age (drā'nĭj) s. drenaje *m.*

drain·pipe (drān'pīp') s. caño de desagüe.

drake (drāk) s. pato (macho).

dram (drăm) s. *(weight)* dracma; *(small drink)* traguito, copita; *(a bit)* pizca.

dra·ma (drä'mə) s. drama *m.*

dra·mat·ic (drə-măt'ĭk) adj. dramático ♦ **dramatics** s.pl. histrionismo; s.sg. TEAT. arte dramático.

dram·a·tist (drăm'ə-tĭst, drä'-) s. dramaturgo.

dram·a·tize (:tīz') tr. TEAT. escenificar; *(an issue, presentation)* dramatizar.

drank (drăngk) cf. **drink.**

drape (drāp) **I.** tr. *(to adorn)* adornar con colgaduras; *(to cover)* cubrir; *(to arrange in folds)* drapear; *(to hang)* colgar; *(arms, legs)* echar —intr. caer II. s. caída ♦ pl. cortinas.

drap·er (drā′pər) s. G.B. pañero.

drap·er·y (:pə-rē) s. *(cloth)* paños; G.B. *(business)* pañería ♦ pl. cortinas.

dras·tic (drăs′tĭk) adj. drástico.

draught (drăft, dräft) G.B. var. de **draft.**

draughts (drăfts) s. G.B. juego de damas.

draw (drô) I. tr. **drew, -n** *(to pull)* tirar de, halar; *(to lead)* conducir, llevar; *(to attract)* atraer; *(liquid, gun, conclusion)* sacar; *(breath)* tomar; *(curtain)* correr; *(lots, straws)* echar (suertes); *(fire, criticism)* provocar; *(salary)* cobrar; *(cards)* robar; *(game, contest)* empatar; *(to stretch taut)* tensar; ARTE. dibujar; MARÍT. calar; COM. *(interest)* ganar, devengar; *(savings)* sacar, retirar ♦ **to d. a blank** no recordar nada • **to d. attention** llamar la atención • **to d. in** *(to retract)* retraer; *(to sketch)* esbozar • **to d. out** *(information)* sonsacar; *(to prolong)* prolongar • **to d. together** unir, juntar • **to d. the line** trazar un límite • **to d. up** redactar, preparar —intr. *(to take in air)* tirar; DEP. *(to tie)* empatar; ARTE. dibujar ♦ **to d. away** apartarse • **to d. back** echarse para atrás • **to d. in** encogerse • **to d. near** acercarse • **to d. on** *(a supply)* servirse de, recurrir a; *(an account)* girar contra • **to d. up** pararse II. s. *(attraction)* atracción *f*; *(air intake)* tiro; *(lottery)* sorteo; *(tie)* empate *m*.

draw·back (′băk′) s. desventaja.

draw·bridge (:brĭj′) s. puente levadizo.

draw·er s. cajón *m*, gaveta ♦ pl. *(women's)* bombachas; *(men's)* calzoncillos.

draw·ing (drô′ĭng) s. dibujo; *(lottery)* lotería, sorteo ♦ **d. card** atractivo, atracción • **d. room** salón.

drawl (drôl) intr. & s. (hablar con) voz lenta y cansina.

drawn (drôn) cf. **drew.**

draw·string (drô′strĭng′) s. cordón *m*.

dread (drĕd) I. s. pavor *m*, terror *m*; *(anticipation)* aprensión II. tr. temer; *(to anticipate)* anticipar (con temor) III. adj. espantoso, terrible.

dread·ful (′fəl) adj. espantoso, terrible.

dread·nought (:nôt′) s. acorazado.

dream (drēm) I. s. sueño; *(daydream)* ensueño II. tr. & intr. **-ed** *o* **-t** soñar *(of, about* con); *(to daydream)* soñar despierto ♦ **to d. up** inventar.

dream·er (drē′mər) s. soñador *m*.

dream·y (:mē) adj. **-i-** como un sueño, de ensueño; FAM. *(wonderful)* maravilloso, precioso.

drea·ry (drîr′ē) adj. **-i-** *(bleak)* deprimente, sombrío; *(dull)* monótono, aburrido.

dredge (drĕj) I. s. draga, rastra II. tr. & intr. dragar, rastrear ♦ **to d. up** desenterrar.

dregs (drĕgz) s.pl. poso, heces *f*; FIG. escoria.

drench (drĕnch) tr. empapar.

dress (drĕs) I. s. *(garment)* vestido, traje *m*; *(apparel)* vestimenta, ropa ♦ **d. ball** baile de etiqueta • **d. code** reglamento de la vestimenta • **d. rehearsal** ensayo general II. tr. vestir; *(to decorate)* decorar; *(hair)* peinar, arreglar; *(wounds)* curar; *(food)* aderezar ♦ **dressed to kill** vestido muy elegantemente • **dressed to the nines** de punta en blanco —intr. vestirse ♦ **to d. down** regañar • **to d. up** vestirse de etiqueta III. adj. *(clothing)* de vestir; *(occasion)*

de etiqueta.

dress·er (′ər) s. cómoda, tocador *m*.

dress·ing (:ĭng) s. MED. vendaje *m*; *(sauce)* aliño, salsa; *(stuffing)* relleno ♦ **d. gown** bata • **d. room** camerino • **d. table** tocador, coqueta.

dress·mak·er (:mā′kər) s. costurera.

dress·mak·ing (:kĭng) s. costura.

dress·y (drĕs′ē) adj. **-i-** elegante.

drew (drōō) cf. **draw.**

drib·ble (drĭb′əl) I. intr. *(to trickle)* gotear; *(to drool)* babear; DEP. *(soccer)* gambetear; *(basketball)* driblear —tr. *(to trickle)* echar a gotas; DEP. gambetear, driblear II. s. *(trickle)* goteo, hilo; *(bit)* gota, pizca; DEP. gambeta, dribling *m*.

dri·er (drī′ər) var. de **dryer.**

drift (drĭft) I. intr. *(off course)* ir a la deriva; *(on a current)* ser arrastrado por la corriente; *(to roam)* vagar, vagabundear; *(snow, sand)* amontonarse —tr. llevar, arrastrar II. s. AVIA., MARÍT. deriva; *(of sand, snow)* pila, montón *m*; *(general idea)* dirección *f*, rumbo ♦ **to get the d.** FAM. caer en la cuenta.

drift·er (drĭf′tər) s. vagabundo.

drift·wood (drĭft′wŏŏd′) s. madera flotante.

drill (drĭl) I. s. *(tool)* torno, taladro; *(oil rig)* perforadora; *(machine)* taladradora; *(exercises)* ejercicios repetitivos; *(cloth)* dril *m* ♦ **d. press** prensa taladradora II. intr. & tr. taladrar, perforar; *(to exercise)* ejercitar; *(to teach)* enseñar por medio de repetición.

drink (drĭngk) I. tr. & intr. **drank, drunk** beber, tomar ♦ **to d. in** devorar • **to d. to** brindar por, beber a la salud de • **to d. up** bebérselo todo II. s. bebida; *(swallow)* trago, buche *m* ♦ **to take to d.** darse a la bebida • **to give someone a d.** dar de beber a alguien.

drink·a·ble (drĭng′kə-bəl) adj. potable, bebible.

drink·er (:kər) s. bebedor *m*.

drink·ing (:kĭng) s. beber *m*; *(habit)* bebida.

drip (drĭp) I. tr. **-pp-** echar (a gotas) —intr. gotear II. s. gota; *(sound)* goteo, goteadero JER. *(bore)* pelma *m*, pesado.

drip-dry (′drī′) adj. que seca rápidamente sin arrugas al estar colgado.

drive (drīv) I. tr. **drove, -n** *(a vehicle)* conducir, guiar; *(passengers)* llevar; *(distance)* recorrer; *(to push)* empujar; *(to compel)* forzar, obligar; *(a nail)* clavar; *(a machine)* hacer funcionar, accionar; *(a stake)* hincar ♦ **to d. away** *o* **off** alejar, apartar • **to d. back** hacer retroceder • **to d. in** clavar, hincar • **to d. out** *(to expel)* echar; *(into the open)* hacer salir —intr. *(a vehicle)* conducir, guiar; *(to travel by car)* ir en coche; *(rain, snow)* azotar ♦ **to d. at** insinuar, querer decir • **to d. by** *o* **through** pasar (por) • **to d. on** seguir el camino II. s. *(ride)* vuelta en coche; *(journey)* viaje *m*; *(road)* carretera, camino; *(campaign)* campaña; *(vigor)* vigor *m*, energía; *(push)* empuje *m*, agresividad *f*; MEC. transmisión *f*; AUTO. tracción *f*; PSIC. impulso; MIL. ofensiva ♦ **d. belt** correa de transmisión • **to go for a d.** dar una vuelta en coche.

drive-in (′ĭn′) s. lugar que atiende a los clientes sin que se bajen del automóvil.

driv·el (drĭv′əl) s. *(saliva)* baba; *(nonsense)* boberías.

driv·en (drĭv′ən) cf. **drive.**

driv·er (:ər) s. chofer *mf*, conductor *m*.

drive·way (drīv′wā′) s. camino de entrada.

driv·ing (drī′vĭng) I. adj. *(impelling)* impulsor,

motriz; *(rain)* torrencial; AUTO. de conducción **II.** s. acción *f* de conducir; *(motoring)* automovilismo.

driz·zle (dríz'əl) **I.** intr. lloviznar, garuar —tr. salpicar **II.** s. llovizna, garúa.

droll (drōl) adj. cómico, gracioso.

drone¹ (drōn) s. *(bee)* zángano; *(aircraft)* aeroplano de control remoto.

drone² **I.** intr. *(to buzz)* zumbar; *(to speak)* hablar monótonamente —tr. decir en forma monótona **II.** s. zumbido; *(bagpipe)* roncón *m.*

drool (drōl) **I.** intr. babosear, babear; FAM. *(to show desire)* caérsele la baba **II.** s. baba, saliva.

droop (drōp) **I.** intr. *(to hang)* inclinarse, doblarse; *(trees, eyelids)* caerse; *(head)* inclinarse; *(shoulders)* encorvarse; *(spirits)* desanimarse **II.** s. caída; *(shoulders)* encorvadura; *(head)* inclinación *f.*

drop (drōp) **I.** s. gota; *(trace)* poco, pizca; *(lozenge)* pastilla; *(fall)* bajada, caída; *(height of fall)* altura; *(in prices)* baja; *(in value, quality)* disminución *f*; *(abyss)* precipicio; *(by parachute)* lanzamiento; *(for messages)* buzón *m* ◆ **a d. in the bucket** una gota de agua en el mar **II.** intr. **-pp-** *(to drip)* gotear; *(to fall)* caer a' tierra, desplomarse; *(wind)* amainar; *(temperature, prices)* bajar; *(value, quality)* disminuir; *(conversation)* terminarse; *(to die)* morir de repente ◆ **to d. behind** quedarse atrás • **to d. in** *o* **by** pasar (por casa de alguien) • **to d. off** *(leaves)* caer; *(part)* caerse, desprenderse; *(to diminish)* disminuir • **to d. out** *(to omit)* omitir; *(to quit)* dejar de participar —tr. *(to let fall)* dejar caer, soltar; *(to let go of)* soltar; *(a letter)* echar; *(conversation)* interrumpir; *(plan)* abandonar; *(to omit)* omitir; *(habit)* dejar de; *(hint)* soltar; *(voice, prices)* bajar; *(bombs)* lanzar ◆ **to d. off** dejar • **to d. someone a line** poner unas líneas a alguien

drop·let ('lĭt) s. gotita.

drop-off (-ôf') s. *(slope)* bajada escarpada; *(decrease)* disminución significativa.

drop·out (:out') s. *(student)* estudiante *mf* que abandona sus estudios; *(from society)* persona que rechaza a la sociedad.

drop·per (:ər) s. gotero, cuentagotas *m.*

drop·pings (:ĭngz) s.pl. excremento de animales.

dross (drôs) s. TEC. escoria; FIG. desperdicio.

drought (drout) s. sequía, seca; FIG. escasez *f.*

drove¹ (drōv) cf. **drive.**

drove² s. *(herd)* manada; FIG. multitud *f* ◆ **in droves** a manadas.

drov·er (drō'vər) s. *(of cattle, mules)* arriero, vaquero; *(of sheep)* pastor *m.*

drown (droun) intr. ahogarse —tr. ahogar; *(to flood)* anegar.

drowse (drouz) intr. adormecerse, estar medio dormido.

drows·y (drou'zē) adj. **-i-** soñoliento, amodorrado.

drub (drŭb) tr. **-bb-** *(to thrash)* apalear; *(to defeat)* derrotar por completo.

drub·bing (:ĭng) s. paliza, zurra; *(defeat)* derrota severa.

drudge (drŭj) s. esclavo del trabajo.

drudg·er·y ('ə-rē) s. faena pesada y aburrida.

drug (drŭg) **I.** s. droga; MED. medicamento; *(narcotic)* narcótico ◆ **d. addict** narcómano, drogadicto **II.** tr. **-gg-** MED. dar medicamento; *(with a narcotic)* drogar, narcotizar; *(food,*

drink) poner una droga en.

drug·gist ('ĭst) s. farmacéutico, boticario.

drug·store s. farmacia, botica.

drum (drŭm) **I.** s. cilindro, tambor *m*; *(barrel)* tonel *m*; MÚS. tambor ◆ pl. batería **II.** intr. & tr. **-mm-** tocar (el tambor); *(fingers)* tamborilear (con) ◆ **to d. into someone's head** meterle a alguien en la cabeza • **to d. out** echar, expulsar • **to d. up** conseguir.

drum·beat ('bēt') s. toque *m* del tambor.

drum·mer (:ər) s. baterista *mf*, tambor *mf.*

drum·stick (:stĭk') s. MUS. baqueta, palillo; CUL. muslo.

drunk (drŭngk) **I.** cf. **drink II.** adj. ebrio, borracho ◆ **to get d.** emborracharse **III.** s. *(drunkard)* borracho; *(bout)* juerga.

drunk·ard (drŭng'kərd) s. borracho.

drunk·en ('kən) adj. borracho, bebido; *(song, brawl)* de borrachos; *(state)* de embriaguez.

dry (drī) **I.** adj. **-i-** *o* **-y-** seco; *(arid)* árido; *(thirsty)* sediento; *(toast)* sin mantequilla; *(boring)* pesado; *(wit, style)* agudo, satírico; *(county, state)* prohibicionista ◆ **d. cleaner's** tintorería, tinte • **d. cleaning** limpieza en seco • **d. dock** carenero • **d. goods** mercería, lencería • **d. land** tierra firme • **d. measure** sistema de medidas para áridos • **d. run** práctica, simulacro • **to run d.** secarse, agotarse **II.** tr. & intr. secar(se), desecar(se) ◆ **d. up!** ¡cállate la boca! • **to d. out** secar(se); *(drunkard)* dejar de beber • **to d. up** desecar(se); *(supply)* esfumarse, desaparecer.

dry-clean (:klēn') tr. limpiar en seco.

dry·er (:ər) s. *(appliance)* secador *m*; *(machine)* secadora *f.*

dry·ness (:nĭs) s. sequedad *f.*

du·al (dōō'əl) adj. dual, doble.

du·al·i·ty (dōō-ăl'ĭ-tē) s. dualidad *f.*

du·al-pur·pose (dōō'əl-pûr'pəs) adj. de doble propósito, de doble función.

dub¹ (dŭb) tr. **-bb-** *(to knight)* armar, hacer caballero; *(to nickname)* apodar.

dub² tr. **-bb-** MÚS. mezclar; CINEM. doblar.

du·bi·ous (dōō'bē-əs) adj. *(doubtful)* dudoso, incierto; *(questionable)* sospechoso.

duch·ess (dŭch'ĭs) s. duquesa.

duch·y (:ē) s. ducado.

duck¹ (dŭk) s. pato; *(female)* pata.

duck² tr. *(head)* agachar; *(to dodge)* eludir, evadir; *(to plunge)* zambullir —intr. agacharse, zambullirse ◆ **to d. out** desaparecer • **to d. out on** eludir.

duck·ling ('lĭng) s. patito, anadón *m.*

duct (dŭkt) s. conducto, tubo; ANAT. canal *m.*

dud (dŭd) s. FAM. *(bomb)* bomba que no estalla; *(failure)* fracaso ◆ pl. FAM. *(clothes)* trapos; *(belongings)* posesiones.

dude (dōōd) s. FAM. hombre *m* de ciudad; *(dandy)* petimetre *m*; JER. *(guy)* tipo, tío.

due (dōō) **I.** adj. *(payable)* pagadero; *(amount)* sin pagar; *(just)* debido, merecido; *(sufficient)* suficiente ◆ **d. date** vencimiento • **d. process** proceso legal correspondiente • **to d. to** debido a, a causa de • **to become** *o* **fall d.** vencer **II.** s. *(comeuppance)* merecido; *(reward)* recompensa ◆ pl. cuota **III.** adv. derecho hacia.

du·el (dōō'əl) intr. & s. (batirse en) duelo.

du·el·er·ist (:ə-lər/ĭst) s. duelista *m.*

du·et (dōō-ĕt') s. dueto, dúo.

duf·fel bag (dŭf'əl) s. bolsa de lona.

dug (dŭg) cf. **dig.**

dug·out (dŭg'out') s. *(boat)* piragua; *(shelter)*

trinchera.

duke (dōōk) s. duque *m*.

dukes (dōōks) s.pl. JER. puños ♦ **put** *o* **stick up your d.!** ¡ponte en guardia!

dul·cet (dŭl′sĭt) adj. suave, dulce.

dull (dŭl) **I.** adj. *(stupid)* tonto, torpe; *(insensitive)* lento, embotado; *(blunt)* desafilado, romo; *(sound, pain)* sordo; *(boring)* aburrido; *(sluggish)* flojo; *(color, sound)* apagado; *(cloudy)* nublado, gris **II.** tr. & intr. *(to blunt)* desafilar(se), enromar(se); *(pain)* aliviar(se); *(feelings)* embotar(se); *(to muffle)* amortiguar(se), apagar(se).

dull·ard (′ərd) s. estúpido, idiota *mf*.

dul(l)·ness (:nĭs) s. *(blade, senses)* embotamiento; *(stupidity)* torpeza; *(flatness)* monotonía, insipidez *f*.

du·ly (dōō′lē) adv. correctamente, debidamente; *(punctually)* al debido tiempo.

dumb (dŭm) adj. *(mute)* mudo; FAM. *(stupid)* tonto, estúpido ♦ **d. show** pantomima • **to strike d.** dejar sin habla.

dumb·bell (′bĕl′) s. *(weight)* pesas; JER. *(dolt)* estúpido, tonto.

dumb·wait·er (:wā′tər) s. montaplatos *m*.

dum(b)·found (:found′) tr. pasmar, asombrar.

dum·my (:ē) **I.** s. *(puppet)* muñeco, títere *m*; *(mannequin)* maniquí *m*; *(front)* testaferro; FAM. *(dolt)* tonto, bobo **II.** adj. falso, ficticio.

dump (dŭmp) **I.** tr. tirar, deshacerse de; *(to empty)* vaciar, descargar; COM. inundar el mercado con; COMPUT. imprimir (información) —intr. caerse, desplomarse ♦ **to d. out** vaciar(se) **II.** s. vertedero, muladar *m*; *(depot)* depósito; JER. *(unkept place)* pocilga ♦ **d. truck** volquete ♦ pl. FAM. abatimiento.

dump·ling (:lĭng) s. bola de masa cocida.

dun¹ (dŭn) tr. **-nn-** apremiar (a un deudor).

dun² s. *(color)* pardo.

dunce (dŭns) s. FAM. zopenco, burro ♦ **d. cap** orejas de burro.

dune (dōōn) s. duna ♦ **d. buggy** automóvil para andar sobre dunas.

dung (dŭng) s. estiércol *m*.

dun·ga·rees (dŭng′gə-rē′z′) s.pl. pantalones vaqueros.

dun·geon (dŭn′jən) s. mazmorra.

dunk (dŭngk) tr. sumergir, hundir; *(food)* ensopar, remojar.

du·o (dōō′ō) s. FAM. *(pair)* pareja; MÚS. dúo.

du·o·dec·i·mal (dōō′ə-dĕs′ə-məl) **I.** adj. duodecimal **II.** s. duodécimo.

du·o·de·num (:dē′nəm) s. [pl. **s** *o* **-na**] duodeno.

dupe (dōōp) **I.** FAM. primo **II.** tr. embaucar, engañar.

du·plex (dōō′plĕks) **I.** adj. doble **II.** s. *(apartment)* apartamento de dos pisos; *(house)* casa de dos viviendas.

du·pli·cate (:plĭ-kĭt) **I.** s. duplicado, copia ♦ **in d.** por duplicado **II.** tr. (:kāt′) copiar, duplicar; *(on a machine)* multicopiar **III.** adj. duplicado.

du·plic·i·ty (dōō-plĭs′ĭ-tē) s. engaño.

du·ra·ble (dōōr′ə-bəl) adj. duradero ♦ **d. goods** productos no perecederos.

du·ra·tion (dōō-rā′shən) s. duración *f*.

du·ress (dōō-rĕs′) s. coerción *f* ♦ **under d.** por coacción.

dur·ing (dōōr′ĭng) prep. durante.

dusk (dŭsk) s. crepúsculo ♦ **at d.** al atardecer.

dusk·y (dŭs′kē) adj. **-i-** oscuro, fusco; *(color)* negruzco, moreno.

dust (dŭst) **I.** s. polvo ♦ **d. cloud** polvareda • **d. jacket** sobrecubierta • **to bite the d.** morirse • **to let the d. settle** dejar que se calme la situación **II.** tr. limpiar el polvo de; *(to cover)* empolvar; *(to sprinkle)* espolvorear —intr. limpiar el polvo.

dust·bin (′bĭn′) s. G.B. basurero.

dust·er (dŭs′tər) s. *(cloth)* trapo (para limpiar); *(with feathers)* plumero; *(smock)* guardapolvo.

dust·ing (:tĭng) s. limpieza de polvo; *(covering)* capa de polvo; G.B., FAM. *(thrashing)* paliza.

dust·man (dŭst′mən) s. [pl. **-men**] G.B. basurero.

dust·pan (:păn′) s. recogedor *m*.

dust·y (dŭs′tē) adj. **-i-** polvoriento.

du·ti·ful (dōō′tĭ-fəl) adj. obediente, cumplidor.

du·ty (dōō′tē) s. deber *m*, obligación *f*; *(task)* función *f*; *(tax)* impuesto, arancel ♦ **in the line of d.** en cumplimiento del deber • **to be on (off) d.** (no) estar de servicio • **to do one's d.** cumplir con su deber.

du·ty-free (:frē′) adj. & adv. exento de derechos de aduana.

du·ty-paid (:pād′) adj. con los derechos de aduana pagados.

dwarf (dwôrf) **I.** adj. & s. [pl. **s** *o* **-ves**] enano **II.** tr. achicar, empequeñecer.

dwell (dwĕl) tr. **-ed** *o* **dwelt** morar, residir; FIG. persistir, existir ♦ **to d. on** *(to focus on)* detenerse en, insistir en; *(to expatiate)* dilatarse sobre.

dwell·er (′ər) s. morador *m*, habitante *mf*.

dwell·ing (:ĭng) s. residencia, morada.

dwin·dle (dwĭn′dl) tr. & intr. disminuir, menguar.

dye (dī) **I.** s. tintura, tinte *m* **II.** tr. **dyeing** teñir, colorar.

dy·er (dī′ər) s. tintorero.

dye·stuff (dī′stŭf′) s. tinte *m*, colorante *m*.

dy·ing (dī′ĭng) **I.** cf. **die¹** **II.** adj. moribundo; *(final)* último.

dy·nam·ic (dī-năm′ĭk) adj. dinámico ♦ **dynamics** s. dinámica.

dy·na·mite (dī′nə-mīt′) **I.** s. dinamita **II.** interj. JER. estupendo, maravilloso.

dy·na·mo (:mō′) s. dínamo *f*.

dy·nas·ty (dī′nə-stē) s. dinastía.

dys·en·ter·y (dĭs′ən-tĕr′ē) s. disentería.

dys·func·tion (dĭs-fŭngk′shən) s. disfunción *f*.

dys·pep·sia (dĭs-pĕp′shə) s. dispepsia.

dys·tro·phy (dĭs′trə-fē) s. distrofia.

E

e, E (ē) s. quinta letra del alfabeto inglés; MÚS. mi *m*.

each (ēch) **I.** adj. cada ♦ **e. and every one** todos sin excepción **II.** pron. cada uno ♦ **e. for himself** cada cual por su cuenta • **e. other** uno a otro, mutuamente • **to e. his own** cada uno con su gusto **III.** adv. por persona, cada uno.

ea·ger (ē′gər) adj. **-er, -est** *(avid)* ansioso, ávido; *(desirous)* deseoso, ardiente ♦ **e. beaver** FAM. persona de exagerado entusiasmo • **to be e. for** ansiar, anhelar.

ea·ger·ness (:nĭs) s. ansia, anhelo.

ea·gle (ē′gəl) s. águila.

ear¹ (îr) s. oreja; *(organ of hearing)* oído ♦ **e. lobe** lóbulo de la oreja • **to fall on deaf ears**

caer en saco roto • **to give an e. to** prestar atención a • **to have a good e. (for)** tener un buen oído (para) • **to have someone's e.** tener la atención de alguien • **to keep** *o* **have one's e. to the ground** mantenerse alerta *o* al corriente • **to listen with half an e.** escuchar a medias • **to play by e.** tocar de oído • **to play it by e.** improvisar sobre la marcha • **to turn a deaf e.** hacerse el sordo.

ear² s. BOT. espiga, mazorca.

ear·ache (îr'āk') s. dolor *m* de oído.

ear·drum (îr'drŭm') s. tímpano.

ear·flap (îr'flăp') s. orejera.

earl (ûrl) s. conde *m*.

earl·dom ('dəm) s. condado.

ear·ly (ûr'lē) -i- I. adj. temprano; *(near the beginning)* primero; *(quick)* rápido, pronto; *(premature)* prematuro; *(primitive)* primitivo • **at an e. date** en fecha cercana • **at the earliest** lo más pronto • **at your earliest convenience** con la mayor brevedad • **e. bird** FAM. *(riser)* madrugador; *(arrival)* persona que llega temprano • **e. show** primera función **II.** adv. *(soon)* temprano, pronto; *(before)* antes; *(in advance)* con tiempo, con anticipación; *(prematurely)* prematuramente • **as e.** as ya en • **as e. as possible** lo más pronto posible • **bright and e.** muy temprano • **e. in** a principios de • **e. in the morning** de madrugada • **e. on** pronto.

ear·mark (îr'märk') I. s. marca característica, señal *f* II. tr. marcar • **to be earmarked for** estar reservado para.

ear·muff (îr'mŭf') s. orejera.

earn (ûrn) tr. *(to make)* ganar; *(to deserve)* ganarse, merecer; *(to acquire)* ganar; *(interest)* devengar.

ear·nest¹ (ûr'nĭst) adj. sincero, serio; *(important)* grave • **in e.** en serio.

ear·nest² s. *(deposit)* arras *f*; *(token)* prenda.

earn·ings (ûr'nĭngz) s.pl. *(salary)* sueldo; COM. *(income)* ingresos; *(profits)* utilidades *f*.

ear·phone (îr'fōn') s. audífono.

ear·ring (îr'ĭng) s. pendiente *m*, arete *m*.

ear·shot (îr'shŏt') s. • **within e.** al alcance del oído.

ear·split·ting (îr'splĭt'ĭng) adj. ensordecedor.

earth (ûrth) s. tierra; *(world)* mundo • **down to e.** sensato, realista • **E.** Tierra • **to come back to e.** volver a la realidad • **who, what on e.** quién, qué diablo.

earth·en (ûr'thən) adj. de tierra.

earth·en·ware (:wâr') I. s. loza II. adj. de barro.

earth·ling (ûrth'lĭng) s. terrícola *mf*.

earth·ly (:lē) adj. mundanal, terreno; FAM. *(conceivable)* concebible, posible • **to be of no e. use** no servir para nada.

earth·quake (:kwāk') s. terremoto, temblor *m*.

earth·shak·ing (:shā'kĭng) adj. importantísimo, de enormes consecuencias.

earth·work (:wûrk') s. terraplén *m*.

earth·worm (:wûrm') s. lombriz *f*.

earth·y (ûr'thē) adj. -i- vulgar, tosco.

ear·wax (îr'wăks') s. cerumen *m*.

ease (ēz) I. s. *(comfort)* comodidad *f*; *(relief)* alivio, desahogo; *(naturalness)* desenvoltura; *(facility)* facilidad *f*, soltura; *(affluence)* afluencia • **at e.** cómodo; MIL. en posición de descanso • **at e.!** ¡descanso! • **to put at e.** poner cómodo • **with e.** fácilmente, sin esfuerzo II. tr. & intr. *(pain)* aliviar(se), mitigar(se); *(pressure)* descargar(se); *(tension)* relajar(se);

(to loosen) aflojar(se) ♦ **to e. in(to)** (hacer) entrar con cuidado ♦ **to e. up** bajar, disminuir • **to e. up on** tratar con menos rigor.

ea·sel (ē'zəl) s. caballete *m*.

ease·ment (ēz'mənt) s. servidumbre *f*.

eas·i·ly (ē'zə-lē) adv. fácilmente; *(possibly)* muy probablemente.

eas·i·ness (ē'zē-nĭs) s. facilidad *f*; *(comfort)* comodidad *f*.

east (ēst) I. s. este *m*, oriente m II. adj. del este, oriental III. adv. al este, hacia el este.

east·bound ('bound') adj. con rumbo al este.

Eas·ter (ē'stər) s. Pascua de Resurrección; *(period)* Semana Santa ♦ **E. Sunday** domingo de Pascua.

east·ern (ē'stərn) adj. oriental, del este.

east·ward (ēst'wərd) I. adv. hacia el este II. adj. oriental, que va al este.

eas·y (ē'zē) -i- I. adj. fácil; *(free from worry)* tranquilo; *(comfortable)* cómodo; *(easygoing)* desenvuelto, natural; *(simple)* sencillo; *(not strict)* suave, leve; *(wanton)* desordenado; *(unhurried)* lento, pausado • **e. chair** sillón • **e. to get along with** acomodadizo • **to be easy-going** • **e. street** vivir acomodado II. adv. fácilmente ♦ **e. does it** con calma • **to come e.** costar poco esfuerzo, resultar fácil • **to go e. on** FAM. *(to use moderately)* usar con moderación; *(to be lenient to)* no tratar con mucha severidad • **to take it e.** FAM. *(to relax)* descansar; *(to stay calm)* no agitarse; *(to enjoy)* deleitarse en • *(to stay calm)* no agitarse; *(to not hurry)* no apurarse.

eas·y·go·ing ('-gō'ĭng) adj. despreocupado; *(tolerant)* tolerante.

eat (ēt) tr. ate, eaten comer; *(lunch, dinner)* tomar (el almuerzo, la cena); *(to corrode)* corroer; JER. *(to annoy)* molestar, fastidiar ♦ **to e. away** corroer, carcomer • **to e. up** *(to devour)* comérselo todo; *(to use up)* consumir, gastar; *(to be credulous)* creer sin crítica; *(to enjoy)* deleitarse en • **what's eating you?** ¿qué mosca te ha picado? —intr. comer, alimentarse ♦ **to e. (away) at** roer, corroer • **to e.** *(in, to corrode)* corroer; *(to use up)* (des)gastar • **to e. out** comer fuera (de casa) • **to e. through** corroer.

eats (ēts) s.pl. JER. comida, alimento.

eaves (ēvz) s.pl. alero.

eaves·drop ('drŏp') intr. -pp- escuchar disimulada *o* secretamente.

ebb (ĕb) I. s. menguante *f* • **e. and flow** flujo y reflujo; FIG. altibajos • **to be at a low e.** tener poca energía II. intr. menguar.

eb·on·y (ĕb'ə-nē) I. s. ébano II. adj. negro.

e·bul·lient (ĭ-bŏŏl'yənt) adj. *(lively)* entusiasta; *(bubbly)* burbujeante.

ec·cen·tric (ĭk-sĕn'trĭk) I. adj. excéntrico II. s. *(person)* excéntrico; MEC. excéntrica.

ec·cen·tric·i·ty (ĕk'sĕn-trĭs'ĭ-tē) s. excentricidad *f*.

ec·cle·si·as·tic (ĭ-klē'zē-ăs'tĭk) adj. & s. eclesiástico.

ech·e·lon (ĕsh'ə-lŏn') s. escalón *m*.

ech·o (ĕk'ō) I. s. [pl. es] eco ♦ **e. chamber** cámara de resonancia II. tr. *(to repeat)* repetir; *(to imitate)* imitar —intr. producir eco, resonar.

e·clec·tic (ĭ-klĕk'tĭk) adj. & s. ecléctico.

e·clipse (ĭ-klĭps') I. s. eclipse *m* II. tr. eclipsar.

e·clip·tic (ĭ-klĭp'tĭk) adj. s. eclíptica.

ec·o·log·i·cal (ĕk'ə-lŏj'ĭ-kəl) adj. ecológico.

e·col·o·gy (ĭ-kŏl'ə-jē) s. ecología.

ec·o·nom·ic (ĕk'ə-nŏm'ĭk, ē'kə-) adj. económico ♦ **economics** s.sg. economía.

ec·o·nom·i·cal (:ĭ-kəl) adj. económico.
e·con·o·mist (ĭ-kŏn′ə-mĭst) s. economista *mf.*
e·con·o·mize (:mīz′) intr. economizar (*on* en).
e·con·o·my (:mē) s. economía *f* ♦ **e. car** automóvil económico.
ec·o·sys·tem (ĕk′ə-sĭs′təm) s. ecosistema *m.*
ec·sta·sy (ĕk′stə-sē) s. éxtasis *m.*
ec·stat·ic (ĕk-stăt′ĭk) adj. extático.
ec·u·men·i·cal (ĕk′yə-mĕn′ĭ-kəl) adj. ecuménico.
ec·ze·ma (ĕk′sə-mə) s. eczema *m.*
ed·dy (ĕd′ē) I. s. remolino II. intr. arremolinarse, remolinar.
edge (ĕj) I. s. (*cutting side*) filo, corte *m*; (*border, rim*) borde *m*; (*shore, hem*) orilla; (*boundary*) límite *m*; (*angle*) arista; (*of table, coin*) canto; (*farthest part*) extremidad *f*; FIG. (*sharpness*) filo, mordacidad *f*; FAM. (*advantage*) ventaja ♦ **e. of town** afueras • **on e.** de canto • **to be on e.** tener los nervios de punta • **to be on the e.** of estar al borde o al punto de • **to set one's teeth** o **nerves on e.** dar dentera, ponerle a uno los pelos de punta • **to take the e. off** (*to blunt*) embotar; (*the appetite*) acallar II. tr. (*to sharpen*) afilar; (*to border*) bordear; (*to trim*) ribetear ♦ **to e. out** vencer por un margen pequeño —intr. andar o moverse cautelosamente ♦ **to e. away, toward** retirarse, adelantarse poco a poco.
edge·wise/ways (ĕj′wīz′ /wāz′) adv. (*on end*) de filo o de canto; (*sideways*) sesgadamente ♦ **I couldn't get a word in e.** no podía meter baza.
edg·y (ĕj′ē) adj. **-i-** nervioso, tenso.
ed·i·ble (ĕd′ə-bəl) adj. & s. comestible *m.*
e·dict (ē′dĭkt′) s. edicto.
ed·i·fi·ca·tion (ĕd′ə-fĭ-kā′shən) s. edificación *f.*
ed·i·fice (ĕd′ə-fĭs) s. edificio.
ed·i·fy (:fī′) tr. edificar.
ed·it (ĕd′ĭt) tr. (*to draft*) redactar; (*to correct*) corregir, editar; (*edition, text*) preparar; (*a publication*) dirigir; CINEM. montar ♦ **to e. out** quitar, suprimir.
ed·it·ing (ĕd′ĭ-tĭng) s. (*of text*) redacción *f*; (*correction*) corrección *f*, revisión *f*; (*of a publication*) dirección *f*; (*of film*) montaje *m.*
e·di·tion (ĭ-dĭsh′ən) s. edición *f*; (*number of copies*) tirada *m*, tirada; FIG. versión *f.*
ed·i·tor (ĕd′ĭ-tər) s. editor *m*; (*supervisor*) redactor jefe *m*; CINEM. montador *m* ♦ **e. in chief** jefe de redacción, redactor en jefe.
ed·i·to·ri·al (′-tôr′ē-əl) adj. & s. editorial *m* ♦ **e. staff** redacción *f.*
ed·i·tor·ship (:tər-shĭp′) s. dirección *f*, redacción *f.*
ed·u·cate (ĕj′ə-kāt′) tr. educar.
ed·u·cat·ed (:kā′tĭd) adj. (*cultured*) culto; (*schooled*) educado.
ed·u·ca·tion (′-′shən) s. educación *f.*
ed·u·ca·tion·al (:shə-nəl) adj. (*institution, staff*) docente; (*instructive*) educativo.
ed·u·ca·tor (ĕj′ə-kā′tər) s. educador *m.*
eel (ēl) s. [pl. inv. o **s**] anguila.
ee·rie/ry (îr′ē) adj. **-i-** (*creepy*) espeluznante; (*mysterious*) sobrenatural, misterioso.
ef·face (ĭ-fās′) tr. borrar ♦ **to e. oneself** comportarse sin llamar la atención.
ef·fect (ĭ-fĕkt′) I. s. efecto; (*result*) resultado ♦ **for e.** para impresionar • **in e.** (*in fact*) efectivamente; (*virtually*) casi, prácticamente; (*in operation*) en vigor, vigente • **to be in e.** estar vigente • **to go into e.** entrar en vigor • **to have no e.** no dar resultado • **to no e.** inútilmente,

sin resultado • **to take e.** (*medication*) surtir efecto; (*laws, schedule*) entrar en vigor ♦ pl. bienes, pertenencias II. tr. efectuar, realizar.
ef·fec·tive (ĭ-fĕk′tĭv) adj. efectivo; (*striking*) impresionante; (*operative*) vigente.
ef·fec·tive·ness (:nĭs) s. eficacia.
ef·fec·tu·al (ĭ-fĕk′chŏō-əl) adj. eficaz.
ef·fem·i·na·cy (ĭ-fĕm′ə-nə-sē) s. afeminación *f.*
ef·fem·i·nate (:nĭt) adj. afeminado.
ef·fer·ves·cent (ĕf′ər-vĕs′ənt) adj. efervescente.
ef·fete (ĭ-fēt′) adj. (*worn-out*) gastado; (*decadent*) decadente.
ef·fi·ca·cy (ĕf′ĭ-kə-sē) s. eficacia.
ef·fi·cien·cy (ĭ-fĭsh′ən-sē) s. eficiencia; FAM. (*apartment*) apartamento de un cuarto con cocina y baño; MEC. rendimiento.
ef·fi·cient (ĭ-fĭsh′ənt) adj. eficaz, eficiente; MEC. de buen o gran rendimiento.
ef·fi·gy (ĕf′ə-jē) s. efigie *f.*
ef·flu·ent (ĕf′lŏō-ənt) I. adj. efluente II. s. chorro.
ef·fort (ĕf′ərt) s. esfuerzo; (*achievement*) obra ♦ **to spare no e.** hacer todo lo posible.
ef·fort·less (:lĭs) adj. fácil, sin esfuerzo.
ef·fron·ter·y (ĭ-frŭn′tə-rē) s. descaro.
ef·fu·sion (ĭ-fyŏō′zhən) s. efusión *f.*
ef·fu·sive (:sĭv) adj. efusivo.
e·gal·i·tar·i·an (ĭ-găl′ĭ-târ′ē-ən) adj. & s. igualitario.
egg (ĕg) I. s. huevo; BIOL. óvulo; JER. (*fellow*) tío, tipo ♦ **bad e.** JER. calavera • **good e.** JER. buen tipo • **to put all one's eggs in one basket** jugárselo todo en una carta • **to walk** o **tread on eggs** andar con extremo cuidado • **with e. on one's face** pasando vergüenza II. tr. ♦ **to e. on** incitar.
egg·beat·er (ĕg′bē′tər) s. batidor *m* de huevos.
egg·head (ĕg′hĕd′) s. JER. intelectual *mf.*
egg·nog (ĕg′nŏg′) s. ronpopo.
egg·plant (ĕg′plănt′) s. berenjena.
egg·shell (ĕg′shĕl′) s. cascarón *m.*
e·go (ē′gō) s. yo, ego; (*egotism*) egoísmo.
e·go·ist (:ĭst) s. egoísta *mf.*
e·go·is·tic/al (′-ĭs′tĭk) adj. egoísta.
e·go·ma·ni·a (:mā′nē-ə) s. preocupación obsesiva con el ego.
e·go·tist (ē′gə-tĭst) s. egotista *mf.*
e·go·tis·tic/al (′-tĭs′tĭk) adj. egotista.
e·gre·gious (ĭ-grē′jəs) adj. atroz, flagrante.
e·gress (ē′grĕs′) s. salida.
e·gret (ē′grĭt) s. airón *m.*
ei·der·down (ī′dər-doun′) s. edredón *m.*
eight (āt) s. & adj. ocho ♦ **e. hundred** ochocientos • **e. o'clock** las ocho.
eight·een (ā-tēn′) s. & adj. dieciocho.
eight·eenth (ā-tēnth′) I. s. dieciocho; (*part*) dieciochava parte II. adj. (*place*) décimoctavo; (*part*) dieciochavo.
eighth (ātth) s. & adj. octavo.
eight·i·eth (ā′tē-ĭth) I. s. ochenta; (*part*) octogésima parte II. adj. octogésimo.
eight·y (ā′tē) s. & adj. ochenta *m.*
ei·ther (ē′thər, ī′-) I. pron. & adj. uno u otro, cualquiera de los dos; (*negative*) ni uno ni otro, ninguno de los dos II. adv. uno u otro, cualquiera de los dos; (*negative*) ni uno ni otro, ninguno de los dos III. conj. o . . . o <*e. we go now, or we stay* o nos vamos ahora o nos quedamos> III. adv. tampoco.
e·jac·u·late (ĭ-jăk′yə-lāt′) tr. & intr. FISIOL. eyacular; (*to exclaim*) exclamar.
e·jac·u·la·tion (′-lā′shən) s. eyaculación *f*; (*exclamation*) exclamación *f*; (*prayer*) jaculatoria.
e·ject (ĭ-jĕkt′) tr. expeler, expulsar —intr.

AVIA. eyectar.
e·jec·tion (ĭ-jĕk'shən) s. expulsión *f*; AER. eyección *f* ♦ **e. seat** asiento eyectable *o* lanzable.
eke (ēk) tr. ♦ **to e. out** suplir para que sea apenas suficiente • **to e. out a living** ganarse la vida a duras penas.
e·lab·o·rate (ĭ-lăb'ər-ĭt) I. adj. *(detailed)* esmerado; *(intricate)* complicado II. tr. (:ə-rāt') elaborar, desarrollar —intr. explicarse ♦ **to e. on** explayarse.
e·lab·o·ra·tion (:ə-rā'shən) s. elaboración *f*; *(explanation)* explicación *f.*
e·lapse (ĭ-lăps') intr. transcurrir, pasar.
e·las·tic (ĭ-lăs'tĭk) adj. elástico.
e·las·tic·i·ty (ĭ-lă-stĭs'ĭ-tē) s. elasticidad *f.*
e·late (ĭ-lāt') tr. regocijar, alborozar.
e·lat·ed (ĭ-lā'tĭd) adj. contento, alborozado.
e·la·tion (:shən) s. regocijo, alegría.
el·bow (ĕl'bō') I. s. codo ♦ **e. grease** FAM. energía física II. tr. dar un codazo ♦ **to e. one's way** abrirse paso a codazos.
el·bow·room (:rōōm') s. espacio suficiente.
eld·er (ĕl'dər) I. adj. mayor ♦ **to be (two) years (his) e.** ser (dos) años mayor que (él) II. s. *(old person)* mayor *m*; *(leader)* anciano.
eld·er·ly (:lē) adj. mayor (de edad).
eld·est (ĕl'dĭst) adj. mayor.
e·lect (ĭ-lĕkt') I. tr. & intr. elegir II. electo ♦ **the e.** los elegidos.
e·lec·tion (ĭ-lĕk'shən) s. *(choice)* elección *f*; POL. elecciones ♦ **e. time** período electoral, electoral.
e·lec·tion·eer (-'shə-nîr') intr. hacer campaña electoral.
e·lec·tive (-'tĭv) I. adj. electivo II. s. curso electivo.
e·lec·tor·al (ĭ-lĕk'tər-əl) adj. electoral.
e·lec·tor·ate (:ĭt) s. electorado.
e·lec·tric/tri·cal (ĭ-lĕk'trĭk) adj. eléctrico; *(thrilling)* emocionante.
e·lec·tri·cian (·trĭsh'ən) s. electricista *mf.*
e·lec·tric·i·ty (:trĭs'ĭ-tē) s. electricidad *f.*
e·lec·tri·fy (ĭ-lĕk'trə-fī') tr. electrizar; *(a building, town)* electrificar.
e·lec·tro·car·di·o·gram (-'trō-kär'dē-ə-grăm') s. electrocardiograma *m.*
e·lec·tro·cute (:trə-kyōōt') tr. electrocutar.
e·lec·trode (:trōd') s. electrodo.
e·lec·tro·dy·nam·ics (-'trō-dī-năm'ĭks) s.sg. electrodinámica.
e·lec·trol·y·sis (--trŏl'ĭ-sĭs) s. electrólisis *f.*
e·lec·tro·lyte (-'trə-līt') s. electrólito.
e·lec·tro·mag·net (-'trō-măg'nĭt) s. electroimán *m.*
e·lec·tro·mag·net·ic (:măg-nĕt'ĭk) adj. electromagnético.
e·lec·tro·mo·tive (:mō'tĭv) s. electromotriz.
e·lec·tron (ĭ-lĕk'trŏn') s. electrón *m.*
e·lec·tron·ic (--trŏn'ĭk) adj. electrónico ♦ **electronics** s.sg. electrónica.
e·lec·tro·plate (:'trə-plāt') tr. galvanizar.
e·lec·tro·shock (:trō-shŏk') s. electrochoque *m.*
e·lec·tro·stat·ic (:stăt'ĭk) adj. electrostático.
e·lec·tro·type (:trō-tīp') s. electrotipo.
el·e·gance (ĕl'ĭ-gəns) s. elegancia.
el·e·gant (:gənt) adj. elegante.
el·e·gi·ac (ĕl'ə-jī'ăk) adj. elegíaco.
el·e·gy (ĕl'ə-jē) s. elegía.
el·e·ment (ĕl'ə-mənt) s. elemento ♦ **an e. of** algo de ♦ pl. *(weather)* los elementos; RELIG. especies eucarísticas.
el·e·men·tal ('-mĕn'tl) adj. elemental.

el·e·men·ta·ry (:tə-rē) adj. elemental ♦ **e. school** escuela primaria.
el·e·phant (ĕl'ə-fənt) s. elefante *m.*
el·e·phan·tine ('-făn'tēn') adj. enorme; *(clumsy)* torpe.
el·e·vate (ĕl'ə-vāt') tr. elevar; *(to promote)* ascender (*to a*).
el·e·vat·ed (:vā'tĭd) I. adj. elevado II. s. FAM. ferrocarril elevado.
el·e·va·tion ('-'shən) s. elevación *f*; GEOG. altitud *f.*
el·e·va·tor ('-'tər) s. ascensor *m*; AGR. elevador *m*; AVIA. timón *m* de profundidad.
el·ev·en (ĭ-lĕv'ən) s. & adj. once *m* ♦ **e. o'clock** las once.
el·ev·enth (:ənth) s. & adj. undécimo; *(part)* onzavo *m.*
elf (ĕlf) s. [pl. **-ves**] duende *m.*
e·lic·it (ĭ-lĭs'ĭt) tr. sonsacar, sacar.
el·i·gi·ble (ĕl'ĭ-jə-bəl) adj. elegible.
e·lim·i·nate (ĭ-lĭm'ə-nāt') tr. eliminar.
e·lim·i·na·tion (-'-nā'shən) s. eliminación *f.*
e·lite *o* **é·lite** (ĭ-lēt', ā-lēt') s. élite *f.*
e·lit·ist (ĭ-lē'tĭst, ā-lē'-) adj. elitista.
elk (ĕlk) s. [pl. inv. *o* **s**] alce *m.*
e·lipse (ĭ-lĭps') s. elipse *f.*
e·lip·sis (ĭ-lĭp'sĭs) s. [pl. **-ses**] elipsis *f.*
el·lip·tic/ti·cal (:tĭk) adj. elíptico.
elm (ĕlm) s. olmo.
el·o·cu·tion (ĕl'ə-kyōō'shən) s. elocución *f.*
e·lon·ga·tion (ĭ-lông'gā'shən) s. extensión *f*, alargamiento.
e·lope (ĭ-lōp') intr. fugarse (con un amante).
e·lope·ment (:mənt) s. fuga.
el·o·quence (ĕl'ə-kwəns) s. elocuencia.
el·o·quent (:kwənt) adj. elocuente.
else (ĕls) adj. & adv. ♦ **all** *o* **everything e.** todo lo demás • **anybody** *o* **anyone e.** cualquier otro, cualquier otra persona; *(negative)* ningún otro, nadie más • **anything e.** cualquier otra cosa, algo más; *(negative)* ninguna otra cosa, nada más • **anywhere e.** *(place)* en cualquier otra parte; *(direction)* a cualquier otra parte; *(negative) (place)* en ningún otro lugar; *(in existence)* en ningún otro lugar • **everyone e.** todos los demás • **everywhere e.** en *o* a todas partes • **how e.?** ¿de qué otro modo? • **much e.** mucho, muchas cosas • **nobody** *o* **no one e.** nadie más, ningún otro • **nothing e.** nada más • **nowhere e.** en *o* a ninguna otra parte • **or e.** si no • **somebody** *o* **someone e.** otro, otra persona • **something e.** otra cosa; *(something additional)* algo más • **somewhere e.** en *o* a otra parte • **what e.** ¿qué más? • **where e.?** ¿en *o* a qué otro sitio? • **who e?** ¿quién más?
else·where ('hwâr') adv. a *o* en otra parte.
e·lu·ci·date (ĭ-lōō'sĭ-dāt') tr. elucidar.
e·lude (ĭ-lōōd') tr. eludir, esquivar; *(to escape understanding)* escapársele a uno.
e·lu·sive (ĭ-lōō'sĭv) adj. evasivo; *(hard to describe)* difícil de describir.
e·ma·ci·at·ed (ĭ-mā'shē-ā'tĭd) adj. demacrado.
em·a·nate (ĕm'ə-nāt') intr. proceder, emanar *(from* de).
e·man·ci·pate (ĭ-măn'sə-pāt') tr. emancipar ♦ **to become emancipated** emanciparse.
e·man·ci·pa·tor (:pə'tər) s. emancipador *m.*
e·mas·cu·late (ĭ-măs'kyə-lāt') tr. emascular; FIG. debilitar, disminuir.
em·balm (ĕm-bäm') tr. *(a corpse)* embalsamar.
em·bank·ment (ĕm-băngk'mənt) s. terraplén *m.*

em·bar·go (ĕm-bär´gō) I. s. [pl. **es**] embargo II. tr. embargar.

em·bark (ĕm-bärk´) tr. & intr. embarcar(se) ♦ **to e. on** lanzarse a.

em·bar·ka·tion (ĕm´bär-kā´shən) s. *(of people)* embarco; *(of goods)* embarque m.

em·bar·rass (ĕm-bär´əs) tr. *(to disconcert)* desconcertar, turbar; *(to shame)* avergonzar; *(to cause trouble for)* poner en aprieto ♦ **to be** o **feel embarrassed** sentirse confuso o avergonzado.

em·bar·rass·ing (:ĭng) adj. *(disconcerting)* desconcertante; *(situation)* violento.

em·bar·rass·ment (:mənt) s. *(shame)* vergüenza, turbación f; *(trouble)* embarazo; *(confusion)* desconcierto.

em·bas·sy (ĕm´bə-sē) s. embajada.

em·bat·tled (ĕm-băt´ld) adj. asediado.

em·bed (ĕm-bĕd´) tr. & intr. **-dd-** implantar(se), incrustar(se); FIG. fijar(se).

em·bel·lish (ĕm-bĕl´ĭsh) tr. embellecer; *(a story)* añadir detalles a.

em·ber (ĕm´bər) s. ascua, brasa.

em·bez·zle (ĕm-bĕz´əl) tr. malversar, desfalcar.

em·bez·zle·ment (:mənt) s. malversación f, desfalco f.

em·bez·zler (ĕm-bĕz´lər) s. malversador m, desfalcador m.

em·bit·ter (ĕm-bĭt´ər) tr. amargar, agriar.

em·blem (ĕm´bləm) s. emblema m.

em·blem·at·ic (ĕm´blə-măt´ĭk) adj. simbólico.

em·bod·i·ment (ĕm-bŏd´ē-mənt) s. personificación f.

em·bod·y (ĕm-bŏd´ē) tr. encarnar, personificar; *(to include)* incorporar.

em·bold·en (ĕm-bōl´dən) tr. alentar.

em·bo·lism (ĕm´bə-lĭz´əm) s. embolia.

em·boss (ĕm-bôs´) tr. grabar en relieve; *(leather, silver)* repujar.

em·brace (ĕm-brās´) I. tr. abrazar; *(to accept eagerly)* aprovecharse de —intr. abrazarse II. s. abrazo; *(acceptance)* adopción f.

em·broi·der (ĕm-broi´dər) tr. bordar; *(a story)* exagerar —intr. hacer bordado.

em·broi·der·y (:də-rē) s. bordado.

em·broil (ĕm-broil´) tr. embrollar, enredar.

em·bry·o (ĕm´brē-ō´) s. embrión m.

em·bry·ol·o·gy (´-ŏl´ə-jē) s. embriología.

em·bry·on·ic (:ŏn´ĭk) adj. embrionario.

em·cee (ĕm´sē´) s. & intr. FAM. (actuar de) maestro de ceremonias.

e·mend (ĭ-mĕnd´) tr. enmendar, corregir.

e·men·da·tion (ē´mĕn-dā´shən) s. enmienda.

em·er·ald (ĕm´ər-əld) s. esmeralda.

e·merge (ĭ-mûrj´) intr. emerger, surgir; *(to come known)* darse a entender.

e·mer·gen·cy (ĭ-mûr´jən-sē) s. emergencia; MED. caso de urgencia; *(need)* necesidad f urgente ♦ **e. landing** aterrizaje forzoso.

e·mer·gent (:jənt) adj. emergente.

em·er·y (ĕm´ə-rē) s. esmeril m ♦ **e. board** lima de uñas.

e·met·ic (ĭ-mĕt´ĭk) adj. & s. emético, vomitivo.

em·i·grant (ĕm´ĭ-grənt) s. & adj. emigrante m.

em·i·grate (grāt´) intr. emigrar.

em·i·nence (ĕm´ə-nəns) s. eminencia.

em·i·nent (:nənt) adj. eminente.

em·is·sar·y (ĕm´ĭ-sĕr´ē) s. emisario.

e·mis·sion (ĭ-mĭsh´ən) s. emisión f.

e·mit (ĭ-mĭt´) tr. **-tt-** emitir.

e·mo·tion (ĭ-mō´shən) s. emoción f.

e·mo·tion·al (:shə-nəl) adj. emocional; *(scene, person)* emotivo.

em·pa·thize (ĕm´pə-thīz´) intr. identificarse.

em·pa·thy (:thē) s. identificación f.

em·per·or (ĕm´pər-ər) s. emperador m.

em·pha·sis (ĕm´fə-sĭs) s. [pl. **-ses**] énfasis m; GRAM. *(stress)* acento.

em·pha·size (:sīz´) tr. enfatizar, hacer hincapié en; GRAM. acentuar.

em·phat·ic (ĕm-făt´ĭk) adj. enfático; *(vigorous)* enérgico; GRAM. acentuado.

em·phy·se·ma (ĕm´fĭ-sē´mə) s. enfisema m.

em·pire (ĕm´pīr´) s. imperio.

em·pir·ic/·i·cal (ĕm-pîr´ĭk) adj. empírico.

em·pir·i·cism (:ĭ-sĭz´əm) s. empirismo.

em·ploy (ĕm-ploi´) I. tr. emplear ♦ **to be employed** tener empleo II. s. empleo ♦ **in the e. of** empleado por.

em·ploy·ee (:ē´) s. empleado.

em·ploy·er (:ər) s. empleador m.

em·ploy·ment (:mənt) s. empleo.

em·po·ri·um (ĕm-pôr´ē-əm) s. [pl. **s** o **-ria**] emporio.

em·pow·er (ĕm-pou´ər) tr. autorizar.

em·press (ĕm´prĭs) s. emperatriz f.

emp·ti·ness (ĕmp´tē-nĭs) s. vacío; *(of a person, words)* vacuidad f.

emp·ty (ĕmp´tē) I. adj. **-i-** vacío; *(unpopulated)* desierto; *(vain)* vano, hueco; *(idle)* ocioso; *(devoid)* falto II. tr. vaciar; *(to vacate)* dejar vacío, desalojar; *(to unload)* descargar —intr. vaciarse ♦ **to e. into** desembocar en III. s. envase vacío.

emp·ty-hand·ed (´-hăn´dĭd) adj. manivacío.

emp·ty-head·ed (:hĕd´ĭd) adj. frívolo.

em·py·re·an (ĕm´pī-rē´ən) s. & adj. empíreo.

em·u·late (ĕm´yə-lāt´) tr. emular.

em·u·la·tor (:lā´tər) s. emulador m.

e·mul·si·fy (ĭ-mŭl´sə-fī´) tr. emulsionar.

e·mul·sion (:shən) s. emulsión f.

en·a·ble (ĕn-ā´bəl) tr. *(to make able)* capacitar; *(to make possible)* posibilitar; DER. autorizar.

en·act (ĕn-ăkt´) tr. promulgar; TEAT. representar.

en·act·ment (:mənt) s. promulgación f; TEAT. representación f.

e·nam·el (ĭ-năm´əl) I. s. esmalte m II. tr. esmaltar.

e·nam·el·ware (:wâr´) s. utensilios de hierro esmaltado.

en·am·or (ĭ-năm´ər) tr. enamorar ♦ **to become enamored of** enamorarse de.

en·camp·ment (ĕn-kămp´mənt) s. campamento.

en·cap·su·late (ĕn-kăp´sə-lāt´) tr. encerrar en una cápsula.

en·case (ĕn-kās´) tr. encerrar, encajonar.

en·ceph·a·li·tis (ĕn-sĕf´ə-lī´tĭs) s. encefalitis f.

en·chant (ĕn-chănt´) tr. encantar.

en·chant·ing (ĕn-chăn´tĭng) adj. encantador.

en·chant·ment (ĕn-chănt´mənt) s. *(bewitchment)* encantamiento; *(charm)* encanto.

en·cir·cle (ĕn-sûr´kəl) tr. rodear, circundar.

en·close (ĕn-klōz´) tr. encerrar; *(a document)* adjuntar; *(to fence in)* cercar ♦ **enclosed herewith** encontrará adjunto.

en·clo·sure (ĕn-klō´zhər) s. encierro; *(land)* cercado; *(document)* adjunto, documento; *(fence)* cerco, valla.

en·code (ĕn-kōd´) tr. codificar.

en·com·pass (ĕn-kŭm´pəs) tr. *(to surround)* rodear; *(to include)* abarcar.

en·core (ŏn'kôr') I. s. repetición f, bis m II. interj. ¡otra!, ¡bis!
en·coun·ter (ĕn-koun'tər) I. s. encuentro; (clash) choque m II. tr. encontrar; MIL. enfrentarse con.
en·cour·age (ĕn-kûr'ĭj) tr. animar, alentar; (to embolden) fortalecer; (to foster) fomentar.
en·cour·age·ment (:mənt) s. ánimo, aliento; (incentive) incentivo.
en·cour·ag·ing (ĕn-kûr'ə-jĭng) adj. alentador.
en·croach (ĕn-krōch') intr. ♦ to e. on meterse en, invadir.
en·crust (ĕn-krŭst') tr. incrustar.
en·crypt (ĕn-krĭpt') tr. codificar.
en·cum·ber (ĕn-kŭm'bər) tr. (to overburden) sobrecargar; (to impede) impedir.
en·cum·brance (:brəns) s. obstáculo, impedimento; DER. gravamen m.
en·cy·clo·p(a)e·di·a (ĕn-sī'klə-pē'dē-ə) s. enciclopedia.
end (ĕnd) I. s. (tip) extremo, punta; (boundary) límite m; (conclusion) fin m, final m; (outcome) desenlace m; (death) fin, muerte f; (goal) propósito; (destruction) destrucción f ♦ at the e. of al cabo de • e. to e. punta con punta • for days on end día tras día • from e. to e. de un extremo al otro • in the e. al fin, al final • odds and ends restos, sobrante • on e. (upright) de pie, derecho; (nonstop) sin parar; (hair) de punta • to bring (come) to an e. terminar(se), acabar(se) • to make ends meet cubrir las necesidades con el dinero que se tiene • to meet one's e. encontrar la muerte • to no e. en vano, inútilmente • to put an e. to poner fin a • to what end? ¿con qué finalidad? II. tr. acabar, concluir; (to destroy) destruir ♦ to e. it all acabar con la vida —intr. terminar(se), acabar(se) ♦ to e. up terminar, ir a parar.
en·dan·ger (ĕn-dān'jər) tr. poner en peligro.
en·dear (ĕn-dîr'ĭng) adj. atractivo.
en·dear·ment (:mənt) s. cariño, afecto.
en·deav·or (ĕn-dĕv'ər) I. s. (effort) esfuerzo; (attempt) intento II. intr. intentar.
en·dem·ic (ĕn-dĕm'ĭk) adj. endémico.
end·ing (ĕn'dĭng) s. conclusión f, fin m; (of a story) desenlace m, final m.
en·dive (ĕn'dīv') s. escarola, endibia.
end·less (ĕnd'lĭs) adj. interminable; (infinite) infinito; (continuous) continuo.
en·do·crine (ĕn'də-krĭn) adj. endocrino.
en·dorse (ĕn-dôrs') tr. endosar; (to support) apoyar; (to approve) sancionar.
en·dors·ee ('-sē') s. endosatario, endosado.
en·dorse·ment (ĕn-dôrs'mənt) s. endoso; (approval) aprobación f; (support) apoyo.
en·dors·er (ĕn-dôr'sər) s. endosante mf.
en·dow (ĕn-dou') tr. dotar.
en·dow·ment (:mənt) s. dotación f; (natural gift) dote m, don m.
en·dur·ance (ĕn-dŏŏr'əns) s. resistencia, aguante m.
en·dure (ĕn-dŏŏr') tr. resistir, aguantar; (to tolerate) tolerar —intr. aguantarse, resistir; (to last) durar.
en·dur·ing (:ĭng) adj. perdurable, duradero; (long-suffering) sufrido.
end·wise/ways (ĕnd'wīz'/wāz') adv. (upright) de punta, de pie; (end foremost) con la punta al frente; (lengthwise) longitudinalmente; (end to end) extremo con extremo.
en·e·ma (ĕn'ə-mə) s. enema.
en·e·my (ĕn'ə-mē) s. & adj. enemigo.

en·er·get·ic (ĕn'ər-jĕt'ĭk) adj. enérgico.
en·er·gize (ĕn'ər-jīz') tr. dar energía a, vigorizar; ELEC. (to charge) excitar.
en·er·gy (ĕn'ər-jē) s. energía.
en·er·vate (ĕn'ər-vāt') tr. enervar.
en·fee·ble (ĕn-fē'bəl) tr. debilitar.
en·fold (ĕn-fōld') tr. (to envelop) envolver; (to surround) rodear; (to embrace) abrazar.
en·force (ĕn-fôrs') tr. (a law) hacer cumplir o respetar; (to impose) imponer.
en·force·a·ble (ĕn-fôr'sə-bəl) adj. (law) aplicable; (contract) ejecutorio.
en·force·ment (ĕn-fôrs'mənt) s. aplicación f, ejecución f.
en·fran·chise (ĕn-frăn'chīz') tr. otorgar el derecho al voto; (to free) libertar, manumitir.
en·gage (ĕn-gāj') tr. (to hire) emplear; (to reserve) contratar, reservar; (to engross) cautivar; (to promise) comprometer, empeñar; MIL. trabar combate con; MEC. (gears) engranar; (clutch) embragar —intr. comprometerse, obligarse (a pagar, ayudar); MIL. trabarse en combate ♦ to e. in ocuparse o tomar parte en.
en·gaged (ĕn-gājd') adj. (employed) empleado; (busy) ocupado; (reserved) contratado; (betrothed) comprometido; MIL. combatiente; MEC. engranado ♦ to be e. (busy) estar ocupado; (betrothed) estar comprometido • to get e. prometerse.
en·gage·ment (ĕn-gāj'mənt) s. compromiso; (appointment) cita; MIL. batalla, combate m; MEC. engranaje m.
en·gag·ing (ĕn-gā'jĭng) adj. atractivo.
en·gen·der (ĕn-jĕn'dər) tr. engendrar.
en·gine (ĕn'jĭn) s. máquina, motor m; F.C. locomotora f ♦ e. block bloque de cilindros.
en·gi·neer (ĕn'jə-nîr') I. s. ingeniero; F.C. maquinista m; FIG. artífice mf II. tr. maniobrar, maquinar.
en·gi·neer·ing (:ĭng) s. ingeniería.
Eng·lish-speak·ing (ĭng'glĭsh-spē'kĭng) adj. de habla inglesa.
en·gorge (ĕn-gôrj') tr. devorar, engullir; MED. congestionar.
en·grave (ĕn-grāv') tr. grabar; (on stone) tallar.
en·grav·er (ĕn-grā'vər) s. grabador m.
en·grav·ing (:vĭng) s. grabado.
en·gross (ĕn-grōs') tr. absorber, cautivar.
en·gross·ing (ĕn-grō'sĭng) adj. absorbente.
en·gulf (ĕn-gŭlf') tr. (to surround) encerrar, rodear; (to swallow up) tragarse.
en·hance (ĕn-hăns') tr. (to increase) aumentar; (to intensify) dar realce a, realzar.
en·hance·ment (:mənt) s. (increase) aumento; (of flavor, beauty) realce m.
e·nig·ma (ĭ-nĭg'mə) s. enigma m.
en·ig·mat·ic (ĕn'ĭg-măt'ĭk) adj. enigmático.
en·join (ĕn-join') tr. (to command) mandar; (to prohibit) prohibir.
en·join·der (:dər) s. mandato.
en·joy (ĕn-joi') tr. gozar (de), disfrutar; (to like) gustar a ♦ to oneself divertirse, pasarlo bien.
en·joy·a·ble (:ə-bəl) adj. agradable, encantador; (fun) divertido.
en·joy·ment (:mənt) s. placer m, goce m; disfrute m.
en·large (ĕn-lärj') tr. agrandar, aumentar; (to magnify) magnificar; FOTOG. ampliar —intr. agrandarse ♦ to e. on explayarse sobre.
en·larg·er (ĕn-lär'jər) s. ampliadora.
en·light·en (ĕn-līt'n) tr. iluminar, ilustrar; (to

inform) aclarar.

en·light·ened (:nd) adj. culto, ilustrado; *(spiritually)* iluminado.

en·light·en·ment (:n-mənt) s. iluminación *f*, ilustración *f* ♦ **the E.** la Ilustración.

en·list (ĕn-lĭst') tr. MIL. alistar; *(to engage)* ganar el apoyo de —intr. alistarse ♦ **enlisted man** soldado de tropa.

en·list·ment (:mənt) s. alistamiento.

en·liv·en (ĕn-lī'vən) tr. alegrar, animar.

en·mesh (ĕn-mĕsh') tr. enredar, enmarañar.

en·mi·ty (ĕn'mĭ-tē) s. enemistad *f*.

en·no·ble (ĕn-nō'bəl) tr. ennoblecer.

en·nui (ŏn-wē') s. lasitud *f*, aburrimiento.

e·nor·mi·ty (ĭ-nôr'mĭ-tē) s. enormidad *f*.

e·nor·mous (:məs) adj. enorme.

e·nough (ĭ-nŭf') I. adj. bastante, suficiente ♦ **to be e.** ser suficiente, bastar II. adv. bastante, suficientemente ♦ **curiously** o **oddly e.** por raro que parezca • **sure e.** en efecto • **well e.** bastante bien III. s. lo bastante, lo suficiente ♦ **e. is e.** basta y sobra • **it is e. to drive you mad** es para volverse loco • **to have had e.** *(to be satisfied)* estar satisfecho; *(to be tired of)* estar harto IV. interj. ¡basta! ♦ **e. of this!** ¡basta ya!

en·rage (ĕn-rāj') tr. enfurecer, encolerizar.

en·rap·ture (ĕn-răp'chər) tr. embelesar.

en·rich (ĕn-rĭch') tr. enriquecer; *(to fertilize)* abonar.

en·rol(l) (ĕn-rōl') tr. & intr. -ll- registrar(se), inscribir(se); *(a student)* matricular(se).

en·rol(l)·ment (:mənt) s. inscripción *f*; *(in school)* matriculación *f*; *(record)* registro.

en·sconce (ĕn-skŏns') tr. ♦ **to e. oneself** establecerse cómodamente.

en·sem·ble (ŏn-sŏm'bəl) s. conjunto; TEAT. compañía.

en·shrine (ĕn-shrīn') tr. guardar en un relicario; FIG. conservar religiosamente.

en·sign (ĕn'sən) s. *(flag)* pabellón *m*; *(officer)* alférez *m*.

en·slave (ĕn-slāv') tr. esclavizar.

en·snare (ĕn-snâr') tr. entrampar.

en·sue (ĕn-sō̄') intr. seguir(se), resultar.

en·su·ing (:ĭng) adj. resultante.

en·sure (ĕn-shŏŏr') tr. asegurar, garantizar.

en·tail (ĕn-tāl') tr. implicar, comportar; DER. vincular.

en·tan·gle (ĕn-tăng'gəl) tr. enmarañar, enredar.

en·tente (ŏn-tŏnt') s. *(agreement)* acuerdo, convenio; *(signatories)* aliados.

en·ter (ĕn'tər) tr. entrar en; *(to penetrate)* penetrar en, perforar; *(to insert)* introducir, insertar; *(to participate in)* participar en; *(to embark upon)* emprender, empezar; *(to join)* afiliarse a; *(to obtain admission to)* ingresar, entrar a; *(a profession)* iniciar, abrazar; *(in a register)* asentar, anotar; DER. entablar, presentar ♦ **to e. one's head** o **mind** ocurrírsele a uno —intr. entrar; *(to gain entry)* ingresar; *(to register)* inscribirse, matricularse; TEAT. salir ♦ **not to e. into it** no figurar para nada • **to e. into** *(a contract)* celebrar, concertar; *(to begin)* iniciar.

en·ter·prise (ĕn'tər-prīz') s. empresa; *(initiative)* iniciativa.

en·ter·pris·ing (:prī'zĭng) adj. emprendedor *m*.

en·ter·tain (ĕn'tər-tān') tr. divertir, entretener; *(to host)* agasajar; *(an idea)* considerar ♦ **to e. oneself** divertirse —intr. recibir invitados.

en·ter·tain·er (:tā'nər) s. artista *mf*.

en·ter·tain·ing (:nĭng) adj. entretenido, diver-

tido.

en·ter·tain·ment (ĕn'tər-tān'mənt) s. entretenimiento, diversion *f*; *(show)* espectáculo.

en·thrall (ĕn-thrôl') tr. cautivar; *(to enslave)* esclavizar.

en·throne (ĕn-thrōn') tr. entronizar.

en·thuse (ĕn-thō̄z') tr. & intr. FAM. entusiasmar(se).

en·thu·si·asm (ĕn-thō̄'zē-ăz'əm) s. entusiasmo.

en·thu·si·ast (:ăst') s. entusiasta *mf*.

en·thu·si·as·tic (-'-ăs'tĭk) adj. entusiástico.

en·tice (ĕn-tīs') tr. atraer, tentar.

en·tire (ĕn-tīr') adj. entero, total; *(in one piece)* intacto.

en·tire·ty (:tē) s. totalidad *f*.

en·ti·tle (ĕn-tīt'l) tr. titular; *(to give a right)* dar derecho a ♦ **to be entitled to** tener derecho a.

en·ti·tle·ment (:mənt) s. derecho.

en·ti·ty (ĕn'tĭ-tē) s. ser *m*; *(thing)* ente *m*.

en·tomb (ĕn-tō̄m') tr. sepultar, enterrar.

en·to·mol·o·gy (ĕn'tə-mŏl'ə-jē) s. entomología.

en·tou·rage (ŏn'tŏŏ-räzh') s. séquito.

en·trails (ĕn'trālz') s.pl. entrañas, vísceras.

en·train (ĕn-trān') intr. subir al tren.

en·trance¹ (ĕn'trəns) s. entrada; TEAT. salida (a escena).

en·trance² (ĕn-trăns') tr. encantar.

en·trant (ĕn'trənt) s. concursante *mf*.

en·trap (ĕn-trăp') tr. -pp- entrampar.

en·treat (ĕn-trēt') tr. implorar, suplicar.

en·treat·y (ĕn-trē'tē) s. pedido, súplica.

en·trée/tree (ŏn'trā') s. *(admittance)* entrada; *(main dish)* plato principal.

en·trench (ĕn-trĕnch') tr. atrincherar ♦ **to e. oneself** atrincherarse.

en·tre·pre·neur (ŏn'trə-prə-nûr') s. empresario.

en·trust (ĕn-trŭst') tr. confiar ♦ **to e. with** encargar, encomendar.

en·try (ĕn'trē) s. entrada; *(in a register)* registro; DEP. *(entrant)* competidor *m*; TEN. asiento.

en·twine (ĕn-twīn') tr. & intr. entrelazar(se).

e·nu·mer·ate (ĭ-nō̄'mə-rāt') tr. enumerar.

e·nun·ci·ate (ĭ-nŭn'sē-āt') tr. enunciar; *(to proclaim)* proclamar.

en·vel·op (ĕn-vĕl'əp) tr. envolver.

en·ve·lope (ĕn'və-lōp', ŏn'-) s. sobre *m*; *(wrapping)* envoltura; *(cover)* cobertura.

en·vi·a·ble (ĕn'vē-ə-bəl) adj. envidiable.

en·vi·ous (ĕn'vē-əs) adj. envidioso.

en·vi·ron·ment (ĕn-vī'rən-mənt) s. medio ambiente; *(atmosphere)* ambiente *m*.

en·vi·rons (:rənz) s.pl. alrededores *m*.

en·vis·age (ĕn-vĭz'ĭj) tr. concebir; *(to imagine)* imaginarse, concebir.

en·voy (ĕn'voi', ŏn'-) s. mensajero; POL. representante diplomático.

en·vy (ĕn'vē) I. s. envidia; *(object)* cosa o persona envidiada II. tr. envidiar, tener envidia de —intr. sentir envidia.

en·zyme (ĕn'zīm') s. enzima.

e·on (ē'ŏn') s. eón *m*.

ep·au·let(te) (ĕp'ə-lĕt') s. charretera.

e·phem·er·al (ĭ-fĕm'ər-əl) adj. efímero.

ep·ic (ĕp'ĭk) I. s. epopeya II. adj. épico.

ep·i·cen·ter (ĕp'ĭ-sĕn'tər) s. epicentro.

ep·i·cure (ĕp'ĭ-kyŏŏr') s. gastrónomo.

ep·i·dem·ic (ĕp'ĭ-dĕm'ĭk) I. adj. epidémico II. s. MED. epidemia; FIG. ola.

ep·i·der·mis (ĕp'ĭ-dûr'mĭs) s. epidermis *f*.

ep·i·gram (ĕp'ĭ-grăm') s. epigrama *m*.

ep·i·graph (ĕp′ĭ-grăf′) s. epígrafe *m.*
ep·i·lep·sy (ĕp′ə-lĕp′sē) s. epilepsia.
ep·i·log(ue) (ĕp′ə-lôg′) s. epílogo.
e·piph·a·ny (ĭ-pĭf′ə-nē) s. revelación *f.*
e·pis·co·pal (ĭ-pĭs′kə-pəl) adj. episcopal.
ep·i·sode (ĕp′ĭ-sōd′) s. episodio.
e·pis·te·mol·o·gy (ĭ-pĭs′tə-mŏl′ə-jē) s. epistemología.
e·pis·tle (ĭ-pĭs′əl) s. epístola.
e·pis·to·lar·y (ĭ-pĭs′tə-lĕr′ē) adj. epistolar.
ep·i·taph (ĕp′ĭ-tăf′) s. epitafio.
ep·i·thet (ĕp′ə-thĕt′) s. epíteto; *(insult)* insulto.
e·pit·o·me (ĭ-pĭt′ə-mē) s. epítome *m; (embodiment)* personificación *f.*
e·pit·o·mize (:mīz′) tr. *(to sum up)* resumir; *(to embody)* personificar.
ep·och (ĕp′ək) s. época; *(milestone)* hito.
ep·ox·y (ĭ-pŏk′sē) s. resina epoxídica.
eq·ua·ble (ĕk′wə-bəl) adj. *(unvarying)* invariable; *(even-tempered)* calmo, tranquilo.
e·qual (ē′kwəl) **I.** adj. igual; *(evenhanded)* equitativo ♦ **all things being e.** si todo sigue igual ♦ **on e. terms** en un plano de igualdad ♦ **to be e. to** *(same as)* ser igual que; *(capable)* ser apto para **II.** s. igual *mf* ♦ **between equals** de igual a igual ♦ **e. sign** signo de igualdad ♦ **without e.** sin par **III.** tr. ser igual a; *(to match)* igualar.
e·qual·i·ty (ĭ-kwŏl′ĭ-tē) s. igualdad *f.*
e·qual·ize (ē′kwə-līz′) tr. & intr. igualar.
e·qual·ly (:lē) adv. igualmente, por igual.
e·qua·nim·i·ty (ē′kwə-nĭm′ĭ-tē, ĕk′wə-) s. ecuanimidad *f.*
e·quate (ĭ-kwāt′) tr. igualar; MAT. poner en ecuación —intr. ser iguales.
e·qua·tion (ĭ-kwā′zhən) s. ecuación *f.*
e·qua·tor (ĭ-kwā′tər) s. ecuador *m.*
e·ques·tri·an (ĭ-kwĕs′trē-ən) **I.** adj. ecuestre **II.** s. jinete *mf.*
e·qui·lat·er·al (ē′kwə-lăt′ər-əl) adj. equilátero.
e·qui·lib·ri·um (:lĭb′rē-əm) s. [pl. **s** *o* **-ia**] equilibrio.
e·qui·nox (:nŏks′) s. equinoccio.
e·quip (ĭ-kwĭp′) tr. **-pp-** equipar; FIG. preparar.
e·quip·ment (:mənt) s. equipo; *(tools)* avíos; FIG. aptitud *f;* AUTO. accesorios.
eq·ui·ta·ble (ĕk′wĭ-tə-bəl) adj. equitativo.
eq·ui·ty (ĕk′wĭ-tē) s. equidad *f,* imparcialidad *f;* FIN. valor líquido.
e·quiv·a·lence/len·cy (ĭ-kwĭv′ə-ləns) s. equivalencia.
e·quiv·a·lent (:lənt) adj. & s. equivalente *m.*
e·quiv·o·cal (ĭ-kwĭv′ə-kəl) adj. equívoco.
e·quiv·o·cate (:kāt′) intr. usar intencionalmente lenguaje equívoco *o* ambiguo.
e·ra (îr′ə, ĕr′ə) s. era.
e·rad·i·cate (ĭ-răd′ĭ-kāt′) tr. erradicar.
e·rase (ĭ-rās′) tr. borrar.
e·ras·er (ĭ-rā′sər) s. goma de borrar, borrador *m.*
e·ra·sure (:shər) s. borradura.
e·rect (ĭ-rĕkt′) **I.** adj. erecto, erguido; *(hair)* erizado **II.** tr. *(to construct)* erigir, construir; *(to raise, establish)* levantar.
e·rec·tion (ĭ-rĕk′shən) s. erección *f; (of a building)* construcción *f.*
erg (ûrg) s. ergio.
er·go (ûr′gō, âr′gō) conj. & adv. por (lo) tanto.
er·go·nom·ics (ûr′gə-nŏm′ĭks) s.sg. ergonomía.
er·mine (ûr′mĭn) s. armiño.
e·rode (ĭ-rōd′) tr. & intr. erosionar(se), desgas-

tar(se); *(to corrode)* corroer(se).
e·rog·e·nous (ĭ-rŏj′ə-nəs) adj. erógeno.
e·ro·sion (ĭ-rō′zhən) s. erosión *f.*
e·rot·ic (ĭ-rŏt′ĭk) adj. erótico.
e·rot·i·cism (:ĭ-sĭz′əm) s. erotismo.
err (ûr, ĕr) intr. errar, equivocarse; *(to sin)* pecar.
er·rand (ĕr′ənd) s. mandado, recado.
er·rant (ĕr′ənt) adj. errante, errabundo.
er·rat·ic (ĭ-răt′ĭk) adj. irregular; *(eccentric)* excéntrico, extravagante.
er·ra·tum (ĭ-rä′təm) s. [pl. **-ta**] errata, error *m.*
er·ro·ne·ous (ĭ-rō′nē-əs) adj. erróneo.
er·ror (ĕr′ər) s. error *m.*
er·satz (ĕr′zäts′) adj. artificial.
er·u·dite (ĕr′yə-dīt′) adj. erudito.
e·rupt (ĭ-rŭpt′) intr. *(to spew)* brotar violentamente; *(emotions, riot)* estallar, explotar; GEOL., MED. hacer erupción; ODONT. salir.
e·rup·tion (ĭ-rŭp′shən) s. erupción *f; (outburst)* estallido.
es·ca·late (ĕs′kə-lāt′) tr. & intr. *(war)* extender(se), intensificar(se); *(prices)* subir.
es·ca·la·tion (′-lā′shən) s. *(of war)* intensificación *f; (of prices)* subida.
es·ca·la·tor (ĕs′kə-lā′tər) s. escalera mecánica.
es·cape (ĭ-skāp′) **I.** intr. escaparse —tr. escapar de, librarse de; *(name, meaning)* eludir, escapársele a uno **II.** s. escapatoria; *(evasion)* evasión *f; (leakage)* escape *m,* salida.
es·cap·ee (ĭ-skā′pē′) s. prófugo, fugitivo.
es·cap·ist (ĭ-skā′pĭst) **I.** adj. escapista **II.** s. persona que se evade de la realidad.
es·carp·ment (ĭ-skärp′mənt) s. escarpa.
es·cha·tol·o·gy (ĕs′kə-tŏl′ə-jē) s. escatología.
es·chew (ĭs-chōō′) tr. evitar.
es·cort **I.** s. (ĕs′kôrt′) escolta; *(companion)* acompañante *m* **II.** tr. (ĭ-skôrt′) acompañar, escoltar.
es·crow (ĕs′krō′) s. plica ♦ **e. account** cuenta en plica ♦ **in e.** en depósito.
e·soph·a·gus (ĭ-sŏf′ə-gəs) s. [pl. **-gi**] esófago.
es·o·ter·ic (ĕs′ə-tĕr′ĭk) adj. esotérico.
es·pe·cial (ĭ-spĕsh′əl) adj. especial.
es·pe·cial·ly (:ə-lē) adv. especialmente.
es·pi·o·nage (ĕs′pē-ə-näzh′) s. espionaje *m.*
es·pla·nade (ĕs′plə-näd′) s. explanada.
es·pous·al (ĭ-spou′zəl) s. adhesión *f,* apoyo.
es·pouse (ĭ-spouz′) tr. casarse con; *(a cause)* adoptar.
es·quire (ĕs′kwīr′) s. G.B. terrateniente *m* ♦ **E.** [abr. **Esq.**] Don, Señor <*John Smith,* Esq. Sr. *John Smith*>.
es·say **I.** tr. (ĕ-sā′) ensayar **II.** s. (ĕs′ā′) ensayo.
es·say·ist (ĕs′ā′ĭst) s. ensayista *mf.*
es·sence (ĕs′əns) s. esencia ♦ **in e.** esencialmente.
es·sen·tial (ĭ-sĕn′shəl) adj. & s. (elemento) esencial ♦ **to get down to the essentials** ir al grano.
es·tab·lish (ĭ-stăb′lĭsh) tr. establecer; *(to prove)* demostrar; *(facts)* verificar ♦ **to e. oneself** establecerse.
es·tab·lished (:lĭsht) adj. establecido; *(custom)* arraigado; *(fact)* conocido; *(business)* de buena fama *o* reputación; *(staff)* de plantilla; *(religion)* oficial.
es·tab·lish·ment (:lĭsh-mənt) s. establecimiento ♦ **E.** RELIG. iglesia oficial; POL. clase dirigente.

es·tate (ĭ-stāt′) s. *(land)* hacienda, finca; *(property)* propiedad *f*; *(inheritance)* herencia; DER. testamentaría ♦ **real e.** bienes raíces • **the fourth e.** la prensa.

es·teem (ĭ-stēm′) **I.** tr. estimar **II.** s. estimación *f*, aprecio ♦ **to hold someone in high e.** tenerle gran estima a alguien.

es·thet·ic (ĕs-thĕt′ĭk) var. de **aesthetic.**

es·ti·mate (ĕs′tə-māt′) **I.** tr. estimar **II.** s. (:mĭt) estimación *f*; *(of costs)* presupuesto; *(opinion)* opinión *f* ♦ **rough e.** cálculo aproximado.

es·ti·ma·tion (′-mā′shən) s. estimación *f*, valoración *f*; *(opinion)* opinión *f*.

es·trange·ment (ĭ-strānj′mənt) s. enajenación *f*, alejamiento.

es·tro·gen (ĕs′trə-jən) s. estrógeno.

es·trus (ĕs′trəs) s. estro.

es·tu·ar·y (ĕs′chŏō-ĕr′ē) s. estuario.

et cet·er·a *o* **et·cet·er·a** (ĕt-sĕt′ər-ə) etcétera.

etch (ĕch) tr. & intr. grabar al agua fuerte.

etch·ing (:ĭng) s. aguafuerte *m*, grabado.

e·ter·nal (ĭ-tûr′nəl) adj. & s. eterno.

e·ter·ni·ty (:nĭ-tē) s. eternidad *f*.

e·ther (ē′thər) s. éter *m*.

e·the·re·al (ĭ-thîr′ē-əl) adj. etéreo.

eth·ic (ĕth′ĭk) s. ética ♦ **ethics** sg. ética.

eth·i·cal (:ĭ-kəl) adj. ético, moral.

eth·nic (ĕth′nĭk) adj. étnico.

eth·nol·o·gy (ĕth-nŏl′ə-jē) s. etnología.

e·thos (ē′thŏs′) s. genio.

eth·yl (ĕth′əl) s. etilo ♦ **e. alcohol** alcohol etílico.

et·i·quette (ĕt′ĭ-kĕt′) s. etiqueta, protocolo.

et·y·mol·o·gy (ĕt′ə-mŏl′ə-jē) s. etimología.

eu·ca·lyp·tus (yōō′kə-lĭp′təs) s. [pl. **es** *o* **-ti**] eucalipto.

eu·lo·gize (yōō′lə-jīz′) tr. elogiar, encomiar.

eu·lo·gy (:jē) s. panegírico.

eu·nuch (yōō′nək) s. eunuco.

eu·phe·mism (yōō′fə-mĭz′əm) s. eufemismo.

eu·pho·ny (yōō′fə-nē) s. eufonía.

eu·pho·ri·a (yōō-fôr′ē-ə) s. euforia.

eu·phor·ic (:ĭk) adj. eufórico.

eu·tha·na·sia (yōō′thə-nā′zhə) s. eutanasia.

e·vac·u·ate (ĭ-văk′yōō-āt′) tr. evacuar —intr. retirarse.

e·vac·u·a·tion (′-ā′shən) s. evacuación *f*.

e·vac·u·ee (:ē′) s. evacuado.

e·vade (ĭ-vād′) tr. evitar, evadir.

e·val·u·ate (ĭ-văl′yōō-āt′) tr. evaluar; *(to appraise)* tasar, valorar.

e·val·u·a·tion (′-ā′shən) s. evaluación *f*, valoración *f*; *(judgment)* opinión *f*.

ev·a·nes·cent (ĕv′ə-nĕs′ənt) adj. evanescente.

e·van·gel·ic/i·cal (ē′văn-jĕl′ĭk) adj. evangélico.

e·van·gel·ist (ĭ-văn′jə-lĭst) s. evangelizador *m*.

e·vap·o·rate (ĭ-văp′ə-rāt′) tr. & intr. evaporar(se).

e·vap·o·ra·tion (′-rā′shən) s. evaporación *f*.

e·va·sion (ĭ-vā′zhən) s. evasión *f*.

e·va·sive (:sĭv) adj. evasivo.

eve (ēv) s. víspera; *(before a feast)* vigilia ♦ **on the e. of** en vísperas de.

e·ven (ē′vən) **I.** adj. *(flat)* plano, llano; *(smooth)* liso; *(level)* a nivel; *(uniform)* regular; *(equally matched)* parejo; *(score)* empatado; *(exact)* justo; *(equal)* igual; *(temper)* sereno; *(fair)* equitativo; MAT. par ♦ **to be e.** estar mano a mano • **to get e.** desquitarse • **to make e.** allanar • **to stay e.** cubrir los gastos **II.** adv. todavía, aun <e. **worse** aun peor>; si-

quiera <he **didn't e. cry** ni siquiera lloró> ♦ **e. as** precisamente, justo cuando • **e. if** *o* **though** aunque, aun cuando • **e. so** aun así • **e. now** ahora mismo **III.** tr. *(to level, smooth)* emparejar, nivelar; *(to make equal)* igualar ♦ **to e. up the score** DEP. igualar; FAM. *(to get revenge)* ajustar cuentas.

e·ven·hand·ed (′-hăn′dĭd) adj. equitativo.

eve·ning (ēv′nĭng) s. tarde *f*; *(dusk)* anochecer *m*, noche *f*; *(entertainment)* velada ♦ **e. class** clase nocturna • **e. dress** *(for men)* traje de etiqueta; *(for women)* traje de noche • **e. performance** función de noche • **good e.!** ¡buenas tardes!; *(after sunset)* ¡buenas noches! • **in the e.** por la tarde.

e·ven·ness (ē′vən-nĭs) s. igualdad *f*; *(of temper, judgment)* ecuanimidad *f*.

e·ven·song (ē′vən-sông′) s. vísperas.

e·vent (ĭ-vĕnt′) s. suceso, acontecimiento; *(outcome)* resultado; DEP. evento ♦ **in any e.** en todo caso • **in the e. of** en caso de (que).

e·vent·ful (:fəl) adj. lleno de acontecimientos; *(momentous)* extraordinario, memorable.

e·ven·tu·al (ĭ-vĕn′chōō-əl) adj. final.

e·ven·tu·al·ly (:ə-lē) adv. con el tiempo, a la larga.

ev·er (ĕv′ər) adv. *(always)* siempre; *(at any time)* alguna vez <have you **e. been to Paris?** ¿estuviste alguna vez en París?>; *(at all)* nunca, jamás <nobody has e. **treated me this way** nunca nadie me trató así> ♦ **as e.** como siempre • **better than e.** mejor que nunca • **e. since** *(from the time)* desde que; *(since then)* desde entonces • **e. so (happy)** tan (feliz) • **e. so little** muy poco • **e. so much** mucho, muchísimo • **for e. and e.** por siempre jamás, para siempre • **hardly e.** casi nunca • **not e.** nunca.

ev·er·chang·ing (′-chān′jĭng) adj. cambiadizo.

ev·er·green (′-grēn′) adj. & s. *(plant, tree m)* de hoja perenne.

ev·er·last·ing (′-lăs′tĭng) adj. eterno; *(longlasting)* perdurable; *(tedious)* interminable.

ev·er·y (ĕv′rē) adj. cada <e. **two hours** cada dos horas>; todo(s) <e. **man** todo hombre> ♦ **e. day** todos los días • **e. one** cada uno, cada cual • **e. one of them** todos (sin excepción) • **e. other day** cada dos días • **e. time** cada vez, siempre • **e. which way** por todas partes; *(in no order)* en total desorden.

eve·ry·bod·y (:bŏd′ē, :bŭd′ē) pron. cada uno, cada cual; *(all)* todos, todo el mundo.

eve·ry·day (:dā′) adj. diario, cotidiano; *(usual)* común; *(clothes)* de todos los días.

eve·ry·one (:wŭn′) pron. cada uno, cada cual; *(all)* todos, todo el mundo ♦ **e. for himself** cada cual por su cuenta.

eve·ry·thing (:thĭng′) pron. todo.

eve·ry·where (:hwâr′) adv. en, a *o* por todas partes; *(wherever)* dondequiera que.

e·vict (ĭ-vĭkt′) tr. expulsar; DER. desahuciar.

e·vic·tion (ĭ-vĭk′shən) s. desahucio.

ev·i·dence (ĕv′ĭ-dəns) s. prueba; *(data)* hechos, datos; *(testimony)* declaración *f* ♦ **to be in e.** estar a la vista • **to give e.** declarar como testigo • **to show e. of** presentar señales de • **to turn state's e.** dar testimonio en contra de los cómplices **II.** tr. evidenciar, probar.

ev·i·dent (:dənt) adj. evidente.

e·vil (ē′vəl) **I.** adj. malo, malvado; *(harmful)* nocivo, perjudicial; *(influence)* pernicioso; *(look)* nefasto ♦ **e. eye** mal de ojo **II.** s. mal, maldad *f*; *(harm)* perjuicio; *(immorality)* perversidad *f*.

e·vil·do·er (:dōō'ər) s. malhechor *m*, malvado.

e·vil-mind·ed ('-mīn'dĭd) adj. malicioso, malintencionado.

e·vis·cer·ate (ĭ-vĭs'ə-rāt') tr. destripar.

e·voc·a·tive (ĭ-vŏk'ə-tĭv) adj. evocador.

e·voke (ĭ-vōk') tr. evocar.

ev·o·lu·tion (ĕv'ə-lōō'shən) s. evolución *f*.

ev·o·lu·tion·ar·y ('-'shə-nĕr'ē) adj. evolutivo.

ev·o·lu·tion·ist (:nĭst) s. evolucionista *mf*.

e·volve (ĭ-vŏlv') tr. & intr. desarrollar(se); BIOL. (hacer) evolucionar.

ewe (yōō) s. oveja hembra.

ew·er (yōō'ər) s. aguamanil *m*.

ex·ac·er·bate (ĭg-zăs'ər-bāt') tr. exacerbar.

ex·act (ĭg-zăkt') I. adj. exacto II. tr. quitar por la fuerza ♦ **to e. from** *o* **of** exigir a.

ex·act·ing (ĭg-zăk'tĭng) adj. *(demanding)* exigente; *(severe)* severo; *(rigorous)* riguroso.

ex·act·ly (ĭg-zăkt'lē) adv. exactamente; *(wholly)* precisamente; *(time)* en punto; *(quite true)* es verdad, así es.

ex·ag·ger·ate (ĭg-zăj'ə-rāt') tr. & intr. exagerar.

ex·ag·ger·a·tion ('-'rā'shən) s. exageración *f*.

ex·alt (ĭg-zôlt') tr. exaltar.

ex·am (ĭg-zăm') s. FAM. examen *m*.

ex·am·i·na·tion (ĭg-zăm'ə-nā'shən) s. examen *m*; DER. interrogatorio; *(inquiry)* investigación *f* ♦ **to take an e.** sufrir un examen.

ex·am·ine (ĭg-zăm'ĭn) tr. examinar; *(to scrutinize)* escudriñar; DER. interrogar.

ex·am·in·er (:ə-nər) s. examinador *m*.

ex·am·ple (ĭg-zăm'pəl) s. ejemplo ♦ **to set an e.** dar ejemplo.

ex·as·per·ate (ĭg-zăs'pə-rāt') tr. exasperar.

ex·ca·vate (ĕk'skə-vāt') tr. *(to dig)* excavar; *(ruins)* desenterrar.

ex·ceed (ĭk-sēd') tr. exceder; *(limits, authority)* propasarse en, excederse en.

ex·ceed·ing·ly (ĭk-sē'dĭng-lē) adv. extremadamente.

ex·cel (ĭk-sĕl') tr. **-ll-** superar, aventajar —intr. distinguirse.

ex·cel·lence (ĕk'sə-ləns) s. excelencia *f*.

Ex·cel·len·cy (:lən-sē) s. Excelencia.

ex·cel·lent (ĕk'sə-lənt) adj. excelente.

ex·cept (ĭk-sĕpt') I. prep. excepto, menos ♦ **e. for** *(were it not for)* si no fuera por, a no ser por; *(apart from)* aparte de II. conj. *(only)* sólo que; *(otherwise than)* sino ♦ **e. that** salvo *o* excepto que III. tr. exceptuar, excluir.

ex·cept·ing (ĭk-sĕp'tĭng) prep. salvo, con excepción de.

ex·cep·tion (:shən) s. excepción *f* ♦ **to take e. to** estar en desacuerdo con, oponerse a • **with the e. of** a excepción de, excepto.

ex·cep·tion·al (:shə-nəl) adj. excepcional.

ex·cerpt I. s. (ĕk'sûrpt') extracto II. tr. (ĭk-sûrpt') extractar ♦ **e. from** citar de.

ex·cess (ĭk-sĕs', ĕk'sĕs') I. s. exceso ♦ **in e. of** más que • **to e.** en *o* con exceso II. adj. excesivo.

ex·ces·sive (ĭk-sĕs'ĭv) adj. excesivo.

ex·change (ĭks-chānj') I. tr. cambiar, intercambiar; *(glances, words)* cruzar; *(prisoners, goods)* canjear ♦ **to e. for** cambiar por II. s. cambio, intercambio; *(of prisoners, goods)* canje *m*; COM. bolsa; TEL. central telefónica ♦ **e. rate** tipo de cambio • **in e. for** a cambio de.

ex·change·a·ble (:chān'jə-bəl) adj. canjeable.

ex·cheq·uer (ĭks-chĕk'ər) s. tesoro público ♦ **E.**

G.B. Ministerio de Hacienda.

ex·cise tax (ĕk'sīz') s. impuesto indirecto.

ex·ci·sion (ĭk-sĭzh'ən) s. excisión *f*.

ex·cite (ĭk-sīt') tr. excitar; *(to thrill)* entusiasmar, emocionar.

ex·cit·ed (ĭk-sī'tĭd) adj. excitado; *(emotions)* agitado; *(thrilled)* entusiasmado ♦ **to get e.** excitarse, agitarse; *(with glee)* entusiasmarse.

ex·cite·ment (ĭk-sīt'mənt) s. emoción *f*, agitación *f*; *(enthusiasm)* entusiasmo.

ex·cit·ing (ĭk-sī'tĭng) adj. emocionante.

ex·claim (ĭk-sklām') intr. exclamar —tr. gritar, proclamar.

ex·cla·ma·tion (ĕk'sklə-mā'shən) s. exclamación *f* ♦ **e. point** signo de admiración.

ex·clude (ĭk-sklōōd') tr. excluir.

ex·clud·ing (ĭk-sklōō'dĭng) prep. excepto, exceptuando a.

ex·clu·sive (:sĭv) I. adj. exclusivo; *(select)* selecto, elegante ♦ **e. rights** exclusividad • **mutually e.** que se excluyen II. s. noticia de exclusividad.

ex·com·mu·ni·cate (ĕks'kə-myōō'nĭ-kāt') I. tr. excomulgar II. s. & adj. (:kĭt) excomulgado.

ex·com·mu·ni·ca·tion ('-'-kā'shən) s. excomunión *f*.

ex·co·ri·ate (ĭk-skôr'ē-āt') tr. *(to abrade)* excoriar; *(to upbraid)* reprochar, recriminar.

ex·cre·ment (ĕk'skrə-mənt) s. excremento.

ex·crete (ĭk-skrēt') tr. excretar.

ex·cre·to·ry (ĭk-skrī-tôr'ē) adj. excretor(io).

ex·cru·ci·at·ing (ĭk-skrōō'shē-ā'tĭng) adj. insoportable, dolorosísimo.

ex·cul·pate (ĕk'skəl-pāt') tr. exculpar.

ex·cur·sion (ĭk-skûr'zhən) s. excursión *f*, paseo; *(digression)* digresión *f*.

ex·cur·sive (:sĭv) adj. digresivo.

ex·cuse (ĭk-skyōōz') I. tr. excusar, disculpar; *(to exempt)* dispensar *(from* de*)* ♦ **e. me** *(I'm sorry!)* ¡discúlpeme!; *(pardon me)* con permiso • **to be excused from** estar dispensado de • **to e. oneself** for disculparse de II. s. (:skyōōs') excusa ♦ **to make excuses (for)** dar excusas (por).

ex·e·cute (ĕk'sĭ-kyōōt') tr. ejecutar; *(to do)* hacer; *(to validate)* formalizar.

ex·e·cu·tion ('-kyōō'shən) s. ejecución *f*; *(validation)* legalización *f*.

ex·e·cu·tion·er (:shə-nər) s. verdugo.

ex·ec·u·tive (ĭg-zĕk'yə-tĭv) I. s. ejecutivo; POL. *(officer)* presidente *m*, jefe *m* de estado; *(branch)* poder ejecutivo II. adj. ejecutivo.

ex·ec·u·tor (:tər) s. (ejecutor) testamentario.

ex·ec·u·trix (:trĭks') s. [pl. **es** *o* **-ices**] (ejecutora) testamentaria.

ex·em·plar (ĭg-zĕm'plər) s. ejemplar *m*.

ex·em·pla·ry (:plə-rē) adj. ejemplar.

ex·em·pli·fy (:plə-fī') tr. ejemplificar.

ex·empt (ĭg-zĕmpt') I. tr. eximir *(from* de*)* II. adj. exento.

ex·emp·tion (ĭg-zĕmp'shən) s. exención *f*.

ex·er·cise (ĕk'sər-sīz') I. s. ejercicio ♦ pl. *(ceremony)* ceremonia II. tr. *(to use)* usar de, proceder con; *(to drill)* ejercitar, entrenar; *(rights)* ejercer —intr. ejercitarse.

ex·ert (ĭg-zûrt') tr. *(strength)* emplear; *(influence)* ejercer ♦ **to e. oneself** esforzarse.

ex·er·tion (ĭg-zûr'shən) s. *(of strength)* empleo; *(of influence)* ejercicio; *(effort)* esfuerzo.

ex·ha·la·tion (ĕks'hə-lā'shən) s. exhalación *f*.

ex·hale (ĕks-hāl') intr. & tr. exhalar.

ex·haust (ĭg-zôst') I. tr. *(to use up)* agotar; *(to*

tire) cansar; *(soil)* empobrecer; *(gases)* vaciar, extraer **II.** s. AUTO. escape *m*, descarga; *(fumes)* gases *m* de escape ♦ **e. pipe** tubo de escape.

ex·haust·i·ble (ĭg-zôs′stə-bəl) adj. agotable.

ex·haus·tion (ĭg-zôs′chən) s. agotamiento.

ex·haus·tive (ĭg-zô′stĭv) adj. exhaustivo.

ex·hib·it (ĭg-zĭb′ĭt) **I.** tr. exhibir; *(at a show)* exponer; *(emotion, trait)* manifestar —intr. exponer **II.** s. *(display)* exhibición *f*; *(object)* objeto exhibido; DER. prueba instrumental.

ex·hi·bi·tion (ĕk′sə-bĭsh′ən) s. exhibición *f*, exposición *f*; G.B. *(scholarship)* beca.

ex·hi·bi·tion·ist (:ə-nĭst) s. exhibicionista *mf*.

ex·hib·i·tor (ĭg-zĭb′ĭ-tər) s. expositor *m*.

ex·hil·a·rant (ĭg-zĭl′ər-ənt) s. estimulante *m*.

ex·hil·a·rate (:ə-rāt′) tr. *(to elate)* alborozar; *(to invigorate)* animar; *(to stimulate)* estimular.

ex·hil·a·rat·ing (:ə-rā′tĭng) adj. *(invigorating)* vigorizante; *(stimulating)* estimulante.

ex·hil·a·ra·tion (-′-′shən) s. entusiasmo, exaltación *f*.

ex·hort (ĭg-zôrt′) tr. exhortar.

ex·hume (ĭg-zyōōm′, ĭk-syōōm′) tr. exhumar.

ex·i·gen·cy (ĕk′sə-jən-sē) s. exigencia; *(emergency)* caso de urgencia.

ex·ile (ĕg′zīl′, ĕk′sīl′) **I.** s. exilio, destierro; *(person)* desterrado **II.** tr. exiliar, desterrar.

ex·ist (ĭg-zĭst′) intr. existir, ser; *(to live)* vivir; *(to subsist)* subsistir.

ex·is·tence (ĭg-zĭs′təns) s. existencia; *(life)* vida *f* ♦ **to come into e.** empezar a existir.

ex·is·tent (:tənt) adj. viviente; *(current)* existente, actual.

ex·is·ten·tial (ĕg′zĭ-stĕn′shəl, ĕk′sĭ-) adj. existencial.

ex·is·ten·tial·ist (:shə-lĭst) s. & adj. existencialista *mf*.

ex·ist·ing (ĭg-zĭs′tĭng) adj. existente.

ex·it (ĕg′zĭt, ĕk′sĭt) **I.** s. salida ♦ **to make one's e.** salir, marcharse **II.** intr. salir.

ex·o·dus (ĕk′sə-dəs) s. éxodo.

ex·on·er·ate (ĭg-zŏn′ə-rāt′) tr. *(from responsibility)* exonerar; *(from blame)* disculpar.

ex·or·bi·tant (ĭg-zôr′bĭ-tnt) adj. exorbitante.

ex·or·cise (ĕk′sôr-sīz′) tr. exorcizar.

ex·or·cist (:sĭst) s. exorcista *mf*.

ex·ot·ic (ĭg-zŏt′ĭk) adj. exótico.

ex·pand (ĭk-spănd′) tr. & intr. extender(se); *(to enlarge)* expandir(se); *(to develop)* desarrollar(se); FÍS. dilatar(se).

ex·panse (ĭk-spăns′) s. extensión *f*.

ex·pan·sion (ĭk-spăn′shən) s. expansión *f*; FÍS. dilatación *f*; *(of a town)* ensanche *m*; *(of an idea)* ampliación *f*; *(of trade)* expansión.

ex·pan·sive (:sĭv) adj. expansivo.

ex·pa·tri·ate (ĕks-pā′trē-āt′) **I.** tr. expatriar **II.** s. (:ĭt, :āt′) exiliado.

ex·pect (ĭk-spĕkt′) tr. *(to await)* esperar; *(to require)* contar con; *(to suppose)* suponer.

ex·pec·tan·cy (ĭk-spĕk′tən-sē) s. expectación *f*, expectativa.

ex·pec·tant (:tənt) adj. expectante; *(pregnant)* embarazada.

ex·pec·ta·tion (ĕk′spĕk-tā′shən) s. expectación *f*, expectativa; *(prospect)* esperanza ♦ **beyond e.** más de lo esperado • **contrary to e.** contrariamente a lo esperado.

ex·pec·to·rate (ĭk-spĕk′tə-rāt′) tr. & intr. expectorar.

ex·pe·di·ence/en·cy (ĭk-spē′dē-əns) s. conveniencia.

ex·pe·di·ent (:ənt) **I.** adj. conveniente **II.** s. expediente *m*, recurso.

ex·pe·dite (ĕk′spĭ-dīt′) tr. apresurar; *(to facilitate)* facilitar; *(to dispatch)* expedir.

ex·pe·di·tion (′-dĭsh′ən) s. expedición *f*.

ex·pel (ĭk-spĕl′) tr. **-ll-** expeler; *(to dismiss)* echar, expulsar.

ex·pend (ĭk-spĕnd′) tr. *(to spend)* gastar; *(to consume)* consumir.

ex·pend·a·ble (ĭk-spĕn′də-bəl) adj. prescindible.

ex·pen·di·ture (:dĭ-chər) s. desembolso, gasto.

ex·pense (ĭk-spĕns′) s. gasto ♦ **at the e. of** a expensas de ♦ pl. expensas • **legal e.** costas ♦ **to meet e.** hacer frente a los gastos.

ex·pen·sive (ĭk-spĕn′sĭv) adj. costoso, caro.

ex·pe·ri·ence (ĭk-spîr′ē-əns) **I.** s. experiencia **II.** tr. *(to undergo)* experimentar; *(to feel)* sentir; *(difficulties)* tener.

ex·pe·ri·enced (:ənst) adj. experimentado.

ex·per·i·ment (ĭk-spĕr′ə-mənt) **I.** s. experimento **II.** intr. experimentar (on en).

ex·per·i·men·tal (′-mĕn′tl) adj. experimental.

ex·pert (ĕk′spûrt′) s. & adj. experto, perito.

ex·per·tise (ĕk′spər-tēz′) s. pericia.

ex·pi·ate (ĕk′spē-āt′) tr. & intr. expiar.

ex·pi·ra·tion (ĕk′spə-rā′shən) s. *(end, death)* expiración *f*; *(lapse)* caducidad *f*; *(breath)* espiración *f*; COM. vencimiento.

ex·pire (ĭk-spîr′) intr. *(to end, die)* expirar; *(to lapse)* vencer, caducar; *(to exhale)* espirar.

ex·plain (ĭk-splān′) tr. explicar —intr. dar explicaciones ♦ **to e. oneself** explicarse.

ex·pla·na·tion (ĕk′splə-nā′shən) s. explicación *f*.

ex·plan·a·to·ry (ĭk-splăn′ə-tôr′ē) adj. explicativo.

ex·ple·tive (ĕk′splĭ-tĭv) s. obscenidad *f*.

ex·pli·cate (ĕk′splĭ-kāt′) tr. explicar.

ex·plic·it (ĭk-splĭs′ĭt) adj. explícito.

ex·plode (ĭk-splōd′) intr. explotar, estallar; FIG. prorrumpir —tr. hacer explotar; *(to detonate)* detonar; *(to disprove)* desbaratar ♦ **exploded view** vista esquemática.

ex·ploit **I.** s. (ĕk′sploit′) hazaña, proeza **II.** tr. (ĭk-sploit′) explotar.

ex·ploit·er (ĭk-sploi′tər) s. explotador *m*.

ex·plo·ra·tion (ĕk′splə-rā′shən) s. exploración *f*.

ex·plore (ĭk-splôr′) tr. explorar; FIG. investigar.

ex·plor·er (:ər) s. explorador *m*.

ex·plo·sion (ĭk-splō′zhən) s. explosión *f*.

ex·plo·sive (:sĭv) adj. & s. explosivo.

ex·po·nent (ĭk-spō′nənt) s. representante *mf*, exponente *mf*; MAT. exponente *m*.

ex·po·nen·tial (ĕk′spə-nĕn′shəl) adj. exponencial.

ex·port **I.** tr. (ĭk-spôrt′) exportar **II.** s. (ĕk′spôrt′) exportación *f*.

ex·por·ta·tion (ĕk′spôr-tā′shən) s. exportación *f*.

ex·port·er (ĭk-spôr′tər) s. exportador *m*.

ex·pose (ĭk-spōz′) tr. exponer; *(to reveal)* revelar; *(to unmask)* desenmascarar ♦ **to be exposed to** estar expuesto a.

ex·po·sé (ĕk′spō-zā′) s. revelación *f*.

ex·po·si·tion (ĕk′spə-zĭsh′ən) s. exposición *f*.

ex·pos·tu·late (ĭk-spŏs′chə-lāt′) intr. objetar ♦ **to e. with** reconvenir a.

ex·po·sure (ĭk-spō′zhər) s. exposición *f*; *(revelation)* revelación *f*, descubrimiento ♦ **e. meter**

exposímetro • **to make an e.** sacar una fotografia.

ex·pound (ĭk-spound') tr. exponer, explicar —intr. hacer una exposición detallada (on de).

ex·press (ĭk-sprĕs') **I.** tr. expresar; (to show) manifestar; (to squeeze) exprimir; COM. enviar por expreso **II.** adj. expreso; (explicit) explícito; (mail) de entrega inmediata **III.** adv. por expreso **IV.** s. transporte rápido; (train) expreso, rápido.

ex·pres·sion (ĭk-sprĕsh'ən) s. expresión f; (sign) señal f; (gesture) gesto.

ex·pres·sion·ist (:ə-nĭst) s. & adj. expresionista mf.

ex·pres·sion·less (:ən-lĭs) adj. inexpresivo.

ex·pres·sive (ĭk-sprĕs'ĭv) adj. expresivo ♦ **e. of** que expresa.

ex·press·ly (:lē) adv. expresamente.

ex·press·way (:wā') s. autopista.

ex·pro·pri·ate (ĕks-prō'prē-āt') tr. expropiar.

ex·pro·pri·a·tion (-'-ā'shən) s. expropiación f.

ex·pul·sion (ĭk-spŭl'shən) s. expulsión f.

ex·punge (ĭk-spŭnj') tr. borrar, tachar.

ex·pur·gate (ĕk'spər-gāt') tr. expurgar.

ex·qui·site (ĕk'skwĭ-zĭt, ĭk-swĭz'ĭt) adj. exquisito; (acute) agudo, vivo.

ex·tant (ĕk'stənt, ĕk-stănt') adj. existente.

ex·tem·po·ra·ne·ous (ĭk-stĕm'pə-rā'nē-əs) adj. improvisado.

ex·tem·po·rize (-'-rīz') tr. & intr. improvisar.

ex·tend (ĭk-stĕnd') tr. extender; (road, visit) prolongar; (hand, arm) alargar; (to enlarge) agrandar, ampliar; (to offer) ofrecer; FIN. (payment) prorrogar ♦ **to e. an invitation** invitar • **to e. oneself** esforzarse —intr. extenderse; (to reach) alcanzar.

ex·ten·sion (ĭk-stĕn'shən) s. extensión f; (expansion) ampliación f; (annex) anexo; (continuation) prolongación f; FIN. prórroga ♦ **e. ladder** escalera extensible.

ex·ten·sive (:sĭv) adj. extensivo, extenso.

ex·tent (ĭk-stĕnt') s. extensión f; (degree) grado ♦ **to a certain e.** hasta cierto punto • **to a large e.** en gran parte • **to what e.?** ¿hasta qué punto?

ex·ten·u·ate (ĭk-stĕn'yōō-āt') tr. atenuar.

ex·ten·u·at·ing (:ā'tĭng) adj. atenuante.

ex·te·ri·or (ĭk-stîr'ē-ər) **I.** adj. (outer) exterior; (external) externo **II.** s. exterior m.

ex·ter·mi·nate (ĭk-stûr'mə-nāt') tr. exterminar.

ex·ter·mi·na·tor (:nā'tər) s. exterminador m.

ex·ter·nal (ĭk-stûr'nəl) **I.** adj. externo; (exterior, foreign) exterior ♦ **e. ear** oreja **II.** s. ♦ pl. apariencia, aspecto exterior.

ex·ter·nal·ize (:nə-līz') tr. exteriorizar.

ex·tinct (ĭk-stĭngkt') adj. extinto, desaparecido; (inactive) inactivo.

ex·tin·guish (ĭk-stĭng'gwĭsh) tr. extinguir, apagar.

ex·tin·guish·er (:gwĭ-shər) s. extintor m.

ex·tir·pate (ĕk'stər-pāt') tr. extirpar.

ex·tol(l) (ĭk-stōl') tr. -ll- alabar.

ex·tort (ĭk-stôrt') tr. (money) extorsionar; (confession) arrancar, sacar por la fuerza.

ex·tor·tion (ĭk-stôr'shən) s. extorsión f; (graft) concusión f.

ex·tra (ĕk'strə) **I.** adj. extra; (additional) adicional **II.** s. extra m; PERIOD. extraordinario; (worker) supernumerario; CINEM., TEAT. extra mf **III.** adv. excepcionalmente.

ex·tract **I.** tr. (ĭk-străkt') extraer; (to excerpt)

extractar **II.** s. (ĕk'străkt') extracto.

ex·trac·tion (ĭk-străk'shən) s. extracción f; (origin) origen m.

ex·tra·cur·ric·u·lar (ĕk'strə-kə-rĭk'yə-lər) adj. extracurricular.

ex·tra·dite ('-dīt') tr. entregar por extradición.

ex·tra·di·tion ('-dĭsh'ən) s. extradición f.

ex·tra·mar·i·tal (:măr'ĭ-tl) adj. adúltero.

ex·tra·mu·ral (:myŏŏr'əl) adj. de o situado extramuros.

ex·tra·ne·ous (ĭk-strā'nē-əs) adj. ajeno.

ex·traor·di·nar·y (ĭk-strôr'dn-ĕr'ē, ĕk'strə-ôr'-) adj. extraordinario.

ex·trap·o·late (ĭk-străp'ə-lāt') tr. extrapolar.

ex·tra·sen·so·ry perception (ĕk'strə-sĕn'sə-rē) adj. percepción f por medios extrasensibles.

ex·tra·ter·res·tri·al (:tə-rĕs'trē-əl) adj. extraterrestre mf.

ex·trav·a·gance (ĭk-străv'ə-gəns) s. extravagancia; (of spending) despilfarro.

ex·trav·a·gant (:gənt) adj. (lavish) pródigo; (wasteful) derrochador; (exorbitant) costoso.

ex·trav·a·gan·za (-'-găn'zə) s. entretenimiento espectacular.

ex·treme (ĭk-strēm') **I.** adj. extremo; (extraordinary) excepcional; (drastic) drástico ♦ **e. unction** extremaunción **II.** s. extremo ♦ **in the e.** en extremo • **to go to extremes** tomar medidas extremas.

ex·treme·ly (:lē) adv. extremadamente.

ex·trem·ist (ĭk-strē'mĭst) adj. & s. extremista mf.

ex·trem·i·ty (ĭk-strĕm'ĭ-tē) s. extremidad f; (utmost degree) extremo; (danger) grave peligro; (distress) adversidad f.

ex·tri·cate (ĕk'strĭ-kāt') tr. (from a difficulty) librar, sacar; (to disengage) desprender.

ex·trin·sic (ĭk-strĭn'sĭk) adj. extrínseco.

ex·tro·vert (ĕk'strə-vûrt') s. extrovertido.

ex·trude (ĭk-strōōd') tr. empujar hacia afuera; TEC. extrudir —intr. sobresalir.

ex·u·ber·ant (ĭg-zōō'bər-ənt) adj. exuberante; (mood, spirits) efusivo.

ex·ude (ĭg-zōōd') intr. & tr. exudar, rezumar.

ex·ult (ĭg-zŭlt') intr. exultar, regocijarse.

ex·ul·tant (ĭg-zŭl'tənt) adj. exultante, jubiloso.

eye (ī) **I.** s. ojo ♦ **e. opener** revelación, sorpresa • **e. shadow** sombreador • **in the twinkling of an e.** en un abrir y cerrar de ojos • **my e.!** ¡de ningún modo! • **to catch someone's e.** llamar la atención de alguien • **to give someone the e.** FAM. lanzar una mirada incitante a alguien • **to keep an e. on** vigilar • **to keep one's eyes open** mantenerse alerta • **to make eyes at** echar miradas a • **to roll one's eyes** poner los ojos en blanco • **to see e. to e.** estar de acuerdo • **to set eyes on** alcanzar a ver • **with an e. to** con miras a • **without batting an e.** sin pestañar **II.** tr. eyeing o eying ojear, mirar.

eye·ball (ī'bôl') s. globo ocular.

eye·brow (ī'brou') s. ceja.

eye·drop·per (ī'drŏp'ər) s. cuentagotas m.

eye·ful (ī'fŏŏl') s. vistazo, ojeada.

eye·glass (ī'glăs') s. monóculo ♦ pl. lentes.

eye·lash (ī'lăsh') s. pestaña.

eye·let (ī'lĭt) s. ojete m.

eye·lid (ī'lĭd') s. párpado.

eye·piece (ī'pēs') s. ocular m.

eye·sight (ī'sīt') s. vista ♦ **within e.** al alcance de la vista.

eye·sore (ī'sôr') s. cosa que ofende la vista.

eye·strain (ī′strān′) s. vista fatigada.
eye·tooth (ī′tōōth′) s. [pl. **-teeth**] colmillo.
eye·wash (ī′wŏsh′) s. colirio; FAM. *(nonsense)* tontería.
eye·wit·ness (ī′wĭt′nəs) s. testigo ocular.
ey·rie (âr′ē, ir′ē) s. aguilera.

F

f, F (ĕf) s. sexta letra del alfabeto inglés; MÚS. fa *m.*
fa·ble (fā′bəl) s. fábula; *(lie)* mentira.
fa·bled (fā′bəld) adj. legendario.
fab·ric (făb′rĭk) s. tela; FIG. estructura.
fab·ri·cate (făb′rĭ-kāt′) tr. fabricar.
fab·ri·ca·tion (′-kā′shən) s. fabricación *f; (falsehood)* mentira.
fab·u·list (făb′yə-lĭst) s. fabulista *mf.*
fab·u·lous (făb′yə-ləs) adj. fabuloso.
fa·çade (fə-säd′) s. fachada.
face (fās) I. s. cara; *(grimace)* mueca, gesto; FIG. apariencia; *(countenance)* rostro; *(façade)* frente *m; (of a clock)* esfera ♦ **f. card** figura (naipe) • **f. cloth** paño • **f. down, up** boca abajo, arriba • **f. of the earth** faz de la tierra • **f. value** FIN. valor nominal; FIG. valor aparente • **in the f.** of frente a • **on the f.** of a primera vista • **to lose f.** desprestigiarse • **to one's f.** en la cara de uno • **to save f.** salvar las apariencias • **to show one's f.** hacer acto de presencia II. tr. *(to turn toward)* ponerse de cara a, mirar hacia; *(to look out on)* estar frente a, dar a; *(to confront)* hacer frente a, arrostrar; TEC. revestir; COST. guarnecer (un borde) ♦ **let's f.** it reconozcámoslo • **to be faced with** enfrentarse con • **to f. down** resistir firmemente —intr. *(to be situated)* estar orientado hacia, mirar hacia; *(to turn)* volverse, voltear la cara ♦ **to f. up to** encararse con, enfrentarse a.
face·less (′lĭs) adj. sin cara; FIG. anónimo.
face-lift (:lĭft′) o **face·lift·ing** (:lĭf′tĭng) s. cirugía estética; FIG. modernización *f,* embellecimiento.
face-off (:ôf′) s. confrontación *f.*
face-sav·ing (:sā′vĭng) adj. que salva la dignidad.
fa·cet (făs′ĭt) s. faceta.
fa·ce·tious (fə-sē′shəs) adj. jocosamente irónico, humorístico.
fa·cial (fā′shəl) adj. & s. *(treatment)* facial.
fac·ile (făs′əl) adj. fácil; *(superficial)* superficial.
fa·cil·i·tate (fə-sĭl′ĭ-tāt′) tr. facilitar.
fa·cil·i·ty (:tē) s. facilidad *f* ♦ pl. COM. facilidades; *(buildings)* instalaciones; *(public toilet)* servicio, baño.
fac·sim·i·le (făk-sĭm′ə-lē) s. & adj. facsímil *m.*
fact (făkt) s. hecho ♦ **in fact** en realidad • **the f. of the matter is** la verdad es • **the f. remains that** a pesar de todo • **to know for a f.** saber a ciencia cierta ♦ pl. datos, información.
fact-find·ing (′f ĭn′dĭng) adj. investigador.
fac·tion (făk′shən) s. facción *f.*
fac·tion·al (:shə-nəl) adj. faccioso.
fac·tor (făk′tər) s. factor *m.*
fac·to·ry (făk′tə-rē) s. fábrica.
fac·tu·al (făk′chōō-əl) adj. verdadero.
fac·ul·ty (făk′əl-tē) s. facultad *f;* EDUC. cuerpo docente, profesorado.
fad (făd) s. manía, novedad *f.*

fad·dish (:ĭsh) adj. que sigue la moda.
fade (fād) intr. *(light)* palidecer, apagarse; *(sound, hope)* desvanecerse; *(flower)* marchitarse; *(strength)* debilitarse; *(color)* desteñirse ♦ **to f. away** *(to waste away)* consumirse; *(to leave gradually)* desvanecerse • **to f. in, out** CINEM. aparecer, desaparecer gradualmente —tr. desvanecer.
fade-in (′ĭn′) s. fundido, aparición *f* gradual.
fade-out (:out′) s. desvanecimiento gradual.
fag¹ (făg) I. s. trabajo, faena II. intr. **-gg-** trabajar duro ♦ **to be tagged out** estar rendido —tr. ♦ **to f. out** fatigar.
fag² s. JER. cigarrillo.
fag·(g)ot (făg′ət) s. haz *m* de leña.
fail (fāl) I. intr. fracasar; *(motor, health, support)* fallar; *(to be inadequate)* faltar; *(to weaken)* decaer, debilitarse; *(in school)* no aprobar, aplazarse; COM. quebrar ♦ **to f. to** *(to be unsuccessful in)* no lograr, no alcanzar a; *(to neglect to)* dejar de —tr. fallar, frustrar; *(course, exam)* salir mal en; *(student)* no aprobar a II. s. ♦ **without f.** sin falta.
fail·ing (fā′lĭng) s. falla, defecto.
fail-safe (fāl′sāf′) adj. que no falla.
fail·ure (fāl′yər) s. fracaso; *(person)* fracasado; *(weakening)* deterioro; *(nonfulfillment)* incumplimiento; *(of crops)* pérdida; ELEC. corte *m;* suspenso; COM. quiebra ♦ **heart f.** ataque al corazón.
faint (fānt) I. adj. *(indistinct)* borroso; *(slight)* vago, ligero; *(pale)* apagado; *(dizzy)* mareado; *(timid)* tímido; *(weak)* débil II. s. desmayo III. intr. desmayarse.
faint-heart·ed (′här′tĭd) adj. tímido.
fair¹ (fâr) I. adj. *(beautiful)* bello; *(blond)* rubio; *(skin)* blanco; *(impartial)* imparcial; *(just)* justo, equitativo; *(reasonable)* razonable; *(mediocre)* regular; *(weather)* bueno; *(sky)* despejado ♦ **f. and square** honrado a carta cabal • **f. enough!** ¡vale!, ¡bien! • **f. game** FIG. presa fácil • **f. play** juego limpio • **f. shake** JER. oportunidad • **f. to middling** regular, bastante bueno • **no f.!** ¡no hay derecho! • **one's f. share** lo que le corresponde a uno • **to give someone f. warning** prevenir a alguien II. adv. honradamente ♦ **to play f.** jugar limpio.
fair² s. *(market)* mercado; *(exhibition)* exposición *f,* feria; *(church bazaar)* tómbola.
fair·ground (′ground′) s. campo para ferias.
fair·ly (:lē) adv. *(justly)* justamente, equitativamente; *(moderately)* bastante.
fair-mind·ed (:mīn′dĭd) adj. imparcial.
fair·ness (:nĭs) s. *(beauty)* belleza; *(justness)* imparcialidad *f* ♦ **in all f.** para ser justo.
fair·y (fâr′ē) s. hada ♦ **f. tale** cuento de hadas.
fair·y·land (:lănd′) s. país *m* de las hadas.
fait ac·com·pli (fā′tä-kôm-plē′) s. [pl. **faits ac·complis**] hecho consumido.
faith (fāth) s. *(confidence)* confianza; *(belief)* fe *f; (set of beliefs)* doctrina ♦ **in good, bad f.** de buena, mala fe • **of every f.** de todas las religiones • **to break f. with** faltar a la palabra dada a • **to have f. in** fiarse de • **to keep f. with** cumplir la palabra dada a.
faith·ful (′fəl) I. adj. fiel; *(reliable)* digno de confianza II. s.pl. ♦ **the f.** los fieles.
faith·less (′lĭs) adj. infiel, desleal.
fake (fāk) I. adj. falso, fraudulento II. s. impostor *m; (fraud)* engaño; *(forgery)* falsificación *f* III. tr. falsificar; *(to feign)* fingir ♦ **to f. out** engañar —intr. engañarse, fingirse.

fak·er (fā′kər) s. falsificador *m*, impostor *m*.
fa·kir (fə-kîr′) s. faquir *m*.
Fa·lan·gist (fə-lăn′jĭst) s. & adj. falangista *mf.*
fal·con (făl′kən, fôl′-) s. halcón *m.*
fal·con·ry (:rē) s. halconería.
fall (fôl) I. intr. **fell, fallen** caer(se); *(light)* dar *(on, across* sobre); *(prices, temperature)* bajar; *(wind, voice)* disminuir; *(to become)* quedarse, volverse <*f. silent* quedarse mudo> ♦ **falling star** estrella fugaz • **to f. away** *(to slope)* descender; *(to come loose)* desprenderse; *(to decline)* declinar • **to f. back** caerse de espaldas; *(to retreat)* replegarse; *(to lag)* quedarse atrás • **to f. behind** quedarse atrás, rezagarse; *(to be late)* atrasarse; *(in payments)* retrasarse; *(in class)* quedar a la zaga • **to f. down** caer(se); *(building)* venirse abajo, derrumbarse • **to f. due** vencer, ser pagadero • **to f. flat** fracasar • **to f. flat on one's face** caer de bruces; *(to fail)* fracasar • **to f. for** FAM. *(person)* volverse loco por; *(trick)* tragarse • **to f. from grace** caer en desgracia • **to f. in** *(roof)* hundirse, venirse abajo; *(soldiers)* formar filas • **to f. into** tocar en • **to f. off** *(to come loose)* desprenderse; *(to decrease)* disminuir, decaer; *(quality)* empeorar • **to f. (up)on** *(head, knees)* caer de; *(duty)* tocar a; *(to attack)* caer sobre • **to f. out** *(of bed)* caerse; *(of a car)* salirse; *(to quarrel)* reñir, pelear • **to f. over** *(to fall)* caerse, volcarse; *(to trip over)* tropezar con • **to f. through** venirse abajo, fracasar • **to f. to** *(to begin to)* empezar a; *(to befall)* tocar a, corresponder a • **to f. within** estar dentro de, estar incluido en II. s. caída; *(autumn)* otoño; *(reduction)* bajada, descenso; *(decline)* decadencia, ruina ♦ **to ride for a f.** ir al fracaso • **to take a bad f.** darse una mala caída, caerse duro ♦ pl. catarata, cascada.
fal·la·cious (fə-lā′shəs) adj. falaz, engañoso.
fal·la·cy (făl′ə-sē) s. idea falsa; LOG. falacia.
fal·li·ble (făl′ə-bəl) adj. falible.
fall·ing-out (fô′lĭng-out′) s. desacuerdo, pelea.
fall·out (fôl′out′) s. lluvia radioactiva; *(side effects)* consecuencias.
fal·low (făl′ō) I. adj. durmiente, inactivo; AGR. barbechado II. tr. barbechar.
false (fôls) I. adj. falso; *(hope)* infundado; *(teeth)* postizo; MÚS. desafinado ♦ **f. arrest** a-'rresto ilegal • **f. pretense** intención fraudulenta • **f. start** salida mala *o* nula • **f. step** paso en falso, desliz II. adv. falsamente, con falsedad; *(wrong)* mal.
false-heart·ed (′här′tĭd) adj. pérfido.
false·hood (:hŏŏd′) s. mentira.
false·ness (:nĭs) s. falsedad *f.*
fal·set·to (fôl-sĕt′ō) adv. & s. (en) falsete *m.*
fal·si·fy (fôl′sə-fī′) tr. falsificar, falsear.
fal·ter (fôl′tər) I. intr. titubear; *(to fail)* fallar II. s. vacilación *f*, titubeo.
fame (fām) s. fama, renombre *m.*
famed (fāmd) adj. famoso.
fa·mil·ial (fə-mĭl′yəl) adj. familiar, de familia.
fa·mil·iar (fə-mĭl′yər) I. adj. familiar; *(well-known)* conocido; *(common)* corriente; *(intimate)* de confianza; *(forward)* confianzudo ♦ **that does not sound f.** eso no me suena • **to be f. with** conocer • **to be on f. terms with** tener confianza con II. s. *(friend)* amigo íntimo; *(spirit)* espíritu *m* protector.
fa·mil·iar·i·ty (-′yăr′ĭ-tē) s. familiaridad *f*; *(impropriety)* atrevimiento ♦ pl. libertades.
fa·mil·iar·ize (-′yə-rīz′) tr. familiarizar.

fam·i·ly (făm′ə-lē) s. familia ♦ **f. doctor** médico de cabecera • **f. name** apellido • **f. planning** planeamiento del tamaño de la familia • **f. skeleton** secreto de familia • **f. tree** árbol genealógico.
fam·ine (făm′ĭn) s. hambre *f.*
fam·ished (:ĭsht) adj. muerto de hambre.
fa·mous (fā′məs) adj. famoso.
fa·mous·ly (:lē) adv. FAM. muy bien.
fan[1] (făn) I. s. *(paper)* abanico; *(electric)* ventilador *m* ♦ **f. belt** correa del ventilador II. tr. **-nn-** abanicar; FIG. avivar, excitar ♦ **to f. out** abrirse en abanico.
fan[2] s. FAM. *(enthusiast)* aficionado ♦ **f. mail** cartas de admiradores.
fa·nat·ic (fə-năt′ĭk) s. & adj. fanático.
fa·nat·i·cal (:ĭ-kəl) adj. fanático.
fa·nat·i·cism (:sĭz′əm) s. fanatismo.
fan·ci·er (făn′sē-ər) s. conocedor, aficionado.
fan·ci·ful (făn′sĭ-fəl) adj. imaginativo.
fan·cy (făn′sē) I. s. imaginación *f*, fantasía; *(whim)* capricho ♦ **to strike one's f.** antojársele a uno • **to take a f. to** tomar cariño *o* gusto a II. adj. **-i-** *(elaborate)* muy adornado; *(superior)* fino, selecto; *(luxurious)* lujoso ♦ **f. dress** disfraz III. tr. imaginar; *(to like)* cobrar afecto por, gustarle a uno; *(to suppose)* suponer ♦ **f. that!** ¡imagínese! • **to f. oneself** imaginarse.
fan·cy-free (:frē′) adj. despreocupado.
fan·cy·work (:wûrk′) s. bordado.
fan·fare (făn′fâr′) s. fanfarria.
fang (făng) s. colmillo; *(of snake)* diente *m.*
fan·ny (făn′ē) s. JER. trasero.
fan·ta·size (făn′tə-sīz′) tr. & intr. fantasear.
fan·tas·tic (făn-tăs′tĭk) adj. fantástico.
fan·ta·sy (făn′tə-sē) s. fantasía.
far (fär) **-ther** *o* **further, -thest** *o* **furthest** I. adv. lejos; *(much)* mucho <*f. more* mucho más>; *(very)* muy <*f. different* muy diferente> ♦ **as f. as** *(up to)* hasta; *(to the extent that)* por lo que • **as f. as I am concerned** por mi parte • **as f. as possible** en lo posible • **by f.** con mucho • **f. and away** con mucho • **f. and wide** por todas partes • **f. away** *o* **f. off** (a lo) lejos • **f. be it from me** no me propongo • **f. from** lejos de • **f. from it** al contrario • **f. into** *(very late)* hasta muy avanzado; *(very deep)* hasta muy adentro de • **how f.?** *(distance)* ¿a qué distancia?; *(place)* ¿hasta dónde?; *(degree)* ¿hasta qué punto? • **so f.** *(place)* hasta aquí; *(up to now)* hasta ahora; *(extent)* hasta cierto punto • **so f. so good** hasta ahora todo va bien • **thus f.** hasta ahora • **to go f.** llegar lejos, realizar mucho; *(money)* rendir • **to go so f. as to** llegar inclusive a • **to go too f.** pasarse de la raya II. adj. lejano; *(side, corner)* otro, opuesto; *(journey)* largo; POL. extremo ♦ **a f. cry** una gran diferencia.
far·a·way (′ə-wā′) adj. lejano, remoto; *(dreamy)* distraído, soñador.
farce (färs) s. farsa.
far·ci·cal (fär′sĭ-kəl) adj. ridículo, absurdo.
fare (fâr) I. intr. ir <*to f. badly* ir mal> II. s. pasaje *m*; *(passenger)* pasajero; *(food)* comida.
fare·well (fâr-wĕl′) s. & interj. adiós *m.*
far-fetched (fär′fĕcht′) adj. tirado de los pelos.
far-flung (:flŭng′) adj. vasto, extenso; *(remote)* remoto, distante.
farm (färm) I. s. granja, finca ♦ **f. hand** peón • **f. machinery** maquinaria agrícola II. tr. cultivar ♦ **to f. out** ceder por contrato —intr. labrar la tierra, ser agricultor.
farm·er (fär′mər) s. granjero, agricultor *m* ♦

　　　　　　　　　　　　　　　　　　farmhouse | **fed**

small f. labrador.
farm·house (färm'hous') s. granja, cortijo.
farm·land (:länd') s. tierra de labrantía.
farm·yard (:yärd') s. corral *m.*
far-off (fär'ôf') adj. remoto.
far-reach·ing (:rē'chǐng) adj. de mucho alcance.
far·row (făr'ō) s. lechigada de cerdos.
far-sight·ed (fär'sī'tǐd) adj. prudente, previsor; OFTAL. présbite.
far·ther (fär'thər) [comp. de **far**] I. adv. *(in space)* más adelante; *(in time)* más adelante; *(degree)* más ♦ **f. on** más adelante II. adj. más lejano.
far·thest (:thǐst) [superl. de **far**] I. adj. más remoto II. adv. más lejos.
fas·ci·nate (făs'ə-nāt') tr. fascinar, encantar.
fas·ci·nat·ing (:nā'tǐng) adj. fascinante.
fas·ci·na·tion ('-'shən) s. fascinación *f,* encanto.
fas·cist (făsh'ǐst) s. fascista *mf.*
fash·ion (făsh'ən) I. s. manera, modo; *(style)* moda ♦ **after a f.** en cierto modo ♦ **f. plate** figurín ♦ **in f.** de moda ♦ **in one's own f.** al estilo personal ♦ **latest f.** la última moda ♦ **to be in f.** estar de moda ♦ **to go out of f.** pasar de moda II. tr. formar, moldear; *(to adapt)* amoldar ♦ **to f. out of** *o* **from** hacer con.
fash·ion·a·ble (:ə-nə-bəl) adj. de moda; *(elegant)* elegante, de buen tono.
fast¹ (făst) I. adj. *(quick)* rápido; *(swift)* veloz; *(clock)* adelantado; *(dissipated)* disipado; *(color)* inalterable; *(secure)* firme (en su lugar); *(stuck)* atascado; *(loyal)* leal ♦ **f. friend** amigo leal ♦ **to pull a f. one** hacer una maldad (a alguien) II. adv. rápidamente, velozmente; *(securely)* firmemente; *(clock)* adelantadamente ♦ **f. and furious** a todo meter ♦ **f. and loose** irresponsablemente ♦ **to make f.** atar, sujetar ♦ **to stand f.** mantenerse firme.
fast² I. intr. ayunar II. s. ayuno.
fas·ten (făs'ən) tr. fijar, sujetar; *(to tie)* atar; *(to close)* cerrar; *blame* echar ♦ **to f. the door** echar el cerrojo —intr. fijarse, afirmarse.
fas·ten·er (:ə-nər) s. sujetador *m.*
fas·tid·i·ous (fă-stǐd'ē-əs) adj. meticuloso.
fat (făt) I. s. grasa; CUL. manteca ♦ **the f. of the land** el meollo de la tierra II. adj. **-tt-** gordo; *(lucrative)* lucrativo; *(thick)* grueso; *(large)* grande ♦ **f. cat** JER. persona rica ♦ **f. chance** JER. ninguna posibilidad ♦ **to get f.** ponerse gordo, engordar.
fa·tal (fāt'l) adj. fatal, mortal.
fa·tal·ist (:ĭst) s. fatalista *mf.*
fa·tal·is·tic ('-ĭs'tǐk) adj. fatalista.
fa·tal·i·ty (fā-tăl'ĭ-tē) s. fatalidad *f; (victim)* muerto, víctima.
fate (fāt) s. destino, sino; *(doom)* fatalidad *f.*
fat·ed (fā'tĭd) adj. predestinado.
fate·ful (fāt'fəl) adj. fatídico, fatal.
fat·head (făt'hĕd') s. JER. imbécil *mf,* estúpido.
fa·ther (fä'thər) I. s. padre *m* ♦ **like f. like son** de tal palo tal astilla II. tr. engendrar.
fa·ther·hood (:hŏŏd') s. paternidad *f.*
fa·ther-in-law (:ĭn-lô') s. [pl. **fathers-**] suegro.
fa·ther·land (:länd') s. patria.
fa·ther·ly (:lē) adj. paternal, paterno.
fath·om (făth'əm) I. s. braza II. tr. comprender a fondo; MARÍT. *(to sound)* sondear.
fa·tigue (fə-tēg') I. s. fatiga; MIL. faena ♦ pl. traje de faena II. tr. fatigar, cansar.
fat·ness (făt'nĭs) s. gordura.

fat·so (:sō) s. [pl. **es**] JER. gordo.
fat·ten (:n) tr. engordar, cebar; FIG. aumentar —intr. engordar.
fat·ten·ing (:ĭng) adj. que engorda.
fat·ty (făt'ē) adj. graso, adiposo.
fat·u·ous (făch'ŏŏ-əs) adj. fatuo.
fau·cet (fô'sĭt) s. grifo, canilla.
fault (fôlt) I. s. culpa; *(shortcoming)* defecto; ELEC., GEOL. falla ♦ **at f.** culpable ♦ **to be at f.** tener la culpa ♦ **to find f.** criticar II. tr. encontrar defectos en.
fault·find·ing (′fōlt′dǐng) adj. criticón.
fault·less (:lĭs) adj. perfecto, impecable.
fault·y (fôl'tē) adj. **-i-** defectuoso, imperfecto.
faun (fôn) s. fauno.
fa·vor (fā'vər) I. s. favor *m; (esteem)* estimación *f,* aprecio; *(approval)* aprobación *f,* apoyo ♦ **in f. of** a favor de; *(made out to)* a nombre de ♦ **to be in (out of) f.** (dejar de) ser popular ♦ **to be in f. of** estar a favor de, ser partidario de II. tr. favorecer; *(to be partial to)* preferir; *(to resemble)* parecerse a.
fa·vor·a·ble (:ə-bəl) adj. favorable.
fa·vored (fā'vərd) adj. favorecido; *(favorite)* preferido; *(blessed)* dotado.
fa·vor·ite (fā'vər-ĭt) I. s. favorito; *(protégé)* privado II. adj. favorito, preferido.
fa·vour (fā'vər) G.B. var. de **favor**.
fawn¹ (fôn) intr. hacer fiestas ♦ **f. on** adular.
fawn² s. cervato; *(color)* color *m* de gamuza.
fawn·ing (′ĭng) adj. adulador, servil.
faze (fāz) tr. perturbar, desconcertar.
fe·al·ty (fē'əl-tē) s. lealtad *f.*
fear (fîr) I. s. miedo, temor *m; (dread)* aprensión *f* ♦ **for f. that** por miedo de que ♦ **to be in f. of** tener miedo de II. tr. & intr. tener miedo (de), temer ♦ **never f.** ¡no hay cuidado!
fear·ful (′fəl) adj. espantoso; *(frightened)* temeroso; *(anxious)* aprehensivo; FAM. *(dreadful)* tremendo ♦ **to be f. of** temer.
fear·less (:lĭs) adj. intrépido, audaz.
fear·some (:səm) adj. *(frightening)* temible, terrible.
fea·si·ble (fē'zə-bəl) adj. factible, viable.
feast (fēst) I. s. banquete *m,* comilona; *(treat)* gozo; RELIG. fiesta ♦ **f. day** día festivo II. tr. & intr. banquetear ♦ **to f. (one's eyes) on** regalarse (la vista) con.
feat (fēt) s. proeza, hazaña.
feath·er (fĕth'ər) I. s. pluma ♦ **a f. in one's cap** un triunfo de uno ♦ **f. bed** colchón de plumas ♦ **in fine f.** de muy buen humor ♦ pl. plumas, plumaje II. tr. emplumar ♦ **to f. one's nest** hacer su agosto.
feath·er·brain (:brān') s. FAM. pelele *m.*
feath·er·weight (:wāt') s. peso pluma.
feath·er·y (fĕth'ə-rē) adj. plumoso.
fea·ture (fē'chər) I. s. característica, rasgo; CINEM. película principal; PERIOD. artículo de primera plana ♦ pl. facciones, rasgos II. tr. *(to showcase)* presentar; *(to be a characteristic of)* tener, incorporar; *(to draw)* representar ♦ **f. that!** ¡imagínate eso!
fea·tured (fē'chərd) adj. *(film)* principal; *(role)* estelar; *(article)* de primera plana.
feb·rile (fĕb'rəl, fē'brəl) adj. febril.
Feb·ru·ar·y (fĕb'rōō-ĕr'ē, fĕb'yōō-) s. febrero.
fe·ces (fē'sēz) s.pl. excrementos, heces *f.*
feck·less (fĕk'lĭs) adj. irresponsable.
fe·cund (fē'kənd) adj. fecundo.
fe·cun·date (fē'kən-dāt') tr. fecundar.
fed (fĕd) I. cf. **feed** II. adj. ♦ **f. up with** harto

de.

fed·er·al (fĕd′ər-əl) adj. federal.

fed·er·al·ist (:ə-lĭst) adj. & s. federalista mf.

fed·er·ate (fĕd′ə-rāt′) I. tr. & intr. federar(se), confederar(se) II. adj. (:ər-ĭt) federado.

fed·er·a·tion (′-rā′shən) s. federación f.

fee (fē) s. honorarios, emolumentos ♦ **admission, membership f.** cuota de admisión, socio • **registration f.** derechos de matrícula.

fee·ble (fē′bəl) adj. -er, -est débil.

fee·ble-mind·ed (:mīn′dĭd) adj. imbécil.

feed (fēd) I. tr. fed dar de comer a; (to nourish, supply) alimentar; (anger, suspicion) avivar; (to breast-feed) amamantar; (to bottle-feed) dar el biberón a ♦ **to f.** on alimentarse con; FIG. derivar satisfacción de —intr. comer ♦ **to f.** oneself alimentarse II. s. (fodder) pienso, forraje m; FAM. (meal) comida; MEC. alimentación f.

feed·back (′băk′) s. información f; ELECTRÓN. realimentación f, retroacción f.

feed·bag (:băg′) s. morral m.

feed·ing (fē′dĭng) s. alimentación f.

feel (fēl) I. tr. felt sentir; (to touch) tocar; (to examine) palpar; (to sense) percibir ♦ **it feels cold, hot** hace frío, calor • **to f. it in one's bones that** FAM. tener el presentimiento que ♦ **to f. out** averiguar, sondear —intr. sentir (por tacto); (physically) ser . . . al tacto <the sheets f. smooth las sábanas son suaves al tacto>; (emotionally) sentirse, estar; (to seem) parecer; (to grope) andar a tientas; (to believe) creer, pensar ♦ **to f. cold, hot** tener o sentir frío, calor • **to f. for** (to sympathize) compadecer; (to grope for) buscar a tientas • **to f. hungry, sleepy** tener hambre, sueño • **to f. like** FAM. (to want to) tener ganas de; (to the touch) parecer (como) • **to f. up to** FAM. sentirse con ánimos para II. s. (touch) tacto; (perception) sensación f; (atmosphere) atmósfera ♦ **to get the f. of** coger el truco de • **to have a f. for** tener sentido para.

feel·er (fē′lər) s. (probe) sondeo; ZOOL. antena, tentáculo ♦ **to put out feelers** sondear.

feel·ing (fē′lĭng) I. s. (touch) tacto; (sensation) sensación f; (emotion) emoción f; (impression) impresión f; (premonition) presentimiento; (passion) pasión f; (opinion) opinión f; (aptitude) sentido ♦ pl. sensibilidades • **hard f.** resentimiento • **ill f.** malos sentimientos II. adj. sensible.

feet (fēt) cf. **foot.**

feign (fān) tr. & intr. aparentar, fingir.

feint (fānt) s. finta; MIL. maniobra fingida.

feist·y (fī′stē) adj. -i- intrépido, arrojado.

feld·spar (fĕld′spär′) s. feldespato.

fe·lic·i·tous (fĭ-lĭs′ĭ-təs) adj. oportuno, apto.

fe·lic·i·ty (:tē) s. felicidad f; (phrase) dicho feliz.

fe·line (fē′līn′) adj. felino.

fell¹ (fĕl) tr. cortar, talar; (to kill) acogotar.

fell² adj. cruel, feroz ♦ **in one f. swoop** de un solo golpe.

fell³ cf. **fall.**

fel·low (fĕl′ō) I. s. (boy) muchacho; (man) hombre m; (friend) compañero; (guy) tipo; (of a society) socio ♦ **poor f.!** ¡pobre! II. adj. ♦ **f. citizens** (con)ciudadanos • **f. man** prójimo • **f. member** (con)socio • **f. worker** compañero de trabajo.

fel·low·ship (:shĭp′) s. comunidad f (de intereses, ideas); (fraternity) fraternidad f; (friendship) compañerismo; EDUC. beca ♦ **good f.** espíritu de paz y concordia.

fel·on (fĕl′ən) s. criminal m, felón m.

fel·o·ny (:ə-nē) s. felonía, delito mayor.

felt¹ (fĕlt) adj. & s. (de) fieltro.

felt² cf. **feel.**

fe·male (fē′māl′) I. adj. femenino; (clothes, manners) de mujer; (group) de mujeres; BIOL., MEC. hembra II. s. mujer; BIOL., BOT. hembra.

fem·i·nine (fĕm′ə-nĭn) adj. & s. femenino.

fem·i·nin·i·ty (′-ĭ-nĭn′ĭ-tē) s. feminidad f.

fem·i·nist (fĕm′ə-nĭst) s. feminista mf.

fem·i·nize (:nīz′) tr. & intr. afeminar(se).

fen (fĕn) s. ciénaga, pantano.

fence (fĕns) I. s. cerca, empalizada; JER. traficante mf de artículos robados ♦ **to sit on the f.** nadar entre dos aguas II. tr. cercar, vallar; (to close off) encerrar ♦ **to f. in** (property) cercar; (animals) encerrar • **to f. off** cercar • **to f. out** excluir —intr. DEP. practicar la esgrima; JER. traficar con artículos robados.

fenc·er (fĕn′sər) s. esgrimista mf.

fence-sit·ting (fĕns′sĭt′ĭng) s. irresolución f.

fend (fĕnd) tr. ♦ **to f. off** (blow) parar; (attack) repeler —intr. ♦ **to f. for oneself** valerse por sí mismo.

fend·er (fĕn′dər) s. AUTO. guardafango; F.C. quitapiedras m; (fireplace screen) pantalla.

fen·es·tra·tion (fĕn′ĭ-strā′shən) s. ventanaje m.

fen·nel (fĕn′əl) s. hinojo.

fer·ment (s. fûr′mĕnt′) fermento; (unrest) agitación f II. tr. & intr. (fər-mĕnt′) fermentar.

fern (fûrn) s. helecho.

fe·ro·cious (fə-rō′shəs) adj. feroz.

fe·roc·i·ty (fə-rŏs′ĭ-tē) s. ferocidad f.

fer·ret (fĕr′ĭt) I. s. hurón m II. tr. ♦ **to f. out** descubrir.

fer·ric (fĕr′ĭk) adj. férrico.

Fer·ris wheel (fĕr′ĭs) s. noria, vuelta al mundo.

fer·rite (fĕr′īt′) s. QUÍM. ferrito; MIN. ferrita.

fer·ro·con·crete (fĕr′ō-kŏn′krēt′) s. hormigón armado.

fer·ro·mag·net·ic (:măg-nĕt′ĭk) adj. ferromagnético.

fer·rous (fĕr′əs) adj. ferroso.

fer·rule (fĕr′əl) s. virola, contera.

fer·ry (fĕr′ē) I. tr. transportar en barco o avión II. s. transbordador m; (pier) embarcadero.

fer·ry·boat (:bōt′) s. transbordador m, ferry m.

fer·ry·man (:mən) s. [pl. -men] barquero.

fer·tile (fûr′tl) adj. fértil; BIOL. fecundo.

fer·til·i·ty (fər-tĭl′ĭ-tē) s. fertilidad f, fecundidad f.

fer·til·ize (fûr′tl-īz′) tr. abonar; BIOL. fecundar.

fer·til·iz·er (:ī′zər) s. fertilizante m, abono.

fer·vent (fûr′vənt) adj. ferviente, fervoroso.

fer·vid (fûr′vĭd) adj. fervoroso.

fer·vor (fûr′vər) s. fervor m.

fes·ter (fĕs′tər) intr. (to rankle) enconarse; (to suppurate) supurar.

fes·ti·val (fĕs′tə-vəl) I. s. fiesta; (art, film) festival m II. adj. festivo, de fiesta.

fes·tive (fĕs′tĭv) adj. festivo, de fiesta.

fes·tiv·i·ty (fĕ-stĭv′ĭ-tē) s. festividad f, fiesta; (merriment) regocijo ♦ pl. diversiones.

fes·toon (fĕ-stōōn′) I. s. festón m II. tr. festonear.

fetch (fĕch) tr. traer, ir a buscar; (a sigh) dar; (blood, tears) hacer brotar; (a price) venderse por —intr. cobrar la presa ♦ **fetch!** ¡tráelo! (a un perro).

fetch·ing (fĕch′ĭng) adj. atractivo, encantador.

fete (fāt, fĕt) I. s. fiesta, festín m II. tr. festejar.

fet·id (fĕt′ĭd) adj. fétido, hediondo.

fet·ish (fĕt′ĭsh) s. fetiche *m* ♦ **to make a f. of** venerar.

fet·ish·ist (:ĭ-shĭst′) s. fetichista *mf*.

fet·ter (fĕt′ər) I. s. *(shackle)* grillete *m; (restraint)* traba II. tr. poner grilletes *o* trabas a.

fet·tle (fĕt′l) s. ♦ **in fine f.** *(condition)* en forma; *(spirits)* de buen humor.

fe·tus (fē′təs) s. [pl. **es**] feto.

feud (fyōōd) I. s. enemistad prolongada II. intr. pelear, contender.

feu·dal (′l) adj. feudal.

fe·ver (fē′vər) s. fiebre *f.*

fe·ver·ish (:ĭsh) adj. febril.

few (fyōō) I. adj. poco ♦ **a f.** unos • **a f. times** varias veces • **every f. (miles)** cada dos o tres (millas) • **the last f. (days)** estos últimos (días) II. s. & pron. pocos ♦ **a f.** unos cuantos • **a f. of** algunos de • **quite a f.** muchos.

few·er (′ər) adj. & pron. menos *(than* de) ♦ **the f. the better** cuantos menos mejor.

few·est (:ĭst) I. adj. menos II. pron. el menor número.

fi·an·cé (fē′än-sā′) s. novio, prometido ♦ **fiancée** novia, prometida.

fi·as·co (fē-ăs′kō) s. [pl. **(e)s**] fiasco.

fi·at (fē′ăt′, fē′ăt′) s. fiat *m.*

fib (fĭb) I. s. mentirillas II. intr. **-bb-** decir mentirillas.

fib·ber (′ər) s. mentirosillo.

fi·ber (fī′bər) s. fibra; FIG. carácter *m,* nervio ♦ **f. glass** fibra de vidrio.

fi·ber·board (:bôrd′) s. madera de bagazo.

fi·brous (fī′brəs) adj. fibroso.

fick·le (fĭk′əl) adj. inconstante, variable.

fic·tion (fĭk′shən) s. ficción *f; (lie)* mentira.

fic·tion·al (:shə-nəl) adj. ficticio; LIT. novelístico, de ficción.

fic·tion·al·ize (:nə-līz′) tr. novelar, novelizar.

fic·ti·tious (fĭk-tĭsh′əs) adj. ficticio.

fid·dle (fĭd′l) FAM. I. s. violín *m* ♦ **fit as a f.** sano como una manzana • **to play second f.** desempeñar un papel secundario II. intr. tocar el violín ♦ **to f. around** perder el tiempo • **to f. with** juguetear con —tr. tocar ♦ **to f. away** perder.

fid·dler (:lər) s. FAM. violinista *mf.*

fid·dle·sticks (:l-stĭks′) interj. ¡tonterías!

fi·del·i·ty (fĭ-dĕl′ĭ-tē) s. fidelidad *f.*

fidg·et (fĭj′ĭt) intr. moverse, no estarse quieto.

fidg·et·y (:ĭ-tē) adj. nervioso, inquieto.

fi·du·cial (fĭ-dōō′shəl) adj. fiducial.

fi·du·ci·ar·y (:shē-ĕr′ē) adj. & s. fiduciario.

fief (fēf) s. feudo.

field (fēld) I. s. campo; *(profession)* profesión *f; (contestants)* competidores *m* ♦ **f. glasses** gemelos • **f. goal** gol de patada • **f. gun** cañón de campaña • **f. hand** peón • **f. marshal** mariscal de campo • **f. of view** campo visual • **f. trip** excursión ♦ **to take the f.** DEP. salir a jugar; MIL. entrar en campaña II. tr. *(team)* poner en el campo; *(question)* manejar.

field·work (′wûrk′) s. trabajo en el terreno.

fiend (fēnd) s. demonio; FAM. *(addict)* vicioso.

fiend·ish (fēn′dĭsh) adj. diabólico.

fierce (fîrs) adj. feroz; *(violent)* violento; *(hard-fought)* reñido; *(ardent)* furioso.

fier·y (fîr′ē) adj. *(blazing)* llameante; *(hot)* abrasador; *(color)* encendido; *(temper)* fogoso; *(words)* enardecido.

fife (fīf) s. pífano, flautín *m.*

fif·teen (fĭf-tēn′) s. & adj. quince *m.*

fif·teenth (:tēnth′) s. & adj. *(place)* decimo-

quinto; *(part)* quinzavo.

fifth (fĭfth) adj. & s. quinto.

fif·ti·eth (fĭf′tē-ĭth) I. s. *(place)* cincuenta; *(part)* quincuagésimo II. adj. *(place)* quincuagésimo; *(part)* cincuentavo.

fif·ty (fĭf′tē) adj. & s. cincuenta *m.*

fif·ty-fif·ty (′-′-) adj. FAM. mitad y mitad ♦ **to go f.** ir a medias.

fig (fĭg) s. higo ♦ **f. leaf** hoja de parra • **not to care a f.** importarle a uno un bledo.

fight (fīt) I. intr. **fought** luchar, pelear; *(to box)* boxear; *(to argue)* reñir ♦ **to f. back** defenderse —tr. luchar con *o* contra; *(to resist, combat)* combatir; *(a battle)* dar, librar; DER. litigar, contender ♦ **to f. it out** decidirlo luchando • **to f. off** rechazar, repeler II. s. lucha; *(combat)* combate *m; (quarrel)* riña, disputa; *(brawl, boxing)* pelea; *(bellicosity)* combatividad *f* ♦ **fair f.** buena lid • **to have a f.** pelearse.

fight·er (fī′tər) s. luchador *m,* combatiente *mf; (boxer)* boxeador *m* ♦ **f. plane** avión de caza.

fig·ment (fĭg′mənt) s. invención *f* ♦ **f. of one's imagination** producto de la imaginación.

fig·u·ra·tive (fĭg′yər-ə-tĭv) adj. figurativo.

fig·ure (fĭg′yər) I. s. figura; *(number)* cifra; *(price)* precio; *(illustration)* diseño, dibujo; *(silhouette)* silueta ♦ **f. of speech** figura, tropo • **f. skating** patinaje artístico • **to cut a fine f.** causar una buena impresión • **to keep one's f.** guardar la línea ♦ pl. cálculos, operaciones • **in round f.** en números redondos • **to be good at f.** ser fuerte en aritmética II. tr. computar, calcular; *(to depict)* figurar, representar; FAM. *(to reckon)* imaginar(se), figurar(se) ♦ **to f. out** *(to solve)* resolver; *(to understand)* comprender —intr. hacer cálculos; *(to appear)* figurar, encontrarse ♦ **to f. as** pasar por • **to f. on** FAM. contar con.

fig·ure·head (:hĕd′) s. *(leader)* testaferro; MARÍT. mascarón *m* de proa.

fig·u·rine (fĭg′yə-rēn′) s. estatuilla.

fil·a·ment (fĭl′ə-mənt) s. filamento.

fil·bert (fĭl′bərt) s. avellana.

filch (fĭlch) tr. hurtar, robar.

file¹ (fīl) I. s. archivo; *(for cards)* fichero; *(dossier)* expediente *m; (folder)* carpeta; MIL. fila, columna ♦ **f. card** ficha • **f. clerk** archivista • **to be on f.** estar archivado II. tr. archivar; *(to put in order)* clasificar, ordenar; *(claim, suit)* entablar; *(complaint)* sentar; *(petition, appeal)* presentar —intr. marchar en fila ♦ **to f. by** *(to parade)* desfilar; *(single file)* pasar uno por uno • **to f. in, out** entrar, salir en fila.

file² I. s. *(tool)* lima II. tr. limar.

fi·let (fĭ-lā′) s. filete *m.*

fil·i·bus·ter (fĭl′ə-bŭs′tər) I. s. maniobra obstruccionista II. tr. obstruir *(moción, propuesta).*

fil·i·gree (fĭl′ĭ-grē′) s. filigrana.

fil·ing (fī′lĭng) s. colocación *f* en un archivo.

fil·ings (fī′lĭngz) s.pl. limaduras.

fill (fĭl) tr. llenar; *(to plug up)* tapar; *(a tooth)* empastar; *(to fulfill)* cumplir con; FARM. preparar *(receta); (to occupy)* ocupar; CONSTR., CUL. rellenar; COM. *(order)* despachar; MARÍT. hinchar *(velas)* ♦ **to f. in** *(a form)* llenar; *(to complete)* completar con *(información, detalles)* • **to f. out** *(to enlarge)* ensanchar; *(a form)* completar; COM. *(order)* despachar • **to f. someone in on** poner a alguien al corriente de • **to f. up** llenar (hasta el tope) —intr. llenarse ♦ **to f. in for** reemplazar a • **to f. out** ensancharse • **to f.**

up llenarse II. s. *(enough)* hartura, hartazgo; CONSTR. terraplén *m*, relleno ♦ **to have had one's f. of** estar harto de.

fill·er (′ər) s. relleno.

fil·let (fĭ-lā′, fĭl′ĭt) I. s. filete *m* II. tr. cortar en filetes.

fill·ing (fĭl′ĭng) s. relleno; ODONT. empaste *m* ♦ **f. station** gasolinera.

fil·ly (fĭl′ē) s. potranca, potra.

film (fĭlm) I. s. película; *(coating)* capa; *(in eyes)* tela; *(cinema)* cinema *m* ♦ **f. studio** estudio cinematográfico II. tr. *(an event)* filmar; *(a scene)* rodar; *(a play)* hacer una versión fílmica de —intr. rodar.

film·mak·er (′mā′kər) s. cineasta *mf*.

film·strip (:strĭp′) s. tira de película.

film·y (fĭl′mē) adj. **-i-** tenue, diáfano.

fil·ter (fĭl′tər) I. s. filtro II. tr. & intr. filtrar(se) ♦ **to f.** in entrar poco a poco.

filth (fĭlth) s. mugre *f*, suciedad *f*.

filth·y (fĭl′thē) adj. **-i-** sucio, mugriento.

fil·trate (fĭl′trāt′) I. tr. filtrar II. s. filtrado.

fin (fĭn) s. aleta; AER. plano de deriva.

fi·na·gle (fə-nā′gəl) JER. tr. agenciarse.

fi·nal (fī′nəl) I. adj. *(last)* último; *(concluding)* final; *(unalterable)* definitivo II. s. DEP. final *f*; EDUC. examen *m* final.

fi·nal·e (fə-nǎl′ē) s. final *m*; TEAT. último acto.

fi·nal·ist (fī′nə-lĭst) s. finalista *mf*.

fi·nal·ize (:līz′) tr. finalizar, concluir.

fi·nal·ly (:lē) adv. finalmente, por último.

fi·nance (fə-năns′, fī′năns′) I. s. finanzas ♦ **f. company** sociedad financiera ♦ pl. finanzas, fondos II. tr. financiar.

fi·nan·cial (fə-năn′shəl, fī-) adj. financiero.

fi·nan·cier (fĭn′ən-sîr′) s. financiero.

fi·nanc·ing (fə-năn′sĭng, fī′-năn′-) s. financiamiento, financiación *f*.

finch (fĭnch) s. pinzón *m*.

find (fīnd) I. tr. **found** encontrar; *(to notice)* hallar; *(to discover)* descubrir; *(a target)* dar en; *(to regain)* recuperar; DER. declarar ♦ **to f. oneself** verse, encontrarse ♦ **to f. out** averiguar, descubrir —intr. ♦ **to f. for** fallar a favor de ♦ **to f. out about** informarse sobre II. s. descubrimiento, hallazgo.

find·ings (fīn′dĭngz) s.pl. *(of research)* resultados; *(of a report)* conclusiones; DER. fallo.

fine¹ (fīn) I. adj. fino; *(skillful)* excelente; *(weather)* lindo; *(sharp)* afilado; *(healthy)* bien; *(subtle)* sutil ♦ **f. arts** bellas artes ♦ **f. print** letra menuda ♦ **(it's) f. with me** FAM. estoy de acuerdo ♦ **one f. day** un buen día ♦ **that's f.!** ¡está bien! II. adv. estupendamente; *(minutely)* finamente; FAM. muy bien.

fine² f. I. s. multa II. tr. multar.

fine·ness (′nĭs) s. fineza, delicadeza; *(excellence)* perfección *f*; *(thinness)* finura.

fin·er·y (fī′nə-rē) s. adornos, galas.

fi·nesse (fə-nĕs′) s. *(skill)* finura, delicadeza; *(subtlety)* delicadeza, tacto.

fine-tune (fīn′tŏŏn′) tr. afinar.

fin·ger (fĭng′gər) I. s. dedo ♦ **index f.** (dedo) índice ♦ **little f.** (dedo) meñique ♦ **not to lift a f.** no mover un dedo ♦ **ring f.** (dedo) anular ♦ **to get one's fingers burned** cogerse los dedos ♦ **to keep one's fingers crossed** esperar que todo salga bien ♦ **to put one's f. on** acertar II. tr. *(to handle, play)* tocar; JER. *(to inform on)* denunciar; *(a victim)* marcar.

fin·ger·board (:bôrd′) s. diapasón *m*.

fin·ger·ing (:ĭng) s. digitación *f*.

fin·ger·nail (:nāl′) s. uña.

fin·ger·print (:prĭnt′) I. s. huella digital II. tr. tomar las huellas digitales.

fin·ger·tip (:tĭp′) s. punta o yema del dedo.

fin·ick·y (fĭn′ĭ-kē) adj. **-i-** quisquilloso.

fin·ish (fĭn′ĭsh) I. tr. acabar (con); *(to terminate)* terminar; *(a journey)* llegar al final de; *(to perfect)* rematar ♦ **to f. off** acabar con; *(to perfect)* rematar ♦ **to f. up** acabar, terminar —intr. acabar, terminar ♦ **to f. (first)** llegar o quedar (en primer lugar) ♦ **to f. with someone** romper (relaciones) con alguien II. s. final *m*, fin *m*; *(substance)* pulimento; *(perfection)* perfección *f*; TEC. acabado ♦ **f. line** línea de llegada.

fin·ished (:ĭsht) adj. acabado; FIG. consumado, excelente; *(ruined)* arruinado.

fin·ish·ing (:ĭsh-ĭng) adj. último ♦ **f. school** colegio para señoritas ♦ **f. touch** último toque.

fi·nite (fī′nīt′) adj. finito.

fink (fĭngk) s. JER. persona odiosa.

fir (fûr) s. abeto.

fire (fīr) I. s. fuego; *(destructive)* incendio ♦ **f. bomb** bomba incendiaria ♦ **f. department** o **brigade** cuerpo de bomberos ♦ **f. drill** ejercicios contra incendios ♦ **f. engine** camión de bomberos ♦ **f. escape** salida de urgencia ♦ **f. wall** muro refractario ♦ **to be on f.** estar en llamas o ardiendo ♦ **to be** o **come under f.** FIG. ser blanco de ataques ♦ **to catch f.** encenderse, coger fuego ♦ **to set on f** o **to set f. to** prenderle o pegarle fuego a II. tr. *(to ignite)* encender; *(to arouse)* enardecer; *(gun, bullet)* disparar; *(a shot)* tirar; *(a rocket)* lanzar; FAM. *(to hurl)* tirar, arrojar; *(from a job)* despedir, echar; CERÁM. cocer ♦ **to f. questions** bombardear a preguntas —intr. disparar *(on* contra*)* ♦ **to f. away** disparar sin cesar ♦ **to get fired up** apasionarse.

fire·arm (′ärm′) s. arma de fuego.

fire·ball (:bôl′) s. bola incandescente.

fire·base (:bās′) s. base *f* de fuego.

fire·boat (:bōt′) s. barco bomba.

fire·brand (:brănd′) s. *(torch)* tizón *m*, tea; FIG. agitador *m*, cizañero.

fire·break (:brāk′) s. cortafuego.

fire·crack·er (:krăk′ər) s. cohete *m*, petardo.

fire·fight·er (:fī′tər) s. bombero.

fire·fly (:flī′) s. luciérnaga.

fire·house (:hous′) s. estación *f* de bomberos.

fire·light (:līt′) s. luz *f* del hogar, lumbre *f*.

fire·man (:mən) s. [pl. **-men**] bombero.

fire·place (:plās′) s. hogar, chimenea *m*.

fire·plug (:plŭg′) s. boca de incendios.

fire·pow·er (:pou′ər) s. potencia de fuego.

fire·proof (:prŏŏf′) adj. a prueba de fuego; *(incombustible)* incombustible.

fire·side (:sīd′) s. hogar *m*.

fire·wa·ter (:wô′tər) s. JER. aguardiente *m*.

fire·wood (:wŏŏd′) s. leña.

fire·works (:wûrks′) s.pl. fuegos artificiales.

fir·ing (:ĭng) s. *(of guns)* disparo, descarga; *(shots)* disparos; FAM. *(from a job)* despido ♦ **f. pin** percusor ♦ **f. squad** pelotón de fusilamiento.

firm¹ (fûrm) adj. & adv. firme ♦ **to stand f.** mantenerse firme.

firm² s. COM. firma, casa.

fir·ma·ment (fûr′mə-mənt) s. firmamento.

firm·ness (fûrm′nĭs) s. firmeza.

first (fûrst) I. adj. primero; *(elementary)* primario; *(outstanding)* sobresaliente; *(principal)*

principal ♦ f. **aid** primeros auxilios • **(at)** f. **hand** de primera mano • f. **mate** segundo oficial • f. **name** nombre de pila • f. **papers** E.U. solicitud de nacionalización • **in the** f. **place** en primer lugar • **not to know the** f. **thing about** no saber absolutamente nada de **II.** adv. primero; *(before anything else)* antes; *(firstly)* en primer lugar; *(for the first time)* por primera vez ♦ **at** f. en un principio • f. **and foremost** antes que nada • f. **of all** ante todo • **to come** f. ser lo más importante • **to go** f. ser el primero **III.** s. primero; *(beginning)* principio; AUTO. primera.

first-born ('bôrn') adj. & s. primogénito.

first-class (:klăs') **I.** adj. de primera clase; *(first-rate)* de primera categoría **II.** adv. en primera.

first-hand (:hănd') adv. & adj. de primera mano.

first·ly (:lē) adv. en primer lugar.

first-rate (:rāt') **I.** adj. de primera categoría *o* clase **II.** adv. FAM. muy bien.

firth (fûrth) s. estuario.

fis·cal (fĭs'kəl) s. & adj. fiscal *m*.

fish (fĭsh) **I.** s. [pl. inv. *o* **es**] pez *m*; *(food)* pescado ♦ **a cold** f. FAM. persona sin sentimientos • **neither** f. **nor fowl** ni chicha ni limonada • **to have other** f. **to fry** FAM. tener otras cosas en que ocuparse **II.** intr. pescar ♦ **to** f. **for** andar a la pesca de • **to go fishing** ir de pesca —tr. pescar; *(from pocket)* buscar, sacar ♦ **to** f. **out** agotar los peces en.

fish·bone (:bōn') s. espina.

fish·bowl (:bōl') s. pecera, FIG. vidriera.

fish·er (:ər) s. pescador *m*.

fish·er·man (:ər-mən) s. [pl. **-men**] pescador *m*.

fish·er·y (:ə-rē) s. pesca; *(place)* pesquería.

fish·eye (:ī') s. fig. de ángulo plano, de 180°.

fish·hook (:hŏŏk') s. anzuelo.

fish·ing (:ĭng) s. pesca ♦ f. **ground** zona de pesca • f. **rod** caña de pescar.

fish·mar·ket (:mär'kĭt) s. pescadería.

fish·mon·ger (:mŭng'gər) s. G.B. pescadero.

fish·net (:nĕt') s. red *f*.

fish·tail (:tāl') intr. colear.

fish·wife (:wīf') s. [pl. **-ves**] FAM. verdulera.

fish·y (:ē) adj. **-i-** a pescado; FAM. sospechoso.

fis·sile (fĭs'əl, fĭs'īl') adj. fisionable, fisil.

fis·sion (fĭsh'ən) s. fisión *f*.

fis·sure (fĭsh'ər) s. fisura.

fist (fĭst) s. puño.

fist·fight (:fīt') s. pelea a puñetazos.

fist·ful (:fŏŏl') s. puñado.

fist·i·cuffs (fĭs'tĭ-kŭfs') s.pl. pelea a puñetazos.

fit¹ (fĭt) **I.** tr. **fit(ted), -tting** *(to go on, in)* entrar en; *(to put on, in)* colocar, meter; *(to alter, adjust, match)* ajustar; *(to suit)* sentar bien ♦ **to** f. **in** tener tiempo para • **to** f. **out** proveer; *(a ship)* armar —intr. caber; *(part, piece)* ajustar, encajar; *(to agree)* concordar; *(clothes)* sentar bien • **to** f. **in(to)** encajar *o* caber en • **to** f. **in with** *(people)* congeniar con; *(things)* cuadrar **II.** adj. **-tt-** oportuno, conveniente; *(healthy)* sano; *(competent)* idóneo; *(suitable)* apropiado, digno ♦ f. **to be tied** FAM. fuera de sí • **to keep** f. mantenerse en buen estado físico • **to see** f. juzgar conveniente **III.** s. ajuste *m*, encaje *m*; *(clothes)* corte *m*, entalladura.

fit² s. ataque *m*; *(convulsion)* convulsión *f* ♦ **by fits and starts** a tropezones.

fit·ful ('fəl) adj. intermitente, irregular.

fit·ness (:nĭs) s. propiedad *f*, conveniencia;

(healthiness) salud *f*, estado físico.

fit·ted (:ĭd) adj. apto, capacitado; *(clothes)* entallado; *(suit)* hecho a la medida.

fit·ting (:ĭng) **I.** adj. apropiado, oportuno; *(proper)* propio, justo **II.** s. *(of clothes)* prueba; MEC. parte suelta.

five (fīv) s. & adj. cinco ♦ f. **hundred** quinientos • f. **o'clock** las cinco.

five-and-ten ('ən-tĕn') *o* **five-and-dime** (:dīm') s. tienda que vende artículos baratos.

fix (fĭks) **I.** tr. fijar; *(to repair)* reparar, componer; *(hair)* arreglar; *(meal)* preparar; FAM. *(to get even with)* ajustarle las cuentas a; *(race, election)* arreglar; *(to solve)* solucionar ♦ **to** f. **up** FAM. *(to repair)* componer; *(to arrange)* organizar; *(to tidy)* arreglar —intr. fijarse ♦ **to** f. **on** decidir **II.** s. apuro, aprieto; RAD. posición *f*; *(bribery)* soborno; JER. dosis *f* de narcótico.

fix·a·tion (fĭk-sā'shən) s. fijación *f*.

fix·a·tive (fĭk'sə-tĭv) s. fijador *m*.

fixed (fĭkst) adj. fijo; *(stationary)* estacionario; FAM. *(contest)* arreglado; QUÍM. estable.

fix·er (fĭk'sər) s. fijador *m*.

fix·ture (fĭks'chər) s. instalación fija; *(appliance)* accesorio, artefacto.

fizz (fĭz) **I.** s. sonido de efervescencia **II.** intr. hacer sonido de efervescencia.

fiz·zle ('əl) **I.** s. FAM. fracaso **II.** intr. chisporrotear ♦ **to** f. **out** FAM. quedarse sin energía.

fjord (fyôrd) s. fiordo.

flab (flăb) s. FAM. carne *o* piel fláccida.

flab·ber·gast (flăb'ər-găst') tr. FAM. asombrar.

flab·by (flăb'ē) adj. **-i-** fláccido.

flac·cid (flăk'sĭd, flăs'ĭd) adj. fláccido.

flag¹ (flăg) **I.** s. bandera **II.** tr. **-gg-** marcar *(con una señal)*; *(taxi, bus)* hacer parar con señales a.

flag² intr. **-gg-** *(to weaken)* debilitarse; *(to falter)* disminuir.

flag·el·lant (flăj'ə-lənt) s. flagelante *mf*.

flag·el·late (:lāt') tr. flagelar.

flag·on (flăg'ən) s. jarra grande, pichel *m*.

flag·pole (flăg'pōl') s. mástil *m*, asta *f*.

fla·gran·cy (flā'grən-sē) s. descaro.

fla·grant (flā'grənt) adj. *(glaring)* descarado; *(shocking)* escandaloso.

flag·ship (flăg'shĭp') s. buque *m* insignia.

flag·stone (flăg'stōn') s. lastra, losa.

flag-wav·ing (flăg'wā'vĭng) s. patriotería.

flail (flāl) **I.** s. mayal *m* **II.** tr. *(to thresh)* desgranar; *(to thrash)* golpear —intr. agitarse.

flair (flâr) s. *(knack)* don *m*; *(style)* elegancia.

flak (flăk) s. MIL. artillería antiaérea; FAM. *(criticism)* crítica excesiva.

flake (flāk) **I.** s. escama, hojuela; *(snowflake)* copo; JER. persona rara **II.** intr. *(skin)* descamarse; *(paint)* desprenderse en escamillas.

flak·y (flā'kē) adj. **-i-** escamoso; JER. raro, loco.

flam·boy·ant (flăm-boi'ənt) **I.** adj. rimbombante, llamativo **II.** s. framboyán *m*.

flame (flām) **I.** s. llama; FAM. *(sweetheart)* novio, -a **II.** intr. arder, llamear ♦ f. **up** *(person)* inflamarse; *(situation)* estallar.

flame·proof ('prŏŏf') adj. incombustible.

flame·throw·er (:thrō'ər) s. lanzallamas *m*.

flam·ing (flā'mĭng) adj. ardiente, llameante.

fla·min·go (flə-mĭng'gō) s. [pl. **(e)s**] flamenco.

flam·ma·ble (flăm'ə-bəl) adj. inflamable.

flank (flăngk) **I.** s. costado **II.** tr. flanquear.

flan·nel (flăn'əl) s. franela ♦ pl. pantalones *o* ropa interior de franela.

flap (flăp) I. s. *(of wings)* aleteo; *(of flags)* ondulación f; *(of envelopes)* solapa; *(of pockets)* cartera; *(of garments)* faldón m; *(of hats)* ala; AVIA. alerón m; JER. *(uproar)* jaleo II. tr. & intr. **-pp-** *(wings)* aletear, batir; *(arms)* agitar; *(sails)* gualdrapear; *(to sway)* sacudir(se).

flare (flâr) I. intr. llamear; *(to glow)* brillar; *(to widen)* acampanarse ♦ **to f. up** llamear; *(in anger)* encolerizarse; *(conflict)* estallar II. s. llamarada; *(signal)* señal luminosa; *(outburst)* arrebato; COST. vuelo; ASTRON. erupción f.

flare-up (ŭp′) s. llamarada repentina; *(outburst)* estallido.

flash (flăsh) I. tr. *(to emit)* lanzar, despedir (luz); *(to reflect)* reflejar; *(to aim)* dirigir; FAM. *(to flaunt, show)* enseñar; *(a smile)* echar —intr. *(to sparkle)* brillar, destellar; *(to flare up)* llamear; *(thought, idea)* pasar o cruzar como un relámpago; *(eyes)* relampaguear *(with* de) ♦ **to f. by** pasar como un rayo II. s. destello, resplandor m; FOTOG. flash m; *(of understanding)* rayo de luz; *(news)* noticia de último momento; *(of lightning)* relámpago; FAM. ostentación f ♦ **a f. in the pan** mucho ruido y pocas nueces • **f. bulb** lámpara de flash • **f. flood** riada ♦ **f. point** punto de inflamación • **in a f.** en un instante • **like a f.** como un rayo.

flash-back (′băk′) s. escena retrospectiva intercalada en la acción presente.

flash-er (:ər) s. destellador m.

flash-ing (:ĭng) adj. centelleante, intermitente.

flash-light (:līt′) s. linterna eléctrica.

flash-y (:ē) adj. -i- llamativo, chillón.

flask (flăsk) s. frasco; QUÍM. matraz m.

flat¹ (flăt) **-tt-** I. adj. *(level)* plano, llano; *(smooth)* liso, raso; *(prone)* tendido; *(definite)* categórico; *(fixed)* fijo; *(dull)* monótono; *(tasteless)* soso; *(tire)* desinflado; *(color)* sin brillo; MÚS. *(key)* bemol; *(pitch)* desafinado II. adv. horizontalmente, de plano; *(completely)* sin más ni más ♦ **f. broke** FAM. pelado • **f. out** a toda velocidad III. s. plano, superficie f; *(tire)* pinchazo; MÚS. bemol m • **the f. of the hand** la palma de la mano ♦ pl. llanura, llano.

flat² s. *(apartment)* apartamento.

flat-boat (′bōt′) s. barca chata, chalana.

flat-car (:kär′) s. vagón m de plataforma.

flat-footed (:fŏot′ĭd) adj. de pies planos.

flat-land (:lănd′) s. llano, llanura.

flat-ten (:n) tr. allanar, achatar; *(to knock down)* derribar —intr. achatarse.

flat-ter (flăt′ər) tr. adular, halagar; *(to suit)* favorecer —intr. emplear lisonjas.

flat-ter-er (:ər) s. adulador m, lisonjero.

flat-ter-y (flăt′ə-rē) s. lisonja, halago.

flat-u-lent (flăch′ə-lənt) adj. flatulento.

flaunt (flônt) tr. hacer ostentación de.

fla-vor (flā′vər) I. s. gusto, sabor m *<mint f. sabor a menta>*; *(flavoring)* condimento II. tr. condimentar, aderezar.

fla-vor-ful (:fəl) adj. sabroso, gustoso.

fla-vor-ing (:ĭng) s. condimento, aderezo.

fla-vour (flā′vər) G.B. var. de **flavor.**

flaw (flô) s. imperfección f, defecto.

flawed (flôd) adj. defectuoso, estropeado.

flaw-less (flô′lĭs) adj. perfecto, sin defecto.

flax (flăks) s. lino; *(fiber)* fibra de lino.

flax-en (flăk′sən) adj. de lino; *(blond)* rubio.

flay (flā) tr. desollar, despellejar.

flea (flē) s. pulga ♦ **f. market** mercado de artículos usados.

fleck (flĕk) I. s. pinta, mota II. tr. motear.

fledg(e)-ling (flĕj′lĭng) s. pajarito; *(novice)* novato.

flee (flē) intr. **fled** huir, escaparse; *(to vanish)* desvanecerse —tr. huir de.

fleece (flēs) I. s. lana; *(sheared)* vellón m; *(lining)* muletón m II. tr. *(to shear)* esquilar; *(to rob)* desplumar, pelar.

fleec-y (flē′sē) adj. -i- lanudo.

fleet¹ (flēt) s. *(of ships)* flota; *(of cars)* escuadra; MIL. armada, fuerza naval.

fleet² adj. *(fast)* rápido, ligero.

fleet-ing (flē′tĭng) adj. fugaz, efímero.

flesh (flĕsh) I. s. carne f; *(fat)* gordura; *(of fruits)* pulpa ♦ **f. wound** herida superficial • **in the f.** en persona II. tr. ♦ **to f. out** extender, completar.

flesh-y (′ē) adj. -i- carnoso; *(fat)* corpulento.

flew (flōo) cf. **fly¹.**

flex (flĕks) I. tr. & intr. doblar(se), encorvar(se) II. s. G.B. flexible m.

flex-i-ble (flĕk′sə-bəl) adj. flexible.

flick¹ (flĭk) I. s. golpecito; *(of tail)* coleada; *(of fingers)* capirotazo II. tr. golpear rápida y ligeramente; *(to snap)* dar un golpecito a —intr. colear ♦ **to f. through** hojear.

flick² s. FAM. *(film)* película, filme m.

flick-er (:ər) I. intr. oscilar, temblar; *(light)* parpadear, vacilar II. s. luz f vacilante.

fli-er (flī′ər) s. aviador m; *(circular)* volante m.

flight¹ (flīt) s. vuelo; *(flock)* bandada; *(swift movement)* paso fugaz; *(floor)* piso; *(of stairs)* tramo ♦ **f. attendant** aeromozo, -a • **f. deck** cubierta de aterrizaje • **to take f.** alzar el vuelo.

flight² s. *(act of fleeing)* huida, fuga.

flight-less (′lĭs) adj. incapaz de volar.

flight-y (flī′tē) adj. -i- frívolo, casquivano.

flim-sy (flĭm′zē) adj. -i- insubstancial, endeble; *(excuse)* flojo.

flinch (flĭnch) I. intr. *(to wince)* sobresaltarse; *(to retreat)* recular II. s. reculada.

fling (flĭng) I. tr. **flung** arrojar, tirar ♦ **to f. about** agitar (brazos) • **to f. aside** abandonar, desechar • **to f. down** echar al suelo • **to f. oneself** precipitarse, lanzarse II. s. lanzamiento; FAM. *(spree)* juerga; *(attempt)* tentativa (breve) ♦ **to have a f.** echar una cana al aire.

flint (flĭnt) s. pedernal m.

flint-lock (′lŏk′) s. llave f o trabuco de chispa.

flip (flĭp) I. tr. **-pp-** lanzar, tirar ♦ *(coin)* echar (a cara o cruz) ♦ **f. over** dar la vuelta a —intr. agitarse, dar vueltas ♦ **to f. out** enloquecerse *(over* por) • **to f. over** voltearse, volcarse • **to f. through** hojear II. s. golpe m; *(shake)* sacudida; *(somersault)* salto mortal ♦ **f. side** reverso (de un disco) III. adj. FAM. descarado.

flip-flop (′flŏp′) s. FAM. cambio brusco.

flip-pant (flĭp′ənt) adj. frívolo, impertinente.

flip-per (flĭp′ər) s. aleta.

flirt (flûrt) I. intr. flirtear, coquetear; *(with danger)* jugar II. s. *(man)* galanteador m; *(woman)* coqueta.

flir-ta-tion (flûr-tā′shən) s. flirteo, coqueteo.

flit (flĭt) intr. **-tt-** revolotear.

float (flōt) I. tr. hacer flotar, poner a flote; FIN. *(a loan)* negociar; *(currency)* dejar fluctuar —intr. flotar; FIN. *(currency)* fluctuar; *(to wander)* vagar, errar II. s. flotador m; *(buoy)* boya; *(platform)* balsa, plataforma flotante.

float-ing (flō′tĭng) adj. flotante, boyante.

flock (flŏk) I. s. *(of birds)* bandada; ZOOL., RELIG. rebaño II. intr. congregarse ♦ **to f.** llegar en tropel a.

floe (flō) s. témpano o masa de hielo flotante.

flog (flŏg) tr. **-gg-** azotar, flagelar.

flog·ging ('ĭng) s. paliza, flagelación f.

flood (flŭd) **I.** s. inundación f; (torrent) torrente m; (floodlight) luz f de proyector ✦ **f. plain** terreno aluvial ✦ **f. tide** pleamar ✦ **the F.** el Diluvio **II.** tr. & intr. inundar(se).

flood·gate ('gāt') s. compuerta de exclusa.

flood·light (:līt') s. luz f de proyector.

floor (flôr) **I.** s. piso m; (of a dance hall) pista; (bottom) fondo; (assembly members) congresistas mf ✦ **f. lamp** lámpara de pie ✦ **f. show** espectáculos ✦ **to ask for** o **take the f.** pedir o tener la palabra ✦ **top f.** piso alto **II.** tr. (to knock down) derribar; FAM. (the accelerator) pisar a fondo; (to stun) apabullar.

floor·board ('bôrd') s. tabla de piso.

floor·walk·er (:wô'kər) s. superintendente m de departamento (en un almacén).

flop (flŏp) **I.** s. sonido sordo; FAM. (failure) fracaso **II.** tr. **-pp-** dejar caer (pesadamente) —intr. dejarse caer; (to move about) agitarse; FAM. (to fail) fracasar.

flop·house ('hous') s. JER. pensión f de mala muerte.

flop·py (:ē) adj. **-i-** FAM. flojo, blando ✦ **f. disk** COMPUT. disco flexible (de memoria auxiliar).

flor·id (flôr'ĭd) adj. (face) rojo; (style) florido.

flor·ist (flôr'ĭst) s. florista mf.

floss (flŏs) s. (waste) borra; COST. seda; (dental) seda vegetal.

flo·ta·tion (flō-tā'shən) s. flotación f.

flot·sam (flŏt'səm) s. pecios.

flounce[1] (flouns) s. COST. volante m, cairel m.

flounce[2] **I.** intr. sacudirse ✦ **f. out** salir enfadado **II.** s. sacudida.

floun·der[1] (floun'dər) intr. luchar o esforzarse inútilmente.

floun·der[2] s. ICT. platija, lenguado.

flour (flour) **I.** s. harina **II.** tr. enharinar.

flour·ish (flûr'ĭsh) **I.** intr. florecer, prosperar —tr. blandir **II.** s. floreo; (signature) rúbrica.

flout (flout) tr. & intr. burlarse (de).

flow (flō) **I.** intr. fluir; ELEC., FIG. correr; (to circulate) circular; (to gush) manar; (tide) subir; (blood, tears) derramar ✦ **to f. from** FIG. provenir de ✦ **to f. into** desaguar ✦ **to f. together** confluir **II.** s. flujo; (of blood, traffic) circulación f; (stream) corriente f; (volume) caudal m; (course) curso ✦ **f. chart** diagrama de fabricación.

flow·er (flou'ər) **I.** s. flor f; FIG. flor y nata ✦ **f. shop** florería **II.** intr. florecer, dar flor.

flow·er·pot (:pŏt') s. maceta.

flow·er·y (flou'ə-rē) adj. florido.

flown (flōn) cf. **fly**[1].

flu (flōo) s. FAM. gripe f.

fluc·tu·ate (flŭk'chōo-āt') intr. fluctuar.

flue (flōo) s. cañón humero.

flu·en·cy (flōo'ən-sē) s. (in a language) dominio; (effortlessness) fluidez f, soltura.

flu·ent (flōo'ənt) adj. perfecto; (fluid) fluyente ✦ **to be f.** in hablar perfectamente, dominar.

flu·ent·ly (:lē) adv. con soltura.

fluff (flŭf) **I.** s. (down) pelusa; (trifle) nadería **II.** tr. mullir; FAM. (to botch) chapucear.

fluff·y ('ē) adj. **-i-** lanoso; (soft) mullido.

flu·id (flōo'ĭd) s. & adj. fluido, líquido ✦ **f. ounce** onza líquida.

fluke[1] (flōok) s. (of anchor) uña; (of whale) aleta (de la cola).

fluke[2] s. (luck) chiripa, tiro de suerte.

flung (flŭng) cf. **fling**.

flunk (flŭngk) intr. FAM. sacar suspenso ✦ **to f. out** ser expulsado (por malas notas) —tr. (a course) sacar suspenso en, fracasar en; (a student) colgar, suspender.

flun·ky (flŭng'kē) s. lacayo.

flu·o·res·cence (flŏō'rĕs'əns) s. fluorescencia.

flu·o·res·cent (:ənt) adj. fluorescente.

fluor·i·da·tion (flôōr'ĭ-dā'shən, flôr'-) s. fluorización f.

fluor·ide ('īd') s. fluoruro.

fluor·ine (:ēn') s. flúor m.

flur·ry (flûr'ē) s. (gust) ráfaga; (snowfall) nevisca; (bustle) fiebre f, frenesí m; FIG. lluvia.

flush[1] (flŭsh) **I.** intr. fluir abundantemente; (to blush) ruborizarse —tr. (to redden) enrojecer; (to excite) exaltar; (to clean) limpiar con agua ✦ **to f. the toilet** apretar el botón del inodoro, tirar la cadena **II.** s. (gush) chorro; (blush) rubor m; (glow) resplandor m; (exhilaration) animación f **III.** adj. copioso, abundante ✦ **f. against** contra, pegado a ✦ **f. with** a nivel con **IV.** adv. al mismo nivel.

flush[2] tr. hacer salir del escondite.

flus·ter (flŭs'tər) tr. poner nervioso.

flute (flōot) s. MÚS. flauta; ARQ. estría.

flut·ing (flōo'tĭng) s. estriado, acanaladura.

flut·ist (flōo'tĭst) s. flautista mf.

flut·ter (flŭt'ər) **I.** intr. revolotear, aletear; (in the wind) ondear, ondular; (to tremble) temblar; (heart) palpitar —tr. agitar, mover **II.** s. revoloteo, aleteo; (waving) ondulación f; (agitation) agitación f; MED. palpitación f ✦ **to be in a f.** estar nervioso.

flux (flŭks) s. flujo; (fluctuation) cambio.

fly[1] (flī) **I.** intr. **flew, flown** volar; (hair, flag) flotar; (to flee) huir, escapar; (to hurry) darse prisa; (to rush by) pasar o irse volando; (sparks, chips) saltar ✦ **to f. at** FAM. lanzarse sobre ✦ **to f. in the face of** ir contra, hacer frente a ✦ **to f. into a rage** encolerizarse ✦ **to f. open** abrirse repentinamente —tr. hacer volar; (to pilot) pilotear; (to transport) transportar en avión; (to cross) atravesar o cruzar en avión; (a flag) desplegar; (kite) remontar **II.** s. (of trousers) bragueta; (tent flap) toldo; G.B. (carriage) coche m de punto ✦ **pl.** TEAT. telares.

fly[2] s. ENTOM. mosca ✦ **f. swatter** matamoscas.

fly·ing ('ĭng) adj. volador; (swift) veloz, ligero ✦ **f. buttress** contrafuerte ✦ **f. saucer** platillo volador ✦ **f. time** duración del vuelo ✦ **to get off to a f. start** empezar muy bien.

fly·leaf (:lēf') s. **pl. -ves** guarda.

fly-o·ver (:ō'vər) s. G.B. cruce elevado.

fly·pa·per (:pā'pər) s. papel m matamoscas.

foal (fōl) **I.** s. potro **II.** intr. parir un potro.

foam (fōm) **I.** s. espuma ✦ **f. rubber** espuma de caucho **II.** intr. hacer espuma ✦ **to f. at the mouth** espumajear, rabiar.

foam·y (fō'mē) adj. **-i-** espumoso.

fob[1] (fŏb) s. (chain) leontina, leopoldina.

fob[2] tr. **-bb-** ✦ **to f. something off on someone** encajarle algo a alguien.

fo·cal (fō'kəl) adj. focal ✦ **f. point** foco.

fo·cus (fō'kəs) **I.** s. **[pl. es** o **-ci]** foco ✦ **in f.** enfocado ✦ **out of f.** desenfocado ✦ **to bring into f.** enfocar **II.** tr. enfocar; (a lens) ajustar; FIG. concentrar —intr. enfocarse ✦ **to f. on** enfocar.

fod·der (fŏd'ər) s. forraje m, pienso ✦ **cannon f.** carne de cañón.

foe (fō) s. enemigo; *(opponent)* adversario.
foe·tus (fē'təs) var. de **fetus**.
fog (fôg) **I.** s. neblina, niebla; *(at sea)* bruma; FOTOG. velo ♦ **f. bank** nube de bruma • **in a f.** confundido **II.** tr. **-gg-** *(glass)* empañar; *(sky, mind)* nublar —intr. ♦ **to f. up** *(glass)* empañarse; *(sky)* nublarse; FOTOG. velarse.
fog·gy (fô'gē) adj. **-i-** neblinoso; *(glass)* empañado; *(bewildered)* ofuscado ♦ **not to have the foggiest idea** no tener ni la más mínima idea.
fog·horn (fôg'hôrn') s. sirena de niebla.
fo·gy (fō'gē) s. persona chapada a la antigua.
foi·ble (foi'bəl) s. punto flaco, debilidad *f.*
foil[1] (foil) tr. frustrar, hacer fracasar.
foil[2] s. *(sheet)* lámina fina de metal; *(contrast)* contraste *m* ♦ **to act as a f.** to servir de contraste a.
foil[3] s. DEP. florete *m.*
foist (foist) tr. ♦ **to f. off on** encajar a.
fold[1] (fōld) **I.** tr. doblar, plegar; *(arms)* cruzar; *(hands)* enlazar; *(wings)* plegar, recoger ♦ **to f. back** doblar • **to f. down** *o* **out** bajar (asiento de silla, mesa plegadiza) • **to f. in** CUL. incorporar • **to f. up** *(to wrap up)* envolver; *(to collapse)* plegar (sillas) —intr. doblarse, plegarse; *(to fail)* fracasar; FAM. *(to give in)* doblegarse ♦ **to f. up** doblarse, plegarse **II.** s. pliegue *m*; *(crease)* doblez *m*, arruga.
fold[2] s. *(corral)* redil *m*; *(flock)* rebaño.
fold·er (fōl'dər) s. carpeta.
fold·ing (fōl'dĭng) adj. plegable, plegadizo ♦ **f. screen** biombo • **f. seat** traspuntín.
fold-out (fōld'out') s. lámina desplegable.
fo·li·age (fō'lē-ĭj) s. follaje *m.*
fo·li·o (fō'lē-ō') s. folio; *(book)* infolio.
folk (fōk) **I.** s. [pl. inv. *o* **s**] pueblo, nación *f* ♦ **country f.** campesinos • **f. dance** baile folklórico • **f. medicine** medicina popular ♦ pl. **folks** gente; FAM. *(relatives)* familia • **the old f.** los viejos **II.** adj. popular.
folk·lore (fōr') s. folklore *m.*
folk·sy (:sē) adj. **-i-** campechano, afable.
folk·tale (:tāl') s. cuento tradicional.
fol·li·cle (fōl'ĭ-kəl) s. folículo.
fol·lies (fōl'ēz) s.pl. revista teatral.
fol·low (fōl'ō) tr. seguir; *(to chase)* perseguir; *(a road, course)* proseguir, continuar por; *(rules)* observar; *(a profession)* dedicarse a; *(speech, book)* prestar atención a; *(to understand)* comprender ♦ **to f. through** *o* **up** llevar a cabo —intr. seguir ♦ **as follows** *(to do)* de la siguiente manera; *(to reply)* lo siguiente • **it follows that** se deduce que.
fol·low·er (:ər) s. *(disciple)* discípulo; *(supporter)* partidario; *(admirer)* admirador *m.*
fol·low·ing (:ĭng) **I.** adj. siguiente **II.** s. adherentes *mf*; *(admirers)* admiradores *m.*
fol·low-up (:ŭp') **I.** adj. complementario **II.** s. complemento (de un proceso); *(continuation)* resultado, consecuencia.
fol·ly (fōl'ē) s. tontería; *(silly idea or action)* disparate *m.*
fo·ment (fō-mĕnt') tr. fomentar.
fond (fōnd) adj. cariñoso; *(doting)* indulgente; *(cherished)* caro ♦ **to be f. of** *(person)* tener cariño a; *(thing)* ser aficionado a.
fon·dle (fōn'dl) tr. & intr. acariciar.
fond·ness (fōnd'nĭs) s. afecto, cariño; *(inclination)* inclinación *f*; *(taste)* afición *f.*
font (fônt) s. fuente *f*; RELIG. pila bautismal.
food (fōōd) s. comida; *(nourishment)* alimento ♦ **f. poisoning** intoxicación alimenticia • **f. pro-**

cessor procesador de alimentos.
food·stuff ('stŭf') s. comestible.
fool (fōōl) **I.** s. tonto, necio; *(jester)* bufón *m*; *(dupe)* simplón *m* ♦ **f.'s errand** empresa inútil • **to make a f. of** *(to deceive)* poner en ridículo a; *(to tease)* tomar el pelo a **II.** tr. *(to trick)* engañar; *(to surprise)* sorprender —intr. jugar ♦ **to fool·har·dy** ('här'dē) adj. **-i-** temerario.
fool·har·dy ('här'dē) adj. **-i-** temerario.
fool·ing (fōō'lĭng) s. broma, chacota ♦ **no f.** hablando en serio • **no f.!** ¡no me digas! • **to be just f.** estar sólo bromeando.
fool·ish (:lĭsh) adj. *(silly)* tonto, absurdo; *(embarrassed)* ridículo.
fool·ish·ness (:nĭs) s. tontería.
fool·proof (fōōl'prōōf') adj. infalible; *(impossible to misuse)* a prueba contra mal uso.
fools·cap (fōōlz'kăp') s. hoja de papel.
foot (fōōt) **I.** s. [pl. **feet**] pie *m*; ZOOL. pata; *(base)* base *f* ♦ **by** *o* **on f.** a pie • **f. brake** freno de pedal • **f. soldier** soldado de infantería • **my f.!** JER. ¡tonterías! • **to drag one's feet** FIG. roncear • **to get cold feet** FAM. coger miedo • **to get one's f. in the door** abrir una brecha • **to land on one's feet** caer de pie • **to put one's f. down** ponerse firme • **to put one's f. in one's mouth** meter la pata • **to stand on one's own two feet** valerse por sí mismo **II.** intr. ♦ **to f. it** andar a pie —tr. ♦ **to f. the bill** pagar la cuenta.
foot·age ('ĭj) s. medida de superficie *o* longitud (expresada en pies); CINEM. metraje *m.*
foot-and-mouth disease ('n-mouth') s. glosopeda, fiebre aftosa.
foot·ball ('bôl') s. fútbol *m*; *(ball)* pelota.
foot·bridge (:brĭj') s. puente *m* para peatones.
foot·hill (:hĭl') s. estribación *f* (de montaña).
foot·hold (:hōld') s. *(support)* lugar *m* de apoyo (para el pie); *(starting point)* posición *f.*
foot·ing (:ĭng) s. pie *m*, equilibrio; *(basis)* base *f* ♦ **on equal f.** en pie de igualdad • **to lose one's f.** perder el pie.
foot·lights (:'lĭts') s.pl. candilejas.
foot·loose (:lōōs') adj. sin obligaciones ♦ **f. and fancy free** libre, ligero *o* contento.
foot·man (:man) s. [pl. **-men**] lacayo.
foot·note (:nōt') **I.** s. anotación *f* **II.** tr. anotar.
foot·path (:păth') s. sendero.
foot·print (:prĭnt') s. huella.
foot·race (:rās') s. carrera pedestre.
foot·sore (:sôr') adj. con los pies cansados.
foot·step (:stĕp') s. pisada.
foot·stool (:stōōl') s. taburete *m.*
foot·wear (:wâr') s. calzado.
foot·work (:wûrk') s. juego de piernas.
fop (fôp) s. petimetre *m.*
fop·per·y (:ə-rē) s. afectación *f.*
fop·pish (:ĭsh) adj. afectado.
for (fôr, fər) **I.** prep. para, por; *(destination)* para, hacia; *(beneficiary)* para; *(exchange)* por; *(duration)* por, desde hace; *(on account of)* de, por; *(in spite of)* a pesar de, con; *(considering)* para ♦ **as f.** en cuanto a • **f. all that** con todo • **to be all f. it** FAM. estar completamente a favor de • **to be f.** estar de parte de • **to be f. someone** tocarle a alguien **II.** conj. ya que, pues, porque.
for·age (fôr'ĭj) **I.** s. forraje *m* **II.** intr. hurgar ♦ **to f. for** buscar hurgando.
for·ay (fôr'ā') s. incursión *f.*
for·bear (fôr-bâr') tr. **-bore, -borne** abstener *o*

desistir de —intr. *(to refrain)* abstenerse; *(to be tolerant)* ser tolerante.

for·bear·ance (:ǝns) s. tolerancia, paciencia.

for·bid (fǝr-bĭd') tr. **-bad(e)**, **-bid(den)**, **-dding** prohibir.

for·bid·ding (:ĭng) adj. amenazante.

force (fôrs) **I.** s. fuerza; *(efficacy)* eficacia, peso; *(corps)* cuerpo; DER. *(effect)* vigencia, validez *f* ✦ **by f.** por la fuerza • **by f. of** a fuerza de • **in f.** DER. vigente, en vigor; *(in numbers)* en masa • **to put in f.** poner en vigor **II.** tr. compeler, obligar; *(to obtain)* obtener por la fuerza; *(to coerce, break open)* forzar; *(to impose)* imponer; AGR. hacer crecer temprano ✦ **to f. back** *(to repel)* rechazar; *(tears)* contener, reprimir • **to f. down** obligar a bajar • **to f. from** echar *o* sacar fuera • **to f. one's way** abrirse paso • **to f. open** forzar • **to f. out** obtener por la fuerza • **to f. up(on)** obligar a tomar *o* aceptar.

forced (fôrst) adj. forzado; *(landing)* forzoso; *(unnatural)* fingido.

force·ful (fôrs'fǝl) adj. fuerte, enérgico.

for·ceps (fôr'sǝps) s.inv. pinzas, fórceps *m.*

forc·i·ble (fôr'sǝ-bǝl) adj. forzado.

forc·i·bly (:blē) adv. a la fuerza.

ford (fôrd) **I.** s. vado **II.** tr. vadear.

fore (fôr) **I.** adj. delantero **II.** s. frente *m*, delantera ✦ **to come to the f.** comenzar a destacarse **III.** adv. hacia el frente.

fore·arm[1] (-ärm') tr. prepararse de antemano.

fore·arm[2] ('ärm') s. antebrazo.

fore·bear (:bâr') s. antepasado.

fore·bod·ing (-bō'dĭng) s. presentimiento.

fore·cast ('kăst') **I.** tr. & intr. **-cast(ed)** pronosticar **II.** s. pronóstico.

fore·cast·er (:kăs'tǝr) s. pronosticador *m.*

fore·cas·tle (fōk'sǝl, fôr'kăs'ǝl) s. castillo de proa.

fore·close (fôr-klōz') intr. privar del derecho de redimir una hipoteca.

fore·clo·sure (:klō'zhǝr) s. pérdida del derecho a redimir una hipoteca.

fore·fa·ther ('fä' thǝr) s. antepasado.

fore·fin·ger (:fĭng'gǝr) s. dedo índice.

fore·foot (:fŏŏt') s. [pl. **-feet**] pata delantera.

fore·front (:frŭnt') s. vanguardia.

fore·go (-gō') tr. **-went**, **-gone** preceder.

fore·gone ('gôn') adj. previo, pasado.

fore·ground (:ground') s. primer plano.

fore·hand (:hănd') adj. & s. (golpe) derecho.

fore·head (:ĭd; :hĕd') s. frente *f.*

for·eign (fôr'ĭn) adj. extranjero; *(trade)* exterior; *(uncharacteristic)* ajeno ✦ **f. exchange** *(currency)* divisas; COM. cambio exterior • **f. office** G.B. Ministerio de Asuntos Exteriores • **f. service** servicio diplomático y consular.

for·eign·er (:ǝ-nǝr) s. extranjero, forastero.

fore·knowl·edge (fôr-nŏl'ĭj) s. presciencia.

fore·leg ('lĕg') s. pata delantera, brazo.

fore·lock (:lŏk') s. mechón *m.*

fore·man (:mǝn) s. [pl. **-men**] capataz *m*; DER. presidente *m* de un jurado.

fore·men·tioned (:mĕn'shǝnd) adj. antedicho.

fore·most (:mōst') adj. primero, delantero; *(paramount)* máximo, supremo.

fo·ren·sic (fǝ-rĕn'sĭk) adj. forense.

fore·run·ner (fôr'rŭn'ǝr) s. precursor *m*, predecesor *m*; *(harbinger)* anunciador *m.*

fore·said (:sĕd') adj. antedicho, susodicho.

fore·see (:sē') tr. **-saw**, **-seen** prever, anticipar.

fore·see·a·ble (:ǝ-bǝl) adj. previsible.

fore·shad·ow (fôr-shăd'ō) tr. presagiar.

fore·short·en·ing (:shôr'tn-ĭng) s. escorzo.

fore·sight ('sīt') s. previsión *f.*

fore·sight·ed (:sī'tĭd) adj. prudente.

fore·skin (:skĭn') s. prepucio.

for·est (fôr'ĭst) **I.** s. bosque *m*, selva ✦ **f. ranger** guardabosque **II.** tr. poblar de árboles **III.** adj. forestal, selvático.

fore·stall (fôr-stôl') tr. impedir, prevenir.

for·est·land (fôr'ĭst-lănd') s. área boscosa.

for·est·ry (:ĭ-strē) s. silvicultura.

fore·taste (fôr'tāst') s. goce anticipado.

fore·tell (-tĕl') tr. **-told** predecir.

fore·thought ('thôt') s. deliberación *f*, premeditación *f.*

for·ev·er (fôr-ĕv'ǝr, fǝr-) adv. por *o* para siempre, eternamente; *(always)* siempre.

for·ev·er·more (-'-môr') adv. para siempre jamás.

fore·warn (fôr-wôrn') tr. prevenir, avisar.

fore·word ('wǝrd') s. prólogo, prefacio.

for·feit (fôr'fĭt) **I.** s. *(penalty)* penalidad *f*; *(loss)* pérdida legal de un derecho; *(forfeiture)* prenda perdida **II.** tr. perder como castigo.

for·fei·ture (:fĭ-chŏŏr') s. pérdida (de título, derecho); *(security)* prenda perdida.

for·gave (fǝr-gāv') cf. **forgive.**

forge[1] (fôrj) **I.** s. *(smithy)* forja, fragua **II.** tr. fraguar, forjar; *(to counterfeit)* falsificar.

forge[2] intr. avanzar ✦ **to f. ahead** adelantar con esfuerzo.

forg·er (fôr'jǝr) s. falsificador *m.*

for·ger·y (:jǝ-rē) s. falsificación *f.*

for·get (fǝr-gĕt') tr. & intr. **-got**, **-got(ten)**, **-tting** olvidar, olvidarse de ✦ **to f. oneself** propasarse, extralimitarse • **to f. to** olvidarse de.

for·get·ful (:fǝl) adj. olvidadizo, desmemoriado; *(negligent)* descuidado.

for·get-me-not (:mē-nŏt') s. nomeolvides *f.*

for·give (fǝr-gĭv') tr. & intr. **-gave**, **-given** perdonar.

for·give·ness (:nĭs) s. perdón *m.*

for·giv·ing (:ĭng) adj. clemente, indulgente.

for·go (fôr-gō') tr. **-went**, **-gone** renunciar, prescindir de.

for·got(·ten) (fǝr-gŏt[n]') cf. **forget.**

fork (fôrk) **I.** s. tenedor *m*; AGR. horca; *(of a road)* bifurcación *f*; *(of a tree)* horqueta; *(in a river)* horcajo ✦ **f. lift** montacargas **II.** tr. levantar con la horca ✦ **to f. over** FAM. aflojar, desembolsar —intr. bifurcarse.

forked (fôrkt) adj. *(fork-shaped)* ahorquillado; *(tail)* hendido.

for·lorn (fǝr-lôrn', fôr-) adj. *(sad)* acongojado; *(deserted)* abandonado, desolado; *(hopeless)* sin esperanzas.

form (fôrm) **I.** s. forma; *(figure)* figura; *(type)* clase *f*, tipo; *(convention)* convencionalismo; *(manners)* conducta, modales *m*; *(formality)* formalidad *f*; *(document)* formulario, EDUC. *(grade)* año, grado ✦ **bad f.** algo que no se hace • **for f.'s sake** por pura fórmula • **f. letter** circular **II.** tr. formar; *(to model)* moldear, modelar; *(to develop)* desarrollar; *(to conceive)* idear, concebir; *(a habit)* contraer, adquirir —intr. formarse, tomar forma.

for·mal (fôr'mǝl) **I.** adj. formal; *(according to conventions)* convencional; *(official)* oficial; *(done in proper form)* en debida forma; *(correct)* muy correcto; *(ceremonious)* ceremonioso; *(dinner, dress)* de etiqueta; *(for the sake of form)* de cumplido, formulario **II.** s. ceremonia de etiqueta; *(attire)* traje *m* de etiqueta.

for·mal·de·hyde (fôr-mǎl′də-hīd′) s. formaldehído.

for·mal·i·ty (fôr-mǎl′ĭ-tē) s. ceremonia; *(requirement)* formalidad *f*, trámite *m*; *(custom)* fórmula ♦ **as a mere f.** para *o* por cumplir ♦ pl. ceremonias, cumplidos.

for·mal·ize (fôr′mə-līz′) tr. formalizar.

for·mal·ly (:lē) adv. formalmente; *(officially)* oficialmente; *(ceremoniously)* protocolariamente, ceremoniosamente.

for·mat (fôr′mǎt′) s. *(plan)* concepción *f*, plan *m*; *(layout)* formato.

for·ma·tion (fôr-mā′shən) s. formación *f*.

for·mer (fôr′mər) adj. *(earlier)* antiguo, pasado; *(of two)* primero, anterior; *(no longer)* antiguo, ex ♦ **the f.** el primero, aquél.

for·mer·ly (:lē) adv. anteriormente, antes.

form·fit·ting (fôrm′fĭt′ĭng) adj. ajustado.

for·mi·da·ble (fôr′mĭ-də-bəl) adj. formidable; *(awesome)* tremendo, impresionante.

form·less (fôrm′lĭs) adj. informe, sin forma.

for·mu·la (fôr′myə-lə) s. [pl. **s** *o* **-lae**] fórmula; *(baby food)* mezcla nutritiva preparada.

for·mu·late (:lāt′) tr. formular.

for·ni·cate (fôr′nĭ-kāt′) intr. fornicar.

for·sake (fər-sāk′) tr. **-sook, -saken** *(to give up)* dejar, renunciar a; *(to abandon)* abandonar.

for·swear (fôr-swâr′) tr. **-swore, -sworn** abjurar de ♦ **to f. oneself** perjurar, jurar en falso.

fort (fôrt) s. fuerte *m*; *(base)* base *f* militar ♦ **to hold down the f.** permanecer en el puesto.

forte (fôrt, fôr′tā′) s. (punto) fuerte *m*.

forth (fôrth) adv. en adelante ♦ **and so f.** y cosas así • **to come f.** aparecer, adelantarse • **to go f.** ir(se) • **to put f.** *(leaves)* echar; *(argument)* adelantar.

forth·com·ing (-kŭm′ĭng) adj. *(upcoming)* próximo, venidero; *(available)* disponible.

forth·right (′rīt′) adj. directo, franco.

for·ti·eth (fôr′tē-ĭth) I. s. *(place)* cuarenta *m*; *(part)* cuadragésimo II. adj. *(place)* cuadragésimo; *(part)* cuarentavo.

for·ti·fy (fôr′tə-fī′) tr. fortificar; *(to invigorate)* fortalecer; *(food)* enriquecer; *(wine)* encabezar.

for·ti·fy·ing (:ĭng) adj. fortificante.

for·ti·tude (fôr′tĭ-tōōd′) s. fortaleza.

fort·night (fôrt′nīt′) s. quincena, quince días *m*.

fort·night·ly (:lē) I. adj. & s. (publicación *f*) quincenal II. adv. quincenalmente.

for·tress (fôr′trĭs) s. fortaleza.

for·tu·i·tous (fôr-tōō′ĭ-təs) adj. fortuito.

for·tu·nate (fôr′chə-nĭt) adj. afortunado ♦ **to be f.** *(person)* tener suerte; *(event)* ser una suerte.

for·tu·nate·ly (:lē) adv. afortunadamente.

for·tune (fôr′chən) s. fortuna; *(good luck)* suerte *f* ♦ **to make a f.** hacerse rico.

for·tune·tell·er (:tĕl′ər) s. adivino.

for·tune·tell·ing (:ĭng) s. adivinación *f*.

for·ty (fôr′tē) adj. & s. cuarenta *m*.

fo·rum (fôr′əm) s. [pl. **s** *o* **-ra**] foro.

for·ward (fôr′wərd) I. adj. *(frontal)* delantero; *(bold)* descarado; *(progressive)* avanzado; *(precocious)* adelantado II. adv. hacia adelante ♦ **looking f. to seeing you** a la espera de volverle a ver • **to bring f.** *(topic)* presentar, ofrecer; TEN. llevar (saldo) • **to come f.** presentarse, ofrecerse • **to look f. to** anticipar III. s. DEP. delantero IV. tr. *(mail)* enviar, reexpedir; *(to help advance)* promover, fomentar.

for·ward·er (:wər-dər) s. agente *m* expedidor.

for·ward·ing (:dĭng) s. envío, expedición *f*.

for·wards (fôr′wərdz) adv. (hacia) adelante.

fos·sil (fŏs′əl) s. & adj. fósil *m*.

fos·ter (fŏs′tər) I. tr. *(to bring up)* criar; *(to promote)* fomentar, promover; *(hope)* abrigar II. adj. adoptivo.

fought (fôt) cf. **fight**.

foul (foul) I. adj. *(revolting)* asqueroso; *(rotten)* podrido; *(dirty)* sucio; *(polluted)* contaminado, viciado; *(obscene)* obsceno, grosero; *(horrible)* atroz ♦ **f. play** maniobra *o* juego sucio • **to fall f. of** ponerse a malas con II. s. DEP. falta III. adv. sucio, contra las reglas IV. tr. ensuciar; *(to obstruct)* obstruir, atascar; *(to entangle)* enredarse en *o* con; DEP. cometer una falta contra ♦ **to f. up** FAM. chapucear —intr. DEP. cometer una falta; *(to tangle)* enredarse ♦ **to f. up** FAM. hacer una chapuceada.

foul-mouthed (′mouthd′) adj. malhablado.

foul-up (:up′) s. FAM. maraña, confusión *f*; MEC. falla mecánica.

found[1] (found) tr. *(to establish)* fundar; *(building, theory)* fundamentar.

found[2] tr. METAL. fundir.

found[3] cf. **find**.

foun·da·tion (foun-dā′shən) s. fundación *f*; *(basis)* fundamento; *(for cosmetics)* base *f*; CONSTR. cimientos ♦ **f. stone** primera piedra • **to lay the foundations** sentar las bases.

foun·der[1] (foun′dər) intr. *(to break down)* fracasar, venirse abajo; VET. despearse; *(to sink)* hundir.

found·er[2] s. fundador *m*.

found·ling (found′lĭng) s. expósito.

foun·dry (foun′drē) s. fundición *f*.

fount (fount) s. fuente *f*.

foun·tain (foun′tən) s. fuente *f*; *(for drinking)* surtidor *m* ♦ **f. pen** estilográfica.

foun·tain·head (:hĕd′) s. fuente *f*.

four (fôr) s. & adj. cuatro ♦ **f. hundred** cuatrocientos • **f. o'clock** las cuatro.

four-foot·ed (:fŏŏt′ĭd) adj. cuadrúpedo.

four-let·ter word (:lĕt′ər) s. palabrota.

four·square (:skwâr′) adj. *(firm)* inequívoco; *(forthright)* franco, sincero.

four·teen (fôr-tēn′) s. & adj. catorce *m*.

four·teenth (:tēnth′) s. & adj. *(place)* decimocuarto; *(part)* catorzavo.

fourth (fôrth) adj. & s. cuarto.

fourth-class (′klǎs′) adj. & adv. (por correo) abierto.

fowl (foul) I. s. [pl. inv. *o* **s**] aves *f* (en general); *(domesticated)* ave de corral; *(meat)* carne *f* de ave II. intr. cazar aves.

fox (fŏks) I. s. zorro II. tr. engañar.

fox·hole (′hōl′) s. pozo de tirador.

fox·hound (:hound′) s. perro raposero.

fox·y (fŏk′sē) adj. **-i-** taimado, astuto.

foy·er (foi′ər, foi′ā′) s. salón *m* de entrada.

fra·cas (frā′kəs) s. riña, reyerta.

frac·tion (frǎk′shən) s. MAT. fracción *f*, quebrado; *(bit)* porción minúscula, pizca.

frac·tion·al (:shə-nəl) adj. fraccionario, fraccionado; *(tiny)* minúsculo.

frac·tious (frǎk′shəs) adj. indócil, rebelde.

frac·ture (frǎk′chər) I. s. fractura II. tr. & intr. fracturar(se).

frag·ile (frǎj′əl, :īl′) adj. frágil.

fra·gil·i·ty (frə-jĭl′ĭ-tē) s. fragilidad *f*.

frag·ment (frǎg′mənt) I. s. fragmento II. tr. & intr. (′mĕnt′) fragmentar.

frag·men·tar·y (frǎg′mən-tĕr′ē) adj. fragmentario.

fra·grance (frā′grəns) s. fragancia, perfume *m*.

fra·grant (:grənt) adj. fragante.

frail (frāl) adj. *(fragile)* frágil; *(weak)* débil.
frail·ty (:tē) s. fragilidad f; *(moral)* flaqueza.
frame (frām) **I.** s. *(structure)* armadura, armazón f; *(border)* cerco, marco; *(body)* estructura corporal; CINEM. fotograma m; JER. *(frame-up)* conspiración f; AUTO. chasis m; *(bicycle)* cuadro; *(glasses)* montura ♦ **f. of mind** estado de ánimo, disposición f **II.** tr. construir, armar; *(to formulate)* formular; *(picture)* enmarcar, encuadrar; JER. *(to incriminate)* acriminar falsamente **III.** adj. de tablas, de madera.
frame-up ('ŭp') s. JER. estratagema m, maquinación f para incriminar a alguien.
frame·work (:wûrk') s. estructura; *(system)* sistema m; CONSTR. armazón f, esqueleto.
franc (frăngk) s. FIN. franco.
fran·chise (frăn'chīz') s. derecho de voto; COM. concesión f, licencia.
frank¹ (frăngk) **I.** adj. franco, sincero **II.** tr. franquear **III.** s. franquicia postal.
frank² tr. & FAM. *(hot dog)* perro caliente.
frank·furt·er ('fər-tər) s. salchicha, perro caliente.
frank·in·cense (frăng'kĭn-sĕns') s. incienso.
frank·ness (frăngk'nĭs) s. franqueza.
fran·tic (frăn'tĭk) adj. desesperado; *(pace)* frenético.
fra·ter·nal (frə-tûr'nəl) adj. fraternal, fraterno ♦ **f. twins** mellizos.
fra·ter·ni·ty (:nĭ-tē) s. (con)fraternidad f; *(organization)* asociación estudiantil masculina.
frat·er·nize (frăt'ər-nīz') intr. fraternizar.
fraud (frôd) s. fraude m; *(person)* impostor m.
fraud·u·lence (frô'yə-ləns) s. fraudulencia.
fraught (frôt) adj. cargado, lleno.
fray¹ (frā) s. *(brawl)* riña, pelea.
fray² tr. & intr. desgastar(se), deshilachar(se).
fraz·zle (frăz'əl) **I.** tr. desgastar, agotar **II.** s. ♦ **worn to a f.** completamente agotado.
freak (frēk) **I.** s. cosa extraña *o* imprevista; *(monstrosity)* fenómeno; *(whim)* capricho; JER. *(drug user)* narcómano; *(fan)* fanático **II.** intr. & tr. ♦ **to f. out** JER. alucinar; *(emotionally)* agitar(se), excitar(se).
freak·ish (frē'kĭsh) adj. extraño, raro; *(abnormal)* anormal; *(capricious)* caprichoso.
freak·y (:kē) adj. **-i-** raro, extraño.
freck·le (frĕk'əl) **I.** s. peca **II.** tr. motear, salpicar —intr. cubrirse de pecas.
freck·led (:əld) adj. pecoso.
free (frē) **I.** adj. libre; *(independent)* independiente; *(gratis)* gratis, gratuito; *(not occupied)* desocupado; *(frank)* franco; *(liberal)* generoso; *(untied)* suelto ♦ **for f.** gratis ♦ **f. and clear** libre de trabas *o* gravámenes ♦ **f. enterprise** libre empresa ♦ **f. from** *o* **of** sin ♦ **f. of charge** gratis ♦ **f. on board** franco a bordo ♦ **f. trade** librecambio ♦ **f. will** libre albedrío ♦ **to be f.** to tener la libertad para, poder ♦ **to break f.** soltarse, librarse ♦ **to feel f. to** sentirse con la libertad de ♦ **to give, have a f. hand** dar, tener carta blanca ♦ **to set f.** poner en libertad; *(slave)* emancipar; *(animal)* soltar **II.** adv. libremente; *(gratis)* gratis **III.** tr. libertar, poner en libertad; *(to emancipate)* emancipar; *(to let loose)* soltar; *(to rid)* liberar, librar; *(to untangle)* desembarazar; *(to exempt)* eximir.
free·base ('bās') intr. inhalar cocaína que ha sido purificada con éter.
free·bie/bee (:bē) s. JER. dádiva.
free·boot·er (:bō'tər) s. pirata m.
free·born (:bôrn') adj. nacido libre.

freed·man (frēd'mən) s. [pl. **-men**] manumiso.
free·dom (frē'dəm) s. libertad f; *(exemption)* exención f; *(immunity)* inmunidad f; *(privilege)* privilegio; *(ease)* soltura.
free-for-all (:fər-ôl') s. refriega, pelea.
free·hand (:hănd') adj. a pulso.
free-lance (:lăns') **I.** intr. trabajar independientemente **II.** adj. independiente.
free-lanc·er (:lăn'sər) *o* **free lance** s. persona que trabaja independientemente.
free·load (:lōd') intr. JER. vivir de arriba.
free·load·er (:lō'dər) s. JER. parásito.
free·ly (:lē) adv. libremente; *(generously)* liberalmente.
free·man (:mən) s. [pl. **-men**] ciudadano.
Free·ma·son (:mā'sən) s. francmasón m.
free-spo·ken (:spō'kən) adj. franco.
free·style (:stīl') s. estilo libre (de natación).
free·think·er (:thĭng'kər) s. librepensador m.
free·way (:wā') s. autopista.
free·will (:wĭl') adj. voluntario.
freeze (frēz) **I.** intr. **froze, frozen** helarse, congelarse; *(person)* tener frío, helarse; *(from fear)* quedarse paralizado ♦ **to f. over** helarse, congelarse ♦ **to f. to death** morirse de frío —tr. helar; *(food, assets)* congelar; *(to chill)* enfriar, refrigerar ♦ **to f. out** excluir **II.** s. congelación f; *(cold snap)* ola de frío.
freeze-dry (:drī') tr. secar por congelación.
freez·er (frē'zər) s. congelador m.
freez·ing (:ĭng) **I.** adj. glacial ♦ **it's f. cold** hace un frío tremendo **II.** s. congelación f.
freight (frāt) **I.** s. carga, flete m ♦ **f. car, train** vagón, tren de carga **II.** tr. *(to transport)* transportar, fletar; *(to load)* cargar.
freight·er (frā'tər) s. carguero, buque m de carga m.
French (frĕnch) ♦ **F. door** puertaventana ♦ **F. fries** patatas fritas ♦ **F. horn** corno francés ♦ **F. window** puertaventana.
fre·net·ic (frə-nĕt'ĭk) adj. frenético.
fren·zied (frĕn'zēd) adj. frenético.
fren·zy (frĕn'zē) s. frenesí m; *(delirium)* desvarío; *(craze)* furor m.
fre·quen·cy (frē'kwən-sē) s. frecuencia.
fre·quent (frē'kwənt) **I.** adj. frecuente **II.** tr. (-kwĕnt') frecuentar.
fres·co (frĕs'kō) s. [pl. **(e)s**] fresco.
fresh (frĕsh) **I.** adj. fresco; *(new, additional)* nuevo; *(water)* dulce; *(air)* puro; *(recent)* reciente ♦ **f. from** recién llegado de ♦ **to be f. out of** FAM. acabarse de quedar sin **II.** adv. recientemente, acabado de.
fresh·en ('ən) intr. *(wind)* refrescar ♦ **to f. up** refrescarse, asearse —tr. refrescar.
fresh·en·er (:ə-nər) s. purificador m.
fresh·et (:ĭt) s. avenida, riada.
fresh·man (:mən) s. [pl. **-men**] estudiante mf de primer año; *(novice)* novato.
fresh·ness (:nĭs) s. frescura; *(novelty)* novedad f; *(purity)* pureza.
fresh·wa·ter (:wô'tər) adj. de agua dulce.
fret¹ (frĕt) intr. **-tt-** *(to worry)* preocuparse; *(to fuss)* quejarse; *(to wear away)* gastar.
fret² s. MÚS. traste m.
fret·ful ('fəl) adj. irritable, molesto.
fret·work (:wûrk') s. calado.
Freu·dian (froi'dē-ən) adj. & s. freudiano.
fri·ar (frī'ər) s. fraile m.
fric·tion (frĭk'shən) s. fricción f ♦ **f. match** fósforo, cerilla ♦ **f. tape** cinta aisladora.
Fri·day (frī'dē) s. viernes m.

fridge (frĭj) s. FAM. refrigerador *m*, nevera.
fried (frīd) pret. y part. p. de **fry¹**.
friend (frĕnd) s. amigo ♦ **a f. of mine** un amigo mío • **f. of the family** un amigo de la casa • **to be (best) friends with** ser (muy) amigo de • **to have friends in high places** tener influencia • **to make friends** ganarse amigos • **to make friends with** trabar amistad con • **to part friends** separarse en buenos términos.
friend·less (′lĭs) adj. sin amigos.
friend·li·ness (:lē-nĭs) s. amigabilidad *f*.
friend·ly (frĕnd′lē) adj. **-i-** amable, simpático; *(warm)* amistoso; *(not hostile)* amigo; *(allied)* aliado; *(favorable)* favorable ♦ **f. advice** consejo de amigo • **f. to** favorable a • **to be f. with** ser muy amigo de • **to become f. (with)** hacerse amigo (de).
friend·ship (:shĭp′) s. amistad *f*.
frieze (frēz) s. *(band)* cenefa; ARQ. friso.
frig·ate (frĭg′ĭt) s. fragata.
fright (frīt) s. miedo, susto; FAM. *(mess)* esperpento.
fright·en (′n) tr. & intr. asustar(se), alarmar(se).
fright·en·ing (:ĭng) adj. espantoso.
fright·ful (frīt′fəl) adj. espantoso, horrible; *(terrifying)* aterrador; FAM. *(awful)* tremendo.
frig·id (frĭj′ĭd) adj. muy frío, helado; *(indifferent)* frío; MED. frígido ♦ **f. zone** zona glacial.
fri·gid·i·ty (frĭ-jĭd′ĭ-tē) s. frialdad *f*.
frill (frĭl) s. faralá *m* ♦ pl. FAM. adornos.
frill·y (′ē) adj. **-i-** con volantes o faralás; *(frivolous)* con muchos adornos.
fringe (frĭnj) s. *(trim)* franja; *(flounce)* fleco, orla; *(border)* ribete *m*; POL. grupo marginal o extremista ♦ **f. benefits** beneficios suplementarios • **on the f.** o **fringes of** al margen de.
frisk (frĭsk) I. intr. retozar, juguetear —tr. FAM. cachear, palpar (de armas) II. s. cacheo, registro (de armas).
frisk·y (frĭs′kē) adj. **-i-** *(playful)* retozón, juguetón; *(horse)* fogoso.
frit·ter¹ (frĭt′ər) tr. ♦ **to f. away** malgastar.
frit·ter² s. CUL. fritura, fritada.
friv·o·lous (frĭv′ə-ləs) adj. frívolo.
frizz (frĭz) I. tr. & intr. rizar(se), encrespar(se) II. s. rizos, bucles *m*.
friz·zle (frĭz′əl) intr. freírse chirriando.
friz·zy (frĭz′ē) adj. **-i-** muy rizado, encrespado.
fro (frō) adv. *(hacia)* atrás ♦ **to and f.** de aquí para allá.
frock (frŏk) s. vestido; *(smock)* guardapolvo; RELIG. vestido talar ♦ **f. coat** levita.
frog (frôg) s. rana; FAM. *(in throat)* ronquera.
frog·man (′măn′) s. [pl. **-men**] *(diver)* buceador *m*, buzo; MIL. hombre *m* rana.
frol·ic (frŏl′ĭk) I. s. jugueteo, diversión *f* II. intr. **-ck-** juguetear, retozar.
from (frŭm, frŏm) prep. *(distance, place)* de, desde; *(time)* de, desde, a partir de; *(origin, reason)* de, (de) parte de, a causa de, por; *(removal)* de, a; *(according to)* por, según; *(against)* de; *(among)* entre.
frond (frŏnd) s. fronda.
front (frŭnt) I. s. frente *m*; *(forefront)* parte delantera; *(first part)* principio, comienzo; *(demeanor)* postura, posición *f*; *(appearance)* apariencia; FAM. *(cover)* pantalla, fachada ♦ **from the f.** por delante, de frente • **in f. of** delante de, frente a, en frente de • **out f.** afuera • **to put on a bold f.** hacer de tripas corazón II. adj. delantero, frontal ♦ **f. door** puerta de entrada •

f. man testaferro • **f. money** depósito o pago inicial • **f. page** primera plana • **f. row** primera fila III. tr. *(to face)* dar frente a, dar a; *(to confront)* hacer frente a, afrontar —intr. ♦ **to f. on(to)** mirar hacia, dar frente a • **to f. for** servir de fachada a.
front·age (frŭn′tĭj) s. anchura de un solar o terreno; *(adjacent land)* terreno frontero ♦ **with f. on** con fachada a.
fron·tal (:tl) adj. frontal.
fron·tier (frŭn-tîr′) I. s. frontera, límite *m*; FIG. campo II. adj. fronterizo.
fron·tiers·man (:tîrz′mən) s. [pl. **-men**] habitante *m* de la frontera.
fron·tis·piece (frŭn′tĭ-spēs′) s. frontispicio.
front-line (frŭnt′lĭn′) adj. de la vanguardia.
front-page (:pāj′) adj. de primera plana.
front-run·ner (:rŭn′ər) s. el que está en ventaja en una competencia (esp. política).
front·ward (:wərd) adj. & adv. [o **-wards**] al frente, hacia el frente.
frost (frôst) I. s. escarcha; *(freezing weather)* helada II. tr. *(window)* empañar; CUL. escarchar; TEC. deslustrar; AGR. quemar —intr. ♦ **to f. over** o **up** cubrir con escarcha, empañar.
frost·bite (′bīt′) I. s. congelación *f* II. tr. **-bit, -biten** congelar.
frost·ed (frô′stĭd) adj. *(ground, cake)* escarchado; *(window)* empañado; *(glassware)* deslustrado; *(foods)* helado, congelado.
frost·ing (:stĭng) s. alcorza, escarchado.
frost·y (:stē) adj. **-i-** muy frío, de helada; *(welcome)* frío, glacial; *(hair)* canoso, cano.
froth (frôth) I. s. espuma; *(saliva)* espumarajo; FIG. trivialidades *f* II. intr. hacer espuma; *(at the mouth)* espumajear.
froth·y (frô′thē) adj. **-i-** espumoso, de espuma; *(frivolous)* frívolo, insubstancial.
frown (froun) I. s. ceño, entrecejo II. intr. fruncir el entrecejo ♦ **to f. at** mirar con ceño • **to f. (up)on** desaprobar.
frow·zy/sy (frou′zē) adj. **-i-** desaseado, desaliñado.
froze (frōz) cf. **freeze**.
fro·zen (frō′zən) I. cf. **freeze** II. adj. helado; *(food, assets)* congelado; *(very cold)* frígido; *(numb)* entumecido; *(with fear)* paralizado.
fruc·tose (frŭk′tōs′) s. fructosa.
fru·gal (frō′gəl) adj. frugal, parco.
fruit (frōt) I. s. [pl. inv. o **s**] fruta; BOT. fruto ♦ **to bear f.** dar fruto; FIG. dar resultado ♦ pl. resultados II. intr. dar fruto.
fruit·cake (′kāk′) s. torta de frutas; JER. *(crazy person)* loco.
fruit·ful (:fəl) adj. fructuoso, fructífero.
fru·i·tion (frō-ĭsh′ən) s. fruición *f* ♦ **to bring (come) to f.** realizar(se).
fruit·less (frōt′lĭs) adj. infructuoso.
fruit·y (frō′tē) adj. **-i-** de olor o sabor de fruta; *(sentimental)* sentimental.
frump·y (frŭm′pē) adj. **-i-** *(dowdy)* desaliñado; *(old-fashioned)* anticuado.
frus·trate (frŭs′trāt′) tr. frustrar.
fry¹ (frī) I. tr. & intr. freír(se) ♦ **frying pan** sartén II. s. fritada ♦ pl. patatas o papas fritas.
fry² s.inv. *(young fish)* pececillos.
fry·er (′ər) s. *(pan)* sartén *f*; *(chicken)* pollo para freír.
fuch·sia (fyō′shə) s. fucsia.
fud·dle (fŭd′l) I. tr. atontar, confundir II. s. confusión *f* ♦ **to be in a f.** estar atontado.
fud·dy-dud·dy (fŭd′ē-dŭd′ē) s. carcamal *m*.

fudge (fŭj) I. s. *(candy)* dulce *m* de chocolate; *(nonsense)* tontería II. tr. falsificar —intr. engañar ♦ to f. on dejar de cumplir con.

fu·el (fyōō'əl) I. s. combustible *m* ♦ f. cell celda electroquímica • f. oil aceite fuel *o* combustible • to add f. to the fire echar leña al fuego • to be f. for dar pábulo a II. tr. *(furnace)* alimentar; *(auto)* echar gasolina a; *(ship, plane)* abastecer de combustible a; FIG. dar pábulo a.

fu·gi·tive (fyōō'jĭ-tĭv) adj. & s. fugitivo.

fugue (fyōōg) s. fuga.

ful·fil(l) (fōŏl-fĭl') tr. -ll- *(requirements)* llenar; *(duty)* desempeñar; *(contract, promise)* cumplir (con); *(need)* satisfacer; *(ambition)* realizar.

full (fōŏl) I. adj. lleno; *(complete)* completo; *(detailed)* detallado; *(maximum)* máximo; *(crowded)* atestado; *(hotel, theater)* completo; *(entire)* entero; *(total)* total; *(figure)* amplio ♦ f. house sala repleta • f. powers plenos poderes • f. sail vela llena • f. stop GRAM. punto • f. swing en plena actividad • f. tilt a todo dar • in f. view of a plena vista de • to be f. *(person)* estar satisfecho; *(hotel)* no tener lugar • to the fullest extent al máximo II. adv. *(very)* extremadamente, muy; *(directly)* directamente, de lleno ♦ in f. swing en plena operación III. s. ♦ in f. completamente, detalladamente • to pay in f. pagar íntegramente.

full-blood·ed ('blŭd'ĭd) adj. *(purebred)* de raza *o* casta; *(vigorous)* robusto.

full-blown (:blōn') adj. BOT. abierto; FIG. desarrollado, maduro.

full-fledged (:flějd') adj. *(having full status)* cabal; ORNIT. de plumaje completo.

full-grown (:grōn') adj. crecido, maduro.

full-length (:lĕngkth') adj. *(portrait)* de cuerpo entero; *(of standard length)* de tamaño normal; *(film)* de largo metraje.

full·ness (:nĭs) s. abundancia, plenitud *f*; *(satiety)* saciedad *f*, hartura.

full-scale (:skāl') adj. *(model)* de tamaño natural; *(all-out)* en gran escala, a todo dar.

full-size(d) (:sīz[d]') adj. de tamaño natural.

full-time (:tīm') adj. de jornada completa.

ful·ly (:ē) adv. *(totally)* completamente, enteramente; *(at least)* por lo menos.

ful·mi·nate (fōŏl'mə-nāt') I. intr. *(to denounce)* tronar; *(to explode)* fulminar II. s. fulminato.

fum·ble (fŭm'bəl) intr. *(to handle)* enredarse; *(to grope)* buscar torpemente ♦ to f. for words buscar las palabras —tr. *(to handle)* manejar torpemente; *(to bungle)* estropear; DEP. *(to drop)* dejar caer ♦ to f. one's way ir a tientas.

fum·bling (:blĭng) adj. torpe.

fume (fyōōm) I. s. humo, tufo ♦ pl. gases, humo II. intr. echar humo, enfurecerse.

fu·mi·gate (fyōō'mĭ-gāt') tr. & intr. fumigar.

fun (fŭn) s. diversión *f*, alegría ♦ for f. *(as a joke)* en broma, bromeando; *(to have fun)* para divertirse • for the f. of it para divertirse • in f. en broma, bromeando • to be f. ser divertido • to have f. divertirse, pasarlo bien • to make f. of reírse *o* burlarse de • to spoil the f. aguar la fiesta • what f.! ¡qué divertido!

func·tion (fŭngk'shən) I. s. función *f*; *(ceremony)* acto, ceremonia ♦ in one's f. as en calidad de • to be a f. of estar en relación con II. intr. funcionar ♦ to f. as servir en la capacidad de.

func·tion·al (:shə-nəl) adj. funcional.

func·tion·ar·y (:nĕr'ē) s. funcionario.

fund (fŭnd) I. s. fondo ♦ pl. fondos, dinero disponible • the f. G.B. deuda pública II. tr. COM. suministrar fondos para; *(to finance)* costear; *(a debt)* consolidar.

fun·da·men·tal (fŭn'də-mĕn'tl) I. adj. fundamental II. s. fundamento.

fun·da·men·tal·ist (:ĭst) s. fundamentalista *mf*.

fund·ing (fŭn'dĭng) s. financiamiento.

fund-rais·ing (fŭnd'rā'zĭng) adj. para recaudar fondos, de recaudación de fondos.

fu·ner·al (fyōō'nər-əl) s. funeral(es) *m*; *(procession)* cortejo fúnebre ♦ f. home funeraria • f. march marcha fúnebre • f. service misa de cuerpo presente.

fu·ner·ar·y (:nə-rĕr'ē) adj. funerario.

fu·ne·re·al (fyōō-nîr'ē-əl) adj. fúnebre.

fun·gi·cide (fŭn'jĭ-sīd', fŭng'gĭ-) s. fungicida *m*.

fun·gous (fŭng'gəs) adj. fungoso.

fun·gus (fŭng'gəs) s. [pl. es *o* -gi] BOT. hongo; MED. fungo.

funk (fŭngk) s. FAM. depresión *f* ♦ to be in a f. estar desanimado.

fun·nel (fŭn'əl) I. s. *(utensil)* embudo; *(stack)* chimenea II. intr. tomar forma de embudo, encañonarse ♦ to f. through encauzarse, pasar por —tr. encauzar, dirigir.

fun·ny (fŭn'ē) I. adj. -i- *(amusing)* divertido, cómico, gracioso; *(odd)* raro, extraño; *(fishy)* sospechoso ♦ f. bone huesito de la alegría; FAM. sentido del humor • f. papers tiras cómicas, muñequitos • that's not f. eso no es ninguna gracia • to try to be f. hacerse el gracioso II. s. ♦ pl. tiras cómicas.

fur (fûr) I. s. pelo, pelaje *m*; *(pelt)* piel *f* ♦ f. coat abrigo de piel(es) II. tr. -rr- cubrir *o* forrar con pieles.

fu·ri·ous (fyōŏr'ē-əs) adj. furioso; *(speed)* vertiginoso ♦ at a f. pace a toda velocidad.

furl (fûrl) tr. & intr. enrollar(se), plegar(se).

fur·long (fûr'lông') s. estadio.

fur·lough (fûr'lō) I. s. permiso ♦ to be on f. estar de permiso II. tr. dar permiso a.

fur·nace (fûr'nĭs) s. horno.

fur·nish (fûr'nĭsh) tr. *(room, house)* amueblar; *(supplies)* suministrar; *(opportunity)* dar; *(proof)* aducir ♦ to f. with proveer de.

fur·nish·ings (:nĭ-shĭngz) s.pl. mobiliario, moblaje *m*.

fur·ni·ture (:chər) s. muebles *m*, mobiliario ♦ a piece of f. un mueble • f. store mueblería.

fu·ror (fyōŏr'ôr') s. furor *m*; *(commotion)* conmoción *f*.

fur·ri·er (fûr'ē-ər) s. peletero.

fur·row (fûr'ō) I. s. surco II. tr. surcar; *(the brow)* arrugar.

fur·ry (fûr'ē) adj. -i- peludo; *(tongue)* sarroso.

fur·ther (fûr'thər) I. adj. [comp. de **far**] *(more distant)* más lejano *o* alejado; *(additional)* otro, más; *(renewed)* nuevo II. adv. [comp. de **far**] *(extent, degree)* más; *(distance)* más lejos, más allá ♦ f. back *(space)* más atrás; *(time)* antes • f. on más adelante III. tr. promover, fomentar.

fur·ther·more (:môr') adv. además.

fur·thest (fûr'thĭst) [superl. de **far**] I. adj. *(more distant)* más lejano; *(remotest)* más remoto II. adv. *(extent, degree)* al extremo; *(distance)* más lejos.

fur·tive (fûr'tĭv) adj. furtivo.

fu·ry (fyōŏr'ē) s. furia ♦ to be in a f. estar furioso.

fuse¹ (fyōōz) s. *(wick)* mecha; ARM. espoleta.

fuse² I. tr. & intr. fundir(se) II. s. ELEC. fusible

m, plomo ♦ f. **box** caja de fusibles *o* plomos • **to blow a f.** ELEC. fundir(se) un plomo; FIG. enfurecerse.

fu·se·lage (fyōͦ'sə-läzh') s. fuselaje *m*.

fu·sil·lade (fyōͦ'sə-läd') s. fusilería *f*.

fu·sion (fyōͦ'zhən) s. fusión *f*.

fuss (fŭs) I. s. *(commotion)* alboroto, bulla; *(concern)* aspavientos; *(formalities)* cumplidos; *(quarrel)* lío ♦ **it's not worth the f.** no vale la pena • **to kick up** *o* **to make a f.** armar un lío • **to make a f. over** *(to worry)* preocuparse por; *(to pamper)* mimar II. intr. inquietarse *(over* por*)*; *(to whimper)* lloriquear; *(to object)* quejarse ♦ **to f. about** *o* **around** andar de acá para allá • **to f. with** jugar con, toquetear.

fuss-budg·et (ˈbŭjˈĭt) s. quisquilloso.

fuss·i·ness (:ē-nĭs) s. carácter quisquilloso *o* melindroso; *(meticulousness)* escrupulosidad *f*.

fuss·y (fŭsˈē) adj. **-i-** *(touchy)* susceptible, irritable; *(baby)* lloricón; *(fastidious)* quisquilloso, melindroso; *(meticulous)* concienzudo.

fu·tile (fyōͦtˈl, fyōͦˈtīlˈ) adj. inútil, vano.

fu·til·i·ty (fyōͦ-tĭlˈĭ-tē) s. inutilidad *f*.

fu·ture (fyōͦˈchər) I. s. futuro, porvenir *m* ♦ **in the f.** en lo sucesivo • **in the near f.** dentro de poco ♦ pl. COM. futuros, bienes de entrega futura II. adj. futuro, venidero.

fu·tur·ist·ic ('chə-rĭsˈtĭk) adj. futurista.

fuzz¹ (fŭz) s. pelusa.

fuzz² s. JER. policía, poli *f*.

fuzz·y (ˈē) adj. **-i-** velloso, velludo; *(indistinct)* borroso; *(confused)* confuso.

G

g, G (jē) s. séptima letra del alfabeto inglés; MÚS. sol *m*; FÍS. signo de la gravedad.

gab (găb) FAM. I. intr. **-bb-** parlotear, picotear II. s. parloteo, palique *m* ♦ **to have the gift of g.** tener mucha labia.

gab·ar·dine (găbˈər-dēnˈ) s. gabardina.

gab·ble (găbˈəl) I. intr. *(to babble)* cotorrear; *(geese)* graznar II. s. *(geese)* cotorreo, graznido.

gab·by (găbˈē) adj. **-i-** FAM. locuaz, hablador.

ga·ble (gāˈbəl) s. aguilón *m*.

gad·fly (gădˈflīˈ) s. moscardón *m*.

gadg·et (găjˈĭt) s. FAM. artilugio, dispositivo.

gadg·et·ry (:ĭ-trē) s. artilugios, dispositivos.

gaff (găf) I. s. *(hook)* garfio, gancho; *(spar)* cangrejo II. tr. enganchar.

gaffe (găf) s. metida de pata.

gag (găg) I. s. mordaza; FAM. *(joke)* chiste *m* II. tr. **-gg-** amordazar; *(to choke)* atorar, ahogar; *(to nauseate)* dar náuseas a —intr. atorarse, ahogarse.

ga·ga (gäˈgä) adj. JER. chocho, chiflado.

gage¹ (gāj) s. *(pledge)* prenda; *(challenge)* reto.

gage² s. BOT. ciruela verdal.

gag·gle (găgˈəl) s. manada (de gansos).

gai·e·ty (gāˈĭ-tē) s. regocijo, alegría.

gain (gān) I. tr. ganar; *(to acquire)* adquirir; *(respect, confidence)* granjearse; *(strenth, momentum)* cobrar; *(clock)* adelantarse; *(to advance)* avanzar —intr. *(to become greater)* aumentar; *(to become better)* mejorar; *(in value)* subir (valor) ♦ **to g. on** ganar terreno, acercarse a II. s. *(profit)* ganancia, beneficio; *(increase)* aumento ♦ pl. *(profits)* ganancias; *(acquisitions)* adquisiciones.

gain·ful ('fəl) adj. ventajoso, lucrativo.

gain·say (gān-sāˈ) tr. **-said** negar.

gait (gāt) s. paso.

gal (găl) s. FAM. muchacha, chica.

ga·la (gāˈlə, gălˈə) adj. & s. (de) gala, (de) fiesta.

ga·lac·tic (gə-lăkˈtĭk) adj. galáctico.

gal·ax·y (gălˈək-sē) s. galaxia; FIG. *(assemblage)* constelación *f*.

gale (gāl) s. *(wind)* vendaval *m*, ventarrón *m*; *(of laughter)* explosión *f*.

gall¹ (gôl) s. FISIOL. hiel *f*; FIG. *(bitterness)* rencor *m*; *(impudence)* descaro.

gall² I. s. *(sore)* matadura, rozadura II. tr. *(to chafe)* rozar; *(to exasperate)* molestar, irritar.

gal·lant (gălˈənt) I. adj. *(courageous)* gallardo, bizarro; *(dashing)* galano; *(chivalrous)* galante; *(flirtatious)* galanteador II. s. galán *m*.

gal·lant·ry ('ən-trē) s. galantería.

gall·blad·der (gôlˈblădˈər) s. vesícula biliar.

gal·ler·y (gălˈə-rē) s. galería ♦ **to play to the g.** actuar para la galería, complacer al vulgo.

gal·ley (gălˈē) s. *(ship)* galera; *(kitchen)* cocina; IMPR. *(proof)* galerada.

gall·ing (gôˈlĭng) adj. irritante, exasperante.

gal·li·vant (gălˈə-văntˈ) intr. callejear.

gal·lon (gălˈən) s. galón *m*.

gal·lop (gălˈəp) I. s. galope *m* ♦ **at a g.** al galope • **at full g.** a galope tendido II. tr. hacer galopar ♦ **to g. through** hacer de prisa —intr. galopar.

gal·lows (gălˈōz) s. [pl. inv. *o* **es**] horca ♦ **g. humor** humor negro.

gall·stone (gôlˈstōnˈ) s. cálculo biliar.

ga·lore (gə-lôrˈ) adj. FAM. en cantidad, a granel.

gal·van·ic (găl-vănˈĭk) adj. galvánico.

gal·va·nize ('və-nīzˈ) tr. galvanizar.

gam·bit (gămˈbĭt) s. *(chess move)* gambito; *(strategy)* estratagema, maniobra.

gam·ble (gămˈbəl) I. intr. *(to bet)* jugar; *(to risk)* arriesgarse ♦ **to g. on** contar con que —tr. *(to bet)* jugar, apostar; *(to risk)* arriesgar ♦ **to g. away** perder en el juego II. s. *(bet)* jugada; *(risk)* riesgo, empresa arriesgada.

gam·bler (:blər) s. jugador *m*.

gam·bling (:blĭng) s. juego.

gam·bol (gămˈbəl) I. intr. brincar, cabriolar II. s. brinco, cabriola.

game¹ (gām) I. s. juego; *(of checkers, etc.)* partida; *(of baseball, etc.)* partido; *(wild animals)* caza; *(quarry)* presa ♦ **big g.** caza mayor • **board g.** juego de mesa • **g. show** concurso televisivo • **the g. is up!** ¡se acabó la jugada! • **to be on to someone's g.** conocer el juego a alguien • **to play games** FIG. jugar, andar con trucos II. adj. *(plucky)* valeroso; FAM. *(willing)* listo.

game² adj. cojo, lisiado.

game·cock (ˈkŏkˈ) s. gallo de pelea.

game·keep·er (:kēˈpər) s. guardabosque *mf*.

games·man·ship (gāmzˈmən-shĭpˈ) s. maestría en juegos.

gam·ut (gămˈət) s. gama ♦ **to run the g.** abarcarlo todo.

gam·y (gāˈmē) adj. **-i-** salvajino.

gan·der (gănˈdər) s. ganso ♦ **to take a g. at** JER. echar una ojeada a.

gang (găng) I. s. pandilla; *(laborers)* cuadrilla; *(tools)* juego II. intr. ♦ **to g. up** formar una pandilla • **to g. up on** atacar en grupo.

gang·bust·er ('bǔs'tər) s. JER. funcionario que combate el crimen organizado ♦ **like gangbusters** FAM. a todo trapo.

gan·gling (găng'glĭng) adj. larguirucho.

gan·gly (:glē) adj. -i- larguirucho.

gang·plank (găng'plăngk') s. plancha.

gan·grene (găng'grēn') s. gangrena.

gan·gre·nous (:grə-nəs) adj. gangrenoso.

gang·ster (găng'stər) s. gángster *m*, bandido.

gang·way (găng'wā') s. *(passageway)* pasillo; *(gangplank)* plancha ♦ **g.!** ¡paso!

gaol (jāl) G.B. var. de **jail.**

gap (găp) I. s. boquete *m*, hueco; *(crack)* hendedura; GEOG. *(pass)* desfiladero; *(blank)* espacio; *(of time)* intervalo; *(disparity)* diferencia, discrepancia; *(void)* vacío; ELEC. separación *f* ♦ **to bridge the g.** salvar las diferencias ♦ **to fill a g.** compensar una deficiencia II. intr. -pp- abrirse, estar abierto.

gape (găp) I. intr. *(to yawn)* bostezar; *(to stare)* quedarse boquiabierto; *(chasm, hole)* abrirse ♦ **to g. at** mirar boquiabierto II. s. *(yawn)* bostezo; *(stare)* mirada atónita; *(hole)* boquete *m*, brecha.

gap·ing (gā'pĭng) adj. muy abierto.

ga·rage (gə-räzh', -räj') s. garaje *m*.

garb (gärb) I. s. vestidura II. tr. vestir.

gar·bage (gär'bĭj) s. basura, desperdicio; FIG. porquería ♦ **g. disposal** aparato triturador para la eliminación de basura.

gar·ble (gär'bəl) tr. *(message)* desvirtuar; *(words)* mezclar.

gar·den (gär'dn) I. s. jardín *m*; *(for vegetables)* huerto, huerta II. intr. trabajar en el jardín, cultivar el huerto III. adj. de jardín, del huerto ♦ **g. apartments** edificios de apartamentos con jardines.

gar·den·er (gärd'nər) s. jardinero; *(of vegetables)* hortelano.

gar·de·nia (gär-dēn'yə) s. gardenia.

gar·den·ing (gärd'nĭng) s. jardinería; *(of vegetables)* horticultura.

gar·gan·tu·an (gär-găn'chōō-ən) adj. enorme.

gar·gle (gär'gəl) I. intr. gargarizar, hacer gárgaras II. s. gárgara; *(medication)* gargarismo.

gar·goyle (gär'goil') s. gárgola.

gar·ish (gär'ĭsh) adj. chillón, charro.

gar·land (gär'lənd) I. s. guirnalda II. tr. enguirnaldar.

gar·lic (gär'lĭk) s. ajo.

gar·ment (gär'mənt) s. vestido, prenda de vestir.

gar·ner (gär'nər) tr. *(to store)* almacenar, acopiar; *(to accumulate)* acumular.

gar·net (gär'nĭt) s. granate *m*.

gar·nish (gär'nĭsh) I. tr. *(to embellish)* adornar; CUL. guarnecer, aderezar; DER. embargar II. s. ornamento; CUL. guarnición *f*.

gar·nish·ment (:mənt) s. DER. embargo.

gar·ret (gär'ĭt) s. buhardilla, desván *m*.

gar·ri·son (gär'ĭ-sən) I. s. guarnición *f* II. tr. *(troops)* poner en guarnición; *(post)* guarnecer.

gar·rot(t)e (gə-rŏt') I. s. garrote *m* II. tr. agarrotar.

gar·ru·lous (gär'ə-ləs) adj. gárrulo, locuaz.

gar·ter (gär'tər) s. liga ♦ **Order of the G.** Orden de la Jarretera.

gas (găs) I. s. [pl. **-(s)es**] gas *m*; *(gasoline)* gasolina; *(asphyxiant)* gas asfixiante; *(anesthetic)* gas anestésico; JER. *(idle talk)* cháchara ♦ **g. mask** máscara antigás ♦ **g. station** gasolinera ♦ **to be a g.** JER. ser divertidísimo ♦ **to step**

on the g. pisar el acelerador II. tr. -ss- asfixiar con gas —intr. JER. chacharear ♦ **to g. up** FAM. llenar el tanque (con gasolina).

gas·e·ous (găs'ē-əs, găsh'əs) adj. gaseoso.

gash (găsh) I. tr. acuchillar II. s. cuchillada.

gas·ket (găs'kĭt) s. junta, arandela.

gas·light (găs'līt') s. luz *f* o lámpara de gas.

gas·o·line/lene (găs'ə-lēn') s. gasolina, nafta.

gasp (găsp) I. intr. *(in surprise)* quedar boquiabierto; *(to pant)* jadear ♦ **to g. for air** hacer esfuerzos para respirar II. s. jadeo.

gas·sy (găs'ē) adj. -i- gaseoso.

gas·tric (găs'trĭk) adj. gástrico.

gas·tro·nom·ic ('trə-nŏm'ĭk) adj. gastronómico.

gas·tron·o·my (gă-strŏn'ə-mē) s. gastronomía.

gas·works (găs'wûrks') s.pl. fábrica de gas.

gate (gāt) s. puerta; *(of iron)* verja; FIG. *(pathway)* camino; MEC. válvula; TEAT. *(attendance)* taquilla ♦ **to get the g.** JER. ser puesto de patitas en la calle.

gate·crash·er (gāt'krăsh'ər) s. JER. calado, persona que entra sin pagar.

gate·keep·er (:kē'pər) s. portero.

gate·way (:wā') s. *(opening)* pórtico; *(access)* puerta, entrada; FIG. *(pathway)* camino.

gath·er (găth'ər) I. tr. reunir, juntar; *(to congregate)* congregar; *(to infer)* deducir; *(flowers)* coger; *(crops, thoughts)* recoger; *(to amass)* acumular; *(speed)* ganar; *(strength)* cobrar; COST. fruncir ♦ **to g. from** concluir • **to g. together** reunir, juntar ♦ **to g. up** recoger —intr. reunirse, congregarse; *(to accumulate)* acumularse, amontonarse; *(to build up)* aumentar ♦ **g. round!** ¡acérquense! • **to g. together** reunirse, juntarse II. s. frunce *m*, pliegue *m*.

gath·er·ing (:ĭng) s. *(collection)* recolección *f*; *(assembly)* asamblea, reunión *f*.

gauche (gōsh) adj. torpe, sin tacto.

gaud·y (gô'dē) adj. -i- llamativo, chillón.

gauge (gāj) I. s. *(measurement)* medida; *(size)* tamaño, extensión *f*; TEC. calibrador *m*; FIG. muestra (de carácter, habilidad); F.C. entrevía; ARM. calibre *m* II. tr. *(to measure)* medir; *(to evaluate)* estimar, evaluar; *(to determine)* determinar.

gaunt (gônt) adj. macilento, demacrado.

gaunt·let[1] (gônt'lĭt) s. *(glove)* guante *m* de manopla ♦ **to throw down, take up the g.** arrojar, recoger el guante.

gaunt·let[2] s. *(punishment)* baqueta ♦ **to run the g.** sufrir una desaprobación general.

gauze (gôz) s. gasa.

gave (gāv) cf. **give.**

gav·el (găv'əl) s. martillo.

gawk (gôk) intr. FAM. papar moscas.

gawk·y (gô'kē) adj. -i- torpe, desgarbado.

gay (gā) I. adj. alegre; *(bright)* vistoso; JER. homosexual II. s. JER. homosexual *mf*.

gaze (gāz) I. intr. mirar con fijeza, contemplar II. s. mirada fija.

ga·ze·bo (gə-zē'bō) s. [pl. **(e)s**] pérgola.

ga·zelle (gə-zĕl') s. gacela.

ga·zette (gə-zĕt') s. gaceta.

gaz·et·teer (găz'ĭ-tîr') s. diccionario geográfico.

gear (gîr) I. s. MEC. rueda dentada, engranaje *m*; AUTO. velocidad *f*, marcha; *(assembly)* tren *m*; *(equipment)* equipo, aparejos; FAM. *(belongings)* cosas ♦ **in g.** engranado • **to change** o **shift gears** AUTO. cambiar de velocidad; FIG. cambiar de objetivo • **to put into g.** engranar II. tr. MEC. engranar ♦ **to g. to** ajustar o adaptar

a • **to g. (oneself) up** prepararse.
gear·box ('bŏks') s. caja de cambios.
gear·ing (:ĭng) s. engranaje m.
gear·shift (:shĭft') s. palanca de cambios.
gear·wheel (:hwēl') s. rueda dentada.
gee (jē) interj. FAM. ¡caramba!
geese (gēs) cf. **goose.**
gee·zer (gē'zər) s. JER. viejo excéntrico, tío.
Gei·ger counter (gī'gər) s. contador m Geiger.
gel (jĕl) s. gel m.
gel·a·tin(e) (jĕl'ə-tn) s. gelatina.
ge·lat·i·nous (jə-lăt'n-əs) adj. gelatinoso.
geld (gĕld) tr. castrar, capar.
geld·ing (gĕl'dĭng) s. caballo castrado.
gem (jĕm) s. piedra preciosa, gema; FIG. tesoro, joya.
gem·stone ('stōn') s. piedra preciosa.
gen·der (jĕn'dər) s. GRAM. género; (sex) sexo.
gene (jēn) s. gene m.
ge·ne·al·o·gy (jē'nē-ŏl'ə-jē) s. genealogía.
gen·er·al (jĕn'ər-əl) I. adj. general • **g. delivery** lista de correos • **g. practitioner** médico general • **g. store** almacén • **in g.** por lo general II. s. general m.
gen·er·al·i·ty ('ə-răl'ĭ-tē) s. generalidad f.
gen·er·al·i·za·tion (jĕn'ər-ə-lĭ-zā'shən) s. generalización f.
gen·er·al·ize ('--līz') tr. generalizar —intr. hacer generalizaciones.
gen·er·al-pur·pose (jĕn'ər-əl-pûr'pəs) adj. de uso general.
gen·er·ate (jĕn'ə-rāt') tr. generar; FIG. (to produce) producir, engendrar.
gen·er·a·tion ('-rā'shən) s. generación f • **the younger g.** los jóvenes.
gen·er·a·tor ('-'tər) s. generador m.
ge·ner·ic (jə-nĕr'ĭk) adj. genérico.
gen·er·os·i·ty (jĕn'ə-rŏs'ĭ-tē) s. generosidad f.
gen·er·ous ('ər-əs) adj. generoso.
gen·e·sis (jĕn'ĭ-sĭs) s. [pl. **-ses**] génesis f.
ge·netic (jə-nĕt'ĭk) adj. genético • **genetics** s.sg. genética.
gen·ial (jēn'yəl) adj. (friendly) afable, simpático; (benign) benigno, suave.
ge·ni·al·i·ty (jē'nē-ăl'ĭ-tē) s. afabilidad f, simpatía; (pleasantness) templanza.
ge·nie (jē'nē) s. genio.
gen·i·tal (jĕn'ĭ-tl) I. adj. genital II. s. • pl. órganos genitales.
gen·i·ta·li·a ('-tā'lē-ə) s.pl. órganos genitales.
gen·ius (jēn'yəs) s. [pl. **es**] genio.
gen·o·cide (jĕn'ə-sīd') s. genocidio.
gen·re (zhän'rə) s. género, clase f.
gent (jĕnt) s. FAM. señor m, individuo.
gen·teel (jĕn-tēl') adj. (refined) fino, cortés; (stylish) gallardo, elegante.
gen·tile (jĕn'tīl') s. gentil m, pagano • **G.** persona no judía.
gen·til·i·ty (jĕn-tĭl'ĭ-tē) s. (gentry) nobleza; (politeness) gentileza, cortesía.
gen·tle (jĕn'tl) adj. **-er, -est** (kind) bondadoso, amable; (tender) dulce; (mild) suave; (tame) manso, dócil • **g. birth** bien nacido.
gen·tle·man (:mən) s. [pl. **-men**] caballero, señor m • **g.'s agreement** pacto de honor • pl. (in letters) míos señores míos o nuestros; (form of address) caballeros, señores.
gen·tle·ness (:nĭs) s. bondad f; (mildness) suavidad f; (tameness) mansedumbre f.
gen·tle·wom·an (:wŏm'ən) s. [pl. **-women**] dama, señora; (attendant) dama de compañía.

gen·try (jĕn'trē) s. personas bien nacidas; G.B. (upper classes) alta burguesía.
gen·u·flect (jĕn'yə-flĕkt') intr. hacer una genuflexión.
gen·u·flec·tion ('-flĕk'shən) s. genuflexión f.
gen·u·ine (jĕn'yōō-ĭn) adj. (real) verdadero; (authentic) genuino; (sincere) sincero.
ge·nus (jē'nəs) s. [pl. **-nera**] género.
ge·o·graph·ic/i·cal (jē'ə-grăf'ĭk) adj. geográfico.
ge·og·ra·phy (jē-ŏg'rə-fē) s. geografía.
ge·o·log·ic/i·cal (jē'ə-lŏj'ĭk) adj. geológico.
ge·ol·o·gist (jē-ŏl'ə-jĭst) s. geólogo.
ge·ol·o·gy (:jē) s. geología.
ge·o·met·ric/ri·cal (jē'ə-mĕt'rĭk) adj. geométrico.
ge·om·e·try (jē-ŏm'ĭ-trē) s. geometría.
ge·o·phys·i·cist (jē'ō-fĭz'ĭ-sĭst) s. geofísico.
ge·o·phys·ics (:fĭz'ĭks) s.sg. geofísica.
ge·o·po·lit·i·cal (:pə-lĭt'ĭ-kəl) adj. geopolítico.
ge·o·pol·i·tics (:pŏl'ĭ-tĭks) s.sg. geopolítica.
ge·o·ther·mal (:thûr'məl) adj. geotérmico.
ge·ra·ni·um (jə-rā'nē-əm) s. geranio.
ger·i·at·ric (jĕr'ē-ăt'rĭk) adj. & s. (paciente mf) geriátrico • **geriatrics** s.sg. geriatría.
germ (jûrm) s. BIOL., FIG. germen m; MED. (microbe) microbio; (bacillus) bacilo.
ger·mane (jər-mān') adj. pertinente.
Ger·man (jûr'mən) • **G. measles** rubéola • **G. shepherd** pastor alemán.
ger·mi·cide (jûr'mĭ-sīd') s. germicida m.
ger·mi·nal (:mə-nəl) adj. germinal.
ger·mi·nate (:nāt') tr. & intr. (hacer) germinar.
ger·mi·na·tion (:nā'shən) s. germinación f.
ger·on·tol·o·gy (jĕr'ən-tŏl'ə-jē) s. gerontología.
ger·ry·man·der (jĕr'ē-măn'dər) tr. dividir (una entidad política) injustamente.
ger·und (jĕr'ənd) s. gerundio.
ges·tate (jĕs'tāt') tr. gestar.
ges·ta·tion (jĕ-stā'shən) s. gestación f.
ges·tic·u·late (jĕ-stĭk'yə-lāt') intr. gesticular.
ges·tic·u·la·tion ('-lā'shən) s. gesticulación f, gesto.
ges·ture (jĕs'chər) I. s. gesto, ademán m; (token) detalle m, muestra II. intr. hacer ademán —tr. expresar con ademán.
get (gĕt) tr. **got, got(ten), -tt-** (to obtain) obtener, conseguir; (to buy) comprar; (to receive) recibir; (to win) sacar; (to attract) atraer; (to seize) agarrar, capturar; (flu, cold) coger, contraer; (to cause to become) hacer que <that got me angry eso hizo que me enfadara>; (a meal) hacer, preparar; (to bring) traer, alcanzar <g. my slippers, please tráeme las pantuflas, por favor>; (to persuade) lograr, hacer que <we got her to come with us logramos que ella viniera con nosotros>; FAM. (to possess) poseer, tener <what have you got in your hand? ¿qué tienes en la mano?>; (must) tener que <we have got to win tenemos que ganar>; (to annoy) molestar, irritar; (to punish) castigar; (to understand) comprender; (to hear) oír bien; (to puzzle) desconcertar, confundir; (to capture) coger, captar <to get the feel of coger el truco de> • **to g. across** hacer comprender • **to g. away (from)** quitar (a) • **to g. back** recuperar, recobrar • **to g. down** poner por escrito • **to g. off** (to send) mandar, enviar; (defendant) lograr la absolución para; (day) tener libre • **to g. out** (to remove) sacar; (news) difundir; (stain) quitar • **to g. out of** (information) sonsacar de; (pleasure, benefit) sacar o obtener de • **to g. over**

(with) acabar con • **to g. up** *(petition)* organizar; *(courage)* armarse —intr. *(to become)* ponerse *<he got well se puso bien>; (to turn)* ponerse, hacer *<it's getting cold empieza a hacer frío>* • **I can't g. over it** no lo puedo creer • **to g. across** cruzar • **to g. along** *(in years)* ponerse viejo; *(to manage)* arreglárselas *(on con); (to be friendly)* llevarse bien *(with con)* • **to g. along without** pasar sin, prescindir de • **to g. around** *(to travel)* viajar; *(socially)* salir mucho; *(news)* difundirse; *(an obstacle)* lograr pasar; *(a person)* engatusar • **to g. around to** encontrar tiempo para • **to g. at** *(the truth)* averiguar, descubrir; *(to mean)* querer decir • **to g. away** *(to escape)* escaparse *(from de); (to leave)* conseguir irse; *(on vacation)* ir de vacaciones • **to g. back** regresar, volver • **to g. back at** vengarse de • **to g. back to** *(to return)* volver a; *(to call back)* volver a llamar • **to g. by** arreglárselas • **to g. down to** *(business)* ponerse a; *(details)* pasar a considerar • **to g. in** *(to arrive)* llegar; *(to gain entry)* entrar; *(to return home)* regresar a casa • **to g. in with** trabar amistad con • **to g. into** *(car)* subir a; *(bed, trouble)* meterse en; *(a habit)* adquirir; FAM. *(to enjoy)* apasionarse por • **to g. off** *(train, horse)* apearse; *(work)* salir (del trabajo); *(to escape punishment)* librarse • **to g. on** *(train, horse)* montar en; *(to be friendly)* llevarse bien *(with con)* • **to g. on with** seguir con • **to g. out** *(to be over)* terminar; *(to manage to leave)* lograr salir • **to g. out of** *(bed, chair)* levantarse de; *(town)* alejarse de; *(obligation)* librarse de; *(trouble)* sacarse de; *(the way)* quitarse (de en medio); *(car)* apearse de • **to g. over** *(to finish)* terminar; *(illness)* reponerse de; *(shyness, disappointment)* superar; *(person)* olvidar; *(difficulty)* vencer; *(loss)* sobreponerse de • **to g. through** *(exam)* aprobar; *(the day, crowd)* pasar; *(to finish)* terminar; *(to manage to arrive)* llegar a su destino *(provisiones, mensaje)* • **to g. through to** *(by phone)* conseguir comunicación con; *(to be understood)* hacer comprender • **to g. to** *(to manage to)* lograr; *(to arrive)* llegar a; FAM. *(to begin)* abordar, comenzar; *(to upset)* molestar a *(alguien); (to affect)* impresionar, conmover • **to g. up** *(to stand up)* levantarse, ponerse de pie; *(out of bed)* levantarse (de la cama) • **what's gotten into him?** ¿qué le pasa?
get·a·way (ˈə-wāʹ) s. fuga, escape *m*.
get-to·geth·er (ˈtə-gĕthʹər) s. FAM. fiestecita.
get-up (gĕtʹŭpʹ) s. atavío, vestimenta.
get-up-and-go (gĕtʹŭp-ən-gōʹ) s. ambición *f*, arrojo.
gey·ser (gīʹzər) s. géiser *m*.
ghast·ly (găstʹlē) adj. -i- horrible, horroroso; *(ghostly)* cadavérico; *(awful)* atroz.
gher·kin (gûrʹkĭn) s. pepinillo.
ghet·to (gĕtʹō) s. [pl. **(e)s**] ghetto.
ghost (gōst) s. fantasma *m*, espectro; *(haunting image)* visión *f*, *(trace)* sombra, asomo ♦ **g. town** pueblo desierto • **not to have a g. of a chance** no tener la más remota posibilidad • **the Holy G.** BÍBL. el Espíritu Santo • **to give up the g.** entregar el alma.
ghost·ly (ˈlē) adj. -i- espectral, fantasmal.
ghost·writ·er (ːrīʹtər) s. escritor *m* que escribe para otro, negro.
ghoul (gōōl) s. demonio necrófago.
ghoul·ish (gōōʹlĭsh) adj. diabólico, malvado.
GI (jēʹī) s. [pl. **s** o **ʼs**] soldado (de los E.U.).
gi·ant (jīʹənt) adj. & s. gigante *m*.

gib·ber (jĭbʹər) intr. farfullar.
gib·ber·ish (ːĭsh) s. galimatías *m*, jerga.
gib·bet (jĭbʹĭt) **I.** s. horca **II.** tr. ahorcar.
gib·bon (gĭbʹən) s. gibón *m*.
gibe (jīb) **I.** intr. & tr. burlarse, mofarse (de) **II.** s. burla, mofa.
gib·lets (jĭbʹlĭts) s.pl. menudos (de ave).
gid·dy (gĭdʹē) adj. -i- *(dizzy)* mareado; *(causing dizziness)* vertiginoso; *(frivolous)* frívolo.
gift (gĭft) s. regalo, obsequio; *(donation)* donación *f*; *(talent)* talento, aptitud *f*.
gift·ed (gĭfʹtĭd) adj. *(person)* dotado, de muchas dotes; *(performance)* excepcional.
gig¹ (gĭg) s. *(carriage)* calesa.
gig² s. *(spear)* arpón *m* de pesca.
gig³ s. JER., MÚS. actuación *f*, presentación *f*.
gi·gan·tic (jī-gănʹtĭk) adj. gigantesco.
gig·gle (gĭgʹəl) **I.** intr. reírse tontamente **II.** s. risita entrecortada y tonta ♦ **to get** o **have the giggles** estar tentado de risa.
gig·gly (ːlē) adj. de risa fácil.
gild (gĭld) tr. **-ed** o **gilt** dorar.
gill¹ (gĭl) s. ICT. agalla, branquia ♦ **to look green about the gills** tener mala cara.
gill² (jĭl) s. E.U. cuatro onzas (líquidas); G.B. cinco onzas (líquidas).
gilt (gĭlt) **I.** cf. **gild II.** adj. dorado **III.** s. lámina *o* chapa de oro.
gilt-edge(d) (ˈĕjʹd]ʹ) adj. de bordes dorados ♦ **g. securities** valores de primer orden.
gim·let (gĭmʹlĭt) s. barrena de mano.
gim·mick (gĭmʹĭk) s. truco *<sales g.* truco publicitario>; *(gadget)* artefacto.
gim·mick·ry (ːĭ-krē) s. *(tricks)* trucos; *(gadgetry)* artefactos innecesarios.
gimp (gĭmp) s. JER. *(limp)* renguera, cojera; *(person)* rengo, paticojo.
gimp·y (gĭmʹpē) adj. JER. rengo, cojo.
gin¹ (jĭn) s. *(liquor)* ginebra.
gin² **I.** s. *(cotton gin)* desmotadora **II.** tr. **-nn-** desmotar (algodón).
gin·ger (jĭnʹjər) s. jengibre *m*; FAM. *(liveliness)* garra, chispa.
gin·ger·bread (ːbrĕdʹ) s. CUL. pan *m* de jengibre; *(decoration)* ornamentación excesiva.
gin·ger·ly (ːlē) **I.** adv. cuidadosamente, cautelosamente **II.** adj. cuidadoso, cauteloso.
gin·ger·snap (ːsnăpʹ) s. galletita con sabor a jengibre.
ging·ham (gĭngʹəm) s. guinga.
gin·gi·vi·tis (jĭnʹjə-vīʹtĭs) s. gingivitis *f*.
gin·seng (jĭnʹsĕngʹ) s. ginseng *m*, ginseng *m*.
gi·raffe (jə-răfʹ) s. [pl. inv. *o* **s**] jirafa.
gird (gûrd) tr. **-ed** o **girt** *(to strap)* ceñir, atar; *(to surround)* rodear ♦ **to g. oneself** prepararse.
gird·er (gûrʹdər) s. viga.
gir·dle (gûrʹdl) **I.** s. *(sash)* faja; *(belt)* cinturón *m*; *(undergarment)* faja **II.** tr. *(to encircle)* rodear; *(to belt)* ceñir, atar.
girl (gûrl) s. muchacha, chica; *(child)* niña; *(unmarried young woman)* joven *f*, señorita; *(daughter)* hija; *(sweetheart)* novia.
girl·friend o **girl friend** (ˈfrĕndʹ) s. amiga; *(sweetheart)* novia.
girl·hood (ːhŏŏdʹ) s. niñez *f*, juventud *f*.
girl·ish (gûrʹlĭsh) adj. de niña.
girth (gûrth) s. circunferencia; *(bulk)* tamaño, dimensiones *f*; *(cinch)* cincha.
gis·mo (gĭzʹmō) s. JER. cosa, artefacto.
gist (jĭst) s. esencia, quid *m*.
► **give** (gĭv) **I.** tr. **gave, given** dar; *(a gift)* regalar; *(to pay)* pagar; *(to bestow)* conferir, otor-

gar; *(to donate)* donar; *(to cause)* ocasionar, causar; *(a speech)* pronunciar; *(an illness)* transmitir, contagiar; *(to supply, provide)* proporcionar, proveer de; *(to dispense)* administrar (medicina, sacramentos); *(to yield)* ceder; *(to host)* dar (baile, fiesta); *(to devote)* dedicar, consagrar ♦ **to g. away** *(bride)* entregar (la novia) al novio; *(awards)* entregar; *(to divulge)* contar, revelar (secreto, trama); *(to sell cheaply)* regalar • **to g. back** devolver • **to g. chase** perseguir • **to g. it to someone** FAM. castigar *o* reprender a alguien • **to g. notice** *(to resign)* renunciar a (empleo); *(to fire)* despedir (de un empleo) • **to g. off** emitir, despedir (olor, vapor) • **to g. oneself up** entregarse (a las autoridades) • **to g. oneself up to** *(vice, despair)* abandonarse a; *(study, work)* dedicarse a • **to g. out** distribuir, repartir —intr. agotarse *(authority, presos)* • **to g. someone his due** reconocer a alguien sus méritos • **to g. up** *(to abandon)* abandonar, renunciar a (intento, tarea); *(to hand over)* entregar; *(business, activity)* retirarse de; *(to stop)* dejar de; *(to consider as lost)* dar por perdido • **to g. warning** prevenir, advertir —intr. hacer regalos, dar; *(to fail)* fallar; *(to yield)* ceder; *(to collapse)* caerse ♦ **to g. as good as one gets** pagar con la misma moneda • **to g. in** *(to collapse)* ceder, caerse; *(to accede)* acceder; *(to admit defeat)* darse por vencido • **to g. on(to)** dar a • **to g. out** *(from exhaustiom)* perder las fuerzas; *(to fail)* fallar, pararse; *(funds, luck)* agotarse • **to g. up** *(to resign oneself)* resignarse; *(to concede defeat)* darse por vencido; *(to lose hope)* perder las esperanzas • **to g. way** *(to yield)* ceder; *(to collapse)* caerse II. s. elasticidad *f*, flexibilidad *f*.

give-and-take ('ɔn-tāk') s. *(compromise)* toma y daca; *(of ideas)* intercambio.

give·a·way ('ə-wā') s. FAM. *(gift)* regalo; *(accidental exposure)* revelación involuntaria.

giv·en (:ɔn) I. cf. GIVE II. adj. dado ♦ **g. name** nombre de pila • **g. that** dado que.

giv·ing (:ĭng) adj. generoso, liberal.

giz·zard (gĭz'ɔrd) s. molleja.

gla·cial (glā'shɔl) adj. glacial.

gla·cier (:shɔr) s. glaciar *m*, ventisquero.

glad (glăd) adj. **-dd-** *(happy)* alegre, contento; *(cheerful)* bueno ♦ **g. to meet you** mucho gusto en conocerle • **to be g.** to alegrarse de.

glad·den ('n) tr. alegrar.

glade (glād) s. claro.

glad·i·a·tor (glăd'ē-ā'tɔr) s. gladiador *m*.

glad·i·o·lus (glăd'ē-ō'lɔs) s. [pl. **es** *o* **-li**] gladiolo, gladiolo.

glam·o(u)r (glăm'ɔr) s. encanto, hechizo.

glam·o(u)r·ize (:ɔ-rīz') tr. *(to beautify)* embellecer; *(to idealize)* idealizar, glorificar.

glam·o(u)r·ous (:ɔr-ɔs) adj. elegante, hechicero.

glance (glăns) I. intr. echar un vistazo *o* una mirada ♦ **to g. off** rozar, rebotar contra • **to g. through** *o* **at** echar un vistazo a, hojear II. s. *(glimpse)* vistazo, mirada; *(deflection)* rebote *m* ♦ **at a g.** de un vistazo • **at first g.** a primera vista • **to cast a g. at** echar una mirada a.

gland (glănd) s. glándula.

glan·du·lar (glăn'jɔ-lɔr) adj. glandular.

glare (glâr) I. intr. *(to stare angrily)* mirar con rabia; *(to dazzle)* relumbrar; *(to stand out)* saltar a la vista —tr. expresar con una mirada furibunda II. s. mirada furibunda; *(blinding light)* deslumbramiento, resplandor *m*.

glar·ing ('ĭng) adj. *(irate)* airado; *(light)* deslumbrador; *(error)* patente, manifiesto.

glass (glăs) s. vidrio, cristal *m*; *(glassware)* cristalería; *(drinking vessel)* vaso; *(mirror)* espejo ♦ pl. *(eyeglasses)* lentes, anteojos; *(binoculars)* gemelos • **dark g.** espejuelos de sol.

glass·ful ('fŏol') s. vaso.

glass·mak·ing (:mā'kĭng) s. vidriería.

glass·ware (:wâr') s. cristalería.

glass·works (:wûrks') s.sg. fábrica de vidrio.

glass·y (:ē) adj. **-i-** vítreo; *(smooth)* liso; *(eyes)* vidrioso.

glau·co·ma (glou-kō'mɔ) s. glaucoma *m*.

glaze (glāz) I. s. *(ice)* capa de hielo; CERÁM. vidriado, barniz *m*; CUL. capa de almíbar, garapiña II. tr. *(a window)* poner vidrios a; CERÁM. barnizar; CUL. garapiñar —intr. ponerse vidrioso, nublarse.

gla·zier (glā'zhɔr) s. vidriero.

gleam (glēm) I. s. destello; *(of intelligence)* chispa, pizca II. intr. destellar.

glean (glēn) tr. espigar.

glean·ings (glē'nĭngz) s.pl. cosecha, acopio.

glee (glē) s. regocijo, alegría ♦ **g. club** orfeón.

glee·ful ('fɔl) adj. regocijado, alegre.

glen (glēn) s. valle estrecho, cañada.

glib (glĭb) adj. **-bb-** *(self-assured)* desenvuelto; *(insincerely eloquent)* locuaz, de mucha labia.

glide (glīd) I. intr. deslizarse; *(furtively)* escurrirse; AVIA. planear —tr. hacer planear II. s. deslizamiento; AVIA. planeo; MÚS. ligadura.

glid·er (glī'dɔr) s. planeador *m*.

glim·mer (glĭm'ɔr) I. s. luz trémula; *(trace)* indicio ♦ **a g. of hope** un rayo de esperanza II. intr. brillar con luz trémula, lucir débilmente.

glimpse (glĭmps) I. s. vistazo, ojeada ♦ **to catch a g. of** vislumbrar II. tr. vislumbrar.

glint (glĭnt) I. s. destello, fulgor *m* II. intr. destellar.

glis·ten (glĭs'ɔn) intr. resplandecer, brillar.

glitch (glĭch) s. JER. malfuncionamiento.

glit·ter (glĭt'ɔr) I. s. centello, destello; COST. lentejuelas II. intr. relucir, centellear.

gloat (glōt) I. intr. regodearse II. s. regodeo.

glob (glŏb) s. gotita; *(lump)* pelota, masa.

glob·al (glō'bɔl) adj. *(spherical)* esférico; *(worldwide)* mundial; *(total)* global.

globe (glōb) s. globo *(terrestre)*.

globe·trot·ter ('trŏt'ɔr) s. trotamundos *mf*.

glob·u·lar (glŏb'yɔ-lɔr) adj. globular.

glob·ule (:yōbl) s. glóbulo.

glob·u·lin (:yɔ-lĭn) s. globulina.

gloom (glōom) s. *(partial)* penumbra; *(total)* tinieblas *f*; *(melancholy)* melancolía, tristeza.

gloom·y (glō'mē) adj. **-i-** *(dark)* oscuro; *(dreary)* lúgubre; *(melancholy)* triste; *(pessimistic)* pesimista.

glop (glŏp) JER. I. s. amasijo, plasta II. tr. **-pp-** de plasta.

glo·ri·fy (glôr'ɔ-fī') tr. glorificar; *(to exalt inordinately)* idealizar, poner por las nubes.

glo·ri·ous (:ē-ɔs) adj. glorioso; FAM. *(magnificent)* esplendoroso; FAM. *(wonderful)* magnífico.

glo·ry (glôr'ē) I. s. gloria ♦ **to be in one's g.** estar en la gloria II. intr. ♦ **to g. in** gloriarse de.

gloss¹ (glôs) I. s. *(luster)* lustre *m*, brillo; *(deceptive appeal)* falso brillo, oropel *m* II. tr. ♦ **to g. over** prestar poca atención a.

gloss² I. s. *(explanation)* glosa; *(glossary)* glosario II. tr. glosar.

glos·sa·ry (glô'sə-rē) s. glosario.
gloss·y (glô'sē) I. adj. -i- lustroso, brillante; *(paper)* glaseado; *(showy)* vistoso II. s. fotografía impresa en papel glaseado.
glove (glŭv) s. guante *m* ✦ **g. compartment** guantera • **hand in g.** inseparables • **to fit like a g.** quedar como anillo al dedo.
glow (glō) I. intr. resplandecer, brillar; *(coals, sky)* arder; *(from passion)* encenderse II. s. resplandor *m*, brillo; *(heat)* calor *m*; *(of sunset)* arrebol *m*; *(blush)* rubor *m*; *(physical warmth)* sensación *f* de bienestar; *(ardor)* ardor *m*, enardecimiento.
glow·er (glou'ər) I. intr. echar chispas por los ojos II. s. mirada furiosa.
glow·ing (glō'ĭng) adj. ardiente, incandescente; *(shining)* resplandeciente; *(face)* radiante; *(enthusiastic)* fervoroso.
glow-worm (:wûrm') s. gusano de luz.
glu·cose (glōō'kōs') s. glucosa.
glue (glōō) I. s. goma de pegar, pegamento; *(for wood)* cola II. tr. pegar.
glu·ey (:ē) adj. pegajoso, viscoso.
glum (glŭm) adj. -mm- *(dejected)* abatido, triste; *(gloomy)* taciturno; *(dismal)* sombrío.
glut (glŭt) I. tr. -tt- hartar, atracar ✦ **to g. the market** inundar el mercado II. s. exceso.
glu·ten (glōōt'n) s. gluten *m*.
glu·ti·nous (:əs) adj. glutinoso, pegajoso.
glut·ton (glŭt'n) s. glotón *m*.
glut·ton·ous (:əs) adj. glotón.
glut·ton·y (:ē) adj. glotonería, gula.
glyc·er·ide (glĭs'ə-rīd') s. glicérido.
glyc·er·in(e) (:ər-ĭn) s. glicerina.
glyc·er·ol (:ə-rôl') s. glicerol *m*.
gly·col (glī'kôl') s. glicol *m*.
G-man (jē'măn') s. [pl. -men] agente *m* del F.B.I.
gnarled (närld) adj. *(wood)* nudoso; *(hands)* rugoso.
gnash (năsh) tr. rechinar (los dientes).
gnat (năt) s. jején *m*.
gnaw (nô) tr. & intr. roer.
gnome (nōm) s. gnomo.
gnos·tic (nŏs'tĭk) adj. & s. gnóstico.
gnu (nōō) s. ñu *m*.
go (gō) I. intr. **went, gone** ir; *(to proceed)* seguir adelante; *(to leave)* irse, marcharse; *(to take its course)* andar, marchar *<how is everything going?* ¿cómo anda todo?>; *(to turn out)* salir, resultar *<to go well salir bien>*; *(to extend)* llegar; *(to function)* funcionar, andar; *(to be acceptable)* aceptarse *<anything goes nowadays todo se acepta hoy en día>*; *(to be sold)* venderse; *(to become)* tornarse, volverse *<he went mad se volvió loco>*; *(to say)* decir; *(to be abolished)* ser suprimido; *(to pass away)* desaparecer *<the pain has gone el dolor desapareció>*; *(to be used up)* gastarse; *(to fail, give out)* fallar; *(to have validity)* valer, ser ley *<whatever he says goes lo que él dice es ley>*; *(inheritance)* pasar; FAM. *(to wait)* esperar *<we still have another hour to go tenemos que esperar otra hora todavía>*; *(to be left)* faltar *<there are ten miles to go before we arrive faltan diez millas para llegar>* ✦ **to go about** hacer, emprender • **to go about one's business** ocuparse en los asuntos propios • **to go after** *(to follow)* seguir a; *(to attack)* caerle a, atacar • **to go around** circular • **to go away** *(to leave)* irse, marcharse; *(to pass)* pasar *(dolor, molestia)* • **to go before** preceder, ir antes • **to go by** *(to pass by)* pasar por; *(time)*

pasar; *(to follow)* ajustarse a (las reglas); *(to be guided by)* juzgar por; *(the name of)* ser conocido por • **to go down** *(to descend)* bajar; *(the sun)* ponerse; *(a ship)* hundirse; *(airplane)* caerse; *(in history)* dejar huella • **to go for** *(to fetch)* ir por, ir a traer; FAM. *(to delight in)* gustar mucho; *(to attack)* atacar; *(to be alloted)* destinarse a • **to go forward** adelantar(se) • **to go in** *(to enter)* entrar en; *(to fit)* caber, encajar • **to go in for** FAM. dedicarse a • **to go into** *(to enter)* entrar en; *(to fit)* caber o encajar en; *(a profession)* dedicarse a; *(to examine)* examinar, investigar • **to go off** *(gun)* dispararse; *(bomb)* hacer explosión; *(to sound)* sonar; *(to turn out)* resultar, salir *<everything went off well todo salió bien>* • **to go on** *(to continue)* continuar, seguir; *(to take place)* suceder, ocurrir; *(to fit)* caber en • **to go out** *(to exit, socially)* salir; *(light)* apagarse; *(fire, matches)* extinguirse • **to go over** *(to examine)* examinar; *(to rehearse)* ensayar; *(to review)* repasar; *(to succeed)* salir bien • **to go through** *(to get approval)* aprobarse; *(to experience)* pasar por, sufrir • **to go to o toward** dirigirse o acercarse a • **to go under** *(to drown)* ahogarse; *(to become bankrupt)* quebrar; *(to fail)* fracasar • **to go up** *(to ascend)* subir; *(building)* levantarse • **to go up to** acercarse a • **to go with** *(to accompany)* acompañar; *(to match)* hacer juego con; *(to date)* salir con —tr. *(to wager)* apostar; *(to tolerate)* tolerar, soportar; *(to follow)* seguir *<to go the same way seguir el mismo camino>* ✦ **to go it alone** obrar solo y sin ayuda II. s. [pl. **es**] *(try)* intento; *(turn)* turno; *(energy)* energía ✦ **to go** en actividad, ocupado • **to have a go at something** intentar algo • **to make a go of something** tener éxito en sacar adelante.
goad (gōd) I. s. aguijada; FIG. *(incentive)* aguijón *m* II. tr. aguijonear.
go-a·head (gō'ə-hĕd') s. FAM. autorización *f*.
goal (gōl) s. meta; DEP. *(structure)* portería; *(score)* gol *m*, tanto ✦ **g. post** poste.
goal·keep·er ('kē'pər) s. portero, guardameta *m*.
goat (gōt) s. cabra, macho cabrío; *(scapegoat)* cabeza de turco ✦ **to get someone's g.** FAM. molestar o enojar a alguien.
goat·ee (gō-tē') s. perilla, barbas de chivo.
goat·skin (gōt'skĭn') s. piel *f* de cabra; *(container)* bota.
gob (gŏb) s. pedazo ✦ pl. FAM. gran cantidad.
gob·ble¹ (gŏb'əl) tr. devorar, engullir ✦ **to g. up** FAM. agotar rápidamente, acabar con.
gob·ble² I. s. gluglú *m*, graznido (del pavo) II. intr. gluglutear.
gob·ble·dy·gook (:dē-gŏŏk') s. FAM. blablablá.
go-be·tween (gō'bĭ-twēn') s. intermediario.
gob·let (gŏb'lĭt) s. copa.
gob·lin (gŏb'lĭn) s. duende *m*, trasgo.
god (gŏd) s. dios; *(idol)* ídolo ✦ **G.** Dios.
god·child ('chīld') s. [pl. -dren] ahijado, -a.
god·daugh·ter (:dô'tər) s. ahijada.
god·dess (:ĭs) s. diosa.
god·fa·ther (:fä'thər) s. padrino.
god·for·sak·en (:fər-sā'kən) adj. remoto; *(desolate)* desolado, abandonado.
god·head (:hĕd') s. divinidad *f* ✦ **G.** Dios.
god·less (:lĭs) adj. descreído, ateo.
god·like (:līk') adj. como dios; *(divine)* divino.
god·li·ness (:lē-nĭs) s. piedad *f*; *(divinity)* divinidad *f*.
god·ly (:lē) adj. -i- piadoso, pío; *(divine)* di-

vino.

god·moth·er (:mŭth′ər) s. madrina.

god·par·ent (:pâr′ənt) s. padrino, madrina.

god·send (:sĕnd′) s. cosa llovida del cielo.

god·son (:sŭn′) s. ahijado.

go·get·ter (gō′gĕt′ər) s. FAM. buscavidas *mf.*

gog·gle (gŏg′əl) I. intr. mirar con los ojos desorbitados II. s. ♦ pl. gafas, anteojos.

gog·gle-eyed (:īd′) adj. do ojos saltones.

go·ing (gō′ĭng) I. s. *(departure)* ida, partida; *(condition underfoot)* piso; FAM. *(progress)* progreso, marcha ♦ **good g.!** ¡muy bien! II. adj. *(working)* que funciona; *(flourishing)* que marcha; *(prevailing)* actual, corriente.

go·ing-o·ver (:ō′vər) s. FAM. inspección *f*; *(beating)* paliza; *(reprimand)* castigo.

go·ings-on (gō′ĭngz-ŏn′) s.pl. actividades *f.*

goi·ter (goi′tər) s. bocio.

gold (gōld) I. s. oro II. adj. *(made of gold)* de oro; *(golden)* dorado.

gold·en (gōl′dən) adj. dorado; *(voice, epoch)* de oro; *(hair)* rubio; *(opportunity)* excelente ♦ **g. mean** justo medio.

gold-filled (gōld′fĭld′) adj. chapado de oro.

gold·finch (:fĭnch′) s. jilguero, cardelina.

gold·fish (:fĭsh′) s. [pl. inv. *o* **es**] pececillo de color.

gold·smith (:smĭth′) s. orfebre *m,* orífice *m.*

golf (gŏlf) I. s. golf *m* II. intr. jugar al golf.

golf·er (gŏl′fər) s. golfista *mf.*

gol·ly (gŏl′ē) interj. FAM. ¡Dios mío!, ¡caramba!

go·nad (gō′năd′) s. gónada.

gon·do·la (gŏn′dl-ə) s. góndola; F.C. batea.

gon·do·lier (′-îr′) s. gondolero.

gone (gôn) I. cf. **go** II. adj. *(past)* pasado, ido; *(dead)* muerto; *(ruined)* arruinado; *(lost)* perdido; *(exhausted)* agotado ♦ **to be g.** *(departed)* haberse ido; *(disappeared)* haber desaparecido, faltar; *(used up)* haberse acabado; *(away)* estar afuera, irse ♦ **to be g. on** FAM. estar loco por.

gon·er (gô′nər) s. FAM. persona condenada *o* arruinada.

gong (gông) s. gong *m,* batintín *m.*

gon·or·rhe·a (gŏn′ə-rē′ə) s. gonorrea.

goo (gᴏᴏ) s. FAM. substancia pegajosa; *(drivel)* sentimentalismo.

goo·ber (gᴏᴏ′bər) s. cacahuete *m,* maní *m.*

good (gᴏᴏd) I. adj. **better, best** *(beneficial)* beneficioso; *(thorough)* completo; *(valid)* válido; *(genuine)* auténtico; *(ample)* abundante; *(full)* más de <*I waited a g. hour* esperé más de una hora>; *(pleasant)* agradable; *(favorable)* favorable; *(reliable)* digno de confianza ♦ **a g.** turn un favor, una bondad • **as g. as** prácticamente, casi • **g. for nothing** inútil • **how g. of you** muy amable de su parte • **g. looks** buen parecer • **in g. standing** de buena reputación • **that's a g. one!** JER. ¡un buen chiste! • **to be g.** at tener capacidad *o* talento para • **to be g. for** *(to last)* durar; *(to have credit)* tener crédito hasta; *(to be beneficial)* hacer bien • **to be g. to someone** ser bueno para con alguien • **to be no g.** ser inútil, no servir para nada • **to be g. enough** to tener la bondad de • **to have a g. time** divertirse, pasarlo bien • **to hold g.** valer, tener validez • **to make g.** *(to prosper)* prosperar; *(a debt)* cubrir; *(a promise)* cumplir II. s. bien *m*; *(goodness)* bondad *f* ♦ **for g.** para siempre • **the g.** lo bueno • **to come to no g.** terminar mal ♦ pl. *(wares, belongings)* bienes; *(merchandise)* mercancías, géneros; *(fabric)* tela • **g. and chattels** muebles y enseres • **to**

deliver the g. cumplir lo prometido • **to have the g. on someone** tener pruebas de culpabilidad contra alguien III. adv. FAM. bien ♦ **g. and proper** por las buenas • **to do one g.** sentarle bien • **to feel g.** *(satisfied)* estar satisfecho; *(well)* sentirse bien; *(pleasurable)* ser agradable, dar gusto IV. interj. ¡bueno!, ¡muy bien!

good-by(e) (-bī′) I. interj. ¡adiós!, ¡hasta luego! II. s. [pl. **(e)s**] adiós, despedida.

good-for-noth·ing (-fər-nŭth′ĭng) I. s. haragán *m,* inútil *m* II. adj. inútil, sin valor.

good-heart·ed (:här′tĭd) adj. bondadoso.

good-hu·mored (:hyᴏᴏ′mərd) adj. jovial, alegre.

good-look·ing (:lᴏᴏk′ĭng) adj. bien parecido.

good·ly (:lē) adj. **-i-** *(attractive)* atractivo, agradable; *(large)* grande, considerable.

good-na·tured (:nā′chərd) adj. afable, amable.

good·ness (:nĭs) I. s. bondad *f* II. interj. ¡Dios mío!, ¡Ave María!

good-sized (:sīzd′) adj. bastante grande.

good-tem·pered (:tĕm′pərd) adj. afable.

good·y (:ē) FAM. I. s. golosina, dulce *m* II. interj. ¡qué bien!

good·y-good·y (:ē;ē) adj. & s. santurrón *m.*

goo·ey (gᴏᴏ′ē) adj. pegajoso, viscoso.

goof (gᴏᴏf) JER. I. s. *(fool)* bobo, simplón *m*; *(mistake)* disparate *m,* pifia II. intr. meter la pata ♦ **to g. off** *o* **around** holgazanear.

goof-off (′-ôf′) s. JER. haragán *m,* holgazán *m.*

goof·y (gᴏᴏ′fē) adj. **-i-** JER. tonto, ridículo.

gook (gᴏᴏk) s. JER. mugre *f,* suciedad *f.*

goon (gᴏᴏn) s. FAM. *(thug)* terrorista pagado; JER. *(stupid person)* estúpido, tonto.

goose (gᴏᴏs) s. [pl. **geese**] ganso ♦ **g. bumps** *o* **flesh** carne de gallina • **to cook one's g.** FAM. malograrle los planes a uno.

goose-step (′stĕp′) intr. **-pp-** ir a paso de ganso.

go·pher (gō′fər) s. ardilla terrestre.

Gor·di·an knot (gôr′dē-ən) s. nudo gordiano.

gore[1] (gôr) tr. cornear.

gore[2] s. *(cloth)* sesga, nesga.

gore[3] s. *(blood)* sangre coagulada.

gorge (gôrj) I. s. *(ravine)* desfiladero; *(throat)* garganta II. tr. hartar, atiborrar —intr. ♦ **to g. oneself** hartarse y atiborrarse.

gor·geous (gôr′jəs) adj. *(beautiful)* hermosísimo; *(magnificent)* magnífico, espléndido.

go·ril·la (gə-rĭl′ə) s. gorila *m.*

go·ry (gôr′ē) adj. **-i-** *(bloody)* ensangrentado; *(fight)* sangriento.

gosh (gŏsh) interj. ¡cielos!, ¡Dios!

gos·ling (gŏz′lĭng) s. ansarino.

gos·pel (gŏs′pəl) s. evangelio ♦ **g. meeting** reunión evangélica.

gos·sa·mer (gŏs′ə-mər) I. s. telaraña fina; *(fabric)* gasa II. adj. muy delgado, muy fino.

gos·sip (gŏs′ĭp) I. s. chismes *m*; *(gossiper)* chismoso ♦ **g. column** noticias sociales II. intr. chismear, chismorrear.

gos·sip·mon·ger (:mŭng′gər) s. chismoso.

gos·sip·y (gŏs′ĭ-pē) adj. chismoso.

got, got·ten (gŏt; gŏt′n) cf. **get.**

Goth·ic (gŏth′ĭk) adj. gótico.

gouge (gouj) I. s. *(tool)* gubia; *(cut)* muesca II. tr. escoplear *o* cortar (con una gubia); JER. *(to overcharge)* estafar ♦ **to g. out** excavar.

gourd (gôrd) s. calabaza.

gour·mand (gᴏᴏr-mänd′) s. goloso, glotón *m.*

gour·met (gᴏᴏr-mā′) s. gastrónomo.

gout (gout) s. gota.

gov·ern (gŭv′ərn) tr. gobernar; *(to determine)* determinar —intr. gobernar.

gov·ern·a·ble (:ər-nə-bəl) adj. gobernable.

gov·er·nance (:nəns) s. gobierno.

gov·ern·ess (:nĭs) s. institutriz *f.*

gov·ern·ment (gŭv′ərn-mənt) s. & adj. (del) gobierno.

gov·ern·men·tal (′-mĕn′tl) adj. gubernamental, gubernativo.

gov·er·nor (gŭv′ər-nər) s. gobernador *m*; MEC. *(regulator)* regulador automático.

gov·er·nor·ship (:shĭp′) s. gobierno.

gown (goun) s. vestido (de etiqueta); *(night-gown)* camisón *m*; *(ceremonial robe)* toga.

grab (grăb) I. tr. **-bb-** *(to seize)* agarrar, coger; *(to snatch)* arrebatar; JER. *(to attract)* cautivar ♦ **to g. a bite to eat** comer algo a la carrera —intr. ♦ **to g.** at tratar de arrebatar II. s. ♦ **to make a g.** at tratar de agarrar • **up for grabs** disponible.

grab·by (ē) adj. **-i-** codicioso.

grace (grās) I. s. gracia; *(reprieve)* plazo; *(at table)* bendición *f* de la mesa ♦ **by the g. of** gracias a • **g. period** plazo de respiro • **to be in the good graces of** gozar del favor de • **to fall from g.** caer en desgracia • **to say g.** bendecir la mesa II. tr. adornar, embellecer ♦ **to g. with** honrar con.

grace·ful (′fəl) adj. agraciado, elegante.

grace·less (:lĭs) adj. sin gracia; *(clumsy)* torpe.

gra·cious (grā′shəs) adj. *(courteous)* amable, cortés; *(kind)* compasivo; *(elegant)* elegante ♦ **goodness g.!** *o* **g. me!** ¡válgame Dios!

grad (grăd) s. FAM. graduado.

gra·date (grā′dāt′) tr. & intr. graduar(se).

gra·da·tion (grā-dā′shən) s. gradación *f*, graduación *f*; *(of colors)* degradación *f.*

grade (grād) I. s. *(degree, rank)* grado; *(quality)* calidad *f*; EDUC. *(class)* año, curso; *(mark)* nota; *(slope)* pendiente *f* ♦ **g. A** de primera • **g. crossing** paso a nivel • **g. school** escuela primaria • **to make the g.** FAM. tener éxito II. tr. *(to classify)* clasificar; *(an exam)* calificar; *(a student)* dar nota a; *(to level)* nivelar.

gra·di·ent (grā′dē-ənt) s. inclinación *f.*

grad·u·al (grăj′ōō-əl) adj. gradual, paulatino.

grad·u·ate (grăj′ōō-āt′) I. tr. & intr. graduar(se) ♦ **to g. as** recibirse de II. adj. & s. graduado, diplomado III. s. graduate ♦ **g. school** escuela para graduados.

grad·u·a·tion (′-′shən) s. graduación *f*; *(commencement)* entrega de diplomas.

graf·fi·ti (grə-fē′tē) s.pl. inscripciónes *f* en las paredes.

graft[1] (grăft) AGR., MED. I. tr. & int. injertar(se) II. s. injerto.

graft[2] I. s. *(crime)* concusión *f*, extorsión *f* II. tr. & intr. extorsionar.

gra·ham (grā′əm) s. harina de trigo entero.

grain (grān) s. grano; *(cereals)* cereales *m*; *(bit)* pizca, asomo; *(in wood)* fibra; *(in leather)* flor *f*; *(texture)* textura ♦ **to go against one's g.** ir contra el carácter de uno • **with a g. of salt** con reservas.

grain·y (grā′nē) adj. **-i-** *(granular)* granoso, granular; *(veined)* veteado.

gram (grăm) s. gramo.

gram·mar (grăm′ər) s. gramática ♦ **g. school** escuela primaria; G.B. escuela secundaria.

gram·mar·i·an (grə-mâr′ē-ən) s. gramático.

gram·mat·i·cal (:măt′ĭ-kəl) adj. gramatical.

gramme (grăm) G.B. var. de **gram**.

gram·o·phone (grăm′ə-fōn′) s. gramófono.

gran·a·ry (grān′ə-rē) s. granero.

grand (grănd) I. adj. grandioso, magnífico; *(principal)* principal; *(sumptuous)* suntuoso; *(dignified)* ilustre, distinguido; *(style)* elevado; *(wonderful)* fenomenal ♦ **g. jury** jurado de acusación • **g. larceny** robo de mayor cuantía • **g. piano** piano de cola • **the g. total** la suma total • **to have a g. time** pasarlo fenomenalmente II. s. piano de cola; JER. mil dólares.

grand·aunt (′ănt′, ′änt′) s. tía abuela.

grand·child (:chīld′) s. [pl. **-dren**] nieto, -a.

grand-dad(·dy) (grăn′dăd′[ē]) s. abuelo, abuelito; *(archetype)* arquetipo.

grand·daugh·ter (:dô′tər) s. nieta.

gran·deur (grăn′jər) s. grandeza.

grand·fa·ther (grănd′fä′thər) s. abuelo ♦ **g. clock** reloj de pie *o* de caja.

gran·dil·o·quence (grăn-dĭl′ə-kwəns) s. grandilocuencia.

gran·dil·o·quent (:kwənt) adj. grandilocuente.

gran·di·ose (grăn′dē-ōs′) adj. grandioso; *(style)* pomposo; *(scheme)* ambicioso.

grand·ma (grăn′mä′) s. FAM. abuelita.

grand·moth·er (grănd′mŭth′ər) s. abuela.

grand·pa (grăn′pä′) s. FAM. abuelo, abuelito.

grand·par·ent (grănd′pâr′ənt) s. abuelo, -a.

grand·son (:sŭn′) s. nieto.

grand·stand (:stănd′) I. s. tribuna II. intr. actuar de manera ostentosa.

grange (grānj) s. G.B. granja, finca.

gran·ite (grăn′ĭt) s. granito.

gran·ny/nie (grăn′ē) s. abuelita; *(fussy person)* persona minuciosa.

grant (grănt) I. tr. *(to concede)* conceder; *(to bestow)* otorgar; *(to admit)* admitir ♦ **granted** *o* **granting that** suponiendo que • **to take it for granted** dar por sentado • **to take someone for granted** no apreciar suficientemente a alguien II. s. concesión *f*; *(donation)* donación *f*; *(scholarship)* beca; DER. *(transfer)* cesión *f.*

gran·u·lar (grăn′yə-lər) adj. granular.

gran·u·late (:lāt′) tr. & intr. granular(se).

gran·ule (grăn′yōōl) s. gránulo.

grape (grāp) s. uva.

grape·fruit (′frōōt′) s. toronja, pomelo.

grape·shot (:shŏt′) s. metralla.

grape·vine (:vīn′) s. vid *f*, parra ♦ **through the g.** por medio de chismes.

graph (grăf) I. s. gráfico, diagrama *m* ♦ **g. paper** papel cuadriculado II. tr. representar mediante un gráfico *o* diagrama.

graph·ic (′ĭk) I. adj. gráfico II. s. ilustración gráfica ♦ **graphics** sg. *o* pl. *(drawing)* dibujo lineal; ARTE. artes gráficas.

graph·ite (grăf′īt′) s. grafito.

grap·ple (grăp′əl) I. s. garfio II. tr. MARÍT. aferrar (con un garfio); *(to grip)* agarrar —intr. luchar cuerpo a cuerpo ♦ **to g. with** afrontar.

grasp (grăsp) I. tr. *(to seize)* agarrar, asir; *(to clasp)* apretar; *(to comprehend)* captar —intr. ♦ **to g.** at tratar de agarrar II. s. *(grip)* apretón *m*; *(embrace)* abrazo; FIG. comprensión *f* ♦ **beyond, within one's g.** fuera del, al alcance de uno • **to have a good g. of** dominar.

grasp·ing (grăs′pĭng) adj. avaricioso.

grass (grăs) s. hierba; *(lawn)* césped *m*; *(pasture)* pasto; JER. *(marijuana)* yerba.

grass·hop·per (′hŏp′ər) s. saltamontes *m.*

grass·land (:lănd′) s. pradera, prado.

grass·roots (:rōōts′) s.pl. nivel *m* local (de la organización política).

grass·y (:ē) adj. **-i-** con mucha hierba.

grate¹ (grāt) I. tr. CUL. rallar; *(teeth)* hacer rechinar, FIG. irritar —intr. rechinar ♦ **to g. on** irritar II. s. *(of metal)* chirrido; *(of teeth)* rechinamiento.

grate² s. *(grill)* reja, verja; *(for coals)* parrilla.

grate·ful (grāt′fəl) adj. agradecido.

grat·er (grā′tər) s. rallador *m*.

grat·i·fi·ca·tion (grăt′ə-fĭ-kā′shən) s. gratificación *f*.

grat·i·fy (grăt′ə-fī′) tr. complacer, satisfacer.

grat·ing (grā′tĭng) adj. *(rasping)* discordante, malsonante; *(irritating)* molesto.

grat·is (grăt′ĭs) adj. & adv. gratis.

grat·i·tude (grăt′ĭ-tōōd′) s. gratitud *f*.

gra·tu·i·tous (grə-tōō′ĭ-təs) adj. gratuito.

gra·tu·i·ty (:tē) s. propina.

grave¹ (grāv) s. tumba, sepultura; *(pit)* fosa.

grave² adj. grave, serio; *(dignified)* solemne.

grave·dig·ger (′dĭg′ər) s. sepulturero.

grav·el (grăv′əl) s. ripio, grava.

grave·stone (grāv′stōn′) s. lápida.

grave·yard (:yärd′) s. cementerio, camposanto.

grav·i·tate (grăv′ĭ-tāt′) intr. gravitar ♦ **to g. toward** tender hacia, ser atraído por.

grav·i·ta·tion (′-tā′shən) s. gravitación *f*.

grav·i·ty (grăv′ĭ-tē) s. gravedad *f*; *(solemnity)* solemnidad *f*.

gra·vy (grā′vē) s. *(juices)* jugo; *(sauce)* salsa; JER. *(easy gain)* breva ♦ **g. boat** salsera.

gray (grā) I. s. gris II. adj. gris; *(hair)* cano ♦ **g. area** zona no definida • **to go** *o* **turn g.** encanecer.

gray·ish (′ĭsh) adj. grisáceo.

graze¹ (grāz) intr. *(to feed)* pacer, pastar —tr. apacentar.

graze² I. tr. & intr. *(to brush against)* rozar II. s. rozadura.

grease (grēs) I. s. grasa ♦ **g. monkey** JER. mecánico • **g. paint** maquillaje II. tr. engrasar, untar.

greas·y (grē′sē, grē′zē) adj. **-i-** *(grease-coated)* engrasado; *(fatty)* grasoso; *(dirty)* grasiento.

great (grāt) I. adj. grande; *(age)* avanzado; FAM. *(very good)* magnífico, bárbaro ♦ **a g. while** mucho tiempo • **to be g. at** FAM. ser un hacha en • **to be g. friends** FAM. ser muy amigos • **to have a g. time** pasarlo en grande II. s. grande *m* III. adv. FAM. muy bien.

great·coat (:kōt′) s. sobretodo, abrigo.

great-grand·child (-grănd′chīld′) s. [pl. **-dren**] bisnieto, -a.

great-grand·daugh·ter (:dô′tər) s. bisnieta.

great-grand·fa·ther (:fä′thər) s. bisabuelo.

great-grand·moth·er (:mŭth′ər) s. bisabuela.

great-grand·par·ent (:pâr′ənt) s. bisabuelo, -a.

great-grand·son (:sŭn′) s. bisnieto.

great·ly (grāt′lē) adv. muy, mucho.

greed (grēd) s. *(for wealth)* codicia, avaricia; *(for food)* gula, glotonería.

greed·y (grē′dē) adj. **-i-** *(avaricious)* codicioso; *(gluttonous)* glotón *m*; *(eager)* ávido.

green (grēn) s. verde *m*; *(verdure)* verdor *m*; *(lawn)* césped *m* ♦ **g. bean** habichuela *o* judía verde • **g. thumb** FAM. habilidad para la jardinería ♦ pl. verduras II. adj. verde; *(sickly)* pálido; *(raw)* inexperto, novato ♦ **he is g. with envy** se le come la envidia.

green·back (′băk′) s. FAM. billete *m*.

green·er·y (grē′nə-rē) s. follaje *m*, verdor *m*.

green·gro·cer (grēn′grō′sər) s. G.B. verdulero.

green·horn (:hôrn′) s. novato, bisoño.

green·house (:hous′) s. invernadero.

green·ish (grē′nĭsh) adj. verdoso.

greet (grēt) tr. dar la bienvenida, saludar; *(news, fact)* recibir; *(one's eyes, ears)* presentarse a.

greet·ing (grē′tĭng) s. saludo ♦ **g. card** tarjeta.

gre·gar·i·ous (grĭ-gâr′ē-əs) adj. *(group-forming)* gregario; *(sociable)* sociable.

grem·lin (grĕm′lĭn) s. duende *mf*.

gre·nade (grə-nād′) s. granada.

grew (grōō) cf. **grow**.

grey (grā) var. de **gray**.

grey·hound (′hound′) s. galgo.

grid (grĭd) s. *(grating)* rejilla; *(on a map)* cuadrícula; ELEC. *(network)* red *f*.

grid·dle (grĭd′l) s. plancha.

grid·i·ron (grĭd′ī′ərn) s. CUL. parrilla; *(football field)* campo de rugby americano.

grid·lock (grĭd′lŏk′) s. embotellamiento de tráfico.

grief (grēf) s. *(sorrow)* pena, congoja; *(trouble)* desgracia ♦ **to come to g.** fracasar, sufrir un desastre.

griev·ance (grē′vəns) s. *(cause)* motivo de queja; *(complaint)* queja.

grieve (grēv) tr. dar pena, afligir —intr. apenarse, afligirse; *(to mourn)* lamentarse.

griev·ous (grē′vəs) adj. *(causing grief)* penoso; *(serious)* serio, grave.

grill (grĭl) I. tr. *(to broil)* asar a la parrilla; FAM. *(to cross-examine)* asar II. s. *(rack)* parrilla; *(food)* asado; *(restaurant)* restaurante *m*.

grill(e) (grĭl) s. *(grate)* reja; *(at window)* verja.

grim (grĭm) adj. **-mm-** *(unrelenting)* implacable; *(forbidding)* imponente, terrible; *(ghastly)* macabro; *(gloomy)* lúgubre ♦ **the g. truth** la escueta verdad.

grim·ace (grĭm′ĭs) I. s. mueca II. intr. hacer muecas.

grime (grīm) s. mugre *f*.

grim·y (grī′mē) adj. **-i-** mugriento.

grin (grĭn) I. intr. **-nn-** sonreír ♦ **to g. and bear it** soportar estoicamente II. s. sonrisa abierta.

grind (grīnd) I. tr. **ground** *(to crush)* triturar, pulverizar; *(to sharpen)* amolar; *(a lens)* pulir; *(glass)* esmerilar; *(teeth)* hacer rechinar; *(coffee, wheat)* moler; *(meat)* picar ♦ **to g. down** *(to wear away)* desgastar; *(to oppress)* agobiar, oprimir • **to g. out** producir rutinariamente • **to g. up** triturar —intr. *(to mill)* molerse; *(brake, gears)* chirriar, ir dando chirridos; FAM. *(to study hard)* quemarse las pestañas estudiando; *(to work hard)* trabajar mucho II. s. FAM. *(student)* empollón *m*; *(task)* trabajo pesado ♦ **to get back to the g.** volver a los libros *o* al trabajo.

grind·stone (′stōn′) s. muela.

grip (grĭp) I. s. *(firm grasp)* asimiento; *(of hands)* apretón *m*; *(control)* control *m*; *(handle)* asidero; *(suitcase)* maleta ♦ **to come to grips with** afrontar, habérselas con • **to get a good g. on** agarrar bien • **to get a g. on oneself** controlarse, calmarse • **to have a good g. on** tener un buen dominio de II. tr. **-pp-** *(to seize)* agarrar; *(to clasp)* apretar; FAM. *(to enthrall)* cautivar —intr. agarrarse.

gripe (grīp) FAM. I. tr. fastidiar —intr. quejarse *(about* de) II. s. queja.

grippe (grĭp) s. gripe *f*, influenza.

gris·ly (grĭz′lē) adj. espantoso, horroroso.
grist (grĭst) s. molienda ♦ **to be g. for the mill** ser provechoso.
gris·tle (grĭs′əl) s. cartílago.
grit (grĭt) I. s. *(granules)* granitos de arena; FAM. *(pluck)* agallas, valor *m* II. tr. **-tt-** ♦ **to g. one's teeth** FAM. apretar las dientes.
grits (grĭts) s.pl. maíz *m* a medio moler.
grit·ty (grĭt′ē) adj. **-i-** arenoso.
griz·zly (grĭz′lē) I. adj. **-i-** grisáceo II. s. oso gris.
groan (grōn) I. intr. *(to moan)* gemir; *(to creak)* crujir (bajo mucho peso) —tr. decir *o* indicar con gemidos II. s. gemido.
gro·cer (grō′sər) s. tendero, almacenero.
gro·cer·y (:sə-rē) s. tienda de comestibles, almacén *m* ♦ **g. store** almacén ♦ pl. comestibles.
grog (grŏg) s. grog *m* (esp. ron con agua).
grog·gy (grŏg′ē) adj. **-i-** *(dazed)* atontado; *(shaky)* tambaleante.
groin (groin) s. ANAT. ingle *f*; ARQ. arista.
groom (grōōm) I. s. mozo de caballos; *(bridegroom)* novio II. tr. *(horses)* cuidar; *(person)* preparar *(for* para) ♦ **grooming** acicaladura ♦ **to g. oneself** arreglarse, acicalarse.
groove (grōōv) I. s. ranura; *(of a record)* surco; *(routine)* rutina ♦ **in the g.** JER. en plena forma ♦ **to get into the g. of things** acostumbrarse II. tr. acanalar —intr. ♦ **to g. on** JER. disfrutar de.
grope (grōp) intr. andar a tientas ♦ **to g. for** buscar a tientas —tr. tentar.
gross (grōs) I. adj. *(income, weight)* bruto; *(error, ignorance)* craso; *(vulgar)* grosero; *(disgusting)* repugnante; *(unrefined)* ordinario, tosco ♦ **g. amount** suma total ♦ **g. injustice** injusticia notoria • **g. national product** producto nacional bruto II. s. total *m*; *(twelve dozen)* gruesa ♦ **by the g.** en gruesas III. tr. recaudar dinero en bruto ♦ **to g. out** JER. dar asco a.
gro·tesque (grō-tĕsk′) adj. grotesco.
grot·to (grŏt′ō) s. [pl. **(e)s**] gruta.
grouch (grouch) I. intr. gruñir, refunfuñar II. s. gruñón *m*.
grouch·y (grou′chē) adj. **-i-** malhumorado.
ground¹ (ground) I. s. tierra, suelo; *(area)* terreno, campo; ELEC. toma de tierra ♦ **from the g. up** completamente • **g. crew** personal de tierra • **g. floor** planta baja • **g. hog** marmota • **g. rule** regla de procedimiento *o* comportamiento • **g. swell** mar de fondo • **g. water** agua subterránea • **g. zero** sitio de una explosión nuclear ♦ **to break g.** empezar (esp. a construir) • **to break new g.** marcar nuevos rumbos • **to cover the g.** *(distance)* recorrer el trecho; FIG. tratar extensamente un tópico • **to get off the g.** tomar vuelo • **to give, gain g.** ceder, ganar terreno • **to hold** *o* **stand one's g.** mantenerse firme, no ceder • **to run into the g.** agotar (un tema) ♦ pl. *(piece of land)* terreno, *(basis)* base; *(cause)* causa, motivo <g. for divorce motivo de divorcio>; *(sediment)* poso II. tr. *(theory)* basar, fundar; AVIA. impedir volar; FAM. *(to punish)* prohibir salir; ELEC. conectar con tierra; MARÍT. hacer varar *o* encallar ♦ **to be well-grounded** in ser versado en.
ground² cf. **grind**.
ground·less (′lĭs) adj. infundado, sin base.
ground·work (:wûrk′) s. fundamento, base *f*.
group (grōōp) I. s. grupo; *(organization)* agrupación *f*; MÚS. conjunto II. tr. & intr. agrupar(se).

group·ing (grōō′pĭng) s. agrupación *f*.
grouse¹ (grous) s.inv. ORNIT. urogallo.
grouse² FAM. I. intr. quejarse, refunfuñar II. s. queja, refunfuño.
grout (grout) s. lechada.
grove (grōv) s. bosquecillo, soto.
grov·el (grōv′əl) intr. *(to cringe)* rebajarse; *(to debase oneself)* envilecerse.
grow (grō) tr. **grew, grown** cultivar <to g. flowers> cultivar flores>; *(beard, hair)* dejar(se) crecer —intr. *(business, industry)* expandirse, agrandarse; *(to increase)* aumentar; *(to mature)* madurar (persona) ♦ **to g. accustomed to** acostumbrarse a • **to g. dark** oscurecerse • **to g. into** llegar a ser • **to g. old** envejecer • **to g. on trees** encontrarse dondequiera • **to g. on one** llegar a gustarle a uno • **to g. out of** *(a habit)* perder; *(to result from)* deberse a • **to g. up** *(physically)* crecer; *(mentally)* madurar, hacerse adulto; *(to be raised)* criarse.
growl (groul) I. s. gruñido II. intr. gruñir —tr. expresar con gruñidos.
grown (grōn) I. cf. **grow** II. adj. *(mature)* mayor, adulto.
grown-up (′ŭp′) adj. & s. adulto.
growth (grōth) s. crecimiento; *(development)* desarrollo; *(increase)* aumento; *(of beard)* barba; *(of grass)* brote *m*; MED. tumor *m*.
grub (grŭb) I. tr. **-bb-** *(to dig up)* desarraigar, JER. *(to sponge)* gorronear —intr. *(to dig)* cavar; *(to rummage)* hurgar II. s. ZOOL. larva, gusano; JER. *(food)* comida.
grub·by (′ē) adj. **-i-** sucio.
grudge (grŭj) I. tr. escatimar, dar a regañadientes II. s. rencor *m* ♦ **to hold a g. against** guardar rencor a.
grudg·ing·ly (′ĭng-lē) adv. de mala gana.
gru·el (grōō′əl) s. gachas *f*, avenate *m*.
gru·el·(l)ing (′ə-lĭng) adj. *(demanding)* abrumador; *(exhausting)* agotador, penoso.
grue·some (grōō′səm) adj. horrible, horrendo.
gruff (grŭf) adj. brusco; *(hoarse)* ronco.
grum·ble (grŭm′bəl) I. intr. quejarse, gruñir II. s. queja, refunfuño.
grum·bler (:blər) s. gruñidor *m*, gruñón *m*.
grum·bling (:blĭng) adj. gruñón, refunfuñón.
grump (grŭmp) I. s. gruñón *m* ♦ pl. mal humor II. intr. quejarse, refunfuñar.
grump·y (grŭm′pē) adj. **-i-** malhumorado.
grunt (grŭnt) I. intr. gruñir II. s. gruñido.
guar·an·tee (găr′ən-tē′) I. s. garantía; *(promise)* palabra, promesa; *(guarantor)* garante *mf* ♦ **to be a g. of** asegurar, garantizar II. tr. garantizar; *(to promise)* prometer; *(someone's actions)* responder de.
guar·an·tor (:tôr′) s. garante *mf*.
guar·an·ty (′-tē′) s. garantía.
guard (gärd) I. tr. guardar; *(to protect)* proteger; *(to watch over)* custodiar —intr. ♦ **to g. against** guardarse de II. s. *(sentinel)* guardia *m*, guardián *m*; *(body of troops)* guardia *f*; *(escort)* escolta; DEP. *(players)* defensa *m*; *(defensive posture)* guardia; *(act of guarding)* custodia, guardia; *(of a prisoner)* vigilancia; *(safeguard)* protección *f* ♦ **off (one's) g.** desprevenido • **on (one's) g.** prevenido, en guardia • **to be on g.** MIL. estar de guardia • **under g.** a buen recaudo.
guard·ed (gär′dĭd) adj. *(cautious)* cauto; *(restrained)* mesurado; *(protected)* protegido.
guard·house (gärd′hous′) s. cuerpo de guardia; *(jail)* cárcel *f* militar.

guard·i·an (gär′dē-ən) s. guardián m, guarda m; (of an orphan) tutor m, curador m.
gua·va (gwä′və) s. guayaba.
gu·ber·na·to·ri·al (gōō′bər-nə-tôr′ē-əl) adj. del gobernador.
guck (gŭk) s. JER. mugre f.
gue(r)·ril·la (gə-rĭl′ə) s. guerrillero ♦ **g. warfare** guerrilla.
guess (gĕs) I. tr. & intr. conjeturar; (to suppose) suponer; (to estimate correctly) adivinar ♦ **I g. so** me imagino que sí • **g. who!** ¡adivina! • **to g. right** adivinar, acertar • **to keep someone guessing** mantener a alguien con suspenso II. s. conjetura, suposición f ♦ **rough g.** cálculo aproximado • **to take a g.** tratar de adivinar.
guess·work (′wûrk′) s. conjetura.
guest (gĕst) s. (at home) invitado; (at hotel) huésped m ♦ **be my g.** FAM. hazlo si quieres • **g. room** cuarto de huéspedes.
guff (gŭf) s. JER. disparate m, tontería.
guf·faw (gə-fô′) I. s. carcajada, risotada II. intr. reírse a carcajadas.
guid·ance (gīd′ns) s. (direction) dirección f; (leadership) gobierno; (counseling) consejo ♦ **under the g.** of guiado por.
guide (gīd) I. s. (leader) guía mf; (book, device) guía f II. tr. guiar; (to steer, govern) dirigir; (to advise) aconsejar ♦ **guided missile** proyectil teledirigido —intr. servir de guía.
guide·book (′bŏŏk′) s. guía.
guide·line (:līn′) s. pauta.
guide·post (:pōst′) s. poste m indicador.
guild (gĭld) s. gremio, asociación f.
guile (gīl) s. engaño.
guile·less (′lĭs) adj. inocente, cándido.
guil·lo·tine (gĭl′ə-tēn′) I. s. guillotina II. tr. guillotinar.
guilt (gĭlt) s. culpabilidad f; (blame, remorse) culpa.
guilt·less (′lĭs) adj. inocente.
guilt·y (gĭl′tē) adj. **-i-** culpable ♦ **not g.** inocente • **to find g.** declarar culpable • **to have a g. conscience** remorderle a uno la conciencia.
guinea pig s. conejillo de Indias.
guise (gīz) s. (aspect) apariencia; (pretext) pretexto; (dress) traje m.
gui·tar (gĭ-tär′) s. guitarra.
gulf (gŭlf) s. golfo; (abyss) abismo.
gul·let (gŭl′ĭt) s. esófago; (throat) garganta.
gul·li·ble (gŭl′ə-bəl) adj. bobo, crédulo.
gul·ly (gŭl′ē) s. badén m, barranco.
gulp (gŭlp) I. tr. tragar, engullir ♦ **to g. down** tragarse —intr. tragar en seco; (in fear) quedar boquiabierto II. s. trago.
gum¹ (gŭm) I. s. (sap, glue) goma; (for chewing) chicle m II. tr. **-mm-** engomar ♦ **to g. up** (to clog) atascar; (to ruin) estropear.
gum² s. ODONT. encía.
gum·bo (gŭm′bō) s. (sopa de) quingombó.
gump·tion (gŭmp′shən) s. FAM. espíritu m.
gun (gŭn) I. s. arma de fuego; (cannon) cañón m; (handgun) pistola; (rifle) fusil m; (shotgun) escopeta; (killer) pistolero m II. tr. **-nn-** disparar; AUTO. acelerar a fondo ♦ **to g. down** matar (a tiros).
gun·boat (′bōt′) s. cañonero.
gun·fight (:fīt′) s. pelea a tiros.
gun·fire (:fīr′) s. disparos, tiros; (from artillery) cañonazos; (shooting) tiroteo.
gunk (gŭnk) s. FAM. mugre f, porquería.
gun·man (gŭn′mən) s. [pl. **-men**] pistolero m.
gun·ner (:ər) s. MIL. artillero.

gun·ner·y (:ə-rē) s. artillería.
gun·ny·sack (gŭn′ē-săk′) s. saco de arpillera.
gun·pow·der (gŭn′pou′dər) s. pólvora.
gun·run·ner (:rŭn′ər) s. traficante mf de armas.
gun·shot (:shŏt′) s. tiro; (artillery) cañonazo; (range) alcance m ♦ **within g.** a tiro de fusil.
gun·shy (shī′) adj. asustadizo, receloso.
gun·sling·er (:slĭng′ər) s. pistolero.
gun·smith (:smĭth′) s. armero.
gun·wale (gŭn′əl) s. regala, borda.
gur·gle (gûr′gəl) I. intr. (water) gorgotear; (baby) gorjear II. s. gorgoteo, gorjeo.
gu·ru (gōōr′ōō) s. maestro.
gush (gŭsh) I. intr. brotar, chorrear; (person) hablar con efusión excesiva II. s. chorro; (display) efusión excesiva.
gush·er (:ər) s. pozo brotante de petróleo.
gust (gŭst) I. s. ventolera, ráfaga; (of anger) acceso II. intr. soplar (el viento).
gus·to (gŭs′tō) s. deleite m, entusiasmo.
gust·y (gŭs′tē) adj. **-i-** ventoso, borrascoso.
gut (gŭt) I. s. intestino, tripa ♦ pl. (entrails) tripas; JER. (courage) agallas II. tr. **-tt-** destripar; FIG. acabar con el interior de III. adj. JER. (feeling) hondo; (reaction) instintivo; (issue) fundamental.
gut·less (′lĭs) adj. JER. sin agallas, cobarde.
guts·y (:sē) adj. **-i-** JER. con agallas, atrevido.
gut·ter (gŭt′ər) I. s. (street) cuneta; (roof) canalón m, canal m ♦ **g. language** lenguaje obsceno • **to come from the g.** venir de lo más bajo II. intr. parpadear (una vela).
guy¹ (gī) I. s. (tether) tirante ♦ II. tr. atirantar.
guy² s. FAM. (fellow) tipo, tío ♦ pl. muchachos.
guz·zle (gŭz′əl) tr. soplarse, beber mucho.
guz·zler (:lər) s. bebedor m, borracho.
gym (jĭm) s. FAM. gimnasio.
gym·na·si·um (jĭm-nā′zē-əm) s. gimnasio.
gym·nast (′năst′) s. gimnasta mf.
gym·nas·tic (:năs′tĭk) adj. gimnástico ♦ **gymnastics** s.sg. gimnasia.
gy·ne·col·o·gist (gī′nĭ-kŏl′ə-jĭst) s. ginecólogo.
gy·ne·col·o·gy (:jē) s. ginecología.
gyp (jĭp) FAM. I. tr. **-pp-** estafar II. s. (swindle) estafa; (swindler) estafador m.
gyp·sum (jĭp′səm) s. yeso.
gyp·sy (jĭp′sē) s. gitano ♦ **G.** gitano.
gy·rate (jī′rāt′) intr. girar, rotar.
gy·ra·tion (jī-rā′shən) s. giro, rotación f.
gyre (jīr) s. espiral m.
gy·ro (jī′rō) s. giroscopio.
gy·ro·scope (jī′rə-skōp′) s. giroscopio.

H

h, H (āch) s. octava letra del alfabeto inglés.
ha (hä) interj. ¡ah!, ¡ja!
ha·be·as cor·pus (hā′bē-əs kôr′pəs) s. hábeas corpus m.
hab·er·dash·er (hăb′ər-dăsh′ər) s. vendedor m de artículos para caballeros.
hab·er·dash·er·y (:ə-rē) s. (tienda de) artículos para caballeros.
hab·it (hăb′ĭt) s. costumbre f; (addiction) dependencia; (dress) hábito ♦ **out of h.** por costumbre • **to be in the h. of** acostumbrarse de • **to kick the h.** FAM. dejar el vicio.
hab·it·a·ble (hăb′ĭ-tə-bəl) adj. habitable.
hab·i·tat (:tăt′) s. hábitat m.

hab·i·ta·tion ('-tā'shən) s. habitación *f.*

hab·it-form·ing (hăb'ĭt-fôr'mĭng) adj. que crea hábito.

ha·bit·u·al (hə-bĭch'ōō-əl) adj. inveterado, empedernido; *(usual)* acostumbrado.

ha·bit·u·ate (:āt') tr. & intr. habituar(se).

hack[1] (hăk) I. tr. *(to chop)* cortar, tajar; FAM. *(to cope)* aguantar —intr. toser II. s. tajo, hachazo; *(cough)* tos seca.

hack[2] I. s. *(nag)* jamelgo, penco; *(hireling)* asalariado; *(carriage)* coche *m* de alquiler; FAM. taxista *mf* II. intr. FAM. trabajar de taxista III. adj. comercializado; *(hackneyed)* trillado.

hack·le (hăk'əl) s. pluma del cuello ♦ pl. pelos del cuello • **to get one's h. up** sacar las garras.

hack·ney (hăk'nē) I. s. *(horse)* trotón *m*, caballo de silla; *(carriage)* coche *m* de alquiler.

hack·neyed (:nēd) adj. gastado, trillado.

hack·saw (hăk'sô') s. sierra para metales.

had (hăd) cf. **have.**

had·dock (hăd'ək) s. [pl. inv. *o* **s**] abadejo.

hag (hăg) s. vieja bruja, arpía.

hag·gard (hăg'ərd) adj. demacrado.

hag·gle (hăg'əl) intr. regatear.

hag·gler (:lər) s. regateador *m.*

hag·gling (:lĭng) s. regateo.

hag·rid·den (hăg'rĭd'n) adj. atormentado.

ha-ha (hä'hä') interj. ¡ja, ja, ja!

hail[1] (hāl) I. s. *(ice)* granizo; *(barrage)* lluvia, andanada II. intr. granizar.

hail[2] I. tr. saludar; *(to acclaim)* aclamar; *(cab)* llamar —intr. ♦ **to h. from** ser de II. s. saludo III. interj. ¡salve! ♦ **h. to** viva.

hail·stone (hāl'stōn') s. granizo.

hail·storm (:stôrm') s. granizada.

hair (hâr) s. pelo, cabello ♦ **gray h.** canas • **h. piece** tupé, peluquín • **h. spray** gomina, laca • **h. style** peinado • **to comb one's h.** peinarse • **h. style** peinado • **to comb one's h.** peinarse • **to get in someone's h.** tener a alguien hasta la coronilla • **to let one's h. down** echar una cana al aire • **to make one's h.** **stand on end** ponerle a uno los pelos de punta • **to tear one's h. out** tirarse de los pelos • **to split hairs** hilar demasiado fino.

hair·brush ('brush') s. cepillo (para el pelo).

hair·cut (:kŭt') s. corte *m* de pelo ♦ **to get a h.** cortarse el pelo.

hair·do (:dōō') s. peinado.

hair·dress·er (:drĕs'ər) s. peluquero.

hair·dress·ing (:ĭng) s. *(occupation)* peluquería; *(act)* peinado.

hair·less (hâr'lĭs) adj. sin pelo; *(face)* lampiño.

hair·line (:līn') s. nacimiento del pelo; *(line)* rayita ♦ **receding h.** entradas.

hair·net (:nĕt') s. redecilla para el cabello.

hair·pin (:pĭn') s. *(pin)* horquilla; *(curve)* curva cerrada (de una carretera).

hair-rais·ing (:rā'zĭng) adj. espeluznante.

hairs·breadth (hârz'brĕdth') s. pelo, tris *m.*

hair·split·ting (hâr'splĭt'ĭng) s. argucias.

hair-trig·ger (hâr'trĭg'ər) adj. impulsivo.

hair·y (hâr'ē) adj. -i- peludo; JER. *(hazardous)* espinoso.

hake (hāk) s. [pl. inv. *o* **s**] merluza.

hal·cy·on (hăl'sē-ən) adj. venturoso.

hale[1] (hāl) adj. robusto, fuerte.

hale[2] tr. llevar a la fuerza, arrastrar.

half (hăf) I. s. [pl. **-ves**] mitad *f; (part)* parte *f;* DEP. tiempo ♦ **and a h.** y medio • **better h.** FAM. cara mitad, costilla • **by h.** a la mitad • **by halves** a medias • **h. brother, sister** hermanas-

tro, -a • **h. note** MÚS. blanca • **h. past (two)** (dos) y media II. adj. & adv. medio, a medias ♦ **h. price** a mitad de precio • **not h. bad** FAM. no tan malo.

half-alive ('ə-līv') adj. medio muerto.

half-and-half ('ən-hăf') I. adj. mitad y mitad II. adv. a medias III. s. leche *f* con crema.

half·back (:băk') s. DEP. medio.

half-baked (:bākt') adj. a medio cocer; FAM. *(ill-conceived)* disparatado, precipitado.

half-breed (:brēd') s. & adj. JER. mestizo.

half-caste (:kăst') s. & adj. mestizo.

half-cocked (:kŏkt') adj. FAM. descabellado.

half-heart·ed (:här'tĭd) adj. sin entusiasmo.

half-hour (:our') s. media hora.

half-life (:līf') s. período de desintegración radioactiva.

half-mast (:măst') s. ♦ **at h.** a media asta.

half-moon (:mōōn') s. media luna.

half-o·pen (:ō'pən) adj. entreabierto.

half-slip (:slĭp') s. enagua corta.

half-truth (:trōōth') s. verdad *f* a medias.

half·way (:wā') I. adj. medio, intermedio; *(measures)* parcial II. adv. a la mitad; *(partially)* a medias ♦ **to meet h.** partir la diferencia, hacer concesiones.

half-wit (:wĭt') s. retrasado mental.

half-wit·ted (-'ĭd) adj. necio, tonto.

hal·i·but (hăl'ə-bət) s. halibut *m.*

hall (hôl) s. corredor *m; (lobby)* vestíbulo; *(auditorium)* sala; EDUC. *(building)* facultad *f* ♦ **h. of fame** museo conmemorativo.

hal·le·lu·jah (hăl'ə-lōō'yə) interj. aleluya.

hall·mark (hôl'märk') s. sello.

hal·low (hăl'ō) tr. santificar; *(to revere)* venerar.

hal·lu·ci·nate (hə-lōō'sə-nāt') tr. & intr. alucinar(se).

hal·lu·ci·na·tion (-'-nā'shən) s. alucinación *f.*

hal·lu·ci·na·to·ry (-'-nə-tôr'ē) adj. alucinante.

hal·lu·ci·no·gen (:nə-jən) s. alucinógeno

hal·lu·ci·no·gen·ic (-'--jĕn'ĭk) adj. alucinógeno.

hall·way (hôl'wā') s. pasillo, corredor *m.*

ha·lo (hā'lō) s. [pl. **(e)s**] halo; *(aura)* aura.

halt[1] (hôlt) I. s. *(stop)* alto, parada; *(pause)* interrupción *f* ♦ **to call a h.** to poner fin a II. tr. & intr. parar(se), detener(se); *(briefly)* interrumpir(se) ♦ **halt!** ¡alto!

halt[2] intr. *(to hobble)* cojear; *(to waver)* titubear.

hal·ter (hôl'tər) I. s. dogal *m; (bodice)* corpiño sin espalda II. tr. encabestrar; *(to restrain)* restringir.

halt·ing (hôl'tĭng) adj. cojo; *(wavering)* titubeante.

halve (hăv) tr. partir *o* reducir a la mitad; *(a number)* dividir por dos.

halves (hăvz) cf. **half.**

ham (hăm) I. s. jamón *m*, pernil *m;* ANAT. corva; FAM. *(performer)* comicastro; RAD. radioaficionado II. tr. **-mm-** exagerar.

ham·burg·er (hăm'bûr'gər) s. hamburguesa.

ham·let (hăm'lĭt) s. aldea, caserío.

ham·mer (hăm'ər) I. s. martillo; *(of gun)* percusor *m; (of piano)* martinete *m* II. tr. martillar ♦ **to h. away at** FAM. *(an opponent)* castigar a; *(a task)* trabajar con ahínco en • **to h. home** FIG. machacar incansablemente • **to h. out** *(dent)* sacar a martillazos; *(contract)* elaborar, llegar a.

ham·mered (:ərd) adj. repujado.

ham·mer·head (:ər-hěd´) s. cabeza de martillo; ICT. pez martillo.

ham·mock (hăm´ək) s. hamaca.

ham·per¹ (hăm´pər) tr. poner trabas a.

ham·per² s. (basket) cesto.

ham·ster (hăm´stər) s. hámster m.

ham·string (hăm´strĭng´) I. s. tendón m de la corva II. tr. **-strung** cortar el tendón de la corva a; (to hinder) incapacitar.

hand (hănd) I. s. mano f; (of clock, gauge) aguja, manecilla; (side) lado; (script) letra; (applause) aplauso; (laborer) obrero, jornalero; (on ship) tripulante m; (expert) perito; (cards) mano; EQUIT. palmo menor; (bananas) racimo ♦ **at the hands of** en manos de • **by h.** a mano • **by the h.** de la mano • **(close) at h.** muy cerca, a mano • **h. in h.** tomados de la mano • **h. over fist** FAM. a manos llenas • **hands down** fácilmente • **hands off!** ¡no tocar! • **on h.** disponible • **on one's hands and knees** a gatas • **on the one (other) h.** por una (otra) parte • **out of h.** fuera de control • **out of my hands** fuera de mi alcance • **the matter at h.** el asunto que se está estudiando • **to be an old h. at** tener mucha experiencia en • **to be someone's right h.** ser el brazo derecho de alguien • **to bite the h. that feeds you** ser mal agradecido • **to change hands** cambiar de dueño • **to clap one's hands** batir palmas • **to get o lay one's hands on** encontrar, localizar • **to give o lend a h. (with)** echar una mano (a) • **to have a h. in** tener parte en • **to have one's hands full** tener mucho que hacer • **to keep one's h. in** no perder la práctica de • **to know like the back of one's h.** conocer como la palma de la mano • **to live from h. to mouth** vivir al día • **to play into someone's hands** hacerle el juego a alguien • **to shake hands** darse la mano • **to take one's life in(to) one's hands** jugarse uno la vida • **to take something off someone's hands** quitarle a alguien algo • **to throw up one's hands** echarse o llevarse las manos a la cabeza • **to wait on someone h. and foot** desvivirse por alguien II. tr. entregar, dar ♦ **to h. down** transmitir; (verdict) dictar • **to h. in** presentar, entregar • **to h. out** (to administer) dar, aplicar; (to distribute) repartir • **to h. over (to)** ceder (a) • **to have to h. it to** JER. tener que felicitar a o reconocer los méritos de.

hand·bag (´băg´) s. cartera, bolso.

hand·ball (:bôl´) s. pelota (vasca).

hand·bill (:bĭl´) s. volante m, octavilla.

hand·book (:bŏŏk´) s. manual m.

hand·car (:kär´) s. zorrilla.

hand·cart (:kärt´) s. carretilla.

hand·cuff (:kŭf´) I. s. esposas II. tr. esposar; FIG. maniatar.

hand·ful (:fŏŏl´) s. puñado ♦ **a real h.** una verdadera lata.

hand·gun (:gŭn´) s. pistola.

hand·i·cap (hăn´dē-kăp´) I. s. hándicap m; (hindrance) obstáculo; (physical) defecto; (mental) retraso II. tr. **-pp-** asignar un hándicap a; (to impede) poner en desventaja.

hand·i·capped (:kăpt´) adj. impedido.

hand·i·craft (hăn´dē-krăft´) s. destreza manual; (occupation, product) (artículo de) artesanía.

hand·i·work (:wûrk´) s. trabajo manual; (doing) obra.

hand·ker·chief (hăng´kər-chĭf) s. pañuelo.

han·dle (hăn´dl) I. tr. tocar, andar con; (conveyance) manejar, dirigir; (to deal with) encargarse de; (to represent) ser el agente de; (to cope with) poder con; (to trade in) comerciar en ♦ **h. with care** frágil • **to h. oneself** comportarse —intr. manejarse II. s. mango; (of door) manija; (grip) asa, asidero; JER. nombre m ♦ **to fly off the h.** perder los estribos.

han·dle·bars (:bärz´) s.pl. manillar m.

han·dler (hănd´lər) s. COM. tratante m; DEP. entrenador m.

han·dling (:lĭng) s. manejo; (treatment) forma de tratar ♦ **shipping and h.** gastos de flete.

hand·made (hănd´mād´) adj. hecho a mano.

hand-me-down (:mē-doun´) s. & adj. (prenda de vestir) de segunda mano.

hand·out (:out´) s. limosna; (leaflet) folleto.

hand-pick (:pĭk´) tr. escoger, seleccionar.

hand·rail (:rāl´) s. pasamano, barandilla.

hand·saw (:sô´) s. serrucho.

hand·shake (:shāk´) s. apretón m de manos.

hands-off (hăndz´ôf´) adj. de no intervención.

hand·some (hăn´səm) adj. **-er,** est guapo, bien parecido; FIG. liberal, generoso.

hands-on (hăndz´ŏn´) adj. práctico.

hand·spring (hănd´sprĭng´) s. DEP. voltereta.

hand·stand (:stănd´) s. parada de cabeza.

hand-to-hand (:tə-hănd´) adj. cuerpo a cuerpo.

hand-to-mouth (:tə-mouth´) adj. precario.

hand·writ·ing (:rī´tĭng) s. escritura; (style) letra.

hand·writ·ten (:rĭt´ən) adj. escrito a mano.

hand·y (hăn´dē) adj. **-i-** mañoso; (accessible) a mano; (useful) conveniente ♦ **to be h. with** saber manejar • **to come in h.** venir bien.

hand·y·man (:măn´) s. [pl. **-men**] hombre m que hace bricolages.

hang (hăng) I. tr. **hung** suspender, colgar; (to execute) ahorcar; (pictures) fijar; (one's head) bajar, inclinar ♦ **h. it up** (to delay) demorar; (telephone) colgar —intr. colgar; (to be executed) ser ahorcado; (in air) flotar; (to droop) inclinarse; (fabric) caer; (paintings) exhibirse ♦ **h. in there!** FAM. ¡ánimo! • **to h. around** o **out** FAM. haraganear • **to h. back** quedarse atrás • **to h. loose** JER. estar tranquilo • **to h. on** (to wait) esperar; (to grasp) asirse de; (to persevere) persistir; (to depend on) depender de • **to h. onto** guardar, quedarse con II. s. caída (de tela, prenda) ♦ **not to give a h.** FAM. importarle a uno un comino • **to get the h. of something** FAM. cogerle el truco a algo.

han·gar (hăng´ər) s. hangar m.

hang·er (hăng´ər) s. colgadero, percha.

hang·er-on (hăng´ər-ŏn´) s. [pl. **hangers-**] parásito, gorrón m.

hang·ing (hăng´ĭng) I. s. ejecución f en la horca II. adj. colgante, pendiente.

hang·out (:out´) s. guarida, punto de reunión.

hang·o·ver (:ō´vər) s. resaca; FIG. vestigio.

hang-up (:ŭp´) s. FAM. complejo, problema m; (obstacle) traba.

hank (hăngk) s. madeja.

han·ker (hăng´kər) intr. anhelar.

han·ker·ing (:ĭng) s. deseo, ganas; (nostalgia) añoranza.

han·kie/ky (hăng´kē) s. FAM. pañuelo.

han·ky-pan·ky (hăng´kē-păng´kē) s. JER. truquitos, jueguitos; (foolishness) boberías ♦ **there's some h. going on** hay algo que no huele bien.

hap·haz·ard (hăp-hăz´ərd) adj. fortuito.

hap·less (hăp´lĭs) adj. desventurado.

hap·pen (hăp'ən) intr. *(to come to pass)* pasar, suceder; *(to take place)* producirse, ocurrir ♦ **how does it h. that...?** ¿cómo es posible que...? • **if you h.** to talk to him si por casualidad hablaras con él • **it (so) happens that** *o* **as it happens** da la casualidad que • **to h. to be** dar la casualidad de ser *o* estar.

hap·pen·stance (:stăns') s. casualidad *f.*

hap·pi·ness (hăp'ē-nĭs) s. felicidad *f*, dicha; *(merriment)* alegría.

hap·py (hăp'ē) adj. **-i-** feliz, dichoso; *(fortunate)* dichoso; *(fulfilled)* contento; *(merry)* alegre; *(fitting)* acertado; *(overly fond of)* obsesionado ♦ **h. birthday!** ¡feliz cumpleaños!, ¡felicidades! • **to be h. for,** to alegrarse por, de.

hap·py-go-luck·y ('-gō-lŭk'ē) adj. despreocupado.

ha·rangue (hə-răng') I. s. arenga II. tr. & intr. arengar.

ha·rass (hə-răs', hăr'əs) tr. acosar; *(to annoy)* molestar; *(to wear out)* agobiar; MIL. hostilizar.

ha·rass·ment (:mənt) s. acoso, hostigamiento.

har·bin·ger (här'bĭn-jər) s. heraldo; *(omen)* presagio; *(forerunner)* precursor *m.*

har·bor (här'bər) I. s. puerto, bahía; *(refuge)* refugio II. tr. proteger; *(hopes)* abrigar; *(resentment)* guardar.

hard (härd) I. adj. duro, sólido; *(firm)* firme; *(resistant)* resistente; *(difficult)* difícil, arduo; *(robust)* fuerte; *(strong-minded)* decidido, resuelto; *(diligent)* diligente; *(inclement)* duro; *(stern)* severo; *(trying)* difícil; *(callous)* cruel, de piedra; *(damaging)* dañino; *(facts)* incontestable; *(liquor)* fuerte ♦ **h. and fast** riguroso, invariable • **h. cash** metálico • **h. core** núcleo, médula • **h. drugs** drogas adictivas • **h. labor** trabajos forzados • **h. line** postura firme • **h. luck** mala suerte II. adv. *(intensely)* mucho; *(vigorously)* con fuerza; *(badly)* gravemente; *(firmly)* fuertemente ♦ **h. on the heels of** pisándole los talones a • **to be h. at it** trabajar con ahínco • **to be h. hit** estar severamente afectado • **to be h. up** encontrarse sin dinero.

hard·back ('băk') adj. & s. (libro) encuadernado.

hard-boiled (:boild') adj. *(egg)* duro; FAM. *(callous)* duro; *(unsentimental)* práctico.

hard·bound (:bound') var. de **hardback.**

hard-core *o* **hard·core** (:kôr') adj. empedernido; *(pornography)* explícito.

hard·cov·er (:kŭv'ər) var. de **hardback.**

hard·en (här'dn) tr. & intr. endurecer(se); *(to inure)* acostumbrar(se).

hard·en·ing (:ĭng) s. endurecimiento.

hard·head·ed (härd'hĕd'ĭd) adj. *(stubborn)* testarudo; *(realistic)* práctico.

hard·heart·ed (:här'tĭd) adj. duro de corazón.

har·di·hood (här'dē-hŏod') s. temeridad *f*; *(impudence)* atrevimiento.

hard-line *o* **hard·line** (härd'līn') adj. firme; *(uncompromising)* intransigente.

hard·lin·er (:lī'nər) s. intransigente *mf.*

hard·ly (:lē) adv. *(just)* apenas <*I had h. closed my eyes* apenas había cerrado los ojos>; *(scarcely)* escasamente, casi no.

hard-nosed (:nōzd') adj. cabezón, obstinado.

hard·ship (:shĭp') s. sufrimiento; *(privation)* penuria.

hard·ware (:wâr') s. (artículos de) ferretería; COMPUT. equipo, maquinaria; FAM. *(weapons)* hierros ♦ **h. store** ferretería.

hard-won (:wŭn') adj. ganado con dificultad.

hard·wood (:wŏod') s. & adj. (árbol *m*) de madera dura.

har·dy (här'dē) adj. robusto, resistente; *(intrepid)* temerario.

hare (hâr) s. liebre *f.*

hare·brained ('brānd') adj. atolondrado.

hare·lip (:lĭp') s. labio leporino.

har·em (hâr'əm) s. harén *m.*

hark (härk) intr. escuchar, prestar atención ♦ **to h. back to** remontarse a.

har·lot (här'lət) s. ramera.

harm (härm) I. s. daño, perjuicio; *(evil)* mal *m* ♦ **out of h.'s way** a salvo II. tr. hacer daño.

harm·ful (:fəl) adj. perjudicial; *(damaging)* dañino.

harm·less (:lĭs) adj. inocuo.

har·mon·ic (här-mŏn'ĭk) adj. & s. armónico.

har·mon·i·ca (:ĭ-kə) s. armónica.

har·mo·ni·ous (här-mō'nē-əs) adj. armonioso.

har·mo·nize ('mə-nīz') tr. & intr. armonizar.

har·mo·ny (:nē) s. armonía.

har·ness (här'nĭs) I. s. arreos II. tr. *(horse)* enjaezar; *(energy)* aprovechar, utilizar.

harp (härp) I. s. arpa II. intr. tocar la arpa ♦ **to h. on** machacar, insistir en.

har·poon (här-pŏon') I. s. arpón *m* II. tr. arponear.

harp·si·chord (härp'sĭ-kôrd') s. clavicémbalo.

har·py (här'pē) s. arpía.

har·row·ing (här'ō-ĭng) adj. espantoso.

har·ry (här'ē) tr. merodear; *(to harass)* atormentar.

harsh (härsh) adj. áspero; *(stern)* cruel, severo.

har·vest (här'vĭst) I. s. cosecha; *(of sugar cane)* zafra; *(of grapes)* vendimia; *(result)* fruto II. tr. & intr. cosechar, hacer la cosecha.

har·vest·er (:vĭ-stər) s. *(of fruit)* recolector *m*; *(of sugar cane)* cortador *m*; *(machine)* segadora.

has (hăz) tercera persona sing. de **have.**

has-been (hăz'bĭn') s. FAM. persona acabada.

hash[1] (hăsh) I. s. CUL. picadillo; *(jumble)* revoltillo II. tr. picar; FAM. *(to mangle)* mutilar ♦ **to h. out** *o* **over** discutir a fondo.

hash[2] s. JER. *(hashish)* hachís *m.*

hash·ish ('ĕsh') s. hachís *m.*

has·sle (hăs'əl) FAM. I. s. reyerta, jaleo II. tr. fastidiar, molestar.

has·sock (hăs'ək) s. cojín *m*, almohadón *m.*

haste (hāst) s. prisa; *(rashness)* precipitación *f* ♦ **in h.** de prisa, precipitadamente • **to make h.** darse prisa.

has·ten (hā'sən) intr. darse prisa, apresurarse —tr. apresurar.

hast·y (hā'stē) adj. **-i-** apresurado; *(rash)* precipitado ♦ **to be h.** precipitarse.

hat (hăt) s. sombrero ♦ **at the drop of a h.** al menor pretexto • **h. in hand** humildemente • **my h.!** ¡naranjas! • **to keep under one's h.** no decir nada de • **to take one's h. off to** reconocer el mérito de • **to throw one's h. into the ring** postularse como candidato.

hatch[1] (hăch) s. trampa; MARÍT. escotilla.

hatch[2] intr. salir del cascarón —tr. *(to produce young)* sacar pollos; *(an egg)* empollar; *(plot)* tramar.

hatch·er·y ('ə-rē) s. criadero (de peces, aves).

hatch·et (hăch'ĭt) s. hachuela ♦ **h. man** JER. matón; *(henchman)* esbirro • **to bury the h.** envainar la espada.

hatch·way (hăch'wā') s. MARÍT. escotilla.

hate (hāt) I. tr. odiar —intr. sentir odio II. s.

odio.

hate·ful ('fəl) adj. odioso; *(full of hatred)* rencoroso.

ha·tred (hā'trĭd) s. odio, aborrecimiento.

hat·ter (hăt'ər) s. sombrerero.

haugh·ty (hô'tē) adj. -i- altivo.

haul (hôl) I. intr. & tr. halar, tirar (de); *(to transport)* transportar ♦ **to h. off** coger impulso II. s. tirada; *(distance)* tramo; *(load)* carga; *(of fish)* redada ♦ **over the long h.** a la larga.

haunch (hônch) s. cuarto trasero; *(hip)* cadera.

haunt (hônt) I. tr. *(ghosts)* aparecer a o en; *(to frequent)* rondar; *(to obsess)* perseguir ♦ **to be haunted** estar embrujado o encantado II. s. lugar predilecto.

haunt·ing (hôn'tĭng) adj. inolvidable.

have I. tr. had tener; *(to possess)* poseer; *(in mind)* retener; *(to acquire)* obtener; *(letter)* recibir; *(disease)* sufrir de; *(good time)* pasar; *(words)* encontrar; *(to cause to be done)* hacer, mandar; *(to permit)* tolerar; *(baby)* dar a luz, alumbrar; *(to be obligated to)* deber <*I h. to get there on time* debo llegar a tiempo> ♦ **to be had** ser engañado ♦ **to h. had it** estar hasta la coronilla ♦ **to h. it in for** FAM. tenérsela jurada a ♦ **to h. it out with** habérselas con ♦ **to h. on** llevar puesto ♦ **to h. to do with** tener que ver con —aux. haber <*he had lost his temper* se había enojado>; hacer <*it has been snowing for a week* hace una semana que está nevando> ♦ **had better** más vale que <*I had better leave* más vale que me vaya> II. s. ♦ **the haves and the have-nots** los ricos y los pobres.

ha·ven (hā'vən) s. puerto; *(shelter)* refugio.

have-not (hăv'nŏt') s. pobre *mf.*

hav·er·sack (hăv'ər-săk') s. mochila.

hav·oc (hăv'ək) s. estragos; *(chaos)* caos *m.*

hawk¹ (hôk) s. halcón *m;* FIG. tiburón *m;* FAM. *(warmonger)* militarista *mf.*

hawk² intr. & tr. *(to peddle)* pregonar.

hawk·er (hô'kər) s. pregonero.

hawk·ish (hô'kĭsh) adj. militarista.

haw·ser (hô'zər) s. guindaleza.

haw·thorn (hô'thôrn') s. espino.

hay (hā) I. s. heno ♦ **h. fever** fiebre del heno ♦ **to hit the h.** FAM. acostarse, irse a roncar II. intr. secar heno.

hay·loft (hā'lôft') s. henil *m.*

hay·seed (hā'sēd') s. JER. patán *m.*

hay·stack (hā'stăk') s. almiar *m.*

hay·wire (hā'wīr') adj. FAM. descontrolado.

haz·ard (hăz'ərd) I. s. riesgo; *(chance)* azar *m;* *(in golf)* obstáculo II. tr. arriesgar; *(a guess)* aventurar.

haz·ard·ous (:ər-dəs) adj. peligroso; *(chancy)* azaroso; *(harmful)* perjudicial.

haze¹ (hāz) s. niebla ligera; *(mental)* ofuscamiento.

haze² tr. someter a ritos de iniciación.

ha·zel (hā'zəl) adj. & s. (de) avellano.

ha·zel·nut (:nŭt') s. avellana.

haz·y (hā'zē) adj. -i- nebuloso; *(unclear)* confuso.

H-bomb (āch'bŏm') s. bomba H.

he (hē) I. pron. él II. s. varón *m.*

head (hĕd) I. s. cabeza; *(sense)* inteligencia; *(ability)* habilidad *f;* *(composure)* aplomo; *(person)* persona; *(chief)* jefe *m;* *(top)* tope *m;* *(of table, bed)* cabecera; *(of steam)* presión *f;* *(on beer)* espuma; *(point)* punta; *(of drum)* parche *m;* *(of page)* principio; *(headline)* titular *m;*

GEOG. cabo; BOT. repollo; MARIT. letrina; AUTO. culata (de cilindro) ♦ **from h. to foot** de arriba abajo ♦ **h. of hair** cabellera ♦ **h. over heels** patas arriba; FIG. locamente ♦ **h. start** ventaja ♦ **h. wind** viento en contra ♦ **off the top of one's h.** sin pensar mucho en ello ♦ **to be over one's h.** estar (algo) fuera de la capacidad de uno ♦ **to be soft in the h.** FAM. estar tocado de la cabeza ♦ **to bring to a h.** forzar el desenlace ♦ **to come to a h.** madurar, definirse ♦ **to get it into one's h. (to)** FAM. metérsele a uno la idea (de) ♦ **to get it through one's h.** comprender algo ♦ **to go to one's h.** subírsele a la cabeza ♦ **to keep one's h. above water** mantenerse a flote ♦ **to stand on one's h. (to)** hacer lo imposible (para) ♦ **to talk one's h. off** FAM. hablar hasta por los codos ♦ pl. cara (de moneda) ♦ **h. or tails** cara o cruz ♦ **not to make h. or tails of** FAM. no encontrar ni pies ni cabeza a II. tr. encabezar; *(to be first)* ir a la cabeza de; *(to turn)* apuntar; DEP. cabecear ♦ **to h. off** prevenir —intr. dirigirse ♦ **to h. back** regresar ♦ **to h. for** ir con rumbo a III. adj. principal, central; *(at the head)* delantero.

head·ache ('āk') s. dolor *m* de cabeza; FAM. *(annoyance)* quebradero de cabeza.

head·band (:bănd') s. cinta.

head·board (:bôrd') s. cabecera (de cama).

head·er (:ər) s. FAM. salto o caída de cabeza.

head·first (:fûrst') adv. de cabeza; *(impetuously)* precipitadamente.

head·gear (:gîr') s. *(headdress)* tocado; *(helmet)* casco.

head·hunt·er (:hŭn'tər) s. cazador *m* de cabezas; JER. *(recruiter)* reclutador *m.*

head·ing (:ĭng) s. encabezamiento; *(section)* apartado; *(course)* derrotero.

head·lamp (:lămp') s. faro, luz delantera.

head·land (:lənd) s. promontorio.

head·light (:līt') s. faro, luz delantera.

head·line (:līn') I. s. titular *m* ♦ pl. sumario de noticias ♦ **to make the h.** aparecer en primera plana II. tr. poner titular a.

head·long (:lông') I. adv. precipitadamente II. adj. precipitado.

head·mas·ter (:măs'tər) s. director *m* (de un colegio).

head·mis·tress (:mĭs'trĭs) s. directora (de un colegio).

head-on (:ŏn') adj. & adv. de frente.

head·phone (:fōn') s. audífono, auricular *m.*

head·quar·ter (:kwôr'tər) tr. acuartelar.

head·quar·ters (:tərz) s.pl. cuartel *m* general; *(police)* jefatura; COM. oficina central.

head·rest (hĕd'rĕst') s. cabecera; AUTO. apoyo para la cabeza.

head·set (:sĕt') s. auriculares *m,* audífonos.

head·stone (:stōn') s. lápida sepulcral.

head·strong (:strông') adj. voluntarioso.

head·wait·er ('wā'tər) s. jefe *m* de comedor.

head·wa·ter (:wô'tər) s. cabecera.

head·way (:wā') s. avance *m,* progreso; *(clearance)* altura libre, espacio sobrante ♦ **to make h.** avanzar, progresar.

head·y (:ē) adj. -i- embriagador.

heal (hēl) tr. curar; *(to remedy)* remediar —intr. sanar.

heal·er (hē'lər) s. curandero.

heal·ing (:lĭng) I. adj. curativo II. s. curación *f.*

health (hĕlth) s. salud *f;* *(of community)* sanidad *f* ♦ **h. food** alimentos naturales ♦ **h. insur-**

ance seguro médico • **h. spa** centro de ejercicios • **to be in bad, good h.** estar mal, bien de salud • **to your h.!** ¡salud!

health·ful ('fəl) adj. sano, saludable.

health·y (:thē) adj. -i- sano; *(air, place)* saludable, salubre; *(appetite)* bueno; *(sizable)* generoso, considerable ♦ **to feel h.** sentirse bien de salud.

heap (hēp) I. s. montón; JER. *(jalopy)* cacharro II. tr. amontonar, apilar.

hear (hîr) tr. **heard** oír; *(to listen to)* escuchar; *(Mass, lecture)* asistir a, oír; *(a faint sound)* sentir; *(to know)* enterarse de; *(legal case)* ver ♦ **to have never heard of no conocer** • **to h. about** oír hablar de • **to h. out** escuchar hasta el final —intr. oír ♦ **I won't h. of it!** ¡ni hablar! • **to h. from** tener noticias de.

hear·ing ('îng) s. oído; *(earshot)* alcance m del oído; DER. audiencia ♦ **hard of h.** duro de oído • **h. aid** audífono • **to give a fair h.** escuchar sin prejuicios.

hear·ken (här'kən) intr. escuchar, atender.

hear·say (hîr'sā') s. rumores m.

hearse (hûrs) s. carroza fúnebre.

heart (härt) s. corazón m; *(cards)* copa; *(of lettuce)* cogollo ♦ **at h.** en el fondo • **by h.** de memoria • **h. and soul** en cuerpo y alma • **h. attack** ataque cardiaco • **h. failure** colapso (cardiaco) • **in the h. of winter** en pleno invierno • **not to have one's h. in something** hacer algo sin entusiasmo • **the h. of the matter** el quid, el meollo • **to be near** *o* **dear to one's h.** tocarle a uno en el alma • **to have h. trouble** no andar bien del corazón • **to have one's h. set on** encapricharse en • **to have the h.** to tener valor para • **to lose h.** descorazonarse • **to one's h.'s content** hasta saciarse • **to take h.** cobrar ánimo • **to take to h.** tomar a pecho • **to wear one's h. on one's sleeve** mostrar fácilmente los sentimientos • **with all** *o* **from one's h.** de todo corazón.

heart·ache ('āk') s. tristeza, pena.

heart·beat (:bēt') s. latido.

heart·break (:brāk') s. angustia, pena; *(disappointment)* decepción f.

heart·bro·ken (:brō'kən) adj. angustiado, apenado; *(disappointed)* decepcionado ♦ **to be h.** tener el corazón destrozado.

heart·burn (:bûrn') s. acedía.

heart·en (här'tn) tr. alentar.

heart·felt (härt'fĕlt') adj. sincero; *(grief, sympathy)* más sentido.

hearth (härth) s. hogar m.

heart·land (härt'lănd') s. región f central.

heart·less (:lĭs) adj. despiadado, cruel.

heart·rend·ing (:rĕn'dĭng) adj. desgarrador.

heart·throb (:thrŏb') s. *(heartbeat)* latido del corazón; *(sweetheart)* enamorado.

heart-to-heart (:tə-härt') adj. cándido.

heart·y (här'tē) adj. -i- cordial, sincero; *(robust)* robusto; *(appetite)* bueno; *(meal)* abundante ♦ **to be a h. eater** ser de buen comer.

heat (hēt) s. calor m; *(for building)* calefacción f; *(estrus)* estro, celo; DEP. carrera; JER. *(police)* jara, poli f ♦ **h. rash** miliaria • **h. stroke** insolación • **the h. of the day** lo más caluroso del día II. tr. & intr. calentar(se); *(to excite)* acalorar(se) ♦ **to h. up** recalentarse.

heat·ed (hē'tĭd) adj. caliente; *(debate)* acalorado.

heat·er (hē'tər) s. radiador calorífero; *(stove)* estufa, calentador m; JER. revólver m.

heath (hēth) s. brezo; *(land)* breñal m.

hea·then (hē'thən) s. [pl. inv. *o* **s**] & adj. pagano; *(savage)* salvaje m.

heath·er (hĕth'ər) s. brezo.

heat·ing (hē'tĭng) I. adj. calentador; FÍS. calorífico II. s. calentamiento; *(system)* calefacción f.

heave (hēv) I. tr. alzar (con esfuerzo); *(to hurl)* arrojar; *(sigh)* exhalar —intr. levantarse; FAM. *(to retch)* nausear II. s. tiro; GEOL. desplazamiento, levantamiento ♦ pl. arcadas.

heav·en (hĕv'ən) s. cielo; *(paradise)* paraíso ♦ **for h.'s sake!** ¡por (amor de) Dios! • **h. forbid that** Dios nos libre de • **h. knows** Dios es testigo • **thank h.!** ¡gracias a Dios! ♦ pl. cielo, firmamento • **good h.!** ¡Dios mío!, ¡cielos!

heav·en·ly (:lē) adj. celestial; *(delightful)* divino, sublime.

heav·y (hĕv'ē) I. adj. -i- pesado; *(thick)* espeso; *(rain)* fuerte; *(sea)* borrascoso; *(clumsy)* torpe; *(excessive)* fuerte; *(grave)* serio; *(arduous)* dificultoso; *(large-scale)* en gran escala; *(onerous)* gravoso; *(coarse)* grueso; *(heart)* oprimido; *(foul)* cargado; *(eyelids)* amodorrado II. adv. pesadamente; *(slowly)* lentamente III. s. TEAT. villano.

heav·y-du·ty ('-dōō'tē) adj. de servicio pesado.

heav·y-hand·ed (:hăn'dĭd) adj. torpe; *(oppressive)* de mano dura.

heav·y-heart·ed (:här'tĭd) adj. afligido.

heav·y·set (:sĕt') adj. corpulento.

heav·y·weight ('-wāt') s. peso pesado; FAM. persona importante.

heck (hĕk) I. interj. ¡diablos! II. s. infierno.

heck·le (hĕk'əl) tr. interrumpir (a un orador).

heck·ler (:lər) s. persona que interrumpe a un orador.

hec·tic (hĕk'tĭk) adj. ajetreado.

hedge (hĕj) I. s. seto (vivo); FIN. inversión defensiva; *(excuse)* evasiva II. tr. encerrar (con seto); *(to limit)* restringir —intr. FIN. hacer operaciones compensatorias; *(to skirt)* andarse con rodeos.

hedge·hog (hĕj'hôg') s. erizo.

hedge·row (hĕj'rō') s. seto (vivo).

he·don·ist (hēd'n-ĭst) s. hedonista mf.

hee·bie-jee·bies (hē'bē-jē'bēz) s.pl. JER. desasosiego, nervios.

heed (hēd) I. intr. & tr. hacer caso (a, de) II. s. atención f ♦ **to pay h.** to prestar atención a.

heed·ful (:fəl) adj. atento, cuidadoso.

heed·less (:lĭs) adj. descuidado, incauto ♦ **to be h.** of no hacer caso a.

hee·haw (hē'hô') s. rebuzno; *(guffaw)* risotada.

heel¹ (hēl) I. s. talón m; *(of shoe)* tacón m; *(of bread)* punta; JER. *(cad)* canalla ♦ **to be on someone's heels** andar pisándole los talones a alguien • **to cool one's heels** hacer antesala larga • **to take to one's heels** poner pies en polvorosa • **to turn on one's h.** dar media vuelta II. tr. poner el tacón a —intr. seguir de cerca.

heel² (hēl) tr. & intr. MARÍT. escorar, inclinar(se).

heft (hĕft) I. s. peso II. tr. *(to test the weight of)* sopesar; *(to lift)* alzar.

heft·y (hĕf'tē) adj. -i- pesado; *(strong)* robusto; *(amount)* cuantioso.

he·gem·o·ny (hĭ-jĕm'ə-nē) s. hegemonía.

heif·er (hĕf'ər) s. novilla.

height (hīt) s. altura, alto; *(summit)* cumbre f; *(of stupidity)* colmo; *(of person)* estatura; *(hill)* colina.

height·en ('n) tr. & intr. *(to increase)* aumentar(se); *(to make higher)* elevar(se).

hei·nous (hā'nəs) adj. atroz, nefando.

heir (âr) s. heredero ♦ **h. apparent** heredero forzoso.

heir·ess (âr'ĭs) s. heredera (de una fortuna).

heir·loom (âr'lōōm') s. reliquia de familia.

heist (hīst) JER. **I.** tr. robar **II.** s. robo.

held (hĕld) cf. **hold**[1].

hel·i·cop·ter (hĕl'ĭ-kŏp'tər) s. helicóptero.

he·li·o·cen·tric (hē'lē-ō-sĕn'trĭk) adj. heliocéntrico.

he·li·o·graph ('ə-grăf') s. heliógrafo.

he·lio·trope (hĕl'yə-trōp') s. heliotropo.

hel·i·port (hĕl'ə-pôrt') s. helipuerto.

he·li·um (hē'lē-əm) s. helio.

he·lix (hē'lĭks) s. [pl. **-es** o **-ces**] hélice *f*.

hell (hĕl) s. infierno ♦ FAM. **a h. of a** *(bad)* más malo que el diablo; *(good)* buenísimo • **a h. of a lot** muchísimo • **come h. or high water** contra viento y marea • **for the h. of it** por puro gusto • **like h.** muchísimo • **to give someone h.** encenderle los pelos a alguien • **to go to h.** echarse a perder • **to h. with it!** ¡al diablo! • **to raise h.** armar una de todos los diablos • **what, who the h. . . .** qué, quién diablos . . .

hell·bent ('bĕnt') adj. empeñado.

hell·cat (:kăt') s. *(shrew)* arpía; *(fiend)* demonio.

hell·fire ('fīr') s. fuego del infierno.

hell·hole (:hōl') s. lugar *m* de mala muerte.

hell·ion (:yən) s. FAM. bribón *m*, diablo.

hell·ish (:ĭsh) adj. infernal.

hel·lo (hĕ-lō', hə-) **I.** interj. ¡hola! **II.** s. ♦ **to say h.** saludar.

helm (hĕlm) s. timón *m*.

hel·met (hĕl'mĭt) s. casco.

help (hĕlp) **I.** tr. ayudar; *(to relieve)* aliviar; *(to save)* auxiliar; *(to prevent)* evitar; *(to serve)* servir ♦ **to h. oneself to** *(food)* servirse; *(to mooch)* mangar —intr. *(to serve)* ser útil; *(to assist)* prestar asistencia ♦ **to h. out** dar una mano **II.** s. ayuda; *(succor)* auxilio; *(relief)* alivio; *(remedy)* remedio; *(employees)* empleados; *(servants)* sirvientes.

help·er (hĕl'pər) s. ayudante *mf*.

help·ful (hĕlp'fəl) adj. útil; *(beneficial)* provechoso; *(kind)* amable.

help·ing (hĕl'pĭng) s. ración *f* ♦ **to have another h.** servirse más, repetir.

help·less (hĕlp'lĭs) adj. indefenso; *(powerless)* incapaz; *(disabled)* inválido.

help·mate (:māt') s. compañero; *(spouse)* esposo.

hel·ter-skel·ter (hĕl'tər-skĕl'tər) **I.** adj. atropellado; *(haphazard)* desordenado **II.** s. desorden *m* III. adv. FAM. a troche y moche.

hem[1] (hĕm) **I.** s. dobladillo **II.** tr. **-mm-** dobladillar; *(to enclose)* encerrar.

hem[2] **I.** interj. ¡ejem! **II.** intr. **-mm-** decir ¡ejem! ♦ **to h. and haw** vacilar al hablar.

he·man (hē'măn') s. [pl. **-men**] FAM. macho.

hem·i·sphere (hĕm'ĭ-sfîr') s. hemisferio.

hem·i·spher·ic/i·cal ('-sfîr'ĭk) adj. hemisférico.

hem·line (hĕm'līn') s. COST. bastilla, ruedo.

hem·lock (hĕm'lŏk') s. abeto, pinabete *m*; *(poisonous plant)* cicuta.

he·mo·glo·bin (hē'mə-glō'bĭn) s. hemoglobina.

he·mo·phil·i·a ('-fĭl'ē-ə) s. hemofilia.

he·mo·phil·i·ac (:ăk') s. hemofílico.

hem·or·rhage (hĕm'ər-ĭj) s. & intr. (sufrir una) hemorragia.

hem·or·rhoid (:ə-roid') s. almorrana.

hemp (hĕmp) s. cáñamo.

hem·stitch (hĕm'stĭch') s. vainica.

hen (hĕn) s. gallina; *(female bird)* hembra.

hence (hĕns) adv. por lo tanto; *(from now)* de aquí a <*a year h.* de aquí a un año>.

hence·forth ('fôrth') adv. de ahora en adelante.

hench·man (hĕnch'mən) s. [pl. **-men**] hombre *m* de confianza; *(supporter)* secuaz *m*.

hen·house (hĕn'hous') s. gallinero.

hen·na (hĕn'ə) s. alcana, alheña.

hen·peck (hĕn'pĕk') tr. FAM. dominar (al marido).

he·pat·ic (hĭ-păt'ĭk) adj. hepático.

hep·a·ti·tis (hĕp'ə-tī'tĭs) s. hepatitis *f*.

hep·ta·gon (hĕp'tə-gŏn') s. heptágono.

her (hər, hûr) **I.** pron. pers. la <*I saw h.* la vi>; le <*I told h.* le dije>; ella <*for h.* para ella> **II.** adj. pos. su, de ella.

her·ald (hĕr'əld) **I.** s. heraldo, anunciador *m*; *(harbinger)* precursor *m* **II.** tr. proclamar.

her·ald·ry (:əl-drē) s. blasón *m*; *(pageantry)* pompa heráldica.

herb (ûrb, hûrb) s. hierba ♦ **pl.** finas hierbas.

her·ba·ceous (hûr-bā'shəs, ûr-) adj. herbáceo.

herb·al (hûr'bəl, ûr'bəl) adj. herbario.

herb·al·ist (:bə-lĭst) s. herbolario.

her·bi·cide (:bĭ-sīd') s. herbicida.

her·biv·o·rous (hûr-bĭv'ər-əs, ûr-) adj. herbívoro.

her·cu·le·an (hûr'kyə-lē'ən) adj. hercúleo.

herd (hûrd) **I.** s. manada; *(crowd)* muchedumbre *f* **II.** tr. & intr. reunir(se) en manada.

herd·er (hûr'dər) s. *(of cattle)* vaquero; *(of sheep)* pastor *m*; *(livestock owner)* ganadero.

here (hîr) **I.** adv. aquí; *(to this place)* acá; *(now)* ahora; *(on this point)* en este punto ♦ **h. we are** ya llegamos • **that's neither h. nor there** eso no viene al caso **II.** adj. este <*my friend h.* este amigo mío>.

here·a·bout(s) ('ə-bout[s]') adv. por aquí.

here·af·ter (:ăf'tər) **I.** adv. en lo sucesivo; *(at a future time)* en un futuro **II.** s. el más allá.

here·by (:bī') adv. por este medio.

he·red·i·tar·y (hə-rĕd'ĭ-tĕr'ē) adj. hereditario.

he·red·i·ty (:tē) s. herencia.

here·in (hîr-ĭn') adv. en esto.

here·of (:ŭv') adv. *(acerca de esto).*

here·on (:ŏn') adv. sobre esto.

her·e·sy (hĕr'ĭ-sē) s. herejía.

her·e·tic (:tĭk) s. hereje *mf*.

he·ret·i·cal (hə-rĕt'ĭ-kəl) adj. herético.

here·to·fore (hîr'tə-fôr') adv. hasta ahora.

here·up·on (:ə-pŏn') adv. a continuación.

here·with (hîr-wĭth') adv. adjunto.

her·i·ta·ble (hĕr'ĭ-tə-bəl) adj. hereditario.

her·i·tage (:tĭj) s. herencia; *(legacy)* patrimonio.

her·maph·ro·dite (hər-măf'rə-dīt') s. hermafrodita *mf*.

her·mit (hûr'mĭt) s. ermitaño.

her·mit·age (:mĭ-tĭj) s. RELIG. ermita.

her·ni·a (hûr'nē-ə) s. [pl. **s** o **-ae**] hernia.

he·ro (hîr'ō) s. [pl. **es**] héroe *m*; LIT. protagonista *m*; JER. *(sandwich)* emparedado grande.

he·ro·ic (hĭ-rō'ĭk) adj. heroico ♦ **heroics** s.pl. rimbombancia.

her·o·in (hĕr'ō-ĭn) s. heroína (narcótico).

her·o·ine (hĕr'ō-ĭn) s. heroína; LIT. protago-

nista.
her·o·ism (:ĭz'əm) s. heroísmo.
her·on (hĕr'ən) s. garza.
her·pes (hûr'pēz) s. herpes *m*.
her·ring (hĕr'ĭng) s. [pl. inv. *o* **s**] arenque *m*.
her·ring·bone (:bōn') s. *(pattern)* espinapez *f*; *(in cloth)* punto de espina.
hers (hûrz) pron. pos. (el) suyo, el de ella.
her·self (hûr-sĕlf') pron. pers. *(reflexive)* se <*she hurt h.* se lastimó>; *(emphatic)* ella misma <*she h.* ella misma>; *(after preposition)* (sí) misma ♦ **by h.** sola.
hes·i·tan·cy (hĕz'ĭ-tn-sē) s. indecisión *f*.
hes·i·tant (:tnt) adj. vacilante.
hes·i·tate (:tāt') intr. vacilar; *(not to dare)* no atreverse.
hes·i·ta·tion ('-tā'shən) s. indecisión *f*; *(vacillation)* titubeo.
het·er·o·dox (hĕt'ər-ə-dŏks') adj. heterodoxo; *(heretic)* herético.
het·er·o·dox·y (:dŏk'sē) s. heterodoxia.
het·er·o·ge·ne·ous ('--jē'nē-əs) adj. heterogéneo.
het·er·o·sex·u·al (hĕt'ə-rō-sĕk'shōō-əl) adj. & s. heterosexual.
het·er·o·sex·u·al·i·ty (:sĕk'shōō-ăl'ĭ-tē) s. heterosexualidad *f*.
hew (hyōō) tr. **-ed**, **-ed** *o* **-n** *(to shape)* tallar; *(to cut down)* talar —intr. conformarse.
hex (hĕks) I. s. embrujo; *(jinx)* aojo II. tr. embrujar.
hex·a·gon (hĕk'sə-gŏn') s. hexágono.
hex·ag·o·nal (hĕk-săg'ə-nəl) adj. hexagonal.
hey (hā) interj. ¡eh!, ¡oiga!
hey·day (hā'dā') s. auge *m*.
hi (hī) interj. ¡oye!, ¡hola!
hi·a·tus (hī-ā'təs) s. [pl. inv. *o* **es**] grieta; *(gap)* laguna; ANAT., FONÉT. hiato.
hi·ber·nate (hī'bər-nāt') intr. hibernar.
hi·ber·na·tion ('-nā'shən) s. hibernación *f*.
hi·bis·cus (hī-bĭs'kəs) s. hibisco.
hic·cup/cough (hĭk'əp) I. s. hipo II. intr. **-pp-** tener hipo, hipar.
hick (hĭk) s. FAM. aldeano.
hick·o·ry (hĭk'ə-rē) s. nogal americano.
hide¹ (hīd) tr. **hid**, **hid(den)** ocultar, esconder; *(to conceal)* disimular; *(to cover up)* tapar —intr. esconderse; *(to seek refuge)* refugiarse.
hide² s. cuero ♦ **not to see h. nor hair of** no ver el pelo de.
hide-and-seek (hīd'n-sēk') s. escondidas.
hide·a·way ('-ə-wā') s. escondite *m*; *(retreat)* retiro.
hid·e·ous (hĭd'ē-əs) adj. espantoso; *(atrocious)* atroz.
hide-out (hīd'out') s. escondite *m*.
hid·ing (hī'dĭng) s. ♦ **h. place** escondite ♦ **in h.** escondido ♦ **to come out of h.** salir de su escondite ♦ **to go into h.** esconderse.
hi·er·ar·chy (hī'ə-rär'kē) s. jerarquía.
hi·er·o·glyph·ic (hī'ər-ə-glĭf'ĭk) adj. & s. jeroglífico.
hi-fi (hī'fī') s. (aparato de) alta fidelidad.
high (hī) I. adj. alto; *(tall)* de altura; *(peaking)* culminante; *(lofty)* grande; *(wind, fever)* fuerte; *(Mass)* mayor; *(voice)* agudo; *(advanced)* avanzado; *(crime)* grave; FAM. *(drunk)* borracho; *(drugged)* drogado ♦ **h. and dry** desam·pa·ra·do ♦ **h. and mighty** FAM. arrogante ♦ **h. jump** salto de altura ♦ **h. noon** pleno mediodía ♦ **h. priority** primera importancia ♦ **h. seas** alta mar ♦ **h. school** escuela secundaria ♦ **h. tide**

pleamar ♦ **to be h. in** tener un alto contenido de ♦ **to be h. time** ya ser hora ♦ **to be in h. spirits** estar de excelente humor II. adv. en lo alto, alto ♦ **h. above** muy por encima de ♦ **h. priced** caro, de lujo ♦ **to look h. and low** buscar por todas partes ♦ **to run h.** estar exaltado ♦ **to sing h.** cantar en un tono alto *o* agudo III. s. altura; *(gear)* directa; METEOR. zona de alta presión ♦ **on h.** en las alturas ♦ **to be on a h.** JER. estar de excelente humor.
high·ball (hī'bôl') s. whisky *m* con gaseosa.
high·born (hī'bôrn') adj. de noble cuna.
high·boy (hī'boi') s. cómoda alta.
high·brow (hī'brou') FAM. I. s. intelectual *mf*; *(pedant)* pedante *mf* II. adj. culto.
high-chair (hī'châr') s. silla alta para niños.
high-class (hī'klăs') adj. de primera clase.
high·er (hī'ər) adj. más alto; *(greater)* mayor; *(advanced)* superior.
high·er-up (hī'ər-ŭp') s. FAM. superior *m*.
high-fa·lu·tin (hī'fə-lōōt'n) adj. FAM. pretencioso.
high-grade (hī'grād') adj. de calidad superior.
high-hand·ed (hī'hăn'dĭd) adj. arrogante; *(dictatorial)* despótico.
high-hat (hī'hăt') adj. desdeñoso, engreido.
high·land (hī'lənd) s. terreno montañoso.
high-lev·el (hī'lĕv'əl) adj. de alto nivel.
high·light (hī'līt') I. s. toque *m* de luz; *(event)* suceso *o* atracción *f* principal II. tr. iluminar; *(to emphasize)* destacar.
high·ly (hī'lē) adv. altamente; *(extremely)* extremadamente; *(well)* muy bien.
high-mind·ed (hī'mīn'dĭd) adj. noble.
high·ness (hī'nĭs) s. altura ♦ **H.** Alteza.
high-per·for·mance (hī'pər-fôr'məns) adj. de alto rendimiento.
high-pitched (hī'pĭcht') adj. agudo; *(voice)* chillón; *(activity)* frenético.
high-pow·er(ed) (hī'pou'ər[d]) adj. de alta potencia, de gran fuerza *o* energía.
high-pres·sure (hī'prĕsh'ər) adj. de alta presión; FAM. *(tenacious)* insistente.
high-rise (hī'rīz') s. edificio de muchos pisos.
high-spir·it·ed (hī'spĭr'ĭ-tĭd) adj. animoso; *(energetic)* vivo.
high-strung (hī'strŭng') adj. muy nervioso.
high-tail (hī'tāl') intr. JER. salir corriendo.
high-tech (hī'tĕk') adj. de tecnología avanzada.
high-test (hī'tĕst') adj. de alta octanaje.
high·way (hī'wā') s. carretera, autopista.
hi·jack (hī'jăk') tr. FAM. *(vehicle)* secuestrar; *(goods)* robarse.
hi·jack·er (:ər) s. secuestrador *m*; *(of plane)* pirata aéreo.
hi·jack·ing (:ĭng) s. secuestro; *(of plane)* piratería aérea.
hike (hīk) I. intr. caminar ♦ **to h. up** subirse —tr. aumentar (precios) II. s. *(walk)* caminata; *(rise)* aumento ♦ **take a h.!** JER. ¡váyase a paseo! ♦ **to go on a h.** ir de excursión.
hik·er (hī'kər) s. excursionista *mf*.
hi·lar·i·ous (hī-lâr'ē-əs) adj. para morirse de risa.
hi·lar·i·ty (:ĭ-tē) s. hilaridad *f*.
hill (hĭl) s. colina; *(heap)* montón *m* ♦ **to be over the h.** FAM. ir cuesta abajo.
hill·bil·ly (hĭl'bĭl'ē) s. FAM. patán *m*.
hill·side (:sīd') s. ladera (de un cerro).
hill·top (:tŏp') s. cima (de un cerro).
hill·y (:ē) adj. **-i-** montuoso.
hilt (hĭlt) s. mango ♦ **to the h.** totalmente.

him (hǐm) pron. pers. le, lo <*they accepted h.* lo aceptaron>; le <*they sent h. a letter* le mandaron una carta>; él <*to h.* a él>.

him·self (:sĕlf′) pron. pers. *(reflexive)* se <*he hit h.* se golpeó>; *(emphatic)* él mismo <*he h.* él mismo>; *(after preposition)* (sí) mismo ♦ **by h.** solo.

hind¹ (hīnd) adj. trasero, posterior.

hind² s. *(deer)* cierva.

hin·der (hǐn′dər) tr. impedir, obstaculizar.

hind·most (hīnd′mōst′) adj. postrero, último.

hin·drance (hǐn′drəns) s. impedimento.

hind·sight (hīnd′sīt′) s. retrospección *f.*

hinge (hǐnj) I. s. bisagra II. tr. poner bisagras a —intr. ♦ **to h. on** depender de.

hint (hǐnt) I. s. insinuación *f*; *(tip)* sugerencia; *(clue)* idea ♦ **not a h. of** ni rastro de • **to drop a h.** tirar una indirecta • **to take a h.** darse por aludido II. tr. insinuar, dar a entender —intr. ♦ **to h. at** insinuar; *(to allude to)* aludir a.

hin·ter·land (hǐn′tər-lănd′) s. interior *m* (de un país).

hip¹ (hǐp) s. ANAT. cadera.

hip² adj. **-pp-** JER. al tanto, informado.

hip³ interj. ♦ **h., h., hurrah!** ¡hurra!, ¡viva!, ¡olé!

hip·bone (′bōn′) s. cía, hueso de la cadera.

hip·pie (hǐp′ē) s. hippie *mf.*

hip·po (hǐp′ō) s. FAM. hipopótamo.

Hip·po·crat·ic oath (hǐp′ə-krăt′ĭk) s. juramento hipocrático.

hip·po·drome (hǐp′ə-drōm′) s. hipódromo.

hip·po·pot·a·mus (hǐp′ə-pŏt′ə-məs) s. [pl. **es** o **-mi**] hipopótamo.

hire (hīr) I. tr. emplear; *(to rent)* alquilar ♦ **now hiring** se necesitan empleados —intr. ♦ **to h. out** as aceptar trabajo de II. s. *(wages)* sueldo; *(rent)* alquiler *m* ♦ **for h.** se alquila.

hire·ling (′lǐng) s. asalariado, alquilón *m.*

hir·ing (:ĭng) s. contratación *f*; *(renting)* alquiler *m.*

hir·sute (hûr′sōōt′) adj. hirsuto.

his (hǐz) I. adj. pos. su, de él II. pron. pos. (el) suyo, el de él.

His·pan·o·phone (hĭ-spăn′ə-fōn′) s. hispanohablante *mf.*

hiss (hǐs) I. s. siseo; *(whistling)* silbido II. tr. & intr. silbar.

his·to·ri·an (hǐ-stôr′ē-ən) s. historiador *m.*

his·to·ric/i·cal (:ĭk) adj. histórico.

his·to·ry (hǐs′tə-rē) s. historia; *(background)* historial *m* ♦ **to go down in h.** pasar a la historia • **to make h.** dejar huella en la historia.

his·tri·on·ic (hǐs′trē-ŏn′ĭk) adj. histriónico ♦ **histrionics** s.pl. histrionismo.

hit (hǐt) I. tr. **hit** golpear; *(to collide with)* chocar contra o con; *(target)* dar en; *(to reach)* alcanzar; FAM. *(idea)* ocurrir ♦ **to h. home** tocar un punto vulnerable • **to h. it off (with)** FAM. hacer buenas migas con • **to h. on** FAM. encontrar, dar con —intr. ocurrir ♦ **to h. below the belt** dar un golpe bajo II. s. golpe *m*; *(collision)* choque *m*; *(shot)* tiro; *(success)* éxito ♦ **h. or miss** al azar ♦ **to be a h. with** caerle simpático a.

hit-and-run (′n-rŭn′) adj. que atropella y huye *(conductor de un vehículo).*

hitch (hǐch) I. tr. enganchar ♦ **to h. a ride** FAM. hacerse llevar en automóvil • **to h. up** uncir —intr. FAM. *(to hitchhike)* viajar a dedo; *(to fasten)* engancharse a ♦ **to get hitched** FAM. casarse II. s. FAM. tropiezo; MIL. período de servicio; *(knot)* vuelta de cabo; *(tug)* tirón *m*;

(device) enganche *m* ♦ **without a h.** sin dificultad.

hitch·hike (′hīk′) intr. hacer autostop.

hitch·hik·er (:hī′kər) s. autostopista *mf.*

hith·er (hǐth′ər) I. adv. (hacia) acá II. adj. citerior, más cercano.

hith·er·to (:tōō′) adv. hasta ahora.

hive (hīv) s. colmena; *(colony)* enjambre *m.*

hives (hīvz) s.pl. urticaria.

ho (hō) interj. ¡eh!, ¡oiga!

hoa·gie (hō′gē) s. FAM. sandwich *m* grande.

hoar (hôr) s. escarcha.

hoard (hôrd) I. s. provisión acumulada II. tr. & intr. acaparar, atesorar.

hoar·frost (hôr′frôst′) s. escarcha.

hoarse (hôrs) adj. ronco.

hoar·y (hôr′ē) adj. **-i-** cano; *(old)* vetusto.

hoax (hōks) s. engaño, trampa.

hob·ble (hŏb′əl) I. intr. cojear —tr. *(an animal)* trabar, manear; *(to hamper)* impedir II. s. *(walk)* cojera; *(device)* maniota.

hob·by (hŏb′ē) s. pasatiempo, afición *f.*

hob·by·horse (:hôrs′) s. caballito de madera; *(topic)* tema favorito.

hob·gob·lin (hŏb′gŏb′lĭn) s. duende *m*; *(bugbear)* espantajo.

hob·nob (hŏb′nŏb′) intr. **-bb-** codearse.

ho·bo (hō′bō) [pl. **(e)s**] vago, vagabundo.

hock¹ (hŏk) s. ZOOL. jarrete *m.*

hock² FAM. I. tr. empeñar II. s. empeño.

hock·ey (hŏk′ē) s. hockey *m* ♦ **ice h.** hockey sobre hielo.

hock·shop (hŏk′shŏp′) s. FAM. casa de empeños.

ho·cus-po·cus (hō′kəs-pō′kəs) I. s. pasapasa *m*; *(trickery)* engaño II. interj. abracadabra.

hodge·podge (hŏj′pŏj′) s. mezcolanza.

hoe (hō) I. s. azada II. tr. & intr. azadonar.

hog (hŏg, hôg) I. s. cerdo, puerco; FAM. *(selfish person)* cochino ♦ **to live high on the h.** FAM. vivir en la abundancia II. tr. **-gg-** acaparar.

hog-tie o **hog·tie** (′tī′) tr. **-tying/-tieing** atar juntas las patas de; *(to impede)* poner trabas.

hog·wash (:wŏsh′) s. *(swill)* bazofia; *(nonsense)* tonterías.

ho-hum (hō′hŭm′) interj. expresa aburrimiento.

hoist (hoist) I. tr. izar II. s. grúa, cabria.

hok·ey (hō′kē) adj. **-i-** JER. *(trite)* banal; *(phony)* falso.

hold¹ (hōld) I. tr. **held** asir, agarrar; *(to take)* tener; *(to support)* sostener; *(to secure)* sujetar; *(to own)* ser dueño de; *(for questioning)* tener bajo custodia; *(to keep)* retener; *(to accommodate)* tener capacidad para; *(to control)* contener; *(to occupy)* ocupar; *(fort)* defender; *(course)* mantener; *(to reserve)* reservar; *(to consider)* creer; *(meeting)* celebrar; *(elections)* convocar; *(title)* poseer; MÚS. sostener; *(room)* reservar; *(one's liquor)* aguantar ♦ **h. everything!** ¡paren! • **h. it!** ¡no se muevan! • **h. the phone!** ¡un momento! • **h. your horses!** FAM. ¡espérate un momento! • **to be left holding the bag** FAM. cargar con el muerto • **to h. a gun on** apuntar con una pistola a • **to h. back** *(to repress)* reprimir, contener; *(to impede)* impedir • **to h. captive** mantener cautivo • **to h. dear** estimar • **to h. down** *(to oppress)* oprimir; *(to pin down)* mantener sujeto; *(prices)* moderar • **to h. down a job** tener un trabajo • **to h. hands** ir cogidos de la mano • **to h. it against** guardar rencor a • **to h. it in** JER. aguantarse • **to h. off** alejar • **to h. one's own** defenderse •

to h. on tight agarrar fuertemente • **to h. on to** *(to grip)* agarrarse a; *(to keep)* seguir con • **to h. over** *(to threaten)* amenazar con; *(to extend)* continuar • **to h. to** hacer cumplir • **to h. up** FAM. *(to delay)* atrasar; *(to rob)* atracar; *(to lift)* levantar; *(to stop)* detener —intr. asirse, agarrar-se; *(to be firm)* sostenerse; *(to be valid)* seguir en vigor ♦ **to h. back** contenerse • **to h. forth** on hablar de • **to h. off** demorarse • **to h. on** *(to grip)* agarrarse bien; *(to continue)* proseguir; *(to wait)* aguardar, esperar • **to h. out** *o* **up** *(to last)* durar; *(to resist)* aguantar • **to h. out on** FAM. tener secretos con • **to h. over** aplazar • **to h. to** seguir firme en II. s. *(grip)* asidero; *(influence)* influencia; *(cell)* celda (de prisión); MÚS. calderón *m* ♦ **to get h. of** *(to grasp)* coger; *(to obtain)* conseguir; *(to find)* encontrar • **to get h. of oneself** controlarse, dominarse.

hold² s. MARÍT. bodega; AER. cabina de carga.

hold·ing (hōl'dĭng) s. inquilinato ♦ pl. propiedades.

hold·out (hōld'out') s. persona que obstaculiza un acuerdo.

hold·o·ver (:ō'vər) s. remanente *m*, resto.

hold·up (:ŭp') s. *(delay)* demora; *(robbery)* asalto, atraco (a mano armada).

hole (hōl) I. s. hueco; *(in ground)* hoyo; *(in road)* bache *m*; *(small)* agujero; *(large)* boquete *m*; *(burrow)* madriguera; *(dwelling)* ratonera; *(flaw)* falla; *(predicament)* aprieto; *(in golf)* hoyo ♦ **in the h.** FAM. endeudado II. tr. agujerear —intr. ♦ **to h. up** esconderse.

hol·i·day (hōl'ĭ-dā') s. día feriado; RELIG. día de fiesta ♦ pl. G.B. vacaciones.

ho·li·er-than-thou (hō'lē-ər-*than*-thou') adj. santurrón.

hol·ler (hōl'ər) I. intr. & tr. gritar II. s. grito.

hol·low (hōl'ō) I. adj. hueco; *(concave)* cóncavo; *(reverberating)* retumbante; *(empty)* vacío II. s. hueco; *(depression)* depresión *f*; *(emptiness)* vacío III. tr. ♦ **to h. out** ahuecar.

hol·ly (hōl'ē) s. acebo.

hol·ly·hock (hōl'ē-hŏk') s. malva loca.

ho·lo·caust (hō'lə-kôst', hŏl'ə-) s. destrucción completa (por el fuego).

ho·lo·gram (hō'lə-grăm', hŏl'ə-) s. holograma *m*.

ho·lo·graph (:grăf') s. ológrafo.

hol·ster (hōl'stər) s. pistolera.

ho·ly (hō'lē) adj. -i- sacro; *(revered)* venerable; *(saintly)* santo, pío ♦ **H. day** fiesta de guardar.

hom·age (hŏm'ĭj, ŏm'-) s. homenaje *m*.

home (hōm) I. s. casa; *(residence)* domicilio; *(household)* hogar *m*; *(headquarters)* sede *f*; *(institution)* asilo ♦ **a h. away from h.** lugar donde uno está como en su propia casa • **at h. and abroad** dentro y fuera del país • **to be away from h.** estar de viaje • **to feel at h.** sentirse a gusto • **to make oneself at h.** ponerse cómodo • **to make one's h.** establecerse II. adj. casero; *(native)* natal; *(team)* de casa; *(game)* en casa ♦ **h. economics** economía doméstica • **h. front** frente civil • **h. port** puerto de origen • **h. run** DEP. jonrón III. adv. ♦ **at h.** en casa • **to be h.** estar (en casa); *(after a trip)* estar de vuelta • **to come, go h.** regresar, irse a casa • **to see h.** acompañar hasta casa • **to hit h.** dar en el blanco IV. intr. volver a casa; *(missile)* autodirigirse ♦ **homing pigeon** paloma mensajera.

home·bod·y (:bŏd'ē) s. persona hogareña.

home·com·ing (:kŭm'ĭng) s. regreso al hogar.

home·grown (:grōn') adj. de cosecha propia.

home·land (:lănd') s. patria.

home·less (:lĭs) adj. sin hogar.

home·ly (:lē) adj. -i- sin atractivo; *(domestic)* casero; *(plain)* sencillo, rústico.

home·made (:mād') adj. hecho en casa.

home·mak·er (:mā'kər) s. ama de casa.

hom·er (hō'mər) s. jonrón *m*.

home·sick (:sĭk') adj. nostálgico.

home·spun (:spŭn') adj. tejido en casa; *(simple)* sencillo.

home·stead (:stĕd') I. s. *(farm)* granja; FAM. casa II. intr. & tr. tomar posesión legalmente (de tierras).

home·stretch (:strĕch') s. etapa final.

home·town (:toun') s. ciudad *f* de origen *o* de residencia.

home·ward (:wərd) I. adj. de vuelta, de regreso II. adv. [*o* -wards] hacia casa.

home·work (:wûrk') s. deberes *m*, tareas escolares; FIG. trabajo preliminar.

hom·ey (hō'mē) adj. -i- FAM. hogareño; *(intimate)* íntimo.

hom·i·cid·al (hŏm'ĭ-sīd'l, hō'mĭ-) adj. homicida.

hom·i·cide ('-sīd') s. homicidio; *(murderer)* homicida *mf*.

hom·i·ly (hŏm'ə-lē) s. homilía, sermón *m*.

ho·mo·ge·ne·ous (hō'mə-jē'nē-əs) adj. homogéneo.

ho·mog·e·nize (hō-mŏj'ə-nīz') tr. homogeneizar.

hom·o·graph (hŏm'ə-grăf') s. homógrafo.

hom·o·nym (:nĭm') s. homónimo.

hom·o·phone (:fōn') s. homófono.

ho·mo·sex·u·al (hō'mō-sĕk'shōō-əl) adj. & s. homosexual *mf*.

ho·mo·sex·u·al·i·ty (:sĕk'shōō-ăl'ĭ-tē) s. homosexualidad *f*.

hon·cho (hŏn'chō) JER. s. jefe *m*.

hone (hōn) I. s. piedra de afilar II. tr. afilar; *(to perfect)* pulir.

hon·est (ŏn'ĭst) I. adj. honesto; *(honorable)* recto; *(truthful)* veraz; *(sincere)* franco; *(genuine)* legítimo II. interj. te lo juro.

hon·es·ty (:ĭ-stē) s. honestidad *f*; *(integrity)* honradez *f*; *(truthfulness)* veracidad *f*; *(sincerity)* franqueza.

hon·ey (hŭn'ē) s. miel *f*; *(sweetness)* dulzura; *(darling)* tesoro, encanto ♦ **a h. of a** una maravilla de.

hon·ey·bee (:bē') s. abeja (melera).

hon·ey·comb (:kōm') I. s. panal *m* II. tr. acribillar.

hon·ey·dew (:dōō') s. secreción dulce de algunos insectos; *(melon)* variedad de melón dulce.

hon·ey·eyed (hŭn'ēd) adj. con miel; *(sweet)* meloso.

hon·ey·moon (:ē-mōōn') s. & intr. (pasar la) luna de miel.

hon·ey·suck·le (:sŭk'əl) s. madreselva.

honk (hôngk) I. s. *(goose)* graznido; *(horn)* bocinazo II. tr. & intr. tocar la bocina.

hon·or (ŏn'ər) I. s. honor *m*, honra; *(decoration)* condecoración *f*; *(probity)* probidad *f* ♦ **on my h.!** ¡palabra de honor! • **to be on one's h.** estar obligado por el honor • **to consider it an h.** tener la honra de • **to do the honors** rendir honores • **your H.** Su Señoría II. tr. honrar; *(check)* aceptar; *(contract)* cumplir.

hon·or·a·ble (:ə-bəl) adj. honorable; *(praiseworthy)* honroso; *(honest)* honrado; *(illustri-*

ous) excelentísimo; *(honorific)* honorífico ♦ **h. mention** accesít.

hon·or·a·bly (:blē) adv. honorablemente.

hon·o·rar·i·um (ŏn´ə-rår´ē-əm) s. [pl. **s** o **-ia**] honorarios.

hon·or·ar·y (´-rĕr´ē) adj. honorario.

hon·or·if·ic (:rĭf´ĭk) adj. honorífico.

hood (hŏd) s. capucha, caperuza; *(of car)* capó.

hood·ed (´ĭd) adj. encapuchado; *(hood-shaped)* con forma de capucha.

hood·lum (hŏd´ləm, hŏd´-) s. *(gangster)* maleante m; *(ruffian)* rufián m.

hood·wink (hŏd´wĭngk´) tr. engañar; *(to trick)* embaucar.

hoo·ey (hŏo´ē) s. JER. tonterías.

hoof (hŏof) I. s. [pl. **s** o **-ves**] pezuña II. tr. ♦ **to h. it** FAM. ir andando —intr. JER. bailar.

hoofed (hŏoft) adj. ungulado.

hook (hŏok) I. s. gancho; *(for fishing)* anzuelo; *(for clothes)* percha ♦ **by h. or by crook** por las buenas o por las malas • **h., line, and sinker** JER. del todo • **off the h.** *(telephone)* descolgado; *(absolved)* eximido II. tr. enganchar; *(to snare)* pescar; JER. *(to steal)* robar; *(to bend)* encorvar ♦ **to get hooked on** JER. enviciarse con • **to h. up** enganchar; ELEC. conectar; *(to assemble)* armar —intr. doblar, torcer; *(to be fastened)* engancharse.

hooked (hŏokt) adj. ganchudo; *(addicted)* adicto; *(trapped)* enviciado ♦ **h. rug** alfombra de nudo.

hook·er (hŏok´ər) s. JER. prostituta.

hook·nosed (:nōzd´) adj. de nariz aguileña.

hook·up (:ŭp´) s. sistema m de conexión.

hook·worm (:wûrm´) s. anquilostoma m.

hook·y (hŏok´ē) s. ♦ **to play h.** hacer novillos.

hoo·li·gan (hŏo´lĭ-gən) s. FAM. rufián m.

hoop (hŏop) s. aro; *(band)* zuncho.

hoop·la (hŏop´lä´) s. alboroto; *(misleading talk)* galimatías.

hoot (hŏot) I. intr. ulular; *(to boo)* abuchear II. s. ululato; *(shout)* risotada ♦ **not to give a h.** no importarle a uno un comino.

hooves (hŏovz) cf. **hoof.**

hop¹ (hŏp) I. intr. -**pp**- brincar; *(to skip)* saltar con un pie ♦ **to h. to it** echar manos a la obra II. brinco; *(rebound)* rebote m; FAM. *(dance)* baile m; *(short trip)* vuelo corto ♦ **h., skip, and a jump** distancia corta.

hop² (hŏp) s. lúpulo ♦ pl. frutos desecados del lúpulo.

hope (hōp) I. intr. esperar ♦ **I should h. so!** ¡eso espero! • **to h. for** tener esperanzas de II. s. esperanza ♦ **to build up one's hopes** hacerse ilusiones.

hope·ful (´fəl) I. adj. esperanzado; *(promising)* prometedor II. s. aspirante m.

hope·ful·ly (:f-lē) adv. esperanzadamente; *(one hopes)* se espera que.

hope·less (:lĭs) adj. desesperado; *(impossible)* imposible ♦ **h. case** caso perdido.

hop·scotch (hŏp´skŏch´) s. rayuela.

horde (hôrd) s. horda, multitud f.

ho·ri·zon (hə-rī´zən) s. horizonte m.

hor·i·zon·tal (hôr´ĭ-zŏn´tl) adj. & s. horizontal f.

hor·mo·nal (hôr-mō´nəl) adj. hormonal.

hor·mone (´mōn´) s. hormona.

horn (hôrn) I. s. cuerno; TEC. bocina; MÚS. trompa; FAM. saxófono, trompeta ♦ **h. of plenty** cornucopia • **to blow one's own h.** echarse flo-

res II. intr. ♦ **to h. in** JER. entremeterse.

horn·bill (´bĭl´) s. cálao.

horned (hôrnd) adj. cornudo.

hor·net (hôr´nĭt) s. avispón m.

horn·y (hôr´nē) adj. -**i**- córneo; *(calloused)* calloso.

hor·o·scope (hôr´ə-skōp´) s. horóscopo.

hor·ren·dous (hô-rĕn´dəs) adj. horrendo.

hor·ri·ble (hôr´ə-bəl) adj. horrible; *(disagreeable)* desagradable.

hor·rid (hôr´ĭd) adj. hórrido; *(offensive)* repulsivo.

hor·rif·ic (hô-rĭf´ĭk) adj. horrendo.

hor·ri·fy (hôr´ə-fī´) tr. horrorizar; *(to shock)* escandalizar.

hor·ror (:ər) s. *(fear)* horror m; *(abhorrence)* aversión f; FAM. *(ugly thing)* espanto ♦ **h. film** película de miedo.

hors d'oeuvre (ôr dûrv´) s. [pl. inv. o **s**] entremés m.

horse (hôrs) I. s. caballo; *(frame)* caballete m; DEP. potro ♦ **a h. of another color** otro cantar • **from the h.'s mouth** de buena tinta • **h. sense** FAM. sentido común II. intr. ♦ **to h. around** jugar alborotosamente III. adj. hípico.

horse·back (´bǎk´) s. ♦ adv. a caballo.

horse·drawn (:drōn´) adj. tirado por caballos.

horse·flesh (:flĕsh´) s. caballos (en general).

horse·fly (:flī´) s. tábano.

horse·hair (:hâr´) s. pelo de caballo; *(cloth)* tela de crin.

horse·man (:mən) s. [pl. **-men**] caballista m; *(breeder)* criador m (de caballos).

horse·play (:plā´) s. FAM. juego rudo.

horse·pow·er (:pou´ər) s. caballo de fuerza.

horse·rad·ish (:rǎd´ĭsh) s. rábano picante.

horse·shoe (:shŏo´) s. herradura ♦ pl. juego en que se tira a un hito con herraduras.

horse·wom·an (:wŏom´ən) s. [pl. **-women**] caballista f; *(breeder)* criadora (de caballos).

hors·(e)y (hôr´sē) adj. -**i**- caballuno, caballar.

hor·ti·cul·ture (hôr´tĭ-kŭl´chər) s. horticultura.

hose (hōz) I. s. [pl. inv.] medias; *(socks)* calcetines m; *(tube)* [pl. **s**] manguera II. tr. regar o lavar (con manguera).

ho·sier·y (hō´zhə-rē) s. medias.

hos·pice (hŏs´pĭs) s. hospicio.

hos·pi·ta·ble (hŏs´pĭ-tə-bəl, hŏ-spĭt´ə-) adj. hospitalario; *(receptive)* receptivo.

hos·pi·tal (hŏs´pĭt´l) s. hospital m.

hos·pi·tal·i·ty (hŏs´pĭ-tǎl´ĭ-tē) s. hospitalidad f.

hos·pi·tal·ize (hŏs´pĭt´l-īz´) tr. hospitalizar.

host¹ (hōst) I. s. *(at a meal, party)* anfitrión m; *(of inn)* mesonero; TELEV. presentador m II. tr. FAM. ser el anfitrión de.

host² (hōst) s. multitud f; *(army)* hueste f.

hos·tage (hŏs´tĭj) s. rehén mf.

hos·tel (hŏs´təl) s. albergue m (para jóvenes); *(inn)* hostería.

hos·tel·ry (:rē) s. hostería.

host·ess (hō´stĭs) s. *(host)* anfitriona; *(waitress)* camarera; *(stewardess)* azafata.

hos·tile (hŏs´təl, -tīl´) adj. hostil; *(antagonistic)* antagónico.

hos·til·i·ty (hŏ-stĭl´ĭ-tē) s. hostilidad f; *(act)* acto hostil ♦ pl. hostilidades, actos de guerra.

hot (hŏt) adj. -**tt**- caliente; *(climate)* cálido; *(sun)* abrasador; *(spicy)* picante; *(temper)* vivo; *(controversial)* muy discutido; *(heated)* acalorado; *(stolen)* robado; *(excellent)* excelente; *(lucky)* con mucha suerte; *(new)* muy rítmico ♦ **h. air** JER. palabrería • **h. dog** salchicha • **h. line** línea de emergencia • **h. off the press**

de última hora • **h. on the trail** sobre la pista • **in h. pursuit** tras los talones • **h. pepper** ají • **h. plate** infiernillo • **h. rod** automóvil modificado • **h. seat** FAM. situación crítica • **in h. water** FAM. en un lío • **to be h.** *(person)* tener calor; *(weather)* hacer calor.

hot·bed (′bĕd′) s. almajara; FIG. semillero.

hot·blood·ed (′blŭd′ĭd) adj. fogoso.

ho·tel (hō-tĕl′) s. hotel *m.*

hot·foot (hŏt′fŏŏt′) intr. ◆ **to h. it** ir de prisa.

hot·head (:hĕd′) s. persona arrebatada.

hot·head·ed (′′ĭd) adj. arrebatado.

hot·house (hŏt′hous′) s. invernadero.

hot·shot (:shŏt′) s. JER. as *mf* (persona brillante).

hot·wa·ter bottle (-wŏ′tər) s. bolsa de agua caliente.

hound (hound) **I.** s. podenco; *(enthusiast)* aficionado **II.** tr. *(to harass)* acosar; *(to nag)* importunar.

hour (our) s. hora.

hour·glass (′glăs′) s. reloj *m* de arena.

hour·ly (:lē) **I.** adj. horario; *(by the hour)* por hora **II.** adv. a cada hora; *(by the hour)* por horas.

house (hous) **I.** s. casa; *(home)* hogar *m; (auditorium)* teatro; *(audience)* público; *(of parliament)* cámara **h. arrest** arresto domiciliario **II.** tr. (houz) alojar; *(to shelter)* proteger; *(to contain)* contener.

house·boat (′bŏt′) s. casa flotante.

house·bro·ken (:brŏ′kən) adj. enseñado en limpieza *(un animal casero).*

house·clean·ing (:klē′nĭng) s. limpieza de la casa.

house·coat (:kōt′) s. bata (de casa).

house·fly (:flī′) s. mosca común.

house·hold (:hōld′) s. casa (establecimiento doméstico).

house·keep·er (:kē′pər) s. ama de llaves.

house·keep·ing (:kē′pĭng) s. manejo de una casa.

house·warm·ing (:wŏr′mĭng) s. fiesta para el estreno de una casa.

house·wife (:wīf′) s. [pl. **-ves**] ama de casa.

house·work (:wûrk′) s. quehaceres domésticos.

hous·ing (hou′zĭng) s. casas *f; (place to live)* vivienda; MEC. cárter *m* ◆ **h. development** unidad vecinal.

hov·el (hŭv′əl, hŏv′-) s. cuchitril *m.*

hov·er (hŭv′ər, hŏv′-) intr. *(soar)* cernerse; *(flutter)* revolotear ◆ **to h. around** rondar • **to h. between** vacilar.

how (hou) **I.** adv. cómo; *(in what condition)* qué tal; *(to what extent)* cuánto, qué ◆ **and h.!** ¡y cómo! • **h. about . . . ?** ¿qué te parece . . . ? • **h. about me?** ¿y yo, qué? • **h. are you?** ¿cómo está usted? • **h. big is it?** ¿cómo es de grande? • **h. come?** FAM. ¿cómo es qué?, ¿cómo es (posible) que? • **h. could you!** ¿no te da vergüenza? • **h. do you do?** ¿cómo está usted? • **h. far?** *(away)* ¿a qué distancia?; *(to what point?)* ¿hasta dónde? • **h. fast?** *(speed)* ¿a qué velocidad?; *(how quickly)* ¿con qué rapidez? • **h. is it (that)** ¿cómo es que? • **h. is that again?** ¿cómo? • **h. long?** *(length)* ¿cómo . . . de largo? *(time)* ¿cuánto tiempo? • **h. many?** ¿cuántos? • **h. much?** ¿cuánto? • **h. old are you?** ¿cuántos años tienes?, ¿qué edad tienes? • **h. so?** ¿cómo? **II.** conj. cómo; *(that)* que **III.** s. ◆ **the h.** el cómo.

how·dy (hou′dē) interj. REG. ¡hola!

how·e·ver (hou-ĕv′ər) **I.** adv. de cualquier modo, como quiera que; *(by what means)* cómo; *(to whatever degree)* por . . . que <h. tired she was por más cansada que estuviera> ◆ **h. it may be** sea lo que sea • **h. much** por más o por mucho que **II.** conj. no obstante.

howl (houl) **I.** intr. aullar; *(with pain)* dar alaridos —tr. gritar **II.** s. aullido; *(of pain)* alarido.

how·so·ev·er (hou′sō-ĕv′ər) adv. de cualquier modo; *(to whatever degree)* por muy.

hub (hŭb) s. cubo; FIG. centro, foco.

hub·bub (hŭb′ŭb′) s. bullicio.

huck·le·ber·ry (hŭk′əl-bĕr′ē) s. BOT. arándano.

huck·ster (hŭk′stər) s. buhonero; JER. *(ad writer)* agente *mf* de publicidad.

hud·dle (hŭd′l) **I.** s. *(crowd)* group, turba; *(conference)* reunión *f* (pequeña o privada) **II.** tr. & intr. apiñar(se) ◆ **to h. up** acurrucarse.

hue (hyŏŏ) s. color *m*, tinte *m; (shade)* matiz *m* ◆ **h. and cry** protesta pública.

huff (hŭf) **I.** s. arranque *m* de furia **II.** intr. resoplar.

huff·y (′ē) adj. **-i-** *(touchy)* quisquilloso; *(indignant)* indignado; *(arrogant)* altivo.

hug (hŭg) **I.** tr. **-gg-** abrazar; *(to cling to)* ceñirse a —intr. abrazarse **II.** s. abrazo.

huge (hyŏŏj) adj. enorme.

huh (hŭ) interj. expresa interrogación, sorpresa o indiferencia.

hulk (hŭlk) **I.** s. carraca; *(hull)* casco; *(large thing)* armatoste *m* **II.** intr. *(to loom)* surgir amenazadoramente.

hulk·ing (hŭl′kĭng) adj. pesado.

hull (hŭl) **I.** s. *(pod)* vaina; *(shell)* cáscara; MARÍT. casco **II.** tr. descascarillar.

hul·la·ba·loo (hŭl′ə-bə-lŏŏ′) s. FAM. alboroto.

hum (hŭm) **I.** intr. **-mm-** tararear; *(bees)* zumbar; FAM. *(to be active)* estar muy activo —tr. tararear **II.** s. zumbido.

hu·man (hyŏŏ′mən) adj. & s. (ser) humano ◆ **h. being** ser humano.

hu·mane (-mān′) adj. compasivo; *(humanistic)* humanístico.

hu·man·ist (′mə-nĭst) s. humanista *mf.*

hu·man·i·tar·i·an (-măn′ĭ-târ′ē-ən) **I.** adj. humanitario **II.** s. filántropo, persona humanitaria.

hu·man·i·ty (-′-tē) s. humanidad *f; (humanness)* naturaleza humana.

hu·man·ize (′mə-nīz′) tr. humanizar.

hu·man·kind (:mən-kīnd′) s. raza humana.

hu·man·oid (:mə-noid′) adj. & s. humanoide.

hum·ble (hŭm′bəl) **I.** adj. **-er, -est** humilde; *(submissive)* sumiso; *(unpretentious)* sin pretensiones ◆ **to eat h. pie** rectractarse, disculparse de manera humillante **II.** tr. humillar.

hum·ble·ness (:nĭs) s. humildad *f.*

hum·bug (hŭm′bŭg′) **I.** s. patraña; *(trickster)* embaucador *m; (nonsense)* tontería **II.** tr. & intr. **-gg-** embaucar.

hum·ding·er (hŭm′dĭng′ər) s. JER. maravilla.

hum·drum (hŭm′drŭm′) adj. monótono.

hu·mer·us (hyŏŏ′mər-əs) s. húmero.

hu·mid (hyŏŏ′mĭd) adj. húmedo.

hu·mid·i·fi·er (-′ə-fī′ər) s. humedecedor *m.*

hu·mid·i·fy (:ə-fī′) tr. humedecer.

hu·mid·i·ty (:ĭ-tē) s. humedad *f.*

hu·mi·dor (hyŏŏ′mĭ-dôr′) s. bote *m* que mantiene húmedo el tabaco.

hu·mil·i·ate (hyōō-mĭl'ē-āt') tr. humillar.
hu·mil·i·a·tion (-'-ā'shən) s. humillación *f.*
hu·mil·i·ty (hyōō-mĭl'ĭ-tē) s. humildad *f.*
hum·ming·bird (hŭm'ĭng-bûrd') s. colibrí *m.*
hu·mor (hyōō'mər) s. humor *m.*
hu·mor·ist (:ĭst) s. humorista *mf.*
hu·mor·less (:lĭs) adj. sin humor, solemne.
hu·mor·ous (:əs) adj. cómico; *(employing humor)* humorista.
hump (hŭmp) s. joroba; *(in the ground)* montecillo ♦ **to be over the h.** haber vencido la mayor dificultad.
hump·back ('băk') s. jorobado; MED. cifosis *f.*
hump·backed (:băkt') adj. jorobado.
humph (hŭmf) interj. ¡puf!, ¡uh!
hunch (hŭnch) I. s. *(feeling)* corazonada; *(hump)* giba II. tr. doblar (la espalda) —intr. agacharse; *(to thrust forward)* adelantarse ♦ **to h. up** estar con el cuerpo encorvado.
hunch·back ('băk') s. jorobado.
hun·dred (hŭn'drĭd) s. [pl. inv. *o* **s**] & adj. cien, ciento; MAT. centena ♦ pl. centenares.
hun·dred·fold (:fōld') adj. & s. céntuplo.
hun·dredth (hŭn'drĭdth) adj. & s. centésimo, centavo.
hung (hŭng) I. cf. **hang** II. adj. ♦ **h. jury** jurado que no llega a un fallo unánime • **h. over** que sufre una resaca ♦ **h. up** FAM. preocupado • **to be h. up on** estar obsesionado con • **to get h. up** demorarse.
hun·ger (hŭng'gər) I. s. hambre *f; (desire)* sed *f* II. intr. tener hambre *o* sed.
hun·gry (:grē) adj. -i- hambriento; *(avid)* ávido; *(look)* de hambre.
hunk (hŭngk) s. FAM. trozo (grande).
hun·ker (hŭng'kər) intr. agacharse.
hun·ky-do·ry (hŭng'kē-dôr'ē) adj. JER. muy bien, estupendo.
hunt (hŭnt) I. tr. cazar; *(to pursue)* perseguir; *(to search for)* buscar ♦ **to h. down** capturar —intr. ♦ **to go hunting** ir de caza II. s. caza; *(pursuit)* persecución *f; (search)* búsqueda.
hunt·er (hŭn'tər) s. cazador *m; (searcher)* buscador *m.*
hunt·ing (:tĭng) I. s. cacería II. adj. de caza.
hur·dle (hûr'dl) I. s. valla; FIG. barrera II. tr. saltar; *(to overcome)* vencer.
hurl (hûrl) I. tr. lanzar II. s. lanzamiento.
hur·rah (hŏŏ-rä') interj. ¡hurra!, ¡ole!
hur·ri·cane (hûr'ĭ-kān') s. huracán *m.*
hur·ried (hûr'ēd) adj. apresurado.
hur·ry (:ē) I. intr. darse prisa, apurarse ♦ **to h. away, back** marcharse, volver de prisa • **to h. up** apresurarse —tr. apurar; *(to rush)* dar prisa a II. s. prisa; *(urgency)* apuro ♦ **in a h.** de prisa • **to be in a h. (to)** tener prisa (por).
hurt (hûrt) I. tr. **hurt** hacer daño; *(to distress)* angustiar; *(to damage)* perjudicar ♦ **to h. someone's feelings** ofenderle a alguien —intr. doler *<my head hurts* me duele la cabeza> ♦ **to get h.** *o* **to h. oneself** lastimarse II. s. *(harm)* daño; *(pain)* dolor *m; (injury)* herida; *(anguish)* angustia.
hurt·ful ('fəl) adj. dañoso; *(wounding)* hiriente; *(detrimental)* perjudicial.
hur·tle (hûr'tl) intr. abalanzarse —tr. arrojar.
hus·band (hŭz'bənd) I. s. marido II. tr. economizar.
hus·band·ry (:bən-drē) s. agricultura; *(livestock)* cría de ganado; *(economy)* economía.
hush (hŭsh) I. tr. & intr. callar(se); *(to calm)* calmar(se) ♦ **to h. up** silenciar(se) II. s. silen-

cio; *(stillness)* quietud *f* III. interj. ¡silencio! ♦ **h. up!** ¡cállate!
hush-hush ('hŭsh') adj. FAM. secreto.
husk (hŭsk) I. s. vaina; *(shell)* cáscara II. tr. desvainar.
husk·y¹ (hŭs'kē) adj. -i- *(hoarse)* ronco.
husk·y² (hŭs'kē) adj. -i- FAM. *(burly)* fornido.
hus·ky³ s. perro esquimal.
hus·sy (hŭz'ē, hŭs'ē) s. *(saucy)* pícara; *(immoral)* mujer libertina.
hus·tle (hŭs'əl) I. tr. empujar; FAM. *(to hurry)* apurar; *(to swindle)* estafar —intr. FAM. *(to hurry)* ajetrearse; *(prostitute)* trabajar de prostituta II. s. FAM. ajetreo; *(swindle)* estafa.
hus·tler (:lər) s. persona enérgica; *(swindler)* estafador *m; (prostitute)* prostituta.
hut (hŭt) s. choza.
hutch (hŭch) s. jaula (para conejos); *(cupboard)* alacena; *(hut)* choza.
hy·a·cinth (hī'ə-sĭnth) s. jacinto.
hy·brid (hī'brĭd) s. híbrido.
hy·drant (hī'drənt) s. boca de agua.
hy·drate (hī'drāt') I. s. hidrato II. tr. & intr. hidratar(se).
hy·drau·lic (hī-drô'lĭk) adj. hidráulico, de la hidráulica ♦ **hydraulics** s.sg. hidráulica.
hy·dro·car·bon (hī'drə-kär'bən) s. hidrocarburo.
hy·dro·ceph·a·lous (hī'drō-sĕf'ə-ləs) adj. hidrocéfalo, hidrocefálico.
hy·dro·chlo·ride (hī'drə-klôr'īd') s. clorhidrato.
hy·dro·e·lec·tric (hī'drō-ĭ-lĕk'trĭk) adj. hidroeléctrico.
hy·dro·gen (hī'drə-jən) s. hidrógeno.
hy·dro·gen·ate (:jə-nāt', hī-drŏj'ə-) tr. hidrogenar.
hy·drol·o·gy (hī-drŏl'ə-jē) s. hidrología.
hy·drol·y·sis (:ĭ-sĭs) s. hidrólisis *f.*
hy·dro·lyze (hī'drə-līz') tr. hidrolizar.
hy·dro·pho·bi·a ('-fō'bē-ə) s. hidrofobia.
hy·dro·plane (:plān') I. s. hidroavión *m; (boat)* hidroplano II. intr. deslizarse sobre agua.
hy·dro·ther·a·py (:-'thēr'ə-pē) s. hidroterapia.
hy·drous (hī'drəs) adj. hidratado.
hy·drox·ide (hī-drŏk'sīd') s. hidróxido.
hy·e·na (hī-ē'nə) s. hiena.
hy·giene (hī'jēn') s. higiene *f.*
hy·gi·en·ic (hī'jē-ĕn'ĭk, hī-jĕn'-) adj. higiénico, de la higiene; *(sanitary)* sanitario.
hy·gien·ist (hī-jēn'ĭst) s. higienista *mf.*
hy·men (hī'mən) s. himen *m.*
hymn (hĭm) s. himno.
hym·nal ('nəl) s. himnario.
hype (hīp) I. s. JER. superchería; *(promotion)* publicidad exagerada II. tr. promocionar (con exageraciones).
hyped-up (hīpt'ŭp') adj. JER. entusiasmado.
hy·per·ac·tive (hī'pər-ăk'tĭv) adj. hiperactivo.
hy·per·bo·la (hī-pûr'bə-lə) s. [pl. **s** *o* **-ae**] hipérbola.
hy·per·bo·le (:lē) s. hipérbole *f.*
hy·per·crit·i·cal (hī'pər-krĭt'ĭ-kəl) adj. hipercrítico.
hy·per·sen·si·tive (:sĕn'sĭ-tĭv) adj. hipersensible.
hy·per·ten·sion (:tĕn'shən) s. hipertensión *f.*
hy·per·ten·sive (:tĕn'sĭv) adj. & s. hipertenso.
hy·per·ther·mi·a (:thûr'mē-ə) s. hipertermia.
hy·phen (hī'fən) s. guión *m.*
hy·phen·ate (:fə-nāt') tr. unir *o* separar con

guión.

hyp·no·sis (hǐp-nō′sǐs) s. [pl. **-ses**] hipnosis f.

hyp·not·ic (:nŏt′ǐk) adj. & s. hipnótico.

hyp·no·tism (′nə-tǐz′əm) s. hipnotismo.

hyp·no·tist (:tǐst) s. hipnotizador m.

hyp·no·tize (:tīz′) tr. hipnotizar; FIG. magnetizar.

hy·po·chon·dri·a (hī′pə-kŏn′drē-ə) s. hipocondría.

hy·po·chon·dri·ac (:ăk′) s. & adj. hipocondríaco.

hy·poc·ri·sy (hǐ-pŏk′rǐ-sē) s. hipocresía.

hyp·o·crite (hǐp′ə-krǐt′) s. hipócrita mf.

hyp·o·crit·i·cal (-′-kəl) adj. hipócrita.

hy·po·der·mic (hī′pə-dûr′mǐk) I. adj. hipodérmico II. s. injección f o jeringa hipodérmica.

hy·po·gly·ce·mi·a (hī′pō-glī-sē′mē-ə) s. hipoglicemia.

hy·po·ten·sion (:tĕn′shən) s. hipotensión f.

hy·pot·e·nuse (hǐ-pŏt′n-ōōs′) s. hypotenusa.

hy·po·thal·a·mus (hī′pō-thăl′ə-məs) s. hipotálamo.

hy·po·ther·mi·a (:thûr′mē-ə) s. hipotermia.

hy·poth·e·sis (hǐ-pŏth′ǐ-sǐs) s. [pl. **-ses**] hipótesis f, suposición f.

hy·poth·e·size (:sīz′) intr. formar una hipótesis.

hy·po·thet·i·cal (hī′pə-thĕt′ǐ-kəl) adj. hipotético; (contingent) dependiente.

hys·ter·ec·to·my (hǐs′tə-rĕk′tə-mē) s. histerectomía.

hys·te·ri·a (hǐ-stĕr′ē-ə, -stîr′-) s. MED. histerismo; FAM. (fit) emoción f incontrolable.

hys·ter·ic (:stĕr′ǐk) s. histérico ♦ **hysterics** s.pl. (fit) paroxismo; (hysteria) ataque m de histeria.

hys·ter·i·cal (:ĭ-kəl) adj. histérico; (emotional) emocional (persona).

I

i, I (ī) s. novena letra del alfabeto inglés.

I (ī) I. pron. yo II. s. [pl. **I's**] yo, ego.

i·bis (ī′bǐs) s. ibis m.

ice (īs) I. s. hielo; (dessert) helado escarchado ♦ **i. age** período glaciar • **i. cap** casquete polar • **i. cream** helado • **i. cube** cubito de hielo • **i. skate** patín de hielo • **to break the i.** (to relax) romper el hielo; (to begin) dar el primer paso • **to cut no i.** FAM. no convencer, no surtir efecto • **to keep on i.** FAM. tener en reserva • **to tread on thin i.** pisar terreno peligroso II. tr. (cake) escarchar; (to freeze) helar; (to chill) congelar —intr. ♦ **to i. over** helarse.

ice·berg (īs′bûrg′) s. iceberg m.

ice·box (īs′bŏks′) s. nevera, refrigerador m.

ice-cold (īs′kōld′) adj. helado.

ice-cream cone (īs′krēm′) s. helado en barquillo o cucurucho.

iced (īst) adj. congelado, helado; (cooled) refrigerado; (cake) escarchado, garapiñado.

ice-skate (īs′skāt′) intr. patinar sobre hielo.

ich·thy·ol·o·gy (ĭk′thē-ŏl′ə-jē) s. ictiología.

i·ci·cle (ī′sĭ-kəl) s. carámbano.

ic·i·ly (ī′sə-lē) adv. fríamente, con frialdad.

ic·ing (ī′sĭng) s. alcorza, escarchado.

i·con (ī′kŏn′) s. icono.

i·con·o·clast (-′ə-klăst′) s. iconoclasta mf.

ic·y (ī′sē) adj. **-i-** helado; (person, look) glacial.

ID card (ī′dē′) s. carnet m de identificación.

i·de·a (ī-dē′ə) s. idea; (plan) proyecto ♦ **bright**

i. idea genial • **that's the i.!** ¡eso es! • **to get an i. of** hacerse una idea de • **to get an i. into one's head** metérsele a uno una idea en la cabeza • **to get ideas** hacerse ilusiones • **to get the i.** darse cuenta • **what's the big i.?** FAM. ¿a qué viene eso?

i·de·al (ī-dē′əl) adj. & s. ideal m.

i·de·al·ist (:ə-lǐst) s. idealista mf.

i·de·al·is·tic (-′-lǐs′tǐk) adj. idealista.

i·de·al·ize (-′-līz′) tr. idealizar.

i·den·ti·cal (ī-dĕn′tǐ-kəl) adj. idéntico.

i·den·ti·fi·a·ble (:fǐ′ə-bəl) adj. identificable ♦ **easily i.** de fácil identificación.

i·den·ti·fi·ca·tion (-′-fǐ-kā′shən) s. identificación f ♦ **i. card, papers** carnet, documentos de identidad.

i·den·ti·fy (ī-dĕn′tə-fī′) tr. & intr. identificar(se).

i·den·ti·ty (ī-dĕn′tǐ-tē) s. identidad f ♦ **i. card, papers** tarjeta, documentos de identidad.

i·de·o·log·i·cal (ī′dē-ə-lŏj′ī-kəl, ǐd′ē-) adj. ideológico.

i·de·o·logue (:lŏg′) s. ideólogo.

i·de·ol·o·gy (ī′dē-ŏl′ə-jē, ǐd′ē-) s. ideología.

id·i·o·cy (ĭd′ē-ə-sē) s. idiotez f; (foolish deed) necedad f.

id·i·om (ĭd′ē-əm) s. (expression) modismo, locución f; (jargon) jerga, idioma m.

id·i·o·mat·ic (′-ə-măt′ĭk) adj. idiomático ♦ **i. expression** modismo.

id·i·o·syn·cra·sy (ĭd′ē-ō-sǐng′krə-sē) s. idiosincrasia.

id·i·o·syn·crat·ic (:sǐn-krăt′ĭk) adj. idiosincrásico.

id·i·ot (ĭd′ē-ət) s. idiota mf; (fool) tonto.

id·i·ot·ic (′-ŏt′ĭk) adj. idiota, tonto.

i·dle (īd′l) I. adj. **-er, -est** ocioso; (unemployed) parado; (threat) vano ♦ **i. gossip** cuentos de viejas • **i. talk** palabras vacías II. intr. (to loaf) haraganear; (machinery) funcionar en vacío —tr. (a worker) dejar parado; (a motor) hacer funcionar en vacío.

i·dol (īd′l) s. ídolo.

i·dol·a·trous (ī-dŏl′ə-trəs) adj. idólatra.

i·dol·a·try (:trē) s. idolatría.

i·dol·ize (īd′l-īz′) tr. idolatrar.

i·dyl(l) (īd′l) s. idilio.

i·dyl·lic (ī-dĭl′ĭk) adj. idílico.

if (ĭf) I. conj. si; (granting that) en caso que; (even though) si bien, aunque ♦ **if and when** siempre y cuando • **if at all** si es que • **if I were you** yo que tú II. s. ♦ **no ifs, ands, or buts** no hay pero que valga.

ig·loo (ĭg′lōō) s. iglú m.

ig·ne·ous (ĭg′nē-əs) adj. ígneo.

ig·nite (ĭg-nīt′) tr. & intr. encender(se).

ig·ni·tion (ĭg-nǐsh′ən) s. ignición f; AUTO. encendido.

ig·no·ble (ĭg-nō′bəl) adj. innoble, bajo.

ig·no·min·i·ous (ĭg′nə-mǐn′ē-əs) adj. ignominioso.

ig·no·min·y (ĭg′nə-mǐn′ē) s. ignominia.

ig·no·ra·mus (ĭg′nə-rā′məs) s. ignorante mf.

ig·no·rance (ĭg′nər-əns) s. ignorancia.

ig·no·rant (:ənt) adj. ignorante.

ig·nore (ĭg-nôr′) tr. (to disregard) no hacer caso de; (to leave out) pasar por alto.

i·gua·na (ĭ-gwä′nə) s. iguana.

ilk (ĭlk) s. clase f, índole f.

ill (ĭl) I. adj. **worse, worst** I. adj. enfermo, malo; (hostile) malo ♦ **i. effects** consecuencias • **i. will** enemistad • **to be in i. health** estar mal de salud • **to feel i.** sentirse mal **II.** adv. *(not well)* mal <*i. paid* mal remunerado>; *(scarcely)* mal, poco <*i. prepared* poco preparado> ♦ **i. at ease** incómodo **III.** s. mal *m.*

ill·ad·vised (ĭl'ăd-vīzd') adj. imprudente.

ill·bred (ĭl'brĕd') adj. mal educado.

ill·con·sid·ered (ĭl'kən-sĭd'ərd) adj. imprudente.

il·le·gal (ĭ-lē'gəl) **I.** adj. ilegal, ilícito **II.** s. inmigrante *mf* ilegal.

il·le·gal·i·ty ('-găl'ĭ-tē) s. ilegalidad *f*; *(unlawful act)* acto ilegal.

il·leg·i·bil·i·ty (ĭ-lĕj'ə-bĭl'ĭ-tē) s. ilegibilidad *f.*

il·leg·i·ble ('-bəl) adj. ilegible.

il·le·git·i·ma·cy (ĭl'ə-jĭt'ə-mə-sē) s. ilegitimidad *f.*

il·le·git·i·mate (ĭl'ə-jĭt'ə-mĭt) adj. *(illegal)* ilegal; *(bastard)* ilegítimo, bastardo.

ill·fat·ed (ĭl'fā'tĭd) adj. malaventurado.

ill·got·ten (ĭl'gŏt'n) adj. mal habido.

ill·hu·mored (ĭl'hyōō'mərd) adj. malhumorado.

il·lic·it (ĭ-lĭs'ĭt) adj. ilícito.

il·lit·er·a·cy (ĭ-lĭt'ər-ə-sē) s. analfabetismo.

il·lit·er·ate (-ĭt) s. & adj. analfabeto; *(ignorant)* ignorante *mf.*

ill·man·nered (ĭl'măn'ərd) adj. mal educado.

ill·ness (ĭl'nĭs) s. enfermedad *f.*

il·log·i·cal (ĭ-lŏj'ĭ-kəl) adj. ilógico.

ill·pre·pared (ĭl'prĭ-pârd') adj. mal preparado.

ill·suit·ed (ĭl'sōō'tĭd) adj. impropio.

ill·tem·pered (ĭl'tĕm'pərd) adj. de mal genio.

ill·treat (ĭl'trēt') tr. maltratar.

il·lu·mi·nate (ĭ-lōō'mə-nāt') tr. iluminar.

il·lu·mi·nat·ing (:nā'tĭng) adj. *(book)* instructivo; *(solution, remark)* revelador.

il·lu·mi·na·tion (-'-nā'shən) s. iluminación *f.*

il·lu·sion (ĭ-lōō'zhən) s. ilusión *f*; *(magic trick)* truco ♦ **to be under an i.** engañarse.

il·lu·sive (ĭ-lōō'sĭv) adj. ilusivo, ilusorio.

il·lu·so·ry (:sə-rē) adj. ilusivo, ilusorio.

il·lus·trate (ĭl'ə-strāt') tr. & intr. ilustrar.

il·lus·tra·tion ('-strā'shən) s. ilustración *f.*

il·lus·tra·tive (ĭ-lŭs'trə-tĭv, ĭl'ə-strā'tĭv) adj. ilustrativo ♦ **to be i. of** ilustrar, ejemplificar.

il·lus·tra·tor (ĭl'ə-strā'tər) s. ilustrador *m.*

il·lus·tri·ous (ĭ-lŭs'trē-əs) adj. ilustre.

im·age (ĭm'ĭj) **I.** s. imagen *f*; *(reputation)* reputación *f* ♦ **in one's own i.** a imagen de uno • **mirror i.** espejo **II.** tr. representar, retratar.

im·age·ry (:rē) s. imágenes *f*; ARTE. imaginería.

i·mag·i·na·ble (ĭ-măj'ə-nə-bəl) adj. imaginable.

i·mag·i·nar·y (:nĕr'ē) adj. imaginario.

i·mag·i·na·tion (ĭ-măj'ə-nā'shən) s. imaginación *f* ♦ **to have no i.** ser una persona sin imaginación.

i·mag·i·na·tive (-'-nə-tĭv) adj. imaginativo.

i·mag·ine (ĭ-măj'ĭn) tr. imaginar; *(to suppose)* imaginarse, suponer ♦ **just i.!** ¡imagínate!

im·bal·ance (ĭm-băl'əns) s. desequilibrio.

im·be·cile (ĭm'bə-sĭl) adj. & s. imbécil *mf.*

im·be·cil·i·ty (-'-'ĭ-tē) s. imbecilidad *f.*

im·bibe (ĭm-bīb') tr. beber; FIG. absorber.

im·bue (ĭm-byōō') tr. imbuir.

im·i·tate (ĭm'ĭ-tāt') tr. imitar.

im·i·ta·tion ('-tā'shən) s. imitación *f* ♦ **i. leather** cuero artificial • **in i. of** a imitación de.

im·mac·u·late (ĭ-măk'yə-lĭt) adj. inmaculado.

im·ma·nent (ĭm'ə-nənt) adj. inmanente.

im·ma·te·ri·al (ĭm'ə-tîr'ē-əl) adj. inmaterial; *(unimportant)* sin importancia ♦ **to be i.** no ve-

nir al caso.

im·ma·ture (ĭm'ə-chŏŏr') adj. inmaduro.

im·ma·tur·i·ty (:ĭ-tē) s. falta de madurez.

im·meas·ur·a·ble (ĭ-mĕzh'ər-ə-bəl) adj. inmensurable; *(vast)* inconmensurable, ilimitado.

im·me·di·a·cy (ĭ-mē'dē-ə-sē) s. *(proximity)* inmediación *f*; *(of a problem)* urgencia.

im·me·di·ate (ĭ-mē'dē-ĭt) adj. inmediato; *(near, soon)* próximo; *(danger)* inminente; *(problem)* urgente ♦ **i. vicinity** inmediaciones.

im·me·mo·ri·al (ĭm'ə-môr'ē-əl) adj. inmemorial.

im·mense (ĭ-mĕns') adj. inmenso, enorme.

im·men·si·ty (ĭ-mĕn'sĭ-tē) s. inmensidad *f.*

im·merse (ĭ-mûrs') tr. sumergir; *(to baptize)* bautizar por inmersión; FIG. absorber.

im·mer·sion (ĭ-mûr'zhən) s. inmersión *f.*

im·mi·grant (ĭm'ĭ-grənt) s. inmigrante *mf.*

im·mi·grate (:grāt') intr. inmigrar.

im·mi·gra·tion ('-grā'shən) s. inmigración *f.*

im·mi·nence (ĭm'ə-nəns) s. inminencia.

im·mi·nent (:nənt) adj. inminente.

im·mo·bile (ĭ-mō'bəl, -bīl') adj. *(not moving)* inmóvil; *(not movable)* inmovible; *(fixed)* fijo.

im·mo·bi·lize (:bə-līz') tr. inmovilizar.

im·mod·er·ate (ĭ-mŏd'ər-ĭt) adj. inmoderado.

im·mod·est (ĭ-mŏd'ĭst) adj. inmodesto; *(boastful)* jactancioso.

im·mo·late (ĭm'ə-lāt') tr. inmolar.

im·mor·al (ĭ-môr'əl) adj. inmoral.

im·mo·ral·i·ty (ĭm'ô-răl'ĭ-tē) s. inmoralidad *f.*

im·mor·tal (ĭ-môr'tl) adj. & s. inmortal *mf.*

im·mor·tal·i·ty (ĭm'ôr-tăl'ĭ-tē) s. inmortalidad *f.*

im·mor·tal·ize (ĭ-môr'tl-īz') tr. inmortalizar.

im·mov·a·ble (ĭ-mōō'və-bəl) adj. *(not movable)* inamovible; *(unyielding)* inflexible.

im·mune (ĭ-myōōn') adj. inmune *(from* de).

im·mu·ni·ty (ĭ-myōō'nĭ-tē) s. inmunidad *f.*

im·mu·ni·za·tion (ĭm'yə-nĭ-zā'shən) s. inmunización *f.*

im·mu·nize ('-nīz') tr. inmunizar.

im·mu·nol·o·gy ('-nŏl'ə-jē) s. inmunología.

im·mure (ĭ-myŏŏr') tr. emparedar.

im·mu·ta·ble (ĭ-myōō'tə-bəl) adj. inmutable.

imp (ĭmp) s. diablillo; *(child)* niño travieso.

im·pact I. s. (ĭm'păkt') impacto, choque *m*; *(influence)* efecto, consecuencias **II.** tr. (-') chocar contra; FAM. *(to affect)* afectar.

im·pair (ĭm-pâr') tr. deteriorar, dañar.

im·pair·ment (:mənt) s. deterioro, daño.

im·pale (ĭm-pāl') tr. empalar.

im·pal·pa·ble (ĭm-păl'pə-bəl) adj. impalpable; *(imperceptible)* imperceptible.

im·pan·el (ĭm-păn'əl) tr. elegir (un jurado).

im·part (ĭm-pärt') tr. *(to bestow)* impartir; *(to disclose)* dar a conocer.

im·par·tial (ĭm-pär'shəl) adj. imparcial.

im·par·ti·al·i·ty (-'shē-ăl'ĭ-tē) s. imparcialidad *f.*

im·pass·a·ble (ĭm-păs'ə-bəl) adj. *(road)* intransitable; *(obstacle)* infranqueable.

im·passe (ĭm'păs') s. *(street)* callejón *m* sin salida; FIG. atolladero, estancamiento.

im·pas·sion (ĭm-păsh'ən) tr. apasionar.

im·pas·sioned (:ənd) adj. apasionado.

im·pas·sive (ĭm-păs'ĭv) adj. impasible.

im·pa·tience (ĭm-pā'shəns) s. impaciencia.

im·pa·tient (:shənt) adj. impaciente ♦ **to be i. with** no tener paciencia con • **to get i.** perder la paciencia • **to make i.** impacientar.

im·peach (ĭm-pēch') tr. *(to charge)* acusar, denunciar; *(to prosecute)* enjuiciar.

im·peach·ment (:mənt) s. *(charging)* acusación *f; (prosecution)* enjuiciamiento.

im·pec·ca·ble (ĭm-pĕk′ə-bəl) adj. impecable.

im·pede (ĭm-pēd′) tr. impedir; *(to delay)* retardar.

im·ped·i·ment (ĭm-pĕd′ə-mənt) s. impedimento; *(defect)* defecto.

im·pel (ĭm-pĕl′) tr. **-ll-** impeler, impulsar.

im·pend (ĭm-pĕnd′) intr. ser inminente.

im·pen·e·tra·ble (ĭm-pĕn′ĭ-trə-bəl) adj. impenetrable.

im·per·a·tive (ĭm-pĕr′ə-tĭv) adj. *(tone)* imperioso; *(urgent)* urgente; GRAM. imperativo.

im·per·cep·ti·ble (ĭm′pər-sĕp′tə-bəl) adj. imperceptible.

im·per·fect (ĭm-pûr′fĭkt) adj. imperfecto.

im·per·fec·tion (ĭm′pər-fĕk′shən) s. imperfección *f.*

im·pe·ri·al (ĭm-pîr′ē-əl) adj. imperial; *(majestic)* augusto, señorial.

im·pe·ri·al·ist (:ə-lĭst) s. imperialista *mf.*

im·pe·ri·al·is·tic (:lĭs′tĭk) adj. imperialista.

im·per·il (ĭm-pĕr′əl) tr. poner en peligro.

im·pe·ri·ous (ĭm-pîr′ē-əs) adj. imperioso.

im·per·ish·a·ble (ĭm-pĕr′ĭ-shə-bəl) adj. imperecedero.

im·per·ma·nent (ĭm-pûr′mə-nənt) adj. no permanente, temporal.

im·per·me·a·ble (ĭm-pûr′mē-ə-bəl) adj. impermeable.

im·per·mis·si·ble (ĭm′pər-mĭs′ə-bəl) adj. no permisible, inadmisible.

im·per·son·al (ĭm-pûr′sə-nəl) adj. impersonal.

im·per·son·ate (ĭm-pûr′sə-nāt′) tr. hacerse pasar por.

im·per·son·a·tion (-′-nā′shən) s. imitación *f.*

im·per·son·a·tor (-′-′tər) s. imitador *m.*

im·per·ti·nence (ĭm-pûr′tn-əns) s. impertinencia.

im·per·ti·nent (:ənt) adj. impertinente.

im·per·turb·a·ble (ĭm′pər-tûr′bə-bəl) adj. imperturbable.

im·per·vi·ous (ĭm-pûr′vē-əs) adj. insensible.

im·pet·u·ous (ĭm-pĕch′ōō-əs) adj. *(rash)* impetuoso.

im·pe·tus (ĭm′pĭ-təs) s. ímpetu *m,* impulso.

im·pinge (ĭm-pĭnj′) intr. ♦ **to i. on** *(to invade)* invadir, violar; *(to affect)* impresionar.

im·pi·ous (ĭm′pē-əs, ĭm-pī′əs) adj. impío.

imp·ish (ĭm′pĭsh) adj. pícaro.

im·plac·a·ble (ĭm-plăk′ə-bəl) adj. implacable.

im·plant I. tr. (ĭm-plănt′) implantar II. s. (″) MED. injerto.

im·plan·ta·tion (ĭm′plăn-tā′shən) s. implantación *f.*

im·plau·si·ble (ĭm-plô′zə-bəl) adj. *(unbelievable)* inverosímil; *(improbable)* improbable.

im·ple·ment I. s. (ĭm′plə-mənt) utensilio, instrumento II. tr. (:mĕnt′) poner en práctica; *(a law)* aplicar.

im·ple·men·ta·tion (′-mən-tā′shən) s. *(of plan)* puesta en práctica; *(of law)* aplicación *f.*

im·pli·cate (ĭm′plĭ-kāt′) tr. implicar.

im·pli·ca·tion (′-kā′shən) s. implicación *f; (inference)* inferencia.

im·plic·it (ĭm-plĭs′ĭt) adj. implícito; *(unquestioning)* absoluto.

im·plied (ĭm-plīd′) adj. implícito.

im·plore (ĭm-plôr′) tr. implorar.

im·ply (ĭm-plī′) tr. *(to entail)* implicar, significar; *(to hint)* dar a entender, insinuar.

im·po·lite (ĭm′pə-līt′) adj. descortés.

im·pol·i·tic (ĭm-pŏl′ĭ-tĭk) adj. imprudente.

im·port I. tr. (ĭm-pôrt′) *(goods)* importar; *(to signify)* significar —intr. tener importancia II. s. (″) *(item)* artículo importado; *(business)* importación *f; (significance)* importancia.

im·por·tance (ĭm-pôr′tns) s. importancia ♦ **to be of i.** ser importante, tener importancia.

im·por·tant (:tnt) adj. importante ♦ **it's not i.** no importa.

im·por·ta·tion (ĭm′pôr-tā′shən) s. importación *f.*

im·port·er (-′tər) s. importador *m.*

im·por·tu·nate (ĭm-pôr′chə-nĭt) adj. importuno, fastidioso.

im·por·tune (ĭm′pôr-tōōn′, ĭm-pôr′chən) tr. importunar, fastidiar.

im·por·tu·ni·ty (′-tōō′nĭ-tē) s. importunidad *f.*

im·pose (ĭm-pōz′) tr. imponer ♦ **to i. oneself** imponerse —intr. ♦ **to i. (up)on** abusar de.

im·pos·ing (ĭm-pō′zĭng) adj. imponente.

im·po·si·tion (ĭm′pə-zĭsh′ən) s. *(act)* imposición *f; (unfair demand)* abuso.

im·pos·si·bil·i·ty (ĭm-pŏs′ə-bĭl′ĭ-tē) s. imposibilidad *f.*

im·pos·si·ble (ĭm-pŏs′ə-bəl) adj. imposible.

im·pos·tor (ĭm-pŏs′tər) s. impostor *m.*

im·po·tence/ten·cy (ĭm′pə-tns) s. impotencia.

im·po·tent (:tnt) adj. impotente.

im·pound (ĭm-pound′) tr. *(to confine)* encerrar; DER. *(to seize)* embargar, confiscar.

im·pov·er·ish (ĭm-pŏv′ər-ĭsh) tr. *(people)* empobrecer; *(resources)* agotar.

im·prac·ti·ca·ble (ĭm-prăk′tĭ-kə-bəl) adj. impracticable.

im·prac·ti·cal (:kəl) adj. poco práctico.

im·prac·ti·cal·i·ty (′-kăl′ĭ-tē) s. impracticabilidad *f.*

im·pre·cise (ĭm′prĭ-sīs′) adj. impreciso.

im·pre·ci·sion (:sĭzh′ən) s. imprecisión *f.*

im·preg·na·ble (ĭm-prĕg′nə-bəl) adj. *(fortress)* inexpugnable; FIG. invulnerable.

im·preg·nate (ĭm-prĕg′nāt′) tr. dejar preñada; *(ovum)* fecundar; *(to permeate)* impregnar.

im·pre·sa·ri·o (ĭm′prĭ-sär′ē-ō′) s. empresario.

im·press¹ (ĭm-prĕs′) I. tr. *(to imprint)* imprimir; *(to affect)* impresionar, causar impresión ♦ **I was not impressed** no me pareció gran cosa II. s. (″) *(mark)* marca, señal *f; (seal)* sello.

im·press² tr. MIL. reclutar a la fuerza.

im·pres·sion (ĭm-prĕsh′ən) s. impresión *f; (memory)* idea; IMPR. tirada ♦ **to be under the i.** **that** tener la impresión de que.

im·pres·sion·a·ble (:ə-nə-bəl) adj. impresionable.

im·pres·sion·is·tic (-′-nĭs′tĭk) adj. ARTE. impresionista; *(subjective)* subjetivo.

im·pres·sive (ĭm-prĕs′ĭv) adj. impresionante.

im·pri·ma·tur (ĭm′prə-mä′tŏr′) s. imprimátur *m.*

im·print (ĭm-prĭnt′) I. tr. imprimir II. s. (″) impresión *f; (influence)* impronta; IMPR. pie *m* de imprenta.

im·pris·on (ĭm-prĭz′ən) tr. aprisionar.

im·pris·on·ment (:mənt) s. aprisionamiento.

im·prob·a·bil·i·ty (ĭm-prŏb′ə-bĭl′ĭ-tē) s. improbabilidad *f.*

im·prob·a·ble (ĭm-prŏb′ə-bəl) adj. improbable.

im·promp·tu (ĭm-prŏmp′tōō) I. adj. improvisado II. adv. improvisadamente.

im·prop·er (ĭm-prŏp′ər) adj. impropio; *(indecorous)* incorrecto, indebido.

im·pro·pri·e·ty (ĭm′prə-prī′ĭ-tē) s. impropiedad *f; (improper act)* falta de corrección.

im·prove (ĭm-prōōv′) tr. mejorar; *(to upgrade)* hacer mejoras en; *(productivity)* aumentar, incrementar; *(skill, product)* perfeccionar; *(one's mind)* desarrollar ♦ **to i. one's appearance** hacerse más presentable —intr. mejorar; *(patient)* mejorar(se) ♦ **to i. (up)on** mejorar.

im·prove·ment (:mənt) s. mejora, mejoramiento; *(in productivity, quality)* aumento; *(of a skill)* perfeccionamiento; *(in attitude)* reforma; *(mental)* desarrollo; *(in school)* adelanto, progreso; *(in health)* mejoría; *(in a building)* reforma; *(in a facility)* ampliación f ♦ **to make improvements in** perfeccionar.

im·prov·i·dent (ĭm-prŏv′ĭ-dənt) adj. imprevisor.

im·pro·vi·sa·tion (ĭm-prŏv′ĭ-zā′shən) s. improvisación f.

im·pro·vise (ĭm′prə-vīz′) tr. & intr. improvisar.

im·pru·dent (ĭm-prōōd′nt) adj. imprudente.

im·pu·dence (ĭm′pyə-dns) s. impudencia.

im·pu·dent (:dnt) adj. impudente, descarado.

im·pugn (ĭm-pyōōn′) tr. impugnar.

im·pulse (ĭm′pŭls′) s. impulso ♦ **on i.** sin reflexionar.

im·pul·sive (ĭm-pŭl′sĭv) adj. impetuoso.

im·pu·ni·ty (ĭm-pyōō′nĭ-tē) s. impunidad f.

im·pure (ĭm-pyŏŏr′) adj. impuro; *(adulterated)* mezclado; *(air)* contaminado.

im·pu·ri·ty (:ĭ-tē) s. impureza; *(contamination)* contaminación f; *(substance)* contaminante m.

im·pute (ĭm-pyōōt′) tr. imputar.

in (ĭn) I. prep. en, dentro de, por; *(time)* a, por, durante, de; *(arrival)* a; *(method)* a, en, por; *(with verbs)* al, mientras <*in running after the bus* mientras corría para tomar el autobús> II. adv. *(inside)* (a)dentro; *(in power)* en el poder; *(in fashion)* de moda ♦ **to be in** estar <*is the doctor in?* ¿está el doctor?>; *(in power)* estar en el poder ♦ **to be in for it** FAM. ir a recibir un castigo (por algo hecho) ♦ **to be in on** *(to participate)* tomar parte en; *(to know)* estar enterado de ♦ **to be in with someone** FAM. gozar del favor de alguien ♦ **to have it in for someone** FAM. tenerle antipatía a alguien III. adj. *(fashionable)* de moda; *(entering)* de entrada ♦ **the in party** FAM. el partido en el poder IV. s. influencia ♦ **the ins and outs** los pormenores, los detalles ♦ **to have an in somewhere** tener influencia en algún sitio.

in·a·bil·i·ty (ĭn′ə-bĭl′ĭ-tē) s. incapacidad f.

in·ac·ces·si·ble (ĭn′ăk-sĕs′ə-bəl) adj. inaccesible.

in·ac·cu·ra·cy (ĭn-ăk′yər-ə-sē) s. inexactitud f; *(error)* error m.

in·ac·cu·rate (:ĭt) adj. inexacto.

in·ac·tive (ĭn-ăk′tĭv) adj. inactivo; MIL. en o de reserva.

in·ac·tiv·i·ty (′-ĭ-tē) s. inactividad f.

in·ad·e·qua·cy (ĭn-ăd′ĭ-kwə-sē) s. inadecuación f; *(insufficiency)* insuficiencia.

in·ad·e·quate (:kwĭt) adj. inadecuado; *(insufficient)* insuficiente.

in·ad·mis·si·ble (ĭn′əd-mĭs′ə-bəl) adj. inadmisible.

in·ad·ver·tent (ĭn′əd-vûr′tnt) adj. *(inattentive)* descuidado; *(unintentional)* accidental.

in·ad·vis·a·ble (ĭn′əd-vī′zə-bəl) adj. imprudente, no aconsejable.

in·al·ien·a·ble (ĭn-āl′yə-nə-bəl) adj. inalienable.

in·al·ter·a·ble (ĭn-ôl′tər-ə-bəl) adj. inalterable.

in·ane (ĭn-ān′) adj. tonto, necio.

in·an·i·mate (ĭn-ăn′ə-mĭt) adj. *(not living)* inanimado; *(dull)* desanimado, apagado.

in·an·i·ty (:ĭ-tē) s. necedad f, insensatez f.

in·ap·pli·ca·ble (ĭn-ăp′lĭ-kə-bəl, ĭn′ə-plĭk′ə-) adj. que no viene al caso.

in·ap·pre·cia·ble (ĭn′ə-prē′shə-bəl) adj. inapreciable, insignificante.

in·ap·pro·pri·ate (ĭn′ə-prō′prē-ĭt) adj. impropio, inadecuado.

in·ar·tic·u·late (ĭn′är-tĭk′yə-lĭt) adj. *(sound)* inarticulado; *(person)* incapaz de expresarse.

in·as·much as (ĭn′əz-mŭch′əz) conj. ya que.

in·at·ten·tion (ĭn′ə-tĕn′shən) s. desatención f.

in·at·ten·tive (:tĭv) adj. desatento, distraído.

in·au·di·ble (ĭn-ô′də-bəl) adj. inaudible.

in·au·gu·ral (ĭn-ô′gyər-əl) adj. inaugural.

in·au·gu·rate (:gyə-rāt′) tr. *(to begin)* inaugurar; POL. investir del cargo a.

in·au·gu·ra·tion (-′-rā′shən) s. inauguración f; POL. investidura, toma de posesión.

in·aus·pi·cious (ĭn′ô-spĭsh′əs) adj. desfavorable, poco propicio.

in·born (ĭn′bôrn′) adj. congénito, innato.

in·bound (ĭn′bound′) adj. que viene, de venida.

in·bred (ĭn′brĕd′) adj. consanguíneo; *(innate)* innato.

in·breed·ing (ĭn′brē′dĭng) s. procreación f en consanguinidad; *(people)* endogamia.

in·cal·cu·la·ble (ĭn-kăl′kyə-lə-bəl) adj. incalculable.

in·can·des·cent (ĭn′kən-dĕs′ənt) adj. incandescente.

in·can·ta·tion (ĭn′kăn-tā′shən) s. invocación f; *(spell)* sortilegio, conjuro.

in·ca·pa·ble (ĭn-kā′pə-bəl) adj. incapaz; *(incompetent)* incompetente.

in·ca·pac·i·tate (ĭn′kə-păs′ĭ-tāt′) tr. incapacitar.

in·ca·pac·i·ty (:tē) s. incapacidad f.

in·car·cer·ate (ĭn-kär′sə-rāt′) tr. encarcelar.

in·car·cer·a·tion (-′-rā′shən) s. encarcelamiento.

in·car·nate (ĭn-kär′nĭt) I. adj. encarnado II. tr. (:nāt′) encarnar.

in·car·na·tion (′-nā′shən) s. encarnación f.

in·cen·di·ar·y (ĭn-sĕn′dē-ĕr′ē) adj. incendiario.

in·cense¹ (ĭn-sĕns′) tr. encolerizar, enfurecer.

in·cense² (′′) s. *(sticks, smoke)* incienso.

in·cen·tive (ĭn-sĕn′tĭv) s. incentivo.

in·cep·tion (ĭn-sĕp′shən) s. principio.

in·ces·sant (ĭn-sĕs′ənt) adj. incesante.

in·cest (ĭn′sĕst′) s. incesto.

in·ces·tu·ous (ĭn-sĕs′chōō-əs) adj. incestuoso.

inch (ĭnch) I. s. pulgada ♦ **every i. of the way** todo el camino • **i. by i.** poco a poco • **to know every i. of** conocer como la palma de la mano • **within an i. of** a un punto de II. intr. avanzar poco a poco —tr. mover poco a poco.

in·ci·dence (ĭn′sĭ-dəns) s. incidencia; *(rate)* frecuencia, índice m.

in·ci·dent (:dənt) adj. & s. incidente m ♦ **without i.** sin novedad.

in·ci·den·tal (′-dĕn′tl) I. adj. *(related)* incidente; *(minor)* secundario; *(expense)* accesorio ♦ **i. to** propio de II. s.pl. imprevistos.

in·cin·er·ate (ĭn-sĭn′ə-rāt′) tr. incinerar.

in·cin·er·a·tor (:rā′tər) s. incinerador m.

in·cip·i·ent (ĭn-sĭp′ē-ənt) adj. incipiente.

in·cise (ĭn-sīz′) tr. cortar; *(to engrave)* tallar.

in·ci·sion (ĭn-sĭzh′ən) s. incisión f.

in·ci·sive (ĭn-sī′sĭv) adj. *(mentally)* penetrante,

agudo; *(biting)* incisivo, mordaz.
in·ci·sor (:zər) s. (diente) incisivo.
in·cite (ĭn-sīt') tr. incitar.
in·cite·ment (:mənt) s. incitación *f.*
in·clem·ent (ĭn-klĕm'ənt) adj. inclemente.
in·cli·na·tion (ĭn'klə-nā'shən) s. inclinación *f;* *(tendency)* tendencia; *(preference)* gusto.
in·cline (ĭn-klīn') I. tr. & intr. inclinar(se) ♦ **if you feel so inclined** si usted desea • **to be inclined** to estar dispuesto a • **to i.** to tender a II. s. ('') inclinación *f,* pendiente *f.*
in·clined (ĭn-klīnd') adj. inclinado ♦ **i.** to dispuesto a • **musically i.** que le atrae la música.
in·clude (ĭn-klōōd') tr. incluir, abarcar.
in·clud·ed (ĭn-klōō'dĭd) adj. incluido, incluso.
in·clu·sion (:zhən) s. inclusión *f.*
in·clu·sive (:sĭv) adj. *(including)* inclusive; *(comprehensive)* inclusivo.
in·cog·ni·to (ĭn-kŏg'nĭ-tō', '-nē'tō) I. adj. & s. incógnito II. adv. de incógnito.
in·co·her·ence (ĭn'kō-hîr'əns) s. incoherencia.
in·co·her·ent (:ənt) adj. incoherente.
in·com·bus·ti·ble (ĭn'kəm-bŭs'tə-bəl) adj. & s. (substancia) incombustible.
in·come (ĭn'kŭm') s. ingresos *m,* entrada; *(on investments)* renta; *(profit)* utilidades *f* ♦ **gross, net i.** entrada bruta, neta • **i. tax** impuesto sobre los ingresos *o* utilidades.
in·com·ing (ĭn'kŭm'ĭng) adj. entrante, que entra; *(new)* nuevo.
in·com·mu·ni·ca·do (ĭn'kə-myōō'nĭ-kä'dō) adj. incomunicado.
in·com·pa·ra·ble (ĭn-kŏm'pər-ə-bəl) adj. incomparable.
in·com·pat·i·bil·i·ty (ĭn'kəm-păt'ə-bĭl'ĭ-tē) s. incompatibilidad *f.*
in·com·pat·i·ble ('-'-bəl) adj. incompatible.
in·com·pe·tence/ten·cy (ĭn-kŏm'pĭ-tns) s. incompetencia, incapacidad *f.*
in·com·pe·tent (:tnt) I. adj. incompetente, incapaz II. s. persona incompetente.
in·com·plete (ĭn'kəm-plēt') adj. incompleto.
in·com·pre·hen·si·ble (ĭn-kŏm'prĭ-hĕn'sə-bəl) adj. incomprensible.
in·con·ceiv·a·ble (ĭn'kən-sē'və-bəl) adj. inconcebible; *(incredible)* increíble.
in·con·clu·sive (ĭn'kən-klōō'sĭv) adj. no concluyente, inconcluyente.
in·con·gru·ent (ĭn'kŏn-grōō'ənt) adj. incongruente.
in·con·gru·i·ty (:ĭ-tē) s. incongruencia.
in·con·gru·ous (ĭn-kŏng'grōō-əs) adj. incongruo, incongruente.
in·con·se·quen·tial (ĭn-kŏn'sĭ-kwĕn'shəl) adj. insignificante, sin trascendencia.
in·con·sid·er·ate (ĭn'kən-sĭd'ər-ĭt) adj. desconsiderado.
in·con·sis·ten·cy (ĭn'kən-sĭs'tən-sē) s. inconsecuencia; *(irregularity)* irregularidad *f.*
in·con·sis·tent (:tənt) adj. inconsecuente; *(irregular)* irregular; *(contradictory)* contradictorio ♦ **i. with** en contradicción con.
in·con·sol·a·ble (ĭn'kən-sō'lə-bəl) adj. inconsolable, desconsolado.
in·con·spic·u·ous (ĭn'kən-spĭk'yōō-əs) adj. no conspicuo, discreto.
in·con·test·a·ble (ĭn'kən-tĕs'tə-bəl) adj. incontestable.
in·con·ti·nent (ĭn-kŏn'tə-nənt) adj. incontinente.
in·con·tro·vert·i·ble (ĭn-kŏn'trə-vûr'tə-bəl) adj. incontrovertible, indiscutible.

in·con·ven·ience (ĭn'kən-vēn'yəns) I. s. inconveniencia; *(bother)* molestia II. tr. incomodar, molestar.
in·con·ven·ient (:yənt) adj. inconveniente; *(bothersome)* molesto.
in·cor·po·rate (ĭn-kôr'pə-rāt') tr. *(to include)* incorporar, incluir; COM. constituir en sociedad —intr. constituirse en sociedad.
in·cor·po·rat·ed (:rā'tĭd) adj. incorporado; COM. constituido en sociedad.
in·cor·rect (ĭn'kə-rĕkt') adj. incorrecto.
in·cor·ri·gi·ble (ĭn-kôr'ĭ-jə-bəl) adj. incorregible.
in·crease (ĭn-krēs') I. tr. & intr. aumentar; *(prices)* subir; *(production)* incrementar, tomar incremento II. s. ('') aumento; *(in prices)* subida, alza; *(in production)* incremento ♦ **to be on the i.** ir en aumento.
in·creas·ing (ĭn-krē'sĭng) adj. creciente.
in·creas·ing·ly (:lē) adv. cada vez más.
in·cred·i·ble (ĭn-krĕd'ə-bəl) adj. increíble.
in·cre·du·li·ty (ĭn'krĭ-dōō'lĭ-tē) s. incredulidad *f.*
in·cred·u·lous (ĭn-krĕj'ə-ləs) adj. incrédulo.
in·cre·ment (ĭng'krə-mənt) s. incremento ♦ **un-earned i.** plusvalía.
in·crim·i·nate (ĭn-krĭm'ə-nāt') tr. incriminar.
in·crim·i·na·tion (-'-nā'shən) s. incriminación *f.*
in·cu·bate (ĭng'kyə-bāt') tr. & intr. incubar.
in·cu·ba·tion (ĭn'kyə-bā'shən) s. incubación *f.*
in·cu·ba·tor ('-'tər) s. incubadora.
in·cul·cate (ĭn-kŭl'kāt') tr. inculcar.
in·cum·bent (ĭn-kŭm'bənt) I. adj. *(resting)* apoyado; POL. actual ♦ **to be i. on** corresponderle a alguien II. s. POL. titular *m.*
in·cur (ĭn-kûr') tr. incurrir.
in·cur·a·ble (ĭn-kyŏŏr'ə-bəl) adj. incurable.
in·cur·sion (ĭn-kûr'zhən) s. incursión *f.*
in·debt·ed (ĭn-dĕt'ĭd) adj. endeudado; *(owing gratitude)* agradecido.
in·de·cen·cy (ĭn-dē'sən-sē) s. indecencia.
in·de·cent (:sənt) adj. indecente ♦ **i. exposure** exhibicionismo.
in·de·ci·pher·a·ble (ĭn'dĭ-sī'fər-ə-bəl) adj. indescifrable.
in·de·ci·sion (ĭn'dĭ-sĭzh'ən) s. indecisión *f.*
in·de·ci·sive (:sī'sĭv) adj. *(inconclusive)* dudoso; *(irresolute)* indeciso, irresoluto.
in·deed (ĭn-dēd') I. adv. *(truly)* verdad, verdaderamente; *(in fact)* en efecto; *(of course)* claro ♦ **i.?** ¿de verdad? • **that is a luxury** eso sí que es lujo • **yes i.!** ¡claro que sí! II. interj. de veras, verdad.
in·de·fen·si·ble (ĭn'dĭ-fĕn'sə-bəl) adj. indefensible; *(inexcusable)* imperdonable.
in·de·fin·a·ble (ĭn'dĭ-fī'nə-bəl) adj. indefinible.
in·def·i·nite (ĭn-dĕf'ə-nĭt) adj. indefinido; *(uncertain)* incierto, impreciso; *(vague)* vago.
in·del·i·ble (ĭn-dĕl'ə-bəl) adj. indeleble.
in·del·i·ca·cy (ĭn-dĕl'ĭ-kə-sē) s. indelicadeza.
in·del·i·cate (:kĭt) adj. indelicado.
in·dem·ni·fy (ĭn-dĕm'nə-fī') tr. *(to insure)* asegurar; *(to compensate)* indemnizar.
in·dem·ni·ty (:nĭ-tē) s. *(security, exemption)* indemnidad *f;* *(compensation)* indemnización *f.*
in·dent (ĭn-dĕnt') I. tr. IMPR. sangrar; *(to serrate)* dentar; *(to notch)* hacer muescas en II. s. ('') IMPR. sangría; *(notch)* muesca.
in·den·ta·tion (ĭn'dĕn-tā'shən) s. *(notch)* muesca; *(recess)* hueco; IMPR. sangría.
in·den·ture (ĭn-dĕn'chər) tr. ligar por contrato.

in·de·pend·ence (ĭn'dĭ-pĕn'dəns) s. independencia.

in·de·pend·ent (:dənt) adj. & s. independiente *mf* ♦ **of i. means** con recursos propios, adinerado • **to be i.** of no depender de.

in-depth (ĭn'dĕpth') adj. profundo.

in·de·scrib·a·ble (ĭn'dĭ-skrī'bə-bəl) adj. indescriptible.

in·de·struc·ti·ble (ĭn'dĭ-strŭk'tə-bəl) adj. indestructible.

in·de·ter·mi·nate (ĭn'dĭ-tûr'mə-nĭt) adj. indeterminado, incierto.

in·dex (ĭn'dĕks') **I.** s. [pl. **es** o **-dices**] índice *m*; *(sign)* indicio; IMPR. *(fist)* manecilla; TEC. *(pointer)* indicador *m*; *(of a cell)* ficha, tarjeta **II.** tr. poner un índice a; *(to indicate)* indicar, señalar; *(to regulate)* regular (precios).

In·di·a (ĭn'dē-ə) ♦ **I. ink** tinta china • **I. rubber** caucho.

in·di·cate (ĭn'dĭ-kāt') tr. indicar.

in·di·ca·tion ('-kā'shən) s. indicación *f*; *(sign)* indicio, seña; *(symptom)* síntoma *m*.

in·dic·a·tive (ĭn-dĭk'ə-tĭv) adj. & s. indicativo ♦ **to be i.** of indicar, ser un indicio de.

in·di·ca·tor (ĭn'dĭ-kā'tər) s. indicador *m*.

in·di·ces (ĭn'dĭ-sēz') cf. **index.**

in·dict (ĭn-dīt') tr. acusar.

in·dict·a·ble (ĭn-dī'tə-bəl) adj. que merece acusación legal.

in·dict·ment (ĭn-dīt'mənt) s. acusación *f*.

in·dif·fer·ence (ĭn-dĭf'ər-əns) s. indiferencia.

in·dif·fer·ent (:ənt) adj. indiferente; *(impartial)* desinteresado; *(mediocre)* regular.

in·di·gence (ĭn'dĭ-jəns) s. indigencia.

in·dig·e·nous (ĭn-dĭj'ə-nəs) adj. indígena.

in·di·gent (ĭn'dĭ-jənt) adj. & s. indigente *mf*.

in·di·gest·i·ble (ĭn'dĭ-jĕs'tə-bəl, ĭn'dī-) adj. indigestible.

in·di·ges·tion (:chən) s. indigestión *f*.

in·dig·nant (ĭn-dĭg'nənt) adj. indignado.

in·dig·na·tion ('-nā'shən) s. indignación *f*.

in·dig·ni·ty (ĭn-dĭg'nĭ-tē) s. indignidad *f*; *(humiliation)* humillación *f*.

in·di·go (ĭn'dĭ-gō') s. [pl. **(e)s**] índigo, añil *m*.

in·di·rect (ĭn'dĭ-rĕkt', ĭn'-dī-) adj. indirecto.

in·dis·cern·i·ble (ĭn'dĭ-sûr'nə-bəl) adj. indiscernible, imperceptible.

in·dis·creet (ĭn'dĭ-skrēt') adj. indiscreto.

in·dis·cre·tion (:skrĕsh'ən) s. indiscreción *f*.

in·dis·crim·i·nate (ĭn'dĭ-skrĭm'ə-nĭt) adj. *(undiscriminating)* sin criterio; *(random)* al azar; *(admiration, praise)* ciego.

in·dis·pens·a·ble (ĭn'dĭ-spĕn'sə-bəl) adj. indispensable, imprescindible.

in·dis·posed (ĭn'dĭ-spōzd') adj. *(slightly ill)* indispuesto; *(averse)* adverso, maldispuesto.

in·dis·po·si·tion (ĭn-dĭs'pə-zĭsh'ən) s. *(aversion)* aversión *f*; *(ailment)* indisposición *f*.

in·dis·put·a·ble (ĭn'dĭ-spyōō'tə-bəl) adj. indisputable.

in·dis·tinct (ĭn'dĭ-stĭngkt') adj. indistinto.

in·dis·tin·guish·a·ble (:stĭng'gwĭsh-ə-bəl) adj. indistinguible.

in·di·vid·u·al (ĭn'də-vĭj'ōō-əl) **I.** adj. individual; *(style, manner)* particular, propio **II.** s. individuo.

in·di·vid·u·al·ist (:ə-lĭst) s. individualista *mf*.

in·di·vid·u·al·is·tic ('-'-ə-lĭs'tĭk) adj. individualista.

in·di·vid·u·al·i·ty (:ăl'ĭ-tē) s. individualidad *f*, particularidad *f*.

in·di·vid·u·al·ize ('-'-ə-līz') tr. individualizar.

in·di·vis·i·ble (ĭn'də-vĭz'ə-bəl) adj. indivisible.

in·doc·tri·nate (ĭn-dŏk'trə-nāt') tr. adoctrinar.

in·doc·tri·na·tion (-'-nā'shən) s. adoctrinamiento.

in·do·lence (ĭn'də-ləns) s. indolencia.

in·do·lent (:lənt) adj. indolente.

in·dom·i·ta·ble (ĭn-dŏm'ĭ-tə-bəl) adj. indomable, indómito.

in·door (ĭn'dôr') adj. *(interior)* interior, interno; *(event)* de puertas adentro.

in·doors (ĭn-dôrz') adv. dentro, bajo techo.

in·duce (ĭn-dōōs') tr. *(to cause)* ocasionar; *(childbirth)* provocar; *(to infer)* inducir ♦ **to i.** to lograr convencer de que.

in·duce·ment (:mənt) s. *(incentive)* incentivo, aliciente *m*; *(lure)* atractivo.

in·duct (ĭn-dŭkt') tr. POL. instalar; MIL. reclutar; *(new member)* admitir.

in·duc·tion (ĭn-dŭk'shən) s. inducción *f*; POL. instalación *f*; *(into a society)* admisión *f*; MIL. incorporación *f* a filas.

in·duc·tive (:tĭv) adj. inductivo.

in·dulge (ĭn-dŭlj') tr. *(to pamper)* consentir, mimar; *(to gratify)* satisfacer ♦ **to i. oneself** darse gusto —intr. ♦ **to i. in** permitirse el lujo de.

in·dul·gence (ĭn-dŭl'jəns) s. *(humoring)* complacencia; *(pampering)* consentimiento; *(in pleasures)* gratificación *f*; *(treat)* gusto, capricho; *(favor)* favor *m*; RELIG. indulgencia.

in·dul·gent (:ənt) adj. indulgente.

in·dus·tri·al (ĭn-dŭs'trē-əl) adj. industrial ♦ **i. park** zona industrial • **i. relations** relaciones laborales **II.** s. ♦ pl. valores industriales.

in·dus·tri·al·ist (:ə-lĭst) s. industrial *m*.

in·dus·tri·al·ize (:ə-līz') tr. & intr. industrializar(se).

in·dus·tri·ous (:əs) adj. industrioso.

in·dus·try (ĭn'də-strē) s. industria; *(management)* empresariado *m*; *(diligence)* diligencia.

in·e·bri·ate (ĭn-ē'brē-āt') **I.** tr. embriagar, emborrachar **II.** adj. & s. (:ĭt) ebrio.

in·e·bri·at·ed (:ā'tĭd) adj. embriagado.

in·e·bri·a·tion (-'-'shən) s. embriaguez *f*.

in·ed·i·ble (ĭn-ĕd'ə-bəl) adj. incomestible.

in·ef·fec·tive (ĭn'ĭ-fĕk'tĭv) adj. ineficaz.

in·ef·fec·tu·al (:chōō-əl) adj. vano, inútil.

in·ef·fi·cien·cy (ĭn'ĭ-fĭsh'ən-sē) s. ineficacia.

in·ef·fi·cient (:ənt) adj. ineficiente, ineficaz.

in·el·i·gi·ble (ĭn-ĕl'ĭ-jə-bəl) adj. inelegible.

in·ept (ĭn-ĕpt') adj. inepto, incapaz.

in·ep·ti·tude (ĭn-ĕp'tĭ-tōōd') s. ineptitud *f*.

in·e·qual·i·ty (ĭn'ĭ-kwŏl'ĭ-tē) s. desigualdad *f*; *(injustice)* injusticia.

in·eq·ui·ty (ĭn-ĕk'wĭ-tē) s. injusticia.

in·ert (ĭn-ûrt') adj. inerte.

in·er·tia (ĭn-ûr'shə) s. inercia.

in·es·cap·a·ble (ĭn'ĭ-skā'pə-bəl) adj. ineludible, inevitable.

in·ev·i·ta·ble (ĭn-ĕv'ĭ-tə-bəl) adj. inevitable.

in·ex·act (ĭn'ĭg-zăkt') adj. inexacto.

in·ex·cus·a·ble (ĭn'ĭk-skyōō'zə-bəl) adj. inexcusable, imperdonable.

in·ex·haust·i·ble (ĭn'ĭg-zô'stə-bəl) adj. inagotable.

in·ex·o·ra·ble (ĭn-ĕk'sər-ə-bəl) adj. inexorable.

in·ex·pen·sive (ĭn'ĭk-spĕn'sĭv) adj. barato.

in·ex·pe·ri·ence (ĭn'ĭk-spîr'ē-əns) s. inexperiencia.

in·ex·pe·ri·enced (:ənst) adj. inexperto.

in·ex·pli·ca·ble (ĭn'ĭk-splĭk'ə-bəl) adj. inexplicable.

in·ex·tin·guish·a·ble (ĭn'ĭk-stĭng'gwĭsh-ə-bəl)

adj. inextinguible.
in·fal·li·ble (ĭn-făl′ə-bəl) adj. infalible.
in·fa·mous (ĭn′fə-məs) adj. infame.
in·fa·my (:mē) s. infamia.
in·fan·cy (ĭn′fən-sē) s. infancia.
in·fant (ĭn′fənt) s. infante *mf*, niño.
in·fan·tile (ĭn′fən-tīl′) adj. infantil.
in·fan·try (ĭn′fən-trē) s. infantería.
in·farct (ĭn′färkt′) s. infarto.
in·fat·u·at·ed (ĭn-făch′ōō-ā′tĭd) adj. locamente enamorado; *(foolish)* encaprichado.
in·fat·u·a·tion (-′-′shən) s. encaprichamiento.
in·fect (ĭn-fĕkt′) tr. infectar; *(to contaminate)* contaminar; *(another person)* contagiar.
in·fec·tion (ĭn-fĕk′shən) s. infección *f*.
in·fec·tious (:shəs) adj. infeccioso.
in·fer (ĭn-fûr′) tr. -rr- inferir, deducir.
in·fer·ence (ĭn′fər-əns) s. inferencia.
in·fer·en·tial (ĭn′fə-rĕn′shəl) adj. que se infiere.
in·fe·ri·or (ĭn-fîr′ē-ər) adj. & s. inferior *m*.
in·fe·ri·or·i·ty (-′-ôr′ĭ-tē) s. inferioridad *f*.
in·fer·nal (ĭn-fûr′nəl) adj. infernal.
in·fer·no (ĭn-fûr′nō) s. infierno.
in·fer·tile (ĭn-fûr′tl) adj. infértil, estéril.
in·fer·til·i·ty (ĭn′fər-tĭl′ĭ-tē) s. infertilidad *f*.
in·fest (ĭn-fĕst′) tr. infestar, plagar.
in·fes·ta·tion (ĭn′fĕ-stā′shən) s. infestación *f*.
in·fi·del (ĭn′fĭ-dəl) s. infiel *mf*.
in·fi·del·i·ty (-′-ĭ-tē) s. infidelidad.
in·fight·ing (ĭn′fī′tĭng) s. lucha interna.
in·fil·trate (ĭn-fĭl′trāt′) tr. infiltrar; *(an organization)* infiltrarse en.
in·fil·tra·tion (-′-trā′shən) s. infiltración *f*.
in·fi·nite (ĭn′fə-nĭt) adj. & s. infinito.
in·fin·i·tes·i·mal (ĭn-fĭn′ĭ-tĕs′ə-məl) adj. infinitesimal.
in·fin·i·tive (ĭn-fĭn′ĭ-tĭv) s. infinitivo.
in·fin·i·ty (:tē) s. infinidad *f*; MAT. infinito.
in·firm (ĭn-fûrm′) adj. débil, enfermizo.
in·fir·ma·ry (ĭn-fûr′mə-rē) s. enfermería.
in·fir·mi·ty (:mĭ-tē) s. *(weakness)* debilidad *f*; *(illness)* enfermedad *f*, achaque *m*.
in·flame (ĭn-flām′) tr. inflamar.
in·flam·ma·ble (ĭn-flăm′ə-bəl) adj. inflamable.
in·flam·ma·tion (ĭn′flə-mā′shən) s. inflamación *f*.
in·flam·ma·to·ry (ĭn-flăm′ə-tôr′ē) adj. *(arousing)* incendiario; MED. inflamatorio.
in·flate (ĭn-flāt′) tr. inflar; FIG. hinchar; ECON., FIN. causar la inflación de —intr. inflarse, hincharse.
in·flat·ed (ĭn-flā′tĭd) adj. inflado, hinchado; *(bombastic)* pomposo; *(wages, prices)* excesivo.
in·fla·tion (:shən) s. inflación *f*.
in·fla·tion·ar·y (:shə-nĕr′ē) adj. inflacionario.
in·flect (ĭn-flĕkt′) tr. *(voice)* modular; GRAM. *(verb)* conjugar; *(noun)* declinar.
in·flec·tion (ĭn-flĕk′shən) s. inflexión *f*.
in·flex·i·ble (ĭn-flĕk′sə-bəl) adj. inflexible.
in·flict (ĭn-flĭkt′) tr. infligir, causar ♦ **to i. (up)on** imponer a.
in·flic·tion (ĭn-flĭk′shən) s. imposición *f*.
in·flow (ĭn′flō′) s. afluencia, flujo.
in·flu·ence (ĭn′flōō-əns) I. s. influencia, influjo ♦ **to be an i. on** tener influencia sobre • **to have i.** ser influyente • **under the i.** embriagado II. tr. influir en, ejercer influencia sobre.
in·flu·en·tial (′-ĕn′shəl) adj. influyente.
in·flu·en·za (ĭn′flōō-ĕn′zə) s. influenza.
in·flux (ĭn′flŭks′) s. afluencia, entrada.
in·form (ĭn-fôrm′) tr. informar, avisar ♦ **to i. someone that** comunicarle a alguien que

—intr. ♦ **to i. on** delatar, denunciar.
in·for·mal (ĭn-fôr′məl) adj. *(casual)* familiar, llano; *(unofficial)* extraoficial; *(agreement)* no legalizado; *(unceremonious)* sin ceremonia; *(dress)* de diario, de calle.
in·for·mal·i·ty (′-măl′ĭ-tē) s. familiaridad *f*, llaneza; *(of occasion)* ausencia de ceremonia.
in·form·ant (ĭn-fôr′mənt) s. informador *m*.
in·for·ma·tion (ĭn′fər-mā′shən) s. información *f*; *(data)* datos; *(knowledge)* conocimientos ♦ **for your i.** para su conocimiento.
in·form·a·tive (ĭn-fôr′mə-tĭv) adj. informativo.
in·formed (ĭn-fôrmd′) adj. informado, enterado ♦ **to keep someone i.** tener a alguien al corriente.
in·form·er (ĭn-fôr′mər) s. delator *m*, soplón *m*.
in·frac·tion (ĭn-frăk′shən) s. infracción *f*.
in·fra·red (ĭn′frə-rĕd′) adj. infarrojo.
in·fra·struc·ture (ĭn′frə-strŭk′chər) s. infraestructura.
in·fre·quent (ĭn-frē′kwənt) adj. infrecuente.
in·fringe (ĭn-frĭnj′) tr. infringir —intr. ♦ **to i. (up)on** usurpar, abusar de.
in·fringe·ment (:mənt) s. *(of law)* infracción *f*; *(of rights)* usurpación *f*.
in·fu·ri·ate (ĭn-fyŏŏr′ē-āt′) tr. enfurecer.
in·fuse (ĭn-fyŏōz′) tr. infundir.
in·fu·sion (ĭn-fyŏō′zhən) s. infusión *f*.
in·gen·ious (ĭn-jēn′yəs) adj. ingenioso.
in·gé·nue (ăn′zhə-nŏō′) s. joven ingenua.
in·ge·nu·i·ty (ĭn′jə-nŏō′ĭ-tē) s. ingenio.
in·gen·u·ous (ĭn-jĕn′yŏō-əs) adj. ingenuo.
in·gest (ĭn-jĕst′) tr. ingerir.
in·ges·tion (ĭn-jĕs′chən) s. ingestión *f*.
in·got (ĭng′gət) s. lingote *m*, barra.
in·grained (ĭn-grānd′) adj. arraigado.
in·gra·ti·ate (ĭn-grā′shē-āt′) tr. congraciarse.
in·grat·i·tude (ĭn-grăt′ĭ-tōōd′) s. ingratitud *f*.
in·gre·di·ent (ĭn-grē′dē-ənt) s. ingrediente *m*.
in·hab·it (ĭn-hăb′ĭt) tr. habitar, vivir en.
in·hab·it·a·ble (:ĭ-tə-bəl) adj. habitable.
in·hab·i·tant (:ĭ-tnt) s. habitante *mf*.
in·ha·la·tion (ĭn′hə-lā′shən) s. inhalación *f*.
in·hale (ĭn-hāl′) tr. aspirar; *(smoke)* tragar; MED. inhalar —intr. aspirar aire.
in·her·ent (ĭn-hĕr′ənt) adj. inherente.
in·her·it (ĭn-hĕr′ĭt) tr. heredar.
in·her·i·tance (:ĭ-tns) s. *(act)* sucesión *f*; *(thing)* herencia; *(heritage)* patrimonio.
in·hib·it (ĭn-hĭb′ĭt) tr. inhibir; *(to prevent)* impedir; *(to prohibit)* prohibir.
in·hi·bi·tion (ĭn′hə-bĭsh′ən) s. inhibición *f*.
in·hos·pi·ta·ble (ĭn-hŏs′pĭ-tə-bəl, ĭn′hŏ-spĭt′ə-) adj. inhospitalario; *(barren)* inhóspito.
in·house (ĭn′hous′) adj. interno, de la casa.
in·hu·man (ĭn-hyŏō′mən) adj. inhumano, cruel; *(monstrous)* no humano.
in·hu·mane (′-mān′) adj. inhumano.
in·im·i·cal (ĭn-ĭm′ĭ-kəl) adj. adverso, hostil.
in·im·i·ta·ble (ĭn-ĭm′ĭ-tə-bəl) adj. inimitable.
in·iq·ui·ty (ĭn-ĭk′wĭ-tē) s. iniquidad *f*.
in·i·tial (ĭ-nĭsh′əl) I. adj. & s. inicial *f* ♦ s.pl. *(person)* iniciales; *(organization)* siglas II. tr. firmar con las iniciales.
in·i·ti·ate (ĭ-nĭsh′ē-āt′) I. tr. iniciar; *(proceedings)* entablar II. adj. & s. (:ĭt) iniciado.
in·i·ti·a·tion (-′-ā′shən) s. iniciación *f*.
in·i·tia·tive (ĭ-nĭsh′ə-tĭv) s. iniciativa.
in·ject (ĭn-jĕkt′) tr. inyectar; *(a patient)* poner una inyección a; FIG. introducir.
in·jec·tion (ĭn-jĕk′shən) s. inyección *f*.
in·junc·tion (ĭn-jŭngk′shən) s. *(command)* or-

den *f*; *(prohibition)* entredicho.
in·jure (ĭn′jər) tr. lastimar, herir; *(to impair)* dañar, averiar; *(to wrong)* injuriar.
in·ju·ri·ous (ĭn-jŏŏr′ē-əs) adj. *(harmful)* dañino, perjudicial; *(offensive)* injurioso.
in·ju·ry (ĭn′jə-rē) s. *(damage, wrong)* daño, perjuicio; *(wound)* herida.
in·jus·tice (ĭn-jŭs′tĭs) s. injusticia.
ink (ĭngk) I. s. tinta II. tr. entintar.
in·kling (ĭng′klĭng) s. *(hint)* indicio; *(suspicion)* sospecha.
ink·well (ĭngk′wĕl′) s. tintero.
in·land (ĭn′lănd′) I. adj. (del) interior II. adv. tierra adentro, hacia el interior.
in·law (ĭn′lô′) s. pariente político.
in·lay I. tr. (ĭn-lā′) -laid incrustar II. s. (′′) incrustación *f*.
in·let (ĭn′lĕt′) s. *(bay)* cala; *(estuary)* estuario.
in·mate (ĭn′māt′) s. *(of asylum)* asilado; *(prisoner)* presidiario, preso.
inn (ĭn) s. posada, hostería; *(tavern)* taberna.
in·nards (ĭn′ərdz) s.pl. FAM. entrañas.
in·nate (ĭ-nāt′) adj. innato.
in·ner (ĭn′ər) adj. interior, interno; *(profound)* profundo, recóndito; *(intimate)* íntimo ♦ **i. circle** esfera de mayor influencia • **i. city** distrito del centro de una ciudad • **i. tube** cámara.
in·ner·most (:mōst′) adj. más interno, más adentro; FIG. más profundo, más íntimo.
in·no·cence (ĭn′ə-səns) s. inocencia.
in·no·cent (:sənt) adj. & s. inocente *mf*.
in·noc·u·ous (ĭ-nŏk′yŏŏ-əs) adj. inocuo.
in·no·vate (ĭn′ə-vāt′) tr. & intr. innovar.
in·no·va·tion (′-vā′shən) s. innovación *f*.
in·no·va·tive (′-′tĭv) adj. innovador.
in·no·va·tor (:tər) s. innovador *m*.
in·nu·en·do (ĭn′yŏŏ-ĕn′dō) s. [pl. **es**] insinuación *f*, indirecta.
in·nu·mer·a·ble (ĭ-nŏŏ′mər-ə-bəl) adj. innumerable.
in·ob·ser·vant (ĭn′əb-zûr′vənt) adj. desatento.
in·ob·tru·sive (ĭn′əb-trŏŏ′sĭv) adj. discreto.
in·oc·u·late (ĭ-nŏk′yə-lāt′) tr. inocular.
in·oc·u·la·tion (′-lā′shən) s. inoculación *f*.
in·of·fen·sive (ĭn′ə-fĕn′sĭv) adj. inofensivo.
in·op·er·a·ble (ĭn-ŏp′ər-ə-bəl) adj. *(not functioning)* que no funciona; CIR. inoperable.
in·op·er·a·tive (:tĭv) adj. *(not in effect)* inoperante; *(not functioning)* que no funciona.
in·op·por·tune (ĭn-ŏp′ər-tŏŏn′) adj. inoportuno.
in·or·di·nate (ĭn-ôr′dn-ĭt) adj. inmoderado.
in·or·gan·ic (ĭn′ôr-găn′ĭk) adj. inorgánico.
in·pa·tient (ĭn′pā′shənt) s. paciente *mf* internado en un hospital.
in·put (ĭn′pŏŏt′) I. s. COMPUT., ELEC. entrada; MEC. energía consumida; FIG. intervención *f* II. tr. COMPUT. entrar, ingresar.
in·quest (ĭn′kwĕst′) s. indagatoria, encuesta.
in·quire (ĭn-kwīr′) intr. preguntar; *(to ask)* preguntar, hacer una pregunta ♦ **to i. about** *(a person)* preguntar por; *(a matter)* pedir informes sobre • **to i. into** investigar (sobre) —tr. preguntar por, averiguar.
in·quir·y (ĭng′kwə-rē) s. pregunta; *(investigation)* investigación *f*, indagación *f*.
in·qui·si·tion (ĭng′kwĭ-zĭsh′ən) s. inquisición *f*.
in·quis·i·tive (ĭn-kwĭz′ĭ-tĭv) adj. *(prying)* preguntón, inquisitivo; *(curious)* curioso.
in·quis·i·tor (:tər) s. inquisidor *m*.
in·road (ĭn′rōd′) s. invasión *f*, incursión *f*.
in·sane (ĭn-sān′) adj. loco, demente; *(absurd)* disparatado ♦ **i. asylum** manicomio.

in·san·i·ty (ĭn-săn′ĭ-tē) s. locura, demencia; *(folly)* insensatez *f*, locura.
in·sa·tia·ble (ĭn-sā′shə-bəl) adj. insaciable.
in·scribe (ĭn-skrīb′) tr. inscribir; *(to dedicate)* dedicar, firmar.
in·scrip·tion (ĭn-skrĭp′shən) s. inscripción *f*; *(dedication)* dedicatoria.
in·scru·ta·ble (ĭn-skrŏŏ′tə-bəl) adj. inescrutable.
in·sect (ĭn′sĕkt′) s. insecto.
in·sec·ti·cide (ĭn-sĕk′tĭ-sīd′) s. insecticida *m*.
in·se·cure (ĭn′sĭ-kyŏŏr′) adj. inseguro.
in·se·cu·ri·ty (:ĭ-tē) s. inseguridad *f*.
in·sem·i·nate (ĭn-sĕm′ə-nāt′) tr. inseminar.
in·sem·i·na·tion (′-nā′shən) s. inseminación *f*.
in·sen·sate (ĭn-sĕn′sāt′) adj. insensible.
in·sen·si·ble (:sə-bəl) adj. insensible.
in·sen·si·tive (:sĭ-tĭv) adj. insensible.
in·sep·a·ra·ble (ĭn-sĕp′ər-ə-bəl) adj. inseparable.
in·sert (ĭn-sûrt′) I. tr. *(into)* insertar, introducir; *(between)* intercalar II. s. (′′) inserción *f*; *(page)* encarte *m*; COST. entredós *m*.
in·ser·tion (ĭn-sûr′shən) s. inserción *f*.
in·side (ĭn-sīd′, ′′) I. s. interior *m*, parte *f* de adentro ♦ **to be on the i.** tener acceso a información confidencial • **to know i. out** conocer a fondo • **to turn i. out** volver al revés ♦ pl. FAM. entrañas, tripas II. adj. *(inner)* interior, interno; *(confidential)* confidencial, secreto ♦ **i. job** delito cometido por un empleado de la casa • **i. track** DEP. pista interior; FIG. ventaja III. adv. *(within)* dentro, adentro; *(on the inner side)* por dentro IV. prep. dentro de ♦ **i. of** FAM. dentro de.
in·sid·er (ĭn-sī′dər) s. miembro de un grupo; *(well-informed person)* persona enterada.
in·sid·i·ous (ĭn-sĭd′ē-əs) adj. insidioso.
in·sight (ĭn′sīt′) s. perspicacia; *(revelation)* revelación *f*, idea.
in·sight·ful (:fəl) adj. perspicaz.
in·sig·ni·a (ĭn-sĭg′nē-ə) s. [pl. inv. **o s**] insignia.
in·sig·nif·i·cant (ĭn′sĭg-nĭf′ĭ-kənt) adj. insignificante.
in·sin·cere (ĭn′sĭn-sîr′) adj. insincero.
in·sin·cer·i·ty (:sĕr′ĭ-tē) s. insinceridad *f*.
in·sin·u·ate (ĭn-sĭn′yŏŏ-āt′) tr. insinuar.
in·sip·id (ĭn-sĭp′ĭd) adj. insípido.
in·sist (ĭn-sĭst′) intr. insistir ♦ **to i. (up)on** insistir en • **to i.** that insistir en que.
in·sis·tence (ĭn-sĭs′təns) s. insistencia.
in·sis·tent (:tənt) adj. insistente.
in·so·far as (ĭn′sō-fär′ ăz) conj. en cuanto a, en la medida en que.
in·sole (ĭn′sōl′) s. plantilla (del zapato).
in·so·lence (ĭn′sə-ləns) s. insolencia, descaro.
in·so·lent (:lənt) adj. insolente, descarado.
in·sol·u·ble (ĭn-sŏl′yə-bəl) adj. insoluble.
in·sol·vent (:vənt) adj. & s. insolvente *mf*.
in·som·ni·a (ĭn-sŏm′nē-ə) s. insomnio.
in·som·ni·ac (:ăk′) adj. & s. (persona) insomne.
in·so·much as (ĭn′sō-mŭch′ ăz) conj. ya que.
in·sou·ci·ant (ĭn-sŏŏ′sē-ənt) adj. despreocupado.
in·spect (ĭn-spĕkt′) tr. inspeccionar; MIL. pasar revista.
in·spec·tion (ĭn-spĕk′shən) s. inspección *f*; MIL. revista.
in·spec·tor (:tər) s. inspector *m*.
in·spi·ra·tion (ĭn′spə-rā′shən) s. inspiración *f* ♦ **to be an i.** to servir de ejemplo a.

in·spi·ra·tion·al (:shə-nəl) adj. inspirador.
in·spire (ĭn-spīr') tr. inspirar, motivar; *(emotion)* suscitar, infundir ♦ **to i. with** infundir, llenar de.
in·spired (ĭn-spīrd') adj. inspirado, de inspiración.
in·spir·ing (ĭn-spīr'ĭng) adj. inspirador.
in·sta·bil·i·ty (ĭn'stə-bĭl'ĭ-tē) s. inestabilidad *f*.
in·stall (ĭn-stôl') tr. instalar.
in·stal·la·tion (ĭn'stə-lā'shən) s. instalación *f*; MIL. base *f*.
in·stall·ment (:mənt) s. *(payment)* plazo, pago; *(of a publication)* entrega ♦ **i. plan** pago a plazos • **monthly i.** mensualidad.
in·stance (ĭn'stəns) s. *(example)* ejemplo, muestra; *(case)* caso ♦ **for i.** por ejemplo • **in many instances** en muchos casos.
in·stant (ĭn'stənt) **I.** s. instante *m*, momento ♦ **the i. (that)** en cuanto • **this i.** al instante, en seguida **II.** adj. inmediato; *(urgent)* apremiante; *(food, success)* instantáneo ♦ **i. replay** repetición inmediata por videocinta.
in·stan·ta·ne·ous (ĭn'stən-tā'nē-əs) adj. instantáneo.
in·stant·ly (ĭn'stənt-lē) adv. instantáneamente, inmediatamente.
in·stead (ĭn-stĕd') adv. en su lugar; *(rather than)* en cambio ♦ **i. of** en lugar de, en vez de.
in·step (ĭn'stĕp') s. empeine *m*.
in·sti·gate (ĭn'stĭ-gāt') tr. fomentar.
in·sti·ga·tion ('-gā'shən) s. instigación *f*.
in·sti·ga·tor ('-'tər) s. instigador *m*.
in·still (ĭn-stĭl') tr. instilar.
in·stinct (ĭn'stĭngkt') s. instinto.
in·stinc·tive (ĭn-stĭngk'tĭv) adj. instintivo.
in·sti·tute (ĭn'stĭ-tōōt') **I.** tr. instituir, establecer; *(to initiate)* iniciar **II.** s. instituto.
in·sti·tu·tion ('-tōō'shən) s. institución *f*; *(asylum)* asilo; *(for the insane)* manicomio.
in·sti·tu·tion·al (:shə-nəl) adj. institucional ♦ **i. care** atención médica (en asilo, manicomio).
in·sti·tu·tion·al·ize (:nə-līz') tr. institucionalizar; *(a person)* meter en un asilo o manicomio.
in·struct (ĭn-strŭkt') tr. instruir; *(to order)* dar instrucciones, mandar.
in·struc·tion (ĭn-strŭk'shən) s. instrucción *f*.
in·struc·tor (:tər) s. instructor *m*.
in·stru·ment (ĭn'strə-mənt) s. instrumento.
in·stru·men·tal ('-mĕn'tl) adj. instrumental ♦ **to be i. in** *o* for ayudar a, contribuir a.
in·sub·or·di·nate (ĭn'sə-bôr'dn-ĭt) adj. insubordinado.
in·sub·stan·tial (ĭn'səb-stăn'shəl) adj. insubstancial; *(flimsy)* flojo.
in·suf·fer·a·ble (ĭn-sŭf'ər-ə-bəl) adj. intolerable.
in·suf·fi·cient (ĭn'sə-fĭsh'ənt) adj. insuficiente.
in·su·lar (ĭn'sə-lər) adj. insular; *(narrow-minded)* estrecho de miras.
in·su·late (ĭn'sə-lāt') tr. aislar.
in·su·la·tion ('-lā'shən) s. aislamiento; *(material)* aislador *m*, material *m* aislante.
in·su·lin (ĭn'sə-lĭn) s. insulina.
in·sult (ĭn-sŭlt') **I.** tr. insultar **II.** s. ('') insulto.
in·sult·ing (ĭn-sŭl'tĭng) adj. insultante.
in·sup·port·a·ble (ĭn'sə-pôr'tə-bəl) adj. insoportable; *(claim)* injustificable.
in·sur·a·ble (ĭn-shōōr'ə-bəl) adj. asegurable.
in·sur·ance (:əns) s. seguro; FIG. seguridad *f* ♦ **to take out i.** sacar(se) un seguro.
in·sure (ĭn-shōōr') tr. asegurar.

in·sured (ĭn-shōōrd') s. asegurado.
in·sur·er (ĭn-shōōr'ər) s. asegurador *m*.
in·sur·gence/·cy (ĭn-sûr'jəns) s. insurrección *f*.
in·sur·gent (:jənt) adj. & s. insurgente *mf*.
in·sur·mount·a·ble (ĭn'sər-moun'tə-bəl) adj. insuperable.
in·sur·rec·tion (ĭn'sə-rĕk'shən) s. insurrección *f*.
in·tact (ĭn-tăkt') adj. intacto.
in·take (ĭn'tāk') s. entrada, toma; *(valve)* admisión *f*.
in·tan·gi·ble (ĭn-tăn'jə-bəl) adj. & s. *(cosa)* intangible.
in·te·ger (ĭn'tĭ-jər) s. *(número)* entero.
in·te·gral (ĭn'tĭ-grəl) **I.** adj. integral; *(part)* integrante **II.** s. integral *f*.
in·te·grate (:grāt') tr. & intr. integrar(se).
in·te·grat·ed (:grā'tĭd) adj. integrado.
in·te·gra·tion ('-'shən) s. integración *f*.
in·teg·ri·ty (ĭn-tĕg'rĭ-tē) s. integridad *f*.
in·tel·lect (ĭn'tl-ĕkt') s. intelecto.
in·tel·lec·tu·al ('-ĕk'chōō-əl) adj. & s. intelectual *mf*.
in·tel·lec·tu·al·ize (:ə-līz') tr. intelectualizar.
in·tel·li·gence (ĭn-tĕl'ĭ-jəns) s. inteligencia; *(information)* información secreta.
in·tel·li·gent (:jənt) adj. inteligente.
in·tel·li·gent·si·a (-'-jĕnt'sē-ə) s. intelectualidad *f*.
in·tel·li·gi·ble (-'-jə-bəl) adj. inteligible.
in·tem·per·ate (ĭn-tĕm'pər-ĭt) adj. intemperante; *(climate)* inclemente.
in·tend (ĭn-tĕnd') tr. *(to plan)* proponerse, tener la intención (de); *(to contemplate)* pensar; *(to mean)* querer decir.
in·tend·ed (ĭn-tĕn'dĭd) **I.** adj. *(planned)* proyectado; *(intentional)* deliberado; *(future)* futuro ♦ **i. for** destinado a, para; *(remark)* dirigido a **II.** s. FAM. prometido, -a.
in·tense (ĭn-tĕns') adj. intenso.
in·ten·si·fy (ĭn-tĕn'sə-fī') tr. & intr. intensificar(se), aumentar(se).
in·ten·si·ty (:sĭ-tē) s. intensidad *f*.
in·ten·sive (:sĭv) adj. intensivo.
in·tent (ĭn-tĕnt') **I.** s. *(purpose)* intención *f*, propósito; *(meaning)* sentido ♦ **for all intents and purposes** en efecto **II.** adj. fijo ♦ **i. (up)on** resuelto a.
in·ten·tion (ĭn-tĕn'shən) s. intención *f*, propósito ♦ **to be one's i.** proponerse.
in·ten·tion·al (:shə-nəl) adj. intencional.
in·ter (ĭn-tûr') tr. **-rr-** enterrar.
in·ter·act (ĭn'tər-ăkt') intr. actuar recíprocamente, influenciar uno a otro.
in·ter·ac·tion (:ăk'shən) s. interacción *f*.
in·ter·breed (:brēd') tr. & intr. **-bred** cruzar(se) animales de especie diferente.
in·ter·cede (:sēd') intr. interceder.
in·ter·cept (ĭn'tər-sĕpt') tr. interceptar.
in·ter·cep·tion (:sĕp'shən) s. interceptación *f*.
in·ter·ces·sion (:sĕsh'ən) s. intercesión *f*.
in·ter·change (:chānj') **I.** tr. intercambiar; *(places)* alternar **II.** s. ('-') intercambio; *(highway junction)* empalme *m*.
in·ter·change·a·ble (:chān'jə-bəl) adj. intercambiable.
in·ter·col·le·giate (:kə-lē'jĭt) adj. interuniversitario.
in·ter·com ('-kŏm') s. sistema *m* de intercomunicación.
in·ter·con·nect ('-kə-nĕkt') intr. & tr. conectar.
in·ter·con·nec·tion (:kə-nĕk'shən) s. inter-

conexión *f.*
in·ter·course ('-kôrs') *s.* relaciones *f* sociales; *(trade)* comercio, tráfico; *(coitus)* coito.
in·ter·de·pend·ent ('-dī-pĕn'dənt) *adj.* interdependiente.
in·ter·dict (:dīkt') interdecir, prohibir.
in·ter·est (ĭn'trĭst, ĭn'tər-ĭst) **I.** *s.* interés *m; (benefit)* beneficio; COM. *(share)* acción *f; (on money)* interés ♦ **in one's own i.** en beneficio propio • **to be in one's best i.** to ser mejor para uno que • **to be of i.** ser interesante • **to take an i. in** interesarse por **II.** *tr.* interesar ♦ **to i. someone in** hacer que alguien se interese en *o* por.
in·ter·est·ed (ĭn'trĭs-tĭd, ĭn'tər-ĭs-tĭd) *adj.* interesado ♦ **to be i. in** interesarle a uno.
in·ter·est·ing (:stĭng) *adj.* interesante.
in·ter·fere (ĭn'tər-fîr') *intr.* interferir; *(to meddle)* entrometerse ♦ **to i. with** obstruir, impedir.
in·ter·fer·ence (:əns) *s.* interferencia.
in·ter·im (ĭn'tər-ĭm) **I.** *s.* interín *m* **II.** *adj.* interino, provisional.
in·te·ri·or (ĭn-tîr'ē-ər) *adj.* & *s.* interior *m.*
in·ter·ject (ĭn'tər-jĕkt') *tr.* interponer.
in·ter·jec·tion (:jĕk'shən) *s.* interposición *f*; GRAM. interjección *f.*
in·ter·lock (:lŏk') *intr.* trabarse.
in·ter·loc·u·tor (:lŏk'yə-tər) *s.* interlocutor *m.*
in·ter·lop·er (ĭn'tər-lō'pər) *s.* entrometido.
in·ter·lude (:lᵫd') *s.* intermedio; TEAT. entremés *m.*
in·ter·mar·ry ('-mär'ē) *intr. (races, religions)* casarse personas de distintos grupos; *(family)* casarse entre parientes.
in·ter·me·di·ar·y (:mē'dē-ĕr'ē) *s.* intermediario.
in·ter·me·di·ate (:ĭt) **I.** *adj.* intermedio **II.** *s.* intermediario.
in·ter·ment (ĭn-tûr'mənt) *s.* entierro.
in·ter·mi·na·ble (ĭn-tûr'mə-nə-bəl) *adj.* interminable.
in·ter·mis·sion (ĭn'tər-mĭsh'ən) *s.* intermisión *f*; TEAT. intermedio, entreacto.
in·ter·mit·tent (:mĭt'nt) *adj.* intermitente.
in·tern (ĭn'tûrn') **I.** *s.* interno, médico residente **II.** *intr.* (-') trabajar como interno —*tr.* internar, recluir (esp. en tiempo de guerra).
in·ter·nal (ĭn-tûr'nəl) *adj.* interno; *(domestic)* interior, nacional ♦ **i. revenue** rentas públicas.
in·ter·nal-com·bus·tion engine (:kəm-bŭs'chən) *s.* motor *m* de explosión.
in·ter·nal·ize (:nə-līz') *tr.* hacer interno.
in·ter·na·tion·al (ĭn'tər-nǎsh'ə-nəl) *adj.* internacional.
in·ter·na·tion·al·ize (:nə-līz') *tr.* internacionalizar.
in·ter·nist (ĭn-tûr'nĭst) *s.* internista *mf.*
in·tern·ment (ĭn-tûrn'mənt) *s.* internamiento.
in·ter·of·fice (ĭn'tər-ô'f ĭs) *adj.* interno.
in·ter·per·son·al (:pûr'sə-nəl) *adj.* personal.
in·ter·play (-'plā') *s.* interacción *f.*
in·ter·po·late (ĭn-tûr'pə-lāt') *tr.* interpolar.
in·ter·pose (ĭn'tər-pōz') *tr.* & *intr.* interponer(se).
in·ter·pret (ĭn-tûr'prĭt) *tr.* interpretar —*intr.* servir de intérprete.
in·ter·pre·ta·tion (-'prĭ-tā'shən) *s.* interpretación *f* ♦ **to bear a different i.** poder entenderse de otro modo.
in·ter·pret·er (:tər) *s.* intérprete *mf.*
in·ter·pre·tive (:tĭv) *adj.* interpretativo.
in·ter·ra·cial (ĭn'tər-rā'shəl) *adj.* entre las razas.

in·ter·re·lat·ed (ĭn'tər-rĭ-lā'tĭd) *adj.* correlativo, mutuamente relacionado.
in·ter·ro·gate (ĭn-tĕr'ə-gāt') *tr.* interrogar.
in·ter·ro·ga·tion (-'-gā'shən) *s.* interrogación *f*; *(close questioning)* interrogatorio.
in·ter·rog·a·tive (ĭn'tə-rŏg'ə-tĭv) *adj.* & *s.* interrogativo.
in·ter·ro·ga·tor (ĭn-tĕr'ə-gā'tər) *s.* interrogador *m.*
in·ter·rupt (ĭn'tə-rŭpt') *tr.* interrumpir.
in·ter·rup·tion (:rŭp'shən) *s.* interrupción *f.*
in·ter·sect (ĭn'tər-sĕkt') *tr. (to cut)* cruzar; *(to cross)* cruzarse con —*intr.* cruzarse.
in·ter·sec·tion (:sĕk'shən) *s.* intersección *f*; *(of streets)* bocacalle *f*; *(of roads)* cruce *m.*
in·ter·sperse (:spûrs') *tr. (to distribute)* entreverar, entremezclar; *(to scatter)* salpicar.
in·ter·state (:stāt') *adj.* entre estados *o* provincias ♦ **i. highway** carretera nacional.
in·ter·twine (:twīn') *tr.* & *intr.* entrelazar(se), entretejer(se).
in·ter·val (ĭn'tər-vəl) *s.* intervalo ♦ **at intervals** a ratos • **at regular intervals** con regularidad.
in·ter·vene (ĭn'tər-vēn') *intr.* intervenir.
in·ter·ven·tion (:vĕn'shən) *s.* intervención *f.*
in·ter·view (ĭn'tər-vyᵫ') **I.** *s.* entrevista **II.** *tr.* & *intr.* entrevistar(se).
in·ter·view·er (:ər) *s.* entrevistador *m.*
in·ter·weave (ĭn'tər-wēv') *tr.* & *intr.* **-wove, -woven** entretejer(se).
in·tes·ta·cy (ĭn-tĕs'tə-sē) *s.* falta de testamento.
in·tes·tate (:tāt') *adj.* & *s.* intestado.
in·tes·ti·nal (ĭn-tĕs'tə-nəl) *adj.* intestinal.
in·tes·tine (:tĭn) *s.* intestino ♦ **large, small i.** intestino grueso, delgado.
in·ti·ma·cy (ĭn'tə-mə-sē) *s.* intimidad *f.*
in·ti·mate¹ (ĭn'tə-mĭt) *adj.* & *s.* intimo ♦ **to become i.** intimar.
in·ti·mate² (:māt') *tr.* dar a entender, insinuar.
in·tim·i·date (ĭn-tĭm'ĭ-dāt') *tr.* intimidar.
in·tim·i·da·tion (-'-dā'shən) *s.* intimidación *f.*
in·ti·ma·tion (ĭn'tə-mā'shən) *s.* insinuación *f.*
in·to (ĭn'tᵫ) *prep.* en, a, dentro de, contra ♦ **well i.** bien entrado *o* avanzado.
in·tol·er·a·ble (ĭn-tŏl'ər-ə-bəl) *adj.* intolerable.
in·tol·er·ant (:ənt) *adj.* intolerante ♦ **to be i. of** no poder tolerar.
in·to·na·tion (ĭn'tə-nā'shən) *s.* entonación *f.*
in·tone (ĭn-tōn') *tr.* recitar melódicamente.
in·tox·i·cate (ĭn-tŏk'sĭ-kāt') *tr.* embriagar.
in·tox·i·ca·tion (-'-kā'shən) *s.* embriaguez *f.*
in·trac·ta·ble (ĭn-trǎk'tə-bəl) *adj.* intratable, obstinado; MED. rebelde.
in·tran·si·gent (ĭn-trǎn'sə-jənt) *adj.* intransigente.
in·tran·si·tive (ĭn-trǎn'sĭ-tĭv) *adj.* & *s.* (verbo) intransitivo.
in·tra·ve·nous (ĭn'trə-vē'nəs) *adj.* intravenoso.
in·trep·id (ĭn-trĕp'ĭd) *adj.* intrépido.
in·tri·ca·cy (ĭn'trĭ-kə-sē) *s.* complejidad *f.*
in·tri·cate (:kĭt) *adj.* complejo, intrincado.
in·trigue (ĭn'trēg') **I.** *s.* intriga; *(love affair)* amorío secreto **II.** *intr.* & *tr.* (-') intrigar.
in·tri·gu·er (ĭn-trēg'ər) *s.* intrigante *mf.*
in·trin·sic (ĭn-trĭn'sĭk) *adj.* intrínseco.
in·tro·duce (ĭn'trə-dᵫs') *tr.* presentar; *(to insert, bring into use)* introducir; *(a product)* lanzar al mercado; *(a topic)* sacar a colación; *(to initiate)* familiarizar (**to** con); *(into a new surrounding)* traer; *(to preface)* prologar.
in·tro·duc·tion (:dŭk'shən) *s.* introducción *f*; *(of people)* presentación *f*; *(of a product)* lanza-

miento.

in·tro·duc·to·ry (:tə-rē) adj. preliminar.

in·tro·mis·sion (ĭn' trə-mĭsh'ən) s. inserción f.

in·tro·spec·tion (:spĕk'shən) s. introspección f.

in·tro·spec·tive (:tĭv) adj. introspectivo.

in·tro·vert (ĭn' trə-vûrt') s. introvertido.

in·tro·vert·ed (:vûr' tĭd) adj. introvertido.

in·trude (ĭn-trōd') tr. meter por fuerza (en) —intr. *(to meddle)* inmiscuirse, entrometerse; *(to interrupt)* molestar, interrumpir.

in·trud·er (ĭn-trō'dər) s. intruso.

in·tru·sion (:zhən) s. intrusión f; *(invasion)* invasión f; *(imposition)* molestia.

in·tru·sive (:sĭv) adj. intruso.

in·tu·it (ĭn-tō'ĭt) tr. intuir.

in·tu·i·tion ('-ĭsh'ən) s. intuición f.

in·tu·i·tive (-'ĭ-tĭv) adj. intuitivo.

in·un·date (ĭn'ŭn-dāt') tr. inundar.

in·un·da·tion (:dā'shən) s. inundación f.

in·ure (ĭn-yŏŏr') tr. curtir, endurecer.

in·vade (ĭn-vād') tr. invadir; *(privacy)* no respetar; *(rights)* violar —intr. hacer una invasión.

in·vad·er (ĭn-vā'dər) s. invasor m.

in·va·lid¹ (ĭn'və-lĭd) adj. & s. inválido.

in·val·id² (ĭn-văl'ĭd) adj. nulo, inválido; *(faulty)* defectuoso, imperfecto.

in·val·i·date (:ĭ-dāt') tr. invalidar.

in·val·i·da·tion (-'-dā'shən) s. invalidación f.

in·va·lid·i·ty (ĭn'və-lĭd'ĭ-tē) s. nulidad f.

in·val·u·a·ble (ĭn-văl'yōō-ə-bəl) adj. inestimable.

in·var·i·a·ble (ĭn-vâr'ē-ə-bəl) adj. invariable.

in·va·sion (ĭn-vā'zhən) s. invasión f; *(of privacy)* entrometimiento; *(of rights)* transgresión f.

in·vec·tive (ĭn-vĕk'tĭv) s. invectiva, vituperio.

in·veigh (ĭn-vā') intr. ♦ **i. against** vituperar.

in·vei·gle (ĭn-vā'gəl) tr. sonsacar.

in·vent (ĭn-vĕnt') tr. inventar.

in·ven·tion (ĭn-vĕn'shən) s. invención f; *(new device)* invento; *(skill)* inventiva.

in·ven·tive (:tĭv) adj. inventivo.

in·ven·tor (:tər) s. inventor m.

in·ven·to·ry (ĭn'vən-tôr'ē) **I.** s. inventario; *(stock)* existencias **II.** tr. inventariar.

in·verse (ĭn'vûrs') adj. & s. (lo) inverso.

in·ver·sion (ĭn-vûr'zhən) s. inversión f.

in·vert (ĭn-vûrt') tr. invertir.

in·ver·te·brate (ĭn-vûr'tə-brĭt) adj. & s. invertebrado.

in·vest (ĭn-vĕst') tr. *(money)* invertir; *(effort)* dedicar; *(to endow)* conferir; *(to install in office)* investir —intr. hacer una inversión.

in·ves·ti·gate (ĭn-vĕs'tĭ-gāt') tr. investigar.

in·ves·ti·ga·tion (-'-gā'shən) s. investigación f.

in·ves·ti·ga·tive (-'-'tĭv) adj. de investigación.

in·ves·ti·ga·tor (:tər) s. investigador m.

in·ves·ti·ture (ĭn-vĕs'tĭ-chŏŏr') s. investidura.

in·vest·ment (ĭn-vĕst'mənt) s. inversión f.

in·ves·tor (ĭn-vĕs'tər) s. inversionista mf.

in·vet·er·ate (ĭn-vĕt'ər-ĭt) adj. *(deep-rooted)* inveterado; *(confirmed)* incorregible.

in·vid·i·ous (ĭn-vĭd'ē-əs) adj. provocador.

in·vig·o·rate (ĭn-vĭg'ə-rāt') tr. dar vigor a.

in·vin·ci·ble (ĭn-vĭn'sə-bəl) adj. invencible.

in·vi·o·la·ble (ĭn-vī'ə-lə-bəl) adj. inviolable.

in·vi·o·late (:lĭt) adj. inviolado.

in·vis·i·ble (ĭn-vĭz'ə-bəl) adj. invisible ♦ **i. ink** tinta simpática.

in·vi·ta·tion (ĭn'vĭ-tā'shən) s. invitación f.

in·vite I. tr. (ĭn-vīt') invitar; *(for food, drink)* convidar; *(a response)* solicitar; *(trouble)* provocar, buscar **II.** s. ('') FAM. invitación f.

in·vit·ing (ĭn-vī'tĭng) adj. atrayente, tentador.

in·vo·ca·tion (ĭn' və-kā'shən) s. invocación f.

in·voice (ĭn'vois') **I.** factura **II.** tr. facturar.

in·voke (ĭn-vōk') tr. invocar.

in·vol·un·tar·y (ĭn-vŏl'ən-tĕr'ē) adj. involuntario.

in·vo·lu·tion (ĭn'və-lōō'shən) s. complicación f.

in·volve (ĭn-vŏlv') tr. *(to include)* comprender, incluir; *(to entail)* implicar, entrañar; *(in a matter)* comprometer, involucrar; *(to engross)* absorber; *(to complicate)* enredar.

in·volved (ĭn-vŏlvd') adj. complicado, enredado ♦ **to be i. in** estar involucrado en • **to get i. in** meterse o involucrarse en.

in·volve·ment (ĭn-vŏlv'mənt) s. *(entanglement)* envolvimiento, comprometimiento; *(in a matter)* participación f; *(engrossment)* abstraimiento; *(intricateness)* intrincación f.

in·vul·ner·a·ble (ĭn-vŭl'nər-ə-bəl) adj. invulnerable.

in·ward (ĭn'wərd) **I.** adj. interior, interno **II.** adv. o **-wards** hacia adentro.

i·o·dine (ī'ə-dīn', :dĭn') s. yodo.

i·o·dize (ī'ə-dīz') tr. yodar.

i·on (ī'ən, ī'ŏn') s. ion.

i·on·ic (ī-ŏn'ĭk) adj. Fís iónico, de los iones.

Ionic order s. ARQ. orden jónico.

i·on·ize (ī'ə-nīz') tr. & intr. ionizar(se).

i·o·ta (ī-ō'tə) s. iota; *(bit)* ápice m, pizca.

IOU (ī'ō-yōō's) [pl. **s** o **'s**] pagaré m, vale m.

IQ o **I.Q.** (ī'kyōō') s. cociente m intelectual.

i·ras·ci·ble (ĭ-răs'ə-bəl) adj. irascible, iracundo.

i·rate (ī-rāt') adj. colérico, airado.

ire (īr) s. ira.

ir·i·des·cence (ĭr'ĭ-dĕs'əns) s. irisación f.

ir·i·des·cent (:ənt) adj. iridiscente, irisado.

i·ris (ī'rĭs) s. [pl. **es** o **irides**] *(of the eye)* iris m; BOT. lirio.

irk (ûrk) tr. irritar, sacar de quicio.

irk·some ('səm) adj. irritante.

i·ron (ī'ərn) **I.** s. hierro; *(for clothes)* plancha ♦ **I. Curtain** cortina de hierro • **i. horse** FAM. locomotora, ferrocarril • **i. lung** pulmón de acero • **i. ore** mineral de hierro ♦ pl. grilletes • **in i.** encadenado **II.** tr. & intr. planchar ♦ **to i. out** allanar, resolver.

i·ron·clad (:klăd') **I.** adj. *(sheathed)* acorazado, blindado; *(strict)* riguroso **II.** s. acorazado.

i·ron·ic/i·cal (ī-rŏn'ĭk) adj. irónico.

i·ron·ing (ī'ər-nĭng) s. planchado ♦ **i. board** tabla de planchar.

i·ro·ny (ī'rə-nē) s. ironía.

ir·ra·di·ate (ĭ-rā'dē-āt') tr. irradiar.

ir·ra·di·a·tion (-'-ā'shən) s. irradiación f.

ir·ra·tion·al (ĭ-răsh'ə-nəl) adj. irracional.

ir·rec·on·cil·a·ble (ĭ-rĕk'ən-sī'lə-bəl) adj. *(differences)* insuperable; *(ideas)* inconciliable.

ir·re·cov·er·a·ble (ĭr'ĭ-kŭv'ər-ə-bəl) adj. irrecuperable; *(irreparable)* irreparable.

ir·re·deem·a·ble (ĭr'ĭ-dē'mə-bəl) adj. *(loan)* irredimible; *(situation)* irremediable.

ir·re·duc·i·ble (ĭr'ĭ-dōō'sə-bəl) adj. irreducible.

ir·ref·u·ta·ble (ĭ-rĕf'yə-tə-bəl) adj. irrefutable.

ir·reg·u·lar (ĭ-rĕg'yə-lər) **I.** adj. irregular; *(uneven)* desigual; *(merchandise)* imperfecto **II.** s. soldado irregular.

ir·reg·u·lar·i·ty (-'-lâr'ĭ-tē) s. irregularidad f; *(of a surface)* desigualdad f; MED. estreñimiento.

ir·rel·e·vance/·cy (ĭ-rĕl'ə-vəns) s. improcedencia, falta de pertinencia.

ir·rel·e·vant (ĭr'ĕl'ə-vənt) adj. inaplicable, improcedente ♦ **to be i.** no venir al caso ♦ **to be i.** to no tener nada que ver con.

ir·re·lig·ious (ĭr'ĭ-lĭj'əs) adj. irreligioso.

ir·re·me·di·a·ble (ĭr'ĭ-mē'dē-ə-bəl) adj. irremediable.

ir·rep·a·ra·ble (ĭ-rĕp'ər-ə-bəl) adj. irreparable.

ir·re·place·a·ble (ĭr'ĭ-plā'sə-bəl) adj. irreemplazable.

ir·re·pres·si·ble (ĭr'ĭ-prĕs'ə-bəl) adj. incontenible.

ir·re·proach·a·ble (ĭr'ĭ-prō'chə-bəl) adj. irreprochable, intachable.

ir·re·sist·i·ble (ĭr'ĭ-zĭs'tə-bəl) adj. irresistible.

ir·res·o·lute (ĭ-rĕz'ə-lōōt') adj. irresoluto.

ir·re·spec·tive (ĭr'ĭ-spĕk'tĭv) adj. ♦ **i.** of sin tener en cuenta, no obstante.

ir·re·spon·si·bil·i·ty (ĭr'ĭ-spŏn'sə-bĭl'ĭ-tē) s. irresponsabilidad f.

ir·re·spon·si·ble ('-'-bəl) adj. irresponsable.

ir·re·triev·a·ble (ĭr'ĭ-trē'və-bəl) adj. (not recoverable) irrecuperable; (mistake) irreparable.

ir·rev·er·ence (ĭ-rĕv'ər-əns) s. irreverencia.

ir·rev·er·ent (:ənt) adj. irreverente.

ir·re·vers·i·ble (ĭr'ĭ-vûr'sə-bəl) adj. irreversible; (damage) irreparable; (decision) irrevocable.

ir·rev·o·ca·ble (ĭ-rĕv'ə-kə-bəl) adj. irrevocable.

ir·ri·gate (ĭr'ĭ-gāt') tr. irrigar.

ir·ri·ga·tion ('-gā'shən) s. irrigación f.

ir·ri·ta·ble (ĭr'ĭ-tə-bəl) adj. irritable.

ir·ri·tant (:tnt) adj. & s. (substancia) irritante.

ir·ri·tate (:tāt') tr. irritar.

ir·ri·tat·ing (:tā'tĭng) adj. irritante, molesto.

ir·ri·ta·tion (:-tā'shən) s. irritación f.

ir·rupt (ĭ-rŭpt') tr. irrumpir.

ir·rup·tion (ĭ-rŭp'shən) s. irrupción f.

is (ĭz) tercera persona sg. de **be.**

Is·lam·ic (ĭs-läm'ĭk, ĭz-) islámico.

is·land (ī'lənd) s. isla; (in a street) isleta.

isle (īl) s. isla; (islet) isleta.

is·let (ī'lĭt) s. isleta, islote m.

i·so·late (ī'sə-lāt') tr. aislar; (a prisoner) incomunicar.

i·so·la·tion (:lā'shən) s. aislamiento; (in prison) incomunicación f; (quarantine) cuarentena.

i·so·la·tion·ist (:shə-nĭst) s. aislacionista mf.

i·so·mer (ī'sə-mər) s. isómero.

i·sos·ce·les (ī-sŏs'ə-lēz') adj. isósceles.

i·so·tope (ī'sə-tōp') s. isótopo.

is·su·ance (ĭsh'ōō-əns) s. emisión f.

is·sue (ĭsh'ōō) I. s. (money, stamps) emisión f; (edition) tirada; (copy) número; (result) consecuencia; (offspring) progenie f; (point under discussion) punto, cuestión f; (problem) problema m; (outlet) salida ♦ **at i.** en discusión ♦ **to force the i.** forzar una decisión ♦ **to raise the i. of** plantear el problema de ♦ **to take i. with** estar en desacuerdo con II. intr. salir; (to emanate) surgir de; (to result) resultar (from de, in en) —tr. (to distribute) repartir; (to publish) publicar; (orders) dar; (decree) promulgar; (stamps, money) emitir.

isth·mus (ĭs'məs) s. istmo.

it (ĭt) pron. lo, la, <do you know this song? yes, I know it ¿conoces esta canción? sí, la conozco>; le <give it a push dale un empujón>; ello, eso <we thought about it pensábamos en eso>; (not translated) él, ella, ello <has the mail come? yes, it just arrived ¿ha llegado el correo? sí, acaba de llegar> ♦ **it is cold** hace frío • **it is good** es

bueno • **it is snowing** está nevando.

i·tal·ic (ĭ-tăl'ĭk, ī-tăl'-) s. & adj. cursiva.

i·tal·i·cize (:-sīz') tr. imprimir en cursiva.

itch (ĭch) I. s. picazón f; (rash) sarna; (desire) comezón f ♦ **to have an i.** to tener el prurito de II. intr. picar <my ear itches me pica el oído> ♦ **to be itching to** estar desesperado por —tr. dar picazón; (to scratch) rascarse.

itch·y (:ē) adj. **-i-** que da picazón; (restless) impaciente.

i·tem (ī'təm) s. artículo; (on an agenda) punto; (of a document) ítem m; (of a form) casilla; TEN. (entry) partida; (of information) detalle m.

i·tem·ize (ī'tə-mīz') tr. enumerar, detallar.

it·er·ate (ĭt'ə-rāt') tr. iterar, repetir.

i·tin·er·ant (ī-tĭn'ər-ənt) adj. & s. (persona) ambulante.

i·tin·er·ar·y (:tĭn'ə-rĕr'ē) s. itinerario.

its (ĭts) adj. pos. su.

it·self (ĭt-sĕlf') pron. se <it turns i. off automatically se apaga automáticamente>; sí mismo <the cat saw i. in the mirror el gato se vio a sí mismo en el espejo>; sólo <the yarn i. cost $20 la lana sóla cuesta 20 dólares>; mismo <the trouble is in the motor i. el problema es el motor mismo> ♦ **(all) by i.** solo • of o en sí.

i·vo·ry (ī'və-rē) s. marfil m ♦ **i. tower** torre de marfil ♦ pl. FAM. (piano keys) teclas; (teeth) colmillos.

i·vy (ī'vē) s. hiedra, yedra.

J

j, J (jā) s. décima letra del alfabeto inglés.

jab (jăb) I. tr. **-bb-** (to poke) hurgonear; (to stab) clavar; (to punch) golpear; (with the elbow) dar un codazo a —intr. ♦ **to i.** at asestar un golpe rápido a II. s. (prick) pinchazo; (with the elbow) codazo; (punch) golpe corto.

jab·ber (jăb'ər) I. intr. parlotear, farfullar II. s. parloteo, farfulla.

jack (jăk) I. s. (in cards) sota; (jackass) burro; (flag) pabellón m; FAM. (fellow) tipo, tío; ELEC. toma de corriente; MEC. gato, cric m ♦ **j. rabbit** liebre norteamericana ♦ pl. tabas II. tr. ♦ **to j. up** alzar con el gato; FAM. (prices) aumentar.

jack·al (jăk'əl) s. chacal m.

jack·ass (jăk'ăs') s. asno, burro.

jack·et (jăk'ĭt) s. saco, chaqueta; (covering) cubierta; (of a book) sobrecubierta; (of a record) envoltura.

jack·ham·mer (jăk'hăm'ər) s. perforadora neumática.

jack-in-the-box ('ĭn-thə-bŏks') s. caja de sorpresa (con muñeco de resorte).

jack·knife (:nīf') I. s. [pl. **-ves**] navaja, cortaplumas m; (dive) salto de carpa II. intr. doblarse como una navaja.

jack-of-all-trades ('əv-ôl'trādz') s. [pl. **jacks-**] persona de muchos oficios.

jack-o'-lantern ('ə-lăn'tərn) s. lámpara hecha con una calabaza o zapallo.

jack·pot (:pŏt') s. premio gordo ♦ **to hit the j.** sacarse el premio gordo; FIG. tener gran suerte.

jade¹ (jād) s. MIN. jade m.

jade² I. s. (horse) jamelgo II. tr. agotar.

jad·ed (jā'dĭd) adj. (wearied) agotado; (sated) harto; (cynical) cínico.

jag¹ (jăg) s. (sharp point) punta saliente.

jag² s. FAM. juerga ♦ **to go on a j.** ir de juerga.

jag·ged (jăg′ĭd) adj. *(notched)* dentado, mellado; *(uneven)* cortado irregularmente.
jag·uar (jăg′wär′) s. jaguar m.
jai a·lai (hī′ lī′, hī′ ə-lī′) s. jai alai m.
jail (jāl) I. s. cárcel f II. tr. encarcelar.
jai·ler/lor (jā′lər) s. carcelero.
ja·lop·y (jə-lŏp′ē) s. FAM. cacharro.
ja·lou·sie (jăl′ə-sē) s. celosía.
jam¹ (jăm) I. tr. **-mm-** *(to lock)* trabar, atascar; *(to fill, crowd)* atestar; *(to clog)* atorar; *(one's finger)* pillarse; RAD. causar interferencias en ♦ **jammed with** atestado o atiborrado de • **to j. in** apretar, forzar • **to j. on the brakes** frenar en seco —intr. atascarse, trabarse; *(firearm)* encasquillarse; *(brakes)* agarrotarse; MÚS. improvisar II. s. *(blockage)* atasco; *(congestion)* aprieto ♦ **j. session** sesión de jazz improvisado • **to be in a j.** FAM. estar en un apuro o aprieto.
jam² s. CUL. mermelada.
jamb (jăm) s. jamba.
jan·gle (jăng′gəl) I. tr. & intr. (hacer) sonar de modo discordante ♦ **to j. one's nerves** irritar a uno II. s. sonido metálico discordante.
jan·i·tor (jăn′ĭ-tər) s. empleado de limpieza.
Jan·u·ar·y (jăn′yōō-ĕr′ē) s. enero.
jar¹ (jär) s. *(jug)* jarra; *(pot)* tarro, pote m.
jar² I. intr. **-rr-** *(to squeal, grate)* chirriar; *(to shake)* sacudirse ♦ **to j. on one's nerves** ponerle a uno los nervios de punta • **to j. with** no concordar con —tr. sacudir; *(to startle)* estremecer ♦ **to j. one's nerves** irritar II. s. *(jolt, shock)* choque m; *(harsh sound)* chirrido.
jar·gon (jär′gən) s. jerga.
jas·mine (jăz′mĭn) s. jazmín m.
jaun·dice (jôn′dĭs) s. ictericia.
jaunt (jônt) I. s. paseo, excursión f II. intr. ir de paseo o de excursión.
jaunt·y (jôn′tē) adj. **-i-** *(sprightly)* vivaz; *(self-confident)* desenvuelto; *(stylish)* apuesto.
jave·lin (jăv′lən) s. jabalina.
jaw (jô) I. s. mandíbula, quijada; JER. *(back talk)* réplica insolente ♦ boca • **the j. of death** las garras de la muerte II. intr. JER. chacharear.
jay (jā) s. arrendajo.
jay·walk (jā′wôk′) intr. cruzar la calle sin prudencia.
jay·walk·er (:ər) s. peatón m imprudente.
jazz (jăz) I. s. jazz m; JER. palabrería, cuentos ♦ **all that j.** FAM. la mar de cosas II. tr. ♦ **to j. up** FAM. avivar, animar.
jaz·zy ('ē) adj. **-i-** de jazz, sincopado; JER. *(showy)* llamativo.
jea·lous (jĕl′əs) adj. celoso; *(suspicious)* receloso; *(envious)* envidioso ♦ **to be j. of** tener celos de.
jeal·ous·y (:ə-sē) s. celos m, envidia.
jeans (jēns) s. pantalones vaqueros.
jeer (jîr) I. intr. *(to mock)* mofarse, burlarse *(at* de); *(to boo)* abuchear —tr. insultar II. s. *(mockery)* mofa, burla; *(boo)* abucheo.
jell (jĕl) I. intr. & tr. coagular(se), cuajar(se); FAM. *(idea, plan)* formar(se).
jel·ly (jĕl′ē) I. s. jalea II. tr. & intr. convertir(se) en jalea.
jel·ly·bean (:bēn′) s. confite m de goma.
jel·ly·fish (:fĭsh′) s. [pl. inv. o **es**] medusa.
jeop·ard·ize (jĕp′ər-dīz′) tr. poner en peligro.
jeop·ard·y (:dē) s. riesgo, peligro.
jerk¹ (jûrk) I. tr. dar un tirón a, tironear de —intr. *(to jolt)* moverse a sacudones; *(to twitch)* moverse espasmódicamente II. s. *(yank)* tirón

m, sacudida; *(twitch)* espasmo; FAM. *(fool)* idiota mf, estúpido.
jerk² tr. CUL. tasajear, charquear.
jerk·y¹ (jûr′kē) adj. **-i-** espasmódico; *(uneven)* desigual; *(ride)* zarandeado.
jerk·y² s. CUL. tasajo, charqui m.
jer·ry·build (jĕr′ē-bĭld′) tr. **-built** construir rápidamente y con mala calidad.
jer·sey (jûr′zē) s. *(fabric)* tejido de jersey; *(garment)* jersey m.
jest (jĕst) I. s. chiste m, broma ♦ **in j.** en broma II. intr. bromear, chancear.
jes·ter (jĕs′tər) s. bufón m, bromista mf.
jet¹ (jĕt) s. MIN. azabache m ♦ **j. black** azabachado.
jet² I. s. *(spurt)* chorro; *(nozzle)* boquilla; *(airplane)* jet m, avión m a reacción; *(engine)* reactor m ♦ **j. lag** cansancio causado por viajar larga distancia en avión II. intr. **-tt-** volar en jet; *(to spurt)* salir a chorro.
jet·lin·er (:lī′nər) avión m de pasajeros a reacción.
jet-pro·pelled (:prə-pĕld′) adj. propulsado por motor a chorro.
jet·ti·son (jĕt′ĭ-sən) tr. *(cargo)* echar al mar; FIG. *(to discard)* desechar.
jet·ty (jĕt′ē) s. desembarcadero, muelle m.
Jew (jōō) s. judío.
jew·el (jōō′əl) I. s. joya, alhaja; *(gem)* gema; *(in watches)* rubí m II. tr. enjoyar, alhajar.
jew·el·(l)er (:ə-lər) s. joyero ♦ **j.'s** joyería.
jew·el·ry (:əl-rē) s. joyas, alhajas.
Jew·ess (jōō′ĭs) s. judía.
Jew·ish (:ĭsh) adj. judío.
jib¹ (jĭb) s. MARÍT. foque m; MEC. aguilón m.
jib² intr. **-bb-** resistirse.
jibe¹ (jĭb) intr. FAM. concordar.
jibe² var. de **gibe**.
jif·fy (jĭf′ē) o **jiff** (jĭf) s. FAM. ♦ **in a j.** en un santiamén.
jig (jĭg) I. s. *(dance)* giga; MEC. patrón m, guía ♦ **the j. is up** JER. se acabó la fiesta II. intr. **-gg-** bailar la giga; *(to bob)* andar a saltitos.
jig·ger¹ (jĭg′ər) s. medida para licores; *(gadget)* chuchería, chisme m.
jig·ger² s. ENTOM. nigua.
jig·gle (jĭg′əl) I. tr. & intr. zangolotear(se), menear(se) II. s. zangoloteo, meneo.
jig·saw (jĭg′sô′) s. sierra de vaivén ♦ **j. puzzle** rompecabezas.
jilt (jĭlt) tr. dejar plantado, dar calabazas.
jim·my (jĭm′ē) I. s. palanca II. tr. forzar con una palanca.
jin·gle (jĭng′gəl) I. tr. & intr. (hacer) cascabelear o tintinear II. s. cascabeleo, tintineo; *(ad)* anuncio rimado y cantado.
jinx (jĭngks) FAM. I. s. *(person, object)* gafe m, cenizo; *(condition)* mala suerte II. tr. traer mala suerte a.
jit·ter (jĭt′ər) I. intr. estar inquieto II. s. ♦ pl. nerviosismo ♦ **to give someone the j.** poner nervioso a alguien • **to have the j.** estar nervioso.
jit·ter·y (:ə-rē) adj. **-i-** FAM. nervioso.
jive (jīv) s. JER., MÚS. jazz m; *(jargon)* jerga de los músicos de jazz; *(empty talk)* cháchara.
job (jŏb) I. s. *(task)* tarea; *(work)* obra, trabajo; *(employment)* empleo <*to look for a j.* buscar un empleo>; *(responsibility)* deber m, responsabilidad f; JER. *(robbery)* golpe m ♦ **by the j.** a destajo • **j. action** huelga • **on the j.**

FAM. en su puesto, vigilante • **to be out of a j.** estar sin trabajo • **to do a j. on** FAM. dañar, arruinar **II.** intr. **-bb-** *(to do piecework)* trabajar a destajo; *(as a jobber)* trabajar como intermediario —tr. ♦ **to j. out** dar a destajo.

job·ber ('ər) s. intermediario.

job·hold·er (:hōl'dər) s. empleado.

job·less (:lĭs) adj. sin trabajo.

jock (jŏk) s. JER. atleta *m.*

jock·ey (jŏk'ē) **I.** s. jockey *mf* **II.** tr. montar (como jockey); FIG. maniobrar, manipular.

jock·strap (:străp) s. suspensorio *m.*

jo·cose (jō-kōs') adj. jocoso, divertido.

joc·u·lar (jŏk'yə-lər) adj. jocoso, humorístico.

jodh·purs (jŏd'pərz) s.pl. pantalones *m* de montar.

jog (jŏg) **I.** tr. **-gg-** *(to push)* empujar levemente; *(to nudge)* dar un codazo a; *(the memory)* refrescar —intr. *(to trot)* cabalgar a trote corto; *(to run)* correr despacio **II.** s. *(push)* empujoncito, codazo; *(slow pace)* paso lento.

jog·ger ('ər) s. persona que corre despacio para hacer ejercicio.

jog·gle (:əl) **I.** tr. sacudir ligeramente, traquetear **II.** s. sacudida, traqueteo.

john (jŏn) s. JER. *(toilet)* retrete *m*; *(customer)* cliente *m* (de una prostituta).

join (join) tr. juntar, unir; *(forces)* aunar; *(land)* lindar con; *(a cause)* abrazar; *(political party)* afiliarse a; *(church, club)* hacerse socio de; *(business firm)* entrar en; *(road, river)* dar o empalmar con; *(people)* encontrarse o reunirse con; MIL. alistarse en ♦ **to j. forces with** aliarse con • **to j. hands** FIG. darse las manos • **to j. in marriage** unir en matrimonio • **to j. together** juntar —intr. juntarse, unirse; *(in marriage)* unirse; *(roads, lines)* empalmar; *(rivers)* confluir ♦ **to j. in** participar en • **to j. up** MIL. alistarse • **to j. up with** reunirse con.

join·er (joi'nər) s. persona que se une a grupos o causas; G.B. *(carpenter)* ebanista *m.*

joint (joint) **I.** s. junta, unión *f*; ANAT. coyuntura; BOT. nudo; CUL. corte *m* para asar; JER. *(marijuana)* cigarrillo de marihuana; *(bar)* tugurio ♦ **out of j.** *(bone)* dislocado; *(disordered)* en desorden; *(grouchy)* de mal humor **II.** adj. (en) común; *(collective)* mutuo ♦ **j. ownership** propiedad en común **III.** tr. juntar, ensamblar.

joist (joist) s. viga.

joke (jōk) **I.** s. chiste *m*; *(amusing remark)* gracia <*not to get the j.* no verle la gracia>; *(prank)* broma <*he can't take a j.* él no sabe tomar una broma> ♦ **as a j.** en broma • **to crack a j.** decir un chiste • **to j. on** hacerle una broma a J. of tomar en broma • **to play a j. on** hacerle una broma a J. intr. contar chistes, bromear ♦ **joking apart** fuera de bromas • **to j. around** bromear • **you must be joking** tú estás bromeando.

jok·er (jō'kər) s. bromista *mf*; *(cards)* comodín *m*; FAM. *(clause)* cláusula engañadora; *(wise guy)* tío, sujeto.

jol·ly (jŏl'ē) **I.** adj. **-i-** *(person)* alegre, jovial; *(occasion)* agradable; G.B. *(very)* muy **II.** tr. complacer, consentir.

jolt (jōlt) **I.** tr. *(to bump)* dar un tumbo o sacudida; *(to shake)* sacudir; *(to shock)* sobresaltar —intr. sacudirse, traquetear **II.** s. *(jerk)* sacudida, tumbo; *(shock)* choque *m.*

josh (jŏsh) tr. & intr. bromear.

jos·tle (jŏs'əl) **I.** tr. & intr. empujar, dar empellones **II.** s. empujón *m*, empellón *m.*

jot (jŏt) **I.** s. pizca, ápice *m* **II.** tr. **-tt-** ♦ **to j.**

down anotar, apuntar.

jounce (jouns) **I.** intr. dar tumbos —tr. sacudir, traquetear **II.** s. tumbo.

jour·nal (jûr'nəl) s. diario; TEN. (libro) diario; *(periodical)* revista, boletín *m.*

jour·nal·ism (:nə-lĭz'əm) s. periodismo.

jour·nal·ist (:nə-lĭst) s. periodista *mf.*

jour·nal·istic ('-lĭs'tĭk) adj. periodístico.

jour·ney (jûr'nē) **I.** s. viaje *m*; *(distance)* jornada **II.** intr. viajar —tr. recorrer.

jour·ney·man (:mən) s. [pl. -men] oficial *m.*

joust (joust) **I.** s. justa **II.** intr. justar, tornear.

jo·vi·al (jō'vē-əl) adj. jovial, alegre.

owl (joul) s. *(jaw)* quijada; *(flesh)* carrillo.

joy (joi) s. alegría, júbilo; *(person, thing)* regocijo, motivo de alegría.

joy·ful (′fəl) adj. alegre, jubiloso.

joy·less (:lĭs) adj. sin alegría.

joy·ous (:əs) adj. alegre, gozoso.

joy·ride (:rīd′) s. FAM. paseo alocado en coche.

ju·bi·lant (jōō′bə-lənt) adj. jubiloso.

ju·bi·la·tion ('-lā'shən) s. júbilo, exultación *f.*

ju·bi·lee (′-lē′) s. *(anniversary)* aniversario (esp. el quincuagésimo); *(celebration)* celebración *f.*

Ju·da·ic (jōō-dā'ĭk) adj. judaico.

Ju·da·ism ('dē-ĭsm) s. judaísmo.

judge (jŭj) **I.** tr. juzgar; *(to determine)* determinar, evaluar; *(innocent, guilty)* declarar —intr. juzgar ♦ **judging from** o **by** a juzgar por **II.** s. juez *mf*; *(in a contest)* árbitro; *(expert)* concedor *m.*

judge·ship ('shĭp') s. magistratura, juzgado.

judg(e)·ment (:mənt) s. *(good sense, opinion)* juicio; *(ruling)* opinión *f*, dictamen *m*; *(estimate)* cálculo aproximado; DER. decisión *f*, fallo ♦ **Last J.** juicio final • **to pass j. on** *(person)* juzgar a; *(issue)* juzgar sobre.

ju·di·ca·ture (jōō'dĭ-kə-chōōr') s. judicatura.

ju·di·cial (jōō-dĭsh'əl) adj. judicial.

ju·di·ci·ar·y (-ē-ĕr'ē) s. *(branch)* el poder judicial *m*; *(judicature)* judicatura, los jueces.

ju·di·cious (:əs) adj. sensato, juicioso.

ju·do (jōō'dō) s. judo.

jug (jŭg) s. *(jar)* jarra, cántaro; JER. cárcel *f*, chirona.

jug·ger·naut (jŭg'ər-nôt') s. fuerza irresistible.

jug·gle (jŭg'əl) tr. hacer malabares con; *(figures)* hacer trampas con —intr. hacer juego de manos.

jug·gler (:lər) s. malabarista *mf.*

jug·u·lar (jŭg'yə-lər) adj. & s. yugular *f.*

juice (jōōs) **I.** s. jugo; *(of fruits, vegetables)* zumo, jugo; JER. *(electricity)* electricidad *f*; *(fuel)* gasolina **II.** tr. exprimir ♦ **to j. up** FAM. animar, vigorizar.

juic·y (jōō'sē) adj. **-i-** zumoso, jugoso; *(gossip)* picante, sabroso; *(lucrative)* lucrativo.

juke box (jōōk) s. tocadiscos *m* automático de moneda.

Ju·ly (jōō-lī') s. julio.

jum·ble (jŭm'bəl) **I.** tr. mezclar; *(to muddle)* embarullar, confundir **II.** s. *(mess)* revoltijo, embrollo; *(state)* mezcolanza, confusión *f.*

jum·bo (jŭm'bō) **I.** s. coloso **II.** adj. muy grande, enorme.

jump (jŭmp) **I.** intr. saltar; *(to be startled)* sobresaltarse; *(to respond quickly)* moverse; *(prices, temperature)* dar un salto; *(to jump)* pasar por alto, saltear; FAM. *(club, party)* animarse ♦ **to j. at** *(a chance)* aprovechar; *(offer, invitation)* apresurarse a aceptar • **to j. down** bajar de un salto • **to j. in(to)** *(a car, water)* saltar a; *(new project)* emprender • **to j. off** saltar de; *(a vehicle)* salir de • **to j. on** subir de un salto a • **to j. on someone (for)** echarse encima de alguien (por) • **to j. out of** saltar de • **to j. over** saltar • **to j. to conclusions** sacar conclusiones precipitadamente • **to j. up** levantarse de un salto —tr. saltar (por encima de); *(to attack)* agredir, atacar; *(prices, stakes)* elevar; *(in checkers)* comer ✦ **j. bail** fugarse estando bajo fianza • **to j. ship** FIG. irse, abandonar • **to j. the gun** adelantarse • **to j. the tracks** descarrillarse **II. s.** salto; *(leap)* brinco; *(sudden movement)* sobresalto; *(checkers)* captura ✦ **j. suit** uniforme de paracaidistas • **to get o have a j. on** llevar o tener una ventaja sobre.

jump·er¹ (jŭm'pər) s. saltador m; ELEC. cable m de empalme.

jump·er² s. *(dress)* vestido sin mangas.

jump-start (jŭmp'stärt') tr. hacer arrancar (un motor) usando un cable de empalme.

jump·y (jŭm'pē) adj. **-i-** nervioso.

junc·tion (jŭngk'shən) s. juntura, conexión f; *(of rivers)* confluencia; F.C., ELEC. empalme m.

junc·ture (:chər) s. juntura, unión f ✦ **at this j.** a estas alturas.

June (jōn) s. junio.

jun·gle (jŭng'gəl) s. selva, jungla; *(tangle)* maraña.

jun·ior (jōn'yər) **I.** adj. *(younger)* más joven; *(for children)* juvenil, para gente joven; *(in rank)* subalterno; *(in school)* de penúltimo año **II. s.** joven mf, menor mf; *(rank)* subordinado; *(student)* estudiante mf de penúltimo año.

ju·ni·per (jōn'nə-pər) s. enebro, junípero.

junk¹ (jŭngk) **I.** s. *(scrap)* chatarra; FAM. *(useless objects)* trastos viejos, cachivaches m; JER. heroína ✦ **j. food** alimentos preparados de poco valor nutritivo • **j. mail** FAM. propaganda no solicitada **II.** tr. *(to discard)* echar a la basura, desechar; *(to scrap)* reducir a chatarra.

junk² s. MARÍT. junco.

junk·et (jŭng'kĭt) s. CUL. crema de leche y cuajo; *(trip)* viaje m (pagado con fondos públicos).

junk·ie (jŭng'kē) s. JER. drogadicto; *(devotee)* adicto.

junk·man (jŭngk'măn') s. [pl. **-men**] trapero, chatarrero.

junk·yard (:yärd') s. depósito de chatarra.

jun·ta (hōn'tə) s. junta militar.

ju·rid·ic/i·cal (jō-rĭd'ĭk) jurídico.

ju·ris·dic·tion (jōr-ĭs-dĭk'shən) s. jurisdicción f.

ju·ris·pru·dence ('-prōōd'ns) s. jurisprudencia.

ju·rist (jōr'ĭst) s. jurista mf.

ju·ror (:ər) s. jurado mf (persona).

ju·ry (:ē) s. jurado, tribunal m ✦ **j. duty** deber cívico de formar parte de un jurado.

jury·man (:mǎn') s. [pl. **-men**] jurado.

just (jŭst) **I.** adj. *(fair, right)* justo; *(equitable)* imparcial; *(legitimate)* justificado; *(accurate)* exacto **II.** adv. *(exactly)* justo, justamente <*j. the right amount* justamente la cantidad correcta>; *(recently)* recién <*j. published* recién publicado>; *(nearby)* no más que, apenas; *(barely)* por muy poco <*you j. missed the bus* perdiste el ómnibus por muy poco>; *(merely)* simplemente, sólo <*j. because* sólo porque>; *(really)* verdaderamente <*it is j. beautiful* es verdaderamente hermoso>; *(possibly)* posiblemente, quizás ✦ **j. about** *(not quite)* casi; *(positively)* ya <*I'm j. about fed up* ya estoy harto>; *(soon)* pronto <*it's j. about dinnertime* pronto será la hora de cenar> • **j. about to** a punto de • **j. as** *(precisely)* lo mismo que; *(in every way)* tal como <*j. as I thought!* ¡tal como pensaba!>; *(when)* justo cuando <*he came j. as I was leaving* llegó justo cuando me iba> • **j. as if** lo mismo que si • **j. in case** por si acaso • **j. in time to** o **for** justo a tiempo para • **j. like** *(same as)* como, igual que; *(typical of)* muy de <*that's j. like him!* ¡eso es muy de él!> • **j. my luck!** ¡qué suerte la mía! • **j. now** en este momento • **j. so** a su gusto, ni más ni menos • **j. the same** sin embargo • **not j. yet** todavía no • **to have j.** acabar de <*I've j. gotten here* acabo de llegar>.

jus·tice (jŭs'tĭs) s. justicia; *(righteousness)* rectitud f; *(judge)* juez mf ✦ **to do j. to** *(to enjoy)* apreciar debidamente; *(to show)* tratar debidamente • **to bring to j.** aprehender y enjuiciar • **j. of the peace** juez de paz.

jus·ti·fi·a·ble (jŭs'tə-fī'ə-bəl) adj. justificable.

jus·ti·fi·ca·tion ('-fi-kā'shən) s. justificación f.

jus·ti·fy ('-fī') tr. justificar.

just·ness (jŭst'nĭs) s. justicia; *(righteousness)* rectitud f; *(fairness)* imparcialidad f.

jut (jŭt) intr. **-tt-** ✦ **to j.** resaltar, sobresalir.

ju·ve·nile (jōō'və-nəl, :nīl') **I.** adj. joven, juvenil; *(immature)* infantil; *(of minors)* de menores **II. s.** joven mf ✦ **j. court** tribunal de menores • **j. delinquent** delincuente juvenil.

jux·ta·pose (jŭk'stə-pōz') tr. yuxtaponer.

jux·ta·po·si·tion ('-pə-zĭsh'ən) s. yuxtaposición f.

K

k, K (kā) s. undécima letra del alfabeto inglés; FAM. *(thousand)* mil m; COMPUT. mil bitios.

kale (kāl) s. col rizada.

ka·lei·do·scope (kə-lī'də-skōp') s. calidoscopio.

ka·lei·do·scop·ic (-'-skōp'ĭk) s. calidoscópico.

kan·ga·roo (kǎng'gə-rōō') s. canguro ✦ **k. court** tribunal desautorizado.

ka·put (kä-pŏŏt') adj. FAM. acabado.

kar·at (kǎr'ət) s. quilate m.

ka·ra·te (kə-rä'tē) s. karate m.

kar·ma (kär'mə) s. karma m; FAM. *(atmosphere)* ambiente m, aura.

ka·ty·did (kā'tē-dĭd') s. saltamontes m.

kay·ak (kī'ăk') s. kayac m.

kay·o (kā-ō') JER. **I.** s. knock-out m **II.** tr. poner fuera de combate.

ka·zoo (kə-zōō') s. chicharra (instrumento).

ke·bab (kə-bŏb') s. carne asada en espetones.

keel (kēl) **I.** s. quilla ✦ **on an even k.** tranquilo **II.** intr. irse a pique ✦ **to k. over** desplomarse.

keel·boat ('bōt') s. chalana fluvial (con quilla).

keen¹ (kēn) adj. agudo; *(blade)* afilado; *(interest)* vivo; *(appetite)* bueno; *(competition)* reñido, fuerte; *(enthusiastic)* entusiasta; JER. *(great)* fantástico ✦ **to be k. on** *(to like)* gustarle a uno; *(to wish to)* tener muchas ganas de.

keen² intr. lamentarse.

keen·ness ('nĭs) s. agudeza; *(of a blade)* filo; *(of emotions)* intensidad f; *(enthusiasm)* entusiasmo.

keep (kēp) **I.** tr. **kept** *(in one's possession)* quedarse con; *(to put aside)* guardar <*k. some for later* guarda algo para más tarde>; *(a family)* sostener, mantener; *(in a place)* guardar <*where do you k. your saw?* ¿en dónde guardas la sierra?>; *(boarders)* dar hospedaje a, alojar; *(garden)* cultivar; *(animals)* criar; *(to manage)* dirigir, llevar; *(to preserve)* conservar <*to k. food fresh* conservar la comida fresca>; *(order, tradition)* mantener; *(diary, accounts)* llevar; *(to detain)* detener <*what is keeping you?* ¿qué es lo que te detiene?>; *(to fulfill)* cumplir, guardar <*to k. one's word* cumplir la palabra de uno>; *(an appointment)* acudir a; *(holiday)* celebrar, observar ♦ **to k. away** mantener alejado • **to k. back** *(tears)* contener; *(information)* ocultar; *(to withhold)* quedarse con • **to k. down** *(to oppress)* oprimir, sojuzgar; *(costs, temperature)* mantener bajo; *(to restrict)* limitar • **to k. from** *(to prevent)* impedir <*they kept me from speaking out* me impidieron expresar mi opinión>; *(to conceal)* ocultar • **to k. house** manejar una casa • **to k. in** no dejar salir, mantener dentro • **to k. on** *(clothing)* no quitarse; *(an employee)* no despedir, retener • **to k. one's head** no perder la cabeza • **to k. out** no dejar entrar • **to k. out of** FIG. no meterse <*k. out of my affairs* no te metas en mis asuntos> • **to k. (someone) quiet** hacer callar a (alguien) • **to k. (someone) waiting** hacer esperar a (alguien) • **to k. up** *(to continue)* continuar, proseguir <*k. up the good work* continúe haciendo tan buen trabajo>; *(to prevent from sleeping)* tener en vela; *(to maintain)* mantener <*to k. up a property* mantener una propiedad> • **to k. up appearances** guardar las apariencias • **to k. up with** *(work)* tener al día; *(the neighbors)* achantar a (los vecinos) • **to k. up with the times** ser muy de su época —intr. *(to stay)* permanecer, quedarse; *(food)* conservarse; *(to continue)* seguir; *(to not stop)* no dejar de <*he kept shouting* no dejó de gritar> ♦ **it can k.** puede esperar • **k. off** prohibido pisar • **k. out** prohibida la entrada • **to k. at it** FAM. perseverar, persistir • **to k. away** mantenerse a distancia • **to k. going** *(to proceed)* seguir; *(to manage)* ir tirando • **to k. on** seguir, continuar <*k. on talking* continúa hablando> • **to k. quiet** quedarse callado • **to k. to** *(promise, word)* cumplir con; *(the right, left)* mantenerse a • **to k. up** ir al paso de, alcanzar **II.** s. *(care)* custodia, protección *f; (of a castle)* torreón *m* ♦ pl. **for keeps** para siempre • **to earn one's k.** ganarse la vida.

keep·er (kē'pər) s. guarda *m,* guardián *m.*

keep·ing (kē'pĭng) s. *(guarding)* guardia, custodia; *(custody)* cuidado, cargo <*in his k.* a cargo suyo> ♦ **in safe k.** a buen recaudo • **to be in (out of) k. with** (no) estar de acuerdo con.

keep·sake (kēp'sāk') s. recuerdo.

keg (kĕg) s. barril *m.*

kelp (kĕlp) s. kelp *m,* varec *m.*

ken (kĕn) s. ♦ **beyond one's k.** fuera de comprensión o alcance.

ken·nel (kĕn'əl) tr. & s. (meter en la) perrera.

kept (kĕpt) cf. **keep.**

ker·chief (kûr'chĭf) s. pañuelo.

ker·nel (kûr'nəl) s. grano; *(of a nut)* masa; FIG. meollo ♦ **k. of truth** un fondo de verdad.

ker·o·sene/sine (kĕr'ə-sēn') s. queroseno.

ketch (kĕch) s. queche *m.*

ketch·up (kĕch'əp, kăch'-) s. salsa de tomate.

ket·tle (kĕt'l) s. *(pot)* marmita, caldera; *(teakettle)* tetera ♦ **a fine k. of fish** un berenjenal.

ket·tle·drum (:drŭm') s. timbal *m.*

key¹ (kē) **I.** s. llave *f; (code, solution)* clave *f;* *(of a piano, typewriter)* tecla; MÚS. tonalidad *f,* tono; TELEG. manipulador *m; (pitch)* tono <*she spoke in a high k.* habló en un tono alto> ♦ **in k.** afinado • **master k.** llave maestra • **off k.** desafinado **II.** adj. clave, importante **III.** tr. *(to encode)* codificar; MÚS. afinar ♦ **to be keyed to** *(to be appropriate for)* ser apropiado para; *(information)* explicarse por medio de una clave • **to be keyed up about** estar entusiasmado o nervioso a causa de.

key² s. GEOG. cayo.

key·board (kē'bôrd') **I.** s. teclado **II.** tr. IMPR. componer (mediante teclado).

key·hole (kē'hōl') s. bocallave *f.*

key·note (kē'nōt') s. MÚS. (nota) tónica; FIG. idea fundamental ♦ **k. address** discurso inaugural.

key·punch (kē'pŭnch') **I.** s. perforadora de tarjetas **II.** tr. procesar en una perforadora de teclado.

key·punch·er (kē'pŭn'chər) s. perforador *m* de tarjetas.

key·stone (kē'stōn') s. clave *f.*

key·stroke (kē'strōk') s. golpe *m* de la tecla.

kha·ki (kăk'ē) **I.** s. caqui *m* ♦ pl. uniforme de color caqui **II.** adj. de color caqui.

kib·itz (kĭb'ĭts) intr. FAM. dar consejos no solicitados.

ki·bosh (kī'bŏsh') s. ♦ **to put the k. on something** FAM. ponerle fin o término a algo.

kick (kĭk) **I.** intr. patear, dar puntapiés; *(animals)* cocear, dar coces; *(firearm)* dar un culatazo; FAM. *(to complain)* quejarse ♦ **to k. around** FAM. andar rodando • **to k. off** DEP. dar el puntapié inicial; FIG. *(to die)* estirar la pata • **to k. oneself** reprocharse —tr. patear, dar un puntapié a; *(animals)* dar coces a; *(firearm)* dar un culatazo en; DEP. patear; *(a goal)* marcar, meter ♦ **to k. around** FAM. *(to abuse)* maltratar; *(idea)* considerar, hablar de • **k. in** *(one's share)* aportar (dinero); *(a door)* derribar a patadas • **to k. off** poner en marcha • **to k. out** echar a patadas **II.** s. patada; *(person)* puntapié *m; (animal)* coz *f; (firearm)* culatazo; JER. *(complaint)* queja; *(of a drink, motor)* fuerza ♦ **to be on a k.** estar obsesionado con • **to get a k. out of** FAM. encontrar placer en ♦ pl. sensación, emoción • **for k.** FAM. por gusto, por diversión.

kick·back ('băk') s. JER. tajada, coima.

kick·er (:ər) s. FAM. sorpresa.

kick·off (:ôf') s. DEP. saque *m* inicial; FIG. comienzo.

kick·stand (:stănd') s. soporte *m* (de bicicleta).

kick·y (:ē) adj. **-i-** JER. excitante.

kid (kĭd) **I.** s. *(goat)* cabrito; *(other animals)* cría; *(leather)* cabritilla; FAM. *(child)* niño; JER. *(pal)* muchachón *m* ♦ **k. brother** hermano menor • **k. stuff** juego de niños • **to handle with k. gloves** tratar con guante blanco **II.** tr. & intr. **-dd-** FAM. bromear o jugar (con) ♦ **are you kidding?** *(really?)* ¿de verdad?; *(of course not)* ¡ni en broma! • **no kidding!** ¡mentira!, ¡no me digas! • **to k. oneself** engañarse.

kid·der (:ər) s. bromista *mf.*

kid·dy/die (:ē) s. FAM. niñito, crío.

kid·nap (:năp') tr. secuestrar, raptar.

kid·nap·(p)er (:ər) s. secuestrador *m,* raptor *m.*

kid·nap·(p)ing (:ĭng) s. secuestro, rapto.

kid·ney (kĭd'nē) s. riñón *m* ♦ **k. bean** frijol colorado • **k. stone** cálculo renal.

kid·skin (kĭd'skĭn') s. cabritilla.

kill (kĭl) **I.** tr. matar; *(to destroy)* destruir; *(to overpower)* arruinar ‹*garlic killed the taste of the meat* el ajo arruinó el sabor de la carne›; FAM. *(motor, light)* apagar; *(bottle)* agotar; *(to veto)* vetar; *(to delete)* suprimir; *(to make laugh)* hacer morir de risa ♦ **to k. off** exterminar • **to k. time** *(to wait)* hacer tiempo; *(to idle)* matar el tiempo —intr. matar; *(to murder)* asesinar **II.** s. *(slaughter)* matanza; *(animal)* cacería; *(final blow)* golpe *m* final, acabamiento.

kill·er (:ər) s. asesino ♦ **k. whale** orca • **to be a k.** ser mortal (una enfermedad).

kill·ing (:ĭng) **I.** s. *(murder)* asesinato; *(slaughter)* matanza ♦ **to make a k.** FAM. ganar gran cantidad de dinero **II.** adj. que mata, mortal; *(exhausting)* agotador; *(funny)* graciosísimo.

kill·joy (:joi′) s. aguafiestas *mf.*

kiln (kĭln, kĭl) s. horno.

ki·lo (kē′lō) s. kilo.

kil·o·cy·cle (kĭl′ə-sī′kəl) s. kilociclo.

kil·o·gram (:grăm′) s. kilogramo.

kil·o·li·ter (:lē′tər) s. kilolitro.

kil·o·me·ter (:mē′tər, kĭ-lŏm′ĭ-tər) s. kilómetro.

kil·o·met·ric (kĭl′ə-mĕt′rĭk) adj. kilométrico.

kil·o·ton (′ə-tŭn′) s. kilotón *m.*

kil·o·watt (′ə-wŏt′) s. kilovatio.

kilt (kĭlt) s. falda escocesa, kilt *m.*

kil·ter (kĭl′tər) s. FAM. buena condición ♦ **to be out of k.** no funcionar bien.

ki·mo·no (kĭ-mō′nō) s. kimono, quimono.

kin (kĭn) s. parientes *m* ♦ **kith and k.** parientes y amigos • **next of k.** pariente más cercano.

kind[1] (kīnd) adj. bueno, afable; *(generous)* generoso, bondadoso; *(courteous)* cortés, amable ‹*it is very k. of you* es muy amable de su parte› ♦ **would you be so k. as to?** ¿tendrá usted la bondad de?

kind[2] s. *(class)* género, especie *f*; *(type)* tipo, clase *f* ‹*what k. of airplane is that?* ¿qué tipo de avión es ése?› ♦ **a k. of** un cierto • **all kinds of** FAM. *(plenty of)* de sobra; *(many different)* de todas clases, toda clase de • **in k.** del mismo modo • **k. of** FAM. un poco ‹*it's k. of cold today* hace un poco de frío hoy› • **nothing of the k.** nada por el estilo • **to repay in k.** pagar con la misma moneda • **two of a k.** un par.

kin·der·gar·ten (kĭn′dər-gär′tn) s. jardín *m* de infantes.

kind·heart·ed (kīnd′här′tĭd) adj. bondadoso.

kin·dle (kĭn′dl) tr. & intr. encender(se).

kin·dling (kĭnd′lĭng) s. leña, astillas.

kind·ly (kīnd′lē) **I.** adj. -i- *(benevolent)* benigno, bondadoso; *(friendly)* amable, agradable **II.** adv. bondadosamente ♦ **k. take a seat** tenga la bondad de sentarse • **to take k. to** aceptar de buena gana.

kind·ness (:nĭs) s. bondad *f*; *(favor)* favor *m* ♦ **have the k. to** tenga la bondad de.

kin·dred (kĭn′drĭd) **I.** s. parientes *m* **II.** adj. afín, similar ♦ **k. spirits** almas gemelas.

kin·e·scope (kĭn′ĭ-skōp′) s. cinescopio.

kin·es·the·sia (kĭn′ĭs-thē′zhə) s. quinestesia.

ki·net·ic (kĭ-nĕt′ĭk) adj. cinético ♦ **kinetics** s.sg. cinética.

kin·folk(s) (kĭn′fōk[s]′) s.pl. parientes *m.*

king (kĭng) s. rey *m*; *(in checkers)* dama ♦ **to live like a k.** vivir a cuerpo de rey.

king·bird (:bûrd′) s. tirano.

king·dom (:dəm) s. reino ♦ **to blow someone to k. come** mandar a alguien de cabeza al otro mundo.

king·fish·er (:fĭsh′ər) s. martín *m* pescador.

king·ly (:lē) adj. -i- real, majestuoso.

king·pin (:pĭn′) s. FAM. persona clave, líder *m.*

king·ship (:shĭp′) s. trono; *(reign)* reinado.

king-size(d) (:sīz[d]′) adj. grande.

kink (kĭngk) **I.** s. *(in a wire)* rosca; *(tight curl)* rizo; *(muscle spasm)* calambre *m*; *(flaw)* falla; *(mental quirk)* extravagancia **II.** tr. & intr. *(a wire)* enroscar(se); *(hair)* rizar(se).

kink·y (kĭng′kē) adj. -i- *(wire)* enroscado; *(hair)* rizado; FAM. *(perverted)* pervertido.

kin·ship (kĭn′shĭp′) s. parentesco.

kins·man (kĭnz′mən) s. [pl. **-men**] *(relative)* pariente *m*; *(compatriot)* compatriota *m.*

kins·wom·an (:wŏm′ən) s. [pl. **-women**] *(relative)* parienta; *(compatriot)* compatriota *m.*

ki·osk (kē′ŏsk′) s. quiosco.

kip·per (kĭp′ər) s. arenque ahumado.

kis·met (kĭz′mĕt′) s. destino.

kiss (kĭs) **I.** tr. besar, dar un beso a; *(to brush against)* rozar ♦ **to k. away** borrar con besos • **to k. off** FAM. despachar, despedir • **to k. something goodbye** FAM. decir adiós a algo —intr. besarse **II.** s. beso; *(slight touch)* roce *m* ♦ **to blow a k.** tirar un beso.

kiss·er (:ər) s. JER. hocico, trompa.

kiss-off (:ôf′) s. FAM. despido.

kit (kĭt) s. *(set of tools)* equipo, conjunto; *(collection of items)* juego; *(container)* estuche *m* ♦ **first-aid k.** botiquín *m* • **model k.** juego de armar • **the whole k. and caboodle** FAM. la colección entera.

kitch·en (kĭch′ən) s. cocina ♦ **k. sink** fregadero.

kitch·en·ette (′ə-nĕt′) s. cocina pequeña.

kitch·en·ware (′ən-wâr′) s. batería de cocina.

kite (kīt) s. *(toy)* cometa; ORNIT. milano ♦ **go fly a k.!** FAM. ¡piérdete!

kit·ten (kĭt′n) s. gatito.

kit·ty[1] (kĭt′ē) s. *(in cards)* puesta del ganador; *(pool of money)* banca.

kit·ty[2] s. FAM. *(cat)* gato; *(kitten)* gatito.

kit·ty-cor·nered (:kôr′nərd) adj. diagonal.

klep·to·ma·ni·a (klĕp′tə-mā′nē-ə) s. cleptomanía.

klep·to·ma·ni·ac (:āk′) s. cleptómano.

klutz (klŭts) s. JER. chambón *m.*

knack (năk) s. *(skill)* facilidad *f* *(for* para*)*; *(natural talent)* don *m* *(for* de*)*.

knap·sack (năp′săk′) s. mochila.

knave (nāv) s. bribón *m*, bellaco.

knav·er·y (nā′və-rē) s. bribonada, bellaquería.

knav·ish (nā′vĭsh) adj. bribón, bellaco.

knead (nēd) tr. amasar, heñir.

knee (nē) **I.** s. rodilla; ZOOL. codillo; *(of garment)* rodillera ♦ **to bring someone to his knees** poner a alguien de rodillas • **to go down on one's knees** caer de hinojos **II.** tr. dar con la rodilla.

knee·cap (nē′kăp′) s. rótula.

knee-deep (nē′dēp′) adj. *(knee-high)* que llega hasta las rodillas; *(submerged)* metido hasta las rodillas.

knee-high (nē′hī′) adj. que llega hasta las rodillas.

kneel (nēl) intr. **-ed** o **knelt** arrodillarse.

knee·pad (nē′păd′) s. rodillera.

knell (nĕl) **I.** intr. sonar lúgubremente **II.** s. toque *m*, tañido ♦ **death k.** toque a muerto • **to sound the death k. of** presagiar el fin de.

knelt (nĕlt) cf. **kneel.**

knew (nō̄o) cf. **know.**

knick·ers (nĭk′ərz) s.pl. *(bloomers)* bragas *f*; *(knee breeches)* calzones *m*, bombachos.

knick·knack (nĭk′năk′) s. chuchería.

knife (nīf) I. s. [pl. **-ves**] cuchillo; *(blade, pocketknife)* cuchilla II. tr. *(to cut)* cortar; *(to stab)* apuñalar; FAM. *(to betray)* apuñalar por la espalda, traicionar.

knife-edge (′ĕj′) s. filo.

knight (nīt) I. s. caballero; *(in chess)* caballo II. tr. armar caballero; G.B. conceder el título de *Sir* a.

knight·hood (′hŏŏd′) s. rango *o* título de caballero; *(chivalry)* caballerosidad *f*.

knit (nĭt) I. tr. & intr. **knit(ted), -tting** tejer, hacer punto; *(to unite)* unir(se); *(brows)* fruncir(se); *(bone)* soldarse II. s. *(garment)* prenda de punto; *(cloth)* género de punto.

knit·ting (′ĭng) s. tejido, labor *f* de punto ♦ **k. needle** aguja de tejer *o* de hacer punto.

knit·wear (′wâr′) s. artículos de punto.

knives (nīvz) cf. **knife.**

knob (nŏb) s. *(of a door)* perilla, tirador *m*; *(dial)* botón *m*; *(bulge)* protuberancia.

knock (nŏk) I. tr. *(to hit)* golpear, pegar; *(to break through)* hacer <*to k. a hole in the wall* hacer un agujero en la pared>; JER. *(to criticize)* criticar, menospreciar ♦ **k. it off!** ¡basta ya! ♦ **to k. around** FAM. *(idea)* considerar; *(to abuse)* maltratar ♦ **to k. down** derribar, tumbar; FAM. *(price)* rebajar ♦ **to k. off** hacer caer, tirar <*to k. the lamp off the table* hacer caer la lámpara de la mesa>; FAM. *(to stop)* parar, suspender (tarea, trabajo); *(to do quickly)* terminar con; *(to deduct)* rebajar en; JER. *(to kill)* liquidar ♦ **to k. out** *(a person)* dejar sin sentido; *(in boxing)* poner fuera de combate; *(to render inoperative)* estropear, inutilizar; *(power)* cortar; FAM. *(to impress)* impresionar ♦ **to k. over** tirar (vaso, lámpara) —intr. *(at the door)* golpear, llamar; AUTO. pistonear *o* detonar (un motor) ♦ **to k. around** FAM. vagar, merodear ♦ **to k. against** chocar contra ♦ **to k. off** salir del trabajo ♦ **to k. oneself out** FAM. matarse II. s. *(blow)* golpe *m*; *(rap)* toque *m*, llamada; AUTO. pistoneo; FAM. *(criticism)* crítica.

knock·down (′doun′) I. adj. demoledor, que derriba II. s. caída.

knock·er (:ər) s. aldaba, picaporte.

knock·ing (:ĭng) s. aldabonazo, llamada (a la puerta); *(sound)* golpeteo.

knock·kneed (:nēd′) adj. patizambo.

knock·out (:out′) s. knock-out *m*; JER. *(person)* maravilla; *(success)* exitazo ♦ **k. punch** golpe demoledor.

knoll (nōl) s. loma, montículo.

knot (nŏt) I. s. nudo; *(group)* grupo, corrillo; *(difficulty)* problema *m* ♦ **to get tied up in knots** FAM. enredarse ♦ **to tie the k.** FAM. casarse II. tr. & intr. **-tt-** anudar(se); *(to entangle)* enredar(se).

knot·hole (:hōl′) s. agujero (que deja un nudo).

knot·ted (:ĭd) adj. anudado; *(intricate)* enredado, enmarañado; *(gnarled)* nudoso.

knot·ty (:ē) adj. **-i-** *(rope)* lleno de nudos; *(wood)* nudoso; *(problem)* enredado.

know (nō) I. tr. **knew, known** saber <*I know arithmetic* sé aritmética>; *(a person, place)* conocer; *(to perceive)* comprender <*I k. how you feel* comprendo cómo te sientes>; *(to recognize)* reconocer; *(to distinguish)* distinguir <*to k. right from wrong* distinguir el bien del mal> ♦ **to get to k. someone** llegar a conocer a alguien ♦ **to let someone k.** hacer saber a alguien ♦ **to make known** hacer saber ♦ **to k. about** saber de ♦ **to k. how to** saber —intr. saber ♦ **as far as I k.** que yo sepa ♦ **how should I k.!** ¡yo qué sé! ♦ **I ought to k.!** ¡lo sabré yo! ♦ **to k. best** saber mejor que nadie ♦ **to k. better** saber lo que debe hacerse ♦ **to k. better than to** saber que no se debe ♦ **to k. each other** conocerse II. s. ♦ **to be in the k.** FAM. estar al tanto.

know·a·ble (nō′ə-bəl) adj. conocible.

know-how (nō′hou′) s. *(ability)* habilidad *f*; *(experience)* experiencia.

know·ing (nō′ĭng) adj. *(shrewd)* astuto, hábil; *(look, smile)* de complicidad.

know·ing·ly (:ĭng-lē) adv. *(shrewdly)* astutamente; *(deliberately)* a sabiendas ♦ **to glance k. at** dirigir una mirada de complicidad a.

know-it-all (nō′ĭt-ôl′) s. FAM. sabelotodo *mf*.

knowl·edge (nŏl′ĭj) s. *(understanding)* conocimiento; *(information)* conocimientos, saber *m* <*k. about genetics* conocimientos sobre la genética>; *(erudition)* erudición *f* ♦ **it is common k.** that todo el mundo sabe que ♦ **it has come to my k. that** me enteré de que ♦ **to have a working k. of** tener conocimientos prácticos de ♦ **to have a thorough k. of** conocer a fondo ♦ **to have no k. of** no saber nada de ♦ **(not) to my k.** (no) que yo sepa ♦ **to the best of my k.** según mi entender ♦ **without my k.** sin saberlo yo.

knowl·edge·a·ble (:ĭ-jə-bəl) adj. instruido, informado ♦ **to be k. about** conocer bien.

known (nōn) I. cf. **know** II. adj. conocido.

know-noth·ing (nō′nŭth′ĭng) s. ignorante *mf*.

knuck·le (nŭk′əl) I. s. nudillo ♦ **to rap someone's knuckles** dar en los nudillos II. intr. ♦ **to k. down** aplicarse duro ♦ **to k. under** ceder.

knuck·le·head (:hĕd′) s. alcornoque *m*.

KO DEP., JER. I. tr. (kā-ō′) **′d, ′ing** noquear II. s. (kā-ō′) [pl. **′s**] knock-out *m*.

ko·a·la (kō-ä′lə) s. koala *m*.

kook (kŏŏk) s. JER. alocado, excéntrico.

kook·y (kŏŏ′kē) adj. **-i-** JER. alocado, excéntrico.

ko·sher (kō′shər) adj. conforme al régimen alimenticio judío; JER. *(proper)* conforme a las reglas; *(genuine)* legítimo.

kow·tow (kou-tou′) intr. hacer una reverencia china; *(to fawn)* humillarse, postrarse.

ku·dos (kyŏŏ′dōz′) s. prestigio, fama.

kum·quat (kŭm′kwŏt′) s. naranjita china.

L

l, L (ĕl) s. duodécima letra del alfabeto inglés.

lab (lăb) s. laboratorio.

la·bel (lā′bəl) I. s. rótulo, etiqueta; *(brand name)* marca de fábrica, FIG. *(epithet)* etiqueta II. tr. rotular, marcar; *(to describe)* describir.

la·bi·al (lā′bē-əl) adj. labial.

la·bor (lā′bər) I. s. trabajo, labor *f*; *(task)* tarea, faena; *(effort)* esfuerzo; *(workers)* mano *f* de obra, obreros; *(union)* sindicato; *(childbirth)* parto ♦ **hard l.** trabajos forzosos ♦ **l. union** sindicato II. intr. trabajar; *(to strive)* esforzarse; *(to plod)* moverse con dificultad; MED. estar de parto ♦ **to l. over** tomarse trabajo en —tr. insistir en III. adj. laboral ♦ **l. camp** campo de trabajo ♦ **l. pains** dolores de parto.

lab·o·ra·to·ry (lăb′rə-tôr′ē) s. laboratorio.

la·bored (lā′bərd) adj. trabajoso, dificultoso;

(strained) forzado.

la·bor·er (lā'bər-ər) s. trabajador *m*, obrero; *(unskilled)* peón *m*, jornalero.

la·bo·ri·ous (lə-bôr'ē-əs) adj. laborioso.

la·bor·sav·ing (lā'bər-sā'vĭng) adj. que conserva mano de obra.

la·bour (lā'bər) G.B. var. de **labor.**

lab·y·rinth (lăb'ə-rĭnth') s. laberinto.

lac (lăk) s. laca.

lace (lās) I. s. encaje *m*; *(trim)* puntilla; *(shoelace)* cordón *m* de zapato II. tr. encordonar; *(a drink)* echar licor a ♦ **to l. into** reprochar.

lac·er·ate (lăs'ə-rāt') tr. lacerar.

lac·er·a·tion ('-rā'shən) s. laceración *f*; *(wound)* rasgón *m*.

lach·ry·mal (lăk'rə-məl) adj. lagrimal.

lack (lăk) I. s. *(deficiency)* falta, carencia; *(need)* escasez *f* ♦ **for l. of** por falta de II. tr. *(to be without)* carecer de, faltar; *(to need)* necesitar; *(to require)* hacer falta, requerir(se); *(to have no)* no tener —intr. hacer falta.

lack·a·dai·si·cal (lăk'ə-dā'zĭ-kəl) adj. indiferente, apático.

lack·ey (lăk'ē) s. lacayo; *(toady)* adulador *m*.

lack·ing (lăk'ĭng) I. adj. deficiente, falto de ♦ **to be l.** faltar II. prep. sin.

lack·lus·ter (:lŭs'tər) adj. deslucido.

la·con·ic (lə-kŏn'ĭk) adj. lacónico.

lac·quer (lăk'ər) I. s. laca II. tr. laquear.

lac·tase (lăk'tās') s. lactasa.

lac·tate (:tāt') I. intr. lactar II. s. lactato.

lac·ta·tion (-tā'shən) s. lactancia.

lac·tic ('tĭk) adj. láctico.

lac·tose (:tōs') s. lactosa.

la·cu·na (lə-kōō'nə) s. [pl. **s** o **-ae**] laguna.

lac·y (lā'sē) adj. **-i-** de encaje; FIG. diáfano.

lad (lăd) s. joven *m*, muchacho.

lad·der (lăd'ər) s. escalera, escala; *(status)* jerarquía; G.B. *(in a stocking)* carrera.

lad·die (lăd'ē) s. joven *m*, chico.

lade (lād) tr. **-d, -d** o **-n** cargar; FIG. agobiar.

lad·en (lād'n) I. cf. **lade** II. adj. cargado; FIG. agobiado, abrumado.

lad·ing (lā'dĭng) s. carga, flete *m*.

la·dle (lād'l) I. s. cucharón *m* II. tr. servir con cucharón.

la·dy (lā'dē) s. dama; *(married woman)* señora ♦ **l. in waiting** dama de honor • **l. of the evening** prostituta • **l. of the house** ama de la casa ♦ **l.'s man** hombre galanteador • **young l.** señorita.

la·dy·bird (:bûrd') s. mariquita.

la·dy·bug (:bŭg') s. mariquita.

la·dy·kill·er (:kĭl'ər) s. JER. tenorio.

la·dy·like (:līk') adj. bien educada.

la·dy·ship (:shĭp') s. excelencia, señoría.

lag (lăg) I. intr. **-gg-** *(to straggle)* rezagarse, retrasarse; *(to flag)* aflojar(se) ♦ **to l. behind** retrasarse II. s. dilación *f*, retraso.

la·ger (lä'gər) s. cerveza de Alemania.

lag·gard (lăg'ərd) adj. & s. rezagado.

la·goon (lə-gōōn') s. laguna.

la·ic·i·cal (lā'ĭk) adj. laico, secular.

laid (lād) cf. **lay**[1].

laid-back (lād-băk') adj. FAM. despreocupado.

lain (lān) cf. **lie**[1].

lair (lâr) s. guarida, madriguera.

lais·sez faire (lĕs'ā fâr') s. doctrina de no intervención.

la·i·ty (lā'ĭ-tē) s. laicos; *(non-professionals)* profanos.

lake (lāk) s. lago.

lam (lăm) JER. I. intr. **-mm-** fugarse, huir II. s. fuga, escape *m* ♦ **to take it on the l.** largarse.

lamb (lăm) s. cordero; *(dear)* cielo, amor *m*; *(dupe)* inocente *mf*.

lam·baste (lăm-bāst') tr. *(to thrash)* dar una paliza; *(to scold)* regañar duramente.

lame (lām) I. adj. cojo, renco; FIG. débil II. tr. lisiar, baldar.

la·mé (lă-mā') s. lamé *m*.

lame·brain (lām'brān') s. tonto.

la·ment (lə-mĕnt') I. tr. lamentar, llorar; *(to regret)* deplorar —intr. lamentarse II. s. lamento; *(elegy)* elegía.

la·men·ta·ble (lə-mĕn'tə-bəl) adj. lamentable.

la·ment·ed (:tĭd) adj. lamentado.

lam·i·na (lăm'ə-nə) s. [pl. **s** o **-ae**] lámina.

lam·i·nate (:nāt') I. tr. laminar II. adj. & s. laminado.

lam·i·nat·ed (:nā'tĭd) adj. laminado.

lam·i·na·tion ('-nā'shən) s. laminación *f*; *(lamina)* lámina.

lamp (lămp) s. lámpara.

lamp·black ('blăk') s. negro de humo.

lamp·light (:līt') s. luz *f* de la lámpara.

lam·poon (lăm-pōōn') I. s. pasquín *m*, sátira II. tr. pasquinar, satirizar.

lamp·post (lămp'pōst') s. poste *m* de farol.

lam·prey (lăm'prē) s. lamprea.

lance (lăns) I. s. lanza; CIR. lanceta II. tr. lancear; CIR. abrir con una lanceta.

lan·cet (lăn'sĭt) s. lanceta.

land (lănd) I. s. tierra; *(soil)* suelo; *(tract)* campo, terreno; *(country)* tierra, país *m*; *(people)* pueblo; *(real estate)* bienes *m* raíces ♦ **l. bank** banco hipotecario • **l. mine** mina terrestre • **l. of milk and honey** tierra de Jauja • **no man's l.** tierra de nadie • **to get the lay of the l.** tantear el terreno ♦ pl. tierras, posesiones II. tr. *(to unload)* desembarcar; *(to bring to earth)* aterrizar; FAM. *(fish)* coger, atrapar; *(to win)* lograr, conseguir; *(a blow)* dar, asestar ♦ **to l. (someone) in** llevar (a alguien) a —intr. *(to arrive)* arribar; *(to disembark)* desembarcar; *(to alight)* posarse; *(to come to rest)* caer; *(plane)* aterrizar ♦ **to l. up** ir a parar.

land·ed (lăn'dĭd) adj. hacendado ♦ **l. gentry** terratenientes.

land·fall (lănd'fôl') s. recalada.

land·fill (:fĭl') s. tierra rehabilitada.

land·hold·er (:hōl'dər) s. terrateniente *mf*.

land·hold·ing (:dĭng) s. tenencia de tierras.

land·ing (lăn'dĭng) s. *(on land)* aterrizaje *m*; *(on the sea)* amaraje *m*; *(on the moon)* alunizaje *m*; *(of passengers)* desembarco; *(of cargo)* desembarque *m*; *(site)* desembarcadero; *(of a staircase)* descanso.

land·la·dy (lănd'lā'dē) s. propietaria, dueña.

land·locked (:lŏkt') adj. sin salida al mar.

land·lord (:lôrd') s. propietario, arrendador *m*.

land·lub·ber (:lŭb'ər) s. FAM. marinero de agua dulce.

land·mark (:märk') s. mojón *m*; *(event)* acontecimiento histórico; *(site)* monumento histórico.

land·mass (:măs') s. área de terreno grande.

land·own·er (:ō'nər) s. terrateniente *mf*.

land·scape (:skāp') I. s. paisaje *m*, panorama *m* II. tr. ornamentar (un terreno).

land·scap·ing (:skā'pĭng) s. jardinería ornamental.

land·slide (:slīd') s. derrumbe *m* (de tierra), corrimiento; POL. triunfo electoral aplastante.

land·ward (:wərd) **I.** adj. más cerca de la tierra **II.** adv. hacia la tierra.

lane (lān) s. *(path)* senda, vereda; *(road)* camino; *(for ships, aircraft)* ruta; *(of a highway)* vía, carril m; DEP. calle f; *(in bowling)* pista.

lan·guage (lăng′gwĭj) s. lenguaje m; *(dialect)* lengua, idioma m; *(of a document)* términos ♦ **strong l.** palabras mayores o fuertes • **to use bad l.** ser mal hablado.

lan·guid (lăng′gwĭd) adj. lánguido.

lan·guish (:gwĭsh) intr. languidecer; *(to dwindle)* decaer; *(to stagnate)* estancarse; *(to waste away)* pudrirse.

lan·guish·ing (′′ĭng) adj. lánguido.

lan·guor (lăng′gər) s. languidez f.

lan·guor·ous (:əs) adj. lánguido.

lank (lăngk) adj. *(gaunt)* delgado; *(limp)* lacio.

lank·y (lăng′kē) adj. -i- larguirucho.

lan·o·lin (lăn′ə-lĭn) s. lanolina.

lan·tern (lăn′tərn) s. linterna; *(in a lighthouse)* fanal m.

lan·yard (lăn′yərd) s. MARÍT. acollador m, cuerda; MIL. cuerda y gancho de disparo.

lap¹ (lăp) s. falda, regazo; *(of a garment)* falda ♦ **in the l. of luxury** rodeado de lujo • **l. dog** perro faldero • **to fall into one's l.** caerle a uno del cielo.

lap² I. tr. **-pp-** *(to fold)* doblar, plegar; *(to overlap)* cubrir parcialmente, traslapar ♦ **to l. over** *(to overlap)* imbricarse, traslaparse; *(to extend out)* sobresalir II. s. *(overlap)* traslapo, solapa; *(of a race)* vuelta a la pista; *(of a swimming pool)* largo; *(segment)* etapa.

lap³ I. tr. **-pp-** *(to drink)* beber a lengüetadas; *(to wash)* bañar, besar ♦ **to l. up** *(to drink)* lamer, beber a lengüetadas; *(to accept)* aceptar con entusiasmo —intr. *(to drink)* lengüetear, sorber; *(waves)* chapotear II. s. chapoteo.

la·pel (lə-pĕl′) s. solapa (de una vestimenta).

lap·i·dar·y (lăp′ĭ-dĕr′ē) s. & adj. lapidario.

lapse (lăps) I. intr. *(to drift)* caer, deslizarse; *(to fail)* faltar; *(to subside)* decaer, desvanecerse; *(to elapse)* pasar, transcurrir; *(to expire)* caducar II. s. *(slip)* desliz m, fallo; *(error, interval)* lapso; *(expiration)* caducidad f.

lapsed (lăpst) adj. *(elapsed)* transcurrido; *(expired)* caduco.

lar·ce·nist (lär′sə-nĭst) s. ladrón m, ratero.

lar·ce·nous (:nəs) adj. culpable de robo.

lar·ce·ny (:nē) s. hurto, robo.

larch (lärch) s. ORNIT. alondra.

lard (lärd) I. s. lardo II. tr. lardar, mechar; FIG. adornar.

lard·er (lär′dər) s. despensa.

large (lärj) I. adj. grande; *(comprehensive)* extenso, amplio ♦ **l. as life** de tamaño natural II. adv. grande ♦ **at l.** *(at liberty)* libre, en libertad; *(at length)* extensamente • **by and l.** por lo general • **l. order** FAM. tarea peliaguda.

large-heart·ed (′här′tĭd) adj. FIG. magnánimo.

large·ly (:lē) adv. en gran parte.

large-scale (:skāl′) adj. en o a gran escala.

lar·gess(e) (lär-zhĕs′) s. largueza, generosidad f; *(gift)* dádiva, donativo.

lar·i·at (lăr′ē-ət) s. lazo.

lark¹ (lärk) s. ORNIT. alondra.

lark² s. *(spree)* calaverada; *(prank)* broma ♦ **to do something for a l.** hacer algo para divertirse.

lar·va (lär′və) s. [pl. **-ae**] larva.

lar·val (:vəl) adj. larval.

lar·yn·gi·tis (lăr′ən-jī′tĭs) s. laringitis f.

lar·ynx (lăr′ĭngks) s. [pl. **es** o **-ges**] laringe f.

las·civ·i·ous (lə-sĭv′ē-əs) adj. lascivo.

lase (lāz) intr. funcionar como láser.

la·ser (lā′zər) s. láser m.

lash¹ (lăsh) I. s. *(blow)* azote m, latigazo; *(whip)* azote, látigo; *(eyelash)* pestaña II. tr. azotar, dar latigazos a; *(tail)* agitar con fuerza; *(to criticize)* fustigar ♦ **to l. out** al fulminar contra, fustigar —intr. dar latigazos, restallar ♦ **to l. out** estallar de ira.

lash² tr. *(to tie)* atar.

lash·ing (′ĭng) s. *(whipping)* azotaina; *(criticism)* fustigación f; *(for binding)* atadura.

lass (lăs) s. muchacha, joven f.

las·sie (′ē) s. muchacha, joven f.

las·si·tude (lăs′ĭ-tōōd′) s. lasitud f.

las·so (lăs′ō, lă-sōō′) I. s. [pl. **(e)s**] lazo II. tr. coger con un lazo.

last¹ (lăst) I. adj. *(final)* último; *(past)* pasado; *(newest)* último; *(authoritative)* definitivo, final; *(least likely)* último ♦ **l. but not least** el último en orden pero no en importancia • **l. name** apellido • **l. night** anoche II. adv. el último; *(most recently)* la última vez; *(finally)* por último, finalmente III. s. el último; *(the end)* final m ♦ **at (long) l.!** ¡por fin!, ¡al fin! • **to the l.** hasta el fin.

last² intr. durar; *(to survive)* sobrevivir; *(to endure)* perdurar; *(to be enough)* bastar, alcanzar —tr. bastar; *(to survive)* resistir, aguantar.

last³ s. horma (de zapato).

last-ditch (′dĭch′) adj. desesperado, último.

last·ing (lăs′tĭng) adj. duradero, perdurable.

last·ly (lăst′lē) adv. por último, finalmente.

last-min·ute (:mĭn′ĭt) adj. de última hora.

latch (lăch) I. s. pestillo, aldabilla II. tr. cerrar con pestillo o aldabilla.

latch·key (′kē′) s. llave f (de picaporte).

late (lāt) I. adj. *(behind schedule)* retrasado, atrasado; *(at an advanced hour)* a una hora avanzada; *(at the end)* a fines de; *(recent)* reciente, último; *(former)* antiguo, anterior; *(dead)* fallecido, difunto ♦ **to get l.** hacerse tarde • **to make someone l.** retrasar a alguien II. adv. tarde; *(at the end)* tardíamente, recientemente; *(recently)* hasta ♦ **l. in life** a una edad avanzada • **of l.** recientemente, últimamente.

late·com·er (′kŭm′ər) s. retrasado; *(newcomer)* recién llegado.

late·ly (:lē) adv. recientemente, últimamente.

la·ten·cy (lāt′n-sē) s. latencia.

late·ness (lāt′nĭs) s. tardanza; *(delay)* demora, retraso.

la·tent (lāt′nt) adj. latente.

lat·er (lā′tər) I. adj. posterior; *(more recent)* más reciente II. adv. más tarde, después ♦ **l. on** luego, después • **(I'll) see you l.** hasta luego.

lat·er·al (lăt′ər-əl) adj. lateral.

lat·est (lā′tĭst) I. adj. último; *(newest)* más reciente II. adv. el último III. s. lo último, lo más reciente ♦ **at the l.** a más tardar • **the very l.** el último grito.

la·tex (lā′tĕks′) s. látex m.

lath (lăth) s. *(wood)* listón m; *(metal)* lata; *(lathing)* listonería, enlistonado.

lathe (lāth) I. s. torno II. tr. tornear.

lath·er (lăth′ər) I. s. *(of soap)* espuma; *(of the mouth)* espumarajo; *(agitation)* agitación f II. tr. enjabonar —intr. espumar.

lat·i·tude (lăt′ĭ-tōōd′) s. amplitud f; *(freedom)* libertad f; ASTRON., GEOG. latitud f.

la·trine (lə-trēn′) s. letrina, retrete m.

lat·ter (lăt′ər) adj. *(second)* éste; *(nearer the end)* último; *(later)* más reciente, último

lat·ter-day (:dā′) adj. reciente.

lat·tice (lăt′ĭs) I. s. enrejado, celosía; *(window)* ventana con celosía II. tr. enrejar.

lat·tice·work (:wûrk′) s. enrejado, celosía.

laud (lôd) tr. *(to glorify)* loar, alabar; *(to give praise to)* elogiar, encomiar.

laud·a·ble (lô′də-bəl) adj. loable, laudable.

laud·a·to·ry (:tôr′ē) adj. laudatorio.

laugh (lăf) I. intr. reír(se) ♦ **to be nothing to l. about** no ser cosa de risa • **to burst out laughing** echarse a reír a carcajadas • **to l. at** *(to show amusement)* reírse con; *(to ridicule)* reírse de, burlarse de • **to l. it up** divertirse • **t l. off** *o* **away** tomar a risa • **to l. one's head off** reírse a más no poder • **to l. out loud** reírse a carcajadas • **to l. up one's sleeve** reírse para los adentros II. s. risa; *(joke)* chiste m, cosa de risa ♦ **for laughs** para hacer reír • **good for a l.** divertido • **to have a good l.** reírse mucho • **to have the last l.** ser el último que ríe.

laugh·a·ble (′ə-bəl) adj. cómico; *(ludicrous)* ridículo, absurdo.

laugh·ing (:ĭng) adj. risueño ♦ **it's no l. matter** no es cosa de risa • **l. gas** gas hilarante.

laugh·ing·stock (:stŏk′) s. hazmerreír m.

laugh·ter (lăf′tər) s. risa(s); *(loud)* carcajadas.

launch¹ (lônch) I. tr. lanzar; *(into the water)* botar; *(to initiate)* iniciar, emprender —intr. lanzarse ♦ **to l. forth** *o* **out** on emprender II. s. lanzamiento; *(into the sea)* botadura ♦ **l. pad** plataforma de lanzamiento.

launch² s. MARIT. lancha.

launch·er (lôn′chər) s. lanzador m.

launch·ing (:chĭng) s. lanzamiento; *(of a ship)* botadura ♦ **l. pad** plataforma de lanzamiento.

laun·der (lôn′dər) tr. & intr. lavar(se).

laun·dered (:dərd) adj. lavado; *(money)* que ha pasado por otras manos.

laun·der·er (:dər-ər) s. lavandero.

laun·dress (:drĭs) s. lavandera.

laun·dry (:drē) s. *(soiled)* ropa sucia; *(clean)* ropa limpia; *(place)* lavandería.

lau·re·ate (lôr′ē-ĭt) adj. & s. laureado.

lau·rel (lôr′əl) s. laurel m ♦ **to rest on one's laurels** dormirse en los laureles.

la·va (lä′və, lăv′ə) s. lava.

lav·a·to·ry (lăv′ə-tôr′ē) s. servicios; *(washbasin)* lavamanos m, lavabo.

lav·en·der (lăv′ən-dər) I. s. lavanda, alhucema II. adj. de color lavanda.

lav·ish (lăv′ĭsh) I. adj. generoso; *(extravagant)* lujoso, espléndido II. tr. prodigar, derrochar ♦ **to l. (something) on someone** colmar a alguien de (algo).

law (lô) s. ley f; *(code)* fuero, código; *(study)* derecho; *(principle)* ley, principio; FAM. *(police)* policía; LÓG., MAT. regla ♦ **case l.** jurisprudencia • **l. and order** orden público • **l. school** facultad de derecho • **to lay down the l.** dictar la ley • **to practice l.** ejercer la abogacía • **to take the l. into one's own hands** tomarse la ley por la propia mano.

law-a·bid·ing (lô′ə-bī′dĭng) adj. respetuoso de la ley.

law·break·er (lô′brā′kər) s. infractor m de la ley.

law·ful (lô′fəl) adj. *(allowed by law)* legal, lícito; *(recognized)* legítimo.

law·less (lô′lĭs) adj. *(conduct)* desordenado; *(region)* sin leyes, ingobernable.

law·mak·er (lô′mā′kər) s. legislador m.

lawn (lôn) s. césped m ♦ **l. mower** cortacéspedes.

law·suit (lô′sōōt′) s. pleito, juicio.

law·yer (lô′yər) s. abogado, jurista mf.

lax (lăks) adj. *(morals)* laxo; *(negligent)* descuidado; *(discipline)* flojo.

lax·a·tive (lăk′sə-tĭv) s. & adj. laxante m.

lax·i·ty (lăk′sĭ-tē) *o* **lax·ness** (lăks′nĭs) s. laxitud f; *(slackness)* flojedad f; *(negligence)* negligencia, descuido.

lay¹ (lā) tr. **laid** poner; *(to cause to lie)* acostar; *(blame)* achacar, atribuir; *(plans)* trazar, hacer; *(to submit)* presentar, someter; *(to wager)* apostar; *(to impose)* imponer; *(eggs)* poner ♦ **to be laid up** guardar cama • **l. an egg** JER. *(to fail)* fracasar • **to l. aside** *(to give up)* abandonar; *(to put aside)* guardar, dejar a un lado • **to l. away, by,** *o* **in** guardar para el futuro • **to l. claim to** reclamar los derechos a • **to l. down** dictar, establecer • **to l. down one's life for** sacrificar la vida por • **to l. hands on** FAM. *(to catch)* coger, atrapar; *(to hit)* poner la mano encima • **to l. into** JER. *(to beat)* apalear; *(to scold)* regañar, reñir • **to l. it on (thick)** JER. exagerar • **to l. off** *(to dismiss)* despedir (esp. temporalmente); *(a habit)* dejar, abandonar • **to l. out** *(to plan)* planear, proyectar; *(to spread out)* preparar; *(to prepare for burial)* amortajar; *(to spend)* gastar • **to l. to rest** *(to bury)* enterrar; *(to refute)* refutar —intr. *(to produce eggs)* poner huevos, aovar; *(to bet)* apostar; MARIT. situarse, colocarse ♦ **to l. over** pararse, detenerse • **to l. to** MARIT. pairar en el barco.

lay² adj. secular, laico; *(not professional)* lego.

lay³ s. *(song)* cantar m.

lay⁴ cf. **lie¹**.

lay·er (lā′ər) I. s. capa; GEOL. estrato II. tr. separar en capas.

lay·ette (lā-ĕt′) s. ajuar m de niño.

lay·man (lā′mən) s. [pl. **-men**] laico, seglar m; *(nonprofessional)* lego.

lay·off (lā′ôf′) s. *(suspension)* suspensión f temporaria de empleados; *(dismissal)* despido.

lay·out (lā′out′) s. disposición f, distribución f; *(sketch)* trazado.

lay·o·ver (lā′ō′vər) s. escala, parada.

laze (lāz) intr. holgazanear, gandulear —tr. ♦ **to l. away** perder, desperdiciar.

la·zi·ness (lā′zē-nĭs) s. pereza.

la·zy (lā′zē) adj. **-i-** perezoso ♦ **l. Susan** bandeja giratoria.

la·zy·bones (:bōnz′) s.pl. JER. remolón m.

leach (lēch) tr. & intr. lixiviar(se).

lead¹ (lēd) tr. **led** *(to guide)* guiar, conducir; *(to command)* dirigir, mandar; *(to induce)* inducir; *(to head)* ser el primero de, encabezar; *(to be ahead of)* llevar una ventaja de; *(to live)* llevar; *(in cards)* salir con ♦ **to l. astray** descarriar • **to l. on** *(to entice)* seducir, tentar; *(to deceive)* engañar —intr. ser primero, estar a la cabeza; *(to go first)* enseñar el camino; *(to command)* mandar; *(to go)* llevar, conducir; *(in cards)* ser mano • **to l. off** empezar, dar comienzo II. s. *(position)* primer lugar m, delantera; *(margin)* ventaja; *(clue)* indicación f, pista; CINEM., TEAT. *(role)* papel m principal; *(actor)* protagonista mf; PERIOD. párrafo introductor; *(news story)* artículo principal; *(in cards)* mano; *(leash)* trailla, correa ♦ **l. in the** l. a la cabeza, primero • **to follow the l. of** seguir el ejemplo de • **to take the l.** tomar la delantera, adelantarse III. adj. principal.

lead² (lĕd) I. s. plomo; (pencil) mina ✦ I. poisoning saturnismo II. tr. cubrir o forrar con plomo; (window) emplomar.

lead·en (lĕd'n) adj. plúmbeo, de plomo; (gray) plomizo; (heavy) pesado; (sluggish) lento; (depressed) deprimido.

lead·er (lē'dər) s. jefe m, líder m; (guide) guía mf; (politician) caudillo; (first) primero; (pipe) canalón m, conducto.

lead·er·ship (:shĭp') s. dirección f, mando; (capacity) dotes f de mando.

lead-in (lĕd'ĭn') I. s. introducción f II. adj. de entrada.

lead·ing¹ (lē'dĭng) adj. (foremost) primero, que va a la cabeza; (main) principal; TEAT. primero ✦ I. edge puesto de avanzada • I. question pregunta capciosa.

lead·ing² (lĕd'ĭng) s. emplomado.

lead-off (lĕd'ôf') s. (move) comienzo, principio; (person) iniciador m.

lead-time (:tīm') s. tiempo requerido para completar un proyecto.

leaf (lēf) I. s. [pl. **-ves**] hoja; (foliage) follaje m, hojas; (page) página; (metal) lámina ✦ gold I. pan de oro • to shake like a I. temblar como una hoja o un azogado • to turn over a new I. empezar una nueva vida II. intr. BOT. echar hojas ✦ to I. through hojear.

leaf·let ('lĭt) s. folleto, panfleto; (flier) volante m.

leaf·y (lē'fē) adj. -i- frondoso, hojoso.

league¹ (lēg) s. liga; (organization) asociación f; DEP. liga ✦ to be in I. with estar aliado con • out of one's I. en competencia desigual.

league² s. (distance) legua.

leak (lēk) I. intr. (container) salirse; (pipe) tener pérdidas; (roof, faucet) gotear; (boat) hacer agua ✦ to I. in filtrarse, colarse • to I. out salirse, escaparse; (to become known) divulgarse —tr. divulgar II. s. (container) agujero; (pipe) pérdida; (faucet, roof) gotera; (boat) vía de agua; (escape) salida, escape; (disclosure) divulgación f.

leak·y (lē'kē) adj. -i- que se sale, que gotea; (boat) que hace agua.

lean¹ (lēn) intr. -ed o -t inclinarse; (to rest on) apoyarse, reclinarse; (to rely) depender de, contar con; (to tend) inclinarse con; (to exert pressure) hacer presión ✦ to I. back (against the wall) recostarse; (in a chair) reclinarse • to I. forward inclinarse • to I. over backwards to FAM. hacer todo lo posible para —tr. (to rest) apoyar, recostar; (to cause to incline) inclinar, ladear.

lean² I. adj. (thin) delgado, flaco; (meat) magro, sin grasa ✦ I. years años de escasez II. s. CUL. carne f sin grasa.

lean·ing (lē'nĭng) s. proclividad f, inclinación f.

lean-to (lēn'tōō') s. cobertizo.

leap (lēp) I. intr. -ed o -t saltar ✦ to I. at the chance no dejar escapar la oportunidad —tr. saltar por encima de; (a horse) hacer saltar II. s. salto, brinco; FIG. paso ✦ by leaps and bounds a grandes pasos • I. year año bisiesto.

leap·frog ('frôg') I. s. pídola II. tr. -gg- saltar por encima de.

learn (lûrn) tr. -ed o -t aprender; (to find out) saber, enterarse de ✦ to I. by heart aprender de memoria —intr. aprender; (from mistakes) escarmentar ✦ to I. how to aprender a.

learn·ed (lûr'nĭd) adj. erudito.

learn·er ('nər) s. principiante mf ✦ to be a fast

I. aprender rápidamente.

learn·ing ('nĭng) s. aprendizaje m; (knowledge) saber m, erudición f ✦ I. disability dificultad de aprendizaje.

lease (lēs) I. s. contrato de arrendamiento; (duration) alquiler m ✦ to get a new I. on life empezar una nueva vida II. tr. arrendar, dar en arriendo; (to rent) alquilar.

lease·hold ('hōld') s. inquilinato, arrendamiento; (property) propiedad arrendada.

lease·hold·er (:hōl'dər) s. inquilino, arrendatario.

leash (lēsh) I. s. correa, traílla II. tr. atraillar; (to control) controlar, dominar.

leas·ing (lē'sĭng) s. alquiler m, arrendamiento.

least (lēst) I. cf. **little** II. adj. menor; (smallest) mínimo, más pequeño ✦ that's the I. of my worries eso es lo de menos III. adv. menos IV. s. lo menos ✦ at I. (not less than) por lo menos; (in any event) al menos • at the very I. por lo mínimo • not in the I. en absoluto, en lo más mínimo • to say the I. sin exagerar; IRÓN. por no decir otra cosa.

least·wise ('wīz') adv. FAM. (anyway) de todas maneras; (at least) por lo menos.

leath·er (lĕth'ər) s. cuero, piel f.

leath·er·y ('ə-rē) adj. parecido al cuero; (weathered) curtido; (meat) correoso, duro.

leave¹ (lēv) tr. **left** salir de; (to forget) olvidar, dejar; (to let stay, result in) dejar; (to bequeath) dejar, legar; (to entrust) encomendar; (to abandon) dejar, abandonar ✦ to I. alone dejar en paz • to I. behind dejar atrás; (to depart without) irse o partir sin • to I. in the dark dejar a oscuras • to I. out omitir, excluir —intr. irse, marcharse; (to depart) salir, partir ✦ to be left quedar • to be left over quedar, sobrar • to I. off dejar, parar.

leave² s. permiso ✦ to take (one's) I. of someone despedirse de alguien.

leav·en (lĕv'ən) I. s. levadura; FIG. estímulo, fermento II. tr. leudar; (to ferment) fermentar.

leav·en·ing (:ə-nĭng) s. levadura.

leaves (lēvz) cf. **leaf.**

leave-tak·ing (lēv'tā'kĭng) s. despedida.

leav·ing (lē'vĭng) s. partida, salida.

lech·er (lĕch'ər) s. libertino, lujurioso.

lech·er·ous (:əs) adj. libertino, lujurioso.

lech·er·y (lĕch'ə-rē) s. libertinaje m, lujuria.

lec·tern (lĕk'tərn) s. atril m, facistol m.

lec·tor (:tər) s. lector m.

lec·ture (:chər) I. s. conferencia; (class) curso, clase f; (reprimand) reprimenda, sermón m II. intr. dictar conferencia —tr. dar una conferencia a; (to scold) reprender, sermonear.

lec·tur·er (:ər) s. conferenciante mf, conferencista mf.

led (lĕd) cf. **lead¹.**

ledge (lĕj) s. (of a wall) repisa, anaquel m; (on a cliff) reborde m, saliente m; (in the ocean) banco de arrecifes.

ledg·er (lĕj'ər) s. libro mayor.

lee (lē) s. MARÍT. sotavento; FIG. abrigo.

leech (lēch) I. s. sanguijuela; FIG. parásito, vividor m II. tr. ✦ to I. off someone pegarse a alguien como parásito.

leek (lēk) s. puerro.

leer (lĭr) I. intr. mirar de reojo II. s. mirada de reojo.

leer·y (:ē) adj. -i- suspicaz, cauteloso.

lees (lēz) s.pl. sedimento de un líquido.

lee·ward (lē'wərd) adj. & s. (de) sotavento.
lee·way (lē'wā') s. *(drift)* deriva; FIG. *(margin)* margen m; *(latitude)* campo, libertad f.
left[1] (lĕft) I. adj. izquierdo II. s. izquierda III. adv. a o hacia la izquierda.
left[2] cf. **leave[1]**.
left-hand ('hănd') adj. *(on the left)* a o de la izquierda; *(left-handed)* para zurdos.
left-hand·ed (:hăn'dĭd) I. adj. *(person)* zurdo; *(utensil)* para zurdos; *(compliment)* de doble filo II. adv. con la mano izquierda.
left·ist (lĕf'tĭst) s. & adj. POL. izquierdista mf.
left·o·ver (lĕft'ō'vər) I. adj. sobrante, restante II. s. ♦ pl. sobras, restos; CUL. plato hecho de restos de comida.
left-wing (:wĭng') adj. izquierdista.
left-wing·er (lĕft'wĭng'ər) s. izquierdista mf.
left·y (lĕf'tē) s. JER. zurdo.
leg (lĕg) s. pierna; *(of an animal)* pata; *(of furniture)* pata, pie m; *(of pants)* pierna, pernera; *(in a journey)* etapa; *(in races)* tramo, trecho ♦ **not to have a l. to stand on** FAM. carecer de una razón válida • **on its last legs** FAM. sin recursos, en las últimas • **to pull someone's l.** FAM. tomarle el pelo a alguien • **to shake a l.** FAM. apresurarse, darse prisa • **to stretch one's legs** *(to stretch)* estirar las piernas; *(to take a walk)* dar un paseo.
leg·a·cy (lĕg'ə-sē) s. herencia.
le·gal (lē'gəl) adj. legal; *(relating to the law)* jurídico; *(statutory)* legítimo ♦ **l. tender** moneda de curso legal • **of l. age** mayor de edad.
le·gal·ese (lē'gə-lēz') s. vocabulario legal.
le·gal·ist ('-lĭst) s. legalista mf.
le·gal·is·tic ('-lĭs'tĭk) adj. legalista.
le·gal·i·ty (lē-găl'ĭ-tē) s. legalidad f ♦ pl. trámites jurídicos.
le·gal·ize (lē'gə-līz') tr. legalizar, legitimar.
leg·ate (lĕg'ĭt) s. legado (enviado papal).
le·ga·tion (lĭ-gā'shən) s. legación f.
leg·end (lĕj'ənd) s. leyenda; *(person)* mito; *(caption)* pie m.
leg·en·dar·y (:ən-dĕr'ē) adj. legendario.
leg·ged (lĕg'ĭd, lĕgd) adj. *(people)* de piernas; *(animals, furniture)* de patas.
leg·gings (lĕg'ĭngz) s.pl. polainas.
leg·gy (:ē) adj. -i- de piernas largas.
leg·i·bil·i·ty (lĕj'ə-bĭl'ĭ-tē) s. legibilidad f.
leg·i·ble (:bəl) adj. legible.
le·gion (lē'jən) s. legión f.
le·gion·ar·y (lē'jə-nĕr'ē) adj. & s. legionario.
le·gion·naire ('-nâr') s. legionario.
leg·is·late (lĕj'ĭ-slāt') intr. legislar —tr. disponer o establecer por.
leg·is·la·tion ('-slā'shən) s. legislación f.
leg·is·la·tive ('-'tĭv) adj. legislativo.
leg·is·la·tor (:tər) s. legislador m.
leg·is·la·ture (:chər) s. legislatura.
le·git (lə-jĭt') adj. JER. legítimo.
le·git·i·ma·cy (:ə-mə-sē) s. legitimidad f.
le·git·i·mate (:mĭt) adj. *(lawful)* lícito; *(reasonable)* válido; *(authentic)* legítimo, auténtico; *(child)* legítimo.
le·git·i·mize (:mīz') tr. legitimar.
leg·ume (lĕg'yōōm') s. legumbre f.
leg·work (lĕg'wûrk') s. FAM. trabajo que requiere caminar mucho.
lei·sure (lē'zhər, lĕzh'ər) s. ocio ♦ **at one's l.** cuando uno tenga tiempo • **l. time** tiempo libre.
lei·sure·ly (:lē) adj. & adv. sin prisa.
lem·ming (lĕm'ĭng) s. lemming m.
lem·on (lĕm'ən) I. s. limón m; FAM. *(car)* ca-

charro ♦ **l. tree** limonero II. adj. limonado.
lem·on·ade ('-nād') s. limonada.
lend (lĕnd) tr. lent prestar; *(to impart)* dar, impartir ♦ **l. itself to** prestarse a • **to l. a hand** ayudar —intr. hacer préstamos.
lend·er (lĕn'dər) s. prestador m; COM. prestamista mf.
length (lĕngkth) s. largo, longitud f; *(quality)* largura, extensión f; *(piece)* pedazo, tramo; *(in a race)* cuerpo; *(duration)* duración f ♦ **at l.** *(eventually)* al cabo, por fin; *(fully)* por extenso, detenidamente • **to go to great lengths** hacer todo lo posible • **to keep somebody at arm's l.** mantener a alguien a distancia.
length·en (lĕngk'thən) tr. & intr. alargar(se), estirar(se); *(time)* prolongar(se).
length·wise (lĕngkth'wīz') adj. & adv. longitudinal(mente).
length·y (lĕngk'thē) adj. -i- prolongado; *(long)* largo.
le·nience/·cy (lĕn'yəns) s. indulgencia.
le·nient (:yənt) adj. indulgente.
lens (lĕnz) s. lente mf.
lent (lĕnt) cf. **lend**.
len·til (lĕn'təl) s. lenteja.
le·o·nine (lē'ə-nīn') adj. leonino.
leop·ard (lĕp'ərd) s. leopardo.
le·o·tard (lē'ə-tärd') s. malla de bailarines.
lep·er (lĕp'ər) s. leproso.
lep·re·chaun (lĕp'rĭ-kŏn') s. duende m.
lep·ro·sy (lĕp'rə-sē) s. lepra.
lep·rous (:rəs) adj. leproso.
les·bi·an (lĕz'bē-ən) s. lesbiana.
le·sion (lē'zhən) s. lesión f.
less (lĕs) I. cf. **little** II. adj. menos; *(not as great)* menor ♦ **in l. than no time** en un abrir y cerrar de ojos • **l. than** menos de (lo que) • **no l. than** *(as much as)* nada menos que; *(at least)* por lo menos • **nothing l. than** nada menos que III. prep. menos IV. adv. menos ♦ **l. and l.** cada vez menos • **l. than** *(not at all)* nada <*you are being l. than honest* no estás siendo nada honesto>; *(far from)* ni mucho menos • **much l.** mucho menos IV. s. menos.
les·see (lĕ-sē') s. locatario, arrendatario.
less·en (lĕs'ən) tr. & intr. disminuir.
less·er (:ər) adj. menor; *(smaller)* más pequeño.
les·son (lĕs'ən) s. lección f ♦ **to learn one's l.** escarmentar • **to take lessons** tomar clases.
les·sor (lĕs'ôr') s. locador m, arrendador m.
lest (lĕst) conj. para (que) no.
let[1] (lĕt) I. tr. let, -tting permitir; *(to allow)* dejar <*l. the water run* deja correr el agua>; *(to rent)* alquilar; *(to lease)* arrendar ♦ **to l. by** o **through** dejar pasar • **to l. down** bajar; *(to lengthen)* alargar; *(hair)* dejar caer; *(to disappoint)* fallar • **to l. go** *(to fire)* despedir; *(to set free)* dejar en libertad; *(to release)* soltar • **to l. in** dejar entrar • **to l. it go at that** dejarlo así • **to l. know** avisar, dar a conocer • **to l. off** *(steam)* dejar salir; *(to exempt)* eximir, dispensar de; *(to forgive)* perdonar • **to l. oneself go** *(to enjoy)* soltarse, desatarse; *(to neglect)* descuidarse • **to l. out** dejar salir; *(to set free)* poner en libertad; *(garments)* ensanchar, extender; *(to divulge)* divulgar; *(scream)* pegar, despedir; *(to rent)* alquilar —intr. *(to be rented)* alquilarse; *(to be leased)* arrendarse ♦ **to l. on** *(to divulge)* soltar, revelar el secreto; *(to pretend)* fingir • **to l. up** FAM. *(to cease)* cesar; *(to slacken)* aflojarse, disminuirse

—aux. <*l. us pray* oremos> <*let's see* veamos> <*l. x equal* y supongamos que x es igual a y> **II. conj. ♦ l. alone** y mucho menos, ni siquiera.

let² s. obstáculo; *(in tennis)* let m.

let·down ('doun') s. disminución f; *(disappointment)* decepción f, desilusión f.

le·thal (lē'thəl) adj. letal, mortífero.

le·thar·gic (lə-thär'jĭk) adj. letárgico.

leth·ar·gy (lĕth'ər-jē) s. letargo.

let·ter (lĕt'ər) **I.** s. *(of alphabet)* letra; *(note)* carta ♦ **capital l.** mayúscula • **l. bomb** carta explosiva • **l. opener** abrecartas • **small l.** minúscula • **to the l.** al pie de la letra ♦ pl. letras, erudición **II.** tr. inscribir letras en.

let·ter·box (:bŏks') s. apartado, buzón m.

let·tered (lĕt'ərd) adj. literato, letrado; *(erudite)* erudito; *(with letters)* rotulado.

let·ter·head (lĕt'ər-hĕd') s. *(heading)* membrete m; *(stationery)* papel membretado.

let·ter·ing (:ĭng) s. rotulado, rótulo.

let·ter·per·fect (:-pûr'fĭkt) adj. preciso.

let·tuce (lĕt'əs) s. lechuga.

let·up (lĕt'ŭp') s. disminución f; *(pause)* pausa, interrupción f.

leu·ke·mi·a (lōō-kē'mē-ə) s. leucemia.

lev·ee (lĕv'ē) s. *(on a river)* ribero, dique m; *(pier)* muelle m fluvial.

lev·el (lĕv'əl) **I.** s. nivel m; *(height)* altura; *(flat land)* llano, llanura; *(rank)* posición f, categoría ♦ **at ground l.** a ras de tierra • **on the l.** FIG. honesto, limpio **II.** adj. plano, llano; *(horizontal)* horizontal, a nivel; *(even)* parejo, igual; *(steady)* uniforme; *(rational)* equilibrado; CUL. *(not heaping)* al ras, raso ♦ **to do one's l. best** FAM. hacer todo lo posible **III.** tr. nivelar; *(to make flat)* allanar, aplanar; *(to make uniform)* emparejar, igualar; *(to raze)* arrasar, echar por tierra; *(gun)* apuntar; *(accusation)* dirigir ♦ **to l. off** nivelar —intr. nivelarse, igualarse ♦ **to l. off** estabilizarse.

lev·el·head·ed (:hĕd'ĭd) adj. equilibrado.

lev·er (lĕv'ər, lē'vər) **I.** s. palanca **II.** tr. apalancar.

lev·er·age (:ĭj) s. apalancamiento; *(power)* fuerza de una palanca; FIG. poder m, influencia.

le·vi·a·than (lə-vī'ə-thən) s. gigante m.

lev·i·tate (lĕv'ĭ-tāt') tr. & intr. mantener(se) en el aire por levitación.

lev·i·ta·tion (':-tā'shən) s. levitación f.

lev·i·ty (lĕv'ĭ-tē) s. ligereza, frivolidad f.

lev·y (lĕv'ē) **I.** tr. *(to impose)* exigir, imponer; *(to collect)* recaudar; *(to draft)* levar, reclutar; *(a war)* hacer **II.** s. *(imposition)* exacción f, imposición f; *(collection)* recaudación f; *(draft)* leva, reclutamiento; *(tax)* impuesto; *(surcharge)* sobretasa.

lewd (lōōd) adj. *(lustful)* lujurioso, lascivo; *(obscene)* obsceno, indecente.

lewd·ness ('nĭs) s. lujuria, lascivia.

lex·i·cal (lĕk'sĭ-kəl) adj. léxico.

lex·i·cog·ra·pher ('-kŏg'rə-fər) s. lexicógrafo.

lex·i·cog·ra·phy (:fē) s. lexicografía.

lex·i·con (lĕk'sĭ-kŏn') s. lexicón m, diccionario; *(vocabulary)* léxico, vocabulario.

li·a·bil·i·ty (lī'ə-bĭl'ĭ-tē) s. responsabilidad f, obligación f; *(to prosecution)* sujeción f; *(debt)* deuda; *(hindrance)* desventaja, inconveniente m; *(tendency)* susceptibilidad f ♦ **l. insurance** seguro de responsabilidad civil ♦ pl. COM. el pasivo.

li·a·ble (lī'ə-bəl) adj. responsable; *(obligated)*

obligado; *(subject)* sujeto; *(tending to)* susceptible; *(likely)* probable.

li·ai·son (lē'ā-zŏn', lē-ā'-) s. enlace m; *(love affair)* romance m.

li·ar (lī'ər) s. mentiroso.

li·ba·tion (lī-bā'shən) s. libación f; *(beverage)* bebida.

li·bel (lī'bəl) **I.** s. libelo, difamación f **II.** tr. difamar.

li·bel·er (lī'bə-lər) s. libelista mf, difamador m.

li·bel·ous (:ləs) adj. difamatorio.

lib·er·al (lĭb'ər-əl) **I.** adj. liberal; *(generous)* generoso; *(abundant)* abundante, amplio; *(not literal)* libre ♦ **l. arts** artes liberales, humanidades **II.** s. liberal mf.

lib·er·al·i·ty ('ə-răl'ĭ-tē) s. liberalidad f.

lib·er·al·ize ('ər-ə-līz') tr. & intr. liberalizar(se).

lib·er·ate (:ə-rāt') tr. liberar, libertar.

lib·er·a·tion ('-rā'shən) s. liberación f.

lib·er·a·tor ('-'-tər) s. liberador m.

lib·er·tar·i·an (lĭb'ər-târ'ē-ən) s. libertario.

lib·er·tine (lĭb'ər-tēn') s. & adj. libertino.

lib·er·ty (lĭb'ər-tē) s. libertad f; MARÍT. permiso, licencia ♦ **at l.** libre, en libertad.

li·bid·i·nous (lĭ-bĭd'n-əs) adj. libidinoso.

li·brar·i·an (lī-brâr'ē-ən) s. bibliotecario.

li·brar·y (lī'brĕr'ē) s. biblioteca.

li·bret·to (lĭ-brĕt'ō) s. [pl. **s** o **-ti**] libreto.

lice (līs) cf. **louse.**

li·cense (lī'səns) **I.** s. licencia, permiso; *(card)* carnet m; *(latitude, freedom)* libertad f ♦ **l. plate** patente, placa (de matrícula) **II.** tr. licenciar, autorizar; *(to accredit)* acreditar.

li·cens·er (lī'sən-sər) s. expedidor m de una licencia.

li·cen·ti·ate (lī-sĕn'shē-ĭt) s. licenciado.

li·cen·tious (:shəs) adj. licencioso.

li·chen (lī'kən) s. liquen m.

lic·it (lĭs'ĭt) adj. lícito.

lick (lĭk) **I.** tr. lamer; *(to beat)* cascar, zurrar; *(to defeat)* vencer; *(to overcome)* superar ♦ **to l. someone's boots** adular servilmente a alguien —intr. lamer **II.** s. lametazo; *(little bit)* pizca, ápice m; *(salt)* salegar m; *(blow)* golpe m.

lick·e·ty·split (lĭk'ĭ-tē-splĭt') adv. FAM. rapidísimamente, a gran velocidad.

lick·ing (lĭk'ĭng) s. JER. *(beating)* paliza; *(defeat)* derrota.

lic·o·rice (lĭk'ər-ĭs, :ĭsh) s. regaliz m.

lid (lĭd) s. tapa; *(eyelid)* pestaña ♦ **to blow the l. off** FAM. descubrir, revelar • **to flip one's l.** JER. pegar el grito en el cielo • **to put the l. on** JER. poner frenos a.

lie¹ (lī) **I.** intr. **lay, lain, lying** *(to recline)* tenderse, acostarse; *(to be stretched out)* estar tendido, yacer; *(to remain)* quedarse; *(to be buried)* estar enterrado; *(to be situated)* estar situado; *(to be admissible)* ser admisible; FIG. *(to consist)* radicar, residir *(in* en) ♦ **to l. back** inclinarse hacia atrás • **to l. low** FAM. esconderse, ocultarse • **to take (it) lying down** FAM. aceptar (algo) sin protestar **II.** s. posición f.

lie² **I.** s. mentira, embuste m ♦ **l. detector** aparato detector de mentiras • **to give the l. to** desmentir **II.** intr. **lying** mentir.

liege (lēj) **I.** s. *(lord)* señor m feudal; *(vassal)* vasallo **II.** adj. leal, fiel.

lien (lēn, lē'ən) s. derecho de retención.

lieu (lōō) s. ♦ **in l. of** en lugar de, en vez de.

lieu·ten·ant (lōō-tĕn'ənt) s. MIL. teniente m; MARÍT. alférez m de navío; *(deputy)* lugarteniente m ♦ **l. commander** capitán de corbeta •

l. governor vice gobernador.
life (lîf) s. [pl. **-ves**] vida; *(usefulness)* duración *f*; *(activity)* animación *f*; *(imprisonment)* cadena perpetua ♦ **for dear l.** *o* **for one's l.** como para salvar la propia vida ♦ **in later l.** en los últimos años • **l. jacket** chaleco salvavidas • **l. of the party** alma de la fiesta • **l. preserver** salvavidas • **not on your l.!** ¡de ninguna manera! • **that's l.!** ¡así es la vida! • **to bring back to l.** reanimar, resucitar • **to have the time of one's l.** divertirse mucho • **to take one's own l.** suicidarse • **true to l.** verosímil.
life·blood (:blŭd') s. sangre *f*; FIG. alma, parte *f* vital.
life·boat (:bōt') s. bote *m* salvavidas.
life·guard (:gärd') s. bañero, salvavidas *mf*.
life·less (:lĭs) adj. inanimado; *(dead)* muerto; *(dull)* sin vida.
life·like (:līk') adj. que parece vivo; *(natural)* natural.
life·long (:lông') adj. de toda la vida.
lif·er (lī'fər) s. JER. presidiario condenado a prisión perpetua.
life·sav·er (lĭf'sā'vər) s. *(life preserver)* salvavidas *m*; FIG salvación *f*.
life·sav·ing (:sā'vĭng) **I.** s. salvamento, socorrismo **II.** adj. de salvamento.
life·size(d) (:sīz[d]') adj. de tamaño natural.
life·style (:stīl') s. estilo de vida.
life-sup·port system (:sə-pôrt') s. sistema *m* de mantenimiento de vida.
life·time (:tīm') s. vida.
life·work (:wûrk') s. obra principal de la vida.
lift (lĭft) **I.** tr. alzar, levantar; *(to hoist)* elevar, izar; *(to revoke)* revocar; *(to steal)* escamotear, birlar; *(to plagiarize)* plagiar —intr. levantarse, ascender; *(fog)* disiparse ♦ **to l. off** AER. despegar **II.** s. alzamiento, levantamiento, *(load)* carga; *(elevation)* elevación *f*; *(elation)* exaltación *f*; AER. fuerza ascensional; MEC. gato; G.B. ascensor *m* ♦ **to give someone a l.** llevar a alguien en un vehículo; *(to cheer up)* levantarle a alguien el ánimo.
lift-off ('ôf') s. despegue *m*.
lig·a·ment (lĭg'ə-mənt) s. ligamento.
li·gate (lī'gāt') tr. ligar.
li·ga·tion (lī-gā'shən) s. ligadura.
lig·a·ture (lĭg'ə-chŏor') s. ligadura.
light[1] (līt) **I.** s. luz *f*; *(flame)* fuego; *(viewpoint)* aspecto, punto de vista; *(luminary)* lumbrera, eminencia; *(gleam)* brillo ♦ **in l.** of en vista de, considerando ♦ **l. bulb** bombilla • **l. meter** fotómetro • **to bring to l.** sacar a luz, revelar • **to shed** *o* **throw l. on** aclarar • **to come to l.** salir a la luz • **to give the green l.** aprobar • **to see the l.** comprender, darse cuenta ♦ pl. FIG. *(opinions)* luces, conocimientos **II.** tr. **-ed** *o* **lit** encender; *(to illuminate)* alumbrar, iluminar ♦ **to l. up** iluminar; *(cigarette)* encender —intr. encenderse ♦ **to l. up** iluminarse **III.** adj. *(colors)* claro; *(complexion)* blanco; *(hair)* rubio; *(bright)* bien iluminado.
light[2] **I.** adj. *(not heavy)* ligero, liviano; *(not forceful)* suave, leve; *(rain)* fino; *(food)* ligero; *(faint)* débil; *(frivolous)* superficial; *(happy)* alegre ♦ **l. in the head** mareado • **to make l.** of no tomar en serio **II.** adv. ligeramente ♦ **to travel l.** viajar con poco equipaje **III.** intr. **-ed** *o* **lit** *(to dismount)* apearse, desmontar; *(to alight)* posarse ♦ **to l. into** atacar • **to l. (up)on** *(to land on)* posarse; *(to come across)* tropezar con • **to l. out** FAM. largarse.

light·en[1] (līt'n) tr. & intr. iluminar(se), aclarar(se).
light·en[2] tr. & intr. *(less heavy)* aligerar(se); *(to relieve)* aliviar(se); *(to gladden)* alegrar(se).
light·er[1] (lī'tər) s. encendedor *m*.
light·er[2] s. MARÍT. barcaza, gabarra.
light-fin·gered (līt'fĭng'gərd) adj. listo de manos, ligero de dedos.
light-foot·ed (:fŏot'ĭd) adj. ligero de pies.
light-head·ed (:hĕd'ĭd) adj. *(dizzy)* mareado; *(frivolous)* frívolo, ligero de cascos.
light-heart·ed (:här'tĭd) adj. despreocupado.
light·house (:hous') s. faro.
light·ing (lī'tĭng) s. iluminación *f*, alumbrado.
light·ly (līt'lē) adv. ligeramente; *(superficially)* levemente; *(nimbly)* ágilmente; *(blithely)* despreocupadamente; *(indifferently)* a la ligera ♦ **to let off l.** dar un castigo leve a • **to take l.** no dar importancia a.
light·ness[1] (līt'nĭs) s. luminosidad *f*, claridad *f*.
light·ness[2] s. ligereza; *(agility)* agilidad *f*, gracia; *(blitheness)* despreocupación *f*.
light·ning (līt'nĭng) **I.** s. rayo, relámpago **II.** intr. descargar un rayo *o* relámpago **III.** adj. *(quick)* relámpago ♦ **l. bug** luciérnaga • **l. rod** pararrayos.
light·weight (:wāt') s. persona de poco peso; *(boxer)* peso ligero; FAM. pelele *m*.
light-year *o* **light year** (:yîr') s. año luz.
lik·a·ble (lī'kə-bəl) adj. agradable, grato.
like[1] (līk) **I.** tr. gustar *<I l. the movies* me gusta el cine>; *(to want)* desear, querer —intr. querer ♦ **as you l.** como usted quiera **II.** s. gusto.
like[2] **I.** prep. como; *(typical of)* típico, propio (de); *(such as)* (tal) como ♦ **l. this** *o* **that** así • **something l.** algo así como • **that's more l. it!** ¡eso es mucho mejor! **II.** adj. similar, parecido **III.** s. semejante *mf*, igual *mf* ♦ **l. and the l.** FAM. y cosas por el estilo • **the likes of** personas como **IV.** conj. como.
like·li·hood ('lē-hŏod') s. probabilidad *f*.
like·ly (:lē) **I.** adj. **-i-** probable; *(plausible)* verosímil; *(promising)* prometedor ♦ **that's a l. story!** ¡vaya cuento! **II.** adv. probablemente.
like-mind·ed (:mīn'dĭd) adj. del mismo parecer.
lik·en (lī'kən) tr. comparar.
like·ness (līk'nĭs) s. semejanza; *(appearance)* apariencia; *(representation)* retrato, imagen *f*.
like·wise (:wīz') adv. del mismo modo, lo mismo; *(also)* además.
lik·ing (lī'kĭng) s. afición *f*; *(taste)* gusto ♦ **to take a l. to** *(something)* aficionarse a; *(someone)* coger *o* tener simpatía a.
li·lac (lī'lək, lī'lăk') s. & adj. *(de color)* lila.
lilt (lĭlt) **I.** s. canción *f* alegre; *(cadence)* ritmo; *(accent)* deje *m* **II.** tr. cantar alegremente.
lil·y (lĭl'ē) s. lirio ♦ **l. of the valley** muguete • **l. pad** hoja de nenúfar.
lil·y-liv·ered ('-lĭv'ərd) adj. cobarde, tímido.
lil·y-white ('-hwīt') adj. blanco como la nieve; *(irreproachable)* intachable.
li·ma bean (lī'mə) s. frijol *m*, haba.
limb (lĭm) **I.** s. BOT. rama; ANAT. miembro, extremidad *f* ♦ **out on a l.** FAM. en una situación precaria • **to tear l. from l.** despedazar.
lim·ber (lĭm'bər) **I.** adj. flexible; *(agile)* ágil **II.** intr. ♦ **to l. up** prepararse haciendo ejercicios.
lim·bo (lĭm'bō) s. nada *f* • **L.** TEOL. limbo.
lime[1] (līm) s. *(tree, fruit)* lima.

lime² I. s. cal *f; (birdlime)* liga II. tr. *(wall, surface)* encalar; *(soil)* abonar con cal.
lime·light (′lĭt′) s. luz *f* de calcio; FIG. centro de atención.
lim·er·ick (lĭm′ər-ĭk) s. poema humorístico.
lime·stone (līm′stōn′) s. (piedra) caliza.
lim·it (lĭm′ĭt) I. s. límite *m; (maximum)* máximo ♦ **the sky's the l.** FAM. todo es posible ♦ pl. límites, confines • **within l.** hasta cierto punto II. tr. limitar.
lim·i·ta·tion (′ĭ-tā′shən) s. limitación *f*, restricción *f* ♦ pl. restricciones; *(shortcomings)* deficiencias.
lim·it·ed (′-tĭd) I. adj. limitado, reducido; *(qualified)* módico ♦ **for a l. time only** por corto plazo solamente • **l. company** COM. sociedad anónima • **of l. means** corto de recursos II. s. (tren) expreso.
lim·it·ing (:tĭng) adj. limitativo.
lim·it·less (lĭm′ĭt-lĭs) adj. ilimitado, sin límites.
lim·o (lĭm′ō) s. limosina.
lim·ou·sine (lĭm′ə-zēn′) s. limosina.
limp (lĭmp) I. intr. cojear II. s. cojera III. adj. fláccido; *(hanging)* caído; *(hair)* lacio; *(weak)* débil.
lim·pid (lĭm′pĭd) adj. límpido, claro.
lin·age (lī′nĭj) s. número de líneas.
linch·pin (lĭnch′pĭn′) s. *(pin)* pezonera; *(essential)* parte *f* esencial.
lin·den (lĭn′dən) s. tilo.
line¹ (līn) I. s. línea; *(mark)* raya; *(wrinkle)* arruga; *(boundary)* frontera, límite *m; (wire)* cable *m; (rope)* cabo; *(cord)* cordón *m*, cordel *m; (fishing)* sedal *m; (transportation)* línea; *(company)* compañía; *(trajectory)* trayectoria; *(method)* línea, curso; *(occupation)* ocupación *f; (specialty)* especialidad *f*, rama; *(merchandise)* surtido; *(row)* hilera, fila; *(queue)* cola; *(verse)* verso; *(brief letter)* letras, líneas ♦ **along the lines of** algo como • **in l. with** de acuerdo con • **down the l.** en el futuro • **l. of work** ocupación • **on the l.** en el teléfono; *(in jeopardy)* en peligro • **the end of the l.** FIG. el final, el fin • **to be in l. for** ser candidato para • **to be out of l.** comportarse incorrectamente • **to draw the l.** fijar límites • **to drop someone a l.** ponerle a alguien unas letras • **to feed, give** *o* **hand someone a l.** embaucar a alguien • **to hold the l.** restringir • **to lay it on the l.** hablar con franqueza • **to step out of l.** salirse de lo que está establecido • **to toe the l.** conformarse II. tr. rayar, trazar líneas en • **to l. up** poner en fila —intr. ♦ **to l. up** hacer cola.
line² tr. *(to put lining in)* forrar; *(to cover)* cubrir; TEC. revestir; *(brakes)* guarnecer ♦ **to l. one's pockets** enriquecerse.
lin·e·age (lĭn′ē-ĭj) s. linaje *m*, estirpe *m*.
lin·e·al (:əl) adj. en línea directa; *(linear)* lineal.
lin·e·ar (:ər) adj. linear, lineal ♦ **l. measure** medida de longitud.
lined (līnd) adj. *(ruled)* rayado; *(with a lining)* forrado.
lin·en (lĭn′ən) I. s. lino, hilo; *(goods)* lencería ♦ pl. ropa de cama II. adj. de lino *o* hilo.
lin·er¹ (lī′nər) s. trasatlántico, barco de travesía; AVIA. avión *m* de línea *o* travesía.
lin·er² s. *(lining)* forro, revestimiento.
lines·man (līnz′mən) s. [pl. **-men**] ELEC. guardalínea *m*; DEP. juez *m* de línea.
line·up *o* **line-up** (līn′ŭp′) s. CRIMIN. fila de personas); DEP. alineación *f*.

lin·ger (lĭng′gər) intr. quedarse; *(to lag behind)* quedarse atrás; *(before dying)* durar; *(to persist)* persistir, subsistir.
lin·ge·rie (län′zhə-rē′, :rā′) s. lencería, ropa interior de mujer).
lin·ger·ing (lĭng′gər-ĭng) adj. persistente.
lin·go (lĭng′gō) s. [pl. **es**] FAM. jerigonza.
lin·gual (lĭng′gwəl) adj. lingual.
lin·guist (:gwĭst) s. políglota; *(specialist)* lingüista *mf*.
lin·guis·tic (-gwĭs′tĭk) adj. lingüístico ♦ **linguistics** s.sg. lingüística.
lin·i·ment (lĭn′ə-mənt) s. linimento, untura.
lin·ing (lī′nĭng) s. forro.
link (lĭngk) I. s. eslabón *m; (element)* enlace *m; (connection)* unión *f*, conexión *f; (bond)* vínculo, lazo ♦ **weak l.** punto débil II. tr. & intr. *(to unite)* unir(se), enlazar(se); *(to connect)* eslabonar(se), conectar(se).
link·age (lĭng′kĭj) s. eslabonamiento; *(bond)* unión *f*, enlace *m*.
linked (lĭngkt) adj. conectado, enlazado; *(united)* vinculado; *(combined)* ligado.
links (lĭngks) s.pl. campo de golf.
li·no·le·um (lĭ-nō′lē-əm) s. linóleo.
lint (lĭnt) s. pelusa, tamo; MED. hilas.
lin·tel (lĭn′tl) s. dintel *m*, lintel *m*.
li·on (lī′ən) s. león *m; (celebrity)* celebridad *f* ♦ **the l.'s share** la mejor parte.
li·on·ess (lī′ə-nĭs) s. leona.
li·on·heart·ed (lī′ən-här′tĭd) adj. muy valiente.
li·on·ize (lī′ə-nīz′) tr. agasajar.
lip (lĭp) s. labio; *(edge)* reborde *m; (rim)* pico; JER. insolencia, impertinencia ♦ **to keep a stiff upper l.** poner a mal tiempo buena cara • **to lick one's lips** FIG. relamerse • **to pay l. service to** fingir estar de acuerdo con • **to smack one's lips** hacer un chasquido con los labios.
lip-read (lĭp′rēd′) intr. **-read** leer los labios.
lip·stick (:stĭk′) s. lápiz *m* labial.
liq·ue·fac·tion (lĭk′wə-fãk′shən) s. licuefacción *f*.
liq·ue·fy (′-fī′) tr. & intr. licuar(se).
li·queur (lĭ-kûr′) s. licor *m*.
liq·uid (lĭk′wĭd) I. s. líquido II. adj. líquido; *(clear)* claro, transparente; *(flowing)* límpido ♦ **l. assets** activo líquido.
liq·ui·date (:wĭ-dāt′) tr. liquidar; *(assets)* convertir en efectivo; FAM. *(to murder)* asesinar.
liq·ui·da·tion (′-dā′shən) s. liquidación *f*.
liq·uid·i·ty (lĭ-kwĭd′ĭ-tē) s. liquidez *f*, fluidez *f*.
liq·ui·fy (lĭk′wə-fī) var. de **liquefy.**
liq·uor (lĭk′ər) s. licor *m*.
lisp (lĭsp) I. s. ceceo II. intr. cecear.
lis·some (lĭs′əm) adj. flexible; *(willowy)* elástico; *(nimble)* ágil.
list¹ (lĭst) I. s. lista II. tr. hacer una lista de, enumerar; *(to register)* poner en una lista.
list² MARÍT. I. s. escora II. intr. escorar.
lis·ten (lĭs′ən) intr. escuchar; *(to heed advice)* prestar atención ♦ **to l. up** escuchar bien.
lis·ten·er (:ə-nər) s. oyente *mf*.
list·ing (lĭs′tĭng) s. alistamiento; *(list entry)* listado; *(list)* lista.
list·less (lĭst′lĭs) adj. apático.
lit (lĭt) cf. **light¹, light².**
lit·a·ny (lĭt′n-ē) s. letanía.
li·ter (lē′tər) s. litro.
lit·er·a·cy (lĭt′ər-ə-sē) s. alfabetismo.
lit·er·al (lĭt′ər-əl) adj. literal; *(true)* escueto, llano; *(by letters)* alfabético.
lit·er·ar·y (lĭt′ə-rĕr′ē) adj. literario.

lit·er·ate (:ər-ĭt) adj. que sabe leer y escribir; *(educated)* letrado, instruido; *(literary)* literato.

lit·er·a·ture (:ə-chŏŏr′) s. literatura; *(printed material)* folletos, impresos.

lithe (līth) adj. flexible, elástico.

lith·i·um (līth′ē-əm) s. litio.

lith·o·graph (līth′ə-grăf′) s. litografía.

li·thog·ra·pher (lĭ-thŏg′rə-fər) s. litógrafo.

li·thog·ra·phy (:fē) s. litografía.

lit·i·gant (lĭt′ĭ-gənt) s. & adj. litigante *mf.*

lit·i·gate (:gāt′) tr. & intr. litigar, pleitear.

lit·i·ga·tion (′-gā′shən) s. litigio, pleito.

li·ti·gious (lĭ-tĭj′əs) adj. litigioso.

lit·mus (lĭt′məs) s. tornasol *m* ♦ **l. test** prueba de acidez; FIG. prueba determinante.

li·tre (lē′tər) G.B. var. de **liter.**

lit·ter (lĭt′ər) I. s. *(conveyance)* litera; *(stretcher)* camilla; *(animal bedding)* lecho de paja; *(animal's young)* camada, cría; *(trash)* basura II. tr. *(with trash)* tirar basura en; *(to cover)* estar esparcido por; *(to scatter)* esparcir, regar —intr. tirar basura.

lit·ter·bug (:bŭg′) s. FAM. persona que arroja basura en lugares públicos.

lit·tle (lĭt′l) I. adj. **-er** *o* **less, -est** *o* **least** *(small)* pequeño; *(short)* bajo; *(brief)* breve; *(not much)* poco; *(petty)* estrecho ♦ **l. ones** niños, gente menuda II. adv. **less, least** *(not much)* poco; *(not at all)* no <*I. did I know that* no me imaginé que>; *(somewhat)* un poco, algo <*she's a l. better* está algo mejor> ♦ **l. by l.** poco a poco III. s. poco; *(short time)* momento.

li·tur·gi·cal (lĭ-tûr′jĭ-kəl) adj. litúrgico.

lit·ur·gy (lĭt′ər-jē) s. liturgia.

liv(e)·a·ble (lĭv′ə-bəl) adj. habitable; *(bearable)* soportable, tolerable.

live¹ (lĭv) intr. vivir ♦ **to l. and learn** vivir para ver • **to l. in** vivir donde se trabaja • **to l. on** vivir, perdurar —tr. vivir, llevar ♦ **to l. down** lograr borrar de la memoria • **to l. it up** FAM. correr las grandes juergas, vivir la vida • **to l. off** *(someone)* vivir a expensas de; *(the land)* vivir de • **to l. through** sobrevivir • **to l. up to** *(to conform with)* actuar en conformidad con; *(to fulfill)* cumplir • **to l. with** tolerar, aceptar.

live² (lĭv) I. adj. vivo; *(of interest)* actual; *(burning)* encendido; ARM. sin estallar; RAD., TELEV. en directo ♦ **l. wire** ELEC. cable con corriente; FIG. persona vivaz y activa II. adv. en directo.

live-in (lĭv′ĭn′) adj. residente, con cama.

live·li·hood (lĭv′lē-hŏŏd′) s. medios de ganarse la vida.

live·li·ness (:nĭs) s. vida, animación *f.*

live·long (lĭv′lông′) adj. entero, completo ♦ **all the l. day** todo el santo día.

live·ly (lĭv′lē) adj. **-i-** lleno de vida, vivaz; *(spirited)* alegre; *(animated)* animado; *(keen)* vivo, grande; *(vivid)* vivo.

liv·en (lĭ′vən) tr. & intr. animar(se).

liv·er¹ (lĭv′ər) s. ANAT., CUL. hígado.

liv·er² s. ♦ **fast l.** juerguista *mf.*

liv·er·wurst (:wûrst′) s. salchicha de hígado.

liv·er·y (lĭv′ə-rē) s. *(uniform)* librea; *(stable)* caballeriza de alquiler.

lives (lĭvz) cf. **life.**

live·stock (lĭv′stŏk′) s. ganado.

liv·id (lĭv′ĭd) adj. lívido; *(pale)* pálido; *(furious)* furioso.

liv·ing (lĭv′ĭng) I. adj. vivo; *(extant)* viviente, contemporáneo; *(vivid)* lleno de vida, vívido ♦ **l. expenses** gastos de manutención ♦ **l. quar-**

ters vivienda, alojamiento • **l. room** sala de estar • **l. wage** salario vital II. s. vida ♦ **to earn** *o* **to make a l.** ganarse la vida.

liz·ard (lĭz′ərd) s. lagarto.

lla·ma (lä′mə) s. llama.

load (lōd) I. s. *(weight)* peso; *(cargo)* carga, cargamento; *(burden)* peso, presión *f* ♦ **get a l. of this!** JER. ¡fíjate!, ¡mira esto! • **to take a l. off one's mind** sacarse un peso de encima ♦ pl. FAM. montón, muchísimo II. tr. *(to fill)* cargar, llenar; *(to burden)* agobiar, abrumar; *(to adulterate)* adulterar —intr. cargar(se).

load·ed (lō′dĭd) adj. *(full)* cargado; *(tricky)* intencionado; *(drunk)* borracho, embriagado; *(rich)* rico, forrado de dinero.

loaf¹ (lōf) s. [pl. **-ves**] pan *m*; *(shaped mass)* hogaza, barra; *(of sugar)* pilón *m.*

loaf² intr. haraganear, holgazanear.

loaf·er (lō′fər) s. holgazán *m*; *(shoe)* mocasín *m.*

loam (lōm) s. mantillo, tierra labrantía.

loan (lōn) I. s. préstamo ♦ **l. shark** FAM. usurero • **on l.** prestado II. tr. prestar.

loath (lōth) adj. poco dispuesto, renuente.

loathe (lōth) tr. aborrecer.

loath·ing (lō′thĭng) s. aborrecimiento.

loath·some (lōth′səm) adj. repugnante.

loaves (lōvz) cf. **loaf¹.**

lob (lŏb) I. tr. **-bb-** volear II. s. volea alta.

lob·by (lŏb′ē) I. s. *(foyer)* vestíbulo; *(waiting room)* sala de espera; POL. grupo de presión II. intr. POL. ejercer presiones.

lobe (lōb) s. lóbulo.

lo·bot·o·my (lō-bŏt′ə-mē) s. lobotomía.

lob·ster (lŏb′stər) s. langosta, bogavante.

lo·cal (lō′kəl) I. adj. local ♦ **l. call** TEL. llamada urbana • **l. government** gobierno municipal • **l. news** noticias de la ciudad II. s. tren *o* ómnibus local; *(chapter)* sección *f* local.

lo·cale (lō-kăl′) s. sitio, lugar *m.*

lo·cal·i·ty (:ĭ-tē) s. localidad *f.*

lo·cal·ize (lō′kə-līz′) tr. & intr. localizar(se).

lo·cate (lō′kāt′) tr. localizar; *(to place)* ubicar, colocar —intr. establecerse, asentarse.

lo·ca·tion (lō-kā′shən) s. lugar *m*, sitio; CINEM. exteriores <*to film on l.* rodar los exteriores>.

lock¹ (lŏk) I. s. *(device)* cerradura; *(of a canal)* esclusa; *(gunlock)* llave *f* ♦ **l., stock, and barrel** FAM. por completo, completamente • **under l. and key** bajo llave II. tr. cerrar con llave; *(to interlock)* trabar ♦ **to l. arms** tomarse del brazo • **to l. horns with** reñir con • **to l. out** *(the house)* cerrar la puerta a; *(employees)* dejar sin trabajo • **to l. up** *(to confine)* encerrar; *(to fasten)* cerrar con llave; *(in jail)* encarcelar —intr. cerrarse; *(to interlock)* trabarse; *(to jam)* agarrotarse; *(a firearm)* encasquillarse ♦ **to be locked out** estar fuera sin llave • **to l. up** echar la llave.

lock² s. *(of hair)* mecha ♦ pl. cabello.

lock·er (′ər) s. ropero, armario; *(trunk)* baúl *m*; *(refrigerator)* cámara frigorífica ♦ **l. room** vestuario (de un gimnasio, club).

lock·et (:ĭt) s. guardapelo, relicario.

lock·jaw (:jô′) s. trismo.

lock·smith (:smĭth′) s. cerrajero.

lock·up (:ŭp′) s. FAM. calabozo.

lo·co (lō′kō) adj. FAM. loco, chiflado.

lo·co·mo·tion (lō′kə-mō′shən) s. locomoción *f.*

lo·co·mo·tive (:tĭv) I. s. locomotora II. adj. locomotor, locomotivo.

lo·cus (lō′kəs) s. [pl. **-ci**] lugar *m*, localidad *f*;

GEOM. lugar geométrico.

lo·cust (lō′kəst) s. ENTOM. langosta, saltamontes *m*; *(cicada)* cigarra; BOT. acacia blanca.

lo·cu·tion (lō-kyōō′shən) s. locución *f.*

lode (lōd) s. veta, filón *m.*

lode·star (:stär′) s. estrella polar; FIG. guía *m.*

lode·stone (:stōn′) s. piedra imán.

lodge (lŏj) **I.** s. *(cabin)* casa de campo; *(inn)* posada; *(meeting hall)* logia **II.** tr. *(to house)* alojar, hospedar; *(to deposit)* depositar; *(to place)* colocar; *(to embed)* alojar, incrustar; *(complaint)* presentar, sentar; *(authority)* conferir —intr. alojarse.

lodg·er (′ər) s. inquilino.

lodg·ing (:ĭng) s. alojamiento.

loft (lôft) **I.** s. *(upper floor)* piso sin dividir; *(attic)* desván *m*; *(gallery)* galería; *(hayloft)* pajar *m* **II.** tr. lanzar (en alto).

loft·y (lôf′tē) adj. -i- alto, elevado; *(noble)* noble; *(arrogant)* arrogante, altanero.

log¹ (lôg) **I.** s. leño, tronco; MARÍT. diario de navegación; AVIA. diario de vuelo ♦ **l. cabin** cabaña de troncos ♦ **to sleep like a l.** dormir como un tronco **II.** tr. **-gg-** *(trees)* aserrar; AVIA., MARÍT. consignar en un diario de navegación *o* de vuelo ♦ **to l. miles** recorrer una distancia de millas —intr. cortar y transportar árboles.

log² s. MAT. logaritmo.

log·a·rithm (lô′gə-rĭth′ əm) s. logaritmo.

log·book (lôg′bŏŏk′) s. AVIA., MARÍT. diario de navegación *o* de vuelo.

loge (lōzh) s. TEAT. *(box)* palco; *(mezzanine)* primer balcón *m* de butacas.

log·ger·head (lô′gər-hĕd′) s. tortuga de mar ♦ **to be at loggerheads** estar en desacuerdo.

log·ic (lŏj′ĭk) s. lógica.

log·i·cal (-ĭ-kəl) adj. lógico.

lo·gi·cian (lō-jĭsh′ən) s. lógico, dialéctico.

lo·gis·tic/ti·cal (lō-jĭs′tĭk) adj. logístico ♦ **logistics** s.sg. *o* pl. logística.

log·jam (lôg′jăm′) s. atasco de troncos flotantes; FIG. *(deadlock)* atolladero.

loin (loin) s. ANAT. lomo; *(flank)* ijada, ijar *m*; CUL. *(of beef)* solomillo; *(of pork)* lomo ♦ pl. ANAT. ingle *f*; *(genitals)* órganos genitales.

loi·ter (loi′tər) intr. holgazanear; *(to delay)* retrasarse; *(to dawdle)* perder el tiempo.

loll (lŏl) intr. *(to slouch)* repantigarse; *(to droop)* pender.

lol·li·pop/ly·pop (lŏl′ē-pŏp′) s. pirulí *m.*

lone (lōn) adj. solo, solitario; *(sole)* único.

lone·li·ness (lōn′lē-nĭs) s. soledad *f.*

lone·ly (:lē) adj. -i- *(alone)* solo; *(isolated)* solitario.

lon·er (lō′nər) s. FAM. solitario.

lone·some (lōn′səm) adj. solo, solitario.

long¹ (lông) **I.** adj. largo; *(in distance)* de largo, de longitud ♦ **in the l. run** a la larga • **l. johns** FAM. calzón interior largo • **l. jump** salto de longitud • **l. shot** *(entry)* competidor con poca probabilidad de ganar; *(bet)* apuesta arriesgada • **l. suit** punto fuerte • **not by a l. shot** ni mucho menos • **to be l. on** tener mucho • **to take a l. time** tardar mucho **II.** adv. mucho tiempo ♦ **as l. as** *(while)* mientras; *(if)* si, siempre y cuando • **how l.?** *(time)* ¿cuánto tiempo?; *(length)* ¿qué largo? • **l. live the king!** ¡viva el rey! • **no longer** ya no, no más • **so l.!** FAM. ¡hasta luego!, ¡adiós! • **so l. as** con tal que, siempre que **III.** s. mucho tiempo ♦ **before l.** dentro de poco **for l.** mucho

tiempo • **the l. and the short of** la esencia de.

long² intr. ♦ **to l. for** añorar, desear con ansia • **to l. to** anhelar, desear ardientemente.

long·bow (′bō′) s. arco.

long-dis·tance (:dĭs′təns) adj. & adv. de larga distancia.

lon·gev·i·ty (lŏn-jĕv′ĭ-tē) s. longevidad *f.*

long·hair (lông′hâr′) s. FAM. bohemio.

long·haired (:hârd′) adj. pelilargo.

long·hand (:hănd′) s. letra cursiva.

long·ing (:ĭng) s. anhelo, deseo.

lon·gi·tude (lŏn′jĭ-tōōd′) s. longitud *f.*

long-lived (lông′līvd′, :lĭvd′) adj. de larga vida.

long-play·ing (:plā′ĭng) adj. de larga duración.

long-range (:rānj′) adj. de largo alcance.

long·shore·man (′shôr′mən) s. [pl. **-men**] estibador *m.*

long-stand·ing (:stăn′dĭng) adj. duradero.

long-suf·fer·ing (:sŭf′ər-ĭng) adj. resignado.

long-term (:tûrm′) adj. a largo plazo.

long-time (:tīm′) adj. antiguo, viejo.

long-wind·ed (:wĭn′dĭd) adj. verboso.

long·wise (:wīz′) adv. a lo largo, longitudinalmente.

look (lŏŏk) **I.** intr. mirar; *(to search)* buscar; *(to seem)* parecer; *(to face)* estar orientado hacia, dar a ♦ **l. alive!** ¡apresúrate! • **l. out!** ¡cuidado! • **to l. alike** parecerse • **to l. away** apartar la mirada • **to l. back** mirar hacia atrás; *(to remember)* recordar el pasado • **to l. down** bajar la mirada, bajar los ojos • **to l. up** levantar la mirada; FIG. ir mejorando, ponerse mejor —tr. mirar ♦ **to l. after** *(someone)* cuidar a, ocuparse de; *(something)* ocuparse de, encargarse de • **to l. around for** estar en busca de, buscar • **to l. back on** recordar • **to l. down on** despreciar • **to l. down one's nose at** FAM. menospreciar • **to l. for** buscar; *(to expect)* esperar • **to l. forward to** anticipar • **to l. in on** pasar por casa de • **to l. into** investigar • **to l. like** parecer(se) • **to l. (up)on** estimar, considerar • **to l. out for** *(to watch for)* estar al acecho de; *(to expect)* esperar; *(to take care of)* cuidar a • **to l. out on** dar a • **to l. over** examinar, repasar • **to l. (someone) up** ir a ver *o* visitar a alguien • **to l. (something) up** buscar • **to l. up to** respetar, tener en estima **II.** s. *(quick glance)* ojeada, vistazo; *(gaze)* mirada; *(aspect)* aspecto, apariencia; *(in fashion)* moda, estilo ♦ **by the l. of things** según parece • **to have a l.** at mirar, echar un vistazo a • **to take a good l.** at mirar bien ♦ pl. *(appearance)* aspecto; *(beauty)* belleza.

look-a·like (′ə-līk′) s. doble *mf.*

look·ing glass (:ĭng) s. espejo.

look·out (:out′) s. *(watch)* vigilancia; *(watchtower)* atalaya; *(vantage point)* mirador *m*; *(outlook)* perspectiva, panorama *m* ♦ **to be on the l. for** estar al acecho de.

loom¹ (lōōm) intr. *(to appear)* aparecer, surgir; *(to impend)* amenazar.

loom² s. telar *m.*

loon¹ (lōōn) s. ORNIT. somorgujo.

loon² s. *(simpleton)* bobo.

loon·y (lōō′nē) FAM. **I.** adj. -i- bobo ♦ **l. bin** manicomio **II.** s. loco, lunático.

loop (lōōp) **I.** s. lazo; *(coil)* vuelta; AVIA. rizo ♦ **to knock** *o* **throw for a l.** desconcertar **II.** tr. hacer un lazo en; *(to coil)* dar una vuelta a; *(to tie)* enlazar —intr. *(length of line)* hacer un lazo; *(to coil)* tener vueltas.

loop·hole (′hōl′) s. MIL. tronera, aspillera; FIG.

escapatoria, pretexto.
loose (lōōs) **I.** adj. *(unfastened)* suelto; *(slack)* flojo; *(not tight)* holgado; *(not compact)* poco compacto; *(vague)* vago, indefinido; *(idle)* irresponsable; *(promiscuous)* ligero, liviano; *(not literal)* libre; *(not packaged)* a granel ♦ **I. end** *(rope)* cabo suelto; FIG. asunto pendiente • **to be at I. ends** FIG. no saber qué hacer • **to tie up I. ends** FIG. atar cabos **II.** adv. ♦ **to come I.** aflojarse, desatarse • **to hang I.** JER. quedarse calmo • **to turn I.** soltar, libertar **III.** tr. soltar, poner en libertad; *(a volley)* disparar —intr. soltarse **IV.** s. ♦ **on the I.** FAM. suelto, en libertad.
loose-leaf ('lēf') adj. de hojas sueltas.
loose·ly (:ē) adv. sueltamente; *(vaguely)* vagamente; *(freely)* libremente.
loos·en (lōō'sən) tr. aflojar; *(to untie)* desatar ♦ **to I. someone's tongue** hacer soltar la lengua a alguien • **to I. up on someone** ser menos riguroso con alguien —intr. aflojarse.
loot (lōōt) **I.** s. botín m, presa; JER. *(money)* dinero **II.** tr. *(to pillage)* pillar, saquear; *(to take as booty)* llevar como botín —intr. entregarse al saqueo.
loot·er (lōō'tər) s. saqueador m.
loot·ing (:tĭng) s. saqueo.
lop (lŏp) tr. **-pp-** *(to trim)* podar; *(to eliminate)* eliminar.
lope (lōp) **I.** intr. correr a paso largo **II.** s. paso largo.
lop·sid·ed (lŏp'sī'dĭd) adj. desproporcionado; *(leaning)* inclinado, ladeado.
lo·qua·cious (lō-kwā'shəs) adj. locuaz.
lo·quac·i·ty (lō-kwăs'ĭ-tē) s. locuacidad f.
lord (lôrd) **I.** s. señor m ♦ **I. and master** dueño y señor • **I. of the manor** señor feudal **II.** intr. ♦ **to I. it over** dominar.
lord·ship ('shĭp') s. *(title)* señoría; *(authority)* señorío.
lore (lôr) s. *(tradition)* tradición f; *(belief)* creencia popular; *(knowledge)* ciencia, saber m.
lor·gnette (lôrn-yĕt') s. impertinentes m.
lor·ry (lôr'ē) s. G.B. camión m.
lose (lōōz) tr. **lost** perder; *(to cost)* costar, hacer perder <*his arrogance lost him his job* su arrogancia le costó el empleo>; *(clock)* atrasar ♦ **to I. oneself** in perderse en —intr. perder ♦ **to I. out** perder, salir perdiendo.
los·er (lōō'zər) s. perdedor m; *(one that fails)* fracasado; *(lost cause)* causa perdida ♦ **to be a good I.** saber perder.
loss (lôs) s. *(defeat)* derrota; *(game)* juego perdido; *(destruction)* estrago, daño ♦ **to be at a I.** *(to be puzzled)* no saber qué hacer; *(for words)* no encontrar palabras con qué expresarse ♦ pl. MIL. bajas; COM. pérdidas • **to cut one's I.** cortar por lo sano.
lost (lôst) **I.** cf. **lose II.** adj. perdido; *(engrossed)* absorto ♦ **get I.!** JER. ¡vete al demonio! • **I. and found** oficina de objetos perdidos • **to get I.** perderse.
lot (lŏt) s. *(drawing)* sorteo; *(share)* parte f, porción f; *(fate)* suerte f, sino; *(people)* grupo de personas; *(articles for sale)* lote m, partida; *(large amount)* gran cantidad, mucho; *(land)* solar m, lote; CINEM. estudio ♦ **by I.** por sorteo • **lots of** cantidades de, mucho • **to draw lots** echar suertes • **to improve one's I.** mejorar la suerte • **to throw in one's I. with** compartir la suerte de.
lo·tion (lō'shən) s. loción f.

lot·ter·y (lŏt'ə-rē) s. lotería.
lo·tus (lō'təs) s. loto m.
loud (loud) **I.** adj. alto, fuerte; *(noisy)* ruidoso, bullicioso; *(gaudy)* chillón, llamativo; *(loud-mouthed)* gritón ♦ **in a I. voice** en voz alta, a gritos **II.** adv. *(to sound, yell, sing)* fuerte ♦ **out I.** en voz alta.
loud·mouth ('mouth') FAM. s. gritón m.
loud·ness (:nĭs) s. volumen m, fuerza.
loud·speak·er (:spē'kər) s. altavoz m, altoparlante m.
lounge (lounj) **I.** intr. repantigarse **II.** s. *(waiting room)* sala de espera; *(bar)* cantina; *(couch)* sofá m ♦ **I. chair** tumbona.
lour (lou'ər) var. de **lower[1]**.
louse (lous) **I.** s. ENTOM. [pl. **lice**] piojo; JER. [pl. **es**] canalla mf, sinvergüenza mf **II.** tr. ♦ **to I. up on** *(to)* estropear, echar a perder —intr. ♦ **to I. up** hacer una pifia.
lous·y (lou'zē) adj. **-i-** piojoso, lleno de piojos; *(unpleasant)* vil, malísimo; *(worthless)* pésimo.
lout (lout) s. patán m, bruto.
lou·ver/vre (lōō'vər) s. *(blind)* persiana; *(slat)* tablilla.
lov·a·ble (lŭv'ə-bəl) adj. adorable; *(endearing)* cautivador.
love (lŭv) **I.** s. amor m, cariño; *(lover)* amor; DEP. cero (en tenis) ♦ **I. o with I.** *(affectionately)* un cariñoso saludo; *(cordially)* un cordial saludo (al terminar una carta) • **I. affair** *(romance)* amorío; *(enthusiasm)* gran entusiasmo • **I. po·tion** filtro amoroso • **I. seat** confidente • **in I.** enamorado • **to fall in I.** enamorarse • **to make I.** hacer el amor **II.** tr. amar, querer; *(to enjoy)* gustarle a uno, encantar ♦ **I'd I. to!** ¡con mucho gusto! —intr. amar, querer.
love·bird ('bûrd') s. periquito.
love·less (:lĭs) adj. sin amor.
love·li·ness (:lē-nĭs) s. belleza, hermosura.
love·lorn (:lôrn') adj. herido de amor.
love·ly (:lē) adj. **-i-** hermoso, bello; *(nice)* encantador.
love·mak·ing (:mā'kĭng) s. *(sexual)* relaciones f sexuales; *(courtship)* galanteo.
lov·er (:ər) s. amante mf, querido; *(devotee)* aficionado.
love·sick (:sĭk') adj. enfermo de amor.
lov·ing (:ĭng) adj. amoroso, cariñoso ♦ **I. cup** *(wine vessel)* copo de la amistad; *(prize)* trofeo, copa.
low[1] (lō) **I.** adj. bajo; *(in quality)* inferior; *(humble)* plebeyo, humilde; *(mean)* vil, malo; *(unfavorable)* desfavorable, malo; *(coarse)* vulgar, grosero ♦ **in I. spirits** abatido, deprimido • **I. relief** bajo relieve • **I. tide** bajamar • **to be I. on** estar escaso de • **to keep a I. profile** comportarse reservadamente • **to lie I.** FAM. esconderse temporalmente **II.** adv. bajo **III.** s. punto más bajo; METEOR. depresión f; AUTO. primera.
low[2] (lō) **I.** s. mugido **II.** intr. mugir.
low·brow (lō'brou') s. ignorante mf, persona inculta.
low-cost (lō'kôst') adj. barato, de bajo costo.
low-cut (lō'kŭt') adj. muy escotado (vestido).
low·down (lō'doun') s. JER. la pura verdad.
low·er[1] (lou'ər) intr. *(to scowl)* fruncir el ceño; *(to cloud over)* nublarse, encapotarse.
low·er[2] (lō'ər) **I.** adj. más bajo, inferior ♦ **I. case** IMPR. minúsculas **II.** tr. & intr. bajar; *(to diminish)* disminuir, reducir.
low·er-case ('-kās') adj. minúscula.
low-grade (lō'grād') adj. de calidad inferior.

low·ing (lō′ĭng) s. mugido.
low-key(ed) (lō′kē[d]′) adj. de baja intensidad.
low·land (lō′lənd) s. tierra baja.
low-lev·el (lō′lĕv′əl) adj. de bajo nivel; *(rank)* de grado inferior, subalterno.
low-life (lō′līf′) s. plebeyo; *(despicable person)* persona ruin, perverso.
low·ly (lō′lē) adj. **-i-** bajo, inferior; *(humble)* humilde; *(prosaic)* prosaico, ordinario.
low·ness (lō′nĭs) s. *(shortness)* falta de altura; *(meanness)* bajeza, vileza.
low-pitched (lō′pĭcht′) adj. *(voice)* grave, bajo; *(roof)* poco inclinado; *(room)* de techo bajo.
low-pres·sure (lō′prĕsh′ər) adj. de baja presión; *(person)* relajado.
low-priced (lō′prīst′) adj. de bajo precio.
low-ten·sion (lō′tĕn′shən) adj. de baja tensión.
lox¹ (lŏks) s. CUL. salmón ahumado.
lox² (lŏks) s. FÍS. oxígeno líquido.
loy·al (loi′əl) adj. leal.
loy·al·ist (:ə-lĭst) s. gubernamental *mf.*
loy·al·ty (:əl-tē) s. lealtad *f.*
loz·enge (lŏz′ənj) s. GEOM. rombo; *(cough drop)* pastilla, tableta.
lu·bri·cant (lōō′brĭ-kənt) s. lubricante *m.*
lu·bri·cate (:kāt′) tr. lubricar.
lu·bri·cious (lōō-brĭsh′əs) adj. lúbrico.
lu·cent (lōō′sənt) adj. luminoso.
lu·cid (lōō′sĭd) adj. lúcido, claro; *(sane)* cuerdo; *(translucent)* translúcido.
lu·cid·i·ty (-′ĭ-tē) s. *(clarity)* lucidez *f*, claridad *f*; *(brilliance)* brillantez *f*, transparencia.
luck (lŭk) I. s. fortuna, suerte *f* ♦ **for l.** para que traiga buena suerte • **good l.!** ¡buena suerte! • **no such l.!** ¡ojalá! • **to be in l.** estar de suerte • **to be out of l.** no tener suerte • **to push one's l.** FAM. arriesgarse innecesariamente • **to try one's l.** probar suerte II. intr. ♦ **to l. out** FAM. tener suerte.
luck·less (′lĭs) adj. desafortunado.
luck·y (:ē) adj. **-i-** afortunado; *(fortuitous)* fortuito, oportuno; *(bringing good luck)* que trae suerte ♦ **l. break** coyuntura favorable • **thank your l. stars!** ¡bendice tu buena estrella!
lu·cra·tive (lōō′krə-tĭv) adj. lucrativo.
lu·cre (:kər) s. lucro, ganancia.
lu·di·crous (lōō′dĭ-krəs) adj. absurdo, ridículo.
luff (lŭf) I. s. orza II. intr. orzar.
lug¹ (lŭg) s. MEC. *(handle)* agarradera, asa; *(nut)* orejera; *(blockhead)* mentecato.
lug² tr. & intr. **-gg-** arrastrar, halar.
lug·gage (lŭg′ĭj) s. equipaje *m.*
lu·gu·bri·ous (lōō-gōō′brē-əs) adj. lúgubre.
luke·warm (lōōk′wôrm′) adj. tibio.
lull (lŭl) I. tr. *(to soothe)* calmar, sosegar; *(to deceive)* embaucar II. s. momento de calma, cese *m* temporal; *(pause)* pausa.
lull·a·by (′ə-bī′) s. canción *f* de cuna, nana.
lum·bar (lŭm′bər) adj. & s. *(parte f)* lumbar.
lum·ber¹ (lŭm′bər) I. s. maderos; *(plank)* tabla; G.B. *(junk)* trastos viejos II. tr. *(to fell timber)* talar; *(to cut wood)* cortar madera.
lum·ber² intr. avanzar pesadamente.
lum·ber·ing (:ĭng) I. adj. *(movement)* pesado, torpe; *(person)* que anda pesadamente *o* ruidosamente II. s., industria maderera.
lum·ber·jack (:jăk′) s. leñador *m.*
lum·ber·yard (:yärd′) s. almacén *m o* depósito de madera.
lu·mi·nance (lōō′mə-nəns) s. luminancia.
lu·mi·nar·y (:nĕr′ē) s. luminar *m.*
lu·mi·nes·cence (′-nĕs′əns) s. luminiscencia.

lu·mi·nes·cent (:nĕs′ənt) adj. luminiscente.
lu·mi·nos·i·ty (:nŏs′ĭ-tē) s. luminosidad *f.*
lu·mi·nous (′-nəs) adj. luminoso; *(illuminated)* iluminado; *(lucid)* lúcido, claro.
lum·mox (lŭm′əks) s. FAM. porro, necio.
lump¹ (lŭmp) I. s. montón *m*, masa; *(of soil, sugar)* terrón *m*; *(glob)* grumo; *(piece)* pedazo, trozo; *(totality)* conjunto; *(dolt)* alcornoque *m*; MED. bulto; *(on the head)* chichón *m* ♦ **to have a l. in one's throat** tener un nudo en la garganta • **to take one's lumps** aguantar II. tr. *(to amass)* amontonar; *(to make into a mass)* apelotonar ♦ **to l. together** juntar.
lump² tr. FAM. soportar, tolerar.
lump·y (lŭm′pē) adj. **-i-** aterronado; *(liquid)* grumoso.
lu·na·cy (lōō′nə-sē) s. locura *f*; *(act)* desatino.
lu·nar (:nər) adj. lunar, de la luna.
lu·na·tic (:nə-tĭk) I. adj. loco; *(for the insane)* de *o* para locos; *(foolish)* disparatado, descabellado II. s. lunático.
lunch (lŭnch) I. s. almuerzo II. intr. almorzar ♦ **out to l.** FAM. chiflado • **to have** *o* **to eat l.** almorzar, comer.
lunch·eon (lŭn′chən) s. almuerzo.
lunch·eon·ette (′chə-nĕt′) s. restaurante pequeño, cafetería.
lunch·room (lŭnch′rōōm′) s. restaurante pequeño.
lunch·time (:tīm′) s. hora de comer.
lung (lŭng) s. pulmón *m.*
lunge (lŭnj) I. s. arremetida, embestida; *(in fencing)* estocada II. intr. lanzarse, arrojarse; *(in fencing)* dar una estocada ♦ **to l. at** arremeter contra.
lu·pine (lōō′pīn) s. lupino.
lurch¹ (lûrch) I. intr. tambalearse, hacer eses; *(of a ship)* guiñar, dar guiñadas II. s. tambaleo, bamboleo; *(of a ship)* guiñada, bandazo.
lurch² s. ♦ **to leave someone in the l.** dejar a alguien plantado *o* en la estacada.
lure (lōōr) I. s. tentación *f*; *(appeal)* atracción *f*; *(bait)* cebo, carnada II. tr. tentar, seducir.
lu·rid (lōōr′ĭd) adj. *(gruesome)* horrible, espeluznante; *(sensational)* sensacional, chocante; *(glowing)* resplandeciente.
lurk (lûrk) intr. estar al acecho; *(to sneak)* andar a hurtadillas, moverse furtivamente.
lus·cious (lŭsh′əs) adj. suculento, exquisito.
lush¹ (lŭsh) adj. *(thick)* lujuriante, exuberante; *(plentiful)* abundante; *(luxurious)* suntuoso.
lush² s. JER. borrachín *m*, borracho.
lust (lŭst) I. s. lujuria, lascivia; *(overwhelming desire)* ansia, anhelo II. intr. ♦ **to l. after** *(something)* codiciar; *(someone)* desear.
lus·ter (lŭs′tər) s. lustre *m.*
lus·ter·less (′lĭs) adj. deslustrado.
lust·ful (lŭst′fəl) adj. lujurioso, lascivo.
lus·trous (lŭs′trəs) adj. lustroso, brillante.
lust·y (lŭs′tē) adj. **-i-** fuerte.
lute¹ (lōōt) s. MÚS. laúd *m.*
lute² s. TEC. zulaque *m*, luten *m.*
lux·u·ri·ant (lŭg-zhŏŏr′ē-ənt) adj. lujuriante.
lux·u·ri·ate (:āt′) intr. crecer con exuberancia ♦ **to l. in** deleitarse con.
lux·u·ri·ous (:əs) adj. lujoso; *(lush)* suntuoso.
lux·u·ry (lŭg′zhə-rē, lŭk′shə-) s. lujo; *(frill)* cosa superflua ♦ **to live in l.** vivir espléndidamente.
ly·ce·um (lī-sē′əm) s. *(hall)* auditorio, sala de conferencias; *(organization)* ateneo.
lye (lī) s. lejía.

ly·ing¹ (lī'ĭng) I. cf. **lie¹** II. adj. *(reclining)* tendido, acostado; *(located)* situado.
ly·ing² (lī'ĭng) I. cf. **lie²** II. adj. mentiroso III. s. mentira; *(lies)* mentiras.
ly·ing-in (lī'ĭng-ĭn') s. parto.
lymph (lĭmf) s. linfa.
lym·phat·ic (lĭm-făt'ĭk) adj. linfático.
lym·pho·cyte ('fə-sīt') s. linfocito.
lym·pho·ma (-fō'mə) s. [pl. **s** o **-mata**] linfoma *m.*
lynch (lĭnch) tr. linchar.
lynx (lĭngks) s. lince *m.*
lyre (līr) s. lira.
lyr·ic (lĭr'ĭk) I. adj. lírico II. s. *(poem)* poema lírico; *(genre)* lírica; *(poet)* lírico ♦ pl. MÚS. letra (de una canción).
lyr·i·cal (:ĭ-kəl) adj. lírico.
lyr·i·cist (:sĭst) s. autor *m* de la letra de una canción.

M

m, M (ĕm) s. decimotercera letra del alfabeto inglés.
ma (mä) s. FAM. mamá.
ma·ca·bre (mə-kä'brə) adj. macabro.
mac·a·ro·ni (măk'ə-rō'nē) s.pl. macarrones *m.*
mac·a·roon (măk'ə-rōōn') s. mostachón *m.*
ma·caw (mə-kô') s. guacamayo.
mace¹ (mās) s. maza; *(staff)* maza ceremonial.
mace² s. *(spice)* macia, macís *f.*
mac·er·ate (măs'ə-rāt') tr. & intr. macerar(se).
ma·chet·e (mə-shĕt'ē) s. machete *m.*
mach·i·nate (măk'ə-nāt', măsh'-) tr. & intr. maquinar.
mach·i·na·tion ('-nā'shən) s. maquinación *f.*
ma·chine (mə-shēn') I. s. máquina; *(device)* mecanismo; *(person)* autómata *mf*; *(political)* maquinaria ♦ **m. gun** ametralladora ♦ **m. shop** taller de maquinaria ♦ **slot m.** tragaperras ♦ **washing m.** lavadora II. tr. labrar a máquina.
ma·chine-gun (:gŭn') tr. **-nn-** ametrallar.
ma·chin·er·y (mə-shē'nə-rē) s. maquinaria; *(working parts)* mecanismo.
ma·chin·ist (:nĭst) s. maquinista *mf.*
mack·er·el (măk'ə-rəl) s. [pl. inv. o **s**] caballa.
mack·i·naw (măk'ə-nô') s. chamarra de lana.
mac(k)·in·tosh (măk'ĭn-tŏsh') s. G.B. impermeable *m.*
mac·ra·mé (măk'rə-mā') s. macramé *m.*
mac·ro·bi·ot·ics (măk'rō-bī-ŏt'ĭks) s.sg. macrobiótica.
mac·ro·code (măk'rə-kōd') s. macrocódigo.
mac·ro·cosm (:kŏz'əm) s. macrocosmo.
mac·ro·scop·ic ('-skŏp'ĭk) adj. macroscópico.
mad (măd) adj. **-dd-** loco; FAM. enojado; *(senseless)* insensato; *(frantic)* frenético; *(dog)* rabioso ♦ **like m.** como un loco ♦ **m. as a hatter** *o* **March hare** más loco que una cabra ♦ **raving m.** loco de atar ♦ **to be mad about** estar loco por; *(angry)* estar enfadado por ♦ **to be m. at** estar enojado con ♦ **to drive someone m.** volver loco a alguien ♦ **to get m.** enfadarse ♦ **to make someone m.** hacer que alguien se enoje.
Mad·am (măd'əm) s. [pl. **Mesdames**] señora ♦ **m.** [pl. **s**] señora; *(of brothel)* patrona.
mad·cap (măd'kăp') I. s. tarambana *mf* II. adj. alocado, atolondrado.
mad·den (măd'n) tr. enloquecer; *(to make angry)* enfurecer —intr. enfurecerse.

mad·den·ing (:ĭng) adj. enloquecedor; *(irritating)* exasperante.
made (mād) I. cf. **make** II. adj. hecho ♦ **to have it m.** tener éxito.
made-to-or·der ('tōō-ôr'dər) adj. hecho a la medida.
made-up ('ŭp') adj. inventado; *(with make-up)* maquillado.
mad·house (măd'hous') s. manicomio; FIG. casa de locos.
mad·man (:măn') s. [pl. **-men**] demente *m.*
mad·ness (:nĭs) s. locura; *(fury)* rabia.
Ma·don·na (mə-dŏn'ə) s. Madona.
mad·wom·an (măd'wŏm'ən) s. [pl. **-women**] demente *f.*
mael·strom (māl'strəm) s. remolino; FIG. torbellino.
mag·a·zine (măg'ə-zēn') s. revista; *(for ammunition)* polvorín *m*; *(of gun)* peine *m* (de balas); FOTOG. depósito (de la película).
ma·gen·ta (mə-jĕn'tə) s. rojo purpúreo.
mag·got (măg'ət) s. gusano.
ma·gi (mā'jī') cf. **magus.**
mag·ic (măj'ĭk) I. s. magia; FIG. encanto II. adj. mágico.
mag·i·cal (:ĭ-kəl) adj. mágico.
ma·gi·cian (mə-jĭsh'ən) s. mago.
mag·is·te·ri·al (măj'ĭ-stîr'ē-əl) adj. magistral; *(authoritarian)* autoritario; *(of a magistrate)* de magistrado.
mag·is·tra·cy ('-strə-sē) s. magistratura; *(district)* jurisdicción *f* de magistrado.
mag·is·trate (:strāt') s. magistrado.
mag·nan·i·mous (măg-năn'ə-məs) adj. magnánimo.
mag·nate (măg'nāt', :nĭt) s. magnate *m.*
mag·ne·si·um (măg-nē'zē-əm) s. magnesio.
mag·net (măg'nĭt) s. FIS. imán *m*; *(something attractive)* persona *o* cosa atractiva.
mag·net·ic (-nĕt'ĭk) adj. magnético.
mag·net·ism (măg'nĭ-tĭz'əm) s. magnetismo.
mag·net·ize (:nī-tīz') tr. magnetizar, imantar.
mag·ni·fi·ca·tion (măg'nə-fĭ-kā'shən) s. ampliación *f*; ÓPT. aumento.
mag·nif·i·cence (măg-nĭf'ĭ-səns) s. magnificencia.
mag·nif·i·cent (:sənt) adj. magnífico.
mag·ni·fi·er (măg'nə-fī'ər) s. lupa; ÓPT. sistema *m* amplificador.
mag·ni·fy (:fī') tr. aumentar; *(to exaggerate)* exagerar; *(to praise)* glorificar ♦ **magnifying glass** lente de aumento.
mag·ni·tude (măg'nĭ-tōōd') s. magnitud *f.*
mag·num (măg'nəm) s. magnum *m* ♦ **m. opus** obra maestra.
mag·pie (măg'pī') s. urraca.
ma·gus (mā'gəs) s. [pl. **-gi**] mago ♦ **the Magi** los Reyes Magos.
ma·hog·a·ny (mə-hŏg'ə-nē) s. caoba.
maid (mād) s. criada; *(unwed girl)* soltera; *(virgin)* doncella ♦ **m. of honor** dama de honor.
maid·en ('n) I. s. doncella II. adj. virginal; *(unmarried)* soltera; *(virgin)* virgen; *(first)* primero ♦ **m. name** apellido de soltera.
maid·en·head (:hĕd') s. virginidad *f*; ANAT. himen *m.*
maid·en·hood (:hōōd') s. doncellez *f.*
maid·ser·vant (măd'sûr'vənt) s. sirvienta.
mail¹ (māl) I. s. correo ♦ **air m.** via aérea ♦ **by return m.** a vuelta de correo II. tr. enviar por correo; *(to post)* echar al correo III. adj. postal.

mail² s. (cota de) malla.
mail·box (māl'bŏks') s. buzón *m*.
mail·ing (mā'lĭng) s. envío.
mail·man (māl'măn') s. [pl. **-men**] cartero.
maim (mām) tr. lisiar; FIG. estropear.
main (mān) I. adj. principal; *(office)* central; *(valve)* maestro; MARÍT. mayor ♦ **the m. thing** lo principal *o* esencial II. s. tubería *o* cable *m* principal; *(might)* fuerzas ♦ **in the m.** principalmente.
main·frame ('frām') s. elaborador *m* central.
main·land (:lănd') s. tierra firme.
main·sail (:səl) s. vela mayor.
main·spring (:sprĭng') s. MEC. muelle *m* real; FIG. causa principal, fuerza motriz.
main·stay (:stā') s. MARÍT. estay *m* mayor; FIG. soporte *m* principal.
main·stream (:strēm') s. corriente *f* principal.
main·tain (mān-tān') tr. mantener; *(silence)* guardar; *(to preserve)* conservar; *(to repair)* cuidar ♦ **to m. one's composure** mantenerse sereno ♦ **to m. one's ground** mantenerse firme.
main·te·nance ('tə-nəns) s. mantenimiento; *(upkeep)* cuidado, conservación *f* ♦ **m. staff** personal de servicio.
maize (māz) s. maíz *m*.
ma·jes·tic (mə-jĕs'tĭk) adj. majestuoso.
maj·es·ty (măj'ĭ-stē) s. majestad *f*; *(splendor)* majestuosidad *f*.
ma·jor (mā'jər) I. adj. mayor; *(chief)* principal; *(extensive)* amplio; *(serious)* grave II. s. MIL. comandante *m*; EDUC. especialidad *f* III. intr. ♦ **to m. in** EDUC. especializarse en.
ma·jor·do·mo ('-dō'mō) s. mayordomo.
ma·jor·i·ty (mə-jôr'ĭ-tē) s. mayoría, mayor parte *f* ♦ **to be in a m.** constituir la mayoría.
ma·jor-league (mā'jər-lēg') adj. FAM. importante, principal.
make (māk) I. tr. **made** hacer; *(to build)* construir; *(to manufacture)* fabricar; *(decision)* tomar; *(payment)* efectuar; *(a speech)* pronunciar; *(agreement)* concertar; *(excuses)* presentar; *(goal)* marcar; FAM. *(train)* alcanzar; *(to appoint)* nombrar; *(problems)* causar; *(food)* preparar; *(to establish)* establecer como; *(to attain)* llegar a; *(team)* entrar en; *(to earn)* ganar; *(money)* producir; *(to compel)* obligar a; *(to be good for)* servir para hacer; *(to become)* ser; *(to think of)* pensar; *(to add up to)* equivaler a; *(to count as)* ser; JER. seducir ♦ **to m. a mistake** cometer un error • **to m. a move** *(to move)* moverse; *(to act)* obrar • **to m. an appointment** citar • **to m. a point** hacer una observación • **to m. clear** poner en claro • **to m. easy** facilitar • **to m. for** ir hacia; *(problems)* crear • **to m. into** convertir en • **to m. it** tener éxito • **to m. out** *(check)* hacer; *(to comprehend)* entender; *(to perceive)* divisar • **to m. ready** preparar • **to m. up** preparar; *(to assemble)* confeccionar; *(story)* inventar; *(to compensate)* recobrar; *(to constitute)* integrar • **to m. worse** empeorar —intr. ♦ **to m. for** contribuir a, servir para • **to m. off** huir • **to m. out** salir (bien, mal); *(to embrace)* abrazar(se) • **to m. up** hacer las paces II. s. fabricación *f*; *(in clothes)* confección *f*; *(style)* corte *m*; *(brand)* marca ♦ **to be on the m.** buscar su propio provecho; JER. *(seduction)* tener intención de seducir.
make-be·lieve ('bĭ-lēv') I. s. fingimiento, simulación *f* II. adj. fingido, simulado.
mak·er (mā'kər) s. fabricante *m* ♦ **M.** Hacedor.

make·shift (māk'shĭft') I. s. reemplazo provisional II. adj. improvisado, temporal.
make-up *o* **make·up** (:ŭp') s. construcción *f*, composición *f*; *(temperament)* carácter *m*; *(cosmetics)* maquillaje *m*.
mak·ing (mā'kĭng) s. creación *f*; *(manufacture)* fabricación *f*; *(of a meal)* preparación *f*; *(of a will)* redacción *f* ♦ **in the m.** *(plans)* en preparación; *(country)* en desarrollo; *(history)* en marcha • **to be of one's own m.** ser obra propia • **to have the makings of** tener los elementos necesarios para llegar a ser.
mal·ad·just·ed (măl'ə-jŭs'tĭd) adj. inadaptado.
mal·a·droit (măl'ə-droit') adj. desmañado.
mal·a·dy (măl'ə-dē) s. dolencia.
mal·aise (mă-lāz') s. malestar *m*.
mal·a·prop·ism (măl'ə-prŏp'ĭz'əm) s. uso cómicamente incorrecto de una palabra.
ma·lar·i·a (mə-lâr'ē-ə) s. malaria, paludismo.
ma·lar·k(e)y (mə-lär'kē) s. JER. charlatanería.
mal·con·tent (măl'kən-tĕnt') I. adj. malcontento II. s. ('-') malcontento.
male (māl) I. adj. varón *m*; *(masculine)* masculino; *(manly)* varonil; *(for men)* de hombres; *(school)* de varones; BIOL., MEC. macho II. s. varón *m*; BIOL. macho.
mal·e·dic·tion (măl'ĭ-dĭk'shən) s. maldición *f*.
mal·e·fac·tor (măl'ə-făk'tər) s. malhechor *m*.
ma·lef·ic (mə-lĕf'ĭk) adj. maléfico.
ma·lev·o·lence (mə-lĕv'ə-ləns) s. malevolencia.
ma·lev·o·lent (:lənt) adj. malévolo.
mal·fea·sance (măl-fē'zəns) s. DER. mala conducta (esp. de un empleado público).
mal·formed (măl-fôrmd') adj. mal formado.
mal·func·tion (:fŭngk'shən) I. intr. funcionar mal II. s. funcionamiento defectuoso.
mal·ice (măl'ĭs) s. malicia; DER. intención maliciosa.
ma·li·cious (mə-lĭsh'əs) adj. malicioso; DER. premeditado, delictuoso.
ma·lign (mə-līn') I. tr. difamar II. adj. maligno.
ma·lig·nan·cy (mə-lĭg'nən-sē) s. malignidad *f*.
ma·lig·nant (:nənt) adj. maligno; *(harmful)* pernicioso.
ma·lin·ger (mə-lĭng'gər) intr. fingirse enfermo.
mall (môl) s. alameda; *(for shopping)* galería.
mal·lard (măl'ərd) s. [pl. inv. *o* **s**] pato silvestre.
mal·le·a·ble (măl'ē-ə-bəl) adj. maleable.
mal·let (măl'ĭt) s. mazo; DEP. mallo.
mal·nour·ished (măl-nûr'ĭsht) adj. desnutrido.
mal·nu·tri·tion ('nōō-trĭsh'ən) s. desnutrición *f*.
mal·prac·tice (-prăk'tĭs) s. MED. tratamiento erróneo; *(misconduct)* conducta inmoral.
malt (môlt) s. malta; *(beer)* cerveza de malta.
mal·treat (măl-trēt') tr. maltratar.
mal·treat·ment (:mənt) s. maltratamiento.
ma(m)·ma (mä'mə) s. mamá, mama.
mam·ma·li·an (mə-mā'lē-ən) adj. mamífero.
mam·ma·ry (măm'ə-rē) adj. mamario.
mam·moth (măm'əth) I. s. mamut *m* II. adj. enorme, gigantesco.
man (măn) I. s. [pl. **men**] hombre *m*; *(male)* varón *m*; *(mankind)* el hombre; *(servant)* sirviente *m*; *(in chess)* pieza ♦ **m. about town** hombre de mundo • **m. and wife** marido y mujer • **m. of his word** hombre de palabra • **men's room** servicio *o* baño para caballeros • **no man's land** tierra de nadie • **the M.** JER. la policía • **to a m.** hasta el último • **to be one's**

own m. ser un hombre independiente ♦ pl. *(workers)* obreros; *(servicemen)* soldados **II.** tr. **-nn-** *(vessel)* tripular; *(station)* manejar **III.** interj. ¡hombre!

man·a·cle (măn′ə-kəl) **I.** s. manilla ♦ pl. esposas; FIG. restricción **II.** tr. esposar; FIG. restringir.

man·age (măn′ĭj) tr. controlar; *(business)* dirigir; *(property)* administrar; *(to handle)* poder con —intr. arreglárselas.

man·age·a·ble (:ĭ-jə-bəl) adj. manejable; *(tame)* dócil; *(task)* realizable ♦ **of m. size** manuable.

man·age·ment (:ĭj-mənt) s. gerencia; *(directors)* gerentes *mf*; *(skill)* habilidad directiva.

man·ag·er (:ĭ-jər) s. gerente *mf*; *(agent)* apoderado.

man·a·ge·ri·al (′ə-jîr′ē-əl) adj. directivo, ejecutivo.

man-at-arms (măn′ət-ärmz′) s. [pl. **men-**] soldado (esp. de caballería).

man·da·rin (măn′də-rĭn) **I.** s. mandarín *m* **II.** adj. ♦ **m. orange** mandarina.

man·date (măn′dāt′) **I.** s. mandato; *(territory)* territorio bajo mandato **II.** tr. ordenar.

man·da·to·ry (:də-tôr′ē) adj. obligatorio; *(holding a mandate)* mandante.

man·do·lin (măn′dl-ĭn′) s. mandolina.

mane (măn) s. *(of horse)* crin *f*; *(of lion)* melena.

man-eat·er (măn′ē′tər) s. animal *m* que come carne humana; *(cannibal)* caníbal *mf*.

ma·neu·ver (mə-nō̄o′vər) **I.** s. maniobra **II.** intr. maniobrar; *(to manipulate)* manipular.

ma·neu·ver·a·ble (:ə-bəl) s. maniobrable.

man·ful (măn′fəl) adj. varonil, masculino.

man·ga·nese (măng′gə-nēz′) s. manganeso.

mange (mānj) s. sarna.

man·ger (măn′jər) s. pesebre *m*.

man·gle[1] (măng′gəl) tr. mutilar.

man·gle[2] s. planchadora a rodillo.

man·go (măng′gō) s. [pl. **(e)s**] mango.

man·grove (măng′grōv′) s. mangle *m*.

mang·y (măn′jē) adj. **-i-** sarnoso; FAM. *(shabby)* sucio.

man·han·dle (măn′hăn′dl) tr. tratar duramente.

man·hole (măn′hōl′) s. boca de acceso.

man·hood (:hŏŏd′) s. madurez *f*; *(manliness)* hombría; *(men)* hombres *m* ♦ **to grow to m.** hacerse hombre.

man·hunt (:hŭnt′) s. búsqueda de un criminal.

ma·ni·a (mā′nē-ə) s. manía.

ma·ni·ac (mā′nē-ăk′) s. & adj. maníaco.

ma·ni·a·cal (mə-nī′ə-kəl) adj. maníaco, maniaco; FIG. loco.

man·ic (măn′ĭk) adj. maníaco, maniaco.

man·ic-de·pres·sive (′-dĭ-prĕs′ĭv) s. maníacodepresivo, maníacodepresivo.

man·i·cure (măn′ĭ-kyŏŏr′) **I.** s. manicura **II.** tr. hacer la manicura a; *(to trim)* recortar.

man·i·cur·ist (:ĭst) s. manicuro.

man·i·fest (măn′ə-fĕst′) **I.** adj. manifiesto **II.** tr. manifestar **III.** s. *(cargo)* manifiesto; *(passengers)* relación *f* de pasajeros.

man·i·fes·ta·tion (′-fĕ-stā′shən) s. manifestación *f*.

man·i·fes·to (:fĕs′tō) s. [pl. **(e)s**] manifiesto.

man·i·fold (măn′ə-fōld′) **I.** adj. diverso; *(of many parts)* variado **II.** s. AUTO. colector *m* de escape **III.** tr. multiplicar, diversificar.

ma·ni·kin (măn′ĭ-kĭn) s. enano; *(model)*

maniquí *m*.

ma·nip·u·late (mə-nĭp′yə-lāt′) tr. manipular.

ma·nip·u·la·tion (-′-lā′shən) s. manipulación *f*; *(deceit)* manipuleo.

ma·nip·u·la·tive (-′-′ tĭv) adj. de manipuleo.

ma·nip·u·la·tor (:tər) s. manipulador *m*.

man·kind (măn′kīnd′) s. género humano; *(men)* los hombres.

man·like (:līk′) adj. parecido al hombre.

man·li·ness (:lē-nĭs) s. hombría; *(masculinity)* masculinidad *f*.

man·ly (:lē) **I.** adj. **-i-** varonil; *(masculine)* masculino **II.** adv. como un hombre.

man·made (:măd′) adj. artificial.

man·na (măn′ə) s. maná *m*.

manned (mănd) adj. tripulado.

man·ne·quin (măn′ĭ-kĭn) s. maniquí *m*.

man·ner (măn′ər) s. manera, modo; *(bearing)* comportamiento ♦ **all m. of** todo tipo de • **in a m. of speaking** por así decirlo ♦ pl. modales; *(politeness)* educación ♦ **man·nered** (:ərd) adj. amanerado ♦ **ill-m.** de malos modales.

man·ner·ism (:ə-rĭz′əm) s. amaneramiento; *(peculiarity)* peculiaridad *f*.

man·ner·ly (:ər-lē) adj. de buenos modales.

man·ni·kin (măn′ĭ-kĭn) var. de **manikin**.

man·nish (măn′ĭsh) adj. hombruno.

man-of-war (măn′ə-wôr′) s. [pl. **men-**] buque *m* de guerra.

man·or (măn′ər) s. *(estate)* finca; *(mansion)* casa solariega; *(fief)* señorío, feudo.

man·pow·er (măn′pou′ər) s. fuerza humana; *(labor)* mano de obra disponible.

manse (măns) s. rectoría.

man·ser·vant (măn′sûr′vənt) s. [pl. **menservants**] sirviente *m*.

man·sion (măn′shən) s. casa grande.

man-size(d) (măn′sīz[d]′) adj. FAM. de gran tamaño, muy grande.

man·slaugh·ter (:slô′tər) s. homicidio impremeditado *o* involuntario.

man·ta (măn′tə) s. chal *m*. ♦ **m. ray** ICT. manta.

man·tel (măn′tl) s. *(facing)* manto (de la chimenea); *(shelf)* repisa de la chimenea.

man·tel·piece (:pēs′) s. repisa de la chimenea.

man·tle (măn′tl) **I.** s. manto **II.** tr. tapar.

man-to-man (măn′tə-măn′) adj. de hombre a hombre.

man·u·al (măn′yŏŏ-əl) **I.** adj. manual **II.** s. manual *m*; MÚS. teclado; MIL. ejercicio de armas.

man·u·fac·ture (măn′yə-făk′chər) **I.** tr. manufacturar; *(clothing)* confeccionar; *(to produce)* fabricar **II.** s. manufactura, fabricación *f*; *(product)* producto manufacturado.

man·u·fac·tured (:chərd) adj. manufacturado.

man·u·fac·tur·er (:chər-ər) s. fabricante *mf*.

man·u·fac·tur·ing (:ĭng) **I.** adj. manufacturero **II.** s. manufactura.

man·u·mit (măn′yə-mĭt′) tr. **-tt-** manumitir.

ma·nure (mə-nŏŏr′) **I.** s. estiércol *m* **II.** tr. estercolar.

man·u·script (măn′yə-skrĭpt′) s. & adj. manuscrito.

man·y (mĕn′ē) **I.** adj. **more, most** muchos ♦ **how m.?** ¿cuántos? • **m. a man** muchos hombres • **m. people** mucha gente • **too m.** demasiado • **twice as m.** dos veces más **II.** s. & pron. muchos ♦ **a great m.** muchísimos • **as m. as** *(the same number)* tantos como; *(up to)* hasta • **the m.** las masas.

map (măp) **I.** s. mapa *m* ♦ **to put on the m.** dar fama a **II.** tr. **-pp-** trazar un mapa de; *(to plan)* planear.

ma·ple (mā′pəl) s. arce *m* ♦ **m. syrup** jarabe de arce.

map·mak·er (măp′mā′kər) s. cartógrafo.

map·mak·ing (:kĭng) s. cartografía.

map·ping (măp′ĭng) s. cartografía.

mar (mär) tr. **-rr-** *(to damage)* dañar, estropear; *(to disfigure)* desfigurar.

mar·a·thon (măr′ə-thŏn′) s. maratón *m*; *(contest)* competencia de resistencia.

ma·raud (mə-rôd′) intr. merodear —tr. pillar.

ma·raud·er (:rô′dər) s. merodeador *m*.

mar·ble (mär′bəl) **I.** s. mármol *m*; *(glass ball)* canica, bolita ♦ **to lose one's marbles** JER. aflojársele a uno un tornillo **II.** tr. jaspear **III.** adj. marmóreo, de mármol.

mar·bled (:bəld) adj. jaspeado.

mar·bling (:blĭng) s. marmoración *f*.

march[1] (märch) **I.** intr. MIL. marchar; *(to walk)* ir a pie; *(to advance)* avanzar ♦ **forward m.!** ¡de frente! ♦ **marching orders** órdenes de movilización • **to m. on** seguir la marcha • **to m. up to** acercarse a —tr. MIL. hacer marchar **II.** s. marcha; *(pace)* paso; *(of time)* transcurso; *(distance)* caminata ♦ **on the m.** en marcha.

march[2] s. *(frontier)* marca.

March (märch) s. marzo.

march·er (mär′chər) s. manifestante *mf*.

mare (mâr) s. yegua.

mar·ga·rine (mär′jər-ĭn) s. margarina.

mar·gin (mär′jĭn) s. margen *mf*; FIN. *(collateral)* garantía.

mar·gin·al (:jə-nəl) adj. marginal; *(barely acceptable)* mínimo.

mar·i·gold (măr′ĭ-gōld′) s. maravilla.

mar·i·jua·na/hua·na (măr′ə-wä′nə) s. mariguana; *(hemp)* cáñamo índico.

ma·ri·na (mə-rē′nə) s. marina.

mar·i·nade (măr′ə-nād′) s. escabeche *m*.

mar·i·nate (:nāt′) tr. escabechar, marinar.

ma·rine (mə-rēn′) **I.** adj. marítimo; *(life)* marino ♦ **m. engineer** ingeniero naval **II.** s. *(fleet)* marina; *(soldier)* soldado de marina ♦ **merchant m.** marina mercante ♦ pl. infantería de marina.

mar·i·ner (măr′ə-nər) s. marinero, marino.

mar·i·o·nette (măr′ē-ə-nĕt′) s. marioneta.

mar·i·tal (măr′ĭ-tl) adj. matrimonial, marital.

mar·i·time (măr′ĭ-tīm′) adj. marítimo.

mar·jo·ram (mär′jər-əm) s. mejorana.

mark[1] (märk) **I.** s. marca; *(punctuation)* signo de puntuación; *(grade)* nota; *(indication)* signo; *(standard)* altura; *(attention)* atención *f*; *(target)* blanco; *(goal)* objetivo; *(reference point)* señal *f*; *(impression)* sello; DEP. *(starting line)* línea de salida; *(record)* récord *m* ♦ **to be off the m.** no alcanzar el fin deseado; *(inaccurate)* estar incorrecto • **to hit the m.** *(to succeed)* tener éxito; *(to be right)* dar en el clavo • **to make one's m.** distinguirse ♦ pl. *(appraisal)* evaluación; *(rating)* calificación **II.** tr. marcar; *(to draw)* dibujar; *(a spot)* señalar; *(to characterize)* caracterizar; *(to grade)* calificar; *(to heed)* prestar atención ♦ **to m. down** *(to write down)* anotar; *(prices)* rebajar • **to m. off** *(to demarcate)* demarcar; *(to note)* apuntar • **to m. time** marcar el paso • **to m. up** *(to deface)* estropear; *(prices)* aumentar.

mark[2] s. FIN. marco.

mark·down (märk′doun′) s. rebaja.

marked (märkt) adj. marcado; *(noticeable)* notable ♦ **a m. man** un hombre señalado.

mark·er (mär′kər) s. marcador *m*; JER. *(promissory note)* pagaré *m*.

mar·ket (mär′kĭt) **I.** s. mercado; *(demand)* salida; *(stock market)* bolsa ♦ **buyer's, seller's m.** mercado que favorece al comprador, vendedor • **foreign exchange m.** mercado de cambios • **m. price** precio corriente *o* de mercado • **m. research** análisis de mercados • **m. value** valor comercial • **to be in the m. for** querer comprar • **to be on the m.** estar en venta • **to find a ready m.** tener fácil salida • **to play the m.** jugar a la bolsa • **to put on the m.** poner en venta **II.** tr. vender —intr. hacer las compras.

mar·ket·a·ble (:kĭ-tə-bəl) adj. vendible.

mar·ket·er (:tər) s. vendedor *m*; *(of new products)* mercantilizador *m*.

mar·ket·ing (:tĭng) s. comercio; *(of new products)* mercadeo.

mar·ket·place (mär′kĭt-plās′) s. *(plaza del)* mercado; *(business world)* mundo mercantil.

mark·ing (mär′kĭng) s. marca; *(act)* marcación *f*; ZOOL. pinta.

marks·man (märks′mən) s. [pl. **-men**] tirador *m* (al blanco).

marks·man·ship (:shĭp′) s. *(buena)* puntería.

mark·up (märk′ŭp′) s. *(of prices)* aumento; *(profit margin)* margen *m* de ganancia bruta.

mar·ma·lade (mär′mə-lād′) s. mermelada.

ma·roon[1] (mə-rōōn′) tr. abandonar; *(to isolate)* aislar.

ma·roon[2] s. & adj. *(color)* marrón *m*, castaño.

mar·quee (mär-kē′) s. *(tent)* tienda de campaña *(grande)*; *(of theater, hotel)* marquesina.

mar·quis (mär′kwĭs, mär-kē′) s. marqués *m*.

mar·quise (mär-kēz′) s. marquesa.

mar·riage (mär′ĭj) s. matrimonio; *(wedding)* boda, casamiento; *(close union)* unión *f* ♦ **m. articles** contrato matrimonial • **m. certificate** partida de matrimonio • **to be related by m.** tener parentesco político • **to take in m.** contraer matrimonio con.

mar·riage·a·ble (:ĭ-jə-bəl) adj. casadero.

mar·ried (:ēd) adj. casado; *(conjugal)* conyugal ♦ **m. couple** matrimonio • **m. name** apellido de casada • **to get m.** casarse.

mar·row (măr′ō) s. médula.

mar·ry (măr′ē) tr. *(to join in marriage)* casar; *(to take in marriage)* casarse con; *(to give in marriage)* dar en casamiento; *(to unite)* unir —intr. casarse; *(to unite)* unirse ♦ **to m. beneath oneself** casarse con alguien de clase inferior • **to m. into** emparentar con.

marsh (märsh) s. pantano; *(salt)* marisma.

mar·shal (mär′shəl) **I.** s. MIL. mariscal *m*; *(chief)* jefe **II.** tr. poner en orden; *(to usher)* acompañar ceremoniosamente ♦ **to m. (forces) against** movilizar *(fuerzas)* en contra de.

marsh·land (märsh′lănd′) s. terreno pantanoso.

marsh·mal·low (märsh′mĕl′ō, :măl′ō) s. bombón *m* de merengue blando.

marsh·y (mär′shē) adj. **-i-** pantanoso.

mar·su·pi·al (mär-sōō′pē-əl) adj. & s. marsupial *m*.

mart (märt) s. mercado.

mar·tial (mär′shəl) adj. marcial; *(military)* militar.

mar·ti·net (mär′tn-ĕt′) s. ordenancista *mf*.

mar·tyr (mär′tər) **I.** s. mártir *mf* **II.** tr. martirizar.

mar·tyr·dom (:dəm) s. martirio.
mar·vel (mär'vəl) I. s. maravilla; *(astonishment)* asombro II. intr. maravillarse.
mar·vel·lous (:və-ləs) adj. maravilloso; *(superb)* excelente.
mas·car·a (mă-skăr'ə) s. rimel *m*.
mas·cot (măs'kŏt') s. mascota.
mas·cu·line (măs'kyə-lĭn) adj. & s. masculino.
mas·cu·lin·i·ty ('-'ĭ-tē) s. masculinidad *f*.
mash (măsh) I. s. malta remojada; *(for animals)* mezcla de granos molidos; *(mixture)* mezcolanza II. tr. *(to crush)* majar; *(to grind)* moler.
mash·er ('ər) s. majador *m*.
mask (măsk) I. s. máscara; *(face covering)* antifaz *m*, careta; *(funeral)* mascarilla; FOTOG. ocultador *m* II. tr. *(to cover)* enmascarar; *(to disguise)* disimular; *(to conceal)* ocultar.
masked (măskt) adj. enmascarado; *(disguised)* disfrazado ♦ **m. ball** baile de máscaras.
masking tape s. cinta adhesiva opaca.
mas·o·chist (măs'ə-kĭst) s. masoquista *mf*.
mas·o·chis·tic ('-kĭs'tĭk) adj. masoquista.
ma·son (mā'sən) s. *(bricklayer)* albañil *m*; *(stonecutter)* cantero ♦ **M.** masón.
ma·son·ry (:rē) s. *(trade)* albañilería; *(brickwork)* obra de albañilería; *(rubblework)* mampostería; *(stonework)* cantería ♦ **M.** masonería.
masque (măsk) s. espectáculo alegórico; *(masked ball)* baile *m* de disfraces.
mas·quer·ade (măs'kə-rād') I. s. mascarada; *(costume)* disfraz *m*; *(pretense)* farsa II. intr. ♦ **to m. as** disfrazarse de; FIG. *(to pose as)* hacerse pasar por.
mass (măs) I. s. masa; *(large amount)* montón *m*; *(majority)* mayor parte *f*; *(physical bulk)* volumen *m* II. tr. amontonar —intr. congregarse en masa III. adj. de la masa ♦ **m. hysteria** histeria colectiva • **m. media** medios de comunicación de masa.
Mass *o* **mass** (măs) s. RELIG. misa ♦ **High, Low M.** misa mayor, rezada.
mas·sa·cre (măs'ə-kər) I. s. masacre *f* II. tr. masacrar.
mas·sage (mə-säzh', mə-säj') I. s. masaje *m* II. tr. dar masajes a, masajear.
mas·seur (mă-sûr') s. masajista *m*.
mas·seuse (mă-soez') s. masajista *f*.
mas·sive (măs'ĭv) adj. masivo; *(huge)* monumental.
mass-pro·duce (măs'prə-dōōs') tr. fabricar en gran escala.
mast (măst) s. mástil *m*; *(pole)* palo.
mas·tec·to·my (mă-stěk'tə-mē) s. mastectomía.
mas·ter (măs'tər) I. s. maestro; *(expert)* perito; *(degree)* maestría (título académico entre la licenciatura y el doctorado); *(owner)* amo; *(of household)* señor *m*; MARÍT. capitán *m* de barco mercante ♦ **M.** señorito II. adj. maestro; *(main)* principal; *(copy)* original III. tr. lograr dominar; *(to overcome)* superar.
mas·ter·ful (:fəl) adj. *(imperious)* dominante; *(skillful)* hábil.
mas·ter·ly (:lē) I. adj. magistral, genial II. adv. magistralmente, genialmente.
mas·ter·mind (:mīnd') I. s. genio creador y director II. tr. ser el cerebro de, dirigir.
mas·ter·piece (:pēs') s. obra maestra.
mas·ter·y (măs'tə-rē) s. *(skill)* maestría; *(rule)* gobierno, hábil.
mast·head (măst'hěd') s. *(of mast)* tope *m*;

IMPR. cabecera.
mas·tic (măs'tĭk) s. mástique *m*.
mas·ti·cate (măs'tĭ-kāt') tr. masticar.
mas·tiff (măs'tĭf) s. mastín *m*.
mas·toid (măs'toid') I. s. mastoides *f* II. adj. mastoideo, mastoidal.
mas·tur·bate (măs'tər-bāt') tr. & intr. masturbar(se).
mas·tur·ba·tion ('-bā'shən) s. masturbación *f*.
mat[1] (măt) I. s. estera; *(doormat)* esterilla; DEP. *(floor pad)* colchoneta; *(tangled mass)* maraña II. tr. & intr. **-tt-** enmarañar(se).
mat[2] I. s. *(border)* marco de cartón; *(finish)* acabado mate II. tr. **-tt-** *(a picture)* poner un marco de cartón a; *(glass, metal)* dar un acabado mate a III. adj. mate.
match[1] (măch) I. s. par *m*; *(pair)* juego; *(marriage)* matrimonio; DEP. partido ♦ **to be a good m.** *(mate)* ser un buen partido; *(to harmonize)* hacer juego ♦ **to be a m. for** poder competir con • **to meet one's m.** hallar un rival digno de uno II. tr. corresponder a; *(to go with)* hacer juego con; *(to pit)* oponer; *(to equal)* igualar —intr. hacer juego.
match[2] s. *(stick)* fósforo.
match·book ('bŏok') s. sobre *m* de fósforos.
match·box (:bŏks') s. caja de fósforos, fosforera.
match·less (măch'lĭs) adj. sin igual, sin par.
match·mak·er (mă'kər) s. casamentero.
mate[1] (māt) I. s. compañero; *(male)* macho; *(female)* hembra; *(buddy)* socio; MARÍT. piloto; *(assistant)* ayudante *m* II. tr. & intr. *(to join)* hermanar(se); *(to marry)* casar(se); ZOOL. aparear(se).
mate[2] I. s. *(chess)* mate *m* (en ajedrez) II. intr. & tr. dar mate (a).
ma·té (mä-tā') s. mate *m*.
ma·te·ri·al (mə-tîr'ē-əl) I. s. material *m*; *(cloth)* tela II. adj. material; *(noticeable)* notable; *(relevant)* pertinente.
ma·te·ri·al·ist (:ə-lĭst) s. materialista *mf*.
ma·te·ri·al·is·tic (:ə-lĭs'tĭk) adj. materialista.
ma·te·ri·al·i·ty (:ăl'ĭ-tē) s. materialidad *f*; DER. pertinencia.
ma·te·ri·al·ize ('-ə-līz') tr. materializar —intr. concretizarse; *(to appear)* materializarse.
ma·te·ri·el/té·ri·el (-'-ēl') s. material *m*, suministros y pertrechos.
ma·ter·nal (mə-tûr'nəl) adj. maternal; *(of one's mother)* materno.
ma·ter·ni·ty (:nĭ-tē) s. maternidad *f*; *(motherliness)* cariño maternal.
math (măth) s. matemática(s).
math·e·mat·i·cal ('ə-măt'ĭ-kəl) adj. matemático.
math·e·ma·ti·cian (:mə-tĭsh'ən) s. matemático.
math·e·mat·ics (:măt'-ĭks) s.sg. matemática(s).
mat·i·nee/née (măt'n-ā') s. matinée *f*.
mat·ing (mā'tĭng) s. *(of persons)* unión *f*; *(of animals)* apareamiento.
ma·tri·arch (mā'trē-ärk') s. matriarca.
ma·tri·ar·chal (-'är'kəl) adj. matriarcal.
ma·tri·ar·chy ('-kē) s. matriarcado.
mat·ri·cide (măt'rĭ-sīd') s. matricidio; *(person)* matricida *mf*.
ma·tric·u·late (mə-trĭk'yə-lāt') tr. & intr. matricular(se).
ma·tric·u·la·tion (-'-lā'shən) s. matriculación *f*, matrícula.
mat·ri·mo·ni·al (măt'rə-mō'nē-əl) adj. matri-

monial.

mat·ri·mo·ny ('-'nē) s. matrimonio.

ma·trix (mā'trĭks) s. [pl. **es** o **-ces**] matriz f.

ma·tron (mā'trən) s. matrona; (head nurse) enfermera jefe; (prison guard) celadora.

ma·tron·ly (:lē) adj. matronal, de matrona.

matte (măt) s. acabado mate.

mat·ted (măt'ĭd) adj. (with mats) esterado; (tangled) enmarañado.

mat·ter (măt'ər) I. s. materia; (concern) cuestión f; (approximate quantity) cosa ♦ **as a m. of course** normalmente, por costumbre • **as a m. of fact** de hecho • **as matters stand** tal y como están las cosas • **for that m.** en cuanto a eso • **in the m. of** en lo tocante a • **no m.** no importa • **no m. how** sea como sea • **no m. what happens** pase lo que pase • **nothing's the m.** no pasa nada • **printed m.** impresos • **small m.** asunto sin importancia • **to be another m.** ser cosa aparte • **to be no laughing m.** no ser cosa de risa • **to make matters worse** para colmo de males • **what's the m.?** ¿qué sucede? II. intr. importar.

mat·ter-of-fact ('əv-făkt') adj. práctico; (factual) realista; (prosaic) prosaico.

mat·ting (măt'ĭng) s. estera.

mat·tress (măt'rĭs) s. colchón m.

mat·u·ra·tion (măch'ə-rā'shən) s. maduración f.

ma·ture (mə-chŏŏr', -tŏŏr', -tŏor') I. adj. **-er, -est** maduro; (considered) meditado; FIN. (due) pagadero II. tr. & intr. madurar.

ma·tu·ri·ty (:ĭ-tē) s. madurez f; FIN. vencimiento ♦ **to reach m.** llegar a la madurez; FIN. ser pagadero, vencer.

maud·lin (môd'lĭn) adj. sensiblero.

maul (môl) I. s. almádena II. tr. (to handle roughly) maltratar; (to injure) lacerar.

mau·so·le·um (mô'sə-lē'əm) s. [pl. **s** o **-lea**] mausoleo.

mauve (mōv) s. & adj. malva m.

mav·er·ick (măv'ər-ĭk) s. res f sin marcar; (dissenter) disidente mf.

maw (mô) s. (of a lion) fauces f; (opening) abertura profunda.

mawk·ish (mô'kĭsh) s. sensiblero.

max·im (măk'sĭm) s. máxima.

max·i·mal (măk'sə-məl) adj. máximo.

max·i·mize (:mīz') tr. llevar al máximo.

max·i·mum (măk'sə-məm) adj. & s. máximo.

may (mā) aux. [pret. **might**] (permission) poder <m. I go? yes, you m. ¿puedo irme? sí, puedes>; (possibility) ser posible (que); (wish) ojalá que ♦ **be that as it m.** sea como fuere • **come what m.** pase lo que pase • **if I m.** si me lo permite • **long m. he live!** ¡que viva muchos años! • **m. as well** más vale que, mejor que • **m. I . . .?** ¿me permite . . .?

May (mā) s. mayo.

may·be (mā'bē) adj. (perhaps) quizá(s); (possibly) tal vez.

may·day (mā'dā') s. señal f de socorro.

may·flow·er (mā'flou'ər) s. espino.

may·hem (mā'hĕm') s. DER. mutilación f criminal; (havoc) estrago.

may·on·naise (mā'ə-nāz') s. mayonesa.

may·or (mā'ər) s. alcalde m.

may·or·al·ty (:əl-tē) s. alcaldía.

maze (māz) s. laberinto.

me (mē) pron. me; (after preposition) mí ♦ **it's me** FAM. soy yo • **with me** conmigo.

mead (mēd) s. aguamiel f, hidromel m.

mead·ow (mĕd'ō) s. pradera.

mea·ger (mē'gər) adj. (lean) magro; (scanty) exiguo; (feeble) pobre.

meal¹ (mēl) s. (ground grain) harina.

meal² s. comida ♦ **m. ticket** JER. sustento.

meal·time (mēl'tīm') s. hora de comer.

meal·y (mē'lē) adj. **-i-** (granular) harinoso; (made of meal) de harina; (sprinkled with meal) enharinado; (pale) pálido.

meal·y-mouthed (:mouthd') adj. meloso, camandulero.

mean¹ (mēn) tr. **meant** (to signify) querer decir; (to intend) tener la intención de; (to allude to) referirse a; (to entail) implicar ♦ **not to m. to do something** hacer algo sin querer • **to m. it** hablar en serio —intr. importar ♦ **to m. well** tener buenas intenciones.

mean² adj. inferior; (base) ruin; (stingy) tacaño; (malicious) mal intencionado; FAM. (illtempered) de malas pulgas; JER. (difficult) malo ♦ **to be m. to** tratar mal a • **to play a m. game of** JER. ser un bárbaro en.

mean³ I. s. (middle) punto medio; MAT. (average) promedio; (arithmetic) media ♦ pl. medios; (method) forma ♦ **by all m.** (certainly) sin duda; (of course) por supuesto • **by any m.** del modo que sea, como sea • **by m. of** por medio de, mediante • **by no m.** (in no way) de ningún modo; (in no sense) nada • **to live beyond one's m.** gastar más de lo que uno tiene II. adj. medio.

me·an·der (mē-ăn'dər) I. intr. serpentear; (to wander) vagar II. s. meandro.

mean·ing (mē'nĭng) s. sentido; (intent) significado ♦ **full of m.** cargado de sentido • **what's the m. of?** (a word) ¿qué significa?, ¿qué quiere decir?; (a look) ¿a qué viene?

mean·ing·ful (:fəl) adj. significativo.

mean·ing·less (:lĭs) adj. insignificante; (senseless) sin sentido.

meant (mĕnt) cf. **mean¹**.

mean·time (mēn'tīm') I. s. ínterin m II. adv. entretanto, mientras tanto.

mean·while (:hwīl') I. s. ínterin m II. adv. entretanto, mientras tanto.

mea·sles (mē'zəlz) s. sarampión m; (German measles) rubéola.

mea·sly (mēz'lē) adj. **-i-** JER. exiguo, ínfimo.

meas·ure (mĕzh'ər) I. s. medida; (unit) unidad f de medida; (system) sistema m (de medidas); (limited amount) cierto <a m. of recognition cierto reconocimiento>; (bounds) límite m; (bill) proyecto de ley; MÚS. compás m ♦ **beyond m.** sin límite • **for good m.** por añadidura • **in great m.** en gran parte • **to take the m. of** poner a prueba II. tr. medir; (to estimate) estimar ♦ **to m. off** medir • **to m. out** repartir (midiendo) —intr. ♦ **to m. up to** estar a la altura de.

meas·ured (:ərd) adj. acompasado; (restrained) mesurado.

meas·ure·ment (:ər-mənt) s. medición f; (unit) medida; (system) sistema m (de medidas).

meat (mēt) s. carne f; (fleshy part) parte f interior de algo comestible; (essence) meollo.

meat·ball ('bôl') s. albóndiga.

meat·less (:lĭs) adj. sin carne.

meat·y (mē'tē) adj. **-i-** carnoso, carnudo; FIG. substancioso.

mec·ca (mĕk'ə) s. meca.

me·chan·ic (mĭ-kăn'ĭk) s. mecánico ♦ **mechanics** sg. o pl. FÍS. mecánica; TEC. mecanismo;

FIG. técnica (de un arte, ciencia, sistema).
me·chan·i·cal (ĭ-kəl) adj. MEC. mecánico, de máquinas; FIG. *(machine-like)* maquinal.
mech·a·nism (mĕk′ə-nĭz′ əm) s. mecanismo.
mech·a·nis·tic (′-nĭs′tĭk) adj. mecanicista; *(mechanical)* mecánico.
mech·a·nize (′-nīz′) tr. mecanizar.
med·al (mĕd′l) s. medalla.
med·al·ist (:ĭst) s. DEP. ganador m.
me·dal·lion (mĭ-dăl′yən) s. medallón m.
med·dle (mĕd′l) intr. entremeterse ♦ to m. with manosear.
med·dler (:lər) s. entremetido.
med·dle·some (:l-səm) adj. entremetido.
me·di·a (mē′dē-ə) [pl. de **medium**] s.pl. medios publicitarios (prensa, radio, televisión) ♦ **advertising m.** medios de publicidad • **broadcast m.** medios de (radio)difusión.
me·di·an (mē′dē-ən) I. adj. mediano; *(value)* medio II. s. punto medio; *(middle value)* valor medio.
me·di·ate (mē′dē-āt′) tr. ser mediador en; *(to negotiate)* negociar como mediador —intr. mediar.
me·di·a·tion (′-ā′shən) s. intervención f; DER. *(arbitration)* mediación f.
me·di·a·tor (′-′ tər) s. mediador m.
med·ic (mĕd′ĭk) s. médico; *(surgeon)* cirujano; *(student)* estudiante mf de medicina; MIL. auxiliar médico.
med·i·cal (ĭ-kəl) adj. médico ♦ **m. examiner** DER. médico forense.
me·dic·a·ment (mĭ-dĭk′ə-mənt, mĕd′ĭ-kə-) s. medicamento.
med·i·cate (mĕd′ĭ-kāt′) tr. medicinar; *(to permeate)* impregnar (de sustancia medicinal).
med·i·ca·tion (′-kā′shən) s. medicamento; *(treatment)* tratamiento médico.
med·i·cine (mĕd′ĭ-sĭn) s. medicina ♦ **m. man** hechicero • **to give someone a taste of his own m.** pagarle a uno con la misma moneda • **to take one's m.** atenerse a las consecuencias.
me·di·e·val (mē′dē-ē′vəl, mĕ-dē′vəl) adj. medieval.
me·di·o·cre (mē′dē-ō′kər) adj. mediocre.
me·di·oc·ri·ty (:ŏk′rĭ-tē) s. mediocridad f.
med·i·tate (mĕd′ĭ-tāt′) tr. & intr. meditar; *(to contemplate)* contemplar.
med·i·ta·tion (′-tā′shən) s. meditación f.
med·i·ta·tive (′-tā′tĭv) adj. meditabundo.
me·di·um (mē′dē-əm) I. s. [pl. **s** o **-ia**] medio; *(spiritualist)* médium mf II. adj. mediano.
med·ley (mĕd′lē) s. mescolanza; MÚS. popurrí m.
meek (mēk) adj. *(humble)* humilde; *(submissive)* manso.
meet (mēt) I. tr. met encontrar(se) con; *(to be present at arrival)* recibir; *(to be introduced)* conocer; *(to confer with)* entrevistarse con; *(to join)* unirse con; *(to confront)* hacer frente a; *(a challenge)* salir adelante; *(requirements)* satisfacer; *(debts)* pagar —intr. encontrarse, verse; *(to join)* unirse; *(to contend)* enfrentarse; *(to make acquaintance)* conocerse; *(to assemble)* reunirse II. s. DEP. encuentro.
meet·ing (mē′tĭng) s. reunión f; *(rally)* mitin m.
meet·ing·house (:hous′) s. templo.
meg·a·lo·ma·ni·a (mĕg′ə-lō-mā′nē-ə) s. megalomanía.
meg·a·lop·o·lis (:lŏp′ə-lĭs) s. megalópolis f.
meg·a·phone (mĕg′ə-fōn′) s. megáfono.

meg·a·ton (:tŭn′) s. megatón m.
meg·a·watt (:wŏt′) s. megavatio.
mel·an·chol·ic (mĕl′ən-kŏl′ĭk) adj. melancólico.
mel·an·chol·y (′-ē) I. s. melancolía II. adj. melancólico; *(depressing)* triste.
meld (mĕld) tr. & intr. fusionar(se).
me·lee o **mê·lée** (mā′lā′) s. refriega; *(tumult)* tumulto.
mel·io·rate (mēl′yə-rāt′) tr. & intr. mejorar(se).
mel·io·ra·tion (′-rā′shən) s. mejoramiento.
mel·lif·lu·ous (mə-lĭf′lŏō-əs) adj. melifluo.
mel·low (mĕl′ō) I. adj. **-er, -est** maduro; *(wine)* añejo; *(tone)* dulce; *(relaxed)* reposado II. tr. & intr. madurar; *(wine)* añejar(se); FIG. suavizar(se).
me·lod·ic (mə-lŏd′ĭk) adj. melódico.
me·lo·di·ous (mə-lō′dē-əs) adj. melodioso.
mel·o·dra·ma (mĕl′ə-drä′mə) s. melodrama m.
mel·o·dra·mat·ic (′-drə-măt′ĭk) adj. melodramático ♦ **melodramatics** s.pl. teatralidad.
mel·o·dy (mĕl′ə-dē) s. melodía.
mel·on (mĕl′ən) s. melón m.
melt (mĕlt) intr. derretirse; *(to dissolve)* disolverse; *(to vanish)* desvanecerse; *(to merge)* fusionarse; *(to soften)* ablandarse —tr. licuar, derretir; *(to dissolve)* disolver; *(to soften)* ablandar.
melt·down (′doun′) s. fusión f del núcleo del reactor nuclear.
mem·ber (mĕm′bər) s. miembro.
mem·ber·ship (:shĭp′) s. *(in group)* calidad f de miembro; *(number)* número total de socios o miembros
mem·brane (mĕm′brān′) s. membrana.
me·men·to (mə-mĕn′tō) s. [pl. **(e)s**] recuerdo.
mem·o (mĕm′ō) s. memorándum m.
mem·oir (mĕm′wär′) s. (auto)biografía ♦ pl. memorias.
mem·o·ra·bil·i·a (mĕm′ər-ə-bĭl′ē-ə) s.pl. eventos memorables; *(mementos)* recuerdos.
mem·o·ra·ble (′--bəl) adj. memorable.
mem·o·ran·dum (mĕm′ə-răn′dəm) s. [pl. **s** o **-da**] nota; *(communiqué)* memorándum m.
me·mo·ri·al (mə-môr′ē-əl) I. s. monumento conmemorativo; *(petition)* memorial m II. adj. conmemorativo.
me·mo·ri·al·ize (:ə-līz′) tr. conmemorar.
mem·o·rize (mĕm′ə-rīz′) tr. memorizar.
mem·o·ry (:rē) s. memoria; *(recollection)* recuerdo ♦ **from m.** de memoria • **if my m. serves me** si no me falla la memoria • **to commit to m.** aprender de memoria.
men (mĕn) cf. **man.**
men·ace (mĕn′ĭs) I. s. amenaza; *(annoying person)* pesado II. tr. & intr. amenazar.
me·nag·er·ie (mə-năj′ə-rē) s. colección f de animales salvajes.
mend (mĕnd) I. tr. remendar; *(to reform)* reformar ♦ **to m. one's ways** enmendarse —intr. sanar II. s. remiendo ♦ **to be on the m.** ir mejorando.
men·da·cious (mĕn-dā′shəs) adj. mendaz.
men·dac·i·ty (:dăs′ĭ-tē) s. mendacidad f.
men·di·cant (mĕn′dĭ-kənt) I. adj. mendicante II. s. *(beggar)* mendigo; RELIG. mendicante mf.
men·folk(s) (mĕn′fōk[s]′) s.pl. hombres m.
me·ni·al (mē′nē-əl) I. adj. doméstico; *(servile)* servil II. s. criado.
men·in·gi·tis (mĕn′ĭn-jī′tĭs) s. meningitis f.
men·o·pause (mĕn′ə-pôz′) s. menopausia.
men·stru·al (mĕn′strōō-əl) adj. menstrual.

men·stru·ate (:āt′) intr. menstruar.

men·stru·a·tion (′-ā′shən) s. menstruación f.

men·su·ra·ble (měn′sə-rə-bəl) adj. mensurable.

men·su·ra·tion (′-rā′shən) s. mensura.

mens·wear (měnz′wâr′) s. ropa para hombres.

men·tal (měn′tl) adj. mental; (hospital) psiquiátrico ♦ **m. derangement** alienación f, enajenación mental.

men·tal·i·ty (měn-tǎl′ĭ-tē) s. mentalidad f; (attitude) modo de pensar.

men·thol (měn′thôl′) s. mentol m.

men·tho·lat·ed (:thə-lā′tĭd) adj. mentolado.

men·tion (měn′shən) I. tr. mencionar II. s. mención f.

men·u (měn′yōō, mā′nyōō) s. menú m, carta.

me·ow (mē-ou′) I. s. maullido II. intr. maullar.

mer·can·tile (mûr′kən-tēl′, :tīl′) adj. mercantil.

mer·ce·nar·y (mûr′sə-něr′ē) adj. & s. mercenario.

mer·chan·dise (mûr′chən-dīz′) I. s. mercancía, mercadería II. tr. (:dīz′) comerciar.

mer·chant (mûr′chənt) I. s. mercader m, comerciante mf; (shopkeeper) tendero II. adj. mercante.

mer·chant·man (:mən) s. [pl. **-men**] buque m mercante.

mer·ci·ful (mûr′sĭ-fəl) adj. misericordioso.

mer·ci·less (:lĭs) adj. cruel, despiadado.

mer·cu·ri·al (mər-kyŏŏr′ē-əl) adj. volátil; QUÍM. mercurial.

mer·cu·ro·chrome (:ə-krōm′) s. mercurocromo.

mer·cu·ry (mûr′kyə-rē) s. mercurio.

mer·cy (mûr′sē) s. clemencia; (compassion) misericordia f; (relief) alivio ♦ **m. killing** eutanasia • **to be at the m. of** estar a (la) merced de • **to have m. on** tener piedad de.

mere (mîr) adj. (simple) puro; (no more than) no más que <he is a m. employee no es más que un empleado>.

mere·ly (′lē) adv. simplemente; (no more than) no más que <she's m. an assistant no es más que una ayudanta.

mer·e·tri·cious (měr′ĭ-trĭsh′əs) adj. (gaudy) llamativo; (insincere) engañoso.

merge (mûrj) tr. & intr. unir(se); COM. fusionar(se).

merg·er (mûr′jər) s. unión f; COM. fusión f.

me·rid·i·an (mə-rĭd′ē-ən) I. s. (apex) cenit m II. adj. meridiano.

me·ringue (mə-rǎng′) s. merengue m.

mer·it (měr′ĭt) I. s. mérito m; (advantage) ventaja ♦ **m. raise** aumento (de sueldo) por excelencia • **on one's merits** según las cualidades de uno ♦ pl. DER. fondo II. tr. & intr. merecer.

mer·i·to·ri·ous (měr′ĭ-tôr′ē-əs) adj. meritorio.

mer·maid (mûr′mād′) s. sirena.

mer·ri·ment (měr′ĭ-mənt) s. alegría; (amusement) diversión f.

mer·ry (měr′ē) adj. -i- alegre; (entertaining) divertido; (brisk) ligero ♦ **M. Christmas** Feliz Navidad • **to make m.** divertirse.

mer·ry-go-round (:gō-round′) s. tiovivo, (whirl) remolino.

mer·ry·mak·ing (:mā′kĭng) s. juerga.

mes·cal (mě-skǎl′) s. mezcal m; (liquor) aguardiente m de mezcal.

mes·ca·line (měs′kə-lēn′) s. mescalina.

mesh (měsh) I. s. malla f; (of gears) engranaje m ♦ pl. malla; (snares) redes II. tr. enredar ♦ **to m. together** enlazar —intr. (to become entangled) enredarse; MEC. engranar; (to harmo-

nize) encajar.

mes·mer·ize (měz′mə-rīz′) tr. hipnotizar; (to enthrall) cautivar.

mes·o·morph (měz′ə-môrf′) s. mesomorfo.

mes·quite (mě-skēt′) s. mezquite m.

mess (měs) I. s. desorden m; (dirty condition) asquerosidad f; (difficulty) lío; (serving) ración f; (meal) rancho ♦ **m. hall** comedor II. tr. ♦ **to m. up** o **make a m. of** (to soil) ensuciar; (to disarrange) desordenar, desarreglar; (to spoil) echar a perder —intr. ♦ **to m. around** FAM. entretenerse • **to m. with** FAM. molestar.

mes·sage (měs′ĭj) s. mensaje m.

mes·sen·ger (měs′ən-jər) s. mensajero.

mess·y (měs′ē) adj. -i- desordenado; (filthy) asqueroso; (slovenly) desaseado; (complicated) complicado.

met (mět) cf. **meet.**

met·a·bol·ic (mět′ə-bŏl′ĭk) adj. metabólico.

me·tab·o·lism (mə-tăb′ə-lĭz′əm) s. metabolismo.

me·tab·o·lize (:līz′) tr. & intr. metabolizar(se).

met·al (mět′l) s. metal m; (mettle) temple m.

me·tal·lic (mə-tăl′ĭk) adj. metálico.

met·al·lur·gy (mět′l-ûr′jē) s. metalurgia.

met·al·work (:wûrk′) s. (craft) metalistería; (things) objetos de metal.

met·a·mor·phic (mět′ə-môr′fĭk) adj. metamórfico.

met·a·mor·phose (mět′ə-môr′fōz′, :fōs′) tr. & intr. metamorfosear(se).

met·a·mor·pho·sis (:fə-sĭs) s. [pl. **-ses**] metamorfosis f.

met·a·phor (mět′ə-fôr′) s. metáfora.

met·a·phor·i·cal (′-ĭ-kəl) adj. metafórico.

met·a·phys·i·cal (mět′ə-fĭz′ĭ-kəl) adj. metafísico.

met·a·phys·ics (:ĭks) s.sg. metafísica.

me·tas·ta·sis (mə-tăs′tə-sĭs) s. [pl. **-ses**] metástasis f.

mete (mēt) tr. ♦ **to m. out** repartir.

me·te·or (mē′tē-ər) s. meteoro.

me·te·or·ic (′-ôr′ĭk) adj. meteórico.

me·te·or·ite (′-ə-rīt′) s. meteorito.

me·te·or·o·log·i·cal (mē′tē-ə-rə-lŏj′ĭ-kəl) adj. meteorológico.

me·te·or·ol·o·gist (:rŏl′ə-jĭst) s. meteorólogo, meteorologista mf.

me·te·or·ol·o·gy (:jē) s. meteorología.

me·ter¹ (mē′tər) s. (measurement, verse) metro; (device) contador m; MÚS. compás m.

meth·ane (měth′ān′) s. metano.

meth·od (měth′əd) s. método; (order) orden m.

me·thod·ic·i·cal (mə-thŏd′ĭk) metódico.

meth·od·ol·o·gy (měth′ə-dŏl′ə-jē) s. metodología.

meth·yl (měth′əl) s. metilo.

me·tic·u·lous (mə-tĭk′yə-ləs) adj. meticuloso; (overscrupulous) minucioso.

mé·tier (mā-tyā′) s. especialidad f.

me·tre (mē′tər) G.B. var. de **meter.**

met·ric (mět′rĭk) adj. métrico.

met·ri·cal (:rĭ-kəl) adj. GRAM. métrico, de la métrica; (of measurement) métrico, del metro.

met·ro·nome (mět′rə-nōm′) s. metrónomo.

me·trop·o·lis (mə-trŏp′ə-lĭs) s. metrópoli f.

met·ro·pol·i·tan (mět′rə-pŏl′ĭ-tn) adj. metropolitano.

met·tle (mět′l) s. (character) entereza; (courage) temple m ♦ **on one's m.** puesto a prueba.

met·tle·some (:səm) adj. animoso.

mew¹ (myōō) s. (small street) callejuela.

mew² I. intr. maullar II. s. maullido.
mewl (myōōl) intr. lloriquear.
mez·za·nine (mĕz'ə-nēn') s. entresuelo.
mi·as·ma (mī-ăz'mə) s. miasma *m.*
mice (mīs) cf. **mouse.**
mi·cro (mī'krō) s. FAM. microcomputadora.
mi·crobe (mī'krōb') s. microbio.
mi·cro·bi·ol·o·gy (mī'krō-bī-ŏl'ə-jē) s. micro-
biología.
mi·cro·bus (-bŭs') s. microbús *m.*
mi·cro·chip (-chĭp') s. microplaqueta.
mi·cro·cir·cuit (:sûr'kĭt) s. microcircuito.
mi·cro·com·put·er (:kəm-pyōō'tər) s. microcomputadora.
mi·cro·cosm (mī'krə-kŏz'əm) s. microcosmo.
mi·cro·ec·o·nom·ics (mī'krō-ĕk'ə-nŏm'ĭks)
s.sg. microeconomía.
mi·cro·fiche ('-fēsh') s. [pl. inv. *o* **s**] microficha.
mi·cro·film (mī'krə-fĭlm') I. s. microfilm *m*
II. tr. reproducir en microfilm.
mi·cron (mī'krŏn') s. [pl. **s** *o* **-cra**] micrón *m.*
mi·cro·or·gan·ism (mī'krō-ôr'gə-nĭz'əm) s.
microorganismo.
mi·cro·phone (mī'krə-fōn') s. micrófono.
mi·cro·proc·es·sor (mī'krō-prŏs'ĕs-ər) s.
microprocesador *m.*
mi·cro·scope (mī'krə-skōp') s. microscopio.
mi·cro·scop·ic/i·cal ('-skŏp'ĭk) adj. microscó-
pico.
mi·cro·sur·ger·y (mī'krō-sûr'jə-rē) s. micro-
cirugía.
mi·cro·wave (mī'krə-wāv') s. microonda.
mid¹ (mĭd) adj. medio ♦ **in mid-April** a mediados de abril ♦ **in m. course** a media carrera.
mid² prep. POÉT. en medio de.
mid·air (mĭd'âr') s. punto en medio del aire ♦
m. collision AVIA. choque en pleno vuelo.
mid·day (:dā') s. mediodía *m.*
mid·dle (mĭd'l) I. adj. medio; *(intermediate)*
intermedio ♦ **M. Ages** Edad Media • **m.
ground** punto de vista intermedio II. s. medio; *(waist)* cintura ♦ **in the m. of** en medio de.
mid·dle-aged ('-ājd') adj. de edad madura.
mid·dle-class (:klăs') adj. de la clase media.
mid·dle·man ('-măn') s. [pl. **-men**] intermediario.
mid·dle-of-the-road ('-əv-thə-rōd') adj. moderado.
mid·dle·weight ('-wāt') s. DEP. peso medio.
mid·dling (mĭd'lĭng) adj. *(medium)* mediano;
(mediocre) ordinario.
midg·et (mĭj'ĭt) s. *(person)* enano; *(object)* objeto pequeño.
mid·land (mĭd'lənd) s. región *f* central.
mid·night (:nīt') s. medianoche *f* ♦ **to burn the
m. oil** quemarse las cejas o pestañas.
mid·point (:point') s. punto céntrico.
mid·riff (:rĭf') s. abdomen *m* superior.
mid·sec·tion (:sĕk'shən) s. sección media.
mid·ship (:shĭp') adj. del medio del barco.
mid·ship·man (:shĭp'mən) s. [pl. **-men**] guar-
diamarina *m.*
mid·ships (:shĭps') adv. en medio del barco.
midst (mĭdst) I. s. medio ♦ **in our m.** entre nosotros • **in the m. of** en medio de II. prep. entre,
en medio de.
mid·stream (mĭd'strēm') s. pleno río.
mid·sum·mer (:sŭm'ər) s. pleno verano; *(summer solstice)* solsticio de verano.
mid·term (:tûrm') s. mitad *f* del semestre;
(exam) examen *m* parcial.
mid·town (:toun') s. centro de una ciudad.

mid·way (:wā') I. s. avenida central (de una feria o exposición) II. adv. & adj. a mitad *o* medio del camino.
mid·week (:wĕk') s. medio de la semana.
mid·wife (:wīf') [pl. **-ves**] I. s. comadrona, partera II. tr. **-f-** *o* **-v-** partear.
mid·wife·ry (:wīf'rē, :wīf'-) s. partería.
mid·win·ter (:wĭn'tər) s. pleno invierno; *(winter solstice)* solsticio de invierno.
mid·year (:yîr') s. mitad *f* del año; *(exam)* examen *m* parcial de mitad del año.
mien (mēn) s. *(bearing)* porte *m;* *(aspect)* aspecto.
miff (mĭf) tr. disgustar.
might¹ (mīt) s. fuerzas.
might² aux. [pret. de **may**] poder <*she m. help
if she knew the truth* ella podría ayudar si su-
piera la verdad>; ser posible que <*it m. rain* es
posible que llueva>.
might·y (mī'tē) I. adj. **-i-** poderoso; *(imposing)*
imponente II. adv. FAM. extremadamente.
mi·graine (mī'grān') s. jaqueca, migraña.
mi·grant (mī'grənt) I. s. emigrante *mf;*
(worker) trabajador *m* ambulante II. adj. migratorio.
mi·grate (mī'grāt') intr. emigrar.
mi·gra·tion (mī-grā'shən) s. migración *f.*
mi·gra·to·ry (mī'grə-tôr'ē) adj. migratorio.
mike (mīk) s. FAM. micrófono.
mild (mīld) adj. suave; *(in character)* apacible;
(climate) templado; *(lenient)* poco severo;
(cold, cough) leve.
mildew (mĭl'dōō') I. s. moho II. tr. & intr.
enmohecer(se).
mile (mīl) s. milla ♦ **to be off by a m.** estar
lejos de la cuenta.
mile·age (mī'lĭj) s. distancia en millas; *(miles
traveled)* recorrido en millas; *(allowance)* gastos de viaje (pagados por millas); FAM. *(usefulness)* rendimiento, utilidad *f.*
mile·stone (mīl'stōn') s. piedra miliaria;
(event) hito.
mi·lieu (mēl-yōō') s. ambiente *m.*
mil·i·tan·cy (mĭl'ĭ-tn-sē) s. belicosidad *f.*
mil·i·tant (:tnt) adj. & s. militante *mf.*
mil·i·ta·rist (:tər-ĭst) s. militarista *mf.*
mil·i·ta·ris·tic (:tə-rĭs'tĭk) adj. militarista.
mil·i·ta·rize ('-tə-rīz') tr. militarizar.
mil·i·tar·y (:tĕr'ē) I. adj. militar II. s. los militares, las fuerzas armadas.
mil·i·tate (:tāt') intr. militar.
mi·li·tia (mə-lĭsh'ə) s. milicia.
mi·li·tia·man (:mən) s. [pl. **-men**] miliciano.
milk (mĭlk) I. s. leche *f* ♦ **chocolate m.** leche
con chocolate • **m. products** productos lácteos •
m. shake batido de leche • **not to cry over
spilled m.** a lo hecho, pecho • **powdered m.**
leche en polvo • **skim m.** leche desnatada •
whole m. leche sin desnatar II. tr. ordeñar; *(to
draw out)* sacar ♦ **to m. dry** exprimir como una
naranja.
milk·weed (:wēd') s. algodoncillo.
milk·y (mĭl'kē) adj. **-i-** lechoso ♦ **M. Way** Vía
Láctea.
mill (mĭl) I. s. molino; *(for spices, coffee)*
molinillo; *(factory)* fábrica ♦ **run of the m.** corriente y moliente • **to go through the m.**
aprender a golpes II. tr. moler; *(to process)*
tratar —intr. arremolinarse.
mil·len·ni·um (mə-lĕn'ē-əm) s. [pl. **s** *o* **-ia**]
milenio; RELIG. reinado de los mil años; *(golden
age)* época de paz y prosperidad.

mill·er (mĭl′ər) s. molinero.
mil·li·gram (mĭl′ə-grăm′) s. miligramo.
mil·li·li·ter (:lē′tər) s. mililitro.
mil·li·me·ter (:mē′tər) s. milímetro.
mil·li·ner (mĭl′ə-nər) s. sombrerero.
mil·li·ner·y (:nĕr′ē) s. sombrerería de señoras.
mil·lion (mĭl′yən) s. [pl. inv. o **s**] millón *m*.
mil·lion·aire (mĭl′yə-nâr′) s. millonario.
mil·li·pede (mĭl′ə-pēd′) s. milpiés *m*.
mill·stone (mĭl′stōn′) s. piedra de molino.
milque·toast (mĭlk′tōst′) s. persona de carácter tímido y reservado.
mime (mīm) **I.** s. pantomima; *(performer)* pantomimo **II.** tr. *(to mimic)* remedar; *(to pantomime)* hacer una pantomima de —intr. actuar en pantomima.
mim·e·o·graph (mĭm′ē-ə-grăf′) **I.** s. mimeógrafo **II.** tr. & intr. mimeografiar.
mim·ic (mĭm′ĭk) **I.** tr. **-ck-** remedar; *(resemble)* simular **II.** s. pantomimo; *(impersonator)* imitador *m*; *(copy)* imitación *f*.
mim·ic·ry (:ĭ-krē) s. mímica; BIOL. mimetismo.
mi·mo·sa (mĭ-mō′sə) s. mimosa.
mince (mĭns) tr. *(meat)* picar; *(words)* abstenerse de usar.
mince·meat (′mēt′) s. mezcla de fruta picada y especias ♦ **to make m. of** JER. hacer pedazos de.
minc·ing (mĭn′sĭng) adj. remilgado.
mind (mīnd) **I.** s. mente *f*; *(intelligence)* inteligencia; *(intellect)* cerebro; *(memory)* memoria; *(psychology)* psicología; *(opinion)* opinión *f*; *(attention)* atención ♦ **to be in one's right m.** estar uno en sus cabales • **to be out of one's m.** haber perdido el juicio • **to bring to m.** recordar • **to change one's m.** cambiar de opinión *o* parecer • **to come to m.** venir a la memoria • **to cross one's m.** ocurrírsele a uno • **to have a (good) m. to** estar dispuesto a • **to have in m.** planear • **to know one's (own) m.** saber lo que uno quiere • **to lose one's m.** perder la razón • **to make up one's m.** decidirse • **to my m.** a mi parecer • **to set one's m. on** estar resuelto a • **to speak one's m.** hablar con franqueza **II.** tr. *(to heed)* prestar atención a; *(to obey)* obedecer; *(to watch out for)* tener cuidado con; *(to dislike)* molestar <they do not m. the cold no les molesta el frío>; *(to look after)* cuidar ♦ **¡m. your own business!** ¡no te entrometas! • **not to m.** no tener inconveniente —intr. *(to give heed)* prestar atención; *(to obey)* obedecer ♦ **never m.** no importa, da igual.
mind·ed (mīnd′dĭd) adj. de mentalidad <commercially m. de mentalidad mercantil>; *(disposed toward)* dispuesto.
mind·ful (mīnd′fəl) adj. atento.
mind·less (:lĭs) adj. estúpido; *(senseless)* sin sentido; *(careless)* descuidado.
mind·set (:sĕt′) s. predisposición *f* mental.
mine¹ (mīn) **I.** s. mina ♦ **land m.** mina terrestre **II.** tr. extraer; *(to dig a mine)* minar, poner minas en ♦ **to m. for** cavar en busca de.
mine² pron. (el) mío.
mine·field (mīn′fēld′) s. campo de minas.
min·er (mī′nər) s. minero.
min·er·al (mĭn′ər-əl) s. & adj. mineral *m*.
min·er·al·ize (:ə-līz′) tr. & intr. mineralizar(se).
min·er·al·o·gy (mĭn′ə-rŏl′ə-jē) s. mineralogía.
min·gle (mĭng′gəl) tr. & intr. mezclar(se).
min·i (mĭn′ē) s. algo más pequeño de lo normal.
min·i·a·ture (:ə-chŏŏr′, :ə-chər) **I.** s. miniatura **II.** adj. en miniatura.
min·i·a·tur·ize (:ə-chə-rīz′) tr. miniaturizar.

min·i·bike (:bīk′) s. pequeña motocicleta.
min·i·bus (:bŭs′) s. microbús *m*.
min·i·com·put·er (′-kəm-pyŏŏ′tər) s. minicomputadora.
min·i·mal (mĭn′ə-məl) adj. & s. mínimo.
min·i·mize (:mīz′) tr. minimizar.
min·i·mum (:məm) s. & adj. [pl. **s** *o* **-ma**] mínimo ♦ **m. wage** salario vital.
min·ing (mī′nĭng) s. (la) minería; MIL. minado, siembra de minas.
min·ion (mĭn′yən) s. favorito; *(sycophant)* paniaguado; *(subordinate)* funcionario subordinado.
min·is·ter (mĭn′ĭ-stər) **I.** s. ministro ♦ **Prime M.** primer ministro **II.** intr. cuidar.
min·is·te·ri·al (′-stîr′ē-əl) adj. POL. ministerial; RELIG. pastoral.
min·is·try (′-strē) s. POL. ministerio; RELIG. sacerdocio ♦ **to enter the m.** hacerse clérigo.
mink (mĭngk) s. [pl. inv. *o* **s**] visón *m*.
min·now (mĭn′ō) s. [pl. inv. *o* **s**] pez pequeño.
mi·nor (mī′nər) **I.** adj. menor; *(not serious)* pequeño; *(secondary)* de poca importancia; *(in age)* menor de edad **II.** s. menor *mf* de edad; EDUC. especialización secundaria **III.** intr. ♦ **to m. in** EDUC. estudiar como especialización secundaria.
mi·nor·i·ty (mə-nôr′ĭ-tē, mī-) s. minoría.
mi·nor-league (mī′nər-lēg′) adj. FAM. de importancia secundaria.
min·ster (mĭn′stər) s. G.B. iglesia de un monasterio; *(cathedral)* catedral *f*.
min·strel (mĭn′strəl) s. trovador *m*; *(performer)* cantor y actor cómico.
mint¹ (mĭnt) **I.** s. casa de moneda; *(fortune)* cantidad *f* grande **II.** tr. acuñar; *(to invent)* idear **III.** adj. sin usar ♦ **in m. condition** como nuevo.
mint² s. BOT. menta, hierbabuena; *(candy)* (pastilla de) menta.
min·u·end (mĭn′yŏŏ-ĕnd′) s. minuendo.
min·u·et (mĭn′yŏŏ-ĕt′) s. minué *m*.
mi·nus (mī′nəs) **I.** prep. MAT. menos; FAM. *(without)* sin **II.** adj. MAT. negativo **III.** s. MAT. (signo) menos *m*.
min·us·cule (mĭn′ə-skyŏŏl′) **I.** s. minúscula **II.** adj. minúsculo.
min·ute¹ (mĭn′ĭt) s. minuto; *(moment)* momento ♦ **any m.** de un momento a otro • **at the last m.** a última hora • **just a m.!** ¡un momento! • **m. hand** minutero • **the m. something happens** en cuanto algo suceda • **this (very) m.** ahora mismo • **to take a m.** detenerse un momento a ♦ pl. acta.
mi·nute² (mī-nōōt′, mĭ-) adj. diminuto; *(insignificant)* insignificante; *(thorough)* minucioso.
min·ute·man (mĭn′ĭt-măn′) s. [pl. **-men**] miliciano (en la guerra de independencia de E.U.).
mi·nu·ti·a (mĭ-nōō′shē-ə) s. [pl. **-iae**] minucias.
minx (mĭngks) s. joven coqueta *o* descarada.
mir·a·cle (mĭr′ə-kəl) s. milagro; FIG. maravilla.
mi·rac·u·lous (mĭ-răk′yə-ləs) adj. milagroso.
mi·rage (mĭ-räzh′) s. espejismo.
mire (mīr) **I.** s. lodazal *m*; *(mud)* fango **II.** tr. & intr. atascar(se).
mir·ror (mĭr′ər) **I.** s. espejo **II.** tr. reflejar.
mirth (mûrth) s. alegría; *(laughter)* hilaridad *f*.
mirth·ful (′fəl) adj. alegre.
mirth·less (:lĭs) adj. sin alegría.
mis·ad·ven·ture (mĭs′əd-vĕn′chər) s. desventura.
mis·ad·vise (:əd-vīz′) tr. aconsejar mal.

mis·a·ligned (:ə-līnd′) adj. mal alineado.

mis·a·lign·ment (:līn′mənt) s. desalineación *f.*

mis·al·li·ance (:lī′əns) s. mala unión; *(marriage)* matrimonio con persona de clase inferior.

mis·an·thrope (mĭs′ən-thrōp′) s. misántropo.

mis·an·throp·ic (′-thrōp′ĭk) adj. misantrópico.

mis·an·thro·pist (mĭs-ăn′thrə-pĭst) s. misántropo.

mis·an·thro·py (:pē) s. misantropía.

mis·ap·pli·ca·tion (mĭs-ăp′lĭ-kā′shən) s. mala aplicación; *(misuse)* uso indebido.

mis·ap·ply (′ə-plī′) tr. aplicar mal.

mis·ap·pre·hend (mĭs-ăp′rĭ-hĕnd′) tr. comprender mal.

mis·ap·pre·hen·sion (:hĕn′shən) s. malentendido.

mis·ap·pro·pri·ate (mĭs′ə-prō′prē-āt′) tr. apropiar erróneamente; *(to embezzle)* malversar.

mis·ap·pro·pri·a·tion (′-′-ā′shən) s. malversación *f.*

mis·be·got·ten (mĭs′bĭ-gŏt′n) adj. ilegítimo; *(ill-conceived)* mal concebido.

mis·be·have (:hāv′) intr. portarse mal.

mis·be·hav·ior (:yər) s. mala conducta.

mis·cal·cu·late (mĭs-kăl′kyə-lāt′) tr. & intr. calcular mal.

mis·cal·cu·la·tion (′-lā′shən) s. cálculo erróneo; *(mistake)* error *m.*

mis·call (mĭs-kôl′) tr. llamar erróneamente.

mis·car·riage (mĭs-kăr′ĭj) s. *(failure)* fracaso; MED. aborto.

mis·car·ry (:ē) intr. *(to fail)* malograrse; MED. abortar.

mis·ceg·e·na·tion (mĭ-sĕj′ə-nā′shən, mĭs′ĭ-jə-) s. cruce *m* de razas.

mis·cel·la·ne·ous (mĭs′ə-lā′nē-əs) adj. misceláneo ♦ m. **assortment** surtido variado.

mis·cel·la·ny (′-nē) s. miscelánea.

mis·chance (mĭs-chăns′) s. infortunio; *(bad luck)* mala suerte.

mis·chief (mĭs′chĭf) s. *(damage)* daño; *(prank)* travesura; *(perverseness)* malicia.

mis·chie·vous (:chə-vəs) adj. malicioso; *(playful)* travieso; *(troublesome)* molesto.

mis·clas·si·fy (mĭs-klăs′ə-fī′) tr. clasificar incorrectamente.

mis·con·ceive (′kən-sēv′) tr. interpretar incorrectamente.

mis·con·cep·tion (:sĕp′shən) s. concepto erróneo.

mis·con·duct (mĭs-kŏn′dŭkt) s. mala conducta; *(mismanagement)* mala administración.

mis·con·strue (′kən-strōō′) tr. interpretar mal.

mis·count I. tr. & intr. (mĭs-kount′) contar mal II. s. (′kount′) recuento erróneo.

mis·cre·ant (mĭs′krē-ənt) I. s. malhechor *m* II. adj. bellaco.

mis·cue (mĭs-kyōō′) I. s. pifia II. intr. pifiar.

mis·deal I. tr. & intr. (mĭs-dēl′) -**dealt** repartir mal (los naipes) II. s. (′dēl′) reparto erróneo.

mis·deed (mĭs-dēd′) s. fechoría.

mis·de·mean·or (′dĭ-mē′nər) s. *(misdeed)* fechoría; DER. delito menor.

mis·di·ag·nose (mĭs-dī′ag-nōs′) tr. diagnosticar incorrectamente.

mis·di·ag·no·sis (′-nō′sĭs) s. [pl. -**ses**] diagnóstico incorrecto.

mis·di·rect (mĭs′dĭ-rĕkt′) tr. dirigir erradamente.

mis·di·rec·tion (:rĕk′shən) s. mala dirección.

mi·ser (mī′zər) s. avaro.

mis·er·a·ble (mĭz′ər-ə-bəl) adj. *(unhappy)* desdichado; *(disagreeable)* desagradable; *(mean)* abyecto; *(inadequate)* miserable; *(inferior)* de mala calidad.

mi·ser·ly (mī′zər-lē) adj. avariento.

mis·er·y (mĭz′ə-rē) s. miseria; *(unhappiness)* desdicha.

mis·es·ti·mate (mĭs-ĕs′tə-māt′) tr. estimar erróneamente.

mis·fea·sance (:fē′zəns) s. DER. ejecución *f* ilegal de un procedimiento lícito.

mis·file (:fīl′) tr. archivar mal.

mis·fire (:fīr′) I. intr. fallar II. s. (′fīr′) fallo de encendido; FIG. fracaso.

mis·fit (′fĭt′) s. cosa *o* prenda que encaja *o* cae mal; *(person)* persona inadaptada.

mis·for·tune (mĭs-fôr′chən) s. mala suerte; *(mischance)* infortunio.

mis·giv·ing (:gĭv′ĭng) s. duda.

mis·gov·ern (:gŭv′ərn) tr. gobernar mal.

mis·guide (:gīd′) tr. dirigir mal.

mis·guid·ed (:gī′dĭd) adj. descaminado.

mis·han·dle (:hăn′dl) tr. *(to botch)* manejar mal; *(to maltreat)* maltratar.

mis·hap (′hăp′) s. desgracia.

mish·mash (mĭsh′mäsh′) s. revoltijo.

mis·i·den·ti·fy (mĭs′ī-dĕn′tə-fī′) tr. identificar mal *o* erróneamente.

mis·in·form (:īn-fôrm′) tr. dar informes erróneos.

mis·in·for·ma·tion (′-fər-mā′shən) s. información errónea.

mis·in·ter·pret (′-tûr′prĭt) tr. interpretar mal.

mis·in·ter·pre·ta·tion (′-′-prĭ-tā′shən) s. mala interpretación.

mis·judge (mĭs-jŭj′) tr. & intr. juzgar mal.

mis·judg·ment (:mənt) s. juicio equivocado.

mis·la·bel (mĭs-lā′bəl) tr. clasificar mal.

mis·lay (:lā′) tr. -**laid** perder.

mis·lead (:lēd′) tr. -**led** descaminar; *(to deceive)* engañar.

mis·lead·ing (:lē′dĭng) adj. engañoso.

mis·led (:lĕd′) cf. **mislead.**

mis·man·age (:măn′ĭj) tr. administrar mal.

mis·man·age·ment (:mənt) s. mala administración.

mis·mar·riage (mĭs-măr′ĭj) s. matrimonio desacertado.

mis·match (:măch′) I. tr. emparejar mal II. s. (′măch′) emparejamiento mal hecho.

mis·name (mĭs-nām′) tr. dar nombre que no corresponde a la realidad.

mis·no·mer (:nō′mər) s. nombre poco apto.

mi·sog·a·my (mĭ-sŏg′ə-mē) s. misogamia.

mi·sog·y·ny (mĭ-sŏj′ə-nē) s. misoginia.

mis·per·ceive (mĭs′pər-sēv′) tr. percibir mal.

mis·place (mĭs-plās′) tr. *(to mislay)* colocar fuera de su lugar; *(to lose)* extraviar; *(to bestow mistakenly)* otorgar indebidamente.

mis·print (mĭs′prĭnt′) s. error *m* de imprenta.

mis·pro·nounce (′prə-nouns′) tr. & intr. pronunciar mal *o* incorrectamente.

mis·quote (-kwōt′) tr. citar incorrectamente.

mis·read (:rēd′) tr. -**read** leer mal; *(to misinterpret)* interpretar mal.

mis·rep·re·sent (:rĕp′rĭ-zĕnt′) tr. tergiversar.

mis·rep·re·sen·ta·tion (:zĕn-tā′shən) s. *(distortion)* tergiversación *f;* *(fraud)* representación fraudulenta.

mis·rule (mĭs-rōōl′) I. tr. desgobernar II. s. desgobierno.

miss¹ (mĭs) I. tr. perder; *(a shot)* errar; *(not to*

meet) no encontrar; *(not to see)* no ver; *(not to perceive)* no darse cuenta de; *(not to achieve)* no conseguir; *(to regret the absence of)* echar de menos, extrañar ♦ **to m. one's turn** perder el turno ♦ **to m. out on** perderse ♦ **to m. the boat** FAM. írsele a uno el tren ♦ **to m. the mark** equivocarse ♦ **to m. the point** no comprender • **you can't miss it** lo encontrarás fácilmente —intr. fallar ♦ **to be missing** faltar • **you can't m.** FAM. no hay forma de perder **II.** s. fallo; *(failure)* fracaso.

miss² s. señorita ♦ **M. Brown** la señorita Brown.

mis·shap·en (mĭs-shā′pən) adj. deformado.

mis·sile (mĭs′əl, -īl′) s. proyectil m; *(guided)* misil teledirigido; *(ballistic)* proyectil balístico.

mis·sile·ry (:əl-rē) s. (ciencia de) cohetes teledirigidos.

miss·ing (mĭs′ĭng) adj. *(lost)* perdido; *(disappeared)* desaparecido; *(absent)* ausente; *(lacking)* que falta ♦ **m. link** eslabón perdido.

mis·sion (mĭsh′ən) s. misión f; DIPL. embajada; *(welfare organization)* beneficencia.

mis·sion·ar·y (:ə-nĕr′ē) s. & adj. misionero.

mis·sis (mĭs′ĭz) s. FAM. esposa, doña.

mis·sive (mĭs′ĭv) s. misiva.

mis·spell (mĭs-spĕl′) tr. **-ed** o **-spelt** ortografiar o deletrear mal.

mis·spend (:spĕnd′) tr. **-spent** malgastar.

mis·state (:stāt′) tr. exponer o relatar mal.

mis·step (:stĕp′) s. tropezón m; *(blunder)* desacierto.

mist (mĭst) **I.** s. *(fog)* neblina; *(at sea)* bruma; *(haze)* calina; FIG. oscuridad f **II.** intr. *(to fog up)* cubrirse de niebla; *(to blur)* empañarse.

mis·take (mĭ-stāk′) **I.** s. error m **II.** tr. **-took, -taken** interpretar mal ♦ **to m. . . . for** confundir . . . con —intr. ♦ **to be mistaken** equivocarse.

mis·tak·en (mĭ-stā′kən) adj. *(wrong)* equivocado, errado; *(inexact)* erróneo.

Mis·ter (mĭs′tər) s. señor m.

mis·tle·toe (mĭs′əl-tō′) s. muérdago.

mis·took (mĭs-stŏŏk′) cf. **mistake**.

mis·treat (mĭs-trēt′) tr. maltratar.

mis·treat·ment (:mənt) s. maltrato.

mis·tress (mĭs′trĭs) s. *(head of household)* señora; *(lover)* amante f; *(controller)* dueña.

mis·tri·al (mĭs-trī′əl) s. juicio nulo (por error de procedimiento o desacuerdo del jurado).

mis·trust (:trŭst′) **I.** s. desconfianza **II.** tr. & intr. desconfiar (de).

mist·y (mĭs′tē) adj. **-i-** nebuloso; *(obscured)* empañado; *(vague)* vago.

mis·un·der·stand (mĭs-ŭn′dər-stănd′) tr. **-stood** entender o interpretar mal.

mis·un·der·stand·ing (:stăn′dĭng) s. malentendido; *(disagreement)* desacuerdo.

mis·use **I.** s. (mĭs-yōōs′) mal empleo; *(mistreatment)* maltrato **II.** tr. (:yōōz′) emplear mal; *(to mistreat)* maltratar.

mite¹ (mīt) s. ENTOM. arador m, acárido.

mite² s. *(money)* suma ínfima; *(object)* pizca.

mi·ter (mī′tər) **I.** s. RELIG. mitra; CARP. inglete m **II.** tr. unir a inglete.

mit·i·gate (mĭt′ĭ-gāt′) tr. mitigar.

mit·i·ga·tion (′-gā′shən) s. mitigación f.

mitt (mĭt) s. *(woman's)* mitón m; *(for baseball)* guante m de béisbol; JER. *(hand)* mano.

mit·ten (mĭt′n) s. manopla.

mix (mĭks) **I.** tr. mezclar; *(a drink)* preparar; *(to crossbreed)* cruzar ♦ **to get mixed up in** me-

terse en • **to m. in** agregar • **to m. it up** JER. llegar a las manos • **to m. up** *(to confuse)* confundir; *(to jumble)* mezclar —intr. mezclarse; *(to go together)* pegar **II.** s. mezcla; *(for a cake)* masa.

mixed (mĭkst) adj. mezclado; *(conflicting)* contradictorio; *(composite)* mixto ♦ **m. drink** trago combinado.

mixed-up (′ŭp′) adj. FAM. confundido, que no sabe lo que quiere.

mix·er (mĭk′sər) s. *(person)* persona sociable; *(machine)* mezcladora; *(appliance)* batidora; *(beverage)* bebida (para mezclar); *(gathering)* fiesta informal para que la gente se conozca.

mix·ture (mĭks′chər) s. mezcla; *(compound)* mixtura.

mix-up (mĭks′ŭp′) s. confusión f, lío.

mne·mon·ic (nĭ-mŏn′ĭk) **I.** adj. mnemotécnico, nemónico **II.** s. fórmula o rima nemónica ♦ **mnemonics** sg. mnemotécnica, nemónica.

moan (mōn) **I.** s. gemido **II.** intr. gemir.

moat (mōt) s. foso de un castillo).

mob (mŏb) **I.** s. turba; *(masses)* populacho; FAM. *(gang)* pandilla **II.** tr. **-bb-** *(to crowd in)* atestar; *(to throng around)* rodear.

mo·bile (mō′bəl, mō-bīl′) **I.** adj. móvil; *(character)* cambiadizo; *(society)* sin divisiones rígidas (de clase) **II.** s. (mō′bēl′) ARTE. móvil m.

mo·bil·i·ty (mō-bĭl′ĭ-tē) s. movilidad f.

mo·bi·lize (mō′bə-līz′) tr. & intr. movilizar(se).

mob·ster (mŏb′stər) s. JER. pandillero.

moc·ca·sin (mŏk′ə-sĭn) s. mocasín m.

mo·cha (mō′kə) s. moca.

mock (mŏk) **I.** tr. mofarse de; *(to imitate)* imitar **II.** adj. simulado.

mock·er·y (′ə-rē) s. mofa; *(object of ridicule)* objeto de burla; *(imitation)* imitación f; *(parody)* parodia ♦ **to make a m. of** parodiar a.

mock·ing·bird (′-bûrd′) s. sinsonte m.

mock·up o **mock-up** (′ŭp′) s. maqueta.

mod (mŏd) **I.** s. moda **II.** adj. de moda.

mo·dal (mōd′l) adj. modal.

mo·dal·i·ty (mō-dăl′ĭ-tē) s. modalidad f.

mode (mōd) s. modo; *(fashion)* moda.

mod·el (mŏd′l) **I.** s. & adj. modelo **II.** tr. modelar; *(fashions)* presentar ♦ **to m. after** o **on** *(thing)* construir según; *(oneself)* tomar como modelo a —intr. modelar; *(to pose)* posar.

mod·el·ing (:ĭng) s. profesión f de modelo; *(production of designs)* creación f de modelos; *(representation)* modelado.

mod·er·ate (mŏd′ər-ĭt) **I.** adj. moderado; *(price)* módico; *(medium)* mediano **II.** s. moderado **III.** tr. (:ə-rāt′) moderar; *(to preside over)* presidir —intr. moderarse; *(to preside)* servir de moderador.

mod·er·a·tion (′ə-rā′shən) s. moderación f.

mod·er·a·tor (′-′tər) s. moderador m.

mod·ern (mŏd′ərn) adj. & s. moderno.

mod·ern·ize (:ər-nīz′) tr. & intr. modernizar(se).

mod·est (mŏd′ĭst) adj. modesto; *(reserved)* recatado; *(in dress)* pudoroso; *(in price)* módico.

mod·es·ty (:ĭ-stē) s. modestia; *(decency)* pudor; *(in price)* modicidad f.

mod·i·cum (mŏd′ĭ-kəm) s. [pl. s o **-ca**] pizca.

mod·i·fi·ca·tion (mŏd′ə-fĭ-kā′shən) s. modificación f.

mod·i·fi·er (′-fī′ər) s. modificador m; GRAM. modificativo.

mod·i·fy (:fī′) tr. modificar; *(to moderate)*

moderar.
mod·ish (mō'dǐsh) adj. de moda.
mod·u·lar (mŏj'ə-lər) adj. modular, del módulo; *(furniture)* de módulos.
mod·u·late (mŏj'ə-lāt') tr. & intr. modular.
mod·u·la·tion ('-lā'shən) s. modulación f.
mod·u·la·tor ('-'tər) s. modulador m.
mod·ule (mŏj'ōōl) s. módulo; ELECTRÓN. componente m.
mod·u·lus (mŏj'ə-ləs) s. [pl. **-li**] módulo.
mo·hair (mō'hâr') s. mohair m.
moist (moist) adj. *(wet)* mojado; *(damp)* húmedo.
mois·ten (moi'sən) tr. & intr. humedecer(se).
moist·ness (moist'nǐs) s. humedad f.
mois·ture (mois'chər) s. humedad f.
mois·tur·ize (:chə-rīz') tr. humedecer.
mois·tur·iz·er (:rī'zər) s. cosa que humedece; *(lotion)* loción f humectante.
mo·lar (mō'lər) s. & adj. molar m.
mo·las·ses (mə-lǎs'ǐz) s. melaza.
mold¹ (mōld) I. s. *(hollow form)* molde m; *(model)* patrón m; *(molded item)* vaciado; *(shape)* forma; *(character)* temple m ♦ **to be cast in the m. of** estar cortado por el patrón de II. tr. moldear ♦ **to m. oneself on** tomar como modelo a.
mold² BIOL. I. s. moho II. intr. enmohecerse.
mold³ s. *(soil)* mantillo.
mold·er (mōl'dər) tr. & intr. desmoronar(se).
mold·ing (mōl'dǐng) s. pieza moldeada; ARQ. moldura.
mold·y (mōl'dē) adj. **-i-** mohoso; *(musty)* enmohecido.
mole¹ (mōl) s. ANAT. lunar m.
mole² s. ZOOL. topo.
mo·lec·u·lar (mə-lěk'yə-lər) adj. molecular.
mol·e·cule (mŏl'ǐ-kyōōl') s. molécula.
mole·hill (mōl'hǐl') s. topera.
mo·lest (mə-lěst') tr. molestar; *(sexually)* abusar sexualmente.
mo·lest·er (mə-lěs'tər) s. molestador m; *(sexually)* persona que comete abusos sexuales.
moll (mŏl) s. JER. querida de un gángster.
mol·li·fy (mŏl'ə-fī') tr. *(to placate)* apaciguar; *(to soften)* molificar.
mol·lusk/lusc (mŏl'əsk) s. molusco.
mol·ly·cod·dle (mŏl'ē-kŏd'l) tr. FAM. mimar.
molt (mōlt) I. tr. & intr. mudar (las plumas o la piel) II. s. muda (de las plumas o la piel).
mol·ten (mōl'tən) adj. *(melted)* derretido; *(made by melting)* fundido.
mom (mŏm) s. FAM. mamá.
mo·ment (mō'mənt) s. momento ♦ **any m.** de un momento a otro • **at the last m.** a última hora • **at the m.** en este momento • **just a m.!** ¡un momento! • **m. of truth** hora de la verdad • **not for a m.!** ¡ni muerto! • **the m. something happens** en cuanto algo suceda • **this very m.** ahora mismo.
mo·men·tar·i·ly (mō'mən-târ'ə-lē) adv. *(for a moment)* momentáneamente; *(at any moment)* de un momento a otro; *(soon)* en un momento.
mo·men·tar·y (mō'-těr'ē) adj. momentáneo.
mo·men·tous (mō-měn'təs) adj. de gran importancia.
mo·men·tum (:təm) s. [pl. **s** o **-ta**] momento; *(impulse)* ímpetu m.
mon·arch (mŏn'ərk) s. monarca m; ENTOM. mariposa de color anaranjado y negro.
mo·nar·chic/chi·cal (mə-när'kĭk) adj. monárquico.

mon·ar·chist (mŏn'ər-kĭst) s. & adj. monárquico.
mon·ar·chy (:kē) s. monarquía.
mon·as·ter·y (mŏn'ə-stěr'ē) s. monasterio.
mo·nas·tic (mə-nǎs'tǐk) adj. monástico.
Mon·day (mǔn'dē) s. lunes m.
mon·e·tar·y (mŏn'ǐ-těr'ē) adj. monetario.
mon·ey (mǔn'ē) s. [pl. **s** o **-ies**] dinero; *(currency)* moneda ♦ **m. order** giro postal • **m. talks** el dinero todo lo puede • **not for all the m. in the world** ni por todo el oro del mundo • **ready m.** dinero disponible • **to be in the m.** estar entre los ganadores • **to be made of m.** ser millonario • **to make m.** ganar dinero • **to put m. on** apostar a • **your m. or your life!** ¡la bolsa o la vida! ♦ pl. fondos.
mon·ey·bag (:bǎg') s. monedero ♦ pl. FAM. ricachón.
mon·ey·chang·er (:chān'jər) s. cambista mf; *(machine)* máquina que cambia monedas.
mon·eyed (mǔn'ēd) adj. adinerado.
mon·ey·lend·er (:ě-lěn'dər) s. prestamista mf.
mon·ey·mak·er (:mā'kər) s. amasador m de dinero; *(thing)* fuente f de dinero.
mon·ey·mak·ing (:kǐng) I. s. enriquecimiento II. adj. lucrativo.
mon·gol·ism (mŏng'gə-lĭz'əm) s. MED. mongolismo.
mon·gol·oid (:loid') adj. & s. MED. mongólico.
mon·goose (mŏng'gōōs') s. mangosta.
mon·grel (mŏng'grəl, mŏng'-) s. & adj. híbrido (esp. perro cruzado).
mon·i·ker (mŏn'ǐ-kər) s. JER. nombre m.
mo·ni·tion (mə-nǐsh'ən) s. admonición f.
mon·i·tor (mŏn'ǐ-tər) I. s. monitor m II. tr. *(signal, quality)* comprobar; *(for radiation)* determinar la contaminación radioactiva de; *(to keep track of)* vigilar (electrónicamente); *(for content)* escuchar —intr. servir de monitor.
mon·i·to·ry (mŏn'ǐ-tôr'ē) adj. admonitorio.
monk (mǔngk) s. monje m.
mon·key (mǔng'kē) I. s. mono II. intr. ♦ **to m. around** hacer payasadas • **to m. (around) with** manosear o jugar con algo.
mon·key·shines (:shīnz') s.pl. JER. payasadas.
monk·hood (mǔngk'hōōd') s. monacato.
monk·ish (mǔng'kǐsh) adj. monacal; *(of friars)* frailesco.
mon·o¹ (mŏn'ō) s. MED. mononucleosis f.
mon·o² adj. monoaural.
mon·o·chro·mat·ic (mŏn'ə-krō-mǎt'ǐk) adj. monocromático.
mon·o·cle (mŏn'ə-kəl) s. monóculo.
mo·noc·u·lar (mə-nŏk'yə-lər) adj. monocular.
mo·nog·a·mist (mə-nŏg'ə-mǐst) s. monógamo.
mo·nog·a·mous (:məs) adj. monógamo.
mo·nog·a·my (:mē) s. monogamia.
mon·o·gram (mŏn'ə-grǎm') I. s. monograma m II. tr. marcar con un monograma.
mon·o·graph (:grǎf') s. monografía.
mon·o·lin·gual ('-lǐng'gwəl) adj. monolingüe.
mon·o·lith ('-lǐth') s. monolito.
mon·o·lith·ic ('-'lǐk') adj. monolítico.
mon·o·log(ue) (mŏn'ə-lôg') s. monólogo.
mon·o·ma·ni·a ('-mā'nē-ə) s. monomanía.
mon·o·mor·phic (mŏn'ō-môr'fǐk) adj. monomórfico.
mon·o·nu·cle·o·sis (:nōō'klē-ō'sǐs) s. mononucleosis f.
mon·o·plane (mŏn'ə-plān') s. monoplano.
mo·nop·o·list (mə-nŏp'ə-lǐst) s. monopolizador m.

mo·nop·o·lis·tic (-'-lǐs'tǐk) adj. monopolizador.

mo·nop·o·lize (-'-līz') tr. monopolizar.

mo·nop·o·ly (:lē) s. monopolio.

mon·o·rail (mŏn'ə-rāl') s. monocarril m.

mon·o·syl·lab·ic ('-sǐ-lǎb'ǐk) adj. (word) monosílabo; (language) monosilábico.

mon·o·tone (mŏn'ə-tōn') s. monotonía.

mo·not·o·nous (mə-nŏt'n-əs) adj. monótono.

mo·not·o·ny (:ē) s. monotonía.

mon·ox·ide (mə-nŏk'sīd') s. monóxido.

mon·soon (mŏn-sōōn') s. monzón m.

mon·ster (mŏn'stər) s. monstruo.

mon·strance (mŏn'strəns) s. custodia.

mon·stros·i·ty (mŏn-strŏs'ĭ-tē) s. monstruosidad f.

mon·strous ('strəs) adj. monstruoso.

mon·tage (mŏn-täzh') s. montaje m.

month (mŭnth) s. [pl. **s**] mes m. ♦ **in a m. of Sundays** nunca.

month·ly ('lē) I. adj. mensual ♦ **m. installment, payment** mensualidad II. adv. mensualmente III. s. publicación f mensual.

mon·u·ment (mŏn'yə-mənt) s. monumento.

mon·u·men·tal ('-měn'tl) adj. monumental.

moo (mōō) I. intr. mugir II. s. mugido.

mooch (mōōch) JER. tr. conseguir gratis —intr. gorronear.

mooch·er (mōō'chər) s. JER. gorrón m.

mood (mōōd) s. humor m; (disposition) disposición f ♦ **to be in a bad, good m.** estar de mal, buen humor • **to be in the m. for** tener ganas de.

mood·y (mōō'dē) adj. -i- malhumorado; (whimsical) caprichoso.

moon (mōōn) I. s. luna; (moonlight) claro de luna ♦ **crescent m.** media luna • **once in a blue m.** de Pascuas a Ramos II. intr. FAM. estar en la luna.

moon·beam ('bēm') s. rayo de luna.

moon·light (:līt') I. s. luz f de la luna II. intr. FAM. tener otro empleo además del principal.

moon·shine (:shīn') s. claro de luna; FAM. (foolishness) pamplinas f; JER. (whiskey) alcohol destilado ilegalmente.

moon·stone (:stōn') s. piedra de la luna.

moon·struck (:strŭk') adj. chiflado, atontado.

moon·walk (:wŏk') s. caminata exploratoria sobre la superficie lunar.

moon·y (mōō'nē) adj. -i- soñador.

moor[1] (mŏōr) tr. MARÍT. amarrar.

moor[2] s. GEOG. terreno pantanoso.

moor·age (mŏōr'ĭj) s. (place) amarradero; (act) amarradura.

moor·ing (:ĭng) s. (cable) amarra; (act) amarradura; (place) amarradero.

moose (mōōs) s.inv. anta.

moot (mōōt) adj. ♦ **m. point** punto debatible.

mop (mŏp) I. s. estropajo; (of hair) greña II. tr. **-pp-** fregar —intr. ♦ **to m. up** FAM. dar cabo a una tarea.

mope (mŏp) intr. estar abatido.

mo·ped (mŏ'pĕd') s. ciclomotor m.

mop·pet (mŏp'ĭt) s. niño.

mor·al (môr'əl) I. adj. moral; (person) recto II. s. moraleja ♦ pl. principios morales • **loose m.** costumbres relajadas.

mo·rale (mə-rāl') s. moral f, estado de ánimo.

mor·al·ist (môr'ə-lĭst) s. moralista mf; (moralizer) moralizador m.

mor·al·is·tic ('-lĭs'tĭk) adj. moralizador.

mor·al·i·ty (mə-rāl'ĭ-tē) s. moralidad f; (morals)

moral f.

mor·al·ize (môr'ə-līz') intr. moralizar.

mo·rass (mə-rās') s. ciénaga; FIG. embrollo.

mor·a·to·ri·um (môr'ə-tôr'ē-əm) s. [pl. **s** o **-ia**] moratoria.

mo·ray (môr'ā) s. morena.

mor·bid (môr'bĭd) adj. morboso.

mor·bid·i·ty (-'ĭ-tē) s. morbosidad f.

mor·dant (môr'dnt) adj. mordaz.

more (môr) I. adj. más; (greater in quantity) superior II. s. más ♦ **the m....the m....** cuanto más...más...• **the m. the merrier** cuanto más, mejor III. pron. más IV. adv. más ♦ **m. and m.** cada vez más • **m. or less** más o menos • **m. than** (with adjectives) más que; (with numbers) más de • **to be no m.** ya no existir.

more·o·ver (:ō'vər) adv. además.

mo·res (môr'āz') s.pl. costumbres f, usos.

morgue (môrg) s. depósito de cadáveres.

mor·i·bund (môr'ə-bənd) adj. moribundo.

morn (môrn) s. POÉT. mañana.

morn·ing (môr'nĭng) s. mañana ♦ **good m.!** ¡buenos días! • **in the m.** por la mañana.

morn·ing-glo·ry (:glôr'ē) s. dondiego de día.

mo·ron (môr'ŏn') s. FAM. imbécil m.

mo·ron·ic (mə-rŏn'ĭk) adj. FAM. imbécil.

mo·rose (mə-rōs') adj. malhumorado.

mor·pheme (môr'fēm') s. morfema m.

mor·phine (môr'fēn') s. morfina.

mor·phol·o·gy (môr-fŏl'ə-jē) s. morfología.

mor·row (môr'ō) s. día m siguiente.

Morse code (môrs) s. morse m.

mor·sel (môr'səl) s. (bite) bocado, pedacito; (delicacy) manjar m.

mor·tal (môr'tl) I. adj. mortal; (human) humano; (terrible) terrible II. s. mortal m.

mor·tal·i·ty (môr-tāl'ĭ-tē) s. mortalidad f.

mor·tar (môr'tər) s. mortero.

mor·tar·board (:bôrd') s. (tool) esparavel m; (hat) birrete m.

mort·gage (môr'gĭj) I. s. hipoteca; (contract) contrato de hipoteca II. tr. hipotecar.

mort·ga·gee ('-gĭ-jē') s. acreedor hipotecario.

mort·ga·gor ('-jər) s. deudor hipotecario.

mor·ti·cian (môr-tĭsh'ən) s. agente funerario.

mor·ti·fi·ca·tion (môr'tə-fĭ-kā'shən) s. mortificación f; (torment) tormento; MED. necrosis f.

mor·ti·fy ('-fī') tr. & intr. mortificar(se).

mor·ti·fy·ing (:ĭng) adj. mortificador.

mor·tise (môr'tĭs) s. mortaja.

mor·tu·ar·y (môr'chōō-ĕr'ē) s. mortuorio.

mo·sa·ic (mō-zā'ĭk) s. mosaico.

mo·sey (mō'zē) intr. FAM. deambular.

mosque (mŏsk) s. mezquita.

mos·qui·to (mə-skē'tō) s. [pl. **(e)s**] mosquito ♦ **m. net** mosquitero.

moss (môs) s. musgo.

moss·y (mô'sē) adj. -i- musgoso; (resembling moss) parecido al musgo.

most (môst) I. adj. (in quantity) más...que todos los demás; (in measure) mayor; (almost all) la mayoría de ♦ **for the m. part** en su mayoría II. s. la mayor parte; (the majority) la mayoría ♦ **at (the) m.** a lo sumo • **the m.** lo más • **to make the m. of** aprovechar al máximo III. pron. la mayoría, la mayor parte IV. adv. más...que todos los demás; (superlative) más; (very) muy ♦ **m. certainly** con toda seguridad • **m. likely** muy probablemente • **m. of all** sobre todo.

most·ly ('lē) adv. en su mayor parte.

mote (mōt) s. *(dust)* partícula; *(speck)* mota.
mo·tel (mō-tĕl′) s. motel *m*.
moth (môth) s. [pl. **s**] mariposa nocturna; *(clothes moth)* polilla.
moth·ball (′bôl′) I. s. bola de naftalina ♦ **in mothballs** en condición de almacenamiento prolongado II. tr. almacenar.
moth-eat·en (:ēt′n) adj. apolillado; *(old)* viejo.
moth·er (mŭth′ər) I. s. madre *f*; *(superior)* superiora II. adj. materno; *(country)* madre III. tr. *(to give birth to)* dar a luz a; *(to protect)* cuidar como una madre.
moth·er·hood (:hŏŏd′) s. maternidad *f*.
moth·er-in-law (:ĭn-lô′) s. [pl. **mothers**-] suegra.
moth·er·land (:lănd′) s. patria; *(of ancestors)* madre patria.
moth·er·ly (:lē) adj. materno, maternal.
moth·er-of-pearl (′-əv-pûrl′) s. madreperla.
moth·proof (môth′prŏŏf′) I. adj. a prueba de polillas II. tr. proteger contra las polillas.
moth·y (mô′thē) adj. -i- apolillado.
mo·tif (mō-tēf′) s. motivo.
mo·tion (mō′shən) I. s. movimiento; *(gesture)* ademán *m*; *(proposal)* moción *f* ♦ **m. picture** película cinematográfica • **m. sickness** mareo • **to set in m.** poner en marcha II. intr. hacer señas *o* una señal.
mo·tion·less (:lĭs) adj. inmóvil.
mo·ti·vate (mō′tə-vāt′) tr. motivar.
mo·ti·va·tion (′-vā′shən) s. motivación *f*.
mo·tive (mō′tĭv) I. s. motivo; *(criminal)* móvil *m* II. adj. motriz; *(impelling)* impulsor.
mot·ley (mŏt′lē) adj. abigarrado.
mo·tor (mō′tər) I. s. motor *m* II. adj. motor; *(driven by a motor)* de motor ♦ **m. home** casa a remolque con motor • **m. inn** *o* **lodge** motel, hotel con estacionamiento • **m. vehicle** vehículo automotor III. intr. ir en automóvil.
mo·tor·bike (:bīk′) s. motocicleta liviana.
mo·tor·boat (:bōt′) s. bote *m* a motor.
mo·tor·cade (:kād′) s. caravana de automóviles.
mo·tor·car (:kär′) s. automóvil *m*, coche *m*.
mo·tor·cy·cle (:sī′kəl) s. motocicleta, moto *f*.
mo·tor·cy·clist (:sī′klĭst) s. motociclista *mf*.
mo·tor·ist (:ĭst) s. automovilista *mf*.
mo·tor·ize (mō′tə-rīz′) tr. motorizar.
mo·tor·man (mō′tər-mən) s. [pl. -men] maquinista *mf* (de tranvía *o* tren eléctrico).
mot·tle (mŏt′l) tr. motear, jaspear.
mot·tled (:ld) adj. moteado, jaspeado.
mot·to (mŏt′ō) s. [pl. (**e**)**s**] lema *m*.
mould (mōld) G.B. var. de **mold**.
mound (mound) s. *(hill)* montículo.
mount[1] (mount) I. tr. *(to climb)* subir (a); *(a horse)* montar; *(to fix in place)* fijar; MEC. montar; *(an attack)* lanzar —intr. *(to move upward)* subir; *(to ride)* montar II. s. montura; *(base)* soporte *m*.
mount[2] s. *(hill)* monte *m*.
moun·tain (moun′tən) s. montaña ♦ **m. lion** león americano • **m. range** cordillera.
moun·tain·eer (′-tə-nîr′) s. *(inhabitant)* montañés *m*; *(climber)* alpinista *mf*, montañero.
moun·tain·ous (′-tə-nəs) adj. montañoso; *(immense)* inmenso.
moun·tain·side (:tən-sīd′) s. ladera *o* falda de una montaña.
moun·tain·top (:tŏp′) s. cima de una montaña.
moun·te·bank (moun′tə-băngk′) s. saltabanco.
mount·ed (moun′tĭd) adj. montado.

mount·ing (:tĭng) s. montura; *(of jewel)* engaste *m*.
mourn (môrn) intr. & tr. llorar; *(a death)* lamentar(se).
mourn·er (môr′nər) s. persona que está de luto; *(at a funeral)* doliente *mf*.
mourn·ful (môrn′fəl) adj. dolorido, triste; *(arousing grief)* penoso.
mourn·ing (môr′nĭng) s. duelo; *(period)* luto ♦ **m. dove** paloma torcaza • **to be in m.** estar de luto.
mouse (mous) s. [pl. **mice**] ZOOL., COMPUT. ratón *m*.
mouse·trap (′trăp′) s. ratonera.
mousse (mŏs) s. postre frío.
mous·tache (mŭs′tăsh′, mə-stăsh′) var. de **mustache**.
mous·y (mou′sē) adj. -i- FAM. *(dull gray)* pardusco; *(timid)* tímido.
mouth (mouth) I. s. [pl. **s**] boca ♦ **not to open one's m.** no decir esta boca es mía • **to be down in the m.** estar deprimido • **to have a big m.** ser un bocazas • **to keep one's m. shut** callar(se) • **to make one's m. water** hacérsele a uno la boca agua • **watch your m.!** FAM. ¡ten cuidado con lo que dices! II. tr. *(mouth)* pronunciar; *(to utter)* decir (de forma afectada); *(soundlessly)* articular en silencio; *(to take into the mouth)* meter en la boca —intr. ♦ **to m. off** hablar con descaro.
mouth·ful (′fŏŏl′) s. bocado; *(of smoke)* bocanada ♦ **you said a m.!** FAM. ¡muy bien dicho!
mouth·piece (:pēs′) s. boquilla; FAM. *(spokesman)* vocero.
mouth-to-mouth (:tə-mouth′) adj. de boca a boca.
mouth·wash (:wŏsh′) s. enjuague *m* bucal.
mouth·y (mou′thē, :thē) adj. -i- bombástico.
mov·a·bil·i·ty (mŏŏ′və-bĭl′ĭ-tē) s. movilidad *f*.
mov(e)·a·ble (′-bəl) adj. movible, móvil.
move (mŏŏv) I. intr. moverse; *(to change position)* cambiar de postura; *(to relocate)* mudarse; *(to act)* entrar en acción; *(to make a motion)* proponer; *(in a game)* jugar ♦ **to m. about** *o* **around** cambiar de sitio • **to m. along** *o* **forward** seguir adelante • **to m. away** alejarse • **to m. in** instalarse • **to m. in on** intentar apoderarse de • **to m. up** ascender —tr. mover; *(to change the place of)* trasladar; *(to prompt)* impulsar; MEC. *(to set in motion)* poner en marcha; *(to stir)* conmover ♦ **to m. up** subir; *(to advance)* adelantar (una fecha); *(to promote)* ascender II. s. movimiento; *(change of residence)* mudanza; *(of a piece)* jugada; *(player's turn)* turno; *(step)* paso ♦ **on the m.** andando de acá para allá; *(active)* activo • **to get a m. on** FAM. empezar a moverse.
move·ment (′mənt) s. movimiento; *(gesture)* gesto; *(trend)* tendencia; *(activity)* actividad *f*; *(of bowels)* evacuación (del vientre) *f*; *(watch)* mecanismo.
mov·er (mŏŏ′vər) s. persona que hace mudanzas ♦ pl. agencia de mudanzas.
mov·ie (:vē) s. película ♦ **m. star** estrella de cine • **m. theater** cine ♦ pl. cine.
mov·ie·go·er (:gō′ər) s. aficionado al cine.
mov·ie·mak·er (:mā′kər) s. cineasta *mf*.
mov·ing (mŏŏ′vĭng) adj. móvil; *(changing residence)* de mudanza; *(in motion)* en marcha; *(touching)* conmovedor.
mow (mō) tr. **-ed, -ed** *o* **-n** segar.
mow·er (mō′ər) s. segador *m*; *(machine)* sega-

dora; *(for lawn)* cortacéspedes *m.*

mow·ing (mō′ĭng) s. AGR. siega; *(lawn)* corte *m* ♦ m. **machine** segadora.

mown (mōn) cf. **mow.**

mox·ie (mŏk′sē) s. *(pluck)* coraje *m*; *(pep)* brío.

Mr. (mĭs′tər) s. [abr. de **Mister**] Sr.

Mrs. (mĭs′ĭz) s. [abr. de **Mistress**] Sra.

much (mŭch) I. adj. **more, most** mucho ♦ **as m. . . . as** tanto . . . como • **how m.?** ¿cuánto? • **three times as m.** tres veces más • **too m.** demasiado II. s. mucho; *(large part)* gran parte *f* ♦ **as m. again** otro tanto • **as m. as** tanto como • **as m. as to say** como si dijera • **I thought as m.** ya me lo figuraba • **it's as m. as anybody can do** es todo lo que se puede hacer • **not so m. as** ni siquiera • **not to be m.** no ser gran cosa • **not to be m. of** no ser gran cosa como • **not to think m. of** no tener un gran concepto de • **so m.** tanto • **so m. for that** borrón y cuenta nueva • **so m. so that** tanto que • **so m. the better** tanto mejor • **there's not m.** to it no es muy complicado • **this, that m.** un tanto así • **to make m. of** dar mucha importancia a • **to say this m. for** decir esto en defensa de • **twice as m.** el doble III. adv. mucho ♦ **however m.** por mucho que • **how m.?** ¿cuánto? • **m. to my amazement** con gran sorpresa mía • **very m.** muchísimo.

mu·ci·lage (myōō′sə-lĭj) s. mucílago; *(adhesive)* goma de pegar (esp. de origen vegetal).

muck (mŭk) I. s. lodo; *(filth)* suciedad *f*; *(manure)* estiércol *m*; *(fertile soil)* mantillo II. tr. ♦ **to m. up** ensuciar; *(to bungle)* chapucear.

muck·a·muck (mŭk′ə-mŭk′) s. JER. persona importante.

muck·rake (mŭk′rāk′) intr. descubrir *o* revelar escándalos.

muck·rak·er (:rā′kər) s. revelador *m* de escándalos públicos.

muck·y (:ē) adj. **-i-** fangoso.

mu·cous (myōō′kəs) adj. mucoso.

mu·cus (:kəs) s. mucosidad *f*, mucus *m.*

mud (mŭd) s. barro, lodo; *(slander)* difamación *f* ♦ **to sling m. at** calumniar a.

mud·dle (mŭd′l) tr. *(to muddy)* enturbiar; *(to jumble)* embrollar; *(to befuddle)* atontar; *(to bungle)* chapucear ♦ **to m. through** salir bien a pesar de torpezas.

mud·dy (mŭd′ē) I. adj. **-i-** fangoso; *(cloudy)* turbio II. tr. enfangar; *(a river)* llenar de fango; *(to make cloudy)* enturbiar ♦ **to m. the waters** complicar una situación.

mud·sling·er (:slĭng′ər) s. difamador *m.*

muff¹ (mŭf) I. tr. hacer mal II. s. chapucería.

muff² s. *(hand covering)* manguito.

muf·fin (mŭf′ĭn) s. mollete *m.*

muf·fle (mŭf′əl) tr. embozar; *(sound)* amortiguar; *(to make vague)* confundir.

muf·fler (mŭf′lər) s. *(scarf)* bufanda; AUTO. silenciador *m.*

mug¹ (mŭg) s. *(cup)* jarra.

mug² I. s. JER. *(face)* jeta; FAM. *(hoodlum)* rufián *m* II. tr. **-gg-** *(to take a mugshot)* fotografiar; *(to assault)* asaltar —intr. JER. exagerar los gestos faciales.

mug·ger (′gər) s. asaltante *mf.*

mug·ging (:ĭng) s. asalto (con intento de robo).

mug·gy (mŭg′ē) adj. **-i-** bochornoso.

mu·lat·to (mə-lä′tō) s. [pl. **(e)s**] mulato.

mul·ber·ry (mŭl′bĕr′ē) s. mora.

mulch (mŭlch) I. s. pajote *m* II. tr. cubrir con pajote.

mule¹ (myōōl) s. mulo; FAM. *(person)* testarudo.

mule² s. *(slipper)* chinela, pantufla.

mule·skin·ner (myōōl′skĭn′ər) s. FAM. arriero.

mu·le·teer (myōō′lə-tîr′) m. mulero.

mul·ish (′lĭsh) adj. terco.

mull¹ (mŭl) tr. CUL. calentar (vino).

mull² tr. & intr. ponderar (sobre).

mul·let (mŭl′ĭt) s. [pl. inv. *o* **s**] mújol *m*, lisa.

mul·ti·col·ored (mŭl′tĭ-kŭl′ərd) adj. multicolor.

mul·ti·di·men·sion·al (′tē-dĭ-mĕn′shə-nəl) adj. multidimensional.

mul·ti·far·i·ous (:tə-fâr′ē-əs) adj. variado.

mul·ti·fold (′-fōld′) adj. doblado varias veces; *(multiple)* múltiple.

mul·ti·form (′fôrm′) adj. multiforme.

mul·ti·lat·er·al (mŭl′tē-lăt′ər-əl) adj. multilátero; POL. multilateral.

mul·ti·lev·el(ed) (:lĕv′əl[d]) adj. de varios niveles.

mul·ti·lin·gual (:lĭng′gwəl) adj. polígloto.

mul·ti·me·di·a (:mē′dē-ə) adj. que incluye el uso de various medios de comunicación.

mul·ti·mil·lion·aire (:mĭl′yə-nâr′) s. multimillonario.

mul·ti·na·tion·al (:năsh′ə-nəl) adj. & s. multinacional *f.*

mul·ti·ple (mŭl′tə-pəl) I. adj. múltiple; MAT. múltiplo II. s. múltiplo.

mul·ti·plex (:plĕks′) adj. múltiple; ELECTRÓN. múltiplex.

mul·ti·pli·cand (′-plī-kănd′) s. multiplicando.

mul·ti·pli·ca·tion (:plī-kā′shən) s. multiplicación *f* ♦ **m. table** tabla de multiplicar.

mul·ti·plic·i·ty (:plĭs′ĭ-tē) s. multiplicidad *f.*

mul·ti·pli·er (′-plī′ər) s. multiplicador *m.*

mul·ti·ply (:plī′) tr. & intr. multiplicar(se).

mul·ti·pur·pose (mŭl′tē-pûr′pəs) adj. multiuso.

mul·ti·tude (′tĭ-tōōd′) s. multitud *f.*

mul·ti·tu·di·nous (′-′n-əs) adj. multitudinario.

mul·ti·va·lent (mŭl′tə-vā′lənt) adj. polivalente.

mum¹ (mŭm) adj. silencioso ♦ **to keep m.** guardar silencio.

mum² s. G.B., FAM. mamá.

mum³ s. BOT., FAM. crisantemo.

mum·ble (mŭm′bəl) I. tr. mascullar —intr. balbucir II. s. refunfuño.

mum·bo jum·bo (mŭm′bō jŭm′bō) s. FAM. galimatías *m.*

mum·mer (mŭm′ər) s. mimo; *(masked person)* máscara *mf.*

mum·mer·y (:ə-rē) s. *(pantomime)* pantomima; *(mascarade)* mascarada.

mum·mi·fy (mŭm′ə-fī′) tr. & intr. momificar(se).

mum·my¹ (:ē) s. *(corpse)* momia.

mum·my² s. FAM. mamá.

mumps (mŭmps) s.pl. paperas *f.*

munch (mŭnch) tr. ronzar.

mun·dane (mŭn′dān′) adj. mundano.

mu·nic·i·pal (myōō-nĭs′ə-pəl) adj. municipal.

mu·nic·i·pal·i·ty (′-′păl′ĭ-tē) s. municipalidad *f.*

mu·nif·i·cence (myōō-nĭf′ĭ-səns) s. munificencia.

mu·nif·i·cent (:sənt) adj. munífico.

mu·ni·tion (myōō-nĭsh′ən) s. municiones *f.*

mu·ral (myōōr′əl) s. pintura mural.

mur·der (mûr′dər) I. s. asesinato; *(massacre)* matanza; JER. *(trouble)* cosa espantosa ♦ **first-, second-degree m.** homicidio premeditado, impremeditado • **to get away with** m. FAM. salirse con la suya **II.** tr. asesinar; *(to destroy)* destrozar; *(to defeat)* aplastar.

mur·der·er (:ər) s. asesino.

mur·der·ess (:ĭs) s. asesina.

mur·der·ous (:əs) adj. asesino; FAM. terrible.

murk (mûrk) s. lobreguez f.

murk·y (mûr'kē) adj. **-i-** lóbrego.

mur·mur (mûr'mər) **I.** s. murmullo; MED. soplo cardiaco **II.** tr. & intr. murmurar.

mus·ca·tel (mŭs'kə-tĕl') s. vino moscatel.

mus·cle (mŭs'əl) **I.** s. ANAT. músculo; *(power)* fuerza **II.** intr. abrirse paso a la fuerza.

mus·cle-bound (:bound') adj. con los músculos abarrotados *o* endurecidos.

mus·cu·lar (mŭs'kyə-lər) adj. muscular; *(strong)* musculoso.

mus·cu·la·ture (:lə-chŏŏr') s. musculatura.

muse (myōōz) intr. meditar.

mu·se·um (myōō-zē'əm) s. museo.

mush (mŭsh) s. CUL. gachas de harina de maíz; *(soft thing)* masa muy blanda; FAM. *(sentimentality)* sentimentalismo.

mush·room (mŭsh'rōōm') **I.** s. BOT. hongo; CUL. champiñón m **II.** intr. crecer rápidamente.

mush·y (mŭsh'ē) adj. **-i-** blando; FAM. *(sentimental)* sensiblero; *(amorous)* enamoradizo.

mu·sic (myōō'zĭk) s. música ♦ **m. hall** sala de conciertos • **to be m. to one's ears** ser lo que uno quiere escuchar • **to face the m.** afrontar las consecuencias • **to set to m.** poner música a.

mu·si·cal (:zĭ-kəl) **I.** adj. de música; *(like music)* musical; *(fond of music)* aficionado a la música ♦ **m. chairs** juego de las sillas vacías **II.** s. comedia musical.

mu·si·cal·i·ty (:-kăl'ĭ-tē) s. musicalidad f.

mu·si·cian (myōō-zĭsh'ən) s. músico.

mu·si·col·o·gy (:'zĭ-kŏl'ə-jē) s. musicología.

mus·ing (myōō'zĭng) **I.** adj. contemplativo **II.** s. contemplación f.

musk (mŭsk) s. almizcle m.

mus·ket (mŭs'kĭt) s. mosquete m.

mus·ket·eer ('kĭ-tîr') s. mosquetero.

mus·ket·ry ('-trē) s. mosquetes m; *(firing)* mosquetazos; *(technique)* mosquetería.

musk·mel·on (mŭsk'mĕl'ən) s. melón m.

musk·rat (mŭsk'răt') s. [pl. inv. *o* **s**] rata almizclera *o* almizclada.

musk·y (mŭs'kē) adj. **-i-** almizcleño.

mus·lin (mŭz'lĭn) s. muselina.

muss (mŭs) **I.** tr. desordenar; *(to rumple)* arrugar **II.** s. desorden m; *(squabble)* riña.

mus·sel (mŭs'əl) s. mejillón m.

muss·y (mŭs'ē) adj. **-i-** FAM. desordenado.

must¹ (mŭst) **I.** aux. deber, tener que; *(indicating probability)* deber de ♦ **it m. not be** eso no debe permitirse **II.** s. FAM. cosa indispensable ♦ **to be a m.** ser para no perdérselo.

must² s. *(juice)* mosto; *(mold)* moho.

mus·tache (mŭs'tăsh', mə-stăsh') s. bigote(s) m.

mus·tang (mŭs'tăng') s. mustang m.

mus·tard (mŭs'tərd) s. mostaza ♦ **to cut the m.** FAM. hacer lo que se espera de uno.

mus·ter (mŭs'tər) **I.** tr. & intr. reunir(se) ♦ **to m. up** armarse de **II.** s. MIL. revista; *(meeting)* asamblea ♦ **to pass m.** ser aceptable.

must·y (mŭs'tē) adj. **-i-** *(moldy)* mohoso; *(smelly)* que huele a cerrado.

mu·ta·ble (myōō'tə-bəl) adj. *(variable)* mudable; *(inconstant)* inconstante.

mu·tant (myōōt'nt) s. mutante m.

mu·tate (myōō'tāt') tr. & intr. mudar(se); BIOL. transformar(se).

mu·ta·tion (-tā'shən) s. alteración f; BIOL. mutación f.

mute (myōōt) **I.** adj. mudo; *(silent)* callado **II.** s. mudo; MÚS. sordina **III.** tr. amortiguar; MÚS. poner sordina a.

mut·ed (myōō'tĭd) adj. sordo.

mu·ti·late (myōōt'l-āt') tr. mutilar.

mu·ti·la·tion ('-ā'shən) s. mutilación f.

mu·ti·neer (myōōt'n-îr') s. amotinador m.

mu·ti·nous ('-əs) adj. amotinador.

mu·ti·ny (:ē) **I.** s. motín m **II.** intr. amotinarse.

mutt (mŭt) s. JER. perro cruzado.

mut·ter (mŭt'ər) **I.** intr. & tr. murmurar; *(to grumble)* refunfuñar **II.** s. murmullo; *(grumbling)* refunfuño.

mut·ton (mŭt'n) s. carne f de carnero.

mu·tu·al (myōō'chōō-əl) adj. mutuo ♦ **by m. agreement** de común acuerdo • **m. fund** fondo mutualista de inversión).

muz·zle (mŭz'əl) **I.** s. *(snout)* hocico; *(restraint)* mordaza; *(gun)* boca (de un arma de fuego) **II.** tr. poner bozal a; *(to restrain)* amordazar.

my (mī) **I.** adj. pos. mi ♦ **my dear sir** muy señor mío **II.** interj. ¡caramba!

my·o·pi·a (mī-ō'pē-ə) s. miopía.

my·op·ic (mī-ŏp'ĭk, mī-ō'pĭk) adj. miope.

myr·i·ad (mîr'ē-əd) **I.** adj. innumerable **II.** s. miríada.

myrrh (mûr) s. mirra.

myr·tle (mûr'tl) s. mirto.

my·self (mī-sĕlf') pron. yo mismo; *(reflexive)* me; *(after proposition)* mí (mismo) ♦ **(all) by m.** completamente solo.

mys·te·ri·ous (mĭ-stîr'ē-əs) adj. misterioso.

mys·ter·y (mĭs'tə-rē) s. misterio; CINEM. película policíaca; LIT. novela policíaca.

mys·tic (:tĭk) adj. & s. místico.

mys·ti·cal (:tĭ-kəl) adj. místico.

mys·ti·fy (:tə-fī') tr. mistificar.

mys·tique (mĭ-stēk') s. misterio secreto.

myth (mĭth) s. mito.

myth·i·cal (mĭth'ĭ-kəl) adj. mítico.

myth·o·log·i·cal ('ə-lŏj'ĭ-kəl) adj. mitológico.

my·thol·o·gist (mĭ-thŏl'ə-jĭst) s. mitologista mf.

my·thol·o·gize (:jīz') tr. convertir en mito —intr. crear un mito.

my·thol·o·gy (:jē) s. mitología.

N

n, N (ĕn) s. decimocuarta letra del alfabeto inglés.

nab (năb) tr. **-bb-** JER. *(to arrest)* arrestar; *(to grab)* coger, agarrar.

na·dir (nā'dər) s. nadir m; FIG. punto más bajo.

nag¹ (năg) **I.** tr. **-gg-** *(to scold)* regañar; *(to pester)* importunar —intr. *(to find fault)* criticar; *(to complain)* quejarse **II.** s. regañón m.

nag² s. *(old horse)* jamelgo.

nail (nāl) **I.** s. clavo; *(finger, toe)* uña ♦ **n. polish** esmalte de uñas • **to be as hard as nails** tener corazón de piedra • **to bite one's nails** comerse las uñas • **to hit the n. on the head** dar en el clavo **II.** tr. clavar, asegurar con clavos; FAM. *(to catch)* coger, atrapar; *(to knock down)*

derribar; *(to hit)* pegar ♦ **to n. down** *(to fasten)* clavar; *(to get)* obtener; *(to establish)* establecer firmemente.
na·ive·íve/ive·té (nä-ēv') adj. cándido, ingenuo.
na·ive·té/íve·té ('-tā') s. ingenuidad *f.*
naked (nā'kĭd) adj. desnudo ♦ **the n. truth** la pura verdad ♦ **to the n. eye** a simple vista.
name (nām) I. s. nombre *m; (surname)* apellido; *(reputation)* fama, reputación *f;* FAM. *(celebrity)* celebridad *f* ♦ **full n.** nombre y apellido • **my n. is** me llamo • **n. brand** FAM. marca conocida • **to call someone names** insultar a alguien • **to go by the n. of** ser conocido por el nombre de • **to make a n. for oneself** hacerse un nombre • **what's your n.?** ¿cómo se llama Ud.? II. tr. llamar; *(a baby)* poner nombre a; *(to identify)* dar el nombre de; *(to mention)* nombrar, mencionar; *(to specify)* dar nombre a; *(time, price)* fijar (hora, precio); *(to appoint)* nombrar ♦ **to be named** llamarse.
name·less ('lĭs) adj. sin nombre, anónimo.
name·ly (:lē) adv. es decir, a saber.
name·plate (:plāt') s. placa *o* letrero con el nombre.
name·sake (:sāk') s. tocayo.
nan·ny (năn'ē) s. niñera.
nap[1] (năp) I. s. siesta ♦ **to take a n.** dormir la siesta II. intr. **-pp-** echar *o* dormir la siesta ♦ **to be napping** FIG. estar desprevenido.
nap[2] s. *(of cloth)* lanilla, peluza.
na·palm (nā'päm') s. napalm *m.*
nape (nāp, năp) s. nuca.
nap·kin (năp'kĭn) s. servilleta.
narc (närk) s. JER. agente *m* de policía que se ocupa de detener a los traficantes de drogas.
nar·cis·sism (när'sĭ-sĭz'əm) s. narcisismo.
nar·cis·sus (när-sĭs'əs) s. [pl. **es** *o* **-si**] narciso.
nar·cot·ic (när-kŏt'ĭk) s. & adj. narcótico.
nar·rate (năr'āt') tr. narrar.
nar·ra·tion (nă-rā'shən) s. narración *f.*
nar·ra·tive (năr'ə-tĭv) I. s. *(mode)* narrativa; *(account)* relato II. adj. narrativo.
nar·ra·tor (:āt'ər) s. narrador *m.*
nar·row (năr'ō) I. adj. **-er, -est** angosto, estrecho; *(mind)* estrecho, rígido; *(interests, interpretation)* limitado; *(barely sufficient)* escaso; *(strict)* estricto; *(intolerant)* intolerante, de miras estrechas ♦ **to have a n. escape** escaparse por un pelo II. tr. estrechar; *(to limit)* limitar, reducir ♦ **to n. down** limitar, reducir • **to n. it down to** reducirse a —intr. estrecharse III. s. ♦ pl. estrecho.
nar·row·ing (:ĭng) s. estrechamiento; FIG. *(limitation)* limitación *f.*
nar·row·mind·ed (:mĭn'dĭd) adj. de miras estrechas.
na·sal (nā'zəl) adj. nasal.
na·sal·i·ty (nā-zăl'ĭ-tē) s. nasalidad *f.*
nas·ty (năs'tē) adj. **-i-** *(filthy)* sucio; *(unpleasant)* asqueroso; *(cruel)* antipático; *(malicious)* malicioso; *(morally offensive)* obsceno, repugnante; *(cough, cold)* molesto; *(accident, fall)* grave; *(problem, affair)* difícil ♦ **to be n. to** tratar mal a • **to have a n. mind** ser un mal pensado.
na·tal (nāt'l) adj. natal.
na·tal·i·ty (nā-tăl'ĭ-tē) s. natalidad *f.*
na·tion (nā'shən) s. nación *f; (people)* pueblo.
na·tion·al (năsh'ə-nəl) adj. & s. nacional.
na·tion·al·ist (:nə-lĭst) s. nacionalista *mf.*
na·tion·al·is·tic ('-nə-lĭs'tĭk) adj. nacionalista.
na·tion·al·i·ty (:năl'ĭ-tē) s. nacionalidad *f,* ciudadanía.

na·tion·al·ize ('-nə-līz') tr. nacionalizar.
na·tion·hood (nā'shən-hŏŏd') s. la condición de ser una nación, independencia.
na·tion·wide ('-wīd') adj. por toda la nación.
na·tive (nā'tĭv) I. adj. *(inborn)* natural, innato; *(inhabitant)* nativo; *(country, town)* natal; *(language)* materno; *(customs)* originario; *(product)* del país ♦ **to be n. to** ser originario de II. s. nativo, indígena *mf* ♦ **to be a n. of** ser nativo de.
na·tiv·i·ty (nə-tĭv'ĭ-tē) s. nacimiento ♦ **N.** natividad (de Cristo).
nat·ty (năt'ē) adj. **-i-** FAM. elegante.
nat·u·ral (năch'ər-əl) I. adj. natural; *(inherent)* nato; *(fitting)* lógico; *(one's own)* propio ♦ **n. resource** recurso natural II. s. MÚS. *(note)* nota natural; *(sign)* becuadro ♦ **to be a n.** tener talento.
nat·u·ral·ist (:ə-lĭst) s. naturalista *mf.*
nat·u·ral·is·tic ('--lĭs'tĭk) adj. naturalista.
nat·u·ral·ize ('--līz') tr. & intr. *(an alien)* naturalizar(se); *(to adapt)* adaptar(se).
nat·u·ral·ly (:lē) adv. naturalmente; *(by nature)* por naturaleza; *(of course)* por supuesto, claro.
na·ture (nā'chər) s. (la) naturaleza, natura; *(character)* índole *f* <*of a confidential n.* de índole confidencial>; *(essence)* naturaleza; *(temperament)* natural *m* ♦ **by n.** por naturaleza • **something in the n. of** algo así como • **to be in someone's n.** ser propio de alguien.
naught (nôt) s. nada; MAT. cero.
naugh·ty (nô'tē) adj. **-i-** *(mischievous)* travieso; *(disobedient)* desobediente; *(joke)* verde.
nau·sea (nô'zhə) s. náusea; *(disgust)* asco.
nau·se·ate (nô'zē-āt') tr. dar náuseas a; *(to disgust)* dar asco a.
nau·se·at·ing (:ā'tĭng) adj. nauseabundo, asqueroso.
nau·seous (nô'shəs) adj. nauseabundo ♦ **to feel n.** tener náuseas.
nau·ti·cal (nô'tĭ-kəl) adj. náutico ♦ **n. mile** milla marina.
na·val (nā'vəl) adj. naval.
nave (nāv) s. nave *f.*
na·vel (nā'vəl) s. ombligo.
nav·i·ga·ble (năv'ĭ-gə-bəl) adj. navegable.
nav·i·gate (năv'ĭ-gāt') intr. & tr. navegar.
nav·i·ga·tion ('-gā'shən) s. navegación *f.*
nav·i·ga·tor ('-' tər) s. navegante *m.*
na·vy (nā'vē) s. marina de guerra, flota; *(color)* azul marino ♦ **n. bean** judía blanca • **the N.** la marina, la armada.
nay (nā) I. adv. no; *(and moreover)* más bien II. s. voto en contra; *(refusal)* negativa.
neap tide (nēp) s. marea muerta.
near (nîr) I. adv. cerca, próximo; *(almost)* casi; *(closely related)* íntimo, cercano ♦ **n. and far** por todas partes • **to come n.** FAM. faltar poco para • **to come** *o* **draw n.** acercarse II. adj. inmediato, próximo; *(relation)* cercano, allegado; *(direct)* directo, corto ♦ **n. and dear** íntimo • **to be a n. miss** fallar por poco III. prep. *(close to)* cerca de; *(almost)* casi IV. tr. & intr. acercarse (a), aproximarse (a).
near·by ('bī') I. adj. cercano, próximo II. adv. cerca.
near·ly (:lē) adv. casi.
near·sight·ed (:sī'tĭd) adj. miope.
neat (nēt) adj. *(tidy)* limpio, pulcro; *(orderly)* ordenado; *(work)* esmerado, bien hecho; *(writing)* claro; *(clever)* ingenioso; *(liquor)* solo; JER. *(terrific)* fantástico.

neb·u·la (nĕb′yə-lə) s. [pl. **s** o **-ae**] nebulosa.
neb·u·lar (:lər) adj. nebuloso.
neb·u·lous (:ləs) adj. nebuloso.
nec·es·sar·y (nĕs′ĭ-sĕr′ē) I. adj. necesario; *(inevitable)* inevitable II. s. cosa necesaria.
ne·ces·si·tate (nə-sĕs′ĭ-tāt′) tr. necesitar.
ne·ces·si·ty (:tē) s. necesidad *f* ♦ **out of n.** por necesidad.
neck (nĕk) I. s. cuello; *(of animals)* pescuezo, cogote *m; (of bottles)* gollete *m; (of land)* istmo ♦ **by a n.** DEP. por una cabeza • **n. and n.** parejos • **n. of the woods** parajes • **to break one's n.** desnucarse; FIG. deslomarse • **to risk** o **stick out one's n.** arriesgarse • **to save someone's n.** salvarle el pellejo a alguien • **up to one's n.** metido hasta el cuello II. intr. JER. besuquearse.
neck·er·chief (′ər-chĭf) s. pañuelo para el cuello.
neck·lace (:lĭs) s. collar *m.*
neck·line (:līn′) s. escote *m.*
neck·tie (:tī′) s. corbata.
ne·crol·o·gy (nə-krŏl′ə-jē) s. necrología.
nec·ro·man·cy (nĕk′rə-măn′sē) s. necromancia, nigromancia.
ne·crop·o·lis (nə-krŏp′ə-lĭs) s. [pl. **es** o **-leis**] necrópolis *f.*
ne·cro·sis (nə-krō′sĭs) s. necrosis *f.*
nec·tar (nĕk′tər) s. néctar *m.*
nec·tar·ine (nĕk′tə-rēn′) s. griñón *m,* pelón *m.*
need (nēd) I. s. necesidad *f; (trouble)* apuro ♦ **if n. be** si fuera necesario • **there's no n. to** no hace falta • **to be in n.** estar necesitado • **to be in n. of** necesitar II. tr. necesitar —intr. estar necesitado ♦ **to n. to** *(to have to)* deber, tener que; *(to be necessary)* ser necesario <*she needs to be told* se necesita decírselo>.
need·ful (′fəl) adj. necesario, requerido.
nee·dle (nēd′l) I. s. aguja II. tr. FAM. hacer rabiar, pinchar.
nee·dle·point (:point′) s. encaje *m* de aguja.
need·less (nēd′lĭs) adj. innecesario, superfluo ♦ **n. to say** huelga decir que.
nee·dle·work (nēd′l-wûrk′) s. costura, labor *f.*
need·y (nē′dē) adj. -i- necesitado, indigente ♦ **the n.** los pobres.
ne'er-do-well (nâr′dōō-wĕl′) s. inútil *mf.*
ne·far·i·ous (nə-fâr′ē-əs) adj. infame, nefario.
ne·gate (nĭ-gāt′) tr. *(to deny)* negar; *(to nullify)* anular.
ne·ga·tion (nĭ-gā′shən) s. negación *f.*
neg·a·tive (nĕg′ə-tĭv) I. adj. negativo II. s. negativa; GRAM. negación *f;* FOTOG. negativo; MAT. término negativo.
ne·glect (nĭ-glĕkt′) I. tr. descuidar ♦ **to n. one's duty** faltar al deber de uno • **to n. to** olvidarse de II. s. descuido, negligencia ♦ **out of** o **through n.** por negligencia.
ne·glect·ful (:fəl) adj. negligente.
neg·li·gee (nĕg′lĭ-zhā′) s. negligé *m.*
neg·li·gence (nĕg′lĭ-jəns) s. negligencia.
neg·li·gent (:jənt) adj. negligente, descuidado.
neg·li·gi·ble (:jə-bəl) adj. insignificante.
ne·go·tia·ble (nĭ-gō′shə-bəl) adj. negociable.
ne·go·ti·ate (:shē-āt′) intr. negociar —tr. negociar; *(obstacle)* franquear.
ne·go·ti·a·tion (-′-ā′shən) s. negociación *f.*
ne·go·ti·a·tor (-′-ā′tər) s. negociador *m.*
Ne·gro (nē′grō) adj. & s. [pl. **es**] negro.
neigh (nā) I. s. relincho II. intr. relinchar.
neigh·bor (nā′bər) I. s. vecino; *(fellow human)* prójimo II. intr. estar contiguo, lindar.

neigh·bor·hood (:hŏod′) s. barrio; *(people)* vecindario ♦ **in the n. of** FAM. cerca de, casi.
neigh·bor·ing (:ĭng) adj. vecino.
neigh·bor·ly (:lē) adj. *(relations)* de buena vecindad; *(person, action)* amable.
nei·ther (nē′thər, nī′-) I. adj. ninguno (de los dos) II. pron. ninguno (de los dos), ni uno ni otro III. conj. & adv. (ni . . .) tampoco <*she doesn't like winter and n. do I* a ella no le gusta el invierno, ni a mí tampoco> ♦ **n. . . . nor** ni . . . ni <*n. you nor I* ni tú ni yo>.
nem·e·sis (nĕm′ĭ-sĭs) s. [pl. **-ses**] nemesis *f.*
ne·o·clas·sic/si·cal (nē′ō-klăs′ĭk) adj. neoclásico.
ne·ol·o·gism (nē-ŏl′ə-jĭz′əm) s. neologismo.
ne·ol·o·gist (:jĭst) s. neólogo.
ne·on (nē′ŏn′) s. neón *m.*
ne·o·phyte (nē′ə-fīt′) s. neófito.
nep·o·tism (nĕp′ə-tĭz′əm) s. nepotismo.
nerve (nûrv) I. s. nervio; *(courage)* valor *m;* FAM. *(boldness)* descaro, tupé *m* ♦ **n. center** centro nervioso • **n. gas** gas neurotóxico • **to get on one's nerves** crispar los nervios a uno • **to lose one's n.** acobardarse ♦ pl. nerviosidad II. tr. animar, dar ánimos a.
nerve·less (′lĭs) adj. sin nervios.
nerve-rack·ing (:răk′ĭng) adj. que crispa los nervios, exasperante.
nerv·ous (nûr′vəs) adj. nervioso; *(high-strung)* irritable, excitable ♦ **n. breakdown** depresión nerviosa • **to be n.** dar motivo atener miedo a.
nerv·ous·ness (:nĭs) s. nerviosidad *f.*
nerv·y (nûr′vē) adj. -i- *(brazen)* descarado; *(daring)* audaz; G.B. *(nervous)* nervioso.
nest (nĕst) I. s. nido; *(of hens)* nidal *m; (of wasps)* avispero ♦ **n. egg** ahorros, economías • **to leave the n.** irse a vivir por su cuenta II. intr. anidar; *(boxes)* encajar —tr. encajar.
nes·tle (nĕs′əl) tr. ♦ **to be nestled among** estar situado en • **to be nestled in** *(a place)* estar al abrigo de; *(someone's arms)* acurrucarse en —intr. acurrucarse.
net[1] (nĕt) I. s. red *f; (fabric)* tul *m* II. tr. -tt- coger o atrapar con una red.
net[2] I. adj. *(after deductions)* neto; *(final)* final II. s. *(profit)* ganancia neta; *(weight)* peso neto III. tr. -tt- *(to yield)* producir; *(to clear)* ganar neto.
neth·er (nĕth′ər) adj. inferior.
neth·er·world (:wûrld′) s. infierno.
net·ting (nĕt′ĭng) s. red *f.*
net·tle (nĕt′l) I. s. ortiga II. tr. irritar.
net·tle·some (:səm) adj. irritante, molesto.
net·work (nĕt′wûrk′) s. red *f.*
neu·ral (nŏor′əl) adj. de los nervios.
neu·ral·gia (nŏo-răl′jə) s. neuralgia.
neu·ral·gic (:jĭk) adj. neurálgico.
neu·ri·tis (nŏo-rī′tĭs) s. neuritis *f.*
neu·rol·o·gist (nŏo-rŏl′ə-jĭst) s. neurólogo.
neu·rol·o·gy (:jē) s. neurología.
neu·ron(e) (nŏor′ŏn′) s. neurona.
neu·ro·sis (nŏo-rō′sĭs) s. [pl. **-ses**] neurosis *f.*
neu·ro·sur·ger·y (nŏor′ō-sûr′jə-rē) s. neurocirujía.
neu·rot·ic (nŏo-rŏt′ĭk) adj. & s. neurótico.
neu·ter (nŏo′tər) I. adj. neutro II. s. GRAM. neutro; VET. animal castrado III. tr. castrar.
neu·tral (nŏo′trəl) I. adj. neutral; FÍS., QUÍM. neutro II. s. neutral *mf;* AUTO. punto muerto.
neu·tral·i·ty (-trăl′ĭ-tē) s. neutralidad *f.*
neu·tral·ize (′trə-līz′) tr. neutralizar.

neu·tral·iz·er (:lī'zər) s. neutralizador m.

neu·tron (nōō'trŏn') s. neutrón m.

nev·er (nĕv'ər) adv. nunca, jamás ♦ **n. again** nunca más • **n. ever** nunca jamás • **n. mind** no importa.

nev·er·more ('-môr') adv. nunca más.

nev·er·the·less (:thə-lĕs') adv. sin embargo, no obstante.

new (nōō) I. adj. nuevo; *(recent)* reciente; *(modern)* moderno; *(additional)* distinto ♦ **what's n.?** ¿qué hay de nuevo? II. adv. recién.

new·born ('bôrn') I. adj. recién nacido; FIG. renacido II. s. niño recién nacido.

new·com·er (:kŭm'ər) s. recién llegado.

new·el (nōō'əl) s. nabo (de una escalera).

new·fan·gled (nōō'făng'gəld) adj. novedoso.

new·found (:found') adj. nuevo.

new·ly·wed (:lē-wĕd') s. recién casado.

news (nōōz) s. noticia *<that's good n.* es una buena noticia>; *(current events)* noticias, actualidades f; *(broadcast)* noticiario ♦ **n. item** noticia • **that's n. to me!** ¡eso para mí es una novedad! • **to break the n.** to dar una noticia a.

news·boy ('boi') s. muchacho vendedor de periódicos.

news·cast (:kăst') s. noticiario.

news·cast·er (:kăs'tər) s. locutor m.

news·let·ter (:lĕt'ər) s. hoja informativa.

news·man (:măn') s. [pl. **-men**] periodista mf.

news·pa·per (:pā'pər) s. periódico, diario.

news·print (:prĭnt') s. papel m de periódico.

news·reel (:rēl') s. noticiario cinematográfico.

news·room (:rōōm') s. sala de redacción.

news·stand (:stănd') s. quiosco (de periódicos).

news·wor·thy (:wûr'thē) adj. de interés periodístico.

news·y (nōō'zē) adj. **-i-** FAM. informativo.

newt (nōōt) s. tritón m.

new·ton (nōōt'n) s. newton m, neutonio m.

next (nĕkst) I. adj. *(in time)* que viene, próximo; *(adjacent)* de al lado; *(following)* siguiente *<the n. day* el día siguiente> ♦ **to be n.** ser el siguiente • **what n.!** ¡y ahora, qué! II. adv. después, luego ♦ **n. door** al lado • **n. to** *(beside)* junto a, al lado de; *(almost)* casi *<n. to nothing* casi nada> • **to come n.** seguir, venir después.

next-door (:dôr') adj. de al lado.

nex·us (nĕk'səs) s. [pl. inv. *o* **es**] nexo.

ni·a·cin (nī'ə-sĭn) s. ácido nicotínico.

nib (nĭb) s. plumilla (de estilográfica).

nib·ble (nĭb'əl) I. tr. mordiscar; *(bait)* morder —intr. comisquear ♦ **to n. at** morder II. s. *(bite)* mordisco; *(morsel)* bocadito; FIG. *(offer)* oferta.

nice (nīs) adj. *(friendly)* amable, bueno; *(pleasant)* agradable; *(attractive)* bonito, lindo; *(well-done)* bien hecho *<n. job* trabajo bien hecho>; *(virtuous)* decente; *(considerate)* delicado ♦ **n. and** FAM. muy, bien *<n. and warm* bien calentito> • **to be n. to** ser amable con • **to have a n. time** pasarlo bien.

ni·ce·ty (nī'sĭ-tē) s. *(exactness)* precisión f; *(subtle detail)* sutileza; *(refinement)* delicadeza.

niche (nĭch, nēsh) s. ARQ. hornacina, nicho; FIG. *(place)* colocación f, lugar m.

nick (nĭk) I. s. mella, muesca; *(wound)* rasguño ♦ **in the n. of time** en el momento crucial II. tr. mellar, hacer muescas en; *(the skin)* cortar.

nick·el (nĭk'əl) s. QUÍM. níquel m; *(U.S. coin)* moneda de cinco centavos.

nick·el-and-dime ('-ən-dīm') adj. FAM. de

poco dinero; *(small-time)* de poca monta.

nick·name (nĭk'năm') I. s. apodo II. tr. apodar.

nic·o·tine (nĭk'ə-tēn') s. nicotina.

niece (nēs) s. sobrina.

nif·ty (nĭf'tē) adj. **-i-** JER. formidable.

nig·gard·ly (nĭg'ərd-lē) adj. *(stingy)* tacaño, avaro; *(meager)* escaso.

nig·gle (nĭg'əl) intr. pararse en pequeñeces.

nig·gling (:lĭng) adj. demasiado meticuloso.

nigh (nī) I. adv. cerca II. adj. próximo III. prep. cerca de.

night (nīt) I. s. noche f; *(nightfall)* anochecer m ♦ **at** *o* **by n.** de noche • **good n.!** ¡buenas noches! • **last n.** anoche, ayer por la noche • **the n. before** la noche anterior • **the n. before last** anteanoche • **to make a n. of it** FAM. pasarse la noche de juerga • **to say good n. (to someone)** dar las buenas noches (a alguien) • **to stay out all n.** trasnochar • **to work nights** trabajar de noche II. adj. nocturno, de la noche ♦ **n. owl** FIG. trasnochador • **n. school** escuela nocturna • **n. shift** turno de noche.

night·cap ('kăp') s. *(cap)* gorro de dormir; FAM. *(drink)* bebida tomada antes de acostarse.

night·club (:klŭb') s. club nocturno.

night·fall (:fôl') s. anochecer m.

night·gown (:goun') s. camisa de dormir, camisón m.

night·hawk (:hôk') s. ORNIT. chotacabras m; FIG., *(person)* noctámbulo.

night·ie (nī'tē) s. FAM. camisón m.

night·in·gale (nīt'n-gāl') s. ruiseñor m.

night·life (nīt'līf') s. vida nocturna.

night·light (:līt') s. lamparilla.

night·ly (:lē) I. adj. nocturno, de noche; *(every night)* de todas las noches II. adv. por la noche; *(every night)* todas las noches.

night·mare (:mâr') s. pesadilla.

night·stick (:stĭk') s. porra de policía.

night·time (:tīm') s. noche f ♦ **in the n.** de noche.

ni·hil·ist (nī'ə-lĭst, nē'-) s. nihilista mf.

ni·hil·is·tic (:-lĭs'tĭk) adj. nihilista.

nil (nĭl) s. nada; *(zero)* cero.

nim·ble (nĭm'bəl) adj. **-er, -est** ágil.

nim·bus (nĭm'bəs) s. [pl. **es** *o* **-bi**] nimbo.

nin·com·poop (nĭn'kəm-pōōp') s. bobo, necio.

nine (nīn) s. & adj. nueve m ♦ **n. hundred** novecientos • **n. o'clock** las nueve.

nine·pins ('pĭnz') s. bolos (juego).

nine·teen (nīn-tēn') s. & adj. diecinueve m.

nine·teenth (:tēnth') s. & adj. decimonoveno.

nine·ti·eth (nīn'tē-ĭth') s. & adj. nonagésimo.

nine·ty (nīn'tē) s. & adj. noventa.

nin·ny (nĭn'ē) s. simplón m, tonto.

ninth (nīnth) s. & adj. noveno.

nip (nĭp) I. tr. **-pp-** *(to pinch)* pellizcar; *(to bite)* morder; *(to chill)* helar; JER. *(to steal)* birlar ♦ **to n. in the bud** cortar de raíz • **to n. off** cortar II. s. *(pinch)* pellizco; *(bite)* mordedura; *(sip)* traguito ♦ **n. and tuck** reñido • **there's a n. in the air** hace fresco.

nip·ple (nĭp'əl) s. pezón m; *(on bottle)* tetilla.

nip·py (nĭp'ē) adj. **-i-** frío.

nit (nĭt) s. liendre f.

nit·er (nī'tər) s. nitro.

nit-pick (nĭt'pĭk') intr. FAM. fijarse en pequeñeces.

ni·trate (nī'trāt') s. nitrato; *(fertilizer)* nitrato de potasio *o* de sodio.

ni·tric (nī'trĭk) adj. nítrico.

ni·trite (nī'trīt') s. nitrito.
ni·tro·gen (nī'trə-jən) s. nitrógeno.
ni·tro·glyc·er·in(e) (nī' trō-glĭs'ər-ĭn) s. nitroglicerina.
ni·trous (nī'trəs) adj. nitroso.
nit·ty-grit·ty (nĭt'ē-grĭt'ē) s. JER. esencia, meollo.
nit·wit (nĭt'wĭt') s. FAM. bobalicón m.
nix (nĭks) FAM. **I.** s. nada **II.** adv. no **III.** tr. prohibir ♦ **n. it!** ¡no lo hagas!
no (nō) **I.** adv. no ♦ **no longer** ya no • **no more** ya no . . . más <*I want no more* ya no quiero más>; *(not any)* no más <*there's no more wine* no queda más vino> • **to say no** decir que no **II.** adj. no; *(not one)* no . . . ninguno <*she has no hope* no tiene ninguna esperanza>; *(not at all)* ninguno <*she is no actress* no es ninguna actriz> ♦ **by no means** de ninguna manera • **in no time** en un abrir y cerrar de ojos • **no admittance** prohibida la entrada • **no matter!** ¡no importa! • **no more, no less** ni más, ni menos • **no other** más <*I see no other way out* no veo más solución> • **no smoking** prohibido fumar • **no way!** ¡nunca!, ¡jamás! • **with no** *<with no chance of* sin la oportunidad de> **III.** s. [pl. **es**] no ♦ pl. votos en contra.
no·ac·count (nō'ə-kount') adj. FAM. inútil.
no·bil·i·ty (nō-bĭl'ĭ-tē) s. nobleza.
no·ble (nō'bəl) adj. & s. **-er, -est** noble *mf.*
no·ble·man (:mən) s. [pl. **-men**] noble *m.*
no·ble·wom·an (:wŏm'ən) s. [pl. **-women**] noble *f.*
no·bod·y (nō'bŏd'ē) **I.** pron. nadie ♦ **to be n.'s fool** no ser tomado por tonto **II.** s. don nadie *m,* nadie *m.*
noc·tur·nal (nŏk-tûr'nəl) adj. nocturno.
nod (nŏd) **I.** intr. **-dd-** balancearse, inclinarse; *(sleepily)* dar cabezadas; *(in agreement)* asentir con la cabeza; *(in greeting)* saludar con la cabeza ♦ **to n. off** dormirse —tr. inclinar *(la cabeza)* ♦ **to n. hello** saludar con la cabeza **II.** s. inclinación *f* de cabeza ♦ **to get the n.** obtener la aprobación ♦ **to give the n.** asentir, aprobar.
nod·al (nōd'l) adj. nodal.
node (nōd) s. protuberancia; BOT. nudo; ANAT., FÍS. nodo.
nod·u·lar (nŏj'ə-lər) adj. nodular.
nod·ule (:ōl) s. nódulo.
no-fault (nō'fôlt') adj. sin responsabilidad.
nog·gin (nŏg'ĭn) s. JER. cabeza, chola.
no-go (nō'gō') adj. JER. que no está listo.
no-good (nō'gŏod') adj. inútil; *(vile)* vil.
noise (noiz) s. ruido; FÍS. interferencia ♦ **to make a lot of n. about** quejarse de.
noise·less ('lĭs) adj. silencioso, sin ruido.
noise·mak·er (:mā'kər) s. matraca.
noi·some (noi'səm) adj. nocivo.
nois·y (noi'zē) adj. **-i-** ruidoso.
no-load (nō'lōd') adj. sin comisión de ventas.
no·mad (nō'măd') s. nómada *mf.*
no·mad·ic (-'ĭk) adj. nómada.
no man's land s. tierra de nadie.
no·men·cla·ture (nō'mən-klā'chər) s. nomenclatura.
nom·i·nal (nŏm'ə-nəl) adj. nominal; *(of shares)* nominativo; *(trifling)* insignificante.
nom·i·nate (:nāt') tr. nombrar; *(as a candidate)* proponer.
nom·i·na·tion ('-nā'shən) s. nombramiento.
nom·i·na·tive ('-nə-tĭv) adj. & s. nominativo.
nom·i·nee ('-nē') s. candidato.
non·ag·gres·sion (nŏn' ə-grĕsh'ən) s. no agresión *f.*

non·a·ligned (:ə-līnd') adj. no alineado.
non·at·ten·dance (:ə-tĕn'dəns) s. ausencia.
non·break·a·ble (-brā'kə-bəl) adj. irrompible.
non·cha·lance (nŏn'shə-läns') s. imperturbabilidad *f.*
non·cha·lant (länt') adj. imperturbable.
non·com·bat·ant (nŏn'kəm-băt'nt) s. & adj. no combatiente *mf.*
non·com·bus·ti·ble (:kəm-bŭs'tə-bəl) adj. incombustible.
non·com·mit·tal (:kə-mĭt'l) adj. evasivo.
non·com·pli·ance (:kəm-plī'əns) s. incumplimiento.
non·con·duc·tor (:kən-dŭk'tər) s. aislante *m.*
non·con·form·ist (:kən-fôr'mĭst) adj. & s. no conformista *mf,* disidente *mf.*
non·con·form·i·ty (:kən-fôr'mĭ-tē) s. no conformidad *f,* disidencia.
non·de·nom·i·na·tion·al (:dĭ-nŏm'ə-nā'shə-nəl) adj. no sectario.
non·de·script (:dĭ-skrĭpt') adj. de poco *o* ningún carácter.
non·dis·crim·i·na·tion (:dĭ-skrĭm'ə-nā'shən) s. ausencia de discriminación.
non·drink·er (-drĭng'kər) s. no bebedor *m.*
none (nŭn) **I.** pron. *(nobody)* nadie, ninguno; *(not any)* ninguno <*n. of them* ninguno de ellos>; *(not any)* nada ♦ **n. but** solamente • **n. other than** nadie *o* nada menos que **II.** adv. no <*he is n. too happy* él no está muy contento>.
non·en·ti·ty (nŏn-ĕn'tĭ-tē) s. nulidad *f.*
non·es·sen·tial (:ĭ-sĕn'shəl) adj. no esencial.
none·such (nŭn'sŭch') s. cosa sin par.
none·the·less ('thə-lĕs') adv. sin embargo.
non·ex·ist·ent (nŏn'ĭg-zĭs'tənt) adj. inexistente.
non·fat ('făt') adj. sin grasa.
non·fea·sance (-fē'zəns) s. incumplimiento.
non·fic·tion (fĭk'shən) s. literatura no novelesca.
non·flam·ma·ble (:flăm'ə-bəl) adj. no inflamable.
non·in·ter·ven·tion (:ĭn'tər-vĕn'shən) s. no intervención *f.*
non·ne·go·tia·ble ('nĭ-gō'shə-bəl) adj. no negociable.
no-no (nō'nō') s. [pl. **'s**] FAM. algo prohibido *o* inadmisible.
no-non·sense (nō'nŏn'sĕns') adj. práctico.
non·pa·reil (nŏn' pə-rĕl') adj. & s. *(persona)* sin igual, *(cosa)* sin par.
non·par·ti·san (-pär'tĭ-zən) adj. independiente.
non·pay·ment (:pā'mənt) s. falta de pago.
non·per·for·mance (:pər-fôr'məns) s. incumplimiento.
non·plus (-plŭs') tr. desconcertar.
non·pro·duc·tive ('prə-dŭk'tĭv) adj. improductivo.
non·pro·fes·sion·al (:prə-fĕsh'ə-nəl) adj. & s. no profesional *mf.*
non·prof·it (-prŏf'ĭt) adj. sin fin lucrativo.
non·res·i·dent (:rĕz'ĭ-dənt) adj. & s. no residente *mf,* transeúnte *mf.*
non·re·stric·tive ('rĭ-strĭk'tĭv) adj. sin restricción.
non·re·turn·a·ble (:rĭ-tûr'nə-bəl) adj. sin devolución.
non·sched·uled (-skĕj'ōŏld) adj. no regular.
non·sec·tar·i·an ('sĕk-târ'ē-ən) adj. no sectario.

non·sense (nŏn'sĕns') s. disparate(s) *m* ♦ n.!
tonterías • **to talk n.** decir tonterías.
non·sen·si·cal (-sĕn'sĭ-kəl) adj. disparatado.
non·stan·dard (nŏn-stăn'dərd) adj. no reglamentario.
non·stop ('stŏp') **I.** adv. sin parar **II.** adj.
(train) directo; (plane) sin escalas.
non·sup·port ('sə-pôrt') s. falta de pago de la
pensión alimenticia.
non·tax·a·ble (-tăk'sə-bəl) adj. no imponible.
non·trans·fer·a·ble ('trăns-fûr'ə-bəl) adj. in-
transferible.
non·un·ion (-yŏon'yən) adj. (labor) no sindi-
cado; (shop) que no emplea miembros de un
sindicato.
non·vi·a·ble (:vī'ə-bəl) adj. no viable.
non·vi·o·lence (:vī'ə-ləns) s. no violencia.
noo·dle (nŏod'l) s. CUL. tallarín *m*, fideo; JER.
(head) coco.
nook (nŏok) s. rincón *m*.
noon (nŏon) **I.** s. mediodía *m* ♦ **at high n.** a
mediodía **II.** adj. de mediodía.
noon·day ('dā') adj. & s. (de) mediodía *m*.
no one *o* **no-one** (nŏ'wŭn') pron. nadie, ninguno.
noon·time (nŏon'tīm') s. mediodía *m*.
noose (nŏos) s. (knot) nudo corredizo; (hangman's rope) dogal *m*.
nor (nôr) conj. ni <he was neither willing n. able
ni quería ni podía>; ni tampoco <n. do I want to
go ni tampoco quiero ir>.
norm (nôrm) s. norma.
nor·mal (nôr'məl) **I.** adj. normal **II.** s. normalidad ♦ **to return to n.** volver a la normalidad.
nor·mal·i·ty (-măl'ĭ-tē) s. normalidad *f*.
nor·mal·ize ('mə-līz') tr. normalizar.
nor·ma·tive (-mə-tĭv) adj. normativo.
north (nôrth) **I.** s. norte *m* ♦ **N.** región septentrional **II.** adj. del norte **III.** adv. hacia el norte.
north·bound ('bound') adj. con rumbo al
norte.
north·east (-ēst') **I.** s. nordeste *m* **II.** adj. del
nordeste **III.** adv. hacia el nordeste.
north·east·ern (:ē'stərn) adj. del nordeste.
north·er·ly (nôr'thər-lē) **I.** adj. (del) norte
II. adv. hacia el norte.
north·ern (:thərn) adj. septentrional, del norte
♦ **n. lights** aurora boreal.
north·ern·er (:thər-nər) s. norteño.
north·land (nôrth'lănd') s. región del norte *f*.
north·ward (:wərd) adv. & adj. hacia el norte.
north·west (-wĕst') **I.** s. noroeste *m* **II.** adj. del
noroeste **III.** adv. hacia el noroeste.
north·west·ern (:wĕs'tərn) adj. del noroeste.
nose (nŏz) **I.** s. nariz *f*; (snout) hocico; (sense
of smell) olfato; (knack) olfato ♦ **as plain as
the n.** on one's face más claro que el agua • **n.
cone** morro • **on the n.** exacto • **right under
one's n.** delante de las narices • **to blow one's
n.** sonarse la nariz • **to follow one's n.** seguir
recto • **to lead by the n.** manejar al antojo de
uno • **to look down one's n. at** FAM. mirar por
encima del hombro a • **to pay through the n.**
FAM. pagar un dineral • **to poke** *o* **stick one's n.
into** FAM. meter la nariz en • **to turn up
one's n. at** FAM. despreciar, desdeñar **II.** tr.
empujar con el hocico —intr. husmear ♦ **to n.
forward** avanzar con cuidado • **to n. around**
husmear.
nose·bleed ('blēd') s. hemorragia nasal.
nosedive (:dīv') s. picado.
nose·gay (:gā') s. ramillete *m* de flores.

nos·tal·gia (nə-stăl'jə) s. nostalgia.
nos·tal·gic (:jĭk) adj. nostálgico.
nos·tril (nŏs'trəl) s. ventana ♦ pl. narices.
nos·trum (nŏs'trəm) s. panacea.
nos·y (nŏ'zē) adj. -i- entrometido.
not (nŏt) adv. no <I will n. go no iré> ♦ **certainly n.!** ¡de ninguna manera! • **n. even** ni
siquiera • **n. to mention** por no mencionar • **n.
yet** ya no, todavía no.
no·ta·bil·i·ty (nŏ'tə-bĭl'ĭ-tē) s. notabilidad *f*.
no·ta·ble (nŏ'tə-bəl) adj. & s. notable *m*.
no·ta·rize (nŏ'tə-rīz') tr. hacer certificar por
notario.
no·ta·ry (:rē) s. notario ♦ **n. public** notario.
no·ta·tion (nŏ-tā'shən) s. MAT., MÚS. notación
f; (brief note) nota, anotación *f*.
notch (nŏch) **I.** s. (cut) muesca, corte *m*; GEOG.
desfiladero; FAM. (level) grado ♦ **to take someone down a n.** FAM. bajar los humos a alguien
II. tr. hacer una muesca en, cortar.
note (nŏt) **I.** s. nota; FIN. billete *m*; (bird call)
trino; (mention) mención *f*; (I.O.U.) pagaré *m*
♦ **of n.** (renowned) de renombre; (important) de
importancia • **to make a n. of** tomar nota de •
to strike a false n. desentonar ♦ pl. notas,
apuntes • **to compare n.** cambiar impresiones
II. tr. (to notice) notar, advertir; (to mention)
señalar; (to observe) fijarse en.
note·book ('bŏok') s. cuaderno.
not·ed (nŏ'tĭd) adj. notable, eminente.
note·pa·per (nŏt'pā'pər) s. papel *m* de escribir.
note·wor·thy (:wûr'thē) adj. notable.
noth·ing (nŭth'ĭng) **I.** pron. nada; (not anything) no . . . nada <she believes in n. no cree
en nada> ♦ **for n.** (for free) por nada; (in vain)
para nada; (for no reason) sin motivo • **n. at all**
nada de nada • **n. but** sólo • **n. doing!** FAM. ¡ni
hablar! • **there's n. to it** es sencillísimo • **to
come to n.** quedar en nada • **to have n. to do
with** no tener nada que ver con • **to make n. of**
no dar importancia a • **to say n. of** por no
hablar de • **to think n. of** no suponer nada
(para uno) **II.** s. nada, nadería; (person) cero a
la izquierda **III.** adv. ♦ **n. less than** nada menos que • **n. like** no . . . nada <she is n. like her
mother no se parece nada a su madre>.
no·tice (nŏ'tĭs) **I.** s. (attention) atención *f*;
(warning) aviso, notificación *f* <without prior n.
sin previo aviso>; (announcement) anuncio;
(review) crítica, reseña; (sign) letrero ♦ **at a
moment's n.** sin previo aviso • **on (such) short
n.** en tan poco tiempo • **to be on n.** estar avisado • **to escape one's n.** escapársele a uno •
to give n. (to resign) renunciar a (un empleo);
(to fire) despedir; (to inform) avisar • **to put on** *o*
serve n. advertir, avisar • **to take n. of** (someone) hacer caso a; (something) hacer caso de,
prestar atención a • **until further n.** hasta nuevo
aviso **II.** tr. (to note) observar; (to see) fijarse
en; (to realize) darse cuenta de, advertir.
no·tice·a·ble (nŏ'tĭ-sə-bəl) adj. notable, sensible; (obvious) evidente ♦ **it is barely n.** casi no
se nota.
no·ti·fi·ca·tion (nŏ'tə-fĭ-kā'shən) s. notificación *f*, aviso.
no·ti·fy (nŏ'tə-fī') tr. notificar, avisar.
no·tion (nŏ'shən) s. noción *f*, idea; (opinion)
opinión *f* ♦ **to have no n.** no tener la más mínima idea • **to have a n. to** estar dispuesto a ♦ pl.
artículos de mercería.
no·to·ri·e·ty (nŏ'tə-rī'ĭ-tē) s. notoriedad *f*.
no·to·ri·ous (nŏ-tôr'ē-əs) adj. de mala fama.

not·with·stand·ing (nŏt´wĭth-stăn´dĭng) prep. & conj. a pesar de (que).

nou·gat (nōō´gət) s. turrón *m* de almendras.

noun (noun) s. sustantivo, nombre *m*.

nour·ish (nûr´ĭsh) tr. nutrir, alimentar; *(to promote)* fomentar; *(hopes)* abrigar.

nour·ish·ment (:mənt) s. alimento.

no·va (nō´və) s. [pl. **s** *o* **-ae**] nova.

nov·el (nŏv´əl) I. s. novela II. adj. nuevo, original.

nov·el·ist (:ə-lĭst) s. novelista *mf*.

nov·el·is·tic (´-lĭs´tĭk) adj. novelístico.

nov·el·la (nō-vĕl´ə) s. cuento, novela corta.

nov·el·ty (nŏv´əl-tē) s. novedad *f*, innovación *f* ✦ pl. chucherías, baratijas.

No·vem·ber (nō-vĕm´bər) s. noviembre *m*.

nov·ice (nŏv´ĭs) s. novato; RELIG. novicio.

no·vi·ti·ate (nō-vĭsh´ē-ĭt) s. noviciado.

now (nou) I. adv. ahora; *(immediately)* ahora mismo; *(at last)* ya; *(as things are)* ahora ya <n. we won't be able to stay ahora ya no podemos quedarnos> ✦ **just n.** *(at present)* ahora mismo; *(recently)* hace un momento • **n. . . . n.** ya . . . ya • **n., n.** vamos, vamos • **n. and again** *o* **n. and then** de vez en cuando • **n. then** ahora bien • **right n.!** ¡ahora mismo! II. conj. ✦ **n. that** ya que, ahora que III. s. ✦ **by n.** ya • **for n.** por ahora • **from n. on** de ahora en adelante • **not n.** ahora no • **until** *o* **up to n.** hasta ahora.

now·a·days (´ə-dāz´) adv. hoy (en) día.

no·way(s) (nō´wā[z]´) adv. de ningún modo.

no·where (nō´hwâr´) I. adv. *(location)* en *o* por ninguna parte; *(direction)* a ninguna parte ✦ **n. near** muy lejos de • **n. near as** ni mucho menos tan • **to get n.** no conseguir nada II. s. ✦ **in the middle of n.** en el quinto pino • **out of n.** de la nada.

no-win (nō´wĭn´) adj. que no se puede ganar.

nox·ious (nŏk´shəs) adj. nocivo, dañino.

noz·zle (nŏz´əl) s. boquilla.

nth (ĕnth) adj. enésimo.

nu·ance (nōō-äns´) s. matiz *m*.

nub (nŭb) s. protuberancia; *(core)* esencia.

nu·bile (nōō´bəl, :bīl´) adj. núbil.

nuclear (nōō´klē-ər) adj. nuclear.

nu·cle·us (:əs) [pl. **es** *o* **-lei**] s. núcleo.

nude (nōōd) s. & adj. desnudo ✦ **in the n.** al desnudo.

nudge (nŭj) I. s. codazo II. tr. dar un codazo a.

nud·ist (nōō´dĭst) s. & adj. nudista *mf*.

nu·di·ty (:dĭ-tē) s. desnudez *f*.

nug·get (nŭg´ĭt) s. pepita.

nui·sance (nōō´səns) s. *(person)* pesado; *(thing)* fastidio, molestia ✦ **to make a n. of oneself** molestar, dar la lata.

null (nŭl) I. adj. nulo ✦ **n. and void** nulo y sin valor II. s. cero.

nul·li·fy (´ə-fī´) tr. anular.

nul·li·ty (:i-tē) s. nulidad *f*.

numb (nŭm) I. adj. entumecido; *(with fear)* paralizado II. tr. entumecer; *(with fear)* paralizar.

num·ber (nŭm´bər) I. s. número ✦ **a n. of** *(several)* varios; *(a lot)* muchos • **any n. of** muchos • **beyond n.** innumerable • **by the numbers** *(mechanically)* mecánicamente; *(strictly)* de uno en uno • **to do a n. on** FAM. dañar, arruinar • **to have someone's n.** FAM. tener a alguien calado • **your n. is up** FAM. te llegó la hora ✦ pl. *(many)* muchos; MAT. números • **n. game** lotería ilegal II. tr. numerar, po-

ner número a; *(to include, restrict)* contar, *(to have)* tener ✦ **to n. among** contar entre —intr. ser <we numbered twenty éramos veinte> ✦ **to n. in** contarse (por).

num·ber·ing (:ĭng) s. recuento, enumeración *f*; *(of pages)* numeración *f*.

num·ber·less (:lĭs) adj. innumerable.

numb·ness (nŭm´nĭs) s. entumecimiento.

nu·men (nōō´mən) s. [pl. **-mina**] numen *f*.

nu·mer·a·ble (nōō´mər-ə-bəl) adj. numerable.

nu·mer·al (:əl) s. número ✦ **Arabic, Roman n.** número arábigo, romano.

nu·mer·ate (nōō´mə-rāt´) tr. enumerar, contar.

nu·mer·a·tion (´-rā´shən) s. numeración *f*.

nu·mer·a·tor (´-´tər) s. numerador *m*.

nu·mer·ic/i·cal (nōō-mĕr´ĭk) adj. numérico.

nu·mer·ol·o·gy (´mə-rŏl´ə-jē) s. numerología.

nu·mer·ous (´mər-əs) adj. numeroso.

nu·mis·mat·ic (nōō´mĭz-măt´ĭk) adj. numismático ✦ **numismatics** s.sg. numismática.

num·skull (nŭm´skŭl´) s. tonto, mentecato.

nun (nŭn) s. monja, religiosa.

nun·ner·y (´ə-rē) s. convento de monjas.

nup·tial (nŭp´shəl) I. adj. nupcial II. s. ✦ pl. nupcias.

nurse (nûrs) I. s. enfermero; *(wet nurse)* nodriza; *(nursemaid)* niñera II. tr. *(infant)* criar; *(patient)* cuidar; *(grudge)* guardar; *(drink)* beber lentamente —intr. *(mother)* dar de mamar; *(infant)* mamar.

nurse·maid (´mād´) s. niñera.

nurs·er·y (nûr´sə-rē) s. cuarto de los niños; *(center)* guardería infantil; AGR. vivero ✦ **n. rhyme** poesía infantil • **n. school** escuela de párvulos.

nurs·ing (:sĭng) s. profesión *f* de enfermero; *(suckling)* lactancia ✦ **n. home** hogar de ancianos.

nur·ture (nûr´chər) I. s. *(feeding)* alimentación *f*; *(rearing)* crianza, educación *f* II. tr. *(to nourish)* alimentar; *(children)* criar; FIG. cultivar.

nut (nŭt) s. fruto seco, nuez *f*; JER. *(odd person)* estrafalario; *(crazy person)* chiflado; *(fan)* entusiasta *mf*; *(head)* coco; MEC. *(for bolts)* tuerca ✦ **a hard n. to crack** un hueso duro de roer.

nut·crack·er (´krăk´ər) s. cascanueces *m*.

nut·meg (nŭt´mĕg´) s. nuez moscada.

nu·tri·ent (nōō´trē-ənt) adj. & s. *(alimento)* nutritivo.

nu·tri·ment (:trə-mənt) s. alimento nutritivo.

nu·tri·tion (nōō-trĭsh´ən) s. nutrición *f*.

nu·tri·tion·al (:ə-nəl) adj. nutritivo.

nu·tri·tion·ist (:ə-nĭst) s. especialista *mf* en problemas de nutrición.

nu·tri·tious (:əs) adj. nutritivo.

nu·tri·tive (nōō´trĭ-tĭv) adj. nutritivo.

nuts (nŭts) FAM. I. adj. chalado, chiflado *(about por)* ✦ **to drive someone n.** volver loco a alguien • **to go n.** volverse loco *(over por)* II. interj. ¡cuernos!

nut·shell (nŭt´shĕl´) s. cáscara de nuez ✦ **in a n.** en pocas palabras.

nut·ty (nŭt´ē) adj. **-i-** *(flavor)* con sabor a nuez; JER. *(crazy)* loco, chiflado.

nuz·zle (nŭz´əl) tr. & intr. hocicar.

ny·lon (nī´lŏn´) s. nilón *m* ✦ pl. medias de nilón.

nymph (nĭmf) s. ninfa.

nym·pho·ma·ni·a (nĭm´fə-mā´nē-ə) s. ninfomanía.

O

o, O (ō) s. (*letter*) decimoquinta letra del alfabeto inglés; (*zero*) cero.
oaf (ōf) s. zoquete *m*, patán *m*.
oak (ōk) s. roble *m*.
oak·en (ō'kən) adj. de roble.
oar (ôr) s. remo.
o·a·sis (ō-ā'sĭs) s. [pl. **-ses**] oasis *m*.
oat (ōt) s. avena ♦ **to feel one's oats** FAM. estar lleno de vigor.
oath (ōth) s. juramento.
oat·meal (ōt'mēl') s. (*uncooked*) copas de avena; (*porridge*) gachas de avena.
ob·du·ra·cy (ŏb'dŏŏ-rə-sē) s. obstinación *f*.
ob·du·rate (:rĭt) adj. (*hardhearted*) insensible; (*obstinate*) obstinado, inflexible.
o·be·di·ence (ō-bē'dē-əns) s. obediencia.
o·be·di·ent (:ənt) adj. obediente.
ob·e·lisk (ŏb'ə-lĭsk) s. obelisco.
o·bese (ō-bēs') adj. obeso.
o·be·si·ty (ō-bē'sĭ-tē) s. obesidad *f*.
o·bey (ō-bā') tr. obedecer; (*the law*) respetar; (*orders*) cumplir, acatar —intr. ser obediente.
ob·fus·cate (ŏb'fə-skāt') tr. ofuscar.
ob·fus·ca·tion ('-skā'shən) s. ofuscación *f*.
o·bit·u·ar·y (ō-bĭch'ōō-ĕr'ē) s. obituario.
ob·ject¹ (əb-jĕkt') intr. hacer objeciones; (*to disapprove*) desaprobar —tr. objetar.
ob·ject² (ŏb'jĭkt) s. objeto; (*purpose*) propósito; (*goal*) fin *m*; GRAM. complemento ♦ **price is no o.** no importa el precio.
ob·jec·tion (əb-jĕk'shən) s. objeción *f*, reparo; DER. protesta; (*disapproval*) inconveniente *m* <*there's no o. to her going* no hay inconveniente en que ella vaya> ♦ **if there are no objections** si no hay nada que objetar • **to raise an o.** poner un reparo.
ob·jec·tion·a·ble (:shə-nə-bəl) adj. (*behavior*) reprobable; (*language*) ofensivo.
ob·jec·tive (:tĭv) I. adj. objetivo; GRAM. complementario ♦ **to be o. about** considerar objetivamente II. s. objetivo.
ob·jec·tiv·i·ty (ŏb'jĕk-tĭv'ĭ-tē) s. objetividad *f*.
ob·jec·tor (əb-jĕk'tər) s. objetor *m*.
ob·li·gate (ŏb'lĭ-gāt') tr. obligar ♦ **to be obligated to** tener la obligación de.
ob·li·ga·tion ('-gā'shən) s. obligación *f*; (*duty*) deber *m*; (*commitment*) compromiso ♦ **to be under an o.** to (*do something*) tener la obligación de; (*someone*) estarle reconocido a • **to feel an o.** to sentirse obligado a.
o·blig·a·to·ry (ə-blĭg'ə-tôr'ē) adj. obligatorio.
o·blige (ə-blīj') tr. obligar <*she is not obliged to do it* nada la obliga a hacerlo>; (*to do a favor for*) hacer un favor a; (*to humor*) complacer ♦ **much obliged** muy agradecido • **to be obliged to** (*do something*) verse obligado a; (*someone*) estarle reconocido a.
o·blig·ing (ə-blī'jĭng) adj. complaciente.
o·blique (ō-blēk') I. adj. oblicuo; (*evasive*) indirecto II. s. línea oblicua.
o·blit·er·ate (ə-blĭt'ə-rāt') tr. (*to erase*) borrar; (*to annihilate*) arrasar, aniquilar.
o·bliv·i·on (ə-blĭv'ē-ən) s. olvido.
o·bliv·i·ous (:əs) adj. (*forgetful*) olvidadizo; (*unmindful*) inconsciente (*to, of* de).
ob·long (ŏb'lông') I. adj. oblongo, rectangular II. s. rectángulo.
ob·nox·ious (ŏb-nŏk'shəs) adj. desagradable, repugnante; (*person*) insoportable.

o·boe (ō'bō) s. oboe *m*.
ob·scene (əb-sēn') adj. obsceno; (*gesture*) grosero; (*loathsome*) repugnante, soez.
ob·scen·i·ty (əb-sĕn'ĭ-tē) s. obscenidad *f*.
ob·scure (əb-skyŏŏr') I. adj. **-er, -est** oscuro; (*faint*) indistinto; (*inconspicuous*) imperceptible; (*meaning*) oculto II. tr. oscurecer; (*to hide*) ocultar; (*to complicate*) enredar ♦ **to o. someone's view** tapar la vista a alguien.
ob·scu·ri·ty (:ĭ-tē) s. oscuridad *f*.
ob·se·qui·ous (əb-sē'kwē-əs) adj. servil.
ob·ser·vance (əb-zûr'vəns) s. (*of law, rule*) observancia, cumplimiento; (*of a holiday*) celebración *f*; (*observation*) observación *f*.
ob·ser·vant (:vənt) adj. observador ♦ **to be o. of** (*the law*) respetar; (*one's duty*) cumplir con.
ob·ser·va·tion (ŏb'zər-vā'shən) s. observación *f* ♦ **to be under o.** estar en observación • **to escape o.** pasar desapercibido.
ob·ser·va·to·ry (əb-zûr'və-tôr'ē) s. observatorio.
ob·serve (əb-zûrv') tr. observar; (*to remark*) decir; (*a contract, duty*) cumplir con; (*law*) acatar; (*silence, a feast*) guardar; (*a holiday*) celebrar.
ob·serv·er (əb-zûr'vər) s. observador *m*.
ob·sess (əb-sĕs') tr. obsesionar.
ob·ses·sion (əb-sĕsh'ən) s. obsesión *f*.
ob·ses·sive (əb-sĕs'ĭv) adj. obsesivo.
ob·so·les·cence (ŏb'sə-lĕs'əns) s. obsolencia.
ob·so·les·cent (:ənt) adj. en desuso.
ob·so·lete (ŏb'sə-lēt') adj. obsoleto; (*outmoded*) anticuado.
ob·sta·cle (ŏb'stə-kəl) s. obstáculo.
ob·ste·tri·cian (ŏb'stĭ-trĭsh'ən) s. obstetra *mf*.
ob·stet·ric/ri·cal (əb-stĕt'rĭk) adj. obstétrico ♦ **obstetrics** s.sg. obstetricia.
ob·sti·na·cy (ŏb'stə-nə-sē) s. obstinación *f*.
ob·sti·nate (:nĭt) adj. obstinado.
ob·strep·er·ous (əb-strĕp'ər-əs) adj. (*noisy*) estrepitoso, ruidoso; (*rebellious*) revoltoso.
ob·struct (əb-strŭkt') tr. obstruir; (*to hinder*) dificultar; (*view*) tapar.
ob·struc·tion (əb-strŭk'shən) s. obstrucción *f*; (*obstacle*) obstáculo, impedimento.
ob·struc·tion·ist (:shə-nĭst) s. obstruccionista *mf*.
ob·tain (əb-tān') tr. obtener, lograr; (*to acquire*) adquirir —intr. prevalecer.
ob·trude (əb-trōōd') tr. imponer, introducir a la fuerza —intr. manifestarse.
ob·tru·sion (əb-trōō'zhən) s. intrusión *f*.
ob·tru·sive (:sĭv) adj. llamativo, que se nota.
ob·tuse (əb-tōōs') adj. obtuso.
ob·verse (ŏb'vûrs') adj. (del) anverso.
ob·vi·ate (ŏb'vē-āt') tr. obviar.
ob·vi·ous (ŏb'vē-əs) adj. obvio, patente.
ob·vi·ous·ly (:lē) adv. evidentemente; (*of course*) claro.
oc·ca·sion (ə-kā'zhən) I. s. ocasión *f*; (*event*) acontecimiento; (*reason*) motivo ♦ **as the o. requires** según el caso • **on o.** ocasionalmente • **to rise to the o.** estar a la altura de las circunstancias II. tr. ocasionar, provocar.
oc·ca·sion·al (:zhə-nəl) adj. ocasional.
oc·ci·dent (ŏk'sə-dĕnt') s. occidente *m*.
oc·clude (ə-klōōd') tr. MED. ocluir; (*to obstruct*) obstruir, tapar.
oc·cult (ə-kŭlt') I. adj. oculto II. s. ciencias ocultas, magia.
oc·cu·pan·cy (ŏk'yə-pən-sē) s. ocupación *f*; (*of house*) residencia; (*of hotel*) estancia.

oc·cu·pant (:pənt) s. *(tenant)* inquilino; *(guest)* huésped *mf*; *(passenger)* pasajero.
oc·cu·pa·tion (ŏk′yə-pā′shən) s. ocupación *f*; *(job)* trabajo; *(pastime)* tarea, pasatiempo.
oc·cu·pa·tion·al (:shə-nəl) adj. ocupacional.
oc·cu·pied (ŏk′yə-pīd′) adj. ocupado.
oc·cu·py (:pī′) tr. *(space)* ocupar; *(time)* emplear ♦ **to o. oneself with** *(to engage in)* ponerse a; *(to busy oneself in)* entretenerse con.
oc·cur (ə-kûr′) intr. **-rr-** ocurrir, suceder; *(in special cases)* darse; *(to be found)* encontrarse ♦ **it occurs to me that** se me ocurre que.
oc·cur·rence (:əns) s. *(incident)* suceso; *(instance)* caso; *(presence)* presencia ♦ **to be an unusual o.** no darse a menudo.
o·cean (ō′shən) s. océano ♦ **o. liner** transatlántico • **oceans of** FIG. la mar de.
o·ce·an·ic (ō′shē-ăn′ĭk) adj. oceánico.
o·cean·og·ra·phy (ō′shə-nŏg′rə-fē) s. oceanografía.
o·cher *o* **o·chre** (ō′kər) s. ocre *m*.
o'clock (ə-klŏk′) adv. ♦ **one o.** la una • **it's ten o.** son las diez.
oc·ta·gon (ŏk′tə-gŏn′) s. octágono, octógono.
oc·tag·o·nal (ŏk-tăg′ə-nəl) adj. octogonal.
oc·tane (ŏk′tān′) s. octano.
Oc·to·ber (ŏk-tō′bər) s. octubre *m*.
oc·to·ge·nar·i·an (ŏk′tə-jə-nâr′ē-ən) adj. & s. octogenario.
oc·to·pus (ŏk′tə-pəs) s. [pl. **es** *o* **-pi**] pulpo.
oc·tu·ple (ŏk′tə-pəl, ŏk-tō͞o′pəl) adj. óctuplo.
oc·u·lar (ŏk′yə-lər) adj. ocular.
oc·u·list (:lĭst) s. oculista *mf*.
OD (ō-dē′) JER. I. s. dosis excesiva de drogas II. intr. **'d, 'ing** darse una dosis excesiva *(on de)*.
odd (ŏd) adj. *(unusual)* raro, extraño; *(strange)* curioso; *(in excess of)* y pico; *(remaining)* de sobra; *(shoe, glove)* suelto; MAT. impar, non ♦ **at o. intervals** de rato en rato • **o. jobs** chapuces • **o. or even?** ¿pares o nones? • **the o. man out** la excepción.
odd·ball (ŏd′bôl′) s. FAM. tipo raro, excéntrico.
odd·i·ty (ŏd′ĭ-tē) s. rareza, singularidad *f*.
odds (ŏdz) s.pl. *(advantage)* ventaja; *(chances)* probabilidades *f* ♦ **o. and ends** retazos • **the o. are against it** no es muy probable • **the o. are that** lo más probable es que • **to be at o. with** *(facts)* no concordar con; *(someone)* estar de punta con.
ode (ōd) s. oda.
o·di·ous (ō′dē-əs) adj. odioso.
o·di·um (:əm) s. odio, rencor *m*.
o·dom·e·ter (ō-dŏm′ĭ-tər) s. odómetro.
o·dor (ō′dər) s. olor *m*.
o·dor·less (ō′dər-lĭs) adj. inodoro.
o·dor·ous (:əs) adj. *(fragrant)* fragante; *(malodorous)* maloliente, pestilente.
o·dour (ō′dər) G.B. var. de **odor**.
od·ys·sey (ŏd′ĭ-sē) s. odisea.
oe·nol·o·gy (ē-nŏl′ə-jē) s. enología.
of (ŏv, ŭv, əv) prep. de; *(time)* menos, para <*it is ten minutes of four* las cuatro menos diez>; *(source)* de . . . parte <*it is very kind of you es* muy gentil de su parte> ♦ **a friend of mine** un amigo mío • **all of them** todos ellos.
off (ôf) I. adv. *(distant)* lejos, a distancia; *(away)* a <*a place five miles o.* un lugar a cinco millas (de distancia)> ♦ **o. and on** de vez en cuando • **o. with you!** ¡lárgate! • **ten per cent o.**

diez por ciento de descuento • **to be o.** irse • **to be (two days) o.** faltar (dos días) para II. adj. *(lights, appliances)* apagado; *(not operating)* desconectado; *(canceled)* cancelado; *(productivity)* más bajo; *(quality, performance)* inferior; *(incorrect)* equivocado ♦ **in the o. position** en posición de cerrado • **o. chance** posibilidad remota • **to be o.** *(mistaken)* estar equivocado; *(from work)* estar libre • **to have an o. day** tener un día malo III. prep. *(from)* de <*take your feet o. my desk* quita los pies de mi escritorio>; *(branching from)* que sale de; *(near)* frente a, a la altura de <*o. the coast* frente a la costa>; *(away from)* fuera, lejos de; *(down from)* desde, por <*to fall o. a cliff* caer por un precipicio>; *(by means of)* gracias a, de <*he lives o. his pension* vive de su pensión>.
of·fal (ô′fəl) s. *(entrails)* menudos; *(refuse)* desperdicios, desecho.
off·beat (ôf′bēt′) I. s. MÚS. tiempo débil II. adj. JER. excéntrico, raro.
off-col·or (ôf′kŭl′ər) adj. *(improper)* de mal gusto; *(in bad spirits)* indispuesto.
of·fence (ə-fĕns′) G.B. var. de **offense**.
of·fend (ə-fĕnd′) tr. ofender ♦ **to be offended at** *o* **by** ofenderse por —intr. ser ofensivo.
of·fend·er (ə-fĕn′dər) s. infractor *m*.
of·fense (ə-fĕns′) s. ofensa; *(crime)* delito; *(attack)* ofensiva; DEP. (ôf′ĕns′) equipo con la pelota ♦ **minor o.** delito leve • **no o. (intended)** sin intención de ofender • **second o.** reincidencia • **to give o.** ofender • **to take o.** de ofenderse por.
of·fen·sive (ə-fĕn′sĭv) I. adj. ofensivo; *(obscene)* grosero; *(unpleasant)* desagradable II. s. ofensiva ♦ **on the o.** a la ofensiva.
of·fer (ô′fər) I. tr. ofrecer; *(to propose)* proponer; *(for sale)* vender; *(resistance)* oponer; *(to provide)* proporcionar; *(to present)* presentar —intr. *(to volunteer)* ofrecerse (a); *(opportunity)* presentarse II. s. oferta.
of·fer·ing (:ĭng) s. oferta, ofrecimiento; *(donation)* donativo; RELIG. oblación *f*, ofrenda.
off·hand (ôf′hănd′) I. adv. sin pensarlo ♦ **I can't recall** no recuerdo en este momento II. adj. improvisado; *(manner)* desenvuelto.
of·fice (ô′fĭs) s. oficina; *(room)* despacho; *(of a doctor)* consultorio; *(of a lawyer)* bufete *m*; *(department)* sección *f*; *(task)* oficio, deber *m*; POL. *(position)* cargo (público); *(Department)* ministerio ♦ **o. building** edificio de oficinas • **o. clerk** *o* **worker** oficinista • **o. hours** horario de oficina *o* consulta • **to be in** *o* **hold o.** ocupar un cargo.
of·fice·hold·er (:hōl′dər) s. funcionario.
of·fi·cer (ô′fĭ-sər) s. oficial *m*, funcionario; *(in a company)* dirigente *m*; MARÍT., MIL. oficial *m*; *(policeman)* agente *m* de policía.
of·fi·cial (ə-fĭsh′əl) I. adj. oficial II. s. oficial *m*, funcionario; *(in a company)* dirigente *mf*; *(referee)* árbitro.
of·fi·cial·ese (-′ə-lēz′) s. lenguaje burocrático.
of·fi·ci·ate (-′ē-āt′) intr. RELIG. oficiar; *(to serve as)* hacer las veces de; DEP. arbitrar.
of·fi·cious (:əs) adj. oficioso.
off·ing (ô′fĭng) s. ♦ **in the o.** a la vista.
off-key (ôf′kē′) adj. desafinado; FIG. fuera de tono.
off-lim·its (ôf′lĭm′ĭts) adj. prohibida la entrada.
off-line (ôf′līn′) adj. COMPUT. fuera de línea.
off-sea·son (ôf′sē′zən) s. baja estación.
off·set I. tr. (ôf-sĕt′) **-set, -tting** compensar; *(to*

counteract) contrarrestar **II.** s. *('')* compensación *f*; IMPR. offset *m* ♦ **o. press** offset.

off·shoot (ôf'shōōt') s. ramal *m*; *(descendant)* vástago; BOT. retoño.

off·shore (ôf'shôr') **I.** adj. de mar adentro; *(coastal)* costanero **II.** adv. mar adentro.

off·side *o* **off side** (ôf'sīd') adj. fuera de juego.

off·spring (ôf'sprîng') s.inv. progenie *f*, prole *f*.

off-the-rack (ôf'thə-rāk') adj. de confección.

off-the-wall (ôf'thə-wôl') adj. FAM. extraño.

off-white (ôf'hwīt') adj. & s. (de) color crudo.

oft (ôft) adv. frecuentemente, a menudo.

of·ten (ô'fən) adv. frecuentemente, a menudo ♦ **as o. as** not no pocas veces • **every so o.** alguna que otra vez • **how o.?** ¿cuántas veces? • **more o. than not** la mayoría de las veces • **not very o.** pocas veces • **too o.** con demasiada frecuencia.

of·ten·times (:tīmz') adv. frecuentemente.

off-the-rec·ord (ôf'thə-rĕk'ərd) adj. *(unofficial)* extraoficial; *(confidential)* confidencial.

o·gle (ō'gəl) tr. mirar con avidez.

o·gre (ō'gər) s. ogro.

oh (ō) interj. *(surprise)* ¡oh!; *(pain)* ¡ay!; *(understanding)* ¡ah! <*oh, I see* ¡ah, ya veo!>.

oil (oil) **I.** s. aceite *m*; *(fuel)* petróleo; *(lubricant)* aceite lubricante; ARTE. óleo ♦ **o. field, well** yacimiento, pozo petrolífero • **o. paint** pintura al óleo **II.** tr. lubricar, aceitar.

oil·can ('kăn') s. aceitera, alcuza.

oil·cloth (:klôth') s. hule *m*, encerado.

oiled (oild) adj. lubricado, aceitado; JER. *(drunk)* borracho.

oil·skin (oil'skĭn') s. *(fabric)* hule *m*; *(garment)* impermeable *m*.

oil·y (oi'lē) adj. **-i-** aceitoso, grasoso; FIG., FAM. *(unctuous)* untuoso.

oink (oingk) s. gruñido del cerdo.

oint·ment (oint'mənt) s. ungüento, pomada.

O.K. *o* **OK** *o* **o·kay** (ō-kā') **I.** s. [pl. **'s**] autorización *f* **II.** tr. **'d, 'ing** aprobar, autorizar **III.** interj. ¡muy bien!, ¡de acuerdo!

o·kra (ō'krə) s. quingombó.

old (ōld) **I.** adj. viejo; *(elderly)* mayor, anciano; *(looking old)* envejecido; *(ancient, former)* antiguo ♦ **any o. thing** cualquier cosa • **any o. way** de cualquier manera • **older** mayor • **oldest** (el) mayor • **o. hat** pasado de moda • **o. maid** solterona • **o. wive's tale** cuento de viejas • **to be (ten years) o.** tener (diez años) de edad **II.** s. ♦ **of o.** de la antigüedad • **the o.** *(something)* lo viejo; *(people)* los ancianos.

old·en (ōl'dən) adj. antiguo, pasado.

old-fash·ioned (ōld'făsh'ənd) adj. anticuado; *(person)* chapado a la antigua.

old-line (:līn') adj. conservador, tradicional.

old·ster (:stər) s. FAM. viejo, anciano.

old-time (:tīm') adj. de antaño.

old-tim·er (:tī'mər) s. FAM. viejo, anciano.

old-world (:wûrld') adj. del viejo mundo.

o·le·o (ō'lē-ō') s. margarina.

o·le·o·mar·ga·rine ('--mär'jə-rĭn) s. oleomargarina.

ol·fac·to·ry (ōl-făk'tə-rē) adj. olfativo.

ol·i·garch (ōl'ĭgärk') s. oligarca *mf*.

ol·i·gar·chy (:gär'kē) s. oligarquía.

ol·ive (ōl'ĭv) s. oliva, aceituna; *(color)* verde *m* oliva ♦ **o. oil** aceite de oliva • **o. tree** olivo *m*.

O·lym·pic (ō-lĭm'pĭk) **I.** adj. olímpico **II.** s. ♦ **pl.** juegos olímpicos.

om·buds·man (ŏm'bŭdz'mən) s. [pl. **-men**] mediador *m* en asuntos de interés público.

om·e·let(te) (ŏm'ə-lĭt) s. tortilla.

o·men (ō'mən) s. presagio, agüero.

om·i·nous (ŏm'ə-nəs) adj. ominoso.

o·mis·sion (ō-mĭsh'ən) s. omisión *f*; *(error)* descuido.

o·mit (ō-mĭt') tr. **-tt-** omitir.

om·ni·bus (ŏm'nĭ-bŭs') **I.** s. ómnibus *m* **II.** adj. incluye varias cosas.

om·nip·o·tence (ŏm-nĭp'ə-tns) s. omnipotencia.

om·nip·o·tent (:tnt) adj. omnipotente.

om·ni·scient (ŏm-nĭsh'ənt) adj. omnisciente.

on (ŏn) **I.** prep. *(general)* en; *(on top of)* sobre; *(to, onto)* a, sobre; *(upon)* al <*on entering the room* al entrar al cuarto>; *(against)* contra; *(according to)* según; *(for)* por <*to travel on business* viajar por negocios>; *(about)* en, sobre ♦ **on July third** el tres de julio • **on my authority** bajo mi autoridad **II.** adv. puesto <*with the lid on* con la tapa puesta> ♦ **on and off** de vez en cuando • **on and on** sin parar **III.** adj. *(appliance, lights)* prendido, encendido; *(gas, electricity)* encendido; *(faucet)* abierto; *(brakes, alarms)* puesto; *(planned)* planeado; *(in progress)* empezado, comenzado.

once (wŭns) **I.** adv. *(one time)* una vez; *(formerly)* en otro tiempo, antes; *(before)* hace tiempo ♦ **at o.** *(immediately)* inmediatamente; *(at the same time)* al mismo tiempo • **o. again** otra vez • **o. and for all** de una vez para siempre • **o. in a while** de vez en cuando • **o. more** otra vez • **o. upon a time** érase una vez **II.** s. una vez ♦ **for o.** una vez siquiera **III.** conj. una vez que, tan pronto como.

once-o·ver (ō'vər) s. JER. revisada a la ligera.

on·col·o·gy (ŏn-kŏl'ə-jē) s. oncología.

on·com·ing (ŏn'kŭm'ĭng) adj. que viene.

one (wŭn) **I.** adj. un, uno; *(sole, only)* solo, único; *(the same)* mismo ♦ **o. and the same** el mismo • **o. hundred** cien • **the o.** and **only** el incomparable **II.** s. uno; *(unit)* unidad *f* ♦ **all in o.** de una sola pieza • **o. o'clock** la una • **to be o. up** tener la ventaja **III.** pron. dem. ♦ **that o.** aquél • **this o.** éste • **which o.?** ¿cuál? **IV.** pron. indef. uno; se <*o. doesn't do such things* esas cosas no se hacen> ♦ **I, for o.** yo, por lo menos • **o. and all** todos • **o.'s** de uno, su.

one-di·men·sion·al ('dĭ-mĕn'shə-nəl) adj. unidimensional.

one-man (:măn') adj. que consiste de un solo miembro; *(for, by one person)* para *o* de una sola persona.

one-piece (:pēs') adj. enterizo.

on·er·ous (ŏn'ər-əs, ō'nər-) adj. oneroso.

one·self (wŭn-sĕlf') pron. sí (mismo), uno (mismo); *(reflexively)* se <*to brace o. for something* prepararse para algo>; *(emphatically)* uno mismo ♦ **by o.** solo • **to be o.** comportarse con naturalidad • **to come to o.** volver en sí.

one-shot ('shŏt') adj. único, que no se repite.

one-sid·ed (:sī'dĭd) adj. *(biased)* parcial; *(unequal)* desigual.

one-time (:tīm') adj. antiguo.

one-time (:tīm') adj. de una sola vez.

one-to-one (:tə-wŭn') adj. MAT. exacto.

one-track (:trăk') adj. ♦ **to have a o. mind** no poder pensar más que en una sola cosa.

one-up·man·ship (-ŭp'mən-shĭp') s. FAM. arte *m* de superar a competidores.

one-way (wā') adj. *(street)* de sentido único; *(ticket)* de ida solamente.

on·go·ing (ŏn′gō′ĭng) adj. *(current)* actual; *(in progress)* en marcha.

on·ion (ŭn′yən) s. cebolla.

on·ion·skin (:skĭn′) s. papel *m* cebolla.

on-line (ŏn′līn′) adj. COMPUT. en línea.

on·look·er (ŏn′lŏŏk′ər) s. espectador *m.*

on·ly (ōn′lē) **I.** adj. *(sole)* único, solo; *(best)* mejor **II.** adv. *(merely)* sólo; *(simply)* simplemente; *(solely)* únicamente; para luego <*they received a raise o. to be laid off* recibieron un aumento para luego ser despedidos> ♦ **if o.** ojalá • **not o.... but also** no sólo ... sino también • **o. too** muy III. conj. *(except that)* sólo que; *(but)* pero <*you may go, o. be careful* puedes ir, pero ten cuidado>.

on·rush (ŏn′rŭsh′) s. arremetida, embestida; *(assault)* ataque *m,* carga.

on·shore (ŏn′shôr′) adj. & adv. (que se dirige) hacia la costa *or* la tierra.

on·slaught (ŏn′slôt′) s. ataque violento.

on·to (ŏn′tŏŏ) prep. *(upon)* sobre, encima de; FAM. *(aware of)* al tanto de, al corriente de.

o·nus (ō′nəs) s. carga, obligación *f.*

on·ward (ŏn′wərd) adj. & adv. hacia adelante.

on·wards (ŏn′wərdz) adv. hacia adelante.

on·yx (ŏn′ĭks) s. ónix *m.*

oo·dles (ŏŏd′lz) s.pl. FAM. montones *m.*

oomph (ŏŏmf) s. JER. vitalidad *f,* energía.

oops (ŏŏps, wŏŏps) interj. usado para expresar sorpresa o consternación.

ooze¹ (ŏŏz) tr. rezumar, supurar; *(confidence, charm)* rebozar de —intr. rezumarse, fluir.

ooze² s. *(soft mud)* cieno, lama.

o·pal (ō′pəl) s. ópalo.

o·pal·es·cence (ō′pə-lěs′əns) s. opalescencia.

o·paque (ō-pāk′) adj. opaco; *(obtuse)* obtuso.

o·pen (ō′pən) **I.** adj. *(fields)* descampado; *(view)* libre, despejado; *(without covering)* descubierto; *(without top)* destapado; *(meeting, court)* público; *(unrestricted)* sin restricción; *(job, post)* vacante, libre; *(question)* pendiente; *(frank)* franco, sincero; *(mind)* sin prejuicios; *(port)* libre, franco ♦ **o. for business** abierto al público • **o. house** recepción general • **o. secret** secreto a voces • **o. sesame!** ¡ábrete sésamo! • **to be o. to** *(ideas, criticism)* estar dispuesto a recibir; *(doubt, interpretation)* admitir, permitir; *(to be vulnerable to)* estar expuesto a **II.** tr. abrir; *(to unfasten)* desatar; *(way, path)* despejar; *(to unblock)* desatascar; *(to uncover)* destapar; *(to unwrap)* desempaquetar; *(to unfold)* desplegar; *(to begin)* iniciar; *(a business)* establecer ♦ **to o. out** ensanchar • **to o. up** *(to make available)* hacer accesible; *(to explore)* explorar —intr. abrirse; *(to come undone)* desatarse; *(halfway)* entreabrirse; *(to unfold)* desplegarse; *(a business)* establecerse; *(to begin)* empezar, comenzar <*we opened with a list of complaints* comenzamos con una lista de quejas>; TEAT. estrenarse ♦ **to o. into** dar a • **to o. on(to)** dar a • **to o. out** *(to unfold)* desplegar(se); *(to extend)* extenderse • **to o. up** *(to spread out)* extenderse; *(to begin)* empezar; *(to speak freely)* desplegarse **III.** s. claro, lugar abierto ♦ **in the o.** *(outdoors)* al aire libre; *(in the country)* en el campo; *(in a clear space)* a campo abierto; *(revealed)* descubierto • **to bring, come into the o.** sacar, salir a la luz.

o·pen-air (′-âr′) adj. al aire libre.

o·pen-and-shut (:ən-shŭt′) adj. simple.

o·pen-end·ed (:-ĕn′dĭd) adj. abierto, ilimitado.

o·pen·er (ō′pə-nər) s. abridor *m;* TEAT. primer

acto ♦ **for openers** para comenzar.

o·pen-hand·ed (ō′pən-hăn′dĭd) adj. maniabierto.

o·pen·ing (ō′pə-nĭng) s. *(aperture)* abertura, orificio; *(breach)* grieta; *(clearing)* claro; *(beginning)* apertura, comienzo; *(of a movie, play)* estreno; *(of a store, exhibition)* inauguración *f;* *(chance)* oportunidad *f;* *(job)* puesto, vacante *f;* POL. apertura ♦ **o. ceremonies** actos de inauguración • **o. night** noche de estreno.

o·pen-mind·ed (ō′pən-mīn′dĭd) adj. receptivo.

op·er·a (ŏp′ər-ə) s. ópera ♦ **o. glasses** gemelos de teatro • **o. house** ópera.

op·er·a·ble (ŏp′ər-ə-bəl) s. operable; *(functional)* que funciona.

op·er·ate (ŏp′ə-rāt′) intr. *(to work)* funcionar; *(to have an effect)* actuar; CIR., MIL. operar; COM. efectuar operaciones —tr. *(to drive)* manejar; *(tool)* usar; *(machinery)* trabajar en, ocuparse de; *(appliance, device)* hacer funcionar, accionar; *(business)* manejar, administrar ♦ **operated by** que funciona con.

op·er·at·ing (ŏp′ə-rā′tĭng) adj. *(operational)* que funciona; *(profit, expenses)* de explotación; *(costs)* de mantenimiento ♦ **o. room** sala de operaciones.

op·er·a·tion (ŏp′ə-rā′shən) s. operación *f;* *(condition)* funcionamiento; *(of vehicles, tools)* manejo; *(management)* administración *f;* *(effect)* acción *f,* efecto; *(undertaking)* maniobra ♦ **method of o.** procedimiento • **to be in o.** estar funcionando.

op·er·a·tion·al (:shə-nəl) adj. de operación; *(in working order)* en condiciones de servicio; *(functioning)* en funcionamiento.

op·er·a·tive (ŏp′ər-ə-tĭv) **I.** adj. *(effective)* operativo, operante; *(functioning)* en condiciones de servicio; *(law)* en vigor; CIR. operatorio **II.** s. *(worker)* operario; *(agent)* agente secreto.

op·er·a·tor (ŏp′ə-rā′tər) s. *(of a machine)* operario; TEL. telefonista *mf;* *(of a vehicle)* conductor *m;* *(manager)* administrador *m;* *(dealer)* agente *m;* FAM. *(clever person)* maquinador *m.*

op·er·et·ta (ŏp′ə-rĕt′ə) s. opereta.

oph·thal·mol·o·gist (ŏf′thăl-mŏl′ə-jĭst, ŏp′-) s. oftalmólogo.

oph·thal·mol·o·gy (:jē) s. oftalmología.

o·pi·ate (ō′pē-ĭt) s. opiato.

o·pine (ō-pīn′) tr. opinar.

o·pin·ion (ə-pĭn′yən) s. opinión *f* ♦ **in my o.** a mi juicio • **in the o. of** según.

o·pin·ion·at·ed (:yə-nā′tĭd) adj. obstinado.

o·pi·um (ō′pē-əm) s. opio.

o·pos·sum (ə-pŏs′əm) s. [pl. inv. *o* **s**] ZOOL. zarigüeya.

op·po·nent (ə-pō′nənt) s. adversario.

op·por·tune (ŏp′ər-tōōn′) adj. oportuno.

op·por·tun·ist (:tōō′nĭst) s. oportunista *mf.*

op·por·tu·ni·ty (:nĭ-tē) s. oportunidad *f.*

op·pose (ə-pōz′) tr. oponerse a; *(to combat)* hacer frente a; *(to set against)* contraponer.

op·po·site (ŏp′ə-zĭt) **I.** adj. opuesto; *(direction)* contrario; *(across from)* de enfrente; *(opinions)* contrario ♦ **on the o. side of** del otro lado de **II.** s. contrario ♦ **it is just the o.** es todo lo contrario **III.** adv. enfrente ♦ **to be directly o.** estar frente a **IV.** prep. enfrente de, frente a.

op·po·si·tion (′-zĭsh′ən) s. oposición *f;* *(resistance)* resistencia; POL. (partido de la) oposición ♦ **to act in o.** obrar en contra de • **to be in o.** estar en contra de.

op·press (ə-prĕs′) tr. *(to subjugate)* oprimir;

(mind, spirit) deprimir; FIG. agobiar.
op·pres·sion (ə-prĕsh'ən) s. opresión *f.*
op·pres·sive (ə-prĕs'ĭv) adj. opresivo; *(tyrannical)* tiránico; *(feeling)* agobiador.
op·pres·sor (:ər) s. opresor *m.*
op·pro·bri·um (ə-prō'brē-əm) s. oprobio.
opt (ŏpt) intr. optar *(for, to* por).
op·tic (ŏp'tĭk) adj. óptico ♦ **optics** s.sg. óptica.
op·ti·cal (ŏp'tĭ-kəl) adj. óptico.
op·ti·cian (ŏp-tĭsh'ən) s. óptico.
op·ti·mal (ŏp'tə-məl) adj. óptimo.
op·ti·mism (ŏp'tə-mĭz'əm) s. optimismo.
op·ti·mist (:mĭst) s. optimista *mf.*
op·ti·mis·tic ('-mĭs'tĭk) adj. optimista ♦ **to feel o.** tener optimismo.
op·ti·mize ('-mīz') tr. mejorar en todo lo posible; *(results)* hacer rendir lo más posible.
op·ti·mum (:məm) I. s. ♦ **the o.** lo óptimo II. adj. óptimo.
op·tion (ŏp'shən) s. opción *f.*
op·tion·al (ŏp'shə-nəl) adj. opcional.
op·tom·e·trist (ŏp-tŏm'ĭ-trĭst) s. optómetra *mf.*
op·tom·e·try (:trē) s. optometría.
op·u·lence (ŏp'yə-ləns) s. opulencia.
op·u·lent (:lənt) adj. opulento.
o·pus (ō'pəs) s. [pl. **es** *o* **opera**] MÚS. opus *m*; LIT. obra.
or (ôr) conj. o; [*before* (h)o] u; [*after negative*] ni <*I don't drink or smoke* ni tomo ni fumo>.
or·a·cle (ôr'ə-kəl) s. oráculo.
o·rac·u·lar (ō-răk'yə-lər) adj. profético.
o·ral (ôr'əl) I. adj. oral ♦ **o. hygiene** higiene bucal II. s. examen *m* oral.
or·ange (ôr'ĭnj) I. s. naranja; *(tree)* naranjo ♦ **o. blossom** azahar • **o. grove** naranjal II. adj. anaranjado.
o·rang·u·tan (ə-răng'ə-tăn') s. orangután *m.*
o·rate (ō-rāt') intr. declamar.
o·ra·tion (ō-rā'shən) s. oración *f.*
or·a·tor (ôr'ə-tər) s. orador *m.*
or·a·tor·i·cal (:-tôr'ĭ-kəl) adj. oratorio.
or·a·to·ry¹ (ôr'ə-tôr'ē) s. *(rhetoric)* oratoria.
or·a·to·ry² s. *(chapel)* oratorio.
orb (ôrb) s. orbe *m.*
or·bit (ôr'bĭt) I. s. órbita ♦ **to go into o.** entrar en órbita II. tr. girar alrededor de; *(a satellite)* poner en órbita —intr. *(to revolve)* girar, dar vueltas; *(to be in orbit)* estar en órbita.
or·bit·al (ôr'bĭ-tl) adj. orbital.
or·chard (ôr'chərd) s. huerto.
or·ches·tra (ôr'kĭ-strə) s. orquesta ♦ **o. seats** butacas de platea.
or·ches·tral (ôr-kĕs'trəl) adj. orquestal.
or·ches·trate (ôr'kĭ-strāt') tr. MÚS. orquestar; *(to organize)* organizar.
or·ches·tra·tion ('-strā'shən) s. orquestación *f.*
or·chid (ôr'kĭd) s. orquídea; *(color)* malva *m.*
or·dain (ôr-dān') tr. ordenar; *(to predestine)* disponer, predestinar.
or·deal (ôr-dēl') s. *(trial)* prueba dura; *(torment)* sufrimiento.
or·der (ôr'dər) I. s. orden *m*; *(arrangement)* disposición *f*; *(procedure)* regla; *(decree, command)* orden *f*; COM. pedido <*to place an o. for* hacer un pedido de>; *(goods)* mercancía; *(of food)* porción *f*; *(organization)* orden *f*, sociedad *f*; *(kind)* tipo, índole *f*; *(rank)* categoría; DER. mandamiento, orden *f* del juez; RELIG. orden *f*; MAT. grado ♦ **in bad o.** desordenado • **in good o.** en buen estado • **in o.** *(in place)* en orden; *(in good condition)* en buenas condiciones; *(in a meeting)* aceptable; *(appropriate)*

pertinente • **in o. that** a fin de que, para que • **in o. to** a fin de, para • **in short o.** pronto • **out of o.** *(out of place)* en desorden; *(not working)* descompuesto; *(in a meeting)* inaceptable; *(inappropriate)* impertinente • **pay to the o. of** páguese a la orden de II. tr. *(to command, arrange)* ordenar; *(to request)* pedir —intr. *(command)* dar una orden; *(request)* hacer un pedido.
or·der·ly (:lē) I. adj. *(neat)* ordenado, en orden; *(conduct)* pacífico II. s. MED. ayudante *m*; MIL. ordenanza *m* III. adv. sistemáticamente.
or·di·nal (ôr'dn-əl) adj. & s. (número) ordinal.
or·di·nance (ôr'dn-əns) s. *(order)* ordenanza; *(statute)* estatuto.
or·di·nar·y (ôr'dn-ĕr'ē) adj. ordinario; *(plain)* corriente, cualquiera; *(average)* medio ♦ **out of the o.** fuera de lo común, extraordinario.
or·di·nate (:ĭt) s. ordenada.
or·di·na·tion (-'ā'shən) s. ordenación *f.*
ord·nance (ôrd'nəns) s. armamentos, equipos de guerra; *(artillery)* artillería.
ore (ôr) s. mineral *m*, mena.
o·reg·a·no (ə-rĕg'ə-nō') s. orégano.
or·gan (ôr'gən) s. órgano; *(agency)* organismo.
or·gan·dy/die (ôr'gən-dē) s. organdí *m.*
or·gan·ic (ôr-găn'ĭk) adj. orgánico.
or·gan·ism (ôr'gə-nĭz'əm) s. organismo.
or·gan·ist (ôr'gə-nĭst) s. organista *mf.*
or·gan·i·za·tion (ôr'gə-nĭ-zā'shən) s. organización *f*; *(group)* organismo.
or·gan·i·za·tion·al (:shə-nəl) adj. de una organización.
or·gan·ize (ôr'gə-nīz') tr. organizar; *(to arrange)* arreglar, ordenar —intr. organizarse.
or·gan·iz·er (:nī'zər) s. organizador *m.*
or·gan·za (ôr-găn'zə) s. organdí *m.*
or·gasm (ôr'găz'əm) s. orgasmo.
or·gi·as·tic (ôr'jē-ăs'tĭk) adj. orgiástico.
or·gy (ôr'jē) s. orgía.
o·ri·ent (ôr'ē-ənt) I. s. oriente *m* II. tr. (:ĕnt') orientar ♦ **to o. oneself** orientarse.
o·ri·en·tal ('-ĕn'tl) adj. & s. oriental *mf.*
o·ri·en·tate (:ĕn-tāt') tr. orientar.
o·ri·en·ta·tion ('--tā'shən) s. orientación *f.*
or·i·fice (ôr'ə-fĭs) s. orificio.
or·i·gin (ôr'ə-jĭn) s. origen *m*; *(of a flight, object)* procedencia ♦ **to have its origins in** originarse en.
o·rig·i·nal (ə-rĭj'ə-nəl) I. adj. original; *(first)* primero; *(authentic)* legítimo; *(inventive)* creativo II. s. persona *o* modelo original; ARTE. original *m.*
o·rig·i·nal·i·ty (-'-năl'ĭ-tē) s. originalidad *f.*
o·rig·i·nate (-'-nāt') tr. *(to introduce)* originar; *(to invent)* crear —intr. *(to start)* originarse, surgir; *(family)* ser originario *u* oriundo de.
o·rig·i·na·tion (-'-nā'shən) s. origen *m.*
o·rig·i·na·tor (-'-tər) s. autor *m*, creador *m.*
o·ri·ole (ôr'ē-ōl') s. oriol *m.*
or·na·ment (ôr'nə-mənt) I. s. ornamento II. tr. ornamentar.
or·na·men·tal ('-mĕn'tl) adj. ornamental.
or·na·men·ta·tion (:mĕn-tā'shən) s. ornamentación *f*; *(decoration)* ornato.
or·nate (ôr-nāt') adj. recargado.
or·ner·y (ôr'nə-rē) adj. **-i-** FAM. terco.
or·ni·thol·o·gy (ôr'nə-thŏl'ə-jē) s. ornitología.
or·phan (ôr'fən) I. s. & adj. huérfano II. tr. dejar huérfano.
or·phan·age (ôr'fə-nĭj) s. orfanato, orfelinato.

or·tho·don·tics (ôr′thə-dŏn′tĭks) s.sg. ortodoncia.

or·tho·dox (ôr′thə-dŏks′) adj. ortodoxo.

or·tho·dox·y (:dŏk′sē) s. ortodoxia.

or·tho·graph·ic (′-grăf′ĭk) adj. ortográfico.

or·thog·ra·phy (ôr-thŏg′rə-fē) s. ortografía.

or·tho·p(a)e·dic (ôr′thə-pē′dĭk) adj. ortopédico ♦ **orthop(a)edics** s.sg. ortopedia.

os·cil·late (ŏs′ə-lāt′) intr. oscilar.

os·cil·la·tion (′-lā′shən) s. oscilación f.

os·mo·sis (ŏz-mō′sĭs) s. ósmosis f.

os·si·fy (ŏs′ə-fī′) tr. & intr. osificar(se).

os·su·ar·y (ŏsh′ōͤ-ĕr′ē) s. osario.

os·ten·si·ble (ŏ-stĕn′sə-bəl) adj. ostensible.

os·ten·ta·tion (ŏs′tĕn-tā′shən) s. ostentación f.

os·ten·ta·tious (:shəs) s. ostentoso.

os·te·o·path (ŏs′tē-ə-păth′) osteópata mf.

os·te·op·a·thy (′-ŏp′ə-thē) s. osteopatía.

os·tra·cism (ŏs′trə-sĭz′əm) s. ostracismo.

os·tra·cize (:sīz′) tr. condenar al ostracismo.

os·trich (ŏs′trĭch) s. [pl. inv. o **es**] avestruz m.

oth·er (ŭth′ər) **I.** adj. otro; (additional) demás; (different) distinto ♦ **o. people** otros **II.** s. otro ♦ **no o.** ningún otro ♦ **no o. than** nadie más que **III.** pron. otro <something or o. una cosa u otra> ♦ **sometime or o.** cualquier día **IV.** adv. ♦ **o. than** (differently) de otro modo; (anything but) otra cosa que.

oth·er·wise (:wīz′) **I.** adv. (differently) de otro modo; (under other circumstances) de lo contrario, si no <o. I would have gone de lo contrario habría ido>; (in other respects) por lo demás, a no ser por eso **II.** adj. diferente, otro.

ot·ter (ŏt′ər) s. [pl. inv. o **s**] nutria.

ot·to·man (ŏt′ə-mən) s. otomana.

ouch (ouch) interj. ¡ay!

ought (ôt) aux. (to be obliged) deber; (to be wise) convenir, ser conveniente <you o. to wear a raincoat conviene que lleves una gabardina>; (to be desirable) tener que; (to be likely) deber de.

ounce (ouns) s. onza; FIG. pizca, poquito.

our (our) adj. pos. nuestro.

ours (ourz) pron. pos. (el) nuestro.

our·selves (:sĕlvz′) pron. nos <we should wash o. debemos lavarnos>; nosotros (mismos) <we did it o. lo hicimos nosotros mismos>.

oust (oust) tr. expulsar.

oust·er (ou′stər) s. expulsión f.

out (out) **I.** adv. (away from) fuera <o. of the office fuera de la oficina>; (outside) afuera; hasta el final <to argue it o. discutirlo hasta el final>; (on strike) en huelga ♦ **all o.** con tesón ♦ **o. and o.** completamente ♦ **o. for** empeñado en ♦ **to be o.** (not at home) no estar en casa; (sun, moon) haber salido; (eliminated) quedar excluido; FUG. estar fuera del poder **II.** adj. (exterior) exterior; (absent) ausente; (used up) agotado; (extinguished) apagado; (impossible) imposible <that's o. eso es imposible>; (not in fashion) fuera de moda **III.** prep. (through) por; (beyond) fuera de, al otro lado de ♦ **o. of** de <to take o. of sacar de>; (without) sin <o. of money sin dinero>; (because of) por <o. of curiosity por curiosidad>; (from among) de cada **IV.** s. FAM. (way out) salida; (excuse) excusa ♦ **on the outs** FAM. enemistado **V.** intr. descubrirse **VI.** interj. ¡fuera!

out·age (ou′tĭj) s. corte m de electricidad.

out-and-out (out′n-out′) adj. completo, total.

out·bid (-bĭd′) tr. **-bid, -bid(den), -dd-** superar a, ofrecer más que.

out·board (′bôrd′) adj. fuera de borda.

out·bound (:bound′) adj. de salida, que sale.

out·break (:brāk′) s. brote m.

out·burst (:bûrst′) s. arranque m, estallido.

out·cast (:kăst′) s. paria mf.

out·class (-klăs′) tr. ser muy superior a.

out·come (′kŭm′) s. resultado, consecuencia.

out·crop (:krŏp′) s. afloramiento.

out·cry (:krī′) s. protesta; (clamor) alboroto.

out·dat·ed (-dā′tĭd) adj. obsoleto, anticuado.

out·dis·tance (:dĭs′təns) tr. dejar atrás.

out·do (:dōō′) tr. **-did, -done** superar.

out·door (′dôr′) adj. al aire libre.

out·doors (-dôrz′) **I.** adv. al aire libre; (outside) (a)fuera **II.** s. el aire libre.

out·doors·man (:mən) s. [pl. **-men**] hombre m que gusta del aire libre, la pesca o la caza.

out·er (ou′tər) ♦ **o.** oído externo ♦ **o. space** espacio exterior.

out·er·most (:mōst′) adj. más alejado.

out·fit (out′fĭt′) **I.** s. (clothing) conjunto; FAM. (military unit) unidad f; (business) empresa **II.** tr. **-tt-** equipar.

out·flank (-flăngk′) tr. desbordar el flanco de; (to outwit) aventajar tácticamente.

out·flow (′flō′) s. flujo.

out·fox (-fŏks′) tr. ganar en astucia, burlar.

out·go·ing (′gō′ĭng) adj. de salida, que sale; (retiring) saliente; (friendly) sociable.

out·grow (-grō′) tr. **-grew, -grown** crecer más que; (interests, ideas) perder ♦ **to o. one's clothes** quedarle la ropa chica a uno.

out·growth (′grōth′) s. brote m; FIG. resultado.

out·guess (-gĕs′) tr. anticipar.

out·house (′hous′) s. excusado, retrete m.

out·ing (:ĭng) s. excursión f.

out·land·ish (-lăn′dĭsh) adj. extravagante.

out·last (:lăst′) tr. durar más que.

out·law (′lô′) **I.** s. malhechor m, criminal m; (fugitive) forajido **II.** tr. prohibir.

out·lay (out′lā′) s. desembolso, gastos.

out·let (′lĕt′) s. salida; (socket) tomacorriente m; (for feelings) forma de desahogar; (for energies) forma de descargar; COM. (market) salida; (store) distribuidor m.

out·line (:līn′) **I.** s. (contour) contorno; (profile) perfil m; (shape) silueta; (summary) resumen m; ARTE. bosquejo; TEC. trazado ♦ **in broad o.** en líneas generales **II.** tr. trazar las líneas o los contornos de; (to profile) perfilar; (to describe) trazar a grandes rasgos; (to summarize) resumir; (to sketch) bosquejar.

out·live (-lĭv′) tr. sobrevivir.

out·look (′lŏŏk′) s. punto de vista; (attitude) actitud f; (prospect) posibilidades f.

out·ly·ing (:lī′ĭng) adj. alejado del centro ♦ **the o. suburbs** las afueras de la ciudad.

out·ma·neu·ver (′mə-nōō′vər) tr. ganar en astucia; AUTO. moverse mejor que.

out·mod·ed (-mō′dĭd) adj. anticuado.

out·num·ber (:nŭm′bər) tr. superar en número.

out-of-date (′əv-dāt′) adj. (outmoded) anticuado; (expired) caducado.

out-of-the-way (:thə-wā′) adj. (remote) apartado; (secluded) solitario; (unusual) insólito.

out·pa·tient (out′pā′shənt) s. paciente mf que no está hospitalizado.

out·post (:pōst′) s. MIL. puesto avanzado; (settlement) puesto fronterizo.

out·pour·ing (:pôr′ĭng) s. efusión f.

out·put (:pŏŏt') I. s. producción f; (energy) potencia; (yield) rendimiento; COMPUT. salida II. COMPUT. imprimir.
out·rage (:rāj') I. s. ultraje m; (destructive act) atropello; (anger) indignación f ♦ **an o. against** un atentado contra II. tr. indignar.
out·ra·geous (-rā'jəs) adj. ultrajante; (flagrant) flagrante; (infuriating) indignante; (exorbitant) excesivo.
out·rank (-răngk') tr. tener un rango superior a; (to surpass) ser superior a.
out·reach ('rēch') s. servicio especial de asistencia pública.
out·right (:rīt') I. adv. (frankly) sin reservas; (obviously) patentemente; (utterly) absolutamente; (straightway) en el acto II. adj. (unqualified) sin reservas; (obvious) patente; (out-and-out) absoluto <o. viciousness maldad absoluta>.
out·run (-rŭn') tr. **-ran, -run, -nn-** (to outstrip) dejar rezagado; (to surpass) librarse de.
out·sell (:sĕl') tr. **-sold** vender más que o mejor que; (a product) venderse mejor que.
out·set ('sĕt') s. principio, inicio.
out·shine (-shīn') tr. **-shone** brillar más que; FIG. superar.
out·side (out-sīd') I. s. exterior m; (appearance) superficie f ♦ **at the o.** como mucho o máximo ♦ **from, on the o.** desde, por fuera II. adj. exterior <o. assistance ayuda exterior>; (estimate) máximo; (influence) de afuera; (chance) remoto III. adv. (a)fuera <to step o. ir afuera>; (outdoors) en o a la calle IV. prep. fuera de ♦ **o. of** fuera de; (except) excepto.
out·sid·er (-sī'dər) s. forastero.
out·skirts ('skûrts') s.pl. afueras.
out·smart (-smärt') tr. ser más astuto que.
out·spo·ken (:-spō'kən) adj. abierto, franco ♦ **to be o.** no tener pelos en la lengua.
out·spread (-sprĕd') I. tr. **-spread** extender, desplegar II. adj. extendido, desplegado.
out·stand·ing (:stăn'dĭng) adj. sobresaliente; (prominent) destacado; (superior) excelente; (not resolved) pendiente.
out·stretched (:strĕcht') adj. extendido.
out·strip (:strĭp') tr. **-pp-** (to leave behind) dejar atrás; (to exceed) sobrepasar.
out·take ('tāk') s. CINEM. toma de película no utilizada.
out·ward (:wərd) I. adj. exterior, externo; (direction) hacia afuera; (superficial) superficial; (journey) de ida II. adv. o **-wards** hacia afuera.
out·weigh (-wā') tr. pesar más que.
out·wit (:wĭt') tr. **-tt-** ser más vivo que, burlar.
o·val (ō'vəl) I. adj. ovalado, oval II. s. óvalo.
o·va·ry (ō'və-rē) s. ovario.
o·va·tion (ō-vā'shən) s. ovación f.
ov·en (ŭv'ən) s. horno.
o·ver (ō'vər) I. prep. sobre; (above) encima de; (across, on, higher than) por encima de <to jump o. the fence saltar por encima de la valla>; (on the other side of) al otro lado de; (throughout) por todo, a través de <so as to cover or close) para tapar o cerrar; (during) durante <o. the past two years durante los dos últimos años>; (more than) más de o que; (in preference to) antes que; (by means of) por <o. the telephone por teléfono> II. adv. (above) (por) encima; (across) al otro lado, enfrente; allá <o. in Europe allá en Europa>; (again) otra vez, de nuevo; (more) más <ten times o. diez veces más> ♦ **o. again** otra vez, de nuevo ♦ **o. and**

above además de ♦ **o. and o.** una y otra vez ♦ **o. here, there** aquí, allá ♦ **o. with** FAM. acabado III. adj. terminado, acabado.
o·ver·a·bun·dance ('-ə-bŭn'dəns) s. exceso.
o·ver·act (:ăkt') tr. & intr. exagerar.
o·ver·all o **o·ver-all** (:ôl') I. adj. total II. adv. en general, generalmente.
o·ver·alls ('-ôlz') s.pl. mono, overol m.
o·ver·bear·ing ('-bâr'ĭng) adj. (overwhelming) avasallador; (arrogant) arrogante.
o·ver·bid ('-bĭd') s. oferta mayor.
o·ver·bite (:bīt') s. oclusión defectuosa.
o·ver·blown ('-blōn') adj. inflado, pomposo.
o·ver·board ('-bôrd') adv. por la borda ♦ **man o.!** ¡hombre al agua! ♦ **to go o.** FAM. irsele la mano.
o·ver·book ('-bŏŏk') tr. & intr. vender más localidades de las que hay disponibles (en).
o·ver·bur·den (:bûr'dn) tr. sobrecargar.
o·ver·cast ('kăst') adj. nublado.
o·ver·cau·tious ('-kô'shəs) adj. demasiado cauteloso.
o·ver·charge I. tr. & intr. ('-chärj') cobrar demasiado II. s. ('-') precio excesivo.
o·ver·coat (-kōt') s. sobretodo, abrigo.
o·ver·come ('-kŭm') tr. **-came, -come** (to defeat) derrotar, conquistar; (to overwhelm) abrumar; (obstacle, difficulty) superar ♦ **to be o. by** estar afectado profundamente por.
o·ver·com·pen·sate ('-kŏm'pən-sāt') tr. & intr. sobrecompensar.
o·ver·con·fi·dent (:kŏn'fĭ-dnt) adj. demasiado confiado.
o·ver·do (:dōō') tr. **-did, -done** hacer demasiado; (diet, exercise) exagerar; (food) cocinar demasiado —intr. hacer demasiado.
o·ver·dose I. s. ('-dōs') dosis excesiva II. tr. & intr. ('-') dar(se) una dosis excesiva (on de).
o·ver·draft ('-drăft') s. giro en descubierto.
o·ver·draw ('-drô') tr. **-drew, -drawn** girar en descubierto.
o·ver·drawn (:drôn') adj. al descubierto.
o·ver·dress (:drĕs') intr. vestirse con más lujo de lo necesario.
o·ver·drive ('-drīv') s. sobremarcha.
o·ver·due ('-dōō') adj. (unpaid) vencido (en el pago); (delayed) retrasado.
o·ver·eat (:ēt') intr. **-ate, -eaten** comer demasiado.
o·ver·em·pha·size (:ĕm'fə-sīz') tr. & intr. dar demasiado énfasis (a).
o·ver·es·ti·mate (:ĕs'tə-māt') tr. sobreestimar.
o·ver·ex·pose (:ĭk-spōz') tr. exponer demasiado; FOTOG. sobreexponer.
o·ver·ex·po·sure (:ĭk-spō'zhər) s. (publicity) publicidad excesiva; FOTOG. sobreexposición f.
o·ver·ex·tend (:ĭk-stĕnd') tr. extender o ampliar demasiado.
o·ver·flow I. intr. ('-flō') desbordarse ♦ **to o. with** rebosar de — desbordar, salirse de; (to flood) inundar II. s. ('-') (flood) inundación f; (excess) exceso; (outlet) desagüe m.
o·ver·grown ('-grōn') adj. cubierto (with de).
o·ver·hang I. tr. ('-hăng') **-hung** sobresalir o colgar por encima de II. s. ('-') saliente m.
o·ver·haul I. tr. ('-hôl') hacer una reparación general de II. s. ('-hôl') reparación f general.
o·ver·head I. adj. de arriba; (light) del techo; (railway) elevado; (wire) aéreo; COM. general II. s. COM. gastos generales III. adv. (above) arriba; (up) para o hacia arriba.

o·ver·hear ('-hîr') tr. **-heard** oír por casualidad.
o·ver·heat (:hēt') tr. & intr. recalentar(se).
o·ver·in·dulge (:ĭn-dŭlj') tr. *(child)* consentir; *(appetite)* saciar —intr. **♦ to o. in** abusar de.
o·ver·in·dul·gence (:ĭn-dŭl'jəns) s. *(permissiveness)* consentimiento excesivo; *(gratification)* exceso, falta de control.
o·ver·joyed (:joid') adj. loco de contento.
o·ver·kill s. ('-kĭl') s. MIL. capacidad excesiva de represalia nuclear; FIG. medidas excesivas.
o·ver·lap ('-lăp') tr. & intr. **-pp-** superponerse (a); *(in time, function)* coincidir en parte (con).
o·ver·lay I. tr. ('-lā') **-laid** cubrir, extender sobre; ARTE. revestir II. s. ('-') revestimiento.
o·ver·load I. tr. ('-lōd') sobrecargar II. s. sobrecarga.
o·ver·look ('-lŏŏk') I. tr. mirar desde lo alto; *(to rise above)* dominar; *(view, window)* dar a, tener vista a; *(to disregard)* pasar por alto; *(to supervise)* supervisar II. s. mirador m.
o·ver·ly (:lē) adv. demasiado.
o·ver·much ('-mŭch') I. adj. demasiado, excesivo II. adv. excesivamente.
o·ver·night (:nīt') I. adj. *(guests)* por la noche; *(sudden)* repentino, inesperado **♦ o. bag** maletín de viaje II. adv. durante o por la noche; *(suddenly)* de la noche a la mañana **♦ to stay o.** pasar la noche.
o·ver·pass ('-păs') s. paso superior, puente m.
o·ver·pay ('-pā') tr. **-paid** pagar demasiado (por).
o·ver·play (:plā') tr. exagerar.
o·ver·pop·u·la·tion (:pŏp'yə-lā'shən) s. superpoblación f.
o·ver·pow·er (:pou'ər) tr. abrumar.
o·ver·pow·er·ing (:ĭng) adj. *(overwhelming)* abrumador; *(irresistible)* irresistible.
o·ver·price (ō'vər-prīs') tr. poner un precio demasiado alto a.
o·ver·pro·duc·tion (:prə-dŭk'shən) s. superproducción f, sobreproducción f.
o·ver·qual·i·fied (:kwŏl'ə-fīd') adj. excesivamente capacitado.
o·ver·rate (:rāt') tr. sobrestimar **♦ to be overrated** tener demasiada fama.
o·ver·reach (:rēch') tr. extralimitarse en.
o·ver·re·act (:rē-ăkt') intr. reaccionar de modo exagerado.
o·ver·ride (:rīd') tr. **-rode, -ridden** *(to prevail over)* imponerse a; *(to nullify)* anular.
o·ver·rule (:rōōl') tr. *(to rule against)* decidir en contra de; *(to declare null)* anular.
o·ver·run I. tr. (:rŭn') **-ran, -run, -nn-** *(to defeat)* destruir; *(to invade)* invadir; *(limit)* pasarse de II. s. ('-') costo por sobre del presupuesto.
o·ver·seas ('-sēz') I. adv. en el o al extranjero II. adj. extranjero; *(trade)* exterior.
o·ver·see (:sē') tr. **-saw, -seen** supervisar.
o·ver·se·er ('-sē'ər) s. capataz m.
o·ver·sen·si·tive ('-sĕn'sĭ-tĭv) adj. hipersensible.
o·ver·shad·ow (:shăd'ō) tr. oscurecer.
o·ver·shoe ('-shōō') s. chanclo.
o·ver·shoot (:shōōt') tr. **-shot** *(to miss)* irse por encima de; *(a runway, goal)* pasarse de.
o·ver·sight (:sīt') s. *(omission)* descuido, omisión f; *(watchful care)* vigilancia.
o·ver·size(d) (:sīz[d]') adj. demasiado grande; *(clothes)* de talla especial.
o·ver·sleep (:slēp') intr. **-slept** quedarse dormido.

o·ver·state (:stāt') tr. exagerar.
o·ver·state·ment (:mənt) s. exageración f.
o·ver·stay (ō'vər-stā') tr. **♦ to o. one's welcome** prolongar demasiado la visita.
o·ver·step (:stĕp') tr. **-pp-** traspasar, pasar de **♦ to o. one's limits** extralimitarse.
o·ver·stock (:stŏk') tr. tener existencias excesivas de, almacenar en exceso.
o·ver·stuff (:stŭf') tr. rellenar abundantemente.
o·ver·sup·ply I. s. ('-sə-plī') suministro excesivo **♦ an o. of** un exceso de II. tr. ('-') suministrar en exceso.
o·vert (ō-vûrt') adj. abierto, público.
o·ver·take (ō'vər-tāk') tr. **-took, -taken** *(to catch up with)* alcanzar; *(to pass)* pasar.
o·ver·tax (:tăks') tr. oprimir con impuestos; FIG. agotar.
o·ver-the-count·er (:thə-koun'tər) adj. *(stock)* que se vende fuera de la bolsa; *(drug)* que se despacha sin receta médica.
o·ver·throw I. tr. ('-thrō') **-threw, -thrown** *(to oust)* derrocar; *(to dethrone)* destronar II. s. ('-') derrocamiento; *(downfall)* caída.
o·ver·time ('-tīm') s. & adv. horas extras.
o·ver·tone (:tōn') s. *(hint)* sugestión f; MÚS. armónico **♦ an o.** o overtones of una nota de.
o·ver·ture (:chŏōr') s. *(proposal)* oferta, propuesta; MÚS. obertura.
o·ver·turn (:tûrn') tr. volcar; *(to upset)* trastornar; *(to revoke)* revocar —intr. volcarse; *(a vehicle)* dar una vuelta.
o·ver·use (:yōōs') s. uso excesivo, abuso.
o·ver·val·ue (:văl'yōō) tr. sobrestimar.
o·ver·view ('-vyōō') s. repaso, resumen m.
o·ver·weight ('-wāt') adj. pasado de peso; *(obese)* obeso, gordo.
o·ver·whelm (:hwĕlm') tr. *(to defeat)* aplastar; *(to overcome)* abrumar; *(with requests)* acosar **♦ to be overwhelmed** *(with joy)* rebosar (de contento); *(by grief)* estar abrumado (de dolor).
o·ver·whelm·ing (:hwĕl'mĭng) adj. *(staggering)* abrumador; *(victory)* arrollador; *(majority)* inmenso; *(passion)* irresistible.
o·ver·work (:wûrk') tr. hacer trabajar demasiado; *(an idea)* abusar de —intr. trabajar demasiado.
o·ver·wrought (:rôt') adj. *(agitated)* muy alterado, sobrexcitado; *(ornate)* recargado.
o·vi·duct (ō'vĭ-dŭkt') s. oviducto.
o·void (ō'void') adj. ovoide.
o·vu·late (ō'vyə-lāt', ŏv'yə-) intr. ovular.
o·vule (ō'vyōōl, ŏv'yōōl) s. óvulo.
o·vum (ō'vəm) s. [pl. **ova**] óvulo.
owe (ō) tr. deber **♦ to o. it to oneself** merecérselo **• to o. someone** deber a alguien.
ow·ing (ō'ĭng) adj. por pagarse **♦ o. to** debido a.
owl (oul) s. lechuza, búho.
own (ōn) I. adj. propio **♦ by their o. admission** según ellos mismos lo reconocieron **• he buys his o. clothes** él mismo se compra la ropa **• it's my o. money** es mi dinero II. pron. lo mío, lo tuyo, lo suyo, lo nuestro, lo vuestro **♦ of one's o.** *(belonging to oneself)* propio; *(peculiar to oneself)* de uno; *(for use by oneself)* para uno **• on one's o.** *(unaided)* sin ayuda de nadie; *(independently)* por cuenta propia **• to be on one's o.** arreglárselas por cuenta propia **• come into one's o.** lograr el éxito merecido **• to get one's o. back** tomar revancha III. tr. ser dueño de, tener **♦ to o. up to** confesar **• who owns this scarf?** ¿de quién es esta bufanda?

—intr. ♦ **to o. up** confesar.
own·er (ō'nər) s. dueño, propietario.
own·er·ship (:shĭp') s. *(state)* posesión f; *(legal right)* propiedad f.
ox (ŏks) s. [pl. **-en**] buey m.
ox·i·dant (ŏk'sĭ-dnt) s. oxidante m.
ox·i·da·tion ('-dā'shən) s. oxidación f.
ox·ide (ŏk'sīd') s. óxido.
ox·i·dize (ŏk'sĭ-dīz') tr. & intr. oxidar(se).
ox·y·gen (ŏk'sĭ-jən) s. oxígeno.
ox·y·gen·ate (ŏk'sĭ-jə-nāt') tr. oxigenar.
oys·ter (oi'stər) s. ostra.
o·zone (ō'zōn') s. ozono ♦ **o. layer** ozonosfera.

P

p, P (pē) s. decimosexta letra del alfabeto inglés ♦ **to mind one's p's and q's** tener cuidado con lo que uno hace.
pa (pä) s. FAM. papá m.
pace (pās) I. s. paso; *(speed)* ritmo, tren m ♦ **at a snail's p.** a paso de tortuga • **to keep p. with** avanzar al mismo paso que; *(to keep abreast of)* mantenerse al corriente de • **to set the p.** fijar el paso, establecer el ritmo • **to put someone through his paces** poner a alguien a prueba II. tr. ir y venir por, pasearse por; *(to measure)* medir a pasos; *(to set the speed)* fijar el paso de ♦ **to p. off** medir a pasos • **to p. oneself** coger el ritmo de uno —intr. pasear.
pace·mak·er (mā'kər) s. corredor m que toma la delantera; MED. marcapasos m.
pace·set·ter (:sĕt'ər) s. el que da la pauta.
pach·y·derm (pāk'ĭ-dûrm') s. paquidermo.
pa·cif·ic (pə-sĭf'ĭk) adj. pacífico.
pac·i·fi·ca·tion (pās'ə-fĭ-kā'shən) s. pacificación f.
pac·i·fi·er ('-fī'ər) s. pacificador m; *(for a baby)* chupete m.
pac·i·fist (:fist) s. pacifista mf.
pac·i·fy (:fī') tr. pacificar, apaciguar.
pack (pāk) I. s. paquete m; *(knapsack)* mochila; *(batch)* lote m; *(heap)* montón m; *(of cigarettes)* cajetilla; *(of matches)* cajita; *(of cards)* baraja; *(of dogs)* jauría; *(of wolves)* manada; *(of people)* banda ♦ **a p. of lies** una sarta de mentiras • **p. animal** animal de carga II. tr. *(to wrap up)* envolver; *(to fill up)* llenar; *(for traveling)* hacer, preparar; *(for shipping)* embalar; *(to put)* poner; *(to package)* empacar, empaquetar; *(to cram)* apiñar, apretar; *(to compact)* prensar; *(a panel)* llenar de partidarios; MED. envolver en paños ♦ **to p. a pistol** FAM. llevar una pistola • **to p. down** prensar, comprimir • **to p. someone off** to despachar a alguien para • **to send someone packing** FAM. mandar a alguien a paseo —intr. *(for traveling)* hacer las maletas; *(people)* apiñarse, apretarse.
pack·age (pāk'ĭj) I. s. paquete m ♦ **p. store** tienda de vinos y licores II. tr. empaquetar.
pack·ag·ing (:ĭ-jĭng) s. embalaje m.
packed (pākt) adj. *(crowded)* lleno, atestado; *(compressed)* apiñado; *(filled with)* lleno de.
pack·et (pāk'ĭt) s. paquete pequeño; *(boat)* paquebote m.
pack·horse (:hôrs') s. caballo de carga.
pack·ing (:ĭng) s. embalaje m, envase m.
pact (pākt) s. pacto, convenio.
pad¹ (pād) I. s. *(cushion)* almohadilla, cojín m; *(stuffing)* relleno; *(of paper)* bloc m; *(leaf)*

hoja grande; *(of animals)* pulpejo; *(apartment)* nido ♦ **launch p.** pista de lanzamiento II. tr. **-dd-** *(to stuff)* rellenar; *(to line)* forrar; FAM. *(speech, report)* hinchar.
pad² intr. **-dd-** *(to walk)* pisar suavemente.
pad·ded ('ĭd) adj. con una almohadilla; *(upholstered)* relleno; *(shoulders)* con hombreras; *(account)* hinchado, aumentado.
pad·ding (:ĭng) s. relleno.
pad·dle¹ (pād'l) I. s. pagaya, canalete m; *(of waterwheel)* paleta, álabe m ♦ **p. boat** vapor de ruedas, hidropedal II. intr. remar con pagaya —tr. *(to propel)* hacer avanzar con pagaya; *(to stir)* mover con una paleta; *(to spank)* azotar.
pad·dle² intr. *(to splash)* chapotear; *(to toddle)* hacer pinitos, andar a gatas.
pad·dock (pād'ək) s. potrero, dehesa.
pad·dy (pād'ē) s. arrozal m.
pad·lock (pād'lŏk') I. s. candado II. tr. cerrar con candado.
pa·gan (pā'gən) s. & adj. pagano.
page¹ (pāj) I. s. paje m; *(in hotel)* botones m II. tr. llamar.
page² I. s. página II. tr. *(to number)* paginar; *(to order)* compaginar —intr. hojear.
pag·eant (pāj'ənt) s. espectáculo; *(procession)* desfile histórico.
pag·eant·ry (:ən-trē) s. espectáculo; *(pomp)* pompa.
pag·i·nate (pāj'ə-nāt') tr. paginar.
pag·i·na·tion (-nā'shən) s. paginación f.
paid (pād) cf. **pay**.
pail (pāl) s. cubo, balde m.
pain (pān) I. s. dolor m; *(distress)* pena, sufrimiento ♦ **on o under p. of** so pena de, bajo pena de • **to be a p. in the neck** FAM. *(somebody)* ser un pesado; *(something)* dar lata • **to be in p.** tener dolores, sufrir • **to take pains** *(efforts)* hacer esfuerzos, empeñarse; *(care)* esmerarse II. tr. & intr. doler.
pain·ful ('fəl) adj. doloroso; *(difficult)* difícil, penoso; *(pitiful)* lastimoso.
pain·kill·er (:kĭl'ər) s. calmante m.
pain·less (:lĭs) adj. indoloro, sin dolor.
pains·tak·ing (pānz'tā'kĭng) adj. esmerado, cuidadoso.
paint (pānt) I. s. pintura II. tr. & intr. pintar ♦ **to p. the town red** JER. irse de juerga.
paint·brush ('brŭsh') s. brocha; ARTE. pincel m.
paint·er (pān'tər) s. pintor m.
paint·ing (:ĭng) s. pintura.
pair (pâr) I. s. [pl. inv. o **s**] par m; *(persons, animals)* pareja; *(of horses, oxen)* yunta; *(in cards)* par ♦ **in pairs** de dos en dos II. tr. *(to match up)* parear, casar; *(to group)* juntar, emparejar; *(to mate)* aparear —intr. hacer pareja ♦ **to p. off** o **up** formar parejas.
pa·ja·mas (pə-jä'məz, -jām'əz) s.pl. piyama m.
pal (pāl) I. s. FAM. amigote m, compinche m II. intr. **-ll-** ♦ **to p. around with** ser amigo de.
pal·ace (pāl'ĭs) s. palacio.
pal·at·a·ble (pāl'ə-tə-bəl) adj. sabroso, apetitoso; *(agreeable)* aceptable.
pal·ate (pāl'ĭt) s. paladar m.
pa·la·tial (pə-lā'shəl) adj. palaciego; *(splendid)* espléndido, magnífico.
pa·lav·er (pə-lāv'ər) s. palabrería.
pale¹ (pāl) s. *(stake)* estaca; *(wooden fence)* empalizada; *(boundary)* límite m, margen m ♦ **to be beyond the p.** FIG. no ser aceptable.
pale² I. adj. *(complexion)* pálido; *(color)* claro;

(dim) tenue, sin brillo **II.** tr. poner pálido —intr. palidecer.

pa·le·og·ra·phy (pǎ'lē-ŏg'rə-fē) s. paleografía.

pa·le·on·tol·o·gy (:ŏn-tŏl'ə-jē) s. paleontología.

pal·ette (pǎl'ĭt) s. paleta; *(colors)* gama de colores.

pal·i·sade (pǎl'ĭ-sād') s. *(fence)* estacada, cerca; *(stake)* estaca ♦ pl. acantilado, risco.

pall¹ (pôl) s. *(of a coffin)* paño mortuorio; *(coffin)* ataúd m; *(covering)* capa, cortina ♦ **to cast a p.** over producir un efecto deprimente en.

pall² intr. *(to become boring)* perder su sabor; *(to become satiated)* saciarse, cansarse.

pall·bear·er ('bâr'ər) s. portador m del ataúd.

pal·let¹ (pǎl'ĭt) s. *(platform)* paleta.

pal·let² s. *(pad)* jergón m.

pal·li·ate (pǎl'ē-āt') tr. paliar, mitigar.

pal·li·a·tive (:ā'tĭv) adj. & s. paliativo.

pal·lid (pǎl'ĭd) adj. pálido.

pal·lor (:ər) s. palidez f.

palm¹ (päm) **I.** s. *(of a hand)* palma; *(measure)* palmo; *(of an oar)* pala ♦ **to grease** o **cross someone's p.** untar la mano a alguien **II.** tr. escamotear ♦ **to p. off** encajar, clavar.

palm² s. palma, palmera; *(emblem)* palma.

palm·is·try (pä'mĭ-strē) s. quiromancia.

pal·pa·ble (pǎl'pə-bəl) adj. palpable.

pal·pate (pǎl'pāt') tr. palpar.

pal·pi·tate (pǎl'pĭ-tāt') intr. palpitar.

pal·pi·ta·tion ('-tā'shən) s. palpitación f.

pal·sied (pôl'zēd) adj. MED. paralítico; *(trembling)* temblante.

pal·sy (:zē) s. parálisis f, perlesía.

pal·try (pôl'trē) adj. **-i-** *(petty)* miserable; *(trivial)* insignificante; *(worthless)* despreciable.

pam·per (pǎm'pər) tr. mimar, consentir.

pam·phlet (pǎm'flĭt) s. folleto.

pan¹ (pǎn) **I.** s. cacerola; *(frying pan)* sartén f; *(on a scale)* platillo **II.** tr. **-nn-** MIN. lavar en una batea; *(to criticize)* poner por los suelos —intr. ♦ **to p. out** FAM. salir bien.

pan² tr. **-nn-** CINEM. girar la cámara para hacer una toma panorámica.

pan·a·ce·a (pǎn'ə-sē'ə) s. panacea.

pa·nache (pə-nǎsh') s. *(plume)* penacho; *(dash)* brío, garbo.

Pan·a·ma hat (pǎn'ə-mä) s. jipijapa m.

Pan-A·mer·i·can (pǎn'ə-mĕr'ĭ-kən) adj. panamericano.

pan·cake (pǎn'kāk') s. panqueque m.

pan·cre·as (pǎng'krē-əs) s. páncreas m.

pan·da (pǎn'də) s. panda m.

pan·dem·ic (pǎn-dĕm'ĭk) adj. pandémico.

pan·de·mo·ni·um (pǎn'də-mō'nē-əm) s. pandemónium m.

pan·der (pǎn'dər) **I.** s. alcahuete m, proxeneta mf **II.** intr. alcahuetear ♦ **to p.** to satisfacer.

pane (pān) s. hoja de vidrio; *(glass)* vidrio.

pan·el (pǎn'əl) **I.** s. panel m; *(of a wall)* entrepaño; *(of a dress)* tabla, paño; *(jury)* jurado; *(group)* grupo **II.** tr. *(a door, wall)* poner paneles en; *(a jury)* elegir.

pan·el·ing (:ə-lĭng) s. revestimiento de madera.

pan·el·ist (:lĭst) s. miembro de un grupo de discusión.

pang (pǎng) s. *(of pain)* punzada, dolor agudo; *(of conscience)* remordimiento.

pan·han·dle¹ (pǎn'hǎn'dl) s. mango de sartén.

pan·han·dle² tr. & intr. FAM. mendigar.

pan·han·dler (:dlər) s. FAM. mendigo.

pan·ic (pǎn'ĭk) **I.** s. pánico; JER. persona chis-

tosa **II.** tr. & intr. **-ck-** aterrar(se), asustar(se).

pan·ick·y (:ĭ-kē) adj. lleno de pánico.

pan·ic-strick·en (:ĭk-strĭk'ən) adj. lleno de pánico.

pan·o·ram·a (pǎn'ə-rǎm'ə) s. panorama m.

pan·o·ram·ic (:ĭk) adj. panorámico.

pan·sy (pǎn'zē) s. BOT. pensamiento.

pant (pǎnt) **I.** intr. jadear **II.** s. jadeo.

pan·the·on (pǎn'thē-ŏn') s. panteón m.

pan·ther (pǎn'thər) s. pantera.

pant·ies (pǎn'tēz) s.pl. bragas, bombachas.

pan·ting (pǎn'tĭng) **I.** s. jadeo **II.** adj. jadeante.

pan·to·mime (pǎn'tə-mīm') **I.** s. pantomima; *(actor)* mimo **II.** tr. representar por gestos —intr. expresarse por medio de gestos.

pan·try (pǎn'trē) s. despensa.

pants (pǎnts) s.pl. pantalones m; *(underpants)* calzoncillos m ♦ **to be caught with one's p. down** FAM. ser sorprendido en una posición embarazosa.

pant·y·hose (pǎn'tē-hōz') s. media pantalón.

pap (pǎp) s. *(food)* papilla; *(something insubstantial)* tonterías.

pa·pa (pä'pə, pə-pä') s. papá m.

pa·pa·cy (pä'pə-sē) s. papado.

pa·pal (pä'pəl) adj. papal.

pa·pa·ya (pə-pī'ə) s. papaya; *(tree)* papayo.

pa·per (pä'pər) **I.** s. papel m; *(document)* documento; *(essay)* ensayo; *(composition)* trabajo escrito; *(in a symposium)* ponencia; *(newspaper)* periódico ♦ **blotting p.** papel secante • **brown p.** papel de empaquetar • **drawing p.** papel de dibujo • **on p.** *(in writing)* por escrito; *(in theory)* sobre el papel • **p. clip** sujetapapeles, presilla • **tissue p.** papel de seda • **tracing p.** papel de calcar • **wax(ed) p.** papel encerado • **wrapping p.** papel de envolver ♦ pl. papeles; *(ship's papers)* patente de navegación **II.** tr. empapelar **III.** adj. de papel; *(theoretical)* teórico, por realizar ♦ **p. cup** vaso de cartón.

pa·per·back (:bǎk') s. libro de bolsillo.

pa·per·board (:bôrd') s. cartón m.

pa·per·weight (:wāt') s. pisapapeles m.

pap·er·work (:wûrk') s. papeleo.

pa·pier-mâ·ché (pǎp'yā-mä-shā') s. cartón m piedra, papel m maché.

pa·pist (pä'pĭst) s. papista mf.

pap·py (pǎp'ē) s. papá m, papi m.

pa·pri·ka (pə-prē'kə) s. paprika, pimentón m.

pa·py·rus (pə-pī'rəs) s. [pl. **es** o **-ri**] papiro.

par (pär) **I.** s. *(average)* promedio; *(equivalence)* igualdad f, paridad f; *(in golf)* par m; *(face value)* valor m nominal; *(parity)* par, paridad ♦ **to be on a p.** with estar en un pie de igualdad con **II.** adj. normal, regular; *(nominal)* nominal; *(at parity)* al o a la par.

par·a·ble (pǎr'ə-bəl) s. parábola.

pa·rab·o·la (pə-rǎb'ə-lə) s. parábola.

par·a·bol·ic (pǎr'ə-bŏl'ĭk) adj. parabólico.

par·a·chute (pǎr'ə-shōōt') **I.** s. paracaídas m **II.** tr. lanzar en paracaídas —intr. saltar en paracaídas.

par·a·chut·ist (:shōō'tĭst) s. paracaidista mf.

pa·rade (pə-rād') **I.** s. desfile m; *(ostentatious display)* ostentación f, alarde m; MIL. desfile de tropas **II.** tr. *(to march)* hacer desfilar; *(to flaunt)* hacer alarde de —intr. desfilar; MIL. formar en parada ♦ **to p. around** FAM. pasearse.

par·a·digm (pǎr'ə-dĭm') s. paradigma m.

par·a·dise (pǎr'ə-dīs') s. *(heaven)* cielo, gloria; *(delight)* paraíso.

par·a·dox (pǎr'ə-dŏks') s. paradoja.

par·a·dox·i·cal ('-dŏk'sĭ-kəl) adj. paradójico.
par·af·fin (păr'ə-fĭn) s. parafina; G.B. *(fuel)* petróleo, queroseno.
par·a·gon (păr'ə-gŏn') s. dechado, modelo.
par·a·graph (păr'ə-grăf') s. párrafo.
par·a·keet (păr'ə-kēt') s. perico, periquito.
par·al·lel (păr'ə-lĕl') I. adj. paralelo; *(corresponding)* correspondiente II. s. GEOM. paralela; *(match)* igual *m; (comparison)* paralelo, analogía; GEOG. paralelo III. tr. extenderse en línea paralela a; *(to match)* ser igual a; *(to compare with)* ser análogo a.
par·al·lel·ism (:ĭz'əm) s. paralelismo.
par·al·lel·o·gram ('-'ə-grăm') s. paralelogramo.
pa·ral·y·sis (pə-răl'ĭ-sĭs) s. [pl. **-ses**] parálisis *f; (stoppage)* paralización *f*, estancamiento.
par·a·lyt·ic (păr'ə-lĭt'ĭk) adj. & s. paralítico.
par·a·lyze (păr'ə-līz') tr. paralizar.
par·a·med·ic (păr'ə-mĕd'ĭk) s. integrante *mf* de la profesión paramédica.
pa·ram·e·ter (pə-răm'ĭ-tər) s. parámetro; FIG. límite *m.*
par·a·mil·i·tar·y (păr'ə-mĭl'ĭ-tĕr'ē) adj. paramilitar.
par·a·mount (păr'ə-mount') adj. principal.
par·a·mour (păr'ə-mŏor') s. amante *mf.*
par·a·noi·a (păr'ə-noi'ə) s. paranoia.
par·a·noi·ac (:ăk') s. & adj. paranoico.
par·a·noid (păr'ə-noid') adj. & s. paranoico.
par·a·pet (păr'ə-pĭt) s. baranda, antepecho; MIL. parapeto.
par·a·pher·na·lia (păr'ə-fər-nāl'yə) s.pl. *(belongings)* avíos; *(equipment)* conjunto de aparatos, accesorios.
par·a·phrase (păr'ə-frāz') I. s. paráfrasis *f* II. tr. & intr. parafrasear.
par·a·ple·gi·a (păr'ə-plē'jē-ə) s. paraplejía.
par·a·ple·gic (:jĭk) adj. & s. parapléjico.
par·a·pro·fes·sion·al (păr'ə-prə-fĕsh'ə-nəl) s. ayudante *mf* auxiliar de un profesional.
par·a·site (păr'ə-sīt') s. parásito.
par·a·sit·ic ('-sĭt'ĭk) adj. parasítico.
par·a·sol (păr'ə-sôl') s. parasol *m*, sombrilla.
par·a·troop·er (păr'ə-trŏo'pər) s. soldado paracaidista.
par·a·troops (:trŏops') s.pl. tropas paracaidistas.
par·boil (păr'boil') tr. sancochar.
par·cel (păr'səl) I. s. paquete *m*, fardo; *(of land)* parcela; *(of things)* partida, lote *m* ♦ **p. post** servicio de encomienda postal II. tr. empaquetar ♦ **to p. out** repartir en lotes.
parch (pärch) tr. resecar; *(to roast)* tostar —intr. resecarse.
parch·ment (pärch'mənt) s. pergamino.
par·don (pär'dn) I. tr. perdonar; *(an offense)* disculpar; *(to excuse)* excusar ♦ **p. me** perdóneme II. s. perdón *m; (exemption)* indulto ♦ **I beg your p.?** ¿cómo?, ¿cómo dijo?
par·don·a·ble (:ə-bəl) adj. perdonable.
pare (pâr) tr. mondar, pelar; *(to clip)* recortar ♦ **to p. down** disminuir, reducir.
par·e·gor·ic (păr'ə-gôr'ĭk) s. elixir paregórico.
par·ent (pâr'ənt) s. *(father)* padre *m; (mother)* madre *f; (forefather)* antepasado; *(cause)* causa, origen *m* ♦ **p. company** casa matriz ♦ **pl.** padres.
par·ent·age (:ĭj) s. linaje *m.*
pa·ren·tal (pə-rĕn'tl) adj. de los padres.
pa·ren·the·sis (pə-rĕn'thĭ-sĭs) s. [pl. **-ses**] paréntesis *m.*

par·en·thet·ic/i·cal (păr'ən-thĕt'ĭk) adj. entre paréntesis.
par·ent·hood (pâr'ənt-hŏod') s. *(father)* paternidad *f; (mother)* maternidad *f.*
pa·ri·ah (pə-rī'ə) s. paria *mf.*
pa·ri·e·tal (pə-rī'ĭ-tl) adj. & s. parietal *m* ♦ s.pl. reglas de conducta en residencias universitarias.
par·ing (pâr'ĭng) s. *(skin)* cáscara; *(peeling)* peladura, mondadura; *(trimming)* recorte *m* ♦ **p. knife** cuchillo para mondar.
par·ish (păr'ĭsh) s. parroquia.
pa·rish·ion·er (pə-rĭsh'ə-nər) s. feligrés *m.*
par·i·ty (păr'ĭ-tē) s. paridad *f.*
park (pärk) I. s. parque *m; (stadium)* estadio; *(preserve)* coto ♦ **car p.** G.B. aparcamiento II. tr. *(a vehicle)* estacionar; FAM. *(to place)* plantar —intr. estacionarse, parquearse.
park·ing (pär'kĭng) s. aparcamiento, estacionamiento ♦ **p. lot** aparcamiento, playa de estacionamiento ♦ **p. meter** parquímetro ♦ **p. place** o **space** plaza de estacionamiento.
park·way (pärk'wā') s. avenida, bulevar *m.*
par·lance (pär'ləns) s. lenguaje *m*, habla *m* ♦ **in common p.** en lenguaje corriente.
par·lay (pär'lā') I. tr. apostar en un *paroli* II. s. *paroli m.*
par·ley (pär'lē) I. s. parlamento, negociaciones *f* II. intr. parlamentar.
par·lia·ment (pär'lə-mənt) s. parlamento.
par·lia·men·tar·i·an ('-mĕn-târ'ē-ən) s. parlamentario.
par·lia·men·ta·ry ('-'tə-rē) adj. parlamentario.
par·lor (pär'lər) s. sala de recibo; *(for business)* salón *m* ♦ **funeral p.** funeraria ♦ **ice-cream p.** heladería.
pa·ro·chi·al (pə-rō'kē-əl) adj. parroquial; *(provincial)* provincial.
par·o·dy (păr'ə-dē) I. s. parodia II. tr. parodiar.
pa·role (pə-rōl') I. s. libertad *f* bajo palabra; *(word of honor)* palabra de honor II. tr. poner en libertad bajo palabra.
pa·rol·ee (pə-rō'lē') s. convicto en libertad condicional.
par·ox·ysm (păr'ək-sĭz'əm) s. paroxismo.
par·quet (pär-kā') I. s. parqué *m*, entarimado II. tr. poner parqué, entarimar.
par·ri·cide (păr'ĭ-sīd') s. *(person)* parricida *mf; (act)* parricidio.
par·rot (păr'ət) I. s. papagayo, loro; *(person)* cotorra, loro II. tr. repetir como un loro.
par·ry (păr'ē) I. tr. *(in fencing)* parar, esquivar; *(to evade)* evadir, eludir II. s. *(in fencing)* parada, quite *m; (evasion)* evasión *f.*
par·si·mo·ni·ous (păr'sə-mō'nē-əs) adj. parsimonioso.
par·si·mo·ny ('-'nē) s. parsimonia.
pars·ley (pär'slē) s. perejil *m.*
par·son (pär'sən) s. pastor *m* protestante.
par·son·age (:sə-nĭj) s. rectoría.
part (pärt) I. s. parte *f; (of a machine)* pieza; *(role)* papel *m; (of the hair)* raya del pelo ♦ **for the most p.** generalmente, por lo general ♦ **p. and parcel** parte integrante ♦ **the best p.** lo mejor ♦ **the greater p.** la mayor parte ♦ **to be p. of** formar parte de ♦ **to do one's p.** hacer lo que le corresponde a uno ♦ **to have no p. in** no tener nada que ver con ♦ **to look the p.** parecerlo, venirle bien el papel a uno ♦ **pl.** ♦ **in these p.** en estas regiones ♦ **private p.** partes pudendas II. tr. *(to divide)* dividir; *(to break)* partir, romper; *(to come between)* apartar ♦ **to**

p. company with romper relaciones con ◆ **to p. with** *(to get rid of)* deshacerse de; *(to spend)* soltar, gastar —intr. separarse, apartarse; *(to leave)* irse **III.** adv. en parte, parcialmente **IV.** adj. parcial.

par·take (pär-tāk′) intr. **-took, -taken** participar, tomar parte —tr. ◆ **to p. in** participar de, tomar parte en ◆ **to p. of** compartir.

par·tial (pär′shəl) adj. parcial ◆ **p. to** partidario de, aficionado a.

par·ti·al·i·ty (′shē-ăl′ĭ-tē) s. parcialidad *f.*

par·tic·i·pant (pär-tĭs′ə-pənt) s. & adj. participante *mf*, partícipe *mf.*

par·tic·i·pate (:pāt′) intr. participar.

par·tic·i·pa·tion (-′-pā′shən) s. participación *f.*

par·tic·i·pa·to·ry (-′-pə-tôr′ē) adj. partícipe.

par·ti·ci·ple (pär′tĭ-sĭp′əl) s. participio.

par·ti·cle (pär′tĭ-kəl) s. partícula.

par·tic·u·lar (pər-tĭk′yə-lər) **I.** adj. particular; *(fussy)* exigente, minucioso ◆ **in p.** especialmente, en particular **II.** s. particularidad *f*, detalle *m* ◆ pl. pormenores.

par·tic·u·lar·i·ty (-′-lär′ĭ-tē) s. particularidad *f.*

par·tic·u·lar·ly (-′-lər-lē) adv. *(especially)* especialmente; *(specifically)* específicamente, en particular; *(individually)* particularmente.

part·ing (pär′tĭng) **I.** s. separación *f*; *(departure)* partida, despedida ◆ **p. of the ways** punto de separación **II.** adj. de partida, de despedida.

par·ti·san (pär′tĭ-zən) **I.** s. partidario, prosélito **II.** adj. *(of a party)* partidista; *(of a supporter)* partidario; *(biased)* parcial.

par·tite (pär′tīt′) adj. partido, dividido.

par·ti·tion (pär-tĭsh′ən) **I.** s. partición *f*; *(wall)* tabique *m*, mampara **II.** tr. dividir, repartir ◆ **to p. off** separar con un tabique.

part·ner (pärt′nər) s. socio; *(spouse)* cónyuge *mf*; *(in a dance, games)* pareja; *(in crime)* cómplice *mf.*

part·ner·ship (:shĭp′) s. sociedad *f.*

par·took (pär-tŏŏk′) cf. **partake.**

par·tridge (pär′trĭj) s. [pl. inv. o **s**] perdiz *f.*

part-time (pärt′tīm′) adj. & adv. por horas.

par·tu·ri·tion (pär′tyŏŏ-rĭsh′ən) s. parto.

part·way (pärt′wā′) adv. FAM. hasta cierto punto, en parte.

par·ty (pär′tē) **I.** s. *(gathering)* fiesta; POL. partido; *(group)* grupo; *(team)* equipo; DER. parte *f* ◆ **p. line** *(telephone)* línea colectiva; POL. línea política ◆ **to be a p. to** *(accessory)* ser cómplice en; *(participant)* participar en, tener algo que ver con **II.** intr. FAM. parrandear.

par·ve·nu (pär′və-nŏŏ′) s. advenedizo.

pass (pǎs) **I.** intr. pasar; *(to cross)* cruzarse; *(to be transferred)* ser traspasado; *(to happen)* acontecer; *(in examination, course)* aprobar ◆ **in passing** de paso ◆ **to be passing through** estar de paso ◆ **to come to p.** suceder ◆ **to p. away** *o* **on** fallecer ◆ **to p. out** desmayarse —tr. pasar; *(to go past)* pasar por delante de; *(to come across)* cruzarse con; *(to exceed)* sobrepasar, superar; *(an examination, student)* aprobar; *(to adopt)* adoptar; *(to approve)* aprobar; DER. dictar; FISIOL. evacuar ◆ **to p. off** *(to palm off)* pasar, colar; *(to present)* hacer pasar ◆ **to p. oneself off as** hacerse pasar por ◆ **to p. on** pasar, transmitir ◆ **to p. out** repartir, distribuir ◆ **to p. over** pasar por alto ◆ **to p. up** *(opportunity)* dejar pasar, desperdiciar; *(offer)* rechazar **II.** s. paso; *(written permit)* pase *m*; *(authorization)* permiso, licencia; *(safe-conduct)*

salvoconducto; *(free ticket)* pase (gratis); *(in a table game)* pase; DEP., TAUR. pase ◆ **to make a p. at** hacer insinuaciones amorosas a.

pass·a·ble (′ə-bəl) adj. *(road)* transitable; *(work)* aceptable; *(satisfactory)* pasable.

pas·sage (pǎs′ĭj) s. paso; POL. *(of a bill)* aprobación *f*, promulgación *f*; *(journey)* pasaje *m*, travesía; *(ticket)* pasaje; *(path)* pasaje, pasadizo; *(corridor)* corredor *m*, pasillo; LIT., MÚS. pasaje.

pas·sage·way (:wā′) s. *(alley)* callejón *m*; *(corridor)* corredor *m.*

pass·book (pǎs′bŏŏk′) s. *(bankbook)* libreta de banco; COM. libro de cuenta y razón.

pas·sé (pǎ-sā′) adj. *(out-of-date)* anticuado, pasado de moda; *(aged)* en decadencia.

pas·sel (pǎs′əl) s. FAM. montón *m.*

pas·sen·ger (pǎs′ən-jər) s. pasajero, viajero.

pass·er·by (′ər-bī′) s. [pl. **passers-**] transeúnte *mf.*

pass·ing (pǎs′ĭng) **I.** adj. pasante, que pasa; *(transitory)* pasajero, transitorio; *(casual)* casual, de pasada ◆ **p. grade** EDUC. calificación aprobatoria **II.** s. pasada, transcurso; *(death)* fallecimiento.

pas·sion (pǎsh′ən) s. pasión *f.*

pas·sion·ate (:ə-nĭt) adj. apasionado; *(ardent)* ardiente, fervoroso.

pas·sive (pǎs′ĭv) **I.** adj. pasivo; *(inert)* inerte, inactivo; COM. que no devenga intereses **II.** s. GRAM. voz pasiva.

pas·siv·i·ty (pǎ-sĭv′ĭ-tē) s. pasividad *f.*

pass·key (pǎs′kē′) s. llave maestra.

Pass·o·ver (pǎs′ō′vər) s. Pascua.

pass·port (:pôrt′) s. pasaporte *m.*

pass·word (:wûrd′) s. contraseña, santo y seña.

past (pǎst) **I.** adj. pasado; *(former)* anterior, último; GRAM. pretérito, pasado ◆ **p. master** experto, perito **II.** s. pasado; *(background)* historia; GRAM. pretérito, pasado **III.** adv. al pasar **IV.** prep. *(by)* por delante de; *(on the far side of)* más allá de; *(later than)* más de; *(beyond)* ya no; *(plus)* y <*it's ten p. two* son las dos y diez> ◆ **I wouldn't put it p. him** no me extrañaría de su parte.

pas·ta (pä′stə) s. masa de harina de trigo; *(dish)* plato de pastas.

paste[1] (pāst) s. engrudo; *(dough)* pasta, masa; *(clay)* barro; JOY. *(glass)* estrás *m*; *(artificial gem)* imitación *f* **II.** tr. *(to stick)* pegar; *(to cover)* engrudar.

paste[2] tr. JER. *(to punch)* pegar.

paste·board (′bôrd′) s. cartón *m.*

pas·tel (pǎ-stĕl′) s. pastel *m.*

paste-up (pāst′ŭp′) s. montaje *m*, collage *m*; IMPR. maqueta.

pas·teur·ize (pǎs′chə-rīz′) tr. paste(u)rizar.

pas·time (pǎs′tīm′) s. pasatiempo.

pas·tor (pǎs′tər) s. pastor *m.*

pas·tor·al (:əl) adj. & s. pastoral *f.*

pas·try (pā′strē) s. *(paste)* pasta; *(cakes)* pasteles *m.*

pas·tur·age (pǎs′chər-ĭj) s. pastura.

pas·ture (pǎs′chər) **I.** s. pastura ◆ **to put out to p.** *(to graze)* apacentar, pastorear; *(to retire)* jubilar, retirar **II.** tr. pastorear, apacentar —intr. pastar, pacer.

past·y[1] (pā′stē) adj. **-i-** *(like paste)* pastoso; *(pale)* pálido.

past·y[2] (pǎs′tē) s. pastel *m*, empanada.

pat (pǎt) **I.** tr. **-tt-** *(to tap)* dar palmaditas *o* golpecitos a; *(to stroke)* acariciar; *(to mold)* moldear a palmaditas ♦ **to p. (oneself) on the back** congratular(se) **II.** s. *(with hand)* palmadita; *(with object)* golpecito; *(sound)* ruido ligero; *(small mass)* porción *f* **III.** adj. *(exactly right)* preciso; *(contrived)* preparado, pronto **IV.** adv. ♦ **to have something down p.** FAM. saberse algo al dedillo • **to stand p.** mantenerse firme.

patch (păch) **I.** s. parche *m*; *(in patchwork)* retazo; *(field)* siembra, bancal *m* **II.** tr. poner un parche a; *(to repair poorly)* remendar *o* arreglar mal ♦ **to p. up a quarrel** hacer las paces.

patch·work (′wûrk′) s. *(needlework)* labor hecha con retazos; *(jumble)* mezcolanza.

patch·y (:ē) adj. -i- de remiendos, remendado; *(uneven)* desigual, irregular.

pate (pāt) s. FAM. cabeza, coronilla.

pâ·té (pä-tā′) s. pasta de carne; *(pastry)* pastel *m*, empanada.

pa·ten·cy (păt′n-sē, pāt′n-) s. evidencia.

pat·ent (păt′nt) **I.** s. patente *f* **II.** adj. *(obvious)* patente, evidente; *(of patents)* de patentes ♦ **p. leather** charol **III.** tr. patentar.

pat·ent·ly (:lē) adv. patentemente.

pa·ter·nal (pə-tûr′nəl) adj. *(fatherly)* paternal; *(on the father's side)* paterno.

pa·ter·nal·is·tic (-′nə-lĭs′tĭk) adj. paternalista.

pa·ter·ni·ty (-′nĭ-tē) s. paternidad *f*.

path (păth) s. [pl. **s**] *(trail)* sendero, senda; *(track)* camino, pista; *(course)* curso; FIG. camino, senda ♦ **to cross someone's p.** cruzarse con alguien.

pa·thet·ic (pə-thĕt′ĭk) adj. patético.

path·find·er (păth′fĭn′dər) s. explorador *m*.

path·o·gen(e) (păth′ə-jən) s. agente *o* microbio patógeno.

path·o·log·ic/i·cal (păth′ə-lŏj′ĭk) adj. patológico.

pa·thol·o·gist (pă-thŏl′ə-jĭst) s. patólogo.

pa·thol·o·gy (:jē) s. patología.

pa·thos (pā′thŏs′) s. pathos *m*, patetismo.

path·way (păth′wā′) s. *(trail)* sendero, senda; *(track)* camino, pista.

pa·tience (pā′shəns) s. paciencia; G.B. solitario.

pa·tient (pā′shənt) adj. & s. paciente *mf*.

pat·i·na (păt′n-ə, pə-tē′nə) s. pátina.

pat·i·o (păt′ē-ō′, pä′tē-ō′) s. patio, terraza.

pat·ois (păt′wä′) s.inv. dialecto regional.

pa·tri·arch (pā′trē-ärk′) s. patriarca *m*.

pa·tri·ar·chal (′-är′kəl) adj. patriarcal.

pa·tri·ar·chy (′-′kē) s. patriarcado.

pa·tri·cian (pə-trĭsh′ən) s. patricio.

pat·ri·cide (păt′rĭ-sīd′) s. *(act)* parricidio; *(person)* parricida *mf*.

pat·ri·mo·ny (:mō′nē) s. patrimonio.

pa·tri·ot (pā′trē-ət) s. patriota *mf*.

pa·tri·ot·ic (′-ŏt′ĭk) adj. patriótico.

pa·tri·ot·ism (′-ə-tĭz′əm) s. patriotismo.

pa·trol (pə-trōl′) **I.** s. *(action)* ronda, patrulla; *(group)* patrulla **II.** tr. & intr. -ll- rondar.

pa·trol·man (:mən) s. [pl. **-men**] policía *mf*, guardia *mf*.

pa·tron (pā′trən) s. benefactor *m*, patrocinador *m*; *(customer)* cliente *m*; *(protector)* protector *m*, defensor *m* ♦ **p. saint** santo patrón.

pa·tron·age (pā′trə-nĭj, păt′rə-) s. patrocinio; *(clientele)* clientela; POL. influencia política.

pa·tron·ize (:nīz′) tr. patrocinar, auspiciar; *(a business)* ser cliente de, frecuentar; *(to condescend to)* tratar con condescendencia.

pat·sy (păt′sē) s. JER. pelele *mf*, simplón *m*.

pat·ter¹ (păt′ər) **I.** intr. golpetear, tamborilear **II.** s. golpeteo, tamborileo.

pat·ter² **I.** intr. charlar, parlotear —tr. farfullar, balbucir **II.** s. parloteo, palique *m*.

pat·tern (păt′ərn) **I.** s. modelo, ejemplo; *(for sewing)* patrón *m*, molde *m*; *(design)* diseño, dibujo; *(on fabrics)* estampado; *(actions)* patrón, norma; *(regularity)* regularidad *f* **II.** tr. adornar con diseños; *(fabrics)* estampar ♦ **to p. after** *o* **on** imitar el ejemplo de.

pat·ty (păt′ē) s. croqueta de carne picada *o* pescado; *(candy)* caramelo.

pau·ci·ty (pô′sĭ-tē) s. *(small number)* número pequeño; *(scarcity)* escasez *f*.

paunch (pônch) s. barriga, vientre *m*.

paunch·y (pôn′chē) adj. -i- panzón, barrigón.

pau·per (pô′pər) s. pobre *mf*, indigente *mf*; *(beggar)* mendigo.

pause (pôz) **I.** intr. *(mentally)* hacer una pausa; *(physically)* pararse, detenerse; *(to hesitate)* vacilar **II.** s. pausa; *(rest)* descanso ♦ **to give p.** hacer preocupar.

pave (pāv) tr. *(with blocks)* adoquinar; *(with asphalt, concrete)* pavimentar; *(with bricks)* enladrillar; *(with cobblestones)* empedrar ♦ **to p. the way for** preparar el camino para.

pave·ment (′mənt) s. pavimento; G.B. acera.

pa·vil·ion (pə-vĭl′yən) s. pabellón *m*.

pav·ing (pā′vĭng) s. pavimentación *f*; *(material)* pavimento.

paw (pô) **I.** s. pata; FAM. *(hand)* manaza, manota **II.** tr. *(to strike)* dar zarpazos a; *(to handle)* manosear, toquetear ♦ **to p. at** manosear.

pawn¹ (pôn) **I.** s. *(object)* prenda; *(act)* empeño, pignoración *f*; *(hostage)* rehén *mf* **II.** tr. empeñar, pignorar; *(to risk)* arriesgar.

pawn² s. peón *m*; FIG. pelele *m*, juguete *m*.

pawn·bro·ker (′brō′kər) s. prestamista *mf*.

pawn·shop (:shŏp′) s. casa de empeños.

pay (pā) **I.** tr. **paid** pagar; *(to yield)* dar, producir; *(to profit)* compensar; *(visit, compliment)* hacer; *(respects)* presentar; *(attention)* prestar ♦ **to p. back** *(money)* devolver, reembolsar; *(someone)* pagar; *(to take revenge on)* vengarse de • **to p. off** *(debts)* saldar, liquidar; *(creditor)* reembolsar; *(mortgage)* redimir; *(employee)* pagar y despedir; FAM. *(to bribe)* sobornar • **to p. out** *(money)* desembolsar; *(rope, cable)* arriar, soltar • **to p. over** pagar • **to p. the piper** pagar las consecuencias • **to p. up** pagar —intr. pagar; *(debt)* saldar una deuda; *(to be profitable)* ser rentable; *(to be worthwhile)* compensar ♦ **it pays** vale la pena • **to p. for it** pagarlas • **to p. off** merecer la pena • **to p. up** pagar una deuda **II.** s. paga, pago; *(of employee)* paga, sueldo; *(of day worker)* jornal *m*; *(of workman)* salario ♦ **to be in the p. of** estar al servicio de **III.** adj. de pago ♦ **p. telephone** teléfono público.

pay·a·ble (pā′ə-bəl) adj. pagadero ♦ **accounts p.** cuentas a pagar • **p. to** a favor de.

pay·check (pā′chĕk′) s. cheque *m* de pago de sueldo.

pay·day (pā′dā′) s. día *m* de pago.

pay·ee (pā-ē′) s. *(of a check)* beneficiario; *(of a draft)* tenedor *m* de una letra.

pay·er (pā′ər) s. pagador *m*.

pay·ing (pā′ĭng) **I.** adj. que paga; *(profitable)* provechoso, rentable **II.** s. pago.

pay·load (pā′lōd′) s. carga útil *o* de pago; MIL. carga explosiva.

pay·mas·ter (pā'măs'tər) s. pagador *m*, cajero.
pay·ment (pā'mənt) s. pago; *(reward)* recompensa, pago ♦ **down p.** desembolso inicial.
pay·off (pā'ôf') s. pago; FAM. *(end result)* resultado final; *(bribe)* soborno, coima.
pay·o·la (pā-ō'lə) s. JER. soborno, coima.
pay·roll (pā'rōl') s. nómina *o* planilla de pagos; *(total)* suma de dinero para pago de sueldos.
pea (pē) s. guisante *m*, arveja ♦ **like two peas in a pod** parecidos como dos gotas de agua.
peace (pēs) s. paz *f*; *(harmony)* armonía; *(law and order)* orden público; *(serenity)* paz, tranquilidad *f* ♦ **at p.** *(serene)* en calma, tranquilo; *(free from strife)* en paz • **to hold** *o* **to keep one's p.** guardar silencio • **to keep the p.** mantener el orden • **to make p.** hacer las paces.
peace·a·ble (pēs'ə-bəl) adj. pacífico.
peace·ful (pēs'fəl) adj. pacífico; *(tranquil)* apacible, tranquilo.
peace-lov·ing (:lŭv'ĭng) adj. pacífico.
peace·mak·er (:mā'kər) s. pacificador *m*; *(mediator)* árbitro.
peach (pēch) s. *(tree)* melocotonero, duraznero; *(fruit)* melocotón *m*, durazno; *(color)* color melocotón *m*; FIG. monada.
pea·cock (pē'kŏk') s. pavo real.
peak (pēk) I. s. punta; *(of a mountain)* cima, cumbre *f*; *(mountain)* pico; *(of a cap)* visera; *(climax)* punto culminante; *(maximum)* tope *m*, máximo II. tr. hacer culminar, traer al máximo —intr. formar un pico; *(to climax)* culminar, llegar al punto culminante; *(to achieve)* llegar al tope *o* al máximo III. adj. máximo.
peaked (pēkt, pē'kĭd) adj. puntiagudo.
peak·ed² (pē'kĭd) adj. demacrado, consumido.
peal (pēl) I. s. repiqueteo, repique *m* ♦ **peals of laughter** carcajadas II. intr. repiquetear, repicar —tr. hacer resonar, tañer.
pea·nut (pē'nət) I. s. cacahuate *m*, maní *m* ♦ pl. (casi) nada II. adj. de maní.
pear (pâr) s. *(tree)* peral *m*; *(fruit)* pera.
pearl (pûrl) I. s. perla, aljófar *m*; *(mother-of-pearl)* madreperla, nácar *m*; FIG. perla, joya II. adj. perlado, de perlas.
pearl·y (pûr'lē) adj. -i- *(in color)* perlino; *(with pearls)* perlado, perlificado ♦ **p. whites** FAM. los dientes.
peas·ant (pĕz'ənt) s. campesino; FIG. patán *m*.
pea·shoot·er (pē'shōō'tər) s. cerbatana.
peat (pēt) s. turba ♦ **p. moss** BOT. musgo de pantano; AGR. turba.
peb·ble (pĕb'əl) I. s. guijarro, canto rodado II. tr. pavimentar con guijas.
pe·can (pĭ-kän', -kăn') s. pacana.
pec·ca·dil·lo (pĕk'ə-dĭl'ō) s. [pl. (e)s] pecadillo, falta leve.
peck¹ (pĕk) I. tr. *(bird)* picotear; *(to pick up)* recoger con el pico; *(to kiss)* besar —intr. picotear ♦ **pecking order** FIG. jerarquía II. s. *(of a bird)* picotazo, picotada; *(kiss)* beso.
peck² s. *(measure)* celemín *m*; FAM. *(large quantity)* montón *m*, sinnúmero.
pec·tin (pĕk'tĭn) s. pectina.
pec·to·ral (pĕk'tər-əl) adj. & s. *(músculo)* pectoral.
pe·cu·liar (pĭ-kyōōl'yər) adj. peculiar; *(odd)* raro, extraño; *(special)* especial, singular.
pe·cu·li·ar·i·ty (pĭ-kyōō'lē-ăr'ĭ-tē) s. peculiaridad *f*; *(eccentricity)* excentricidad *f*.
pe·cu·ni·ar·y (pĭ-kyōō'nē-ĕr'ē) adj. pecuniario.
ped·a·gog·ic/i·cal (pĕd'ə-gŏj'ĭk) adj. pedagógico.

ped·a·gogue ('-gŏg') s. pedagogo.
ped·a·go·gy (:gō'jē, :gŏj'ē) s. pedagogía.
ped·al (pĕd'l) I. s. pedal *m* II. adj. del pie, del pedal III. intr. pedalear.
ped·ant (pĕd'nt) s. pedante *mf*.
pe·dan·tic (pə-dăn'tĭk) adj. pedante.
ped·ant·ry (pĕd'n-trē) s. pedantería.
ped·dle (pĕd'l) tr. *(to sell)* ir vendiendo de puerta en puerta; *(to disseminate)* difundir, diseminar —intr. vender de puerta en puerta.
ped·dler (:lər) s. vendedor *m* ambulante.
ped·er·ast (pĕd'ə-răst') s. pederasta *m*.
ped·es·tal (pĕd'ĭ-stəl) s. pedestal *m*.
pe·des·tri·an (pə-dĕs'trē-ən) I. s. peatón *m*, caminante *mf* II. adj. pedestre.
pe·di·at·ric (pē'dē-ăt'rĭk) adj. pediátrico ♦ **pediatrics** s.sg. pediatría.
pe·di·a·tri·cian (:ə-trĭsh'ən) s. pediatra *mf*.
ped·i·cure (pĕd'ĭ-kyŏŏr') s. pedicura.
ped·i·gree (pĕd'ĭ-grē') s. *(lineage)* linaje *m*, ascendencia; *(animal's)* pedigrí *m*.
pe·dom·e·ter (pĭ-dŏm'ĭ-tər) s. pedómetro.
peek (pēk) I. intr. *(to glance)* echar una ojeada; *(to look furtively)* atisbar, mirar a hurtadillas II. s. atisbo, ojeada.
peek·a·boo (pē'kə-bōō') s. escondite *m*, cucú *m*.
peel (pēl) I. s. cáscara, mondadura II. tr. *(to pare)* pelar, mondar; *(to unpaste)* despegar; *(to strip away)* quitar —intr. pelarse; *(to shed skin)* despellejarse; *(to lose bark)* descortezarse; *(to become unpasted)* despegarse.
peel·er (pē'lər) s. pelador *m*.
peel·ing (pē'lĭng) s. peladura, mondadura.
peep¹ (pēp) I. intr. pipiar, piar II. s. pío, piada ♦ **I don't want to hear a p. out of you!** FAM. ¡no digas ni pío!
peep² I. intr. *(to glance)* echar una ojeada; *(to peer from behind)* mirar a hurtadillas II. s. *(glance)* ojeada; *(furtive look)* atisbo.
peep·er¹ (pē'pər) s. *(frog)* rubeta, rana; *(bird)* pollito.
peep·er² s. *(person)* mirón *m*; JER. *(eye)* ojo.
peep·hole (pēp'hōl') s. mirilla.
peer¹ intr. *(to look)* mirar curiosamente, mirar con atención; *(to peep out)* aparecer, asomar.
peer² s. *(equal)* semejante *mf*; *(nobleman)* par *m*; G.B. noble *m* inglés.
peer·age ('ĭj) s. rango de par.
peer·less (:lĭs) adj. sin par, sin igual.
peeve (pēv) I. tr. irritar II. s. *(vexation)* queja; *(bad mood)* malhumor *m*, enojo ♦ **pet p.** motivo de enojo.
pee·vish (pē'vĭsh) adj. irritable, picajoso; *(ill-tempered)* malhumorado.
peg (pĕg) I. s. *(plug, spike)* clavija; *(wooden stake)* estaca; *(clothes hook)* percha, gancho; *(degree)* grado, escalón *m*; *(pretext)* pretexto; MÚS. clavija ♦ **to take down a p.** bajar los humos II. tr. **-gg-** *(to fasten)* sujetar con una clavija; *(to plug)* tapar con una clavija; *(to mark)* marcar con clavijas ♦ **to have someone pegged** FAM. conocer el juego de alguien —intr. ♦ **to p. away at** machacar, afanarse por.
peg·board ('bôrd') s. tabla de madera prensada perforada.
pe·jo·ra·tive (pĭ-jôr'ə-tĭv) adj. peyorativo.
pel·i·can (pĕl'ĭ-kən) s. pelicano, pelícano.
pel·let (pĕl'ĭt) s. *(small ball)* bolita, pelotilla; *(pill)* píldora; *(bullet)* bala; *(shot)* perdigón *m*.
pell-mell *o* **pell·mell** (pĕl'mĕl') adv. *(helter-skelter)* en desorden; *(headlong)* atropelladamente.

pelt¹ (pĕlt) s. *(skin)* piel *f*, pellejo.
pelt² I. tr. *(to bombard)* lanzar, arrojar; *(to strike)* apedrear —intr. golpear con fuerza repetidamente II. s. golpe *m*.
pel·vic (pĕl'vĭk) adj. pélvico, pelviano.
pel·vis (:vĭs) s. [pl. **es** *o* **-ves**] pelvis *f*.
pen¹ (pĕn) I. s. pluma; *(ball-point)* bolígrafo ♦ **p. name** seudónimo de autor • **p. pal** amigo epistolar II. tr. -**nn**- escribir, redactar.
pen² I. s. *(corral)* corral *m*; *(coop)* gallinero; *(sty)* pocilga II. tr. -**nn**- acorralar, encerrar.
pen³ s. JER. *(jail)* chirona, prisión *f*.
pe·nal (pē'nəl) adj. penal.
pe·nal·ize (pē'nə-līz', pĕn'ə-) tr. penalizar.
pen·al·ty (pĕn'əl-tē) s. pena; *(fine)* multa; *(consequences)* consecuencias; FIN. descuento; DEP. castigo, penalty *m* ♦ **on** *o* **under p. of** so pena de, bajo pena de.
pen·ance (pĕn'əns) s. penitencia.
pen·chant (pĕn'chənt) s. propensión *f*.
pen·cil (pĕn'səl) I. s. lápiz *m* ♦ **p. sharpener** sacapuntas II. tr. escribir con un lápiz; *(to sketch)* esbozar a lápiz ♦ **to p. someone in** FAM. hacer planes tentativos con alguien.
pen·dant/dent (pĕn'dənt) I. s. colgante *m*; *(earring)* pendiente *m* II. adj. pendiente, colgante.
pend·ing (pĕn'dĭng) I. adj. pendiente II. prep. *(during)* durante; *(until)* hasta.
pen·du·lar (pĕn'jə-lər) adj. pendular.
pen·du·lous (:ləs) adj. colgante, pendiente.
pen·du·lum (:ləm) s. péndulo.
pen·e·tra·bil·i·ty (pĕn'ĭ-trə-bĭl'ĭ-tē) s. penetrabilidad *f*.
pen·e·tra·ble ('--bəl) adj. penetrable.
pen·e·trant (pĕn'ĭ-trənt) adj. penetrante.
pen·e·trate (:trāt') tr. penetrar; *(to understand)* entender, descubrir; *(to affect deeply)* conmover —intr. penetrar.
pen·e·trat·ing (:trā'tĭng) adj. penetrante.
pen·e·tra·tion ('-'shən) s. penetración *f*.
pen·guin (pĕng'gwĭn) s. pingüino.
pen·i·cil·lin (pĕn'ĭ-sĭl'ĭn) s. penicilina.
pen·in·su·la (pə-nĭn'syə-lə) s. península.
pe·nis (pē'nĭs) s. [pl. **es** *o* **-nes**] pene *m*.
pen·i·tence (pĕn'ĭ-təns) s. penitencia.
pen·i·tent (:tənt) adj. & s. penitente.
pen·i·ten·tial ('-tĕn'shəl) adj. penitencial.
pen·i·ten·tia·ry (:shə-rē) s. penitenciaría.
pen·knife (pĕn'nīf') s. [pl. **-ves**] navaja, cortaplumas *m*.
pen·man·ship (pĕn'mən-shĭp') s. caligrafía.
pen·nant (pĕn'ənt) s. pendón *m*, gallardete *m*.
pen·ni·less (pĕn'ə-lĭs) adj. sin dinero.
pen·ny (pĕn'ē) s. G.B. penique *m*; *(cent)* centavo ♦ **p. pincher** FAM. tacaño, mezquino • **to cost a pretty p.** costar un ojo de la cara.
pen·ny-wise (:wīz') adj. ♦ **to be p. and pound-foolish** hacer economías de chicha y nabo.
pe·nol·o·gy (pē-nŏl'ə-jē) s. penología.
pen·sion (pĕn'shən) I. s. pensión *f*, jubilación *f* II. tr. pensionar ♦ **to p. off** jubilar.
pen·sion·er (:shə-nər) s. pensionado.
pen·sive (pĕn'sĭv) adj. pensativo.
pen·ta·gon (pĕn'tə-gŏn') s. pentágono.
Pen·te·cost (pĕn'tĭ-kôst') s. Pentecostés *m*.
pent·house (pĕnt'hous') s. ático.
pent-up (pĕnt'ŭp') adj. reprimido, contenido.
pe·nul·ti·mate (pĭ-nŭl'tə-mĭt) adj. & s. penúltimo.
pe·num·bra (pĭ-nŭm'brə) s. [pl. **s** *o* **-ae**] penumbra.

pe·nu·ri·ous (pə-nŏŏr'ē-əs) adj. *(stingy)* tacaño, avaro; *(needy)* pobre, indigente.
pen·u·ry (pĕn'yə-rē) s. penuria.
pe·on (pē'ŏn') s. peón *m*; *(servant)* criado.
pe·o·ny (pē'ə-nē) s. peonía.
peo·ple (pē'pəl) I. s.pl. gente *f*; *(nation)* pueblo; *(in definite numbers)* personas <**ten p.** diez personas>; *(family)* familia; *(ancestors)* antepasados; *(human beings)* personas, seres humanos —s.sg. [pl. **s**] pueblo ♦ **p.'s republic** república popular • **the (common) p.** el pueblo, la gente común y corriente II. tr. poblar.
pep (pĕp) FAM. I. s. ánimo, empuje *m* ♦ **p. pill** JER. píldora de anfetamina • **p. talk** exhortación II. tr. -**pp**- ♦ **to p. up** animar, vigorizar.
pep·per (pĕp'ər) I. s. *(plant)* pimentero; *(condiment)* pimienta; *(fruit)* pimiento II. tr. sazonar con pimienta; *(to pelt)* acribillar; *(to enliven)* salpicar.
pep·per·corn (:kôrn') s. grano de pimienta.
pep·per·mint (:mĭnt') s. *(plant)* hierbabuena, menta; *(candy)* pastilla de menta.
pep·per·y (pĕp'ə-rē) adj. picante.
pep·py (pĕp'ē) adj. -**i**- FAM. lleno de vida, vivaz.
pep·tic (pĕp'tĭk) adj. péptico.
per (pûr) prep. por; *(according to)* según ♦ **as p. usual** como de costumbre • **p. capita** por cabeza • **p. se** por sí mismo.
per·am·bu·la·tor (pə-răm'byə-lā'tər) s. G.B. cochecito de niño.
per·cale (pər-kāl') s. percal *m*.
per·ceive (pər-sēv') tr. percibir; *(to notice)* notar, percatarse de; *(to understand)* comprender.
per cent *o* **per·cent** (pər-sĕnt') I. adv. por ciento II. s.inv. por ciento; *(percentage)* tanto por ciento, porcentaje *m*.
per·cent·age (:sĕn'tĭj) s. porcentaje *m*; FAM. *(gain)* provecho, ventaja.
per·cen·tile (:tīl') s. percentil *m*.
per·cept (pûr'sĕpt') s. percepción *f*.
per·cep·ti·ble (pər-sĕp'tə-bəl) adj. perceptible.
per·cep·tion (:shən) s. percepción *f*.
per·cep·tive (:tĭv) adj. perceptivo.
per·cep·tu·al (:chŏŏ-əl) adj. de percepción.
perch¹ (pûrch) I. s. percha; *(high place)* posición *f*, sitio II. intr. *(to roost)* posarse; *(to balance)* balancearse en un sitio elevado —tr. situar en un sitio elevado.
perch² s. [pl. inv. *o* **es**] ICT. perca.
per·chance (pər-chăns') adv. *(perhaps)* quizás, acaso; *(by chance)* por casualidad.
per·cip·i·ent (pər-sĭp'ē-ənt) adj. perceptor.
per·co·late (pûr'kə-lāt') tr. & intr. filtrar(se).
per·co·la·tor (:lā'tər) s. cafetera de filtro.
per·cuss (pər-kŭs') tr. MED. percutir.
per·cus·sion (:kŭsh'ən) s. percusión *f*.
per·cus·sion·ist (:ə-nĭst) s. músico que toca instrumentos de percusión.
per·cus·sive (pər-kŭs'ĭv) adj. de percusión.
per di·em (pər dē'əm) I. adv. diariamente II. s. dieta III. adj. diario.
per·di·tion (pər-dĭsh'ən) s. perdición *f*.
per·emp·to·ry (pə-rĕmp'tə-rē) adj. perentorio; *(dictatorial)* dictatorial.
per·en·ni·al (pə-rĕn'ē-əl) adj. & s. (planta) perenne.
per·fect (pûr'fĭkt) I. adj. perfecto; *(ideal)* ideal II. (pər-fĕkt') tr. perfeccionar.
per·fec·tion (pər-fĕk'shən) s. perfección *f*; *(perfecting)* perfeccionamiento ♦ **to p.** a la perfección.
per·fec·tion·ism (:shə-nĭz'əm) s. perfeccio-

nismo.

per·fec·tion·ist (:nĭst) s. perfeccionista *mf.*

per·fect·ly (pûr′fĭkt-lē) adv. perfectamente; *(completely)* completamente; *(utterly)* absolutamente.

per·fid·i·ous (pər-fĭd′ē-əs) adj. pérfido.

per·fi·dy (pûr′fĭ-dē) s. perfidia.

per·fo·rate (pûr′fə-rāt′) tr. perforar, agujerear.

per·fo·rat·ed (:rā′tĭd) adj. perforado.

per·fo·ra·tion (′-rā′shən) s. perforación *f.*

per·force (pər-fôrs′) adv. por fuerza.

per·form (pər-fôrm′) tr. *(to do)* ejecutar, hacer; *(a function)* desempeñar; TEAT. *(a role)* interpretar; *(a play)* representar; MÚS. ejecutar —intr. *(to function)* funcionar, trabajar; *(to fulfill an obligation)* cumplir; TEAT. *(to act)* actuar; *(to do tricks)* hacer trucos; *(to sing)* cantar.

per·form·ance (pər-fôr′məns) s. *(doing)* ejecución *f*; *(of a function)* ejecución, desempeño; *(of a play)* representación *f*; *(of a role, musical composition)* interpretación *f*; *(in a competition)* actuación *f*; *(functioning)* funcionamiento; *(of an engine)* rendimiento; *(show)* función *f.*

per·form·er (:mər) s. *(actor)* artista *m*; *(musician)* músico; *(dancer)* bailarín *m.*

per·fume I. s. (pûr′fyōōm′, pər-fyōōm′) perfume II. tr. (pər-fyōōm′) perfumar.

per·func·to·ry (pər-fŭngk′tə-rē) adj. rutinario.

per·fuse (pər-fyōōz′) tr. *(to suffuse)* inundar, bañar; *(to diffuse)* introducir, hacer penetrar.

per·fu·sion (:fyōō′zhən) s. perfusión *f.*

per·haps (pər-hăps′) adv. quizá(s).

per·il (pĕr′əl) s. peligro.

per·il·ous (:ə-ləs) adj. peligroso, arriesgado.

pe·rim·e·ter (pə-rĭm′ĭ-tər) s. perímetro.

pe·ri·od (pîr′ē-əd) s. período, periodo; *(term)* plazo; *(age, stage)* época; *(class)* hora, clase *f*; *(playing time)* tiempo; *(menstruation)* período, regla; *(punctuation mark)* punto.

pe·ri·od·ic (′-ŏd′ĭk) adj. periódico.

pe·ri·od·i·cal (:ĭ-kəl) I. adj. periódico; *(of a journal)* de revistas II. s. publicación periódica, revista.

per·i·o·don·tal (pĕr′ē-ō-dŏn′tl) adj. periodontal.

pe·riph·er·al (pə-rĭf′ər-əl) adj. periférico.

pe·riph·er·y (:ə-rē) s. periferia.

per·i·scope (pĕr′ĭ-skōp′) s. periscopio.

per·ish (pĕr′ĭsh) intr. perecer; *(to spoil)* echarse a perder.

per·ish·a·ble (′ĭ-shə-bəl) I. adj. perecedero II. s. ♦ pl. artículos de fácil deterioro.

per·i·to·ni·tis (pĕr′ĭ-tə-nī′tĭs) s. peritonitis *f.*

per·jure (pûr′jər) tr. perjurar.

per·ju·ri·ous (pər-jŏŏr′ē-əs) adj. perjurador.

per·ju·ry (pûr′jə-rē) s. perjurio.

perk¹ (pûrk) intr. proyectarse, sobresalir ♦ to p. up animarse, reanimarse —tr. alzar, levantar ♦ to p. up *(to cheer up)* animar, reanimar; *(to spruce up)* adornar, engalanar; *(to improve)* ir mejor, ir mejorando • to p. up one's ears aguzar el oído.

perk² s. FAM. *(privilege)* privilegio que corresponde a ciertos puestos.

perk·y (pûr′kē) adj. -i- animado, vivaz.

perm (pûrm) I. s. permanente *f* II. tr. & intr. hacer(se) una permanente.

per·ma·nence (pûr′mə-nəns) s. permanencia.

per·ma·nen·cy (:nən-sē) s. permanencia.

per·ma·nent (:nənt) I. adj. permanente II. s. permanente *f.*

per·me·a·bil·i·ty (pûr′mē-ə-bĭl′ĭ-tē) s. permeabilidad *f.*

per·me·a·ble (′--bəl) adj. permeable.

per·me·ate (pûr′mē-āt′) tr. & intr. penetrar, infiltrar(se).

per·mis·si·ble (pər-mĭs′ə-bəl) adj. permisible.

per·mis·sion (:mĭsh′ən) s. permiso.

per·mis·sive (:ĭv) adj. permisivo; *(indulgent)* indulgente.

per·mit I. tr. (pər-mĭt′) -tt- permitir; *(to give consent to)* dar permiso a, dejar II. s. (pûr′mĭt) permiso.

per·mu·ta·tion (pûr′myōō-tā′shən) s. permutación *f.*

per·mute (pər-myōōt′) tr. permutar.

per·ni·cious (pər-nĭsh′əs) adj. pernicioso.

per·o·rate (pĕr′ə-rāt′) intr. perorar.

per·o·ra·tion (′-rā′shən) s. peroración *f.*

per·ox·ide (pə-rŏk′sīd′) I. s. peróxido; *(hydrogen peroxide)* peróxido de hidrógeno II. tr. *(to treat)* tratar con peróxido; *(to bleach)* aclarar con peróxido de hidrógeno.

per·pen·dic·u·lar (pûr′pən-dĭk′yə-lər) I. adj. perpendicular; *(vertical)* vertical II. s. perpendicular *f.*

per·pe·trate (pûr′pĭ-trāt′) tr. perpetrar.

per·pe·tra·tion (′-trā′shən) s. perpetración *f.*

per·pe·tra·tor (′-′ tər) s. perpetrador *m.*

per·pet·u·al (pər-pĕch′ōō-əl) adj. perpetuo; *(constant)* constante; *(eternal)* eterno.

per·pet·u·ate (:āt′) tr. perpetuar.

per·pet·u·a·tion (-′-ā′shən) s. perpetuación *f.*

per·pe·tu·i·ty (pûr′pĭ-tōō′ĭ-tē) s. perpetuidad *f.*

per·plex (pər-plĕks′) tr. desconcertar.

per·plexed (:plĕkst′) adj. perplejo, confuso.

per·plex·i·ty (:plĕk′sĭ-tē) s. perplejidad *f.*

per·qui·site (pûr′kwĭ-zĭt) s. ganancia extra.

per·se·cute (pûr′sĭ-kyōōt′) tr. perseguir; *(to harass)* acosar, atormentar.

per·se·cu·tion (′-kyōō′shən) s. persecución *f.*

per·se·cu·tor (′-′ tər) s. perseguidor *m.*

per·se·ver·ance (pûr′sə-vîr′əns) s. perseverancia.

per·se·vere (:vîr′) intr. perseverar.

per·sim·mon (pər-sĭm′ən) s. caqui *m.*

per·sist (pər-sĭst′) intr. persistir.

per·sist·ence/en·cy (:sĭs′təns) s. persistencia, empeño.

per·sist·ent (:tənt) adj. persistente.

per·snick·e·ty (pər-snĭk′ĭ-tē) s. puntilloso, quisquilloso.

per·son (pûr′sən) s. persona.

per·son·a·ble (:sə-nə-bəl) adj. agradable.

per·son·age (:nĭj) s. personaje *m.*

per·son·al (pûr′sə-nəl) adj. personal; *(private)* particular; *(in person)* en persona; *(for one's use)* de uso personal ♦ p. property bienes muebles • to get p. hacer comentarios de carácter personal.

per·son·al·i·ty (′-năl′ĭ-tē) s. personalidad *f*; *(celebrity)* personaje *m*, figura.

per·son·al·ize (:nə-līz′) tr. personalizar.

per·son·i·fi·ca·tion (pər-sŏn′ə-fĭ-kā′shən) s. personificación *f.*

per·son·i·fy (′-fī′) tr. personificar.

per·son·nel (pûr′sə-nĕl′) s. personal *m.*

per·spec·tive (pər-spĕk′tĭv) s. perspectiva ♦ to put things in p. apreciar las cosas en su justo valor.

per·spi·ca·cious (pûr′spĭ-kā′shəs) adj. perspicaz.

per·spi·cac·i·ty (:kăs′ĭ-tē) s. perspicacia.

per·spic·u·ous (pər-spĭk′yōō-əs) adj. perspicuo.

per·spi·ra·tion (pûr′spə-rā′shən) s. sudor *m*, transpiración *f.*

per·spire (pər-spīr′) tr. & intr. sudar, transpirar.

per·suade (pər-swād′) tr. persuadir.

per·sua·sion (:swā′zhən) s. persuasión *f*, persuasiva; *(conviction)* convicción *f*, creencia.

per·sua·sive (:sĭv) adj. persuasivo.

per·sua·sive·ness (:nĭs) s. persuasión *f.*

pert (pûrt) adj. *(saucy)* impertinente; *(lively)* vivaz; *(jaunty)* alegre, gracioso.

per·tain (pər-tān′) intr. pertenecer; *(to relate to)* concernir.

per·ti·na·cious (pûr′tn-ā′shəs) adj. pertinaz; *(obstinate)* porfiado, obstinado.

per·ti·nence/nen·cy (′-əns) s. pertinencia.

per·ti·nent (:ənt) adj. pertinente.

per·turb (pər-tûrb′) tr. perturbar.

per·tur·ba·tion (pûr′tər-bā′shən) s. perturbación *f.*

per·tus·sis (pər-tŭs′ĭs) s. tos ferina.

pe·rus·al (pə-rōō′zəl) s. lectura cuidadosa.

pe·ruse (pə-rōōz′) tr. leer cuidadosamente.

per·vade (pər-vād′) tr. penetrar, impregnar.

per·va·sive (:vā′sĭv) adj. penetrante.

per·verse (pər-vûrs′) adj. perverso; *(willful)* terco.

per·ver·sion (:vûr′zhən) s. perversión *f.*

per·ver·si·ty (:sĭ-tē) s. *(perversion)* perversión *f*; *(willfulness)* terquedad *f.*

per·vert I. tr. (pər-vûrt′) pervertir; *(to misuse)* abusar de II. s. (pûr′vûrt′) pervertido.

per·vert·ed (pər-vûr′tĭd) adj. pervertido.

pes·ky (pĕs′kē) adj. -i- FAM. molesto.

pes·si·mism (pĕs′ə-mĭz′əm) s. pesimismo.

pes·si·mist (:mĭst) s. pesimista *mf.*

pes·si·mis·tic (′-mĭs′tĭk) adj. pesimista.

pest (pĕst) s. *(insect)* insecto; *(person)* pelmazo, persona molesta; *(plant, animal)* plaga, peste *f.*

pes·ter (pĕs′tər) tr. molestar, fastidiar.

pes·ti·cide (pĕs′tĭ-sīd′) s. pesticida, insecticida.

pes·tif·er·ous (pĕ-stĭf′ər-əs) adj. pestífero.

pes·ti·lence (pĕs′tə-ləns) s. pestilencia, peste *f.*

pes·ti·lent/len·tial (pĕs′tə-lənt/lĕn′shəl) adj. pestilente; *(annoying)* molesto.

pes·tle (pĕs′əl, pĕs′təl) mano *f* (de mortero).

pet (pĕt) I. s. animal domesticado; *(person)* favorito, preferido II. adj. domesticado; *(favorite)* favorito III. tr. **-tt-** *(to caress)* acariciar; *(to pamper)* mimar.

pet·al (pĕt′l) s. pétalo.

pe·ter (pē′tər) intr. ♦ **to p. out** disminuir.

pe·tite (pə-tēt′) adj. pequeña, chiquita.

pe·ti·tion (pə-tĭsh′ən) I. s. petición *f* II. tr. suplicar, pedir a.

pe·ti·tion·er (:ə-nər) s. peticionario.

pet·ri·fy (pĕt′rə-fī′) tr. & intr. petrificar(se).

pet·ro·chem·i·cal (pĕt′rō-kĕm′ĭ-kəl) s. producto petroquímico.

pet·rol (pĕt′rəl) s. G.B. gasolina.

pe·tro·le·um (pə-trō′lē-əm) s. petróleo ♦ **p. jelly** petrolato.

pet·ti·coat (pĕt′ē-kōt′) I. s. enaguas II. adj. femenino, de mujeres.

pet·ti·ness (pĕt′ē-nĭs) s. *(smallness)* pequeñez *f*; *(behavior)* mezquindad *f.*

pet·ting (pĕt′ĭng) s. FAM. besuqueo.

pet·ty (pĕt′ē) adj. **-i-** *(insignificant)* insignificante, trivial; *(narrow-minded)* mezquino; *(spiteful)* rencoroso ♦ **p. cash** caja chica • **p.**

lar·ce·ny hurto menor, ratería.

pet·u·lance (pĕch′ə-ləns) s. malhumor *m.*

pet·u·lant (:lənt) adj. malhumorado.

pe·tu·nia (pĭ-tōōn′yə) s. petunia.

pew (pyōō) s. banco de iglesia.

pew·ter (pyōō′tər) s. & adj. (de) peltre *m.*

pha·lanx (fā′lăngks′) s. [pl. **es** *o* **-ges**] falange *f.*

phal·lic (făl′ĭk) adj. fálico.

phal·lus (:əs) s. [pl. **es** *o* **-li**] falo.

phan·tasm (făn′tăz′əm) s. fantasma *m.*

phan·tom (:təm) I. s. fantasma *m* II. adj. fantasmal.

phar·aoh (fâr′ō) s. faraón *m.*

phar·i·see (fâr′ĭ-sē) s. fariseo.

phar·ma·ceu·ti·cal (fär′mə-sōō′tĭ-kəl) adj. & s. farmacéutico ♦ **pharmaceutics** s.sg. farmacia.

phar·ma·cist (′-sĭst) s. farmacéutico.

phar·ma·col·o·gy (′-kŏl′ə-jē) s. farmacología.

phar·ma·co·poe·ia (:kə-pē′ə) s. farmacopea.

phar·ma·cy (fär′mə-sē) s. farmacia.

phar·ynx (fâr′ĭngks) s. [pl. **es** *o* **-ges**] faringe *f.*

phase (fāz) I. s. fase ♦ **in p.** en fase, sincronizado • **out of p.** desfasado II. tr. *(to plan)* planear por fases, escalonar; ELEC., FIS. poner en fase ♦ **to p. in** introducir progresivamente • **to p. out** eliminar progresivamente.

phase·out (′out′) s. eliminación *f* gradual.

pheas·ant (fĕz′ənt) s. [pl. inv. *o* **s**] faisán *m.*

phe·nom·e·na (fĭ-nŏm′ə-nə) cf. **phenomenon.**

phe·nom·e·nal (:nəl) adj. fenomenal.

phe·nom·e·non (fĭ-nŏm′ə-nŏn′) s. [pl. **s** *o* **-na**] fenómeno.

phew (fyōō) interj. ¡uy!, ¡puf!

phi·al (fī′əl) s. frasco pequeño.

phi·lan·der (fĭ-lăn′dər) intr. galantear.

phi·lan·der·er (:ər) s. galanteador *m*, tenorio.

phil·an·throp·ic/i·cal (fĭl′ən-thrŏp′ĭk) adj. filantrópico.

phi·lan·thro·pist (fĭ-lăn′thrə-pĭst) s. filántropo.

phi·lan·thro·py (:pē) s. filantropía.

phi·lat·e·ly (fĭ-lăt′l-ē) s. filatelia.

phil·har·mon·ic (fĭl′här-mŏn′ĭk) adj. & s. (orquesta) filarmónica.

Phil·is·tine (fĭl′ĭ-stēn) s. filisteo.

phil·o·den·dron (fĭl′ə-dĕn′drən) s. [pl. **s** *o* **-dra**] filodendro.

phi·lol·o·gy (fĭ-lŏl′ə-jē) s. filología.

phi·los·o·pher (fĭ-lŏs′ə-fər) s. filósofo.

phil·o·soph·ic/i·cal (fĭl′ə-sŏf′ĭk) adj. filosófico.

phi·los·o·phize (f ĭ-lŏs′ə-fīz′) intr. filosofar.

phi·los·o·phy (:fē) s. filosofía.

phil·ter (fĭl′tər) s. filtro, poción *f.*

phle·bi·tis (flĭ-bī′tĭs) s. flebitis *f.*

phle·bot·o·my (:bŏt′ə-mē) s. flebotomía.

phlegm (flĕm) s. flema.

phleg·mat·ic (flĕg-măt′ĭk) adj. flemático.

pho·bi·a (fō′bē-ə) s. fobia.

phoe·nix (fē′nĭks) s. fénix *m.*

phone (fōn) FAM. I. s. teléfono II. tr. & intr. telefonear, llamar por teléfono.

pho·neme (fō′nēm) s. fonema *m.*

pho·net·ic (fə-nĕt′ĭk) adj. fonético ♦ **phonetics** s.sg. fonética.

pho·ne·ti·cian/net·i·cist (fō′nĭ-tĭsh′ən/fə-nĕt′ĭ-sĭst) s. fonetista *mf.*

phon·ic (fŏn′ĭk) adj. fónico ♦ **phonics** s.sg. fonética.

pho·no·graph (fō′nə-grăf′) s. fonógrafo.

pho·nog·ra·phy (fə-nŏg′rə-fē) s. fonografía.

pho·nol·o·gy (fə-nŏl′ə-jē) s. fonología.

pho·ny (fō′nē) FAM. I. adj. **-i-** falso; *(fake)*

postizo **II.** s. *(object)* camelo; *(person)* farsante *mf*, camelista *mf*.

phoo·ey (fo͞o′ē) interj. ¡puf!

phos·phate (fŏs′fāt′) s. fosfato.

phos·phor (:fər) s. substancia fosforescente.

phos·pho·res·cent (′fə-rĕs′ənt) adj. fosforescente.

phos·phor·ic (-fôr′ĭk) adj. fosfórico.

phos·pho·rus (′fər-əs) s. fósforo.

pho·to (fō′tō) s. foto, fotografía.

pho·to·cell (:sĕl′) s. fotocélula.

pho·to·cop·i·er (fō′tə-kŏp′ē-ər) s. fotocopiadora.

pho·to·cop·y (:ē) **I.** tr. fotocopiar **II.** s. fotocopia.

pho·to·e·lec·tric/tri·cal (fō′tō-ĭ-lĕk′trĭk) adj. fotoeléctrico.

pho·to·en·grave (:ĕn-grāv′) tr. fotograbar.

pho·to·gen·ic (fō′tə-jĕn′ĭk) adj. fotogénico.

pho·to·graph (fō′tə-grăf′) **I.** s. fotografía, foto *f* **II.** tr. fotografiar, sacar una fotografía —intr. ♦ **to p. well** salir bien en las fotografías.

pho·tog·ra·pher (fə-tŏg′rə-phər) s. fotógrafo.

pho·to·graph·ic (fō′tə-grăf′ĭk) adj. fotográfico.

pho·tog·ra·phy (fə-tŏg′rə-fē) s. fotografía.

pho·ton (fō′tŏn′) s. fotón *m*.

pho·to·sen·si·tive (fō′tō-sĕn′sĭ-tĭv) adj. fotosensible.

pho·to·stat (fō′tə-stăt′) s. fotostato.

pho·to·syn·the·sis (fō′tō-sĭn′thĭ-sĭs) s. fotosíntesis *f*.

phrase (frāz) **I.** s. frase *f* ♦ **p. book** diccionario de expresiones • **set p.** frase hecha **II.** tr. *(in speaking)* expresar; *(in writing)* redactar.

phra·se·ol·o·gy (frā′zē-ŏl′ə-jē) s. fraseología.

phras·ing (frā′zĭng) s. *(wording)* estilo, lenguaje *m*; *(phraseology)* fraseología.

phre·nol·o·gy (frĭ-nŏl′ə-jē) s. frenología.

phy·lum (fī′ləm) s. [pl. **-la**] filum *m*.

phys·ic (fĭz′ĭk) s. catártico.

phys·i·cal (fĭz′ĭ-kəl) **I.** adj. físico **II.** s. reconocimiento médico, chequeo.

phy·si·cian (fĭ-zĭsh′ən) s. médico, facultativo.

phys·i·cist (fĭz′ĭ-sĭst) s. físico.

phys·ics (fĭz′ĭks) s.sg. física.

phys·i·o·log·ic/i·cal (fĭz′ē-ə-lŏj′ĭk) adj. fisiológico.

phys·i·ol·o·gist (:ŏl′ə-jĭst) s. fisiólogo.

phys·i·ol·o·gy (:jē) s. fisiología.

phys·i·o·ther·a·py (fĭz′ē-ō-thĕr′ə-pē) s. fisioterapia.

phy·sique (fĭ-zēk′) s. físico.

pi·an·ist (pē-ăn′ĭst, pē′ə-nĭst) s. pianista *mf*.

pi·an·o (pē-ăn′ō) s. piano.

pi·az·za (pē-ăz′ə, -ä′zə) s. [pl. **s** o **-ze**] plaza; *(verandah)* galería, terraza.

pi·ca (pī′kə) s. IMPR. pica.

pic·a·resque (pĭk′ə-rĕsk′) adj. picaresco.

pic·a·yune (pĭk′ē-yōōn′) adj. *(paltry)* insignificante; *(petty)* mezquino.

pic·co·lo (pĭk′ə-lō′) s. flautín *m*.

pick¹ (pĭk) **I.** tr. escoger, elegir; *(to gather)* recoger; *(to strip clean)* mondar; *(to pluck)* desplumar; *(to tear off)* sacar, arrancar; *(to break up)* cavar; *(to open)* abrir; *(to peck)* picar, picotear ♦ **to p. a fight** buscar bronca • **to p. apart** *(to tear)* destrozar, despedazar; *(to refute)* echar por tierra • **to p. off** matar de un solo tiro • **to p. oneself up** levantarse • **to p. one's nose** hurgarse la nariz • **to p. one's teeth** mondarse los dientes • **to p. out** *(to choose)* escoger, seleccionar; *(to distinguish)* distinguir • **to p. over**

inspeccionar • **to p. someone's brains** FIG. explotar los conocimientos de alguien • **to p. someone's pocket** robar algo del bolsillo de alguien • **to p. up** *(to lift)* coger; *(fallen object)* recoger; *(to tidy)* recoger; *(to stop for)* recoger; FAM. *(to buy)* comprar; *(to learn)* aprender; *(to notice)* encontrar; *(a habit)* coger, adquirir; *(to pay)* pagar; *(a disease)* coger, pescar; RAD., TELEV. coger, captar; *(speed)* cobrar; JER. *(to arrest)* pescar, coger; *(to continue)* reanudar, proseguir • **to p. up on** darse cuenta de —intr. picar; *(to decide)* decidir cuidadosamente ♦ **to p. at** *(food)* picar, picotear; FAM. *(to nag)* cogerla con • **to p. on** *(to tease)* atormentar; *(to bully)* abusar de • **to p. up** *(to resume)* continuar; FAM. *(to improve)* mejorar **II.** s. elección *f*, selección *f* ♦ **the p. of the crop** o **of the litter** la flor y nata.

pick² s. *(tool)* piqueta, pico; *(picklock)* ganzúa; MÚS. plectro, púa.

pick·a·back (pĭk′ə-băk′) **I.** adv. a cuestas, sobre los hombros **II.** s. paseo a cuestas.

pick·ax(e) (pĭk′ăks′) s. piqueta, zapapico.

picked (pĭkt) adj. escogido, selecto.

pick·et (pĭk′ĭt) **I.** s. estaca; MIL. piquete *m*; *(strikers)* piquete **II.** tr. *(to enclose)* cercar con estacas; *(to guard)* guardar o vigilar con piquetes —intr. vigilar, estar de guardia.

pick·ing (pĭk′ĭng) s. *(harvest)* cosecha, recolección *f*; *(choice)* selección *f* ♦ pl. sobras, restos.

pick·le (pĭk′əl) **I.** s. *(food)* encurtido; *(solution)* salmuera, escabeche *m*; FAM. *(plight)* lío **II.** tr. encurtir.

pick·led (:əld) adj. *(food)* en salmuera o escabeche; *(person)* borracho, bebido.

pick·pock·et (pĭk′pŏk′ĭt) s. carterista *mf*.

pick·up (pĭk′ŭp′) s. *(collection)* recogida; *(acceleration)* poder *m* de aceleración; *(truck)* camioneta; *(increase)* aumento; *(improvement)* mejora; *(casual acquaintance)* ligue *m*.

pick·y (pĭk′ē) adj. **-i-** quisquilloso.

pic·nic (pĭk′nĭk) **I.** s. picnic *m* ♦ **to be no p.** FAM. no ser fácil **II.** intr. **-ck-** comer al aire libre.

pic·to·ri·al (pĭk-tôr′ē-əl) adj. pictórico.

pic·ture (pĭk′chər) **I.** s. *(painting)* cuadro, pintura; *(illustration)* ilustración *f*; *(photograph)* fotografía; *(portrait)* retrato; *(mental image)* imagen *f*, idea; *(description)* descripción *f*, cuadro; *(physical image)* retrato, imagen; *(film)* película, filme *m*; *(television)* imagen ♦ **p. book** libro ilustrado • **p. tube** TELEV. pantalla • **p. window** ventanal • **pretty as a p.** una monada • **to be out of the p.** quedar fuera del juego • **to come into the p.** aparecer • **to give somebody the general p.** dar a alguien una idea general **II.** tr. *(to paint)* pintar; *(to draw)* dibujar; *(to visualize)* imaginar; *(to describe)* pintar.

pic·tur·esque (′chə-rĕsk′) adj. pintoresco.

pid·dling (pĭd′lĭng) adj. insignificante, trivial.

pidg·in (pĭj′ĭn) s. lengua franca.

pie (pī) s. *(with meat)* empanada; *(with fruit)* pastel *m* ♦ **as easy as p.** FAM. muy fácil • **p. in the sky** ilusiones • **to have a finger in the p.** estar metido en el asunto.

piece (pēs) **I.** s. pedazo; *(in a set)* pieza; *(specimen)* muestra; *(firearm)* arma; *(distance)* tramo; LIT., MÚS. obra *f* ♦ **p.** *(object)* en buen estado; *(person)* sano y salvo • **to give someone a p. of one's mind** cantar a alguien las cuarenta • **to say one's p.** decir lo que uno piensa ♦ pl. **in p.** *(unassembled)* desarmado; *(shattered)* hecho añicos • **to go to p.** FAM. no poderse dominar II. tr. ♦ **to p. together** *(to put together)* armar; *(to rearrange)* rehacer; *(to figure out)* llegar a entender.

piece·meal (′mēl′) adv. *(bit by bit)* a trozos; *(gradually)* poco a poco.

piece·work (:wûrk′) s. trabajo a destajo.

pier (pîr) s. muelle *m,* embarcadero; *(of a bridge)* pila; *(of an arch)* pilar *m;* *(between windows)* entreventana; *(buttress)* contrafuerte *m.*

pierce (pîrs) tr. *(to puncture)* traspasar; *(to perforate)* perforar; *(to penetrate)* atravesar, abrirse paso por ♦ **to have** ○ **get one's ears pierced** hacerse agujeros en las orejas.

pierc·ing (pîr′sĭng) adj. *(sharp)* agudo; *(look)* penetrante; *(wind)* cortante.

pi·e·ty (pī′ĭ-tē) s. piedad *f.*

pig (pĭg) I. s. cerdo, puerco; *(pork)* lechón *m;* FAM. *(glutton)* tragón *m,* glotón *m;* *(slob)* cochino, puerco; METAL. lingote *m* ♦ **a p. in a poke** algo (comprado) sin saber exactamente qué es • **p. iron** hierro en lingotes II. intr. **-pp-** ♦ **to p. out** comer como un puerco.

pi·geon (pĭj′ən) s. paloma; *(dupe)* tonto.

pi·geon·hole (:hōl′) I. s. *(cubbyhole)* casilla; *(category)* clasificación *f* II. tr. *(to file)* archivar; *(to categorize)* clasificar; *(to shelve)* dar carpetazo a.

pi·geon-toed (:tōd′) adj. de pies que apuntan hacia adentro.

pig·gish (pĭg′ĭsh) adj. *(greedy)* glotón; *(pigheaded)* testarudo.

pig·gy (:ē) s. cerdito ♦ **p. bank** alcancía.

pig·gy·back (:băk′) I. adv. a cuestas; *(in transportation)* en vagón plataforma II. adj. ♦ **p. ride** paseo a cuestas.

pig·head·ed (pĭg′hĕd′ĭd) adj. testarudo, terco.

pig·let (:lĭt) s. cochinillo, lechón *m.*

pig·ment (pĭg′mənt) s. pigmento.

pig·men·ta·tion (′mən-tā′shən) s. pigmentación *f.*

pig·pen (pĭg′pĕn′) s. pocilga.

pig·skin (:skĭn′) s. piel *f* ○ cuero de cerdo; *(football)* pelota.

pig·sty (:stī′) s. pocilga.

pig·tail (:tāl′) s. coleta, trenza.

pike¹ (pīk) s. *(spear)* pica.

pike² s. [pl. inv. ○ **s**] *(fish)* lucio.

pike³ s. *(turnpike)* carretera de peaje.

pike⁴ s. *(sharp point)* punta.

pile¹ (pīl) I. s. pila, montón *m;* *(funeral pyre)* pira funeraria; FORTUNE fortuna; FÍS. pila atómica II. tr. apilar, amontar; *(to fill)* llenar ♦ **to p. it on** exagerar • **to p. up** apilar, amontonar —intr. amontonarse ♦ **to p. in** entrar en tropel • **to p. up** acumularse.

pile² (pīl) s. *(furry surface)* pelo.

piles (pīlz) s.pl. hemorroides *f,* almorranas.

pile·up (pīl′ŭp′) s. accidente *m* entre varios vehículos.

pil·fer (pĭl′fər) tr. & intr. robar.

pil·fer·age (:ĭj) s. robo.

pil·grim (pĭl′grĭm) s. *(devotee)* peregrino; *(traveler)* viajante *mf.*

pil·grim·age (:grə-mĭj) s. peregrinación *f.*

pil·ing (pī′lĭng) s. *(foundation)* cimentación *f* con pilotes; *(piles)* pilotaje *m.*

pill (pĭl) I. s. píldora; *(contraceptive)* píldora anticonceptiva; *(person)* pelmazo II. intr. formar pelotillas ○ bolitas.

pil·lage (pĭl′ĭj) I. tr. & intr. pillar, saquear II. s. pillaje *m,* saqueo.

pil·lag·er (:ĭ-jər) s. pillador *m,* saqueador *m.*

pil·lar (pĭl′ər) s. pilar *m* ♦ **from p. to post** de la Ceca a la Meca.

pill·box (pĭl′bŏks′) s. cajita para píldoras; *(hat)* pequeño sombrero sin ala; MIL. fortín *m.*

pil·lo·ry (pĭl′ə-rē) I. s. picota II. tr. poner en la picota.

pil·low (pĭl′ō) I. s. almohada; *(for decoration)* almohadón *m* II. tr. *(to rest)* hacer descansar sobre una almohada; *(to support)* servir de almohada.

pil·low·case (:kās′) s. funda de almohada.

pi·lot (pī′lət) I. s. AVIA. piloto; MARÍT. *(in a port)* práctico del puerto; *(helmsman)* piloto, timonel *m;* *(leader)* guía *mf,* director *m;* TELEV. programa *m* de introducción de una serie ♦ **p. light** llama piloto II. tr. pilotear III. adj. *(trial)* piloto, experimental; *(guiding)* modelo.

pi·men·to (pĭ-mĕn′tō) s. pimiento, ají *m.*

pi·mien·to (pĭ-mĕn′tō, -myĕn′-) s. pimiento morrón.

pimp (pĭmp) I. s. alcahuete *m* II. intr. alcahuetear.

pim·ple (pĭm′pəl) s. grano.

pim·ply (:plē) adj. granujiento, espinilloso.

pin (pĭn) I. s. alfiler *m;* *(badge)* insignia; *(brooch)* broche *m;* *(cotter)* pasador *m,* chaveta; *(bolt)* perno; *(peg)* clavija; *(in bowling)* bolo ♦ **to hear a p. drop** oír el vuelo de una mosca II. tr. **-nn-** prender con alfileres; *(in wrestling)* sujetar ♦ **to p. down** sujetar, asegurar; *(to immobilize)* inmovilizar; *(to establish)* determinar, precisar; *(to force to be specific)* hacer que (alguien) sea más preciso • **to p. on** prender en; *(hopes)* cifrar en; *(to blame)* echar la culpa a • **to p. up** *(hair)* sujetar con horquillas; *(a notice)* clavar con chinchetas.

pin·a·fore (pĭn′ə-fôr′) s. delantal *m.*

pin·ball (pĭn′bôl′) s. billar romano.

pince-nez (păns′nā′, pĭns′-) s.inv. quevedos *m.*

pin·cer (pĭn′sər) s. pinza ♦ pl. pinzas, tenazas.

pinch (pĭnch) I. tr. pellizcar; *(to catch)* cogerse, pillarse; *(shoes)* apretar; *(to cause hardship)* poner en aprietos a; JER. *(to steal)* ratear, mangar; *(to arrest)* pescar, prender ♦ **to p. pennies** andar con tacañerías, escatimar gastos —intr. *(shoes)* apretar; *(to economize)* escatimar gastos II. s. pellizco; *(of seasoning)* pizca; *(of snuff)* pulgarada ♦ **in a p.** en caso de apuro ○ de necesidad • **to feel the p.** pasar apuros, verse apretado.

pin·cush·ion (pĭn′kŏsh′ən) s. alfiletero.

pine¹ (pīn) s. pino ♦ **p. cone** piña.

pine² intr. ♦ **to p. away** consumirse, languidecer • **to p. for** suspirar por, anhelar.

pine·ap·ple (pīn′ăp′əl) s. piña, ananás *m.*

ping (pĭng) I. s. sonido metálico II. intr. producir un sonido metálico.

pin·head (pĭn′hĕd′) s. cabeza de alfiler; *(stupid person)* tonto, bobo.

pink¹ (pĭngk) I. s. clavel *m;* *(color)* rosado, rosa ♦ **in the p.** rebosante de salud • **in the p. of** en perfecto estado de II. adj. rosado, rosa.

pink² tr. *(to decorate)* festonear; *(to perforate)* picar ♦ **pinking shears** tijeras dentadas.

pink·eye ○ **pink eye** (′) s. conjuntivitis aguda.

pink·ie (pĭng′kē) s. FAM. dedo meñique.

pink·ish (pĭng′kĭsh) adj. rosáceo.

pink·o (:kō) s. JER. rojillo, comunacho.

pink·y (pĭng′kē) s. FAM. dedo meñique.

pin·na·cle (pĭn′ə-kəl) s. ARQ. pináculo; *(peak)* pico, cima; FIG. cumbre *f.*

pi·noc(h)·le (pē′nŭk′əl) s. juego de naipes.
pin·point (pĭn′point′) I. s. punta de alfiler II. tr. localizar con precisión III. adj. exacto.
pin·prick (:prĭk′) s. alfilerazo; *(minor annoyance)* molestia.
pin·stripe (:strīp′) I. s. raya fina II. adj. de rayas finas.
pint (pīnt) s. pinta.
pint·size(d) (′sīz[d]′) adj. FAM. pequeño.
pin·up (pĭn′ŭp′) s. *(picture)* fotografía de una mujer atractiva; *(woman)* mujer atractiva.
pin·wheel (:hwēl′) s. molinillo; *(fireworks)* girándula.
pi·o·neer (pī′ə-nîr′) I. s. pionero II. adj. *(innovating)* innovador; *(of settlers)* de pionero III. tr. *(to explore)* iniciar la exploración de; *(to open up)* marcar nuevos rumbos en; *(to settle)* colonizar.
pi·ous (pī′əs) adj. piadoso; *(hypocritical)* beato; *(commendable)* digno de alabanza.
pip (pĭp) s. *(seed)* pepita.
pipe (pīp) I. s. *(for liquids, gas)* tubería, cañería; *(for tobacco)* pipa ♦ **exhaust p.** tubo de escape • **p. cleaner** limpiapipas • **p. dream** ilusión, castillos en el aire • **p. wrench** llave para tubos • **put that in your p. and smoke it!** FAM. ¡chúpate ésa! ♦ pl. *(tubes)* tubería, cañería; *(bagpipe)* gaita II. tr. *(liquids, gas)* conducir por tuberías; *(to provide with pipes)* instalar tuberías o cañerías en —intr. MÚS. tocar; *(to screech)* chillar; *(bird)* cantar ♦ **to p. down** JER. cerrar el pico, callarse la boca • **to p. up** prorrumpir chillando.
pipe·line (′līn′) s. *(gas)* gasoducto; *(oil)* oleoducto; *(information)* conducto; *(supply)* línea.
pip·er (pī′pər) s. *(flutist)* flautista mf; *(bagpiper)* gaitero.
pi·pet(te) (pī-pĕt′) s. pipeta, probeta.
pip·ing (pī′pĭng) I. s. *(pipes)* tubería, cañería; *(on clothing)* ribete m II. adj. ♦ **p. hot** muy caliente.
pip-squeak (pĭp′skwēk′) s. cero a la izquierda.
pi·quant (pē′kənt) adj. *(spicy)* picante; *(provocative)* provocativo.
pique (pēk) I. s. pique m ♦ **in a fit of p.** por resentimiento II. tr. *(to vex)* picar, molestar; *(interest)* despertar.
pi·ra·cy (pī′rə-sē) s. piratería.
pi·rate (pī′rĭt) I. s. pirata m; *(thief)* persona que comete fraudes II. tr. *(to rob)* robar, pillar; *(books, records)* hacer una edición pirata de.
pir·ou·ette (pĭr′ōō-ĕt′) I. s. pirueta, cabriola II. intr. piruetear, hacer cabriolas.
pis·ta·chi·o (pī-stăsh′ē-ō′) s. *(tree)* pistachero, alfóncigo; *(nut)* pistacho, alfóncigo.
pis·tol (pĭs′təl) s. pistola.
pis·ton (pĭs′tən) s. pistón m.
pit¹ (pĭt) I. s. *(hole)* hoyo, pozo; *(for cockfights)* reñidero; *(pockmark)* picadura de viruela; *(of a stock exchange)* sección f de la bolsa dedicada a una sola mercancía; *(for a mechanic)* foso; *(at a racecourse)* puesto ♦ **in the p. of one's stomach** en la boca del estómago • **orchestra p.** foso de la orquesta • **the pits** JER. lo peor de lo peor II. tr. **-tt-** *(to make holes in)* llenar de hoyos; *(by a disease)* llenar de picaduras ♦ **to p. against** oponer —intr. *(surface)* llenarse de hoyos; *(skin)* llenarse de picaduras o de marcas.
pit² I. s. hueso (de frutas) II. tr. **-tt-** deshuesar.
pit·a·pat (pĭt′ə-păt′) I. intr. **-tt-** *(to move)* moverse con paso ligero; *(to beat)* latir rápidamente II. s. *(steps)* paso ligero; *(beats)* latido,

palpitación f III. adv. ♦ **to go p.** latir rápidamente.
pitch¹ (pĭch) I. s. *(sticky substance)* pez f; *(bitumen)* alquitrán m, brea; *(resin)* resina II. tr. embrear, embetunar.
pitch² I. tr. *(to throw)* lanzar, tirar; *(hay)* echar; *(tent)* montar, armar; *(speech)* ajustar; *(a product)* pregonar las virtudes de; *(to incline)* inclinar ♦ **to p. camp** acampar —intr. *(to fall)* caer(se); *(to lurch)* tambalearse, dar tumbos; *(plane, ship)* cabecear; *(to slope)* inclinarse ♦ **to p. in** FAM. dar una mano II. s. *(throw)* lanzamiento, tiro; *(intensity)* grado; *(of a ship)* cabeceo; *(slope)* inclinación f; *(of a roof)* pendiente f; JER. *(talk)* charlatanería; MÚS. tono ♦ **p. pipe** diapasón.
pitch-black (′blăk′) adj. *(dark)* oscuro como boca de lobo; *(black)* negro como el carbón.
pitch-dark (:därk′) adj. oscuro como boca de lobo.
pitch·er¹ (pĭch′ər) s. DEP. lanzador m.
pitch·er² s. jarra, cántaro.
pitch·fork (pĭch′fôrk′) s. horquilla, horca.
pit·e·ous (pĭt′ē-əs) adj. lastimoso, lastimero; *(pathetic)* patético.
pit·fall (pĭt′fôl′) s. *(trap)* trampa; *(difficulty)* dificultad f.
pith (pĭth) s. BOT. médula; *(essence)* meollo.
pith·y (′ē) adj. **-i-** meduloso, medular; *(substantial)* substancial.
pit·i·a·ble (pĭt′ē-ə-bəl) adj. lastimoso.
pit·i·ful (pĭt′ĭ-fəl) adj. lastimoso; *(contemptible)* despreciable.
pit·i·less (:lĭs) adj. despiadado.
pit·tance (pĭt′ns) s. miseria.
pit·ter-pat·ter (pĭt′ər-păt′ər) I. s. *(tapping)* golpeteo; *(of rain)* tamborileo II. intr. *(to tap)* golpetear; *(to rain)* tamborilear.
pi·tu·i·tar·y (pĭ-tōō′ĭ-tĕr′ē) s. & adj. *(glándula)* pituitaria.
pit·y (pĭt′ē) I. s. piedad f; *(regrettable fact)* lástima, pena II. intr. & tr. compadecer(se de).
piv·ot (pĭv′ət) I. s. *(shaft)* pivote m; *(center)* eje m; *(turn)* pivote II. tr. hacer girar ♦ **to p. on** *(to turn)* girar sobre; *(to depend on)* depender de —intr. girar sobre un eje.
piv·o·tal (′ə-tl) adj. *(turning)* giratorio, de giro; *(essential)* fundamental, cardinal.
pix·y/ie (pĭk′sē) s. duendecillo, hada traviesa.
piz·za (pēt′sə) s. pizza.
plac·ard (plăk′ärd′) I. s. cartel m, letrero II. tr. *(to announce)* anunciar por medio de carteles; *(to post)* poner carteles.
pla·cate (plā′kāt′, plăk′āt′) tr. apaciguar.
place (plās) I. s. lugar m; *(locale)* sitio, local m; *(house)* casa; *(seat)* asiento; *(place setting)* cubierto; *(in a book)* página por donde uno va; *(function)* función f; *(rank)* posición f social; *(in a line)* puesto ♦ **all over the p.** por todas partes • **any p.** en o a dondequiera • **if I were in your p.** yo que tú • **in high places** en las altas esferas • **in p.** en orden • **in p. of** en lugar de, en vez de • **not to be one's p.** to no corresponderle a uno • **out of p.** fuera de lugar • **p. mat** mantelito individual • **p. setting** cubierto • **to go places** FAM. llegar lejos • **to know one's p.** saber guardar las distancias • **to put someone in his p.** poner a alguien en su lugar • **to take p.** *(to happen)* tener lugar; *(to be held)* celebrarse • **to take the p. of** sustituir II. tr. colocar, poner; *(to situate)* situar, ubicar; *(to estimate)* calcular; *(to bet)* hacer; *(to call)* pedir ♦ **to be**

able to p. saber dónde uno ha visto • to p. an order tener un pedido —intr. clasificarse entre los tres primeros.

pla·ce·bo (plə-sē'bō) s. [pl. (e)s] placebo.

place·ment (plās'mənt) s. colocación f.

pla·cen·ta (plə-sĕn'tə) s. [pl. s o -ae] placenta.

plac·id (plăs'ĭd) adj. tranquilo, apacible.

pla·gia·rism (plā'jə-rĭz'əm) s. plagio.

pla·gia·rize (:rīz') tr. & intr. plagiar.

plague (plāg) I. s. (disease) peste f; (nuisance) molestia, fastidio; (outbreak) plaga II. tr. atormentar.

plaid (plăd) s. tela a cuadros; (pattern) diseño a cuadros.

plain (plān) I. adj. (obvious) claro, evidente; (simple) sencillo; (straightforward) claro, sin rodeos; (unmixed) puro, solo; (unaffected) llano, corriente; (unpatterned) sin adornos; (unattractive) nada atractivo; (utter) puro, absoluto ♦ in p. sight a la vista de todos • the p. truth la pura verdad II. s. llanura, llano ♦ pl. praderas III. adv. (bluntly) claro; (utterly) absolutamente.

plain·song ('sòng') s. canto llano.

plaint (plānt) s. (complaint) queja; (lamentation) lamento, quejido.

plain·tiff (plān'tĭf) s. demandante mf.

plain·tive (:tĭv) adj. quejumbroso.

plait (plăt, plăt) I. s. (hair) trenza; (pleat) pliegue m II. tr. trenzar.

plan (plăn) I. s. plan m; (schedule) programa m; (intention) intención f; (project) proyecto; (outline) esquema m; (diagram) plano II. tr. -nn- planear, proyectar; (to project) planificar; (to draw) hacer el plano de; (to design) diseñar ♦ to p. to pensar • to p. for esperar —intr. hacer planes ♦ to p. on (to count on) contar con, hacerse la idea de; (to intend to) pensar; (to expect) esperar.

plane (plān) I. s. MAT. plano; (surface) superficie plana; (level) nivel m; (airplane) avión m; CARP. cepillo II. tr. CARP. cepillar.

plan·et (plăn'ĭt) s. planeta m.

plan·e·tar·i·um ('ĭ-târ'ē-əm) s. [pl. s o -ia] planetario.

plan·e·tar·y ('-tĕr'ē) adj. planetario.

plank (plăngk) I. s. tablón m; POL. punto II. tr. (to cover) entablar; (to broil) cocinar a la plancha ♦ to p. down FAM. (to lay down) tirar con violencia; (to pay out) desembolsar.

plank·ton (plăngk'tən) s. plancton m.

plan·ning (plăn'ĭng) I. s. planificación f II. adj. planificador.

plant (plănt) I. s. planta; (factory) fábrica; (installation) instalación f; (spy) espía mf II. tr. plantar; (to found) fundar; (to implant) infundir, inculcar; (spies) apostar; (a blow) asestar.

plan·tain¹ (plăn'tən) s. plantaina.

plan·tain² s. (plant) plátano; (fruit) banano.

plan·ta·tion (plăn-tā'shən) s. plantación f; (estate) hacienda.

plant·er (plăn'tər) s. plantador m; (pot) tiesto; (machine) sembradora.

plaque (plăk) s. placa.

plas·ma (plăz'mə) s. plasma m.

plas·ter (plăs'tər) I. s. yeso; (of a cast) escayola; (poultice) emplasto, cataplasma ♦ p. cast ESCULT. vaciado en yeso; MED. enyesado • p. of Paris sulfato de cal, yeso mate II. tr. enyesar, enlucir; (to repair) tapar con yeso; FIG. (to cover) llenar; (a limb) escayolar; (to smear) untar; FAM. (to inflict damage on) hacer daño a.

plas·ter·board (:bôrd') s. cartón m de yeso.

plas·tered (plăs'tərd) s. JER. borracho.

plas·ter·ing (:tər-ĭng) s. enyesado.

plas·tic (plăs'tĭk) I. adj. plástico; (artificial) artificial ♦ p. surgery cirugía plástica o estética II. s. plástico; JER. (credit card) tarjeta de crédito.

plas·tic·i·ty (plă-stĭs'ĭ-tē) s. plasticidad f.

plat (plăt) I. tr. -tt- entrelazar II. s. trenza.

plate (plāt) I. s. (dish) plato; (service and food) cubierto; (tableware) vajilla; (plaque) placa; (of metal) plancha, lámina; (coating) revestimiento; (illustration) grabado, lámina; ARM. plancha de blindaje; FOTOG. placa; (of teeth) dentadura postiza; (in baseball) base f del bateador ♦ p. glass vidrio cilindrado, luna II. tr. (with metal) chapar; (with gold) dorar; (with silver) platear; (for armor) blindar.

pla·teau (plă-tō') s. [pl. s o -x] meseta, altiplanicie f.

plat·ed (plā'tĭd) adj. (coated) enchapado; (armored) blindado.

plate·let (plāt'lĭt) s. plaqueta.

plat·form (plăt'fôrm') s. plataforma; (railroad) andén m; POL. programa político.

plat·ing (plā'tĭng) s. enchapado; (of gold) dorado; (of silver) plateado; (armor plate) blindaje m.

plat·i·num (plăt'n-əm) s. platino.

pla·ton·ic (plə-tŏn'ĭk) adj. platónico.

plat·ter (plăt'ər) s. fuente f; (record) disco.

plau·dits (plô'dĭts) s.pl. aplausos.

plau·si·bil·i·ty (plô'zə-bĭl'ĭ-tē) s. plausibilidad f.

plau·si·ble (plô'zə-bəl) adj. plausible.

play (plā) I. intr. jugar; (to jest) bromear; (to pretend to be) fingirse; (to be performed) poner, dar; MÚS. tocar; (light) bailar ♦ to p. along cooperar • to p. around (to joke) bromear, tomar el pelo; (to flirt) flirtear, coquetear; (to have fun) retozar, juguetear • to p. fair jugar limpio • to p. for (money) jugar por; (a team) jugar con • to p. on aprovecharse de • to p. up to FAM. adular, halagar • to p. with (to fiddle with) jugar con; (to consider) darle vueltas en la cabeza —tr. jugar (a); TEAT. (a role) desempeñar; (to act as) hacer de; (to give performances in) representar obras en, actuar en; (to compete against) jugar contra; (a card) jugar; (game piece) mover; (to bet) jugarse, apostar; (water, light) dirigir; MÚS. tocar ♦ to p. back volver a poner (algo grabado) • to p. both ends against the middle meter discordia entre los rivales • to p. down quitar importancia a • to p. hardball FIG. jugar duro • to p. havoc causar estragos (with con, en) • to p. out (to exhaust) agotar; (to finish) acabar • to p. possum hacerse el muerto • to p. the field FIG. salir o andar con más de una persona • to p. the fool hacerse el tonto • to p. up resaltar II. s. juego; (drama) obra, pieza; (performance) teatro, representación f; (move) jugada; (turn) turno; (dealings) jugada • to bring into p. poner en juego • to come into p. entrar en el juego • in p. (in jest) en broma; DEP. en juego • on words juego de palabras • to make a p. for FAM. hacer proposiciones a.

play·act ('ăkt') intr. (to act) desempeñar un papel, actuar; (to pretend) fingir; (to overreact) hacer la comedia.

play·back (:băk') s. (of a tape) reproducción f; (sound) sonido pregrabado.

play·bill (:bĭl′) s. *(poster)* cartel *m*; *(program)* programa *m*.

play·boy (:boi′) s. hombre *m* de mundo.

play·er (:ər) s. jugador *m*; *(actor)* actor *m*; *(actress)* actriz *f*; *(musician)* ejecutante *mf*, músico ♦ **p. piano** pianola, piano mecánico.

play·ful (plā′fəl) adj. juguetón; *(humorous)* humorístico.

play·go·er (:gō′ər) s. aficionado al teatro.

play·ground (:ground′) s. jardín *m* para jugar.

play·house (:hous′) s. *(theater)* teatro; *(for children)* casita para juego de niños.

play·mate (plā′māt′) s. compañero de juego.

play·off (:ôf′) s. DEP. partido de desempate.

play·pen (:pĕn′) s. corralito para niños.

play·room (:rōōm′) s. cuarto de jugar.

play·thing (:thĭng′) s. juguete *m*.

play·time (:tīm′) s. recreo.

play·wright (:rīt′) s. dramaturgo.

pla·za (plä′zə, plăz′ə) s. plaza.

plea (plē) s. súplica; *(excuse)* pretexto; DER. alegato ♦ **to cop a p.** FAM. declararse culpable de un delito menos grave a cambio de no ser acusado de otro más serio.

plead (plēd) intr. **-ed** *o* **pled** suplicar, implorar; *(to argue for)* abogar, interceder; DER. *(to enter a plea)* contestar a los cargos; *(to address a court)* hacer un alegato ♦ **to p. guilty** declararse culpable ♦ **to p. not guilty** declararse inocente —tr. alegar; *(a case, cause)* defender.

pleas·ant (plĕz′ənt) adj. agradable.

pleas·ant·ry (:ən-trē) s. gracia, chiste *m* ♦ **pl.** conversación amena.

please (plēz) tr. agradar, gustar; *(to satisfy)* contentar, complacer ♦ **hard to p.** muy exigente • **p.** *(polite)* por favor; *(formal)* se ruega; *(yes)* por supuesto • **to be pleased** alegrarse de que • **to be pleased to** tener mucho gusto en • **to be pleased with** estar contento con • **to p. oneself** hacer uno lo que quiere —intr. agradar, gustar; *(to wish)* querer ♦ **if you p.** *(if you will)* por favor, haga el favor de; *(if you can imagine)* ¡figúrate!

pleas·ing (plē′zĭng) adj. agradable.

pleas·ur·a·ble (plĕzh′ər-ə-bəl) adj. agradable.

pleas·ure (plĕzh′ər) s. placer *m*, gusto; *(wish)* voluntad *f* ♦ **p. cruise** crucero de excursión • **to take p.** in gustarle a uno • **with p.** con gusto.

pleat (plēt) I. s. pliegue *m* II. tr. plisar.

ple·be·ian (plĭ-bē′ən) adj. & s. plebeyo.

pleb·i·scite (plĕb′ĭ-sīt′) s. plebiscito.

pled (plĕd) cf. **plead**.

pledge (plĕj) I. s. promesa; *(obligation)* compromiso, obligación *f*; *(pawn)* prenda; *(as security)* entrega de prenda ♦ **p. of allegiance** voto de lealtad • **to take** *o* **make a p.** FAM. comprometerse a II. tr. prometer; *(to vow)* hacer voto de; *(to bind)* exigir; *(to pawn)* dar en prenda, empeñar —intr. hacer una promesa.

ple·na·ry (plē′nə-rē, plĕn′ə-) adj. plenario.

plen·i·po·ten·ti·ar·y (plĕn′ə-pə-tĕn′shē-ĕr′ē) adj. & s. plenipotenciario.

plen·i·tude (plĕn′ĭ-tōōd′) s. plenitud *f*.

plen·te·ous (:tē-əs) adj. abundante, copioso.

plen·ti·ful (:tĭ-fəl) adj. abundante, copioso.

plen·ty (plĕn′tē) I. s. abundancia; *(affluence)* afluencia II. adj. abundante; *(sufficient)* suficiente, bastante ♦ **p. of** bastante; *(more than enough)* de sobra III. adv. FAM. muy.

pleth·o·ra (plĕth′ər-ə) s. plétora.

pleu·ri·sy (plŏōr′ĭ-sē) s. pleuresía.

pli·a·ble (plī′ə-bəl) adj. flexible.

pli·ant (:ənt) adj. flexible.

pli·ers (plī′ərz) s. alicates *m*, tenazas.

plight[1] (plīt) s. apuro, situación *f* difícil.

plight[2] tr. ♦ **to p. one's troth** dar palabra de matrimonio.

plod (plŏd) intr. **-dd-** ♦ **to p. (along)** *(to walk)* andar trabajosamente; *(to work)* trabajar lentamente • **to p. away at** perseverar en.

plop (plŏp) I. intr. **-pp-** ♦ **to p. down** caerse de golpe, desplomarse —tr. dejar caer con ruido apagado II. s. ruido apagado.

plot (plŏt) I. s. *(of land)* parcela; *(patch)* cuadro; *(story line)* trama, argumento; *(conspiracy)* complot *m* II. tr. **-tt-** *(to chart)* trazar; *(to scheme)* tramar; MAT. marcar, trazar —intr. conspirar.

plot·ter (:ər) s. intrigante *mf*, conspirador *m*.

plow (plou) I. s. arado; *(snowplow)* quitanieves *m* II. tr. *(a field)* arar; *(to clear)* abrir ♦ **to p. through** *(a crowd)* abrirse paso a través de; *(to read)* leer con dificultad • **to p. under** *(to overwhelm)* agobiar, abrumar; *(to bury)* enterrar • **to p. up** arar, roturar —intr. arar la tierra ♦ **to p. into** FAM. *(to strike)* arremeter *o* precipitarse contra; *(to undertake)* acometer • **to p. through** *(a crowd)* abrirse paso a través de; *(to read)* leer con dificultad.

plow·share (:shâr′) s. reja del arado.

ploy (ploi) s. truco, estratagema.

pluck (plŭk) I. tr. *(to pick)* coger; *(eyebrows)* pelar; *(a chicken)* desplumar; *(to pull out)* arrancar; MÚS. pulsar, puntear ♦ **to p. up one's courage** armarse de valor II. s. tirón *m*; *(courage)* valor *m*, arrojo.

pluck·y (:ē) adj. **-i-** resuelto, valeroso.

plug (plŭg) I. s. tapón *m*; ELEC. enchufe *m*; *(spark plug)* bujía; *(fireplug)* boca de incendio; *(publicity)* propaganda, publicidad *f*; *(gunshot)* balazo II. tr. **-gg-** tapar; JER. *(to shoot)* pegar un tiro a; *(to publicize)* hacer propaganda de ♦ **to p. in** enchufar • **to p. up** tapar —intr. ♦ **to p. away** FAM. trabajar obstinadamente • **to p. away at** perseverar en • **to p. for** afanarse por.

plum (plŭm) I. s. *(tree)* ciruelo; *(fruit)* ciruela; *(color)* color *m* ciruela; FIG. breva, chollo II. adj. de color ciruela.

plum·age (plōō′mĭj′) s. plumaje *m*.

plumb (plŭm) I. s. plomada II. adj. *(vertical)* a plomo, vertical; *(utter)* completo III. adv. a plomo; *(utterly)* completamente IV. tr. MARÍT. sondar; CONSTR. aplomar.

plumb·er (:ər) s. plomero.

plumb·ing (:ĭng) s. *(pipes)* cañería, tubería; *(trade)* plomería.

plume (plōōm) I. s. pluma; *(on a helmet)* penacho; *(of smoke)* penacho II. tr. *(to adorn)* emplumar; *(to preen)* arreglarse las plumas.

plum·met (plŭm′ĭt) intr. *(object)* caer a plomo; *(plane)* caer en picado.

plump[1] (plŭmp) I. adj. rechoncho, regordete II. tr. engordar —intr. ponerse regordete.

plump[2] I. intr. caer *o* dejarse caer pesadamente —tr. dejar caer pesadamente II. s. *(fall)* caída pesada; *(sound)* ruido sordo III. adv. *(with an impact)* con un ruido sordo; *(straight down)* a plomo; *(directly)* rotundamente, sin rodeos.

plun·der (plŭn′dər) I. tr. saquear —intr. robar II. s. *(booty)* botín *m*; *(plundering)* saqueo.

plun·der·er (:ər) s. saqueador *m*.

plunge (plŭnj) I. tr. hundir —intr. hundirse; *(to dive)* zambullirse; *(into an activity)* meterse de cabeza *(into* en); *(to rush)* precipitarse; *(to* *descend)* bajar vertiginosamente; *(to take a chance)* jugarse el todo por el todo ♦ **to p. ahead** *o* **forward** precipitarse a II. s. *(dive)* zambullida; *(fall)* caída; *(in prices)* baja vertiginosa; *(swim)* chapuzón *m*, baño ♦ **to take a p.** bajar vertiginosamente • **to take the p.** dar el paso decisivo.

plung·er (plŭn′jər) s. *(piston)* émbolo; *(for pipes, drains)* desatascador *m*.

plunk (plŭngk) I. tr. MÚS. puntear ♦ **to p.** *o* **p. down** dejar caer pesadamente —intr. hacer un ruido sordo II. s. *(twang)* rasgueo, punteo; *(hollow sound)* ruido sordo.

plu·ral (plŏor′əl) adj. & s. plural *m*.

plu·ral·ism (:ə-lĭz′əm) s. pluralismo.

plu·ral·i·ty (plŏo-răl′ĭ-tē) s. pluralidad *f*; *(large part)* mayor parte *f*, mayoría.

plus (plŭs) I. prep. más; *(besides)* además de II. adj. positivo; *(extra)* adicional, extra; FAM. *(and more)* extraordinario III. s. [pl. **-(s)es**] ventaja IV. conj. y además.

plush (plŭsh) I. s. felpa II. adj. afelpado, de felpa; *(luxurious)* lujoso.

plu·toc·ra·cy (plŏo-tŏk′rə-sē) s. plutocracia.

plu·to·crat (′tə-krăt′) s. plutócrata *mf*.

plu·to·ni·um (plŏo-tō′nē-əm) s. plutonio.

plu·vi·al (plŏo′vē-əl) adj. pluvial.

ply[1] (plī) I. tr. *(to twist)* enrollar; *(to fold)* doblar II. s. *(of cloth)* capa; *(of wool)* cabo; *(of wood)* chapa; *(of paper)* pliego.

ply[2] tr. *(to wield)* manejar; *(to practice)* ejercer; *(to traverse)* hacer el trayecto de.

ply·wood (plī′wŏod′) s. madera terciada.

pneu·mat·ic (nŏo-măt′ĭk) adj. neumático ♦ **pneumatics** s.sg. neumática.

pneu·mo·nia (nŏo-mōn′yə) s. pulmonía.

poach[1] (pōch) tr. cocer a fuego lento, escalfar.

poach[2] intr. cazar *o* pescar en vedado.

poach·er (pō′chər) s. cazador *o* pescador furtivo.

pock (pŏk) I. s. pústula; *(pockmark)* cicatriz *f* de viruela II. tr. picar de viruelas.

pock·et (pŏk′ĭt) I. s. bolsillo; *(pouch)* bolsa pequeña; *(of a pool table)* tronera; *(area, group)* foco; *(of air)* bache *m*; *(of gas, oil)* bolsa; *(of ore)* filón *m* ♦ **p. edition** edición de bolsillo • **p. money** dinero para gastos personales • **to line one's pockets** forrarse de dinero II. adj. de bolsillo III. tr. meterse en el bolsillo; *(to steal)* robarse.

pock·et·book (:bŏok′) s. *(billfold)* billetera; *(purse)* cartera de mano, monedero; *(financial resources)* recursos; *(book)* libro de bolsillo.

pock·et·knife (:nīf′) s. [pl. **-ves**] navaja, cortaplumas *m*.

pock·et-size(d) (:sīz[d]′) adj. de bolsillo.

pock·mark (pŏk′märk′) I. s. cicatriz *f* de viruela II. tr. picar de viruelas.

pod (pŏd) s. vaina.

po·di·a·trist (pə-dī′ə-trĭst) s. podiatra *m*.

po·di·a·try (:trē) s. podiatría.

po·di·um (pō′dē-əm) s. [pl. **s** *o* **-ia**] podio.

po·em (pō′əm) s. poema *m*.

po·et (pō′ĭt) s. poeta *mf*.

po·et·ess (pō′ĭ-tĭs) s. poetisa.

po·et·ic (pō-ĕt′ĭk) adj. poético.

po·et·ry (pō′ĭ-trē) s. poesía.

poign·ance/an·cy (poin′yəns) s. patetismo.

poign·ant (:yənt) adj. *(painful)* agudo, intenso; *(sad)* patético; *(touching)* conmovedor.

poin·set·ti·a (poin-sĕt′ē-ə) s. flor *f* de Pascua.

point (point) I. s. punto; *(sharp tip)* punta;

(spot) lugar *m*; *(subject)* tema *m* <**stick to the p.** no te salgas del tema>; *(reason)* motivo, razón *f*; DEP. punto, tanto; FIN. entero; GEOG. punta; MAT. coma <**one p. five** uno coma cinco>; ELEC. contacto ♦ **at the p. of** a punto de • **at this p.** a estas alturas • **in p. of fact** en realidad • **p. of order** cuestión de orden • **that's just the p.!** ¡eso es! • **that's not the p.** eso no tiene nada que ver • **to come to the p.** ir al grano • **to make one's p.** salirse con la suya • **to make a p. of** poner empeño en • **to miss the p.** no comprender • **to reach the p. of no return** no poder volver atrás • **to stretch the p.** ir más allá del límite • **to the p.** pertinente • **what's the p.?** ¿para qué? II. tr. *(to aim)* apuntar; *(to show)* indicar; *(to sharpen)* sacar punta a, afilar; *(a dog)* parar; CONSTR. unir con mortero, rellenar ♦ **to p. out** señalar • **to p. up** poner de relieve —intr. apuntar; *(dogs)* pararse; *(ships)* navegar de bolina ♦ **to p. at** señalar (con el dedo) • **p. to** *(to show)* señalar; *(to suggest)* indicar que.

point-blank (′blăngk′) I. adj. directo; *(at a close range)* a quemarropa; *(blunt)* categórico II. adv. directamente, a quemarropa; *(without hesitation)* sin rodeos.

point·ed (poin′tĭd) adj. *(sharp)* puntiagudo, afilado; *(critical)* mordaz; *(intended)* intencional; *(conspicuous)* evidente, obvio.

point·er (:tər) s. indicador *m*; *(of a scale)* fiel *m*; *(of a watch)* manecilla; *(stick)* puntero; *(dog)* perro de muestra; *(tip)* consejo útil.

point·less (point′lĭs) adj. *(meaningless)* sin sentido; *(useless)* inútil.

point·y (poin′tē) adj. **-i-** puntiagudo.

poise (poiz) I. tr. poner en equilibrio —intr. estar en equilibrio II. s. equilibrio; *(composure)* aplomo, serenidad *f*; *(bearing)* porte *m*.

poi·son (poi′zən) I. s. veneno, ponzoña; *(insecticide)* insecticida ♦ **p. ivy** zumaque venenoso II. tr. envenenar; *(to pollute)* contaminar III. adj. venenoso, envenenado.

poi·son·ing (poi′zə-nĭng) s. envenenamiento.

poi·son·ous (:nəs) adj. venenoso.

poke (pōk) I. tr. *(to jab)* pinchar, aguijonear; *(with elbow)* dar codazo; *(with finger)* dar con la punta del dedo; *(to thrust)* meter ♦ **to p. a hole** hacer un hueco • **to p. out** *(to gouge)* sacar; *(to stick out)* sacar —intr. meterse ♦ **to p. along** caminar lentamente • **to p. around** *(to search)* hurgar; *(to look around)* curiosear • **to p. at** *(an animal)* pinchar, aguijonear; *(a fire)* atizar • **to p. out** asomar II. s. *(jab)* pinchazo; *(with elbow)* codazo; *(dawdler)* vago.

pok·er[1] (pō′kər) s. atizador *m*, hurgón *m*.

pok·er[2] s. póker *m*, póquer *m*.

po·key (pō′kē) s. JER. prisión *f*, cárcel *f*.

pok(e)·y (pō′kē) FAM. adj. **-i-** lerdo.

po·lar (pō′lər) adj. polar; *(opposite)* opuesto ♦ **p. bear** oso blanco.

po·lar·i·ty (pō-lăr′ĭ-tē) s. polaridad *f*.

po·lar·ize (pō′lə-rīz′) tr. polarizar.

pole[1] (pōl) s. *(axis)* polo ♦ **North, South P.** polo ártico, antártico.

pole[2] I. s. *(post)* poste *m*, palo II. tr. empujar con una pértiga.

pole·cat (:kăt′) s. zorrillo.

po·lem·ic (pə-lĕm′ĭk) I. s. polémica ♦ **polemics** s.sg. polémica II. adj. /**i·cal** polémico.

po·lem·i·cist (:ĭ-sĭst) s. polemista *mf*.

pole·star (pōl′stär′) s. estrella polar; FIG. principio orientador.

pole-vault (pōl′vôlt′) **I.** s. salto con garrocha **II.** intr. saltar con garrocha.

po·lice (pə-lēs′) **I.** s.inv. policía; MIL. limpieza ◆ **p. force** fuerza pública • **p. officer** agente de policía • **p. record** antecedentes penales • **p. state** estado policial • **p. station** jefatura de policía **II.** tr. *(to patrol)* patrullar; *(to keep in order)* mantener el orden en; MIL. limpiar.

po·lice·man (:mən) s. [pl. -men] policía *m.*

po·lice·wom·an (:wŏm′ən) s. [pl. -women] mujer *f* policía.

pol·i·cy¹ (pŏl′ĭ-sē) s. *(of a government)* política; *(of a business)* norma; *(course of action)* sistema *m*, táctica.

pol·i·cy² s. *(written contract)* póliza.

pol·i·cy·hold·er (:hōl′dər) s. asegurado.

po·li·o (pō′lē-ō′) s. polio *f*, poliomielitis *f*.

pol·ish (pŏl′ĭsh) **I.** tr. *(to wax)* encerar; *(to shine)* limpiar; *(metals)* bruñir; *(nails)* esmaltar, pintar; *(to refine)* pulir ◆ **to p. off** FAM. despachar —intr. pulirse **II.** s. *(shininess)* brillo, lustre *m*; *(wax)* cera; *(for metals)* líquido de bruñir; *(for nails)* esmalte *m; (act)* pulimento; *(manners)* refinamiento ◆ **shoe p.** betún.

pol·ished (:ĭsht) adj. pulido; *(shoes)* brilloso, lustroso; *(metals)* bruñido; *(refined)* refinado.

pol·ish·er (:ĭ-shər) s. pulidor *m.*

po·lite (pə-līt′) adj. **-er, -est** *(courteous)* cortés; *(refined)* educado, fino.

po·lite·ness (:nĭs) s. cortesía.

pol·i·tic (pŏl′ĭ-tĭk) adj. *(artful)* diplomático; *(clever)* astuto.

po·lit·i·cal (pə-lĭt′ĭ-kəl) adj. político.

po·lit·i·cian (pŏl′ĭ-tĭsh′ən) s. político.

po·lit·i·cize (pə-lĭt′ĭ-sīz′) tr. politizar.

pol·i·tick (pŏl′ĭ-tĭk′) intr. politiquear.

pol·i·ti·co (pə-lĭt′ĭ-kō′) s. politiquero.

pol·i·tics (pŏl′ĭ-tĭks) s.sg. política.

pol·ka (pōl′kə) **I.** s. polca ◆ **p. dots** lunares **II.** intr. bailar la polca.

poll (pōl) **I.** s. *(votes)* votación *f; (survey)* encuesta; *(head)* coronilla ◆ pl. urnas, centro electoral • **to go to the p.** ir a las urnas, votar **II.** tr. *(to get votes)* obtener, recibir; *(to register)* registrar los votos de; *(to question)* hacer una encuesta de; *(hair, horns)* cortar.

pol·len (pŏl′ən) s. polen *m.*

pol·li·nate (:ə-nāt′) tr. polinizar.

pol·li·na·tion (:′-nā′shən) s. polinización *f.*

poll·ing (pō′lĭng) s. votación *f.*

pol·li·wog (pŏl′ē-wŏg′) s. renacuajo.

poll·ster (pōl′stər) s. encuestador *m.*

pol·lut·ant (pə-lŏt′nt) s. agente *m* contaminador.

pol·lute (pə-lŏt′) tr. *(to corrupt)* corromper; *(to contaminate)* contaminar.

pol·lu·tion (pə-lŏ′shən) s. contaminación *f.*

po·lo (pō′lō) s. polo ◆ **p. shirt** polo.

pol·ter·geist (pōl′tər-gīst′) s. duende *m.*

pol·y·es·ter (pŏl′ē-ĕs′tər) s. poliéster *m.*

pol·y·eth·yl·ene (′-ĕth′ə-lēn′) s. polietileno.

po·lyg·a·mist (pə-lĭg′ə-mĭst) s. polígamo.

po·lyg·a·mous (:məs) adj. polígamo.

po·lyg·a·my (:mē) s. poligamia.

pol·y·gon (pŏl′ē-gŏn′) s. polígono.

pol·y·graph (:grăf′) s. polígrafo.

pol·y·mer (pŏl′ə-mər) s. polímero.

pol·y·no·mi·al (pŏl′ē-nō′mē-əl) **I.** adj. polinómico **II.** s. polinomio.

pol·yp (pŏl′ĭp) s. pólipo.

pol·y·tech·nic (pŏl′ē-tĕk′nĭk) **I.** adj. politécnico **II.** s. instituto politécnico.

pol·y·un·sat·u·rat·ed (:ŭn-săch′ə-rā′tĭd) adj. que contiene muchos enlaces no saturados.

pol·y·u·re·thane (:yŏŏr′ə-thān′) s. poliuretano.

po·made (pō-mād′) s. pomada.

po·man·der (pō′măn′dər) s. *(bag)* almohadilla perfumada; *(box)* cajita de perfumes.

pome·gran·ate (pŏm′grăn′ĭt) s. *(tree)* granado; *(fruit)* granada.

pom·mel (pŭm′əl, pŏm′-) **I.** s. *(of a weapon)* pomo; *(of a saddle)* perilla **II.** tr. aporrear.

pomp (pŏmp) s. pompa.

pom·pa·dour (pŏm′pə-dôr′) s. copete.

pom·pom/pon (pŏm′pŏm′/pŏn′) s. borla.

pom·pos·i·ty (pŏm-pŏs′ĭ-tē) s. pomposidad *f.*

pom·pous (pŏm′pəs) adj. pomposo; *(pretentious)* presumido; *(ceremonious)* ceremonioso.

pond (pŏnd) s. charca, estanque *m.*

pon·der (pŏn′dər) tr. examinar, sopesar —intr. meditar.

pon·der·ous (:əs) adj. voluminoso; *(heavy)* pesado; *(labored)* laborioso.

pon·tiff (pŏn′tĭf) s. pontífice *m.*

pon·tif·i·cal (-tĭf′ĭ-kəl) adj. & s. pontifical *m.*

pon·tif·i·cate **I.** s. (:kĭt) pontificado **II.** intr. (:kāt′) pontificar.

pon·toon (pŏn-tōōn′) s. pontón *m.*

po·ny (pō′nē) s. poney *m*, jaca.

po·ny·tail (:tāl′) s. cola de caballo.

pooch (pōōch) s. JER. perro.

poo·dle (pōōd′l) s. perro de lanas, caniche *m.*

pooh (pōō) interj. ¡bah!

pooh-pooh (pōō′pōō′) tr. FAM. desdeñar.

pool¹ (pōōl) s. *(small pond)* charca; *(puddle)* charco; *(for swimming)* piscina.

pool² **I.** s. *(betting fund)* banco, bolsa; *(team)* equipo; *(of vehicles)* parque *m* móvil; *(common fund)* fondos comunes; *(billiards)* billar americano **II.** tr. & intr. reunir(se), juntar(se).

poop¹ (pōōp) s. *(stern)* popa; *(deck)* toldilla.

poop² tr. dejar sin resuello ◆ **to be pooped** FAM. estar exhausto.

poop³ s. JER. información *f.*

poor (pōŏr) adj. pobre; *(mediocre)* malo, mediocre; *(scarce)* escaso; *(judgment)* escaso, poco ◆ **p. thing!** ¡pobrecito! • **to be in p. health** no estar bien de salud • **to be p. at** no ser bueno en.

poor·house (′hous′) s. casa de beneficencia, asilo para los pobres.

poor·ly (:lē) adv. pobremente ◆ **to be feeling p.** FAM. estar indispuesto.

pop¹ (pŏp) **I.** intr. **-pp-** estallar; *(cork)* saltar; *(eyes)* abrirse; *(firearm)* disparar ◆ **to p. in** entrar de sopetón • **to p. off** *(to leave)* salir disparado; *(to speak)* vociferar • **to p. out** *(cork, eyes)* saltar; *(to step out)* salir un momento; *(to spring)* salir de sopetón • **to p. up** *(to appear)* aparecer de repente; *(to come up)* surgir, suscitarse —tr. *(balloon)* hacer estallar; *(cork)* hacer saltar; *(corn)* hacer; *(to put)* meter; *(to hit)* pegar ◆ **to p. open** abrir haciendo sonar • **to p. out** asomar • **to p. the question** FAM. pedir la mano **II.** s. estallido; *(of a cork)* taponazo; *(of a firearm)* tiro, disparo; *(soda pop)* gaseosa **III.** adv. con un estallido; *(abruptly)* de súbito, de repente ◆ **to go p.** explotar.

pop² s. FAM. papi *m*, papá *m.*

pop³ adj. FAM. popular.

pop·corn (′kôrn′) s. rosetas de maíz.

pope o **Pope** (pōp) s. papa *m.*

pop·gun (pŏp′gŭn′) s. pistola de aire comprimido.

pop·in·jay (pŏp′ĭn-jā′) s. pedante *mf.*
pop·lar (pŏp′lər) s. álamo.
pop·lin (pŏp′lĭn) s. popelín *m*, popelina.
pop·pa (pä′pə) s. papá *m.*
pop·py (pŏp′ē) s. amapola.
pop·py·cock (pŏp′ē-kŏk′) s. tonterías.
pop·u·lace (pŏp′yə-lĭs) s. *(the masses)* populacho; *(population)* población *f.*
pop·u·lar (pŏp′yə-lər) adj. popular; *(election)* democrático; *(in vogue)* de moda; *(prevalent)* generalizado, común.
pop·u·lar·i·ty (′-lâr′ĭ-tē) s. popularidad *f.*
pop·u·lar·ize (′-lə-rīz′) tr. popularizar.
pop·u·late (:lāt′) tr. *(to people)* poblar; *(to inhabit)* habitar.
pop·u·la·tion (′-lā′shən) s. polación *f*; *(neighborhood)* vecindario.
pop·u·lism (′-lĭz′əm) s. populismo.
pop·u·list (:lĭst) s. & adj. populista *mf.*
pop·u·lous (:ləs) adj. populoso.
por·ce·lain (pôr′sə-lĭn) s. porcelana.
porch (pôrch) s. porche *m.*
por·cine (pôr′sīn′) adj. porcino.
por·cu·pine (pôr′kyə-pīn′) s. puercoespín *m.*
pore¹ (pôr) intr. ♦ **to p. over** examinar detenidamente; *(to ponder)* meditar sobre.
pore² s. ANAT. poro.
pork (pôrk) s. cerdo, carne *f* de cerdo.
por·no (pôr′nō) o **porn** (pôrn) s. JER. pornografía.
por·nog·ra·pher (pôr-nŏg′rə-fər) s. pornógrafo.
por·no·graph·ic (′nə-grăf′ĭk) adj. pornográfico.
por·nog·ra·phy (-nŏg′rə-fē) s. pornografía.
po·rous (pôr′əs) adj. poroso.
por·poise (pôr′pəs) s. [pl. inv. o **s**] marsopa.
por·ridge (pôr′ĭj) s. gachas de avena.
port¹ (pôrt) I. s. puerto ♦ **p. of call** puerto de escala II. adj. portuario.
port² (pôrt) s. MARÍT. babor *m* II. adj. a *o* de babor III. tr. girar a babor.
port³ s. *(porthole)* portilla; *(opening)* orificio.
port⁴ s. *(wine)* oporto.
por·ta·ble (pôr′tə-bəl) adj. & s. *(máquina)* portátil.
por·tage (:tĭj) I. s. porteo, transporte *m*; *(route)* ruta de porteo II. tr. transportar.
por·tal (pôr′tl) s. portal *m.*
por·tend (pôr-tĕnd′) tr. presagiar; *(to indicate)* indicar.
por·tent (pôr′tĕnt′) s. *(omen)* augurio; *(significance)* significado; *(prodigy)* portento.
por·ten·tous (-tĕn′təs) adj. *(foreboding)* de mal agüero; *(prodigious)* portentoso.
por·ter¹ (pôr′tər) s. mozo.
por·ter² s. G.B. *(doorman)* portero.
por·ter³ s. *(beer)* cerveza negra.
port·fo·li·o (pôrt-fō′lē-ō′) s. cartera; *(folder)* carpeta.
port·hole (pôrt′hōl′) s. portilla.
por·ti·co (pôr′tĭ-kō′) s. [pl. **(e)s**] pórtico.
por·tion (pôr′shən) I. s. *(part)* porción *f*, parte *f*; *(dowry)* dote *f*; *(fate)* suerte *f*, destino II. tr. dividir ♦ **to p. out** repartir, distribuir.
port·ly (pôrt′lē) adj. -**i**- *(stout)* corpulento.
por·trait (pôr′trĭt) s. retrato.
por·trai·ture (:trĭ-chŏr′) s. pintura de retratos.
por·tray (pôr-trā′) tr. *(to represent)* retratar; *(to depict)* describir; TEAT. representar.
por·tray·al (:əl) s. *(portrait)* retrato; *(description)* descripción *f*; TEAT. representación *f.*

pose (pōz) I. intr. posar; *(to affect an attitude)* asumir una pose ♦ **to p. as** hacerse pasar por —tr. posar, colocar; *(question)* plantear; *(threat)* representar II. s. pose *f.*
posh (pŏsh) adj. FAM. *(fashionable)* elegante; *(luxurious)* de lujo; *(exclusive)* selecto.
pos·it (pŏz′ĭt) tr. proponer, postular.
po·si·tion (pə-zĭsh′ən) I. s. posición *f*; *(place)* lugar *m*, sitio; *(post)* puesto; *(point of view)* postura, actitud *f*; *(status)* posición social; *(job)* puesto II. tr. colocar, poner ♦ **to p. oneself** ponerse en un lugar favorable.
pos·i·tive (pŏz′ĭ-tĭv) I. adj. positivo; *(emphatic)* tajante; *(express)* explícito, expreso; *(irrefutable)* categórico, rotundo; *(sure)* seguro, cierto II. s. positivo; ELEC. polo positivo; FOTOG. positiva.
pos·sess (pə-zĕs′) tr. poseer; *(to control)* dominar; *(to obsess)* obsesionar; *(to drive)* impulsar <*what possessed him to do it?* ¿qué lo impulsó a hacerlo?>.
pos·sessed (pə-zĕst′) adj. poseído, poseso; *(by an idea)* obsesionado; *(calm)* dueño de sí mismo ♦ **to be p. of** poseer, tener; *(to be blessed with)* estar dotado de.
pos·ses·sion (pə-zĕsh′ən) s. posesión *f*; *(holding)* tenencia; *(self-control)* dominio de sí mismo ♦ **in one's p.** en manos de uno • **to be in full p. of one's faculties** tener pleno dominio de sus facultades • **to be in p. of** poseer • **to come into p. of** adquirir • **to get** *o* **take p. of** apoderarse de ♦ pl. posesiones.
pos·ses·sive (pə-zĕs′ĭv) I. adj. posesivo; *(jealous)* celoso II. s. GRAM. posesivo.
pos·ses·sor (:ər) s. poseedor *m*, dueño.
pos·si·bil·i·ty (pŏs′ə-bĭl′ĭ-tē) s. posibilidad *f* ♦ **to have possibilities** ser prometedor • **within the realm of p.** dentro de lo posible.
pos·si·ble (pŏs′ə-bəl) adj. posible ♦ **as much as p.** todo lo posible • **as soon as p.** lo antes posible • **if p.** si es posible.
pos·sum (pŏs′əm) var. de **opossum**.
post¹ (pōst) I. s. *(pole)* poste *m*; *(stake)* palo, estaca; *(starting line)* línea de salida II. tr. *(to fasten up)* pegar, fijar; *(to announce)* anunciar.
post² I. s. MIL. *(base)* base *f*; *(position)* puesto; *(job)* puesto, cargo II. tr. *(a guard)* apostar; *(an officer)* enviar, destinar; *(bail)* dar.
post³ I. s. G.B. *(mail)* correo; *(delivery)* reparto; *(collection)* recogida ♦ **p. card** tarjeta postal • **p. office** (oficina de) correos II. intr. viajar de prisa —tr. *(to mail)* echar al correo; *(to inform)* poner al corriente ♦ **to keep someone posted** tener a alguien al corriente.
post·age (pō′stĭj) s. franqueo ♦ **p. stamp** sello (postal), estampilla.
post·al (pō′stəl) adj. & s. postal *f* ♦ **p. service** servicio de correos.
post·date (pōst-dāt′) tr. posfechar.
post·er (pō′stər) s. cartel *m*, afiche *m.*
pos·te·ri·or (pŏ-stîr′ē-ər) I. adj. posterior II. s. FAM. trasero.
pos·ter·i·ty (pŏ-stĕr′ĭ-tē) s. posteridad *f.*
post·grad·u·ate (pōst-grăj′ōō-ĭt) adj. & s. postgraduado.
post·haste (pōst′hāst′) adv. a toda prisa.
post·hu·mous (pŏs′chə-məs) adj. póstumo.
post·man (pōst′mən) s. [pl. -**men**] cartero.
post·mark (:märk′) I. s. matasellos II. tr. matasellar.
post·mas·ter (:măs′tər) s. administrador *m* de correos ♦ **p. general** director general de co-

rreos.

post·mis·tress (pōst′mĭs′trĭs) s. administradora de correos.

post·mor·tem (pōst-môr′təm) I. adj. postmórtem II. s. autopsia.

post·na·sal (:nā′zəl) adj. postnasal.

post·na·tal (:nāt′l) adj. postnatal.

post·op·er·a·tive (:ŏp′ər-ə-tĭv) adj. postoperatorio.

post·paid (pōst′pād′) adj. con franqueo pagado.

post·par·tum (pōst-pär′təm) adj. de después del parto.

post·pone (pōst-pōn′) tr. (to delay) posponer; (to put off) diferir, aplazar.

post·pone·ment (:mənt) s. aplazamiento.

post·script (pōst′skrĭpt′) s. posdata.

pos·tu·late (pŏs′chə-lāt′) I. tr. postular II. s. postulado.

pos·tu·la·tion (′-lā′shən) s. postulación f.

pos·ture (pŏs′chər) I. s. postura II. intr. posar, asumir una pose ♦ to p. as darse tono de.

post·war (pōst′wôr′) adj. de la postguerra.

po·sy (pō′zē) s. flor f; (bunch) ramillete m de flores.

pot (pŏt) I. s. (for cooking) cazuela, olla; (flowerpot) maceta, tiesto; (in cards) platillo, puesta; FAM. (common fund) fondo común; (potbelly) panza; (marijuana) yerba ♦ pots and pans batería de cocina • p. shot (shot) tiro al azar; (criticism) crítica ♦ to go to p. FAM. echarse a perder II. tr. -tt- plantar en una maceta.

po·ta·ble (pō′tə-bəl) adj. potable.

pot·ash (pŏt′ăsh′) s. potasa.

po·tas·si·um (pə-tăs′ē-əm) s. potasio.

po·ta·to (pə-tā′tō) s. [pl. es] patata, papa ♦ p. chips papas fritas.

pot·bel·ly (pŏt′bĕl′ē) s. panza, barriga; (stove) salamandra.

pot·boil·er (:boi′lər) s. obra artística de calidad mediocre hecha con fin de lucro.

po·ten·cy (pōt′n-sē) s. potencia.

po·tent (:nt) adj. potente.

po·ten·tate (:n-tāt′) s. potentado.

po·ten·tial (pə-tĕn′shəl) I. adj. potencial, posible II. s. posibilidad f; FÍS., GRAM., MAT. potencial m; ELEC. voltaje m.

pot·hold·er (pŏt′hōl′dər) s. agarrador m para utensilios calientes.

pot·hole (:hōl′) s. bache m.

po·tion (pō′shən) s. poción f.

pot·pour·ri (pō′pŏŏ-rē′) s. popurrí m; (sachet) pebete m.

pot·tage (pŏt′ĭj) s. sopa, potaje m.

pot·ted (pŏt′ĭd) adj. (plant) en maceta; JER. (drunk) borracho; (stoned) drogado.

pot·ter (pŏt′ər) s. alfarero ♦ p.'s field fosa común • p.'s wheel rueda o torno de alfarero.

pot·ter·y (:ə-rē) s. alfarería.

pot·ty¹ (pŏt′ē) G.B. adj. -i- (trivial) trivial; (intoxicated) levemente borracho; (silly) chiflado.

pot·ty² s. FAM. orinal m para niños.

pouch (pouch) s. bolsa pequeña, valija; (for game) morral m; (for ammunition) cartuchera; (for tobacco) petaca; ZOOL. bolsa.

poul·tice (pōl′tĭs) s. cataplasma.

poul·try (pōl′trē) s. aves f de corral

pounce (pouns) I. intr. (to spring) saltar sobre; (to attack) abalanzarse sobre —tr. ♦ to p. on (to attack) saltar sobre; (an opportunity) no perder II. s. ataque repentino; (jump) salto repentino.

pound¹ (pound) s. [pl. inv o s] FIN., FÍS. libra.

pound² I. tr. golpear; (to grind) moler; (to crush) machacar; FIG. inculcar —intr. dar golpes; (to move heavily) andar con paso pesado; (the heart) palpitar, latir violentamente; (waves) batir II. s. golpe m; (sound) ruido de golpes.

pound³ s. (for dogs) perrera; (for cats, property) depósito.

pound·age (poun′dĭj) s. peso.

pour (pôr) tr. echar; (to serve) servir; (to spill) verter, derramar ♦ to p. out (a liquid) verter, echar; (feelings) dar rienda suelta a • to p. one's heart out to someone abrirse a alguien —intr. (to flow) manar, correr; (to gush) salir a chorros; (to rain) llover a cántaros; (to serve) servir bebidas ♦ to p. in (people) entrar en tropel; (letters) llegar en abundancia • to p. out (liquid) salir a chorros; (people) salir en tropel.

pout (pout) intr. hacer pucheros; (to sulk) poner mala cara.

pov·er·ty (pŏv′ər-tē) s. pobreza; (deficiency) carencia, escasez f.

pov·er·ty-strick·en (:strĭk′ən) adj. indigente, muy pobre.

pow·der (pou′dər) I. s. polvo; (cosmetic, medicinal) polvos; (gunpowder) pólvora; (snow) nieve seca ♦ p. keg (cask) tonel, cuñete de pólvora; (situation) polvorín • p. puff mota, borla • p. room tocador, servicios II. tr. hacer polvo, pulverizar; (to sprinkle) espolvorear ♦ to p. one's face ponerse polvos.

pow·er (pou′ər) I. s. poder m; (capacity) capacidad f; (strength) fuerza; (person) fuerza, influencia; (nation) potencia; (energy) energía; (electricity) electricidad f, corriente f; FIG., ÓPT. potencia ♦ p. brake servofreno • p. drill taladro eléctrico • p. line línea de transmisión eléctrica • p. of attorney poder (legal) • p. steering servodirección • p. tool herramienta eléctrica • the powers that be las autoridades • to come to p. subir al poder ♦ pl. poder, capacidad II. tr. TEC. suministrar energía a ♦ to be powered by funcionar con.

pow·er·boat (:bōt′) s. bote m a motor.

pow·er·ful (:fəl) adj. poderoso; (potent) potente; (strong) fuerte; (convincing) convincente.

pow·er·house (:hous′) s. central f de energía eléctrica f; (person) persona de mucha energía.

pow·er·less (:lĭs) adj. impotente; (helpless) indefenso; (ineffectual) inútil; (lacking authority) sin autoridad.

pox (pŏks) s. (smallpox) viruela; (chicken pox) varicela; (syphilis) sífilis f.

prac·ti·cal (prăk′tĭ-kəl) adj. práctico ♦ for all p. purposes prácticamente, a fin de cuentas • p. joke broma pesada.

prac·ti·cal·i·ty (′-kăl′ĭ-tē) s. carácter práctico.

prac·ti·cal·ly (prăk′tĭk-lē) adv. de modo práctico; (almost) prácticamente, casi.

prac·tice (prăk′tĭs) I. tr. practicar; (to train in) ejercitarse o entrenarse en; (to use) ejercer, proceder con; (a profession) ejercer ♦ to p. what one preaches actuar según la doctrina de uno —intr. hacer prácticas; (to train) ejercitarse, entrenarse; (a professional) ejercer II. s. práctica; (training) ejercicios; (custom) costumbre f; (of a profession) ejercicio; (of a doctor) clientela; (of a lawyer) bufete m • to be out of p. no estar en forma • to make a p. of tener por costumbre • **to set up a p.** *(as a doctor)* poner un consultorio; *(as a lawyer)* poner un bufete ♦ pl. procedimientos.

prac·ticed (:tĭst) adj. experimentado, experto.

prac·tic·ing (:tĭ-sĭng) adj. *(professional)* que ejerce; RELIG. practicante, devoto.

prac·ti·tion·er (-tĭsh'ə-nər) s. profesional *mf* ♦ **general p.** médico general.

prag·mat·ic/i·cal (prăg-măt'ĭk) adj. pragmático.

prag·ma·tism ('mə-tĭz'əm) s. pragmatismo.

prag·ma·tist (:tĭst) s. pragmatista *mf.*

prai·rie (prâr'ē) s. llanura, planicie *f* ♦ **p. dog** marmota de las praderas.

praise (prāz) I. s. alabanza ♦ **to sing the praises of** cantar las alabanzas de II. tr. alabar ♦ **to p. to the skies** poner por las nubes.

praise·wor·thy (:wûr'thē) adj. elogiable.

pram (prăm) s. G.B. cochecito de niño.

prance (prăns) intr. EQUIT. cabriolar; FIG. pavonearse.

prank (prăngk) s. jugarreta, travesura; *(joke)* broma.

prank·ster (:stər) s. bromista *mf.*

prate (prāt) I. intr. parlotear II. s. parloteo.

prat·tle (prăt'l) I. intr. parlotear II. s. parloteo.

prawn (prôn) s. camarón *m*, gamba.

pray (prā) intr. rezar, orar; *(to plead)* rogar, suplicar —tr. rogar ♦ **praying mantis** mantis religiosa.

prayer (prâr) s. oración *f*; *(request)* ruego.

preach (prēch) tr. predicar; *(to exhort)* exhortar; *(to deliver)* pronunciar —intr. predicar ♦ **to p.** at sermonear a.

preach·er (prē'chər) s. RELIG. pastor *m*; *(one who preaches)* predicador *m.*

pre·ad·o·les·cence (prē'ăd'l-ĕs'əns) s. preadolescencia.

pre·am·ble (prē'ăm'bəl) s. preámbulo.

pre·ar·range (prē'ə-rānj') tr. preparar de antemano.

pre·as·signed (:ə-sīnd') adj. asignado de antemano.

pre·car·i·ous (prĭ-kâr'ē-əs) adj. precario.

pre·cau·tion (prĭ-kô'shən) s. precaución *f.*

pre·cau·tion·ar·y (:shə-nĕr'ē) adj. preventivo.

pre·cau·tious (:shəs) adj. precavido.

pre·cede (prĭ-sēd') tr. & intr. preceder.

prec·e·dence (prĕs'ĭ-dns, prĭ-sēd'ns) s. precedencia; *(priority)* prioridad *f* ♦ **to take p. over** tener prioridad sobre.

prec·e·dent (prĕs'ĭ-dnt) adj & s. precedente.

pre·ced·ing (prĭ-sē'dĭng) adj. *(antecedent)* precedente; *(previous)* previo.

pre·cept (prē'sĕpt') s. precepto.

pre·cep·tor (prĭ-sĕp'tər) s. preceptor *m.*

pre·ces·sion (prē-sĕsh'ən) s. precedencia.

pre·cinct (prē'sĭngkt') s. *(police district)* zona de patrulla; *(police station)* jefatura de policía, comisaría; *(election district)* distrito electoral; *(area)* recinto ♦ pl. *(area)* recinto; *(boundary)* limites; FIG. campo, esfera.

pre·cious (prĕsh'əs) I. adj. precioso; *(cherished)* valioso, preciado; *(beloved)* querido II. adv. muy.

prec·i·pice (prĕs'ə-pĭs) s. precipicio.

pre·cip·i·tant (prĭ-sĭp'ĭ-tnt) I. adj. precipitado; *(sudden)* repentino II. s. QUÍM. precipitado.

pre·cip·i·tate (prĭ-sĭp'ĭ-tāt') I. tr. *(to bring on)* provocar; *(to hurl)* precipitar; QUÍM. precipitar —intr. METEOR. condensarse; *(to fall)* precipitarse II. adj. (:tĭt) precipitado III. s. (:tāt',

:tĭt) QUÍM. precipitado.

pre·cip·i·ta·tion (-'-tā'shən) s. precipitación *f.*

pre·cip·i·tous (-'-təs) adj. *(steep)* escarpado; *(hasty)* precipitado.

pré·cis (prā-sē') s.inv. resumen *m.*

pre·cise (prĭ-sīs') adj. preciso.

pre·ci·sion (:sĭzh'ən) s. precisión *f.*

pre·clude (prĭ-klōōd') tr. *(to exclude)* excluir; *(to avoid)* evitar; *(to prevent)* prevenir.

pre·clu·sion (:klōō'zhən) s. *(exclusion)* exclusión *f*; *(prevention)* prevención *f.*

pre·co·cious (prĭ-kō'shəs) adj. precoz.

pre·coc·i·ty (:kŏs'ĭ-tē) s. precocidad *f.*

pre·cog·ni·tion (prē'kŏg-nĭsh'ən) s. precognición *f.*

pre·Co·lum·bi·an (:kə-lŭm'bē-ən) adj. precolombino.

pre·con·ceive (:kən-sēv') tr. preconcebir.

pre·con·cep·tion (:kən-sĕp'shən) s. preconcepción *f*; *(prejudice)* prejuicio.

pre·con·di·tion (:kən-dĭsh'ən) s. condición previa; *(requisite)* requisito previo.

pre·cook (-kōōk') tr. precocer.

pre·cur·sor (prĭ-kûr'sər) s. precursor *m.*

pre·cur·so·ry (:sə-rē) adj. precursor.

pre·date (prē-dāt') tr. preceder; *(to give prior date to)* poner una fecha anterior a.

pred·a·tor (prĕd'ə-tər) s. predator *m.*

pred·a·to·ry (:tôr'ē) adj. *(predacious)* de rapiña; *(plundering)* depradador.

pre·de·cease (prē'dĭ-sēs') tr. morir antes que.

pred·e·ces·sor (prĕd'ĭ-sĕs'ər) s. predecesor *m*; *(ancestor)* antepasado.

pre·des·ti·na·tion (prē-dĕs'tə-nā'shən) s. *(act, condition)* predestinación *f*; *(destiny)* destino.

pre·des·tine (-'tĭn) tr. predestinar.

pre·de·ter·mine (prē'dĭ-tûr'mĭn) tr. predeterminar.

pre·dic·a·ment (prĭ-dĭk'ə-mənt) s. apuro.

pred·i·cate (prĕd'ĭ-kāt') I. tr. fundar, basar; *(to affirm)* afirmar II. s. (:kĭt) GRAM. predicado III. adj. (:kĭt) GRAM. predicativo.

pred·i·ca·tion (-'kā'shən) s. afirmación *f.*

pre·dict (prĭ-dĭkt') tr. predecir; *(to forecast)* pronosticar.

pre·dict·a·bil·i·ty (-dĭk'tə-bĭl'ĭ-tē) s. carácter *m* previsible

pre·dict·a·ble (-'-bəl) adj. previsible; *(behavior)* invariable, constante.

pre·dic·tion (prĭ-dĭk'shən) s. predicción *f*; *(forecast)* pronóstico.

pre·dic·tor (:tər) s. pronosticador *m.*

pred·i·lec·tion (prĕd'l-ĕk'shən, prēd'-) s. predilección *f.*

pre·dis·pose (prē'dĭ-spōz') tr. predisponer.

pre·dis·po·si·tion (:dĭs'pə-zĭsh'ən) s. predisposición *f*; *(tendency)* tendencia.

pre·dom·i·nance (prĭ-dŏm'ə-nəns) s. predominio; *(preponderance)* preponderancia.

pre·dom·i·nant (:nənt) adj. predominante.

pre·dom·i·nate (:nāt') intr. predominar; *(to prevail)* prevalecer —tr. predominar sobre; *(to prevail over)* prevalecer.

pre·em·i·nence *o* **pre·em·i·nence** (prē-ĕm'ə-nəns) s. preeminencia.

pre·em·i·nent *o* **pre·em·i·nent** (:nənt) adj. preeminente.

pre·empt *o* **pre·empt** (prē-ĕmpt') tr. *(to displace)* supeditar; *(to appropriate)* apropiarse de; TELEV. substituir.

pre·emp·tive *o* **pre·emp·tive** (:ĕmp'tĭv) adj. MIL. preventivo.

preen (prēn) tr. arreglar, limpiar ♦ **to p. one-self** pavonearse —intr. pavonearse.

pre·ex·ist o **pre·ex·ist** (prē´ĭg-zĭst´) tr. existir antes que —intr. preexistir.

pre·fab·ri·cate (-făb´rĭ-kāt´) tr. prefabricar.

pref·ace (prĕf´ĭs) I. s. prefacio, prólogo II. tr. prologar; *(remarks)* servir de prólogo a.

pref·a·to·ry (prĕf´ə-tôr´ē) adj. introductorio.

pre·fect (prē´fĕkt´) s. prefecto.

pre·fer (prĭ-fûr´) tr. **-rr-** preferir.

pref·er·a·ble (prĕf´ər-ə-bəl) adj. preferible.

pref·er·ence (:əns) s. preferencia ♦ **to have no p.** serle igual.

pref·er·en·tial (prĕf´ə-rĕn´shəl) adj. preferente.

pre·fer·ment (prĭ-fûr´mənt) s. *(advancement)* adelanto; *(promotion)* ascenso.

pre·fig·ure (prē-fĭg´yər) tr. prefigurar; *(to imagine)* figurarse de antemano.

pre·fix (prē´fĭks´) I. tr. anteponer II. s. prefijo.

preg·na·ble (prĕg´nə-bəl) adj. MIL. expugnable.

preg·nan·cy (prĕg´nən-sē) s. embarazo.

preg·nant (:nənt) adj. encinta, embarazada; *(animal)* preñada; *(meaningful)* significativo.

pre·heat (prē-hēt´) tr. precalentar.

pre·hen·sile (prē-hĕn´səl, :sīl´) adj. prensil.

pre·his·tor·ic/i·cal (prē´hĭ-stôr´ĭk) adj. prehistórico.

pre·judge (prē-jŭj´) tr. prejuzgar.

prej·u·dice (prĕj´ə-dĭs) I. s. prejuicio II. tr. crear prejuicios a; *(to injure)* perjudicar.

prej·u·di·cial (´-dĭsh´əl) adj. perjudicial.

prej·u·di·cious (:əs) adj. perjudicial.

prel·ate (prĕl´ĭt) s. prelado.

pre·lim·i·nar·y (prĭ-lĭm´ə-nĕr´ē) adj. & s. preliminar *m.*

prel·ude (prĕl´yōōd´, prā´lōōd´) s. preludio.

pre·mar·i·tal (prē-măr´ĭ-tl) adj. premarital.

pre·ma·ture (prē´mə-chŏŏr´) adj. prematuro.

pre·med (prē-mĕd´) FAM. I. adj. preparatorio para el ingreso a la facultad de medicina II. s. estudiante *mf* que se prepara para el ingreso a la facultad de medicina.

pre·med·i·tate (prē-mĕd´ĭ-tāt´) tr. premeditar.

pre·med·i·tat·ed (:tā´tĭd) adj. premeditado.

pre·med·i·ta·tion (´-´-shən) s. premeditación *f.*

pre·men·stru·al (prē-mĕn´strōō-əl) adj. premenstrual.

pre·mier (prē´mē-ər, prĭ-mîr´) I. adj. *(first)* primero; *(chief)* principal II. s. primer ministro; *(Canadian)* presidente *m.*

pre·mière (prĭ-mîr´, prĭm-yâr´) I. s. estreno II. tr. & intr. estrenar III. adj. primero.

prem·ise (prĕm´ĭs) I. s. premisa ♦ pl. *(site)* local; *(building)* edificio II. tr. sentar como premisa —intr. formular una premisa.

pre·mi·um (prē´mē-əm) s. *(prize)* premio, recompensa; *(fee)* prima; *(installment)* prima (de un seguro) ♦ **to be at a p.** *(to cost more)* costar más; *(in demand)* tener mucha demanda • **to put a p. on** valorar mucho.

pre·mo·ni·tion (prē´mə-nĭsh´ən, prĕm´ə-) s. premonición *f.*

pre·na·tal (prē-nāt´l) adj. prenatal.

pre·oc·cu·pa·tion (prē-ŏk´yə-pā´shən) s. preocupación *f.*

pre·oc·cu·pied (´-pīd´) adj. preocupado; *(absorbed)* absorto.

pre·oc·cu·py (:pī´) tr. preocupar; *(to engross)* absorber.

pre·or·dain (prē´ôr-dān´) tr. preordinar.

prep (prĕp) FAM. I. adj. preparatorio ♦ **p. school** escuela secundaria privada II. tr. &

intr. preparar(se).

pre·pack·age (prē-păk´ĭj) tr. preempaquetar.

pre·paid (:pād´) I. cf. **prepay** II. adj. pagado por adelantado; *(letter)* franqueado.

prep·a·ra·tion (prĕp´ə-rā´shən) s. preparación *f; (medicine)* preparado ♦ pl. preparativos.

pre·par·a·to·ry (prĭ-păr´ə-tôr´ē) adj. preparatorio.

pre·pare (prĭ-pâr´) tr. & intr. preparar(se) ♦ **to be prepared for** estar preparado para • **to be prepared to** estar dispuesto a.

pre·par·ed·ness (:ĭd-nĭs) s. estado de preparación.

pre·pay (prē-pā´) tr. **-paid** pagar por adelantado.

pre·pay·ment (:mənt) s. pago adelantado.

pre·pon·der·ance (prĭ-pŏn´dər-əns) s. preponderancia.

pre·pon·der·ant (:ənt) adj. preponderante.

prep·o·si·tion (prĕp´ə-zĭsh´ən) s. preposición *f.*

pre·pos·sess (prē´pə-zĕs´) tr. *(to influence)* predisponer (a favor); *(to impress)* impresionar (favorablemente).

pre·pos·sess·ing (:ĭng) adj. agradable.

pre·pos·ter·ous (prĭ-pŏs´tər-əs) adj. absurdo.

prep·pie/py (prĕp´ē) s. FAM. alumno de una escuela preparatoria.

pre·pu·bes·cence (prē´pyōō-bĕs´əns) s. prepubescencia.

pre·puce (prē´pyōōs´) s. prepucio.

pre·req·ui·site (prē-rĕk´wĭ-zĭt) I. s. condición previa II. adj. requerido de antemano.

pre·rog·a·tive (prĭ-rŏg´ə-tĭv) s. prerrogativa.

pres·age (prĕs´ĭj) I. s. presagio II. tr. presagiar.

pre·school (prē´skōōl´) I. adj. preescolar II. s. jardín *m* de infantes.

pre·science (prē´shəns, prĕsh´əns) s. presciencia.

pre·scient (:shənt) adj. presciente.

pre·scribe (prĭ-skrīb´) tr. prescribir; MED. *(a drug)* recetar; *(treatment)* mandar —intr. establecer, dictar; MED. hacer recetas.

pre·scrip·tion (:skrĭp´shən) s. prescripción *f;* MED. receta; *(medicine)* remedio.

pre·scrip·tive (:tĭv) adj. establecido, *(establishing rules)* preceptivo.

pres·ence (prĕz´əns) s. presencia; *(bearing)* porte *m,* talle *m; (confidence)* seguridad *f* ♦ **p. of mind** presencia de ánimo.

pres·ent[1] (prĕz´ənt) I. s. presente *m* ♦ **for the p.** por ahora II. adj. presente; *(month)* corriente; *(year)* en curso ♦ **at the p. time** en este momento • **to be p.** asistir • **to be p. at** *(to be)* haber en; *(to witness)* presenciar.

pre·sent[2] I. tr. (prĭ-zĕnt´) presentar; *(to give)* regalar, obsequiar; *(a case)* exponer; *(a problem)* plantear; *(an invoice)* pasar; *(arms)* presentar; *(charges)* formular II. s. (prĕz´ənt) presente *m,* regalo.

pre·sent·a·ble (prĭ-zĕn´tə-bəl) adj. presentable.

pres·en·ta·tion (prĕz´ən-tā´shən) s. presentación *f; (of a play)* representación *f; (of a case, argument)* exposición *f.*

pres·ent-day (prĕz´ənt-dā´) adj. actual.

pre·sen·ti·ment (prĭ-zĕn´tə-mənt) s. presentimiento.

pres·ent·ly (prĕz´ənt-lē) adv. *(soon)* dentro de poco; *(now)* actualmente.

pres·er·va·tion (prĕz´ər-vā´shən) s. preservación *f; (of customs, food)* conservación *f.*

pre·ser·va·tive (prĭ-zûr'və-tĭv) I. adj. preservativo II. s. conservante *m*, preservador *m*.
pre·serve (prĭ-zûrv') I. tr. preservar; *(to maintain)* conservar; *(food)* conservar; *(game)* proteger II. s. coto, vedado; FIG. terreno ◆ pl. confitura.
pre·serv·er (:zûr'vər) s. preservador *m*.
pre·side (prĭ-zīd') intr. presidir.
pres·i·den·cy (prĕz'ĭ-dən-sē) s. presidencia.
pres·i·dent (:dənt) s. presidente *m*.
pres·i·dent-e·lect ('-ĭ-lĕkt') s. presidente electo.
pres·i·den·tial (prĕz'ĭ-dĕn'shəl) adj. presidencial.
pre·sid·i·um (prĭ-sĭd'ē-əm) s. [pl. **s** o **-ia**] presidium *m*.
pre·sort (prē-sôrt') tr. clasificar en zonas postales antes de llevarlas al correo.
press (prĕs) I. tr. *(to bear down on)* apretar; *(to squeeze)* prensar; *(to compress)* comprimir; *(to iron)* planchar; *(to entreat)* instar; *(to harass)* hostigar, acosar; *(to hurry)* apremiar; *(to insist on)* insistir en ◆ **to be pressed for** estar con apuros de • **to p. one's luck** forzar la suerte —intr. apretar, ejercer presión; *(to trouble)* pesar, abrumar; *(to be urgent)* apremiar; *(to crowd)* apiñarse ◆ **to p. ahead** o **forward** avanzar con determinación • **to p. for** pedir con insistencia • **to p. on** seguir adelante II. s. prensa; *(for printing)* imprenta; *(journalists)* prensa; *(urgency)* urgencia.
press·ing ('ĭng) adj. urgente.
press·room (:rōōm') s. taller *m* de imprenta.
press·run (:rŭn') s. tirada.
pres·sure (prĕsh'ər) I. s. presión *f*; *(compression)* compresión *f* ◆ **blood p.** presión arterial • **p. cooker** *(pot)* olla de presión; FIG. situación en atmósfera de apremio y urgencia • **to bring p. to bear on** o **to put p. on** ejercer presión sobre II. tr. ejercer presión sobre.
pres·sur·ize (:ə-rīz') tr. presurizar.
pres·ti·dig·i·ta·tion (prĕs'tĭ-dĭj'ĭ-tā'shən) s. prestidigitación *f*.
pres·tige (prē-stēzh', -stēj') s. prestigio.
pres·ti·gious (prē-stē'jəs, -stĭj'əs) adj. prestigioso.
pre·sum·a·ble (prĭ-zōō'mə-bəl) adj. presumible.
pre·sume (prĭ-zōōm') tr. suponer; *(to dare)* tener el atrevimiento de; *(to pretend)* pretender, creerse —intr. presumir ◆ **to p. on** abusar de.
pre·sum·ing (-zōō'mĭng) adj. presumido.
pre·sump·tion (:zŭmp'shən) s. presunción *f*, suposición *f*; *(effrontery)* osadía.
pre·sump·tive (:tĭv) adj. presuntivo; *(presumed)* presunto.
pre·sump·tu·ous (:chōō-əs) adj. presuntuoso; *(rash)* atrevido, osado.
pre·sup·pose (prē'sə-pōz') tr. presuponer.
pre·tend (prĭ-tĕnd') tr. *(to feign)* fingir; *(illness, deafness)* hacerse; *(to oneself)* imaginarse; *(to claim)* pretender —intr. *(to feign)* fingir; *(to dissemble)* disimular ◆ **to p. to the throne** pretender al trono.
pre·tend·er (:tĕn'dər) s. fingidor *m*; *(claimant)* pretendiente *mf*.
pre·tense (prē-tĕns', prĭ-tĕns') s. fingimiento; *(pretext)* pretexto; *(claim)* pretensión *f*; *(affectation)* ostentación *f*; *(pretentiousness)* presunción *f* ◆ **to make no p.** to no pretender • **under false pretenses** por fraude • **under the p. of** con el pretexto de.

pre·ten·tious (prĭ-tĕn'shəs) adj. pretencioso.
pre·ter·nat·u·ral (prē'tər-năch'ər-əl) adj. preternatural; *(supernatural)* sobrenatural.
pre·test (prē'tĕst') s. prueba preliminar.
pre·text (prē'tĕkst') s. pretexto.
pret·ty (prĭt'ē) I. adj. **-i-** lindo; FAM. considerable ◆ **a p. penny** mucho dinero II. adv. bastante ◆ **p. much** más o menos • **to be sitting p.** FAM. tener una buena posición.
pre·vail (prĭ-vāl') intr. prevalecer; *(to win)* triunfar; *(to predominate)* predominar ◆ **to p. on** o **upon** convencer a.
pre·vail·ing (:vā'lĭng) adj. prevaleciente; *(predominant)* predominante; *(current)* corriente; *(widespread)* común.
prev·a·lence (prĕv'ə-ləns) s. predominio.
prev·a·lent (:lənt) adj. común; *(general)* generalizado.
pre·var·i·cate (prĭ-văr'ĭ-kāt') intr. *(to twist)* tergiversar; *(to lie)* mentir.
pre·vent (prĭ-vĕnt') tr. *(to avoid)* evitar; *(to impede)* impedir.
pre·vent·a·ble (:vĕn'tə-bəl) adj. evitable.
pre·ven·ta·tive (:tĭv) var. de **preventive**.
pre·ven·tion (prĭ-vĕn'shən) s. prevención *f*.
pre·ven·tive (:tĭv) adj. preventivo.
pre·view (prē'vyōō') I. s. exhibición *f* preliminar; CINEM. avance *m* II. tr. *(to view)* ver antes que otros; *(to show)* exhibir previamente.
pre·vi·ous (prē'vē-əs) adj. previo ◆ **p. to** antes de.
prey (prā) I. s. presa; FIG. víctima II. tr. ◆ **to p. on** *(to hunt)* cazar; *(to victimize)* hacer víctima de; *(to weigh)* abrumar.
price (prīs) I. s. precio; FIN. cotización *f* ◆ **full p.** precio sin descuento • **list p.** precio de lista • **opening p.** cotización inicial • **p. tag** *(tag)* etiqueta de precio; *(cost)* costo • **to pay a high** o **heavy p.** pagar caro II. tr. *(to establish)* poner precio a; *(to find out)* averiguar el precio de.
price·less ('lĭs) adj. sin precio, de gran valor; *(amusing)* muy divertido.
prick (prĭk) I. s. pinchazo; *(of an insect)* picadura; *(of jealousy, curiosity)* punzada, aguijón *m*; *(pointed object)* aguijón, pincho II. tr. pinchar; *(conscience)* remorder; *(jealousy, curiosity)* picar ◆ **to p. up one's ears** *(a dog)* erguir las orejas; FIG. aguzar el oído —intr. *(to hurt)* picar; *(ears)* erguirse.
prick·er ('ər) s. punzón *m*, púa.
prick·le (:əl) I. s. *(thorn)* espina; *(spine)* pincho; *(sensation)* picazón *f* II. tr. *(to prick)* pinchar; *(to tingle)* picar —intr. sentir picazón.
prick·ly (:lē) adj. **-i-** *(with prickles)* espinoso; *(stinging)* que causa picazón; *(vexatious)* erizado; *(irritable)* quisquilloso ◆ **p. heat** salpullido causado por el calor.
pride (prīd) I. s. orgullo; *(self-respect)* amor propio; *(best)* flor *f*; *(of cats)* manada de leones ◆ **to take p. in** estar orgulloso de II. tr. ◆ **to p. oneself on** estar orgulloso de.
priest (prēst) s. sacerdote *m*, cura *m*; *(minister)* presbítero, pastor *m*.
priest·ess (prē'stĭs) s. sacerdotisa.
priest·hood (prēst'hŏŏd') s. sacerdocio; *(clergy)* clerecía, clero.
prig (prĭg) s. mojigato.
prim (prĭm) adj. **-mm-** estirado, remilgado.
pri·ma·cy (prī'mə-sē) s. primacía.
pri·mal (:məl) adj. original; *(fundamental)* fundamental; *(primary)* primario.

pri·mar·i·ly (prī-mâr′ə-lē) adv. principalmente.
pri·mar·y (prī′mĕr′ē, :mə-rē) **I.** adj. primario; *(primitive)* primitivo; *(foremost)* fundamental **II.** s. *(in order)* lo primero; *(in importance)* lo principal; *(election)* elección primaria.
pri·mate (prī′māt′) s. RELIG. primado; ZOOL. primate *m*.
prime (prīm) **I.** adj. primero; *(main)* fundamental; *(choice)* de primera (calidad); MAT. primo ♦ **of p. importance** de la mayor importancia **II.** s. *(dawn)* alba; *(spring)* primavera; *(age)* flor *f* de la vida, plenitud *f*; *(pick)* flor y nata, lo mejor; MAT. número primo ♦ **p. meridian** primer meridiano ♦ **p. minister** primer ministro ♦ **p. mover** fuerza motriz ♦ **p. rate** tasa preferida **III.** tr. preparar; *(gun, motor)* cebar, cargar; *(walls)* dar una primera mano de pintura a ♦ **to p. the pump** FAM. estimular.
prim·er (prĭm′ər) s. texto elemental; *(manual)* manual *m*.
prim·er² (prī′mər) s. cebador *m*; *(detonator)* detonador *m*; PINT. primera mano.
pri·me·val (prī-mē′vəl) adj. primordial.
prim·i·tive (prĭm′ĭ-tĭv) adj. & s. primitivo.
pri·mo·gen·i·tor (prī′mō-jĕn′ĭ-tər) s. primogenitor *m*.
pri·mo·gen·i·ture (:chŏr′) s. primogenitura.
pri·mor·di·al (prī-môr′dē-əl) adj. primordial.
primp (prĭmp) tr. & intr. emperejilar(se).
prim·rose (prĭm′rōz′) s. primavera, prímula.
prince (prĭns) s. príncipe *m* ♦ **crown p.** príncipe heredero ♦ **p. charming** el príncipe azul.
prin·cess (prĭn′sĭs) s. princesa.
prin·ci·pal (prĭn′sə-pəl) **I.** adj. principal **II.** s. *(of a school)* director *m*; *(performer)* primera figura; COM., FIN. principal *m*.
prin·ci·pal·i·ty (prĭn′sə-păl′ĭ-tē) s. principado.
prin·ci·ple (prĭn′sə-pəl) s. principio ♦ **a matter of p.** una cuestión de principios ♦ **in p.** en principio ♦ **on p.** por principio.
prin·ci·pled (:pəld) adj. de principios.
print (prĭnt) **I.** s. *(impression)* impresión *f*, huella; *(stamp, seal)* estampa, cuño; *(letters)* letra, tipo; FOTOG. copia; *(engraving)* grabado, estampa; *(fabric)* estampado ♦ **in p.** impreso, publicado ♦ **out of p.** agotado **II.** tr. imprimir; *(edition)* tirar, hacer una tirada; *(to publish)* publicar; FOTOG. copiar; *(to write)* escribir con letras de imprenta *o* de molde —intr. *(to be a printer)* trabajar como impresor; *(to write plainly)* escribir con letras de imprenta *o* de molde; *(book, publication)* imprimirse.
print·er (prĭn′tər) s. *(person)* impresor *m*; *(machine)* impresora.
print·ing (:tĭng) s. *(art, business)* imprenta; *(act, quality of run)* impresión *f*; *(run)* tiraje *m*; *(written characters)* letra de imprenta; *(layout)* tipografía ♦ **p. press** prensa.
print-out (prĭnt′out′) s. salida impresa.
pri·or¹ (prī′ər) adj. previo ♦ **p. to** antes de.
pri·or² s. RELIG. prior *m*.
pri·or·ess (:ĭs) s. RELIG. priora.
pri·or·i·ty (prī-ôr′ĭ-tē) s. prioridad *f*; *(time precedence)* anterioridad *f*.
prism (prĭz′əm) s. prisma *m*.
pris·on (prĭz′ən) s. cárcel *f*, prisión *f* ♦ **to put in** *o* **send to p.** encarcelar.
pris·on·er (:ə-nər) s. prisionero, preso; *(under arrest)* detenido; *(accused)* acusado.
pris·sy (prĭs′ē) adj. -i- remilgado.
pris·tine (prĭs′tēn′) adj. prístino; *(pure)* puro.
pri·va·cy (prī′və-sē) s. *(seclusion)* intimidad *f*;

(isolation) aislamiento; *(secrecy)* secreto.
pri·vate (prī′vĭt) **I.** adj. privado; *(not public)* particular; *(secluded)* solitario ♦ **p. citizen** particular ♦ **p. enterprise** *(sector)* sector privado; *(business)* empresa particular **II.** s. soldado raso.
pri·va·tion (prī-vā′shən) s. privación *f*.
priv·i·lege (prĭv′ə-lĭj) s. privilegio ♦ **to have the p. of** tener el honor de.
priv·i·leged (:lĭjd) adj. privilegiado ♦ **p. communication** comunicación confidencial ♦ **to be p. to** tener el privilegio de.
priv·y (prĭv′ē) **I.** adj. privado ♦ **p. seal** G.B. sello real ♦ **to be p. to** estar enterado de **II.** s. excusado, retrete rústico.
prize¹ (prīz) **I.** s. premio **II.** adj. de premio; *(given a prize)* premiado; *(outstanding)* de primera categoría **III.** tr. valorar.
prize² s. MARÍT. presa.
prize³ **I.** tr. ♦ **to p. open** *o* **up** abrir *o* levantar con una palanca **II.** s. *(leverage)* apalancamiento; *(lever)* palanca.
prize·fight (′fīt′) s. pelea profesional de boxeo.
prize·fight·er (:fī′tər) s. boxeador *m* profesional.
pro¹ (prō) **I.** s. ♦ **the pros and cons** el pro y el contra **II.** adv. a favor **III.** prep. a favor de **IV.** adj. partidario.
pro² s. & adj. FAM. profesional *mf*.
prob·a·bil·i·ty (prŏb′ə-bĭl′ĭ-tē) s. probabilidad *f*.
prob·a·ble (prŏb′ə-bəl) adj. probable; *(plausible)* verosímil ♦ **p. cause** motivo presunto.
pro·bate (prō′bāt′) DER. **I.** s. legalización *f* (de un testamento) ♦ **p. court** tribunal sucesorio **II.** tr. legalizar.
pro·ba·tion (-bā′shən) s. período de prueba; *(freedom)* libertad *f* condicional ♦ **on p.** a prueba.
probe (prōb) **I.** s. *(device)* sonda; *(exploration)* sondeo; *(investigation)* investigación *f* **II.** tr. *(to explore)* sondar; *(to investigate)* investigar —intr. indagar.
pro·bi·ty (prō′bĭ-tē) s. probidad *f*.
prob·lem (prŏb′ləm) **I.** s. problema *m* **II.** adj. difícil.
prob·lem·at·ic/·i·cal (prŏb′lə-măt′ĭk) adj. problemático.
pro·bos·cis (prō-bŏs′ĭs) s. [pl. **es** *o* **-cides**] ZOOL. trompa; ENTOM. probóscide *f*.
pro·ce·dur·al (prə-sē′jər-əl) adj. de procedimiento.
pro·ce·dure (:jər) s. procedimiento.
pro·ceed (prə-sēd′) intr. proceder; *(to continue)* proseguir, continuar; *(to go forward)* avanzar; *(to move along)* ir, desarrollar.
pro·ceed·ing (:sē′dĭng) s. procedimiento, acción *f* ♦ **pl.** acontecimientos; *(minutes)* actas; DER. proceso.
pro·ceeds (prō′sēdz′) s.pl. ganancias.
proc·ess (prŏs′ĕs′, prō′sĕs′) **I.** s. *(treatment)* procedimiento; *(method)* proceso; DER. proceso; *(summons)* citación *f*; BIOL. apéndice *m* ♦ **in p.** en marcha ♦ **in the p.** al hacerlo ♦ **to be in (the) p. of** estar en vías de **II.** tr. *(an application)* tramitar; *(to treat)* tratar; *(to convert)* transformar; FOTOG. revelar; COMPUT., DER. procesar.
proc·ess·ing (:ĭng) s. *(of food)* tratamiento; *(of raw materials)* transformación *f*; FOTOG. revelado; COMPUT. procesamiento ♦ **data p.** procesamiento de datos; *(science)* informática.

pro·ces·sion (prə-sĕsh′ən) s. procesión f, desfile m; *(orderly course)* progresión f.

pro·ces·sion·al (:ə-nəl) s. *(book)* procesionario; *(hymn)* himno procesionario.

proc·es·sor (prŏs′ĕs′ər) s. procesador m.

pro·claim (prō-klām′) tr. proclamar.

proc·la·ma·tion (prŏk′lə-mā′shən) s. proclamación f; *(announcement)* proclama.

pro·cliv·i·ty (prō-klĭv′ĭ-tē) s. propensión f.

pro·cras·ti·nate (prō-krăs′tə-nāt′) intr. aplazar una decisión —tr. aplazar, postergar.

pro·cras·ti·na·tion (-′-nā′shən) s. dilación f, retraso.

pro·cras·ti·na·tor (-′-′tər) s. persona dada a la postergación.

pro·cre·ate (prō′krē-āt′) tr. & intr. procrear.

pro·cre·a·tion (-′-ā′shən) s. procreación f.

pro·cre·a·tive (′-′tĭv) adj. procreador.

proc·tol·o·gy (prŏk-tŏl′ə-jē) s. proctología.

proc·tor (prŏk′tər) I. s. vigilante mf II. tr. vigilar.

proc·u·ra·tor (prŏk′yə-rā′tər) s. procurador m.

pro·cure (prō-kyr′) tr. obtener; *(a woman)* alcahuetear —intr. dedicarse al proxenetismo.

pro·cure·ment (:mənt) s. obtención f, logro.

pro·cur·er (:ər) s. alcahuete m.

prod (prŏd) tr. **-dd-** pinchar; *(to goad)* estimular.

prod·i·gal (prŏd′ĭ-gəl) adj. & s. pródigo.

pro·di·gious (prə-dĭj′əs) adj. enorme; *(marvelous)* prodigioso.

prod·i·gy (prŏd′ə-jē) s. prodigio.

pro·duce I. tr. (prə-ds′) producir; *(to manufacture)* fabricar; *(to give rise to)* causar; *(to show)* exhibir, mostrar —intr. producir II. s. (prŏd′ds) producto.

pro·duc·er (prə-ds′ər) s. productor m.

prod·uct (prŏd′əkt) s. producto.

pro·duc·tion (prə-dŭk′shən) s. producción f.

pro·duc·tive (:tĭv) adj. productivo.

pro·duc·tiv·i·ty (prō′dŭk-tĭv′ĭ-tē, prŏd′ək-) s. productividad f.

prof (prŏf) s. FAM. profe m, profesor m.

pro·fane (prə-fān′) I. adj. profano; *(vulgar)* vulgar II. tr. profanar.

pro·fan·i·ty (:făn′ĭ-tē) s. profanidad f; *(language)* lenguaje obsceno.

pro·fess (prə-fĕs′) tr. *(to affirm)* declarar, proclamar; *(to pretend)* pretender; RELIG. profesar.

pro·fessed (:fĕst′) adj. declarado; *(pretended)* supuesto; RELIG. profeso.

pro·fes·sion (:fĕsh′ən) s. profesión f.

pro·fes·sion·al (:ə-nəl) adj. & s. profesional mf; *(expert)* perito, experto.

pro·fes·sor (prə-fĕs′ər) s. profesor m; *(university)* catedrático.

pro·fes·sor·ship (:shĭp′) s. profesorado, cátedra.

prof·fer (prŏf′ər) tr. ofrecer, proponer.

pro·fi·cien·cy (prə-fĭsh′ən-sē) s. competencia.

pro·fi·cient (:ənt) adj. capaz, competente.

pro·file (prō′fīl′) I. s. perfil m; *(biography)* retrato; *(description)* descripción f ♦ **to keep a low p.** no llamar la atención II. tr. perfilar.

prof·it (prŏf′ĭt) I. s. beneficio ♦ **p. sharing** participación en los beneficios • **to make a p.** *(person)* ganar dinero; *(business)* rendir ganancias • **to show a p.** ganar dinero • **to turn something to p.** sacar provecho de algo ♦ pl. *(from investments)* rentas; *(gains)* ganancias, utilidades II. intr. servir ♦ **to p. by** o **from** COM. sacar dinero; *(to benefit from)* sacar provecho de.

prof·it·a·bil·i·ty (′ĭ-tə-bĭl′ĭ-tē) s. COM. carácter lucrativo.

prof·it·a·ble (′--bəl) adj. beneficioso, provechoso; COM. lucrativo.

prof·i·teer (prŏf′ĭ-tîr′) I. s. aprovechón m II. intr. aprovecharse.

prof·li·gate (prŏf′lĭ-gĭt) adj. disoluto; *(wasteful)* derrochador.

pro·found (prə-found′) adj. **-er, -est** profundo.

pro·fun·di·ty (prə-fŭn′dĭ-tē) s. profundidad f.

pro·fuse (prə-fys′) adj. profuso; *(extravagant)* pródigo.

pro·fu·sion (:fy′zhən) s. profusión f.

pro·gen·i·tor (prō-jĕn′ĭ-tər) s. *(ancestor)* antepasado; *(parent)* progenitor m.

prog·e·ny (prŏj′ə-nē) s. progenie m.

pro·ges·ter·one (prō-jĕs′tə-rōn′) s. progesterona.

prog·no·sis (prŏg-nō′sĭs) s. [pl. **-ses**] pronóstico.

prog·nos·tic (:nŏs′tĭk) augurio, presagio.

prog·nos·ti·cate (:tĭ-kāt′) tr. pronosticar.

prog·nos·ti·ca·tion (-′-kā′shən) s. pronosticación f; *(forecast)* pronóstico.

pro·gram (prō′grăm′, :grəm) I. s. programa m II. tr. programar.

pro·gram·(m)er (:ər) s. programador m.

pro·gram·(m)ing (:ĭng) s. programación f.

prog·ress I. s. (prŏg′rĕs′, :rĭs) progreso; *(development)* desarrollo; *(of events)* marcha, curso ♦ **in p.** en curso • **to make p.** progresar; *(to improve)* mejorar II. intr. (prə-grĕs′) progresar; *(to improve)* mejorar.

pro·gres·sion (prə-grĕsh′ən) s. progreso; MAT., MÚS. progresión f.

pro·gres·sive (:grĕs′ĭv) I. adj. progresivo; POL. progresista II. s. POL. progresista mf.

pro·hib·it (prō-hĭb′ĭt) tr. prohibir.

pro·hi·bi·tion (prō′ə-bĭsh′ən) s. prohibición f.

pro·hib·i·tive/to·ry (′-tĭv/tôr′ē) adj. prohibitivo.

proj·ect I. s. (prŏj′ĕkt′) proyecto II. tr. (prə-jĕkt′) *(to protrude)* hacer sobresalir, sacar; *(missile, image)* proyectar; *(to convey)* sugerir; *(to plan)* proyectar, planear —intr. *(to protrude)* sobresalir, salir; *(to speak)* hablar claramente.

pro·jec·tile (prə-jĕk′təl, :tīl′) s. proyectil m.

pro·jec·tion (:shən) s. proyección f; *(of a mood)* sugestión f; *(protuberance)* saliente m, punta; *(estimate)* cálculo, pronóstico.

pro·jec·tion·ist (:shə-nĭst) s. operador m de cine que proyecta las películas.

pro·jec·tor (:tər) s. proyector m.

pro·le·tar·i·an (prō′lĭ-târ′ē-ən) adj. & s. proletario.

pro·le·tar·i·at (:ĭt) s. proletariado.

pro·lif·er·ate (prə-lĭf′ə-rāt′) intr. proliferar —tr. hacer crecer o aumentar.

pro·lif·er·a·tion (-′-rā′shən) s. proliferación f.

pro·lif·ic (prə-lĭf′ĭk) adj. prolífico.

pro·log(ue) (prō′lôg′) s. prólogo.

pro·long (prə-lông′) tr. prolongar.

pro·lon·gate (:gāt′) tr. prolongar.

pro·lon·ga·tion (′-gā′shən) s. prolongación f.

prom·e·nade (prŏm′ə-nād′, :näd′) I. s. paseo II. intr. pasearse —tr. pasear.

prom·i·nence (prŏm′ə-nəns) s. prominencia.

prom·i·nent (:nənt) adj. prominente; *(eminent)* notable.

pro·mis·cu·i·ty (prŏm′ĭ-sky′ĭ-tē) s. promiscuidad f.

pro·mis·cu·ous (prə-mĭs′ky-əs) adj. promiscuo.

prom·ise (prŏm'ĭs) **I.** s. promesa **♦ to break one's p.** faltar a su palabra • **to keep one's p.** cumplir su promesa • **to show p.** ser prometedor **II.** tr. prometer —intr. hacer una promesa.

prom·is·ing (:ĭ-sĭng) adj. prometedor.

prom·is·so·ry (:sôr'ē) adj. promisorio **♦ p. note** pagaré.

prom·on·to·ry (prŏm'ən-tôr'ē) s. promontorio.

pro·mote (prə-mōt') tr. *(employee, officer)* ascender; *(student)* adelantar de año; *(to further)* promover, fomentar; *(to advocate)* apoyar; *(to advertise)* promocionar; *(to finance)* financiar.

pro·mot·er (:mō'tər) s. promotor m.

pro·mo·tion (:shən) s. ascenso; *(furtherance)* fomento.

prompt (prŏmpt) **I.** adj. puntual; *(without delay)* pronto, rápido **II.** tr. *(to incite)* incitar; *(to inspire)* inspirar; TEAT. apuntar.

prompt·er (prŏmp'tər) s. TEAT. apuntador m.

prompt·ness (prŏmpt'nĭs) s. prontitud f.

prom·ul·gate (prŏm'əl-gāt', prō'məl-) tr. promulgar.

prom·ul·ga·tion (:gā'shən) s. promulgación f.

prom·ul·ga·tor ('-'tər) s. promulgador m.

prone (prōn) adj. & adv. boca abajo **♦ to be p. to** ser propenso a.

prong (prŏng) s. punta; *(of a fork)* diente m.

pro·noun (prō'noun') s. pronombre m.

pro·nounce (prə-nouns') tr. pronunciar; *(to declare)* declarar —intr. pronunciarse.

pro·nounced (:nounst') adj. pronunciado.

pro·nounce·ment (:nouns'mənt) s. declaración f.

pro·nun·ci·a·tion (prə-nŭn'sē-ā'shən) s. pronunciación f; FONÉT. transcripción fonética.

proof (prōōf) **I.** s. prueba f; *(alcoholic content)* grado **II.** tr. *(to proofread)* corregir las pruebas de; *(to make resistant to)* hacer resistente a.

proof·read ('·rēd') tr. **·read** corregir —intr. corregir pruebas.

proof·read·er (:rē'dər) s. corrector m de pruebas.

prop[1] (prŏp) **I.** s. puntal m; FIG. sostén m **II.** tr. **·pp·♦ to p. open** mantener abierto • **to p. up** apuntalar.

prop[2] s. TEAT. accesorio.

prop[3] s. FAM. hélice f.

prop·a·gan·da (prŏp'ə-găn'də) s. propaganda.

prop·a·gan·dist (:dĭst) s. propagandista mf.

prop·a·gan·dize (:dīz') tr. & intr. hacer propaganda (de).

prop·a·gate (prŏp'ə-gāt') tr. & intr. propagar(se).

prop·a·ga·tion ('-gā'shən) s. propagación f.

pro·pane (prō'pān') s. propano.

pro·pel (prə-pĕl') tr. **·ll·** propulsar, impeler.

pro·pel·ler/lor (:ər) s. hélice f.

pro·pen·si·ty (prə-pĕn'sĭ-tē) s. propensión f.

prop·er (prŏp'ər) adj. apropiado; *(right)* debido; *(itself)* propio, mismo; *(correct)* correcto; *(characteristic)* característico; GRAM., MAT. propio.

prop·er·ly (:lē) adv. apropiadamente; *(strictly)* propiamente; *(correctly)* correctamente.

prop·er·ty (prŏp'ər-tē) s. propiedad f; *(possessions)* bienes m; TEAT. accesorio **♦ personal p.** bienes muebles.

proph·e·cy (prŏf'ĭ-sē) s. profecía.

proph·e·sy (:sī') tr. & intr. profetizar.

proph·et (prŏf'ĭt) s. profeta m.

proph·et·ess (:ĭ-tĭs) s. profetisa.

pro·phet·ic/i·cal (prə-fĕt'ĭk) adj. profético.

pro·phy·lac·tic (prō'fə-lăk'tĭk) adj. & s. profiláctico.

pro·phy·lax·is (:sĭs) s. [pl. **-xes**] profilaxis f.

pro·pin·qui·ty (prə-pĭng'kwĭ-tē) s. proximidad f; *(kinship)* parentesco.

pro·pi·ti·ate (prə-pĭsh'ē-āt') tr. propiciar.

pro·pi·tious (:əs) adj. propicio.

pro·po·nent (prə-pō'nənt) s. proponente mf.

pro·por·tion (prə-pôr'shən) **I.** s. proporción f; *(part)* parte f, porción f **♦ in p.** proporcionado • **out of p.** desproporcionado **♦** pl. dimensiones, tamaño **II.** tr. proporcionar.

pro·por·tion·al (:shə-nəl) adj. proporcional.

pro·por·tion·ate (:nĭt) adj. proporcional.

pro·pos·al (prə-pō'zəl) s. propuesta; *(of marriage)* propuesta matrimonial.

pro·pose (prə-pōz') tr. proponer; *(to intend)* tener intención de —intr. proponerse; *(marriage)* ofrecer matrimonio.

prop·o·si·tion (prŏp'ə-zĭsh'ən) **I.** s. proposición f; FAM. *(matter)* asunto, problema m; *(immoral)* proposición deshonesta **II.** tr. FAM. hacer una propuesta deshonesta a.

pro·pound (prə-pound') tr. proponer.

pro·pri·e·tar·y (prə-prī'ĭ-tĕr'ē) adj. propietario; *(patented)* patentado.

pro·pri·e·tor (:tər) s. propietario.

pro·pri·e·tor·ship (:shĭp') s. (derecho de) propiedad f.

pro·pri·e·tress (prə-prī'ĭ-trĭs) s. propietaria.

pro·pri·e·ty (:tē) s. conveniencia; *(decency)* decencia **♦** pl. convenciones.

pro·pul·sion (prə-pŭl'shən) s. propulsión f.

pro·rate (prō-rāt') tr. prorratear.

pro·sa·ic (prō-zā'ĭk) adj. prosaico.

pro·sce·ni·um (prō-sē'nē-əm) s. proscenio.

pro·scribe (prō-skrīb') tr. proscribir.

pro·scrip·tion (:skrĭp'shən) s. proscripción f.

prose (prōz) s. prosa.

pros·e·cute (prŏs'ĭ-kyōōt') tr. proseguir; DER. *(a person)* procesar; *(claim, case)* entablar —intr. entablar una acción judicial.

pros·e·cu·tion ('-kyōō'shən) s. procesamiento; *(trial)* proceso; *(attorney)* fiscal mf.

pros·e·cu·tor ('-'tər) s. fiscal mf.

pros·e·ly·tize (prŏs'ə-lĭ-tīz') intr. ganar prosélitos —tr. convertir.

pros·o·dy (prŏs'ə-dē) s. *(study)* métrica; *(system)* prosodia.

pros·pect (prŏs'pĕkt') **I.** s. perspectiva; *(expectation)* expectativa; *(customer)* cliente m probable; *(candidate)* candidato probable; *(exposure)* orientación f; *(view)* vista **♦** pl. perspectivas **II.** tr. prospectar **♦ to p. for** buscar.

pro·spec·tive (prə-spĕk'tĭv) adj. *(expected)* esperado; *(likely to be)* presunto.

pros·pec·tor (prŏs'pĕk'tər) s. buscador m.

pro·spec·tus (prə-spĕk'təs) s. prospecto.

pros·per (prŏs'pər) intr. prosperar.

pros·per·i·ty (prŏ-spĕr'ĭ-tē) s. prosperidad f.

pros·per·ous (prŏs'pər-əs) adj. próspero; *(favorable)* favorable.

pros·tate (prŏs'tāt') s. próstata.

pros·the·sis (prŏs-thē'sĭs) s. [pl. **-ses**] prótesis f.

pros·ti·tute (prŏs'tĭ-tōōt') **I.** s. prostituta **II.** tr. prostituir **♦ to p. oneself** prostituirse.

pros·ti·tu·tion ('-tōō'shən) s. prostitución f.

pros·trate (prŏs'trāt') **I.** tr. postrar **II.** adj. postrado.

pros·tra·tion (prŏ-strā'shən) s. postración f.
pro·tag·o·nist (prō-tăg'ə-nĭst) s. protagonista mf.
pro·te·an (prō'tē-ən) adj. proteico.
pro·tect (prə-tĕkt') tr. proteger.
pro·tect·er (:tĕk'tər) s. protector m.
pro·tec·tion (:shən) s. protección f.
pro·tec·tion·ist (:shə-nĭst) s. proteccionista mf.
pro·tec·tive (:tĭv) adj. & s. protector m.
pro·tec·tor (:tər) s. protector m.
pro·tec·tor·ate (:ĭt) s. protectorado.
pro·té·gé (prō'tə-zhā') s. protegido.
pro·tein (prō'tēn') s. proteína.
pro·test I. tr. (prə-tĕst') protestar contra; (to affirm) protestar de —intr. protestar II. s. (prō'tĕst') protesta; (statement) protesto ♦ under p. contra su voluntad.
Prot·es·tant (prŏt'ĭ-stənt) s. & adj. protestante mf.
prot·es·ta·tion (prŏt'ĭ-stā'shən) s. protesta.
pro·test·er (prə-tĕs'tər) s. persona que protesta; (demonstrator) manifestante mf.
pro·to·col (prō'tə-kôl') s. protocolo.
pro·ton (prō'tŏn') s. protón m.
pro·to·type (prō'tə-tīp') s. prototipo.
pro·tract (prō-trăkt') tr. prolongar.
pro·trac·tion (:trăk'shən) s. prolongación f.
pro·trac·tor (:tər) s. transportador m.
pro·trude (prō-trōōd') tr. sacar —intr. sobresalir, resaltar.
pro·tru·sion (:trōō'zhən) s. acción f de sacar; (state) prominencia; (projection) saliente m.
pro·tru·sive (:trōō'sĭv) adj. sobresaliente.
pro·tu·ber·ance (prō-tōō'bər-əns) s. protuberancia.
pro·tu·ber·ant (:ənt) adj. protuberante.
proud (proud) adj. orgulloso; (of oneself) satisfecho; (memorable) memorable; (arrogant) soberbio; (honorable) honorable; (spirited) animoso ♦ to be p. to tener el honor de.
prove (prōōv) tr. **-d, -d** o **-n** probar; (to test) poner a prueba ♦ **proving ground** campo de pruebas —intr. salir, resultar.
prov·en (prōō'vən) I. cf. **prove** II. adj. probado.
prov·e·nance (prŏv'ə-nəns) s. origen m.
prov·en·der (prŏv'ən-dər) s. (fodder) forraje m; (food) comida.
prov·erb (prŏv'ûrb') s. proverbio.
pro·ver·bi·al (prə-vûr'bē-əl) adj. proverbial.
pro·vide (prə-vīd') tr. (to supply) suministrar; (to make available) proveer; (to stipulate) estipular —intr. proveer ♦ **provided** o **providing that** con tal que.
prov·i·dence (prŏv'ĭ-dəns) s. providencia.
prov·i·dent (:dənt) adj. providente; (economical) económico.
prov·i·den·tial ('-dĕn'shəl) adj. providencial.
pro·vid·er (prə-vī'dər) s. proveedor m.
prov·ince (prŏv'ĭns) s. provincia; (field) esfera, campo; (jurisdiction) competencia.
pro·vin·cial (prə-vĭn'shəl) I. adj. provincial; (unsophisticated) provinciano; (narrow) de miras estrechas II. s. provinciano.
pro·vi·sion (prə-vĭzh'ən) I. s. provisión f; (stipulation) estipulación f ♦ **to make provisions for** (the future) prever; (family) mantener II. tr. proveer.
pro·vi·sion·al (:ə-nəl) adj. provisional.
pro·vi·so (prə-vī'zō) s. [pl. **(e)s**] condición f.
pro·vi·so·ry (:zə-rē) adj. condicional.
pro·vo·ca·teur (prō-vŏk'ə-tûr') s. agente m provocador.
prov·o·ca·tion (prŏv'ə-kā'shən) s. provocación f.
pro·voc·a·tive (prə-vŏk'ə-tĭv) adj. provocativo.
pro·voke (prə-vŏk') tr. provocar.
prow (prou) s. proa.
prow·ess (prou'ĭs) s. (skill) habilidad f, destreza; (courage) valor m.
prowl (proul) I. tr. & intr. merodear, rondar II. s. merodeo, ronda ♦ **on the p.** buscando algo.
prox·i·mate (prŏk'sə-mĭt) adj. próximo.
prox·im·i·ty (-sĭm'ĭ-tē) s. proximidad f.
prox·y (prŏk'sē) s. (person) apoderado; (authority) poder m ♦ **by p.** por poder.
prude (prōōd) s. mojigato, gazmoño.
pru·dence (prōōd'ns) s. prudencia.
pru·dent (:nt) adj. prudente.
pru·den·tial (prōō-dĕn'shəl) adj. prudencial.
prune¹ (prōōn) s. (fruit) ciruela pasa.
prune² tr. & intr. (to trim) podar; (to remove) cortar, cercenar; (to reduce) reducir.
pru·ri·ent (prōōr'ē-ənt) adj. lascivo, libidinoso.
pry¹ (prī) intr. fisgar, curiosear.
pry² tr. ♦ **to p. open** abrir con una palanca • **to p. out of** arrancar.
pry·ing (:ĭng) adj. fisgón, entremetido.
psalm (säm) s. salmo.
pseu·do·nym (sōōd'n-ĭm') s. seudónimo.
pso·ri·a·sis (sə-rī'ə-sĭs) s. psoriasis f.
psy·che (sī'kē) s. psique f.
psy·che·del·ic (sī'kĭ-dĕl'ĭk) adj. psicodélico.
psy·chi·at·ric (sī'kē-ăt'rĭk) adj. psiquiátrico.
psy·chi·a·trist (sĭ-kī'ə-trĭst, sī-) s. psiquiatra mf.
psy·chi·a·try (:trē) s. psiquiatría.
psy·chic (sī'kĭk) I. adj. psíquico II. s. medium m.
psy·cho·a·nal·y·sis (sī'kō-ə-năl'ĭ-sĭs) s. psicoanálisis m.
psy·cho·an·a·lyze (:ăn'ə-līz') tr. psicoanalizar.
psy·cho·log·i·cal (sī'kə-lŏj'ĭ-kəl) adj. psicológico.
psy·chol·o·gist (sī-kŏl'ə-jĭst) s. psicólogo.
psy·chol·o·gy (:jē) s. psicología.
psy·cho·path (sī'kə-păth') s. psicópata mf.
psy·cho·pa·thy (sī-kŏp'ə-thē) s. psicopatía.
psy·cho·sis (sī-kō'sĭs) s. [pl. **-ses**] psicosis f.
psy·cho·so·mat·ic (sī'kə-sō-măt'ĭk) adj. & s. psicosomático.
psy·cho·ther·a·py (sī'kō-thĕr'ə-pē) s. psicoterapia.
psy·chot·ic (sī-kŏt'ĭk) I. s. psicópata mf II. adj. psicopático.
pto·maine poisoning (tō'mān') s. envenenamiento por tomainas.
pub (pŭb) s. taberna, cantina.
pu·ber·ty (pyōō'bər-tē) s. pubertad f.
pu·bes·cence (-bĕs'əns) s. pubescencia.
pu·bes·cent (:ənt) adj. pubescente.
pu·bic (pyōō'bĭk) adj. pubiano, púbico.
pu·bis (:bĭs) s. [pl. **-bes**] pubis m.
pub·lic (pŭb'lĭk) adj. & s. público ♦ **p. defender** defensor de oficio in • **p. school** (U.S.) escuela pública; (G.B.) colegio particular • **p. servant** funcionario • **p. television** televisión no comercial • **p. utility** empresa de servicio público • **to make p.** publicar.
pub·li·ca·tion (pŭb'lĭ-kā'shən) s. publicación f.
pub·li·cist (:sĭst) s. publicista mf.
pub·lic·i·ty (pŭ-blĭs'ĭ-tē) s. publicidad f.
pub·li·cize (pŭb'lĭ-sīz') tr. publicar.

pub·lic-spir·it·ed (pŭb′lĭk-spĭr′ĭ-tĭd) adj. de espíritu cívico.
pub·lish (pŭb′lĭsh) tr. & intr. publicar.
pub·lish·er (:ĭ-shər) s. editor m.
puck (pŭk) s. disco.
puck·er (pŭk′ər) I. tr. fruncir —intr. ♦ **to p. up** arrugarse II. s. arruga, fruncido.
pud·ding (pōōd′ĭng) s. budín m.
pud·dle (pŭd′l) s. charco.
pudg·y (pŭj′ē) adj. **-i-** regordete.
pu·er·ile (pyōō′ər-əl) adj. pueril.
puff (pŭf) I. s. (of breath) resoplido; (of air) soplo; (of wind) soplido; (of smoke, steam) bocanada; (on a cigarette) fumada; (swelling) hinchazón f; (pastry) buñuelo; (for powder) borla; (flattery) bombo II. intr. (to blow) soplar; (to breathe) resoplar, resollar; (to emit smoke) echar bocanadas; (to smoke) fumar ♦ **to p. up** (to swell) hincharse; (to become vain) engreírse —tr. (to blow) soplar; (to smoke) fumar; (to praise) dar bombo a ♦ **to p. up** (to swell) hinchar; (to make vain) engreír.
puffed-up (pŭft′ŭp′) adj. engreído.
puf·fin (pŭf′ĭn) s. frailecillo.
puff·y (pŭf′ē) adj. **-i-** hinchado.
pu·gi·lism (pyōō′jə-lĭz′əm) s. pugilismo.
pu·gi·list (:lĭst) s. pugilista m.
pug·na·cious (pŭg-nā′shəs) adj. belicoso.
pug·nac·i·ty (:năs′ĭ-tē) s. belicosidad f.
pug-nosed (pŭg′nōzd′) adj. braco.
puke (pyōōk) JER. I. intr. & tr. vomitar II. s. vómito.
pull (pōōl) I. tr. (to move) tirar de; (to extract) sacar, extraer; (to tug at) tirar de, halar; (trigger) apretar; (to stretch) estirar; (muscle) torcerse; FAM. (to attract) traer; (to do) hacer; JER. (gun) sacar ♦ **to p. apart** (to rend) desgarrar, rasgar; (to criticize) criticar • **to p. down** (to demolish) echar abajo, derribar; (to lower) bajar; (to reduce) rebajar; FAM. (salary) cobrar • **to p. for** (to cheer) animar; (to support) apoyar • **to p. in** (to restrain) contener; FAM. (to arrest) detener; (to attract) atraer • **to p. off** (to take off) quitar; (to carry out) llevar a cabo • **to p. on** (clothes) ponerse; (to tug at) tirar de • **to p. punches** (boxer) no pegar a fondo; (to hold back) andarse con rodeos • **to p. oneself together** componerse, dominarse • **to p. strings** conseguir algo por influencias • **to p. the rug out from under someone** dejar a alguien en la estacada • **to p. the wool over someone's eyes** engañar a alguien • **to p. up** (socks) subirse; (a chair) acercar —intr. (to tug) tirar; (to row) remar ♦ **to p. ahead** destacarse • **to p. away** dejar atrás • **to p. in** (train) entrar en la estación; (to arrive) llegar • **to p. out** (to depart) salir; (to withdraw) retirarse • **to p. over** AUTO. parar • **to p. through** (to survive) salir de una enfermedad o apuro • **to p. together** aunar los esfuerzos • **to p. up** pararse, detenerse II. s. (tug) tirón m; (effort) esfuerzo; (knob, cord) tirador m; (inhalation) chupada; JER. (influence) enchufe m, palanca; FAM. (appeal) atracción f.
pull·back (′băk′) s. retirada (de tropas).
pul·let (pōōl′ĭt) s. pollo, polla.
pul·ley (pōōl′ē) s. polea, roldana.
pull·out (pōōl′out′) s. retirada.
pull·o·ver (:ō′vər) s. jersey m, suéter m.
pul·mo·nar·y (pōōl′mə-něr′ē) adj. pulmonar.
pulp (pŭlp) s. pulpa; BOT. médula.
pul·pit (pōōl′pĭt, pŭl′-) s. púlpito.
pul·sar (pŭl′sär′) s. púlsar m.

pul·sate (:sāt′) intr. pulsar.
pul·sa·tion (-sā′shən) s. pulsación f.
pulse (pŭls) I. s. pulso; (amplification) pulsación f II. intr. pulsar.
pul·ver·ize (pŭl′və-rīz′) tr. & intr. pulverizar(se).
pu·ma (pyōō′mə, pōō′-) s. puma m.
pum·ice (pŭm′ĭs) s. piedra pómez.
pum·mel (pŭm′əl) tr. aporrear, apuñear.
pump¹ (pŭmp) I. s. MEC. bomba; AUTO. surtidor m II. tr. bombear; (blood) impulsar; (to move up and down) mover de arriba abajo ♦ **to p. for information** sonsacar información.
pump² s. (shoe) escarpín m.
pump·kin (pŭmp′kĭn) s. calabaza.
pun (pŭn) I. s. juego de palabras II. intr. **-nn-** hacer juegos de palabras.
punch¹ (pŭnch) I. s. punzón m; (for paper) perforadora; (for tickets) máquina de picar billetes ♦ **p. card** tarjeta perforada II. tr. (tickets) picar; (metal, leather) taladrar ♦ **to p. in, out** marcar la hora de llegada, salida del trabajo.
punch² I. tr. dar un puñetazo II. s. puñetazo; (in boxing) pegada; (vigor) vigor m, fuerza ♦ **p. line** gracia de un chiste.
punch³ s. (beverage) ponche m ♦ **p. bowl** ponchera.
punch-drunk (′drŭngk′) adj. aturdido; (in boxing) aturdido por los golpes.
punch·y (pŭn′chē) adj. **-i-** aturdido.
punc·til·i·ous (pŭngk-tĭl′ē-əs) adj. puntilloso.
punc·tu·al (pŭngk′chōō-əl) adj. puntual.
punc·tu·al·i·ty (′-ăl′ĭ-tē) s. puntualidad f.
punc·tu·ate (′-āt′) tr. puntuar; (to interrupt) interrumpir; (to stress) acentuar.
punc·tu·a·tion (′-ā′shən) s. puntuación f.
punc·ture (pŭngk′chər) I. tr. perforar; (a tire) pinchar; (to deflate) rebajar II. s. perforación f; (in a tire) pinchazo.
pun·dit (pŭn′dĭt) s. (in India) pandit m; (learned person) erudito; (authority) experto.
pun·gent (pŭn′jənt) adj. acre; (piquant) picante; FIG. mordaz.
pun·ish (pŭn′ĭsh) tr. castigar; (to injure) maltratar —intr. imponer castigo.
pun·ish·a·ble (:ĭ-shə-bəl) adj. castigable.
pun·ish·ment (:ĭsh-mənt) s. castigo; (mistreatment) maltrato.
pu·ni·tive (pyōō′nĭ-tĭv) adj. punitivo.
punk¹ (pŭngk) s. (tinder) yesca.
punk² JER. I. s. joven mf sin experiencia II. adj. sin mérito.
pun·ster (pŭn′stər) s. aficionado a los juegos de palabras.
punt¹ (pŭnt) I. s. batea II. tr. impeler una batea.
punt² DEP. I. s. patada II. tr. & intr. dar una patada (a.
pu·ny (pyōō′nē) adj. **-i-** débil, enclenque.
pup (pŭp) s. (puppy) cachorro; (young animal) cría; (youth) mocoso ♦ **p. tent** pequeña tienda de campaña.
pu·pa (pyōō′pə) s. [pl. s o **-ae**] crisálida.
pu·pil¹ (pyōō′pəl) s. (student) alumno.
pu·pil² s. ANAT. pupila.
pup·pet (pŭp′ĭt) s. marioneta, títere m; FIG. títere, pelele m.
pup·pet·eer (′-ĭ-tîr′) s. titiritero.
pup·pet·ry (′-trē) s. arte m del titiritero.
pup·py (pŭp′ē) s. cachorro; (youth) joven inexperto ♦ **p. love** amor juvenil.
pur·chase (pûr′chĭs) I. tr. comprar II. s.

compra ♦ **p. order** orden de compra.

pur·chas·er (:chĭ-sǝr) s. comprador *m*.

pure (pyŏŏr) adj. puro; *(clean)* limpio; *(chaste)* casto, virgen.

pure·blood(·ed) ('blŭd'[ĭd]) adj. de pura sangre *o* raza.

pure·bred ('brĕd') I. adj. de pura sangre II. s. animal *m* de pura sangre.

pu·rée (pyŏŏ-rā') I. tr. **-réed, -réeing** hacer un puré de II. s. puré *m*.

pur·ga·tion (pûr-gā'shǝn) s. purgación *f*.

pur·ga·tive ('gǝ-tĭv) adj. & s. purgante *m*.

pur·ga·to·ry (:tôr'ē) s. purgatorio.

purge (pûrj) I. tr. purgar II. s. purga.

pu·ri·fi·er (pyŏŏr'ǝ-fī'ǝr) s. purificador *m*; TEC. depurador *m*.

pu·ri·fy (:fī') tr. purificar; *(to refine)* refinar —intr. purificarse.

pur·ist (pyŏŏr'ĭst) s. purista *mf*.

Pu·ri·tan (:ĭ-tn) s. & adj. puritano.

pu·ri·tan·i·cal ('ĭ-tăn'ĭ-kǝl) adj. puritano.

pu·ri·ty ('-tē) s. pureza.

purl[1] (pûrl) I. intr. *(to murmur)* susurrar, murmurar II. s. susurro, murmullo.

purl[2] I. tr. hacer punto al revés —intr. hacer con puntos al revés II. s. punto al revés.

pur·ple (pûr'pǝl) I. s. violeta, morado; *(cloth)* púrpura II. adj. purpúreo, morado; *(royal)* imperial.

pur·port I. tr. (pǝr-pôrt') pretender II. s. (pûr'pôrt') lo que parece significar.

pur·port·ed (pǝr-pôr'tĭd) adj. supuesto.

pur·pose (pûr'pǝs) I. s. objetivo; *(intention)* propósito *f* ♦ **for all intents and purposes** para todos los efectos • **for the p. of** con el objeto de • **on p.** a propósito, adrede • **to no p.** para nada II. tr. tener intención de.

pur·pose·ful (:fǝl) adj. *(person)* resuelto; *(activity)* útil.

pur·pose·less (:lĭs) adj. sin propósito; *(pointless)* inútil.

pur·pose·ly (:lē) adv. adrede, a propósito.

purr (pûr) I. s. ronroneo; *(of an engine)* zumbido II. intr. ronronear; *(an engine)* zumbar.

purse (pûrs) I. s. *(moneybag)* portamonedas *m*; *(handbag)* bolso; *(money)* bolsa; *(prize)* premio II. tr. apretar.

purs·er (pûr'sǝr) s. MARÍT. contador *m*.

pur·su·ant (pǝr-sōō'ǝnt) adj. ♦ **p. to** según.

pur·sue (pǝr-sōō') tr. perseguir; *(to strive for)* aspirar a; *(to follow)* seguir, continuar; *(to devote oneself to)* dedicarse a.

pur·suit (:sōōt') s. persecución *f*; *(striving)* búsqueda; *(activity)* pasatiempo ♦ **in p. of** en búsqueda de.

pu·ru·lent (pyŏŏr'ǝ-lǝnt) adj. purulento.

pur·vey (pǝr-vā') tr. proveer, abastecer.

pur·vey·or (:ǝr) s. proveedor *m*, abastecedor *m*; *(distributor)* distribuidor *m*.

pur·view (pûr'vyōō') s. *(scope)* alcance *m*, esfera; *(outlook)* perspectiva.

pus (pŭs) s. pus *m*.

push (pŏŏsh) I. tr. empujar; *(to urge forward)* hacer adelantar; *(to press)* ejercer presión; *(to extend)* extender; JER. *(to sell)* vender; *(to promote)* promover; *(to recommend)* recomendar ♦ **to p. around** FAM. intimidar • **to p. aside** *o* **away** apartar • **to p. back** empujar; *(to repel)* hacer retroceder • **to p. down** apretar; *(someone)* hacer caer • **to p. over** *(something)* volcar; *(someone)* hacer caer • **to p. through** pasar por, sacar por; *(to carry out)* llevar a cabo; *(a*

bill) hacer aceptar • **to p. up** *(to lift)* levantar; *(prices)* hacer subir —intr. empujar; *(to put pressure on)* ejercer presión; *(to advance)* abrirse paso a empujones; *(to expend great effort)* esforzarse ♦ **to p. ahead** avanzar • **to p. back** retroceder • **to p. forward** avanzar • **to p. off** FAM. largarse • **to p. on** seguir adelante, continuar II. s. empujón *m*; *(drive)* empuje *m*; *(effort)* empujón *m*; MIL. ofensiva ♦ **p. button** pulsador, botón de contacto.

push·cart (:kärt') s. carretilla de mano.

push·er (:ǝr) s. empujador *m*; *(ambitious person)* arribista *mf*; JER. *(of drugs)* vendedor *m* de drogas.

push·o·ver (:ō'vǝr) s. *(easy thing)* ganga; *(dupe)* pelele *m*.

push·up (:ŭp') s. plancha.

push·y (:ē) adj. -**i**- FAM. insistente.

pu·sil·lan·i·mous (pyōō'sǝ-lăn'ǝ-mǝs) adj. pusilánime.

puss[1] (pŏŏs) s. FAM. *(cat)* minino, gatito.

puss[2] s. JER. *(mouth)* hocico; *(face)* jeta.

puss·y ('ē) s. gatito ♦ **p. willow** sauce común.

puss·y·cat (:kăt') s. gato; FAM. *(amiable person)* persona afable.

puss·y·foot (:fŏŏt') intr. andar cautelosamente; FIG. andarse con tiento.

pus·tu·lar (pŭs'chǝ-lǝr) adj. pustuloso.

pus·tule (:chōōl) s. pústula.

put (pŏŏt) I. tr. **put, -tting** poner; *(to insert)* meter; *(to add)* echar; *(question)* formular, hacer; *(to subject)* someter; *(to attribute)* dar; *(blame)* echar; *(to estimate)* calcular; *(to impose)* gravar con; *(to bet, invest)* poner; *(to say)* decir; *(to hurl)* lanzar, tirar ♦ **to p. across** hacer comprender • **to p. aside** poner a un lado; *(to save)* guardar • **to p. away** FAM. *(to imprison)* encarcelar; *(to institutionalize)* meter en un manicomio; *(to consume)* zamparse • **to p. back** volver a poner en su sitio • **to p. before** *(to submit)* someter a; *(to place before)* anteponer • **to p. down** *(to let go of)* soltar; *(to suppress)* reprimir; *(to write down)* apuntar; *(to include)* poner en la lista; *(to criticize)* poner por los suelos; *(to attribute)* achacar; *(down payment)* hacer un desembolso inicial de • **to p. forth** *(to sprout)* brotar; *(to offer)* presentar, proponer • **to p. in** meter; *(to install)* poner • **to p. in a good word for** hablar por *o* en favor de • **to p. into words** expresar • **to p. it mildly** sin exagerar • **to p. off** *(to postpone)* aplazar, diferir; *(to offend)* dar asco, asquear; *(to make wait)* hacer esperar • **to p. on** TEAT. poner en escena; *(clothes)* ponerse; *(to affect)* afectar; *(to turn on)* encender • **to p. on the brakes** echar el freno • **to p. one over on** engañar • **to p. one's house in order** arreglar uno sus asuntos • **to p. out** *(to extinguish)* apagar; *(to inconvenience)* molestar; *(to publish)* publicar; *(to display)* sacar, mostrar • **to p. through** *(to accomplish)* llevar a cabo; *(to enact)* hacer aprobar; *(to cause)* hacer pasar; TEL. poner con • **to p. together** atar cabos • **to p. up** *(to build)* levantar, construir; *(to can)* envasar; *(to nominate)* proponer; *(to provide)* poner, adelantar; *(to offer)* poner; *(to lodge)* hospedar, alojar; *(to hang up)* colgar • **to p. up to** incitar a • **to p. upon** abusar de —intr. ♦ **to p. in** MARÍT. hacer escala en un puerto • **to p. up** *o* **shut up** FAM. aguantar • **to p. up with** aguantar II. s. tiro, lanzamiento III. adj. ♦ **to be hard p. to** serle a uno difícil • **to stay p.** quedarse en su sitio.

put-down ('doun') s. JER. desdén m.
put-on (:ŏn') I. adj. fingido II. s. JER. engaño.
pu·tre·fac·tion (pyŏʊ'trə-făk'shən) s. putrefacción f; *(condition)* podredumbre f.
pu·tre·fy ('fī') tr. & intr. pudrir(se).
pu·trid (pyŏʊ'trĭd) adj. pútrido; *(rotten)* podrido; MED. gangrenoso; *(vile)* asqueroso.
putt (pŭt) DEP. I. s. tiro al hoyo II. tr. & intr. tirar al hoyo.
put·ter (pŭt'ər) intr. no hacer nada de particular —tr. ♦ **to p. away** perder.
put·ty (pŭt'ē) s. masilla.
puz·zle (pŭz'əl) I. tr. desconcertar, dejar perplejo ♦ **to p. out** resolver, descifrar —intr. ♦ **to p. over** reflexionar, meditar II. s. enigma m, misterio; *(riddle)* acertijo; *(bewilderment)* perplejidad f ♦ **crossword p.** crucigrama • **jigsaw p.** rompecabezas.
puz·zle·ment (:mənt) s. perplejidad f.
pyg·my (pĭg'mē) adj. & s. pigmeo.
py·ja·mas (pə-jä'məz) G.B. var. de **pajamas**.
py·lon (pī'lŏn') s. *(gateway)* pilón m; AVIA. torre marcadora del curso del vuelo; ELEC. poste m.
py·or·rhe·a (pī'ə-rē'ə) s. piorrea.
pyr·a·mid (pĭr'ə-mĭd') s. pirámide f.
pyre (pīr) s. pira, hoguera.
py·rite (pī'rīt') s. pirita (de hierro).
py·ro·ma·ni·a (pī'rō-mā'nē-ə) s. piromanía.
py·ro·ma·ni·ac (:ăk') s. & adj. pirómano.
py·ro·tech·nic (pī'rə-tĕk'nĭk) adj. pirotécnico ♦ **pyrotechnics** s.sg. pirotecnia.
Pyr·rhic victory (pĭr'ĭk) s. victoria pírrica.
py·thon (pī'thŏn') s. pitón m.

Q

q, Q (kyŏʊ) s. decimoséptima letra del alfabeto inglés.
q.t. (kyŏʊ'tē') s. ♦ **on the q.t.** JER. calladamente.
quack[1] (kwăk) I. s. graznido II. intr. graznar.
quack[2] s. *(doctor)* curandero.
quack·er·y ('ə-rē) s. curandería, charlatanería.
quad[1] (kwŏd) s. ARQ. patio cuadrangular.
quad[2] s. *(quadruplet)* cuatrillizo.
quad·ran·gle ('răng'gəl) s. cuadrángulo; ARQ. plaza, patio (de una universidad).
quad·rant (:rənt) s. cuadrante m.
quad·rate (:rāt') adj. & s. cuadrado.
quad·rat·ic (kwŏ-drăt'ĭk) adj. cuadrático.
quad·ri·ceps (kwŏd'rĭ-sĕps') s. cuadriceps m.
quad·ri·lat·er·al ('rə-lăt'ər-əl) s. & adj. cuadrilátero.
qua·drille (kwə-drĭl') s. cuadrilla.
quad·ri·ple·gi·a (kwŏd'rə-plē'jē-ə) s. cuadriplejía.
quad·ri·ple·gic (:jĭk) adj. & s. cuadripléjico.
quad·roon (kwŏ-drŏʊn') s. cuarterón m.
quad·ru·ped (kwŏd'rə-pĕd') s. cuadrúpedo.
quad·ru·ple (kwŏ-drŏʊ'pəl) I. adj. cuádruple II. tr. & intr. cuadruplicar(se).
quad·ru·plet (:plĭt) s. *(group of four)* cuádruplo; *(offspring)* cuatrillizo.
quad·ru·pli·cate (:plĭ-kĭt) adj. & s. cuádruplo ♦ **in q.** por cuadruplicado.
quaff (kwŏf) tr. & intr. beber a grandes tragos.
quag·gy (kwăg'ē) adj. **-i-** pantanoso.
quag·mire (:mīr') s. pantano.
quail[1] (kwāl) s. [pl. inv. *o* **s**] codorniz f.
quail[2] intr. acobardarse.
quaint (kwānt) adj. pintoresco.

quaint·ness ('nĭs) s. carácter pintoresco.
quake (kwāk) I. intr. temblar; *(with fear)* estremecerse II. s. temblor m.
qual·i·fi·ca·tion (kwŏl'ə-fĭ-kā'shən) s. calificación m; *(requirement)* requisito; *(restriction)* reserva ♦ **pl.** credenciales.
qual·i·fied (kwŏl'ə-fīd') adj. *(competent)* capacitado; *(certified)* acreditado; *(restricted)* con reservas.
qual·i·fi·er (:fī'ər) s. calificativo.
qual·i·fy (:fī') tr. calificar, caracterizar; *(to train)* capacitar; *(to entitle)* dar derecho a; *(to certify)* acreditar; *(to moderate)* atenuar; GRAM. modificar —intr. *(for a position)* tener las capacidades necesarias; DEP. clasificarse ♦ **to q. as** merecer el título de.
qual·i·fy·ing (:ĭng) adj. eliminatorio.
qual·i·ta·tive (kwŏl'ĭ-tā'tĭv) adj. cualitativo.
qual·i·ty (kwŏl'ĭ-tē) s. *(nature, excellence)* calidad f; *(property)* característica; *(attribute)* cualidad f; *(high status)* categoría.
qualm (kwäm, kwŏm) s. *(doubt)* duda; *(scruple)* remordimiento ♦ **to have no qualms about** no vacilar en.
quan·da·ry (kwŏn'də-rē) s. dilema m.
quan·ti·fy (kwŏn'tĭ-fī') tr. determinar la cantidad de.
quan·ti·ta·tive (:tā'tĭv) adj. cuantitativo.
quan·ti·ty (kwŏn'tĭ-tē) s. cantidad f ♦ **in q.** en grandes cantidades • **unknown q.** incógnita.
quan·tum (kwŏn'təm) s. [pl. **-ta**] FÍS. cuanto, quantum m ♦ **q. jump** FÍS. transición cuántica; FIG. desviación repentina • **q. mechanics,** theory mecánica, teoría cuántica.
quar·an·tine (kwŏr'ən-tēn') I. s. cuarentena II. tr. poner en cuarentena.
quark (kwôrk) s. quark m.
quar·rel (kwôr'əl) I. s. pelea, discusión f ♦ **to have no q. with** no tener nada en contra de II. intr. *(to argue)* pelear, discutir; *(with an issue)* estar en desacuerdo ♦ **to q. over** discutir.
quar·rel·er (:ə-lər) s. pendenciero.
quar·rel·ing (:ə-lĭng) s. disputas f.
quar·rel·some (:əl-səm) adj. pendenciero.
quar·ry[1] (kwôr'ē) s. *(prey)* presa.
quar·ry[2] I. s. *(pit)* cantera II. tr. *(stone)* sacar de una cantera; *(land)* excavar.
quart (kwôrt) s. cuarto de galón).
quar·ter (kwôr'tər) I. s. *(fourth part)* cuarto, cuarta parte; *(of a dollar)* veinticinco centavos; *(of an hour, mile)* cuarto; *(of a year)* trimestre m; *(direction)* dirección f; *(neighborhood)* barrio; GEOM. cuadrante m; DEP. *(period)* tiempo ♦ **(a) q. past** y cuarto • **(a) q. to** *o* **of** menos cuarto • **q. note** negra f ♦ pl. *(residence)* residencia; *(barracks)* cuartel • **at close q.** *(at close range)* de cerca; *(fighting)* cuerpo a cuerpo • **from all q.** de todas partes II. tr. dividir en cuartos, cuartear; *(to lodge)* alojar; MIL. acuartelar ♦ **to draw and q.** descuartizar —intr. *(troops)* acuartelarse; *(to lodge)* alojarse III. adj. cuarto de <a q. inch un cuarto de pulgada>.
quar·ter·back (:băk') I. s. jugador m que dirige la jugada II. tr. dirigir.
quar·ter·deck (:dĕk') s. alcázar m.
quar·ter·fi·nal ('fī'nəl) s. cuarto de final.
quar·ter·hour (:our') s. cuarto de hora.
quar·ter·ly ('-lē) I. s. & adj. *(publication f)* trimestral II. adv. trimestralmente, cada tres meses.
quar·ter·mas·ter (:măs'tər) s. MIL. oficial m de

intendencia; MARÍT. cabo de mar.

quar·ter·staff (:stăf´) s. [pl. **-ves**] vara.

quar·tet(te) (kwôr-tĕt´) s. cuarteto.

quar·to (´tō) s. [pl. **-tos**] libro en cuarto.

quartz (kwôrts) s. cuarzo.

quartz·ite (kwôrt´sīt´) s. cuarcita.

qua·sar (kwā´zär´) s. cuásar *m.*

quash (kwŏsh) tr. *(to annul)* anular; *(uprising, feeling)* sofocar.

qua·si (kwā´zī´, kwä´zē) adj. cuasi, casi.

quat·rain (kwŏt´rān´) s. cuarteto.

qua·ver (kwā´vər) I. intr. temblar; *(to trill)* trinar —tr. decir con voz trémula II. s. *(of voice)* temblor *m*; *(trill)* trino.

quay (kē, kā) s. muelle *m.*

quay·age (kē´ĭj, kā´-) s. derechos de muelle.

quea·si·ness (kwē´zē-nĭs) s. náusea.

quea·sy (kwē´zē) adj. **-i-** *(nauseous)* con náuseas; *(stomach)* débil; *(uneasy)* inquieto.

queen (kwēn) s. reina; *(in cards, chess)* dama ♦ **q. mother** reina madre.

queen·ly (´lē) adj. **-i-** de reina, majestuoso.

queen-size (:sīz´) adj. muy grande.

queer (kwîr) I. adj. *(strange)* raro; *(odd)* curioso; *(eccentric)* estrafalario; *(suspicious)* sospechoso ♦ **to feel q.** no sentirse bien II. tr. JER. arruinar.

queer·ness (´nĭs) s. rareza, extrañeza.

quell (kwĕl) tr. *(a riot)* sofocar; *(emotions)* dominar.

quench (kwĕnch) tr. *(fire)* apagar; *(enthusiasm, thirst)* matar; *(metals)* templar.

quench·a·ble (kwĕn´chə-bəl) adj. apagable.

quer·u·lous (kwĕr´ə-ləs) adj. quejumbroso.

que·ry (kwîr´ē) I. s. pregunta; *(doubt)* duda; *(mark)* signo de interrogación II. tr. poner en duda; *(to question)* preguntar.

quest (kwĕst) s. búsqueda.

ques·tion (kwĕs´chən) I. s. pregunta; *(issue)* cuestión *f*; *(problem)* problema *m*; *(proposition)* moción *f*; *(doubt)* duda <*there is no q.* about no hay duda alguna de> ♦ **beyond q.** fuera de duda • **in q.** en cuestión • **q. mark** signo de interrogación • **to be out of the q.** ser imposible • **to call into q.** poner en tela de juicio • **to raise the q. of** plantear la cuestión de II. tr. preguntar, hacer una pregunta a; DER. interrogar; *(to dispute)* poner en tela de juicio.

ques·tion·a·ble (:chə-nə-bəl) adj. *(debatable)* cuestionable; *(dubious)* dudoso.

ques·tion·er (:nər) s. interrogador *m.*

ques·tion·ing (:nĭng) I. s. interrogación *f* II. adj. interrogativo; *(inquisitive)* inquisitivo.

ques·tion·naire (´-nâr´) s. cuestionario.

queue (kyō͞o) I. s. cola, fila II. intr. ♦ **to q. up** hacer cola.

quib·ble (kwĭb´əl) I. intr. andar con sutilezas II. s. sutileza.

quiche (kēsh) s. pastel *m* de queso y huevos.

quick (kwĭk) I. adj. *(fast)* rápido; *(bright)* listo; *(mind)* despierto; *(temper)* irascible ♦ **to be q. about** hacer rápidamente • **to be q. to act** obrar sin perder tiempo • **to be q. to take offense** ofenderse por nada II. s. médula ♦ **the q. and the dead** los vivos y los muertos • **to cut to the q.** herir en lo más vivo III. adv. rápido, rápidamente.

quick-and-dirt·y (´ən-dûr´tē) adj. de mala calidad.

quick·en (´ən) tr. *(pace)* apresurar, acelerar; *(pulse)* acelerar; *(appetite, interest)* reavivar —intr. apresurarse, acelerarse; *(to revive)* resucitar.

quick-freeze (:wĭk´frēz´) tr. **-froze, -frozen** congelar rápidamente.

quick·ie (:ē) s. FAM. cosa hecha rápidamente.

quick·ness (:nĭs) s. rapidez *f*; *(of mind)* viveza.

quick·sand (:sănd´) s. arena movediza.

quick·sil·ver (:sĭl´vər) I. s. mercurio, azogue *m* II. adj. caprichoso.

quick·step (:stĕp´) s. marcha militar.

quick-tem·pered (:tĕm´pərd) adj. irascible.

quick-wit·ted (:wĭt´ĭd) adj. listo, agudo.

quid[1] (kwĭd) s. mascada (de tabaco).

quid[2] s. [pl. inv. o **s**] JER., G.B. libra esterlina.

quid·di·ty (kwĭd´ĭ-tē) s. quid *m*, esencia.

qui·es·cent (kwī-ĕs´ənt) adj. quieto.

qui·et (kwī´ĭt) I. adj. **-er, -est** *(silent)* callado, silencioso; *(calm)* tranquilo; *(not showy)* discreto ♦ **be q.!** ¡cállate! • **to be q.** *(not noisy)* no hacer ruido; *(to stop talking)* callarse II. s. *(calm)* quietud *f*; *(silence)* silencio; *(rest)* reposo III. tr. *(to silence)* hacer callar; *(to calm)* tranquilizar —intr. ♦ **to q. down** calmarse.

qui·et·ness (:nĭs) s. silencio; *(calmness)* tranquilidad *f*, quietud *f.*

qui·e·tude (kwī´ĭ-tōo̅d´) s. quietud *f.*

qui·e·tus (kwī-ē´təs) s. muerte *f*; *(of a debt)* finiquito.

quill (kwĭl) s. *(feather, pen)* pluma; *(stem)* cañón *m* (de una pluma); *(of a porcupine)* púa.

quilt (kwĭlt) I. s. colcha II. tr. acolchar.

quilt·ing (kwĭl´tĭng) s. acolchado.

quince (kwĭns) s. membrillo.

qui·nine (kwī´nīn´) s. quinina ♦ **q. water** agua de quina.

quin·sy (kwĭn´zē) s. amigdalitis *f.*

quint (kwĭnt) s. quintillizo.

quin·tes·sence (kwĭn-tĕs´əns) s. quintaesencia.

quin·tet(te) (:tĕt´) s. quinteto.

quin·tu·plet (:tŭp´lĭt) s. *(group of five)* quíntuplo; *(offspring)* quintillizo.

quip (kwĭp) I. s. ocurrencia II. intr. **-pp-** decir sarcásticamente; *(to gibe)* tirar pullas.

quip·ster (´stər) s. persona ocurrente.

quire (kwîr) s. mano *f* (de papel).

quirk (kwûrk) s. *(twist)* vuelta; *(idiosyncracy)* peculiaridad *f*; *(vagary)* capricho.

quirk·y (kwûr´kē) adj. **-i-** *(peculiar)* peculiar, singular; *(capricious)* caprichoso.

quirt (kwûrt) s. cuarta, fusta.

quis·ling (kwĭz´lĭng) s. colaboracionista *mf.*

quit (kwĭt) I. tr. **quit(ted), -tting** *(to leave)* salir de <*to q. work at five* salir del empleo a las cinco>; *(a school, job)* abandonar, dejar; *(to stop)* dejar de <*to q. smoking* dejar de fumar> —intr. *(to stop)* parar <*I q. at five* paro a las cinco>; *(to give up)* desistir; *(to resign)* renunciar II. adj. ♦ **to be q. of** estar libre de.

quit·claim (´klām´) s. renuncia.

quite (kwīt) adv. totalmente <*we are q. satisfied* estamos totalmente satisfechos>; *(altogether)* del todo <*it is not q. finished* no está del todo terminado>; *(absolutely)* absolutamente; *(exactly)* exactamente; *(rather)* bastante <*q. long* bastante largo>; FAM. *(very)* muy, bastante ♦ **q. a bit** bastante • **q. a while** un buen rato • **q. so!** ¡así es! • **to be q.** a ser un gran.

quits (kwĭts) adj. ♦ **to be q.** estar iguales *o* en paz • **to call it q.** dejarlo así.

quit·tance (kwĭt´ns) s. quita.

quit·ter (:ər) s. ♦ **to be a q.** darse por vencido fácilmente.

quiv·er¹ (kwĭv′ər) **I.** intr. temblar, estremecerse **II.** s. temblor *m*, estremecimiento.

quiv·er² s. *(for arrows)* aljaba.

quix·ot·ic (kwĭk-sŏt′ĭk) adj. quijotesco.

quiz (kwĭz) **I.** tr. **-zz-** interrogar; *(to test)* examinar **II.** s. interrogatorio; *(test)* prueba, examen *m* ♦ **q. show** concurso de televisión.

quiz·zi·cal (kwĭz′ĭ-kəl) adj. perplejo.

quoin (koin, kwoin) s. piedra angular.

quo·rum (kwôr′əm) s. quórum *m*.

quo·ta (kwō′tə) s. cuota.

quot·a·ble (kwō′tə-bəl) adj. digno de citarse.

quo·ta·tion (kwō-tā′shən) s. cita; *(of prices)* cotización *f* ♦ **q. marks** comillas.

quote (kwōt) **I.** tr. *(words, source)* citar; *(example, price)* dar; FIN. cotizar —intr. hacer una cita ♦ **and I q.** y cito sus palabras **II.** s. FAM. cita; *(mark)* comilla <in quotes entre comillas> ♦ **q. unquote** entre comillas.

quo·tid·i·an (kwō-tĭd′ē-ən) adj. *(daily)* diario, cotidiano; *(commonplace)* común.

quo·tient (kwō′shənt) s. MAT. cociente *m*.

R

r, R (är) s. decimoctava letra del alfabeto inglés.

rab·bi (răb′ī) s. rabino.

rab·bit (răb′ĭt) s. [pl. inv. *o* **s**] conejo.

rab·ble (răb′əl) s. gentío, chusma.

rab·ble-rous·er (:rou′zər) s. demagogo.

rab·id (răb′ĭd) adj. rabioso; *(fanatic)* fanático.

ra·bies (rā′bēz) s. rabia.

rac·coon (ră-kōōn′) s. [pl. inv. *o* **s**] mapache *m*.

race¹ (rās) s. *(people)* raza.

race² **I.** s. *(contest)* carrera; *(of water)* corriente *f* ♦ **r. car** coche de carreras • **r. car driver** corredor **II.** intr. correr; *(to compete)* competir; *(engine)* embalarse ♦ **to r. around** ajetrearse —tr. competir con, correr contra; *(engine)* acelerar al máximo ♦ **I'll r. you** te echo una carrera • **to r. after** perseguir.

race·course (:kôrs′) s. *(horse)* hipódromo; *(auto)* autódromo.

race·horse (:hôrs′) s. caballo de carreras.

rac·er (rā′sər) s. corredor *m*.

race·track (rās′trăk′) s. pista; *(horse)* hipódromo.

ra·cial (rā′shəl) adj. racial.

rac·ism (rā′sĭz′əm) s. racismo.

ra·cist (rā′sĭst) adj. & s. racista *mf*.

rack (răk) **I.** s. *(in a train, car)* portaequipajes *m*; *(for hats, coats)* percha; *(for feed)* comedero; *(for torture)* potro; *(of pain)* tormento ♦ **r. and pinion steering** engranaje de cremallera y piñón • **to be on the r.** FAM. estar atormentado • **to go to r. and ruin** venirse abajo **II.** tr. hacer sufrir ♦ **to be racked by** *o* **with** estar atormentado por • **to r. up** FAM. acumular.

rack·et¹ (răk′ĭt) s. DEP. raqueta.

rack·et² s. *(uproar)* alboroto; *(illegal business)* negocio ilegal; *(fraud)* timo, estafa.

rack·et·eer (răk′ĭ-tîr′) s. persona que hace negocios deshonestos.

rack·et·eer·ing (:ĭng) s. negocio ilegal; *(bribery)* soborno; *(blackmail)* chantaje *m*.

rac·on·teur (răk′ŏn-tûr′) s. cuentista *mf*.

rac·y (rā′sē) adj. **-i-** *(joke)* picante; *(lively)* animado.

ra·dar (rā′där′) s. radar *m*.

ra·di·al (rā′dē-əl) **I.** adj. radial **II.** s. *(radius)* radio; *(tire)* neumático radial.

ra·di·ance/an·cy (rā′dē-əns) s. resplandor *m*.

ra·di·ant (:ənt) adj. radiante.

ra·di·ate (:āt′) intr. *(to shine)* brillar; *(to spread out)* radiar, FÍS. irradiar, emitir —tr. (ir)radiar.

ra·di·a·tion (′-ā′shən) s. radiación *f*.

ra·di·a·tor (′-′tər) s. radiador *m*.

rad·i·cal (răd′ĭ-kəl) adj. & s. radical *m*.

rad·i·cle (răd′ĭ-kəl) s. radícula.

ra·di·o (rā′dē-ō′) **I.** s. radio *f* ♦ **r. network** red de emisoras • **r. station** emisora **II.** tr. & intr. transmitir (un mensaje) por radio.

ra·di·o·ac·tive (′-−äk′tĭv) adj. radiactivo.

ra·di·o·ac·tiv·i·ty (:äk-tĭv′ĭ-tē) s. radiactividad *f*.

ra·di·o·broad·cast (:brôd′kăst′) *o* **ra·di·o·cast** (:kăst′) tr. & intr. **-cast(ed)** radiar.

ra·di·o·gram (:grăm′) s. radiograma *m*.

ra·di·o·graph (:grăf′) **I.** s. radiografía **II.** tr. radiografiar.

ra·di·ol·o·gist (rā′dē-ŏl′ə-jĭst) s. radiólogo.

ra·di·ol·o·gy (:jē) s. radiología.

ra·di·om·e·try (rā′dē-ŏm′ĭ-trē) s. radiometría.

ra·di·o·ther·a·py (:ō-thĕr′ə-pē) s. radioterapia.

rad·ish (răd′ĭsh) s. rábano.

ra·di·um (rā′dē-əm) s. radio.

ra·di·us (rā′dē-əs) s. [pl. **es** *o* **-dii**] radio.

ra·don (rā′dŏn′) s. radón *m*.

raff·ish (răf′ĭsh) adj. vulgar; *(showy)* ostentoso.

raf·fle (răf′əl) **I.** s. rifa **II.** tr. & intr. rifar.

raft¹ (răft) **I.** s. balsa **II.** intr. ♦ **to go rafting** ir en balsa.

raft² s. FAM. *(great number)* montón *m*.

raft·er (răf′tər) s. par *m* (de un techo).

rag¹ (răg) s. *(cloth)* trapo; JER. *(newspaper)* periodicucho ♦ pl. harapos.

rag² tr. **-gg-** *(to scold)* regañar; JER. *(to tease)* tomar el pelo a.

rag·a·muf·fin (răg′ə-mŭf′ĭn) s. golfo.

rage (rāj) **I.** s. furia ♦ **to be all the r.** estar en boga • **to fly into a r.** enfurecerse **II.** intr. *(storm)* bramar; *(plague, fire)* propagarse.

rag·ged (răg′ĭd) adj. *(beggar)* andrajoso; *(sleeve)* raido; *(edge)* mellado; *(performance)* desigual.

rag·time (răg′tīm′) s. jazz *m* de ritmo sincopado.

rag·weed (răg′wēd′) s. ambrosia.

rah (rä) interj. ¡hurra!

raid (rād) **I.** s. MIL. incursión *f*, ataque sorpresivo; *(by police)* redada **II.** tr. atacar por sorpresa; *(police)* hacer una redada en.

raid·er (rā′dər) s. invasor *m*.

rail¹ (rāl) s. *(banister)* barandilla; *(at racetrack)* cerca; F.C. riel *m* ♦ **by r.** por ferrocarril ♦ pl. ferrocarriles.

rail² s. ORNIT. rascón *m*.

rail³ intr. ♦ **to r. against** denostar contra.

rail·ing (rā′lĭng) s. *(of balcony)* baranda; *(of stairs)* pasamanos.

rail·road (rāl′rōd′) **I.** s. ferrocarril *m* ♦ **r. car** vagón • **r. crossing** cruce de ferrocarril • **r. station** estación ferroviaria **II.** tr. transportar por ferrocarril; FAM. *(bill, law)* hacer votar apresuradamente; *(person)* encarcelar falsamente.

rail·way (:wā′) s. ferrocarril *m*; *(track)* vía.

rain (rān) **I.** s. lluvia ♦ **(come) r. or shine** pase lo que pase • **in the r.** bajo la lluvia • **r. forest**

selva tropical **II.** intr. llover ♦ **it never rains but it pours** las desgracias nunca vienen solas —tr. ♦ **to r. cats and dogs** llover a cántaros.

rain·bow ('bō') s. arco iris.

rain·coat (:kōt') s. impermeable *m.*

rain·drop (:drŏp') s. gota de lluvia.

rain·fall (:fôl') s. *(shower)* aguacero; *(precipitation)* precipitación *f.*

rain·storm (:stôrm') s. tempestad *f* de lluvia.

rain·wa·ter (:wô'tər) s. agua de lluvia.

rain·wear (:wâr') s. ropa impermeable.

rain·y (rā'nē) adj. **-i-** lluvioso.

raise (rāz) **I.** tr. levantar; *(window, prices)* subir; *(land)* divisar; *(flag)* izar; *(a ship)* sacar a flote; *(welt, blister)* producir; *(the dead)* resucitar; *(voice)* alzar; *(rank, level)* ascender; *(children, animals)* criar; *(crop)* cultivar; *(point)* hacer, formular; *(an issue)* plantear; *(doubts)* suscitar; *(to arouse)* sublevar; *(money)* recaudar; *(an army)* reclutar; MARÍT. levar; CUL. hacer subir; MAT. elevar ♦ **to be raised** criarse **II.** s. aumento.

raised (rāzd) adj. *(in relief)* en relieve; *(embossed)* repujado.

rai·sin (rā'zĭn) s. pasa (de uva).

rake¹ (rāk) **I.** s. *(tool)* rastrillo **II.** tr. rastrillar; *(leaves)* recoger con el rastrillo; *(to sweep)* rastrear; *(with gunfire)* ametrallar ♦ **to r. in** ganar mucho • **to r. over the coals** censurar duramente • **to r. up** *(gossip)* sacar a relucir; *(money)* reunir.

rake² s. libertino, Don Juan.

ral·ly (rǎl'ē) **I.** tr. *(to assemble)* reunir; *(to revive)* recobrar —intr. reunirse; *(to recover)* recuperarse ♦ **to r. round** o **to** dar apoyo a, adherirse a **II.** s. reunión *f*; COM., MED. recuperación *f*; AUTO. rally *m.*

ram (rǎm) **I.** s. ZOOL. carnero; MAQ., MEC. pisón *m*; MIL. ariete *m*; MARÍT. espolón *m* **II.** tr. **-mm-** *(to stuff)* meter a la fuerza; *(to crash into)* chocar con.

ram·ble (rǎm'bəl) **I.** intr. *(to walk)* pasear; *(to digress)* divagar **II.** s. paseo.

ram·bler (:blər) s. vagabundo.

ram·bling (:blĭng) adj. sin orden ni concierto.

ram·bunc·tious (rǎm-bǔngk'shəs) adj. alborotador.

ram·i·fi·ca·tion (rǎm'ə-fĭ-kā'shən) s. ramificación *f.*

ramp (rǎmp) s. rampa.

ram·page (rǎm'pāj') s. alboroto ♦ **to go on a r.** andar como loco, ir destrozándolo todo.

ram·pant (rǎm'pənt) adj. desenfrenado.

ram·part (rǎm'pärt') **I.** s. muralla; FIG. amparo **II.** tr. amurallar.

ram·rod (rǎm'rŏd') s. *(loading)* taco; *(cleaning)* baqueta.

ram·shack·le (rǎm'shǎk'əl) adj. desvencijado.

ran (rǎn) cf. **run.**

ranch (rǎnch) **I.** s. hacienda ♦ **r. house** casa de una sola planta **II.** intr. llevar una hacienda.

ranch·er (rǎn'chər) s. estanciero, hacendado.

ran·cid (rǎn'sĭd) adj. rancio.

ran·cor (rǎng'kər) s. rencor *m.*

ran·cor·ous (:əs) adj. rencoroso.

ran·dom (rǎn'dəm) adj. hecho al azar, fortuito ♦ **at r.** al azar.

rang (rǎng) cf. **ring².**

range (rānj) **I.** s. *(reach)* alcance *m*; *(scope)* extensión *f*; *(variety)* gama; *(stove)* cocina; *(of merchandise)* surtido; AER. radio de acción; *(firing range)* campo de tiro; *(for livestock)* te-

rreno de pasto; *(habitat)* habitat *m*; GEOG. cordillera, cadena; MÚS. registro; MIL. distancia (del blanco) ♦ **close r.** de cerca, a quemarropa • **r. of vision** campo visual • **within firing r.** a tiro **II.** tr. *(in rows)* alinear; *(to classify)* ordenar, clasificar; *(to traverse)* recorrer; *(livestock)* apacentar —intr. extenderse; *(to explore)* recorrer ♦ **to r. from . . . to** ir de . . . a.

rang·er (rān'jər) s. *(of a forest)* guardabosques *m*; *(mounted policeman)* policía *m.*

rang·y (:jē) adj. **-i-** alto y delgado.

rank¹ (rǎngk) **I.** s. *(row)* fila; *(in society)* clase *f*; *(high status)* rango; *(quality)* categoría; MIL. grado ♦ **r. and file** MIL. soldados rasos; *(ordinary people)* gente común; *(of a union)* miembros ♦ pl. filas • **to break r.** romper filas • **to close (the) r.** cerrar las filas • **to join the r. of** unirse con **II.** tr. *(in rows)* alinear; *(in order)* clasificar ♦ **to r. above** ser superior a • **to r. among** figurar entre —intr. clasificarse ♦ **to r. high** ocupar una alta posición.

rank² adj. *(growth)* tupido; *(smell)* rancio.

rank·ing (rǎng'kĭng) adj. superior.

ran·kle (rǎng'kəl) intr. doler, enconarse.

ran·sack (rǎn'sǎk') tr. *(to search)* registrar; *(to plunder)* saquear.

ran·som (rǎn'səm) **I.** s. rescate *m* **II.** tr. rescatar, liberar.

rant (rǎnt) tr. & intr. vociferar.

rap¹ (rǎp) **I.** s. golpe seco ♦ **to beat the r.** JER. librarse de una condena • **to take the r.** JER. cargar con la culpa *(for* de) **II.** tr. **-pp-** *(to strike)* golpear; *(to criticize)* criticar —intr. ♦ **to r. on** *(door)* llamar a; *(table)* golpear.

rap² JER. **I.** intr. **-pp-** conversar **II.** s. conversación *f.*

ra·pa·cious (rə-pā'shəs) adj. rapaz.

ra·pac·i·ty (rə-pǎs'ĭ-tē) s. rapacidad *f.*

rape¹ (rāp) **I.** s. violación *f*; *(abduction)* rapto **II.** tr. violar.

rape² s. BOT. colza.

rap·id (rǎp'ĭd) **I.** adj. rápido ♦ **r. transit** sistema de transporte urbano **II.** s. ♦ pl. rápidos.

ra·pid·i·ty (rə-pĭd'ĭ-tē) s. rapidez *f.*

rap·ine (rǎp'ĭn) s. rapiña, saqueo.

rap·ist (rā'pĭst) s. violador *m.*

rap·port (rǎ-pôr') s. relación *f.*

rap·proche·ment (rǎ'prōsh-mä') s. acercamiento.

rapt (rǎpt) adj. *(enraptured)* extasiado; *(engrossed)* absorto.

rap·ture (rǎp'chər) s. éxtasis *m.*

rap·tur·ous (:əs) adj. extasiado.

rare¹ (râr) adj. raro; *(special)* poco común.

rare² adj. CUL. jugoso, poco hecho.

rar·e·fied (râr'ə-fīd') adj. esotérico, refinado.

rar·e·fy (:fī') tr. & intr. enrarecer(se).

rar·ing (râr'ĭng) adj. FAM. impaciente.

rar·i·ty (râr'ĭ-tē) s. rareza.

ras·cal (rǎs'kəl) s. tunante *m*, bribón *m.*

rash¹ (rǎsh) adj. *(act)* precipitado; *(person)* impetuoso.

rash² s. MED. sarpullido; FIG. ola.

rash·er (rǎsh'ər) s. lonja de jamón, tocino.

rasp (rǎsp) **I.** tr. escofinar **II.** s. escofina; *(sound)* chirrido.

rasp·ber·ry (rǎz'bĕr'ē) s. *(plant)* frambueso; *(fruit)* frambuesa; JER. abucheo.

rasp·y (rǎs'pē) adj. **-i-** áspero.

rat (rǎt) **I.** s. rata; JER. canalla *m*, traidor *m* ♦ **to smell a r.** FAM. sospechar algo **II.** intr. **-tt-** ♦ **to r. on** JER. delatar a.

ratch·et (răch´ĭt) s. MEC. trinquete *m*, uña.
rate[1] (rāt) **I.** s. *(speed)* velocidad *f*; *(of change)*
coeficiente *m*; *(of occurence)* índice *m*; *(percent-age)* porcentaje *m*; *(of pay)* tipo; FIN. interés *m*
♦ **at any r.** de todos modos • **at this r.** a este
paso • **postal r.** tarifa postal • **r. of exchange**
cambio **II.** tr. *(to estimate)* estimar; *(to value)*
valorar; *(to classify)* clasificar; *(to deserve)* merecer —intr. ♦ **to be rated (as)** ser considerado
como • **to r. high** ocupar una alta posición.
rate[2] tr. & intr. *(to berate)* regañar.
rath·er (răth´ər) adv. *(more exactly)* mejor dicho; *(quite)* bastante; *(somewhat)* un poco ♦
but r. sino (que) • **I would r.** preferiría • **I
would r. not** mejor no • **r. than** en vez de.
rat·i·fy (răt´ə-fī´) tr. ratificar.
rat·ing (rā´tĭng) s. *(standing)* clasificación *f*;
(credit rating) solvencia; TELEV. popularidad *f*.
ra·tio (rā´shō) s. proporción *f*; MAT. razón *f*.
ra·ti·oc·i·nate (răsh´ē-ŏs´ə-nāt´) tr. raciocinar.
ra·tion (răsh´ən, rā´shən) **I.** s. ración *f*, porción *f*
♦ pl. MIL. provisiones **II.** tr. racionar.
ra·tion·al (răsh´ə-nəl) adj. racional; *(sensible)*
razonable.
ra·tion·ale (´-năl´) s. *(reason)* razón *f* fundamental; *(explanation)* explicación *f*.
ra·tion·al·i·ty (:năl´ĭ-tē) s. racionalidad *f*.
ra·tion·al·i·za·tion (:nə-lĭ-zā´shən) s. raciona-
lización *f*.
ra·tion·al·ize (´--līz´) tr. racionalizar.
ra·tion·ing (răsh´ə-nĭng) s. racionamiento *m*.
rat·tan (ră-tăn´) s. rota, junco de Indias.
rat·tle (răt´l) **I.** intr. *(vehicle)* traquetear; *(window, door)* golpetear; *(teeth)* castañetear ♦ **to r.
on** seguir parloteando —tr. *(to shake)* sacudir; FAM. *(to unnerve)* poner nervioso ♦ **to r. off**
decir rápidamente **II.** tr. traqueteo; *(of door,
window)* golpe *m*; *(of teeth)* castañeteo; *(of
baby)* sonajero.
rat·tler (´lər) s. serpiente *f* de cascabel.
rat·tle·snake (:l-snāk´) s. serpiente *f* de cascabel.
rat·tle·trap (:l-trăp´) s. cacharro (vehículo).
rat·trap (răt´trăp´) s. ratonera; FIG. pocilga.
rat·ty (răt´ē) adj. -i- ratonil; JER. *(dilapidated)*
destartalado; *(shabby)* andrajoso.
rau·cous (rô´kəs) adj. estridente.
raun·chy (rôn´chē) adj. -i- JER. *(grimy)* sucio;
(obscene) vulgar.
rav·age (răv´ĭj) **I.** tr. destrozar; *(by army)* saquear **II.** s. destrozo ♦ pl. estragos.
rave (rāv) **I.** intr. delirar, desvariar ♦ **to r. about**
estar loco por **II.** s. ♦ **to get r. reviews** FAM.
recibir críticas entusiastas.
rav·el (răv´əl) tr. & intr. deshilar(se).
ra·ven (rā´vən) **I.** s. cuervo **II.** adj. negro.
rav·en·ous (răv´ə-nəs) adj. hambriento; *(voracious)* voraz.
ra·vine (rə-vēn´) s. barranco.
rav·ing (rā´vĭng) **I.** adj. FAM. extraordinario ♦ **to
be r. mad** estar loco de atar **II.** s. ♦ pl. desva-
ríos.
rav·ish (răv´ĭsh) tr. *(to seize)* raptar; *(to rape)*
violar.
rav·ish·ing (:ĭ-shĭng) adj. encantador.
raw (rô) adj. crudo; *(not refined)* bruto;
(weather) frío y húmedo; *(inexperienced)* novato; *(socially coarse)* tosco; *(throat)* inflamado; *(wound)* en carne viva ♦ **in the r.** FAM.
desnudo • **r. material** materia prima • **to get a
r. deal** JER. recibir un tratamiento injusto.
raw·hide (rô´hīd´) s. cuero sin curtir.

ray[1] (rā) s. rayo; MAT., BOT. radio.
ray[2] s. ICT. raya.
ray·on (rā´ŏn´) s. rayón *m*.
raze (rāz) tr. arrasar, demoler.
ra·zor (rā´zər) s. navaja de afeitar ♦ **r. blade**
cuchilla *u* hoja de afeitar.
razz (răz) tr. JER. tomar el pelo a, burlarse de.
reach (rēch) **I.** tr. alcanzar; *(as far as)* llegar
hasta; *(to arrive at)* llegar a; *(on the phone)* comunicarse con; *(to get through to)* impresionar;
(in length, height) llegar a, extenderse hasta; *(in
age)* cumplir; FAM. *(to pass an object)* pasar,
llegar ♦ **to r. out** extender, alargar —intr. llegar ♦ **to r. down** inclinarse, agacharse • **to r. for**
tratar de coger *o* agarrar • **to r. for the stars**
aspirar a lo inalcanzable • **to r. in(to)** meter la
mano (en) • **to r. out** extender la mano • **to r.
up** alzar la mano **II.** s. alcance *m*; *(comprehension)* comprensión *f*; *(of cord, arm)* extensión *f* ♦ **within r.** *(of the hand)* al alcance de la
mano; *(by transportation)* cerca.
re·act (rē-ăkt´) intr. reaccionar.
re·ac·tion (rē-ăk´shən) s. reacción *f*.
re·ac·tion·ar·y (:shə-nĕr´ē) adj. & s. reacciona-
rio.
re·ac·ti·vate (:tə-vāt´) tr. reactivar.
re·ac·tive (:tĭv) adj. reactivo.
re·ac·tor (:tər) s. QUÍM. reactivo; ELEC., FÍS.
reactor *m*.
read (rēd) **I.** tr. read leer; *(thoughts, the future)*
adivinar; G.B. *(to study)* cursar, estudiar; RAD.
oír; TEC. *(an instrument)* marcar <*the dial reads
32°* la esfera marca 32°> ♦ **to r. into** atribuir
(a) • **to r. out** leer en voz alta • **to r. over** *(to go
over)* repasar; *(to reread)* releer • **to r. someone like a book** saber lo que alguien está pen-
sando • **to r. up on** informarse acerca de
—intr. leer; *(to be worded)* rezar, decir ♦ **to r.
between the lines** leer entre líneas **II.** s. lectura **III.** adj. ♦ **well-read** *(book)* muy leído;
(person) instruido.
read·a·ble (rē´də-bəl) adj. *(legible)* legible; *(interesting)* interesante.
read·er (rē´dər) s. lector *m*; *(schoolbook)* libro
de lecturas; *(anthology)* antología.
read·i·ly (rĕd´l-ē) adv. *(willingly)* de buena
gana; *(easily)* con facilidad.
read·i·ness (:ē-nĭs) s. buena disposición.
read·ing (rē´dĭng) s. lectura; *(of a situation)* interpretación *f*; *(of a text)* versión *f*; TEC. indicación *f*; COMPUT. transferencia ♦ **r. room** sala de
lectura • **the r. public** el público lector • **to take
a r.** TEC. medir.
re·ad·just (rē´ə-jŭst´) tr. reajustar, readaptar.
re·ad·just·ment (:mənt) s. reajuste *m*.
read·out (rēd´out´) s. información impresa.
read·y (rĕd´ē) **I.** adj. *(willing)* dispuesto; *(about to)* a punto de; *(clever)* agudo,
vivo; *(answer)* rápido; *(available)* disponible ♦
r. cash *o* **money** dinero contante *o* sonante **II.**
tr. *(to prepare)* preparar(se); *(to fix up)* arre-
glar(se) **II.** tr. preparar.
read·y-made (´-mād´) adj. hecho.
read·y-to-wear (:tə-wâr´) **I.** adj. hecho, confec-
cionado **II.** s. ropa hecha.
re·af·firm (rē´ə-fûrm´) tr. reafirmar.
real (rē´əl) **I.** adj. real; *(true)* verdadero; *(objective)* cierto; *(serious)* de verdad ♦ **for r.** FAM.
de verdad • **r. estate** bienes inmuebles *o* raíces
II. adv. FAM. muy, mucho.
re·a·lign (rē´ə-līn´) tr. *(tires)* realinear; *(people)*
reagrupar.

re·al·ism (rē′ə-lĭz′əm) s. realismo.

re·al·ist (:lĭst) s. realista *mf*.

re·al·is·tic (′-lĭs′tĭc) adj. realista.

re·al·i·ty (rē-ăl′ĭ-tē) s. realidad *f*; *(fact)* hecho.

re·al·i·za·tion (rē′ə-lĭ-zā′shən) s. *(understanding)* comprensión *f*; *(fulfillment)* realización *f*.

re·al·ize (rē′ə-līz′) tr. *(to comprehend)* darse cuenta de; *(to attain)* realizar, hacer realidad; *(a profit)* obtener.

re·al·ly (rē′ə-lē, rē′lē) adv. *(in reality)* en realidad; *(truly)* verdaderamente; *(very)* muy ♦ **r.!** ¡hay que ver! • **r.?** ¿de veras?

realm (rĕlm) s. reino.

re·al·tor (rē′əl-tər) s. corredor *m* de bienes raíces.

re·al·ty (:tē) s. bienes *m* raíces.

ream[1] (rēm) s. resma *f*. FIG. montones.

ream[2] tr. *(to enlarge)* agrandar; *(to squeeze)* exprimir.

reap (rēp) tr. & intr. cosechar; *(to cut)* segar.

reap·er (rē′pər) s. *(person)* segador *m*; *(machine)* segadora.

re·ap·pear (rē′ə-pîr′) intr. reaparecer.

re·ap·pear·ance (:əns) s. reaparición *f*.

re·ap·point (rē-ə-point′) tr. nombrar de nuevo.

re·ap·point·ment (:mənt) s. nuevo nombramiento.

re·ap·por·tion (rē′ə-pôr′shən) tr. repartir de nuevo.

re·ap·por·tion·ment (:mənt) s. nueva distribución.

re·ap·prais·al (rē′ə-prā′zəl) s. revaluación *f*.

rear[1] (rîr) **I.** s. parte trasera; *(of a house)* fondo; FAM. *(buttocks)* nalgas ♦ **at the r. of** detrás de **II.** adj. trasero, de atrás ♦ **r. guard** retaguardia.

rear[2] tr. *(animals)* criar; *(children)* cuidar, educar —intr. *(horse)* encabritarse.

rear·ing (′ĭng) s. crianza, cría.

re·arm (rē-ärm′) tr. & intr. rearmar(se).

re·ar·ma·ment (rē-är′mə-mənt) s. rearme *m*.

re·ar·range (rē′ə-rānj′) tr. volver a arreglar, disponer de otro modo; *(plans)* cambiar.

re·ar·range·ment (:mənt) s. nuevo arreglo, nueva disposición.

rear·view mirror (rîr′vyōō′) s. retrovisor *m*.

rea·son (rē′zən) **I.** s. razón *f* ♦ **all the more r. (to)** razón de más (para) • **by r. of** en virtud de • **for no r.** sin ningún motivo • **the r. why** el porqué • **to be within r.** ser razonable • **to have r. to** tener motivos para • **to listen to r.** avenirse a razones • **to stand for r.** ser evidente **II.** tr. & intr. razonar ♦ **to r. out** resolver.

rea·son·a·ble (rē′zə-nə-bəl) adj. razonable.

rea·son·ing (:nĭng) s. razonamiento.

re·as·sess (rē′ə-sĕs′) tr. valorar de nuevo.

re·as·sur·ance (rē′ə-shŏŏr′əns) s. *(confidence)* confianza; *(promise)* promesa.

re·as·sure (rē′ə-shŏŏr′) tr. dar confianza.

re·bate (rē′bāt′) **I.** s. rebaja; *(repayment)* reembolso **II.** tr. rebajar, reembolsar.

re·bel (rĭ-bĕl′) **I.** intr. *(rī-bĕl′)* **-ll-** rebelarse **II.** s. *(rĕb′əl)* rebelde *mf*.

re·bel·lion (rĭ-bĕl′yən) s. rebelión *f*.

re·bel·lious (:yəs) adj. rebelde.

re·birth (rē-bûrth′) s. renacimiento.

re·bound (rĭ-bound′) **I.** intr. rebotar; FIG. recuperarse **II.** s. (′′) rebote *m* ♦ **to marry on the r.** casarse por despecho.

re·buff (rĭ-bŭf′) **I.** s. *(refusal)* rechazo; *(snub)* desaire *m* **II.** tr. rechazar, desairar.

re·build (rē-bĭld′) tr. & intr. **-built** reconstruir.

re·buke (rĭ-byōōk′) **I.** tr. reprender **II.** s. reprimenda.

re·but (rĭ-bŭt′) tr. & intr. **-tt-** refutar.

re·but·tal (:l) s. refutación *f*.

re·cal·ci·trant (rĭ-kăl′sĭ-trənt) adj. recalcitrante.

re·call I. tr. (rĭ-kôl′) *(to remember)* recordar, acordarse de; *(workers)* hacer volver; *(diplomat)* retirar; *(product)* retirar del mercado **II.** s. (rē′-kôl′) *(withdrawal)* retiro; *(recollection)* recuerdo.

re·cant (rĭ-kănt′) tr. & intr. retractar(se).

re·cap (rē′kăp′) FAM. **I.** tr. **-pp-** recapitular **II.** s. recapitulación *f*.

re·ca·pit·u·late (rē′kə-pĭch′ə-lāt′) tr. recapitular —intr. resumir.

re·ca·pit·u·la·tion (′-′-lā′shən) s. recapitulación *f*.

re·cap·ture (rē-kăp′chər) **I.** s. reconquista **II.** tr. *(the past)* hacer revivir; *(prisoner)* volver a capturar; MIL. reconquistar.

re·cede (rĭ-sēd′) intr. retroceder; *(to become distant)* alejarse.

re·ceipt (rĭ-sēt′) s. recibo ♦ **on r. of** al recibir ♦ **pl.** ingresos.

re·ceiv·a·ble (rĭ-sē′və-bəl) adj. a cobrar.

re·ceive (rĭ-sēv′) tr. recibir; *(salary)* percibir, cobrar; *(members)* aceptar; *(to shelter)* acoger ♦ **receiving line** fila de recepción —intr. recibir ♦ **to be well received** recibir una buena acogida.

re·ceiv·er (rĭ-sē′vər) s. receptor *m*; DER. síndico; TEL. auricular *m*.

re·cent (rē′sənt) adj. reciente.

re·cep·ta·cle (rĭ-sĕp′tə-kəl) s. receptáculo; ELEC. enchufe *m* hembra.

re·cep·tion (rĭ-sĕp′shən) s. recepción *f*.

re·cep·tion·ist (:shə-nĭst) s. recepcionista *mf*.

re·cep·tive (:tĭv) adj. receptivo.

re·cep·tor (:tər) s. receptor *m*.

re·cess (rē′sĕs′, rĭ-sĕs′) **I.** s. *(in school)* recreo; *(in meeting)* interrupción *f*; *(in wall)* hueco, nicho ♦ **to be in r.** *(Congress)* estar clausurado; *(school)* estar cerrada por vacaciones **II.** tr. hacer un hueco en —intr. *(Congress)* suspender; *(school)* cerrar.

re·ces·sion (rĭ-sĕsh′ən) s. retirada; ECON. recesión *f*.

re·ces·sive (rĭ-sĕs′ĭv) adj. BIOL. recesivo.

re·charge (rē-chärj′) tr. recargar.

re·cid·i·vism (rĭ-sĭd′ə-vĭz′əm) s. reincidencia.

rec·i·pe (rĕs′ə-pē) s. receta.

re·cip·i·ent (rĭ-sĭp′ē-ənt) adj. & s. receptor *m*.

re·cip·ro·cal (rĭ-sĭp′rə-kəl) adj. recíproco.

re·cip·ro·cate (:kāt′) tr. corresponder a; *(to exchange)* intercambiar —intr. corresponder.

rec·i·proc·i·ty (rĕs′ə-prŏs′ĭ-tē) s. reciprocidad *f*.

re·cit·al (rĭ-sīt′l) s. recital *m*.

rec·i·ta·tion (rĕs′ĭ-tā′shən) s. recitación *f*; *(narration)* narración *f*, relato.

re·cite (rĭ-sīt′) tr. & intr. *(poem)* recitar; *(story)* narrar; *(list)* enumerar.

reck·less (rĕk′lĭs) adj. *(careless)* imprudente; *(rash)* precipitado.

reck·on (rĕk′ən) tr. calcular; *(to regard)* considerar; FAM. *(to assume)* suponer ♦ **to r. on** contar con —intr. calcular ♦ **to r. with** tener en cuenta.

reck·on·ing (:ə-nĭng) s. cálculo ♦ **day of r.** día de ajuste de cuentas.

re·claim (rĭ-klām′) tr. *(land)* recobrar; *(swamp)* sanear; *(from waste)* recuperar.

re·cline (rĭ-klīn') tr. & intr. reclinar(se).
re·cluse (rĕk'lōōs', rĭ-klōōs') s. solitario.
re·clu·sive (rĭ-klōō'sĭv) adj. solitario.
rec·og·ni·tion (rĕk'əg-nĭsh'ən) s. reconocimiento.
rec·og·niz·a·ble ('-nī'zə-bəl) adj. reconocible.
rec·og·nize (rĕk'əg-nīz') tr. reconocer; *(speaker)* dar la palabra a.
re·coil I. intr. (rĭ-koil') *(firearm)* dar un culatazo; *(cannon)* retroceder ♦ **to r. at** *(in fear)* tener horror a; *(in disgust)* tener asco a II. s. (rē'koil') *(of firearm)* culatazo; *(of cannon)* retroceso.
rec·ol·lect (rĕk'ə-lĕkt') tr. & intr. acordarse (de).
rec·ol·lec·tion (:lĕk'shən) s. recuerdo.
rec·om·mend (rĕk'ə-mĕnd') tr. recomendar.
rec·om·men·da·tion (:mĕn-dā'shən) s. recomendación f.
rec·om·pense (rĕk'əm-pĕns') I. tr. recompensar II. s. recompensa.
rec·on·cil·a·ble (rĕk'ən-sī'lə-bəl) adj. reconciliable; *(compatible)* compatible.
rec·on·cile ('-sīl') tr. *(people)* reconciliar; *(differences)* conciliar ♦ **to r. oneself to** resignarse a.
rec·on·cil·i·a·tion ('-sīl'ē-ā'shən) s. reconciliación f; *(settlement)* conciliación f.
re·con·di·tion (rē'kən-dĭsh'ən) tr. arreglar.
re·con·firm (rē'kən-fûrm') tr. reconfirmar.
re·con·nais·sance (rĭ-kŏn'ə-səns) s. reconocimiento.
re·con·noi·ter (rē'kə-noi'tər, rĕk'ə-) tr. reconocer —intr. hacer un reconocimiento.
re·con·sid·er (rē'kən-sĭd'ər) tr. & intr. reconsiderar.
re·con·sti·tute (rē-kŏn'stĭ-tōōt') tr. reconstituir; CUL. hidratar.
re·con·struct (rē'kən-strŭkt') tr. reconstruir.
re·con·vene (rē'kən-vēn') tr. convocar de nuevo —intr. reunirse de nuevo.
re·cord I. tr. (rĭ-kôrd') *(facts, data)* registrar; *(impression, idea)* apuntar, anotar; *(to tally)* consignar, llevar cuenta de; *(instrument)* indicar; TEC. grabar —intr. grabar II. s. (rĕk'ərd) *(evidence)* constancia f; *(account)* relación f; *(tally)* cuenta; *(testimony)* testimonio; *(of conduct, health)* historial m; *(dossier)* expediente m; *(of an employee)* hoja de servicios; *(of a criminal)* antecedentes m; *(best performance)* récord m; *(for a phonograph)* disco; *(recording)* grabación f ♦ **for the r.** para que así conste • **in r. time** en un tiempo récord • **in r. numbers** en cantidades sin precedentes • **r. player** tocadiscos • **to be off the r.** ser extraoficial • **to break the r.** batir el récord • **to go on r.** hacer constar • **to have a clean r.** no tener antecedentes penales ♦ pl. archivos.
re·cord·er (rĭ-kôr'dər) s. *(device)* grabadora; MÚS. flauta dulce.
re·cord·ing (:dĭng) s. grabación f.
re·count (rĭ-kount') tr. relatar.
re·count I. tr. (rē-kount') volver a contar II. s. ('') recuento.
re·coup (rĭ-kōōp') tr. recuperar.
re·course (rē'kôrs', rĭ-kôrs') s. recurso ♦ **to have r. to** recurrir a.
re·cov·er (rĭ-kŭv'ər) tr. *(to regain)* recuperar; *(damages)* cobrar —intr. recuperarse.
re·cov·er·y (:ə-rē) s. recuperación f.
re·cre·ate (rē'krē-āt') tr. recrear.
rec·re·a·tion (rĕk'rē-ā'shən) s. recreo.

rec·re·a·tion·al (:shə-nəl) adj. recreativo.
re·crim·i·nate (rĭ-krĭm'ə-nāt') tr. recriminar.
re·crim·i·na·tion (-'-nā'shən) s. recriminación f.
re·cruit (rĭ-krōōt') I. tr. *(workers)* contratar; MIL. reclutar —intr. MIL. reclutar II. s. recluta m; *(new member)* socio nuevo.
re·cruit·er (rĭ-krōō'tər) s. reclutador m.
re·cruit·ment (:mənt) s. reclutamiento.
rec·tal (rĕk'təl) adj. rectal.
rec·tan·gle (rĕk'tăng'gəl) s. rectángulo.
rec·tan·gu·lar (-'gyə-lər) adj. rectangular.
rec·ti·fy (rĕk'tə-fī') tr. rectificar.
rec·ti·tude (rĕk'tĭ-tōōd') s. rectitud f.
rec·tor (rĕk'tər) s. *(of a parish)* cura párroco; *(of a school)* director m; *(of a university)* rector m.
rec·to·ry (:tə-rē) s. rectoría.
rec·tum (rĕk'təm) s. [pl. **s** o **-ta**] recto.
re·cum·bent (rĭ-kŭm'bənt) adj. recostado.
re·cu·per·ate (rĭ-kōō'pə-rāt') tr. & intr. recuperar(se).
re·cu·per·a·tion (-'-rā'shən) s. recuperación f.
re·cu·per·a·tive (-'-'tĭv) adj. recuperativo.
re·cur (rĭ-kûr') intr. **-rr-** repetirse; *(symptom)* reaparecer ♦ **to r. to** recurrir a.
re·cur·rence (:əns) s. repetición f, reaparición f; *(return)* vuelta.
re·cur·rent (:ənt) adj. que se repite; *(periodic)* periódico; ANAT., MAT. recurrente.
re·cur·ring (:ĭng) adj. periódico.
re·cy·cle (rē-sī'kəl) tr. reciclar.
red (rĕd) I. s. rojo, colorado ♦ **R.** POL. rojo • **to be in the r.** tener pérdidas • **to see r.** ponerse furioso II. adj. **-dd-** rojo, colorado; *(wine)* tinto ♦ **r. tape** trámites, papeleo.
re·dact (rĭ-dăkt') tr. redactar.
red-blood·ed (rĕd'blŭd'ĭd) adj. vigoroso.
red·cap (:kăp') s. mozo de equipajes.
red·den (:n) intr. enrojecer; *(a person)* ruborizarse.
red·dish (:ĭsh) adj. rojizo.
re·deem (rĭ-dēm') tr. redimir; *(situation)* salvar; *(to make up for)* compensar.
re·deem·a·ble (rĭ-dē'mə-bəl) adj. redimible.
re·deem·er (:mər) s. redentor m.
re·demp·tion (rĭ-dĕmp'shən) s. redención f; *(of a mortgage)* cancelación f.
red-hand·ed (rĕd'hăn'dĭd) adj. & adv. con las manos en la masa.
red·head (:hĕd') s. pelirrojo.
red-hot (:hŏt') adj. *(very hot)* candente; *(excited)* animado; *(new)* muy reciente.
re·di·rect (rē'dĭ-rĕkt') tr. *(letter)* mandar a otra dirección; *(to reroute)* mostrar otro camino.
re·dis·cov·er (rē'dĭ-skŭv'ər) tr. redescubrir.
re·dis·trib·ute (rē'dĭ-strĭb'yōōt) tr. redistribuir.
red-let·ter (rĕd'lĕt'ər) adj. memorable.
red-light district (:līt') s. barrio de burdeles.
re·do (rē-dōō') tr. **-did, -done** volver a hacer, rehacer; *(to redecorate)* decorar de nuevo.
red·o·lent (rĕd'l-ənt) adj. *(aromatic)* fragante, oloroso; *(suggestive)* evocador.
re·dou·ble (rē-dŭb'əl) tr. & intr. redoblar.
re·doubt·a·ble (rĭ-dou'tə-bəl) adj. formidable.
re·dound (rĭ-dound') intr. redundar (to en).
re·dress (rĭ-drĕs') I. tr. *(to remedy)* reparar; *(to rectify)* rectificar II. s. reparación f, enmienda.
re·duce (rĭ-dōōs') tr. reducir; COM. rebajar —intr. disminuir, reducirse; *(to lose weight)* adelgazar.
re·duc·tion (rĭ-dŭk'shən) s. reducción f, disminución f; *(discount)* descuento.

re·dun·dant (rĭ-dŭn′dənt) s. superfluo; GRAM. redundante.

red·wood (rĕd′wŏod′) s. secoya.

reed (rēd) s. *(plant, stalk)* caña; MÚS. (instrumento de) lengüeta.

re·ed·u·cate (rē-ĕj′ə-kāt′) tr. reeducar.

reef[1] (rēf) s. GEOL. arrecife *m*, escollo.

reef[2] MARÍT. I. s. rizo (de vela) II. tr. arrizar.

reef·er (rē′fər) s. JER. cigarrillo de marihuana.

reek (rēk) I. intr. *(to stink)* apestar; *(to smell)* oler *(of a)* II. s. olor *m*.

reel[1] (rēl) I. s. *(spool)* carrete *m*; CINEM., FOTOG. rollo II. tr. enrollar en un carrete ♦ **to r. off** recitar de un tirón.

reel[2] intr. *(to stagger)* tambalear(se); *(to feel dizzy)* tener vértigo.

re·e·lect (rē′ĭ-lĕkt′) tr. reelegir.

re·en·act (rē′ĕn-ăkt′) tr. *(law)* aprobar de nuevo; *(play)* volver a representar.

re·en·list (rē′ĕn-lĭst′) intr. reengancharse.

re·en·try (rē-ĕn′trē) s. reingreso; *(space vehicle)* reentrada.

re·es·tab·lish (rē′ĭ-stăb′lĭsh) tr. restablecer.

re·ex·am·ine (rē′ĭg-zăm′ĭn) tr. reexaminar.

re·fec·to·ry (rĭ-fĕk′tə-rē) s. comedor *m*.

re·fer (rĭ-fûr′) tr. **-rr-** *(to direct to)* remitir; *(to send to)* enviar; *(to submit to)* someter a —intr. referirse; *(to apply)* aplicarse.

ref·e·ree (rĕf′ə-rē′) I. s. árbitro II. tr. & intr. arbitrar.

ref·er·ence (rĕf′ər-əns) s. referencia; *(allusion)* alusión *f*, mención *f*; *(person)* fiador *m* ♦ **r. book** libro de consulta ♦ **r. mark** llamada ♦ **with r. to** *(a letter)* con relación a; *(as regards)* en cuanto a.

ref·er·en·dum (rĕf′ə-rĕn′dəm) s. [pl. **s** o **-da**] referéndum *m*, plebiscito.

re·fer·ral (rĭ-fûr′əl) s. referencia.

re·fill I. tr. (rē-fĭl′) rellenar II. s. (′′) recambio.

re·fine (rĭ-fīn′) tr. refinar.

re·fined (rĭ-fīnd′) adj. *(pure)* refinado; *(elegant)* fino.

re·fine·ment (rĭ-fīn′mənt) s. *(oil, sugar)* refinación *f*; *(person)* refinamiento.

re·fin·er·y (rĭ-fī′nə-rē) s. refinería.

re·flect (rĭ-flĕkt′) tr. reflejar; *(to manifest)* revelar —intr. reflejarse; *(to think)* reflexionar, meditar ♦ **to r. on** pensar (sobre).

re·flec·tion (rĭ-flĕk′shən) s. *(image)* reflejo; *(contemplation)* reflexión *f* ♦ **on r.** pensándolo bien.

re·flec·tive (:tĭv) adj. que refleja; *(meditative)* pensativo.

re·flec·tor (:tər) s. reflector *m*.

re·flex (rē′flĕks′) adj. & s. reflejo.

re·flex·ive (rĭ-flĕk′sĭv) adj. reflexivo.

re·form (rĭ-fôrm′) I. tr. & intr. reformar(se) II. s. reforma ♦ **r. school** reformatorio.

ref·or·ma·tion (rĕf′ər-mā′shən) s. reforma.

re·for·ma·to·ry (rĭ-fôr′mə-tôr′ē) s. reformatorio.

re·formed (rĭ-fôrmd′) adj. reformado.

re·form·er (rĭ-fôr′mər) s. reformador *m*.

re·form·ist (:mĭst) s. reformista *mf*.

re·fract (rĭ-frăkt′) tr. refractar.

re·frac·tion (rĭ-frăk′shən) s. refracción *f*.

re·frac·to·ry (:tə-rē) adj. obstinado, indócil; FÍS. refractario; MED. intratable.

re·frain[1] (rĭ-frān′) intr. abstenerse *(from* de).

re·frain[2] s. MÚS., POET. estribillo.

re·fresh (rĭ-frĕsh′) tr. & intr. refrescar(se).

re·fresh·er course (:ər) s. curso de repaso.

re·fresh·ing (:ĭng) adj. refrescante; *(restorative)* reparador; *(pleasant)* placentero.

re·fresh·ment (:mənt) s. refresco ♦ pl. refrigerio, colación.

re·frig·er·ant (rĭ-frĭj′ər-ənt) s. refrigerante *m*.

re·frig·er·ate (:ə-rāt′) tr. refrigerar.

re·frig·er·a·tion (-′-rā′shən) s. refrigeración *f*.

re·frig·er·a·tor (-′-′tər) s. nevera, frigorífico.

re·fu·el (rē-fyōō′əl) tr. echar gasolina a *o* en —intr. reabastecerse (de gasolina).

ref·uge (rĕf′yōōj) s. refugio ♦ **to take r. in** refugiarse en.

ref·u·gee (′yōō-jē′) s. refugiado.

re·ful·gent (rĭ-fŏol′jənt) adj. refulgente.

re·fund I. tr. (rĭ-fŭnd′) reembolsar II. s. (rē′fŭnd′) reembolso.

re·fund·a·ble (rĭ-fŭn′də-bəl) adj. reembolsable.

re·fur·bish (rē-fûr′bĭsh) tr. restaurar.

re·fur·nish (rē-fûr′nĭsh) tr. amueblar de nuevo.

re·fus·al (rĭ-fyōō′zəl) s. negativa.

re·fuse[1] (rĭ-fyōōz′) tr. *(offer)* no aceptar; *(permission)* negar —intr. negarse *(to* a).

ref·use[2] (rĕf′yōōs) s. desperdicios, basura.

ref·u·ta·tion (rĕf′yōō-tā′shən) s. refutación *f*.

re·fute (rĭ-fyōōt′) tr. refutar.

re·gain (rē-gān′) tr. recuperar, recobrar.

re·gal (rē′gəl) adj. real, regio.

re·gale (rĭ-gāl′) tr. agasajar, entretener.

re·ga·lia (rĭ-gāl′yə) s.pl. *(of royalty)* insignias reales; *(finery)* adornos.

re·gard (rĭ-gärd′) I. tr. *(to watch)* observar, mirar; *(to consider)* considerar; *(to esteem)* apreciar; *(to concern)* referirse a, concernir ♦ **as regards** con respecto a II. s. *(gaze)* mirada; *(attention)* consideración *f*; *(esteem)* aprecio ♦ **in** *o* **with r. to** con respecto a ♦ **in (this, that) r.** por lo que a (esto, eso) se refiere ♦ **to send one's regards** dar recuerdos a alguien ♦ **to have r. for** respetar ♦ **with best regards** saludos cordiales de ♦ **without r. to** sin tomar en consideración.

re·gard·ing (:ĭng) prep. con respecto a.

re·gard·less (rĭ-gärd′lĭs) adv. *(anyway)* a pesar de todo; *(come what may)* pase lo que pase ♦ **r. of** *(without regard to)* sin tener en cuenta; *(in spite of)* a pesar de.

re·gat·ta (rĭ-gä′tə, -gät′ə) s. regata.

re·gen·cy (rē′jən-sē) s. regencia.

re·gen·er·ate (rĭ-jĕn′ə-rāt′) I. tr. & intr. regenerar(se) II. adj. *(:ər-ĭt)* renovado.

re·gen·er·a·tion (-′-rā′shən) s. regeneración *f*.

re·gen·er·a·tive (-′-′tĭv) adj. regenerador.

re·gent (rē′jənt) s. regente *mf* ♦ **board of regents** EDUC. junta directiva.

re·gime *o* **ré·gime** (rā-zhēm′) s. régimen *m*.

reg·i·men (rĕj′ə-mən) s. régimen *m*.

reg·i·ment (:mənt) I. s. regimiento II. tr. regimentar.

reg·i·men·ta·tion (′-mĕn-tā′shən) s. reglamentación estricta.

re·gion (rē′jən) s. región *f*.

re·gion·al (rē′jə-nəl) adj. regional.

reg·is·ter (rĕj′ĭ-stər) I. s. registro; *(cash register)* registradora; *(meter)* contador *m*; *(for heat)* regulador *m* II. tr. registrar; *(a birth, death)* declarar; *(students)* matricular; *(vehicle)* sacar la matrícula de; *(complaint)* presentar; *(on a scale)* marcar; *(emotion)* manifestar, expresar; *(mail)* certificar —intr. *(at the polls, hotel)* inscribirse; *(at school)* matricularse.

reg·is·tered (:stərd) adj. *(trademark)* registrado; *(student, vehicle)* matriculado; *(certified)* titulado ♦ **r. mail** correo certificado.

reg·is·trar (:strär′) s. *(registry)* jefe *m* de registros civiles; *(university)* secretario general.
reg·is·tra·tion ('-strä′shǝn) s. *(of voters)* inscripción *f*; *(of students, cars)* matrícula; *(for the draft)* alistamiento.
reg·is·try ('-strē) s. registro.
re·gress I. intr. (rĭ-grĕs′) retroceder II. s. (rē′grĕs′) retroceso.
re·gres·sion (rĭ-grĕsh′ǝn) s. retroceso.
re·gres·sive (rĭ-grĕs′ĭv) adj. regresivo.
re·gret (rĭ-grĕt′) I. tr. **-tt-** *(to be sorry for)* arrepentirse de; *(to be sorry about)* lamentar II. s. *(sorrow)* pena; *(remorse)* arrepentimiento ♦ to have no regrets no arrepentirse de nada ♦ pl. excusas.
re·gret·ful·ly (:fǝ-lē) adv. sentidamente.
re·gret·ta·ble (:ǝ-bǝl) adj. lamentable.
re·gret·ta·bly (:ǝ-blē) adv. desafortunadamente.
re·group (rē-grꚍp′) tr. & intr. reagrupar(se).
reg·u·lar (rĕg′yǝ-lǝr) I. adj. regular; *(usual)* normal <*during r. office hours* durante las horas normales de oficina>; *(customary)* habitual, de costumbre; *(work)* fijo; *(customer)* habitual, fijo; FAM. *(nice)* decente, bueno ♦ to make r. use of emplear con regularidad II. s. MIL. regular *m*; FAM. cliente fijo.
reg·u·lar·i·ty ('-lăr′ĭ-tē) s. regularidad *f*.
reg·u·lar·ize ('-lǝ-rīz′) tr. regularizar.
reg·u·late (:lāt′) tr. *(to control)* reglamentar; *(to adjust)* regular.
reg·u·la·tion ('-lā′shǝn) s. *(act)* regulación *f*; *(rule)* regla ♦ pl. reglamento.
reg·u·la·tor ('-lā′tǝr) s. regulador *m*.
reg·u·la·to·ry (:lǝ-tôr′ē) adj. regulador.
re·gur·gi·tate (rē-gûr′jĭ-tāt′) intr. regurgitar —tr. vomitar.
re·ha·bil·i·tate (rē′hǝ-bĭl′ĭ-tāt′) tr. rehabilitar; *(building, neighborhood)* restaurar.
re·ha·bil·i·ta·tion ('-'-tā′shǝn) s. rehabilitación *f*; *(restoration)* restauración *f*.
re·hash I. tr. (rē-hăsh′) volver a repetir, machacar II. s. ('') repetición *f*.
re·hears·al (rĭ-hûr′sǝl) s. ensayo.
re·hearse (rĭ-hûrs′) tr. & intr. ensayar.
reign (rān) I. s. reinado; *(dominance)* dominio ♦ r. of terror régimen de terror II. intr. reinar.
re·im·burse (rē′ĭm-bûrs′) tr. reembolsar.
re·im·burse·ment (:mǝnt) s. reembolso.
rein (rān) I. s. rienda ♦ to give free r. to dar rienda suelta a • to keep a tight r. on atar corto a II. tr. poner riendas a ♦ to r. in refrenar.
re·in·car·nate (rē′ĭn-kär′nāt′) tr. reencarnar.
re·in·car·na·tion ('-'-nā′shǝn) s. reencarnación *f*.
rein·deer (rān′dîr′) s. [pl. inv. o ♦ s] reno.
re·in·force (rē′ĭn-fôrs′) tr. reforzar ♦ reinforced concrete concreto armado.
re·in·force·ment (:mǝnt) s. *(strengthening)* refuerzo ♦ pl. MIL. refuerzos.
re·in·state (rē′ĭn-stāt′) tr. *(to restore to office)* restituir, reintegrar; *(to reestablish)* restablecer.
re·in·sure (rē′-ĭn-shꚍr′) tr. reasegurar.
re·in·vest (rē′ĭn-vĕst′) tr. reinvertir.
re·in·vest·ment (:mǝnt) s. reinversión *f*.
re·is·sue (rē-ĭsh′ꚍ) I. tr. reeditar II. s. reedición *f*.
re·it·er·ate (rē-ĭt′ǝ-rāt′) tr. reiterar.
re·it·er·a·tion (:ǝ-rā′shǝn) s. reiteración *f*.
re·ject I. tr. (rĭ-jĕkt′) *(to refuse)* rechazar, rehusar; *(to discard)* desechar II. s. (rē′jĕkt′) *(thing)* desecho; *(person)* persona rechazada.

re·jec·tion (rĭ-jĕk′shǝn) s. rechazo.
re·joice (rĭ-jois′) tr. & intr. regocijar(se).
re·joic·ing (rĭ-joi′sĭng) s. regocijo.
re·join (rĭ-join′) I. tr. & intr. responder, replicar.
re·join (rē-join′) tr. & intr. juntar(se) de nuevo.
re·join·der (rĭ-join′dǝr) s. respuesta.
re·ju·ve·nate (rĭ-jꚍ′vǝ-nāt′) tr. rejuvenecer.
re·ju·ve·na·tion (-'-nā′shǝn) s. rejuvenecimiento.
re·kin·dle (rē-kĭn′dl) tr. volver a encender.
re·lapse I. intr. (rĭ-lăps′) recaer II. (rē′lăps′) recaída.
re·late (rĭ-lāt′) tr. *(to tell)* relatar, contar; *(to associate)* relacionar, asociar —intr. estar relacionado *(to* con); *(to interact)* relacionarse *(with,* to con).
re·lat·ed (rĭ-lā′tĭd) adj. relacionado *(to* con); *(by blood, marriage)* emparentado.
re·la·tion (rĭ-lā′shǝn) s. relación *f*; *(kinship)* parentesco; *(relative)* pariente *mf* ♦ in r. to en relación a.
re·la·tion·ship (:shĭp′) s. relación *f*; *(kinship)* parentesco; *(tie)* vínculo.
rel·a·tive (rĕl′ǝ-tĭv) I. adj. relativo II. s. pariente *mf*.
rel·a·tiv·i·ty ('-'-ĭ-tē) s. relatividad *f*.
re·lax (rĭ-lăks′) tr. & intr. relajar(se) ♦ r.! ¡cálmate!
re·lax·a·tion (rē′lăk-sā′shǝn) s. relajación *f*; *(of efforts)* disminución *f*; *(state)* descanso, reposo; *(recreation)* distracción *f*.
re·laxed (rĭ-lăkst′) adj. relajado; *(calm)* tranquilo.
re·lay (rē′lā′) I. s. relevo; *(of messages)* transmisión *f*; *(of news)* difusión *f*; ELEC. relevador *m* ♦ r. race carrera de relevos II. tr. transmitir, difundir; RAD., TELEV. retransmitir.
re·lease (rĭ-lēs′) I. tr. *(from captivity)* poner en libertad; *(from one's grip)* soltar; *(from debt, promise)* descargar; *(for sale)* poner en venta; *(film)* estrenar; *(record)* sacar II. s. liberación *f*; *(of film)* estreno; *(record)* disco, grabación *f*; *(communiqué)* anuncio.
rel·e·gate (rĕl′ĭ-gāt′) tr. relegar.
re·lent (rĭ-lĕnt′) intr. ceder.
re·lent·less (:lĭs) adj. *(without pity)* implacable; *(persistent)* incesante.
rel·e·vance/van·cy (rĕl′ǝ-vǝns) s. pertinencia.
rel·e·vant (:vǝnt) adj. pertinente.
re·li·a·bil·i·ty (rĭ-lī′ǝ-bĭl′ĭ-tē) s. fiabilidad *f*.
re·li·a·ble (rĭ-lī′ǝ-bǝl) adj. *(person)* de confianza; *(machine)* fiable; *(data, source)* fidedigno.
re·li·ance (:ǝns) s. confianza.
re·li·ant (:ǝnt) adj. confiado.
rel·ic (rĕl′ĭk) s. reliquia ♦ pl. restos mortales.
re·lief (rĭ-lēf′) s. alivio; *(assistance)* ayuda; *(replacement)* relevo; ARTE., GEOG. relieve *m* ♦ in r. en relieve • what a r.! ¡qué alivio!
re·lieve (rĭ-lēv′) tr. *(to alleviate)* aliviar; *(to aid)* auxiliar; *(from worry)* liberar; *(of duties)* destituir; *(to replace)* reemplazar; *(boredom)* disipar.
re·li·gion (rĭ-lĭj′ǝn) s. religión *f*.
re·li·gious (:ǝs) adj. religioso; *(pious)* devoto.
re·lin·quish (rĭ-lĭng′kwĭsh) tr. abandonar; *(to renounce)* renunciar a; *(to release)* soltar.
rel·ish (rĕl′ĭsh) I. s. *(liking)* gusto, afición *f*; *(pleasure)* placer *m*; CUL. condimento II. tr. gustar, encantar.
re·live (rē-lĭv′) tr. volver a vivir, recordar.
re·load (rē-lōd′) tr. & intr. recargar.

re·lo·cate (rē-lō′kāt′) tr. & intr. establecer(se) en un nuevo lugar.

re·lo·ca·tion (′-kā′shən) s. ubicación nueva.

re·luc·tance/tan·cy (:lŭk′təns) s. desgana.

re·luc·tant (:tənt) adj. (reticent) reacio; (unwilling) poco dispuesto.

re·ly (rĭ-lī′) intr. ♦ **to r. (up)on** (to depend) depender de; (to trust) contar con.

re·main (rĭ-mān′) intr. (to keep being) seguir; (to stay) permanecer, quedarse; (to be left) quedar ♦ **to r. to be (seen)** quedar por (ver).

re·main·der (:dər) s. resto, residuo.

re·main·ing (rĭ-mā′nĭng) adj. restante.

re·mains (rĭ-mānz′) s.pl. restos; (corpse) restos mortales.

re·make (rē-māk′) **I.** tr. -made rehacer, hacer de nuevo **II.** s. (′′) nueva versión.

re·mand (rĭ-mănd′) tr. (to prison) encarcelar; (to a lower court) remitir al tribunal inferior.

re·mark (rĭ-märk′) **I.** tr. & intr. (to comment) comentar (on sobre); (to notice) observar **II.** s. comentario, observación f.

re·mark·a·ble (rĭ-mär′kə-bəl) adj. notable; (admirable) extraordinario, admirable.

re·mar·ry (rē-măr′ē) intr. volver a casarse.

re·me·di·al (rĭ-mē′dē-əl) adj. MED. correctivo; (class, studies) de estudiantes atrasados.

rem·e·dy (rĕm′ĭ-dē) **I.** s. remedio **II.** tr. remediar.

re·mem·ber (rĭ-mĕm′bər) tr. (to recall) acordarse de, recordar; (to bear in mind) tener en cuenta; (in greeting) dar recuerdos o saludos de —intr. acordarse.

re·mem·brance (:brəns) s. recuerdo ♦ **in r. of** en conmemoración de.

re·mind (rĭ-mīnd′) tr. recordar ♦ **that reminds me!** ¡a propósito!

re·mind·er (rĭ-mīn′dər) s. (of a date) recordatorio; (notice) aviso, notificación f.

rem·i·nisce (rĕm′ə-nĭs′) intr. recordar el pasado.

rem·i·nis·cent (:ənt) adj. evocador.

re·miss (rĭ-mĭs′) adj. negligente, descuidado.

re·mis·sion (rĭ-mĭsh′ən) s. remisión f.

re·mit (rĭ-mĭt′) tr. -tt- (money) remitir; (obligation) rescindir.

re·mit·tal (:l) s. remisión f.

re·mit·tance (:ns) s. remesa, envío.

rem·nant (rĕm′nənt) s. (remainder) resto; (of fabric) retazo; (trace) vestigio.

re·mod·el (rē-mŏd′l) tr. reconstruir, reformar.

re·mon·strate (rĭ-mŏn′strāt′) intr. protestar.

re·morse (rĭ-môrs′) s. remordimiento.

re·mote (rĭ-mōt′) adj. remoto; (relative) lejano ♦ **r. control** control a distancia.

re·mov·al (rĭ-mōō′vəl) s. (elimination) eliminación f; (transfer) traslado; (from a job) despido; MED. extirpación f.

re·move (rĭ-mōōv′) **I.** tr. (to take off, away) quitar(se); (to eliminate) eliminar; (from a job) despedir; CIR. extirpar —intr. mudarse, trasladarse **II.** s. distancia.

re·moved (rĭ-mōōvd′) adj. distante ♦ **first cousin once r.** primo segundo.

re·mu·ner·ate (rĭ-myōō′nə-rāt′) tr. remunerar.

re·mu·ner·a·tion (-′-rā′shən) s. remuneración f.

ren·ais·sance (rĕn′ə-säns′) **I.** s. renacimiento **II.** adj. renacentista.

re·nal (rē′nəl) adj. renal.

rend (rĕnd) tr. -ed o rent desgarrar.

ren·der (rĕn′dər) tr. (help) dar; (homage) rendir; (to depict) representar; (to perform) interpretar; (to translate) traducir; (verdict) pronunciar; (to cause to become) dejar; CUL. derretir ♦ **for services rendered** por servicios prestados.

ren·dez·vous (rän′dā-vōō′) **I.** s.inv. (place) lugar m de reunión; (meeting) cita **II.** intr. reunirse.

ren·di·tion (rĕn-dĭsh′ən) s. presentación f; (translation) versión f; MÚS. interpretación f.

ren·e·gade (rĕn′ĭ-gād′) s. renegado.

re·nege (rĭ-nĭg′, -nĕg′) intr. volverse atrás; (in cards) renunciar ♦ **to r. on** no cumplir.

re·new (rĭ-nōō′) tr. renovar; (to resume) reanudar; (to replenish) volver a llenar.

re·new·al (:əl) s. renovación f; (of negotiations) reanudación f.

re·nounce (rĭ-nouns′) tr. & intr. renunciar (a).

ren·o·vate (rĕn′ə-vāt′) tr. renovar, restaurar.

ren·o·va·tion (′-vā′shən) s. renovación f; (restoration) restauración f.

re·nown (rĭ-noun′) s. renombre m.

re·nowned (rĭ-nound′) adj. renombrado.

rent¹ (rĕnt) **I.** s. alquiler m <one month's r. un mes de alquiler> ♦ **for r.** se alquila **II.** tr. & intr. alquilar(se).

rent² **I.** cf. rend **II.** s. rasgadura.

rent·al (rĕn′tl) **I.** s. (amount) alquiler m; (property) propiedad alquilada **II.** adj. de alquiler.

rent·er (:tər) s. inquilino.

re·nun·ci·a·tion (rĭ-nŭn′sē-ā′shən) s. renuncia.

re·or·gan·i·za·tion (rē-ôr′gə-nĭ-zā′shən) s. reorganización f.

re·or·gan·ize (-′-nīz′) tr. & intr. reorganizar(se).

rep (rĕp) s. FAM. representante mf.

re·pair¹ (rĭ-pâr′) **I.** tr. reparar; (clothes) remendar **II.** s. reparación f ♦ **closed for repairs** cerrado por reformas • **in bad r.** en mal estado • **to be beyond r.** no tener arreglo.

re·pair² intr. (to go) ir, acudir.

re·pair·man (:măn′) s. [pl. -men] reparador m.

rep·a·ra·ble (rĕp′ər-ə-bəl) adj. reparable.

rep·a·ra·tion (rĕp′ə-rā′shən) s. reparación f ♦ pl. indemnización.

rep·ar·tee (rĕp′ər-tē′) s. conversación f con réplicas agudas.

re·past (rĭ-păst′) s. comida.

re·pa·tri·ate (rē-pā′trē-āt′) **I.** tr. repatriar **II.** s. (:ĭt) repatriado.

re·pay (rē-pā′) tr. -paid (loan) pagar; (favor) devolver; (to compensate) compensar ♦ **to r. in kind** pagar con la misma moneda.

re·pay·ment (:mənt) s. pago, reembolso; (reward) recompensa.

re·peal (rĭ-pēl′) **I.** tr. (to revoke) revocar; (to annul) anular **II.** s. revocación f, anulación f.

re·peat (rĭ-pēt′) **I.** tr. & intr. repetir ♦ **to r. one-self** repetirse **II.** s. repetición f; RAD., TELEV. segunda difusión f.

re·peat·ed (rĭ-pē′tĭd) adj. repetido.

re·peat·ing (:tĭng) adj. de repetición.

re·pel (rĭ-pĕl′) tr. -ll- repeler; (advances) rechazar ♦ **to r. each other** repelerse.

re·pel·lent (:ənt) **I.** adj. repelente; (repulsive) repugnante **II.** s. ♦ **insect r.** producto contra los insectos.

re·pent (rĭ-pĕnt′) intr. & tr. arrepentirse (de).

re·pen·tance (rĭ-pĕn′təns) s. arrepentimiento.

re·pen·tant (:tənt) adj. arrepentido.

re·per·cus·sion (rē′pər-kŭsh′ən, rĕp′ər-) s. repercusión f.

rep·er·toire (rĕp′ər-twär′) s. repertorio.
rep·er·to·ry (:tôr′ē) s. repertorio; *(theater)* teatro de repertorio; *(repository)* depósito.
rep·e·ti·tion (rĕp′ĭ-tĭsh′ən) s. repetición *f.*
rep·e·ti·tious (:əs) adj. repetitivo.
re·pet·i·tive (rĭ-pĕt′ĭ-tĭv) adj. repetitivo.
re·place (rĭ-plās′) tr. *(to put back)* reponer; *(to substitute)* reemplazar, suplir.
re·place·ment (:mənt) s. reposición *f;* *(substitution)* reemplazo; *(person)* relevo ♦ **r. part** repuesto.
re·play I. tr. (rē-plā′) *(game)* volver a jugar; *(videotape)* volver a poner; *(to repeat)* repetir II. s. (′′) repetición *f.*
re·plen·ish (rĭ-plĕn′ĭsh) tr. volver a llenar; *(to restore)* llenar, restaurar.
re·plete (rĭ-plēt′) adj. repleto.
rep·li·ca (rĕp′lĭ-kə) s. copia.
rep·li·cate (:kāt′) tr. & intr. duplicar(se).
re·ply (rĭ-plī′) I. tr. & intr. contestar, responder II. s. respuesta, contestación *f.*
re·port (rĭ-pôrt′) I. s. *(account)* relato; *(official account)* informe *m;* *(of news)* reportaje *m;* *(rumor)* rumor *m;* *(noise)* detonación *f* ♦ **r. card** boletín de notas • **weather r.** boletín meteorológico II. tr. *(to recount)* relatar; *(to tell of)* informar; *(to denounce)* denunciar ♦ **it is reported that** se dice que —intr. presentar un informe ♦ **to r. for** *(military duty)* incorporarse a; *(work)* presentarse a • **to r. on** hacer un informe sobre; *(news)* escribir una crónica de.
re·port·ed·ly (rĭ-pôr′tĭd-lē) adv. según se dice.
re·port·er (:tər) s. reportero, periodista *mf.*
re·pose¹ (rĭ-pōz′) I. s. *(rest)* reposo; *(sleep)* sueño; *(calm)* tranquilidad *f* II. intr. & tr. descansar.
re·pose² depositar (confianza).
re·pos·i·to·ry (rĭ-pŏz′ĭ-tôr′ē) s. depósito.
re·pos·sess (rē′ pə-zĕs′) tr. recuperar.
rep·re·hend (rĕp′rĭ-hĕnd′) tr. reprender.
rep·re·hen·si·ble (:hĕn′sə-bəl) adj. reprensible.
rep·re·hen·sion (:shən) s. reprensión *f.*
rep·re·sent (rĕp′rĭ-zĕnt′) tr. representar.
rep·re·sen·ta·tion (:zĕn-tā′shən) s. representación *f;* DER. declaración *f;* POL. delegación *f.*
rep·re·sen·ta·tive (′-tə-tĭv) I. s. representante *mf* II. adj. representativo; *(typical)* típico.
re·press (rĭ-prĕs′) tr. & intr. reprimir.
re·pres·sion (rĭ-prĕsh′ən) s. represión *f.*
re·pres·sive (rĭ-prĕs′ĭv) adj. represivo.
re·prieve (rĭ-prēv′) I. tr. *(execution)* suspender la ejecución de; *(sentence)* conmutar la pena de II. s. alivio temporal; *(of an execution)* suspensión *f;* *(of a sentence)* conmutación *f.*
rep·ri·mand (rĕp′rə-mănd′) I. tr. reprender II. s. reprimenda.
re·print I. s. (rē′prĭnt′) *(of book)* reimpresión *f;* *(of article)* tirada aparte II. tr. (-′) reimprimir.
re·pri·sal (rĭ-prī′zəl) s. represalia.
re·prise (rĭ-prēz′) s. repetición *f.*
re·proach (rĭ-prōch′) I. tr. reprochar II. s. reproche *m* ♦ **to be beyond r.** ser intachable.
rep·ro·bate (rĕp′rə-bāt′) s. & adj. réprobo.
re·proc·ess (rē-prŏs′ĕs′, -prō′sĕs′) tr. someter de nuevo a algún procedimiento.
re·pro·duce (rē′prə-dōōs′) tr. & intr. reproducir(se).
re·pro·duc·tion (:dŭk′shən) s. reproducción *f.*
re·pro·duc·tive (:tĭv) adj. reproductivo.
re·proof (rĭ-prōōf′) s. reprobación *f.*

re·prove (rĭ-prōōv′) tr. reprobar.
rep·tile (rĕp′təl, :tīl′) s. reptil *m;* FIG. rastrero.
rep·til·i·an (rĕp-tĭl′ē-ən) adj. & s. reptil *m.*
re·pub·lic (rĭ-pŭb′lĭk) s. república.
re·pub·li·can (:lĭ-kən) adj. & s. republicano.
re·pu·di·ate (rĭ-pyōō′dē-āt′) tr. repudiar.
re·pug·nance (rĭ-pŭg′nəns) s. repugnancia.
re·pug·nant (:nənt) adj. repugnante.
re·pulse (rĭ-pŭls′) I. tr. repeler, rechazar II. s. *(act)* repulsión *f;* *(rejection)* rechazo.
re·pul·sion (rĭ-pŭl′shən) s. repulsión *f;* *(aversion)* repugnancia, aversión *f.*
re·pul·sive (:sĭv) adj. repulsivo.
rep·u·ta·ble (rĕp′yə-tə-bəl) adj. respetable.
rep·u·ta·tion (′-tā′shən) s. reputación *f.*
re·pute (rĭ-pyōōt′) I. tr. ♦ **to be reputed to be** tener fama de II. s. reputación *f,* fama.
re·put·ed (rĭ-pyōō′tĭd) adj. supuesto.
re·quest (rĭ-kwĕst′) I. tr. solicitar II. s. solicitud *f* ♦ **available on r.** disponible a petición.
re·quire (rĭ-kwīr′) tr. *(to need)* requerir, necesitar; *(to demand)* exigir.
re·quire·ment (:mənt) s. *(prerequisite)* requisito; *(need)* necesidad *f.*
req·ui·site (rĕk′wĭ-zĭt) I. adj. necesario, indispensable II. s. requisito.
req·ui·si·tion (′-zĭsh′ən) I. s. solicitud *f;* MIL. requisa II. tr. requisar.
re·quit·al (rĭ-kwīt′l) s. compensación *f.*
re·run (rē′rŭn′) s. CINEM., TELEV. reestreno; FIG. repetición *f.*
re·sale (rē′sāl′) s. reventa.
re·sched·ule (rē-skĕj′ōōl) tr. *(event)* volver a programar; *(debt)* reestructurar.
re·scind (rĭ-sĭnd′) tr. rescindir, anular.
re·scis·sion (rĭ-sĭzh′ən) s. rescisión *f.*
res·cue (rĕs′kyōō) I. tr. rescatar, salvar II. s. rescate *m,* salvamento ♦ **to come to someone's r.** acudir en auxilio de alguien.
re·search (rĭ-sûrch′, rē′sûrch′) I. s. investigación *f* II. tr. & intr. hacer una investigación (sobre).
re·search·er (:ər) s. investigador *m.*
re·sell (rē-sĕl′) tr. -**sold** revender.
re·sem·blance (rĭ-zĕm′bləns) s. parecido.
re·sem·ble (:bəl) tr. parecerse a.
re·sent (rĭ-zĕnt′) tr. resentirse por.
re·sent·ful (:fəl) adj. resentido.
re·sent·ment (:mənt) s. resentimiento.
res·er·va·tion (rĕz′ər-vā′shən) s. *(of room, table)* reservación *f;* *(condition, land)* reserva.
re·serve (rĭ-zûrv′) I. tr. reservar II. s. reserva ♦ **in r.** de reserva ♦ pl. MIL. reserva • **cash r.** reservas en metálico III. adj. de reserva.
re·served (rĭ-zûrvd′) adj. reservado.
res·er·voir (rĕz′ər-vwär′) s. embalse *m;* FIG. fondo.
re·shape (rē-shāp′) tr. rehacer, reformar.
re·side (rĭ-zīd′) intr. residir.
res·i·dence (rĕz′ĭ-dəns) s. residencia ♦ **in r.** residente.
res·i·den·cy (:dən-sē) s. residencia.
res·i·dent (:dənt) I. s. residente *mf;* MED. interno II. adj. *(residing)* residente; *(permanent)* fijo ♦ **r. alien** extranjero residente.
res·i·den·tial (′-dĕn′shəl) adj. residencial.
re·sid·u·al (rĭ-zĭj′ōō-əl) I. adj. residual II. s. residuo.
res·i·due (rĕz′ĭ-dōō′) s. residuo.
re·sign (rĭ-zīn′) tr. renunciar, dimitir ♦ **to r. oneself to** resignarse a —intr. dimitir.
res·ig·na·tion (rĕz′ĭg-nā′shən) s. *(act)* renun-

cia; *(acceptance)* resignación *f.*
re·signed (rǐ-zīnd') adj. resignado.
re·sil·ience/ien·cy (rǐ-zǐl'yəns) s. elasticidad *f;*
MEC. resiliencia.
re·sil·ient (:yənt) adj. flexible.
res·in (rĕz'ǐn) I. s. resina II. tr. untar con resina.
res·in·ous (rĕz'ə-nəs) adj. resinoso.
re·sist (rǐ-zǐst') tr. & intr. resistir.
re·sis·tance (rǐ-zǐs'təns) s. resistencia.
re·sis·tant (:tənt) adj. resistente.
re·sist·i·ble (:tə-bəl) adj. resistible.
re·sis·tor (:tər) s. resistor *m.*
res·o·lute (rĕz'ə-lōōt') adj. resuelto.
res·o·lu·tion ('-lōō'shən) s. resolución *f* ♦ to
show r. mostrarse resuelto.
re·solve (rǐ-zŏlv') I. tr. resolver —intr. decidir II. s. resolución *f.*
re·solved (rǐ-zŏlvd') adj. resuelto.
res·o·nance (rĕz'ə-nəns) s. resonancia.
res·o·nant (:nənt) adj. resonante.
res·o·nate (:nāt') tr. & intr. (hacer) resonar.
re·sort (rǐ-zôrt') I. intr. ♦ to r. to recurrir a
II. s. lugar *m* de temporada ♦ as a last r. como
último recurso.
re·sound (rǐ-zound') intr. *(sound)* resonar;
(fame) tener resonancia.
re·sound·ing (rǐ-zoun'dǐng) adj. resonante.
re·source (rē'sôrs', rǐ-sôrs') s. recurso, medio.
re·source·ful (rǐ-sôrs'fəl) adj. listo, ingenioso.
re·spect (rǐ-spĕkt') I. tr. *(to esteem)* respetar;
(to concern) referirse a II. s. respeto ♦ **in other
respects** por lo demás ♦ **in every r.** en todos
los aspectos ♦ **in that r.** en cuanto a eso ♦ **out of
r. for** por respeto a ♦ **to command r.** hacerse
respetar ♦ **to pay one's respects** presentar los
respetos ♦ **with r. to** con relación a.
re·spect·a·ble (rǐ-spĕk'tə-bəl) adj. respetable;
(sum) considerable; *(clothes)* presentable.
re·spect·ful (rǐ-spĕkt'fəl) adj. respetuoso.
re·spect·ing (rǐ-spĕk'tǐng) prep. respecto a.
re·spec·tive (:tǐv) adj. respectivo.
res·pi·ra·tion (rĕs'pə-rā'shən) s. respiración *f.*
res·pi·ra·tor ('-tər) s. respirador *m.*
res·pi·ra·to·ry (rĕs'pər-ə-tôr'ē) adj. respirato-
rio.
re·spire (rǐ-spīr') tr. & intr. respirar.
res·pite (rĕs'pǐt) s. respiro; DER. suspensión *f.*
re·splen·dent (rǐ-splĕn'dənt) adj. resplandeciente, reluciente.
re·spond (rǐ-spŏnd') intr. responder.
re·spon·dent (rǐ-spŏn'dənt) I. adj. respondedor II. s. respondedor *m;* DER. demandado.
re·sponse (rǐ-spŏns') s. respuesta; *(to a proposal)* acogida; *(to a stimulus)* reacción *f.*
re·spon·si·bil·i·ty (rǐ-spŏn'sə-bǐl'ǐ-tē) s. responsabilidad *f* ♦ **on one's own r.** bajo su propia responsabilidad ♦ **that is not my r.** eso no es
asunto mío.
re·spon·si·ble (-'-bəl) adj. responsable *(for de,
to* ante); *(position)* de responsabilidad; *(person)*
digno de confianza.
re·spon·sive (rǐ-spŏn'sǐv) adj. sensible *(to* a).
rest¹ (rĕst) I. s. descanso; *(peace)* tranquilidad
f; (sleep) sueño; *(death)* paz *f; (respite)* respiro; *(support)* soporte *m;* MÚS. pausa ♦ **at r.**
(asleep) dormido; *(quiet)* tranquilo; *(motionless)* quieto ♦ **r. home** *(for sick people)* sanatorio; *(for the aged)* asilo de ancianos ♦ **r. room**
baño ♦ **to come to r.** pararse ♦ **to lay to r.** enterrar ♦ **to put to r.** olvidarse de ♦ **to take a r.**
descansar un rato II. intr. descansar; *(to re-

main)* quedarse; *(to stop)* pararse ♦ **let it r.** déjalo estar ♦ **may he r. in peace** que en paz
descanse ♦ **to r. on** *(a support)* apoyarse en; *(to
depend)* depender de —tr. dejar descansar;
(to place, lean) apoyar, descansar *(on, against*
en); *(hopes)* poner; *(defense)* basar ♦ **God r. his
soul** que Dios le tenga en su gloria ♦ **to r. one's
case** DER. terminar el alegato.
rest² I. s. ♦ **the r.** *(remainder)* el resto; *(others)*
los demás II. intr. quedarse <*you can r. assured*
puedes quedarte tranquilo>.
res·tau·rant (rĕs'tə-ränt') s. restaurante *m.*
res·tau·ra·teur (rĕs'tər-ə-tûr') s. dueño de un
restaurante.
rest·ful (rĕst'fəl) adj. quieto, sosegado.
res·ti·tute (rĕs'tǐ-tōōt') tr. restituir.
res·ti·tu·tion ('-tōō'shən) s. restitución *f; (compensation)* indemnización *f.*
res·tive (rĕs'tǐv) adj. *(uneasy)* inquieto; *(unruly)*
indócil.
rest·less (rĕst'lǐs) adj. inquieto, agitado.
res·to·ra·tion (rĕs'tə-rā'shən) s. restauración *f;*
(of order, relations) reintegro.
re·stor·a·tive (rǐ-stôr'ə-tǐv) adj. & s. reconstitu-
yente *m,* fortificante *m.*
re·store (rǐ-stôr') tr. *(order, relations)* restablecer; *(painting, monarch)* restaurar.
re·strain (rǐ-strān') tr. *(to repress)* reprimir; *(to
limit)* restringir; *(to confine)* encerrar.
re·strained (rǐ-strānd') adj. *(restricted)* restrin-
gido; *(reserved)* reservado, discreto.
re·straint (rǐ-strānt') s. *(limitation)* restricción *f;*
(moderation) moderación *f; (self-control)* dominio (de uno mismo).
re·strict (rǐ-strǐkt') tr. restringir, limitar.
re·strict·ed (rǐ-strǐk'tǐd) adj. *(limited)* restrin-
gido, limitado; *(access)* prohibido.
re·stric·tion (:shən) s. restricción *f.*
re·stric·tive (:tǐv) adj. restrictivo.
re·sult (rǐ-zŭlt') I. intr. ♦ **to r. from, in** resultar
de, en II. s. resultado ♦ **as a r. of** a causa de.
re·sul·tant (rǐ-zŭl'tənt) adj. & s. resultante *f.*
re·sume (rǐ-zōōm') tr. *(talking)* reanudar;
(working) reasumir ♦ **to r. one's seat** volver
a sentarse —intr. *(working)* reanudar; *(talking)*
proseguir.
rés·u·mé (rĕz'ə-mā') s. currículum vitae *m.*
re·sump·tion (rǐ-zŭmp'shən) s. reanudación *f;*
(continuation) continuación *f.*
re·sur·gence (rǐ-sûr'jəns) s. resurgimiento.
re·sur·gent (:jənt) adj. renaciente.
res·ur·rect (rĕz'ə-rĕkt') tr. & intr. resucitar.
res·ur·rec·tion (:rĕk'shən) s. *(revival)* restablecimiento; RELIG. resurrección *f.*
re·sus·ci·tate (rǐ-sŭs'ǐ-tāt') tr. resucitar.
re·sus·ci·ta·tion (-'-tā'shən) s. *(revival)* renacimiento; MED. resucitación *f.*
re·tail (rē'tāl') COM. I. s. venta al por menor *o*
al detalle II. adj. & adv. al por menor, al detalle III. tr. & intr. vender(se) al por menor.
re·tail·er (:ər) s. minorista *mf,* detallista *mf.*
re·tail·ing (:lǐng) s. venta al por menor.
re·tain (rǐ-tān') tr. retener; *(lawyer)* contratar;
(sense of humor) conservar.
re·tain·er (rǐ-tā'nər) s. *(servant)* criado; *(employee)* empleado; *(fee)* anticipo.
re·tal·i·ate (rǐ-tăl'ē-āt') intr. tomar represalias.
re·tal·i·a·tion ('-ā'shən) s. venganza.
re·tal·i·a·to·ry (rǐ-tăl'ē-ə-tôr'ē) adj. vengativo.
re·tard (rǐ-tärd') tr. retardar, retrasar.
re·tar·dant (rǐ-tär'dənt) adj. que retarda.
re·tar·da·tion (rē'tär-dā'shən) s. atraso, re-

traso; MED. atraso mental.
re·tard·ed (rĭ-tär'dĭd) adj. atrasado.
retch (rĕch) intr. tener náuseas —tr. vomitar.
re·ten·tion (rĭ-tĕn'shən) s. retención *f.*
re·ten·tive (:tĭv) adj. retentivo.
ret·i·cence (rĕt'ĭ-səns) s. reserva, reticencia.
ret·i·cent (:sənt) adj. reservado, reticente.
ret·i·cle (rĕt'ĭ-kəl) s. retículo.
ret·i·na (rĕt'n-ə) s. [pl. **s** o **-ae**] retina.
ret·i·nue (rĕt'n-ōō') s. séquito.
re·tire (rĭ-tīr') intr. *(to go to bed)* acostarse; *(to stop working)* jubilarse; *(to retreat)* retirarse —tr. retirar; *(employee)* jubilar.
re·tired (rĭ-tīrd') adj. jubilado.
re·tir·ee (rĭ-tīr'ē') s. jubilado.
re·tire·ment (rĭ-tīr'mənt) s. jubilación *f* ♦ **to go into r.** *(worker)* jubilarse; *(artist)* retirarse.
re·tir·ing (:ĭng) adj. tímido, retraído.
re·tort[1] (rĭ-tôrt') I. tr. replicar II. s. réplica.
re·tort[2] s. QUÍM. retorta.
re·touch (rē-tŭch') tr. retocar —intr. hacer retoques II. s. ('') retoque *m.*
re·trace (rē-trās') tr. trazar de nuevo ♦ **to r. one's steps** volver sobre los pasos.
re·tract (rĭ-trăkt') tr. & intr. *(to disavow)* retractar(se); *(to draw back)* retraer(se).
re·tract·a·ble/i·ble (rĭ-trăk'tə-bəl) adj. *(remark)* retractable; *(part)* retráctil.
re·trac·tile (rĭ-trăk'tĭl, :tīl') adj. retráctil.
re·trac·tion (:shən) s. *(disavowal)* retractación *f*; *(drawing back)* retracción *f.*
re·tread I. tr. (rē-trĕd') recauchutar II. s. ('') neumático recauchutado.
re·treat (rĭ-trēt') I. s. retirada; *(signal)* retreta; *(refuge)* refugio; RELIG. retiro ♦ **to beat a hasty r.** FAM. batirse en retirada II. intr. retirarse.
re·trench (rĭ-trĕnch') intr. hacer economías.
re·tri·al (rē-trī'əl) s. nuevo juicio.
ret·ri·bu·tion (rĕt'rə-byōō'shən) s. castigo.
re·triev·al (rĭ-trē'vəl) s. recuperación *f*; *(in hunting)* cobranza ♦ **beyond r.** irreparable.
re·trieve (rĭ-trēv') tr. recuperar; *(damage)* reparar; *(thought)* recordar; *(in hunting)* cobrar.
re·triev·er (rĭ-trē'vər) s. perro cobrador.
ret·ro·ac·tive (rĕt'rō-ăk'tĭv) adj. retroactivo.
ret·ro·cede (:sēd') intr. retroceder.
ret·ro·grade (rĕt'rə-grād') adj. retrógrado.
ret·ro·gress (:grĕs') intr. degenerar.
ret·ro·gres·sion ('-grĕsh'ən) s. regresión *f.*
ret·ro·rock·et (rĕt'rō-rŏk'ĭt) s. retrocohete *m.*
ret·ro·spect (rĕt'rə-spĕkt') s. ♦ **in r.** retrospectivamente.
ret·ro·spec·tion ('-spĕk'shən) s. retrospección *f.*
ret·ro·spec·tive (:tĭv) adj. retrospectivo.
re·turn (rĭ-tûrn') I. intr. volver, regresar; *(to respond)* responder; *(to revert)* revertir —tr. devolver; *(to put back)* volver a colocar; *(profits, interest)* producir; *(love, kindness)* corresponder; *(lost, stolen property)* restituir II. s. *(coming back)* regreso; *(giving back)* devolución *f*; *(repayment)* pago; *(response)* respuesta; *(profits)* ganancia; *(of income tax)* declaración *f* ♦ **by r. mail** a vuelta de correo • **in r. (for)** *(as a reward)* en pago; *(in exchange)* a cambio • **many happy returns** que cumpla(s) muchos años más • **r. address** dirección del remitente • **r. ticket** billete de ida y vuelta • **r. trip** viaje de regreso ♦ pl. *(income)* ingresos; *(in an election)* resultados.
re·un·ion (rē-yōōn'yən) s. reunión *f.*
re·u·nite (rē'yōō-nīt') tr. & intr. reunir(se).

re·us·a·ble (rē-yōō'zə-bəl) adj. que puede volverse a usar.
re·use tr. (rē-yōōz') volver a usar.
rev (rĕv) FAM. I. s. revolución *f* (de un motor) II. tr. **-vv-** ♦ **to r. up** acelerar —intr. ♦ **to r. up** *(engine)* embalarse.
re·val·u·ate (rē-văl'yōō-āt') tr. revalorizar.
re·val·ue (:yōō) tr. revalorizar.
re·vamp (rē-vămp') tr. renovar, modernizar.
re·veal (rĭ-vēl') tr. revelar.
rev·eil·le (rĕv'ə-lē) s. MIL. diana.
rev·el (rĕv'əl) I. intr. jaranear ♦ **to r. in** gozar de II. s. ♦ pl. jarana, juerga.
rev·e·la·tion (rĕv'ə-lā'shən) s. revelación *f.*
rev·el·ry (rĕv'əl-rē) s. jarana, juerga.
re·venge (rĭ-vĕnj') I. tr. vengar, vengarse de II. s. venganza ♦ **to take r.** vengarse *(on* de).
rev·e·nue (rĕv'ə-nōō') s. ingreso, renta; *(of a government)* rentas públicas.
re·ver·ber·ate (rĭ-vûr'bə-rāt') intr. resonar.
re·ver·ber·a·tion ('-rā'shən) s. eco.
re·vere (rĭ-vîr') tr. reverenciar, venerar.
rev·er·ence (rĕv'ər-əns) I. s. reverencia ♦ **to hold in r.** reverenciar II. tr. reverenciar.
rev·er·end (:ənd) adj. & s. reverendo.
rev·er·ent (:ənt) adj. reverente.
rev·er·en·tial (rĕv'ə-rĕn'shəl) adj. reverencial.
rev·er·ie (rĕv'ə-rē) s. ensueño.
re·ver·sal (rĭ-vûr'səl) s. *(of direction, opinion)* cambio; *(setback)* revés *m*; DER. revocación *f.*
re·verse (rĭ-vûrs') I. adj. *(opposite)* opuesto, contrario; *(inverse)* inverso <in r. order en orden inverso> ♦ **the r. side** *(of cloth)* revés, vuelta; *(of a form)* dorso; *(of a page, coin)* reverso II. s. *(opposite)* lo opuesto, lo contrario; *(setback)* revés *m*; AUTO. marcha atrás ♦ **just the r.** todo lo contrario ♦ **to put in(to) r.** poner en marcha atrás III. tr. *(order)* invertir; *(to turn inside out)* volver al revés; *(to transpose)* transponer; *(policy, direction)* cambiar; DER. revocar —intr. AUTO. dar marcha atrás.
re·vers·i·bil·i·ty (-'-bĭl'ĭ-tē) s. reversibilidad *f.*
re·vers·i·ble (rĭ-vûr'sə-bəl) adj. reversible.
re·ver·sion (rĭ-vûr'zhən) s. reversión *f.*
re·vert (rĭ-vûrt') intr. ♦ **to r. to** *(to return to)* volver a; DER. revertir a.
re·view (rĭ-vyōō') I. tr. *(volver a)* examinar; *(lesson, text)* repasar; *(film, book)* reseñar, criticar; DER. revisar; MIL. pasar revista a —intr. *(to study)* repasar *(for* para); *(to write reviews)* escribir críticas II. s. examen *m*; *(of lesson)* repaso; *(critique)* crítica; *(report)* análisis *m*; MIL., PERIOD. revista; DER. revisión *f.*
re·view·er (:ər) s. crítico.
re·vile (rĭ-vīl') tr. injuriar, insultar.
re·vise (rĭ-vīz') tr. *(to correct)* revisar, corregir; *(to modify)* modificar.
re·vi·sion (rĭ-vĭzh'ən) s. corrección *f*; *(modification)* modificación *f*; *(of views)* revisión *f.*
re·vi·sion·ist (:ə-nĭst) s. revisionista *mf.*
re·vis·it (rē-vĭz'ĭt) tr. visitar de nuevo.
re·vi·tal·ize (rē-vīt'l-īz') tr. revitalizar.
re·viv·al (rĭ-vī'vəl) s. *(reanimation)* revitalización *f*; *(of interest)* renacimiento *m*; ECON. reactivación *f*; TEAT. reposición *f* ♦ **r. meeting** asamblea evangelista.
re·vive (rĭ-vīv') tr. resucitar; *(spirits)* reanimar; *(custom)* restablecer; *(interest)* renovar; *(economy)* reactivar; *(hopes)* despertar; *(play)* reponer —intr. resucitar; *(to feel better)* reanimarse, volver en sí.
rev·o·ca·ble (rĕv'ə-kə-bəl) adj. revocable.
re·voke (rĭ-vōk') tr. revocar.

re·volt (rĭ-vōlt′) **I.** intr. rebelarse —tr. repugnar **II.** s. rebelión *f* ♦ **in r.** en rebeldía.

re·volt·ing (rĭ-vōl′tĭng) adj. repugnante.

rev·o·lu·tion (rĕv′ə-lōō′shən) s. revolución *f*; *(around axis)* rotación *f.*

rev·o·lu·tion·ar·y (:shə-nĕr′ē) adj. & s. revolucionario.

rev·o·lu·tion·ize (:nīz′) tr. revolucionar.

re·volve (rĭ-vōlv′) tr. hacer girar —intr. girar ♦ **to r. around** girar alrededor de • **to r. on** girar sobre.

re·volv·er (rĭ-vōl′vər) s. revólver *m.*

re·vue (rĭ-vyōō′) s. TEAT. revista.

re·vul·sion (rĭ-vŭl′shən) s. repugnancia, asco.

re·ward (rĭ-wôrd′) **I.** s. recompensa, premio **II.** tr. recompensar, premiar.

re·ward·ing (rĭ-wôr′dĭng) adj. *(remunerative)* remunerador; *(useful)* provechoso, útil.

re·wind (rē-wīnd′) tr. **-wound** rebobinar.

re·word (rē-wûrd′) tr. expresar con otras palabras.

re·work (rē-wûrk′) tr. revisar (discurso, obra).

re·write (rē-rīt′) -wrote, -written escribir de nuevo **II.** s. (″) ♦ **to do a r.** escribir de nuevo.

rhap·so·dize (răp′sə-dīz′) intr. ♦ **to r. about** *o* **over** poner por las nubes.

rhap·so·dy (:dē) s. rapsodia ♦ **to go into rhapsodies over** *o* **about** poner por las nubes.

rhet·o·ric (rĕt′ər-ĭk) s. retórica.

rhe·tor·i·cal (rĭ-tôr′ĭ-kəl) adj. retórico.

rheum (rōōm) s. lagaña.

rheu·mat·ic (rōō-măt′ĭk) adj. & s. reumático ♦ **r. fever** fiebre reumática.

rheu·ma·tism (rōō′mə-tĭz′əm) s. reumatismo.

rheu·ma·toid arthritis (:toid′) s. reúma *m* articular.

rhine·stone (rīn′stōn′) s. diamante falso.

rhi·noc·er·os (rī-nŏs′ər-əs) s. [pl. inv. *o* **es**] rinoceronte *m.*

rho·do·den·dron (rō′də-dĕn′drən) s. rododendro.

rhom·bus (rŏm′bəs) s. [pl. **es** *o* **-bi**] rombo.

rhu·barb (rōō′bärb′) s. BOT. ruibarbo; JER. *(quarrel)* riña.

rhyme (rīm) **I.** s. rima ♦ **without r. or reason** a tontas y a locas **II.** intr. & tr. rimar.

rhythm (rĭth′əm) s. ritmo.

rhyth·mic/mi·cal (rĭth′mĭk) adj. rítmico.

rib (rĭb) **I.** s. costilla; BOT. nervio; *(of an umbrella)* varilla; *(in fabric)* cordoncillo **II.** tr. **-bb-** proveer de costillas; JER. *(to tease)* tomar el pelo a.

rib·ald (rĭb′əld) adj. verde, obsceno.

rib·bing (rĭb′ĭng) s. JER. tomadura de pelo.

rib·bon (rĭb′ən) s. cinta; MIL. galón *m* ♦ **to tear to ribbons** hacer jirones.

rice (rīs) s. arroz *m* ♦ **r. field** *o* **paddy** arrozal.

rich (rĭch) adj. rico; *(food)* con mucha (materia) grasa; *(voice)* potente; *(color)* vivo; FAM. *(amusing)* gracioso ♦ **to be r. in** abundar en • **to get r.** hacerse rico.

rich·es (′ĭz) s.pl. riquezas.

rick·ets (rĭk′ĭts) s. raquitismo.

rick·et·y (rĭk′ĭ-tē) adj. **-i-** *(shaky)* desvencijado; MED. raquítico.

ric·o·chet (rĭk′ə-shā′) **I.** intr. rebotar **II.** s. rebote *m.*

rid (rĭd) tr. **rid(ded), -dding** librar ♦ **to be r. of** estar libre de • **to r. oneself of** librarse de.

rid·dance (:ns) s. liberación *f* ♦ **good r.!** ¡al fin me lo quité de encima!

rid·dle¹ (rĭd′l) tr. acribillar; FIG. llenar.

rid·dle² s. *(puzzle)* acertijo; *(mystery)* enigma *m* ♦ **to talk in riddles** hablar en clave.

ride (rīd) **I.** intr. **rode, ridden** montar; *(to move)* andar; *(to travel)* ir, viajar; *(in a car)* pasearse; *(to float)* flotar ♦ **to be riding high** estar en plena forma • **to let r.** dejar tranquilo • **to r. on** depender de • **to r. up** *(clothing)* subirse —tr. *(a horse)* montar a; *(a bicycle)* montar en; *(to travel over)* recorrer; *(to tease)* ridiculizar ♦ **to r. out** aguantar, soportar **II.** s. *(on horse, car)* paseo; *(trip)* viaje *m*; *(tour)* vuelta; *(means for transportation)* medio de transporte ♦ **to give someone a r.** llevar a alguien • **to go for a r.** dar un paseo • **to take for a r.** JER. dar gato por liebre.

rid·er (rī′dər) s. *(horse)* jinete *m*; *(bicycle)* ciclista *mf*; *(passenger)* viajero; DER. cláusula añadida.

ridge (rĭj) s. *(of earth)* lomo; *(of a hill)* cresta; *(of hills)* cordillera; *(of roof)* caballete *m.*

rid·i·cule (rĭd′ĭ-kyōōl′) **I.** s. ridículo ♦ **object of r.** blanco de burlas **II.** tr. ridiculizar, poner en ridículo.

ri·dic·u·lous (rĭ-dĭk′yə-ləs) adj. ridículo.

rife (rīf) adj. corriente ♦ **r. with** repleto de.

riff·raff (rĭf′răf′) s. gentuza, chusma.

ri·fle¹ (rī′fəl) **I.** s. rifle *m*; MIL. fusil *m* ♦ **r. range** campo de tiro **II.** tr. rayar.

ri·fle² tr. *(to ransack)* saquear.

rift (rĭft) s. *(in a breach)* ruptura; *(in a political party)* escisión *f*; GEOL. falla.

rig (rĭg) **I.** tr. **-gg-** *(to equip)* equipar; *(an election)* amañar; *(a contest)* arreglar; MARÍT. aparejar ♦ **the fight was rigged** hubo tongo en el combate • **to be rigged out as, in** vestirse de, con • **to r. up** preparar rápidamente **II.** s. *(gear)* equipo; FAM. *(truck)* camión *m*; *(outfit)* traje *m*; MARÍT. aparejo ♦ **oil r.** torre de perforación.

rig·ging (:ĭng) s. MARÍT. aparejo, jarcia.

right (rīt) **I.** adj. *(just, fair)* justo; *(ethical)* bueno, correcto; *(correct)* correcto; *(exact)* exacto (palabra, hora); *(appropriate)* más indicado; *(ideal)* ideal; *(proper)* debido <**in its r. place** en su debido sitio>; *(conditions)* bueno, favorable; *(in order)* en orden; *(opposite the left)* derecho; POL. de derecha, derechista; GEOM. recto ♦ **all r.** *(fine)* bastante bien; *(reliable)* de confianza; *(well)* bien <**are you all r.?** ¿te encuentras bien?> • **all r.?** ¿está bien? • **all r.!** ¡perfecto! • **is that r.?** ¿de verdad? • **it's all r.** no pasa nada • **r.!** ¡eso es! • **r. angle** ángulo recto • **r. wing** POL. derecha • **to be r.** tener razón • **to feel r.** *(well)* sentirse bien; *(pleasurable)* dar gusto (a uno) • **to put r.** arreglar • **to turn out all r.** salir bien **II.** s. *(justice)* justicia; *(good)* (lo) bueno, bien *m*; *(side, hand)* derecha; *(in boxing)* derechazo; *(claim)* derecho <**the r. to vote** el derecho al voto>; POL. derecha ♦ **by rights** de derecho • **in its own r.** de por sí • **in one's own r.** por derecho propio • **r. of way** derecho de paso • **to be in the r.** tener razón • **to be within one's rights** estar uno en su derecho • **to have a r.** to tener derecho a • **to make a r.** doblar a la derecha **III.** adv. *(directly)* derecho, directamente <**they came r. home** vinieron derecho a casa>; *(well, correctly)* bien <**it doesn't work r.** no funciona bien>; *(exactly)* exactamente, justo <**r. at the end** justo al final>; *(squarely)* en pleno; *(to the* *right)* a la derecha; FAM. *(very)* muy, bien ♦ **go r. ahead** siga, continúe • **if I remember r.** si mal no recuerdo • **r. and left** a diestra y siniestra • **r. behind** justo detrás • **r. face!** ¡derecha! • **r. off** inmediatamente • **r. now** ahora mismo • **r. (over) here, there** aquí, ahí mismo • **r. through** *(continuously)* sin parar; *(from side to side)* de lado a lado • **to do r.** by portarse bien con • **to get r.** *(to do)* hacer bien; *(to understand)* entender bien; *(to answer)* contestar bien • **to go r. on...** seguir... como si nada IV. tr. & intr. enderezar(se).

right·eous (rī′chəs) adj. *(morally right)* recto; *(honest)* honrado; *(just)* justo.

right·ful (rīt′fəl) adj. legítimo.

right-hand (:hănd′) adj. a la derecha ♦ **on the r. side** al lado derecho • **r. man** brazo derecho.

right-hand·ed (:hăn′dĭd) adj. que usa la mano derecha; *(tool)* para la mano derecha.

right·ly (:lē) adv. correctamente; *(properly)* con derecho • **r. or wrongly** con razón o sin ella, mal que bien.

rig·id (rĭj′ĭd) adj. rígido.

ri·gid·i·ty (rĭ-jĭd′ĭ-tē) s. rigidez *f.*

rig·ma·role (rĭg′mə-rōl′) s. galimatías *m.*

rig·or (rĭg′ər) s. rigor *m.*

rig·or·ous (:əs) adj. riguroso.

rile (rīl) tr. irritar.

rim (rĭm) I. s. borde *m*; *(coin)* canto; *(barrel)* aro; *(wheel)* llanta II. tr. **-mm-** bordear.

rind (rīnd) s. *(fruits)* cáscara; *(cheese)* corteza.

ring¹ (rĭng) I. s. anillo; *(hoop)* aro, argolla; *(circle)* círculo; *(on finger)* anillo, sortija; *(at circus)* pista; *(for bullfights)* ruedo; *(in boxing)* ring *m*, cuadrilátero; *(of criminals)* organización *f*; *(of spies)* red *f*; MEC. aro; QUÍM. cadena ♦ **key r.** llavero II. tr. *(to encircle)* rodear; *(to shape)* anillar.

ring² I. intr. **rang, rung** *(bells)* sonar, repicar; *(telephone, doorbell)* sonar; *(to jingle)* tintinear; *(to resound)* resonar; *(ears)* zumbar ♦ **to r. false, true** sonar a falso, cierto • **to r. out** oírse —tr. *(a bell, buzzer)* tocar; *(to telephone)* llamar, telefonear; *(the hour)* dar ♦ **to r. up** G.B. telefonear II. s. *(sound)* sonido (metálico); *(of telephone, buzzer, voice)* timbre *m*; *(of bell)* tañido; *(tinkle)* tintineo; *(telephone call)* telefonazo; *(quality)* tono <a suspicious r. un tono sospechoso> ♦ **it has a familiar r.** me suena.

ring·ing (:ĭng) I. adj. sonoro, resonante II. s. *(of bells)* tañido; *(of buzzer, alarm)* toque *m*; *(of phone)* timbre *m*; *(in the ears)* zumbido.

ring·lead·er (:lē′dər) s. cabecilla *m.*

ring·let (:lĭt) s. bucle *m*, rizo.

ring·mas·ter (:măs′tər) s. maestro de ceremonias.

ring·worm (:wûrm′) s. tiña.

rink (rĭngk) s. pista ♦ **ice-skating, roller-skating r.** pista de hielo, patinaje.

rinse (rĭns) I. tr. enjuagar II. s. enjuague *m.*

ri·ot (rī′ət) I. s. *(disturbance)* disturbio, tumulto; *(insurrection)* motín *m*, alboroto; *(profusion)* derroche *m* ♦ **r. act** ley de orden público • **r. police** guardia de asalto • **to be a r.** FAM. ser divertidísimo II. intr. alborotarse, amotinarse.

ri·ot·er (rī′ə-tər) s. alborotador *m.*

ri·ot·ous (:əs) adj. *(living)* desenfrenado; *(crowd)* alborotado; *(growth)* exuberante.

rip (rĭp) I. tr. **-pp-** rasgar, desgarrar ♦ **to r. apart** desgarrar • **to r. off** arrancar, quitar; JER.

(to rob) robar, limpiar • **to r. open** abrir de un tirón • **to r. out** arrancar; *(a seam)* descoser • **to r. up** desgarrar, destrozar —intr. rasgarse, desgarrarse; *(seam)* descoserse ♦ **to r. by** ir volando • **to r. into** regañar II. s. *(tear)* rasgón *m*, desgarrón *m*; *(split seam)* descosido ♦ **r. tide** corriente turbulenta.

rip·cord (:kôrd′) s. cuerda de apertura.

ripe (rīp) adj. maduro; *(cheese)* hecho; *(age)* avanzado ♦ **r. for** listo para • **the time is r. for** ha llegado el momento de.

rip·en (rī′pən) tr. & intr. madurar.

rip-off (rĭp′ôf′) s. FAM. *(swindle)* timo; *(imitation)* imitación *f* ♦ **r. artist** engañador.

rip·ple (rĭp′əl) I. tr. & intr. *(water)* rizarse; *(wheat)* ondular II. s. *(small wave)* rizo, onda; *(of laughter)* carcajada general.

rise (rīz) I. intr. **rose, risen** *(person, wind, dough)* levantarse; *(buildings, hills, spirits)* elevarse; *(temperature, prices, land)* subir; *(in rank, position)* ascender; *(water level)* crecer; *(voice)* alzarse; *(sun)* salir; *(pressure)* aumentar; *(stock market)* estar en alza; *(from the dead)* resucitar; *(in rebellion)* sublevarse ♦ **to r. above** *(to overcome)* sobreponerse a; *(to loom over)* surgir • **to r. to one's feet** ponerse de pie • **to r. to power** subir al poder • **to r. to the surface** salir a la superficie II. s. *(ascension)* subida, ascensión *f*; *(elevation)* elevación *f*; *(of prices, temperature, land)* subida; *(in water level)* crecida; *(of value, salary)* aumento; *(in rank)* ascenso; *(in pressure, rate, pitch)* elevación; *(of sun, moon)* salida; COM. alza ♦ **r. and fall** MARÍT. flujo y reflujo; HIST. grandeza y decadencia • **to give r. to** ocasionar, dar lugar a.

ris·er (rī′zər) s. ♦ **early r.** madrugador • **late r.** dormilón.

ris·ing (rī′zĭng) adj. ascendente; *(tide, anger)* creciente; *(promising)* prometedor; *(sun, moon)* naciente; *(prices, temperature)* que sube.

risk (rĭsk) I. s. riesgo II. tr. arriesgarse a.

risk·y (rĭs′kē) adj. -i- arriesgado.

ris·qué (rĭ-skā′) adj. escabroso.

rite (rīt) s. rito ♦ **funeral rites** exequias • **last rites** extremaunción.

rit·u·al (rĭch′o͞o-əl) s. ritual *m.*

rit·u·al·is·tic (′-ə-lĭs′tĭk) adj. ritualista.

ritz·y (rĭt′sē) adj. -i- JER. lujoso.

ri·val (rī′vəl) I. adj & s. rival *m* II. tr. rivalizar con.

ri·val·ry (:rē) s. rivalidad *f.*

riv·er (rĭv′ər) s. río.

riv·er·bank (:băngk′) s. ribera, orilla.

riv·er·bed (:bĕd′) s. cauce *m.*

riv·er·boat (:bōt′) s. barco, embarcación *f* de río.

riv·er·side (:sīd′) s. ribera, orilla.

riv·et (rĭv′ĭt) I. s. roblón *m* II. tr. *(attention)* cautivar; *(eyes)* fijar; MAQ. remachar.

roach¹ (rōch) s. [pl. inv. o **es**] ICT. gobio.

roach² s. ENTOM. cucaracha.

road (rōd) s. *(highway)* carretera; *(route, path)* camino; *(way, track)* vía ♦ **r. map** mapa de carreteras • **to be on the r.** TEAT. estar de gira • **to hit the r.** FAM. largarse.

road·bed (:bĕd′) s. F.C. terraplén *m.*

road·block (:blŏk′) s. *(by police, military)* barricada; FIG. obstáculo, impedimento.

road·house (:hous′) s. taberna.

road·side (:sīd′) s. borde *m* de la carretera.

road·way (:wā′) s. carretera.

roam (rōm) intr. & tr. vagar (por).

roan (rōn) adj. & s. (caballo) ruano.

roar (rôr) I. intr. (people) vociferar; (lion) rugir; (bull, wind) bramar ♦ **to r. by** o **past** pasar zumbando • **to r. with laughter** reírse a carcajadas —tr. decir a gritos, vociferar II. s. rugido, bramido; (of traffic) estruendo; (of the crowd) clamor m; (of laughter) carcajada.

roast (rōst) I. tr. (meat) asar; (coffee, nuts) tostar; FAM. (to criticize) poner por los suelos —intr. asarse, tostarse; (to feel hot) asarse II. s. asado; (cut) carne f para asar III. adj. asado ♦ **r. beef** rosbif.

roast·er (rō′stər) s. asador m.

rob (rŏb) tr. & intr. **-bb-** robar ♦ **to r. of** (reputation) quitar, robar; (strength) dejar sin.

rob·ber (:ər) s. (thief) ladrón m; (highwayman) salteador m; (bandit) bandido.

rob·ber·y (:ə-rē) s. robo.

robe (rōb) s. (judge) toga; (priest) sotana; (bathrobe) bata ♦ pl. vestiduras.

rob·in (rŏb′ĭn) s. tordo norteamericano; (Old World) petirrojo.

ro·bot (rō′bət, :bŏt′) s. robot m, autómata m.

ro·bot·ics (rō-bŏt′ĭks) s. técnica de los robots.

ro·bust (rō-bŭst′) adj. robusto, fuerte.

rock¹ (rŏk) s. roca; (stone) piedra; (cliff, crag) peñasco, peña; FIG. base f, soporte m; JER. diamante m ♦ **on the rocks** FAM. con hielo • **r. bottom** fondo • **r. salt** sal gema • **to be on the rocks** FAM. andar mal.

rock² I. intr. (to sway) balancearse; (to shake) estremecerse —tr. (baby, cradle) mecer; (to shake) sacudir; (to upset) dejar estupefacto ♦ **don't r. the boat** JER. deja las cosas como están • **to r. to sleep** mecer II. s. balanceo; MÚS. rock 'n' roll m.

rock·er (:ər) s. (chair) mecedora; (curved piece) arco ♦ **to be off one's r.** JER. estar chalado.

rock·et (rŏk′ĭt) I. s. cohete m; (weapon) proyectil m II. intr. subir rápidamente.

rock·et·ry (:ĭ-trē) s. técnica de los cohetes.

rock·ing (rŏk′ĭng) I. adj. ♦ **r. chair** mecedora • **r. horse** caballito de balancín II. s. balanceo.

rock 'n' roll (rŏk′ən-rōl′) s. rock 'n' roll m.

rock·y¹ (rŏk′ē) adj. **-i-** (stony) rocoso; FIG. difícil.

rock·y² adj. **-i-** (shaky) bamboleante, débil.

rod (rŏd) s. (stick) vara; (staff) bastón m; MEC. barra; JER. (pistol) pistolón m ♦ **divining r.** varita adivinatoria • **piston r.** biela.

rode (rōd) cf. **ride**.

ro·dent (rōd′nt) adj. & s. roedor m.

ro·de·o (rō′dē-ō′, rō-dā′ō) s. rodeo.

roe¹ (rō) s. (fish eggs) hueva.

roe² s. (deer) corzo.

rogue (rōg) s. pícaro.

role o **rôle** (rōl) s. papel m.

roll (rōl) I. intr. rodar; (to wallow) revolcarse; (prairie, hills) ondular; (thunder) retumbar; (drum) redoblar; AVIA., MARÍT. balancearse ♦ **to get rolling** FAM. ponerse en marcha • **to r. by** o **on** pasar • **to r. down** (tears) correr por; (ball) rodar por, bajar rodando por • **to r. in** llegar en abundancia • **to r. off** caerse rodando • **to r. over** dar una vuelta —tr. (to hacer) rodar; (to wheel) empujar; (a cigarette) liar; CINEM. rodar ♦ **rolling pin** rodillo • **to r. back** bajar, reducir • **to r. down** (to push) empujar por; (car windows) bajar • **to r. into** envolver en • **to r. out** (a map, scroll) desenrollar; (dough) extender con el rodillo • **to r. over** (object) voltear; (to destroy) derribar • **to r. up** (paper, rug) enro-

llar; (sleeves) arremangar II. s. (of paper, film) rollo; (of plane, boat) balanceo; (of the ocean) oleaje m; (of thunder) retumbo; (of money) fajo; (bread) bollo, panecillo ♦ **drum r.** redoble • **r. call** acto de pasar lista • **to call the r.** pasar lista ♦ pl. (records) archivos; (register) listas.

roll·er (rō′lər) s. (cylinder) rodillo; (small wheel) ruedecilla; (for the hair) rulo ♦ **r. coaster** montaña rusa • **r. skate** patín de ruedas.

rol·lick·ing (rŏl′ĭ-kĭng) adj. animado.

ro·ly·po·ly (rō′lē-pō′lē) adj. rechoncho.

Ro·man numeral (rō′mən) s. número romano.

Roman Catholic adj. & s. católico romano.

ro·mance (rō-măns′, ′′) I. s. romance m; (novel) novela romántica; (spirit) lo romántico; (love affair) amores m; (adventure) aventura II. tr. & intr. FAM. galantear.

ro·man·tic (rō-măn′tĭk) adj. & s. romántico.

ro·man·ti·cize (:tĭ-sīz′) tr. hacer romántico —intr. tener ideas románticas.

romp (rŏmp) I. intr. juguetear, retozar II. s. (play) retozo; (victory) triunfo fácil.

roof (rōof, rŏof) I. s. techo, tejado; (of the mouth) paladar m ♦ **to hit the r.** poner el grito en el cielo II. tr. techar.

roof·top (′tŏp′) s. tejado.

rook¹ (rŏok) I. s. ORNIT. grajo II. tr. JER. timar.

rook² s. (chess) torre f.

rook·ie (rŏok′ē) s. JER. (recruit) recluta mf; (in sports, police) novato.

room (rōom, rŏom) I. s. habitación f, cuarto; (for meetings) sala; (space, a spot) sitio ♦ **r. and board** pensión completa • **to make r. for** hacer sitio para • **to take up r.** ocupar sitio ♦ pl. alojamiento II. intr. alojarse ♦ **to r. together** o **with** compartir la habitación (con) • **rooming house** pensión.

room·er (′ər) s. huésped m.

room·mate (:māt′) s. compañero de cuarto.

room·y (:ē) adj. **-i-** espacioso, amplio.

roost (rōost) I. s. (perch) percha, palo; (coop) gallinero II. intr. posarse para dormir ♦ **to rule the r.** llevar la voz cantante.

roost·er (rōo′stər) s. gallo.

root¹ (rōot, rŏot) I. s. raíz f ♦ **r. canal** ODONT. empaste de la raíz • **r. cellar** bodega en la que se guardan legumbres • **to be at the r. of** ser la raíz de • **to put down roots** radicarse • **to take r.** echar raíces II. intr. echar raíces —tr. arraigar ♦ **to r. out** extirpar.

root² tr. (to dig) hocicar —intr. (to rummage) rebuscar.

root³ intr. ♦ **to r. for** animar a.

rope (rōp) I. s. soga, cuerda; (lasso) lazo ♦ **at the end of one's r.** en un aprieto • **to know the ropes** estar al tanto (de las cosas) • **to learn the ropes** ponerse al tanto II. tr. (to tie) amarrar, atar; (to lasso) coger con lazo ♦ **to r. in** embaucar • **to r. off** acordonar.

rose¹ (rōz) I. s. rosa ♦ **r. garden** rosaleda • **r. water** agua de rosas ♦ **to come up roses** salir bien II. adj. (de color) rosa.

rose² (rōz) cf. **rise**.

ro·sé (rō-zā′) s. rosado, clarete m.

rose·bud (rōz′bŭd′) s. capullo.

rose·bush (:bŏosh′) s. rosal m.

rose·mar·y (:mĕr′ē) s. romero.

ro·sette (rō-zĕt′) s. rosa, rosetón m.

rose·wood (rōz′wŏod′) s. palisandro.

ros·in (rŏz′ĭn) s. colofonia.

ros·ter (rŏs′tər) s. lista, registro.

ros·trum (rŏs′trəm) s. [pl. s o **-tra**] estrado.

ros·y (rō′zē) adj. **-i-** *(pink)* rosado; *(skin)* sonrosado; *(future)* prometedor; *(view)* optimista.

rot (rŏt) **I.** tr. & intr. **-tt-** pudrir(se) **II.** s. putrefacción *f*; *(substance)* podredumbre *f*; *(nonsense)* tontería.

ro·ta·ry (rō′tə-rē) **I.** adj. rotatorio **II.** s. *(device)* rotativa; *(traffic circle)* glorieta circular.

ro·tate (rō′tāt′) tr. & intr. *(hacer)* girar; *(crops, wheels)* alternar; *(workers)* turnarse.

ro·ta·tion (rō-tā′shən) s. *(turning)* giro, rotación *f*; *(turn)* revolución *f.*

rote (rōt) s. rutina ♦ **by r.** por repetición.

ro·tis·ser·ie (rō-tĭs′ə-rē) s. CUL. asador *m*.

ro·tor (rō′tər) s. rotor *m.*

rot·ten (rŏt′n) adj. **-er, -est** *(meat, fruit)* estropeado; *(wood)* carcomido; *(smell, egg)* podrido; *(trick)* malo; *(weather)* pésimo.

ro·tund (rō-tŭnd′) adj. rotundo.

ro·tun·da (rō-tŭn′də) s. rotonda.

rou·ble (rōō′bəl) s. var. de **ruble**.

rouge (rōōzh) s. colorete *m.*

rough (rŭf) **I.** adj. *(not smooth)* áspero; *(terrain)* accidentado; *(coarse)* basto, burdo; *(seas)* agitado; *(stormy)* tempestuoso; *(trying)* difícil, malo; *(rowdy)* alborotador; *(rude)* tosco; *(work)* duro; *(idea, guess)* aproximado ♦ **r. draft** borrador ♦ **r. sketch** boceto ♦ **to be r. on** *(person)* tratar con dureza; *(situation)* ser una mala suerte para **II.** s. terreno accidentado ♦ **in the r.** JOY. en bruto **III.** tr. poner áspero ♦ **to r. it** vivir sin comodidades ♦ **to r. out** bosquejar ♦ **to r. up** *(hair, feathers)* erizar, arrugar; *(someone)* darle una paliza a **IV.** adv. rudamente, toscamente ♦ **to play r.** jugar duro.

rough·age (:ĭj) s. alimento difícil de digerir que contribuye al movimiento peristáltico.

rough·en (:ən) tr. & intr. poner áspero.

rough·house (:hous′) intr. armar una trifulca.

rou·lette (rōō-lĕt′) s. ruleta.

round (round) **I.** adj. redondo; *(complete)* completo, bueno; *(sum)* considerable; *(voice, tone)* sonoro; *(plump)* regordete ♦ **r. trip** viaje de ida y vuelta **II.** s. *(circle)* círculo; *(of a ladder)* peldaño; *(series)* serie *f*; *(of talks, drinks)* ronda; *(of applause)* salva; ARM. descarga; DEP. *(of golf)* partido; *(in boxing)* asalto ♦ **to make one's rounds** *(police, patrol)* hacer la ronda; *(salesperson)* hacer el recorrido; *(doctor)* hacer las visitas **III.** tr. redondear; *(corner)* doblar, dar la vuelta a ♦ **to r. off** *(object, number)* redondear; *(to finish off)* rematar ♦ **to r. out** completar ♦ **to r. up** *(animals)* acorralar, rodear; *(people)* reunir **IV.** adv. *(around)* alrededor; *(everywhere)* por todas partes; *(here and there)* aquí y allá ♦ **all r.** para todos ♦ **all year r.** durante todo el año ♦ **r. about** a eso de ♦ **r. and r.** dando vueltas a la redonda **V.** prep. *(the world)* alrededor de; *(the corner)* a la vuelta de.

round·a·bout (roun′də-bout′) adj. indirecto, con rodeos ♦ **to take a r. route** dar un rodeo.

round·ed (:dĭd) adj. redondo, esférico.

round·up (round′ŭp′) s. *(of cattle)* rodeo; *(by the police)* redada; *(of news)* resumen *m.*

rouse (rouz) tr. & intr. despertar(se).

rous·ing (rou′zĭng) adj. conmovedor, animado.

roust (roust) tr. despertar, suscitar.

rout¹ (rout) **I.** s. *(retreat)* desbandada; *(defeat)* derrota completa **II.** tr. derrotar.

rout² tr. ♦ **to r. out** *(from hiding)* hacer salir; *(to dig up)* hocicar; *(to uncover)* descubrir.

route (rōōt, rout) **I.** s. *(course)* ruta, vía; *(road)* carretera; *(for delivery)* recorrido; *(means)* ca-

mino **II.** tr. mandar, encaminar.

rou·tine (rōō-tēn′) **I.** s. rutina; TEAT. número **II.** adj. rutinario, habitual.

rove (rōv) intr. vagar, errar.

rov·er (rō′vər) s. vagabundo.

row¹ (rō) s. línea, fila ♦ **in a r.** *(in succession)* seguidos; *(in a line)* en fila ♦ **in rows** en filas ♦ **r. house** casa en hilera.

row² (rō) intr. remar —tr. *(a boat)* conducir remando; *(passengers)* llevar.

row³ (rou) s. *(quarrel)* pelea; *(noise)* jaleo.

row·boat (rō′bōt′) s. bote *m* de remos.

row·dy (rou′dē) **I.** s. camorrista *mf*, pendenciero **II.** adj. **-i-** pendenciero, camorrista.

roy·al (roi′əl) adj. real.

roy·al·ist (:ə-lĭst) s. monárquico, realista *mf.*

roy·al·ty (:əl-tē) s. familia real; *(rank, power)* realeza; *(payment)* derechos de autor.

rub (rŭb) **I.** tr. **-bb-** frotar *(against* contra); *(to massage)* friccionar, dar friegas; *(one's hands)* frotarse; *(to irritate)* irritar; *(to chafe)* rozar; *(to polish)* limpiar frotando; *(to scour)* fregar ♦ **to r. down** friccionar ♦ **to r. elbows with** codearse con ♦ **to r. in u** on frotar con ♦ **to r. it in** FAM. machacar ♦ **to r. off** quitar frotando ♦ **to r. off** on *(good qualities)* transmitírsele a uno; *(bad qualities)* pegársele a uno ♦ **to r. out** borrar ♦ **to r. the wrong way** irritar, molestar —intr. rozar ♦ **to r. off** quitarse frotando ♦ **to r. (up) against** rozar contra **II.** s. *(rubbing)* frotamiento; *(massage)* fricción *f*; *(difficulty)* dificultad *f.*

rub·ber (rŭb′ər) s. caucho; *(synthetic)* goma; *(eraser)* goma de borrar ♦ **r. band** goma ♦ **r. stamp** sello de goma; *(approval)* aprobación automática.

rub·ber·ize (:ə-rīz′) tr. cauchutar.

rub·ber·neck (rŭb′ər-nĕk′) intr. curiosear.

rub·ber·stamp ('-stămp′) tr. aprobar automáticamente.

rub·ber·y (rŭb′ə-rē) adj. elástico.

rub·bish (rŭb′ĭsh) s. basura; FIG. tonterías.

rub·ble (rŭb′əl) s. escombros.

rub·down (rŭb′doun′) s. masaje *m.*

rube (rōōb) s. JER. patán *m*, palurdo.

ru·bel·la (rōō-bĕl′ə) s. rubéola.

ru·ble (rōō′bəl) s. FIN. rublo.

ru·bric (rōō′brĭk) s. rúbrica.

ru·by (rōō′bē) s. rubí *m.*

ruck·sack (rŭk′săk′) s. mochila.

ruck·us (rŭk′əs) s. FAM. trifulca, jaleo.

rud·der (rŭd′ər) s. timón *m..*

rud·dy (rŭd′ē) adj. **-i-** *(healthy)* rubicundo; G.B., FAM. maldito.

rude (rōōd) adj. *(crude)* crudo, rudo; *(humble)* humilde; *(discourteous)* grosero, descortés.

ru·di·ment (rōō′də-mənt) s. rudimento.

ru·di·men·ta·ry ('-mĕn′tə-rē) adj. rudimentario.

rue¹ (rōō) tr. arrepentirse de, lamentar.

rue² s. BOT. ruda.

rue·ful (′fəl) adj. pesaroso.

ruff (rŭf) s. *(collar)* gola; ZOOL. collar *m.*

ruf·fi·an (rŭf′ē-ən) s. rufián *m.*

ruf·fle (rŭf′əl) **I.** s. volante *m*, frunce *m* **II.** tr. *(to disturb)* agitar; *(cloth)* plegar; *(feathers)* erizar; *(a person)* aturdir ♦ **to get ruffled** fastidiarse.

rug (rŭg) s. alfombra.

rug·ged (rŭg′ĭd) adj. *(terrain)* escabroso; *(mountains)* escarpado; *(features)* duro; *(climate)* riguroso; *(hardy)* robusto.

ru·in (rōō'ĭn) I. s. ruina ♦ **to go to r.** caer en ruinas II. tr. arruinar; *(crops, party)* estropear; *(plans)* echar abajo; *(morally)* deshonrar.
ru·in·a·tion ('ə-nā'shən) s. ruina.
ru·in·ous ('ə-nəs) adj. ruinoso.
rule (rōōl) I. s. regla; *(control)* dominio, mando *<under foreign r.* bajo dominio extranjero>; *(power)* poder m; *(reign)* reinado ♦ **as a (general) r.** por lo regular • **as a r. of thumb** de forma práctica • **to be the r.** ser normal • **to make it a r. to** ser un deber para uno • **to play by the rules** obrar como es debido ♦ pl. reglamento • **r. of the road** reglamento del tránsito II. tr. *(to govern)* gobernar; *(to control)* dominar; *(to decree)* decretar; *(to decide)* decidir; *(to declare)* declarar; *(with lines)* rayar ♦ **to r. out** *(to exclude)* excluir, descartar; *(to make impossible)* hacer imposible —intr. gobernar, mandar; *(to decide)* decidir; DER. fallar ♦ **to r. against** DER. fallar en contra • **to r. over** gobernar.
rul·er (rōō'lər) s. gobernante m; *(strip)* regla.
rul·ing (:lĭng) I. adj. *(class, party)* gobernante; *(passion)* (pre)dominante II. s. DER. decisión f, fallo.
rum[1] (rŭm) s. ron m.
rum[2] adj. **-mm-** G.B. raro, extraño.
rum·ble (rŭm'bəl) I. intr. *(vehicle)* rodar con estrépito; *(gunfire, thunder)* retumbar II. s. retumbo; *(of protest)* rumor m; JER. *(fight)* pelea callejera.
ru·mi·nant (rōō'mə-nənt) adj. & s. rumiante m.
ru·mi·nate (:nāt') tr. & intr. rumiar.
ru·mi·na·tion ('nā'shən) s. rumia; *(meditation)* reflexión f.
rum·mage (rŭm'ĭj) I. tr. & intr. revolver, hurgar II. s. búsqueda desordenada ♦ **r. sale** venta benéfica.
rum·my[1] (rŭm'ē) s. *(game)* rami m.
rum·my[2] s. JER. *(drunkard)* borracho.
ru·mor (rōō'mər) I. s. rumor m II. tr. ♦ **to be rumored** rumorearse.
rump (rŭmp) s. *(of an animal)* ancas, grupa; *(of beef)* cuarto trasero; *(of a person)* nalgas.
rum·ple (rŭm'pəl) tr. & intr. arrugar(se).
rum·pus (rŭm'pəs) s. jaleo ♦ **r. room** cuarto de juegos.
run (rŭn) I. intr. **ran, run, -nn-** correr; *(to flee)* echar a correr, huir; *(to extend)* extenderse; *(to keep company)* andar *(with* con); *(to function)* andar, marchar; *(to be in operation)* estar en marcha, andar; *(to be in service)* circular, estar en servicio; *(wound)* supurar; *(nose)* moquear; *(eyes)* llorar; *(to melt)* derretirse; *(to spread)* correrse *(color, tinta)*; *(stockings)* correrse; *(contract)* ser válido; *(to last)* durar; *(to stretch)* estar colocado *<shelves ran along the walls* los estantes estaban colocados a lo largo de las paredes>; POL. presentarse como candidato; *(to tend)* inclinarse; ZOOL. *(to migrate)* emigrar ♦ **to come** *o* **go running** to acudir a • **to r. along** irse *<r. along!* ¡vete!> • **to r. around** *(to roam)* andar; *(to rush)* ajetrearse; *(to be unfaithful)* ser infiel • **to r. around (shouting, singing)** ir (gritando, cantando) • **to r. away** *(to flee)* fugarse; *(from home)* abandonar el hogar • **to r. down** parar • **to r. in the family** venir de familia • **to r. loose** andar suelto • **to r. low (on)** *o* **short (of)** andar escaso (de), quedar poco • **to r. off** *(to flee)* fugarse; *(liquid)* irse • **to r. on** *(to chatter)* hablar sin cesar; *(to elapse)* pasar (el tiempo) • **to r. out** *(to be exhausted)* acabarse,

agotarse; *(to expire)* expirar • **to r. over** *(to overflow)* rebosar; *(to go beyond)* durar más de lo previsto • **to r. smoothly** ir sobre ruedas, ir bien • **to r. up** *o* **over** acercarse corriendo —tr. *(race, risk)* correr; *(distance)* recorrer, cubrir; *(errand, experiment)* hacer; *(as candidate)* presentar de candidato; *(to operate)* hacer funcionar; *(to transport)* llevar; *(to smuggle)* pasar de contrabando; *(blockade)* romper; *(tap water)* dejar correr *o* salir; *(film)* dar, poner; *(to publish)* publicar; *(business, campaign)* dirigir; *(household)* llevar; *(to follow)* seguir *<to r. its course* seguir su curso> • **to r. a red light** pasar con la luz roja • **to r. a temperature** *o* **fever** tener fiebre • **to r. after** perseguir, ir detrás de • **to r. against** ir en contra de • **to r. around with** andar con • **to r. away with** llevarse • **to r. down** *(to knock down)* atropellar; *(to capture)* dar con, encontrar; *(to disparage)* poner por los suelos; *(to exhaust)* agotar; *(to review)* repasar • **to r. into** *(to meet by chance)* encontrarse con; *(to collide with)* chocar contra; *(difficulties)* tropezar con; *(to amount to)* llegar a • **to r. off** *(to print)* tirar; *(to force off)* echar *<he ran us off the road* nos echó de la carretera> • **to r. off with** *(to steal)* llevarse; *(to elope)* fugarse con • **to r. out of** acabársele a uno, quedarse uno sin • **to r. out on** abandonar, dejar • **to r. over** atropellar • **to r. the length of** correr de un extremo a otro de • **to r. through** *(to stab)* traspasar (con arma blanca); *(to squander)* despilfarrar; *(to rehearse)* ensayar • **to r. up** *(prices)* hacer subir; *(charges)* dejar que se accumulen; *(flag)* izar • **to r. up against** tropezar con II. s. *(route)* recorrido, trayecto; *(race)* carrera; *(quick trip)* visita *<a r. into town* una visita a la ciudad>; *(printing)* tirada; *(sudden demand)* gran demanda *(on* de); *(flow)* flujo; *(duration)* duración f; *(stream)* arroyo; *(enclosure)* corral m; *(in stockings)* carrera; *(series)* serie f; *(of luck)* racha; *(in cards)* escalera; *(trend)* dirección f, curso; DEP. *(slope)* pista; MÚS. carrerilla; MIN. veta, filón m; ICT. migración f ♦ **at a r.** corriendo • **on the r.** *(hurrying)* corriendo; *(fleeing)* huyendo; *(without pausing)* a la carrera • **to give someone the r. of the house** poner la casa a disposición de alguien • **to give someone a r. for his money** *(competition)* hacer competencia a alguien; *(satisfaction)* dar satisfacción a alguien • **to have a long r.** permanecer mucho tiempo en el cartel • **to have the r. of a place** tener libre acceso a un lugar • **to make a r. for it** correr.
run-a·round ('ə-round') s. evasiva ♦ **to give someone the r.** FAM. dar excusas.
run·a·way (:ə-wā') I. s. *(slave)* fugitivo; *(child)* niño desertor II. adj. fugitivo; *(horse)* desbocado; *(child)* desertor; *(victory)* fácil, abrumador; *(inflation)* galopante.
run-down (:doun') I. s. informe detallado II. adj. en estado de deterioro; *(person)* agotado.
rung[1] (rŭng) s. *(step)* peldaño; *(crosspiece)* barrote m.
rung[2] (rŭng) cf. **ring**[2].
run-in (rŭn'ĭn') s. riña.
run·ner (rŭn'ər) s. *(racer)* corredor m; *(messenger)* mensajero; *(of a skate)* cuchilla; *(of a sled)* patín m; *(of sliding door)* guía; *(cloth)* tapete m; *(carpet)* alfombra; BOT. planta trepadora.
run·ner-up ('-ŭp') s. segundo.
run·ning (rŭn'ĭng) I. s. *(of a business)* dirección

f; *(of a machine, household)* manejo ♦ **to be in the r.** tener posibilidades de ganar • **to be out of the r.** no tener ninguna posibilidad de ganar II. adj. *(water)* corriente; *(knot)* corredizo; *(sore)* que supura ♦ **r. start** salida lanzada III. adv. seguido.

run·ny (:ē) adj. **-l-** líquido; *(nose)* que gotea.

run-off (:ôf´) s. *(overflow)* derrame *m*; *(competition)* carrera de desempate.

run-of-the-mill adj. corriente y moliente.

runt (rŭnt) s. *(animal)* animal pequeño; DESPEC. *(person)* enano, renacuajo.

run-through (rŭn´thrōō´) s. ensayo.

run·way (:wā´) s. *(ramp)* rampa; AVIA. pista.

rup·ture (rŭp´chər) I. s. ruptura; *(hernia)* hernia II. tr. & intr. romper; *(an organ)* reventar(se).

ru·ral (rŏŏr´əl) adj. rural.

ruse (rōōs, rōōz) s. artimaña, treta.

rush[1] (rŭsh) I. intr. *(to run)* ir de prisa; *(to hurry)* apresurarse, darse prisa; *(to flow)* correr ♦ **to r. around** ajetrearse • **to r. in, off** entrar, marcharse corriendo • **to r. (right) over** acudir, ir corriendo • **to r. through** hacer de prisa —tr. *(a person)* dar prisa, apurar; *(a job)* hacer de prisa; *(an order)* ejecutar urgentemente; *(a package, to the hospital)* llevar de prisa o con urgencia; *(to attack)* atacar ♦ **to r. things** precipitar las cosas II. s. *(of activity)* gran demanda; *(haste)* prisa; *(attack)* acometida; *(onslaught)* fiebre *f* <*the gold r.* la fiebre del oro>; *(bustle)* bullicio, ajetreo; *(of wind)* ráfaga; *(of water)* torrente *m*; *(of emotion)* arrebato; *(narcotic high)* sensación eufórica ♦ **in a mad r.** precipitadamente • **r. hour** hora punta • **there's no r.** no corre prisa • **there was a (mad) r. to** la gente se apresuró • **to be in a r.** andar con prisa III. adj. urgente.

rush[2] s. BOT. junco.

rus·set (rŭs´ĭt) adj. & s. (color *m*) rojizo.

rust (rŭst) I. s. herrumbre *f*; *(on plants)* tizón *m* II. tr. & intr. oxidar(se), enmohecer(se).

rus·tic (rŭs´tĭk) adj. & s. rústico.

rus·tle (rŭs´əl) I. tr. & intr. *(leaves)* (hacer) susurrar; *(paper, fabric)* (hacer) crujir; *(cattle)* robar (ganado) II. s. susurro.

rust·y (rŭs´tē) adj. **-l-** oxidado, mohoso; *(color)* rojizo ♦ **to be r.** *(person)* estar falto de práctica.

rut[1] (rŭt) I. s. carril *m*; FIG. rutina <*to be in a r.* ser esclavo de la rutina> II. tr. **-tt-** surcar.

rut[2] s. ZOOL. *(heat)* celo.

ru·ta·ba·ga (rōō´tə-bā´gə) s. nabo sueco.

ruth·less (rōōth´lĭs) adj. despiadado, cruel.

rye (rī) s. centeno; *(whiskey)* whisky *m* de centeno.

S

s, S (ĕs) s. decimonovena letra del alfabeto inglés.

Sab·bath (săb´əth) s. *(Jewish)* sábado; *(Christian)* domingo.

sab·bat·i·cal (sə-băt´ĭ-kəl) s. licencia sabática.

sa·ber (sā´bər) s. sable *m*.

sa·ble (sā´bəl) I. s. ZOOL. marta cebellina II. adj. negro.

sab·o·tage (săb´ə-täzh´) I. s. sabotaje *m* II. tr. sabotear.

sab·o·teur (´-tûr´) s. saboteador *m*.

sac (săk) s. saco.

sac·cha·rin (săk´ər-ĭn) s. sacarina.

sac·cha·rine (:ĭn) adj. empalagoso; QUÍM. sacarino.

sa·chet (să-shā´) s. almohadilla perfumada.

sack[1] (săk) I. s. *(bag)* saco; JER. *(bed)* cama ♦ **to get the s.** JER. ser despedido II. tr. ensacar; *(to fire)* despedir.

sack[2] I. tr. *(to loot)* saquear II. s. saqueo.

sack·cloth (săk´klôth´) s. tela de arpillera.

sac·ra·ment (săk´rə-mənt) s. sacramento.

sa·cred (sā´krĭd) adj. sacro, sagrado; *(venerable)* venerable; *(holy)* consagrado ♦ **nothing is s.** no se respeta nada • **s.** to consagrado a.

sac·ri·fice (săk´rə-fīs´) I. s. sacrificio ♦ **at a s.** COM. con pérdida • **to make a s.** to ofrecer un sacrificio a II. tr. sacrificar; COM. vender con pérdida —intr. ofrecer un sacrificio.

sac·ri·fi·cial (´-fĭsh´əl) adj. de sacrificio.

sac·ri·lege (săk´rə-lĭj) s. sacrilegio.

sac·ri·le·gious (´-lē´jəs, :lĭj´əs) adj. sacrílego.

sac·ro·il·i·ac (săk´rō-ĭl´ē-ăk´, sā´krō-) I. adj. sacroilíaco II. s. región sacroilíaca.

sac·ro·sanct (săk´rō-săngkt´) adj. sacrosanto.

sa·crum (sā´krəm) s. [pl. **-cra**] sacro.

sad (săd) adj. **-dd-** triste; *(regrettable)* lamentable ♦ **s. to say that** la triste verdad es que.

sad·den (săd´n) tr. entristecer.

sad·dle (săd´l) I. s. silla de montar; *(of bicycle)* sillín *m*; *(cut of meat)* cuarto trasero II. tr. ensillar ♦ **to s. with** cargar con —intr. ♦ **to s. up** montar en la silla.

sad·dle·bag (:băg´) s. alforja.

saddle horse s. caballo de silla.

sa·dism (sā´dĭz´əm, săd´ĭz´-) s. sadismo.

sa·dist (sā´dĭst, săd´ĭst) s. sádico.

sa·dis·tic (sə-dĭs´tĭk) adj. sádico.

sad·ness (săd´nĭs) s. tristeza.

safe (sāf) I. adj. seguro ♦ **have a s. trip!** ¡ten cuidado! • **is it s.?** ¿no es peligroso? • **it is s. to say that** se puede decir con seguridad que • **s. and sound** sano y salvo • **s. from** a salvo de • **to be on the s. side** para mayor seguridad • **to be s.** estar a salvo • **to play it s.** actuar con precaución II. s. caja de caudales.

safe-con·duct (´kŏn´dŭkt) s. salvoconducto.

safe·crack·er (:krăk´ər) s. ladrón *m* de cajas fuertes.

safe-de·pos·it box (´dĭ-pŏz´ĭt) s. caja de seguridad.

safe·guard (´gärd´) I. s. salvaguarda ♦ **to be a s. against** proteger contra II. tr. salvaguardar.

safe·keep·ing (:kē´pĭng) s. *(act)* depósito; *(state)* protección *f*.

safe·ly (:lē) adv. *(without harm)* sin accidente; *(driving)* con cuidado.

safe·ty (:tē) s. seguridad *f*; ARM. seguro ♦ **s. belt, valve** cinturón, válvula de seguridad • **s. pin** imperdible • **to get to s.** ponerse a salvo.

saf·flow·er (săf´lou´ər) s. alazor *m*.

saf·fron (săf´rən) s. azafrán *m*; *(color)* color *m* azafrán.

sag (săg) I. intr. **-gg-** *(skin, clothes)* colgar; *(plank)* combarse; *(clothesline)* aflojarse; *(production, sales)* decaer; *(prices)* bajar II. s. *(decline)* caída; *(in board)* comba.

sa·ga (sä´gə) s. saga.

sa·ga·cious (sə-gā´shəs) adj. sagaz.

sa·gac·i·ty (sə-găs´ĭ-tē) s. sagacidad *f*.

sage[1] (sāj) s. & adj. sabio.

sage[2] s. BOT. salvia.

sage·brush (´brŭsh´) s. artemisa.

sag·ging (săg´ĭng) adj. *(sunken)* hundido; *(de-*

clining) decreciente.
said (sĕd) I. cf. **say** II. adj. (ante)dicho.
sail (sāl) I. s. vela; *(trip)* viaje *m* en barco; *(of windmill)* brazo ♦ **to make s.** desplegar las velas • **to set s.** hacerse a la vela • **under full s.** a toda vela • **under s.** con las velas alzadas II. intr. navegar; *(to travel)* ir en barco; *(to set out)* zarpar —tr. *(an ocean)* atravesar; *(one's boat)* botar ♦ **to s. around** *(a cape)* doblar; *(the world)* dar la vuelta a • **to s. the seas** surcar los mares • **to s. through** pasar fácil y rápidamente por.
sail·boat ('bōt') s. barco de vela.
sail·cloth (:klŏth') s. lona para velas.
sail·fish (:fĭsh') s. [pl. inv. o **es**] pez *m* vela.
sail·ing (sā'lĭng) s. navegación *f*; *(sport)* vela; *(departure)* salida ♦ **to be smooth s.** ser fácil.
sail·or (sā'lər) s. marinero.
saint (sānt) I. s. santo II. tr. canonizar.
saint·ed (sān'tĭd) adj. santo.
saint·hood (sānt'hŏŏd') s. santidad *f*.
saint·ly (:lē) adj. **-i-** santo.
sake[1] (sāk) s. ♦ **for God's o goodness' o heaven's s.!** ¡por (el amor de) Dios! • **for one's own s.** por el propio bien de uno • **for the s. of** por.
sa·ke[2] o sa·ki (sä'kē, :kĕ) s. sake *m*, saki *m*.
sal·a·ble (sāl'ə-bəl) adj. vendible.
sa·la·cious (sə-lā'shəs) adj. salaz.
sal·ad (săl'əd) s. ensalada ♦ **s. dressing** aderezo • **s. days** días de juventud.
sal·a·man·der (săl'ə-măn'dər) s. salamandra.
sal·a·ried (săl'ə-rēd) adj. *(person)* salariado; *(work)* a sueldo.
sal·a·ry (săl'ə-rē) s. salario.
sale (sāl) s. venta; *(clearance)* liquidación *f* ♦ **for s.** se vende • **on s.** *(available)* en venta; *(reduced)* en liquidación • **s. price** precio de saldo • **to have a s.** estar de liquidación • **to put up for s.** poner en venta ♦ pl. venta • **s. tax** impuesto a las ventas.
sales·clerk (sālz'klûrk') s. dependiente *m*.
sales·girl (:gûrl') s. vendedora.
sales·man (:mən) s. [pl. -men] vendedor *m*.
sales·man·ship (:shĭp') s. arte *m* de vender.
sales·per·son (sālz'pûr'sən) s. vendedor, -a.
sales·wom·an ('wŏŏm'ən) s. [pl. -women] vendedora.
sa·li·ent (sā'lē-ənt) adj. *(projecting)* saliente; *(prominent)* sobresaliente.
sa·line (sā'lēn', :līn') adj. salino.
sa·li·va (sə-lī'və) s. saliva.
sal·i·var·y (săl'ə-vĕr'ē) adj. salival.
sal·i·vate (:vāt') intr. salivar.
sal·low (săl'ō) adj. **-er, -est** cetrino.
sal·ly (săl'ē) I. intr. ♦ **to s. forth** salir II. s. salida; *(outburst)* arranque; *(jaunt)* paseo.
salm·on (săm'ən, să'mən) s. [pl. inv. o **s**] salmón *m*; *(color)* color *m* salmón.
sal·mo·nel·la (săl'mə-nĕl'ə) s. [pl. inv. o **s** o **-ae**] salmonela.
sa·lon (sə-lŏn') s. salón *m*.
sa·loon (sə-lōōn') s. taberna; *(hall, lounge)* salón *m*.
salt (sôlt) I. s. sal *f* ♦ **not to be worth one's s.** no valer gran cosa • **old s.** viejo lobo de mar • **s. water** agua salada II. tr. echar sal a; *(to preserve)* salar; *(writing)* salpicar.
salt·pe·ter ('pē'tər) s. nitrato de sodio o potasio.
salt·shak·er (:shā'kər) s. salero.
salt·wa·ter (:wô'tər) adj. de agua salada.
salt·y (sôl'tē) adj. **-i-** *(saline)* salino; *(with salt)*

salado; *(witty)* agudo; *(lively)* picante.
sa·lu·bri·ous (sə-lōō'brē-əs) adj. salubre.
sal·u·tar·y (săl'yə-tĕr'ē) adj. saludable; *(beneficial)* benéfico.
sal·u·ta·tion (săl'yə-tā'shən) s. saludo.
sa·lu·ta·to·ry (sə-lōō'tə-tôr'ē) adj. de saludo.
sa·lute (sə-lōōt') I. tr. saludar —intr. hacer un saludo II. s. saludo.
sal·vage (săl'vĭj) I. s. MARÍT. salvamento; *(things)* objetos salvados; *(compensation)* prima de salvamento II. tr. salvar.
sal·vage·a·ble (:vĭ-jə-bəl) adj. salvable.
sal·va·tion (săl-vā'shən) s. salvación *f*.
salve (săv, säv) I. s. ungüento; FIG. bálsamo II. tr. apaciguar.
sal·ver (săl'vər) s. bandeja.
sal·vo (săl'vō) s. [pl. **(e)s**] salva.
same (sām) I. adj. mismo; *(similar)* igual ♦ **at the s. time** sin embargo • **s. difference o thing** FAM. lo mismo • **the s. old story** la historia de siempre • **to be of the s. mind** pensar igual II. adv. igual III. pron. el mismo; *(thing)* lo mismo ♦ **all the s.** sin embargo • **everything is the s.** todo sigue igual • **it's all the s. to me** me da igual o lo mismo • **the s. to you!** ¡igualmente!; *(in anger)* ¡te deseo lo mismo!
same·ness (:nĭs) s. igualdad *f*; *(monotony)* monotonía.
sam·ple (săm'pəl) I. s. muestra; CIENT. espécimen *m* II. tr. tomar una muestra de; CUL. catar.
sam·pler (:plər) s. COST. dechado.
sam·pling (:plĭng) s. muestra.
san·a·tive (săn'ə-tĭv) adj. sanativo.
san·a·to·ri·um (săn'ə-tôr'ē-əm) s. [pl. **s** o **-ia**] sanatorio.
sanc·ti·fy (săngk'tə-fī') tr. santificar.
sanc·ti·mo·ni·ous ('-mō'nē-əs) adj. santurrón.
sanc·tion (săngk'shən) I. s. sanción *f* II. tr. sancionar.
sanc·ti·ty (săngk'tĭ-tē) s. santidad *f*.
sanc·tu·ar·y (:chōō-ĕr'ē) s. santuario; *(refuge)* asilo; *(game preserve)* coto.
sand (sănd) I. s. arena ♦ **s. dune** médano ♦ pl. *(land)* arenales; FIG. *(of time)* tiempo II. tr. & intr. *(road)* enarenar; *(wood)* lijar.
san·dal (săn'dl) s. sandalia.
san·dal·wood (:wŏŏd') s. sándalo.
sand·bag (sănd'băg') I. s. saco de arena II. tr. **-gg-** proteger con sacos de arena.
sand·bank (:băngk') s. banco de arena.
sand·bar (:bär') s. arrecife *m* de arena.
sand·blast (:blăst') I. s. chorro de arena II. tr. limpiar con chorro de arena.
sand·box (:bŏks') s. cajón *m* de arena.
sand·er (săn'dər) s. persona o aparato que esparce arena; *(tool)* lijadora.
sand·lot (sănd'lŏt') s. solar *m*, baldío.
sand·pa·per (:pā'pər) I. s. papel *m* de lija II. tr. lijar.
sand·pi·per (:pī'pər) s. aguzanieves *f*.
sand·stone (:stōn') s. arenisca.
sand·storm (:stôrm') s. tempestad *f* de arena.
sand·wich (:wĭch') s. emparedado, sandwich *m*.
sand·y (săn'dē) adj. **-i-** arenoso.
sane (sān) adj. cuerdo; *(reasonable)* razonable.
sang (săng) cf. **sing.**
san·guine (săng'gwĭn) adj. sanguíneo; *(optimistic)* optimista.
san·i·tar·i·um (săn'ĭ-târ'ē-əm) s. [pl. **s** o **-ia**] sanatorio.
san·i·tar·y (săn'ĭ-tĕr'ē) adj. sanitario ♦ **s. nap-**

kin paño higiénico.
san·i·ta·tion ('-tā'shən) s. saneamiento.
san·i·tize ('-tīz') tr. sanear.
san·i·ty (săn'ĭ-tē) s. cordura; *(sense)* sensatez *f.*
sank (săngk) cf. **sink.**
sap¹ (săp) s. BOT. savia; *(vitality)* vitalidad *f;* JER. *(dupe)* bobo.
sap² tr. **-pp-** *(to deplete)* agotar; *(to undermine)* socavar.
sa·pi·ent (sā'pē-ənt) adj. sapiente.
sap·ling (săp'lĭng) s. árbol *m* joven.
sap·phire (săf'īr') s. zafiro; *(color)* color *m* zafiro.
sap·py (săp'ē) adj. **-i-** lleno de savia; *(foolish)* tontuelo.
sar·casm (sär'kăz'əm) s. sarcasmo.
sar·cas·tic (sär-kăs'tĭk) adj. sarcástico.
sar·dine (sär-dēn') s. sardina.
sar·don·ic (sär-dŏn'ĭk) adj. sardónico.
sash¹ (săsh) s. *(band)* fajín *m.*
sash² s. *(frame)* marco.
sa·shay (să-shā') intr. FAM. pavonearse.
sass (săs) FAM. I. s. impertinencia II. tr. hablar con insolencia a.
sas·sa·fras (săs'ə-frăs') s. sasafrás *f.*
sas·sy (săs'ē) adj. **-i-** descarado.
sat (săt) cf. **sit.**
sa·tan·ic/i·cal (sā-tăn'ĭk) adj. satánico.
satch·el (săch'əl) s. cartapacio.
sate (sāt) tr. saciar; *(to glut)* hartar.
sat·el·lite (săt'l-īt') s. satélite *m.*
sa·tia·ble (sā'shə-bəl) adj. saciable.
sa·ti·ate (sā'shē-āt') tr. saciar; *(to glut)* hartar.
sa·ti·a·tion ('-ā'shən) s. saciedad *f.*
sa·ti·e·ty (sə-tī'ĭ-tē) s. hartura.
sat·in (săt'n) s. raso, satén *m.*
sat·ire (săt'īr') s. sátira.
sa·tir·ic/i·cal (sə-tĭr'ĭk) adj. satírico.
sat·i·rist (săt'ər-ĭst) s. *(writer)* satírico.
sat·i·rize (:ə-rīz') tr. satirizar.
sat·is·fac·tion (săt'ĭs-făk'shən) s. satisfacción *f; (compensation)* compensación *f.*
sat·is·fac·to·ry (:tə-rē) adj. satisfactorio.
sat·is·fy (săt'ĭs-fī') tr. satisfacer; *(requirements)* cumplir con; *(to content)* contentarse; *(to assure)* convencer —intr. dar satisfacción.
sat·is·fy·ing (:ĭng) adj. satisfactorio; *(experience)* agradable; *(food)* sustancioso.
sat·u·rate (săch'ə-rāt') tr. saturar.
sat·u·rat·ed (::răt'ĭd) adj. saturado.
sat·u·ra·tion ('-'shən) s. saturación *f.*
Sat·ur·day (săt'ər-dē) s. sábado.
sauce (sôs) I. s. salsa; *(compote)* compota; *(impudence)* descaro II. tr. echar salsa a; FAM. insolentarse con.
sauce·pan (sôs'păn') s. cacerola.
sau·cer (sô'sər) s. platillo.
sauc·y (sô'sē) adj. **-i-** descarado.
sau·na (sô'nə) s. sauna.
saun·ter (sôn'tər) I. intr. pasearse II. s. paseo.
sau·sage (sô'sĭj) s. embutido; *(pork)* salchicha.
sau·té (sō-tā', sô-) tr. **-(e)d** saltear.
sav·age (săv'ĭj) I. adj. salvaje; *(ferocious)* feroz; *(cruel)* cruel II. s. salvaje *mf.*
sav·age·ry (:rē) s. salvajismo.
sa·van·na(h) (sə-văn'ə) s. sabana.
sa·vant (sə-vänt') s. sabio.
save¹ (sāv) I. tr. *(to rescue)* salvar; *(to keep)* guardar; *(to conserve)* ahorrar ♦ **to s.** one's breath ahorrar saliva • **to s.** oneself the trouble ahorrarse la molestia • **to s. the day** salvar

la situación —intr. ahorrar II. s. DEP. parada.
save² I. prep. salvo II. conj. a no ser que ♦ **s. for** salvo por • **s. that** si no fuera porque.
sav·er (sā'vər) s. salvador *m; (of money)* ahorrador *m.*
sav·ing (sā'vĭng) s. salvamento; *(economy)* ahorro ♦ pl. ahorros • **s. account, bank** cuenta, caja de ahorros.
sav·ior (sāv'yər) s. salvador.
sa·vor (sā'vər) I. s. sabor *m* II. intr. ♦ **to s. of** saber a —tr. gozar del sabor de.
sa·vor·y (sā'və-rē) adj. sabroso; *(piquant)* picante.
sav·vy (săv'ē) JER. I. intr. entender II. s. sentido común.
saw¹ (sô) I. s. *(handsaw)* serrucho; *(machine)* sierra II. tr. **-ed, -ed** *o* **-n** (a)serrar.
saw² s. proverbio ♦ **old s.** viejo dicho.
saw³ cf. **see¹.**
saw·dust (sô'dŭst') s. (a)serrín *m.*
saw·horse (sô'hôrs') s. CARP. burro.
saw·mill (sô'mĭl') s. aserradero, serrería.
sax (săks) FAM. saxo, saxófono.
sax·o·phone (săk'sə-fōn') s. saxófono.
say (sā) I. tr. **said** decir; *(prayer)* rezar; *(to indicate)* marcar; *(to suppose)* suponer ♦ **enough said!** ¡basta! • **I'll s.!** ¡ya lo creo! • **it goes without saying** huelga decir • **easier said than done** más fácil decirlo que hacerlo • **it is said** se dice • **let us s.** digamos • **no sooner said than done** dicho y hecho • **not to s.** por no decir • **s.!** ¡oiga! • **s. no more!** ¡no me digas más! • **that is to s.** o sea, es decir • **to s. nothing of** por no hablar de • **to s. again** volver a decir • **to s. the least** por lo menos • **to s. the word** dar la orden • **to s. to oneself** decir para sí • **what do you s.?** ¿qué te parece? • **when all is said and done** al fin y al cabo • **you can s. that again!** ¡ya lo creo! • **you don't s.!** ¡no me digas! • **you said it!** ¡dímelo a mí! II. s. *(opinion)* voz *f; (turn to speak)* uso de la palabra.
say·ing (sā'ĭng) s. dicho.
say-so (sā'sō') s. FAM. afirmación *f; (authority)* autoridad *f.*
scab (skăb) I. s. postilla; BOT. escabro; FAM. *(strikebreaker)* esquirol *m* II. intr. **-bb-** formar costra; FAM. *(to take a job)* sustituir a un huelguista.
scab·bard (skăb'ərd) s. vaina (de una espada).
scab·by (skăb'ē) adj. **-i-** costroso; VET. roñoso.
sca·bies (skā'bēz') s.inv. sarna.
scab·rous (skăb'rəs, skā'brəs) adj. escabroso.
scads (skădz) s.pl. FAM. montones *m.*
scaf·fold (skăf'əld) s. andamio; *(for executions)* patíbulo.
scaf·fold·ing (:əl-dĭng) s. andamiaje *m.*
scal·a·wag (skăl'ə-wăg') s. FAM. bribón *m.*
scald (skôld) I. tr. escaldar; *(milk)* calentar casi hasta el hervor II. s. escaldadura.
scald·ing (skôl'dĭng) adj. hirviente.
scale¹ (skāl) I. s. *(flake)* escama; *(of pipe)* incrustaciones *f* II. tr. escamar —intr. ♦ **to s. off** *(skin)* pelarse; *(paint)* descascararse.
scale² I. s. escala II. tr. *(to climb)* escalar; *(to adjust)* adaptar ♦ **to s. down, up** reducir, aumentar a escala.
scale³ s. *(balance)* báscula; *(tray)* platillo (de balanza).
scal·lion (skăl'yən) s. cebollino.
scal·lop (skŏl'əp, skăl'-) I. s. ZOOL. vieira; *(shell)* venera; *(border)* festón *m,* onda II. tr. COST. ondular; CUL. guisar al gratén.

scalp (skălp) **I.** s. *(trophy)* escalpe *m*; ANAT. cuero cabelludo **II.** tr. escalpar; FAM. *(tickets)* revender.
scal·pel (skăl′pəl) s. escalpelo.
scalp·er (skăl′pər) s. revendedor *m*.
scal·y (skă′lē) adj. **-i-** escamoso.
scam (skăm) s. JER. estafa.
scam·per (skăm′pər) **I.** intr. corretear **II.** s. correteo.
scan (skăn) **I.** tr. **-nn-** *(to examine)* escudriñar; *(to look around)* recorrer con la mirada; *(to glance at)* echar un vistazo a; *(verse)* escandir; ELECTRÓN. registrar, explorar —intr. ELECTRÓN. registrar, explorar; POÉT. escandir **II.** s. escudriñamiento.
scan·dal (skăn′dl) s. escándalo; *(gossip)* chismorreo.
scan·dal·ize (:īz′) tr. escandalizar.
scan·dal·ous (:əs) adj. escandaloso; *(defamatory)* difamatorio.
scan·ner (skăn′ər) s. ELECTRÓN. dispositivo explorador; MED. tomógrafo.
scant (skănt) adj. escaso **II.** tr. escatimar.
scant·y (skăn′tē) adj. **-i-** escaso.
scape·goat (skāp′gōt′) s. cabeza de turco.
scar (skär) **I.** s. cicatriz *f* **II.** tr. **-rr-** *(to mark)* señalar; *(the skin)* dejar una cicatriz en —intr. cicatrizar(se).
scar·ab (skăr′əb) s. escarabajo.
scarce (skârs) adj. raro; *(insufficient)* escaso ♦ **to become s.** escasear.
scarce·ly (′lē) adv. apenas; *(hardly)* casi no; *(surely not)* seguramente no.
scar·ci·ty (skâr′sĭ-tē) s. escasez *f*.
scare (skâr) **I.** tr. & intr. asustar(se) ♦ **to be scared of** asustarse de • **to be scared stiff** *o* **to death** estar muerto de miedo • **to s. away** *o* **off** ahuyentar • **to s. to death** dar un miedo espantoso **II.** s. susto.
scare·crow (′krō′) s. espantapájaros *m*.
scarf (skärf) s. [pl. **s** *o* **-ves**] bufanda; *(kerchief)* pañuelo; *(runner)* tapete *m*.
scar·let (skär′lĭt) s. & adj. escarlata ♦ **s. fever** escarlatina • **s. woman** mujer de mala vida.
scar·y (skâr′ē) adj. **-i-** asustador.
scath·ing (skā′thĭng) adj. severísimo.
sca·tol·o·gy (skă-tŏl′ə-jē) s. escatología.
scat·ter (skăt′ər) tr. dispersar; *(to strew)* esparcir —intr. dispersarse.
scat·ter·brain (:brān′) s. cabeza de chorlito.
scat·ter·brained (:brānd′) adj. ligero de cascos.
scat·ter·ing (:ĭng) s. dispersión *f*.
scav·enge (skăv′ənj) tr. encontrar entre la basura —intr. buscar en la basura.
scav·en·ger (skăv′ən-jər) s. trapero; ZOOL. animal *m* que se alimenta de carroña.
sce·nar·i·o (sĭ-nâr′ē-ō′) s. TEAT. argumento; CINEM. guión *m*; *(events)* situación *f*.
scene (sēn) s. escena; *(place)* lugar; JER. *(sphere)* mundo; *(situation)* situación *f* ♦ **behind the scenes** *(backstage)* entre bastidores; *(in private)* en privado • **to come on the s.** aparecer.
scen·er·y (sē′nə-rē) s. *(landscape)* paisaje *m*; TEAT. decorado.
sce·nic (sē′nĭk) adj. del paisaje; *(picturesque)* pintoresco; TEAT. escénico.
scent (sĕnt) **I.** s. *(smell)* olor *m*; *(trail)* pista ♦ **to pick up the s.** encontrar la pista • **to throw off the s.** despistar **II.** tr. olfatear; *(to perfume)* perfumar.

scep·ter (sĕp′tər) s. cetro.
sched·ule (skĕj′ool) **I.** s. *(timetable)* horario; *(agenda)* calendario; *(plan)* plan *m*; *(list)* inventario ♦ **to be behind s.** *(plane)* llevar retraso; *(work)* estar atrasado • **to go according to s.** desarrollarse como estaba previsto • **on s.** a la hora **II.** tr. *(train)* fijar el horario de; *(meeting)* programar ♦ **to be scheduled** estar previsto.
sche·mat·ic (skē-măt′ĭk) adj. esquemático.
scheme (skēm) **I.** s. *(plan)* proyecto; *(plot)* ardid *m*; *(arrangement)* combinación *f* **II.** tr. tramar —intr. conspirar.
schem·er (skē′mər) s. intrigante *mf*.
schism (sĭz′əm, skĭz′-) s. escisión *f*; RELIG. cisma *m*.
schiz·oid (skĭt′soid′) adj. & s. esquizofrénico.
schiz·o·phre·ni·a (skĭt′sə-frē′nē-ə) s. esquizofrenia.
schol·ar (skŏl′ər) s. erudito; *(specialist)* especialista *mf*; *(student)* estudiante *mf*.
schol·ar·ly (:lē) adj. erudito.
schol·ar·ship (:shĭp′) s. erudición *f*; *(financial aid)* beca.
scho·las·tic (skə-lăs′tĭk) adj. escolar.
school[1] (skool) **I.** s. escuela; *(for teens)* colegio; *(department)* facultad *f*; *(class)* clase *f*; *(students)* alumnado, estudiantado ♦ **driving s.** escuela para aprender a conducir • **military s.** academia militar • **night s.** escuela nocturna • **s. of thought** escuela filosófica • **secretarial s.** escuela de secretariado • **summer s.** curso(s) de verano • **Sunday s.** RELIG. escuela dominical • **to teach s.** ser maestro **II.** tr. educar; *(to train)* disciplinar.
school[2] s. *(fish)* cardumen *m*.
school·book (skool′book′) s. libro de texto.
school·boy (:boi′) s. alumno.
school·girl (:gûrl′) s. alumna.
school·house (:hous′) s. colegio, escuela.
school·ing (skoo′lĭng) s. instrucción *f*; *(training)* entrenamiento.
school·mas·ter (skool′măs′tər) s. maestro.
school·mate (:māt′) s. compañero de escuela.
school·mis·tress (:mĭs′trĭs) s. maestra.
school·room (:room′) s. sala de clase.
school·teach·er (:tē′chər) s. maestro, -a.
schoo·ner (skoo′nər) s. goleta.
sci·at·i·ca (sī-ăt′ĭ-kə) s. ciática.
sci·ence (sī′əns) s. ciencia ♦ **s. fiction** ciencia ficción.
sci·en·tif·ic (sī′ən-tĭf′ĭk) adj. científico.
sci·en·tist (′-tĭst) s. científico.
scin·til·late (sĭn′tl-āt′) intr. chispear; *(to twinkle)* centellear.
sci·on (sī′ən) s. vástago; BOT. púa.
scis·sors (sĭz′ərz) s.pl. tijeras *f* ♦ **a pair of s.** tijeras • **s. hold** DEP. tijereta.
scle·ro·sis (sklə-rō′sĭs) s. esclerosis *f*.
scoff (skŏf) intr. mofarse *(at* de).
scoff·law (′lô′) s. persona que burla la ley.
scold (skōld) **I.** intr. & tr. regañar **II.** s. regañón *m*.
scold·ing (skōl′dĭng) s. regaño ♦ **to give a s.** regañar.
scone (skōn, skŏn) s. bizcocho, galleta.
scoop (skoop) **I.** s. *(ladle)* cucharón *m*; *(amount)* cucharadas; PERIOD. noticia exclusiva; MAQ. *(of shovel)* cuchara; *(of dredge)* cangilón *m* **II.** tr. ♦ **to s. into** meter en • **to s. out** excavar • **to s. up** *(by hand)* coger; *(with spoon)* sacar.

scoot (skōōt) intr. andar rápidamente.

scoot·er (skōō'tər) s. *(child's)* monopatín *m*, patineta; *(motor vehicle)* motoneta.

scope (skōp) s. *(range)* ámbito; *(extent)* amplitud *f*; *(reach)* alcance *m*; *(freedom)* libertad *f*.

scorch (skôrch) I. tr. & intr. quemar(se) II. s. quemadura.

scorch·er (skôr'chər) s. FAM. día *m* abrasador.

score (skôr) I. s. *(notch)* muesca; *(line)* raya; *(twenty)* veintena; DEP. tanteo; EDUC. calificación *f*; MÚS. partitura ◆ **final s.** DEP. resultado ◆ **on that s.** en cuanto a eso • **to keep s.** apuntar los tantos • **to know the score** conocer el percal • **to settle a s.** ajustar cuentas II. tr. *(to mark off)* apuntar *(mediante rayas)* en; *(to scratch)* rayar; DEP. marcar; *(to count as)* valer; *(to win)* lograr; FAM. *(to get)* conseguir; EDUC. sacar; MÚS. orquestar —intr. FAM. tener éxito; DEP. marcar un tanto; *(to keep score)* tantear.

score·board (skôr'bôrd') s. marcador *m*.

scor·er (:ər) s. tanteador *m*; *(player)* jugador *m* que marca tantos; *(in soccer)* goleador *m*.

scorn (skôrn) I. s. desprecio II. tr. despreciar ◆ **to s. to** no dignarse.

scorn·ful (skôrn'fəl) adj. desdeñoso.

scor·pi·on (skôr'pē-ən) s. escorpión *m*.

scotch (skŏch) tr. poner fin a.

Scotch (skŏch) s. escocés *m*.

scot-free (skŏt'frē') adj. sin pagar o castigo.

scoun·drel (skoun'drəl) s. canalla *m*.

scour[1] (skour) tr. fregar, restregar.

scour[2] tr. *(to search)* batir; *(to range over)* recorrer —intr. *(to run)* correr.

scourge (skûrj) I. s. azote *m* II. tr. azotar.

scout[1] (skout) I. tr. explorar; *(talent)* evaluar —intr. buscar ◆ **to s. around for** hacer una batida por II. s. FAM. *(fellow)* sujeto; MIL. explorador *m* ◆ **Boy Scout** niño explorador • **s. plane** avión de reconocimiento.

scout[2] tr. rechazar con desprecio, desdeñar.

scowl (skoul) I. intr. fruncir el ceño II. s. ceño.

scrag·gly (skrăg'lē) adj. -i- *(unkempt)* desaseado; *(sparse)* ralo.

scram (skrăm) intr. **-mm-** FAM. largarse.

scram·ble (skrăm'bəl) I. intr. gatear; *(struggle)* pelearse ◆ **to s. out** salir a gatas • **to s. up** trepar —tr. revolver; ELECTRÓN. perturbar ◆ **scrambled eggs** huevos revueltos • **s. into one's clothes** vestirse rápidamente • **s. together** mezclar II. s. lucha.

scram·bler (:blər) s. aparato para perturbar las emisiones radiofónicas.

scrap[1] (skrăp) I. s. *(of paper)* pedazo; *(of evidence)* pizca; *(metal)* chatarra; *(waste)* desperdicios; *(of fabric)* retazo ◆ **pl.** *(of food)* restos; *(waste)* desechos II. tr. **-pp-** desechar; *(ships)* desguazar; *(machines)* desmontar.

scrap[2] JER. I. intr. **-pp-** pelearse II. s. pelea.

scrap·book (skrăp'bŏŏk') s. álbum *m* de recortes.

scrape (skrāp) I. tr. raspar ◆ **to s. off** o **out** quitar (raspando) • **to s. together** o **up** lograr reunir —intr. *(to graze)* rozar; *(to scrimp)* hacer economías ◆ **to s. by** ir tirando II. s. raspado; *(sound)* chirrido; *(on skin)* rasguño.

scrap·er (skrā'pər) s. rascador *m*, raspador *m*.

scrap·py (skrăp'ē) adj. -i- JER. *(crazy)* chiflado;

scratch (skrăch) I. tr. & intr. rayar(se); *(to claw)* arañar; *(to rub)* rascarse ◆ **to s. out** tachar • **to s. the surface** no profundizar mucho II. s. raya; *(on skin)* arañazo; *(sound)* chirrido ◆ **from s.** de la nada • **to come up to s.** satisfa-

cer los requisitos III. adj. al azar ◆ **s. paper** papel (de) borrador.

scratch·pad ('păd') s. bloc *m* para apuntes; COMPUT. memoria auxiliar.

scratch·y (:ē) adj. -i- *(surface)* rayado; *(fabric)* que pica; *(sound)* chirriante; *(pen)* que raspa.

scrawl (skrôl) I. tr. & intr. garabatear II. s. garabateo.

scraw·ny (skrô'nē) adj. -i- flacucho.

scream (skrēm) I. intr. chillar ◆ **it's enough to make you s.** es para pegarse un tiro • **to s. in pain** gritar de dolor II. s. chillido ◆ **to be a s.** ser divertidísimo.

scream·er (skrē'mər) s. chillón *m*.

scream·ing (:ĭng) I. s. grito(s) II. adj. chillón; *(funny)* divertidísimo.

screech (skrēch) I. intr. *(to scream)* chillar; *(to make a shrill noise)* chirriar II. s. chillido.

screen (skrēn) I. s. pantalla; *(for privacy)* biombo; *(for windows)* alambrera; *(for sifting)* criba; *(of troops)* cobertura; *(of planes)* protección *f* ◆ **s. door** puerta de tela metálica II. tr. *(to hide)* ocultar; *(to protect)* resguardar; *(to sift)* cribar; *(a porch)* poner una alambrera a; *(applicants)* pasar por el tamiz; CINEM. proyectar ◆ **to s. out** descartar.

screen·play ('plā') s. guión *m*.

screen·writ·er ('rī'tər) s. guionista *mf*.

screw (skrōō) I. s. CARP. tornillo ◆ **to have a s. loose** tener flojos los tornillos • **to put the screws to someone** apretarle las clavijas a alguien II. tr. JER. *(to cheat)* estafar ◆ **to have one's head screwed on right** FAM. tener la cabeza bien puesta • **to s. down** o **on** CARP. atornillar (en) • **to s. on** tapar • **to s. open** o **off** destapar • **to s. up** FAM. arruinar, desbaratar.

screw·ball ('bôl') adj. & s. JER. estrafalario.

screw·driv·er (:drī'vər) s. destornillador *m*.

screwed-up (skrōōd'ŭp') adj. JER. desbaratado.

screw-up (skrōō'ŭp') s. JER. metedura de pata.

screw·y (:ē) adj. -i- JER. *(crazy)* chiflado; *(amiss)* errado.

scrib·ble (skrĭb'əl) I. tr. & intr. garabatear II. s. garabato.

scribe (skrīb) s. FAM. *(writer)* escritorzuelo; HIST. *(clerk, copyist)* escribiente *m*.

scrim·mage (skrĭm'ĭj) I. s. DEP. entrenamiento II. intr. entrenarse.

scrimp (skrĭmp) intr. hacer economías ◆ **to s. and save** apretarse el cinturón.

scrip[1] (skrĭp) s. *(money)* vale *m*.

scrip[2] s. título provisional de propiedad.

script (skrĭpt) s. letra cursiva; CINEM. guión *m*.

scrip·tur·al (skrĭp'chər-əl) adj. bíblico.

scrod (skrŏd) s. bacalao inmaduro.

scroll (skrōl) s. rollo de pergamino.

scro·tum (skrō'təm) s. [pl. **s** o **-ta**] escroto.

scrounge (skrounj) tr. JER. juntar ◆ **to s. up** conseguir de gorra —intr. gorronear ◆ **to s. around for** juntar.

scrub[1] (skrŭb) I. tr. **-bb-** fregar; *(clothes)* restregar; JER. *(mission)* cancelar —intr. fregar II. s. fregado ◆ **s. brush** cepillo.

scrub[2] s. *(shrub)* árbol achaparrado; *(thicket)* matorral *m*; FAM. *(animal pequeño; *(nobody)* don *m* nadie; DEP. jugador *m* suplente.

scrub·bing (skrŭb'ĭng) s. fregado.

scrub·by (skrŭb'ē) adj. -i- cubierto de maleza; *(stunted)* achaparrado.

scrub·wom·an (skrŭb'wŏŏm'ən) s. [pl. **-women**] fregona.

scruff (skrŭf) s. cogote m.

scruf·fy (skrŭf′ē) adj. -**i**- desaliñado.

scrump·tious (skrŭmp′shəs) adj. FAM. de rechupete.

scru·ple (skrōō′pəl) s. escrúpulo; (bit) pizca.

scru·pu·lous (:pyə-ləs) adj. escrupuloso.

scru·ti·nize (skrōōt′n-īz′) tr. escudriñar.

scru·ti·ny (:ē) s. escrutinio.

scu·ba (skōō′bə) s. escafandra autónoma.

scuff (skŭf) I. intr. estropear —tr. (feet) arrastrar; (shoes, floor) estropear II. s. arrastre m de los pies; (slipper) chancleta.

scuf·fle (skŭf′əl) I. intr. pelearse; (to scuff) arrastrar los pies II. s. refriega.

scull (skŭl) I. s. (long oar) espadilla; (oar) remo; (boat) bote m de remo II. tr. impulsar con remo o espadilla —intr. remar.

scul·ler·y (skŭl′ə-rē) s. trascocina.

sculpt (skŭlpt) tr. esculpir.

sculp·tor (skŭlp′tər) s. escultor m.

sculp·tress (:trĭs) s. escultora.

sculp·tur·al (:chər-əl) adj. escultural.

sculp·ture (skŭlp′chər) I. s. escultura II. tr. esculpir.

scum (skŭm) s. (on pond) verdín m; (on liquids) telilla; (on milk) nata; (on metal) escoria; JER. (people) escoria.

scurf (skûrf) s. (dry skin) caspa; (scab) costra.

scur·ri·lous (skûr′ə-ləs) adj. grosero.

scur·ry (skûr′ē) intr. correr.

scur·vy (skûr′vē) I. s. escorbuto II. adj. -**i**- vil.

scut·tle¹ (skŭt′l) I. s. trampilla; MARÍT. escotilla II. tr. FAM. desechar; MARÍT. barrenar.

scut·tle² (for coal) balde m.

scut·tle³ intr. (to run) correr.

scythe (sīth) I. s. guadaña II. tr. guadañar.

sea (sē) I. s. mar mf ♦ **at s.** en el mar ♦ **by the s.** a (la) orilla del mar ♦ **heavy s.** marejada ♦ **on the high seas** en alta mar ♦ **s. gull** gaviota ♦ **s. urchin** erizo de mar ♦ **s. wall** rompeolas II. adj. marino; (saltwater) de mar.

sea·bed (sē′bĕd′) s. fondo del mar.

sea·board (sē′bôrd′) s. litoral m.

sea·coast (sē′kōst′) s. litoral m.

sea·dog (sē′dôg′) s. FAM. lobo de mar.

sea·far·er (sē′fâr′ər) s. marinero.

sea·far·ing (:ĭng) I. s. marinería II. adj. marinero.

sea·food (sē′fōōd′) s. mariscos; (fish) pescado.

sea·go·ing (sē′gō′ĭng) adj. de mar; (people) marinero.

seal¹ (sēl) I. s. sello; (pledge) garantía; (sticker) precinto; (closure) cierre m II. tr. sellar; (with wax) lacrar; (envelope) cerrar; (fate) determinar ♦ **sealing wax** lacre ♦ **to s. in** encerrar ♦ **to s. off** acordonar; (pipe) cerrar ♦ **to s. up** (hole) tapar; (envelope) cerrar.

seal² I. s. ZOOL. foca; (pelt) piel f de foca II. intr. cazar focas.

seal·ant (sē′lənt) s. sellador m.

seal·er¹ (sē′lər) s. pintura o barniz utilizado para sellar una superficie.

seal·er² s. cazador m de focas.

seal·skin (sēl′skĭn′) s. piel f de foca.

seam (sēm) I. s. costura; (crease) arruga; MIN. veta ♦ **to be bursting at the seams** (with feelings) rebosar (with de); (with people) rebosar de gente II. tr. unir; (to line) marcar.

sea·man (sē′mən) s. [pl. -men] marinero.

sea·man·ship (:shĭp′) s. pericia náutica.

seam·stress (sēm′strĭs) s. costurera.

seam·y (sē′mē) adj. -**i**- sórdido.

sé·ance (sā′äns′) s. sesión f de espiritismo.

sea·plane (sē′plān′) s. hidroavión m.

sea·port (sē′pôrt′) s. puerto marítimo.

sear (sîr) tr. & intr. marchitar(se).

search (sûrch) I. tr. & intr. registrar; (conscience) examinar ♦ **s. me!** FAM. ¡yo qué sé! ♦ **to s. for** buscar ♦ **to s. out** descubrir II. s. búsqueda; (by police) registro; (of person) cacheo; (of ship) visita ♦ **in s. of** en busca de ♦ **s. party** partida de buscadores ♦ **s. warrant** mandamiento de registro.

search·er (sûr′chər) s. buscador m.

search·light (sûrch′līt′) s. reflector m.

sea·scape (sē′skāp′) s. (vista) marina.

sea·shell (sē′shĕl′) s. concha marina.

sea·shore (sē′shôr′) s. (beach) orilla del mar; (coast) litoral m.

sea·sick (sē′sĭk′) adj. mareado ♦ **to get s.** marearse.

sea·sick·ness (:nĭs) s. mareo.

sea·side (sē′sīd′) s. (beach) playa; (coast) litoral m ♦ **s. resort** estación balnearia.

sea·son (sē′zən) I. s. (of year) estación f; (time) temporada; (of animals) época ♦ **in s.** (produce) en sazón; (animals) en celo ♦ **off s.** temporada baja ♦ **s. ticket** abono II. tr. (food) sazonar; (to enliven) amenizar; (wood) secar; (to accustom) habituar —intr. (wood) secarse.

sea·son·a·ble (sē′zə-nə-bəl) adj. propio de la estación; (timely) a su tiempo.

sea·son·al (sē′zə-nəl) adj. estacional; (unemployment) temporal; (worker) temporero.

sea·son·ing (:nĭng) s. aderezo.

seat (sēt) I. s. asiento; (for an event) localidad f; (of trousers) fondillos; (of bicycle) sillín m; (of government) sede f; (of learning) centro; POL. escaño; (buttocks) trasero ♦ **by the s. of one's pants** FAM. por los pelos ♦ **s. belt** cinturón de seguridad II. tr. sentar; (to accommodate) tener sitio para ♦ **be seated** siéntense.

seat·ing (sē′tĭng) s. (places) asientos; (placement) colocación f.

sea·ward (sē′wərd) I. adj. que da al mar II. adv. hacia el mar.

sea·way (sē′wā′) s. ruta marítima.

sea·weed (sē′wēd′) s. alga.

sea·wor·thy (sē′wûr′thē) adj. -**i**- en condiciones de navegar.

se·cede (sĭ-sēd′) intr. separarse.

se·ces·sion (sĭ-sĕsh′ən) s. secesión f.

se·clude (sĭ-klōōd′) tr. recluir ♦ **to s. oneself** apartarse.

se·clud·ed (sĭ-klōō′dĭd) adj. aislado.

se·clu·sion (:zhən) s. reclusión f ♦ **in s.** apartado.

sec·ond¹ (sĕk′ənd) s. (time unit) segundo; FAM. momento ♦ **s. hand** segundero.

sec·ond² I. adj. segundo; (another) otro ♦ **every s.** (uno de) cada dos ♦ **on s. thought** pensándolo bien ♦ **s. floor** primer piso (en países hispánicos) ♦ **s. nature** costumbre arraigada ♦ **s. sight** clarividencia ♦ **s. thoughts** dudas ♦ **to be s. to none** no tener igual ♦ **to get one's s. wind** recobrar las fuerzas II. s. segundo; (in duel) padrino; MEC. segunda ♦ pl. (food) una porción más; COM. artículos con pequeños desperfectos III. tr. (to attend) secundar; (motion) apoyar IV. adv. en segundo lugar.

sec·ond·ar·y (sĕk′ən-dĕr′ē) adj. secundario ♦ **s. education** enseñanza media.

sec·ond-best (sĕk′ənd-bĕst′) adj. segundo.

sec·ond-class (:kläs') I. adj. de segunda clase II. adv. en segunda (clase).

sec·ond-gen·er·a·tion ('-jěn'ə-rā'shən) adj. de segunda generación.

sec·ond-guess (:gěs') tr. *(to criticize)* criticar; *(to anticipate)* anticiparse a.

sec·ond·hand (:hănd') adj. & adv. de segunda mano.

sec·ond-rate (:rāt') adj. de segunda categoría.

se·cre·cy (sē'krĭ-sē) s. secreto.

se·cret (sē'krĭt) I. adj. secreto; *(secluded)* oculto II. s. secreto ♦ **as a s.** confidencialmente • **to keep a s.** guardar un secreto.

sec·re·tar·i·al (sěk'rĭ-târ'ē-əl) adj. de secretario.

sec·re·tar·i·at (:ĭt) s. secretariado.

sec·re·tar·y (sěk'rĭ-těr'ē) s. secretario; *(desk)* secreter m; *(minister)* ministro.

sec·re·tar·y-gen·er·al ('-'-jěn'ər-əl) s. [pl. -taries-] secretario general.

se·crete¹ (sĭ-krēt') tr. FISIOL. secretar.

se·crete² tr. *(to hide)* esconder.

se·cre·tion (sĭ-krē'shən) s. secreción f.

se·cre·tive (sē'krĭ-tĭv) adj. sigiloso.

sect (sěkt) s. secta.

sec·tar·i·an (sěk-târ'ē-ən) s. & adj. sectario.

sec·tion (sěk'shən) I. s. sección f, parte f; *(of orange)* gajo; *(of track)* tramo; *(of town)* barrio; DER. aparte m II. tr. dividir en secciones.

sec·tion·al (:shə-nəl) adj. *(local)* regional; *(furniture)* desmontable.

sec·tor (sěk'tər) s. sector m.

sec·u·lar (sěk'yə-lər) adj. mundano; *(music)* profano; *(school)* laico; *(clergy)* secular.

sec·u·lar·ism (:lə-rĭz'əm) s. laicismo.

sec·u·lar·ize (:rīz') tr. secularizar.

se·cure (sĭ-kyŏŏr') I. adj. -er, -est seguro; *(stable)* asegurado ♦ **s. from** protegido contra II. tr. asegurar; *(to obtain)* conseguir; *(boat)* amarrar ♦ **to s. from** proteger contra.

se·cu·ri·ty (:ĭ-tē) s. seguridad f, *(of loan)* garantía ♦ **s. guard** guardia ♦ pl. FIN. valores.

se·dan (sĭ-dăn') s. *(automobile)* sedán m; *(chair)* silla de manos.

se·date¹ (sĭ-dāt') adj. sosegado.

se·date² tr. MED. administrar calmantes.

se·da·tion (sĭ-dā'shən) s. sedación f.

sed·a·tive (sěd'ə-tĭv) s. & adj. sedante m.

sed·en·tar·y (sěd'n-těr'ē) adj. sedentario.

sedge (sěj) s. juncia.

sed·i·ment (sěd'ə-mənt) s. sedimento.

sed·i·men·ta·ry ('-měn'tə-rē) adj. sedimentario.

sed·i·men·ta·tion (:mən-tā'shən) s. sedimentación f.

se·di·tion (sĭ-dĭsh'ən) s. sedición f.

se·di·tious (:əs) adj. sedicioso.

se·duce (sĭ-dōōs') tr. seducir.

se·duc·er (sĭ-dōō'sər) s. seductor m.

se·duc·tion (sĭ-dŭk'shən) s. seducción f.

se·duc·tive (:tĭv) adj. seductivo, seductor.

se·duc·tress (:trĭs) s. seductora.

sed·u·lous (sěj'ə-ləs) adj. asiduo.

see¹ (sē) tr. **saw, seen** ver; *(to understand)* entender; *(to ensure)* asegurarse de; *(to visit with)* encontrarse con; *(to date)* salir con; *(to socialize with)* verse; *(to consult)* consultar; *(to attend)* recibir; *(to escort)* acompañar; *(to experience)* conocer ♦ **as I s.** it por lo que veo • **I saw it in his eyes** se lo vi en la cara • **it is worth seeing** merece la pena verse • **seeing is**

believing ver para creer • **s. you later!** ¡hasta luego! • **s. you (on) Saturday!** ¡hasta el sábado! • **that remains to be seen** eso está por verse • **there's nothing to s.** no hay nada que merezca la pena verse • **to go (and) s.** ir a ver • **to s. off** ir a despedirse de • **to s. red** echar chispas • **to s. the light** comprender • **to s. through** *(person)* ayudar a pasar por; *(task)* llevar a cabo • **to s. things** ver visiones • **to s.** to atender a —intr. ver; *(to understand)* comprender ♦ **as far as the eye can s.** hasta donde alcanza la vista • **let's s.** a ver, veamos • **s.?** ¿ves? • **s. for yourself!** ¡vea usted mismo! • **s. here!** ¡mire! • **s. if I care!** ¡a mí no me importa! • **seeing that...** ya que... • **to s. fit** creer conveniente • **to wait and s.** ver • **you s...** es que... • **you'll s.!** ¡ya verás! • **we'll s. about that!** ¡ya (lo) veremos!

see² s. RELIG. sede f ♦ **Holy S.** Santa Sede.

seed (sēd) I. s. [pl. inv. o s] semilla; *(source)* germen m; *(pip)* pepita; *(progeny)* descendencia; *(sperm)* semen m ♦ **to go to s.** BOT. ir a granar; FIG. echarse a perder II. tr. sembrar; *(fruit)* despepitar.

seed·bed ('běd') s. semillero.

seed·ling (:lĭng) s. plantón m.

seed·y (sē'dē) adj. -i- *(clothing)* raído; *(place)* sórdido; BOT. granado.

see·ing (sē'ĭng) conj. ♦ **s. that** visto que.

seek (sēk) tr. **sought** buscar; *(fame)* anhelar; *(advice)* solicitar ♦ **to be (highly) sought after** *(person)* ser (muy) solicitado; *(things)* ser (muy) cotizado • **to s. out** ir en busca de • **to s.** to tratar de —intr. buscar.

seek·er (sē'kər) s. buscador m.

seem (sēm) intr. parecer ♦ **incredible as it may s.** aunque parezca increíble • **it hardly seems possible that** parece mentira que • **what seems to be the trouble?** ¿pasa algo?

seem·ing (sē'mĭng) adj. aparente.

seem·ly (sēm'lē) adj. -i- apropiado.

seen (sēn) cf. **see¹**.

seep (sēp) intr. rezumarse.

seep·age (sē'pĭj) s. filtración f.

seer (sîr, sē'ər) s. vidente mf.

seer·suck·er (sîr'sŭk'ər) s. tejido rayado en relieve.

see·saw (sē'sô') I. s. subibaja m; *(movement)* vaivén m II. intr. columpiarse; *(to oscillate)* oscilar.

seethe (sēth) intr. hervir; *(person)* estar agitado ♦ **seething with anger** ardiendo de cólera.

see-through (sē'thrōō') adj. transparente.

seg·ment (sěg'mənt) I. s. segmento II. tr. & intr. (-měnt') segmentar(se).

seg·men·ta·tion ('mən-tā'shən) s. segmentación f.

seg·ment·ed (sěg'měn'tĭd) adj. dividido en segmentos.

seg·re·gate (sěg'rĭ-gāt') tr. & intr. segregar(se).

seg·re·ga·tion ('-gā'shən) s. segregación f.

seine (sān) s., tr. & intr. *(to fish)* pescar con jábega.

seis·mic (sīz'mĭk) adj. sísmico.

seis·mo·graph (:mə-grăf') s. sismógrafo.

seis·mol·o·gy (:mŏl'ə-jē) s. sismología.

seize (sēz) tr. agarrar; *(to possess)* apoderarse de; *(to arrest)* detener; *(to confiscate)* incautarse de; *(opportunity)* aprovechar ♦ **to be seized by, with** *(fear)* estar sobrecogido por; *(desire)* entrarle a uno • **to s. upon** aprovecharse de —intr. ♦ **to s. (up)** MEC. agarrotarse.

sei·zure (sē'zhər) s. detención f; *(of goods)* embargo; *(of power)* toma; MED. ataque m.
sel·dom (sĕl'dəm) adv. rara vez.
se·lect (sĭ-lĕkt') I. tr. & intr. escoger; DEP. seleccionar II. adj. selecto; *(club)* exclusivo; *(merchandise)* de primera calidad.
se·lec·tion (sĭ-lĕk'shən) s. selección f; *(collection)* surtido.
se·lec·tive (:tĭv) adj. selectivo.
se·lec·tiv·i·ty (-'ĭ-tē) s. selectividad f.
se·lect·man (sĭ-lĕkt'măn') s. [pl. **-men**] concejal m.
self (sĕlf) s. [pl. **-ves**] uno mismo; *(ego)* ego ♦ **to be back to one's old s.** volver a ser el mismo de siempre.
self-ad·dressed ('ə-drĕst') adj. con la dirección del remitente
self-ag·gran·dize·ment (:ə-grăn'dĭz-mənt) s. exaltación f de sí mismo.
self-ap·point·ed (:ə-poin'tĭd) adj. nombrado por sí mismo.
self-as·ser·tive (:ə-sûr'tĭv) adj. agresivo.
self-as·sured (:ə-shŏŏrd') adj. seguro de sí mismo.
self-cen·tered (:sĕn'tərd) adj. egocéntrico.
self-com·posed ('kəm-pōzd') adj. dueño de sí mismo.
self-con·fessed (:kən-fĕst') adj. reconocido por uno mismo.
self-con·fi·dence ('kŏn'fĭ-dəns) s. confianza en sí mismo.
self-con·scious (:kŏn'shəs) adj. cohibido.
self-con·tained ('kən-tānd') adj. *(self-sufficient)* autónomo; *(reserved)* reservado.
self-con·trol (:kən-trōl') s. dominio de sí mismo ♦ **to lose one's s.** perder la calma.
self-de·feat·ing (:dĭ-fē'tĭng) adj. contraproducente.
self-de·fense (:dĭ-fĕns') s. autodefensa; DER. legítima defensa ♦ **in s.** en defensa propia.
self-de·ni·al (:dĭ-nī'əl) s. abnegación f.
self-de·struct (:dĭ-strŭkt') intr. autodestruirse.
self-de·struc·tion (:dĭ-strŭk'shən) s. autodestrucción f.
self-de·ter·mi·na·tion (:dĭ-tûr'mə-nā'shən) s. autodeterminación f.
self-dis·ci·pline ('dĭs'ə-plĭn) s. autodisciplina.
self-doubt (:dout') s. desconfianza en sí mismo.
self-ed·u·cat·ed (:ĕj'ə-kā'tĭd) adj. autodidacta.
self-ef·fac·ing ('ĭ-fā'sĭng) adj. humilde.
self-em·ployed (:ĕm-ploid') adj. que trabaja por cuenta propia.
self-es·teem (:ĭ-stēm') s. amor propio.
self-ev·i·dent ('ĕv'ĭ-dənt) adj. evidente.
self-ex·plan·a·to·ry ('ĭk-splăn'ə-tôr'ē) adj. obvio.
self-ex·pres·sion (:ĭk-sprĕsh'ən) s. expresión f de la propia personalidad.
self-ful·fill·ing (:fŏŏl-fĭl'ĭng) adj. que llega a cumplirse.
self-gov·ern·ment ('gŭv'ərn-mənt) s. autonomía.
self-grat·i·fi·ca·tion ('grăt'ə-fĭ-kā'shən) s. satisfacción f de los deseos propios.
self-help ('hĕlp') s. esfuerzo propio.
self-im·age (:ĭm'ĭj) s. representación f de sí mismo.
self-im·por·tance ('ĭm-pôr'tns) s. presunción f.
self-im·posed (:ĭm-pōzd') adj. que uno se impone a sí mismo.

self-im·prove·ment (:ĭm-prŏŏv'mənt) s. superación propia.
self-in·crim·i·na·tion (:ĭn-krĭm'ə-nā'shən) s. autoincriminación f.
self-in·duced (:ĭn-dŏŏst') adj. que uno se hace a sí mismo.
self-in·dul·gence (:ĭn-dŭl'jəns) s. desenfreno.
self-in·flict·ed (:ĭn-flĭk'tĭd) adj. que uno se inflige a sí mismo.
self-in·ter·est ('ĭn'trĭst) s. interés propio; *(selfishness)* egoísmo.
self-in·volved ('ĭn-vŏlvd') adj. que piensa en su propio interés.
self·ish (sĕl'fĭsh) adj. egoísta.
self·ish·ness (:nĭs) s. egoísmo.
self·less (sĕlf'lĭs) adj. desinteresado.
self-love (:lŭv') s. egoísmo; PSIC. narcisismo.
self-made (:măd') adj. logrado por propio esfuerzo.
self-pit·y (:pĭt'ē) s. compasión f de sí mismo.
self-por·trait (:pôr'trĭt) s. autorretrato.
self-pres·er·va·tion (:prĕz'ər-vā'shən) s. instinto de la propia conservación.
self-pro·claimed (:prō-klāmd') adj. supuesto.
self-re·gard (:rĭ-gärd') s. amor propio; *(self-respect)* dignidad f.
self-re·li·ance (:rĭ-lī'əns) s. confianza en sí mismo.
self-re·spect (:rĭ-spĕkt') s. dignidad f.
self-re·straint (:rĭ-strānt') s. control m, dominio de sí mismo.
self-righ·teous ('rī'chəs) adj. santurrón.
self-ris·ing (:rī'zĭng) adj. que no necesita levadura.
self-rule (:rŏŏl') s. autonomía.
self-sac·ri·fice (:săk'rə-fīs') s. sacrificio de sí mismo.
self·same (:sām') adj. mismísimo.
self-seek·ing (:sē'kĭng) I. adj. egoísta II. s. egoísmo.
self-serv·ice (:sûr'vĭs) adj. de autoservicio.
self-serv·ing (:sûr'vĭng) adj. egoísta.
self-suf·fi·cient (:sə-fĭsh'ənt) adj. autosuficiente.
self-sup·port (:sə-pôrt') s. independencia económica.
self-sus·tain·ing (:sə-stā'nĭng) adj. que se mantiene por sus propios medios.
self-taught (:tôt') adj. autodidacta.
sell (sĕl) I. tr. **sold** vender ♦ **to be sold on** estar convencido de • **to s. off** COM. liquidar • **to s. short** subestimar —intr. venderse ♦ **to be sold out** estar agotado • **to s. like hot cakes** venderse como pan caliente • **to s. out** liquidar todo; *(cause)* venderse II. s. ♦ **hard, soft s.** publicidad agresiva, discreta.
sell·er ('ər) s. vendedor m; *(dealer)* comerciante mf ♦ **quick s.** artículo que se vende fácilmente • **s.'s market** mercado favorable al vendedor.
sell·out (:out') s. COM. liquidación f total; TEAT. lleno; FAM. *(traitor)* traidor m.
selt·zer (sĕlt'sər) s. agua de seltz.
sel·vage/vedge (sĕl'vĭj) orillo.
se·man·tic (sĭ-măn'tĭk) adj. semántico ♦ **semantics** s.sg. semántica.
sem·a·phore ('sĕm'ə-fôr') I. s. semáforo II. tr. transmitir por semáforo.
sem·blance (sĕm'bləns) s. apariencia; *(copy)* copia.
se·men (sē'mən) s. semen m.
se·mes·ter (sə-mĕs'tər) s. semestre m.

sem·i·an·nu·al (sĕm'ē-ăn'yŏo-əl) adj. semestral.

sem·i·au·to·mat·ic (:ô'tə-măt'ĭk) adj. semiautomático.

sem·i·cir·cle (sĕm'ĭ-sûr'kəl) s. semicírculo.

sem·i·cir·cu·lar ('-'kyə-lər) adj. semicircular.

sem·i·co·lon (sĕm'ĭ-kō'lən) s. punto y coma.

sem·i·con·duc·tor ('ē-kən-dŭk'tər) s. semiconductor m.

sem·i·fi·nal DEP. I. s. (sĕm'ē-fī'nəl) semifinal f II. adj. ('-'nəl) semifinalista.

sem·i·month·ly (sĕm'ē-mŭnth'lē) I. adj. bimensual II. adv. dos veces al mes III. s. publicación f bimensual.

sem·i·nal (sĕm'ə-nəl) adj. seminal; (creative) creativo.

sem·i·nar (sĕm'ə-när') s. seminario; (conference) reunión f.

sem·i·nar·y (:nĕr'ē) s. seminario.

sem·i·pre·cious (sĕm'ē-prĕsh'əs) adj. semiprecioso ♦ s. stone piedra fina.

sem·i·pri·vate (:prī'vĭt) adj. para dos o tres personas.

sem·i·skilled (:skĭld') adj. poco entrenado.

sem·i·week·ly (:wēk'lē) I. s. & adj. (publicación f) bisemanal II. adv. dos veces por semana.

sem·i·year·ly (:yîr'lē) I. s. & adj. (publicación f) semestral II. adv. dos veces al año.

sen·ate (sĕn'ĭt) s. senado.

sen·a·tor (sĕn'ə-tər) s. senador m.

sen·a·to·ri·al ('-tôr'ē-əl) adj. senatorial.

send (sĕnd) tr. **sent** mandar; (letter) enviar; (to propel) hacer <the blow sent him staggering el golpe lo hizo tambalear>; RAD. transmitir ♦ **to s. away** echar ♦ **to s. away for** ordenar por correo • **to s. back** (person) hacer regresar; (object) devolver • **to s. chills down one's spine** darle a uno escalofríos • **to s. down** hacer bajar • **to s. in** (an entry) mandar; (a person) hacer pasar • **to s. into** lanzar • **to s. off** (letter) echar al buzón; (person) ir a despedir • **to s. on** reexpedir • **to s. out** (invitations) enviar; (leaves) echar; (heat) emitir • **to s. (out) for** enviar a alguien a buscar • **to s. up** (to jail) meter en la cárcel; (prices) hacer subir; (spacecraft) lanzar —intr. enviar.

send·er (sĕn'dər) s. remitente mf.

send-off (sĕnd'ôf') s. despedida afectuosa.

send-up (sĕnd'ŭp') s. FAM. imitación graciosa.

se·nes·cent (sĭ-nĕs'ənt) adj. senescente.

se·nile (sē'nīl', sĕn'īl') adj. senil.

se·nil·i·ty (sĭ-nĭl'ĭ-tē) s. senectud f.

sen·ior (sēn'yər) I. adj. (father) padre; (partner) principal; (senator) más antiguo; (officer) superior; (in school) del último año ♦ s. citizen anciano II. s. anciano; (student) estudiante mf del último año ♦ to be someone's s. ser mayor que alguien • to be five years someone's s. llevarle cinco años a alguien.

sen·ior·i·ty (sēn-yôr'ĭ-tē) s. antigüedad f; (priority) precedencia.

sen·sa·tion (sĕn-sā'shən) s. sensación f.

sen·sa·tion·al (:shə-nəl) adj. sensacional.

sen·sa·tion·al·ism (:nə-lĭz'əm) s. sensacionalismo.

sen·sa·tion·al·ize (:līz') tr. exagerar.

sense (sĕns) I. s. sentido; (feeling) sensación f; (consciousness) sentimiento; (judgment) sentido común ♦ good s. sentido común • in a s. en cierto sentido • to come to one's senses recobrar el juicio • to have the s. to tener la

cordura de • to make s. tener sentido • to make s. of comprender el sentido de • to talk s. hablar con sentido común II. tr. (to perceive) darse cuenta de; (to detect) detectar.

sense·less ('lĭs) adj. sin sentido; (foolish) insensato; (unconscious) inconsciente.

sen·si·bil·i·ty (sĕn'sə-bĭl'ĭ-tē) s. sensibilidad f.

sen·si·ble (sĕn'sə-bəl) adj. sensato; (perceptible) sensible ♦ to be s. of darse cuenta de.

sen·si·tive (:sĭ-tĭv) adj. sensible; (delicate) delicado ♦ to be s. to o about ser susceptible a.

sen·si·tiv·i·ty ('-tĭv'ĭ-tē) s. sensibilidad f; (susceptibility) susceptibilidad f.

sen·si·tize ('-tīz') tr. & intr. sensibilizar(se).

sen·sor (sĕn'sər, :sôr') s. sensor m.

sen·so·ry (:sə-rē) adj. sensorio.

sen·su·al (:shŏo-əl) adj. sensual.

sen·su·al·i·ty ('-ăl'ĭ-tē) s. sensualidad f.

sen·su·ous ('-əs) adj. sensual.

sent (sĕnt) cf. **send**.

sen·tence (sĕn'təns) I. s. GRAM. oración f, frase f; DER. sentencia ♦ death s. pena de muerte • life s. condena perpetua • to be under s. of death estar condenado a muerte • to pass s. on sentenciar • to serve out one's s. cumplir la sentencia II. tr. sentenciar.

sen·ten·tious (sĕn-tĕn'shəs) adj. sentencioso.

sen·tient (sĕn'shənt) adj. consciente.

sen·ti·ment (sĕn'tə-mənt) s. sentimiento; (sentimentality) sentimentalismo; (view) opinión f.

sen·ti·men·tal ('-mĕn'tl) adj. sentimental.

sen·ti·men·tal·i·ty ('--tăl'ĭ-tē) s. sentimentalismo.

sen·ti·men·tal·ize ('-'tl-īz') tr. hablar con sentimentalismo de —intr. ponerse sentimental.

sen·ti·nel (sĕn'tə-nəl) s. centinela m.

sen·try (sĕn'trē) s. centinela m ♦ to stand s. estar de guardia.

sep·a·rate I. tr. & intr. (sĕp'ə-rāt') separar(se) ♦ to s. from separar(se) de; (to distinguish) distinguir(se) entre • to s. into dividir(se) en II. adj. (:ər-ĭt) (detached) separado; (loose) suelto; (different) distinto; (another) otro III. s. (:ər-ĭt) ♦ pl. prendas de vestir que se compran por separado.

sep·a·ra·tion ('-rā'shən) s. separación f.

sep·a·ra·tist (sĕp'ər-ə-tĭst) s. separatista mf.

Sep·tem·ber (sĕp-tĕm'bər) s. septiembre m.

sep·tic (sĕp'tĭk) adj. séptico ♦ s. tank fosa séptica, pozo séptico.

sep·ul·cher (sĕp'əl-kər) s. sepulcro.

se·pul·chral (sə-pŭl'krəl) adj. sepulcral.

se·quel (sē'kwəl) s. continuación f; (consequence) consecuencia, resultado.

se·quence (sē'kwəns) s. sucesión f; (arrangement) orden m; (series) serie f.

se·quent (sē'kwənt) adj. subsiguiente; (consequent) consecuente.

se·quen·tial (sĭ-kwĕn'shəl) adj. consecutivo.

se·ques·ter (sĭ-kwĕs'tər) tr. secuestrar; (jury) aislar ♦ to s. oneself retirarse.

se·quin (sē'kwĭn) s. lentejuela.

sere (sîr) adj. marchito.

ser·e·nade (sĕr'ə-nād') I. s. serenata II. tr. dar una serenata a.

ser·en·dip·i·ty (sĕr'ən-dĭp'ĭ-tē) s. hallazgo afortunado.

se·rene (sə-rēn') adj. sereno ♦ His S. Highness Su Alteza Serenísima.

se·ren·i·ty (sə-rĕn'ĭ-tē) s. serenidad f.

serf (sûrf) s. siervo.

serge (sûrj) s. sarga.

ser·geant (sär'jənt) s. sargento ♦ **s. at arms** ujier.

se·ri·al (sîr'ē-əl) I. adj. *(program)* seriado; *(novel, story)* por capítulos; *(order)* consecutivo ♦ **s. number** número de serie II. s. serial *m.*

se·ri·al·ize (:ə-līz') tr. publicar por capítulos.

se·ries (sîr'ēz) s.inv. serie *f.*

se·ri·ous (sîr'ē-əs) adj. serio; *(illness)* grave ♦ **are you s.?** ¿en serio? ♦ **to be s. about** tomar en serio.

se·ri·ous-mind·ed ('--mīn'dĭd) adj. serio.

se·ri·ous·ness ('--nĭs) s. seriedad *f.*

ser·mon (sûr'mən) s. sermón *m.*

ser·mon·ize (:mə-nīz') tr. & intr. sermonear.

ser·pent (sûr'pənt) s. serpiente *f.*

ser·pen·tine (:pən-tēn', :tīn') adj. serpentino.

ser·rate/rat·ed (sĕr'āt'/ā'tĭd) adj. serrado.

se·rum (sîr'əm) s. [pl. **s** *o* **-ra**] suero.

ser·vant (sûr'vənt) s. sirviente *m;* *(public)* funcionario.

serve (sûrv) I. tr. servir; *(in a store)* atender; *(Mass)* ayudar a; *(to aid)* ser útil a ♦ **if (my) memory serves me** si la memoria no me falla ♦ **it serves you right!** ¡lo tienes bien merecido! ♦ **to s. as** *o* **for** servir de ♦ **to s. no purpose** no servir para nada ♦ **to s. on** ser miembro de —intr. servir; *(to carry out duties)* desempeñar los deberes; *(to satisfy)* ser suficiente II. s. DEP. saque *m.*

serv·ice (sûr'vĭs) I. s. servicio; *(benefit)* utilidad *f;* *(to customers)* atención *f;* *(set)* juego; DEP. saque *m* ♦ **at your s.** a sus órdenes ♦ **diplomatic** ♦ **in s.** funcionando ♦ **s. charge** recargo por servicios ♦ **to be of s. (to)** servir (a) ♦ **to be out of s.** no funcionar ♦ **to take into one's** ♦ emplear II. adj. de servicio; *(military)* militar III. tr. *(to maintain)* mantener; *(to repair)* reparar.

serv·ice·a·ble (:vĭ-sə-bəl) adj. servible.

serv·ice·man (:vĭs-măn') s. [pl. **-men**] militar *m;* *(repairman)* mecánico.

ser·vile (:vəl, :vīl') adj. servil.

ser·vil·i·ty (sər-vĭl'ĭ-tē) s. servilismo.

serv·ing (sûr'vĭng) s. CUL. porción *f.*

ser·vi·tude (:vĭ-tōod') s. servidumbre *f.*

ses·a·me (sĕs'ə-mē) s. sésamo, ajonjolí *m.*

ses·sion (sĕsh'ən) s. sesión *f;* *(of legislature)* reunión *f* ♦ **summer s.** EDUC. curso(s) de verano ♦ **to be in s.** estar en reunión.

set¹ (sĕt) I. tr. **set, -tting** poner; *(to locate)* situar; *(bone)* encajar; *(watch)* poner en hora; *(type)* componer; *(stage)* montar; *(precedent)* sentar; *(date, price)* fijar; *(record)* establecer; *(example)* dar; *(pearl)* montar ♦ **to be s. back from** estar a cierta distancia de ♦ **to be s. in** TEAT. desarrollarse en ♦ **to s. about** ponerse a ♦ **to s. above** anteponer ♦ **to s. against** *(to pit)* enfrentar con; *(to compare)* contraponer a ♦ **to s. apart** separar ♦ **to s. aside** hacer a un lado; *(for future use)* guardar; *(one's feelings)* dejar de lado; *(decision)* anular ♦ **to s. at liberty** poner en libertad ♦ **to s. back** atrasar; FAM. costar ♦ **to s. down** poner en el suelo; *(to record)* poner por escrito; *(to attribute)* achacar; *(to establish)* fijar ♦ **to s. forth** exponer ♦ **to s. free** liberar ♦ **to s. off** *(reaction)* iniciar; *(bomb)* hacer estallar; *(alarm)* hacer sonar; *(to distinguish)* hacer sobresalir; *(to accentuate)* hacer resaltar ♦ **to s. oneself up** se dárselas de ♦ **to s. one's house in order** arreglar los asuntos de uno ♦ **to s. out** *(to lay out)* disponer; *(to*

display) desplegar ♦ **to s. out to** proponerse ♦ **to s. (work)** ponerse a (trabajar) ♦ **to s. (to) thinking** dar que pensar a ♦ **to s. up** *(to raise, set upright)* levantar; *(machine)* montar; *(in power)* instaurar; *(to trick)* engañar ♦ **to s. up in** ayudar a establecerse en (un negocio) ♦ **to s. upon** acometer —intr. *(sun)* ponerse; *(hen)* empollar; *(cement)* endurecerse; *(bone)* encajarse; *(gelatin)* cuajar; *(dye)* fijarse; FAM. *(to sit)* sentarse ♦ **to s. down** AVIA. aterrizar ♦ **to s. forth** *o* **off** *o* **out** salir, encaminarse ♦ **to s. in** *(winter, night)* cerrar; *(rains)* llegar; *(discontent)* arraigar ♦ **to s. up** establecerse II. adj. *(agreed upon)* señalado; *(price)* fijo; *(procedure)* reglamentario; *(customs)* arraigado; *(opinion)* firme; *(face)* inmóvil; *(determined)* resuelto; *(ready)* listo ♦ **all s.** listo ♦ **dead s. against** resueltamente en contra de ♦ **get ready, get s., go** preparados, listos, ya ♦ **to be s. in one's ways** tener costumbres muy arraigadas ♦ **to be s. on** *(doing something)* estar empeñado en; *(idea)* estar aferrado a ♦ **to get s.** prepararse III. s. *(of shoulders)* postura, porte *m;* *(hardening)* endurecimiento.

set² s. *(of items)* juego; *(of rules)* serie *f;* *(clothes)* muda; *(people)* grupo; *(works)* colección *f;* TEAT. decorado; RAD. aparato; MAT. conjunto; DEP. set *m* ♦ **generating s.** grupo electrógeno ♦ **s. of dishes** vajilla ♦ **s. of teeth** dentadura ♦ **television s.** televisor ♦ **the smart s.** la gente elegante.

set·back (sĕt'băk') s. revés *m.*

set·tee (sĕ-tē') s. sofá *m.*

set·ter (sĕt'ər) s. perro de muestra.

set·ting (sĕt'ĭng) s. *(place)* marco; *(of action)* escenario; *(scenery)* decorado; *(of gem)* engastadura.

set·tle (sĕt'l) tr. *(affairs)* arreglar; *(claim)* satisfacer; *(debt)* saldar; *(problem)* resolver; *(person)* instalar; *(territory)* colonizar; *(in business)* establecer; *(nerves)* calmar; *(stomach)* asentar; DER. asignar ♦ **that settles it!** ¡no hay más que hablar! ♦ **to s. accounts** ajustar cuentas ♦ **to s. for** contentarse con ♦ **to s. (up)on** decidirse por —intr. *(bird, gaze)* posarse; *(dust)* asentarse; *(in a city)* establecerse; *(disease)* localizarse; *(in dispute)* arreglarse ♦ **to s. down** establecerse; *(a child)* calmarse; *(conditions)* normalizarse; *(in marriage)* casarse ♦ **to s. down to** ponerse a ♦ **to s. in** instalarse; *(at a job)* acostumbrarse ♦ **to s. up** ajustar cuentas.

set·tled (:ld) adj. *(established)* arraigado; *(stabilized)* estable; *(paid)* pagado.

set·tle·ment (:l-mənt) s. *(of dispute)* arreglo; *(of problem)* solución *f;* *(agreement)* acuerdo; *(colony)* poblado.

set·tler (:lər) s. poblador *m.*

set·to (:tōo') s. disputa; *(fight)* refriega.

set·up (:ŭp') s. *(organization)* organización *f;* *(plan)* plan *m;* JER. combate amañado.

sev·en (sĕv'ən) s. & adj. siete ♦ **s. hundred** setecientos ♦ **s. o'clock** las siete.

sev·en·teen ('tēn') s. & adj. diecisiete *m.*

sev·en·teenth (:tēnth') I. s. *(place)* diecisiete *m;* *(part)* diecisieteava parte II. adj. *(place)* decimoséptimo; *(part)* diecisieteavo.

sev·enth (sĕv'ənth) s. & adj. séptimo.

sev·en·ti·eth (:ən-tē-ĭth) I. s. *(place)* setenta *m;* *(part)* setentava parte II. adj. septuagésimo.

sev·en·ty (sĕv'ən-tē) s. & adj. setenta *m.*

sev·er (sĕv'ər) tr. cortar; *(ties)* romper ♦ **to s.**

from separar de.

sev·er·al (sĕv′ər-əl) **I.** adj. varios; *(distinct)* distintos **II.** s. varios.

sev·er·ance (sĕv′ər-əns) s. separación *f*; *(breakup)* ruptura ♦ **s. pay** indemnización por despido.

se·vere (sə-vîr′) adj. **-er, -est** severo; *(harsh)* riguroso; *(intense)* intenso.

se·ver·i·ty (sə-vĕr′ĭ-tē) s. severidad *f*.

sew (sō) tr. & intr. **-ed, -ed** *o* **-n** coser ♦ **to s. up** *(deal)* cerrar; *(market)* monopolizar.

sew·age (sō′ĭj) s. aguas cloacales.

sew·er (sō′ər) s. alcantarilla, cloaca.

sew·er·age (:ĭj) s. *(system)* alcantarillado; *(sewage)* aguas cloacales *o* residuales.

sew·ing (sō′ĭng) s. costura ♦ **s. circle** grupo de costureras • **s. machine** máquina de coser.

sewn (sōn) cf. **sew**.

sex (sĕks) s. sexo ♦ **s. life** vida sexual • **to have s.** tener relaciones sexuales.

sex·ist (sĕk′sĭst) adj. & s. (persona) que tiene prejuicios sexuales.

sex·less (sĕks′lĭs) adj. asexual, asexuado.

sex·tant (sĕk′stənt) s. sextante *m*.

sex·u·al (sĕk′shōō-əl) adj. sexual ♦ **s. intercourse** coito.

sex·u·al·i·ty (′-ăl′ĭ-tē) s. sexualidad *f*.

sex·y (sĕk′sē) adj. **-i-** excitante; *(erotic)* erótico.

sh! (sh) interj. ¡chitón!

shab·bi·ness (shăb′ē-nĭs) s. aspecto andrajoso.

shab·by (shăb′ē) adj. **-i-** *(clothing, upholstery)* raído; *(beggar)* andrajoso; *(house, neighborhood)* derruido; *(treatment)* malo, mezquino.

shack (shăk) s. choza.

shack·le (shăk′əl) **I.** s. grillete *m* **II.** tr. poner grilletes a.

shad (shăd) s. [pl. inv. *o* **s**] sábalo.

shade (shād) **I.** s. sombra; *(for lamp)* pantalla; *(for window)* persiana; *(hue)* tono; *(of meaning)* matiz *m*; *(bit)* pizca ♦ **s. tree** árbol que da sombra ♦ pl. JER. anteojos de sol **II.** tr. *(from light)* resguardar; *(to obscure)* dar sombra a; *(a picture)* sombrear; *(a meaning)* matizar.

shad·ing (shā′dĭng) s. DIB., PINT. *(of darkness)* sombreado; *(of color)* degradación *f*.

shad·ow (shăd′ō) **I.** s. sombra ♦ **beyond the s. of a doubt** sin lugar a dudas • **to cast a s. (on)** hacer sombra (sobre) • **to cast a s. over** ensombrecer ♦ pl. oscuridad **II.** tr. sombrear; *(to trail)* seguir (la pista de) ♦ **to s. forth** *o* **out** presentir **III.** adj. POL. fantasma.

shad·ow·y (:ē) adj. **-i-** *(dark)* obscuro; *(vague)* vago.

shad·y (shā′dē) adj. **-i-** sombreado; *(person)* sospechoso.

shaft (shăft) **I.** s. *(of spear)* asta; *(of arrow)* astil *m*; *(arrow)* flecha; *(of light)* rayo; *(of tool)* mango; *(of vehicle)* varal *m*; *(mine)* pozo; *(elevator)* hueco; MEC. eje *m* ♦ **to get the s.** JER. salir perjudicado **II.** tr. JER. perjudicar.

shag·gy (shăg′ē) adj. **-i-** *(hairy)* peludo; *(woolly)* lanudo; *(unkempt)* desgreñado.

shake (shāk) **I.** tr. **shook, -n** sacudir; *(house)* hacer temblar; *(bottle)* agitar; *(faith)* hacer vacilar; *(habit)* librarse de ♦ **to s. down** FAM. sacar dinero a; *(to search)* registrar • **to s. hands** darse la mano • **to s. hands with** dar la mano • **to s. off** liberarse de • **to s. one's head** negar con la cabeza • **to s. out** sacudir • **to s. up** *(bottle)* agitar; *(person)* sacudir; *(organization)* reorganizar —intr. temblar ♦ **to s. with** *(fear,*

cold) temblar de *(miedo, frío)* **II.** s. sacudida; *(tremble)* temblor *m*; *(beverage)* batido ♦ **to be no great shakes** JER. no valer gran cosa • **to have the shakes** FAM. tener escalofríos.

shake·down ('doun') **I.** s. prueba; FAM. extorsión *f*; *(search)* registro **II.** adj. de prueba.

shak·er (shā′kər) s. *(for cocktails)* coctelera; *(for salt)* salero; *(for pepper)* pimentero.

shake·up (shāk′ŭp′) s. reorganización *f*.

shak·y (shā′kē) adj. **-i-** tembloroso; *(unstable)* inestable; *(dubious)* discutible ♦ **to feel s.** sentirse débil.

shale (shāl) s. esquisto.

shall (shăl) aux. [pret. **should**] <*I s. be 28 tomorrow* cumpliré 28 años mañana> <*the penalty s. not exceed two years in prison* el castigo no excederá más de dos años de cárcel> <*shall I call?* ¿quiere que llame por teléfono?>.

shal·lot (shə-lŏt′, shăl′ət) s. chalote *m*.

shal·low (shăl′ō) **I.** adj. poco profundo; *(dish)* llano; FIG. superficial **II.** s. ♦ pl. MARÍT. bajíos.

sham (shăm) **I.** s. falsificación *f*; *(fraud)* farsa; *(impostor)* impostor *m* **II.** adj. falso; *(feigned)* fingido **III.** tr. & intr. **-mm-** fingir.

sham·bles (shăm′bəlz) s. caos *m* ♦ **to make a s. of** convertir en caos.

shame (shām) **I.** s. vergüenza; *(pity)* lástima ♦ **a crying s.** una verdadera lástima • **s. on you!** ¡qué vergüenza! • **to bring s. on** deshonrar a • **to put to shame** avergonzar **II.** tr. avergonzar; *(to dishonor)* deshonrar.

shame·ful ('fəl) adj. vergonzoso ♦ **how s.!** ¡qué vergüenza!

shame·less (:lĭs) adj. *(person)* descarado, sinvergüenza; *(behavior)* vergonzoso.

sham·poo (shăm-pōō′) **I.** s. champú *m* ♦ **II.** tr. dar un champú a —intr. lavarse la cabeza con champú.

sham·rock (shăm′rŏk′) s. trébol *m*.

shang·hai (shăng-hī′) tr. obligar a hacer algo por la fuerza.

shank (shăngk) s. *(lower leg)* espinilla; *(of horse)* caña; *(of meat)* pierna; *(of pin)* tija.

shan·ty (shăn′tē) s. choza.

shan·ty·town (:toun′) s. villa miseria.

shape (shāp) **I.** s. forma; *(body)* figura; *(guise)* aspecto; *(condition)* estado ♦ **to be in no s. to** no estar en condiciones de *o* para • **to be out of s.** DEP. no estar en forma • **to knock out of s.** deformar • **to take s.** formarse **II.** tr. formar; *(object)* dar forma a; *(idea)* concebir; *(one's life)* adaptar ♦ **shaped** en forma de <*mushroom-shaped* en forma de hongo> • **to s. into** dar forma de —intr. ♦ **to s. up** FAM. ponerse en condiciones.

shape·less ('lĭs) adj. informe; *(misshapen)* deforme.

shape·ly (:lē) adj. **-i-** bien proporcionado.

shard (shärd) s. fragmento; *(pottery)* casco.

share¹ (shâr) **I.** s. parte *f*; *(of stock)* acción *f* ♦ **to go shares in** ir a partes iguales en **II.** tr. compartir ♦ **to s. and s. alike** compartir por partes iguales • **to s. in** tener parte en • **to s. out** repartir.

share² s. AGR. reja de arado.

share·crop·per (shâr′krŏp′ər) s. aparcero.

share·hold·er (:hōl′dər) s. accionista *mf*.

shark (shärk) s. tiburón *m*; JER. usurero.

sharp (shärp) **I.** adj. *(cutting)* afilado; *(pointed)* puntiagudo; *(image)* nítido; *(feature)* anguloso; *(contrast)* marcado; *(abrupt)* repentino;

(curve) cerrado; *(acute)* agudo; *(alert)* atento; *(biting)* mordaz; *(tongue)* de víbora; *(tone)* áspero; *(strong)* fuerte; *(pungent)* acre; MÚS. sostenido; JER. *(stylish)* elegante ♦ **to be s. at** ser un hacha en • **to have a s. temper** enojarse fácilmente II. adv. en punto ♦ **to look s.** estar atento III. s. FAM. *(cheater)* fullero; MÚS. sostenido.

sharp·en (shär′pən) tr. afilar; *(pencil)* sacar punta a; *(senses, appetite)* aguzar.

sharp·en·er (:pə-nər) s. *(for pencil)* sacapuntas m; *(machine)* afiladora.

sharp-eyed (shärp′īd′) adj. que tiene ojos de lince; *(observant)* observador.

sharp·ness (:nĭs) s. *(of knife)* filo; *(of cliff)* lo puntiagudo; *(of increase)* brusquedad f; *(of image)* nitidez f; *(acuteness)* agudeza; *(of tone)* aspereza; *(of criticism)* mordacidad f; *(of curve)* lo cerrado; *(of taste)* acritud f.

sharp·shoot·er (:shōō′tər) s. tirador m de primera.

sharp-sight·ed (:sī′tĭd) adj. que tiene ojos de lince; *(observant)* observador.

sharp-wit·ted (:wĭt′ĭd) adj. perspicaz.

shat·ter (shăt′ər) tr. & intr. hacer(se) añicos.

shat·ter·proof (:prōōf′) adj. inastillable.

shave (shāv) I. tr. **-ed, -ed** *o* **-n** afeitar; *(hair)* rapar; *(wood)* cepillar; *(cheese)* cortar en tajadas finas —intr. afeitarse II. s. afeitado ♦ **to get a s.** afeitarse • **to have a close s.** librarse por los pelos.

shav·er (shā′vər) s. afeitadora; FAM. *(boy)* mozalbete m.

shav·ing (:vĭng) s. afeitado; *(sliver)* viruta; TEC. cepillado ♦ **s. cream** crema de afeitar.

shawl (shôl) s. chal m.

she (shē) I. pron. ella II. s. hembra.

sheaf (shēf) s. [pl. **-ves**] fajo.

shear (shîr) tr. **-ed, -ed** *o* **shorn** *(sheep)* esquilar; *(fabric)* tundir; *(metal)* cizallar; *(hedge)* cortar con tijeras ♦ **to s. of** despojar de • **to s. off** cortar —intr. ♦ **to s. off** TEC. romperse por cizallamiento.

shears (shîrz) s.pl. tijeras; *(for metal)* cizalla.

sheath (shēth) s. vaina.

sheathe (shēth) tr. *(knife)* enfundar; *(sword)* envainar; *(claws)* retraer; *(cable)* forrar.

shed[1] (shĕd) tr. **shed, -dding** *(tears)* derramar; *(water)* verter; *(skin)* mudar; *(leaves)* despojarse de ♦ **to s. light on** iluminar —intr. mudar.

shed[2] s. cobertizo.

sheen (shēn) s. brillo; *(of silk)* viso.

sheep (shēp) s.inv. oveja ♦ **s. dog** perro pastor.

sheep·ish (shē′pĭsh) adj. tímido; *(bashful)* vergonzoso.

sheep·skin (shēp′skĭn′) s. piel f de carnero; *(leather)* badana; *(parchment)* pergamino.

sheer[1] (shîr) intr. desviarse.

sheer[2] I. adj. *(fabric)* transparente; *(drop)* vertical; *(utter)* puro II. adv. perpendicularmente.

sheet[1] (shēt) s. *(for bed)* sábana; *(paper)* hoja; *(glass)* lámina; *(ice)* capa ♦ **s. metal** metal en chapa.

sheet[2] s. escota ♦ pl. espacios en la proa y popa de un bote • **three s. to the wind** FAM. borracho.

shelf (shĕlf) s. [pl. **-ves**] *(in closet)* tabla, anaquel m; *(shelving)* estante m; GEOL. arrecife m ♦ **on the s.** arrinconado.

shell (shĕl) s. concha; *(of crustaceans)* caparazón m; *(of nuts, eggs)* cáscara; *(of peas)* vaina; MARIT. bote m para regatas; ARM. proyectil m; *(for firearm)* casquillo ♦ **s. shock** trauma psicológico causado por la guerra II. tr. *(peas)* desvainar; *(nuts)* descascarar; MIL. bombardear ♦ **to s. out** FAM. soltar, pagar.

shel·lac (shə-lăk′) I. s. laca II. tr. **-ck-** laquear; JER. *(to defeat)* derrotar completamente.

shell·fire (shĕl′fīr′) s. cañoneo.

shell·fish (shĕl′fĭsh′) s. [pl. inv. *o* **es**] molusco; *(crustacean)* crustáceo; CUL. mariscos.

shel·ter (shĕl′tər) I. s. cobertizo; *(refuge)* refugio ♦ **to take s.** ponerse a cubierto II. tr. proteger; *(to harbor)* acoger —intr. refugiarse.

shel·tered (:tərd) adj. protegido.

shelve (shĕlv) tr. poner en un estante; *(to put aside)* dar carpetazo a —intr. estar en declive.

shelv·ing (shĕl′vĭng) s. estantería.

she·nan·i·gan (shə-năn′ĭ-gən) s. FAM. engaño ♦ pl. travesuras.

shep·herd (shĕp′ərd) I. s. pastor m II. tr. cuidar.

shep·herd·ess (:ər-dĭs) s. pastora.

sher·bet (shûr′bĭt) s. sorbete m.

sher·iff (shĕr′ĭf) s. sheriff m.

sher·ry (shĕr′ē) s. jerez m.

shield (shēld) I. s. escudo II. tr. escudar; *(to conceal)* tapar.

shift (shĭft) I. tr. *(load)* pasar; *(to switch)* cambiar de —intr. cambiar; *(person)* moverse; AUTO. cambiar de velocidad II. s. cambio; *(of workers)* turno; *(dress)* traje recto ♦ **in shifts** por turnos.

shift·less (shĭft′lĭs) adj. perezoso.

shift·y (shĭf′tē) adj. **-i-** evasivo.

shill (shĭl) s. JER. cómplice m.

shil·ly-shal·ly (shĭl′ē-shăl′ē) intr. titubear.

shim·mer (shĭm′ər) I. intr. destellar II. s. destello.

shim·mer·ing (:ĭng) adj. *(light)* destellante; *(tint)* tornasolado.

shim·my (shĭm′ē) I. s. shimmy m; AUTO. trepidación f oscilante II. intr. AUTO. oscilar.

shin (shĭn) s. espinilla.

shin·bone (′bōn′) s. tibia.

shin·dig (shĭn′dĭg′) s. JER. fiesta.

shine (shīn) I. intr. **-d** *o* **shone** brillar ♦ **to s. on** iluminar —tr. *(to polish)* sacar brillo a; *(light)* dirigir II. s. brillo; *(shoeshine)* brillo de zapatos ♦ **rain or s.** llueva o truene.

shin·er (shī′nər) s. JER. ojo a la funerala.

shin·gle[1] (shĭng′gəl) I. s. CONSTR. tablilla ♦ **to hang out one's s.** FAM. establecerse II. tr. cubrir con tablillas.

shin·gle[2] s. *(beach)* playa de guijarros; *(gravel)* cascajo.

shin·gles (shĭng′gəlz) s.inv. MED. herpes mf.

shin·ny (shĭn′ē) intr. trepar.

shin·y (shī′nē) adj. **-i-** brillante; *(glossy)* lustroso.

ship (shĭp) I. s. barco; *(boat)* buque m; *(crew)* tripulación f; *(aircraft)* aeronave f II. tr. **-pp-** *(goods)* enviar; *(oars)* desarmar; *(water)* hacer agua ♦ **to s. off** enviar a —intr. ♦ **to s. (out) as** enrolarse de.

ship·build·er (′bĭl′dər) s. constructor m naval.

ship·build·ing (:dĭng) s. construcción f naval.

ship·ment (shĭp′mənt) s. embarque m; *(cargo)* cargamento.

ship·per (:ər) s. expedidor m.

ship·ping (:ĭng) s. embarque m; *(ships)* barcos.

ship·shape (:shāp′) adj. en orden.

ship·wreck (:rĕk´) I. s. naufragio II. tr. hacer naufragar; FIG. hundir ◊ **to be shipwrecked** naufragar.

ship·yard (:yärd´) s. MARÍT. astillero.

shirk (shûrk) tr. & intr. esquivar.

shirt (shûrt) s. camisa ◊ **stuffed s.** FAM. persona estirada • **to keep one's s. on** JER. no sulfurarse • **to lose one's s.** JER. perder hasta la camisa.

shirt·tail (shûrt´tāl´) s. faldón m de camisa.

shiv·er¹ (shĭv´ər) I. intr. tiritar II. s. escalofrío.

shiv·er² intr. & tr. (to break) hacer(se) astillas.

shiv·er·y (shĭv´ə-rē) adj. tembloroso.

shoal¹ (shōl) I. s. bajío II. intr. hacerse menos profundo III. adj. poco profundo.

shoal² I. s. (of fish) banco II. intr. ir en bancos.

shock¹ (shŏk) I. s. choque m; (mental) golpe m; (of earthquake) sacudida ◊ **s. absorber** amortiguador II. tr. & intr. chocar ◊ **to be shocked at** escandalizarse por.

shock² s. (of hair) greña; AGR. tresnal m.

shock·er (shŏk´ər) s. cosa horrible.

shock·ing (:ĭng) adj. (disturbing) horroroso; (offensive) indecente.

shod (shŏd) cf. **shoe.**

shod·dy (shŏd´ē) I. s. (cloth) lana regenerada; (goods) mercancía de mala calidad II. adj. -i- regenerado; (goods) de mala calidad.

shoe (shōō) I. s. zapato; (for horses) herradura; (of brake) zapata; (of tire) cubierta ◊ **leather s.** suela de zapato • **s. polish** betún • **s. store** zapatería • **to be in another's shoes** estar en el lugar de otro • **to fill someone's shoes** ocupar el lugar de otro II. tr. shod (person) calzar; (horse) herrar.

shoe·horn (´hôrn´) s. calzador m.

shoe·lace (:lās´) s. cordón m.

shoe·mak·er (:mā´kər) s. zapatero.

shoe·string (:strĭng´) s. cordón m ◊ **on a s.** con poco dinero.

shoe·tree (:trē´) s. horma.

shone (shōn) cf. **shine.**

shoo (shōō) interj. ¡fuera!

shook (shŏŏk) cf. **shake.**

shook-up (-ŭp´) adj. JER. perturbado.

shoot (shōōt) I. tr. shot (a weapon) disparar; (to wound) herir; (to kill) matar a tiros; (to hit) pegar un tiro; (to execute) fusilar; (to send) lanzar; (to film) rodar; (to photograph) fotografiar ◊ **to s. down** derribar • **to s. forth** BOT. echar • **to s. out** resolverlo a tiros • **to s. off** disparar • **to s. the breeze** o **bull** FAM. charlar • **to s. the works** FAM. jugarse el todo por el todo • **to s. dead** o **to death** matar a tiros • **to s. up** JER. inyectar (drogas) —intr. (to fire) disparar; (to hunt) cazar; DEP. tirar ◊ **to s. across, through** pasar rápidamente • **to s. ahead** tomar rápidamente la delantera • **to s. at** tirar a • **to s. for** tratar de lograr • **to s. from the hip** hablar a tontas y a locas • **to s. in** entrar como un torbellino • **to s. off** o **out** salir disparando • **to s. off one's mouth** hablar demasiado • **to s. out** brotar; (projection) sobresalir • **to s. past** o **by** pasar como un rayo • **to s. up** (to grow) espigar; (prices) subir de repente; (sparks) brotar; JER. (drugs) inyectar drogas II. s. BOT. retoño; (contest) tiro III. interj. ¡miércoles!

shoot·er (shōō´tər) s. tirador m; DEP. goleador m.

shoot·ing (:tĭng) I. s. (firing) tiro; (shoot-out) tiroteo; (execution) fusilamiento; (killing) matanza; (murder) asesinato; (filming) rodaje m II. adj. ◊ **s. pain** dolor punzante.

shoot-out o **shoot·out** (shōōt´out´) s. tiroteo.

shop (shŏp) I. s. tienda; (workshop) taller m ◊ **s. window** escaparate • **to set up s.** poner un negocio • **to talk s.** hablar del trabajo II. intr. -pp- ir de compras ◊ **to s. around (for)** buscar • **to s. for** ir a comprar.

shop·keep·er (´kē´pər) s. tendero.

shop·lift·er (:lĭf´tər) s. ratero de tiendas.

shop·per (:ər) s. comprador m.

shop·ping (:ĭng) s. compras ◊ **s. bag** bolsa • **s. center** centro comercial • **to go s.** ir de compras.

shop·talk (:tôk´) s. conversación f sobre el trabajo.

shop·worn (:wôrn´) adj. gastado.

shore¹ (shôr) s. (coast) orilla; (beach) playa ◊ pl. tierra.

shore² tr. ◊ **to s. up** apuntalar.

shore·line (shôr´lĭn´) s. ribera.

shor·ing (shôr´ĭng) s. puntales m.

shorn (shôrn) cf. **shear.**

short (shôrt) I. adj. corto; (in height) bajo; (in amount) poco; (brusque) seco; GRAM. breve; FIN. al descubierto; CUL. crujiente ◊ **a s. distance from** a poca distancia de • **a s. way off** a corta distancia • **in s. order** sin demora • **in s. supply** escaso • **s. and sweet** FAM. corto y bueno • **s. circuit** ELEC. cortocircuito • **s. story** cuento • **to be (a dollar) s.** faltarle a uno (un dólar) • **to be s. of** (money) andar escaso de; (breath) faltarle a uno • **to be s. on** tener poco • **to be (a foot) too s.** tener (un pie) de menos • **to get the s. end (of the stick)** llevar la peor parte • **to have a s. memory** fallarle a uno la memoria • **to have a s. temper** o **fuse** enojarse fácilmente • **to run s. of** agotársele (a uno) II. adv. (abruptly) en seco; (near) cerca ◊ **nothing s.** of nada menos que • **to catch s.** cogerle a uno desprevenido • **to come up s.** quedarse corto • **to cut s.** (to cut off) cortar en seco; (to abbreviate) acortar • **to fall s. (of)** no alcanzar • **to sell s.** (commodities) vender al descubierto; (person) subestimar III. s. cortocircuito ◊ **for s. de mote** • **in s.** en resumen ◊ pl. pantalones cortos; (underpants) calzoncillos IV. tr. & intr. ◊ **to s.** poner(se) en cortocircuito.

short·age (shôr´tĭj) s. falta.

short·change (shôrt´chānj´) tr. dar de menos en el cambio.

short-cir·cuit (:sûr´kĭt) tr. & intr. poner(se) en cortocircuito.

short·com·ing (:kŭm´ĭng) s. defecto.

short·cut (:kŭt´) s. atajo.

short·en (shôr´tn) tr. & intr. acortar(se).

short·en·ing (:ĭng) s. CUL. materia grasa; (abbreviation) acortamiento.

short·fall (shôrt´fôl´) s. déficit m.

short·hand (:hānd´) s. taquigrafía.

short·hand·ed (:hăn´dĭd) adj. falto de mano de obra.

short-lived (:līvd´, :lĭvd´) adj. de breve duración.

short·ly (:lē) adv. dentro de poco; (succinctly) brevemente.

short·ness (:nĭs) s. cortedad f; (in height) pequeñez f; (in duration) brevedad f; (of breath) falta; (of manner) sequedad f.

short-range (:rānj´) adj. de alcance reducido.

short·sight·ed (:sī´tĭd) adj. corto de vista.

short·tem·pered (:tĕm′pərd) adj. que se enoja fácilmente.

short-term (:tûrm′) adj. a corto plazo.

short-wave (:wāv′) adj. de onda corta.

short-wind·ed (:wĭn′dĭd) adj. corto de resuello.

shot[1] (shŏt) s. disparo; *(marksman)* tirador m; *(drink)* trago; DEP. *(ball)* peso; *(try)* tiro; *(in pool)* golpe m; CINEM. *(view)* plano; FOTOG. foto f; MED. inyección f; *(pellets)* perdigones m ♦ **like a s.** como una bala • **not by a long s.** ni mucho menos • **s. in the arm** estímulo • **s. in the dark** conjetura • **to call the shots** llevar la voz cantante • **to take a s. at** tratar de (hacer algo) • **without firing a s.** sin pegar un tiro.

shot[2] adj. FAM. *(day)* perdido; *(clothes)* gastado ♦ **her nerves are s.** tiene los nervios destrozados.

shot[3] cf. shoot.

shot·gun (shŏt′gŭn′) s. escopeta.

shot-put (:pŏŏt′) s. lanzamiento de peso.

should (shŏŏd) aux. [pret. de shall] *(obligation)* deber; *(expectation)* deber de; *(conditional)* <if he s. fall, so would I si él se cayera, me caería yo también> ♦ **how s. I know?** ¿cómo iba yo a saber?

shoul·der (shōl′dər) I. s. hombro; *(of meat)* paletilla; *(of road)* orilla ♦ **s. bag** bolsa de bandolera • **s. blade** omóplato • **s. strap** tirantes • **s. to s.** hombro con hombro • **to give the cold s.** tratar con frialdad • **to shrug one's shoulders** encogerse de hombros II. tr. echarse al hombro; *(blame)* cargar con.

shout (shout) I. s. grito II. tr. & intr. gritar.

shove (shŭv) I. tr. empujar a —intr. dar empujones ♦ **to s. off** JER. largarse II. s. empujón m.

shov·el (shŭv′əl) I. s. pala; *(shovelful)* palada II. tr. *(snow)* quitar con la pala; *(steps)* limpiar con la pala ♦ **to s. food into one's mouth** FAM. zamparse la comida.

show (shō) I. tr. **-ed, -ed** o **-n** mostrar; *(to guide)* llevar; *(to present)* presentar; *(to grant)* conceder; *(to prove)* demostrar; *(to manifest)* manifestar; *(to point out)* indicar; *(to exhibit)* exponer ♦ **to have nothing to s. for something** no sacar ningún beneficio • **to s. around** mostrar • **to s. how to** enseñar a • **to s. in** hacer entrar • **to s. off** hacer alarde de • **to s. one's hand** poner las cartas boca arriba • **to s. oneself** dejarse ver • **to s. out** acompañar a la puerta • **to s. someone the door** echar de la casa • **to s. up** revelar —intr. verse; FAM. *(to come)* aparecer ♦ **it just goes to s.** sirve para demostrar • **to s. off** alardear • **to s. up** aparecer • **to s. up (against)** destacarse II. s. demostración f; *(pretense)* alarde m; TELEV. programa m; TEAT. espectáculo ♦ **by a s. of hands** a mano alzada • **fashion s.** desfile de modelos • **for s.** para impresionar a los demás • **horse s.** concurso hípico • **one-man s.** exposición individual • **s. business** mundo del espectáculo • **s. room** sala de exposición • **to put on, make a s. of** hacer gala o alarde de • **to run the s.** llevar la voz cantante • **to steal the s.** llevarse todos los aplausos.

show·case (″kās′) I. s. vitrina II. tr. poner bien a la vista.

show·down (:doun′) s. momento decisivo; *(confrontation)* confrontación f.

show·er (shou′ər) I. s. *(rain)* chaparrón m; *(snow)* nevada; *(outpouring)* avalancha; *(party)* fiesta a la que se llevan regalos; *(bath)* ducha II. tr. *(to sprinkle)* salpicar; *(to pour)* derramar —intr. ducharse.

show·ing (shō′ĭng) s. exposición f; *(performance)* actuación f.

show·man (:mən) s. [pl. **-men**] TEAT. comediante m.

show·man·ship (:shĭp′) s. teatralidad f.

show-off (shō′ôf′) s. FAM. presumido.

show·piece (:pēs′) s. obra maestra.

show·y (:ē) adj. **-i-** llamativo.

shrank (shrăngk) cf. shrink.

shrap·nel (shrăp′nəl) s.inv. *(shell)* granada de metralla; *(fragments)* metralla.

shred (shrĕd) I. s. jirón m; *(particle)* fragmento ♦ **to rip** o **tear to shreds** hacer trizas II. tr. **-dd-** hacer trizas.

shred·der (′ər) s. desfibradora.

shrew (shrōō) s. *(rodent)* musaraña; FAM. mujer regañona.

shrewd (shrōōd) adj. astuto.

shrew·ish (shrōō′ĭsh) adj. regañón.

shriek (shrēk) I. s. chillido II. intr. chillar ♦ **to s. with laughter** reírse a carcajadas.

shrill (shrĭl) I. adj. chillón II. intr. chillar.

shrimp (shrĭmp) s. [pl. inv. o **s**] camarón m; JER. *(small fry)* renacuajo.

shrine (shrīn) s. relicario; *(tomb)* sepulcro; *(site)* lugar santo.

shrink (shrĭngk) I. intr. **shrank** o **shrunk, shrunk(en)** encoger(se); *(to dwindle)* mermar; *(to recoil)* retroceder ♦ **to s. away, back** echarse atrás —tr. encoger II. s. JER. psiquiatra mf.

shrink·age (shrĭng′kĭj) s. encogimiento; *(reduction)* disminución f; *(loss)* merma.

shriv·el (shrĭv′əl) tr. & intr. *(to shrink)* encoger(se); *(to wrinkle)* arrugar(se); *(to lose vitality)* marchitar(se); *(to waste away)* consumir(se).

shroud (shroud) I. s. sudario; *(veil)* velo; MARÍT. obenque m II. tr. tapar.

shrub (shrŭb) s. matorral m.

shrub·ber·y (′ə-rē) s. matorrales m.

shrug (shrŭg) I. intr. **-gg-** encogerse de hombros —tr. ♦ **to s. off** *(to minimize)* no hacer caso de; *(to get rid of)* echar de lado con una sacudida II. s. encogimiento de hombros.

shrunk (shrŭngk), **shrunk·en** (shrŭng′kən) cf. shrink.

shuck (shŭk) I. s. *(of nuts)* cáscara; *(of corn)* espata II. tr. *(nuts)* pelar; *(corn)* quitar la espata de; *(peas)* desvainar III. interj. ♦ **shucks** ¡diablos!

shud·der (shŭd′ər) I. intr. estremecerse II. s. estremecimiento.

shuf·fle (shŭf′əl) I. tr. *(to move)* cambiar de sitio; *(to stir)* mezclar; *(cards)* barajar —intr. ♦ **to s. along** arrastrar los pies • **to s. off** irse II. s. arrastramiento de los pies; *(of cards)* barajada.

shun (shŭn) tr. **-nn-** rehuir.

shunt (shŭnt) I. s. desviación f; F.C. maniobras II. tr. & intr. desviar(se); F.C. cambiar de vía.

shush (shŭsh, shŏŏsh) interj. ¡chitón!

shut (shŭt) tr. & intr. **shut, -tting** cerrar(se) ♦ **to s. away** guardar bajo llave; *(to imprison)* encerrar • **to s. in** encerrar • **to s. off** *(to isolate)* aislar; *(to turn off)* desconectar • **to s. out** no admitir • **to s. up** encerrar; *(to silence)* hacer callar; *(to be silent)* callarse la boca.

shut·down (′doun′) s. cierre m.

shut·eye (:ī′) s. JER. sueño.

shut·ter (:ər) s. contraventana; FOTOG. obturador *m*.

shut·tle (shŭt'l) I. s. lanzadera; *(vehicle)* vehículo que hace trayectos cortos entre dos puntos ♦ **space s.** transbordador espacial II. intr. hacer trayectos cortos y regulares.

shut·tle·cock (:kŏk') s. volante *m*.

shy (shī) I. adj. **-er, -est** *o* **-i-** tímido; *(bashful)* vergonzoso; *(wary)* cauteloso; FAM. *(lacking)* escaso ♦ **s. of** falto de • **to be s. of** desconfiar de II. intr. sobresaltarse; *(to draw back)* echarse atrás asustado ♦ **to s. away** espantarse • **to s. away (from)** huir (de).

shy·lock (shī'lŏk') s. usurero.

shy·ness (shī'nĭs) s. timidez *f*; *(caution)* cautela.

shy·ster (shī'stər) s. JER. picapleitos *m*.

sib·ling (sĭb'lĭng) s. hermano, -a.

sick (sĭk) adj. enfermo; *(disturbed)* trastornado; *(morbid)* morboso; *(disgusted)* asqueado; *(tired)* cansado; *(longing)* anhelante ♦ **s. leave** baja por enfermedad • **to be s.** vomitar • **to be s. and tired of** estar harto de • **to feel s.** tener náuseas • **to be s. at heart** estar desesperado • **to get s.** *(seasick)* marearse; *(to take sick)* ponerse enfermo • **to make s.** dar asco a.

sick·bay ('bā') s. enfermería.

sick·bed (:bĕd') s. lecho de enfermo.

sick·en (:ən) tr. & intr. enfermar(se).

sick·en·ing (:ə-nĭng) adj. nauseabundo; *(distressing)* deprimente.

sick·le (sĭk'əl) s. hoz *f*.

sick·ly (sĭk'lē) adj. **-i-** enfermizo; *(weak)* enclenque; *(unhealthy)* malsano.

sick·ness (sĭk'nĭs) s. enfermedad *f*; *(nausea)* náusea.

side (sīd) I. s. lado; *(of hill)* ladera; *(of boat)* costado; *(of coin)* cara; *(edge)* borde *m*; *(lineage)* parte *f*; *(team)* facción *f* ♦ **by the s. of** al lado de • **from all sides** de todas partes • **on all, both sides** por todas, ambas partes • **on either s.** de cada lado • **on every s.** por todas partes • **on one's s.** de costado • **on the s.** aparte de la ocupación habitual • **on this s.** por este lado • **s. by s.** juntos • **the other s. of the coin** el reverso de la medalla • **the right s.** el derecho; *(correct)* el lado bueno; *(right-hand)* la derecha • **to be on the safe s.** para estar tranquilo • **to change sides** cambiar de partido • **to get on the right** *o* **good s. of** granjearse la simpatía de • **to have on one's s.** tener de parte de uno • **to keep on the right s. of the law** mantenerse dentro de la ley • **to move to one s.** apartarse • **to take sides** tomar partido • **to take sides with** ponerse de parte de • **to turn over on its s.** volcar • **wrong s. out** al *o* del revés II. adj. lateral; *(indirect)* indirecto; *(supplementary)* adicional ♦ **s. arm** arma de mano • **s. effect** efecto secundario • **s. view** vista de perfil III. intr. ♦ **to s. with** ponerse del lado de.

side·board ('bôrd') s. aparador *m*.

side·burns (:bûrnz') s.pl. patillas.

side·car (:kär') s. sidecar *m*.

side·kick (:kĭk') s. JER. amigo, compañero.

side·line (:līn') s. actividad suplementaria; DEP. línea de banda.

side·long (:lông') I. adj. lateral; *(sideways)* de soslayo II. adv. *(obliquely)* oblicuamente.

side·sad·dle (:săd'l) I. s. silla de amazona II. adv. a la amazona.

side·show (:shō') s. atracción secundaria.

side·split·ting (:splĭt'ĭng) adj. divertidísimo.

side·step (:stĕp') tr. **-pp-** esquivar, evitar; *(to evade)* eludir —intr. dar un paso lateral.

side·swipe (:swīp') I. tr. chocar de refilón contra II. s. golpe *m* de refilón.

side·track (:trăk') I. tr. desviar; *(an issue)* dejar de lado II. s. desvío.

side·walk (:wôk') s. acera.

side·ways (:wāz') I. adv. de lado; *(to step)* hacia un lado II. adj. lateral, de lado.

sid·ing (sī'dĭng) s. F.C. apartadero; CONSTR. tablas de forro.

si·dle (sīd'l) tr. & intr. mover(se) furtiva y lateralmente.

siege (sēj) s. MIL. sitio; FIG. calvario.

sieve (sĭv) I. s. tamiz *m* II. tr. tamizar.

sift (sĭft) tr. cerner; *(to separate)* separar; *(to examine)* examinar.

sift·er (sĭf'tər) s. cedazo.

sigh (sī) intr. suspirar.

sight (sīt) I. s. vista; *(vision)* visión *f*; *(thing to see)* lugar *m* de interés; *(of device)* mira; *(quantity)* gran cantidad ♦ **a s. for sore eyes** FAM. persona grata • **on s.** a primera vista • **s. draft** COM. letra a la vista • **s. unseen** sin haberlo visto • **to be (with)in s.** of estar a la vista de • **to catch s. of** vislumbrar • **to come into s.** aparecer, asomar • **to lose s. of** perder de vista ♦ pl. meta • **to set one's s. on** tener el ojo puesto en II. tr. ver; *(to aim)* apuntar.

sight·ed (sī'tĭd) adj. de vista normal.

sight·less (sīt'lĭs) adj. ciego.

sight·ly (:lē) adj. **-i-** agradable a la vista.

sight·see (:sē') intr. **-saw, -seen** visitar lugares de interés.

sight·see·ing (:ĭng) s. visita a lugares de interés.

sight·se·er (:ər) s. turista *mf*.

sign (sīn) I. s. signo; *(gesture)* gesto; *(poster)* letrero; *(symbol)* símbolo; *(trace)* huella; *(presage)* presagio ♦ **s. language** lenguaje por señas • **to make no s.** no dar señales • **to show signs of** dar muestras de II. tr. firmar; *(to express)* indicar ♦ **to s. away** *o* over ceder • **to s. on** *o* up contratar —intr. hacer señas; *(to write)* firmar ♦ **to s. in** inscribirse • **to s. on** *o* up alistarse • **to s. off** acabar el programa • **to s. out** firmar y salir.

sig·nal (sĭg'nəl) I. s. señal *f* ♦ **s. flare** bengala de señales II. adj. señalado III. tr. dar la señal de *o* para; *(to make known)* indicar —intr. hacer señales.

sig·na·to·ry (:nə-tôr'ē) adj. & s. signatario.

sig·na·ture (:chər) s. firma; *(act)* signatura; MÚS. armadura.

sign·er (sī'nər) s. firmante *mf*.

sig·net (sĭg'nĭt) s. sello ♦ **s. ring** sortija de sello.

sig·nif·i·cance (sĭg-nĭf'ĭ-kəns) s. significación *f*.

sig·nif·i·cant (:kənt) adj. significativo.

sig·ni·fy (sĭg'nə-fī') tr. significar; *(to intimate)* expresar —intr. significar.

sign·post (sīn'pōst') s. poste *m* indicador.

si·lage (sī'lĭj) s. ensilaje *m*.

si·lence (sī'ləns) I. s. silencio II. tr. hacer callar; *(to suppress)* reprimir.

si·lenc·er (sī'lən-sər) s. silenciador *m*.

si·lent (sī'lənt) adj. silencioso; *(mute)* mudo; *(tacit)* tácito ♦ **s. partner** COM. socio comanditario • **to be s.** callar.

sil·hou·ette (sĭl'ōō-ĕt') I. s. silueta II. tr. siluetear.

sil·i·con (sĭl'ĭ-kŏn') s. silicio.

sil·i·cone (sĭl'ĭ-kŏn') s. silicona.

silk (sĭlk) s. seda ♦ **s. cotton** seda vegetal • **s. hat** sombrero de copa • **s. screen** serigrafía.

silk·en (sĭl'kən) adj. de seda.

silk·worm (sĭlk'wûrm') s. gusano de seda.

silk·y (sĭl'kē) adj. -i- sedoso; *(suave)* suave.

sill (sĭl) s. *(door)* umbral m; *(window)* alféizar m.

sil·li·ness (sĭl'ē-nĭs) s. tontería.

sil·ly (sĭl'ē) adj. -i- tonto, bobo; *(ridiculous)* ridículo.

si·lo (sī'lō) s. silo.

silt (sĭlt) I. s. cieno II. tr. & intr. enarenar(se); *(canal)* encenagar(se).

sil·ver (sĭl'vər) I. s. plata; *(coins)* monedas de plata; *(color)* plateado II. adj. de plata; *(like silver)* plateado; *(melodious)* argentino ♦ **s. plate** platería • **s. screen** CINEM. pantalla • **s. tongue** pico de oro III. tr. platear.

sil·ver·smith (:smĭth') s. platero.

sil·ver·ware (:wâr') s. *(vajilla de)* plata.

sim·i·an (sĭm'ē-ən) I. adj. símico II. s. simio.

sim·i·lar (sĭm'ə-lər) adj. similar.

sim·i·lar·i·ty (-lăr'ĭ-tē) s. similitud f.

sim·mer (sĭm'ər) intr. hervir a fuego lento; *(to seethe)* fermentar ♦ **to s. down** sosegarse —tr. hervir a fuego lento.

sim·per (sĭm'pər) I. intr. sonreír tontamente o con afectación II. s. sonrisa tonta.

sim·ple (sĭm'pəl) adj. -er, -est simple; *(not elaborate)* sencillo; *(sincere)* sincero.

sim·ple-mind·ed (-mīn'dĭd) adj. *(artless)* ingenuo; *(silly)* tonto; *(stupid)* simple.

sim·ple·ton ('-tn) s. simplón m.

sim·plic·i·ty (sĭm-plĭs'ĭ-tē) s. sencillez f; *(foolishness)* simpleza.

sim·pli·fi·ca·tion ('plə-fī-kā'shən) s. simplificación f.

sim·pli·fy ('-fī') tr. simplificar.

sim·ply (sĭm'plē) adv. simplemente, sencillamente; *(really)* absolutamente.

sim·u·late (sĭm'yə-lāt') tr. simular.

sim·u·la·tion ('-lā'shən) s. simulación f.

sim·u·la·tor ('-'-tər) s. TEC. simulador m.

si·mul·cast (sī'məl-kăst', sĭm'əl-) s. transmisión simultánea por radio y televisión.

si·mul·ta·ne·ous (:'-tā'nē-əs) adj. simultáneo.

sin (sĭn) I. s. pecado II. intr. -nn- pecar.

since (sĭns) I. adv. desde entonces; *(ago)* hace *<five days s.* hace cinco días> ♦ **ever s.** desde entonces • **how long s.?** ¿cuánto tiempo hace? • **long s.** hace mucho tiempo • **s. when?** ¿desde cuándo? II. prep. desde ♦ **s. that time** desde entonces III. conj. desde que; *(inasmuch as)* ya que ♦ **ever s.** desde que.

sin·cere (sĭn-sîr') adj. -er, -est sincero.

sin·cer·i·ty (sĭn-sĕr'ĭ-tē) s. sinceridad f.

si·ne·cure (sī'nĭ-kyŏŏr', sĭn'ĭ-) s. sinecura.

sin·ew (sĭn'yōō) s. tendón m; FIG. vigor m.

sin·ew·y (sĭn'yōō-ē) adj. nervudo; *(strong)* fuerte.

sin·ful (sĭn'fəl) adj. *(deed)* pecaminoso; *(person)* pecador.

sing (sĭng) intr. **sang, sung** cantar ♦ **to s. to sleep** arrullar • **to s. a different tune** cambiar de tono.

singe (sĭnj) tr. chamuscar.

sing·er (sĭng'ər) s. cantante mf.

sin·gle (sĭng'gəl) I. adj. solo; *(for one)* individual; *(unmarried)* soltero ♦ **every s. one** todos •

not a s. one ni uno • **s. bed** cama para una persona • **s. file** hilera II. s. *(person)* individuo; *(accommodation)* alojamiento individual; *(unmarried person)* soltero, -a; *(bill)* billete m de un dólar ♦ pl. DEP. individual, simple (tenis) III. tr. ♦ **to s. out** *(to choose)* escoger; *(to distinguish)* distinguir.

sin·gle-hand·ed ('-hăn'dĭd) adj. solo, sin ayuda.

sin·gle-mind·ed (:mīn'dĭd) adj. resuelto.

sing·song (sĭng'sông') s. tono monótono.

sin·gu·lar (sĭng'gyə-lər) adj. & s. singular m.

sin·gu·lar·i·ty ('-lär'ĭ-tē) s. singularidad f.

sin·is·ter (sĭn'ĭ-stər) adj. siniestro.

sink (sĭngk) I. intr. **sank** o **sunk, sunk** descender; *(to incline)* inclinarse; *(to submerge)* hundirse; FIG. debilitarse ♦ **his heart sank** se le cayó el alma a los pies • **to s. in** penetrar • **to s. into** caer en • **to s.** or **swim** triunfar o fracasar —tr. hundir; *(to force down)* echar al fondo; *(into the ground)* echar abajo; COM. *(to invest)* invertir ♦ **to be sunk in** estar sumido en II. s. *(bathroom)* lavabo; *(kitchen)* fregadero; *(cesspool)* pozo negro.

sink·er (sĭng'kər) s. plomo.

sink·ing (:kĭng) s. hundimiento.

sin·ner (sĭn'ər) s. pecador m.

sin·u·ous (sĭn'yōō-əs) adj. sinuoso.

si·nus (sī'nəs) s. seno.

sip (sĭp) I. tr. & intr. -pp- sorber II. s. sorbo.

si·phon (sī'fən) I. s. sifón m II. tr. sacar con sifón.

sir (sûr) s. señor m, caballero ♦ **Dear S.** muy señor mío • **S.** sir *(título)*.

sire (sīr) s. padre m; *(animal)* semental m; ANT. progenitor m; *(title)* mi Señor.

si·ren (sī'rən) s. sirena.

sir·loin (sûr'loin') s. solomillo.

sis·sy (sĭs'ē) s. mariquita m; *(timid person)* timorato.

sis·ter (sĭs'tər) s. hermana; G.B. *(nurse)* enfermera ♦ **s. ships** buques gemelos.

sis·ter·hood (:hŏŏd') s. hermandad f; RELIG. comunidad f de monjas.

sis·ter-in-law (:ĭn-lô') s. [pl. sisters-] *(spouse's sister, brother's wife)* cuñada, hermana política; *(spouse's brother's wife)* concuñada.

sis·ter·ly (:lē) adj. de hermana.

sit (sĭt) intr. **sat** sentarse; *(to be at rest)* estar sentado; *(to perch)* posarse (pájaro); *(to brood)* empollar; *(to lie)* estar situado; *(to pose)* posar; *(to convene)* reunirse; *(to be inactive)* quedarse; *(to babysit)* cuidar a niños ♦ **to be sitting pretty** FAM. estar en posición ventajosa • **to s. back** sentarse cómodamente • **to s. down** sentarse • **to s. in** participar; *(to protest)* tomar parte en una sentada • **to s. for an examination** G.B. presentarse a un examen • **to s. in for** reemplazar • **to s. on** ser miembro de • **to s. on one's hands** no hacer nada • **to s. still** no moverse • **to s. tight** FAM. no moverse • **to s. up** incorporarse; *(to stay up)* quedarse levantado; *(to become alert)* prestar atención —tr. sentar; *(to ride)* montar (un caballo) ♦ **to s. out** *(to remain seated)* quedarse sentado durante (baile) • **to s. through** quedarse hasta el final de.

site (sīt) I. s. sitio; *(location)* ubicación f II. tr. situar.

sit·ter (sĭt'ər) s. persona que cuida niños.

sit·ting (:ĭng) s. asentada; *(session)* sesión f ♦ **s. duck** víctima fácil • **s. room** sala de estar.

sit·u·ate (sĭch'ōō-āt') tr. ubicar.

sit·u·a·tion ('-ā'shən) s. situación *f*; *(position)* puesto.

six (sĭks) s. & adj. seis *m* ♦ **at sixes and sevens** en desorden • **s. hundred** seiscientos • **s. o'clock** las seis.

six-gun ('gŭn') s. revólver *m* de seis tiros.

six-pack (:păk') s. caja de seis botellas *o* latas.

six-shoot·er (:shōō'tər) s. FAM. revólver *m* de seis tiros.

six·teen (sĭk-stēn') s. & adj. dieciséis *m*.

six·teenth (:stēnth') I. s. *(place)* dieciséis *m*; *(part)* dieciseisavo II. adj. *(place)* decimosexto; *(part)* dieciseisavo.

sixth (sĭksth) s. & adj. sexto.

six·ti·eth (sĭk'stē-ĭth) I. s. *(place)* sesenta *m*; *(part)* sesentavo II. adj. sexagésimo.

six·ty (sĭk'stē) s. & adj. sesenta *m*.

siz·a·ble (sī'zə-bəl) adj. considerable.

size[1] (sīz) I. s. tamaño *f*; *(of shoes)* número; *(of persons, garments)* talla; *(magnitude)* magnitud *f* ♦ **that's about the s.** of it es más o menos eso • **to cut down to s.** bajarle los humos a • **to cut to s.** cortar algo del tamaño que se necesita • **to try on for s.** probar II. tr. clasificar según el tamaño ♦ **to s. up** evaluar.

size[2] I. s. *(paste)* cola II. tr. encolar.

siz·ing (sī'zĭng) s. apresto, cola.

siz·zle (sĭz'əl) I. intr. chisporrotear; FIG. *(to be furious)* hervir II. s. chisporroteo.

skate[1] (skāt) I. s. patín *m* II. intr. patinar.

skate[2] s. ICT. raya.

skate·board (skāt'bôrd') s. tabla de patinar sobre ruedas.

skat·er (skā'tər) s. patinador *m*.

skein (skān) s. madeja.

skel·e·tal (skĕl'ĭ-tl) adj. esquelético.

skel·e·ton (skĕl'ĭ-tn) s. esqueleto; *(outline)* bosquejo.

skep·tic (skĕp'tĭk) s. escéptico.

skep·ti·cal (:tĭ-kəl) adj. escéptico.

skep·ti·cism (:sĭz'əm) s. escepticismo.

sketch (skĕch) I. s. esbozo; *(outline)* bosquejo; LIT. obra corta; MÚS. pieza corta II. tr. esbozar —intr. hacer un croquis.

sketch·book ('bŏok') s. bloc *m* de dibujo.

sketch·y (:ē) adj. -i- sin detalles; *(superficial)* superficial.

skew (skyōō) I. intr. torcerse —tr. *(to cut)* sesgar; *(to distort)* tergiversar II. s. sesgo.

skew·er (skyōō'ər) I. s. brocheta II. tr. ensartar.

ski (skē) I. s. esquí *m* ♦ **s. jump** salto con esquís • **s. lift** telesquí • **ski run** *o* **slope** pista de esquí II. intr. & tr. esquiar.

skid (skĭd) I. s. patinazo; *(chock)* calzo; *(ramp)* rampa de descarga; AVIA. patín *m* ♦ **s. row** barrio bajo ♦ pl. MARÍT. varadera • **to be on** *o* **hit the s.** estar de capa caída II. intr. -dd- patinar, resbalar (rueda, automóvil).

ski·er (skē'ər) s. esquiador *m*.

ski·ing (:ĭng) s. esquí *m* (deporte).

skill (skĭl) s. maña; *(art)* técnica; *(experience)* experiencia; *(trade)* oficio.

skilled (skĭld) adj. mañoso; *(qualified)* especializado.

skil·let (skĭl'ĭt) s. sartén *f*.

skill·ful (skĭl'fəl) adj. hábil, mañoso.

skill·ful·ness (:nĭs) s. habilidad *f*, maña.

skim (skĭm) I. tr. -mm- *(liquid)* espumar; *(milk)* desnatar; *(to brush)* rozar; *(book)* hojear ♦ **to s. along** volar a ras de • **to s. over** pasar rozando; *(a subject)* tratar superficial-

mente • **to s. through** echar una ojeada a —intr. hojear (libro) II. s. ♦ **s. milk** leche desnatada.

skimp (skĭmp) tr. escatimar —intr. economizar.

skimp·y (skĭm'pē) adj. -i- *(scanty)* escaso; *(small)* pequeño.

skin (skĭn) I. s. piel *f* ♦ **by the s. of one's teeth** por los pelos • **he is nothing but s. and bones** está en los huesos • **it's no s. off my nose** esto no es asunto mío • **s. diving** buceo • **to get under one's s.** irritarle a uno; *(obsession)* ser una obsesión • **to have a thick s.** ser insensible • **to jump out of one's s.** llevarse un susto tremendo • **to save one's s.** salvar el pellejo • **under the s.** en el fondo II. tr. -nn- despellejar; *(to peel)* pelar; *(to scrape)* desollar ♦ **to s. alive** desollar vivo a; *(to scold)* regañar mucho.

skin-deep ('dēp') I. adj. superficial II. adv. superficialmente.

skin-dive (:dīv') intr. bucear.

skin-flint (:flĭnt') s. tacaño.

skin·ny (:ē) adj. -i- flaco.

skin·ny-dip (:dĭp') intr. -pp- FAM. nadar desnudo.

skin·tight (skĭn'tīt') adj. ceñido.

skip (skĭp) I. intr. -pp- saltar; *(engine)* fallar; EDUC. saltar un curso ♦ **to s. out** FAM. desaparecer —tr. saltar; *(class, meeting)* dejar de ir a ♦ **s. it!** ¡olvídalo! • **to s. over** saltar por encima de • **to s. town** FAM. largarse II. s. salto.

skip·per (skĭp'ər) s. MARÍT. capitán *m*.

skir·mish (skûr'mĭsh) I. s. escaramuza; *(dispute)* pelea II. intr. escaramuzar.

skirt (skûrt) I. s. falda II. tr. & intr. bordear; *(to pass around)* faldear; *(to elude)* eludir.

skit (skĭt) s. TEAT. escena satírica.

skit·ter (skĭt'ər) intr. pasar rozando el agua.

skit·tish (skĭt'ĭsh) adj. asustadizo; *(undependable)* caprichoso.

skiv·vies (skĭv'ēz) s.pl. JER. calzoncillo y camiseta ♦ **in one's s.** en paños menores.

skulk (skŭlk) intr. *(to lurk)* esconderse; *(to steal)* pasar furtivamente.

skull (skŭl) s. cráneo ♦ **s. and crossbones** calavera • **to be out of one's s.** FAM. estar loco.

skull·dug·ger·y (skŭl-dŭg'ə-rē) s. engaños.

skunk (skŭngk) I. s. ZOOL. mofeta; JER. *(person)* canalla *m* II. tr. JER. derrotar.

sky (skī) s. cielo ♦ **out of the clear blue s.** en el momento menos pensado • **to praise to the skies** poner por las nubes.

sky·cap ('kăp') s. changador *m* de un aeropuerto.

sky·dive (:dīv') intr. lanzarse en paracaídas.

sky·jack (:jăk') tr. secuestrar en vuelo.

sky·light (:līt') s. claraboya.

sky·line (:līn') s. horizonte *m*; *(of city)* perfil *m*.

sky·rock·et (:rŏk'ĭt) I. s. cohete *m* II. tr. & intr. subir rápidamente.

sky·scrap·er (:skrā'pər) s. rascacielos *m*.

sky·ward (:wərd) I. adj. dirigido hacia el cielo II. adv. hacia el cielo.

slab (slăb) s. *(piece)* trozo; *(of stone)* losa; *(of cake)* porción *f*; *(of wood)* costero.

slack (slăk) I. adj. *(sluggish)* lento; *(not busy)* de poca actividad; *(loose)* flojo; *(negligent)* negligente II. tr. aflojar; *(to slake)* apagar —intr. aflojarse; *(to be remiss)* ser negligente ♦ **to s. off** disminuir III. s. *(loose part)* parte floja; *(lull)* período de poca actividad ♦ **there is a lot of s. in the rope** la cuerda está muy floja • **to take up the s.** in a rope tensar una cuerda ♦ pl. pantalones.

slack·en ('ən) tr. *(to slow)* aminorar; *(to loosen)* aflojar —intr. *(to slow down)* amainar; *(to loosen)* aflojarse.

slack·er (:ər) s. haragán *m*.

slag (slăg) s. escoria.

slain (slān) cf. **slay.**

slake (slāk) tr. aplacar; *(lime)* apagar.

slam¹ (slăm) **I.** tr. **-mm-** *(to shut)* cerrar de golpe; *(to move)* hacer golpear; *(to hit)* golpear con estrépito ♦ **to s. something down on** poner algo violentamente en • **to s. the door** dar un portazo • **to s. the door** on cerrar la puerta a —intr. cerrarse de golpe; *(to crash)* chocar **II.** s. golpe *m* fuerte; *(of door)* portazo.

slam² (in bridge) slam *m*.

slan·der (slăn'dər) **I.** s. calumnia; DER. difamación *f* **II.** tr. calumniar; DER. difamar.

slan·der·ous (:əs) adj. calumnioso; DER. difamador.

slang (slăng) s. jerga.

slang·y (slăng'ē) adj. **-i-** vulgar.

slant (slănt) **I.** tr. inclinar; *(a problem)* enfocar de modo parcial —intr. inclinarse **II.** s. inclinación *f*; *(point of view)* parecer *m*.

slap (slăp) **I.** s. palmada; *(on face)* bofetada; *(on head)* cachetada ♦ **a s. in the face** FIG. un insulto • **a s. on the back** un espaldazo **II.** tr. **-pp-** *(to strike)* dar una palmada; *(the face)* abofetar; *(the head)* dar una cachetada; FIG. insultar ♦ **to s. down** prohibir.

slap·hap·py ('hăp'ē) adj. **-i-** JER. aturdido.

slash (slăsh) **I.** tr. acuchillar; *(to hack)* dar un tajo a; *(prices)* rebajar —intr. tirar o dar tajos **II.** s. tajo; *(slit)* cuchillada; *(virgule)* vírgula.

slat (slăt) s. tablilla.

slate (slāt) **I.** s. pizarra; *(list)* lista de candidatos elegibles ♦ **to clear the s.** borrar los antecedentes • **to have a clean s.** no tener antecedentes **II.** tr. empizarrar; *(to appoint)* designar.

slath·er (slăth'ər) tr. FAM. extender en gran cantidad.

slaugh·ter (slô'tər) **I.** s. matanza **II.** tr. *(animals)* matar; *(to kill brutally)* matar brutalmente.

slaugh·ter·house (:hous') s. matadero.

slave (slāv) **I.** s. esclavo ♦ **s. labor** trabajo de esclavo **II.** intr. trabajar como esclavo.

slav·er¹ (slăv'ər) **I.** intr. babear **II.** s. baba.

slav·er² (slā'vər) s. *(ship)* buque *m* traficante de esclavos; *(person)* traficante *m* de esclavos.

slav·er·y (:və-rē, slăv'rē) s. esclavitud *f* ♦ **white s.** trata de blancas.

slay (slā) tr. **slew, slain** matar.

slea·zy (slē'zē) adj. **-i-** ligero; *(cheap)* de mala calidad; *(vulgar)* vulgar.

sled (slĕd) **I.** s. trineo **II.** tr. **-dd-** llevar en trineo —intr. ir en trineo.

sled·ding ('ĭng) s. transporte por trineo.

sledge (slĕj) s. trineo.

sledge·ham·mer (slĕj'hăm'ər) s. almádena.

sleek (slēk) adj. suave y brillante; *(well-groomed)* elegante.

sleep (slēp) **I.** s. sueño ♦ **in one's s.** durante el sueño • **to drop off to s.** quedarse dormido • **to go to s.** dormirse • **to put to s.** *(animal)* sacrificar • **to walk in one's s.** ser sonámbulo **II.** intr. **slept** dormir ♦ **to s.** in dormir hasta tarde • **to s. like a log** dormir como un tronco

—tr. pasar durmiendo; *(to accommodate)* tener cabida para ♦ **not to s. a wink** no pegar ojo • **to s. off** dormir hasta que pase (dolor de cabeza, borrachera) • **to s. on it** consultar con la almohada.

sleep·er (slē'pər) s. persona que duerme; *(sleeping car)* coche *m* cama; FAM. *(success)* éxito inesperado ♦ **to be a heavy, light s.** tener el sueño pesado, ligero.

sleep·ing (:pĭng) adj. dormido, durmiendo ♦ **s. bag** saco de dormir • **s. car** coche cama • **s. pill** somnífero.

sleep·less (slēp'lĭs) adj. en blanco.

sleep·walk·ing (:wô'kĭng) s. sonambulismo.

sleep·y (slē'pē) adj. **-i-** soñoliento.

sleep·y·head (:hĕd') s. FAM. dormilón *m*.

sleet (slēt) **I.** s. aguanieve *f* **II.** intr. cellisquear.

sleeve (slēv) s. manga; *(of record)* funda ♦ **up one's s.** FAM. escondido.

sleeve·less ('lĭs) adj. sin mangas.

sleigh (slā) **I.** s. trineo **II.** intr. ir en trineo.

sleight (slīt) s. habilidad *f*; *(stratagem)* estratagema ♦ **s. of hand** juego de manos.

slen·der (slĕn'dər) adj. **-er, -est** delgado; *(svelte)* esbelto; *(meager)* escaso.

slen·der·ize (:də-rīz') intr. & tr. adelgazar.

slept (slĕpt) cf. **sleep.**

sleuth (slōōth) **I.** s. FAM. detective *m* **II.** intr. hacer de detective.

slew¹ (slōō) s. FAM. montón *m*.

slew² cf. **slay.**

slice (slīs) **I.** s. *(of meat)* tajada; *(of bread)* rebanada; *(of ham)* lonja; *(of fish)* raja; *(share)* parte *f*; DEP. golpe *m* que da efecto a la pelota **II.** tr. cortar, tajar; *(bread)* rebanar; DEP. golpear con efecto ♦ **to s. off** cortar.

slic·er (slī'sər) s. máquina de cortar.

slick (slĭk) **I.** adj. resbaladizo; *(adroit)* diestro; *(wily)* astuto **II.** s. superficie resbaladiza; *(tool)* herramienta para alisar ♦ **oil s.** capa de petróleo **III.** tr. alisar.

slick·er ('ər) s. impermeable *m*; FAM. *(swindler)* estafador *m*.

slide (slīd) **I.** intr. **slid** resbalar; *(to coast)* deslizarse; *(to glide)* pasar suavemente ♦ **to let things s.** dejar pasar las cosas sin hacer nada • **to s. down** bajar deslizándose por —tr. hacer resbalar ♦ **to s. over** pasar por alto **II.** s. deslizamiento, desliz *m*; *(surface)* superficie resbaladiza; *(playground)* tobogán *m*; *(track)* resbaladero; *(microscope)* portaobjeto; *(avalanche)* desprendimiento; FOTOG. diapositiva ♦ **s. rule** regla de cálculo.

slight (slīt) **I.** adj. escaso; *(trifling)* insignificante; *(slender)* delgado **II.** tr. menospreciar; *(to shirk)* desatender **III.** s. desaire *m*.

slim (slĭm) **I.** adj. **-mm-** delgado; *(scant)* escaso **II.** tr. & intr. **-mm-** adelgazar.

slime (slīm) s. *(mud)* limo; *(animal substance)* babaza.

slim·y (slī'mē) adj. **-i-** viscoso; *(mucous)* baboso.

sling (slĭng) **I.** s. *(weapon)* honda; *(for rifle)* portafusil *m*; MED. cabestrillo; MARÍT. eslinga **II.** tr. **slung** *(to throw)* arrojar; *(to hang)* colgar ♦ **to s. hash** JER. trabajar en un restaurante barato.

sling·shot ('shŏt') s. tirador *m*.

slink (slĭngk) intr. **slunk** escabullirse.

slink·y (slĭng'kē) adj. **-i-** *(stealthy)* sigiloso; FAM. sinuoso.

slip¹ (slĭp) **I.** intr. **-pp-** deslizarse; *(to steal)* es-

cabullirse; *(to lose one's balance)* resbalar; *(to escape)* soltarse; *(to fall behind)* retrasarse; *(to make a mistake)* equivocarse; FAM. *(to fall off)* empeorar ♦ **my foot slipped** se me fue el pie • **to let an opportunity slip by** dejar pasar una oportunidad • **to let s.** decir sin querer • **to s. away** escabullirse; *(time)* correr • **to s. by** *(time)* correr; *(unnoticed)* pasar inadvertido • **to s. down** dejarse caer • **to s. in** introducirse • **to s. off** escabullirse • **to s. out** salir inadvertido; *(to become known)* saberse • **to s. through** escabullirse por • **to s. through one's fingers** escapársele de las manos • **to s. up** FAM. equivocarse —tr. librarse *(from* de) ♦ **to s. in** introducir • **to s. into** *(to don)* ponerse; *(to enter)* entrar • **to s. off** quitarse (ropa) • **to s. on** ponerse (ropa) • **to s. one over on** FAM. pegársela a • **to s. one's mind** írsele de la memoria a uno II. s. resbalón *m; (false step)* paso en falso; *(error)* equivocación *f; (lapse)* desliz *m; (undergarment)* combinación *f; (pillowcase)* funda; MARÍT. *(pier)* muelle *m; (slipway)* grada ♦ **s. of the tongue** lapsus linguae.
slip² s. *(cutting)* esqueje *m; (of paper)* papeleta ♦ **a s. of a girl** una chiquilla.
slip·cov·er ('kŭv'ər) s. funda.
slip·knot (:nŏt') s. nudo corredizo.
slip·page (:ĭj) s. resbalamiento; MEC. pérdida de fuerza de transmisión.
slip·per (:ər) s. zapatilla.
slip·per·y (:ə-rē) adj. -i- resbaladizo; *(evasive)* evasivo.
slip·shod (:shŏd') adj. descuidado.
slip·stream (:strēm') s. estela.
slip-up (:ŭp') s. FAM. error *m*.
slit (slĭt) I. s. corte *m* II. tr. **slit, -tting** hender ♦ **to someone's throat** degollar a alguien.
slith·er (slĭth'ər) I. intr. resbalar; *(to crawl)* deslizarse, culebrear II. s. deslizamiento.
sliv·er (slĭv'ər) I. s. *(splinter)* astilla; *(slice)* tajada II. tr. cortar en rodajas —intr. astillarse.
slob (slŏb) s. DESPEC., FAM. palurdo.
slob·ber (slŏb'ər) I. intr. babear II. s. baboseo.
slog (slŏg) tr. **-gg-** golpear —intr. *(to plod)* andar pesadamente; *(to work)* trabajar como un burro.
slo·gan (slō'gən) s. lema *m; (in advertising)* slogan *m*.
sloop (slōp) s. balandro.
slop (slŏp) I. s. *(mud)* fango; *(food)* aguachirle *f* ♦ pl. *(swill)* bazofia II. intr. & tr. **-pp-** *(to splash)* salpicar; *(to spill)* derramar(se).
slope (slōp) I. tr. & intr. inclinar(se) ♦ **to s. down** bajar • **to s. up** subir II. s. *(incline)* cuesta; *(of roof)* vertiente *f; (inclination)* inclinación *f* ♦ **on a s.** en declive.
slop·pi·ness (slŏp'ē-nĭs) s. falta de cuidado.
slop·py (slŏp'ē) adj. -i- FAM. *(messy)* desordenado; *(careless)* chapucero.
slosh (slŏsh) tr. salpicar —intr. chapotear.
slot (slŏt) s. *(groove)* ranura; *(on roster)* puesto en el escalafón; FAM. *(niche)* rincón *m* ♦ **s. machine** máquina tragaperras.
sloth (slôth, slŏth) s. indolencia; ZOOL. perezoso.
sloth·ful (′fəl) adj. perezoso, indolente.
slouch (slouch) I. intr. *(to sit)* repantigarse; *(to stand)* tener una postura desgarbada ♦ **to s. around** gandulear —tr. echar hacia adelante II. s. postura desgarbada; *(person)* perezoso ♦ **to walk with a s.** caminar con los hombros caí-

dos.
slough¹ (slŏ, slou) s. fangal *m; (state of despair)* estado de abatimiento.
slough² (slŭf) I. s. ZOOL. camisa II. intr. caerse; MED. desprenderse (costra) —tr. abandonar (hábito) ♦ **to s. off** deshacerse de.
slov·en (slŭv'ən) s. persona desaseada.
slov·en·ly (:lē) adj. desaseado.
slow (slō) I. adj. lento; *(clock)* atrasado; *(tardy)* atrasado; *(dense)* torpe; FAM. *(boring)* aburrido ♦ **business is s.** hay poca actividad • **my watch is five minutes s.** mi reloj tiene cinco minutos de retraso • **s. motion** cámara lenta • **to be s.** to tardar en II. adv. lentamente, despacio III. tr. *(to make slow)* reducir la marcha de; *(to retard)* retrasar —intr. ir más despacio ♦ **s. down!** ¡más despacio!
slow·down ('doun') s. retraso.
slow·ness (:nĭs) s. lentitud *f; (boredom)* pesadez *f; (stupidity)* torpeza.
slow·poke (:pōk') s. FAM. tortuga (persona).
slow-wit·ted (:wĭt'ĭd) adj. lento, torpe.
sludge (slŭj) s. cieno; *(sewage)* fango de alcantarillado; *(sediment)* sedimento.
slug¹ (slŭg) s. *(bullet)* bala; *(metal disk)* ficha; *(lump of metal)* trozo de metal; FAM. *(drink)* trago.
slug² s. ZOOL. babosa.
slug³ I. tr. **-gg-** pegar un porrazo II. s. porrazo.
slug·gish (slŭg'ĭsh) adj. *(slow)* lento; *(lazy)* perezoso; *(inactive)* flojo.
sluice (slōs) I. s. canal *m; (gate)* esclusa II. tr. *(to flush)* regar; *(to send down)* transportar por un canal.
slum (slŭm) I. s. barrio bajo II. intr. **-mm-** ♦ **to go slumming** visitar los barrios bajos.
slum·ber (slŭm'bər) I. intr. dormir; *(to doze)* dormitar II. s. sueño; *(dormancy)* sopor *m*.
slum·ber·ous/brous (:bər-əs/brəs) adj. *(asleep)* dormido; *(quiet)* tranquilo.
slump (slŭmp) I. intr. desplomarse; *(to slouch)* repantigarse II. s. disminución brusca; *(depression)* depresión *f*.
slung (slŭng) cf. **sling.**
slunk (slŭngk) cf. **slink.**
slur (slûr) I. tr. **-rr-** *(to treat lightly)* hacer poco caso de; *(to pronounce indistinctly)* pronunciar mal; *(to slander)* difamar; MÚS. ligar II. s. *(aspersion)* difamación *f; (blot)* mancha; MÚS. ligado.
slurp (slûrp) tr. & intr. *(to eat)* comer haciendo ruido; *(to drink)* beber haciendo ruido.
slush (slŭsh) s. *(melted snow)* aguanieve *f; (mud)* lodo.
slut (slŭt) s. mujerzuela.
sly (slī) adj. **-er, -est** o **-i-** *(cunning)* astuto; *(deceitful)* malicioso; *(roguish)* travieso.
smack¹ (smăk) I. tr. hacer un chasquido con los labios; *(to kiss)* besar sonoramente; *(to strike)* dar una palmada —intr. chasquear; *(to kiss)* dar un beso sonoro II. s. chasquido; *(kiss)* beso sonoro; *(blow)* golpe *m* III. adv. de lleno.
smack² I. s. *(flavor)* sabor *m; (trace)* indicio II. intr. saber ♦ **to s. of** oler a.
small (smôl) I. adj. pequeño; *(minor)* insignificante; *(petty)* mezquino; *(humiliated)* humillado ♦ **in a s. way** en pequeña escala • **s. fry** gente menuda • **s. letters** minúsculas • **s. talk** charloteo • **to feel s.** sentir vergüenza II. s. parte pequeña ♦ **the s. of the back** la región lumbar.

small·pox ('pŏks') s. viruela.
smart (smärt) **I.** adj. *(intelligent)* listo; *(witty)* ingenioso; *(impertinent)* impertinente; *(quick)* rápido; *(fashionable)* de moda **II.** intr. *(to sting)* escocer.
smart·en (smär'tn) intr. despabilarse.
smash (smăsh) **I.** tr. romper; *(to shatter)* destrozar; *(to throw)* estrellar; *(to crush)* aplastar —intr. romperse; *(to crash)* estrellarse; *(to be crushed)* hacerse pedazos **II.** s. *(breakage)* rotura; *(sound)* estrépito; *(collision)* choque *m*; FAM. *(hit)* éxito **III.** adj. ◆ **a s. hit** un gran éxito.
smash·up ('ŭp') s. choque *m*.
smat·ter·ing (smăt'ər-ĭng) s. conocimiento superficial.
smear (smîr) **I.** tr. untar; *(to dirty)* embadurnar; *(to vilify)* difamar **II.** s. mancha.
smell (smĕl) **I.** tr. **-ed** *o* **smelt, -lling** oler; *(to detect)* olfatear ◆ **I s. a rat** FAM. hay gato encerrado • **to s. out** olfatear —intr. oler; *(to stink)* apestar ◆ **smelling salts** sales aromáticas **II.** s. *(act)* olfateo; *(sense)* olfato; *(odor)* olor *m*.
smell·y ('ē) adj. **-i-** FAM. maloliente.
smelt[1] (smĕlt) tr. & intr. fundir.
smelt[2] s. [pl. inv. *o* **s**] ICT. eperlano.
smid·gen/gin (smĭj'ən) s. FAM. pizca.
smile (smīl) **I.** s. sonrisa **II.** intr. sonreír(se) —tr. expresar con una sonrisa ◆ **to s. on** favorecer.
smirch (smûrch) tr. manchar.
smirk (smûrk) **I.** intr. sonreír con afectación **II.** s. sonrisa afectada.
smite (smīt) tr. **smote, smitten** *o* **smote** golpear; *(to destroy)* destruir ◆ **to be smitten with** *(a girl)* estar encaprichado por.
smith (smĭth) s. herrero.
smith·y ('ē, smĭth'ē) s. herrería.
smock (smŏk) **I.** s. guardapolvo **II.** tr. COST. fruncir.
smog (smŏg) s. mezcla de humo y niebla.
smog·gy ('ē) adj. **-i-** lleno de humo y niebla.
smoke (smōk) **I.** s. humo; FAM. *(cigarette)* pitillo ◆ **s. bomb** bomba de humo • **s. detector** ahumadero • **s. screen** cortina de humo • **to go up in s.** irse en humo • **where there's there's fire** cuando el río suena, agua lleva **II.** intr. humear; *(tobacco)* fumar —tr. fumar; *(to preserve)* ahumar ◆ **to s. out** desalojar con humo; *(to reveal)* descubrir.
smoke·stack ('stăk') s. chimenea.
smok·y (smō'kē) adj. **-i-** *(fire)* humeante; *(room)* lleno de humo; *(color, taste)* ahumado.
smol·der (smōl'dər) **I.** intr. arder (sin llama); FIG. estar latente **II.** s. humo espeso.
smooch (smōōch) JER. **I.** s. beso **II.** intr. besuquearse.
smooth (smōōth) **I.** adj. *(fine)* liso; *(soft)* suave; *(calm)* tranquilo; *(fluid)* fluido; *(uneventful)* sin novedad; *(ingratiating)* meloso; *(refined)* refinado; *(unwrinkled)* sin arrugas ◆ **s. talk** zalamerías **II.** tr. *(to level)* alisar; *(to polish)* pulir; *(to soothe)* aliviar ◆ **to s. the way for** preparar el terreno para • **to s. things over** limar asperezas —intr. alisarse.
smooth-tongued ('tŭngd') adj. zalamero.
smote (smōt) cf. **smite**.
smoth·er (smŭth'ər) **I.** tr. sofocar; *(to conceal)* enterrar; *(to cover)* cubrir —intr. asfixiarse.
smoul·der (smōl'dər) var. de **smolder**.
smudge (smŭj) **I.** tr. *(to dirty)* manchar; *(to blur)* emborronar —intr. manchar(se) **II.** s. mancha; *(against insects)* humo para fumigar.
smug (smŭg) adj. **-gg-** presumido.
smug·gle (smŭg'əl) tr. pasar de contrabando —intr. contrabandear.
smug·gler (:lər) s. contrabandista *mf*.
smug·gling (:lĭng) s. contrabando.
smug·ness (smŭg'nĭs) s. presunción *f*.
smut (smŭt) s. *(particle)* hollín *m*; *(smudge)* mancha de tizne; *(obscenity)* obscenidad *f*.
smut·ty ('ē) adj. **-i-** *(dirty)* manchado; *(obscene)* obsceno.
snack (snăk) **I.** s. bocado ◆ **s. bar** cafetería **II.** intr. tomar(se) un bocado.
snag (snăg) **I.** s. protuberancia; *(submerged tree)* tronco sumergido; *(obstacle)* tropiezo **II.** tr. **-gg-** *(to tear)* rasgar; FAM. *(to catch)* agarrar —intr. rasgarse.
snail (snāl) s. caracol *m*.
snake (snāk) **I.** s. serpiente *f*; FIG. traidor *m* ◆ **s. in the grass** traidor **II.** tr. & intr. serpentear.
snake·skin ('skĭn') s. piel *f* de serpiente.
snap (snăp) **I.** intr. **-pp-** *(to click)* chasquear; *(to break)* quebrarse; *(to bite)* morder ◆ **s. out of it!** ¡anímate! • **to s. at** *(dog)* intentar morder; *(to speak harshly to)* hablar con brusquedad a • **to s. off** desprenderse • **to s. open, shut** abrirse, cerrarse de golpe —tr. *(to break)* quebrar; *(to utter)* decir bruscamente; *(fingers, whip)* chasquear ◆ **to s. up** llevarse **II.** s. *(sound)* chasquido; *(breaking)* rotura; *(of fingers)* castañeteo; *(clasp)* broche de presión; *(cookie)* galleta; *(brief spell)* ola (de frío); *(effortless task)* cosa fácil ◆ **put some s. into it!** ¡muévase! **III.** adj. rápido.
snap·per ('ər) s. [pl. inv. *o* **s**] cubera.
snap·py (:ē) adj. **-i-** FAM. *(brisk)* vivo, animado; *(smart)* elegante.
snap·shot (:shŏt') s. instantánea.
snare[1] (snâr) **I.** s. trampa **II.** tr. tender trampas; *(to trap)* cazar con trampa.
snare[2] s. MÚS. cuerda ◆ **s. drum** tambor.
snarl[1] (snärl) **I.** intr. gruñir; *(to speak angrily)* refunfuñar **II.** s. gruñido; *(hostile utterance)* refunfuño.
snarl[2] **I.** s. *(tangle)* maraña; *(predicament)* enredo **II.** tr. & intr. enredar(se).
snatch (snăch) **I.** tr. agarrar, arrebatar; *(illicitly)* secuestrar —intr. arrebatar **II.** s. arrebatamiento; *(fragment)* pedacito ◆ **in snatches** a ratos.
snaz·zy (snăz'ē) adj. **-i-** JER. llamativo.
sneak (snēk) **I.** intr. andar a hurtadillas —tr. hacer furtivamente **II.** s. persona cobarde; *(exit)* salida disimulada ◆ **s. thief** ratero.
sneak·er (snē'kər) s. zapato de lona.
sneak·y (:kē) adj. **-i-** furtivo; *(surreptitious)* solapado.
sneer (snîr) **I.** s. gesto de desprecio **II.** intr. hacer un gesto de desprecio.
sneeze (snēz) **I.** intr. estornudar **II.** s. estornudo.
sneez·ing (snē'zĭng) s. estornudo.
snick·er (snĭk'ər) **I.** intr. reírse disimuladamente **II.** s. risita.
snide (snīd) adj. sarcástico.
sniff (snĭf) **I.** intr. aspirar por la nariz; *(in contempt)* despreciar —tr. *(odor)* olfatear; *(drug)* inhalar **II.** s. aspiración *f*; *(smelling)* olfateo.
snif·fle ('əl) **I.** intr. resollar; *(to whimper)* lloriquear **II.** s. resuello; *(whimper)* lloriqueo ◆ pl.

FAM. resfriado.
snif·ter (snĭf´tər) s. copa para coñac.
snig·ger (snĭg´ər) I. s. risa disimulada II. intr. reír disimuladamente.
snip (snĭp) I. tr. & intr. **-pp-** tijeretear II. s. *(action)* tijeretazo; *(piece)* recorte m.
snipe (snĭp) I. s. [pl. inv. o **s**] agachadiza II. intr. *(shots)* tirar desde una posición emboscada; *(remarks)* atacar solapadamente.
snip·er (snī´pər) s. francotirador m.
snip·pet (snĭp´ĭt) s. recorte m.
snip·py (snĭp´ē) adj. **-i-** FAM. impertinente.
snit (snĭt) JER. s. arranque m de cólera ♦ **to be in a s.** estar enfadado.
snitch (snĭch) JER. I. tr. birlar —intr. soplar II. s. soplón m.
sniv·el (snĭv´əl) intr. gimotear; *(to run at the nose)* moquear.
snob (snŏb) s. snob m.
snob·ber·y (´ə-rē) s. snobismo.
snob·bish (:ĭsh) adj. como un snob.
snood (snō͞od) s. redecilla.
snoop (snō͞op) FAM. I. intr. entrometerse ♦ **to s. around** husmear II. s. curioso, entrometido.
snoop·y (snō͞o´pē) adj. **-i-** FAM. entrometido.
snoot (snō͞ot) s. JER. *(snout)* hocico; *(nose)* nariz f; *(snob)* snob m.
snoot·y (snō͞o´tē) adj. **-i-** JER. altanero.
snooze (snō͞oz) FAM. I. intr. dormitar II. s. sueño ligero.
snore (snôr) I. intr. roncar II. s. ronquido.
snor·kel (snôr´kəl) I. s. tubo de respiración II. intr. bucear con tubo de respiración.
snort (snôrt) I. s. bufido; JER. *(a drink)* trago II. intr. bufar —tr. JER. *(drugs)* inhalar.
snot (snŏt) s. JER. moco; *(person)* mocoso.
snot·ty (´ē) adj. **-i-** FAM. mocoso; *(angry)* de mal humor.
snout (snout) s. hocico; JER. *(nose)* nariz f.
snow (snō) I. s. nieve f; *(snowfall)* nevada ♦ **s. job** JER. engaño ♦ **s. tire** neumático para nieve II. intr. nevar —tr. *(to cover)* cubrir con nieve; JER. *(to flatter)* adular; *(to deceive)* embaucar ♦ **to s. under** abrumar.
snow·ball (´bôl´) I. s. bola de nieve II. intr. aumentar rápidamente.
snow·bank (:băngk´) s. montón m de nieve.
snow·drift (:drĭft´) s. ventisquero.
snow·fall (:fôl´) s. nevada.
snow·man (:măn´) s. [pl. **-men**] muñeco de nieve.
snow·mo·bile (:mō-bēl´) s. vehículo automotor para ir por la nieve.
snow·plow (:plou´) s. quitanieves m.
snow·shoe (:shō͞o´) I. s. raqueta II. intr. caminar sobre la nieve con raquetas.
snow·storm (:stôrm´) s. tormenta de nieve.
snow·suit (:sō͞ot´) s. traje m que usan los niños en la nieve.
snow·y (:ē) adj. **-i-** nevado; *(subject to snow)* nevoso; *(white)* blanco como la nieve.
snub (snŭb) I. tr. **-bb-** *(to slight)* desairar; *(to stop)* parar bruscamente II. s. desaire m; *(stop)* parada brusca.
snub-nosed (´nōzd´) adj. de nariz chata.
snuff¹ (snŭf) tr. & intr. aspirar; *(to sniff)* oler.
snuff² I. s. *(of candle)* pabilo II. tr. despabilar; *(to extinguish)* apagar ♦ **to s. out** destruir.
snuff³ s. *(tobacco)* rapé m ♦ **to be up to s.** FAM. ser satisfactorio.
snuff·box (´bŏks´) s. caja de rapé.
snuf·fle (snŭf´əl) I. intr. resollar II. s. resuello

♦ pl. FAM. resfrío.
snug (snŭg) adj. **-gg-** *(cozy)* cómodo; *(warm)* calentito; *(tight)* ajustado ♦ **to be as s. as a bug in a rug** estar muy cómodo.
snug·gle (snŭg´əl) tr. & intr. acurrucar(se).
so (sō) I. adv. *(thus)* así, de esta manera; *(to such an extent)* de tal manera, tan; *(consequently)* por eso; *(approximately)* así de <the wound was so wide la herida era así de ancha>; *(likewise)* también <you were on time and so was I tú llegaste a tiempo y yo también>; *(so much)* tanto; *(then)* así que ♦ **and so on and so forth** y así sucesivamente • **how so?** ¿cómo es eso? • **if so** si es así • **I hope so** eso espero, espero que sí • **is that so?** ¿es verdad?, ¿ah, sí? • **I think so** creo que sí • **I told you so!** ¡ya te lo dije! • **it just so happens that** pues resulta que • **just so** ni más ni menos • **not so** no es así • **not so much as** ni siquiera • **or so** más o menos • **so as to** a fin de • **so far** hasta aquí; *(point)* hasta cierto punto • **so far as** hasta donde • **so far as I'm concerned** por lo que a mí respecta • **so far as I know** que yo sepa • **so far so good** por ahora, bien • **so it is!** ¡así es! • **so long** tanto (tiempo); *(good-bye)* hasta luego • **so long as** mientras que • **so many** tantos • **so much for** vaya • **so so** así, así • **so that** de manera que • **so then** así pues • **so to speak** por decirlo así • **so what?** ¿y qué? • **to be so kind as to** tener la bondad de II. adj. así III. conj. así que ♦ **so that** para que, a fin de que IV. pron. lo mismo.
soak (sōk) I. tr. empapar; *(to immerse)* remojar; *(to absorb)* absorber; JER. *(to overcharge)* cobrar demasiado ♦ **to s. to the skin** calar hasta los huesos —intr. remojarse; *(to penetrate)* infiltrarse ♦ **to s. through** penetrar; *(to drench)* calar II. s. remojo.
soak·ing (sō´kĭng) I. s. remojón m II. adj. empapado ♦ **s. wet** calado hasta los huesos.
so-and-so (sō´ən-sō´) s. Fulano de Tal.
soap (sōp) I. s. jabón m ♦ **s. opera** serial m II. tr. (en)jabonar.
soap·stone (´stōn´) s. esteatita.
soap·y (sō´pē) adj. **-i-** jabonoso.
soar (sôr) intr. *(to rise)* remontarse; *(to ascend)* elevarse súbitamente; AER. planear.
sob (sŏb) I. intr. **-bb-** sollozar II. s. sollozo.
so·ber (sō´bər) I. adj. **-er, -est** sobrio; *(serious)* grave; *(reasonable)* cuerdo II. tr. desembriagar —intr. ♦ **to s. up** pasársele a uno la embriaguez.
so·bri·e·ty (sō-brī´ĭ-tē) s. sobriedad f; *(seriousness)* seriedad f.
so·bri·quet (sō´brĭ-kā´) s. apodo.
so-called (sō´kôld´) adj. llamado.
soc·cer (sŏk´ər) s. fútbol m.
so·cia·ble (sō´shə-bəl) s. sociable; *(friendly)* amistoso.
so·cial (sō´shəl) I. adj. social; *(sociable)* sociable ♦ **s. climber** arribista • **s. column** ecos de sociedad • **s. disease** enfermedad venérea • **s. services** programa de asistencia social • **s. work** asistencia social II. s. reunión f.
so·cial·ist (sō´shə-lĭst) s. & adj. socialista mf.
so·cial·is·tic (´-lĭs´tĭk) adj. socialista.
so·cial·ite (´-līt´) s. persona de alta sociedad.
so·cial·ize (:līz´) I. tr. socializar; *(to make sociable)* volver sociable ♦ **socialized medicine** medicina estatal —intr. alternar.
so·ci·e·tal (sə-sī´ĭ-tl) adj. social.
so·ci·e·ty (sə-sī´ĭ-tē) s. sociedad f; *(upper class)*

alta sociedad; *(companionship)* compañía ♦ **high s.** alta sociedad • **s.** page noticias de la sociedad • **to go into s.** ser presentada en sociedad.

so·ci·o·ec·o·nom·ic (sō'sē-ō-ĕk'ə-nŏm'ĭk) adj. socioeconómico.

so·ci·o·log·i·cal (:ə-lŏj'ĭ-kəl) adj. sociológico.

so·ci·ol·o·gist (:ŏl'ə-jĭst) s. sociólogo.

so·ci·ol·o·gy (:jē) s. sociología.

so·ci·o·path (sō'sē-ə-păth') s. persona antisocial.

so·ci·o·po·lit·i·cal ('-ō-pə-lĭt'ĭ-kəl) adj. sociopolítico.

sock¹ (sŏk) I. s. [pl. **s** o **sox**] calcetín m II. tr. ♦ **to s. away** FAM. guardar (dinero).

sock² JER. I. tr. golpear II. s. puñetazo.

sock·et (sŏk'ĭt) s. hueco; *(of bulb)* casquillo; *(connection)* enchufe m (hembra); *(eye)* cuenca.

sod (sŏd) I. s. *(lawn)* césped m; *(piece)* tepe m II. tr. **-dd-** cubrir de césped.

so·da (sō'də) s. carbonato de sodio; *(sodium oxide)* sosa; *(water)* gaseosa; *(refreshment)* soda ♦ **s. fountain** mostrador en el que se despachan bebidas gaseosas y helados • **s. pop** FAM. soda, gaseosa.

so·dal·i·ty (sō-dăl'ĭ-tē) s. RELIG. cofradía; *(fellowship)* asociación f.

sod·den (sŏd'n) adj. *(wet)* empapado; *(food, mind)* pesado.

so·di·um (sō'dē-əm) s. sodio ♦ **s. bicarbonate, chloride** bicarbonato, cloruro de sodio.

sod·om·y (sŏd'ə-mē) s. sodomía.

so·fa (sō'fə) s. sofá m.

soft (sôft) adj. *(not hard)* blando; *(not loud)* bajo; *(gentle, smooth)* suave; *(tender)* tierno; *(lenient)* indulgente; *(weak)* débil; FAM. *(easy)* fácil <a s. job un trabajo fácil> ♦ **s. drink** gaseosa • **s. in the head** estúpido • **to be s. on** ser indulgente con.

soft-boiled ('boild') adj. *(egg)* pasado por agua; FAM. *(sentimental)* sensiblero.

soft·en (sô'fən) tr. & intr. ablandar(se).

soft·heart·ed (sôft'här'tĭd) adj. compasivo.

soft·ness (:nĭs) s. suavidad f, blandura; *(weakness)* debilidad f; *(tenderness)* dulzura.

soft-spo·ken (:spō'kən) adj. de voz suave; *(genial)* afable.

soft·ware (:wâr') s. software m.

sog·gy (sŏg'ē) adj. **-i-** empapado.

soil¹ (soil) s. *(land)* tierra.

soil² I. tr. *(to dirty)* ensuciar; *(to disgrace)* manchar II. s. *(dirtiness)* suciedad f; *(stain)* mancha; *(excrement)* excremento.

soiled (soild) adj. sucio, manchado.

so·journ (sō'jûrn') I. intr. residir temporalmente II. s. residencia temporal, estada.

sol·ace (sŏl'ĭs) I. s. consuelo II. tr. consolar.

so·lar (sō'lər) adj. solar.

so·lar·i·um (sō-lâr'ē-əm) s. [pl. **s** o **-ia**] solana.

sold (sōld) cf. **sell.**

sol·der (sŏd'ər) I. s. soldadura II. tr. soldar.

sol·dier (sōl'jər) I. s. soldado ♦ **s. of fortune** mercenario II. intr. servir como soldado.

sold-out (sōld'out') adj. agotado.

sole¹ (sōl) I. s. *(of foot)* planta; *(of shoe)* suela II. tr. poner suela a (zapato, bota).

sole² adj. *(single)* único <his s. aim su único propósito>; *(rights, ownership)* exclusivo.

sole³ s. [pl. inv. o **-s**] ICT. lenguado.

sol·emn (sŏl'əm) adj. solemne; *(sacred)* sagrado.

so·lem·ni·ty (sə-lĕm'nĭ-tē) s. solemnidad f.

so·lic·it (sə-lĭs'ĭt) tr. solicitar; *(prostitute)* abordar —intr. hacer una petición.

so·lic·i·ta·tion (-'ĭ-tā'shən) s. solicitación f.

so·lic·i·tor (-'-tər) s. *(chief law officer)* procurador m; G.B. *(lawyer)* abogado.

so·lic·i·tous (:təs) adj. solícito, atento.

so·lic·i·tude (:tōōd') s. solicitud f, cuidado.

sol·id (sŏl'ĭd) I. adj. sólido; *(not hollow)* macizo <s. gold de oro macizo>; *(line)* continuo; *(fact)* seguro; *(citizen)* modelo; *(unanimous)* unánime; *(of color)* uniforme ♦ **s. as a rock** firme como una roca II. s. sólido.

sol·i·dar·i·ty (sŏl'ĭ-dăr'ĭ-tē) s. solidaridad f.

so·lid·i·fy (sə-lĭd'ə-fī') tr. & intr. solidificar(se).

so·lid·i·ty (:ĭ-tē) s. solidez f.

sol·id·ly (sŏl'ĭd-lē) adv. sólidamente; *(unanimously)* unánimemente; *(non-stop)* sin parar.

so·lil·o·quy (sə-lĭl'ə-kwē) s. soliloquio.

sol·i·taire (sŏl'ĭ-târ') s. solitario.

sol·i·tar·y (sŏl'ĭ-tĕr'ē) I. adj. solitario; *(single)* solo ♦ **s. confinement** incomunicación II. s. solitario; FAM. *(prison)* incomunicación f.

sol·i·tude (:tōōd') s. soledad f.

so·lo (sō'lō) I. adj. & s. solo II. adv. a solas III. intr. volar solo.

so·lo·ist (:ĭst) s. solista mf.

sol·stice (sŏl'stĭs) s. solsticio.

sol·u·ble (sŏl'yə-bəl) adj. soluble.

sol·ute (:yōōt') s. soluto, substancia disuelta.

so·lu·tion (sə-lōō'shən) s. solución f.

solv·a·ble (sŏl'və-bəl) adj. soluble.

solve (sŏlv) tr. resolver, solucionar.

sol·ven·cy (sŏl'vən-sē) s. solvencia.

sol·vent (:vənt) I. adj. COM. solvente; QUÍM. disolvente II. s. solvente m, disolvente m.

som·ber (sŏm'bər) adj. sombrío.

some (sŭm) I. adj. alguno(s); *(s. people* algunas personas>; *(a little)* algo de, un poco de; cierto <after s. time después de cierto tiempo>; unos (cuantos), varios <s. days ago hace varios días>; IRÓN. menudo <s. advice! ¡menudo consejo!>; *(remarkable)* extraordinario ♦ **s. luck!** ¡vaya suerte! • **s. other time** otro día, otro momento • **s. way or other** de una manera u otra II. pron. *(several)* algunos; *(a little)* un poco, algo ♦ **and then s.** y más todavía III. adv. unos <s. forty people unas cuarenta personas>; FAM. *(somewhat)* un poco, algo.

some·bod·y ('bŏd'ē) I. pron. alguien II. s. FAM. alguien m, personaje m <he thinks he's s. se cree alguien>.

some·day (:dā') adv. algún día, un día de éstos.

some·how (:hou') adv. de algún modo, de alguna manera; *(for some reason)* por alguna razón.

some·one (:wŭn') cf. **somebody.**

some·place (:plās') adv. en o a alguna parte.

som·er·sault (sŭm'ər-sôlt') I. s. salto mortal; FIG. cambio total (de opinión) II. intr. dar un salto mortal.

some·thing (sŭm'thĭng) I. pron. & s. algo ♦ **or s.** o algo por el estilo • **s. or another** una cosa u otra • **to be quite s.** ser algo extraordinario • **to be s.** ser de alguna importancia • **to be s. of a . . .** tener algo de . . . • **to have a certain s.** tener un no sé qué II. adv. algo; *(extremely)* sumamente.

some·time (:tīm') I. adv. alguna vez, algún día ♦ **s. soon** pronto II. adj. *(former)* ex, antiguo.

some·times (:tīmz′) adv. de vez en cuando, a veces.

some·way (:wā′) adv. de alguna manera.

some·what (:hwŏt′) adv. algo.

some·where (:hwâr′) adv. en *o* a alguna parte; *(approximately)* más o menos, entre ♦ **s. near here** por aquí • **s. or other** en alguna parte.

som·nam·bu·list (sŏm-năm′byə-lĭst) s. sonámbulo.

som·no·lence (sŏm′nə-ləns) s. somnolencia.

som·no·lent (:lənt) adj. soñoliento.

son (sŭn) s. hijo.

so·nar (sō′när′) s. sonar m.

song (sông) s. canción *f*; *(act)* canto, cantar *m*; *(poetry)* canto ♦ **for a s.** por poca cosa • **same old s.** FAM. (la misma) cantilena • **to give someone a s. and dance** FAM. contarle a alguien toda una historia.

song·bird ('bûrd′) s. cantor *m*, ave canora.

song·ster (:stər) s. cantante *mf*.

song·writ·er (:rī′ tər) s. compositor *m*.

son·ic (sŏn′ĭk) adj. sónico, acústico ♦ **s. boom** estampido supersónico.

son-in-law (sŭn′ĭn-lô′) s. [pl. **sons-**] yerno, hijo político.

son·net (sŏn′ĭt) s. soneto.

son·ny (sŭn′ē) s. FAM. hijito.

so·nor·i·ty (sə-nôr′ĭ-tē) s. sonoridad *f.*

so·no·rous (sə-nôr′əs, sŏn′ər-) adj. sonoro.

soon (sōōn) adv. pronto; *(early)* temprano <*back so s.?* ¿de vuelta tan temprano?> ♦ **as s. as** en cuanto, tan pronto como • **had sooner** preferiría • **how s.?** ¿cuándo (a más tardar)? • **no sooner said than done** dicho y hecho • **s. after** poco después • **the sooner the better** cuanto más pronto, mejor • **sooner or later** tarde o temprano.

soot (sŏt) s. hollín *m*, tizne *m.*

soothe (sōōth) tr. calmar, tranquilizar; *(pain)* aliviar.

sooth·ing (sōō′thĭng) adj. tranquilizador.

sooth·say·er (sōōth′sā′ ər) s. adivino.

soot·y (sŏt′ē) adj. -i- tiznado; *(dark)* ennegrecido.

sop (sŏp) I. tr. & intr. -pp- remojar(se) ♦ **to s. up** absorber II. s. dádiva (para apaciguar).

so·phis·ti·cate (sə-fĭs′tĭ-kĭt) s. persona sofisticada.

so·phis·ti·cat·ed (:kā′tĭd) adj. sofisticado; *(complicated)* complejo.

so·phis·ti·ca·tion (-′-′shən) s. sofisticación *f.*

soph·is·try (sŏf′ĭ-strē) s. sofistería.

soph·o·more (sŏf′ə-môr′) s. estudiante *mf* de segundo año.

soph·o·mor·ic ('-′ĭk) adj. inmaduro.

sop·o·rif·ic (sŏp′ə-rĭf′ĭk) adj. & s. soporífico.

sop·ping (sŏp′ĭng) I. adj. empapado II. adv. ♦ **s. wet** *(thing)* empapado; *(person)* calado hasta los huesos.

so·pran·o (sə-prăn′ō) s. soprano *mf.*

sor·cer·er (sôr′sər-ər) s. hechicero, brujo.

sor·cer·ess (:ĭs) s. hechicera, bruja.

sor·cer·y (sôr′sə-rē) s. hechicería, brujería.

sor·did (sôr′dĭd) adj. sórdido.

sore (sôr) I. adj. dolorido; FAM. *(offended)* molesto ♦ **s. point** asunto delicado • **s. throat** dolor de garganta • **to be s.** doler <*my throat is s.* me duele la garganta>; FAM. *(mad)* estar enfadado *(at* con) • **to get s.** ofenderse II. s. *(wound)* llaga; *(pain)* dolor *m.*

sore·ly (′lē) adv. *(a lot)* mucho; *(very)* muy.

sor·ghum (sôr′gəm) s. sorgo.

so·ror·i·ty (sə-rôr′ĭ-tē) s. asociación estudiantil femenina.

sor·rel¹ (sôr′əl) s. BOT. acedera.

sor·rel² s. *(color, horse)* alazán *m.*

sor·row (sôr′ō) I. s. *(sadness)* pesar *m*, dolor *m*; *(grieving)* duelo II. intr. sentir pena.

sor·row·ful (sôr′ə-fəl) adj. *(person)* pesaroso; *(news)* doloroso.

sor·ry (sôr′ē) I. adj. -i- *(sad)* triste; *(wretched)* infeliz; *(paltry)* insignificante ♦ **I'm s.** lo siento • **to be s.** sentir <*I'm s. to be late* siento llegar tarde> • **to feel s. for** compadecer • **to feel s. for oneself** sentirse desgraciado • **you'll be s.!** ¡te arrepentirás! II. interj. ¡perdón!

sort (sôrt) I. s. *(class)* clase *f*, tipo; *(type)* especie *f*; *(person)* tipo ♦ **after a s.** de mala manera • **it's s. of big** es más bien grande • **nothing of the s.!** ¡nada de eso! • **of sorts** una especie de • **out of sorts** de mal humor • **something of the s.** algo por el estilo II. tr. *(to classify)* clasificar; *(to put in order)* ordenar ♦ **to s. out** *(to separate)* separar; *(problems)* resolver.

sor·tie (sôr′tē) s. MIL. salida.

so-so (sō′sō′) adj. & adv. regular.

sot (sŏt) s. borracho.

sought (sôt) cf. **seek.**

soul (sōl) s. alma; personificación *f* <*the s. of honor* la personificación del honor> ♦ **poor s.** pobre • **to search one's s.** examinar la conciencia.

soul·ful ('fəl) adj. sentimental.

soul-search·ing (:sûr′chĭng) s. examen *m* de conciencia.

sound¹ (sound) I. s. sonido ♦ **from the s. of it** al parecer • **I don't like the s. of it** no me huele bien • **to the s. of** al son de • **s. barrier** barrera del sonido • **s. effects** efectos sonoros • **s. stage** estudio para filmar con sonido II. intr. sonar; *(to seem)* parecer ♦ **to s. off** MIL. marcar el paso; *(to express)* protestar a voz en grito —tr. *(instrument)* tocar; *(alarm)* dar; MED. auscultar.

sound² adj. en buenas condiciones; *(healthy)* sano; *(firm)* firme; *(economy)* fuerte; *(reason)* válido; *(knowledge)* completo; *(sleep)* profundo; *(defeat)* total; *(trustworthy)* de confianza; *(advice)* razonable; DER. válido ♦ **to be s. of mind** estar uno en su sano juicio.

sound³ s. MARÍT. estrecho, brazo de mar.

sound⁴ tr. *(to fathom)* sondear ♦ **to s. out** sondear —intr. sondear; *(whale)* sumergirse.

sound·ing¹ (soun′dĭng) s. GEOL., MARÍT. sondeo.

sound·ing² adj. resonante ♦ **s. board** MÚS. tabla de armonía; *(spokesman)* portavoz.

sound·less (:lĭs) adj. silencioso, mudo.

sound·ly (:lē) adv. *(solidly)* sólidamente; *(deeply)* profundamente; *(thoroughly)* del todo.

sound·ness (:nĭs) s. *(solidity)* solidez *f*; *(validity)* validez *f*; *(good sense)* sensatez *f.*

sound·proof (:prōōf′) I. adj. insonoro, a prueba de sonido II. tr. insonorizar.

sound·track (:trăk′) s. pista *o* banda sonora.

soup (sōōp) s. sopa ♦ **from s. to nuts** de cabo a rabo • **s. kitchen** comedor de beneficencia • **to be in the s.** JER. estar en un apuro • **to s. up** AUTO. aumentar la potencia de.

soup·spoon ('spōōn′) s. cuchara de sopa.

soup·y (sōō′pē) adj. -i- *(liquid)* espeso; *(foggy)* con niebla espesa.

sour (sour) I. adj. agrio; *(milk)* cortado; *(smell)* acre ♦ **to turn** *o* **go s.** *(wine, mood)* agriarse; *(milk)* cortarse; *(deal)* fracasar **II.** tr. & intr. *(wine, mood)* agriar(se); *(milk)* cortar(se); *(person)* amargar(se).

source (sôrs) s. origen *m; (of river)* manantial *m; (of supply, information)* fuente *f.*

sour·dough (sour'dō') s. *(leaven)* levadura; JER. *(prospector)* cateador *m.*

souse (sous) **I.** tr. *(to drench)* empapar; JER. *(to make drunk)* emborrachar **II.** s. CUL. carne conservada en vinagre; JER. *(drunkard)* borracho.

south (south) **I.** s. sur *m* **II.** adj. del sur, austral **III.** adv. hacia el sur.

south·bound ('bound') adj. con rumbo al sur.

south·east (-ēst') **I.** s. sudeste *m* **II.** adj. del sudeste **III.** adv. hacia el sudeste.

south·east·ern (:ē'stərn) adj. del sudeste.

south·er·ly (sŭth'ər-lē) adj. del sur.

south·ern (:ərn) adj. del sur.

south·ern·er (:ər-nər) s. habitante *mf* del sur, sureño; HIST. sudista *mf.*

south·paw (south'pô') s. JER. zurdo.

south·ward (:wərd) adv. hacia el sur.

south·west (-wĕst') **I.** s. suroeste *m,* sudoeste *m* **II.** adj. del sudoeste **III.** adv. hacia el sudoeste.

south·west·ern (:wĕs'tərn) adj. del sudoeste.

sou·ve·nir (sōō'və-nîr') s. recuerdo.

sov·er·eign (sŏv'ər-ĭn) adj. & s. soberano.

sov·er·eign·ty (:tē) s. soberanía.

sow¹ (sō) tr. **-ed, -ed** *o* **-n** sembrar.

sow² (sou) s. *(female hog)* cerda.

soy (soi) s. soja ♦ **s. sauce** salsa de soja.

soy·a (':ə) s. soja *(semilla).*

soy·bean (:bēn') s. soja.

spa (spä) s. *(mineral spring)* manantial *m* de agua mineral; *(resort)* balneario.

space (spās) **I.** s. espacio; *(blank)* espacio en blanco; *(place)* sitio, lugar *m <it takes up too much s.* ocupa demasiado sitio> ♦ **outer s.** espacio exterior • **s. age, suit** era, traje espacial • **s. bar** espaciador • **s. shuttle** transbordador espacial • **to stare into s.** tener la mirada perdida **II.** tr. espaciar, distanciar ♦ **to s. out** separar, distanciar —intr. **to s. out** JER. abstraerse.

space·craft ('krăft') s.inv. astronave *f.*

space·flight (:flīt') s. vuelo espacial.

space·man (:măn') s. [pl. **-men**] astronauta *mf.*

space·ship (:shĭp') s. nave *f* espacial.

spac·ing (spā'sĭng) s. espaciamiento.

spa·cious (:shəs) adj. espacioso, amplio.

spa·cy (:ē) adj. **-i-** JER. *(vacant)* vago, abstraído; *(weird)* extraño.

spade¹ (spād) **I.** s. *(digging tool)* pala ♦ **to call a s. a s.** llamar al pan pan y al vino vino **II.** tr. remover con pala.

spade² s. *(cards)* espada, pico.

spa·ghet·ti (spə-gĕt'ē) s. espagueti *m.*

span¹ (spăn) **I.** s. *(breadth)* anchura; *(of wings)* envergadura; *(of bridge)* ojo; *(arched support)* arcada; *(of hand)* palmo; *(period of time)* duración *f* **II.** tr. **-nn-** *(to extend across)* cruzar, atravesar; *(to measure by hand)* medir en palmos; *(in time)* durar.

span² pareja de caballos o bueyes).

span·gle (spăng'gəl) s. lentejuela.

span·gled (:gəld) adj. *(costume)* adornado con lentejuelas, *(star-studded)* estrellado.

span·iel (spăn'yəl) s. perro de aguas.

Span·ish-speak·ing (spăn'ĭsh-spē'kĭng) adj. hispanoparlante, hispanohablante.

spank (spăngk) **I.** tr. dar una zurra a, zurrar —intr. ir de prisa **II.** s. zurra.

spank·ing (spăng'kĭng) **I.** adj. FAM. *(breeze)* fresco **II.** s. zurra.

spar¹ (spär) s. MARÍT. palo.

spar² intr. **-rr-** *(in boxing)* entrenarse; *(to dispute)* discutir, pelear.

spare (spâr) **I.** s. *(expenses, efforts)* escatimar; *(strength)* reservar; *(to avoid)* evitar *<they spared him the trouble* le evitaron la molestia de hacerlo>; *(not to destroy)* perdonar; *(to save)* salvar; *(to do without)* prescindir de; *(to afford)* dar, dedicar *<I can't s. the time* no puedo dedicar el tiempo>; *(feelings)* no herir ♦ **to s.** de sobra • **to s. oneself** ahorrarse trabajos **II.** adj. *(part)* de repuesto, de recambio; *(extra)* sobrante, de sobra *<s. cash* dinero sobrante>; *(unoccupied)* libre *<in my s. time* en mis ratos libres>; *(thin)* delgado, enjuto ♦ **s. room** cuarto en desuso **III.** s. pieza de repuesto.

spare·ribs ('rĭbz') s.pl. costillas de cerdo.

spar·ing (:ĭng) adj. *(frugal)* frugal, económico; *(scarce)* parco; *(lenient)* indulgente.

spark¹ (spärk) **I.** s. chispa ♦ **to give off sparks** echar chispas **II.** intr. echar chispas, chispear —tr. provocar ♦ **to s. off** provocar.

spark² s. *(dandy)* petimetre *m,* pisaverde *m; (gallant)* galán *m* **II.** tr. & intr. galantear.

spar·kle (spär'kəl) **I.** intr. *(to glitter)* centellear, brillar; *(with wit)* chispear; *(to effervesce)* burbujear **II.** s. *(glitter)* centelleo, destello; *(vivacity)* viveza, burbujeo.

spar·kler (:klər) s. cohete chispero.

spark·plug (spärk'plŭg') s. AUTO. bujía.

spar·row (spăr'ō) s. gorrión *m.*

sparse (spärs) adj. disperso, infrecuente.

spasm (spăz'əm) s. espasmo; FIG. arrebato.

spas·mod·ic (spăz-mŏd'ĭk) adj. espasmódico.

spas·tic (spăs'tĭk) adj. & s. espástico.

spat¹ (spăt) adj.) cf. **spit¹.**

spat² s. *(gaiter)* polaina ♦ pl. polainas.

spat³ **I.** s. *(quarrel)* riña, pelea **II.** intr. **-tt-** reñir, pelear.

spa·tial (spā'shəl) adj. espacial.

spat·ter (spăt'ər) **I.** tr. & intr. salpicar **II.** s. salpicadura.

spat·u·la (spăch'ə-lə) s. espátula.

spawn (spôn) **I.** s. *(of fish)* freza, hueva; *(outcome)* resultado; *(offspring)* engendro **II.** intr. ICT. frezar —tr. FIG. engendrar, producir.

spay (spā) tr. VET. quitar los ovarios.

speak (spēk) intr. **spoke, spoken** hablar; *(to express oneself)* expresarse; *(in assembly)* tomar la palabra; FIG. decir, expresar *<facts s. more than words* los hechos dicen más que las palabras> ♦ **so to s.** por así decirlo • **to be on speaking terms** hablarse, tener buenas relaciones • **to s. of** mencionar *<there is nothing to s. of* no hay nada que mencionar> • **to s. out** hablar claro • **to s. up** *(louder)* hablar más fuerte; *(to be heard)* decir lo que uno piensa —tr. *(to tell)* decir *<I s. the truth* digo la verdad>; *(a language)* hablar; *(to reveal)* revelar, expresar ♦ **to s. for** *(to recommend)* hablar en favor de; *(on behalf of)* hablar en nombre de • **to s. for itself** ser evidente • **to s. well, ill of** hablar bien, mal de.

speak·er (spē'kər) s. persona que habla; *(spokesperson)* portavoz *m; (orator)* orador *m; (lecturer)* conferenciante *mf,* conferencista *mf; (loudspeaker)* altoparlante *m,* altavoz *m.*

spear (spîr) **I.** s. lanza; *(for fishing)* arpón *m;* BOT. brizna **II.** tr. traspasar, atravesar (con

una lanza); *(fish)* arponear.
spear·head ('hĕd') I. s. punta de lanza; MIL., FIG. vanguardia II. tr. encabezar.
spear·mint (:mĭnt') s. hierbabuena.
spe·cial (spĕsh'əl) I. adj. especial; *(in particular)* de particular <*nothing s.* nada de particular>; *(superior)* superior; *(friend)* íntimo; *(edition, flight)* extraordinario ♦ s. delivery entrega inmediata II. s. TELEV. programa *m* especial.
spe·cial·ist (:ə-lĭst) s. especialista *mf.*
spe·ci·al·i·ty ('ĕ-ăl'ĭ-tē) s. especialidad *f.*
spe·cial·i·za·tion (:ə-lĭ-zā'shən) s. especialización *f.*
spe·cial·ize (spĕsh'ə-līz') intr. especializarse; BIOL. diferenciarse.
spe·cial·ly (:ə-lē) adv. especialmente, en particular.
spe·cial·ty (:əl-tē) s. especialidad *f.*
spe·cie (spē'shē, :sē) s. metálico, efectivo.
spe·cies (spē'shēz, :sēz) s.inv. especie *f.*
spe·cif·ic (spĭ-sĭf'ĭk) I. adj. específico ♦ s. gravity peso específico II. s. cualidad específica.
spec·i·fi·ca·tion (spĕs'ə-fĭ-kā'shən) s. especificación *f.*
spec·i·fy (spĕs'ə-fī') tr. especificar.
spec·i·men (spĕs'ə-mən) s. *(sample)* muestra, ejemplar *m;* BIOL. espécimen *m.*
spe·cious (spē'shəs) adj. especioso.
speck (spĕk) I. s. *(small spot)* mancha, mota; *(particle)* partícula II. tr. motear.
speck·le (spĕk'əl) I. s. *(speck)* mancha, mota; *(freckle)* peca II. tr. motear, salpicar de manchas.
speck·led (:əld) adj. *(spotted)* moteado, salpicado de manchas; *(freckled)* pecoso.
specs (spĕks) s.pl. FAM. *(eyeglasses)* gafas; *(specifications)* especificaciones *f.*
spec·ta·cle (spĕk'tə-kəl) s. espectáculo ♦ to make a s. of oneself ponerse en ridículo ♦ pl. gafas.
spec·tac·u·lar (:tăk'yə-lər) I. adj. espectacular, grandioso II. s. TEAT. espectáculo.
spec·ta·tor (spĕk'tā'tər) s. espectador *m.*
spec·ter (spĕk'tər) s. espectro.
spec·tral (:trəl) adj. espectral.
spec·tro·graph (:trə-grăf') s. espectrógrafo.
spec·u·late (spĕk'yə-lāt') intr. especular.
spec·u·la·tion ('-lā'shən) s. especulación *f.*
spec·u·la·tive ('-lə-tĭv) adj. especulativo.
spec·u·la·tor (:lā'tər) s. especulador *m.*
spec·u·lum (spĕk'yə-ləm) s. [pl. **s** *o* **-la**] ÓPT. espejo; CIR., ZOOL. espéculo.
sped (spĕd) cf. **speed.**
speech (spēch) s. habla; *(conversation)* conversación *f;* *(address)* discurso; *(language)* lenguaje *m* ♦ free s. libertad de expresión • s. impediment defecto de pronunciación • to deliver *o* make a s. pronunciar un discurso.
speech·less ('lĭs) adj. mudo, sin habla ♦ to be *o* be left s. quedarse mudo.
speech·mak·er (:mā'kər) s. orador *m.*
speed (spēd) I. s. velocidad *f;* JER. *(drug)* anfetamina ♦ at full *o* top s. a toda velocidad • s. limit velocidad máxima • to pick up s. acelerar II. intr. -ed *o* sped ir de prisa, ir corriendo; *(to drive fast)* conducir con exceso de velocidad ♦ to s. along ir a gran velocidad • to s. up *(faster)* acelerar; *(to hurry)* apresurarse —tr. ♦ to s. up acelerar.
speed·boat ('bōt') s. lancha motora.
speed·ing (spē'dĭng) I. adj. veloz, rápido II. s.

AUTO. exceso de velocidad.
speed·om·e·ter (spĭ-dŏm'ĭ-tər) s. velocímetro.
speed·y (spē'dē) adj. -i- rápido, veloz; *(prompt)* pronto.
spell¹ (spĕl) tr. -ed *o* spelt *(with letters)* deletrear; *(to write)* escribir <*how do you s. his name?* ¿cómo se escribe su nombre?>; FIG. significar ♦ to s. out deletrear; *(to explain)* explicar —intr. escribir.
spell² s. *(trance)* sortilegio; FIG. fascinación *f,* encanto ♦ to be under a s. estar hechizado • to cast a s. on hechizar.
spell³ I. s. *(of time)* temporada; *(of work)* turno; FAM. *(of weather)* racha; *(of illness)* ataque *m* II. tr. *(to relieve)* relevar, reemplazar.
spell·bind·ing ('bĭnd'-ĭng) adj. hechizante.
spell·bound (:bound') adj. hechizado.
spell·er (:ər) s. *(person)* deletreador *m;* *(book)* abecedario.
spell·ing (:ĭng) s. *(orthography)* ortografía; *(action)* deletreo.
spe·lunk·er (spĭ-lŭng'kər) s. espeleólogo.
spend (spĕnd) tr. spent *(money)* gastar; *(time)* pasar, dedicar; *(force, anger)* agotar, consumir; *(to use)* emplear —intr. gastar dinero.
spend·ing (spĕn'dĭng) I. s. gasto ♦ s. money dinero para gastos menudos II. adj. para gastar.
spend·thrift (spĕnd'thrĭft') s. & adj. derrochador *m,* manirroto.
spent (spĕnt) I. cf. **spend** II. adj. *(consumed)* gastado; *(passed)* acabado; *(exhausted)* agotado.
sperm¹ (spûrm) s. [pl. inv. *o* **s**] BIOL. esperma.
sperm² s. *(whale oil)* esperma de ballena ♦ s. whale cachalote.
spew (spyōō) tr. & intr. vomitar; *(to eject)* arrojar; *(words)* soltar.
sphere (sfîr) s. esfera.
spher·i·cal ('ĭ-kəl) adj. esférico.
sphinc·ter (sfĭngk'tər) s. esfínter *m.*
sphinx (sfĭngks) s. esfinge *f.*
spice (spīs) I. s. especia; FIG. sabor *m,* interés *m* II. tr. sazonar; FIG. salpimentar.
spick-and-span (spĭk'ən-spăn') adj. *(spotless)* inmaculado; *(brand-new)* flamante.
spic·y (spī'sē) adj. -i- picante.
spi·der (spī'dər) s. araña.
spiel (spēl) JER. I. s. rollo, perorata II. intr. & tr. perorar.
spig·ot (spĭg'ət) s. *(faucet)* grifo; *(tap)* espita.
spike¹ (spīk) I. s. *(nail)* clavo, estaca; *(spine)* púa; *(sharp point)* punta ♦ s. heel tacón alto y puntiagudo II. tr. *(to impale)* empalar, perforar; *(to nail)* clavar; *(to block)* impedir, frustrar; *(a drink)* echar licor a.
spike² s. *(ear of grain)* espiga.
spike·nard (spīk'närd') s. nardo.
spill (spĭl) I. tr. -ed *o* spilt *(liquid)* derramar, verter; *(blood)* derramar; *(a container)* volcar; *(to divulge)* revelar ♦ to s. the beans descubrir el pastel —intr. *(liquid)* derramarse, verterse; *(rider)* caerse ♦ to s. out salir, desbordar • to s. over salirse II. s. *(of liquid)* derrame *m;* *(fall)* caída.
spill·age ('ĭj) s. *(amount)* derrame *m.*
spill·way (:wā') s. derramadero, aliviadero.
spin (spĭn) I. tr. spun *(thread)* hilar; *(web)* tejer; *(to twirl)* hacer girar, dar vueltas a; *(story)* contar; *(a ball)* dar efecto a ♦ to s. off derivar • to s. out alargar, prolongar —intr. *(to make thread)* hilar; *(to whirl)* girar, dar vueltas; *(to*

reel) tener vértigo; *(wheels)* patinar ♦ **my head was spinning** me daba vueltas la cabeza • **to s. along** ir volando **II.** s. *(motion)* giro, vuelta; *(on a ball)* efecto; **EOM.** *(short drive)* vuelta, paseo ♦ **to be in a s.** estar aturdido • **to go for a s.** dar una vueltecita (en coche) • **to go into a s.** AVIA. entrar en barrena; FIG. aturdirse.

spin·ach (spĭn′ĭch) s. espinaca.

spi·nal (spī′nəl) **I.** adj. espinal, vertebral ♦ **s. column** columna vertebral • **s. cord** médula espinal **II.** s. anestesia por conducto vertebral.

spin·dle (spĭn′dl) s. TEJ. huso; MEC. eje *m.*

spin·dly (spĭnd′lē) adj. **-i-** FAM. larguirucho.

spine (spīn) s. ANAT. espina dorsal; *(of a book)* lomo; BOT., ZOOL. espina, púa.

spine·less (′lĭs) adj. invertebrado; *(without will power)* blando, débil.

spin·ner (spĭn′ər) s. *(person)* hilador *m;* *(needle)* aguja giratoria.

spin·ner·et (′ə-rĕt′) s. hilera.

spin·ning (′ĭng) s. *(act)* hilado; *(art)* hilandería ♦ **s. wheel** rueca, torno de hilar.

spin-off (:ôf′) s. subproducto, derivado.

spi·nose (spī′nōs′) adj. espinoso.

spin·ster (spĭn′stər) s. solterona.

spin·y (spī′nē) adj. **-i-** espinoso.

spi·ral (spī′rəl) **I.** s. espiral *f* **II.** adj. espiral ♦ **s. staircase** escalera de caracol **III.** intr. moverse en espiral.

spire[1] (spīr) s. *(pinnacle)* cúspide *f,* cima; *(steeple)* aguja.

spire[2] s. *(whorl)* vuelta, rosca.

spir·it (spĭr′ĭt) **I.** s. *(person)* espíritu *m;* *(soul)* alma; *(mood)* humor *m;* *(courage)* ánimo; QUÍM. alcohol *m* ♦ **in a friendly s.** de manera amistosa • **in s.** para sus adentros • **s. lamp** lámpara de alcohol ♦ pl. *(mood)* humor; *(alcohol)* alcohol, licor • **in high o good s.** de buen humor • **in poor o low s.** desanimado • **to keep up one's s.** no perder el ánimo • **to raise someone's s.** animar a alguien **II.** tr. alentar, animar ♦ **to s. away** o **off** llevarse, hacer desaparecer.

spir·it·ed (:ĭ-tĭd) adj. *(animated)* animado; *(vigorous)* enérgico; *(horse)* brioso.

spir·i·tu·al (:ĭ-cho͞o-əl) adj. & s. espiritual *m.*

spir·i·tu·al·ist (:o-lĭst) s. *(medium)* espiritista *mf;* FILOS., RELIG. espiritualista *mf.*

spit[1] (spĭt) **I.** s. saliva; *(act)* escupitajo; ENTOM. espuma **II.** tr. **spat** o **spit, -tting** *(escupir* —intr. escupir; *(to sputter)* chisporrotear; *(to rain)* chispear ♦ **to s. at** despreciar.

spit[2] **I.** s. *(pointed rod)* espetón *m;* GEOG. punta; *(of sand)* banco **II.** tr. **-tt-** espetar.

spite (spīt) **I.** s. rencor *m,* ojeriza ♦ **in s. of** a pesar de, no obstante • **out of s.** por despecho **II.** tr. fastidiar, despechar.

spite·ful (′fəl) adj. rencoroso.

spit·fire (spĭt′fīr′) s. persona colérica.

spit·tle (spĭt′l) s. saliva; ENTOM. espuma.

spit·toon (spĭ-to͞on′) s. escupidera.

splash (splăsh) **I.** tr. *(to spatter)* salpicar *(with* de); *(to wet)* chapotear —intr. salpicar; *(in o through water)* chapotear ♦ **to s. about** chapotear • **to s. down** amerizar **II.** s. salpicadura; *(sound)* chapoteo; *(of light, color)* mancha ♦ **to make a s.** causar sensación.

splash·down (′doun′) s. amerizaje *m.*

splash·y (:ē) adj. **-i-** llamativo.

splat (splăt) s. ruido sordo.

splat·ter (splăt′ər) **I.** tr. & intr. salpicar **II.** s. salpicadura.

splay (splā) tr. & intr. extender(se).

spleen (splēn) s. ANAT. bazo; *(ill temper)* mal humor *m.*

splen·did (splĕn′dĭd) adj. espléndido.

splen·dor (:dər) s. esplendor *m.*

splice (splīs) **I.** tr. empalmar **II.** s. empalme *m.*

splint (splĭnt) s. tablilla.

splin·ter (splĭn′tər) **I.** s. astilla; *(of bone)* esquirla ♦ **s. group** grupo disidente **II.** tr. & intr. astillar.

split (splĭt) **I.** tr. **split, -tting** *(in two)* partir, dividir; *(to crack)* hender; *(to rip)* desgarrar; *(to share)* compartir; QUÍM. descomponer; FÍS. desintegrar ♦ **splitting headache** dolor de cabeza fuertísimo • **to s. off** separar • **to s. one's sides laughing** partirse de risa • **to s. up** *(to divide)* dividir, repartir; *(to separate)* separar —intr. *(in two)* partirse; *(to crack)* henderse; *(cloth)* desgarrarse; JER. largarse ♦ **to s. off** o **up** separarse **II.** s. *(crack)* grieta; *(tear)* desgarrón *m;* *(in a group)* ruptura **III.** adj. partido; *(cracked)* agrietado; *(torn)* desgarrado ♦ **s. personality** personalidad doble • **s. second** fracción de segundo.

splotch (splŏch) **I.** s. manchón *m,* borrón *m* **II.** tr. manchar.

splotch·y (:ē) adj. **-i-** manchado.

splurge (splûrj) **I.** tr. & intr. derrochar **II.** s. derroche *m.*

splut·ter (splŭt′ər) **I.** intr. & tr. farfullar **II.** s. farfulla.

spoil (spoil) **I.** tr. **-led** o **-t** *(to damage)* estropear; *(to impair)* dañar; *(appearance)* afear; *(child)* mimar ♦ **to s. someone's fun** aguarle la fiesta a alguien —intr. estropearse **II.** s. ♦ pl. *(of war)* botín; *(of political party)* prebendas.

spoil·age (spoi′lĭj) s. putrefacción *f.*

spoil·sport (spoil′spôrt′) s. aguafiestas *mf.*

spoke[1] (spōk) s. *(of a wheel)* radio; *(rung)* peldaño.

spoke[2] (spōk) cf. **speak.**

spo·ken (spō′kən) **I.** cf. **speak II.** adj. hablado.

spokes·man (spōks′mən) s. [pl. **-men**] portavoz *m,* vocero.

spokes·per·son (:pûr′sən) s. portavoz *mf.*

spokes·wom·an (:wŏm′ən) s. [pl. **-women**] vocera, portavoz *f.*

spo·li·a·tion (spō′lē-ā′shən) s. saqueo.

sponge (spŭnj) **I.** s. esponja; FIG. *(person)* gorrón *m* ♦ **s. bath** lavado con esponja o toalla • **s. cake** bizcocho • **to throw in the s.** FAM. darse por vencido **II.** tr. limpiar con esponja; FIG. *(to obtain free)* gorronear ♦ **to s. up** absorber —intr. *(to borrow money)* sablear ♦ **to s. off** o vivir a costa de.

spong·er (spŭn′jər) s. gorrón *m.*

spong·y (:jē) adj. **-i-** esponjoso.

spon·sor (spŏn′sər) **I.** s. patrocinador *m;* *(godparent)* padrino, madrina **II.** tr. patrocinar; *(as godparent)* apadrinar, amadrinar.

spon·sor·ship (:shĭp′) s. patrocinio ♦ **under the s. of** patrocinado por.

spon·ta·ne·i·ty (spŏn′tə-nē′ĭ-tē, :nā′-) s. espontaneidad *f.*

spon·ta·ne·ous (spŏn-tā′nē-əs) adj. espontáneo ♦ **s. combustion** combustión espontánea.

spoof (spo͞of) **I.** s. *(hoax)* engaño; *(parody)* broma **II.** tr. engañar, bromear.

spook (spo͞ok) FAM. **I.** s. *(specter)* espectro; *(spy)* espía *mf* **II.** tr. asustar.

spook·y (spo͞o′kē) adj. **-i-** FAM. *(eerie)* espectral; *(skittish)* asustadizo.

spool (spōol) **I.** s. carrete *m*, bobina **II.** tr. encanillar, enrollar.
spoon (spōon) **I.** s. cuchara; *(spoonful)* cucharada **II.** tr. sacar con cuchara —intr. FAM. acariciarse, besuquearse.
spoor (spŏŏr) s. rastro.
spo·rad·ic (spə-răd′ĭk) adj. esporádico.
spore (spôr) s. espora.
sport (spôrt) **I.** s. deporte *m*; *(active pastime)* juego; *(hunting)* caza; *(jest)* broma, burla ♦ **athletic sports** atletismo • **in s.** en broma • **to be a good s.** *(about losing)* ser buen perdedor; *(to be a good person)* ser buena persona • **to make s. of** burlarse de **II.** intr. jugar, divertirse —tr. lucir <*she is sporting a new dress* luce un nuevo vestido> **III.** adj. de sport.
sport·ing (spôr′tĭng) adj. deportivo; *(gambling-related)* jugador.
spor·tive (:tĭv) adj. juguetón.
sports (spôrts) adj. de sport <*s. jacket* chaqueta de sport> ♦ **s. car** automóvil deportivo.
sports·cast (′kăst′) s. programa deportivo.
sports·man (:mən) s. [pl. -men] deportista *m*; *(gentleman)* jugador *m* que se conforma con las reglas.
sports·man·ship (:shĭp′) s. deportividad *f*.
sports·wom·an (spôrts′wŏŏm′ən) s. [pl. -women] deportista *f*.
sports·writ·er (:rī′tər) s. cronista *mf* deportivo.
sport·y (spôr′tē) adj. -i- FAM. casual; *(for sport)* deportivo.
spot (spŏt) **I.** s. lugar *m*; *(stain)* mancha; *(dot)* lunar *m*; TELEV. anuncio ♦ **beauty s.** lunar • **black s.** mancha (en la reputación) • **in a bad o tight s.** en apuros • **in spots** de vez en cuando • **night s.** sala de fiestas • **on the s.** allí mismo; *(pressed)* en situación precaria • **s. price** precio actual en el mercado • **s. remover** quitamanchas • **tender o sore s.** punto sensible • **to hit the s.** FAM. venirle muy bien a uno • **to put on the s.** poner en un aprieto • **to touch a sore s.** poner el dedo en la llaga **II.** tr. -tt- manchar; *(to detect)* notar —intr. mancharse **III.** adj. *(random)* al azar; COM., FIN. *(paid immediately)* contante; *(delivered immediately)* para entrega inmediata.
spot-check (′chĕk′) tr. & intr. inspeccionar al azar.
spot·less (:lĭs) adj. inmaculado; *(irreproachable)* intachable.
spot·light (:līt′) **I.** s. foco; *(attention)* atención pública **II.** tr. **-ed** *o* **-lit** iluminar; *(to focus attention on)* destacar.
spot·ty (:ē) adj. -i- irregular.
spou·sals (spou′zəlz) s.pl. desposorios.
spouse (spous, spouz) s. esposo, -a.
spout (spout) **I.** intr. chorrear; *(whale)* resoplar ♦ **to s. off** FAM. perorar —tr. *(to gush)* echar, arrojar; *(nonsense)* soltar **II.** s. *(for pouring)* pico; *(tube)* caño; *(stream)* chorro.
sprain (sprān) **I.** s. torcedura **II.** tr. torcer.
sprang (sprăng) cf. **spring.**
sprawl (sprôl) **I.** intr. *(to sit)* repantigarse; *(to spread out)* extenderse **II.** s. postura desgarbada; *(disorderly growth)* extensión *f* ♦ **urban s.** urbanización desordenada.
spray[1] (sprā) **I.** s. *(of liquid)* rociada; *(atomizer)* vaporizador *m*; MARÍT. espuma ♦ **s. paint** pintura para atomizador • **s. can** lata de atomizador • **s. gun** pistola para pulverizar **II.** tr. rociar —intr. vaporizarse.
spray[2] s. *(bouquet)* ramo, ramillete *m*.

spray·er (sprā′ər) s. vaporizador *m*.
spread (sprĕd) **I.** tr. **spread** extender; *(to move apart)* separar; *(butter)* untar; *(religion)* propagar; *(to sow)* sembrar; *(table)* poner ♦ **to s. oneself thin** dedicarse a muchas actividades • **to s. out** esparcir —intr. esparcirse; *(to extend)* extenderse; *(to propagate)* propagarse; *(to become known)* difundirse; *(to move apart)* separarse ♦ **to s. out** extenderse; *(to get wider)* ensancharse **II.** s. difusión *f*; *(expanse)* extensión *f*; *(ranch)* rancho; *(bedspread)* colcha; *(food)* comida (para untar); FAM. *(meal)* comida (sobre la mesa); IMPR. artículo a dos *o* más columnas; *(difference)* diferencia.
spread·er (′ər) s. *(for butter)* untador *m*; *(farm implement)* esparcidora; *(beam)* viga cepo.
spree (sprē) s. borrachera; *(party)* parranda ♦ **to go on a shopping** *o* **spending s.** hacer muchas compras.
sprig (sprĭg) s. ramito.
spright·ly (sprīt′lē) adj. -i- vivo.
spring (sprĭng) **I.** intr. **sprang, sprung** *(to jump)* saltar; *(to emerge)* brotar; *(to arise)* surgir; *(to warp)* alabearse ♦ **to s. back** volver a su posición original • **to s. forth** brotar • **to s. open, shut** abrirse, cerrarse de un golpe • **to s. to one's feet** levantarse de un salto • **to s. up** levantarse; *(to grow)* espigarse; *(to emerge)* surgir • **to s. at** lanzarse sobre —tr. *(trap)* hacer funcionar; *(to jump)* saltar; *(to release)* soltar; *(a surprise)* echar ♦ **to s. a leak** empezar a hacer agua **II.** s. *(coil)* resorte *m*; *(resilience)* elasticidad *f*; *(jump)* salto; *(season)* primavera; *(source)* fuente *f* ♦ **s. cleaning** limpieza general • **s. fever** desasosiego ocasionado por la llegada de la primavera.
spring·board (′bôrd′) s. trampolín *m*.
spring·time (:tīm′) s. primavera.
spring·y (:ē) adj. -i- elástico.
sprin·kle (sprĭng′kəl) **I.** tr. rociar —intr. rociar; *(to drizzle)* lloviznar **II.** s. rociada; *(drizzle)* llovizna; *(small amount)* pizca.
sprin·kler (:klər) s. regadera; *(fire extinguisher)* extintor *m*.
sprin·kling (:klĭng) s. *(spray)* aspersión *f*; *(small amount)* pizca.
sprint (sprĭnt) **I.** s. sprint *m* **II.** intr. sprintar.
sprint·er (sprĭn′tər) s. sprinter *m*.
sprite (sprīt) s. duende *m*; *(specter)* espectro.
sprock·et (sprŏk′ĭt) s. diente *m*.
sprout (sprout) **I.** intr. brotar; *(to burgeon)* crecer rápidamente —tr. hacer crecer **II.** s. brote *m*.
spruce[1] (sprōos) s. BOT. picea.
spruce[2] **I.** adj. ordenado **II.** tr. & intr. ♦ **to s. up** acicalar(se).
sprung (sprŭng) cf. **spring.**
spry (sprī) adj. **-er, -est** *o* **-i-** activo.
spud (spŭd) s. *(tool)* escarda; JER. *(potato)* papa.
spume (spyōom) s. espuma.
spun (spŭn) cf. **spin.**
spunk (spŭngk) s. yesca; FAM. *(pluck)* valor *m*.
spunk·y (spŭng′kē) adj. -i- valiente.
spur (spûr) **I.** s. espuela; *(incentive)* incentivo; ORNIT. espolón *m*; F.C. vía muerta ♦ **on the s. of the moment** sin pensarlo **II.** tr. **-rr-** espolear.
spu·ri·ous (spyŏŏr′ē-əs) adj. espurio.
spurn (spûrn) tr. rechazar (con desdén).
spurt (spûrt) **I.** s. chorro; *(outbreak)* arrebato **II.** intr. salir a chorros —tr. echar.

sput·ter (spŭt'ər) I. intr. chisporrotear; *(to stammer)* farfullar —tr. farfullar II. s. farfulla; *(of particles)* chisporroteo.
sput·ter·ing (:ĭng) s. chisporroteo.
spu·tum (spyōō'təm) s. [pl. **-ta**] esputo.
spy (spī) I. s. espía *mf* II. tr. *(to watch)* espiar; *(to see)* divisar —intr. ♦ **to s. (on)** espiar.
spy·glass ('glăs') s. catalejo ♦ pl. prismáticos.
spy·ing (:ĭng) s. espionaje *m*.
squab (skwŏb) s. pichón *m* implume.
squab·ble (skwŏb'əl) I. intr. pelearse II. s. riña.
squad (skwŏd) s. cuadrilla; *(team)* equipo; MIL. pelotón *m* ♦ **s. car** coche patrulla.
squad·ron ('rən) s. MARÍT. escuadra; MIL. escuadrón *m*; AER. escuadrilla.
squal·id (skwŏl'ĭd) adj. escuálido; *(repulsive)* asqueroso; *(sordid)* sórdido.
squall[1] (skwôl) I. s. chillido II. intr. chillar.
squall[2] (skwôl) s. racha.
squal·or (skwŏl'ər) s. escualidez *f*.
squan·der (skwŏn'dər) tr. derrochar; *(time)* desperdiciar.
square (skwâr) I. s. cuadrado; *(design)* cuadro; *(tool)* escuadra; *(in town)* plaza; JER. *(fogy)* convencionalista *mf* II. adj. cuadrado; *(in a right angle)* a escuadra; *(just)* equitativo; *(paid-up)* saldado; JER. *(old-fashioned)* convencional ♦ **s. dance** baile de figuras • **s. deal** FAM. trato justo • **s. knot** nudo de envergue o de rizo • **s. meal** comida completa III. tr. cuadrar; *(to adapt)* ajustar; *(to settle)* saldar ♦ **to s. accounts with** ajustarle las cuentas a • **to s. away** dejar en orden —intr. cuadrar ♦ **to s. off** ponerse de guardia (para pelear).
square·ly ('lē) adv. a escuadra; *(firmly)* firmemente; *(face to face)* de frente; *(honestly)* honradamente; *(exactly)* justo, exactamente.
squash[1] (skwŏsh, skwôsh) s. BOT. calabaza.
squash[2] I. tr. & intr. *(to crush)* aplastar(se); *(to squeeze)* apretar(se) II. s. DEP. juego de pelota.
squat (skwŏt) I. intr. **-tt-** ponerse en cuclillas; *(to settle)* ocupar ilegalmente un lugar II. adj. **-tt-** regordete III. s. posición *f* en cuclillas.
squat·ter (:ər) s. persona que ocupa ilegalmente un lugar.
squaw (skwô) s. india norteamericana.
squawk (skwôk) I. intr. graznar; *(to complain)* quejar(se) II. s. graznido; *(protest)* protesta.
squeak (skwēk) I. intr. chirriar ♦ **to s. through** *o* **by** pasar dificultosamente II. s. chirrido ♦ **a narrow s.** un escape apenas.
squeak·y (skwē'kē) adj. **-i-** chirriante.
squeal (skwēl) I. intr. chirriar; JER. *(to betray)* chivatear II. s. chillido.
squeal·er (skwē'lər) s. FAM. chivato.
squea·mish (skwē'mĭsh) adj. *(easily offended)* delicado; *(prudish)* pudibundo; *(oversensitive)* remilgado ♦ **to feel s.** sentir náuseas.
squeeze (skwēz) I. tr. *(to compress)* apretar; *(to crush)* exprimir; *(to extract)* extraer; *(to extort)* sonsacar; *(to cram)* forzar ♦ **to s. out** sacar; *(to exclude)* excluir —intr. ♦ **to s. in, out** meterse, salir con dificultad ♦ **to s. by** pasar a duras penas • **to s. together** apretujarse II. s. presión *f*; *(embrace)* abrazo; *(shortage)* escasez *f*.
squelch (skwĕlch) I. tr. despachurrar II. s. *(sound)* chapoteo; *(answer)* réplica.
squid (skwĭd) s. [pl. inv. *o* **s**] calamar *m*.
squig·gle (skwĭg'əl) I. s. garabato II. intr. re-

torcerse.
squint (skwĭnt) I. intr. entrecerrar los ojos; *(to glance)* mirar de reojo; OFTAL. bizquear II. s. mirada bizca; *(side-glance)* mirada de reojo; OFTAL. estrabismo.
squire (skwīr) I. s. HIST. escudero; G.B. *(country gentleman)* terrateniente *m*; *(dignitary)* señor *m*; *(gallant)* galán *m* II. tr. acompañar.
squirm (skwûrm) I. intr. retorcerse; *(to feel humiliation)* avergonzarse II. s. retorcimiento.
squir·rel (skwûr'əl) s. ardilla.
squirt (skwûrt) I. intr. salir a chorros —tr. dejar salir a chorros; *(to wet)* echar agua a II. s. chorro; *(device)* jeringa; FAM. *(brat)* mequetrefe *m*.
stab (stăb) I. tr. **-bb-** apuñalar; *(to wound)* herir con un cuchillo ♦ **to s. to death** matar a puñaladas II. s. puñalada; *(wound)* herida ♦ **to take a s. at** intentar.
stab·bing ('ĭng) I. s. puñalada, asesinato a puñaladas II. adj. punzante (dolor).
sta·bil·i·ty (stə-bĭl'ĭ-tē) s. estabilidad *f*; *(steadfastness)* firmeza.
sta·bi·li·za·tion (stā'bə-lĭ-zā'shən) s. estabilización *f*.
sta·bi·lize ('-līz') tr. & intr. estabilizar(se).
sta·bi·liz·ing ('lī'zĭng) adj. estabilizador.
sta·ble[1] (stā'bəl) adj. **-er, -est** estable; *(enduring)* duradero; *(balanced)* equilibrado.
sta·ble[2] I. s. *(building)* establo; *(horses)* cuadra II. tr. poner en un establo.
stack (stăk) I. s. *(pile)* pila, hacina; *(smokestack)* chimenea; FAM. montón *m* ♦ **to blow one's s.** reventar de ira ♦ pl. estantes II. tr. amontonar, hacinar ♦ **to s. the deck** hacer trampas • **to s. up** amontonar; FIG. comparar.
sta·di·um (stā'dē-əm) s. [pl. **s** *o* **-ia**] estadio.
staff (stăf) I. s. [pl. **s**] *(personnel)* personal *m*; *(aides)* cuerpo de administración; [pl. **s** *o* **-ves**] *(walking stick)* bastón *m*; *(cudgel)* garrote *m*; *(flagpole)* asta; MÚS. pentagrama ♦ **editorial s.** redacción • **s. of life** alimento básico • **teaching s.** cuerpo docente • **to be on the s.** estar en plantilla II. tr. proveer de personal.
staff·er ('ər) s. FAM. empleado.
stag (stăg) I. s. ciervo II. adj. ♦ **s. party** reunión de hombres solos III. adv. solo (sin compañera).
stage (stāj) I. s. plataforma; *(setting)* escena, escenario; *(phase)* etapa; *(stagecoach)* diligencia; TEAT. escena; *(boards)* tablas; FIG. teatro; ASTRONAUT. cuerpo ♦ **by stages** progresivamente • **in stages** por etapas • **s. door** entrada de artistas • **s. fright** miedo al público • **s. manager** regidor de escena • **to go on the s.** dedicarse al teatro II. tr. TEAT. representar; *(to arrange)* organizar.
stage·hand ('hănd') s. tramoyista *mf*.
stage-struck (:strŭk') adj. apasionado por el teatro.
stag·ger (stăg'ər) I. intr. tambalearse —tr. hacer tambalearse; *(to overwhelm)* asombrar; *(to alternate)* escalonar II. s. tambaleo.
stag·ger·ing (:ĭng) adj. tambaleante; *(overwhelming)* asombroso.
stag·ing (stā'jĭng) s. TEAT. puesta en escena.
stag·nant (stăg'nənt) adj. estancado; *(foul)* rancio; *(sluggish)* inactivo.
stag·nate (:nāt') intr. estancarse.
stag·na·tion (-nā'shən) s. estancamiento.
staid (stād) adj. serio.
stain (stān) I. tr. manchar; *(to dye)* teñir; *(to*

taint) mancillar ♦ **stained glass** vidrio con dibujos coloreados —intr. mancharse II. s. mancha; *(dye)* tinte m.

stain·less ('lĭs) adj. limpio; *(corrosion-resistant)* inoxidable; *(unblemished)* inmaculado.

stair (stâr) s. escalón m ♦ pl. escalera.

stair·case ('kās) s. escalera.

stair·way (:wā') s. escalera.

stair·well (:wĕl') s. caja de la escalera.

stake (stāk) I. s. *(stick)* estaca; *(post)* poste m; *(interest)* intereses m; *(for burning)* hoguera ♦ **at s.** en juego • **to pull up stakes** irse ♦ pl. *(bet)* apuesta; *(prize)* premio II. tr. *(to secure)* estacar; *(to tether)* amarrar a un poste; *(a plant)* rodrigar; *(to gamble)* apostar; *(to risk)* jugarse; *(to finance)* financiar ♦ **to s. a claim** delimitar una propiedad con estacas.

stake·out ('out') s. vigilancia.

sta·lac·tite (stə-lăk'tīt') s. estalactita.

sta·lag·mite (stə-lăg'mīt') s. estalagmita.

stale (stāl) I. adj. *(food)* rancio; *(bread)* duro; *(wine)* picado; *(news)* viejo; *(trite)* trillado; *(run-down)* decaído II. intr. echarse a perder.

stale·mate ('māt') I. s. *(deadlock)* estancamiento; *(chess)* ahogado II. tr. estancar; *(chess)* ahogar.

stale·ness (:nĭs) s. ranciedad f, rancidez f.

stalk¹ (stôk) s. *(plant stem)* tallo; *(flower stem)* pedúnculo m; *(leaf stem)* pecíolo.

stalk² intr. *(to walk)* caminar con paso impresionante —tr. *(to pursue)* acechar.

stall (stôl) I. s. *(in barn)* pesebre m; *(booth)* caseta; *(pew)* banco de iglesia; *(delaying tactic)* evasiva; G.B. *(seat)* butaca; MEC. calado (de motor) II. tr. *(to delay)* demorar; AUTO. calar —intr. *(to delay)* andar con rodeos; AUTO. calarse.

stal·lion (stăl'yən) s. semental m.

stal·wart (stôl'wərt) I. adj. robusto; *(uncompromising)* firme II. s. persona fuerte.

sta·men (stā'mən) s. estambre m.

stam·i·na (stăm'ə-nə) s. aguante m.

stam·mer (stăm'ər) I. intr. tartamudear II. s. tartamudez f, tartamudeo.

stam·mer·ing (:ĭng) s. tartamudeo.

stamp (stămp) I. tr. *(to crush)* pisotear; *(to imprint)* estampar; *(to affix stamp)* poner un sello a; *(to impress)* marcar ♦ **to s. on** pisar • **to s. one's feet** patear • **to s. out** *(fire)* apagar con el pie, *(rebellion)* acabar con, sofocar —intr. patear; *(to walk)* caminar con pasos pesados II. s. sello; *(postage)* sello, estampilla; *(official)* timbre m; TEC. *(die)* cuño ♦ **s. collector** filatelista • **trading s.** cupón.

stam·pede (stăm-pēd') I. s. espantada II. tr. espantar *(animales)* —intr. abalanzarse.

stance (stăns) s. postura.

stanch¹ (stônch, stŏnch) tr. restañar (sangre).

stanch² var. de **staunch¹**.

stan·chion (stăn'chən, :shən) s. poste m.

stand (stănd) I. intr. **stood** estar de pie; *(to rise)* ponerse de pie; *(to place oneself)* ponerse; *(to remain valid)* tener vigencia; *(to be committed)* mantenerse; *(to be situated)* erguirse; *(to rank)* ser ♦ **to s. alone** ser el único • **to s. aside** retirarse • **to s. at attention** cuadrarse • **to s. back** retroceder • **to s. by** estar listo; *(to look on)* mirar y no hacer nada • **to s. down** retirarse del estrado • **to s. fast** no cejar • **to s. in** o **on line** hacer cola • **to s. in the way (of)** estorbar • **to s. off** apartarse • **to s. on end** *(hair)* erizarse; *(thing)* ponerse de punta • **to s.**

out resaltar • **to s. still** estarse quieto • **to s. to reason** ser lógico • **to s. to (win, lose)** tener la probabilidad de (ganar, perder) • **to s. together** mantenerse unidos • **to s. up** ponerse de pie • **where do you s.?** ¿qué opinión tienes? —tr. poner de pie; *(to place)* colocar; *(to withstand)* tolerar; *(to resist)* resistir ♦ **to s. against** hacer frente a • **to s. by** permanecer fiel a • **to s. for** representar; *(to support)* abogar por; *(to tolerate)* soportar • **to s. in for** reemplazar • **to s. on end** poner derecho • **to s. one's ground** mantenerse firme • **to s. the test** pasar por la prueba • **to s. up** FAM. dejar plantado a • **to s. up for** sacar la cara por • **to s. up to** hacer frente a; *(to last)* resistir II. s. *(halt)* parada; *(dais)* estrado; *(booth)* quiosco; *(counter)* mostrador m; *(pedestal)* pie m; *(for coats, hats)* perchero; *(for umbrellas)* paragüero ♦ **to make a s. against** oponerse a • **to take a s. for** declararse a favor de • **to take a (firm) s.** adoptar una actitud (firme) • **to take the (witness) s.** DER. subir a la barra de los testigos ♦ pl. graderías.

stan·dard (stăn'dərd) I. s. *(flag)* estandarte m; *(criterion)* criterio; *(model)* patrón m; *(level)* nivel m ♦ **s. of living** nivel de vida ♦ pl. normas II. adj. standard; *(accepted)* normal, corriente; *(trite)* trillado ♦ **s. time** hora civil.

stan·dard-bear·er (:'bâr'ər) s. abanderado.

stan·dard·ize (stăn'dər-dīz') tr. estandarizar.

stand·by (stănd'bī') s. [pl. **-bys**] *(dependable person)* persona de confianza; *(substitute)* substituto ♦ **s. list** lista de espera • **s. passenger** pasajero que está en la lista de espera.

stand-in (:ĭn') s. TEAT. suplente mf; CINEM. doble m; *(substitute)* substituto.

stand·ing (stăn'dĭng) I. s. *(reputation)* reputación f; *(length of time)* antigüedad f II. adj. de pie, parado; *(permanent)* permanente; *(stationary)* fijo; *(stagnant)* estancado ♦ **s. room** sitio donde la gente permanece de pie.

stand·off (stănd'ôf') s. empate m.

stand·off·ish (-ô'fĭsh) adj. distante, reservado.

stand·point ('point') s. punto de vista.

stand·still (:stĭl') s. parada.

stank (stăngk) cf. **stink**.

stan·za (stăn'zə) s. estrofa, estancia.

staph·y·lo·coc·cus (stăf'ə-lō-kŏk'əs) s. [pl. **-ci**] estafilococo.

sta·ple¹ (stā'pəl) s. *(commodity)* producto básico (de una región); *(trade item)* producto principal; *(feature)* elemento básico; *(raw material)* materia prima; *(fiber)* fibra.

sta·ple² I. s. *(metal fastener)* grapa II. tr. sujetar con una grapa.

sta·pler (stā'plər) s. grapador m.

star (stär) I. s. estrella; *(asterisk)* asterisco ♦ **shooting s.** estrella fugaz • **to thank one's lucky stars** dar las gracias a Dios ♦ pl. ASTROL. astros II. tr. **-rr-** *(to adorn)* estrellar; *(with asterisk)* poner un asterisco en; *(to feature)* presentar como protagonista —intr. protagonizar; *(to perform well)* destacarse III. adj. estelar ♦ **s. sapphire** zafiro estrellado.

star·board (stär'bərd) I. s. estribor m II. adj. de estribor III. adv. a estribor.

starch (stärch) I. s. *(foodstuff)* fécula; *(stiffener)* almidón m II. tr. almidonar.

starch·y (stär'chē) adj. **-i-** feculento; *(like starch)* almidonado.

star·dom (stär'dəm) s. estrellato.

stare (stâr) I. intr. mirar fijamente ♦ **to s.**

down hacer bajar la vista a **II.** s. mirada fija.
star·fish (stär′fĭsh′) s. [pl. inv. o **es**] estrella de mar.
star·gaze (:gāz′) intr. mirar las estrellas; *(to daydream)* mirar a las telarañas.
stark (stärk) **I.** adj. *(bleak)* desolado; *(truth, facts)* desnudo; *(complete)* total **II.** adv. totalmente.
stark·ness (′nĭs) s. *(bleakness)* desolación f; *(bareness)* austeridad f.
star·let (stär′lĭt) s. actriz f joven.
star·light (:līt′) s. luz f de las estrellas.
star·ling (stär′lĭng) s. estornino.
star·lit (stär′lĭt′) adj. iluminado por las estrellas.
star·ry (:ē) adj. -i- estrellado.
star·ry-eyed (:īd′) adj. soñador.
start (stärt) **I.** intr. empezar; *(to set out)* salir; *(motor)* arrancar; *(to jerk)* sobresaltarse ♦ **to s. back** emprender el regreso • **to s. in** o **off** o **out** empezar • **to s. up** arrancar • **to s. with** para comenzar —tr. empezar; *(car, machine)* poner en marcha; *(to initiate)* iniciar; *(to found)* establecer **II.** s. *(beginning)* principio; *(startle)* sobresalto; *(place)* salida, punto de partida ♦ **flying s.** salida lanzada • **to get off to a good s.** empezar bien • **to give someone a s.** *(to help)* ayudar a alguien; *(to startle)* dar un susto a alguien • **to make a fresh s.** empezar de nuevo • **with a s.** sobresaltando.
start·er (stär′tər) s. iniciador m; AUTO. arranque m; DEP. *(official)* juez m de salida.
star·tle (stär′tl) **I.** tr. & intr. sobresaltar(se) **II.** s. sobresalto.
start-up (stärt′ŭp′) s. puesta en marcha; *(beginning)* principio.
star·va·tion (stär-vā′shən) s. hambre f; MED. inanición f ♦ **s. wages** sueldos de hambre.
starve (stärv) intr. *(to be hungry)* pasar hambre; *(to die)* morirse de hambre —tr. no dar de comer; *(to kill)* matar de hambre ♦ **to be starved** o **starving for** *(to need)* carecer de; *(to desire)* anhelar.
starv·ing (stär′vĭng) adj. hambriento.
stash (stăsh) FAM. **I.** tr. esconder **II.** s. *(cache)* escondrijo; *(hidden thing)* cosa escondida.
sta·sis (stā′sĭs) s. [pl. **-ses**] estasis f.
state (stāt) **I.** s. estado; *(social position)* rango; *(pomp)* pompa ♦ **the s. of the art** últimos adelantos • **the States** los Estados Unidos • **to be in a s.** agitarse • **to lie in s.** estar en capilla ardiente **II.** tr. declarar **III.** adj. estatal; *(ceremonious)* solemne; *(official)* oficial.
state·li·ness (′lē-nĭs) s. majestuosidad f.
state·ly (:lē) adj. -i- majestuoso.
state·ment (stāt′mənt) s. declaración f; COM. *(bill)* cuenta; *(report)* estado de cuenta.
states·man (stāts′mən) s. [pl. **-men**] estadista m.
states·man·ship (:shĭp′) s. arte m de gobernar.
state·wide (stāt′wīd′) adj. por todo el estado.
stat·ic (stăt′ĭk) **I.** adj. estático **II.** s. RAD. parásitos; JER. *(back talk)* insolencias.
sta·tion (stā′shən) **I.** s. estación f; *(post)* puesto; *(social position)* rango ♦ **military s.** guarnición • **police s.** comisaría • **service s.** estación de servicio • **s. wagon** camioneta **II.** tr. estacionar; *(to post)* apostar.
sta·tion·ar·y (:shə-nĕr′ē) adj. estacionario; *(fixed)* fijo.
sta·tion·er (stā′shə-nər) s. papelero.

sta·tion·er·y (:nĕr′ē) s. papel y sobres m; *(office supplies)* objetos de escritorio; *(store)* papelería.
sta·tion·mas·ter (stā′shən-măs′tər) s. jefe m de estación.
sta·tis·tic (stə-tĭs′tĭk) s. estadística ♦ **statistics** sg. *(science)* estadística.
sta·tis·ti·cal (:tĭ-kəl) adj. estadístico.
stat·is·ti·cian (stăt′ĭ-stĭsh′ən) s. estadístico.
stat·u·ar·y (stăch′ōō-ĕr′ē) s. estatuas; *(art)* estatuaria.
stat·ue (stăch′ōō) s. estatua.
stat·u·esque (:-ĕsk′) adj. escultural.
stat·u·ette (:ĕt′) s. estatuilla.
stat·ure (stăch′ər) s. estatura; FIG. categoría.
sta·tus (stā′təs, stăt′əs) s. DER. estado; *(position)* posición social f; *(situation)* situación f.
stat·ute (stăch′ōōt) s. estatuto ♦ **s. mile** milla terrestre • **s. of limitations** ley de prescripción.
stat·u·to·ry (:ə-tôr′ē) adj. estatutario.
staunch[1] (stônch, stänch) adj. *(steadfast)* constante; *(true)* fiel; *(strong)* fuerte.
staunch[2] var. de **stanch**[1].
stave (stāv) **I.** s. *(of barrel)* duela; *(stanza)* estrofa ♦ pl. cf. **staff II.** tr. -**d** o **stove** ♦ **to s. in** desfondar • **to s. off** rechazar.
stay[1] (stā) **I.** intr. quedarse; *(to sojourn)* alojarse; *(to stop)* detenerse; *(to wait)* esperar; *(to last)* durar; *(to keep up)* mantenerse, seguir ♦ **it is here to s.** se ha establecido • **to s. away** ausentarse • **to s. away from** evitar • **to s. in** quedarse en casa • **to s. in bed** guardar cama • **to s. on** quedarse • **to s. over** pasar la noche • **to s. out** no entrar; *(all night)* no venir a casa • **to s. put** no moverse • **to s. up late** acostarse tarde —tr. detener; *(to postpone)* aplazar; *(to appease)* apaciguar ♦ **to s. the course** continuar hasta el final **II.** s. *(halt)* parada f; *(visit)* estancia; DER. aplazamiento.
stay[2] s. *(support)* apoyo; *(of corset)* ballena.
stay[3] s. MARÍT. estay m.
stead (stĕd) s. lugar m ♦ **in someone's, something's s.** en lugar de alguien, algo • **to stand someone in good s.** serle útil a alguien.
stead·fast (stĕd′făst′) adj. *(fixed)* fijo; *(unchanging)* constante; *(loyal)* leal.
stead·i·ness (stĕd′ē-nĭs) s. estabilidad f; *(firmness)* firmeza.
stead·y (stĕd′ē) **I.** adj. -i- firme; *(stable)* estable; *(sure)* seguro; *(continuous)* constante; *(calm)* tranquilo; *(reliable)* seguro **II.** tr. & intr. estabilizar(se); *(to calm)* calmar(se).
steak (stāk) s. bistec m; *(fish)* filete m.
steal (stēl) **I.** tr. & intr. stole, stolen robar ♦ **to s. away** escabullirse • **to s. in, out** entrar, salir furtivamente **II.** s. robo; JER. *(bargain)* ganga.
steal·ing (stē′lĭng) s. robo.
stealth (stĕlth) s. sigilo ♦ **by s.** furtivamente.
stealth·y (stĕl′thē) adj. -i- *(person)* cauteloso; *(action)* furtivo.
steam (stēm) **I.** s. vapor m; *(mist)* vaho, humo; *(heating)* calefacción f; *(energy)* energía ♦ **s. engine** máquina a vapor • **s. shovel** pala mecánica • **to let off s.** descargar vapor; FIG. desahogarse **II.** intr. echar vapor; *(to rise)* humear; *(ship)* avanzar; *(to fog up)* empañarse; FAM. *(to fume)* echar humo —tr. *(to fog)* empañar; CUL. cocer al vapor.
steam·boat (′bōt′) s. vapor m.
steam·er (stē′mər) s. *(ship)* vapor m; CUL. olla de vapor ♦ **s. trunk** baúl (de camarote).
steam·roll·er (:rō′lər) **I.** s. apisonadora **II.** tr.

apisonar; FIG. aplastar.
steam·ship (:shǐp´) s. vapor *m.*
steam·y (stē´mē) adj. **-i-** vaporoso; JER. *(erotic)* apasionado.
steed (stēd) s. corcel *m.*
steel (stēl) I. s. acero II. adj. de acero ♦ **s. industry** la industria siderúrgica • **s. mill** acería III. tr. acerar ♦ **to s. one's heart** volverse insensible • **to s. oneself** endurecerse.
steel·y (stē´lē) adj. **-i-** *(of steel)* de acero; *(like steel)* acerado ♦ **s. eyes** mirada penetrante.
steel·yard (stēl´yärd´) s. romana.
steep¹ (stēp) adj. *(high)* empinado; *(precipitous)* escarpado; *(price)* excesivo.
steep² tr. remojar —intr. estar en remojo.
stee·ple (stē´pəl) s. torrecilla; *(spire)* aguja.
stee·ple·chase (:chās´) s. carrera de obstáculos.
steer¹ (stîr) tr. *(boat)* gobernar; *(car)* conducir; FIG. dirigir, guiar —intr. gobernar, conducir; *(to handle)* conducirse ♦ **steering wheel** volante • **to s. clear of** evitar • **to s. for** poner rumbo a.
steer² s. *(ox)* novillo.
steer·age (stîr´ĭj) s. MARÍT. gobierno; *(accommodation)* entrepuente *m.*
stein (stīn) s. jarra de cerveza).
stel·lar (stĕl´ər) adj. estelar.
stem¹ (stĕm) I. s. *(trunk)* tronco; *(stalk)* tallo; *(of goblet)* pie *m; (of pipe)* cañón *m;* FILOL. radical *m* ♦ **from s. to stern** de proa a popa II. intr. **-mm-** ♦ **to s. from** ser el resultado de.
stem² tr. **-mm-** *(to hold back)* contener.
stench (stĕnch) s. hedor *m.*
sten·cil (stĕn´səl) I. s. estarcido II. tr. estarcir.
ste·nog·ra·pher (stə-nŏg´rə-fər) s. estenógrafo.
ste·nog·ra·phy (:fē) s. estenografía.
sten·to·ri·an (stĕn-tôr´ē-ən) adj. estentóreo.
step (stĕp) I. s. paso; *(sound)* pisada; *(measure)* medida; *(degree)* escalón ♦ **in s. with** de acuerdo con • **out of s. with** en desacuerdo con • **s. by s.** paso a paso • **to keep in s.** llevar el paso • **to take a s.** dar un paso • **watch your step!** ¡vaya con cuidado! ♦ pl. *(staircase)* escaleras II. intr. **-pp-** pisar; *(to take a step)* dar un paso ♦ **s. this way!** ¡pase por aquí! • **to s. aside** hacerse a un lado • **to s. back** retroceder • **to s. down** bajar; *(to resign)* renunciar • **to s. forward** *o* **up** avanzar • **to s. in** entrar; *(to intervene)* intervenir • **to s. out** salir; *(of vehicle)* apearse • **to s. up** subir —tr. ♦ **s. on it!** ¡date prisa! • **to s. on** pisar • **to s. up** acelerar; *(to increase)* aumentar.
step·broth·er (stĕp´brŭth´ər) s. hermanastro.
step·child (:chīld´) s. [pl. **-dren**] hijastro.
step·daugh·ter (:dô´tər) s. hijastra.
step·fa·ther (:fä´thər) s. padrastro.
step·lad·der (stĕp´lăd´ər) s. escalera de tijera.
step·moth·er (stĕp´mŭth´ər) s. madrastra.
step·par·ent (:pâr´ənt) s. padrastro, madrastra.
steppe (stĕp) s. estepa.
step·ping·stone (stĕp´ĭng-stōn´) s. pasadera; FIG. *(springboard)* trampolín *m.*
step·sis·ter (stĕp´sĭs´tər) s. hermanastra.
step·son (:sŭn´) s. hijastro.
step-up (stĕp´ŭp´) s. *(acceleration)* aceleración *f; (increase)* aumento.
ster·e·o (stĕr´ē-ō´) I. s. equipo estereofónico; *(sound)* sonido estereofónico II. adj. estéreo.
ster·e·o·phon·ic (´-fŏn´ĭk) adj. estereofónico.
ster·e·o·type (stĕr´ē-ə-tīp´) I. s. estereotipo

II. tr. estereotipar.
ster·ile (stĕr´əl, :īl´) adj. estéril.
ste·ril·i·ty (stə-rĭl´ĭ-tē) s. esterilidad *f.*
ster·il·i·za·tion (stĕr´ə-lĭ-zā´shən) s. esterilización *f.*
ster·il·ize (stĕr´ə-līz´) tr. esterilizar.
ster·ling (stûr´lĭng) I. s. FIN. libra esterlina; *(tableware)* plata II. adj. FIN. de la libra esterlina; *(silver)* de plata de ley; FIG. de primera calidad ♦ **s. silver** *(artículos de)* plata de ley.
stern¹ (stûrn) adj. firme; *(severe)* severo; *(gloomy)* sombrío; *(relentless)* implacable.
stern² s. MARÍT. popa.
ster·num (stûr´nəm) s. [pl. **s** *o* **-na**] esternón *m.*
ster·oid (stĕr´oid´, stîr´-) s. esteroide *m.*
steth·o·scope (stĕth´ə-skōp´) s. estetoscopio.
ste·ve·dore (stē´və-dôr´) s. estibador *m.*
stew (stōō) I. tr. guisar —intr. cocerse; FAM. *(to worry)* agitarse II. s. guiso; FAM. agitación *f* ♦ **in a s.** agitado.
stew·ard (stōō´ərd) s. administrador *m; (household manager)* mayordomo; MARÍT. *(attendant)* camarero; *(officer)* despensero ♦ **shop s.** enlace sindical.
stew·ard·ess (:ər-dĭs) s. azafata.
stew·ard·ship (:ərd-shĭp´) s. gerencia.
stewed (stōōd) adj. CUL. guisado; JER. *(drunk)* borracho.
stick (stĭk) I. s. vara, palo; *(twig)* ramita; *(walking stick)* bastón *m; (wand)* varilla; *(of dynamite)* cartucho; *(of chocolate)* barra; *(adhesiveness)* adhesión *f;* AVIA. palanca de mando ♦ **s. shift** AUTO. cambio manual • **the sticks** región apartada II. tr. **stuck** *(to push into)* introducir, meter; *(to pin)* prender (con alfileres); *(to glue)* pegar; *(to impale)* clavar ♦ **to s. by** ser fiel a • **to s. down** pegar • **to s. it out** aguantar hasta el fin • **to s. out** *(tongue)* mostrar; *(head)* asomar • **to s. up** atracar • **to s. up for** defender —intr. *(nail, pin)* clavarse; *(to cling)* pegarse; *(to persevere)* perseverar; *(to jam)* atascarse • **to s. around** quedarse • **to s. close** mantenerse juntos • **to s. out** sobresalir • **to s. to** *(promise)* cumplir; *(friend)* ser fiel a; *(facts)* ceñirse a • **to s. to business** dejarse de rodeos • **to s. to it** perseverar • **to s. to one's guns** mantenerse uno en sus treces • **to s. together** mantenerse unidos.
stick·er (´ər) s. *(label)* etiqueta adhesiva; *(prickle)* espina.
stick-in-the-mud (:ĭn-thə-mŭd´) s. FAM. persona sin iniciativa.
stick·ler (stĭk´lər) s. persona rigorista.
stick·pin (stĭk´pĭn´) s. alfiler *m* de corbata.
stick-up (:ŭp´) s. FAM. atraco.
stick·y (stĭk´ē) adj. **-i-** pegajoso; *(muggy)* húmedo; FAM. *(difficult)* difícil.
stiff (stĭf) I. adj. rígido; *(not limber)* tieso; *(joint)* anquilosado; *(taut)* tenso; *(formal)* formal; *(thick)* espeso; *(unyielding)* inflexible; *(drink)* fuerte; *(difficult)* difícil; *(punishment)* duro; *(prices)* excesivo II. adv. ♦ **to be bored s.** estar muy aburrido • **to be scared s.** estar muerto de miedo III. s. JER. *(corpse)* fiambre *m; (drunk)* borracho.
stiff·en (´ən) tr. & intr. poner(se) rígido.
stiff·ness (stĭf´nĭs) s. rigidez *f,* inflexibilidad *f; (toughness)* dureza; *(thickness)* consistencia; *(of drink)* fuerza; *(of knee)* anquilosamiento; *(of muscle)* agarrotamiento.
sti·fle¹ (stī´fəl) tr. & intr. sofocar(se).
sti·fle² s. ZOOL. babilla.

stig·ma (stĭg′mə) s. [pl. **s** o **-mata**] estigma *m.*

stig·ma·tize (:tīz′) tr. estigmatizar.

sti·let·to (stə-lĕt′ō) s. [pl. **(e)s**] estilete *m.*

still¹ (stĭl) **I.** adj. *(silent)* silencioso; *(at rest)* inmóvil; *(tranquil)* sosegado; *(waters)* manso; FOTOG. fija ♦ **s. life** naturaleza muerta **II.** s. silencio; FOTOG. foto fija **III.** adv. *(motionlessly)* quieto; *(yet)* todavía, aún; *(even)* aun; *(nevertheless)* sin embargo **IV.** tr. tranquilizar; *(to silence)* (hacer) callar; *(to stop)* detener; *(to calm)* calmar.

still² s. alambique *m*; *(distillery)* destilería.

still·born (:bôrn′) adj. nacido muerto.

stilt (stĭlt) s. zanco; *(support)* pilote *m.*

stilt·ed (stĭl′tĭd) adj. afectado.

stim·u·lant (stĭm′yə-lənt) s. *(drug)* estimulante *m*; *(stimulus)* estímulo.

stim·u·late (:lāt′) tr. estimular.

stim·u·la·tion (′-lā′shən) s. estímulo.

stim·u·lus (′-ləs) s. [pl. **-li**] estímulo.

sting (stĭng) **I.** tr. **stung** picar; *(to hurt)* escocer; FIG. herir —intr. *(to prick)* picar; *(to cause pain)* hacer escocer **II.** s. picadura; *(pain)* escozor *m*; ZOOL. aguijón *m.*

sting·er (′ər) s. aguijón *m.*

stin·gy (stĭn′jē) adj. **-i-** tacaño; *(scant)* escaso.

stink (stĭngk) **I.** intr. **stank** o **stunk, stunk** heder, apestar; FIG. *(person, policy)* tener mala fama; *(performance)* estar fatal ♦ **to s. of money** estar podrido de dinero • **to s. up** dar mal olor **II.** s. hedor *m* ♦ **to make** o **raise a s.** armar un escándalo.

stink·er (stĭng′kər) s. JER. canalla *mf.*

stink·ing (:ĭng) adj. hediondo, apestoso.

stint (stĭnt) **I.** tr. restringir, limitar ♦ **to s. on** escatimar **II.** s. faena, trabajo.

sti·pend (stī′pĕnd′) s. estipendio.

stip·ple (stĭp′əl) **I.** tr. puntear **II.** s. punteado.

stip·u·late (stĭp′yə-lāt′) tr. & intr. estipular.

stip·u·la·tion (′-lā′shən) s. estipulación *f.*

stir (stûr) **I.** tr. **-rr-** *(to mix)* revolver; *(to move)* agitar; *(liquid, memory)* remover; *(fire)* atizar; *(to incite)* incitar; *(to affect)* conmover ♦ **to s. up** *(to revive)* despertar; *(trouble)* provocar —intr. moverse **II.** s. movimiento; *(disturbance)* conmoción *f*; *(flurry)* sensación *f.*

stir·rer (stûr′ər) s. agitador *m.*

stir·ring (:ĭng) adj. *(rousing)* bullicioso; *(moving)* conmovedor; *(lively)* animado.

stir·rup (stûr′əp) s. estribo.

stitch (stĭch) **I.** s. COST. puntada; *(decorative)* punto; MED. punzada ♦ **a s. in time saves nine** más vale prevenir que curar • **to be in stitches** estar muerto de risa • **without a s. on** en cueros **II.** tr. coser; *(to bind)* encuadernar.

stock (stŏk) **I.** s. *(inventory)* existencias, stock *m*; *(supply)* surtido; *(livestock)* ganado; *(shares)* acciones *f*; *(lineage)* linaje *m*; *(broth)* caldo; *(of rifle)* culata; *(repertoire)* repertorio ♦ **in s.** en existencia • **out of s.** agotado • **surplus s.** excedentes • **to put s. in** darle importancia a • **to take s. of** evaluar ♦ pl. *(pillory)* cepo **II.** tr. *(to supply)* surtir; *(to keep in supply)* tener existencias de ♦ **to s. up on** abastecerse de **III.** adj. en existencia, de surtido; *(standard)* trillado ♦ **s. certificate** título de acciones • **s. company** sociedad anónima • **s. exchange** o **market** bolsa.

stock·ade (stŏ-kād′). empalizada.

stock·bro·ker (stŏk′brō′kər) s. corredor *m* de bolsa.

stock·hold·er (:hōl′dər) s. accionista *mf.*

stock·ing (stŏk′ĭng) s. media.

stock·pile (stŏk′pīl′) **I.** s. reservas **II.** tr. acumular.

stock-still (stŏk′stĭl′) adj. completamente inmóvil.

stock·y (stŏk′ē) adj. **-i-** *(solid)* fuerte, robusto; *(plump)* rechoncho.

stock·yard (stŏk′yärd′) s. corral *m* de ganado.

stodg·y (stŏj′ē) adj. **-i-** *(dull)* aburrido; *(pompous)* pomposo.

sto·ic/i·cal (stō′ĭk) adj. & s. estoico.

sto·i·cism (:ĭ-sĭz′əm) s. estoicismo.

stoke (stōk) tr. & intr. echar combustible a.

stok·er (stō′kər) s. fogonero; *(device)* cargador mecánico.

stole¹ (stōl) s. estola.

stole², sto·len (stōl, stō′lən) cf. **steal.**

stol·id (stŏl′ĭd) adj. impasible.

stom·ach (stŭm′ək) **I.** s. estómago; *(abdomen)* vientre *m*; *(appetite)* apetito **II.** tr. aguantar.

stom·ach·ache (:āk′) s. dolor *m* de estómago.

stomp (stŏmp) tr. & intr. pisotear.

stone (stōn) **I.** s. piedra; *(pebble)* guijarro; *(gem)* piedra preciosa; G.B. *(weight unit)* peso que equivale a 6,350 kg; *(pit)* hueso; MED. cálculo ♦ **within a s.'s throw** a dos pasos • **to leave no s. unturned** remover Roma con Santiago **II.** tr. apedrear, lapidar.

stoned (stōnd) adj. JER. *(drunk)* borracho; *(drugged)* drogado, intoxicado.

stone-deaf (stōn′dĕf′) adj. sordo como una tapia.

stone·ware (:wâr′) s. gres *m.*

stone·work (:wûrk′) s. cantería.

ston·y (stō′nē) adj. **-i-** pedregoso; *(like stone)* pétreo; *(unemotional)* frío.

stood (stŏŏd) cf. **stand.**

stooge (stōōj) s. *(follower)* secuaz *mf*; TEAT. actor *m* que da pie a un cómico.

stool (stōōl) s. taburete *m*; *(footrest)* escabel *m*; *(toilet bowl)* taza; FISIOL. deposiciones *f* ♦ **s. pigeon** JER. soplón.

stoop¹ (stōōp) **I.** intr. *(to bend)* encorvarse; *(to lower oneself)* rebajarse; *(to condescend)* condescender **II.** s. inclinación *f* de hombros.

stoop² s. *(porch)* pórtico.

stop (stŏp) **I.** tr. **-pp-** *(to halt)* parar, detener; *(to cease)* dejar de; *(to end)* acabar; *(to prevent)* impedir; *(to plug)* tapar; *(to obstruct)* bloquear; *(to staunch)* restañar; *(a check)* cancelar ♦ **s. it!** ¡basta! • **to s. one's ears** taparse los oídos • **to s. up** taponar —intr. detenerse; *(to cease)* cesar; *(to visit)* hacer alto ♦ **to s. at nothing** no pararse en barras • **to s. by** o **in** hacer una visita corta • **to s. dead** o **short** pararse en seco • **to s. off** pararse • **to s. over** alojarse **II.** s. *(act)* detención *f*; *(cessation)* cesación *f*; *(finish)* término; *(stay)* estancia; *(place)* parada; *(en route)* escala; *(plug)* tapón *m*; *(on check)* orden *f* de suspensión de pago; MÚS. *(organ)* registro ♦ **full s.** punto • **s. sign** señal de alto • **to come to a s.** pararse • **to pull out all the stops** tocar todos los registros • **to put a s. to** poner fin a.

stop·gap (′găp′) s. substituto.

stop·light (:līt′) s. *(traffic signal)* semáforo; *(brake light)* luz *f* de frenado.

stop·o·ver (:ō′vər) s. AVIA., MARÍT. escala; *(place)* lugar visitado.

stop·page (:ĭj) s. *(stop)* parada, detención *f*; *(work halt)* paro; *(blockage)* obstrucción *f.*

stop·per (:ər) s. tapón *m.*

stop·watch (:wŏch') s. cronómetro.
stor·age (stôr'ĭj) s. almacenamiento; *(space)* almacén *m; (fee)* almacenaje *m;* ELEC. acumulación *f* ♦ **s. battery** o **cell** acumulador.
store (stôr) **I.** s. *(shop)* tienda; *(supply)* surtido; *(warehouse)* almacén *m; (abundance)* acopio ♦ **department s.** gran almacén • **to be in s. for** one esperarle a uno • **to have in s.** tener guardado • **to set s. by** dar importancia a ♦ pl. MIL. *(equipment)* pertrechos; *(supplies)* provisiones **II.** tr. almacenar ♦ **to s. away** guardar • **to s. up** acumular.
store·house ('hous') s. almacén *m,* depósito.
store·keep·er (:kē'pər) s. *(shopkeeper)* tendero.
store·room (:rōōm') s. despensa, bodega.
sto·ried (stôr'ēd) adj. celebrado por la historia.
stork (stôrk) s. cigüeña.
storm (stôrm) **I.** s. tormenta; *(wind)* vendaval *m; (outburst)* arrebato; *(attack)* asalto; *(of protest)* lluvia ♦ **s. cellar** refugio contra los ciclones • **s. cloud** nubarrón • **s. door** contrapuerta • **s. trooper** miliciano nazi • **s. window** contraventana • **to ride out** o **weather a s.** capear el temporal **II.** intr. haber tormenta; *(to rant)* vociferar ♦ **to s. in, out** entrar, salir violentamente —tr. tomar por asalto.
storm·y (stôr'mē) adj. **-i-** tempestuoso; *(violent)* turbulento.
sto·ry¹ (stôr'ē) s. cuento, relato; *(plot)* trama; *(version)* versión *f; (article)* artículo; *(anecdote)* anécdota; *(lie)* mentira.
sto·ry² s. *(of a building)* piso.
sto·ry·book (:bŏŏk') s. libro de cuentos.
sto·ry·tell·er (:tĕl'ər) s. *(author)* cuentista *mf; (narrator)* narrador *m;* FAM. *(liar)* mentiroso.
stout (stout) **I.** adj. *(bulky)* corpulento; *(determined)* resuelto; *(brave)* valiente; *(sturdy)* fornido; *(substantial)* sólido; *(powerful)* enérgico; *(staunch)* firme **II.** s. cerveza de malta.
stout·heart·ed ('här'tĭd) adj. valiente.
stove¹ (stōv) s. cocina; *(heater)* estufa.
stove² cf. **stave.**
stow (stō) tr. guardar ♦ **to s. away** *(to put away)* guardar; *(on board)* viajar de polizón.
stow·a·way ('ə-wā') s. polizón *m.*
strad·dle (străd'l) **I.** tr. sentarse a horcajadas sobre o en; *(an issue)* no tomar ningún partido en ♦ **to s. the fence** nadar entre dos aguas **II.** s. posición *f* a horcajadas.
strafe (strāf) tr. bombardear.
strag·gle (străg'əl) intr. *(to fall behind)* rezagarse; *(to spread out)* desparramarse.
strag·gly (:lē) adj. desordenado.
straight (strāt) **I.** adj. *(line)* recto; *(upright, not bent)* derecho; *(frank)* franco; *(uninterrupted)* seguido; *(orderly)* arreglado; *(in sequence)* en orden; *(undiluted)* puro; *(honorable)* honrado; JER. *(conventional)* convencional; *(sober)* sobrio; *(not gay)* heterosexual ♦ **s. face** cara seria • **s. hair** pelo lacio • **s. razor** navaja de afeitar • **s. talk** lenguaje franco • **to keep a s. face** mantenerse impávido **II.** adv. en línea recta; *(erect)* derecho; *(without delay)* directamente; *(candidly)* sinceramente; *(continuously)* continuamente ♦ **s. ahead** en frente; *(forward)* todo seguido • **s. away** o **off** sin interrupción • **to get** o **put s.** poner en claro • **to go s.** enmendarse • **to look someone s. in the eye** mirar a alguien a los ojos • **to read s. through** leer de un tirón • **to set s.** corregir; *(to set right)* poner bien • **to tell something s.** decirle algo sin rodeos **III.** s. *(straight part)* recta; *(card se-*

quence) escalera ♦ **the s. and narrow** el buen camino.
straight·a·way ('ə-wā') s. recta.
straight·edge (:ĕj') s. regla (recta).
straight·en (:n) tr. & intr. enderezar(se) ♦ **to s. out** *(to put in order)* ordenar; *(to solve)* resolver; *(to rectify)* rectificar.
straight·for·ward (:-fôr'wərd) adj. *(direct)* directo; *(honest)* sincero.
straight·way (strāt'wā') adv. en seguida.
strain¹ (strān) **I.** tr. *(to stretch)* estirar; *(nerves)* agotar; *(limb)* torcer; *(to sieve)* colar; TEC. deformar ♦ **to s. one's eyes** cansar la vista —intr. *(to strive)* esforzarse; *(to stretch)* tenderse; *(to filter)* filtrarse ♦ **to s. under** soportar con gran esfuerzo **II.** s. *(effort)* esfuerzo; *(stress)* tensión *f; (burden)* peso; *(twisting)* torcedura; TEC. deformación *f.*
strain² s. *(race)* raza; *(descent)* cepa; *(tendency)* tendencia; *(tenor)* sentido; *(tune)* melodía.
strained (strānd) adj. colado; *(forced)* forzado; *(relations)* tirante.
strain·er (strā'nər) s. filtro; *(colander)* colador *m; (sieve)* cedazo.
strait (strāt) s. estrecho ♦ pl. *(narrows)* estrecho; *(jam)* aprieto.
strait·jack·et ('jăk'ĭt) s. camisa de fuerza.
strait-laced (:lāst') adj. puritano.
strand¹ (strănd) **I.** s. playa **II.** tr. & intr. *(to run aground)* encallar; *(to abandon)* dejar desamparado.
strand² s. *(of rope)* ramal *m; (single thread)* hebra; *(of pearls)* sarta.
strange (strānj) adj. *(unfamiliar)* desconocido; *(odd)* extraño, raro; *(peculiar)* peculiar; *(exotic)* exótico; *(uncommon)* desacostumbrado ♦ **strangest of all** lo más extraño del caso es que.
strang·er (strān'jər) s. *(unknown person)* desconocido; *(foreigner)* extranjero; *(outsider)* forastero ♦ **to be no s.** to conocer muy bien.
stran·gle (străng'gəl) tr. estrangular; *(to smother)* sofocar; FIG. sofocar, limitar.
stran·gu·late (:gyə-lāt') tr. & intr. estrangular(se).
stran·gu·la·tion (-lā'shən) s. estrangulación *f.*
strap (străp) **I.** s. *(strip)* tira, correa; *(band)* banda; *(of a dress)* tirante *m* **II.** tr. **-pp-** *(to fasten)* atar; *(to whip)* azotar; *(razor)* suavizar.
strap·less ('lĭs) adj. sin tiras; *(dress)* sin tirantes.
strapped (străpt) adj. FAM. sin un centavo.
strap·ping (străp'ĭng) adj. fornido.
stra·ta (strā'tə, străt'ə) cf. **stratum.**
strat·a·gem (străt'ə-jəm) s. estratagema.
stra·te·gic (strə-tē'jĭk) adj. estratégico.
strat·e·gist (străt'ə-jĭst) s. estratega *m.*
strat·e·gy (străt'ə-jē) s. estrategia.
strat·i·fi·ca·tion (străt'ə-fĭ-kā'shən) s. estratificación *f.*
strat·i·fy ('-fī') tr. & intr. estratificar(se).
strat·o·sphere (străt'ə-sfîr') s. estratósfera.
stra·tum (strā'təm) s. [pl. **s** o **-ta**] estrato.
straw (strô) **I.** s. BOT. paja; *(trifle)* comino ♦ **a s. in the wind** un indicio • **the last s.** la última gota • **to grasp at straws** agarrarse a un pelo • **to draw straws** echar suertes **II.** adj. de paja; *(color)* pajizo; FIG. insignificante.
straw·ber·ry (strô'bĕr'ē) s. fresa.
stray (strā) **I.** intr. *(to roam)* errar; *(to go astray)* descarriarse **II.** s. animal *m* callejero **III.** adj. *(lost)* perdido <**s. bullet** bala perdida>; *(lone)* aislado; *(scattered)* disperso.

streak (strēk) **I.** s. *(stripe)* raya; *(trait)* fondo; *(of luck)* racha; *(of lightning)* rayo **II.** tr. rayar —intr. pasar como un rayo.

streak·y (strē'kē) adj. **-i-** *(streaked)* rayado; *(veined)* veteado.

stream (strēm) **I.** s. arroyo; *(flow)* chorro; *(of insults)* sarta; *(of tears)* torrente m; *(of people)* oleada ♦ **to go with the s.** seguir la corriente **II.** intr. correr; *(to wave)* ondear ♦ **to s. in** entrar a raudales • **to s. out** *(people)* salir en tropel; *(liquid)* salir a torrentes.

stream·er (strē'mər) s. *(pennant)* gallardete m; *(long strip)* serpentina; *(headline)* titular m.

stream·line (strēm'līn') tr. construir en forma aerodinámica; *(to modernize)* modernizar.

stream·lined (:līnd') s. aerodinámico; FIG. modernizado.

street (strēt) s. calle f.

street·car ('kär') s. tranvía m.

street·walk·er (:wô'kər) s. prostituta.

strength (strĕngkth) s. fuerza; *(of material)* resistencia; *(vigor)* fortaleza; *(solidity)* solidez f; *(intensity)* intensidad f; *(validity)* validez f; *(efficacy)* eficacia; *(potency)* potencia ♦ **by sheer s.** a fuerza viva • **on the s. of** en virtud de • **s. of character** entereza • **to be present in great s.** estar en gran número.

strength·en (strĕngk'thən) tr. *(to reinforce)* reforzar; *(physically)* fortalecer; *(ties)* estrechar; *(relations)* intensificar —intr. fortalecerse, intensificarse.

stren·u·ous (strĕn'yo͞o-əs) adj. *(active)* vigoroso; *(energetic)* enérgico.

strep·to·coc·cus (strĕp'tə-kŏk'əs) s. [pl. **-ci**] estreptococo.

stress (strĕs) **I.** s. *(significance)* hincapié m; *(tension)* tensión f; MED. fatiga nerviosa; GRAM. énfasis m; MEC. fatiga ♦ **to lay s. on** insistir en **II.** tr. hacer hincapié en; MEC. someter a un esfuerzo; GRAM. acentuar.

stretch (strĕch) **I.** tr. estirar; *(to reach)* extender; *(wings)* desplegar; *(wire)* tender; *(shoes)* ensanchar ♦ **to s. a point** excederse • **to s. it** exagerar • **to s. oneself** desperezarse • **to s. the rules** hacer una excepción —intr. estirarse; *(shoes)* ensancharse ♦ **to s. out** estirarse; *(to lie down)* tumbarse **II.** s. *(lengthening)* alargamiento; *(elasticity)* elasticidad f; *(of road)* tramo; *(of track)* recta; *(of time)* período; *(of imagination)* esfuerzo ♦ **at a s.** seguido • **home s.** última etapa.

stretch·er ('ər) s. *(litter)* camilla; *(for canvas)* bastidor m.

stretch·er-bear·er (:bâr'ər) s. camillero.

strew (stro͞o) tr. **-ed, -ed** o **-n** *(to scatter)* esparcir, desparramar; *(to cover)* cubrir (with de).

stri·a·tion (strī-ā'shən) s. estriación f.

strick·en (strĭk'ən) **I.** cf. **strike II.** adj. afligido.

strict (strĭkt) adj. estricto.

strict·ly ('lē) adv. estrictamente; *(severely)* severamente ♦ **s. speaking** en realidad.

stric·ture (strĭk'chər) s. censura; MED. estrechez f.

stride (strīd) **I.** intr. **strode, stridden** caminar a grandes pasos **II.** s. zancada ♦ **to take in one's s.** tomarse con calma ♦ pl. progreso • **to make great s.** progresar a grandes pasos.

stri·dent (strīd'nt) adj. estridente.

strife (strīf) s. disensión f; *(conflict)* conflicto.

strike (strīk) **I.** tr. **struck, struck** o **stricken** golpear; *(to inflict)* asestar; *(to crash into)* cho-

car con; *(to attack)* atacar; *(coins)* acuñar; *(lightning)* caer en; *(hour)* dar; *(match)* encender; *(to expunge)* tachar; *(oil)* hallar; *(terror)* infundir; *(a pose)* adoptar; *(camp)* desmontar; *(employer)* declararse en huelga contra ♦ **to s. a jury** elegir jurado • **to s. an average** encontrar el término medio • **to s. blind** cegar • **to s. down** derribar; *(disease)* abatir • **to s. off** *(to expunge)* sacar; *(to cross out)* tachar; *(to deduct)* deducir • **to s. one as** dar la impresión de • **to s. out** tachar • **to s. roots** echar raíces • **to s. through** atravesar • **to s. up** *(friendship)* trabar; *(music)* empezar a tocar; *(conversation)* entablar • **to s. upon** ocurrírsele a uno • **to s. with admiration** llenar de admiración • **to s. with terror** sobrecoger de terror —intr. golpear, dar golpes; *(to attack)* atacar; *(bell)* sonar; *(to set out)* dirigirse hacia; *(to stop work)* declararse en huelga ♦ **to s. back** devolver golpe por golpe • **to s. home** dar en el blanco • **to s. out** *(to hit out)* pegar; *(to start out)* tomar una resolución; *(to fail)* fallar • **to s. out (for)** ponerse en marcha (hacia) • **to s. up** MÚS. empezar a tocar **II.** s. *(act)* golpe m; *(attack)* ataque m; *(labor)* huelga <on s. en huelga>; *(discovery)* descubrimiento ♦ **a lucky s.** FAM. un golpe de suerte • **to go on s.** declararse en huelga • **to have two strikes against one** FAM. estar uno en posición desventajosa.

strike·break·er ('brā'kər) s. rompehuelgas mf.

strik·er (strī'kər) s. huelguista mf.

strik·ing (:kĭng) adj. notable.

string (strĭng) **I.** s. cuerda; *(row)* hilera; *(series)* serie f ♦ **s. bean** CUL. judía verde • **s. of beads** rosario; *(necklace)* collar • **s. orchestra, quartet** orquesta, cuarteto de cuerdas • **to have on a s.** tener en un puño ♦ pl. MÚS. instrumentos de cuerda; *(conditions)* estipulaciones **II.** tr. **strung** *(to fit with strings)* encordar; *(to thread)* ensartar; *(to fasten)* atar con una cuerda; *(to stretch)* tender ♦ **high strung** muy nervioso • **to s. along with** acompañar a • **to s. someone along** dejar a alguien pendiente; *(to deceive)* engañar.

strin·gen·cy (strĭn'jən-sē) s. *(severity)* rigor m; *(scarcity)* escasez f.

strin·gent (:jənt) adj. riguroso; *(strict)* estricto; *(pressing)* apurado.

string·y (strĭng'ē) adj. **-i-** fibroso; *(with strings)* lleno de fibras.

strip¹ (strĭp) tr. **-pp-** *(to undress)* desnudar; *(bed)* deshacer; *(fruit)* pelar; *(tree)* descortezar; *(to dismantle)* desmantelar; *(gear)* estropear ♦ **to s. down** *(paint)* raspar; *(motor)* desmontar • **s. mine** mina a cielo abierto • **to s. of** despojar de • **to s. off** quitar —intr. desvestirse ♦ **to s. off** desnudarse.

strip² s. faja; AER. pista de aterrizaje.

stripe (strīp) **I.** s. raya; *(chevron)* galón m; *(kind)* calaña **II.** tr. rayar.

striped (strīpt, strī'pĭd) adj. a rayas, rayado.

strip·ling (strĭp'lĭng) s. mozalbete m.

strip-mine (:mīn') tr. explotar una mina a cielo abierto.

strip·per (:ər) s. bailarina de strip-tease.

strive (strīv) intr. **-ed** o **strove, -ed** o **-n** esforzarse; *(to struggle)* luchar.

strobe (strōb) s. FOTOG. estroboscopio; *(light)* luz estroboscópica ♦ **s. light** luz estroboscópica.

strode (strōd) cf. **stride.**

stroke (strōk) **I.** s. golpe m; *(of bell)* campanada; *(apoplexy)* apoplejía; *(in rowing)* palada; *(in swimming)* brazada; *(with brush)* pincelada; *(with pen)* trazo ♦ **at the s. of . . .** al dar las . . . • **finishing s.** golpe de gracia • **s. of luck** suerte • **s. of genius** idea genial • **with one s.** de un plumazo II. tr. acariciar.

stroll (strōl) I. intr. pasearse II. s. paseo.

stroll·er (strō′lər) s. paseante *mf*; *(pram)* cochecito de niño.

strong (strông) adj. fuerte; *(powerful)* poderoso; *(persuasive)* persuasivo; *(language)* subido de tono *or* color ♦ **s. point** fuerte • **to be going s.** FAM. marchar bien • **to be s. in numbers** ser numerosos • **to have a s. character** tener mucho carácter • **to have a s. stomach** tener un buen estómago • **to have s. feelings about** tener ideas muy firmes sobre.

strong-arm (′ärm′) FAM. I. adj. de mano dura ♦ **s. tactics** fuerza II. tr. intimidar.

strong·box (:bŏks′) s. caja fuerte.

strong·hold (:hōld′) s. fortaleza.

strong-mind·ed (:mīn′dĭd) adj. determinado.

strop (strŏp) I. s. suavizador *m* (de navajas) II. tr. **-pp-** suavizar.

strove (strōv) cf. **strive.**

struck (strŭk) I. cf. **strike** II. adj. cerrado (por huelga).

struc·tur·al (strŭk′chər-əl) adj. estructural.

struc·ture (strŭk′chər) I. s. estructura II. tr. estructurar.

struc·tured (:chərd) adj. estructurado.

strug·gle (strŭg′əl) I. intr. luchar II. s. lucha; *(effort)* esfuerzo.

strug·gling (:lĭng) adj. que lucha.

strum (strŭm) MÚS. I. tr. & intr. **-mm-** rasguear II. s. rasgueo.

strung (strŭng) cf. **string.**

strut (strŭt) I. intr. **-tt-** pavonearse II. s. *(gait)* pavoneo; *(rod)* puntal *m*.

strych·nine (strĭk′nīn′) s. estricnina.

stub (stŭb) I. s. tocón *m*; *(check)* talón *m*; *(ticket)* resguardo II. tr. **-bb-** *(toe)* tropezar con; *(cigarette)* apagar.

stub·ble (′əl) s. rastrojo; *(beard)* barba incipiente ♦ **s. field** campo de rastrojos.

stub·born (stŭb′ərn) adj. testarudo; *(persistent)* tenaz; *(resistant)* duro.

stub·born·ness (:nĭs) s. testarudez *f*.

stub·by (stŭb′ē) adj. **-i-** rechoncho.

stuc·co (stŭk′ō) I. s. [pl. **(e)s**] estuco II. tr. estucar.

stuck (stŭk) cf. **stick.**

stuck-up (′ŭp′) adj. FAM. engreído.

stud¹ (stŭd) I. s. ARQ. montante *m*; *(ornament)* tachón *m*; *(brace)* travesaño; *(spindle)* espiga II. tr. **-dd-** tachonar; *(to strew)* salpicar.

stud² s. semental *m* ♦ **at s.** de cría.

stu·dent (stōōd′nt) s. estudiante *mf*; *(observer)* observador *m* ♦ **s. body** estudiantado.

stud·ied (stŭd′ēd) adj. afectado.

stu·di·o (stōō′dē-ō′) s. estudio; *(of artist)* taller *m* ♦ **s. apartment** departamento de una habitación, baño y cocina.

stu·di·ous (:əs) adj. estudioso; *(diligent)* aplicado.

stud·y (stŭd′ē) I. s. estudio II. tr. & intr. estudiar ♦ **to s. a part** aprender un papel • **to s. to be** estudiar para • **to s. under** ser alumno de.

stuff (stŭf) I. s. material *m*; FAM. *(belongings)* cosas; *(nonsense)* disparates; *(junk)* basura; *(capability)* pasta; G.B. *(fabric)* género ♦ **do your s.!** ¡muestra lo que sabes! • **same old s.**

lo mismo de siempre • **to be hot s.** ser fenomenal • **to know one's s.** conocer el percal II. tr. rellenar; *(to plug)* tapar; *(to gorge)* atiborrar ♦ **s. it!** FAM. ¡vete a paseo! • **to s. oneself** atiborrarse.

stuffed (stŭft) adj. relleno.

stuff·ing (stŭf′ĭng) s. relleno.

stuff·y (stŭf′ē) adj. **-i-** sofocante, mal ventilado; *(congested)* tupido; FAM. pomposo.

stul·ti·fy (stŭl′tə-fī′) tr. *(to dispirit)* desanimar; *(to disable)* anular; *(to ridicule)* ridiculizar.

stum·ble (stŭm′bəl) I. intr. *(to trip)* tropezar; *(to flounder)* balbucear; *(to blunder)* cometer un desliz ♦ **to s. across** *o* **upon** tropezar con • **stumbling block** tropiezo II. s. *(act)* tropiezo, traspié *m*; *(mistake)* desliz *m*.

stump (stŭmp) I. s. *(of tree)* tocón *m*; *(limb)* muñón *m*; *(tooth)* raigón *m*; *(place)* tribuna política ♦ **up a s.** perplejo II. tr. FAM. dejar perplejo —intr. POL. hacer giras políticas.

stump·y (stŭm′pē) adj. **-i-** *(person)* rechoncho; *(land)* lleno de tocones.

stun (stŭn) I. tr. **-nn-** dejar sin sentido; *(to astound)* dejar estupefacto II. s. choque *m*.

stung (stŭng) cf. **sting.**

stunk (stŭngk) cf. **stink.**

stun·ning (stŭn′ĭng) adj. imponente.

stunt¹ (stŭnt) tr. impedir el crecimiento de.

stunt² s. *(feat)* proeza; *(publicity trick)* truco publicitario.

stu·pe·fac·tion (stōō′pə-făk′shən) s. estupefacción *f*.

stu·pe·fy (′fī′) tr. *(to dull)* atontar; *(to amaze)* dejar estupefacto.

stu·pen·dous (stōō-pĕn′dəs) adj. estupendo; *(amazing)* asombroso.

stu·pid (stōō′pĭd) adj. **-er, -est** estúpido, tonto.

stu·pid·i·ty (:′ĭ-tē) s. estupidez *f*, tontería.

stu·por (stōō′pər) s. estupor *m*; *(daze)* atontamiento.

stur·di·ness (stûr′dē-nĭs) s. *(firmness)* firmeza; *(strength)* robustez *f*.

stur·dy (stûr′dē) adj. robusto; *(firm)* firme.

stur·geon (stûr′jən) s. esturión *m*.

stut·ter (stŭt′ər) I. intr. tartamudear II. s. tartamudeo.

stut·ter·er (:ər) s. tartamudo.

stut·ter·ing (:ĭng) I. s. tartamudeo II. adj. tartamudo.

sty¹ (stī) s. *(for swine)* pocilga.

sty² s. MED. orzuelo.

style (stīl) I. s. estilo; *(vogue)* moda; *(cut)* hechura; *(type)* modelo, tipo; *(title)* tratamiento; *(stylus)* aguja ♦ **in s.** con estilo; *(in vogue)* de moda II. tr. *(to stylize)* estilizar; *(to design)* diseñar; *(to designate)* titular.

styl·ish (stī′lĭsh) adj. a la moda.

styl·ist (:lĭst) s. diseñador *m*; *(hairdresser)* peluquero; LIT. estilista *mf*.

sty·lis·tic (-lĭs′tĭk) adj. estilístico.

styl·ize (′līz′) tr. estilizar.

sty·lus (stī′ləs) s. [pl. **es** *o* **-li**] estilo; *(needle)* aguja (de fonógrafo); *(tool)* punzón *m*.

sty·mie (stī′mē) tr. obstaculizar.

styp·tic (stĭp′tĭk) adj. astringente.

suave (swäv) adj. afable.

sub (sŭb) FAM. I. s. *(submarine)* submarino; *(substitute)* sustituto; *(sandwich)* emparedado grande II. intr. **-bb-** substituir.

sub·a·tom·ic (sŭb′ə-tŏm′ĭk) adj. subatómico.

sub·com·mit·tee (′kə-mĭt′ē) s. subcomité *m*.

sub·com·pact (-kŏm′păkt′) s. automóvil pequeño.

sub·con·scious ('kŏn'shəs) adj. & s. subconsciente m.

sub·con·ti·nent (:kŏn'tə-nənt) s. subcontinente m.

sub·con·tract (-kŏn'trăkt') I. s. subcontrato II. tr. (kən-trăkt') subcontratar.

sub·cu·ta·ne·ous (' kyoō-tā'nē-əs) adj. subcutáneo.

sub·di·vide (:dĭ-vīd') tr. & intr. subdividir(se).

sub·di·vi·sion ('vĭzh'ən) subdivisión f.

sub·due (səb-dōō') tr. sojuzgar; *(to make tractable)* amansar; *(to tone down)* suavizar.

sub·group (sŭb'groōp') s. subgrupo.

sub·hu·man (-hyoō'mən) adj. infrahumano.

sub·ject (sŭb'jĭkt) I. adj. dominado ♦ **s. matter** materia ♦ **s. to** *(prone to)* propenso a; *(exposed to)* expuesto a; *(dependent on)* sujeto a II. s. sujeto; *(of country)* súbdito; *(theme)* tema; *(course)* asignatura ♦ **on the s. of** a propósito de ♦ **to keep off a s.** no tocar el tema III. tr. (səb-jĕkt') someter ♦ **to s. to** exponer a; *(to make dependent on)* supeditar a.

sub·jec·tion (səb-jĕk'shən) s. sujeción f.

sub·jec·tive (:tĭv) adj. subjetivo.

sub·jec·tiv·i·ty (sŭb'jĕk-tĭv'ĭ-tē) s. subjetividad f.

sub·ju·gate (sŭb'jə-gāt') tr. subyugar.

sub·ju·ga·tion ('-gā'shən) s. dominación f.

sub·lease (sŭb-lēs') I. tr. subarrendar II. s. ('lēs') subarrendamiento.

sub·let (:lĕt') I. tr. **let, -tting** subalquilar II. s. ('lĕt') FAM. subarrendamiento.

sub·li·mate (sŭb'lə-māt') tr. sublimar.

sub·li·ma·tion ('-mā'shən) s. sublimación f.

sub·lime (sə-blīm') I. adj. sublime II. tr. & intr. sublimar(se).

sub·lim·i·nal (sə-blĭm'ə-nəl) adj. subconsciente.

sub·ma·chine gun (sŭb'mə-shēn') s. pistola ametralladora, metralleta.

sub·ma·rine (sŭb'mə-rēn') I. adj. submarino II. s. submarino; JER. sandwich m grande.

sub·merge (səb-mûrj') tr. sumergir.

sub·mer·gence (:mûr'jəns) s. sumersión f.

sub·merse (:mûrs') tr. sumergir.

sub·mis·sion (:mĭsh'ən) s. *(act)* sometimiento; *(meekness)* sumisión f; *(proposal)* proposición f.

sub·mis·sive (:mĭs'ĭv) adj. sumiso.

sub·mit (səb-mĭt') tr. someter; *(evidence)* presentar; *(to propose)* proponer; *(to suggest)* sugerir —intr. *(to give in)* someterse; *(meekly)* conformarse.

sub·nor·mal (sŭb-nôr'məl) adj. subnormal.

sub·or·di·nate (sə-bôr'dn-ĭt) I. adj. & s. subordinado II. tr. (:āt') subordinar.

sub·or·di·na·tion (-'-ā'shən) s. subordinación f.

sub·orn (sə-bôrn') tr. sobornar.

sub·poe·na (sə-pē'nə) DER. I. s. citación f II. tr. citar.

sub·scribe (səb-scrīb') tr. subscribir —intr. subscribirse; *(to magazines)* abonarse.

sub·scrib·er (:skrī'bər) s. subscriptor m.

sub·scrip·tion (:skrĭp'shən) s. firma; *(purchase)* subscripción f, abono.

sub·se·quent (sŭb'sĭ-kwěnt') adj. subsiguiente.

sub·ser·vi·ent (səb-sûr'vē-ənt) adj. subordinado; *(servile)* servil.

sub·side (səb-sīd') intr. *(to sink)* hundirse; *(to settle)* asentarse; *(to abate)* apaciguarse.

sub·sid·i·ar·y (səb-sĭd'ē-ĕr'ē) I. adj. auxiliar; *(secondary)* secundario; *(of subsidy)* subsidiario II. s. *(company)* sucursal f.

sub·si·dize (sŭb'sĭ-dīz') tr. subvencionar.

sub·si·dy (:dē) s. subsidio; *(monetary aid)* subvención f.

sub·sist (səb-sĭst') intr. subsistir; *(to maintain life)* sustentarse *(on con, de).*

sub·sis·tence (-sĭs'təns) s. subsistencia; *(sustenance)* sustento.

sub·soil (sŭb'soil') s. subsuelo.

sub·stance (sŭb'stəns) s. substancia; *(essence)* esencia; *(solidity)* solidez f; *(body)* cuerpo; *(goods)* caudal m ♦ **man of s.** hombre acaudalado.

sub·stan·dard (sŭb-stăn'dərd) adj. inferior a lo normal.

sub·stan·tial (səb-stăn'shəl) adj. material; *(real)* verdadero; *(strong)* sólido; *(meal)* sustancioso; *(important)* sustancial; *(considerable)* considerable; *(well-to-do)* adinerado.

sub·stan·ti·ate (:shē-āt') tr. establecer.

sub·stan·ti·a·tion (-'-ā'shən) s. justificación f.

sub·stan·tive (sŭb'stən-tĭv) I. adj. real; *(essential)* esencial II. s. GRAM. sustantivo.

sub·sti·tute (sŭb'stĭ-tōōt') I. s. substituto II. tr. & intr. substituir.

sub·sti·tu·tion ('-tōō'shən) s. substitución f.

sub·sume (səb-soōm') tr. incluir en una categoría.

sub·ter·fuge (sŭb'tər-fyoōj') s. subterfugio.

sub·ter·ra·ne·an (sŭb'tə-rā'nē-ən) adj. subterráneo.

sub·ti·tle ('tīt'l) I. s. subtítulo II. tr. subtitular.

sub·tle (sŭt'l) adj. **-er, -est** *(elusive)* sutil; *(keen)* agudo; *(clever)* astuto; *(devious)* taimado.

sub·tle·ty (:tē) s. *(cleverness)* astucia; *(distinction)* sutileza.

sub·to·tal (sŭb'tōt'l) I. s. subtotal m II. tr. ('l) sumar parte de una serie de números.

sub·tract (səb-trăkt') tr. sustraer.

sub·trac·tion (:trăk'shən) s. sustracción f.

sub·urb (sŭb'ûrb') s. suburbio ♦ **pl.** afueras.

sub·ur·ban (sə-bûr'bən) adj. suburbano.

sub·ur·ban·ite (:bə-nīt') s. habitante mf de las afueras.

sub·ven·tion (səb-věn'shən) s. subvención f.

sub·ver·sion (səb-vûr'zhən) s. subversión f.

sub·ver·sive (:sĭv) adj. subversivo.

sub·vert (səb-vûrt') tr. *(to corrupt)* corromper; *(to overthrow)* derrocar.

sub·way (sŭb'wā') s. subterráneo, metro; *(passage)* paso subterráneo.

suc·ceed (sək-sēd') intr. tener éxito; *(to turn out well)* salir bien; *(to follow)* suceder ♦ **to s. to the throne** heredar el trono —tr. suceder a; *(to follow)* seguir.

suc·cess (:sěs') s. éxito; *(person)* persona que tiene éxito.

suc·cess·ful (:fəl) adj. de éxito, exitoso.

suc·ces·sion (sək-sěsh'ən) s. sucesión f ♦ **in s.** seguido ♦ **in s. to** como sucesor de.

suc·ces·sive (:sěs'ĭv) adj. sucesivo; *(consecutive)* consecutivo.

suc·ces·sor (:ər) s. sucesor m.

suc·cinct (sək-sĭngkt') adj. sucinto.

suc·cor (sŭk'ər) I. s. socorro II. tr. socorrer.

suc·cu·lence (sŭk'yə-ləns) s. suculencia.

suc·cu·lent (:lənt) I. adj. suculento; BOT. carnoso II. s. planta carnosa.

suc·cumb (sə-kŭm′) intr. sucumbir; *(to die)* morir.

such (sŭch) I. adj. *(of this nature)* tal, semejante; *(of this kind)* de este tipo; *(so extreme)* tanto, semejante; *(so big)* tan, tan grande; *(so much)* tanto ♦ **one s.** un tal • **s. and s.** tal y cual • **s. as it is** tal cual es II. adv. tan III. pron. los que; *(so great)* tal; *(the like)* cosas por el estilo ♦ **as s.** *(of itself)* en sí; *(as what one is)* como tal • **s. is life** así es la vida.

such·like (′lïk′) I. adj. de esta clase, de este tipo II. pron. cosas *or* personas semejantes.

suck (sŭk) I. tr. chupar; *(a liquid)* sorber; *(air)* aspirar —intr. dar chupadas II. s. chupada.

suck·er (′ər) I. s. chupador *m*; FAM. *(dupe)* primo, incauto; *(lollipop)* pirulí *m*; *(mouth part)* ventosa; BOT. chupón *m*.

suck·le (:əl) tr. amamantar; *(to rear)* criar —intr. tomar el pecho.

suck·ling (:lïng) s. mamón *m*.

su·crose (sōō′krōs′) s. sucrosa.

suc·tion (sŭk′shən) s. succión *f*; *(aspiration)* aspiración ♦ **s. pump** bomba aspirante.

sud·den (sŭd′n) adj. *(unforeseen)* imprevisto; *(abrupt)* brusco; *(swift)* súbito, repentino ♦ **all of a s.** de repente.

sud·den·ly (:lē) adv. de repente.

suds (sŭdz) s.pl. *(soapy water)* jabonaduras; *(lather)* espuma; FAM. *(beer)* cerveza.

sue (sōō) tr. suplicar; DER. demandar ♦ **to s. for divorce** presentar demanda de divorcio —intr. entablar acción judicial.

suede *o* **suède** (swād) s. gamuza, ante *m*.

su·et (sōō′ĭt) s. sebo.

suf·fer (sŭf′ər) intr. ser dañado —tr. sufrir ♦ **to s. from** adolecer de.

suf·fer·ance (əns) s. tolerancia; *(tacit assent)* consentimiento tácito.

suf·fice (sə-fīs′) intr. bastar ♦ **s. it to say** basta (con) decir.

suf·fi·cien·cy (sə-fĭsh′ən-sē) s. suficiencia.

suf·fi·cient (:ənt) adj. bastante, suficiente.

suf·fi·cient·ly (:lē) adv. bastante.

suf·fix (sŭf′ĭks′) s. sufijo.

suf·fo·cate (sŭf′ə-kāt′) tr. & intr. sofocar(se); *(to stifle)* reprimir(se).

suf·fo·ca·tion (′-kā′shən) s. asfixia.

suf·frage (sŭf′rĭj) s. sufragio; *(right)* derecho al voto.

suf·fuse (sə-fyōōz′) tr. extenderse por.

suf·fu·sion (sə-fyōō′zhən) s. difusión *f*.

sug·ar (shōōg′ər) I. s. azúcar *mf* ♦ **s. bowl** azucarero • **s. cane** caña de azúcar • **s. loaf** pan de azúcar • **s. mill** ingenio II. tr. azucarar ♦ **to s. the pill** FIG. dorar la píldora.

sug·ar-coat (:kōt′) tr. endulzar.

sug·ar·y (shōōg′ə-rē) adj. -i- azucarado; *(tasting like sugar)* dulzón; FAM. *(cloyingly)* meloso.

sug·gest (səg-jĕst′) tr. sugerir; *(to evoke)* hacer pensar en; *(to imply)* insinuar.

sug·ges·tion (:jĕs′chən) s. sugerencia; *(hint)* indicación *f*; PSIC. sugestión *f*.

sug·ges·tive (:tĭv) adj. sugestivo; *(indicative)* evocador; *(insinuating)* insinuante.

su·i·cid·al (sōō′ĭ-sīd′l) adj. suicida.

su·i·cide (sōō′ĭ-sīd′) s. suicidio; *(person)* suicida *mf* ♦ **to commit s.** suicidarse.

suit (sōōt) I. s. traje *m*; *(set)* conjunto; *(cards)* palo; *(legal)* pleito; *(courtship)* galanteo ♦ **to bring s.** entablar un pleito • **to follow s.** *(in cards)* jugar el mismo palo; FIG. seguir el ejemplo II. tr. satisfacer; *(to look good)* quedar bien

♦ **to s. oneself** hacer lo que uno quiere • **to s. to** adaptar a.

suit·a·bil·i·ty (sōō′tə-bĭl′ĭ-tē) s. conveniencia.

suit·a·ble (′-bəl) adj. conveniente; *(compatible)* compatible.

suit·case (sōōt′kās′) s. maleta.

suite (swēt) s. *(retinue)* séquito; *(apartment)* suite *f*; *(furniture)* juego; MÚS. suite.

suit·or (sōō′tər) s. peticionario; *(wooer)* pretendiente *m*.

sul·fate (sŭl′fāt′) s. sulfato.

sul·fide (:fīd′) s. sulfuro.

sul·fite (:fīt′) s. sulfito.

sulfur (:fər) s. azufre *m* ♦ **s. dioxide** dióxido de azufre.

sul·fu·ric (-fyŏōr′ĭk) adj. sulfúrico.

sul·fur·ous (′fər-əs) adj. sulfuroso; *(from burning sulfur)* azufroso.

sulk (sŭlk) I. intr. estar de malhumor II. s. mal humor *m*.

sulk·y¹ (sŭl′kē) adj. -i- malhumorado.

sulk·y² s. *(vehicle)* tílburi *m*, sulky *m*.

sul·len (sŭl′ən) adj. -er, -est *(ill-humored)* resentido; *(gloomy)* sombrío.

sul·ly (sŭl′ē) tr. manchar.

sul·phur¹ (sŭl′fər) s. mariposa anaranjada *o* amarilla.

sul·phur² var. de **sulfur**.

sul·tan (sŭl′tən) s. sultán *m*.

sul·try (sŭl′trē) adj. -i- bochornoso; *(torrid)* tórrido; *(voluptuous)* voluptuoso.

sum (sŭm) I. s. suma; *(total)* total *m*; *(of money)* cantidad *f* ♦ **in s.** en resumen ♦ pl. aritmética II. tr. -mm- sumar ♦ **to s. up** resumir.

su·mac(h) (sōō′măk′) s. zumaque *m*.

sum·ma·rize (sŭm′ə-rīz′) tr. resumir.

sum·ma·ry (:rē) I. adj. sumario; *(fast)* rápido II. s. resumen *m*.

sum·ma·tion (sə-mā′shən) s. recapitulación *f*.

sum·mer (sŭm′ər) I. s. verano ♦ **s. squash** calabaza II. intr. veranear *(at, in* en).

sum·mer·house (:hous′) s. cenador *m*.

sum·mer·time (:tīm′) s. verano, estío.

sum·mit (sŭm′ĭt) s. cúspide *f*.

sum·mon (sŭm′ən) tr. convocar; *(to send for)* llamar; DER. citar ♦ **to s. up** armarse de.

sum·mons (sŭm′ənz) I. s. [pl. **es**] notificación *f*; DER. *(to defendant)* citación *f* judicial; *(to juror)* requerimiento judicial II. tr. citar ante la justicia.

sump·tu·ous (sŭmp′chōō-əs) adj. suntuoso.

sun (sŭn) I. s. sol *m* ♦ **in the s.** al sol • **a place in the s.** una buena situación • **s. lamp** lámpara de rayos ultravioletas • **under the s.** en el mundo II. tr. & intr. -nn- asolear(se).

sun·bathe (′bāth′) intr. tomar el sol.

sun·bon·net (:bŏn′ĭt) s. cofia, papalina.

sun·burn (:bûrn′) I. quemadura de sol II. tr. & intr. **-ed** *o* **-burnt** quemar(se) al sol.

sun·burst (:bûrst′) s. sol *m* resplandeciente.

sun·dae (sŭn′dē) s. helado con frutas, nueces y almíbar.

Sun·day (sŭn′dē) s. domingo.

sun·der (sŭn′dər) tr. & intr. separar(se).

sun·di·al (sŭn′dī′əl) s. reloj *m* de sol.

sun·down (:doun′) s. ocaso.

sun·dries (sŭn′drēz) s.pl. artículos diversos.

sun·dry (sŭn′drē) adj. diversos.

sun·fish (sŭn′fĭsh′) s. [pl. inv. *o* **es**] pez *m* luna.

sun·flow·er (:flou′ər) s. girasol *m*.

sung (sŭng) cf. **sing**.

sun·glass·es (sŭn′glăs′ĭz) s.pl. gafas de sol.
sunk (sŭngk) cf. **sink.**
sunk·en (sŭng′kən) adj. hundido.
sun·less (sŭn′lĭs) adj. sin sol; *(gloomy)* sombrío.
sun·light (:līt′) s. luz *f* del sol.
sun·lit (:līt′) adj. iluminado por el sol.
sun·ny (:ē) adj. **-i-** soleado; *(cheerful)* risueño.
sun·rise (:rīz′) s. amanecer *m.*
sun·roof (:rōōf′) s. capota.
sun·set (:sĕt′) s. ocaso.
sun·shine (:shīn′) s. luz *f* del sol; *(happiness)* alegría.
sun·spot (:spŏt′) s. mancha solar.
sun·stroke (:strōk′) s. insolación *f.*
sun·tan (:tăn′) s. bronceado.
sun·up (:ŭp′) s. salida del sol.
sup (sŭp) intr. **-pp-** cenar.
su·per (sōō′pər) FAM. I. s. conserje *m* II. adj. estupendo.
su·per·a·ble (sōō′pər-ə-bəl) adj. superable.
su·per·an·nu·at·ed (sōō′pər-ăn′yōō-ā′tĭd) adj. *(retired)* jubilado; *(obsolete)* anticuado.
su·perb (sōō-pûrb′) adj. excelente, soberbio.
su·per·cil·i·ous (sōō′pər-sĭl′ē-əs) adj. desdeñoso.
su·per·fi·cial (sōō′pər-fĭsh′əl) adj. superficial.
su·per·fi·ci·al·i·ty (-′-ē-ăl′ĭ-tē) s. superficialidad *f.*
su·per·flu·ous (sōō-pûr′flōō-əs) adj. superfluo.
su·per·high·way (sōō′pər-hī′wā′) s. autopista.
su·per·hu·man (:hyōō′mən) adj. sobrehumano.
su·per·im·pose (:ĭm-pōz′) tr. sobreponer.
su·per·in·tend (:ĭn-tĕnd′) tr. supervisar.
su·per·in·ten·dent (:ĭn-tĕn′dənt) s. superintendente *m; (of building)* conserje *m.*
su·pe·ri·or (sōō-pîr′ē-ər) adj. & s. superior *m.*
su·pe·ri·or·i·ty (-′-ôr′ĭ-tē) s. superioridad *f.*
su·per·la·tive (sōō-pûr′lə-tĭv) adj. & s. superlativo.
su·per·man (sōō′pər-măn′) s. [pl. **-men**] superhombre *m.*
su·per·mar·ket (:mär′kĭt) s. supermercado.
su·per·nat·u·ral (′-năch′ər-əl) adj. sobrenatural.
su·per·nu·mer·ar·y (:nōō′mə-rĕr′ē) I. adj. supernumerario II. s. supernumerario; TEAT. figurante *m.*
su·per·pow·er (′-pou′ər) s. superpotencia.
su·per·sat·u·rate (′-săch′ə-rāt′) tr. supersaturar.
su·per·script (′-skrĭpt′) I. adj. sobrescrito II. s. signo *o* índice sobrescrito.
su·per·sede (′-sēd′) tr. suplantar.
su·per·sen·si·tive (:sĕn′sĭ-tĭv) adj. hipersensible.
su·per·son·ic (:sŏn′ĭk) adj. supersónico.
su·per·star (′-stär′) s. gran estrella.
su·per·sti·tion (sōō′pər-stĭsh′ən) s. superstición *f.*
su·per·sti·tious (:əs) adj. supersticioso.
su·per·struc·ture (sōō′pər-strŭk′chər) s. superestructura.
su·per·vene (′-vēn′) intr. sobrevenir.
su·per·vise (′-vīz′) tr. supervisar.
su·per·vi·sion (′-vĭzh′ən) s. supervisión *f.*
su·per·vi·sor (′-vī′zər) s. supervisor *m.*
su·per·vi·so·ry (′-′zə-rē) adj. de supervisión, de supervisor.
su·pine (sōō-pīn′) adj. supino; *(passive)* indolente.

sup·per (sŭp′ər) s. cena ♦ **to have s.** cenar.
sup·plant (sə-plănt′) tr. suplantar.
sup·ple (sŭp′əl) adj. **-er, -est** flexible.
sup·ple·ment (sŭp′lə-mənt) I. s. suplemento II. tr. suplir; *(to add to)* aumentar.
sup·ple·men·ta·ry/tal (′-mĕn′tə-rē/tl) adj. suplementario.
sup·pli·cant (sŭp′lĭ-kənt) s. & adj. suplicante *m.*
sup·pli·cate (:kāt′) tr. & intr. suplicar.
sup·pli·ca·tion (′-kā′shən) s. súplica.
sup·pli·er (sə-plī′ər) s. suministrador *m.*
sup·ply (sə-plī′) I. tr. suministrar; *(to satisfy)* satisfacer II. s. suministro; *(stock)* surtido; ECON. oferta ♦ **in short s.** escaso ♦ pl. provisiones; MIL. pertrechos • **office s.** artículos de oficina.
sup·port (sə-pôrt′) I. tr. sostener; *(to bear)* soportar; *(doubts)* confirmar; *(a child)* mantener; *(with money)* ayudar ♦ **to s. oneself** ganarse la vida II. s. apoyo; ARQ., TEC. soporte *m; (maintenance)* mantenimiento.
sup·port·er (sə-pôr′tər) s. soporte *m; (advocate)* partidario.
sup·por·tive (:tĭv) adj. sustentador.
sup·pose (sə-pōz′) I. tr. suponer; *(to believe)* creer ♦ **s. we dine together** ¿qué tal si cenamos juntos? —intr. imaginarse.
sup·posed (sə-pōzd′, -pō′zĭd) adj. *(presumed)* presunto; *(required)* supuesto.
sup·pos·ing (sə-pō′zĭng) conj. en el supuesto de que.
sup·po·si·tion (sŭp′ə-zĭsh′ən) s. suposición *f.*
sup·pos·i·to·ry (sə-pŏz′ĭ-tôr′ē) s. supositorio *m.*
sup·press (sə-prĕs′) tr. suprimir; *(to prohibit)* prohibir; *(to restrain)* contener.
sup·pres·sion (sə-prĕsh′ən) s. supresión *f; (repression)* represión *f.*
sup·pres·sive (sə-prĕs′ĭv) adj. represivo.
sup·pu·rate (sŭp′yə-rāt′) intr. supurar.
sup·pu·ra·tion (′-rā′shən) s. supuración *f.*
su·prem·a·cy (sə-prĕm′ə-sē) s. supremacía.
su·preme (sōō-prēm′) adj. supremo ♦ **s. court** corte supremo.
sur·charge (sûr′chärj′) I. s. sobrecarga; *(overcharge)* recargo II. tr. sobrecargar, recargar.
sure (shŏr) I. adj. seguro; *(infallible)* certero; *(hand)* firme ♦ **s. thing!** ¡claro! • **to be s.** sin duda • **to make s.** asegurarse II. adv. seguramente; *(of course)* claro ♦ **for s.** con toda seguridad • **s. enough** efectivamente.
sure-fire (′fīr′) adj. FAM. de éxito seguro.
sure-foot·ed (:fŏŏt′ĭd) adj. de pie firme.
sure·ty (:ĭ-tē) s. seguridad *f; (pledge)* garantía; *(person)* garante *mf.*
surf (sûrf) I. s. oleaje *m* II. intr. hacer surfing.
sur·face (sûr′fəs) I. s. superficie *f* ♦ **on the s.** en apariencia II. adj. superficial III. intr. salir a la superficie.
surf·board (sûrf′bôrd′) s. tabla hawaiana.
sur·feit (sûr′fĭt) I. tr. hartar II. s. hartura; *(indigestion)* empacho; *(excess)* exceso.
surf·ing (sûr′fĭng) s. surfing *m,* deporte *m* de la tabla hawaiana.
surge (sûrj) I. intr. *(the sea)* encresparse; *(energy, enthusiasm)* subir súbitamente II. s. *(of waves)* oleada; *(billow)* mar *mf* de fondo; *(onrush)* arranque *m;* ELEC. sobretensión *f.*
sur·geon (sûr′jən) s. cirujano.
sur·ger·y (:jə-rē) s. intervención quirúrgica; *(room)* quirófano; *(work)* cirugía.
sur·gi·cal (:jĭ-kəl) adj. quirúrgico.

sur·ly (sûr'lē) adj. **-i-** malhumorado.
sur·mise (sər-mīz') I. tr. conjeturar II. s. conjetura.
sur·mount (sər-mount') tr. superar; *(to climb)* escalar.
sur·name (sûr'nām) s. apellido.
sur·pass (sər-păs') tr. sobrepasar; *(to exceed)* superar.
sur·pass·ing (:ĭng) adj. incomparable.
sur·plice (sûr'plĭs) s. sobrepelliz *f.*
sur·plus (sûr'pləs) I. adj. excedente II. s. excedente *m;* COM. superávit *m.*
sur·prise (sər-prīz') I. tr. sorprender ♦ **to be surprised at** sorprenderse de *o* con II. s. sorpresa ♦ **s. attack** ataque por sorpresa ♦ **s. visit** visita inesperada ♦ **to take by s.** coger desprevenido.
sur·pris·ing (:prī'zĭng) adj. sorprendente.
sur·re·al (sə-rē'əl) adj. surrealista.
sur·re·al·is·tic (-'ə-lĭs'tĭk) adj. surrealista.
sur·ren·der (sə-rĕn'dər) I. tr. entregar; *(to give up)* ceder; *(to abandon)* abandonar ♦ **to s. one-self** entregarse —intr. rendirse II. s. rendición *f;* *(abandonment)* abandono.
sur·rep·ti·tious (sûr'əp-tĭsh'əs) adj. subrepticio.
sur·ro·gate (sûr'ə-gĭt, :gāt') I. s. substituto; DER. juez *m* de testamentarías II. adj. substituto.
sur·round (sə-round') tr. rodear.
sur·round·ings (sə-roun'dĭngz) s.pl. alrededores *m.*
sur·tax (sûr'tăks') s. recargo.
sur·veil·lance (sər-vā'ləns) s. vigilancia.
sur·vey (sər-vā') I. tr. examinar; *(to inspect)* inspeccionar; *(to measure)* medir —intr. hacer una encuesta II. s. (sûr'vā') inspección *f;* *(review)* repaso; *(measurement)* medición *f;* *(map)* mapa fotográfico.
sur·vey·ing (sər-vā'-ĭng) s. agrimensura.
sur·vey·or (:ər) s. agrimensor *m;* *(inspector)* inspector *m.*
sur·viv·al (sər-vī'vəl) s. supervivencia.
sur·vive (sər-vīv') tr. & intr. sobrevivir ♦ **to s. on** subsistir con.
sur·vi·vor (sər-vī'vər) s. sobreviviente *mf.*
sus·cep·ti·bil·i·ty (sə-sĕp'tə-bĭl'ĭ-tē) s. susceptibilidad *f;* *(sensitivity)* sensibilidad *f.*
sus·cep·ti·ble (-'-bəl) adj. susceptible; *(sensitive)* sensible ♦ **to be s. of** permitir ♦ **to be s. to** ser propenso a.
sus·pect (sə-spĕkt') I. tr. sospechar II. s. & adj. (sŭs'pĕkt') sospechoso.
sus·pend (sə-spĕnd') tr. & intr. suspender.
sus·pend·ers (sə-spĕn'dərz) s.pl. tirantes *m.*
sus·pense (sə-spĕns') s. suspensión *f;* *(doubt)* incertidumbre *f;* CINEM. suspenso.
sus·pen·sion (sə-spĕn'shən) s. suspensión *f* ♦ **s. bridge** puente colgante.
sus·pi·cion (sə-spĭsh'ən) s. sospecha; *(pinch)* pizca ♦ **above s.** fuera de toda sospecha • **on s.** como sospechoso • **to come under s. of** ser sospechado de.
sus·pi·cious (:əs) adj. sospechoso.
sus·pi·cious·ness (:nĭs) s. suspicacia.
sus·tain (sə-stān') tr. sostener; *(to encourage)* animar; *(to maintain)* mantener; *(an idea)* apoyar; *(injury)* sufrir.
sus·tain·a·ble (sə-stā'nə-bəl) adj. sostenible.
sus·tain·ment (sə-stān'mənt) s. sostenimiento.
sus·te·nance (sŭs'tə-nəns) s. sustento; *(nourishment)* alimento; *(livelihood)* medios de sub-

sistencia.
su·ture (sōō'chər) I. s. sutura II. tr. suturar.
svelte (svĕlt) adj. esbelto.
swab (swŏb) I. s. tapón *m;* *(mop)* estropajo; JER. *(sailor)* marinero II. tr. **-bb-** limpiar con tapón; *(to mop)* fregar con estropajo.
swad·dle (swŏd'l) tr. envolver; *(to diaper)* poner los pañales a.
swag (swăg) s. JER. *(loot)* botín *m.*
swag·ger (swăg'ər) I. intr. pavonearse; *(to boast)* vanagloriarse II. s. *(strut)* pavoneo; *(manner)* jactancia.
swain (swān) s. *(country youth)* zagal *m;* *(suitor)* pretendiente *m.*
swal·low¹ (swŏl'ō) I. tr. tragar; FIG. *(insults, pride)* tragarse; *(feelings)* reprimir ♦ **to s. one's words** comerse sus palabras • **to s. up** destruir —intr. tragar II. s. deglución *f;* *(of drink)* trago; *(of food)* bocado ♦ **at** *o* **with one s.** de un trago.
swal·low² s. ORNIT. golondrina.
swam (swăm) cf. **swim.**
swamp (swŏmp, swŏm) I. s. pantano II. tr. *(to inundate)* inundar, anegar; *(to sink)* hundir; FIG. *(to overwhelm)* sumergir.
swamp·land ('lănd') s. ciénaga.
swamp·y (swŏm'pē, swŏm'-) adj. **-i-** pantanoso.
swan (swŏn) s. cisne *m* ♦ **s. dive** salto del ángel • **s. song** canto del cisne.
swank (swăngk) I. adj. lujoso; *(ostentatious)* ostentoso II. s. elegancia.
swap (swŏp) FAM. I. tr. & intr. **-pp-** canjear II. s. canje *m.*
swarm (swôrm) I. s. enjambre *m;* *(of people)* muchedumbre *f* II. intr. pulular, hormiguear; *(bees)* salir en enjambre —tr. inundar ♦ **to s. with** bullir de.
swar·thy (swôr'thē) adj. **-i-** prieto.
swash (swŏsh, swôsh) I. s. chapoteo II. intr. chapotear.
swas·ti·ka (swŏs'tĭ-kə) s. esvástica.
swat (swŏt) I. tr. **-tt-** aplastar II. s. golpe repentino.
swatch (swŏch) s. muestra (de un tejido).
swath (swŏth, swôth) s. golpe *m* de guadaña; *(path)* ringlera ♦ **to cut a wide s.** hacer un gran papel.
swathe (swōth, swôth) tr. vendar.
swat·ter (swŏt'ər) s. matamoscas *m.*
sway (swā) I. tr. hacer oscilar; *(to influence)* ejercer influencia en ♦ **to s. somebody from** apartar a alguien de —intr. balancearse; *(to move unsteadily)* tambalearse II. s. oscilación *f;* *(power)* dominio ♦ **to be under the s. of** estar dominado por • **to hold s. over** dominar.
sway·back ('băk') s. lomo hundido.
swear (swâr) tr. & intr. **swore, sworn** jurar ♦ **to s. at** maldecir • **to s. in** investir de un cargo bajo juramento • **to s. off** FAM. prometer renunciar a • **to s. someone to secrecy** hacer que alguien jure guardar un secreto • **to s. to** afirmar bajo juramento • **to s. up and down** FAM. jurar y perjurar.
swear·word ('wûrd') s. palabrota.
sweat (swĕt) I. intr. **sweat(ed)** sudar; *(to exude)* rezumar —tr. sudar; *(to cause to perspire)* hacer sudar; *(to overwork)* explotar (obreros) ♦ **to s. it out** JER. pasar un mal rato II. s. sudor *m;* *(moisture)* humedad *f* ♦ **no s.** no es ningún problema • **s. shirt** jersey • **s. suit** chandal • **to be in a s.** estar angustiado.
sweat·er (swĕt'ər) s. suéter *m.*

sweat·shop (:shŏp′) s. fábrica en la que se explota al obrero.
sweat·y (swĕt′ē) adj. -i- sudoroso; *(laborious)* agotador.
sweep (swēp) I. tr. swept barrer; *(to remove)* llevarse; *(to traverse)* recorrer ♦ to s. a constituency llevarse la mayoría de los votos ♦ to s. off one's feet hacerle perder la cabeza a uno • to s. the board FAM. llevarse todo ♦ to s. up recoger —intr. barrer; *(to flow)* pasar rápidamente; *(to trail)* arrastrarse; *(to extend)* extenderse ♦ to s. along andar rápidamente II. s. *(sweeping)* barrido; *(motion)* movimiento amplio; *(reach)* alcance m; *(curve)* curva; *(chimney sweep)* deshollinador m; *(victory)* victoria aplastante ♦ at one s. de una vez • to make a clean s. hacer tabla rasa.
sweep·er (swē′pər) s. barrendero; *(machine)* barredora; *(for streets)* barredera.
sweep·ing (:pĭng) I. adj. extenso; *(dramatic)* dramático; *(gesture)* amplio II. s. ♦ pl. basura.
sweep·stake(s) (swēp′stāk[s]) s. lotería.
sweet (swēt) I. adj. dulce; *(gratifying)* agradable; *(lovable)* encantador; *(fresh)* fresco; *(potable)* potable ♦ s. oil aceite de oliva • s. one querido • s. pepper pimiento morrón • s. potato batata, boniato • s. sixteen quince abriles • s. talk lisonjas • s. tooth gusto por la confitura • to be s. on estar enamorado de • to take one's own s. time no darse prisa • to taste s. estar dulce II. s. dulce m; *(person)* cariño.
sweet·bread (′brĕd′) s. mollejas.
sweet·en (:n) tr. & intr. endulzar(se).
sweet·en·er (:ər) s. dulcificante m.
sweet·en·ing (:ĭng) s. endulzamiento; *(sweetener)* dulcificante m.
sweet·heart (swĕt′härt′) s. enamorado; *(lovable person)* persona adorable.
sweet·meat (:mēt′) s. dulce m, confitura.
sweet·ness (:nĭs) s. dulzura.
swell (swĕl) I. intr. -ed, -ed o swollen hincharse; *(to increase)* aumentar; *(with emotion)* hincharse ♦ to s. up o out hincharse —tr. hinchar; *(increase)* hacer aumentar ♦ to get a swollen head FAM. engreírse II. s. *(act)* inflamiento; *(wave)* oleada; FAM. *(handsome person)* guapo III. adj. FAM. *(stylish)* elegante; *(fine)* fenomenal.
swell·ing (′ĭng) s. inflamiento; *(swollen part)* hinchazón f.
swel·ter (swĕl′tər) intr. sofocarse de calor.
swel·ter·ing (:ĭng) adj. *(day)* abrasador; *(person)* sudando a mares.
swept (swĕpt) cf. **sweep.**
swerve (swûrv) I. tr. & intr. desviar(se) II. s. desviación f.
swift (swĭft) I. adj. veloz; *(quick)* rápido II. s. ORNIT. vencejo.
swift·ness (′nĭs) s. rapidez f, velocidad f.
swig (swĭg) FAM. I. s. trago II. tr. & intr. -gg- beber a tragos.
swill (swĭl) I. tr. *(to drink)* beber a tragos; *(to flood)* empapar II. s. bazofia; *(refuse)* basura.
swim (swĭm) I. intr. swam, swum nadar; *(to glide)* deslizarse; *(to float)* flotar; *(to be immersed)* estar cubierto; *(to whirl)* dar vueltas ♦ swimming pool piscina • to s. with the tide seguir la corriente —tr. nadar; *(to swim across)* atravesar a nado ♦ swimming in lleno de II. s. natación f; *(period of swimming)* baño ♦ to go for o to take a s. ir a nadar.
swim·ming·ly (′ĭng-lē) adv. espléndidamente.

swim·suit (:sōōt′) s. traje m de baño.
swin·dle (swĭn′dl) I. tr. & intr. timar II. s. timo.
swin·dler (swĭnd′lər) s. timador m.
swine (swīn) s.inv. cerdo.
swine·herd (′hûrd′) s. porquerizo.
swing (swĭng) I. intr. swung oscilar; *(on a swing)* columpiarse; *(on hinges)* girar; JER. *(to be up to date)* estar al día; MÚS. tocar con ritmo ♦ to s. clear dar un viraje para evitar un choque • to s. to cerrarse • to s. to and fro balancearse —tr. hacer girar; *(on swing)* hacer balancear; JER. *(to manage)* lograr ♦ to s. an election ganar una elección • to s. around a corner AUTO. doblar una esquina • to s. at dirigir un golpe a II. s. oscilación f; *(swoop)* descenso rápido; *(for children)* columpio; MÚS. ritmo.
swing·er (′ər) s. oscilador m; JER. *(person)* persona a la última moda y sin inhibiciones.
swing·ing (:ĭng) JER. I. s. libertinaje m II. adj. muy moderno; *(spirited)* alegre; MÚS. rítmico.
swin·ish (swī′nĭsh) adj. cochino.
swipe (swīp) I. s. golpetazo II. tr. *(to hit)* dar un tortazo; JER. *(to steal)* robar, birlar.
swirl (swûrl) I. intr. dar vueltas —tr. girar II. s. giro; *(whorl)* espiral m.
swish (swĭsh) s. I. intr. *(cane, whip)* silbar; *(fabric)* crujir —tr. *(tail)* menear II. s. silbido; *(rustle)* crujido.
switch (swĭch) I. s. ELEC. interruptor m; *(rod)* látigo; *(lashing)* latigazo; *(shift)* cambio; *(false hair)* trenza postiza; F.C. cambio (de vías) II. tr. *(to whip)* azotar; *(to shift)* cambiar de; *(to exchange)* intercambiar; F.C. desviar ♦ to s. off desconectar; *(lights)* apagar ♦ to s. on conectar; *(lights)* encender —intr. cambiar.
switch·blade (′blād′) s. navaja de muelle.
switch·board (:bôrd′) s. ELEC. tablero de distribución; TEL. centralita de teléfonos ♦ s. operator telefonista mf.
switch·man (:mən) s. [pl. -men] guardagujas m.
swiv·el (swĭv′əl) I. s. *(link)* eslabón giratorio; *(pivot)* pivote m II. intr. & tr. (hacer) girar.
swiz·zle stick (swĭz′əl) s. varilla de cóctel.
swol·len (swō′lən) cf. **swell.**
swoon (swōōn) I. intr. desmayarse II. s. desmayo.
swoop (swōōp) I. intr. abalanzarse II. s. calada ♦ in one fell s. de un solo golpe.
sword (sôrd) s. espada; *(instrument)* arma; *(power)* poder m militar ♦ to be at s.'s points estar a punto de matarse • to cross swords with habérselas con alguien • to put to the s. pasar a cuchillo.
sword·fish (′fĭsh′) s. [pl. inv. o s] pez m espada.
sword·play (:plā′) s. esgrima.
swords·man (sôrdz′mən) s. [pl. -men] *(fencer)* esgrimista mf; *(fighter)* espadachín m.
swore (swôr), **sworn** (swôrn) cf. **swear.**
swum (swŭm) cf. **swim.**
swung (swŭng) cf. **swing.**
syb·a·rite (sĭb′ə-rīt′) s. sibarita mf.
syc·a·more (sĭk′ə-môr′) s. sicómoro.
syc·o·phant (sĭk′ə-fənt) s. adulón m.
syl·lab·ic (sĭ-lăb′ĭk) adj. silábico.
syl·lab·i·cate (:ĭ-kāt′) tr. silabear.
syl·lab·i·ca·tion (-′-kā′shən) s. silabeo.
syl·lab·i·fy (-′-fī′) tr. silabear.
syl·la·ble (sĭl′ə-bəl) s. sílaba.
syl·la·bus (sĭl′ə-bəs) s. [pl. es o -bi] programa

m de estudios; *(summary)* resumen *m.*
syl·lo·gism (sĭl′ə-jĭz′ əm) s. silogismo.
syl·lo·gis·tic (′-jĭs′tĭk) adj. silogístico.
syl·van (sĭl′vən) adj. silvestre.
sym·bi·o·sis (sĭm′bē-ō′sĭs) s. simbiosis *f.*
sym·bi·ot·ic (:ŏt′ĭk) adj. simbiótico.
sym·bol (sĭm′bəl) s. símbolo.
sym·bol·ic/i·cal (-bŏl′ĭk) adj. simbólico.
sym·bol·ism (′bə-lĭz′əm) s. simbolismo.
sym·bol·ize (:līz′) tr. simbolizar.
sym·met·ric/ri·cal (sĭ-mĕt′rĭk) simétrico.
sym·me·try (sĭm′ĭ-trē) s. simetría.
sym·pa·thet·ic (sĭm′pə-thĕt′ĭk) adj. *(compassionate)* compasivo; *(favorable)* favorable; *(supporting)* simpatizante; ANAT. simpático.
sym·pa·thize (′-thīz′) intr. compadecerse; *(to understand)* comprender.
sym·pa·thiz·er (:′thī′ zər) s. simpatizante *mf.*
sym·pa·thy (sĭm′pə-thē) s. simpatía; *(compatibility)* compatibilidad *f; (understanding)* comprensión *f; (expression of sorrow)* pésame *m; (compassion)* compasión *f* ♦ **her sympathies lie with** simpatiza con • **message of s.** pésame • **to be in s. with** estar de acuerdo con.
sym·phon·ic (sĭm-fŏn′ĭk) adj. sinfónico.
sym·pho·ny (sĭm′fə-nē) s. MÚS. sinfonía; *(orchestra)* orquesta sinfónica; *(harmony)* armonía.
sym·po·si·um (sĭm-pō′zē-əm) s. [pl. **s** *o* **-ia**] simposio; *(collection)* colección *f.*
symp·tom (sĭmp′təm) s. *(indication)* indicio; MED. síntoma *m.*
symp·to·mat·ic (′tə-măt′ĭk) adj. sintomático.
syn·a·gog(ue) (sĭn′ə-gŏg′) s. sinagoga.
syn·apse (sĭn′ăps′) s. sinapsis *f.*
sync(h) (sĭngk) FAM. I. s. sincronización *f* ♦ **to be out of s.** no estar sincronizado II. tr. sincronizar.
syn·chro·ni·za·tion (sĭng′krə-nĭ-zā′shən) s. sincronización *f.*
syn·chro·nize (′-nīz′) intr. coincidir; *(to operate in unison)* sincronizar —tr. sincronizar.
syn·chro·niz·er (:′nī′ zər) s. sincronizador *m.*
syn·chro·nous (:nəs) adj. sincrónico; MEC. sincrono.
syn·co·pa·tion (sĭng′kə-pā′shən) s. síncopa.
syn·di·cate (sĭn′dĭ-kĭt) I. s. sindicato; *(of newspapers)* cadena de periódicos II. tr. (:kāt′) sindicar; PERIOD. vender a través de una agencia —intr. sindicarse.
syn·di·ca·tion (′-kā′shən) s. sindicalización *f.*
syn·drome (sĭn′drōm′) s. síndrome *m.*
syn·er·gism/gy (sĭn′ər-jĭz′əm/jē) sinergia.
syn·od (sĭn′əd) s. sínodo.
syn·o·nym (sĭn′ə-nĭm′) s. sinónimo.
syn·on·y·mous (sĭ-nŏn′ə-məs) adj. sinónimo.
syn·on·y·my (:mē) s. sinonimia.
syn·op·sis (sĭ-nŏp′sĭs) s. [pl. **-ses**] sinopsis *f.*
syn·tac·tic/ti·cal (sĭn-tăk′tĭk) adj. sintáctico.
syn·tax (sĭn′tăks′) s. sintaxis *f.*
syn·the·sis (sĭn′thĭ-sĭs) s. [pl. **-ses**] síntesis *f.*
syn·the·size (:sīz′) tr. sintetizar.
syn·the·siz·er (:sī′zər) s. sintetizador *m.*
syn·thet·ic (sĭn-thĕt′ĭk) adj. & s. *(material)* sintético.
syph·i·lis (sĭf′ə-lĭs) s. sifilis *f.*
syph·i·lit·ic (′-lĭt′ĭk) adj. & s. sifilítico.
sy·ringe (sə-rĭnj′, sĭr′ĭnj) s. jeringa.
syr·up (sĭr′əp) s. CUL. almíbar *m.*
sys·tem (sĭs′təm) s. sistema *m; (human body)* organismo; ANAT. aparato.
sys·tem·at·ic (′tə-măt′ĭk) adj. sistemático.

sys·tem·a·tize (′-mə-tīz′) tr. sistematizar.
sys·tem·ic (sĭ-stĕm′ĭk) adj. sistemático; *(of the body)* que afecta al organismo.
sys·tem·ize (sĭs′tə-mīz′) tr. sistematizar.
sys·to·le (sĭs′tə-lē) s. sístole *f.*

T

t, T (tē) s. vigésima letra del alfabeto inglés ♦ **to a T** a la perfección.
tab (tăb) s. lengüeta; *(at a restaurant)* cuenta; *(of a typewriter)* tabulador *m* ♦ **to keep tabs on** observar detalladamente.
tab·by (tăb′ē)s. *(striped)* gato atigrado; *(female cat)* gata.
tab·er·na·cle (tăb′ər-năk′ əl) s. tabernáculo.
ta·ble (tā′bəl) I. s. mesa; *(data)* tabla, cuadro ♦ **t. of contents** índice • **to turn the tables on someone** volver las tornas a alguien • **under the t.** *(covertly)* bajo la mesa; *(drunk)* completamente borracho II. tr. *(to place)* poner sobre una mesa; *(to shelve)* dar carpetazo a; *(to tabulate)* tabular; FIG. *(to present)* presentar.
tab·leau (tăb′lō′, tă-blō′) s. [pl. **s** *o* **-x**] cuadro ♦ **t. vivant** TEAT. cuadro vivo.
ta·ble·cloth (tā′bəl-klôth′) s. mantel *m.*
ta·ble·land (:lănd′) s. meseta.
ta·ble·spoon (:spōōn′) s. cuchara de sopa; *(quantity)* cucharada.
tab·let (tăb′lĭt) s. tableta, tablilla; *(writing pad)* taco, bloc *m; (pill)* pastilla.
ta·ble·ware (tā′bəl-wâr′) s. servicio de mesa.
tab·loid (tăb′loid′) s. periódico de formato reducido.
ta·boo (tă-bōō′) s. & adj. tabú *m.*
tab·u·lar (tăb′yə-lər) adj. tabular.
tab·u·late (:lāt′) tr. tabular.
tab·u·la·tion (′-lā′shən) s. tabulación *f.*
tab·u·la·tor (′-′ tər) s. *(person, key)* tabulador *m; (machine)* tabuladora.
tac·it (tăs′ĭt) adj. tácito; *(implicit)* implícito.
tac·i·turn (:ĭ-tûrn′) adj. taciturno.
tack (tăk) I. s. tachuela; *(direction)* dirección *f,* línea; COST. hilván *m;* MARÍT. puño de la amura ♦ **to get down to brass tacks** ir al grano II. tr. clavar con tachuelas; *(to stitch)* hilvanar; MARÍT. virar por avante ♦ **to t. on** añadir, agregar —intr. MARÍT. cambiar de bordada.
tack·le (tăk′əl) I. s. *(gear)* equipo, avíos *m; (harness)* arreos; MARÍT. aparejo, jarcias II. tr. atacar, abordar; DEP. agarrar.
tack·y[1] (tăk′ē) adj. **-i-** *(sticky)* pegajoso.
tack·y[2] adj. **-i-** FAM. *(shabby)* descuidado; *(lacking style)* cursi; *(vulgar)* vulgar.
tact (tăkt) s. tacto.
tact·ful (′fəl) adj. discreto.
tac·tic (tăk′tĭk) s. táctica ♦ **tactics** s.sg. táctica.
tac·ti·cal (:tĭ-kəl) adj. táctico.
tac·ti·cian (-tĭsh′ən) s. táctico.
tac·tile (tăk′tʌl, :tīl′) adj. táctil.
tact·less (tăkt′lĭs) adj. falto de tacto.
tad·pole (tăd′pōl′) s. renacuajo.
taf·fy (tăf′ē) s. melcocha.
tag[1] (tăg) I. s. *(label)* etiqueta; *(aglet)* herrete *m; (cliché)* cliché *m; (characterization)* etiqueta, epíteto ♦ **t. line** TEAT. gracia, punto; *(slogan)* slogan II. tr. **-gg-** etiquetar; *(to identify)* identificar; *(to characterize)* denominar; *(to follow)* seguir de cerca —intr. ♦ **to t. along** seguir, acompañar.

tag² s. *(game)* mancha, pillarse *m*.

tag·a·long (′ə-lông′) s. persona que sigue a otra persistentemente.

tail (tāl) I. s. cola; *(backside)* trasero; *(of a shirt)* faldón *m*; FAM. *(spy)* espía *mf* ♦ **from head to t.** de pies a cabeza • **t. end** *(rear)* parte trasera; *(end)* fin, final • **t. pipe** MEC. tubo de escape • **t. wind** viento de cola • **to be on someone's t.** *(to trail)* seguirle el rastro a alguien ♦ pl. *(of a coin)* cruz, reverso; *(tailcoat)* frac II. tr. FAM. *(to follow)* seguir de cerca, espiar —intr. ♦ **to t. away** *o* **off** ir disminuyendo.

tail·gate (′gāt′) I. s. compuerta de cola II. tr. & intr. seguir demasiado cerca a (otro vehículo).

tail·light (:līt′) s. luz trasera *o* de cola.

tai·lor (tā′lər) I. s. sastre *m* II. tr. hacer a la medida; *(to adapt)* adaptar.

tai·lored (tā′lərd) adj. *(trim)* de corte prolijo; *(custom-made)* hecho a medida.

tai·lor-made (tā′lər-mād′) adj. hecho a medida; *(perfect)* perfecto.

tail·piece (:pēs′) s. pieza de cola.

tail·spin (:spĭn′) s. *(collapse)* colapso emocional; AER. barrena.

taint (tānt) I. tr. manchar; *(to spoil)* contaminar; *(to corrupt)* corromper —intr. mancharse; *(to rot)* corromperse II. s. *(moral defect)* mácula, defecto; *(influence)* mala influencia.

take (tāk) I. tr. **took, taken** tomar; *(to confiscate, steal)* apoderarse de; *(to arrest)* detener, capturar; *(to win)* ganar; *(to buy)* comprar; *(to cost)* costar; *(to swindle)* engañar; *(to carry along)* llevarse; *(to captivate)* cautivar, encantar; *(to admit)* recibir; *(to accept)* aceptar; *(to withstand)* aguantar, soportar; *(film, clothing)* usar; *(in shoes)* calzar; *(to study)* estudiar; *(in chess, checkers)* comerse, capturar; *(to remove)* sacar; *(to subtract)* sustraer ♦ **as I t.** it a mi entender • **t. it from me!** ¡créame! • **t. a bow** agradecer el aplauso • **t. along** llevar consigo, llevarse • **to t. amiss** tomar mal • **to t. an oath** prestar juramento • **to t. apart** *(to disassemble)* desarmar, desmontar; *(to analyze)* analizar; *(to wreck)* hacer pedazos • **to t. a trip** hacer un viaje • **to t. away** *(to remove)* quitar, sacar; *(to subtract)* restar; *(to carry away)* llevarse • **to t. back** *(to return)* devolver; *(to receive back)* recibir de vuelta; *(person)* volver a recibir; *(former employee)* volver a emplear; *(to retract)* retractar; *(to bring to mind)* hacer recordar, hacer pensar en • **to t. chances** arriesgarse • **to t. down** *(to write down)* anotar; *(to disassemble)* desarmar; *(to knock down)* derribar • **to t. hold of** agarrar • **to t. in** *(to accept)* aceptar; *(to lodge)* alojar; *(to understand)* comprender; *(to include)* incluir; *(to realize)* percatarse de; *(to deceive)* engañar; *(to earn)* ganar; *(a seam)* embeber, meter; *(a dress)* achicar • **to t. it out** on desahogarse con • **to t.** it that suponer que, inferir que • **to t. notes** hacer apuntes • **to t. off** quitar; *(clothes, hat)* quitarse; *(time)* tomarse; *(to deduct)* rebajar • **to t. on** *(to characteristic, attitude)* asumir, tomar; *(responsibility)* encargarse de; *(employee)* contratar; *(passengers)* recibir a bordo; *(bet, challenge)* aceptar; *(adversary)* enfrentarse a; *(client, patient)* aceptar • **to t. out** llevar afuera, poner afuera; *(to remove)* sacar; *(license, policy)* sacar; *(stain, spot)* quitar, extraer; *(tooth)* extraer • **to t. over** hacerse cargo

de • **to t. pity on** tener lástima de • **to t. up** *(to raise)* llevar arriba; *(to pick up)* levantar, alzar; *(time, space)* ocupar, llenar; *(challenge, bet)* aceptar; *(career, profession)* dedicarse a; *(study)* empezar; *(residence)* establecer; COST. acortar • **to t. upon oneself** encargarse de • **to t. up with** asociarse con —intr. *(to stick)* adherirse; *(to succeed)* tener éxito; *(to set)* cuajar; *(plants)* arraigar; *(vaccination)* prender ♦ **to t. after** parecerse a • **to t. off** *(to leave)* irse, partir; *(aircraft)* despegar • **to t. over** asumir la autoridad • **to t. to** empezar a • **to t. to someone** tomarle simpatía a alguien • **to t. to something** aficionarse a algo II. s. *(receipts)* entrada, ingresos; *(in hunting)* presa; *(in fishing)* pesca; *(in chess, checkers)* captura, toma; CINEM. toma.

take-home pay (′hōm′) s. sueldo neto.

take·off (:ôf′) s. AVIA. despegue *m*; FAM. *(imitation)* caricatura.

take·o·ver (:ō′vər) s. toma de poder.

tak·ing (tā′kĭng) I. adj. atractivo II. s. toma; *(catch)* presa, pesca ♦ pl. ingresos.

talc (tălk) I. s. talco II. tr. **-c(k)-** poner talco a.

tal·cum (tăl′kəm) s. talco; *(powder)* polvos de talco.

tale (tāl) s. cuento; *(lie)* mentira; *(gossip)* chisme *m* ♦ **old wives' t.** cuento de viejas.

tal·ent (tăl′ənt) s. talento; *(aptitude)* aptitud *f*, don *m*; *(persons)* talento.

tal·ent·ed (:ən-tĭd) adj. talentoso.

tal·is·man (tăl′ĭs-mən) s. talismán *m*.

talk (tôk) I. tr. hablar; *(to speak)* decir ♦ **to t. a blue streak** FAM. hablar por los codos • **to t. sense** hablar sensatamente • **to t. into** persuadir a • **to t. out of** disuadir a • **to t. turkey** no andarse con rodeos —intr. hablar; *(to chatter)* charlar ♦ **look who's talking!** ¡mira quién habla! • **now you're talking!** ¡así se habla! • **to t. away** hablar sin parar • **to t. back** replicar • **to t. behind someone's back** hablar (mal) de alguien a sus espaldas • **to t. down to** hablar con altivez a II. s. conversación *f*; *(speech)* discurso; *(jargon)* habla; *(rumor)* rumor *m*; *(subject of conversation)* chisme *m*, comidilla; *(empty speech)* palabrería ♦ pl. negociaciones.

talk·a·tive (tô′kə-tĭv) adj. hablador, locuaz.

talk·er (tô′kər) s. hablador *m*.

talk·ing (tô′kĭng) adj. parlante, que habla; *(movie)* sonora.

talk·ing-to (:-tōō′) s. FAM. bronca.

tall (tôl) I. adj. alto; *(of certain height)* de alto, de altura; FAM. *(tale)* exagerado; *(difficult)* difícil ♦ **how t. are you?** ¿cuánto mide usted? II. adv. ♦ **to walk t.** caminar con porte altivo.

tal·low (tăl′ō) s. sebo.

tal·ly (tăl′ē) I. s. *(stick)* tarja, tara; *(score)* cuenta; *(receipt)* talón *m*; COM. lista II. tr. *(to record)* tarjar; *(to score)* llevar la cuenta; *(to cause to agree)* hacer cuadrar —intr. cuadrar.

tal·on (tăl′ən) s. garra.

ta·lus (tā′ləs) s. [pl. **-li**] astrágalo.

tam·bour (tăm′bŏŏr′) s. tambor *m*.

tam·bou·rine (tăm′bə-rēn′) s. pandereta.

tame (tām) I. adj. domesticado; *(gentle)* manso; *(docile)* dócil; FAM. insípido II. tr. domesticar; *(to break)* domar; *(to subdue)* dominar; *(to soften)* suavizar.

tam-o'-shan·ter (tăm′ə-shăn′tər) s. boina escocesa.

tamp (tămp) tr. apisonar, pisonear.

tam·per (tăm′pər) intr. ♦ **t. with** interferir en; *(to meddle)* entrometerse en.

tam·pon (tăm′pŏn′) s. tapón *m*, tampón *m*.
tan (tăn) **I.** tr. **-nn-** *(leather)* curtir; *(skin)* broncear; FAM. *(to beat)* zurrar —intr. broncearse, tostarse **II.** s. & adj. (color) tostado *o* bronceado.
tan·dem (tăn′dəm) s. & adv. (en) tándem *m*.
tang (tăng) s. *(flavor)* gusto fuerte; *(odor)* olor *m* penetrante; *(of a tool)* cola.
tan·gent (tăn′jənt). adj. & s. tangente *f*.
tan·gen·tial (tăn-jĕn′shəl) adj. tangencial.
tan·ger·ine (tăn′jə-rēn′) s. *(color)* anaranjado rojizo; *(tree)* mandarino; *(fruit)* mandarina.
tan·gi·ble (tăn′jə-bəl) adj. tangible; *(real)* real.
tan·gle (tăng′gəl) **I.** tr. & intr. *(to snarl)* enredar(se), enmarañar(se); *(to entangle)* embrollar(se) ♦ **to t. with** meterse con **II.** s. enredo, embrollo; *(confusion)* confusión *f*.
tan·gled (:gəld) adj. enredado, embrollado.
tan·go (tăng′gō) **I.** s. tango **II.** intr. bailar el tango.
tang·y (tăng′ē) adj. **-i-** fuerte, penetrante.
tank (tăngk) s. tanque *m*; JER. *(jail)* cárcel *f*.
tank·ard (tăng′kərd) s. jarra de cerveza.
tank·er (tăng′kər) s. buque *m* tanque; *(truck)* camión *m* tanque; *(plane)* avión *m* tanque.
tan·ner (tăn′ər) s. curtidor *m*.
tan·ner·y (:ə-rē) s. curtiduría, curtiembre *f*.
tan·nic (tăn′ĭk) adj. tánico.
tan·nin (tăn′ĭn) s. tanino.
tan·ning (tăn′ĭng) s. *(leather)* curtimiento; *(skin bronzing)* bronceado; FAM. *(beating)* zurra.
tan·ta·lize (tăn′tə-līz′) tr. tentar.
tan·ta·liz·ing (:ĭng) adj. tentador.
tan·ta·mount (tăn′tə-mount′) adj. ♦ **t. to** equivalente a.
tan·trum (tăn′trəm) s. rabieta, pataleta.
tap¹ (tăp) **I.** tr. **-pp-** golpear ligeramente; *(to rap)* dar golpecitos con; *(shoes)* poner tapas a —intr. dar golpes ligeros; *(with the fingers)* tamborilear; *(with the feet)* zapatear **II.** s. golpe ligero; *(sole)* media suela; *(metal tip)* chapa ♦ **t. dance** zapateo americano.
tap² (tăp) s. *(faucet)* grifo; *(spigot)* canilla, espita; *(beer)* cerveza de barril; MED. drenaje *m*; MEC. macho de roscar; ELEC. toma de corriente **II.** tr. **-pp-** *(to put a tap on)* espitar; *(to pierce)* horadar; *(tree)* sangrar; *(to draw)* sacar de un barril; *(to make use of)* utilizar; *(to connect)* hacer una conexión en; *(to wiretap)* interceptar; ELEC. desviar; MEC. roscar; MED. drenar.
tap-dance (′dăns′) intr. zapatear.
tape (tāp) **I.** s. *(strip)* cinta; *(adhesive)* cinta adhesiva; *(magnetic)* cinta magnética; *(measure)* cinta métrica; *(recording)* grabación *f* en cinta magnética; DEP. cinta de llegada ♦ **red t.** papeleo ♦ **t. player** grabadora ♦ **t. recorder** grabadora magnetofónica ♦ **t. recording** cinta grabada **II.** tr. *(to fasten)* asegurar con cinta; *(to glue)* pegar con cinta adhesiva; *(to measure)* medir; *(to record)* grabar.
ta·per (tā′pər) **I.** s. vela delgada; *(gradual decrease)* ahusamiento **II.** tr. & intr. ♦ **to t. off** disminuir.
tape-re·cord (tāp′rĭ-kôrd′) tr. grabar en cinta magnetofónica.
tap·es·try (tăp′ĭ-strē) s. tapiz *m*.
tape·worm (tāp′wûrm′) s. tenia, solitaria.
tap·i·o·ca (tăp′ē-ō′kə) s. tapioca.
ta·pir (tā′pər) s. tapir *m*.
tap·room (tăp′rōōm′) s. bar *m*.
taps (tăps) s. MIL. toque *m* de queda.
tar¹ (tär) **I.** s. alquitrán *m* **II.** tr. **-rr-** alquitra-

nar.
tar² s. FAM. *(sailor)* marinero.
ta·ran·tu·la (tə-răn′chə-lə) s. tarántula.
tar·dy (tär′dē) adj. **-i-** *(late)* tardío; *(delayed)* demorado; *(slow)* lento ♦ **to be t.** llegar tarde.
tar·get (tär′gĭt) **I.** s. blanco; *(goal)* meta ♦ **to be on t.** dar en el blanco **II.** tr. fijar como objetivo.
tar·iff (tär′ĭf) s. tarifa.
tar·mac (tär′măk′) s. asfalto; *(runway)* pista.
tar·na·tion (tär-nă′shən) s. & interj. FAM. maldición *f*.
tar·nish (tär′nĭsh) **I.** tr. & intr. empañar(se), descolorar(se); *(to spoil)* estropear(se) **II.** s. empañamiento, deslustre *m*; *(besmirchment)* mancha.
tar·ot (tär′ō) s. naipe *m* de dibujos alegóricos que se usa en la adivinación.
tar·pa·per (tär′pā′pər) s. papel alquitranado.
tar·pau·lin (tär-pô′lĭn, tär′pə-) s. alquitranado.
tar·ra·gon (tär′ə-gŏn′) s. estragón *m*.
tar·ry¹ (tär′ē) intr. *(to delay)* demorar; *(to linger)* rezagarse.
tar·ry² (tär′ē) adj. **-i-** alquitranado.
tar·sal (tär′səl) adj. tarsal.
tar·sus (tär′səs) s. tarso.
tart¹ (tärt) adj. *(taste)* acre; *(tone)* hiriente.
tart² s. *(pie)* pastelillo; *(prostitute)* prostituta.
tar·tan (tär′tn) s. tartán *m*.
tar·tar (tär′tər) s. QUIM. tártaro; ODONT. sarro ♦ **t. sauce** salsa tártara.
task (tăsk) s. tarea; *(difficult undertaking)* faena ♦ **t. force** fuerza operante • **to take to t.** reprender **II.** tr. agobiar con tareas.
task·mas·ter (′măs′tər) s. capataz *m* exigente.
tas·sel (tăs′əl) s. borla.
taste (tāst) **I.** tr. probar; *(to discern flavors)* notar un sabor a; *(to sample)* catar; *(to experience)* experimentar —intr. *(to distinguish flavors)* sentir sabor; *(to have a flavor)* tener sabor **II.** s. gusto, *(small portion)* pizca; *(experience)* experiencia ♦ **in good t.** de buen gusto • **t. bud** papila del gusto.
taste·ful (′fəl) adj. de buen gusto.
taste·less (:lĭs) adj. *(flat)* sin sabor; *(insipid)* insípido; *(tacky)* cursi.
tast·y (tā′stē) adj. **-i-** sabroso.
tat (tăt) tr. **-tt-** hacer encaje de frivolité —intr. tejer.
tat·ter (tăt′ər) **I.** s. andrajo, jirón *m* ♦ pl. harapos **II.** tr. convertir en harapos —intr. deshilacharse.
tat·tered (:ərd) adj. andrajoso.
tat·ting (tăt′ĭng) s. encaje *m* de hilo.
tat·tle (tăt′l) intr. *(to gossip)* chismear, comadrear; *(to prattle)* charlar, cotorrear.
tat·tler (:lər) s. *(gossip)* chismoso; *(prattler)* parlanchín *m*.
tat·tle·tale (:l-tāl′) s. *(gossip)* chismoso; *(informer)* acusón *m*.
tat·too¹ (tă-tōō′) s. MIL. *(parade)* desfile *m* militar; *(drumming)* tamboreo.
tat·too² **I.** s. tatuaje *m* **II.** tr. tatuar.
taught (tôt) cf. **teach.**
taunt (tônt) **I.** tr. mofarse de, burlarse de **II.** s. burla.
taupe (tōp) s. gris pardo.
taut (tôt) adj. *(tight)* tirante; *(strained)* tenso; *(trim)* aseado, prolijo.
taut·en (′tn) tr. & intr. tensar(se).
tav·ern (tăv′ərn) s. taberna; *(inn)* posada.
taw·dry (tô′drē) adj. **-i-** charro.

taw·ny (tô'nē) adj. **-i-** pardo.

tax (tăks) **I.** s. impuesto; *(strain)* carga **II.** tr. *(to charge)* gravar; *(to make demands on)* agotar.

tax·a·ble (tăk'sə-bəl) adj. gravable.

tax·a·tion (-sā'shən) s. fijación *f* de impuestos.

tax-de·duct·i·ble (tăks'dĭ-dŭk'tə-bəl) adj. que se puede deducir como gasto.

tax-ex·empt (-ĭg-zĕmpt') adj. libre de impuestos.

tax-free (-frē') adj. libre de impuestos.

tax·i (tăk'sē) **I.** s. [pl. **(e)s**] taxi *m* ◆ **t. driver** taxista **II.** intr. **-iing** o **-ying** ir en taxi; *(airplane)* carretear.

tax·i·cab (:kăb') s. taxi *m*.

tax·i·der·my (tăk'sĭ-dûr'mē) s. taxidermia.

tax·ing (tăk'sĭng) adj. pesado.

tax·pay·er (tăks'pā'ər) s. contribuyente *mf*.

tea (tē) s. *(drink)* té *m*; *(gathering)* reunión *f* social en la cual se sirve té.

teach (tēch) tr. **taught** enseñar; *(students)* dar clases a; *(a subject)* dar clases de —intr. ser maestro.

teach·er (tē'chər) s. maestro, profesor *m*.

teach·ing (tē'chĭng) s. enseñanza.

tea·cup (tē'kŭp') s. taza de té.

teak (tēk) s. *(tree, wood)* teca.

tea·ket·tle (tē'kĕt'l) s. caldero, hervidor *m*.

teak·wood (tēk'wŏod') s. madera de teca.

teal (tēl) s. [pl. inv. o **s**] *(duck)* cerceta; *(color)* verde azuloso.

team (tēm) **I.** s. equipo; *(of animals)* yunta **II.** tr. enyugar ◆ **to t. up with** unir fuerzas con.

team·mate (:māt') s. compañero de equipo.

team·ster (:stər) s. carretero; *(truck driver)* camionero profesional.

team·work (:wûrk') s. trabajo de equipo.

tea·pot (tē'pŏt') s. tetera.

tear¹ (târ) **I.** tr. **tore, torn** *(to rend)* desgarrar, rasgar; *(to rip)* despedazar; *(to pull)* arrancar; *(to wound)* herir; *(to wrench)* distender; *(to distress)* angustiar ◆ **to t. apart** *(to rip)* romper; *(to disunite)* dividir ◆ **to t. off** o **out** arrancar ◆ **to t. down** *(to demolish)* demoler; *(to denigrate)* denigrar ◆ **to t. in** o **to pieces** despedazar ◆ **to t. up** hacer pedazos; *(to uproot)* desarraigar —intr. desgarrarse, rasgarse ◆ **to t. around** correr como un loco ◆ **to t. into** acometer **II.** s. desgarradura, rasgadura.

tear² (tîr) **I.** s. lágrima; *(drop)* gota ◆ **t. gas** gas lacrimógeno ◆ pl. lágrimas, llanto ◆ **in t.** llorando ◆ **to be bored to t.** aburrirse como una ostra ◆ **to move to t.** hacer llorar ◆ **to shed t.** llorar **II.** intr. llenarse de lágrimas.

tear·drop (tîr'drŏp') s. lágrima.

tear·ful (:fəl) adj. lacrimoso.

tear-jerk·er (:jûr'kər) s. JER. drama *m* sentimentaloide.

tea·room (tē'rōōm') s. salón *m* de té.

tease (tēz) **I.** tr. *(to annoy)* fastidiar; *(to make fun of)* tomar el pelo a; *(to tantalize)* tentar; *(wool)* cardar **II.** s. bromista *mf*.

teas·er (tē'zər) s. *(joker)* bromista *mf*; *(puzzle)* rompecabezas *m*.

tea·spoon (tē'spōōn') s. cucharita de té; *(content)* cucharadita.

teat (tēt, tĭt) s. teta.

tech·ni·cal (tĕk'nĭ-kəl) adj. técnico; *(specialized)* especializado; *(scientific)* científico; *(technological)* tecnológico; *(theoretical)* teórico.

tech·ni·cal·i·ty (-'kăl'ĭ-tē) s. tecnicidad *f*; *(expression)* expresión técnica.

tech·ni·cian (tĕk-nĭsh'ən) s. técnico.

tech·nique (:nēk') s. técnica.

tech·no·log·ic·i·cal ('nə-lŏj'ĭk) s. tecnológico.

tech·nol·o·gist (-nŏl'ə-jĭst) s. tecnólogo.

tech·nol·o·gy (:jē) s. tecnología.

ted·dy bear (tĕd'ē) s. osito de juguete.

te·di·ous (tē'dē-əs) adj. tedioso.

te·di·um (:əm) s. tedio.

tee¹ DEP. **I.** s. tee *m* **II.** tr. colocar sobre un tee ◆ **to t. off** *(to hit)* pegarle a la pelota desde el tee; *(to start)* comenzar.

tee² s. meta ◆ **to a t.** a la perfección.

teem (tēm) intr. hervir, abundar.

teen (tēn) adj. & s. adolescente *mf*, joven *mf*.

teen-age(d) ('āj[d]') adj. adolescente.

teen-ag·er (:ā'jər) s. joven *mf*, adolescente *mf*.

teens (tēnz) s.pl. *(numbers)* números entre 13 y 19; *(age)* adolescencia.

tee·ny (tē'nē) o **teen·sy** (tēn'sē) adj. **-i-** pequeñito.

tee·ter (tē'tər) intr. FAM. bambolearse; *(to vacilate)* vacilar.

tee·ter-tot·ter (:tŏt'ər) s. columpio, subibaja *m*.

teeth (tēth) cf. **tooth.**

teethe (tēth) intr. echar los dientes.

tee·to·tal·(l)er (tē'tōt'l-ər) s. abstemio.

tel·e·cast (tĕl'ĭ-kăst') **I.** tr. & intr. **-cast(ed)** televisar **II.** s. transmisión *f* de television.

tel·e·com·mu·ni·ca·tion ('-kə-myōō'nĭ-kā'shən) s. telecomunicación *f* ◆ **telecommunica-tions** s.sg. la ciencia de las telecomunicaciones.

tel·e·gram ('-grăm') s. telegrama *m*.

tel·e·graph (:grăf') **I.** s. telégrafo; *(telegram)* telegrama *m* **II.** tr. telegrafiar —intr. mandar un telegrama.

tel·e·graph·ic ('-grăf'ĭk) adj. telegráfico.

te·leg·ra·phy (tə-lĕg'rə-fē) s. telegrafía.

tel·e·ki·ne·sis (tĕl'ĭ-kĭ-nē'sĭs) s. telequinesis *f*.

tel·e·me·ter ('ə-mē'tər) s. telémetro.

te·lem·e·try (tə-lĕm'ĭ-trē) s. telemetría.

tel·e·path·y (tə-lĕp'ə-thē) s. telepatía.

tel·e·phone (tĕl'ə-fōn') **I.** s. teléfono **II.** tr. telefonear, llamar por teléfono —intr. comunicarse por teléfono.

tel·e·pho·to (:-fō'tō) adj. telefotográfico.

tel·e·pho·to·graph (:tə-grăf') **I.** s. telefotografía **II.** tr. fotografiar con una lente telefotográfica.

tel·e·print·er (tĕl'ə-prĭn'tər) s. teletipo.

tel·e·proc·ess·ing ('-prŏs'ĕs'ĭng) s. teleproceso.

tel·e·scope (tĕl'ĭ-skōp') **I.** s. telescopio **II.** tr. extender; *(to compress)* comprimir —intr. extenderse.

tel·e·scop·ic ('-skŏp'ĭk) adj. telescópico.

tel·e·thon (:-thŏn') s. programa *m* de televisión destinado para recaudar fondos.

tel·e·vise (:-vīz') tr. & intr. televisar.

tel·e·vi·sion (:vĭzh'ən) s. televisión *f*; *(set)* televisor *m*.

tel·ex (tĕl'ĕks') **I.** s. télex *m* **II.** intr. enviar un télex.

tell (tĕl) tr. **told** decir; *(to inform)* comunicar; *(to reveal)* revelar; *(to discriminate)* distinguir; *(to assure)* asegurar; *(to know)* adivinar, saber; *(to explain)* explicar ◆ **all told** en total ◆ **I t. you what** se me ocurre una idea ◆ **I told you so!** ¡te lo dije! ◆ **to t. off** FAM. cantar las cuarenta —intr. relatar, contar; *(to have an effect)* producir efecto.

tell·er ('ər) s. narrador *m*; *(bank employee)* ca-

jero.
tell·ing (:ĭng) adj. *(effective)* efectivo; *(significant)* significante.
tell·tale (:tāl′) s. *(informer)* soplón *m; (gossip)* chismoso.
te·mer·i·ty (tə-mĕr′ĭ-tē) s. temeridad *f.*
tem·per (tĕm′pər) I. tr. & intr. templar(se) II. s. *(disposition)* temperamento; *(composure)* compostura; *(tendency toward anger)* mal genio; *(anger)* ira; *(of metal)* temple *m* ♦ **to keep one's t.** dominarse ♦ **to lose one's t.** enfadarse.
tem·per·a·ment (:prə-mənt) s. temperamento.
tem·per·a·men·tal (′-mĕn′tl) adj. temperamental; *(moody)* caprichoso; *(unpredictable)* impredecible.
tem·per·ance (tĕm′pər-əns) s. templanza; *(abstinence)* abstinencia.
tem·per·ate (:ĭt) adj. moderado; *(tempered)* templado; *(weather)* templado.
tem·per·a·ture (:ə-chŏŏr′) s. temperatura.
tem·pered (tĕm′pərd) adj. *(disposed)* dispuesto; *(moderated)* moderado; METAL., MÚS. templado.
tem·pest (tĕm′pĭst) s. tempestad *f;* FIG. alboroto.
tem·pes·tu·ous (-pĕs′chŏŏ-əs) adj. tempestuoso; FIG. turbulento.
tem·plate (tĕm′plĭt) s. plantilla, patrón *m.*
tem·ple¹ (tĕm′pəl) s. templo; *(synagogue)* sinagoga.
tem·ple² s. ANAT. sien *f.*
tem·po (tĕm′pō) s. [pl. **s** o **-pi**] ritmo; MÚS. tempo.
tem·po·ral¹ (tĕm′pər-əl) adj. temporal; *(secular)* secular.
tem·po·ral² adj. ANAT. temporal.
tem·po·rar·y (tĕm′pə-rĕr′ē) I. adj. transitorio; *(worker)* temporero, temporario; *(position)* interino II. s. temporero.
tempt (tĕmpt) tr. tentar; *(to seduce)* seducir; *(to provoke)* provocar.
temp·ta·tion (tĕmp-tā′shən) s. tentación *f.*
tempt·ing (′tĭng) adj. tentador.
ten (tĕn) s. & adj. diez *m* ♦ **t. o'clock** las diez.
ten·a·ble (tĕn′ə-bəl) adj. sostenible, defensible.
te·na·cious (tə-nā′shəs) adj. tenaz; *(adhesive)* adhesivo; *(retentive)* retentivo.
te·nac·i·ty (tə-năs′ĭ-tē) s. tenacidad *f.*
ten·an·cy (tĕn′ən-sē) s. tenencia legal; *(time period)* tiempo de posesión.
ten·ant (tĕn′ənt) s. inquilino.
tend¹ (tĕnd) intr. *(to head)* dirigirse; *(to be likely)* tender; *(to be inclined)* propender a.
tend² tr. *(to look after)* cuidar, atender; *(to serve)* servir —intr. *(to serve)* atender; FAM. *(to pay attention)* prestar atención a.
ten·den·cy (tĕn′dən-sē) s. tendencia.
ten·der¹ (tĕn′dər) adj. **-er, -est** frágil; *(soft)* tierno; *(delicate)* delicado; *(young)* joven; *(sensitive)* sensible; *(painful)* dolorido; *(affectionate)* cariñoso.
ten·der² I. s. *(offer)* oferta de pago; *(bid)* propuesta ♦ **legal t.** dinero II. tr. ofrecer.
ten·der·heart·ed (′-här′tĭd) adj. compasivo.
ten·der·ize (tĕn′də-rīz′) tr. ablandar.
ten·der·iz·er (:rī′zər) s. condimento ablandador de carne.
ten·der·loin (tĕn′dər-loin′) s. lomo, filete *m.*
ten·der·ness (:nĭs) s. ternura.
ten·don (tĕn′dən) s. tendón *m.*
ten·dril (tĕn′drəl) s. zarcillo.

ten·e·ment (tĕn′ə-mənt) s. residencia con departamentos de alquiler; *(rundown building)* conventillo; G.B. *(apartment)* departamento.
ten·et (tĕn′ĭt) s. principio.
ten·fold (tĕn′fōld′) I. adj. décuplo II. adv. diez veces.
ten·nis (tĕn′ĭs) s. tenis *m.*
ten·on (tĕn′ən) s. CARP. espiga, barbilla.
ten·or (tĕn′ər) s. sentido, tono; MÚS. tenor *m.*
ten·pin (tĕn′pĭn′) s. bolo ♦ pl. bolos.
tense¹ (tĕns) I. adj. *(stretched)* estirado; *(taut)* tirante; *(strained)* tenso II. tr. tensar —intr. ponerse tenso.
tense² s. GRAM. tiempo.
ten·sile (tĕn′səl, :sĭl′) adj. tensivo; *(extensible)* extensible.
ten·sion (tĕn′shən) s. tensión *f.*
ten·sor (tĕn′sər, :sôr′) s. tensor *m.*
tent (tĕnt) s. tienda.
ten·ta·cle (tĕn′tə-kəl) s. tentáculo.
ten·ta·tive (tĕn′tə-tĭv) adj. *(experimental)* experimental; *(provisional)* provisorio; *(uncertain)* indeciso.
ten·ter·hook (tĕn′tər-hŏŏk′) s. gancho de bastidor ♦ **to be on tenterhooks** estar en ascuas.
tenth (tĕnth) s. & adj. décimo.
ten·u·ous (tĕn′yŏŏ-əs) adj. tenue; *(slender)* delgado; *(weak)* débil.
ten·ure (tĕn′yər) s. *(occupation)* ocupación *f,* ejercicio; *(terms)* condiciones *f; (period)* período; *(permanence)* permanencia.
tep·id (tĕp′ĭd) adj. tibio.
te·qui·la (tə-kē′lə) s. tequila *mf.*
term (tûrm) I. s. *(time period)* período, plazo; *(school year)* período académico; *(deadline)* término, fin *m; (of an official)* mandato; *(court session)* período de sesión; GRAM. voz *f,* vocablo; LÓG., MAT. término ♦ **in no uncertain terms** muy claramente ♦ **in terms of** en cuanto a • **in the long t.** a la larga ♦ pl. *(conditions)* condiciones; *(terminology)* términos; *(relations)* relaciones ♦ **to bring to t.** hacer ceder, obligar a convenir • **to come to t.** *(to agree)* llegar a un arreglo; *(to accept)* aceptar II. tr. calificar de, llamar.
ter·mi·nal (tûr′mə-nəl) I. adj. *(fatal)* fatal; *(final)* final; *(periodic)* periódico, recurrente; II. s. *(end point)* término; *(station)* terminal *f;* ELEC., COMPUT. terminal *m.*
ter·mi·nate (:nāt′) tr. terminar; *(employment)* dejar cesante —intr. terminar ♦ **to t.** in tener como resultado.
ter·mi·na·tion (:nā′shən) s. terminación *f; (end)* final *m.*
ter·mi·nol·o·gy (tûr′mə-nŏl′ə-jē) s. terminología.
ter·mi·nus (tûr′mə-nəs) s. [pl. **es** o **-ni**] *(end)* fin *m,* final *m; (terminal)* estación *f* terminal.
ter·mite (tûr′mīt′) s. termita, comején *m.*
tern (tûrn) s. golondrina de mar.
ter·race (tĕr′ĭs) I. s. terraza; *(balcony)* balcón *m; (roof)* azotea; *(embankment)* bancal *m* II. tr. terraplenar.
ter·ra cot·ta (tĕr′ə kŏt′ə) s. terracota.
ter·rain (tə-rān′) s. terreno.
ter·rar·i·um (tə-râr′ē-əm) s. [pl. **s** o **-ia**] terrario.
ter·res·tri·al (tə-rĕs′trē-əl) adj. terrestre; *(mundane)* mundano.
ter·ri·ble (tĕr′ə-bəl) adj. terrible; *(tremendous)* tremendo; *(disagreeable)* desagradable.
ter·ri·er (tĕr′ē-ər) s. terrier *m.*
ter·ri·fic (tə-rĭf′ĭk) adj. terrorífico; *(extraor-*

dinary) extraordinario.

ter·ri·fy (tĕr′ə-fī′) tr. aterrorizar.

ter·ri·to·ri·al (tĕr′ĭ-tôr′ē-əl) adj. territorial.

ter·ri·to·ri·al·i·ty (′-′-ăl′ĭ-tē) s. territorialidad *f.*

ter·ri·to·ry (tĕr′ĭ-tôr′ē) s. *(region)* región *f*; *(jurisdiction)* territorio; *(sphere)* esfera, sector *m.*

ter·ror (tĕr′ər) s. terror *m* ♦ **t.** *o* **holy t.** FAM. niño travieso.

ter·ror·ism (:ə-rĭz′əm) s. terrorismo.

ter·ror·ist (:rĭst) s. terrorista *mf.*

ter·ror·is·tic (:rĭs′tĭk) adj. terrorista.

ter·ror·ize (:rīz′) tr. aterrorizar.

ter·ry (tĕr′ē) s. ♦ **t.** **cloth** tela de toalla.

terse (tûrs) adj. conciso.

ter·ti·ar·y (tûr′shē-ĕr′ē) adj. & s. tercero; CIENT., ORNIT., RELIG. terciario.

test (tĕst) I. s. examen *m*, prueba; *(criterion)* criterio ♦ **t.** **case** DER. caso prueba ♦ **t.** **flight** vuelo de prueba ♦ **t.** **tube** tubo de ensayo, probeta ♦ **to put to the t.** poner a prueba ♦ **to stand the t.** **of time** resistir el paso del tiempo II. tr. examinar; *(to subject to a test)* someter a prueba.

tes·ta·cy (tĕs′tə-sē) s. la condición de haber hecho testamento antes de morir.

tes·ta·ment (:mənt) s. credo; DER. testamento; RELIG. convenio entre el hombre y Dios ♦ **Old, New T.** Antiguo, Nuevo Testamento.

tes·tate (tĕs′tāt′) adj. testado.

test·er (tĕs′tər) s. probador *m*, ensayador *m.*

tes·ti·cle (tĕs′tĭ-kəl) s. testículo.

tes·ti·fy (tĕs′tə-fī′) intr. ser testigo; DER. atestiguar bajo juramento —tr. testimoniar, revelar; DER. atestiguar bajo juramento ♦ **t. to** evidenciar.

tes·ti·mo·ni·al (′-mō′nē-əl) I. s. testimonio; *(recommendation)* recomendación *f*; *(tribute)* homenaje *m* II. adj. testimonial.

tes·ti·mo·ny (tĕs′tə-mō′nē) s. evidencia, prueba; DER., RELIG. testimonio.

tes·tis (tĕs′tĭs) s. [pl. **-tes**] teste *m*, testículo.

tes·tos·ter·one (tĕ-stŏs′tə-rōn′) s. testosterona.

tes·ty (tĕs′tē) adj. -i- irritable.

tet·a·nus (tĕt′n-əs) s. tétano(s).

teth·er (tĕth′ər) I. s. traílla, correa ♦ **at the end of one's t.** *(financially)* en las últimas; *(patience)* harto II. tr. atar.

tet·ra·cy·cline (tĕt′rə-sī′klēn′) s. tetraciclina.

text (tĕkst) s. texto; *(theme)* tema *m.*

text·book (′bŏŏk′) s. libro de texto.

tex·tile (tĕk′stīl′, :stəl) s. & adj. textil *m.*

tex·tu·al (tĕks′chŏŏ-əl) adj. textual.

tex·tur·al (tĕks′chər-əl) adj. de textura.

tex·ture (tĕks′chər) s. textura.

tex·tured (:chərd) adj. de textura.

thal·a·mus (thăl′ə-məs) s. [pl. **-mi**] tálamo.

tha·lid·o·mide (thə-lĭd′ə-mīd′) s. talidomida.

than (thăn, thən) conj. que <*she is a better athlete t. I* ella es mejor atleta que yo>; de <*more t. half* más de la mitad>; del que, de lo que <*more complex t. I had anticipated* más complejo de lo que había previsto> ♦ **other t.** aparte de, fuera de ♦ **rather t.** antes que.

thank (thăngk) tr. agradecer, dar las gracias a ♦ **t. you** *(for)* gracias (por).

thank·ful (′fəl) adj. agradecido.

thank·less (:lĭs) adj. *(ungrateful)* desagradecido; *(not appreciated)* ingrato.

thanks (thăngks) s.pl. gracias; *(acknowledgment)* reconocimiento; *(gratitude)* gratitud *f* ♦ **no t. to** a pesar de ♦ **t. to** gracias a.

thanks·giv·ing (:gĭv′ĭng) s. acción *f* de gracias.

that (thăt, thət) I. adj. dem. [pl. **those**] *(near)* ese; *(distant)* aquel ♦ **t. one** *(near)* ése; *(distant)* aquél ♦ **t. way** *(direction)* por aquel camino; *(manner)* de ese modo II. pron. dem. [pl. **those**] *(near)* ése; *(distant)* aquél; *(neuter)* eso, aquello ♦ **and t.'s that!** ¡eso es todo! ♦ **like t.** así ♦ **t.'s it!** ¡eso es! III. pron. rel. [pl. **that**] que <*the house t. I sold* la casa que vendí>; quien <*the person t. you've heard from* la persona de quien recibiste noticias>; el que, la que <*the closet t. you keep your clothes in* el armario en el que guardas tu ropa>; lo que <*all t. they knew* todo lo que ellos sabían> ♦ **at t.** *(without further elaboration)* así, sin más; *(nevertheless)* sin embargo; *(furthermore)* todavía ♦ **for all t.** a pesar de eso IV. adv. *(so)* tan; así de <*the steps were t. high* los escalones eran así de alto> ♦ **t. many** tantos ♦ **t. much** tanto V. conj. que ♦ por cuanto ♦ **oh, t. . . .!** ¡ojalá (que) . . .! ♦ **so t.** para que.

thatch (thăch) I. s. paja II. tr. cubrir con paja.

thaw (thô) I. intr. derretirse; *(to become warm)* ponerse tibio; *(to relax)* relajarse —tr. ♦ **to t. out** *(food)* descongelar; *(snow)* derretir II. s. derretimiento; *(warm period)* tiempo tibio.

the (thē antes de vocal, thə antes de consonante) I. art. def. el, la, lo, las, los II. adv. ♦ **t. less . . . t. better** cuanto menos . . . mejor ♦ **t. more . . . t. more** cuanto más . . . más ♦ **t. sooner t. better** cuanto antes mejor.

the·a·ter/tre (thē′ə-tər) s. teatro; *(auditorium)* auditorio; *(setting)* local *m*; MIL. teatro ♦ **operating t.** quirófano.

the·at·ri·cal (-ăt′rĭ-kəl) adj. teatral.

the·at·rics (:rĭks) s.s.g. arte escénico —s.pl. *(effects)* efectos teatrales.

thee (thē) pron. ANT., POÉT. te, ti.

theft (thĕft) s. robo.

their (thâr) pron. pos. su, suyo, suya, de ellos, de ellas.

theirs (thârz) pron. pos. (el) suyo, (la) suya, (los) suyos, (las) suyas, de ellos, de ellas.

them (thĕm, thəm) pron. *(as direct object)* los, las; *(as indirect object)* les; *(as object of preposition)* ellos, ellas.

the·mat·ic (thĭ-măt′ĭk) adj. temático.

theme (thēm) s. tema *m*; *(composition)* ensayo.

them·selves (thĕm-sĕlvz′, thəm-) pron. *(object)* se <*they prepared t.* ellos se prepararon>; *(subject)* mismos, mismas; *(object of preposition)* si mismos, sí mismas <*they are always bragging about t.* están siempre haciendo alarde de sí mismos> ♦ **among t.** entre ellos.

then (thĕn) I. adv. *(at that time)* entonces; *(afterward)* después; *(in that case)* entonces; *(in addition)* además; *(consequently)* en consecuencia ♦ **t. and there** ahí mismo II. s. entonces *m* ♦ **from t. on** desde entonces • **since t.** desde entonces • **until t.** hasta entonces III. adj. entonces, de entonces.

the·oc·ra·cy (thē-ŏk′rə-sē) s. teocracia.

the·o·lo·gian (thē′ə-lō′jən) s. teólogo.

the·o·log·i·cal (:lŏj′ĭ-kəl) adj. teológico.

the·ol·o·gy (thē-ŏl′ə-jē) s. teología.

the·o·rem (thē′ər-əm) s. teorema *m.*

the·o·ret·ic/i·cal (′ə-rĕtĭk) adj. teórico.

the·o·re·ti·cian (:ər-ə-tĭsh′ən) s. teórico.

the·o·rist (′-ĭst) s. teórico.

the·o·rize (thē′ə-rīz′) intr. teorizar.

the·o·ry (:rē) s. teoría.

ther·a·peu·tic/ti·cal (thĕr′ə-pyŏŏ′tĭk) adj. tera-

péutico ♦ **therapeutics** s.sg. terapéutica.
ther·a·pist ('-pĭst) s. terapeuta *mf.*
ther·a·py (thĕr'ə-pē) s. MED. terapia; PSIC. psicoterapia.
there (thâr) I. adv. allí, allá, ahí; *(in that matter)* en eso ♦ **here and t.** aquí y allá II. pron. ♦ **t. are** hay • **t. is** hay • **t. was** había, hubo • **t. were** habían, hubo • **t. will be** habrá III. interj. ¡vaya! ♦ **t. now!** ¡ya está! • **t.,** t. ya, ya.
there·a·bout(s) ('ə-bout[s]) adv. aproximadamente.
there·af·ter (-ăf'tər) adv. de allí en adelante.
there·by (:bī') adv. *(by that means)* por medio de eso; *(in a specified connection)* por eso.
there·fore ('fôr') adv. por lo tanto.
there·in (-ĭn') adv. *(in that place)* allí dentro; *(in that circumstance)* en eso.
there·of (:ŭv', :ŏv') adv. de eso.
there·on (:ŏn') adv. *(on that)* sobre eso; *(thereupon)* inmediatamente después.
there·to·fore ('tə-fôr') adv. hasta entonces.
there·up·on (:ə-pŏn') adv. *(upon this)* sobre eso; *(directly following)* luego; *(therefore)* en consecuencia.
there·with (-wĭth') adv. *(with that)* con eso; *(thereafter)* inmediatamente después.
ther·mal (thûr'məl) adj. termal.
ther·mo·dy·nam·ic ('mō-dī-năm'ĭk) adj. termodinámico ♦ **thermodynamics** s.sg. termodinámica.
ther·mo·e·lec·tric/tri·cal (:ī-lĕk'trĭk) adj. termoeléctrico.
ther·mom·e·ter (thər-mŏm'ĭ-tər) s. termómetro.
ther·mom·e·try (:trē) s. termometría.
ther·mo·nu·cle·ar (thûr'mō-nōō'klē-ər) adj. termonuclear.
ther·mo·plas·tic (:mə-plăs'tĭk) adj. termoplástico.
ther·mo·stat ('-stăt') s. termostato.
the·sau·rus (thĭ-sôr'əs) s. [pl. **es** o **-ri**] *(dictionary)* diccionario; *(book of synonyms)* libro de sinónimos.
these (thēz) cf. **this.**
the·sis (thē'sĭs') s. [pl. **-ses**] tesis *f.*
they (thā) pron. ellos, ellas ♦ **t. say** se dice.
thi·a·min(e) (thī'ə-mĭn, :mēn') s. tiamina.
thick (thĭk) I. adj. grueso; *(not watery)* espeso; *(in thickness)* de grosor; *(stuffy)* sofocante; *(full of)* atestado *(with* de); *(clouds)* impenetrable; *(indistinct)* poco claro, confuso; *(accent)* fuerte; *(crowd)* denso; *(beard)* tupido; *(lips)* grueso; FAM. *(stupid)* bruto; *(intimate)* íntimos II. adv. grueso ♦ **t. as thieves** inseparables • **to lay it on t.** exagerar al dar cumplidos III. s. ♦ **in the t. of** en lo más reñido de • **through t. and thin** contra viento y marea.
thick·en ('ən) tr. & intr. espesar(se); *(to complicate)* complicar(se).
thick·en·ing (:ə-nĭng) s. espesamiento.
thick·et (thĭk'ĭt) s. bosquecillo.
thick·head·ed (thĭk'hĕd'əd) adj. torpe.
thick·ness (:nĭs) s. grosor *m,* espesor *m.*
thick·set (:sĕt') adj. corpulento.
thick-skinned (:skĭnd') adj. de piel gruesa; *(not easily offended)* de mucho estómago; *(insensitive)* insensible.
thief (thēf) s. [pl. **-ves**] ladrón *m.*
thieve (thēv) tr. & intr. robar, hurtar.
thiev·er·y (thē'və-rē) s. robo, hurto.
thigh (thī) s. muslo.
thigh·bone ('bōn') s. fémur *m.*

thim·ble (thĭm'bəl) s. dedal *m.*
thin (thĭn) I. adj. **-nn-** delgado; *(fine)* fino; *(sparse)* escaso; *(hair)* ralo; *(air)* enrarecido; *(soup)* aguado; *(weak)* débil ♦ **to be as t. as a rail** estar en los huesos • **to disappear into t. air** hacerse humo II. adv. débilmente, escasamente III. tr. **-nn-** hacer adelgazar; *(to dilute)* diluir, aguar; *(to cut away)* entresacar; *(to reduce)* reducir —intr. adelgazar; *(to diminish)* reducirse; *(to fade)* disiparse.
thine (thīn) pron. ANT. tuyo.
thing (thĭng) s. cosa; *(object)* objeto; *(creature)* criatura; *(commodity)* artículo; *(obsession)* obsesión *f;* *(situation)* asunto, cuestión *f;* *(dislike)* manía ♦ **a t. or two** unas cuantas cosas • **first t.** a primera hora • **first things first** cada cosa a su debido tiempo • **for another t.** además • **for one t.** en primer lugar • **it's a good t. that** menos mal que • **sure t.!** ¡seguro! • **the latest t.** *(fashions)* el último grito; *(latest development)* la última palabra • **to do one's own t.** JER. hacer lo que uno quiere ♦ pl. *(stuff, conditions)* cosas; *(equipment)* equipo.
thing·a·ma·jig ('ə-mə-jĭg') s. FAM. cómo se llama *m.*
think (thĭngk) tr. **thought** pensar (en); *(to regard)* creer, parecerle a uno; *(to remember)* recordar; *(to imagine)* imaginarse ♦ **come to t. of it** pensándolo bien • **to be well thought of** *(person)* ser tenido en mucho; *(actions)* ser visto con buenos ojos • **to t. about** pensar (en) • **to t. nothing of it** molestarle nada a uno • **to t. of** pensar (en); *(to recall)* recordar; *(to have regard for)* pensar en • **to t. of oneself as** creerse • **to t. out** pensar bien; *(a theory, plan)* elaborar; *(a problem)* resolver; *(a solution)* encontrar • **to t. over** o **through** pensar bien • **to t. up** inventar —intr. pensar; *(to believe)* creer, parecerle a uno • **just t.!** ¡imagínese!, ¡figúrese! • **not to know what to t.** no saber a qué atenerse • **not to t. much of** *(a thing)* no parecerle a uno gran cosa; *(a person)* no tener un gran concepto de • **to make one t.** dar que pensar a uno • **to t. again** o **twice** pensarlo bien, reconsiderar • **to t. back** recordar • **to t. better of it** cambiar de parecer • **to t. of** *(to conceive of)* ocurrírsele a uno; *(to believe)* parecerle a uno; *(to imagine)* imaginarse, figurarse.
think·er (thĭng'kər) s. pensador *m.*
think·ing (:kĭng) I. s. *(thought)* pensamiento; *(judgment)* juicio, opinión *f* II. adj. pensante, racional.
thin-skinned (thĭn'skĭnd') adj. suceptible.
third (thûrd) I. s. tercero; *(part)* tercio, tercera parte; MÚS., AUTO. tercera; ASTRON., GEOM. tercero II. adj. tercero.
third-class ('klăs') I. adj. de tercera clase, de tercera II. adv. en tercera clase, en tercera.
thirst (thûrst) I. s. sed *f;* FIG. deseo ardiente, ansia II. intr. tener sed ♦ **to t. after** o **for** ansiar.
thirst·y (thûr'stē) adj. **-i-** sediento; *(arid)* seco ♦ **to be t.** tener sed • **to make t.** dar sed.
thir·teen (thûr-tēn') s. & adj. trece *m.*
thir·teenth (:tēnth') I. s. trece *m;* *(part)* trezavo, decimotercera parte II. adj. decimotercero; *(part)* trezavo.
thir·ti·eth (thûr'tē-ĭth) I. s. *(place)* treinta *m;* *(part)* treintavo, trigésima parte II. adj. *(place)* trigésimo; *(part)* treintavo.
thir·ty (thûr'tē) adj. & s. treinta *m.*
this (thĭs) [pl. **these**] I. pron. éste, ésta, esto II. adj. este, esta ♦ **t. way** *(direction)* por aquí,

por acá; *(manner)* de este modo, así **III.** adv. *(so)* tan; así de <*it was t. long* era así de largo> ♦ **t. much** tanto.

this·tle (thǐs'əl) s. cardo.

this·tle·down (:doun') s. vilano del cardo.

thong (thông) s. *(strip)* tira de cuero, correa; *(sandal)* sandalia de tiras.

tho·rac·ic (thə-răs'ǐk) adj. torácico.

tho·rax (thôr'ăks') s. [pl. **es** o **-ces**] tórax *m.*

thorn (thôrn) s. espina; *(plant)* espino, endrino; FIG. espina.

thorn·y (thôr'nē) adj. **-i-** espinoso.

thor·ough (thûr'ō) adj. completo; *(detailed)* detallado, minucioso; *(total)* total.

thor·ough·bred (:ə-brĕd') **I.** s. *(animal)* pura sangre *mf*; *(person)* persona bien nacida **II.** adj. de pura sangre.

thor·ough·fare (:fâr') s. *(highway)* carretera, camino principal; *(street)* calle *f*, vía publica.

thor·ough·go·ing ('-gō'ǐng) adj. *(complete)* cabal, completo; *(unmitigated)* rematado.

thor·ough·ness ('-nǐs) s. minuciosidad *f.*

those (thōz) cf. **that.**

thou¹ (thou) pron. ANT., POÉT. tú.

thou² (thou) s. JER. mil *m* (dólares).

though (thō) **I.** conj. aunque ♦ **as t.** como si ♦ **even t.** aunque **II.** adv. sin embargo, no obstante.

thought (thôt) **I.** cf. **think II.** s. pensamiento; *(idea)* idea; *(philosophy)* filosofía; *(consideration)* consideración *f*; *(intention, purpose)* intención *f*, propósito; *(opinion)* opinión *f*, punto de vista ♦ **at the t. of** al pensar en • **on second t.** pensándolo bien • **that's a t.!** ¡buena idea! • **the mere t. of it** sólo en pensarlo • **to be lost in t.** estar absorto en meditación • **to collect one's thoughts** pensar, concentrarse • **to give t. to** considerar.

thought·ful ('fəl) adj. pensativo; *(well thought out)* bien pensado; *(considerate)* atento, solícito.

thought·less (:lǐs) adj. *(unthinking)* irreflexivo, imprudente; *(careless)* descuidado; *(inconsiderate)* falto de consideración.

thou·sand (thou'zənd) **I.** s. mil *m* ♦ **by the t.** por millar • **in** o **by the thousands** a millares **II.** adj. mil.

thou·sandth (:zəndth) **I.** s. mil *m*; *(part)* milésimo, milésima parte **II.** adj. milésimo.

thrall (thrôl) s. *(slave)* esclavo, siervo; *(slavery)* esclavitud *f*, servidumbre.

thrash (thrăsh) tr. *(to flog)* azotar; *(to flail)* agitar; *(to vanquish)* derrotar; AGR. trillar ♦ **to t. out** discutir a fondo —intr. agitarse.

thrash·ing ('ǐng) s. *(flogging)* azotaina; AGR. trilla.

thread (thrĕd) **I.** s. hilo; *(fiber)* fibra; *(strand)* hebra; *(of light)* rayo; MEC. filete *m*, rosca ♦ **to be hanging by a t.** estar pendiente de un hilo • **to lose the t.** perder el hilo • **to pick up the t. again** coger el hilo ♦ pl. JER. ropa, trapos **II.** tr. *(a needle)* ensartar, enhebrar; *(beads)* ensartar; *(film, tape)* cargar con; *(screw, nut)* filetear, roscar ♦ **to t. one's way through** abrirse paso por.

thread·bare ('bâr') adj. *(cloth)* raído, gastado; *(trite)* trillado.

threat (thrĕt) s. amenaza.

threat·en ('n) tr. & intr. amenazar.

three (thrē) s. & adj. tres *m* ♦ **t. hundred** trescientos • **t. o'clock** las tres.

three-di·men·sion·al ('dǐ-mĕn'shə-nəl) adj.

tridimensional.

three·fold ('fōld') **I.** adj. triple **II.** adv. tres veces.

three-piece (:pēs') adj. de tres piezas.

three-quar·ter (:kwôr'tər) adj. de tres cuartos.

three-ring circus (:rǐng') s. circo de tres arenas; FIG. confusión *f*, caos *m.*

three·some (:səm) **I.** adj. triple **II.** s. trío.

thresh (thrĕsh) tr. trillar.

thresh·old (thrĕsh'ōld', :hōld') s. umbral *m.*

threw (thrō͞o) cf. **throw.**

thrice (thrīs) adv. tres veces.

thrift (thrǐft) s. economía, ahorro ♦ **t. shop** tienda de gangas.

thrift·less ('lǐs) adj. despilfarrador.

thrift·y (:tē) adj. **-i-** económico, ahorrativo.

thrill (thrǐl) **I.** tr. *(to excite)* excitar, emocionar; *(to delight)* encantar, deleitar —intr. estremecerse, temblar **II.** s. emoción *f*; *(quiver)* temblor *m*, estremecimiento; MED. tremor *m.*

thrill·er ('ər) s. FAM. novela o película de aventuras excitantes.

thrive (thrīv) intr. **-d** o **throve, -d** o **-n** *(to prosper)* prosperar, medrar; *(to flourish)* crecer.

throat (thrōt) s. garganta; *(neck)* cuello ♦ **to clear one's t.** aclararse la voz • **to cut one's own t.** arruinarse a sí mismo • **to ram down someone's t.** meterle a alguien por las narices.

throat·y (thrō'tē) adj. **-i-** gutural, ronco.

throb (thrŏb) **I.** intr. **-bb-** *(to beat)* latir, palpitar; *(with pain)* dar punzadas; *(motors)* vibrar; *(engines)* zumbar **II.** s. *(beat)* latido, palpitación *f*; *(of pain)* punzada; *(of engines)* zumbido; *(vibration)* vibración *f.*

throe (thrō) s. espasmo, punzada ♦ pl. *(of death)* agonía; *(of childbirth)* dolores • **in the t. of** en los dolores o suplicio de.

throne (thrōn) s. trono.

throng (thrông) **I.** s. gentío, muchedumbre *f* **II.** tr. *(to crowd into)* atestar, llenar; *(to press in on)* apretar, aplastar —intr. *(to gather)* amontonarse, apiñarse; *(to flock)* afluir.

throt·tle¹ (thrŏt'l) s. *(windpipe)* tráquea; TEC. válvula de admisión o de estrangulación.

throt·tle² tr. FAM. *(to choke)* estrangular, ahogar; *(to suppress)* suprimir; TEC. estrangular, obturar ♦ **to t. back** reducir la velocidad de.

through (thrō͞o) **I.** prep. o cf. *(among)* a través de; *(by the agency of)* por medio de, a través de; *(during)* durante; *(between)* entre; de . . . a, desde . . . hasta <*open Monday t. Friday* abierto de lunes a viernes>; *(thanks to)* gracias a ♦ **to have been t. it all** haberlas pasado **II.** adv. *(from one end to another)* de un lado al otro; *(from beginning to end)* hasta el final; *(completely)* completamente ♦ **t. and t.** *(completely)* completamente; *(throughout)* hasta los tuétanos • **to carry something t.** llevar algo a cabo • **to fall t.** fracasar **III.** adj. directo; *(street)* de paso libre, de vía libre; *(washed-up)* acabado ♦ **to be t.** *(to have finished)* haber terminado; *(not to be able to take it)* no poder más • **to be t. with** *(to have finished)* haber terminado con; *(to be fed up with)* no querer ver más a.

through·out (:out') **I.** prep. por todo, en todo; *(during every part of)* durante todo **II.** adv. por todas partes; *(completely)* completamente; *(during the entire time)* todo el tiempo.

throve (thrōv) cf. **thrive.**

throw (thrō) **I.** tr. **threw, thrown** tirar, arrojar; *(punches, jabs)* dar, asestar; *(to the ground, floor)* desmontar, echar por tierra; *(opponent)* derribar, tumbar; *(pottery)* modelar; *(dice)* tirar, echar; *(glance)* echar, dirigir; *(party)* dar; *(switch)* echar, conectar; FAM. *(to lose a contest)* perder adrede ♦ **to t. a fit** enfurecerse • **to t. aside** echar a un lado, desechar • **to t. away** *(to waste)* malgastar; *(to miss)* desaprovechar; *(to discard)* tirar, desechar • **to t. back** *(to return)* devolver; *(to delay)* retrasar • **to t. down** echar por tierra, derribar • **to t. in** añadir • **to t. off** *(to reject)* desechar, deshacerse de; *(to emit)* despedir; *(to mislead)* engañar; *(to disconcert)* desconcertar • **to t. on** echarse encima, ponerse rápidamente • **to t. oneself at** lanzarse sobre • **to t. oneself into** lanzarse en • **to t. out** *(to reject)* rechazar; *(to throw away)* tirar • **to t. over** *(to abandon)* abandonar; *(to overthrow)* derrocar • **to t. up** *(to raise)* alzar; *(hands)* echarse a la cabeza; *(building)* construir rápidamente —intr. arrojar, lanzar ♦ **to t. up** vomitar, devolver **II.** s. lanzamiento, tiro; *(of dice)* lance *m*; *(coverlet)* colcha, cobertor *m*; *(rug)* alfombra pequeña.

throw·a·way ('ə-wā') adj. desechable.

throw·back (:băk') s. retroceso.

thrown (thrōn) cf. **throw.**

thru (thrōō) FAM. cf. **through.**

thrush (thrŭsh) s. tordo, zorzal *m.*

thrust (thrŭst) **I.** tr. **thrust** *(to push)* meter con fuerza; *(to stab)* clavar; *(to put in)* meter; *(to force oneself into)* meterse en ♦ **to t. at** asestar un golpe a • **to t. upon** imponer —intr. *(to push)* empujar; *(to stab)* dar una puñalada; *(to force one's way)* abrirse paso **II.** s. empujón *m*, embestida; *(stab)* puñalada, estocada; *(direction)* dirección *f*; *(impetus)* ímpetu *m*, energía; ASTRONÁUT., FÍS. empuje *m.*

thru·way (thrōō'wā') s. autopista.

thud (thŭd) **I.** s. *(sound)* ruido sordo; *(blow)* batacazo **II.** intr. **-dd-** dar un batacazo.

thug (thŭg) s. maleante *m*, matón *m.*

thumb (thŭm) **I.** s. pulgar *m* ♦ **t. index** uñeros • **thumbs up!** FAM. ¡buena suerte! • **to be all thumbs** ser torpe *o* desmañado **II.** tr. manosear; FAM. *(a ride)* hacer dedo a —intr. hacer autostop ♦ **to t. one's nose** hacer un palmo de narices • **to t. through** hojear.

thumb·nail (:nāl') **I.** s. uña del pulgar **II.** adj. *(small)* pequeño; *(brief)* breve ♦ **t. sketch** cuadro conciso.

thumb·screw (:skrōō') s. tornillo de mariposa.

thumb·tack (:tăk') s. chinche *f*, chincheta.

thump (thŭmp) **I.** s. puñetazo, porrazo; *(noise)* ruido sordo, baque *m* **II.** tr. golpear, aporrear —intr. golpear, aporrear; *(to throb)* latir violentamente.

thun·der (thŭn'dər) **I.** s. trueno; *(roar)* estruendo, estrépito **II.** intr. tronar; *(to vociferate)* vociferar, tronar —tr. vociferar.

thun·der·bolt (:bōlt') s. rayo.

thun·der·cloud (:kloud') s. nubarrón *m.*

thun·der·head (:hĕd') s. masa de nubes.

thun·der·ous (:əs) adj. que truena; *(loud)* atronador; *(deafening)* ensordecedor.

thun·der·show·er (:shou'ər) s. borrasca con truenos y lluvia.

thun·der·storm (:stôrm') s. tormenta.

thun·der·struck (:strŭk') adj. atónito.

Thurs·day (thûrz'dē) s. jueves *m.*

thus (thŭs) adv. así, de esta manera; *(therefore)* así que, por eso ♦ **t. far** hasta ahora.

thwack (thwăk) **I.** tr. golpear, aporrear **II.** s. golpe fuerte y sonoro.

thwart (thwôrt) tr. frustrar.

thy (thī) adj. pos. ANT. tu.

thyme (tīm) s. tomillo.

thy·mus (thī'məs) s. timo.

thy·roid (thī'roid') adj. & s. tiroides *f.*

thy·self (thī-sĕlf') pron. reflex. ANT. *(yourself)* te; *(emphatic)* tú mismo, ti mismo.

ti·ar·a (tē-ăr'ə, -ä'rə) s. *(papal crown)* tiara; *(woman's headdress)* diadema.

tib·i·a (tĭb'ē-ə) s. [pl. **s** *o* **-iae**] tibia.

tic (tĭk) s. tic *m.*

tick¹ (tĭk) **I.** s. *(sound)* tictac *m*; *(mark)* marca, señal *f*; G.B. *(moment)* instante *m* **II.** intr. hacer tictac ♦ **to t. away** transcurrir —tr. contar, registrar ♦ **to t. off** *(item)* marcar; JER. *(person)* enojar, irritar.

tick² ENTOM. s. garrapata.

tick³ s. *(case)* funda; *(ticking)* cotí *m.*

tick·er ('ər) s. TELEG. teletipo, teleimpresor *m*; FAM. *(watch)* reloj *m*; JER. *(heart)* corazón *m* ♦ **t. tape** cinta de teleimpresor.

tick·et (tĭk'ĭt) **I.** s. *(for transport)* billete *m*, boleto; *(for movies, theater)* entrada, boleto; *(permit)* pase *m*; *(price)* etiqueta; *(summons)* boleta <*speeding t.* boleta por exceso de velocidad>; *(coupon)* cupón *m* ♦ **one-way t.** boleto de ida • **round-trip t.** boleto de ida y vuelta • **that's the t.!** ¡eso es! • **t. agent** *(travel agent)* agente de viajes; *(seller)* taquillero • **t. office** *o* **window** taquilla **II.** tr. vender billete a; *(to label)* etiquetar; *(a motorist)* darle una boleta a.

tick·ing (tĭk'ĭng) s. cotí *m.*

tick·le (tĭk'əl) **I.** tr. hacer cosquillas, cosquillear; *(to titillate)* excitar agradablemente; *(to delight)* deleitar ♦ **tickled pink** *o* **to death** FAM. contentísimo, encantado —intr. sentir cosquillas **II.** s. cosquilleo.

tick·lish (:lĭsh) adj. cosquilloso; FIG. *(touchy)* quisquilloso; *(situation)* delicado.

tick-tack-toe (tĭk'tăk'tō') s. tres en raya *m.*

tick·tock (tĭk'tŏk') s. tictac *m.*

tid·al (tīd'l) adj. de marea ♦ **t. wave** marejada.

tid·bit (tĭd'bĭt') s. bocado; *(gossip)* chisme *m.*

tide (tīd) **I.** s. marea; *(current)* corriente *f*, flujo; *(wave)* ola, corriente; *(season)* estación *f* **II.** tr. ♦ **to t. one over** bastarle a uno.

tide·land (:lănd') s. marisma.

tide·wa·ter (:wô'tər) s. agua de marea; *(land)* tierras bajas del litoral.

tid·ings (tī'dĭngz) s.pl. nuevas, noticias.

ti·dy (tī'dē) **I.** adj. **-i-** *(neat)* ordenado, arreglado; *(clean)* limpio; *(substantial)* considerable **II.** tr. & intr. ♦ **to t. up** ordenar.

tie (tī) **I.** tr. **tying** atar; *(to knot)* anudar; *(to link)* ligar; *(a contest)* empatar ♦ **to t. down** atar, sujetar • **to t. in** conectar, relacionar • **to t. up** atar; *(to confine)* restringir, limitar; *(traffic)* obstruir; *(boat)* amarrar; *(capital)* invertir —intr. atarse; *(contestants)* empatar ♦ **to t. in (with)** relacionarse (con) **II.** s. *(cord)* cuerda, atadura; *(necktie)* corbata; *(rail support)* traviesa; *(draw)* empate *m*; *(tie beam)* tirante *m*; FIG. *(bond)* lazo, vínculo; *(attachment)* atadura.

tie-in (tī'ĭn') s. relación *f*, conexión *f.*

tie·pin (tī'pĭn') s. alfiler *m* de corbata.

tier (tîr) **I.** s. fila, hilera; *(at a theater)* fila de palcos; *(of a cake)* piso **II.** tr. disponer en filas.

tie-up (tī'ŭp') s. interrupción *f.*

tiff (tĭf) s. *(irritation)* pique *m*; *(quarrel)* riña.

ti·ger (tī'gər) s. tigre *m* ♦ **t. lily** lirio de tigre.

tight (tīt) **I.** adj. *(screw, knot)* apretado; *(sealed)* hermético; *(faucet, lid)* bien cerrado; *(clothes, shoes)* ajustado; *(opening)* estrecho; *(rope, situation)* tenso; *(strict)* estricto; *(stingy)* tacaño; *(money, credit)* escaso; *(closely contested)* reñido, disputado ♦ **t. as a drum** muy tirante • **to be in a t. spot** estar en un aprieto • **to be t.** JER. estar borracho • **to get t.** JER. emborracharse **II.** adv. *(firmly)* bien, fuertemente; *(soundly)* profundamente ♦ **hold t.!** ¡agárrense bien! • **to sit t.** cruzarse de brazos.

tight·en (´n) tr. apretar; *(a cord)* tensar; *(bonds)* estrechar ♦ **to t. one's belt** FIG. apretarse el cinturón —intr. apretarse.

tight·fist·ed (:fĭs´tĭd) adj. FAM. tacaño, avaro.

tight·lipped (:lĭpt´) adj. con los labios apretados; *(reticent)* callado.

tight·rope (:rōp´) s. cuerda floja.

tights (tīts) s.pl. malla.

tight·wad (tīt´wŏd´) s. JER. tacaño, avaro.

ti·gress (tī´grĭs) s. tigresa.

tile (tīl) **I.** s. *(of a roof)* teja; *(of a floor)* losa, baldosa; *(of a wall)* azulejo; *(tiling)* enlosado; *(of a game)* pieza **II.** tr. *(a roof)* tejar; *(a floor)* embaldosar; *(a wall)* azulejar.

till¹ (tĭl) tr. AGR. labrar, cultivar.

till² prep. hasta (donde) **II.** conj. hasta que.

till³ s. *(for money)* caja, cajón m.

tilt (tĭlt) **I.** tr. inclinar —intr. inclinarse; HIST. *(to joust)* participar en una justa ♦ **to t. over** *(to lean)* inclinarse; *(to fall)* volcarse, caer **II.** s. inclinación f; *(joust)* torneo, justa ♦ **(at) full t. a toda velocidad • on** *o* **at t.** inclinado.

tim·ber (tĭm´bər) **I.** s. árboles m maderables; *(lumber)* maderamen m; *(beam)* viga; MARÍT. cuaderna, FIG. material m **II.** tr. enmaderar.

tim·ber·land (:lănd´) s. bosque m maderable.

tim·ber·line (:līn´) s. altitud f límite de la vegetación arbórea.

tim·bre (tăm´bər, tĭm´-) s. timbre m.

time (tīm) **I.** s. tiempo; *(moment)* momento; *(instant)* instante m; *(period)* período; *(season)* estación f, temporada; *(era)* era, época; *(a specified time)* hora; *(occasion)* ocasión f; *(instance)* vez f; *(lifetime)* vida; *(prison sentence)* condena; MÚS. tiempo; *(tempo)* compás m; *(duration)* duración f; GRAM. tiempo ♦ **all in good t.** todo a su tiempo • **all the t.** *(every moment)* todo el tiempo; *(always)* siempre • **a long t. ago** hace mucho tiempo • **(at) any t.** en cualquier momento • **a short t.** un rato • **at all times** en todo momento • **at a t.** a la vez • **at no t.** nunca • **at one t.** en cierta época • **at the present t.** en la actualidad • **at the same t.** a la vez, al mismo tiempo • **at times** a veces • **behind the times** anticuado • **by that t.** para entonces • **each** *o* **every t.** cada vez • **for the t. being** por el momento • **from this t. on** desde ahora en adelante • **from t. to t.** de vez en cuando • **hard t.** mal rato • **hard times** tiempos difíciles • **have a good t.!** ¡diviértanse! • **in a short t.** dentro de poco • **in due t.** en su día • **in no t. (at all)** en un abrir y cerrar de ojos • **in t.** *(on time)* a tiempo; MÚS. al compás • **many a time** *o* **many times** muchas veces • **on t.** a tiempo • **t. and t. again** repetidas veces • **t. off** tiempo libre • **time's up!** ¡es la hora! • **to keep good t.** andar bien (un reloj) • **to keep t.** *(clock)* marcar la hora; MÚS. llevar el compás • **to keep up with the times** estar al tanto de las cosas • **to make t.** ganar tiempo • **to pass the t.** pasar el tiempo • **to pass** *o* **while the t. away** matar el tiempo • **to serve** *o* **do t.** cumplir una condena

• **to take one's t.** tomarse tiempo • **to waste t.** perder el tiempo • **what t. is it?** ¿qué hora es? **II.** adj. del tiempo; *(on installment)* a plazos ♦ **t. clock** reloj registrador • **t. zone** huso horario **III.** tr. fijar la hora *o* el tiempo de; *(to record)* cronometrar.

time·card (´kärd´) s. tarjeta de marcar.

timed (tīmd) adj. de duración limitada.

time-hon·ored (tīm´ŏn´ərd) adj. tradicional.

time·keep·er (:kē´pər) s. *(timepiece)* cronómetro, reloj m; DEP. cronometrador m.

time-lapse (:lăps´) adj. FOTOG. a intervalos.

time·less (:lĭs) adj. *(eternal)* eterno; *(ageless)* sin limitación de tiempo.

time·li·ness (:lē-nĭs) s. *(punctuality)* puntualidad f; *(fitness of time)* oportunidad f.

time·ly (:lē) **I.** adj. **-i-** *(opportune)* oportuno; *(punctual)* puntual **II.** adv. oportunamente.

time-out *o* **time out** (:out´) s. DEP. interrupción f temporal; *(break)* descanso.

time·piece (:pēs´) s. reloj m, cronómetro.

tim·er (tī´mər) s. *(timekeeper)* cronometrador m; *(timepiece)* cronómetro, cronógrafo; TEC., ELEC. regulador eléctrico; AUTO. distribuidor m del encendido.

times (tīmz) prep. multiplicado (por).

time-sav·ing (tīm´sā´vĭng) adj. que ahorra tiempo.

time-shar·ing (:shâr´ĭng) s. COMPUT. tiempo compartido.

time·ta·ble (:tā´bəl) s. horario.

time·worn (:wôrn´) adj. *(used)* usado, gastado; *(trite)* trillado.

tim·id (tĭm´ĭd) adj. **-er, -est** *(hesitant)* temeroso; *(shy)* tímido.

ti·mid·i·ty (tĭ-mĭd´ĭ-tē) s. timidez f.

tim·ing (tī´mĭng) s. oportunidad f; MÚS. compás m; DEP. coordinación f; TEC., AUTO. regulación f de tiempo.

tim·or·ous (tĭm´ər-əs) adj. timorato.

tin (tĭn) **I.** s. estaño; *(container)* lata; *(for baking)* molde m **II.** tr. **-nn-** estañar; G.B. *(to can)* enlatar.

tinc·ture (tĭngk´chər) **I.** s. colorante m, pigmento; *(hue)* tinte m; *(trace)* vestigio; QUÍM., FARM. tintura **II.** tr. teñir.

tin·der (tĭn´dər) s. yesca, mecha.

tin·der·box (:bŏks´) s. yesquero; FIG. polvorín m.

tine (tīn) s. *(of a pitchfork)* punta; *(of a fork)* diente m.

tin·foil *o* **tin foil** (tĭn´foil´) s. papel m de estaño.

ting (tĭng) **I.** s. tintineo **II.** intr. tintinear.

tinge (tĭnj) **I.** tr. **-(e)ing** matizar, teñir **II.** s. matiz m, tinte m; *(trace)* vestigio.

tin·gle (tĭng´gəl) **I.** intr. sentir picazón —tr. picar, causar picazón a **II.** s. picazón f; *(quiver)* estremecimiento.

tin·ker (tĭng´kər) **I.** s. calderero remendón; *(bungler)* chapucero ♦ **it's not worth a t.'s damn** JER. no vale un comino **II.** intr. remendar como calderero; *(to play)* entretenerse ♦ **to t. with** jugar con, juguetear.

tin·kle (tĭng´kəl) **I.** intr. tintinear —tr. hacer tintinear **II.** s. tintineo.

tin·kling (:klĭng) s. tintineo.

tin·ny (tĭn´ē) adj. **-i-** *(sound)* metálico; *(flimsy)* frágil.

tin-plate (:plāt´) tr. estañar.

tin·sel (tĭn´səl) **I.** s. oropel m **II.** adj. de oropel.

tin·smith (tĭn´smĭth´) s. estañero.

tint (tĭnt) **I.** s. tinte m; *(hue)* matiz m; *(trace)* huella; ARTE. media tinta **II.** tr. matizar.

ti·ny (tī'nē) adj. **-i-** minúsculo.

tip¹ (tĭp) s. *(end)* punta, cabo; *(extremity)* extremidad *f*; *(apex)* ápice *m*; *(of a cigarette)* filtro ♦ **from t. to toe** de pies a cabeza • **to have it on the t. of one's tongue** tenerlo en la punta de la lengua.

tip² **I.** tr. **-pp-** volcar, derribar; *(to tilt)* inclinar ♦ **to t. one's hat to** saludar (con el sombrero) a • **to t. over** volcar, derribar —intr. volcar, derribar; *(to lean)* inclinarse ♦ **to t. off** caerse • **to t. over** volcarse **II.** s. inclinación *f*.

tip³ **I.** tr. **-pp-** golpear ligeramente **II.** s. golpe ligero.

tip⁴ **I.** s. *(gratuity)* propina; *(information)* información *f*; *(advice)* consejo **II.** tr. **-pp-** *(with money)* dar una propina; *(with information)* dar una información ♦ **to t. one's hand** revelar uno sus verdaderas intenciones —intr. dar propinas.

tip-off (·'ôf') s. FAM. información *f*, soplo.

tip·ple (tĭp'əl) intr. FAM. empinar el codo.

tip·pler (:lər) s. FAM. borrachín *m*.

tip·sy (tĭp'sē) adj. **-i-** *(slightly drunk)* achispado; *(unsteady)* tambaleante.

tip·toe (tĭp'tō') **I.** intr. andar de puntillas; *(stealthily)* andar sigilosamente **II.** s. punta del pie **III.** adj. & adv. de puntillas.

tip·top ('tŏp') **I.** s. cumbre *f*, cima; *(highest quality)* calidad *f* superior **II.** adj. de calidad superior **III.** adv. perfectamente.

ti·rade (tī'rād') s. perorata.

tire¹ (tīr) tr. & intr. cansar(se); *(to bore)* aburrir(se).

tire² s. AUTO. llanta, neumático.

tired (tīrd) adj. cansado; *(bored)* aburrido; *(hackneyed)* trillado.

tire·less (tīr'lĭs) adj. incansable.

tire·some (:səm) adj. cansado, tedioso.

tis·sue (tĭsh'ōō) s. BIOL. tejido; *(disposable towel)* pañuelo de papel; *(web)* red *f* ♦ **t. paper** papel de seda.

tit¹ (tĭt) s. ORNIT. paro.

tit² s. teta; *(nipple)* pezón *m* ♦ **to give t. for tat** FIG. pagar con la misma moneda.

ti·tan·ic (tī-tăn'ĭk) adj. gigantesco, colosal; *(powerful)* poderoso.

tithe (tīth) **I.** s. RELIG. diezmo; *(tenth part)* décima parte **II.** tr. diezmar —intr. pagar el diezmo.

tit·il·late (tĭt'l-āt') tr. *(to tickle)* cosquillear; *(to stimulate)* estimular.

ti·tle (tīt'l) **I.** s. título; CINEM. subtítulo; DEP. campeonato ♦ **t. page** portada • **t. role** papel principal **II.** tr. conferir título a; *(to entitle)* titular.

ti·tled (:ld) adj. titulado; *(person)* con título.

ti·tle·hold·er (:l-hōl'dər) s. titular *mf*; *(champion)* campeón *m*.

tit·mouse (tĭt'mous') s. [pl. **-mice**] paro.

tit·ter (tĭt'ər) **I.** intr. reír entre dientes **II.** s. risa entre dientes.

tit·tle (tĭt'l) s. pizca, ápice *m*.

tit·tle-tat·tle (tĭt'l-tăt'l) **I.** s. chismorreo, chismes **II.** intr. chismear.

tit·u·lar (tĭch'ə-lər) adj. titular; *(nominal)* nominal.

tit·u·lar·y (:lĕr'ē) s. titular *mf*.

tiz·zy (tĭz'ē) s. JER. agitación *f*.

to (tōō, tə) prep. a; *(direction)* hacia; *(as far as)* hasta; *(against)* contra; *(of, for)* de, para; *(constituting)* por; *(in accord with)* según, de

acuerdo con; *(as compared with)* comparado a; *(before)* menos, para; *(until)* hasta; *(for the purpose of)* para, en; *(in honor of)* por, en honor a; *(with the result)* para, ante; *(toward)* con; *(not translated)* ‹tell him if you want to díselo si quieres›.

toad (tōd) s. sapo; FIG. persona repulsiva.

toad·stool ('stōōl') s. hongo venenoso.

toad·y (tō'dē) **I.** s. adulador *m*, cobista *mf* **II.** intr. adular (a).

toast¹ (tōst) **I.** tr. tostar; *(body, hands)* calentar —intr. tostarse **II.** s. tostada.

toast² **I.** s. *(drink)* brindis *m* ♦ **the t. of the town** el héroe de la ciudad • **to drink a t. to** brindar por **II.** tr. & intr. brindar (a).

toast·er (tō'stər) s. tostadora.

toast·mas·ter (tōst'măs'tər) s. maestro de ceremonias en un banquete.

to·bac·co (tə-băk'ō) s. [pl. **(e)s**] tabaco.

to·be (tōō-bē') adj. futuro.

to·bog·gan (tə-bŏg'ən) s. tobogán *m*.

to·day *o* **to-day** (tə-dā') **I.** adv. hoy; *(at the present time)* actualmente **II.** s. hoy *m*; *(the present time)* hoy (en) día.

tod·dle (tŏd'l) **I.** intr. hacer pinitos **II.** s. pino, pinito.

tod·dler (:lər) s. niño que empieza a andar.

tod·dy (tŏd'ē) s. ponche *m*.

to-do (tə-dōō') s. FAM. alboroto, jaleo.

toe (tō) **I.** s. dedo del pie; *(of a shoe, sock)* puntera ♦ **from head to t.** de pies a cabeza • **to be on one's toes** estar alerta • **to step on someone's toes** herir los sentimientos de alguien **II.** tr. tocar con la punta del pie ♦ **to t. the line** *o* **mark** conformarse —intr. ♦ **to t. in, out** andar con los pies hacia adentro, hacia afuera.

toed (tōd) adj. ZOOL. de … dedos en el pie; CARP. metido oblicuamente.

toe·hold (tō'hōld') s. hendidura para apoyar la punta del pie; FIG. asidero.

toe·nail (tō'nāl') s. uña del dedo del pie.

tof·fee (tŏf'ē) s. melcocha, arropía.

tog (tŏg) FAM. **I.** s. *(jacket)* chaqueta; *(cloak)* capa ♦ pl. ropa **II.** tr. **-gg-** vestir.

to·ga (tō'gə) s. toga.

to·geth·er (tə-gĕth'ər) adv. juntos; *(in total)* en total, todos (juntos) ♦ **getting along t.** llevándose bien • **to bring t.** *(to reunite)* reunir; *(to reconcile)* reconciliar • **to come t.** FIG. tener buen éxito • **to come** *o* **to get t.** juntarse, reunirse • **to go t.** *(to go out)* salir juntos; *(colors, flavors)* armonizar.

to·geth·er·ness (:nĭs) s. solidaridad *f*, unión *f*.

tog·gle (tŏg'əl) s. MARÍT. cabilla; MEC. *(pin)* fiador atravesado; *(joint)* rótula; *(button)* alamar *m* ♦ **t. switch** interruptor eléctrico.

toil¹ (toil) **I.** intr. trabajar duro; *(to move)* moverse con dificultad **II.** s. esfuerzo, trabajo.

toil² s. *(net)* red *f* ♦ pl. FIG. red, trampa.

toi·let (toi'lĭt) s. retrete *m*, lavabo; *(toilette)* arreglo, aseo ♦ **t. paper** papel higiénico • **t. water** agua de tocador.

toi·let·ry (toi'lĭ-trē) s. artículo de tocador.

toi·lette (twä-lĕt') s. arreglo, aseo.

to·ken (tō'kən) **I.** s. señal *f*, prueba; *(symbol)* símbolo; *(souvenir)* recuerdo; *(chip)* ficha ♦ **by the same t.** igualmente **II.** adj. simbólico.

told (tōld) cf. **tell.**

tol·er·a·ble (tŏl'ər-ə-bəl) adj. tolerable; *(passable)* mediano, pasable.

tol·er·ance (:əns) s. *(acceptance)* tolerancia;

(patience) paciencia.
tol·er·ant (:ənt) adj. tolerante.
tol·er·ate (tŏl′ə-rāt′) tr. tolerar; *(suffering, pain)* sufrir, aguantar.
tol·er·a·tion (′-rā′shən) s. tolerancia.
toll[1] (tōl) s. peaje *m*; *(on a phone call)* tasa, recargo; *(loss)* bajas, número de víctimas.
toll[2] **I.** tr. & intr. *(to ring)* tañer, tocar **II.** s. tañido.
toll·booth (′bōōth′) s. caseta de peaje.
toll·gate (:gāt′) s. barrera de peaje.
toll·house (:hous′) s. garita de peaje.
tom (tŏm) s. macho.
tom·a·hawk (tŏm′ə-hôk′) s. hacha de guerra de los indios norteamericanos.
to·ma·to (tə-mā′tō, -mä′-) s. [pl. **es**] tomate *m* ♦ **t. plant** tomatera.
tomb (tōōm) s. tumba; *(place)* sepultura.
tom·boy (tŏm′boi′) s. FAM. marimacho.
tomb·stone (tŏm′stōn′) s. lápida.
tom·cat (tŏm′kăt′) s. gato macho.
tome (tōm) s. tomo; *(huge book)* libraco.
tom·fool·er·y (tŏm-fōō′lə-rē) s. tonterías, disparate *m*.
tom·my·rot (tŏm′ē-rŏt′) s. JER. disparate *m*.
to·mor·row (tə-môr′ō) **I.** s. mañana ♦ **the day after t.** pasado mañana **II.** adv. mañana.
tom-tom (tŏm′tŏm′) s. tantán *m*, tamtam *m*.
ton (tŭn) s. tonelada ♦ pl. FAM. montones.
to·nal (tō′nəl) adj. tonal.
to·nal·i·ty (tō-năl′ĭ-tē) s. tonalidad *f.*
tone (tōn) **I.** s. tono **II.** tr. dar tono a, modificar el tono de; *(colors)* matizar ♦ **to t. down** bajar, suavizar ♦ **to t. up** *(color)* intensificar; *(muscle)* tonificar.
tone·less (′lĭs) adj. apagado.
tongs (tŏngz) s.pl. tenacillas; *(fire tool)* tenazas.
tongue (tŭng) **I.** s. lengua; *(language)* idioma *m*; *(of a shoe)* lengüeta; *(of a bell)* badajo ♦ **to hold o bite one's t.** morderse la lengua, callarse ● **to stick out one's t.** sacar la lengua ● **t. twister** trabalenguas **II.** tr. lamer; CARP. ensamblar, machihembrar.
tongue-in-cheek (′ĭn-chēk′) adj. irónico.
tongue-lash·ing (′lăsh′ĭng) s. FAM. reprimenda, regaño.
tongue-tied (:tīd′) adj. con la lengua atada.
ton·ic (tŏn′ĭk) s. tónico; MÚS., FONÉT. tónica; *(quinine water)* agua tónica.
to·night (tə-nīt′) adv. & s. esta noche.
ton·nage (tŭn′ĭj) s. tonelaje *m.*
ton·sil (tŏn′səl) s. amígdala.
ton·sil·lec·to·my (′ sə-lĕk′tə-mē) s. tonsilectomía, amigdalectomía.
ton·sil·li·tis (:lī′tĭs) s. amigdalitis *f.*
ton·so·ri·al (tŏn-sôr′ē-əl) adj. barberil.
ton·sure (tŏn′shər) s. tonsura.
too (tōō) adv. *(also)* también; *(as well as)* además; *(excessively)* demasiado; *(very)* muy ♦ **not t.** FAM. no muy, nada ● **to be t. much** ser demasiado ● **t. little** *(amount)* demasiado poco; *(size)* muy pequeño ● **t. many** demasiados.
took (tŏŏk) cf. **take.**
tool (tōōl) **I.** s. herramienta; *(utensil)* utensilio, útil *m*; FIG. instrumento **II.** tr. *(to shape)* labrar; *(to equip)* equipar con herramientas —intr. ♦ **to t. around** FAM. pasear (en coche).
tool·box (′bŏks′) s. caja de herramientas.
toot (tōōt) **I.** intr. sonar, emitir sonidos —tr. tocar, hacer sonar ♦ **to t. one's own horn** FAM. echarse flores **II.** s. pitazo, bocinazo.

tooth (tōōth) s. [pl. **teeth**] diente *m*; *(molar)* muela; *(of a saw)* diente; *(of a comb)* púa ♦ **by the skin of one's teeth** por poco, por un pelo ● **to cut one's teeth on** iniciarse en ● **to fight t. and nail** luchar a brazo partido ● **to get one's teeth into** meterse bien en ● **to have a sweet t.** ser goloso ● **to show one's teeth** mostrar los dientes ● **wisdom t.** muela del juicio.
tooth·ache (′āk′) s. dolor *m* de muelas.
tooth·brush (:brŭsh′) s. cepillo de dientes.
toothed (tōōtht, tōōthd) adj. dentado; de dientes <*saw-toothed* de dientes aserrados>.
tooth·less (tōōth′lĭs) adj. sin dientes, desdentado; *(ineffectual)* ineficaz.
tooth·paste (:pāst′) s. pasta dentífrica.
tooth·pick (:pĭk′) s. mondadientes *m.*
tooth·pow·der (:pou′dər) s. polvo dentífrico.
tooth·some (:səm) adj. sabroso, apetitoso; *(attractive)* atractivo.
tooth·y (tōō′thē) adj. **-i-** dentudo.
top[1] (tŏp) **I.** s. parte *f* superior o de arriba; *(of the head)* coronilla; *(of a container)* borde *m*; *(of a mountain)* cumbre *f*; *(of a house)* techo; *(of a tree, hat)* copa; *(of a bottle, pan)* tapa; *(of a page)* cabeza; *(of liquids)* superficie *f*; *(of plants)* tallo; *(blouse)* blusa; *(jacket)* chaqueta; *(of a bikini)* sostén *m*; *(peak)* cumbre *f* ♦ **at the t. of** a la cabeza de ● **at the t. of one's form** en plena forma ● **from t. to bottom** de arriba abajo ● **on t.** encima ● **on t. of** además de ● **on t. of it all** para colmo de males ● **to come out on t.** salir ganando ● **to blow one's t.** FAM. salirse de sus casillas **II.** adj. de arriba; *(topmost)* último; *(highest)* más alto; *(great)* de categoría; *(best)* mejor; *(maximum)* máximo ♦ **t. hat** sombrero de copa **III.** tr. **-pp-** *(to form a top of)* coronar, rematar; *(to reach a top)* llegar a la cumbre de; *(to cover)* cubrir; *(to surpass)* superar; *(to be at the head of)* estar a la cabeza de; *(to be bigger than)* medir más que, ser más alto que; *(trees)* desmochar ♦ **to t. it all off** por si fuera poco ● **to t. off** rematar, coronar.
top[2] s. *(toy)* peonza, trompo.
to·paz (tō′păz′) s. topacio.
top·coat (:kōt′) s. abrigo, sobretodo.
top-drawer (:drôr′) FAM. adj. *(first-class)* de la más alta categoría; *(people)* de la alta sociedad.
top-flight (:flīt′) adj. de primera categoría.
top-heav·y (:hĕv′ē) adj. más pesado arriba que abajo.
to·pi·ar·y (tō′pē-ĕr′ē) s. *(art)* jardinería; *(garden)* jardín *m* ornamental.
top·ic (tŏp′ĭk) s. tópico, tema *m.*
top·i·cal (:ĭ-kəl) adj. tópico; *(contemporary)* corriente, actual; MED. tópico.
top·knot (tŏp′nŏt′) s. *(of hair)* moño alto; *(of feathers, bows)* copete *m.*
top·less (:lĭs) adj. sin la parte superior; *(woman)* con el busto desnudo.
top·most (:mōst′) adj. *(highest)* más alto, más elevado; *(uppermost)* máximo.
top·notch (:nŏch′) adj. FAM. de primera clase.
to·pog·ra·phy (tə-pŏg′rə-fē) s. topografía.
to·pol·o·gy (tə-pŏl′ə-jē) s. topología.
top·ping (tŏp′ĭng) s. *(sauce)* salsa; *(frosting)* cobertura, garapiña; *(garnish)* aderezo.
top·ple (tŏp′əl) tr. derribar; *(government)* volcar —intr. *(to fall)* volcarse; *(to totter)* tambalearse.
tops (tŏps) adj. JER. fantástico, buenísimo.
top-se·cret (tŏp′sē′krĭt) adj. absolutamente se-

creto.

top·soil (:soil′) s. tierra, capa superficial del suelo.

top·sy-tur·vy (tŏp′sē-tûr′vē) **I.** adv. patas arriba, al revés; *(in disorder)* en desorden **II.** adj. desordenado.

torch (tôrch) s. antorcha; *(for welding)* soplete *m*; G.B. *(flashlight)* linterna ♦ **to carry a t. for someone** estar enamorado de alguien sin ser correspondido ♦ **t. song** canción de amor.

torch·bear·er ('bâr′ər) s. abanderado.

tore (tôr) cf. **tear¹.**

tor·e·a·dor (tôr′ē-ə-dôr′) s. toreador *m.*

tor·ment I. s. (tôr′mĕnt′) tormento; *(torture)* tortura **II.** tr. (-′) atormentar; *(to torture)* torturar; *(to pester)* molestar.

tor·men·tor/ment·er (tôr-mĕn′tər) s. atormentador *m*, torturador *m.*

torn (tôrn) cf. **tear¹.**

tor·na·do (tôr-nā′dō) s. [pl. **(e)s**] tornado.

tor·pe·do (tôr-pē′dō) **I.** s. [pl. **es**] torpedo **II.** tr. torpedear.

tor·pid (tôr′pĭd) adj. tórpido; *(lethargic)* letárgico; *(apathetic)* apático.

tor·por (:pər) s. *(dullness)* torpor *m*; *(apathy)* apatía.

torque (tôrk) s. momento *o* fuerza de torsión, par *m* de torsión.

tor·rent (tôr′ənt) s. torrente *m.*

tor·ren·tial (tô-rĕn′shəl) adj. torrencial.

tor·rid (tôr′ĭd) adj. tórrido; *(scorching)* abrasado, FIG. ardiente.

tor·sion (tôr′shən) s. torsión *f.*

tor·so (tôr′sō) s. [pl. **s** *o* **-si**] torso.

tort (tôrt) s. DER. agravio.

tor·ti·lla (tôr-tē′yə) s. tortilla (de maíz).

tor·toise (tôr′tĭs) s. tortuga de tierra.

tor·toise-shell (:shĕl′) s. concha de carey.

tor·tu·ous (tôr′chŏŏ-əs) adj. tortuoso; *(complex)* complicado.

tor·ture (tôr′chər) **I.** s. tortura **II.** tr. torturar.

tor·tur·er (:ər) s. torturador *m.*

tor·tur·ous (:əs) adj. atormentador.

toss (tôs) **I.** tr. tirar, lanzar; *(one's head, hair)* echar hacia atrás; *(rider)* dejar caer; *(salads)* revolver; *(coin)* echar a cara o cruz ♦ **to t. aside** echar a un lado • **to t. down** beber de un trago • **to t. off** hacer fácilmente • **to t. out** desechar —intr. *(to be flung to and fro)* ser agitado, volverse; *(to flip a coin)* echar una moneda a cara o cruz ♦ **to t. and turn** dar vueltas en la cama **II.** s. lanzamiento, tiro; *(rapid movement)* sacudida; *(fall)* caída ♦ **to win the t.** ganar a cara o cruz.

toss·up ('ŭp′) FAM. s. lanzamiento de una moneda a cara o cruz; *(odds)* probabilidad pareja.

tot¹ (tŏt) s. *(child)* nene *m*; *(drop)* trago.

tot² tr. **-tt-** ♦ **to t. up** sumar.

to·tal (tōt′l) **I.** s. total *m*; *(entirety)* totalidad *f* **II.** adj. total **III.** tr. & intr. totalizar ♦ **to t. up to** ascender a.

to·tal·i·tar·i·an (tō-tăl′ĭ-târ′ē-ən) adj. totalitario.

to·tal·i·ty (-′-tē) s. totalidad *f.*

tote (tōt) **I.** tr. llevar **II.** s. carga, peso ♦ **t. bag** bolsa grande.

to·tem (tō′təm) s. tótem *m* ♦ **t. pole** poste de un tótem.

tot·ter (tŏt′ər) intr. tambalearse.

tot·ter·ing (:ĭng) adj. tambaleante.

tou·can (tō̄′kăn′, -kän′) s. tucán *m.*

touch (tŭch) **I.** tr. tocar; *(to taste)* probar, to-

car; *(to disturb)* toquetear, manosear; *(to border)* lindar con; *(to equal)* igualarse a; *(to mention)* referirse a; *(to concern)* concernir a; *(to move)* conmover ♦ **to t. bottom** tocar fondo • **to t. off** desencadenar, provocar • **to t. up** *(to add touches to)* corregir, retocar; *(to finish off)* dar los últimos toques a —intr. tocarse; *(to be in contact)* estar en contacto ♦ **to t. down** AVIA. aterrizar **II.** s. toque *m*; *(sense)* tacto; *(mild attack)* ataque ligero; *(dash)* pizca, poquito; *(facility)* mano <to lose one's t. perder la mano>; *(contact)* contacto, comunicación *f*; JER. *(approach for a loan)* sablazo ♦ **by t.** al tacto • **final** *o* **finishing t.** último toque • **to be out of t. with** *(people)* haber perdido el contacto con; *(things)* no estar al corriente *o* al tanto de • **to keep in t.** mantenerse en contacto.

touch-and-go ('ən-gō′) adj. arriesgado.

touch·down ('doun′) s. AER. aterrizaje *m*; DEP. tanto, gol *m.*

touched (tŭcht) adj. *(moved)* conmovido; FAM. *(mentally unbalanced)* tocado de la cabeza.

touch·ing (tŭch′ĭng) adj. conmovedor.

touch·stone ('stōn′) s. piedra de toque; *(criterion)* criterio de prueba.

touch-type (:tīp′) intr. mecanografiar al tacto.

touch·up (:ŭp′) s. retoque *m.*

touch·y (:ē) adj. **-i-** *(oversensitive)* susceptible, quisquilloso; *(requiring speed)* delicado.

tough (tŭf) **I.** adj. duro; *(physically hardy)* fuerte, robusto; *(harsh)* severo, áspero; *(aggressive)* agresivo; *(difficult)* difícil; *(resolute)* decidido; *(rough)* tosco, bruto; *(unyielding)* inflexible ♦ **t!** *o* **t. luck!** FAM. ¡mala suerte! **II.** s. matón *m.*

tough·en ('ən) tr. & intr. endurecer(se).

tough-mind·ed (:mīn′dĭd) adj. duro (de carácter).

tou·pee (tŏŏ-pā′) s. peluquín *m.*

tour (tŏŏr) **I.** s. excursión *f*, viaje *m*; *(visit)* visita; TEAT. gira **II.** tr. recorrer, hacer un viaje por; TEAT. presentar en gira —intr. ir de viaje.

tour·ing ('ĭng) **I.** s. turismo **II.** adj. de turismo; *(theatrical company)* que está de gira.

tour·ism (:ĭz′əm) s. turismo.

tour·ist (:ĭst) **I.** s. turista *m/f* **II.** adj. de turista.

tour·na·ment (tŏŏr′nə-mənt) s. torneo.

tour·ney (:nē) **I.** intr. tornear **II.** s. torneo.

tour·ni·quet (:nĭ-kĭt) s. torniquete *m.*

tou·sle (tou′zəl) tr. *(hair)* desordenar; *(clothes)* arrugar, desarreglar.

tout (tout) FAM. **I.** s. vendedor *m* de informaciones sobre caballos de carrera **II.** tr. *(to recommend)* recomendar; *(to solicit)* solicitar; *(to importune)* importunar.

tow¹ (tō) **I.** tr. remolcar **II.** s. remolque *m*; *(tow truck)* camión *m* remolcador; *(tugboat)* remolcador *m*; *(rope, cable)* remolque, sirga.

tow² s. *(fiber)* estopa.

tow·age (tō′ĭj) s. remolque *m*; *(fee)* derechos de remolque.

to·ward(s) (tôrd[z], tə-wôrd[z]′) prep. hacia; *(facing)* próximo a; *(for)* para; *(with)* con, para con; *(near in time)* alrededor de.

tow·el (tou′əl) **I.** s. toalla, paño ♦ **to throw in the t.** DEP. tirar la esponja; FIG. darse por vencido **II.** tr. & intr. secar(se) *o* frotar(se) con una toalla.

tow·er (tou′ər) **I.** s. torre *f*; *(fortress)* torreón *m*, fortaleza; *(watch tower)* atalaya; AER. torre de control **II.** intr. elevarse ♦ **to t. over** *o* **above** dominar, destacarse sobre.

tow·er·ing (:ĭng) adj. *(very high)* altísimo; *(outstanding)* sobresaliente; *(intense)* intenso.
tow·head (tō′hĕd′) s. persona rubia.
tow·line (tō′līn′) s. remolque *m*, sirga.
town (toun) **I.** s. *(city)* ciudad *f*; *(village)* pueblo; *(commercial center)* centro; *(residents)* gente *f*, pueblo ♦ **to be out of t.** estar fuera, estar de viaje • **to go out on the t.** FAM. salir a divertirse • **to go to t. on** FAM. hacer con toda el alma • **to paint the t. red** JER. ir de juerga **II.** adj. urbano ♦ **t. crier** pregonero • **t. hall** ayuntamiento, municipalidad
town·ship (′shĭp′) s. municipio.
towns·peo·ple (tounz′pē′pəl) s.pl. habitantes *mf* de una ciudad.
tow·rope (tō′rōp′) s. remolque *m*, sirga.
tox·e·mi·a (tŏk-sē′mē-ə) s. toxemia.
tox·ic (tŏk′sĭk) s. tóxico.
tox·i·cant (:sĭ-kənt) s. & adj. tóxico.
tox·ic·i·ty (-sĭs′ĭ-tē) s. toxicidad *f*.
tox·i·col·o·gist (′sĭ-kŏl′ə-jĭst) s. toxicólogo.
tox·i·col·o·gy (:jē) s. toxicología.
tox·in (tŏk′sĭn) s. toxina.
toy (toi) **I.** s. juguete *m*; *(trifle)* nadería; *(bauble)* chuchería, baratija **II.** adj. de juguete ♦ **t. poodle** perro de lanas enano • **t. soldier** soldadito de plomo **III.** intr. jugar, juguetear ♦ **to t. with** *(to play with)* jugar con; *(an idea)* dar vueltas a.
trace[1] (trās) **I.** s. *(mark)* pista; *(footprint)* huella, rastro; *(sign)* señal *f*, indicio; *(bit)* pizca **II.** tr. *(to sketch)* dibujar, trazar; *(to follow a trail)* seguir; *(to locate)* localizar.
trace[2] s. *(strap)* tirante *m*, tiradera.
trace·a·ble (trā′sə-bəl) adj. fácil de seguir.
trac·er (:sər) s. *(investigator)* investigador *m*; *(instrument)* tiralíneas *m*; COST. patrón *m*; *(bullet)* bala trazadora; QUÍM. indicador *m*.
tra·che·a (trā′kē-ə) s. [pl. **s** o **-ae**] tráquea.
tra·che·ot·o·my (′-ŏt′ə-mē) s. traqueotomía.
track (trăk) **I.** s. *(path)* camino, senda; *(footprint)* huella; *(of a person)* pista; *(of things)* vestigio, rastro; *(of a tape recorder)* pista; *(of a bullet)* trayectoria; *(railway)* vía (férrea); DEP. *(for running)* pista; *(sport)* atletismo en pista ♦ **in one's tracks** allí mismo • **to be off the t.** *(train)* estar descarrilado; *(person)* estar despistado • **to be on the right t.** ir por buen camino • **to be on somebody's t.** estar sobre la pista de alguien • **to cover one's tracks** no dejar rastro • **to keep t. of** *(to stay informed about)* seguir con atención, estar al día con; *(to follow)* vigilar de cerca • **to lose t. of** *(people)* perder de vista; *(time)* perder la noción de; *(thought, conversation)* perder el hilo de • **to make tracks** JER. irse, marcharse • **t. meet** concurso de atletismo **II.** tr. *(to trail)* seguir, rastrear; *(to observe)* seguir ♦ **t. down** localizar —intr. seguir una huella.
track·er (′ər) s. *(person)* perseguidor *m*; *(dog)* rastreador *m*.
track·ing (:ĭng) s. localización *f* ♦ **t. station** estación de seguimiento.
track·suit (:sōot′) s. chandal *m*.
tract[1] (trăkt) s. tracto; ANAT. sistema.
tract[2] s. *(pamphlet)* folleto, opúsculo.
trac·ta·ble (trăk′tə-bəl) adj. tratable, dócil; *(malleable)* maleable, dúctil.
trac·tile (:təl, :tīl′) adj. dúctil, maleable.
trac·tion (:shən) s. tracción *f*.
trac·tor (:tər) s. tractor *m*.
trade (trād) **I.** s. ocupación *f*; *(commerce)* co-

mercio, negocio; *(industry)* industria; *(transaction)* transacción *f*; *(exchange)* cambio; *(businessmen)* comerciantes *m*; *(customers)* clientela ♦ **by t.** de profesión • **t. name** nombre comercial • **t. school** escuela vocacional • **t. union** sindicato, gremio **II.** intr. comerciar, negociar; *(to be a customer)* ser cliente ♦ **to t. on** aprovecharse de —tr. cambiar, trocar ♦ **to t. in** dar un artículo usado como pago inicial por otro nuevo ♦ **to t. off** trocar.
trade-in (′ĭn′) s. artículo entregado como pago parcial de una compra.
trade·mark (:märk′) s. marca registrada *o* de fábrica; FIG. sello distintivo.
trade·off *o* **trade-off** (:ôf′) s. trueque *m*.
trad·er (trā′dər) s. comerciante *mf*; *(ship)* buque *m* mercante; FIN. bolsista *mf*.
trades·man (trādz′mən) s. [pl. **-men**] comerciante *mf*.
trad·ing (trā′dĭng) **I.** s. comercio **II.** adj. comercial.
tra·di·tion (trə-dĭsh′ən) s. tradición *f*.
tra·di·tion·al (:ə-nəl) adj. tradicional.
tra·di·tion·al·ist (:nə-lĭst) s. & adj. tradicionalista *mf*.
tra·duce (trə-dōos′) tr. calumniar, difamar.
traf·fic (trăf′ĭk) **I.** s. tráfico; COM. *(trade)* comercio, negocio; *(exchange)* cambio; *(of ideas)* intercambio ♦ **t. jam** embotellamiento **II.** intr. **-ck-** traficar.
traf·fick·er (:ĭ-kər) s. negociante *mf*; *(of drugs)* traficante *mf*.
tra·ge·di·an (trə-jē′dē-ən) s. trágico.
tra·ge·di·enne (:ĕn′) s. trágica.
trag·e·dy (trăj′ĭ-dē) s. tragedia.
trag·ic (′ĭk) adj. trágico.
trag·i·com·e·dy (′ĭ-kŏm′ĭ-dē) s. tragicomedia.
trag·i·com·ic (:ĭk) adj. tragicómico.
trail (trāl) **I.** tr. *(to drag)* arrastrar; *(to track)* rastrear; *(to follow)* seguir; *(to lag behind)* rezagar —intr. arrastrarse; *(a plant)* trepar ♦ **to t. behind** quedarse a la zaga • **to t. off** desvanecerse **II.** s. *(trace)* huella, rastro; *(of a person)* pista; *(of smoke)* estela; *(path)* camino, sendero; FIG. estela ♦ **to be on the t. of** seguir la pista de • **to lose, to pick up the t.** perder, encontrar la pista.
trail·blaz·er (′blā′zər) s. pionero.
trail·er (trā′lər) s. *(person)* rastreador *m*; *(vehicle)* remolque *m*; *(furnished van)* casa-remolque *m* ♦ **t. truck** camión de remolque.
train (trān) **I.** s. tren *m*; *(succession)* sucesión *f*, serie *f*; *(of people)* séquito, cortejo; *(of a dress)* cola ♦ **to lose one's t. of thought** perder el hilo de lo que uno iba a decir **II.** tr. *(a person)* enseñar; *(a child)* disciplinar, educar; *(an animal)* domar, amaestrar; *(an athlete)* entrenar; *(a plant)* guiar —intr. prepararse, formarse; *(an athlete)* entrenarse.
trained (trānd) adj. *(educated)* entrenado; *(physically)* preparado; *(animals)* amaestrado ♦ **to have a t. eye** tener un ojo experto.
train·ee (trā-nē′) s. aprendiz *mf*.
train·er (′nər) s. DEP. entrenador *m*; *(of horses)* preparador *m*; *(of animals)* amaestrador *m*.
train·ing (:nĭng) s. instrucción *f*, enseñanza; *(apprenticeship)* aprendizaje *m*; *(of animals)* amaestramiento; DEP. entrenamiento.
train·man (trān′mən) s. [pl. **-men**] ferroviario.
traipse (trāps) intr. FAM. andar.
trait (trāt) s. rasgo distintivo, característica.
trai·tor (trā′tər) s. traidor *m*.

trai·tor·ous (:əs) adj. traidor, traicionero.
tra·jec·to·ry (trə-jĕk'tə-rē) s. trayectoria.
tram (trăm) s. G.B. *(streetcar)* tranvía *m*; *(tramway)* rieles *m*, carriles *m*; *(cable car)* telefèrico; *(small wagon)* vagoneta.
tram·car ('kär', ' s. G.B. *(streetcar)* tranvía *m*; *(coal car)* vagoneta.
tram·mel (trăm'əl) I. s. traba ♦ pl. trabas, obstáculos II. tr. poner trabas a.
tramp (trămp) I. intr. *(to trudge)* andar con pasos pesados; *(to hike)* caminar, ir a pie; *(to wander)* vagar, errar —tr. pisotear con fuerza II. s. *(footfall)* ruido; *(hike)* caminata, paseo largo; *(vagrant)* vagabundo; JER. *(prostitute)* fulana, ramera.
tram·ple (trăm'pəl) I. tr. pisotear ♦ to t. on pisotear —intr. pisar rudamente II. s. pisoteo; *(sound)* ruido de pisadas.
tram·po·line (trăm'pə-lēn') s. trampolín *m*.
trance (trăns) s. trance *m*.
tran·quil (trăng'kwəl) adj. tranquilo.
tran·quil·(l)ize (:kwə-līz') tr. & intr. tranquilizar(se).
tran·quil·iz·er (:ər) s. tranquilizante *m*.
tran·quil·(l)i·ty (trăng-kwĭl'ĭ-tē) s. tranquilidad *f*.
trans·act (trăn-săkt') tr. llevar a cabo, ejecutar.
trans·ac·tion (:săk'shən) s. *(act)* negociación *f*; *(deal)* transacción *f* ♦ pl. actas.
trans·ac·tion·al (:shən-əl) adj. de transacción.
trans·ac·tor (:tər) s. negociante *mf*.
trans·at·lan·tic (trăns'ət-lăn'tĭk) adj. transatlántico.
trans·ceiv·er (trăn-sē'vər) s. transceptor *m*.
trans·cend (trăn-sĕnd') tr. transcender; *(to surpass)* sobrepasar —intr. trascender.
tran·scen·dence/den·cy (trăn-sĕn'dəns) s. trascendencia.
tran·scen·dent (:dənt) adj. trascendente.
tran·scen·den·tal (:dĕn'tl) adj. trascendental.
trans·con·ti·nen·tal (trăns'kŏn-tə-nĕn'tl) adj. transcontinental.
tran·scribe (trăn-skrīb') tr. transcribir; MÚS. adaptar, arreglar.
tran·scrib·er (-skrī'bər) s. transcriptor *m*.
tran·script (trăn'skrĭpt') s. transcripción *f*.
tran·scrip·tion (-skrĭp'shən) s. transcripción *f*; *(recording)* grabación *f*; RAD., TELEV. emisión diferida.
trans·duc·er (trăns-dōō'sər) s. transductor *m*.
tran·sect (trăn-sĕkt') tr. cortar transversalmente.
trans·fer (trăns-fûr') I. tr. -**rr-** *(to convey)* trasladar; *(to shift)* transferir —intr. *(to move)* trasladarse; *(to change carrier)* transbordar II. s. ('fər) *(ticket)* boleto de transbordo; *(of money)* transferencia; *(of power)* transmisión *f*.
trans·fer·a·ble (:ə-bəl) adj. transferible.
trans·fer·al (:əl) s. transferencia.
trans·fer·ence (:əns) s. transferencia.
trans·fig·u·ra·tion (trăns-fĭg'yə-rā'shən) s. transfiguración *f*.
trans·fig·ure (-'yər) tr. *(to alter radically)* transfigurar; *(to exalt)* exaltar, glorificar.
trans·fix (trăns-fĭks') tr. traspasar, atravesar; FIG. paralizar, inmovilizar.
trans·form (trăns-fôrm') tr. transformar.
trans·for·ma·tion ('fər-mā'shən) s. transformación *f*.
trans·form·er (-fôr'mər) s. transformador *m*.
trans·fuse (trăns-fyōōz') tr. *(to transfer)* transvasar, trasegar; *(to permeate)* impregnar; MED.

hacer una transfusión de *o* a.
trans·fu·sion (:fyōō'zhən) s. trasiego; MED. transfusión *f*.
trans·gress (trăns-grĕs') tr. *(a limit)* traspasar; *(the law)* infringir —intr. *(to sin)* pecar; *(to break the law)* cometer una infracción.
trans·gres·sion (:grĕsh'ən) s. *(of a law)* infracción *f*; *(of a rule)* transgresión *f*; *(of limits)* traspaso; *(sin)* pecado.
trans·gres·sor (:grĕs'ər) s. *(offender)* transgresor *m*; *(sinner)* pecador *m*.
tran·sience (trăn'shəns) transitoriedad *f*.
tran·sient (:shənt) I. adj. transitorio; *(passing through)* transeúnte II. s. transeúnte *mf*.
tran·sis·tor (trăn-zĭs'tər) s. transistor *m*.
tran·sis·tor·ize (:tə-rīz') tr. equipar con transistores a.
tran·sit (trăn'sĭt) s. tránsito; *(transport)* transporte *m*; *(transition)* transición *f*.
tran·si·tion (trăn-zĭsh'ən) s. transición *f*.
tran·si·tion·al (:ə-nəl) adj. de transición.
tran·si·tive (trăn'sĭ-tĭv) adj. transitivo.
tran·si·to·ry (trăn'sĭ-tôr'ē) adj. transitorio.
trans·late (trăns-lāt', '') tr. traducir; *(to explain)* explicar; *(to convert)* convertir.
trans·la·tion (-lā'shən) s. traducción *f*.
trans·la·tor (:lā'tər) s. traductor *m*.
trans·lit·er·ate (trăns-lĭt'ə-rāt') tr. traducir de un alfabeto a otro.
trans·lu·cent (trăns-lōō'sənt) adj. translúcido.
trans·lu·cid (:sĭd) adj. translúcido.
trans·mi·grate (trăns-mī'grāt') intr. transmigrar.
trans·mi·gra·tion ('-grā'shən) s. transmigración *f*.
trans·mis·sion (trăns-mĭsh'ən) s. transmisión *f* ♦ **automatic t.** AUTO. cambio automático.
trans·mit (trăns-mĭt') tr. & intr. -**tt-** transmitir.
trans·mit·tal (:l) s. transmisión *f*.
trans·mit·ter (:ər) s. *(apparatus)* transmisor *m*; *(station)* emisora.
trans·mu·ta·tion (trăns'myōō-tā'shən) s. transmutación *f*.
trans·mute (trăns-myōōt') tr. transmutar.
trans·o·ce·an·ic (trăns'ō-shē-ăn'ĭk) adj. transoceánico.
tran·som (trăn'səm) s. *(window)* montante *m*, listón *m*; *(crosspiece)* travesaño.
tran·son·ic (trăn-sŏn'ĭk) adj. transónico.
trans·par·ence (trăns-pâr'əns) s. transparencia.
trans·par·en·cy (:ən-sē) s. transparencia; *(slide)* diapositiva.
trans·par·ent (:ənt) adj. transparente.
trans·pi·ra·tion (trăn'spə-rā'shən) adj. transpiración *f*.
tran·spire (trăn-spīr') tr. transpirar —intr. *(to exude)* transpirar; *(to reveal)* revelarse; *(to happen)* acontecer.
trans·plant I. tr. (trăns-plănt') trasplantar II. s. ('') trasplante *m*.
trans·port I. tr. (trăns-pôrt') transportar; *(to enrapture)* embelesar II. s. ('') transporte *m*; *(rapture)* embeleso; *(ship)* buque *m* de transporte; *(aircraft)* avión *m* de transporte.
trans·por·ta·tion (trăns'pər-tā'shən) s. transportación *f*; *(state)* transporte *m*.
trans·pose (trăns-pōz') tr. transponer; *(to transform)* transformar.
trans·po·si·tion ('pə-zĭsh'ən) s. transposición *f*; MÚS. transporte *m*.
trans·ship (trăns-shĭp') tr. -**pp-** transbordar.

tran·sub·stan·ti·ate (trăn′səb-stăn′shē-āt′) tr. transubstanciar.

trans·ver·sal (trăns-vûr′səl) adj. & s. transversal f.

trans·verse (:vûrs′) adj. & s. transversal f.

trap (trăp) I. s. trampa; TEC. sifón m, bombillo; DEP. lanzaplatos; (in golf) hoyo de arena ♦ **shut your t.!** JER. ¡cierra el pico! • **t. door** escotillón • **t. rock** basalto II. tr. **-pp-** (to ensnare) coger en una trampa; (to catch) atrapar; (to seal off) detener —intr. poner trampas.

tra·peze (tră-pēz′) s. trapecio ♦ **t. artist** trapecista.

trap·per (trăp′ər) s. trampero.

trap·ping (trăp′ĭng) s. ♦ pl. adornos, atavíos; (for a horse) jaeces, arreos.

trap·shoot·ing (trăp′shōō′tĭng) s. tiro al plato.

trash (trăsh) I. s. desechos, desperdicios; (people) gentuza II. tr. (to discard) desechar; JER. (to smash) destrozar.

trash·y (′ē) adj. **-i-** malo.

trau·ma (trô′mə) s. [pl. **s** o **-ata**] trauma m.

trau·mat·ic (-măt′ĭk) adj. traumático.

trau·ma·tize (′mə-tīz′) tr. traumatizar.

tra·vail (trə-vāl′) s. (weariness) fatiga; (anguish) congoja; (childbirth) dolores m de parto.

trav·el (trăv′əl) I. intr. viajar; (to be a salesman) ser viajante; (light, sound) propagarse; (to spread) extenderse; (to associate) frecuentar ♦ **to t. light** viajar con poco equipaje • **traveling salesman** viajante de comercio —tr. viajar por II. s. viajar m; (traffic) tráfico ♦ pl. viajes.

tra·vel(l)ed (:əld) adj. que ha viajado mucho; (frequented) frecuentado.

trav·el·(l)er (:ə-lər) s. viajero; G.B. (salesman) viajante m ♦ **t.'s check** cheque de viajero.

trav·e·log(ue) (:ə-lôg′) s. documental m o conferencia ilustrada sobre un viaje.

tra·vers·al (trə-vûr′səl) s. travesía.

tra·verse (trə-vûrs′) I. tr. cruzar; (to move along) recorrer —intr. cruzar II. s. (trăv′ərs) travesía; (route) ruta sinuosa; (crosspiece) travesaño III. adj. (trăv′ərs, trə-vûrs′) transversal.

trav·es·ty (trăv′ĭ-stē) I. s. parodia II. tr. parodiar.

trawl (trôl) MARÍT. I. s. red barredera II. tr. & intr. pescar con red barredera.

trawl·er (trô′lər) s. (boat) jábega; (fisherman) jabeguero.

tray (trā) s. bandeja.

treach·er·ous (trĕch′ər-əs) adj. traicionero; (dangerous) peligroso.

treach·er·y (:ə-rē) s. traición f.

trea·cle (trē′kəl) s. melaza.

tread (trĕd) I. s. trod, trod(den) pisar; (to trample) pisotear; (to crush) aplastar ♦ **t. water** pedalear en el agua • **well-trodden path** camino trillado —intr. pisar; (to walk) andar, caminar ♦ **to t. lightly** andar con tiento II. s. pisada; (horizontal step) huella (de un escalón); (of a tire) banda de rodadura.

tread·le (′l) I. s. pedal m II. intr. pedalear.

tread·mill (:mĭl′) s. rueda de andar; (routine) rutina.

trea·son (trē′zən) s. traición f.

trea·son·a·ble (:zə-nə-bəl) adj. traicionero.

trea·son·ous (:nəs) adj. traicionero.

treas·ure (trĕzh′ər) I. s. tesoro II. tr. (to accumulate) atesorar; (to appreciate) estimar.

treas·ur·er (:ər) s. tesorero.

treas·ure-trove (trōv′) s. tesoro hallado; (discovery) hallazgo.

treas·ur·y (trĕzh′ə-rē) s. (office) tesorería; (public funds) erario público.

treat (trēt) I. tr. tratar; (to invite) convidar, invitar; (to consider) tomar ♦ **to t. oneself to** darse el lujo de —intr. invitar, convidar II. s. (present) regalo; (invitation) invitación f; (delight) placer m.

treat·a·ble (trē′tə-bəl) adj. tratable.

trea·tise (trē′tĭs) s. tratado.

treat·ment (trēt′mənt) s. tratamiento.

trea·ty (trē′tē) s. convenio, tratado.

treb·le (trĕb′əl) I. adj. MAT. triple; MÚS. de soprano, de tiple II. s. MÚS. soprano, tiple m III. tr. & intr. triplicar(se).

tree (trē) I. s. árbol m; (for shoes) horma; (post) poste m ♦ **to bark up the wrong t.** equivocarse • **to be up a t.** estar en un aprieto II. tr. (animal) hacer refugiarse en un árbol; FIG. poner en un aprieto.

tree·top (:tŏp′) s. copa.

tre·foil (trē′foil′, trĕf′oil) s. trébol m.

trek (trĕk) I. s. viaje largo y difícil II. intr. **-kk-** hacer un viaje largo.

trel·lis (trĕl′ĭs) s. (frame) enrejado; (arbor) parra.

trem·ble (trĕm′bəl) I. intr. temblar II. s. temblor m.

tre·men·dous (trĭ-mĕn′dəs) adj. terrible; (enormous) tremendo; (marvelous) extraordinario.

trem·or (trĕm′ər) s. temblor m.

trem·u·lous (trĕm′yə-ləs) adj. trémulo, tembloroso; (timid) tímido.

trench (trĕnch) s. (furrow) zanja; (ditch) cuneta, foso; MIL. trinchera ♦ **t. coat** impermeable • **t. mouth** inflamación de las encías.

trench·ant (trĕn′chənt) adj. vigoroso; (incisive) mordaz.

trend (trĕnd) I. s. (direction) dirección f; (tendency) tendencia; (fashion) moda II. intr. tender a, inclinarse a.

trend·set·ter (′sĕt′ər) s. persona que dicta una moda.

trend·y (trĕn′dē) adj. **-i-** FAM. que sigue la última moda.

trep·i·da·tion (trĕp′ĭ-dā′shən) s. aprensión f.

tres·pass (trĕs′pəs, :păs′) I. intr. (to infringe upon) infringir; (to enter) entrar ilegalmente; RELIG. pecar II. s. violación f; DER. transgresión f ♦ **no trespassing** prohibido el paso ♦ pl. RELIG. pecados.

tres·pass·er (trĕs′pə-sər) s. intruso; DER. infractor m; RELIG. pecador m.

tress (trĕs) s. mechón f ♦ pl. cabellera.

tres·tle (trĕs′əl) s. caballete m.

tri·ad (trī′ăd′) s. tríada.

tri·al (trī′əl) I. s. (testing) prueba, ensayo; (experiment) experimento; (attempt) tentativa; (hardship) dificultad f; (test) prueba; DER. proceso, juicio ♦ **on t.** (being judged) enjuiciado, procesado; (being tested) a título de prueba • **to bring to t.** encausar, enjuiciar • **to do something by t. and error** hacer algo por un método de tanteos • **to go on t.** ser procesado II. adj. DER. procesal; (testing) de prueba ♦ **t. run** experimento.

tri·an·gle (trī′ăng′gəl) s. triángulo.

tri·an·gu·lar (trī-ăng′gyə-lər) adj. triangular.

tri·an·gu·late (:lāt′) I. tr. triangular II. adj. triangulado.

trib·al (trī′bəl) adj. tribal.

tribe (trīb) s. tribu f; FAM. familia numerosa.

tribes·man (trībz′mən) s. [pl. **-men**] miembro

de una tribu.

trib·u·la·tion (trĭb′yə-lā′shən) s. tribulación f.

tri·bu·nal (trī-byōō′nəl) s. tribunal m.

trib·une (trĭb′yōōn′) s. HIST. tribuno; (protector) defensor m de los derechos.

trib·u·tar·y (trĭb′yə-tĕr′ē) I. adj. tributario II. s. (river) afluente m; (person) tributario.

trib·ute (trĭb′yōōt) s. tributo; (gift) ofrenda.

trice (trīs) s. instante m ♦ **in a t.** en un abrir y cerrar de ojos.

tri·cen·ten·ni·al (trī′sĕn-tĕn′ē-əl) I. adj. de trescientos años II. s. tricentenario.

tri·ceps (trī′sĕps′) s. [pl. inv. o **es**] tríceps m.

trich·i·no·sis (trĭk′ə-nō′sĭs) s. triquinosis f.

trick (trĭk) I. s. truco; (swindle) estafa; (prank) travesura; (special skill) maña; (of cards) baza ♦ **a dirty t.** una trastada ♦ **not to miss a t.** no perder una ♦ **to be up to one's old tricks** volver a las andadas ♦ **to do the t.** resolver el problema, surtir efecto II. tr. engañar, burlar; (to swindle) estafar III. adj. de truco ♦ **t. photography** trucaje ♦ **t. question** pregunta de pega.

trick·er·y (′ə-rē) s. engaño.

trick·le (trĭk′əl) I. intr. gotear ♦ **to t. in** llegar en pequeñas cantidades II. s. goteo; (small amount) gota.

trick·ster (trĭk′stər) s. burlador m.

trick·y (:ē) adj. -I- (wily) astuto; (situation, problem) delicado.

tri·col·or (trī′kŭl′ər) s. bandera tricolor.

tri·corn(e) (:kôrn′) s. tricornio.

tri·cot (trē′kō) s. tricot m.

tri·cy·cle (trī′sĭ-kəl) s. triciclo.

tri·dent (trīd′nt) s. tridente m.

tried (trīd) adj. I. cf. **try** II. adj. probado.

tried-and-true (′n-trōō′) adj. seguro.

tri·fle (trī′fəl) I. s. nadería; (small amount) poquito; (dessert) bizcocho borracho ♦ **a t.** un poquito, algo II. intr. (to jest) bromear; (to play) jugar (with con).

tri·fling (:flĭng) adj. insignificante, frívolo.

trig·ger (trĭg′ər) I. s. (of a firearm) gatillo; (of a mechanism) disparador m; (provocation) provocación f II. tr. poner en funcionamiento.

trig·ger-hap·py (:hăp′ē) adj. pronto a disparar; JER. impulsivo.

trig·o·nom·e·try (trĭg′ə-nŏm′ĭ-trē) s. trigonometría.

trike (trīk) s. FAM. triciclo.

tri·lat·er·al (trī-lăt′ər-əl) s. trilátero.

trill (trĭl) s. gorjeo; MÚS. trino.

tril·lion (trĭl′yən) s. E.U. [10^12] billón m; G.B. [10^18] trillón m.

tril·o·gy (trĭl′ə-jē) s. trilogía.

trim (trĭm) I. tr. -mm- (to make tidy) ordenar; (hair, nails) recortar; (branches) podar; (to ornament) decorar; (to reduce) reducir; (sails) orientar; AVIA., MARÍT. (to balance) equilibrar —intr. estar equilibrado II. s. condición f; (ornamentation) adorno; (cuttings) recorte m; (of a ship) asiento; (of sails) orientación f; AVIA. equilibrio ♦ **in good t.** en forma ♦ **out of t.** (person) en baja forma; (boat) mal estibado III. adj. -mm- (in good order) arreglado; (elegant) elegante; (looking well) bien parecido.

tri·mes·ter (trī-mĕs′tər) s. trimestre m.

trim·ming (trĭm′ĭng) s. adorno; FAM. (beating) paliza, zurra ♦ pl. (accesories) accesorios; CUL. guarnición; (scraps) recortes.

trin·i·ty (trĭn′ĭ-tē) s. trío.

trin·ket (trĭng′kĭt) s. (ornament) dije m; (trifle) chuchería.

tri·o (trē′ō) s. trío.

trip (trĭp) I. s. viaje m; (excursion) excursión f; (stumble) tropezón m, traspié m; (mistake) error m ♦ **round t.** viaje de ida y vuelta II. intr. -pp- (to stumble) dar un traspié; (to move nimbly) andar con paso ligero; (to make a mistake) equivocarse —tr. (a person) hacer tropezar o caer; (an alarm) hacer sonar; (a catch, spring) soltar, disparar ♦ **to t. up** hacer confundir.

tripe (trīp) s. CUL. callos; FAM. tonterías.

tri·ple (trĭp′əl) I. adj. & s. triple m II. tr. & intr. triplicar(se).

tri·ple-space (′-spās′) tr. & intr. escribir a máquina dejando dos líneas en blanco.

tri·plet (trĭp′lĭt) s. trío; (baby) trillizo.

tri·pod (trī′pŏd′) s. trípode m.

tri·sect (trī′sĕkt′) tr. trisecar.

tri·sec·tion (-sĕk′shən) s. trisección f.

trite (trīt) adj. trillado.

tri·umph (trī′əmf) I. intr. triunfar; (to exult) regocijarse II. s. triunfo; (exultation) regocijo.

tri·um·phal (-ŭm′fəl) adj. triunfal.

tri·um·phant (:fənt) adj. triunfante.

tri·um·vi·rate (trī-ŭm′vər-ĭt) s. triunvirato.

triv·et (trĭv′ĭt) s. (for cooking) trébedes m; (for the table) salvamantel m.

triv·i·a (trĭv′ē-ə) s.pl. trivialidades f.

triv·i·al (:əl) adj. insignificante, trivial.

triv·i·al·i·ty (′əl′ĭ-tē) s. trivialidad f.

trod (trŏd), **trod·den** (trŏd′n) cf. **tread**.

troll[1] (trōl) I. tr. (to fish) pescar con cebo de cuchara; (to sing) cantar en canon II. s. (lure) cebo de cuchara; MÚS. canon m.

troll[2] s. (creature) duende m, gnomo.

trol·ley (trŏl′ē) s. tranvía m; (carriage) carretilla; (electric device) colector m de corriente.

trol·lop (trŏl′əp) s. (slattern) mujer sucia; (prostitute) prostituta.

trom·bone (trŏm-bōn′) s. trombón m.

troop (trōōp) I. s. (group) grupo; (of animals) manada; (of soldiers) escuadrón m; (scouts) grupo ♦ pl. tropas II. intr. ir en grupo.

troop·er (trōō′pər) s. (cavalryman) soldado de caballería; (horse) caballo; (policeman) policía montado; (state police) patrullero ♦ **to be a t.** FAM. ser un profesional.

tro·phy (trō′fē) s. trofeo.

trop·ic (trŏp′ĭk) I. s. trópico II. adj. tropical.

trop·i·cal (:ĭ-kəl) adj. tropical.

trot (trŏt) I. s. (gait) trote m; (jog) paso corto; FAM. (translation) traducción f II. intr. -tt- (to move) trotar; (to hurry) apurarse —tr. hacer trotar ♦ **to t. out** FAM. (to bring out) sacar a relucir; (to show off) hacer alarde de.

troth (trŏth, trōth) s. (fidelity) fidelidad f; (betrothal) compromiso ♦ **to plight one's t.** dar palabra de matrimonio.

trot·ter (trŏt′ər) s. trotón m.

trou·ba·dour (trōō′bə-dôr′) s. trovador m.

trou·ble (trŭb′əl) I. s. (affliction) pena; (misfortune) desgracia; (distress) apuro, aprieto; (worry) preocupación f; (annoyance) disgusto; (difficulty) dificultad f; (hindrance) estorbo; (bother) molestia; (effort) esfuerzo; (dispute) conflicto; (disturbance) disturbios ♦ **no t. at all** con mucho gusto ♦ **to ask** o **look for t.** FAM. buscarse líos ♦ **to be in t.** estar en un aprieto ♦ **to be worth the t.** valer la pena ♦ **to get into t.** meterse en líos ♦ **to start t.** dar problemas ♦ **to stay out of t.** no meterse en líos ♦ **to take the t. to** tomarse la molestia de ♦ **what's the t.?** ¿cuál es el problema? II. tr. (to disturb) agitar, turbar; *(to affect)* afligir; *(to worry)* preocupar; *(to afflict)* afligir; *(to bother)* molestar —intr. *(to be worried)* preocuparse; *(to take pains)* molestarse.

trou·ble·mak·er (:mā′kər) s. perturbador *m*.

trou·ble·shoot·er (:shō͞o′tər) s. mediador *m*.

trou·ble·some (:səm) adj. *(worrisome)* inquietante; *(difficult)* dificultoso.

trough (trôf) s. *(for drinking)* abrevadero; *(for feeding)* pesebre *m*; *(gutter)* canalón *m*; *(depression)* depresión *f*; *(low point)* mínimo; METEOR. zona de presiones bajas.

trounce (trouns) tr. zurrar; *(to defeat)* derrotar rotundamente.

troupe (trōo͞p) s. TEAT. compañía.

troup·er (trō͞o′pər) s. TEAT. actor *m*.

trou·sers (trou′zərz) s.pl. pantalones *m*.

trous·seau (trōo͞′sō) s. [pl. **s** *o* **-x**] ajuar *m*.

trout (trout) s. [pl. inv. *o* **s**] trucha *f*.

trove (trōv) s. hallazgo.

trow·el (trou′əl) s. *(for leveling)* palustre *m*; *(for digging)* desplantador.

troy (troi) adj. troy.

tru·an·cy (trō͞o′ən-sē) s. falta a clase.

tru·ant (:ənt) s. & adj. (persona) que hace novillos.

truce (trōo͞s) s. tregua.

truck¹ (trŭk) I. s. camión *m*; *(barrow)* carretilla; G.B., F.C. vagón raso II. tr. transportar en camión —intr. conducir un camión.

truck² I. tr. *(to barter)* trocar; *(to peddle)* vender de puerta en puerta —intr. comerciar II. s. *(garden produce)* hortalizas; *(exchange)* trueque *m*; FAM. *(business)* comercio ♦ t. **farm** huerto, huerta.

truck·age (′ĭj) s. transporte *m* por camión.

truck·er (:ər) s. camionero.

truck·ing (:ĭng) s. transporte *m* por camión.

truc·u·lent (trŭk′yə-lənt) adj. *(fierce)* feroz; *(pugnacious)* belicoso.

trudge (trŭj) I. intr. caminar con dificultad II. s. caminata larga y penosa.

true (trōo͞) I. adj. verdadero; *(loyal)* leal; *(legitimate)* legítimo; *(accurate)* exacto ♦ **to come t.** realizarse, cumplirse • **t. to life** conforme a la realidad II. adv. verdaderamente; *(exactly)* exactamente III. s. verdad *f* ♦ **to be out of t.** estar desalineado IV. tr. rectificar, corregir.

true·blue (′blōo͞′) s. & adj. (persona) leal.

true·love (:lŭv′) s. amor *m*.

truf·fle (trŭf′əl) s. trufa.

tru·ism (trōo͞′ĭz′əm) s. perogrullada.

tru·ly (:lē) adv. verdaderamente; *(sincerely)* sinceramente; *(properly)* propiamente ♦ **yours t.** suyo atentamente, su seguro servidor.

trump (trŭmp) I. s. triunfo II. tr. matar con un triunfo —intr. ♦ **to t. up** inventar.

trum·pet (trŭm′pĭt) I. s. MÚS. trompeta; *(sound)* trompetilla II. intr. tocar la trompeta —tr. pregonar.

trun·cate (trŭng′kāt′) tr. truncar.

trun·cat·ed (:kā′tĭd) adj. truncado.

trun·cheon (trŭn′chən) s. cachiporra, porra.

trun·dle (trŭn′dl) I. s. carriola II. intr. rodar.

trunk (trŭngk) s. tronco; *(of an elephant)* trompa; *(luggage)* baúl *m*; *(of a car)* portaequipaje *m*, maletera ♦ pl. pantalones cortos • **swimming t.** traje de baño.

truss (trŭs) I. s. MED. braguero; *(framework)* armazón *mf* II. tr. *(to tie up)* atar; *(to support)* apuntalar.

trust (trŭst) I. s. confianza; *(charge)* custodia;

(duty) deber *m*; *(hope)* fe *f*, esperanza; *(credit)* crédito; DER. fideicomiso; COM., FIN. trust *m*, consorcio ♦ **in t.** DER. en depósito • **to take on t.** creer a ojos cerrados • **t. fund** fondo fiduciario II. intr. *(to rely)* depender; *(to hope)* esperar, confiar —tr. tener confianza en, fiarse de; *(to believe)* creer; *(to hope)* esperar; *(to entrust)* confiar; COM., FIN. dar crédito a.

trus·tee (trŭs-tē′) s. *(administrator)* fideicomisario; *(member of a board)* síndico ♦ **board of trustees** consejo de administración.

trus·tee·ship (:shĭp′) s. *(position)* cargo de síndico; *(territory)* fideicomiso.

trust·ful (trŭst′fəl) adj. confiado.

trust·ing (trŭs′tĭng) adj. confiado.

trust·wor·thy (trŭst′wûr′thē) adj. **-i-** de confianza.

trust·y (trŭs′tē) adj. **-i-** de confianza.

truth (trōo͞th) s. [pl. **s**] verdad *f*; *(exactitude)* exactitud *f*; *(reality)* realidad *f*; *(veracity)* veracidad *f*; *(sincerity)* sinceridad *f*.

truth·ful (′fəl) adj. *(honest)* sincero; *(true)* verídico.

truth·ful·ness (:nĭs) s. veracidad *f*.

try (trī) I. tr. *(to test, taste)* probar; *(to make an effort at)* tratar <to t. to ski tratar de esquiar>; DER. *(a case)* someter a juicio; *(a person)* juzgar, procesar ♦ **to t. on** probarse • **to t. one's best** hacer todo lo posible • **to t. one's hand at** probar uno su habilidad en • **to t. out** probar —intr. esforzarse II. s. tentativa, intento.

try·ing (′ĭng) adj. irritante, molesto.

try·out (:out′) s. prueba de aptitud; *(audition)* audición *f*.

tryst (trĭst) s. *(date)* cita; *(place)* lugar *m* de cita.

tsar (tsär) var. de czar.

tset·se fly (tsĕt′sē, tsĕt′-) s. mosca tse-tsé.

T-shirt (tē′shûrt′) s. camiseta.

T-square (tē′skwâr′) s. escuadra en T, regla T.

tub (tŭb) s. *(vessel)* tonel *m*; *(bathtub)* bañera; FAM. *(bath)* baño; *(ship)* carraca.

tu·ba (tōo͞′bə) s. tuba.

tu·bal (tōo͞′bəl) adj. tubárico, tubario.

tub·by (tŭb′ē) adj. **-i-** rechoncho.

tube (tōo͞b) s. tubo; ANAT. trompa; FAM. *(television)* tele *f*; G.B. *(subway)* metro.

tu·ber (tōo͞′bər) s. tubérculo.

tu·ber·cle (:kəl) s. tubérculo.

tu·ber·cu·lar (tōo͞-bûr′kyə-lər) adj. & s. tuberculoso.

tu·ber·cu·lin (:lĭn) s. tuberculina.

tu·ber·cu·lo·sis (-′-lō′sĭs) s. tuberculosis *f*.

tu·ber·cu·lous (-′-ləs) adj. tuberculoso.

tube·rose (tōo͞b′rōz′) s. tuberosa.

tu·ber·ous (tōo͞′bər-əs) adj. tuberoso.

tub·ing (tōo͞′bĭng) s. tubería.

tu·bu·lar (:byə-lər) adj. tubular.

tu·bule (:byōo͞l) s. tubo pequeño.

tuck (tŭk) I. tr. plegar ♦ **to t. away** esconder • **to t. in** *(to put in)* meter; *(in bed)* arropar —intr. hacer pliegues II. s. pliegue *m*.

tuck·er (tŭk′ər) tr. FAM. agotar.

Tues·day (tōo͞z′dē) s. martes *m*.

tuft (tŭft) s. mechón *m*; *(crest)* copete *m*.

tug (tŭg) I. tr. **-gg-** *(to pull)* tirar de; *(to drag)* arrastrar; *(to tow)* remolcar —intr. tirar fuerte II. s. tirón *m*; *(tugboat)* remolcador *m* ♦ **t. of war** DEP. juego de la cuerda; FIG. lucha.

tug·boat (′bōt′) s. remolcador *m*.

tu·i·tion (tōo͞-ĭsh′ən) s. matrícula; *(instruction)* enseñanza.

tu·lip (tōō′lĭp) s. tulipán m.
tulle (tōōl) s. tul m.
tum·ble (tŭm′bəl) I. intr. (to roll) rodar; (to fall) caerse; (to collapse) derrumbarse ♦ **to t. down** derrumbarse • **to t. out** salir a montones —tr. (to knock down) derribar; (a government) derrocar ♦ **to t. on** dar con II. s. (fall) caída; (somersault) voltereta ♦ **to take a t.** caerse.
tum·ble-down (:doun′) adj. destartalado.
tum·bler (tŭm′blər) s. (acrobat) volatinero; (glass) vaso; (of a lock) seguro, guarda.
tum·ble·weed (:bəl-wēd′) s. planta rodadora.
tum·bling (:blĭng) s. acrobacia.
tu·me·fac·tion (tōō′mə-făk′shən) s. tumefacción f.
tu·mes·cence (tōō-mĕs′əns) s. tumescencia.
tu·mid (tōō′mĭd) adj. hinchado.
tum·my (tŭm′ē) s. FAM. barriga.
tum·my·ache (:āk′) s. FAM. dolor m de estómago.
tu·mor (tōō′mər) s. tumor m.
tu·mult (tōō′mŭlt′) s. (crowd) tumulto; (agitation) agitación f; (riot) motín m.
tu·mul·tu·ous (-mŭl′chōō-əs) adj. tumultuoso.
tu·na (tōō′nə) s. [pl. inv. o **s**] atún m.
tun·dra (tŭn′drə) s. tundra.
tune (tōōn) I. s. (melody) melodía; (pitch) tono; FIG. armonía ♦ **in t.** afinado • **in t. with** FIG. de acuerdo con • **out of t.** desafinado • **to carry a t.** cantar afinado • **to change one's t.** FIG. cambiar de tono • **to the t. of** FIG. por la cantidad de II. tr. MÚS. afinar; MEC. poner a punto ♦ **to t. in** RAD., TELEV. sintonizar • **to t. out** JER. (to ignore) no prestar atención • **to t. up** MÚS. afinar; MEC. poner a punto —intr. ♦ **to t. up** afinar los instrumentos.
tune·ful (′fəl) adj. melodioso.
tun·er (tōō′nər) s. (person) afinador m; (device) sintonizador m.
tune-up (tōōn′ŭp′) s. puesta a punto.
tung·sten (tŭng′stən) s. tungsteno.
tu·nic (tōō′nĭk) s. túnica.
tun·nel (tŭn′əl) I. s. túnel m II. tr. construir un túnel en; (to dig) cavar —intr. hacer un túnel.
tun·ny (tŭn′ē) s. [pl. inv. o **-ies**] atún m.
tur·ban (tûr′bən) s. turbante m.
tur·bid (tûr′bĭd) adj. (muddy) turbio; (dense) espeso; (confused) confuso.
tur·bine (tûr′bĭn) s. turbina.
tur·bo·charg·er (tûr′bō-chär′jər) s. turbocompresor m.
tur·bo·jet (:jĕt′) s. turborreactor m.
tur·bo·prop (:prŏp′) s. turbopropulsor m.
tur·bot (tûr′bət) s. [pl. inv. o **s**] rodaballo.
tur·bu·lence (tûr′byə-ləns) s. turbulencia.
tur·bu·lent (:lənt) adj. turbulento.
tu·reen (tōō-rēn′) s. sopera.
turf (tûrf) s. (sod) césped m; (piece of earth) tepe m; (peat) turba; JER. (territory) territorio; DEP. (track) hipódromo; (sport) hipismo.
tur·gid (tûr′jĭd) adj. MED. hinchado; FIG. ampuloso.
tur·key (tûr′kē) s. pavo; (failure) fracaso; (person) fracasado.
tur·mer·ic (tûr′mər-ĭk) s. cúrcuma.
tur·moil (tûr′moil′) s. confusión f.
turn (tûrn) I. tr. (to revolve) dar vueltas a; (to flip) pasar, volver; (to rotate) girar; (corner) dar la vuelta a, doblar; (to shape) tornear; (a phrase) construir; (to twist) torcer; (stomach) revolver; (to deflect) desviar; (to direct) dirigir; (age) cumplir; (to change color) cambiar el color de; (to transform) convertir, transformar ♦ **to t. against** volverse en contra de • **to t. a profit** producir una ganancia • **to t. around** (words) tergiversar, desvirtuar; (to turn over) dar vuelta a • **to t. aside** desviar • **to t. away** (to send away) negar la entrada a; (to deflect) rechazar; (head) volver; (eyes) desviar • **to t. back** hacer retroceder; (the clock) retrasar • **to t. down** (to diminish) bajar; (to reject) rechazar; (to fold) doblar, plegar • **to t. in** (to give over) entregar; (to betray) entregar a la policía; (to produce) hacer • **to t. inside out** poner al revés • **to t. into** volverse • **to t. loose** soltar • **to t. off** (radio, light) apagar; (tap, gas) cerrar; (electricity, water) cortar; (an engine) parar; JER. (to disgust) disgustar • **to t. on** (water, gas) abrir la llave; (radio) poner; (light) encender; (an engine) poner en marcha; (a tap) abrir; (stove, fire) encender, prender; (electrical current) conectar; (to become hostile) volverse en contra de; JER. (to excite) excitar • **to t. one's back on** volver la espalda a • **to t. out** (light) apagar; (to shut off) cerrar; (to manufacture) producir; (to evict) expulsar • **to t. over** (to reverse in position) invertir, volcar; (to think about) considerar; (to transfer) entregar • **to t. over to** (to transfer) traspasar; (to entrust) dejar a cargo de • **to t. the tide of** cambiar el curso o el rumbo de • **to t. up** (to find) encontrar; (radio, television) subir, poner más fuerte; (the collar) alzar • **to t. upside down** poner patas arriba —intr. (to rotate) girar; (to change direction) dar la vuelta; (to change) cambiar; (to devote oneself) dedicarse; (to become transformed) transformarse, convertirse en; (to change color) cambiar de color; (to become) ponerse, volverse; (to curdle) cortarse; (to ferment) avinagrarse; (to sour) ponerse rancio ♦ **to t. around** darse vuelta • **to t. aside** desviarse • **to t. away** (to begin to leave) alejarse; (to turn one's back) volver la cara o la espalda • **to t. back** retroceder • **to t. in** FAM. (to go to bed) acostarse; (to point inward) estar vuelto hacia adentro • **to t. off** desviarse • **to t. out** (to be found to be) resultar; (to point outward) estar vuelto hacia afuera • **to t. over** (car, truck) volcar; (to shift position) voltearse • **to t. to** recurrir a <who can I t. to? ¿a quién puedo recurrir?>; (to begin) empezar • **to t. up** aparecer II. s. vuelta; (rotation) rotación f; (change) cambio; (opportunity) oportunidad f; (adeptness) aptitud f; (inclination) inclinación; (deed) proceder m; (advantage) provecho; (twist in shape) torcedura; (shock) susto, sobresalto ♦ **at every t.** a cada instante • **at the t. of the century** al final del siglo pasado • **to take a t. for the better, worse** mejorarse, empeorarse • **to take turns** at turnarse.
turn·a·bout (tûrn′ə-bout′) s. cambio radical.
turn·a·round (:ə-round′) s. vuelta.
turn·buck·le (:bŭk′əl) s. tensor m.
turn·coat (:kōt′) s. traidor m.
turn·down (:doun′) s. rechazo.
turned-up (tûrnd′ŭp′) adj. (nose) respingada; (folded up) doblado hacia arriba; (collar) alto.
turn·ing (tûr′nĭng) s. viraje m ♦ **t. point** momento crucial.
tur·nip (tûr′nĭp) s. nabo.
turn·key (tûrn′kē′) s. carcelero.
turn·off (:ôf′) s. desvío; JER. (disappointment) decepción f.
turn·out (:out′) s. (attendance) concurrencia;

(spectators) entrada; *(outfit)* atuendo.

turn·o·ver (:ō′vər) s. *(upset)* vuelco; *(reversal)* cambio brusco; *(pastry)* empanada; COM. *(of stock)* movimiento de mercancías; *(of business)* volumen m de negocios; *(of sales)* volumen de ventas; *(of staff)* cambio de personal.

turn·pike (:pīk′) s. autopista de peaje.

turn·screw (:skrōō′) s. destornillador m.

turn·stile (:stīl′) s. torniquete m.

turn·ta·ble (:tā′bəl) s. *(platform)* plataforma giratoria; *(of a phonograph)* plato.

tur·pen·tine (tûr′pən-tīn′) s. trementina.

tur·pi·tude (tûr′pĭ-tōōd′) s. bajeza.

tur·quoise (tûr′kwoiz′, :koiz′) adj. & s. turquesa.

tur·ret (tûr′ĭt) s. torreón m; MIL. torre blindada.

tur·tle (tûr′tl) s. tortuga.

tur·tle·dove (tûr′tl-dŭv′) s. tórtola.

tur·tle·neck (tûr′tl-nĕk′) s. cuello vuelto o alto; *(sweater)* suéter m con cuello vuelto.

tusk (tŭsk) s. colmillo grande.

tus·sle (tŭs′əl) I. intr. forcejear II. s. forcejeo.

tut (tŭt) interj. ¡vaya!, ¡basta!

tu·te·lage (tōōt′l-ĭj) s. tutela.

tu·te·lar·y/lar (:ĕr′ē/-ər) adj. tutelar.

tu·tor (tōō′tər) I. s. profesor m particular; *(in a family)* ayo; *(in universities)* tutor m II. tr. dar clases particulares a —intr. ser tutor.

tu·to·ri·al (-tôr′ē-əl) I. adj. de tutor II. s. clase f particular

tu·tu (tōō′tōō) s. tutú m.

tu·xe·do (tŭk-sē′dō) s. [pl. **(e)s**] smoking m.

TV (tē′vē′) s. [pl. **(′)s**] televisión f; *(set)* televisor m..

twad·dle (twŏd′l) s. tonterías.

twang (twăng) I. intr. *(string)* vibrar; *(voice)* ganguear —tr. hacer vibrar II. s. sonido vibrante; *(of guitar)* tañido; *(voice)* gangueo.

twang·y (′ē) adj. gangoso.

tweak (twēk) s. I. tr. pellizcar II. s. pellizco.

tweed (twēd) s. tejido de lana ♦ pl. traje de lana.

tweed·y (twē′dē) adj. **-i-** parecido a la lana; *(wearing tweeds)* que viste con traje de lana.

tweet (twēt) I. intr. piar II. s. pío pío.

tweeze (twēz) tr. sacar con pinzas.

tweez·ers (twē′zərz) s.pl. pinzas.

twelfth (twĕlfth) I. s. doce m; *(part)* doceavo II. adj. *(place)* duodécimo; *(part)* doceava.

twelve (twĕlv) s. & adj. doce m ♦ **t. o'clock** las doce.

twen·ti·eth (twĕn′tē-ĭth) I. s. veinte m; *(part)* vigésimo II. adj. vigésimo.

twen·ty (twĕn′tē) adj. & s. veinte m.

twerp (twûrp) s. JER. imbécil mf, idiota mf.

twice (twīs) adv. dos veces, el doble.

twid·dle (twĭd′l) tr. hacer girar —intr. ♦ **to t. one's thumbs** matar el tiempo.

twig (twĭg) s. ramita.

twi·light (twī′līt′) I. s. *(time)* crepúsculo; *(light)* media luz; *(decline)* ocaso II. adj. crepuscular.

twill (twĭl) s. tela asargada.

twin (twĭn) I. s. gemelo; *(counterpart)* doble m ♦ **Siamese twins** hermanos siameses II. adj. gemelo ♦ **t. bed** cama separada o gemela.

twine (twīn) I. s. cordel m, bramante m II. tr. *(to intertwine)* trenzar; *(to encircle)* ceñir —intr. enroscarse.

twinge (twĭnj) I. s. *(pain)* punzada; *(remorse)* remordimiento II. tr. & intr. dar punzadas.

twin·kle (twĭng′kəl) I. intr. centellear, parpadear; *(eyes)* brillar II. s. centelleo,

parpadeo; *(of eyes)* brillo.

twin·kling (:klĭng) s. centelleo; FIG. instante m.

twin-screw (twĭn′skrōō′) adj. de dos hélices.

twin-size (:sīz′) adj. de cama gemela.

twirl (twûrl) tr. girar —intr. *(to spin around)* dar vueltas; *(to whirl)* girar en redondo.

twist (twĭst) I. tr. torcer; *(to twine)* enrollar; *(a cork, jar top)* dar vueltas a; *(meanings)* tergiversar, desvirtuar ♦ **to t. off** romper retorciendo —intr. torcerse, retorcerse; *(to coil)* enrollarse; *(to meander)* dar vueltas ♦ **to t. and turn** *(road)* serpentear; *(in bed)* dar vueltas II. s. torcimiento; *(of wire)* vuelta; *(of a road, river)* vuelta, recodo; *(of an ankle)* torcedura; *(unexpected change)* giro imprevisto.

twist·er (twĭs′tər) s. ciclón m, tornado.

twit (twĭt) I. tr. **-tt-** burlarse de II. s. burla; JER. imbécil mf.

twitch (twĭch) I. tr. tirar bruscamente de —intr. crisparse II. s. tic m; *(tug)* tirón m.

twit·ter (twĭt′ər) I. intr. *(to chirp)* gorjear; *(to chatter)* parlotear II. s. *(chirp)* gorjeo; *(flutter)* agitación f.

two (tōō) s. & adj. dos m ♦ **to be t. of a kind** ser tal para cual • **to put t. and t. together** atar cabos • **t. cents worth** FAM. opinión • **t. hundred** doscientos • **t. o'clock** las dos.

two-bit (′bĭt′) adj. JER. de poca monta.

two-by-four (:bī-fôr′) s. madera de dos por cuatro pulgadas.

two-di·men·sion·al (′dĭ-mĕn′shə-nəl, ′dī-) adj. de dos dimensiones.

two-edged (′ĕjd′) adj. de doble filo.

two-faced (:fāst′) adj. de dos caras; *(false)* falso.

two-fist·ed (:fĭs′tĭd) adj. FAM. viril.

two·fold (:fōld′) I. adj. doble II. adv. dos veces.

two·pence (tŭp′əns) s. [pl. inv. o **s**] G.B. dos peniques m; FIG. comino.

two·pen·ny (tŭp′ə-nē, tōō′pĕn′ē) adj. de dos peniques; *(cheap)* barato.

two-piece (tōō′pēs′) adj. de dos piezas.

two·some (:səm) s. pareja.

two-time (:tīm′) tr. JER. engañar.

two-tim·er (:tīm′ər) s. JER. traidor m.

two-way (:wā′) adj. de doble dirección; TEL. emisor y receptor.

ty·coon (tī-kōōn′) s. magnate m.

tyke (tīk) s. FAM. chiquillo travieso; *(dog)* perro que no es de raza.

tym·pan (tĭm′pən) s. tímpano.

tym·pa·nist (:pə-nĭst) s. timbalero.

tym·pa·num (:nəm) s. [pl. **s** o **-na**] tímpano.

tym·pa·ny (:nē) s. timpanos.

type (tīp) I. s. tipo II. tr. *(with a typewriter)* escribir a máquina; *(blood)* determinar el grupo sanguíneo de; *(to classify)* clasificar —intr. escribir a máquina.

type·cast (′kăst′) tr. **-cast** TEAT. encasillar.

type·face (:fās′) s. tipografía.

type·script (:skrĭpt′) s. texto mecanografiado.

type·set (:sĕt′) tr. **-set, -tting** componer.

type·set·ter (:sĕt′ər) s. tipógrafo.

type·set·ting (:sĕt′ĭng) s. composición f.

type·write (:rīt′) tr. **-wrote, -written** mecanografiar —intr. escribir a máquina.

type·writ·er (tīp′rī′tər) s. máquina de escribir.

type·writ·ing (:tĭng) s. mecanografía.

ty·phoid (tī′foid′) adj. tifoideo.

ty·phoon (tī-fōōn′) s. tifón m.

ty·phus (tī′fəs) s. tifus m.

typ·i·cal (tĭp′ĭ-kəl) adj. típico.
typ·i·fy (:fī′) tr. *(to embody)* representar el tipo de; *(to symbolize)* simbolizar.
typ·ing (tī′pĭng) s. mecanografía.
typ·ist (tī′pĭst) s. mecanógrafo.
ty·po (tī′pō) s. FAM. error tipográfico.
ty·pog·ra·pher (tī-pŏg′rə-fər) s. tipógrafo.
ty·pog·ra·phy (:fē) s. tipografía.
ty·pol·o·gy (tī-pŏl′ə-jē) s. tipología.
ty·ran·ni·cal (tĭ-răn′ĭ-kəl) adj. tiránico.
tyr·an·nize (tĭr′ə-nīz′) tr. tiranizar.
tyr·an·nous (:nəs) adj. tiránico.
tyr·an·ny (:nē) s. tiranía.
ty·rant (tī′rənt) s. tirano.
ty·ro (tī′rō) s. aprendiz *m*, principiante *mf*.
tzar (tsär) var. de **czar.**
tza·ri·na (tsä-rē′nə) var. de **czarina.**

U

u, U (yōō) s. vigésima primera letra del alfabeto inglés.
u·biq·ui·tous (yōō-bĭk′wĭ-təs) adj. ubicuo.
u·biq·ui·ty (:tē) s. ubicuidad *f.*
U-boat (yōō′bōt′) s. submarino alemán.
ud·der (ŭd′ər) s. ubre *f.*
UFO (yōō′ĕf-ō′) s. [pl. **(')s**] AER. ovni.
ugh (ŭg, ŭk) interj. ¡uf!
ug·li·ness (ŭg′lē-nĭs) s. fealdad *f.*
ug·ly (ŭg′lē) adj. -**i**- feo; *(unpleasant)* desagradable; *(bad)* malo; *(sky)* amenazante.
uh-huh (ə-hŭ′) interj. FAM. sí, ajá.
u·ku·le·le (yōō′kə-lā′lē) s. ukelele *m.*
ul·cer (ŭl′sər) s. úlcera; FIG. cáncer *m.*
ul·cer·ate (ŭl′sə-rāt′) tr. & intr. ulcerar(se).
ul·cer·ous (ŭl′sər-əs) adj. ulceroso.
ul·na (ŭl′nə) s. [pl. **s** o **-ae**] ANAT. cúbito.
ul·ster (ŭl′stər) s. abrigo amplio y largo.
ul·te·ri·or (ŭl-tîr′ē-ər) adj. ulterior ◆ **u. motive** motivo oculto.
ul·ti·mate (ŭl′tə-mĭt) **I.** adj. último; *(final)* final; *(fundamental)* fundamental; *(maximum)* máximo **II.** s. lo último.
ul·ti·ma·tum ('-mā′təm) s. [pl. **s** o **-ta**] ultimátum *m.*
ul·tra (ŭl′trə) adj. excesivo, extremado.
ul·tra·con·ser·va·tive ('-kən-sûr′və-tĭv) adj. & s. ultraconservador m.
ul·tra·ma·rine (:mə-rēn′) **I.** s. azul ultramarino **II.** adj. de color azul ultramarino; *(beyond the sea)* ultramarino.
ul·tra·mod·ern (:mŏd′ərn) adj. ultramoderno.
ul·tra·son·ic (:sŏn′ĭk) adj. ultrasónico.
ul·tra·sound ('-sound') s. ultrasonido.
ul·tra·vi·o·let ('-vī′ə-lĭt) **I.** adj. ultravioleta **II.** s. luz *f* ultravioleta.
ul·u·late (ŭl′yə-lāt′) intr. ulular.
um·bil·i·cal (ŭm-bĭl′ĭ-kəl) **I.** adj. umbilical ◆ **u. cord** cordón umbilical **II.** s. ASTRONÁUT. línea de abastecimiento.
um·bil·i·cus (:kəs) s. [pl. **-ci**] ombligo.
um·brage (ŭm′brĭj) s. ofensa ◆ **to take u. at** ofenderse por.
um·brel·la (ŭm-brĕl′ə) s. paraguas *m* ◆ **u. organization** POL. cuerpo coordinador.
um·pire (ŭm′pīr′) **I.** s. árbitro **II.** tr. arbitrar.
ump·teen (ŭmp′tēn′) adj. FAM. innumerables.
ump·teenth (-tēnth′) adj. enésimo.
un·a·bat·ed (ŭn′ə-bā′tĭd) adj. no disminuido.
un·a·ble (ŭn-ā′bəl) adj. incapaz.

un·a·bridged (ŭn′ə-brĭjd′) adj. no abreviado.
un·ac·cent·ed (ŭn-ăk′sĕn-tĭd) adj. sin acento.
un·ac·cept·a·ble (ŭn′ăk-sĕp′tə-bəl) adj. inaceptable.
un·ac·com·pa·nied (ŭn′ə-kŭm′pə-nēd) adj. solo.
un·ac·com·plished (ŭn′ə-kŏm′plĭsht) adj. falto de aptitudes *o* cualidades.
un·ac·count·a·ble (ŭn′ə-koun′tə-bəl) adj. inexplicable; *(not responsible)* no responsable.
un·ac·count·ed (ŭn′ə-koun′tĭd) adj. ◆ **u. for** desaparecido; *(unexplained)* inexplicado.
un·ac·cus·tomed (ŭn′ə-kŭs′təmd) adj. no acostumbrado; *(unusual)* insólito.
un·ac·knowl·edged (ŭn′ăk-nŏl′ĭjd) adj. no reconocido; *(unanswered)* no contestado.
un·ac·quaint·ed (ŭn′ə-kwān′tĭd) adj. ◆ **u. with** ignorante de.
un·a·dorned (ŭn′ə-dôrnd′) adj. sin adorno.
un·a·dul·ter·at·ed (ŭn′ə-dŭl′tə-rā′tĭd) adj. no adulterado.
un·ad·vised (ŭn′əd-vīzd′) adj. no informado; *(imprudent)* irreflexivo.
un·af·fect·ed (ŭn′ə-fĕk′tĭd) adj. no afectado; *(natural)* sin afectación.
un·a·fraid (ŭn′ə-frād′) adj. sin temor.
un·aid·ed (ŭn-ā′dĭd) adj. sin ayuda.
un·al·loyed (ŭn′ə-loid′) adj. no mezclado.
un·am·big·u·ous (ŭn′ăm-bĭg′yōō-əs) adj. sin ambigüedad.
u·na·nim·i·ty (yōō′nə-nĭm′ĭ-tē) s. unanimidad *f.*
u·nan·i·mous (yōō-năn′ə-məs) adj. unánime.
un·an·nounced (ŭn′ə-nounst′) adj. sin ser anunciado.
un·an·swer·a·ble (ŭn-ăn′sər-ə-bəl) adj. incontestable.
un·ap·pe·tiz·ing (ŭn-ăp′ĭ-tī′zĭng) adj. poco apetitoso; *(not interesting)* poco apetecible.
un·ap·proach·a·ble (ŭn′ə-prō′chə-bəl) adj. inaccesible.
un·armed (ŭn-ärmd′) adj. desarmado; *(defenseless)* indefenso.
un·asked (ŭn-ăskt′) adj. no solicitado; *(question)* sin formular; *(guest)* no convidado.
un·as·sail·a·ble (ŭn′ə-sā′lə-bəl) adj. inexpugnable.
un·as·sist·ed (ŭn′ə-sĭs′tĭd) adj. sin ayuda.
un·as·sum·ing (ŭn′ə-sōō′mĭng) adj. modesto.
un·at·tached (ŭn′ə-tăcht′) adj. suelto; *(not married)* soltero.
un·at·tain·a·ble (ŭn′ə-tā′nə-bəl) adj. inalcanzable.
un·at·tend·ed (ŭn′ə-tĕn′dĭd) adj. desatendido.
un·at·test·ed (ŭn′ə-tĕs′tĭd) adj. no atestiguado.
un·at·trac·tive (ŭn′ə-trăk′tĭv) adj. inatractivo.
un·au·thor·ized (ŭn-ô′thə-rīzd′) adj. desautorizado, sin autorización.
un·a·vail·a·ble (ŭn′ə-vā′lə-bəl) adj. *(not available)* no disponible; *(busy)* ocupado.
un·a·vail·ing (ŭn′ə-vā′lĭng) adj. ineficaz.
un·a·void·a·ble (ŭn′ə-voi′də-bəl) adj. inevitable.
un·a·ware (ŭn′ə-wâr′) **I.** adj. ignorante ◆ **to be u. of** no darse cuenta de ◆ **to be u. that** ignorar que **II.** adv. de improviso.
un·a·wares (ŭn′ə-wârz′) adv. desprevenido.
un·bal·anced (ŭn-băl′ənst) adj. desequilibrado.
un·bar (ŭn-bär′) tr. -**rr**- desatrancar; FIG. abrir.
un·bear·a·ble (ŭn-bâr′ə-bəl) adj. insoportable.
un·beat·a·ble (ŭn-bē′tə-bəl) adj. invencible.

un·beat·en (ŭn-bēt'n) adj. invicto.
un·be·com·ing (ŭn'bĭ-kŭm'ĭng) adj. indecoroso.
un·be·known(st) (ŭn'bĭ-nōn[st]') adj. ♦ u. to me sin saberlo yo.
un·be·lief (ŭn'bĭ-lēf') s. incredulidad f.
un·be·liev·a·ble (:lē'və-bəl) adj. increíble.
un·be·liev·er (:vər) s. no creyente mf.
un·be·liev·ing (:vĭng) adj. incrédulo.
un·bend (ŭn-bĕnd') tr. & intr. -bent desencorvar(se); (to relax) relajar(se).
un·bend·ing (ŭn-bĕn'dĭng) adj. inflexible.
un·bi·as(s)ed (ŭn-bī'əst) adj. imparcial.
un·bid(·den) (ŭn-bĭd'[n]) adj. no pedido.
un·bind (ŭn-bīnd') tr. -bound desatar.
un·blink·ing (ŭn-blĭng'kĭng) adj. sin pestañear; (unmoved) impasible; (rigorous) riguroso.
un·blush·ing (ŭn-blŭsh'ĭng) adj. que no se ruboriza; (shameless) desvergonzado.
un·bolt (ŭn-bōlt') tr. desatrancar.
un·born (ŭn-bôrn') adj. no nacido aún; (future) venidero.
un·bound·ed (ŭn-boun'dĭd) adj. ilimitado.
un·bowed (ŭn-boud') adj. recto; FIG. (not subdued) no sometido.
un·break·a·ble (ŭn-brā'kə-bəl) adj. irrompible.
un·breath·a·ble (ŭn-brē'thə-bəl) adj. irrespirable.
un·bri·dled (ŭn-brīd'ld) adj. desembridado; (unrestrained) desenfrenado.
un·bro·ken (ŭn-brō'kən) adj. sin romper; (inviolate) inviolado; (uninterrupted) ininterrumpido; (untamed) no domado.
un·buck·le (ŭn-bŭk'əl) tr. deshebillar.
un·bur·den (ŭn-bûr'dn) tr. descargar; FIG. desahogar.
un·but·ton (ŭn-bŭt'n) tr. & intr. desabotonar(se).
un·caged (ŭn-kājd') adj. libre, suelto.
un·called-for (ŭn-kôld'fôr') adj. (undeserved) inmerecido; (out of place) inapropiado.
un·can·ny (ŭn-kăn'ē) adj. -i- inexplicable.
un·cap (ŭn-kăp') tr. -pp- destapar.
un·ceas·ing (ŭn-sē'sĭng) adj. incesante.
un·cer·e·mo·ni·ous (ŭn-sĕr'ə-mō'nē-əs) adj. informal; (abrupt) brusco.
un·cer·tain (ŭn-sûr'tn) adj. incierto, dudoso; (undecided) indeciso; (variable) cambiable.
un·cer·tain·ty (ŭn-sûr'tn-tē) s. incertidumbre f.
un·chain (ŭn-chān') tr. desencadenar.
un·change·a·ble (ŭn-chān'jə-bəl) adj. invariable, inalterable.
un·changed (ŭn-chānjd') adj. inalterado.
un·chang·ing (ŭn-chān'jĭng) adj. invariable.
un·char·i·ta·ble (ŭn-chăr'ĭ-tə-bəl) adj. severo.
un·chart·ed (ŭn-chär'tĭd) adj. inexplorado; (unknown) desconocido.
un·chaste (ŭn-chāst') adj. impúdico.
un·cir·cum·cised (ŭn-sûr'kəm-sīzd') adj. no circuncidado.
un·civ·il (ŭn-sĭv'əl) adj. incivil.
un·civ·i·lized (ŭn-sĭv'ə-līzd') adj. incivilizado.
un·clad (ŭn-klăd') adj. desnudo.
un·claimed (ŭn-klāmd') adj. no reclamado.
un·clasp (ŭn-klăsp') tr. desabrochar; (hands, embrace) separar.
un·clas·si·fied (ŭn-klăs'ə-fīd') adj. sin clasificar.
un·cle (ŭng'kəl) s. tío ♦ cry u.! ¡ríndete!
un·clean (ŭn-klēn') adj. -er, -est sucio.
un·clean·li·ness (ŭn-klĕn'lē-nĭs) s. suciedad f.

un·clean·ly (ŭn-klĕn'lē) adj. -i- sucio.
un·clear (ŭn-klîr') adj. -er, -est confuso.
un·clench (ŭn-klĕnch') tr. & intr. relajar(se).
un·cloak (ŭn-klōk') tr. desencapotar; FIG. desenmascarar.
un·clog (ŭn-klŏg') tr. -gg- desatascar.
un·close (ŭn-klōz') tr. & intr. abrir(se).
un·clothe (ŭn-klōth') tr. desvestir.
un·coil (ŭn-koil') tr. & intr. desenrollar(se).
un·col·lect·ed (ŭn'kə-lĕk'tĭd) adj. no cobrado.
un·com·fort·a·ble (ŭn-kŭm'fər-tə-bəl) adj. incómodo; (disquieting) inquietante.
un·com·mit·ted (ŭn'kə-mĭt'ĭd) adj. no comprometido.
un·com·mon (ŭn-kŏm'ən) adj. -er, -est poco común, raro; (remarkable) excepcional.
un·com·mu·ni·ca·tive (ŭn'kə-myōō'nĭ-kā'tĭv, :kə-tĭv) adj. taciturno, reservado.
un·com·plain·ing (ŭn'kəm-plā'nĭng) adj. que no protesta, resignado.
un·com·pli·cat·ed (ŭn-kŏm'plĭ-kā'tĭd) adj. sencillo, simple.
un·com·pli·men·ta·ry (ŭn-kŏm'plə-mĕn'tə-rē) adj. despectivo.
un·com·pro·mis·ing (ŭn-kŏm'prə-mī'zĭng) adj. intransigente.
un·con·cern (ŭn'kən-sûrn') s. indiferencia; (lack of worry) despreocupación f.
un·con·cerned (:sûrnd') adj. despreocupado.
un·con·di·tion·al (:kən-dĭsh'ə-nəl) adj. incondicional.
un·con·di·tioned (:dĭsh'ənd) adj. incondicional; PSIC. no condicionado.
un·con·fined (ŭn'kən-fīnd') adj. libre.
un·con·firmed (:kən-fûrmd') adj. no confirmado.
un·con·nect·ed (ŭn'kə-nĕk'tĭd) adj. inconexo.
un·con·quer·a·ble (ŭn-kŏng'kər-ə-bəl) adj. inconquistable.
un·con·scion·a·ble (ŭn-kŏn'shə-nə-bəl) adj. sin consciencia; (unscrupulous) inescrupuloso.
un·con·scious (:shəs) I. adj. inconsciente; MED. sin sentido II. s. inconsciente m.
un·con·sid·ered (ŭn'kən-sĭd'ərd) adj. inconsiderado; (rash) irreflexivo.
un·con·sti·tu·tion·al (ŭn-kŏn'stĭ-tōō'shə-nəl) adj. inconstitucional.
un·con·trol·la·ble (ŭn'kən-trō'lə-bəl) adj. incontrolable.
un·con·trolled (:trōld') adj. desenfrenado.
un·con·ven·tion·al (:vĕn'shə-nəl) adj. poco convencional, desacostumbrado.
un·con·vinc·ing (:vĭn'sĭng) adj. poco convincente.
un·cooked (ŭn-kŏŏkt') adj. crudo.
un·cork (ŭn-kôrk') tr. descorchar; (to let out) dar rienda suelta a.
un·cor·rupt·ed (ŭn'kə-rŭp'tĭd) adj. incorrupto.
un·count·ed (ŭn-koun'tĭd) adj. innumerable.
un·cou·ple (ŭn-kŭp'əl) tr. desacoplar.
un·couth (ŭn-kōōth') adj. tosco.
un·cov·er (ŭn-kŭv'ər) tr. destapar; FIG. revelar.
un·cov·ered (ŭn-kŭv'ərd) adj. destapado.
un·cross (ŭn-krôs') tr. descruzar.
unc·tion (ŭngk'shən) s. unción f; (ointment) ungüento; (balm) bálsamo; FIG. untuosidad f.
unc·tu·ous (ŭngk'chōō-əs) adj. (greasy) untuoso; (syrupy) meloso.
un·cul·ti·vat·ed (ŭn-kŭl'tə-vā'tĭd) adj. (land) sin cultivar; (person) inculto.
un·cut (ŭn-kŭt') adj. sin cortar; (stones) en bruto; (pages) intonso; (unabridged) entero.

un·dam·aged (ŭn-dăm'ĭjd) adj. libre de daño.
un·daunt·ed (ŭn-dôn'tĭd) adj. impávido.
un·de·ceive (ŭn'dĭ-sēv') tr. desengañar.
un·de·cid·ed (ŭn'dĭ-sī'dĭd) adj. *(not settled)* no resuelto; *(uncommitted)* no comprometido.
un·de·feat·ed (ŭn'dĭ-fē'tĭd) adj. invicto.
un·de·mon·stra·tive (ŭn'dĭ-mŏn'strə-tĭv) adj. poco expresivo, reservado.
un·de·ni·a·ble (ŭn'dĭ-nī'ə-bəl) adj. innegable.
un·der (ŭn'dər) **I.** prep. (por) debajo de (de); *(beneath)* bajo; *(less than)* menos de; *(during)* durante el reinado de; *(with)* con ♦ **u. repair** en reparación • **u. the care of** al cuidado de • **u. the circumstances** dadas las circunstancias **II.** adv. bajo, debajo; *(less)* menos **III.** adj. bajo; *(subordinate)* subalterno.
un·der·a·chieve ('-ə-chēv') intr. rendir *o* lograr menos de lo que se espera de uno.
un·der·age (:āj') adj. menor de edad.
un·der·arm ('-ärm') s. axila.
un·der·bel·ly (:bĕl'ē) s. bajo vientre; FIG. parte *f* vulnerable.
un·der·bid ('-bĭd') tr. **-bid, -dding** COM. ofrecer menos que —intr. rebajar innecesariamente.
un·der·brush ('-brŭsh') s. maleza.
un·der·car·riage (:kăr'ĭj) s. AUTO. chasis *m*; AVIA. tren *m* de aterrizaje.
un·der·charge ('-chärj') tr. COM. cobrar menos de lo debido.
un·der·class·man (:klăs'mən) s. [pl. **-men**] estudiante *mf* de primer *o* segundo año.
un·der·clothes (:klōthz') s.pl. ropa interior.
un·der·cloth·ing (:klō'thĭng) s. ropa interior.
un·der·coat (:kōt') **I.** s. *(jacket)* chaqueta interior; *(paint)* primera capa; AUTO. capa anticorrosiva **II.** tr. aplicar una primera capa a.
un·der·cov·er ('-kŭv'ər) adj. clandestino.
un·der·cur·rent ('-kûr'ənt) s. corriente submarina; FIG. fondo.
un·der·cut (ŭn'dər-kŭt') tr. **-cut, -tting** socavar; *(to sell)* vender más barato que.
un·der·de·vel·oped (:dĭ-vĕl'əpt) adj. insuficientemente desarrollado; ECON. subdesarrollado.
un·der·dog ('-dôg') s. el que no es favorito.
un·der·done ('-dŭn') adj. poco hecho.
un·der·dressed (:drĕst') adj. vestido de forma inapropiada.
un·der·em·ployed (:ĕm-ploid') adj. que no utiliza toda la capacidad obrera.
un·der·es·ti·mate (:ĕs'tə-māt') **I.** tr. subestimar **II.** s. (:mĭt) subestimación *f.*
un·der·es·ti·ma·tion (:ĕs'tə-mā'-shən) s. subestimación *f.*
un·der·ex·pose (:ĭk-spōz') tr. subexponer.
un·der·ex·po·sure (:ĭk-spō'zhər) s. subexposición *f.*
un·der·foot (:fŏŏt') adv. bajo los pies; *(in the way)* en el camino.
un·der·gar·ment ('-gär'mənt) s. prenda interior.
un·der·go ('-gō') tr. **-went, -gone** *(to experience)* experimentar; *(to endure)* sufrir.
un·der·grad·u·ate (:grăj'ŏŏ-ĭt) s. & adj. (de *o* para) estudiante universitario no graduado.
un·der·ground ('-ground') **I.** adj. subterráneo; *(clandestine)* clandestino; *(avant-garde)* de vanguardia **II.** s. movimiento clandestino; *(resistance)* resistencia; G.B. *(subway)* subterráneo **III.** adv. bajo tierra.
un·der·growth (:grōth') s. maleza.
un·der·hand·ed ('-hăn'dĭd) adj. solapada.

un·der·lie (:lī') tr. **-lay, -lain, -lying** estar *o* extenderse debajo de; FIG. ser la base de.
un·der·line ('-līn') **I.** tr. subrayar **II.** s. raya.
un·der·ling (:lĭng) s. subalterno.
un·der·ly·ing (:lī'ĭng) adj. subyacente; *(basic)* fundamental.
un·der·mine ('-mīn') tr. socavar.
un·der·most ('-mōst') adj. más bajo, último.
un·der·neath ('-nēth') **I.** adv. (por) debajo; *(on the lower part)* en la parte inferior **II.** prep. bajo, debajo de **III.** s. parte *f* inferior.
un·der·nour·ish (:nûr'ĭsh) tr. desnutrir.
un·der·nour·ish·ment (:mĭnt) s. desnutrición *f.*
un·der·paid (ŭn'dər-pād') s. mal pagado.
un·der·pants ('-pănts') s.pl. calzoncillos.
un·der·pass (:păs') s. paso por debajo.
un·der·pay ('-pā') tr. **-paid** pagar poco.
un·der·pin (:pĭn') tr. **-nn-** apuntalar.
un·der·pin·ning ('-pĭn'ĭng) s. apuntalamiento ♦ pl. base; FAM. *(the legs)* las piernas.
un·der·play ('-plā') tr. & intr. minimizar.
un·der·priv·i·leged (:prĭv'ə-lĭjd) adj. desamparado.
un·der·pro·duc·tion (:prə-dŭk'shən) s. producción baja *o* insuficiente.
un·der·rate (:rāt') tr. subestimar.
un·der·score ('-skôr') tr. subrayar.
un·der·sea (:sē') **I.** adj. submarino **II.** adv. bajo la superficie del mar.
un·der·sec·re·tar·y ('-sĕk'rĭ-tĕr'ē) s. subsecretario.
un·der·sell (:sĕl') tr. **-sold** vender más barato que.
un·der·shirt ('-shûrt') s. camiseta.
un·der·shorts (:shôrts') s.pl. calzoncillos.
un·der·side (:sīd') s. parte *f* de abajo.
un·der·signed (:sīnd') s.inv. ♦ **the u.** el suscrito, el abajo firmante.
un·der·size(d) (:sīz[d]') adj. *(person)* de talla baja; *(small)* pequeño.
un·der·skirt ('-skûrt') s. enagua.
un·der·stand (:stănd') tr. & intr. **-stood** entender, comprender; *(to infer)* sobreentender.
un·der·stand·a·ble (:stăn'də-bəl) adj. comprensible.
un·der·stand·ing (:dĭng) **I.** s. comprensión *f*; *(intelligence)* entendimiento; *(opinion)* opinión *f*; *(agreement)* acuerdo **II.** adj. comprensivo.
un·der·state (ŭn'dər-stāt') tr. subestimar.
un·der·state·ment (:mənt) s. exposición exageradamente modesta.
un·der·stood (ŭn'dər-stŏŏd') **I.** cf. **understand II.** adj. entendido; *(implied)* sobreentendido ♦ **to make oneself u.** hacerse comprender.
un·der·stud·y ('-stŭd'ē) s. suplente *mf.*
un·der·take (:tāk') tr. **-took, -taken** *(task)* emprender; *(duty)* encargarse de; *(to promise)* prometer.
un·der·tak·er ('-tā'kər) s. agente funerario.
un·der·tak·ing (:tā'kĭng) s. empresa; *(promise)* promesa; *(trade)* pompas fúnebres.
un·der-the-count·er ('-thə-koun'tər) adj. ilegal.
un·der·tone ('-tōn') s. voz baja; *(color)* color apagado de fondo; *(underlying meaning)* fondo.
un·der·tow ('-tō') s. resaca.
un·der·val·ue ('-văl'yŏŏ) tr. apreciar en menos; *(to underrate)* desapreciar.
un·der·wa·ter (:wô'tər) adj. subacuático.
un·der·wear (:wâr') s. ropa interior.
un·der·weight (:wāt') adj. de peso insuficiente

o menor que el normal.

un·der·world ('-wûrld') s. el otro mundo; *(criminal world)* hampa *m.*

un·der·write (:rīt') tr. **-wrote, -written** subscribir; *(to finance)* financiar; *(to insure)* asegurar.

un·der·writ·er (:rī' tɜr) s. asegurador *m.*

un·de·served (ŭn'dĭ-zûrvd') adj. inmerecido.

un·de·sir·a·ble (ŭn'dĭ-zīr'ə-bəl) adj. & s. (persona) indeseable.

un·dies (ŭn'dēz) s. FAM. ropa interior.

un·dig·ni·fied (ŭn-dĭg'nə-fīd') adj. indecoroso.

un·di·rect·ed (ŭn'dĭ-rĕk'tĭd, :dī-) adj. no dirigido.

un·dis·ci·plined (ŭn-dĭs'ə-plĭnd) adj. indisciplinado.

un·dis·cov·ered (ŭn'dĭ-skŭv'ərd) adj. no descubierto; *(unknown)* desconocido.

un·dis·guised (ŭn'dĭs-gīzd') adj. sincero.

un·dis·put·ed (ŭn'dĭ-spyōō'tĭd) adj. indisputable.

un·dis·tin·guished (:gwĭsht) adj. ordinario.

un·dis·turbed (ŭn'dĭ-stûrbd') adj. tranquilo; *(untouched)* sin tocar.

un·do (ŭn-dōō') tr. **-did, -done** anular; *(to untie)* desatar; *(to open)* desenvolver; *(to destroy)* arruinar; *(to unsettle)* trastornar.

un·do·ing (:ĭng) s. *(of damage)* reparación *f;* *(loosening)* aflojamiento; *(downfall)* ruina.

un·done (ŭn-dŭn') I. cf. **undo** II. adj. no hecho; *(untied)* desatado; *(emotionally)* deshecho ♦ **to leave u.** dejar sin hacer.

un·doubt·ed (ŭn-dou'tĭd) adj. indudable.

un·dress (ŭn-drĕs') I. tr. & intr. desvestir(se) II. s. desnudez *f.*

un·dressed (ŭn-drĕst') adj. desnudo.

un·due (ŭn-dōō') adj. indebido; *(improper)* impropio.

un·du·lant (ŭn'jə-lənt) adj. ondulante.

un·du·late (:lāt') intr. ondular; *(in form)* ser ondulado.

un·du·la·tion ('-lā'shən) s. ondulación *f.*

un·du·ly (ŭn-dōō'lē) adv. indebidamente; *(improperly)* impropiamente.

un·dy·ing (ŭn-dī'ĭng) adj. eterno.

un·earned (ŭn-ûrnd') adj. *(undeserved)* inmerecido; COM. no devengado.

un·earth (ŭn-ûrth') tr. desenterrar; FIG. descubrir.

un·earth·ly (:lē) adj. **-i-** extraterreno; *(terrifying)* aterrador; *(absurd)* absurdo.

un·eas·i·ness (ŭn-ē'zē-nĭs) s. inquietud *f.*

un·eas·y (:zē) adj. **-i-** inquieto; *(worried)* ansioso; *(awkward)* incómodo.

un·ed·u·cat·ed (ŭn-ĕj'ə-kā'tĭd) adj. inculto.

un·em·ployed (ŭn'ĕm-ploid') adj. desempleado; *(idle)* no usado.

un·em·ploy·ment (:ploi'mənt) s. desempleo.

un·en·cum·bered (ŭn'ĕn-kŭm'bərd) adj. ♦ **u. by** sin las trabas de.

un·end·ing (ŭn-ĕn'dĭng) adj. sin fin.

un·e·qual (ŭn-ē'kwəl) adj. desigual; *(asymmetric)* asimétrico; *(fluctuating)* fluctuante; *(inadequate)* inadecuado.

un·e·qualed (ŭn-ē'kwəld) adj. sin igual.

un·e·quiv·o·cal (ŭn'ĭ-kwĭv'ə-kəl) adj. inequívoco.

un·err·ing (ŭn-ûr'ĭng) adj. infalible.

un·es·sen·tial (ŭn'ĭ-sĕn'shəl) adj. no esencial.

un·e·ven (ŭn-ē'vən) adj. **-er, -est** desigual.

un·e·ven·ness (:nĭs) s. desigualdad *f.*

un·e·vent·ful (ŭn'ĭ-vĕnt'fəl) adj. sin novedad.

un·ex·cep·tion·al (ŭn'ĭk-sĕp'shə-nəl) adj.

usual.

un·ex·pect·ed (ŭn'ĭk-spĕk'tĭd) adj. inesperado.

un·ex·plored (ŭn'ĭk-splôrd') adj. inexplorado.

un·ex·posed (ŭn'ĭk-spōzd') adj. no expuesto.

un·ex·pres·sive (ŭn'ĭk-sprĕs'ĭv) adj. inexpresivo.

un·fail·ing (ŭn-fā'lĭng) adj. constante; *(inexhaustible)* inagotable; *(infallible)* infalible.

un·fair (ŭn-fâr') adj. **-er, -est** injusto.

un·fair·ness (:nĭs) s. injusticia.

un·faith·ful (ŭn-fāth'fəl) adj. infiel; *(adulterous)* adúltero; *(inaccurate)* inexacto.

un·faith·ful·ness (:nĭs) s. infidelidad *f.*

un·fa·mil·iar (ŭn'fə-mĭl'yər) adj. desconocido ♦ **u. with** no familiarizado con.

un·fa·mil·iar·i·ty ('--yär'ĭ-tē) s. falta de familiaridad.

un·fash·ion·a·ble (ŭn-făsh'ə-nə-bəl) adj. fuera de moda; *(not elegant)* poco elegante.

un·fas·ten (ŭn-făs'ən) tr. & intr. desatar(se).

un·fath·om·a·ble (ŭn-făth'ə-mə-bəl) adj. insondable.

un·fa·vor·a·ble (ŭn-fā'vər-ə-bəl) adj. desfavorable; *(negative)* negativo.

un·feel·ing (ŭn-fē'lĭng) adj. *(numb)* insensible; *(callous)* duro de corazón.

un·fet·ter (ŭn-fĕt'ər) tr. destrabar; FIG. libertar.

un·fin·ished (ŭn-fĭn'ĭsht) adj. incompleto.

un·fit (ŭn-fĭt') adj. incapaz (for, to de); *(unsuitable)* inadecuado; *(unqualified)* incompetente.

un·flag·ging (ŭn-flăg'ĭng) adj. incansable.

un·flap·pa·ble (ŭn-flăp'ə-bəl) adj. impasible.

un·flat·ter·ing (ŭn-flăt'ər-ĭng) adj. poco halagüeño.

un·fledged (ŭn-flĕjd') adj. ORNIT. sin plumas; FIG. inmaduro.

un·flinch·ing (ŭn-flĭn'chĭng) adj. resuelto.

un·fo·cus(s)ed (ŭn-fō'kəst) adj. sin enfocar.

un·fold (ŭn-fōld') tr. & intr. desdoblar(se); *(plot)* desarrollar(se); *(to open out)* abrir(se).

un·fore·seen (ŭn'fər-sēn') adj. imprevisto.

un·for·get·ta·ble (ŭn'fər-gĕt'ə-bəl) adj. inolvidable.

un·for·giv·a·ble (ŭn'fər-gĭv'ə-bəl) adj. imperdonable.

un·formed (ŭn-fôrmd') adj. *(shapeless)* informe; *(uncreated)* no formado aún.

un·for·tu·nate (ŭn-fôr'chə-nĭt) I. adj. desafortunado; *(disastrous)* desastroso; *(regrettable)* lamentable II. s. desgraciado.

un·found·ed (ŭn-foun'dĭd) adj. infundado.

un·friend·li·ness (ŭn-frĕnd'lē-nĭs) s. hostilidad *f.*

un·friend·ly (:lē) adj. **-i-** hostil.

un·fruit·ful (ŭn-frōōt'fəl) adj. infructuoso.

un·furl (ŭn-fûrl') tr. & intr. desplegar(se).

un·fur·nished (ŭn-fûr'nĭsht) adj. desamueblado.

un·gain·ly (ŭn-gān'lē) adj. **-i-** desmañado.

un·glued (ŭn-glōōd') adj. JER. trastornado.

un·god·ly (ŭn-gŏd'lē) adj. **-i-** impío; *(wicked)* perverso; FAM. *(outrageous)* atroz.

un·gov·ern·a·ble (ŭn-gŭv'ər-nə-bəl) adj. ingobernable.

un·gra·cious (ŭn-grā'shəs) adj. brusco.

un·grate·ful (ŭn-grāt'fəl) adj. desagradecido.

un·ground·ed (ŭn-groun'dĭd) adj. infundado.

un·guard·ed (ŭn-gär'dĭd) adj. sin defensa; *(incautious)* incauto.

un·guent (ŭng'gwənt) s. ungüento.

un·gu·late (ŭng'gyə-lĭt) adj. & s. ungulado.

un·hand (ŭn-hănd') tr. desasir.

un·hap·pi·ness (ŭn-hăp′ē-nĭs) s. desgracia.
un·hap·py (ŭn-hăp′ē) adj. **-i-** infeliz; *(unlucky)* desafortunado; *(inappropriate)* impropio.
un·health·y (ŭn-hĕl′thē) adj. **-i-** enfermizo; *(unwholesome)* insalubre; *(corruptive)* malsano.
un·heard (ŭn-hûrd′) adj. no oído; *(not considered)* desatendido.
un·heard-of (:ŭv′, :ŏv′) adj. inaudito.
un·hinge (ŭn-hĭnj′) tr. desgoznar; *(the mind)* desquiciar.
un·hitch (ŭn-hĭch′) tr. desenganchar.
un·ho·ly (ŭn-hō′lē) adj. profano; *(wicked)* impío; FAM. infernal.
un·hook (ŭn-hŏŏk′) tr. desenganchar.
u·ni·corn (yōō′nĭ-kôrn′) s. unicornio.
u·ni·cy·cle (:sī′ kəl) s. monociclo.
un·i·den·ti·fied flying object (ŭn′ī-dĕn′tə-fīd′) s. objeto volador no identificado (ovni).
u·ni·fi·ca·tion (yōō′nə-fĭ-kā′shən) s. unificación *f.*
u·ni·form (yōō′nə-fôrm′) adj. & s. uniforme *m.*
u·ni·for·mi·ty (′-fôr′mĭ-tē) s. uniformidad *f.*
u·ni·fy (′-fī′) tr. & intr. unificar(se).
u·ni·lat·er·al (′-lăt′ər-əl) adj. unilateral.
un·i·mag·i·na·ble (ŭn′ĭ-măj′ə-nə-bəl) adj. inimaginable.
un·im·peach·a·ble (ŭn′ĭm-pē′chə-bəl) adv. irreprochable; *(unquestionable)* irrecusable.
un·im·por·tant (ŭn′ĭm-pôr′tnt) adj. poco importante.
un·in·form·a·tive (ŭn′ĭn-fôr′mə-tĭv) adj. nada informativo.
un·in·formed (:fôrmd′) adj. mal informado.
un·in·hab·it·a·ble (:hăb′ĭ-tə-bəl) adj. inhabitable.
un·in·hab·it·ed (:tĭd) adj. inhabitado.
un·in·hib·it·ed (ŭn′ĭn-hĭb′ĭ-tĭd) adj. sin inhibiciones.
un·in·jured (ŭn-ĭn′jərd) adj. indemne.
un·in·spired (ŭn′ĭn-spīrd′) adj. sin inspiración.
un·in·sured (ŭn′ĭn-shŏŏrd′) adj. no asegurado.
un·in·tel·li·gent (ŭn′ĭn-tĕl′ə-jənt) adj. poco inteligente.
un·in·tel·li·gi·ble (:jə-bəl) adj. ininteligible.
un·in·ter·est·ed (ŭn-ĭn′trĭs-tĭd) adj. desinteresado; *(indifferent)* apático.
un·in·ter·est·ing (:trĭ-stĭng) adj. falto de interés.
un·in·ter·rupt·ed (ŭn-ĭn′tə-rŭp′tĭd) adj. ininterrumpido.
un·ion (yōō′nyən) s. unión *f; (labor)* gremio, sindicato ♦ **student u.** centro estudiantil ♦ **u. jack** bandera.
un·ion·ist (:yə-nĭst) s. sindicalista *mf.*
un·ion·ize (:nīz′) tr. & intr. sindicar(se).
u·nique (yōō-nēk′) adj. único en su género; *(unparalleled)* sin igual.
u·ni·sex (yōō′nĭ-sĕks′) adj. unisexo.
u·ni·sex·u·al (′-sĕk′shōŏ-əl) adj. unisexual.
u·ni·son (yōō′nĭ-sən) s. unísono; *(agreement)* armonía ♦ **in u.** al unísono.
u·nit (yōō′nĭt) s. unidad *f; (part)* parte *f; (device)* aparato.
u·ni·tar·y (:nĭ-tĕr′ē) adj. unitario; *(whole)* íntegro.
u·nite (yōō-nīt′) tr. & intr. unir(se); *(to combine)* combinar(se).
u·ni·ty (yōō′nĭ-tē) s. unidad *f; (unification)* unificación *f; (continuity)* continuidad *f.*
u·ni·va·lent (′-vā′lənt) adj. univalente.
u·ni·valve (:-vălv′) adj. univalvo.
u·ni·ver·sal (yōō′nə-vûr′səl) adj. universal.

u·ni·ver·sal·i·ty (:vər-săl′ĭ-tē) s. universalidad *f.*
u·ni·verse (′-vûrs′) s. universo.
u·ni·ver·si·ty (′-vûr′sĭ-tē) s. universidad *f.*
un·just (ŭn-jŭst′) adj. injusto.
un·jus·ti·fi·a·ble (ŭn-jŭs′tə-fī′ə-bəl) adj. injustificable.
un·kempt (ŭn-kĕmpt′) adj. despeinado; *(messy)* desarreglado.
un·kind (ŭn-kīnd′) adj. **-er, -est** poco amable.
un·know·ing (ŭn-nō′ĭng) adj. ignorante.
un·known (ŭn-nōn′) **I.** adj. desconocido **II.** s. desconocido; MAT. incógnita.
un·lace (ŭn-lās′) tr. desenlazar.
un·lade (ŭn-lād′) tr. & intr. descargar.
un·la·dy·like (ŭn′lā′dē-līk′) adj. impropio de una dama.
un·lash (ŭn-lăsh′) tr. desamarrar.
un·latch (ŭn-lăch′) tr. abrir levantando el picaporte.
un·law·ful (ŭn-lô′fəl) adj. ilegal.
un·lead·ed (ŭn-lĕd′ĭd) adj. sin plomo.
un·learn·ed (ŭn-lûr′nĭd) adj. inculto.
un·leash (ŭn-lēsh′) tr. soltar; FIG. desencadenar.
un·leav·ened (ŭn-lĕv′ənd) adj. ázimo.
un·less (ŭn-lĕs′) conj. a menos que.
un·let·tered (ŭn-lĕt′ərd) adj. analfabeto.
un·like (ŭn′līk′) **I.** adj. *(not alike)* nada parecido; *(not equal)* desigual **II.** prep. diferente de; *(not typical of)* no característico de.
un·like·li·hood (-′lē-hŏŏd′) s. improbabilidad *f.*
un·like·ly (ŭn-līk′lē) adj. **-i-** improbable; *(likely to fail)* poco prometedor.
un·lim·ber (ŭn-lĭm′bər) tr. & intr. alistar(se) para la acción.
un·list·ed (ŭn-lĭs′tĭd) adj. *(not on a list)* que no figura en la lista; FIN. no cotizado.
un·load (ŭn-lōd′) tr. descargar; FIG. desahogar; *(to dispose of)* deshacerse de —intr. descargar.
un·lock (ŭn-lŏk′) tr. & intr. abrir(se).
un·loos·en (ŭn-lōō′sən) tr. soltar.
un·luck·y (ŭn-lŭk′ē) adj. **-i-** desgraciado; *(inauspicious)* aciago ♦ **to be u.** tener mala suerte.
un·make (ŭn-māk′) tr. **-made** deshacer.
un·man·age·a·ble (ŭn-măn′ĭ-jə-bəl) adj. inmanejable.
un·man·ly (ŭn-măn′lē) adj. **-i-** *(cowardly)* cobarde; *(effeminate)* afeminado.
un·manned (ŭn-mănd′) adj. sin tripulación.
un·man·nered (ŭn-măn′ərd) adj. descortés.
un·man·ner·ly (:ər-lē) adj. grosero.
un·marked (ŭn-märkt′) adj. sin marcar.
un·mar·ket·a·ble (ŭn-mär′kĭ-tə-bəl) adj. no comerciable.
un·mar·ried (ŭn-măr′ēd) adj. soltero.
un·mask (ŭn-măsk′) tr. desenmascarar; *(to expose)* descubrir —intr. quitarse la máscara.
un·matched (ŭn-măcht′) adj. sin par.
un·meant (ŭn-mĕnt′) adj. involuntario.
un·men·tion·a·ble (ŭn-mĕn′shə-nə-bəl) **I.** adj. que no debe mencionarse **II.** s. ♦ pl. FAM. ropa interior.
un·mer·ci·ful (ŭn-mûr′sĭ-fəl) adj. despiadado; *(excessive)* excesivo.
un·mind·ful (ŭn-mīnd′fəl) adj. olvidadizo ♦ **u. of** descuidando.
un·mis·tak·a·ble (ŭn′mĭ-stā′kə-bəl) adj. evidente.
un·mit·i·gat·ed (ŭn-mĭt′ĭ-gā′tĭd) adj. implacable; *(absolute)* absoluto.

un·mor·al (ŭn-môr′əl) adj. amoral.
un·named (ŭn-nāmd′) adj. anónimo.
un·nat·u·ral (ŭn-năch′ər-əl) adj. no natural.
un·nec·es·sar·y (ŭn-nĕs′ĭ-sĕr′ē) adj. innecesa-rio.
un·nerve (ŭn-nûrv′) tr. amilanar.
un·no·tice·a·ble (ŭn-nō′tĭ-sə-bəl) adj. imper-ceptible.
un·no·ticed (:tĭst) adj. inadvertido.
un·num·bered (ŭn-nŭm′bərd) adj. innume-rable; *(lacking a number)* sin número.
un·ob·served (ŭn′əb-zûrvd′) adj. desaperci-bido.
un·ob·tain·a·ble (:tā′nə-bəl) adj. inasequible.
un·ob·tru·sive (:trōō′sĭv) adj. discreto.
un·oc·cu·pied (ŭn-ŏk′yə-pīd′) adj. *(vacant)* desocupado; *(idle)* desempleado.
un·of·fi·cial (ŭn′ə-fĭsh′əl) adj. extraoficial.
un·or·gan·ized (ŭn-ôr′gə-nīzd′) adj. no organi-zado; *(not unionized)* sin sindicar.
un·or·tho·dox (ŭn-ôr′thə-dŏks′) adj. poco or-todoxo.
un·pack (ŭn-păk′) tr. desempacar; *(to unload)* descargar —intr. deshacer las maletas.
un·paid (ŭn-pād′) adj. no remunerado.
un·par·al·leled (ŭn-păr′ə-lĕld′) adj. sin igual.
un·par·don·a·ble (ŭn-pär′dn-ə-bəl) adj. im-perdonable.
un·pa·tri·ot·ic (ŭn-pā′trē-ŏt′ĭk) adj. antipatrió-tico.
un·pleas·ant (ŭn-plĕz′ənt) adj. desagradable.
un·pleas·ant·ness (ŭn-plĕz′ənt-nĭs) s. desa-grado, disgusto.
un·plug (ŭn-plŭg′) tr. **-gg-** destapar; ELEC. de-senchufar.
un·pol·ished (ŭn-pŏl′ĭsht) adj. FIG. rudo.
un·pol·lut·ed (ŭn′pə-lōō′tĭd) adj. no contami-nado.
un·pop·u·lar (ŭn-pŏp′yə-lər) adj. impopular.
un·pop·u·lar·i·ty (-′-lăr′ĭ-tē) s. impopularidad f.
un·prac·ticed (ŭn-prăk′tĭst) adj. inexperto.
un·prec·e·dent·ed (ŭn-prĕs′ĭ-dĕn′tĭd) adj. sin precedente.
un·pre·dict·a·ble (ŭn′prĭ-dĭk′tə-bəl) adj. que no se puede predecir o pronosticar.
un·prej·u·diced (ŭn-prĕj′ə-dĭst) adj. imparcial.
un·pre·pared (ŭn′prĭ-pârd′) adj. desprevenido.
un·pre·pos·sess·ing (ŭn-prē′pə-zĕs′ĭng) adj. poco impresionante.
un·pre·ten·tious (ŭn′prĭ-tĕn′shəs) adj. sin pre-tenciones.
un·prin·ci·pled (ŭn-prĭn′sə-pəld) adj. falto de principios, sin escrúpulos.
un·print·a·ble (ŭn-prĭn′tə-bəl) adj. impubli-cable.
un·pro·duc·tive (ŭn′prə-dŭk′tĭv) adj. impro-ductivo; *(attempt)* infructuoso.
un·pro·fes·sion·al (ŭn′prə-fĕsh′ə-nəl) adj. no profesional.
un·prof·it·a·ble (ŭn-prŏf′ĭ-tə-bəl) adj. impro-ductivo; *(useless)* infructuoso.
un·pro·voked (ŭn′prə-vōkt′) adj. no provo-cado.
un·qual·i·fied (ŭn-kwŏl′ə-fīd′) adj. incompe-tente; *(without reservations)* incondicional.
un·ques·tion·a·ble (ŭn-kwĕs′chə-nə-bəl) adj. incuestionable.
un·ques·tioned (ŭn-kwĕs′chənd) adj. incues-tionable.
un·qui·et (ŭn-kwī′ĭt) adj. **-er, -est** inquieto.
un·quote (ŭn-kwōt′) interj. fin de la cita.

un·rav·el (ŭn-răv′əl) tr. & intr. desenredar(se), desenmarañar(se).
un·read (ŭn-rĕd′) adj. no leído; *(ignorant)* poco leído, inculto.
un·read·a·ble (ŭn-rē′də-bəl) adj. ilegible.
un·re·al (ŭn-rē′əl) adj. irreal.
un·re·al·is·tic (ŭn-rē′ə-lĭs′tĭk) adj. no realista.
un·re·al·i·ty (ŭn′rē-ăl′ĭ-tē) s. irrealidad f.
un·rea·son·a·ble (ŭn-rē′zə-nə-bəl) adj. irra-zonable; *(excessive)* excesivo.
un·rea·son·ing (ŭn-rē′zə-nĭng) adj. irracional.
un·rec·og·niz·a·ble (ŭn-rĕk′əg-nī′zə-bəl) adj. irreconocible.
un·re·gen·er·ate (ŭn′rĭ-jĕn′ər-ĭt) adj. incorre-gible.
un·re·hearsed (ŭn′rĭ-hûrst′) adj. improvisado.
un·re·lat·ed (ŭn′rĭ-lā′tĭd) adj. inconexo ♦ **to be u.** no ser de la misma familia.
un·re·lent·ing (ŭn′rĭ-lĕn′tĭng) adj. implacable.
un·re·li·a·ble (ŭn′rĭ-lī′ə-bəl) adj. que no es de fiar.
un·re·mark·a·ble (ŭn′rĭ-mär′kə-bəl) adj. ordi-nario.
un·re·mit·ting (ŭn′rĭ-mĭt′ĭng) adj. incesante.
un·re·served (ŭn′rĭ-zûrvd′) adj. libre; *(unquali-fied)* sin reservas; *(candid)* franco.
un·re·spon·sive (ŭn′rĭ-spŏn′sĭv) adj. insensi-ble.
un·rest (ŭn-rĕst′) s. desasosiego.
un·re·strained (ŭn′rĭ-strānd′) adj. suelto.
un·re·strict·ed (ŭn′rĭ-strĭk′tĭd) adj. libre.
un·ripe (ŭn-rīp′) adj. inmaduro; BOT. verde.
un·ri·valed (ŭn-rī′vəld) adj. sin rival.
un·roll (ŭn-rōl′) tr. & intr. desenrollar(se).
un·ruf·fled (ŭn-rŭf′əld) adj. tranquilo.
un·ru·ly (ŭn-rōō′lē) adj. **-i-** indócil.
un·sad·dle (ŭn-săd′l) tr. desensillar.
un·safe (ŭn-sāf′) adj. peligroso.
un·said (ŭn-sĕd′) adj. sin decir.
un·sal(e)·a·ble (ŭn-sā′lə-bəl) adj. invendible.
un·san·i·tar·y (ŭn-săn′ĭ-tĕr′ē) adj. antihigié-nico.
un·sat·is·fac·to·ry (ŭn-săt′ĭs-făk′tə-rē) adj. in-satisfactorio.
un·sat·u·rat·ed (ŭn-săch′ə-rā′tĭd) adj. sin gra-sas saturadas.
un·sa·vor·y (ŭn-sā′və-rē) adj. *(insipid)* soso; *(distasteful)* desabrido; *(offensive)* ofensivo.
un·scathed (ŭn-skāthd′) adj. ileso.
un·schooled (ŭn-skōōld′) adj. sin instrucción.
un·sci·en·tif·ic (ŭn-sī′ən-tĭf′ĭk) adj. poco cien-tífico.
un·scram·ble (ŭn-skrăm′bəl) tr. *(to straighten out)* arreglar; *(to decipher)* descifrar.
un·screw (ŭn-skrōō′) tr. destornillar; *(to loosen)* desenroscar —intr. destornillarse.
un·scru·pu·lous (ŭn-skrōō′pyə-ləs) adj. sin es-crúpulos, inescrupuloso.
un·seal (ŭn-sēl′) tr. romper el sello de.
un·sea·son·a·ble (ŭn-sē′zə-nə-bəl) adj. fuera de temporada o tiempo.
un·seat (ŭn-sēt′) tr. *(from horse)* derribar; *(from office)* destituir.
un·seem·ly (ŭn-sēm′lē) adj. **-i-** indecoroso.
un·seen (ŭn-sēn′) adj. invisible.
un·sel·fish (ŭn-sĕl′fĭsh) adj. generoso.
un·set·tle (ŭn-sĕt′l) tr. trastornar.
un·set·tled (ŭn-sĕt′ld) adj. inestable; *(not re-solved)* pendiente; *(not paid)* sin liquidar; *(re-gion)* despoblado; *(not fixed)* inconstante.
un·shack·le (ŭn-shăk′əl) tr. quitar los grillos.
un·shak·a·ble (ŭn-shā′kə-bəl) adj. inquebran-

table.
un·shak·en (ŭn-shā′kən) adj. inconmovible.
un·shaped (ŭn-shāpt′) adj. sin forma.
un·shape·ly (ŭn-shāp′lē) adj. **-I-** desproporcionado.
un·shav·en (ŭn-shā′vən) adj. sin afeitar.
un·sheathe (ŭn-shē*th*′) tr. desenvainar.
un·sight·ly (ŭn-sīt′lē) adj. **-I-** feo.
un·skilled (ŭn-skĭld′) adj. inexperto, sin entrenamiento; *(work)* no especializado; *(worker)* no cualificado.
un·snap (ŭn-snăp′) tr. **-pp-** desabrochar.
un·snarl (ŭn-snärl′) tr. desenredar.
un·so·cia·ble (ŭn-sō′shə-bəl) adj. insociable.
un·sold (ŭn-sōld′) adj. sin vender.
un·so·lic·it·ed (ŭn′sə-lĭs′ĭ-tĭd) adj. sin solicitar.
un·solved (ŭn-sōlvd′) adj. sin resolver.
un·so·phis·ti·cat·ed (ŭn′sə-fĭs′tĭ-kā′tĭd) adj. ingenuo.
un·sound (ŭn-sound′) adj. **-er, -est** poco firme; *(defective)* defectuoso; *(unhealthy)* enfermizo.
un·spar·ing (ŭn-spâr′ĭng) adj. generoso; *(cruel)* despiadado.
un·speak·a·ble (ŭn-spē′kə-bəl) adj. indescriptible; *(atrocious)* abominable.
un·spent (ŭn-spĕnt′) adj. sin gastar.
un·spo·ken (ŭn-spō′kən) adj. tácito.
un·spot·ted (ŭn-spŏt′ĭd) adj. inmaculado.
un·sta·ble (ŭn-stā′bəl) adj. inestable.
un·stead·i·ness (ŭn-stĕd′ē-nĭs) s. inestabilidad *f*; *(inconstancy)* inconstancia.
un·stead·y (ŭn-stĕd′ē) adj. **-I-** inestable; *(hands)* temblorosa; *(variable)* variable.
un·stick (ŭn-stĭk′) tr. **-stuck** despegar.
un·stint·ing (ŭn-stĭn′tĭng) adj. generoso.
un·stop (ŭn-stŏp′) tr. **-pp-** destapar.
un·stop·pa·ble (:ə-bəl) adj. irrefrenable.
un·strap (ŭn-străp′) tr. **-pp-** aflojar las correas a.
un·stressed (ŭn-strĕst′) adj. sin acento; *(not emphasized)* sin énfasis.
un·struc·tured (ŭn-strŭk′chərd) adj. falto de estructura.
un·strung (ŭn-strŭng′) adj. desatado; *(unnerved)* trastornado.
un·stud·ied (ŭn-stŭd′ēd) adj. sin afectación.
un·sub·stan·tial (ŭn′səb-stăn′shəl) adj. insubstancial; *(flimsy)* ligero.
un·suc·cess·ful (ŭn′sək-sĕs′fəl) adj. fracasado; *(futile)* infructuoso ◆ **to be u.** no tener éxito.
un·suit·a·ble (ŭn-sōō′tə-bəl) adj. inadecuado; *(inconvenient)* inconveniente; *(unbecoming)* inapropiado.
un·sung (ŭn-sŭng′) adj. no cantado; *(uncelebrated)* no celebrado, olvidado.
un·sus·pect·ed (ŭn′sə-spĕk′tĭd) adj. insospechado.
un·sus·pect·ing (:tĭng) adj. confiado.
un·sym·pa·thet·ic (ŭn-sĭm′pə-thĕt′ĭk) adj. indiferente; *(hostile)* hostil.
un·sys·tem·at·ic (ŭn-sĭs′tə-măt′ĭk) adj. poco metódico.
un·tamed (ŭn-tāmd′) adj. indomado.
un·tan·gle (ŭn-tăng′gəl) tr. desenredar.
un·tapped (ŭn-tăpt′) adj. sin explotar.
un·taught (ŭn-tôt′) adj. sin instrucción; *(natural)* natural.
un·ten·a·ble (ŭn-tĕn′ə-bəl) adj. indefensible.
un·thank·ful (ŭn-thăngk′fəl) adj. ingrato.
un·think·a·ble (ŭn-thĭng′kə-bəl) adj. impensable.

un·think·ing (:kĭng) adj. irreflexivo.
un·ti·di·ness (ŭn-tī′dē-nĭs) s. desorden *m*.
un·ti·dy (ŭn-tī′dē) adj. **-I-** desordenado.
un·tie (ŭn-tī′) tr. **-tying** desatar; *(to free)* soltar —intr. desatarse.
un·til (ŭn-tĭl′) prep. & conj. hasta (que).
un·time·ly (ŭn-tīm′lē) adj. **-I-** inoportuno.
un·tir·ing (ŭn-tīr′ĭng) adj. incansable.
un·to (ŭn′tōō) prep. a.
un·told (ŭn-tōld′) adj. nunca antes dicho; *(beyond measure)* incalculable.
un·touch·a·ble (ŭn-tŭch′ə-bəl) adj. & s. intocable *m*.
un·to·ward (ŭn-tôrd′, ŭn′tə-wôrd′) adj. desfavorable; *(obstinate)* obstinado.
un·trav·eled (ŭn-trăv′əld) adj. poco frecuentado; *(person)* que no ha viajado.
un·tried (ŭn-trīd′) adj. no probado.
un·trod·den (ŭn-trŏd′n) adj. no hollado.
un·true (ŭn-trōō′) adj. **-er, -est** falso; *(inaccurate)* inexacto; *(unfaithful)* desleal.
un·trust·wor·thy (ŭn-trŭst′wûr′*the*) adj. **-I-** indigno de confianza.
un·truth (ŭn-trōōth′) s. falsedad *f*.
un·truth·ful (:fəl) adj. falso; *(lying)* mendaz.
un·tu·tored (ŭn-tōō′tərd) adj. sin instrucción.
un·twist (ŭn-twĭst′) tr. & intr. desenrollar(se).
un·used (ŭn-yōōzd′) adj. sin usar; *(new)* nuevo ◆ **u. to** (ŭn-yōōst′) no acostumbrado a.
un·u·su·al (ŭn-yōō′zhōō-əl) adj. fuera de lo común; *(exceptional)* extraordinario.
un·ut·ter·a·ble (ŭn-ŭt′ər-ə-bəl) adj. inexpresable.
un·var·nished (ŭn-vär′nĭsht) adj. sin barnizar; FIG. puro <*u. truth* la pura verdad>.
un·veil (ŭn-vāl′) tr. quitar el velo a; *(to reveal)* revelar —intr. descubrirse.
un·voiced (ŭn-voist′) adj. no expresado.
un·want·ed (ŭn-wŏn′tĭd) adj. no deseado.
un·war·rant·ed (ŭn-wôr′ən-tĭd) adj. injustificado.
un·war·y (ŭn-wâr′ē) adj. **-I-** incauto.
un·washed (ŭn-wŏsht′) adj. desaseado.
un·wed (ŭn-wĕd′) adj. soltero.
un·wel·come (ŭn-wĕl′kəm) adj. inoportuno; *(news)* desagradable.
un·well (ŭn-wĕl′) adj. enfermo, indispuesto.
un·whole·some (ŭn-hōl′səm) adj. malsano; *(harmful)* nocivo.
un·wield·y (ŭn-wēl′dē) adj. **-I-** difícil de manejar.
un·will·ing (ŭn-wĭl′ĭng) adj. no dispuesto.
un·will·ing·ness (:nĭs) s. desgana, desgano.
un·wind (ŭn-wīnd′) tr. **-wound** desenrollar —intr. desenrollarse; *(to relax)* relajarse.
un·wise (ŭn-wīz′) adj. **-er, -est** desaconsejado.
un·wit·ting (ŭn-wĭt′ĭng) adj. *(unaware)* inconsciente; *(unintentional)* sin intención.
un·wont·ed (ŭn-wŏn′tĭd) adj. inusitado.
un·world·ly (ŭn-wûrld′lē) adj. **-I-** espiritual; *(naive)* ingenuo.
un·wor·thy (ŭn-wûr′*the*) adj. **-I-** despreciable ◆ **u. of** no digno de.
un·wound·ed (ŭn-wōōn′dĭd) adj. ileso.
un·wrap (ŭn-răp′) tr. **-pp-** desenvolver.
un·writ·ten (ŭn-rĭt′n) adj. no escrito; *(traditional)* tradicional.
un·yield·ing (ŭn-yēl′dĭng) adj. inflexible.
un·yoke (ŭn-yōk′) tr. desuncir.
un·zip (ŭn-zĭp′) tr. **-pp-** bajar la cremallera de.
up (ŭp) **I.** adv. hacia arriba, en lo alto; arriba <*I put it up there* lo puse allí arriba>; para arriba

<*from ten dollars up* de diez dólares para arriba> ♦ **close up** cerca • **high up** muy arriba • **to be u.** haberse levantado (de la cama); *(to be finished)* estar terminado, acabarse • **to be up all night** no acostarse en toda la noche • **to come** *o* **go up to** acercarse a • **to feel up to** sentirse capaz de • **to get up** levantarse • **up!** *o* **get up!** ¡arriba! • **up above** arriba • **up against** junto a • **up and down** de arriba abajo • **up north** hacia *o* en el norte • **up to** hasta • **up to date** al día II. adj. *(moving upward)* que va hacia arriba; *(out of bed)* levantado ♦ **it is up to you** decídelo tú • **to be up against** tener que hacer frente a • **to be up against it** estar en apuros • **to be up and around** estar de nuevo en pie • **to be up for** *(office)* ser candidato a; *(to feel like)* tener ganas de • **to be up on** estar bien enterado sobre • **to be up to standard** satisfacer los requisitos • **to be up to something** estar tramando algo • **up in arms** furioso • **up to** hasta; *(capable of)* capacitado para • **what are you up to?** ¿en qué andas? • **¿qué pasa?** III. prep. arriba IV. s. ♦ **on the up and up** honesto, legal • **to be on an up** FAM. estar eufórico • **to be on the up** COM. estar en subida • **ups and downs** altibajos V. tr. **-pp-** *(to increase)* aumentar; *(to raise)* elevar —intr. levantarse.

up·and·com·ing (ŭp′ən-kŭm′ĭng) adj. prometedor.

up·and·down (:doun′) adj. variante; *(vertical)* vertical.

up·beat (ŭp′bēt′) adj. FAM. optimista.

up·braid (ŭp-brād′) tr. reprochar.

up·bring·ing (ŭp′brĭng′ĭng) s. crianza.

up·com·ing (ŭp′kŭm′ĭng) adj. futuro.

up·coun·try (ŭp′kŭn′trē) I. s. interior *m* II. adj. del interior III. adv. hacia el interior.

up·date (ŭp-dāt′) I. tr. poner al día II. s. (″) información actualizada.

up·draft (ŭp′drăft′) s. corriente *f* ascendente.

up·end (ŭp-ĕnd′) tr. poner de punta; *(to overturn)* derribar.

up·front (ŭp′frŭnt′) adj. franco; *(in advance)* por adelantado.

up·grade (ŭp′grād′) I. tr. mejorar la calidad de; *(to promote)* ascender II. s. cuesta.

up·heav·al (ŭp-hē′vəl) s. levantamiento; *(disruption)* trastorno; GEOL. solevantamiento.

up·hill (ŭp′hĭl′) I. adj. ascendente; *(difficult)* arduo II. s. cuesta III. adv. cuesta arriba.

up·hold (ŭp-hōld′) tr. **-held** levantar; *(to support)* sostener; *(to sustain)* defender.

up·hol·ster (ŭp-hōl′stər) tr. tapizar.

up·hol·ster·y (:stə-rē) s. tapicería.

up·keep (ŭp′kēp′) s. mantenimiento; *(cost)* gastos de mantenimiento.

up·land (ŭp′lənd) s. altiplanicie *f.*

up·lift (ŭp-lĭft′) I. tr. (ŭp-lĭft′) alzar; *(to elevate)* elevar II. s. (″) alzamiento.

up·most (ŭp′mōst′) adj. más alto.

up·on (ə-pŏn′) prep. sobre.

up·per (ŭp′ər) I. adj. superior ♦ **to have the u. hand** llevar ventaja • **u. case** mayúsculas • **u. crust** FAM. la flor y nata II. s. *(of a shoe)* pala; JER. *(drug)* pepa (anfetamina).

up·per·case (′-kās′) adj. en mayúsculas.

up·per·class (:klăs′) adj. de la clase alta.

up·per·class·man (:′mən) s. [pl. **-men**] estudiante *mf* del tercer *o* cuarto año.

up·per·cut (ŭp′ər-kŭt′) s. gancho (en boxeo).

up·per·most (:mōst′) I. adj. más alto II. adv. en primer lugar.

up·pi·ty (ŭp′ĭ-tē) adj. FAM. presumido.

up·raise (ŭp-rāz′) tr. levantar.

up·right (ŭp′rīt′) I. adj. vertical; *(honorable)* recto II. adv. verticalmente III. s. montante *m.*

up·ris·ing (ŭp′rī′zĭng) s. insurrección *f.*

up·riv·er (ŭp′rĭv′ər) adj. & adv. río arriba.

up·roar (ŭp′rôr′) s. alboroto.

up·roar·i·ous (-′ē-əs) adj. tumultuoso; *(boisterous)* ruidoso; *(hilarious)* hilarante.

up·root (ŭp-rōōt′) tr. arrancar; FIG. desarraigar.

up·set (ŭp-sĕt′) I. tr. **-set, -tting** *(to tip over)* volcar; *(to throw into disorder)* desordenar; *(to trouble)* afectar; *(physically, mentally)* perturbar; *(the stomach)* caer mal a; *(an opponent)* vencer inesperadamente II. s. (″) vuelco; *(trouble)* molestia; *(defeat)* derrota inesperada III. adj. *(disordered)* desordenado; *(worried)* preocupado ♦ **don't be u.** *(worried)* no te preocupes; *(angry)* no te enojes • **to have an u. stomach** estar descompuesto del estómago.

up·shot (ŭp′shŏt′) s. resultado.

up·side-down (ŭp′sīd-doun′) adj. al revés; FIG. patas arriba ♦ **to turn u.** volcar(se); FIG. trastornar(se).

up·stage (ŭp′stāj′) I. adv. en *o* hacia el fondo del escenario II. tr. TEAT. robar la escena; FAM. eclipsar.

up·stairs (ŭp′stârz′) I. adv. arriba; *(on upper floor)* en el piso superior II. adj. del piso superior III. s.inv. piso de arriba.

up·stand·ing (ŭp-stăn′dĭng) adj. erguido; *(honest)* recto.

up·start (ŭp′stärt′) s. advenedizo.

up·state (ŭp′stāt′) adv. hacia la parte norte del estado.

up·stream (ŭp′strēm′) adv. aguas arriba.

up·surge (ŭp-sûrj′) I. intr. subir repentinamente II. s (″) subida repentina.

up·swing (ŭp′swĭng′) s. alza.

up·take (ŭp′tāk′) s. canal *m* de salida de la chimenea ♦ **quick on the u.** que comprende muy rápidamente.

up·tight (ŭp′tīt′) adj. JER. tenso.

up-to-date (ŭp′tə-dāt′) adj. al día; *(keeping up)* al tanto.

up-to-the-min·ute (:thə-mĭn′ĭt) adj. de última hora.

up·town (ŭp′toun′) adv. & s. (hacia) la parte alta de una ciudad.

up·turn (ŭp′tûrn′) s. alza.

up·ward (ŭp′wərd) I. adj. ascendente II. adv. *o* **-wards** hacia *o* para arriba ♦ **u. of** en exceso de, más de.

up·wind (ŭp′wĭnd′) adj. contra el viento.

u·ra·ni·um (yŏŏ-rā′nē-əm) s. uranio.

ur·ban (ûr′bən) adj. urbano.

ur·bane (ûr-bān′) adj. urbano, cortés.

ur·ban·ite (ûr′bə-nīt′) s. habitante *mf* de una ciudad.

ur·ban·i·ty (ûr-băn′ĭ-tē) s. finura.

ur·ban·ize (ûr′bə-nīz′) tr. urbanizar.

ur·chin (ûr′chĭn) s. golfillo.

u·re·a (yŏŏ-rē′ə) s. urea.

u·re·mi·a (:mē-ə) s. uremia.

u·re·ter (yŏŏr′ĭ-tər) s. uréter *m.*

u·re·thra (yŏŏ-rē′thrə) s. [pl. **s** *o* **-ae**] uretra.

urge (ûrj) I. tr. *(to impel)* incitar; *(to exhort)* exhortar; *(to advocate)* propugnar II. s. im-

pulso; *(desire)* deseo.
ur·gen·cy (ûr′jən-sē) s. urgencia.
ur·gent (ûr′jənt) adj. urgente.
u·ric (yŏŏr′ĭk) adj. úrico.
u·ri·nal (:ə-nəl) s. *(fixture)* urinal *m*, urinario; *(receptacle)* orinal *m*.
u·ri·nal·y·sis (′-năl′ĭ-sĭs) s. [pl. **-ses**] análisis *m* de orina.
u·ri·nar·y (′-nĕr′ē) adj. urinario.
u·ri·nate (:nāt′) intr. orinar.
u·rine (yŏŏr′ĭn) s. orina.
urn (ûrn) s. urna; *(for tea, coffee)* recipiente *m* grande.
u·ro·gen·i·tal (yŏŏr′ō-jĕn′ĭ-tl) adj. urogenital.
u·rol·o·gy (yŏŏ-rŏl′ə-jē) s. urología *m*.
us (ŭs) pron. nos <*the movie impressed us la película nos impresionó*>; nosotros, nosotras <*to us a nosotros*>.
us·a·ble (yŏŏ′zə-bəl) adj. utilizable.
us·age (yŏŏ′sĭj) s. uso; *(customary practice)* usanza; *(parlance)* lenguaje *m*.
use (yŏŏz) I. tr. usar; *(to treat)* tratar; *(drugs)* tomar ♦ **to be used as, for** servir de, para ♦ **to u. up** agotar —intr. [ú. solamente en la forma imperfecta **used** (yŏŏst)] soler <*I used to go to Florida every winter yo solía ir a la Florida todos los inviernos*> ♦ **to get used to** acostumbrarse a II. s. (yŏŏs) uso; *(usefulness)* utilidad *f* ♦ **it's no u.** es inútil • **to be of no u.** no servir para nada • **to have no u. for** no necesitar; *(to dislike)* no gustarle a uno • **to have the u. of** tener uno a su disposición • **to put to good u.** sacar partido de • **what's the u.!** ¡para qué!
used (yŏŏzd) adj. usado.
use·ful (yŏŏs′fəl) adj. útil.
use·ful·ness (:nĭs) s. utilidad *f*.
use·less (yŏŏs′lĭs) adj. ineficaz; *(futile)* inútil.
use·less·ness (:nĭs) s. inutilidad *f*.
us·er (yŏŏ′zər) s. usuario; *(addict)* adicto.
ush·er (ŭsh′ər) I. s. acomodador *m*; *(doorkeeper)* ujier *mf* II. tr. acomodar; *(to escort)* acompañar ♦ **to u. in** anunciar.
ush·er·ette (′ə-rĕt′) s. acomodadora.
u·su·al (yŏŏ′zhŏŏ-əl) adj. usual; *(customary)* acostumbrado ♦ **as u.** como de costumbre • **the u. thing** lo de siempre.
u·su·rer (yŏŏ′zhər-ər) s. usurero.
u·su·ri·ous (-zhŏŏr′ē-əs) adj. usurario.
u·surp (yŏŏ-sûrp′) tr. & intr. usurpar.
u·sur·pa·tion (′-sûr-pā′shən) s. usurpación *f*.
u·surp·er (-′pər) s. usurpador *m*.
u·su·ry (yŏŏ′zhə-rē) s. usura.
u·ten·sil (yŏŏ-tĕn′səl) s. utensilio.
u·ter·ine (yŏŏ′tər-ĭn) adj. uterino.
u·ter·us (:əs) s. útero.
u·til·i·tar·i·an (yŏŏ-tĭl′ĭ-târ′ē-ən) I. adj. utilitario; FILOS. utilitarista II. s. utilitarista *mf*.
u·til·i·ty (yŏŏ-tĭl′ĭ-tē) s. utilidad *f*; *(service)* servicio público.
u·til·iz·a·ble (yŏŏt′l-ī′zə-bəl) adj. utilizable.
u·til·i·za·tion (′-ī-zā′shən) s. utilización *f*.
u·til·ize (yŏŏt′l-īz′) tr. utilizar.
ut·most (ŭt′mōst′) I. adj. máximo; *(farthest)* más lejano II. s. máximo ♦ **to do one's u.** hacer todo lo posible • **to the u.** hasta más no poder.
u·to·pi·a (yŏŏ-tō′pē-ə) s. utopía.
u·to·pi·an (:ən) I. adj. utópico II. s. utopista *mf*.
ut·ter¹ (ŭt′ər) tr. decir; *(to pronounce)* pronunciar; *(sigh, cry)* dar.
ut·ter² adj. total, absoluto.

ut·ter·a·ble (ŭt′ər-ə-bəl) adj. decible.
ut·ter·ance (:əns) s. pronunciación *f*; *(expression)* expresión *f*; *(of a sound)* emisión *f*.
ut·ter·ly (ŭt′ər-lē) adv. totalmente.
ut·ter·most (:mōst′) adj. extremo.
U-turn (yŏŏ′tûrn′) s. AUTO. media vuelta.
u·vu·la (yŏŏ′vyə-lə) s. úvula, campanilla.
ux·o·ri·ous (ŭk-sôr′ē-əs) adj. perdidamente enamorado de la esposa.

V

v, V (vē) s. vigésima segunda letra del alfabeto inglés.
va·can·cy (vā′kən-sē) s. vacío; *(unfilled position)* vacante *f*; *(in a hotel)* habitación *f* libre.
va·cant (vā′kənt) adj. *(empty)* vacío; *(not occupied)* libre; *(position)* vacante; *(look, stare)* inexpresivo, vago.
va·cate (vā′kāt′) tr. dejar vacante; *(house)* desocupar; DER. anular —intr. irse, marcharse.
va·ca·tion (vā-kā′shən) I. s. vacaciones *f* <*on v. de vacaciones*> II. intr. tomar las vacaciones.
vac·ci·nate (văk′sə-nāt′) tr. & intr. vacunar.
vac·ci·na·tion (′-nā′shən) s. vacunación *f*.
vac·cine (văk-sēn′, ′′) s. vacuna.
vac·il·late (văs′ə-lāt′) intr. vacilar.
vac·il·la·tion (′-lā′shən) s. vacilación *f*.
va·cu·i·ty (vă-kyŏŏ′ĭ-tē) s. vacuidad *f*; *(remark)* vaciedad *f*.
vac·u·ous (văk′yŏŏ-əs) adj. *(empty)* vacío; *(inane)* vacuo; *(look)* vago, perdido.
vac·u·um (văk′yŏŏm) I. s. [pl. **s** *o* **-ua**] vacío; *(isolation)* aislamiento ♦ **v. cleaner** aspiradora II. tr. & intr. pasar la aspiradora (por).
vac·u·um-packed (′-păkt′) adj. envasado al vacío.
vag·a·bond (văg′ə-bŏnd′) s. & adj. vagabundo.
va·ga·ry (vā′gə-rē) s. capricho.
va·gi·na (və-jī′nə) s. [pl. **s** *o* **-ae**] vagina.
vag·i·nal (văj′ə-nəl) adj. vaginal.
va·gran·cy (vā′grən-sē) s. vagancia.
va·grant (vā′grənt) I. s. *(vagabond)* vagabundo; *(bum)* vago II. adj. vagabundo.
vague (văg) adj. vago; *(reply)* ambiguo; *(shape, idea)* impreciso.
vain (vān) adj. *(fruitless)* vano, inútil; *(conceited)* vanidoso ♦ **in v.** en vano, vanamente.
vain·glo·ri·ous (-glôr′ē-əs) adj. vanaglorioso.
vain·glo·ry (:ē) s. vanagloria.
val·ance (văl′əns) s. doselera.
vale (vāl) s. valle *m*.
val·e·dic·to·ri·an (văl′ĭ-dĭk-tôr′ē-ən) s. alumno que da el discurso de fin de curso.
val·e·dic·to·ry (′-′tə-rē) adj. & s. (discurso de) despedida.
va·lence/len·cy (vā′ləns) s. valencia.
val·en·tine (văl′ən-tīn′) s. tarjeta del día de los enamorados; *(sweetheart)* novio, -a.
val·et (văl′ĭt, vă-lā′) s. ayuda de cámara.
val·iance (văl′yəns) s. valentía, bravura.
val·iant (:yənt) adj. & s. valiente *mf*.
val·id (văl′ĭd) adj. válido; DER. *(in effect)* vigente ♦ **to be no longer v.** haber caducado.
val·i·date (:ī-dāt′) tr. validar; *(to verify)* verificar.
val·i·da·tion (′-dā′shən) s. validación *f*; *(verification)* verificación *f*.
va·lid·i·ty (və-lĭd′ĭ-tē) s. validez *f*.
va·lise (və-lēs′) s. maleta, valija.

val·ley (văl'ē) s. valle m.

val·or (văl'ər) s. valor m, valentía.

val·or·ous (văl'ər-əs) adj. valeroso, valiente.

val·u·a·ble (văl'yŏō-ə-bəl) I. adj. valioso, de valor; (information, assistance) importante, de valor ♦ **to be v.** valer mucho II. s. ♦ pl. objetos de valor.

val·u·ate (:āt') tr. valorar, tasar.

val·u·a·tion ('-ā'shən) s. valoración f, tasación f; (value) valor estimado.

val·ue (văl'yŏō) I. s. valor m; (importance) importancia ♦ **market** o **commercial v.** valor comercial • **to attach little v. to** dar poco valor a • **to be of (no) v.** (no) ser valioso • **to lose v.** desvalorizarse • **to set a v. on** estimar, valuar II. tr. (to appraise) valorizar, tasar; (to rate) estimar, valorar; (to esteem) estimar, apreciar.

val·ued (:yŏōd) adj. estimado, apreciado.

valve (vălv) s. ANAT., TEC. válvula; MÚS. llave f.

val·vu·lar (văl'vyə-lər) adj. valvular.

va·moose (vă-mŏōs') intr. JER. largarse.

vamp¹ (vămp) s. (shoe part) empeine m; MÚS. acompañamiento improvisado.

vamp² s. vampiresa, seductora.

vam·pire (văm'pīr') s. vampiro.

van¹ (văn) s. (truck) camioneta, furgoneta; G.B., F.C. vagón m de carga.

van² s. vanguardia.

van·dal·ism (văn'dl-īz'əm) s. vandalismo.

van·dal·ize (:īz') tr. destrozar, destruir.

vane (văn) s. (weathercock) veleta; (of a propeller) paleta; (of a windmill) aspa; (of a rocket) estabilizador m.

van·guard (văn'gärd') s. vanguardia.

va·nil·la (və-nĭl'ə) s. (extracto de) vainilla.

van·ish (văn'ĭsh) intr. desaparecer; (to fade) desvanecerse ♦ **to v. into thin air** esfumarse.

van·i·ty (văn'ĭ-tē) s. vanidad f; (conceit) presunción f; (table) tocador m ♦ **v. case** neceser.

van·quish (văng'kwĭsh) tr. derrotar, vencer.

van·tage (văn'tĭj) s. ventaja ♦ **v. point** posición de ventaja, lugar ventajoso.

vap·id (văp'ĭd, vā'pĭd) adj. insípido, soso.

va·por (vā'pər) s. vapor m; (mist) niebla, bruma; (fumes) humo, vapor.

va·por·ize (vā'pə-rīz') tr. & intr. vaporizar(se).

va·por·iz·er (:rī'zər) s. vaporizador m.

va·por·ous (vā'pər-əs) adj. vaporoso.

var·i·a·bil·i·ty (vâr'ē-ə-bĭl'ĭ-tē) s. variabilidad f.

var·i·a·ble (vâr'ē-ə-bəl) I. adj. variable; (fickle) inconstante II. s. variable f.

var·i·ance (:əns) s. (act) variación f; (deviation) desviación f ♦ **at v.** en desacuerdo.

var·i·ant (:ənt) I. adj. (differing) variante, diferente; (variable) variable II. s. variante f.

var·i·a·tion ('-ā'shən) s. variación f.

var·i·cose (vâr'ĭ-kōs') adj. varicoso.

var·ied (vâr'ēd) adj. variado.

var·i·e·gat·ed (vâr'ē-ĭ-gā'tĭd) adj. (varicolored) abigarrado, jaspeado; (diversified) variado.

va·ri·e·ty (və-rī'ĭ-tē) s. variedad f; (assortment) surtido ♦ **in a v. of** en varios • **v. show** espectáculo de variedades.

var·i·ous (vâr'ē-əs) adj. (several) varios; (varied) vario; (different) diferente.

var·mint (vär'mĭnt) s. FAM. sabandija.

var·nish (vär'nĭsh) I. s. barniz m; (coating) capa de barniz ♦ **v. remover** quitaesmalte II. tr. barnizar; (the truth) embellecer.

var·si·ty (vär'sĭ-tē) s. equipo universitario; G.B. universidad f.

var·y (vâr'ē) tr. variar —intr. variar, cambiar.

(to differ) diferir; (to deviate) desviarse.

var·y·ing (:ĭng) adj. variante, variable.

vas·cu·lar (văs'kyə-lər) adj. vascular.

vase (vās, vāz, väz) s. jarrón m, florero.

va·sec·to·my (və-sĕk'tə-mē) s. vasectomía.

vas·sal (văs'əl) s. vasallo.

vast (văst) adj. vasto, inmenso ♦ **by a v. majority** por una abrumadora mayoría.

vast·ness (:nĭs) s. vastedad f, inmensidad f.

vat (văt) s. cuba.

va·tic·i·na·tion (və-tĭs'ə-nā'shən) s. vaticinio.

vaude·ville (vōd'vĭl') s. vodevil m.

vault¹ (vôlt) I. s. ARQ. bóveda; (cellar) sótano; (of a bank) cámara acorazada; (burial chamber) cripta II. tr. abovedar.

vault² I. s. & intr. saltar II. s. salto.

vault·ing¹ (vôl'tĭng) s. ARQ. bóveda.

vault·ing² adj. saltador; (ambition, pride) desmesurado.

vaunt (vônt) I. tr. & intr. jactarse (de) II. s. alarde m, jactancia.

veal (vēl) s. (carne f de) ternera.

vec·tor (vĕk'tər) s. vector m.

veep (vēp) s. FAM. vicepresidente m.

veer (vîr) I. intr. (to swerve) desviarse; (the wind) cambiar; (a boat) virar —tr. desviar; (a boat) virar II. s. desvío, viraje m.

veg·e·ta·ble (vĕj'tə-bəl) I. s. verdura, legumbre f; (inactive person) vegetal m II. adj. vegetal ♦ **v. oil** aceite vegetal.

veg·e·tal (:ĭ-tl) adj. vegetal.

veg·e·tar·i·an ('-târ'ē-) s. vegetariano.

veg·e·tate ('-tāt') intr. vegetar.

veg·e·ta·tion ('-tā'shən) s. vegetación f.

ve·he·mence (vē'ə-məns) s. vehemencia.

ve·he·ment (:mənt) adj. vehemente.

ve·hi·cle (vē'ĭ-kəl) s. vehículo.

ve·hic·u·lar (vē-hĭk'yə-lər) adj. de o para vehículos.

veil (vāl) I. s. velo; FIG. velo, capa ♦ **under a v. of secrecy** en secreto II. tr. velar.

vein (vān) I. s. vena; BOT., ENTOM. nervio; GEOL., MIN. veta, filón m; (in wood, marble) vena, veta ♦ **in the same v.** del mismo estilo II. tr. vetear.

veined (vānd) adj. venoso; (streaked) veteado.

vel·lum (vĕl'əm) s. vitela, pergamino.

ve·loc·i·ty (və-lŏs'ĭ-tē) s. velocidad f.

ve·lour(s) (və-lŏor') s. veludillo.

ve·lum (vē'ləm) s. [pl. **-la**] velo del paladar.

vel·vet (vĕl'vĭt) I. s. terciopelo; (on antlers) vello II. adj. de terciopelo; (velvety) aterciopelado.

vel·vet·een ('-vĭ-tēn') s. veludillo, velludo.

vel·vet·y ('-tē) adj. aterciopelado.

ve·nal (vē'nəl) adj. venal.

ve·nal·i·ty (vē-năl'ĭ-tē) s. venalidad f.

vend (vĕnd) tr. vender ♦ **vending machine** distribuidor automático, máquina vendedora.

vend·er (vĕn'dər) s. vendedor m.

ven·det·ta (vĕn-dĕt'ə) s. vendetta, venganza.

vend·i·ble (vĕn'də-bəl) s. artículo vendible.

ve·neer (və-nîr') I. s. chapa, enchapado; FIG. apariencia, barniz m II. tr. chapear, enchapar.

ven·er·a·ble (vĕn'ər-ə-bəl) adj. venerable.

ven·er·ate (vĕn'ə-rāt') tr. venerar.

ven·er·a·tion ('-rā'shən) s. veneración f.

ve·ne·re·al (və-nîr'ē-əl) adj. venéreo ♦ **v. disease** enfermedad venérea.

Ve·ne·tian blind (və-nē'shən) s. persiana veneciana, celosías.

ven·geance (vĕn'jəns) s. venganza, vindicta ♦

to take v. on vengarse de • **with a v.** *(furiously)* con violencia; *(excessively)* con creces.
venge·ful (vĕnj′fəl) adj. vengativo.
ve·ni·al (vē′nē-əl) adj. venial.
ven·i·son (vĕn′ĭ-sən) s. *(carne f de)* venado.
ven·om (vĕn′əm) s. veneno.
ven·om·ous (:ə-məs) adj. venenoso.
vent (vĕnt) I. s. *(for air)* respiradero; *(outlet)* salida; *(hole)* agujero, abertura ◆ **to give v. to** dar rienda suelta a II. tr. abrir un agujero en; *(to discharge)* dar salida a, descargar; *(feelings, words)* desahogar, dar rienda suelta a.
ven·ti·late (vĕn′tl-āt′) tr. ventilar.
ven·ti·la·tion (′-ā′shən) s. *(system)* ventilación f; *(air circulation)* aeración f.
ven·ti·la·tor (′-ā′tər) s. ventilador m.
ven·tral (vĕn′trəl) adj. ventral, abdominal.
ven·tri·cle (vĕn′trĭ-kəl) s. ventrículo.
ven·tril·o·quism (vĕn-trĭl′ə-kwĭz′əm) s. ventriloquia.
ven·tril·o·quist (:kwĭst) s. ventrílocuo.
ven·ture (vĕn′chər) I. s. *(undertaking)* aventura; *(stake)* riesgo; COM. empresa o negocio arriesgado ◆ **at a v.** a la (buena) ventura • **v. capital** capital de inversión II. tr. *(money, opinion)* aventurar; *(to dare)* atreverse a ◆ **nothing ventured nothing gained** el que no arriesga no gana —intr. *(to dare)* atreverse; *(to go)* ir ◆ **to v. forth o v. forth** tr, salir.
ven·ture·some (:səm) adj. aventurado, arriesgado; *(enterprising)* emprendedor.
ven·tur·ous (:əs) adj. valiente, arrojado.
ven·ue (vĕn′yōō) s. *(of a crime)* lugar m; DER. jurisdicción f.
ve·ra·cious (və-rā′shəs) adj. veraz, verídico.
ve·rac·i·ty (və-rǎs′ĭ-tē) s. veracidad f; *(accuracy)* exactitud f.
ve·ran·da(h) (və-rǎn′də) s. terraza, veranda.
verb (vûrb) s. verbo.
ver·bal (vûr′bəl) adj. verbal.
ver·bal·ize (:bə-līz′) tr. expresar con palabras.
ver·ba·tim (vər-bā′tĭm) I. adj. literal II. adv. palabra por palabra, literalmente.
ver·bi·age (vûr′bē-ĭj) s. palabrería, verborrea.
ver·bose (vər-bōs′) adj. verboso.
ver·bos·i·ty (-bŏs′ĭ-tē) s. verbosidad f.
ver·dant (vûr′dnt) adj. verde.
ver·dict (vûr′dĭkt) s. veredicto; *(judgment)* dictamen m.
verge¹ (vûrj) I. s. *(edge, rim)* borde m, margen m; *(boundary)* límite m; *(staff)* cetro ◆ **to be on the v. of** estar a punto de II. intr. ◆ **to v. (up)on** *(to come near)* rayar en; *(to tend towards)* estar al borde de.
verge² intr. ◆ **to v. into** o **on** *(to pass into)* rayar en, acercarse a.
ver·i·fi·ca·tion (vĕr′ə-fĭ-kā′shən) s. verificación f.
ver·i·fi·er (′-fī′ər) s. verificador m.
ver·i·fy (vĕr′ə-fī′) tr. verificar.
ver·i·ly (vĕr′ə-lē) adv. verdaderamente.
ver·i·si·mil·i·tude (vĕr′ə-sĭ-mĭl′ĭ-tōōd′) s. verosimilitud f.
ver·i·ta·ble (vĕr′ĭ-tə-bəl) adj. verdadero.
ver·i·ty (vĕr′ĭ-tē) s. verdad f.
ver·mi·cel·li (vûr′mə-chĕl′ē, :sĕl′ē) s. fideos delgados.
ver·mi·cide (vûr′mĭ-sīd′) s. vermicida m.
ver·mi·form (vûr′mə-fôrm′) adj. vermiforme ◆ **v. appendix** apéndice vermiforme.
ver·mi·fuge (:fyōōj′) s. & adj. vermífugo.
ver·mil(l)·ion (vər-mĭl′yən) I. s. bermellón m

II. adj. bermejo.
ver·min (vûr′mĭn) s.inv. *(pest)* bicho(s), sabandija(s); *(person)* sabandija.
ver·mouth (vər-mōōth′) s. vermut m.
ver·nac·u·lar (vər-nǎk′yə-lər) I. s. *(language)* lengua vernácula; *(popular speech)* lenguaje m popular; *(jargon)* jerga ◆ **to put in the v.** expresar en lenguaje popular II. adj. vernáculo.
ver·nal (vûr′nəl) adj. vernal.
ver·sa·tile (vûr′sə-tl) adj. *(person)* de talentos variados; *(object)* de muchos usos.
ver·sa·til·i·ty (′-tĭl′ĭ-tē) s. *(of an object)* varios usos; *(of a person)* varios talentos.
verse¹ (vûrs) s. *(poetry)* verso; *(stanza)* estrofa; *(of a song)* cuplé m; BÍBL. versículo.
verse² tr. familiarizarse con ◆ **to be versed in** estar familiarizado en.
versed (vûrst) adj. versado.
ver·si·fy (vûr′sə-fī′) tr. & intr. versificar.
ver·sion (vûr′zhən) s. versión f; *(adaptation)* adaptación f.
ver·sus (vûr′səs) prep. contra <*conjecture v. evidence* la conjetura contra la evidencia>.
ver·te·bra (vûr′tə-brə) s. [pl. **s** o **-ae**] vértebra.
ver·te·bral (:brəl) adj. vertebral.
ver·te·brate (:brāt′) adj. & s. vertebrado.
ver·tex (vûr′tĕks′) s. [pl. **es** o **-tices**] *(apex)* ápice m; ANAT., GEOM. vértice m.
ver·ti·cal (vûr′tĭ-kəl) adj. & s. vertical f.
ver·ti·go (vûr′tĭ-gō′) s. [pl. **(e)s**] vértigo.
verve (vûrv) s. brío, ánimo.
ver·y (vĕr′ē) I. adv. muy; *(truly)* de veras <*it's the v. best de es veras mejor*>; *(indeed)* mucho <*are you tired? v.* ¿estás cansado? mucho>; *(precisely)* precisamente, exactamente <*the v. same one* exactamente el mismo>; *(an intensive)* muy, tan <*he is so v. poor* es tan pobre> ◆ **at the v. latest** a más tardar • **at the v. least** como mínimo • **at the v. most** a lo más, a lo sumo • **not v.** poco <*it was not v. interesting* fue poco interesante> • **the v. best** el o lo mejor • **v. much (so)** muchísimo II. adj. **-i-** absoluto, puro <*the v. truth* la verdad absoluta>; *(selfsame, exact)* mismo <*at that v. moment* en ese mismo momento>; *(mere)* mero, simple <*the v. thought frightens us* el mero pensamiento nos espanta> ◆ **at the v. end** al final de todo • **the v. idea!** ¡vaya idea! • **to be the v. image of** ser el vivo retrato de • **to shudder at the v. thought of it** temblar con sólo pensarlo.
ves·pers (vĕs′pərz) s.pl. vísperas.
ves·sel (vĕs′əl) s. *(container)* vaso, vasija; MARÍT. nave f, embarcación f; ANAT., BOT. vaso.
vest (vĕst) I. s. chaleco; G.B. *(undershirt)* camiseta II. tr. ◆ **to v. in** *(rights, property)* conceder, conferir; *(authority, power)* investir.
ves·tal (vĕs′təl) adj. & s. vestal f.
vest·ed (vĕs′tĭd) adj. DER. concedido, establecido ◆ **v. interest** intereses creados.
ves·ti·bule (vĕs′tə-byōōl′) s. vestíbulo, zaguán m.
ves·tige (vĕs′tĭj) s. vestigio.
ves·tig·i·al (vĕ-stĭj′ē-əl) adj. rudimentario.
vest·ment (vĕst′mənt) s. vestidura; *(robe)* toga; RELIG. vestimenta.
ves·try (vĕs′trē) s. sacristía, vestuario.
vet (vĕt) s. FAM. *(veterinarian)* veterinario; *(veteran)* veterano.
vet·er·an (vĕt′ər-ən) adj. & s. veterano.
vet·er·i·nar·i·an (vĕt′ər-ə-nâr′ē-ən) s. veterinario.
vet·er·i·nar·y (′--nĕr′ē) adj. & s. veterinario.

ve·to (vē'tō) I. s. [pl. **es**] veto II. tr. vetar; *(to prohibit)* prohibir.
vex (věks) tr. *(to bother)* fastidiar, molestar; *(to baffle)* confundir.
vex·a·tion (věk-sā'shən) s. fastidio, molestia.
vex·a·tious (:shəs) adj. fastidioso, molesto.
vexed (věkst) adj. *(person)* enfadado, irritado; *(question, matter)* controvertido.
vi·a (vī'ə, vě'ə) prep. vía ♦ **v. air mail** por vía aérea.
vi·a·bil·i·ty (vī'ə-bĭl'ĭ-tē) s. viabilidad f.
vi·a·ble (vī'ə-bəl) adj. viable.
vi·a·duct (vī'ə-dŭkt') s. viaducto.
vi·al (vī'əl) s. frasco.
vi·and (vī'ənd) s. vianda ♦ pl. provisiones.
vibes (vībz) s. FAM. *(vibraphone)* s. vibráfono; JER. *(vibrations)* vibraciones f.
vi·bran·cy (vī'brən-sē) s. viveza, animación f.
vi·brant (vī'brənt) adj. vibrante; *(energetic)* enérgico, animado.
vi·bra·phone (vī'brə-fōn') s. vibráfono.
vi·brate (vī'brāt') intr. vibrar; *(to resonate)* resonar; *(to thrill)* estremecerse —tr. vibrar.
vi·bra·tion (vī-brā'shən) s. vibración f; *(quiver)* temblor m, estremecimiento ♦ pl. JER. vibraciones.
vi·bra·tor ('-tər) s. vibrador m.
vic·ar (vĭk'ər) s. vicario.
vic·ar·age (:ĭj) s. vicaría.
vi·car·i·ous (vī-kâr'ē-əs) adj. *(punishment)* sufrido por otro; *(pleasure)* indirecto.
vice¹ (vīs) s. vicio ♦ **v. squad** dependencia policial que combate el vicio.
vice² var. de **vise**.
vice³ I. s. *(used as a prefix)* vice ♦ **v. chancellor** vicecanciller • **v. president** vice presidente II. prep. en lugar de ♦ **v. versa** viceversa.
vice·roy (vīs'roi') s. virrey m.
vice·roy·al·ty ('-tē) s. virreinato.
vi·cin·i·ty (vī-sĭn'ĭ-tē) s. proximidad f; *(area)* vecindad f ♦ **in the v. of** aproximadamente.
vi·cious (vĭsh'əs) adj. *(addicted to vice)* vicioso; *(malicious)* malicioso, rencoroso; *(storm, attack)* violento, fuerte; *(animal, crime)* salvaje, atroz ♦ **v. circle** círculo vicioso.
vi·cis·si·tude (vī-sĭs'ĭ-tōōd') s. vicisitud f.
vic·tim (vĭk'tĭm) s. víctima ♦ **to fall (a) v.** to sucumbir a.
vic·tim·ize (:tə-mīz') tr. hacer víctima; *(to swindle)* estafar, embaucar.
vic·tor (vĭk'tər) s. vencedor m, triunfador m.
Vic·to·ri·an (vĭk-tôr'ē-ən) adj. & s. victoriano.
vic·to·ri·ous (vĭk-tôr'ē-əs) adj. triunfante, vencedor.
vic·to·ry (vĭk'tə-rē) s. victoria, triunfo.
vic·tuals (vĭt'lz) s.pl. vituallas.
vid·e·o (vĭd'ē-ō') adj. & s. vídeo.
vid·e·o·cas·sette ('-kə-sĕt') s. videocasete mf.
vid·e·o·con·fer·ence (:kŏn'fər-əns) s. teleconferencia.
vid·e·o·disc/disk ('--dĭsk') s. videodisco.
vid·e·o·tape (:tāp') I. s. videocinta II. tr. grabar en videocinta.
vie (vī) intr. vying competir, contender.
view (vyōō) I. s. *(sight, vista)* vista; *(examination)* examinación f, inspección f; *(systematic survey)* panorama m; *(opinion)* opinión f; *(approach)* enfoque m <*our v. of the problem* nuestro enfoque del problema>; *(intention)* propósito <*with a v. to doing something* con el propósito de hacer algo>; *(chance)* posibilidad f, perspectiva ♦ **in v. of** en vista de, conside-

rando • **point of v.** punto de vista • **to be on v.** estar a la vista • **to come into v.** aparecer • **to have in v.** *(a project)* tener a la vista; *(to keep in mind)* tener presente • **to keep in v.** no perder de vista • **to take the v. that** pensar que • **v. finder** visor II. tr. ver, mirar; *(to examine)* examinar; *(to consider)* considerar, enfocar.
view·er ('ər) s. espectador m; *(television viewer)* televidente mf; FOTOG. visor m.
view·point (:'point') s. punto de vista.
vig·il (vĭj'əl) s. vigilia ♦ **to keep v.** velar.
vig·i·lance (:ə-ləns) s. vigilancia.
vig·i·lant (:lənt) adj. vigilante, alerto.
vig·i·lan·te (vĭj'ə-lăn'tē) s. vigilante mf, miembro de una junta que actúa como policía.
vi·gnette (vĭn-yĕt') s. IMPR. viñeta; FOTOG. retrato con bordes esfumados; LIT. bosquejo corto; CINEM. escena corta.
vig·or (vĭg'ər) s. vigor m.
vig·or·ous (:əs) adj. *(strong)* vigoroso, fuerte; *(energetic)* enérgico.
vig·our (vĭg'ər) G.B. var. de **vigor**.
vile (vīl) adj. *(despicable)* vil, ruin; *(loathsome)* odioso; *(food)* desagradable; *(weather)* pésimo.
vil·i·fy (vĭl'ə-fī') tr. difamar, denigrar.
vil·la (vĭl'ə) s. villa, quinta; G.B. *(residence)* chalet m.
vil·lage (vĭl'ĭj) s. *(hamlet)* aldea; *(town)* pueblo; *(inhabitants)* población f.
vil·lag·er (:ĭ-jər) s. aldeano.
vil·lain (vĭl'ən) s. villano, canalla m; FIG. causa.
vil·lain·ous (:ə-nəs) adj. *(vile)* vil; *(wicked)* villano, malvado.
vil·lain·y (:ə-nē) s. villanía, vileza.
vim (vĭm) s. energía, brío.
vin·ai·grette (vĭn'ĭ-grĕt') s. *(container)* vinagrera; *(sauce)* vinagreta.
vin·di·cate (vĭn'dĭ-kāt') tr. vindicar, exculpar; *(to justify)* justificar.
vin·di·ca·tion ('-kā'shən) s. vindicación f.
vin·dic·tive (vĭn-dĭk'tĭv) adj. vengativo.
vine (vīn) s. enredadera; *(grapevine)* parra, vid f ♦ **clinging v.** persona pegajosa.
vin·e·gar (vĭn'ĭ-gər) s. vinagre m.
vine·stock (vīn'stŏk') s. cepa (de la vid).
vine·yard (vĭn'yərd) s. viñedo, viña.
vin·tage (vĭn'tĭj) I. s. *(season)* vendimia; *(crop, year)* cosecha II. adj. *(wine)* añejo, de calidad; *(classic)* clásico; *(of the best)* excelente <*a v. year for us* un año excelente para nosotros>.
vint·ner (vĭnt'nər) s. vinatero.
vi·nyl (vī'nəl) s. vinilo.
vi·ol (vī'əl) s. viola.
vi·o·la¹ (vē-ō'lə) s. MÚS. viola.
vi·o·la² (vī-ō'lə, vī'ə-lə) s. BOT. viola, violeta.
vi·o·la·ble (vī'ə-lə-bəl) adj. violable.
vi·o·late (vī'ə-lāt') tr. violar.
vi·o·la·tion ('-lā'shən) s. violación f.
vi·o·la·tor ('-lā'tər) s. violador m.
vi·o·lence (vī'ə-ləns) s. violencia ♦ **to do v. to** violar, ir en contra de.
vi·o·lent (:lənt) adj. violento; *(pain)* intenso; *(feeling)* profundo ♦ **to become v.** mostrarse violento.
vi·o·let (vī'ə-lĭt) I. s. *(plant)* violeta; *(color)* violeta m II. adj. violado.
vi·o·lin (vī'ə-lĭn') s. violín m.
vi·o·lin·ist (:ĭst) s. violinista mf.
vi·o·lon·cel·lo (vē'ə-lən-chĕl'ō) s. violoncelo.
VIP (vē'ī-pē') s. FAM. personalidad f (impor-

tante).

vi•per (vī'pər) s. víbora.

vi•ral (vī'rəl) s. causado por un virus, virulento.

vir•gin (vûr'jĭn) **I.** s. virgen ♦ **The V.** la Virgen María **II.** adj. virgen; *(initial)* inicial, primero; *(unsullied)* puro, intacto.

vir•gin•al¹ (vûr'jə-nəl) adj. virginal.

vir•gin•al² s. MÚS. espineta.

vir•gin•i•ty (vər-jĭn'ĭ-tē) s. virginidad *f.*

vir•gule (vûr'gyōol) s. vírgula.

vir•ile (vîr'əl, :īl') adj. viril, varonil.

vi•ril•i•ty (və-rĭl'ĭ-tē) s. virilidad *f.*

vi•rol•o•gy (vī-rŏl'ə-jē) s. virología.

vir•tu•al (vûr'chōo-əl) adj. virtual.

vir•tu•al•ly (:ə-lē) adv. prácticamente, casi <*it is v. impossible* es casi imposible>.

vir•tue (vûr'chōo) s. virtud *f*; *(chastity)* castidad *f*, honra; *(advantage)* ventaja ♦ **by** *o* **in v. of** en virtud de • **of easy v.** fácil.

vir•tu•os•i•ty (vûr'chōo-ŏs'ĭ-tē) s. virtuosismo.

vir•tu•o•so (:ō'sō) s. [pl. **s** *o* **-si**] virtuoso.

vir•tu•ous (vûr'chōo-əs) adj. *(righteous)* virtuoso; *(chaste)* casto, puro.

vir•u•lence (vîr'yə-ləns) s. virulencia.

vir•u•lent (:lənt) adj. virulento.

vi•rus (vī'rəs) s. virus *m.*

vi•sa (vē'zə) s. visa, visado.

vis•age (vĭz'ĭj) s. cara, semblante *m.*

vis-à-vis (vē'zə-vē') **I.** adv. frente a frente, cara a cara **II.** prep. *(opposite to)* frente a, enfrente de; *(compared with)* comparado con, con relación a.

vis•cer•a (vĭs'ər-ə) s.pl. vísceras.

vis•cer•al (:əl) adj. ANAT. visceral; *(profound)* profundo, íntimo; *(instinctive)* instintivo.

vis•cos•i•ty (vĭ-skŏs'ĭ-tē) s. viscosidad *f.*

vis•count (vī'kount') s. vizconde *m.*

vis•count•ess (vī'koun'tĭs) s. vizcondesa.

vis•cous (vĭs'kəs) adj. viscoso.

vise (vīs) s. tornillo de banco.

vis•i•bil•i•ty (vĭz'ə-bĭl'ĭ-tē) s. visibilidad *f.*

vis•i•ble (:'-bəl) adj. visible; *(apparent)* manifiesto; *(evident)* evidente.

vi•sion (vĭzh'ən) **I.** s. *(sight)* vista, visión *f*; *(foresight)* clarividencia, previsión *f*; *(mental image)* visión, fantasía ♦ **a person of v.** una persona clarividente.

vi•sion•ar•y (:ə-nĕr'ē) **I.** adj. *(foresighted)* visionario; *(dreamy)* de ensueño; *(utopian)* utópico **II.** s. visionario.

vis•it (vĭz'ĭt) **I.** tr. visitar; *(as a guest)* pasar una temporada en; *(punishment, misfortune)* infligir, enviar —intr. hacer una visita, ir de visita; FAM. *(to chat)* charlar **II.** s. visita; *(stay)* estadía (como invitado) ♦ **to be on a v. to** estar de visita en • **to pay a v. to** visitar a.

vis•i•tant (:ĭ-tnt) s. *(guest)* invitado; *(ghost)* aparecido.

vis•i•ta•tion (:-tā'shən) s. visita; *(calamity)* desgracia, calamidad *f* ♦ **v. rights** derecho de visita (a hijos después del divorcio).

vis•it•ing (:'-tĭng) adj. *(card, hours)* de visita; *(person)* visitante.

vis•i•tor (vĭz'ĭ-tər) s. visitante *mf*, visita; *(tourist)* turista *mf.*

vi•sor (vī'zər) s. visera.

vis•ta (vĭs'tə) s. vista, perspectiva.

vi•su•al (vĭzh'ōo-əl) adj. visual; *(inspection, proof)* ocular ♦ **v. aids** medios visuales.

vi•su•al•ize (:ə-līz') tr. & intr. visualizar.

vi•tal (vīt'l) adj. vital ♦ **v. statistics** estadística demográfica.

vi•tal•i•ty (vī-tăl'ĭ-tē) s. vitalidad *f.*

vi•tal•ize (vīt'l-īz') tr. vitalizar.

vi•tals (vīt'lz) s.pl. órganos vitales; FIG. partes *f* esenciales.

vi•ta•min (vī'tə-mĭn) s. vitamina.

vi•ti•ate (vĭsh'ē-āt') tr. viciar.

vit•i•cul•ture (vĭt'ĭ-kŭl'chər) s. viticultura.

vit•re•ous (vĭt'rē-əs) adj. vítreo.

vit•ri•fy (vĭt'rə-fī') tr. & intr. vitrificar(se).

vit•ri•ol (vĭt'rē-əl) s. vitriolo; FIG. virulencia, veneno.

vit•ri•ol•ic ('-ŏl'ĭk) adj. vitriólico; FIG. mordaz.

vi•tu•per•ate (vī-tōo'pə-rāt') tr. vituperar.

vi•tu•per•a•tion (-'pə-rā'shən) s. vituperación *f.*

vi•tu•per•a•tive (-'pər-ə-tĭv) adj. vituperante.

vi•va•cious (vĭ-vā'shəs, vī-) adj. vivaz.

vi•vac•i•ty (vĭ-văs'ĭ-tē, vī-) s. vivacidad *f.*

viv•id (vĭv'ĭd) adj. vívido; *(memory)* vivo.

viv•i•fy (vĭv'ə-fī') tr. vivificar; FIG. animar.

viv•i•sect (vĭv'ĭ-sĕkt') tr. hacer la vivisección de.

viv•i•sec•tion ('-sĕk'shən) s. vivisección *f.*

vix•en (vĭk'sən) s. zorra; FIG. arpía.

vo•cab•u•lar•y (vō-kăb'yə-lĕr'ē) s. vocabulario.

vo•cal (vō'kəl) adj. vocal; *(clamorous)* ruidoso; *(outspoken)* que dice lo que piensa ♦ **v. cords** cuerdas vocales.

vo•cal•ist (vō'kə-lĭst) s. vocalista *mf.*

vo•cal•ize (:līz') tr. articular —intr. vocalizar.

vo•ca•tion (vō-kā'shən) s. vocación *f.*

vo•ca•tion•al (:shə-nəl) adj. vocacional ♦ **v. school** escuela vocacional.

vo•cif•er•ate (vō-sĭf'ə-rāt') tr. & intr. vociferar.

vo•cif•er•ous (:ər-əs) adj. vociferador.

vogue (vōg) s. moda, boga ♦ **in v.** en boga.

voice (vois) **I.** s. voz *f*; *(timbre)* voz <*a gentle v.* un tono dulce> ♦ **at the top of one's v.** a voz en cuello • **in a loud, low v.** en voz alta, baja • **to give v. to** expresar • **to have a v. in** tener voz en • **to lose, raise one's v.** perder, alzar la voz • **v. box** laringe **II.** tr. *(to utter)* expresar; FONÉT. sonorizar.

voice•less (:lĭs) adj. mudo; FONÉT. sordo.

voice-o•ver (:ō'vər) s. CINEM. voz *f* del comentador *o* narrador que no aparece en la imagen.

void (void) **I.** adj. *(empty)* vacío; *(vacant)* vacante; DER. nulo, inválido ♦ **v. of** desprovisto de **II.** s. vacío **III.** tr. *(to invalidate)* invalidar, anular; *(to empty)* vaciar; FISIOL. evacuar.

vol•a•tile (vŏl'ə-tl, :tīl') adj. volátil; FIG. inestable, explosivo.

vol•a•til•i•ty ('-tĭl'ĭ-tē) s. volatilidad *f.*

vol•can•ic (vŏl-kăn'ĭk) adj. volcánico.

vol•ca•no (vŏl-kā'nō) s. [pl. **(e)s**] volcán *m.*

vo•li•tion (və-lĭsh'ən) s. volición *f*, voluntad *f.*

vol•ley (vŏl'ē) **I.** s. *(of missiles, bullets)* descarga, andanada; *(of stones)* lluvia; *(of oaths, insults)* torrente *m*; *(in tennis)* voleo **II.** tr. MIL. lanzar —intr. DEP. volear.

vol•ley•ball (:bôl') s. balonvolea *m*, voleibol *m*; *(ball)* balón *m.*

volt¹ (vōlt) s. ELEC. voltio.

volt² s. EQUIT. vuelta; ESGR. esquiva.

volt•age (vōl'tĭj) s. voltaje *m*, tensión *f.*

vol•ta•ic (-tā'ĭk) adj. voltaico.

vol•u•ble (vŏl'yə-bəl) adj. locuaz.

vol•ume (vŏl'yōom) s. volumen *m* ♦ **v. control** botón del volumen ♦ pl. montones.

vo•lu•mi•nous (və-lōō'mə-nəs) adj. voluminoso; *(information, detail)* abundante.

vol•un•tar•y (vŏl'ən-tĕr'ē) adj. voluntario; *(spontaneous)* espontáneo.

vol·un·teer ('-tûr') I. s. voluntario II. adj. voluntario; *(police, army)* de voluntarios III. tr. & intr. ofrecer(se) voluntariamente; MIL. alistar(se) como voluntario.

vo·lup·tu·ous (və-lŭp'chōō-əs) adj. voluptuoso, sensual.

vom·it (vŏm'ĭt) I. tr. & intr. vomitar II. s. vómito.

voo·doo (vōō'dōō) s. vodú, vudú f.

vo·ra·cious (vô-rā'shəs) adj. voraz.

vor·tex (vôr'tĕks) s. [pl. **es** o **-tices**] vórtice m; FIG. vorágine f.

vo·ta·ry (vō'tə-rē) s. devoto.

vote (vōt) I. s. voto; *(act, result)* votación f; *(right)* derecho de voto; *(bloc)* votos <*the labor v.* los votos de los obreros> ♦ **by a majority v.** por una mayoría de votos • **popular, secret v.** votación popular, secreta • **to take a v. on** poner o someter a votación • **to put to the v.** poner o someter a votación • **unanimous v.** votación por unanimidad • **v. of confidence** voto de confianza II. intr. votar —tr. votar; *(to select)* elegir; FAM. *(to suggest)* sugerir, proponer ♦ **to v. down** votar en contra de, rechazar • **to v. in** elegir (por votación).

vot·er (vō'tər) s. votante mf, elector m.

vot·ing (vō'tĭng) I. s. votación f II. adj. *(person, public)* votante; *(campaign)* electoral.

vo·tive (vō'tĭv) adj. votivo.

vouch (vouch) tr. verificar, comprobar —intr. ♦ **to v. for** avalar, responder por.

vouch·er (vou'chər) s. *(person)* fiador m; *(document)* comprobante m, vale m.

vouch·safe (vouch-sāf') tr. dignarse a dar.

vow (vou) I. s. promesa; RELIG. voto ♦ **to take vows** hacer votos monásticos II. tr. *(to pledge)* jurar; *(to promise)* prometer.

vow·el (vou'əl) s. vocal f.

voy·age (voi'ĭj) I. s. viaje m, travesía II. intr. hacer un viaje, viajar.

vul·ca·nize (vŭl'kə-nīz') tr. vulcanizar.

vul·gar (vŭl'gər) adj. vulgar; *(joke, story)* indecente, verde; *(rude)* grosero; *(taste)* cursi.

vul·gar·i·an (-gâr'ē-ən) s. persona vulgar.

vul·gar·ism ('gə-rĭz'əm) s. vulgarismo.

vul·gar·i·ty (-gâr'ĭ-tē) s. vulgaridad f, grosería.

vul·gar·ize (gə-rīz') tr. vulgarizar.

Vul·gate ('gāt') s. lenguaje m popular ♦ **V.** Vulgata.

vul·ner·a·bil·i·ty (vŭl'nər-ə-bĭl'ĭ-tē) s. vulnerabilidad f.

vul·ner·a·ble ('--bəl) adj. vulnerable ♦ **to be v. to** ser susceptible a.

vul·ture (vŭl'chər) s. buitre m, gallinazo.

vul·va (vŭl'və) s. [pl. **-ae**] vulva.

W

w, W (dŭb'əl-yōō) s. vigésima tercera letra del alfabeto inglés.

wack·y (wăk'ē) adj. **-l-** JER. loco.

wad (wŏd) s. taco, fajo; *(of papers)* lío; FAM. dineral m.

wad·ding ('ĭng) s. taco, fajo.

wad·dle (wŏd'l) I. intr. contonearse II. s. contoneo.

wade (wād) intr. caminar en; *(to struggle)* avanzar con dificultad —tr. vadear.

wad·er (wā'dər) s. vadeador m; ORNIT. ave zancuda ♦ pl. botas altas de vadeo.

wa·fer (wā'fər) s. barquillo; RELIG. hostia.

waf·fle[1] (wŏf'əl) s. panqueque m al estilo de barquillo.

waf·fle[2] intr. FAM. *(to waver)* vacilar.

waft (wăft, wäft) I. tr. llevar por el aire o sobre el agua —intr. flotar II. s. soplo.

wag[1] (wăg) I. intr. **-gg-** agitarse —tr. menear II. s. meneo; *(of a tail)* coleo.

wag[2] s. *(joker)* bromista mf.

wage (wāj) I. s. pago, sueldo ♦ pl. *(pay)* salario; FIG. fruto II. tr. *(war)* hacer; *(a campaign)* emprender.

wa·ger (wā'jər) I. s. apuesta II. tr. & intr. apostar.

wag·ger·y (wăg'ə-rē) s. broma.

wag·gle (wăg'əl) tr. menear rápidamente —intr. agitarse.

wag·on (wăg'ən) s. *(vehicle)* carro; *(railway car)* vagón m; *(station wagon)* furgoneta ♦ **to be** o **to go on the w.** JER. no beber, dejar de beber.

waif (wāf) s. *(child)* expósito; *(animal)* animal abandonado.

wail (wāl) I. intr. lamentarse; *(to howl)* aullar II. s. *(cry)* lamento; *(howl)* aullido.

wain·scot (wān'skət, :skŏt') I. s. revestimiento de madera II. tr. revestir con madera.

wain·wright (wān'rīt') s. carretero.

waist (wāst) s. cintura; *(of garment)* talle m.

waist·band ('bănd') s. cinturón m.

waist·coat (wĕs'kĭt, wāst'kōt') s. G.B. chaleco.

waist·line (wāst'līn') s. cintura, talle m.

wait (wāt) I. intr. esperar ♦ **to w. up** esperar sin acostarse ♦ **waiting list, room** lista, sala de espera —tr. esperar; *(to delay)* retrasar ♦ **to w. for** esperar • **to w. on** *(tables)* servir, atender II. s. espera ♦ **to lie in w.** estar al acecho.

wait·er (wā'tər) s. camarero.

wait·ress (wā'trĭs) s. camarera.

waive (wāv) tr. *(to relinquish)* renunciar a; *(to dispense with)* suspender; *(to put off)* postergar.

waiv·er (wā'vər) s. DER. renuncia.

wake[1] (wāk) I. intr. **-oke** o **-oke, -ed** o **woken** despertarse; *(to be awake)* estar despierto —tr. despertar; *(to alert)* alertar; *(to revive)* resucitar ♦ **to w. up** despertar II. s. velatorio.

wake[2] s. *(track)* huella; *(of a ship)* estela ♦ **in the w. of** inmediatamente después de.

wake·ful ('fəl) adj. desvelado; *(alert)* alerta.

wak·en (wā'kən) tr. & intr. despertar(se).

wale (wāl) s. verdugón m.

walk (wôk) I. intr. caminar, andar; *(to go on foot)* ir a pie; *(to stroll)* pasear ♦ **to w. around** pasear(se) • **to w. away** o **off** irse • **to w. in** entrar • **to w. out** *(on strike)* declararse en huelga; *(to leave)* irse • **walking papers** FAM. nota de despido —tr. caminar por; *(a distance)* caminar, andar; *(a horse)* llevar al paso; *(to escort)* acompañar ♦ **to w. away from** alejarse de; *(problems)* evitar; *(accident)* salir ileso de • **to w. away** o **off with** llevarse • **to w. in on** aparecérsele inesperadamente a • **to w. into** entrar en; *(wall)* chocar contra; *(trap)* caer en • **to w. out on** FAM. dejar abandonado II. s. paseo; *(hike)* caminata; *(pace)* paso ♦ **people from all walks of life** todo tipo de gente • **to go for** o **to take a w.** dar un paseo.

walk·a·way (wô'kə-wā') s. victoria fácil.

walk·er (wô'kər) s. *(pedestrian)* peatón m; *(stroller)* paseante mf; *(for infants)* andador m.

walk·ie-talk·ie (wô'kē-tô'kē) s. radioteléfono portátil.

walk-in (wôk'ĭn') adj. tan grande que uno

puede entrar en él; *(services)* que no requiere cita previa.

walk·out (:out') s. *(strike)* huelga; *(quitting)* renuncia.

walk·o·ver (:ō'vər) s. victoria fácil.

walk·up o **walk-up** (:ŭp') s. *(building)* edificio sin ascensor; *(apartment)* departamento en un edificio sin ascensor.

walk·way (:wā') s. pasillo.

wall (wôl) I. s. pared *f; (around a house)* muro; *(of city)* muralla; *(of garden)* tapia; *(obstacle)* barrera ♦ **to drive up the w.** FAM. volver loco II. tr. poner un muro o una pared a ♦ **to w. in** o **up** *(house, town)* amurallar; *(garden)* tapiar • **to w. off** separar con una pared III. adj. de pared, mural.

wall·board ('bôrd') s. madera prensada.

wal·let (wôl'ĭt) s. billetera, cartera.

wall·eye (wôl'ī') s. ojo albino.

wall·flow·er (:flou'ər) s. *(flower)* alhelí *m; (person)* persona que no participa.

wal·lop (wôl'əp) I. tr. pegar con fuerza II. s. *(blow)* golpe *m* fuerte; *(force)* fuerza, impacto.

wal·lop·ing (:ə-pĭng) FAM. I. adj. enorme; *(impressive)* impresionante II. s. paliza.

wal·low (wôl'ō) I. intr. revolcarse II. s. *(act)* revuelco; *(of animals)* bañadero.

wall·pa·per (wôl'pā'pər) I. s. papel *m* de empapelar II. tr. & intr. empapelar.

wall-to-wall (:tə-wôl') adj. de pared a pared; *(all-inclusive)* total.

wal·nut (wôl'nŭt) s. nuez *f; (tree, wood)* nogal *m.*

wal·rus (wôl'rəs) s. [pl. inv. o **es**] morsa.

waltz (wôlts) I. s. vals *m* II. intr. bailar el vals ♦ **to w. through** FAM. pasar como si tal cosa.

wan (wŏn) adj. **-nn-** pálido; *(weary)* pesaroso.

wand (wŏnd) s. varita mágica; *(rod)* vara.

wan·der (wŏn'dər) intr. *(to roam)* vagar; *(to go astray)* desviarse —tr. vagar por.

wan·der·er (:ər) s. vagabundo.

wan·der·ing (:ĭng) I. adj. nómada II. s. vagabundeo.

wan·der·lust (:lŭst') s. deseos de viajar.

wane (wān) I. intr. disminuir; *(to decline)* declinar; ASTRON. menguar II. s. disminución *f;* ASTRON. cuarto menguante.

wan·gle (wăng'gəl) FAM. tr. conseguir tramposamente —intr. hacer trampa.

wan·ing (wā'nĭng) s. mengua, disminución *f.*

want (wŏnt, wônt) I. tr. querer; *(to desire)* desear; *(to lack)* carecer de; *(to need)* necesitar ♦ **to w. out** FAM. querer irse • **wanted** se busca; *(by an employer)* necesítase —intr. querer ♦ **to w. for** carecer de II. s. *(lack)* falta; *(poverty)* pobreza; *(wish)* deseo.

want·ing (wŏn'tĭng, wôn'-) I. adj. ausente; *(deficient)* deficiente II. prep. *(without)* sin; *(minus)* menos.

wan·ton (wŏn'tən) adj. *(lewd)* sensual; *(unjust)* sin piedad; *(unrestrained)* desenfrenado; *(excessive)* excesivo; *(playful)* juguetón.

war (wôr) I. s. guerra II. adj. de guerra III. intr. **-rr-** guerrear.

war·ble (wôr'bəl) I. intr. trinar II. s. trino.

war·bler (:blər) s. silvido; *(European)* curruca.

ward (wôrd) I. s. distrito, barrio; *(of hospital)* sala; *(of jail)* pabellón *m; (minor)* pupilo; *(custody)* tutela II. tr. ♦ **to w. off** prevenir.

war·den (wôr'dn) s. *(prison official)* director *m; (custodian)* guardián *m.*

ward·er (wôr'dər) s. guardia.

ward·robe (wôr'drōb') s. armario; *(garments)* vestuario.

ward·room (wôrd'rōōm') s. MARÍT. comedor *m* de oficiales.

ware (wâr) s. *(articles)* artículos; *(ceramics)* cerámica ♦ pl. mercancías.

ware·house ('hous') I. s. almacén *m* II. tr. almacenar.

war·fare (wôr'fâr') s. guerra.

war·head (:hĕd') s. ojiva de proyectil.

war-horse (:hôrs') s. caballo de guerra; FAM. veterano.

war·like (:līk') adj. belicoso; *(of war)* guerrero.

war·lock (wôr'lŏk') s. brujo.

war·lord (wôr'lôrd') s. jefe *m* militar.

warm (wôrm) I. adj. tibio, caliente; *(weather)* cálido, caluroso; *(clothing)* que mantiene abrigado; *(enthusiastic)* entusiasta; *(cordial)* cordial; *(loving)* cariñoso; *(fresh)* fresco; FAM. *(dangerous)* peligroso ♦ **to be w.** *(weather)* hacer calor; *(person)* tener calor; *(thing)* estar caliente II. tr. calentar; *(to cheer)* alegrar ♦ **to w. up** *(food)* recalentar; *(body)* hacer entrar en calor; *(debate)* avivar —intr. calentarse.

warm-blood·ed (:blŭd'ĭd) adj. de sangre caliente; FIG. ardiente.

warm-heart·ed (:här'tĭd) adj. cariñoso.

war·mon·ger (wôr'mŭng'gər) s. belicista *mf.*

warmth (wôrmth) s. calor *m; (affection)* afecto; *(ardor)* ardor *m.*

warm-up (wôrm'ŭp') s. DEP. calentamiento.

warn (wôrn) tr. & intr. advertir.

warn·ing (wôr'nĭng) I. s. advertencia; *(signal)* señal *f; (advice)* aviso ♦ **without w.** de repente II. adj. de advertencia; *(device)* de alarma.

warp (wôrp) I. tr. alabear, deformar; *(to pervert)* pervertir; *(to twist)* torcer —intr. deformarse, torcerse; *(to deviate)* pervertirse II. s. alabeo, deformación *f; (perversion)* perversión *f;* TEJ. urdimbre *f.*

war·path (wôr'păth') s. ♦ **to be on the w.** estar propenso a pelear.

war·plane (:plān') s. avión *m* de guerra.

war·rant (wôr'ənt) I. s. autorización *f; (guarantee)* garantía; *(grounds)* justificación *f; (search, arrest)* orden *f* judicial II. tr. garantizar; *(to justify)* justificar; *(to authorize)* autorizar.

war·ran·tor (:ən-tər, :tôr') s. garante *mf.*

war·ran·ty (:tē) s. garantía; *(grounds)* justificación *f; (authorization)* autorización *f.*

war·ren (wôr'ən) s. conejera.

war·ri·or (wôr'ē-ər) s. guerrero.

war·ship (wôr'shĭp') s. buque *m* de guerra.

wart (wôrt) s. verruga ♦ **w. hog** jabalí verrugoso.

war·time (wôr'tīm') s. época de guerra.

war·y (wâr'ē) adj. **-i-** *(guarded)* cauteloso; *(watchful)* cuidadoso.

was (wŏz, wŭz, wəz) pret. de **be.**

wash (wŏsh) I. tr. lavar; *(to moisten)* mojar; *(to lap)* bañar; *(wound, eyes)* bañar; *(to erode)* erosionar ♦ **to w. away** o **out** *(grease, stains)* quitar; *(to carry away)* llevarse • **w. down** limpiar; *(to gulp down)* tragar; *(with wine, beer)* rociar • **to w. off** quitar —intr. lavarse; *(clothes)* lavar ropa ♦ **to w. away** derrumbarse • **to w. off** salir en el lavado • **to w. out** *(colors)* desteñirse; *(to fail)* fracasar • **to w. up** lavarse; *(the dishes)* lavar los platos II. s. lavado; *(clothes)* ropa para lavar; *(waste liquid)* desperdicio; *(coating)* baño; *(rush of water)* golpe *m*

de agua; *(sound of water)* rumor *m* ♦ **it will all come out in the w.** al final todo se arreglará.
wash·a·ble ('ə-bəl) adj. lavable.
wash-and-wear (:ən-wâr') adj. que no se plancha.
wash·ba·sin (:bā'sĭn) s. lavabo.
wash·board (:bôrd') s. tabla de lavar.
wash·bowl (:bōl') s. lavabo.
wash·cloth (:klôth') s. [pl. **s**] toallita para lavarse.
wash·day (:dā') s. día *m* para lavar.
washed-out (wŏsht'out') adj. descolorido; *(exhausted)* agotado.
washed-up (:ŭp') adj. acabado.
wash·er (wŏsh'ər) s. lavador *m;* *(disc)* arandela; *(machine)* máquina de lavar.
wash·er·wom·an (:wŏŏm'ən) s. [pl. **-women**] lavandera.
wash·ing (wŏsh'ĭng) s. lavado; *(clothes to be done)* ropa para lavar; *(residue)* residuo.
wash·out (:out') s. derrubio; *(failure)* fracaso.
wash·room (:rŏŏm') s. baño.
wash·stand (:stănd') s. lavabo.
wash·tub (:tŭb') s. tina de lavar.
wasp (wŏsp) s. avispa.
wasp·ish (wŏs'pĭsh) adj. irascible.
was·sail (wŏs'əl) s. brindis *m*.
wast·age (wā'stĭj) s. desperdicio.
waste (wāst) I. tr. *(money)* despilfarrar; *(time)* perder; *(talent)* desperdiciar; *(to exhaust)* agotar; JER. *(to kill)* matar —intr. *(goods)* desperdiciarse; *(time)* perderse; *(strength, vigor)* debilitarse ♦ **to w. away** consumirse II. s. despilfarro; *(wastage)* desperdicios; *(of time, energy)* pérdida; *(residue)* residuos; *(garbage)* basura ♦ **to go to w.** desperdiciarse III. adj. desperdiciado; *(residual)* residual.
waste·bas·ket (:băs'kĭt) s. cesto de papeles.
wast·ed (wā'stĭd) adj. desperdiciado; *(superfluous)* innecesario; JER. *(stoned)* drogado.
waste·ful (wāst'fəl) adj. despilfarrador.
waste·land (:lănd') s. páramo.
wast·rel (wā'strəl) s. derrochador *m;* *(idler)* vagabundo.
watch (wŏch) I. intr. mirar; *(to keep vigil)* vigilar ♦ **to w. out** tener cuidado —tr. mirar; *(to see)* ver; *(to pay attention to)* fijarse en; *(to guard)* vigilar; *(to take care of)* cuidar; *(to stand vigil over)* velar; *(to be careful with)* tener cuidado con ♦ **to w. for** esperar • **to w. one's step** tener cuidado • **to w. over** vigilar II. s. *(timepiece)* reloj *m;* *(act)* vigilia, vela; *(group of persons)* ronda, guardia; MIL. centinela *m;* *(lookout)* vigía *m* ♦ **to keep w.** estar de guardia.
watch·dog ('dôg') s. perro guardián; FIG. guardián *m*.
watch·ful (:fəl) adj. alerta, vigilante.
watch·mak·er (:mā'kər) s. relojero.
watch·man (:mən) s. [pl. **-men**] sereno.
watch·tow·er (:tou'ər) s. atalaya, garita.
watch·word (:wûrd') s. contraseña.
wa·ter (wŏ'tər) I. s. agua; *(urine)* orina; *(of a fabric)* aguas ♦ **like w.** en gran abundancia • **to be in deep** *o* **hot w.** estar en un gran aprieto • **to hold w.** ser lógico • **to keep one's head above w.** mantenerse a flote • **to pass w.** orinar • **to throw cold w.** on echar un jarro de agua fría sobre • **w. bed** cama con colchón de agua • **w. buffalo** búfalo de India • **w. closet** inodoro, wáter • **w. color** acuarela • **w. cooler** refrigerador de agua • **w. hole** charco • **w. lily**

ninfea II. tr. *(a garden)* regar; *(animals)* abrevar; *(to make wet)* mojar; *(to dilute)* diluir ♦ **to w. down** *(a drink)* aguar; FIG. suavizar, moderar —intr. *(eyes)* llorar ♦ **to make one's mouth w.** hacérsele agua la boca a uno.
wa·ter·borne (:bôrn') adj. flotante.
wa·ter·col·or (:kŭl'ər) adj. & s. (de) acuarela.
wa·ter·course (:kôrs') s. vía navegable; *(channel)* canal *m*.
wa·ter·cress (:krĕs') s. berro, mastuerzo.
wa·ter·fall (:fôl') s. catarata, cascada.
wa·ter·fowl (:foul') s. [pl. inv. *o* **s**] ave acuática.
wa·ter·front (:frŭnt') s. *(land)* costanera; *(dock zone)* muelles *m*.
wa·ter·ing (:ĭng) I. s. riego II. adj. de riego; *(eyes)* lloroso ♦ **w. can** regadera • **w. hole** *(hole)* charco; *(bar)* bar.
wa·ter·logged (:lôgd') adj. saturado de agua.
wa·ter·loo (wŏ'tər-lŏō') s. ♦ **to meet one's w.** sufrir una derrota terminante.
wa·ter·mark (wŏ'tər-märk') s. marca de nivel de agua; *(in paper)* marca de agua.
wa·ter·mel·on (:mĕl'ən) s. sandía.
wa·ter·pow·er (:pou'ər) s. energía hidráulica.
wa·ter·proof (:prŏōf') I. adj. impermeable II. tr. impermeabilizar.
wa·ter·re·pel·lent (:rĭ-pĕl'ənt) adj. que repele el agua.
wa·ter·re·sis·tant (:rĭ-zĭs'tənt) adj. resistente al agua.
wa·ter·shed (:shĕd') s. línea divisoria; *(area)* cuenca; *(critical point)* momento crítico.
wa·ter·side (:sīd') s. costa, ribera.
wa·ter·ski (:skē') I. intr. hacer esquí acuático II. s. [pl. inv. *o* **s**] esquí acuático.
wa·ter·spout (:spout') s. *(tornado)* tromba marina; *(pipe)* boquilla (de surtidor).
wa·ter·tight (:tīt') adj. a prueba de agua; *(irrefutable)* irrefutable.
wa·ter·way (:wā') s. vía fluvial.
wa·ter·works (:wûrks') s. s.inv. sistema *m* de abastecimiento de agua; JER. *(tears)* lágrimas.
wa·ter·y (wŏ'tə-rē) adj. -i- acuoso; *(liquid)* líquido; *(diluted)* aguado; *(without force)* sin fuerza.
watt (wŏt) s. vatio, watt *m*.
watt·age ('ĭj) s. potencia en vatios.
wat·tle (wŏt'l) s. *(branches)* zarzo, estera; ZOOL. carnosidad *f*.
wave (wāv) I. intr. ondear; *(with the hand)* agitar la mano —tr. agitar; *(hair)* ondular ♦ **to w. good-bye** decir adiós II. s. ola; *(on a surface, hair)* ondulación *f*; *(of a hand)* movimiento; *(gesture)* gesto, ademán *m*; *(series)* serie *f*; *(of people)* oleadas; FÍS., RAD. onda.
wave·band (:bănd') s. banda de ondas.
wave·length (:lĕngth') s. longitud *f* de onda ♦ **to be on the same w.** estar en la misma onda.
wa·ver (wā'vər) I. intr. oscilar; *(to vacillate)* vacilar II. s. oscilación *f*; *(vacillation)* vacilación *f*.
wav·y (wā'vē) adj. -i- ondulante, onduloso; *(curly)* ondulado.
wax[1] (wăks) I. s. cera ♦ **w. paper** papel encerado II. tr. encerar.
wax[2] intr. *(to increase)* crecer.
wax·en (wăk'sən) adj. céreo, ceroso.
wax·work (wăks'wûrk') s. figura de cera ♦ pl. museo de cera.
wax·y (wăk'sē) adj. -i- ceroso; *(made of wax)* céreo.
way (wā) I. s. *(street)* camino; *(passage)* pasaje

m; (direction) dirección *f; (method)* manera, modo; *(means)* método; *(mode)* estilo; *(aspect)* aspecto; *(talent)* facilidad *f; (condition)* situación *f; (behavior)* manera de ser ♦ **all the w.** hasta el final; *(completely)* en todo • **by the w.** a propósito • **by w. of** pasando por; *(as a means of)* a manera de • **in a big, small w.** en gran, pequeña escala • **in a w.** en cierto modo • **in every w.** en todos los aspectos • **in my own w.** a mi manera • **(in) no w.** de ninguna manera • **on the w.** en camino • **out of the w.** lejano • **right of w.** derecho de paso • **that w.** por allí; *(manner)* así • **the other w. around** al contrario • **this w.** por aquí; *(thus)* así • **to be in the w.** estar en el camino • **to be set in one's ways** estar acostumbrado a la forma de uno • **to clear the w.** despejar el camino • **to come one's w.** FAM. caerle a uno • **to feel one's w.** tantear el camino • **to get one's w.** salirse con la suya • **to get out of the w.** quitar(se) de en medio • **to get under w.** *(to progress)* progresar; *(to set out)* ponerse en camino; *(to weigh anchor)* zarpar • **to give w.** *(to be replaced by)* ceder el paso a; *(to give in to)* ceder ante; *(despair)* entregarse a • **to go out of one's w.** tomarse la molestia de • **to have a w. with** tener el don de • **to lead the w.** enseñar el camino • **to look the other w.** hacer la vista gorda • **to make one's w.** abrirse paso • **to mend one's ways** cambiar de vida • **to pave the w. for** preparar el terreno para • **to stand in the w. of** obstaculizar • **to take the easy w. out** tomar el camino más fácil • **w. down** bajada • **w. in** entrada • **w. out** salida; *(escape)* escapatoria • **w. up** subida • **ways and means** medios y arbitrios • **which w.?** ¿por dónde? **II.** adv. allá.

way·bill (wā′bĭl′) s. COM. itinerario.

way·far·er (wā′fâr′ər) s. caminante *m.*

way·lay (wā′lā′) tr. **-laid** *(to lie in wait)* acechar; *(to accost)* abordar; *(to delay)* demorar.

way·side (wā′sīd′) s. borde *m* del camino.

way·ward (wā′wərd) adj. *(naughty)* desobediente; *(unpredictable)* caprichoso.

we (wē) pron. nosotros, nosotras.

weak (wēk) adj. débil; *(fragile)* frágil; *(lacking skill)* flojo; *(unconvincing)* poco convincente.

weak·en (wē′kən) tr. & intr. debilitar(se).

weak-kneed (wēk′nēd′) adj. tímido.

weak·ling (wēk′lĭng) s. enclenque *m;* FIG. tímido.

weak·ly (:lē) adj. **-i-** enclenque.

weak·ness (:nĭs) s. debilidad *f.*

weal[1] (wēl) s. *(welfare)* bienestar *m* general.

weal[2] s. *(welt)* cardenal *f,* roncha.

wealth (wĕlth) s. *(riches)* riqueza; *(profusion)* abundancia; ECON. caudal *m.*

wealth·y (wĕl′thē) adj. **-i-** rico.

wean (wēn) tr. destetar ♦ **to w. oneself of** dejar de.

weap·on (wĕp′ən) s. arma.

weap·on·ry (:rē) s. armamento, armas.

wear (wâr) **I.** tr. **wore, worn** llevar; *(to damage)* deteriorar; *(to exhaust)* agotar ♦ **to w. away** desgastar • **to w. down** *(to damage)* desgastar; *(to exhaust)* agotar • **to w. off** gastar • **to w. out** *(to consume)* consumir; *(to tire)* cansar —intr. *(to last)* durar; *(to deteriorate)* desgastarse ♦ **to w. off** disiparse • **to w. thin** disminuir • **to w. out** gastarse **II.** s. uso; *(clothing)* ropa; *(damage)* desgaste *m;* *(durability)* durabilidad *f* ♦ **w. and tear** deterioro.

wea·ried (wîr′ēd) adj. fatigado.

wea·ri·some (:ē-səm) adj. tedioso.

wea·ry (wîr′ē) **I.** adj. **-i-** fatigado **II.** tr. & intr. fatigar(se); *(to annoy)* fastidiar(se).

wea·sel (wē′zəl) **I.** s. ZOOL. comadreja; JER. chivato **II.** intr. ser evasivo.

weath·er (wĕth′ər) **I.** s. tiempo; *(bad)* mal tiempo ♦ **under the w.** FAM. indispuesto; *(drunk)* borracho **II.** tr. *(to expose)* exponer a la intemperie; *(to outride)* aguantar —intr. deteriorarse; *(the skin)* curtirse; *(wood)* curarse; *(to resist)* resistir **III.** adj. meteorológico ♦ **w. stripping** burlete • **w. vane** veleta.

weath·er-beat·en (:bēt′n) adj. deteriorado por la intemperie.

weath·ered (wĕth′ərd) adj. curtido por la intemperie.

weath·er·man (:ər-măn′) s. [pl. **-men**] FAM. meteorólogo.

weath·er·proof (:prōof′) **I.** adj. impermeable **II.** tr. impermeabilizar.

weave (wēv) **I.** tr. **wove, woven** tejer; *(to interlace)* entrelazar —intr. tejer; *(to become interlaced)* entrelazarse; *(through traffic)* zigzaguear **II.** s. tejido.

weav·er (wē′vər) s. tejedor *m.*

web (wĕb) s. tejido, tela; *(of a spider)* telaraña; *(net)* red *f; (of lies)* sarta; ANAT. membrana.

webbed (wĕbd) o **web-foot·ed** (wĕb′fŏŏt′ĭd) adj. palmeado.

wed (wĕd) tr. **-dded, wed(ded), -dd-** casarse con; FIG. unir —intr. casarse.

wed·ding (:ĭng) **I.** s. boda, casamiento; *(anniversary)* bodas; FIG. enlace *m,* unión *f* **II.** adj. de boda, nupcial.

wedge (wĕj) **I.** s. cuña; *(slice)* trozo; *(for securing)* calce *m* **II.** tr. *(to split)* partir; *(to fix in place)* calzar; FIG. *(to crowd)* apretar.

wed·lock (wĕd′lŏk′) s. matrimonio ♦ **out of w.** ilegítimo.

Wednes·day (wĕnz′dē) s. miércoles *m.*

wee (wē) adj. pequeñito.

weed[1] (wēd) **I.** s. mala hierba, maleza **II.** tr. desherbar ♦ **to w. out** extirpar, eliminar —intr. arrancar la maleza.

weed[2] s. ♦ pl. ropa de luto de una viuda.

week (wēk) s. semana.

week·day (′dā) s. día *m* de trabajo.

week·end (:ĕnd′) **I.** s. fin *m* de semana **II.** intr. pasar el fin de semana.

week·ly (:lē) **I.** adj. & adv. semanal(mente) **II.** s. semanario.

weep (wēp) **I.** tr. **wept** llorar; *(to lament)* lamentar —intr. llorar; *(to grieve)* dolerse; *(to drip)* gotear **II.** s. ♦ pl. llanto.

weep·ing (wē′pĭng) adj. lloroso ♦ **w. willow** sauce llorón.

wee·vil (wē′vəl) s. gorgojo, mordihuí *m.*

weft (wĕft) s. trama; *(fabric)* tela tejida.

weigh (wā) tr. pesar; *(anchor)* levar ♦ **to w. down** sobrecargar; *(to oppress)* abrumar —intr. pesar.

weight (wāt) **I.** s. peso; *(measured heaviness)* pesa; *(authority)* autoridad *f* ♦ **to gain** o **put on w.** engordar • **to lose w.** adelgazar • **to pull one's w.** hacer su parte • **to throw one's w. around** darse importancia **II.** tr. añadir peso a; *(to hold down)* sujetar con un peso; *(to burden)* cargar; *(statistically)* ponderar.

weight·less (′lĭs) adj. sin peso, ingrávido.

weight·lift·ing (:lĭf′tĭng) s. levantamiento de pesas.

weight·y (wā′tē) adj. **-i-** *(heavy)* pesado; *(burdensome)* gravoso.

weird (wîrd) adj. misterioso.

weird·o (wîr'dō) s. [pl. **es**] JER. persona estrafalaria.

wel·come (wĕl'kəm) **I.** adj. bienvenido; *(agreeable)* agradable ♦ **you're w.!** ¡no hay de qué!, ¡de nada! • **you are w. to it** está a su disposición **II.** s. saludo de bienvenida **III.** tr. dar la bienvenida a; *(to accept)* aceptar con beneplácito **IV.** interj. ¡bienvenido!

weld (wĕld) **I.** tr. soldar; FIG. unir, juntar —intr. soldarse **II.** s. soldadura.

weld·er (wĕl'dər) s. soldador *m.*

wel·fare (wĕl'fâr') s. bienestar *m; (benefits)* asistencia social.

well[1] **I.** s. pozo; *(spring)* fuente *f; (for stairs)* caja **II.** intr. manar —tr. verter.

well[2] (wĕl) **better, best I.** adv. bien ♦ **as w.** también • **as w. as** además de; *(just as)* así como • **that is just as w.** es mejor así • **to do w.** prosperar • **to do w. by** tratar bien • **w. done!** ¡bien hecho! **II.** adj. bien ♦ **to get w.** mejorar • **w. and good** tanto mejor **III.** interj. ¡bueno!

well-ap·point·ed (' ə-poin'tĭd) adj. bien amueblado.

well-bal·anced (:băl'ənst) adj. bien equilibrado.

well-be·haved (:bĭ-hāvd') adj. bien educado.

well-be·ing ('bē'ĭng) s. bienestar *m.*

well-born ('bôrn') adj. bien nacido.

well-bred (:brĕd') adj. bien criado.

well-de·fined ('dĭ-fīnd') adj. bien definido.

well-dis·posed (:dĭ-spōzd') adj. bien dispuesto.

well-done ('dŭn') adj. bien hecho; *(cooked)* bien cocido.

well-fixed (:fĭkst') adj. FAM. acomodado.

well-found·ed (:foun'dĭd) adj. bien fundado.

well-groomed (:grōmd') adj. bien arreglado.

well-ground·ed (:groun'dĭd) adj. bien fundado.

well·head (wĕl'hĕd') s. manantial *m.*

well-heeled (wĕl'hēld') adj. JER. rico.

well-in·ten·tioned ('ĭn-tĕn'shənd) adj. bien intencionado.

well-known ('nōn') adj. bien conocido.

well-man·nered (:măn'ərd) adj. de buenos modales.

well-mean·ing (:mē'nĭng) adj. bien intencionado.

well-meant (:mĕnt') adj. honesto.

well-off (:ôf') adj. acomodado.

well-read (:rĕd') adj. leído, ilustrado.

well-round·ed (:roun'dĭd) adj. acabado.

well-spo·ken (:spō'kən) adj. bienhablado.

well·spring (wĕl'sprĭng') s. fuente *f.*

well-thought-of (wĕl-thôt'ŭv') adj. de buena reputación.

well-timed ('tīmd') adj. oportuno.

well-to-do (' tə-dō') adj. próspero.

well-turned ('tûrnd') adj. bien torneado; *(sentence)* bien construido.

well-wish·er (:wĭsh'ər) s. persona que desea el bien de otra.

well-worn (:wôrn') adj. *(worn-out)* desgastado; *(hackneyed)* trillado.

welsh (wĕlsh, wĕlch) intr. ♦ **to w. on** JER. estafar.

welt (wĕlt) **I.** s. *(of a shoe)* vira; *(cord)* ribete *m; (injury)* verdugón *m,* roncha **II.** tr. levantar un verdugón en; COST. ribetear.

wel·ter (wĕl'tər) **I.** intr. revolcarse; *(the sea)* hincharse **II.** s. confusión *f.*

wel·ter·weight (:wāt') s. welter *m.*

wench (wĕnch) s. *(girl)* moza; *(servant)* criada; *(prostitute)* prostituta.

wend (wĕnd) tr. ♦ **to w.** one's way dirigirse a.

went (wĕnt) cf. **go.**

wept (wĕpt) cf. **weep.**

were (wûr) pret. de **be.**

were·wolf (wîr'wŏolf') s. [pl. **-ves**] hombre lobo.

west (wĕst) **I.** s. oeste *m,* occidente *m* **II.** adj. del oeste, occidental **III.** adv. al oeste.

west·bound ('bound') adj. con rumbo al oeste.

west·ern (wĕs'tərn) **I.** adj. occidental, del oeste **II.** s. película del oeste.

west·ern·er (:tər-nər) s. habitante *m* del oeste.

west·ern·ize (:nīz') tr. occidentalizar.

west·ward (wĕst'wərd) adv. hacia el oeste.

wet (wĕt) adj. **-tt-** mojado; *(rainy)* lluvioso; *(paint)* fresco ♦ **all w.** JER. totalmente equivocado • **soaking w.** calado hasta los huesos • **to be w. behind the ears** ser un imberbe • **w. blanket** FAM. aguafiestas • **w. nurse** nodriza **II.** s. mojadura **III.** tr. **wet(ted), -tting** mojar ♦ **to w.** one's whistle FAM. beber un trago —intr. mojarse.

wet·land ('lănd') s. tierra húmeda.

whack (hwăk) FAM. **I.** tr. pegar **II.** s. golpe *m* fuerte; *(attempt)* intento ♦ **out of w.** averiado.

whale[1] (hwāl) s. ZOOL. ballena.

whale[2] tr. zurrar —intr. vapulear.

whale·boat (:bōt') s. bote ballenero.

whale·bone (:bōn') s. barba de ballena.

whal·er (hwā'lər) s. ballenero.

wham (hwăm) **I.** s. *(blow)* golpe *m* fuerte; *(thud)* ruido sordo **II.** tr. **-mm-** golpear con fuerza resonante.

wham·my (hwăm'ē) s. FAM. hechizo.

wharf (hwôrf) s. [pl. **s** o **-ves**] muelle *m.*

wharf·age (hwôr'fĭj) s. muellaje *m.*

what (hwŏt, hwŭt, hwət) **I.** pron. interrog. qué; *(which)* cuál ♦ **so w.?** ¿y qué? • **w. for?** ¿para qué? • **w. of it?** ¿y eso qué importa? **II.** pron. rel. el que ♦ **to know what's w.** estar bien enterado • **w. is more** más aún • **w. it takes** lo que es necesario **III.** adj. interrog. qué; *(which)* cuál **IV.** adj. rel. que **V.** adv. cuánto, cómo **VI.** interj. ¡cómo!

what·ev·er (-ĕv'ər) **I.** pron. *(anything that)* lo que; *(all of what)* todo lo que; *(no matter what)* cualquier cosa; FAM. qué <w. does he mean? ¿qué quiere decir?> **II.** adj. *(any)* cualquiera que; *(of any kind at all)* de ninguna clase.

what·not ('nŏt') s. cualquier cosa.

what·so·ev·er ('sō-ĕv'ər) var. de **whatever.**

wheat (hwēt) s. trigo.

whee·dle (hwēd'l) tr. engatusar —intr. lisonjear.

wheel (hwēl) **I.** s. rueda; *(steering)* volante *m; (of ship)* timón *m; (of potter)* torno; FAM. bicicleta; *(of turning)* vuelta ♦ **fifth w.** persona superflua • **to be behind** o **at the w.** manejar el coche; *(in charge)* dirigir • **to grease the wheels** FAM. dar coimas ♦ pl. TÉC. engranaje; JER. *(car)* automóvil; *(forces)* mecanismos **II.** tr. *(to carry)* llevar sobre ruedas; *(to rotate)* hacer rodar —intr. *(to rotate)* girar; *(to roll)* rodar; *(to pivot)* dar una vuelta.

wheel·bar·row ('băr'ō) s. carretilla.

wheel·chair (hwēl'châr') s. silla de ruedas.

wheeled (hwēld) adj. que tiene ruedas.

wheel·er-deal·er (hwē'lər-dē'lər) s. FAM. persona que anda en tramoyas.

wheeze (hwēz) I. intr. respirar con dificultad II. s. resuello ronco.

wheez·y (hwē'zē) adj. -i- jadeante.

whelp (hwĕlp) I. s. ZOOL. cachorro; FIG. granuja II. tr. & intr. parir.

when (hwĕn) I. adv. cuándo II. conj. cuando; *(as soon as)* al, en cuanto; *(if)* si III. pron. cuándo IV. s. fecha, momento.

whence (hwĕns) I. adv. de dónde II. conj. de donde, de lo cual.

when·ev·er (hwĕn-ĕv'ər) adv. & conj. cuando quiera (que); *(when)* cuando; *(every time that)* siempre que.

where (hwâr) I. adv. dónde; *(from where)* de dónde; *(to where)* adónde II. conj. donde, en donde; *(to where)* a donde III. s. lugar *m*.

where·a·bouts ('ə-bouts') I. adv. dónde, por dónde II. s. paradero, ubicación *f*.

where·as (-ăz') conj. *(since)* visto que; *(while)* mientras (que).

where·at (-ăt') conj. a lo cual, con lo cual.

where·by (-bī') conj. por o según el cual.

where·fore ('fôr') I. adv. por qué II. s. porqué *m*.

where·in (-ĭn') I. adv. en dónde II. conj. donde, en que.

where·of (-ŏv') conj. *(of what)* de que, de lo que; *(of which, whom)* del que.

where·to ('tŏŏ') I. adv. adónde II. conj. a lo que.

where·up·on (-ə-pŏn') conj. con lo cual.

wher·ev·er (-ĕv'ər) I. adv. dondequiera que; FAM. dónde diablos II. conj. dondequiera que.

where·with ('wĭth') conj. con que, con lo cual.

where·with·al (-wĭth-ôl') s. recursos.

whet (hwĕt) tr. -tt- *(to sharpen)* afilar; *(appetite)* abrir; *(curiosity)* estimular.

wheth·er (hwĕth'ər) conj. *(if)* si; *(for alternatives)* sea . . . o ♦ **w. or not** de todos modos.

whet·stone (hwĕt'stōn') s. piedra de afilar.

whew (hwŏŏ, hyŏŏ) interj. ¡vaya!

whey (hwā) s. suero de la leche.

which (hwĭch) I. pron. interrog. cuál II. pron. rel. que *<take those w. are yours* toma aquellos que son tuyos>; el cual *<my house, w. is small and old* mi casa, la cual es pequeña y vieja>; lo cual, lo que *<he acted very rudely, w. did not surprise me* se portó muy groseramente, lo que no me sorprendió>; el que, el cual *<the subject on w. he spoke* el tema sobre el cual él habló> III. adj. interrog. qué, cuál ♦ **w. one(s)?** ¿cuál(es)? ♦ **w. way?** ¿por dónde? IV. adj. rel. cuyo; *(any)* cualquier.

which·ev·er ('ĕv'ər) I. pron. cualquiera; *(any one)* el que, lo que II. adj. cualquier, cualquiera que sea.

whiff (hwĭf) I. s. soplo; *(smell)* olor *m*; *(of smoke)* bocanada II. intr. soplar —tr. exhalar.

while (hwīl) I. s. rato, tiempo ♦ **once in a w.** de vez en cuando • **to be worth (one's) w.** valer la pena II. conj. *(as long as)* mientras (que); *(although)* aunque, si bien III. tr. pasar.

whim (hwĭm) s. capricho, antojo.

whim·per (hwĭm'pər) I. intr. lloriquear II. s. gemido, quejido.

whim·si·cal (-zĭ-kəl) adj. *(capricious)* caprichoso; *(fanciful)* extravagante.

whim·s(e)y (-zē) s. capricho.

whine (hwīn) I. intr. gimotear; *(to complain)* quejarse II. s. gimoteo; *(complaint)* quejido.

whin·ny (hwĭn'ē) I. intr. relinchar II. s. relin-

cho.

whip (hwĭp) I. tr. -t- o -pped, -pping azotar; *(cream, eggs)* batir; FAM. *(to outdo)* dar una paliza a ♦ **to w. out** sacar de repente • **to w. up** estimular; FAM. preparar rápidamente —intr. *(to dart)* precipitarse; *(to snap about)* restallar II. s. azote *m*; *(dessert)* batido.

whip·lash ('lăsh') s. latigazo.

whip·per·snap·per (hwĭp'ər-snăp'ər) s. mequetrefe *m*.

whip·pet (hwĭp'ĭt) s. lebrel *m*.

whip·poor·will (hwĭp'ər-wĭl') s. chotacabras *m*.

whir (hwûr) I. intr. -rr- zumbar II. s. zumbido.

whirl (hwûrl) I. intr. *(to spin)* dar vueltas; *(to turn)* dar una vuelta; *(dust, water)* arremolinarse —tr. hacer girar II. s. giro; *(of dust, water)* remolino; *(tumult)* tumulto; *(of events)* torbellino; *(dizziness)* vértigo ♦ **to give it a w.** FAM. intentar hacerlo.

whirl·i·gig ('lĭ-gĭg') s. *(toy)* molinete *m*; *(carousel)* tiovivo; *(spinning thing)* torbellino.

whirl·pool (hwûrl'pŏŏl') s. remolino.

whirl·wind (-wĭnd') I. s. torbellino, remolino II. adj. intenso y rápido.

whirl·y·bird (-lē-bûrd') s. JER. helicóptero.

whisk (hwĭsk) I. tr. sacudir; CUL. batir —intr. moverse rápidamente ♦ **to w. past** pasar a toda velocidad II. s. movimiento rápido; *(whisk-broom)* cepillo de ropa; CUL. batidor *m*.

whisk·broom ('brŏŏm') s. cepillo de ropa.

whisk·er (hwĭs'kər) s. pelo ♦ pl. *(of man)* barbas; *(of animal)* bigotes.

whis·k(e)y (hwĭs'kē) s. whisky *m*.

whis·per (hwĭs'pər) I. s. susurro II. intr. susurrar —tr. decir en secreto.

➤**whis·tle** (hwĭs'əl) I. intr. silbar; *(with a device)* pitar; *(birds)* piar ♦ **to w. in the dark** intentar cobrar ánimo —tr. silbar II. s. *(instrument)* pito, silbato; *(act, sound)* silbido, pitido.

whit (hwĭt) s. pizca.

white (hwīt) I. s. blanco; *(of an egg)* clara II. adj. blanco; *(pale)* pálido; *(pure)* puro ♦ **as w. as a sheet** o **ghost** blanco como el papel • **w. lie** mentirilla • **w. water** agua espumosa.

white·col·lar (kŏl'ər) adj. de oficina.

white·fish (-fĭsh') s. [pl. inv. o **es**] pescado blanco.

white·hot (-hŏt') adj. *(fervid)* candente; FÍS. al rojo blanco.

whit·en (-n) tr. & intr. blanquear(se).

white·wall tire (-wôl') s. AUTO. neumático de banda blanca.

white·wash (-wŏsh') I. s. cal *f*; *(concealing)* encubrimiento II. tr. enjalbegar; FIG. encubrir.

whith·er (hwĭth'ər) adv. *(where)* adónde; *(to which)* adonde; *(wherever)* dondequiera.

whit·tle (hwĭt'l) tr. *(to carve)* tallar; *(to reduce)* reducir —intr. tallar.

whiz(z) (hwĭz) I. intr. -zz- zumbar II. s. [pl. -zes] zumbido ♦ **to be a w.** FAM. ser un as.

who (hŏŏ) I. pron. interrog. quién II. pron. rel. quien; que *<the man w. came to see you* el hombre que vino a verte>; el cual *<my parents, w. built this business* mis padres, los cuales establecieron este negocio>.

whoa (hwō) interj. ¡jo!, ¡cho!

who·dun·it (hŏŏ-dŭn'ĭt) s. FAM. novela o película policial.

who·ev·er (hŏŏ-ĕv'ər) pron. quienquiera que; *(the one who)* el que, quien; FAM. ¿quién diablos?

whole (hōl) I. adj. entero, todo; *(total)* total; *(healthy)* sano; *(undamaged)* intacto ♦ **a w. lot of** muchísimo • **w. note** redonda II. s. todo, totalidad *f*; *(complete entity)* suma ♦ **as a w.** en conjunto • **on the w.** en general III. adv. FAM. completamente.

whole·heart·ed (:här'tĭd) adj. incondicional.

whole·ness (:nĭs) s. integridad *f*.

whole·sale (:sāl') I. s. venta al por mayor II. adj. al por mayor; *(general)* general III. adv. al por mayor; *(extensively)* en general IV. tr. & intr. vender(se) al por mayor.

whole·some (:səm) adj. sano.

whole·wheat (:hwēt') adj. de trigo entero.

whom (hōōm) I. pron. interrog. **a quién** <*w. did you see?* ¿a quién viste?>; de quién <*from w. did you get it?* ¿de quién lo recibiste?> II. pron. rel. que, quien.

whom·ev·er (-ĕv'ər) pron. a quienquiera.

whom·so·ev·er (:sō-ĕv'ər) var. de *whomever*.

whoop (hōōp, hwōōp) I. s. *(shout)* grito; *(bird's cry)* graznido; *(cough)* estertor *m* de la tos ferina ♦ **whooping cough** tos ferina *o* convulsa • **whooping crane** grulla blanca II. intr. gritar; *(to hoot)* graznar; *(to cough)* toser ahogándose ♦ **to w. it up** armar jaleo.

whoops (hwōōps, hwōōps) interj. ¡epa!

whoosh (hwōōsh, hwōōsh) I. intr. pasar como un silbido II. s. silbido.

whop (hwŏp) I. tr. **-pp-** derrotar II. s. golpe *m*.

whop·per ('ər) s. *(something big)* cosa enorme; *(lie)* mentira colosal.

whop·ping (:ĭng) adj. FAM. enorme.

whore (hôr) s. prostituta.

whore·house ('hous') s. prostíbulo.

whorl (hwôrl, hwûrl) s. espiral *f*; BOT. verticilo.

whose (hōōz) I. pron. & adj. interrog. de quién II. pron. rel. cuyo.

why (hwī) I. adv. por qué, para qué II. conj. por que, por lo que III. s. [pl. **s**] (la) causa, (el) porqué IV. interj. ¡vaya!, ¡toma!

wick (wĭk) s. mecha.

wick·ed (wĭk'ĭd) adj. malvado; *(mischievous)* travieso; *(offensive)* desagradable.

wick·ed·ness (:nĭs) s. maldad *f*.

wick·er (wĭk'ər) I. s. mimbre *m*; *(wickerwork)* artículos de mimbre II. adj. de mimbre.

wick·et (wĭk'ĭt) s. *(small gate)* portillo; *(small window)* ventanilla.

wide (wīd) I. adj. ancho; *(in width)* de ancho; *(extensive)* extenso; *(large)* amplio; *(eyes)* muy abiertos ♦ **w. of the mark** lejos del blanco II. adv. *(completely)* de par en par; *(to the full extent)* bien abierto ♦ **far and w.** por todas partes • **w. open** de par en par.

wide-an·gle lens ('ăng'gəl) s. objetivo gran angular.

wide-a·wake ('ə-wāk') adj. despierto.

wide-eyed ('īd') adj. con los ojos muy abiertos; *(innocent)* inocente.

wide·ly (:lē) adv. *(very)* muy; *(much)* mucho; *(extensively)* extensamente.

wid·en (:n) tr. & intr. ensanchar(se).

wide-o·pen (:ō'pən) adj. abierto de par en par.

wide·spread (:sprĕd') adj. extendido; *(prevalent)* general.

wid·ow (wĭd'ō) I. s. viuda II. tr. dejar viuda ♦ **to be widowed** quedar viuda.

wid·ow·er (:ər) s. viudo.

width (wĭdth) s. anchura, ancho.

wield (wēld) tr. *(weapon)* blandir; *(tool)* mane-

jar; *(influence)* ejercer.

wie·ner (wē'nər) s. salchicha de Viena.

wife (wīf) s. [pl. **-ves**] esposa, mujer *f*.

wig (wĭg) s. peluca.

wig·gle (wĭg'əl) I. intr. & tr. menear(se) II. s. meneo.

wild (wīld) I. adj. salvaje; *(plant)* silvestre; *(unruly)* desordenado; *(crazy)* loco, extraviado; *(frenzied)* frenético; *(extravagant)* extravagante; *(stormy)* tormentoso; *(guess)* al azar ♦ **to be w. about** FAM. estar loco por • **to run w.** propagarse desmesuradamente • **to sow one's w. oats** correr sus mocedades • **wild-goose chase** búsqueda inútil II. s. región *f* salvaje ♦ **in the w.** en estado natural • **the wilds** región inexplorada III. adv. alocadamente; *(without being planted)* sin cultivo.

wild·cat ('kăt') I. s. fiera; ZOOL. gato montés; TEC. sondeo de exploración II. adj. arriesgado ♦ **w. strike** huelga no aprobada por el sindicato.

wil·de·beest (wĭl'də-bēst', vĭl'-) s. ñú *m*.

wil·der·ness (wĭl'dər-nĭs) s. región *f* sin cultivar.

wild-eyed (wīld'īd') adj. de mirada furiosa.

wild·fire (:fīr') s. incendio descontrolado ♦ **to spread like w.** propagarse rápidamente.

wild·flow·er (:flou'ər) s. flor *f* silvestre.

wild·fowl (:foul') s. [pl. inv. *o* **s**] ave *f* silvestre.

wild·life (:līf') s. fauna.

wile (wīl) I. s. ardid *m*; *(cunning)* astucia II. tr. atraer ♦ **to w. away the time** pasar el tiempo.

will¹ (wĭl) I. s. voluntad *f*; DER. testamento *o* **good, ill w.** buena, mala voluntad • **last w. and testament** última voluntad • **of one's own free w.** por voluntad propia • **w. power** fuerza de voluntad II. tr. querer; *(to order)* ordenar; DER. legar.

will² I. aux. [pret. **would**] *(simple futurity)* <*they w. come later* vendrán más tarde>; *(likelihood, certainty)* ir a <*you w. regret this* lo vas a lamentar>; *(willingness)* querer; *(requirement, command)* deber; *(habitual action)* soler <*she would spend hours in the kitchen* solía pasar horas en la cocina>; *(emphasis)* <*I w. do it!* ¡sí, lo haré!> II. tr. & intr. querer.

will·ful (wĭl'fəl) adj. *(deliberate)* deliberado; *(obstinate)* obstinado.

wil·lies (wĭl'ēz) s.pl. escalofrío, pelos de punta.

will·ing (wĭl'ĭng) adj. de buena voluntad.

will·ing·ness (:nĭs) s. buena voluntad.

will-o'-the-wisp (wĭl'ə-thə-wĭsp') s. fuego fatuo; *(delusive goal)* quimera.

wil·low (wĭl'ō) s. sauce *m*.

wil·low·y (:ē) adj. **-i-** esbelto.

wil·ly-nil·ly (wĭl'ē-nĭl'ē) adv. de grado o por fuerza.

wilt (wĭlt) intr. & tr. marchitar(se); *(to weaken)* debilitar(se).

wil·y (wī'lē) adj. **-i-** astuto.

wimp (wĭmp) s. JER. mentecato.

wim·ple (wĭm'pəl) s. griñón *m*.

win (wĭn) I. intr. **won, -nning** ganar, triunfar; ♦ **to w. out** salir victorioso —tr. ganar; *(to obtain)* conseguir; *(to gain)* alcanzar; *(affection, sympathy)* conquistar ♦ **to w. over** ganarse el apoyo de II. s. victoria, triunfo.

wince (wĭns) I. intr. respingar II. s. respingo.

winch (wĭnch) s. *(hoist)* torno, cabrestante *m*; *(crank)* manivela, cigüeña.

wind¹ (wĭnd) I. s. viento; *(air)* aire *m*; *(ver-*

biage) palabrería; *(breath)* respiración *f*; *(flatulence)* flatulencia ♦ **head w.** viento en contra • **there's something in the w.** algo flota en el aire • **to break w.** FAM. ventosear • **to get w. of** enterarse de • **to have the w. knocked out of one** quedar sin aliento ♦ pl. MÚS. instrumentos de viento II. tr. dejar sin aliento.

wind² (wīnd) I. tr. wound envolver; *(to entwine)* enrollar; *(wool, cotton)* devanar; *(to bend)* torcer; *(a watch)* dar cuerda a; *(to lift)* levantar con cabrestante ♦ **to be wound up** estar muy nervioso • **to w. down** disminuir • **to w. up** enrollar; FAM. concluir, terminar —intr. *(road)* serpentear; *(rope)* enrollarse; *(to twist)* torcerse; *(to bend)* encorvarse II. s. vuelta.

wind·bag (wīnd′băg′) s. JER. charlatán *m*.

wind·break (:brāk′) s. protección *f* contra el viento.

wind·ed (wĭn′dĭd) adj. jadeante.

wind·fall (wīnd′fôl′) s. suerte inesperada.

wind·flow·er (:flou′ər) s. anémona.

wind·ing (wīn′dĭng) I. s. enrollamiento; ELEC. bobinado II. adj. sinuoso; *(spiral)* en espiral.

wind·jam·mer (wīnd′jăm′ər) s. *(ship)* velero; *(sailor)* marinero.

wind·lass (wīnd′ləs) s. torno, molinete *m*.

wind·mill (wīnd′mĭl′) s. molino de viento.

win·dow (wĭn′dō) s. ventana; *(small)* ventanilla; *(pane of glass)* cristal *m*; *(of a shop)* escaparate *m*.

win·dow-pane (:pān′) s. cristal *m* de ventana.

win·dow-shop (:shŏp′) intr. -pp- comprar con los ojos.

win·dow·sill (:sĭl′) s. alféizar *m*.

wind·pipe (wĭnd′pīp′) s. tráquea.

wind·shield (:shēld′) s. parabrisas *m* ♦ **w. wiper** limpiaparabrisas.

wind·sock (:sŏk′) s. manga de aire.

wind·storm (:stôrm′) s. vendaval *m*.

wind·swept (:swĕpt′) adj. barrido por el viento.

wind-up (wīnd′ŭp′) s. conclusión *f*, final *m*.

wind·ward (wīnd′wərd) s. & adj. (de) barlovento.

wind·y (wĭn′dē) adj. -i- ventoso; *(unsheltered)* expuesto al viento; *(verbose)* verboso.

wine (wīn) I. s. vino II. tr. ♦ **to w. and dine** agasajar.

wine·glass (′glăs′) s. copa para vino.

wine·grow·er (:grō′ər) s. viticultor *m*.

wine·press (:prĕs′) s. trujal *m*, lagar *m*.

win·er·y (wī′nə-rē) s. vinería, lagar *m*.

wine·skin (wīn′skĭn′) s. odre *m*, pellejo de vino.

wing (wĭng) I. s. ala; *(of a chair)* oreja; FAM. *(arm)* brazo ♦ **on the w.** volando ♦ pl. TEAT. bastidores II. intr. volar —tr. *(to empower)* dar alas a; *(to speed along)* atravesar volando; *(to wound)* herir ♦ **to w. it** FAM. improvisar.

wing·ding (wĭng′dĭng′) s. FAM. fiesta animada.

winged (wĭngd, wĭng′ĭd) adj. alado; *(flying)* volador; *(sublime)* sublime.

wing·span/spread (wĭng′spăn′/sprĕd′) s. envergadura.

wink (wĭngk) I. intr. pestañear; *(lights)* parpadear; *(stars)* centellear ♦ **to w. at** guiñar el ojo a; FIG. hacer la vista gorda a II. s. *(blink)* pestañeo; *(hint)* guiño; *(of light)* parpadeo ♦ **in a w.** en un abrir y cerrar de ojos • **not to sleep a w.** no pegar los ojos, pasar la noche en blanco • **to get forty winks** FAM. echarse un sueñecito.

win·ner (wĭn′ər) s. ganador *m*; IRÓN. *(loser)* perdedor *m*.

win·ning (:ĭng) I. adj. victorioso; *(book, ticket)* premiado; *(charming)* encantador II. s. victoria ♦ pl. ganancias.

win·now (wĭn′ō) tr. *(grain)* aventar; FIG. *(to separate)* separar; *(to select)* seleccionar.

win·some (wĭn′səm) adj. simpático.

win·ter (wĭn′tər) I. s. invierno II. intr. invernar.

win·ter·green (:grēn′) s. gaultería.

win·ter·ize (wĭn′tə-rīz′) tr. preparar para el invierno.

win·ter·time (:tər-tīm′) s. invierno.

win·try/te·ry (:trē/tə-rē) adj. -i- invernal; FIG. helado.

wipe (wīp) I. tr. limpiar; *(to dry)* secar ♦ **to w. away** *o* **off** quitar • **to w. the slate clean** hacer borrón y cuenta nueva • **to w. out** destruir; *(a debt)* cancelar; FAM. asesinar II. s. limpieza.

wire (wīr) I. s. alambre *m*, hilo; *(finish line)* línea de llegada; ELEC. cable *m*; *(telegraph)* telegrafía; *(telegram)* telegrama *m* ♦ **under the w.** al último momento II. tr. alambrar; *(a house)* instalar el alambrado de; TELEG. telegrafiar —intr. poner un telegrama.

wired (wīrd) adj. ELEC. con instalación de alambres; JER. nervioso.

wire·less (wīr′lĭs) I. adj. sin alambres II. s. radio *mf*.

wire·tap (:tăp′) TEL. I. s. dispositivo interceptor II. tr. & intr. -pp- interceptar.

wir·ing (:ĭng) s. instalación eléctrica.

wir·y (:ē) adj. -i- *(kinky)* ensortijado, crespo; *(lean)* enjuto y fuerte.

wis·dom (wĭz′dəm) s. *(knowledge)* sabiduría; *(common sense)* cordura; *(learning)* erudición *f* ♦ **w. tooth** muela del juicio.

wise¹ (wīz) I. adj. sabio; *(judicious)* juicioso; *(sensible)* sensato ♦ **to get w.** JER. *(to understand)* caer en el chiste; *(to become insolent)* ponerse impertinente • **w. guy** FAM. sabelotodo II. tr. & intr. ♦ **to w. up** JER. poner(se) al tanto.

wise² s. manera, modo.

wise·a·cre (wīz′ā′kər) s. FAM. sabelotodo *mf*.

wise·crack (:krăk′) s. JER. ocurrencia.

wish (wĭsh) I. s. deseo II. tr. querer, desear; *(to like to)* gustar; *(to bid)* dar.

wish·bone (′bōn′) s. espoleta.

wish·ful (:fəl) adj. deseoso ♦ **w. thinking** ilusiones.

wish·y-wash·y (wĭsh′ē-wŏsh′ē) adj. FAM. -i- ni fu ni fa.

wisp (wĭsp) s. *(small bunch)* manojo, hacecillo; *(hair)* mechón *m*; *(trace)* vestigio.

wis·ter·i·a/tar·i·a (wĭ-stîr′ē-ə/-stâr′-) s. glicina.

wist·ful (wĭst′fəl) adj. nostálgico.

wit¹ s. inteligencia; *(good sense)* juicio; *(imagination)* imaginación *f*; *(cleverness)* ingenio; *(person)* persona ingeniosa ♦ **to be at w.'s end** no saber qué hacer ♦ pl. juicio; *(ingenuity)* ingenio • **to collect one's w.** serenarse • **to keep one's w. about one** no perder la cabeza • **to live by one's w.** vivir uno de su ingenio.

wit² intr. ♦ **to w.** es decir, a saber.

witch (wĭch) s. bruja; FAM. *(young woman)* hechicera ♦ **w. hazel** agua de hamamelis.

witch·craft (′krăft′) s. brujería.

witch·er·y (:ə-rē) s. brujería.

witch-hunt (:hunt′) s. persecución *f* de brujas; POL. investigación falsa para sacar ventaja.

witch·ing (:ĭng) adj. hechicero, mágico.

with (wĭth, wĭth) prep. con; *(next to)* junto a; *(in the employ of)* en, para; *(according to)* de

drug medicamento milagroso **II.** intr. *(to ponder)* pensar; *(to be doubtful)* dudar ♦ **to w. at** asombrarse de —tr. preguntarse.

won·der·ful (:fəl) adj. *(astonishing)* asombroso; *(excellent)* maravilloso.

won·der·land (:länd') s. *(imaginary)* país *m* de las maravillas; *(real)* lugar bellísimo.

won·der·ment (:mənt) s. *(astonishment)* asombro; *(marvel)* maravilla.

won·drous (wŭn'drəs) adj. maravilloso.

wont (wŏnt, wōnt) **I.** adj. acostumbrado; *(apt)* propenso **II.** s. costumbre *f.*

wont·ed (wŏn'tĭd, wōn'-) adj. habitual.

woo (wōō) tr. cortejar, galantear; *(to seek)* buscar; *(to solicit)* solicitar —intr. cortejar.

wood (wŏŏd) **I.** s. madera; *(firewood)* leña ♦ pl. bosque **II.** tr. *(to fuel)* alimentar con leña; *(to forest)* poblar con árboles.

wood·block ('blŏk') s. grabado en madera.

wood·chuck (:chŭk') s. marmota de Norteamérica.

wood·cock (:kŏk') s. [pl. inv. *o* **s**] coalla.

wood·craft (:kräft') s. artesanía en madera.

wood·cut (:kŭt') s. grabado en madera.

wood·cut·ter (:kŭt' ər) s. leñador *m.*

wood·ed (:ĭd) adj. arbolado, boscoso.

wood·en (:n) adj. de madera; *(leg)* de palo; *(stiff)* tieso; *(expressionless)* sin expresión.

wood·land (:lənd, :länd') s. bosque *m.*

wood·peck·er (:pĕk' ər) s. pájaro carpintero.

wood·pile (:pīl') s. montón *m* de leña.

wood·shed (:shĕd') s. leñera.

woods·man (wŏŏdz'mən) s. [pl. **-men**] habitante *m* de los bosques.

woods·y (wŏŏd'zē) adj. **-i-** boscoso.

wood·wind (wŏŏd'wĭnd') s. instrumento de viento de madera.

wood·work (:wûrk') s. maderaje *m.*

wood·worm (:wûrm') s. carcoma.

wood·y (:ē) adj. **-i-** leñoso; *(smell, taste)* a madera; *(land)* arbolado.

woof¹ (wŏŏf, wōōf) s. *(fibers)* trama; *(texture)* tejido.

woof² (wŏŏf) s. *(bark)* ladrido.

wool (wŏŏl) s. lana ♦ **steel w.** lana de acero.

wool·en (:ən) **I.** adj. de lana **II.** s. ♦ pl. prendas de lana.

wool·gath·er·ing (:găth' ər-ĭng) s. distracción *f.*

wool·ly (:ē) adj. **-i-** de lana; *(fleecy)* lanoso, lanudo; *(unclear)* borroso.

woo·zy (wŏŏ'zē, wōōz'ē) adj. **-i-** *(dazed)* aturdido; *(dizzy)* mareado.

word (wûrd) s. palabra; *(order)* orden *f*; *(password)* santo y seña; *(news)* información *f* ♦ **by w. of mouth** verbalmente • **in other words** mejor dicho • **mark my words** tome nota de lo que digo • **my w.!** ¡válgame Dios! • **on my w.** bajo mi palabra • **play on words** juego de palabras • **take my w. for it** se lo aseguro • **to eat one's words** retractarse • **to have the last w.** decir la última palabra • **to have o exchange words with someone** reñir de palabra con alguien • **to keep one's w.** cumplir la palabra • **to leave w. that** dejar dicho que • **to put in a good w. for** decir unas palabras en favor de • **to take the words out of someone's mouth** quitarle a alguien la palabra de la boca • **w. processing** procesamiento de palabras • **w. processor** procesador de palabras ♦ pl. *(speech)* discurso; *(quarrel)* disputa; MÚS. letra.

word·ing (wûr'dĭng) s. redacción *f.*

word·y (:dē) adj. **-i-** verboso.

wore (wôr) cf. **wear.**

---

acuerdo con, según; *(in comparison)* a; *(against)* contra; *(because of)* de; *(added to)* junto con; *(among)* entre ♦ **w. child** embarazada • **w. herself** *o* **himself** consigo • **w. me** conmigo • **w. you** contigo, con usted(es).

with·al (:ôl') adv. además, también.

with·draw (:drô') tr. **-drew, -n** sacar, quitar; *(to retract)* retractar —intr. *(to retreat)* retraerse; *(to draw away)* apartarse.

with·draw·al (:drô'əl) s. *(retreat)* retiro; *(removal)* retirada; *(termination)* abandono; FISIOL. síntomas *m* de reajuste.

with·drawn (:drôn') adj. remoto; *(shy)* tímido.

with·er (wĭth'ər) intr. secarse; *(to droop)* marchitarse —tr. marchitar; *(to stun)* fulminar.

with·hold (wĭth-hōld', wĭth-) tr. **-held** *(to restrain)* retener, contener; *(to refuse)* rehusar ♦ **withholding tax** impuesto retenido.

with·in (:ĭn') **I.** adv. dentro; *(indoors)* adentro; *(inwardly)* internamente **II.** prep. dentro de; *(distance)* a menos de; *(time)* antes de; *(not beyond)* dentro de los límites de **III.** s. adentro.

with·it (wĭth'ĭt) adj. FAM. moderno, al día.

with·out (-out') **I.** adv. fuera **II.** prep. sin; *(on the outside of)* (a)fuera de ♦ **it goes w. saying** se sobreentiende • **to do w.** pasar(se) sin.

with·stand (wĭth-stănd', wĭth-) tr. **-stood** resistir a —intr. resistirse.

wit·less (wĭt'lĭs) adj. tonto.

wit·ness (:nĭs) **I.** s. *(person)* testigo; *(act)* testimonio ♦ **to bear false w.** perjurarse • **to bear w.** atestiguar **II.** tr. atestiguar; *(to provide evidence of)* dar prueba de —intr. atestiguar.

wit·ti·cism (:ĭ-sĭz'əm) s. salida graciosa.

wit·ty (:ē) adj. **-i-** *(clever)* ingenioso; *(humorous)* gracioso.

wiz·ard (wĭz'ərd) s. hechicero; FIG. as *m.*

wiz·ard·ry (:ər-drē) s. magia, hechicería.

wiz·ened (wĭz'ənd) adj. arrugado.

wob·ble (wŏb'əl) intr. bambolearse; *(to shake)* temblar; *(to waver)* vacilar.

wob·bly (:lē) adj. **-i-** *(shaky)* bamboleante; *(unsteady)* tembloroso; *(uncertain)* vacilante.

woe (wō) **I.** s. pesar *m*; *(misfortune)* infortunio **II.** interj. ♦ **w. is me** ¡ay de mí!

woe·be·gone (wō'bĭ-gôn') adj. triste.

wo(e)·ful (wō'fəl) adj. *(mournful)* apenado; *(pitiful)* lamentable.

woke (wōk), **wo·ken** (wō'kən) cf. **wake¹.**

wolf (wŏŏlf) **I.** s. [pl. **-ves**] lobo; FIG. persona rapaz y feroz; JER. don Juan *m* ♦ **lone w.** persona solitaria • **to cry w.** dar la alarma sin causa • **w. in sheep's clothing** hipócrita **II.** tr. ♦ **to w. down** comer vorazmente.

wolf·hound ('hound') s. galgo ruso.

wol·ver·ine (wŏŏl'və-rēn') s. ZOOL. glotón *m.*

wom·an (wŏŏm'ən) s. [pl. **women**] mujer *f*; *(servant)* criada.

wom·an·hood (:hŏŏd') s. feminidad *f.*

wom·an·ish (wŏŏm'ə-nĭsh) adj. femenino; *(effeminate)* afeminado.

wom·an·kind (:ən·kīnd') s. las mujeres.

wom·an·ly (:lē) adj. femenino.

womb (wŏŏm) s. matriz *f*; FIG. cuna.

wom·bat (wŏm'băt') s. oso australiano.

wom·en (wĭm'ĭn) cf. **woman.**

wom·en·folk(s) (:fōk[s]') s.pl. las mujeres.

won (wŭn) cf. **win.**

won·der (wŭn'dər) **I.** s. maravilla; *(miracle)* milagro; *(astonishment)* asombro ♦ **no w.** no es de extrañar • **to do** *o* **to work wonders** hacer milagros • **w. child** niño prodigio • **w.**

work (wûrk) I. s. trabajo; *(job)* empleo; *(result, deed)* obra ♦ **let's get to w.!** ¡manos a la obra! • **the works** JER. todo, de todo • **to make short w. of** terminar rápidamente • **w. force** mano de obra ♦ pl. *(output)* obra; *(factory)* taller; *(mechanism)* mecanismo II. intr. trabajar; *(to be employed)* tener trabajo; *(to operate)* funcionar; *(to be effectual)* surtir efecto; *(to contort)* torcerse • **to w. out** *(to go well)* salir bien; *(to do exercises)* hacer gimnasia —tr. producir; *(to handle)* manejar; *(metal)* forjar; *(to solve)* resolver; *(to arrange)* arreglárselas; *(to cultivate)* cultivar; *(to drive)* hacer trabajar; *(to persuade)* influir en ♦ **to w. at** ocuparse de • **to w. in** introducir • **to w. out** resolver, solucionar; • **to w. over** alterar • **to w. up** *(to excite)* estimular; *(to develop)* desarrollar.

work·a·ble (wûr'kə-bəl) adj. factible.

work·a·day (:kə-dā') adj. laborable; *(everyday)* cotidiano.

work·a·hol·ic (:hô'lĭk) s. trabajador compulsivo.

work·bench (wûrk'bĕnch') s. mesa de trabajo.

work·book (:bŏŏk') s. cuaderno de ejercicios; *(manual)* manual *m* de instrucciones.

work·day (:dā') s. día *m* laborable.

work·er (wûr'kər) s. trabajador *m*.

work·horse (wûrk'hôrs') s. caballo de tiro; *(person)* persona muy trabajadora.

work·house (:hous') s. correccional *m*.

work·ing (wûr'kĭng) I. adj. que trabaja; *(class)* obrero; *(hours)* de trabajo; *(expenses)* de explotación; *(day)* laborable; *(knowledge)* básico; *(model)* operativo; MEC. móvil ♦ **to be in w. order** estar funcionando • **w. capital** capital activo II. s. trabajo; *(operation)* funcionamiento; *(of metals, land)* labrado; *(of a mine)* explotación *f*.

work·ing·man (:măn') s. [pl. **-men**] trabajador *m*, obrero.

work·load (wûrk'lōd') s. carga de trabajo.

work·man (:mən) s. [pl. **-men**] trabajador *m*.

work·man·like (:līk) adj. hecho a conciencia.

work·man·ship (:shĭp') s. destreza.

work·out (wûrk'out') s. ejercicio.

work·room (:rŏŏm') s. taller *m*.

work·shop (:shŏp') s. taller *m*.

work·ta·ble (:tā'bəl) s. mesa de trabajo.

work·week (:wĕk') s. semana laboral.

world (wûrld) s. mundo ♦ **a w. of** la mar de • **for all the w.** ni más ni menos • **not to be long for this w.** quedarle poco a uno • **on top of the w.** FAM. en el séptimo cielo • **out of this w.** FAM. increíble • **to bring into the w.** traer al mundo • **to come down in the w.** venir a menos • **to come into the w.** venir al mundo • **to have the best of both worlds** tenerlo todo al mismo tiempo • **to move up in the w.** prosperar • **to see the w.** ver mundo • **to think the w. of** poner por las nubes a • **where, what in the w.?** ¿dónde, qué diablos? • **w. war** guerra mundial.

world·ly ('lē) adj. -i- secular; *(worldly-wise)* sofisticado; *(material)* material.

world·ly-wise (:wīz') adj. sofisticado.

world·wide (wûrld'wīd') adj. mundial.

worm (wûrm) I. s. gusano; *(parasite)* helminto; *(tormenting force)* gusanillo; *(vile person)* canalla *m* ♦ pl. MED. helmintiasis II. tr. *(to make way)* colarse; *(to elicit)* sacar; *(to cure)* librar de gusanos —intr. arrastrarse.

worm-eat·en ('ēt'n) adj. agusanado; *(decayed)* podrido; *(antiquated)* anticuado.

worm·wood (:wŏŏd') s. amargura; BOT. absintio, ajenjo.

worm·y (wûr'mē) adj. -i- agusanado; *(wormeaten)* carcomido.

worn (wôrn) I. cf. **wear** II. adj. *(used)* gastado; *(exhausted)* agotado; *(trite)* trillado.

worn-out ('out') adj. *(used)* gastado; *(exhausted)* agotado.

wor·ri·er (wûr'ē-ər) s. aprensivo.

wor·ri·ment (:mənt) s. preocupación *f*.

wor·ri·some (:səm) adj. inquietante.

wor·ry (wûr'ē) I. intr. preocupar —tr. *(to distress)* preocupar; *(to bother)* molestar; *(to toy with)* jugar con II. s. preocupación *f*.

wor·ry·wart (:wôrt') s. persona aprensiva.

worse (wûrs) I. adj. [comp. de **bad, ill**] peor; *(more severe)* más fuerte ♦ **to get w. and w.** ir de mal en peor • **to get w.** empeorar • **to make matters w.** para empeorar las cosas II. s. ♦ **and w.** y cosas peores • **to take a turn for the w.** empeorar • **so much the w.** tanto peor • **to be none the w. for it** no perjudicarle a uno • **to think none the w. of** no tener en menos III. adv. peor; *(more severely)* más ♦ **to be w. off** estar peor.

wors·en (wûr'sən) tr. & intr. empeorar(se).

wor·ship (wûr'shĭp) I. s. adoración *f*; *(devotion)* devoción *f* II. tr. RELIG. venerar; FIG. adorar —intr. venerar.

wor·ship·(p)er (:shī-pər) s. devoto, adorador *m*; RELIG. fiel *mf*.

wor·ship·ful (:shĭp-fəl) adj. reverente; *(adoring)* adorador.

worst (wûrst) I. adj. [superl. de **bad, ill**] peor; *(most severe)* más fuerte ♦ **in the w. way** FAM. de mala manera II. adv. peor; *(most severely)* más ♦ **w. of all** peor aún III. tr. derrotar, vencer IV. s. ♦ **at w.** *o* **if w. comes to w.** en el peor de los casos.

wor·sted (wŏŏs'tĭd, wûr'stĭd) s. *(yarn)* estambre *m*; *(fabric)* tela de estambre.

worth (wûrth) I. s. valor *m*; *(wealth)* fortuna; *(merit)* mérito ♦ **to get one's money's w.** sacar provecho de lo pagado II. adj. que vale ♦ **for what it is w.** por si sirve de algo • **to be w.** valer; *(in value)* tener un valor de; *(to be the equivalent of)* valer por • **to be w. it** valer la pena.

worth·less ('lĭs) adj. sin valor; *(contemptible)* despreciable.

worth·while ('hwīl') adj. que vale la pena.

wor·thy (wûr'thē) I. adj. -i- meritorio; *(useful)* útil; *(deserving)* digno II. s. persona ilustre.

would (wŏŏd) cf. **will²**.

would-be ('bē') adj. aspirante.

wound¹ (wŏŏnd) I. s. herida II. tr. & intr. herir.

wound² (wound) cf. **wind²**.

wove (wōv), **wo·ven** (wō'vən) cf. **weave**.

wow (wou) FAM. I. interj. ¡increíble!, ¡cáspita! II. s. gran éxito III. tr. asombrar.

wrack (răk) s. despojo, ruina ♦ **to go to w. and ruin** echarse a perder.

wraith (rāth) s. fantasma *m*, espectro.

wran·gle (răng'gəl) I. intr. pelear —tr. obtener arguyendo II. s. pelea.

wran·gler (:glər) s. *(quarreler)* pendenciero; *(cowboy)* vaquero.

wrap (răp) I. tr. **-t** *o* **-pped, -pping** envolver; *(rope, chain)* enrollar ♦ **to be wrapped up in** estar absorto en • **to w. up** *(to end)* cerrar; *(to summarize)* resumir —intr. enrollarse II. s.

(cloak) manto; *(wrapper)* envoltura ♦ **to keep under wraps** mantener en secreto.
wrap·a·round ('ə-round') s. manto.
wrap·per (:ər) s. *(person)* empaquetador *m*; *(wrap)* envoltura; *(robe)* bata.
wrap·ping (:ĭng) s. envoltura.
wrap-up (:ŭp') s. resumen *m*.
wrath (răth, räth) s. *(anger)* ira; *(fury)* furia.
wrath·ful (:fəl) adj. furioso.
wreak (rēk) tr. infligir; *(anger)* descargar ♦ **to w. havoc** hacer estragos.
wreath (rēth) s. [pl. **s**] guirnalda; *(spiral)* espiral *m*.
wreathe (rēth) tr. hacer una guirnalda de; *(to crown)* coronar con guirnalda; *(to surround)* rodear —intr. *(to curl)* enroscarse.
wreck (rĕk) I. s. destrucción *f*; *(crash)* choque *m*; *(shipwreck)* naufragio; *(collision remains)* destrozos; *(heap)* cascajo ♦ **to be a w.** estar hecho un cascajo II. tr. destrozar; *(to tear down)* derrumbar; *(to ruin)* arruinar —intr. destrozarse.
wreck·age ('ĭj) s. restos, despojos.
wreck·er (:ər) s. destructor *m*; *(demolition expert)* demoledor *m*; *(truck)* grúa.
wren (rĕn) s. reyezuelo, abadejo.
wrench (rĕnch) I. s. *(injury)* torcedura; MEC. llave *f* II. tr. torcer; *(to grieve)* doler.
wrest (rĕst) I. tr. arrebatar; *(to extract)* arrancar II. s. torción violenta.
wres·tle (rĕs'əl) intr. & tr. luchar (con *o* contra).
wres·tler (:lər) s. luchador *m*.
wres·tling (:lĭng) s. lucha.
wretch (rĕch) s. *(unhappy person)* desgraciado; *(base person)* canalla *m*.
wretch·ed ('ĭd) adj. desgraciado, miserable.
wrig·gle (rĭg'əl) I. intr. *(to squirm)* menearse; *(to proceed)* culebrear; *(to get out)* escabullirse; *(to get into)* insinuarse II. s. meneo, culebreo.
wring (rĭng) tr. **wrung** escurrir; *(to wrench)* torcer.
wring·er ('ər) s. escurridor *m*.
wrin·kle (rĭng'kəl) I. s. arruga; FAM. método nuevo II. tr. arrugar; *(brow)* fruncir —intr. arrugarse.
wrist (rĭst) s. puño; ANAT. muñeca ♦ **w. watch** reloj de pulsera.
wrist·band ('bănd') s. muñequera.
writ (rĭt) s. DER. mandato, orden *f*.
write (rīt) tr. **wrote, written** escribir; *(a will, contract)* redactar; *(a check)* extender, hacer; *(insurance)* preparar ♦ **to w. down** poner por escrito; *(to make a note of)* anotar • **to w. off** *(a person)* dar por perdido; *(to depreciate)* amortizar; *(a debt)* cancelar • **to w. out** poner por escrito; *(in full)* escribir con todas las letras —intr. escribir ♦ **to be nothing to w. home about** no ser nada del otro mundo.
write-in ('ĭn') s. candidato no oficial.
writ·er (rī'tər) s. escritor *m*.
write-up (rīt'ŭp') s. crítica.
writhe (rīth) intr. retorcerse.
writ·ing (rī'tĭng) s. escritura; *(inscription)* inscripción *f*; *(handwriting)* letra; *(written work)* escrito ♦ **in w.** por escrito • **to see the w. on the wall** vérsela venir.
writ·ten (rĭt'n) cf. **write.**
wrong (rông) I. adj. malo; *(unfair)* injusto; *(incorrect)* erróneo; *(mistaken)* equivocado; *(not suitable)* inadecuado ♦ **to be w.** hacer mal; *(to be mistaken)* equivocarse; *(to be amiss)* andar mal • **to get up on the w. side of the bed**

levantarse con el pie izquierdo II. adv. mal ♦ **to do someone w.** ser injusto con • **to do, get w.** hacer, tener mal • **to go w.** *(morally)* ir por mal camino; *(to act mistakenly)* fallar; *(to go amiss)* salir mal • **to have it all w.** estar totalmente equivocado • **you can't go w.** FAM. no hay forma de equivocarse III. s. mal *m*; *(unjust act)* injusticia; *(bad deed)* maldad *f*; *(fault)* error *m* ♦ **to be in the w.** no tener razón • **to right a w.** deshacer un entuerto IV. tr. ser injusto con; *(to treat dishonorably)* agraviar; *(to malign)* calumniar.
wrong·do·er ('dōō'ər) s. maleante *mf*.
wrong·do·ing (:dōō'ĭng) s. mal *m*.
wrong·ful (:fəl) adj. injusto.
wrong-head·ed (:hĕd'ĭd) adj. obstinado.
wrote (rōt) cf. **write.**
wrought (rôt) adj. armado; *(shaped)* formado; *(elaborate)* labrado ♦ **w. iron** hierro forjado • **w. up** agitado.
wrung (rŭng) cf. **wring.**
wry (rī) adj. **-er, -est** *o* **-i-** *(crooked)* torcido; *(twisted)* forzado; *(ironical)* irónico.
wurst (wûrst, wŏŏrst) s. salchicha, embutido.

X

x, X (ĕks) s. vigésima cuarta letra del alfabeto inglés; MAT. incógnita ♦ **x amount of** una cantidad equis de • **to x out** tachar.
x-ax·is ('ăk'sĭs) s. [pl. **-es**] eje *m* horizontal.
X-chro·mo·some (:krō'mə-sōm') s. cromosoma X *m*.
xen·o·phile (zĕn'ə-fīl', zē'nə-) s. xenófilo.
xen·o·phil·i·a ('-fīl'ē-ə) s. afición *f* a lo extranjero.
xen·o·phobe ('-fōb') s. xenófobo.
xen·o·pho·bi·a ('-fō'bē-ə) s. xenofobia.
xen·o·pho·bic (:bĭk) adj. xenófobo.
Xe·rox (zîr'ŏks') I. s. marca registrada de un proceso rápido de reproducción; *(copy)* xerocopia II. tr. xerografiar.
X·mas (krĭs'məs, ĕks'məs) s. FAM. Navidad *f*.
x-ra·di·a·tion (ĕks'rā'dē-ā'shən) s. MED. tratamiento con rayos X; FÍS. radiación *f* de rayos X.
X-rat·ed ('rā'tĭd) adj. no apto para menores de 16 años.
x-ray *o* **X-ray** (:rā') I. s. radiografía; FÍS. rayo X II. tr. examinar con rayos X; *(to radiograph)* radiografiar.
xy·lo·phone (zī'lə-fōn') s. xilófono.

Y

y, Y (wī) s. vigésima quinta letra del alfabeto inglés.
yacht (yät) s. yate *m*.
yacht·ing (yä'tĭng) s. navegación *f* (en yate).
ya·hoo (yä'hōō) s. FAM. bruto, bestia.
yak¹ (yăk) s. ZOOL. yac *m*.
yak² intr. **-kk-** JER. parlotear, cotorrear.
yam (yăm) s. *(root)* ñame *f*; *(sweet potato)* batata.
yam·mer (yăm'ər) intr. *(to whimper)* lloriquear; *(to talk)* parlotear.
yank (yăngk) I. tr. & intr. tironear (de), dar un tirón (a) II. s. tirón *m*.
Yan·kee (yăng'kē) adj. & s. yanqui *mf*.

yap (yăp) **I.** intr. **-pp-** ladrar; JER. *(to jabber)* cotorrear **II.** s. ladrido; JER. *(jabber)* charla; *(mouth)* hocico.

yard¹ (yärd) s. *(measure)* yarda; MARÍT. verga ♦ **y. goods** tela vendida por yardas; géneros.

yard² s. *(enclosed grounds)* patio; *(surrounding grounds)* jardín *m*; *(work area)* depósito, taller *m*; *(corral)* corral *m*; F.C. estación *f* de depósito.

yard·age (yär′dĭj) s. medida en yardas; *(cloth)* tela.

yard·stick (yärd′stĭk′) s. vara de una yarda de largo; *(standard)* patrón *m*, norma.

yarn (yärn) s. hilo; FAM. *(story)* cuento, historia.

yaw (yô) **I.** intr. *(a ship)* guiñar; AER. desviarse **II.** s. guiñada, desvío.

yawl (yôl) s. yola.

yawn (yôn) **I.** intr. bostezar; *(cave, chasm)* abrirse **II.** s. bostezo.

yawn·ing (yô′nĭng) adj. abierto, cavernoso.

y-ax·is (wī′ăk′sĭs) s. [pl. **-es**] eje *m* vertical.

Y-chro·mo·some (wī′krō′mə-sōm′) s. cromosoma Y *m.*

ye (yē) pron. pers. ANT. vosotros, ustedes.

yea (yā) adv. & s. sí *m.*

yeah (yě′ə, yă′ə) adv. FAM. sí.

year (yîr) s. año ♦ **a y.** por año, anualmente • **financial** *o* **fiscal y.** año económico ♦ **from y. to y.** año tras año • **once a y.** una vez al año • **school y.** año escolar • **y. in y. out** año tras año ♦ pl. *(age)* edad <*she feels her y.* ya siente su edad>; *(long period)* una eternidad.

year·book (′bŏŏk′) s. anuario.

year-end *o* **year·end** (:ěnd′) adj. & s. (de) fin *m* de año económico.

year·ling (:lĭng) s. animal *m* de un año de edad.

year·long (:lông′) adj. de un año de duración.

year·ly (:lē) **I.** adj. anual **II.** adv. anualmente **III.** s. anuario (revista, libro).

yearn (yûrn) intr. añorar; *(to feel compassion)* sentir compasión ♦ **to y. for** añorar.

yearn·ing (yûr′nĭng) s. anhelo, añoranza.

year-round (yîr′round′) adj. de todo el año.

yeast (yēst) s. levadura; *(froth)* espuma; *(ferment)* fermento.

yell (yěl) **I.** tr. & intr. gritar ♦ **to y. for help** pedir auxilio a gritos **II.** s. grito.

yel·low (yěl′ō) **I.** s. amarillo; *(yolk)* yema ♦ pl. ictericia **II.** adj. *(color)* amarillo; *(hair)* rubio; JER. *(cowardly)* cobarde ♦ **to turn y.** amarillear • **y. jacket** avispa **III.** tr. & intr. volver(se) amarillo.

yel·low-bel·lied (:běl′ēd) adj. JER. cobarde.

yel·low·ish (:ĭsh) adj. amarillento.

yelp (yělp) **I.** intr. gañir **II.** s. gañido.

yen¹ (yěn) **I.** intr. **-nn-** anhelar **II.** s. anhelo ♦ **to have a y. for** desear • **to have a y. to** tener ganas de.

yen² (yěn) s.inv. FIN. yen *m.*

yeo·man (yō′mən) **I.** s. [pl. **-men**] MARÍT. oficial *m* oficinista; G.B. *(landholder)* pequeño terrateniente **II.** adj. *(workmanlike)* sólido.

yeo·man·ry (:rē) s. terratenientes pequeños.

yep (yěp) adv. FAM. sí.

yes (yěs) **I.** adv. sí ♦ **to say y.** dar el sí • **y. indeed** claro que sí • **y. of course!** ¡por supuesto! **II.** s. [pl. **-es**] sí *m* ♦ **y. man** FAM. subordinado servil.

yes·ter·day (yěs′tər-dā′) **I.** adv. ayer ♦ **I wasn't born y.** no soy tonto • **late y.** ayer a última hora **II.** s. (el día de) ayer *m* ♦ **the day before y.** anteayer ♦ pl. pasado.

yes·ter·year (:yîr′) s. el año pasado; *(yore)* antaño.

yet (yět) **I.** adv. todavía, aún; *(thus far)* ya; *(still more)* aún más; *(eventually)* probablemente ♦ **as (of) y.** hasta ahora • **not y.** todavía no • **y. again** una vez más • **y. more** aún más **II.** conj. *(nevertheless)* sin embargo; *(but)* pero.

yield (yēld) **I.** tr. dar, producir; *(profit)* rendir; *(to give up)* ceder ♦ **to y. up** entregar; *(secret)* revelar —intr. rendirse; *(in traffic)* ceder el paso ♦ **to y. to** ceder a **II.** s. INDUS. rendimiento; AGR. cosecha; COM. *(profit)* beneficio.

yield·ing (yēl′dĭng) adj. flexible; *(docile)* dócil.

yip (yĭp) **I.** s. ladrido agudo **II.** intr. **-pp-** ladrar.

yip·pee (yĭp′ē) interj. ¡yupi!, ¡huija!

yo·del (yōd′l) **I.** tr. & intr. cantar a la tirolesa **II.** s. canto tirolés.

yo·ga (yō′gə) s. yoga *m.*

yo·gurt (yō′gərt) s. yogur *m.*

yoke (yōk) **I.** s. yugo; *(pair of oxen)* yunta; *(carried by a person)* balancín *m*; *(clamp)* brida; *(of garment)* canesú *m* ♦ **to throw off the y.** sacudir el yugo **II.** tr. *(to join)* uncir; *(to bind)* unir.

yo·kel (yō′kəl) s. paleto.

yolk (yōk) s. yema.

yon·der (yŏn′dər) **I.** adj. aquel **II.** adv. allá **III.** pron. aquél.

yoo-hoo (yŏŏ′hŏŏ) interj. ¡eh!, ¡hola!

yore (yôr) s. antaño.

you (yŏŏ) pron. pers. [sujeto] *(familiar)* tú, vosotros, vosotras; *(formal)* usted, ustedes; [complemento] *(familiar, direct and indirect)* te, os <*I'll call you later* te llamo más tarde> <*I handed it to you* te lo di>; *(formal, direct)* lo, la, los, las <*I'll see you tomorrow* la veo mañana> <*they invited you* los invitaron>; *(formal, indirect)* le, les, se <*I give you the book* le doy el libro> <*I give it to you* se lo doy>; [después de preposición] *(familiar)* ti, vosotros, vosotras <*the book is for you* el libro es para ti> <*he'll go with you* irá con vosotras> <*the book is for you* el libro es para ti> ; *(formal)* usted, ustedes <*the book is for you* el libro es para usted> <*he'll go with you* irá con ustedes> ♦ **all of y.** todos vosotros, todos ustedes • **between y. and me** entre tú y yo • **if I were y.** yo que tú • **with y.** contigo, con usted(es), con vosotros • **y. can't do that** eso no se permite • **y. never know** uno nunca sabe.

you-all (yŏŏ-ôl′) pron. FAM. vosotros.

young (yŭng) **I.** adj. joven; *(early life)* de juventud ♦ **in my younger days** en mi juventud • **y. lady** señorita • **y. man, woman** joven **II.** s.pl. jóvenes *mf*; *(offspring)* cría (de animal) ♦ **with y.** preñada.

young·ish (′ĭsh) adj. bastante joven.

young·ster (yŭng′stər) s. jovencito.

your (yŏŏr, yər) adj. pos. *(familiar, sg.)* tu(s); *(formal, sg.)* su(s), de usted; *(familiar, pl.)* vuestro(s), vuestra(s); *(formal, pl.)* su(s), de ustedes.

yours (yŏŏrz) pron. pers. *(familiar, sg.)* (el) tuyo, (la) tuya; *(formal, sg.)* (el o la) de usted, el suyo, la suya; *(familiar, pl.)* (el) vuestro, (la) vuestra; *(formal, pl.)* (el o la) de ustedes, (el) suyo, (la) suya.

your·self (yŏŏr-sělf′, yər-) **I.** pron. pers. *(familiar)* tú (mismo, misma) <*write it down y.* escríbelo tú mismo>; *(formal)* usted (mismo, misma) <*you said it y.* usted misma lo dijo> II. pron. reflex. *(familiar)* te <*please, don't hurt y.* por favor, no te hagas daño>; *(formal)* se <*prepárese ahora* prepare yourself now>.

your·selves (:sĕlvz′) I. pron. pers. *(familiar)* vosotros (mismos), vosotras (mismas) <*you y. wanted it* vosotras mismas lo quisisteis>; *(formal)* ustedes (mismos, mismas) <*you did it to y.* se lo buscaron ustedes mismos> II. pron. reflex. *(familiar)* os <*have you dressed y. yet?* ¿os habéis vestido ya?>; *(formal)* se <*give y. plenty of time* dense suficiente tiempo>.

youth (yo͞oth) s. [pl. **s**] juventud *f*; *(young person)* joven *mf*.

youth·ful (′fəl) adj. joven, juvenil.

yowl (youl) I. intr. dar aullidos, aullar II. s. aullido.

yo-yo (yō′yō′) I. s. *(toy)* yoyó; JER. *(dope)* tonto, patán *m* II. intr. vacilar.

yuc·ca (yŭk′ə) s. yuca.

yum·my (yŭm′ē) adj. -i- FAM. delicioso, rico.

Z

z, Z (zē) s. vigésima sexta letra del alfabeto inglés.

za·ny (zā′nē) I. s. persona cómica y estrafalaria; TEAT. bufón *m* II. adj. -i- *(comical)* estrafalario; *(clownish)* bufo.

zap (zăp) JER. I. tr. **-pp-** *(to kill)* matar; *(to destroy)* destruir II. interj. ¡zas!

zeal (zēl) s. celo, ahínco.

zeal·ot·ry (zĕl′ə-trē) s. fanatismo.

zeal·ous (:əs) adj. celoso, fervoroso.

ze·bra (zē′brə) s. cebra.

ze·nith (zē′nĭth) s. cenit *m*.

zeph·yr (zĕf′ər) s. brisa; TEJ. céfiro.

zep·pe·lin (zĕp′ə-lĭn) s. zepelín *m*.

ze·ro (zîr′ō) I. s. [pl. **(e)s**] cero; *(nothing)* nada; METEOR. cero grado II. adj. nulo III. tr. & intr. ♦ **to z. in on** afinar la puntería hacia; *(to*

close in) apuntar hacia.

ze·ro-base(d) (:băs[t]′) que justifica los gastos en términos de necesidad *o* costo.

zest (zĕst) s. gusto, sabor *m*; *(enjoyment)* brío; *(rind)* cáscara.

zest·ful (′fəl) adj. sabroso; *(spirited)* lleno de vida.

zig·zag (zĭg′zăg′) I. s. zigzag *m* II. adj. en zigzag III. adv. zigzagueando IV. intr. **-gg-** ir zigzagueando —tr. poner en zigzag.

zilch (zĭlch) s. JER. nada, cero.

zil·lion (zĭl′yən) s. FAM. número astronómico.

zinc (zĭngk) s. cinc *m*.

zing (zĭng) I. s. zumbido II. intr. FAM. zumbar.

zing·er (′ər) s. observación *f* mordaz.

zin·ni·a (zĭn′ē-ə) s. cinnia.

zip (zĭp) I. s. silbido; *(energy)* vigor *m* II. intr. **-pp-** zumbar ♦ **to z. by** pasar como una bala • **to z. up** subir *o* cerrar la cremallera —tr. cerrar la cremallera de.

zip·per (′ər) s. cremallera.

zip·py (:ē) adj. -i- vivaz, enérgico.

zir·con (zûr′kŏn′) s. circón *m*.

zith·er (zĭth′ər, zĭth′-) s. cítara.

zo·di·ac (zō′dē-ăk′) s. zodíaco.

zom·bi(e) (zŏm′bē) s. cadáver resucitado; FIG. autómata *m*.

zo·nal (zō′nəl) adj. zonal.

zone (zōn) I. s. zona II. tr. dividir en zonas.

zon·ing (zō′nĭng) s. restricciones *f* para edificar en un barrio de una ciudad.

zonked (zŏngkt) adj. JER. mamado.

zoo (zo͞o) s. ZOO; FIG. confusión *f*.

zo·o·log·i·cal (zō′ə-lŏj′ĭ-kəl) adj. zoológico.

zo·ol·o·gist (zō-ŏl′ə-jĭst) s. zoólogo.

zo·ol·o·gy (:jē) s. zoología.

zoom (zo͞om) I. intr. *(to buzz)* zumbar; AVIA. subir verticalmente; FOTOG. *(in)* acercarse; *(out)* alejarse ♦ **to z. away** salir zumbando II. s. *(sound)* zumbido; AVIA. subida vertical.

zounds (zoundz) interj. ¡cáspita!

zuc·chi·ni (zo͞o-kē′nē) s.inv. zapallito italiano.

zwie·back (swē′băk′, swī′-) s. tostada de pan ligeramente azucarada.